LEONARDO
DA VINCI

WALTER
ISAACSON

Simon & Schuster Paperbacks

NEW YORK   LONDON   TORONTO   SYDNEY   NEW DELHI

Simon & Schuster Paperbacks
An Imprint of Simon & Schuster, Inc.
1230 Avenue of the Americas
New York, NY 10020

First Simon & Schuster trade paperback edition October 2018

SIMON & SCHUSTER PAPERBACKS and colophon are registered trademarks
of Simon & Schuster, Inc.

For information about special discounts for bulk purchases, please contact
Simon & Schuster Special Sales at 1-866-506-1949
or business@simonandschuster.com.

The Simon & Schuster Speakers Bureau can bring authors to your
live event. For more information or to book an event contact the
Simon & Schuster Speakers Bureau at 1-866-248-3049 or
visit our website at www.simonspeakers.com.

Interior design by Paul Dippolito

Manufactured in the United States of America

1   3   5   7   9   10   8   6   4   2

The Library of Congress has cataloged the hardcover edition as follows:
Title: Leonardo da Vinci / Walter Isaacson.
Description: New York : Simon & Schuster, 2017. |
Includes bibliographical references and index.
Identifiers: LCCN 2017020817 (print) | LCCN 2017021625 (ebook) |
ISBN 9781501139178 (ebook) | ISBN 9781501139154 (hardback) |
ISBN 9781501139161 (trade paperback)
Subjects: LCSH: Leonardo, da Vinci, 1452-1519. |
Artists--Italy--Biography. | Scientists--Italy--Biography. | Gifted persons--Italy--Biography. |
BISAC:
BIOGRAPHY & AUTOBIOGRAPHY / Artists, Architects, Photographers. |
BIOGRAPHY & AUTOBIOGRAPHY / Science & Technology. | BIOGRAPHY &
AUTOBIOGRAPHY / Historical.
Classification: LCC N6923.L33 (ebook) | LCC N6923.L33 I827 2017 (print) |
DDC 709.2 [B] --dc23
LC record available at https://lccn.loc.gov/2017020817

ISBN 978-1-5011-3915-4
ISBN 978-1-5011-3916-1 (pbk)
ISBN 978-1-5011-3917-8 (ebook)

"Isaacson uses his subject's contradictions to give him humanity and depth."

—*The New York Times*

"A captivating narrative about art and science, curiosity and discipline."

—Adam Grant, #1 *New York Times* bestselling author of *Originals*

"I've read a lot about Leonardo over the years, but I had never found one book that satisfactorily covered all the different facets of his life and work. . . . More than any other Leonardo book I've read, this one helps you see him as a complete human being and understand just how special he was."

—Bill Gates

"Leonardo gets the biographer he deserves—an author capable of comprehending his often frenetic, frequently weird quest to understand. This is not just a joyful book; it's also a joy to behold. . . . A very human portrait of a genius."

—*The Times of London*

"Leonardo led an astonishingly interesting, eventful life. And Isaacson brilliantly captures its essence."

—*The Toronto Star*

"A monumental tribute to a titanic figure."

—*Publishers Weekly* (starred review)

"Majestic . . . Isaacson takes on another complex, giant figure and transforms him into someone we can recognize. . . . Totally enthralling, masterful, and passionate."

—*Kirkus Reviews* (starred review)

"Encompassing in its coverage, robust in its artistic explanations, yet written in a smart, conversational tone, this is both a solid introduction to the man and a sweeping saga of his genius."

—*Booklist* (starred review)

"Absorbing, enlightening and always engaging."

—Miranda Seymour, author of *Mary Shelley*

"Isaacson, to his credit, helps us see Leonardo's artistic vision with fresh eyes. . . . We finish the book with a renewed conviction that the world's most famous Renaissance man was, in essence, inimitable."

—*The Christian Science Monitor*

"Exuberant . . . a richly illustrated ride through the artist's life . . . a fascinating, bonbon-size tribute to the man who thought to ask."

—*Newsday*

"An ideal match of author and subject. . . . Fascinated by Leonardo's genius, Isaacson lucidly and lovingly captures his stunning powers of observation that spanned so many disciplines. . . . Magnificent."

—*Tulsa World*

"In some ways this is Walter Isaacson's most ambitious book. He uses the life he recounts in a wonderful way to speculate on the source of geniuses . . . always you are informed, entertained, stimulated, satisfied."

—Fareed Zakaria, *GPS*

"[A] splendid work that provides an illuminating guide to the output of one of the last millennium's greatest minds."

—*The Guardian US*

"Leonardo da Vinci's prowess as a polymath—driven by insatiable curiosity about everything from the human womb to deadly weaponry—still stuns. In this copiously illustrated biography, we feel its force all over again. Walter Isaacson wonderfully conveys how Leonardo's genius unified science and art."

—*Nature*

"Dazzling."

—*The Harvard Gazette*

"Luminous."

—*The Daily Beast*

"A full and engrossing profile of the artist."

—*The East Hampton Star*

ALSO BY WALTER ISAACSON

*The Innovators: How a Group of Hackers, Geniuses,
and Geeks Created the Digital Revolution*

Steve Jobs

American Sketches

Einstein: His Life and Universe

A Benjamin Franklin Reader

Benjamin Franklin: An American Life

Kissinger: A Biography

The Wise Men: Six Friends and the World They Made
(with Evan Thomas)

Pro and Con

CONTENTS

Acknowledgments   ix

Main Characters   xi

Currency in Italy in 1500   xiii

Note Regarding the Cover   xiii

Primary Periods of Leonardo's Life   xiii

Timeline   xiv

INTRODUCTION   I Can Also Paint   I

CHAPTER 1   Childhood   11

CHAPTER 2   Apprentice   23

CHAPTER 3   On His Own   68

CHAPTER 4   Milan   91

CHAPTER 5   Leonardo's Notebooks   105

CHAPTER 6   Court Entertainer   112

CHAPTER 7   Personal Life   129

CHAPTER 8   *Vitruvian Man*   140

CHAPTER 9   The Horse Monument   160

CHAPTER 10   Scientist   170

CHAPTER 11   Birds and Flight   181

CHAPTER 12   The Mechanical Arts   190

CHAPTER 13   Math   200

CHAPTER 14   The Nature of Man   212

CHAPTER 15   *Virgin of the Rocks*   223

CHAPTER 16   The Milan Portraits   236

CHAPTER 17   The Science of Art   260

CHAPTER 18   *The Last Supper*   279

CHAPTER 19   Personal Turmoil   293

CHAPTER 20   Florence Again   299

CHAPTER 21   Saint Anne   315

CHAPTER 22   Paintings Lost and Found   325

CHAPTER 23   Cesare Borgia   335

CHAPTER 24   Hydraulic Engineer   347

CHAPTER 25   Michelangelo and the Lost *Battles*   355

CHAPTER 26   Return to Milan   380

CHAPTER 27   Anatomy, Round Two   394

CHAPTER 28   The World and Its Waters   425

CHAPTER 29   Rome   444

CHAPTER 30   Pointing the Way   463

CHAPTER 31   The *Mona Lisa*   475

CHAPTER 32   France   495

CHAPTER 33   Conclusion   517

CODA   Describe the tongue of the woodpecker   525

Abbreviations of Frequently Cited Sources   527

Notes   533

Illustration Credits   571

Index   573

ACKNOWLEDGMENTS

Marco Cianchi professionally read the manuscript of this book, made many suggestions, helped with translations, and was a guide in Italy. A professor at the Accademia di Belle Arti in Florence, he has degrees in art history from the universities of Florence and Bologna. He is a longtime collaborator with Carlo Pedretti and is the author of many books, including *Le macchine di Leonardo* (Becocci, 1981), *Leonardo, I Dipinti* (Giunti, 1996), and *Leonardo, Anatomia* (Giunti, 1997). He has become a delightful friend.

Juliana Barone of Birkbeck College, University of London, was also a professional reader of much of the manuscript. She wrote her doctoral dissertation on Leonardo at Oxford and is the author of *Leonardo: The Codex Arundel* (British Library, 2008), *Studies of Motion: Drawings by Leonardo from the Codex Atlanticus* (De Agostini, 2011), *The Treatise on Painting* (De Agostini, 2014), and the forthcoming books *Leonardo, Poussin and Rubens* and *Leonardo in Britain*.

Dr. Barone was recommended to me by Martin Kemp, emeritus professor of art history at Oxford University and one of the great Leonardo scholars of our era. Over the past fifty years, he has authored or co-authored seventy-two books and scholarly articles on Leonardo. He graciously spent time with me at Trinity College, Oxford, shared with me his research findings and an early manuscript of his co-authored book *Mona Lisa: The People and the Painting* (Oxford University Press, 2017), and in countless emails offered his opinions on a variety of issues.

Frederick Schroeder, the curator of the Codex Leicester for Bill Gates, and Domenico Laurenza, an author of many books on Leonardo's engineering and inventions, read my sections on the Codex Leicester and provided me with their own updated translations from that work, scheduled for publication in 2018. David Linley took me to Windsor Castle to see the Leonardo drawings there and introduced me to the curator and Leonardo scholar Martin Clayton.

Other Leonardo scholars and curators who read parts of the manuscript, gave me access to collections, provided assistance, or offered ideas include Luke Syson, formerly of the National Gallery in London and now at the Metropolitan Museum of Art in New York City; Vincent Delieuvin and Ina Giscard d'Estaing of the Louvre; David Alan Brown of the National Gallery of Art in Washington, DC; Valeria Poletto of the Gallerie dell'Accademia in Venice; Pietro Marani of the Politecnico di Milano; Alberto Rocca of the Biblioteca Ambrosiana in Milan; and Jacqueline Thalmann of Christ Church, Oxford. I am also grateful to the staffs of the Villa I Tatti in Florence, the Dumbarton Oaks Library in Washington, DC, and the Harvard Fine Arts Library. Getty Images, led by Dawn Airey, adopted this book as a special project; the team overseeing the acquisition of images included David Savage, Eric Rachlis, Scott Rosen, and Jill Braaten. At the Aspen Institute, my deep thanks go to Pat Zindulka, Leah Bitounis, Eric Motley, Chloe Tabah, and other indulgent colleagues.

I also want to thank Filippo Dal Corno, an Aspen Italia Board Member and Milan's Councilor for Culture, who arranged a private tour of the Leonardo exhibition at Palazzo Reale with its renowned curator Pietro Marani, as well as the other delightful colleagues at Aspen Italia who helped me get access to Leonardo resources in Florence, Venice, and Milan.

All of my books for more than three decades have been published by Simon & Schuster, and that is because the team there is extraordinarily talented: Alice Mayhew, Carolyn Reidy, Jonathan Karp, Stuart Roberts (who shepherded this book and its illustrations), Richard Rhorer, Stephen Bedford, Jackie Seow, Kristen Lemire, Judith Hoover, Julia Prosser, Lisa Erwin, Jonathan Evans, and Paul Dippolito. During my entire writing career, Amanda Urban has been my agent, adviser, wise counselor, and friend. Strobe Talbott, my colleague from when I joined *Time* in 1979, has read the drafts of every one of my books, beginning with *The Wise Men*, made incisive comments, and offered encouragement; as we enter the dessert course of our careers, I savor the procession of memories that began when we were in our salad days.

As usual, my greatest gratitude goes to my wife, Cathy, and our daughter, Betsy, who are wise, smart, supportive, and very loving. Thank you.

MAIN CHARACTERS

Cesare Borgia (c. 1475–1507). Italian warrior, illegitimate son of Pope Alexander VI, subject of Machiavelli's *The Prince*, Leonardo employer.

Donato Bramante (1444–1514). Architect, friend of Leonardo in Milan, worked on Milan Cathedral, Pavia Cathedral, and St. Peter's in the Vatican.

Caterina Lippi (c. 1436–1493). Orphaned peasant girl from near Vinci, mother of Leonardo; later married Antonio di Piero del Vaccha, known as Accattabriga.

Charles d'Amboise (1473–1511). French governor of Milan from 1503 to 1511, Leonardo patron.

Beatrice d'Este (1475–1497). From Italy's most venerable family, married Ludovico Sforza.

Isabella d'Este (1474–1539). Beatrice's sister, the Marchesa of Mantua, tried to get Leonardo to paint her portrait.

Francesco di Giorgio (1439–1501). Artist-engineer-architect who worked with Leonardo on Milan's cathedral tower, traveled with him to Pavia, translated Vitruvius, and drew a version of Vitruvian man.

Francis I (1494–1547). King of France from 1515, last patron of Leonardo.

Pope Leo X, Giovanni de' Medici (1475–1521). Son of Lorenzo de' Medici, elected pope in 1513.

Louis XII (1462–1515). King of France from 1498, conquered Milan in 1499.

Niccolò Machiavelli (1469–1527). Florentine diplomat and writer, became envoy to Cesare Borgia and friend of Leonardo in 1502.

Giuliano de' Medici (1479–1516). Son of Lorenzo, brother of Pope Leo X, Leonardo's patron in Rome.

Lorenzo "the Magnificent" de' Medici (1449–1492). Banker, art patron, and de facto ruler of Florence from 1469 until his death.

Francesco Melzi (c. 1493–c. 1568). From a noble Milan family, joined Leonardo's household in 1507 and became a surrogate son and heir.

Michelangelo Buonarroti (1475–1564). Florentine sculptor and rival of Leonardo.

Luca Pacioli (1447–1517). Italian mathematician, friar, and friend of Leonardo.

Piero da Vinci (1427–1504). Florentine notary, father of Leonardo, did not marry Leonardo's mother, subsequently had eleven other children with four wives.

Andrea Salai, born Gian Giacomo Caprotti da Oreno (1480–1524). Entered Leonardo's household at age ten and was dubbed Salai, meaning "Little Devil."

Ludovico Sforza (1452–1508). De facto ruler of Milan from 1481, Duke of Milan from 1494 until his ouster by the French in 1499, patron of Leonardo.

Andrea del Verrocchio (c. 1435–1488). Florentine sculptor, goldsmith, and artist in whose workshop Leonardo trained and worked from 1466 to 1477.

CURRENCY IN ITALY IN 1500

The ducat was the gold coin of Venice. The florin was the gold coin of Florence. Both contained 3.5 grams (0.12 ounces) of gold, which would make them worth about $138 in 2017. One ducat or florin was worth approximately 7 lire or 120 soldi, which were silver coins.

NOTE REGARDING THE COVER

The cover is a detail of an oil painting in Florence's Uffizi Gallery that was once thought to be a self-portrait painted by Leonardo. Based on recent X-ray analysis, it is now considered to be a portrait of Leonardo by an unknown artist done in the 1600s. It is based on, or is the basis for, a similar portrait rediscovered in Italy in 2008, called the Lucan portrait of Leonardo da Vinci. It has been copied many times. A watercolor-on-ivory version painted in the 1770s by Giuseppe Macpherson is in the British Royal Collection and in 2017 was in the show "Portrait of the Artist" in the Queen's Gallery of Buckingham Palace.

PRIMARY PERIODS OF LEONARDO'S LIFE

Vinci
1452–1464

Florence
1464–1482

Milan
1482–1499

Florence
1500–1506

Milan
1506–1513

Rome
1513–1516

France
1516–1519

Becomes a member of the painters' guild; first known drawing is a landscape

c.1473

Collaborated with Verrocchio on the *Baptism of Christ*

c.1478

Portrait of Ginevra de' Benci, daughter of a wealthy Florentine banker

c.1475

1452

Born on April 15

End 100 Years' War; fall of Constantinople

Michelangelo is born

Ludovico Sforza becomes ruler of Milan
Magellan is born

Gutenberg prints the Bible

Machiavelli is born;
Lorenzo de' Medici takes power

Copernicus is born

Johannes de Spira starts publishing house in Venice

Raphael is born

Becomes an apprentice in Verrocchio's studio in Florence

The *Adoration of the Magi* commissioned

1482

Moves to Milan and begins keeping notebooks

1481

c.1468

The *Annunciation*: youthful experiment with perspective is flawed, but heralds brilliance

c.1472

science life world art

Lady with an Ermine; clay model for the horse monument is put on display in Milan

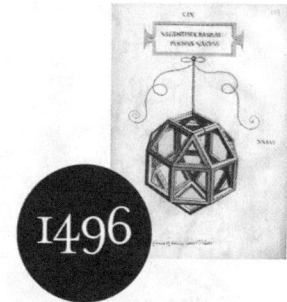

Does the drawings for Pacioli's *De divina proportione*

1496

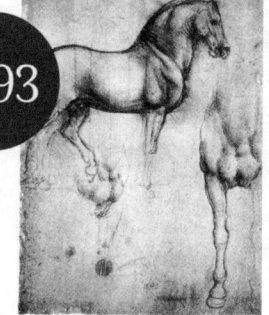

1493

1498

First attempt at a flying machine

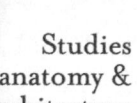

Studies anatomy & architecture

1489

Dias of Portugal rounds the southern tip of Africa

Christopher Columbus sails to the New World; Lorenzo de' Medici dies; Rodrigo Borgia becomes Pope Alexander VI

Vasco da Gama finds a sea route to India; Louis XII becomes King of France; Savonarola's Bonfire of the Vanities; France conquers Milan

Süleyman I, of the Ottoman Empire, is born; Ludovico officially becomes Duke

Savonarola deposes the Medici in Florence; King Charles VIII of France invades Italy

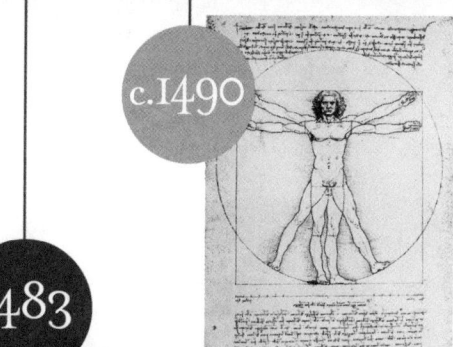

c.1490

Vitruvian Man; *Feast of Paradise* is presented for the wedding feast of the duke's nephew; Salai comes to live with Leonardo

1483

Begins *The Last Supper* in the refectory in the convent of Santa Maria delle Grazie

1495

Commissioned, along with the de Predis brothers, to paint *Virgin of the Rocks*

1499

Leaves Milan

1503

Returns to Florence, begins painting the *Mona Lisa* and works on it for the rest of his life

Studies the flight of birds; second unsuccessful attempt to fly; struggles to paint the *Battle of Anghiari*, a major commission in Florence that is eventually abandoned, unfinished.

1505

Michelangelo's statue of David; young Raphael comes to Florence to study with Leonardo and Michelangelo

Leonardo's friend, Amerigo Vespucci, publishes his account of sailing to the New World

The architect Donato Bramante is hired by the pope to rebuild St. Peter's church in Rome

1502

Returns to Milan, where he remains, on and off, for seven years

1506

1507

Painter and engineer to Louis XII

Begins to work for Cesare Borgia as military engineer

1513

c.1508

Divides his time between Milan and Florence; studies of waterworks; designs the Trivulzio monument; second *Virgin of the Rocks*

Moves to Rome; the iconic Turin drawing, a possible self-portrait done in the preceding years, often defines our image of Leonardo

Michelangelo finishes painting the Sistine Chapel; Gerardus Mercator, who produces the first map of the world, is born; Medici return to power in Florence

Andreas Vesalius, who publishes the first accurate book on human anatomy, is born in Brussels

Martin Luther launches Protestant Reformation

King Henry VIII becomes king of England

Vasari is born

Giovanni de' Medici becomes Pope Leo X

Francis I becomes king of France

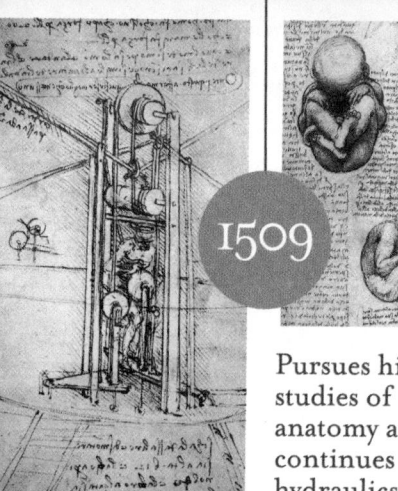

1509

1516

Moves to Amboise as a guest of Francis I

1514

Pursues his studies of anatomy and continues with hydraulics

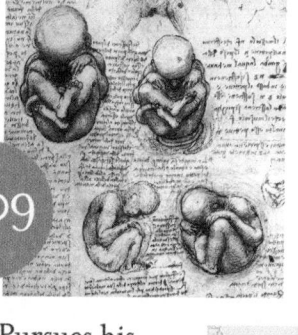

Visits Parma and Florence; Plans to drain the Pontine Marshes

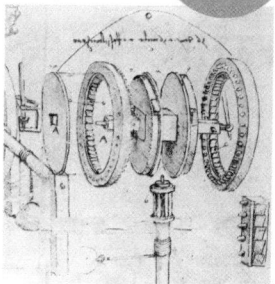

dies on May 2

1519

LEONARDO
DA VINCI

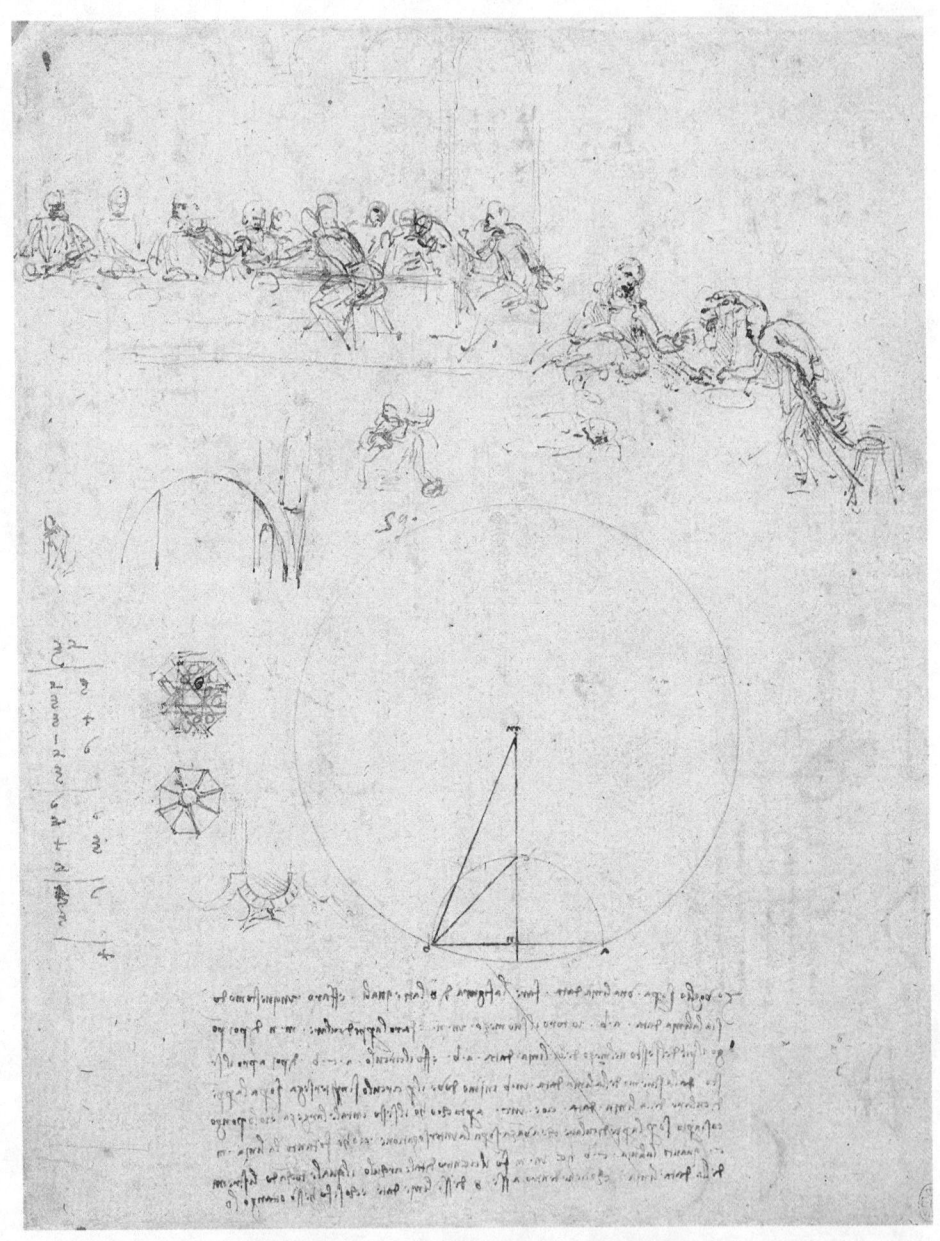

From Leonardo's notebooks c. 1495: a sketch for *The Last Supper*,
geometric studies for squaring a circle, octagonal church designs,
and a passage in his mirror-script writing.

I Can Also Paint

Around the time that he reached the unnerving milestone of turning thirty, Leonardo da Vinci wrote a letter to the ruler of Milan listing the reasons he should be given a job. He had been moderately successful as a painter in Florence, but he had trouble finishing his commissions and was searching for new horizons. In the first ten paragraphs, he touted his engineering skills, including his ability to design bridges, waterways, cannons, armored vehicles, and public buildings. Only in the eleventh paragraph, at the end, did he add that he was also an artist. "Likewise in painting, I can do everything possible," he wrote.[1]

Yes, he could. He would go on to create the two most famous paintings in history, *The Last Supper* and the *Mona Lisa*. But in his own mind, he was just as much a man of science and engineering. With a passion that was both playful and obsessive, he pursued innovative studies of anatomy, fossils, birds, the heart, flying machines, optics, botany, geology, water flows, and weaponry. Thus he became the archetype of the Renaissance Man, an inspiration to all who believe that the "infinite works of nature," as he put it, are woven together in a unity filled with marvelous patterns.[2] His ability to combine art and science, made iconic by his drawing of a perfectly proportioned man spread-eagle inside a circle and square, known as *Vitruvian Man*, made him history's most creative genius.

His scientific explorations informed his art. He peeled flesh off the faces of cadavers, delineated the muscles that move the lips, and then painted the world's most memorable smile. He studied human skulls, made layered drawings of the bones and teeth, and conveyed the skeletal agony of *Saint Jerome in the Wilderness*. He explored the mathematics of optics, showed how light rays strike the retina, and produced magical illusions of changing visual perspectives in *The Last Supper*.

By connecting his studies of light and optics to his art, he mastered the use of shading and perspective to model objects on a two-dimensional surface so they look three-dimensional. This ability to "make a flat surface display a body as if modeled and separated from this plane," Leonardo said, was "the first intention of the painter."[3] Largely due to his work, dimensionality became the supreme innovation of Renaissance art.

As he aged, he pursued his scientific inquiries not just to serve his art but out of a joyful instinct to fathom the profound beauties of creation. When he groped for a theory of why the sky appears blue, it was not simply to inform his paintings. His curiosity was pure, personal, and delightfully obsessive.

But even when he was engaged in blue-sky thinking, his science was not a separate endeavor from his art. Together they served his driving passion, which was nothing less than knowing everything there was to know about the world, including how we fit into it. He had a reverence for the wholeness of nature and a feel for the harmony of its patterns, which he saw replicated in phenomena large and small. In his notebooks he would record curls of hair, eddies of water, and whirls of air, along with some stabs at the math that might underlie such spirals. While at Windsor Castle looking at the swirling power of the "Deluge drawings" that he made near the end of his life, I asked the curator, Martin Clayton, whether he thought Leonardo had done them as works of art or of science. Even as I spoke, I realized it was a dumb question. "I do not think that Leonardo would have made that distinction," he replied.

I embarked on this book because Leonardo da Vinci is the ultimate example of the main theme of my previous biographies: how the ability to make connections across disciplines—arts and sciences, humanities and technology—is a key to innovation, imagination, and genius. Benjamin Franklin, a previous subject of mine, was a Leonardo of his era: with no formal education, he taught himself to become an imaginative polymath who was Enlightenment America's best scientist, inventor, diplomat, writer, and business strategist. He proved by flying a kite that lightning is electricity, and he invented a rod to tame it. He devised bifocal glasses, enchanting musical instruments, clean-burning stoves, charts of the Gulf Stream, and America's unique style of homespun humor. Albert Einstein, when he was stymied in his pursuit of his theory of relativity, would pull out his violin and play Mozart, which helped him reconnect with the harmonies of the cosmos. Ada Lovelace, whom I profiled in a book on innovators, combined the poetic sensibility of her father, Lord Byron, with her mother's love of the beauty of math to envision a general-purpose computer. And Steve Jobs climaxed his product launches with an image of street signs showing the intersection of the liberal arts and technology. Leonardo was his hero. "He saw beauty in both art and engineering," Jobs said, "and his ability to combine them was what made him a genius."[4]

Yes, he was a genius: wildly imaginative, passionately curious, and creative across multiple disciplines. But we should be wary of that word. Slapping the "genius" label on Leonardo oddly minimizes him by making it seem as if he were touched by lightning. His early biographer, Giorgio Vasari, a sixteenth-century artist, made this mistake: "Sometimes, in supernatural fashion, a single person is marvelously endowed by heaven with beauty, grace, and talent in such abundance that his every act is divine and everything he does clearly comes from God rather than from human art."[5] In fact, Leonardo's genius was a human one, wrought by his own will and ambition. It did not come from being the divine recipient, like Newton or Einstein, of a mind with so much processing power that we mere mortals cannot fathom it. Leonardo had almost no schooling and could barely read Latin or do long division. His genius was of the type we can understand, even take lessons from. It was based on skills we can aspire to improve in ourselves, such as curiosity and intense observation. He had an imagination so excitable that it flirted with the edges of fantasy, which is also something we can try to preserve in ourselves and indulge in our children.

Leonardo's fantasies pervaded everything he touched: his theatrical productions, plans to divert rivers, designs for ideal cities, schemes for flying machines, and almost every aspect of his art as well as engineering. His letter to the ruler of Milan is an example, since his military engineering skills then existed mainly in his mind. His initial role at the court was not building weapons but conjuring up festivals and pageants. Even at the height of his career, most of his fighting and flying contraptions were more visionary than practical.

At first I thought that his susceptibility to fantasia was a failing, revealing a lack of discipline and diligence that was related to his propensity to abandon artworks and treatises unfinished. To some extent, that is true. Vision without execution is hallucination. But I also came to believe that his ability to blur the line between reality and fantasy, just like his sfumato techniques for blurring the lines of a painting, was a key to his creativity. Skill without imagination is barren. Leonardo knew how to marry observation and imagination, which made him history's consummate innovator.

My starting point for this book was not Leonardo's art masterpieces but his notebooks. His mind, I think, is best revealed in the more than 7,200 pages of his notes and scribbles that, miraculously, survive to this day. Paper turns out to be a superb information-storage technology, still readable after five hundred years, which our own tweets likely won't be.

Fortunately, Leonardo could not afford to waste paper, so he crammed every inch of his pages with miscellaneous drawings and looking-glass jottings that seem random but provide intimations of his mental leaps. Scribbled alongside each other, with rhyme if not reason, are math calculations, sketches of his devilish young boyfriend, birds, flying machines, theater props, eddies of water, blood valves, grotesque heads, angels, siphons, plant stems, sawed-apart skulls, tips for painters, notes on the eye and optics, weapons of war, fables, riddles, and studies for paintings. The cross-disciplinary brilliance whirls across every page, providing a delightful display of a mind dancing with nature. His notebooks are the greatest record of curiosity ever created, a wondrous guide to the person whom the eminent art historian Kenneth Clark called "the most relentlessly curious man in history."[6]

My favorite gems in his notebooks are his to-do lists, which sparkle with his curiosity. One of them, dating from the 1490s in Milan, is that day's list of things he wants to learn. "The measurement of Milan and its suburbs," is the first entry. This has a practical purpose, as revealed by an item later in the list: "Draw Milan." Others show him relentlessly seeking out people whose brains he could pick: "Get the master of arithmetic to show you how to square a triangle. . . . Ask Giannino the Bombardier about how the tower of Ferrara is walled. . . . Ask Benedetto Protinari by what means they walk on ice in Flanders. . . . Get a master of hydraulics to tell you how to repair a lock, canal and mill in the Lombard manner. . . . Get the measurement of the sun promised me by Maestro Giovanni Francese, the Frenchman."[7] He is insatiable.

Over and over again, year after year, Leonardo lists things he must do and learn. Some involve the type of close observation most of us rarely pause to do. "Observe the goose's foot: if it were always open or always closed the creature would not be able to make any kind of movement." Others involve why-is-the-sky-blue questions about phenomena so commonplace that we rarely pause to wonder about them. "Why is the fish in the water swifter than the bird in the air when it ought to be the contrary since the water is heavier and thicker than the air?"[8]

Best of all are the questions that seem completely random. "Describe the tongue of the woodpecker," he instructs himself.[9] Who on earth would decide one day, for no apparent reason, that he wanted to know what the tongue of a woodpecker looks like? How would you even find out? It's not information Leonardo needed to paint a picture or even to understand the flight of birds. But there it is, and, as we shall see, there are fascinating things to learn about the tongue of the woodpecker. The reason he wanted to know was because he was Leonardo: curious, passionate, and always filled with wonder.

Oddest of all, there is this entry: "Go every Saturday to the hot bath where you will see naked men."[10] We can imagine Leonardo wanting to do that, for reasons both anatomical and aesthetic. But did he really need to remind himself to do it? The next item on the list is "Inflate the lungs of a pig and observe whether they increase in width and in length, or only in width." As the *New Yorker* art critic Adam Gopnik once wrote, "Leonardo remains weird, matchlessly weird, and nothing to be done about it."[11]

To wrestle with these issues, I decided to write a book that used these notebooks as its foundation. I started by making pilgrimages to see the originals in Milan, Florence, Paris, Seattle, Madrid, London, and Windsor Castle. That followed Leonardo's injunction to begin any investigation by going to the source: "He who can go to the fountain does not go to the water-jar."[12] I also immersed myself in the little-tapped trove of academic articles and doctoral dissertations on Leonardo, each of which represents years of diligent work on very specific topics. In the past few decades, especially since the rediscovery of his Codices Madrid in 1965, there have been great advances in the analysis and interpretation of his writings. Likewise, modern technology has revealed new information about his painting and techniques.

After immersing myself in Leonardo, I did the best I could to be more observant of phenomena that I used to ignore, making a special effort to notice things the way he did. When I saw sunlight hitting drapes, I pushed myself to pause and look at the way the shadows caressed the folds. I tried to see how light that was reflected from one object subtly colored the shadows of another object. I noticed how the glint of a lustrous spot on a shiny surface moved when I tilted my head. When I looked at a distant tree and a near one, I tried to visualize the lines of perspective. When I saw an eddy of water, I compared it to a ringlet of hair. When I couldn't understand a math concept, I did the best I was able to visualize it. When I saw people at a supper, I studied the relationship of their motions to their emotions. When I saw the hint of a smile come across someone's lips, I tried to fathom her inner mysteries.

No, I did not come anywhere close to being Leonardo, mastering his insights, or mustering a modicum of his talents. I did not get a millimeter closer to being able to design a glider, invent a new way to draw maps, or paint the *Mona Lisa*. I had to push myself to be truly curious about the tongue of the woodpecker. But I did learn from Leonardo how a desire to marvel about the world that we encounter each day can make each moment of our lives richer.

There are three major early accounts of Leonardo by writers who were almost contemporaries. The painter Giorgio Vasari, born in 1511 (eight years before Leonardo died), wrote the first real art history book, *Lives of the Most Eminent Painters, Sculptors, and Architects*, in 1550 and came out with a revised version in 1568 that included corrections based on further interviews with people who knew Leonardo, including his pupil Francesco Melzi.[13] A Florentine chauvinist, Vasari gave Leonardo and especially Michelangelo the most fulsome treatments for creating what he dubbed, for the first time in print, a "renaissance" in art.[14] As Huckleberry Finn said of Mark Twain, there were things that Vasari stretched, but he told the truth, mainly. The remainder is a mix of gossip, embellishments, inventions, and unintentional errors. The problem is knowing which picturesque anecdotes—such as Leonardo's teacher throwing down his own brush in awe of his pupil—fall into which category.

An anonymous manuscript written in the 1540s, known as the "Anonimo Gaddiano" after the family that once owned it, contains colorful details about Leonardo and other Florentines. Once again, some of the assertions, such as that Leonardo lived and worked with Lorenzo de' Medici, may be embellished, but it provides colorful details that ring true, such as that Leonardo liked to wear rose-colored tunics that reached only to his knee even though others wore long garments.[15]

A third early source is by Gian Paolo Lomazzo, a painter who became a writer when he went blind. He wrote an unpublished manuscript called *Dreams and Arguments* in about 1560 and then published a voluminous treatise on art in 1584. He was the student of a painter who had known Leonardo, and he interviewed Leonardo's pupil Melzi, so he had access to some firsthand stories. Lomazzo is especially revealing about Leonardo's sexual proclivities. In addition, there are shorter accounts contained in writings by two Leonardo contemporaries, Antonio Billi, a Florentine merchant, and Paolo Giovio, an Italian physician and historian.

Many of these early accounts mention Leonardo's looks and personality. He is described as a man of eye-catching beauty and grace. He had flowing golden curls, a muscular build, remarkable physical strength, and an elegance of bearing when he was walking through town in his colorful garb or riding on a horse. "Beautiful in person and aspect, Leonardo was well-proportioned and graceful," according to the Anonimo. In addition, he was a charming conversationalist and a lover of nature, renowned for being sweet and gentle to both people and animals.

There is less agreement about certain specifics. In the course of my research I discovered that many facts about Leonardo's life, from the site of his birth to the scene at his death, have been the subject of debate, mythology, and mystery. I try to give my best assessment and then describe the controversies and counterarguments in the notes.

I also discovered, at first to my consternation and then to my pleasure, that Leonardo was not always a giant. He made mistakes. He went off on tangents, literally, pursuing math problems that became time-sucking diversions. Notoriously, he left many of his paintings unfinished, most notably the *Adoration of the Magi, Saint Jerome in the Wilderness*, and the *Battle of Anghiari*. As a result, there exist now at most fifteen paintings fully or mainly attributable to him.[16]

Although generally considered by his contemporaries to be friendly and gentle, Leonardo was at times dark and troubled. His notebooks and drawings are a window into his fevered, imaginative, manic, and sometimes elated mind. Had he been a student at the outset of the twenty-first century, he may have been put on a pharmaceutical regimen to alleviate his mood swings and attention-deficit disorder. One need not subscribe to the artist-as-troubled-genius trope to believe we are fortunate that Leonardo was left to his own devices to slay his demons while conjuring up his dragons.

In one of the quirky riddles in his notebooks is this clue: "Huge figures will appear in human shape, and the nearer you get to them, the more their immense size will diminish." The answer: "The shadow cast by a man at night with a light."[17] Although the same may be said of Leonardo, I believe he is, in fact, not diminished by being discovered to be human. Both his shadow and his reality deserve to loom large. His lapses and oddities allow us to relate to him, to feel that we might emulate him, and to appreciate his moments of triumph even more.

The fifteenth century of Leonardo and Columbus and Gutenberg was a time of invention, exploration, and the spread of knowledge by new technologies. In short, it was a time like our own. That is why we have much to learn from Leonardo. His ability to combine art, science, technology, the humanities, and imagination remains an enduring recipe for creativity. So, too, was his ease at being a bit of a misfit: illegitimate, gay, vegetarian, left-handed, easily distracted, and at times heretical. Florence flourished in the fifteenth century because it was comfortable with such people. Above all, Leonardo's relentless curiosity and experimentation should remind us of the importance of instilling, in both ourselves and our children, not just received knowledge but a willingness to question it—to be imaginative and, like talented misfits and rebels in any era, to think different.

The town of Vinci and the church where Leonardo was baptized.

CHAPTER 1

Childhood

Vinci, 1452–1464

DA VINCI

Leonardo da Vinci had the good luck to be born out of wedlock. Otherwise, he would have been expected to become a notary, like the firstborn legitimate sons in his family stretching back at least five generations.

His family roots can be traced to the early 1300s, when his great-great-great-grandfather, Michele, practiced as a notary in the Tuscan hill town of Vinci, about seventeen miles west of Florence.* With the rise of Italy's mercantile economy, notaries played an important role drawing up commercial contracts, land sales, wills, and other legal documents in Latin, often garnishing them with historical references and literary flourishes.

---

* Leonardo da Vinci is sometimes incorrectly called "da Vinci," as if that were his last name rather than a descriptor meaning "from Vinci." However, the usage is not as egregious as some purists proclaim. During Leonardo's lifetime, Italians increasingly began to regularize and register the use of hereditary surnames, and many of these, such as Genovese and DiCaprio, derived from family hometowns. Both Leonardo and his father, Piero, frequently appended "da Vinci" to their names. When Leonardo moved to Milan, his friend the court poet Bernardo Bellincioni referred to him in writing as "Leonardo Vinci, the Florentine."

Because Michele was a notary, he was entitled to the honorific "Ser" and thus became known as Ser Michele da Vinci. His son and grandson were even more successful notaries, the latter becoming a chancellor of Florence. The next in line, Antonio, was an anomaly. He used the honorific Ser and married the daughter of a notary, but he seems to have lacked the da Vinci ambition. He mostly spent his life living off the proceeds from family lands, tilled by sharecroppers, that produced a modest amount of wine, olive oil, and wheat.

Antonio's son Piero made up for the lassitude by ambitiously pursuing success in Pistoia and Pisa, and then by about 1451, when he was twenty-five, establishing himself in Florence. A contract he notarized that year gave his work address as "at the Palazzo del Podestà," the magistrates' building (now the Bargello Museum) facing the Palazzo della Signoria, the seat of government. He became a notary for many of the city's monasteries and religious orders, the town's Jewish community, and on at least one occasion the Medici family.[1]

On one of his visits back to Vinci, Piero had a relationship with an unmarried local peasant girl, and in the spring of 1452 they had a son. Exercising his little-used notarial handwriting, the boy's grandfather Antonio recorded the birth on the bottom of the last page of a notebook that had belonged to his own grandfather. "1452: There was born to me a grandson, the son of Ser Piero my son, on the 15th day of April, a Saturday, at the third hour of the night [about 10 p.m.]. He bears the name Leonardo."[2]

Leonardo's mother was not considered worth mentioning in Antonio's birth notation nor in any other birth or baptism record. From a tax document five years later, we learn only her first name, Caterina. Her identity was long a mystery to modern scholars. She was thought to be in her mid-twenties, and some researchers speculated that she was an Arab slave, or perhaps a Chinese slave.[3]

In fact, she was an orphaned and impoverished sixteen-year-old from the Vinci area named Caterina Lippi. Proving that there are still things to be rediscovered about Leonardo, the art historian Martin Kemp of Oxford and the archival researcher Giuseppe Pallanti of Florence produced evidence in 2017 documenting her background.[4]

Born in 1436 to a poor farmer, Caterina was orphaned when she was fourteen. She and her infant brother moved in with their grandmother, who died a year later, in 1451. Left to fend for herself and her brother, Caterina had a relationship in July of that year with Piero da Vinci, then twenty-four, who was prominent and prosperous.

There was little likelihood they would marry. Although described by one earlier biographer as "of good blood,"[5] Caterina was of a different social class, and Piero was probably already betrothed to his future wife, an appropriate match: a sixteen-year-old named Albiera who was the daughter of a prominent Florentine shoemaker. He and Albiera were wed within eight months of Leonardo's birth. The marriage, socially and professionally advantageous to both sides, had likely been arranged, and the dowry contracted, before Leonardo was born.

Keeping things tidy and convenient, shortly after Leonardo was born Piero helped to set up a marriage for Caterina to a local farmer and kiln worker who had ties to the da Vinci family. Named Antonio di Piero del Vacca, he was called Accattabriga, which means "Troublemaker," though fortunately he does not seem to have been one.

Leonardo's paternal grandparents and his father had a family house with a small garden right next to the walls of the castle in the heart of the village of Vinci. That is where Leonardo may have been born, though there are reasons to think not. It might not have been convenient or appropriate to have a pregnant and then breast-feeding peasant woman living in the crowded da Vinci family home, especially as Ser Piero was negotiating a dowry from the prominent family whose daughter he was planning to marry.

Instead, according to legend and the local tourist industry, Leonardo's birthplace may have been a gray stone tenant cottage next to a farmhouse two miles up the road from Vinci in the adjacent hamlet of Anchiano, which is now the site of a small Leonardo museum. Some of this property had been owned since 1412 by the family of Piero di Malvolto, a close friend of the da Vincis. He was the godfather of Piero da Vinci and, in 1452, would be a godfather of Piero's newborn son, Leonardo—which would have made sense if Leonardo had been born on his property. The families were very close. Leonardo's grandfather Antonio had served as a witness to a contract involving some parts of Piero di Malvolto's property. The notes describing the exchange say that Antonio was at a nearby house playing backgammon when he was asked to come over for that task. Piero da Vinci would buy some of the property in the 1480s.

At the time of Leonardo's birth, Piero di Malvolto's seventy-year-old widowed mother lived on the property. So here in the hamlet of Anchiano, an easy two-mile walk from the village of Vinci, living alone in a farmhouse that had a run-down cottage next door, was a widow who was a trusted friend to at least two generations of the da Vinci family. Her dilapidated cottage (for tax purposes the family claimed it as uninhabitable) may have been the ideal place to shelter Caterina while she was pregnant, as per local lore.[6]

Leonardo was born on a Saturday, and the following day he was baptized by the local priest at the parish church of Vinci. The baptismal font is still there. Despite the circumstances of his birth, it was a large and public event. There were ten godparents giving witness, including Piero di Malvolto, far more than the average at the church, and the guests included prominent local gentry. A week later, Piero da Vinci left Caterina and their infant son behind and returned to Florence, where that Monday he was in his office notarizing papers for clients.[7]

Leonardo left us no comment on the circumstances of his birth, but there is one tantalizing allusion in his notebooks to the favors that nature bestows upon a love child. "The man who has intercourse aggressively and uneasily will produce children who are irritable and untrustworthy," he wrote, "but if the intercourse is done with great love and desire on both sides, the child will be of great intellect, witty, lively, and lovable."[8] One assumes, or at least hopes, that he considered himself in the latter category.

He split his childhood between two homes. Caterina and Accattabriga settled on a small farm on the outskirts of Vinci, and they remained friendly with Piero da Vinci. Twenty years later, Accattabriga was working in a kiln that was rented by Piero, and they served as witnesses for each other on a few contracts and deeds over the years. In the years following Leonardo's birth, Caterina and Accattabriga

had four girls and a boy. Piero and Albiera, however, remained childless. In fact, until Leonardo was twenty-four, his father had no other
children. (Piero would make up for it during his third and fourth
marriages, having at least eleven children.)

With his father living mainly in Florence and his mother nurturing a growing family of her own, Leonardo by age five was primarily
living in the da Vinci family home with his leisure-loving grandfather
Antonio and his wife. In the 1457 tax census, Antonio listed the dependents residing with him, including his grandson: "Leonardo, son
of the said Ser Piero, *non legittimo*, born of him and of Caterina, who
is now the woman of Achattabriga."

Also living in the household was Piero's youngest brother, Francesco, who was only fifteen years older than his nephew Leonardo.
Francesco inherited a love of country leisure and was described in
a tax document by his own father, in a pot-calling-the-kettle way,
as "one who hangs around the villa and does nothing."[9] He became
Leonardo's beloved uncle and at times surrogate father. In the first
edition of his biography, Vasari makes the telling mistake, later corrected, of identifying Piero as Leonardo's uncle.

"A GOLDEN AGE FOR BASTARDS"

As Leonardo's well-attended baptism attests, being born out of
wedlock was not a cause for public shame. The nineteenth-century
cultural historian Jacob Burckhardt went so far as to label Renaissance Italy "a golden age for bastards."[10] Especially among the ruling
and aristocratic classes, being illegitimate was no hindrance. Pius II,
who was the pope when Leonardo was born, wrote about visiting
Ferrara, where his welcoming party included seven princes from the
ruling Este family, among them the reigning duke, all born out of
wedlock. "It is an extraordinary thing about that family," Pius wrote,
"that no legitimate heir has ever inherited the principate; the sons of
their mistresses have been so much more fortunate than those of their
wives."[11] (Pius himself fathered at least two illegitimate children.)
Pope Alexander VI, also during Leonardo's lifetime, had multiple
mistresses and illegitimate children, one of whom was Cesare Borgia,

who became a cardinal, commander of the papal armies, an employer of Leonardo, and the subject of Machiavelli's *The Prince*.

For members of the middle classes, however, illegitimacy was not as readily accepted. Protective of their new status, merchants and professionals formed guilds that enforced moral strictures. Although some of the guilds accepted the illegitimate sons of their members, that was not the case with the Arte dei Giuduci e Notai, the venerable (founded in 1197) guild of judges and notaries to which Leonardo's father belonged. "The notary was a certified witness and scribe," Thomas Kuehn wrote in *Illegitimacy in Renaissance Florence*. "His trustworthiness had to be above reproach. He had to be someone fully in the mainstream of society."[12]

These strictures had an upside. Illegitimacy freed some imaginative and free-spirited young men to be creative at a time when creativity was increasingly rewarded. Among the poets, artists, and artisans born out of wedlock were Petrarch, Boccaccio, Lorenzo Ghiberti, Filippo Lippi, his son Filippino, Leon Battista Alberti, and of course Leonardo.

Being born out of wedlock was more complex than merely being an outsider. It created an ambiguity of status. "The problem with bastards was that they were part of the family, but not totally," wrote Kuehn. That helped some be, or forced them to be, more adventurous and improvisational. Leonardo was a member of a middle-class family but separate from it. Like so many writers and artists, he grew up feeling a part of the world but also detached. This limbo extended to inheritance: a combination of conflicting laws and contradictory court precedents left it unclear whether a son born out of wedlock could be an heir, as Leonardo was to find out in legal battles with his half-brothers many years later. "Management of such ambiguities was one of the hallmarks of life in a Renaissance city-state," explained Kuehn. "It was related to the more celebrated creativity of a city like Florence in the arts and humanism."[13]

Because Florence's guild of notaries barred those who were *non legittimo*, Leonardo was able to benefit from the note-taking instincts that were ingrained in his family heritage while being free to pursue his own creative passions. This was fortunate. He would have made a poor notary: he got bored and distracted too easily, especially when a project became routine rather than creative.[14]

DISCIPLE OF EXPERIENCE

Another upside for Leonardo of being born out of wedlock was that he was not sent to one of the "Latin schools" that taught the classics and humanities to well-groomed aspiring professionals and merchants of the early Renaissance.[15] Other than a little training in commercial math at what was known as an "abacus school," Leonardo was mainly self-taught. He often seemed defensive about being an "unlettered man," as he dubbed himself with some irony. But he also took pride that his lack of formal schooling led him to be a disciple of experience and experiment. "Leonardo da Vinci, disscepolo della sperientia,"[16] he once signed himself. This freethinking attitude saved him from being an acolyte of traditional thinking. In his notebooks he unleashed a blast at what he called the pompous fools who would disparage him for this:

> I am fully aware that my not being a man of letters may cause certain presumptuous people to think that they may with reason blame me, alleging that I am a man without learning. Foolish folk! . . . They strut about puffed up and pompous, decked out and adorned not with their own labors, but by those of others. . . . They will say that because I have no book learning I cannot properly express what I desire to describe—but they do not know that my subjects require experience rather than the words of others.[17]

Thus was Leonardo spared from being trained to accept dusty Scholasticism or the medieval dogmas that had accumulated in the centuries since the decline of classical science and original thinking. His lack of reverence for authority and his willingness to challenge received wisdom would lead him to craft an empirical approach for understanding nature that foreshadowed the scientific method developed more than a century later by Bacon and Galileo. His method was rooted in experiment, curiosity, and the ability to marvel at phenomena that the rest of us rarely pause to ponder after we've out-grown our wonder years.

To that was added an intense desire and ability to observe the wonders of nature. He pushed himself to perceive shapes and shadows with wondrous precision. He was particularly good at apprehending movement, from the motions of a flapping wing to the emotions flickering across a face. On this foundation he built experiments, some conducted in his mind, others with drawings, and a few with physical objects. "First I shall do some experiments before I proceed further," he announced, "because my intention is to consult experience first and then with reasoning show why such experience is bound to operate in such a way."[18]

It was a good time for a child with such ambitions and talents to be born. In 1452 Johannes Gutenberg had just opened his publishing house, and soon others were using his moveable-type press to print books that would empower unschooled but brilliant people like Leonardo. Italy was beginning a rare forty-year period during which it was not wracked by wars among its city-states. Literacy, numeracy, and income were rising dramatically as power shifted from titled landowners to urban merchants and bankers, who benefited from advances in law, accounting, credit, and insurance. The Ottoman Turks were about to capture Constantinople, unleashing on Italy a migration of fleeing scholars with bundles of manuscripts containing the ancient wisdom of Euclid, Ptolemy, Plato, and Aristotle. Born within about a year of Leonardo were Christopher Columbus and Amerigo Vespucci, who would lead an era of exploration. And Florence, with its booming merchant class of status-seeking patrons, had become the cradle of Renaissance art and humanism.

CHILDHOOD MEMORIES

The most vivid memory Leonardo had of his infancy was one he recorded fifty years later, when he was studying the flight of birds. He was writing about a hawk-like bird called a kite, which has a forked tail and elegant long wings that allow it to soar and glide. Observing it with his typical acuity, Leonardo perceived precisely how it opened its wings and then spread and lowered its tail when it landed.[19] This aroused a memory from when he was a baby: "Writing about the kite seems to be my destiny since among the first recollections of my infancy, it seemed to me that, as I was in my cradle, a kite came to me and opened my mouth with its tail and struck me several times with its tail inside my lips."[20] Like much of what came from Leonardo's mind, there was probably some fantasy and fabulism in the brew. It is hard to imagine a bird actually landing in a cradle and prying open a baby's mouth with its tail, and Leonardo appears to acknowledge this by using the phrase "it seemed to me," as if it were perhaps partly a dream.

All of this—a childhood with two mothers, an often absent father, and a dreamlike oral encounter with a flapping tail—would provide great fodder for a Freudian analyst. And it did—from Freud himself. In 1910 Freud used the kite tale as the foundation for a short book, *Leonardo da Vinci and a Memory of His Childhood.*[21]

Freud got off to a stumbling start by using a poor German translation of Leonardo's note that mistakenly called the bird a vulture rather than a kite. This sent him into a long tangential explanation about the symbolism of vultures in ancient Egypt and the etymological relationship of the words for *vulture* and *mother*, all of which was irrelevant and, Freud later admitted, embarrassing.[22] Leaving aside the bird mix-up, the main thrust of Freud's analysis was that the word for *tail* in many languages, including Italian (*coda*), is slang for "penis" and that Leonardo's memory was related to his homosexuality. "The situation contained in the fantasy, that a vulture opened the mouth of the child and forcefully belabored it with its tail, corresponds to the idea of fellatio," Freud wrote. Leonardo's repressed desires, he speculated, were channeled into his feverish creativity, but he left many works unfinished because he was inhibited.

These interpretations have prompted some devastating critiques, most famously by art historian Meyer Schapiro,[23] and they seem, at least to me, to reveal more about Freud than about Leonardo. Biographers should be cautious about psychoanalyzing someone who lived five centuries earlier. Leonardo's dreamlike memory may have simply reflected his lifelong interest in the flight of birds, which is how he framed it. And it does not take a Freud to understand that sexual drives can be sublimated into ambition and other passions. Leonardo said so himself. "Intellectual passion drives out sensuality," he wrote in one of his notebooks.[24]

A better source for insight into Leonardo's formative character and motivations is another personal memory he recorded, this one about hiking near Florence. The recollection involved chancing upon a dark cave and pondering whether he should enter. "Having wandered some distance among gloomy rocks, I came to the mouth of a great cavern, in front of which I stood some time, astonished," he recalled. "Bending back and forth, I tried to see whether I could discover anything inside, but the darkness within prevented that. Suddenly there arose in me two contrary emotions, fear and desire—fear of the threatening dark cave, desire to see whether there were any marvelous thing within."[25]

Desire won. His unstoppable curiosity triumphed, and Leonardo went into the cave. There he discovered, embedded in the wall, a fossil whale. "Oh mighty and once-living instrument of nature," he wrote, "your vast strength was to no avail."[26] Some scholars have assumed that he was describing a fantasy hike or riffing on some verses by Seneca. But his notebook page and those surrounding it are filled with descriptions of layers of fossil shells, and many fossilized whale bones have in fact been discovered in Tuscany.[27]

The whale fossil triggered a dark vision of what would be, throughout his life, one of his deepest forebodings, that of an apocalyptic deluge. On the next side of the sheet he described at length the furious power once held by the long-dead whale: "You lashed with swift, branching fins and forked tail, creating in the sea sudden tempests that buffeted and submerged ships." Then he turned philosophical. "Oh time, swift despoiler of all things, how many kings, how many nations hast thou undone, and how many changes of states and of circumstances have happened since this wondrous fish perished."

By this point Leonardo's fears were about a realm far different from whatever dangers might be lurking inside the cave. Instead they were driven by an existential dread in the face of the destructive powers of nature. He began scribbling rapidly, using a silverpoint on a red-tinted page, describing an apocalypse that begins with water and ends with fire. "The rivers will be deprived of their waters, the earth will no longer put forth her greenery; the fields will no more be decked with waving corn; all the animals, finding no fresh grass for pasture, will die," he wrote. "In this way the fertile and fruitful earth will be forced to end with the element of fire; and then its surface will be left burnt up to cinder and this will be the end of all earthly nature."[28]

The dark cave that Leonardo's curiosity compelled him to enter offered up both scientific discoveries and imaginative fantasies, strands that would be interwoven throughout his life. He would weather storms, literally and psychologically, and he would encounter dark recesses of the earth and soul. But his curiosity about nature would always impel him to explore more. Both his fascinations and his forebodings would be expressed in his art, beginning with his depiction of Saint Jerome agonizing near the mouth of a cave and culminating in his drawings and writings about an apocalyptic deluge.

Florence in the 1480s, the cathedral with Brunelleschi's dome in the center
and the Palazzo della Signoria, the seat of government, to its right.

CHAPTER 2

Apprentice

THE MOVE

Until he was twelve, Leonardo had a life in Vinci that, despite the complexities of being part of an extended family, was quite settled. He lived primarily with his grandparents and his idle uncle Francesco in the family house in the heart of Vinci. His father and stepmother were listed as living there when Leonardo was five, but after that their primary residence was in Florence. Leonardo's mother and her husband lived with their growing brood of children, along with Accattabriga's parents and his brother's family, in a farmhouse an easy walk from town.

But in 1464 this world was disrupted. His stepmother, Albiera, died in childbirth, along with what would have been her first child. Leonardo's grandfather Antonio, the head of the Vinci household, also had recently died. So just as Leonardo was reaching the age when he needed to prepare for a trade, his father, living alone and probably lonely, brought him to Florence.[1]

Leonardo rarely wrote in his notebooks about his own emotions, so it is hard to know what he felt about the move. But the fables he recorded sometimes give a glimpse of his sentiments. One described the sad odyssey of a stone perched on a hill surrounded by colorful flowers and a grove of trees—in other words, a place like Vinci. Looking at the crowd of stones along the road below, it decided it wanted to join them. "What am I doing here among these plants?" the stone asked. "I want to live in the company of my fellow stones." So it rolled down to the others. "After a while," Leonardo recounted, "it found itself in continual distress from the wheels of the carts, the iron hoofs of horses, and the feet of the passers-by. One rolled it over, another trod upon it. Sometimes the stone raised itself up a little as it lay covered with mud or the dung of some animal, but it was in vain that it looked up at the spot whence it had come as a place of solitude and tranquil peace." Leonardo drew a moral: "This is what happens to those who leave a life of solitary contemplation and choose to come to dwell in cities among people full of infinite evil."[2]

His notebooks have many other maxims praising the countryside and solitude. "Leave your family and friends and go over the mountains and valleys into the country," he instructed aspiring painters. "While you are alone you are entirely your own master."[3] These paeans to country living are romantic and, for those who cherish the image of lonely genius, quite appealing. But they are infused with fantasy. Leonardo would spend almost all of his career in Florence, Milan, and Rome, crowded centers of creativity and commerce, usually surrounded by students, companions, and patrons. He rarely retreated alone to the countryside for an extended period of solitude. Like many artists, he was stimulated by being with people of diverse interests and (willing to contradict himself in his notebooks) declared, "Drawing in company is much better than alone."[4] The impulses of his grandfather and uncle, who both practiced the quiet country life, were imprinted in Leonardo's imagination but not practiced in his life.

During his early years in Florence, Leonardo lived with his father, who arranged for him to get a rudimentary education and would soon help him get a good apprenticeship and commissions. But there is one significant thing that Ser Piero did not do, which would have been easy enough for a well-connected notary: go through the legal process of having his son legitimated. This could be accomplished by the father and child appearing before a local official known as a "count palatine," usually a dignitary who had been granted power to act on such matters, and presenting a petition as the child knelt.[5] Piero's decision not to do this for Leonardo is particularly surprising, since he then had no other children of his own.

Perhaps one reason that Piero did not legitimate Leonardo was that he hoped to have as his heir a son who would follow family tradition and become a notary, and it was already clear, by the time Leonardo turned twelve, that he was not so inclined. According to Vasari, Piero noticed that his son "never ceased drawing and sculpting, pursuits which suited his fancy more than any other." In addition, the notary guild had a rule, which may have been difficult to circumvent, that denied membership even to out-of-wedlock sons who had been legitimated. So Piero apparently saw no reason to go through the process. By not legitimating Leonardo, he could hope to have another son who would be his heir as a notary. A year later Piero married the daughter of another prominent Florence notary, but it would only be after his third marriage, in 1475 to a woman six years younger than Leonardo, that he would produce a legitimate heir who indeed became a notary.

FLORENCE

There was no place then, and few places ever, that offered a more stimulating environment for creativity than Florence in the 1400s. Its economy, once dominated by unskilled wool-spinners, had flourished by becoming one that, like our own time, interwove art, technology, and commerce. It featured artisans working with silk makers and merchants to create fabrics that were works of art. In 1472 there were eighty-four wood-carvers, eighty-three silk workers, thirty master painters, and forty-four goldsmiths and jewelry craftsmen working in Florence. It was also a center of banking; the florin, noted for its gold purity, was the dominant standard currency in all of Europe, and the adoption of double-entry bookkeeping that recorded debits and credits permitted commerce to flourish. Its leading thinkers embraced a Renaissance humanism that put its faith in the dignity of the individual and in the aspiration to find happiness on this earth through knowledge. Fully a third of Florence's population was literate, the highest rate in Europe. By embracing trade, it became a center of finance and a cauldron of ideas.

"Beautiful Florence has all seven of the fundamental things a city requires for perfection," the essayist Benedetto Dei wrote in 1472, when Leonardo was living there. "First of all, it enjoys complete liberty; second, it has a large, rich, and elegantly dressed population; third, it has a river with clear, pure water, and mills within its walls; fourth, it rules over castles, towns, lands and people; fifth, it has a university, and both Greek and accounting are taught; sixth, it has masters in every art; seventh, it has banks and business agents all over the world."[6] Each one of those assets was valuable for a city, just as they are today: not only the "liberty" and "pure water," but also that the population was "elegantly dressed" and that the university was renowned for teaching accounting as well as Greek.

The city's cathedral was the most beautiful in Italy. In the 1430s it had been crowned with the world's largest dome, built by the architect Filippo Brunelleschi, which was a triumph of both art and engineering, and linking those two disciplines was a key to Florence's creativity. Many of the city's artists were also architects, and its fabric industry had been built by combining technology, design, chemistry, and commerce.

This mixing of ideas from different disciplines became the norm as people of diverse talents intermingled. Silk makers worked with goldbeaters to create enchanted fashions. Architects and artists developed the science of perspective. Wood-carvers worked with architects to adorn the city's 108 churches. Shops became studios. Merchants became financiers. Artisans became artists.[7]

When Leonardo arrived, Florence's population was 40,000, which is about what it had been for a century but down from the 100,000 or so who lived there in 1300, before the Black Death and subsequent waves of plague. There were at least a hundred families that could be considered very wealthy, plus some five thousand guild members, shopkeepers, and merchants who were part of a prosperous middle class. Because most of them were new to wealth, they had to establish and assert their status. They did so by commissioning distinctive

works of art, buying luxurious clothes of silk and gold, building palatial mansions (thirty went up between 1450 and 1470), and becoming
patrons of literature, poetry, and humanist philosophy. Consumption
was conspicuous but tasteful. By the time Leonardo arrived, Florence
had more wood-carvers than butchers. The city itself had become a
work of art. "There is no place more beautiful in all the world," the
poet Ugolino Verino wrote.[8]

Unlike some city-states elsewhere in Italy, Florence was not ruled
by hereditary royalty. More than a century before Leonardo arrived,
the most prosperous merchants and guild leaders crafted a republic whose elected delegates met at the Palazzo della Signoria, now
known as the Palazzo Vecchio. "The people were kept amused every
day by shows, festivals, and novelties," the fifteenth-century Florentine historian Francesco Guicciardini wrote. "They were well fed from
the provisions with which the city abounded. Industry of every sort
flourished. Talented and able men were maintained, and a welcome
and a position secured to all teachers of literature, art, and every liberal pursuit."[9]

The republic was not, however, democratic or egalitarian. In fact,
it was barely a republic. Exercising power from behind its façade was
the Medici family, the phenomenally wealthy bankers who dominated
Florentine politics and culture during the fifteenth century without
holding office or hereditary title. (In the following century they became hereditary dukes, and lesser family members became popes.)

After Cosimo de' Medici took over the family bank in the 1430s,
it became the largest in Europe. By managing the fortunes of the
continent's wealthy families, the Medici made themselves the wealthiest of them all. They were innovators in bookkeeping, including the
use of debit-and-credit accounting that became one of the great spurs
to progress during the Renaissance. By means of payoffs and plotting,
Cosimo became the de facto ruler of Florence, and his patronage
made it the cradle of Renaissance art and humanism.

A collector of ancient manuscripts who had been schooled in
Greek and Roman literature, Cosimo supported the rebirth of interest in antiquity that was at the core of Renaissance humanism. He
founded and funded Florence's first public library and the influential

but informal Platonic Academy, where scholars and public intellectuals discussed the classics. In art, he was a patron of Fra Angelico, Filippo Lippi, and Donatello. Cosimo died in 1464, just as Leonardo arrived in Florence from Vinci. He was succeeded by his son and then, five years later, his famous grandson, Lorenzo de' Medici, aptly dubbed Lorenzo the Magnificent.

Lorenzo had been tutored in humanist literature and philosophy under the watchful eye of his mother, an accomplished poet, and he patronized the Platonic Academy, launched by his grandfather. He was also an accomplished sportsman, distinguishing himself in jousting, hunting, falconry, and breeding horses. All of this made him a better poet and patron than he was a banker; he took more delight in using wealth than in making it. During his twenty-three-year reign, he would sponsor innovative artists, including Botticelli and Michelangelo, as well as patronize the workshops of Andrea del Verrocchio, Domenico Ghirlandaio, and Antonio del Pollaiuolo, which were producing paintings and sculptures to adorn the booming city.

Lorenzo de' Medici's patronage of the arts, autocratic rule, and ability to maintain a peaceful balance of power with rival city-states helped to make Florence a cradle of art and commerce during Leonardo's early career there. He also kept his citizenry amused with dazzling public spectacles and grandly produced entertainments, ranging from Passion Plays to pre-Lenten carnivals. The work done for these pageants was ephemeral, but it was lucrative and stimulated the creative imagination of many of the artists involved, most notably young Leonardo.

Florence's festive culture was spiced by the ability to inspire those with creative minds to combine ideas from disparate disciplines. In narrow streets, cloth dyers worked next to goldbeaters next to lens crafters, and during their breaks they went to the piazza to engage in animated discussions. At the Pollaiuolo workshop, anatomy was being studied so that the young sculptors and painters could better understand the human form. Artists learned the science of perspective and how angles of light produce shadows and the perception of depth. The culture rewarded, above all, those who mastered and mixed different disciplines.

BRUNELLESCHI AND ALBERTI

The legacy of two such polymaths had a formative influence on Leonardo. The first was Filippo Brunelleschi (1377–1446), the designer of the cathedral dome. Like Leonardo, he was the son of a notary. Desiring a more creative life, he trained to become a goldsmith. Fortunately for his wide-ranging interests, goldsmiths were lumped together with other artisans as members of the guild of silk weavers and merchants, which also included sculptors. Brunelleschi's interests soon embraced architecture as well, and he traveled to Rome to study classical ruins with his friend Donatello, another young Florentine goldsmith, who later achieved fame as a sculptor. They measured the Pantheon dome, studied other great buildings, and read the works of ancient Romans, most notably Vitruvius's paean to classical proportions, *De Architectura.* Thus they became embodiments of the multidisciplinary interests and rebirth of classical knowledge that shaped the early Renaissance.

To build his cathedral dome—a self-supporting structure of close to four million bricks that is still the largest masonry dome in the world—Brunelleschi had to develop sophisticated mathematical modeling techniques and invent an array of hoists and other engineering tools. In an example of the diverse forces that were animating creativity in Florence, some of these hoists were then used to stage Lorenzo de' Medici's magnificent theatrics involving flying characters and moving scenery.[10]

Brunelleschi also rediscovered and greatly advanced the classical concepts of visual perspective, which had been missing in the art of the Middle Ages. In an experiment that foreshadowed the work of Leonardo, he painted a panel that depicted the view of the Florence Baptistery across the plaza from the cathedral. After drilling a small hole in the panel, he put the back of it up to his eye while he faced the Baptistery. Then he took a mirror and held it at arm's length, reflecting back on the painting. As he moved the mirror in and out of his line of sight, he would compare the reflection of his painting to the real Baptistery. The essence of realistic painting, he thought, was to render a three-dimensional view onto a two-dimensional surface. After accomplishing this trick on a painted panel, Brunelleschi showed how parallel lines seemed to converge in the distance toward a vanishing point. His formulation of linear perspective transformed art and also influenced the science of optics, the craft of architecture, and the uses of Euclidean geometry.[11]

Brunelleschi's successor as a theorist of linear perspective was another of the towering Renaissance polymaths, Leon Battista Alberti (1404–1472), who refined many of Brunelleschi's experiments and extended his discoveries about perspective. An artist, architect, engineer, and writer, Alberti was like Leonardo in many ways: both were illegitimate sons of prosperous fathers, athletic and good-looking, never-married, and fascinated by everything from math to art. One difference is that Alberti's illegitimacy did not prevent him from being given a classical education. His father helped him get a dispensation from the Church laws barring illegitimate children from taking holy orders or holding ecclesiastical offices, and he studied law at Bologna, was ordained as a priest, and became a writer for the pope. During his early thirties, Alberti wrote his masterpiece analyzing painting and perspective, *On Painting*, the Italian edition of which was dedicated to Brunelleschi.

Alberti had an engineer's instinct for collaboration and, like Leonardo, was "a lover of friendship" and "open-hearted," according to the scholar Anthony Grafton. He also honed the skills of courtiership. Interested in every art and technology, he would grill people from all walks of life, from cobblers to university scholars, to learn their secrets. In other words, he was much like Leonardo, except in one respect: Leonardo was not strongly motivated by the goal of furthering human knowledge by openly disseminating and publishing his findings; Alberti, on the other hand, was dedicated to sharing his work, gathering a community of intellectual colleagues who could build on each other's discoveries, and promoting open discussion and publication as a way to advance the accumulation of learning. A maestro of collaborative practices, he believed, according to Grafton, in "discourse in the public sphere."

When Leonardo was a teenager in Florence, Alberti was in his sixties and spending much of his time in Rome, so it is unlikely they spent time together. Alberti was a major influence nonetheless. Leonardo studied his treatises and consciously tried to emulate both his writing and his demeanor. Alberti had established himself as "an avatar of grace in every word or movement," a style that very much appealed to Leonardo. "One must apply the greatest artistry in three things," Alberti wrote, "walking in the city, riding a horse, and speaking, for in each of these one must try to please everyone."[12] Leonardo mastered all three.

Alberti's *On Painting* expanded on Brunelleschi's analysis of perspective by using geometry to calculate how perspective lines from distant objects should be captured on a two-dimensional pane. He also suggested that painters hang a veil made of thin thread between themselves and the objects they are painting, then record where each element falls on the veil. His new methods improved not only painting but endeavors ranging from mapmaking to stage designs. By applying mathematics to art, Alberti elevated the painter's status and advanced the argument that the visual arts deserve a standing equal to that of other humanist fields, a cause that Leonardo would later champion.[13]

EDUCATION

Leonardo's only formal learning was at an abacus school, an elementary academy that emphasized the math skills useful in commerce. It did not teach how to formulate abstract theories; the focus was on practical cases. One skill that was emphasized was how to draw analogies between cases, a method that Leonardo would use repeatedly in his later science. Analogies and spotting patterns became for him a rudimentary method of theorizing.

His enthusiastic early biographer Vasari wrote, with what seems to be typical exaggeration, "In arithmetic, during the few months that he studied it, he made so much progress, that, by continually suggesting doubts and difficulties to the master who was teaching him, he would very often bewilder him." Vasari also noted that Leonardo was interested in so many things that he got easily distracted. He turned out to be good in geometry, but he never mastered the use of equations or the rudimentary algebra that existed at the time. Nor did he learn Latin. In his thirties he would still be trying to remedy this deficiency by drawing up lists of Latin words, painstakingly writing out awkward translations, and wrestling with grammar rules.[14]

A left-hander, Leonardo wrote from right to left on a page, the opposite direction of the words on this and other normal pages, and drew each letter facing backward. "They are not to be read save with a mirror," as Vasari described these pages. Some have speculated that he adopted this script as a code to keep his writings secret, but that is not true; it can be read, with or without a mirror. He wrote that way because when using his left hand he could glide leftward across the page without smudging the ink. The practice was not completely uncommon. When his friend the mathematician Luca Pacioli described Leonardo's mirror writing, he made the point that some other left-handers wrote likewise. A popular fifteenth-century calligraphy book even shows left-handed readers the best way to do *lettera mancina*, or mirror script.[15]

Being left-handed also affected Leonardo's method of drawing. As with his writing, he drew from right to left so as not to smudge the lines with his hand.[16] Most artists draw hatching strokes that slope upward to the right, like this: ////. But Leonardo's hatching was distinctive because his lines started on the lower right and moved upward to the left, like this: \\. Today this style has an added advantage: the left-handed hatching in a drawing is evidence that it was made by Leonardo.

When viewed in a mirror, Leonardo's writing is somewhat similar to that of his father, indicating that Piero probably helped Leonardo learn to write. However, many of his numerical calculations are written in conventional fashion, showing that the abacus school probably did not indulge his use of mirror script for math.[17] Being left-handed was not a major handicap, but it was considered a bit of an oddity, a trait that conjured up words like *sinister* and *gauche* rather than *dexterous* and *adroit*, and it was one more way in which Leonardo was regarded, and regarded himself, as distinctive.

VERROCCHIO

Around the time Leonardo was fourteen, his father was able to secure for him an apprenticeship with one of his clients, Andrea del Verrocchio, a versatile artist and engineer who ran one of the best workshops in Florence. Vasari wrote, "Piero took some of his drawings and carried them to Andrea del Verrocchio, who was his good friend, and asked if he thought it would be profitable for the boy to study drawing." Piero knew Verrocchio well, and he notarized at least four legal settlements and rental documents for him around this time. But Verrocchio probably gave the boy an apprenticeship on merit, not just as a favor to his father. He was, Vasari reported, "astonished" at the boy's talent.[18]

Verrocchio's workshop, which was nestled in a street near Piero's notarial office, was the perfect place for Leonardo. Verrocchio conducted a rigorous teaching program that involved studying surface anatomy, mechanics, drawing techniques, and the effects of light and shade on material such as draperies.

When Leonardo arrived, Verrocchio's workshop was creating an ornate tomb for the Medici, sculpting a bronze statue of Christ and Saint Thomas, designing banners of white taffeta gilded with flowers of silver and gold for a pageant, curating the Medici's antiques, and generating Madonna paintings for merchants who wanted to display both their wealth and their piety. An inventory of his shop showed that it had a dining table, beds, a globe, and a variety of books in Italian, including translated classical poetry by Petrarch and Ovid as well as humorous short stories by the fourteenth-century popular Florentine writer Franco Sacchetti. The topics of discussion in his shop included math, anatomy, dissection, antiquities, music, and philosophy. "He applied himself to the sciences, and particularly geometry," according to Vasari.[19]

Verrocchio's bottega, like those of his five or six main competitors in Florence, was more like a commercial shop, similar to the shops of the cobblers and jewelers along the street, than a refined art studio. On the ground floor was a store and workroom, open to the street, where the artisans and apprentices mass-produced products from their easels, workbenches, kilns, pottery wheels, and metal grinders. Many of the workers lived and ate together in the quarters upstairs. The paintings and objects were not signed; they were not intended to be works of individual expression. Most were collaborative efforts, including many of the paintings commonly attributed to Verrocchio himself. The goal was to produce a constant flow of marketable art and artifacts rather than nurture creative geniuses yearning to find outlets for their originality.[20]

With their lack of Latin schooling, the artisans in such shops were not considered to be part of the cultural elite. But the status of artists was beginning to change. The rebirth of interest in the ancient Roman classics had revived the writings of Pliny the Elder, who extolled classical artists for representing nature so accurately that their grapes could fool birds. With the help of the writings of Alberti and the development of mathematical perspective, the social and intellectual standing of painters was rising, and a few were becoming sought-after names.

Trained as a goldsmith, Verrocchio left much of the brushwork of painting to others, most notably a crop of young artists that included Lorenzo di Credi. Verrocchio was a kind master; students such as Leonardo often continued to live with and work for him after their apprenticeships were completed, and other young painters, including Sandro Botticelli, became part of his circle.

Verrocchio's collegial nature did have one downside: he was not a tough taskmaster and his workshop was not renowned for delivering commissions on time. Vasari noted that Verrocchio once made preparatory drawings for a battle scene of nude figures and other narrative works of art, "but for some reason, whatever it may have been, they remained unfinished." Verrocchio held on to some paintings for years before completing them. Leonardo would far exceed his master in all things, including in his propensity to get distracted, walk away from projects, and linger over paintings for years.

One of Verrocchio's most captivating sculptures was a four-foot bronze of the young warrior David standing in triumph over the head of Goliath (fig. 1). His smile is tantalizing and a bit mysterious— What exactly is he thinking?—like the ones Leonardo would later

Fig. 1. Verrocchio's *David*.

Fig. 3. Drawing possibly of Leonardo modeling for Verrocchio's *David*.

Fig. 2. Presumed self-portrait by Leonardo in the *Adoration of the Magi*.

paint. It quavers between expressing a childlike glory and a dawning realization of future leadership; a cocky smile is caught in the moment of being transformed into resolution. Unlike Michelangelo's iconic marble statue of a muscular David as a man, Verrocchio's David seems to be a slightly effeminate and strikingly pretty boy of about fourteen.

That was the age of Leonardo, newly apprenticed in the studio, when Verrocchio probably began work on the statue.[21] Artists of Verrocchio's era typically blended the classical ideal with more naturalistic features, and it is unlikely that his statues are exact portraits of a particular model. Nevertheless there are reasons to think that Leonardo posed for Verrocchio's *David*.[22] The face is not the usual broad type that Verrocchio had previously favored. He clearly used a new model, and the recently arrived boy in the shop was the obvious candidate, especially because, according to Vasari, young Leonardo had "a beauty of body beyond description, a splendor that rejoiced the most sorrowful souls." Such praises of young Leonardo's loveliness are echoed by his other early biographers. Another piece of evidence: David's face is similar (strong nose and chin, soft cheeks and lips) to that of a young boy Leonardo drew on the edge of the *Adoration of the Magi* that is presumed to be a self-portrait (fig. 2) as well as other supposed likenesses.

So with just a little imagination, we can look at Verrocchio's transfixing statue of the pretty boy David and envision what the young Leonardo looked like when he stood modeling on the ground floor of the studio. In addition, there is a drawing by one of Verrocchio's students that is probably a copy of a study made for the statue. It shows the boy model in exactly the same pose, down to his finger placement on his hip and the little hollow where his neck hits his collarbone, but nude (fig. 3).

Verrocchio's art was sometimes criticized as workmanlike. "The style of his sculpture and painting tended to be hard and crude, since it came from unremitting study rather than any inborn gift," Vasari wrote. But his statue of David is a beautiful gem that influenced the young Leonardo. David's curls and those of the hair and beard of Goliath's head are luxurious spirals of the type that would become a signature feature of Leonardo's art. In addition, Verrocchio's statue (unlike, say, Donatello's version in 1440) displays a care and mastery of anatomical details. For example, the two veins visible in David's right arm are accurately rendered and pop in just the precise way to show that, despite his seeming nonchalance, he is gripping his dagger-like sword very tightly. Likewise, the muscle connecting David's left forearm to his elbow is flexed in a way that comports with the twisting of his hand.

That ability to convey the subtleties of motion in a piece of still art was among Verrocchio's underappreciated talents, one that Leonardo would adopt and then far surpass in his paintings. More than most previous artists, Verrocchio imbued his statues with twists, turns, and flows. In his bronze *Christ and Saint Thomas*, begun while Leonardo was an apprentice, Saint Thomas turns to his left to touch the wound of Jesus, who is twisting to his right as he lifts his arm. The sense of motion turns the statue into a narrative. It conveys not merely a moment but a story, the one told in the Gospel of John, when Thomas doubts the resurrection of Jesus and responds to his injunction "Reach hither thy hand, and thrust it into my side." Kenneth Clark called it "the first instance in the Renaissance of that complicated flow of movement through a composition, achieved by contrasted axes of the figures, which Leonardo made the chief motif of all his constructions."[23] We can also see Verrocchio's love of movement and flow in the hair of Saint Thomas and beard of Jesus, which again feature a sensuous profusion of spiraling curls and tight coils.

Leonardo had studied the use of math for commercial purposes at his abacus school, but from Verrocchio he learned something more profound: the beauty of geometry. After Cosimo de' Medici died, Verrocchio designed a marble-and-bronze slab for his tomb, which was finished in 1467, a year after Leonardo became his apprentice. Instead of religious imagery, the tomb slab featured geometrical patterns dominated by a circle inside a square, as Leonardo would use for his drawing *Vitruvian Man*. Inside the design, Verrocchio and his workshop carved carefully proportioned rectangles and half-circles in colors that were based on harmonic ratios and the Pythagorean musical scale.[24] There was harmony in proportions, Leonardo learned, and math was nature's brushstroke.

Geometry and harmony combined again two years later, when Verrocchio's studio was given a monumental engineering task: mounting a two-ton ball on top of Brunelleschi's dome of Florence's cathedral. It was a triumph of both art and technology. The crowning moment, which was accompanied by trumpet fanfare and hymns of praise, occurred in 1471, when Leonardo was nineteen. The project, which he would still refer to decades later in his notebook, ingrained in him a sense of the interplay between artistry and engineering; he made loving, meticulous drawings of the hoists and gear mechanisms that Verrocchio's studio used, some of which had originally been devised by Brunelleschi.[25]

The construction of the ball, which was made of stone that was clad with eight sheets of copper and then gilded, also kindled in Leonardo a fascination with optics and the geometry of light rays. There were no welding torches at the time, so the triangular sheets of copper had to be soldered together using concave mirrors, about three feet wide, that would concentrate sunlight into a point of intense heat. An understanding of geometry was needed to calculate the precise angle of the rays and grind the curve of the mirrors accordingly. Leonardo became mesmerized—at times obsessed—by what he called "fire mirrors"; over the years he would make almost two hundred drawings in his notebooks that show how to make concave mirrors that will focus light rays from varying angles. Close to forty years later, when working in Rome on huge curved mirrors that might turn the heat of the sun into a weapon, he jotted in his notebook, "Remember how the ball of Santa Maria del Fiore was soldered together in sections?"[26]

Leonardo was also influenced by Verrocchio's primary commercial competitor in Florence, Antonio del Pollaiuolo. Even more than Verrocchio, Pollaiuolo was experimenting with the expression of moving and twisting bodies, and he performed surface dissections of humans to study anatomy. He was, wrote Vasari, "the first master to skin many human bodies in order to investigate the muscles and understand the nude in a more modern way." In his engraving *Battle of the Nudes* and his sculpture and painting *Hercules and Antaeus*, Pollaiuolo depicted warriors contorted in powerful yet realistic ways as they struggle to stab or subdue each other. The anatomy of muscles and nerves informs the grimaces on faces and the twists of limbs.[27]

Leonardo's father came to appreciate, and in one case profit from, his son's fevered imagination and ability to connect art to the wonders of nature. A peasant who worked in Vinci one day made a small shield of wood and asked Piero to take it to Florence and have it painted.

Piero gave the task to Leonardo, who decided to create a terrifying image of a dragon-like monster breathing fire and belching poison. To make it naturalistic, he assembled parts from real lizards, crickets, snakes, butterflies, grasshoppers, and bats. "He labored over it so long that the stench of the dead animals was past bearing, but Leonardo did not notice it, so great was the love that he bore towards art," Vasari wrote. When Piero finally came to get it, he recoiled in shock from what in the dim light appeared at first to be a real monster. Piero decided to keep his son's creation and buy another shield for the peasant. "Later, Ser Piero sold the buckler of Leonardo secretly to some merchants in Florence, for a hundred ducats; and in a short time it came into the hands of the Duke of Milan, having been sold to him by the merchants for three hundred ducats."

The shield, perhaps Leonardo's first recorded piece of art, displayed his lifelong talent for combining fantasy with observation. In the notes for his proposed treatise on painting, he would later write, "If you wish to make an imaginary animal invented by you appear natural, let us say a dragon, take for the head that of a mastiff or hound, for the eyes a cat, and for the ears a porcupine, and for the nose a greyhound, and the brows of a lion, the temple of an old cock, the neck of a terrapin."[28]

DRAPERIES, CHIAROSCURO, AND SFUMATO

One of the exercises in Verrocchio's studio was the drawing of "drapery studies," most done with delicate brushstrokes of black and white washes on linen. According to Vasari, Leonardo "would make clay models of figures, draping them with soft pieces of cloth dipped in plaster, and would then draw them patiently on thin sheets of cambric or linen, in black and white, with the point of the brush." The velvety renderings of the folds and waves of drapery featured deft depictions of light, nuanced gradations of shadow, and the occasional glint of luster (fig. 4).

Some of the drapery drawings from Verrocchio's studio appear to be studies for paintings. Others were probably done just as learning exercises. The drawings have given rise to a vibrant academic industry

Fig. 4. Drapery study from Verrocchio's studio,
attributed to Leonardo, c. 1470.

that tries to sort out which were done by Leonardo and which were
more likely by Verrocchio, Ghirlandaio, or their coworkers.[29] The fact
that the attributions are difficult to resolve is evidence of the collegial
nature of Verrocchio's bottega.

For Leonardo, the drapery studies helped foster one of the key
components of his artistic genius: the ability to deploy light and shade
in ways that would better produce the illusion of three-dimensional
volume on a two-dimensional surface. They also helped him hone his
ability to observe how light subtly caresses an object, causing a glis-
tening of luster, a sharpened contrast on a fold, or a hint of reflected
glow creeping into the heart of a shadow. "The first intention of the
painter," Leonardo later wrote, "is to make a flat surface display a
body as if modeled and separated from this plane, and he who sur-
passes others in this skill deserves most praise. This accomplishment,
with which the science of painting is crowned, arises from light and

shade, or we may say chiaroscuro."[30] That statement could stand as his artistic manifesto, or at least a key element of it.

Chiaroscuro, from the Italian for "light/dark," is the use of contrasts of light and shadow as a modeling technique for achieving the illusion of plasticity and three-dimensional volume in a two-dimensional drawing or painting. Leonardo's version of the technique involved varying the darkness of a color by adding black pigments rather than making it a more saturated or richer hue. In his *Benois Madonna*, for example, he painted the Virgin Mary's blue dress in shades ranging from almost white to almost black.

When mastering drapery drawings in Verrocchio's studio, Leonardo also pioneered sfumato, the technique of blurring contours and edges. It is a way for artists to render objects as they appear to our eye rather than with sharp contours. This advance caused Vasari to proclaim Leonardo the inventor of the "modern manner" in painting, and the art historian Ernst Gombrich called sfumato "Leonardo's famous invention, the blurred outline and mellowed colors that allow one form to merge with another and always leave something to our imagination."[31]

The term *sfumato* derives from the Italian word for "smoke," or more precisely the dissipation and gradual vanishing of smoke into the air. "Your shadows and lights should be blended without lines or borders in the manner of smoke losing itself in the air," he wrote in a series of maxims for young painters.[32] From the eyes of his angel in the *Baptism of Christ* to the smile of the *Mona Lisa,* the blurred and smoke-veiled edges allow a role for our own imagination. With no sharp lines, enigmatic glances and smiles can flicker mysteriously.

WARRIORS WITH HELMETS

In 1471, around the time the copper ball was placed atop the Duomo, Verrocchio & Co. was involved, as were most of the other artisans of Florence, in the festivities organized by Lorenzo de' Medici for the visit of Galeazzo Maria Sforza, the cruel and authoritarian (and soon-to-be-assassinated) Duke of Milan. Accompanying Galeazzo was his swarthy and charismatic younger brother Ludovico Sforza, who was nineteen, the same age as Leonardo. (It was to him that Leonardo would address his famous job-seeking letter eleven years later.) Verrocchio's shop had two major tasks for the festivities: redecorating the Medici's guest quarters for the visitors and crafting a suit of armor and an ornate helmet as a gift.

The Duke of Milan's cavalcade was dazzling even to Florentines who were used to Medicean public spectacles. It included two thousand horses, six hundred soldiers, a thousand hunting hounds, falcons, falconers, trumpeters, pipers, barbers, dog trainers, musicians, and poets.[33] It's hard not to admire an entourage that travels with its own barbers and poets. Because it was Lent, there were three religious spectacle plays in place of public jousts and tournaments. But the overall atmosphere was far from Lenten. The visit marked the climax of the Medici practice of using public pageants and spectacles to dissipate popular discontent.

To Machiavelli, who wrote a history of Florence in addition to his famous how-to manual for authoritarian princes, the penchant for pageantry was related to a decadence that infected Florence during its period of relative peace, when Leonardo was a young artist there: "The youth having become more dissolute than before, more extravagant in dress, feasting, and other licentiousness, and being without employment, wasted their time and means on gaming and women; their principal study being how to appear splendid in apparel, and attain a crafty shrewdness in discourse. These manners derived additional encouragement from the followers of the duke of Milan, who, with his duchess and the whole ducal court, came to Florence, where he was received with pomp and respect." One church burned to the ground during the festivities, which was considered divine retribution for the fact that, as Machiavelli wrote, "during Lent, when the church commands us to abstain from animal food, the Milanese, without respect for either God or his church, ate of it daily."[34]

Leonardo's most famous early drawing may have been inspired by or related to this visit by the Duke of Milan.[35] It is of a craggy Roman warrior in profile wearing an ornate helmet (fig. 5), and it was derived from a drawing by Verrocchio, whose studio had designed a helmet as one of Florence's gifts to the duke. Intricately drawn with a

Fig. 5. A warrior.

silverpoint stylus on tinted paper, Leonardo's warrior sports a helmet adorned by a frightfully realistic bird wing and the flourishes of curls and spirals that he adored. On the breastplate is a ludicrous but loveable growling lion. The warrior's face is subtly modeled with delicate shadings made by patiently drawn hatch lines, but his jowls and brows and lower lip are exaggerated to the edge of caricature. The hooked nose and jutting jaw create a profile that became a leitmotif in Leonardo's drawings, that of a gruff old warrior, noble but faintly farcical.

The influence of Verrocchio can be clearly seen. From Vasari's *Lives* we know that Verrocchio created sculptured reliefs of "two heads in metal, one representing Alexander the Great in profile, and the other a fanciful portrait of Darius," the ancient Persian king. These are now lost but are known through various copies made at the time. Most notably, in Washington, DC's National Gallery there is a marble relief of a young Alexander the Great, attributed to Verrocchio and his workshop, which features a similar ornate helmet with a winged dragon, a breastplate adorned with a roaring face, and the profusion of curls and fluttering swirls that the master imparted to his apprentice. In his own drawing, Leonardo eliminated a large-jawed animal that Verrocchio had perched atop the helmet, turned the dragon into swirls of plants, and generally made the design less complicated. "What Leonardo's simplifications achieved was to make the beholder's eye focus on the profile heads of the warrior and lion, i.e., on the relationship between the man and the animal," according to Martin Kemp and Juliana Barone.[36]

As with his paired carvings of Darius and Alexander, Verrocchio occasionally juxtaposed a profile of a craggy old warrior with that of a pretty boy, a theme that would become a favorite of Leonardo's, both in his drawings and in random notebook doodles. One example is in Verrocchio's *Beheading of Saint John the Baptist*, a silver relief he did for Florence's Baptistery, where a young warrior and an old one are juxtaposed on the far right. By the time this sculpture was made, starting around 1477, when Leonardo was twenty-five, it is unclear who was influencing whom; the young and old warriors facing each other, as well as an angelic young boy on the far left, have the vibrant movement and emotion-laden facial expressions that make it seem possible Leonardo had a hand in them.[37]

PAGEANTS AND PLAYS

For the artists and engineers in Florence's bottegas, working on the Medici pageants and spectacles was a significant component of their job. For Leonardo it was also a joy. He was already making a name as a colorful dresser, fond of brocade doublets and rose tunics, and as a showman adept at imaginative theatrics. Over the years, both in Florence and especially after he moved to Milan, he spent time devising costumes, theatrical scenery, stage machinery, special effects, floats, banners, and entertainments. His theatrical productions were ephemeral, and they linger only in sketches in his notebooks. They can be dismissed as diversions, but they were also an enjoyable way for him to combine art and engineering, and thus they became a formative influence on his personality.[38]

The artisans who created the sets for theatrical events became masters of the rules of artistic perspective that had been refined in the

1400s. The painted scenery and backdrops had to be unified with the three-dimensional stage settings, props, moving objects, and actors. Reality and illusions were blended. We can see the influence of these plays and pageants on both Leonardo's art and his engineering. He studied how to make the rules of perspective work for different vantage points, loved mixing illusion with reality, and delighted in devising the special effects, costumes, scenery, and theatrical machinery. All of this helps to explain many of the sketches and fantasy writings in his notebooks that scholars sometimes find mystifying.

For example, some of the gears and cranks and mechanisms that Leonardo rendered in his notebooks were, I think, theatrical machinery that he encountered or contrived. Florentine impresarios had created ingenious mechanisms, called *ingegni*, for changing scenery, propelling dazzling props, and turning stages into living paintings. Vasari praises a Florentine carpenter and engineer who climaxed a festival show with a scene of "Christ carried upward from a mountain carved of wood and borne to heaven by a cloud filled with angels."

Likewise, some of the flying contraptions that we find in Leonardo's notebooks were probably for the amusement of theatrical audiences. The Florentine plays often involved characters and props descending from the heavens or being magically suspended in air. Some of Leonardo's flying machines were, as we will see, clearly aimed at real human flight. Others, however, are on notebook pages from the 1480s and seem to have a theatrical purpose. They feature wings with limited range moved by cranks, and they could not possibly have been propelled into the skies by a human pilot. Similar pages include notes on how to project lights onto a scene and drawings of a hook-and-pulley system to raise actors.[39]

Even Leonardo's famous drawing of an aerial screw (fig. 6), often touted as the design for the first helicopter, falls into this category of *ingegni* devised for a theatrical spectacle, I believe. Its spiral mechanism of linen, wire, and cane was, in theory, supposed to turn and bore upward into the air. Leonardo specified certain details, like making sure the linen has "its pores stopped up with starch," but he showed no method for a human to operate it. It is big enough to be amusing but probably not enough to carry a human. In one model,

Fig. 6. A flying machine, probably for the theater.

he specified that the "axis will be made of a fine steel blade, bent by force, and when released it will turn the screw." There were toys at the time that used similar mechanisms. Like some of his mechanical birds, the aerial screw was probably made to transport spectators' imaginations rather than their bodies.[40]

THE ARNO LANDSCAPE

Leonardo enjoyed the collegial and familial atmosphere in Verrocchio's workshop so much that, when his apprenticeship ended in 1472, at the age of twenty, he decided to continue to work and live there. He remained on friendly terms with his father, who lived nearby with his second wife and still had no other children. When Leonardo registered as a member of the Florentine painters' confraternity, the Compagnia di San Luca, he affirmed his relationship by signing himself "Leonardo di Ser Piero da Vinci."

The Compagnia was not a guild but a club-like mutual aid society or fraternity. Other members who registered and paid dues in 1472 included Botticelli, Pietro Perugino, Ghirlandaio, Pollaiuolo, Filippino Lippi, and Verrocchio himself.[41] The Compagnia had been in existence for a century, but it was undergoing a revitalization partly because artists were reacting against Florence's antiquated guild system. Under the old guild structure, they were lumped into the Arte dei Medici e Speziali, which had been founded in 1197 for physicians and pharmacists. By the late 1400s they were eager to assert a more distinctive status for themselves.

Months after becoming a master painter, Leonardo escaped the bustling narrow streets and crammed workshops of Florence and took a trip back to the rolling green hills around Vinci. "I, staying with Antonio, am contented," he scribbled in his notebook in the summer of 1473, when he was twenty-one.[42] His grandfather Antonio had died, so the reference is perhaps to his mother's husband, Antonio Buti (Accattabriga). One can picture him content as he stays with his mother and his large stepfamily in the hills just outside of Vinci; it conjures up his tale of the stone that willed itself to roll down to the crowded road but later yearned to be back up on the quiet hill.

On the reverse of that notebook page is what may be Leonardo's earliest surviving art drawing, the shimmering start of a career of combining scientific observation with artistic sensibility (fig. 7). In his mirror script he has dated it "day of Holy Mary of the Snows on the 5th August 1473."[43] The drawing is an impressionistic panorama, sketched with quick pen strokes on paper, evoking the rocky hills and verdant valley surrounding the Arno River near Vinci. There are a few familiar landmarks from the area—a conical hill, perhaps a castle—but the aerial view seems to be, typical of Leonardo, a mix of the actual and the imagined, viewed as if by a soaring bird. The glory of being an artist, he realized, was that reality should inform but not constrain. "If the painter wishes to see beauties that would enrapture him, he is master of their production," he wrote. "If he seeks valleys, if he wants to disclose great expanses of countryside from the summits of mountains, and if he subsequently wishes to see the horizon of the sea, he is lord of all of them."[44]

Other artists had drawn landscapes as backdrops, but Leonardo

Fig. 7. Leonardo's Arno Valley landscape, 1473.

was doing something different: depicting nature for its own sake. That makes his Arno Valley drawing a contender for the first such landscape in European art. The geological realism is striking: the craggy rock outcroppings eroded by the river reveal accurately rendered layers of stratified rock, a subject that was to fascinate Leonardo for the rest of his life. So, too, is the near-precision of linear perspective and the way the atmosphere blurs the distant horizon, an optical phenomenon that he would later call "aerial perspective."

Even more arresting is the young artist's ability to convey motion. The leaves of the trees and even their shadows are drawn with quick curved lines that make them seem to tremble in the breeze. The water falling into a pool is made vibrant with flutters of quick strokes. The result is a delightful display of the art of observing movement.

TOBIAS AND THE ANGEL

While working as a master painter in Verrocchio's shop during his late teens and early twenties, Leonardo contributed elements to two paintings: he was responsible for the scampering dog and shiny fish in *Tobias and the Angel* (fig. 8) and for the angel on the far left in the *Baptism of Christ*. These collaborations show what he learned from Verrocchio and how he then surpassed him.

The biblical tale of Tobias, which was popular in late fifteenth-

Fig. 8. *Tobias and the Angel* by Verrocchio with Leonardo.

century Florence, tells of a boy who is sent by his blind father to collect a debt, accompanied by his guardian angel, Raphael. On the journey they catch a fish, the guts of which turn out to have healing powers, including that of restoring the father's sight. Raphael was the patron saint of travelers and of the guild of physicians and apothecaries. The tale of him and Tobias was particularly appealing to the wealthy merchants who had become art patrons in Florence, especially those with traveling sons.[45] Among the Florentines who painted it were Pollaiuolo, Verrocchio, Filippino Lippi, Botticelli, and Francesco Botticini (seven times).

Pollaiuolo's version (fig. 9) was produced in the early 1460s for the church of Orsanmichele. It was well known to Leonardo and Verrocchio, who was sculpting his statue of Christ and Saint Thomas for a niche of that church's wall. In producing his own *Tobias and the Angel* a few years later, Verrocchio engaged in an explicit competition with Pollaiuolo.[46]

The version that came out of Verrocchio's shop includes the exact same elements as Pollaiuolo's: Tobias and the angel walking hand in hand, a Bolognese terrier scampering alongside, Tobias holding a carp on a stick and strings, and Raphael holding a tin with the fish's guts, all in front of a meandering river landscape with clumps of grass and clusters of trees. And yet it is a fundamentally different painting, in both its impact and detail, in ways that reveal what Leonardo was learning.

One difference is that Pollaiuolo's version is stiff, while Verrocchio's conveys movement. As a sculptor, he had mastered the twists and thrusts that impart dynamism to a body. His Tobias leans in as he strides, his cloak billowing out behind him while tassels and threads flutter. He and Raphael turn to each other naturally. Even the way they hold hands is more dynamic. Whereas Pollaiuolo's faces seem vacuous, the body motions in the Verrocchio version connect to emotional expressions, conveying mental as well as physical movements.

Verrocchio, who was more of a sculptor than a painter, developed a reputation for not being a master at portraying nature. True, there is a good raptor sweeping down in his *Baptism of Christ*, but his way with animals was generally considered "indifferent" and "deficient."[47]

Fig. 9. Antonio del Pollaiuolo's *Tobias and the Angel.*

So it is not surprising that to paint the fish and dog he would turn to his pupil Leonardo, whose eye for nature was proving to be astonishing. Both animals are painted on what was already a finished background landscape; we know this because, as sometimes happened with Leonardo's experimental mixtures, his paint has become somewhat transparent.

The shiny and shimmery scales of the fish show that Leonardo was already mastering the magic of how light strikes an object and dances to our eyes. Each scale is a gem. The sunshine coming from the top left of the picture produces a mix of light and shade and sparkle. Both behind the gill and at the front of the liquidy eye is a spot of luster. Unlike other painters, Leonardo even took care to render the blood dripping from the fish's cut belly.

As for the dog prancing just under Raphael's feet, it has an expression and personality that matches in its charm that of Tobias. In stark contrast to Pollaiuolo's stiff terrier, Leonardo's trots naturally and watches alertly. Most notable are its curls. Their painstaking design and lustrous lighting match that of the curls above Tobias's ear, which (an analysis of the left-handed style shows) were also drawn by Leonardo.[48] Swirling and flowing curls, perfectly lit and coiled, were becoming a Leonardo signature.

In this deeply pleasing and sprightly painting, we can see the power of a master-pupil collaboration. Leonardo was already an extreme observer of nature, and he was perfecting the ability to convey the effects of light on objects. Added to that, he had imbibed from Verrocchio, the master sculptor, the excitement of conveying motion and narrative.

BAPTISM OF CHRIST

The culmination of Leonardo's collaborations with Verrocchio came in the mid-1470s with the completion of the *Baptism of Christ*, which shows John the Baptist pouring water over Jesus while two angels kneeling beside the River Jordan watch (fig. 10). Leonardo painted the radiant, turning angel on the far left of the scene, and Verrocchio was so awed when he beheld it that he "resolved never again to touch a brush"—or at least that's what Vasari tells us. Even allowing for Vasari's penchant to mythologize and trot out clichéd themes, there was probably some truth to the tale. Afterward Verrocchio never completed any new painting on his own.[49] More to the point, a comparison between the parts of the *Baptism of Christ* that Leonardo painted with those done by Verrocchio shows why the older artist would have been ready to defer.

Fig. 10. *Baptism of Christ* by Verrocchio with Leonardo.

An X-ray analysis of the painting confirms that the angel on the left and much of the background landscape and the body of Jesus were painted with multiple thin layers of oil paint, the pigments highly diluted, stroked on with great delicacy and sometimes dabbed and smoothed by fingertips, a style that Leonardo was developing in the 1470s. Oil painting had come to Italy from the Netherlands, and Pollaiuolo's workshop was using it, as was Leonardo. Verrocchio, on the contrary, never embraced the use of oils, and instead continued to use tempera, a mix of water-soluble pigments bound with egg yolks.[50]

The most striking trait of Leonardo's angel is the dynamism of his pose. Shown from slightly behind in a twisted three-quarter profile, his neck turns to the right as his torso twists slightly to the left. "Always set your figures so that the side to which the head turns is not the side to which the breast faces, since nature for our convenience has made us with a neck which bends with ease in many directions," Leonardo wrote in one of his notebooks.[51] As evident in his *Christ and Saint Thomas*, Verrocchio was a master of depicting motion in sculptures, and Leonardo became an expert in its painterly conveyance.

A comparison of the two angels shows how Leonardo was surpassing his master. Verrocchio's angel seems vacant, his face flat, and his only emotion seems to be a sense of wonder that he happens to find himself next to a much more expressive angel. "He seems to look with astonishment at his companion, as at a visitant from another world," Kenneth Clark wrote, "and, in fact, Leonardo's angel belongs to a world of the imagination which Verrocchio's never penetrated."[52]

Like most artists, Verrocchio drew lines to delineate the contours of his angel's head and face and eyes. But in Leonardo's angel, there are no clear edges that delineate the features. The curls dissolve gently into each other and the face, rather than creating a hairline. Look at the shadow underneath the jaw of Verrocchio's angel, done with visible brushstrokes of tempera paint that create a sharp jaw line. Then look at Leonardo's; the shadow is more translucent and blends more smoothly, something that's easier done with oil. The almost imperceptible strokes are fluid, thinly layered, and occasionally smoothed by hand. The contours of the angel's face are soft. There are no perceptible edges.

We can also see this beauty in the body of Jesus. Compare his legs, painted by Leonardo, with those of Verrocchio's John the Baptist. The latter have sharper lines, unlike what a careful observer would see in reality. Leonardo even minutely blurs the curls of Jesus' exposed pubic hair.

This use of sfumato, the smokiness that blurs sharp contours, was by now a hallmark of Leonardo's art. Alberti in his treatise on painting had advised that lines should be drawn to delineate edges, and Verrocchio did just that. Leonardo took care to observe the real world, and he noticed the opposite: when we look at three-dimensional objects, we don't see sharp lines. "Paint so that a smoky finish can be seen, rather than contours and profiles that are distinct and crude," he wrote. "When you paint shadows and their edges, which cannot be perceived except indistinctly, do not make them sharp or clearly defined, otherwise your work will have a wooden appearance."[53] Verrocchio's angel has this wooden appearance. Leonardo's does not.

X-ray analysis shows that Verrocchio, with his lesser feel for nature, had originally begun the background by drawing a few rounded clumps of trees and bushes, more wooden than sylvan. When Leonardo took over, he used oils to paint a richly natural view of a languid but sparkling river flowing through rocky cliffs, echoing his Arno River drawing and foreshadowing the *Mona Lisa*. Other than Verrocchio's pedestrian palm tree, the backdrop displays a magical mix of natural realism and creative fantasia.

The geological striations of the rock (except those on the far right, which someone else must have painted) are carefully rendered, though not with the subtlety that Leonardo would later display. As the scene recedes, it gradually blurs, as our eyes would naturally have it, into a hazy horizon where the blue of the sky whitens into the mists just above the hills. "The edges of the mist will be indistinct against the blue of the sky, and towards the earth it will look almost like dust blown up," Leonardo wrote in one of his notebooks.[54]

In painting the background and foreground, Leonardo created the organizing theme of the picture, which is a narrative united by the meandering river. He portrayed the water's movement with scientific mastery and spiritual profundity, imbuing it with metaphorical power as the lifeblood connecting the macrocosm of the earth and the micro-cosm in humans. The water flows from the heavens and distant lakes, cuts through rocks to form dramatic cliffs and smooth pebbles, and pours from the cup of the Baptist, as if connecting to the blood of his veins. Finally, it swaddles the feet of Jesus and ripples to the edge of the picture, reaching us and making us feel a part of the flow.

There is an inexorable impetus to the water's flow, and when it is obstructed by the ankles of Jesus it forms swirls and eddies as it proceeds along its course. In these acutely observed vortexes and sci-entifically accurate ripples, Leonardo delights in what will become his favorite pattern: nature's spirals. The curls flowing down his angel's neck look like cascades of water, as if the river had flowed over his head and transformed into hair.

At the center of the picture is a small waterfall, one of many such depictions Leonardo would produce, in his paintings and notebooks, of water falling into a swirling pool or stream. Sometimes these renderings are scientific, at other times darkly hallucinatory. In this case the falling water seems sprightly; it causes splashes that prance around the eddies like Tobias's puppy.

With the *Baptism of Christ*, Verrocchio went from being Leonar-do's teacher to being his collaborator. He had helped Leonardo learn the sculptural elements of painting, especially modeling, and also the way a body twists in motion. But Leonardo, with thin layers of oil both translucent and transcendent, and his ability to observe and imagine, was now taking art to an entirely different level. From the mist on the distant horizons to the shadow under the angel's chin to the water at the feet of Christ, Leonardo was redefining how a painter transforms and transmits what he observes.

THE ANNUNCIATION

In addition to the collaborations he did with Verrocchio in the 1470s, the twentysomething Leonardo produced at least four paintings pri-marily on his own while working at the studio: an Annunciation, two small devotional paintings of the Madonna and Child, and a pioneer-ing portrait of a Florentine woman, *Ginevra de' Benci*.

Paintings of the Annunciation, which portray the moment when the angel Gabriel surprised the Virgin Mary by telling her that she would become the mother of Christ, were very popular in the Renaissance. Leonardo's version depicts the announcement and reaction as a narrative occurring in a walled garden of a stately country villa as Mary looks up from reading a book (fig. 11). Although ambitious, the painting is so flawed that its attribution to Leonardo has been debated; some experts contend that it was the product of an awkward collaboration with Verrocchio and others in his shop.[55] But a variety of evidence shows that Leonardo was the primary if not sole artist. He made a preparatory drawing of Gabriel's sleeve, and the painting exhibits his trademark style of dabbing the oil paint with his hands. His finger smudges can be seen, on very close inspection, on the Virgin Mary's right hand and on the leaves of the base of the lectern.[56]

Among the problematic elements of the picture is the bulky garden wall, which seems to be viewed from a slightly higher vantage point than the rest of the picture and distracts from the visual connection between the angel's pointing fingers and Mary's raised hand.

Fig. 11. Leonardo's *The Annunciation*.

It has an odd angle at its opening, which makes it look like it is being viewed from the right, and is jarring when compared to the wall of the house. The cloths covering the Virgin's lap have a rigidity, as if Leonardo had worked on his drapery studies a little too fastidiously, and the odd configuration of what I assume is her armchair makes it seem as if she has three knees. Her pose makes her look like a mannequin, an effect that is compounded by the blankness of her expression. The flatly rendered cypress trees are the same size, yet the one on the right, next to the house, seems closer to us and thus should be bigger. A spindly trunk of one of the cypresses seems to sprout from the angel's fingers, and the botanical exactness of the Madonna lily that the angel holds contrasts with a generic treatment of the other plants and grasses that is untypical of Leonardo.[57]

The most discomforting lapse involves the awkward positioning of Mary in relation to the ornate lectern, which was based on a tomb Verrocchio designed for the Medici. The lectern's base is a few feet closer to the viewer than Mary is, which makes it seem that she is too far away for her right arm to reach the book, yet her arm extends across it, appearing oddly elongated. This is clearly the work of a young artist. *The Annunciation* gives us an insight into what type of painter Leonardo would have been had he not gone on to immerse himself in observations of perspective and studies of optics.

On careful examination, however, the picture is not quite as bad as it looks. Leonardo was experimenting with the trick known as anamorphosis, in which some elements of a work may look distorted when viewed straight on but appear accurate when viewed from another angle. Leonardo occasionally made sketches of the technique in his notebooks. At the Uffizi, guides will suggest that you take a few steps to the right of *The Annunciation* and look again. That helps, but only partly. The angel's arm looks a bit less odd, as does the angle of the opening of the garden wall. It gets slightly better if you also squat down and view the painting from slightly lower. Leonardo was trying to create a piece that would look good to someone walking into the church from the right. He was also nudging us to the right so that we see the act of Annunciation more from Mary's vantage.[58] It almost works. His tricks of perspective display a youthful brilliance, but one that has not yet been refined.

The greatest strength of the picture is Leonardo's depiction of the angel Gabriel. He has the androgynous beauty that Leonardo was perfecting, and his birdlike wings (ignoring the lamentable light brown extension added by someone else) grow out of his shoulders with Leonardo's wondrous blend of naturalism and fantasy. Leonardo is able to convey Gabriel in motion: he is leaning forward, as if he has just landed, and the ribbon tied around his sleeve is fluttering back (unlike in the preparatory drawing), while the wind from his arrival stirs the grass and flowers beneath him.

Another glorious feature of *The Annunciation* is Leonardo's tinting of the shadows. As the setting sun shines from the left side of the painting, it casts a pale yellow glow on the top of the garden wall and the lectern. But where the sun's glow is blocked, the resulting shadows pick up the blue hue of the sky. The front of the white lectern has a slight blue tinge, since it is lit mainly by the refracted light of the sky rather than the yellowish direct glow of the setting sun.[59] "Shadows will vary," Leonardo explained in his notebooks. "The side of an object that receives a reflected light from the azure of the air will be tinged with that hue, and this is particularly observable in white objects. That side that receives the light from the sun will partake of that color. This may be particularly observed in the evening, when the sun is setting between the clouds, which it reddens."[60]

Leonardo was helped in his subtle coloring by his growing mastery of oil paint. By using pigments that were highly diluted, he could apply them in thin translucent layers, subtly allowing the shades to evolve with each fine stroke or dabbing from his fingers. This is most notable in the face of the Virgin Mary. Bathed in the glow of the setting sun, it seems to radiate light with an incandescence not found in Gabriel's flesh. She has a luminosity that causes her to stand out from the rest of the painting, despite her vacant expression.[61]

The Annunciation shows Leonardo, still in his early twenties, experimenting with light, perspective, and narratives involving human reactions. In the process, he made some mistakes. But even the mistakes, which came from innovating and experimenting, heralded his genius.

MADONNAS

Small devotional paintings and sculptures of the Madonna with the infant Jesus were a staple of the Verrocchio workshop, turned out with regularity. Leonardo did at least two such paintings, *Madonna of the Carnation* (fig. 12), also known as the Munich Madonna because of its current location, and the Hermitage Museum's *Madonna and Child with Flowers* (fig. 13), known as the Benois Madonna after a collector who once owned it.

The most interesting aspect of both is the squirming, chubby

Fig. 12. *Madonna of the Carnation* (Munich Madonna).

baby Jesus, whose folds of fat give Leonardo the chance to go beyond the drapery studies in using modeling, light, and shadows to convey realistic three-dimensionality. They become an early example of his use of chiaroscuro, the forceful contrasts of light and shade that use black pigments to alter the tone and brightness of pictorial elements rather than relying on the deepening color hues. "For the first time his chiaroscuro creates, throughout a picture, fully three-dimensional forms rivaling the roundness of sculpture," wrote David Alan Brown of Washington's National Gallery.[62]

The realistic depiction of the baby Jesus in each painting is an early example of Leonardo's art being informed by anatomical observation. "In little children, all the joints are slender and the portions between them are thick," he wrote in his notebook. "This happens

Fig. 13. *Madonna and Child with Flowers* (Benois Madonna).

because nothing but the skin covers the joints without any other flesh and has the character of sinew, connecting the bones like a ligature. And the fat fleshiness is laid on between one joint and the next."[63] This contrast is noticeable in both pictures when comparing the wrists of the Madonna with those of the infant Jesus.

In the Munich *Madonna of the Carnation*, the focus of the picture is the reaction of the newborn Jesus to the flower. The actions of his chubby arms and the emotions shown on his face are connected. He sits on a cushion adorned with crystal balls, a symbol used by the Medici family and an indication that they may have commissioned the work. The landscape seen through the windows shows Leonardo's love of combining observation with fantasy; the hazy atmospheric perspective gives a gauze of reality to jagged rocks that are purely imaginary.

The *Madonna and Child with Flowers* in Russia's Hermitage Museum also shows the lively emotions and reactions that Leonardo had learned to capture in a scene, thus turning a moment into a narrative. In this case, the baby Jesus is absorbed by the cross-shaped flower Mary is handing him, as if he is, as Brown says, "a budding botanist."[64] Leonardo had been studying optics, and he depicts Jesus carefully focusing on the flower, as if he were just learning to discern the form of an object from its background. He gently guides his mother's hands into his focus of sight. Mother and child are integrated by a narrative of reactions: that of Jesus to the flower and that of Mary delighting in the curiosity of her son.

The power of the pictures comes from the premonition that both mother and child seem to have of the crucifixion. The carnation, according to one Christian legend, sprang from the tears Mary shed at the crucifixion. In the Hermitage Museum's Benois Madonna, the symbolism is starker; the flower itself is shaped like a cross. But the psychological impact of the pictures is disappointing. Neither one shows much emotion other than curiosity on the face of Jesus and love on the face of Mary. In Leonardo's later variations on the theme, most notably his *Madonna of the Yarnwinder* and then the *Virgin and Child with Saint Anne* and its variations, he would turn the scene into a much more intense drama and emotional narrative.

Leonardo had two squirming baby models to observe when painting these pictures. After two childless marriages, his father married
a third time, in 1475, and was promptly blessed with two sons, Antonio in 1476 and Giuliano in 1479. Leonardo's notebooks of the
time are filled with drawings and sketches of infants in various active
situations: squirming with a mother, poking at a face, trying to grab
objects or pieces of fruit, and (especially) grappling in many configurations with a cat. Depictions of the Madonna trying to restrain her
restless baby would become an important theme in Leonardo's art.

GINEVRA DE' BENCI

Leonardo's first nonreligious painting is the portrait of a melancholy
young woman with a moonlike face glowing against the backdrop of a
spiky juniper tree (fig. 14). Although somewhat listless and unengag-
ing on first glance, *Ginevra de' Benci* has wonderful Leonardo touches,
such as the lustrous, tightly curled ringlets of hair and unconventional
three-quarters pose. More important, the picture presages the *Mona
Lisa*. As he had done in Verrocchio's *Baptism of Christ*, Leonardo
depicts a meandering river flowing from the misty mountains and
seeming to connect to a human body and soul. With her earth-tone
dress laced by blue thread, Ginevra is unified with the earth and the
river that joins them.

Ginevra de' Benci was the daughter of a prominent Florentine
banker whose aristocratic family was allied with the Medici and
second only to them in wealth. In early 1474, when she was sixteen,
she married Luigi Niccolini, who at thirty-two was a recent widower.
His family, which was in the cloth-weaving business, was politically
prominent but not as wealthy; he soon became the chief magistrate of
the republic, but in a 1480 tax return he declared that he had "more
debts than property." The return also said that his wife was ill and had
been "in the hands of doctors for a long time," which could account
for the unnerving pallor of her complexion in the portrait.

It is likely that Leonardo's father helped him get the commission, probably around the time of Ginevra's 1474 marriage. Piero da

Fig. 14. *Ginevra de' Benci.*

Vinci had served as notary for the Benci family on many occasions, and Leonardo had become friends with Ginevra's older brother, who lent him books and would end up as a temporary custodian of his unfinished *Adoration of the Magi.* But it does not seem that *Ginevra de' Benci* was commissioned as a wedding or betrothal portrait. It shows a three-quarter pose rather than the side profile that was typical of the genre, and she is dressed in a starkly plain brown dress unadorned by jewelry rather than one of the elaborate dresses with luxurious jewels and brocades that was then common for an upper-class wedding painting. Her black shawl is an unlikely adornment for a celebration of a marriage.

In an oddity of Renaissance culture and mores, the picture may not have been commissioned by the Benci family but instead by Bernardo Bembo, who became Venice's ambassador to Florence at the beginning of 1475. He was forty-two at the time and had both a wife and a mistress, but he struck up a proudly public Platonic relationship with Ginevra that made up in effusive adoration what it likely lacked in sexual consummation. This was a type of elevated romance that, at that time, was not only sanctioned but celebrated in poems. "It is with these flames and with such a love that Bembo is on fire and burns, and Ginevra dwells in the midst of his heart," the Florentine Renaissance humanist Cristoforo Landino wrote in a verse extolling their love.[65]

Leonardo painted Bembo's emblem of a laurel and palm wreath on the reverse of the portrait, and it encircles a sprig of juniper, in Italian *ginepro* and thus a reference to Ginevra's name. Woven through the wreath and juniper sprig is a banner proclaiming, "Beauty Adorns Virtue," which attests to her virtuous nature, and an infrared analysis shows Bembo's motto, "Virtue and Honor," had been written beneath it. Suffused with the muted and misty dusk light that Leonardo loved, the painting shows Ginevra looking pale and melancholy. There is a vacant trance-like quality to her, echoed by the dreamlike quality of the distant landscape, that seems to go deeper than merely the physical illness her husband reported.

The portrait, which is more closely focused and sculptural than others of the era, resembles a bust sculpted by Verrocchio, *Lady with Flowers*. The comparison would be even closer except that the bottom portion of Leonardo's painting, perhaps as much as one-third, was at some later date lopped off, which removed what writers from the period described as gracious hands with ivory-white fingers. Fortunately we perhaps can imagine how they looked, since a silverpoint drawing by Leonardo, showing folded hands holding a sprig, which may be related to his painting, exists in the collection at Windsor.[66]

As with the other paintings he did in Verrocchio's shop during the 1470s, Leonardo used thin layers of oil gently blended and blurred, sometimes with his fingers, to create smoky shadows and avoid sharp lines or abrupt transitions. If you stand close enough to the painting at the National Gallery in Washington, DC, you can see his finger-print just to the right of Ginevra's jaw, where her ringlets of hair blur into the background juniper tree and a distinct little spiky sprig juts out. Another can be found just behind her right shoulder.[67]

The most arresting features of the portrait are Ginevra's eyes. The lids are studiously modeled to appear three-dimensional, but this also makes them feel heavy, adding to her somber demeanor. Her gaze looks distracted and indifferent, as if she's looking through us and seeing nothing. Her right eye seems to wander to the distance. At first her gaze seems diverted and looking down and to her left. But the more you stare at each eye separately, the more each seems to focus back on you.

Also noticeable when staring at her eyes is the shiny liquid qual-ity that Leonardo was able to achieve with his oils. Just to the right of each pupil is a tiny spot of luster, showing the sparkling glint from the sunlight coming from the front left. The same use of luster can be seen on her curls.

This perfect glint of luster—the white sparkle caused by a light hitting a smooth and shiny surface—was another of Leonardo's sig-nature marks. It is a phenomenon we see every day but do not often contemplate closely. Unlike reflected light, which "partakes of the color of the object," Leonardo wrote, a spot of luster "is always white," and it moves when the viewer moves. Look at the lustrous glimmer of the curls of *Ginevra de' Benci*, then imagine walking around her. As Leonardo knew, those spots of luster would shift and "appear in as many different places on the surface as different positions are taken by the eye."[68]

After you interact with *Ginevra de' Benci* long enough, what at first seem like a vacant face and distant stare begin to appear suffused with a haunting tinge of emotion. She seems pensive and ruminating, perhaps about her marriage or the departure of Bembo, or because of some deeper mystery. Her life was sad; she was sickly and remained childless. But she also had an inner intensity. She wrote poetry, one line of which survives: "I ask your forgiveness; I am a mountain tiger."[69]

In painting her, Leonardo created a psychological portrait, one that renders hidden emotions. That would become one of his most important artistic innovations. It set him on a trajectory that would culminate three decades later in the greatest psychological portrait in history, the *Mona Lisa*. The tiny hint of a smile that is visible on the right side of Ginevra's lips would be refined into the most memorable smile ever painted. The water flowing from the distant landscape that seems to connect to the soul of Ginevra would become, in the *Mona Lisa*, the ultimate metaphor of the connection between earthly and human forces. *Ginevra de' Benci* is not the *Mona Lisa*, not even close. But it is recognizably the work of the man who would paint it.

CHAPTER 3

On His Own

L'AMORE MASCULINO

In April 1476, a week before his twenty-fourth birthday, Leonardo was accused of engaging in sodomy with a male prostitute. It happened around the time that his father finally had another child, a legitimate son who would become his heir. The anonymous allegation against Leonardo was placed in a *tamburo*, one of the letter drums designated for receipt of morals charges, and involved a seventeen-year-old named Jacopo Saltarelli, who worked in a nearby goldsmith shop. He "dresses in black," the accuser wrote of Saltarelli, "is party to many wretched affairs, and consents to please those persons who request such wickedness of him." Four young men were accused of engaging his sexual services, among them "Leonardo di Ser Piero da Vinci, who lives with Andrea de Verrocchio."

The Officers of the Night, who policed such charges, launched an investigation and may have imprisoned Leonardo and the others for a day or so. The charges could have led to serious criminal penalties if any witnesses were willing to come forward. Fortunately, one of the other four young men was a member of a prominent family that had married into the Medici clan. The case was dismissed "with the condition that no further accusations are made." But a few weeks later, a new accusation was made, this one written in Latin. It said that the four had engaged in multiple sexual engagements with Saltarelli. Because it too was an anonymous allegation and no witnesses came forth to corroborate it, the charges were once again set aside with the same conditions. That, apparently, was the end of the matter.[1]

Thirty years later, Leonardo wrote a bitter comment in a notebook: "When I made a Christ-child you put me in prison, and now if I show him grown up you will do worse to me." The comment is cryptic. Perhaps Saltarelli had modeled for one of his depictions of a young Jesus. At the time, Leonardo felt abandoned. "As I have told you before, I am without any of my friends," he wrote in a note. On the reverse is this: "If there is no love, what then?"[2]

Leonardo was romantically and sexually attracted to men and, unlike Michelangelo, seemed to be just fine with that. He made no effort either to hide or proclaim it, but it probably contributed to his sense of being unconventional, someone who wasn't geared to be part of a family procession of notaries.

Over the years, he would have many beautiful young men as part of his studio and household. Two years after the Saltarelli incidents, on a page with one of his many notebook doodles of an older man and a beautiful boy facing each other in profile, he wrote, "Fioravante di Domenico of Florence is my most beloved friend, as though he were my . . ."[3] The sentence is unfinished, but it leaves the impression that Leonardo had found an emotionally satisfying companion. Shortly after this note, the ruler of Bologna wrote to Lorenzo de' Medici about another young man, who had worked with Leonardo and even adopted his name, Paulo de Leonardo de Vinci da Firenze.* Paulo had been sent away from Florence because of the "wicked life he had led there."[4]

One of Leonardo's earliest male companions was a young musi-

---

* That type of name change was not uncommon for apprentices. A contemporary of Leonardo, the Florentine painter Piero di Cosimo, for example, took his name from his master, Cosimo Rosselli. Leonardo, tellingly, did not do the same and always used his own father's name as part of his full name, Leonardo di ser Piero da Vinci.

cian in Florence named Atalante Migliorotti, whom he taught to play the lyre. Atalante was thirteen in 1480, and around that time Leonardo drew what he described as "a portrait of Atalante raising his face" as well as a full-length sketch of a nude boy from behind playing the lyre.[5] Two years later, Atalante would accompany him to Milan and eventually go on to a successful music career. He would star in a 1491 opera production in Mantua and then make for that city's ruling family a twelve-stringed lyre of "unusual shape."[6]

Leonardo's most serious longtime companion, who joined Leonardo's household in 1490, was angelic looking but devilish in personality, and thus acquired the nickname Salai, the Little Devil. Vasari described him as "a graceful and beautiful youth with fine curly hair in which Leonardo greatly delighted," and he was the subject of many sexual comments and innuendos, as we shall see.

Leonardo was never known to have had a relationship with a woman, and he occasionally recorded his distaste for the idea of heterosexual copulation. He wrote in one of his notebooks, "The sexual act of coitus and the body parts employed for it are so repulsive that, if it were not for the beauty of the faces and the adornment of the actors and the pent-up impulse, nature would lose the human species."[7]

Homosexuality was not uncommon in the artistic community of Florence or in Verrocchio's circle. Verrocchio himself never married, nor did Botticelli, who was also charged with sodomy. Other artists who were gay included Donatello, Michelangelo, and Benvenuto Cellini (who was twice convicted of sodomy). Indeed, *l'amore masculino*, as Lomazzo quoted Leonardo calling it, was so common in Florence that the word *Florenzer* became slang in Germany for "gay." When Leonardo worked for Verrocchio, a cult of Plato was arising among some Renaissance humanists, and it included an idealized view of erotic love for beautiful boys. Homosexual love was celebrated in both uplifting poems and bawdy songs.

Nevertheless, sodomy was a crime, as Leonardo became painfully aware, and it was sometimes prosecuted. During the seventy years following the creation of the Officers of the Night in 1432, an average of four hundred men per year were accused of sodomy, and about sixty per year were convicted and sentenced to prison, exile, or even death.[8] The Church considered homosexual acts a sin. A 1484 papal bull likened sodomy to "carnal knowledge with demons," and preachers regularly railed against it. Dante, whose *Divine Comedy* was beloved by Leonardo and illustrated by Botticelli, consigned sodomites, along with blasphemers and usurers, to the seventh circle of hell. However, Dante displayed Florence's conflicted feelings about homosexuals by praising in the poem one of the denizens he put into this circle, his own mentor, Brunetto Latini.

Some writers, following Freud's unsubstantiated assertions that Leonardo's "passive homosexual" desires were "sublimated," have speculated that his desires were repressed and channeled into his work. One of his maxims seems to give support to the theory that he believed in controlling his sexual urges: "Whoever does not curb lustful desires puts himself on the level of beasts."[9] But there is no reason to believe that he remained celibate. "Those who wish, in the interest of morality, to reduce Leonardo, that inexhaustible source of creative power, to a neutral or sexless agency, have a strange idea of doing service to his reputation," wrote Kenneth Clark.[10]

On the contrary, in his life and in his notebooks, there is much evidence that he was not ashamed of his sexual desires. Instead he seemed amused by them. In a section of his notebooks called "On the Penis," he described quite humorously how the penis had a mind of its own and acted at times without the will of the man: "The penis sometimes displays an intellect of its own. When a man may desire it to be stimulated, it remains obstinate and goes its own way, sometimes moving on its own without the permission of its owner. Whether he is awake or sleeping, it does what it desires. Often when the man wishes to use it, it desires otherwise, and often it wishes to be used and the man forbids it. Therefore it appears that this creature possesses a life and an intelligence separate from the man." He found it curious that the penis was often a source of shame and that men were shy about discussing it. "Man is wrong to be ashamed of giving it a name or showing it," he added, "always covering and concealing something that deserves to be adorned and displayed with ceremony."[11]

How was this reflected in his art? In his drawings and notebook sketches, he showed a far greater fascination for the male body than the female. His drawings of male nudes tend to be works of tender beauty, many rendered in full length. By contrast, almost all of the women he painted, with the exception of a now lost *Leda and the Swan*, are clothed and shown from the waist up.*

Nevertheless, unlike Michelangelo, Leonardo was a master at painting women. From *Ginevra de' Benci* to the *Mona Lisa*, his portraits of women are deeply sympathetic and psychologically insightful. His *Ginevra* is innovative, at least for Italy, by ushering in a three-quarter view for women's poses rather than the full profile that was standard. This allows viewers to look at the eyes of the woman, which, as Leonardo declared, are "the window of the soul." With *Ginevra* women were no longer presented as passive mannequins but were shown as people with their own thoughts and emotions.[12]

On a deeper level, Leonardo's homosexuality seems to have been manifest in his sense of himself as somewhat different, an outsider who didn't quite fit in. By the time he was thirty, his increasingly successful father was an establishment insider and a legal adviser to the Medici, the top guilds, and churches. He was also an exemplar of traditional masculinity; by then he'd had at least one mistress, three wives, and five children. Leonardo, on the contrary, was essentially an outsider. The birth of his half-siblings reinforced the fact that he was not considered legitimate. As a gay, illegitimate artist twice accused of sodomy, he knew what it was like to be regarded, and to regard yourself, as different. But as with many artists, that turned out to be more an asset than a hindrance.

---

* Another possible exception, in addition to the probable *Leda and the Swan*, may have been a half-nude version of the *Mona Lisa*, which does not survive in his own hand but exists in versions by others in his studio. In his series of anatomical drawings, he drew a woman's anatomy, which has a crude and flawed depiction of female genitalia, looking like a forbidding and dark cave. This was a case of not letting experience be a mistress, or vice versa.

SAINT SEBASTIAN

Around the time of the Saltarelli allegations, Leonardo was working on a devotional portrait of Saint Sebastian, the third-century martyr who was tied to a tree, shot with arrows, and later clubbed to death during the Roman emperor Diocletian's persecution of Christians. According to a list of possessions that Leonardo compiled, he drew eight studies for the work, which he apparently never painted.

The image of Sebastian was considered a protection against the plague, but he was also portrayed with homoerotic undertones by some fifteenth-century Italian artists. Vasari wrote that a Saint Sebastian portrait by Bartolommeo Bandinelli was so erotically charged that "parishioners admitted in the confessional that the beautiful nude prompted unclean thoughts."[13]

The surviving Leonardo drawings of Sebastian fall into that category of being beautiful and somewhat charged. The boyish-looking saint is depicted nude with a hand tied behind him to a tree, his face filled with emotion. In one of the drawings, now in Hamburg, you can see how Leonardo wrestled with the movements and contortions and twists of Sebastian's body, sketching his feet in different positions.[14]

Miraculously, one of his missing Saint Sebastian drawings turned up at the end of 2016, when a retired French doctor brought some old artworks that had been collected by his father to an auction house for appraisal. Thaddée Prate, a director at the auction house, spotted one as a possible Leonardo, an attribution that was confirmed by Carmen Bambach, a curator at New York's Metropolitan Museum of Art. "My eyes jumped out of their sockets," Bambach said. "The attribution is quite incontestable. My heart will always pound when I think about that drawing." The newly discovered drawing shows Sebastian's torso and chest modeled by Leonardo's left-handed hatching, but as in the Hamburg version he was still trying different options for the placement of the saint's legs and feet. "It has so many changes of ideas, so much energy in the way he explores the figure," Bambach said. "It has a furious spontaneity. It's like glancing over his shoulder."[15] In addition to showing us Leonardo energetically exploring ideas on paper, the discovery signifies that, even today, there are things about Leonardo that we can find anew.

ADORATION OF THE MAGI

In the accusations against him, Leonardo was described as still living in Verrocchio's workshop. He was twenty-four, and most former apprentices would have flown their master's nest by then. But Leonardo was not only still living with his teacher but was producing Madonnas so lacking in distinctiveness that it is hard to tell whether they were painted by him or someone else in the workshop.

Perhaps prodded by the Saltarelli affair, Leonardo finally broke away and opened a workshop of his own in 1477. Commercially, it was a failure. During the subsequent five years before he headed off to Milan, he would receive only three known commissions, one of which he never started and the other two he left unfinished. Nevertheless, even two unfinished paintings would be enough to enhance his reputation and influence the practice of art.

Leonardo's first commission, which he received in 1478, was to paint an altarpiece for the chapel in the Palazzo della Signoria. His father served as a notary to the Signoria, Florence's governing council, and was thus in a position to help him get the assignment. Some preparatory drawings Leonardo made indicate that he was planning to paint a scene of the shepherds who came to pay their respects to the infant Jesus in Bethlehem.[16]

There is no evidence that he started on the work. However, some of the sketches were inspirations for a painting that he soon began on a related theme, the *Adoration of the Magi* (fig. 15). It was destined to remain unfinished, but it became the most influential unfinished painting in the history of art and, in the words of Kenneth Clark, "the most revolutionary and anti-classical picture of the fifteenth century."[17] The *Adoration of the Magi* thus encapsulates Leonardo's frustrating genius: a pathbreaking and astonishing display of brilliance that was abandoned once it was conceptualized.

The *Adoration* was commissioned in March 1481, when Leonardo was twenty-nine, by the monastery of San Donato, which was just

Fig. 15. *Adoration of the Magi.*

outside the walls of Florence. Once again his father helped. Piero
da Vinci was a notary for the monks and bought his firewood from
them. That year he was given two chickens for work he had done,
which included negotiating a complex contract for his son to paint
the *Adoration* as well as to decorate the face of the monastery's clock.[18]

His father was clearly worried, like the parents of many twenty-
somethings over the ages, about his talented child's work habits. The
monks were as well. The elaborate contract was designed to force
Leonardo, already known for leaving paintings unfinished, to buckle

down and produce a completed work. It stipulated that he had to supply from his own pocket "the colors, the gold and all other costs arising." The painting had to be delivered "within thirty months at the most," or Leonardo would be forced to forfeit whatever he had done and get no compensation. Even the payment plan was odd: Leonardo would receive some property near Florence that had been donated to the monastery, have the right to sell it back to the monastery for 300 florins, but would also have to pay a young woman's dowry of 150 florins that had been part of the land bequest.

It was clear within three months that these badly laid plans were going awry. Leonardo was unable to pay the first installment on the dowry, and he thus went into debt to the monastery for it. He also had to borrow money to buy paint. He was paid a bundle of sticks and logs for decorating the monastery's clock, but his account was debited for "one barrel of vermilion wine" that he got on credit.[19] Thus one of history's most creative artists found himself decorating a clock for firewood, borrowing money for paint, and cadging wine.

The scene Leonardo set out to paint in the *Adoration of the Magi* was one of the most popular in Renaissance Florence: the moment when the three wise men, or kings, who have followed a guiding star to Bethlehem, present the newborn Jesus with gifts of gold, frankincense, and myrrh. The Feast of the Epiphany, which commemorates the revelation of the divinity of Jesus Christ and the adoration of him by the Magi, was marked every January in Florence by a day of pageants and reenactments of the procession. The festivities reached a peak in 1468, when Leonardo was a fifteen-year-old apprentice working on such Medici extravaganzas. The entire city became a stage, and the processional included close to seven hundred riders, the young ones each wearing a mask carved with their father's face.[20]

Many others had painted the Adoration scene, most notably Botticelli, who produced at least seven versions. His most famous was done in 1475 for a church near where Leonardo lived. Like most other versions of the scene before Leonardo, Botticelli's were stately affairs, with dignified kings and courtly princes comporting themselves with reverence and decorum.

Botticelli, whose workshop turned out devotional Madonnas at a faster clip than even Verrocchio's, was seven years older than Leonardo and had won far greater patronage from the Medici. He was good at courting such favor. His greatest *Adoration* incorporates portraits of Cosimo de' Medici, his sons Piero and Giovanni, and his grandsons Lorenzo and Giuliano.

Leonardo was often critical of Botticelli, whose version of an Annunciation scene, painted in 1481, was probably what prompted Leonardo to write, "I recently saw an Annunciation in which the angel looked as if she wished to chase Our Lady out of the room with movement of such violence that she might have been a hated enemy; and Our Lady seemed in such despair that she was about to throw herself out of the window."[21] Leonardo later noted, correctly, that Botticelli "makes very dull landscapes" and, lacking a feel for aerial perspective, painted both close and distant trees the same shade of green.[22]

Despite his disdain, Leonardo closely studied Botticelli's versions of the *Adoration of the Magi* and adopted some of his ideas.[23] But then he set out to make one that, unlike Botticelli's, was filled with energy, emotion, agitation, and messiness. His concept, which showed how he was influenced by pageants and public spectacles, was to produce a vortex—that spiral form he loved—centered on the infant Jesus, with a frenzied procession of at least sixty people and animals swirling around and engulfing him. This was supposed to be, after all, a tale of the Epiphany, and Leonardo wanted to convey the full power of the astonishment and awe of the wise men and accompanying throngs as they are seized by the revelation that Jesus is the Christ child, God incarnate.

Leonardo made multiple preparatory drawings, which were sketched with a stylus and then refined with a quill and ink. In them he explores various gestures, body turns, and expressions that convey a wave of emotion meant to ripple through the work. Many of the figures in his preparatory drawings are nude; he had come to believe in Alberti's advice that an artist should build a picture of a human body from the inside out, first conceiving of the skeleton, then the skin, then the clothing.[24]

The most famous preparatory drawing is a sheet that lays out
Leonardo's initial conception for the entire picture (fig. 16). On it he
plots his perspective lines, following the methods used by Brunelleschi and Alberti. As the scene recedes to the vanishing point, the
horizontal lines, which he drew with a ruler, are compressed with
incredible precision, far more than necessary for a finished painting.

Combined with this meticulous grid are quick, spectral sketches
of twisting and scrambling humans, rearing and frenzied horses, and
an ultimate bit of Leonardo fantasia: a resting camel twisting his neck
to regard the scene with a wild surmise. Mathematically delineated,
precise lines work in concert with frenzied motion and emotion. It is
a remarkable combination of optical science and imaginative art, and
it shows how he constructed his art on a scaffold of science.[25]

As he completed this preparatory drawing, Leonardo had his assistants assemble a large panel, eight-foot square, out of ten planks
of poplar wood. Instead of using the traditional method of pricking

Fig. 16. Preparatory study for the *Adoration of the Magi*.

the preparatory drawing and transferring it to the panel, Leonardo made many modifications to the design and then sketched a new version directly on the panel, which he had treated with a chalky white primer coat. This became his underdrawing.[26]

A technical investigation was done in 2002 for the Uffizi Museum by art analyst Maurizio Seracini, who used high-resolution scans along with ultrasound, ultraviolet, and infrared imaging techniques.[27] The resulting images allow us to appreciate this superb underdrawing and the steps Leonardo took as he created his dramatic scene.

First he put a nail near the center of the panel, right in what became the trunk of the tree, and attached a string so that he could etch perspective lines with a fine stylus onto the white priming coat. Then he drew the architectural background, which included steps leading up to a ruined ancient Roman palace, symbolizing the crumbling of classical paganism. The scientific analysis shows that the underdrawing at one point had sketches of construction workers repairing the ruins in the background.[28] The little scene became a metaphorical expression of the ruined house of David, which Christ would reestablish, and of the rebirth of classical works.

Once he had completed the background, Leonardo began to work on the human figures. By using a fine-tipped black chalk to sketch them lightly, he could revise and retouch them, which allowed him to perfect the gestures until he was satisfied that they conveyed the proper emotions.

We are again lucky that Leonardo described in his notebook the artistic principles that he put into practice, in this case the use of light sketching and revisions to capture mental states. It helps us better appreciate his works as well as the thinking that went into them. "Do not draw the limbs of your figure with hard contours or the same fate will happen to you as has happened to many painters who wished every little stroke of charcoal to be definite," he advised. By drawing fixed lines, these artists create figures that "do not move their limbs in a manner that reflects the motions of their mind." A good painter, he continued, should "decide broadly upon the position of the limbs and attend first to the movement appropriate to the mental attitudes of the creatures in the narrative."[29]

When he was satisfied with his chalk sketches, Leonardo inked them with a thin brush and then filled in the proper shadows with a light blue wash. This was a departure from the brown wash he and other painters traditionally used. Through his study of optics, he knew that a dusty and misty atmosphere gave a blue tint to shadows. Once he had finished this underdrawing on the panel, he covered it with a thin layer of white primer so that it was faintly visible. Then he started, very slowly, to paint.

In the center of his composition for the *Adoration of the Magi*, Leonardo placed the Virgin Mary with a squirming infant Jesus on her lap. His hand reaches out, and from it the narrative swirls in a clockwise spiral. As the viewer's eye moves around this frenzied vortex, the painting becomes not merely a moment but a dramatic narrative. Jesus is accepting a gift from one of the kings, while another of the kings, having already given his gift, is bowing his head to the ground in reverence.

Leonardo rarely featured Mary's husband, Joseph, in his paintings, including those of the Holy Family, and it is not immediately clear in the *Adoration* which if any figure is supposed to be him. But Joseph is in one of Leonardo's preparatory drawings, and it seems to me that he is the similar bald and bearded man behind Mary's shoulder holding the lid and peering into the container of the first gift.[30]

Almost all the characters in the picture, the infant Jesus included, are engaged in motions that are—as they would be in *The Last Supper*—connected to emotions: handing a gift, opening one, bowing to the ground, slapping a forehead in amazement, pointing upward. Leaning on a rock are some younger travelers engaged in animated conversation, while just in front of them an awed onlooker raises his palm to the heavens. We are witnessing the physical and mental response, including amazement and reverence and curiosity, to an epiphany. Only the Virgin seems still, the calm in the vortex.

Portraying the swirl of characters was a daunting task, perhaps too much so. Each had to have a unique pose and set of emotions. As Leonardo later wrote in his notebook, "Do not repeat the same movements in the same figure, be it limbs, hands or fingers, nor should the same pose be repeated in one narrative painting."[31] Among the characters he originally considered were a group of fighters on horseback near the top of the picture. They appear in the preparatory sketch and the underdrawing, where they are modeled with careful shadowing, but Leonardo had trouble integrating them into the swirl. They are partly abandoned in the unfinished painting, though they foreshadow the horses he would later use in his (also unfinished) *Battle of Anghiari.*

The result is a whirlwind of drama and emotion. Not only did Leonardo render each of the reactions of those first beholding the Christ child, but he turned the Epiphany into a swirl in which each character is swept by the others' emotions, and then so is the viewer.

ABANDONED

Leonardo went on to paint the sky in the *Adoration of the Magi* and some highlights of the human figures and parts of the architectural ruins. Then he stopped.

Why? One possible reason is that the task he undertook became overwhelming for a perfectionist. As Vasari explained about Leonardo's unfinished works, he was stymied because his conceptions were "so subtle and so marvelous" that they were impossible to execute faultlessly. "It seemed to him that the hand was not able to attain to the perfection of art in carrying out the things which he imagined." According to Lomazzo, the other early biographer, "he never finished any of the works he began because, so sublime was his idea of art, he saw faults even in the things that to others seemed miracles."[32]

Perfecting the *Adoration of the Magi* must have been especially daunting. There were originally more than sixty characters in his underdrawing. As he went along, he reduced this number by turning some groups of fighters or builders in the background into fewer large-scale characters, but that still left more than thirty to be rendered. He was intent on making sure each one reacted emotionally to the others so that the painting would feel like a coherent narrative and not a random assortment of isolated characters.

Even more complex were the lighting challenges, made all the more difficult by his obsession with optics. On the bottom of a note-book page from around 1480 that shows the mechanisms of the crane that Brunelleschi used to erect Florence's cathedral dome, Leonardo sketched a diagram of how light rays hit the surface of a human eye and are focused inside the eyeball.[33] In painting the *Adoration of the Magi*, he wanted to convey the power of the light that shone down from heaven with the Epiphany and how each rebound of reflected light affected the coloration and gradation of each shadow. "He must have faltered at the thought of how to balance the reflections that bounce from one figure to another and to control the myriad variables of light, shade, and emotions for such a multitude," according to the art historian Francesca Fiorani. "Unlike any other artist, he could not ignore an optical problem."[34]

It was an unnerving set of iterative tasks. All thirty characters had to reflect light and project shade that would influence, and be influenced by, the light and shadows of those around them. They also had to initiate and reflect emotions, which in turn affected, and were affected by, the emotions emanating from those around them.

There was another reason, one even more fundamental, that Leonardo did not complete the painting: he preferred the conception to the execution. As his father and others knew when they drew up the strict contract for his commission, Leonardo at twenty-nine was more easily distracted by the future than he was focused on the present. He was a genius undisciplined by diligence.

He seems to have illustrated this personal trait, consciously or not, in an apparent self-portrait he drew on the far right side of the painting (figs. 2 and 15). A boyish character, pointing toward Jesus but looking away, is in the location often used by Renaissance artists to insert a likeness of themselves. (Botticelli portrays himself in the same location in his *Adoration* of 1475.) The boy's nose and curls and other attributes match the description and other presumed depictions that exist of Leonardo.[35]

This boy is what Alberti referred to as "the commentator," the person who is in a picture but out of it, who is not part of the action but instead connects to the world beyond the frame. His body is facing Jesus, his arm points that way, and his right foot is angled as if he had been moving in that direction. But his head is turned sharply to the left, looking toward something else, as if he had become distracted. He has paused before walking into the action. His eyes are looking far away. He is part of the scene but detached from it, an observer and commentator who is immersed but marginalized. He is, like Leonardo, of this world but apart from it.

Seven months after Leonardo was commissioned to create the painting, his payments ended. He had stopped work. When he departed Florence for Milan shortly thereafter, he left the unfinished painting with his friend Giovanni de' Benci, the brother of Ginevra.

The monks of San Donato subsequently commissioned Botticelli's protégé Filippino Lippi to paint a substitute. The young Lippi had learned from Botticelli the fine art of flattery; as in Botticelli's earlier version, Lippi's *Adoration of the Magi* features likenesses of many members of the Medici family. Leonardo, who lacked that instinct to cater to patrons when painting, had paid no such homage to the Medici in his unfinished *Adoration* or in any of his other works. That was likely one reason Botticelli, Filippino Lippi, and his father, Filippo Lippi, all enjoyed the generous Medici patronage that eluded Leonardo.

In some ways, Filippino Lippi tried to follow Leonardo's original design in the *Adoration* he painted as a substitute. The kings kneel before the Holy Family with their gifts, while a cavalcade of onlookers swirl around. Lippi even includes a portrait of a commentator character on the far right, with the exact pose Leonardo had used. But Lippi's commentator is a calm, older sage, not a dreamy and distracted young man. And even though Lippi tried to give his characters some interesting gestures, there is little of the excitement, energy, passions, or movements of the soul that Leonardo had envisaged.

SAINT JEROME IN THE WILDERNESS

Leonardo's dedication to connecting movements of the body with movements of the soul was manifest in the other great painting he probably began around that time,[36] *Saint Jerome in the Wilderness* (fig. 17). The unfinished work shows Saint Jerome, a fourth-century scholar who translated the Bible into Latin, during his retreat as a hermit in the desert. With an outstretched and twisted arm, he holds a rock that he will beat to his chest in penance; at his feet is the lion that became his companion after he pulled a thorn from its paw. The saint is haggard and emaciated, exuding shame as he seems to implore forgiveness, yet his eyes show his inner strength. The background is filled with Leonardo's signature designs, including a rocky outcropping and a misty landscape.

All of Leonardo's paintings are psychological, and all give vent to his desire to portray emotions, but none more intensely than *Saint Jerome*. The saint's entire body, through its twists and uncomfortable kneeling, conveys passion. The painting also represents Leonardo's first anatomical drawing and—as he fiddled with and revised it over the years—shows the intimate connection between his anatomical and artistic endeavors. He became typically obsessive as he carried forward Alberti's injunction that artists should conceive a body from the inside out. Leonardo wrote, "It is necessary for the painter, in order to be good at arranging the parts of the body in attitudes and gestures which can be represented in the nude, to know the anatomy of the sinews, bones and muscles and tendons."[37]

There is one puzzling detail about the anatomy in *Saint Jerome*, which when unpacked helps us better understand Leonardo's art. He began work on the painting around 1480, yet it seems to accurately reflect the anatomical knowledge that he gleaned later, including from dissections he made in 1510. Most notable is the neck. In Leonardo's early anatomical works and in a drawing he made of Judas around 1495 in preparation for *The Last Supper* (fig. 18), he mistakenly showed the sternocleidomastoid, which goes from the collarbone up the side of the neck, as a single muscle, when in fact it is a pair of muscles. But in his 1510 drawings based on human dissections, which are in the Royal Collection at Windsor, he would get it right (fig. 19).[38] It is somewhat puzzling that his depiction of Saint Jerome, with his neck correctly showing two muscles, includes an anatomical detail that he did not know in the 1480s and discovered only in 1510.[39]

Fig. 17. *Saint Jerome in the Wilderness.*

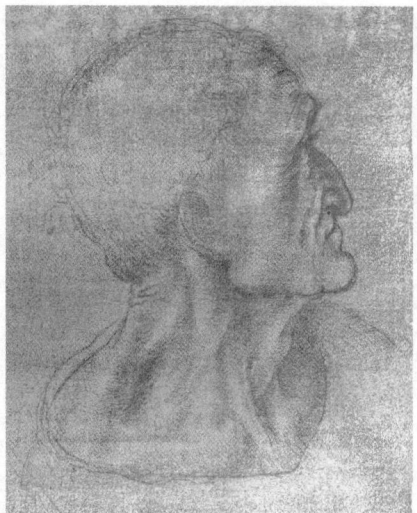 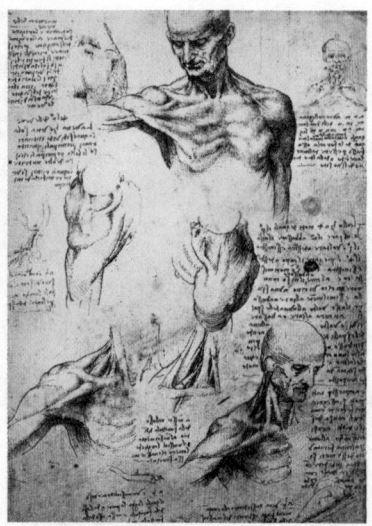

Fig. 18. Drawing in 1495 with neck   Fig. 19. Anatomy drawing c. 1510
muscle incorrect.   with neck muscle correct.

The curator of drawings at Windsor, Martin Clayton, came up with the most convincing explanation. He posited that the painting was done in two phases, the first around 1480 and the other following the dissection studies he made in 1510. Clayton's theory was supported by infrared analysis, which showed that the dual neck muscles were not part of the original underdrawing and that they were painted with a technique different from the other parts. "Significant parts of the modeling of the *Saint Jerome* were added twenty years after his first outlining of the figure," said Clayton, "and that modeling incorporates the anatomical discoveries that Leonardo made during his dissections of the winter of 1510."[40]

The significance of this goes beyond helping us understand the anatomical aspects of the *Saint Jerome*. It shows that Leonardo's record of unreliability was not simply because he decided to give up on certain paintings. He wanted to perfect them, so he kept hold of many of them for years, making refinements.

Even some of his commissions that were completed, or almost so—*Ginevra de' Benci* and the *Mona Lisa*, for example—were never delivered to clients. Leonardo clung to his favorite works, carried them with him when he moved, and returned to them when he had new ideas. He certainly did that with the *Saint Jerome*, and he may have planned to do the same with the *Adoration of the Magi*, which he entrusted to Ginevra's brother for safekeeping but never sold or gave away. He did not like to let go. That is why he would die with some of his masterpieces still near his bedside. As frustrating as it is to us today, there was a poignant and inspiring aspect to Leonardo's unwillingness to declare a painting done and relinquish it: he knew that there was always more he might learn, new techniques he might master, and further inspirations that might strike him. And he was right.

MOTIONS OF THE MIND

Even unfinished, the *Adoration of the Magi* and *Saint Jerome* show that Leonardo was pioneering a new style that treated narrative paintings and even portraits as psychological expositions. This approach to art was partly informed by his love of pageants, theatrical productions, and court amusements; he knew how actors feign sentiments, and he recognized the tells on the lips and in the eyes of audience members that indicate their reactions. It probably also helped that the Italians, then as now, were expressive in their gestures, which Leonardo loved to capture in his notebooks.

He sought to portray not only *moti corporali*, the motions of the body, but also how they related to what he called "atti e moti mentali," the attitudes and motions of the mind.[41] More important, he was a master at connecting the two. This is most noticeable in his action-packed and gesture-filled narrative works, such as the *Adoration* and *The Last Supper*. But it is also the genius behind his most serene portraits, most notably the *Mona Lisa*.

Portraying the "motions of the mind" was not a new concept. Pliny the Elder complimented the fourth-century BC painter Aristides of Thebes by saying he was "the first to express the mentality, sentiments, character, and passions of a subject."[42] Alberti, in *On Painting*, emphasized the importance of the idea in a clear and crisp sentence: "Movements of the soul are made known by movements of the body."[43]

Leonardo was deeply influenced by Alberti's book, and he repeatedly echoed that injunction in his own notebooks. "The good painter has to paint two principal things, man and the intention of his mind," he wrote. "The first is easy and the second is difficult, because the latter has to be represented through gestures and movements of the limbs."[44] He expanded on this concept in a long passage in his notes for his planned treatise on painting: "The movement which is depicted must be appropriate to the mental state of the figure. The motions and postures of figures should display the true mental state of the originator of these motions, in such a way they can mean nothing else. Movements should announce the motions of the mind."[45]

Leonardo's dedication to portraying the outward manifestations of inner emotions would end up driving not only his art but some of his anatomical studies. He needed to know which nerves emanated from the brain and which from the spinal cord, which muscles they activated, and which facial movements were connected to others. He would even try, when dissecting the brain, to figure out the precise location where the connections were made between sensory perceptions, emotions, and motions. By the end of his career, his pursuit of how the brain and nerves turned emotions into motions became almost obsessive. It was enough to make the *Mona Lisa* smile.

DESPAIR

Leonardo's portrayal of emotions may have been enhanced by the fact that he was wrestling with his own inner turmoil. His inability to finish the *Adoration of the Magi* and *Saint Jerome* may have been caused by, and in turn contributed to, melancholy or depression. His notebooks from around 1480 are filled with expressions of gloom, even anguish. On a page that includes a drawing of a water clock and sundial, he lets loose a lament that touches on the sadness of unfinished work: "We do not lack devices for measuring these miserable days of ours, in which it should be our pleasure that they be not frittered away without leaving behind any memory of ourselves in the mind of men."[46] He began scribbling the same phrase over and over again, every time he needed to try a new pen nib or to fritter away a moment: "Tell me if anything was ever done . . . Tell me . . . Tell me."[47]

And at one point he jotted a cry of anguish: "While I thought that I was learning how to live, I have been learning how to die."[48]

Also in his notebooks from around this time are quotes from others that Leonardo found worth recording. One is from a friend who wrote a very personal poem addressed to him. "Leonardo, why so troubled?" the friend writes.[49] On another page is a quote from someone named Johannes: "There is no perfect gift without great suffering. Our glories and our triumphs pass away."[50] On the same sheet is a transcription from Dante's *Inferno*:

> *"Put off this sloth," the master said, "for shame!*
> *Sitting on feather-pillows, lying reclined*
> *Beneath the blanket is no way to fame—*
> *Fame, without which man's life wastes out of mind,*
> *Leaving on earth no more memorial*
> *Than foam in water or smoke upon the wind."*[51]

While he was despairing about, as he saw it, sitting on feather pillows, lying beneath the blanket, and leaving no legacy more lasting than smoke upon the wind, his rivals were enjoying great success. Botticelli, who was definitely not suffering from an inability to churn out finished work, had become the favored painter of the Medici; he was commissioned by them to do two major works, *Spring* and *Pallas and the Centaur*. In 1478 Botticelli painted a damning public depiction of the conspirators who had assassinated Giuliano de' Medici and wounded his brother Lorenzo. When the final plotter was captured a year later, Leonardo did a careful sketch of his hanging and jotted details in his notebook, as if hoping to do a companion painting (fig. 20). But the Medici gave the commission to someone else. Botticelli was again among the chosen in 1481, when Pope Sixtus IV summoned prominent Florentine and other artists to come to Rome to fresco the walls of the Sistine Chapel; Leonardo was not selected.

As he approached his thirtieth birthday, Leonardo had established his genius but had remarkably little to show for it publicly. His only known artistic accomplishments were some brilliant but peripheral contributions to two Verrocchio paintings, a couple of devotional Madonnas that were hard to distinguish from others being produced in the workshop, a portrait of a young woman that he had not delivered, and two unfinished would-be masterpieces.

"When a man has learned in Florence as much as he can, if he wishes to do more than live from day to day like an animal, and instead desires to become rich, he must take his departure from that place," Vasari wrote. "For Florence treats her craftsmen as time treats its own works, which, when perfected, it destroys and consumes little by little."[52] It was time for Leonardo to move on. The fact that he was feeling consumed and was in a fragile mental state, filled with fantasies and fears, was reflected in his willingness to leave Florence and in a letter he would write to the person he hoped would be his next patron.

Fig. 20. The hanging of Bernardo Baroncelli.

CHAPTER 4

Milan

CULTURAL DIPLOMAT

In 1482, the year he turned thirty, Leonardo da Vinci left Florence for Milan, where he would end up spending the next seventeen years. Traveling with him was his companion Atalante Migliorotti, now fifteen, the aspiring musician who learned from Leonardo how to play the lyre and became one of the many young men who floated in and out of his retinue over the years.[1] Leonardo estimated in his notebook that the trip was 180 miles long, which was quite accurate; he had devised a type of odometer that measured distance by counting the turns of a vehicle wheel, and he may have experimented with one on the way. It would have taken him and his companions about a week.

With him he carried a *lira da braccio* (lyre for the arm), roughly akin to a fiddle or violin. "He was sent by Lorenzo the Magnificent, along with Atalante Migliorotti, to the Duke of Milan to present him a lyre, since he was unique in playing this instrument," the Anonimo Gaddiano reports. It was made partly of silver, and Leonardo had crafted it in the shape of a horse's skull.

The lyre and Leonardo's services were a diplomatic gift. Lorenzo de' Medici, eager to navigate the swirling rivalries and alliances among the Italian city-states, saw Florence's artistic culture as a source of influence. Botticelli and some of his other favorite artists went to Rome to please the pope, Verrocchio and others to Venice.

Leonardo and Atalante were probably part of a February 1482 diplomatic delegation headed by Bernardo Rucellai, a wealthy banker, arts patron, and philosophy enthusiast who was married to Lorenzo's older sister and had just been made Florence's ambassador to Milan.[2] In his writings, Rucellai introduced the term *balance of power* to describe the continuous conflicts and shifting alliances involving Florence, Milan, other Italian city-states, plus a pride of popes, French kings, and Holy Roman emperors. The competition among the various rulers was not only military but cultural, and Leonardo sought to be useful on both fronts.

Packing almost all of his belongings, Leonardo embarked for Milan with the thought that he might move there indefinitely. The list he made of his possessions sometime after his arrival in Milan seems to encompass most of his work that could be transported. In addition to the drawing of Atalante with his face raised, there were sketches of "many flowers copied from nature . . . some Saint Jeromes . . . designs of furnaces . . . a head of Christ done in pen . . . eight Saint Sebastians . . . many compositions of angels . . . a head in profile with beautiful hair . . . gadgets for ships . . . gadgets for water . . . many necks of old women and heads of old men . . . many complete nudes . . . a Madonna finished . . . another almost finished that is in profile . . . the head of an old man with an enormous chin . . . a narrative of the Passion made in relief" and much more.[3] The inclusion on the list of designs for furnaces and gadgets for ships and for water shows that he was already engaged with engineering as well as art.

Milan, with 125,000 citizens, was three times the size of Florence. More important for Leonardo, it had a ruling court. The Medici in Florence were generous supporters of the arts, but they were bankers who operated behind the scenes. Milan was different. For two hundred years, it had been not a merchant republic but a city-state ruled by militaristic strongmen who crowned themselves hereditary dukes, first the heads of the Visconti family and then the Sforza family. Because their ambitions were grand but their claims to their titles tenuous, their castles were filled with courtiers, artists, performers, musicians, huntmasters, statecrafters, animal trainers, engineers, and any other helpers or ornaments who could burnish their prestige and legitimacy. In other words, Milan's castle provided a perfect environment for Leonardo, who had a fondness for strong leaders, loved the diversity of talent they attracted, and aspired to be on a comfortable retainer.

When Leonardo arrived, Milan was ruled by Ludovico Sforza, who was also thirty. A dark-skinned and burly man nicknamed "Il Moro" (the Moor), he was not actually the Duke of Milan yet, though he exercised the authority and would soon grab the title. His father, Francesco Sforza, one of seven illegitimate sons of a military mercenary, had seized power and made himself duke in 1450, after the Visconti dynasty dissolved. Upon his death, Ludovico's older brother became duke, but he was soon assassinated, leaving the title to his seven-year-old son. Ludovico eased aside the boy's mother as regent, thus effectively taking control of Milan in 1479. He set about beguiling and bullying his hapless nephew, usurping his powers, executing his supporters, and probably poisoning him. He officially invested himself the Duke of Milan in 1494.

Ruthless in a pragmatic way, Ludovico cloaked his calculated cruelty with pretenses of courtesy, culture, and civility. Tutored by the distinguished Renaissance humanist Francesco Filelfo in painting and writing, he sought to legitimize his power and prestige, along with that of Milan, by attracting great scholars and artists to the Sforza court. He had long dreamed of building a massive equestrian monument to his father, partly as a way to enshrine the family's power.

Unlike Florence, Milan was not well-stocked with master artists. That made it more fertile territory for Leonardo. Because he was an aspiring polymath, he also enjoyed that Milan was filled with scholars and intellectuals in a wide variety of fields, partly due to the esteemed university in nearby Pavia, which was officially founded in 1361 but had roots stretching back to 825. It boasted some of Europe's best lawyers, philosophers, medical researchers, and mathematicians.

Ludovico spent profligately on his personal desires: 140,000 ducats to refurbish the rooms of his palace and 16,000 ducats for his hunting hawks, hounds, and horses.* He was stingier with the intellectual and entertainment retainers in his court: his astrologer had an annual stipend of 290 ducats, high-level government officials got 150 ducats, and the artist-architect Donato Bramante, who would become Leonardo's friend, complained of getting only 62 ducats.[4]

THE JOB APPLICATION

It was probably soon after his arrival in Milan that Leonardo drafted the letter to Ludovico described at the beginning of this book. Some historians have supposed that he wrote the letter from Florence, but this seems unlikely. He mentioned the park adjoining Ludovico's castle and the proposed equestrian monument to his father, indications that he had already spent time in Milan and then sent a letter.[5]

Leonardo did not, of course, write it in his usual mirror script. The copy that survives in his notebooks is a draft, marked up with a few changes, that was composed in the conventional left-to-right manner by a scribe or one of his assistants with good penmanship.[6] It reads:

Most illustrious Lord,

Having now sufficiently studied the inventions of all those who proclaim themselves skilled contrivers of instruments of war, and having found that these instruments are no different than those in common use, I shall be bold enough to offer, with all due respect to the others, my own secrets to your Excellency and to demonstrate them at your convenience.

1) I have designed extremely light and strong bridges, adapted to be easily carried, and with them you may pursue and at any time flee from the enemy; and others, indestructible by fire and battle, easy to lift and place. Also methods of burning and destroying those of the enemy.

2) I know how, during a siege, to take the water out of the trenches, and make an infinite variety of bridges, covered ways, ladders, and other machines suitable to such expeditions.

* About $19 million worth of gold in 2017.

3) If a place under siege cannot be reduced by bombardment, because of the height of its banks or the strength of its position, I have methods for destroying any fortress even if it is founded upon solid rock.

4) I have kinds of cannons, convenient and easy to carry, that can fling small stones almost resembling a hailstorm; and the smoke of these will cause great terror to the enemy, to his great detriment and confusion.

9) [Leonardo moved up this item in the draft.] And when the fight is at sea, I have many kinds of efficient machines for offense and defense, and vessels that will resist the attack of the largest guns, and powder and fumes.

5) I have ways of making, without noise, underground tunnels and secret winding passages to arrive at a desired point, even if it is necessary to pass underneath trenches or a river.

6) I will make unassailable armored chariots that can penetrate the ranks of the enemy with their artillery, and there is no body of soldiers so great that it could withstand them. And behind these, infantry could follow quite unhurt.

7) In case of need I will make cannons and artillery of beautiful and useful design that are different from those in common use.

8) Where bombardment will not work, I can devise catapults, mangonels, caltrops and other effective machines not in common use.

10) In times of peace I can give perfect satisfaction and be the equal of any other in architecture and the composition of buildings public and private; and in guiding water from one place to another.

Also, I can execute sculpture in marble, bronze and clay. Likewise in painting, I can do everything possible, as well as any other man, whosoever he may be.

Moreover, work could be undertaken on the bronze horse, which will be to the immortal glory and eternal honor of His Lordship, your father, and of the illustrious house of Sforza. And if any of the above-mentioned things seem impossible or impracticable to anyone, I am most readily disposed to demonstrate them in your park or in whatsoever place shall please Your Excellency.

Leonardo mentioned none of his paintings. Nor did he refer to the talent that ostensibly caused him to be sent to Milan: an ability to design and play musical instruments. What he mainly pitched was a pretense of military engineering expertise. Partly this was to appeal to Ludovico, whose Sforza dynasty had taken power by force and was faced with the constant threat of a local revolt or French invasion. In addition, Leonardo cast himself as an engineer because he was going through one of his regular bouts of being bored or blocked by the prospect of picking up a brush. As his mood swung between melancholy and exultation, he fantasized and boasted about being an accomplished weapons designer.

These boasts were aspirational. He had never been to a battle nor actually built any of the weapons he described. All he had produced thus far were some elegant sketches of concepts for weapons, many of them more fanciful than practical.

His letter to Ludovico is thus best regarded not as a reliable catalogue of his actual engineering accomplishments but instead as a glimpse into his hopes and ambitions. Nevertheless, his boasts were not completely hollow. Had they been, he would have been easily exposed in a city where weapon design was a deadly serious endeavor. After settling into Milan, he would in fact begin to pursue military engineering earnestly and come up with some innovative concepts for machines, even as he continued to dance around the line between ingenuity and fantasy.[7]

MILITARY ENGINEER

While still living in Florence, Leonardo had sketched a few proposals for clever military devices. One was a mechanism for knocking down the ladders of enemy invaders trying to scale a castle wall (fig. 21).[8] The defenders inside would pull large levers connected to rods that poked through holes in the wall. His drawing includes enlarged details showing how the rods would be attached to the levers plus lively sketches of four soldiers pulling ropes and keeping an eye on the enemy. A related idea was for a propeller-like device that would slash away at those who made it to the top of the castle wall. Gears and shafts turned blades, like those of a helicopter, that would swing just above the wall, chopping down unfortunate soldiers trying to climb over. For when it was time to be on the offense, he designed a rolling armored siege machine that placed a covered bridge over the fortified walls of a castle.[9]

The spread of printing presses helped Leonardo pursue additional military ideas after he arrived in Milan. He borrowed some of his concepts from a book by the thirteenth-century scientist Roger Bacon that had a list of ingenious weapons, including "carts and wagons that could move without animal power; devices used to walk on water and

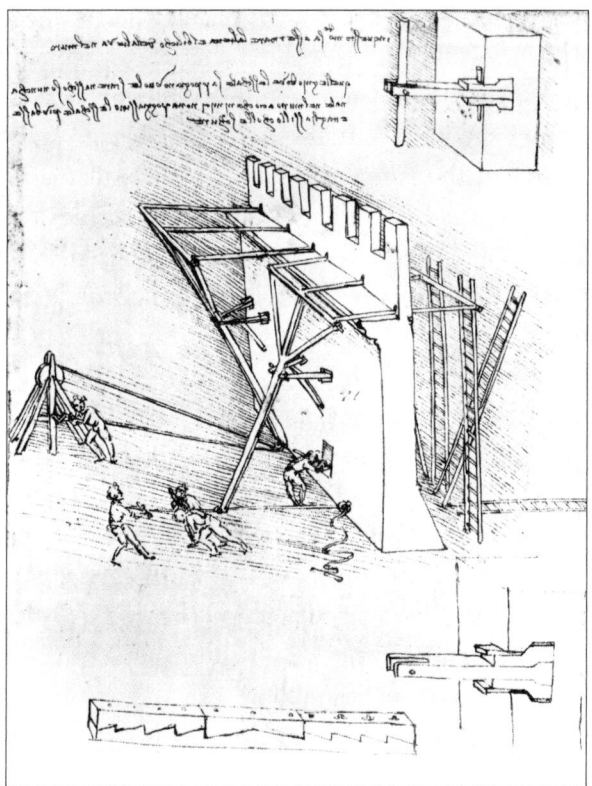

Fig. 21. Machine for pushing away ladders.

to move underneath the water, and contrivances capable of putting man in flight, having a person placed in the center of a mechanical device with artificial wings."[10] Leonardo embellished on all of these ideas. He also studied Roberto Valturio's *On the Military Arts*, a treatise filled with woodcuts of ingenious weapons. It was published in Latin in 1472 and in Italian in 1483, the year after Leonardo arrived in Milan. He bought both versions, annotated them, and struggled to improve his rudimentary Latin by making lists of the terms in the original book alongside their Italian translations.

Valturio's book became a springboard for Leonardo's creativity. For example, Valturio included a drawing of a cart with rotating scythes that was rather tame; each wheel of the clunky cart had only one small, unintimidating blade attached.[11] With his fevered imagination, Leonardo kicked the concept up multiple notches for a fearsome scythed chariot that became one of his most famous—and disconcerting—pieces of military engineering.[12]

Leonardo's drawings of this scythed chariot, which he made soon after he moved to Milan, feature truly frightening whirling blades jutting out from the wheels. It also has a four-bladed spinning shaft that can project in the front or be dragged behind the chariot. He meticulously drew the connection of the gears and cogs to the shafts and wheels, creating artwork so beautiful as to be jarring. The galloping horses and the riders with their billowing capes are dazzling studies of motion, while his hatching strokes create shade and modeling worthy of a museum piece.

One sheet of scythed chariot drawings is especially vivid (fig. 22).[13] On the near side of the moving chariot two bodies lie on the ground, their legs sliced off and the pieces scattered. On the far side he depicts two soldiers just at the moment they are being sliced in half. Here is our gentle and beloved Leonardo, who became a vegetarian because of his fondness for all creatures, wallowing in horrifying depictions of death. It is, perhaps, yet another glimpse of his inner turmoil. Within his dark cave was a demon imagination.

Another of his imagined but unbuilt weapons, which likewise blurs the border between practicality and fantasy, is a giant crossbow (fig. 23) that he drew in Milan around 1485.[14] The proposed machine is huge:

Fig. 22. Scythed chariot.

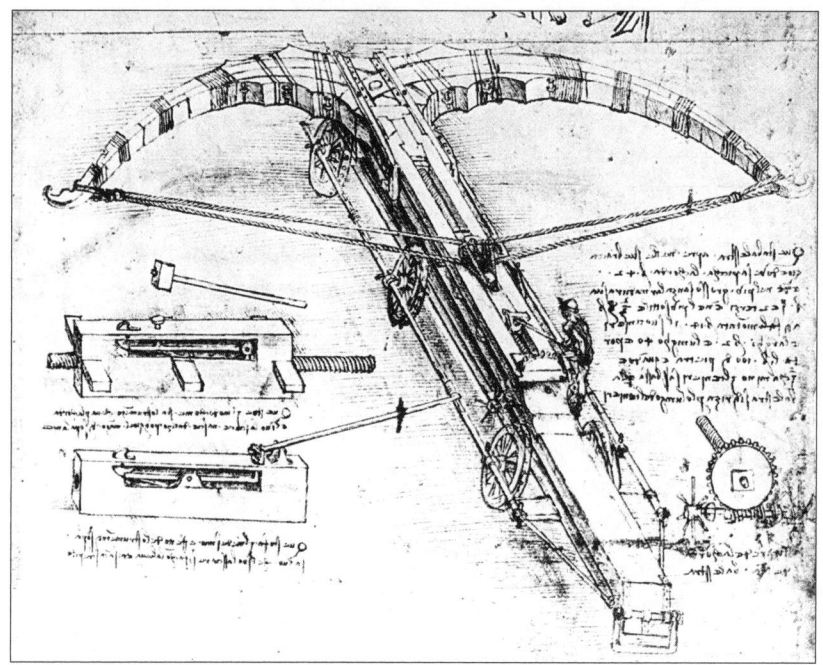

Fig. 23. Giant crossbow.

its armature is eighty feet across, and so is the carriage that would roll it onto the battlefield. To put it in perspective, he shows the weapon dwarfing a soldier who is preparing to unleash the trigger.

Leonardo was a pioneer in propounding laws of proportion: how one quantity, such as force, rises in proportion to another, such as the length of a lever. A super-sized crossbow should, he correctly surmised, be able to hurl projectiles that were bigger or went farther. He tried to figure out the correlation between the distance the bowstring was pulled and the force it exerted on the projectile. At first he thought that a bowstring pulled back twice as far would exert twice the force. But he realized that rate was thrown off by the bending of the bow as the string was pulled. After various calculations, he finally concluded that the force is proportional to the angle of the string at the point where it is pulled back. Pull the string back hard, and it will make (say) a 90-degree angle; pull back even harder, and perhaps you can get the angle down to 45 degrees. A 45-degree angle, he theorized, would deliver twice the force of 90 degrees. That doesn't turn out to be exactly right; Leonardo did not know trigonometry and thus couldn't refine the theory. But in concept he was close. He was learning to use geometric shapes as analogues for nature's forces.

In Leonardo's design, the bow was to be made with interlocking layers of wood, an early example of lamination. That would make it flexible, springy, and less likely to crack. Its string was pulled back by ropes attached to a large gear-and-screw mechanism, which he detailed in a side drawing. Cocked in such a fashion, he wrote, the device should be able to fling "one hundred pounds of stones." Gunpowder was in common use by then, which would seem to make a mechanical crossbow obsolete. However, if the crossbow had worked, it could have been cheaper, easier, and certainly quieter than cannons using gunpowder.

As with the scythed chariot, a question arises: How serious was Leonardo? Was he merely being clever on paper and trying to impress Ludovico? Was the giant crossbow another example of his ingenuity blurring into fantasy? I believe his proposal was serious. He made more than thirty preparatory drawings, and he detailed with precision the gears, worm screws, shafts, triggers, and other mechanisms. Nevertheless, the crossbow should be classified as a work of imagination rather than invention. It was never constructed by Ludovico Sforza. When it was finally built for a television special in 2002, the contemporary engineers were unable to get it to work. During his career, Leonardo would be known for paintings, monuments, and inventions that he conceived but never brought to fruition. The giant crossbow falls into that category.[15]

That was also true, it turned out, for most of the military devices he conceived and drew during the 1480s. "I will make unassailable armored chariots," he promised in his letter to Ludovico. He did in fact design one, at least on paper. His drawing of an armored tank, which looks like a cross between a turtle and a flying saucer, shows metal plates slanted on an angle that would cause it to deflect enemy projectiles. Inside would be eight men, some of them turning cranks to cause the tank to inch ahead, the others firing cannons that project out in all directions. There is one design flaw: a careful look at the crank and gears shows that they would turn the front wheels and the back wheels in opposite directions. Did he draw it that way intentionally so that it could not be easily constructed without his modification? Perhaps. But the issue was moot; the machine was never built.

He had also promised Ludovico, "I will make cannons and artillery of beautiful and useful design that are different from those in common use." One such attempt was a steam cannon, or *architronito*, an idea that Leonardo attributed to Archimedes and that was also in Valturio's book. The concept was that the breach of a cannon would be heated in burning coals until it was super-hot, then a small amount of water would be injected just behind the cannon ball. If the ball was held in place for a second or so, enough steam pressure would build up to fire it a few hundred yards when released.[16] Another proposal he drew was for a machine with many cannons, one with racks of eleven cannons each. While one set of cannons was cooling off and being reloaded, the other sets could be firing. It was the precursor to the machine gun.[17]

Only one of Leonardo's military conceptions is known to have made it off the pages of his notebooks and onto the battlefield, and he arguably deserves priority as its inventor. The wheellock, or wheel lock, which he devised in the 1490s, was a way to create a spark for igniting the gunpowder in a musket or similar hand-carried weapon. When the trigger was pulled, a metal wheel was set spinning by a spring. As it scraped against a stone, it sparked enough heat to ignite the gunpowder. Leonardo used components of some of his previous devices, which included spring-powered wheels. One of the assistants who lived in Leonardo's household at the time was a technician and locksmith named Giulio Tedesco, known as Jules the German, who returned to Germany around 1499 and spread Leonardo's idea there. The wheellock came into use in Italy and Germany around that time and proved to be influential in facilitating both warfare and the personal use of guns.[18]

Leonardo's wondrously imaginative giant crossbows and turtle-like tanks show his ability to let fantasy drive invention. But he had not lashed his imagination to practicality. None of his big machines would be deployed in battle by Ludovico Sforza, who did not face a serious confrontation until the French invaded Milan in 1499, at which time he fled the city. As it turned out, Leonardo would not be involved in military activity until 1502, when he went to work for a more difficult and tyrannical strongman, Cesare Borgia.[19]

The only military project Leonardo actually delivered to Ludovico was a survey of the castle's defenses. He expressed approval of the thickness of the walls, but he warned that the small apertures were directly connected to secret passageways in the castle, which could permit attackers to swarm the castle if breached. While at it, he also noted the proper method for preparing the bath for Ludovico's young new wife: "four parts of cold water to three parts of hot water."[20]

THE IDEAL CITY

Near the end of his job application to Ludovico Sforza, Leonardo touted himself as someone who could "be the equal of any other in architecture and the composition of buildings." But for his first few years in Milan, he had trouble getting any such commissions. So for the time being, he pursued his architectural interests the way he did his military interests: mainly on paper as imaginative visions never to be implemented.

The best example was his set of plans for a utopian city, which was a favorite subject for Italian Renaissance artists and architects. Milan had been ravaged in the early 1480s by three years of the bubonic plague, which killed close to one-third of its inhabitants. With his scientific instincts, Leonardo realized that the plague was spread by unsanitary conditions and that the health of the citizens was related to the health of their city.

He did not focus on marginal improvements in engineering and design. Instead, on multiple pages composed in 1487, he proposed a radical concept, one that combined his artistic sensibilities with his visions as an urban engineer: the creation of entirely new "ideal cities" planned for health and beauty. The population of Milan would be relocated to ten new towns, designed and built from scratch along the river, in order to "disperse its great congregation of people which are packed like goats one behind the other, filling every place with fetid smells and sowing seeds of pestilence and death."[21]

He applied the classic analogy between the microcosm of the human body and the macrocosm of the earth: cities are organisms that breathe and have fluids that circulate and waste that needs to move. He had recently begun studying blood and fluid circulation in the body. Thinking by analogy, he considered what would be the best circulation systems for urban needs, ranging from commerce to waste removal.

The glory of Milan was that it had an ample water supply and a long tradition of channeling the flow of mountain streams and melting snows. Leonardo's idea was to combine the streets and canals into a unified circulation system. The utopian city he envisioned would have two levels: an upper level designed for beauty and pedestrian life, and a level hidden below for canals, commerce, sanitation, and sewage.

"Let only that which is good looking be seen on the upper level of the city," he decreed. The wide streets and arcaded walkways on this level would be reserved for pedestrians and be flanked by beautiful homes and gardens. Unlike the cramped streets of Milan, which Leonardo realized led to the spread of disease, the boulevards in the new town would be at least as wide as the height of the houses. To keep these boulevards clean, they would be sloped to the middle to allow rainwater to drain through central slits into a sewer circulation system below. These were not merely general suggestions; Leonardo got very specific. "Each road must be 20 braccia wide and have ½ braccio slope from the sides towards the middle," he wrote, "and in the middle let there be at every braccio an opening, one braccio long and one finger wide, where the rain water may run off into hollows."*

The lower level, beneath the visible surface, would have canals and roads for deliveries, storage areas, alleys for carts, and a sewerage system to carry away refuse and "fetid substances." Homes would have main entries on the upper level and tradesmen's entrances on the lower level, which would be lit by air shafts and connected to the upper level "at each arch by a winding stair." He specified that these stairs should be spiral, both because he loved that form and because he was a fastidious man. Corners provided a place for men to urinate. "The corners of square ones are always fouled," he wrote. "At the first vault there must be a door entering into public privies." Once again he delved into the details: "The seat of the latrine should be able to swivel like the turnstile in a convent and return to its initial position by the use of a counterweight. The ceiling should have many holes in it so that one can breathe."[22]

As with so many other of Leonardo's visionary designs, he was ahead of what was practical for his time. Ludovico did not adopt his vision of the city, but in this case Leonardo's proposals were sensible as well as brilliant. If even part of his plan had been implemented, it might have transformed the nature of cities, reduced the onslaught of plagues, and changed history.

---

* A braccio is approximately 2.3 feet.

CHAPTER 5

Leonardo's Notebooks

THE COLLECTIONS

As the offspring of a long line of notaries, Leonardo da Vinci had an instinct for keeping records. Jotting down observations, lists, ideas, and sketches came naturally. In the early 1480s, shortly after his arrival in Milan, he began his lifelong practice of keeping notebooks on a regular basis. Some of them began as loose sheets the size of a tabloid newspaper. Others were little volumes bound in leather or vellum, the size of a paperback or even smaller, which he carried around to make field notes.

One purpose of these notebooks was to record interesting scenes, especially those involving people and emotions. "As you go about town," he wrote in one of them, "constantly observe, note, and consider the circumstances and behavior of men as they talk and quarrel, or laugh, or come to blows."[1] For that purpose, he kept a small notebook hanging from his belt. According to the poet Giovanni Battista Giraldi, whose father knew Leonardo:

When Leonardo wished to paint a figure, he first considered what social standing and emotion it was to represent; whether noble or plebeian, joyful or severe, troubled or serene, old or young, irate or quiet, good or evil; and when he had made up his mind, he went to places where he knew that people of that kind assembled and observed their faces, their manners, dresses, and gestures; and when he found what fitted his purpose, he noted it in a little book which he was always carrying in his belt.[2]

These little books on his belt, along with the larger sheets in his studio, became repositories for all of his manifold passions and obsessions, many of them sharing a page. As an engineer, he honed his technical skills by drawing mechanisms he encountered or imagined. As an artist, he sketched ideas and made preparatory drawings. As a court impresario, he jotted down designs for costumes, contrivances for moving scenery and stages, fables to be enacted, and witty lines to be performed. Scribbled in the margins were to-do lists, records of expenses, and sketches of people who caught his imagination. Over the years, as his scientific study got more serious, he filled pages with outlines and passages for treatises on topics such as flight, water, anatomy, art, horses, mechanics, and geology. About the only things missing are intimate personal revelations or intimacies. These are not Saint Augustine's *Confessions* but rather the outward-looking enthrallments of a relentlessly curious explorer.

In collecting such a medley of ideas, Leonardo was following a practice that had become popular in Renaissance Italy of keeping a commonplace and sketch book, known as a *zibaldone*. But in their content, Leonardo's were like nothing the world had ever, or has ever, seen. His notebooks have been rightly called "the most astonishing testament to the powers of human observation and imagination ever set down on paper."[3]

The more than 7,200 pages now extant probably represent about one-quarter of what Leonardo actually wrote,[4] but that is a higher percentage after five hundred years than the percentage of Steve Jobs's emails and digital documents from the 1990s that he and I were able to retrieve. Leonardo's notebooks are nothing less than an astonishing windfall that provides the documentary record of applied creativity.

As usual with Leonardo, however, there is an element of mystery involved. He rarely put dates on his pages, and much of their order has been lost. After his death, many of the volumes were disassembled and the interesting pages were sold or reorganized into new codices by various collectors, most notably the sculptor Pompeo Leoni, who was born in 1533.

For example, one of the many repackaged collections is the Codex Atlanticus, now in Milan's Biblioteca Ambrosiana, which consists of 2,238 pages assembled by Leoni from different notebooks Leonardo used from the 1480s to 1518. The Codex Arundel, now in the British Library, contains 570 pages of Leonardo's writings from the same long time span and was assembled by an unknown collector in the seventeenth century. In contrast, the Codex Leicester contains 72 pages, mainly on geology and water studies, that have remained together since Leonardo composed them around 1508 to 1510; it is now owned by Bill Gates. There are twenty-five codices and manuscript collections of notebook pages in Italy, France, England, Spain, and the United States. (See list of Leonardo's Notebooks in Frequently Cited Sources.) Modern scholars, most notably Carlo Pedretti, have tried to determine the order and dates of many of the pages, a task made more difficult because Leonardo sometimes went back to fill in the unused parts of a page or add to an old notebook he had put aside.[5]

Early on, Leonardo primarily recorded ideas that he considered useful to his art and engineering. For example, the early notebook known as Paris Ms. B, begun around 1487, contains drawings of possible submarines, black-sailed stealth ships, and steam-powered cannons, as well as some architectural designs for churches and ideal cities. Later notebooks show Leonardo pursuing curiosity for its own sake, and that in turn evolved into glimmerings of profound scientific inquiry. He became interested not only in how things work but why.[6]

Because good paper was costly, Leonardo tried to use every edge and corner of most pages, cramming as much as possible on each sheet and jumbling together seemingly random items from diverse fields. Often he would go back to a page, months or even years later, to add another thought, just as he would go back to his painting of Saint Jerome, and later his other paintings, to refine his work as he evolved and matured.

The juxtapositions can seem haphazard, and to some extent they are; we watch his mind and pen leap from an insight about mechanics, to a doodle of hair curls and water eddies, to a drawing of a face, to an ingenious contraption, to an anatomical sketch, all accompanied by mirror-script notes and musings. But the joy of these juxtapositions is that they allow us to marvel at the beauty of a universal mind as it wanders exuberantly in free-range fashion over the arts and sciences and, by doing so, senses the connections in our cosmos. We can extract from his pages, as he did from nature's, the patterns that underlie things that at first appear disconnected.

The beauty of a notebook is that it indulges provisional thoughts, half-finished ideas, unpolished sketches, and drafts for treatises not yet refined. That, too, suited Leonardo's leaps of the imagination, in which brilliance was often unfettered by diligence or discipline. He occasionally declared an intent to organize and refine his notebook jottings into published works, but his failure to do so became a companion to his failure to complete artworks. As he did with many of his paintings, he would hang on to the treatises that he was drafting, occasionally make a few new strokes and refinements, but never see them through to being released to the public as complete.

ONE SHEET

One way to appreciate the notebooks is to focus on just one sheet of paper. Let's pick a large one, twelve-by-eighteen inches, that he composed in about 1490, dubbed by Pedretti a "theme sheet" because it encompasses so many of Leonardo's interests.[7] (See fig. 24 to follow along.)

On the center-left is a figure Leonardo loved to draw or doodle: a semiheroic, craggy old man with a long nose and jutting chin. Wearing a toga, he looks both noble and slightly comic. In the list of possessions he had brought to Milan in 1482, Leonardo described one drawing as "the head of an old man with an enormous chin," and we will see variations of this craggy character reappearing often in his notebooks.

Just below the old man are the trunk and branches of a leafless

Fig. 24. A notebook sheet c. 1490.

tree, which blend into his toga and suggest the aorta and arteries of his blood system. Leonardo believed that analogy was a way to appreciate the unity of nature, and among the analogous forms he explored was the branching pattern that could be found in trees, in the arteries of the human body, and in rivers and their tributaries. He studied carefully the rules governing these branching systems, such as how the size of each branch relates to the size of the main trunk, artery, or river. On this notebook sheet, he hints at the similarity of such branching patterns in humans and in plants.

Flowing out of the man's back is a geometrical drawing of a conical shape that contains some equilateral triangles. Leonardo was beginning his long attempt to solve the ancient mathematical challenge of "squaring the circle," constructing a square that has the same area as a given circle using only a compass and straightedge. He was not great at algebra or even arithmetic, but he had a feel for how geometry could be used to transform one shape into another while keeping the area constant. Scattered on the sheet are geometrical drawings with shaded portions that have the same area.

The conical drawing attached to the man's back resembles a hill, and Leonardo has it flow into a sketch of a mountainous landscape. The result is a seamless connection of geometry to nature and a glimpse into Leonardo's art of spatial thinking.

A clear theme emerges as we look at the flow of this part of the drawing from right to left (the direction in which Leonardo drew). The branches of the leafless tree merge into the man's body, then into the conical geometrical pattern, and finally into the mountainous landscape. What Leonardo probably began as four distinct elements ended up woven together in a way that illustrates a fundamental theme in his art and science: the interconnectedness of nature, the unity of its patterns, and the analogy between the workings of the human body and those of the earth.

Just below these elements is something simpler to fathom. It's a quick but energetic sketch of his vision for Ludovico Sforza's horse monument. With just a few strokes, he is able to convey motion and vitality. Farther down are two heavy-looking mechanical devices, unexplained by any notes, perhaps some system for casting the horse. Barely visible at the bottom of the right half of the sheet is a faint little sketch of a walking horse.

Next to the centerfold at the bottom are two leafy stems, which have such precise botanical detail that they seem to have been drawn from direct observation. Vasari wrote that Leonardo studiously drew plants, and his surviving drawings show how sharp his eye was in observing nature. His botanical correctness is evident in his paintings, most notably the Louvre version of the *Virgin of the Rocks*.[8] Continuing his theme of merging patterns in nature and geometry, one of the grass shoots curving from the base of the stems merges into a perfect semicircle drawn with a compass.

On the far right are studies of fluffy cumulus clouds, each with different patterns of light and shading. Below them is a drawing of a column of falling water stirring up turbulence as it plunges into a placid pool; this was a subject that he would still be drawing at the end of his life. And scattered about on the sheet are doodles of other subjects that he would return to often: a bell tower for a church, curls of hair, shimmering branches of foliage, and a lily emerging from swirls of grass.

There is one note on the page that seems disconnected from everything else. It is a recipe for making blond-brown hair dye: "To make hair tawny, take nuts and boil them in lye and immerse the comb in it, then comb the hair and let it dry in the sun." This may have been a notation in preparation for a court pageant. But it is more likely, I think, that the recipe is a rare intimate jotting. Leonardo was deep into his thirties by now. Perhaps he was resisting going gray.

CHAPTER 6

Court Entertainer

PLAYS AND PAGEANTS

Leonardo da Vinci's entrée into the court of Ludovico Sforza came not as an architect or engineer but as a producer of pageants. As a spectacle-loving apprentice in Verrocchio's Florence workshop, he had become enthralled by staging fantasies, a talent that also happened to be much in demand in Sforza's Milan court, which thrived on plays and public entertainments. There were many elements, both artistic and technical, involved in producing such festivities, and all of them appealed to Leonardo: stage designs, costumes, scenery, music, mechanisms, choreography, allegorical allusions, automatons, and gadgets.

From our vantage centuries later, the time and creativity Leonardo applied to such ephemeral affairs seem wasted. There is nothing to show for the dazzling displays except snippets of reports that recount the fleeting moments of splendor. The time he spent could have been more usefully applied, it might seem, to finishing the *Adoration of the Magi* or *Saint Jerome*. But just as today we love halftime shows and Broadway extravaganzas, fireworks displays and choreographed performances, the events staged by the Sforza court were considered vital, and their producers, including Leonardo, were highly valued.

The entertainments were even educational at times, like an ideas festival; there were demonstrations of science, debates over the relative merits of various art forms, and displays of ingenious devices, all of which were a precursor to the public science and edifying discourse that later became popular during the Enlightenment.

By calling on historical and religious imagery, these shows served to legitimize Sforza family rule, which is why Ludovico turned them into an industry. Architects, mechanics, musicians, poets, performers, and military engineers were all engaged in executing them. For Leonardo, who thought of himself as a member of all of these categories, it was the perfect way to earn a role in the Sforza court.

Ludovico's grander pageants served to amuse and distract not only Milan's populace but also his young nephew Gian Galeazzo Sforza, the titular duke until his mysterious death in 1494. Through a combination of feigned solicitousness and intimidation, Ludovico was able to beguile his nephew and induce him to crave his uncle's affection. He encouraged the young man's debauchery, indulged his drinking, and allowed him to preside over the pageants that were performed at court. One festivity Leonardo worked on was the extravaganza that Ludovico orchestrated in 1490 for his nephew's marriage, at age twenty, to Isabella of Aragon, the Princess of Naples.

The centerpiece of the wedding celebration was a performance and feast, filled with sounds and lights and pageantry, of a theatrical extravaganza entitled *The Feast of Paradise*, which climaxed with a stage piece, *The Masque of the Planets*. It had a libretto by one of Ludovico's favorite poets, Bernardo Bellincioni, who later wrote that the scenery was "made with great brilliance and skill by Maestro Leonardo Vinci, the Florentine." Leonardo created panels that depicted inspiring moments of the Sforza family reign, decorated the silk-clad walls of the long hall of the Sforza Castle with symbol-laden foliage, and designed the fanciful costumes.

The play was an allegorical pageant that began with a masked procession in which the players were introduced and then greeted by a Turkish cavalcade. The bride was serenaded by a procession of actors playing ambassadors from Spain, Poland, Hungary, and other exotic lands, and the appearance of each one became a cause for dancing. The music drowned out most of the whirring of the mechanical devices moving the scenery.

At midnight, after much dancing by the players and spectators, the music stopped and the curtain rose on a celestial curved vault that Leonardo had constructed in the shape of a half egg that was gilded with gold on the inside. Torches served as the stars, and in the background the signs of the Zodiac were illuminated. Actors portrayed the seven known planets, turning and revolving in the proper orbits. "You will see great things in honor of Isabella and her virtues," an angel announced. In his notebooks, Leonardo recorded the expenses for "gold and the glue to affix the gold" and twenty-five pounds of wax "to make the stars." It culminated with gods—led by Jupiter and Apollo and followed by the Graces and Virtues—descending from their pedestals to shower verses of praise on the new duchess.[1]

Leonardo's triumph designing *The Masque of the Planets* brought him a modest amount of fame—more than he had received as a painter of unfinished panels and certainly more than he had ever earned as a military engineer. It also delighted him. His notebooks show the interest he took in the mechanism of the automated props and scenery changes. The interplay of fantasy and machinery was something he was born to choreograph.

Another extravaganza was staged the following year, when Ludovico married the politically connected and culturally savvy Beatrice d'Este, a member of one of Italy's most prominent families. A great jousting tournament was planned, and Leonardo arranged the pageant that accompanied it. He recorded in his notebook visiting the site in order to help some of the footmen, who were going to play the role of primitive savages, try on the loincloths he had designed as their costume.

For the pageant, Leonardo again combined his theatrical skills with his love of allegories. "First a wonderful steed appeared, all covered with gold scales which the artist has colored like peacock eyes," Ludovico's secretary recorded. "Hanging from the warrior's golden helmet was a winged serpent, whose tail touched the horse's back." Leonardo described his allegorical intentions in a notebook: "Above the helmet place a half globe, which is to signify our hemisphere. Every ornament belonging to the horse should be of peacock feathers on a gold background, to signify the beauty which comes of the grace bestowed on him who is a good servant."[2] The steed was followed by the horde of cavemen and savages. It was typical of Leonardo's desire to indulge in the scary and exotic; he had an affinity for bizarre demons and dragons.

Leonardo's technical and artistic talents were again combined in January 1496, when he staged one of the most extravagant plays of the era, a five-act comedy titled *La Danae* written by Ludovico's chancellor and court poet, Baldassare Taccone. Leonardo's notes included a list of the actors and their scenes, a drawing of the stage set, and mechanical diagrams of the machinery for changing scenery and creating special effects. His floor plan shows two elevation drawings done in perspective, and he made a sketch of one scene that depicts a god sitting in a flaming niche. The play was filled with special effects and mechanical feats that Leonardo designed: Mercury descended from above using an intricate system of ropes and pulleys; Jupiter was transformed into a rain of gold dust to impregnate Danae; and at one point the sky was lit "by an infinite number of lamps like stars."[3]

His most complex mechanical designs were of the revolving stages for a theatrical scene that he labeled "Pluto's Paradise." A mountain was opened up in halves to display Hades. "When Pluto's paradise is opened, there will be devils who are playing on twelve pots like openings into hell, creating infernal noises," Leonardo wrote. "Here will be Death, the Furies, ashes, many naked children weeping; living fires made of various colors." Then comes a pithy stage direction: "Dances follow."[4] His moveable stages included two semicircular amphitheaters that were initially facing each other and closed into a sphere, and then were swung open and rotated so they would be back to back.

The mechanical elements of the theatrical events interested Leonardo as much as the artistic ones, and he saw them as connected. He delighted in making ingenious contraptions that would fly, descend, and animate in ways that would excite his audiences. Before he had fully begun his writings on the flight of birds, he made a light sketch in his notebook of a mechanical bird, wings outstretched, attached to a guide string, with the caption "A bird for a comedy."[5]

Leonardo's work producing theatrical pageants was enjoyable and remunerative, but it also served a larger purpose. It required him to execute his fantasies. Unlike paintings, performances had real deadlines. They had to be ready when the curtains parted. He could not cling to them and seek to perfect them indefinitely.

Some of the devices that he made, most notably mechanical birds and wings for actors suspended above the stage, spurred him on to more serious scientific studies, including observing birds and envisioning real flying machines. In addition, his love of stage gestures was reflected in his narrative paintings. The time he spent engaged with theatrical amusements stimulated his imagination in both art and engineering.

MUSIC

Leonardo had originally come to the Sforza court partly as a musical envoy bearing his own specially designed version of an instrument that was popular among court entertainers. It was a type of lyre to be held like a fiddle, with five strings meant to be played with a bow and two that were to be plucked. "It had a very bizarre and unusual design that he had made with his own hands," Vasari wrote, "mainly out of silver, in the shape of a horse skull, made so that the harmony might be fuller and more sonorous in tone." Poets used the *lira da braccio* as an accompaniment when they sang their verses, and it was featured in paintings of angels by Raphael and others.

Leonardo knew how to play the lyre "with rare distinction," according to the Anonimo, "and also taught lyre playing to Atalante Migliorotti." His repertoire ranged from the classical love poems of Petrarch to witty lyrics he concocted himself, and he won a contest in Florence with one of his performances. The humanist and physician Paolo Giovio, a near contemporary who met Leonardo in Milan, wrote, "He was a connoisseur and marvelous inventor of all beautiful things, especially in the field of stage performances, and sang masterfully to his own accompaniment on the lyre. When he played the lyre with the bow, he miraculously pleased all princes."[6]

There are no musical compositions in his notebooks. Rather than reading music or composing lyrics, he improvised when performing at the Sforza court. "Since by nature he possessed a lofty and graceful spirit," Vasari explained, "he sang divinely, improvising his own accompaniment on the lyre."

Vasari recounted one special performance that Leonardo gave at the Milan court in 1494, when Ludovico was officially crowned duke after the death of his nephew: "Leonardo, with great fanfare, was brought to the duke to play for him, since the duke had a great liking for the sound of the lyre, and Leonardo brought the instrument which he had built with his own hands. With this, he surpassed all the musicians who came there to play. In addition, he was the best improviser of verses of his time."

Leonardo also dreamed up new instruments as part of his role as a producer of pageants. His notebooks are filled with sketches both innovative and fanciful. As usual, his creativity came from his combinatory imagination. After sketching a few conventional instruments on a page, he concocted one that drew together elements from a variety of different animals to make a dragon-like creature. Another page shows a three-string violin-like instrument that had a goat's skull, a bird's beak, and some feathers, with the strings fastened to teeth carved at one end.[7]

His musical inventions were the product of both his engineering instincts and his fancy for entertainment. He came up with innovative ways to control the vibrations, and thus the pitch and tones, produced by bells, drums, or strings. On one of his notebook pages, for example, he drew a mechanized ringing instrument (fig. 25) composed of a stationary metal bell flanked by two hammers and four dampers on levers that could be operated by keys to touch the bell at different places. Leonardo knew that a bell has different areas that, depending on their shape and thickness, produce different tones. By dampening up to four of these in different combinations, he could turn a bell into a keyboard instrument that played a variety of pitches. "When struck by the hammers, there will be a change of tones like in an organ," he wrote.[8]

Fig. 25. Keyboard-operated bell.

He likewise tried to create instruments based on drums with different pitches. Some of his sketches involve combining drum skins stretched to various levels of tension. In other cases, he proposed ways to use levers and screws to change the tension of the drum skin while it was being played.[9] He also drew a snare drum with a long cylinder that had holes in its side, like a flute. "Closing of the various holes while beating the skin results in clear pitch differences," he explained.[10] Another method was simpler: he lashed together twelve kettle drums of different sizes and devised a keyboard that allowed each to be hit with a mechanical hammer; the result was a cross between a drum set and a harpsichord.[11]

The most complex of Leonardo's musical instruments, which he drew in many variations on ten different pages of his notebooks, was the *viola organista*, a cross between a violin and an organ.[12] Like a violin, its sound was produced by moving a bow back and forth across some strings, but in this case the bow was moved mechanically. Like an organ, it was played by pressing keys on a keyboard to determine which notes should be produced. In his final and most complex version, a set of wheels turned bowstrings that were looped like the fan belt in a car; pushing a key would cause one of the violin strings to be pressed down onto one of the looping bows, thus producing the desired tone. Multiple strings could be played at once, creating chords. Unlike with a regular bow, the tone produced by the fan belt could be sustained indefinitely. The *viola organista* was a brilliant idea that attempted to combine, in a way that is still not done today, the multitude of notes and chords that a keyboard can produce with the timbre, or tone color, that comes from a stringed instrument.[13]

What started as ways to amuse the Sforza court soon became serious attempts to make better musical instruments. "Leonardo's instruments are not merely diverting devices for performing magic tricks," according to Emanuel Winternitz, a curator of musical instruments at the Metropolitan Museum in New York. "Instead, they are systematic efforts by Leonardo to realize some basic aims."[14] These include new ways to use keyboards, play faster, and increase the range of available tones and sounds. In addition to earning him financial stipends and an entrée at court, his musical pursuits launched him onto more substantive paths: they laid the ground for his work on the science of percussion—how striking an object can produce vibrations, waves, and reverberations—and exploring the analogy between sound waves and water waves.

ALLEGORICAL DRAWINGS

Ludovico Sforza loved complex coats of arms, clever heraldic displays, and family emblems with metaphorical meanings. He owned ornate helmets and shields adorned with personal symbols, and his courtiers created ingenious designs to exalt his virtues, allude to his triumphs, and play with puns on his name. This led to a series of allegorical drawings made by Leonardo that were intended, I think, to be shown at court accompanied by his spoken explanations and tales. Some were designed to justify Ludovico's role as de facto ruler and protector of his feckless nephew. In one, the titular young duke is pictured as a cockerel (the word for cockerel, *galleto*, is a play on the boy's name, Galeazzo) being attacked by a swarm of birds, foxes, and a two-horned fantasy satyr. Protecting him, and serving as representations of Ludovico, are two beautiful virtues, Justice and Prudence. Justice holds a brush and a serpent, which were heraldic symbols of the Sforzas, and Prudence holds a mirror.[15]

Although the allegorical sketches he made while serving Ludovico ostensibly portray the traits of others, a few seem to reveal Leonardo's own inner turmoil. Most notable are the dozen or so drawings depicting Envy. "No sooner is Virtue born than Envy comes into the world to attack it," he wrote on one of them. In his written description of Envy, he seems to have confronted her, in himself and in his competitors: "Envy should be represented with an obscene gesture of the hand towards heaven," he wrote. "Victory and truth are odious to her. Many thunderbolts should proceed from her to signify her evil speaking. Let her be lean and haggard because she is in perpetual torment. Make her heart gnawed by a swelling serpent."[16]

Leonardo portrayed Envy along these lines in several allegorical drawings. He showed her as a wizened hag with sagging breasts on the back of a crawling skeleton accompanied by the explanation "Make her ride upon death, because Envy never dies."[17] Another drawing on the same page portrays her intertwined with Virtue, a serpent springing forth from her tongue, while Virtue tries to stab her in the eyes with an olive branch. Not surprisingly, Ludovico is sometimes depicted as her nemesis. He is shown holding out a pair of eyeglasses to unmask her lies as she cowers away from him. "Il Moro with spectacles, and Envy depicted with False Report," Leonardo captioned the drawing.[18]

THE GROTESQUES

Another set of drawings that Leonardo produced for the amusement of the Sforza court were pen-and-ink caricatures of funny-looking people he dubbed "visi mostruosi" (monstrous faces), which are now commonly called his "grotesques." Most are small, just under the size of a credit card. Satirical in intent, they were, like his allegorical drawings, probably accompaniments to spoken tales, jokes, or performances at the castle. At least two dozen originals survive (fig. 26), and there are many close copies produced by the students in his studio (fig. 27).[19] The grotesques were reproduced or mimicked by later artists, most notably the seventeenth-century Bohemian etcher Wenceslaus Hollar and the nineteenth-century British illustrator John Tenniel, who used them as models for the Ugly Duchess and other characters in *Alice's Adventures in Wonderland*.

With his finely honed ability to see both beauty and ugliness, Leonardo was able to create a satirical combination in his grotesques.

Fig. 26. Leonardo's craggy warrior and a grotesque.

Fig. 27. Copy of a grotesque from Leonardo's studio.

As he wrote in his notes for his treatise on painting, "If the painter wishes to see beauties that charm him, it lies within his power to create them; and if he wishes to see monstrosities that are frightful, buffoonish, or ridiculous, or pitiable, he can be lord thereof."[20]

The grotesques are examples of how Leonardo's observational skills became fodder for his imagination. He would walk the streets with a notebook dangling from his belt, find a group of people with exaggerated features who would make good models, and invite them over for supper. "Sitting close to them," his early biographer Lomazzo recounted, "Leonardo then proceeded to tell the maddest and most ridiculous tales imaginable, making them laugh uproariously. He observed all their gestures very attentively and those ridiculous things they were doing, and impressed them on his mind; and after they had left, he retired to his room and there made a perfect drawing." Lomazzo indicated that part of the purpose was to amuse his patrons at the Sforza court. The drawings "moved those who looked at them to laughter, as if they had been moved by Leonardo's stories at the feast!"[21]

In notes for his treatise on painting, Leonardo recommended to young artists this practice of walking around town, finding people to use as models, and recording the most interesting ones in a portable notebook: "Take a note of them with slight strokes in a little book which you should always carry with you," he wrote. "The positions of the people are so infinite that the memory is incapable of retaining them, which is why you should keep these sketches as your guides."[22]

Sometimes Leonardo used a pen on such face-hunting excursions, and when that was not practical in an outdoor setting he used a stylus. The sharp silverpoint of the stylus made lines on paper that had been coated with ground chicken bones, soot, or other chalky powders, sometimes colored with pulverized minerals. The metal point oxidized this coating, producing silvery gray lines. He also occasionally used chalk, charcoal, or lead. As was his nature, he was constantly experimenting with drawing methods.[23]

These face-finding excursions, along with the sketches that resulted, helped Leonardo in his quest to find ways to relate facial features to inner emotions. At least since the time of Aristotle, who declared, "It is possible to infer character from features,"[24] people had tried to find ways to assess people's innate personality from their head shapes and facial characteristics, a study known as physiognomy. With his empirical mind, Leonardo rejected the scientific validity of this method and dismissed it as akin to astrology and alchemy. "I will not dwell on false physiognomy and palm-reading, because there is no truth in them, and illusions of this kind have no scientific foundation," he insisted.

But even though he did not consider physiognomy a science, he did believe that facial expressions indicate underlying causes. "Characteristics of the face partly reveal the character of men, their vices and temperaments," he wrote. "If the features which separate the cheeks from the lips, or the nostrils from the cavities of the eyes, are strongly pronounced, they belong to cheerful and good-humored men." Those without such distinctive lines are more contemplative, he added, and those "whose facial features stand out in great relief are brutal, bad-tempered, and men of little reason." He went on to associate heavy lines between the eyebrows with bad temper, strong lines on the forehead with regrets, and concluded, "It is possible to discuss many features this way."[25]

He developed a trick for noting these features of a face so that he could draw them later. It involved a shorthand for ten types of nose ("straight, bulbous, hollow . . ."), eleven types of facial shape, and various other characteristics that could be categorized. When he found a person he wished to draw, he would use this shorthand so that he could re-create him or her when he got back to his studio. With the grotesque faces, however, that was not necessary because they were so memorable. "Of grotesque faces I need say nothing, because they are kept in mind without difficulty," he declared.[26]

The most memorable of Leonardo's grotesque drawings is one of five heads that he did around 1494 (fig. 28). The central figure is an

Fig. 28. Five heads.

old man, with the aquiline nose and jutting jaw that Leonardo fa-vored for his typical aging warrior character. He is wearing a wreath of oak leaves and trying to maintain a dignified pose while in fact looking a bit gullible and foolish. The four characters surrounding him are laughing maniacally or smirking.

Leonardo likely drew the scene as part of a facetious tale that he recounted for the amusement of the Sforza court, but no notes survive. That is fortunate, because it allows us to apply our own imagination to the drawing and to Leonardo. Perhaps the man is about to marry the "pug-faced crone" depicted in one of Leonardo's other drawings from the same time, and his friends are showing a mix of derision and com-passion. Maybe the drawing is an exaggerated illustration of human traits, such as lunacy and dementia and megalomania.

A more plausible explanation, since this was probably for a per-formance at court, is that there was a narrative story involved. The man on the right seems to be holding the hand of the wreathed central character, while the man on the left is reaching around his back toward his pocket. Could it be a scene of a man having his palm read and being pickpocketed by gypsies, as Windsor's curator Martin Clayton suggests?[27] Gypsies from the Balkans had spread throughout Europe in the fifteenth century and become such a nuisance in Milan that they were banished by a decree in 1493. In his notebooks, Leo-nardo mentioned a portrayal of a gypsy in a list of his drawings, and he also recorded spending 6 soldi for a fortune-teller. All of this is speculative, and that is one of the many things that make Leonardo's works, including those with a bit of mystery, so wonderful: his fanta-sia is infectious.

LITERARY AMUSEMENTS

Another contribution that Leonardo made to life at the Sforza court were little literary amusements, which were also primarily intended to be read aloud or performed. There are at least three hundred of them in his notebooks, in a variety of forms: fables, facetious tales, prophe-cies, pranks, and riddles. These are scattered in the margins of pages or next to unrelated items, so we know they were not intended to be collections on their own. Instead, they were produced to provide entertainment whenever the occasion warranted.

Oral performances and declamations of riddles and fables were a popular form of amusement at Renaissance courts. Leonardo even included stage directions on some; next to one cryptic prophecy he directed that it should be delivered "in a frenzied or berserk way, as of mental lunacy."[28] He was a clever conversationalist and storyteller, according to Vasari, and that served him well with these slight entertainments that might seem, in retrospect, trivial endeavors. He had not yet been established as one of history's great geniuses, so he was hustling to curry favor at a crowded ducal court.[29]

The fables are pithy moral tales involving animals or objects that take on a personality. They have common themes, most notably the rewards due to virtue and prudence versus the penalties engendered by greed and haste. Although they bear some similarity to Aesop's fables, they are shorter. Most are not particularly clever or even easily comprehensible, at least out of the context of whatever was happening at court that evening. For example, "The mole has very small eyes and it always lives underground; it lives as long as it is in the dark, but when it comes into the light it dies immediately, because it becomes known—and so it is with lies."[30] More than fifty of these fables were jotted in his notebooks during the seventeen years he spent in Milan.

Closely related are the entries in his bestiary, a compendium of short tales of animals and moral lessons based on their traits. Bestiaries were popular among the ancients and in the Middle Ages, and the spread of printing presses meant that many were reprinted in Italy beginning in the 1470s. Leonardo had a copy of the bestiary written by Pliny the Elder and three others by medieval compilers. In contrast to the entries in these collections, Leonardo's tended to be pithy and unadorned with religious trappings. They were probably connected to emblems, heraldic shields, and performances that he created for those in the Sforza circle. "The swan is white without any spot, and it sings sweetly as it dies, its life ending with that song," one of them states. Occasionally Leonardo appended a moral lesson to the entry, such as this: "The oyster, when the moon is full, opens itself wide, and when the crab looks in he throws in a stone or seaweed and the oyster cannot close again, whereby it serves for food to that crab. This is what happens to him who opens his mouth to tell his secret. He becomes the prey of the treacherous hearer."[31]

A third type of literary amusement was one that Leonardo pioneered in the 1490s. He called them "prophecies," and they were often little riddles or trick questions. He was particularly fond of describing some scene of darkness and destruction, in a style that mocked the prophets and doomsayers who hung around the court, then revealing that he was actually referring to something far less apocalyptic. For example, one prophecy begins, "Many people by puffing out a breath with too much haste will thereby lose their sight and soon after all consciousness," but then Leonardo reveals that the description refers to people "blowing out the candlelight when going to bed."

Many of the prophecy-riddles reflect Leonardo's love for animals. "Countless numbers will have their little children taken away and their throats shall be cut," is one prophecy, as if describing a brutal act of war and genocide. But then Leonardo, who had become a vegetarian, reveals that this prophecy refers to the sheep and cows that humans eat. "Winged creatures will support people with their feathers," he wrote in another example, and then revealed that he was not referring to flying machines but "the feathers used to stuff mattresses."[32] As they say in show business, you had to be there.

Leonardo accompanied these literary amusements with pranks and tricks on occasion, such as flash explosions. "Boil ten pounds of brandy to evaporate, but see that the room is completely closed, and throw up some powdered varnish among the fumes," he wrote in his notebook. "Then enter the room suddenly with a lighted torch, and at once it will be set ablaze."[33] Vasari described how Leonardo took a lizard captured by an assistant, pasted on a beard and wings, and kept it in a box to frighten his friends. He also took the intestines of a steer and "made them so fine that they could be compressed into the palm of one hand. Then he would fix one end of them to a pair of bellows lying in another room, and when they were inflated they filled the room in which they were and forced anyone standing there into a corner."[34]

Puns were popular then, and Leonardo often created visual versions of them, such as when he painted a juniper in the portrait of

Ginevra de' Benci. One way he played with puns was by creating for the court cryptograms, pictographs, and rebuses, in which pictures were lined up to create a message that had to be decoded while Leonardo watched. For example, he drew an ear of corn for grain (*grano* in Italian) and a magnetic rock (*calamita*) to make a punning version of the phrase "great calamity" (*gran calimità*). Using both sides of a large notebook sheet, he drew more than 150 of these little puzzles, sketching them quickly, as if he were creating them in front of an audience.[35]

Leonardo's notebooks also contain drafts of fantasy novellas, sometimes in the form of letters describing mysterious lands and adventures. More than a century earlier, the Florentine writer and humanist Giovanni Boccaccio had popularized tales, most notably *The Decameron*, that skated between fantasia and realism. Leonardo did likewise in at least two sustained drafts of long stories.

One of these was probably performed at a farewell party in 1487 for Benedetto Dei, a fellow Florentine who was part of the Sforza court in Milan. It was cast as a letter to Dei, who traveled extensively and spun wondrous (and occasionally embellished) tales. The villain is a black giant, with bloodshot eyes and a "face most horrible," who terrorizes the inhabitants of North Africa. "He lived in the sea and fed on whales, leviathans, and ships," Leonardo wrote. The men of the area swarm all over the giant like ants, but to no avail. "He shook his head and sent the men flying through the air like hail."[36]

The tale is an early example of a theme that Leonardo would return to repeatedly until the end of his life: cataclysmic scenes of destruction and deluge that consume all earthly life. Leonardo's narrator is swallowed by the giant and finds himself swimming in a dark void. The story ends with a lament that describes those nightmarish demons, unleashed from the shadowy cave, that plagued and drove and stymied Leonardo throughout his life. "I do not know what to say or what to do, for everywhere I seem to find myself swimming head downwards through that mighty throat and remaining buried in that huge belly, in the confusion of death."

This dark side of Leonardo's genius is also evident in the other fantasy novella he sketched out while working at the Milan court, which foreshadows the deluge drawings and descriptions he did near the end of his life. This one is composed as a series of letters, written by a prophet and water engineer who is clearly Leonardo himself, to "the Devatdar of Syria, Lieutenant of the Sacred Sultan of Babylon."[37] Once again the narrative involves deluge and destruction:

> First we were assailed by the fury of the winds; and then followed the avalanches from the great mountains of snow which filled up all these valleys and destroyed a great part of our city. And, not content with this, the tempest with a sudden deluge of water has submerged all the lower part of this city. Added to this there came a sudden rain, or rather a ruinous storm full of water, sand, mud, and stones all mingled together with roots, stems, and branches of trees; and every kind of thing came hurtling through the air and descended upon us. Finally there came a great fire—not brought by the wind but carried, it would seem, by thirty thousand devils—completely burnt up and destroyed the country.[38]

The tale shows his fantasies about being a hydraulic engineer. The Syrian storm, Leonardo's narrator recounts, is tamed by building a huge drainage tunnel through the Taurus Mountains.

Some Leonardo scholars have interpreted these writings as a sign that he was suffering bouts of madness. Others have concluded that he actually went to Armenia and had the experience of the deluge he described. I think a more reasonable explanation is that these tales, like many of the odd things Leonardo wrote, were intended for performance at court. But even if merely designed to amuse his patrons, they hint at something deeper, providing a glimpse into the psychological torments swirling in the psyche of the artist playing the entertainer.[39]

CHAPTER 7

Personal Life

OUTSTANDING BEAUTY
AND INFINITE GRACE

Leonardo became known in Milan not only for his talents but also for his good looks, muscular build, and gentle personal style. "He was a man of outstanding beauty and infinite grace," Vasari said of him. "He was striking and handsome, and his great presence brought comfort to the most troubled soul."

Even discounting for the effusiveness of sixteenth-century biographers, it is clear that Leonardo was charming and attractive and had many friends. "His disposition was so lovable that he commanded everyone's affection," according to Vasari. "He was so pleasing in conversation that he attracted to himself the hearts of men." Paolo Giovio, a near contemporary who met Leonardo in Milan, similarly remembered his pleasant nature. "He was friendly, precise, and generous, with a radiant, graceful expression," Giovio wrote. "His genius for invention was astounding, and he was the arbiter of all questions relating to beauty and elegance, especially in pageantry."[1] All of this made him a man with many close friends. In the letters and writings of dozens of other prominent intellectuals in Milan and Florence, ranging from the mathematician Luca Pacioli to the architect Donato Bramante and the poet Piattino Piatti, there are references to Leonardo as a valued and beloved companion.

Leonardo dressed colorfully, sometimes sporting, according to the Anonimo, "a rose-colored cloak, which came only to his knees, though at the time long vestments were the custom." As he grew older, he grew a long beard, which "came to the middle of his breast and was well-dressed and curled."

Most notably, he was known for his willingness to share his blessings. "He was so generous that he sheltered and fed all his friends, rich or poor," according to Vasari. He was not motivated by wealth or material possessions. In his notebooks, he decried "men who desire nothing but material riches and are absolutely devoid of the desire for wisdom, which is the sustenance and truly dependable wealth of the mind."[2] As a result, he spent more time pursuing wisdom than working on jobs that would make him money beyond what he needed to support his growing household retinue. "He possessed nothing and worked little, but he always kept servants and horses," Vasari wrote.

The horses brought him "much delight," Vasari wrote, as did all animals. "Often when passing the places where birds were sold, he would take them with his own hand out of their cages, and having paid to those who sold them the price that was asked, he let them fly away into the air, restoring to them their lost liberty."

Because of his love for animals, Leonardo was a vegetarian for much of his life, although his shopping lists show that he often bought meat for others in his household. "He would not kill a flea for any reason whatsoever," a friend wrote. "He preferred to dress in linen, so as not to wear something dead." A Florentine traveler to India recorded that the people there "do not feed on anything that has blood, nor will they allow anyone to hurt any living thing, like our Leonardo da Vinci."[3]

In addition to his prophecy tales that include dire descriptions of the practice of slaying animals for food, Leonardo's notebooks contain other literary passages assailing meat eating. "If you are, as you have described yourself, the king of the animals," he wrote of humans, "why do you help other animals only so that they may be able to give you their young in order to gratify your palate?" He referred to a vegetable diet as "simple" food and urged its adoption. "Does not nature bring forth enough simple food things to satisfy your hunger? Or if you cannot content yourself with simple things can you not do so by blending these simple foods together to make an infinite number of compounds?"[4]

His rationale for avoiding meat derived from a morality based on science. Unlike plants, animals could feel pain, Leonardo realized. His studies led him to believe that this was because animals had the ability to move their bodies. "Nature has given sensibility to pain to living organisms that have the power of movement, in order to preserve those parts which might be destroyed by movement," he surmised. "Pain is not necessary in plants."[5]

SALAI

Among the young men who became Leonardo's companions, by far the most important was the scamp known as Salai, who arrived on July 22, 1490, when Leonardo was thirty-eight. "Giacomo came to live with me" is the way he recorded the event in his notebook.[6] It is an oddly elusive formulation, in contrast to saying that the young man had become his student or assistant. Then again, it was an oddly elusive relationship.

Gian Giacomo Caprotti was then ten years old, the son of an impoverished peasant from the nearby village of Oreno. Leonardo would soon be referring to him, for good reason, as Salai, or "Little Devil."[7] Soft and languid, with angelic curls and a devilish little smile, he would feature in dozens of Leonardo's drawings and notebook sketches, and for most of the rest of Leonardo's life, Salai would be his companion. He was the one, as noted earlier, described by Vasari as "a graceful and beautiful youth with fine curly hair in which Leonardo greatly delighted."

It was not unusual for a servant boy to go to work at age ten, but Salai was something more. Leonardo would later occasionally refer to him as "my pupil," but that was misleading; he never was more than a mediocre artist and produced few original paintings. Instead he was Leonardo's assistant, companion, and amanuensis, and probably at some point he became a lover. In one of Leonardo's notebooks, another of the students in the studio, perhaps a rival, drew a coarse caricature showing a large penis with two legs poking toward an object on which "Salai" is scribbled.

In an unpublished "Book of Dreams" written in 1560, Lomazzo, who knew one of Leonardo's students, imagined a dialogue between the ancient Greek sculptor Phidias and Leonardo, who confesses to loving Salai. Phidias asks bluntly whether they had engaged in sex. "Did you perhaps play with him that backside game that Florentines love so much?"

"Many times!" Leonardo merrily responds. "You should know that he was a most beautiful young man, especially at about fifteen," which is perhaps an indication of when their relationship may have become physical.

"Are you not ashamed to say this?" asks Phidias.

Leonardo, or at least Lomazzo's fictionalized version, is not. "Why ashamed? Among men of worth there is scarcely greater cause for pride. . . . Understand that masculine love is solely the product of merit [*virtù*] which joins together men of diverse feelings of friendship so that they may, from a tender age, arrive at manhood as stronger friends."[8]

As soon as he moved in with Leonardo, Salai began earning his nickname. "The second day I had two shirts cut out for him, a pair of hose, and a leather jacket, and when I put aside some money to pay for these things he stole the money," Leonardo recorded. "I could never make him confess, although I was quite certain of it." Nevertheless, he began taking Salai to dinner parties as his companion, which indicates that he was more than a sticky-fingered assistant or student. Two days after he arrived, Leonardo took him to a dinner at the home of the architect Giacomo Andrea da Ferrara, where he proved unmannerly. "[Salai] supped for two and did mischief for four, for he broke three cruets and spilled the wine," Leonardo wrote in his notebook.

Leonardo, who rarely revealed much of a personal nature in his notebooks, mentioned Salai dozens of times, often in tones of exasperation that also betrayed amusement and affection. This included at least five times when he stole things. "On the seventh day of September he stole a stylus worth 22 soldi from Marco, who was staying with me. It was of silver and he took it from his studio, and when

Marco had searched for it a long time he found it hidden in the box of Giacomo." During the wedding pageant for Ludovico Sforza and Beatrice d'Este in 1491, Leonardo noted, "When I was in the house of Messer Galeazzo da San Severino to arrange the festival for his tournament, and certain footmen had undressed to try on some of the costumes of the savages which were to appear at the festival, Giacomo went to the wallet of one of them as it lay on the bed with other clothes and took out whatever money he found there."[9]

As the tales pile up, one can be amused not only by Salai but also by Leonardo for continuing to tolerate and record his transgressions. "Maestro Agostino of Pavia gave me a Turkish hide in order to make a pair of boots, and Giacomo stole it from me within a month and sold it to a cobbler for 20 soldi and with this money, by his own confession, he bought aniseed candy," reads yet another example. The lines of accounting are written in a small, impassive hand, but next to one entry Leonardo's words in the margin are twice as big and scrawled in annoyance: "Thief, liar, obstinate, greedy."

Their bickering would persist over the years. A shopping list that Leonardo dictated to an assistant in 1508 dissolves into "Salai, I want peace, not war. No more wars, I give in."[10] Leonardo nevertheless continued, throughout his life, to indulge Salai and dress him in colorful and dandy clothes, many of them pink, the costs of which (including at least twenty-four pairs of fancy shoes and a pair of stockings so expensive they must have been jeweled) would routinely be recorded in his notebooks.

DRAWINGS OF OLD AND YOUNG MEN

Even before Salai moved in with him, Leonardo began what would be a lifelong pattern of juxtaposing sketches of an androgynous, curly-haired pretty boy facing a craggy older man like the one on the "theme sheet," with a jutting chin and aquiline nose (fig. 24). As he later instructed, "In narrative paintings you should closely intermingle direct opposites, because they offer a great contrast to each other, especially when they are adjacent. Thus, have the ugly one next to the beautiful, the large next to the small, the old next to the young."[11]

The pairing was a motif that he picked up from his mentor Verrocchio, who specialized in virile old warriors and pretty boys, and facing off the two types became a regular feature in his sketchbooks. Kenneth Clark described the combination:

> Most typical of such creations is the bald, clean-shaven man, with formidable frown, nutcracker nose and chin, who appears sometimes in the form of a caricature, more often as an ideal. His strongly accentuated features seem to have typified for Leonardo vigor and resolution, and so he becomes the counterpart of that other profile which came with equal facility from Leonardo's pen—the epicene youth. These are, in fact, the two hieroglyphs of Leonardo's unconscious mind, the two images his hand created when his attention was wandering. . . . Virile and effeminate, they symbolize the two sides of Leonardo's nature.[12]

Leonardo's earliest known pair of such profiles appears on a notebook page from 1478, when he was still in Florence (fig. 29). The old man has a long pointed nose curving down, a sunken upper lip, and an exaggerated jutting chin curving up, forming the nutcracker facial type Leonardo often used. The head of wavy hair hints that Leonardo may be drawing a caricature of his older self. Facing him, rendered

Fig. 29. Nutcracker man and young man, 1478.

in a few simple strokes, is a rather featureless slender boy who gazes up languidly, with a subtle twisting of his neck and bending of his body. The lithe and boyish figure, reminiscent of Verrocchio's statue of David that Leonardo likely modeled for, hints that Leonardo may have, consciously or not, been drawing a reflection of his younger self, juxtaposing his boyish and manly sides. There was also a hint of companionship in these face-offs. It is on this page from 1478 that Leonardo inscribed the words "Fioravante di Domenico of Florence is my most beloved friend, as though he were my . . ."[13]

After Salai moved into his household in 1490, Leonardo's doodles and drawings began to feature a boy who is softer, fleshier, and a bit more sultry. This character, who we can safely assume is Salai, slowly matures over the years. A good example is a version of the craggy jut-jawed man facing a young boy that Leonardo drew in the 1490s (fig. 30). Unlike in his 1478 version, this time the young boy has bounti-

Fig. 30. Old man and probably Salai, 1490s.

ful curls, pouring like a deluge from his head and cascading down his long neck. The eyes are big but more vacant. The chin is fleshy. The full lips are shaped into what may be, on second glance, a *Mona Lisa* smile, though a bit more mischievous. He looks angelic yet also devilish. The older man's arm reaches to the boy's shoulder, but the forearm and the torsos are left partly blank, as if the two bodies are melding. Though not a self-portrait of Leonardo, who was then only in his mid-forties, the older man seems to be a caricature he uses over the years that conveys his own emotions as he faces the prospect of aging.[14]

Throughout his career, Leonardo would repeatedly and lovingly draw Salai. We see him age slowly while remaining, at each stage, soft and sensuous. When Salai is in his early twenties, Leonardo draws him with red chalk and pen, standing in the nude (fig. 31). His lips and chin are still boyish, his hair exuberantly curled, but his body and slightly spread arms have the musculature that we will see in *Vitruvian Man* and some of the anatomical drawings. Another full-length nude drawing, this one from behind, also shows him with arms and legs spread, his body strong with just a hint of fleshiness (fig. 32).

A few years later, around 1510, Leonardo made another chalk drawing of Salai's head in profile, this time facing to our right (fig. 33). It has all of the same features, from the swanlike neck to the fleshy chin and languid eyes, but he is now portrayed as just a touch older, though remembered as still boyish. His top lip is full and thrusting, his lower one soft and receding, forming yet again that hint of a devilish smile.

Even in the last years of his life, Leonardo still seemed to be mesmerized by the Salai image. In one drawing from about 1517, he created a tender sketch of a remembered youthful Salai in profile (fig. 34). His heavy-lidded eyes are still sultry and slightly vacant, his hair is still tightly curled in the way, as Vasari reported, "in which Leonardo greatly delighted."[15]

Leonardo's many drawings of an old and a young man juxtaposed in profile are evoked, in a telling way, in a haunting allegorical draw-

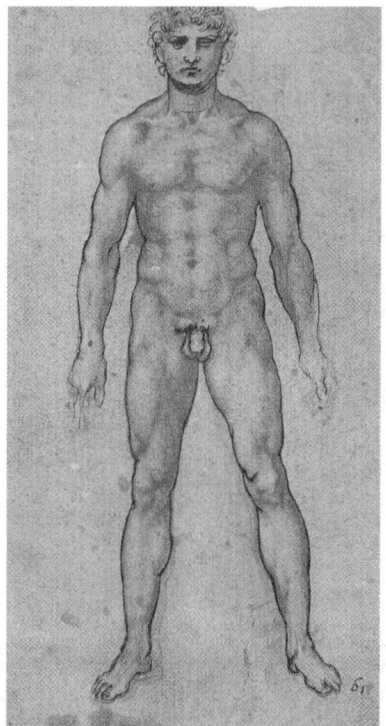

Fig. 31. Salai c. 1504.

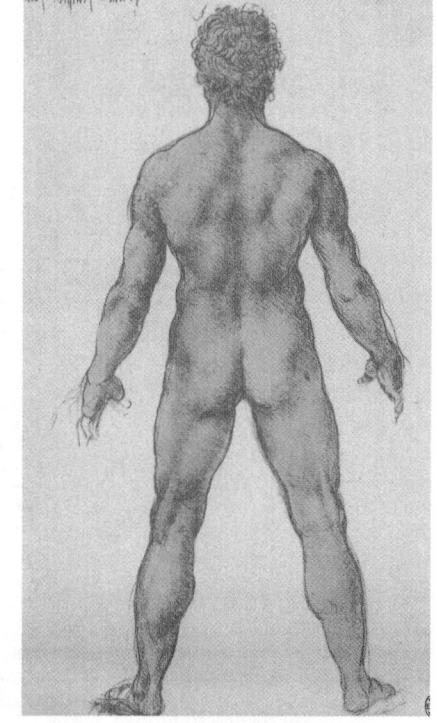

Fig. 32. c. 1504.

Fig. 33. c. 1510.

Fig. 34. c. 1517.

Fig. 35. Allegorical drawing of Pleasure and Pain.

ing that he made of figures representing Pleasure and Pain (fig. 35). The young character depicting Pleasure has some of Salai's looks. He is standing back-to-back and intertwined with the older man, who is the depiction of Pain. Their bodies merge as their arms entangle. "Pleasure and Pain are represented as twins," Leonardo wrote on the drawing, "because there never is one without the other."

As usual with Leonardo's allegorical drawings, there are symbols and puns. Pain stands on mud, while Pleasure stands on gold. Pain is dropping little spiked balls known as *tribolo*, a play on the word *tribolatione*, for "tribulation." Pleasure drops coins and holds a reed. Leonardo explained why the reed evokes the "evil pleasures" that are the source of pain: "Pleasure is here represented with a reed in his right hand which is useless and without strength, and the wounds it inflicts are poisoned. In Tuscany they are used to support beds, to signify that it is here that vain dreams come."

His notion of "vain dreams" appears to include sexual fantasies, and he went on to lament that they can distract a person from getting on with his work. "It is here that much precious time is wasted and many vain pleasures are enjoyed," he wrote of a bed, "both by the mind in imagining impossible things and by the body in partaking of those pleasures that are often the cause of the failing of life." Did this mean that Leonardo believed that some of the vain pleasures he indulged or imagined while in bed were a cause of his own failings? As he warned in his description of the phallic and "useless" reed that Pleasure holds, "If you take Pleasure know that he has behind him one who will deal you Tribulation and Repentance."[16]

CHAPTER 8

Vitruvian Man

A *TIBURIO* FOR MILAN'S CATHEDRAL

When Milan's authorities in 1487 were seeking ideas for building a lantern tower, known as a *tiburio*, atop their cathedral, Leonardo seized the opportunity to establish his credentials as an architect. That year he had completed his plans for an ideal city, but they had engendered little interest. The competition to design the tiburio was a chance to show that he could do something more practical.

Milan's cathedral (fig. 36) was a century old, but it still did not have the traditional tiburio on the roof at the crossing of the nave and transept. The challenge, which had defeated a few previous architects, was to conform with the building's Gothic style and overcome the structural weakness of its crossing area. At least nine architects entered the 1487 competition, approaching the task in a somewhat collaborative fashion, sharing ideas.[1]

The Italian Renaissance was producing artist-engineer-architects who straddled disciplines, in the tradition of Brunelleschi and Alberti, and the tiburio project gave Leonardo the opportunity to work with two of the best: Donato Bramante and Francesco di Giorgio. They became his close friends, and their collaboration produced some interesting church designs. Far more important, it also led to a set of drawings, based on the writings of an ancient Roman architect, that

Fig. 36. Milan Cathedral, with tiburio.

sought to harmonize the proportions of a human to that of a church, an effort that would culminate with an iconic drawing by Leonardo that came to symbolize the harmonious relationship between man and the universe.

Bramante served as the initial expert judging the tiburio submissions. Eight years older than Leonardo, he was a farmer's son from near Urbino with grand ambitions and appetites. He moved to Milan in the early 1470s to make a name for himself, and he carved out roles that ranged from entertainer to engineer. Like Leonardo, he began his work at the Sforza court by being an impresario of pageants and performances. He also wrote witty verses, offered up clever riddles, and occasionally accompanied his performances by playing a lyre or lute.

Some of Leonardo's allegorical tales and prophecies were complements to Bramante's, and by the late 1480s they were working together on fantasias performed for special occasions and other effu-

sions of the Sforza entertainment industry. Both men displayed dazzling brilliance and effortless charm, despite which they became close
friends. In his notebooks Leonardo affectionately called the architect
"Donnino," and Bramante dedicated a book of poems about Roman
antiquities to Leonardo, calling him a "cordial, dear, and delightful
associate."[2]

A few years after he and Leonardo became friends,[3] Bramante
painted a fresco that featured two ancient philosophers, Heraclitus
and Democritus (fig. 37). Democritus, known to be amused by the
human condition, is laughing, while Heraclitus is crying. Round-faced
and balding, the former appears to be a self-portrait of Bramante,
while the portrait of Heraclitus seems to be based on Leonardo. He
has a profusion of flowing, tightly curled hair, rose-colored tunic,
prominent eyebrows and chin, and a manuscript book in front of him
with the characters in right-to-left mirror script. Thus we can imagine
how Leonardo, still clean-shaven, looked in his prime.

Bramante moved on from the role of impresario to being on retainer as an artist-engineer-architect of the Sforza court, thus shaping the role and paving the way for Leonardo. In the mid-1480s,
when he and Leonardo were working together, Bramante displayed
his combination of art and architecture talents by designing a fake
apse, or choir area, behind the altar of Milan's Church of Santa
Maria presso San Satiro. Because space was cramped, there was no
room for a full apse. Using the knowledge of perspective that was
spreading among Renaissance painters, Bramante conjured up a
trompe l'œil, a painted optical illusion that made it seem as if the
space had more depth.

Within a few years, he and Leonardo would together work on a
similar feat of engineering and perspective, when Ludovico Sforza
commissioned Bramante to rework the convent of Santa Maria delle
Grazie by adding a new dining hall, and Leonardo was hired to paint
on its wall a depiction of the Last Supper. Both Bramante and Leonardo favored church designs that were based on strict symmetry. This
led them to prefer central temple-like plans that featured overlapping
squares, circles, and other regular geometric shapes, as can be seen in
many of Leonardo's church sketches (fig. 38).

Fig. 37. Bramante's *Heraclitus and Democritus*, Leonardo on the left.

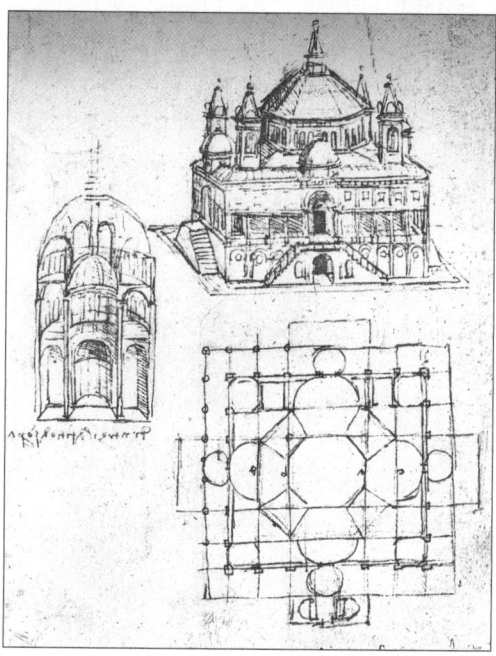

Fig. 38. Church drawings.

Bramante presented his written opinion on the tiburio design ideas in September 1487. One issue was whether the tower should have four sides, which would fit more securely on the support beams of the roof, or eight sides. "I maintain that the square is far stronger and better than the octagon, because it matches the rest of the building far better," he concluded.

Leonardo received six payments in July through September 1487 for his work on the project, which probably included consulting with Bramante as he wrote his opinion. In one of his presentations, Leonardo made a philosophical pitch that drew on the analogy, of which he was so fond, between human bodies and buildings. "Medicines, when properly used, restore health to invalids, and a doctor will make the right use of them if he understands the nature of man," he wrote. "This too is what the sick cathedral needs—it needs a doctor-architect, who understands the nature of the building and the laws on which correct construction is based."[4]

He filled pages of his notebooks with drawings and descriptions of what caused structural weaknesses in buildings, and he was the first to do a systematic study on the origins of fissures in walls. "The cracks that are vertical are caused by the joining of new walls with old ones," he wrote, "for the indentations cannot bear the great weight of the wall added on to them, so it is inevitable that they should break."[5]

To shore up the unsteady parts of the Milan Cathedral, Leonardo devised a system of buttresses to stabilize the area around his proposed tower and, always a believer in experiment, designed a simple test to show how they would work:

An Experiment to show that a weight placed on an arch does not discharge itself entirely on its columns; on the contrary, the greater the weight placed on the arches, the less the arch transmits the weight to the columns: Let a man be placed on a weighing-device in the middle of a well-shaft, then have him push out his hands and feet against the walls of the well. You will find that he weighs much less on the scales. If you put weights on his shoulders you will see for yourselves that the more weight you put on him, the greater will be the force with which he spreads his arms and legs and presses against the wall, and the less will be his weight on the scales.[6]

With the help of a carpenter's assistant he hired, Leonardo made a wooden model of his design for the tiburio, for which he received a series of payments early in 1488. He did not try to have his tiburio blend in with the cathedral's Gothic design and ornate exterior. Instead, he displayed his inbred fondness for Florence's Duomo; his many sketches for a Tuscan-style cupola seem more inspired by Brunelleschi's dome than the Gothic flying buttresses of Milan's cathedral. His most ingenious proposal was to create a double-shelled dome, like Brunelleschi's. It would be four-sided on the outside, as Bramante had recommended, but on the inside it would be octagonal.[7]

FRANCESCO DI GIORGIO IS CALLED IN

After receiving Bramante's opinion along with proposals from Leonardo and other architects, the Milanese authorities seemed baffled about what to do, so in April 1490 they convened a meeting of all who had been involved. The result was to call in yet another expert, Francesco di Giorgio from Siena.[8]

Thirteen years older than Leonardo, he was another exemplar of an artisan who combined art, engineering, and architecture. He had begun as a painter, moved as a young man to Urbino to work as an architect, returned to Siena to run the underground aqueduct system, and was a sculptor in his spare time. He was also interested in military weaponry and fortifications. In other words, he was the Leonardo of Siena.

Like Leonardo, Francesco kept pocket-size notebooks of design ideas, and in 1475 he began collecting them for a treatise on architecture intended as a successor to the one by Alberti. Written in unpolished Italian rather than Latin, Francesco's was designed as a manual for builders rather than a scholarly work. He tried to ground design in math as well as in art. The range of his ideas was similar to those in Leonardo's notebooks. Spilling across its pages were drawings and discussions of machinery, temple-like churches, weapons, pumps, hoists, urban designs, and fortified castles. In church design, he shared with Leonardo and Bramante a preference for a symmetrical Greek cross interior, in which the central plan has the same length for the nave and transept.

An official cultural diplomacy request was sent from Milan's ducal court to the council of Siena describing the importance of the tiburio project and asking that Francesco be permitted to come work on it. The response was reluctant acquiescence. The Siena councilors insisted that his work in Milan be done quickly, because he had many incomplete projects in Siena. By early June, Francesco was in Milan working on a new model for the tiburio.

A grand meeting was held later that month in the presence of Ludovico Sforza and the deputies of the cathedral. After inspecting three alternatives, they accepted Francesco's recommendations and chose two local architect-engineers who had been part of the competition. The result was an ornate, octagonal Gothic tower (fig. 36). It was very different from Leonardo's more graceful and Florentine approach, and he withdrew from the process.

Leonardo nevertheless remained interested in church design, and he made more than seventy other drawings of beautiful domes and idealized plans for church interiors at the same time that he was studying the transformations of shapes and ways to square a circle. His most interesting church designs featured floor plans that imbedded circles inside squares to form a variety of shapes, with the altar in the center, which were intended to evoke a harmonious relationship between man and the world.[9]

A TRIP WITH FRANCESCO TO PAVIA

While they were working together on the Milan Cathedral's tiburio project in June 1490, Leonardo and Francesco di Giorgio took a trip to the town of Pavia, twenty-five miles away, where a new cathedral was being built (fig. 39). The authorities in Pavia, knowing of the work that Leonardo and Francesco were doing in Milan, had asked Ludovico Sforza to send them as consultants. Ludovico wrote to

Fig. 39. Pavia Cathedral.

his secretary, "The building supervisors of this city's cathedral have requested that we agree to provide them with that Sienese engineer employed by the building supervisors of the cathedral in Milan." He was referring to Francesco, whose name he apparently could not remember. In a postscript, he added that "Master Leonardo of Florence" should also be sent.

Ludovico's secretary replied that Francesco could leave Milan in eight days, after his preliminary report on the tiburio was in hand. "Master Leonardo the Florentine," he added, "is always ready, whenever he is asked." Apparently Leonardo was eager to travel with Francesco. "If you send the Sienese engineer, he will come too," the secretary reported. The expense accounts of the Pavia authorities list a hotel payment on June 21: "Paid to Giovanni Agostino Berneri, host of Il Saracino, in Pavia, for expenses he incurred because of Masters Francesco of Siena and Leonardo of Florence, the engineers with their colleagues, attendants and horses, both of whom were summoned for a consultation about the building."[10]

Their friend and collaborator in Milan, Donato Bramante, had given advice a few years earlier on the design for Pavia's proposed cathedral. In contrast to Milan's cathedral, the resulting plan was decidedly non-Gothic, which made it more to Leonardo's taste. It had a simple façade and a very symmetrical interior design based on the Greek cross layout, with both the nave and the transept having the same length. That produced a balanced and equally proportioned geometric elegance. Like the churches that Bramante designed, most notably Saint Peter's Basilica in the Vatican, as well as the ones that Leonardo sketched in his notebooks, the plan featured circles and squares forming very harmonious and balanced areas.[11]

Francesco was at that time revising the manuscript of his treatise on architecture, and he discussed it with Leonardo as they traveled together. Leonardo would eventually acquire a lavishly illustrated copy. They also discussed another, more venerable book. In the thousand-volume Visconti library in the castle in Pavia there was a beautiful manuscript copy of an architectural treatise by Vitruvius, a Roman military officer and engineer from the first century BC. For years Francesco had been struggling to compile a translation of Vitruvius from Latin into Italian. There were many variations in the manuscript copies made of Vitruvius over the centuries, and he wanted to study the fourteenth-century copy that existed in Pavia. So did Leonardo.[12]

VITRUVIUS

Marcus Vitruvius Pollio, born around 80 BC, served in the Roman army under Caesar and specialized in the design and construction of artillery machines. His duties took him to what are now Spain and France and as far away as North Africa. Vitruvius later became an architect and worked on a temple, no longer in existence, in the town of Fano in Italy. His most important work was literary, the only surviving book on architecture from classical antiquity: *De Architectura*, known today as *The Ten Books on Architecture*.[13]

For many dark centuries, Vitruvius's work had been forgotten, but in the early 1400s it was one of the many pieces of classical writing, including Lucretius's epic poem *On the Nature of Things* and Cicero's orations, that were rediscovered and collected by the pioneering Italian humanist Poggio Bracciolini. At a monastery in Switzerland, Poggio found an eighth-century copy of Vitruvius's opus, and he sent it back to Florence. There it became part of the firmament of rediscovered classical works that birthed the Renaissance. Brunelleschi used it as a reference when he traveled to Rome as a young man to measure and study the ruins of classical buildings, and Alberti quoted it extensively in his treatise on architecture. A Latin edition was published in the late 1480s by one of Italy's new print shops, and Leonardo wrote in a notebook, "Enquire at the stationers about Vitruvius."[14]

What made Vitruvius's work appealing to Leonardo and Francesco was that it gave concrete expression to an analogy that went back to Plato and the ancients, one that had become a defining metaphor of Renaissance humanism: the relationship between the microcosm of man and the macrocosm of the earth.

This analogy was a foundation for the treatise that Francesco was composing. "All the arts and all the world's rules are derived from a well-composed and proportioned human body," he wrote in the foreword to his fifth chapter. "Man, called a little world, contains in himself all the general perfections of the whole world."[15] Leonardo likewise embraced the analogy in both his art and his science. He famously wrote around this time, "The ancients called man a lesser world, and certainly the use of this name is well bestowed, because his body is an analog for the world."[16]

Applying this analogy to the design of temples, Vitruvius decreed that the layout should reflect the proportions of a human body, as if the body were laid out flat on its back upon the geometric forms of the floor plan. "The design of a temple depends on symmetry," he wrote at the outset of his third book. "There must be a precise relation between its components, as in the case of those of a well-shaped man."[17]

Vitruvius described in great detail the proportions of this "well-shaped man" that should inform the design of a temple. The distance from his chin to the top of his forehead should be one-tenth of his whole height, he began, and proceeded with many other such notations. "The length of the foot is one sixth of the height of the body; of the forearm, one fourth; and the breadth of the breast is also one fourth. The other members, too, have their own symmetrical proportions, and it was by employing them that the famous painters and sculptors of antiquity attained to great and endless renown."

Vitruvius's descriptions of human proportions would inspire Leonardo, as part of the anatomy studies he had just begun in 1489, to compile a similar set of measurements. More broadly, Vitruvius's belief that the proportions of man are analogous to those of a well-conceived temple—and to the macrocosm of the world—became central to Leonardo's worldview.

After detailing human proportions, Vitruvius went on to describe, in a memorable visualization, a way to put a man in a circle and square in order to determine the ideal proportion of a church:

> In a temple there ought to be harmony in the symmetrical relations of the different parts to the whole. In the human body, the central point is the navel. If a man is placed flat on his back, with his hands and feet extended, and a compass centered at his navel, his fingers and toes will touch the circumference of a circle thereby described. And just as the human body yields a circular outline, so too a square may be found from it. For if we measure the distance from the soles of the feet to the top of the head, and then apply that measure to the outstretched arms, the breadth will be found to be the same as the height, as in the case of a perfect square.[18]

It was a powerful image. But as far as we know, no one of note had made a serious and precise drawing along these lines in the fifteen centuries since Vitruvius composed his description. Then, around 1490, Leonardo and his friends proceeded to tackle this depiction of man spread-eagle amid a church and the universe.

Francesco produced at least three such drawings that were designed to accompany his treatise and translation of Vitruvius. One
of them shows a sweet and dreamy image of a man in a circle and
a square (fig. 40). It is a suggestive rather than precise drawing. The
circle, square, and body do not attempt to show proportions and are
instead rendered casually. Two other drawings that Francesco made
(figs. 41 and 42) depict a man more carefully proportioned inside a
design of circles and squares in the shape of a church floor plan. None

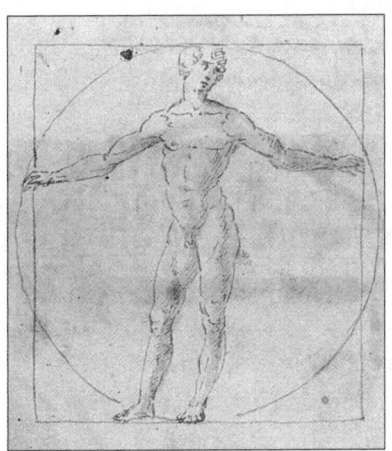

Fig. 40

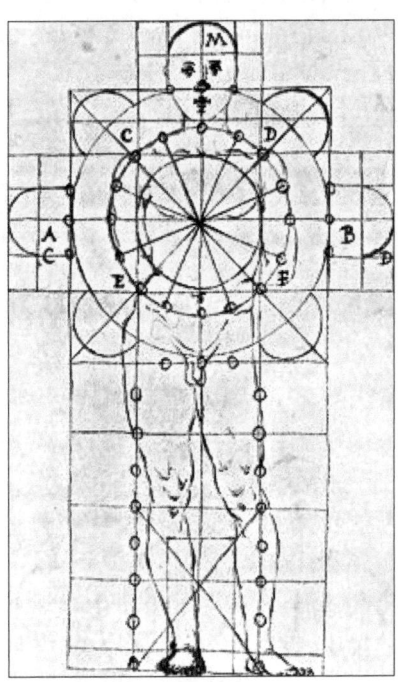

Fig. 41

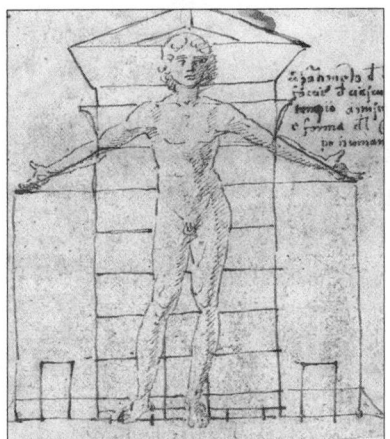

Fig. 42

Francesco di Giorgio's drawings
of Vitruvian Man.

of his drawings is a memorable work of art, but they show that Francesco and Leonardo, at the time of their 1490 trip to Pavia, were both enchanted by the image Vitruvius had conceived.

DINNER WITH GIACOMO ANDREA

Around the same time, another dear friend of Leonardo produced a drawing based on Vitruvius's passage. Giacomo Andrea was part of the collaborative circle of architects and engineers gathered by Ludovico at the court of Milan. Luca Pacioli, a mathematician at the court and another close friend of Leonardo, wrote a dedication to an edition of his book *On Divine Proportion* that listed the distinguished members of that court. After hailing Leonardo, Pacioli adds, "There was also Giacomo Andrea da Ferrara, as dear to Leonardo as a brother, a keen student of Vitruvius's works."[19]

We have met Giacomo Andrea before. He was the host of the dinner that Leonardo went to with Salai two days after the ten-year-old scamp had become his assistant, at which Salai "supped for two and did mischief for four," including breaking three cruets and spilling the wine.[20] That dinner happened on July 24, 1490, just four weeks after Leonardo and Francesco returned from their trip to Pavia. It was one of those priceless historical dinners that makes you yearn for a time machine. The conversation, when not being distracted by Salai's antics, was evidently about the manuscript of Vitruvius that Leonardo and Francesco had just seen at the university.

Andrea decided to try his own hand at illustrating Vitruvius's idea, and one can imagine him discussing it over dinner with Leonardo, hoping that Salai didn't spill wine on their sketches. Andrea produced a simple version of a spread-armed man in a circle and a square (fig. 43). Notably, the circle and square are not centered; the circle rises higher than the square, which allows the man's navel to be in the center of the circle and his genitals to be in the center of the square, like Vitruvius had suggested. The man's arms are stretched outward, Christ-like, and his feet are close together.

Andrea would end up being killed and brutally quartered by French troops when they captured Milan nine years later. Shortly

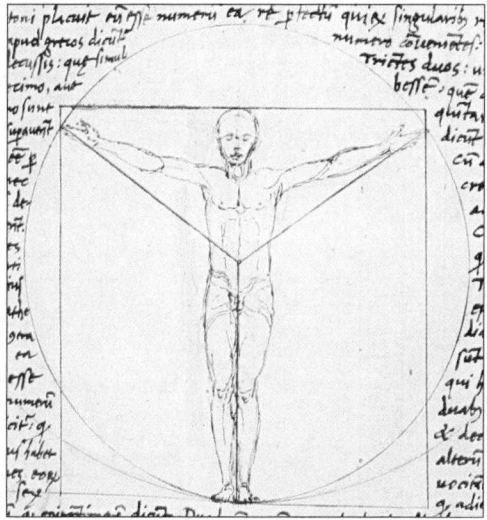

Fig. 43. Giacomo Andrea's drawing of Vitruvian Man.

thereafter, Leonardo would search for and find his manuscript copy of Vitruvius's work. "Messer Vincenzio Aliprando, who lives near the Inn of the Bear, has Giacomo Andrea's Vitruvius," he declared in a notebook entry.[21]

In the 1980s, Andrea's drawing was rediscovered. Architectural historian Claudio Sgarbi found a heavily illustrated manuscript copy of Vitruvius's tome that was languishing in an archive in Ferrara, Italy.[22] He determined that manuscript had been compiled by Andrea. Among its 127 illustrations was Andrea's version of Vitruvian Man.

LEONARDO'S VERSION

There are two key differences that distinguish Leonardo's version of *Vitruvian Man* from those done around the same time by his two friends, Francesco di Giorgio and Giacomo Andrea. In both scientific precision and artistic distinction, Leonardo's is in an entirely different realm (fig. 44).

Rarely on display, because prolonged exposure to light would cause it to fade, it is kept in a locked room on the fourth floor of the Gallerie dell'Accademia in Venice. When a curator brought it out and

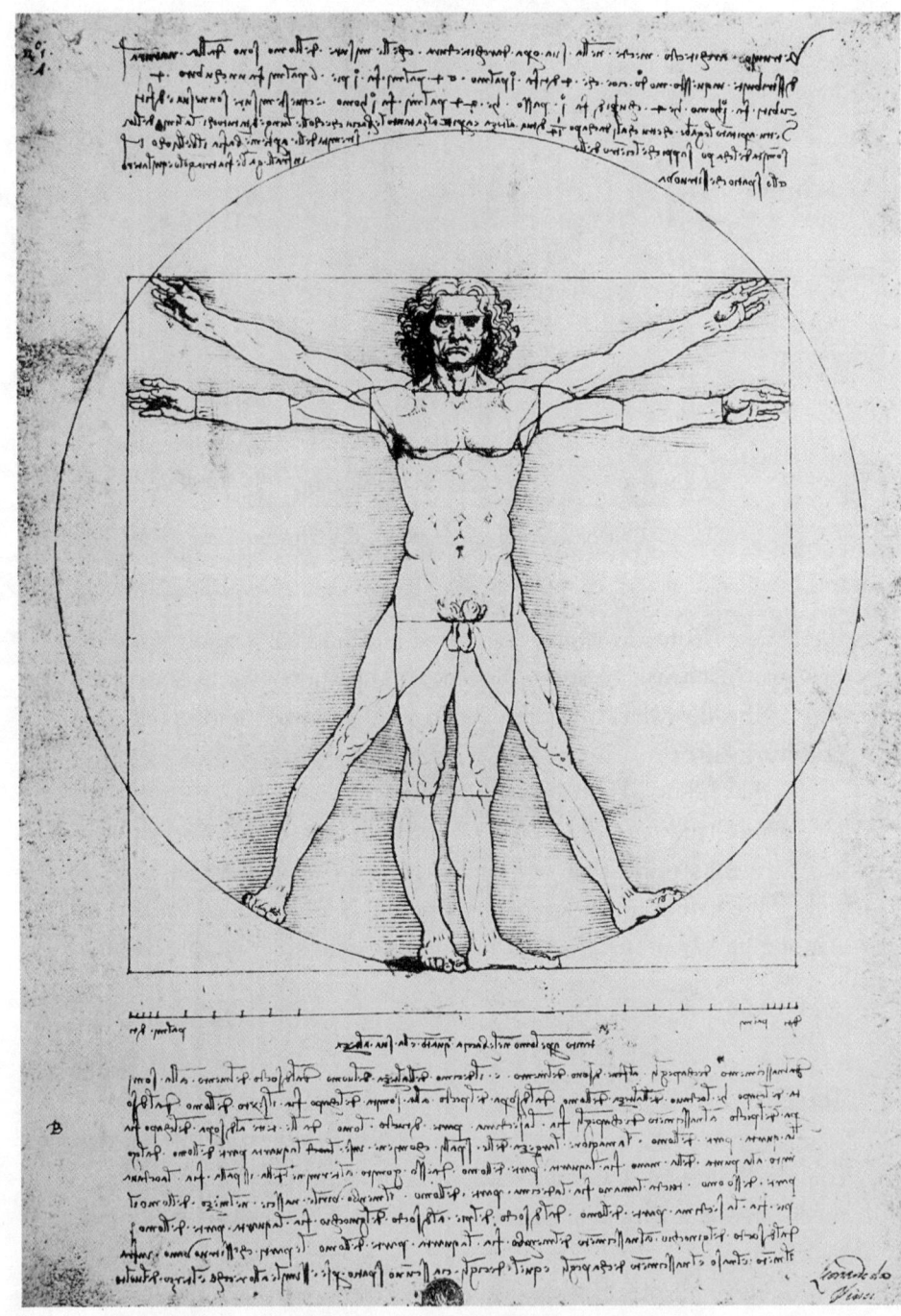

Fig. 44. Leonardo's *Vitruvian Man*.

placed it before me on a table, I was struck by the indentations made by the stylus of Leonardo's metalpoint pen and the twelve pricks made by the point of his compass. I had the eerie and intimate sensation of seeing the hand of the master at work more than five centuries earlier.

Unlike those of his friends, Leonardo's drawing is meticulously done. His lines are not sketchy and tentative. Instead, he dug hard with his stylus, carving the lines confidently into the page as if he were making an etching. He had planned this drawing very carefully and knew precisely what he was doing.

Before he began, he had determined exactly how the circle would rest on the base of the square but extend out higher and wider. Using a compass and a set square, he drew the circle and the square, then allowed the man's feet to rest comfortably on them. As a result, per Vitruvius's description, the man's navel is in the precise center of the circle, and his genitals are at the center of the square.

In one of the notes below the drawing, Leonardo described additional aspects of the positioning: "If you open your legs enough that your head is lowered by one-fourteenth of your height and raise your hands enough that your extended fingers touch the line of the top of your head, know that the center of the extended limbs will be the navel, and the space between the legs will be an equilateral triangle."

Other notes on the page provide more detailed measurements and proportions, which he attributed to Vitruvius:

Vitruvius, architect, writes in his work on architecture that the measurements of man are distributed in this manner:

The length of the outspread arms is equal to the height of a man.

From the hairline to the bottom of the chin is one-tenth of the height of a man.

From below the chin to the top of the head is one-eighth of the height of a man.

From above the chest to the top of the head is one-sixth of the height of a man.

From above the chest to the hairline is one-seventh of the height of a man.

The maximum width of the shoulders is a quarter of the height of a man.

From the breasts to the top of the head is a quarter of the height of a man.

From the elbow to the tip of the hand is a quarter of the height of a man.

From the elbow to the armpit is one-eighth of the height of a man.

The length of the hand is one-tenth of the height of a man.

The root of the penis [*Il membro virile*] is at half the height of a man.

The foot is one-seventh of the height of a man.

Despite what he stated, instead of accepting what Vitruvius had written, Leonardo relied on his own experience and experiments, as per his creed. Fewer than half of the twenty-two measurements that Leonardo cited are the ones Vitruvius handed down. The rest reflect the studies on anatomy and human proportion that Leonardo had begun recording in his notebooks. For example, Vitruvius puts the height of a man at six times the length of his foot, but Leonardo records it as seven times.[23]

In order to make his drawing an informative work of science, Leonardo could have used a simplified figure of a man. Instead, he used delicate lines and careful shading to create a body of remarkable and unnecessary beauty. With its intense but intimate stare and the curls of hair that Leonardo loved to draw, his masterpiece weaves together the human and the divine.

The man seems to be in motion, vibrant and energetic, just like the four-winged dragonflies that Leonardo studied. Leonardo has made us sense, almost see, one leg and then the other being pushed out and pulled back, the arms flapping as if in flight. There is nothing static except the calm torso, with subtle cross-hatch shadings behind it. Yet despite the sense of motion, there is a natural and comfortable feel to the man. The only slightly awkward positioning is of his left foot, which is twisted outward to provide a measurement guide.

To what extent might *Vitruvian Man* be a self-portrait? Leonardo was thirty-eight when he drew it, about the age of the man in the picture. Contemporary descriptions emphasize his "beautiful curling hair" and "well-proportioned" body. *Vitruvian Man* echoes features seen in many assumed portraits of him, especially Bramante's depiction of Heraclitus (fig. 37), which shows Leonardo still beardless at about that age. Leonardo once warned against falling prey to the axiom "Every painter paints himself," but in a section in his proposed treatise on painting called "How Figures Often Resemble Their Masters," he accepted that it was natural to do so.[24]

The stare of Vitruvian Man is as intense as someone looking in a mirror, perhaps literally. According to Toby Lester, who wrote a book about the drawing, "It's an idealized self-portrait in which Leonardo, stripped down to his essence, takes his own measure, and in doing so embodies a timeless human hope: that we just might have the power of mind to figure out how we fit into the grand scheme of things. Think of the picture as an act of speculation, a kind of metaphysical self-portrait in which Leonardo—as an artist, a natural philosopher, and a stand-in for all of humanity—peers at himself with furrowed brow and tries to grasp the secrets of his own nature."[25]

Leonardo's *Vitruvian Man* embodies a moment when art and science combined to allow mortal minds to probe timeless questions about who we are and how we fit into the grand order of the universe. It also symbolizes an ideal of humanism that celebrates the dignity, value, and rational agency of humans as individuals. Inside the square and the circle we can see the essence of Leonardo da Vinci, and the essence of ourselves, standing naked at the intersection of the earthly and the cosmic.

COLLABORATION AND *VITRUVIAN MAN*

Both the creation of *Vitruvian Man* and the design process for the tiburio of Milan's cathedral have engendered much scholarly dispute over which artists and architects deserve the most credit and should be accorded priority. Some of these discussions ignore the role that collaboration and the sharing of ideas played.

When Leonardo drew his *Vitruvian Man*, he had a lot of inter-related ideas dancing in his imagination. These included the mathematical challenge of squaring the circle, the analogy between the microcosm of man and the macrocosm of earth, the human proportions to be found through anatomical studies, the geometry of squares and circles in church architecture, the transformation of geometric shapes, and a concept combining math and art that was known as "the golden ratio" or "divine proportion."

He developed his thoughts about these topics not just from his own experience and reading; they were formulated also through conversations with friends and colleagues. Conceiving ideas was for Leonardo, as it has been throughout history for most other cross-disciplinary thinkers, a collaborative endeavor. Unlike Michelangelo and some other anguished artists, Leonardo enjoyed being surrounded by friends, companions, students, assistants, fellow courtiers, and thinkers. In his notebooks we find scores of people with whom he wanted to discuss ideas. His closest friendships were intellectual ones.

This process of bouncing around thoughts and jointly formulating ideas was facilitated by hanging around a Renaissance court like the one in Milan. In addition to the troupes of musicians and pageant performers, those on stipend at the Sforza court included architects, engineers, mathematicians, medical researchers, and scientists of various stripes who helped Leonardo with his continuing education and indulged his insatiable curiosity. The court poet Bernardo Bellincioni, who was more accomplished as a sycophant than as a versifier, celebrated the diverse collection that Ludovico curated. "Of artists his court is full," he wrote. "Here like the bee to honey comes every man of learning." He compared Leonardo to the greatest of the ancient Greek painters: "From Florence he has brought here an Apelles."[26]

Ideas are often generated in physical gathering places where people with diverse interests encounter one another serendipitously. That is why Steve Jobs liked his buildings to have a central atrium and why the young Benjamin Franklin founded a club where the most interesting people of Philadelphia would gather every Friday. At the court of Ludovico Sforza, Leonardo found friends who could spark new ideas by rubbing together their diverse passions.

CHAPTER 9

The Horse Monument

A RESIDENCE AT THE COURT

As he was consulting on the Milan Cathedral in the spring of 1489, Leonardo got the job he had requested at the end of his letter to Ludovico Sforza seven years earlier: designing the proposed monument "to the immortal glory and eternal honor of His Lordship, your father." The plan was for a mammoth equestrian statue. "Prince Ludovico is planning to erect a worthy monument to his father," Florence's ambassador in Milan reported back to Lorenzo de' Medici in July of that year. "In accordance with his orders, Leonardo has been asked to make a model in the form of a large horse ridden by Duke Francesco in full armor."[1]

The commission, along with his service as an impresario and designer of court pageants, finally earned Leonardo an official appointment at court, with a salary and accommodations. He was described as "Leonardo da Vinci, engineer and painter," and listed as one of the four primary ducal engineers. It was the situation he had yearned for.

The job came with rooms for himself and his assistants, plus a studio for making the model for the horse monument, at the Corte Vecchia, the old castle in the center of town next to the cathedral. Once the home of the Visconti dukes, it was a medieval castle, replete with towers and moats, which had recently been renovated. Ludovico preferred the newer, more strongly fortified palace on the west side of town, which became the Sforza Castle, and he used the old palace as a place to house favored courtiers and artists, such as Leonardo.

Leonardo's stipend was generous enough to cover the costs of his retinue, including two assistants and three or four students, at least during those periods when he actually got paid. Ludovico, whose costs for defense were rising, was at times short of funds, and in the late 1490s Leonardo had to send him a plea for overdue payments to cover his costs and those of "the two skilled workmen who are continually in my pay and at my expense."[2] Ludovico eventually made good by giving Leonardo an income-producing vineyard just outside of Milan, which he kept for the rest of his life.

Leonardo's quarters were on two floors facing the smaller of the two courtyards. In one of the larger upstairs rooms, leading out onto a roof, he built one of his attempts at a flying machine. We can imagine what his studio looked like, in reality or at least in Leonardo's imagination, from a description he wrote of an artist at work: "The painter sits in front of his work at perfect ease. He is well dressed and wields a very light brush dipped in delicate color. He adorns himself with the clothes he fancies; his home is clean and filled with delightful pictures, and he is often accompanied by music or by the reading of various beautiful works."

His engineering instincts led him to envision some ingenious conveniences: the windows of the studio should have adjustable blinds so the light could be easily controlled, and the painting easels should be on platforms that could be raised and lowered with pulleys, "so that it would be the painting, not the painter, that would move up and down." He also devised and drew plans for a system to protect his works at night. "You would be able to put your work away and close it, like those chests that can be used as seats when they are closed."[3]

DESIGNING THE MONUMENT

Since his power was not based on long dynastic heritage, Ludovico sought monumental ways to assert his family's glory, and Leonardo's design for an equestrian statue catered to that desire. It was intended to be a bronze horse and rider weighing seventy-five tons, which would have been the biggest one yet made. Verrocchio and Donatello had recently created large equestrian monuments that were twelve or so feet high; Leonardo planned to build one at least twenty-three feet high, three times larger than life.

Although the original purpose was to honor the late Duke Francesco by glorifying him atop a steed, Leonardo focused more on the horse than the rider. In fact, he seemed to lose all interest in the Duke Francesco component, and the monument soon was being referred to, by himself and others, as *il cavallo* (the horse). In preparation, he threw himself into a detailed anatomical study of horses that included making precise measurements and, later, dissections.

Even though it was typical of him, we still should marvel that he would decide that before sculpting a horse he had to dissect one. Once again his compulsion to engage in anatomical investigations for his art eventually led him to pursue the science for its own sake. We can see this process unfold as he worked on the horse: careful measurements and observations are recorded in his notes, which lead to scores of diagrams, charts, sketches, and beautiful drawings in which art and science are interwoven. This eventually leads him into comparative anatomy; in a later set of drawings of human anatomy, he renders the muscles, bones, and tendons of a man's left leg next to those of a dissected back leg of a horse.[4]

Leonardo got so deeply immersed in these studies that he decided to begin an entire treatise on the anatomy of horses. Vasari claimed that it was actually completed, though that seems unlikely. As usual, Leonardo was easily distracted by related topics. While studying horses, he began plotting methods to make cleaner stables; over the years he would devise multiple systems for mangers with mechanisms to replenish feed bins through conduits from an attic and to remove manure using water sluices and inclined floors.[5]

When Leonardo was studying the horses in the royal stables, he became particularly interested in a Sicilian thoroughbred owned by Galeazzo Sanseverino, the Milanese commander who was married

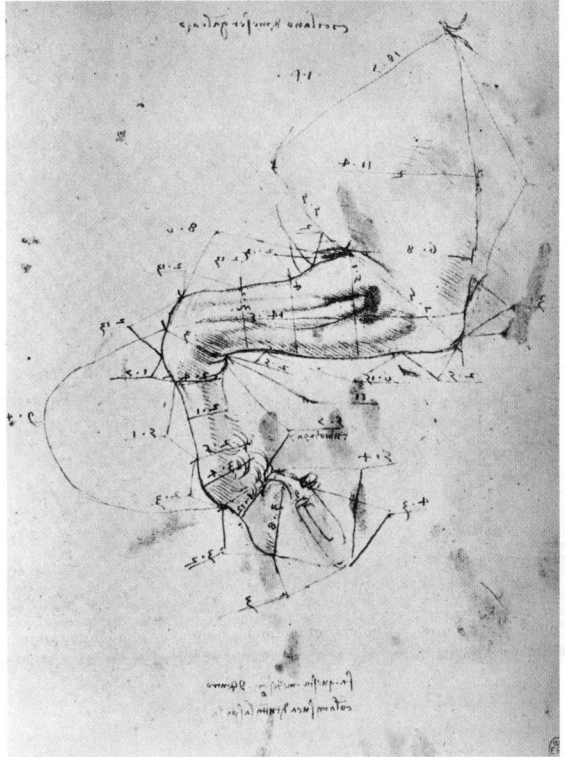

Fig. 45. Leg of horse.

to Ludovico's daughter. He drew it from a variety of angles, and in one detail of its foreleg included twenty-nine precisely diagrammed measurements, from the length of its hoof to the width of its calf in different places (fig. 45). Another drawing, this one using metalpoint and ink on blue prepared paper, is the equestrian version of the *Vitruvian Man*, aesthetically beautiful yet scientifically annotated. In the Royal Collection at Windsor alone, there are more than forty such pieces of his equine anatomical art.[6]

At first Leonardo planned to have the horse rearing on its hind legs, with the left foreleg atop a trampled soldier. In one drawing, he shows the horse's head turning and its muscled legs appearing to move as its tail flutters behind (fig. 46). But even Leonardo was practical enough to realize, eventually, that such a large monument

Fig. 46 Study for the Sforza monument.

so precariously balanced was not a good idea, so he settled for a horse that would be fancifully prancing.

As was often the case, Leonardo's mix of diligence and distraction, focus and delay, made his patrons nervous. The July 1489 report written by Florence's ambassador to Milan mentioned a request from Ludovico that Lorenzo de' Medici "kindly send him one or two Florentine artists who specialize in this kind of work." Apparently Ludovico did not trust Leonardo to complete the task. "Although he has given the commission to Leonardo, it seems that he is not confident that he will succeed," the ambassador explained.

Sensing that he might lose the commission, Leonardo launched a public relations campaign. He enlisted his friend the humanist poet Piattino Piatti to write an epigram for the base of the statue and a poem to celebrate his work on its design. Piatti was not a favorite of the Sforzas, but he had considerable influence with the humanist scholars who formed public opinion around the court. In August 1489, a month after Ludovico solicited suggestions from another sculptor, Piatti sent a letter to his uncle asking him to have "one of your servants deliver as soon as possible the enclosed tetrastich [four-line verse] to Leonardo the Florentine, an excellent sculptor, who requested it some time ago." Piatti told his uncle that he was one of many participants in a public-support campaign: "This task is for me somewhat of an obligation because Leonardo is indeed a good friend of mine. I do not doubt that the same request was made by the same artist to many others, who are probably better qualified than myself to express the same thing." Nevertheless, Piatti persevered in the task. In one poem he wrote of the grandeur of Leonardo's proposed horse: "Art imitating the immortal actions / of the duke, made the horse under the duke a supernatural one." Another of the poems portrayed "Leonardo da Vinci, a most noble sculptor and painter," in humanist terms as an "admirer of the Ancients and their grateful disciple."[7]

Leonardo was successful in hanging on to the commission. "On the 23rd of April 1490, I began this notebook and recommenced the horse," he wrote at the beginning of a new journal.[8]

On his trip to Pavia with Francesco di Giorgio two months later, Leonardo studied one of the few remaining ancient Roman equestrian sculptures. He was struck by how a statue could convey the impression of motion. "The movement is more praiseworthy than anything else," he wrote in his notebook. "The trot almost has the quality of a free horse."[9] He realized that a monument of a horse in a prancing high-stepping walk could be as lively as that of a rearing horse, and it would be far easier to execute. His new design was similar to the monument in Pavia.

Leonardo succeeded in creating a full-size clay model, which was put on display in November 1493 at the celebration for the marriage of Ludovico's niece Bianca Sforza to the future Holy Roman emperor Maximilian I. The mammoth and glorious model occasioned effusions from the court poets. "Neither Greece nor Rome ever saw anything grander," wrote Baldassare Taccone. "See how beautiful this horse is; Leonardo da Vinci alone has created it. Sculptor, fine painter, fine mathematician, so great an intellect rarely does Heaven bestow."[10] Many poets celebrating the colossal scale and beauty of the clay model played on Leonardo's name to herald the Vincian victory over all previous designs, including those of the ancients. They also praised its vitality. Paolo Giovio described it as "vehemently aroused and snorting." The model would, at least for a while, bring Leonardo renown not just as a painter but also as a sculptor and, he hoped, an engineer.[11]

CASTING

Even before he finished the clay model, Leonardo was working on the even greater challenge of casting such a huge monument. With precision and ingenuity, he spent more than two years sketching out plans. "Here a record shall be kept of everything related to the bronze horse, presently under execution," he wrote at the beginning of a new notebook in May 1491.[12]

The traditional way to cast a large monument was in pieces. A separate mold would be made for the head, legs, and torso; the pieces would then be welded together and polished. The result was never perfect, but it was practical. Because Leonardo's monument was so much larger than any ever done, this piecemeal method would seem to be all the more necessary.

Leonardo, however, was dedicated to achieving feats of engineering that would match in beauty and audacity the obsessive perfection he had pursued as an artist. So he decided to cast his huge horse all in one mold. On a captivating page in his notebook, he sketched out many of the mechanisms that would be necessary (fig. 47). His drawings are exuberant and yet detailed, as though a futurist were designing a launch pad for a rocket ship.[13]

Using the clay model he built, Leonardo planned to cast a mold and then coat its inside with a mix of clay and wax. "Dry it in layers," he specified. He would fit the mold around a core made of clay and rubble; the molten bronze would be poured into holes of the mold and displace the wax mixture, then the rubble core would be removed from what would become the hollow inside of the statue. A "little door with hinges" atop the horse, which would eventually be covered by the rider, would serve as a panel through which he could extract the rubble of the core after the bronze had cooled.[14]

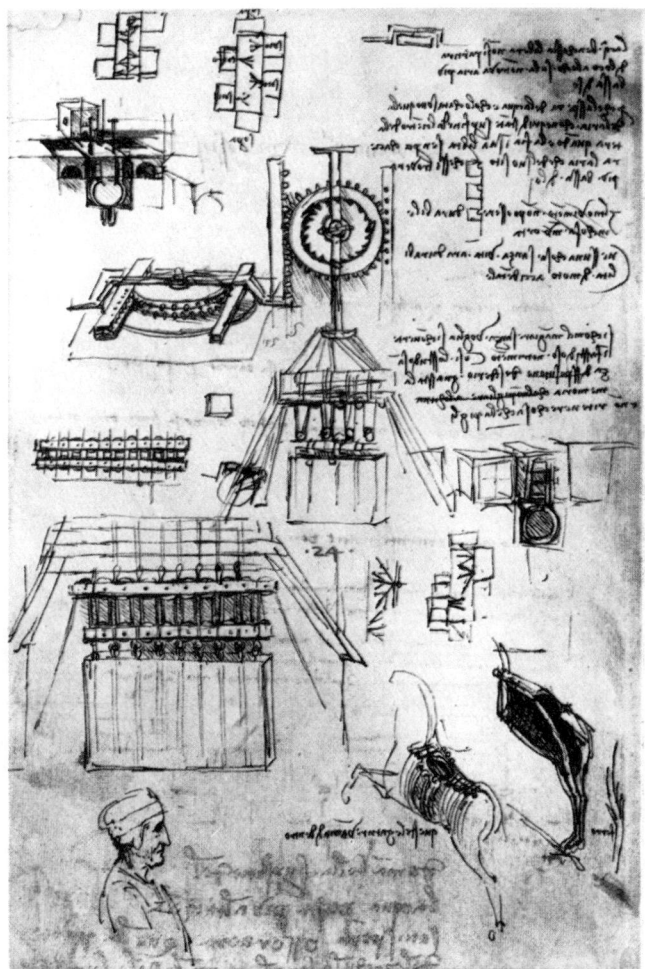

Fig. 47. Plans for casting the monument.

Leonardo then tailored a "casting hood," a lattice iron frame that would be strapped around the outside of the mold like a corset to hold it together and keep it in shape. The hood was not just an ingenious engineering scheme but also a red-chalk piece of art of eerie beauty, with the horse's head gently twisting and latticework elegantly shaded (fig. 48). Crossbars and struts would bolt together the casting hood to the inner core, providing firm support for the entire system. "These are the pieces of the form of the head and neck of the horse with their armatures and irons," he wrote.

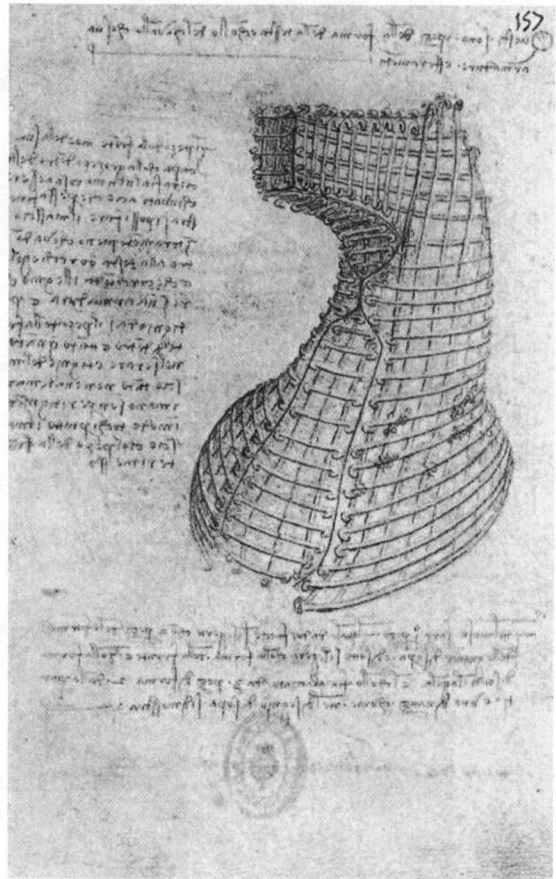

Fig. 48. Casting hood for the monument.

The plan was to pour the molten bronze into the mold through many holes so that it would be distributed evenly. Four furnaces would be arrayed around a pit so that the process could happen quickly and the metal could cool more uniformly. "For the casting, let every man keep his furnace closed with a red-hot iron bar and let the furnaces be opened simultaneously; and let fine iron rods be used to stop any of the holes from becoming blocked by a piece of metal; and let there be four rods kept in reserve at red heat to replace one of the others if they should be broken."

Leonardo experimented with different materials and mixes to get the right components for the casting process. "First of all, test every ingredient and choose the best." For example, he tried out ingredients for the clay-and-rubble mix that formed the inner core. "Try it first," he wrote next to a recipe that included "a mixture of coarse river sand, ash, crushed brick, egg white, and vinegar together with your clay." To keep the mold from being damaged by the damp when it was underground, he concocted many potential coatings. "Let the inside of all the molds be wetted with linseed oil or turpentine, and then take a handful of powdered borax and Greek pitch with distilled alcohol."[15]

At first he considered digging a deep hole and placing the mold in it upside down, with the feet sticking up. The hot metal would be poured into the horse's belly with the steam escaping through holes in the feet. The drawing (fig. 47) shows the hoists, levers, and machinery he planned to use. But by the end of 1493, he had abandoned this approach after realizing that the pit would be so deep that it would hit the water table. Instead, he decided that the mold should be laid sideways in the pit. "I have decided to cast the horse without the tail and on its side," he wrote in December 1493.

Shortly thereafter the project ended. Defense expenditures took precedence over artistic ones. In 1494 the troops of the French king Charles VIII swept through Italy, and the bronze intended for the horse was sent by Ludovico to his father-in-law Ercole d'Este in the town of Ferrara to make three small cannons. In a draft of a letter to Ludovico a few years later, Leonardo seemed dejected but resigned. "Of the horse I will say nothing," he wrote, "for I know the times."[16]

The cannons would end up doing little good, for the French would easily conquer Milan in 1499. And when they did, the French archers used Leonardo's huge clay model for target practice, destroying it. Ercole d'Este, who made the cannons, may have felt bad, because two years later he instructed his agent in Milan to ask the French authorities for the unused mold: "Seeing that there exists in Milan the mold of a horse that Lord Ludovico intended to have cast, made by a certain Messer Leonardo, an excellent master of such things, we believe that if we were granted the use of the mold, it would be a good and desirable thing serving to make our own horse."[17] But his request was never met. Through no fault of his own, Leonardo's horse joined other of his potential masterpieces in the realms of unfulfilled dreams.

CHAPTER 10

Scientist

TEACHING HIMSELF

Leonardo da Vinci liked to boast that, because he was not formally educated, he had to learn from his own experiences instead. It was around 1490 when he wrote his screed about being "a man without letters" and a "disciple of experience," with its swipe against those who would cite ancient wisdom rather than make observations on their own. "Though I have no power to quote from authors as they have," he proclaimed almost proudly, "I shall rely on a far more worthy thing—on experience."[1] Throughout his life, he would repeat this claim to prefer experience over received scholarship. "He who has access to the fountain does not go to the water-jar," he wrote.[2] This made him different from the archetypal Renaissance Man, who embraced the rebirth of wisdom that came from rediscovered works of classical antiquity.

The education that Leonardo was soaking up in Milan, however, began to soften his disdain for handed-down wisdom. We can see a turning point in the early 1490s, when he undertook to teach himself Latin, the language not only of the ancients but also of serious scholars of his era. He copied page after page of Latin words and conjugations from textbooks of his time, including one that was used by Ludovico Sforza's young son. It appears not to have been an enjoyable exercise; in the middle of one notebook page where he copied 130 words, he drew his nutcracker man scowling and grimacing more than usual (fig. 49). Nor did he ever master Latin. For the most part his notebooks are filled with notes and transcriptions from works available in Italian.

In that regard, Leonardo was born at a fortunate moment. In 1452 Johannes Gutenberg began selling Bibles from his new printing press, just when the development of rag processing was making paper more readily available. By the time Leonardo became an apprentice in Florence, Gutenberg's technology had crossed the Alps into Italy. Alberti marveled in 1466 about "the German inventor who has made it pos-

Fig. 49. Trying to learn Latin, with a grimace.

sible, by certain pressings down of characters, to have more than two hundred volumes written out in a hundred days from the original, with the labor of no more than three men." A goldsmith from Gutenberg's hometown of Mainz named Johannes de Spira (or Speyer) moved to Venice and started Italy's first major commercial publishing house in 1469; it printed many of the classics, starting with Cicero's letters and Pliny's encyclopedic *Natural History*, which Leonardo bought. By 1471 there were printing shops also in Milan, Florence, Naples, Bologna, Ferrara, Padua, and Genoa. Venice became the center of Europe's publishing industry, and by the time Leonardo visited in 1500, there were close to a hundred printing houses there, and two million volumes had come off their presses.[3] Leonardo thus was able to become the first major European thinker to acquire a serious knowledge of science without being formally schooled in Latin or Greek.

His notebooks are filled with lists of books he acquired and passages he copied. In the late 1480s he itemized five books he owned: the Pliny, a Latin grammar book, a text on minerals and precious stones, an arithmetic text, and a humorous epic poem, Luigi Pulci's *Morgante*, about the adventures of a knight and the giant he converted to Christianity, which was often performed at the Medici court. By 1492 Leonardo had close to forty volumes. A testament to his universal interests, they included books on military machinery, agriculture, music, surgery, health, Aristotelian science, Arabian physics, palmistry, and the lives of famous philosophers, as well as the poetry of Ovid and Petrarch, the fables of Aesop, some collections of bawdy doggerels and burlesques, and a fourteenth-century operetta from which he drew part of his bestiary. By 1504 he would be able to list seventy more books, including forty works of science, close to fifty of poetry and literature, ten on art and architecture, eight on religion, and three on math.[4]

He also recorded at various times the books that he hoped to borrow or find. "Maestro Stefano Caponi, a physician, lives at the Piscina, and has Euclid," he noted. "The heirs of Maestro Giovanni Ghiringallo have the works of Pelacano." "Vespucci will give me a book of Geometry." And on a to-do list: "An algebra, which the Marliani have, written by their father . . . A book, treating of Milan and its churches,

which is to be had at the last stationers on the way to Corduso." Once
he discovered the University of Pavia, near Milan, he used it as a resource: "Try to get Vitolone, which is in the library at Pavia and deals
with mathematics." On the same to-do list: "A grandson of Gian Angelo's, the painter, has a book on water which was his father's. . . . Get
the Friar di Brera to show you *de Ponderibus*." His appetite for soaking
up information from books was voracious and wide-ranging.

In addition, he liked to pick people's brains. He was constantly
peppering acquaintances with the type of questions we should all
learn to pose more often. "Ask Benedetto Portinari how they walk
on ice in Flanders," reads one memorable and vivid entry on a to-do
list. Over the years there were scores of others: "Ask Maestro Antonio how mortars are positioned on bastions by day or night. . . . Find
a master of hydraulics and get him to tell you how to repair a lock,
canal and mill in the Lombard manner. . . . Ask Maestro Giovannino
how the tower of Ferrara is walled without loopholes."[5]

Thus Leonardo became a disciple of both experience and received
wisdom. More important, he came to see that the progress of science
came from a dialogue between the two. That in turn helped him realize that knowledge also came from a related dialogue: that between
experiment and theory.

CONNECTING EXPERIMENT TO THEORY

Leonardo's devotion to firsthand experience went deeper than just
being prickly about his lack of received wisdom. It also caused him, at
least early on, to minimize the role of theory. A natural observer and
experimenter, he was neither wired nor trained to wrestle with abstract
concepts. He preferred to induce from experiments rather than deduce
from theoretical principles. "My intention is to consult experience first,
and then with reasoning show why such experience is bound to operate
in such a way," he wrote. In other words, he would try to look at facts
and from them figure out the patterns and natural forces that caused
those things to happen. "Although nature begins with the cause and
ends with the experience, we must follow the opposite course, namely
begin with the experience, and by means of it investigate the cause."[6]

As with so many things, this empirical approach put him ahead of his time. Scholastic theologians of the Middle Ages had fused Aristotle's science with Christianity to create an authorized creed that left little room for skeptical inquiry or experimentation. Even the humanists of the early Renaissance preferred to repeat the wisdom of classical texts rather than test it.

Leonardo broke with this tradition by basing his science primarily on observations, then discerning patterns, and then testing their validity through more observations and experiments. Dozens of times in his notebook he wrote some variation of the phrase "this can be proved by experiment" and then proceeded to describe a real-world demonstration of his thinking. Foreshadowing what would become the scientific method, he even prescribed how experiments must be repeated and varied to assure their validity: "Before you make a general rule of this case, test it two or three times and observe whether the tests produce the same effects."[7]

He was aided by his ingenuity, which enabled him to devise all sorts of contraptions and clever methods for exploring a phenomenon. For example, when he was studying the human heart around 1510, he came up with the hypothesis that blood swirled into eddies when it was pumped from the heart to the aorta, and that was what caused the valves to close properly; he then devised a glass device that he could use to confirm his theory with an experiment (see chapter 27). Visualization and drawing became an important component of this process. Not comfortable wrestling with theory, he preferred dealing with knowledge that he could observe and draw.

But Leonardo did not remain merely a disciple of experiments. His notebooks show that he evolved. When he began absorbing knowledge from books in the 1490s, it helped him realize the importance of being guided not only by experiential evidence but also by theoretical frameworks. More important, he came to understand that the two approaches were complementary, working hand in hand. "We can see in Leonardo a dramatic attempt to appraise properly the mutual relation of theory to experiment," wrote the twentieth-century physicist Leopold Infeld.[8]

His proposals for the Milan Cathedral tiburio show this evolution.

To understand how to treat an aging cathedral with structural flaws, he wrote, architects need to understand "the nature of weight and the propensities of force." In other words, they need to understand physics theories. But they also need to test theoretical principles against what actually works in practice. "I shall endeavor," he promised the cathedral administrators, "to satisfy you partly with theory and partly with practice, sometimes showing effects from causes, sometimes affirming principles with experiments." He also pledged, despite his early aversion to received wisdom, to "make use, as is convenient, of the authority of the ancient architects." In other words, he was advocating our modern method of combining theory, experiment, and handed-down knowledge—and constantly testing them against each other.[9]

His study of perspective likewise showed him the importance of joining experience with theories. He observed the way objects appear smaller as they get more distant. But he also used geometry to develop rules for the relationship between size and distance. When it came time to describe the laws of perspective in his notebooks, he wrote that he would do so "sometimes by deduction of the effects from the causes, and sometimes arguing the causes from the effects."[10]

He even came to be dismissive of experimenters who relied on practice without any knowledge of the underlying theories. "Those who are in love with practice without theoretical knowledge are like the sailor who goes onto a ship without rudder or compass and who never can be certain whither he is going," he wrote in 1510. "Practice must always be founded on sound theory."[11]

As a result, Leonardo became one of the major Western thinkers, more than a century before Galileo, to pursue in a persistent hands-on fashion the dialogue between experiment and theory that would lead to the modern Scientific Revolution. Aristotle had laid the foundations, in ancient Greece, for the method of partnering inductions and deductions: using observations to formulate general principles, then using these principles to predict outcomes. While Europe was mired in its dark years of medieval superstition, the work of combining theory and experiment was advanced primarily in the Islamic world. Muslim scientists often also worked as scientific instrument makers, which made them experts at measurements and applying theories. The Arab physicist Ibn al-Haytham, known as Alhazen, wrote a seminal text on optics in 1021 that combined observations and experiments to develop a theory of how human vision works, then devised further experiments to test the theory. His ideas and methods became a foundation for the work of Alberti and Leonardo four centuries later. Meanwhile, Aristotle's science was being revived in Europe during the thirteenth century by scholars such as Robert Grosseteste and Roger Bacon. The empirical method used by Bacon emphasized a cycle: observations should lead to a hypothesis, which should then be tested by precise experiments, which would then be used to refine the original hypothesis. Bacon also recorded and reported his experiments in precise detail so that others could independently replicate and verify them.

Leonardo had the eye and temperament and curiosity to become an exemplar of this scientific method. "Galileo, born 112 years after Leonardo, is usually credited with being the first to develop this kind of rigorous empirical approach and is often hailed as the father of modern science," the historian Fritjof Capra wrote. "There can be no doubt that this honor would have been bestowed on Leonardo da Vinci had he published his scientific writings during his lifetime, or had his Notebooks been widely studied soon after his death."[12]

That goes a step too far, I think. Leonardo did not invent the scientific method, nor did Aristotle or Alhazen or Galileo or any Bacon. But his uncanny abilities to engage in the dialogue between experience and theory made him a prime example of how acute observations, fanatic curiosity, experimental testing, a willingness to question dogma, and the ability to discern patterns across disciplines can lead to great leaps in human understanding.

PATTERNS AND ANALOGIES

In lieu of possessing abstract mathematical tools to extract theoretical laws from nature, the way Copernicus and Galileo and Newton later did, Leonardo relied on a more rudimentary method: he was able to see patterns in nature, and he theorized by making analogies. With his keen observational skills across multiple disciplines, he discerned recurring themes. As the philosopher Michel Foucault noted, the "protoscience" of Leonardo's era was based on similarities and analogies.[13]

Because of his intuitive feel for the unity of nature, his mind and eye and pen darted across disciplines, sensing connections. "This constant search for basic, rhyming, organic form meant that when he looked at a heart blossoming into its network of veins he saw, and sketched alongside it, a seed germinating into shoots," Adam Gopnik wrote. "Studying the curls on a beautiful woman's head he thought in terms of the swirling motion of a turbulent flow of water."[14] His drawing of a fetus in a womb hints at the similarity to a seed in a shell.

When he was inventing musical instruments, he made an analogy between how the larynx works and how a glissando recorder could perform similarly. When he was competing to design the tower for Milan's cathedral, he made a connection between architects and doctors that reflected what would become the most fundamental analogy in his art and science: that between our physical world and our human anatomy. When he dissected a limb and drew its muscles and sinews, it led him to also sketch ropes and levers.

We saw an example of this pattern-based analysis on the "theme sheet," where he made the analogy between a branching tree and the arteries in a human, one that he applied also to rivers and their tributaries. "All the branches of a tree at every stage of its height when put together are equal in thickness to the trunk below them," he wrote elsewhere. "All the branches of a river at every stage of its course, if they are of equal rapidity, are equal to the body of the main stream."[15] This conclusion is still known as "da Vinci's rule," and it has proven true in situations where the branches are not very large: the sum of the cross-sectional area of all branches above a branching point is equal to the cross-sectional area of the trunk or the branch immediately below the branching point.[16]

Another analogy he made was comparing the way that light, sound, magnetism, and the percussion reverberations caused by a hammer blow all disseminate in a radiating pattern, often in waves. In one of his notebooks he made a column of small drawings showing how each force field spreads. He even illustrated what happened when each type of wave hits a small hole in the wall; prefiguring the studies done by Dutch physicist Christiaan Huygens almost two centuries later, he showed the diffraction that occurs as the waves go through the aperture.[17] Wave mechanics were for him merely a passing curiosity, but even in this his brilliance is breathtaking.

The connections that Leonardo made across disciplines served as guides for his inquiries. The analogy between water eddies and air turbulence, for example, provided a framework for studying the flight of birds. "To arrive at knowledge of the motions of birds in the air," he wrote, "it is first necessary to acquire knowledge of the winds, which we will prove by the motions of water."[18] But the patterns he discerned were more than just useful study guides. He regarded them as revelations of essential truths, manifestations of the beautiful unity of nature.

CURIOSITY AND OBSERVATION

In addition to his instinct for discerning patterns across disciplines, Leonardo honed two other traits that aided his scientific pursuits: an omnivorous curiosity, which bordered on the fanatical, and an acute power of observation, which was eerily intense. Like much with Leonardo, these were interconnected. Any person who puts "Describe the tongue of the woodpecker" on his to-do list is overendowed with the combination of curiosity and acuity.

His curiosity, like that of Einstein, often was about phenomena that most people over the age of ten no longer puzzle about: Why is the sky blue? How are clouds formed? Why can our eyes see only in a straight line? What is yawning? Einstein said he marveled about questions others found mundane because he was slow in learning to talk as a child. For Leonardo, this talent may have been connected to growing up with a love of nature while not being overly schooled in received wisdom.

Other topics of his curiosity that he listed in his notebooks are more ambitious and require an instinct for observational investigation. "Which nerve causes the eye to move so that the motion of one eye moves the other?" "Describe the beginning of a human when it is in the womb."[19] And along with the woodpecker, he lists "the jaw of the crocodile" and "the placenta of the calf" as things he wants to describe. These inquiries entail a lot of work.[20]

His curiosity was aided by the sharpness of his eye, which focused on things that the rest of us glance over. One night he saw lightning flash behind some buildings, and for that instant they looked smaller, so he launched a series of experiments and controlled observations to verify that objects look smaller when surrounded by light and look larger in the mist or dark.[21] When he looked at things with one eye closed, he noticed that they appeared less round than when seen with both eyes, so he went on to explore the reasons why.[22]

Kenneth Clark referred to Leonardo's "inhumanly sharp eye." It's a nice phrase, but misleading. Leonardo was human. The acuteness of his observational skill was not some superpower he possessed. Instead, it was a product of his own effort. That's important, because it means that we can, if we wish, not just marvel at him but try to learn from him by pushing ourselves to look at things more curiously and intensely.

In his notebook, he described his method—almost like a trick—for closely observing a scene or object: look carefully and separately at each detail. He compared it to looking at the page of a book, which is meaningless when taken in as a whole and instead needs to be looked at word by word. Deep observation must be done in steps: "If you wish to have a sound knowledge of the forms of objects, begin with the details of them, and do not go on to the second step until you have the first well fixed in memory."[23]

Another gambit he recommended for "giving your eye good practice" at observations was to play this game with friends: one person draws a line on a wall, and the others stand a distance away and try to cut a blade of straw to the exact length of the line. "He who has come nearest with his measure to the length of the pattern is the winner."[24]

Leonardo's eye was especially sharp when it came to observing motion. "The dragonfly flies with four wings, and when those in front are raised those behind are lowered," he found. Imagine the effort it took to watch a dragonfly carefully enough to notice this. In his notebook he recorded that the best place to observe dragonflies was by the moat surrounding the Sforza Castle.[25] Let's pause to marvel at Leonardo walking out in the evening, no doubt dandily dressed, standing at the edge of a moat, intensely watching the motions of each of the four wings of a dragonfly.

His keenness at observing motion helped him overcome the difficulty of capturing it in a painting. There is a paradox, which goes back to Zeno in the fifth century BC, involving the apparent contradiction of an object being in motion yet also being at a precise place at a given instant. Leonardo wrestled with the concept of depicting an arrested instant that contains both the past and the future of that moment.

He compared an arrested instant of motion to the concept of a single geometrical point. The point has no length or width. Yet if it moves, it creates a line. "The point has no dimensions; the line is the transit of a point." Using his method of theorizing by analogy, he wrote, "The instant does not have time; and time is made from the movement of the instant."[26]

Guided by this analogy, Leonardo in his art sought to freeze-frame an event while also showing it in motion. "In rivers, the water that you touch is the last of what has passed, and the first of that which comes," he observed. "So with time present." He came back to this theme repeatedly in his notebooks. "Observe the light," he instructed. "Blink your eye and look at it again. That which you see was not there at first, and that which was there is no more."[27]

Leonardo's skill at observing motion was translated by the flicks of his brush into his art. In addition, while working at the Sforza court, he began channeling his fascination with motion into scientific and engineering studies, most notably his investigations into the flight of birds and machines for the flight of man.

CHAPTER II

Birds and Flight

THEATRICAL FLIGHTS OF FANCY

"Study the anatomy of the wings of a bird together with the breast muscles that move those wings," Leonardo wrote in his notebook. "Do the same for man to show the possibility that man could sustain himself in the air by the flapping of wings."[1]

For more than two decades, beginning around 1490, Leonardo investigated, with an unusual degree of diligence, the flight of birds and the possibility of designing machines that would enable humans to fly. He produced more than five hundred drawings and thirty-five thousand words scattered over a dozen notebooks on these topics. The endeavor wove together his curiosity about nature, his observational skills, and his engineering instincts. It was also an example of his method of using analogy to discover nature's patterns. But in this case the analogy process extended even further: it took him closer than most of his other investigations into the realm of pure theory, including fluid dynamics and the laws of motion.

Leonardo's interest in flying machines began with his work on theatrical pageants. From his early days in Verrocchio's workshop until his final days in France, he threw himself into such spectacles with enthusiasm. His mechanical birds were first used—and last used—as court amusements.[2]

It was at such pageants that he first saw ingenious devices for allowing actors to rise, descend, and float as if they were flying. Brunelleschi, his predecessor as an artist-engineer in Florence, was the "master of effects" at a dazzling production of an *Annunciation* in the 1430s, which was revived using the same machinery in 1471, when Leonardo was nineteen and working in Florence. Suspended from the rafters was a ring holding twelve boys dressed as angels. Contraptions made of large pulleys and hand winches kept everything moving and soaring. Mechanical devices allowed the gilt-winged angels, holding harps and flaming swords, to fly down from heaven and rescue the saved souls, while from below the stage the realm of hell shot forth devils. Gabriel then arrived for the Annunciation. "As the angel ascended amongst the voices of jubilation," one spectator wrote, "he moved his hands up and down, and flapped his wings as if he were truly flying."

Another play performed at the time, *The Ascension*, also featured flying characters. "The sky opened and the Heavenly Father appeared, miraculously suspended in air," according to a report, "and the actor playing Jesus seems to have truly ascended on his own, and without tottering reached a great height." Christ's ascension was accompanied by a group of winged angels, who had been suspended in the make-believe clouds above the stage.[3]

Leonardo's first studies of flight were for such theatrical extravaganzas. One set of drawings that he made just before he left Florence for Milan in 1482 shows bat-like wings, with cranks that would create motion but not actual flight, connected to what appear to be theatrical mechanisms.[4] Another shows a featherless wing connected to gears, pulleys, cranks, and cables: the configuration of the crank and the size of the gears indicate that the whole system is designed for the theater and not for an actual flying machine. But even for his theater designs, he was carefully observing nature. On the back of this sheet he drew a jagged downward line with the caption "This is the manner in which birds descend."[5]

There is one other clue that these drawings from his Florence days were meant for the theater rather than actual flight: in all of the ingenious military devices he says he can build in his job application letter to Ludovico Sforza, there is no boast about being able to make machines for human flight. It was only after he got to Milan that his attention turned from theatrical fantasy to real-world engineering.

BIRD-WATCHING

Here's a test. All of us have looked at birds in flight, but have you ever stopped to look closely enough to see whether a bird moves its wing upward at the same speed as it flaps it down? Leonardo did, and he was able to observe that the answer differs based on species. "There are some birds that move their wings more swiftly when they lower them than when they raise them, and this is the case with doves and such birds," he recorded in a notebook. "There are others which lower their wings more slowly than they raise them, and this is seen with crows and similar birds." And some, such as magpies, raise and lower at the same speed.[6]

Leonardo had a strategy he used to refine his observational skills. He would write down marching orders to himself, determining how he would sequence his observations in a methodical step-by-step way. "First define the motion of the wind and then describe how the birds steer through it with only the simple balancing of the wings and tail," he wrote in one example. "Do this after the description of their anatomy."[7]

He recorded in his notebooks scores of such observations, most of which we find amazing mainly because we never make the effort, in our daily lives, to observe ordinary phenomena so closely. On a trip to the vineyard he had been given by Ludovico in Fiesole, a village just north of Florence, he watched a chukar partridge take flight. "When a bird with a wide wingspan and a short tail wants to take off," he reported, "it will lift its wings with force and turn them to receive the wind beneath them."[8] From observations like that he was able to make a generalization about the relationship between a bird's tail and its wings: "Birds with short tails have very wide wings, which by their width take the place of the tail; and they make considerable use of the helms set on the shoulders when they wish to turn." And later: "When birds are descending near the ground and the head is below the tail, they lower the tail, which is spread wide open, and take short strokes with the wings; consequently, the head is raised above the tail, and the speed is checked so that the bird can alight on the ground without a shock."[9] Ever notice all that?

After twenty years of observing, he decided to compile his notes into a treatise. Much of the work was gathered into an eighteen-folio notebook, now known as the Codex on the Flight of Birds.[10] It begins by exploring the concepts of gravity and density, and it ends by envisioning the launch of a flying machine he had designed and comparing its components with the body parts of a bird. But like much of Leonardo's work, the treatise remained unfinished. He was more interested in nailing concepts than he was in polishing them for publication.

When he was compiling his bird treatise, Leonardo began a section of another notebook with a directive to put them into a broader con-text. "To explain the science of the flight of birds, it is necessary to explain the science of the winds, which we shall prove by the motion of the waters," he wrote. "The understanding of this science of water will serve as a ladder to arrive at the knowledge of things flying in the air."[11] He not only got the basic principles of fluid dynamics correct, but he was able to turn his insights into rudimentary theories that foreshadowed those of Newton, Galileo, and Bernoulli.

No scientist before Leonardo had methodically shown how birds stay aloft. Most had simply embellished on Aristotle, who mistakenly thought that birds were supported by air the way ships were by water.[12] Leonardo realized that keeping aloft in air requires fundamentally different dynamics than doing so in water, because birds are heavier than air and are thus subject to being pulled down by gravity. The first two folios of his Codex on the Flight of Birds deal with the laws of gravity, which he calls the "attraction of one object to another." The force of gravity, he wrote, acts in the direction of "an imaginary line between the centers of each object."[13] He then described how to calculate the center of gravity of a bird, a pyramid, and other complex shapes.

One important observation he made ended up informing his studies of flight and of the flow of water. "Water cannot be compressed like air," he wrote.[14] In other words, a wing beating down on air will compact the air into a smaller space, and as a result the air pressure underneath the wing will be higher than the pressure of the rarefied air above it. "If the air could not be compressed, the birds would not be able to support themselves upon the air that is struck by their wings."[15] The downward flap of the wing pushes the bird higher and thrusts it forward.

He also realized that the pressure the bird puts on the air is met by an equal and opposite pressure that the air puts on the bird. "See how the wings, striking against the air, sustain the heavy eagle in the thin air on high," he noted, then added, "As much force is exerted by the object against the air as by the air against the object."[16] Two hundred years later, Newton would state a refined version of this as his third law of motion: "To every action there is always opposed an equal reaction."

Leonardo accompanied this concept with a precursor to Galileo's principle of relativity: "The effect of moving air on a stationary object is as great as it is when the object is moving and the air is stationary."[17] In other words, the forces that would act upon a bird flying through air are the same as the forces acting on a bird that is stationary but has air rushing past it (such as a bird in a wind tunnel or one hovering on a windy day over a spot on the ground). He drew an analogy from his studies of water flow, which he had recorded earlier in the same notebook: "The action of a pole drawn through still water resembles that of running water against a stationary pole."[18]

Even more presciently, he had an intimation of what became known, more than two hundred years later, as Bernoulli's principle: when air (or any fluid) flows faster, it exerts less pressure. Leonardo drew a cross section of a bird's wing, which shows that the top is curved more than the underside. (This is also true of airplane wings, which make use of this principle.) The air flowing over the curved top of the wing has farther to travel than the air flowing under the bottom. Therefore, the air on top has to travel faster. The difference in speed means that the air on the top of the wing exerts less pressure than the air on the bottom, thus helping the bird (or airplane) to stay aloft. "The air above birds is thinner than the usual thinness of the other air," he wrote.[19] Leonardo thus realized, before other scientists, that a bird stays aloft not merely because the wings beat downward against the air but also because the wings propel the bird forward and the air lessens in pressure as it rushes over the wing's curved top surface.

FLYING MACHINES

Both his observations on anatomy and his analysis of the physics convinced Leonardo that it was possible to build a winged mechanism that would allow humans to fly. "A bird is an instrument working according to mathematical law, and it is in the capacity of man to reproduce such an instrument," he wrote. "A man with wings large enough and duly attached might learn to overcome the resistance of the air and raise himself upon it."[20]

Combining engineering with physics and anatomy, Leonardo began in the late 1480s to devise contraptions to accomplish this. His first design (fig. 50) looks like a big bowl with four oar-like blades that were to alternate in pairs moving up and down, like the four-winged dragonfly he had studied earlier. To overcome the relative weakness of human breast muscles, this cross between a flying saucer and a health club torture chamber has the operator use his legs to push pedals, his arms to crank a gear-and-pulley mechanism, his head to pump a piston, and his shoulders to pull cables. It is unclear how he would manage to steer the machine.[21]

Seven pages later in the same notebook, Leonardo produced an elegant drawing (fig. 51) of an experiment that used a bat-like wing, its thin bones covered with a membrane of skin rather than feathers, that was similar to those he had drawn for theatrical productions back in Florence. The wing is attached to a thick wooden plank, which, he specified, should weigh 150 pounds, like an average man, and to a lever mechanism that would pump the wing. Leonardo even drew an amusing man in motion, jumping up and down on top of the end of the long lever. A little sketch below shows a clever element: when the

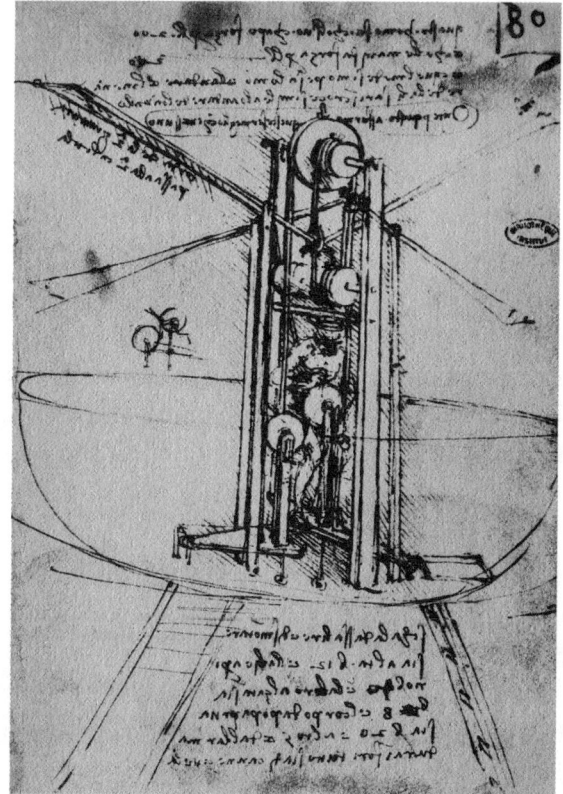

Fig. 50. A human-powered flying machine.

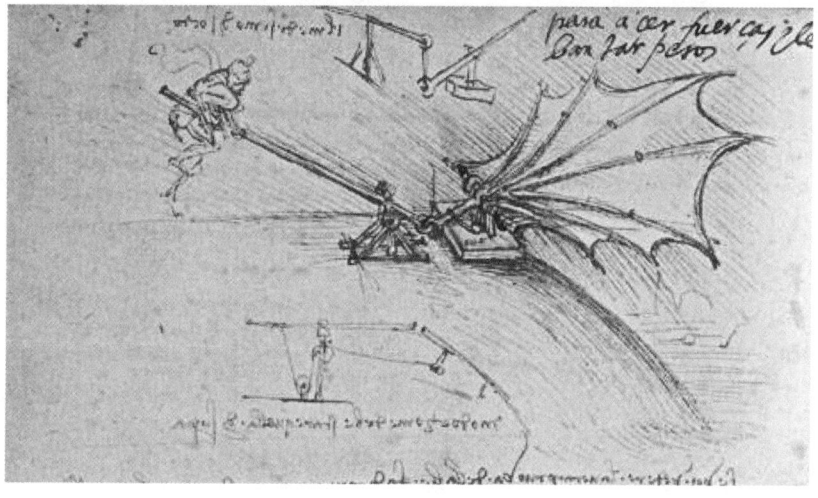

Fig. 51. A wing with hinges.

wing is swinging upward a hinge allows it to point its tips downward and encounter less resistance, then slowly be moved by a spring and pulley back into a rigid position.[22] Later ideas included devising skin flaps in the wings that would be closed on the downswing but fly open on the upswing to minimize air resistance.

At times, Leonardo abandoned the hope of achieving self-propelled flight and designed gliders instead. One of these was shown to be basically workable in a reconstruction done five hundred years later by the ITN television network in Britain.[23] However, for most of his career he remained committed to achieving human-powered flight in birdlike devices with flapping wings. He drew more than a dozen variations, using pedals and levers with the pilot prone or standing, and began referring to his machine as the *uccello*, or bird.

In his spacious accommodations at the Corte Vecchia, Leonardo had what he called "la mia fabrica" (my factory). In addition to being the room where he had worked on the ill-fated horse monument for the Sforzas, it provided space for experimenting with flying machines. At one point he wrote himself a note about how to conduct a flight experiment on the roof without being seen by the workers constructing a tower—the tiburio that he had failed in the competition to design—on the cathedral next door. "Make a large and tall model, and you will have a room on the upper roof," he wrote. "If you stand on the roof at the side of the tower, the men at work upon the tiburio will not see you."[24]

At other times, he envisioned testing a machine over water while wearing a life-preserver. "You will experiment with this machine over a lake and you will wear as a belt a long wineskin, so that if you fall in, you will not drown."[25] And finally, when all of his experiments were nearing an end, he mingled his plans with fantasies. "The large bird will take its first flight from the back of the great Swan," he wrote on the last folio of his Codex on the Flight of Birds, referring to Swan Mountain (Monte Ceceri) near Fiesole, "filling the universe with amazement, filling all writings with its fame, and bringing eternal glory to the nest where it was born."[26]

With beautiful little drawings, Leonardo portrayed the elegance of birds as they twisted, turned, shifted their center of gravity, and maneuvered the winds. He also pioneered the use of vector-like lines and swirls to show invisible currents. But for all the beauty of his art and all the ingenuity of his designs, he was never able to create a human-powered flying machine that could take off on its own. To be fair, it took almost five hundred years before any human did so.

Late in his life, Leonardo sketched a cylinder with two feeble wings, clearly meant as a toy. Look closely, and you can see that it's attached to a wire line. In what may be his last drawing of a mechanical bird, he reverted, in a poignant and slightly sad fashion, to the way he began drawing them thirty years earlier: as dazzling but ephemeral little contraptions for the momentary amusement of audiences at court theatricals and public pageants.[27]

CHAPTER 12

The Mechanical Arts

MACHINES

Leonardo's interest in machinery was linked to his fascination with motion. He saw both machines and humans as apparatuses designed to move, with analogous components such as cords and sinews. As he did with his anatomy drawings of dissected bodies, he drew machines disassembled—using exploded and layered views—to show how motion is transferred from gears and levers to wheels and pulleys, and his cross-disciplinary interests allowed him to connect concepts from anatomy to engineering.

Other Renaissance technologists drew machines, but they did so by presenting them in completed form, without discussing the role and efficiency of each component. Leonardo, on the other hand, was interested in a part-by-part analysis of the transfer of motion. Rendering each of the moving parts—ratchets, springs, gears, levers, axles, and so on—was a method to help him understand their functions and engineering principles. He used drawing as a tool for thinking. He experimented on paper and evaluated concepts by visualizing them.

Take, for example, his drawing, beautifully shaded and in perfect perspective, of a hoist in which a lever can be rocked to ratchet up toothed wheels and lift a heavy load (fig. 52). It shows how an up-and-down cranking motion can be converted into a continuous rotary

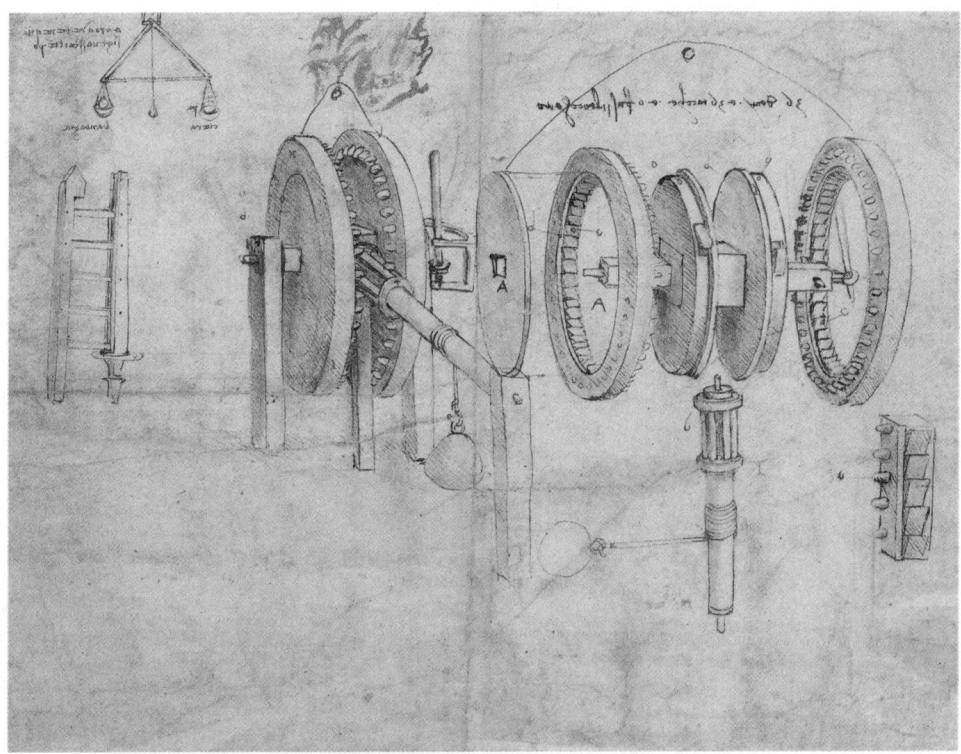

Fig. 52. A hoist with view of components.

motion. The assembled mechanism is on the left side of the page, and to the right is an exploded view of each of the components.[1]

Many of his most beautiful and meticulous drawings explore how to make sure that motion stays at a constant pace, without slowing down, when a coiled spring slowly unwinds. In the beginning, a tightly wound spring transmits a lot of power and causes a mechanism to move quickly, but after a while it has less power and the mechanism slows down. This can be a serious problem for many devices, especially clocks. A major enterprise of the late Renaissance was finding a way to equalize the power of an unwinding spring. Leonardo pioneered the depiction of gears that solve this challenge by using the spiral forms that fascinated him throughout his life. One particularly elegant drawing (fig. 53) shows a spiral gear equalizing the speed of an unwinding barrel spring and transmitting the

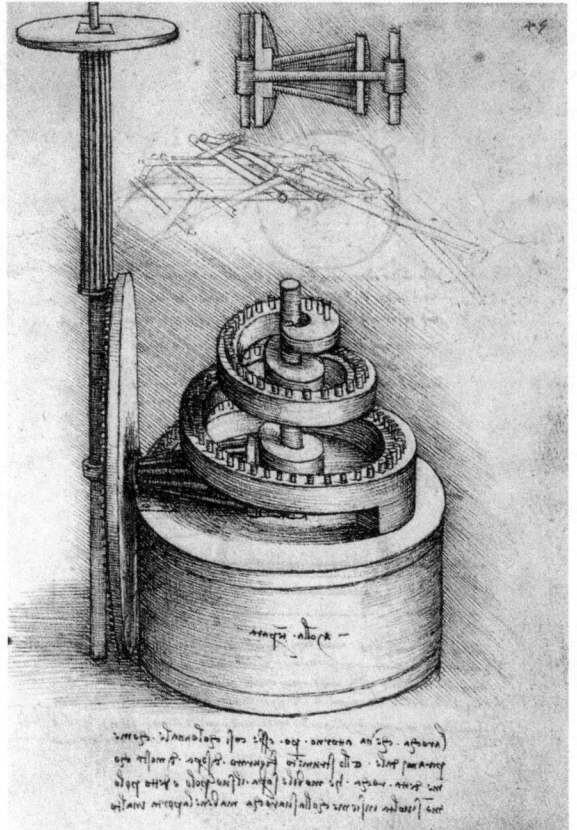

Fig. 53. A spiral gear for equalizing spring power.

constant power to a wheel that pushes a shaft steadily upward.[2] The drawing is one of his most gorgeous works. He used his left-handed hatches to show form and shading, with curved hatchings for the barrel. His mechanical ingenuity is combined with his artistic passion for spirals and curls.

The key purpose of machinery, then as now, is to harness energy and turn it into movements that accomplish useful tasks. For example, Leonardo showed how the energy of humans could be used to pump a treadmill or turn a crank; that power could then be transmitted by gears and pulleys to perform a function. To capture human energy most efficiently, he broke the human body into components; he illustrated how each muscle works, calculated its power, and showed methods for leveraging it. In a notebook from the 1490s, he calculated how much weight a man can lift with his biceps, legs, shoulders, and other muscle groups.[3] "The greatest force a man can apply," he wrote, "will be when he sets his feet on one end of the balance and then leans his shoulders against some stable support. This will raise, at the other end of the balance, a weight equal to his own plus as much weight as he can carry on his shoulders."[4]

These studies were helpful for determining which muscles, if any, would be best at propelling a manned flying machine. But he also applied his findings to other tasks and sources of power. At one point he listed the many practical applications that could come from harnessing the power of the Arno River: "Saw mills, wool-cleaning machines, paper mills, hammers for forges, flour mills, knife grinding and sharpening, burnishing arms, manufacture of gunpowder, the silk spinning power of a hundred women, ribbon weaving, shaping vases made from jasper," and more.[5]

One of the practical applications he explored was using machinery to drive piles in the banks of a river to regulate its flow. His initial concept was to use a drop hammer that was raised by pulleys and ropes. Later he came up with an idea for raising the hammer more efficiently by having men climb a ladder and descend in a stirrup.[6] Likewise, when studying how to harness the power of falling water using a waterwheel, he realized correctly that it would be efficient to have the water fill buckets that would be pulled by gravity down one side of the wheel. He then designed a ratchet system so that the water would be dumped out of each bucket just as it got to the bottom of the turn. In a further modification, he designed a wheel with buckets in the shape of curved scoops.[7]

Leonardo also invented a machine designed to grind needles, which would have been a valuable contribution to the textile industries of Italy. It used human power to revolve a turntable attached to small grinding gears and polishing strips (fig. 54). He thought it might make him rich. "Tomorrow morning on January 2, 1496, I shall try out the broad belt," he wrote in a notebook. He estimated that a hundred such machines could turn out forty thousand needles an hour, each of which could be sold for 5 soldi. With a labored set of

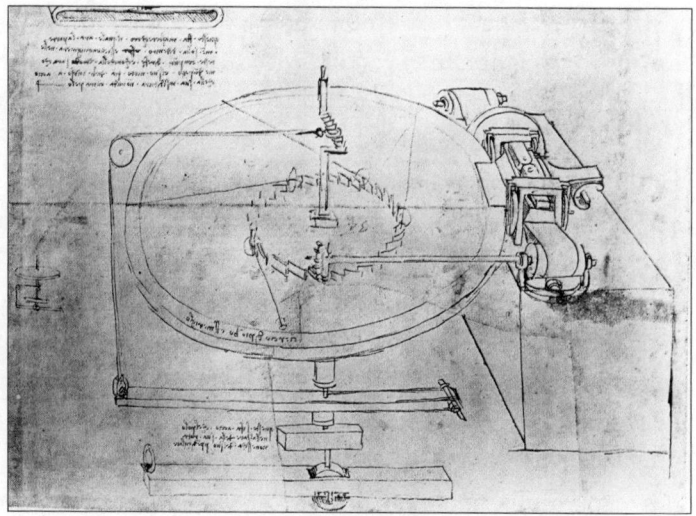

Fig. 54. Needle-grinding machine.

calculations, and a tenfold error in multiplication, he figured that he could reap an annual revenue of 60,000 ducats, the gold equivalent of more than $8 million in 2017. Even allowing for his miscalculation, 6,000 ducats of revenue should have been enticing enough to lure him away from the trade of painting Madonnas and altarpieces. But needless to say, Leonardo never finished executing his plan. Coming up with the conception was enough for him.[8]

PERPETUAL MOTION

Leonardo understood the concept of what he called impetus, which is what happens when a force pushes an object and gives it momentum. "A body in motion desires to maintain its course in the line from which it started," he wrote. "Every movement tends to maintain itself; or, rather, every body in motion continues to move so long as the influence of the force that set it in motion is maintained in it."[9] Leonardo's insights were a precursor to what Newton, two hundred years later, would make his first law of motion: that a body in motion will stay in the same motion unless acted upon by another force.[10]

If you were able to eliminate all forces slowing down an object in motion, then it should be possible, Leonardo thought, for a body to stay in motion forever. So during the 1490s, he used twenty-eight pages of a notebook to explore the possibility of a perpetual-motion machine. He looked for ways to prevent the momentum of an object from draining away, and he studied ways that a system could create or replenish its own impetus. He considered many mechanisms: wheels

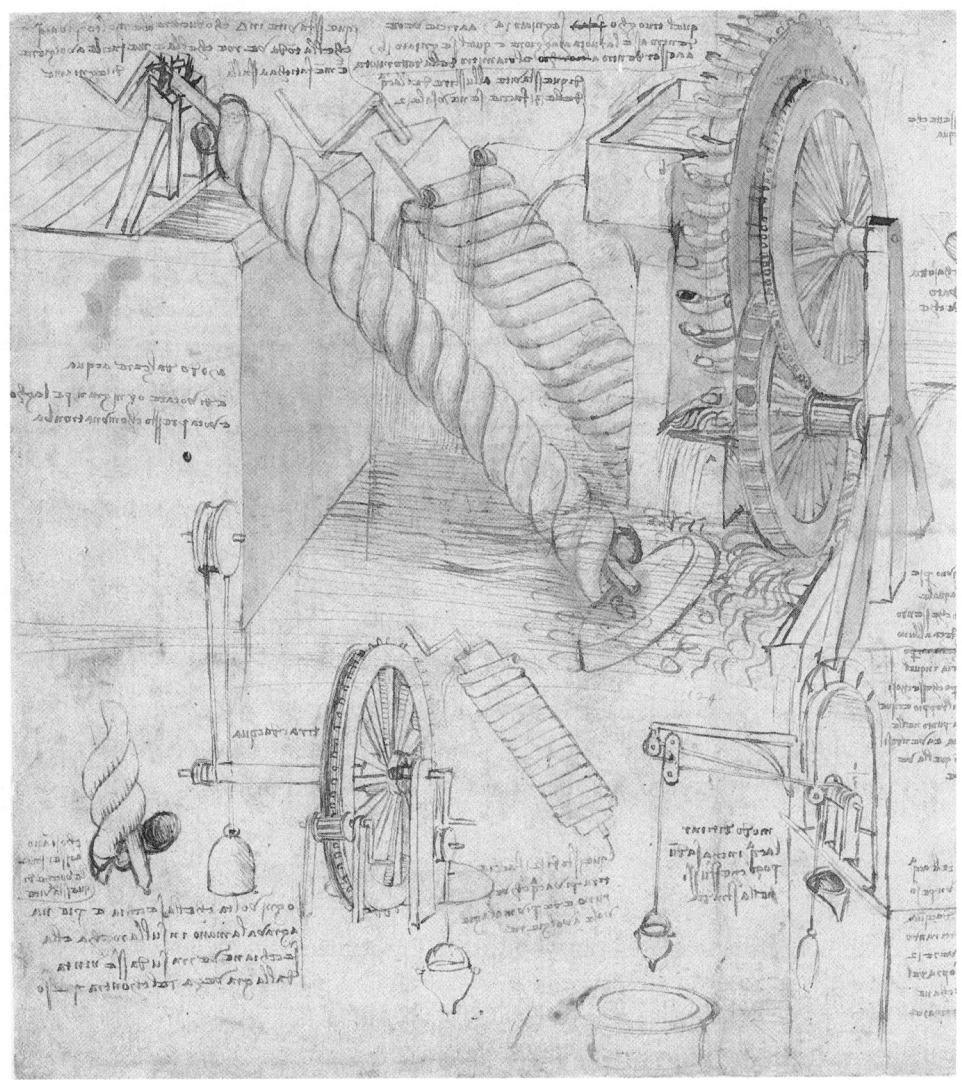

Fig. 55. A perpetual-motion machine using a water screw.

with hammers on hinges that would swing out when their part of the wheel was heading down, ways to hang weights on wheels that would keep them turning, spiral screws that form a double helix, and curved compartments on a wheel with balls that roll to the lowest point when they are heading downward.[11]

He was especially intrigued by the possibility that water devices might be a way to achieve perpetual motion. One such attempt (fig. 55) envisions the use of moving water to turn a coiled tube known as an Archimedes screw, which would carry water upward and then continue turning the screw as it flows downward. Was it possible for the downward flow of water, he asked, to turn the screw with enough power to raise enough water to keep the process going indefinitely? Even though technologists would try ways of accomplishing that trick for the next three centuries, Leonardo concluded, clearly and correctly, that it was impossible. "Descending water will never raise from its resting place an amount of water equal to its weight."[12]

His drawings served as visual thought experiments. By rendering the mechanisms in his notebooks rather than actually constructing them, he could envision how they would work and assess whether they would achieve perpetual motion. He eventually concluded, after looking at many different methods, that none of them would. In reasoning so, he showed that, as we go through life, there is a value in trying to do such tasks as designing a perpetual-motion machine: there are some problems that we will never be able to solve, and it's useful to understand why. "Among the impossible delusions of man is the search for continuous motion, called by some perpetual wheel," he wrote in the introduction to his Codex Madrid I. "Speculators on perpetual motion, how many vain chimeras you have created in this quest!"[13]

FRICTION

What prevents perpetual motion, Leonardo realized, is the inevitable loss of momentum in a system when it rubs against reality. Friction causes energy to be lost and prevents motion from being perpetual. So do air and water resistance, as he knew from his studies of bird flight and fish movement.

Thus he began a methodical study of friction, which resulted in some impressive insights. Through a set of experiments with heavy objects moving down a slope, he discovered the relationship among three determinants of friction: the weight of the object, the smoothness or roughness of the incline's surface, and the steepness of the incline. He was among the first to figure out that the amount of friction is not dependent on the size of the area of contact between the object and the surface. "The friction made by the same weight will be of equal resistance at the beginning of its movement although the contact may be of different breadths and lengths," he wrote. These laws of friction, and in particular the realization that friction is independent of the contact surface area, were an important discovery, but Leonardo never published them. They had to be rediscovered almost two hundred years later by the French scientific instrument maker Guillaume Amontons.[14]

Leonardo then went on to perform experiments to quantify the effects of each factor. To measure the power of an object sliding down an incline, he devised an instrument, now known as a tribometer, that would not be reinvented until the eighteenth century. Using the device, he analyzed what we now call the coefficient of friction, which is the ratio between the force it takes to move one surface over another and the pressure between the surfaces. For a piece of wood sliding against another piece of wood, he calculated this ratio as 0.25, which is about right.

He found that by lubricating the incline, he reduced friction, so he was among the first engineers to include points for the insertion of oil into his mechanical devices. He also devised ways to use ball bearings and roller bearings, techniques that were not commonly used until the late 1800s.[15]

In his Codex Madrid I, which is largely devoted to the design of more efficient machinery, Leonardo drew a new type of screw jack (fig. 56), one of those devices in which a big screw is turned to push upward on a heavy object. These were widely used in the fifteenth century. One drawback is that there is a lot of friction when a heavy load is pressing down. Leonardo's solution, which was likely the first of its kind, was to put some ball bearings between the plate and the

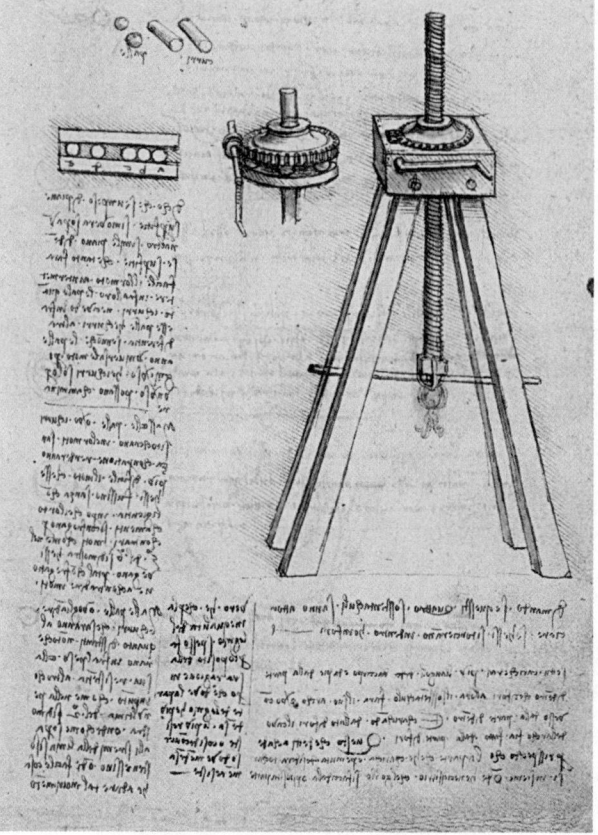

Fig. 56. A screw jack with ball bearings.

gear, which he drew in an exposed view just to the left of the jack. An even closer schematic view is to the left of that. "If a weight of a flat surface moves on a similar surface, its movement will be facilitated by interposing balls or rollers between them," he wrote in the accompanying text. "If the balls or rollers touch each other in their motion, they will make the movement more difficult than if there were no contact between them, because when they touch the friction causes a contrary motion and the movements counteract each other. But if the balls or rollers are kept at a distance from each other . . . it will be easy to generate this movement."[16] Being Leonardo, he then produced many pages of sketched thought experiments in which he varied the size and arrangements of the ball bearings. Three balls are better than four, he determined, because three points define a plane, and thus the three balls will always touch a flat surface, whereas a fourth ball may be out of alignment.

Leonardo was also the first person to record the best mix of metals to produce an alloy that reduces friction. It should be "three parts of copper and seven of tin, melted together," which was similar to the alloy he was using to make mirrors. "Leonardo's formula gives a perfectly working anti-friction composition," wrote Ladislao Reti, the historian of technology who played a role in discovering and publishing the Madrid Codices in 1965. Once again, Leonardo was about three centuries ahead of his time. The first antifriction alloy is usually credited to the American inventor Isaac Babbitt, who patented an alloy containing copper, tin, and antimony in 1839.[17]

Through his work on machinery, Leonardo developed a mechanistic view of the world foreshadowing that of Newton. All movements in the universe—of human limbs and of cogs in machines, of blood in our veins and of water in rivers—operate according to the same laws, he concluded. These laws are analogous; the motions in one realm can be compared to those in another realm, and patterns emerge. "Man is a machine, a bird is a machine, the whole universe is a machine," wrote Marco Cianchi in an analysis of Leonardo's devices.[18] As Leonardo and others led Europe into a new scientific age, he ridiculed astrologers, alchemists, and others who believed in nonmechanistic explanations of cause and effect, and he relegated the idea of religious miracles to the purview of priests.

CHAPTER 13

Math

GEOMETRY

Leonardo increasingly came to realize that mathematics was the key to turning observations into theories. It was the language that nature used to write her laws. "There is no certainty in sciences where mathematics cannot be applied," he declared.[1] He was correct. Using geometry to understand the laws of perspective taught him how math could extract from nature the secrets of its beauty and reveal the beauty of its secrets.

With his visual acuity, Leonardo had a natural feel for geometry, and that branch of math helped him formulate some rules for how nature works. However, his facility with shapes was not matched by one for numbers, so arithmetic did not come naturally. In his notebooks are entries where, for example, he doubles 4,096 to get 8,092, forgetting to carry the 1.[2] As for algebra—that wonderful tool for using numbers and letters to codify nature's laws and variables, bequeathed to later Renaissance scholars by the Arabs and Persians—Leonardo was clueless, which hindered his ability to use equations as brushstrokes for painting the patterns he discerned in nature.

What Leonardo liked about geometry, as opposed to arithmetic, was that geometric shapes are continuous quantities, whereas numbers are discrete digits and thus discontinuous units. "Arithmetic deals with discontinuous quantities, geometry with continuous ones," he wrote.[3] In modern parlance we would say that he was more comfortable with analog tools, including the use of shapes as analogies (yes, that's where the word *analog* comes from), rather than being a digital native. As he wrote, "Arithmetic is a computational science in its calculation, with true and perfect units, but it is of no avail in dealing with continuous quantity."[4]

Geometry also had the advantage of being a visual endeavor. It engaged the eye and the imagination. "When he looked at the way that shells assumed a helical shape," Martin Kemp wrote, "at how leaves and petals originated from stems, and at the reasons why a heart valve worked with perfect economy, geometrical analysis delivered the results he desired."[5]

Not having access to algebra, he instead used geometry to describe the rate of change caused by a variable. For example, he used triangles and pyramids to represent rates of change in the velocity of falling objects, the volume of sounds, and the perspective view of distant objects. "Proportion is not only to be found in number and measure, but also in sounds, weights, times and places and every force that exists," he wrote.[6]

LUCA PACIOLI

One of Leonardo's close friends at Milan's court was Luca Pacioli, a mathematician who developed the first widely published system for double-entry bookkeeping. Like Leonardo, he was born in Tuscany and attended only an abacus school, which provided a trade education in arithmetic but no Latin. He worked as a wandering tutor to boys from wealthy families and then became a Franciscan friar who never moved into a monastery. He wrote a math textbook in Italian, rather than Latin, which was published in Venice in 1494; it thus became part of the explosive spread of learning in vernacular languages triggered by the printing press in the late fifteenth century.

Leonardo bought a copy as soon as it was published, recording the rather high cost (more than twice what he paid for a Bible) in his notebook,[7] and he may have helped recruit Pacioli to become part of the Milan court. The mathematician arrived there in about 1496 and had living quarters along with Leonardo at the Corte Vecchia. They shared a love of geometric shapes. A portrait painted of Pacioli (fig. 57) shows him and a student in front of a table with a protractor, compass, and stylus; a polyhedron of eighteen squares and eight triangles half filled with water dangles from the ceiling.

A lesser-known but important component of Pacioli's work at court involved contributing, alongside Leonardo, to its ephemeral amusements and performances. In a notebook he began just after his arrival, "On the Powers of Numbers," Pacioli compiled riddles, mathematical brain-twisters, magic tricks, and parlor games designed to be presented and solved at court parties. His tricks include how to make an egg walk across a table (it involves wax and strands of hair), how to make a coin go up and down in a glass (vinegar and magnetic powder), and how to make a chicken jump (quicksilver). His parlor

Fig. 57. Luca Pacioli.

games included the first published version of the standard card trick of guessing which card someone has picked from a deck (it involves an accomplice), brain-teasers such as one in which a man has to figure out how to ferry a wolf and a goat and a cabbage across a river, and math games in which a spectator thinks of a number which can then be discovered by asking the result of a few operations performed on it. Particularly appealing to Leonardo were Pacioli's games involving creating circles around triangles and squares using only a ruler and a compass.

Pacioli and Leonardo bonded over their shared fondness for such stimulating amusements and entertainments. Leonardo's name crops up often in Pacioli's notes. After writing the basics of one trick, for instance, Pacioli declares, "Well Leonardo, you can do more of this on your own."[8]

More seriously, Leonardo learned math from Pacioli, a great tutor, who taught him the subtleties and beauties of Euclid's geometry and tried to teach him, with less success, how to multiply squares and square roots. At times when he found a concept difficult to comprehend, Leonardo would copy passages of Pacioli's explanations verbatim into his notebooks.[9]

Leonardo returned the favor by drawing a set of mathematical illustrations, of astonishing artistic beauty and grace, for the book Pacioli began writing upon his arrival in Milan, *On Divine Proportion*, which examines the role of proportions and ratios in architecture, art, anatomy, and math. Given Leonardo's appreciation for the intersection of arts and sciences, he was fascinated by the topic.

Most of Leonardo's drawings for Pacioli's book, which was finished in 1498, are variations of the five shapes known as Platonic solids. These are polyhedrons that have the same number of faces meeting at each vertex: pyramids, cubes, octahedrons (eight faces), dodecahedrons (twelve), and icosahedrons (twenty). He also illustrated more complex shapes, such as a rhombicuboctahedron, which has twenty-six facets, eight of them equilateral triangles that are bordered by squares (fig. 58). He pioneered a new method for making such shapes understandable: instead of drawing them as solids, he made them see-through skeletons, as if constructed of wooden beams.

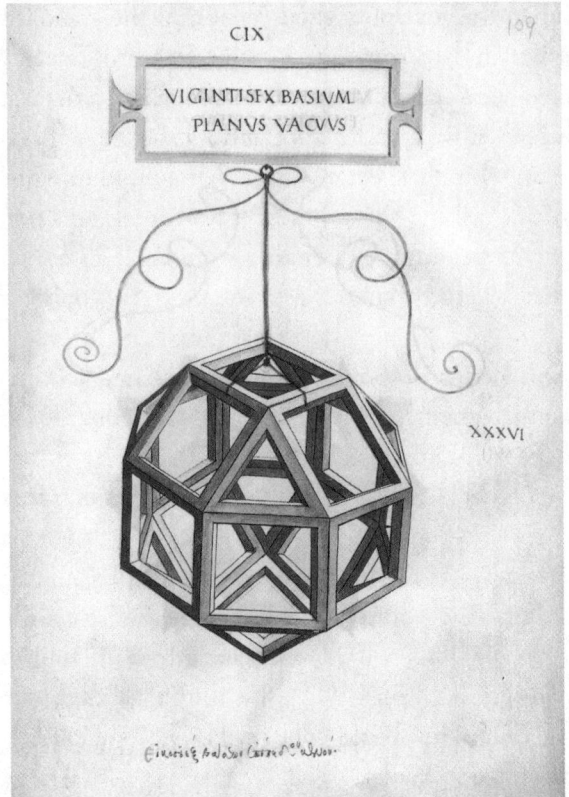

CIX

VIGINTISEX BASIVM
PLANVS VACVVS

XXXVI

Fig. 58. Leonardo's rhombicuboctahedron
for Pacioli's book.

His sixty illustrations for Pacioli were the only drawings he published
during his lifetime.

Part of Leonardo's genius is in the lighting and shading of these
illustrations, which make the geometric renderings seem like actual
objects dangling before our eyes. The light comes in from an angle,
casting shadows both bold and subtle. Each of the object's faces becomes a windowpane. Leonardo's mastery of perspective added to the
three-dimensional look. He could envision the shapes in his head as
real objects, then convey them on the page. But he probably also used
actual wooden models that he hung on a string, like the dangling
polyhedron in the portrait of Pacioli. Using both observation and
mathematical reasoning, and combining his study of geometric shapes

with his inquiries into the flight of birds, Leonardo became the first person to discover the center of gravity of a triangular pyramid (one-quarter of the way up a line from the base to the peak).

In his book, Pacioli gratefully acknowledged that the drawings were "made and formed by the ineffable left hand, so well versed in all the mathematical disciplines, by the prince among mortals today, by the first Florentine, our Leonardo da Vinci, who, in that happy time, together with me, on the same stipends, was in the marvelous city of Milan." Pacioli later called Leonardo the "most worthy of painters, perspectivists, architects and musicians, one endowed with every perfection," and he recalled "that happy time when we were both in the employ of the most illustrious Duke of Milan, Ludovico Maria Sforza Anglo, in the years of Our Lord 1496 to 1499."[10]

Pacioli's book focused on the golden ratio, or divine proportion, an irrational number that expresses a ratio that pops up often in number series, geometry, and art. It is approximately 1.61803398, but (being irrational) has decimals that stretch on randomly forever. The golden ratio occurs when you divide a line into two parts in such a way that the ratio between the whole length and the longer part is equal to the ratio between the longer part and the shorter part. For example, take a line that's 100 inches long and divide it into two parts of 61.8 inches and 38.2 inches. That comes close to the golden ratio, because 100 divided by 61.8 is about the same as 61.8 divided by 38.2; in both cases, it's approximately 1.618.

Euclid wrote about this ratio in around 300 BC, and it has fascinated mathematicians ever since. Pacioli was the first to popularize the name *divine proportion* for it. In his book by that title, he described the way it turns up in studies of geometric solids such as cubes and prisms and polyhedrons. In popular lore, including in Dan Brown's *The Da Vinci Code*, the golden ratio is found throughout Leonardo's art.[11] If so, it is doubtful it was intentional. Although it is possible to draw diagrams of the *Mona Lisa* and *Saint Jerome* asserting this notion, the evidence that Leonardo consciously made use of the precise mathematical ratio is not convincing.

Nevertheless, Leonardo's interest in harmonic ratios was reflected in his intense studies of the ways that ratios and proportions are manifest in anatomy, science, and art. It led him to search for analogies between the proportions of the body, the notes of musical harmonies, and other ratios that underpin the beauty manifest in the works of nature.

TRANSFORMATION OF SHAPES

As an artist, Leonardo was particularly interested in how the shapes of objects transformed when they moved. From his observations on the flow of water, he developed an appreciation for the idea of the conservation of volume: as a quantity of water flows, its shape changes, but its volume remains exactly the same.

Understanding the transformation of volumes was useful for an artist, especially one such as Leonardo, who specialized in portraying bodies in motion. It helped him picture how an object's shape could be distorted or transformed while keeping its volume unchanged. "Of everything that moves," he wrote, "the space which it acquires is as great as that which it leaves."[12] This applies not only to quantities of water, but to a bending arm and twisting torso of a human.

As he became more interested in how geometry could provide analogies for phenomena in nature, Leonardo began to explore more theoretical cases where the conservation of volume held true as one geometric shape morphed into another. An example would be if you took a square and transformed it into a circle with the exact same area. A three-dimensional example would be showing how a sphere could be transformed into a cube with the same volume.

By grappling with these transformations and persistently record-ing his insights, Leonardo helped to pioneer the field of topology, which looks at how shapes and objects can undergo transformations while keeping some of the same properties. Throughout his notebooks we can see him—sometimes with obsessive focus, at other times dis-tracted and doodling—taking curved shapes and transforming them into rectangular shapes of the same size, or doing the same for pyra-mids and cones.[13] He could visualize and draw such transformations, and he sometimes replicated them experimentally using soft wax. But he was not good at the math tools of geometry, which involve being able to multiply the squares of numbers, square roots, cubes, and cube roots. "Learn the multiplication of roots from Maestro Luca," he wrote in his notebook, referring to Pacioli. But he never mastered the math and instead spent his career trying to figure out geometrical transformations using drawings rather than equations.[14]

He started collecting his studies on this topic and in 1505 declared his intention to write "a book entitled transformation, namely of one body into another without diminishing or increasing the material."[15] Like his other treatises, it produced brilliant notebook pages but not a published book.

SQUARING THE CIRCLE

One topic related to the conservation of volume that particularly intrigued Leonardo, and would eventually obsess him, came from the ancient Greek mathematician Hippocrates. It involves a lune, a geometric shape that looks like the crescent of a quarter-moon. Hippocrates discovered a delightful mathematical fact: if you create a lune by overlapping a large half-circle with a smaller one, you can construct a right triangle inside the larger half-circle that has the exact same area as the lune. This was the first way discovered to calculate the exact area inside a curved shape, such as a circle or a lune, and to replicate that area in a straight-sided shape, such as a triangle or rectangle.

That fascinated Leonardo. He filled his notebooks with shaded drawings in which he overlapped two half-circles and then created triangles and rectangles that had the same area as the resulting crescents. Year after year, he relentlessly pursued ways to create circular shapes with areas equivalent to triangles and rectangles, as if addicted to the game. Though he never gave the precise dates of any milestones he reached when making a painting, he treated these geometric studies as if each little success was a moment in history worthy of a notarial record. One night he wrote momentously, "Having for a long time searched to square the angle to two equal curves . . . now in the year 1509 on the eve of the Calends of May [April 30] I have found the solution at the 22nd hour on Sunday."[16]

His pursuit of equivalent areas was aesthetic as well as intellectual. After a while, his experimental geometric shapes, such as his curved triangles, became artistic patterns. On one set of pages (fig. 59) he drew 180 diagrams of overlapping circular and straight-sided shapes, each one annotated with how the shaded and unshaded portions relate to each other in area.[17]

As usual, he decided to put together a treatise on the topic—*De Ludo Geometrico*, he called it (On the Game of Geometry)—and it filled page after page of his notebooks. Not surprisingly, it joined his other treatises in never being finished for publication.[18] His choice of the word *ludo* is interesting; it implies a diversion or pastime that is engrossing but like a game. Indeed, the distraction that came from playing with lunes seemed to drive him to lunacy at times. But to him it was an enthralling mind game, one that he believed would get him closer to the secrets of nature's beautiful patterns.

These obsessions led Leonardo to an ancient riddle described by Vitruvius, Euripides, and others. Faced with a plague in the fifth century BC, the citizens of Delos consulted the oracle of Delphi. They were told that the plague would end if they found a mathematical way to precisely double the size of the altar to Apollo, which was shaped as a cube. When they doubled the length of each side, the plague worsened; the Oracle explained that by doing so they had increased the size of the cube eightfold rather than doubling it. (For example, a cube with two-foot sides has eight times the volume of a cube with one-foot sides.) To solve the problem geometrically required multiplying the length of each side by the cube root of 2.

Despite his note to himself to "learn the multiplication of roots from Maestro Luca," Leonardo was never good at square roots, much less cube roots. Even if he had been, however, neither he nor the plague-stricken Greeks had the tools to solve the problem with numerical calculations, because the cube root of 2 is an irrational number. But Leonardo was able to come up with a visual solution. The answer can be found by drawing a cube that is constructed on a plane that cuts diagonally through the original cube, just as a square

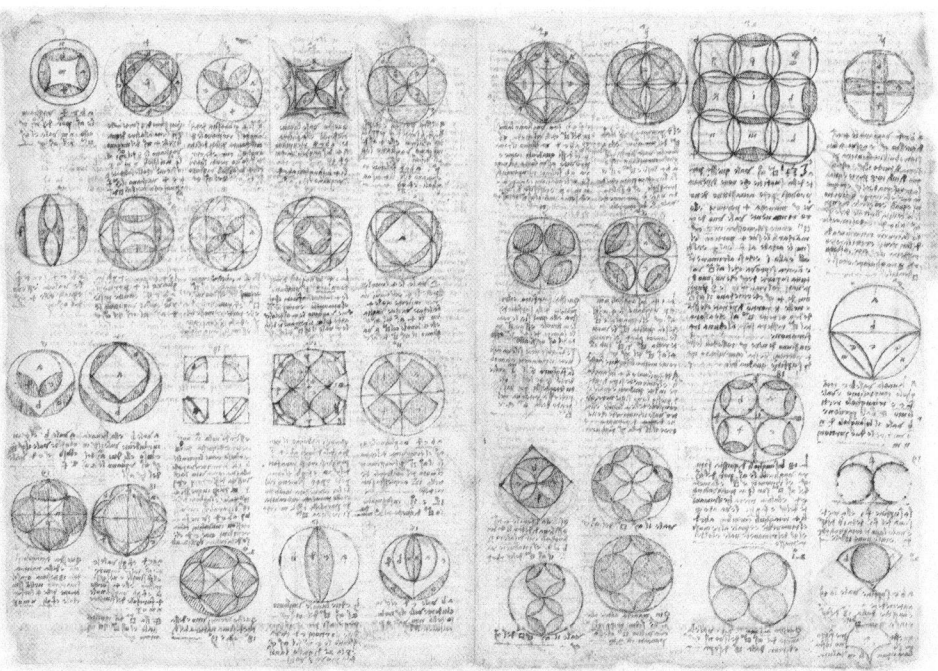

Fig. 59. Finding equivalent geometric areas.

can be doubled in size by constructing a new square on a line cutting it in half diagonally, thus squaring the hypotenuse.[19]

Leonardo also wrestled with a related riddle, the most famous of the ancient math puzzles: squaring the circle. The challenge is to take a circle and, using only a compass and ruler, construct a square that has the exact same area. That quest was what led Hippocrates to work on ways to turn a circular shape into a triangular one with the same volume. For more than a decade, Leonardo became obsessed by the effort.

We now know that a mathematical process for squaring a circle requires use of a transcendental number, in this case π, which cannot be expressed as a fraction and is not the root of any polynomial with rational coefficients.[20] So it's not possible to accomplish with just a compass and ruler. But Leonardo's persistent efforts show the brilliance of his thought process. At one point, exhausted but excited after an all-night effort, he scribbled one of the momentous entries he used for what he thought were mathematical breakthroughs: "On the night of St Andrew [November 30] I reached the end of squaring the circle; and at the end of the light of the candle, of the night, and of the paper on which I was writing, it was completed."[21] But it was a false celebration, and he was soon back at work on different methods.

One approach he took was to calculate the area of a circle experimentally. He sliced a circle into thin triangular wedges and tried to measure the size of each. He also unrolled the circumference to figure out its length. A more sophisticated approach came from his love of lunes. He cut a circle into many rectangles that could be easily measured and then used the methods of Hippocrates to find areas comparable to the remaining curved parts.

Yet another prolonged attempt involved dividing a circle into many sectors, which he then subdivided into triangles and semicircles. He arranged these slices into a rectangle and repeated the process with smaller and smaller slices, approaching the limit of infinitely small triangles. His impulses prefigured those that would lead to the development of calculus, but Leonardo did not have the skills that allowed Leibniz and Newton to devise this mathematical study of change two centuries later.

Throughout his life, Leonardo would remain enchanted by the transformation of shapes. The margins of his notebooks, and sometimes entire pages, would be filled with triangles inside semicircles inside squares inside circles as he played with tricks for turning one geometrical form into another with the same area or volume. He came up with 169 formulas for squaring a circular shape, and on one sheet drew so many examples that it looks like a page from a pattern book. Even the very last notebook page that he is known to have written near the end of his life—a famous one ending with the phrase "the soup is getting cold"—is filled with triangles and rectangles as he tried to calculate comparable areas.

Kenneth Clark once called them "calculations which are of no interest to mathematicians, and of even less interest to the art historian."[22] Yes, but they were interesting to Leonardo. Compulsively so. They may not have led to historic breakthroughs in mathematics, but they were integral to his ability to perceive and portray motion—of bird wings and water, of a squirming baby Jesus and a breast-beating Saint Jerome—like no other artist before him.

CHAPTER 14

The Nature of Man

ANATOMICAL DRAWINGS
(FIRST PERIOD, 1487–1493)

As a young painter in Florence, Leonardo studied human anatomy primarily to improve his art. His forerunner as an artist-engineer, Leon Battista Alberti, had written that anatomical study was essential for an artist because properly depicting people and animals requires beginning with an understanding of their insides. "Isolate each bone of the animal, on this add its muscles, then clothe all of it with its flesh," he wrote in *On Painting*, which became a bible for Leonardo. "Before dressing a man we first draw him nude, then we enfold him in draperies. So in painting the nude, we place first his bones and muscles which we then cover with flesh so that it is not difficult to understand where each muscle is beneath."[1]

Leonardo embraced the advice with an enthusiasm that any other artist, or for that matter most anatomists, would have found unimaginable. And in his notebooks he preached the same sermon: "It is necessary for a painter to be a good anatomist, so that he may be able to design the naked parts of the human frame and know the anatomy of the sinews, nerves, bones, and muscles."[2] Following another part of Alberti's creed, Leonardo wanted to know how psychological emotions led to physical motions. As a result, he would also become interested in the way the nervous system works and how optical impressions are processed.

The most basic anatomical knowledge for a painter is the understanding of muscles, and in this Florence's artists were pioneers. Antonio del Pollaiuolo made an influential copperplate engraving of a battle scene of nude men, showing their muscles in more-than-full glory, around 1470, when Leonardo was associated with Verrocchio's nearby workshop. Vasari wrote that Pollaiuolo "dissected many bodies to study their anatomy," though it's likely these were merely surface studies. Leonardo, who probably observed some of these dissections, naturally soon became interested in exploring even more deeply, and he began what would be a lifelong association with Florence's hospital of Santa Maria Nuova.[3]

When he moved to Milan, he discovered that the study of anatomy there was pursued primarily by medical scholars rather than by artists.[4] The city's culture was more intellectual than artistic, and the University of Pavia was a center for medical research. Prominent anatomical scholars were soon tutoring him, lending him books, and then teaching him dissection. Under their influence, he began pursuing anatomy as a scientific as well as an artistic endeavor. But he did not regard these as separate. In anatomy, as in so many of his studies, he saw the art and science as interwoven. Art required a deep understanding of anatomy, which in turn was aided by a profound appreciation for the beauty of nature. As with his study of the flight of birds, Leonardo went from seeking knowledge that could be of practical use and began seeking knowledge for its own sake, out of pure curiosity and joy.

This was evident when he sat down after seven years in Milan with a clean notebook sheet and made a list of the topics he wished to investigate. On top he wrote the date, "on the second of April 1489," which was unusual for him and an indication that he was embarking on an important endeavor. On the left-hand page he drew, with delicate strokes of a pen, two views of a human skull with veins. On the right-hand page, he listed topics to explore:

What nerve is the cause of the eye's movement and makes the movement of one eye move the other?

Of closing the eyelid.

Of raising the eyebrows. . . .

Of parting the lips with teeth clenched.

Of bringing the lips to a point.

Of laughing.

Of expressing wonder.

Set yourself to describe the beginning of man when he is created in the
womb and why an infant of eight months does not live.

What sneezing is.

What yawning is.

Epilepsy.

Spasm.

Paralysis. . . .

Fatigue.

Hunger.

Sleep.

Thirst.

Sensuality. . . .

Of the nerve that causes the movement of the thigh.

And from the knee to the foot and from the ankle to the toes.[5]

The list begins with inquiries, such as how eyes move and lips smile,
that could be useful for his art. But by the time the list gets to an infant in a womb and the cause of sneezing, it is clear that he's looking
for more than information that might help his brush.

That intermingling of artistic and scientific interests is even more evident on another page that he began writing around the same time. With a sweeping scope, ranging from conception to mirth to music, that would have seemed audacious for anyone other than Leonardo, he outlined a treatise on anatomy that he hoped to produce:

This work should begin with the conception of man, and describe the nature of the womb and how the fetus lives in it, up to what stage it resides there, and in what way it quickens into life and gets food. Also its growth and what interval there is between one stage of growth and another. What forces it out from the body of the mother, and for what reasons it sometimes comes out of the mother's womb before the due time. Then I will describe which parts grow more than the others after the baby is born, and determine the proportions of a child of one year. Then describe the fully grown man and woman, with their proportions, and the nature of their complexions, color, and physiognomy. Then how they are composed of veins, tendons, muscles and bones. Then, in four drawings, represent four universal conditions of men. That is, Mirth, with various acts of laughter, and describe the cause of laughter. Weeping in various aspects with its causes. Fighting, with various acts of killing; flight, fear, ferocity, boldness, murder and everything pertaining to such cases. Then represent Labor, with pulling, thrusting, carrying, stopping, supporting and such like things. Then perspective, concerning the functions and effects of the eye; and of hearing—here I will speak of music—and describe the other senses.[6]

In subsequent notes he described how tissue, veins, muscles, and nerves should be shown from a variety of angles: "Every part will be drawn, using all means of demonstrations, from three different points of view; for when you have seen a limb from the front, with any muscles, sinews, or veins which take their rise from the opposite side, the same limb will be shown to you in a side view or from behind, exactly as if you had that same limb in your hand and were turning it from side to side until you had acquired a full comprehension of all

you wished to know."[7] Thus did Leonardo pioneer a new form of anatomical drawing, perhaps better described in his case as anatomical
art, that is still in use today.

THE SKULL DRAWINGS

Leonardo's initial anatomy studies of 1489 focused on human skulls.
He started with a skull that had been sawed in half, top to bottom
(fig. 60). Then the front of the left half was sawed off. His groundbreaking technique of drawing the two halves together made it easy
to see how the inner cavities were positioned relative to the face. For
example, the frontal sinus, which Leonardo is the first person to correctly depict, is shown to rest just behind the eyebrow.

To appreciate how ingenious this pictorial technique is, cover the
right side of the picture with your hand and notice how much less informative the drawing becomes. "The originality of the skull drawings
of 1489 is so fundamentally different and superior to all other extant
illustrations of the time that they are completely out of character with
the age," according to Francis Wells, a surgeon and an expert on the
anatomical drawings.[8]

To the left of the face Leonardo drew each of the four types of
human teeth, with a note saying that a human typically has thirty-
two, including the wisdom teeth. With this, as far as is now known,
he became the first person in history to describe fully the human
dental elements, including a depiction of the roots that is almost
perfect.[9] "The six upper molars have three roots each, of which two
roots are on the outer side of the jaw and one on the inner," he
wrote, evidence that he had cut through the wall of a sinus to determine the position of the roots. If there were not so much else to remember him for, Leonardo could have been celebrated as a pioneer
of dentistry.

In one of the accompanying drawings, Leonardo showed a skull
from the left side with a top quarter section and then the entire left
side sawed off (fig. 61). What's most striking in the pen-and-ink
drawing is its artistic beauty: fine lines, elegant contours, sfumato
effects, trademark left-handed cross-hatching, and subtle shadings

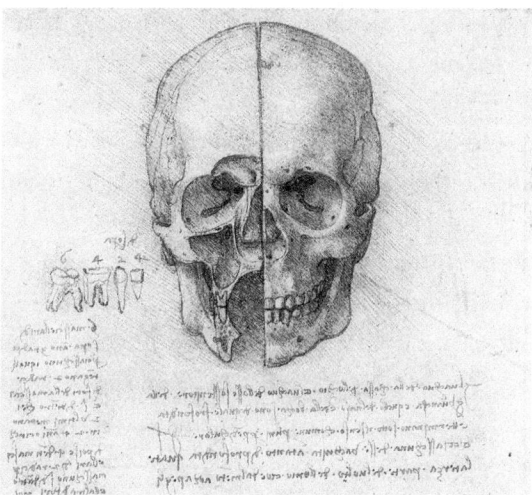

Fig. 60

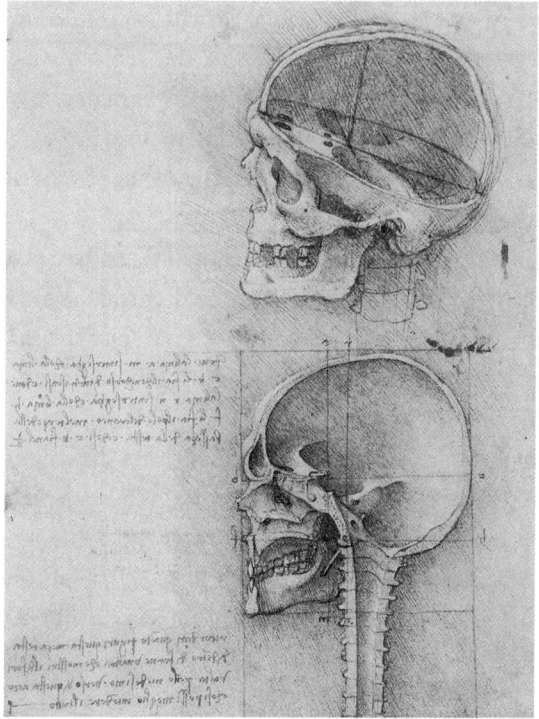

Fig. 61

Skull drawings, 1489.

and shadows adding three-dimensionality. Among Leonardo's many contributions to science was showing how concepts could be developed through drawing. Beginning with the drapery studies done in Verrocchio's studio, Leonardo mastered the art of rendering light hitting rounded and curved objects. Now he was deploying that art to transform, and make beautiful, the study of anatomy.[10]

On this and another of his skull drawings, Leonardo drew a set of axis lines. At their intersection near the center of the brain, he located the cavity that he thought contained the *senso comune*, or confluence of the senses. "The soul seems to reside in the judgment, and the judgment would seem to be seated in that part where all the senses meet; and this is called the *senso comune*," he wrote.[11]

In order to link the movements of the mind to the movements of the body, showing how emotions become motions, Leonardo wanted to locate where that phenomenon occurred. In a series of drawings, he attempted to show how visual observations come in through the eye, are processed, and then are sent to the *senso comune*, where the mind can act on them. The resulting brain signals, he surmised, are transported through the nervous system to the muscles. In most of his drawings, he gave primacy to sight; the other senses did not have a ventricle of their own.[12]

On one drawing from this period showing the bones and nerves of an arm, he drew a faint sketch of the spinal cord and nerves emerging from it. Appended is a note about his experience pithing a frog, the first scientist to record doing what is now a staple of biology classes. "The frog dies instantly when its spinal cord is perforated," he wrote. "And previously it lived without head, without heart or any interior organs, or intestines or skin. Here therefore it appears lies the foundation of movement and life." He repeated the experiment on a dog. His drawings of the nerves and spinal cord are clearly labeled; it was not until 1739 that this pithing experiment would again be illustrated and described correctly.[13]

In the mid-1490s Leonardo put aside his work on anatomy; he would not return to the subject for another decade. Although he was neither fully original nor correct in his description of a *senso comune*, he was right in his general view that the human brain receives visual and other stimuli, processes them into perceptions, then transmits reactions through the nervous system to the muscles. More important, his fascination with the connection between the mind and the body became a key component of his artistic genius: showing how inner emotions are manifest in outward gestures. "In painting, the actions of the figures are, in all cases, expressive of the purpose of their minds," he wrote.[14] As he was finishing his first round of anatomical studies, he was beginning work on what would be the greatest expression in the history of art of that maxim, *The Last Supper*.

STUDIES OF HUMAN PROPORTION

While studying Vitruvius for his work on the Milan and Pavia cathedrals, Leonardo became captivated by the ancient Roman architect's detailed studies of human proportions and measurements. In addition, when he was measuring horses for the Sforza monument, he became interested in how they related to human proportions. Comparative anatomy appealed to his instinct for finding patterns across different subjects. So in 1490 he began measuring and drawing the proportions of the human body.

Using at least a dozen young men as models in his Corte Vecchia studios, he measured each body part from head to toe and produced more than forty drawings and six thousand words. His descriptions included both the average size of body parts and the proportional relationships between different parts. "The space between the mouth and the base of the nose is one-seventh of the face," he wrote. "The space from the mouth to the bottom of the chin is one-fourth of the face and equal to the width of the mouth. The space from the chin to the base of the nose is one-third of the face and equal to the length of the nose and to the forehead." These descriptions and others were accompanied by detailed drawings and diagrams with letters denoting the different measurements (figs. 62 and 63).

Page after page of his notebooks—fifty-one sections in all—are

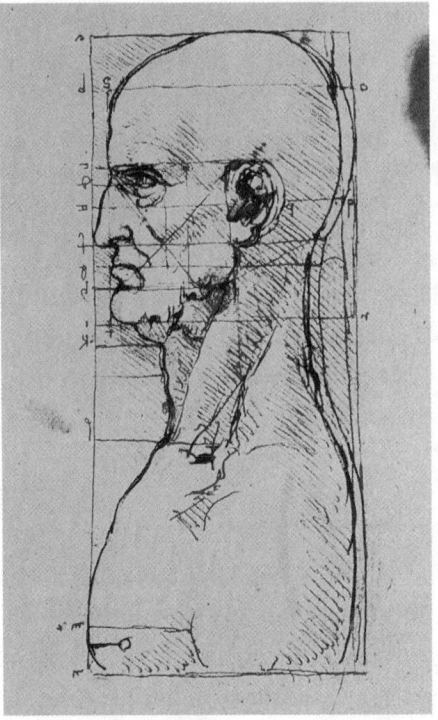

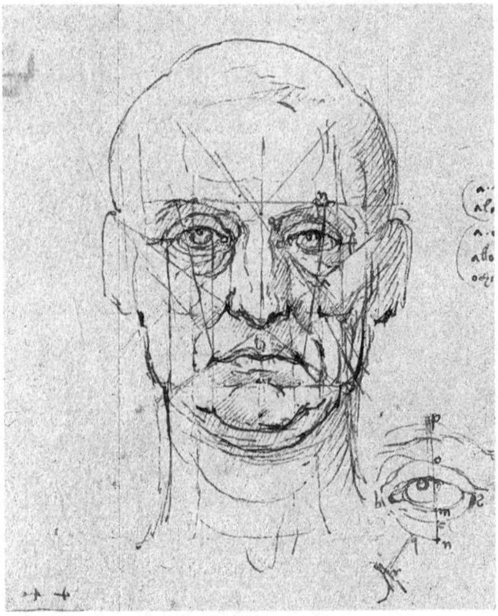

Fig. 63

Proportions of the face.

Fig. 62

filled with ever more precise detail. His descriptions were inspired by Vitruvius, but they went far deeper and were based on his own observations. A small sample of his findings:

> The distance from the top of the nose to the bottom of the chin is two-thirds of the face. . . . The width of the face is equal to the space between the mouth and the roots of the hair and is one-twelfth of the whole height. . . . From the top of the ear to the top of the head is equal to the distance from the bottom of the chin to the duct of the eye and also equal to the distance from the angle of the chin to that of the jaw. . . . The hollow of the cheek bone occurs half way between the tip of the nose and the top of the jaw bone. . . . The great toe is the sixth part of the foot, taking the measure in profile. . . . From the joint of one shoulder

to the other is the length of two faces. . . . From the navel to the genitals is a face's length.[15]

I am tempted to quote him at even greater length because the enormity of his feat, and what it says about his compulsive mind, is evident not in each measurement but in the staggering accumulation of them. He goes on and on, relentlessly. In one entry alone there are at least eighty such calculations or proportions. It becomes both dazzling and dizzying. One tries to imagine him in his studio with measuring string and a handful of compliant assistants dutifully having every body part recorded. Such obsession is a component of genius.

Leonardo was not content merely to measure every aspect of every body part. In addition, he felt compelled to record what occurs when each of these parts moves. What happens to the relative shape of each human feature when a joint moves or a person twists? "Observe how the position of the shoulder changes when the arm moves up and down, inwards and outwards, to the back and to the front, and also in circular movements and any others," he instructs himself in his notebook. "And do the same with reference to the neck, hands and feet and the breast."

We can picture him in his studio, as he made his models move, turn, squat, sit, and lie down. "When the arm is bent, the fleshy part shrinks to two-thirds of its length," he recorded. "When a man kneels down he will diminish by the fourth part of his height. . . . When a heel is raised, the tendon and ankle get closer to each other by a finger's breadth. . . . When a man sits down, the distance from his seat to the top part of his head will be half of his height plus the thickness and length of the testicles."[16]

Plus the thickness and length of the testicles? Once again it is useful to pause and marvel. Why the obsessiveness? Why the need for reams of data? Partly, at least initially, it was to help him paint humans, or horses, in various poses and movements. But there was something grander involved. Leonardo had set for himself the most magnificent of all tasks for the mind of mankind: nothing less than knowing fully the measure of man and how he fits into the cosmos. In his notebook, he proclaimed his intention to fathom what he called "universale misura del huomo," the universal measure of man.[17] It was the quest that defined Leonardo's life, the one that tied together his art and his science.

CHAPTER 15

Virgin of the Rocks

THE COMMISSION

When Leonardo first came to Milan in 1482, he had hopes of working primarily as a military and civil engineer, as he had proposed in his letter to the de facto duke, Ludovico Sforza. That did not happen. Most of his work for the court during the ensuing decade was as a theatrical impresario, then as the sculptor of the unfinished horse monument and a consultant on church designs. Yet his primary talent remained that of a painter, as had been the case in Florence and would be so until his final days.

For his first few years in Milan, before he was given space in the Corte Vecchia, he probably shared a studio with Ambrogio de Predis, one of Ludovico's favorite portrait artists, and his half-brothers, Evangelista and Cristoforo, who was deaf and did not speak. Leonardo later wrote that observing how the deaf communicate was a good way to study the relation between human gestures and thoughts: "Let your figures have actions appropriate to what they are intended to think or say, and these will be well learned by imitating the deaf, who by the motion of their hands, eyes, eyebrows, and the whole body, endeavor to express the sentiments of their mind."[1]

Soon after Leonardo began working with the de Predis brothers, they were jointly given a commission by the Confraternity of the Immaculate Conception, a worship group of rich laymen, to paint altarpieces for the Franciscan church that it used. To Leonardo fell the task of painting the central frame, and his instructions were explicit: it was to feature the Virgin Mary ("her skirt shall be of gold brocade over crimson, in oil, varnished with fine lacquer") and baby Jesus surrounded by "angels done in oil to complete perfection, with the two Prophets." Ignoring these instructions, he decided to paint the Virgin Mary, the baby Jesus, a young John the Baptist, one angel, and no prophets. The scene he chose came from Apocrypha and medieval stories of the Holy Family meeting John on the road to Egypt as they fled Bethlehem after King Herod ordered the Massacre of the Innocents.

Leonardo ended up producing two similar versions of the painting, which became known as the *Virgin of the Rocks*. Reams of scholarship have been produced debating the timing and backstories of these paintings. The most convincing narrative, I believe, is that the first version, done in the 1480s, led to a price dispute with the confraternity and was sold or sent elsewhere; it is now in the Louvre (fig. 64). Leonardo then helped to paint a replacement version, in collaboration with Ambrogio de Predis and his studio, completed sometime around 1508; it is the one now in the National Gallery of London (fig. 65).[2]

The confraternity wanted a painting that would celebrate the Immaculate Conception, a doctrine pushed by the Franciscans asserting that the Virgin Mary was conceived free from all stain of original sin.[3] Some of the iconography in the *Virgin of the Rocks* supports that idea, most notably the setting: a grotto of barren and dramatic rock formations that magically spawns flowering plants and four holy figures. We feel we are looking into the womb of the earth. The figures in front of the cave are bathed in warm light, but the shadowy inside is dark and intimidating. The locale harks back to Leonardo's recollection about coming across the mouth of a mysterious cave while hiking.

The scene is not, however, an obvious evocation of the Immaculate Conception. Even though the Virgin Mary is the central figure, the narrative of the picture centers on John the Baptist, who was the patron saint of Florence and one of Leonardo's favorite subjects. The focus on John is especially true in the first (Louvre) version of the picture, where the angel is dramatically pointing to him, and that may have been one source of the friction between Leonardo and the confraternity.

THE FIRST VERSION (LOUVRE)

Leonardo was a master at storytelling and conveying a sense of dramatic motion, and like many of his paintings, beginning with the *Adoration of the Magi,* the *Virgin of the Rocks* is a narrative. In his first version of the painting, the androgynous curly-haired angel begins the narrative by looking out directly from the scene, catching our eye, smiling enigmatically, and pointing to make us look at the baby Saint John. John in turn is dropping to his knees and clasping his hands in reverence toward the baby Jesus, who returns the gesture with a sign of blessing. The Madonna, her body twisted in motion, glances down at John and grasps his shoulder protectively while hovering her other hand over Jesus. And as our eyes finish a clockwise rotation of the scene, we notice the left hand of the angel holding Jesus as he leans on the rocky precipice over a pond, his hand touching the ledge. Taken in as a whole, it becomes a sequential medley of hand gestures presaging *The Last Supper.*

The angel's pointing finger is the main feature that distinguishes the first version from the second. Thanks to modern technology, we know that Leonardo wrestled with the question of including this gesture. In 2009 technicians at the Louvre deployed an advanced set of infrared imaging techniques on the first version of the *Virgin of the Rocks,* which revealed an underdrawing that Leonardo used to compose the painting. It shows that when he began, he did not plan to have the angel pointing at John. That gesture was added only after most of the background rocks had been painted.[4] Leonardo twice reversed himself, perhaps under pressure from his patrons. The pointing gesture is not in the original underdrawing, is in the first version of the painting, and is not in the second version.

His hesitancy is understandable. The pointing gesture is awkward,

Fig. 64. *Virgin of the Rocks* (first version, Louvre).

Fig. 65. *Virgin of the Rocks* (second version, London).

and Leonardo seems to have sensed it when he did his second version. The angel's bony finger disrupts, in a jarring way, the connection between the Madonna's hovering hand and the head of her baby. The medley of hands becomes a cacophony of competing gestures.[5]

The narrative flow is rescued by the fluid areas of light, which give the painting a sense of unity. In this masterpiece, Leonardo ushered in a new era of art in which light and shade are juxtaposed in a manner that produces a powerful sense of flow.

In Florence, Leonardo had edged away from using mainly tempera paints and had begun to rely more on oils, as had become the practice in the Netherlands, and in Milan he perfected his use of that medium. The ability to slowly apply thin layer upon layer of translucent color allowed him to create the shadings and gentle blurring of outlines that characterized his chiaroscuro and sfumato techniques. It also allowed him to produce luminous tones. The light would pass through the layers and reflect back from the primer coat, making it seem as if the light was emanating from the figures and objects themselves.[6]

Most artists prior to Leonardo differentiated the brightly lit areas of a painting from the shaded areas by adding more white pigment to their colors. But Leonardo knew that light doesn't merely brighten a color; it also reveals better its true and deep tones. Look at where the sunlight strikes the angel's red cloak and the Madonna's blue gown and golden drapery; the colors are saturated and the tones richer. In his notes for a treatise on painting, Leonardo explained, "Since the quality of color is revealed by means of light, where there is more light will be seen more of the true quality of the illuminated color."[7]

The first version of the *Virgin of the Rocks* is a vivid example of Leonardo's using his knowledge of science to inform his art. Its subject is both the Virgin and the rocks. As Ann Pizzorusso pointed out in her study "Leonardo's Geology," the components of the grotto "are rendered with astounding geological accuracy."[8] Most of the formations are of weathered sandstone, a sedimentary rock. But just above the Virgin's head, and also at the top right of the picture, are jutting hard-edged rock formations, with facets that glimmer in the sun. These are diabase, an intrusive igneous rock formed by the cooling of volcanic lava. Even the vertical cracks caused by the cooling are rendered precisely. So is the seam between the sandstone and igneous formation, running horizontally just above the Virgin's head. This is not merely a case of Leonardo's faithfully rendering a scene he saw in nature. The grotto is clearly a product of his imagination, not an actual place he visited. It took a deep appreciation of geology to conjure up a vision that was both so imaginative and so real.

The plants in the picture are located, as they would be in nature, only in the sandstone regions that have weathered sufficiently to permit roots to take hold, both at the top and the floor of the grotto, but not in the hard igneous rocks. The species chosen are botanically and seasonally correct: he depicted only those that would be found in a moist grotto at the same time of year. Yet within these constraints, he was able to choose plants that conveyed his symbolic and artistic aims. As William Emboden demonstrated in his study *Leonardo da Vinci on Plants and Gardens*, "he introduced them into his paintings for their symbolic language, and yet he was careful to portray them in their proper setting."[9]

For example, a white rose is often used to symbolize the purity of Christ, but it would not have grown in such a grotto; so Leonardo instead paints underneath Christ's raised arm a primrose (*Primula vulgaris*), regarded as a sign of virtue because of its white flowers. Faintly discernible above the Virgin's left hand is a swirl of *Galium verum*. "The plant has long been known as Our Lady's Bedstraw and is traditionally the plant of the manger," Emboden wrote. Joseph used it to make Mary's bed, and its white leaves turned to gold when Jesus was born. Leonardo, who was obsessed with spirals and swirls, sometimes slightly altered plants to suit his artistic tastes. For example, at the lower left of the picture is a yellow flag iris (*Iris pseudacorus*) that is depicted with its sword-like leaves not lined up like a fan but slightly contorted to show a spiral pattern, twisting to reflect the subtle turning motions of Saint John and the Virgin.

By the time this first version of the painting was finished, in 1485, Leonardo and his partners had received payments totaling around

800 lire. But a prolonged dispute began when the painters insisted they had spent more than that on materials, especially the gold gilding, and that the work was worth far more. The confraternity balked, and the painting was probably never installed in their church. Instead, it was either sold to another client, perhaps the French king Louis XII, or paid for by Ludovico Sforza as a wedding gift for his niece Bianca and the future Holy Roman emperor Maximilian I. It eventually made its way into the Louvre.

THE SECOND VERSION (LONDON)

During the 1490s, Leonardo worked with Ambrogio de Predis on a new version of *Virgin of the Rocks* for the Confraternity of the Immaculate Conception, to replace the one that had not been delivered. According to the technical studies reported in 2009, Leonardo began with a far different underdrawing. It featured a kneeling Virgin Mary in a posture of adoration, with one hand across her breast. But then Leonardo changed his mind. He covered the new underdrawing with primer and drew another, one that very closely resembles the first version of *Virgin of the Rocks*, except that (as in the original underdrawing for the first version) the angel is not pointing at John the Baptist.[10] In addition, the angel is not peering out from the picture at the viewer. Instead, his dreamy gaze seems to take in the whole scene.

As a result, the narrative is not as distracting. The Virgin Mary becomes the unchallenged center of attention. Our eyes start on her serene face as she watches John kneel, and her hand hovers protectively over her child, this time not interrupted by the angel's intruding finger. The scene becomes one that features the gestures and emotions of the Virgin rather than the angel or John.

Another subtle difference is that the grotto is more closed and there is less sky above. The light is therefore not as diffused but instead comes in directionally as a beam from the left side of the painting, selectively falling upon and highlighting the four characters. As a result, the modeling, plasticity, and three-dimensionality of the shapes are deeply enhanced. Between the first and second versions, Leonardo had been studying light and optics, and the result is an artistic use of light that was new in the history of art. "In its dynamic qualities of variability and selectivity, in contrast to the static, even universal light of the Louvre version, it is the light of a new era," wrote the art historian John Shearman.[11]

The composition of this second version was clearly the work of Leonardo. The question arises, however, how much of the actual painting, which may have been done over the course of almost fifteen years, was by him and how much was delegated to Ambrogio and the assistants at the studio.

One indication that Leonardo delegated some of the work is that the plants are not as authentic as in the first version. "It's very striking, because they go against everything that Leonardo's always done in terms of his botanical art," according to horticulturalist John Grimshaw. "They're not real flowers. They're odd concoctions, like a half-imagined aquilegia."[12] The same divergences can be found in the geology. "The rocks in the National Gallery painting are synthetic, stilted, grotesque characterizations," Pizzorusso wrote. "The rocks in the foreground are not finely bedded but are roughly weathered and massive, giving the appearance of limestone rather than sandstone. The presence of limestone would be incongruous in this geological setting."[13]

Up until 2010, London's National Gallery had stated that its version was not primarily from Leonardo's hand. But after a thorough cleaning and restoration of the painting, the gallery's then-curator Luke Syson and other experts declared that it was in fact painted mainly by Leonardo. Syson conceded that there are lapses in the accuracy of some of the plants and rocks, but he claimed this reflects a more mature and "metaphysical" way of depicting nature that Leonardo began to pursue in the 1490s: "This is no longer a picture just about devout naturalism. Leonardo combined those ingredients he regarded as essential (sometimes simply the most beautiful) to generate things—plants, landscapes, people—which were even more perfect, more completely themselves, than Nature had made."[14]

Especially when viewed after its recent cleaning, the London version does indeed display hallmarks that appear to be by Leonardo's hand. This is true of the angel, whose characteristic radiant curls seem distinctively his, and whose sheer sleeve caught by the sun rays is rendered with a remarkable translucence that comes from Leonardo's talent for applying thin layers of oil. "No one who has looked at it closely can doubt who was responsible for the mouth and chin, and the characteristic curves of the golden hair," Kenneth Clark wrote of the angel.[15] It is also true of the Virgin's head, which like that of the angel suggests the use of Leonardo's characteristic finger blending of paint. "All these effects lie definitively outside Ambrogio's range, or that of any other known pupil," according to Martin Kemp.[16]

This second version of the painting, like the first, was caught up in contractual disputes with the confraternity, and the prolonged negotiation offers further evidence that Leonardo was personally involved in finishing the painting. It was still deemed incomplete by the time he left Milan in 1499, and in 1506 there was another tussle over whether a final payment was due. Leonardo ended up coming back to put finishing touches on the painting. Only then was it finally deemed complete, after which he and Ambrogio received their concluding payment from the confraternity.

TEAMWORK

The questions about what contributions Leonardo's colleagues made to the second *Virgin of the Rocks* highlight the role that collaboration played in his studio. We tend to think of artists as lone creators, holed in a garret, waiting for inspiration to strike. But as evident in his notebooks and in the process that led to his drawing of *Vitruvian Man*, much of Leonardo's thinking was collegial. Ever since his salad days in the art-production bottega run by Verrocchio, Leonardo knew the joys and advantages of having a team. According to Larry Keith, who led the restoration of the National Gallery's *Virgin of the Rocks*, "Leonardo's need to quickly create a studio capable of producing paintings, sculpture, courtly entertainments and other activities meant that he worked closely with established Milanese painters as well as training his own apprentices."[17]

In order to make money, Leonardo at times helped his apprentices produce pieces as if on an assembly line, as had been the practice in

Verrocchio's studio. "Designs circulated between master and pupil using a kind of cut and paste technique involving master drawings and cartoons," Syson explained.[18] Leonardo would create the compositions, cartoons, studies, and sketches. His students would copy them with pinpricks and work together on painting the finished version, often with Leonardo adding his own touches and making corrections. There were sometimes many variations, and different styles can be discerned in a single painting. One visitor to his studio described how "two of Leonardo's pupils were doing some portraits and he from time to time put a touch on them."[19]

Leonardo's apprentices and students did not merely copy his designs. A show at the Louvre in 2012 featured paintings that students and assistants in his workshop did of his masterpieces. Many were variations that were produced alongside his original, indicating that he and his colleagues were together exploring various alternative approaches to the planned painting. While Leonardo worked on the master version, other versions were being painted under his supervision.[20]

HEAD OF A YOUNG WOMAN

Depending on which religious stories you take as the text, the angel in *Virgin of the Rocks* is supposed to be either Gabriel or Uriel. (He's identified on the Louvre website as Gabriel, but the description next to the painting in the museum itself calls him Uriel, proving there is no consensus even within that museum.) Either way, Leonardo's drawing of him is so feminine that even some art critics have referred to him as a female.[21]

The angel, like the one he painted for Verrocchio's *Baptism of Christ*, is an example of Leonardo's proclivity for gender fluidity. Some nineteenth-century critics saw it as a mark of his homosexuality, especially since the positioning and outward gaze of the disturbingly alluring angel make him seem a proxy for the artist.[22]

The androgynous nature of the figure is heightened by comparing the angel to what is generally regarded as a preparatory study for it, a drawing by Leonardo, called *Head of a Young Woman* (fig. 66).[23] The

Fig. 66. Study for *Virgin of the Rocks*.

facial features of the young woman are virtually identical to those of Uriel/Gabriel.

The drawing is fascinating because it is one of the best displays of Leonardo's genius as a draftsman. With a few simple lines and brilliant strokes, concise and precise, he is able to create a sketch of unsurpassed beauty. At first glance it captivates you, then its deceptive simplicity draws you into a prolonged and profound engagement. The pioneering Renaissance art historian Bernard Berenson called it "one of the finest achievements of all draftsmanship," and his protégé Kenneth Clark proclaimed it "one of the most beautiful, I dare say, in the world."[24]

Leonardo sometimes used ink or chalk for his drawings, but in this case he used a silverpoint stylus to incise lines on paper that he had coated with a pale pigment. The grooves are still visible. For highlights, such as the luster on her left cheekbone, he used a white gouache, or watercolor.

The drawing is an exquisite example of Leonardo's use of hatching to create shadows and texture. These parallel strokes are delicate and tight in some places (the shadow on her left cheek) and bold and spacious in others (her back shoulder). The variations in the hatching allow, with just simple strokes, wondrous gradations of shadow and subtle blurring of contours. Look at the nose and marvel at how the hatching models the left nostril. Then look how slightly wider lines make the contour and shadow of her left cheek. The two strong lines creasing her neck and the three strokes delineating the front of her neck seem hasty, but they also convey motion. The free-form curves to the left and right of her head look modernist, yet what they reveal is Leonardo's brainstorming process as it flows through his pen. As the abstract lines cascade down the back of her neck, they hint at the signature curls that he will paint.

And then there are the eyes, which Leonardo made magically liquid. Her right eye has a rounded pupil with a full-on stare, but her left eyelid is heavy, pushing down over the pupil, as if she's dreamily disengaged. Like the angel in the Louvre's *Virgin of the Rocks*, she stares out at us even as her left eye drifts. As you walk back and forth, her eyes follow you. She drinks you in.

CHAPTER 16

The Milan Portraits

PORTRAIT OF A MUSICIAN

Among the many intriguing things about Leonardo are the mysteries that surround much of his work. Take, for example, *Portrait of a Musician* (fig. 67), painted in the mid-1480s. His only known portrait of a man, there are no surviving records or contemporary mentions of it. It is unclear who the subject is and whether the work was commissioned or if it was ever delivered. It is even not certain that Leonardo painted all of it. And like far too many of his pieces, it is unfinished, though it is not known why.

Painted on a walnut panel, which Leonardo had begun to favor, the portrait is of a young man with tightly coiled curls (no surprise there), seen in three-quarter profile, holding a folded sheet of music. His torso, brown vest, and hands are unfinished. Even parts of his face seem missing some of the final layers Leonardo usually applied. And unlike Leonardo's other works, his body faces in the same direction as his gaze, with no sense of movement.

The rigidity is one reason some have doubted that Leonardo painted it. But other elements—the curls, the expressive and liquid eyes, the use of light and shadow—have led most scholars to believe that he at least painted the face, and perhaps one of his students or

Fig. 67. *Portrait of a Musician.*

assistants, such as Giovanni Antonio Boltraffio, added the unfinished and unimpressive torso.[1] What most distinguishes the face as a Leonardo creation is the sense that this is an emotion-laden, real person, with inner thoughts and a whiff of melancholy, whose motions of the mind are about to trigger a movement of the lips.

There is no evidence that the painting was done as a paid commission, nor is it of a notable dignitary. It seems that Leonardo simply decided, on his own, to paint the young man. Perhaps Leonardo was moved by his delicate beauty and golden curls or had a personal connection to him. Some have suggested the subject was Leonardo's friend Franchino Gaffurio, who had become the conductor of the Cathedral choir in Milan in 1484, around the time the portrait was painted. But the portrait does not look like others known to be of Gaffurio, who would have been in his mid-thirties at the time, older than the man portrayed.

I prefer to believe that the portrait is of Atalante Migliorotti, the young musician who accompanied Leonardo a few years earlier from Florence to Milan, bearing the lyre.[2] He would go on to be a distinguished performer, but at the time he was in his early twenties and still working in the Sforza court along with Leonardo. If he was in fact the subject, it would make the *Musician* a personal work that Leonardo undertook for his own satisfaction. We know that Leonardo was taken by Atalante's looks. In his inventory from 1482, there is that item "a portrait of Atalante with his face raised." Perhaps that was a study for this portrait, or even the beginnings of the painting itself.

Although the *Musician* does not have "his face raised," he is gazing out into the light. Leonardo's treatment of the light on his face is the most striking feature of the painting. The spots of luster in the liquid eyeballs show how the light is falling. The illumination is stronger than in other paintings by Leonardo, who wrote that muted light is better for a portrait. But the strong light in this case allowed him to provide a brilliant demonstration of how light hits the contours of a face. The shadows beneath the cheekbone and chin and even the right eyelid make the portrait more lifelike than others of his era. In fact, one flaw in the painting is that the shadows are too harsh, especially under the nose. Leonardo would later warn about the crudeness produced by the use of sharp light:

> An object will display the greatest difference of light and shade when it is seen in the strongest light. . . . But this should not be much used in painting, because the works would be crude and ungraceful. An object seen in a moderate light displays little difference in its light and shade, and this is the case towards evening or when the day is cloudy; works painted then are tender, and every kind of face becomes graceful. Thus, in everything extremes are to be avoided: Too much light gives crudeness; too little prevents our seeing.[3]

The *Musician* illustrates the effects of light and the perils of too much of it. Perhaps the flaw can be explained by the fact that the painting is not fully finished. Parts of the face do not have as many thin layers of oil as Leonardo usually used. If he had continued to perfect the painting, a process that often took him years, there likely would have been a few more strokes, and a bit subtler texture, at least under the nose.

There is one other notable feature about the light. "The pupil of the eye dilates and contracts as it sees a less or greater light," Leonardo noted early on in his studies of the human eye and optics.[4] He also observed how the changes in pupil size take a few moments, as the eyes adjust to the light. Almost eerily, Leonardo has the two pupils of the musician dilated to different degrees: his left eye, which faces the light more directly, has a smaller pupil. Leonardo incorrectly believed that the pupils of the eye dilate separately, when in fact they dilate in unison, and I suspect that he is trying to convey a sense of the passing of a moment as our eyes sweep across the face of the musician, from his left eye to his right.

CECILIA GALLERANI, THE *LADY WITH AN ERMINE*

Cecilia Gallerani was a striking beauty who was born into Milan's educated middle class. Her father was a diplomat and financial agent for the duke, and her mother was the daughter of a noted law professor. They were not exceedingly wealthy; her father died when she was seven, and she had six brothers who divided up the inheritance. But they were cultured and educated. Cecilia composed poetry, delivered orations, wrote letters in Latin, and would later have two novels by Matteo Bandello dedicated to her.[5]

In 1483, when she was ten, her brothers were able to arrange a promising marriage contract for her to Giovanni Stefano Visconti, a member of the family that once ruled Milan. But four years later, before the wedding took place, the contract was dissolved. The brothers had not kept up with the dowry payments. The dissolution agreement noted that the marriage had not been consummated, protecting her virtue.

There may have been another reason the contract was dissolved and the stipulation made about her virtue. Around that time, she attracted the notice of Ludovico Sforza. The de facto Duke of Milan was a ruthless man, but he had good taste. He was attracted to Cecilia for both her mind and her beauty. By 1489, when she was fifteen, she was living not with her family but in rooms provided by Ludovico. The following year she was pregnant with his son.

There was one big problem with their relationship. Since 1480 Ludovico had been contracted to marry Beatrice d'Este, the daughter of Ercole d'Este, the Duke of Ferrara. The arrangement, which represented a major alliance for Ludovico with one of Italy's most ancient noble dynasties, had been made when Beatrice was five, and their wedding was scheduled to take place when she turned fifteen, in 1490. It was to be an occasion marked by great pomp and pageantry.

But Ludovico, enamored with Cecilia, was unenthusiastic. In late 1490 the Duke of Ferrara's ambassador to Milan sent back a candid report. Ludovico was besotted with an "inamorata," he told Beatrice's father. "He keeps her with him at the castle, and wherever he goes, and wants to give her everything. She is pregnant, and as beautiful as a flower, and often he brings me with him to visit her." As a result, the wedding between Ludovico and Beatrice was delayed. It finally took place the following year, with glorious celebrations in Pavia and then Milan.

Over time, Ludovico would come to respect Beatrice and, as we will see, be deeply bereaved when she died. But initially he continued his relationship with Cecilia, who stayed in a suite of rooms in the Sforza Castle. In those days before the pretense of sexual discretion was required of rulers, Ludovico continued to confide his feelings to the ever-informative Ferrara ambassador, who reported them back to Beatrice's father. Ludovico told the ambassador that "he wished he could go and make love to Cecilia, and be with her in peace, and this was what his wife wanted too, because she did not want to submit to him." Finally, after Cecilia gave birth to their son, who was fulsomely celebrated in sonnets by the court poets, Ludovico arranged for her to be married to a wealthy count, and she settled into the life of a respected literary patron.

Cecilia Gallerani's alluring beauty would be captured for the ages. At the height of their relationship, around 1489, when she was fifteen, Ludovico commissioned Leonardo to paint her portrait (fig. 68). It was his first painting assignment for Leonardo, who had been in Milan for seven years, had earned a role at court as an impresario, and had just begun work on the horse monument. The result is a stunning and innovative masterpiece, in many ways the most delightful and charming of Leonardo's paintings. Other than the *Mona Lisa*, it is my favorite of his works.

Painted in oil on a walnut panel, the portrait of Cecilia, now known as *Lady with an Ermine*, was so innovative, so emotionally charged and alive, that it helped to transform the art of portraiture. The twentieth-century art historian John Pope-Hennessy called it the "first modern portrait" and "the first painting in European art to introduce the idea that a portrait may express the sitter's thoughts through posture and gestures."[6] Instead of being shown in profile, as was traditional, she is in three-quarters view. Her body is turned to our left, but her head has seemingly snapped to our right to look at something, presumably Ludovico, coming from the direction of the light. The ermine she is holding also seems to have gone on alert, ears cocked. Exceedingly alive, neither have the vacant or undirected stare found in other portraits of the time, including Leonardo's only previous portrait of a woman, *Ginevra de' Benci*. Something is happening in the scene. Leonardo has captured a narrative contained in an instant,

Fig. 68. *Lady with an Ermine*, Cecilia Gallerani.

one involving outward lives and inner lives. In the medley of hands, paws, eyes, and a mysterious smile, we see both motions of the body and motions of the mind.

Leonardo loved puns, including visual ones, and just as the juniper plays on Ginevra de' Benci's name, so does the ermine (in Greek, *galée*) evoke the name of Gallerani. A white ermine also was a symbol of purity. "The ermine would die rather than soil itself," Leonardo wrote in one of his bestiary entries. And also: "The ermine out of moderation never eats but once a day, and it would rather let itself be captured by hunters than take refuge in a dirty lair, in order not to stain its purity." In addition, the ermine is a reference to Ludovico, who had been bestowed the Order of the Ermine by the king of Naples, prompting a court poet to lyricize him as "the Italian moor, the white ermine."[7]

The twisting head and body, a form of contrapposto, had become one of Leonardo's lively signatures, such as in the angel of *Virgin of the Rocks*. The writhing but poised ermine mimics Cecilia's movement, spiraling in synch with her. Both Cecilia's wrist and that of the ermine are gently cocked, protectively. Their shared vitality makes it seem that they are not merely characters in a picture but players in a real-life situation, part of a scene involving a third participant, the off-scene Ludovico who has caught their eye.

At the time, Leonardo was formulating his theories of how the mind works. There is clearly a lot going on in Cecilia's. We see it not only in her eyes but in her hint of a smile. Yet as would be the case with the *Mona Lisa*, the smile is mysterious. Look at Cecilia a hundred times, and you will sense a hundred different emotions. How happy is she to see Ludovico? Okay, now look again. The same is even true for her pet. Leonardo had such skill that he could make an ermine look intelligent.

Leonardo took exquisite care with each detail, from the knuckles and tendons of Cecilia's hand to her braided and gauze-veiled hair. The coiffure and its sheathing, known as a *coazzone*, and her Spanish-style dress, became fashionable in Milan in 1489, when Isabella of Aragon married the hapless Gian Galeazzo Sforza.

The light on Cecilia is softer than that Leonardo used for the *Mu-*

sician. The shadow under her nose is subtler. The greatest intensity of light, as Leonardo demonstrated in his optics studies, comes when a beam hits a surface head-on rather than at an oblique angle. This occurs on the top of Cecilia's left shoulder and right cheek. The illumination levels on the other contours of her face are done with delicate precision according to formulas he had developed for the proportional variations of light intensities at various angles of incidence. His scientific understanding of optics thus enhanced the three-dimensional illusion of the painting.[8]

Some of the shadows are softened by reflected or secondary radiance. For example, the lower edge of her right hand catches a glow from the ermine's white fur, and underneath her cheek the shadow is softened by light reflected from her chest. "When the arms cross in front of the breast," Leonardo wrote in his notebook, "you should show, between the shadow cast by the arms on the breast and the shadow on the arms themselves, a little light seeming to fall through a space between the breast and the arms; and the more you wish the arm to look detached from the breast the broader you must make the light."[9]

To truly appreciate Leonardo's genius, look at the spot in the painting where the ermine's furry head is set in front of the soft flesh of Cecilia's chest. The ermine's head is a marvel of modeling, rendered with three-dimensional clarity as the light strikes each strand of fur covering the subtly contoured skull. Cecilia's flesh is a soft blend of pale tones and reds, and its texture contrasts with that of the hard beads catching spots of lustrous light.[10]

The portrait was celebrated in a sonnet by the court poet Bernardo Bellincioni with his usual orotund exuberance, in this case justified:

> *Why are you angry? whom do you envy, Nature?*
> *Vinci, who has portrayed one of your stars;*
> *Cecilia, now so beautiful, is she*
> *Whose lovely eyes cast the sun into dim shadow. . . .*
> *He's made her seem to listen, but not to speak. . . .*
> *Therefore you may now thank Ludovico,*
> *And the genius and skill of Leonardo,*
> *Who want her to belong to posterity.*[11]

By noting that she seems to listen but not speak, Bellincioni conveyed what makes the portrait so momentous: it captures the sense of an inner mind at work. Her emotions seem to be revealed, or at least hinted at, by the look in her eyes, the enigma of her smile, and the erotic way she clutches and caresses the ermine. She is visibly thinking, and her face flickers with emotions. As Leonardo portrayed the motions of her mind and soul, he played with our own inner thoughts in a way that no portrait had done before.

LA BELLE FERRONNIÈRE

Leonardo's experimentation with light and shadow is seen in another portrait from this period of a woman in the Sforza court, known as *La Belle Ferronnière* (fig. 69). The subject is most likely Lucrezia Crivelli, who succeeded Cecilia as Ludovico's *maîtresse-en-titre* (official mistress), even though such duties would seem to conflict (or perhaps not) with her role as the lady-in-waiting to Ludovico's new wife, Beatrice d'Este.[12] Like Cecilia, Lucrezia bore Ludovico a son and apparently was similarly rewarded with a portrait of herself by Leonardo. Indeed, the walnut panel on which Leonardo painted it was likely from the same tree as the panel for Cecilia's portrait.

Leonardo's depiction of reflected light is most evident under Lucrezia's left cheek. Her chin and neck are in gentle muted shadows. But the light, which comes from the top left of the painting, falls directly on the smooth and flat plane of her shoulder, and then it bounces up and causes a streak of light—almost exaggerated and of a strange mottled hue—on her left jawbone. As Leonardo wrote in his notebook, "Reverberations are caused by bodies of bright nature with flat and semi-opaque surfaces; when struck by light they rebound it back like the bounce of a ball."[13]

Leonardo was then deeply immersed in his scientific study of how light varies according to the angle at which it strikes a curved surface, and his notebooks are filled with carefully measured and annotated diagrams (figs. 71 and 72). No painter captured so perfectly how shadows and highlights on a face can make it appear three-

Fig. 69. *La Belle Ferronnière.*

dimensional and perfectly modeled. The problem is that the streak of light on Lucrezia's cheekbone is so glaring that it seems unnatural, causing some to speculate that it was later painted by an overeager pupil or restorer. That seems unlikely. I think it's more probable that Leonardo was so intent on showing light reflected into a shadow that he overdid it slightly, daring to be unsubtle.

In this portrait, Leonardo also continued to experiment with his haunting method of creating a stare or gaze that seems to follow a viewer around a room. This "*Mona Lisa* effect" is not magical; it simply comes from drawing a realistic set of eyes staring directly at the viewer with proper perspective, shading, and modeling. But Leonardo discovered that the effect works best when the gaze is intense and the eyes slightly off-kilter, thus making it more noticeable. He was refining the technique he had used in *Ginevra de' Benci*. Ginevra's stare seems slightly averted and distant, until you look at each eye individually and directly; then you see that each in its own way is looking at you.

Likewise, in *La Belle Ferronnière*, Lucrezia seems to be staring so directly that it can make us uncomfortable. When you look at each eye individually, it seems to be looking right at you, and this seems true even as you walk back and forth in front of the painting. But when you try to engage both of her eyes at the same time, they seem slightly unaligned. Her left eye appears to be looking off into the distance, perhaps drifting a bit to the left, partly because the eyeball is shifted. It is hard to meet her gaze in both eyes.

La Belle Ferronnière is not in the same league as *Lady with an Ermine* or the *Mona Lisa*. There's a hint of a smile, but it's not truly alluring or mysterious. The reflected light on the left jawbone seems too studied. The hair is so flat and uninspired, especially compared to Leonardo's usual standards, that it seems to have been painted by others. The head is turned but the body is rigid rather than having even a hint of a Leonardesque twist. The headband and necklace display no mastery of modeling; in fact, they look somewhat unfinished. Only the ribbons on her shoulders flow and catch the light in a masterful way.

The great Bernard Berenson wrote in 1907, "One would regret to have to accept this as Leonardo's own work," though Berenson ultimately did. His protégé Kenneth Clark suggested that it was churned out to please the duke but not captivate the ages. "I am now inclined to think that the picture is by Leonardo, and shows how in these years he was willing to subdue his genius to the needs of the court." There is enough evidence, I think, to support an attribution, in whole or part, to Leonardo: the use of a walnut panel similar in grain to that of *Lady with an Ermine*, the existence of some court sonnets that seem to refer to his painting such a work, and the fact that some aspects of the painting have a beauty worthy of the master. Perhaps it was a collaborative work of his studio, produced to fulfill a ducal commission, with some involvement from Leonardo's brush but not his heart and soul.[14]

PORTRAIT OF A YOUNG FIANCÉE, ALSO KNOWN AS *LA BELLA PRINCIPESSA*

In early 1998 a profile of a young woman drawn with colored chalk on vellum was put up for auction at Christie's in Manhattan (fig. 70). The artist and subject were unknown, and it was described in the catalogue as the work of one of the early nineteenth-century Germans who imitated the style of the Italian Renaissance.[15] A collector named Peter Silverman, who had an eye for spotting hidden treasures, saw it in the catalogue and was so intrigued that he went to inspect it at the showroom. "This is really good," he later recalled thinking. "I don't understand why it's catalogued as nineteenth century." He sensed that it had actually been made during the Renaissance. So he submitted a bid of $18,000, double the minimum estimate set by the auction house. It was not quite enough. His bid was topped by one of $21,850, and Silverman assumed that he would never see the portrait again.[16]

But nine years later Silverman happened into a gallery on Manhattan's Upper East Side owned by Kate Ganz, a respected dealer who specialized in Italian Old Master drawings. On an easel in the middle of a table near the door sat the beguiling portrait. Once again he became convinced it was by a Renaissance master. "The young woman seemed alive and breathing, every feature perfect," he recalled. "Her mouth was serene, her lips gently parted with the subtlest hint of expression, but her eye in profile was radiant with emotion. The formality of the portrait could not mask her blushing youth.

Fig. 70. *Portrait of a Young Fiancée*, also known as *La Bella Principessa*.

She was exquisite."[17] Feigning nonchalance, he asked Ganz the price. She offered to sell it for about what it had sold for nine years earlier. Silverman's wife hastily arranged for a wire transfer of the money, and he walked out of the gallery with the picture wrapped in an envelope under his arm.

As a work of art, the picture is alluring but not extraordinary. The subject is portrayed in conventional profile, body rigid, with little of Leonardo's usual sense of coiled movements of the body and mind. Its primary artistic distinction is the subject's hint of a smile that changes slightly based on the viewer's angle and distance, thus prefiguring that of the *Mona Lisa*.

What is most interesting about the portrait is Silverman's quest to prove that it was by Leonardo. Like most artists of his time, Leonardo never signed his works nor kept a record of them. So the question of authentication—figuring out which truly deserve to be called autograph works by Leonardo—becomes yet another fascinating aspect of grappling with his genius. In the case of the portrait that Silverman bought, the saga involved a combination of detective work, technical wizardry, historical research, and connoisseurship. The interdisciplinary effort, which wove together art and science, was worthy of Leonardo, who would have appreciated the interplay between those who love the humanities and those who love technology.

The process began with connoisseurs, people with a deep intuition about works of art based on years of studied appreciation. Many of the attributions made during the nineteenth and twentieth century were driven by the connoisseurship of art authorities such as Walter Pater, Bernard Berenson, Roger Fry, and Kenneth Clark. But connoisseurship can be controversial. It was put on trial, for example, in a 1920s case involving the authenticity of another purported Leonardo work, a copy of *La Belle Ferronnière* that had turned up in Kansas City. "This is not for beginners," Berenson explained as an expert witness. "It takes a very long time before you get a sort of sixth sense that comes from accumulated experience." He declared that the picture in question was not by Leonardo, prompting the owner to dismiss him as "the majordomo of picture guessers." After fifteen hours, the jury declared it could not reach a verdict, and the case was later settled with a compromise. In this instance the connoisseurs were right. The picture in question was not by Leonardo. But the case became a rallying point for populists who felt the world of art connoisseurs was an elitist cabal.[18]

The connoisseurs who initially saw the drawing that Silverman purchased, including the experts at Christie's and those consulted by the dealer Kate Ganz, summarily dismissed the idea that it might be a true Renaissance work. But Silverman was convinced that it was. He brought it to Paris, where he had an apartment, and showed it to the art historian Mina Gregori. She told him, "This drawing shows dual influences: Florentine in its delicate beauty and Lombard in the costume and braid, or coazzone, which were typical of a court lady of the late fifteenth century. Of course, the most obvious artist to come to mind is Leonardo, one of the few artists who made the transition from Florentine to Milanese." She encouraged Silverman to investigate further.[19]

One day Silverman was at the Louvre admiring a portrait by Giovanni Antonio Boltraffio, who worked in Leonardo's studio. There he ran into Nicholas Turner, a former curator at the British Museum and the Getty in Los Angeles. Silverman pulled out his digital camera and showed him a photograph of the portrait. "I saw a transparency of this not long ago," Turner said, calling the work "remarkable." At that point Silverman still assumed the work was by one of Leonardo's pupils or disciples. Turner surprised him by disagreeing. Pointing out the left-handed slanted hatchings that were Leonardo's hallmark, he said that it was likely by the master himself. "All aspects of the shading of this portrait provide visual testimony of Leonardo's theories of illumination," Turner later pronounced.[20]

The problem with relying on connoisseurs is that in any difficult case there is usually an equal and opposite cadre of them. Among the most prominent naysayers were Thomas Hoving, director of New York's Metropolitan Museum, and Carmen Bambach, the curator of drawings there. Hoving, a charismatic showman, called the picture too "sweet," and Bambach, a respected and diligent scholar, invoked her intuition to declare, "It does not look like a Leonardo."[21]

Bambach also pointed out that there was no known case of Leonardo drawing on vellum. That is true for the four thousand known autograph drawings he made on his own, but the geometrical illustrations he made for two of the editions of Luca Pacioli's *On Divine Proportion* were on vellum. That would turn out to be a clue: it indicated that, if the portrait of the young woman was by Leonardo, then it may have been done for a book produced by someone else.

Ganz, the art dealer who had sold the picture to Silverman, not surprisingly agreed with the skeptical New York connoisseurs. "At the end of the day," she told the *New York Times*, "when you talk about connoisseurship, it comes down to whether something is beautiful enough to be a Leonardo, whether it resonates with all of the qualities that define his handwriting—sublime modeling, exquisite delicacy, an unparalleled understanding of anatomy—and to me this drawing has none of those things."[22]

With connoisseurs divided, the next step was to set up a Leonardesque interplay between intuition and scientific experimentation. Silverman began by having the vellum dated by a carbon-14 test, which measures the decay of carbon in organic material to determine how old it is. The results indicated that the vellum came from sometime between 1440 and 1650. That proved little, since a forger or copier could have found a piece of old vellum. But at least it didn't eliminate Leonardo.

Silverman then took the picture to Lumiere Technology, a Paris-based company that specializes in digital, infrared, and multispectral analysis of artworks. He rode there on the back of a friend's Vespa, clutching the portrait in his arms. Pascal Cotte, the firm's founder and chief technology officer, made a series of super-high-resolution digital photographs that could capture 1,600 pixels per square millimeter. That enabled the image to be magnified hundreds of times, showing each strand of hair.

The magnified images allowed a precise comparison of the picture's details with works known to be by Leonardo. The interlace ornamentation of the young woman's costume, for example, had loops and knotwork that were twined in the same way as the ornamentation in *Lady with an Ermine*, and they were even done with the shadows meticulously drawn and the proper perspective as the ornamentation receded.[23] As Vasari wrote of Leonardo, "He even went so far as to waste his time in drawing knots of cords." Another example was the iris of the eye. The comparison to *Lady with an Ermine*, Silverman said, "showed a thrillingly identical treatment of each detail, including the outer corner of the eyelid, the fold of the upper eyelid, the contour of the iris, the lower eyelashes, the upper eyelashes, and the juxtaposition of the edge of the lower eyelid with the bottom edge of the iris."[24]

Silverman and Cotte showed the high-resolution studies to other experts. The first was Cristina Geddo, a Leonardo scholar at the University of Geneva. She was struck by the use of three-color (black, white, red) pastel crayons, a technique that Leonardo pioneered and discussed in his notebooks. "Close examination of the portrait's surface reveals it is extensively drawn with fine, left-handed shading (slanting from top left to bottom right), which may be seen both with the naked eye and, far more effectively, in the digital scans made under infra-red light," she wrote in a scholarly journal.[25]

The dean of Leonardo scholars, Carlo Pedretti, also weighed in, writing, "The sitter's profile is sublime, and the eye is drawn exactly as it is in so many of Leonardo's drawings of this period."[26] For example, the proportions of the head and neck, along with the details of the way the eyes are delineated, correspond very closely to a drawing from around 1490, now in the Royal Collection at Windsor, called *Portrait of a Young Woman in Profile*,[27] and of a drawing he would do of Isabella d'Este in Mantua in 1500.[28]

At that point, Silverman and Cotte turned to Martin Kemp, an Oxford don of impeccable integrity whose career was focused on studying Leonardo. Kemp, who regularly received missives asking him to authenticate purported Leonardo works, was not optimistic when he opened, in March 2008, the email of a high-resolution of the portrait from Lumiere Technology. "Oh, dear, another bout of painful correspondence," he thought. But as he magnified the image on his computer and carefully studied the left-handed hatching and details, he felt a shiver of excitement. "If you look at the hair band, it pulls this little dip in the back of her hair," he said. "Leonardo always had that wonderful feeling for the stiffness of materials, for how they react under pressure."[29]

Kemp, who took no money or expenses for his expert opinions, agreed to travel to see the original, by then stored in a Zurich bank vault. He was cautious, but after studying the portrait for a few hours from every angle, he became more positive. "Her ear plays a subtle game of hide-and-seek below the gentle waves of her hair," he noticed. "The iris of her pensive eye retains the translucent radiance of a living, breathing person."[30]

Kemp became a believer. "After forty years in the Leonardo business, I thought I'd seen it all," he told Silverman. "But I had not. The delight I had when I first saw it has been reinforced enormously. I'm absolutely convinced." He partnered with Cotte to accumulate more evidence and publish it as a book, *La Bella Principessa: The Story of the New Masterpiece by Leonardo Da Vinci*.[31]

The subject's dress and her *coazzone* hairstyle indicate that she was connected to Ludovico Sforza's court in Milan in the 1490s. Leonardo had already painted two of Ludovico's mistresses, Cecilia Gallerani in *Lady with an Ermine* and Lucrezia Crivelli in *La Belle Ferronnière*. Who might this third woman be? Through a process of elimination, Kemp identified her as Bianca Sforza, the duke's illegitimate (but later legitimated) daughter. In 1496, when she was about thirteen, she was married to one of the most important members of the court: Galeazzo Sanseverino, the commander of Ludovico's military and a close friend of Leonardo, who spent time at his stables making drawings for his horse monument. A few months after she married, Bianca died of what may have been a problem pregnancy. Kemp decided to name the portrait *La Bella Principessa*, even though the duke's daughters weren't officially princesses.[32]

There was one other key piece of scientific evidence that sealed the authentication, or at least initially seemed to do so. Cotte had uncovered in his scans a fingerprint on the top of the portrait. If it could be matched to a fingerprint on another work by Leonardo, who often used his hands and fingers to smooth his colors, that would come close to being dispositive.

Cotte gave an image of the fingerprint to Christophe Champod, a professor at the Institute of Criminology and Criminal Law in Lausanne. Finding it almost impossible to read, he crowdsourced the task, posting it on a website and getting close to fifty people offering their annotations. Alas, the result was inconclusive. No patterns could be determined. "I consider this mark as being of no value," Champod declared.[33]

At this point a controversial character entered the tale. Peter Paul Biro, a forensic art examiner based in Montreal, specialized in finding and using fingerprints to authenticate art. He had done so, or claimed to have, with artists ranging from J. M. W. Turner to Jackson Pollock, shaking up the insular club of art connoisseurs in the process. Kemp, Cotte, and Silverman contacted him in early 2009 to render his verdict on *La Bella Principessa*.

Using a digital enlargement of the picture, Biro claimed that he was able to discern ridge-path details of the fingerprint, and he compared it to a fingerprint that Leonardo was known to have left on *Saint Jerome in the Wilderness*. He declared that there were at least eight points of similarity, and he also claimed that these were compatible with a fingerprint on Leonardo's *Ginevra de' Benci*.

Biro demonstrated his discoveries to David Grann, a respected best-selling author and staff writer at the *New Yorker*, who was writing a profile of him. Biro zoomed in on the blurry lines and then showed a series of images taken by multispectral cameras. That still did not make the prints clear enough. He told Grann that he had then applied a "proprietary" technique, which he didn't demonstrate, to produce a clearer image. This new image allowed him, he said, to pinpoint the eight points of similarity with the *Saint Jerome* print. "For a moment, Biro stared at the prints in silence, as if still awed by what he had found," Grann reported. "The discovery, he said, was a validation of his life's work."[34]

Biro detailed his claims in a chapter he wrote for the book by Kemp and Cotte, which was published in 2010. "The correspondence between the fingerprints on Leonardo's *Saint Jerome* and *La Bella Principessa* provides a highly valuable piece of evidence among the numerous other analyses presented in this book," Biro concluded.

Though he said that the evidence was not strong enough to decide a criminal legal case, "the coincidence of the eight marked characteristics is strongly supportive of Leonardo's authorship."[35]

The fingerprint evidence made headlines worldwide when it was released in October 2009. "The art world is abuzz with the recent discovery that a portrait thought to be the drawing of an unknown nineteenth century German artist is now being attributed to the Italian master Leonardo da Vinci," *Time* magazine reported. "And the way the revelation was made is straight out of a Sherlock Holmes novel: researchers traced the portrait to the artist using a 500-year-old fingerprint." The *Guardian* announced, "Art experts believe a new portrait by Leonardo da Vinci may have been discovered thanks to a 500-year-old fingerprint," and the BBC headline was "Finger Points to New da Vinci Art." Silverman gave the inside story to a friend at *Antiques Trade Gazette*, which reported, "*ATG* have had exclusive access to that scientific evidence and can reveal that it literally reveals the hand—and fingerprint—of the artist in the work." The picture that Silverman had bought for around $20,000 was now estimated to be worth close to $150 million.[36]

Then, as with any good detective tale, there was a twist. In July 2010, less than a year after the big headlines, David Grann's colorful and deeply reported profile of Biro appeared in the *New Yorker*. "Somewhere along the way," Grann wrote about the image Biro had been trying to project of himself, "I began to notice small, and then more glaring, imperfections in this picture."[37]

Grann's 16,000-word narrative painted a troubling portrait of Biro, his methods, and his motives. It pointed to discrepancies in his story about analyzing paint samples of Jackson Pollock, recounted the various lawsuits and allegations of fraud Biro had faced, and quoted people alleging that he had tried to milk them for money when authenticating a picture. It also raised questions about the reliability of his "enhanced" fingerprint images, and it quoted a renowned fingerprint examiner who said that the eight similarities Biro had identified didn't exist. Even more explosively, the article reported that the prints Biro claimed to be of Pollock seemed so uniform that an investigator thought it was possible that someone had fabricated them with a rubber stamp. The fingerprints "screamed forgery," the investigator told Grann.[38] Biro vigorously denied the charges and implications in the article. He sued Grann and the *New Yorker* for libel, but his suit was dismissed by a federal judge, whose ruling was later affirmed by an appeals court.[39]

The *New Yorker*'s attack on Biro's credibility undermined his assessment that Leonardo's fingerprints were on *La Bella Principessa*. Kemp and Cotte deleted the chapter of their book written by Biro when an Italian edition was published. Although they insisted that Biro's fingerprint evidence was just one element of the case, it had been a very public element. Opinion seemed to turn back in favor of the doubters.

Then, like a Leonardo spiral, the story took yet another twist. Cotte had noticed on the left side of the picture signs that someone had used a sharp knife to cut the tough vellum, making a couple of small slips, and that there were three tiny holes along the edge. Kemp began to explore the theory that the picture had once been bound in a book. That might also account for why the picture was on vellum, which was used for books at the time. "My hypothesis, at this stage, is that it was in a volume of poetry dedicated to Bianca," Kemp recalled, "and that it may have been a frontispiece."[40]

Kemp then received an email from David Wright, a retired professor of art history at the University of South Florida, telling him about a volume in Warsaw's National Library of Poland. It was a history of the Sforza family, richly illustrated on vellum, that was made to commemorate the wedding of Bianca Sforza. Each of the original versions had a different frontispiece illustration of whomever it was dedicated to. The edition in Warsaw, made in 1496, had been owned by the king of France, who gave it in 1518 to the king of Poland when he married Bona Sforza, a child of Ludovico's hapless nephew Gian Galeazzo Sforza.[41]

By this point there was enough public interest in the story that *National Geographic*, working with PBS, sent a camera crew to accompany Kemp and Cotte to the Polish National Library in 2011 to see what they would find. Using a high-resolution camera to trace how each folio was bound into the volume, they discovered that one sheet was apparently cut out. The vellum of that sheet matched the vellum of *La Bella Principessa*. The missing page would have been right after the introductory texts, just where an illustration was likely to have been located. In addition, the three holes in the picture aligned with three of the five stitching holes in the bound volume. The different number of holes, they surmised, could be explained by the untidy way the portrait was cut out or because two additional stitches were added when the book was rebound in the eighteenth century.[42]

Few things are ever completely certain in the misty realms surrounding Leonardo, and there are still skeptics who doubt that *La Bella Principessa* is by Leonardo.[43] The shapes in the drawing are too delineated, lacking Leonardo's sfumato, and the outlines of the eyeball and contours of the face are too sharp. The facial features are devoid of deep emotion, and the hair lacks luster or curls. "*La Bella Principessa* is not a Leonardo," the *Guardian* art critic Jonathan Jones wrote in 2015. "I honestly don't know how anyone who loves his art could make that mistake. There is a deadness to this woman's eye, a coldness to the way she is posed and drawn that has no resemblance to Leonardo da Vinci's energy or vitality." Referring jokingly to a very dubious claim by a noted art forger that he faked the piece in the 1970s using as a model a girl he knew from Bolton, England, Jones concluded, "She looks so miserable she may well be on a break from working at a Bolton supermarket in the 1970s."[44] The drawing was pointedly excluded when London's National Gallery held a major exhibition focused on Leonardo's work in Milan. "There was never a question that the so-called Principessa could be hung among Leonardo's masterworks," said one of the curators, Arturo Galansino.

On the other side, Kemp became increasingly convinced that it is "close to an open-and-shut case" that *La Bella Principessa* was drawn by Leonardo. "The dating of the portrait to 1496 and the identification of the sitter as Bianca are thus confirmed to a high level of probability," he and Cotte wrote after their examination of the Sforza book in Poland. "The authorship of the portrait by Leonardo is also powerfully supported. Assertions that it is a modern forgery, a

19th-century pastiche, or a copy of a lost Leonardo are all effectively eliminated."[45]

Whichever assessments are correct, the tale of *La Bella Principessa* provides us with some insights into what we do and do not know about Leonardo's art. The intense human and scientific drama surrounding attempts to authenticate the picture, and to debunk it, helps us better understand what makes something an autograph Leonardo.

CHAPTER 17

The Science of Art

THE *PARAGONE*

On February 9, 1498, Leonardo starred in an evening of debates at the Sforza Castle that involved the relative merits of geometry, sculpture, music, painting, and poetry. He gave a rigorous scientific and aesthetic defense of painting, which was then considered a mechanical art, arguing that it should instead be regarded as the highest of the liberal arts, transcending poetry and music and sculpture. The court mathematician Luca Pacioli, who was there to argue for the primacy of geometry, wrote that the audience included cardinals, generals, courtiers, and "eminent orators, expert in the noble arts of medicine and astrology." Most of Pacioli's praise was lavished on Leonardo. "One of the most illustrious participants," he wrote, was the "ingenious architect and engineer and inventor Leonardo, who with each accomplishment in sculpture, casting and painting proves true his name." Not only was this a pun on his name (Vinci, the victor), but it also showed that Leonardo was viewed by others, and not just himself, as an engineer and architect as well as a painter.[1]

This type of staged debate on the comparative value of various intellectual endeavors, ranging from math to philosophy to art, was a staple of evenings at the Sforza Castle. Known as a *paragone*, from the Italian word for "comparison," such a discourse was a way for artists and scholars to attract patrons and elevate their social status during the Italian Renaissance. This was another field in which Leonardo, with his love of both stagecraft and intellectual discussion, could excel as an ornament of the court.

The relative merit of painting in comparison to other forms of art and craft had been debated since the dawn of the Renaissance with a seriousness that transcended our current-day debates on such things as, say, the merit of television versus cinema. Cennino Cennini in his treatise *The Book of Art* wrote, in about 1400, about the skill and imagination required for painting and argued, "It justly deserves to be enthroned next to theory and crowned with poetry."[2] Alberti provided a similar panegyric on the primacy of painting in his 1435 treatise, *On Painting*. A counterargument was made in 1489 by Francesco Puteolano, who argued that poetry and historical writing were most important. The reputations and memories of the great rulers, including Caesar and Alexander the Great, came from historians rather than sculptors or painters, he said.[3]

Leonardo's *paragone*, which he seems to have written and revised multiple times, occasionally rambles, but it is important to remember that this polemic, like many of his prophecies and parables, was designed to be performed rather than published. Scholars sometimes analyze the *paragone* as an essay rather than another example of the importance that the staging of theatrical events played in Leonardo's life, art, and engineering. We should imagine him declaiming the words in front of an admiring ducal court audience.[4]

The goal of Leonardo's argument was to elevate the work of painters—and their social status—by linking their art to the science of optics and the mathematics of perspective. By exalting the interplay between art and science, Leonardo wove an argument that was integral to understanding his genius: that true creativity involves the ability to combine observation with imagination, thereby blurring the border between reality and fantasy. A great painter depicts both, he said.

One premise for his argument was the supremacy of sight over the other senses. "The eye, which is said to be the window of the soul, is the principal means by which the brain's sensory receptor may fully and magnificently contemplate the infinite works of nature." The sense of hearing was less useful, because sounds disappear after they are made. "Hearing is less noble than sight; as soon as it is born it dies, and its death is as swift as its birth. This does not apply to the sense of sight, because if you represent to the eye a beautiful human body composed of proportionately beautiful parts, this beauty . . . has great permanence and remains to be seen."[5]

As for poetry, it is less noble than painting, Leonardo argued, because it takes many words to convey what a single picture can:

> If you, O poet, tell a story with your pen, the painter with his brush can tell it more easily, with simpler completeness, and less tedious to follow. Take a poet who describes the charms of a woman to her lover, and a painter who represents her, and you will see where nature leads the enamored critic. You have classed painting among the mechanical arts, but, truly, if painters were as apt at praising their own works in writing as you are, it would not lie under the stigma of so unhonored a name.[6]

He admitted, yet again, that he was a man "without letters," and thus could not read all of the classic books, but as a painter he did something more glorious, which was to read nature.

Painting is also more elevated than sculpture, he argued. The painter has to depict "light, shade, and color," which the sculptor can generally ignore. "Therefore sculpture has fewer considerations and consequently requires less ingenuity than painting."[7] In addition, sculpting is a messier endeavor, one not suitable for a gentleman of the court. The sculptor is "pasted and smeared all over with marble powder . . . his dwelling is dirty and filled with dust and chips of stone," whereas the painter "sits before his work at the greatest of ease, well dressed and applying delicate colors with his light brush."

Creative endeavors had been divided since antiquity into two categories: the mechanical arts and the more exalted liberal arts. Painting had been classified as mechanical because it was a craft based on handiwork, like that of goldsmiths and tapestry weavers. Leonardo refuted this by arguing that painting is not only an art but also a science. In order to convey three-dimensional objects on a flat surface, the painter needs to understand perspective and optics. These are sciences that are grounded in mathematics. Therefore, painting is a creation of the intellect as well as the hands.

Leonardo then went one step further. Painting requires not only intellect, he said, but also imagination. This element of fantasia makes painting creative, thus more exalted. It allows not only the depiction of reality but also the conjuring up of imaginative inventions, such as dragons, monsters, angels with wondrous wings, and landscapes that are more magical than any that exist in reality. "Thus it was wrong, O writers, to have omitted painting from the category of the liberal arts, since she embraces not only the works of nature but also infinite things that nature never created."[8]

FANTASIA AND REALITY

That, in a nutshell, was Leonardo's signature talent: the ability to convey, by marrying observation with imagination, "not only the works of nature but also infinite things that nature never created."

Leonardo believed in basing knowledge on experience, but he also indulged his love of fantasy. He relished the wonders that can be seen by the eye but also those seen only by the imagination. As a result, his mind could dance magically, and sometimes frenetically, back and forth across the smudgy line that separates reality from fantasia.

Take, for example, his advice about looking at a wall that is "spotted with stains or has a mix of stones." Leonardo could stare at such a wall and observe with precision the striations of each stone and other factual details. But he also knew how to use the wall as a springboard for his imagination and as a "way to stimulate and arouse the mind to various inventions." He wrote in his advice for young artists:

> You may discover in the patterns on the wall a resemblance to various landscapes, adorned with mountains, rivers, rocks, trees, plains, wide valleys and hills in varied arrangement; or again you may see battles and figures in action; or strange faces and costumes, and an endless variety of objects, which you could turn

into complete and well-drawn forms. The effect produced by these mottled walls is like that of the sound of bells, in which you may recognize any name or word you choose to imagine. . . . It should not be hard for you to look at stains on walls, or the ashes of a fire, or the clouds, or mud, and if you consider them well you will find marvelous new ideas, because the mind is stimulated to new inventions by obscure things.[9]

Leonardo was one of history's most disciplined observers of nature, but his observation skills colluded rather than conflicted with his imaginative skills. Like his love of art and science, his ability to both observe and imagine were interwoven to become the warp and woof of his genius. He had a combinatory creativity. Just as he could festoon a real lizard with various animal parts to turn it into a dragonlike monster, for either a parlor trick or a fanciful drawing, he was able to perceive the details and patterns of nature and then remix them in imaginative combinations.[10]

Not surprisingly, Leonardo tried to find a scientific explanation for this ability. When he mapped the human brain during his anatomy investigations, he located the talent for fantasia in a ventricle where it could interact closely with the capacity for rational thinking.

THE TREATISE

Leonardo's *paragone* presentation was so impressive that, according to his early biographer Lomazzo, the Duke of Milan suggested he write it as a treatise. Leonardo set out to do so, and apparently some of the drafts in his notebook were pulled together in a coherent enough fashion that Lomazzo referred to it as a book.[11] Likewise, Leonardo's friend Pacioli reported in 1498, "Leonardo with all diligence has finished his praiseworthy book on Painting and Human Motion." But as with many of his paintings and all of his treatises, Leonardo had a higher standard for using the word *finished*, and he never released his *paragone* nor any treatise on painting for publication. Pacioli was being overly kind when he ascribed to Leonardo the virtue of diligence.

Instead of publishing his notes on painting, Leonardo fiddled with them for the rest of his career, just as he did with many of his paintings. More than a decade later, he was still adding thoughts and making new outlines for a treatise. The result is a medley of notes in a variety of forms: entries he made in two notebooks during the early 1490s, known as Paris Manuscripts A and C; a set of ideas compiled around 1508, later repackaged in what is now called the Codex Atlanticus; and a lost compilation from the 1490s, Libro W. After Leonardo's death, his assistant and heir, Francesco Melzi, drew on these notebook pages to produce in the 1540s what is known, in various versions and lengths, as Leonardo's *Treatise on Painting*.[12] In most editions of that work, Leonardo's *paragone* was published as the opening section.

Most of the passages that Melzi collected were written by Leonardo between 1490 and 1492, around the time he was beginning the second (London) version of *Virgin of the Rocks* and had built up a studio that included young students and apprentices.[13] It is therefore useful to read Leonardo's words as if many of them had been intended to be studied in his workshop as he collaborated with his colleagues on that painting and tried to get the complex lighting challenges right.

In these writings, we can see how Leonardo treated art as a science. The title that Pacioli used for Leonardo's proposed treatise, "On Painting and Human Motion," indicates the connections his mind made. The topics he wove together include shadows, lighting, color, tone, perspective, optics, and the perception of movements. As with his study of anatomy, he began his work on these subjects to help perfect his painting techniques, but then proceeded to immerse himself in the complexities of science for the pure joy of understanding nature.

SHADOWS

Leonardo's power of observation was especially acute when it came to discerning the effects of light and shade. He studied how different types of shadows were caused by varying types of light, and he deployed these as his primary modeling tool to give his painted objects an impression of volume. He noticed how light bouncing off an object could subtly enliven a nearby shadow or cast a glow on the underside of a face. He could see how the color of an object was affected by a shadow cast over it. And he engaged in the interplay between observation and theory that characterized his science.

He had first tackled the complexities of shadows when drawing draperies as an exercise in Verrocchio's studio. He came to understand that the use of shadows, not lines, was the secret to modeling three-dimensional objects on a two-dimensional surface. The primary goal of a painter, Leonardo declared, "is to make a flat surface display a body as if modeled and separated from this plane." This crowning achievement of painting "arises from light and shade." He knew that the essence of good painting, and the key to making an object look three-dimensional, is getting the shadows right, and that's why he spent more time studying and writing about shadows than he did on any other artistic topic.

He felt that shadows were so important to art that, in the outline for his treatise, he planned that the longest section would be on that topic. "Shadows appear to me to be of supreme importance in perspective, because, without them opaque and solid bodies will be ill defined," he wrote. "Shadow is the means by which bodies display their form. The forms of bodies could not be understood in detail but for shadow."[14]

This emphasis on the use of shadows as the key to modeling three-dimensional objects in a painting was a break from common practice of the time. Following Alberti, most artists emphasized the primacy of contour lines. "Which is the most important, the Shadows or Outlines in Painting?" Leonardo asked in his notes for his treatise. The correct answer, he believed, was the former. "It requires much more observation and study to perfect the shadowing of a picture than in merely drawing the lines of it." Typically he used an experiment to show why shading is more subtle than line drawing. "The proof of this is that the lines may be traced upon a veil or a flat glass placed between the eye and the object to be imitated. But that cannot be of any use in shadowing, because of the infinite gradation of shades and the blending of them, which does not allow of any precise borders."[15]

Leonardo proceeded to write obsessively about shadows. A torrent of more than fifteen thousand words on the topic, which would fill thirty pages of a book, still survives, and that is probably less than half of what he originally wrote. His observations, charts, and diagrams became increasingly complex (figs. 71 and 72). Using his feel for proportional relations, he calculated the effects of light striking contoured objects at varying angles. "If the body is larger than the light, the shadow resembles a truncated and inverted pyramid, and its length has also no defined termination. But if the body is smaller than the light, the shadow will resemble a pyramid and come to an end, as is seen in eclipses of the moon."

The deft use of shadows became a unifying force in Leonardo's paintings, distinguishing them from those of other artists of the time. He was especially ingenious in the way he used gradations of color

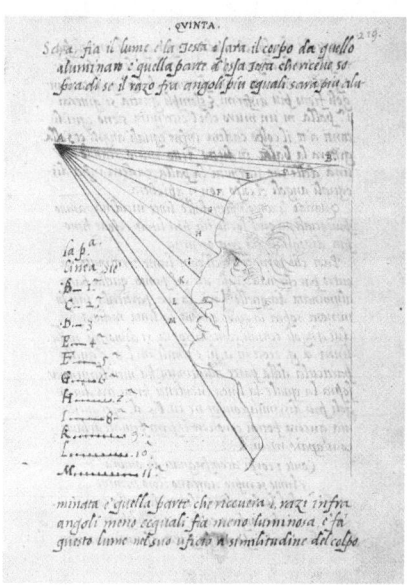

Fig. 71. Study of light hitting a head.

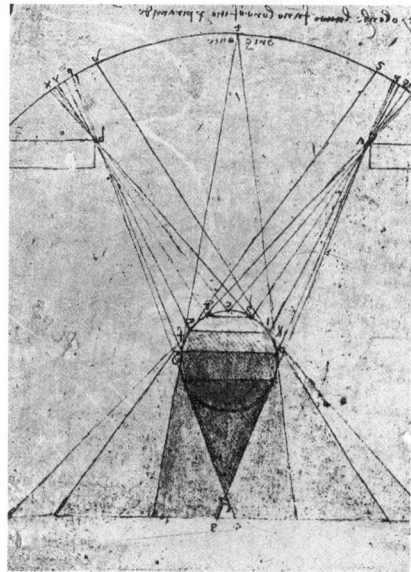

Fig. 72. Study of shadows.

tones to create shadows. The parts of a scene that get the most direct light have the greatest saturated color. This understanding of the relationship between shadows and color tones created a unified coherence to his art.

Having become, by now, a lover of received knowledge as well as a disciple of experience, Leonardo studied Aristotle's work on shadows and combined it with a variety of ingenious experiments involving different sizes of lamps and objects. He came up with multiple categories of shadows and plotted chapters on each: primary shadows that are caused by direct light hitting an object, derived shadows that result from ambient light diffused through the atmosphere, shadows that are subtly tinged with light reflected from nearby objects, compound shadows cast by multiple sources of light, shadows made by the subdued light at dawn or sunset, shadows made by light that has been filtered through linen or paper, and many other variations. With each category, he included striking observations, such as this: "There is always a space where the light falls and then is reflected back towards its cause; it meets the original shadow and mingles with it and modifies it somewhat."[16]

Reading his studies on reflected light provides us with a deeper appreciation for the subtleties of the light-dappled shadow on the edge of Cecilia's hand in *Lady with an Ermine* or the Madonna's hand in *Virgin of the Rocks*, and it reminds us why these are innovative masterpieces. Studying the paintings, in turn, leads to a more profound understanding of Leonardo's scientific inquiry into rebounding and reflected light. This iterative process was true for him as well: his analysis of nature informed his art, which informed his analysis of nature.[17]

SHAPES WITHOUT LINES

Leonardo's reliance on shadows, rather than contour lines, to define the shape of most objects stemmed from a radical insight, one that he derived from both observation and mathematics: there was no such thing in nature as a precisely visible outline or border to an object. It was not just our way of perceiving objects that made their borders look blurred. He realized that nature itself, independent of how our eyes perceive it, does not have precise lines.

In his mathematical studies, he made a distinction between numerical quantities, which involve discrete and indivisible units, and continuous quantities of the sort found in geometry, which involve measurements and gradations that are infinitely divisible. Shadows are in the latter category; they come in continuous, seamless gradations rather than in discrete units that can be delineated. "Between light and darkness there is infinite variation, because their quantity is continuous," he wrote.[18]

That was not a radical proposition. But Leonardo then took a further step. Nothing in nature, he realized, has precise mathematical lines or boundaries or borders. "Lines are not part of any quantity of an object's surface, nor are they part of the air which surrounds this surface," he wrote. He realized that points and lines are mathematical constructs. They do not have a physical presence. They are infinitely small. "The line has in itself neither matter nor substance and may rather be called an imaginary idea than a real object; and this being its nature it occupies no space."

This theory—based on a Leonardesque blend of observation, optics, and mathematics—reinforced his belief that artists should not use lines in their paintings. "Do not edge contours with a definite outline, because the contours are lines, and they are invisible, not only from a distance, but also close at hand," he wrote. "If the line and also the mathematical point are invisible, the outlines of things, also being lines, are invisible, even when they are near at hand." Instead an artist needs to represent the shape and volume of objects by relying on light and shadow. "The line forming the boundary of a surface is of invisible thickness. Therefore, O painter, do not surround your bodies with lines."[19] This was an upending of the Florentine tradition known as *disegno lineamentum*, praised by Vasari, which was founded on linear precision in drawing and the use of lines to create forms and designs.

Leonardo's insistence that all boundaries, both in nature and in art, are blurred led him to become the pioneer of sfumato, the technique of using hazy and smoky outlines such as those so notable in the *Mona Lisa*. Sfumato is not merely a technique for modeling reality more accurately in a painting. It is an analogy for the blurry distinction between the known and the mysterious, one of the core themes of Leonardo's life. Just as he blurred the boundaries between art and science, he did so to the boundaries between reality and fantasy, between experience and mystery, between objects and their surroundings.

OPTICS

Leonardo's realization that there are no precise boundary lines visible in nature was prompted by the observations he made as a painter and by his mathematical knowledge. There was one other cause: his study of optics. Like much of his science, his optics research was begun to help inform his art, but by the 1490s he was pursuing it with a relentless, seemingly insatiable and pure curiosity.

He had originally thought, along with others, that rays of light converged at a single point inside the eye. But he soon became uncomfortable with this idea. A point, like a line, is a mathematical concept that has no size or physical existence in the real world. "If all the images which come to the eye converged in a mathematical point, which is proved to be indivisible," he wrote, "then all the things in the universe would appear to be one and indivisible." Instead, he came to believe, correctly, that visual perception occurs along the entire area of the retina. It was an idea he developed from simple experiments as well as dissections of the eye. And it helped him explain why sharp lines are not visible in nature. "The true outlines of opaque bodies are never seen with sharp precision," he wrote. "This happens because the visual faculty does not occur in a point; it is diffused throughout the pupil [actually the retina] of the eye."[20]

One experiment he did, which was drawn from the work of the eleventh-century Arab mathematician Alhazen, was to move a needle closer and closer to one eye. As it gets near, it does not completely block the vision from the eye, as it would if sight were processed in only a single point on the retina. Instead the needle becomes blurry, a transparent fog. "If you place a sewing needle in front of the pupil as near to the eye as possible, you will see that the perception of any object placed behind this needle at however great a distance will not be impeded."[21] That is because the needle is narrower than the pupil (the hole in the center of the eye that allows light to come in) and the retina (the layer at the back of the eyeball that passes light impulses to the brain). The far left and right of the eye can still pick up light coming from objects behind the needle. Likewise, the eye cannot see a border of an object even if it is up close because different parts of the eye catch the light from the object and its surroundings slightly differently.

One question that stymied him was why images do not appear to be reversed and inverted in our brains. He had studied a device known as a camera obscura, and he knew that the image it produces is upside down and reversed because the lines from the object cross as they go through the aperture. Mistakenly, he assumed that somewhere deep in the eye or brain is another aperture that rights the image. He did not realize that the brain itself can make that adjustment, although his own ability to write and read in mirror script should have provided a clue.

The question of how images turn right-side up after passing through the eye prompted Leonardo to pursue dissections of human and cow eyes and then map the path of visual perceptions from the eyeball to the brain. In one astonishing page of drawings and notes (fig. 73), he shows a view looking down into a skull with its top sawed open. It has the eyeballs in front, and below them are the optic nerves and the x-shaped optic chiasma formed by the nerves on their way to the brain. On the sheet, he described his method:

> Ease away the brain substance from the borders of the dura mater [the hardest of the three membranes surrounding the brain]. . . . Then note all the places where the dura mater penetrates the basilar bone with nerves ensheathed in it, together with the pia mater [the innermost of the three membranes surrounding the brain]. And you will acquire such knowledge with certainty when

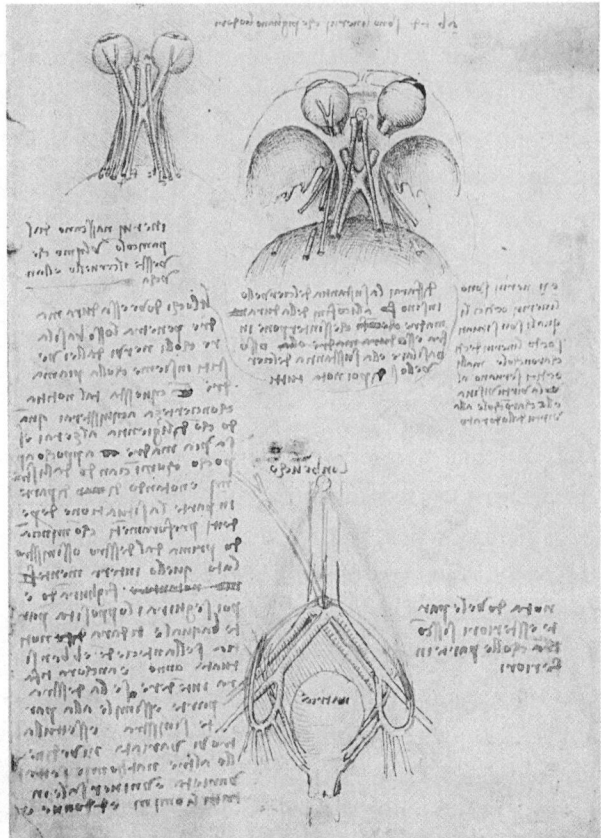

Fig. 73. A view into the skull.

you diligently raise the pia mater, little by little, commencing from the edges and noting bit by bit, the situation of the perforations, commencing first from the right or left side, and drawing this in its entirety.[22]

One problem he faced in dissecting an eyeball was that it tended to change shape when cut. So he came up with an inventive way to solve the problem: "One should place the whole eye in an egg white, boil it until it becomes solid, and cut the egg and the eye transversely in order that none of the middle portion of the eye be poured out."

Leonardo's optics experiments produced discoveries that would not be rediscovered for another century.[23] In addition, they were important in honing his ability to match theory with experiment, and they became an underpinning of his studies on perspective.

PERSPECTIVE

Leonardo realized that the art of painting and the science of optics were inseparable from the study of perspective. Along with the proper ability to deploy shadows, the mastery of various types of perspective allowed painters to convey a three-dimensional beauty on a flat surface. A true understanding of perspective involved more than merely a formulaic approach to sizing objects correctly; he knew it also required studying the science of optics. "Painting is based on perspective," he wrote, "and perspective is nothing else than a thorough knowledge of the function of the eye." So while he was composing his planned treatises on painting and optics, he also gathered ideas for one on perspective.[24]

The field had been well studied. Alhazen had written on the optical science of perspective, and the application of perspective theory to painting had been refined by Leonardo's artistic predecessors, including Giotto, Ghiberti, Masaccio, Uccello, and Donatello. The most important advances came from Brunelleschi, with his famous experiment using a mirror to compare his painting of Florence's Baptistery with the real view, and were codified by Alberti in his masterful *On Painting*.

In his early days in Florence, Leonardo had wrestled with the mathematics of perspective in his preparatory drawing for the *Adoration of the Magi*. The grid he sketched was such a rigorous application of Alberti's concepts that it looks labored, especially in contrast to the delightfully fanciful motions of the sketched horse and camel. Not surprisingly, when he began work on what was supposed to be the final painting, he adjusted the proportions to present a more imaginative picture in which the linear perspective does not constrain the sense of motion and fantasy.

As with many other subjects, Leonardo's serious work on perspective was stimulated in the early 1490s when he became a full participant in the intellectual hothouse surrounding the ducal court in Milan. On his visit to the university in nearby Pavia in 1490 (the same trip that resulted in *Vitruvian Man*), he discussed optics and perspective with Fazio Cardano, a professor who had edited the first printed edition of the study of perspective written by John Peckham in the thirteenth century.

Leonardo's notes on perspective are mixed in with his notes on optics and painting, but he seemed to be considering a separate treatise on the subject. The sixteenth-century artist Benvenuto Cellini said that he owned a manuscript on perspective by Leonardo, which he described as "the most beautiful a man ever made, showing how objects foreshorten not only in depth but also in breadth and height." Lomazzo called it "written very obscurely." Many of his precepts on perspective have survived, but alas, not this manuscript.[25]

Leonardo's most important contribution to the study of perspective was to broaden the concept to include not just linear perspective, which uses geometry to figure out the relative sizes of objects in the foreground and background of a painting, but also ways of conveying depth through changes in color and clarity. "There are three branches of perspective," he wrote. "The first deals with the apparent diminution of objects as they recede from the eye. . . . The second addresses the way colors vary as they recede from the eye. The third is concerned with how the objects in a picture ought to be less detailed as they become more remote."[26]

For linear perspective, he accepted the standard rule of proportion: an object that is twice as far from the eye as another object "will appear half the size of the first, though they be of the same size really, and as the space doubles the diminution will double." He realized that this rule applies to a painting of normal size, one in which the edges are not significantly farther away from the viewer than is the center. But what about a big fresco or mural? One edge might be twice as far from the viewer as the center of the picture is. "Complex perspective," as he called it, occurs when "no surface can be seen exactly as it is because the eye that sees it is not equally remote from all its edges." A wall-size painting, as he would soon show, requires a mix of natural perspective with "artificial perspective." He drew a diagram and explained, "In artificial perspective when objects of unequal size are placed at various distances, the smallest is nearer to the eye than the largest."[27]

His work on linear perspective was not groundbreaking; Alberti had explained much the same. But Leonardo was more innovative when he focused on acuity perspective, which describes how objects far away become less distinct. "You must diminish the sharpness of those objects in proportion to their increasing distance from the eye of the spectator," he instructed. "The parts that are near in the fore-ground should be finished in a bold determined manner; but those in the distance must be unfinished, and confused in their outlines." Be-cause things appear smaller at a distance, he explained, the tiny details of an object vanish, and then even larger details begin to vanish. At a great distance, the outlines of the forms are indistinct.[28]

He used the examples of cities and towers behind walls, where the viewer does not see the base and may not know the size. By making their outlines blurrier, acuity perspective helps to indicate that these structures are in the distance. "How many, in the representation of towns and other objects remote from the eye, express every part of the buildings in the same manner as if they were very near," he wrote. "It is not so in nature, because it is not possible to perceive at any great distance the precise form of objects. The painter therefore who delin-eates the outlines and the tiny details of parts, as several have done, will not accurately depict distant objects, but by this error will make them appear exceedingly near."[29]

In a small notebook sketch done late in his life, which historian James Ackerman called "a token of one of the most consequential changes in the history of Western art," Leonardo shows a receding row of trees. Each one loses a little detail, until the ones near the horizon are just a simple shape devoid of individual branches. Even in his botanical drawings and the depiction of plants in some of his paintings, leaves in the foreground are more distinct than those in the background.[30]

Acuity perspective is related to what Leonardo called aerial perspec-tive: things become blurrier in the distance not only because their details disappear as they become smaller but also because the air and mists soften distant objects. "When objects are distant, there is a great deal of air interposed, which weakens the appearance of forms, and prevents our seeing distinctly the minute parts of such objects," he wrote. "It behooves the painter therefore to touch those parts slightly, in an unfinished manner."[31]

We can see Leonardo experimenting with this concept in many of his drawings. A preliminary sketch of a stampede of horses done for the *Battle of Anghiari* shows those in the foreground drawn with great clarity and sharp focus, while those in the background are softer and less distinct. The effect, as often with Leonardo, is to convey a perception of movement in a still piece of art.

Just as details diminish as objects get more distant, so do colors. To render a scene correctly requires attending to both. "The eye can never arrive at a perfect knowledge of the interval between two objects by means of the linear perspective alone, if not assisted by the perspective of colors," he wrote. "Let the colors vanish in proportion as the objects diminish in size, according to the distance."[32]

Once again he blended theory and experiment. Using a pane of glass, he traced the outline of a nearby tree and then on paper colored it precisely. Then he did the same for a tree at a distance and then another one at double the distance. It will thus be possible, he wrote, to see how color diminishes in tandem with size.[33]

Leonardo's investigations of light and color were successful because he cared about the science of optics. Other perspective theorists, such as Brunelleschi and Alberti, wanted to know how objects could be projected onto a flat panel. Leonardo pursued that knowledge as well, but it led him to another level: he wanted to know how light from objects that enters the eye and is processed by the mind.

By pursuing science that went well beyond its utility for painting a picture, Leonardo could have fallen prey to academism. Some critics have suggested that his excess of diagrams showing light hitting contoured objects and his deluge of notes about shadows were at best a waste of time and at worst led him to be too studied in some later works. To disprove that, you only need to look at *Ginevra de' Benci* and then the *Mona Lisa* to see how a profound understanding of light and shadow, both intuitive and scientific, led to the latter being the historic masterpiece. And to be convinced that he could be flexible and clever in bending the rules of perspective given the needs of a complex situation, one only has to look at, and marvel at, *The Last Supper*.[34]

Fig. 74. *The Last Supper.*

CHAPTER 18

The Last Supper

THE COMMISSION

When Leonardo was painting *The Last Supper* (fig. 74), spectators would visit and sit quietly just so they could watch him work. The creation of art, like the discussion of science, had become at times a public event. According to the account of a priest, Leonardo would "come here in the early hours of the morning and mount the scaffolding," and then "remain there brush in hand from sunrise to sunset, forgetting to eat or drink, painting continually." On other days, however, nothing would be painted. "He would remain in front of it for one or two hours and contemplate it in solitude, examining and criticizing to himself the figures he had created." Then there were dramatic days that combined his obsessiveness and his penchant for procrastination. As if caught by whim or passion, he would arrive suddenly in the middle of the day, "climb the scaffolding, seize a brush, apply a brush stroke or two to one of the figures, and suddenly depart."[1]

Leonardo's quirky work habits may have fascinated the public, but they eventually began to worry Ludovico Sforza. Upon the death of his nephew, he had become the official Duke of Milan in early 1494, and he set about enhancing his stature in a time-honored way, through art patronage and public commissions. He also wanted to create a holy mausoleum for himself and his family, choosing a small but elegant church and monastery in the heart of Milan, Santa Maria delle Grazie, which he had Leonardo's friend Donato Bramante reconstruct. For the north wall of the new dining hall, or refectory, he had commissioned Leonardo to paint a Last Supper, one of the most popular scenes in religious art.

At first Leonardo's procrastination led to amusing tales, such as the time the church prior became frustrated and complained to Ludovico. "He wanted him never to lay down his brush, as if he were a laborer hoeing the Prior's garden," Vasari wrote. When Leonardo was summoned by the duke, they ended up having a discussion of how creativity occurs. Sometimes it requires going slowly, pausing, even procrastinating. That allows ideas to marinate, Leonardo explained. Intuition needs nurturing. "Men of lofty genius sometimes accomplish the most when they work least," he told the duke, "for their minds are occupied with their ideas and the perfection of their conceptions, to which they afterwards give form."

Leonardo added that there were two heads left to paint: that of Christ and of Judas. He was having trouble finding a model for Judas, he said, but he would use the image of the prior if he insisted on continuing to hound him. "The Duke was moved to wondrous laughter, saying that Leonardo had a thousand reasons on his side," Vasari wrote. "The poor prior was confounded and went back to worrying about his garden, leaving Leonardo in peace."

The duke, however, eventually began to get impatient, especially after his wife, Beatrice, died in early 1497, at age twenty-two. Even though he had a series of mistresses, he was bereft; he had come to admire Beatrice and depend on her counsel. She was buried in Santa Maria delle Grazie, and the duke started dining once a week in its refectory. In June of that year, he instructed his secretary "to urge Leonardo the Florentine to finish the work already begun in the Refectory of Santa Maria delle Grazie so that he can then attend to the other wall of the Refectory; and make him sign the contract with his own hand to oblige him to finish within the time to be agreed upon."[2]

It turned out to be worth the wait. The result is the most spellbinding narrative painting in history, displaying multiple elements of

Leonardo's brilliance. His ingenious composition shows his mastery of complex rules of natural and artificial perspective, but it also shows his flexibility at fudging those rules when necessary. His ability to convey motion is evident in the gestures of each of the apostles, and so is his famed ability to follow Alberti's injunction to make movements of the soul—emotions—known through movements of the body. In the same way that he used sfumato to blur hard lines delineating objects, Leonardo blurred the preciseness of perspective and of instants in time.

By conveying ripples of motions and emotions, Leonardo was able not merely to capture a moment but to stage a drama, as if he were choreographing a theatrical performance. *The Last Supper*'s artificial staging, exaggerated movements, tricks of perspective, and theatricality of hand gestures demonstrate the influence of Leonardo's work as a court impresario and producer.

A MOMENT IN MOTION

Leonardo's painting depicts the reactions just after Jesus tells his assembled apostles, "One of you will betray me."[3] At first it looks like a freeze-frame moment, as if Leonardo had used the quickness of his eye, which could make a stop-action image of dragonfly wings, to frame-grab a specific instant. Even Kenneth Clark, who called *The Last Supper* "the keystone of European art," was disconcerted by what he felt was a stationary snapshot of crafted gestures: "The movement is frozen . . . rather terrifying."[4]

I think not. Look longer at the picture. It vibrates with Leonardo's understanding that no moment is discrete, self-contained, frozen, delineated, just as no boundary in nature is sharply delineated. As with the river that Leonardo described, each moment is part of what just passed and what is about to come. This is one of the essences of Leonardo's art: from the *Adoration of the Magi* to *Lady with an Ermine* to *The Last Supper* and the *Mona Lisa*, each moment is not distinct but instead contains connections to a narrative.

The drama begins the second after Jesus' words have been spoken. His head is bowed in silence even as his hands are continuing their movement toward the bread. Like a stone thrown into a pond, his pronouncement causes ripples outward, spreading from him to the edges of the picture and creating a narrative reaction.

As Jesus' words reverberate, subsequent moments from the gospel become part of the drama. The next verses in Matthew are "And they were exceedingly sorrowful, and each of them began to say to him, 'Lord, is it I?'" And from John: "The disciples began to look at one another, perplexed as to which of them he meant."[5] Even as the three apostles on the far left are still reacting, the others are beginning to respond or ask each other questions.

In addition to portraying the motion contained in a moment, Leonardo was masterful at conveying *moti dell'anima*, motions of the soul. "A picture of human figures ought to be done in such a way as that the viewer may easily recognize, by means of their attitudes, the intentions of their minds," he wrote. *The Last Supper* is the grandest and most vibrant example of this in the history of art.[6]

Leonardo's primary method for showing the intentions of the mind was through gestures. Italy was then, as now, a nation of hand-gesture enthusiasts, and Leonardo in his notebooks recorded a variety of them. Here, for example, is his description of how to portray someone making an argument:

Let the speaker, with the fingers of the right hand, hold one finger of the left hand, having the two smaller ones closed; and his face alert and turned towards the people with mouth a little open, to look as though he spoke. If he is sitting, let him appear as though about to rise, with his head forward. If you represent him standing, make him lean slightly forward with body and head towards the people. These you must represent as silent and attentive, all looking at the orator's face with gestures of admiration; and make some old men in astonishment at the things they hear, with the corners of their mouths pulled down and drawn in, their cheeks full of furrows, and their eyebrows raised, and wrinkling the forehead where they meet.[7]

He had learned how much could be communicated by gestures by watching Cristoforo de' Predis, the deaf brother of his painting partners in Milan. Gestures were also important to the monks who ate in the Santa Maria delle Grazie dining hall because they were obliged to observe silence many hours of the day, including at most meals. In one of his pocket notebooks he carried as he walked around town, Leonardo wrote a description of a group of people at a table making gestures as they talked:

> One who was drinking has left his glass in its position and turned his head towards the speaker. Another twists the fingers of his hands together and turns with a frown to his companion. Another with hands spread open showing the palm, shrugs his shoulders up to his ears and makes a grimace of astonishment. Another speaks into his neighbor's ear and the listener turns to him to lend an ear, while he holds a knife in one hand and in the other the loaf half cut through by the knife; and in turning round another, who holds a knife, upsets with his hand a glass on the table. Another lays his hand on the table and is looking. Another blows his mouthful. Another leans forward to see the speaker shading his eyes with his hand.[8]

These read like stage directions, and in *The Last Supper*, which includes many of these gestures, we can see Leonardo choreographing the action.

The twelve apostles are clustered into groups of three. Starting on our left, we can sense the flow of time, as if the narrative moves from left to right. On the far left is the cluster of Bartholomew, James the Minor, and Andrew, all still showing the immediate reaction of surprise at Jesus' announcement. Bartholomew, alert and tough, is in the process of leaping to his feet, "about to rise, his head forward," as Leonardo wrote.

The second trio from the left is Judas, Peter, and John. Dark and ugly and hook-nosed, Judas clutches in his right hand the bag of silver he has been given for promising to betray Jesus, whose words he knows are directed at him. He rears back, knocking over a salt cellar (which is clearly visible in early copies but not the current painting) in a gesture that becomes notorious. He leans away from Jesus and is painted in shadow. Even as his body recoils and twists, his left hand reaches for the incriminating bread that he and Jesus will share. "He that dippeth his hand with me in the dish shall betray me," Jesus says, according to Matthew. Or as in the gospel according to Mark, "Behold, the hand of him that betrayeth me is with me on the table."[9]

Peter is pugnacious and agitated, elbowing forward in indignation. "Who is it of whom he speaks?" he asks. He seems ready to take action. In his right hand is a long knife; he would, later that evening, slice off the ear of a servant of the high priest while trying to protect Jesus from the mob that came to arrest him.

By contrast, John is quiet, knowing that he is not suspect; he seems saddened by yet resigned to what he knows cannot be prevented. Traditionally, John is shown asleep or lying on Jesus' breast. Leonardo shows him a few seconds later, after Jesus' pronouncement, wilting sadly.

Dan Brown in his novel *The Da Vinci Code*, which draws on *The Templar Revelation* by Lynn Picknett and Clive Prince, wove a conspiracy theory that has as one piece of evidence the assertion that the effeminate-looking John is actually secretly meant to be Mary Magdalene, the faithful follower of Jesus. Although a wonderful plot twist for a rollicking novel, it is not supported by the facts. One character in the novel argues that the feminine look of the character was meant to be a clue because "Leonardo was skilled at painting the difference between the sexes." But Ross King points out in a book on *The Last Supper*, "On the contrary: Leonardo was skilled at blurring the differences between the sexes."[10] His alluring androgynous figures begin with his angel in Verrocchio's *Baptism of Christ* and continue through *Saint John the Baptist*, painted in his final years.

Jesus, sitting alone in the center of *The Last Supper*, his mouth still slightly open, has finished making his pronouncement. The expressions of the other figures are intense, almost exaggerated, as if they are players in a pageant. But Jesus' expression is serene and resigned. He looks calm, not agitated. He is slightly larger than the apostles, although Leonardo cleverly disguised the fact that he has used this trick. The open window with the bright landscape beyond forms a natural halo. His blue cloak is painted with ultramarine, the most expensive of pigments. In his studies of optics, Leonardo had discovered that objects against a light background look larger than when against a dark background.

The trio to the right of Jesus includes Thomas, James the Greater, and Philip. Thomas raises his index finger with his hand turned inward in a pointing gesture closely associated with Leonardo. (It appears in many of his paintings, such as *Saint John the Baptist*, and Raphael used it in his depiction of Plato that is believed to be based on Leonardo.) Later he will be known as doubting Thomas because he demanded proof of Jesus' resurrection, which Jesus provided by letting Thomas place a finger in his wounds. Preparatory drawings for Philip and James have survived; the former of them, very androgynous, appears to have also served as a model for the Virgin Mary in the London version of *Virgin of the Rocks*.

The final trio on the right comprises Matthew, Thaddeus, and Simon. They are already in a heated discussion about what Jesus may have meant. Look at the cupped right hand of Thaddeus. Leonardo was a master of gestures, but he also knew how to make them mysterious, so that the viewer could become engaged. Is he slapping his hand down as if to say, I knew it? Is he jerking his thumb toward Judas? Now look at Matthew. Are his two upturned palms gesturing toward Jesus or Judas? The viewer need not feel bad about being confused; in their own ways Matthew and Thaddeus are also confused about what has just occurred, and they are trying to sort it out and turning to Simon for answers.

Jesus' right hand is reaching out to a stemless glass one-third filled with red wine. In a dazzling detail, his little finger is seen through the glass itself. Just beyond the glass are a dish and a piece of bread. His left hand is palm up, gesturing at another piece of bread, which he gazes at with downcast eyes. The perspective and composition of the painting, especially as seen from the door that the monks would use to enter the hall, guide the viewer's eyes to follow those of Jesus, down his left arm to the piece of bread.

That gesture and glance create the second moment that shimmers in the narrative of the painting: that of the institution of the Eucharist. In the gospel of Matthew, it occurs in the moment after the announcement of the betrayal: "Jesus took bread, and blessed it, and broke it, and gave it to the disciples, and said, 'Take, eat; this is my body.' And he took the cup, and gave thanks, and gave it to them, saying, 'Drink ye all of it, for this is my blood of the new testament, which is shed for many for the remission of sins.'" This part of the narrative reverberates outward from Jesus, encompassing both the reaction to his revelation that Judas will betray him and the institution of the holy sacrament.[11]

PERSPECTIVE IN *THE LAST SUPPER*

The only thing straightforward about the perspective in *The Last Supper* is the vanishing point, where all the lines of sight "tend and converge," in Leonardo's words. These receding lines, or orthogonals, point to the forehead of Jesus (fig. 75). When he began his work, Leonardo hammered a small nail in the center of the wall. We can see that hole in Jesus' right temple. Then he cut thin incisions in the wall radiating

Fig. 75. Perspective lines of *The Last Supper*.

out. These would help to guide the lines that were parallel in the imaginary room, such as the beams in the ceiling and the tops of the tapestries, as they receded toward the vanishing point in the painting.[12]

To understand how Leonardo brilliantly manipulated the perspective, look at the tapestries hanging along the two walls. The tops of these tapestries form lines that recede to Jesus' forehead, just as all the perspective lines do. These tapestries were painted in a way that made them appear to be in line with the real tapestries in the actual dining hall, thus creating the illusion that the painting was an extension of the room. Yet it was not a perfect trompe l'oeil of an extended room, nor could it be. Because of the painting's size, the perspective is different depending on the viewer's vantage point (fig. 76). If you stand on the left side of the room, the wall next to you will appear

Fig. 76. The refectory with *The Last Supper*.

to flow seamlessly into the left wall of the painting, but if you look across the room at the right wall, you will notice it doesn't quite align with the painting.

This was just one of many clever manipulations Leonardo used to accommodate the fact that the painting would be seen from different parts of the room. When Alberti wrote about perspective in his treatise, he assumed that all viewers would look at a painting from the same vantage point. But with a painting as large as *The Last Supper*, the viewer might see it from the front or the side or while walking past. That required what Leonardo called "complex perspective," which is a mix of natural and artificial perspective. The artificial part was needed to adjust for the fact that a person looking at a very large painting would be closer to some parts of it than to other parts. "No surface can be seen exactly as it is," Leonardo wrote, "because the eye that sees it is not equally remote from all its edges."[13]

If you stand far enough away from a picture, even a large one, the problem of the edges being at a different distance from you diminishes. Leonardo determined that a proper vantage point for a large picture should be ten to twenty times its width or height. "Stand back until your eye is at least twenty times as far off as the greatest height and width of your work," he wrote at one point. "This will make so little difference when the eye of the spectator moves, that it will be hardly appreciable."[14]

In the case of *The Last Supper*, which is fifteen feet high and twenty-nine feet wide, that would mean the proper vantage would be three hundred to six hundred feet back—clearly not possible. So Leonardo created an artificial ideal vantage point that was about thirty feet from the wall. In addition, he made it fifteen feet off the ground, at eye level with Jesus. No friar would ever view it from such a location, of course. But after making that spot the ideal vantage point, Leonardo proceeded to use optical tricks to make it seem less distorted from a variety of other places in the room from which it would actually be viewed.

Most cleverly, he adjusted and fudged slightly so that the perspective looks natural when viewed from a door in the right wall from which the monks entered. This meant that their first striking perception was that of Jesus' left hand, palm up, directed right at them, as if welcoming them to the room. The angles of the ceiling are slightly higher on the right side. That makes the plane of the picture appear as if it is at eye level of the viewer coming in the door. Because the right wall of the painting is closer to the viewer entering from the door and is lit brighter, it looks bigger and feels a natural continuation of the refectory.[15]

Leonardo used a few tricks to disguise the fact that he had manipulated the perspective. The lines where the floor hits the back and side walls are completely hidden by the table. If you look at the picture carefully and try to imagine the floor lines, you can sense that they would have appeared distorted. In addition, a painted cornice disguises the fact that the ceiling does not extend all the way out to above the table. Otherwise viewers would have noticed that Leonardo slightly accelerated the perspective of the ceiling.

This use of accelerated perspective, in which the walls and ceiling recede toward the vanishing point more quickly than normal, was one of the many tricks that Leonardo learned from the theatrical events he produced. In Renaissance productions, the stage would contain not a rectangular room but one that rapidly became narrower and shorter, to give the illusion of greater depth. It sloped downward toward the audience, and the artificial nature of the scenery was disguised by a decorated cornice, just like the one Leonardo used atop *The Last Supper*. His use of such artifices is another example of why his work on plays and pageants was not time squandered.

In *The Last Supper*, the painted room diminishes in size so quickly that the back wall is just large enough to have three windows showing the landscape outside. The tapestries are not proportional. The table is too narrow for a comfortable supper, and the apostles are all on one side of it, where there are not enough places for them to sit. The floor is raked forward, like a stage, and the table is slanted a bit toward us as well. The characters are all at the forefront, as if in a play, and even their gestures are theatrical.

The tricks of perspective are accompanied by other clever contrivances, including little touches to make the scene appear as if it is connected to the monks eating in the refectory. The light in the painting appears to come from the actual window that is high on the left wall of the refectory, blending reality with imagination (fig. 76). Look at the right wall in the painting; it's bathed in afternoon light as if from the actual window. Also notice the legs of the table: their shadows are cast as if from this source.

The tablecloth shows alternating concave and convex folds, as if it had been pressed and stored in the monk's laundry room before being put on the table. Two little serving platters have eels garnished with fruit slices. They have no obvious religious or iconographic meaning; however, river eels were popular in Italy at the time, and we know that Leonardo, although usually a vegetarian, put "eels and apricots" on at least one of his shopping lists.[16]

All told, *The Last Supper* is a mix of scientific perspective and theatrical license, of intellect and fantasy, worthy of Leonardo. His study of perspective science had not made him rigid or academic as a painter. Instead, it was complemented by the cleverness and ingenuity he had picked up as a stage impresario. Once he knew the rules, he became a master at fudging and distorting them, as if creating perspectival sfumato.

DETERIORATION AND RESTORATION

When Leonardo used oil paint, he would apply a stroke or two, touch and retouch, meditate for a while, then add a few more layers until he had it perfect. This permitted him to show subtle gradations in shadows and blur the borders of objects. His strokes were so light and layered that individual brushstrokes are imperceptible, and he sometimes waited hours or days before gently adding more thin layers and retouchings.

Unfortunately, this leisurely process was not a luxury allowed the painter of a typical wall fresco, which required that the paint be applied onto wet plaster in order to remain fixed. Once a patch of plaster had been put on the wall, that area of the painting had to be completed in one day's session, before it dried, and could not easily be reworked later.

Verrocchio, who did not paint frescoes, never taught the technique to his pupils, and it was clearly unsuited to Leonardo's unhurried style. Instead, he decided to paint directly on the dry plaster wall, which he coated with a layer of ground white stone and then white lead primer. He used tempera paint, in which pigments were mixed into water and egg yolk, along with oil paint, in which pigments were mixed into walnut or linseed oil. Recent scientific analysis of *The Last Supper* shows that he experimented with varying oil-tempera proportions in different parts of the painting. Mixing water-based and oil-based pigments allowed him—or so he thought—to indulge in adding layer after layer of subtle strokes, building them up over weeks to create the shapes and tones he wanted.[17]

Leonardo finished the painting by early 1498, and the duke rewarded him with a bonus of a vineyard near the church, which he owned for the rest of his life. But after only twenty years, the paint began to flake, and it became evident that Leonardo's experimental technique was a failure. When Vasari published his biography of Leonardo in 1550, he reported that the painting was "ruined." By 1652 the painting was so faint and dissipated that the monks felt comfortable breaking a doorway through the wall at the bottom, cutting off the feet of Jesus, which were probably crossed in a manner prefiguring the crucifixion.

Over the years, there have been at least six major attempts to restore the painting, many of which only made the situation worse. The first recorded effort was in 1726 by a curator who used oil paint to fill in missing sections and then put a coat of varnish on top. Less than fifty years later, another restorer stripped away all that the first had done and started repainting the faces on his own; a public outcry forced him to stop with only three faces left to be done. During the French Revolution, anticlerical forces scratched out the eyes of the apostles, and then the refectory was used as a prison. A subsequent restorer tried to remove the painting from the wall, mistakenly thinking it was a fresco. In the early twentieth century, two cleanings were done that avoided further damaging the painting and slowed its deterioration. Allied bombs hit the refectory during World War II, but the painting was protected by sandbags.

The latest restoration, which began in 1978 and lasted twenty-one years, was the most extensive ever. Chief curator Pinin Brambilla Barcilon and her team began by using infrared reflectoscopy and microscopic samples to try to discover, as best as possible, the original elements of the painting. She also had her restorers study Leonardo's drawings and the copies of the painting made during his lifetime. The original intention was to have the wall display only what could be known to be done by Leonardo's hand, but that turned out to be unsatisfying because so little remained. So the restorers reconstructed the missing areas in a way that indicated what was and wasn't original; where it was not possible to discern the original artwork, the team used subtle watercolors with a lighter hue to give a sense of the original while indicating that these sections were speculative.[18]

Not everyone was pleased. Art critic Michael Daley wrote that the result was "a distinctly mongrel work showing alarmingly little original paint and very much alien 'compensatory' and 'reintegrating' new paint." But Brambilla Barcilon generally drew praise for creating and re-creating what is, in fact, a piece of art that seems to be as deeply faithful to the original as is possible. "Not only was the original color recovered, but also the clarity of the architectural structure, the perspective devices, and the physiognomies," she said. "The faces, burdened with grotesque features from so many restorations, again manifest a genuine expressiveness. Now the faces of the apostles seem to genuinely participate in the drama of the moment and evoke the gamut of emotional responses intended by Leonardo to Christ's revelation."[19]

As a result, *The Last Supper*, both in its creation and in its current state, becomes not just an example of Leonardo's genius but also a metaphor for it. It was innovative in its art and too innovative in its methods. The conception was brilliant but the execution flawed. The emotional narrative is profound but slightly mysterious, and the current state of the painting adds another thin veil of mystery to the ones that so often shroud Leonardo's life and work.

CHAPTER 19

Personal Turmoil

CATERINA'S DEATH

On the rare occasions when he recorded a family event in his notebooks, Leonardo sometimes displayed a notarial tic of repeating the date. Thus he recorded the arrival of his mother, Caterina, now widowed and in her sixties, to live with him in Milan:

On the 16th day of July.
Caterina came on the 16th day of July 1493.[1]

During her years with her husband, Accattabriga, Caterina had four daughters and a son. But sometime around 1490 her husband died and their son was killed by a shot from a crossbow. In his notebook shortly after that, Leonardo jotted, "Can you tell me what la Caterina wishes to do?" Apparently, she wanted to come live with him.

On a page adjoining the one in his notebook where he records Caterina's arrival, Leonardo writes a rudimentary family tree that she likely helped him make, listing the names of his father and grandparents. In June 1494 she is included in an accounting of his expenses: he gives 3 soldi to Salai and 20 soldi to her.[2]

She apparently died later that month. A record in the state archives of Milan reports, "On Thursday 26 June at the Parish of the

Saints Nabore and Felix at Porta Vercellina, Caterina from Florence, 60 years old, died of malaria." The evidence from the earlier archival records is that she was actually about fifty-eight, which is close enough to be in accord given the vagaries of records at the time.[3]

Leonardo sublimated whatever emotions he felt; he records nothing about her death, only an accounting of the cost of her funeral. On the listing of soldis he spent, he even crossed out the word "death" and wrote "burial."[4]

Expenses for Caterina's ~~death~~. burial:

For 3 pounds of candle wax	s. 27
For the bier	s. 8
A pall for the bier	s. 12
For bearing and placing a cross	s. 4
For the bearers	s. 8
For 4 priests and 4 clerks	s. 20
Bell, book, sponge,	s. 2
For the gravediggers	s. 16
For the dean	s. 8
For the license	s. 1
	s. 106

[Earlier expenses]

Doctor	s. 5
Sugar and candles	s. 12
	s. 123

The detachment seems odd, and some have argued that the expenses seem low for a mother's funeral. He would spend four times as much in 1497 on the silver cloth, velvet trim, and tailoring for a cloak for Salai.[5] But a careful look shows that it was, in fact, a funeral suitable for his mother rather than a household servant. It was brightly lit, featured four priests, and was carefully planned and recorded for posterity.[6]

CAREER STRUGGLES

When he began painting *The Last Supper* around 1495, Leonardo was at a high point in his career. With his official appointment as artist and engineer of the Sforza court, he was comfortably ensconced at Milan's old palace, the Corte Vecchia, with his retinue of assistants and students. He was renowned as a painter, admired as the sculptor of the mammoth clay model for the horse monument, beloved as a pageant impresario, and respected as a student of optics, flight, hydraulics, and anatomy.

But his life became unsettled in the late 1490s, after Caterina's death and the completion of *The Last Supper*. The bronze for his horse monument had been redirected in 1494 to make cannon to defend against a possible French invasion, and it soon became clear that Ludovico was not going to replace it. Instead of major new commissions or portraits of ducal mistresses, he found himself doing interior design work and engaging in disputes over pay and performance. All the while, Duke Ludovico became increasingly preoccupied, and rightly so, by the French threats to his tenuous hold on power.

One of Leonardo's projects was doing the decorative painting for a set of small rooms in the Sforza Castle, known as the *camerini*, that the duke planned to use as his private retreat. One of the vaulted wood-paneled rooms, the Sala delle Asse, was designed by Leonardo as an enchanted painted forest with sixteen trees, figuratively serving as an architectural fantasia of columns. Their branches intertwined in complex patterns worthy of his mathematical mind, and woven through this caprice was a golden rope that twisted into beautifully complex knots, a lifelong love of his. "In the trees we find a beautiful invention by Leonardo, where all the branches transform themselves into bizarre knots," wrote Lomazzo.[7]

The execution did not go as well as the conception, as was often the case with Leonardo. There was a dispute, and one of the duke's secretaries wrote in June 1496, "The painter who is decorating the camerini caused something of a scandal today, and for this reason he has left."[8] The secretary asked if someone could be sent from Venice to finish the work.

That never happened, and Leonardo resumed the commission in early 1498, just as he was finishing work on *The Last Supper*. But there were other disputes that are revealed in letters drafted in his notebooks. One angry missive from 1497 has been ripped in half, so we have only fragments of sentences that express his frustration. "You remember the commission to paint the camerini" reads one phrase. "Of the horse I will say nothing because I know the times are bad," is another. Then comes a tumult of complaints, including "two years of my salary still not received."[9] In another letter drafted for the duke, Leonardo again complained about money and seems to imply that he had to put aside work on *The Last Supper* to make money by decorating the Sala delle Asse. "Perhaps your Excellency did not give further orders to [pay me], believing that I had money enough," he wrote. "It vexes me greatly that having to earn my living has forced me to interrupt the work and to attend to small matters, instead of following up the work which your Lordship entrusted to me."[10]

As with *The Last Supper*, Leonardo was too slow-paced in painting the Sala delle Asse to put up with using the traditional fresco method that required each section to be executed rapidly on wet plaster before it dried. Instead, he again used a tempera-oil mixture on a dry wall (the wood panels of the room had been removed, unfortunately). The dry plaster did not absorb the pigments, resulting in the same deterioration as suffered by *The Last Supper*. It was restored badly around 1901, salvaged in the 1950s, and in 2017 was in the midst of a more careful, laser-guided restoration.

After his temperamental disputes involving the Sala delle Asse, Leonardo hit a low point. He found himself drafting job applications, including a letter written in the third person to the council of the nearby town of Piacenza, which was commissioning brass doors for the cathedral there. He wrote the letter extolling himself as if he planned to have a supporter send it on his behalf. "Open your eyes and look carefully that your money is not spent as to purchase your own shame," the letter reads. "There is not a man who is capable—and you may believe me—except Leonardo the Florentine, who is making the bronze horse of the Duke Francesco."[11]

Larger forces intervened to rescue Leonardo from his employment concerns. In the summer of 1499, an invasion force sent by the new French king, Louis XII, was bearing down on Milan. Leonardo added up the money in his cash box, 1,280 lire, distributed some to Salai (20 lire) and others, and then proceeded to hide the rest in paper packets around his studio to keep it safe from invaders and looters. At the beginning of September, Duke Ludovico fled the city, which the French king entered a month later. As Leonardo feared, mobs destroyed the homes of many of his friends and looted their treasures. His studio was spared, but the French troops destroyed the clay model of his unbuilt horse monument by shooting arrows at it.

The French were, it turned out, protective of Leonardo. The day after his arrival, the king went to see *The Last Supper,* and he even asked whether it might be possible to cart it back to France. Fortunately, his engineers told him it was impossible. Instead of fleeing, Leonardo spent the next few months working with the French. He made a note to contact one of the painters who had arrived in Milan with King Louis and to get from him "the method of using dry colors and the white salt method and how to make coated paper." On the same page, he laid out a leisurely set of preparations for the long trip from Milan back to Florence and Vinci, which he would not begin until December. "Have two covered boxes made to be carried on mules. One of which leave at Vinci. Buy some tablecloths, napkins, cloaks, caps, and shoes, four pair of hose, a chamois jerkin and skins to make new ones. Sell what you cannot take with you." In other words, he was not scurrying to escape from the French.

In fact, he had forged a secret deal with the new French governor of Milan, the Count of Ligny, to meet him in Naples and act as a military engineer inspecting fortifications. In one of the most curious entries in his notebooks, on the same page as his list preparing for his trip, Leonardo writes not only in his mirror script but using a simplistic code in which he spells names and cities backward: "Go and find ingil [Ligny] and tell him you will wait for him at amor [Roma] and that you will go with him to ilopan [Napoli]."[12]

That plot never came to fruition. What made Leonardo finally leave Milan was the news that his former patron Ludovico was plotting a comeback. In late December, Leonardo made arrangements to transfer 600 florins from his Milanese bank to an account in Florence, then left with his retinue of assistants and his friend the mathematician Luca Pacioli. Eighteen years after he had arrived in Milan with a lute and a letter for Ludovico proclaiming his talents as an engineer and artist, Leonardo da Vinci was returning home to Florence.

CHAPTER 20

Florence Again

THE RETURN

Leonardo's first stop on his journey back to Florence in early 1500 was the town of Mantua. There he was hosted by Isabella d'Este, the sister of Ludovico's late wife, Beatrice. An avid and spoiled art collector from one of Italy's most venerable families, Isabella was eager to have a portrait of her done by Leonardo, and during his short stay he dutifully made a preparatory chalk drawing.

From there he went to Venice, where he offered military advice on defending against a threatened Turkish invasion. Always interested in the flow of water and its military uses, he devised a mobile wooden lock that he believed could allow the Isonzo River to flood a valley that would be used by any invaders.[1] Like many of his visionary schemes, it was never implemented.

He also dreamed up ideas for protecting a port such as Venice by equipping a corps of underwater defenders with diving suits, breathing gear, goggles, a mask, and wineskin airbags. The mask was attached to cane tubes that led up to a diving bell floating on the surface. After sketching some of these items in his notebook, he wrote that he was keeping a few of his plans secret: "Why is it that I do not describe my method for remaining underwater and how long I can remain there without coming up for air? I do not wish to publish this because of the evil nature of men, who might use it for murder on the sea bed."[2] As with many of his inventions, his scuba gear was, at least during his time, just over the edge of practicality. It would be centuries before his ideas came to fruition.

When Leonardo reached Florence in late March 1500, he found a city that had just lived through a reactionary spasm that threatened to destroy its role in the vanguard of Renaissance culture. In 1494 a radical friar named Girolamo Savonarola had led a religious rebellion against the ruling Medici and instituted a fundamentalist regime that imposed strict new laws against homosexuality, sodomy, and adultery. Some transgressions were punished by stoning and burning. A militia of young boys was organized to patrol the streets and enforce morals. On Mardi Gras of 1497 Savonarola led what became known as the "Bonfire of the Vanities," in which books, art, clothing, and cosmetics were set aflame. The following year, popular opinion turned on him, and he was hanged and burned in the central square of Florence. By Leonardo's return, the city had again become a republic that celebrated the classics and art, but its confidence was shaken, its exuberance dampened, and the finances of its government and guilds drained.

Leonardo would make Florence his base for most of 1500 to 1506, boarding comfortably with his entourage at the church of Santissima Annunziata. In many ways, it would be the most productive period of his life. There he began two of his greatest panel paintings, the *Mona Lisa* and *Virgin and Child with Saint Anne*, as well as an image of Leda and the swan that is now lost. As an engineer, he would find work consulting on buildings, such as a structurally challenging church, and serving the military aims of Cesare Borgia. And in his spare time, he would immerse himself again in mathematical and anatomical studies.

LIFE AT FIFTY

As Leonardo approached the age of fifty, living again in Florence, where he and his family were well-known, he was comfortable being a distinctive character. Rather than try to conform, he made a point of being different, dressing and carrying himself as a dandy. At one point he made an inventory in his notebook of clothing he had stored in a trunk. "One gown made of taffeta," he began. "One velvet lining that can be used as a gown. One Arab burnouse. One gown of dusty rose. One rose-colored Catalan gown. One cape of dark purple with wide collar and velvet hood. One coat of dark purple satin. One coat of crimson satin. One pair of dark purple stockings. One pair of dusty-rose stockings. One pink cap."[3] These might seem like costumes from one of his plays or masquerades, but we know from contemporary accounts that he actually dressed like this when walking about town. It is a delightful image: Leonardo in an Arab hooded cloak or strolling in purple and pink garb, heavy on the satin and velvet. He was tailor-made for a Florence that had rebelled against Savonarola's Bonfire of the Vanities and was again willing to embrace flamboyant, eccentric, and artistic free spirits.

Leonardo made sure that his companion Salai, then twenty-four, was dressed with similar brio, usually also in pink and rose. In one entry Leonardo noted, "On this day I paid Salai three gold ducats which he said he wanted for a pair of rose-colored hose with their trimming." The trimmings on the stocking must have been jewels. Four days later, he bought Salai a cloak of silver cloth with green velvet trim.[4]

In the list Leonardo made of the clothing he had stored in a trunk, it is telling that his own clothes and those of Salai are mixed together, unlike the possessions of anyone else in the household. The clothes included "a cape in the French mode, once owned by Cesare Borgia, belonging to Salai." Apparently Leonardo had cloaked his young companion in a cape given to him by the notoriously vicious warlord who was briefly his father figure. If Freud had only known. The trunk also contained "a tunic laced in the French fashion, belonging to Salai," and "a tunic of gray Flemish cloth, belonging to Salai."[5] These are not the types of garment that Leonardo, or anyone else of the time, bought for an ordinary house servant.

It's reassuring to discover that Leonardo spent as much on books as he did on clothes. In the inventories he made in 1504, he listed 116 volumes. These included Ptolemy's *Cosmography*, which he later cited in describing the human circulation and respiratory system as a microcosm of the earth's. He also acquired more books on math, including a three-volume translation of Euclid and a book he described as being about "the squaring of the circle," which was probably a text by Archimedes. There are many more texts on surgery, medicine, and architecture, but his tastes also ran to more popular fare. By then he owned three editions of Aesop's fables and multiple volumes of bawdy verse. He had also acquired the book on architecture written by his friend from Milan, Francesco di Giorgio, who had been a collaborator in conceiving *Vitruvian Man*. He made annotations throughout and copied some passages and drawings into his note-book.[6]

ISABELLA D'ESTE'S UNPAINTED PORTRAIT

We can get an impression of Leonardo's life in Florence at this time by looking at the amusing tale of a commission he did not take. Soon after he arrived, he was besieged by entreaties from Isabella d'Este to fulfill his promise to paint a picture for her, either a portrait based on the chalk drawing he had made of her when he passed through Mantua or, short of that, any other subject he chose. The saga of the two willful people, with a beleaguered friar caught in the middle, turned out to be so prolonged that it became, at least in retrospect, humorous as well as revealing of Leonardo's unwillingness to fulfill commissions that bored him. It also tells us about his interests in Florence, dilatory style, and aloof attitude toward wealthy patrons.

Isabella, a strong-willed first lady of Mantua and a stronger-willed patron of art, was twenty-six at the time. She was the daughter of the Duke of Ferrara and a scion of the Este family, the richest and oldest noble clan in Italy. She had received a rigorous classical education in Latin, Greek, history, and music. From the age of six, she had been betrothed to Francesco Gonzaga, the Marquess of Mantua. Isabella brought a dowry of 25,000 gold ducats (worth more than $3 million at 2017 gold prices), and her wedding in 1491 was lavish. After arriving in Mantua from Ferrara in a flotilla of more than fifty boats, she rode through the streets in a gold chariot cheered by seventeen thousand spectators and accompanied by ambassadors from a dozen realms.[7]

In an era of conspicuous consumption and competitive collecting, Isabella became the most conspicuous and competitive. She also triumphed in a tumultuous marriage. Her husband was a weak leader who was often away, at one point held hostage for three years in Venice, and she served as regent and took command of the city's military, holding off enemies. In return, her ungrateful husband conducted a long, passionate, and public affair with the notoriously beautiful and evil Lucrezia Borgia, who was married to Isabella's brother. (It was Lucrezia's third marriage. Her own brother, the brutal Cesare Borgia, had ordered her second husband to be strangled before her eyes.)

Isabella channeled her emotions into collecting art and, more specifically, seeking suitable portraits of herself. That proved difficult, because artists made the mistake of trying to produce passable likenesses, all of which she decried as making her look too fat. The respected Mantua court artist Andrea Mantegna tried in 1493, but Isabella pronounced, "The painter has done it so badly that it does not look like us in the least."

After a couple of other unsatisfactory portraits, she tried again with a painter who worked for her family in Ferrara, but when she sent it to Milan as a gift, she apologized to Ludovico Sforza. "I am afraid that I shall weary, not only Your Highness, but all Italy with the sight of my portraits," she wrote. "I send this one, which is not really very good and makes me look fatter than I am." Ludovico, who apparently did not know the proper response to a woman who said a portrait made her look fat, responded that he thought the picture was a good likeness. At one point Isabella lamented, "We only wish that we could be as well served by painters as we are by men of letters." Presumably, the many poets who dedicated poems to her could take more literary license with a subject than a painter could.[8]

In her continuing quest for the right artist to paint her, Isabella turned her sights on Leonardo. In 1498, soon after the death of her sister Beatrice, who had been married to Ludovico, Isabella wrote to Ludovico's mistress Cecilia Gallerani, the subject of Leonardo's *Lady with an Ermine*. She wanted to compare that portrait to ones done by the Venetian painter Giovanni Bellini to determine which of the two artists would be her next target. "Having seen today some fine portraits by the hand of Giovanni Bellini, we began to discuss the works of Leonardo, and wished we could compare them with these paintings," she wrote. "And since we remember that he painted your likeness, we beg you to be so good as to send us your portrait by this messenger whom we have dispatched on horseback, so that we may not only be able to compare the works of the two masters, but also have the pleasure of seeing your face again." She promised to return it. "I send it without delay," Cecilia replied, adding that it was no longer a good likeness. "But Your Highness must not think this proceeds from any defect in the master, for indeed I think there is no other painter to equal him in the world, but merely because the portrait was painted when I was much younger." Isabella liked the painting, but she kept her word and returned it to Cecilia.[9]

When Leonardo made his chalk drawing of Isabella on his way from Milan to Florence in early 1500, he also made a copy. He took it with him and showed it to a friend, who reported back to Isabella, "[The] portrait is exactly like you, and it could not be done better."[10] Leonardo had left the original drawing with Isabella, who in her flurry of subsequent correspondence asked him to send a replacement because her husband had given it away. "Will you also beg him to send us another drawing of our portrait," she wrote her agent, "since His Lordship our consort has given away the one which he left here?"[11]

The copy that Leonardo carried with him, which was large enough to be a preparatory cartoon for a painting, is likely the same drawing that is now in the Louvre (fig. 77). The portraits that Leonardo had painted in Milan show the sitters in Spanish-influenced dress, which had been the fashion. But Isabella was a trendsetter, and Leonardo drew her dressed in the very latest from France. That had an advantage: the loose sleeves and bodice hid her plumpness, though Leonardo gave her the hint of a double chin only slightly disguised by his chalky sfumato. There is a willfulness to her mouth and a dignified formality in the choice of a profile pose, which was the standard for portraits of royalty.

In most of his portraits, and all of those that were fully painted, Leonardo avoided the conventional approach of the period, which was to portray subjects in profile. Instead, he preferred to show his subjects facing the viewer or in three-quarters view, which allowed him to imbue them with a sense of motion and psychological engage-

Fig. 77. Drawing of Isabella d'Este.

ment. Ginevra de' Benci, Cecilia Gallerani, Lucrezia Crivelli, and Mona Lisa are posed this way.

But these women were not royalty; two were mistresses of Ludovico and two were upper-class wives. Isabella instead insisted on being portrayed in the classical profile that conveyed courtly decorum. As a result, Leonardo's drawing of her is lackluster. We cannot see into her eyes or mind or soul. She seems to be posing. No thoughts or emotions seem to be churning inside. The fact that she could have viewed Cecilia's *Lady with an Ermine* and then asked Leonardo for a conventional pose indicates that she had more money than taste. That may be one reason Leonardo had no desire to turn the drawing into a painting.[12]

Even though this drawing was pricked for transferring onto a panel, Leonardo showed no signs of fulfilling Isabella's request to produce a portrait painting. She was used to getting what she wanted, however, and after waiting a full year, she decided to launch a lobbying campaign. Caught in the middle was a well-connected friar named Pietro da Novellara, who had been Isabella's confessor.

"If Leonardo the Florentine, the painter, is to be found in Florence, we beg you will inform us what he is doing and whether he has begun any work," she wrote Pietro in late March 1501. "Your Reverence might find out, as you best know how, if he would undertake to paint a picture for our studio."[13]

The friar's reply, sent on April 3, gives a glimpse into what Leonardo was doing and his reluctance to make commitments. "From what I hear, Leonardo's life is very irregular and uncertain, and he seems to live for the day only," Pietro wrote. His only art, the friar reported, was a preparatory drawing for what would eventually become his great painting of the *Virgin and Child with Saint Anne*. "He has done nothing else, excepting that two of his apprentices are painting portraits to which he sometimes adds a few touches."

As usual, Leonardo was distracted by other pursuits. As the friar said at the end of his letter, "He devotes much of his time to geometry, and has no fondness at all for the paintbrush." He repeated that message after Salai arranged for him to meet with Leonardo. "I have succeeded in learning the intentions of the painter Leonardo by means of his pupil, Salai, and some of his other friends, who took me to see him on Wednesday," Pietro wrote on April 14. "In truth, his mathematical experiments have absorbed his thoughts so entirely that he cannot bear the sight of a paintbrush."

As always, Leonardo was charming, even when he was not being accommodating. One issue was that, when Louis XII of France took Milan, Leonardo had committed to do some paintings for him and his secretary, Florimond Robertet. "If he can get free from his engagement with the King of France without displeasing him, which he hopes to do by the end of a month at latest, he would rather serve Your Excellency than any other person in the world," Pietro wrote, stretching the truth. "But, in any case, as soon as he has finished a little picture which he is doing for a certain Robertet, a favorite of the King of France, he will do your portrait immediately." The friar described a painting Leonardo was working on that would become *Madonna of the Yarnwinder*. He ended with a note of resignation: "This is all that I could get from him."[14]

Had he wished to comply with Isabella, it would have been a lucrative commission, one that he could have mostly delegated to his assistants. But Leonardo, although not wealthy, was beyond that. He occasionally led his patrons on—perhaps he even thought he might eventually gratify their wishes—but he rarely allowed himself to be subservient to them. When Isabella wrote to him directly in July 1501, he didn't even deign to send back a formal answer. "I gave him to understand that if he wished to reply I could forward his letters on to Your Ladyship and thus save his costs," reported Isabella's agent. "He read your letter and said he would do so, but hearing nothing more from him I finally sent one of my men to him to learn what he wished to do. He sent back the answer that for now he was not in a position to send another reply to Your Ladyship, but that I should advise you that he has already begun work on that which Your Ladyship wanted from him." He ended his letter with the same resigned lament as Pietro had used. "In short, this is as much as I have been able to get from the said Leonardo."[15]

Three years later, despite all the entreaties, Leonardo had not sent a painting, nor is there any evidence that he had begun one. Finally, in May 1504, Isabella changed tactics and asked him to paint for her instead a picture of the young Jesus. "When you were in this city and drew our portrait in chalk, you promised us that you would some day paint it in colors," she wrote. "But because this would be almost impossible, since you are unable to come here, we beg you to keep your promise by converting our portrait into another figure, which would be still more acceptable to us, that is to say, a youthful Christ of about twelve years old."[16]

Although she implied she would pay whatever he wanted, Leonardo was unmoved. Salai, not surprisingly, was more mercenary, and in January 1505 he offered his own services to do such a painting. "A pupil of Leonardo Vinci, Salai by name, young in years but very talented . . . has a great wish to do some gallant thing for Your Excellency," her agent reported, "so if you desire a little picture from him, you have only to tell me the price you are ready to pay."[17] Isabella declined the offer.

The final chapter came in 1506, when Isabella personally went to Florence. She was not able to meet with Leonardo, who was staying in the countryside doing studies on the flight of birds, but she did meet with Alessandro Amadori, the brother of Leonardo's stepmother, Albiera. He promised to use his influence. "Here in Florence, I act at all hours as the representative of Your Excellency with Leonardo da Vinci, my nephew," he wrote in May, after she returned to Mantua, "and I do not cease to urge him by every argument in my power to satisfy your desire and paint the figure for which you asked him. This time he has really promised me that he will soon begin the work and satisfy your wish."[18]

Needless to say, Leonardo did not. He was pursuing more ambitious paintings as well as his endeavors in anatomy, engineering, math, and science. Painting a conventional portrait for a pushy patron did not interest him. Nor did money motivate him. He painted portraits if the subject struck his fancy, such as the *Musician*, or if a powerful ruler demanded it, as in the case of Ludovico with his mistresses. But he didn't dance to the music of patrons.

MADONNA OF THE YARNWINDER

Friar Pietro, in one of his letters to the persistent Isabella, described a painting that Leonardo was doing at the request of Louis XII's secretary, Florimond Robertet. "The little picture he is working on is of a Madonna who is seated as if she were about to spin yarn," he wrote, "and the child has placed his foot in the basket of yarns and has grasped the yarnwinder, and stares attentively at the four spokes, which are in the form of a cross, and he smiles and grips it tightly, as if he were longing for this cross, not wishing to yield it to his mother, who appears to want to take it away from him."[19]

Dozens of versions of this picture, either by Leonardo or his assistants and followers, still exist, and there has been much debate by experts, as well as some advocacy by owners and dealers, regarding which might be the one Leonardo himself painted and sent to Robertet. Two of the surviving versions, known as the Buccleuch Madonna and the Lansdowne Madonna (fig. 78), are considered most likely to reflect the most involvement of Leonardo's own hand. But the quest to designate the "real" or "original" Leonardo version actually misses the larger meaning of the tale of the *Yarnwinder*s. When he returned to Florence in 1500, Leonardo set up a collaborative workshop, and production of some pictures, especially small devotional ones, became a team effort, just as it had been in Verrocchio's studio.[20]

The emotional power of the *Yarnwinder* scene comes from the psychological complexity and intensity of the baby Jesus as he contemplates and grapples with the yarnwinder, which is in the shape of a cross. Other painters had shown Jesus looking at objects that foretold the Passion, as Leonardo had done in the devotional paintings of the Madonna and Child he had made Benois Madonna and other little paintings in his early years. But the *Yarnwinder* paintings are energized by what had become Leonardo's special ability to convey a psychological narrative.

There is a flow of physical motions as Jesus reaches toward the cross-like object, his finger pointed heavenward, the gesture that Leonardo loved. His moist eyes are shiny with a tiny sparkle of luster, and they have their own narrative: he is just the age when a baby can

Fig. 78. *Madonna of the Yarnwinder* (Lansdowne version).

discern objects and focus on them, and he is doing so with a concerted effort that combines his sight with his sense of touch. We sense that his ability to focus on the cross causes a premonition of his fate. He looks innocent and at first playful, but if you look at his mouth and eyes you sense a resigned and even loving comfort with what will be his destiny. By comparing *Madonna of the Yarnwinder* to the Benois Madonna (fig. 13), we can see the historic leap Leonardo made by turning static scenes into emotion-laden narratives.

Our eyes swirl counterclockwise as the narrative continues with Mary's motions and emotions. Her face and her hand indicate anxiety, a desire to intervene, but also an understanding and an acceptance of what shall be. In the *Virgin of the Rocks* paintings (figs. 64 and 65), Mary's hovering hand offers a serene benediction; in the *Yarnwinders*, her gesture is more conflicted, as if coiled to grasp her child while also recoiling from the temptation to intervene. She reaches out nervously, as if trying to decide whether to restrain him from his fate.

The *Yarnwinder* paintings are only the size of a page of a tabloid newspaper, but they include, especially in the Lansdowne version, Leonardo's marks of genius. There are the tightly coiled and lustrous curls on both mother and child. There is the river winding down from the mystical and misty mountains as if it were an artery connecting the macrocosm of the earth to the veins of the two human bodies. He knew how to have the light play on her thin veil, making it look lighter than her skin but still letting the sunlight hit the top of her forehead and reflect back a shine. The sun highlights the leaves on the closest tree next to her knee, but as the trees recede so does their distinctness, as Leonardo prescribed in his writings on acuity perspective. Also reflecting his scientific exactitude are the sedimentary layers of rocks on which Jesus leans.

Leonardo's picture arrived at the French court in 1507, and Salai possessed a similar picture when he died, according to an accounting of his estate. But there is no clear historical documentation that connects either of these to the Lansdowne and Buccleuch versions, or to any of the at least forty existing versions of the picture that have some claim to have been produced by Leonardo's studio.

Given the lack of a historical record or documentary trail, people have used other methods to try to determine which of the *Yarnwinder* contenders is the "original." One approach is connoisseurship, the ability of a true art expert with a refined eye to discern paintings by the master. Unfortunately, connoisseurship over the years, both in this case and others, has created more disagreements than it has resolved, and it has sometimes been proven wrong when new evidence arises.

Another approach is scientific and technical analysis, which has been made more potent recently with infrared reflectography and other tools using multispectral imagery. Oxford professor Martin Kemp and his graduate student Thereza Crowe Wells began such a process of analysis in the early 1990s on the Buccleuch and then the Lansdowne Madonnas. One of their surprising discoveries is that both paintings have underdrawings that seem to have been made by Leonardo directly on the wood panel. In other words, they were not copied or transferred from a master preparatory drawing. The two underdrawings are similar. But interestingly, they were significantly modified in the course of creating the paintings.

For example, in both underdrawings there is a faint group of figures that includes Joseph making a baby walker for Jesus. It appears that Leonardo decided, as both paintings were being done, that the little scene was too much of a distraction, so it was left out. This and other bits of technical evidence point to the likelihood that the Lansdowne and Buccleuch versions were painted in the studio at the same time, with Leonardo overseeing and probably using his own hand on both. He probably had more of a hand in the Lansdowne, and saw it to completion, given that it has the more Leonardesque landscape and lustrous curls.

At least five of the surviving versions of the painting include the little scene of Joseph building the baby walker. This indicates that these versions were being painted in Leonardo's studio before he decided to eliminate that scene. In other words, the best way to make sense of the versions and variations of the painting is to imagine Leonardo in his studio creating and modifying the painting while his assistants are producing copies.

This aligns with the impression we get from Pietro da Novellara's letter to Isabella d'Este, in which he describes the scene in Leonardo's studio, where "two of his apprentices are painting portraits to which he sometimes adds a few touches." In other words, we should put aside our romantic image of the artist alone in his studio creating works of genius. Instead, Leonardo's studio was like a shop in which he devised a painting and his assistants worked with him to make multiple copies. This is similar to the way it had been in Verrocchio's bottega. "The process of production is more in keeping with the commissioning of a superbly made chair from a major designer-craftsman," Kemp wrote after the results of the technical analysis. "We do not ask if a certain glued joint in the chair was made by the head of the workshop or one of his assistants—providing the joint holds and looks good."

In the case of the *Madonna of the Yarnwinder*, as it was with the two versions of the *Virgin of the Rocks*, we should modify the traditional questions asked by art historians: Which version is the "authentic" or "autograph" or "original" one? Which are mere "copies"? Instead, the proper and more interesting questions to ask are: How did the collaboration occur? What was the nature of the team and the teamwork? As with so many examples in history where creativity was turned into products, Leonardo's Florence studio involved individual genius combined with teamwork. Both vision and execution were required.

Because it was delivered to the French court and extensively copied, *Madonna of the Yarnwinder* turned out to be one of Leonardo's most influential paintings. Leonardo's followers, such as Bernardino Luini and Raphael, and soon painters throughout Europe, upended the genre of staid Madonna-and-child devotional paintings, creating instead narratives of emotional drama. Raphael's 1507 painting *Madonna of the Pinks*, for example, is often compared to Leonardo's Benois Madonna, which it closely mimics, but in fact we can see that Raphael has also picked up on Leonardo's ability in the *Yarnwinder* to imbue a work with psychological movements. The same is true of

Luini's *Madonna of the Carnation* and *Madonna with Child and Young Saint John.*

In addition, the *Yarnwinder* set the stage for one of the most richly layered of Leonardo's masterpieces, another depiction of the emotional swirl that occurs when the baby Jesus apprehends his destiny, this one adding Mary's mother, Saint Anne, to the drama.

CHAPTER 21

Saint Anne

THE COMMISSION

When Friar Pietro da Novellara was floundering in his mission to convince Leonardo to paint a portrait for Isabella d'Este, he wrote to her in April 1501 to explain the situation: "Since he has been in Florence, he has only made one sketch—a cartoon of a child Christ, about a year old, almost jumping out of his mother's arms to seize hold of a lamb. The mother is in the act of rising from Saint Anne's lap and holds back the child from the lamb, which is a symbol of the Passion."[1]

The cartoon that the friar described was a full-size preparatory drawing for what would become one of Leonardo's greatest masterpieces, the *Virgin and Child with Saint Anne* (fig. 79), featuring Mary sitting on the lap of her mother. The final painting combines many elements of Leonardo's artistic genius: a moment transformed into a narrative, physical motions that match mental emotions, brilliant depictions of the dance of light, delicate sfumato, and a landscape informed by geology and color perspective. It was proclaimed to be "Leonardo da Vinci's ultimate masterpiece" (*l'ultime chef d'oeuvre*) in the title of the catalogue published by the Louvre for a 2012 exhibition celebrating its restoration—this from the museum that also owns the *Mona Lisa*.[2]

Fig. 79. *Virgin and Child with Saint Anne.*

The story of the commissioning of the painting probably began when Leonardo returned to Florence from Milan in 1500 and took up residence at the church of Santissima Annunziata. The monks there regularly provided accommodation to distinguished artists, and Leonardo was given five rooms for himself and his assistants. It was wonderfully convenient: the monastery had a library with five thousand volumes, and it was only three blocks from the Santa Maria Nuova hospital, where Leonardo performed his dissections.

The monks had commissioned an altarpiece by Filippino Lippi, the Florentine painter who had painted an *Adoration of the Magi* for a nearby church after Leonardo had abandoned that commission. Leonardo let it be known that he would gladly take on the job of painting the altarpiece himself, and, as Vasari wrote, "when Filippino heard this, like the good-hearted person he was, he decided to withdraw." Another factor working in Leonardo's favor: his father was the notary for the church.

DIFFERENT VERSIONS

Once he got the commission, Leonardo typically procrastinated. "He kept them waiting a long time without even starting anything," Vasari wrote, "then he finally did the cartoon showing Our Lady with Saint Anne and the Infant Christ." The cartoon was a sensation, evidence that Leonardo was now wildly famous in his hometown and that he was leading the way for artists to rise from being nameless artisans to being individual public stars. "Men and women, young and old, continued for two days to flock for a sight of it to the room where it was, as if to a grand festival, to gaze at the marvels of Leonardo," Vasari recorded.

Vasari was presumably referring to the cartoon that Friar Pietro had described to Isabella d'Este. Unfortunately, Vasari confused matters by reporting that the drawing also included "Saint John, depicted as a little boy playing with a lamb." The fact that Vasari's description does not comport exactly with that of the friar, who makes no mention of Saint John, is not surprising. It was probably just a mistake. Vasari, whose accuracy was invariably well below perfect, was writing

fifty years later, and he never saw the cartoon in question. But his in-
jection of Saint John into the picture reflects an interesting historical
mystery that Leonardo scholars still wrestle with, because some of
Leonardo's versions and variations on the drawing did indeed include
Saint John in place of (not playing with) the lamb.

The cartoon that Friar Pietro wrote about—comprising Anne,
Mary, Jesus, and a lamb—has the same four elements as the paint-
ing now in the Louvre. But here's the wrinkle: the only surviving
cartoon by Leonardo related to this project is a drawing now in
London known as the Burlington House cartoon (because of the
Royal Academy headquarters where it was long displayed; fig. 80).
Beautiful and haunting and large, it features Saint Anne, the Virgin
Mary, and the baby Jesus, but with a young Saint John and no lamb.
In other words, it is not the cartoon that Friar Pietro saw in 1501.

Scores of Leonardo scholars have puzzled over the sequencing of
the various versions of the arrangement: there is the cartoon described
by Friar Pietro that was publicly displayed and then apparently lost,
the surviving Burlington House cartoon, and the Louvre painting. In
which order did Leonardo create these?

For much of the late twentieth century, the consensus among
scholars—including Arthur Popham, Philip Pouncey, Kenneth Clark,
and Carlo Pedretti—was that Leonardo began with the cartoon described by Friar Pietro (with a lamb but no Saint John) in 1501, then
changed his mind and drew the Burlington House cartoon a few
years later (with Saint John but no lamb), and then changed his mind
again and reverted to a final painted version that resembled the 1501
drawing (lamb and no Saint John). That theory was based on stylistic
grounds and because some mechanical drawings on the reverse of a
sketch for the Burlington House cartoon seem to have been done
around 1508.[3]

This contorted sequencing began to be revised in 2005, when
a note by Agostino Vespucci, who was Machiavelli's secretary and
Leonardo's friend, was found in the margin of a book by Cicero he
was reading. The ancient Roman philosopher had written that the
painter Apelles "perfected the head and bust of his Venus with the

Fig. 80. Burlington House cartoon for *Saint Anne*.

most elaborate art but left the rest of her body in the rough." Vespucci wrote next to this passage, "So Leonardo da Vinci does in all his paintings, such as the head of Lisa del Giocondo, and Anne, Mother of the Virgin." His note is dated October 1503. Thus in one little discovery there is confirmation that in 1503 Leonardo had started painting the *Mona Lisa*, and that he had already begun work on the *Saint Anne* painting.[4]

If Leonardo was already working on his final painting in 1503, it makes little sense to think that the Burlington House cartoon was done after that. Instead, it may have been done shortly after his return to Florence or perhaps even as early as 1499, before he left Milan. He could have been planning the painting before he got the commission, and indeed might have volunteered for the commission because he had a composition that he had initially intended to do for some other patron. "It seems likely that Leonardo began the Burlington House cartoon while he was still in Milan," wrote Luke Syson in the catalogue for a 2011 London exhibition that included the cartoon. "His patron may well have been the French king Louis XII, whose wife was Anne of Brittany."[5]

That theory that the Burlington House cartoon was the first in the sequence was reinforced in a masterful 2012 exhibition at the Louvre celebrating the completion of a twelve-year restoration of the *Saint Anne* painting. The exhibition brought together the painting and the Burlington House cartoon for the first time since Leonardo's death, along with compositional sketches, preparatory drawings, and copies made by Leonardo's students and other painters. In addition, technical studies, including multispectral analysis, of the painting and cartoon were presented. The conclusion was unequivocal, according to the curator, Vincent Delieuvin: "After working through, then abandoning the solution shown in the Burlington House cartoon, Leonardo developed a different conception and drew a second cartoon in 1501 . . . in which Saint John the Baptist had been replaced by a lamb—the one that Fra Pietro de Novellera described in a letter to Isabella d'Este." The final painted version is based on the 1501 cartoon, but with one change: the figures are reversed. In the painting and in its underdrawing, discovered by an infrared reflectographic analysis, the lamb and the young Jesus are on the right side, not the left.[6]

By looking at some of the smaller sketches Leonardo made, we can see him working out options for showing how the young Jesus would squirm off his mother's lap and wrestle with the lamb. He thinks by sketching. It is a process he called "componimento inculto," an uncultivated composition that helps work out ideas through an intuitive process. It's also instructive to look at the copies of the painting made in his workshop. "It has always been thought that Leonardo's pupils and assistants created these works by copying Leonardo's painting or his cartoons or even his drawings," Francesca Fiorani noted, "but these 'copies' were actually produced while the original was in the making and they reflect alternative solutions Leonardo imagined for it."[7]

THE PAINTING

It is important, Leonardo wrote, to "have a movement of a person's limbs appropriate to that person's mental movements." His painting of the *Virgin and Child with Saint Anne* shows what he meant. Mary's right arm is stretched as she tries to restrain the Christ child, showing a protective but gentle love. But he is intent on wrestling with the lamb, his leg over its neck and his hands grappling with its head. The lamb, as Friar Pietro told us, represents the Passion, Jesus' fate, and he will not be restrained from it.

Both Mary and her mother look young, almost as if they were sisters, even though the apocryphal tale is that Saint Anne was past childbearing age when Mary was born through a miracle. In the cartoon that Friar Pietro described, Leonardo portrayed Saint Anne looking older. We know this because, even though that cartoon was lost, there was a good copy of it. The copy was itself lost in Budapest during World War II, but photographs and etchings of it exist. They show that Leonardo had conceived of Saint Anne as an older woman wearing a matronly cloth headdress.[8] By the time he got around to executing the final painting, he had changed his mind. He made Saint Anne look much younger. In the painting, her torso and that of her daughter seem fused as they dote on the young child.

The image of a squirming boy with what looks like two mothers conjures up Leonardo's own childhood being raised by both his birth mother, Caterina, and his slightly younger stepmother. Freud made much of this, writing, "Leonardo gave the boy two mothers, the one who stretched out her arms after him and another who is seen in the background, both are represented with the blissful smile of maternal happiness. Leonardo's childhood was precisely as remarkable as this picture. He had two mothers." Freud goes on to discern the shape of a vulture lying sideways in the picture composition, but since he got the name of the bird wrong it seems to reflect Freud's fantasy more than Leonardo's.[9]

Underneath the feet and elegant toes of Saint Anne we can see, as in the Louvre version of *Virgin of the Rocks*, how Leonardo's studies of geology informed his paintings. In one of his notebooks, he described what is now known as "graded bedding" in layers of sedimentary rock: "Each layer is composed of heavier and lighter parts, the lowest being the heaviest. And the reason for this is that these layers are formed by the sediments from the waters discharged into the sea by the current of the rivers that flow into it. The heaviest part of this sediment was the part that was discharged first in the sequence."[10] The stratified rock formations and perfectly variegated pebbles beneath Saint Anne's feet portray this phenomenon accurately.

Leonardo had also been wrestling with the question of why the sky appears blue, and around that time he had correctly concluded that it had to do with the water vapor in the air. In the *Saint Anne* painting, he portrays the sky's luminous and misty gradations of blue as no other painter had done. The recent cleaning of the painting fully reveals the magical realism, veiled in vapors, of his distant mountains and skyline.

Most significant, the painting conveys the paramount theme in Leonardo's art: the spiritual connection and analogy between the earth and humans. Echoing so many of his paintings—*Ginevra de' Benci, Virgin of the Rocks, Madonna of the Yarnwinder*, and of course the *Mona Lisa*—a river curls from the distant horizon of the macrocosm of the earth and seems to flow into the veins of the Holy Family, ending with the lamb that foreshadows the Passion. The curving flow of the river connects to the flowing composition of the characters.

As Vespucci's marginal note informs us, Leonardo had completed the central part of the painting by 1503. But he never delivered it to the church of Santissima Annunziata. Instead, he carried it with him for the rest of his life, making improvements on it for more than a decade. During those years, his assistants and students made copies based on the work in progress and on Leonardo's sketches. Some are actually more finished than the painting Leonardo left us, and they allow us to see various details, such as jeweled sandals on the feet of Saint Anne and ornate embroidery on her clothes, that Leonardo was considering or had sketched but never got around to painting.[11]

The *Saint Anne* is the most complex and layered of Leonardo's panel paintings, and many see it as a masterpiece on a par with the *Mona Lisa*, perhaps even surpassing it because it is more complex in its composition and motion. "We are always discovering new felicities of movement and harmony, growing more and more intricate, yet subordinate to the whole," wrote Kenneth Clark, "and, as with Bach, this is not only an intellectual performance; it is charged with human feeling."[12]

Perhaps. The painting's grandeur, brilliant color, and narrative movement are wondrous to behold. But a few elements of the masterpiece make it less than perfectly satisfying, at least to me. There is a slight artificiality in the poses. The bodies seem to swivel unnaturally, with the Virgin Mary awkwardly draped onto her mother's lap. Saint Anne's jutting left arm seems uncomfortably cocked, and Mary's sunlit right shoulder is too broad and prominent. As I stand before the brightly restored painting in the Louvre, I find myself respecting and admiring it, but not being mesmerized the way I am by the two nearby masterpieces, *Saint John the Baptist* and the *Mona Lisa*. There's a profound beauty to the picture, but Leonardo at his best also produces emotional connections tinged with mystery. In the *Saint Anne*, the eyes of the characters do not seem to be windows into their souls; their smiles do not linger with us, hinting at elusive emotions.

Then something interesting happens. I go back to London to see the Burlington House cartoon again in the soft-lit grotto where it is kept in the National Gallery. Even without the misty blue mountains and watery landscape, it has elements that, to me at least, are more interesting. In it, Saint Anne's left arm is not unnaturally cocked but instead her sketched hand points to heaven, Leonardo's quintessential and exhilarating gesture. After a few experimental lines, he has succeeded in rendering the Virgin's right shoulder masterfully. As Saint Anne glances lovingly yet quizzically at the Virgin, who is in turn glancing lovingly but warily at her child, there seems to be a greater depth of emotion than in the final painting.

So maybe there was another reason Leonardo decided not to finish some of his works. The unpainted renderings of the *Adoration of the Magi* and the Burlington House *Saint Anne* cartoon both have an unfinished perfection to them. For most people, "unfinished perfection" would seem to be a contradiction in terms, but sometimes it suits Leonardo. Among other things, he was the master of the unfinished. Vespucci was correct when he said that Leonardo was the new Apelles in that regard.

CHAPTER 22

Paintings Lost and Found

LEDA AND THE SWAN

One of the veils blurring our knowledge of Leonardo is the mystery surrounding the authenticity and dates of some of his paintings, including ones we think are lost and others we think are finds. Like most artist-craftsmen of his era, he did not sign his work. Although he copiously documented trivial items in his notebooks, including the amount he spent on food and on Salai's clothes, he did not record what he was painting, what he had completed, and where his works went. For some paintings we have detailed contracts and disputes to inform us; for others we have to rely on a snippet from the sometimes reliable Vasari or other early chroniclers.

That means we need to look at copies done by his followers to envision works now lost, such as the *Battle of Anghiari*, and to analyze what were thought to be works by his followers to see if they might actually be autograph Leonardos. These endeavors can be frustrating, but even when they do not produce certainty, they can lead to a better understanding of Leonardo, as we saw in the case of *La Bella Principessa.*

Leda and the Swan is the most tantalizing of Leonardo's lost paintings. The existence of multiple copies, including from students in his workshop, makes it seem likely that he actually finished his own version. Lomazzo says that a "nude Leda" was one of Leonardo's few finished paintings, and there seems to be a report of it in 1625 at the French royal chateau of Fontainebleau, where a visitor described "a standing figure of Leda almost totally naked [*quasi tutta ignuda*], with the swan at her side and two eggs, from whose broken shells come forth four babies." That sounds like Leonardo's purported painting, except that Leda, in both his own surviving preparatory drawing and in painted copies, was wholly naked.[1] One tale, which is so delicious that it's a shame it's probably untrue, is that it was destroyed by Madame de Maintenon, the mistress and secret second wife of Louis XIV, because she found it too salacious.

The myth of Leda and the swan tells how the Greek god Zeus assumed the form of a swan and seduced the beautiful mortal princess Leda. She produced two eggs, from which hatched two sets of twins Helen (later known as Helen of Troy) and Clytemnestra, and Castor and Pollux. Leonardo's depiction focuses more on fertility than sex; instead of painting the seduction scene, as others had done, he chose to portray the moment of the births, showing Leda caressing the swan as the four children squirm from their shells. One of the most vivid copies is by his pupil Francesco Melzi (fig. 81).

When Leonardo was working on this painting during his second period in Florence in the early 1500s, he was doing his most intense studies on the flight of birds and also planning a test flight of one of his flying machines, which he hoped to launch from the top of nearby Swan Mountain (Monte Ceceri). His note about his childhood memory of a bird flying into his crib and flapping its tail in his mouth is also from this period.

Leonardo produced a preparatory sketch of his planned painting sometime around 1505 (fig. 82). It shows Leda kneeling and her body twisting as if writhing with joy as the swan nuzzles her. Leonardo's signature left-handed hatch lines are curved, a technique he started using in his machinery drawings of the 1490s and now used to show volume and modeling of curved surfaces. The technique is especially pronounced in Leda's opulent belly and the swan's breast. As usual with Leonardo, the drawing conveys a narrative. As the swan seductively nuzzles Leda, she points to what they have wrought: the children hatching amid the dynamic spirals of the plants. The drawing swirls with motion and energy; no element seems static.

When Leonardo developed the drawing into a full painting, he changed the pose so that Leda was standing and her nude body appeared more lithe and gentle. She is turning her head slightly away from the swan and looking down demurely, yet at the same time she twists her upper body toward him. She caresses his neck; he wraps a

Fig. 81. Francesco Melzi copy of *Leda and the Swan*.

Fig. 82. Leonardo's preparatory drawing for *Leda and the Swan*.

wing firmly around her buttocks. Both exude a sensuous and sinuous beauty.

That earthly and earthy sexuality makes the picture atypical. A nonreligious narrative panel painting (assuming you do not consider the sexual exploits of Greek gods to be a religious subject), it was Leonardo's only overtly sexual or erotic scene.

And yet, at least in the copies available to us today, it is not actually very erotic. Leonardo is not Titian. He never painted romance or eros. Instead, two themes dominate. The painting conveys a domestic and familial harmony, a pleasant portrayal of a couple at home by their lake, cuddling as they admire their newborns. It also goes beyond the erotic to focus on the tale's procreative aspects. From the lushness of the seeding plants, to the fecundity of the soil and the hatching of the eggs, the painting is a celebration of the fertility of nature. Unlike the usual depictions of the Leda myth, Leonardo's is not about sex but birth.[2]

These themes of generational and natural renewal apparently resonated with him now that he was in his mid-fifties, with no heirs. Around the time he began to paint *Leda*, he adopted Francesco Melzi, who painted the *Leda* copy shown as figure 81, to be his surrogate son and heir.

SALVATOR MUNDI

In 2011 a newly rediscovered painting by Leonardo surprised the art world. Each decade, a dozen or so pieces are proposed or pushed as having a reasonable claim to be previously unknown Leonardos, but only twice before in modern times had such assertions ended up generally accepted: the Benois Madonna oil painting in St. Petersburg's Hermitage that was publicly revealed in 1909 and the chalk drawing *La Bella Principessa* that Kemp and others asserted as authentic a century later.

This 2011 addition to the list of autograph works is a painting known as *Salvator Mundi* (Savior of the World), with Jesus gesturing in blessing with his right hand while holding a solid crystal orb in his left (fig. 83). The Salvator Mundi motif, which features Christ with an orb topped by a cross, known as a *globus cruciger*, had become very popular by the early 1500s, especially among northern European painters. Leonardo's version contains some of his distinctive features: a figure that manages to be at once both reassuring and unsettling, a mysterious straight-on stare, an elusive smile, cascading curls, and sfumato softness.

Before the painting was authenticated, there was historic evidence that one like it existed. In the inventory of Salai's estate was a painting of "Christ in the Manner of God the Father." Such a piece was catalogued in the collections of the English king Charles I, who was beheaded in 1649, and also Charles II, who restored the monarchy

Fig. 83. *Salvator Mundi.*

in 1660. The historical trail of Leonardo's version was lost after the painting passed from Charles II to the Duke of Buckingham, whose son sold it in 1763. But a historic reference remained: the widow of Charles I had commissioned Wenceslaus Hollar to make an etching of the painting. There were also at least twenty copies painted by some of Leonardo's followers.

The trail of the painting reappeared in 1900, when it was acquired by a British collector who did not suspect that it was by Leonardo. It had been damaged, overpainted, and so heavily varnished that it was unrecognizable, and it was attributed to Leonardo's student Boltraffio. The work was later catalogued as a copy of Boltraffio's copy. When the collector's estate sold it at auction in 1958, it fetched less than one hundred dollars.

The painting was sold again in 2005, to a consortium of art dealers and collectors who believed that it might be more than just a copy of a copy of a Leonardo painting. As with the tale of *La Bella Principessa*, the subsequent authentication process reveals a lot about Leonardo's work. The consortium brought it to a Manhattan art historian and dealer named Robert Simon, who oversaw a five-year process of cleaning it carefully and quietly showing it to experts.

Among those consulted were Nicholas Penny, then director of London's National Gallery, and Carmen Bambach of New York's Metropolitan Museum. It was brought to London in 2008 so that it could be directly compared with the National Gallery's version of *Virgin of the Rocks* by other experts, including Luke Syson, who was then curator of Italian paintings at the gallery, David Alan Brown of Washington's National Gallery of Art, and Pietro Marani, professor of art history at the Politecnico di Milano. And, of course, a call went out to Martin Kemp, who was also then authenticating *La Bella Principessa*. "We've got something I think you would want to look at," Penny told Kemp. When Kemp saw it, he was struck by the orb and hair. "It had that kind of presence that Leonardos have," he recalled.[3]

But it was not merely gut, intuition, and connoisseurship that authenticated *Salvator Mundi*. The painting duplicated almost precisely the 1650 Wenceslaus Hollar engraving that had been made from the original; it had the same snaking and lustrous curls, the same Leonardesque knot pattern on the sashes, and the irregular pleats on Christ's blue cloak that are also in Leonardo's preparatory drawings.

These similarities, however, were not dispositive. There were many copies made by Leonardo's followers; was it possible that this newly rediscovered painting was also a copy? Technical analysis helped to answer that. After the picture was cleaned, high-resolution photos and X-rays helped reveal a pentimento showing that the thumb of Jesus' right hand had originally been placed differently. That is not something a copyist would need to do. In addition, shining an infrared light that reflected off the white priming of the panel showed that the painter had pressed his palm against the wet paint above Christ's left eye to achieve a sfumato blurring, which was a distinctive Leonardo technique. The work had been painted on walnut, just like other Leonardos of the period, in many very thin layers of almost translucent paint. By that point most of the experts agreed that it was an authentic Leonardo. As a result, the art consortium was able to sell it for close to $80 million in 2013 to a Swiss art dealer, who then resold it to a Russian fertilizer billionaire for $127 million.[4]

Unlike other *Salvator Mundi* paintings, Leonardo's offers the viewer shifting emotional interactions, similar to those found in the *Mona Lisa*. The misty aura and blurred sfumato lines, especially of the lips, produces a psychological mystery and an ambiguous smile that seems to change slightly with each new look. Is there a hint of a smile? Look again. Is Jesus staring at us or into the distance? Move from side to side and ask again.

The curling hair, coiled with energy, seems to spring into motion as it reaches the shoulders, as if Leonardo were painting the eddies of a flowing stream. They become more distinct and less soft as they reach the chest. This stems from his studies of acuity perspective: objects that are closer to a viewer are less blurred.

Around the time he was working on *Salvator Mundi*, Leonardo was doing his optics studies that explored how the eyes focus.[5] He knew that he could create the illusion of three-dimensional depth in a painting by making the objects in the foreground sharper. The two fingers on Christ's right hand that are closest to us are drawn with a crisper delineation. It makes the hand pop out toward us, as if it's in motion and giving us a blessing. Leonardo would reuse this technique a few years later with the pointing hands in two depictions of Saint John the Baptist.

There is, however, a puzzling anomaly in the painting, one that seems to be an unusual lapse or unwillingness by Leonardo to link art and science. It involves the clear crystal orb that Jesus is holding. In one respect, it is rendered with beautiful scientific precision. There are three jagged bubbles in it that have the irregular shape of the tiny gaps in crystal called inclusions. Around that time, Leonardo had evaluated rock crystals as a favor for Isabella d'Este, who was planning to purchase some, and he captured accurately the twinkle of inclusions. In addition, he included a deft and scientifically accurate touch, showing he had tried to get the image correct: the part of Jesus' palm pressing into the bottom of the orb is flattened and lighter, as it would indeed appear in reality.

But Leonardo failed to paint the distortion that would occur when looking through a solid clear orb at objects that are not touching the orb. Solid glass or crystal, whether shaped like an orb or a lens, produces magnified, inverted, and reversed images. Instead, Leonardo painted the orb as if it were a hollow glass bubble that does not refract or distort the light passing through it. At first glance it seems as if the heel of Christ's palm displays a hint of refraction, but a closer look shows the slight double image occurs even in the part of the hand not behind the orb; it is merely a pentimento that occurred when Leonardo decided to shift slightly the hand's position.

Christ's body and the folds of his robe are not inverted or distorted when seen through the orb. At issue is a complex optical phenomenon. Try it with a solid glass ball (fig. 84). A hand touching the orb will not appear to be distorted. But things viewed through the orb that are an inch or so away, such as Christ's robes, will be seen as inverted and reversed. The distortion varies depending on the distance of the objects from the orb. If Leonardo had accurately depicted the distortions, the palm touching the orb would have remained the way he painted it, but hovering inside the orb would be a reduced and inverted mirror image of Christ's robes and arm.[6]

Fig. 84. Image through a crystal orb.

Why did Leonardo not do this? It is possible that he had not no-ticed or surmised how light is refracted in a solid sphere. But I find that hard to believe. He was, at the time, deep into his optics stud-ies, and how light reflects and refracts was an obsession. Scores of notebook pages are filled with diagrams of light bouncing around at different angles. I suspect that he knew full well how an object seen through a crystal orb would appear distorted, but he chose not to paint it that way, either because he thought it would be a distraction (it would indeed have looked very weird), or because he was subtly trying to impart a miraculous quality to Christ and his orb.

CHAPTER 23

Cesare Borgia

RUTHLESS WARRIOR

Ludovico Sforza, Leonardo's patron in Milan, had a reputation for ruthlessness that included, among other alleged acts, poisoning his nephew in order to seize the ducal crown. But Ludovico was a choir boy compared to Leonardo's next patron, Cesare Borgia. Name any odious activity and Borgia was the master of it: murder, treachery, incest, debauchery, wanton cruelty, betrayal, and corruption. He had a brutal tyrant's hunger for power combined with a sociopath's thirst for blood. Once, when he felt he had been libeled, he had the offender's tongue cut out, his right hand chopped off, and the hand with the tongue attached to its little finger hung from a church window. His only sliver of historical redemption, which is undeserved, came when Machiavelli used him as a model of cunning in *The Prince* and taught that his ruthlessness was a tool for power.[1]

Cesare Borgia was the son of the Spanish-Italian cardinal Rodrigo Borgia, soon to become Pope Alexander VI, who vies for the hotly contested title of most libertine Renaissance pope. "He had in the fullest measure all the vices of the flesh and of the spirit," the pope's contemporary Francesco Guicciardini wrote. He was the first pope to recognize openly his illegitimate children—ten in all, including Cesare and Lucrezia, by multiple mistresses—and he was able to get Cesare a dispensation from his illegitimacy so he could hold church offices. He made Cesare the bishop of Pamplona at fifteen and a cardinal three years later, even though the son showed less than zero predilection for piety. In fact, he had not even taken holy orders. Preferring to be a ruler rather than a religious figure, Cesare became the first person in history to fully resign from the cardinalate, and he likely had his brother stabbed to death and thrown into the Tiber so that he could replace him as the commander of the papal forces.

In that capacity, he forged an alliance with the French, and he was with King Louis XII marching into Milan in 1499. The day after their arrival, they went to see *The Last Supper*, and there Borgia first met Leonardo. Knowing Leonardo, it is likely that during the next few weeks he showed Borgia his military engineering designs.

Borgia subsequently launched a plan to carve out his own principality in the politically tumultuous Romagna region that stretched east of Florence to the Adriatic coast. These lands were supposed to be under his father, the pope, but the towns were controlled by their own independent princes, little tyrants, and vicars. Their violent rivalries regularly erupted into frenzied sieges and sackings accompanied by rampant rape and murder. By the spring of 1501, Borgia had conquered Imola, Forlì, Pesaro, Faenza, Rimini, and Cesena.[2]

Borgia next set his sights on Florence, which cowered in dread. Its treasury was depleted, and it had no military to defend it. In May 1501, as his forces neared Florence's walls, the ruling Signoria of the city capitulated by agreeing to pay Borgia 36,000 florins a year as protection money and permitting his army to cross Florentine territory at will as he conquered more towns.

NICCOLÒ MACHIAVELLI

The bribe bought Florence peace for a year, but in June 1502 Borgia was back. As his army sacked more surrounding towns, he commanded the leaders in Florence to send a delegation to hear his latest demands. Two people were selected to try to deal with him. The elder was Francesco Soderini, a wily Church leader who led one of the anti-Medici factions in Florence. Accompanying him was the son of a bankrupt lawyer, well-educated but poor, whose writing skills and savvy understanding of power games had established him as Florence's cleverest young diplomat: Niccolò Machiavelli.

Machiavelli had a smile right out of a Leonardo painting: enigmatic, at times laconic, always appearing to hide a secret. He shared with Leonardo the trait of being a sharp observer. He was not yet a famous author, but already he was known for his ability to produce lucid reports informed by insights into power balances, tactics, and personal motivations. He became a valued civil servant and secretary of Florence's chancery.

As soon as he left Florence, Machiavelli received word that Borgia was in Urbino, a town east of Florence between the Apennine Mountains and Adriatic coast. Borgia had captured Urbino through trickery, by feigning friendship and then striking unexpectedly. "He arrives in one place before anyone knows he has left the other," Machiavelli reported in a dispatch, and is able "to install himself in someone else's house before anyone else noticed it."

As soon as they arrived in Urbino, Soderini and Machiavelli were ushered into the ducal palace. Borgia knew how to put on a power show. He was seated in a dark room, his bearded and pockmarked face lit by a single candle. He insisted that Florence show him respect and support. Once again a vague accommodation seems to have been reached, and Borgia did not attack. A few days later, probably as part of his arrangement with Florence that Machiavelli had helped to negotiate, Borgia secured the services of the city's most famous artist and engineer, Leonardo da Vinci.[3]

LEONARDO AND BORGIA

Leonardo may have gone to work with Borgia at the behest of Machiavelli and Florence's leaders as a gesture of goodwill, similar to the way he had been dispatched twenty years earlier to Milan as a diplomatic gesture to Ludovico Sforza. Or he may have been sent as a way for Florence to have an agent embedded with Borgia's forces. Maybe it was both. But either way, Leonardo was no mere pawn or agent. He would not have gone to work for Borgia unless he wanted to.

On the first page of a pocket-size notebook he took on his journey in service of Borgia, Leonardo listed the equipment he packed: a pair of compasses, a sword belt, a light hat, a book of white paper for drawing, a leather vest, and a "swimming belt." The last item was something he had earlier described among his military inventions. "Have a coat made of leather, which must be double across the breast, that is having a hem on each side of about a finger breadth," he wrote. "When you want to leap into the sea, blow out the skirt of your coat through the double hems."[4]

Even though Borgia was in Urbino, Leonardo first headed southwest from Florence to Piombino, a coastal town that was occupied by Borgia's army. Apparently he had received orders from Borgia to make an inspection tour of the forts in Borgia's control. In addition to studying the fortifications, he looked at ways to drain the marshes and—easily gliding back and forth between practical engineering and pure scientific curiosity—made a study of the movement of the waves and tides.

From there, he headed eastward across the Apennine Mountains to the other side of the Italian peninsula, gathering topographical data for maps and observing landscapes and bridges that would later be reflected in the *Mona Lisa*. Finally, in midsummer 1502, he arrived in Urbino to join Borgia, almost three years after first meeting him in Milan.

Leonardo sketched the staircase of Urbino's palace and the dovecote, and he made a series of three red-chalk drawings that were likely of Borgia (fig. 85). The left-handed hatch lines of the drawing accentuate the shadows under Borgia's eyes; he looks pensive and subdued, his ringlets of curly beard covering a face that has become thickened with age and perhaps pockmarked by his syphilis. He no longer looks like "the handsomest man in Italy," as he was once called.[5]

Perhaps Borgia looked pensive because he was worried, rightly, that the king of France, Louis XII, was hedging his support for Borgia and promising protection to the Florentines. Swirling around the French court and the Vatican were intriguers who had been betrayed or divorced by various Borgias and were now seeking revenge. A week

Fig. 85. Leonardo's sketches probably of Cesare Borgia.

or so after his arrival in Urbino, Leonardo jotted in his notebook, "Where is Valentino?,"[6] using a nickname for Borgia, who had been made the Duke of Valentinois by the French king. Borgia, it turned out, had disguised himself as a Knight Hospitaller and snuck away with three trusted guards to ride north at a furious pace to reinstate himself in the good graces of Louis, which he did.

Borgia had not forgotten Leonardo. When he reached Pavia, where Louis was then holding court, he issued a floridly written "passport" for Leonardo, giving him special privileges and rights of passage, dated August 18, 1502:

> To all our lieutenants, castellans, captains, condottieri, soldiers, and subjects, who may be shown this document: You are hereby ordered and commanded on behalf of our most eminent and well-beloved familial friend [*dilectissimo familiare*], the architect and engineer general Leonardo Vinci, bearer of these documents, who has received our commission to inspect all the strongpoints and fortresses in our dominion, so that he may, according to their needs, provide for their maintenance. He shall be given free passage and be relieved of all public tax, both for himself and for his party, and shall be welcomed amicably, and may make measurements and examine whatever he pleases. For this purpose, provide

him with as many men as he requisitions, and grant him all the help, succor and favor he may demand, for it is our will that every engineer in our dominions shall be bound to confer with him and follow his advice. And let no man dare to do the contrary, if he does not wish to incur our extreme displeasure.[7]

Borgia's passport described Leonardo as he had fancied himself ever since his letter to the Duke of Milan twenty years earlier: as a military engineer and innovator rather than a painter. He had been warmly embraced, in fulsome and familial terms, by the most vibrant warrior of the age. For the moment, the man who had been described as no longer able to bear the sight of a brush got to play the role of a man of action.

Borgia left Pavia to rejoin his army in September, and Leonardo traveled with him eastward as he captured Fossombrone, using a combination of trickery, betrayal, and surprise. That taught Leonardo a lesson about designs for the interiors of castles and fortresses: "Be sure that the escape tunnel does not lead to the inner fortress, lest the fortress be captured by treachery or betrayal of the lord."[8] He also suggested that fortress walls be curved because that would reduce the impact of cannonballs. "Percussion is less strong the more oblique it is," he wrote.[9] He then accompanied Borgia's army as it marched toward the Adriatic coast.

In the town of Rimini, he was enthralled by "the harmony of the different falls of water."[10] A few days later, in the port of Cesenatico, he sketched the harbor and drew up plans for defending the dykes "so that they are not vulnerable to artillery fire." He also directed that the harbor be dredged so that it would stay linked to the sea. Always enthralled by ambitious water projects, he looked at ways the harbor canal could be extended ten miles inland to Cesena.[11]

While in Cesena, which Borgia had made the capital of his Romagna region conquests, Leonardo made a drawing of the fortress. But by then his mind was wandering from military matters. He sketched a house window with a quarter-circle pane on top, which reflected his interest in curved and rectilinear geometric shapes, and a hook with two bunches of grapes. "This is how they carry grapes in

Cesena," he explained.[12] He also combined the compositional eye of
a painter with that of an engineer to note how the workmen digging
a ditch array themselves in a pyramid. He was not impressed with the
engineering intelligence of the locals, at one point drawing a cart and
saying of the Cesena region, "In Romagna, the chief realm of all stupidity [*capo d'ogni grossezza d'ingegno*], vehicles with four wheels are
used, in which the two in front are small and the two high ones behind, an arrangement that is very unfavorable to motion, because on
the front wheels more weight is laid than on those behind."[13] Ideas
for building better wheelbarrows was a topic he had covered in one of
his draft treatises on mechanics.

The mathematician Luca Pacioli later recounted a tale of Leonardo in action. "One day Cesare Borgia . . . found himself and his
army at a river that was twenty-four paces wide, and could find no
bridge, nor any material to make one except for a stack of wood all
cut to a length of 16 paces," Pacioli wrote, probably based on hearing
the story from Leonardo. "From this wood, using neither iron nor
rope nor any other construction, his noble engineer made a bridge
sufficiently strong for the army to pass over."[14] A sketch for such a
self-supporting bridge in Leonardo's notebook (fig. 86, with a fainter

Fig. 86. Self-supporting bridge.

version in fig. 53) has seven short poles and ten longer, each notched so they can be fit together at the scene.[15]

As the fall of 1502 approached, Borgia moved his court to the highly fortified town of Imola, thirty miles inland from Cesena on the road to Bologna. Leonardo made drawings of the fortress compound, noting that its moat was forty feet deep and its walls fifteen feet thick. In front of the only entrance through the walls surrounding the town was a moat split by a man-made island; anyone trying to invade had to cross two bridges and be exposed to a defensive barrage. Borgia's plan was to turn the town into his permanent military headquarters by having Leonardo make it even more impregnable.[16]

Machiavelli arrived on October 7, sent by Florence to be an emissary and informant. In his daily dispatches back to Florence, which he knew were being read by Borgia's intelligence agents, Machiavelli apparently refers to Leonardo only as "another who is also acquainted with Cesare's secrets" and as a "friend" whose knowledge is "worthy of attention."[17] Imagine the scene. For three months during the winter of 1502–3, as if in a historical fantasy movie, three of the most fascinating figures of the Renaissance—a brutal and power-crazed son of a pope, a sly and amoral writer-diplomat, and a dazzling painter yearning to be an engineer—were holed up in a tiny fortified walled town that was approximately five blocks wide and eight blocks long.

While he was in Imola with Machiavelli and Borgia, Leonardo made what may be his greatest contribution to the art of war. It is a map of Imola, but not any ordinary map (fig. 87).[18] It is a work of beauty, innovative style, and military utility. It combines, in his inimitable manner, art and science.

Drawn in ink with colored washes and black chalk, the Imola map was an innovative step in cartography. The moat around the fortified town is tinted a subtle blue, the walls are silvery, and the roofs of the houses brick red. The aerial view is from directly overhead, unlike most maps of the time. On the edges he has specified the distances to nearby towns, useful information for military campaigns, but written in his elegant mirror script, indicating that the version that survives is a copy he made for himself rather than Borgia.

Leonardo used a magnetic compass, and the eight major direc-

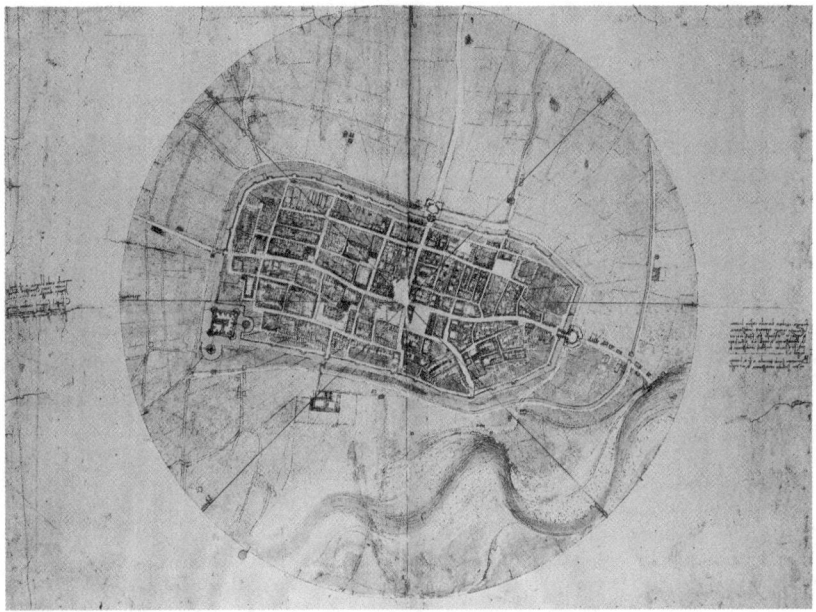

Fig. 87. Leonardo's map of Imola.

tional lines (north, northwest, west, southwest, etc.) are shown with fine strokes. On a preliminary sketch, he marked the position and size of each house. The map is folded many times, indicating he tucked it in his pocket or pouch as he and his assistants paced off the distances.

Around this time, he perfected the odometer he had been developing to measure long distances (fig. 88).[19] On a cart he mounted a vertical cog wheel, which looks like the front wheel of a wheelbarrow, that intersects with a horizontal cog wheel. Every time the vertical wheel completed a revolution, it would move the horizontal wheel a notch, and that would cast a stone into a container. On his drawing of the device, Leonardo noted that it "makes the ear hear the sound of a little stone falling into a basin."[20]

The Imola map and others Leonardo made at the time would have been of great use to Borgia, whose victories came from conducting lightning strikes and, in the words of Machiavelli, being able "to install himself in someone else's house before anyone else noticed it." Acting as an artist-engineer, Leonardo had devised a new military weapon: accurate, detailed, and easily read maps. Over the years, visu-

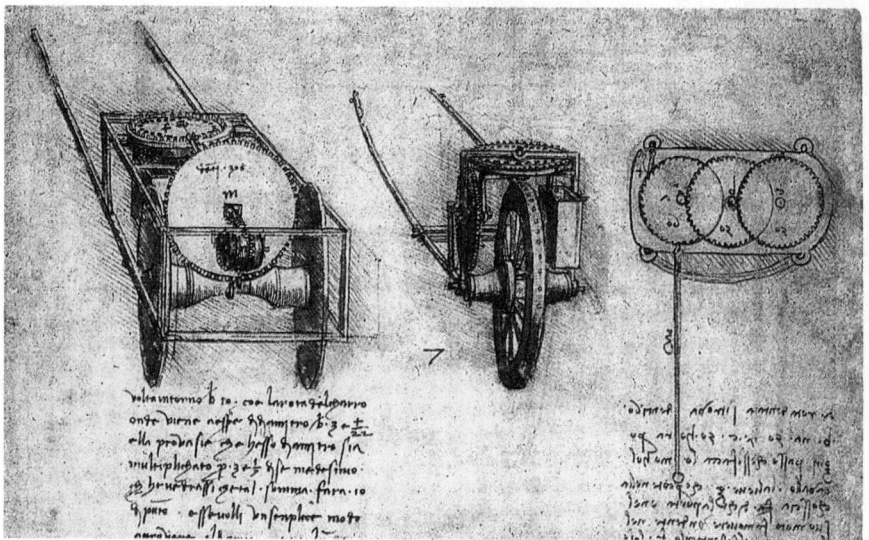

Fig. 88. An odometer.

ally clear maps would become a key component of warfare. For example, the U.S. National Geospatial-Intelligence Agency (originally known as the Defense Mapping Agency) had 14,500 employees and an annual budget exceeding $5 billion in 2017. Projected on the walls of its headquarters are maps combining accuracy with beauty, some of which bear a striking resemblance to Leonardo's map of Imola.

In a larger sense, Leonardo's maps are another example of one of his greatest, though underappreciated, innovations: devising new methods for the visual display of information. In his illustrations for Pacioli's book on geometry, Leonardo was able to show models of a variety of polyhedrons that were perfectly shaded to look three-dimensional. In his notebook entries on engineering and mechanics, he drew pieces of machinery with subtlety and precision, adding cutaway shots of various components. He was among the first to deconstruct complex mechanisms and make separate drawings of each element. Likewise, in his anatomy drawings, he drew muscles, nerves, bones, organs, and blood vessels from different angles, and he pioneered the method of depicting them in multiple layers, like the transparencies of body layers found in encyclopedias centuries later.

LEAVING BORGIA

In December 1502, Cesare Borgia committed a typical act of brutality. He had empowered a deputy, Ramiro de Lorca, to tyrannize Cesena and the surrounding territories with unremitting cruelty and gruesome slaughter to intimidate the populace. But once Ramiro had inspired enough fear, Borgia realized that it would be useful to sacrifice him. The day after Christmas, he had Ramiro brought to the central square in Cesena and sliced in two. The pieces of his body remained there on display. "Cesare Borgia decided that there was no more need for this excessive power," Machiavelli later explained in *The Prince*. "To purge the minds of the people and to win them over, Cesare determined to show the people that Ramiro's cruelties were inflicted by him and not Cesare. One morning, Ramiro's body was found cut in two pieces on the piazza at Cesena, with a block of wood and a bloody knife beside it. The brutality of this spectacle kept the people of the Romagna appeased and stupefied." The coldness of Borgia's brutality impressed Machiavelli, who called it "an example that deserves close study and imitation by others."[21]

Borgia then marched on the coastal town of Senigallia, where local leaders had rebelled against his occupation. He offered them a meeting to negotiate a reconciliation, and he promised that they could keep their leadership roles if they pledged to be loyal. They agreed. But when Borgia arrived, he had the men seized and strangled to death, then ordered that the town be pillaged. By this point even the cold-blooded and calculating Machiavelli was getting a bit squeamish. "The sack of the town continues although it is now the twenty-third hour," he scribbled in a dispatch. "I am much troubled."

One of the strangled men was a friend of Leonardo, Vitellozzo Vitelli, who had lent him a book by Archimedes. Leonardo traveled with Borgia's army for the conquest of Siena a few weeks later, but his notebooks suggest that he had mentally tuned out Borgia's horrors by focusing on other matters. He made a sketch of the church bell at Siena, twenty feet in diameter, and described "the manner of its movement and the position of the attachment of its clapper."[22]

A few days later, shortly after Machiavelli had been recalled to Florence, Leonardo left Borgia's service. By March 1503 he was settled back in Florence and withdrawing money from his bank account at the hospital of Santa Maria Nuova.

"Save me from strife and battle, a most beastly madness," Leonardo once wrote. Yet for eight months he had put himself at Borgia's service and traveled with his armies. Why would a person whose notebook aphorisms decry killing and whose personal morality led him to be a vegetarian go to work for the most brutal murderer of the era? Partly this choice reflects Leonardo's pragmatism. In a land where the Medici, Sforzas, and Borgias jostled for power, Leonardo was able to time his patronage affiliations well and know when to move on. But there is more. Even as he remained aloof from most current events, he seemed to be attracted to power.

It would take a Freudian analyst to explain Leonardo's affinity for attaching himself to strong men, and once again Freud himself tried to do so. He believed that Leonardo gravitated to them as substitutes for the manly but often absent father of his childhood. A simpler explanation is that Leonardo, who had just turned fifty, had dreamed for more than two decades of being a military engineer. As Isabella d'Este's agent reported, he was tired of painting. Borgia had just turned twenty-six. He combined bravado and elegance. "This lord is truly splendid and magnificent, and in war there is no enterprise so great that it does not seem small to him," Machiavelli wrote after meeting him.[23] Indifferent to the shifting political agendas of Italy yet attracted to military engineering and strongmen, Leonardo had a chance to live out his military fantasies, which he did until he realized they could become nightmares.

CHAPTER 24

Hydraulic Engineer

DIVERTING THE ARNO

In his job application to Ludovico Sforza, Leonardo had boasted of his talent for "guiding water from one place to another." That was, at best, an exaggeration. When he first arrived in Milan, in 1482, he had done no hydraulic engineering. But like many of his fantasy aspirations, he willed this one into reality. During his years in Milan, he diligently studied the city's system of canals, and he recorded in his notebooks details of the mechanisms of the locks and other feats of water engineering. In particular, he was fascinated by the city's artificial canals, including the Naviglio Grande, begun in the twelfth century, and the Naviglio Martesana, which was under construction while he lived there.[1]

Milan's waterworks had existed for centuries, even before the Romans built their famed aqueducts in the Po Valley around 200 BC. The flow of water each spring from the melting snow of the Alps was carefully managed in accordance with rules devised by ancient tribes to create controlled floods for the grain fields. Irrigation networks were created, and canals were built that both channeled water and facilitated barge shipping. By the time Leonardo moved to Milan, the system of large canals was three centuries old, and the duchy there raised much of its revenue from the sale of water allocations. Leonardo himself was at one point compensated with a water allocation, and his design for an ideal city near Milan was based on using man-made canals and waterways.[2]

In Florence, by contrast, there had been no major hydraulic works since ancient times. The city had few canals, drainage projects, irrigation systems, or river diversions. With the knowledge he had soaked up in Milan and his fascination with the flow of water, he set out to change that. In his notebooks, he began sketching ways that Florence could copy Milan.

Florence had controlled the town of Pisa, just over fifty miles down the Arno River toward the coast of the Mediterranean, for much of the fifteenth century. This was critical for Florence, which had no other outlet to the sea. But in 1494 Pisa managed to wriggle away and become a free republic. Florence's middling army was incapable of breaching Pisa's walls, and it could not successfully blockade the town because the Arno gave it access to supplies from the sea.

Just before Pisa broke away, a major world event made Florence even more eager to control a sea outlet. In March 1493 Christopher Columbus returned safely from his first voyage across the Atlantic Ocean, and the report of his discoveries quickly spread throughout Europe. This was soon followed by a flurry of other accounts of amazing explorations. Amerigo Vespucci, whose cousin Agostino worked with Machiavelli in the Florentine chancery, helped supply Columbus's third voyage in 1498, and the following year he made his own voyage across the Atlantic, landing in what is now Brazil. Unlike Columbus, who thought he was finding a route to India, Vespucci correctly reported to his Florentine patrons that he had "arrived at a new land which for many reasons . . . we observed to be a continent." His correct surmise led to its being named America, after him. The excitement over what portended to be a new age of exploration made Florence's desire to regain Pisa more urgent.[3]

In July 1503, a few months after he left Borgia's service, Leonardo was sent to join Florence's army at the fortress of Verruca, a square fortification atop a rocky outcropping (*verruca* means "wart") overlooking the Arno seven miles east of Pisa.[4] "Leonardo da Vinci himself came here with his companions, and we showed him everything, and we think that he likes La Verruca very much," a field commissary reported back to the Florentine authorities. "He said that he was thinking of making it impregnable."[5] An entry for an account book in Florence that month lists a set of expenses and then adds, "This money has been spent to provide six horse coaches and to pay the board expenses for the expedition with Leonardo in the territory of Pisa to divert the Arno from its course and take it away from Pisa."[6]

Diverting the Arno River from its course and taking it away from Pisa? It was an audacious way to reconquer the city without storming the wall or wielding any weapons. If the river could be channeled somewhere else, Pisa would be cut off from the sea and lose its source of supply. The primary advocates of the idea included the two clever friends who had been holed up together that past winter in Imola, Leonardo da Vinci and Niccolò Machiavelli.

"The river that is to be diverted from one course to another must be coaxed and not treated roughly or with violence," Leonardo wrote in his notebook. His plan was to dig a huge ditch, thirty-two feet deep, upriver from Pisa and use dams to divert the water from the river into the ditch. "To do this a sort of dam must be inserted into the river, then another one further downstream jutting out beyond it, and similarly third, fourth, and fifth dams, so that the river may discharge itself into the channel made for it."[7]

This would require moving a million tons of earth, and Leonardo calculated the man-hours necessary by doing a detailed time-and-motion study, one of the first in history. He figured out everything from the weight of one shovel-load of dirt (twenty-five pounds) to how many shovel-loads would fill a wheelbarrow (twenty). His answer: it would take approximately 1.3 million man-hours, or 540 men working 100 days, to dig the Arno diversion ditch.

At first he considered ways to use wheeled carts to carry the dirt away, showing why those with three wheels were more efficient than those with four. But he realized that it would be very difficult to push carts up the banks of a ditch. So he designed one of his ingenious machines (fig. 89), which features two crane-like arms that would move lines with twenty-four buckets. When a bucket deposited its dirt on top of the bank of the ditch, a worker would get in it and ride down to keep the weights counterbalanced. Leonardo also designed a tread-mill system to harness human power to move the cranes.[8]

When digging began on the diversion ditch in August 1504, it was overseen by a new waterworks engineer, who revised Leonardo's plans and decided not to build the dirt-moving machine. Instead of one deep ditch, as Leonardo designed, the new engineer decided to dig two ditches and to make them shallower than the bed of the Arno, which Leonardo knew would not work. In fact, the ditches ended up being only fourteen feet deep rather than the thirty-two feet that Leonardo had specified. After consulting Leonardo in Florence, Machiavelli wrote a blunt warning to the engineer: "We fear that the bed of the ditch is shallower than the bed of the Arno; this would have negative effects and in our opinion it would not direct the project to the end we wish."

The warning was ignored, but it turned out to be well founded. When the ditch was opened to the Arno, Machiavelli's assistant on the scene reported, "the waters never went through the ditches except when the river was in flood, and as soon as it subsided the water flowed

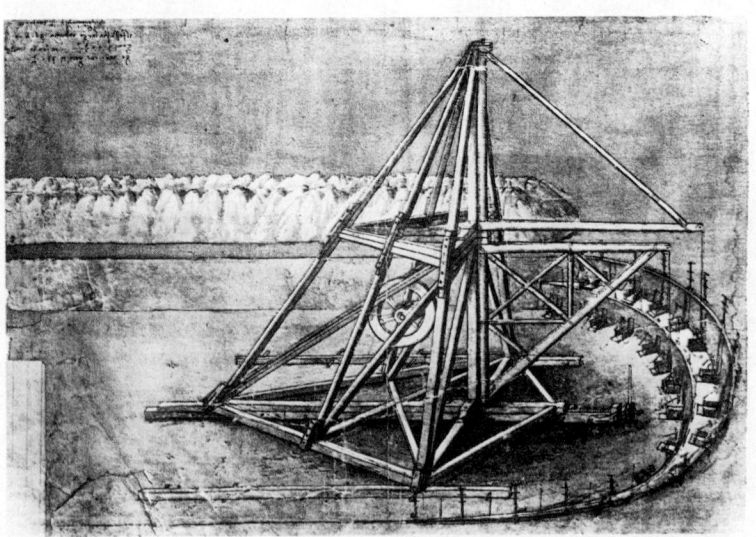

Fig. 89. Machine for digging canals.

back." A few weeks later, in early October, a violent storm caused the walls of the ditches to collapse, flooding the nearby farms but still not diverting the main course of the Arno. The project was abandoned.[9]

Even though it failed, the project to divert the Arno rekindled Leonardo's interest in a larger scheme: creating a navigable waterway between Florence and the Mediterranean Sea. Near Florence the Arno River often silted up, and it also had a series of waterfalls and rapids that kept boats from passing. Leonardo's solution was to bypass that part of the river with a canal. "Sluices should be made in the valley of la Chiana at Arezzo, so that when, in the summer, the Arno lacks water, the canal may not remain dry," he wrote. "Let this canal be twenty braccia [forty feet] wide." The plan would help mills and agriculture in the surrounding region, he suggested, so other towns would likely fund it.[10]

Leonardo drew a variety of maps in 1504 showing how the canal would work. One of them, done with brush and ink, was pricked with pins, evidence that he had made copies.[11] Another, done in delicate color with arresting details of tiny towns and fortifications, showed his plan to turn the swampy marshes of the Val di Chiana into a reservoir (fig. 90).[12] The fiasco of the Arno diversion project prob-

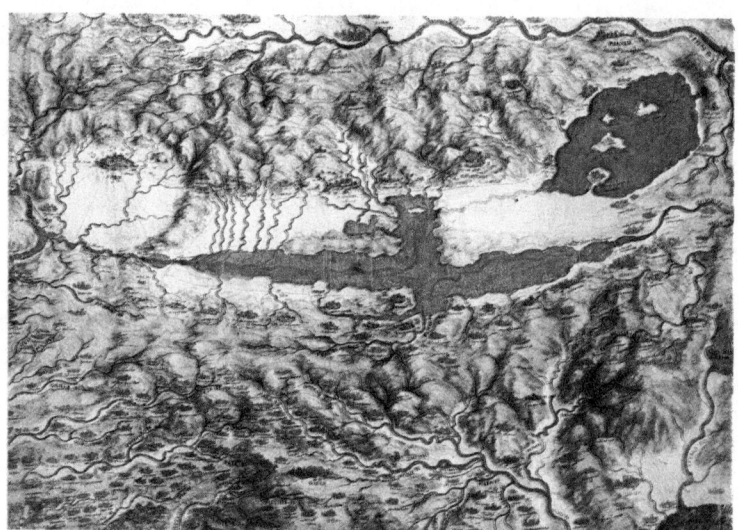

Fig. 90. Topographic view of the Chiana Valley.

ably persuaded the cash-strapped Florentine leaders not to attempt something even more ambitious, so Leonardo's canal proposals were shelved.

DRAINING THE PIOMBINO MARSHES

The failure of these projects did not immediately persuade Leonardo to give up hydraulic engineering, nor did his patrons want him to. At the end of October 1504, just weeks after the Arno diversion was abandoned, he was sent by the Florentine authorities, at Machiavelli's request, to provide technical assistance to the ruler of Piombino, a port city sixty miles south of Pisa that Florence was seeking to turn into an ally. Leonardo had been to Piombino two years earlier, while in the service of Cesare Borgia, and had studied the fortifications and looked at ways to drain the surrounding marshes. On this second visit, he spent two months designing a series of fortifications, moats, and secret passageways that could be used if the ruler was betrayed, "as happened at Fossombrone," a reference to Borgia's use of treachery in capturing that town.

The centerpiece of Leonardo's design was a circular fortress. Inside it had three rings of walls, with spaces between them that could be flooded and turned into moats during an attack. Leonardo had been studying the force exerted by objects hitting a wall at different angles, and he knew that the potency of a strike diminished as the angle became more oblique. Rounded walls, rather than straight ones, were thus more likely to deflect a cannonball. "It was Leonardo's most remarkable conception in the field of military engineering, and represented a total rethinking of the principles of fortification," Martin Kemp wrote. "Nowhere are Leonardo's theoretical principles, his sense of form, and his observational acumen more brilliantly combined than in the circular fortress designs."[13]

Leonardo's hydraulic challenge at Piombino was draining the marshlands surrounding the castle. His first idea was to divert some muddy water from the river into the marsh and allow the silt, dirt, and pebbles to settle to build up the land, similar to what is now being attempted with the marshes in southern Louisiana. Shallow channels would drain away the clear surface water, allowing more muddy water to enter.

Then he came up with another approach that was far more ambitious. At first glance, his plan may seem to skirt his blurred border with fantasy, but like many of his fantasies the basic idea is a good one ahead of its time. Drawing on his love of vortexes and eddies and swirling water, he sketched a way to create a "centrifugal pump" in the sea that was near the marsh. The idea was to stir the seawater in a circular way and thus create an artificial whirlpool. Tubes could then be used to siphon the water from the swamp and have it be sucked into the vortex of the whirlpool, which would be lower than the level of the marsh. In two separate notebooks, Leonardo described and drew a "method for drying up the swamps which border on the sea." The artificial whirlpool in the sea would be created by a "board that is turned by an axle," and "the siphon would expel its water at the back of the turning board." His drawings are extremely detailed and even include the width and speed that would be required of the artificial whirlpool.[14] Although it proved impractical, the theory was correct.

Typical of Leonardo, he also jotted down some observations on color and painting while in Piombino, observing closely the way sunlight and the reflected light from the sea colored the hull of a ship: "I saw the greenish shadows cast by the ropes, mast and spars on a white wall, as the sunlight struck it. The wall surface which was not lit by the sun took on the color of the sea."[15]

The Arno projects, the circular fortress, and the draining of the Piombino swamps had one thing in common with many of Leonardo's grandest projects, and even some of his less grand ones: they never came to fruition. They showed Leonardo at his most fantastical, dreaming up schemes that darted back and forth across the boundaries of practicality. Like the construction of his flying machines, they were too fanciful to execute.

This inability to ground his fantasies in reality has generally been regarded as one of Leonardo's major failings. Yet in order to be a true visionary, one has to be willing to overreach and to fail some of the time. Innovation requires a reality distortion field. The things he envisioned for the future often came to pass, even if it took a few centuries. Scuba gear, flying machines, and helicopters now exist. Suction pumps now drain swamps. Along the route of the canal that Leonardo drew there is now a major highway. Sometimes fantasies are paths to reality.

CHAPTER 25

Michelangelo and the Lost *Battles*

THE ASSIGNMENT

The commission that Leonardo received in October 1503 to paint a sprawling battle scene for Florence's Council Hall in the Palazzo della Signoria could have become one of the most important of his life. Had he completed the mural along the lines of the preparatory drawings he made, the result would have been a narrative masterpiece as captivating as *The Last Supper*, but one in which the motions of the bodies and the emotions of the minds would not have been constrained by the confined setting of a Passover Seder, as *The Last Supper* was. The finished work might have matched the emotional whirlwind that the *Adoration of the Magi* hinted at being, except wrought much larger.

But as with so many of his projects, Leonardo ended up not finishing the *Battle of Anghiari*, and what he painted is now lost. We can envision it mainly through copies. The best, which shows only the central part of what would have been a much larger mural, is by Peter Paul Rubens (fig. 91), which was made from other copies in 1603, after Leonardo's unfinished work was covered up.

Fig. 91. Peter Paul Rubens' copy of Leonardo's *Battle of Anghiari*.

Heightening the significance of the commission was the fact that Leonardo would end up pitted against his personal and professional young rival, Michelangelo, who was chosen in early 1504 to paint the other large mural in the hall. Even though neither painting was finished—like Leonardo's, Michelangelo's work is known to us only through copies and preparatory drawings—the saga provides a fascinating look at how the contrasting styles of Leonardo, then fifty-one, and Michelangelo, twenty-eight, each transformed the history of art.[1]

Florence's leaders wanted Leonardo's mural to be a celebration of a 1440 victory over Milan, one of the few examples of Florence's triumph on the battlefield. Their intent was to exalt the glory of their warriors. But Leonardo aimed to create something more profound. He had intense, conflicted feelings about war. After long fancying himself a military engineer, he had recently gained his first close-up experiences of war in the service of the brutal Cesare Borgia. At one point in his notebooks he called war "a most beastly madness," and some of his parables espouse pacifist sentiments. On the other hand, he had always been captivated and even beguiled by the martial arts. As we can see from his preparatory drawings, he planned to convey the enthralling passion that made war so gripping as well as the brutality that made it so abhorrent. The result would have been neither a commemoration of conquest like the *Bayeux Tapestry* nor an antiwar statement like Picasso's *Guernica*. In his own nature and in his art, Leonardo's attitude toward war was complex.

The location for the proposed painting was immense. It was to adorn almost one-third of the length of a 174-foot wall that was in the imposing meeting chamber for Florence's Signoria, or ruling council, on the second floor of what is now called the Palazzo Vecchio (fig. 92). The hall had been expanded in 1494 by Savonarola so that it would seat all five hundred members of the Grand Council. With Savonarola gone, the leader of the council was known as the *gonfaloniere*, or standard-bearer. That helped Leonardo determine what would be the central element of his *Battle of Anghiari* mural: the fight for the standard at the climax of the battle.

Leonardo was given workshop space for himself and his assistants in the "Popes' Room" in the cloisters of the Church of Santa Maria Novella, which was large enough to accommodate his full-size preparatory drawing. Machiavelli's secretary Agostino Vespucci provided Leonardo with a long narrative description of the original battle, including a blow-by-blow chronicle involving forty squadrons of cavalry and two thousand foot soldiers. Leonardo dutifully placed the account in his notebook (using a spare bit of the page to draw a new idea for hinged wings of a flying machine), and then proceeded to ignore it.[2] He decided instead to focus on an intimate struggle of a few horsemen flanked by scenes of two other tight skirmishes.

Fig. 92. Florence's Palazzo della Signoria, now the Palazzo Vecchio,
in 1498 during the burning of Savonarola. The Duomo is on the left.

THE CONCEPTION

The idea of painting a battle scene that was both glorious and horrifying was not new for Leonardo. He had written a long description
more than ten years earlier, when he was in Milan, of how it should
be done. He paid particular attention to the colors of the dust and
smoke. "First you must represent the smoke of artillery mingling in
the air with the dust tossed up by the movement of horses and the
combatants," he instructed. "The finest part of the dust rises high-

est; hence that part will be least visible and will look almost the same color as the air. . . . At the top, where the smoke is more separate from the dust, the smoke will assume a bluish tinge." He even specified how the dust clouds would be kicked up by the horses: "Make the little clouds of dust distant from each other in proportion to the strides made by the galloping horses; and the clouds which are furthest removed from the horses should be least visible; make them high and spreading and thin, and the nearer ones will be more conspicuous and smaller and denser."

He went on to describe, with his conflicted mix of fascination and repulsion, how to portray the brutality of battle: "If you show a man who has fallen to the ground, show the place where he has been dragged as bloody mud. A horse will drag the body of its dead rider, leaving traces of the corpse's blood in the dust and mud. Make the vanquished look pale and panic-stricken, their eyebrows raised high or knitted in grief, their faces stricken with painful lines." His account, more than a thousand words long, got more lurid as he warmed to his task. The brutality of war didn't repulse him as much as it seemed to mesmerize him, and the goriness he described would be reflected in the drawings he made for his battle mural:

> You must make the dead covered with dust, which is changed into crimson mire where it has mingled with the blood issuing in a stream from the corpse. The dying will be grinding their teeth, their eyeballs rolling heavenward as they beat their bodies with their fists and twist their limbs. Some might be shown disarmed and beaten down by the enemy, turning upon the foe to take an inhuman and bitter revenge with teeth and nails. . . . Some maimed warrior may be seen fallen to the earth, covering himself with his shield, while the enemy, bending over him, tries to deal him a deadly blow.

Just the thought of war brought out Leonardo's dark side and transformed the gentle artist. "There must not be a level spot that is not trampled and saturated with blood," he concluded.[3] His passion is visible in the frenzied sketches he drew in 1503 as he threw himself into his new commission.

THE DRAWINGS

Leonardo's initial drawings for the *Battle of Anghiari* show various moments of the battle, including one of cavalcades of infantry swarming to the scene, another of the Florentine troops arriving, and one showing them racing away with the battle standard that the Milanese carried. But gradually he tightened his focus on a single skirmish. The scene he finally chose for his central section was of three Florentine horsemen grappling the standard away from Milan's defeated but still-defiant general.[4]

In one preparatory drawing in the series (fig. 93), Leonardo used quick and sharp brown-ink strokes to show the fury of the four horses and riders struggling. On the lower half of the page he sketched nine versions of a nude soldier in frenzied twists as he swings a lance. Another drawing in the series shows soldiers being trampled, dragged, and lanced by the furious horsemen, just as he had described in his notebook. His depictions of the frantic clash of men and horses are messily tangled yet also gruesomely precise. One shows massive steeds rearing up and crashing down on naked soldiers squirming on the ground. The riders clinging atop the horses thrust lances into the bodies of the fallen. On another sheet he sketched a soldier beating a writhing enemy warrior who is also being lanced by a horseman. The brutality is frenzied, the savagery chaotic. Leonardo's astonishing ability to use simple pen strokes to capture movement has reached its peak. If you stare long enough at the pages, the horses and bodies seem as vibrant as a video.

He planned the expressions on the faces with great care. In one preparatory chalk drawing, he focused on the face of an old warrior, his bulging brows furrowed and nose wrinkled, as he stares down and shouts with rage (fig. 94). From the brows to the eyes to the mouth, Leonardo displayed his mastery of conveying emotions with every element of a face. His anatomy studies had taught him which of the facial muscles that move the lips also affect nostrils and brows. That allowed him to follow his own directions, written a decade earlier, on how to show an angry, anguished face: "The sides of the nose should have certain furrows, going in an arch from the nose and terminating

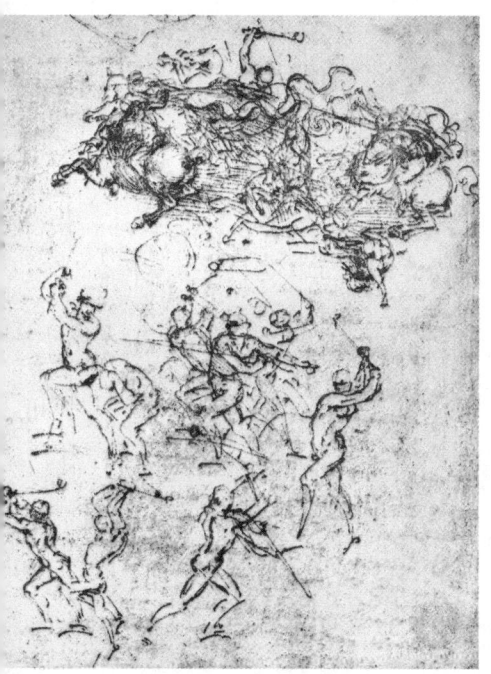

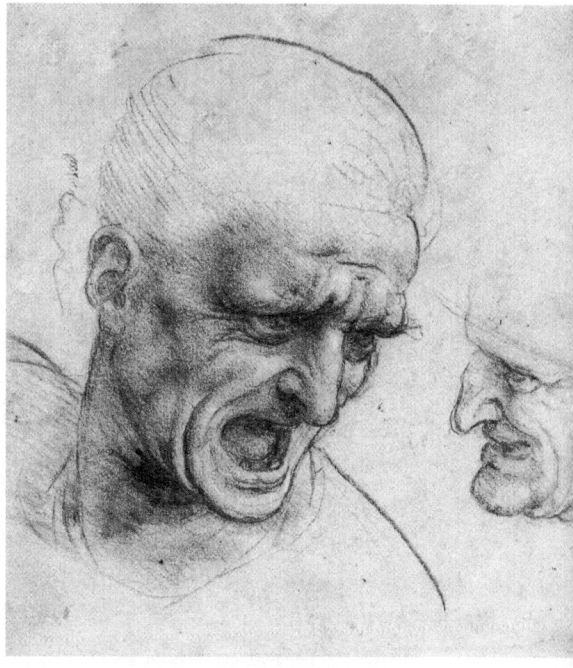

Fig. 93. Study for the
Battle of Anghiari.

Fig. 94. A warrior for the
Battle of Anghiari.

Fig. 95. Conveying the motion of horses.

at the edge of the eyes. Make the nostrils drawn up, causing these furrows, and the lips arched to disclose the upper teeth, with the teeth
parted in order to shriek lamentations."[5] This sketch ended up being
the model for the central warrior in his final full-size drawing for the
painting.

Leonardo had long been fascinated by horses, which he obsessively drew and even dissected when he worked on the equestrian
monument for Ludovico Sforza in Milan. In his preparatory drawings
for the *Anghiari* mural, he reengaged in the subject. His possessions
at the time included "a book of horses sketched for the cartoon,"[6] and
they display the same intensity of motion and emotion as the human
faces he drew. Vasari was among those impressed by how Leonardo
was able to make the horses as much a part of the physical and emotional battle as the humans: "Rage, fury, and revenge are perceived as
much in the men as in the horses, two of which have their forelegs interlocked and are fighting no less fiercely with their teeth than those
who are riding them."

In one of these drawings (fig. 95), Leonardo used a frenzy of
chalk strokes to combine two sequential instants, like a stop-action
photographer or a precursor to Duchamp. The technique allowed him
to convey the horse's wild lurching and lunging as it engaged in the
battle with an intensity equal to that of its rider. In his best drawings,
Leonardo amazes us by capturing the world precisely as an observant
eye would see it; in the case of the wildly charging horses, he goes
even further by capturing motion in a way that our eye cannot see.
"They are among the greatest evocations of movement in the entire
history of art," the British art critic Jonathan Jones wrote. "Movement, something that had obsessed Leonardo ever since he had tried
to catch the blur of a cat's squirming limbs in an early drawing, is here
clarified as a theme with blood-red intensity."[7]

On another page from his book of horses, he demonstrated how a
horse could display emotion like a human (fig. 96). There are six horse
heads, each showing a different degree of anger. Some bare their teeth
and, like the old warrior, furrow their brow and flare their nostrils. In
the midst of these boldly drawn horses, he lightly sketched, as if for
comparison, the head of a man and of a lion with analogous expres-

Fig. 96. Horses showing fury, with an angry lion and man in the center.

sions of fury, their teeth bared and furrowed brow thrust forward. Here we have a cross between a piece of art and a study in comparative anatomy. What began as a preparatory drawing—and indeed had elements that found their way into the battle scene he began to paint—also became, in inimitable Leonardo fashion, an investigation into muscles and nerves.

For a final reminder of how varied his passions and curiosities were, we can turn over the page of horse sketches to see what else he was thinking about at the time. The reverse of the sheet also has an energetic sketch of a horse's head, but above it is a carefully rendered schematic of the solar system, showing the earth and sun and moon with projection lines explaining why we see the various phases of the moon. In a note, he analyzed the illusion of why the moon appears larger when it is on the horizon than when overhead. Look at an object through a lens and it will seem bigger, he wrote, and "by this means you will have produced an exact imitation of the atmosphere." On the bottom of the page are some geometrical illustrations of a square and slices of a circle, as Leonardo pursued his never-ending quest to transform geometric shapes into other shapes of the same area and to solve the challenge of squaring a circle. Even the horse seems a bit awed and reverential, as if it is marveling at how Leonardo has scattered around it the evidence of his amazing mind.[8]

THE PAINTING

Leonardo's immersion in his preparatory studies, which were driven by his passionate curiosity more than the mere utility of sketching out a painting, meant that he was not progressing as fast as the Signoria would have liked. At one point a pay dispute erupted. When he went to get his monthly fee, the cashier gave it to him in small coins. Leonardo refused the money. "I am no penny-painter," he objected. As the tension escalated, he raised money from some friends so he could pay back his fee and abandon the project, but the *gonfaloniere* of the Signoria, Piero Soderini (brother of the diplomat who had negotiated with Borgia), refused the repayment and convinced Leonardo to go back to work.

A revised contract was signed by Leonardo and witnessed by his friend Machiavelli in May 1504. By then the Florentines were beginning to worry about Leonardo's proclivity to procrastinate, so they wrote into the new contract that he would have to repay all his fees and forfeit all the work he had done if he did not finish by February 1505. The document declared:

> Several months ago Leonardo, son of Ser Piero da Vinci, and a Florentine citizen, undertook to do a painting for the Sala del Consiglio Grande, and seeing that this painting has already been begun as a cartoon by the said Leonardo, he moreover having received on such account 35 florins, and desiring that the work be concluded as soon as possible . . . the Signoria have resolved that Leonardo da Vinci is to have completely finished painting and brought it wholly to perfection by the end of next February without quibble or objection. . . . And in the event that Leonardo shall not have finished in the stipulated time, then the Signoria can compel him by whatever means appropriate to repay all the money received in connection with this work and Leonardo would be obliged to make over to the said Signoria as much as had been done.[9]

Soon after signing this new contract, Leonardo constructed a scissors-like platform that, Vasari reported, "was raised by contracting it and lowered by expanding." He requisitioned eighty-eight pounds of flour to make a paste with which to stick up his preparatory cartoon and the ingredients for whitewash to prepare the wall. After spending a few months at the end of the year on his swamp-draining and military mission to Piombino, he returned to the *Battle of Anghiari* in early 1505.

As with *The Last Supper*, Leonardo wanted to paint his mural using oil-based pigments and glazes, which enabled him to create luminous illusions. Oil permitted him to paint more slowly, with finer brush-strokes and greater nuance of color and shadow transitions, which would have been particularly suited for the hazy and dusty atmospheric effects he intended for the *Battle of Anghiari*.[10] Because there were already signs that his use of oil on dry plaster was causing *The Last Supper* to flake away, Leonardo experimented with new techniques. Unfortunately, painting on walls was one endeavor where his quest for innovation and scientific experimentation repeatedly failed him.

For the *Battle of Anghiari*, he treated the plaster wall with what he called Greek pitch ("pece grecha per la pictura"), probably a dark residue of distilled turpentine or a mix of resin and wax. His list of provisions also included almost twenty pounds of linseed oil. His small experiments with these materials seemed to work, so he became confident he could use them for the entire mural. But almost immediately he noticed that his mixtures were not sticking well. One early biographer said that Leonardo was cheated by his supplier and that the linseed oil was faulty. To dry the pigments and perhaps concentrate the oil, Leonardo lit a fire below his painting.

The February 1505 deadline came and went with the painting not close to completion. He was still making his delicate oil brushstrokes on the wall in June when all was almost ruined by a torrential rainstorm. "Friday the 6th of June, 1505, at the stroke of the thirteenth hour I began to paint in the palace," he recorded in a notebook. His brief description of the scene is unclear, but it seems to indicate that the storm caused great leaks that overwhelmed the vessels used to remove the water. "As I lowered the brush, the weather changed for the worse and the bell started to toll, calling the men to the court. The cartoon was torn, water poured down, and the vessel of water that was being carried broke. Suddenly the weather became even worse and it rained very heavily till nightfall."[11]

This entry is considered by some a notarial recording of the momentous day he first began painting the *Battle of Anghiari*, but I think not. He had signed his new contract and requisitioned materials a year earlier, and he had probably been working on and off since then. There is no other case when he recorded the moment of starting or finishing a painting, but he regularly wrote about storms, deluges, and other weather phenomena that stimulated his apocalyptic imagination. I suspect his notebook entry was prompted by the storm rather than some painting milestone.

Vasari, who saw Leonardo's unfinished painting, described it vividly:

> An old soldier in a red cap, crying out, grips the staff with one hand, and, raising a scimitar with the other, furiously aims a blow to cut off both the hands of those who, gnashing their teeth in the struggle, are striving in utmost fierceness to defend their banner. On the ground, between the legs of the horses, there are two figures that are fighting together, and the one on the ground has over him a soldier who has raised his arm as high as possible, that thus with greater force he may plunge a dagger into his throat, in order to end his life; while the other, struggling with his legs and arms, is doing what he can to escape death. It is not possible to describe the invention that Leonardo showed in the garments of the soldiers, all varied by him in different ways, and likewise in the helmet crests and other ornaments; not to mention the incredible mastery that he displayed in the forms and lineaments of the horses, which Leonardo, with their fiery spirit, muscles, and shapely beauty, drew better than any other master.

In trying to complete this painting and make it stick to the wall that summer of 1505, Leonardo could feel the presence of a younger man looking over his shoulder, both literally and figuratively. Preparing to paint a competing mural in the room was the rising star of Florence's art world, Michelangelo Buonarroti.

MICHELANGELO

When Leonardo left Florence for Milan in 1482, Michelangelo was only seven years old. His father was a member of Florence's minor nobility who subsisted on small public appointments, his mother had died, and he was living in the countryside with the family of a stone-cutter. During the seventeen years that Leonardo was away in Milan, Michelangelo became Florence's hot new artist. He was apprenticed to the thriving Florence workshop of the painter Domenico Ghirlandaio, won the patronage of the Medici, and traveled to Rome in 1496, where he carved his *Pietà*, showing Mary grieving over the body of Jesus.

By 1500 the two artists were back in Florence. Michelangelo, then twenty-five, was a celebrated but petulant sculptor, and Leonardo, forty-eight, was a genial and generous painter who had a following of friends and young students. It is enticing to think of what might have occurred if Michelangelo had treated him as a mentor. But that did not happen. As Vasari reported, he displayed instead "a very great disdain" toward Leonardo.

One day Leonardo was walking with a friend through one of the central piazzas of Florence wearing one of his distinctive rose-pink (*rosato*) tunics. There was a small group discussing a passage from Dante, and they asked Leonardo his opinion of its meaning. At that moment Michelangelo came by, and Leonardo suggested that he might be able to explain it. Michelangelo took offense, as if Leonardo were mocking him. "No, explain it yourself," he shot back. "You are the one who modelled a horse to be cast in bronze, was unable to do it, and was forced to give up the attempt in shame." He then turned and walked away. On another occasion when Michelangelo encountered Leonardo, he again referred to the fiasco of the Sforza horse monument, saying, "So those idiot [*caponi*] Milanese actually believed in you?"[12]

Unlike Leonardo, Michelangelo was often contentious. He had once insulted the young artist Pietro Torrigiano, who was drawing alongside him in a Florence chapel; Torrigiano recalled "clenching my

fist and giving him such a blow on the nose that I felt bone and cartilage go down like biscuit beneath my knuckles." Michelangelo had
a disfigured nose for the rest of his life. Combined with his slightly
hunched back and unwashed appearance, that made him a contrast to
the handsome, muscular, and stylish Leonardo. Michelangelo's rivalries extended to many other artists, including Pietro Perugino, whom
he called a "clumsy [*goffo*] artist"; Perugino unsuccessfully sued him
for defamation.

"Leonardo was handsome, urbane, eloquent and dandyishly
well dressed," wrote Michelangelo's biographer Martin Gayford.
"In contrast, Michelangelo was neurotically secretive." He was also
"intense, disheveled, and irascible," according to another biographer,
Miles Unger. He had powerful feelings of love and hate toward those
around him but few close companions or protégés. "My delight is in
melancholy," Michelangelo once confessed.[13]

Whereas Leonardo was disinterested in personal religious practice,
Michelangelo was a pious Christian who found himself convulsed by
the agony and the ecstasy of faith. They were both gay, but Michelangelo was tormented and apparently imposed celibacy on himself,
whereas Leonardo was quite comfortable and open about having male
companions. Leonardo took delight in clothes, sporting colorful short
tunics and fur-lined cloaks. Michelangelo was ascetic in dress and
demeanor; he slept in his dusty studio, rarely bathed or removed his
dog-skin shoes, and dined on bread crusts. "How could he fail to envy
and detest the easy charm, the elegance, refinement, amiable sweetness of manner, dilettantism, and above all the skepticism of Leonardo, a man of another generation, said to be without religious faith,
around whom there constantly strutted a crowd of beautiful pupils,
led by the insufferable Salai?" wrote Serge Bramly.[14]

Soon after his return to Florence, Michelangelo was commissioned
to turn a hulking and imperfect piece of white marble into a statue of
the biblical Goliath-slayer, David. Working with his usual secrecy, by
early 1504 he had produced the most famous statue ever carved (fig.
97). Seventeen feet high and dazzlingly bright, it instantly eclipsed all
previous statues of David, including the pretty-boy version by Verroc-

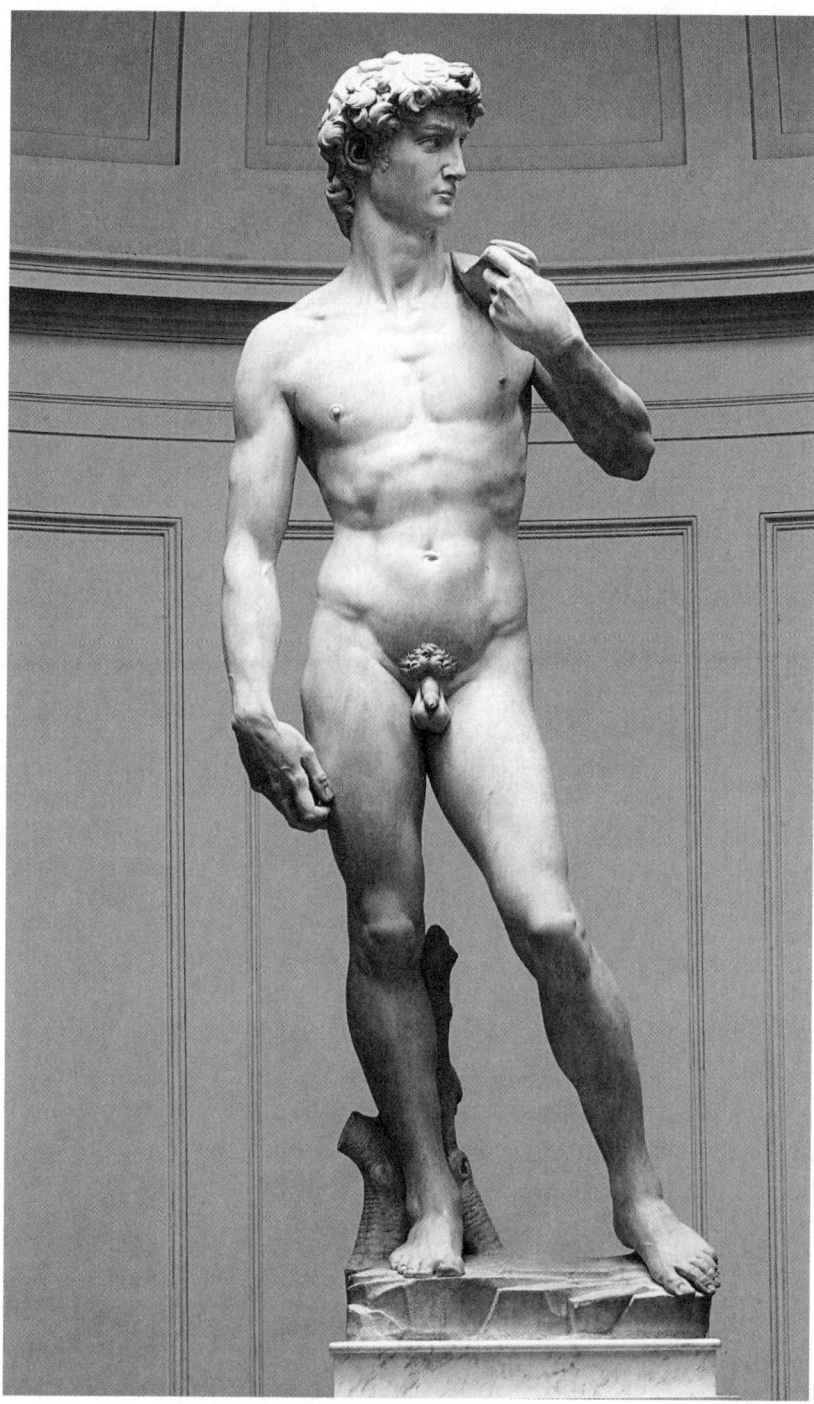

Fig. 97. Michelangelo's *David*.

chio for which the youthful Leonardo served as a model. Verrocchio and others had portrayed David as a young boy in triumph, often with Goliath's head at his feet. But Michelangelo showed him as a man, starkly nude, as he prepared to go into the fight. His stare is alert, his brow determined. He stands, with an air of affected casualness, in a *contrapposto* position, his weight on one leg, the other thrust forward. As Leonardo did in painting, Michelangelo showed the body in motion, torso twisting gently to the right, neck to the left. Though David seems relaxed, we can sense the tension in the muscles of his neck and see the veins bulging on the back of his right hand.

Florence's leaders were then faced with the question of where to place this astonishing colossus. The issue was so contentious that there was even an outbreak of stone-throwing by some protestors. Being a republic, Florence formed a committee. Thirty or so artists and civic leaders were convened to discuss the issue, including Filippino Lippi, Perugino, Botticelli, and of course Leonardo. They gathered on January 25, 1504, in a meeting room near the Duomo, in sight of the finished statue, and considered nine locations, two of which became finalists.

Michelangelo originally hoped that his statue would stand outside the entrance to the cathedral on the Piazza del Duomo, but he soon realized that it was better as a civic symbol of Florence and urged that it be placed in the piazza in front of the Palazzo della Signoria. Giuliano da Sangallo, who was one of Florence's best architects as well as a sculptor, favored a site underneath the wide-arched Loggia della Signoria, a building on the corner of the piazza. He and his supporters made the argument that tucking the *David* there would best protect it from the elements, but that choice also had the effect of making it less prominent, dominant, and visible. "We will go to see it, and not have the figure come to see us," said another supporter of the loggia location.

Not surprisingly, Leonardo came down on the side of stashing it inside the portico. When it was his turn to speak, he said, "I agree that it should be in the Loggia, as Giuliano has said, but on the parapet where they hang the tapestries." Clearly, he preferred that Michelangelo's statue be put in an inconspicuous space.[15]

Leonardo went on to add something surprising. He argued that the statue be installed "with decent ornament [*chon ornamento decente*]." It was clear what he meant. Michelangelo had sculpted David unabashedly naked, with prominent pubic hair and genitalia. Leonardo suggested that a decent ornament should be attached "in such a way that it does not spoil the ceremonies of the officials." In his notebook at the time, he drew a small sketch based on Michelangelo's *David* (fig. 98). Look carefully, and you can see what he is suggest-

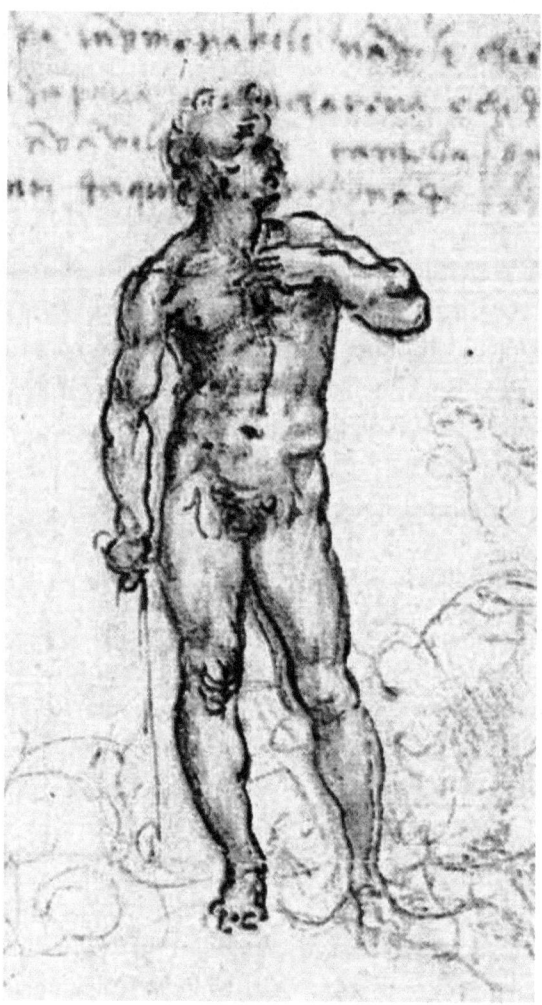

Fig. 98. Leonardo's notebook sketch of Michelangelo's *David.*

ing; he has discreetly covered David's genitals with what looks like a bronze leaf.[16]

Leonardo was not generally prudish about nudity. From his *Vitruvian Man* to his portraits of Salai, he merrily drew naked men, and in his notebooks he once wrote that the penis should be displayed unashamedly. Indeed, a red-chalk and ink nude he drew in 1504, around the time of the statue placement discussions, seems to combine, in a psychologically interesting way, the fleshy face of Salai, then twenty-four, with the muscular physiognomy of Michelangelo's David (fig.31).[17] He also did sketches of a nude and muscular Hercules, front and back, that were probably for a statue he hoped someday to make as a counterpoint to *David*.[18] Yet there was something about Michelangelo's version of muscular, intrusive male nudity that Leonardo found disagreeable.

Michelangelo won the battle of placement. His *David* was carefully rolled from his workshop over a four-day period and installed at the entrance of the Palazzo della Signoria. It stayed there until 1873, when it was moved inside the Accademia Gallery, and in 1910 a replica was placed in front of what had by then been renamed the Palazzo Vecchio. But Leonardo won his argument that a "decent ornament" should be added. A gilded garland made of brass and twenty-eight copper leaves was strapped on, covering David's genitals. It stayed there for at least forty years.[19]

THE COMPETITION

As soon as his statue of David was placed in the most prominent spot in Florence's civic plaza, Michelangelo was commissioned to paint a battle scene that would be a companion to Leonardo's in the great hall. To the Signoria and its leader Soderini, the decision was a conscious effort to play off the rivalry between the era's two greatest artists. Accounts from the time all use the same word for it: *concorrenza*, or competition. At the funeral of Soderini years later, a eulogist praised him by saying, "To stage a competition with Leonardo, he assigned Michelangelo that other wall, where Michelangelo, to conquer him, began to paint." The near contemporary artist and writer Benvenuto Cellini, in praising Michelangelo's cartoon, stated, "He made it in competition with another artist, Leonardo da Vinci."[20] And Vasari used the same word: "While that rarest of painters Leonardo da Vinci was painting in the Great Council Hall, Piero Soderini, then Gonfalonier, because of the great ability he saw in Michelangelo, got part of that Hall allocated to him; which was how it came about that he did the other façade in competition with Leonardo."

The subject assigned to Michelangelo was another of Florence's rare battlefield victories, this one over Pisa in the Battle of Cascina in 1364. Like Leonardo, he failed to complete his painting, and once again we know it only through copies of the full-scale preparatory cartoon he drew, including one made by his pupil Bastiano da Sangallo (fig. 99).

Rather than focusing on a climactic event, as Leonardo did with his battle for the standard, Michelangelo chose to portray an oddly tangential scene, one that featured more than a dozen muscular and naked men. This is the moment when Florence's soldiers were bathing in the Arno River and received an alarm that the enemy was attack-

Fig. 99. A copy of Michelangelo's lost *Battle of Cascina*.

ing, causing them to scramble up the banks and grab their clothes. A rare event in military history that centered on nude wet men, it was a scene suited for Michelangelo, who had never been to war or seen a battle but was infatuated with the male body. "In all his works Michelangelo was drawn to the nude," Jonathan Jones wrote. "Here, he flaunted it as an obsession—drew attention to his habit, dramatized his penchant. . . . Anyone who hadn't registered before that young Michelangelo was utterly besotted with the bodies of men was certainly going to notice now."[21]

Leonardo rarely criticized other painters,[22] but after seeing Michelangelo's bathing nudes he repeatedly disparaged what he called the "anatomical painter." Clearly referring to his rival, he mocked those who "draw their nude figures looking like wood, devoid of grace, so that you would think you were looking at a sack of walnuts rather than the human form, or a bundle of radishes rather than the muscles of figures." The phrase *un sacco di noce* amused him; he used it more than once in his attacks on Michelangelo's muscular nudes. "You should not make all the muscles of the body too conspicuous . . . otherwise you will produce a sack of walnuts rather than a human figure."[23]

Therein lay another difference between the two artists. Michelangelo tended to specialize in muscular male nudes; even when he painted the ceiling of the Sistine Chapel a few years later he included twenty *ignudi*, athletic nude males, as corner figures. Leonardo, on the contrary, prided himself on the "universal" nature of his subjects. He believed "The painter should aim at universality, because there is a great want of self-respect in doing one thing well and another badly, as many do who study only the nude figure and do not seek after variety," Leonardo wrote. "This is a defect that demands stern reprehension."[24] He could certainly draw and paint male nudes, but his virtuosity came from his imagination and inventiveness, which required diversity and fantasy. "Let the painter composing narrative pictures take pleasure in variety," he directed.[25]

Leonardo's broader critique of Michelangelo was his argument that painting is a higher form of art than sculpture. In a passage written just after the showdown of battles in the Florentine hall, Leonardo argued:

Painting embraces and contains within itself all things perceptible in nature, which the poverty of sculpture cannot do, such as show the colors of all things and their diminution. The painter will demonstrate various distances by the variation of color of the air interposed between objects and the eye. He will demonstrate how the species of objects penetrate mists with difficulty. He will demonstrate how mountains and valleys are seen through clouds in the rain. He will demonstrate dust itself, and how the combatants raise a commotion in it.[26]

Leonardo, of course, was referring to Michelangelo's sculptures, but judging from the extant copies his criticism also applied to Michelangelo's *Battle of Cascina* and even some of his finished paintings. In other words, he painted like a sculptor. Michelangelo was good at delineating forms with the use of sharp lines, but he showed little skill with the subtleties of sfumato, shadings, refracted lights, soft visuals, or changing color perspectives. He freely admitted that he preferred the chisel to the brush. "I am not in the right place, and I am not a painter," he confessed in a poem when he embarked on the ceiling of the Sistine Chapel a few years later.[27]

A look at Michelangelo's oil and tempera panel painting *Doni Tondo* (fig.100), done around the time of the Signoria competition, shows the difference between the styles of the two men. Michelangelo seems to have been influenced by the cartoon Leonardo had done for the *Virgin and Child with Saint Anne*, which had caused a sensation when displayed in Florence. Michelangelo's version has a similar narrative feel, with the characters twisting in a tight configuration. But there the similarities end. Michelangelo prominently includes Joseph; for reasons best left to Freud, Leonardo never conspicuously featured Joseph in any of his art. Though vividly colored, Michelangelo's three main figures seem sculpted rather than painted; they are lifeless, and their expressions lack charm or mystery. His background features not nature but his favorite motif: male nudes, lounging languorously and a bit pointlessly, even though there is no river for them to bathe in. They are in sharp focus, with no sign of Leonardo's understanding of atmospheric or distance perspective. "He had no use for Leonardo's

Fig. 100. Michelangelo's *Doni Tondo*.

famous sfumato," writes Unger. Gayford calls *Doni Tondo* "almost a rebuttal in paint of Leonardo's ideas."[28]

Michelangelo's painting has the sharp, delineated outlines that Leonardo, with his love of sfumato and blurred borders, scorned as a matter of philosophy, optics, mathematics, and aesthetics. To define objects, Michelangelo used lines rather than following Leonardo's practice of using shadows, which is why Michelangelo's look flat rather than three-dimensional. The sharply lined contours are also featured in his *Battle of Cascina*, as shown in some of his preparatory studies. It is as if he had looked at Leonardo's method of creating a dusty and hazy battle scene blurred by motion, as well as the *sfumatura* in Leonardo's other works, and decided to do just the opposite.

Their divergent approaches represent two schools in Florentine art: that of Leonardo, Andrea del Sarto, Raphael, Fra Bartolomeo, and others who emphasized the use of sfumato and chiaroscuro, and the more traditional approach taken by Michelangelo, Agnolo Bronzino, Alessandro Allori, and others who favored a *disegno* based on outlined contours.[29]

ABANDONED

In the spring of 1505, with his painting for Florence's council hall not yet begun, Michelangelo accepted a summons from Pope Julius II to Rome to sculpt a tomb. As if energized by Michelangelo's absence, Leonardo threw himself into painting his battle scene. But then the temperamental Michelangelo had a temporary falling out with the pope, who he felt was not being deferential enough. (Artists such as Leonardo and Michelangelo were reaching such a status that popes and marchesas had to defer to them on occasion.) "You can tell the pope that if he wants me from now on, he can seek me elsewhere," Michelangelo declared, and returned to Florence around April 1506.

His presence back in Florence unnerved Leonardo, who as usual was both procrastinating and having difficulty getting his oil-based paint mixtures to adhere to the wall. He would eventually move back to Milan, consigning the *Anghiari* mural to his long list of abandoned projects. Michelangelo too would leave again, kneeling to ask the pope's forgiveness and then returning to Rome. He would stay there for another decade and paint the ceiling of the Sistine Chapel.[30]

So neither painting was ever finished. The final loss of both men's work came at the hand, ironically, of Vasari, the painter-biographer who lionized them. He was commissioned in the 1560s to renovate the great hall, where he painted six battle scenes of his own. In recent years, a group of experts, including the high-technology art diagnostician Maurizio Seracini, discovered some evidence that Leonardo's partial painting may still exist under one of Vasari's. Tiny holes drilled into Vasari's work revealed pigments on the wall underneath that may be from Leonardo's painting. But authorities have resisted requests to allow further investigations that might harm Vasari's mural.[31]

Once again we have to wrestle with the reasons Leonardo decided to leave a work unfinished. The proximate cause was the problems he had with his materials. "Conceiving the wish to color on the wall in oils," Vasari reported, "he made a composition of so gross an admixture to act as a binder on the wall, that when he painted, it began to peel off in such a manner that in a short time he abandoned it, seeing it spoiling."[32] Added to that was the unnerving specter of Michelangelo hovering behind him; Leonardo did not have a competitive personality, so he likely did not relish the contest.

There was also a more artistic challenge, I think, that contributed to Leonardo's decision to abandon the commission. When painting *The Last Supper*, he became immersed in the difficulty of getting the proper visual perspective in a large mural that would be seen from multiple vantage points in a room. A conventional central-point perspective scheme would have made parts of the scene appear distorted. Other painters would not have noticed, or would have chosen to ignore, the way figures in a large painting could seem disproportionate when viewed from different parts of the room. But Leonardo was obsessed by the optics, mathematics, and art of perspective.

For *The Last Supper* he had come up with tricks and illusions and artifices to make his work appear realistic from different vantages. He was able to make a preferred vantage point that was far away from the painting; he calculated it would ideally be located ten to twenty times as far away as the painting was wide. But the area that he was supposed to paint in Florence's council hall was fifty-five feet long, twice that of *The Last Supper*, and his mural would be viewed from at most seventy feet away, far less than twice its width.

In addition, his painting was supposed to be an outdoor scene lit by broad daylight, unlike *The Last Supper*, which depicted an enclosed dining room on the wall of an enclosed dining room. The challenges of how to get all of the perspectives from each angle to look believable were combined with the difficulties of showing direct and reflected lighting and shadows in an open-air scene that was to be viewed inside a room. Leonardo had the authorities cut four more windows in the hall, but that did not eliminate the challenge.[33]

He was a perfectionist faced with challenges other artists would have disregarded but that he could not. So he put down his brushes. That behavior meant he would never again receive a public commission. But it is also what allowed him to go down in history as an obsessed genius rather than merely a reliable master painter.

"SCHOOL OF THE WORLD"

The unfinished battle scenes turned out to be two of the most influential lost paintings in history, and they helped to shape the High Renaissance. "These battle cartoons of Leonardo and Michelangelo are the turning point of the Renaissance," according to Kenneth Clark.[34] They were kept on display in Florence until 1512, and young artists flocked to see them. One of those was the sculptor Cellini, who described the competing display in his autobiography: "These cartoons stood one in the Medici Palace and the other in the Pope's Hall, and so long as they remained there, they served as the school of the world."[35]

Raphael traveled to Florence just to see the two cartoons that had caused such a sensation, Vasari reported, and he drew versions of them. The animated details of both unfinished works spurred the imaginations, and the mannerism, of subsequent generations. "Frenzied faces, monstrous armor, twisting bodies, convoluted poses, masks, and mad horses—between them the two great Council Hall images provided sixteenth-century artists with a banquet of oddities," Jonathan Jones wrote. "In these fantastical works, two geniuses tried to outdo one another in sheer quiddity."[36]

The showdown did more than any paragone could have to raise the status of artists. Leonardo and Michelangelo had become luminaries, paving the way for other artists—who until then had rarely even signed their work—to do the same. When the pope summoned Michelangelo, and when the Milanese vied with the Florentines over the services of Leonardo, it was recognition that super-artists had their own recognizable style, artistic personality, and individual genius. Instead of being treated as somewhat interchangeable members of the craftsman's class, the best artists were now treated as singular stars.

CHAPTER 26

Return to Milan

THE DEATH OF SER PIERO

In the midst of Leonardo's struggle to paint the *Battle of Anghiari*, his father died.

Their relationship had been complex. Piero da Vinci never legitimated Leonardo, but perhaps that was an act of intentional or unintentional kindness as well as coldness. Had he done so, Leonardo may have been expected to become a notary, despite guild rules that made that difficult, and Piero knew that vocation would not suit him. He helped his son get at least three major painting commissions, but he also drew up stringent contracts designed to force him to deliver. When Leonardo failed to do so, it likely caused strain between them.

After not marrying Leonardo's mother, Piero had four wives. The last two were much younger than Leonardo, and with them Piero had nine sons and two daughters, many of them sired when he was in his seventies. Leonardo's half-siblings were all young enough to be his children, and they didn't regard him as a potential family heir.

The difficult family dynamics became evident when Piero died. Leonardo, imperfectly displaying his notarial heritage, recorded the event in his notebook. He seemed agitated. On a page filled with lists of his expenditures in July 1504, including "one florin to Salai to spend on the house," he wrote the following: "On Wednesday at seven o'clock died Ser Piero da Vinci on the 9th of July 1504."[1] There was one little oddity: July 9 that year was a Tuesday.

Then Leonardo did something even more unusual. On the top right of another page, which contains some typical geometric drawings and a few columns of added numbers, he had the information repeated in a sloping script written in the conventional left-to-right manner. If you look at the manuscript carefully, you see that the note is in a different ink from the rest of the page; the fact that it is carefully scribed in a normal direction indicates that it may have been dictated to one of his assistants. It begins, "Wednesday at 7 o'clock." The next word would likely have been "died," but the line breaks off and is crossed out. On the next line the text begins anew: "On the 9th of July 1504 Wednesday at seven o'clock died Ser Piero da Vinci notary at the Palazzo del Popolo, my father, at seven o'clock, being eighty years old, leaving behind ten sons and two daughters." Again there is something wrong with the day, and this time he has stated the hour twice. He also got his father's age wrong by two years; Piero was only seventy-eight.[2]

In saying that Piero had ten sons, Leonardo was counting himself. Nevertheless, his father did not bequeath him any inheritance. Despite his advanced age and the fact that he was a notary, Piero had not made a will. Although he may not have made an active decision to disinherit Leonardo, he knew that dying intestate meant his property would be divided among only his legitimate sons. Perhaps he felt that leaving money to Leonardo wasn't necessary because he was already successful, though in fact he was never comfortably wealthy. Or maybe Piero thought an inheritance would make his son even more negligent about completing commissions. More likely is that Leonardo was not legally an heir and, with their relationship strained, Piero felt no reason to change that. He had brought Leonardo into this world as an *illegitimo*, had not legitimated him as a child, and on his death delegitimized him yet again.[3]

LEAVING FLORENCE

The first time he moved away from Florence to Milan, in 1482, Leonardo left the *Adoration of the Magi* as merely a cartoon. When he decided to move the second time, in 1506, he left with the *Battle of Anghiari* similarly promising but unpainted. He would end up making Milan his home base for seven years, with only temporary visits back to Florence.

His excuse for going to Milan this time was to resolve the dispute over the second version of *Virgin of the Rocks*. He and his partner on the work, Ambrogio de Predis, had not been paid, and they had taken the matter to court. An arbitrator in April 1506 ruled against them, saying that the painting was *imperfetto*, a word connoting "unfinished" as well as "imperfect." Specifically, the judgment was that there was not enough of Leonardo's hand in it, so he was required to come add his own finishing touches before payment would be made.

If he had wished, Leonardo could have deflected the demand that he return to Milan by forfeiting any more payments for the *Virgin of the Rocks*. Money had never dictated his actions, plus he would have earned just as much if he stayed in Florence and finished the *Battle of Anghiari*. He heeded the summons to Milan because he wanted to go there. He had no desire to continue to struggle with his battle scene, compete with a younger artist who painted like a sculptor, or live in a town with his half-siblings.

The Florentine authorities reluctantly let him leave at the end of May 1506 partly for diplomatic reasons. Florence had been protected from Borgia and then other potential invaders by the French king, Louis XII, who then controlled Milan and admired *The Last Supper* and its artist. Louis expressed his desire to have Leonardo return to Milan, at least temporarily, and Florence's leaders were afraid to refuse. However, they did want Leonardo's stay to be temporary, so they required him to sign a notarized document pledging to return in three months. His bank manager had to cosign and commit to pay a penalty of 150 florins if he failed to do so. (The final payment for *Virgin of the Rocks*, when he did collect it, was only 35 florins.)

When Leonardo's three months were almost up, it became clear that he would not be returning to Florence anytime soon. To stave off Florentine demands or a forfeiture of his florins, he had his French patrons launch a protracted and amusing barrage of diplomatic démarches. In August 1506 Charles d'Amboise, the French governor of Milan, sent two missives, one polite and the other more abrupt, saying that "in spite of all previous promises" Leonardo needed an extension of his leave from Florence because he had not finished all of the projects the king wanted. Florence's leaders acquiesced with the understanding that he would come back at the end of September.

Unsurprisingly, that did not occur, and in early October Florence's *gonfaloniere* Soderini lost patience. He sent a letter that attacked Leonardo's honor and threatened Florence's relations with Milan. "Leonardo has not behaved as he should have done towards the Republic, because he has taken a large sum of money and only made a small beginning on the great work he was commissioned to carry out," he wrote. "We do not wish any further requests to be made on this matter, for this great work is for the benefit of all our citizens, and for us to release him from his obligations would be a failure of our duty."[4]

But Leonardo stayed in Milan. Charles d'Amboise sent a flowery and polite rebuke to the Florentines, asserting, with some merit, that Leonardo was loved in Milan and, by implication, underappreciated in Florence, especially when it came to his engineering skills. "We were among those who loved him even before our eyes had rested upon him, and now, since we have known him and been much in his company, and have had personal experience of his various gifts, we truly see that his name, famous in painting, is relatively obscure so far as those other branches of knowledge in which he has reached so great a height." Although he agreed that Leonardo would be free to return to Florence if he wanted, he added a reproach couched as a mischievous recommendation that the Florentines should treat their native son better: "If it be fitting to give a man of such talent a recommendation to his fellow citizens, we recommend him to you as strongly as we can and assure you that everything you can do to increase either his fortune and well-being, or those honors to which he is entitled, would give us, as well as him, the greatest pleasure, and we should be much obliged to you."[5]

At that point King Louis, who had by then appointed Leonardo his "official painter and engineer" (*nostre peintre et ingeneur ordinaire*), intervened personally from the French court at Blois. Summoning Florence's ambassador, he firmly requested that Leonardo stay in Milan until his own arrival there. "Your Signoria must render me a service," he insisted. "He is an excellent master, and I desire to have several things from his hand, certain little Madonnas and other things, according to my fancy, and perhaps I shall ask him to do a portrait of me," he told the ambassador. Florence's leaders realized they had no choice but to please their military protector. The Signoria replied, "[Florence] cannot have any greater pleasure than to obey his wishes. . . . Not only the said Leonardo but all other citizens are at the service of his wishes and needs."[6]

Leonardo was therefore still in Milan in May 1507, when Louis made a triumphant visit, having quelled a rebellion in Genoa on the way. The procession was led by three hundred armored soldiers and "a triumphal chariot bearing the cardinal Virtues and the god Mars holding in one hand an arrow [and] in the other a palm."[7]

To celebrate the king's arrival, there were days of festivals and pageants, and Leonardo was, of course, involved in choreographing them. A tournament was held in the plaza, and Isabella d'Este, her desire for a Leonardo portrait still unfulfilled, was at the masked ball.[8] After Savonarola, the republic of Florence was restrained in its indulgence of such fetes, but Milan still relished them, which was another reason Leonardo loved Milan.

FRANCESCO MELZI

While in Milan in 1507, Leonardo met a fourteen-year-old named Francesco Melzi (fig. 101). He was the son of a distinguished nobleman who was a captain in the Milanese militia and later a civil engineer who worked to reinforce the city's fortifications, endeavors that fascinated Leonardo. The Melzis lived in the largest villa in the town of Vaprio, on a river overlooking Milan, and Leonardo often stayed there, making it a second home.[9]

Leonardo was then fifty-five, and he had no son or heir. Young Francesco was an aspiring artist, pretty in the slightly soft way of Salai, and possessing some talent. With his father's permission, he was effectively adopted by Leonardo, either through an informal agreement or a legal contract, one that would be honored in Leonardo's will a decade later. Leonardo became a mix of legal guardian, godfather,

Fig. 101. Francesco Melzi by Boltraffio.

adoptive father, teacher, and employer of the young Melzi. Although the decision may seem strange in our day, it was an opportunity for the Melzis to have their son become the pupil, heir, and amanuensis of a charming and beloved family intimate who also happened to be the most creative artist of the time. Afterward, Leonardo stayed close to the entire Melzi family, even helping to design improvements to the family's villa.

For the rest of Leonardo's life, Francesco Melzi would be by his side. He worked as Leonardo's personal assistant and scribe, drafted his letters, kept his papers, and preserved them after his death. He wrote in a graceful italic, and his notations are to be found throughout Leonardo's notebooks. He also was Leonardo's art student. Though never a master painter, he was a good artist and draftsman who made some respectable drawings, including a famous one of Leonardo, and copied many of Leonardo's works. With his talent, efficiency, and steady temperament, he was a devoted companion to Leonardo, and a less complicated and devilish one than Salai.

Years later, the biographer Vasari got to know Melzi and wrote that he "was a very beautiful boy [*bellissimo fanciullo*] and much loved by [*molto amato da*] Leonardo." Those are similar to the words Vasari wrote of Salai, but it is unclear whether in this case there was any romantic or sexual relationship. I doubt there was. It is unlikely that Melzi's father would have given him over to Leonardo for such an association, and we know that after Leonardo's death Melzi married a prominent noblewoman and had eight children. Like much of Leonardo's life, there is a cloak of mist over the truth about the full extent of their relationship.

What is clear is that their relationship was not only close but familial. Leonardo drafted a letter to him in early 1508 that displays both fondness and vulnerability:

Good day, Master [*Messer*, a salutation that respects his noble rank] Francesco,
      Why in God's name have you not answered a single one of all the letters I sent you? You just wait till I get there, and by God I'll make you write so much you'll be sorry.[10]

There follows another draft of a letter to Melzi that is slightly more reserved. It describes a question that needed to be resolved about the water rights the king had granted Leonardo as a payment, and notes, "I wrote to the superintendent and to you, and then I repeated it, and never had an answer. So you will have the goodness to answer me as to what happened."

The letter mentioned that Leonardo was sending the messages by the hand of Salai, who was then twenty-seven. That raises the question of what Leonardo's longtime companion thought of this new, younger, aristocratic, and far more polished member of the household. We know that both stayed by Leonardo's side for the next decade of his life and that Melzi made a higher salary. There is a clue that Leonardo needed to work at keeping peace with Salai. It was around this time, in 1508, that the dictated note mentioned earlier appeared in one of his notebooks: "Salai, I want peace, not war. No more wars, I give in."[11]

Whether or not Melzi was ever a lover, he became something more significant. Leonardo loved him as a son, and he needed a son to love. It helped that Melzi was appealing and pretty, which was no doubt one reason Leonardo liked to have him in his retinue. But he was also a loyal and caring companion to whom Leonardo could pass along his papers, his estate, his knowledge, and his wisdom. He could help mold him as he would have a son.

By 1508 that was all the more important to Leonardo. As he passed through his fifties, his notebooks show intimations of his awareness of his mortality. His father had died. His mother had died. He was estranged from his half-brothers. He had no family, other than Francesco Melzi.

FLORENCE INTERLUDE: AN INHERITANCE BATTLE

It was an inheritance dispute with his half-brothers rather than the exhortations of the Signoria or any desire to resume painting the *Battle of Anghiari* that brought Leonardo back to Florence temporarily in August 1507.

After he failed to inherit anything from his father, his beloved uncle Francesco da Vinci, a gentle and unambitious country squire who had been like a doting brother or surrogate father, decided to make up for it. With no children of his own, Uncle Francesco changed his will and, when he died in early 1507, left his estate to Leonardo. This apparently contradicted an understanding that his property would go to Piero's legitimate children, and they sued Leonardo. The main issue was over a piece of farmland with two houses four miles east of Vinci.

For Leonardo, it was a matter of principle as well as property. He had lent his uncle money to improve the farmhouse, and he occasionally visited there to conduct experiments and make drawings of the surrounding landscape. The result was another of the angry draft letters to be found in his notebooks. It was addressed to his half-brothers but was written partly in the third person, perhaps because he had someone send it on his behalf. "You wished the utmost evil to Francesco," he wrote. "You do not wish to repay his heir the money he lent for the property." You have treated Leonardo "not as a brother but as a complete alien."[12]

The king of France came to Leonardo's aid, hoping to speed his return to Milan. He wrote to the Signoria of Florence, "We have been informed that our dear and much-beloved Leonardo da Vinci, official painter and engineer, has some dispute and litigation pending in Florence against his brothers over certain inheritances." Emphasizing that it was important for Leonardo to be "in our entourage and in our presence," the king urged the Florentines to "bring the said dispute and litigation to an end and see that true justice is done with as little delay as possible; and you will give us very agreeable pleasure by doing so."[13] The letter was countersigned and probably arranged and written by the king's secretary Robertet, for whom Leonardo had painted *Madonna of the Yarnwinder*.

The king's letter did not have much effect. By September, Leonardo's inheritance case was still pending, so he tried pulling another string. He composed a letter, which was then scribed for him by Machiavelli's secretary Agostino Vespucci, to Cardinal Ippolito d'Este, the brother of Isabella and Beatrice. The cardinal was a friend of the judge. "I entreat you, as urgently as I know how," Leonardo pleaded, "to write a letter to Ser Raphaello [the judge] in that skillful and affectionate manner which you know so well, recommending to him Leonardo Vincio, Your Lordship's most abject servant, requesting him and urging him not only to do me justice but to do so with propitious urgency."[14]

Leonardo eventually won a partial victory based on a settlement he had proposed in his angry letter to his half-brothers: "Oh why don't you let him [Leonardo] enjoy the property and its proceeds during his life, as long as they would return to your children?" That is probably what happened. Leonardo was given possession of the property and the money it made, but when he died he left it not to Melzi but to his half-brothers.[15]

The litigation settled, Leonardo was ready to return to Milan. He had not, during his eight months back in Florence, set brush to his unfinished *Battle of Anghiari*, nor did he have any desire to do so. He had not figured out how to make the painting work to his satisfaction, I think, and he was eager to abandon it and move back to a city more suited to his wide variety of interests.

But he was worried that he may have lost the favor of Milan's French rulers. He had been away longer than expected, his requests to secure some water rights the king had given him had proven problematic, and some of his letters to Charles d'Amboise, the king's governor in Milan, had gone unanswered. So he sent Salai to Milan to assess the situation and deliver another letter to Charles. "I suspect that my feeble recognition of the great benefits I have received from your Excellency may have made you annoyed with me, and for this reason you have not answered the many letters I have addressed to you," he wrote. "I am now sending Salai to you to inform Your Excellency that I am almost at an end of my litigation with my brothers and I hope to be in Milan this Easter." He would come bearing gifts. "I shall bring with me two pictures of the Madonna, different in size, intended for the Most Christian King or for anyone else that your lordship may choose."

Then he turned somewhat plaintive. He had previously stayed in the palace of the governor, but now he wanted an apartment of his own. "I would like to know where I am to have my living quarters when I return, as I wish no longer to incommode your Excellency." He also inquired whether his salary from the king would continue and if the governor could straighten out the matter of the water rights he had been granted. As he had done in his famous letter to Milan's previous ruler when he first went there in 1482, Leonardo made a point of noting that he was not merely a painter. "I hope when I come to make machines and other things which will give great pleasure to our Most Christian King."[16]

All worked out, and by the end of April 1508 Leonardo was back in Milan, with a home in a parish church; regular payments began arriving from the king, and a final payment for *Virgin of the Rocks* came in October. Both Salai and Melzi were with him, and all was again right with his world. Over the next decade, he would return to Florence only for brief personal visits, but he would never work there again. His heart and his home were once again in Milan.

MILAN'S DELIGHTFUL DIVERSIONS

To understand Leonardo, it is necessary to understand why he moved away from Florence, this time for good. One reason is simple: he liked Milan better. It had no Michelangelo, no cadre of half-brothers suing him, no ghost of his father hovering. It had royalty rather than republicans, with jubilant pageants rather than the after-stench of bonfires of the vanities. It had doting patrons rather than oversight committees. And the foremost patron there was the one who loved Leonardo the most, Charles d'Amboise, the French royal governor who had written a flowery letter reminding the Florentines how brilliant their native son was.

But there was more to Leonardo's move than merely a preference for life in Milan. The first time he went there, he did so to recast himself as an engineer, scientist, and inventor. Now, more than twenty-five years later, he was fleeing not only Florence but also life as a public artist, a man defined mainly by his painting. As Isabella d'Este's agent had reported, "He cannot bear the sight of a paintbrush."

Florence was the artistic center of the Italian Renaissance, but Milan and its nearby university town of Pavia had become more intellectually diverse. Charles d'Amboise was dedicated to creating a court like that of the Sforzas, which included painters, entertainers, scientists, mathematicians, and engineers. Leonardo was the most valued jewel because he embodied all of those vocations.

During his sojourn back in Florence for his inheritance battle, he had focused mainly on scientific endeavors rather than painting commissions. He dissected the corpse of a man who claimed to be a hundred, planned a test of one of his flying machines, began a treatise on geology and water, devised a glass tank to examine the way flowing water deposits sediment, and swam underwater to compare the propulsion of a fish tail to a bird's wing, jotting his conclusions on the same notebook page where he drafted his angry letter to his half-brothers. These interests, he believed, could be better pursued amid the intellectual ferment of Milan.

"Begun in Milan on the day of September 12, 1508," he wrote on the opening page of a new notebook shortly after his return.[17] It is filled with studies of geology, water, birds, optics, astronomy, and architecture. He also busied himself drawing a bird's-eye schematic map of the city, suggesting the proper choir stalls to build in the Duomo, and devising military machinery that could be used against Venice.

In addition to its intellectual ferment, Milan had dazzling pageants and festivities that far surpassed those now to be found in republican Florence. When King Louis came for another visit, in July 1509, the procession included five chariots representing the towns recently conquered by France, followed by a triumphal chariot with three costumed allegorical figures, of the type Leonardo loved to design, representing Victory, Fame, and Happiness. To herald the king's arrival, Leonardo built a mechanical lion. One observer wrote, "Leonardo da Vinci, the famous painter and our Florentine, devised the following intervention: he created a lion above the gate, which was lying down, and then got onto its feet when the King entered the city, and with its paw it opened up its chest and pulled out blue balls full of golden lilies, which he threw and scattered on the ground." The lion, also described by Vasari, became a standard feature at future extravaganzas choreographed or inspired by Leonardo, including the entry of Francis I into Lyons in 1515 and into Argentan in 1517.[18]

Leonardo even had the joy of combining pageantry and architecture. For the palace of his patron Charles d'Amboise, he drew up plans for expanding a great hall so that it could better accommodate masquerades and performances. "The hall for the festival should be situated so that you come first into the presence of the lord, and then of the guests," he wrote. "On the other side should be the entrance of the hall and a convenient staircase, which should be wide, so that the people in passing along them do not push against the masqueraders and damage their costumes."[19]

In imagining a "garden of delights" for the estate, Leonardo indulged his love of water, proposing it as both an aesthetic feature and a method for cooling. "In the summer I shall make the water spring up fresh and bubbling and flow along in the space between the tables," he wrote, drawing how the tables would be arranged. The water would power a mill, which would be used to force breezes. "By means of the mill I shall be able at any time to produce a current of air," he promised, and "many water-conduits through the house, and springs in various places, and a certain passage where, when anyone passes, the water will leap up from all sides below, and so it will be there ready in case anyone should wish to give a shower-bath from below to the women or others who pass there." The flowing water would power a large clock, copper mesh netting would cover the garden to make it an aviary, and "with the help of the mill I will make unending sounds from all sorts of instruments, which will sound for so long as the mill shall continue to move."[20]

Neither the villa additions nor the garden of delights was ever built, which could reinforce the perception that the time Leonardo spent on engineering was to some extent wasted. Kenneth Clark was dismissive after rattling off a list of these nonpainterly passions: "One day he could be deciding on the form of the choir stalls in the Duomo; another, acting as military engineer in the war against

Venice; another, arranging pageants for the entry of Louis XII into Milan." Clark added sorrowfully, "It was a variety of employment which Leonardo enjoyed, but which has left posterity the poorer."[21]

Perhaps Clark is right, in that our store of art does not include a *Battle of Anghiari* or other potential masterpieces. But if posterity is poorer because of the time Leonardo spent immersed in passions from pageantry to architecture, it is also true that his life was richer.

CHAPTER 27

Anatomy, Round Two

THE CENTENARIAN

Shortly before he left Florence in 1508, Leonardo was at the hospital of Santa Maria Nuova, where he struck up a conversation with a man who said he was more than a hundred years old and had never been ill. A few hours later, the old man quietly passed away "without any movement or sign of distress."[1] Leonardo proceeded to dissect his body, launching what would be, from 1508 to 1513, his second round of anatomical studies.

We should pause to imagine the dandy-dressing Leonardo, now in his mid-fifties and at the height of his fame as a painter, spending his night hours at an old hospital in his neighborhood talking to patients and dissecting bodies. It is another example of his relentless curiosity that would astonish us if we had not become so used to it.

Twenty years earlier, while living in Milan, he had filled notebooks with his first round of anatomy drawings, including beautiful renderings of the human skull. Now he picked up the work again, and on one of the pages, above a set of drawings of muscles and veins in a partially skinned cadaver, he drew a respectful little drawing of his centenarian's peaceful face, eyes closed, moments after his death (fig. 102).[2] Then, on thirty more pages, he proceeded to record his dissection.

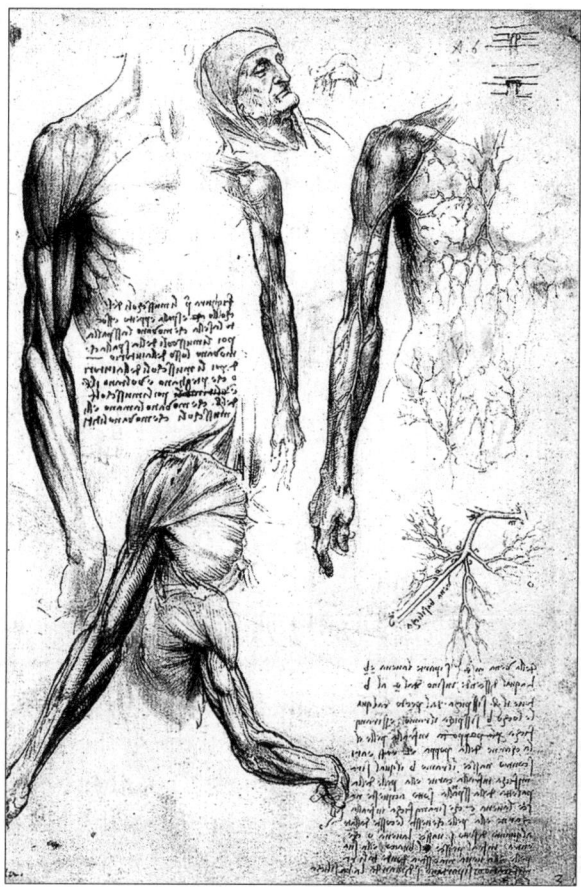

Fig. 102. The centenarian and his muscles.

Leonardo's hand was deft with both pen and scalpel. His close observation plus the strength of his visual memory made his drawings strikingly better than those in any anatomy texts before him. Mustering all of his draftsman's techniques, he made detailed underdrawings in black chalk, then finished them with different colors of ink and washes. With his left-handed curved hatching lines, he gave shape and volume to the form of bones and muscles and with light lines added the tendons and fibers. Each bone and muscle was shown from three or four angles, sometimes in layers or in an exploded view, as if it were a piece of machinery he was deconstructing and delineating. The results are triumphs of both science and art.

His rudimentary dissecting tools took him down layer by layer even as the body, untreated, decomposed. First he showed the surface muscles of the old man, then the inside muscles and veins as he pulled off the skin. He started with the right arm and neck, then the torso. He noted how the spine was curved, then he got to the abdominal wall, the intestines, the stomach, and the membranes connecting them all. Finally he exposed the liver, which he said "resembled frozen bran both in color and substance." He never reached the legs, perhaps because by then the body had decomposed too badly to make it bearable to handle. But there would be other dissections, probably twenty more, and by the time he finished his anatomy studies he would have beautifully illustrated every body part and limb.

In his quest to figure out how the centenarian died, Leonardo made a significant scientific discovery: he documented the process that leads to arteriosclerosis, in which the walls of arteries are thickened and stiffened by the accumulation of plaque-like substances. "I made an autopsy in order to ascertain the cause of so peaceful a death, and found that it proceeded from weakness through the failure of blood and of the artery that feeds the heart and the other lower members, which I found to be very dry, shrunken and withered," he wrote. Next to a drawing of the veins in the right arm, he compared the centenarian's blood vessels to those of a two-year-old boy who also died at the hospital. He found those of the boy to be supple and unconstricted, "contrary to what I found in the old man." Using his skill of thinking and describing through analogies, he concluded, "The network of vessels behaves in man as in oranges, in which the peel becomes tougher and the pulp diminishes the older they become."[3]

The constriction of blood flow had caused, among other things, the centenarian's liver to become so dry that "when it is subjected to even the slightest friction its substance falls away in tiny flakes like sawdust and leaves behind the veins and arteries." It also led to his flesh becoming "the color of wood or dried chestnut, because the skin is almost completely deprived of sustenance." The noted medical historian and cardiologist Kenneth Keele called Leonardo's analysis "the first description of arteriosclerosis as a function of time."[4]

DISSECTIONS

By Leonardo's day, the Church no longer completely prohibited dissections, although its attitude was murky and depended on local authorities. In Florence and Milan, though not in Rome, the practice had become common as Renaissance science progressed. The Florentine physician Antonio Benivieni, born nine years before Leonardo, was a pioneer of autopsies, performing more than 150 of them. Leonardo, who was not strongly religious, pushed back on the fundamentalists who considered dissection heretical. He believed it was a way to appreciate God's handiwork. "You should not be distressed that your discoveries come through another's death; rather you should rejoice that our Creator has provided an instrument of such excellence," he wrote on a tinted blue notebook page on which he drew the muscles and bones of the neck.[5]

Traditional anatomy instructors would stand at a lectern and read aloud from their texts while an assistant dissected a corpse and held up its components for students to view. Leonardo insisted that his drawings were even better than watching a live dissection: "You who say it is better to watch an anatomist at work than to see these drawings would be right, if it were possible to see all those things which are shown in these drawings." The reason it was possible to see more in the drawings, he said, was because they had been based on multiple dissections and also showed views from multiple angles. "I have dissected more than ten human bodies," he wrote, and after making that statement he would dissect even more, working on each as long as possible, until they decomposed so badly he was forced to move on. "As one body did not last so long, it was necessary to proceed by stages with as many bodies as would render my knowledge complete." He then performed even more dissections so that he could ascertain the variances between humans.[6]

When Leonardo began this second round of anatomy studies in 1508, he made a to-do list that surely must rank as one of the quirkiest and most enchanting such lists in the history of intellectual inquiry.[7] On one side of the page are a few sketches of dissecting instruments and, on the other side, some small drawings of veins and nerves found in the brain of the centenarian, with writing crammed all around them. "Have Avicenna's book on useful inventions translated," he wrote, referring to a book by the eleventh-century Persian polymath. Having drawn various surgical tools, he jotted down some of the equipment he needed: "Spectacles with case, firestick, fork, curved knife, charcoal, boards, sheets of paper, white chalk, wax, forceps, pane of glass, finetooth bone saw, scalpel, inkhorn, pen-knife, and get hold of a skull."

Then comes my favorite item on any Leonardo list: "Describe the tongue of the woodpecker." This is not just a random entry. He mentioned the woodpecker's tongue again on a later page, where he described and drew the human tongue. "Make the motions of the woodpecker," he wrote. When I first saw his entry about the woodpecker, I regarded it, as most scholars have, as an entertaining oddity—an *amuse-bouche*, so to speak—evidence of the eccentric nature of Leonardo's relentless curiosity. That it indeed is. But there is more, as I discovered after pushing myself to be more like Leonardo and drill down into random curiosities. Leonardo, I realized, had become fascinated by the muscles of the tongue. All of the other muscles he studied acted by pulling rather than pushing a body part, but the tongue seemed to be an exception. This was true in humans and in other animals. The most notable example is the tongue of the woodpecker. Nobody had drawn or fully written about it before, but Leonardo with his acute ability to observe objects in motion knew that there was something to be learned from it.[8]

On the same list, Leonardo instructed himself to describe "the jaw of the crocodile." Once again, if we follow his curiosity, rather than merely be amused by it, we can see that he was on to an important topic. A crocodile, unlike any mammal, has a second jaw joint, which spreads out the force when it snaps shut its mouth. That gives the crocodile the most forceful bite of any animal. It can exert 3,700 pounds per square inch of force, which is more than thirty times that of a human bite.

Leonardo engaged in dissections before proper fixatives and preservatives had been invented, so alongside his to-do list he issued a warning directed at those who would undertake such a task. It doubles as a subtle boast about the talents—a strong stomach, good drawing skills, knowledge of perspective, an understanding of the math underlying mechanics, along with an obsessive curiosity—that he uniquely brought to his work as an anatomist:

> You will perhaps be deterred by your stomach; and if this does not deter you, you may be deterred by the fear of living through the night hours in the company of quartered and flayed corpses, fearful to behold. And if this does not deter you, perhaps you will lack the good draftsmanship that such a depiction requires; and even if you have skill in drawing, it may not be accompanied by a knowledge of perspective; and if it were so accompanied, you may lack the methods of geometrical demonstration and of calculating the forces and strengths of the muscles; or perhaps you will lack patience so that you will not be diligent.[9]

There is an echo in this passage of Leonardo's memory of coming across the mouth of a cave as a young man. As in that tale, he had to overcome his fear to go into a dark and fearful space. Although at times he was irresolute and willing to abandon tasks, his powerful curiosity tended to overcome any hesitations when it came to exploring nature's wonders.

Leonardo's anatomy studies were another example of the influence of the printing press, which was spawning publishing houses throughout Italy. By then Leonardo owned 116 books, including Johannes de Ketham's *Fasciculus Medicinae*, published in Venice in 1498; Bartolomeo Montagnana's *Tractatus de Urinarum*, published in Padua in 1487; and *Anatomice*, by Leonardo's contemporary Alessandro Benedetti, printed in Venice in 1502. He had an edition of the standard dissection guide by the Bologna physician Mondino de Luzzi, which had been written in about 1316 and was printed in Italian in 1493. He used Mondino's book as a manual for his early dissections, and he even replicated one of Mondino's mistakes in identifying some of the muscles of the abdomen.[10]

But, true to form, Leonardo preferred learning from experiment rather than from established authority. His most important hands-on inquiries came during the winter of 1510–11, when he collaborated with Marcantonio della Torre, a twenty-nine-year-old anatomy professor at the University of Pavia. "Each helped and was helped by the other," Vasari wrote of their relationship. The young professor provided the human cadavers—probably twenty of them were dissected that winter—and lectured while his students did the actual cutting and Leonardo made notes and drawings.[11]

During this period of intense anatomical study, Leonardo made 240 drawings and wrote at least thirteen thousand words of text, illustrating and describing every bone, muscle group, and major organ in the human body for what would have been, if it had been published, his most historic scientific triumph. On an elegant drawing showing a man's muscular calf and the tendons of his foot, modeled and shaded with his signature curved cross-hatchings, Leonardo wrote, "This winter of 1510 I believe I will finish all this anatomy."[12]

It was not to be. Marcantonio died in 1511 of the plague that was devastating Italy that year. It is enticing to imagine what he and Leonardo could have accomplished. One of the things that could have most benefited Leonardo in his career was a partner who would help him follow through and publish his brilliant work. Together he and Marcantonio could have produced a groundbreaking illustrated treatise on anatomy that would have transformed a field still dominated by scholars who mainly regurgitated the notions of the second-century Greek physician Galen. Instead, Leonardo's anatomy studies became another example of how he was disadvantaged by having few rigorous and disciplined collaborators along the lines of Luca Pacioli, whose text on geometric proportions Leonardo had illustrated. With Marcantonio dead, Leonardo retreated to the country villa of Francesco Melzi's family to ride out the plague.

ANALOGIES

In most of his studies of nature, Leonardo theorized by making analogies. His quest for knowledge across all the disciplines of arts and sciences helped him see patterns. Occasionally this mode of thinking misled him, and it sometimes substituted for reaching more profound scientific theories. But this cross-disciplinary thinking and pattern-seeking was his hallmark as the quintessential Renaissance Man, and it made him a pioneer of scientific humanism.

For example, when he looked at the veins and arteries he was dissecting, he compared their flow and branching to that of the human digestive, urinary, and respiratory systems. He made analogies with the flows of rivers, the movements of air, and the branching of plants. On one of his detailed depictions of the human blood circulation system, based on his dissection of the centenarian in 1508, he made a large drawing of the great vessels of the heart, with the aorta and vena cava connecting to increasingly smaller offshoots of veins and arteries and capillaries (fig. 103). Then he moved to his left to make a smaller drawing of a seed, which he labeled "nut," with its roots stretching into the ground and its branches stretching upward. "The heart is the nut which generates the tree of the veins," he wrote on the page.[13]

Another analogy Leonardo made was between the human body and machines. He compared the movement of muscles and the body to the mechanical rules he had learned from his engineering stud-

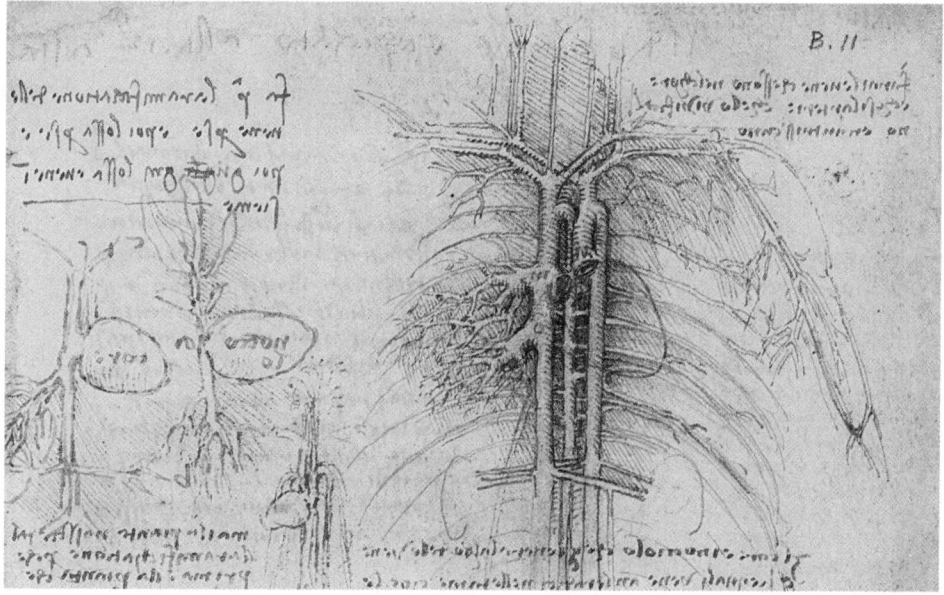

Fig. 103. The heart and arteries juxtaposed with a sprouting seed.

ies. As he had done with machines, he illustrated body parts using exploded views, multiple angles, and stacked-up layers (fig. 104). He studied the movements of various muscles and bones, as if they operated like strings and levers, and layered the muscles on top of the bones to show the mechanics of each joint. "Muscles always arise and end in bones adjoining one another," he explained. "They never arise and end on one and the same bone because nothing would be able to move." It all added up to an ingenious mechanism of moving parts: "The joints between bones obey the tendon, and the tendon obeys the muscle, and the muscle the nerve."[14]

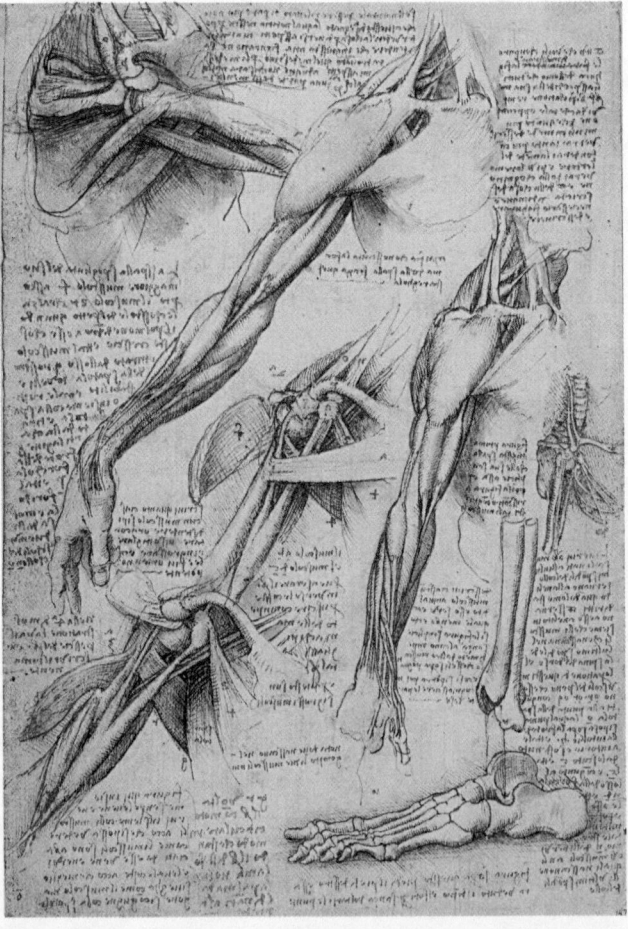

Fig. 104. Multiple layers of bone and muscle.

His comparisons between man-made machinery and the handiwork of nature produced in him a deep reverence for the latter. "Though human ingenuity may make various inventions," he wrote, "it will never devise an invention more beautiful, more simple, more direct than does Nature; because in her inventions nothing is lacking and nothing is superfluous."[15]

Just as Leonardo's anatomy informed his art, so was the reverse true: his artistic, sculpting, drawing, and engineering skills crossed disciplines and aided his anatomical studies. In a groundbreaking experiment, he used sculpture and casting techniques to map the hollow cavities, known as cerebral ventricles, in the human brain (fig. 105). From his studies of ways to cast the great horse monument in Milan, Leonardo knew how to inject molten wax into the brain and provide ventilation holes for the air and fluids in the cavities to escape. "Make two vent-holes in the horns of the greater ventricles, and insert

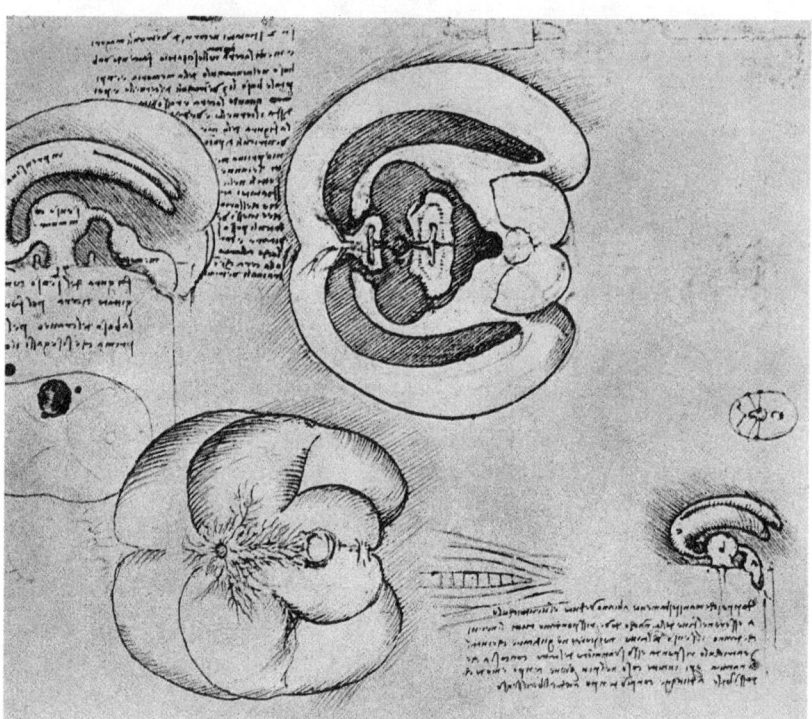

Fig. 105. Method for making a wax cast of the brain.

melted wax with a syringe, making a hole in the ventricle of memory; and through such a hole fill the three ventricles of the brain. Then when the wax has set, take apart the brain, and you will see the shape of the ventricles exactly." A small sketch on the bottom-right of the page illustrates the technique.[16]

Leonardo did the experiment using the brain of a cow, since it was easier to get than a human brain. But from his readings and earlier human dissections, he knew how to modify his findings and apply them to a human brain, which he did with impressive accuracy on

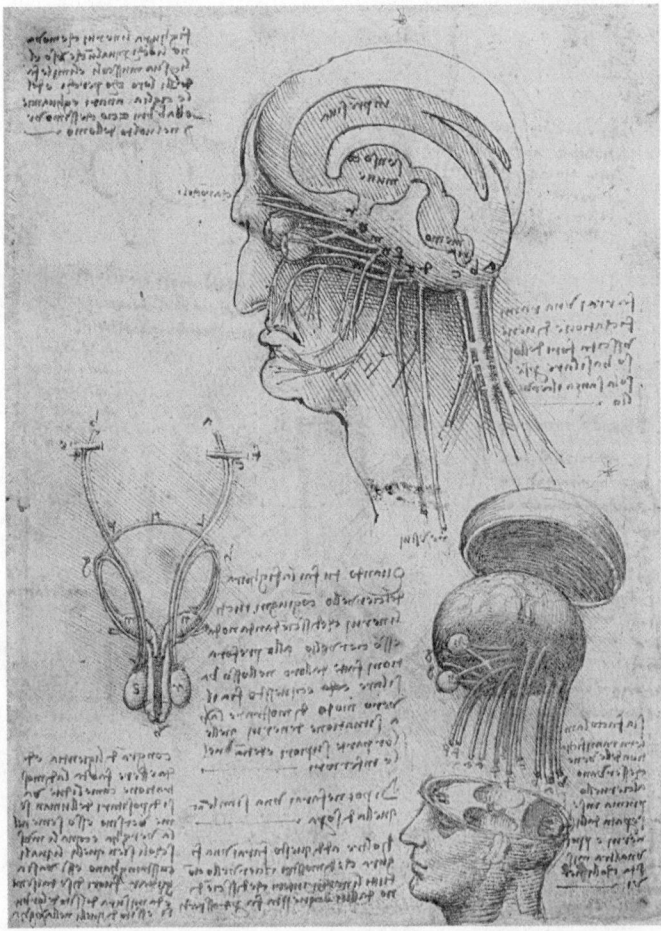

Fig. 106. Nerves and ventricles of the brain.

a set of drawings that display it in an exploded view (fig. 106).[17] His only mistakes were that the middle ventricle is slightly enlarged because of the pressure of the wax, and the ends of the lateral ventricles were not completely filled by the wax. Otherwise, the results were extraordinary. Leonardo had for the first time in history injected a molding material into a human cavity. It was a technique that would not be replicated until the studies by the Dutch anatomist Frederik Ruysch more than two centuries later. Along with his discoveries about heart valves, it was Leonardo's most important anatomical breakthrough, and it happened because he was a sculptor as well as a scientist.

MUSCLES AND BONES

Leonardo's methods as well as his art are displayed on a page on which he depicted the muscles of the shoulder (fig. 107). "Before you form the muscles," he wrote, "make in their place threads that should demonstrate their positions." He did just that in the schematic sketch of threads in the shoulder on the top right of the page (which is the first drawing he made on the page since in his left-handed fashion he starts on the right). Directly to the left and below his sketch of threads we can see the centenarian in two different poses, his skin peeled off to show the muscles of his right shoulder. Leonardo then moved to the top left of the page, where he correctly drew and labeled with letters the pectoralis major, latissimus dorsi, rhomboid, and other muscles.[18]

Leonardo began his studies of human muscles, as with most of his scientific work, to serve his art, but he was soon pursuing them out of pure curiosity. In the former category is a drawing he made that shows the muscles of a right arm in four different views. Understanding how they change shape as they move, he wrote, "will be an advantage for artists who have to exaggerate the muscles that cause the movements of limbs more than the ones that are not employed in such movement."[19] Another anatomy drawing that appears to be related to his *Battle of Anghiari* cartoon is a forceful-looking frontal

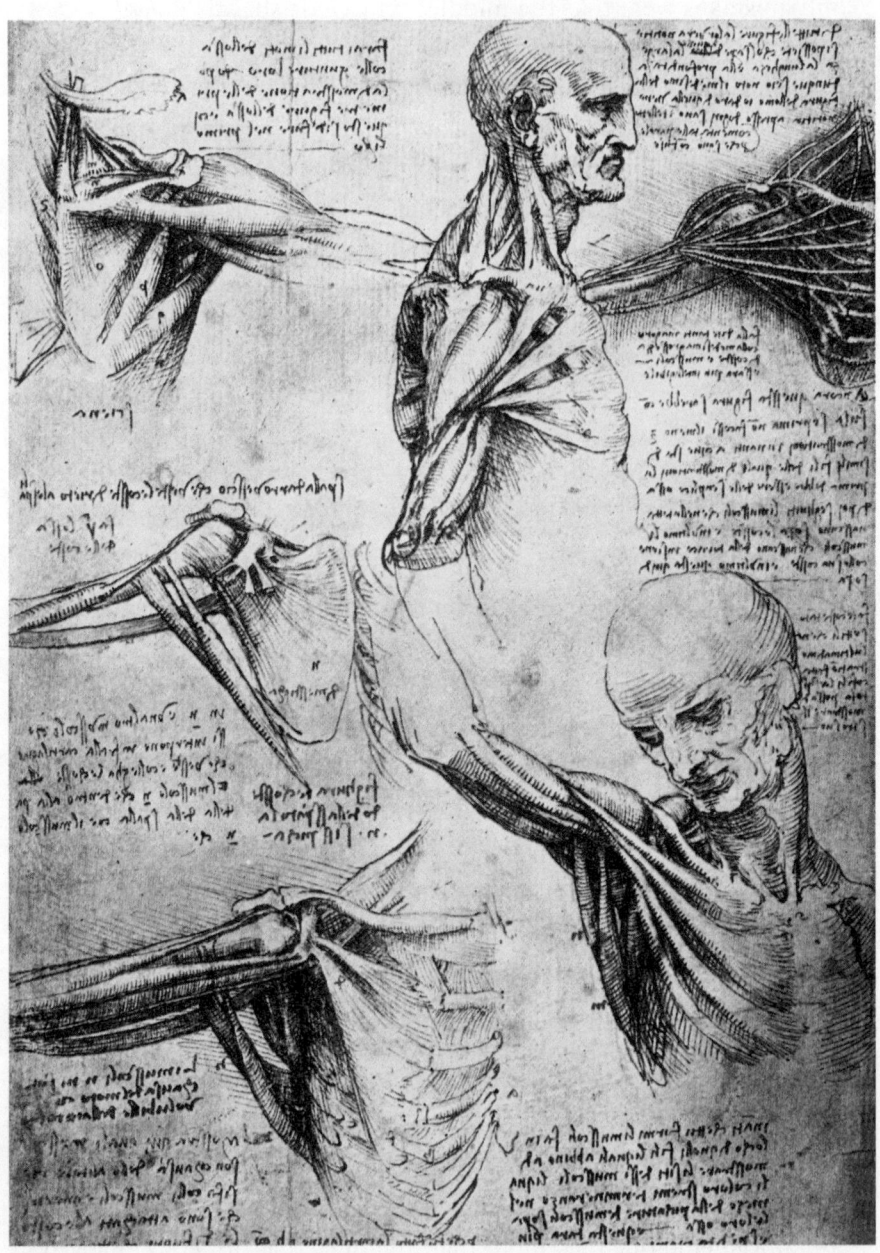

Fig. 107. Muscles of the shoulder.

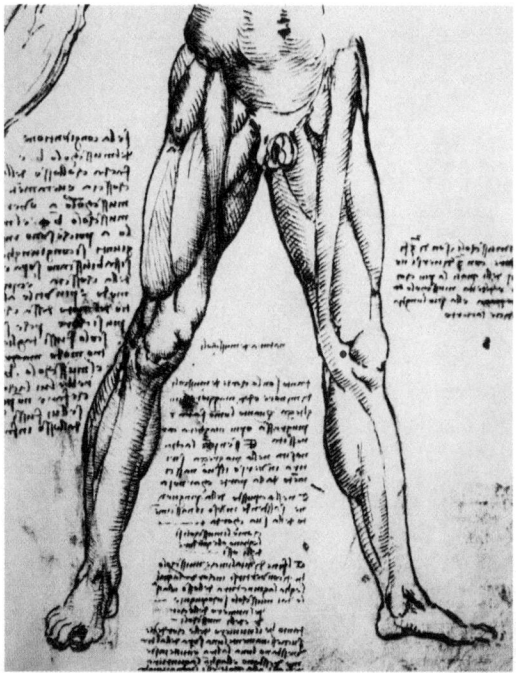

Fig. 108. Muscles of the leg.

view of a man's leg muscles, artistically modeled and shaded with fine cross-hatch strokes (fig. 108). In a note titled "Nature of Muscles," he described the way body fat is distributed in muscular men: "A man will be fatter or leaner in proportion to the greater or lesser lengths of the tendons of muscles."[20]

By the time Leonardo got around to studying and drawing the human spine, he had been captivated by curiosity and the joy of research rather than merely the pursuit of practical painting knowledge. His page showing the spine accurately rendered and notated from a variety of angles is a masterpiece of both anatomy and draftsmanship (fig. 109). Through the use of light and shadows, he was able to make each of the vertebrae seem three-dimensional, and he conveyed a sense of twisting motion in the curved spine at the top middle of the page. Complexity is magically transformed into an elegance that is unrivaled by any anatomical drawings of his time—or ours.

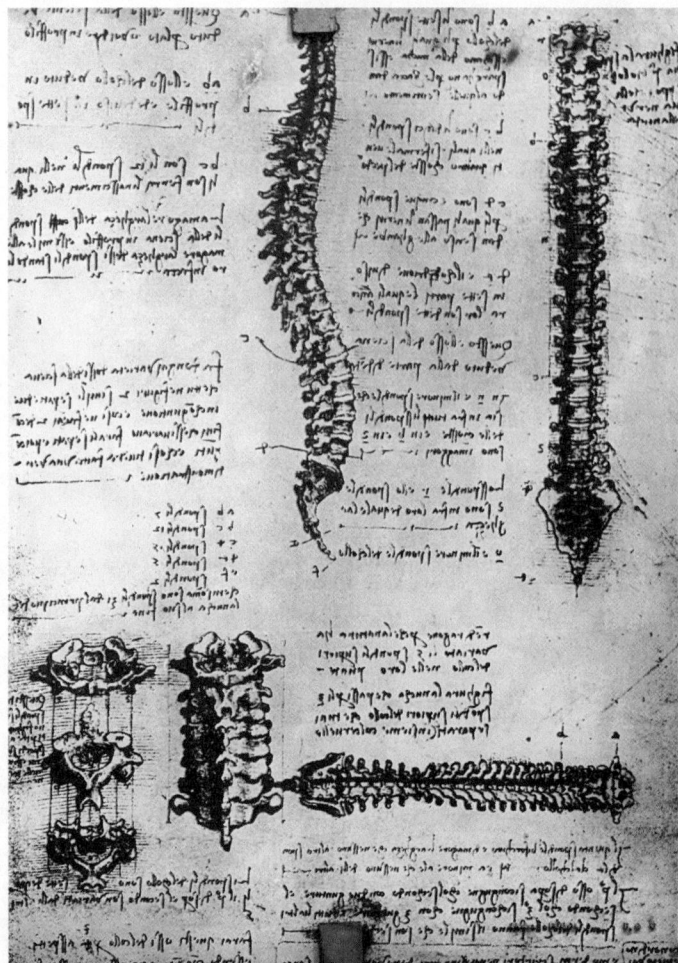

Fig. 109. The spine, with exploded view.

His precise renderings of the five sets of vertebrae are marked with letters, listed in a table, and explained in his notes. This led him to ask questions about details that most people would not have noticed. "Explain why nature has varied the five superior vertebrae of the neck at their extremities," he instructed himself.

The last drawing he made on this sheet, at the bottom left of the page, is one of his exploded views, of the kind he made of machines, showing the first three cervical vertebrae, with their interlocking mechanisms rendered masterfully. It was important, he said, to depict the spine "separate and then joined together," with views from the front, back, side, above, and below. At the bottom of the page, when he had finished, he could not refrain from a bit of boasting about his method, which he declared would produce "knowledge that neither ancient writers nor the moderns would ever have been able to give without an immense, tiresome, and confused amount of writing and time."[21]

LIPS AND SMILE

Leonardo was especially interested in how the human brain and nervous system translate emotions into movements of the body. On one drawing, he showed the spinal cord sawed in half and he delineated all the nerves that ran down to it from the brain. "The spinal cord is the source of the nerves that gives voluntary movement to the limbs," he explained.[22]

Of all these nerves and related muscles, the ones controlling the lips were the most important to Leonardo. Dissecting them was exceedingly difficult, because lip muscles are small and plentiful and originate deep in the skin. "The muscles which move the lips are more numerous in man than in any other animal," he wrote. "One will always find as many muscles as there are positions of the lips and many more that serve to undo these positions." Despite these difficulties, he depicted the facial muscles and nerves with remarkable accuracy.

On one delightfully crammed anatomical sheet (fig. 110), Leonardo drew the muscles of two dissected arms and hands, and he placed between them two partially dissected faces in profile. The faces show the muscles and nerves that control the lips and other elements of expression. In the one on the left, Leonardo has removed part of the jawbone to expose the buccinator muscle, which pulls back the angle of the mouth and flattens the cheek as a smile begins to form. Here we can see, exposed with scalpel cuts and then pen strokes, the actual mechanisms that transmit emotions into facial expressions. He wrote next to one of the faces, "Represent all the causes of motion possessed by the skin, flesh and muscles of the face and see if these

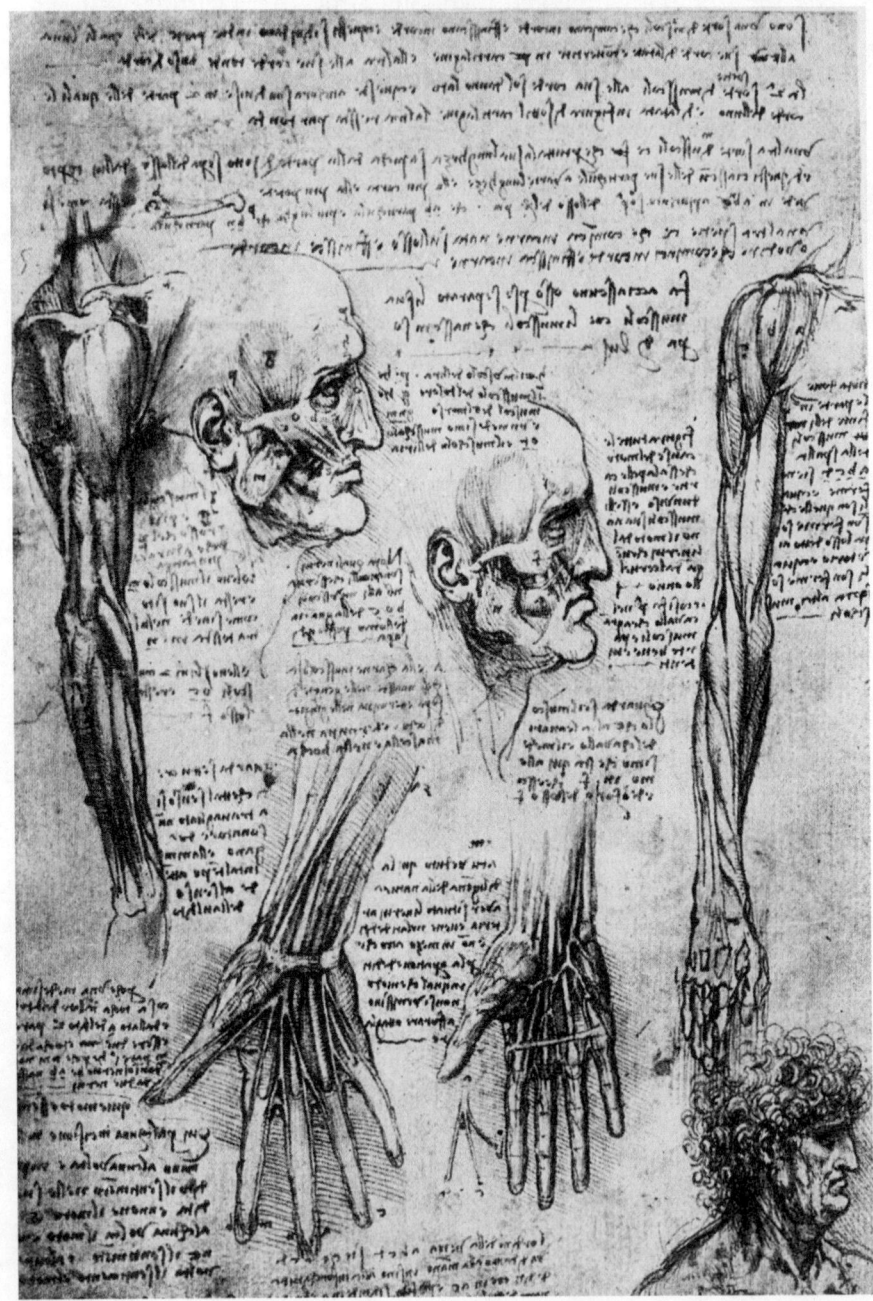

Fig. 110. Dissections of arms and face.

muscles receive their motion from nerves which come from the brain or not."

He labeled one of the muscles in the left-hand drawing "H" and called it "the muscle of anger." Another is labeled "P" and designated as the muscle of sadness or pain. He showed how these muscles not only move the lips but also serve to move the eyebrows downward and together, causing wrinkles.

On this page of dissected faces and lips, we can also see Leonardo pursuing the comparative anatomy he needed for his *Battle of Anghiari* drawings, in which the anger on the faces of the humans is matched by that on the faces of the horses. After his note about representing the causes of motion of the human face, he added, "And do this first for the horse that has large muscles. Notice whether the muscle that raises the nostrils of the horse is the same as that which lies here in man."[23] So here is another secret to Leonardo's unique ability to paint a facial expression: he is probably the only artist in history ever to dissect with his own hands the face of a human and that of a horse to see if the muscles that move human lips are the same ones that can raise the nostrils of the nose.

Finally, as he got to the bottom of the crammed page, Leonardo's mind began to wander, to our delight. He paused to draw his favorite doodle: that of a curly haired man with nutcracker nose and chin. This one seems to hover between being a portrait of a younger version of himself and an older version of Salai. The man's lips are set in a way that displays resolve but also a touch of melancholy.

After his excursion into comparative anatomy, Leonardo proceeded to delve deeper into the mechanisms of humans as they smile or grimace (fig. 111). He focused on the role of various nerves in sending signals to the muscles, and he asked a question that was central to his art: Which of these are cranial nerves originating in the brain, and which are spinal nerves?

His notes begin as if he were focused on a battle scene filled with angry expressions: "Make the nostrils drawn up, causing furrows in the side of the nose, and the lips arched to disclose the upper teeth, with the teeth parted in order to shriek lamentations." But he then

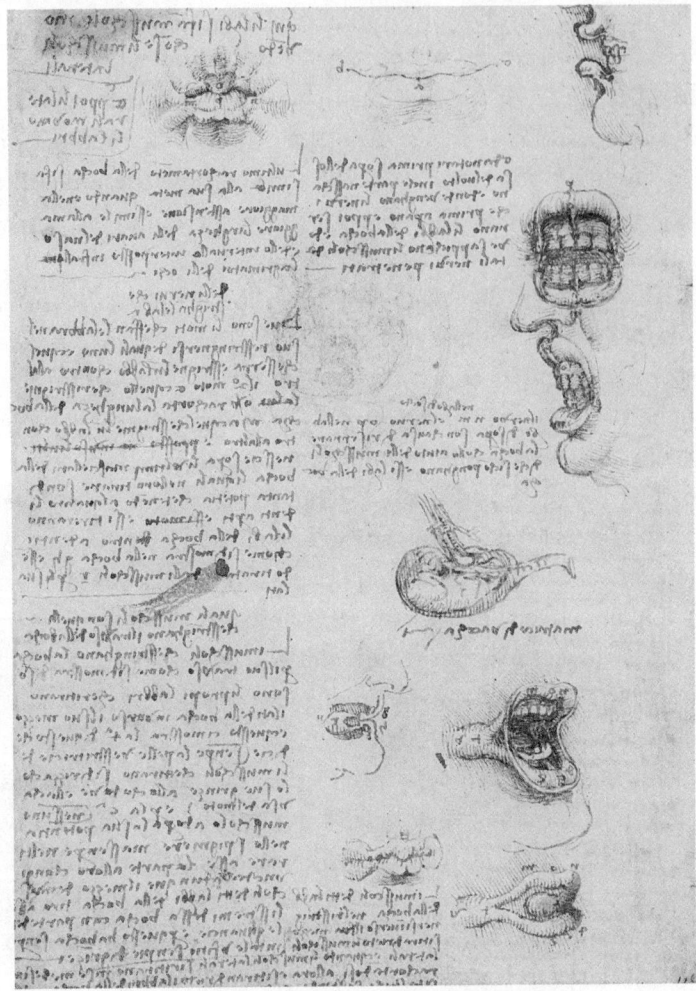

Fig. 111. Nerves and muscles of the mouth.

began to explore other expressions. On the top left are lips tightly pursed, underneath which he wrote, "The maximum shortening of the mouth is equal to half its maximum extension, and it is equal to the greatest width of the nostrils of the nose and to the interval between the ducts of the eye." He tested on himself and on the cadaver how each muscle of the cheek could move the lips, and how the muscle of the lips can also pull the lateral muscles of the wall of the cheek. "The muscle shortening the lips is the same muscle forming the lower lip itself. Other muscles are those which bring the lips to a point, others which spread them, others which curl them back, others which straighten them out, others which twist them transversely, and others which return them to their first position." On the top right of the page are front and profile drawings of retracted lips with the skin still on; at the bottom of the page, he made the drawings after removing the facial skin, showing the muscles that pull the lips. These are the first known examples of the scientific anatomy of the human smile.[24]

Floating above the grotesque grimaces on the top of the page is a faint sketch of a simple set of lips drawn in a way that is artistic rather than anatomical. The lips peek out of the page directly at us with just a hint—flickering and haunting and alluring—of a mysterious smile. At the time, Leonardo was working on the *Mona Lisa*.

THE HEART

On one of Leonardo's pages of drawings of the human heart (fig. 112), done in ink on blue paper, is a reminder of the humanity, and even humanness, that suffuse his anatomical studies.[25] At the top is a drawing of the heart's papillary muscle and a description of how it shortens and elongates when the heart beats. Then, as if he were being too clinical, he let his mind wander and pen begin to doodle. And there, in loving profile, is a drawing of Salai, his beautiful curls flowing down his long neck, his signature receding chin and fleshy throat softly modeled with Leonardo's left-handed hatching. In his chest is a section of a heart, with its muscles sketched in. An analysis of the drawing shows that the heart was sketched first. It seems as if Leonardo drew it, then sketched Salai around it.

Leonardo's studies of the human heart, conducted as part of his overall anatomical and dissection work, were the most sustained and successful of his scientific endeavors.[26] Informed by his love of hydraulic engineering and his fascination with the flow of liquids, he made discoveries that were not fully appreciated for centuries.

In the early 1500s the European understanding of the heart was

Fig. 112. The heart with Salai.

not all that different from that described in the second century AD by Galen, whose work was revived during the Renaissance. Galen believed that the heart was not merely a muscle but was made of a special substance that gave it a vital force. Blood was made in the liver, he taught, and distributed through the veins. Vital spirits were produced by the heart and distributed through arteries, which Galen and his successors considered a separate system. Neither the blood nor vital spirits circulated, he thought; instead, they pulsed back and forth in the veins and arteries.

Leonardo was among the first to fully appreciate that the heart, not the liver, was the center of the blood system. "All the veins and arteries arise from the heart," he wrote on the page that includes the drawings comparing the branches and roots of a seed with the veins and arteries emanating from the heart. He proved this by showing, in both words and a detailed drawing, "that the largest veins and arteries are found where they join with the heart, and the further they are removed from the heart, the finer they become, dividing into very small branches." He became the first to analyze how the size of the branches diminish with each split, and he traced them down to tiny capillaries that were almost invisible. To those who would respond that the veins are rooted in the liver the way a plant is rooted in the soil, he pointed out that a plant's roots and branches emanate from a central seed, which is analogous to the heart.[27]

Leonardo was also able to show, contrary to Galen, that the heart is simply a muscle rather than some form of special vital tissue. Like all muscles, the heart has its own blood supply and nerves. "It is nourished by an artery and veins, as are other muscles," he found.[28]

He also corrected the Galenic belief that the heart has only two ventricles. His dissections showed that there are two upper and two lower ventricles. These must have distinct functions, he argued, because they were separated by valves and membranes. "If they were one and the same, there would be no need for the valves that separate them." In order to figure out how the ventricles work, Leonardo opened up a pig whose heart was still beating. The upper and lower ventricles open at different times, he discovered. "The upper ventricles of the heart are different in their functions and nature from those below, and they are separated by gristle and various substances."[29]

Leonardo did accept Galen's incorrect theory that blood is warm because it is heated by the heart, and he wrestled with many theories of how this happened. He finally settled on the supposition that the heat is generated by the friction of the moving heart and the blood rubbing against the heart walls. "The whirling round of the blood in different eddies, and the friction it makes with the walls, and the percussions in the recesses, are the cause of the heating of the blood," he concluded. In order to test his theory by analogy, as he often did, he considered whether milk became heated when it was churned. "Observe whether the revolution of milk when butter is made heats it" he put on his to-do list.[30]

THE AORTIC VALVE

Leonardo's greatest achievement in his heart studies, and indeed in all of his anatomical work, was his discovery of the way the aortic valve works, a triumph that was confirmed only in modern times. It was birthed by his understanding, indeed love, of spiral flows. For his entire career, Leonardo was fascinated by the swirls of water eddies, wind currents, and hair curls cascading down a neck. He applied this knowledge to determining how the spiral flow of blood through a part of the aorta known as the sinus of Valsalva creates eddies and swirls that serve to close the valve of a beating heart. His analysis filled six pages, crammed with twenty drawings and hundreds of words of notations.[31]

On top of one of the first of these pages he wrote a dictum, derived from the maxim Plato inscribed over the door of his Academy: "Let no one who is not a mathematician read my work."[32] This did not mean that his study of the heart's blood flow would involve rigorous equations; his study of the math describing swirls and curls had not gone beyond a bit of dabbling with the Fibonacci sequence of numbers. Instead, the injunction was an expression of his belief that nature's actions obey physical laws and math-like certainties.

His discoveries about the heart valve derived from the intense inquiries into fluid dynamics he was doing around 1510, including an analysis of how water flowing from pipes into a tank creates eddies. One phenomenon that interested him was fluid drag. When a current flows through a pipe or a channel or a river, he discovered, the water that is closest to the sides flows slower than the water in the middle. This is because the water on the sides rubs up against the wall of the pipe or the banks of the river, and the friction slows it down. The layer of water right next to this will also slow down a little bit; the water flowing at the center of the pipe or river will be slowed the least. When the water flows out of the pipe into a tank, or out of the river into a pool, the difference in speed between the fast central flow and the slower side flow causes whirlpools and eddies. "Of the water that pours out of a horizontal pipe, the part that originates nearer the center of the mouth will go further away from the mouth of the pipe," he wrote. He also described how vortexes and eddies are formed by fluids that flow past curved surfaces or in a channel that gets wider. He applied this to his study of the erosion of riverbanks, his depiction in his art of flowing water, and his inquiries into how blood is pumped out of the heart.[33]

Specifically, Leonardo focused on the blood that was pumped upward from the heart through a triangle-shaped opening into the root of the aorta, which is the large vessel that carries blood from the heart to the body. "The middle of the blood that spouts up through the triangle acquires much more height than that which rises up along the sides," he declared. He went on to describe how that causes it to form spiraling eddies as it pours into the blood that is already in the widened sections of the aorta. These sections are now known as the sinuses of Valsalva, after the Italian anatomist Antonio Valsalva, who wrote about them in the early 1700s. By right they should be called the sinuses of Leonardo, and they probably would have been if Leonardo had published the discoveries he had made about them two centuries before Valsalva.[34]

This swirling action of the blood after it is pumped into the aorta causes the leaflets of the triangular valves between the heart and the aorta to spread out and then cover the opening. "The revolving blood beats against the sides of the three valves and closes them so that the blood cannot descend." It was like wind swirls spreading out the corners of a triangular sail, an analogy Leonardo employed in explaining his discovery. On a drawing that shows how the eddies of blood pull open the cusps of the valve, he wrote, "Give names to the cords that open and shut the two sails."

The common view, which was held by most heart specialists until the 1960s, was that the valve is pushed shut from above once enough blood has rushed into the aorta and begun to back up. Most other kinds of valve work that way, swinging shut when the flow begins to reverse. For more than four centuries, heart researchers paid little attention to Leonardo's argument that the valve would not be properly closed by pressure from above: "The blood which turns back when the heart reopens is not that which closes the valves of the heart. This would be impossible, because if the blood beats against the valves of the heart while they are wrinkled and folded, the blood that presses from above would press down and crumple the membrane." On the top of the last of the six pages, he sketched how the crumpled valve would scrunch up if a backflow of blood pressured it from above (fig. 113).[35]

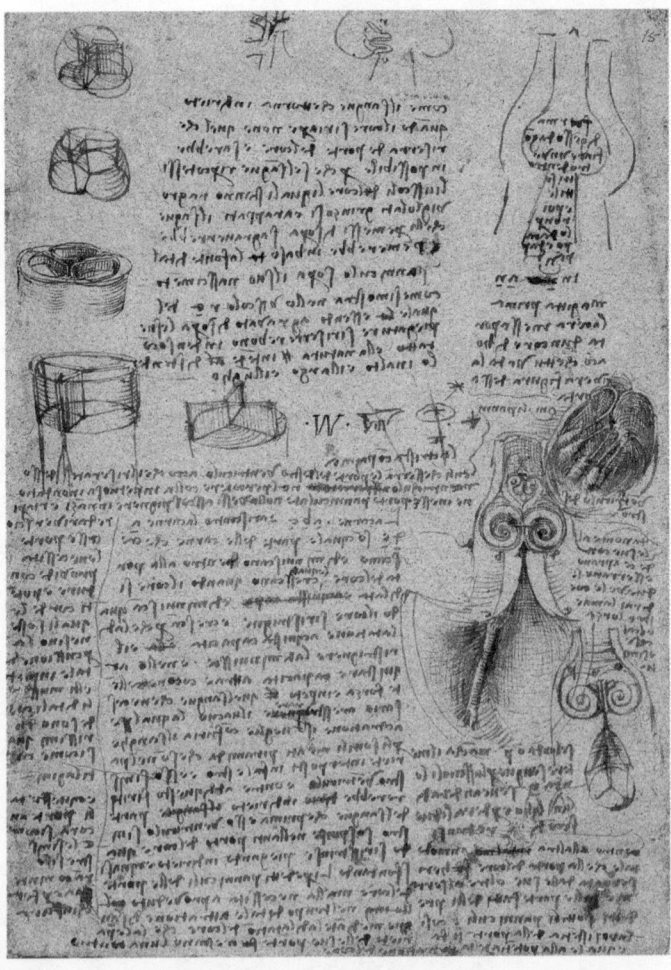

Fig. 113. The aortic valve.

Leonardo had developed his hypothesis through analogy: using what he knew about eddies of water and air, he surmised how the blood would spiral into the aorta. But then he devised an ingenious way to test his idea. On the top of this crammed notebook page, he described and drew a way to make a glass model of the heart. When filled with water, it would allow him to observe the way blood would swirl as it passed into the aorta. He used a bull's heart as a model, filling it with wax using the sculptor's technique he had used in creating a model of the brain. When the wax hardened, he made a mold to build a glass model of the heart chamber, valve, and aorta. By sprinkling in grass seeds, he made the flow of water more visible. "Make this test in the glass and put water and panic-grass seed inside it," he directed.[36]

It took 450 years for anatomists to realize that Leonardo was correct. In the 1960s a team of medical researchers led by Brian Bellhouse at Oxford used dyes and radiography methods to observe blood flows. As Leonardo had done, they used a transparent model of the aorta filled with water to observe the swirls and flow. The experiments showed that the valve required "a fluid dynamic control mechanism which positions the cusps away from the wall of the aorta, so that the slightest reversed flow will close the valve." That mechanism, they realized, was the vortex or swirling flow of blood that Leonardo had discovered in the aorta root. "The vortices produce a thrust on both the cusp and the sinus wall, and the closure of the cusps is thus steady and synchronized," they wrote. "Leonardo da Vinci correctly predicted the formation of vortices between the cusp and its sinus and appreciated that these would help close the valve." The surgeon Sherwin Nuland declared, "Of all the amazements that Leonardo left for the ages, this one would seem to be the most extraordinary."

In 1991 Francis Robicsek of the Carolina Heart Institute showed how closely the Bellhouse experiments resembled the ones that Leonardo described in his notebooks. And in 2014 another Oxford team was able to study blood flow in a living human to prove conclusively that Leonardo was right. To do so they used magnetic resonance techniques to view in real time the complex blood flow patterns in the aortic root of a living person. "We confirm in a human *in vivo* that Leonardo's prediction of systolic flow vortices was accurate and that he provided a strikingly precise depiction of these vortices in proportion to the aortic root," they concluded.[37]

Leonardo's breakthroughs on heart valves were followed, however, by a failure: not discovering that the blood in the body circulates. His understanding of one-way valves should have made him realize the flaw in the Galenic theory, universally accepted during his time, that the blood is pulsed back and forth by the heart, moving to-and-fro. But Leonardo, somewhat unusually, was blinded by book learning. The "unlettered" man who disdained those who relied on received wisdom and vowed to make experiment his mistress failed to do so in this case. His genius and creativity had always come from proceeding without preconceptions. His study of blood flow, however, was one of the rare cases where he had acquired enough textbooks and expert tutors that he failed to think differently. A full explanation of blood circulation in the human body would have to wait for William Harvey a century later.

THE FETUS

Leonardo's anatomical studies culminated with his depiction of the beginning of life. On a cluttered notebook page (fig. 114), he carefully rendered in ink over subtle red chalk his iconic image of a fetus in the womb.[38] The drawing rivals *Vitruvian Man* as an emblem of Leonardo's combination of art and science. It is good as an anatomical study, but purely divine, almost literally so, as a work of art. Drawn with meticulous curved hatchings that are designed to dazzle our eyes as much as inform our minds, it captures the human condition with a spiritual beauty that is at once unnerving and ennobling. We can see ourselves embodied in the wonder of creation: innocent, miraculous, mysterious. Though the drawing is usually parsed and analyzed as a work of anatomy, the *Guardian* art critic Jonathan Jones got closer to its essence when he wrote, "It is for me the most beautiful work of art in the world."[39]

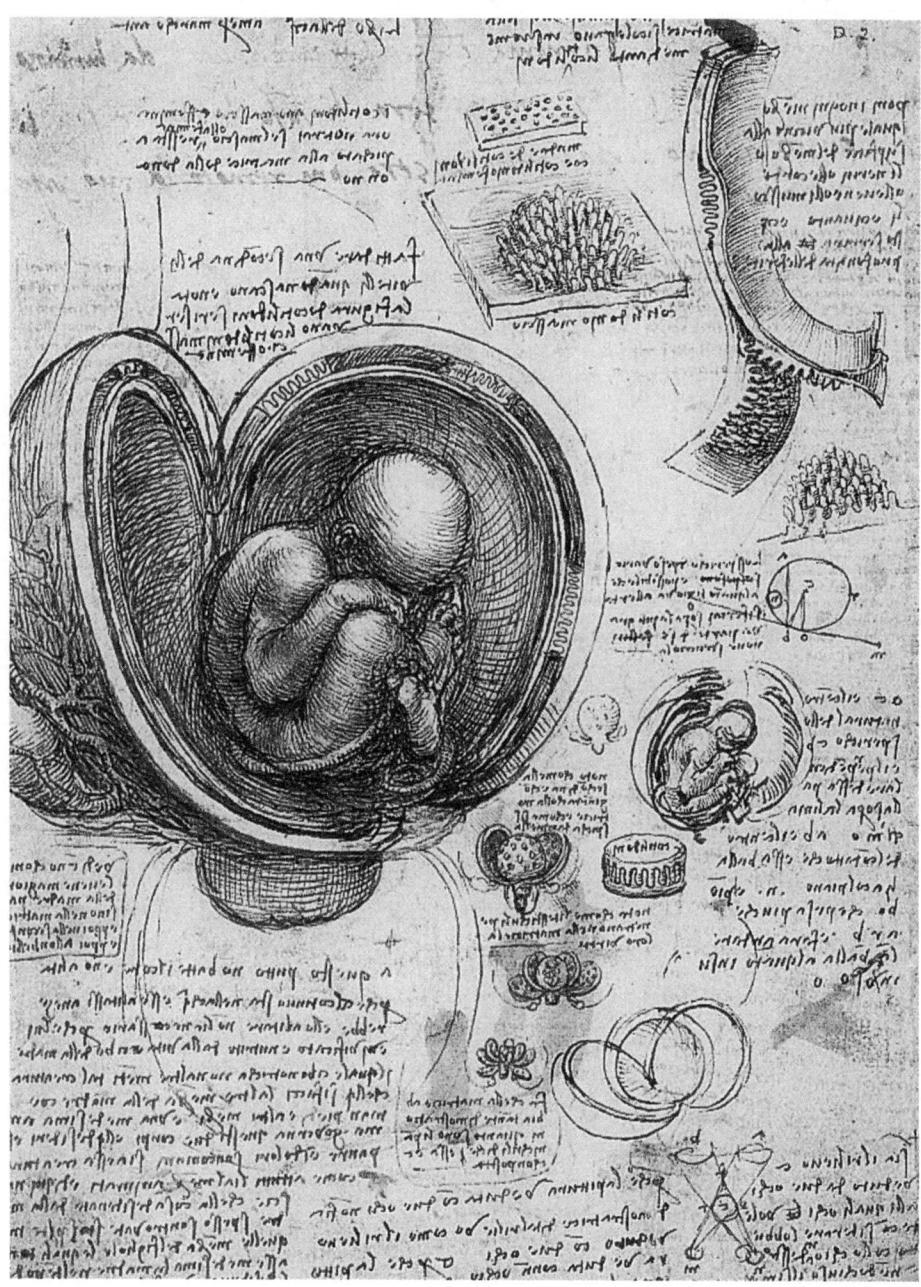

Fig. 114. Fetus in the womb.

Leonardo did not have a female cadaver to dissect, so some of the elements are drawn from a cow dissection. The womb is therefore spherical, unlike in a human. But he did improve on the conventional wisdom of his era. He correctly drew the uterus with one chamber, in contrast to contemporary belief that it had multiple chambers. His depictions of the uterine artery, vascular system of the vagina, and blood vessels in the umbilical cord are also groundbreaking.

As usual, Leonardo saw patterns across disciplines and used analogies as a method of inquiry. At the time of his fetus drawing, he had reengaged in his study of plants. Just as he had made an analogy between the branching of plants and rivers and blood vessels, so he noticed the similarities between the way plant seeds and human embryos develop. Plants have a stalk, known as a funiculus, that connects the seed to the wall of its ovule until the seed becomes ripe, and Leonardo realized that it served the same purpose as an umbilical cord. "All seeds have an umbilical cord, which is broken when the seed is ripe," he wrote on one of his anatomical drawings of a human fetus.[40]

Leonardo was aware that his fetus drawing had a spiritual quality that transcended his other anatomical studies. A few years later, he returned to the sketch to write a paragraph at the bottom of the page. It is more essay than dissection notes. He began scientifically by arguing that the embryo does not breathe in the womb because it is surrounded by fluids. "If it breathed it would drown," he explained, "and breathing is not necessary because it is nourished by the life and food of the mother." Then he added some thoughts that the Church, which believed that individual human life begins at conception, would have considered heretical. The embryo is still as much a part of the mother as her hands and feet are. "One and the same soul governs these two bodies," he added, "and one and the same soul nourishes both."

Leonardo's rejection of Church teachings on the soul was done without drama or angst. He was naturally comfortable with scientific humanism and tended to look at facts. He believed in the glorious and awe-inspiring nature of creation, but for him these were things to be studied and appreciated through science and art, not through the dogmas handed down by the Church.

LOST IMPACT

Leonardo dedicated himself to his anatomy studies with a persistence and diligence that were often lacking in his other endeavors. During his frenzied years of work from 1508 to 1513, he seemed never to tire of it and kept digging deeper, even though it meant nights spent amid cadavers and the stench of decaying organs.

He was mainly motivated by his own curiosity. He may have considered, as well, that he was making a contribution to public knowledge, but here it gets murky. He wrote that he intended his findings to be published, but when it came to editing and organizing his notes he was once again dilatory rather than diligent. He was more interested in pursuing knowledge than in publishing it. And even though he was collegial in his life and work, he made little effort to share his findings.

This is true for all of his studies, not just his work on anatomy. The trove of treatises that he left unpublished testifies to the unusual nature of what motivated him. He wanted to accumulate knowledge for its own sake, and for his own personal joy, rather than out of a desire to make a public name for himself as a scholar or to be part of the progress of history. Some have even said that he wrote in mirror script partly to guard his discoveries from prying eyes; I do not think that is true, but it is indisputable that his passion for gathering knowledge was not matched by one for sharing it widely. As the Leonardo scholar Charles Hope has pointed out, "He had no real understanding of the way in which the growth of knowledge was a cumulative and collaborative process."[41] Although he would occasionally let visitors glimpse his work, he did not seem to realize or care that the importance of research comes from its dissemination.

Years later, when he was living in France in 1517, a visitor reported that Leonardo had dissected more than thirty bodies and "written a treatise on anatomy, showing the limbs, muscles, nerves, veins, joints, intestines, and everything that can be explained in the body of men and women, in a way that has never been done by anyone before." He added that Leonardo had "also written on the nature of water, and has filled an infinite number of volumes with treatises on machines and other subjects, all written in the vulgar tongue, which, when published, will be of the greatest profit and delight."[42] But when he died, Leonardo would leave to Melzi only piles of unedited notebook pages and drawings.

Modern anatomy instead began twenty-five years after Leonardo's death, when Andreas Vesalius published his epochal and beautifully produced *On the Fabric of the Human Body*. That was the book that Leonardo—perhaps in conjunction with Marcantonio della Torre, had he not died young from the plague—could have preceded and surpassed. Instead, Leonardo's anatomical work had minimal influence. Over the years, and even centuries, his discoveries had to be rediscovered by others. The fact that he didn't publish served to diminish his impact on the history of science. But it did not diminish his genius.

CHAPTER 28

The World and Its Waters

THE MICROCOSM AND THE MACROCOSM

During the period when he was probing the human body, Leonardo was also studying the body of the earth. True to form, he made analogies between the two. He was skillful at discerning how patterns resonate in nature, and the grandest and most encompassing of these analogies, in both his art and his science, was the comparison between the body of man and the body of the earth. "Man is the image of the world," he wrote.[1]

Known as the microcosm-macrocosm relationship, it harkened back to the ancients. Leonardo first discussed this analogy in a notebook entry from the early 1490s:

The ancients called man a lesser world, and certainly the use of this name is well bestowed, because his body is an analog for the world. As man has in him bones that support his flesh, the world has its rocks that support the earth. As man has a pool of blood in which the lungs rise and fall in breathing, so the body of the earth has its ocean tide which likewise rises and falls every six hours, as if the world breathed. As the blood veins originate in that pool

and spread all over the human body, so likewise the ocean sea fills
the body of the earth with infinite springs of water.[2]

This echoed what Plato had written in the *Timaeus*, where he argued
that just as the body is nourished by blood, so the earth draws water
to replenish itself. Leonardo also drew on theorists of the Middle
Ages, in particular a compendium by the thirteenth-century Italian
monk and geologist Restoro d'Arezzo.

As a painter who marveled at nature's patterns, Leonardo embraced the microcosm-macrocosm connection as more than merely
an analogy. He viewed it as having a spiritual component, which he
expressed in his drawing of *Vitruvian Man*. As we have seen, this
mystical connection between humans and the earth is reflected in
many of his masterpieces, from *Ginevra de' Benci* to *Saint Anne* to
Madonna of the Yarnwinder and eventually the *Mona Lisa*. It also became an organizing principle for his scientific inquiries. When he was
immersed in his anatomical research on the human digestive system,
he instructed himself, "First give the comparison with the water of the
rivers; then with that of the bile which goes to the stomach against
the course of the food."[3]

Around 1508, while simultaneously pursuing his anatomy and
earth studies in Milan, Leonardo returned to the analogy in a fascinating notebook, the Codex Leicester.* More focused than most
of his other notebooks, it contains seventy-two pages jammed with
long written passages and 360 drawings on geology, astronomy, and
the dynamics of flowing water. His goal was the one that Renaissance
thinkers, himself foremost among them, bequeathed to the subsequent ages of science and enlightenment: understanding the causes
and effects that rule our cosmos, ranging from the mechanics of our
muscles to the movement of the planets, from the flow in our arteries to that in the earth's rivers.[4] Among the questions it addresses:

---

* It was named after the Earl of Leicester, who purchased it in 1717. In 1980 it was
purchased by the industrialist Armand Hammer, who renamed it the Codex Hammer.
When Bill Gates bought it in 1994, his ego was not that intrusive, and he let the name
revert to the Codex Leicester.

What causes springs of water to emerge from mountains? Why do valleys exist? What makes the moon shine? How did fossils get on mountains? What causes water and air to swirl in a vortex? And, most emblematically, why is the sky blue?

As he embarked on the Codex Leicester, Leonardo reached back to the microcosm-macrocosm analogy as his framework. "The body of the earth, like the bodies of animals, is interwoven with ramifications of veins, which are all joined together and are formed for the nutrition and vivification of this earth and of its creatures," he wrote, echoing his words from almost two decades earlier.[5] And on the following page he added, "Its flesh is the soil, its bones are the arrangements of the connections of the rocks of which the mountains are composed, its cartilage is the porous rock, its blood is the veins of waters; the lake of the blood, which is throughout the heart, is the ocean; its breathing and the increase and decrease of the blood through the pulses in the earth is thus: it is the flow and ebb of the sea."[6]

The analogy helped him look at the earth in a pioneering way. Rather than assuming that it had been static since its creation, Leonardo realized that the earth had a dynamic history in which powerful forces caused it to change and mature over the centuries. "We might say that the earth has a vegetative soul," he declared.[7] By regarding the earth as a living organism, he was inspired to explore the way it aged and evolved: how mountains laced with fossils arose from the sea, how rocks became layers, how rivers cut valleys, and how rugged outcroppings eroded.[8]

But even though Leonardo embraced the microcosm-macrocosm analogy, he did not do so blindly. He tested it against experience and experiments, engaging in the great dialogue that shaped his understanding of the world. By the time he finished the Codex Leicester, he would discover that the comparison between the earth and the human body was not always useful. Instead, he came to fathom how nature had two traits that sometimes appeared to be in conflict: there was a unity to nature that resonated in its patterns and analogies, but there was also a wondrously infinite variety.

WATER

The primary focus of the Codex Leicester is the topic that Leonardo regarded as the most fundamental force in the life of the planet and in our bodies: the role and movements of fluids and, in particular, water. More than any other subject except the human body, hydrodynamics engaged his artistic and scientific and engineering interests, and he addressed it on various levels: detailed observations, practical inventions, grand projects, beautiful paintings, and cosmic analogies.[9] One of his earliest drawings was of the landscape carved by the cascading Arno River. In Verrocchio's *Baptism of Christ*, Leonardo painted flowing water as it passed over the feet of Jesus with a combination of beauty and sharply observed realism that had never been seen. In an early notebook, he drew an array of mechanical devices—including pumps, hydraulic tubes, water screws, and bucket wheels—designed to move water to different levels. In his job-seeking letter to Ludovico Sforza, he boasted of his abilities "to take the water out of the trenches" and "in guiding water from one place to another." While in Milan, he studied that city's large network of canals, including the grand canal dug in 1460 to Lake Como, as well as its well-tended waterways, dams, locks, fountains, and irrigation systems.[10] He drilled holes in a barrel to study the trajectory and pressure of the water jets at differing heights.[11] He devised grandiose schemes and practical devices for diverting the Arno River and draining swamps. And by using his knowledge of how water pouring from a pipe causes water eddies, he was able to envision the vortexes inside the human heart and how they would close a valve.

Leonardo's studies of water began with practical and artistic purposes in mind, but as with his studies of anatomy and flight, he became enthralled by the beauty of the science. Water provided the perfect manifestation of Leonardo's fascination with how shapes are transformed when in motion. How can something change its shape—a square becoming a circle, a torso narrowing as it twists—and keep the exact same area or volume? Water provides an answer. Leonardo learned early on that it cannot be compressed; a given quantity always has the exact same volume, whatever the shape of the river or container. So flowing water is constantly going through perfect geometric transformations. No wonder he loved it.

In the 1490s Leonardo began a treatise on hydraulics, which included notes on the speed of river currents at various depths, studies of whirlpools formed by the friction of the banks, and the turbulence caused when different currents collide. Not surprisingly, he never finished it, but in 1508 he tackled the topic again. In the Codex Leicester, he made an outline, as he often did, for the proposed tract. It was to have fifteen chapters, starting with "Of the Waters in Themselves," followed by "Of the Sea" and "Of Underground Rivers," and concluding with "Of Making Water to Rise" and "Of Things Consumed by the Waters." One of the topics he planned to explore arose from his scheme to redirect the Arno River: "How with a few stones a river can be diverted, if one understands the line of its current."[12]

His studies at times became such a deluge of details that they reveal more about his passion than about water's dynamics. He spent hours fixated on flowing water, sometimes observing it and at other times manipulating it to test out his theories. In one part of the Codex Leicester he crammed 730 conclusions about water onto eight pages, causing Martin Kemp to comment, "We may feel that the boundary between dedication and obsession has been overstepped."[13] In another notebook, he made a list of different words that can be used to describe concepts involving the flow of water: "risaltazione, circolazione, revoluzione, ravvoltamento, raggiramento, sommergimento, surgimento, declinazione, elevazione, cavamento." By the end, he had listed sixty-seven of them.[14]

He was able to avoid pedantry by regularly bringing his theories down to earth, so to speak, and tying them to practical applications. As he instructed himself in a typical notebook jotting, "When you put together the science of the motions of water, remember to include under each proposition its application, in order that this science may not be useless."[15]

As usual, he combined experience and experiment; in fact he used the same word, *esperienza*, for both. While in Florence, he devised a pair of goggles for his dives in the Arno so he could study the water as it flowed past a weir. He threw oak apples or corks into a river and counted "beats of time" to study how long it took those in the center and those nearer the banks to move two hundred feet. He made floats that could hover at different depths to see how the currents changed from the surface to the bottom, and he crafted instruments that could measure a river's downhill course so he could determine the "rate of fall of a river per mile."

He also devised studio experiments so that he could test in a controlled environment the concepts he had observed in nature. These included making vessels of varying shapes and sizes so that he could see how water reacted when he disturbed it. He was especially interested in re-creating the eddies that he found in nature, so he built himself a glass tank, which he also used to test his theories of erosion. Make this experiment "in a square glass vessel like a box," he wrote, "and you will see the revolution of this water."[16]

To observe the movements of water, he used millet seeds, leaves, wooden rods, dyes, and colored inks.[17] "Drop a few grains of panic-grass because the movement of these grains can quickly let you know the movement of the water that carries them. From this experiment you will be able to proceed to investigate many beautiful movements which result from one element penetrating into another."[18] Pause for a moment on that word *beautiful*. You have to love Leonardo for realizing that there is beauty in the way different water currents mingle. In another example, he instructed, "Let the water that strikes there have millet or fragments of papyrus mixed in it, so that you can better see its course." In each case, he varied the conditions, such as using a gravel bed, then a bed of sand, then a smooth bed.

Some of the tests he proposed were merely thought experiments, to be conducted in his imagination or on paper. In one of his friction studies, for example, he wrote of doing an experiment "to increase or decrease in my imagination and to find out what is willed by the laws of nature." He did the same type of thought experiments regarding the world and its water. What would happen to nearby underground streams, he asked, if the air were sucked out of a cave?

The primary tool he used, however, was simple observation, though his acute visual focus meant that he saw things the rest of us would miss. When we watch water flowing into a glass or coursing by in a river, we tend not to marvel the way he did at the many types of swirls and movements it makes. But he saw that "running water has within itself an infinite number of movements."[19]

An "infinite number"? For Leonardo, that was not just a figure of speech. When he spoke of the infinite variety in nature, and especially of phenomena such as flowing water, he was making a distinction based on his preference for analog over digital systems. In an analog system, there are infinite gradations. That applies to most of the things that fascinated him: sfumato shadows, colors, movement, waves, the passage of time, the flow of fluids. That is why he believed that geometry was better than arithmetic at describing nature, and even though calculus had not yet been invented, he seemed to sense the need for such a mathematics of continuous quantities.

DIVERSIONS, EDDIES, WHIRLPOOLS, AND VORTEXES

From his care at depicting how the River Jordan would ripple past the ankles of Christ to his schemes for changing the course of the Arno, Leonardo had a keen interest in what happens when a flow of water is obstructed. The dynamics of water, he realized, are connected to the two proto-Newtonian ideas about motion that he embraced: impetus and percussion.

Impetus, a concept developed in the Middle Ages and adopted by Leonardo, describes how a body set in motion tends to keep moving in the same direction. It is a rudimentary precursor to the concepts of inertia, momentum, and Newton's first law. Percussion involves what happens when a body in motion hits another object; it will be reflected or deflected at an angle and with a force that can be calculated. Leonardo's understanding of fluid dynamics was also informed by his studies of transformations; when water is deflected, it changes path and shape, but it always remains the exact same volume.

In the margins of one crammed page of the Codex Leicester, Leonardo drew fourteen exquisite examples of what different obstacles do to the flow of water.[20] Combining the pictures with text, he explored ways that a diversion could influence the erosion of riverbanks and how obstacles affect river flows below the surface. His studies informed his artistic renderings of water flow as well as his engineering aspirations to alter the course of rivers. But as he became more immersed, he began indulging his curiosity about water flow for its own sake.

A display of this can be seen on a stunning page, now at Windsor Castle, that starts with ink and red-chalk drawings of diversions of rivers and then proceeds to a sketch of water falling into a pond (fig. 115). This combination of scientific curiosity and artistic virtuosity begins with drawings of boards placed on an angle to obstruct the flow of a current, one of many such drawings he made after he studied ways to divert the Arno. The interlacing curves of the water

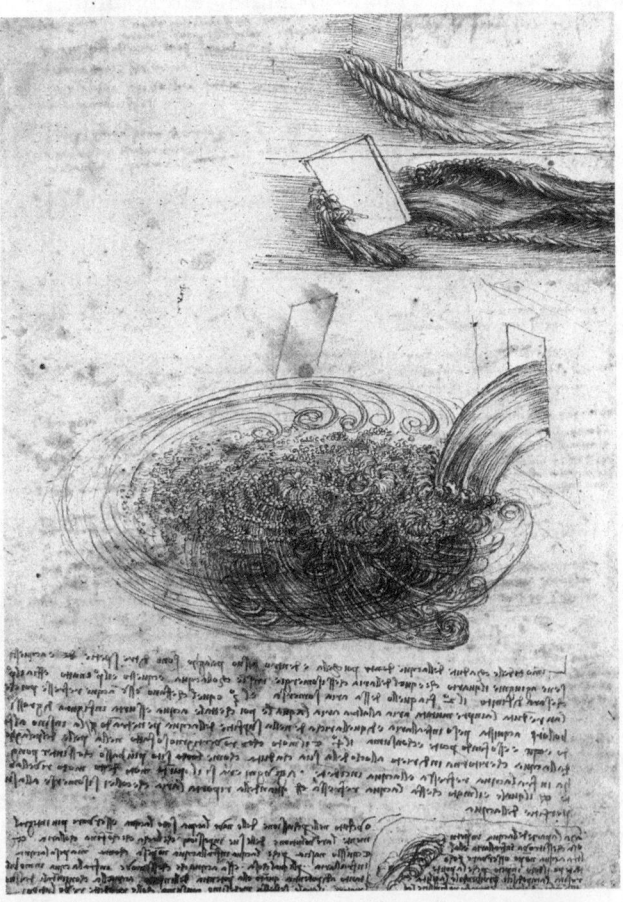

Fig. 115. Water passing obstacles and falling into a pool.

as it rushes past the obstacles are drawn with the gusto Leonardo displayed whenever he drew spirals and curls. The currents look like pennants twisting together at a windy pageant, or the mane of a galloping horse, or the angelic curls of hair Leonardo loved to draw in his paintings of women and sketches of Salai.

As usual, he made an analogy, comparing the forces that create water eddies to those that create a hair curl: "The curling motion of the surface of water resembles the behavior of hair, which has two motions, one of which depends on the weight of the strands, the other on the direction of its revolving; thus water makes eddies, one part of which is due to the impetus of the principal current, and the other is due to the incidental motion and return flow."[21] This brief notation captures the essence of what motivated Leonardo: a joy in seeing the patterns that connect two things that delighted him, in this case ringlets of hair and eddies of water.

After drawing the two obstacles in a river, Leonardo drew a stream of water gushing out of an opening and forming complex patterns as it falls into a pond. These patterns resemble not only his renderings of human curls but also many of his drawings of plants, such as his beautiful rendering of a Star of Bethlehem (fig. 116).[22] His depiction of water falling into a pond does not merely try to capture a moment; like his greatest paintings, it conveys movement.

As always, Leonardo observed details that most of us overlook. He drew and described the effect of the column of water hitting the surface, the waves that emanate from the impact, the percussions of the water in the pool, the movement of the air bubbles that are submerged by the falling water, and the way the bubbles pop into floral-like rosettes when they reach the surface. He noticed that eddies containing bubbles are short-lived because they dissipate as the bubbles rise, but he drew the eddies that have no bubbles with longer lines. "The eddies that begin on the surface are filled with air," he saw. "Those that have their origin within the water are filled with water and these are more lasting because water within water has no weight."[23] Try noticing all that when you next fill a sink.

Leonardo was especially interested in eddies that form when flowing water is deflected from its path. As his drawings show, the water

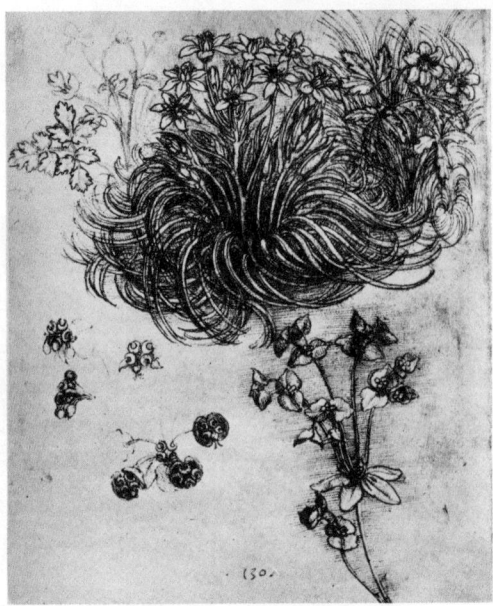

Fig. 116. Star of Bethlehem flower.

flowing past an obstacle curves toward the area directly behind the obstacle, where there is less water, forming a vortex. To this he applied his understanding of impetus and percussion; the water would attempt to continue moving in the same direction, but it would do so in a curved and spiraling manner because of the percussive force of hitting the obstacle.[24]

He realized that vortexes likewise occur in air when it blows past an object or when a beating wing causes an area of low air pressure. Like curls of hair, these swirls of water or air form geometric patterns—a spiral—that follow mathematical laws. It is another example of willfully noticing something in nature, discovering its pattern, and applying it to other aspects of nature. The result was so powerful and beautiful that spiraling vortexes would become an obsession, one that would reach its ultimate expression in a final set of drawings he did near the end of his life.

Leonardo's studies of water movements also led him to understand the concept of waves. He realized that waves do not actually involve water moving forward. Waves in the sea and ripples emanating from a pebble falling into a pond progress in a certain direction, but these "tremors," as he called them, merely cause the water to move up for a moment before returning to where it had been. He compared them to waves caused by a breeze in a field of grain. By the time he wrote the Codex Leicester and other, concurrent notebook pages on the movement of water, Leonardo had a deep feel for how waves propagate in a medium, and he correctly assumed that sound and light travel in waves. With his gift for analogy and ability to notice movement, he even viewed emotions as traveling in waves. At the core of the narrative in *The Last Supper* are the waves of emotion that emanate from the disturbance caused by the utterance of Jesus.

REVISING THE ANALOGY

One mark of a great mind is the willingness to change it. We can see that in Leonardo. As he wrestled with his earth and water studies during the early 1500s, he ran into evidence that caused him to revise his belief in the microcosm-macrocosm analogy. It was Leonardo at his best, and we have the great fortune of being able to watch that evolution as he wrote the Codex Leicester. There he engaged in a dialogue between theories and experience, and when they conflicted he was receptive to trying a new theory. That willingness to surrender preconceptions was key to his creativity.

The evolution of Leonardo's thinking about the microcosm-macrocosm analogy began with his curiosity about why water, which should in theory tend to settle on the earth's surface, emerges from springs and flows into rivers at the top of mountains. The veins of the earth, he wrote, carry "the blood that keeps the mountains alive."[25] He noticed a similar pattern involving plants as well as humans. Just as the blood in the human body goes up to the head and can flow out from cuts and nosebleeds, the sap of plants rises to the top leaves and branches. This pattern is found in both the microcosm and the macrocosm. "The waters circulate with continuous motion from the lowest depths of the seas to the highest summits of the mountains, not obeying the nature of heavy things," he wrote. "And in this case they act like the blood in animals; which always moves from the sea of the heart and flows to the summit of their heads; and if a vein breaks here, as one sees a vein ruptured in the nose, all of the blood rises from below to the height of the broken vein."[26]

Assuming that similar effects have similar causes, he began his quest to figure out what force impels liquids to move upward to become mountain springs. "The same cause which moves the fluids in all kinds of living bodies against the natural course of gravity also propels the water through the veins of the Earth," he surmised. "As the blood rises from below and pours out through the broken veins of the forehead, and as the water rises from the lower part of the vine to the branches that are cut, so from the lowest depth of the sea the water rises to the summits of the mountains where, finding the veins broken, it pours down."[27]

What was the force that did this? Over the years Leonardo considered several explanations. He initially thought the heat of the sun causes the water to rise inside the mountains, either as vapor that is then condensed or through some other method. "Where there is heat there is movement of vapor," he noted, then made this analogy:

> Just as the natural heat of the blood in the veins keeps it in the head of man—for when the man is dead the cold blood sinks to the lower parts—when the sun is hot on the head of a man the blood increases and rises so much that by pressuring the veins often causes headaches; in the same way that veins ramify through the body of the earth, and by the natural heat which is distributed throughout the containing body, the water is raised through the veins to the tops of mountains.[28]

He also considered whether the water may be sucked up, as in a siphon. His interest in water management and swamp drainage had led him over the years to experiment with different kinds of siphons and distillation equipment. On one large sheet of the Codex Leicester folded into folios (fig. 117), each possibility is sketched out in drawings and explained in words.[29] He used drawings as tools to help him think. For example, on this page he made twelve pen-and-ink sketches of siphons to imagine how they could be connected to lift

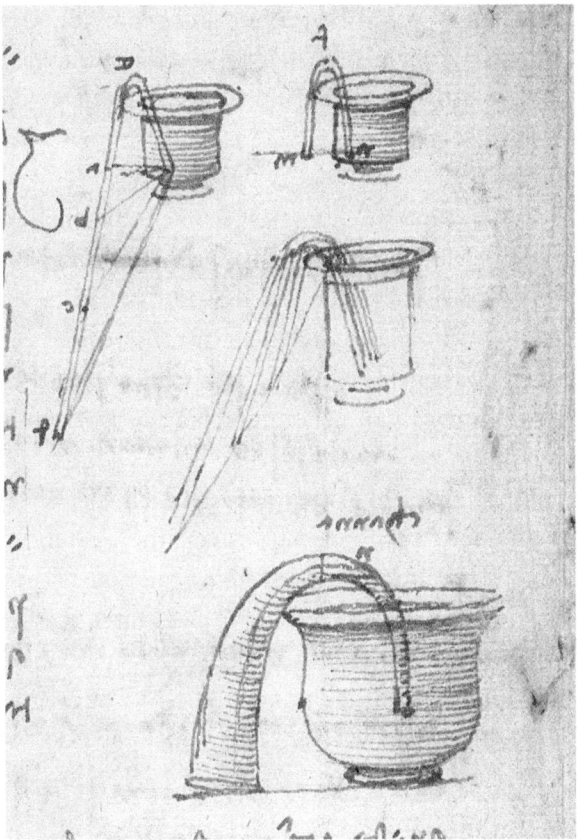

Fig. 117. Thought experiment using siphons.

water to the top of mountains, but none of his configurations worked. It cannot be done, he concluded.

Leonardo proceeded to dismiss all of the explanations for why the earth's water circulates to the top of mountains, including theories he had once accepted. Most notably, he cast away his long-standing belief that heat draws water up inside mountains just like (he thought) it draws blood up to the human head, because he realized that mountain streams are just as prevalent in cold climes and months as they are in warm. "If you said that the heat of the sun draws it up high from the caverns of the mountains as far as the summit of the mountains, thereby drawing it up from the uncovered lakes and seas in the form of vapor for the composition of clouds," he wrote in the Codex

Leicester, "then there would be greater and more abundant veins of waters where the heat is greater than in colder countries, but we see the contrary." He also noted that the veins of humans narrow with age, but the springs and rivers of the earth continually enlarge their channels.[30]

In other words, experience and experiment taught him that the received wisdom from the analogy between the macrocosm of the earth and the microcosm of man was flawed. The analogy had misled him about geology. So, like a good scientist, he revised his thinking. "The ocean does not penetrate under the earth," he wrote in one of his other notebooks, "and cannot penetrate from the roots to the summits of mountains."[31]

Only after pitting various theories against experience did Leonardo eventually get to the correct answer: the existence of springs and mountain rivers, indeed the entire circulation of water on the earth, results from the evaporation of surface water, the formation of clouds, and the subsequent rains. On one of his anatomical drawings from around 1510, written at the same time as he was revising his geological thoughts in his Codex Leicester, Leonardo jotted down a note "on the nature of veins" that declared, "The origin of the sea is contrary to the origin of the blood . . . [because] all the rivers are caused solely by the water vapors raised up into the air." The amount of water on the earth is constant, he concluded, and it is "constantly circulating and returning."[32]

Leonardo's willingness to question and then abandon the enticing analogy between the circulation of water on the earth and the circulation of blood in the human body shows his curiosity and ability to be open-minded. Throughout his life, he was brilliant at discerning patterns and abstracting from them a framework that could be applied across disciplines. His geology studies show an even greater talent: not letting these patterns blind him. He came to appreciate not only nature's similarities but also its infinite variety. Yet even as he abandoned the simplistic version of the microcosm-macrocosm analogy, he retained the aesthetic and spiritual concept underlying it: the harmonies of the cosmos are reflected in the beauty of living creatures.

FLOODS AND FOSSILS

Leonardo's experience as an engineer and enthusiast of flowing water helped him understand erosion, which he realized is caused when water currents carve away dirt from riverbanks. He applied that knowledge to determining how valleys are created: "Rivulets will originate in the lowest parts of a surface, and these will begin to hollow out and form receptacles for other surrounding waters. In this way, every part of their course will become wider and deeper."[33] The rivers thus eventually wear away the earth and create valleys.

Part of his evidence came from sharp observations. The rock strata on one side of a valley, he noticed, has the same sequence of sedimentation as that on the other side. "One sees the strata on one side of the river corresponding with those on the other," he wrote in the Codex Leicester. "With this argument, Leonardo was two hundred years ahead of his time," the science historian Fritjof Capra asserted. "The superposition of rock strata would not be recognized and studied in similar detail until the second half of the seventeenth century."[34]

These observations led Leonardo to consider how fossils—especially those of sea animals—ended up in these high stratified layers of rock. "Why are the bones of great fishes and oysters and corals and other various shells and sea-snails found on the tops of mountains?" he asked. Writing more than 3,500 words on the topic in the Codex Leicester, he described his detailed observations of fossils and argued that the biblical story of the Flood was incorrect. Showing no fear of combining heresy with blasphemy, he wrote "of the foolishness and simple-mindedness of those who require that these animals should be carried by the Deluge to these places, far from the sea."[35]

Because fossils appear in several sediment layers that were deposited at different times, he argued, their location cannot be explained by a single flood. He also provided evidence from his close studies that the fossils did not come from a great swelling of the seas. "If the Deluge had carried the shells three hundred and four hundred miles far from the sea, it would have carried them there mixed up with different species, amassed together. But we see, at such distances, the oysters, and the shells, and the squids and all the other shells which stay congregated together."[36]

His conclusion, which is correct, was that there had been enormous shifts and fluctuations in the crust of the earth that had given rise to mountains. "From time to time the bottom of the sea was raised, depositing these shells in layers," he declared. He had seen it for himself as he hiked on Collegonzi Road near the Arno River south of Vinci, where the river had eroded the mountains and layers of shells were plainly visible in the bluish clay.[37] As he later noted, "The ancient bottoms of the sea have become mountain ridges."[38]

Among the evidence he cited was his discovery of what are now called "trace fossils." These are formed not by the remains of animals but by the tracks and traces that animals left in the sediment when they were still alive. "In rock layers are still found the tracks of the worms, which proceeded through them when they were not yet dried out," he wrote in the Codex Leicester.[39] That proved, Leonardo said, that the sea animals had not been washed up by a deluge to the mountain but instead had been alive, at what was then the bottom of the sea, when the strata were formed. Leonardo thus became a pioneer of ichnology, the study of fossil traces, a field that did not come into full existence for another three hundred years.

When he examined the fossils of shellfish, he noticed a pattern that would help determine how long they had lived: "We can count in the crusts of cockles and snails the years and months of their life, as we do in the horns of oxen and sheep, and in the branches of trees."[40] It was a leap that was far ahead of its time. "That he was able to associate the annual rings in the branches of trees with the growth rings in the horns of sheep is remarkable enough," Capra wrote. "To use the same analysis to infer the lifespan of a fossilized shell is extraordinary."[41]

ASTRONOMY

Il sole nó si muóve. The sun does not move.

These words of Leonardo are written in unusually large letters on the top left of one of his notebook pages that is filled with geometric sketches, mathematical transformations, a cross section of the brain, a drawing of the male urinary tract, and doodles of his old warrior.[42] Is this statement a brilliant leap decades ahead of Copernicus, Galileo, and the realization that the sun does not revolve around the earth? Or is it merely a random thought, perhaps a note for a pageant or play?

Leonardo leaves us in the dark, providing no elaboration. But when he wrote the sentence, around 1510, his geological studies had led him to pursue questions about the earth's place in the cosmos and other wonders of astronomy. He does not seem to have discovered that the movements of the sun and stars are caused by the earth's rotation (a young Copernicus was just formulating this theory at the time),[43] but he did come to the realization that the earth is only one of many cosmic bodies, and not necessarily the central one. "The earth is not in the center of the sun's orbit nor at the center of the universe, but in the center of its companion elements, and united with them,"[44] he wrote. And he understood that gravity kept the seas from falling off the earth. "Let the earth turn on whichever side it may, the surface of the waters will never move from its spherical form, but will always remain equidistant from the center of the globe."[45]

More impressive was his realization that the moon does not emit light but reflects the light of the sun, and that a person standing on the moon would see that the earth reflects light in the same way. "Anyone standing on the moon would see our earth just as we see the moon, and the earth would light it, just as the moon lights us." That earthshine is what gives a new moon its faint glow, he realized. Drawing on the fastidious attention he paid to reflected secondhand light in the shadowed parts of his paintings, he wrote that when we can dimly see the dark part of the moon, it is because the parts not lit by the sun can catch the reflected light from the earth. He erred, however, in applying this theory to stars, which he also thought emitted no light of their own but instead merely reflected light from the sun. "The sun gives light to all celestial bodies," he wrote.[46]

As with so many topics, he said that he was planning to write a treatise on astronomy, but he never did so. "In my book, I propose to show how the oceans and seas must, by means of the sun, make our world shine with the appearance of a moon, and to the remoter worlds it looks like a star."[47] It would have been an ambitious project.

In a memo to himself he wrote, "I have first to demonstrate the distance of the sun from the earth, then to find its true size with one of its rays passed through a small hole into a dark place, and besides this, to find the size of the earth."[48]

BLUE SKY

In pursuing his studies on the perspective of color and later on geology and astronomy, Leonardo pondered a question that seems so ordinary and mundane that most of us forget to marvel about it after age eight or so. But the greatest geniuses, from Aristotle to Leonardo, Newton, Rayleigh, and Einstein, have studied it: Why is the sky blue?

Leonardo worked on many explanations but finally settled on one, basically correct, that he recorded amid the geology and astronomy notes in his Codex Leicester: "I say that the azure in which the air shows itself is not its own color, but it is caused by warm humidity, evaporated in very minute and insensible atoms, which catches behind itself the percussion of the solar rays and makes itself luminous under the vast shades." Or, as he put it more succinctly, "The air takes the azure through the corpuscles of humidity, which catch the luminous rays of the sun."[49]

A similar theory had been handed down from Aristotle, but Leonardo refined it based on personal observations. After climbing to the top of Monte Rosa in the Italian Alps, he noticed how much bluer the sky looked. "If you go to the top of a high mountain the sky will look proportionately darker above you as the atmosphere becomes rarer between you and the outer darkness; and this will be more visible at each degree of increasing height till at last we should find darkness."

He also conducted experiments to test this explanation. First, he re-created the blue by painting a misty white wash over a dark background. "Anyone who wants to see the ultimate proofs, let him tint a board with various colors, among which a most beautiful black should be included, and over all let a thin and transparent white lead be applied; then it will be seen that the brightness of this white lead will nowhere show itself as a more beautiful azure than over the black."[50] Another experiment involved smoke. "Let smoke be made out of a small quantity of dry wood, and let the solar rays percuss this smoke; and behind this smoke place a piece of black velvet, which is not exposed to the sun, and you will see that all the smoke between the eye and the darkness of the velvet shows itself to be of a very fine blue color."[51] He reproduced the phenomenon with "water violently ejected in a fine spray and in a dark chamber." Showing his diligence as an experimenter, he used regular water filled with impurities and then water that had been purified. He discovered that the process "makes the sunbeam blue, and particularly if it is distilled water."[52]

Leonardo found himself stymied by a related question: What causes a rainbow? That would have to wait for Newton, who showed how white light can be scattered by a water mist into its component colors based on wavelengths. Nor did Leonardo figure out that light of shorter wavelengths, at the blue end of the spectrum, scatters more than light of longer wavelengths; that would have to wait for Lord Rayleigh in the late nineteenth century and then for Einstein to calculate the exact formula for the scattering.

CHAPTER 29

Rome

VILLA MELZI

The ongoing hostilities involving the French and their shifting alliances with Italian city-states often resembled pageantry and processionals more than war. "A march through Italy was an occasion for feasts, spectacles, firework displays, jousts, the expropriation of estates, and occasional massacres," wrote Robert Payne. "The French aristocracy acquired new titles, new experiences, new mistresses, new diseases."[1]

In the latest episode, the French in 1512 were losing their grip on Milan, which they had held since expelling Duke Ludovico Sforza thirteen years earlier. By the end of the year, his son Maximilian (Massimiliano) Sforza would retake the city, holding it for three years.

Leonardo had the ability to float above such political disruptions, usually by leaving town, though he also tried to catch the currents that would bring him to powerful patrons of whatever stripe. As a young man in Florence, he had been a second-tier recipient of Medici patronage before moving to Milan and aligning himself with the Sforzas. When they were ousted by the French, Leonardo switched allegiances, then enlisted with Cesare Borgia, and finally found a reliable patron in Charles d'Amboise, the French governor of Milan. But after Charles died in 1511 and the Sforzas were poised to retake the dukedom, Leonardo decided to leave Milan. With no desire to move back to Florence, where both the *Adoration of the Magi* and the *Battle of Anghiari* loomed unfinished, he began a four-year period during which he wandered in search of new patronage, carrying with him some paintings that he had been slowly perfecting.

For most of 1512, he resided comfortably in the family home of his student and surrogate son, Francesco Melzi, who turned twenty-one that year. It was an odd familial menagerie: Francesco had been adopted as a ward by Leonardo, and they were staying with his biological father, Girolamo Melzi. Also there was the still-beloved Salai, now thirty-two. The home was a stately square villa on a bluff over-looking the Adda River nineteen miles from Milan, just far enough away that Leonardo could avoid being swirled into the vortex of the geopolitics there.

Leonardo got to pursue, in a leisurely and broad fashion, all of his curiosities and passions at the Melzi villa. Though he no longer had access to human corpses, he dissected animals, including the rib cages of oxen and still-beating hearts of pigs. He completed his geology writings in the Codex Leicester, analyzing the nearby rock formations and eddies of the Adda. "Flux and reflux of water as demonstrated at the mill of Vaprio," he captioned one sheet. He also offered the Melzi family some architectural suggestions. In his notebooks he drew ground plans of the estate and possible cupolas to be built, and on a page containing anatomical sketches, he added a sketch of the villa and a note about a tower room that likely was his study. He did not, however, use the time to collate his geography, anatomy, flight, or hydraulics studies into publishable treatises. He was still Leonardo, always pursuing a curiosity, less passionate about tying up loose ends.[2]

PORTRAITS OF LEONARDO

While at Villa Melzi, surrounded by the closest thing he had to a family, Leonardo turned sixty. What did he look like? How had his handsome face and flowing curls responded to age? A few portraits and possible portraits of Leonardo exist from this period. What they have in common is that they tend to make him look old, perhaps prematurely old, and they treat him as an iconic venerable sage, beard flowing and brows furrowed.

There is one tantalizing sketch that was drawn by Leonardo himself (fig. 118).[3] The hatchings are left-handed, the notes are in mirror script, and the architectural studies on the verso side are of Villa Melzi, so we know he drew it around 1512. It shows an old man with a walking stick sitting on a rock, his left hand held up to his head as if in contemplation or perhaps feeling melancholy. His balding hair

Fig. 118. Old man and studies of moving water.

is wispy on top, though still curly. His beard flows down almost to his chest. His eye stares alertly, though with signs of fatigue. His lips are turned down—as is the case with most other possible Leonardo portraits—and his nose is distinguished and hooked, like those of his oft-doodled nutcracker man.

The melancholy man seems to be staring across the page at one of Leonardo's many drawings of swirling water forming turbulent eddies that look like curls. Indeed, it is in the note at the bottom of this sheet where Leonardo makes his comparison between water eddies and curls of hair. But this image of the aging artist contemplating the vortexes of water may be more figurative than real; the folio page is folded, and the drawing of the man may have been done separately from that of the turbulent water. As always there is a bit of mystery with Leonardo. Is he imagining himself ruefully contemplating flowing water? Is the connection across the folded sheet subconscious, or is it mere coincidence?

And is Leonardo, consciously or not, sketching himself? The man in the drawing looks older than sixty, but maybe that is how Leonardo actually looked at sixty. Many of the possible portraits make him look older than his age at the time, so it's likely that he had prematurely aged into a bearded sage. Or maybe that is how he imagined he looked. As Kenneth Clark wrote, "Even if this is not strictly a self-portrait, we may call it a self-caricature, using the word to mean a simplified expression of essential character."[4]

Leonardo's contemplative sketch bears some resemblance to a profile portrait we can be pretty confident depicts him: a red-chalk drawing usually attributed to Melzi, probably done sometime between 1512 and 1518, and labeled "Leonardo Vinci" in capital letters (fig. 119).[5] The similarities are tantalizing: Melzi's portrait shows a still-handsome Leonardo with wavy hair tumbling to his shoulders, a bushy beard almost to his chest, and a distinguished nose that is pointed though not quite as hooked as a nutcracker caricature. The forehead looks similar, as does the eye. Most comparable is the overall iconography of the distinguished aging sage with flowing hair and beard.

Fig. 119. Melzi's drawing of Leonardo.

If indeed both Melzi's red-chalk drawing and Leonardo's note-book sketch of an old man are portraits of Leonardo, then master and pupil have portrayed him in different ways. Leonardo made his subject look older, as perhaps he envisioned himself becoming. Melzi, on the other hand, made his subject look younger, still vibrant and barely wrinkled, his face and gaze strong, as he no doubt liked to remember him.

Over the years, Leonardo was often depicted as an iconic bearded philosopher, which was probably based both on reality and on some mythmaking. A prime example of this is a Vatican fresco by Raphael, the Italian artist who was Leonardo's young follower. His *School of Athens*, painted around the time that Leonardo was turning sixty, depicts two dozen ancient philosophers standing in discourse. At the center is Plato, striding alongside Aristotle (fig. 120). Raphael used his contemporaries as models for most of the philosophers, and Plato looks to be a depiction of Leonardo. He wears a rose-colored toga, matching the colorful tunics that Leonardo famously sported. As in the Melzi portrait and others of Leonardo, Plato is balding, with wisps of curly hair on top and curls flowing in waves from the side of his head to his shoulder. There is also the curly beard, coming down to the top of his chest. And he is making a gesture characteristic of Leonardo: his right index finger is pointing up to the heavens.[6]

Another probable portrait of Leonardo, likely by one of his students, is sketched faintly on a page of horse drawings that Leonardo had done in his notebook (fig. 121).[7] We can tell from the left-

Fig. 120. Raphael's pointing Plato, possibly based on Leonardo.

handed hatching and beautiful modeling that Leonardo did the horse legs on the other side of the sheet, but the faint sketch of a man is done with right-hand hatching in a different style. His beard is wavy, and he seems to be wearing a cap. Sweetly, there is a fainter portrait just below of a very young man with a similar cap and curly hair, perhaps the student himself.

A cap is a feature found in many sixteenth-century portraits of Leonardo done after his death, such as the woodcut used to illustrate Vasari's lives in the 1560s (fig. 122). Another disputed example, discovered in 2008 and known as the Lucan portrait (fig. 123), shows the subject in three-quarter profile with a cloth hat that has long been associated with him. It seems to be the model for, or based on, many similar paintings and engravings of a man with a hat and flowing beard, usually identified as Leonardo, such as a famous one in Florence's Uffizi Museum (fig. 124), which appears on the cover of this book.

Fig. 121. A student sketch possibly
of Leonardo.

Fig. 122. Portrait of Leonardo
in Vasari's book.

Fig. 123. The Lucan portrait.

Fig. 124. Portrait in the Uffizi.

The most glorious and famous of all the possible portraits is a haunting red-chalk drawing done by Leonardo himself with his left-handed hatching. The Turin portrait (fig. 125), so called because of where it resides, has been reproduced so often that it defines our image of Leonardo, whether or not it is truly a self-portrait. It shows an old man with flowing beard, waves of curly hair, and bushy eyebrows. Crisp lines of hair are juxtaposed with the sfumato softness of the cheeks. The nose, subtly shaded and modeled with curved and

Fig. 125. The Turin portrait.

straight hatch lines, is distinctively hooked, though not as pronounced as in Leonardo's nutcracker-man sketches. Like many Leonardo works, the face displays different mingled emotions each time you look at it: strength and vulnerability, resignation and impatience, fatalism and resolve. The tired eyes are contemplative, the down-turned lips are melancholy.

Oddly, the eyes do not look at us but downward and to the left. Leonardo was experimenting with mirrors at the time, and he built some that connected at angles, resembling the three flapped mirrors that can be found on a modern medicine cabinet; he even devised an octagonal enclosure of mirrors that a person could stand in. So perhaps he made the drawing while in his studio using hinged mirrors to view himself obliquely. With its averted gaze, the Turin portrait echoes a recently discovered faint sketch by Leonardo, another possible self-portrait, that was largely obscured and covered by notes in his Codex on the Flight of Birds (fig. 126).[8]

But is the Turin drawing really a self-portrait? Like Leonardo's notebook drawing of an old man seeming to gaze at torrents of water, the man in the Turin portrait looks older than sixty. The hair has receded more, the eyebrows are bushier, and the mustache is sparser than in the portrait drawn by Melzi. Did Leonardo by then actually

Fig. 126. Possible self-portrait in notebook.

look older than his age? There is evidence that he did; a traveler who later visited him in France reported his age as ten years older than he really was at the time. Or did Leonardo, when being self-reflective, tend to portray himself as he envisioned he might become? Perhaps it is an extension of his nutcracker-man doodles and drawings of grotesques. Then again, maybe Leonardo is portraying in the Turin drawing someone else, such as his father or uncle, who both lived to around eighty.[9]

If we consider the Turin portrait in conjunction with the various other possible portraits and self-portraits, including the likely ones by Raphael and Melzi, we can see a pattern that probably approximates reality. Taken together, these drawings and paintings circumscribe the image of Leonardo as an iconic bearded genius and noble Renaissance seeker: intense yet also distracted, passionate yet also melancholy. In this he fits the description offered by his near contemporary, the sixteenth-century Italian painter and art writer Gian Paolo Lomazzo: "He had long hair and such long eyelashes and beard that he seemed to embody the true nobility of learning, like the druid Hermes and ancient Prometheus did in the past."[10]

TO ROME

Leonardo was always on the lookout for powerful patrons, and in 1513, with Milan still controlled by his former patrons the Sforzas, a new one appeared in Rome. In March of that year, Giovanni de' Medici was elected to become Pope Leo X. The son of Lorenzo "the Magnificent" de' Medici, the Florentine ruler who was a halfhearted patron to Leonardo and sent him off to Milan as a young man, Giovanni was the last non-priest to maneuver himself into the papacy. Much of his time was spent tending to the Vatican's uncertain alliance with France, which was again aiming to retake Milan and was making pacts with various other Italian cities. The new pope would also later face the threat of Martin Luther and his Reformation. But in 1513 he had time to be a profligate arts patron and indulge his love of theater, music, verse, and art. "Let us enjoy the papacy since God has given it to us," he said, and he did so with gusto.

In his free-spending support of the arts, Pope Leo was aided by his brother Giuliano, who moved from Florence to Rome and established an intellectual court. A lover of both art and science, he was an ideal patron for Leonardo, whom he courted and offered a stipend; Leonardo, tired of having to support himself by completing commissions, accepted. For a few years, the two sons of Lorenzo "the Magnificent" would make up for their father's relative indifference toward him.[11]

"I left Milan for Rome on 24 September 1513, in the company of Giovan, Francesco de Melzi, Salai, Lorenzo and Il Fanfoia," Leonardo recorded on the opening page of a new notebook. Melzi was then twenty-two; Salai was thirty-three. He also recorded that he had paid to ship five hundred pounds of personal belongings from Milan to Rome. The trove included more than a hundred books, his growing but unsorted assortment of notebooks, anatomical drawings, scientific instruments, art equipment, clothes, and furniture. Most important, it included five or six paintings that he was still obsessing over, trying to perfect.[12]

As he traveled across the mountains, Leonardo looked for fossils. "I found some shells in the rocks of the high Apennines and mostly at the rock of La Verna," he recorded.[13] Once on the other side, he made a brief stop in Florence and checked on some relatives. He made a note to inquire "whether Alessandro Amadori, the priest, is alive or not," referring to the brother of his stepmother, Albiera.[14] He was. But the city of his early years held little allure for Leonardo, even though it was back under Medici control. It had too many ghosts.

Rome was a new city for him, a place he had never lived. It was teeming with great architects, including his friend Donato Bramante, who was modernizing vast swatches of roads and buildings. Among his other projects, Bramante was building a formal, terraced courtyard, flanked by arched corridors, that would connect the Vatican to the elegant papal summer palace, the Villa Belvedere. The villa, built less than thirty years earlier, caught the summer breezes on high ground overlooking Rome. It had been designed by Antonio del Pollaiuolo, whom Leonardo knew well from Florence.

In this villa, which housed favorites of Pope Leo and Giuliano,

Leonardo was given his living quarters. It was the perfect place for him. Slightly aloof and secluded, but containing a court of artists and scientists, the Belvedere and its grounds encompassed a mix of great architecture and natural wonders, including a menagerie, a botanical garden, orchards, a fish pond, and classical sculptures collected by the recent popes, such as *Laocoön and His Sons* and the *Apollo Belvedere*.

To make matters even better, the pope ordered one of his architects to modernize quarters in the Villa Belvedere "for the rooms of Master Leonardo da Vinci." The work included the widening of a window and the addition of wooden partitions, a chest for grinding colors, and four dining tables—an indication that Leonardo supported a large household of assistants and students.[15]

In the Belvedere gardens was a sanctuary containing rare plants from different parts of the world. Leonardo studied how a wide variety of leaves grew in spiral arrangements, known as phyllotactic spirals, as they sought to maximize exposure to the sun and rain. The gardens were also a stage for the pranks that he loved. One day a vine keeper in the garden showed him a strange lizard. "Leonardo made some wings of the scales of other lizards and fastened them on its back with a mixture of quicksilver, so that they trembled when it walked," Vasari wrote. "Having made for it eyes, horns, and a beard, he tamed it and kept it in a box, but all his friends to whom he showed it used to run away from fear." Another trick was making animals out of wax and blowing air into them so they would fly, a parlor trick that amused the pope.

Leonardo's relationships with his half-brothers had improved since the resolution of the family's inheritance disputes, and when he got to Rome he sought out his father's oldest legitimate son, Giuliano da Vinci, who, not surprisingly, was a notary. Giuliano had been promised a benefice—a Church appointment that came with a stipend—but there had been a glitch, and Leonardo offered to intercede on his behalf. He personally went to check the registry, and finding that the appointment was not yet in the works he asked for help from the datary, the officer in charge of papal benefices. There ensued a discussion about costs and difficulties, apparently a solicitation for a bribe. However the case got settled, Giuliano's wife seemed pleased. In a letter she wrote to her husband, she appended a postscript: "I forgot to ask you to remember me to your brother Lionardo, a most excellent and singular man [*vuomo eccellentissimo e singhularissimo*]."[16] Giuliano gave the letter to Leonardo, who kept it among his papers for the rest of his life.

Leonardo's conflicted feelings about fathers, sons, and family ties were expressed with a dash of wry humor when another of his half-brothers, Domenico, celebrated the birth of a son. The letter Leonardo sent him is suffused with irony and feigned condolences that may have been only half-joking. "My beloved brother," he wrote. "A short time ago I received a letter from you saying that you have an heir, which I understand has afforded you a great deal of pleasure. Insofar as I had judged you to be prudent, I am now entirely convinced that I am as far removed from having accurate judgment as you are from prudence; seeing that you have been congratulating yourself on having created a watchful enemy, who will strive with all his energies seeking liberty, which can only come into being at your death."[17]

Even though the pope and his brother were liberally commissioning works of art, including from Raphael and Michelangelo, Leonardo had not regained his desire to be a painter. It must have been a test of his impressive stubbornness not to be prodded into painting while being pampered by patrons who were so hungry for art. Baldassare Castiglione, an author and courtier who knew Leonardo in Rome, described him as one "of the world's finest painters, who despises the art for which he has so rare a talent and has set himself to learn philosophy [meaning the sciences]."[18] He received one commission from the pope but apparently did not finish it. As Leonardo lingered over the process of distilling the varnish he planned to use to coat the painting when it was complete, the pope complained, "Alas, this man will never get anything done, for he is thinking about the end before he begins."[19]

Other than that, Leonardo seems to have received no new commission or started any new artwork. His only encounters with the brush involved perfecting, in a slow and studied manner, paintings he had long been working on and resisted relinquishing.

Leonardo instead was still more interested in science and engineering. He accepted the job of devising a way to drain the Pontine Marshes, fifty miles southeast of Rome, for Giuliano de' Medici, who had been assigned the task of reclaiming the land by his brother. Leonardo visited the area and drew one of his subtly colored aerial maps, the lettering done by Melzi, which shows plans for the creation of two new canals that would drain the mountain streams into the sea before they reached the marshes.[20] He also devised for Giuliano a mill for minting coins with good edges.

Leonardo's most intense technology interest while in Rome involved mirrors. Ever since he was nineteen and part of Verrocchio's team that soldered a copper ball and placed it on top of the dome of Florence's cathedral, Leonardo had been fascinated by ways to make concave mirrors that would concentrate light from the sun to produce heat. During his career, he made close to two hundred drawings of ways to focus light and construct such mirrors, calculated the math of how light rays reflect from a curved surface, and studied the technology of using grinding stones to shape and polish metal.[21] One of his drawings from the late 1470s in Florence (fig. 127) shows designs for a furnace, a mechanism to grind a mold, a press using the mold to shape a piece of metal, and a geometric drawing of curved shapes inside a cone.[22] Another shows a machine that turns a large metal bowl and raises it to press up against a curved grindstone, with accompanying text on how "to make a concave sphere to throw fire."[23]

Over the years, Leonardo became increasingly interested in the mathematics involved in focusing a mirror, drawing scores of diagrams of light rays from different directions hitting a curved surface and showing the angles at which they would be reflected. He tackled the problem identified by Ptolemy in AD 150 and studied by the eleventh-century Arab mathematician Alhazen of finding the point on a concave mirror where light coming from a certain source will be reflected to a designated spot (akin to finding the spot on the edge of a circular billiard table where you have to hit a cue ball so that it will bounce

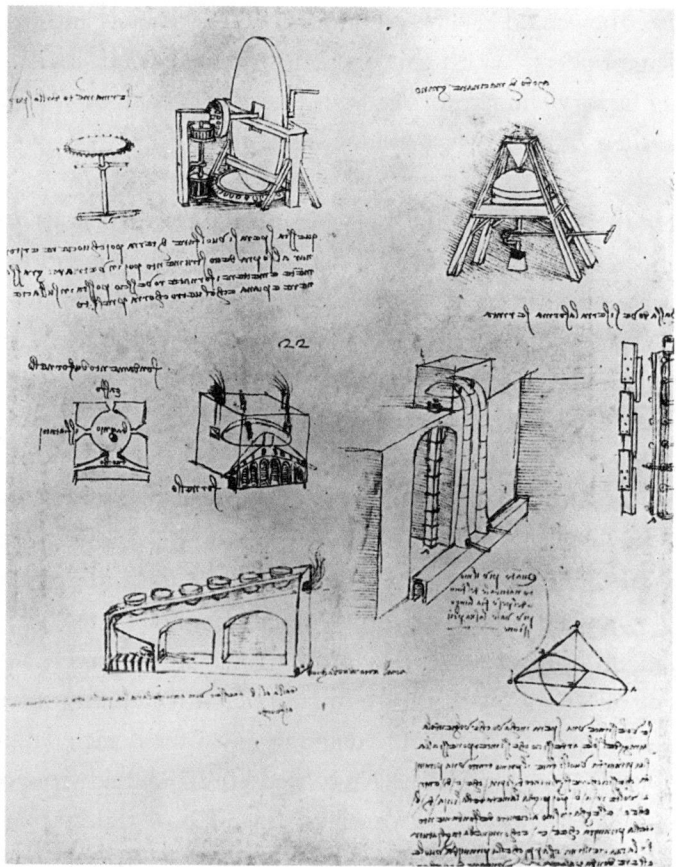

Fig. 127. Machine for making mirrors.

and hit your target). Leonardo failed to solve this using pure math. So in a series of drawings, he made a device that could solve the problem mechanically. He was better at using visualizations than equations.

During his time in Rome, he filled at least twenty more pages with ideas about the mathematics and construction techniques of concave mirrors, especially very large ones.[24] Part of his interest by then was related to his astronomy studies; he was seeking ways to better observe the moon. But primarily he was still interested in using mirrors to focus sunlight into heat. He continued to think of himself as a military engineer, and the mirrors could serve as a weapon, as Archimedes had reportedly done against the Roman ships besieging

Syracuse. They could also be useful for soldering metals and for pow-
ering large boilers. "With this one can supply heat for any boiler in
a dyeing factory," he wrote. "And with this a pool can be warmed up,
because there will be always boiling water."[25]

Living with Leonardo at the Belvedere was a German assistant who
was supposed to be helping him construct his mirrors and produce
some for the wardrobe rooms of the pope and Giuliano. But he was
disloyal, lazy, and erratic, causing Leonardo to go into a tailspin of
rage. He became physically ill as well as petulant, and his psychological unhinging was splayed out in three long drafts of complaining letters intended for Giuliano.

This was not the first time that Leonardo's bouts of torment
seemed to spiral out of control. Back when he was in Milan, he had
walked off the job of decorating rooms for the duke, drafted a fiery
letter of complaint, and then torn it in half. But the letters he drafted
for Giuliano were of a different order of megatonnage. He told the
stories of his clashes with the German in lengthy and disjointed diatribes that verged on the paranoid and were cluttered with details and
digressions that would likely have baffled Giuliano. He wrote of "the
wickedness of that German deceiver" and of how the boy betrayed
him by building his own workshop so he could do jobs for other people. Leonardo also denounced him for wasting his days bird-hunting
with the Swiss guards. This is not the sweet Leonardo we usually see,
tending to young acolytes and twinkling fondly at the transgressions
of the rascally Salai.

Leonardo's other nemesis was another German staying at the
Belvedere, a rival mirror-maker named Giovanni. Leonardo wrote in
a draft letter, "That German, Giovanni the mirror-maker, was in the
workshop every day, wanting to see everything that I was doing and
then broadcasting it around, and criticizing whatever he could not
understand." He accused Giovanni of being jealous, then rambled on
semicoherently about how Giovanni had turned the young assistant
against him.[26]

During this time, Leonardo continued his anatomical studies, dissecting at least three corpses in Rome, probably at the Hospital of the Holy Spirit (Santo Spirito), and refining his drawings of the human heart. Dissections were not illegal, but Leonardo was stopped from continuing with them. "The pope has found out that I have skinned three corpses," he wrote, and he blamed it on the jealous Giovanni. "This person has hindered me in anatomy, denouncing it before the Pope and also at the hospital."[27]

Leonardo's foul mood and his lack of artistic productivity, in stark contrast to Michelangelo and Raphael at the time, served to alienate him from the Medici orbit. The situation worsened when Giuliano's influence declined; he was sent off in early 1515 to marry the daughter of a French duke and then died a year later after a long bout with tuberculosis. It was time for Leonardo to move on once again.

He found a new opportunity when he was invited to be part of Pope Leo's entourage to Florence and Bologna. The Medici pope triumphantly entered his native Florence in November 1515. One observer reported, "All the chief citizens went in procession to meet him and among others about fifty youths, only the richest and foremost, dressed in a livery of clothing of purple cloth with fur collars, going on foot, and each with a type of small, silvered lance in his hands—a most beautiful thing." Leonardo drew in his notebook the temporary arch that had been built for the procession. When the pope arrived at the Council Hall for a gathering of cardinals, the remnants of Leonardo's unfinished *Battle of Anghiari* was still visible on the wall.

In Florence the pope also convened a gaggle of top artists and architects to discuss renewing Florence the way Bramante was Rome. Leonardo made drawings of his ideas for completely reworking and expanding the plaza in the Medici quarters and demolishing the houses in front of the church of San Lorenzo, which would have destroyed many of the streets and alleys of his younger days, and drew the Medici Palace with a new façade that faced the new grand plaza.[28]

But Leonardo did not stay in Florence. Instead, he followed the papal procession to Bologna, where the pope had scheduled a secret parley with the new king of France, Francis I, who had just turned twenty-one. Francis had wrested control of Milan from the Sforzas in September 1515, which convinced the pope he had to make peace with him.

The parley did not settle the French-Italian wars, but it would eventually result in finding Leonardo a new patron. He was at the meetings between the pope and the king, and at one session he made a black-pencil sketch of Artus Gouffier, the king's tutor and chamber master. It is likely that, in Bologna, the king first tried to entice Leonardo to come to France.

CHAPTER 30

Pointing the Way

THE WORD BECOMES FLESH

During the decade of 1506–16, as he wandered between Milan and Rome pursuing his passions and seeking patronage, Leonardo worked on three paintings that have an elegiac and spiritual quality, as if he realized that his days were numbered and was contemplating what lay on the road ahead. These include two sensuous paintings of Saint John the Baptist, one of them converted into a rendering of Bacchus by someone many years later, and a painting of an angel of the Annunciation that has been lost. They feature, as do their related drawings, a sweetly androgynous young man with an enigmatic aura, looking (or perhaps even leering) directly at the viewer and pointing a finger. Despite his immersion into science, or perhaps because of it, Leonardo had developed an ever-deepening appreciation for the profound spiritual mystery of our place in the cosmos. And as Kenneth Clark noted, "Mystery to Leonardo was a shadow, a smile and a finger pointing into darkness."[1]

What distinguishes these paintings is not that they have a religious theme; like the work of every other Renaissance master, most of Leonardo's paintings did. Nor are they the only times that Leonardo used a pointing gesture; Saint Anne in the Burlington House cartoon and Saint Thomas in *The Last Supper* both point upward. What makes

this late trio of paintings distinctive is that the spiritual pointing gesture is directed personally to us, the viewer. When this late-career version of the angel of the Annunciation delivers his divine message, he
is speaking and gesturing not to the Virgin Mary but to us. Likewise,
in both pictures of Saint John, he is looking intimately at us, pointing
the way to our own salvation.

Some critics over the centuries have asserted that Leonardo
marred the spiritual nature of these pieces—perhaps heretically and
intentionally so—by giving them an erotic allure. A cataloguer of the
French royal collection complained in 1625 that the Saint John painting "does not please because it does not arouse feelings of devotion."
In a similar vein, Kenneth Clark wrote, "Our whole sense of propriety
is outraged," adding that the depiction of Saint John is "almost blas-
phemously unlike the fiery ascetic of the Gospels."[2]

I doubt Leonardo thought he was being blasphemous or heretical,
nor should we. The seductive and sensuous elements of these works
enhance rather than lessen the powerful spiritual intimacy that Leonardo intended them to convey. Saint John comes across as less the
Baptist than the Seducer, but in portraying him this way Leonardo
connected the spiritual to the sensual. By highlighting the ambiguity
between spirit and flesh, Leonardo gave his own charged meaning to
"the Word became flesh and dwelt among us."[3]

SAINT JOHN THE BAPTIST

From sketches in his notebook, we know that Leonardo had already
begun working on his portrait of Saint John the Baptist (fig. 128)
while in Milan in 1509.[4] But as with many of his late paintings, most
of which he ended up working on out of personal passion rather than
to fulfill a commission, he carried it around with him and intermittently enhanced it until the end of his life. His focus was on the
saint's eyes, mouth, and gesture. The close-up of him emerging from
the darkness confronts us starkly. There are no distracting landscapes
or lights, and only the Leonardesque ringlets of hair provide any ornamentation.

As he gestures heavenward in a recognition of divine providence,

Fig. 128. *Saint John the Baptist.*

John is also pointing toward the source of the light that radiates on him, thus fulfilling his biblical role "to bear witness of the Light."[5] Leonardo's use of chiaroscuro, contrasting deep shadows with striking illumination, not only enhances the sense of mystery of the scene; it also conveys a powerful feeling of John's role as witness to the true Light.[6]

John wears one of the enigmatic smiles that became a Leonardo signature, but it has a come-hither naughtiness to it that is missing in the smiles of Saint Anne and the *Mona Lisa*. His smile beckons in ways that are sultry and seductive as well as spiritual. That gives the picture its erotic frisson, as does John's androgynous appearance. His shoulders and chest are broad yet feminine. The model seems to be Salai, with his soft face and cascade of curls.

Leonardo's oil-painting technique, which involved applying multiple thin layers of translucent glazes, was by now even more painstaking and slow. He rushed no painting, to a fault. In *Saint John the Baptist*, this pace enhanced the delicacy of his sfumato. The contours are soft, the lines are blurred, and the transitions between light and dark are exceedingly subtle.

There is, however, one exception. Leonardo has painted John's hand with a greater sharpness and clarity, just as he had done with the blessing hand of Christ in *Salvator Mundi*. The line separating John's pointing index finger from his second finger is as distinct as any line in any of Leonardo's paintings, almost like one of Michelangelo's. It is possible this is due to a misguided restoration at some point. But I suspect it was intentional on Leonardo's part, especially since he uses a similar sharp delineation for the pointing hand in what became the Bacchus version of the painting. With his theory of acuity perspective, Leonardo knew that such sharpness would make the hand appear nearer, as if in a different plane. There is a visual disjuncture: the hand is positioned at the same distance as the softly delineated arm, but because it is sharper it seems to pop out toward us and be more in focus.[7]

SAINT JOHN WITH THE ATTRIBUTES OF BACCHUS

The other variation of this theme to emerge from Leonardo's studio—probably based on a drawing by Leonardo and partly painted by him, but also the product of others in his workshop—shows a full-length Saint John sitting on a dark rock formation with a sunny landscape of a mountain and a river to his right (fig. 129). In an inventory of Salai's estate in 1525, it is referred to as a large-scale painting of Saint John,

Fig. 129. Saint John converted to a Bacchus.

and it is identified this way in an inventory of the French royal art collection at Fontainebleau in 1625. But in a subsequent inventory of that collection done in 1695, the designation of Saint John is crossed out and replaced by "Bacchus in a landscape." From this we can surmise that, sometime in the late 1600s, the painting was altered, perhaps for reasons of religious and sexual propriety, to turn Saint John into Bacchus, the Roman god of wine and revelry.[8]

There was once a beautiful red-chalk preparatory drawing by Leonardo for this painting housed in a small museum at a mountaintop religious sanctuary above the town of Varese, north of Milan. It showed Saint John sitting on a rocky ledge, his left leg crossed atop his right, his body muscular but a bit fleshy, like Salai's, his eyes set deep in shadow and staring at us intensely. "I have seldom seen an original Leonardo of more revealing character," Carlo Pedretti wrote in the early 1970s after making a pilgrimage to view it.[9] Sadly, the drawing was stolen from the little museum in 1973, and it has not been publicly seen since. In this drawing, Leonardo had depicted Saint John completely nude, and there is evidence that is the way he was originally rendered in the painting. But when he was converted from a Baptist to a Bacchus, a leopard-skin cloth was placed over his crotch, a wreath of ivy was put on his head, and his staff or cross was turned into a thyrsus. Leonardo's discomforting ambiguity between spirit and flesh was thus replaced by a less jarring depiction of a pagan god whose lustiness is not heretical.[10]

In both Leonardo's drawing and in the painting, the most striking element is the pointing gesture. Instead of pointing heavenward, as in Leonardo's starker rendition of the saint, this time he is pointing off into the darkness to his left, out of the scene of the picture. As with *The Last Supper*, the viewer can almost hear the words that accompany the gesture, in this case John heralding the arrival of "he who cometh after me, whose sandals I am not worthy to carry."[11]

The smile is not as seductive and the body is more muscular and masculine than in Leonardo's other treatment of Saint John, but the face is just as androgynous and the curls just as Salaicious. Once again, the pointing hand as well as the left leg are more sharply delineated than is typical of Leonardo, whose signature sfumato is evident in other parts of the picture. It is unclear whether this is because the leg and hand were retouched or were the work of a student, or because Leonardo made their lines sharper so they would feel closer to the viewer. I suspect it was the latter.

ANGEL OF THE ANNUNCIATION AND *ANGEL INCARNATE*

Around this time, Leonardo painted another pointing figure, an angel of the Annunciation making a gesture that was similar to that in *Saint John the Baptist*. The painting is now lost, but we know what it looked like from copies made by some of Leonardo's followers, including one by Bernardino Luini (fig. 130). There is also a charcoal

Fig. 130. Copy of the lost *Angel of the Annunciation.*

drawing of it (fig. 131) by a student on one of Leonardo's notebook
pages, which is surrounded by Leonardo's own drawings of horses and
men and geometrical figures. On the student's sketch, Leonardo used
his left-handed hatches to correct the pointing arm to put it in the
proper foreshortened perspective.

The scene of the Annunciation, in which the angel Gabriel announces to the Virgin Mary that she will become the mother of
Christ, was the subject of the first painting that Leonardo did mainly
on his own during the early 1470s, while working in Verrocchio's studio (fig. 11). This time, however, there is no Virgin Mary in the picture for the angel to address. Instead, he looks directly at us, and his
upward-pointing gesture seems addressed to us. Like Saint John, he is
heralding the impending arrival of Christ the savior in human form, a
miraculous union of spirit and flesh.

Fig. 131. Student sketch of *Angel of the Annunciation*,
corrected by Leonardo.

The angel and Saint John are depicted in the exact same pose, with the same come-hither stare, enigmatic smile, seductive cocking of the head and twisting of the neck, and glorious curls lustrously lit. Only the arm of the hand pointing to heaven has changed. Saint John is turning to the left, so the upraised arm is seen going across the body. Then as now, Leonardo's boy angels are feminine to the point of being androgynous; it is true of the angel in his early *Annunciation* and also of the one in *Virgin of the Rocks*. In this new *Annunciation*, the androgyny is more pronounced than ever. The angel has budding breasts, and his face is even more girlish.

There is another drawing of the angel, one that is astonishing and still controversial. Made around 1513, while Leonardo was in Rome, it

Fig. 132. *Angel Incarnate*, with breasts and erection.

shows a lewdly leering transgender version of the *Angel of the Annuncia-tion* with female breasts and a large erect penis (fig. 132). Known as the *Angel Incarnate* or *Angel in the Flesh*, it is the extreme example of Leo-nardo's dance around what he viewed as the ambiguous border between flesh and spirit as well as the one between feminine and masculine.

Although it is on one of Leonardo's sheets of blue-tinted paper, which he used for many of his anatomical studies and drawings of mirrors, it is unlikely that he was the primary draftsman of this *Angel Incarnate*. It is not rendered beautifully, and it is delineated and shaded clumsily, without Leonardo's distinctive left-handed hatch-ing. It seems to have been drawn by the same student—probably Salai—who drew the notebook sketch of the *Angel of the Annunciation* that Leonardo corrected; the smile, the gesture, the hollow eyes, the pose, and even the flawed foreshortening of the raised arm are simi-lar. Since it was done on Leonardo's paper, it was likely done for his amusement and perhaps with a few corrections by him, just as he had corrected the *Angel of the Annunciation* drawing.

The result looks like a catamite, eager to please, signaling a will-ingness for an assignation. The juxtaposition of the angel's female-nippled breasts and girlish face with its prominent erection and dangling balls makes the drawing a cross between playful caricature and hermaphroditic pornography. The drawing echoes the theme from Leonardo's Saint John drawings: it combines the angelic and the devilish, and it links spiritual aspiration with sexual arousal. At one point someone apparently tried to erase the penis but succeeded mainly in rubbing away the blue tint of the paper and leaving some erasure marks.[12]

The history of the drawing is a bit mysterious, perhaps because the British royal family, in whose collection it once resided, was embar-rassed by it. One story is that a German scholar came to view it at the Royal Library and whisked it away under his cape; whether or not that is true, it was rediscovered in 1990 in the private collection of an aristocratic German family.[13]

A counterpoint to the gesturing androgynous angels and saints is a poetic and sweet drawing known as the *Pointing Lady* (fig. 133), which the renowned scholar Carlo Pedretti called "perhaps the most beautiful drawing by Leonardo."[14] The subject has the same mysterious and enticing smile as her male counterparts, and she likewise is looking directly at us, directing our attention to a mystery unseen. But unlike Leonardo's various angels of the period, there is nothing devilish about her.

The black-chalk drawing is simple, but it encompasses many facets of Leonardo's life and work: his love of plays and pageants, his feel for fantasy, his mastery of enigmatic smiles, his ability to make women come alive, and the twisting movement. It is filled with the curls and

Fig. 133. *Pointing Lady.*

spirals that Leonardo loved: there is a hint of a stream and waterfall creating eddies, and there are flowers and reeds whose curves echo those of the lady's diaphanous dress and blowing hair.

Most notably, the lady is pointing. In his last decade, Leonardo is mesmerized by that gesture, the signal of tidings borne by a mysterious guide who has come to show us the way. The drawing may have been meant as an illustration for Dante's *Purgatorio*, showing the beautiful Matelda, who guides the poet through ritual bathings in a forest, or it could have been a drawing for a costume pageant. But whatever was the original intent, it became more. It is a profoundly expressive and poetic drawing by a man entering the twilight and still searching for guidance about the eternal mysteries that his science and his art have not, and cannot, explain.

CHAPTER 31

The *Mona Lisa*

THE CULMINATION

And now, the *Mona Lisa* (fig. 134). The discussion of Leonardo's pièce de résistance could have come earlier in this book. He began working on it in 1503, when he returned to Florence after serving Cesare Borgia. But he had not finished it when he moved back to Milan in 1506. In fact, he carried it with him, and continued to work on it, throughout his second period in Milan and then during his three years in Rome. He would even take it to France on the final leg of his life journey, adding tiny strokes and light layers through 1517. It would be in his studio there when he died.

So it makes sense to consider the *Mona Lisa* near the end of his career, exploring it as the culmination of a life spent perfecting an ability to stand at the intersection of art and nature. The poplar panel with multiple layers of light oil glazes, applied over the course of many years, exemplifies the multiple layers of Leonardo's genius. What began as a portrait of a silk merchant's young wife became a quest to portray the complexities of human emotion, made memorable through the mysteries of a hinted smile, and to connect our nature to that of our universe. The landscape of her soul and of nature's soul are intertwined.

Fig. 134. The *Mona Lisa*.

Forty years before he put his last touches on the *Mona Lisa*, while still working in Verrocchio's shop in Florence, a young Leonardo had painted another commissioned portrait of a woman, *Ginevra de' Benci* (fig. 14). On the surface, the two pictures have similarities. Both are of new wives of Florentine cloth merchants portrayed against a river landscape, their bodies in a three-quarters pose. But more striking are the differences between the two paintings. They show the development of Leonardo's painterly skills and, more important, his maturation as a scientist, philosopher, and humanist. *Ginevra de' Benci* was made by a young artist with astonishing skills of observation. The *Mona Lisa* is the work of a man who had used those skills to immerse himself in a lifetime of intellectual passions. The inquiries chronicled on his thousands of notebook pages—of light rays striking curved objects, dissections of human faces, geometrical volumes being transformed into new shapes, flows of turbulent water, the analogies between the earth and human bodies—had helped him fathom the subtleties of depicting motion and emotion. "His insatiable curiosity, his restless leaps from one subject to another, have been harmonized in a single work," Kenneth Clark wrote of the *Mona Lisa*. "The science, the pictorial skill, the obsession with nature, the psychological insight are all there, and so perfectly balanced that at first we are hardly aware of them."[1]

THE COMMISSION

Vasari provided a vivid description of the *Mona Lisa* in his life of Leonardo, first published in 1550. Facts were not Vasari's forte, and it is unlikely that he ever saw the painting (though it is conceivable that he could have if Salai had brought it back to Milan after Leonardo's death, as the confusing inventory of his estate made in 1525 possibly suggests, before it was sold to the king of France). It is more probable that Vasari had seen, at best, a copy or was writing from secondhand descriptions and allowing himself some literary license. Whatever the case, subsequent discoveries have tended to confirm much of his account, so it provides a good starting point for chronicling the masterpiece:

Leonardo undertook to paint, for Francesco del Giocondo, the portrait of Mona Lisa, his wife. . . . Whoever wished to see how nearly art could imitate nature was able to comprehend it when he saw this portrait. . . . The eyes had that luster and watery sheen which are seen in life, and around them were rosy and pearly tints, together with the eyelashes, that cannot be represented without the greatest subtlety. . . . The nose, with its beautiful nostrils, rosy and tender, appeared to be alive. The mouth, with its opening, and with the ends united by the red of the lips to the flesh tints of the face, seemed in truth to be not colors but flesh. In the pit of the throat, if one gazed upon it most intensely, could be seen the beating of the pulse.

Vasari was referring to Lisa del Giocondo, who was born in 1479 into a minor branch of the distinguished Gherardini family, whose roots as landowners stretched from feudal times but whose money had not survived quite so long. At fifteen, she married into the wealthy but not quite so prominent Giocondo family, which had made its riches in the silk trade. Her father had to cede one of their farms as a dowry since they had little cash, but the marriage between frayed landed gentry and rising merchant class turned out to be beneficial to all concerned.

Her new husband, Francesco del Giocondo, had lost his first wife eight months earlier and had a two-year-old son to raise. Having become the purveyor of silks to the Medici, he was increasingly prosperous, with clients throughout Europe, and he bought a few women Moors from North Africa to serve as his household slaves. From all indications he was in love with Lisa, which was not usually a factor in the arrangement of such marriages. He helped support her family, and by 1503 she had borne him two sons. Until then they had been living at his parents' house, but with a growing family and financial prospects he bought a home of their own and around that time commissioned Leonardo to paint a portrait of his wife, who was turning twenty-four.[2]

Why did Leonardo accept the assignment? He was at the time fending off the incessant pleadings of the far wealthier and more prominent art patron Isabella d'Este, and he was so engrossed in his scientific explorations that he was known to pick up a brush only reluctantly.

Perhaps one reason Leonardo accepted was out of family friendship. His father had long served as a notary for Francesco del Giocondo and had represented him in legal disputes several times. Their families shared a close connection to the church of Santissima Annunziata. Leonardo had moved into the church's cloistered complex with his entourage three years earlier, when he returned to Florence from Milan. His father was the notary for the church, and Francesco del Giocondo worshipped there, lent it money, and would eventually endow a family chapel. Given his nature as a sharp and sometimes contentious merchant, Giocondo occasionally got into disputes with the church, and it fell to Piero da Vinci to work them out. One of them in 1497 involved a bill from Giocondo that the friars of Santissima Annunziata disputed; Piero drew up a settlement in the Giocondo silk workshop.[3]

So the aging Piero, then seventy-six, likely had his hand in helping to arrange for his famous son to accept the commission. In addition to doing a favor for a family friend and client, Piero was probably also looking after his son. Although Leonardo was now widely celebrated as an artist and engineer, he had begun to withdraw regularly from his bank account the savings he had brought with him from Milan.

But I suspect the main reason that Leonardo decided to paint Lisa del Giocondo is that he wanted to paint her. Because she was somewhat obscure, not a famed noble or even the mistress of one, he could portray her as he wished. There was no need to cater to or take directions from a powerful patron. Most important, she was beautiful and enticing—and she had an alluring smile.

BUT IS IT REALLY LISA?

The assertion by Vasari and others, including the sixteenth-century Florentine writer Raffaello Borghini, that the *Mona Lisa* is a portrait of Lisa del Giocondo seems straightforward. Vasari knew Francesco and Lisa, who were still alive when he made numerous visits to Florence between 1527 and 1536, and he became friends with their children, who likely were the source for some of his information. When the first edition of his book was printed in 1550, the children were still alive, and Vasari lived diagonally across from the church complex of Santissima Annunziata. If he was incorrect about Lisa being the subject of the painting, there were a lot of her family members and friends who could have corrected him for his second edition in 1568. Yet even though he made a lot of other corrections, the *Mona Lisa* story remained the same.[4]

But this being Leonardo, there have been some mysteries and disputes. Questions arose even before Leonardo finished the painting. In 1517 he was visited at his studio in France by Antonio de Beatis, secretary to Cardinal Luigi of Aragon, who recorded in his diary that he saw three paintings: *Saint John the Baptist*, the *Virgin and Child with Saint Anne*, and a portrait of "a certain Florentine lady." So far, so good. De Beatis apparently was told this by Leonardo, which would comport with the portrait's not being of some rich marchesa or notable mistress, whom de Beatis might know, but of a person such as Lisa del Giocondo, who was not famous enough to mention by name.

There follows, however, a confusing sentence. The painting, de Beatis reported, was "done from life at the instigation [*instantia*] of the late Giuliano de' Medici." This is baffling. When Leonardo started the painting, Giuliano had not yet moved to Rome or become Leonardo's patron. In 1503 he had been exiled by the republican leaders of Florence and was living in Urbino and Venice. If Giuliano "instigated" the portrait, might it have been of one of his mistresses, as some have suggested? But none of his known mistresses was a "Florentine lady," and the ones he had were famous enough that de Beatis would have recognized them if any were the model for the painting.

There is, however, a plausible and delightful possibility that Giuliano was somehow involved in urging Leonardo to paint or keep working on a portrait of Lisa del Giocondo. Giuliano and Lisa were born the same year, 1479, and knew each other through their interrelated families in the small world of the Florentine elite. Among other connections, Lisa's stepmother was Giuliano's cousin. Lisa and Giuliano were both fifteen when he was forced to leave Florence, and a few months later she married the older widower Francesco. Perhaps, as in a Shakespeare play, they were star-crossed lovers. Giuliano may have been Lisa's pining teenage lover or, as Bernardo Bembo was to Ginevra de' Benci, a wistfully Platonic one. Perhaps when Leonardo passed through Venice in 1500, Giuliano asked him to report back, when he got to Florence, on how the beautiful Lisa was faring and what she now looked like. He may have even expressed the desire for a portrait of her. Or, when Leonardo arrived in Rome with the painting unfinished, his new patron Giuliano may have recognized its potential universal beauty and urged him to complete it. These explanations need not replace the narrative that Francesco del Giocondo commissioned the painting. Instead they could supplement it, perhaps add a reason Leonardo accepted the assignment, and even help explain why he never actually delivered the painting to Francesco.[5]

Another wrinkle in the narrative is that the name *Mona Lisa*, a contraction of "Madonna (Madam) Lisa," which was widely adopted based on Vasari's account, is not the only name used for the painting. It is also called *La Gioconda* (in French, *La Joconde*). That is how it, or a copy of it, was listed in the settlement of Salai's estate in 1525,[6] which seems to strengthen the case that the *Mona Lisa* and *La Gioconda* are one and the same. It would be a pun on her last name, which would appeal to Leonardo; the word means "jocund" or "jocular." But some have argued that there might be two different paintings, citing the fact that Lomazzo, writing in the 1580s, mentioned "the portrait of La Gioconda and Mona Lisa," as if they were separate works. Various theorists have scurried down rabbit holes trying to figure out who the jocund lady might be if she is not the *Mona Lisa*. It's more likely, however, either that Lomazzo was mistaken or that an early transcription of his text substituted "and" for "or" in his sentence.[7]

What should put an end to any mystery or confusion is the evidence discovered in 2005, mentioned earlier in my discussion of the *Saint Anne* chronology, of the note scribbled by Agostino Vespucci in 1503 in the margin of an edition of Cicero, which mentions "the head of Lisa del Giocondo" as one of the paintings Leonardo was working on at the time.[8] Sometimes, even with Leonardo, what seems like a mystery isn't. Instead, a straightforward explanation suffices. I am confident that is true in this case. The *Mona Lisa* is Mona Lisa. It is Lisa del Giocondo.

That said, the painting became more than a portrait of a silk-merchant's wife and certainly more than a mere commission. After a few years, and perhaps from the outset, Leonardo was painting it as a universal work for himself and for eternity rather than for Francesco del Giocondo.[9] He never delivered the painting and, judging from his bank records, never collected any money for it. Instead, he kept it with him in Florence, Milan, Rome, and France until he died, sixteen years after he began. Over that period, he added thin layer after layer of little glaze strokes as he perfected it, retouched it, and imbued it with new depths of understanding about humans and nature. Some new insight, new appreciation, new inspiration would strike him, and the brush would alight gently on the poplar panel yet again. As it was with Leonardo, who became more profoundly layered with each step of his journey, so it was with the *Mona Lisa*.

THE PAINTING

The mysterious allure of the *Mona Lisa* begins with Leonardo's preparation of its wood panel. On a thin-grained plank cut from the center of a trunk of poplar, larger than usual for a household portrait, he applied a thick primer coat of lead white rather than a more typical mix of gesso, chalk, and white pigment. That undercoat, he knew, would be better at reflecting back the light that made it through his fine layers of translucent glazes and thereby enhance the impression of depth, luminosity, and volume.[10]

As a result, light penetrates the layers, and some of it reaches the white undercoat to be reflected back through the layers. Our eyes see an interplay between light rays that bounce from the colors on the surface and those that dance back from the depths. This creates shifting and elusive subtleties of modeling. The contours of her cheeks and smile are created by soft transitions of tone that seem veiled by the glaze layers, and they vary as the light in the room and the angle of our gaze changes. The painting comes alive.

Like the fifteenth-century Netherlandish painters such as Jan van Eyck, Leonardo used glazes that had a very small proportion of pigment mixed into the oil. For the shadows on Lisa's face, he pioneered the use of an iron and manganese mix to create a pigment that was burnt umber in color and absorbed oil well. He applied it with brushstrokes so delicate that they are imperceptible, brushing on, over time, up to thirty fine layers. "The thickness of a brown glaze placed over the pink base of the Mona Lisa's cheek grades smoothly from just two to five micrometers to around thirty micrometers in the deepest shadow," according to an X-ray fluorescence spectroscopy study published in 2010. That analysis showed that the strokes were applied in an intentionally irregular way that serves to make the grain of the skin look more lifelike.[11]

Leonardo shows Lisa sitting on a loggia, the base of its columns barely visible at the edges, with her hands folded in the foreground, resting on the arm of her chair. Her body and especially her hands feel unusually close to us, while the jagged mountain landscape recedes into a faraway and misty distance. An analysis of the underpainting shows that he initially drew her left hand grasping the chair arm as if she were about to rise, but then thought better of it. Nevertheless, she still appears to be in motion. We have caught her in the act of turning, as if we had just walked onto the loggia and captured her attention. Her torso twists slightly as her head rotates to look and smile directly at us.

Throughout his career, Leonardo had immersed himself in the study of light, shade, and optics. In a passage in his notebooks, he wrote an analysis that comports closely to the way he let light strike Lisa's face: "When you want to make a portrait, do it in dull weather, or as evening falls. Note in the streets, as evening falls, the faces of the men and women, and when the weather is dull, what softness and delicacy you may perceive in them."[12]

In the *Mona Lisa*, he made the light shine from on high and slightly from the left. To do this, he had to resort to a little sleight of hand, but he did it so subtly that it takes some scrutiny to notice. Judging from the columns, the loggia on which she is sitting is covered; therefore, the light should be coming from the landscape behind her. Instead, it shines on her from the front. Perhaps we are meant to think that the loggia is open on its side, but even that would not explain the full effect. It's an artificial arrangement employed by Leonardo to allow him to use his mastery of shading to create the contours and modeling he needs. His understanding of optics and how light strikes curved surfaces is so brilliant, so convincing, that his trick in the *Mona Lisa* is not conspicuous.[13]

There is another small anomaly about the way light strikes Lisa's face. In his optics writings, Leonardo was studying how long it takes the pupils of an eye to become smaller when exposed to more light. In the *Musician*, the eyes are dilated differently in a way that gives the painting a sense of movement and accords with Leonardo's use of bright light in that painting. In the *Mona Lisa*, the pupil of her right eye is slightly larger. Leonardo incorrectly believed that our eyes dilate separately when exposed to light, but in this case he shows the pupil of the eye facing the light as being smaller. This seems confusing. Was he observant enough to notice a case of anisocoria, in which one eye is more dilated than the other, which occurs in 20 percent of humans? Or was it that he knew that pleasure also causes eyes to widen and was indicating, by showing one of her eyes dilating faster than the other, that Lisa was pleased to see us?

Then again, maybe this is being too obsessive about a tiny, perhaps irrelevant, observation. Call it the Leonardo Effect. His skill of observation was so acute that even an obscure anomaly in his paintings, such as an uneven dilation of pupils, causes us to wrestle, perhaps too much, with what he might have noticed and thought. If so, it is a good thing. By being around him, viewers are stimulated to observe the little details of nature, like the cause of a dilated pupil, and to regain our sense of wonder about them. Inspired by his desire to notice every detail, we try to do the same.

Also a bit puzzling is the issue of Lisa's eyebrows, or lack thereof. In Vasari's fulsome description, he makes a point of lavishing praise on them: "The eyebrows, because he has shown the manner in which the hairs spring from the flesh, growing thickly in one place and lightly in another and curving according to the pores of the skin, could not be more natural." That seems to be another example of Vasari's effusiveness and of Leonardo's brilliant combination of art, observation, and anatomy—until we notice that *Mona Lisa* has no eyebrows. Indeed, a description of the painting from 1625 notes that "this lady, in other respects beautiful, is almost without eyebrows." This has fueled some of the farfetched theories that the painting now in the Louvre is a different work than the one Vasari saw.

One explanation is that Vasari never saw the painting and embellished parts of his account, as he was wont to do. But his description is so precise that this seems improbable. A more plausible explanation is based on what seems to be two faint and blurry oblong patches where the eyebrows should have been, which suggest that they were painted as Vasari described, each hair meticulous, but Leonardo took so long to do them that he painted them over a layer of oil that had completely dried. This would mean that the first time the painting was cleaned, they could have been wiped away. This explanation was supported in 2007 by high-resolution scans made by the French art technician Pascal Cotte. Using light filters, he found tiny indications of eyebrows that originally existed.[14]

Although Lisa is sparsely adorned, without the jewels or fancy costuming that would indicate aristocratic status, her clothing is rendered with dazzling care and scientific astuteness. Ever since he was an apprentice drawing drapery studies in Verrocchio's studio, Leonardo had been observant of the folds and flows of fabric. Her dress billows gently, the light catching the vertical waves and pleats. Most noticeable are the mustard-copper sleeves, rippling and shining with a silky luster that would have dazzled Verrocchio.

Because he was painting a portrait that, at least in theory, was for a merchant of the finest silk, it's not surprising that he included delightful details in Lisa's layers of clothing. To appreciate the exquisite care that Leonardo took, look at an enlarged high-resolution reproduction, many of which can be found in books and online,[15] and study the neckline of her dress. It begins with two rows of braided spirals, the pattern in nature most beloved by Leonardo, between which are interlocked golden rings that catch the light as if in three-dimensional relief. The next row is a series of knots, like those Leonardo loved to draw in his notebooks. They form the shape of crosses, each separated by two hexagonal coils. But there is one place, in the center of the neckline of the dress, where the pattern is slightly broken and there seem to be three hexagonals in a row. Only on very close examination of high-resolution and infrared images does it become clear that Leonardo did not make a mistake; instead, he was very subtly depicting a fold in the bodice right below her cleavage. The infrared images reveal something that is likewise amazing but also, because we are dealing with Leonardo, not surprising: he painted the embroidered patterns on the bodice even in the places where he would later cover it by painting another layer of garment, so that we can faintly sense its presence even where we cannot see it.[16]

Covering Lisa's hair is a gossamer veil, worn as a mark of virtue (not mourning), which is so transparent that it would be almost unnoticeable were it not for the line it makes across the top of her forehead. Look carefully at how it drapes loosely over her hair near her right ear; it is evident that Leonardo was meticulous enough to paint the background landscape first and then used almost-transparent glazes to paint the veil over it. Also look at where her hair comes out from under her veil at her right forehead. Although the veil is almost transparent, the hair underneath is painted to look a tiny bit gauzier and lighter than the hair flowing from underneath it and covering her right ear. When the unveiled hair cascades over her chest on both sides, Leonardo is back to creating the swirling curls he adored.

Depicting veils came naturally to Leonardo. He had a fingertip feel for the elusive nature of reality and the uncertainties of perception. Understanding that light hits multiple points on the retina, he wrote that humans perceive reality as lacking razor-sharp edges and lines; instead, we see everything with a sfumato-like softness of the edges. This is true not only of the misty landscape stretching out to infinity; it applies even to the outlines of Lisa's fingers that seem so close we think we can touch them. We see everything, Leonardo knew, through a veil.

The portrayal of the landscape behind Lisa contains other tricks of the eye. We see it from high above, as if from a bird's-eye view. The geological formations and misty mountains incorporate a mix, as did much of what Leonardo produced, of science and fantasy. The barren jaggedness evokes prehistoric eons, but it is connected to the present by a faint arched bridge (perhaps a depiction of the thirteenth-century Ponte Buriano over the Arno River near Arezzo)[17] spanning the river just above Lisa's left shoulder.

The horizon on the right side seems higher and more distant than the one on the left, a disjuncture that gives the painting a sense of dynamism. The earth seems to twist like Lisa's torso does, and her head seems to cock slightly when you shift from focusing on the left horizon to the right horizon.

The flow of the landscape into the image of Lisa is the ultimate expression of Leonardo's embrace of the analogy between the macrocosm of the world and the microcosm of the human body. The landscape shows the living and breathing and pulsing body of the earth: its veins as rivers, its roads as tendons, its rocks as bones. More than being merely the backdrop for Lisa, the earth flows into her and becomes a part of her.

Follow with your eye the winding path of the river on the right as it passes under the bridge; it seems to flow into the silky scarf draped over her left shoulder. The scarf's folds are straight until they reach her breast, where they start gently twisting and twirling in a way that looks almost exactly like Leonardo's drawings of water flows. On the left side of the picture, the winding road coils as if it will connect to her heart. Her dress just below the neckline ripples and flows down her torso like a waterfall. The background and her garments have the same streaked highlights, reinforcing what has progressed from being an analogy into a union. This is the heart of Leonardo's philosophy: the replication and relationships of the patterns of nature, from the cosmic to the human.

More than that, the painting conveys this unity not only across nature but across time. The landscape shows how the earth and its offspring have been shaped and carved and replenished by flows, from the distant mountains and valleys created eons ago, through the bridges and roads created during human history, to the pulsing throat and inner currents of a young Florentine mother. And thus she is transported into an icon that is eternal. As Walter Pater wrote in his famous effusion of praise of the *Mona Lisa* in 1893, "Hers is the head upon which all the ends of the world are come . . . a perpetual life, sweeping together ten thousand experiences."[18]

THE EYES AND THE SMILE

There are many portraits, including Leonardo's earlier *La Belle Fer-ronnière*, in which the subject's eyes appear to move as the viewer moves. It works even with a good reproduction of that painting or of the *Mona Lisa*. Stand in front, and the subject is staring at you; move from side to side, and the stare still seems direct. Even though Leonardo was not the first to create the appearance that the eyes of a portrait are following you around the room, the effect is so closely associated with him that it is sometimes called "the *Mona Lisa* effect."

Dozens of experts have studied the *Mona Lisa* to determine the scientific reasons for this effect. One is that in the three-dimensional real world, shadows and light on a face shift as our vantage changes, but in a two-dimensional portrait this is not the case. Consequently, we have the perception that eyes staring straight out are looking at us, even if we are not directly in front of the painting. Leonardo's mastery of shadows and lighting helps make the phenomenon more pronounced in the *Mona Lisa*.[19]

And finally, there is the *Mona Lisa*'s most mystical and engaging element of all: her smile. "In this work of Leonardo," wrote Vasari, "there was a smile so pleasing that it was more divine than human." He even told a tale of how Leonardo kept the real Lisa smiling during the portrait sessions: "While painting her portrait, he employed people to play and sing for her, and jesters to keep her merry, to put an end to the melancholy that painters often succeed in giving to their portraits."

There is a mystery to the smile. As we stare, it flickers. What is she thinking? Our eyes move a bit, and her smile seems to change.

The mystery compounds. We look away, and the smile lingers in our minds, as it does in the collective mind of humanity. Never in a painting have motion and emotion, the paired touchstones of Leonardo's art, been so intertwined.

At the time when he was perfecting Lisa's smile, Leonardo was spending his nights in the depths of the morgue under the hospital of Santa Maria Nuova, peeling the flesh off cadavers and exposing the muscles and nerves underneath. He became fascinated about how a smile begins to form and instructed himself to analyze every possible movement of each part of the face and determine the origin of every nerve that controls each facial muscle. Tracing which of those nerves are cranial and which are spinal may not have been necessary for painting a smile, but Leonardo needed to know.

The *Mona Lisa's* smile makes it worth revisiting the remarkable page of anatomical drawings from around 1508, discussed in chapter 27, that shows a pair of lips in an open-mouth grimace and then drawn pursed (fig. 111). The muscle that purses the lips is the same muscle that forms the lower lip, he discovered. Pucker your lower lip and you can see that this is true; it can pucker on its own, with or without the upper lip, but it is impossible to pucker the upper lip alone. It was a tiny discovery, but for an anatomist who was also an artist, especially one who was in the midst of painting the *Mona Lisa*, it was worth noting. Other movements of the lips involve different muscles, including "those which bring the lips to a point, others which spread them, and others which curl them back, others which straighten them out, others which twist them transversely, and others which return them to their first position." Then he drew a row of lips with the skin layer peeled off.[20] At the top of this page is something delightful: a simpler drawing of a gentle smile, sketched lightly in black chalk. Even though the fine lines at the ends of the mouth turn down almost imperceptibly, the impression is that the lips are smiling. Here amid the anatomy drawings we find the makings of *Mona Lisa's* smile.

There is other science involved in the smile. From his optics studies, Leonardo realized that light rays do not come to a single point in the eye but instead hit the whole area of the retina. The central area of the retina, known as the fovea, is best at seeing color and small details; the area surrounding the fovea is best at picking up shadows and shadings of black and white. When we look at an object straight on, it appears sharper. When we look at it peripherally, glimpsing it out of the corner of our eye, it is a bit blurred, as if it were farther away.

With this knowledge, Leonardo was able to create an uncatchable smile, one that is elusive if we are too intent on seeing it. The very fine lines at the corner of Lisa's mouth show a small downturn, just like the mouth floating atop the anatomy sheet. If you stare directly at the mouth, your retina catches these tiny details and delineations, making her appear not to be smiling. But if you move your gaze slightly away from the mouth, to look at her eyes or cheeks or some other part of the painting, you will catch sight of her mouth only peripherally. It will be a bit blurrier. The tiny delineations at the corners of the mouth become indistinct, but you still will see the shadows there. These shadows and the soft sfumato at the edge of her mouth make her lips seem to turn upward into a subtle smile. The result is a smile that flickers brighter the less you search for it.

Scientists recently found a technical way to describe all of this. "A clear smile is much more apparent in the low spatial frequency [blurrier] images than in the high spatial frequency image," according to Harvard Medical School neuroscientist Margaret Livingstone. "Thus, if you look at the painting so that your gaze falls on the background or on Mona Lisa's hands, your perception of her mouth would be dominated by low spatial frequencies, so it would appear much more cheerful than when you look directly at her mouth." A study at Sheffield Hallam University showed that Leonardo used the same technique not only on *La Belle Ferronnière* but also on the recently discovered drawing *La Bella Principessa*.[21]

So the world's most famous smile is inherently and fundamentally elusive, and therein lies Leonardo's ultimate realization about human nature. His expertise was in depicting the outer manifestation of inner emotions. But here in the *Mona Lisa* he shows something more important: that we can never fully know true emotion from outer manifestations. There is always a sfumato quality to other people's emotions, always a veil.

OTHER VERSIONS

Even as Leonardo was perfecting the *Mona Lisa*, his followers and some of his students were making copies, perhaps with an occasional helping hand from the master. Some are very good, including those known as the Vernon *Mona Lisa* and the Isleworth *Mona Lisa*, prompting claims that they may have been painted wholly or mostly by Leonardo, though most academic experts are skeptical.

The most beautiful copy is one in Madrid's Prado Museum, which was cleaned and restored in 2012 (fig. 135). It provides a glimpse of

Fig. 135. The Prado copy.

what the original looked like before its varnish became yellowed and cracked.[22] In addition to showing a wispy line of eyebrows, the copy displays the vibrant copper tones of Lisa's sleeves, the vividness of the blue-misty landscape, the gold embroidered into her neckline, the transparency of the thin shawl over her left shoulder, and the luster highlighting her ringlets of curls.

That raises the question, considered heretical by some, of whether the original *Mona Lisa* should be cleaned and restored, as the Louvre did its *Virgin and Child with Saint Anne* and *Saint John the Baptist*. Vincent Delieuvin, *Mona Lisa's* insightful curator at the Louvre, has described the sensation he feels on the one day a year when the painting is removed from behind its glass and taken out of its frame for careful inspection. The impressions of movement are even more vibrant. He knows that just by removing most of the varnish, and not touching the paint itself, the *Mona Lisa*, which has gotten noticeably darker even in modern times, could be seen in more of its original glory. But the painting is such an icon, and so beloved in its varnished darkness, that even the lightest amount of cleaning would spark huge controversy. French governments have fallen over less.

Perhaps the most interesting derivatives of the *Mona Lisa* made by Leonardo's followers are the seminude variations often called *Monna Vanna*, of which there remain at least eight, one of them attributed to Salai (fig. 136). Given that there were so many of these seminude versions done at the time, Leonardo probably approved of them, found them amusing, and may even have provided a preparatory drawing or a now-lost original. One cartoon in the Chateau of Chantilly, which is pricked as if used as the basis for a painting, is of high quality and has some left-handed hatching, indicating that Leonardo may have contributed to it and even conceived it.[23]

FOR THE AGES

When the British needed to contact their allies in the French Resistance during World War II, they used a code phrase: *La Joconde garde un sourire*. The *Mona Lisa* keeps her smile. Even though it may seem to flicker, her smile contains the immutable wisdom of the ages. Her

Fig. 136. The *Monna Vanna*.

portrait is a profound expression of our human connections, both to our inner selves and to our universe.

The *Mona Lisa* became the most famous painting in the world not just due to hype and happenstance but because viewers were able to feel an emotional engagement with her. She provokes a complex series of psychological reactions, which she herself seems to exhibit as well. Most miraculously, she seems aware—conscious—both of us and of herself. That is what makes her seem alive, the most alive of any portrait ever painted. It is also what makes her unique, one of humankind's unsurpassed creations. As Vasari said, "It was painted in a way to make every brave artist tremble and lose heart."

Stand before the *Mona Lisa*, and the historical discussions about how it was commissioned fade into oblivion. As Leonardo worked on it for most of the last sixteen years of his life, it became more than a portrait of an individual. It became universal, a distillation of his accumulated wisdom about the outward manifestations of our inner lives and about the connections between ourselves and our world. Like *Vitruvian Man* standing in the square of the earth and the circle of the heavens, Lisa sitting on her balcony against the backdrop of geological eons is Leonardo's profound meditation on what it means to be human.

And what about all of the scholars and critics over the years who despaired that Leonardo squandered too much time immersed in studying optics and anatomy and the patterns of the cosmos? The *Mona Lisa* answers them with a smile.

CHAPTER 32

France

FINAL JOURNEY

Much of Leonardo's career was consumed by his quest for patrons who would be unconditionally paternalistic, supportive, and indulgent in ways that his own father had only occasionally been. Although Piero da Vinci got his son a good apprenticeship and helped him get commissions, his behavior was variable from beginning to end: he declined to legitimate his son and excluded him from his will. His primary bequest to his son was to give him an insatiable drive for an unconditional patron.

So far all of Leonardo's benefactors had fallen short. When he was a young painter in Florence, the city was ruled by one of history's super-patrons, but Lorenzo de' Medici gave him few if any commissions and sent him away carrying a lyre as a diplomatic gift. As for Ludovico Sforza, it was many years after Leonardo's arrival in Milan before he was invited to become part of the ducal court, and his most important commission, the horse monument, was scuttled by the duke. After France captured Milan in 1499, Leonardo tried to curry favor with a variety of powerful men, including the French governor of Milan Charles d'Amboise, the brutal Italian warrior Cesare Borgia, and the hapless papal brother Giuliano de' Medici. But in each case the fit was not perfect.

Then, on his trip to Bologna with Pope Leo X in December 1515, Leonardo met the new king of France, Francis I, who had just turned twenty-one (fig. 137). At the beginning of that year, he had succeeded his father-in-law, Louis XII, who admired Leonardo, collected his works, and was among the few who could entice him to paint. Right before he met Leonardo in Bologna, Francis had wrested control of Milan from the Sforzas, just as Louis had done in 1499.

When they were in Bologna together, Francis probably invited Leonardo to come to France. Leonardo instead returned to Rome, but only briefly, perhaps to get his affairs in order. During that period, Francis and his court kept up efforts to recruit him, encouraged in that task by Francis's mother, Louise de Savoie. "I beg you to urge Master Leonardo that he should come to the King's presence," a

Fig. 137. King Francis I of France,
Leonardo's final patron.

member of Francis's court wrote to their ambassador in Rome in March 1516, adding that Leonardo should be "wholeheartedly assured that he will be most welcome both by the King and by Madame his mother."[1]

That month, Giuliano de' Medici died. Beginning during his early career in Florence, Leonardo's relationship to the Medici family had been uncomfortable. "The Medici made me and destroyed me," he wrote cryptically in his notebook at the time of Giuliano's death.[2] He then accepted the French invitation, and in the summer of 1516, before the snows made the Alps impassable, he left Rome to join the court of the king who would be his final and most devoted patron.

Leonardo had never been out of Italy before. He was sixty-four but looked older and knew this was likely to be his last journey. His entourage was accompanied by several mules that carried his household furniture, trunks of clothing and manuscripts, and at least three paintings he was still obsessively perfecting: the *Virgin and Child with Saint Anne*, *Saint John the Baptist*, and the *Mona Lisa*.

Along the way, he and his traveling party stopped in Milan. Salai decided to stay there, at least temporarily. He was then thirty-six, solidly middle-aged and no longer playing the role of Leonardo's pretty-boy companion or competing for attention with the aristocratic Melzi, who was still only twenty-five and remained at Leonardo's side. Salai would settle down at the vineyard and house on the edge of Milan that had been given to Leonardo by Ludovico Sforza. Over the next three years, until Leonardo's death, he would visit Leonardo in France but spend little time there: he received only one stipend payment, which was one-eighth the total of the regular ones that Melzi received.

Perhaps another reason Salai stayed behind was that Leonardo had a new manservant, Battista de Vilanis, who traveled with him from Rome to France. He would soon replace Salai in Leonardo's affections. Salai would end up inheriting only half of the Milan vineyard and its rights; Battista would get the other half.[3]

FRANCIS I

King Francis I was six feet tall, had broad shoulders, and displayed the charisma and courage that appealed to Leonardo. He loved leading his troops into battle. With his standard flying high, he would ride directly to the front lines. He was also, unlike Borgia and some of Leonardo's previous patrons, a civilized and decent man. When Francis captured Milan, instead of killing or even imprisoning its duke, Maximilian Sforza, he let him live at the French court.

Through his cultured mother, Louise de Savoie, and his bevy of dedicated and accomplished tutors, Francis was inculcated with a love of the Italian Renaissance. Unlike the Italian dukes and princes, French kings had collected very few paintings and almost no sculpture, and French art was greatly overshadowed by that of the Italians and Flemish. Francis set out to change that. He had the ambition, which he largely fulfilled, of launching in France the Renaissance that had been sweeping Italy.

He was also a voracious seeker of knowledge, with interests as universal as Leonardo's. He loved science and math, geography and history, poetry and music and literature. He learned Italian, Latin, Spanish, and Hebrew. Personally gregarious and with women lascivious, he cut a dashing figure as a graceful dancer, expert hunter, and powerful wrestler. After spending a few hours each morning on affairs of state, he would have someone read to him the great writers of ancient Rome and Greece. He also put on plays and pageants in the evening. Leonardo was the perfect recruit for his court.[4]

Likewise, Francis proved to be the perfect patron for Leonardo. He would admire Leonardo unconditionally, never pester him about finishing paintings, indulge his love of engineering and architecture, encourage him to stage pageants and fantasias, give him a comfortable home, and pay him a regular stipend. Leonardo was given the title "First Painter, Engineer, and Architect to the King," but his value to Francis was his intellect and not his output. Francis had an unquenchable thirst for learning, and Leonardo was the world's best source of experiential knowledge. He could teach the king about almost any subject there was to know, from how the eye works to why the moon shines. In turn, Leonardo could learn from the erudite and graceful young king. As Leonardo once wrote in his notebooks, referring to Alexander the Great and his tutor, "Alexander and Aristotle were teachers of one another."[5]

Francis became "completely enamored" with Leonardo, according to the sculptor Cellini. "He took such pleasure in hearing him discourse that there were few days in the year when he was parted from him, which was one of the reasons why Leonardo did not manage to pursue to the end his miraculous studies." Cellini later quoted Francis declaring that he "could never believe there was another man born in this world who knew as much as Leonardo, and not only of sculpture, painting and architecture, and that he was truly a great philosopher."[6]

Francis gave Leonardo something he had continually sought: a comfortable stipend that was not dependent on producing any paintings. In addition, he was given the use of a small red-brick manor house, with sandstone trimming and playful spires, next to Francis's castle in the Loire Valley village of Amboise. Known as the Château de Cloux, and now called Clos Lucé, Leonardo's house (fig. 138) was

Fig. 138. Château de Cloux, now called Clos Lucé.

set amid almost three acres of gardens and vineyards and connected
by an underground tunnel to the king's Château d'Amboise, about
five hundred yards away.

The large hall on the ground floor was spacious without being cold
and formal. There Leonardo ate with his retinue and visitors. Above it
was Leonardo's large bedroom (fig. 139), which had thick oak beams,
a stone fireplace, and a view over a grassy slope to the king's château.
Melzi probably had the other room on the second floor; he drew a
sketch of the view from one of its windows. He kept a list of books
that Leonardo, ever curious, wanted him to procure, among them
a study of the formation of the fetus in the womb, which had just
been published in Paris, and a printed volume by Roger Bacon, the
thirteenth-century friar from Oxford who was a forerunner of Leonardo as a scientific experimenter.

As he had for his previous patrons, Leonardo designed and staged
pageants for King Francis. In May 1518, for example, there were celebrations at Amboise to mark the baptism of the king's son and the
marriage of his niece. The preparations included the construction of
an arch topped by a salamander and an ermine, symbolizing the rap-

Fig. 139. Leonardo's last bedroom.

prochement between France and Italy. The piazza was transformed into a theatrical fortress with fake artillery "firing air-inflated balls with great blasting and smoking effects," according to a dispatch from one diplomat. "These balls, falling on the piazza, bounced all over to everyone's delight and without any damage." (A Leonardo drawing from 1518 showing a mechanical device to hurl balls is usually regarded as an example of his military engineering, but it was, I think, for this pageant.)[7]

At an open-air banquet and dance for the king in the gardens of the Château de Cloux the following month, Leonardo helped to re-create scenes from the performance he had staged almost thirty years earlier in Milan for the wedding of Gian Galeazzo Sforza to Isabella of Aragon: the play *Paradiso* by the poet Bernardo Bellincioni, with players costumed as each of the seven known planets and the mechanical marvel of an egg-shaped orb opening up to reveal paradise. "The courtyard was entirely covered with sky-blue sheets with golden-hued stars to look like the sky," one ambassador reported. "There must have been four hundred two-branched candelabras,

Fig. 140. Drawing for a masquerade.

which gave so much light that it was as if the night had been chased away."[8] The plays and masquerades were fleeting, but some of Leonardo's drawings for them remain. One beautiful sheet (fig. 140) shows a young man on horseback holding a lance and wearing an elaborate costume with helmet, feathers, and multiple layers of garment.

THE DE BEATIS VISIT

In October 1517, after Leonardo had been in Amboise for a year, he received a distinguished visitor, Cardinal Luigi of Aragon, who was taking a prolonged trip through Europe accompanied by more than forty members of his entourage. They had known each other in Rome, where the cardinal entertained grandly and was renowned for his gorgeous mistress, with whom he had a daughter. Accompanying him was his chaplain and secretary, Antonio de Beatis, whose diary provides us with our final close-up scene of Leonardo as a lion in winter.[9]

De Beatis referred to Leonardo as "the most eminent painter of our time," which was certainly true but provides evidence that he was regarded as such by his contemporaries, even though the *Mona Lisa*, the *Saint Anne*, and the *Saint John* had not been widely seen, and many of his public commissions, from the *Adoration of the Magi* to the *Battle of Anghiari*, had been left unfinished.

De Beatis described Leonardo, then sixty-five, as "a greybeard of more than seventy years." This is interesting, because many of the possible portraits of Leonardo, including the one in red chalk in Turin widely considered a self-portrait, are sometimes dismissed because they show a subject who seems to be older than Leonardo was. Perhaps, however, Leonardo did in fact look older than he was. By the time he reached his sixties, his despairs and demons may have wizened him.

We can imagine the scene. The visitors are welcomed into the large oak-beamed hall of the manor house, are served drinks by Leonardo's cook, Mathurine, and Leonardo then proceeds to play the role of the venerable icon of art and science, hosting the guests in his upstairs studio chamber. He begins by showing the cardinal and his retinue three easel paintings that he had carried with him on his travels: "One of a certain Florentine lady, done from life at the instigation of the late Giuliano de' Medici, the second is of the youthful Saint John the Baptist, and a third of the Madonna with the Child placed on the lap of Saint Anne, all of the highest perfection." Other than launching a subcult of scholars who have come up with alternative theories about the *Mona Lisa* based on de Beatis's account, the scene is sweetly reassuring. Here is Leonardo, in a comfortable room with a large fireplace, nurturing the paintings he loves and showing them off as his private treasures.

De Beatis also reported that Leonardo's ailments now included an apparent stroke: "Because of a paralysis in his right hand, one can no longer expect any masterpieces from him. He has trained a Milanese disciple [Melzi] who works very well, for if Master Leonardo is no longer capable of painting with the gentleness of touch which was his, he nevertheless continues to draw and teach." There is a typical Leonardo mystery here: he is left-handed, so perhaps the paralysis did not affect him much; we know that he was still drawing in Amboise, and while there he reworked the face and the blue drapery clothing on the left side of his *Saint Anne*.[10]

Leonardo's carefully staged tour also included some glimpses of his notebooks and treatises. "This gentleman has written a great deal about anatomy," de Beatis reported, "with many illustrations of the parts of the body, such as the muscles, nerves, veins and the coilings of intestines, and this makes it possible to understand the bodies of both men and women in a way that has never been done before. All this we saw with our own eyes, and he told us he had already dissected more than thirty bodies, both men and women, of all ages."

Leonardo also described, but apparently did not put on display, the work he had done on science and engineering. "He has also written, as he himself put it, an infinity of volumes on the nature of waters, on various machines, and on other things, all in the vernacular, and if these were to be brought to light they would be both useful and delightful." De Beatis recorded that the books were in Italian ("the vernacular"), but he does not mention the very notable fact that they were written in mirror script; he probably was shown the anatomy drawings but not the actual notebook pages. He is right about one thing: if they were to be published, they would be "both useful and delightful." Alas, Leonardo was not spending his final years at Amboise preparing them for publication.

ROMORANTIN

Rather than commissioning a big piece of public art, the king offered Leonardo an ideal assignment for the culmination of his career: designing a new town and palace complex for the royal court at the village of Romorantin, on the Sauldre River in the center of France, some fifty miles from Amboise. It would, if it came to pass, allow the expression of many of Leonardo's passions: architecture, urban planning, waterworks, engineering, even pageantry and spectacle.

In late 1517 he accompanied the king to Romorantin, where they stayed until January 1518. Drawing on the ideas and fantasies he had developed for an ideal city while living in Milan thirty years earlier, Leonardo began sketching in his notebook his radical and utopian aspirations for inventing a town from scratch.

The plan was for an idyllic palace rather than a fortress-like castle; his interest in military engineering and fortifications had waned. Melzi took charge of pacing the measurements of the existing streets and recording them. Then Leonardo sketched several designs. One is centered on a three-story palace with arched walkways facing the river. Another imagines two castles, one of which would be for the king's mother, with part of the river between them. Featured in all the designs are a profusion of different types of staircases: double doglegs, triple spirals, and various other curves and twists. For Leonardo, staircases were locations for complex flows and twisting motions, which he always loved.[11]

All of the plans were conceived with great outdoor spectacles and water pageants in mind. The galleries facing the river could serve as tiered viewing areas accommodating the entire French court, and there are broad steps that gently lead down to the water level. His drawings show small boats parading on the river and on man-made lakes for aquatic spectacles. "The jousters are to be on the boats," he writes next to one.

Leonardo's lifelong fascination with water suffuses all aspects of his plans for Romorantin, which feature a variety of aquatic engineering both practical and decorative. As with the earth, the waterways serve, both metaphorically and in reality, as the veins of the palace complex. Leonardo envisioned their use for irrigation, street cleaning, flushing out horse stables, carrying away rubbish, and as wonderful displays and decorations. "There should be fountains in every plaza," he declared. There should be "four mills where the water enters the town and four at the outlet, and this may be done by damming the water above Romorantin."[12]

Leonardo had soon expanded his watery dreams to include the entire region. He envisioned a system of canals that would connect the Sauldre to the Loire and Saône rivers, irrigate the region, and drain its marshes. Ever since he had marveled at the locks and canals that tamed the waters of Milan, he had tried to conquer the flow of water. He failed to do it with his plan for diverting the Arno near Florence or draining the Pontine Marshes near Rome. Now he hoped to succeed at Romorantin. "If the tributary of the Loire River were turned with its muddy waters into the river of Romorantin, it would fatten the land it waters, make the land fertile, supply food to the inhabitants, and serve as a navigable canal for commerce," he wrote.[13]

It was not to be. The project was abandoned in 1519, the year Leonardo died. Instead, the king decided to build his new château at Chambord, in the Loire Valley between Amboise and Romorantin. There the ground was less marshy and fewer canals were required.

THE DELUGE DRAWINGS

Leonardo's interest in the art and science of movement, and in particular the flow and swirl of water and wind, climaxed in a series of turbulent drawings that he made during his final years in France.[14] Sixteen of them are known to still exist, eleven of which were done together as a series using black chalk sometimes finished with ink; they are now part of the Windsor collection (for example, figs. 141 and 142).[15] Deeply personal yet coolly analytic in parts, they provide a powerful and dark expression of many of the themes of his life: the

Fig. 141.

Fig. 142.

Deluge drawings.

melding of art and science, the blurred line between experience and fantasy, and the frightful power of nature.

The drawings also convey, I believe, his own emotional turmoil as he faced his final days, partly hobbled by a stroke. They became an outlet for his feelings and fears. "They are an outpouring of something really personal," according to Windsor curator Martin Clayton, "a kind of crescendo at a time when his concerns are more strongly expressed."[16]

Throughout his life he had been obsessed with water and its movements. One of his first drawings, the landscape of the Arno done when he was twenty-one, shows a placid river, calm and life-giving as it meanders gently past fertile land and tranquil villages. It displays no signs of turbulence, just a few gentle ripples. Like a vein, it nourishes life. In his notebooks, there are dozens of references to water as the life-giving fluid that forms the vein that nourishes the earth. "Water is the vital humor [*vitale umore*] of the arid earth," he wrote. "Flowing with unceasing vehemence through the ramifying veins, it replenishes all the parts."[17] In the Codex Leicester he described, by his own count, "657 cases of water and its depths."[18] His mechanical engineering work included close to a hundred devices for moving and diverting water. Year after year he devised plans involving hydrodynamics, which included improving Milan's canal system, flooding the plains around Venice to defend against a Turkish invasion, channeling a direct link from Florence to the sea, diverting the Arno River around Pisa, draining the Pontine Marshes for Pope Leo X, and creating a canal system at Romorantin for King Francis I. But now, near the end of his life, he depicted water and its swirls not as calm or tamed but as filled with fury.

The deluge drawings are powerful works of art. The pages contain framing lines, and the back side of each is blank, signaling that they were drawn for display, or perhaps as artistic accompaniments to a reading of an apocalyptic tale, not just as scientific illustrations in a notebook. Some of the most vivid are done in chalk, then lined with ink and tinted with a color wash. Especially for those who love curls and swirls, as Leonardo did, the drawings are an artistic expression of great aesthetic power. They remind us of the curls cascading down the back of the angel in his *Annunciation*, the painting he made some forty years earlier. Indeed, the underdrawing of the angel's curls, as revealed by a spectrographic analysis, is strikingly similar to the spirals of the deluge drawings.[19]

The careful and detailed observation of motion was one of Leonardo's specialties, and so too was extending his observations into the realm of fantasy. His deluge drawings are based on storms he had witnessed and described in his notebooks, but they are also the product of a fevered and frenzied imagination. He was a master at blurring lines, and in his deluge drawings he did so between reality and fantasia.

Leonardo liked to use both words and drawings to depict his ideas, and this was especially true of the deluge. In three very long passages totaling more than two thousand words, he wrote "of the deluge and how to represent it in a picture." Much of this was intended for his planned treatise on painting. He wrote as if he were instructing both himself and students:

> Let the dark and gloomy air be seen buffeted by the rush of contrary winds and dense from the continued rain mingled with hail and bearing hither and thither an infinite number of branches torn from the trees and mixed with numberless leaves. All round may be seen venerable trees, uprooted by the fury of the winds; and fragments of mountains, already scoured bare by the torrents, falling into those torrents and choking their valleys till the swollen rivers overflow and submerge the wide lowlands and their inhabitants. You might see on many of the hill-tops terrified animals of different kinds, collected together and subdued to tameness, in company with men and women who had fled there with their children.

Leonardo's description continues for two closely written pages of his notebook, and by halfway through he is no longer instructing how to paint a scene. Instead, he has whipped himself into a frenzy describing the apocalyptic deluge and the emotions of the humans as they are thrashed. Perhaps parts were intended to be performed for the king, accompanied by the pictures. Whatever its purpose, the description descends into the darkest of all Leonardo's fantasia scenes:

> Others, with desperate act, took their own lives, hopeless of being able to endure such suffering; and of these, some flung themselves from lofty rocks, others strangled themselves with their own hands, other seized their own children and violently slew them at a blow; some wounded and killed themselves with their own weapons; others, falling on their knees recommended themselves to God. Ah! how many mothers wept over their drowned sons, holding them upon their knees, with arms raised spread out towards heaven and with words and various threatening gestures, upbraiding the wrath of the gods. Others with clasped hands and fingers clenched gnawed them and devoured them till they bled, crouching with their breast down on their knees in their intense and unbearable anguish.[20]

Mixed in with the gloomy fantasy are careful observations about how flowing water when diverted forms swirls and eddies: "The swollen waters will sweep around the pool that contains them, striking in eddying whirlpools against the different obstacles." Even amid the darkest passages there are specific scientific injunctions. "If the heavy masses of large mountains or grand buildings fall into the vast pools of water, a great quantity will be flung into the air and its movement will be in a contrary direction to that of the object which struck the water; the angle of reflection will be equal to the angle of incidence."[21]

The deluge drawings conjure up the story of the Flood in Genesis, a topic treated by Michelangelo and many other artists over the years, but Leonardo makes no mention of Noah. He was conveying more than a biblical tale. At one point he adds Greek and Roman classical gods to the fray: "Neptune will be seen in the midst of the water with his trident, and let Aeolus with his winds be shown entangling the trees floating uprooted and whirling in the huge waves."[22] He drew on Virgil's *Aeneid*, Ovid's *Metamorphoses*, and the thunderous natural phenomena in book 6 of Lucretius's *On the Nature of Things*. The drawings and text also conjure up the tale he wrote in Milan in the 1490s, ostensibly addressed to "the Devatdar of Syria." In that story, performed at Ludovico Sforza's court, Leonardo vividly described "a sudden rain, or rather a ruinous storm full of water, sand, mud, and stones all mingled together with roots, stems, and branches of various trees; and every kind of thing came hurtling through the air and descended upon us."[23]

Leonardo did not focus on, or for that matter even hint at, the wrath of God in his deluge writings and drawings. He conveyed instead his belief that chaos and destruction are inherent in the raw power of nature. The psychological effect is more harrowing than if he were merely depicting a tale of punishment from an angry God. He was imparting his own emotions and thereby tapping into ours. Hallucinatory and hypnotic, the deluge drawings are the unnerving bookend to a life of nature drawing that began with a sketch of the placid Arno flowing near his native village.

THE END

On what may be the last page he wrote in his notebooks, Leonardo drew four right triangles with bases of differing lengths (fig. 143). Inside of each he fit a rectangle, and then he shaded the remaining areas of the triangle. In the center of the page he made a chart with boxes labeled with the letter of each rectangle, and below it he described what he was trying to accomplish. As he had done obsessively over the years, he was using the visualization of geometry to help him understand the transformation of shapes. Specifically, he was trying to understand the formula for keeping the area of a right triangle the same while varying the lengths of its two legs. He had fussed with this problem, explored by Euclid, repeatedly over the years. It was a puzzle that, by this point in his life, as he turned sixty-seven and his health faded, might seem unnecessary to solve. To anyone other than Leonardo, it may have been.

Then abruptly, almost at the end of the page, he breaks off his writing with an "et cetera." That is followed by a line, written in the same meticulous mirror script as the previous lines of his analysis,

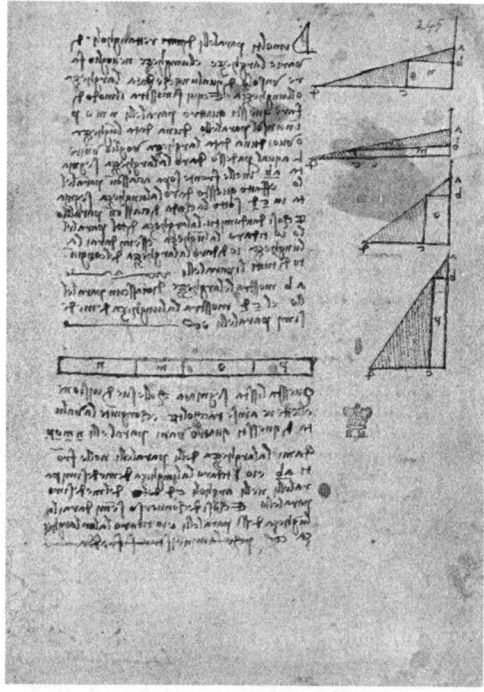

Fig. 143. Studies of right triangle areas,
ending with "the soup is getting cold."

explaining why he is putting down his pen. "Perché la minestra si fredda," he writes. Because the soup is getting cold.[24]

It is the final piece of writing we have by Leonardo's hand, our last scene of him working. Picture him in the upstairs study of his manor house, with its beamed ceiling and fireplace and the view of his royal patron's Château d'Amboise. Mathurine, his cook, is down in the kitchen. Perhaps Melzi and others of the household are already at the table. After all these years, he is still stabbing away at geometry problems that have not yielded the world very much but have given him a profound appreciation of the patterns of nature. Now, however, the soup is getting cold.

There is one final document. On April 23, 1518, eight days after his sixty-seventh birthday, Leonardo had his last will and testament drawn up by a notary in Amboise, witnessed, and signed. He had been ill, and like a good son of a notary he began getting his affairs in order. It begins, "Be it known to all persons, present and to come, that at the court of our Lord the King at Amboise before ourselves in person, Messer Leonardo da Vinci, painter to the King, at present staying at the place known as Cloux near Amboise, duly considering the certainty of death and the uncertainty of its time . . ."

In his will, Leonardo commended his "soul to our Lord, Almighty God, and to the glorious Virgin Mary," but that seems to have been merely a literary flourish. His science led him to adopt many heretical beliefs, including that the fetus in the womb does not have a soul of its own and that the biblical Flood did not happen. Unlike Michelangelo, a man consumed at times with religious fervor, Leonardo made a point of not expounding much on religion during his lifetime. He said that he would not endeavor "to write or give information of those things of which the human mind is incapable and which cannot be proved by an instance of nature," and he left such matters "to the minds of friars, fathers of the people, who by inspiration possess the secrets."[25]

The first items in his will prescribe what shall be his funeral services. His body will be carried to the church at Amboise by its chaplains. "In the said church of Saint Florentin," he specified, "three high masses shall be celebrated by the deacon and sub-deacon and on the same day thirty low masses shall also be performed at Saint Gregory." This will be followed by three masses at the nearby church of Saint Denis. He wanted "sixty candles carried by sixty poor men, to whom shall be given money for carrying them."

To Mathurine, the serving woman who made the soup, he bequeathed "a cloak of good black woolen cloth lined with fur" and 2 ducats. To his half-brothers, he fulfilled what had probably been the legal settlement of their earlier dispute by giving them a sizable cash payment and the property he had inherited from his uncle Francesco.

As Leonardo's de facto and perhaps legally adopted son and heir, Francesco Melzi was named the executor and bequeathed most of the estate. This included Leonardo's pension, all sums of money owed to him, his clothes, books, writings, and "all the instruments and portraits pertaining to his art and calling as a painter." To his most recently hired house servant and companion, Battista de Vilanis, Leonardo left the water rights that had been granted him in Milan as well as half of the vineyard given to him by Ludovico Sforza. He also gave Battista "each and all of the articles of furniture and utensils in his house at Cloux."

And then there was Salai. He was designated to get the other half of the vineyard. Since he was already living there and had built a house on a portion of the land, it would be hard for Leonardo to have done otherwise with the property. But that was all Salai was bequeathed in the will. There had apparently been an estrangement, one that had grown with the ascent of Melzi and the arrival of Battista. Salai was no longer at Leonardo's side when he made the will. Nevertheless, he lived up to his reputation as a sticky-fingered little devil, one who was somehow able to get his hands on things. When he was killed five years later by a crossbow, the inventory of his estate showed that, perhaps during a visit to France, he had been given or had taken many copies of Leonardo's paintings and possibly some of the originals, perhaps including the *Mona Lisa* and *Leda and the Swan*. Always the con artist, it is unclear whether the prices listed in his estate are true values, thus making it hard to know which were copies. Except for the *Leda*, which was lost, whatever original paintings Salai had were returned to France, perhaps having previously been sold by him to the king, and eventually ended up in the Louvre.[26]

"As a well-spent day brings a happy sleep," Leonardo had written thirty years earlier, "so a well-employed life brings a happy death."[27] His came on May 2, 1519, less than three weeks after he turned sixty-seven.

In his biographical essay on Leonardo, Vasari describes a final scene that, as with many of his passages, is likely a mix of truth and his own wishful imagination. Leonardo, he wrote, "feeling himself near to death, asked to have himself diligently informed of the teaching of the Catholic faith, and of the good way and holy Christian religion; and then, with many moans, he confessed and was penitent;

and although he could not raise himself well on his feet, supporting himself on the arms of his friends and servants, he was pleased to take devoutly the most holy Sacrament."

This trope of a deathbed confession feels like something Vasari, who was not there, would invent, or at least embellish. He was more eager to have Leonardo embrace faith than Leonardo himself probably was. As Vasari knew, Leonardo was not conventionally religious. In the first edition of his biography, he wrote that Leonardo "formed in his mind a doctrine so heretical that he depended no more on any religion, perhaps placing scientific knowledge higher than Christian faith." He eliminated that passage in the second edition of the book, presumably to protect Leonardo's reputation.

Vasari goes on to recount that King Francis, "who was in the habit of making frequent affectionate visits to him," arrived in Leonardo's chambers just as the priest who had performed the last rites was leaving. Leonardo then summoned the strength to sit up and give a description of his illness and its symptoms. Of all parts of Vasari's deathbed account, that is the most believable. It is easy to imagine Leonardo explaining to the smart and curious young king the intricacies of a failing heart and blood vessels.

"Thereupon he was seized by a paroxysm, the messenger of death," Vasari reports, "the King having risen and having taken his head, in order to assist him and show him favor to the end, in the hope of alleviating his sufferings, the spirit of Leonardo, which was most divine, conscious that it could attain to no greater honor, breathed its last in the arms of the King."

It was a moment so perfect that it was later portrayed by many admiring painters, most notably Jean-Auguste-Dominique Ingres (fig. 144). And thus we have a fitting and beautiful final scene: Leonardo cradled on his deathbed by a powerful and doting patron in a comfortable house surrounded by his favorite paintings.

But with Leonardo, nothing is quite so simple. The image of him dying in the arms of the king may, or may not, be another sentimental myth. We know that King Francis issued a proclamation on May 3 at Saint-Germain-en-Laye, which was a two-day ride from Amboise. So it seems that he could not have actually been with Leonardo the

Fig. 144. Jean-Auguste-Dominique Ingres, *The Death of Leonardo.*

day before. Or then again, perhaps he could have been. The proclamation in question was issued by the king but was not signed by him.
Instead it was signed by his chancellor, and the records coming out of
the council do not mention the king's presence. So there remains the
possibility that the king stayed in Amboise to cradle the head of his
dying genius.[28]

Leonardo was buried in the church of the Château d'Amboise, but
the current location of his remains is another mystery. That church
was demolished in the early nineteenth century, and sixty years later
the site was excavated and a collection of bones found that may have
been those of Leonardo. The bones were reburied at the chapel of
Saint-Hubert adjoining the château, and a tomb slab was installed
saying it was the site of his "presumed remains" (*restes présumés*).

As always with Leonardo, in his art and in his life, in his birthplace and now even in his death, there is a veil of mystery. We cannot portray him with crisp sharp lines, nor should we want to, just as he would not have wanted to portray Mona Lisa that way. There is something nice about leaving a little to our imagination. As he knew, the outlines of reality are inherently blurry, leaving a hint of uncertainty that we should embrace. The best way to approach his life is the way he approached the world: filled with a sense of curiosity and an appreciation for its infinite wonders.

Chapter 33

Conclusion

GENIUS

In the introduction to this book, I suggested that it was unhelpful to toss around the word *genius* as if it were a superhuman trait, bestowed by heaven and not within the ken of mere mortals. As I hope you will by now agree, Leonardo was a genius, one of the few people in history who indisputably deserved—or, to be more precise, *earned*—that appellation. Yet it is also true that he was a mere mortal.

The most obvious evidence that he was human rather than superhuman is the trail of projects he left unfinished. Among them were a horse model that archers reduced to rubble, an Adoration scene and battle mural that were abandoned, flying machines that never flew, tanks that never rolled, a river that was never diverted, and pages of brilliant treatises that piled up unpublished. "Tell me if anything was ever done," he repeatedly scribbled in notebook after notebook. "Tell me. Tell me. Tell me if ever I did a thing. . . . Tell me if anything was ever made."[1]

Of course, the things he did finish were enough to prove his genius. The *Mona Lisa* alone does that, as do all of his art masterpieces as well as his anatomical drawings. But by the end of writing this book, I even began to appreciate the genius inherent in his designs left unexecuted and masterpieces left unfinished. By skirting the edge of fantasy with his flying machines and water projects and military devices, he envisioned what innovators would invent centuries later. And by refusing to churn out works that he had not perfected, he sealed his reputation as a genius rather than a master craftsman. He enjoyed the challenge of conception more than the chore of completion.

One reason that he was reluctant to relinquish some of his works and declare them completed was that he relished a world in flux. He had an uncanny ability to convey movements—of the body and the mind, of machines and horses, and of rivers and everything else that flows. No instant, he wrote, is self-contained, just as no action in a theatrical pageant nor any drop in a flowing river is self-contained. Each moment incorporates what came right before and what is coming right after. Similarly, he looked upon his art and engineering and his treatises as a part of a dynamic process, always receptive to a refinement by the application of a new insight. He updated *Saint Jerome in the Wilderness* after thirty years, when his anatomy experiments taught him something new about neck muscles. If he had lived another decade, he likely would have continued to refine the *Mona Lisa* for that much longer. Relinquishing a work, declaring it finished, froze its evolution. Leonardo did not like to do that. There was always something more to be learned, another stroke to be gleaned from nature that would make a picture closer to perfect.

What made Leonardo a genius, what set him apart from people who are merely extraordinarily smart, was creativity, the ability to apply imagination to intellect. His facility for combining observation with fantasy allowed him, like other creative geniuses, to make unexpected leaps that related things seen to things unseen. "Talent hits a target that no one else can hit," wrote the German philosopher Arthur Schopenhauer. "Genius hits a target no one else can see."[2] Because they "think different," creative masterminds are sometimes considered misfits, but in the words that Steve Jobs helped craft for an Apple advertisement, "While some may see them as the crazy ones, we see genius. Because the people who are crazy enough to think they can change the world are the ones who do."[3]

What also distinguished Leonardo's genius was its universal nature. The world has produced other thinkers who were more profound or logical, and many who were more practical, but none who was as creative in so many different fields. Some people are geniuses in a particular arena, such as Mozart in music and Euler in math. But Leonardo's brilliance spanned multiple disciplines, which gave him a profound feel for nature's patterns and crosscurrents. His curiosity impelled him to become among the handful of people in history who tried to know all there was to know about everything that could be known.

There have been, of course, many other insatiable polymaths, and even the Renaissance produced other Renaissance Men. But none painted the *Mona Lisa*, much less did so at the same time as producing unsurpassed anatomy drawings based on multiple dissections, coming up with schemes to divert rivers, explaining the reflection of light from the earth to the moon, opening the still-beating heart of a butchered pig to show how ventricles work, designing musical instruments, choreographing pageants, using fossils to dispute the biblical account of the deluge, and then drawing the deluge. Leonardo was a genius, but more: he was the epitome of the universal mind, one who sought to understand all of creation, including how we fit into it.

LEARNING FROM LEONARDO

The fact that Leonardo was not only a genius but also very human— quirky and obsessive and playful and easily distracted—makes him more accessible. He was not graced with the type of brilliance that is completely unfathomable to us. Instead, he was self-taught and willed his way to his genius. So even though we may never be able to match his talents, we can learn from him and try to be more like him. His life offers a wealth of lessons.

Be curious, relentlessly curious. "I have no special talents," Einstein once wrote to a friend. "I am just passionately curious."[4] Leonardo actually did have special talents, as did Einstein, but his distinguishing and most inspiring trait was his intense curiosity. He wanted to know what causes people to yawn, how they walk on ice in Flanders, methods for squaring a circle, what makes the aortic valve close, how light is processed in the eye and what that means for the perspective in a painting. He instructed himself to learn about the placenta of a calf, the jaw of a crocodile, the tongue of a woodpecker, the muscles of a face, the light of the moon, and the edges of shadows. Being relentlessly and randomly curious about everything around us is something that each of us can push ourselves to do, every waking hour, just as he did.

Seek knowledge for its own sake. Not all knowledge needs to be useful. Sometimes it should be pursued for pure pleasure. Leonardo did not need to know how heart valves work to paint the *Mona Lisa*, nor did he need to figure out how fossils got to the top of mountains to produce *Virgin of the Rocks*. By allowing himself to be driven by pure curiosity, he got to explore more horizons and see more connections than anyone else of his era.

Retain a childlike sense of wonder. At a certain point in life, most of us quit puzzling over everyday phenomena. We might savor the beauty of a blue sky, but we no longer bother to wonder why it is that color. Leonardo did. So did Einstein, who wrote to another friend, "You and I never cease to stand like curious children before the great mystery into which we were born."[5] We should be careful to never outgrow our wonder years, or to let our children do so.

Observe. Leonardo's greatest skill was his acute ability to observe things. It was the talent that empowered his curiosity, and vice versa. It was not some magical gift but a product of his own effort. When he visited the moats surrounding Sforza Castle, he looked at the four-wing dragonflies and noticed how the wing pairs alternate in motion. When he walked around town, he observed how the facial expressions of people relate to their emotions, and he discerned how light bounces off differing surfaces. He saw which birds move their wings faster on the upswing than on the downswing, and which do the opposite. This, too, we can emulate. Water flowing into a bowl? Look, as he did, at exactly how the eddies swirl. Then wonder why.

Start with the details. In his notebook, Leonardo shared a trick for observing something carefully: Do it in steps, starting with each detail. A page of a book, he noted, cannot be absorbed in one stare; you need to go word by word. "If you wish to have a sound knowledge of the forms of objects, begin with the details of them, and do not go on to the second step until you have the first well fixed in memory."[6]

See things unseen. Leonardo's primary activity in many of his formative years was conjuring up pageants, performances, and plays. He mixed theatrical ingenuity with fantasy. This gave him a combinatory creativity. He could see birds in flight and also angels, lions roaring and also dragons.

Go down rabbit holes. He filled the opening pages of one of his notebooks with 169 attempts to square a circle. In eight pages of his Codex Leicester, he recorded 730 findings about the flow of water; in another notebook, he listed sixty-seven words that describe different types of moving water. He measured every segment of the human body, calculated their proportional relationships, and then did the same for a horse. He drilled down for the pure joy of geeking out.

Get distracted. The greatest rap on Leonardo was that these passionate pursuits caused him to wander off on tangents, literally in the case of his math inquiries. It "has left posterity the poorer," Kenneth Clark lamented. But in fact, Leonardo's willingness to pursue whatever shiny subject caught his eye made his mind richer and filled with more connections.

Respect facts. Leonardo was a forerunner of the age of observational experiments and critical thinking. When he came up with an idea, he devised an experiment to test it. And when his experience showed that a theory was flawed—such as his belief that the springs within the earth are replenished the same way as blood vessels in humans—he abandoned his theory and sought a new one. This practice became common a century later, during the age of Galileo and Bacon. It has, however, become a bit less prevalent these days. If we want to be more like Leonardo, we have to be fearless about changing our minds based on new information.

Procrastinate. While painting *The Last Supper*, Leonardo would sometimes stare at the work for an hour, finally make one small stroke, and then leave. He told Duke Ludovico that creativity requires time for ideas to marinate and intuitions to gel. "Men of lofty genius sometimes accomplish the most when they work least," he explained, "for their minds are occupied with their ideas and the perfection of their conceptions, to which they afterwards give form." Most of us don't need advice to procrastinate; we do it naturally. But procrastinating like Leonardo requires work: it involves gathering all the possible facts and ideas, and only after that allowing the collection to simmer.

Let the perfect be the enemy of the good. When Leonardo could not make the perspective in the *Battle of Anghiari* or the interaction in the *Adoration of the Magi* work perfectly, he abandoned them rather than produce a work that was merely good enough. He carried around masterpieces such as his *Saint Anne* and the *Mona Lisa* to the end, knowing there would always be a new stroke he could add. Likewise, Steve Jobs was such a perfectionist that he held up shipping the original Macintosh until his team could make the circuit boards inside look beautiful, even though no one would ever see them. Both he and Leonardo knew that real artists care about the beauty even of the parts unseen. Eventually, Jobs embraced a countermaxim, "Real artists ship," which means that sometimes you ought to deliver a product even when there are still improvements that could be made. That is a good rule for daily life. But there are times when it's nice to be like Leonardo and not let go of something until it's perfect.

Think visually. Leonardo was not blessed with the ability to formulate math equations or abstractions. So he had to visualize them, which he did with his studies of proportions, his rules of perspective, his method for calculating reflections from concave mirrors, and his ways of changing one shape into another of the same size. Too often, when we learn a formula or a rule—even one so simple as the method for multiplying numbers or mixing a paint color—we no longer visualize how it works. As a result, we lose our appreciation for the underlying beauty of nature's laws.

Avoid silos. At the end of many of his product presentations, Jobs displayed a slide of a sign that showed the intersection of "Liberal Arts" and "Technology" streets. He knew that at such crossroads lay creativity. Leonardo had a free-range mind that merrily wandered across all the disciplines of the arts, sciences, engineering, and humanities. His knowledge of how light strikes the retina helped inform the perspective in *The Last Supper*, and on a page of anatomical drawings depicting the dissection of lips he drew the smile that would reappear in the *Mona Lisa*. He knew that art was a science and that science was an art. Whether he was drawing a fetus in the womb or the swirls of a deluge, he blurred the distinction between the two.

Let your reach exceed your grasp. Imagine, as he did, how you would build a human-powered flying machine or divert a river. Even try to devise a perpetual-motion machine or square a circle using only a ruler and a compass. There are some problems we will never solve. Learn why.

Indulge fantasy. His giant crossbow? The turtle-like tanks? His plan for an ideal city? The man-powered mechanisms to flap a flying machine? Just as Leonardo blurred the lines between science and art, he did so between reality and fantasy. It may not have produced flying machines, but it allowed his imagination to soar.

Create for yourself, not just for patrons. No matter how hard the rich and powerful marchesa Isabella d'Este begged, Leonardo would not paint her portrait. But he did begin one of a silk-merchant's wife named Lisa. He did it because he wanted to, and he kept working on it for the rest of his life, never delivering it to the silk merchant.

Collaborate. Genius is often considered the purview of loners who retreat to their garrets and are struck by creative lightning. Like many myths, that of the lone genius has some truth to it. But there's usually more to the story. The Madonnas and drapery studies produced in Verrocchio's studio, and the versions of *Virgin of the Rocks* and *Madonna of the Yarnwinder* and other paintings from Leonardo's studio, were created in such a collaborative manner that it is hard to tell whose hand made which strokes. *Vitruvian Man* was produced after sharing ideas and sketches with friends. Leonardo's best anatomy studies came when he was working in partnership with Marcantonio della Torre. And his most fun work came from collaborations on theatrical productions and evening entertainments at the Sforza court. Genius starts with individual brilliance. It requires singular vision. But executing it often entails working with others. Innovation is a team sport. Creativity is a collaborative endeavor.

Make lists. And be sure to put odd things on them. Leonardo's to-do lists may have been the greatest testaments to pure curiosity the world has ever seen.

Take notes, on paper. Five hundred years later, Leonardo's notebooks are around to astonish and inspire us. Fifty years from now, our own notebooks, if we work up the initiative to start writing them, will be around to astonish and inspire our grandchildren, unlike our tweets and Facebook posts.

Be open to mystery. Not everything needs sharp lines.

Describe the tongue of the woodpecker

The tongue of a woodpecker can extend more than three times the length of its bill. When not in use, it retracts into the skull and its cartilage-like structure continues past the jaw to wrap around the bird's head and then curve down to its nostril. In addition to digging out grubs from a tree, the long tongue protects the woodpecker's brain. When the bird smashes its beak repeatedly into tree bark, the force exerted on its head is ten times what would kill a human. But its bizarre tongue and supporting structure act as a cushion, shielding the brain from shock.[1]

There is no reason you actually need to know any of this. It is information that has no real utility for your life, just as it had none for Leonardo. But I thought maybe, after reading this book, that you, like Leonardo, who one day put "Describe the tongue of the woodpecker" on one of his eclectic and oddly inspiring to-do lists, would want to know. Just out of curiosity. Pure curiosity.

ABBREVIATIONS OF FREQUENTLY CITED SOURCES

Leonardo's Notebooks

Codex Arundel = Codex Arundel (c. 1492–c. 1518), British Library, London. Contains 238 pages taken from different original Leonardo notebooks, mainly on architecture and machinery.

Codex Ash. = Codex Ashburnham, vols. 1 (1486–90) and 2 (1490–92), l'Institut de France, Paris, formerly (and now once again) parts of Paris Mss. A and B. In the 1840s, folios 81–114 of Paris Ms. A and folios 91–100 of Paris Ms. B were stolen by Count Guglielmo Libri. He sold them to Lord Ashburnham in 1875, who returned them to Paris in 1890. J. P. Richter, in his notebook compilation, cites the Codices Ashburnham, but later literature tends to cite the folio numbers from the restored Paris Ms. A and Ms. B. (See below on the Paris manuscripts.)

Codex Atl. = Codex Atlanticus (1478–1518), Biblioteca Ambrosiana, Milan. The largest compilation of Leonardo's papers, now arranged in twelve volumes. The folios were given new numbers in a restoration in the late 1970s. Folios are usually cited in the old style/new style.

Codex Atl./Pedretti = Carlo Pedretti, *Leonardo da Vinci Codex Atlanticus: A Catalogue of Its Newly Restored Sheets* (Giunti, 1978).

Codex Forster = Codex Forster, vols. 1–3 (1487–1505), Victoria and Albert Museum, London. The three volumes comprise five pocket notebooks, mainly on machinery, geometry, and the transformation of volumes.

Codex Leic. = Codex Leicester (1508–12), Bill Gates's home near Seattle, Washington. Contains seventy-two pages mainly on the earth and its waters.

Codex Madrid = Codex Madrid, vols. 1 (1493–99) and 2 (1493–1505), Biblioteca Nacional de España, Madrid. Rediscovered in 1966.

Codex on Flight = Codex on the Flight of Birds (c. 1505), Biblioteca Reale, Turin. Originally part of Paris Ms. B. A facsimile with translation is on the website of the Smithsonian Air and Space Museum at https://airandspace .si.edu/exhibitions/codex.

Codex Triv. = Codex Trivulzianus (c. 1487–90), Castle Sforza, Milan. One of Leonardo's earliest manuscripts, now contains fifty-five sheets.

Codex Urb. = Codex Urbinas Latinus, Vatican Library. Contains selections from various manuscripts copied and compiled by Francesco Melzi around 1530. An abbreviated version was published in Paris in 1651 as *Trattato della Pittura* or *Treatise on Painting*.

Leonardo on Painting = *Leonardo on Painting*, selected and translated by Martin Kemp and Margaret Walker (Yale, 2001). An anthology, based partly on the Codex Urbinas, of the writings that Leonardo intended to be in his *Treatise on Painting*.

Leonardo Treatise/Pedretti = Leonardo da Vinci, *Libro di Pittura*, edited by Carlo Pedretti, critical transcription by Carlo Vecce (Giunti, 1995). A two-volume facsimile, transcription, and anotation of the Codex Urbinas. Numbers refer to sections assigned by Pedretti.

Leonardo Treatise/Rigaud = Leonardo da Vinci, *A Treatise on Painting*, translated by John Francis Rigaud (Dover, 2005; originally published 1651). Based on the Codex Urbinas. Numbers refer to the numbered entries in the book.

Notebooks/Irma Richter = *Leonardo da Vinci Notebooks*, selected by Irma A. Richter, new edition edited by Thereza Wells with a preface by Martin Kemp (Oxford, 2008; first published 1939). Irma Richter was the daughter of J. P. Richter (see below). This edition includes her refinement and selection from her father's work, further updated with commentary by Wells and Kemp.

Notebooks/J. P. Richter = *The Notebooks of Leonardo da Vinci*, compiled and edited by Jean Paul Richter, 2 vols. (Dover, 1970; first published in 1883). These volumes contain Italian transcriptions and English translations side by side, with many of Leonardo's illustrations plus notes and commentary. I cite the passage numbers used by Richter, 1–1566, which remain consistent in the many editions of his seminal compilation. The two-volume dual-language Dover edition also gives the name and folio number of the original Leonardo notebook.

Notebooks/MacCurdy = Edward MacCurdy, *The Notebooks of Leonardo da Vinci* (Cape, 1938). Numerous editions are available online. Numbers refer to the passage number given by MacCurdy.

Paris Ms. = Manuscripts in l'Institut de France, which include A (written 1490–92), B (1486–90), C (1490–91), D (1508–9), E (1513–14), F (1508–13), G (1510–15), H (1493–94), I (1497–1505), K1, K2, K3 (1503–8), L (1497–1502), M (1495–1500).

Windsor = Royal Collection, Windsor Castle. The Royal Collection Inventory Number (RCIN) entries for Leonardo have a 9 before the catalogue number.

Other Frequently Cited Sources

Anonimo Gaddiano = The Anonimo Gaddiano or Anonimo Magliabecchiano, in "Life of Leonardo," translated by Kate Steinitz and Ebria Feinblatt (Los Angeles County Museum, 1949), 37, and in Ludwig Goldscheider, *Leonardo da Vinci: Life and Work* (Phaidon, 1959), 28.

Arasse = Daniel Arasse, *Leonardo da Vinci* (Konecky, 1998).

Bambach *Master Draftsman* = Carmen C. Bambach, ed., *Leonardo da Vinci Master Draftsman* (Metropolitan Museum of New York, 2003).

Bramly = Serge Bramly, *Leonardo: The Artist and the Man* (HarperCollins, 1991).

Brown = David Alan Brown, *Leonardo da Vinci: Origins of a Genius* (Yale, 1998).

Capra *Learning* = Fritjof Capra, *Learning from Leonardo* (Berrett-Koehler, 2013).

Capra *Science* = Fritjof Capra, *The Science of Leonardo* (Doubleday, 2007).

Clark = Kenneth Clark, *Leonardo da Vinci* (Penguin, 1939; revised edition edited by Martin Kemp, 1988).

Clayton = Martin Clayton, *Leonardo da Vinci: The Divine and the Grotesque* (Royal Collection, 2002).

Clayton and Philo = Martin Clayton and Ron Philo, *Leonardo da Vinci: Anatomist* (Royal Collection, 2012).

Delieuvin = Vincent Delieuvin, ed., *Saint Anne: Leonardo da Vinci's Ultimate Masterpiece* (Louvre, 2012). Catalogue of the exhibition at the Louvre, 2012.

Fiorani and Kim = Francesca Fiorani and Anna Marazeula Kim, "Leonardo da Vinci: Between Art and Science," University of Virginia, March 2014, http://faculty.virginia.edu/Fiorani/NEH-Institute/essays/.

Keele and Roberts = Kenneth Keele and Jane Roberts, *Leonardo da Vinci: Anatomical Drawings from the Royal Library, Windsor Castle* (Metropolitan Museum of New York, 2013).

Keele Elements = Kenneth Keele, *Leonardo da Vinci's Elements of the Science of Man* (Academic, 1983).

Kemp Leonardo = Martin Kemp, *Leonardo* (Oxford, 2004; revised 2011).

Kemp Marvellous = Martin Kemp, *Leonardo da Vinci: The Marvellous Works of Nature and Man* (Harvard, 1981; revised edition Oxford, 2006).

King = Ross King, *Leonardo and the Last Supper* (Bloomsbury, 2013).

Laurenza = Domenico Laurenza, *Leonardo's Machines* (David and Charles, 2006).

Lester = Toby Lester, *Da Vinci's Ghost* (Simon and Schuster, 2012).

Marani = Pietro C. Marani, *Leonardo da Vinci: The Complete Paintings* (Abrams, 2000).

Marani and Fiorio = Pietro C. Marani and Maria Teresa Fiorio, *Leonardo da Vinci: The Design of the World* (Skira, 2015). Catalogue of the Palazzo Reale exhibition, Milan, 2015.

Moffatt and Taglialagamba = Constance Moffatt and Sara Taglialagamba, *Illuminating Leonardo: A Festschrift for Carlo Pedretti Celebrating His 70 Years of Scholarship* (Brill, 2016).

Nicholl = Charles Nicholl, *Leonardo da Vinci: Flights of the Mind* (Viking, 2004).

O'Malley = Charles D. O'Malley, ed., *Leonardo's Legacy* (University of California, 1969).

Payne = Robert Payne, *Leonardo* (Doubleday, 1978).

Pedretti *Chronology* = Carlo Pedretti, *Leonardo: A Study in Chronology and Style* (University of California, 1973).

Pedretti *Commentary* = Carlo Pedretti, *The Literary Works of Leonardo da Vinci: Commentary* (Phaidon, 1977). A two-volume set of notes and comments on Leonardo's notebooks and J. P. Richter's compilation.

Reti *Unknown* = Ladislao Reti, ed., *The Unknown Leonardo* (McGraw-Hill, 1974).

Syson = Luke Syson, *Leonardo da Vinci, Painter at the Court of Milan* (National Gallery of London, 2011).

Vasari = Giorgio Vasari, *Lives of the Most Eminent Painters, Sculptors, and Architects* (first published in 1550, revised in 1568). Available in multiple print and online editions. Margot Pritzker provided me with an original copy of the corrected edition and some scholarship surrounding it.

Wells = Francis Wells, *The Heart of Leonardo* (Springer, 2013).

Zöllner = Frank Zöllner, *Leonardo da Vinci: The Complete Paintings and Drawings*, 2 vols. (Taschen, 2015). Vol. 1 for paintings, vol. 2 for drawings.

NOTES

INTRODUCTION

1 Codex Atl., 391r-a/1082r; Notebooks/J. P. Richter, 1340. The issue of the date of this letter is addressed in chapter 4. Only a draft that he made in his notebook still survives, not the final version he sent.

2 Kemp *Leonardo*, vii, 4; Kemp's theme in this and other works is the unifying patterns that lie below Leonardo's diverse endeavors.

3 Codex Urb., 133r-v; Leonardo Treatise/Rigaud, ch. 178; *Leonardo on Painting*, 15.

4 Author's interview with Steve Jobs, 2010.

5 Vasari, vol. 4.

6 Clark, 258; Kenneth Clark, *Civilization* (Harper & Row, 1969), 135.

7 Codex Atl., 222a/664a; Notebooks/J. P. Richter, 1448; Robert Krulwich, "Leonardo's To-Do List," *Krulwich Wonders*, NPR, November 18, 2011. Portinari was a Milanese merchant who had been to Flanders.

8 Notebooks/Irma Richter, 91.

9 Windsor, RCIN 919070; Notebooks/J. P. Richter, 819.

10 Paris Ms. F, 0; Notebooks/J. P. Richter, 1421.

11 Adam Gopnik, "Renaissance Man," *New Yorker*, January 17, 2005.

12 Codex Atl., 196b/586b; Notebooks/J. P. Richter, 490.

13 I would like to thank Margot Pritzker for an original of the second edition and some scholarship surrounding it. Vasari's book is available in many places online.

14 Vasari declared that his theme was "the rise of the arts to perfection [during the era of ancient Rome], their decline, and their restoration or rather renaissance."

15 Anonimo Gaddiano.

16 Depending on definitions and standards, different scholars put this number as low as twelve and as high as eighteen. According to Luke Syson, curator at the National Gallery of London and then the Metropolitan Museum of New York: "He started probably no more than 20 pictures in a career that lasted nearly half a century and only 15 surviving pictures are currently agreed to be entirely his, of which at least four are to some degree incomplete." A running discussion of the changing expert attributions and disputes over Leonardo autograph paintings can be found at "List of Works by Leonardo da Vinci," *Wikipedia*, https://en.wikipedia.org/wiki/List_of_works_by_Leonardo_da_Vinci.

17 Paris Ms. K, 2:1b; Notebooks/J. P. Richter, 1308.

1. CHILDHOOD

1 Alessandro Cecchi, "New Light on Leonardo's Florentine Patrons," in Bambach *Master Draftsman*, 123.·

2 Nicholl, 20; Bramly, 37. The sun set in Florence on that date at 6:40 p.m. The "hour of the night" was usually counted from the bell ringing after vespers.

3 Francesco Cianchi, *La Madre di Leonardo era una Schiava?* (Museo Ideale Leonardo da Vinci, 2008); Angelo Paratico, *Leonardo Da Vinci: A Chinese Scholar Lost in Renaissance Italy* (Lascar, 2015); Anna Zamejc, "Was Leonardo Da Vinci's Mother Azeri?," Radio Free Europe, November 25, 2009.

4 Martin Kemp and Giuseppe Pallanti, *Mona Lisa* (Oxford, 2017), 87. I am grateful to Prof. Kemp for sharing their findings and to Pallanti for discussing them with me.

5 Anonimo Gaddiano.

6 Author's communications with archival researcher Giuseppe Pallanti, 2017; Alberto Malvolti, "In Search of Malvolto Piero: Notes on the Witnesses of the Baptism of Leonardo da Vinci," *Erba d'Arno*, no. 141 (2015), 37. Kemp and Pallanti, *Mona Lisa*, do not believe that Leonardo was born in this cottage because it is listed on a tax document as being uninhabitable. However, that description may have been to minimize taxes on a dilapidated cottage that was, most of the time, left vacant.

7 Kemp and Pallanti, *Mona Lisa*, 85.

8 Leonardo, "Weimar Sheet," recto, Schloss-Museum, Weimar; Pedretti, *Commentary*, 2:110.

9 James Beck, "Ser Piero da Vinci and His Son Leonardo," *Notes in the History of Art* 5.1 (Fall 1985), 29.

10 Jacob Burckhardt, *The Civilization of the Renaissance in Italy* (Dover, 2010; originally published in English in 1878 and German in 1860), 51, 310.

11 Jane Fair Bestor, "Bastardy and Legitimacy in the Formation of a Regional State in Italy: The Estense Succession," *Comparative Studies in Society and History* 38.3 (July 1996), 549–85.

12 Thomas Kuehn, *Illegitimacy in Renaissance Florence* (University of Michigan, 2002), 80. See also Thomas Kuehn, "Reading between the Patrilines: Leon Battista Alberti's 'Della Famiglia' in Light of His Illegitimacy," *I Tatti Studies in the Italian Renaissance* 1 (1985), 161–87.

13 Kuehn, *Illegitimacy*, 7, ix.

14 Kuehn, *Illegitimacy*, 80. See Brown; Beck, "Ser Piero da Vinci and His Son Leonardo," 32.

15 Charles Nauert, *Humanism and the Culture of Renaissance Europe* (Cambridge, 2006), 5.

16 Codex Atl., 520r/191r-a; Notebooks/MacCurdy, 2:989.

17 Notebooks/J. P. Richter, 10–11; Notebooks/Irma Richter, 4; Codex Atl., 119v, 327v.

18 Paris Ms. E, 55r; Notebooks/Irma Richter, 8; Capra, *Science*, 161, 169.

19 Paris Ms. L, 58v; Notebooks/Irma Richter, 95.

20 Codex Atl., 66v/199b; Notebooks/J. P. Richter, 1363; Notebooks/Irma Richter, 269.

21 Original German title: *Eine Kindheiterinnerung des Leonardo da Vinci*. Translated by Abraham Brill in 1916 and available in multiple online editions.

22 *Sigmund Freud–Lou Andreas-Salomé Correspondence*, ed. Ernst Pfeiffer (Frankfurt: S. Fischer, 1966), 100.

23 Meyer Schapiro, "Leonardo and Freud," *Journal of the History of Ideas* 17.2 (April 1956), 147. For defenses of Freud and a discussion of the *Envy* drawing's connection to the kite, see Kurt Eissler, *Leonardo da Vinci: Psychoanalytic Notes on the Enigma* (In-

ternational Universities, 1961) and Alessandro Nova, "The Kite, Envy and a Memory of Leonardo da Vinci's Childhood," in Lars Jones, ed., *Coming About* (Harvard, 2001), 381.

24 Codex Atl., 358v; Notebooks/MacCurdy, 1:66; Sherwin Nuland, *Leonardo da Vinci* (Viking, 2000), 18.

25 Codex Arundel, 155r; Notebooks/J. P. Richter, 1339; Notebooks/Irma Richter, 247.

26 Codex Arundel, 156r; Notebooks/J. P. Richter, 1217; Notebooks/Irma Richter, 246.

27 Kay Etheridge, "Leonardo and the Whale," in Fiorani and Kim.

28 Codex Arundel, 155b; Notebooks/J. P. Richter, 1218, 1339n.

2. APPRENTICE

1 Nicholl, 161. Among those arguing that Leonardo began his apprenticeship around 1466 are Beck, "Ser Piero da Vinci and His Son Leonardo," 29; Brown, 76. Piero da Vinci's 1469 tax return lists Leonardo as one of his dependents in Vinci, but this was not a specific claim of residence; Piero himself did not live there, and it was not accepted by the tax authorities, who crossed out Leonardo's name.

2 Notebooks/Irma Richter, 227.

3 Nicholl, 47; Codex Urb., 12r; Notebooks/J. P. Richter, 494.

4 Codex Ash., 1:9a; Notebooks/Richter, 495. (Richter claims that the two quotes are not contradictory, for the latter refers to students, but I think they do express conflicting sentiments and that the latter is closer to Leonardo's reality.)

5 Kuehn, *Illegitimacy*, 52; Robert Genestal, *Histoire de la legitimation des enfants naturels en droit canonique* (Paris: Leroux, 1905), 100.

6 Stefano Ugo Baldassarri and Arielle Saiber, *Images of Quattrocento Florence* (Yale, 2000), 84.

7 John M. Najemym, *A History of Florence 1200–1575* (Wiley, 2008), 315; Eric Weiner, *Geography of Genius* (Simon and Schuster, 2016), 97.

8 Lester, 71; Gene Brucker, *Living on the Edge in Leonardo's Florence* (University of California, 2005), 115; Nicholl, 65.

9 Francesco Guicciardini, *Opere Inedite: The Position of Florence at the Death of Lorenzo*, (Bianchi, 1857), 3:82.

10 Paul Robert Walker, *The Feud That Sparked the Renaissance: How Brunelleschi and Ghiberti Changed the Art World* (William Morrow, 2002); Ross King, *Brunelleschi's Dome: The Story of the Great Cathedral of Florence* (Penguin, 2001).

11 Antonio Manetti, *The Life of Brunelleschi*, trans. Catherine Enggass (Pennsylvania State, 1970; originally published in the 1480s), 115; Martin Kemp, "Science, Nonscience and Nonsense: The Interpretation of Brunelleschi's Perspective," *Art History* 1:2, June 1978, 134.

12 Anthony Grafton, *Leon Battista Alberti: Master Builder of the Italian Renaissance* (Harvard, 2002), 27, 21, 139. See also Franco Borsi, *Leon Battista Alberti* (Harper & Row, 1975), 7–11.

13 Samuel Y. Edgerton, *The Mirror, the Window, and the Telescope: How Renaissance Linear Perspective Changed Our Vision of the Universe* (Cornell, 2009); Richard McLanathan, *Images of the Universe* (Doubleday, 1966), 72; Leon Rocco Sinisgalli, *Battista Alberti: On Painting. A New Translation and Critical Edition* (Cambridge, 2011), 3; Grafton, *Leon Battista Alberti*, 124. Sinisgalli argues that Alberti's Italian (Tuscan) vulgate version was written first and his Latin version came a year later.

14 Arasse, 38, 43. Arasse notes, "As the codex Trivulziano and the Manuscript B show, Leonardo transcribed almost half of Luigi Pulci's 'All Latin Words in order.' . . . The

list in codex Trivulziano follows almost to the letter pages 7–10 of *De Re Militari* by Valturio." The Codex Trivulziano dates from around 1487–90.

15 Carmen Bambach, "Leonardo: Left-Handed Draftsman and Writer," in Bambach *Master Draftsman*, 50.

16 Bambach, "Leonardo: Left-Handed Draftsman and Writer," 48; Thomas Micchelli, "The Most Beautiful Drawing in the World," *Hyperallergic*, November 2, 2013.

17 Geoffrey Schott, "Some Neurological Observations on Leonardo da Vinci's Handwriting," *Journal of Neurological Science* 42.3 (August 1979), 321.

18 Cecchi, "New Light on Leonardo's Florentine Patrons," 121; Bramly, 62.

19 Evelyn Welch, *Art and Society in Italy 1300–1500* (Oxford, 1997), 86; Richard David Serros, "The Verrocchio Workshop: Techniques, Production, and Influences," PhD dissertation, University of California, Santa Barbara, 1999.

20 J. K. Cadogan, "Verrocchio's Drawings Reconsidered," *Zeitschrift fikr Kunstgeschichte* 46.1 (1983), 367; Kemp *Marvellous*, 18.

21 There is a record of the Lords of Florence paying Lorenzo de' Medici 150 florins for the statue in 1476, but most experts now date its actual creation to between 1466 and 1468. See Nicholl, 74; Brown, 8; Andrew Butterfield, *The Sculptures of Andrea del Verrocchio* (Yale, 1997), 18.

22 Many scholars believe that Leonardo was the model for David. Martin Kemp is among those more skeptical. "Seems to be a romantic fantasy to me," he told me, "but I am austere about evidence! They exploit statements of naturalism, but their statues would not have been 'portraits' of their models."

23 John 20:27; Clark, 44.

24 Kim Williams, "Verrocchio's Tombslab for Cosimo de' Medici: Designing with a Mathematical Vocabulary," in *Nexus I* (Florence: Edizioni dell'Erba, 1996), 193.

25 Carlo Pedretti, *Leonardo: The Machines* (Giunti, 2000), 16; Bramly, 72.

26 Pedretti *Commentary*, 1:20; Pedretti, *The Machines*, 18; Paris Ms. G, 84v; Codex Atl., fols. 17v, 879r, 1103v; Sven Dupré, "Optic, Picture and Evidence: Leonardo's Drawings of Mirrors and Machinery," *Early Science and Medicine* 10.2 (2005), 211.

27 Bernard Berenson, *The Florentine Painters of the Renaissance* (Putnam, 1909), section 8.

28 Leonardo Treatise/Rigaud, 353; Codex Ash. 1:6b; Notebooks/J. P. Richter, 585.

29 Brown, 82; Carmen Bambach, "Leonardo and Drapery Studies on 'Tela sottilissima di lino,'" *Apollo*, January 1, 2004; Jean K. Cadogan, "Linen Drapery Studies by Verrocchio, Leonardo and Ghirlandaio," *Zeitschrift für Kunstgeschichte* 46 (1983), 27–62; Francesca Fiorani, "The Genealogy of Leonardo's Shadows in a Drapery Study," Harvard Center for Italian Renaissance Studies at Villa I Tatti, Series no. 29 (Harvard, 2013), 267–73, 840–41; Françoise Viatte, "The Early Drapery Studies," in Bambach *Master Draftsman*, 111; Keith Christiansen, "Leonardo's Drapery Studies," *Burlington Magazine* 132.1049 (1990), 572–73; Martin Clayton, review of Bambach *Master Draftsman* catalogue, *Master Drawings* 43.3 (Fall 2005), 376.

30 Codex Urb., 133r-v; Leonardo Treatise/Rigaud, ch. 178; *Leonardo on Painting*, 15.

31 Ernst Gombrich, *The Story of Art* (Phaidon, 1950), 187.

32 Alexander Nagel, "Leonardo and Sfumato," *Anthropology and Aesthetics* 24 (Autumn 1993), 7; Leonardo Treatise/Rigaud, ch. 181.

33 "Visit of Galeazzo Maria Sforza and Bona of Savoy," *Mediateca Medicea*, http://www.palazzo-medici.it/mediateca/en/Scheda_1471_-_Visita_di_Galeazzo_Maria_Sforza_e_di_Bona_di_Savoia; Nicholl, 92.

34 Niccolò Machiavelli, *History of Florence* (Dunne, 1901; originally written 1525), bk. 7, ch. 5.

35 Many scholars date the drawing to circa 1472, which I think is correct, but the British Museum, where it is located, dates it to 1475–80.

36 Martin Kemp and Juliana Barone, *I disegni di Leonardo da Vinci e della sua cerchia: Collezioni in Gran Bretagna* (Giunti, 2010), item 6. There are various versions and copies of reliefs done by Verrocchio's workshop. The *Alexander the Great* in the National Gallery of Washington, DC, can be seen at http://www.nga.gov/content/ngaweb/Collection /art-object-page.43513.html. For a discussion of these works, see Brown, 72–74, 194nn103 and 104. See also Butterfield, *The Sculptures of Andrea Del Verrocchio*, 231.

37 Gary Radke makes the argument that Leonardo was involved in sculpting the *Beheading of Saint John*. See Gary Radke, ed., *Leonardo da Vinci and the Art of Sculpture* (Yale, 2009); Carol Vogel, "Indications of a Hidden Leonardo," *New York Times*, April 23, 2009; Ann Landi, "Looking for Leonardo," *Smithsonian*, October 2009. For the dating of Leonardo's drawing and Verrocchio's sculptures, and who was influencing whom by the late 1470s, see Brown, 68–72.

38 Javier Berzal de Dios, "Perspective in the Public Sphere," Renaissance Society of America conference, Montreal, 2011; George Kernodle, *From Art to Theatre: Form and Convention in the Renaissance* (University of Chicago, 1944), 177; Thomas Pallen, *Vasari on Theatre* (Southern Illinois University, 1999), 21.

39 Codex Atl., 75r-v.

40 Paris Ms. B, 83r; Laurenza, 42; Pedretti, *The Machines*, 9; Kemp *Marvellous*, 104.

41 Nicholl, 98.

42 "Io morando dant sono chontento," he wrote. Serge Bramly is among those who assumes that "dant" is a contraction for "d'Antonio" (84). Carlo Pedretti, in his commentary on Richter's translations of Leonardo's notebooks, has a totally different interpretation, interpreting the words as "Jo Morando dant sono contento" ("I, Morando d'Antonio, agree as to") and suggesting that it was a draft for some agreement (*Commentary*, 314).

43 Uffizi, Cabinet of Prints and Drawings, no. 8P. His drawing of a helmeted warrior may have been earlier, circa 1472; see note 35 above.

44 Codex Urb., 5r; *Leonardo on Painting*, 32.

45 Ernst Gombrich, "Tobias and the Angel," in *Symbolic Images: Studies in the Art of the Renaissance* (Phaidon, 1972), 27; Trevor Hart, "Tobit in the Art of the Florentine Renaissance," in Mark Bredin, ed., *Studies in the Book of Tobit* (Bloomsbury, 2006), 72–89.

46 Brown, 47–52; Nicholl, 88.

47 The argument is made most forcefully by David Alan Brown (51). For a pushback, see Jill Dunkerton, "Leonardo in Verrocchio's Workshop: Re-examining the Technical Evidence," *National Gallery Technical Bulletin* 32 (2011), 4–31: "That he was capable of making observant studies of nature in his paintings as well as his sculpture is confirmed by the bright-eyed raptor that swoops down over the head of the Baptist. . . . It is important never to underestimate the painting skills of Verrocchio." Luke Syson, who once had *Tobias* in his care as a curator, told me he thought that Verrocchio was in fact very good with nature and may have painted the dog and fish.

48 Nicholl, 89.

49 Vasari, 1486. Verrocchio subsequently was commissioned to paint the altar in the Pistoia Cathedral, but he delegated most of the work to Lorenzo di Credi. Jill Dunkerton and Luke Syson, "In Search of Verrocchio the Painter," *National Gallery Technical Bulletin* 31 (2010), 4; Zöllner, 1:18; Brown, 151.

50 The evidence shows that Verrocchio started the painting in the 1460s, then put it aside. Work on it was resumed in the mid-1470s, with Leonardo reworking the landscape,

finishing the body of Christ (though the loincloth had already been done by Verrocchio), as well as painting his angel. Dunkerton, "Leonardo in Verrocchio's Workshop," 21; Brown, 138, 92; Marani, 65.

51 Codex Ash., 1:5b; Notebooks/J. P. Richter, 595.

52 Clark, 51.

53 Codex Ash., 1:21a; Notebooks/J. P. Richter 236; Janis Bell, "Sfumato and Acuity Perspective," in Claire Farago, ed., *Leonardo da Vinci and the Ethics of Style* (Manchester Univ., 2008), ch. 6.

54 Codex Arundel, 169a; Notebooks/J. P. Richter, 305.

55 See, for example, Cecil Gould, *Leonardo* (Weidenfeld & Nicolson, 1975), 24. For a listing of differing opinions, see Brown, 195nn6, 7, and 8.

56 Zöllner, 1:34; Brown, 64; Marani, 61.

57 Brown, 88. See also Leonardo's "Study of a Lily" drawing, Windsor, RCIN 912418.

58 Matt Ancell, "Leonardo's *Annunciation* in Perspective," in Fiorani and Kim; Lyle Massey, *Picturing Space, Displacing Bodies* (Pennsylvania State, 2007), 42–44.

59 Francesca Fiorani, "The Shadows of Leonardo's *Annunciation* and Their Lost Legacy," in Roy Eriksen and Magne Malmanger, eds., *Imitation, Representation and Printing in the Italian Renaissance* (Pisa: Fabrizio Serra, 2009), 119; Francesca Fiorani, "The Colors of Leonardo's Shadows," *Leonardo* 41.3 (2008), 271.

60 Leonardo Treatise/Rigaud, section 262.

61 Jane Long, "Leonardo's Virgin of the Annunciation," in Fiorani and Kim.

62 Brown, 122.

63 Codex Ash., 1:7a; Notebooks/J. P. Richter, 367; Leonardo Treatise/Rigaud, 34.

64 Brown, 150.

65 Jennifer Fletcher, "Bernardo Bembo and Leonardo's Portrait of Ginevra de' Benci," *Burlington Magazine*, no. 1041 (1989), 811; Mary Garrard, "Who Was Ginevra de' Benci? Leonardo's Portrait and Its Sitter Recontextualized," *Artibus et Historiae* 27.53 (2006), 23; John Walker, "Ginevra de' Benci," in *Report and Studies in the History of Art* (Washington National Gallery, 1967), 1:32; David Alan Brown, ed., *Virtue and Beauty* (Princeton, 2003); Brown, 101–21; Marani, 38–48.

66 Leonardo, "A Study of a Woman's Hands," Windsor, RCIN 912558; Butterfield, *The Sculptures of Andrea Del Verrocchio*, 90.

67 Andrea Kirsh and Rustin Levenson, *Seeing through Paintings: Physical Examination in Art Historical Studies* (Yale, 2002), 135; Leonardo da Vinci, *Ginevra de' Benci*, oil on panel, National Gallery, Washington, DC, https://www.nga.gov/kids/ginevra.htm.

68 Notebooks/J. P. Richter, 132, 135; Paris Ms. A, 113v; Codex Ash., 1:3a.

69 Brown, 104.

3. ON HIS OWN

1 Louis Crompton, *Homosexuality and Civilization* (Harvard, 2006), 265; Payne, 747.

2 Notebooks/Irma Richter, 271.

3 Notebooks/J. P. Richter, 1383. Jean Paul Richter surmises in brackets that Leonardo was going to write "brother," but Richter is being polite. There is no word at the end of the sentence.

4 Nicholl, 131.

5 Anonimo Gaddiano; Notebooks/Irma Richter, 258; Leonardo, "Sketches and Figures for a Last Supper and a Hydrometer," Louvre Inv. 2258r.; Zöllner, item 130, 2:335; Bambach *Master Draftsman*, 325.

6 Anthony Cummings, *The Maecenas and the Madrigalist* (American Philosophical So-

ciety, 2004), 86; Donald Sanders, *Music at the Gonzaga Court in Mantua* (Lexington, 2012), 25.

7 Pedretti *Commentary*, 112; Windsor, RCIN 919009r; Keele *Elements*, 350.

8 Michael Rocke, *Forbidden Friendships: Homosexuality and Male Culture in Renaissance Florence* (Oxford, 1998), 4.

9 Paris Ms. H, 1:12a; Notebooks/J. P. Richter, 1192.

10 Clark, 107.

11 Windsor, RCIN 919030r; Kenneth Keele and Carlo Pedretti, *Corpus of the Anatomical Studies by Leonardo da Vinci: The Queen's Collection at Windsor Castle* (Johnson, 1978), 71v–72r; Keele *Elements*, 350; Notebooks/MacCurdy, section 120.

12 Patricia Simons, "Women in Frames: The Gaze, the Eye, the Profile in Renaissance Portraiture," *History Workshop* 25 (Spring, 1988), 4.

13 Robert Kiely, *Blessed and Beautiful: Picturing the Saints* (Yale, 2010), 11; James Saslow, *Pictures and Passions: A History of Homosexuality in the Visual Arts* (Viking, 1999), 99.

14 *Saint Sebastian Tied to a Tree*, Hamburger Kunsthalle, inv. 21489; Bambach *Master Draftsman*, 342.

15 Scott Reyburn, "An Artistic Discovery Makes a Curator's Heart Pound," *New York Times*, December 11, 2016.

16 Syson, 16. For a more tentative opinion about the subject, see Bambach *Master Draftsman*, 323.

17 Clark, 80.

18 Beck, "Ser Piero da Vinci and His Son Leonardo," 29.

19 Nicholl, 169.

20 Zöllner, 1:60.

21 Leonardo Treatise/Rigaud, 35; Codex Urb., 32v; *Leonardo on Painting*, 200.

22 Leonardo Treatise/Rigaud, 93; Codex Urb., 33v; *Leonardo on Painting*, 36.

23 Michael Kwakkelstein, "Did Leonardo Always Practice What He Preached?," in S. U. Baldassarri, ed., *Proxima Studia* (Fabrizio Serra Editore, 2011), 107; Michael Kwakkelstein, "Leonardo da Vinci's Recurrent Use of Patterns of Individual Limbs, Stock Poses and Facial Stereotypes," in Ingrid Ciulisova, ed., *Artistic Innovations and Cultural Zones* (Peter Lang, 2014), 45.

24 Carmen Bambach, "Figure Studies for the *Adoration of the Magi*," in Bambach *Master Draftsman*, 320; Bulent Atalay and Keith Wamsley, *Leonardo's Universe* (National Geographic, 2009), 85.

25 Clark, 74; Richard Turner, *Inventing Leonardo* (University of California, 1992), 27; Clark, 124.

26 Francesca Fiorani, "Why Did Leonardo Not Finish the *Adoration of the Magi*?," in Moffatt and Taglialagamba, 137; Zöllner, 1:22–35.

27 Melinda Henneberger, "The Leonardo Cover-Up," *New York Times*, April 21, 2002; "Scientific Analysis of the *Adoration of the Magi*," Museo Galileo, http://brunelleschi.imss.fi.it/menteleonardo/emdl.asp?c=13419&k=1470&rif=14071&xsl=1.

28 Alexandra Korey interview with Cecilia Frosinini, art historian on the Uffizi project, Art Trav, http://www.arttrav.com/art-history-tools/leonardo-da-vinci-adoration/.

29 *Leonardo on Painting*, 222; Fiorani, "Why Did Leonardo Not Finish the *Adoration of the Magi*?"

30 Larry Feinberg, *The Young Leonardo* (Santa Barbara Museum, 2011), 177, and Zöllner, 1:58, agree that the figure behind Mary is Joseph. Kemp *Marvellous*, 46, and Nicholl, 171, are among those who say Joseph is hard to identify in the final version. Nicholl wrote, "The father is unidentified, submerged into the periphery. One might resist

540   *Notes for pages 81–92*

a psychoanalytical interpretation of this, but it is a motif too recurrent to ignore—
Leonardo always excises Joseph from the Holy Family."

31   *Leonardo on Painting*, 220.
32   Bambach *Master Draftsman*, 54.
33   Codex Atl., 847r.
34   Fiorani, "Why Did Leonardo Not Finish the *Adoration of the Magi*?," 22. See also
      Francesca Fiorani and Alessandro Nova, eds., *Leonardo da Vinci and Optics: Theory and
      Pictorial Practice* (Marsilio Editore, 2013), 265.
35   Carlo Pedretti, "The Pointing Lady," *Burlington Magazine*, no. 795 (June 1969), 338.
36   Some scholars have suggested a later date, including the late 1480s, based on the
      similarity of the pose to the *Virgin of the Rocks*, the use of walnut panel, and the resem-
      blance of the church to sketches he made while in Milan. I think (following Juliana
      Barone, Martin Clayton, Frank Zöllner, and others) that he made the drawing around
      1480 and then modified it over the years, including while in Milan and then after he
      did his anatomy studies of 1510. See Syson (with essay by Scott Nethersole), 139; Ju-
      liana Barone, "Review of *Leonardo da Vinci, Painter at the Court of Milan*," *Renaissance
      Studies* 27.5 (2013), 28; Luke Syson and Rachel Billinge, "Leonardo da Vinci's Use of
      Underdrawing in the 'Virgin of the Rocks' in the National Gallery and 'St Jerome' in
      the Vatican," *Burlington Magazine*, no. 147 (2005), 450.
37   Paris Ms. L, 79r; Notebooks/J. P. Richter, 488; Notebooks/MacCurdy, 184.
38   Windsor, RCIN 919003.
39   Keele and Roberts, 28.
40   Martin Clayton, "Leonardo's Anatomical Drawings and His Artistic Practice," lecture,
      September 18, 2015, https://www.youtube.com/watch?v=KLwnN2g2Mqg.
41   Leonardo da Vinci, *Libro di Pittura*, ed. Carlo Vecce and Carlo Pedretti (Giunti, 1995),
      285b, 286a; Bambach *Master Draftsman*, 328.
42   Frank Zöllner, "The Motions of the Mind in Renaissance Portraits: The Spiritual
      Dimension of Portraiture," *Zeitschrift für Kunstgeschichte* 68 (2005), 23–40; Pliny the
      Elder, *Historia Naturalis*, section 35.
43   Leon Battista Alberti, *On Painting*, trans. John Spencer (Yale, 1966; originally written
      1435), 77; Paul Barolsky, "Leonardo's Epiphany," *Notes in the History of Art* 11.1 (Fall
      1991), 18.
44   Codex Urb., 60v; Pietro Marani, "Movements of the Soul," in Marani and Fiorio, 223;
      Pedretti *Commentary*, 2:263, 1:219; Paris Ms. A, 100; *Leonardo on Painting*, 144.
45   Codex Urb., 110r; *Leonardo on Painting*, 144.
46   Codex Atl., 42v; Kemp *Marvellous*, 66.
47   Kemp *Marvellous*, 67.
48   Codex Atl., 252r; Notebooks/MacCurdy, 65.
49   Nicholl, 154. The friend is Antonio Cammelli, known as "Il Pistoiese," a popular poet
      of the day.
50   Windsor, RCIN 912349; Notebooks/J. P. Richter, 1547; Notebooks/MacCurdy, 86.
51   Windsor, RCIN 912349; Dante, *Inferno* XXIV, trans. Dorothy L. Sayers (Penguin
      Classics, 1949), 46–51.
52   Vasari, "Pietro Perugino," in *Lives of the Most Eminent Painters*.

4. MILAN

1   Anonimo Gaddiano; Notebooks/Irma Richter, 258.
2   Felix Gilbert, "Bernardo Rucellai and the Orti Oricellari," *Journal of the Warburg and
      Courtauld Institutes* 12 (1949), 101.

3　Codex Atl., 888r; Kemp *Marvellous*, 22. Because the list includes what seems to be a drawing of the head of the Duke of Milan, I think he wrote the list in his notebook after he arrived in Milan.

4　David Mateer, *Courts, Patrons, and Poets* (Yale, 2000), 26.

5　For the letter and discussions of its probable date, see Notebooks/J. P. Richter, 1340; Kemp *Marvellous*, 57; Nicholl, 180; Kemp *Leonardo*, 442; Bramly, 174; Payne, 1349; Matt Landrus, *Leonardo da Vinci's Giant Crossbow* (Springer, 2010), 21; Richard Schofield, "Leonardo's Milanese Architecture," *Journal of Leonardo Studies* 4 (1991); Hannah Brooks-Motl, "Inventing Leonardo, Again," *New Republic*, May 2, 2012.

6　Codex Atl., 382a/1182a; Notebooks/J. P. Richter, 1340.

7　Ladislao Reti and Bern Dibner, *Leonardo da Vinci, Technologist* (Burndy, 1969); Bertrand Gille, *The Renaissance Engineers* (MIT, 1966).

8　Codex Atl., 139r/49v-b; Zöllner, 2:622.

9　Codex Atl., 89r/32v-a, 1084r/391v-a; Zöllner, 2:622.

10　Roger Bacon, *Letter on the Secret Workings of Art and Nature and on the Vanity of Magic*, ch. 4; Domenico Laurenza, *Leonardo on Flight* (Giunti, 2004), 24.

11　Roberto Valturio, *On the Military Arts*, fol. 146v–147r, Bodleian Library, Oxford University, http://bodley30.bodley.ox.ac.uk:8180/luna/servlet/detail/ODLodl~1~1~36082~121456?printerFriendly=1.

12　Zöllner, 2:636.

13　Biblioteca Reale, Turin, inv. 15583r; Zöllner, 2:638.

14　Codex Atl., 149b-r/53v-b; Zöllner, 2:632.

15　Landrus, *Leonardo da Vinci's Giant Crossbow*, 5 and passim; Matthew Landrus, "The Proportional Consistency and Geometry of Leonardo's Giant Crossbow," *Leonardo* 41.1 (2008), 56; Kemp *Leonardo*, 48.

16　Dennis Simms, "Archimedes' Weapons of War and Leonardo," *British Journal for the History of Science* 21.2 (June 1988), 195.

17　Codex Atl., 157r/56v-a.

18　Vernard Foley, "Leonardo da Vinci and the Invention of the Wheellock," *Scientific American*, January 1998; Vernard Foley et al., "Leonardo, the Wheel Lock, and the Milling Process," *Technology and Culture* 24.3 (July 1983), 399. Giulio Tedesco came to live with Leonardo in March 1493, and he fixed two locks in Leonardo's studio in September 1494. Codex Forster 2:88v; Paris Ms. H, 106v; Notebooks/J. P. Richter, 1459, 1460, 1462; *Leonardo on Painting*, 266–67.

19　Pascal Brioist, *Leonard de Vinci, l'homme de Guerre* (Alma, 2013).

20　Paris Ms. I, 32a, 34a; Codex Atl., 22r; Notebooks/J. P. Richter, 1017–18; Notebooks/MacCurdy, 1042.

21　Codex Atl., 64b/197b; Notebooks/J. P. Richter, 1203; Paris Ms. B, 15v, 16r, 36r.

22　Paris Ms. B, 15v, 37v; Notebooks/J. P. Richter, 741, 746, 742; Richard Schofield, "Reality and Utopia in Leonardo's Thinking about Architecture," in Marani and Fiorio, 325; Paolo Galluzzi, ed., *Leonardo Da Vinci: Engineer and Architect* (Montreal Museum, 1987), 258.

5. LEONARDO'S NOTEBOOKS

1　Codex Ash., 1:8a, 2:27; Notebooks/J. P. Richter, 571; Notebooks/Irma Richter, 208.

2　Notebooks/Irma Richter, 301.

3　Lester, 120. See also Clark, 258; Charles Nicholl, *Traces Remain* (Penguin, 2012), 135.

4　The collection of writings on art compiled by his pupil Francesco Melzi has one thousand passages; only one-quarter of these are in Leonardo notebook pages known to exist today, so we can roughly estimate that at least three-quarters of his manuscripts have been lost. Martin Kemp, *Leonardo da Vinci: Experience, Experiment, and Design*, catalogue for Victoria and Albert Collection (2006), 2.

5 Pedretti *Commentary*.

6 Clark, 110.

7 Windsor, RCIN 912283; Carlo Pedretti, *Studi di Natura* (Giunti Barbera, 1982), 24; Kenneth Clark and Carlo Pedretti, *The Drawings of Leonardo da Vinci in the Collection of Her Majesty the Queen at Windsor Castle* (Phaidon, 1968), introduction; Kemp *Marvellous*, 3–19.

8 Francis Ames-Lewis, "Leonardo's Botanical Drawings," *Achademia Leonardo da Vinci* 10 (1997), 117.

6. COURT ENTERTAINER

1 The primary description of *The Feast of Paradise* comes from a report by Jacopo Trotti, the ambassador of Ferrara to Milan: "The Party of Leonardo da Vinci's *Paradise* and Bernardo Bellincore (January 13, 1490)," *Journal of the Historical Society of Lombard*, quarta series, 1 (1904), 75–89; Bernardo Bellincioni, "Chiamata Paradiso che fece Il Signor Ludovico," ACNR, http://www.nuovaricerca.org/leonardo_inf_e_par/BELLINCIONI.pdf; Kate Steinitz, "Leonardo Architetto Teatrale e Organizzatore di Feste," *Lettura Vinciana* 9 (April 15, 1969); Arasse, 227; Bramly, 221; Kemp *Marvellous*, 137, 152; Nicholl, 259.

2 Codex Arundel, 250a; Arasse, 235; Notebooks/J. P. Richter, 674.

3 Codex Atl., 996v; Leonardo da Vinci, "Design for a Stage Setting," Metropolitan Museum of New York, Accession #17.142.2v, with notes by Carmen Bambach; Pedretti *Commentary*, 1:402; Carlo Vecce, "The Sculptor Says," in Moffatt and Taglialagamba, 229; Marie Herzfeld, *La Rappresentazione della "Danai" Organizzata da Leonardo* (Raccolta Vinciana XI, 1920), 226–28.

4 Codex Arundel, 231v, 224r; Notebooks/J. P. Richter, 678; Kemp *Marvellous*, 154. There is no consensus on the dating of the Pluto's Paradise drawings.

5 Codex Atl., 228b/687b; Notebooks/J. P. Richter, 703.

6 Vasari; Anonimo Gaddiano; Emanuel Winternitz, *Leonardo da Vinci as a Musician* (Yale, 1982), 39; Emanuel Winternitz, "Musical Instruments in the Madrid Notebooks of Leonardo da Vinci," *Metropolitan Museum Journal* 2 (1969), 115; Emanuel Winternitz, "Leonardo and Music," in Reti *Unknown*, 110.

7 Codex Ash., 1:Cr; Winternitz, *Leonardo da Vinci as a Musician*, 40; Nicholl, 158, 178.

8 Codex Madrid, 2:folio 75; Winternitz, "Musical Instruments in the Madrid Notebooks of Leonardo da Vinci," 115; Winternitz, "Leonardo and Music," 110; Michael Eisenberg, "Sonic Mapping in Leonardo's *Disegni*," in Fiorani and Kim.

9 Codex Arundel, 175r.

10 Codex Atl., 118r.

11 Codex Atl., 355r.

12 Codex Atl., 34r-b, 213v-a, 218r-c; Paris Ms. H, 28r, 28v, 45v, 46r, 104v; Paris Ms. B, 50v; Codex Madrid, 2:76r.

13 Stawomir Zubrzycki, *Viola Organista* website, 2002, http://www.violaorganista.com.

14 Winternitz, "Leonardo and Music," 112.

15 Notebooks/J. P. Richter, ch. 10 introduction; Zöllner, 2:94, 2:492; Christ Church, Oxford, inv. JBS 18r.

16 Christ Church, Oxford; Notebooks/J. P. Richter, 677.

17 Leonardo, "Two Allegories of Envy," 1490–94, Christ Church, Oxford, inv. JBS 17r; Zöllner, catalogue #394, 2:494.

18 Leonardo, "The Unmasking of Envy," c. 1494, Musee Bonnat, Bayonne; *Leonardo on Painting*, 241.

19 Windsor, RCIN 912490, 912491, 912492, 912493, and others at Windsor; Carmen Bambach, "Laughing Man with Busy Hair," "Old Woman with Beetling Brow," Snub-Nosed Old Man," "Old Woman with Horned Dress," "Four Fragments with Grotesque Heads," "Old Man Standing to the Right," "Head of an Old Man or Woman in Profile," all in Bambach *Master Draftsman*, 451–65, and for copies, 678–722; Johannes Nathan, "Profile Studies, Character Heads, and Grotesques," in Zöllner, 2:366. See also Clark and Pedretti, *The Drawings of Leonardo da Vinci in the Collection of Her Majesty the Queen at Windsor Castle*, 84; Katherine Roosevelt Reeve Losee, "Satire and Medicine in Renaissance Florence: Leonardo da Vinci's Grotesque Drawings," Master's thesis, American University, 2015; Ernst Gombrich, "Leonardo da Vinci's Method of Analysis and Permutation: The Grotesque Heads," in *The Heritage of Apelles* (Cornell, 1976), 57–75; Michael Kwakkelstein, *Leonardo as a Physiognomist: Theory and Drawing Practice* (Primavera, 1994), 55; Michael Kwakkelstein, "Leonardo da Vinci's Grotesque Heads and the Breaking of the Physiognomic Mould," *Journal of the Warburg and Courtauld Institutes* 54 (1991), 135; Varena Forcione, "Leonardo's Grotesques: Originals and Copies," in Bambach *Master Draftsman*, 203.

20 Codex Urb., 13; Notebooks/Irma Richter, 184; Jonathan Jones, "The Marvellous Ugly Mugs," *The Guardian*, December 4, 2002; Clayton, 11; Turner, *Inventing Leonardo*, 158.

21 Notebooks/Irma Richter, 286.

22 Codex Ash., 1:8a; Notebooks/J. P. Richter, 571.

23 Carmen Bambach, introduction to Bambach *Master Draftsman*, 12; King.

24 Aristotle, *Prior Analytics*, 2:27.

25 Codex Urb., 109v; *Leonardo on Painting*, 147.

26 Codex Urb., 108v–109r; Notebooks/J. P. Richter, 571–72; Notebooks/Irma Richter, 208.

27 These interpretations reflect those in Kemp *Marvellous*, 146; Nicholl, 263; Clayton, 96; Windsor, RCIN 912495.

28 Codex Atl., 1033r/370r-a.

29 Filomena Calabrese, "Leonardo's Literary Writings: History, Genre, Philosophy," PhD dissertation, University of Toronto, 2011.

30 Notebooks/J. P. Richter, 1265, 1229.

31 Notebooks/J. P. Richter, 1237, 1239, 1234, 1241.

32 Notebooks/J. P. Richter, 1297–312.

33 Notebooks/J. P. Richter, 649.

34 Capra *Science*, 26.

35 Nicholl, 219.

36 Codex Atl., 265r, 852r; Notebooks/Irma Richter, 253; Kemp *Marvellous*, 145.

37 Some commentators, including Edward MacCurdy (Notebooks/MacCurdy, 388), speculate that Leonardo may have actually gone to Syria in the 1480s, but there is no evidence of this, and it seems highly unlikely.

38 Codex Atl., 393v/145v-b; Notebooks/Irma Richter, 252; Notebooks/J. P. Richter, 1336.

39 Codex Atl., 96v/311r; Notebooks/MacCurdy, 265; Notebooks/J. P. Richter, 1354; Nicholl, 217.

7. PERSONAL LIFE

1 Paolo Giovio, "A Life of Leonardo," c. 1527, in Notebooks/J. P. Richter, revised edition of 1939, 1:2.
2 Codex Atl., 119v-a/327v; Notebooks/J. P. Richter, 10.
3 Lester, 2014; Nicholl, 43.
4 Notebooks/J. P. Richter, 844; Notebooks/MacCurdy, 84.
5 Paris Ms. H, 60r; Notebooks/MacCurdy, 130.
6 Paris Ms. C, 15b; Notebooks/J. P. Richter, 1458.
7 Leonardo first refers to him as Salai in 1494; Paris Ms. H, 2:16v. The term is usually translated as "little devil," but it has the connotation of someone a bit unclean as well as devilish, like a little rascal or scamp. It derives from a Tuscan word meaning "limb of the devil." His name is sometimes written Salaì, with an accent creating a third syllable, thus making the pronunciation sah-lie-yee. The name comes from a demon in Luigi Pulci's epic poem *Il Morgante*, a work that Leonardo owned; in the poem, the name is given as Salai, without an accent on the *i*.
8 Pedretti, *Chronology*, 141.
9 Paris Ms. C, 15b; Notebooks/J. P. Richter, 1458; Notebooks/Irma Richter, 291.
10 Codex Atl., 663v/244r; Pedretti *Chronology*, 64; Notebooks/Irma Richter, 290, 291; Bramly, 223, 228; Nicholl, 276.
11 John Garton, "Leonardo's Early Grotesque Head of 1478," in Fiorani and Kim; Notebooks/Irma Richter, 289; *Leonardo on Painting*, 220; Codex Urb., 61r-v; Jens Thus, *The Florentine Years of Leonardo and Verrocchio* (Jenkins, 1913).
12 Clark, 121.
13 Uffizi, Florence, inv. 446E; Notebooks/J. P. Richter, 1383.
14 Pedretti *Chronology*, 140.
15 Windsor, RCIN 912557, 912554, 912594, 912596.
16 Leonardo, "Allegorical Drawing of Pleasure and Pain," c. 1480, Christ Church Picture Gallery, Oxford; Notebooks/J. P. Richter, 676; Nicholl, 204.

8. *VITRUVIAN MAN*

1 Frances Ferguson, "Leonardo da Vinci and the Tiburio of the Milan Cathedral," in Claire Farago, ed., *An Overview of Leonardo's Career and Projects until c. 1500* (Taylor & Francis, 1999), 389; Richard Schofield, "Amadeo, Bramante, and Leonardo and the Tiburio of Milan Cathedral," *Journal of Leonardo Studies* 2 (1989), 68.
2 Ludwig Heydenreich, "Leonardo and Bramante: Genius in Architecture," in O'Malley, 125; King, 129; Notebooks/J. P. Richter, 1427; Carlo Pedretti, "Newly Discovered Evidence of Leonardo's Association with Bramante," *Journal of the Society of Architectural Historians* 32 (1973), 224. Nicholl, 309, discusses alternate attributions for the poems.
3 Bramante's piece has been given many dates, but the authoritative Milan exhibit of 2015 dated it to 1486–87 (Milan catalogue, 423).
4 Codex Atl., 270r/730r; Notebooks/Irma Richter, 282; Nicholl, 223.
5 Codex Arundel, 158a; Notebooks/J. P. Richter, 773.
6 Paris Ms. B, 27r; Notebooks/J. P. Richter, 788; Nicholl, 222.
7 Codex Atl., 310r-b/850r; Heydenreich, "Leonardo and Bramante," 139; Schofield, "Amadeo, Bramante, and Leonardo and the Tiburio of Milan Cathedral," 68; Schofield, "Leonardo's Milanese Architecture," 111; Jean Guillaume, "Léonard et Bramante L'emploi des ordres à Milan à la fin du XV e siècle," *Arte Lombarda* 86–87 (1988), 101; Carlo Pedretti, *Leonardo Architect* (Rizzoli, 1985), 42; Francesco P. Di Teodoro,

"Leonardo da Vinci: The Proportions of the Drawings of Sacred Buildings in Ms. B," *Architectural Histories* 3.1 (2015), 1.

8 Allen Weller, *Francesco di Giorgio* (University of Chicago, 1943), 366; Pietro Marani, "Leonardo, Francesco di Giorgio e il tiburio del Duomo di Milano," *Arte Lombarda* 62.2 (1982), 81; Pari Rahi, *Ars et Ingenium: The Embodiment of Imagination in Francesco di Giorgio Martini's Drawings* (Routledge, 2015), 45.

9 Teodoro, "Leonardo da Vinci: The Proportions of the Drawings of Sacred Buildings in Ms. B," 9.

10 Lester, 2, 207; Heydenreich, "Leonardo and Bramante," 135.

11 Ludwig Heydenreich and Paul Davies, *Architecture in Italy, 1400–1500* (Yale, 1974), 110.

12 Lester, 11.

13 Indra Kagis McEwen, *Vitruvius: Writing the Body of Architecture* (MIT Press, 2004); Vitruvius, *The Ten Books on Architecture*, trans. Morris Hicky Morgan (Harvard, 1914).

14 Paris Ms. F, 0; Notebooks/J. P. Richter, 1471.

15 Elizabeth Mays Merrill, "The Trattato as Textbook," *Architectural Histories* 1 (2013); Lester, 290; Keele *Elements*, 22; Kemp *Leonardo*, 115; Feinberg, *The Young Leonardo*, 696; Walter Kruft, *History of Architectural Theory* (Princeton, 1994), 57.

16 Paris Ms. A, 55v; Notebooks/J. P. Richter, 929.

17 Vitruvius, *Ten Books on Architecture*, bk. 3, para. 1; Morgan translation, 96.

18 Vitruvius, *Ten Books on Architecture*, bk. 3, para. 3; Morgan translation, 97.

19 Lester, 201.

20 Paris Ms. C, 15b; Notebooks/J. P. Richter, 1458.

21 Paris Ms. K, 3:29b; Notebooks/J. P. Richter, 1501.

22 Claudio Sgarbi, "A Newly Discovered Corpus of Vitruvian Images," *Anthropology and Aesthetics*, no. 23 (Spring 1993), 31–51; Claudio Sgarbi, "Il Vitruvio Ferrarese, alcuni dettagli quasi invisibili e un autore—Giacomo Andrea da Ferrara," in Pierre Gros, ed., *Giovanni Giocondo* (Marsilio, 2014), 121; Claudio Sgarbi, "All'origine dell'Uomo Ideale di Leonardo," *Disegnarecon*, no. 9 (June 2012), 177; Richard Schofield, "Notes on Leonardo and Vitruvius," in Moffatt and Taglialagamba, 129; Toby Lester, "The Other Vitruvian Man?," *Smithsonian*, February 2012.

23 Lester, 208.

24 Codex Urb., 157r; *Leonardo da Vinci on Painting*, ed. Carlo Pedretti (University of California, 1964), 35.

25 Toby Lester interview, *Talk of the Nation*, NPR, March 8, 2012; Lester, xii, 214.

26 Edward MacCurdy, *The Mind of Leonardo da Vinci* (Dodd, Mead, 1928), 35.

9. THE HORSE MONUMENT

1 Notebooks/Irma Richter, 286; Kemp *Marvellous*, 191.

2 Codex Atl., 328b/983b; Notebooks/J. P. Richter, 1345.

3 Codex Ash, 1:29a; Notebooks/J. P. Richter, 512.

4 Leonardo da Vinci, "The Leg Muscles and Bones of Man and Horse," Windsor, RCIN 912625.

5 Codex Atl., 96v; Codex Triv., 21; Paris Ms. B, 38v.

6 Windsor, RCIN 912285 to RCIN 91327.

7 Evelyn Welch, *Art and Authority in Renaissance Milan* (Yale, 1995), 201; Andrea Gamberini, ed., *Companion to Late Medieval and Early Modern Milan* (Brill, 2014), 186.

8 Paris Ms. C, 15v; Notebooks/J. P. Richter, 720.

9 Codex Atl., 399r; Kemp *Marvellous*, 194.

10   Bramly, 232.

11   Kemp *Marvellous*, 194.

12   Codex Madrid, 2:157v.

13   Windsor, RCIN 912349.

14   Notebooks/J. P. Richter, 711.

15   Codex Madrid, 2:143, 149, 157; Notebooks/J. P. Richter, 710–11; Windsor, RCIN 912349; Bramly, 234; Kemp *Marvellous*, 194.

16   Codex Atl., 914ar/335v; Notebooks/J. P. Richter, 723.

17   Ercole d'Este to Giovanni Valla, September 19, 1501.

10. SCIENTIST

1   Codex Atl., 119v/327v; Notebooks/J. P. Richter, 10–11; Notebooks/Irma Richter, 4. In his commentaries, Carlo Pedretti (1:110) dates this page to circa 1490.

2   Codex Atl., 196b/596b; Notebooks/J. P. Richter, 490.

3   Brian Richardson, *Printing, Writers and Readers in Renaissance Italy* (Cambridge, 1999), 3; Lotte Hellinga, "The Introduction of Printing in Italy," unpublished ms., University of Manchester Library, undated.

4   A fuller description can be found in Nicholl, 209, and Kemp *Marvellous*, 240.

5   Notebooks/J. P. Richter, 1488, 1501, 1452, 1496, 1448. Vitolone is a text on optics by a Polish scientist.

6   Paris Ms. E, 55r; Notebooks/Irma Richter, 8; James Ackerman, "Science and Art in the Work of Leonardo," in O'Malley, 205.

7   Paris Ms. A, 47r; Capra *Science*, 156, 162.

8   For more, see Leopold Infeld, "Leonardo Da Vinci and the Fundamental Laws of Science," *Science & Society* 17.1 (Winter 1953), 26–41.

9   Codex Atl., 730r; *Leonardo on Painting*, 256.

10   Codex Atl., 200a/594a; Notebooks/J. P. Richter, 13.

11   Paris Ms. G, 8a; Codex Urb., 39v; Notebooks/J. P. Richter, 19; Pedretti *Commentary*, 114.

12   Capra *Learning*, 5.

13   James S. Ackerman, "Leonardo Da Vinci: Art in Science," *Daedalus* 127.1 (Winter 1998), 207.

14   Gopnik, "Renaissance Man."

15   Paris Ms. I, 12b; Notebooks/J. P. Richter, 394.

16   Ryoko Minamino and Masakai Tateno, "Tree Branching: Leonardo da Vinci's Rule versus Biomechanical Models," *PLoS One* 9.4 (April, 2014).

17   Codex Atl., 126r-a; Winternitz, "Leonardo and Music," 116.

18   Paris Ms. E, 54r; Capra *Learning*, 277.

19   Windsor, RCIN 919059; Notebooks/J. P. Richter, 805.

20   Windsor, RCIN 919070; Notebooks/J. P. Richter, 818–19.

21   Codex Atl., 124a; Notebooks/J. P. Richter, 246.

22   Paris Ms. H, 1a; Notebooks/J. P. Richter, 232.

23   Codex Ash., 1:7b; Notebooks/J. P. Richter, 491.

24   Codex Ash., 1:9a; Notebooks/J. P. Richter, 507.

25   Codex Atl., 377v/1051v; Notebooks/Irma Richter, 98; Stefan Klein, *Leonardo's Legacy* (Da Capo, 2010), 26.

26   Codex Arundel, 176r.

27   Paris Ms. B, 1:176r, 131r; Codex Triv., 34v, 49v, Codex Arundel, 190v; Notebooks/Irma Richter, 62–63; Nuland, *Leonardo da Vinci*, 47; Keele *Elements*, 106.

11. BIRDS AND FLIGHT

1   Codex Atl. 45r/124r, 178a/536a; Notebooks/J. P. Richter, 374.
2   Laurenza, 10.
3   Laurenza, 8–10; Pallen, *Vasari on Theater*, 15; Paul Kuritz, *The Making of Theater History* (Prentice Hall, 1988), 145; Alessandra Buccheri, *The Spectacle of Clouds, 1439–1650: Italian Art and Theatre* (Ashgate, 2014), 31.
4   Codex Atl., 858r, 860r.
5   Uffizi Museum, inv. 447Ev.
6   Paris Ms. L, 58; Notebooks/Irma Richter, 95.
7   Windsor, RCIN 912657; Notebooks/Irma Richter, 84.
8   Codex on Flight, fol. 17v.
9   Paris Ms. E, 53r; Paris Ms. L, 58v; Notebooks/Irma Richter, 95, 89.
10 Biblioteca Reale, Turin, Italy. A facsimile with translation is available on the website of the Smithsonian National Air and Space Museum, https://airandspace.si.edu /exhibitions/codex/. For a discussion of the structure of the codex, see Martin Kemp and Juliana Barone, "What Is Leonardo's Codex on the Flight of Birds About?," in Jeannine O'Grody, ed., *Leonardo da Vinci: Drawings from the Biblioteca Reale in Turin* (Birmingham [Ala.] Museum of Fine Arts, 2008), 97.
11 Paris Ms. E, 54r; Notebooks/Irma Richter, 84.
12 Aristotle, *Movement of Animals*, ch. 2.
13 Codex on Flight, fol. 1r–2r.
14 Codex Atl., 20r/64r; Notebooks/Irma Richter, 25.
15 Paris Ms. F, 87v; Notebooks/Irma Richter, 87.
16 Codex Atl., 381v/1051v; Notebooks/Irma Richter, 99.
17 Notebooks/Irma Richter, 86.
18 Codex Atl., 79r/215r.
19 Paris Ms. E, 45v; Richard Prum, "Leonardo and the Science of Bird Flight," in O'Grody, *Leonardo da Vinci: Drawings from the Biblioteca Reale in Turin*; Capra *Learning*, 266.
20 Codex Atl., 161/434r, 381v/1058v; Notebooks/Irma Richter, 99.
21 Paris Ms. B, 80r; Laurenza, 45.
22 Paris Ms. B, 88v; Laurenza, 41; Pedretti, *The Machines*, 8.
23 Martin Kemp, "Leonardo Lifts Off," *Nature* 421.792 (February 20, 2003).
24 Codex Atl., 1006v; Laurenza, 32.
25 Paris Ms. B, 74v.
26 Codex on Flight, fol. 18v and inside back cover; Notebooks/J. P. Richter, 1428.
27 Codex Atl., 231av.

12. THE MECHANICAL ARTS

1   Codex Atl., 8v/30v; Ladislao Reti, "Elements of Machines," in Reti *Unknown*, 264; Marco Cianchi, *Leonardo da Vinci's Machines* (Becocci, 1988), 69; Arasse, 11.
2   Codex Madrid, 1:45r.
3   Paris Ms. H, 43v, 44r; Lynn White Jr., *Medieval Technology and Social Change* (Oxford, 1962); Ladislao Reti, "Leonardo da Vinci the Technologist," in O'Malley, 67.
4   Paris Ms. A, 30v.
5   Codex Atl., 289r.
6   Paris Ms. H, 80v; Codex Leic., 28v; Reti, "Leonardo da Vinci the Technologist," 75.
7   Paris Ms. B, 33v–34r; Codex Atl., 207v-b, 209v-b; Codex Forster, 1:50v.
8   Codex Atl., 318v; Bern Dibner, "Leonardo: Prophet of Automation,' in O'Malley, 104.

9   Codex on Flight, 12r.

10   Infeld, "Leonardo da Vinci and the Fundamental Laws of Science," 26.

11   Codex Forster, vol. 1; Allan Mills, "Leonardo da Vinci and Perpetual Motion," *Leonardo* 41.1 (February 2008), 39; Benjamin Olshin, "Leonardo da Vinci's Investigations of Perpetual Motion," *Icon* 15 (2009), 1. Leonardo's most interesting wheels with pinballs are in Codex Forster, 2:91r; Codex Atl., 1062r. Wheels with crescent-shaped pieces are in Codex Arundel, 263; Codex Forster, 2:91v, 34v; Madrid, 1:176r. Those of wheels with weights on arms are in Codex Atl., 778r; Madrid, 1:147r, 148r. Archimedean water screws are in Codex Atl., 541v; Codex Forster, 1:42v.

12   Codex Atl., 7v-a/147v-a; Reti, "Leonardo da Vinci the Technologist," 87.

13   Codex Madrid, 1:flysheet; Ladislao Reti, "Leonardo on Bearings and Gears," *Scientific American*, February 1971, 101.

14   Valentin Popov, *Contact Mechanics and Friction* (Springer, 2010), 3.

15   Codex Madrid, 1:122r, 176a; Codex Forster, 2:85v; Codex Forster, 3:72r; Codex Atl., 72r; Keele *Elements*, 123; Ian Hutchings, "Leonardo da Vinci's Studies of Friction," *Wear*, August 15, 2016, 51; Angela Pitenis, Duncan Dowson, and W. Gregory Sawyer, "Leonardo da Vinci's Friction Experiments," *Tribology Letters* 56.3 (December 2014), 509.

16   Codex Madrid, 1:20v, 26r.

17   Ladislao Reti, "The Leonardo da Vinci Codices in the Biblioteca Nacional of Madrid," *Technology and Culture* 84 (October 1967), 437.

18   Cianchi, *Leonardo da Vinci's Machines*, 16.

13. MATH

1   Paris Ms. G, 95b; Notebooks/J. P. Richter, 1158, 3; James McCabe, "Leonardo da Vinci's De Ludo Geometrico," PhD dissertation, UCLA, 1972.

2   Codex Madrid, 1:75r.

3   Codex Madrid, 2:62r; Keele *Elements*, 158.

4   Codex Atl., 183v-a.

5   Kemp *Leonardo*, 969.

6   Paris Ms. K, 49r.

7   Codex Atl., 228r/104r.

8   King, 164; Lucy McDonald, "And That's Renaissance Magic," *The Guardian*, April 10, 2007; Tiago Wolfram Nunes dos Santos Hirth, "Luca Pacioli and His 1500 Book De Viribus Quantitatis," PhD dissertation, University of Lisbon, 2015.

9   Codex Atl., 118a/366a; Notebooks/J. P. Richter, 1444.

10   McCabe, "Leonardo da Vinci's De Ludo Geometrico"; Nicholl, 304.

11   Dan Brown, *The Da Vinci Code* (Doubleday, 2003), 120–24; Gary Meisner, "Da Vinci and the Divine Proportion in Art Composition," *Golden Number*, July 7, 2014, online.

12   Paris Ms. M, 66v; Codex Atl., 152v; Capra *Science*, 267; Keele *Elements*, 100.

13   Codex Arundel, 182v, Codex Atl., 252r, 264r, 471r, among many examples.

14   McCabe, "Leonardo da Vinci's De Ludo Geometrico."

15   Codex Forster, 1:3r.

16   Windsor, RCIN 919145; Kemp *Marvellous*, 290.

17   Codex Atl., 471.

18   Codex Atl., 124v.

19   McCabe, "Leonardo da Vinci's De Ludo Geometrico," 45.

20   Squaring a circle in this manner is even more mathematically complex than doubling a cube. It was not until 1882 that it was proven impossible. That is because π is a tran-

scendental number, rather than merely being an algebraic irrational number. It is not the root of any polynomial with rational coefficients, and it is impossible to construct its square root with a compass and ruler.

21 Kemp *Leonardo,* 247; Codex Madrid, 2:12r.

22 Kenneth Clark, "Leonardo's Notebooks," *New York Review of Books,* December 12, 1974.

14. THE NATURE OF MAN

1 Alberti, *On Painting,* bk. 2.

2 Codex Urb., 118v; Notebooks/J. P. Richter, 488; *Leonardo on Painting,* 130.

3 Domenica Laurenza, *Art and Anatomy in Renaissance Italy* (Metropolitan Museum of New York, 2012), 8.

4 Laurenza, *Art and Anatomy in Renaissance Italy,* 9.

5 Windsor, RCIN 919059v; Notebooks/J. P. Richter, 805.

6 Windsor, RCIN 919037v; Notebooks/J. P. Richter, 797.

7 Notebooks/J. P. Richter, 798.

8 Windsor, RCIN 919058v; Clayton and Philo, 58; Keele and Roberts, 47; Wells, 27.

9 Peter Gerrits and Jan Veening, "Leonardo da Vinci's 'A Skull Sectioned': Skull and Dental Formula Revisited," *Clinical Anatomy* 26 (2013), 430.

10 Windsor, RCIN 919057r; Frank Fehrenbach, "The Pathos of Function: Leonardo's Technical Drawings," in Helmar Schramm, ed., *Instruments in Arts and Science* (Theatrum Scientarum, 2008), 81; Carmen Bambach, "Studies of the Human Skull," in Bambach *Master Draftsman;* Clark, 129.

11 Notebooks/J. P. Richter, 838.

12 Martin Clayton, "Anatomy and the Soul," in Marani and Fiorio, 215; Jonathan Pevsner, "Leonardo da Vinci's Studies of the Brain and Soul," *Scientific American Mind* 16: (2005), 84.

13 Windsor, RCIN 912613; Clayton and Philo, 37; Kenneth Keele, "Leonardo da Vinci's 'Anatomia Naturale,'" *Yale Journal of Biology and Medicine* 52 (1979), 369. Leonardo's experiment was not described and illustrated again until the Scottish physician Alexander Stuart did it in 1739.

14 Martin Kemp, "'Il Concetto dell'Anima' in Leonardo's Early Skull Studies," *Journal of the Warburg and Courtauld Institutes* 34 (1971), 115.

15 Notebooks/J. P. Richter, 308–59; Zöllner, 2:108.

16 Notebooks/J. P. Richter, 348–59.

17 Notebooks/J. P. Richter, preface to ch. 7.

15. *VIRGIN OF THE ROCKS*

1 Leonardo Treatise/Rigaud, ch. 165.

2 My narrative comports with these sources: Martin Kemp, "Beyond Compare," *Artforum International* 50.5 (January 2012), 68; Zöllner, 1:223; W. S. Cannell, "The *Virgin of the Rocks*: A Reconsideration of the Documents and a New Interpretation," *Gazette des Beaux-Arts* 47 (1984), 99; Syson, 63, 161, 170; Larry Keith, Ashok Roy, et al., "Leonardo da Vinci's *Virgin of the Rocks*: Treatment, Technique and Display," *National Galler (London) Technical Bulletin* 32 (2011); Marani, 137; the web page materials of the Louvre and National Gallery (London); personal interview with Vincent Delieuvin. For a contrary view, holding that the London version was painted first, see Tamsyn Taylor, "A Different Opinion," *Leonardo da Vinci and "the Virgin of the Rocks,"* November 8, 2011, http://leonardovirginoftherocks.blogspot.com/. For another take

on when each picture was painted, see Charles Hope, "The Wrong Leonardo?," *New York Review of Books*, February 9, 2012. After going through what we know of the commission and legal disputes, Hope argues, "This suggests that the real problem was something different, namely that when the patrons said that the picture had not been finished, they meant that it had not been completed according to the terms of the contract. Instead of showing the Virgin and Child with angels, as was required, it showed the Virgin and Child with an angel and Saint John." He contends, "It has been argued therefore that the Paris picture was removed from the church, probably in the 1490s, and that the London picture was a substitute. But the documents exclude this possibility. They make it clear beyond reasonable doubt that the picture commissioned in 1483 was still in the church in 1508. Had the patrons disposed of it before that time, the painters would have had no contractual obligation to provide a new version, and no payment was made to them for one. Equally, the documents indicate that the patrons did not return the picture to Leonardo. In order to make a second version, he needed access to the original, and this was not provided before 1508. Accordingly, one picture, evidently the one in the Louvre, was supplied between 1483 and 1490, and the London version cannot have been painted before 1508."

3 Regina Stefaniak, "On Looking into the Abyss: Leonardo's *Virgin of the Rocks*," *Journal of Art History* 66.1 (1997), 1.

4 Larry Keith, "In Pursuit of Perfection," in Syson, 64; Syson, 162n; Claire Farago, "A Conference on Leonardo da Vinci's Technical Practice," *Leonardo da Vinci Society Newsletter*, no. 38 (May 2012); Vincent Delieuvin et al., "The Paris *Virgin of the Rocks*: A New Approach Based on Scientific Analysis," in Michel Menu, ed., *Leonardo da Vinci's Technical Practice* (Hermann, 2014), ch. 9.

5 Michael Thomas Jahosky, "Some Marvelous Thing: Leonardo, Caterina, and the *Madonna of the Rocks*," Master's thesis, University of South Florida, 2010; Julian Bell, "Leonardo in London," *Times Literary Supplement*, November 23, 2011.

6 Bramly, 106; Capra *Science*, 46.

7 Kemp *Marvellous*, 75; Codex Urb., 67v; Edward J. Olszewski, "How Leonardo Invented Sfumato," *Notes in the History of Art* 31.1 (Fall 2011), 4–9.

8 Ann Pizzorusso, "Leonardo's Geology: The Authenticity of the *Virgin of the Rocks*," *Leonardo* 29.3 (Fall 1996). See also Ann Pizzorusso, *Tweeting Da Vinci* (Da Vinci Press, 2014); Bas den Hond, "Science Offers New Clues about Paintings by Munch and da Vinci," *Eos* 98 (April 2017).

9 William Emboden, *Leonardo da Vinci on Plants and Gardens* (Timber Press, 1987), 1, 125.

10 Luke Syson and Rachel Billinge, "Leonardo da Vinci's Use of Underdrawing in the 'Virgin of the Rocks' in the National Gallery and 'St. Jerome' in the Vatican," *Burlington Magazine* 147 (July 2005), 450; Keith et al., "Leonardo da Vinci's *Virgin of the Rocks*"; Francesca Fiorani, "Reflections on Leonardo da Vinci Exhibitions in London and Paris," in *Studiolo revue d'histoire de l'art de l'Académie de France à Rome* (Somogy, 2013); Larry Keith, "In Pursuit of Perfection," in Syson, 64; Kemp, "Beyond Compare," 68; "The Hidden Leonardo," National Gallery (London) website, https://www.national gallery.org.uk/paintings/learn-about-art/paintings-in-depth/the-hidden-leonardo.

11 John Shearman, "Leonardo's Colour and Chiaroscuro," *Zeitschrift für Kunstgeschichte* 25 (1962), 13.

12 Dalya Alberge, "The Daffodil Code: Doubts Revived over Leonardo's *Virgin of the Rocks* in London," *The Guardian*, December 9, 2014.

13 Pizzorusso, "Leonardo's Geology," 197. For a compilation of the attacks on the Na-

tional Gallery's pronouncement, see Michael Daley, "Could the Louvre's 'Virgin and St. Anne' Provide the Proof That the (London) National Gallery's 'Virgin of the Rocks' Is Not by Leonardo da Vinci?," *ArtWatch UK*, June 12, 2012.

14 Syson, 36.

15 Clark, 204.

16 Kemp *Marvellous*, 274.

17 Keith, "In Pursuit of Perfection," in Syson, 64

18 Christine Lin, "Inside Leonardo Da Vinci's Collaborative Workshop," *Epoch Times*, March 31, 2015; Luke Syson, "Leonardo da Vinci: Singular and Plural," lecture, Metropolitan Museum, New York, March 6, 2013; author's interview with Syson.

19 Clark, 171; Fra Pietro da Novellara to Isabella d'Este, April 3, 1501.

20 Fiorani, "Reflections on Leonardo da Vinci Exhibitions in London and Paris"; Delieuvin.

21 Jonathan Jones, "The *Virgin of the Rocks*: Da Vinci decoded," *The Guardian*, July 13, 2010.

22 Andrew Graham-Dixon, "The Mystery of Leonardo's Two Madonnas," *The Telegraph* (London), October 23, 2011.

23 The drawing is almost identical in most traits to the painted angel, and it is considered by most critics to be a study. But in Bambach *Master Draftsman* there is one essay (Carlo Pedretti, 96) that calls it a study and another essay (Pietro Marani, 160) that argues it is not.

24 Clark, 94.

16. THE MILAN PORTRAITS

1 Zöllner, 2:225; Marani, 160; Syson, 86, 95.

 2 Syson, 86.

 3 Codex Ash., 1:2a; Notebooks/J. P. Richter, 516.

 4 Codex Arundel, 64b; Notebooks/J. P. Richter, 830; Codex Forster, 3:158v.

 5 Janice Shell and Grazioso Sironi, "Cecilia Gallerani: Leonardo's *Lady with an Ermine*," *Artibus et Historiae* 13.25 (1992), 47–66; David Alan Brown, "Leonardo and the Ladies with the Ermine and the Book," *Artibus et Historiae* 11.22 (1990), 47–61; Syson, 11; Nicholl, 229; Gregory Lubkin, *A Renaissance Court: Milan under Galleazzo Maria Sforza* (University of California, 1994), 50.

 6 John Pope-Hennessy, *The Portrait in the Renaissance* (Pantheon, 1963), 103; Brown, "Leonardo and the Ladies with the Ermine and the Book," 47.

 7 Paris Ms. H, 1:48b, 12a; Notebooks/J. P. Richter, 1263, 1234; Syson, 111.

 8 Kemp *Marvellous*, 188; Codex Atl., 87r, 88r.

 9 Codex Ash., 1:14a; Notebooks/J. P. Richter, 552; Bell, "Sfumato and Acuity Perspective"; Marani, "Movements of the Soul," 230; Clayton, "Anatomy and the Soul," 216; Jackie Wullschlager, "Leonardo As You'll Never See Him Again," *Financial Times*, November 11, 2011.

10 Bull, "Two Portraits by Leonardo," 67.

11 Shell and Sironi, "Cecilia Gallerani," 47

12 Most scholars now agree that it is Lucrezia Crivelli, and that seems to comport with three court poet sonnets in praise of such a painting. However, Luke Syson, who organized the London 2011 show of Leonardo's Milan paintings, suggests in the catalogue (105) that "it is not impossible" that the subject may actually be Beatrice d'Este, even though there is scant resemblance to other portrayals of her and no poems of praise that almost surely would have accompanied such a painting.

13   Leonardo Treatise/Rigaud, ch. 213; Codex Ash., 2:14v.

14   Bernard Berenson, *North Italian Painters* (Putnam, 1907), 260; Clark, 101.

15   "Head of a Young Girl in Profile to the Left in Renaissance Dress, German School, Early 19th Century," Christie's sale 8812, lot 402, January 30, 1998, http://www.christies .com/LotFinder/lot_details.aspx?intObjectID=473187.

16   Peter Silverman interview, in "Mystery of a Masterpiece," NOVA/National Geographic/PBS, January 25, 2012; Peter Silverman, *Leonardo's Lost Princess: One Man's Quest to Authenticate an Unknown Portrait by Leonardo Da Vinci* (Wiley, 2012), 6. The owner who consigned the picture for auction sued Christie's for breaches of fiduciary duty and negligence. The suit was dismissed because the statute of limitations had expired.

17   Silverman, *Leonardo's Lost Princess*, 8.

18   John Brewer, "Art and Science: A Da Vinci Detective Story," *Engineering & Science* 1.2 (2005); John Brewer, *The American Leonardo* (Oxford, 2009); Carol Vogel, "Not by Leonardo, but Sotheby's Sells a Work for $1.5 Million," *New York Times*, January 28, 2010; Silverman, *Leonardo's Lost Princess*, 44.

19   Silverman, *Leonardo's Lost Princess*, 16.

20   Nicholas Turner, introduction to Martin Kemp and Pascal Cotte, *La Bella Principessa* (Hodder & Stoughton, 2010), 16; Nicholas Turner, "Statement concerning the Portrait on Vellum," Lumiere Technology, September 2008, http://www.lumiere-technology .com/images/Download/Nicholas_Turner_Statement.pdf; Silverman, *Leonardo's Lost Princess*, 19.

21   David Grann, "The Mark of a Masterpiece," *New Yorker*, July 12, 2010.

22   Elisabetta Povoledo, "Dealer Who Sold Portrait Joins Leonardo Debate," *New York Times*, August 29, 2008.

23   Pascal Cotte, "Further Comparisons with Cecilia Gallerani," in Kemp and Cotte, *La Bella Principessa*, 176.

24   Silverman, *Leonardo's Lost Princess*, 64; "Mystery of a Masterpiece"; Lumiere Technology studies on *La Bella Principessa*, http://www.lumiere-technology.com.

25   Christina Geddo, "The 'Pastel' Found: A New Portrait by Leonardo da Vinci?," in *Artes*, no. 14 (2009), 63; Christina Geddo, "Leonardo da Vinci: The Extraordinary Discovery of the Last Portrait," lecture, Société genevoise d'études italiennes Geneva, October 2, 2012.

26   Carlo Pedretti, abstract of the introduction to *Leonardo Infinito: La vita, l'opera completa, la modernità* by Alessandro Vezzosi, Lumiere Technology, 2008, http://www .lumiere-technology.com/images/Download/Abstract_Pr_Pedretti.pdf.

27   Windsor, RCIN 912505. The Royal Collection dates the drawing to c. 1490.

28   See chapter 21.

29   Grann, "The Mark of a Masterpiece"; "Mystery of a Masterpiece"; author's interview with Martin Kemp; Silverman, *Leonardo's Lost Princess*, 73.

30   Kemp and Cotte, *La Bella Principessa*, 24; Silverman, *Leonardo's Lost Princess*, 74; Grann, "The Mark of a Masterpiece."

31   Silverman, *Leonardo's Lost Princess*, 103.

32   Kemp and Cotte, *La Bella Principessa*, 72; Pascal Cotte and Martin Kemp, "*La Bella Principessa* and the Warsaw Sforziad, 2011," Lumiere Technology, http://www .lumiere-technology.com//news/Study_Bella_Principessa_and_Warsaw_Sforziad.pdf; Martin Kemp, *La Bella Principessa*, exhibition catalogue, Palazzo Ducale, Urbino, 2014; Silverman, *Leonardo's Lost Princess*, 75; Grann, "The Mark of a Masterpiece"; author's interview with Kemp.

33 "Mystery of a Masterpiece."

34 Grann, "The Mark of a Masterpiece."

35 Peter Paul Biro, "Fingerprint Examination," in Kemp and Cotte, *La Bella Principessa*, 148.

36 Jeff Israely, "How a 'New' da Vinci Was Discovered, *Time*, October 15, 2009; Helen Pidd, "New Leonardo da Vinci Painting 'Discovered,'" *The Guardian*, October 13, 2009; "Fingerprint Unmasks Original da Vinci Painting," CNN, October 13, 2009; "Finger Points to New da Vinci Art," BBC, October 13, 2009; Simon Hewitt, "Fingerprint Points to $19,000 Portrait Being Revalued as £100m Work by Leonardo da Vinci," *Antiques Trade Gazette*, October 12, 2009.

37 Grann, "The Mark of a Masterpiece."

38 The article is worth reading in its entirety: Grann, "The Mark of a Masterpiece," www .newyorker.com/magazine/2010/07/12/the-mark-of-a-masterpiece.

39 Barbara Leonard, "Art Critic Loses Libel Suit against the *New Yorker*," *Courthouse News Service*, December 8, 2015.

40 "Mystery of a Masterpiece."

41 "New Leonardo da Vinci *Bella Principessa* Confirmed," Lumiere Technology website, September 28, 2011; Cotte and Kemp, "*La Bella Principessa* and the Warsaw Sforziad"; "Mystery of a Masterpiece."

42 Cotte and Kemp, "*La Bella Principessa* and the Warsaw Sforziad"; Simon Hewitt, "New Evidence Strengthens Leonardo Claim for Portrait," *Antiques Trade Gazette*, October 3, 2011.

43 Scott Reyburn, "An Art World Mystery Worthy of Leonardo," *New York Times*, December 4, 2015; Katarzyna Krzyzagórska-Pisarek, "*La Bella Principessa*: Arguments against the Attribution to Leonardo," *Artibus et Historiae* 36 (June 2015), 61; Martin Kemp, "Errors, Misconceptions, and Allegations of Forgery," Lumiere Technology, 2015, http://www.lumiere-technology.com/A&HresponseMK.pdf; "Problems with La Bella Principessa, Part III: Dr. Pisarek Responds to Prof. Kemp," *ArtWatch UK*, 2016, artwatch.org.uk/problems-with-la-bella-principessa-part-iii-dr-pisarek-responds-to -prof-kemp/; Martin Kemp, "Attribution and Other Issues," *Martin Kemp's This and That*, May 16, 2015, martinkempsthisandthat.blogspot.com/; Josh Boswell and Tim Rayment, "It's Not a da Vinci, It's Sally from the Co-op," *Sunday Times* (London), November 29, 2015; Lorena Muñoz-Alonso, "Forger Claims Leonardo da Vinci's *La Bella Principessa* Is Actually His Painting of a Supermarket Cashier," *Artnet News*, November 30, 2015; "Some of the Many Inconsistencies and Dubious Assertions in Greenhalgh's 'A Forger's Tale,'" Lumiere Technology, http://www.lumiere-technology .com/Some%20of%20the%20Many%20Inconsistencies.pdf; Vincent Noce, "*La Bella Principessa*: Still an Enigma," *Art Newspaper*, May 2016, from The Authentication in Art Congress, Louwman Museum, The Hague, May 11, 2016.

44 Jonathan Jones, "This Is a Leonardo da Vinci?," *The Guardian*, November 30, 2015.

45 Cotte and Kemp, "*La Bella Principessa* and the Warsaw Sforziad"; author's interview with Martin Kemp.

17. THE SCIENCE OF ART

1 Zöllner, 2:108; Monica Azzolini, "Anatomy of a Dispute: Leonardo, Pacioli and Scientific Courtly Entertainment in Renaissance Milan," *Early Science and Medicine* 9.2 (2004), 115.

2 Cennino d'Andrea Cennini, *Il Libro dell' Arte*, trans. Daniel V. Thompson Jr. (Dover, 1933).

3   Carlo Dionisotti, "Leonardo uomo di lettere," *Italia Medioevale e Umanistica* 5 (1962), 209.

4   Claire Farago, *Leonardo da Vinci's Paragone: A Critical Interpretation* (Leiden: Brill Studies, 1992). Most of the quotations I use come from her new translation. The primary source of Leonardo's *paragone* and his proposed treatise on painting is a manuscript, probably compiled by Melzi, that is known as the Codex Urbinas 1270 and is in the Vatican. The *paragone* forms the opening section of the treatise; it originated in Paris Ms. A and what is known as the lost Libro A, which has been reconstructed by Carlo Pedretti from passages in the Codex Urbinas. See note 12 below.

5   Codex Ash., 2:19r-v.

6   Codex Ash., 2:20r; Notebooks/Irma Richter, 189; Notebooks/J. P. Richter, 654.

7   Codex Urb., 21v.

8   Codex Urb., 15v.

9   Codex Ash., 1:13a, 2:22v; Codex Urb., 66; Notebooks/J. P. Richter, 508; Notebooks/ Irma Richter, 172. See also Kenneth Clark, "A Note on the Relationship of His Science and Art," *History Today*, May 1, 1952, 303; Kemp *Marvellous*, 145; Martin Kemp, "Analogy and Observation in the Codex Hammer," in Mario Pedini, ed., *Studi Vinciani in Memoria di Nando di Toni* (Brescia, 1986), 103.

10 For an example, see Windsor, RCIN 912371.

11 The early biographer Gian Paolo Lomazzo is the source for the assertion that the treatise was written at Ludovico Sforza's request. Pedretti *Commentary*, 1:76; Farago, *Leonardo da Vinci's Paragone*, 162.

12 For a full chronology of manuscripts and a history of *Treatise* versions, see Carlo Pedretti, *Leonardo da Vinci on Painting* (University of California, 1964), which reassembles a version of the *Treatise* from the Melzi manuscript known as the Codex Urbinas 1270 and other codices (see p. 9 for the Pacioli quote). Melzi listed eighteen manuscripts of Leonardo that he drew upon, but only seven are still known to exist. For a comparison of the manuscripts, see the website *Leonardo da Vinci and His "Treatise on Painting,"* www.treatiseonpainting.org. See also Claire Farago, *Re-reading Leonardo: The Treatise on Painting across Europe, 1550–1900* (Ashgate, 2009), and essays in that book by Martin Kemp and Juliana Barone, "What Might Leonardo's Own Trattato Have Looked Like?" and Claire Farago, "Who Abridged Leonardo da Vinci's Treatise on Painting?"; Monica Azzolini, "In Praise of Art: Text and Context of Leonardo's 'Paragone' and Its Critique of the Arts and Sciences," *Renaissance Studies* 19.4 (September 2005), 487; Fiorani, "The Shadows of Leonardo's *Annunciation* and Their Lost Legacy," 119; Fiorani, "The Colors of Leonardo's Shadows," 271. Claire Farago has raised questions about whether Melzi was the editor.

13 Claire Farago, "A Short Note on Artisanal Epistemology in Leonardo's Treatise on Painting," in Moffatt and Taglialagamba, 51.

14 Codex Urb., 133r-v; Codex Atl., 246a/733a; Leonardo Treatise/Rigaud, ch. 178; *Leonardo on Painting*, 15; Notebooks/J. P. Richter, 111, 121.

15 Leonardo Treatise/Rigaud, ch. 177.

16 Notebooks/J. P. Richter 160, 111–18; Nagel, "Leonardo and Sfumato," 7; Janis Bell, "Aristotle as a Source for Leonardo's Theory of Colour Perspective after 1500," *Journal of the Warburg and Courtauld Institutes* 56 (1993), 100; Codex Atl., 676r; Codex Ash., 2:13v.

17 Jürgen Renn, ed., *Galileo in Context* (Cambridge, 2001), 202.

18 Notebooks/J. P. Richter, 121; Nagel, "Leonardo and Sfumato."

19 Leonardo Treatise/Pedretti, ch. 443, p. 694; Notebooks/J. P. Richter, 49, 47; Bell, "Sfu-

mato and Acuity Perspective"; Carlo Vecce, "The Fading Evidence of Reality: Leonardo and the End," lecture, University of Durham, November 4, 2015.

20 Leonardo da Vinci, *A Treatise on Painting*, trans. A. Philip McMahon (Princeton, 1956), 1:806 (based on the Codex Urbinas); Martin Kemp, "Leonardo and the Visual Pyramid," *Journal of the Warburg and Courtauld Institutes* 40 (1977); James Ackerman, "Leonardo's Eye," *Journal of the Warburg and Courtauld Institutes* 41 (1978).

21 Notebooks/MacCurdy, 224.

22 Leonardo da Vinci, "The Cranial Nerves," Windsor, RCIN 919052; Keele and Roberts, 54.

23 Notebooks/MacCurdy, 253; Rumy Hilloowalla, "Leonardo da Vinci, Visual Perspective and the Crystalline Sphere (Lens): If Only Leonardo Had Had a Freezer," *Vesalius* 10.5 (2004); Ackerman, "Leonardo's Eye," 108. For less laudatory assessments of his optical studies, see David C. Lindberg, *Theories of Vision from Al-kindi to Kepler* (University of Chicago, 1981), ch. 8; Dominique Raynaud, "Leonardo, Optics, and Ophthalmology," in Fiorani and Nova, *Leonardo da Vinci and Optics*, 293.

24 Codex Atl., 200a/594a; Paris Ms. A, 3a; Notebooks/J. P. Richter, 50, 13.

25 Ackerman, "Leonardo's Eye"; Anthony Grafton, *Cardano's Cosmos* (Harvard, 1999), 57.

26 Codex Urb., 154v; Notebooks/J. P. Richter, 14–16.

27 Notebooks/J. P. Richter, 100, 91, 109.

28 Paris Ms. E., 79b; Notebooks/J. P. Richter, 225; Leonardo Treatise/Rigaud, chs. 309, 315; Janis Bell, "Leonardo's prospettiva delle ombre," in Fiorani and Nova, *Leonardo da Vinci and Optics*, 79.

29 Leonardo Treatise/Rigaud, ch. 305.

30 Bell, "Sfumato and Acuity Perspective"; Ackerman, "Leonardo Da Vinci: Art in Science," 207; Paris Ms. G, 26v,

31 Leonardo Treatise/Rigaud, 306.

32 Leonardo Treatise/Rigaud, 283, 286; Notebooks/J. P. Richter, 296.

33 Codex Ash., 1:13a; Notebooks/J. P. Richter, 294.

34 Ackerman, "Leonardo's Eye"; Kemp, "Leonardo and the Visual Pyramid," 128.

18. THE LAST SUPPER

1 Matteo Bandello, *Tutte le Opere*, ed. Francesco Flora (Mondadori, 1934; originally published 1554), 1:646; Norman Land, "Leonardo da Vinci in a Tale by Matteo Bandello," *Discoveries* 2006, 1; King, 145; Kemp *Marvellous*, 166.

2 Pinin Brambilla Barcilon and Pietro Marani, *Leonardo's* Last Supper (University of Chicago, 1999), 2.

3 Matthew 26:21.

4 Clark, 149, 153.

5 Matthew 26:22–23; John 13:22.

6 Codex Atl., 137a/415a; Notebooks/J. P. Richter, 593; Marani, "Movements of the Soul," 233.

7 Codex Atl., 383r; Notebooks/J. P. Richter, 593–94.

8 Codex Forster, 2:62v/1v-2r; Notebooks/J. P. Richter, 665–66.

9 Matthew 26:23, 26:25; Luke 22:21; Matthew Landrus, "The Proportions of Leonardo's *Last Supper*," *Raccolta Vinciana* 32 (December 2007), 43.

10 Brown, *The Da Vinci Code*, 263; King, 189.

11 Matthew 26:26–28; Leonardo Steinberg, *Leonardo's Incessant* Last Supper (Zone, 2001), 38; Jack Wasserman, "Rethinking Leonardo da Vinci's *Last Supper*," *Artibus et Historiae* 28.55 (2007), 23; King, 216. Charles Hope, "The Last 'Last Supper,'" *New*

York Review of Books, August 9, 2001, argues against Steinberg and others who believe that Leonardo means to portray the Eucharist: "Leonardo omitted the one indispensable element of the Eucharist, namely the chalice, which was regularly included in depictions of the Institution. The table is full of fruit, rolls, and wine glasses, so Christ's hands had to be in proximity to them; but it is difficult to believe that Renaissance Christians would have associated the Eucharist with a half-drunk wine tumbler. In any case, the eucharistic theme, though regularly shown in altarpieces for obvious reasons, was not regarded as appropriate for refectories."

12 Notebooks/J. P. Richter, 55; King, 142.

13 Notebooks/J. P. Richter, 100, 91, 109.

14 Notebooks/J. P. Richter, 545.

15 Lillian F. Schwartz, "The Staging of Leonardo's *Last Supper*: A Computer-Based Exploration of Its Perspective," *Leonardo*, supplemental issue, 1988, 89–96; Kemp *Leonardo*, 1761; Kemp *Marvellous*, 182.

16 Ernst Gombrich, "Paper Given on the Occasion of the Dedication of *The Last Supper* (after Leonardo)," Magdalen College, Oxford, March 10, 1993 (includes his translation of Goethe); Kemp, *Marvellous*, 186; John Varriano, "At Supper with Leonardo," *Gastronomica* 8.1 (2014).

17 Barcilon and Marani, *Leonardo's* Last Supper, 327; Claire J. Farago, "Leonardo's *Battle of Anghiari*: A Study in the Exchange between Theory and Practice," *Art Bulletin* 76.2 (June 1994), 311; Pietro Marani, *The Genius and the Passions: Leonardo's Last Supper* (Skira, 2001).

18 Alessandra Stanley, "After a 20-Year Cleanup, a Brighter, Clearer 'Last Supper' Emerges," *New York Times*, May 27, 1999; Hope, "The Last 'Last Supper.'"

19 Michael Daley, "The Perpetual Restoration of Leonardo's *Last Supper*," part 2, *ArtWatch UK*, March 14, 2012; Barcilon and Marani, *Leonardo's* Last Supper, 341.

19. PERSONAL TURMOIL

1 Codex Forster, 3:88r; Notebooks/J. P. Richter, 1384. Some scholars, including Richter, assume that Caterina was a servant; more recent research, including the discovery of a hospital death notice for "Caterina of Florence," provides evidence that she was his mother. See Angelo Paratico, *Beyond Thirty-Nine* blog, May 18, 2015; Vanna Arrighi, Anna Bellinazzi, and Edoardo Villata, *Leonardo da Vinci: La vera immagine. Documenti E Testimonianze Sulla Vita E Sull'opera* (Giunti, 2005), 79.

2 Codex Forster, 3:74v, 88v; Notebooks/J. P. Richter, 1517; Bramly, 242; Nicholl, 536.

3 Arrighi et al., *Leonardo du Vinci: La vera immagine*.

4 Codex Forster, 2:95a; Notebooks/J. P. Richter, 1522.

5 Notebooks/J. P. Richter, 1523.

6 Bramly, 243.

7 Patrizia Costa, "The Sala Delle Asse in the Sforza Castle," Master's thesis, University of Pittsburgh, 2006. The rooms are currently being renovated and are open to visitors and researchers.

8 MacCurdy, *The Mind of Leonardo da Vinci*, 35.

9 Codex Atl., 335v; MacCurdy, *The Mind of Leonardo da Vinci*, 25; Notebooks/J. P. Richter, 1345.

10 Codex Atl., 866r/315v; Notebooks/J. P. Richter, 1345.

11 Codex Atl., 323v; Notebooks/Irma Richter, 302; Notebooks/J. P. Richter, 1346; Pedretti *Commentary*, 2:332.

12 Codex Atl., 243a/669r; *Leonardo on Painting*, 265; Notebooks/J. P. Richter, 1379.

20. FLORENCE AGAIN

1 Codex Atl., 638bv; Bramly, 313.
2 Codex Leic., 22b.
3 Codex Madrid, 2:4b; Pedretti *Commentary*, 2:332.
4 Codex Arundel, 229b; Notebooks/J. P. Richter, 1425, 1423; Notebooks/Irma Richter, 325.
5 Codex Madrid, 2:4b; Codex Atl., 312b/949b.
6 It is in the Biblioteca Medicea Laurenziana, Florence.
7 Julia Cartwright, *Isabella d'Este* (Dutton, 1905), 15.
8 Cartwright, *Isabella d'Este*, 92, 150; Brown, "Leonardo and the Ladies with the Ermine and the Book," 47.
9 Brown, "Leonardo and the Ladies with the Ermine and the Book," 49; Shell and Sironi, "Cecilia Gallerani," 48.
10 Brown, "Leonardo and the Ladies with the Ermine and the Book," 50.
11 All of the letters, in Italian with English translations, are in Francis Ames-Lewis, *Isabella and Leonardo* (Yale, 2012), 223–40, and discussed in chapters 4 and 6 of that book. The letters and story are also in Cartwright, *Isabella d'Este*, 92; Nicholl, 326–36. Nicholl retranslated all of the letters and provides a full account of the saga.
12 Ames-Lewis, *Isabella and Leonardo*, 109. Titian painted two portraits of Isabella in a more frontal view, but those were not done until 1529 and 1534.
13 Isabella d'Este to Pietro da Novellara, March 1501.
14 Pietro da Novellara to Isabella d'Este, April 14, 1501.
15 Manfredo de' Manfredi to Isabella d'Este, July 31, 1501.
16 Isabella d'Este to Leonardo and to Angelo del Tovaglia, May 14, 1504.
17 Aloisius Ciocca to Isabella d'Este, January 22, 1505.
18 Alessandro Amadori to Isabella d'Este, May 3, 1506.
19 Pietro da Novellara to Isabella d'Este, April 14, 1501; Nicholl, 337; Cristina Acidini, Roberto Bellucci, and Cecilia Frosinini, "New Hypotheses on the *Madonna of the Yarnwinders* Series," in Michel Menu, ed., *Leonardo da Vinci's Technical Practice: Paintings, Drawings and Influence, Proceedings of the Charisma Conference* (Paris: Hermann), 114–25. None of the primary versions or known copies actually shows the basket of yarn at Christ's feet.
20 Martin Kemp and Thereza Wells, *Leonardo da Vinci's* Madonna of the Yarnwinder (National Gallery of Scotland, 1992); Martin Kemp, "The *Madonna of the Yarn Winder* in the Buccleuch Collection Reconsidered in the Context of Leonardo's Studio Practice," in Pietro Marani and Maria Teresa Fiorio, eds., *I Leonardeschi a Milano: Fortuna e collezionismo* (Milan, 1991), 35–48; Acidini et al., "New Hypotheses on the *Madonna of the Yarnwinders* Series," 114.

21. SAINT ANNE

1 Pietro da Novellara to Isabella d'Este, April 3, 1501; Ames-Lewis, *Isabella and Leonardo*, 224; Nicholl, 333.
2 Delieuvin. The French edition calls it "l'ultime chef d'oeuvre," which could also connote "last masterpiece." The catalogue is a good guide for exploring the sequence of Leonardo's drawings and paintings as well as the copies made of them.
3 Those who thought it likely that the Burlington House cartoon was done after the 1501 drawing include Arthur Popham, *The Drawings of Leonardo da Vinci* (Harcourt, 1945), 102; Arthur Popham and Philip Pouncey, *Italian Drawings in the British Mu-*

seum (British Museum, 1950); Clark, 164; Pedretti *Chronology*, 120; Nicholl, 334, 424; Eric Harding, Allan Braham, Martin Wyld, and Aviva Burnstock, "The Restoration of the Leonardo Cartoon," *National Gallery Technical Bulletin* 13 (1989), 4. See also Virginia Budny, "The Sequence of Leonardo's Sketches for *The Virgin and Child with Saint Anne and Saint John the Baptist*," *Art Bulletin* 65.1 (March 1983), 34; Johannes Nathan, "Some Drawing Practices of Leonardo da Vinci: New Light on the St. Anne," *Mitteilungen des Kunsthistorischen Institutes in Florenz* 36.1 (1992), 85.

4 The marginal note was first published by Armin Schlecter in a 2005 catalogue of an exhibition of books in Heidelberg University Library. See Jill Burke, "The Bureaucrat, the *Mona Lisa*, and Leaving Things Rough," *Leonardo da Vinci Society Newsletter*, May 2008.

5 Jack Wasserman, "The Dating and Patronage of Leonardo's Burlington House Cartoon," *Art Bulletin* 53.3 (September 1971), 312; Luke Syson, "The Rewards of Service," in Syson, 44.

6 Delieuvin, 49, 56; Louvre press release, December 1, 2011; author's interview with Delieuvin, 2016.

7 Fiorani, "Reflections on Leonardo da Vinci Exhibitions in London and Paris."

8 The copy was called the Resta-Esterházy Cartoon. It disappeared in Budapest in World War II. Photographs and copies of it still exist. Delieuvin, 108.

9 Sigmund Freud, *Leonardo da Vinci, and a Memory of His Childhood* (Norton, 1990), 72.

10 Codex Arundel, 138r.

11 Author's interview with Delieuvin.

12 Clark, 217.

22. PAINTINGS LOST AND FOUND

1 Barbara Hochstetler Meyer, "Leonardo's Hypothetical Painting of Leda and the Swan," *Mitteilungen des Kunsthistorischen Institutes in Florenz* 34.3 (1990), 279.

2 Kemp *Marvellous*, 265; Zöllner, 1:188, 1:246; Nicholl, 397.

3 Martin Kemp, "Sight and Sound," *Nature* 479 (November 2011), 174; Andrew Goldstein, "The Male *Mona Lisa*?," *Blouin Artinfo*, November 17, 2011; Kemp *Leonardo*, 208; Milton Esterow, "A Long Lost Leonardo," *Art News*, August 15, 2011; Syson, 300; Scott Reyburn and Robert Simon, "Leonardo da Vinci Painting Discovered," PR Newswire, July 7, 2011.

4 Graham Bowley and William Rashbaum, "Sotheby's Tries to Block Suit over a Leonardo Sold and Resold at a Big Markup," *New York Times*, November 8, 2016; Sam Knight, "The Bouvier Affair," *New Yorker*, February 8, 2016.

5 Paris Ms. D, written around 1507.

6 André J. Noest, "No Refraction in Leonardo's Orb," and Martin Kemp's reply, *Nature* 480 (December 22, 2011), 457. Noest correctly points out the lack of distortion or inversion of the robes and body, but I think he is incorrect in saying that the palm that is touching the glass would be subject to a similar distortion.

23. CESARE BORGIA

1 Rafael Sabatini, *The Life of Cesare Borgia* (Stanley Paul, 1912), 311; Machiavelli, *The Prince*, ch. 7.

2 Paul Strathern, *The Artist, the Philosopher, and the Warrior: The Intersecting Lives of Da Vinci, Machiavelli, and Borgia and the World They Shaped* (Random House, 2009), 83–90. (Cardinal Ardicino Della Porta the Younger tried to resign a few years earlier, but returned.)

3 Ladislao Reti, "Leonardo da Vinci and Cesare Borgia," *Viator*, January 1973, 333; Strathern, *The Artist, the Philosopher, and the Warrior*, 1, 59; Nicholl, 343; Roger Masters, *Fortune Is a River* (Free Press, 1998), 79.

4 Paris Ms. L, 1b; Paris Ms. B, 81b; Notebooks/J. P. Richter, 1416, 1117.

5 Strathern, *The Artist, the Philosopher, and the Warrior*, 112.

6 Codex Arundel, 202b; Notebooks/J. P. Richter, 1420. Oddly, tantalizingly, perhaps even tellingly, Cesare Borgia is not mentioned any other time in Leonardo's notebooks.

7 Bramly, 324.

8 Codex Atl., 121v/43v-b; Kemp *Marvellous*, 225; Strathern, *The Artist, the Philosopher, and the Warrior*, 138.

9 Strathern, *The Artist, the Philosopher, and the Warrior*, 138; Codex Atl., 43v, 48r.

10 Paris Ms. L, 78a; Notebooks/J. P. Richter, 1048.

11 Paris Ms. L, 66b; Notebooks/J. P. Richter, 1044, 1047; Codex Atl., 3, 4.

12 Paris Ms. L, 47a, 77a; Notebooks/J. P. Richter, 1043, 1047.

13 Paris Ms. L, 72r; Notebooks/J. P. Richter, 1046.

14 Nicholl, 348.

15 Codex Atl., 22a/69r; see also 71v.

16 Klein, *Leonardo's Legacy*, 91; Nicholl, 349; Codex Atl., 133r/48r-b; Paris Ms. L, 29r.

17 Strathern, *The Artist, the Philosopher, and the Warrior*, 163.

18 Windsor, RCIN 912284.

19 Codex Atl., f.1.r.

20 Codex Atl., 1.1r; Laurenza, 231; Schofield, "Notes on Leonardo and Vitruvius," 129; Klein, *Leonardo's Legacy*, 91; Keele *Elements*, 134.

21 Machiavelli, *The Prince*, ch. 7.

22 Paris Ms. L, 33v; Notebooks/J. P. Richter, 1039; Notebooks/Irma Richter, 320.

23 Strathern, *The Artist, the Philosopher, and the Warrior*, 105.

24. HYDRAULIC ENGINEER

1 Claudio Giorgione, "Leonardo da Vinci and Waterways in Lombardy," lecture at UCLA, May 20, 2016.

2 Carlo Zammattio, *Leonardo the Scientist* (London, 1961), 10.

3 Masters, *Fortune Is a River*, 102.

4 Now called Rocca della Verruca, it is not to be confused with Castello della Verrucola, north of Pisa. See Carlo Pedretti, "La Verruca," *Renaissance Quarterly* 25.4 (Winter 1972), 417.

5 Pier Francesco Tosinghi to the Florentine Republic, June 21, 1503, in Pedretti, "La Verruca," 418; Masters, *Fortune Is a River*, 95; Nicholl, 358.

6 Signoria of Florence account book, July 26, 1503, in Masters, *Fortune Is a River*, 96.

7 Codex Leic., 13a; Notebooks/J. P. Richter, 1008.

8 Codex Atl., 4r/1v-b (machine drawing) and 562r/210r-b; Nicholl, 358; Strathern, *The Artist, the Philosopher, and the Warrior*, 318; Kemp *Marvellous*, 224; Masters, *Fortune Is a River*, 123; Codex Madrid, 2:22v.

9 Machiavelli to Colombino, September 21, 1504; Strathern, *The Artist, the Philosopher, and the Warrior*, 320; Nicholl, 359; Masters, *Fortune Is a River*, 132.

10 Codex Atl., 127r/46r-b; Notebooks/J. P. Richter, 774, 1001.

11 Windsor, RCIN 912279. See also other maps: RCIN 912678, 912680, 912683.

12 Leonardo, "A Map of the Valdichiana," Windsor, RCIN 912278; Notebooks/J. P. Richter, 1001; Pedretti *Commentary*, 2:174.

13 Kemp *Marvellous*, 225; Codex Atl., 121v, 133r; Codex Madrid, 2:125r.

14 Paris Ms. F, 13 r-v, 15r–16r; Codex Arundel, 63v; Reti, "Leonardo da Vinci the Technologist," 90.

15 Codex Madrid, 2:125r.

25. MICHELANGELO AND THE LOST *BATTLES*

1 Jonathan Jones, *The Lost Battles: Leonardo, Michelangelo, and the Artistic Duel That Defines the Renaissance* (Knopf, 2010); Michael Cole, *Leonardo, Michelangelo, and the Art of the Figure* (Yale, 2104); Paula Rae Duncan, "Michelangelo and Leonardo: The Frescoes for the Palazzo Vecchio," Master's thesis, University of Montana, 2004; Clark, 198.

2 Codex Atl., 74rb-vc/202r; Notebooks/J. P. Richter, 669.

3 Codex Ash., 30v–31r; Notebooks/J. P. Richter, 601.

4 Günther Neufeld, "Leonardo da Vinci's *Battle of Anghiari*: A Genetic Reconstruction," *Art Bulletin* 31.3 (September 1949), 170–183; Farago, "Leonardo's *Battle of Anghiari*"; Claire J. Farago, "The *Battle of Anghiari*: A Speculative Reconstruction of Leonardo's Design Process," *Achademia Leonardi Vinci* 9 (1996), 73–86; Barbara Hochstetler Meyer, "Leonardo's *Battle of Anghiari*: Proposals for Some Sources and a Reflection," *Art Bulletin* 66.3 (September 1984), 367–82; Cecil Gould, "Leonardo's Great Battlepiece: A Conjectural Reconstruction," *Art Bulletin* 36.2 (June 1954), 117–29; Paul Joannides, "Leonardo da Vinci, Peter Paul Rubens, Pierre-Nolasque Bergeret and the Fight for the Standard," *Achademia Leonardo da Vinci* 1 (1988), 76–86; Kemp *Marvellous*, 225; Jones, *The Lost Battles*, 227.

5 Codex Ash., 2:30v; Kemp *Marvellous*, 235.

6 Codex Madrid, 2:2.

7 Jones, *The Lost Battles*, 138.

8 Windsor, RCIN 912326.

9 Contract of "The Magnificent and Sublime Signoria, the priors of Liberty and the Standardbearer of Justice of the Florentine People," May 4, 1504.

10 Cole, *Leonardo, Michelangelo, and the Art of the Figure*, 31.

11 Codex Madrid, 2:1r; Anna Maria Brizio, "The Madrid Notebooks," *The UNESCO Courier,* October 1974, 36.

12 The tale is in the Anonimo Gaddiano. See also Notebooks/Irma Richter, 356; Nicholl, 376, 380.

13 Martin Gayford, "Was Michelangelo a Better Artist Than Leonardo da Vinci?," *The Telegraph*, November 16, 2013; Martin Gayford, *Michelangelo: His Epic Life* (Penguin, 2015), 252; Miles Unger, *Michelangelo: A Life in Six Masterpieces* (Simon & Schuster, 2014), 112.

14 Bramly, 343.

15 The notes of the meeting were taken by Luca Landucci, a spice dealer and diarist. Saul Levine, "The Location of Michelangelo's *David*: The Meeting of January 25, 1504," *Art Bulletin* 56.1 (March 1974), 31–49; Rona Goffen, *Renaissance Rivals: Michelangelo, Leonardo, Raphael, Titian* (Yale, 2002), 124; N. Randolph Parks, "The Placement of Michelangelo's *David*: A Review of the Documents," *Art Bulletin* 57.4 (December 1975), 560–70; John Paoletti, *Michelangelo's David* (Cambridge, 2015), 345; Nicholl, 378; Bramly, 343.

16 Windsor, RCIN 912591; Jones, *The Lost Battles*, 82; Jonathan Jones, "Leonardo and the Battle of Michelangelo's Penis," *The Guardian*, November 16, 2010; David M. Gunn, "Covering David," Monash University, Melbourne, Australia, July 2001, www.gunnzone.org/KingDavid/CoveringDavid.html. Leonardo's sketch on the Windsor

sheet (and a similar one he did on the reverse of that sheet) very closely resembles the pose of Michelangelo's *David*. Leonardo has very lightly drawn what seems to be a seahorse on a leash, thus suggesting that he was thinking of transforming the figure into a Neptune.

17 Windsor, RCIN 912594.

18 Bambach *Master Draftsman*, catalogue entries 101v-r and 102, pp. 538–48; "Studies for Hercules Holding a Club Seen in Frontal and Rear View," Metropolitan Museum (New York), Accession #2000.328a,b.

19 Anton Gill, *Il Gigante: Michelangelo, Florence, and the* David (St. Martin's, 2004), 295; Victor Coonin, *From Marble to Flesh: The Biography of Michelangelo's* David (Florentine Press, 2014), 90–93; Jones, *The Lost Battles*, 82.

20 Goffen, *Renaissance Rivals*, 143.

21 Jones, *The Lost Battles*, 186.

22 Botticelli being another notable exception.

23 Codex Madrid, 2:128r; Paris Ms. L, 79r; Notebooks/J. P. Richter, 488.

24 Paris Ms. G, 5b; Notebooks/J. P. Richter, 503; Clark, 200.

25 Codex Urbina, 61r.

26 Leonardo Treatise/Rigaud, ch. 40; Claire Farago, *Leonardo's Treatise on Painting: A Critical Interpretation with a New Edition of the Text in the Codex Urbinas* (Brill, 1992), 273. Farago provides a new translation and critical interpretation, and she discusses the dating of this passage on p. 403. Similar descriptions by Leonardo are in chapters 20 and 41 of the *paragone*.

27 Michelangelo, "To Giovanni Da Pistoia When the Author Was Painting the Vault of the Sistine Chapel" (1509), in Andrew Graham-Dixon, *Michelangelo and the Sistine Chapel* (Skyhorse, 2009), ii, 65; modified translation in Joel Agee, *New York Review of Books*, June 19, 2014; modified translation in Gail Mazur, Poetry Foundation, http://www.poetryfoundation.org/poems-and-poets/poems/detail/57328.

28 Gayford, *Michelangelo*, 251; Unger, *Michelangelo*, 117.

29 Cole, *Leonardo, Michelangelo, and the Art of the Figure*, 17, 34, 77, and passim.

30 John Addington Symonds, *The Life of Michelangelo Buonarroti* (Nimmo, 1893), 129, 156.

31 Rab Hatfield, *Finding Leonardo* (Florentine Press, 2007); "Finding the Lost da Vinci," *National Geographic*, March 2012, nationalgeographic.com/explorers/projects/lost-da-vinci/.

32 Farago, "Leonardo's *Battle of Anghiari*," 312; Kemp *Marvellous*, 224; Bramly, 348.

33 Farago, "Leonardo's *Battle of Anghiari*," 329.

34 Clark, 198.

35 *The Life of Benvenuto Cellini, Written by Himself*, many versions on the Internet.

36 Jones, *The Lost Battles*, 256.

26. RETURN TO MILAN

1 Codex Atl., 70b/208b; Notebooks/J. P. Richter, 1526, 1373.

2 Codex Arundel, 272r; Notebooks/J. P. Richter, 1372. See Richter's footnote for documentation of Piero's age.

3 Beck, "Ser Piero da Vinci and His Son Leonardo," 29; Bramly, 356.

4 Soderini letter, October 9, 1506, in Farago, "Leonardo's *Battle of Anghiari*," 329; Nicholl, 407.

5 Charles d'Amboise letter, December 16, 1506; Eugène Müntz, *Leonardo da Vinci* (Parkstone, 2012; original French edition 1898), 2:197; Nicholl, 408.

6   Florentine envoy Francesco Pandolfino, January 7, 1507; Müntz, *Leonardo da Vinci*, 2:200; Kemp *Marvellous*, 209.

7   The king arrived on May 24, 1507, not in April, as some accounts say. Nicholl, 409; Ella Noyes, *The Story of Milan* (Dent, 1908), 380; Arthur Tilley, *The Dawn of the French Renaissance* (Cambridge, 1918), 122.

8   Julia Cartright, "The Castello of Milan," *Monthly Review*, August 1901, 117.

9   This section draws from Nicholl, 412ff.; Bramly, 368ff.; Payne, Kindle loc. 4500ff.; Marrion Wilcox, "Francesco Melzi, Disciple of Leonardo," *Art & Life* 11.6 (December 1919).

10 Notebooks/J. P. Richter, 1350; Codex Atl., 1037v/372v-a.

11 Paris Ms. C; Notebooks/Irma Richter, 290, 291; Bramly, 223, 228; Codex Atl., 663v; Nicholl, 276.

12 Codex Atl., 571a-v/214r-a; Pedretti *Commentary*, 1:298. Carlo Pedretti transcribed the property in question as "Il botro," but others see the meaning of the phrase as "your property."

13 Louis, by the grace of God King of France, to the Perpetual Gonfalonier and the Signoria of Florence, July 26, 1507; Müntz, 186; Payne, Kindle loc. 4280.

14 Leonardo letter, September 18, 1507, in Notebooks/Irma Richter, 336.

15 Melzi's letter to Leonardo's half brothers on June 1, 1519, informing them of Leonardo's death, refers to property in Fiesole, which would not seem to be the same property. However, it seems most probable that Francesco da Vinci's property in question was used by Leonardo, then went to his half brothers.

16 Codex Atl., 317r; Notebooks/J. P. Richter, 1349.

17 Paris Ms. F.

18 Jill Burke, "Meaning and Crisis in the Early Sixteenth Century: Interpreting Leonardo's Lion," *Oxford Art Journal* 29.1 (2006), 79–91.

19 Codex Atl., 214r-b; Notebooks/MacCurdy, 1036; Carlo Pedretti, *Chronology of Leonardo Da Vinci's Architectural Studies after 1500* (Droz, 1962), 41; Sabine Frommel, "Leonardo and the Villa of Charles d'Amboise," in Carlo Pedretti, ed., *Leonardo da Vinci and France* (Amboise, 2019), 117.

20 Windsor, RCIN 912688, 912716; Sara Taglialagamba, "Leonardo da Vinci's Hydraulic Systems and Fountains for His French Patrons Louis XII, Charles d'Amboise, and Francis I," in Moffatt and Taglialagamba, 301.

21 Clark, 211.

27. ANATOMY, ROUND TWO

1   Windsor, RCIN 919027v; Notebooks/Irma Richter, 325; Keele and Roberts, 69; Keele *Elements*, 37.

2   Windsor, RCIN 919005r.

3   Windsor, RCIN 919027v.

4   Windsor, RCIN 919027v; Bauth Boon, "Leonardo da Vinci on Atherosclerosis and the Function of the Sinuses of Valsalva," *Netherland Heart Journal*, December 2009, 496; Keele, "Leonardo da Vinci's 'Anatomia Naturale,'" 369. Atherosclerosis is the thickening of the artery wall caused by the buildup of plaque, fats, cholesterol, and other substances. It is a specific form of arteriosclerosis, but the terms are sometimes used interchangeably.

5   Windsor, RCIN 919075; Leonardo Treatise/Rigaud, 199; Keele and Roberts, 91.

6   Notebooks/J. P. Richter, 796; Clayton and Philo, 18.

7   Windsor, RCIN 919070; "Previously unexhibited page from Leonardo's notebooks includes artist's 'to do' list," Royal Collection press release, April 5, 2012.

8 Windsor, RCIN 919070v, RCIN 919115r; Charles O'Malley and J. B. Saunders, *Leonardo on the Human Body* (Dover, 1983; first published 1952), 122; Notebooks/J. P. Richter, 819.

9 Windsor, RCIN 919070v; Notebooks/J. P. Richter, 796.

10 Keele *Elements*, 200; Windsor, RCIN 919031v.

11 Martin Clayton, "Leonardo's Anatomy Years," *Nature* 484 (April 2012), 314; Nicholl, 443.

12 Windsor, RCIN 919016.

13 Windsor, RCIN 919028r; Wells, 191.

14 Keele *Elements*, 268; Windsor, RCIN 919035v, 919019r.

15 Windsor, RCIN 919115r.

16 Jonathan Pevsner, "Leonardo da Vinci's Contributions to Neuroscience," *Scientific American Mind* 16.1 (2005), 217; Clayton and Philo, 144; Keele and Roberts, 54; Windsor, RCIN 919127.

17 Leonardo, "Weimar Sheet."

18 Windsor, RCIN 919003v; Keele and Roberts, 101.

19 Windsor, RCIN 919005v.

20 Windsor, RCIN 919014r; Keele *Elements*, 344; O'Malley and Saunders, *Leonardo on the Human Body*, 164; Clayton and Philo, 188.

21 Windsor, RCIN 919007v; Keele and Roberts, 82; O'Malley and Saunders, *Leonardo on the Human Body*, 44.

22 Windsor, RCIN 919040r.

23 Windsor, RCIN 919012v; Keele and Roberts, 110; O'Malley and Saunders, *Leonardo on the Human Body*, 156.

24 Windsor, RCIN 919055v; Keele and Roberts, 66; Clayton and Philo, 188. Grace Glueck, "Anatomy Lessons by Leonardo," *New York Times*, January 20, 1984; O'Malley and Saunders, *Leonardo on the Human Body*, 186, 414.

25 Windsor, RCIN 919093.

26 Windsor, RCIN 919093. This section draws on Mohammadali Shoja, Paul Agutter, et al., "Leonardo da Vinci's Studies of the Heart," *International Journal of Cardiology* 167 (2013), 1126; Morteza Gharib, David Kremers, Martin Kemp, et al., "Leonardo's Vision of Flow Visualization," *Experiments in Fluids* 33 (July 2002), 219; Larry Zaroff, "Leonardo's Heart," *Hektoen International Journal*, Spring 2013; Wells, Capra *Learning*, 288; Kenneth Keele, "Leonardo da Vinci and the Movement of the Heart," *Proceedings of the Royal Society of Medicine* 44 (1951), 209. I am grateful to David Linley and Martin Clayton for showing me some of the drawings at Windsor.

27 Windsor, RCIN 919028r.

28 Windsor, RCIN 919050v; Paris Ms. G, 1v; Keele, "Leonardo da Vinci's 'Anatomia Naturale,'" 376; Nuland, *Leonardo da Vinci*, 142.

29 Windsor, RCIN 919062r; Keele, "Leonardo da Vinci's 'Anatomia Naturale,'" 376; Wells, 202.

30 Windsor, RCIN 919063v, RCIN 919118; Wells, 83, 195; Nuland, *Leonardo da Vinci*, 143; Capra *Learning*, Kindle loc. 4574.

31 Windsor, RCIN 919082r, and also 919116r&v, 919117v, 919118r, 919083v. This section draws on Wells, 229–36; Keele and Roberts, 124, 131; Keele *Elements*, 316; Capra *Learning*, 290.

32 Windsor, RCIN 919118r.

33 Windsor, RCIN 912666; Keele *Elements*, 315.

34 Windsor, RCIN 919116r.

35 Windsor, RCIN 919082r; Capra *Learning*, 290; O'Malley and Saunders, *Leonardo on the Human Body*, 269.
36 Windsor, RCIN 919082r, 919116v; Clayton and Philo, 242.
37 Brian Bellhouse et al., "Mechanism of the Closure of the Aortic Valve," *Nature*, 217 (January 6, 1968), 86; Francis Robicsek, "Leonardo da Vinci and the Sinuses of Valsalva," *Annals of Thoracic Surgery* 52.2 (August 1991), 328; Malenka Bissell, Erica Dall'Armellina, and Robin Choudhury, "Flow Vortices in the Aortic Root," *European Heart Journal*, February 3, 2014, 1344; Nuland, *Leonardo da Vinci*, 147. The paper by Bellhouse and his team is interesting because it is a rare scholarly piece with only one reference note, and that reference is to a paper written almost five hundred years before. See also Brian Bellhouse and L. Talbott, "The Fluid Mechanics of the Aortic Valve," *Journal of Fluid Mechanics* 35.4 (1969), 721; Wells, xxii.
38 Windsor, RCIN 919102.
39 Windsor, RCIN 919102r; Jonathan Jones, "The Ten Greatest Works of Art Ever," *The Guardian*, March 21, 2014.
40 Windsor, RCIN 919103; Notebooks/Irma Richter, 166.
41 Hope, "The Last 'Last Supper.'"
42 Antonio de Beatis, *The Travel Journal* (Hakluyt/Routledge, 1979, originally written c. 1518), 132–34.

28. THE WORLD AND ITS WATERS

1 Codex Arundel, 156v; Notebooks/J. P. Richter, 1162.
2 Paris Ms. A, 55v; Notebooks/J. P. Richter, 929.
3 Windsor, RCIN 919102v.
4 Kemp, "Analogy and Observation in the Codex Hammer," 103; T. J. Fairbrother, C. Ishikawa, et al., *Leonardo Lives: The Codex Leicester and Leonardo da Vinci's Legacy of Art and Science* (Seattle Art Museum, 1997); Claire Farago, ed., *Leonardo da Vinci: The Codex Leicester* (American Museum of Natural History, 1996); Claire Farago, "The Codex Leicester," in Bambach *Master Draftsman*, 191. I am grateful to Bill Gates's curator, Frederick Schroeder, for displaying and discussing the Codex Leicester with me and for arranging for me to use a new and unpublished translation by Martin Kemp and Domenico Laurenza, as noted below.
5 Codex Leic., 33v; Notebooks/MacCurdy, 350. The quotations from the Codex Leicester in this chapter, unless otherwise noted, are based on a new translation, edited by Martin Kemp and Domenico Laurenza, to be published by Oxford University Press in 2018.
6 Codex Leic., 34r; Notebooks/J. P. Richter, 1000.
7 Codex Leic., 34r.
8 Domenico Laurenza, "Leonardo's Theory of the Earth," in Fabio Frosini and Alessandro Nova, eds., *Leonardo on Nature* (Marsilio, 2015), 257.
9 Irving Lavin, "Leonardo's Watery Chaos," paper, Institute for Advanced Study, April 21, 1993; Leslie Geddes, "Infinite Slowness and Infinite Velocity: The Representation of Time and Motion in Leonardo's Studies of Geology and Water," in Frosini and Nova, *Leonardo on Nature*, 269.
10 Bramly, 335.
11 Codex Madrid, 1:134v.
12 Codex Leic., 15v, 27v; Kemp *Marvellous*, 302; Nicholl, 431.
13 Codex Leic., 26v; Kemp *Marvellous*, 305.
14 Paris Ms. I, 72r–71u.

15 Paris Ms. F, 2b; Notebooks/J. P. Richter, 2.

16 Codex Leic., 29v.

17 Codex Triv., 32r; Windsor, RCIN 919108v; Keele *Elements*, 135.

18 Paris Ms. F, 34v; Notebooks/MacCurdy, 2:681, 724.

19 Paris Ms. G, 93r; Kemp *Marvellous*, 304.

20 Codex Leic., 14r; Bambach *Master Draftsman*, 624.

21 Windsor, RCIN 912579; Notebooks/J. P. Richter, 389.

22 Windsor, RCIN 912424.

23 Codex Atl., 118a-r; Kemp *Marvellous*, 305.

24 E. H. Gombrich, "The Form of Movement in Water and Air," in O'Malley, 171.

25 Paris Ms. H, 77r; Kemp *Leonardo*, 155.

26 Codex Leic., 21v; Notebooks/J. P. Richter 963.

27 Codex Atl., fol. 468.

28 Paris Ms. A, folio 56r; Notebooks/J. P. Richter, 941, 968.

29 Codex Leicester's sheet 3 is folded into folios, the most important of which is 34v, showing siphons and other ways to move water. See also Bambach *Master Draftsman*, 619.

30 Codex Leic., 28r, 3v; Keele *Elements*, 81, 102; Kemp *Marvellous*, 313.

31 Paris Ms. G, 38r, 70r.

32 Windsor, RCIN 919003r.

33 Paris Ms. F, 11v.

34 Capra *Learning*, Kindle loc. 1201; Codex Leic., 10r. Capra attributes the rediscovery of this type of rock stratification to the seventeenth-century Danish geologist Nicolas Steno.

35 Codex Leic., 10r; Notebooks/J. P. Richter, 990.

36 Codex Leic., 9v; Notebooks/Irma Richter, 28.

37 Codex Leic., 8b; Notebooks/J. P. Richter, 987.

38 Paris Ms. E, 4r; Notebooks/Irma Richter, 349.

39 Codex Leic., 10r; Notebooks/J. P. Richter, 990.

40 Codex Leic., 10r; Notebooks/J. P. Richter, 990. In this case, I have used the Richter translation rather than the one prepared by Domenico Laurenza and the Bill Gates team.

41 Paris Ms. E, 4r; Codex Leic., 10r; Notebooks/J. P. Richter, 990; Capra *Learning*, 70, 83; Stephen Jay Gould, *Leonardo's Mountain of Clams and the Diet of Worms* (Harmony, 1998), 17; Andrea Baucon, "Leonardo da Vinci, the Founding Father of Ichnology," *Palaios* 25 (2010), 361.

42 Windsor, RCIN 912669v; Notebooks/J. P. Richter, 886.

43 Copernicus in his *Commentariolus*, written c. 1510–14, first proposed his heliocentric theory that the apparent movements of heavenly bodies came from the Earth's rotation and movements.

44 Paris Ms. F, 41b; Notebooks/J. P. Richter, 858.

45 Paris Ms. F, 22b; Notebooks/J. P. Richter, 861.

46 Paris Ms. F, 41b; 4b; Notebooks/J. P. Richter, 858, 880.

47 Paris Ms. F, 94b; Notebooks/J. P. Richter, 874.

48 Codex Leic., 1a; Notebooks/J. P. Richter, 864.

49 Codex Leic., 4r; Notebooks/J. P. Richter, 300; Notebooks/MacCurdy, 128.

50 Codex Leic., 4r; Notebooks/J. P. Richter, 300; Notebooks/MacCurdy, 128.

51 Codex Leic., 36r.

52 Codex Leic., 36r; Notebooks/J. P. Richter, 300–301; Bell, "Aristotle as a Source for Leonardo's Theory of Colour Perspective after 1500," 100.

29. ROME

1 Payne, Kindle loc. 3204.
2 Nicholl, 110; Clayton and Philo, 23.
3 Windsor, RCIN 912579.
4 Clark, 237.
5 Windsor, RCIN 912726. Although most scholars attribute the drawing to Melzi, it is possible that it was by another student.
6 Bramly, 6, n7.
7 Windsor, RCIN 912300v.
8 Nick Squires, "Leonardo da Vinci Self Portrait Discovered Hidden in Manuscript," *The Telegraph* (London), February 28, 2009.
9 Scholars are divided. "I continue to believe in it as a potent and unflinching portrait of himself at the end of his life," Charles Nicholl wrote (Nicholl, 493). On the other hand, Martin Kemp says it "is generally but incorrectly taken to be a self-portrait." Some skeptics say the style more resembles Leonardo's work from just after 1500, which would make it less likely as a self-portrait given that the drawing is of an older man.
10 Gian Paolo Lomazzo, *Idea of the Temple of Painting* (Pennsylvania State, 2013; originally published 1590), 92.
11 Clark, 235; Carmen Bambach, "Leonardo and Raphael in Rome," in Miguel Falomir, ed., *Late Raphael* (Museo del Prado, 2013), 26.
12 Carmen Bambach, "Leonardo and Raphael, circa 1513–16," Museo Nacional del Prado lecture, June 2011; Nicholl, 450–65.
13 Windsor, RCIN 919084r; Notebooks/Irma Richter, 349; Notebooks/J. P. Richter, 1064.
14 Codex Atl., 225r.
15 Nicholl, 459.
16 Alessandro da Vinci to Giuliano da Vinci, December 14, 1514.
17 Notebooks/MacCurdy, 2:438.
18 Syson, "The Rewards of Service," 48.
19 Vasari, *Lives*; Notebooks/Irma Richter, 349.
20 Windsor, RCIN 912684.
21 Pedretti *Commentary*, 1:20; Pedretti, *The Machines*, 18; Paris Ms. G, 84v; Codex Atl., f. 17v; Dupré, "Optic, Picture and Evidence," 211.
22 Codex Atl., f. 87r.
23 Codex Atl., f. 17v.
24 Codex Atl., folios 96r, 257r, 672r, 672v, 750r, 751a-v, 751b-r, 751b-v, 1017r, 1017v, 1036a-r, 1036a-v, 1036b-r, 1036b-v; Dupré, "Optic, Picture and Evidence," 221.
25 Codex Atl., 1036a-v; Pedretti *Commentary*, 1:19; Dupré, "Optic, Picture and Evidence," 223.
26 Codex Atl., 247r/671r; Notebooks/J. P. Richter, 1351; Notebooks/Irma Richter, 380.
27 Codex Atl., 182v-c/500; Keele *Elements*, 38.
28 Nicholl, 484.

30. POINTING THE WAY

1 Clark, 248.
2 Clark, 250.
3 John 1:14.

4   Codex Atl., 179r-a, from May 1509, shows a pupil's sketch of the pointing hand. Carlo Pedretti, who dated the Codex Atlanticus sheet, also believes that the *Saint John* was begun about 1509 and provided the inspiration for some copies in Italy beginning then (*Chronology*, 166). Martin Kemp agrees (*Marvellous*, 336). Luke Syson suggests it may have been begun in Milan in 1499 and viewed in 1506 in Florence, where it may have provided the inspiration for an altarpiece there ("The Rewards of Service," 44). Kenneth Clark dated the picture to 1514–15 (248). Frank Zöllner suggests it was 1513–16 (2:248).

5   John 1:7.

6   Paul Barolsky, "The Mysterious Meaning of Leonardo's *Saint John the Baptist*," *Notes in the History of Art* 8.3 (Spring 1989), 14.

7   See Kemp *Marvellous*, 336, for the argument that this is the result of an overzealous restoration.

8   Syson, 249; Janice Shell and Grazioso Sironi, "Salai and Leonardo's Legacy," *Burlington Magazine*, February 1991, no. 104; Zöllner, 2:9.

9   Pedretti *Chronology*, 165. It was in the Baroffio Museum of the Sanctuary of Sacro Monte.

10 Clark, 251; Zöllner, 2:91.

11 Matthew 3:11.

12 Andre Green, *Revelations de l'inachevement* (Flammarion, 1992), 111; Carlo Pedretti, ed., *Angel in the Flesh* (Cartei & Bianchi, 2009).

13 Brian Sewell, *Sunday Telegraph*, April 5, 1992, quoted in Nicholl, 562n26. Sewell once worked in the Royal Library.

14 Pedretti, "The Pointing Lady," 339.

31. THE *MONA LISA*

1   Kenneth Clark, "Mona Lisa," *Burlington Magazine* 115.840 (March 1973), 144.

2   Kemp and Pallanti, *Mona Lisa*, 10; Giuseppe Pallanti, Mona Lisa *Revealed* (Skira, 2006); Dianne Hales, Mona Lisa: *A Life Discovered* (Simon & Schuster, 2014). Some writers have asserted that Francesco had been married twice before, but there is no evidence for this.

3   Pallanti, Mona Lisa *Revealed*, 89–92.

4   Jack Greenstein, "Leonardo, *Mona Lisa*, and La Gioconda," *Artibus et Historiae* 25.50 (2004), 17; Pallanti, Mona Lisa *Revealed*, 75, 96; Kemp and Pallanti, *Mona Lisa*, 50; Zöllner, 1:241, 1:251.

5   Nicholl, 366; Kemp and Pallanti, *Mona Lisa*, 110; Kemp *Marvellous*, 261.

6   Shell and Sironi, "Salai and Leonardo's Legacy," 95.

7   Kemp and Pallanti, *Mona Lisa*, 118.

8   Jill Burke, "Agostino Vespucci's Marginal Note about Leonardo da Vinci in Heidelberg," *Leonardo da Vinci Society Newsletter* 30 (May 2008), 3; Martin Kemp, *Christ to Coke* (Oxford, 2011), 146.

9   For an argument that the portrait from the very outset was a project initiated by Leonardo rather than by Francesco del Giocondo, and that Lisa's plain clothing and grooming make it unlikely that it was a commissioned portrait, see Joanna Woods-Marsden, "Leonardo da Vinci's *Mona Lisa*: A Portrait without a Commissioner?," in Moffatt and Taglialagamba, 169.

10 Laurence de Viguerie, Philippe Walter, et al., "Revealing the Sfumato Technique of Leonardo da Vinci by X-Ray Fluorescence Spectroscopy," *Angewandte Chemie* 49.35 (August 16, 2010), 6125; Sandra Šustić, "Paint Handling in Leonardo's *Mona Lisa*,"

CeROArt, January 13, 2014; Philip Ball, "Behind the *Mona Lisa*'s smile," *Nature*, August 5, 2010; Hales, Mona Lisa: *A Life Discovered*, 158; Alasdair Palmer, "How Leonardo Did It," *Spectator*, September 16, 2006, describing the work of Jacques Franck, a French artist and art historian who studied how to replicate Leonardo's technique.

11 Elisabeth Martin, "The Painter's Palette," in Jean-Pierre Mohen et al., eds., *The* Mona Lisa: *Inside the Painting* (Abrams, 2006), 62. This volume has twenty-five essays along with high-resolution pictures that detail the findings of multispectral imaging techniques.

12 Codex Ash., 1:15a; Notebooks/J. P. Richter, 520.

13 Z. Zaremba Filipczak, "New Light on *Mona Lisa*: Leonardo's Optical Knowledge and His Choice of Lighting," *Art Bulletin* 59.4 (December 1977), 518; Zöllner, 1:160; Klein, *Leonardo's Legacy*, 32.

14 Clark, "Mona Lisa," 144; Pascal Cotte, *Lumiere on the* Mona Lisa (Vinci Editions, 2015); "New Technology Sheds Light On Centuries-Old Debate about *Mona Lisa*," PR Newswire, October 17, 2007; "High Resolution Image Hints at 'Mona Lisa's' Eyebrows," CNN, October 18, 2007.

15 Good books include Mohen et al., *The* Mona Lisa; Cotte, *Lumiere on the* Mona Lisa; Zöllner. The best online versions are from the Paris research firm C2RMF, available on its website, http://en.c2rmf.fr/, and also at *Wikimedia Commons*, https://commons.wikimedia.org/wiki/File:Mona_Lisa,_by_Leonardo_da_Vinci,_from_C2RMF_natural_color.jpg.

16 Bruno Mottin, "Reading the Image," in Mohen et al., *The* Mona Lisa, 68.

17 Carlo Starnazzi, *Leonardo Cartografo* (Istituto geografico militare, 2003), 76.

18 Walter Pater, *The Renaissance* (University of California, 1980; originally published 1893), 79.

19 Takao Sato and Kenchi Hosokawa, "*Mona Lisa* Effect of Eyes and Face," *i-Perception* 3.9 (October 2012), 707; Sheena Rogers, Melanie Lunsford, et al., "The *Mona Lisa* Effect: Perception of Gaze Direction in Real and Pictured Faces," in Sheena Rogers and Judith Effken, eds., *Studies in Perception and Action VII* (Lawrence Erlbaum, 2003), 19; Evgenia Boyarskaya, Alexandra Sebastian, et al., "The *Mona Lisa* Effect: Neural Correlates of Centered and Off-centered Gaze," *Human Brain Mapping* 36.2 (February 2015), 415.

20 Windsor, RCIN 919055v.

21 Margaret Livingstone, "Is It Warm? Is It Real? Or Just Low Spatial Frequency?," *Science* 290.5495 (November 17, 2000), 1299; Alessandro Soranzo and Michelle Newberry, "The Uncatchable Smile in Leonardo da Vinci's *La Bella Principessa* Portrait," *Vision Research*, June 4, 2015, 78; Isabel Bohrn, Claus-Christian Carbon, and Florian Hutzler, "*Mona Lisa*'s Smile: Perception or Deception?," *Psychological Science*, March 2010, 378.

22 Mark Brown, "The Real *Mona Lisa*? Prado Museum Finds Leonardo da Vinci Pupil's Take," *The Guardian*, February 1, 2012.

23 Kemp and Pallanti, *Mona Lisa*, 171.

32. FRANCE

1 Jan Sammer, "The Royal Invitation," in Carlo Pedretti, ed., *Leonardo da Vinci in France* (CB Edizioni, 2010), 32.

2 Codex Atl., 471r/172v-a; Notebooks/J. P. Richter, 1368A.

3 Nicholl, 486–93; Bramly, 397–99; Notebooks/J. P. Richter, 1566.

4 Robert Knecht, *Renaissance Warrior and Patron: The Reign of Francis I* (Cambridge, 1994), 427 and passim; Robert Knecht, *The French Renaissance Court* (Yale, 2008).

5   Bramly, 401; Codex Madrid, 2:24a.

6   Notebooks/Irma Richter, 383.

7   Codex Atl., 106r-a/294v; Luca Garai, "The Staging of *The Besieged Fortress*," in Pedretti, *Leonardo da Vinci in France*, 141.

8   Pedretti, *Leonardo da Vinci in France*, 24, 154.

9   De Beatis, *The Travel Journal*, 132–34.

10 Author's interview with Delieuvin.

11 Taglialagamba, "Leonardo da Vinci's Hydraulic Systems and Fountains for His French Patrons," 300; Carlo Pedretti, *Leonardo da Vinci: The Royal Palace at Romorantin* (Harvard, 1972); Pascal Brioist, "The Royal Palace in Romorantin," and Pascal Brioist and Romano Nanni, "Leonardo's French Canal Projects," in Pedretti, *Leonardo da Vinci in France*, 83, 95; Pedretti, *A Chronology of Leonardo's Architectural Studies after 1500*, 140; Matthew Landrus, "Evidence of Leonardo's Systematic Design Process for Palaces and Canals in Romorantin," in Moffatt and Taglialagamba, 100; Ludwig Heydenreich, "Leonardo da Vinci, Architect of Francis I," *Burlington Magazine* 595.94 (October 1952), 27; Jean Guillaume, "Leonardo and Architecture," in *Leonardo da Vinci: Engineer and Architect* (Montreal Museum, 1987), 278; Hidemichi Tanaka, "Leonardo da Vinci, Architect of Chambord?," *Artibus et Historiae* 13.25 (1992), 85.

12 Notebooks/J. P. Richter, 747.

13 Codex Atl., f. 76v-b/209r., 336v-b/920r; Codex Arundel, 270v.

14 Most of the drawings are in Windsor, which officially dates them to 1517–18, during his period in France. That date was accepted by the Milan exhibition of 2015. Others, including Carmen Bambach (in *Master Draftsman*, 630), have suggested a slightly earlier date of 1515–17. Whenever he started them, Leonardo had them with him when he died in France in 1519, and they were part of the bequest to Francesco Melzi.

15 Windsor, RCIN 912377, 912378, 912380, 912382, 912383, 912384, 912385, 912386.

16 Margaret Mathews-Berenson, *Leonardo da Vinci and the "Deluge Drawings": Interviews with Carmen C. Bambach and Martin Clayton* (Drawing Society, 1998), 7.

17 Codex Atl., 171r-a; Notebooks/J. P. Richter, 965 (the translation of *vitale umore* as "vital human" is a mistake).

18 Codex Leic., sheets 12r and 26v.

19 Brown, 86.

20 Windsor, RCIN 912665; Notebooks/J. P. Richter, 608; Gombrich, "The Form of Movement in Water and Air," 171.

21 Notebooks/J. P. Richter, 609.

22 Paris Ms. G, 6b; Notebooks/J. P. Richter, 607.

23 Codex Atl., 393v/145v-b; Notebooks/Irma Richter, 252; Notebooks/J. P. Richter, 1336; Beth Stewart, "Interesting Weather Ahead: Thoughts on Leonardo's 'Deluge' Drawings," UCLA lecture, May 21, 2016.

24 Codex Arundel, 245v; Pedretti *Commentary*, 2:325 and plate 44; Carlo Pedretti, introduction to *Leonardo's Codex Arundel* (British Library/Giunti, 1998); Nicholl, 1.

25 Windsor, RCIN 919084r, 919115r.

26 Shell and Sironi, "Salai and Leonardo's Legacy," 95; Laure Fagnart, "The French History of Leonardo da Vinci's Paintings," in Pedretti, *Leonardo da Vinci in France*, 113; Bertrand Jestaz, "François I, Salai et les tableaux de Léonard," *Revue de l'art* 4 (1999), 68.

27 Notebooks/J. P. Richter, 1173.

28 Pedretti *Chronology*, 171; Arsène Houssaye, "The Death-Bed of Leonardo," in Mrs. Charles Heaton, *Leonardo da Vinci and His Works* (Macmillan, 1874), 192.

570 Notes for pages 517-525

33. CONCLUSION

1 Notebooks/J. P. Richter, 1360, 1365, 1366.
2 Arthur Schopenhauer, *The World as Representation* (1818), vol. 1, ch. 3, para. 31.
3 Steve Jobs, Rob Siltanen, Lee Clow, and others, Apple print and television advertisement, 1998.
4 Albert Einstein to Carl Seelig, March 11, 1952, Einstein Archives 39-013, online.
5 Albert Einstein to Otto Juliusburger, September 29, 1942, Einstein Archives 38-238, online.
6 Codex Ash., 1:7b; Notebooks/J. P. Richter, 491.

CODA

1 Sang-Hee Yoon and Sungmin Park, "A Mechanical Analysis of Woodpecker Drumming," *Bioinspiration & Biomimetics* 6.1 (March 2011). The first good illustrations of the tongue of the woodpecker were done by Dutch anatomist Volcher Coiter in 1575.

ILLUSTRATION CREDITS

INDEX

Page numbers in *italics* refer to illustrations.

abacus schools, 17, 31, 32, 37, 201
Accademia Gallery, 372
Accattabriga (Antonio di Piero del
    Vaccha), 13, 14–15, 23, 47, 293
    death of, 293
Ackerman, James, 275
Adda River, 445
Adoration of the Magi (Lippi), 83, 317
Aenid (Virgil), 509
Aesop, 125, 172, 302
air, 196
    flight and, 178, 185–86, 196
Alberti, Leon Battista, 16, 30–31, 34,
    55, 77, 82, 84, 140, 176, 266, 281
    architectural treatise of, 145
    on Gutenberg, 171–72
    illegitimacy of, 30
    as influence on Leonardo, 30–31,
        87–88
    On Painting, 30, 31, 87–88, 212, 261,
        273
    perspective and, 30, 31, 78, 273, 275,
        276, 288
Alexander VI, Pope, 15, 335–36
Alexander the Great, 43, 44, 261, 499
algebra, 31–32, 110, 200, 201
Alhazen (Ibn al-Haytham), 176, 270,
    273, 458
Alice's Adventures in Wonderland
    (Carroll), 120

allegorical drawings, 119–20
    of Pleasure and Pain, 136–39, *138*
Allori, Alessandro, 377
Amadori, Alessandro, 308, 455
Amboise, 499, 502, 504, 505, 512
Amboise, Charles d', xi, 383–84,
    389–92, 444, 495
    Leonardo's plans for palace of, 392
Americas, 348
Amontons, Guillaume, 197
analog and digital systems, 201, 431
analogies, 109, 176–78, 181, 201, 206,
    400–405
    arteriosclerosis and, 396
    heart and arteries, and sprouting
        seed, 401, *401,* 415
    human body and buildings, 140–41,
        144, 149–50, *151,* 177
    machines and nature, 199, 401–3
    microcosm of man and macrocosm
        of earth, 109, 110, 149, 158, 302,
        322, 425–27
    in *Ginevra de' Benci,* 63, 67, 322,
        426
    in *Madonna of the Yarnwinder,*
        311, 322, 426
    in *Mona Lisa,* 322, 426, 487
    revision of analogy, 435–38
    in *Virgin and Child with Saint
        Anne,* 322, 426

analogies (*cont.*)
  water and air, 178, 419
  water eddies and hair curls, 433, 434,
    447, 507–8
  water on earth and blood in body,
    435–38
anamorphosis, 58
Anatomice (Benedetti), 399
anatomy, 2, 61–62, 84–86, 88, 158,
    212–22, 295, 300, 308, 344,
    394–424, 494, 503
  analogous forms in nature and, 109,
    110, 401, *401*, 415, 435–38
    see also analogies
  arteriosclerosis and, 396
  of bones, 402, *402*, 405–9
  of brain, 264
    nerves and ventricles, 404–5, *404*
    wax cast of, 403–4, *403*, 419
  branching systems in, 109
  comparative, 162, 219, 363, 411
  dental, 216
  dissections, 2, 162, 177, 213, 270,
    271–72, 317, 397–400, 445,
    460–61, 503
    arms, 409–11, *410*
    centenarian, 391, 394–96, *395*,
      397–98
    Church and, 397
    eye, 270, 271–72
    face, 409–11, *410*
    Leonardo's warning to others on,
      398–99
    veins and arteries, 401
  of eye, 270, 271–72
  female, 72*n*
  of fetus, 177, 215, 420–22, *421*, 500
    compared to seed, 177, 422
  of heart, 174, 201, 401, 405, 413–16,
    414, 428, 461
    aortic valve, 416–20, *418*
    with arteries, compared with
      sprouting seed, 401, *401*, 415
    blood and, 415–20
    glass model of, 419
    ventricles, 415

  of horses, 162, 163, *163*
  of lips and smile, 409–13, *412*, 489
  of liver, 396, 414
  lost impact of Leonardo's work on,
    423–24
  medical scholars and, 213
  muscles, 213, 218, 219, 401–2, *402*,
    405–9
    leg, 405–7, *407*
    mouth, 409–13, *412*
    neck, 84–86, *86*
    shoulder, 405, *406*
  outline for treatise on, 215
  proportions, 219–22
    of face, 219–21, *220*
    see also Vitruvian Man
  skull, 216–19, *217*, 271–72, *272*
  spine and spinal cord, 218, 407–9,
    408
  Vesalius and, 424
Anchiano, 13–14
Andrea da Ferrara, Giacomo, 132,
    152–53
  death of, 152
  Vitruvian Man drawing of, 152–53,
    153
Andrea del Sarto, 377
Anne of Brittany, 320
Annunciation (theatrical production),
    182
Anonimo Gaddiano, 7, 8, 91, 116, 130
Antiques Trade Gazette (*ATG*), 256
aorta, 417
aortic valve, 416–20, *418*
Apelles, 158, 318–20, 324
Apple, 518
Apollo Belvedere, 456
Archimedes, 101, 302, 345, 459–60
Archimedes screw, 196
architecture, 30, 102–3
  Alberti's treatise on, 145
  analogy between human body and
    buildings, 140–41, 144, 149–50,
    151, 177
  buttresses, 144–45
  experiment and theory in, 175

Francesco's treatise on, 145, 148
Leonardo's comparison of doctors
   and architects, 144, 177
Vitruvius's treatise on, 29, 148, 149
see also churches
Aristides of Thebes, 87
Aristotle, 18, 122, 174, 175, 176, 184,
   268, 442
   in Raphael's *School of Athens*, 449,
   449
arithmetic, 3, 31–32, 110, 200–201, 431
arms, dissections of, 409–11, *410*
Arno River, 373, 428, 429, 440, 487
   diverting course of, 347–52, 353, 428,
      429, 431, 432, 505, 507
   harnessing power of, 193
Arno Valley, drawing of, 47–48, *48, 55,*
   507, 510
art:
   anamorphosis in, 58
   chiaroscuro in, 40–41, 61, 228, 377,
      466
   dimensionality in, 2, 40–41, 263, 266,
      273
   Florentine, two schools of, 377
   landscapes, 47–48
   light in, 2, 80, 82, 230–31, 238–39,
      243–44, 245–47
   lines in, 79, 266–67, 377, 466, 486
      Michelangelo and, 375, 376, 466
   oil painting, 54
   perspective in, *see* perspective
   science and, 1, 2, 47, 61–62, 78, 157,
      203, 213, 215, 228, 239, 260–77,
      333, 405, 507, 522–23
      Leonardo's *paragone* and, 260–63,
         264, 265
   sfumato in, 41, 55, 228, 258, 269–70,
      281, 332, 375–77, 466, 468–69,
      486–87, 490
Arte dei Giuduci e Notai, 16
Arte dei Medici e Speziali, 47
arteriosclerosis, 396, 562*n*4
artists:
   disciplines straddled by, 26, 140
   status of, 31, 34, 260–61, 379

Ascension, The (play), 182
astronomy, 440–42, 459
autopsies, 397
Avicenna, 398

Babbitt, Isaac, 199
Bach, Johann Sebastian, 323
Bacon, Francis, 17, 521
Bacon, Roger, 97–98, 176, 500, 521
Bambach, Carmen, 73, 251–52, 331
Bandello, Matteo, 240
Bandinelli, Bartolommeo, 73
Baptism of Christ (Verrocchio with
      Leonardo), 41, 48–49, 50, 52–56,
      53, 63, 233, 284, 428, 537*n*50
Baroncelli, Bernardo, hanging of, 89,
   90
Barone, Juliana, 44
Bartolomeo, Fra, 377
Battista de Vilanis, 497, 513
Battle of Cascina (Michelangelo), 373–74,
      373, 375, 376, 379
Bayeux Tapestry, 357
BBC, 256
Beheading of Saint John the Baptist
      (Verrocchio), 44
*Bella Principessa, La: The Story of the New
      Masterpiece by Leonardo Da Vinci*
      (Kemp and Cotte), 254–57
Bellhouse, Brian, 419, 564*n*37
Bellincioni, Bernardo, 11*n,* 113, 158,
      244–45, 501
Bellini, Giovanni, 304
Bembo, Bernardo, 65, 66, 481
Benci, Ginevra de', 63–64, 83
   Bembo and, 65, 66, 481
   Leonardo's portrait of, 56, 63–67,
      64, 72, 86, 126–27, 241, 243, 255,
      276–77, 306
   earthly and human forces
      connected in, 63, 67, 322, 426
   gaze in, 66, 247
   Mona Lisa compared with, 477
Benci, Giovanni de', 64, 83, 87
Benedetti, Alessandro, 399
Benivieni, Antonio, 397

Berenson, Bernard, 234, 248, 250
Berneri, Giovanni Agostino, 148
Bernoulli, Daniel, 184
Bernoulli's principle, 185
bestiaries, 125
   of Leonardo, 125–26, 243
Bible, 49, 84, 171, 201, 368
   Flood story in, 439, 509, 512
Biblioteca Ambrosiana, 107
Billi, Antonio, 8
birds and flight, 4, 18–20, 178, 180,
   181–89, 204–5, 213, 295, 308,
   326, 391
   air and, 178, 185–86, 196
   bird-watching, 183–86
   Codex on the Flight of Birds, 184,
     188, 453
   flying machines, 45, 98, 180, 181,
     184, 186–89, *187,* 193, 326, 353,
     354, 357, 391
     aerial screw (helicopter), 45–46,
       46, 354
     experiments with, 161, 188
     theatrical, 45–46, *46,* 115–16,
       181–83, 186, 189
   gliders, 188
Biro, Peter Paul, 255–57
blood, 415–20, 425–26
   circulation of, and circulation of
     water on earth, 435–38
Boccaccio, Giovanni, 16, 127
Bologna, 461, 462, 496
Boltraffio, Giovanni Antonio, 238, 251,
   331
   portrait of Melzi by, *385*
bones, 402, *402,* 405–9
Bonfire of the Vanities, 300, 301, 390
Book of Art, The (Cennini), 261
bookkeeping, 25, 27, 201
Borgia, Cesare, xi, 15–16, 301, 303,
   335–46, 382, 498
   conquests of, 336, 337, 340, 352
   Leonardo employed by, 16, 102, 300,
     301, 337–46, 348, 352, 357, 444,
     495
   Leonardo's sketches of, 338, *339*
   Machiavelli and, 16, 335, 336–37,
     342, 343, 345, 346
   ruthlessness and brutality of, 301,
     303, 335–36, 345
Borgia, Lucrezia, 303, 336
Borgia, Rodrigo (Pope Alexander VI),
   15, 335–36
Borgia family, 346
Botticelli, Sandro, 28, 34, 47, 50, 70, 71,
   77, 89, 92, 370
   Adoration paintings of, 76, 77, 82,
     83
   Leonardo's criticism of, 77
   Medici family and, 77, 83, 89
Botticini, Francesco, 50
Bracciolini, Poggio, 149
brain, 264
   emotions and, 409–11
   nerves and ventricles of, 404–5, *404*
   vision and, 218–19, 261–62, 271
   wax cast of, 403–4, *403,* 419
Bramante, Donato, xi, 94, 129, 141,
   455
   church designs of, 142, 146, 148
   equestrian monument of, 162
   fresco of Heraclitus and Democritus,
     142, *143,* 157
   Leonardo's collaborations with,
     141–42
   in Milan Cathedral tiburio project,
     140, 141, 144, 145
   Pavia Cathedral project and, 148
   Santa Maria delle Grazie and, 142,
     280
   Santa Maria presso San Satiro apse
     designed by, 142
   at Sforza court, 141, 142
Brambilla Barcilon, Pinin, 292
Bramly, Serge, 368, 537*n*42
bridge, self-supporting, 341–42, *341*
British Library, 107
British Museum, 251
Bronzino, Agnolo, 377
Brown, Dan, 205, 284
Brown, David Alan, 61, 62, 331,
   537*n*47

Brunelleschi, Filippo, 26, 29–30, 140, 182
   cathedral dome of, 26, 29, 82, 145
     ball mounted atop, 37–38, 41, 458
   as influence on Leonardo, 29
   perspective and, 29–30, 31, 78, 273, 276
Burckhardt, Jacob, 15
buttresses, 144–45
Byron, George Gordon, Lord, 3

Caesar, Julius, 261
calculus, 210, 431
camera obscura, 271
canals, 340, 349–50, *350*, 458, 505
   of Milan, 347–48, 428, 505, 507
cannonballs, 340
Capra, Fritjof, 176, 439, 440
Cardano, Fazio, 274
Carolina Heart Institute, 419
Castiglione, Baldassare, 457
castles, 340
Cellini, Benvenuto, 70, 274, 372–73, 379, 499
Cennini, Cennino, 261
centenarian, 391, 394–96, *395*, 397–98
Cesena, 340–41, 342, 345
Cesenatico, 340
Champod, Christophe, 255
change, rates of, 201
Charles I of England, 329, 331
Charles II of England, 329–30
Charles VIII of France, 169
Château d'Amboise, 499, 500, 511, 515
Château de Cloux (now Clos Lucé), 499–501, *499, 500,* 513
Chiana Valley, 351, *351*
chiaroscuro, 40–41, 61, 228, 377, 466
Christ and Saint Thomas (Verrocchio), 37, 54
Christianity, 174
Christie's, 248, 251
Church, *see* religion and Church
churches, 158, 223
   Bramante's designs for, 142, 146, 148

   double-shelled dome for, 145
   Francesco's designs for, 146
   human body proportions and, 140–41, 149–50, *151*
   Leonardo's drawings for, *xxii,* 142, *143,* 146, 148
   Florence Cathedral dome, 26, 29, 82, 145
     ball mounted atop, 37–38, 41, 458
   Milan Cathedral, 146–47, 160
     buttresses for, 144
     tiburio for, 140–48, *141,* 158, 174–75, 177, 188
     Pavia Cathedral, 146–48, *147*
Church of Santa Maria Novella, 357
Church of Santa Maria presso San Satiro, 142
Cianchi, Marco, 199
Cicero, 149, 172, 318–20
circle, squaring, *xxii,* 109–10, 158, 209–10, 302, 363, 548*n*20
city plan, 102–4, 140
Clark, Kenneth, 5, 37, 54, 71, 74, 134, 179, 210–11, 232, 234, 248, 250, 281, 318, 323, 379, 392–93, 447, 463, 464, 477, 521
Clayton, Martin, 2, 86, 124, 507
Codices Madrid, 6
Codex Arundel, 107
Codex Atlanticus, 107, 567*n*4
Codex Leicester, 107, 426–29, 431, 435–40, 442, 445, 507, 521
Codex on the Flight of Birds, 184, 188
coins, xiii
   minting of, 458
collaboration, and genius, 523
color, 276
   distance and, 276
   light and, 80, 228, 266, 267–68
   of sky, 2, 178, 322, 442–43
Columbus, Christopher, 9, 18, 348
Compagnia di San Luca, 46–47
componimento inculto, 321
Confraternity of the Immaculate Conception, 223–24, 230, 232
Constantinople, 18

contrapposto, 243, 370

Copernicus, Nicolaus, 176, 441

Corte Vecchia, 160–61, 188, 202, 219, 223, 295

Cosmography (Ptolemy), 301–2

Cotte, Pascal, 252–59, 485

Crivelli, Lucrezia, 245
    La Belle Ferronnière, 245–48, *246,* 254, 306, 488, 490
    copy of, 250

crocodile, 398

curiosity, cultivating, 519–20

currency, xiii

Daley, Michael, 292

Danae, La (Taccone), 115

Dante Alighieri, 71, 89, 367, 474

Darius, 43, 44

David (Michelangelo), 35, 368–72, *369*
    Leonardo's sketch of, 371–72, *371*

David (Verrocchio), 34–36, *35,* 135, 368–70, 536*n*21
    Leonardo as model for, 35–36, *35,* 368–70, 536*n*22

da Vinci, Albiera (stepmother), 13, 15, 23, 308, 322, 455

da Vinci, Antonio (grandfather), 12–15, 23, 24, 47

da Vinci, Antonio (half-brother), 63

da Vinci, Domenico (half-brother), 457

da Vinci, Francesco (uncle), 15, 23, 24, 388, 512

da Vinci, Giuliano (half-brother), 63, 456–57

da Vinci, Leonardo, *see* Leonardo da Vinci

da Vinci, Michele (great-great-great-grandfather), 11, 12

da Vinci, Piero (father), xii, 11*n,* 12–16, 32, 33, 72, 346, 380, 479, 495, 535*n*1
    and commissions for Leonardo, 63–64, 74, 75, 82, 380, 479, 495
    death of, 380–81, 387
    estate of, 381, 388, 495

Leonardo's illegitimacy and, 24–25, 380, 381, 495
    marriages and children of, 13, 15, 25, 63, 68, 72, 380, 381
    as notary, 12, 14, 16, 24–25, 33, 63–64, 74, 75, 317, 479
    painted shield and, 38–39

Da Vinci Code, The (Brown), 205, 284

da Vinci's rule, 177

Death of Leonardo, The (Ingres), 514, *515*

de Beatis, Antonio, 480, 502–4

Decameron, The (Boccaccio), 127

Dei, Benedetto, 26, 127

Delieuvin, Vincent, 320, 492

Delphi, oracle of, 208

del Vaccha, Antonio di Piero, *see* Accattabriga

Democritus, Bramante's fresco of Heraclitus and, 142, *143,* 157

de Predis, Ambrogio, 223, 224, 230, 231, 232, 382

de Predis, Cristoforo, 223, 282–83

de Predis, Evangelista, 223

desegno lineamentum, 269

di Credi, Lorenzo, 34

digestive system, 426

di Malvolto, Piero, 13–14

dimensionality in art, 2, 40–41, 263, 266, 273

Diocletian, 73

dissections:
    autopsies by Benivieni, 397
    by Leonardo, 2, 162, 177, 213, 270, 271–72, 317, 397–400
    arms, 409–11, *410*
    centenarian, 391, 394–96, *395,* 397–98
    Church and, 397
    eye, 270, 271–72
    face, 409–11, *410*
    veins and arteries, 401
    Leonardo's warning to others on, 398–99

distraction, embracing, 521

Divine Comedy (Dante), 71

Donatello, 28, 29, 36, 70, 273
Doni Tondo (Michelangelo), 375–76, 376
dragonflies, 156, 179–80
drawings by Leonardo, 8, 106
  allegorical, 119–20
    of Pleasure and Pain, 136–39, 138
  anatomical, *see* anatomy
  Angel Incarnate, 471–72, 471
  Arno Valley landscape, 47–48, 48, 55, 507, 510
  attributions of, 39–40, 73, 259–59
  for *Battle of Anghiari,* 276, 355, 357, 359, 360–64, 361, 363, 379, 405–7, 411
  La Bella Principessa (*Portrait of a Young Fiancée*), 248–59, 249, 325, 329, 331, 490
  of Cesare Borgia, 338, 339
  church designs, *xxii,* 142, 143, 146, 148
  deluge, 2, 21, 128, 505–10, 506
  drapery, 39–40, 40, 41, 218, 266, 485
  face-finding excursions and, 121–22
  facial characteristics and, 123
  first art drawing, 47
  geometrical, for Pacioli's *On Divine Proportion,* 203–5, 204, 252, 344
  grotesques, 120–24, 121, 123, 454
    five heads, 123–24, 123
  Head of a Young Woman, 233–35, 234
  horse monument studies, 163–64, 164
  horses for *Battle of Anghiari,* 360–64, 361, 363
  of Isabella d'Este, 253, 299, 302, 304–6, 305, 308
  The Last Supper sketch, *xxii*
  Leda and the Swan preparatory drawing, 326–28, 328
  left-handed hatching in, 32, 73, 192, 251, 253, 326, 395, 470
  light, 267
  lion, 362–63, 363

  machines, 106, 190–96, 191, 192, 194, 195
  map of Chiana Valley, 351, 351
  map of Imola, 342–43, 343, 344
  for masquerade, 501, 502
  nudes, 72, 137, 372
  nutcracker man, 134, 134, 171, 171, 410, 411, 447, 453, 454
  of old and young men juxtaposed, 44, 133–39, 134, 135, 138
  old man and studies of moving water, 446
  Pointing Lady, 472–74, 473
  Portrait of a Young Woman in Profile, 253
  Saint Sebastian, 73–74
  of Salai, 135–36, 135, 137, 372, 410, 411, 413, 414, 433
  shadows, 267
  techniques used in, 122, 253
  Virgin and Child with Saint Anne and Saint John the Baptist (Burlington House cartoon), 318–20, 319, 323–24, 375, 463
  in visualizing scientific concepts, 174, 218
  Vitruvian Man, 1, 37, 136, 140–41, 152, 153–57, 154, 274
    collaboration and, 158–59
    notes on measurements and proportions in, 155–56
    as self-portrait, 157
  warriors, 42–44, 43, 121, 360–62, 361
Dreams and Arguments (Lomazzo), 7
Dunkerton, Jill, 537n47

earth:
  as living organism, 427
  macrocosm of, and microcosm of man, 109, 110, 149, 158, 302, 311, 322, 425–27
    in *Ginevra de' Benci,* 63, 67, 322, 426
    in *Madonna of the Yarnwinder,* 311, 322, 426

earth (*cont.*)
    in *Mona Lisa*, 322, 426, 487
    revision of analogy, 435–38
    in *Virgin and Child with Saint
        Anne*, 322, 426
    placement in cosmos, 363, 441
Einstein, Albert, 3, 178, 442, 443, 519, 520
Emboden, William, 229
embryo and fetus, 177, 215, 420–22,
    421, 500
    compared to seed, 177, 422
    soul of, 422, 512
emotions:
    brain and, 409–11
    facial expressions and, 360–62
    depiction of, through movement, 50,
        79, 83, 84, 87–88, 238, 241–43,
        245, 281, 282
        in *Adoration of the Magi*, 80
        in *The Last Supper*, 80, 282
    movement and, 212–13, 218, 219,
        409–11, 435
    sfumato and, 490
energy, 192–93
engineering and mechanical arts, 180,
    190–99, 300, 308, 341, 503
    artist studio and, 161
    bridge, 341–42, *341*
    casting of horse monument, 166–69,
        167, 168, 403
    flying machines, 45, 98, 180, 181,
        184, 186–89, *187*, 193, 326, 353,
        354, 357, 391
        aerial screw (helicopter), 45–46,
        46, 354
        building of, 161
        theatrical, 45–46, *46*, 115–16,
        181–83, 186, 189
    for horse stables, 162
    hydraulic, 347–54, 413, 429
        canals, 340, 349–50, *350*
        creating waterway between
        Florence and Mediterranean,
        351
        diverting the Arno River, 347–52,
        353, 428, 429, 431, 505, 507

    draining the Piombino marshes,
        352–54, 365
    harnessing the power of the Arno
        River, 193
    military uses of, 299
    perpetual motion devices, *195*, 196
machines, 190–94, 344
    analogies and, 199, 401–3
    drawings of, 106, 190–96, *191,
        192, 194, 195*
    energy and, 192–93
    friction and, 196–99
    hoist with view of components,
        190–91, *191*
    needle-grinding, 193–94, *194*
    odometer, 91, 343, *344*
    perpetual motion, 194–96, *195*
    screw jack with ball bearings,
        197–99, *198*
    spiral gear for equalizing spring
        power, 191–92, *192*
    transfer of motion in, 190–91
    water power, 193
    wheelbarrows, 341
military, 1, 4, 96–102, 336, 346, 357,
    459–60
    cannons, 101
    giant crossbow, 98–101, *99*
    for pushing away ladders, 96–97, *97*
    scythed chariot, 98, *99*, 100
    wheellock, 101–2
    odometer, 91
    theatrical, 45
    flying machines, 45–46, *46*, 115–16,
        181–83, 186, 189
Enlightenment, 3, 113
Ercole I d'Este, Duke of Ferrara, 169,
    240, 302
ermines, 243
    Lady with an Ermine, 239–45, *242*,
        247, 248, 252, 253, 254, 268, 281,
        304, 306
erosion, 439–40
Este, Beatrice d', xi, 114, 133, 240–41,
    245, 299, 551*n*12
    death of, 280, 304

Este, Ercole d', 169, 240, 302
Este, Ippolito d', 388–89
Este, Isabella d', xi, 299, 302–3, 309,
    313, 315, 317, 320, 333, 346, 384,
    391, 479
    Leonardo's drawing of, 253, 299, 302,
      304–6, *305,* 308
    Leonardo's unpainted portrait of,
      299, 302–8, 315, 523
Este family, 15, 302
Euclid, 18, 30, 172, 203, 205, 302,
    510
Euler, Leonhard, 519
Euripides, 208
exploration, age of, 9, 18, 348
eyes and vision, 176, 218, 219, 261–62,
    270–71, 276
    brain and, 218–19, 261–62, 271
    dissections of, 270, 271–72
    focus and, 332
    "*Mona Lisa* effect" and, 247, 488
    pupils in, 239, 484
    retina in, 270–71, 489–90
    see also light and optics

face:
    dissections of, 409–11, *410*
    emotions conveyed by, 360–62
    lips and smile, 409–13, *412,* 489
      of *Mona Lisa,* 475, 488–90, 492,
      494
    proportions of, 219–21, *220*
fantasy, indulging, 523
Fasciculus Medicinae (Ketham), 399
Feast of the Epiphany, 76
Ferrara, 15
Ferrara, Ercole I d'Este, Duke of, 169,
    240, 302
fetus, 177, 215, 420–22, *421,* 500
    compared to seed, 177, 422
    soul of, 422, 512
Filelfo, Francesco, 93
Fiorani, Francesca, 82
fish, 196, 391
    fossils of, 439
flash explosion prank, 126

flight, *see* birds and flight
floods:
    in Bible, 439, 509, 512
    deluge drawings, 2, 21, 128, 505–10,
      506
    deluge writings, 20–21, 127–28, 366,
      508–10
    fossils and, 439–40
Florence, xiii, 9, 11, 12, 14, 16, 18, *22,*
    23, 25–28, 42, 90, 91–93, 348,
    382, 391, 455, 461, 507
    in balance of power, 92
    banking and bookkeeping in, 25,
      27
    Baptistery in, 44, 273
    Borgia and, 336–38
    Cathedral dome in, 26, 29, 82, 145
      ball mounted atop, 37–38, 41,
        458
    homosexuality in, 70–71
    Leonardo in, 23–24, 26–28, 30,
      299–314, 444, 495
      for inheritance battle, 387–90,
        391
    Leonardo's departures from, 90, 91,
      382–84, 390
    Leonardo's return to, 297–98, 299–300,
      317, 320, 475, 479
    Michelangelo in, 367, 368, 377
    Milan victory of, 356–57
    Palazzo della Signoria in, 27, 74,
      358
      battle scene commissions for,
        355–57, 364, 366, 372–79
      David in, 370, 372
    Pisa and, 348–49
    renewal plans for, 461
    Santissima Annunziata in, 300, 317,
      323, 479, 480
    Savonarola in, 300, 301, 357, *358,*
      384
    two schools of art in, 377
fluid dynamics, 181, 184, 413, 416–17,
    419
fortresses, 340, 342
    circular, 352, 353

fossils, 20, 439–40, 455
  trace, 440
  whale, 20
Fossombrone, 340, 352
Foucault, Michel, 177
Fra Angelico, 28
France:
  Italy and, 102, 152, 169, 295, 297,
    307, 336, 444, 454, 461–62, 495,
    496, 498, 500–501
  Leonardo in, 462, 475, 495–516
  Renaissance in, 498
  Revolution in, 291
Francesco di Giorgio, xi, 145–46, 165,
    302
  architectural treatise of, 145, 148
  in Milan Cathedral tiburio project,
    140, 145–46
  in Pavia Cathedral project, 146–48
  Vitruvian Man drawings of, 150–52,
    151, 153
  Vitruvius and, 149
Francis I of France, xi, 392, 461–62,
    496–502, *496,* 504, 505, 507, 512,
    514–15
Franklin, Benjamin, 3, 159
French Revolution, 291
friction, 196–99, 430
  fluids and, 416
Freud, Sigmund, 19–20, 71, 301, 322,
    346
Fry, Roger, 250

Gaffurio, Franchino, 238
Galansino, Arturo, 258
Galen, 400, 414, 415, 420
Galileo Galilei, 17, 175, 176, 184, 185,
    441, 521
Gallerani, Cecilia, 239–40, 304
  Lady with an Ermine, 239–45, *242,*
    247, 248, 252, 253, 254, 268, 281,
    304, 306
  Ludovico Sforza and, 240–41, 243,
    245
Gallerie dell'Accademia, 153
Ganz, Kate, 248–52

Gates, Bill, 107, 426*n*
Gayford, Martin, 368, 376
Geddo, Cristina, 253
genius:
  collaboration and, 523
  of Leonardo, 3, 261, 264, 313, 379,
    420, 475, 517–19
Genoa, 384
geology, 228–29, 231, 322, 391, 438,
    441, 445
geometric studies, 207–8, *209,* 210
geometry, 30, 37, 38, 110, 180, 203, 260,
    269, 431, 511
  and conservation of volume,
    206–7
  golden ratio, 158, 205
  notebook studies and drawings,
    207–8, *209,* 210
  Pacioli and, *see* Pacioli, Luca
  perspective and, 31, 34, 175, 200,
    201, 261, 274
  rates of change and, 201
  shapes, 203–5
    squaring the circle, *xxii,* 109–10,
      158, 209–10, 302, 548*n*20
  transformation of, 206–10, 363,
      428–29, 431, 510
gestures, 223, 285
  hand, 223, 282–83
    pointing, *see* pointing figures
Getty Museum, 251
Gherardini family, 478
Ghiberti, Lorenzo, 16, 273
Ghirlandaio, Domenico, 28, 40, 47,
    367
Giocondo, Francesco del, 478–82
Giocondo, Lisa del, 478–80
  Giuliano de' Medici and, 480–81
  Mona Lisa as portrait of, 479–82
Giocondo family, 478
Giotto, 273
Giovio, Paolo, 8, 116–17, 129, 166
Giraldi, Giovanni Battista, 105–6
globus cruciger, 329
golden ratio, 158, 205
Gombrich, Ernst, 41

Gonzaga, Francesco, 302–3
good vs. perfect, 522
Gopnik, Adam, 6, 177
Gouffier, Artus, 462
Grafton, Anthony, 30
Grann, David, 255–57
gravity, 184, 441
Gregori, Mina, 251
Grimshaw, John, 231
Grosseteste, Robert, 176
grotesques, 120–24, *121, 123,* 454
    five heads, 123–24, *123*
Guardian, 256, 258
Guernica (Picasso), 357
Guicciardini, Francesco, 27, 335
Gutenberg, Johannes, 9, 18, 171–72

hair dye recipe, 111
Hammer, Armand, 426*n*
hand gestures, 223, 282–83
    pointing, *see* pointing figures
Harvard Medical School, 490
Harvey, William, 420
hearing, 262
heart, 174, 201, 401, 405, 413–16, *414,*
        428, 461
    aortic valve and, 416–20, *418*
    and arteries, compared with
        sprouting seed, 401, *401,* 415
    blood and, 415–20
    glass model of, 419
    ventricles in, 415
Heraclitus, Bramante's fresco of
        Democritus and, 142, *143,* 157
Hippocrates, 207, 209, 210
hoist with view of components, 190–91,
    191
Hollar, Wenceslaus, 120, 331
homosexuality, 70–71
    of Leonardo, 8, 19, 68–72, 2333, 368
    of Michelangelo, 69, 70, 368
    Saint Sebastian images and, 73
    Savonarola and, 300
Hope, Charles, 423
horses, 362
    anatomy of, 162, 163, *163*

in *Battle of Anghiari* drawings, 360–64,
    361, 363
Leonardo's Sforza monument, 110,
    160–69, 188, 223, 241, 295, 296,
    362, 367, 495
    casting plans for, 166–69, *167,*
        168, 403
    clay model of, 165–66, 169, 297
    design of, 161–66, *164*
    French troops and, 169, 297
    stables for, 162
    statues of, 162, 165
Hoving, Thomas, 251
humanism, 20, 18, 70, 149, 157, 174, 401
Huygens, Christiaan, 178

illegitimacy, 15–16, 30
    of Alberti, 30
    of Leonardo, 11, 12, 15, 16, 17,
        24–25, 72, 380, 381, 495
Illegitimacy in Renaissance Florence
    (Kuehn), 16
Immaculate Conception, 224
Imola, 342, 349
    map of, 342–43, *343,* 344
impetus, 194, 431, 434
Infeld, Leopold, 174
Inferno (Dante), 89
Ingres, Jean-Auguste-Dominique, 514,
    515
Institute of Criminology and Criminal
    Law, 255
inventions, *see* engineering and
    mechanical arts
Isabella of Aragon, 113–14, 243, 501
Islamic world, 175–76
Isonzo River, 299
Italy, 18, 346
    balance of power and, 92
    currency in, xiii
    France and, 102, 152, 169, 295, 297,
        307, 336, 444, 454, 461–62, 495,
        496, 498, 500–501
    plagues in, 26, 103, 400
    Renaissance in, *see* Renaissance
ITN, 188

Jobs, Steve, 3, 106, 159, 518, 522
Johannes de Spira, 172
John the Baptist, 224–25
Jones, Jonathan, 258, 362, 374, 379
Julius II, Pope, 377, 379

Keele, Kenneth, 396
Keith, Larry, 232
Kemp, Martin, 12, 44, 201, 232, 312,
     313, 331, 352, 429, 536n22,
     566n9, 567n4
   La Bella Principessa and, 253–59,
     329
Ketham, Johannes de, 399
King, Ross, 284
knowledge for its own sake, 520
Kuehn, Thomas, 16

Lady with Flowers (Verrocchio), 65
Landino, Cristoforo, 65
Laocoön and His Sons, 456
Latin, 3, 11, 17, 32, 34, 172, 201
   Leonardo's study of, 170–71, *171,*
     172
Latini, Brunetto, 71
Leda and the swan:
   Leda and the Swan, 72, 300, 325–29,
     513
     Melzi's copy of, 326, *327, 329*
     preparatory drawing for, 326–28,
     328
   myth of, 326, 329
Leibnitz, Gottfried, 210
Leo X, Pope (Giovanni de' Medici), xi,
     454–56, 457, 458, 460, 461–62,
     507
Leonardo and the Last Supper (King),
     284
Leonardo da Vinci:
   animals loved by, 98, 126, 130
   artworks of, *see* drawings by
     Leonardo; paintings by Leonardo
   baptism of, *10,* 14, 15
   biographical accounts of, 3, 7–8, 36
     in Anonimo Gaddiano, 7, 8, 91,
     116, 130

   by Lomazzo, 7–8, 70, 81, 121,
     132, 264, 295, 326, 454, 481
   by Vasari, *see* Vasari, Giorgio, on
     Leonardo
   bird memory of, 18–19, 326
   beard of, 130
   birth of, 11–14
   birthplace of, 13
   books of, 172–73, 174, 301–2, 399,
     420, 500
   burial of, 515
   career struggles of, 295–98
   cave memory of, 20, 21, 224, 399
   Château de Cloux residence of,
     499–501, *499, 500,* 513
   childhood of, 11–21, 23, 322, 346
   clothing and style of, 7, 44, 129, 130,
     300–301, 367, 368, 394, 449
   collaboration and, 158–59, 232–33,
     247, 248, 265, 309, 313, 321,
     523
   Corte Vecchia studios of, 160–61,
     188, 202, 219, 223, 295
   curiosity and observation of, 3, 5, 9,
     18, 173, 178–80, 183, 263–64,
     394, 398, 405, 423, 430, 433, 477,
     484, 500, 516, 518–20
   dark moods of, 8, 88–89, 460, 461
   death of, 505, 513–15
   distractibility and procrastination of,
     17, 31, 34, 82, 162, 164, 279, 280,
     317, 364, 377 , 519, 521, 521–22
   drawings by, *see* drawings by
     Leonardo
   education of, 3, 17, 24, 31–32, 37,
     178, 262
   failing health of, 503, 510, 511–12,
     514
   family of, 11–17, 23, 47
   father of, *see* da Vinci, Piero
   first commission of, 74
   friendships of, 129, 158, 159
   funeral for, 512
   generosity of, 130
   as genius, 3, 261, 264, 313, 379, 420,
     475, 517–19

horses of, 130

iconic image of, 454

illegitimacy of, 11, 12, 15, 16, 17, 24–25, 72, 380, 381, 495

imagination and fantasies of, 3–4, 9, 19, 21, 39, 116, 263–64, 353–54, 507, 508, 517–18, 521, 523

influence of, 313–14, 423–24

influences on:

    Alberti, 30–31, 87–88

    Brunelleschi, 29

    Pollaiuolo, 38

    Verrocchio, 36–37, 43, 52, 56

inheritance of, 16, 381, 387–90, 391, 456

lapses and oddities of, 8, 9

learning from, 3, 6–7, 9, 173, 179, 398, 484, 519–24

left-handedness of, 32, 503

    drawing and, 32, 73, 192, 251, 253, 326, 395, 470, 503

life in his fifties, 300–302, 329, 346, 385, 387, 394

lyre played by, 70, 116–17

mother of, *see* Lippi, Caterina

as musician, 116–19

name of, 11*n*, 69*n*

notary tradition in family of, 11–12, 14, 16–17, 25, 69, 456

notebooks of, *see* notebooks of Leonardo

own workshop opened by, 74

paintings by, *see* paintings by Leonardo

paragone of, 260–63, 264, 265

patrons and, 83, 308, 346, 444, 454–55, 457, 462, 495–98, 523

personality of, 8, 129

personal life of, 129–39, 293–98

physical appearance of, 8, 36, 129, 130, 368

portraits and depictions of, xv, 157, 445–54, 502

    in Bramante's fresco of Heraclitus and Democritus, 142, *143,* 157

    Lucan portrait, xv, 450, *451*

    by Melzi, 447–48, *448,* 449, 453, 454

    in Raphael's *School of Athens,* 448–49, *449,* 454

    self-portraits, *35,* 36, 82, 157, 446–47, *446,* 452–54, *452, 453, 453,* 502

    student sketch, 449–50, *450*

    Turin portrait, 452–54, *452,* 502

    in Uffizi Museum, 450, *451*

    in Vasari's book, 450, *451*

    Verrochio's *David,* 35–36, *35,* 536*n*22

Santissima Annunziata residence of, 300, 317, 323

as self-taught, 17, 170–73, 519

sexuality and relationships of, 8, 19, 68–72, 233, 368

    see also Salai, Andrea

sexuality as viewed by, 70, 71–72

shield painted by, 39

sodomy accusations against, 68–70, 72–74

stroke suffered by, 503, 507

strong men and, 346

theatrical work of, *see* theatrical productions

timeline for, xvi–xix

unfinished projects of, 8, 86–87, 517

vegetarianism of, 98, 126, 130–31, 290, 346

Villa Belvedere residence of, 455–56

vineyard of, 161, 183, 291, 497, 513

war as viewed by, 357, 359

will and estate of, 385, 389, 424, 511–13

Leonardo da Vinci and a Memory of His Childhood (Freud), 19

Leonardo da Vinci on Plants and Gardens (Emboden), 229

"Leonardo's Geology" (Pizzorusso), 228

Leoni, Pompeo, 107

Lester, Toby, 157

light and optics, 30, 58, 176, 177, 213, 228,
　　245, 261, 263, 270–73, 276–77,
　　285, 295, 494
　art and, 2, 80, 82, 230–31, 238–39,
　　　243–44, 245–47
　color, 276
　　distance and, 276
　　light and, 80, 228, 266, 267–68
　　of sky, 2, 178, 322, 442–43
　diagrams on, 245
　mirrors and, 38, 458–60
　Mona Lisa and, 483–84
　perspective and, 273
　rainbows, 443
　shadows, 165–68, 228, *267*, 269, 273,
　　276–77, 376
　see also eyes and vision
Ligny, Louis de, 297
lines:
　in art, 79, 266–67, 377, 466, 486
　　Michelangelo and, 375, 376, 466
　in nature, 269, 270, 281
　shapes without, 268–70
lions:
　drawing of, 362–63, *363*
　mechanical, 391–92
Lippi, Caterina (mother), xi, 12–15, 23,
　　47, 293, 322, 380, 556n1
　death of, 293–94, 295, 387
　funeral costs for, 294
Lippi, Filippino, 16, 47, 50, 83, 370
　Adoration of the Magi, 83, 317
Lippi, Filippo, 16, 28, 83
lips and smile:
　anatomy of, 409–13, *412*, 489
　of *Mona Lisa*, 475, 488–90, 492,
　　494
lists, making, 523
literary amusements, 124–28
　fables, 125
liver, 396, 414
*Lives of the Most Eminent Painters,
　　Sculptors, and Architects* (Vasari),
　　7, 43, 480
　portrait of Leonardo in, 450, *451*
　see also Vasari, Giorgio

Livingstone, Margaret, 490
lizards, 126, 456
Loire River, 505
Lomazzo, Gian Paolo, 7–8, 70, 81,
　　121, 132, 264, 295, 326, 454,
　　481
Louis XII of France, xii, 230, 297, 307,
　　309, 320, 336, 382, 384, 388,
　　391–92, 393, 496
　Borgia and, 338–39
Louis XIV of France, 326
Louise de Savoie, 496–97, 498
Louvre, 233, 315, 320, 492
Lovelace, Ada, 3
Lucretius, 149, 509
Luigi of Aragon, 480, 502
Luini, Bernardino, 313–14
　copy of *Angel of the Annunciation* by,
　　469, *469*
Lumiere Technology, 252–53
lunes, 207–8
Luther, Martin, 454
lyre, 70
　lira da braccio, 91, 116

MacCurdy, Edward, 543n37
Machiavelli, Niccolò, xii, 16, 42, 318,
　　364
　Arno River project and, 349, 350
　Borgia and, xii, 16, 335, 336–37, 342,
　　343, 345, 346
　Piombino marshes project and, 352
machines, *see* engineering and
　　mechanical arts
Macpherson, Giuseppe, xv
macrocosm of earth and microcosm of
　　man, 109, 110, 149, 158, 302, 311,
　　322, 425–27
　in *Ginevra de' Benci*, 63, 67, 322,
　　426
　in *Madonna of the Yarnwinder*, 311,
　　322, 426
　in *Mona Lisa*, 322, 426, 487
　revision of analogy, 435–38
　in *Virgin and Child with Saint Anne*,
　　322, 426

Madonna of the Carnation (Luini), 313–14

Madonna of the Pinks (Raphael), 313

Madonna with Child and Young Saint John (Luini), 314

Maintenon, Madame de, 326

Mantegna, Andrea, 303

Mantua, 70, 299

maps, 343–44
  of Chiana Valley, 351, *351*
  of Imola, 342–43, *343, 344*

Marani, Pietro, 331

Marcantonio della Torre, 400, 424, 523

marshes and swamps, 354, 428, 505
  Piombino, 352–54, 365
  Pontine, 458, 505, 507

Masaccio, 273

mathematics, 8, 37, 200–211, 263, 300, 308, 459
  abacus schools for, 17, 31, 32, 37, 201
  algebra, 31–32, 110, 200, 201
  arithmetic, 3, 31–32, 110, 200–201, 431
  calculus, 210, 431
  geometry, *see* geometry
  lines and, 268–69, 270
  nature and, 200, 416
  of optics, 2
  Pacioli and, *see* Pacioli, Luca
  perspective and, 34, 175
  points in, 269, 270
  science and, 200
  square and cube roots, 208–9

Mathurine, 502, 511, 512

Maximilian I, Holy Roman Emperor, 165, 230

mechanical art(s):
  liberal arts vs., 262–63
  painting as, 260, 262–63
  see also engineering and mechanical arts

Medici, Cosimo de', 27–28, 77
  tomb for, 37

Medici, Giovanni de' (son of Cosimo), 77

Medici, Giovanni de' (son of Lorenzo), *see* Leo X, Pope

Medici, Giuliano de' (son of Lorenzo), xii, 455, 457, 458, 460, 461, 495, 503
  death of, 497
  Mona Lisa and, 480–81

Medici, Giuliano de' (son of Piero), 77, 89

Medici, Lorenzo "the Magnificent" de', xii, 7, 28, 41, 69, 77, 89, 91–92, 160, 454, 455, 495
  horse monument and, 164
  theatrical productions of, 28, 29

Medici, Piero de', 77

Medici family, 12, 27, 68, 72, 83, 92, 337, 346, 455, 461, 478
  Botticelli and, 77, 83, 89
  Leonardo and, 83, 89, 444, 497
  Michelangelo and, 367
  pageants and spectacles of, 42, 44–46, 76
  Savonarola and, 300
  Verrocchio's workshop and, 33

Melzi, Francesco, xii, 7, 385–87, 389, 400, 424, 455, 458, 497, 500, 503, 504, 511, 512, 541*n*4
  Boltraffio's portrait of, *385*
  copy of *Leda and the Swan* by, 326, *327, 329*
  Leonardo's adoption of, 329, 385–87, 445
  Leonardo's life at home of, 445
  portrait of Leonardo by, 447–48, *448,* 449, 453, 454
  Salai and, 387, 497, 513

Melzi, Girolamo, 445

metal alloys, 199

Metamorphoses (Ovid), 509

Metropolitan Museum of Art, 73, 119, 251, 331

Michelangelo Buonarroti, xii, 7, 28, 72, 158, 367–72, 457, 461, 509, 512
  Battle of Cascina, 373–74, *373,* 375, 376, 379

Michelangelo Buonarroti (*cont.*)
David, 35, 368–72, *369*
Leonardo's sketch of, 371–72, *371*
Doni Tondo, 375–76, *376*
in Florence, 367, 368, 377
homosexuality of, 69, 70, 368
Julius and, 377, 379
Leonardo and, 367–68, 374, 375–77
lines in paintings of, 375, 376, 466
Medici and, 367
nudes in paintings of, *373,* 374, 375, 376
in Palazzo della Signoria competition with Leonardo, 356, 372–79
Perugino and, 368
physical appearance of, 368
Pietà, 367
Sistine Chapel, 374, 375, 377
Torrigiano and, 367–68
microcosm of man and macrocosm of earth, 109, 110, 149, 158, 302, 311, 322, 425–27
in *Ginevra de' Benci,* 63, 67, 322, 426
in *Madonna of the Yarnwinder,* 311, 322, 426
in *Mona Lisa,* 322, 426, 487
revision of analogy, 435–38
in *Virgin and Child with Saint Anne,* 322, 426
Migliorotti, Atalante, 69–70, 91–92, 116, 238
Milan, 92–93, 170, 391, 454, 461–62, 497
in balance of power, 92
canals and waterworks of, 347–48, 428, 505, 507
Cathedral of, 146–47, 160
buttresses for, 144
tiburio for, 140–48, *141,* 158, 174–75, 177, 188
Church of Santa Maria presso San Satiro in, 142
Florence's victory over, 356–57

French hostilities with, 102, 152, 169, 295, 297, 307, 336, 454
gypsies in, 124
Leonardo in, 24, 44, 74, 91–104, 213, 223, 382–93, 444, 475
Leonardo's departure from, 297–98, 445, 479
Leonardo's plan for utopian alternative to, 102–4, 140
Leonardo's returns to, 382–83, 388–90, 475
plague in, 103
rulers in, 92–93
military devices, 1, 4, 96–102
cannons, 101
giant crossbow, 98–101, *99*
for pushing away ladders, 96–97, *97*
scythed chariot, 98, *99,* 100
wheellock, 101–2
milk, 415–16
mirrors, 38, 453, 458–60
machine for making, 458, *459*
Mondino de Luzzi, 399
Montagnana, Bartolomeo, 399
Monte Ceceri, 188, 326
moon, 441, 459
in solar system, 363
Morgante (Pulci), 172
motion, movement, 508, 518
in animals, 131
arrested instants of, 180
in *Battle of Anghiari,* 362
in *Last Supper,* 281–86
in river analogy, 180, 281
changes in human anatomy with, 221
depiction of, 37, 44, 48, 55, 73, 80–81, 165, 211
depiction of emotion and thoughts through, 50, 79, 83, 84, 87–88, 238, 241–43, 245, 281, 282
in *Adoration of the Magi,* 80
in *The Last Supper,* 80, 282
emotions leading to, 212–13, 218, 219, 409–11, 435
impetus and, 194, 431, 434

laws of, 181, 185, 194, 431
in machinery, 192
percussion and, 119, 177, 340, 431, 434
perpetual, 194–96, *195*
transfer of, 190–91
Mozart, Wolfgang Amadeus, 3, 519
muscles:
anatomy of, 213, 218, 219, 401–2, *402*, 405–9
leg, 405–7, *407*
mouth, 409–13, *412*
neck, 84–86, *86*
shoulder, 405, *406*
energy and, 192–93
music, 117–18, *118*, 177, 206
keyboard-operated bell, 117–18, *118*
lyre, 70
lira da braccio, 91, 116
viola organista, 118
Muslim scientists, 175–76
mystery, 524

Naples, 297
National Gallery (London), 258, 331
National Gallery of Art (Washington, DC), 43, 61, 66, 331
National Geographic, 257
National Library of Poland, 257–58
Natural History (Pliny), 172
nature, 2, 17, 18, 21, 507
lines in, 269, 270, 281
mathematics and, 200, 416
metaphysical portrayals of, 231
patterns in, 176–78, 181, 400–405, 427, 433, 438, 487, 519
branching systems, 109, 177, 422
comparative anatomy, 162, 219, 363
spirals, *see* spirals
see also analogies
variety in, 427, 431, 438
Naviglio Grande, 347
Naviglio Martesana, 347

needle-grinding machine, 193–94, *194*
nervous system, 213, 218, 219, 409
Newton, Isaac, 3, 176, 184, 185, 194, 199, 210, 431, 442, 443
New Yorker, 6, 255–57
New York Times, 252
Niccolini, Luigi, 63
notaries, 11, 16
in Leonardo's family, 11–12, 14, 16–17, 25, 69, 456
Leonardo's father, 12, 14, 16, 24–25, 33, 63–64, 74, 75, 317, 479
notebooks of Leonardo, 2, 4–6, 8, 45, 58, 69, 72, 87–89, 91, 105–11, 114, 158, 325, 344, 386, 387, 499, 517, 521, 524
Brunelleschi dome project and, 37–38
Codices Madrid, 6
Codex Arundel, 107
Codex Atlanticus, 107, 567*n*4
Codex Leicester, 107, 426–29, 431, 435–40, 442, 445, 507, 521
Codex on the Flight of Birds, 184, 188, 453
final piece of writing in, 510–11, *511*
interesting scenes, 105–6
juxtapositions in, 107–8
Madrid Codices, 196, 197, 199
mirror script in, *xxii*, 32, 297, 342, 423, 503
pages from, *xxii*, 108–11, *109*
percentage of pages extant, 106
quotes from others, 89
repackaged collections of, 106–7
Salai in, 131–33
science and, 174, 176
theme sheet from, 108–11, *109*, 133, 177
notes, taking, 524
Nuland, Sherwin, 419

observation, cultivating powers of, 520
odometer, 91, 343, *344*

On Divine Proportion (Pacioli), 152, 203
   Leonardo's drawings for, 203–5, *204,*
      252
On Painting (Alberti), 30, 31, 87–88,
   212, 261, 273
On the Fabric of the Human Body
   (Vesalius), 424
On the Military Arts (Valturio), 98, 101
On the Nature of Things (Lucretius), 149,
   509
optics, *see* light and optics
oracle of Delphi, 208
orbs:
   glass or crystal, *334*
      in *Salvator Mundi,* 333–34, 484
   globus cruciger, 329
Ovid, 33, 172, 509
Oxford University, 419–20

Pacioli, Luca, xii, 32, 129, 201–8, 260,
   264, 265, 298, 341, 400
   On Divine Proportion, 152, 203
      Leonardo's drawings for, 203–5,
         204, 252, 344
   parlor games of, 202–3
   portrait of, 202, *202*
   at Sforza court, 201, 202–3, 205
painting:
   debates on merit of, 261–62
      Leonardo's *paragone,* 260–63,
         264, 265
   as mechanical art, 260, 262–63
paintings by Leonardo:
   Adoration of the Magi, 8, *35,* 36, 64,
      74–83, *75,* 87, 88, 112, 225, 281,
      324, 355, 382, 445, 502, 522
      commentator in, *35,* 36, 82–83
      preparatory drawings for, 77–80,
         78, 81, 273
   Angel of the Annunciation, 463, 464,
      469–71, *469*
      Luini's copy of, 469, *469*
      student sketch of, 469–70, *470,*
         472
   The Annunciation, 56–60, *57,* 470,
      471, 508

attributions of, 8, 57, 236, 248, 250,
   325, 329, 331–32, 533n16
Baptism of Christ (Verrocchio with
   Leonardo), 41, 48–49, 50, 52–56,
   53, 63, 233, 284, 428, 537n50
Battle of Anghiari, 8, 81, 325, 355–79,
   382, 387, 389, 393, 445, 461, 502,
   522
   commission for, 355–57, 364, 366,
      378–79
   conception of, 358–59
   drawings for, 276, 355, 357, 359,
      360–64, *361, 363,* 379, 405–7,
      411
   perspective in, 378
   plaster wall and, 365–66, 377, 378
   rainstorm and, 365–66
   Rubens' copy of, 355, *356*
La Belle Ferronnière (Lucrezia
   Crivelli), 245–48, *246,* 254, 306,
   488, 490
   copy of, 250
Ginevra de' Benci, 56, 63–67, *64,*
   72, 86, 126–27, 241, 243, 255 ,
   276–77, 306, 322, 426
   gaze in, 66, 247
   Mona Lisa compared with, 477
Joseph rarely depicted in, 80, 375,
   539n30
Lady with an Ermine (Cecilia
   Gallerani), 239–45, *242,* 247,
   248, 252, 253, 254, 268, 281, 304,
   306
The Last Supper, 1, 2, 80, 142, 142, 219,
   225, *278,* 279–92, 295, 296, 336,
   355, 365, 435, 463, 468, 521, 522
   commission for, 279–81, 291
   deterioration and restoration of,
      290–92, 365
   Eucharist and, 556n11
   as moment in motion, 281–86
   perspective in, 277, 281, 286–90,
      286, 287, 378
   placement in refectory, 287–90,
      287
   sketch for, *xxii*

Leda and the Swan, 72, 300, 325–29, 513

Melzi's copy of, 326, *327,* 329

preparatory drawing for, 326–28, *328*

lost and found, 325–34

Madonna and Child with Flowers (Benois Madonna), 41, 60–63, *61,* 311, 313, 329

Madonna of the Carnation (Munich Madonna), 56, 60–63, *60*

Madonna of the Yarnwinder, 62, 307, 309–14, 322, 388, 426, 523

Buccleuch, 309, 311–12

Lansdowne, 309, *310,* 311–12

underdrawings in, 312

Milan portraits, 236–59

Mona Lisa, 1, 41, 55, 63, 67, 72, 86–88, 205, 241, 243, 247, 250, 269–70, 276–77, 281, 300, 306, 315, 320, 322, 323, 332, 338, 413, 426, 466, 475–94, *476,* 497, 502, 503, 513, 516, 517–20, 522, 523

cleaning and restoration considered, 492

clothing in, 485–86

commission for, 477–79

copies of, 491–92, *491*

eyebrows in, 484–85

eyes in, 488

Ginevra de' Benci compared with, 477

hair and veil in, 486

iconic status of, 492–94

La Gioconda title for, 481

landscape in, 487–88

light in, 483–84

as Lisa del Giocondo, 479–82

and macrocosm of world and microcosm of man, 322, 426, 487

Prado copy of, 491–92, *491*

seminude *Monna Vanna* versions of, 72*n,* 492, *493*

smile in, 475, 488–90, 492, 494

undercoat and glazes in, 482–83

Vasari on, 477–81, 484–85, 488, 493

"*Mona Lisa* effect" in, 247, 488

pointing gestures in, *see* pointing figures

Portrait of a Musician, 236–39, *237,* 243–44, 308, 484

psychological engagement in, 62, 67, 72, 84, 87, 305–6, 309–11, 313, 332, 493

Saint Jerome in the Wilderness, 2, 8, 21, 83–87, *85,* 88, 112, 205, 255, 540*n*36

anatomy in, 84–86, 518

Saint John the Baptist, 284, 285, 323, 463, 464–66, *465,* 480, 492, 497, 502, 503

Saint John with the Attributes of Bacchus, 463, 464, 466, 467–69, *467*

Salvator Mundi, 329–34, *330,* 466

orb in, 333–34, 484

techniques in, 40–41, 51, 54–57, 59, 61, 66, 228, 232, 290, 365, 466

chiaroscuro, 40–41, 61, 228, 377, 466

luster, 66, 238

sfumato, 41, 55, 228, 258, 269–70, 281, 332, 375–77, 466, 468–69, 486–87, 490

Tobias and the Angel (Verrocchio with Leonardo), 48–52, *49*

unfinished, 8, 81, 86–87

Virgin and Child with Saint Anne, 62, 300, 306, 314, 315–24, *316,* 466, 480, 481, 492, 497, 502, 503, 522

analogy between earth and humans in, 322, 426

Burlington House cartoon for, 318–20, *319,* 323–24, 375, 463

commission for, 315–17

rocks in, 322

sky in, 322

versions of, 317–21, *319*

paintings by Leonardo (*cont.*)
  Virgin of the Rocks, 223–35, 243,
      268, 311, 322, 471, 520, 523,
      540*n*36
    angel in, 225–28, 230–33, 235
    collaboration in, 231–32
    commission for, 223–25, 229–30,
      332
    first version of (Louvre), 110,
      224–30, *226,* 235, 313, 322
    Head of a Young Woman, 233–35,
      234
    plants in, 110, 229, 231
    restoration of, 231, 232
    rock formations in, 228–29,
      231
    second version of (London), 224,
      227, 230–32, 265, 285, 313,
      331, 382
    visual puns in, 65, 126–27, 243
Palazzo della Signoria (now Palazzo
      Vecchio), 27, 74, *358*
    battle scene commissions for, 355–57,
      364, 366, 372–79
    David in, 370, 372
Pallanti, Giuseppe, 12
Paradiso (play), 501
paragones, 260–61
    of Leonardo, 260–63, 264, 265
Paris Ms. B, 107
Pater, Walter, 250, 488
patrons, creating for, 523
Pavia, 93, 152, 165, 339–40, 391
    Cathedral of, 146–48, *147*
    University of, 173, 213, 274, 400
Payne, Robert, 444
PBS, 257
Peckham, John, 274
Pedretti, Carlo, 107, 108, 253, 318, 468,
      473, 537*n*42, 567*n*4
Penny, Nicholas, 331
percussion, 119, 177, 340, 431, 434
perfect vs. good, 522
perpetual motion, 194–96, *195*
perspective, 26, 44–45, 263
    accelerated, 289

acuity, 275, 311, 466
aerial, 48, 275–76
Alberti and, 30, 31, 78, 273, 275, 276,
      288
artificial, 274–75, 288
Bramante and, 142
Brunelleschi and, 29–30, 31, 78, 273,
      276
complex, 274, 288
geometry and, 31, 34, 175, 200, 201,
      261, 274
Leonardo's use of, 2, 45, 48, 58,
      59, 175, 204, 273–77, 311, 375,
      466
    in *Adoration of the Magi,* 78, *78,*
      273
    in *Battle of Anghiari,* 378
    in *The Last Supper,* 277, 281,
      286–90, *286, 287,* 378
linear, 274–76
optics and, 273
shadows and, 266
Perugino, Pietro, 47, 368, 370
Petrarch, 16, 33, 116, 172
Phidias, 132
Philadelphia, 159
physiognomy, 122
Piacenza, 296
Piatti, Piattino, 129
    horse monument and, 164–65
Picasso, Pablo, 357
Picknett, Lynn, 284
Piero di Cosimo, 69*n*
Pietà (Michelangelo), 367
Pietro da Novellara, Friar, 306–7, 309,
      313, 315, 317, 318, 320, 321
Piombino, 338, 352, 353
    marshes of, 352–54, 365
Pisa, 348–49
    Battle of Cascina, 373
    diverting the Arno River around,
      347–52, 353, 428, 429, 431, 505,
      507
Pius II, Pope, 15
Pizzorusso, Ann, 228
plague, 26, 103, 104, 208, 400

plants:
    embryo compared with seed of, 177,
        422
    heart and arteries compared with,
        401, *401,* 415
    spiral arrangements of leaves in,
        456
    Star of Bethlehem, 433, *434*
    in *Virgin of the Rocks,* 110, 229,
        231
Plato, 18, 70, 149, 285, 416, 426
    in Raphael's *School of Athens,* 449,
        449
Platonic Academy, 27–28
Platonic solids, 203–5
Pliny the Elder, 34, 87, 125, 172
poetry, 262
pointing figures, 463–74
    Angel Incarnate, 471–72, *471*
    Angel of the Annunciation, 463, 464,
        469–71, *469*
        Luini's copy of, 469, *469*
        student sketch of, 469–70, *470,*
            472
    in *Madonna of the Yarnwinder,*
        309
    Pointing Lady, 472–74, *473*
    Saint John the Baptist, 284, 285, 323,
        463, 464–66, *465,* 480, 492, 497,
        502, 503
    *Saint John with the Attributes of
        Bacchus,* 463, 464, 466, 467–69,
        467
    in *Virgin and Child with Saint Anne,*
        324
    in *Virgin of the Rocks,* 225–28, 230
points, 269, 270
Politecnico di Milano, 331
Pollaiuolo, Antonio del, 28, 38, 47, 54,
        213, 455
    as influence on Leonardo, 38
    Tobias and the Angel, 50, *51,* 52
Pollock, Jackson, 255, 256–57
Ponte Buriano, 487
Pontine Marshes, 458, 505, 507
Pope-Hennessy, John, 241

Popham, Arthur, 318
Portinari, Benedetto, 173
possible self-portrait of Leonardo, 453,
        453
Pouncey, Philip, 318
Po Valley, 347
Prado Museum, 491–92, *491*
Prate, Thaddée, 73
Prince, Clive, 284
Prince, The (Machiavelli), 16, 42, 335,
        345
printing presses, 18, 97, 125, 171–72,
        399
procrastination, embracing, 521–22
proportions and ratios, 203, 205–6
    golden ratio, 158, 205
    human, 219–22, *220*
        see also Vitruvian Man
    perspective and, 274
Ptolemy, Claudius, 18, 301–2, 458
publishing industry, 172, 399
    printing presses, 18, 97, 125, 171–72,
        399
Pulci, Luigi, 172
puns, 126, 481
    visual, 65, 126–27, 138, 243
Purgatorio (Dante), 474
Puteolano, Francesco, 261
puzzles, 127

Radke, Gary, 537*n*37
rainbows, 443
Ramiro de Lorca, 345
Raphael, 116, 285, 313, 377, 379, 457,
        461
    School of Athens, 448–49, *449,*
        454
Rayleigh, Lord, 442, 443
reach to exceed grasp, 523
Reformation, 454
religion and Church, 512
    dissection and, 397
    embryo and, 422
    science and, 174, 199
    and Vasari's account of Leonardo's
        death, 513–14

Renaissance, 2, 7, 18, 34, 37, 103, 261,
    379, 391, 426, 498, 519
  classical works and, 149
  cult of Plato in, 70
  in France, 498
  humanism in, 20, 18, 70, 149, 157,
    174, 401
  illegitimacy during, 15
  Savonarola and, 300
  straddling of disciplines in, 26, 140
  technologists in, 190
  turning point in, 379
Renaissance Man archetype, 1, 170, 401,
    519
Restoro d'Arezzo, 426
Reti, Ladislao, 199
rhombicuboctahedron, 203, *204*
Richter, Jean Paul, 538*n*3
Rimini, 340
Robertet, Florimond, 307, 309, 388
Robicsek, Francis, 419
rocks, 322, 445
  erosion and, 439–40
Romagna, 336, 340, 341
Romans, ancient, 34, 148–49, 509
  aqueducts of, 347
  equestrian sculptures of, 165
Rome, 29, 92, 496, 497
  Leonardo in, 24, 444–62, 475
  Michelangelo in, 367
  Sistine Chapel in, 89
    Michelangelo's painting of, 374,
      375, 377
  Vatican in, 148, 338, 448,
    454, 455
Romorantin, 504–5, 507
Rosselli, Cosimo, 69*n*
Rubens, Peter Paul, copy of Leonardo's
    Battle of Anghiari by,
    355, *356*
Rucellai, Bernardo, 92
Ruysch, Frederik, 405

Sacchetti, Franco, 33
Saint Peter's Basilica, 148
Sala delle Asse, 295–96

Salai, Andrea (Gian Giacomo Caprotti
    da Oreno), xii, 70, 131–33, 135,
    152, 293, 294, 297, 311, 368, 387,
    389, 445, 455, 466, 468, 472, 492,
    497
  clothing of, 301, 325
  death of, 311, 475
  estate of, 311, 329, 467, 477, 481,
    513
  Isabella d'Este and, 306–7, 308
  Leonardo's drawings of, 135–36,
    135, 137, 372, *410,* 411, 413,
    414, 433
  Leonardo's estate and, 513
  Leonardo's paintings owned by, 513
  Melzi and, 387, 497, 513
  name of, 70, 131, 544*n*7
  Vasari on, 70, 131, 386
Saltarelli, Jacopo, 68–69, 73, 74
San Donato, monastery of, 74–76, 83
Sangallo, Bastiano da, 373
Sanseverino, Galeazzo, 162–63, 254
Santa Maria delle Grazie, 142, 280,
    283
  The Last Supper in, 1, 2, 80, 142, 142,
    219, 225, *278,* 279–92, 295, 296,
    336, 355, 365, 435, 463, 468, 521,
    522
  commission for, 279–81, 291
  deterioration and restoration of,
    290–92, 365
  Eucharist and, 556*n*11
  as moment in motion, 281–86
  perspective in, 277, 281, 286–90,
    286, 287, 378
  placement in refectory, 287–90,
    287
  sketch for, *xxii*
Santa Maria Nuova, 213, 317, 346, 394,
    489
Santissima Annunziata, 300, 317, 323,
    479, 480
Saône River, 505
Sauldre River, 504, 505
Savonarola, Girolamo, 300, 301, 357,
    358, 384

Schapiro, Meyer, 19

School of Athens (Raphael), 448–49, *449*, 454

Schopenhauer, Arthur, 518

science, 1–2, 17, 21, 31, 106, 107, 170–80, 199, 308, 391, 426, 463, 479, 503

   art and, 1, 2, 47, 61–62, 78, 157, 203, 213, 215, 228, 239, 260–77, 333, 405, 507, 522–23

      Leonardo's *paragone* and, 260–63, 264, 265

   curiosity and observation in, 178–80, 200

   in Islamic world, 175–76

   and Leonardo as self-taught, 170–73

   mathematics and, 200

   religion and, 174, 199

   scientific method, 174, 176

   Scientific Revolution, 175

   theory in, 181, 200

      experience and, 173–76, 273, 435, 521

   visualization and drawing in, 174, 218

   see also nature; *specific subjects*

screw jack with ball bearings, 197–99, *198*

scuba gear, 299–300, 354

sculpture:

   David (Michelangelo), 35, 368–72, *369*

      Leonardo's sketch of, 371–72, *371*

   David (Verrochio), 34–36, *35*, 135, 368–70, 536*n*21

      Leonardo as model for, 35–36, *35*, 368–70, 536*n*22

   horse statues, 162, 165

   Leonardo on, 262, 374–75

   Leonardo's Sforza monument, 110, 160–69, 188, 223, 241, 295, 296, 362, 367, 495

      casting plans for, 166–69, *167*, *168*, 403

      clay model of, 165–66, 169, 297

      design of, 161–66, *164*

      French troops and, 169, 297

sea animals, 439–40

Sebastian, Saint, 73

seed:

   embryo compared with, 177, 422

   heart and arteries compared with, 401, *401*, 415

Seneca, 20

Senigallia, 345

senso commune, 218–19

Seracini, Maurizio, 79, 377

Sforza, Bianca, 165, 230, 254, 257

Sforza, Bona, 257

Sforza, Francesco, 93

   horse monument and, 160, 162

Sforza, Galeazzo Maria, 41–42, 119

Sforza, Gian Galeazzo, 113, 257

   marriage of, 113–14, 243, 501

Sforza, Ludovico, xii, 41–42, 93–94, 152, 158–59, 230, 264, 279–80, 308, 497, 510, 521

   Beatrice d'Este's marriage to, xi, 114, 133, 240–41, 245, 299, 304

   Beatrice's death and, 280

   La Bella Principessa and, 254

   Bramante and, 141, 142

   Cecilia Gallerani and, 240–41, 243, 245

   French invasion and, 102, 169, 295, 297–98, 444

   Isabella d'Este's portrait and, 303, 304

   The Last Supper commissioned by, 279–81, 291

   Leonardo appointed to court of, 160–61

   Leonardo given vineyard by, 161, 183, 291, 497, 513

   Leonardo's disputes with, 295–96

   Leonardo's job application letter to, 1, 4, 42, 94–96, 102, 160, 183, 298, 340, 347, 390, 428

      text of, 94–96, 223

   Leonardo's military devices and, 94–96, 100–102

Sforza, Ludovico (*cont.*)
  Lucrezia Crivelli and, 245
  Milan Cathedral and, 146–47
  Pacioli and, 201, 202–3, 205
  ruthlessness of, 335
  Sforza Castle rooms and, 295–96
Sforza, Ludovico, Leonardo's work for,
    112–28, 141–42, 180, 223, 241,
    295, 337, 495
  allegorical drawings, 119–20
  grotesque drawings, 120–24, *121,
    123*
  horse monument, 110, 160–69, 188,
    223, 241, 295, 296, 362, 367, 495
    casting plans for, 166–69, *167,
      168,* 403
    clay model of, 165–66, 169, 297
    design of, 161–66, *164*
    French troops and, 169, 297
  literary amusements, 124–28
    fables, 125
  music, 91, 116–19
  plays and pageants, 4, 112–16, 117,
    223, 289, 290, 295
    La Danae, 115
    The Masque of the Planets, 113–14
    "Pluto's Paradise," 115
  pranks and tricks, 126
Sforza, Maximilian (Massimiliano), 171,
    444, 498
Sforza Castle, 161, 180, 241, 260
  camerini in, 295–96
Sforza family, 92, 93, 96, 257, 346, 391,
    444–45, 454, 461–62, 496
sfumato, 41, 55, 228, 258, 269–70,
    281, 332, 375–77, 466, 468–69,
    486–87, 490
Sgarbi, Claudio, 153
shadow, 165–68, 228, *267,* 269, 273,
    276–77, 376
shapes, 203–5
  squaring the circle, *xxii,* 109–10, 158,
    209–10, 302, 363, 548*n*20
  transformation of, 206–10, 363,
    428–29, 431, 510
  without lines, 268–70

Shearman, John, 231
sheep, 440
Sheffield Hallam University, 490
shellfish, 439–40
shells, 20, 455
Siena, 345
silos, avoiding, 522
Silverman, Peter, 248–55
Simon, Robert, 331
siphons, 436–37, *437*
Sistine Chapel, 89
  Michelangelo's painting of, 374, 375,
    377
Sixtus IV, Pope, 89
skull, 216–19, *217,* 271–72, *272*
sky, color of, 2, 178, 322, 442–43
smile:
  anatomy of, 409–13, *412,* 489
  of *Mona Lisa,* 475, 488–90, 492, 494
Soderini, Francesco, 336–37
Soderini, Piero, 364, 372–73, 383
solar system, 363
spine and spinal cord, 218, 407–9, *408*
spiral gear for equalizing spring power,
    191–92, *192*
spirals, 2, 36, 56, 433, 434, 486
  blood flow and, 416, 417
  of leaves, 456
  water eddies and hair curls, 433, 434,
    447, 507–8
squaring the circle, *xxii,* 109–10, 158,
    209–10, 302, 363, 548*n*20
staircases, 504
Star of Bethlehem, 433, *434*
stars, 441
structural weaknesses in buildings, 144
studies of right triangle areas, ending
    with "the soup is getting cold,"
    510–11, *511*
sun, 436, 440–42
  in solar system, 363
Swan Mountain, 188, 326
swimming belt, 338
Syria, 128, 510
Syson, Luke, 231, 233, 320, 331,
    533*n*16, 537*n*47, 551*n*12, 567*n*4

Taccone, Baldassare, 115, 165
Tedesco, Giulio, 102
teeth, 216
Templar Revelation, The (Picknett and
  Prince), 284
Tenniel, John, 120
textile industries, 193
theatrical productions, 4, 44–46, 87
  accelerated perspective in, 289
  flying machines for, 45–46, *46,*
    115–16, 181–83, 186, 189
  plays and pageants, 4, 112–16, 117,
    223, 289, 290, 295
  La Danae, 115
  for King Francis, 500–502
  The Masque of the Planets,
    113–14
  "Pluto's Paradise," 115
thought experiments, 430
  using siphons, 436–37, *437*
Timaeus (Plato), 426
Time, 256
Titian, 328
Tobias and the Angel (Verrocchio with
  Leonardo), 48–52, *49*
to-do lists, making, 523
tongue, 398
  of woodpecker, 5, 178, 398, 525
topology, 206
Torrigiano, Pietro, 367–68
Tractatus de Urinarum (Montagnana),
  399
tribometer, 197
trompe l'œil, 142, 287
Turner, J. M. W., 255
Turner, Nicholas, 251
Twain, Mark, 7

Uccello, Paolo, 273
Uffizi Museum, 79
  Leonardo portrait in, 450, *451*
underwater defense gear, 299–300,
  354
Unger, Miles, 368, 376
University of Geneva, 253
University of South Florida, 257

Urbino, 337, 338–39
U.S. National Geospatial-Intelligence
  Agency, 344

Valsalva, Antonio, 417
Valturio (Valturius), Robert, 98, 101
van Eyck, Jan, 483
Vasari, Giorgio, 7, 45, 73, 90, 269, 367,
  379, 480
  on Leonardo, 7, 25, 110, 125, 162,
    253, 325, 373, 392, 400
  arithmetic, 31
  Battle of Anghiari, 362, 365, 366,
    373, 378
  character, 129, 130
  deathbed confession, 513–14
  father and uncle, 15, 25
  genius, 3
  The Last Supper, 280, 291
  mirror writing, 32
  Mona Lisa, 477–81, 484–85, 488,
    493
  music and lyre, 116, 117
  physical beauty, 36, 129
  portrait, 450, *451*
  pranks, 126, 456
  sfumato, 41
  shield decoration, 39
  unfinished works, 81
  and Verrocchio, 52
  Virgin and Child with Saint Anne,
    317–18
  on Marcantonio, 400
  on Melzi, 386
  Palazzo della Signoria mural of,
    377
  on Pollaiuolo, 38, 213
  on Salai, 70, 131, 386
  on Verrocchio, 33, 34, 36, 43, 52
Vatican, 148, 338, 448, 454, 455
Venice, xiii, 92, 299, 507
  publishing industry in, 172
Verino, Ugolino, 27
Verrochio, Andrea del, xii, 28, 33–44, 47,
  50, 70, 77, 92, 134, 290–91, 309,
  313, 523

Verrochio, Andrea del (*cont.*)
  Baptism of Christ (with Leonardo),
    41, 48–49, 50, 52–56, *53*, 63, 233,
    284, 428, 537*n*50
  Beheading of Saint John the Baptist,
    44
  Christ and Saint Thomas, 37, 54
  David, 34–36, *35*, 135, 368–70,
    536*n*21
    Leonardo as model for,
      35–36, *35*, 368–70,
      536*n*22
  drapery studies at workshop of, 33,
    39–40, *40*, 41, 218, 266, 485
  equestrian monument of, 162
  Florence cathedral ball project,
    37–38, 41, 458
  as influence on Leonardo, 36–37, 43,
    52, 56
  Lady with Flowers, 65
  Leonardo at workshop of, 33–44,
    46, 48–57, 60, 66, 68, 70, 74,
    112, 181, 213, 218, 232–33, 470,
    477
  Medici tomb slab designed by, 37
  nature depictions, 50–51, 55,
    537*n*47
  style of, 36
  Tobias and the Angel (with
    Leonardo), 48–52, *49*
Verruca, 348–49
Vesalius, Andreas, 424
Vespucci, Agostino, 172, 318–20,
  323, 324, 348, 357, 388–89,
  481–82
Vespucci, Amerigo, 18, 348
Villa Belvedere, 455–56
Villa Melzi, 445, 446
Vinci, *10*, 297
  Leonardo's childhood in, 11–21,
    23
Virgil, 509
Visconti, Giovanni Stefano, 240
Visconti family, 92, 93
vision, *see* eyes and vision
visual thinking, 344, 522

Vitelli, Vitellozzo, 345
Vitruvian Man, 149–50, 219, 220
  Andrea's drawing of, 152–53, *153*
  Francesco di Giorgio's drawings of,
    150–52, *151*, 153
  Leonardo's *Vitruvian Man*, 1, 37,
    136, 140–41, 152, 153–57, *154*,
    274, 372, 426, 494
    collaboration and, 158–59, 232,
      302, 523
    notes on measurements and
      proportions in, 155–56
    as self-portrait, 157
Vitruvius, 148–53, 208
  architectural treatise of, 29, 148, 149
  on human proportions, *see* Vitruvian
    Man
volume, conservation of, 206–7

warriors, 42–44, *43*, *121*, 360–62, *3
  61*
water, 177, 178, 184, 196, 391, 428–31,
  445, 507
  canals, 340, 349–50, *350*, 458, 505
    of Milan, 347–48, 428, 505,
      507
  circulation on earth, and blood in
    human body, 435–38
  and conservation of volume, 206
  diversions, eddies, whirlpools, and
    vortexes, 431–35, *432*, 447
  erosion by, 439–40
  floods
    in Bible, 439, 509, 512
    deluge drawings, 2, 21, 128,
      505–10, *506*
    deluge writings, 20–21, 127–28,
      366, 508–10
  fossils and, 439–40
  fluid dynamics and, 181, 184, 431
  hydraulic engineering, 347–54, 413,
    429
    canals, 340, 349–50, *350*
    creating waterway between
      Florence and Mediterranean,
      351

diverting the Arno River, 347–52, 353, 428, 429, 431, 432, 505, 507

draining the Piombino marshes, 352–54, 365

harnessing the power of the Arno River, 193

military uses of, 299

perpetual motion devices, *195,* 196

moving, drawings of, *446*

Romorantin plans and, 504–5, 507

studio experiments on, 430

thought experiment using siphons, 436–37, *437*

underwater defense gear, 299–300

wave mechanics, 177–78, 434–35

Wells, Francis, 216

Wells, Thereza Crowe, 312

whale, fossil, 20

wheelbarrows, 341

Windsor Castle, 2, 65, 84–86, 124, 163, 253, 432, 505

Winternitz, Emanuel, 119

wonder, sense of, 520

woodpecker's tongue, 5, 178, 398, 525

World War II, 291, 321, 492

Wright, David, 257

writings of Leonardo, 24, 47, 54, 55, 59, 69

on anatomy, 61–62

on artist at work, 161

bestiary, 125–26, 243

on books, 172–73

on countryside and solitude, 24

on deluge, 20–21, 127–28, 366, 508–10

description of gestures, 283

fables, 23–24, 125

fantasy novellas, 127–28

on his lack of schooling, 17, 170

on illegitimate children, 14

on looking at mottled walls, 263–64

on material possessions, 130

on meat eating, 130–31

on meeting with Ligny, 297

on microcosm-macrocosm relationship, 425–26

on motion, 180

on observation, 179, 180, 183, 520

on painting and artistic principles, 39–41, 79–81, 84, 88, 121–22, 157, 228, 264–66, 374

on perpetual motion, 195

prophecies, 126, 130

riddles, 8–9, 126

on sculpture, 262, 374–75

on sexuality, 70, 71, 372

topics of curiosity, 178–79, 213–14

Treatise on Painting, 39, 88, 121–22, 228, 264–66, 508

on war, 357

on water, 429, 507

on woodpecker's tongue, 5, 178, 398, 525

Zeno, 180

About the Author

Walter Isaacson, University Professor of History at Tulane, has been CEO of the Aspen Institute, chairman of CNN, and editor of *Time* magazine. He is the author of *The Innovators*; *Steve Jobs*; *Einstein: His Life and Universe*; *Benjamin Franklin: An American Life*; and *Kissinger: A Biography* and the coauthor, with Evan Thomas, of *The Wise Men: Six Friends and the World They Made*.

Facebook: Walter Isaacson

Twitter: @WalterIsaacson

More bestselling biographies from
WALTER ISAACSON

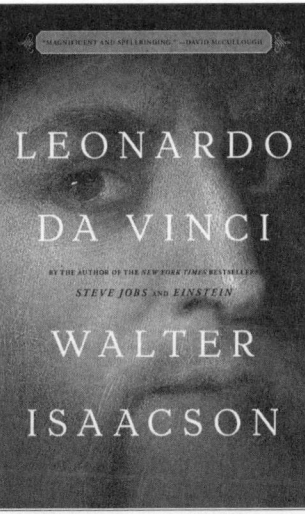

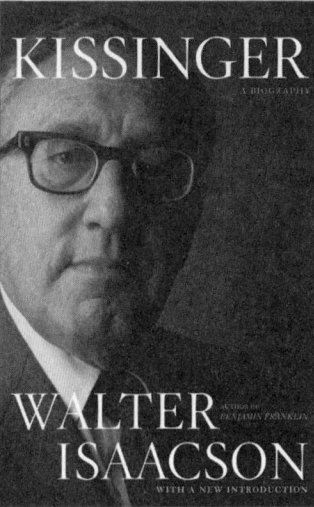

"For the generation that's grown up in a world where computers are the norm, smartphones feel like fifth limbs and music comes from the Internet rather than record and CD stores, *Steve Jobs* is must-read history. . . . The intimate chapters, where Jobs's personal side shines through, with all his faults and craziness, leave a deep impression. There's humor, too . . . it's a rich portrait of one of the greatest minds of our generation."

—*Associated Press*

"Isaacson's biography can be read in several ways. It is on the one hand a history of the most exciting time in the age of computers, when the machines first became personal and later, fashionable accessories. It is also a textbook study of the rise and fall and rise of Apple and the brutal clashes that destroyed friendships and careers. And it is a gadget lover's dream, with fabulous, inside accounts of how the Macintosh, iPod, iPhone and iPad came into being. But more than anything, Isaacson has crafted a biography of a complicated, peculiar personality—Jobs was charming, loathsome, lovable, obsessive, maddening—and the author shows how Jobs's character was instrumental in shaping some of the greatest technological innovations of our time."

—*The Washington Post*

"A wonderfully robust biography that not only tracks Jobs's life but also serves as a history of digital technology. What makes the book come alive, though, is Isaacson's ability to shape the story as a kind of archetypal fantasy: the flawed hero, the noble quest, the holy grail, the death of the king."

—*Booklist*

"A nuanced, balanced portrait that is sure to become mandatory reading for anyone with an interest in big business and popular culture . . . Isaacson is to be commended for explaining the genius of Jobs in fascinating fashion, launching a discussion that could reach infinity and beyond."

—*The Christian Science Monitor*

"Walter Isaacson's biography of Steve Jobs comes as a breath of fresh air . . . a reliable and captivating guide to a man who reshaped the computing industry and more."

—CNET.com

"It's a testament to Isaacson's skill as a biographer that readers can at last obtain the picture of Steve Jobs as a human being rather than a legend . . . anyone who's ever wondered how so very much about the technology landscape has changed so fundamentally in just thirty-five years, owes it to themselves to read this book."

—TUAW.com

"Walter Isaacson's book is an unflinching biography of a manifestly great man. . . . Steve Jobs's life was a great story with a near mythic arc, and Isaacson captures it well . . . the book moves at a fast pace with a great eye for detail. . . . Isaacson is perceptive and original."

—CultofMac.com

"Isaacson's biography lives up to the hype, showing readers the private turbulence that spurred Jobs to public greatness."

—ShelfAwareness.com

"A scrupulously fair chronicle."

—*The New York Review of Books*

"Isaacson's book is studded with moments that make you go 'wow.'"

—*The Guardian*

"If you are interested in the history of the digital age and the emergence of digital culture, Isaacson's book is a must read."

—Technorati.com

"An irresistible glimpse into his complex and often contradictory life."

—*San Francisco Chronicle*

"A riveting book, with as much to say about the transformation of modern life in the information age as about its supernaturally gifted and driven subject."

—*The Telegraph*

STEVE JOBS

WALTER
ISAACSON

SIMON & SCHUSTER PAPERBACKS

New York   London   Toronto   Sydney   New Delhi

Simon & Schuster Paperbacks
An Imprint of Simon & Schuster, Inc.
1230 Avenue of the Americas
New York, NY 10020

This Simon & Schuster paperback edition September 2015

SIMON & SCHUSTER PAPERBACKS and colophon are registered
trademarks of Simon & Schuster, Inc.

Illustration credits appear on page 632.

For information about special discounts for bulk purchases,
please contact Simon & Schuster Special Sales at
1-866-506-1949 or business@simonandschuster.com.

The Simon & Schuster Speakers Bureau can bring authors to your live event.
For more information or to book an event contact the
Simon & Schuster Speakers Bureau at 1-866-248-3049
or visit our website at www.simonspeakers.com.

Designed by Joy O'Meara

Manufactured in the United States of America

5   7   9   10   8   6

The Library of Congress has cataloged the hardcover edition as follows:

Isaacson, Walter.
Steve Jobs / Walter Isaacson.
p. cm.
1. Jobs, Steve, 1955–2011. 2. Computer engineers—United States—Biography.
3. Businesspeople—United States—Biography. 4. Apple Computer, Inc.—History.
I. Title.
QA76.2.J63I83 2011
621.39092—dc23
[B]
2011045006

ISBN 978-1-4516-4853-9
ISBN 978-1-5011-2762-5 (pbk)
ISBN 978-1-4516-4855-3 (ebook)

The people who are crazy enough
to think they can change
the world are the ones who do.

—Apple's "Think Different" commercial, 1997

CONTENTS

Characters   xiii

Introduction: *How This Book Came to Be*   xvii

CHAPTER ONE
Childhood: *Abandoned and Chosen*   1

CHAPTER TWO
Odd Couple: *The Two Steves*   21

CHAPTER THREE
The Dropout: *Turn On, Tune In . . .*   31

CHAPTER FOUR
Atari and India: *Zen and the Art of Game Design*   42

CHAPTER FIVE
The Apple I: *Turn On, Boot Up, Jack In . . .*   56

CHAPTER SIX
The Apple II: *Dawn of a New Age*   71

CHAPTER SEVEN
Chrisann and Lisa: *He Who Is Abandoned . . .*   86

CHAPTER EIGHT
Xerox and Lisa: *Graphical User Interfaces*   92

CHAPTER NINE

Going Public: *A Man of Wealth and Fame*   102

CHAPTER TEN

The Mac Is Born: *You Say You Want a Revolution*   108

CHAPTER ELEVEN

The Reality Distortion Field: *Playing by His Own Set of Rules*   117

CHAPTER TWELVE

The Design: *Real Artists Simplify*   125

CHAPTER THIRTEEN

Building the Mac: *The Journey Is the Reward*   135

CHAPTER FOURTEEN

Enter Sculley: *The Pepsi Challenge*   148

CHAPTER FIFTEEN

The Launch: *A Dent in the Universe*   159

CHAPTER SIXTEEN

Gates and Jobs: *When Orbits Intersect*   171

CHAPTER SEVENTEEN

Icarus: *What Goes Up . . .*   180

CHAPTER EIGHTEEN

NeXT: *Prometheus Unbound*   211

CHAPTER NINETEEN

Pixar: *Technology Meets Art*   238

CHAPTER TWENTY

A Regular Guy: *Love Is Just a Four-Letter Word*   250

CHAPTER TWENTY-ONE

Family Man: *At Home with the Jobs Clan*   267

CHAPTER TWENTY-TWO
Toy Story: *Buzz and Woody to the Rescue* 284

CHAPTER TWENTY-THREE
The Second Coming:
What Rough Beast, Its Hour Come Round at Last . . . 293

CHAPTER TWENTY-FOUR
The Restoration: *The Loser Now Will Be Later to Win* 305

CHAPTER TWENTY-FIVE
Think Different: *Jobs as iCEO* 327

CHAPTER TWENTY-SIX
Design Principles: *The Studio of Jobs and Ive* 340

CHAPTER TWENTY-SEVEN
The iMac: *Hello (Again)* 348

CHAPTER TWENTY-EIGHT
CEO: *Still Crazy after All These Years* 358

CHAPTER TWENTY-NINE
Apple Stores: *Genius Bars and Siena Sandstone* 368

CHAPTER THIRTY
The Digital Hub: *From iTunes to the iPod* 378

CHAPTER THIRTY-ONE
The iTunes Store: *I'm the Pied Piper* 394

CHAPTER THIRTY-TWO
Music Man: *The Sound Track of His Life* 411

CHAPTER THIRTY-THREE
Pixar's Friends: *. . . and Foes* 426

CHAPTER THIRTY-FOUR
Twenty-first-century Macs: *Setting Apple Apart* 444

CHAPTER THIRTY-FIVE

Round One: *Memento Mori*   452

CHAPTER THIRTY-SIX

The iPhone: *Three Revolutionary Products in One*   465

CHAPTER THIRTY-SEVEN

Round Two: *The Cancer Recurs*   476

CHAPTER THIRTY-EIGHT

The iPad: *Into the Post-PC Era*   490

CHAPTER THIRTY-NINE

New Battles: *And Echoes of Old Ones*   511

CHAPTER FORTY

To Infinity: *The Cloud, the Spaceship, and Beyond*   525

CHAPTER FORTY-ONE

Round Three: *The Twilight Struggle*   538

CHAPTER FORTY-TWO

Legacy: *The Brightest Heaven of Invention*   560

Epilogue   573

Acknowledgments   578

Sources   579

Notes   583

Index   603

CHARACTERS

Al Alcorn. Chief engineer at Atari, who designed Pong and hired Jobs.

Gil Amelio. Became CEO of Apple in 1996, bought NeXT, bringing Jobs back.

Bill Atkinson. Early Apple employee, developed graphics for the Macintosh.

Chrisann Brennan. Jobs's girlfriend at Homestead High, mother of his daughter Lisa.

Lisa Brennan-Jobs. Daughter of Jobs and Chrisann Brennan, born in 1978; became a writer in New York City.

Nolan Bushnell. Founder of Atari and entrepreneurial role model for Jobs.

Bill Campbell. Apple marketing chief during Jobs's first stint at Apple and board member and confidant after Jobs's return in 1997.

Edwin Catmull. A cofounder of Pixar and later a Disney executive.

Kobun Chino. A Sōtō Zen master in California who became Jobs's spiritual teacher.

Lee Clow. Advertising wizard who created Apple's "1984" ad and worked with Jobs for three decades.

Deborah "Debi" Coleman. Early Mac team manager who took over Apple manufacturing.

Tim Cook. Steady, calm, chief operating officer hired by Jobs in 1998; replaced Jobs as Apple CEO in August 2011.

Eddy Cue. Chief of Internet services at Apple, Jobs's wingman in dealing with content companies.

Andrea "Andy" Cunningham. Publicist at Regis McKenna's firm who handled Apple in the early Macintosh years.

MICHAEL EISNER. Hard-driving Disney CEO who made the Pixar deal, then clashed with Jobs.

LARRY ELLISON. CEO of Oracle and personal friend of Jobs.

TONY FADELL. Punky engineer brought to Apple in 2001 to develop the iPod.

SCOTT FORSTALL. Chief of Apple's mobile device software.

ROBERT FRIEDLAND. Reed student, proprietor of an apple farm commune, and spiritual seeker who influenced Jobs, then went on to run a mining company.

JEAN-LOUIS GASSÉE. Apple's manager in France, took over the Macintosh division when Jobs was ousted in 1985.

BILL GATES. The other computer wunderkind born in 1955.

ANDY HERTZFELD. Playful, friendly software engineer and Jobs's pal on the original Mac team.

JOANNA HOFFMAN. Original Mac team member with the spirit to stand up to Jobs.

ELIZABETH HOLMES. Daniel Kottke's girlfriend at Reed and early Apple employee.

ROD HOLT. Chain-smoking Marxist hired by Jobs in 1976 to be the electrical engineer on the Apple II.

ROBERT IGER. Succeeded Eisner as Disney CEO in 2005.

JONATHAN "JONY" IVE. Chief designer at Apple, became Jobs's partner and confidant.

ABDULFATTAH "JOHN" JANDALI. Syrian-born graduate student in Wisconsin who became biological father of Jobs and Mona Simpson, later a food and beverage manager at the Boomtown casino near Reno.

CLARA HAGOPIAN JOBS. Daughter of Armenian immigrants, married Paul Jobs in 1946; they adopted Steve soon after his birth in 1955.

ERIN JOBS. Middle child of Laurene Powell and Steve Jobs.

EVE JOBS. Youngest child of Laurene and Steve.

PATTY JOBS. Adopted by Paul and Clara Jobs two years after they adopted Steve.

PAUL REINHOLD JOBS. Wisconsin-born Coast Guard seaman who, with his wife, Clara, adopted Steve in 1955.

REED JOBS. Oldest child of Steve Jobs and Laurene Powell.

RON JOHNSON. Hired by Jobs in 2000 to develop Apple's stores.

JEFFREY KATZENBERG. Head of Disney Studios, clashed with Eisner and resigned in 1994 to cofound DreamWorks SKG.

ALAN KAY. Creative and colorful computer pioneer who envisioned early personal computers, helped arrange Jobs's Xerox PARC visit and his purchase of Pixar.

DANIEL KOTTKE. Jobs's closest friend at Reed, fellow pilgrim to India, early Apple employee.

JOHN LASSETER. Cofounder and creative force at Pixar.

DAN'L LEWIN. Marketing exec with Jobs at Apple and then NeXT.

MIKE MARKKULA. First big Apple investor and chairman, a father figure to Jobs.

REGIS MCKENNA. Publicity whiz who guided Jobs early on and remained a trusted advisor.

MIKE MURRAY. Early Macintosh marketing director.

PAUL OTELLINI. CEO of Intel who helped switch the Macintosh to Intel chips but did not get the iPhone business.

LAURENE POWELL. Savvy and good-humored Penn graduate, went to Goldman Sachs and then Stanford Business School, married Steve Jobs in 1991.

GEORGE RILEY. Jobs's Memphis-born friend and lawyer.

ARTHUR ROCK. Legendary tech investor, early Apple board member, Jobs's father figure.

JONATHAN "RUBY" RUBINSTEIN. Worked with Jobs at NeXT, became chief hardware engineer at Apple in 1997.

MIKE SCOTT. Brought in by Markkula to be Apple's president in 1977 to try to manage Jobs.

JOHN SCULLEY. Pepsi executive recruited by Jobs in 1983 to be Apple's CEO, clashed with and ousted Jobs in 1985.

JOANNE SCHIEBLE JANDALI SIMPSON. Wisconsin-born biological mother of Steve Jobs, whom she put up for adoption, and Mona Simpson, whom she raised.

MONA SIMPSON. Biological full sister of Jobs; they discovered their relationship in 1986 and became close. She wrote novels loosely based on her mother Joanne (*Anywhere but Here*), Jobs and his daughter Lisa (*A Regular Guy*), and her father Abdulfattah Jandali (*The Lost Father*).

ALVY RAY SMITH. A cofounder of Pixar who clashed with Jobs.

BURRELL SMITH. Brilliant, troubled hardware designer on the original Mac team, afflicted with schizophrenia in the 1990s.

AVADIS "AVIE" TEVANIAN. Worked with Jobs and Rubinstein at NeXT, became chief software engineer at Apple in 1997.

JAMES VINCENT. A music-loving Brit, the younger partner with Lee Clow and Duncan Milner at the ad agency Apple hired.

RON WAYNE. Met Jobs at Atari, became first partner with Jobs and Wozniak at fledgling Apple, but unwisely decided to forgo his equity stake.

STEPHEN WOZNIAK. The star electronics geek at Homestead High; Jobs figured out how to package and market his amazing circuit boards and became his partner in founding Apple.

DEL YOCAM. Early Apple employee who became the General Manager of the Apple II Group and later Apple's Chief Operating Officer.

INTRODUCTION

How This Book Came to Be

In the early summer of 2004, I got a phone call from Steve Jobs. He had been scattershot friendly to me over the years, with occasional bursts of intensity, especially when he was launching a new product that he wanted on the cover of *Time* or featured on CNN, places where I'd worked. But now that I was no longer at either of those places, I hadn't heard from him much. We talked a bit about the Aspen Institute, which I had recently joined, and I invited him to speak at our summer campus in Colorado. He'd be happy to come, he said, but not to be onstage. He wanted instead to take a walk so that we could talk.

That seemed a bit odd. I didn't yet know that taking a long walk was his preferred way to have a serious conversation. It turned out that he wanted me to write a biography of him. I had recently published one on Benjamin Franklin and was writing one about Albert Einstein, and my initial reaction was to wonder, half jokingly, whether he saw himself as the natural successor in that sequence. Because I assumed that he was still in the middle of an oscillating career that had many more ups and downs left, I demurred. Not now, I said. Maybe in a decade or two, when you retire.

I had known him since 1984, when he came to Manhattan to have lunch with *Time*'s editors and extol his new Macintosh. He was petulant even then, attacking a *Time* correspondent for having wounded him with a story that was too revealing. But talking to him afterward, I found myself rather captivated, as so many others have been over the years, by his engaging intensity. We stayed in touch, even after he was ousted from Apple. When he had something to pitch, such as a NeXT computer or Pixar movie, the beam of his charm would suddenly refocus on me, and he would take me to a sushi restaurant in Lower Manhattan to tell me that whatever he was touting was the best thing he had ever produced. I liked him.

When he was restored to the throne at Apple, we put him on the cover of *Time*, and soon thereafter he began offering me his ideas for a series we were doing on the most influential people of the century. He had launched his "Think Different" campaign, featuring iconic photos of some of the same people we were considering, and he found the endeavor of assessing historic influence fascinating.

After I had deflected his suggestion that I write a biography of him, I heard from him every now and then. At one point I emailed to ask if it was true, as my daughter had told me, that the Apple logo was an homage to Alan Turing, the British computer pioneer who broke the German wartime codes and then committed suicide by biting into a cyanide-laced apple. He replied that he wished he had thought of that, but hadn't. That started an exchange about the early history of Apple, and I found myself gathering string on the subject, just in case I ever decided to do such a book. When my Einstein biography came out, he came to a book event in Palo Alto and pulled me aside to suggest, again, that he would make a good subject.

His persistence baffled me. He was known to guard his privacy, and I had no reason to believe he'd ever read any of my books. Maybe someday, I continued to say. But in 2009 his wife, Laurene Powell, said bluntly, "If you're ever going to do a book on Steve, you'd better do it now." He had just taken a second medical leave. I confessed to her that when he had first raised the idea, I hadn't known he was sick. Almost nobody knew, she said. He had called me right before he was going to be operated on for cancer, and he was still keeping it a secret, she explained.

I decided then to write this book. Jobs surprised me by readily acknowledging that he would have no control over it or even the right to see it in advance. "It's your book," he said. "I won't even read it." But later that fall he seemed to have second thoughts about cooperating and, though I didn't know it, was hit by another round of cancer complications. He stopped returning my calls, and I put the project aside for a while.

Then, unexpectedly, he phoned me late on the afternoon of New Year's Eve 2009. He was at home in Palo Alto with only his sister, the writer Mona Simpson. His wife and their three children had taken a quick trip to go skiing, but he was not healthy enough to join them. He was in a reflective mood, and we talked for more than an hour. He began by recalling that he had wanted to build a frequency counter when he was twelve, and he was able to look up Bill Hewlett, the founder of HP, in the phone book and call him to get parts. Jobs said that the past twelve years of his life, since his return to Apple, had been his most productive in terms of creating new products. But his more important goal, he said, was to do what Hewlett and his friend David Packard had done, which was create a company that was so imbued with innovative creativity that it would outlive them.

"I always thought of myself as a humanities person as a kid, but I liked electronics," he said. "Then I read something that one of my heroes, Edwin Land of Polaroid, said about the importance of people who could stand at the intersection of humanities and sciences, and I decided that's what I wanted to do." It was as if he were suggesting themes for his biography (and in this instance, at least, the theme turned out to be valid). The creativity that can occur when a feel for both the humanities and the sciences combine in one strong personality was the topic that most interested me in my biographies of Franklin and Einstein, and I believe that it will be a key to creating innovative economies in the twenty-first century.

I asked Jobs why he wanted me to be the one to write his biography. "I think you're good at getting people to talk," he replied. That was an unexpected answer. I knew that I would have to interview scores of people he had fired, abused, abandoned, or otherwise infuriated, and I feared he would not be comfortable with my getting them to talk. And indeed he did turn out to be skittish when word trickled back to him of people that I was interviewing. But after a couple of months, he began encouraging people to talk to me, even foes and former girlfriends. Nor did he try to put anything off-limits. "I've done a lot of things I'm not proud of, such as getting my girlfriend pregnant when

I was twenty-three and the way I handled that," he said. "But I don't have any skeletons in my closet that can't be allowed out." He didn't seek any control over what I wrote, or even ask to read it in advance. His only involvement came when my publisher was choosing the cover art. When he saw an early version of a proposed cover treatment, he disliked it so much that he asked to have input in designing a new version. I was both amused and willing, so I readily assented.

I ended up having more than forty interviews and conversations with him. Some were formal ones in his Palo Alto living room, others were done during long walks and drives or by telephone. During my two years of visits, he became increasingly intimate and revealing, though at times I witnessed what his veteran colleagues at Apple used to call his "reality distortion field." Sometimes it was the inadvertent misfiring of memory cells that happens to us all; at other times he was spinning his own version of reality both to me and to himself. To check and flesh out his story, I interviewed more than a hundred friends, relatives, competitors, adversaries, and colleagues.

His wife also did not request any restrictions or control, nor did she ask to see in advance what I would publish. In fact she strongly encouraged me to be honest about his failings as well as his strengths. She is one of the smartest and most grounded people I have ever met. "There are parts of his life and personality that are extremely messy, and that's the truth," she told me early on. "You shouldn't whitewash it. He's good at spin, but he also has a remarkable story, and I'd like to see that it's all told truthfully."

I leave it to the reader to assess whether I have succeeded in this mission. I'm sure there are players in this drama who will remember some of the events differently or think that I sometimes got trapped in Jobs's distortion field. As happened when I wrote a book about Henry Kissinger, which in some ways was good preparation for this project, I found that people had such strong positive and negative emotions about Jobs that the Rashomon effect was often evident. But I've done the best I can to balance conflicting accounts fairly and be transparent about the sources I used.

This is a book about the roller-coaster life and searingly intense personality of a creative entrepreneur whose passion for perfection and ferocious drive revolutionized six industries: personal computers, animated movies, music, phones, tablet computing, and digital publishing. You might even add a seventh, retail stores, which Jobs did not quite revolutionize but did reimagine. In addition, he opened the way for a new market for digital content based on apps rather than just websites. Along the way he produced not only transforming products but also, on his second try, a lasting company, endowed with his DNA, that is filled with creative designers and daredevil engineers who could carry forward his vision. In August 2011, right before he stepped down as CEO, the enterprise he started in his parents' garage became the world's most valuable company.

This is also, I hope, a book about innovation. At a time when the United States is seeking ways to sustain its innovative edge, and when societies around the world are trying to build creative digital-age economies, Jobs stands as the ultimate icon of inventiveness, imagination, and sustained innovation. He knew that the best way to create value in the twenty-first century was to connect creativity with technology, so he built a company where leaps of the imagination were combined with remarkable feats of engineering. He and his colleagues at Apple were able to think differently: They developed not merely modest product advances based on focus groups, but whole new devices and services that consumers did not yet know they needed.

He was not a model boss or human being, tidily packaged for emulation. Driven by demons, he could drive those around him to fury and despair. But his personality and passions and products were all interrelated, just as Apple's hardware and software tended to be, as if part of an integrated system. His tale is thus both instructive and cautionary, filled with lessons about innovation, character, leadership, and values.

Shakespeare's *Henry V*—the story of a willful and immature prince who becomes a passionate but sensitive, callous but sentimental, inspiring but flawed king—begins with the exhortation "O for a Muse of fire, that would ascend / The brightest heaven of invention." For Steve Jobs, the ascent to the brightest heaven of invention begins with a tale of two sets of parents, and of growing up in a valley that was just learning how to turn silicon into gold.

The Los Altos house with the garage where Apple was born

Paul Jobs with Steve, 1956

In the Homestead High yearbook, 1972

With the "SWAB JOB" school prank sign

CHAPTER ONE

CHILDHOOD

Abandoned and Chosen

The Adoption

When Paul Jobs was mustered out of the Coast Guard after World War II, he made a wager with his crewmates. They had arrived in San Francisco, where their ship was decommissioned, and Paul bet that he would find himself a wife within two weeks. He was a taut, tattooed engine mechanic, six feet tall, with a passing resemblance to James Dean. But it wasn't his looks that got him a date with Clara Hagopian, a sweet-humored daughter of Armenian immigrants. It was the fact that he and his friends had a car, unlike the group she had originally planned to go out with that evening. Ten days later, in March 1946, Paul got engaged to Clara and won his wager. It would turn out to be a happy marriage, one that lasted until death parted them more than forty years later.

Paul Reinhold Jobs had been raised on a dairy farm in Germantown, Wisconsin. Even though his father was an alcoholic and sometimes abusive, Paul ended up with a gentle and calm disposition under his leathery exterior. After dropping out of high school, he wandered through the Midwest picking up work as a mechanic until, at age nineteen, he joined the Coast Guard, even though he didn't know how

1

to swim. He was deployed on the USS *General M. C. Meigs* and spent much of the war ferrying troops to Italy for General Patton. His talent as a machinist and fireman earned him commendations, but he occasionally found himself in minor trouble and never rose above the rank of seaman.

Clara was born in New Jersey, where her parents had landed after fleeing the Turks in Armenia, and they moved to the Mission District of San Francisco when she was a child. She had a secret that she rarely mentioned to anyone: She had been married before, but her husband had been killed in the war. So when she met Paul Jobs on that first date, she was primed to start a new life.

Like many who lived through the war, they had experienced enough excitement that, when it was over, they desired simply to settle down, raise a family, and lead a less eventful life. They had little money, so they moved to Wisconsin and lived with Paul's parents for a few years, then headed for Indiana, where he got a job as a machinist for International Harvester. His passion was tinkering with old cars, and he made money in his spare time buying, restoring, and selling them. Eventually he quit his day job to become a full-time used car salesman.

Clara, however, loved San Francisco, and in 1952 she convinced her husband to move back there. They got an apartment in the Sunset District facing the Pacific, just south of Golden Gate Park, and he took a job working for a finance company as a "repo man," picking the locks of cars whose owners hadn't paid their loans and repossessing them. He also bought, repaired, and sold some of the cars, making a decent enough living in the process.

There was, however, something missing in their lives. They wanted children, but Clara had suffered an ectopic pregnancy, in which the fertilized egg was implanted in a fallopian tube rather than the uterus, and she had been unable to have any. So by 1955, after nine years of marriage, they were looking to adopt a child.

Like Paul Jobs, Joanne Schieble was from a rural Wisconsin family of German heritage. Her father, Arthur Schieble, had immigrated to the outskirts of Green Bay, where he and his wife owned a mink farm and dabbled successfully in various other businesses, including real estate and photoengraving. He was very strict, especially regarding his daughter's relationships, and he had strongly disapproved of her first love, an artist who was not a Catholic. Thus it was no surprise that he threatened to cut Joanne off completely when, as a graduate student at the University of Wisconsin, she fell in love with Abdulfattah "John" Jandali, a Muslim teaching assistant from Syria.

Jandali was the youngest of nine children in a prominent Syrian family. His father owned oil refineries and multiple other businesses, with large holdings in Damascus and Homs, and at one point pretty much controlled the price of wheat in the region. His mother, he later said, was a "traditional Muslim woman" who was a "conservative, obedient housewife." Like the Schieble family, the Jandalis put a premium on education. Abdulfattah was sent to a Jesuit boarding school, even though he was Muslim, and he got an undergraduate degree at the American University in Beirut before entering the University of Wisconsin to pursue a doctoral degree in political science.

In the summer of 1954, Joanne went with Abdulfattah to Syria. They spent two months in Homs, where she learned from his family to cook Syrian dishes. When they returned to Wisconsin she discovered that she was pregnant. They were both twenty-three, but they decided not to get married. Her father was dying at the time, and he had threatened to disown her if she wed Abdulfattah. Nor was abortion an easy option in a small Catholic community. So in early 1955, Joanne traveled to San Francisco, where she was taken into the care of a kindly doctor who sheltered unwed mothers, delivered their babies, and quietly arranged closed adoptions.

Joanne had one requirement: Her child must be adopted by college graduates. So the doctor arranged for the baby to be placed with a lawyer and his wife. But when a boy was born—on February 24, 1955—the designated couple decided that they wanted a girl and backed out. Thus it was that the boy became the son not of a lawyer but of a high school dropout with a passion for mechanics and his salt-of-the-earth wife who was working as a bookkeeper. Paul and Clara named their new baby Steven Paul Jobs.

When Joanne found out that her baby had been placed with a couple who had not even graduated from high school, she refused to sign the adoption papers. The standoff lasted weeks, even after the baby had settled into the Jobs household. Eventually Joanne relented, with the stipulation that the couple promise—indeed sign a pledge—to fund a savings account to pay for the boy's college education.

There was another reason that Joanne was balky about signing the adoption papers. Her father was about to die, and she planned to marry Jandali soon after. She held out hope, she would later tell family members, sometimes tearing up at the memory, that once they were married, she could get their baby boy back.

Arthur Schieble died in August 1955, after the adoption was finalized. Just after Christmas that year, Joanne and Abdulfattah were married in St. Philip the Apostle Catholic Church in Green Bay. He got his PhD in international politics the next year, and then they had another child, a girl named Mona. After she and Jandali divorced in 1962, Joanne embarked on a dreamy and peripatetic life that her daughter, who grew up to become the acclaimed novelist Mona Simpson, would capture in her book *Anywhere but Here*. Because Steve's adoption had been closed, it would be twenty years before they would all find each other.

Steve Jobs knew from an early age that he was adopted. "My parents were very open with me about that," he recalled. He had a vivid memory of sitting on the lawn of his house, when he was six or seven years old, telling the girl who lived across the street. "So does that mean your real parents didn't want you?" the girl asked. "Lightning bolts went off in my head," according to Jobs. "I remember running into the house, crying. And my parents said, 'No, you have to understand.' They were very serious and looked me straight in the eye. They said, 'We specifically picked you out.' Both of my parents said that and repeated it slowly for me. And they put an emphasis on every word in that sentence."

Abandoned. Chosen. Special. Those concepts became part of who Jobs was and how he regarded himself. His closest friends think that the knowledge that he was given up at birth left some scars. "I think his desire for complete control of whatever he makes derives directly from his personality and the fact that he was abandoned at birth," said one longtime colleague, Del Yocam. "He wants to control his environment, and he sees the product as an extension of himself." Greg Calhoun, who became close to Jobs right after college, saw another effect. "Steve talked to me a lot about being abandoned and the pain that caused," he said. "It made him independent. He followed the beat of a different drummer, and that came from being in a different world than he was born into."

Later in life, when he was the same age his biological father had been when he abandoned him, Jobs would father and abandon a child of his own. (He eventually took responsibility for her.) Chrisann Brennan, the mother of that child, said that being put up for adoption left Jobs "full of broken glass," and it helps to explain some of his behavior. "He who is abandoned is an abandoner," she said. Andy Hertzfeld, who worked with Jobs at Apple in the early 1980s, is among the few who remained close to both Brennan and Jobs. "The key question about Steve is why he can't control himself at times from being so reflexively cruel and harmful to some people," he said. "That goes back to being abandoned at birth. The real underlying problem was the theme of abandonment in Steve's life."

Jobs dismissed this. "There's some notion that because I was abandoned, I worked very hard so I could do well and make my parents wish they had me back, or some such nonsense, but that's ridiculous," he insisted. "Knowing I was adopted may have made me feel more independent, but I have never felt abandoned. I've always felt special. My parents made me feel special." He would later bristle whenever anyone referred to Paul and Clara Jobs as his "adoptive" parents or implied that they were not his "real" parents. "They were my parents 1,000%," he said. When speaking about his biological parents, on the other hand, he was curt: "They were my sperm and egg bank. That's not harsh, it's just the way it was, a sperm bank thing, nothing more."

Silicon Valley

The childhood that Paul and Clara Jobs created for their new son was, in many ways, a stereotype of the late 1950s. When Steve was two they adopted a girl they named Patty, and three years later they moved to a tract house in the suburbs. The finance company where Paul worked as a repo man, CIT, had transferred him down to its Palo Alto office, but he could not afford to live there, so they landed in a subdivision in Mountain View, a less expensive town just to the south.

There Paul tried to pass along his love of mechanics and cars. "Steve, this is your workbench now," he said as he marked off a section of the table in their garage. Jobs remembered being impressed by his father's focus on craftsmanship. "I thought my dad's sense of design was pretty good," he said, "because he knew how to build anything. If we needed a cabinet, he would build it. When he built our fence, he gave me a hammer so I could work with him."

Fifty years later the fence still surrounds the back and side yards of the house in Mountain View. As Jobs showed it off to me, he caressed the stockade panels and recalled a lesson that his father implanted deeply in him. It was important, his father said, to craft the backs of cabinets and fences properly, even though they were hidden. "He loved doing things right. He even cared about the look of the parts you couldn't see."

His father continued to refurbish and resell used cars, and he festooned the garage with pictures of his favorites. He would point out the detailing of the design to his son: the lines, the vents, the chrome, the trim of the seats. After work each day, he would change into his dungarees and retreat to the garage, often with Steve tagging along. "I figured I could get him nailed down with a little mechanical ability, but he really wasn't interested in getting his hands dirty," Paul later recalled. "He never really cared too much about mechanical things."

"I wasn't that into fixing cars," Jobs admitted. "But I was eager to hang out with my dad." Even as he was growing more aware that he had been adopted, he was becoming more attached to his father. One day when he was about eight, he discovered a photograph of his father from his time in the Coast Guard. "He's in the engine room, and he's got his shirt off and looks like James Dean. It was one of those *Oh wow* moments for a kid. *Wow, oooh,* my parents were actually once very young and really good-looking."

Through cars, his father gave Steve his first exposure to electronics. "My dad did not have a deep understanding of electronics, but he'd encountered it a lot in automobiles and other things he would fix. He showed me the rudiments of electronics, and I got very interested in that." Even more interesting were the trips to scavenge for parts. "Every weekend, there'd be a junkyard trip. We'd be looking for a generator, a carburetor, all sorts of components." He remembered watching his father negotiate at the counter. "He was a good bargainer, because he knew better than the guys at the counter what the parts should cost." This helped fulfill the pledge his parents made when he was adopted. "My college fund came from my dad paying $50 for a Ford Falcon or some other beat-up car that didn't run, working on it for a few weeks, and selling it for $250—and not telling the IRS."

The Jobses' house and the others in their neighborhood were modeled on ones built by the real estate developer Joseph Eichler, whose company spawned more than eleven thousand homes in various California subdivisions between 1950 and 1974. Inspired by Frank Lloyd Wright's vision of simple modern homes for the American "everyman," Eichler built inexpensive houses that featured floor-to-ceiling glass walls, open floor plans, exposed post-and-beam construction, concrete slab floors, and lots of sliding glass doors. "Eichler did a great thing," Jobs said on one of our walks around the neighborhood. "His houses were smart and cheap and good. They brought clean design and simple taste to lower-income people. They had awesome little features, like radiant heating in the floors. You put carpet on them, and we had nice toasty floors when we were kids."

Jobs said that his appreciation for Eichler homes instilled in him a passion for making nicely designed products for the mass market. "I love it when you can bring really great design and simple capability to something that doesn't cost much," he said as he pointed out the clean elegance of the houses. "It was the original vision for Apple. That's what we tried to do with the first Mac. That's what we did with the iPod."

Across the street from the Jobs family lived a man who had become successful as a real estate agent. "He wasn't that bright," Jobs recalled, "but he seemed to be making a fortune. So my dad thought, 'I can do that.' He worked so hard, I remember. He took these night classes, passed the license test, and got into real estate. Then the bottom fell out of the market." As a result, the family found itself financially strapped for a year or so while Steve was in elementary school. His mother took a job as a bookkeeper for Varian Associates, a company that made scientific instruments, and they took out a second mortgage. One day his fourth-grade teacher asked him, "What is it you don't understand about the universe?" Jobs replied, "I don't understand why all of a sudden my dad is so broke." He was proud that his father never adopted a servile attitude or slick style that may have made him a better salesman. "You had to suck up to people to sell real estate, and he wasn't good at that and it wasn't in his nature. I admired him for that." Paul Jobs went back to being a mechanic.

His father was calm and gentle, traits that his son later praised more than emulated. He was also resolute. Jobs described one example:

> Nearby was an engineer who was working at Westinghouse. He was a single guy, beatnik type. He had a girlfriend. She would babysit me sometimes. Both my parents worked, so I would come here right after school for a couple of hours. He would get drunk and hit her a couple of times. She came over one night, scared out of her wits, and he came over drunk, and my dad stood him down—saying "She's here, but you're not coming in." He stood right there. We like to think everything was idyllic in the 1950s, but this guy was one of those engineers who had messed-up lives.

What made the neighborhood different from the thousands of other spindly-tree subdivisions across America was that even the ne'er-do-wells tended to be engineers. "When we moved here, there were apricot and plum orchards on all of these corners," Jobs recalled. "But it was beginning to boom because of military investment." He soaked up the history of the valley and developed a yearning to play his own role. Edwin Land of Polaroid later told him about being asked by Eisenhower to help build the U-2 spy plane cameras to see how real the Soviet threat was. The film was dropped in canisters and returned to the NASA Ames Research Center in Sunnyvale, not far from where Jobs lived. "The first computer terminal I ever saw was when my dad brought me to the Ames Center," he said. "I fell totally in love with it."

Other defense contractors sprouted nearby during the 1950s. The Lockheed Missiles and Space Division, which built submarine-launched ballistic missiles, was founded in 1956 next to the NASA Center; by the time Jobs moved to the area four years later, it employed twenty thousand people. A few hundred yards away, Westinghouse built facilities that produced tubes and electrical transformers for the missile systems. "You had all these military companies on the cutting edge," he recalled. "It was mysterious and high-tech and made living here very exciting."

In the wake of the defense industries there arose a booming economy based on technology. Its roots stretched back to 1938, when David Packard and his new wife moved into a house in Palo Alto that had a shed where his friend Bill Hewlett was soon ensconced. The house had a garage—an appendage that would prove both useful and iconic in the valley—in which they tinkered around until they had their first product, an audio oscillator. By the 1950s, Hewlett-Packard was a fast-growing company making technical instruments.

Fortunately there was a place nearby for entrepreneurs who had outgrown their garages. In a move that would help transform the area into the cradle of the tech revolution, Stanford University's dean of engineering, Frederick Terman, created a seven-hundred-acre industrial park on university land for private companies that could commercialize the ideas of his students. Its first tenant was Varian Associates, where Clara Jobs worked. "Terman came up with this great idea that did more than anything to cause the tech industry to grow up here," Jobs said. By the time Jobs was ten, HP had nine thousand employees and was the blue-chip company where every engineer seeking financial stability wanted to work.

The most important technology for the region's growth was, of course, the semiconductor. William Shockley, who had been one of the inventors of the transistor at Bell Labs in New Jersey, moved out to Mountain View and, in 1956, started a company to build transistors using silicon rather than the more expensive germanium that was then commonly used. But Shockley became increasingly erratic and abandoned his silicon transistor project, which led eight of his engineers—most notably Robert Noyce and Gordon Moore—to break away to form Fairchild Semiconductor. That company grew to twelve thousand employees, but it fragmented in 1968, when Noyce lost a power struggle to become CEO. He took Gordon Moore and founded a company that they called Integrated Electronics Corporation, which they soon smartly abbreviated to Intel. Their third employee was Andrew Grove, who later would grow the company by shifting its focus from memory chips to microprocessors. Within a few years there would be more than fifty companies in the area making semiconductors.

The exponential growth of this industry was correlated with the phenomenon famously discovered by Moore, who in 1965 drew a graph of the speed of integrated circuits, based on the number of transistors that could be placed on a chip, and showed that it doubled about every two years, a trajectory that could be expected to continue. This was reaffirmed in 1971, when Intel was able to etch a complete central processing unit onto one chip, the Intel 4004, which was dubbed a "microprocessor." Moore's Law has held generally true to this day, and its reliable projection of performance to price allowed two generations of young entrepreneurs, including Steve Jobs and Bill Gates, to create cost projections for their forward-leaning products.

The chip industry gave the region a new name when Don Hoefler, a columnist for the weekly trade paper *Electronic News*, began a series in January 1971 entitled "Silicon Valley USA." The forty-mile Santa Clara Valley, which stretches from South San Francisco through Palo Alto to San Jose, has as its commercial backbone El Camino Real, the royal road that once connected California's twenty-one mission churches and is now a bustling avenue that connects companies and startups accounting for a third of the venture capital investment in the United States each year. "Growing up, I got inspired by the history of the place," Jobs said. "That made me want to be a part of it."

Like most kids, he became infused with the passions of the grownups around him. "Most of the dads in the neighborhood did really neat stuff, like photovoltaics and batteries and radar," Jobs recalled. "I grew up in awe of that stuff and asking people about it." The most important of these neighbors, Larry Lange, lived seven doors away. "He was my model of what an HP engineer was supposed to be: a big ham radio operator, hard-core electronics guy," Jobs recalled. "He would bring me stuff to play with." As we walked up to Lange's old house, Jobs pointed to the driveway. "He took a carbon microphone and a battery and a speaker, and he put it on this driveway. He had me talk into the carbon mike and it amplified out of the speaker." Jobs had been taught by his father that microphones always required an electronic amplifier. "So I raced home, and I told my dad that he was wrong."

"No, it needs an amplifier," his father assured him. When Steve protested otherwise, his father said he was crazy. "It can't work without an amplifier. There's some trick."

"I kept saying no to my dad, telling him he had to see it, and finally he actually walked down with me and saw it. And he said, 'Well I'll be a bat out of hell.'"

Jobs recalled the incident vividly because it was his first realization that his father did not know everything. Then a more disconcerting discovery began to dawn on him: He was smarter than his parents. He had always admired his father's competence and savvy. "He was not an educated man, but I had always thought he was pretty damn smart. He didn't read much, but he could do a lot. Almost everything mechanical, he could figure it out." Yet the carbon microphone incident, Jobs said, began a jarring process of realizing that he was in fact more clever and quick than his parents. "It was a very big moment that's burned into my mind. When I realized that I was smarter than my parents, I felt tremendous shame for having thought that. I will never forget that moment." This discovery, he later told friends, along with the fact that he was adopted, made him feel apart—detached and separate—from both his family and the world.

Another layer of awareness occurred soon after. Not only did he discover that he was brighter than his parents, but he discovered that they knew this. Paul and Clara Jobs were loving parents, and they were willing to adapt their lives to suit a son who was very smart—and also willful. They would go to great lengths to accommodate him. And soon Steve discovered this fact as well. "Both my parents got me. They felt a lot of responsibility once they sensed that I was special. They found ways to keep feeding me stuff and putting me in better schools. They were willing to defer to my needs."

So he grew up not only with a sense of having once been abandoned, but also with a sense that he was special. In his own mind, that was more important in the formation of his personality.

School

Even before Jobs started elementary school, his mother had taught him how to read. This, however, led to some problems once he got to school. "I was kind of bored for the first few years, so I occupied myself by getting into trouble." It also soon became clear that Jobs, by both nature and nurture, was not disposed to accept authority. "I encountered authority of a different kind than I had ever encountered before, and I did not like it. And they really almost got me. They came close to really beating any curiosity out of me."

His school, Monta Loma Elementary, was a series of low-slung 1950s buildings four blocks from his house. He countered his boredom by playing pranks. "I had a good friend named Rick Ferrentino, and we'd get into all sorts of trouble," he recalled. "Like we made little posters announcing 'Bring Your Pet to School Day.' It was crazy, with dogs chasing cats all over, and the teachers were beside themselves." Another time they convinced some kids to tell them the combination numbers for their bike locks. "Then we went outside and switched all of the locks, and nobody could get their bikes. It took them until late that night to straighten things out." When he was in third grade, the pranks became a bit more dangerous. "One time we set off an explosive under the chair of our teacher, Mrs. Thurman. We gave her a nervous twitch."

Not surprisingly, he was sent home two or three times before he finished third grade. By then, however, his father had begun to treat him as special, and in his calm but firm manner he made it clear that he expected the school to do the same. "Look, it's not his fault," Paul Jobs told the teachers, his son recalled. "If you can't keep him interested, it's your fault." His parents never punished him for his transgressions at school. "My father's father was an alcoholic and whipped him with a belt, but I'm not sure if I ever got spanked." Both of his parents, he added, "knew the school was at fault for trying to make me memorize stupid stuff rather than stimulating me." He was already starting to show the admixture of sensitivity and insensitivity, bristliness and detachment, that would mark him for the rest of his life.

When it came time for him to go into fourth grade, the school decided it was best to put Jobs and Ferrentino into separate classes. The teacher for the advanced class was a spunky woman named Imogene Hill, known as "Teddy," and she became, Jobs said, "one of the saints of my life." After watching him for a couple of weeks, she figured that the best way to handle him was to bribe him. "After school one day, she gave me this workbook with math problems in it, and she said, 'I want you to take it home and do this.' And I thought, 'Are you nuts?' And then she pulled out one of these giant lollipops that seemed as big as the world. And she said, 'When you're done with it, if you get it mostly right, I will give you this and five dollars.' And I handed it back within two days." After a few months, he no longer required the bribes. "I just wanted to learn and to please her."

She reciprocated by getting him a hobby kit for grinding a lens and making a camera. "I learned more from her than any other teacher, and if it hadn't been for her I'm sure I would have gone to jail." It reinforced, once again, the idea that he was special. "In my class, it was just me she cared about. She saw something in me."

It was not merely intelligence that she saw. Years later she liked to show off a picture of that year's class on Hawaii Day. Jobs had shown up without the suggested Hawaiian shirt, but in the picture he is front and center wearing one. He had, literally, been able to talk the shirt off another kid's back.

Near the end of fourth grade, Mrs. Hill had Jobs tested. "I scored at the high school sophomore level," he recalled. Now that it was clear, not only to himself and his parents but also to his teachers, that he was intellectually special, the school made the remarkable proposal that he skip two grades and go right into seventh; it would be the easiest way to keep him challenged and stimulated. His parents decided, more sensibly, to have him skip only one grade.

The transition was wrenching. He was a socially awkward loner who found himself with kids a year older. Worse yet, the sixth grade was in a different school, Crittenden Middle. It was only eight blocks from Monta Loma Elementary, but in many ways it was a world apart, located in a neighborhood filled with ethnic gangs. "Fights were a daily occurrence; as were shakedowns in bathrooms," wrote the Silicon Valley journalist Michael S. Malone. "Knives were regularly brought to school as a show of macho." Around the time that Jobs arrived, a group of students were jailed for a gang rape, and the bus of a neighboring school was destroyed after its team beat Crittenden's in a wrestling match.

Jobs was often bullied, and in the middle of seventh grade he gave his parents an ultimatum. "I insisted they put me in a different school," he recalled. Financially this was a tough demand. His parents were barely making ends meet, but by this point there was little doubt that they would eventually bend to his will. "When they resisted, I told them I would just quit going to school if I had to go back to Crittenden. So they researched where the best schools were and scraped together every dime and bought a house for $21,000 in a nicer district."

The move was only three miles to the south, to a former apricot orchard in Los Altos that had been turned into a subdivision of cookie-cutter tract homes. Their house, at 2066 Crist Drive, was one story with three bedrooms and an all-important attached garage with a roll-down door facing the street. There Paul Jobs could tinker with cars and his son with electronics.

Its other significant attribute was that it was just over the line inside what was then the Cupertino-Sunnyvale School District, one of the safest and best in the valley. "When I moved here, these corners were still orchards," Jobs pointed out as we walked in front of his old house. "The guy who lived right there taught me how to be a good organic gardener and to compost. He grew everything to perfection. I never had better food in my life. That's when I began to appreciate organic fruits and vegetables."

Even though they were not fervent about their faith, Jobs's parents wanted him to have a religious upbringing, so they took him to the Lutheran church most Sundays. That came to an end when he was thirteen. In July 1968 *Life* magazine published a shocking cover showing a pair of starving children in Biafra. Jobs took it to Sunday school and confronted the church's pastor. "If I raise my finger, will God know which one I'm going to raise even before I do it?"

The pastor answered, "Yes, God knows everything."

Jobs then pulled out the *Life* cover and asked, "Well, does God know about this and what's going to happen to those children?"

"Steve, I know you don't understand, but yes, God knows about that."

Jobs announced that he didn't want to have anything to do with worshipping such a God, and he never went back to church. He did, however, spend years studying and trying to practice the tenets of Zen Buddhism. Reflecting years later on his spiritual feelings, he said that religion was at its best when it emphasized spiritual experiences rather than received dogma. "The juice goes out of Christianity when it becomes too based on faith rather than on living like Jesus or seeing the world as Jesus saw it," he told me. "I think different religions are different doors to the same house. Sometimes I think the house exists, and sometimes I don't. It's the great mystery."

Paul Jobs was then working at Spectra-Physics, a company in nearby Santa Clara that made lasers for electronics and medical products. As a machinist, he crafted the prototypes of products that the engineers were devising. His son was fascinated by the need for perfection. "Lasers require precision alignment," Jobs said. "The really sophisticated ones, for airborne applications or medical, had very precise features. They would tell my dad something like, 'This is what we want, and we want it out of one piece of metal so that the coefficients of expansion are all the same.' And he had to figure out how to do it." Most pieces had to be made from scratch, which meant that Paul had to create custom tools and dies. His son was impressed, but he rarely went to the machine shop. "It would have been fun if he had gotten to teach me how to use a mill and lathe. But unfortunately I never went, because I was more interested in electronics."

One summer Paul took Steve to Wisconsin to visit the family's dairy farm. Rural life did not appeal to Steve, but one image stuck with him. He saw a calf being born, and he was amazed when the tiny animal struggled up within minutes and began to walk. "It was not something she had learned, but it was instead hardwired into her," he recalled. "A human baby couldn't do that. I found it remarkable, even though no one else did." He put it in hardware-software terms: "It was as if something in the animal's body and in its brain had been engineered to work together instantly rather than being learned."

In ninth grade Jobs went to Homestead High, which had a sprawling campus of two-story cinderblock buildings painted pink that served two thousand students. "It was designed by a famous prison architect," Jobs recalled. "They wanted to make it indestructible." He had developed a love of walking, and he walked the fifteen blocks to school by himself each day.

He had few friends his own age, but he got to know some seniors who were immersed in the counterculture of the late 1960s. It was a time when the geek and hippie worlds were beginning to show some overlap. "My friends were the really smart kids," he said. "I was interested in math and science and electronics. They were too, and also into LSD and the whole counterculture trip."

His pranks by then typically involved electronics. At one point he wired his house with speakers. But since speakers can also be used as microphones, he built a control room in his closet, where he could listen in on what was happening in other rooms. One night, when he had his headphones on and was listening in on his parents' bedroom, his father caught him and angrily demanded that he dismantle the system. He spent many evenings visiting the garage of Larry Lange, the engineer who lived down the street from his old house. Lange eventually gave Jobs the carbon microphone that had fascinated him, and he turned him on to Heathkits, those assemble-it-yourself kits for making ham radios and other electronic gear that were beloved by the soldering set back then. "Heathkits came with all the boards and parts color-coded, but the manual also explained the theory of how it operated," Jobs recalled. "It made you realize you could build and understand anything. Once you built a couple of radios, you'd see a TV in the catalogue and say, 'I can build that as well,' even if you didn't. I was very lucky, because when I was a kid both my dad and the Heathkits made me believe I could build anything."

Lange also got him into the Hewlett-Packard Explorers Club, a group of fifteen or so students who met in the company cafeteria on Tuesday nights. "They would get an engineer from one of the labs to come and talk about what he was working on," Jobs recalled. "My dad would drive me there. I was in heaven. HP was a pioneer of light-emitting diodes. So we talked about what to do with them." Because his father now worked for a laser company, that topic particularly interested him. One night he cornered one of HP's laser engineers after a talk and got a tour of the holography lab. But the most lasting impression came from seeing the small computers the company was developing. "I saw my first desktop computer there. It was called the 9100A, and it was a glorified calculator but also really the first desktop computer. It was huge, maybe forty pounds, but it was a beauty of a thing. I fell in love with it."

The kids in the Explorers Club were encouraged to do projects, and Jobs decided to build a frequency counter, which measures the number of pulses per second in an electronic signal. He needed some parts that HP made, so he picked up the phone and called the CEO. "Back then, people didn't have unlisted numbers. So I looked up Bill Hewlett in Palo Alto and called him at home. And he answered and chatted with me for twenty minutes. He got me the parts, but he also got me a job in the plant where they made frequency counters." Jobs worked there the summer after his freshman year at Homestead High. "My dad would drive me in the morning and pick me up in the evening."

His work mainly consisted of "just putting nuts and bolts on things" on an assembly line. There was some resentment among his fellow line workers toward the pushy kid who had talked his way in by calling the CEO. "I remember telling one of the supervisors, 'I love this stuff, I love this stuff,' and then I asked him what he liked to do best. And he said, 'To fuck, to fuck.'" Jobs had an easier time ingratiating himself with the engineers who worked one floor above. "They served doughnuts and coffee every morning at ten. So I'd go upstairs and hang out with them."

Jobs liked to work. He also had a newspaper route—his father would drive him when it was raining—and during his sophomore year spent weekends and the summer as a stock clerk at a cavernous electronics store, Haltek. It was to electronics what his father's junkyards were to auto parts: a scavenger's paradise sprawling over an entire city block with new, used, salvaged, and surplus components crammed onto warrens of shelves, dumped unsorted into bins, and piled in an outdoor yard. "Out in the back, near the bay, they had a fenced-in area with things like Polaris submarine interiors that had been ripped and sold for salvage," he recalled. "All the controls and buttons were right there. The colors were military greens and grays, but they had these switches and bulb covers of amber and red. There were these big old lever switches that, when you flipped them, it was awesome, like you were blowing up Chicago."

At the wooden counters up front, laden with thick catalogues in tattered binders, people would haggle for switches, resistors, capacitors, and sometimes the latest memory chips. His father used to do that for auto parts, and he succeeded because he knew the value of each better than the clerks. Jobs followed suit. He developed a knowledge of electronic parts that was honed by his love of negotiating and turning a profit. He would go to electronic flea markets, such as the San Jose swap meet, haggle for a used circuit board that contained some valuable chips or components, and then sell those to his manager at Haltek.

Jobs was able to get his first car, with his father's help, when he was fifteen. It was a two-tone Nash Metropolitan that his father had fitted out with an MG engine. Jobs didn't really like it, but he did not want to tell his father that, or miss out on the chance to have his own car. "In retrospect, a Nash Metropolitan might seem like the most wickedly cool car," he later said. "But at the time it was the most uncool car in the world. Still, it was a car, so that was great." Within a year he had saved up enough from his various jobs that he could trade up to a red Fiat 850 coupe with an Abarth engine. "My dad helped me buy and inspect it. The satisfaction of getting paid and saving up for something, that was very exciting."

That same summer, between his sophomore and junior years at Homestead, Jobs began smoking marijuana. "I got stoned for the first time that summer. I was fifteen, and then began using pot regularly." At one point his father found some dope in his son's Fiat. "What's this?" he asked. Jobs coolly replied, "That's marijuana." It was one of the few times in his life that he faced his father's anger. "That was the only real fight I ever got in with my dad," he said. But his father again bent to his will. "He wanted me to promise that I'd never use pot again, but I wouldn't promise." In fact by his senior year he was also dabbling in LSD and hash as well as exploring the mind-bending effects of sleep deprivation. "I was starting to get stoned a bit more. We would also drop acid occasionally, usually in fields or in cars."

He also flowered intellectually during his last two years in high school and found himself at the intersection, as he had begun to see it, of those who were geekily immersed in electronics and those who were into literature and creative endeavors. "I started to listen to music a whole lot, and I started to read more outside of just science and technology—Shakespeare, Plato. I loved *King Lear*." His other favorites included *Moby-Dick* and the poems of Dylan Thomas. I asked him why he related to King Lear and Captain Ahab, two of the most willful and driven characters in literature, but he didn't respond to the connection I was making, so I let it drop. "When I was a senior I had this phenomenal AP English class. The teacher was this guy who looked like Ernest Hemingway. He took a bunch of us snowshoeing in Yosemite."

One course that Jobs took would become part of Silicon Valley lore: the electronics class taught by John McCollum, a former Navy pilot who had a showman's flair for exciting his students with such tricks as firing up a Tesla coil. His little stockroom, to which he would lend the key to pet students, was crammed with transistors and other components he had scored.

McCollum's classroom was in a shed-like building on the edge of the campus, next to the parking lot. "This is where it was," Jobs recalled as he peered in the window, "and here, next door, is where the auto shop class used to be." The juxtaposition highlighted the shift from the interests of his father's generation. "Mr. McCollum felt that electronics class was the new auto shop."

McCollum believed in military discipline and respect for authority. Jobs didn't. His aversion to authority was something he no longer tried to hide, and he affected an attitude that combined wiry and weird intensity with aloof rebelliousness. McCollum later said, "He was usually off in a corner doing something on his own and really didn't want to have much of anything to do with either me or the rest of the class." He never trusted Jobs with a key to the stockroom. One day Jobs needed a part that was not available, so he made a collect call to the manufacturer, Burroughs in Detroit, and said he was designing a new product and wanted to test out the part. It arrived by air freight a few days later. When McCollum asked how he had gotten it, Jobs described—with defiant pride—the collect call and the tale he had told. "I was furious," McCollum said. "That was not the way I wanted my students to behave." Jobs's response was, "I don't have the money for the phone call. They've got plenty of money."

Jobs took McCollum's class for only one year, rather than the three that it was offered. For one of his projects, he made a device with a photocell that would switch on a circuit when exposed to light, something any high school science student could have done. He was far more interested in playing with lasers, something he learned from his father. With a few friends, he created light shows for parties by bouncing lasers off mirrors that were attached to the speakers of his stereo system.

CHAPTER TWO

ODD COUPLE

The Two Steves

Jobs and Wozniak in the garage, 1976

Woz

While a student in McCollum's class, Jobs became friends with a graduate who was the teacher's all-time favorite and a school legend for his wizardry in the class. Stephen Wozniak, whose younger brother had been on a swim team with Jobs, was almost five years older than Jobs and far more knowledgeable about electronics. But emotionally and socially he was still a high school geek.

Like Jobs, Wozniak learned a lot at his father's knee. But their lessons were different. Paul Jobs was a high school dropout who, when fixing up cars, knew how to turn a tidy profit by striking the right deal on parts. Francis Wozniak, known as Jerry, was a brilliant engineering graduate from Cal Tech, where he had quarterbacked the football team, who became a rocket scientist at Lockheed. He exalted engineering and looked down on those in business, marketing, and sales. "I remember him telling me that engineering was the highest level of importance you could reach in the world," Steve Wozniak later recalled. "It takes society to a new level."

One of Steve Wozniak's first memories was going to his father's workplace on a weekend and being shown electronic parts, with his dad "putting them on a table with me so I got to play with them." He watched with fascination as his father tried to get a waveform line on a video screen to stay flat so he could show that one of his circuit designs was working properly. "I could see that whatever my dad was doing, it was important and good." Woz, as he was known even then, would ask about the resistors and transistors lying around the house, and his father would pull out a blackboard to illustrate what they did. "He would explain what a resistor was by going all the way back to atoms and electrons. He explained how resistors worked when I was in second grade, not by equations but by having me picture it."

Woz's father taught him something else that became ingrained in his childlike, socially awkward personality: Never lie. "My dad believed in honesty. Extreme honesty. That's the biggest thing he taught me. I never lie, even to this day." (The only partial exception was in the service of a good practical joke.) In addition, he imbued his son with an aversion to extreme ambition, which set Woz apart from Jobs. At an Apple product launch event in 2010, forty years after they met, Woz reflected on their differences. "My father told me, 'You always want to be in the middle,'" he said. "I didn't want to be up with the high-level people like Steve. My dad was an engineer, and that's what I wanted to be. I was way too shy ever to be a business leader like Steve."

By fourth grade Wozniak became, as he put it, one of the "electronics kids." He had an easier time making eye contact with a transistor than with a girl, and he developed the chunky and stooped look of a guy who spends most of his time hunched over circuit boards. At the same age when Jobs was puzzling over a carbon microphone that his dad couldn't explain, Wozniak was using transistors to build an intercom system featuring amplifiers, relays, lights, and buzzers that connected the kids' bedrooms of six houses in the neighborhood. And at an age when Jobs was building Heathkits, Wozniak was assembling a transmitter and receiver from Hallicrafters, the most sophisticated radios available.

Woz spent a lot of time at home reading his father's electronics journals, and he became enthralled by stories about new computers, such as the powerful ENIAC. Because Boolean algebra came naturally to him, he marveled at how simple, rather than complex, the computers were. In eighth grade he built a calculator that included one hundred transistors, two hundred diodes, and two hundred resistors on ten circuit boards. It won top prize in a local contest run by the Air Force, even though the competitors included students through twelfth grade.

Woz became more of a loner when the boys his age began going out with girls and partying, endeavors that he found far more complex than designing circuits. "Where before I was popular and riding bikes and everything, suddenly I was socially shut out," he recalled. "It seemed like nobody spoke to me for the longest time." He found an outlet by playing juvenile pranks. In twelfth grade he built an electronic metronome—one of those tick-tick-tick devices that keep time in music class—and realized it sounded like a bomb. So he took the labels off some big batteries, taped them together, and put it in a school locker; he rigged it to start ticking faster when the locker opened. Later that day he got called to the principal's office. He thought it was because he had won, yet again, the school's top math prize. Instead he was confronted by the police. The principal had been summoned when the device was found, bravely ran onto the football field clutching it to his chest, and pulled the wires off. Woz tried and failed to suppress his laughter. He actually got sent to the juvenile detention center, where he spent the night. It was a memorable experience. He taught the other prisoners how to disconnect the wires leading to the ceiling fans and connect them to the bars so people got shocked when touching them.

Getting shocked was a badge of honor for Woz. He prided himself on being a hardware engineer, which meant that random shocks were routine. He once devised a roulette game where four people put their thumbs in a slot; when the ball landed, one would get shocked. "Hardware guys will play this game, but software guys are too chicken," he noted.

During his senior year he got a part-time job at Sylvania and had the chance to work on a computer for the first time. He learned FORTRAN from a book and read the manuals for most of the systems of the day, starting with the Digital Equipment PDP-8. Then he studied the specs for the latest microchips and tried to redesign the computers using these newer parts. The challenge he set himself was to replicate the design using the fewest components possible. Each night he would try to improve his drawing from the night before. By the end of his senior year, he had become a master. "I was now designing computers with half the number of chips the actual company had in their own design, but only on paper." He never told his friends. After all, most seventeen-year-olds were getting their kicks in other ways.

On Thanksgiving weekend of his senior year, Wozniak visited the University of Colorado. It was closed for the holiday, but he found an engineering student who took him on a tour of the labs. He begged his father to let him go there, even though the out-of-state tuition was more than the family could easily afford. They struck a deal: He would be allowed to go for one year, but then he would transfer to De Anza Community College back home. After arriving at Colorado in the fall of 1969, he spent so much time playing pranks (such as producing reams of printouts saying "Fuck Nixon") that he failed a couple of his courses and was put on probation. In addition, he created a program to calculate Fibonacci numbers that burned up so much computer time the university threatened to bill him for the cost. So he readily lived up to his bargain with his parents and transferred to De Anza.

After a pleasant year at De Anza, Wozniak took time off to make some money. He found work at a company that made computers for the California Motor Vehicle Department, and a coworker made him a wonderful offer: He would provide some spare chips so Wozniak could make one of the computers he had been sketching on paper. Wozniak decided to use as few chips as possible, both as a personal challenge and because he did not want to take advantage of his colleague's largesse.

Much of the work was done in the garage of a friend just around the corner, Bill Fernandez, who was still at Homestead High. To lubricate their efforts, they drank large amounts of Cragmont cream soda, riding their bikes to the Sunnyvale Safeway to return the bottles, collect the deposits, and buy more. "That's how we started referring to it as the Cream Soda Computer," Wozniak recalled. It was basically a calculator capable of multiplying numbers entered by a set of switches and displaying the results in binary code with little lights.

When it was finished, Fernandez told Wozniak there was someone at Homestead High he should meet. "His name is Steve. He likes to do pranks like you do, and he's also into building electronics like you are." It may have been the most significant meeting in a Silicon Valley garage since Hewlett went into Packard's thirty-two years earlier. "Steve and I just sat on the sidewalk in front of Bill's house for the longest time, just sharing stories—mostly about pranks we'd pulled, and also what kind of electronic designs we'd done," Wozniak recalled. "We had so much in common. Typically, it was really hard for me to explain to people what kind of design stuff I worked on, but Steve got it right away. And I liked him. He was kind of skinny and wiry and full of energy." Jobs was also impressed. "Woz was the first person I'd met who knew more electronics than I did," he once said, stretching his own expertise. "I liked him right away. I was a little more mature than my years, and he was a little less mature than his, so it evened out. Woz was very bright, but emotionally he was my age."

In addition to their interest in computers, they shared a passion for music. "It was an incredible time for music," Jobs recalled. "It was like living at a time when Beethoven and Mozart were alive. Really. People will look back on it that way. And Woz and I were deeply into it." In particular, Wozniak turned Jobs on to the glories of Bob Dylan. "We tracked down this guy in Santa Cruz who put out this newsletter on Dylan," Jobs said. "Dylan taped all of his concerts, and some of the people around him were not scrupulous, because soon there were tapes all around. Bootlegs of everything. And this guy had them all."

Hunting down Dylan tapes soon became a joint venture. "The two of us would go tramping through San Jose and Berkeley and ask about Dylan bootlegs and collect them," said Wozniak. "We'd buy brochures of Dylan lyrics and stay up late interpreting them. Dylan's words struck chords of creative thinking." Added Jobs, "I had more than a hundred hours, including every concert on the '65 and '66 tour," the one where Dylan went electric. Both of them bought high-end TEAC reel-to-reel tape decks. "I would use mine at a low speed to record many concerts on one tape," said Wozniak. Jobs matched his obsession: "Instead of big speakers I bought a pair of awesome headphones and would just lie in my bed and listen to that stuff for hours."

Jobs had formed a club at Homestead High to put on music-and-light shows and also play pranks. (They once glued a gold-painted toilet seat onto a flower planter.) It was called the Buck Fry Club, a play on the name of the principal. Even though they had already graduated, Wozniak and his friend Allen Baum joined forces with Jobs, at the end of his junior year, to produce a farewell gesture for the departing seniors. Showing off the Homestead campus four decades later, Jobs paused at the scene of the escapade and pointed. "See that balcony? That's where we did the banner prank that sealed our friendship." On a big bedsheet Baum had tie-dyed with the school's green and white colors, they painted a huge hand flipping the middle-finger salute. Baum's nice Jewish mother helped them draw it and showed them how to do the shading and shadows to make it look more real. "I know what that is," she snickered. They devised a system of ropes and pulleys so that it could be dramatically lowered as the graduating class marched past the balcony, and they signed it "SWAB JOB," the initials of Wozniak and Baum combined with part of Jobs's name. The prank became part of school lore—and got Jobs suspended one more time.

Another prank involved a pocket device Wozniak built that could emit TV signals. He would take it to a room where a group of people were watching TV, such as in a dorm, and secretly press the button so that the screen would get fuzzy with static. When someone got up and whacked the set, Wozniak would let go of the button and the picture would clear up. Once he had the unsuspecting viewers hopping up and down at his will, he would make things harder. He would keep the picture fuzzy until someone touched the antenna. Eventually he would make people think they had to hold the antenna while standing on one foot or touching the top of the set. Years later, at a keynote presentation where he was having his own trouble getting a video to work, Jobs broke from his script and recounted the fun they had with the device. "Woz would have it in his pocket and we'd go into a dorm . . . where a bunch of folks would be, like, watching *Star Trek*, and he'd screw up the TV, and someone would go up to fix it, and just as they had the foot off the ground he would turn it back on, and as they put their foot back on the ground he'd screw it up again." Contorting himself into a pretzel onstage, Jobs concluded to great laughter, "And within five minutes he would have someone like this."

The Blue Box

The ultimate combination of pranks and electronics—and the escapade that helped to create Apple—was launched one Sunday afternoon when Wozniak read an article in *Esquire* that his mother had left for him on the kitchen table. It was September 1971, and he was about to drive off the next day to Berkeley, his third college. The story, Ron Rosenbaum's "Secrets of the Little Blue Box," described how hackers and phone phreakers had found ways to make long-distance calls for free by replicating the tones that routed signals on the AT&T network. "Halfway through the article, I had to call my best friend, Steve Jobs, and read parts of this long article to him," Wozniak recalled. He knew that Jobs, then beginning his senior year, was one of the few people who would share his excitement.

A hero of the piece was John Draper, a hacker known as Captain Crunch because he had discovered that the sound emitted by the toy whistle that came with the breakfast cereal was the same 2600 Hertz tone used by the phone network's call-routing switches. It could fool the system into allowing a long-distance call to go through without extra charges. The article revealed that other tones that served to route calls could be found in an issue of the *Bell System Technical Journal*, which AT&T immediately began asking libraries to pull from their shelves.

As soon as Jobs got the call from Wozniak that Sunday afternoon, he knew they would have to get their hands on the technical journal right away. "Woz picked me up a few minutes later, and we went to the library at SLAC [the Stanford Linear Accelerator Center] to see if we could find it," Jobs recounted. It was Sunday and the library was closed, but they knew how to get in through a door that was rarely locked. "I remember that we were furiously digging through the stacks, and it was Woz who finally found the journal with all the frequencies. It was like, holy shit, and we opened it and there it was. We kept saying to ourselves, 'It's real. Holy shit, it's real.' It was all laid out—the tones, the frequencies."

Wozniak went to Sunnyvale Electronics before it closed that evening and bought the parts to make an analog tone generator. Jobs had built a frequency counter when he was part of the HP Explorers Club, and they used it to calibrate the desired tones. With a dial, they could replicate and tape-record the sounds specified in the article. By midnight they were ready to test it. Unfortunately the oscillators they used were not quite stable enough to replicate the right chirps to fool the phone company. "We could see the instability using Steve's frequency counter," recalled Wozniak, "and we just couldn't make it work. I had to leave for Berkeley the next morning, so we decided I would work on building a digital version once I got there."

No one had ever created a digital version of a Blue Box, but Woz was made for the challenge. Using diodes and transistors from Radio Shack, and with the help of a music student in his dorm who had perfect pitch, he got it built before Thanksgiving. "I have never designed a circuit I was prouder of," he said. "I still think it was incredible."

One night Wozniak drove down from Berkeley to Jobs's house to try it. They attempted to call Wozniak's uncle in Los Angeles, but they got a wrong number. It didn't matter; their device had worked. "Hi! We're calling you for free! We're calling you for free!" Wozniak shouted. The person on the other end was confused and annoyed. Jobs chimed in, "We're calling from California! From California! With a Blue Box." This probably baffled the man even more, since he was also in California.

At first the Blue Box was used for fun and pranks. The most daring of these was when they called the Vatican and Wozniak pretended to be Henry Kissinger wanting to speak to the pope. "Ve are at de summit meeting in Moscow, and ve need to talk to de pope," Woz intoned.

He was told that it was 5:30 a.m. and the pope was sleeping. When he called back, he got a bishop who was supposed to serve as the translator. But they never actually got the pope on the line. "They realized that Woz wasn't Henry Kissinger," Jobs recalled. "We were at a public phone booth."

It was then that they reached an important milestone, one that would establish a pattern in their partnerships: Jobs came up with the idea that the Blue Box could be more than merely a hobby; they could build and sell them. "I got together the rest of the components, like the casing and power supply and keypads, and figured out how we could price it," Jobs said, foreshadowing roles he would play when they founded Apple. The finished product was about the size of two decks of playing cards. The parts cost about $40, and Jobs decided they should sell it for $150.

Following the lead of other phone phreaks such as Captain Crunch, they gave themselves handles. Wozniak became "Berkeley Blue," Jobs was "Oaf Tobark." They took the device to college dorms and gave demonstrations by attaching it to a phone and speaker. While the potential customers watched, they would call the Ritz in London or a dial-a-joke service in Australia. "We made a hundred or so Blue Boxes and sold almost all of them," Jobs recalled.

The fun and profits came to an end at a Sunnyvale pizza parlor. Jobs and Wozniak were about to drive to Berkeley with a Blue Box they had just finished making. Jobs needed money and was eager to sell, so he pitched the device to some guys at the next table. They were interested, so Jobs went to a phone booth and demonstrated it with a call to Chicago. The prospects said they had to go to their car for money. "So we walk over to the car, Woz and me, and I've got the Blue Box in my hand, and the guy gets in, reaches under the seat, and he pulls out a gun," Jobs recounted. He had never been that close to a gun, and he was terrified. "So he's pointing the gun right at my stomach, and he says, 'Hand it over, brother.' My mind raced. There was the car door here, and I thought maybe I could slam it on his legs and we could run, but there was this high probability that he would shoot me. So I slowly handed it to him, very carefully." It was a weird sort of robbery. The guy who took the Blue Box actually gave Jobs a phone number and said he would try to pay for it if it worked. When Jobs later called the number, the guy said he couldn't figure out how to use it. So Jobs, in his felicitous way, convinced the guy to meet him and Wozniak at a public place. But they ended up deciding not to have another encounter with the gunman, even on the off chance they could get their $150.

The partnership paved the way for what would be a bigger adventure together. "If it hadn't been for the Blue Boxes, there wouldn't have been an Apple," Jobs later reflected. "I'm 100% sure of that. Woz and I learned how to work together, and we gained the confidence that we could solve technical problems and actually put something into production." They had created a device with a little circuit board that could control billions of dollars' worth of infrastructure. "You cannot believe how much confidence that gave us." Woz came to the same conclusion: "It was probably a bad idea selling them, but it gave us a taste of what we could do with my engineering skills and his vision." The Blue Box adventure established a template for a partnership that would soon be born. Wozniak would be the gentle wizard coming up with a neat invention that he would have been happy just to give away, and Jobs would figure out how to make it user-friendly, put it together in a package, market it, and make a few bucks.

CHAPTER THREE

THE DROPOUT

Turn On, Tune In . . .

Chrisann Brennan

Toward the end of his senior year at Homestead, in the spring of 1972, Jobs started going out with a girl named Chrisann Brennan, who was about his age but still a junior. With her light brown hair, green eyes, high cheekbones, and fragile aura, she was very attractive. She was also enduring the breakup of her parents' marriage, which made her vulnerable. "We worked together on an animated movie, then started going out, and she became my first real girlfriend," Jobs recalled. As Brennan later said, "Steve was kind of crazy. That's why I was attracted to him."

Jobs's craziness was of the cultivated sort. He had begun his lifelong experiments with compulsive diets, eating only fruits and vegetables, so he was as lean and tight as a whippet. He learned to stare at people without blinking, and he perfected long silences punctuated by staccato bursts of fast talking. This odd mix of intensity and aloofness, combined with his shoulder-length hair and scraggly beard, gave him the aura of a crazed shaman. He oscillated between charismatic and creepy. "He shuffled around and looked half-mad," recalled Brennan. "He had a lot of angst. It was like a big darkness around him."

Jobs had begun to drop acid by then, and at one point he turned on with Brennan in a wheat field just outside Sunnyvale. "It was great," he recalled. "I had been listening to a lot of Bach. All of a sudden the wheat field was playing Bach. It was the most wonderful feeling of my life up to that point. I felt like the conductor of this symphony with Bach coming through the wheat."

That summer of 1972, after his graduation, he and Brennan moved to a cabin in the hills above Los Altos. "I'm going to go live in a cabin with Chrisann," he announced to his parents one day. His father was furious. "No you're not," he said. "Over my dead body." They had recently fought about marijuana, and once again the younger Jobs was willful. He just said good-bye and walked out.

Brennan spent a lot of her time that summer painting; she was talented, and later she did a picture of a clown for Jobs that he kept on the wall. Jobs wrote poetry and played guitar. He could be brutally cold and rude to her at times, but he was also entrancing and able to impose his will. "He was an enlightened being who was cruel," she recalled. "That's a strange combination."

Midway through the summer, Jobs was almost killed when his red Fiat caught fire. He was driving on Skyline Boulevard in the Santa Cruz Mountains with a high school friend, Tim Brown, who looked back, saw flames coming from the engine, and casually said to Jobs, "Pull over, your car is on fire." Jobs did. His father, despite their arguments, drove out to the hills to tow the Fiat home.

In order to find a way to make money for a new car, Jobs got Wozniak to drive him to De Anza College to look on the help-wanted bulletin board. They discovered that the Westgate Shopping Center in San Jose was seeking college students who could dress up in costumes and amuse the kids. So for $3 an hour, Jobs, Wozniak, and Brennan donned heavy full-body costumes to play Alice in Wonderland, the Mad Hatter, and the White Rabbit. Wozniak, in his earnest and sweet way, found it fun. "I said, 'I want to do it, it's my chance, because I love children.' I think Steve looked at it as a lousy job, but I looked at it as a fun adventure." Jobs did indeed find it a pain. "It was hot, the costumes were heavy, and after a while I felt like I wanted to smack some of the kids." Patience was never one of his virtues.

Reed College

Seventeen years earlier, Jobs's parents had made a pledge when they adopted him: He would go to college. So they had worked hard and saved dutifully for his college fund, which was modest but adequate by the time he graduated. But Jobs, becoming ever more willful, did not make it easy. At first he toyed with not going to college at all. "I think I might have headed to New York if I didn't go to college," he recalled, musing on how different his world—and perhaps all of ours—might have been if he had chosen that path. When his parents pushed him to go to college, he responded in a passive-aggressive way. He did not consider state schools, such as Berkeley, where Woz then was, despite the fact that they were more affordable. Nor did he look at Stanford, just up the road and likely to offer a scholarship. "The kids who went to Stanford, they already knew what they wanted to do," he said. "They weren't really artistic. I wanted something that was more artistic and interesting."

Instead he insisted on applying only to Reed College, a private liberal arts school in Portland, Oregon, that was one of the most expensive in the nation. He was visiting Woz at Berkeley when his father called to say an acceptance letter had arrived from Reed, and he tried to talk Steve out of going there. So did his mother. It was far more than they could afford, they said. But their son responded with an ultimatum: If he couldn't go to Reed, he wouldn't go anywhere. They relented, as usual.

Reed had only one thousand students, half the number at Homestead High. It was known for its free-spirited hippie lifestyle, which combined somewhat uneasily with its rigorous academic standards and core curriculum. Five years earlier Timothy Leary, the guru of psychedelic enlightenment, had sat cross-legged at the Reed College commons while on his League for Spiritual Discovery (LSD) college tour, during which he exhorted his listeners, "Like every great religion of the past we seek to find the divinity within. . . . These ancient goals we define in the metaphor of the present—turn on, tune in, drop out."

Many of Reed's students took all three of those injunctions seriously; the dropout rate during the 1970s was more than one-third.

When it came time for Jobs to matriculate in the fall of 1972, his parents drove him up to Portland, but in another small act of rebellion he refused to let them come on campus. In fact he refrained from even saying good-bye or thanks. He recounted the moment later with uncharacteristic regret:

> It's one of the things in life I really feel ashamed about. I was not very sensitive, and I hurt their feelings. I shouldn't have. They had done so much to make sure I could go there, but I just didn't want them around. I didn't want anyone to know I had parents. I wanted to be like an orphan who had bummed around the country on trains and just arrived out of nowhere, with no roots, no connections, no background.

In late 1972, there was a fundamental shift happening in American campus life. The nation's involvement in the Vietnam War, and the draft that accompanied it, was winding down. Political activism at colleges receded and in many late-night dorm conversations was replaced by an interest in pathways to personal fulfillment. Jobs found himself deeply influenced by a variety of books on spirituality and enlightenment, most notably *Be Here Now,* a guide to meditation and the wonders of psychedelic drugs by Baba Ram Dass, born Richard Alpert. "It was profound," Jobs said. "It transformed me and many of my friends."

The closest of those friends was another wispy-bearded freshman named Daniel Kottke, who met Jobs a week after they arrived at Reed and shared his interest in Zen, Dylan, and acid. Kottke, from a wealthy New York suburb, was smart but low-octane, with a sweet flower-child demeanor made even mellower by his interest in Buddhism. That spiritual quest had caused him to eschew material possessions, but he was nonetheless impressed by Jobs's tape deck. "Steve had a TEAC reel-to-reel and massive quantities of Dylan bootlegs," Kottke recalled. "He was both really cool and high-tech."

Jobs started spending much of his time with Kottke and his girlfriend, Elizabeth Holmes, even after he insulted her at their first meeting by grilling her about how much money it would take to get her to have sex with another man. They hitchhiked to the coast together, engaged in the typical dorm raps about the meaning of life, attended the love festivals at the local Hare Krishna temple, and went to the Zen center for free vegetarian meals. "It was a lot of fun," said Kottke, "but also philosophical, and we took Zen very seriously."

Jobs began sharing with Kottke other books, including *Zen Mind, Beginner's Mind* by Shunryu Suzuki, *Autobiography of a Yogi* by Paramahansa Yogananda, and *Cutting Through Spiritual Materialism* by Chögyam Trungpa. They created a meditation room in the attic crawl space above Elizabeth Holmes's room and fixed it up with Indian prints, a dhurrie rug, candles, incense, and meditation cushions. "There was a hatch in the ceiling leading to an attic which had a huge amount of space," Jobs said. "We took psychedelic drugs there sometimes, but mainly we just meditated."

Jobs's engagement with Eastern spirituality, and especially Zen Buddhism, was not just some passing fancy or youthful dabbling. He embraced it with his typical intensity, and it became deeply ingrained in his personality. "Steve is very much Zen," said Kottke. "It was a deep influence. You see it in his whole approach of stark, minimalist aesthetics, intense focus." Jobs also became deeply influenced by the emphasis that Buddhism places on intuition. "I began to realize that an intuitive understanding and consciousness was more significant than abstract thinking and intellectual logical analysis," he later said. His intensity, however, made it difficult for him to achieve inner peace; his Zen awareness was not accompanied by an excess of calm, peace of mind, or interpersonal mellowness.

He and Kottke enjoyed playing a nineteenth-century German variant of chess called Kriegspiel, in which the players sit back-to-back; each has his own board and pieces and cannot see those of his opponent. A moderator informs them if a move they want to make is legal or illegal, and they have to try to figure out where their opponent's pieces are. "The wildest game I played with them was during a lashing rainstorm sitting by the fireside," recalled Holmes, who served as moderator. "They were tripping on acid. They were moving so fast I could barely keep up with them."

Another book that deeply influenced Jobs during his freshman year was *Diet for a Small Planet* by Frances Moore Lappé, which extolled the personal and planetary benefits of vegetarianism. "That's when I swore off meat pretty much for good," he recalled. But the book also reinforced his tendency to embrace extreme diets, which included purges, fasts, or eating only one or two foods, such as carrots or apples, for weeks on end.

Jobs and Kottke became serious vegetarians during their freshman year. "Steve got into it even more than I did," said Kottke. "He was living off Roman Meal cereal." They would go shopping at a farmers' co-op, where Jobs would buy a box of cereal, which would last a week, and other bulk health food. "He would buy flats of dates and almonds and lots of carrots, and he got a Champion juicer and we'd make carrot juice and carrot salads. There is a story about Steve turning orange from eating so many carrots, and there is some truth to that." Friends remember him having, at times, a sunset-like orange hue.

Jobs's dietary habits became even more obsessive when he read *Mucusless Diet Healing System* by Arnold Ehret, an early twentieth-century German-born nutrition fanatic. He believed in eating nothing but fruits and starchless vegetables, which he said prevented the body from forming harmful mucus, and he advocated cleansing the body regularly through prolonged fasts. That meant the end of even Roman Meal cereal—or any bread, grains, or milk. Jobs began warning friends of the mucus dangers lurking in their bagels. "I got into it in my typical nutso way," he said. At one point he and Kottke went for an entire week eating only apples, and then Jobs began to try even purer fasts. He started with two-day fasts, and eventually tried to stretch them to a week or more, breaking them carefully with large amounts of water and leafy vegetables. "After a week you start to feel fantastic," he said. "You get a ton of vitality from not having to digest all this food. I was in great shape. I felt I could get up and walk to San Francisco anytime I wanted."

Vegetarianism and Zen Buddhism, meditation and spirituality, acid and rock—Jobs rolled together, in an amped-up way, the multiple impulses that were hallmarks of the enlightenment-seeking campus subculture of the era. And even though he barely indulged it at Reed, there was still an undercurrent of electronic geekiness in his soul that would someday combine surprisingly well with the rest of the mix.

Robert Friedland

In order to raise some cash one day, Jobs decided to sell his IBM Selectric typewriter. He walked into the room of the student who had offered to buy it only to discover that he was having sex with his girlfriend. Jobs started to leave, but the student invited him to take a seat and wait while they finished. "I thought, 'This is kind of far out,'" Jobs later recalled. And thus began his relationship with Robert Friedland, one of the few people in Jobs's life who were able to mesmerize him. He adopted some of Friedland's charismatic traits and for a few years treated him almost like a guru—until he began to see him as a charlatan.

Friedland was four years older than Jobs, but still an undergraduate. The son of an Auschwitz survivor who became a prosperous Chicago architect, he had originally gone to Bowdoin, a liberal arts college in Maine. But while a sophomore, he was arrested for possession of 24,000 tablets of LSD worth $125,000. The local newspaper pictured him with shoulder-length wavy blond hair smiling at the photographers as he was led away. He was sentenced to two years at a federal prison in Virginia, from which he was paroled in 1972. That fall he headed off to Reed, where he immediately ran for student body president, saying that he needed to clear his name from the "miscarriage of justice" he had suffered. He won.

Friedland had heard Baba Ram Dass, the author of *Be Here Now*, give a speech in Boston, and like Jobs and Kottke had gotten deeply into Eastern spirituality. During the summer of 1973, he traveled to India to meet Ram Dass's Hindu guru, Neem Karoli Baba, famously known to his many followers as Maharaj-ji. When he returned that fall, Friedland had taken a spiritual name and walked around in sandals and flowing Indian robes. He had a room off campus, above a garage, and Jobs would go there many afternoons to seek him out. He was entranced by the apparent intensity of Friedland's conviction that a state of enlightenment truly existed and could be attained. "He turned me on to a different level of consciousness," Jobs said.

Friedland found Jobs fascinating as well. "He was always walking around barefoot," he later told a reporter. "The thing that struck me was his intensity. Whatever he was interested in he would generally carry to an irrational extreme." Jobs had honed his trick of using stares and silences to master other people. "One of his numbers was to stare at the person he was talking to. He would stare into their fucking eyeballs, ask some question, and would want a response without the other person averting their eyes."

According to Kottke, some of Jobs's personality traits—including a few that lasted throughout his career—were borrowed from Friedland. "Friedland taught Steve the reality distortion field," said Kottke. "He was charismatic and a bit of a con man and could bend situations to his very strong will. He was mercurial, sure of himself, a little dictatorial. Steve admired that, and he became more like that after spending time with Robert."

Jobs also absorbed how Friedland made himself the center of attention. "Robert was very much an outgoing, charismatic guy, a real salesman," Kottke recalled. "When I first met Steve he was shy and self-effacing, a very private guy. I think Robert taught him a lot about selling, about coming out of his shell, of opening up and taking charge of a situation." Friedland projected a high-wattage aura. "He would walk into a room and you would instantly notice him. Steve was the absolute opposite when he came to Reed. After he spent time with Robert, some of it started to rub off."

On Sunday evenings Jobs and Friedland would go to the Hare Krishna temple on the western edge of Portland, often with Kottke and Holmes in tow. They would dance and sing songs at the top of their lungs. "We would work ourselves into an ecstatic frenzy," Holmes recalled. "Robert would go insane and dance like crazy. Steve was more subdued, as if he was embarrassed to let loose." Then they would be treated to paper plates piled high with vegetarian food.

Friedland had stewardship of a 220-acre apple farm, about forty miles southwest of Portland, that was owned by an eccentric millionaire uncle from Switzerland named Marcel Müller. After Friedland became involved with Eastern spirituality, he turned it into a commune called the All One Farm, and Jobs would spend weekends there with Kottke, Holmes, and like-minded seekers of enlightenment. The farm had a main house, a large barn, and a garden shed, where Kottke and Holmes slept. Jobs took on the task of pruning the Gravenstein apple trees. "Steve ran the apple orchard," said Friedland. "We were in the organic cider business. Steve's job was to lead a crew of freaks to prune the orchard and whip it back into shape."

Monks and disciples from the Hare Krishna temple would come and prepare vegetarian feasts redolent of cumin, coriander, and turmeric. "Steve would be starving when he arrived, and he would stuff himself," Holmes recalled. "Then he would go and purge. For years I thought he was bulimic. It was very upsetting, because we had gone to all that trouble of creating these feasts, and he couldn't hold it down."

Jobs was also beginning to have a little trouble stomaching Friedland's cult leader style. "Perhaps he saw a little bit too much of Robert in himself," said Kottke. Although the commune was supposed to be a refuge from materialism, Friedland began operating it more as a business; his followers were told to chop and sell firewood, make apple presses and wood stoves, and engage in other commercial endeavors for which they were not paid. One night Jobs slept under the table in the kitchen and was amused to notice that people kept coming in and stealing each other's food from the refrigerator. Communal economics were not for him. "It started to get very materialistic," Jobs recalled. "Everybody got the idea they were working very hard for Robert's farm, and one by one they started to leave. I got pretty sick of it."

Many years later, after Friedland had become a billionaire copper and gold mining executive—working out of Vancouver, Singapore, and Mongolia—I met him for drinks in New York. That evening I emailed Jobs and mentioned my encounter. He telephoned me from California within an hour and warned me against listening to Friedland. He said that when Friedland was in trouble because of environmental abuses committed by some of his mines, he had tried to contact Jobs to intervene with Bill Clinton, but Jobs had not responded. "Robert always portrayed himself as a spiritual person, but he crossed the line from being charismatic to being a con man," Jobs said. "It was a strange thing to have one of the spiritual people in your young life turn out to be, symbolically and in reality, a gold miner."

. . . Drop Out

Jobs quickly became bored with college. He liked being at Reed, just not taking the required classes. In fact he was surprised when he found out that, for all of its hippie aura, there were strict course requirements. When Wozniak came to visit, Jobs waved his schedule at him and complained, "They are making me take all these courses." Woz replied, "Yes, that's what they do in college." Jobs refused to go to the classes he was assigned and instead went to the ones he wanted, such as a dance class where he could enjoy both the creativity and the chance to meet girls. "I would never have refused to take the courses you were supposed to, that's a difference in our personality," Wozniak marveled.

Jobs also began to feel guilty, he later said, about spending so much of his parents' money on an education that did not seem worthwhile. "All of my working-class parents' savings were being spent on my college tuition," he recounted in a famous commencement address at Stanford. "I had no idea what I wanted to do with my life and no idea how college was going to help me figure it out. And here I was spending all of the money my parents had saved their entire life. So I decided to drop out and trust that it would all work out okay."

He didn't actually want to leave Reed; he just wanted to quit paying tuition and taking classes that didn't interest him. Remarkably, Reed tolerated that. "He had a very inquiring mind that was enormously attractive," said the dean of students, Jack Dudman. "He refused to accept automatically received truths, and he wanted to examine everything himself." Dudman allowed Jobs to audit classes and stay with friends in the dorms even after he stopped paying tuition.

"The minute I dropped out I could stop taking the required classes that didn't interest me, and begin dropping in on the ones that looked interesting," he said. Among them was a calligraphy class that appealed to him after he saw posters on campus that were beautifully drawn. "I learned about serif and sans serif typefaces, about varying the amount of space between different letter combinations, about what makes great typography great. It was beautiful, historical, artistically subtle in a way that science can't capture, and I found it fascinating."

It was yet another example of Jobs consciously positioning himself at the intersection of the arts and technology. In all of his products, technology would be married to great design, elegance, human touches, and even romance. He would be in the fore of pushing friendly graphical user interfaces. The calligraphy course would become iconic in that regard. "If I had never dropped in on that single course in college, the Mac would have never had multiple typefaces or proportionally spaced fonts. And since Windows just copied the Mac, it's likely that no personal computer would have them."

In the meantime Jobs eked out a bohemian existence on the fringes of Reed. He went barefoot most of the time, wearing sandals when it snowed. Elizabeth Holmes made meals for him, trying to keep up with his obsessive diets. He returned soda bottles for spare change, continued his treks to the free Sunday dinners at the Hare Krishna temple, and wore a down jacket in the heatless garage apartment he rented for $20 a month. When he needed money, he found work at the psychology department lab maintaining the electronic equipment that was used for animal behavior experiments. Occasionally Chrisann Brennan would come to visit. Their relationship sputtered along erratically. But mostly he tended to the stirrings of his own soul and personal quest for enlightenment.

"I came of age at a magical time," he reflected later. "Our consciousness was raised by Zen, and also by LSD." Even later in life he would credit psychedelic drugs for making him more enlightened. "Taking LSD was a profound experience, one of the most important things in my life. LSD shows you that there's another side to the coin, and you can't remember it when it wears off, but you know it. It reinforced my sense of what was important—creating great things instead of making money, putting things back into the stream of history and of human consciousness as much as I could."

CHAPTER FOUR

ATARI AND INDIA

Zen and the Art of Game Design

Atari

In February 1974, after eighteen months of hanging around Reed, Jobs decided to move back to his parents' home in Los Altos and look for a job. It was not a difficult search. At peak times during the 1970s, the classified section of the *San Jose Mercury* carried up to sixty pages of technology help-wanted ads. One of those caught Jobs's eye. "Have fun, make money," it said. That day Jobs walked into the lobby of the video game manufacturer Atari and told the personnel director, who was startled by his unkempt hair and attire, that he wouldn't leave until they gave him a job.

Atari's founder was a burly entrepreneur named Nolan Bushnell, who was a charismatic visionary with a nice touch of showmanship in him—in other words, another role model waiting to be emulated. After he became famous, he briefly sported a Rolls-Royce and occasionally held staff meetings in a hot tub while his staff smoked dope. As Friedland had done and as Jobs would learn to do, he was able to turn charm into a cunning force, to cajole and intimidate and distort reality with the power of his personality. His chief engineer was Al Alcorn, beefy and jovial and a bit more grounded, the house grown-up trying to implement the vision and curb the enthusiasms of Bushnell. Their big hit thus far was a video game called Pong, in which two players tried to volley a blip on a screen with two movable lines that acted as paddles. (If you're under thirty, ask your parents.)

When Jobs arrived in the Atari lobby wearing sandals and demanding a job, Alcorn was the one who was summoned. "I was told, 'We've got a hippie kid in the lobby. He says he's not going to leave until we hire him. Should we call the cops or let him in?' I said bring him on in!"

Jobs thus became one of the first fifty employees at Atari, working as a technician for $5 an hour. "In retrospect, it was weird to hire a dropout from Reed," Alcorn recalled. "But I saw something in him. He was very intelligent, enthusiastic, excited about tech." Alcorn assigned him to work with a straitlaced engineer named Don Lang. The next day Lang complained, "This guy's a goddamn hippie with b.o. Why did you do this to me? And he's impossible to deal with." Jobs clung to the belief that his fruit-heavy vegetarian diet would prevent not just mucus but also body odor, even if he didn't use deodorant or shower regularly. It was a flawed theory.

Lang and others wanted to let Jobs go, but Bushnell worked out a solution. "The smell and behavior wasn't an issue with me," he said. "Steve was prickly, but I kind of liked him. So I asked him to go on the night shift. It was a way to save him." Jobs would come in after Lang and others had left and work through most of the night. Even thus isolated, he became known for his brashness. On those occasions when he happened to interact with others, he was prone to informing them that they were "dumb shits." In retrospect, he stands by that judgment. "The only reason I shone was that everyone else was so bad," Jobs recalled.

Despite his arrogance (or perhaps because of it) he was able to charm Atari's boss. "He was more philosophical than the other people I worked with," Bushnell recalled. "We used to discuss free will versus determinism. I tended to believe that things were much more determined, that we were programmed. If we had perfect information, we could predict people's actions. Steve felt the opposite." That outlook accorded with his faith in the power of the will to bend reality.

Jobs helped improve some of the games by pushing the chips to produce fun designs, and Bushnell's inspiring willingness to play by his own rules rubbed off on him. In addition, he intuitively appreciated the simplicity of Atari's games. They came with no manual and needed to be uncomplicated enough that a stoned freshman could figure them out. The only instructions for Atari's *Star Trek* game were "1. Insert quarter. 2. Avoid Klingons."

Not all of his coworkers shunned Jobs. He became friends with Ron Wayne, a draftsman at Atari, who had earlier started a company that built slot machines. It subsequently failed, but Jobs became fascinated with the idea that it was possible to start your own company. "Ron was an amazing guy," said Jobs. "He started companies. I had never met anybody like that." He proposed to Wayne that they go into business together; Jobs said he could borrow $50,000, and they could design and market a slot machine. But Wayne had already been burned in business, so he declined. "I said that was the quickest way to lose $50,000," Wayne recalled, "but I admired the fact that he had a burning drive to start his own business."

One weekend Jobs was visiting Wayne at his apartment, engaging as they often did in philosophical discussions, when Wayne said that there was something he needed to tell him. "Yeah, I think I know what it is," Jobs replied. "I think you like men." Wayne said yes. "It was my first encounter with someone who I knew was gay," Jobs recalled. "He planted the right perspective of it for me." Jobs grilled him: "When you see a beautiful woman, what do you feel?" Wayne replied, "It's like when you look at a beautiful horse. You can appreciate it, but you don't want to sleep with it. You appreciate beauty for what it is." Wayne said that it is a testament to Jobs that he felt like revealing this to him. "Nobody at Atari knew, and I could count on my toes and fingers the number of people I told in my whole life. But I guess it just felt right to tell him, that he would understand, and it didn't have any effect on our relationship."

India

One reason Jobs was eager to make some money in early 1974 was that
Robert Friedland, who had gone to India the summer before, was urging him to take his own spiritual journey there. Friedland had studied
in India with Neem Karoli Baba (Maharaj-ji), who had been the guru
to much of the sixties hippie movement. Jobs decided he should do
the same, and he recruited Daniel Kottke to go with him. Jobs was not
motivated by mere adventure. "For me it was a serious search," he said.
"I'd been turned on to the idea of enlightenment and trying to figure
out who I was and how I fit into things." Kottke adds that Jobs's quest
seemed driven partly by not knowing his birth parents. "There was a
hole in him, and he was trying to fill it."

When Jobs told the folks at Atari that he was quitting to go search
for a guru in India, the jovial Alcorn was amused. "He comes in and
stares at me and declares, 'I'm going to find my guru,' and I say, 'No
shit, that's super. Write me!' And he says he wants me to help pay, and
I tell him, 'Bullshit!' " Then Alcorn had an idea. Atari was making kits
and shipping them to Munich, where they were built into finished
machines and distributed by a wholesaler in Turin. But there was a
problem: Because the games were designed for the American rate of
sixty frames per second, there were frustrating interference problems
in Europe, where the rate was fifty frames per second. Alcorn sketched
out a fix with Jobs and then offered to pay for him to go to Europe to
implement it. "It's got to be cheaper to get to India from there," he said.
Jobs agreed. So Alcorn sent him on his way with the exhortation, "Say
hi to your guru for me."

Jobs spent a few days in Munich, where he solved the interference
problem, but in the process he flummoxed the dark-suited German
managers. They complained to Alcorn that he dressed and smelled like
a bum and behaved rudely. "I said, 'Did he solve the problem?' And
they said, 'Yeah.' I said, 'If you got any more problems, you just call
me, I got more guys just like him!' They said, 'No, no we'll take care
of it next time.' " For his part, Jobs was upset that the Germans kept

trying to feed him meat and potatoes. "They don't even have a word for vegetarian," he complained (incorrectly) in a phone call to Alcorn.

He had a better time when he took the train to see the distributor in Turin, where the Italian pastas and his host's camaraderie were more simpatico. "I had a wonderful couple of weeks in Turin, which is this charged-up industrial town," he recalled. "The distributor took me every night to dinner at this place where there were only eight tables and no menu. You'd just tell them what you wanted, and they made it. One of the tables was on reserve for the chairman of Fiat. It was really super." He next went to Lugano, Switzerland, where he stayed with Friedland's uncle, and from there took a flight to India.

When he got off the plane in New Delhi, he felt waves of heat rising from the tarmac, even though it was only April. He had been given the name of a hotel, but it was full, so he went to one his taxi driver insisted was good. "I'm sure he was getting some baksheesh, because he took me to this complete dive." Jobs asked the owner whether the water was filtered and foolishly believed the answer. "I got dysentery pretty fast. I was sick, really sick, a really high fever. I dropped from 160 pounds to 120 in about a week."

Once he got healthy enough to move, he decided that he needed to get out of Delhi. So he headed to the town of Haridwar, in northern India near the source of the Ganges, which was having a festival known as the Kumbh Mela. More than ten million people poured into a town that usually contained fewer than 100,000 residents. "There were holy men all around. Tents with this teacher and that teacher. There were people riding elephants, you name it. I was there for a few days, but I decided that I needed to get out of there too."

He went by train and bus to a village near Nainital in the foothills of the Himalayas. That was where Neem Karoli Baba lived, or had lived. By the time Jobs got there, he was no longer alive, at least in the same incarnation. Jobs rented a room with a mattress on the floor from a family who helped him recuperate by feeding him vegetarian meals. "There was a copy there of *Autobiography of a Yogi* in English that a previous traveler had left, and I read it several times because there was not a lot to do, and I walked around from village to village and re-

covered from my dysentery." Among those who were part of the community there was Larry Brilliant, an epidemiologist who was working
to eradicate smallpox and who later ran Google's philanthropic arm
and the Skoll Foundation. He became Jobs's lifelong friend.

At one point Jobs was told of a young Hindu holy man who was
holding a gathering of his followers at the Himalayan estate of a wealthy
businessman. "It was a chance to meet a spiritual being and hang out
with his followers, but it was also a chance to have a good meal. I could
smell the food as we got near, and I was very hungry." As Jobs was eating, the holy man—who was not much older than Jobs—picked him
out of the crowd, pointed at him, and began laughing maniacally. "He
came running over and grabbed me and made a tooting sound and
said, 'You are just like a baby,'" recalled Jobs. "I was not relishing this
attention." Taking Jobs by the hand, he led him out of the worshipful
crowd and walked him up to a hill, where there was a well and a small
pond. "We sit down and he pulls out this straight razor. I'm thinking
he's a nutcase and begin to worry. Then he pulls out a bar of soap—
I had long hair at the time—and he lathered up my hair and shaved my
head. He told me that he was saving my health."

Daniel Kottke arrived in India at the beginning of the summer, and
Jobs went back to New Delhi to meet him. They wandered, mainly by
bus, rather aimlessly. By this point Jobs was no longer trying to find
a guru who could impart wisdom, but instead was seeking enlightenment through ascetic experience, deprivation, and simplicity. He was
not able to achieve inner calm. Kottke remembers him getting into a
furious shouting match with a Hindu woman in a village marketplace
who, Jobs alleged, had been watering down the milk she was selling
them.

Yet Jobs could also be generous. When they got to the town of
Manali, Kottke's sleeping bag was stolen with his traveler's checks in it.
"Steve covered my food expenses and bus ticket back to Delhi," Kottke
recalled. He also gave Kottke the rest of his own money, $100, to tide
him over.

During his seven months in India, he had written to his parents
only sporadically, getting mail at the American Express office in New

Delhi when he passed through, and so they were somewhat surprised when they got a call from the Oakland airport asking them to pick him up. They immediately drove up from Los Altos. "My head had been shaved, I was wearing Indian cotton robes, and my skin had turned a deep, chocolate brown-red from the sun," he recalled. "So I'm sitting there and my parents walked past me about five times and finally my mother came up and said 'Steve?' and I said 'Hi!'"

They took him back home, where he continued trying to find himself. It was a pursuit with many paths toward enlightenment. In the mornings and evenings he would meditate and study Zen, and in between he would drop in to audit physics or engineering courses at Stanford.

The Search

Jobs's interest in Eastern spirituality, Hinduism, Zen Buddhism, and the search for enlightenment was not merely the passing phase of a nineteen-year-old. Throughout his life he would seek to follow many of the basic precepts of Eastern religions, such as the emphasis on experiential *prajñā*, wisdom or cognitive understanding that is intuitively experienced through concentration of the mind. Years later, sitting in his Palo Alto garden, he reflected on the lasting influence of his trip to India:

> Coming back to America was, for me, much more of a cultural shock than going to India. The people in the Indian countryside don't use their intellect like we do, they use their intuition instead, and their intuition is far more developed than in the rest of the world. Intuition is a very powerful thing, more powerful than intellect, in my opinion. That's had a big impact on my work.
>
> Western rational thought is not an innate human characteristic; it is learned and is the great achievement of Western civilization. In the villages of India, they never learned it. They learned something else, which is in some ways just as valuable but in other ways is not. That's the power of intuition and experiential wisdom.

Coming back after seven months in Indian villages, I saw the craziness of the Western world as well as its capacity for rational thought. If you just sit and observe, you will see how restless your mind is. If you try to calm it, it only makes it worse, but over time it does calm, and when it does, there's room to hear more subtle things—that's when your intuition starts to blossom and you start to see things more clearly and be in the present more. Your mind just slows down, and you see a tremendous expanse in the moment. You see so much more than you could see before. It's a discipline; you have to practice it.

Zen has been a deep influence in my life ever since. At one point I was thinking about going to Japan and trying to get into the Eihei-ji monastery, but my spiritual advisor urged me to stay here. He said there is nothing over there that isn't here, and he was correct. I learned the truth of the Zen saying that if you are willing to travel around the world to meet a teacher, one will appear next door.

Jobs did in fact find a teacher right in his own neighborhood. Shunryu Suzuki, who wrote *Zen Mind, Beginner's Mind* and ran the San Francisco Zen Center, used to come to Los Altos every Wednesday evening to lecture and meditate with a small group of followers. After a while he asked his assistant, Kobun Chino Otogawa, to open a full-time center there. Jobs became a faithful follower, along with his occasional girlfriend, Chrisann Brennan, and Daniel Kottke and Elizabeth Holmes. He also began to go by himself on retreats to the Tassajara Zen Center, a monastery near Carmel where Kobun also taught.

Kottke found Kobun amusing. "His English was atrocious," he recalled. "He would speak in a kind of haiku, with poetic, suggestive phrases. We would sit and listen to him, and half the time we had no idea what he was going on about. I took the whole thing as a kind of lighthearted interlude." Holmes was more into the scene. "We would go to Kobun's meditations, sit on zafu cushions, and he would sit on a dais," she said. "We learned how to tune out distractions. It was a magical thing. One evening we were meditating with Kobun when it was raining, and he taught us how to use ambient sounds to bring us back to focus on our meditation."

As for Jobs, his devotion was intense. "He became really serious and self-important and just generally unbearable," according to Kottke. He began meeting with Kobun almost daily, and every few months they went on retreats together to meditate. "I ended up spending as much time as I could with him," Jobs recalled. "He had a wife who was a nurse at Stanford and two kids. She worked the night shift, so I would go over and hang out with him in the evenings. She would get home about midnight and shoo me away." They sometimes discussed whether Jobs should devote himself fully to spiritual pursuits, but Kobun counseled otherwise. He assured Jobs that he could keep in touch with his spiritual side while working in a business. The relationship turned out to be lasting and deep; seventeen years later Kobun would perform Jobs's wedding ceremony.

Jobs's compulsive search for self-awareness also led him to undergo primal scream therapy, which had recently been developed and popularized by a Los Angeles psychotherapist named Arthur Janov. It was based on the Freudian theory that psychological problems are caused by the repressed pains of childhood; Janov argued that they could be resolved by re-suffering these primal moments while fully expressing the pain—sometimes in screams. To Jobs, this seemed preferable to talk therapy because it involved intuitive feeling and emotional action rather than just rational analyzing. "This was not something to think about," he later said. "This was something to do: to close your eyes, hold your breath, jump in, and come out the other end more insightful."

A group of Janov's adherents ran a program called the Oregon Feeling Center in an old hotel in Eugene that was managed by Jobs's Reed College guru Robert Friedland, whose All One Farm commune was nearby. In late 1974, Jobs signed up for a twelve-week course of therapy there costing $1,000. "Steve and I were both into personal growth, so I wanted to go with him," Kottke recounted, "but I couldn't afford it."

Jobs confided to close friends that he was driven by the pain he was feeling about being put up for adoption and not knowing about his birth parents. "Steve had a very profound desire to know his physical parents so he could better know himself," Friedland later said. He had learned from Paul and Clara Jobs that his birth parents had both been graduate students at a university and that his father might be Syrian. He had even thought about hiring a private investigator, but he decided not to do so for the time being. "I didn't want to hurt my parents," he recalled, referring to Paul and Clara.

"He was struggling with the fact that he had been adopted," according to Elizabeth Holmes. "He felt that it was an issue that he needed to get hold of emotionally." Jobs admitted as much to her. "This is something that is bothering me, and I need to focus on it," he said. He was even more open with Greg Calhoun. "He was doing a lot of soul-searching about being adopted, and he talked about it with me a lot," Calhoun recalled. "The primal scream and the mucusless diets, he was trying to cleanse himself and get deeper into his frustration about his birth. He told me he was deeply angry about the fact that he had been given up."

John Lennon had undergone the same primal scream therapy in 1970, and in December of that year he released the song "Mother" with the Plastic Ono Band. It dealt with Lennon's own feelings about a father who had abandoned him and a mother who had been killed when he was a teenager. The refrain includes the haunting chant "Mama don't go, Daddy come home." Jobs used to play the song often.

Jobs later said that Janov's teachings did not prove very useful. "He offered a ready-made, buttoned-down answer which turned out to be far too oversimplistic. It became obvious that it was not going to yield any great insight." But Holmes contended that it made him more confident: "After he did it, he was in a different place. He had a very abrasive personality, but there was a peace about him for a while. His confidence improved and his feelings of inadequacy were reduced."

Jobs came to believe that he could impart that feeling of confidence to others and thus push them to do things they hadn't thought possible. Holmes had broken up with Kottke and joined a religious cult in San Francisco that expected her to sever ties with all past friends. But Jobs rejected that injunction. He arrived at the cult house in his Ford Ranchero one day and announced that he was driving up to Friedland's apple farm and she was to come. Even more brazenly, he said she would have to drive part of the way, even though she didn't know how to use the stick shift. "Once we got on the open road, he made me get behind the wheel, and he shifted the car until we got up to 55 miles per hour," she recalled. "Then he puts on a tape of Dylan's *Blood on the Tracks*, lays his head in my lap, and goes to sleep. He had the attitude that he could do anything, and therefore so can you. He put his life in my hands. So that made me do something I didn't think I could do."

It was the brighter side of what would become known as his reality distortion field. "If you trust him, you can do things," Holmes said. "If he's decided that something should happen, then he's just going to make it happen."

Breakout

One day in early 1975 Al Alcorn was sitting in his office at Atari when Ron Wayne burst in. "Hey, Stevie is back!" he shouted.

"Wow, bring him on in," Alcorn replied.

Jobs shuffled in barefoot, wearing a saffron robe and carrying a copy of *Be Here Now*, which he handed to Alcorn and insisted he read. "Can I have my job back?" he asked.

"He looked like a Hare Krishna guy, but it was great to see him," Alcorn recalled. "So I said, sure!"

Once again, for the sake of harmony, Jobs worked mostly at night. Wozniak, who was living in an apartment nearby and working at HP, would come by after dinner to hang out and play the video games. He had become addicted to Pong at a Sunnyvale bowling alley, and he was able to build a version that he hooked up to his home TV set.

One day in the late summer of 1975, Nolan Bushnell, defying the prevailing wisdom that paddle games were over, decided to develop a single-player version of Pong; instead of competing against an opponent, the player would volley the ball into a wall that lost a brick whenever it was hit. He called Jobs into his office, sketched it out on his little blackboard, and asked him to design it. There would be a bonus, Bushnell told him, for every chip fewer than fifty that he used. Bushnell knew that Jobs was not a great engineer, but he assumed, correctly, that he would recruit Wozniak, who was always hanging around. "I looked at it as a two-for-one thing," Bushnell recalled. "Woz was a better engineer."

Wozniak was thrilled when Jobs asked him to help and proposed splitting the fee. "This was the most wonderful offer in my life, to actually design a game that people would use," he recalled. Jobs said it had to be done in four days and with the fewest chips possible. What he hid from Wozniak was that the deadline was one that Jobs had imposed, because he needed to get to the All One Farm to help prepare for the apple harvest. He also didn't mention that there was a bonus tied to keeping down the number of chips.

"A game like this might take most engineers a few months," Wozniak recalled. "I thought that there was no way I could do it, but Steve made me sure that I could." So he stayed up four nights in a row and did it. During the day at HP, Wozniak would sketch out his design on paper. Then, after a fast-food meal, he would go right to Atari and stay all night. As Wozniak churned out the design, Jobs sat on a bench to his left implementing it by wire-wrapping the chips onto a breadboard. "While Steve was breadboarding, I spent time playing my favorite game ever, which was the auto racing game Gran Trak 10," Wozniak said.

Astonishingly, they were able to get the job done in four days, and Wozniak used only forty-five chips. Recollections differ, but by most accounts Jobs simply gave Wozniak half of the base fee and not the bonus Bushnell paid for saving five chips. It would be another ten years before Wozniak discovered (by being shown the tale in a book on the history of Atari titled *Zap*) that Jobs had been paid this bonus. "I think that Steve needed the money, and he just didn't tell me the truth," Wozniak later said. When he talks about it now, there are long pauses, and he admits that it causes him pain. "I wish he had just been honest. If he had told me he needed the money, he should have known I would have just given it to him. He was a friend. You help your friends." To Wozniak, it showed a fundamental difference in their characters.

"Ethics always mattered to me, and I still don't understand why he would've gotten paid one thing and told me he'd gotten paid another," he said. "But, you know, people are different."

When Jobs learned this story was published, he called Wozniak to deny it. "He told me that he didn't remember doing it, and that if he did something like that he would remember it, so he probably didn't do it," Wozniak recalled. When I asked Jobs directly, he became unusually quiet and hesitant. "I don't know where that allegation comes from," he said. "I gave him half the money I ever got. That's how I've always been with Woz. I mean, Woz stopped working in 1978. He never did one ounce of work after 1978. And yet he got exactly the same shares of Apple stock that I did."

Is it possible that memories are muddled and that Jobs did not, in fact, shortchange Wozniak? "There's a chance that my memory is all wrong and messed up," Wozniak told me, but after a pause he reconsidered. "But no. I remember the details of this one, the $350 check." He confirmed his memory with Nolan Bushnell and Al Alcorn. "I remember talking about the bonus money to Woz, and he was upset," Bushnell said. "I said yes, there was a bonus for each chip they saved, and he just shook his head and then clucked his tongue."

Whatever the truth, Wozniak later insisted that it was not worth rehashing. Jobs is a complex person, he said, and being manipulative is just the darker facet of the traits that make him successful. Wozniak would never have been that way, but as he points out, he also could never have built Apple. "I would rather let it pass," he said when I pressed the point. "It's not something I want to judge Steve by."

The Atari experience helped shape Jobs's approach to business and design. He appreciated the user-friendliness of Atari's insert-quarter-avoid-Klingons games. "That simplicity rubbed off on him and made him a very focused product person," said Ron Wayne. Jobs also absorbed some of Bushnell's take-no-prisoners attitude. "Nolan wouldn't take no for an answer," according to Alcorn, "and this was Steve's first impression of how things got done. Nolan was never abusive, like Steve sometimes is. But he had the same driven attitude. It made me cringe, but dammit, it got things done. In that way Nolan was a mentor for Jobs."

Bushnell agreed. "There is something indefinable in an entrepreneur, and I saw that in Steve," he said. "He was interested not just in engineering, but also the business aspects. I taught him that if you act like you can do something, then it will work. I told him, 'Pretend to be completely in control and people will assume that you are.'"

CHAPTER FIVE

THE APPLE I

Turn On, Boot Up, Jack In . . .

Daniel Kottke and Jobs with the Apple I at
the Atlantic City computer fair, 1976

Machines of Loving Grace

In San Francisco and the Santa Clara Valley during the late 1960s, various cultural currents flowed together. There was the technology revolution that began with the growth of military contractors and soon included electronics firms, microchip makers, video game designers, and computer companies. There was a hacker subculture—filled with wireheads, phreakers, cyberpunks, hobbyists, and just plain geeks— that included engineers who didn't conform to the HP mold and their kids who weren't attuned to the wavelengths of the subdivisions. There were quasi-academic groups doing studies on the effects of LSD; participants included Doug Engelbart of the Augmentation Research Center in Palo Alto, who later helped develop the computer mouse and graphical user interfaces, and Ken Kesey, who celebrated the drug with music-and-light shows featuring a house band that became the Grateful Dead. There was the hippie movement, born out of the Bay Area's beat generation, and the rebellious political activists, born out of the Free Speech Movement at Berkeley. Overlaid on it all were various self-fulfillment movements pursuing paths to personal enlightenment: Zen and Hinduism, meditation and yoga, primal scream and sensory deprivation, Esalen and est.

This fusion of flower power and processor power, enlightenment and technology, was embodied by Steve Jobs as he meditated in the mornings, audited physics classes at Stanford, worked nights at Atari, and dreamed of starting his own business. "There was just something going on here," he said, looking back at the time and place. "The best music came from here—the Grateful Dead, Jefferson Airplane, Joan Baez, Janis Joplin—and so did the integrated circuit, and things like the *Whole Earth Catalog*."

Initially the technologists and the hippies did not interface well. Many in the counterculture saw computers as ominous and Orwellian, the province of the Pentagon and the power structure. In *The Myth of the Machine*, the historian Lewis Mumford warned that computers were sucking away our freedom and destroying "life-enhancing values." An injunction on punch cards of the period—"Do not fold, spindle or mutilate"—became an ironic phrase of the antiwar Left.

But by the early 1970s a shift was under way. "Computing went from being dismissed as a tool of bureaucratic control to being embraced as a symbol of individual expression and liberation," John Markoff wrote in his study of the counterculture's convergence with the computer industry, *What the Dormouse Said*. It was an ethos lyrically expressed in Richard Brautigan's 1967 poem, "All Watched Over by Machines of Loving Grace," and the cyberdelic fusion was certified when Timothy Leary declared that personal computers had become the new LSD and years later revised his famous mantra to proclaim,

"Turn on, boot up, jack in." The musician Bono, who later became a friend of Jobs, often discussed with him why those immersed in the rock-drugs-rebel counterculture of the Bay Area ended up helping to create the personal computer industry. "The people who invented the twenty-first century were pot-smoking, sandal-wearing hippies from the West Coast like Steve, because they saw differently," he said. "The hierarchical systems of the East Coast, England, Germany, and Japan do not encourage this different thinking. The sixties produced an anarchic mind-set that is great for imagining a world not yet in existence."

One person who encouraged the denizens of the counterculture to make common cause with the hackers was Stewart Brand. A puckish visionary who generated fun and ideas over many decades, Brand was a participant in one of the early sixties LSD studies in Palo Alto. He joined with his fellow subject Ken Kesey to produce the acid-celebrating Trips Festival, appeared in the opening scene of Tom Wolfe's *The Electric Kool-Aid Acid Test*, and worked with Doug Engelbart to create a seminal sound-and-light presentation of new technologies called the Mother of All Demos. "Most of our generation scorned computers as the embodiment of centralized control," Brand later noted. "But a tiny contingent—later called hackers—embraced computers and set about transforming them into tools of liberation. That turned out to be the true royal road to the future."

Brand ran the Whole Earth Truck Store, which began as a roving truck that sold useful tools and educational materials, and in 1968 he decided to extend its reach with the *Whole Earth Catalog*. On its first cover was the famous picture of Earth taken from space; its subtitle was "Access to Tools." The underlying philosophy was that technology could be our friend. Brand wrote on the first page of the first edition, "A realm of intimate, personal power is developing—power of the individual to conduct his own education, find his own inspiration, shape his own environment, and share his adventure with whoever is interested. Tools that aid this process are sought and promoted by the *Whole Earth Catalog*." Buckminster Fuller followed with a poem that began: "I see God in the instruments and mechanisms that work reliably."

Jobs became a *Whole Earth* fan. He was particularly taken by the final issue, which came out in 1971, when he was still in high school, and he brought it with him to college and then to the All One Farm. "On the back cover of their final issue" Jobs recalled, "was a photograph of an early morning country road, the kind you might find yourself hitchhiking on if you were so adventurous. Above it were the words: 'Stay Hungry. Stay Foolish.'" Brand sees Jobs as one of the purest embodiments of the cultural mix that the catalog sought to celebrate. "Steve is right at the nexus of the counterculture and technology," he said. "He got the notion of tools for human use."

Brand's catalog was published with the help of the Portola Institute, a foundation dedicated to the fledgling field of computer education. The foundation also helped launch the People's Computer Company, which was not a company at all but a newsletter and organization with the motto "Computer power to the people." There were occasional Wednesday-night potluck dinners, and two of the regulars, Gordon French and Fred Moore, decided to create a more formal club where news about personal electronics could be shared.

They were energized by the arrival of the January 1975 issue of *Popular Electronics*, which had on its cover the first personal computer kit, the Altair. The Altair wasn't much—just a $495 pile of parts that had to be soldered to a board that would then do little—but for hobbyists and hackers it heralded the dawn of a new era. Bill Gates and Paul Allen read the magazine and started working on a version of BASIC, an easy-to-use programming language, for the Altair. It also caught the attention of Jobs and Wozniak. And when an Altair kit arrived at the People's Computer Company, it became the centerpiece for the first meeting of the club that French and Moore had decided to launch.

The Homebrew Computer Club

The group became known as the Homebrew Computer Club, and it encapsulated the *Whole Earth* fusion between the counterculture and technology. It would become to the personal computer era something akin to what the Turk's Head coffeehouse was to the age of Dr. Johnson, a place where ideas were exchanged and disseminated. Moore wrote the flyer for the first meeting, held on March 5, 1975, in French's

Menlo Park garage: "Are you building your own computer? Terminal, TV, typewriter?" it asked. "If so, you might like to come to a gathering of people with like-minded interests."

Allen Baum spotted the flyer on the HP bulletin board and called Wozniak, who agreed to go with him. "That night turned out to be one of the most important nights of my life," Wozniak recalled. About thirty other people showed up, spilling out of French's open garage door, and they took turns describing their interests. Wozniak, who later admitted to being extremely nervous, said he liked "video games, pay movies for hotels, scientific calculator design, and TV terminal design," according to the minutes prepared by Moore. There was a demonstration of the new Altair, but more important to Wozniak was seeing the specification sheet for a microprocessor.

As he thought about the microprocessor—a chip that had an entire central processing unit on it—he had an insight. He had been designing a terminal, with a keyboard and monitor, that would connect to a distant minicomputer. Using a microprocessor, he could put some of the capacity of the minicomputer inside the terminal itself, so it could become a small stand-alone computer on a desktop. It was an enduring idea: keyboard, screen, and computer all in one integrated personal package. "This whole vision of a personal computer just popped into my head," he said. "That night, I started to sketch out on paper what would later become known as the Apple I."

At first he planned to use the same microprocessor that was in the Altair, an Intel 8080. But each of those "cost almost more than my monthly rent," so he looked for an alternative. He found one in the Motorola 6800, which a friend at HP was able to get for $40 apiece. Then he discovered a chip made by MOS Technologies that was electronically the same but cost only $20. It would make his machine affordable, but it would carry a long-term cost. Intel's chips ended up becoming the industry standard, which would haunt Apple when its computers were incompatible with it.

After work each day, Wozniak would go home for a TV dinner and then return to HP to moonlight on his computer. He spread out the parts in his cubicle, figured out their placement, and soldered them onto his motherboard. Then he began writing the software that would get the microprocessor to display images on the screen. Because he could not afford to pay for computer time, he wrote the code by hand. After a couple of months he was ready to test it. "I typed a few keys on the keyboard and I was shocked! The letters were displayed on the screen." It was Sunday, June 29, 1975, a milestone for the personal computer. "It was the first time in history," Wozniak later said, "anyone had typed a character on a keyboard and seen it show up on their own computer's screen right in front of them."

Jobs was impressed. He peppered Wozniak with questions: Could the computer ever be networked? Was it possible to add a disk for memory storage? He also began to help Woz get components. Particularly important were the dynamic random-access memory chips. Jobs made a few calls and was able to score some from Intel for free. "Steve is just that sort of person," said Wozniak. "I mean, he knew how to talk to a sales representative. I could never have done that. I'm too shy."

Jobs began to accompany Wozniak to Homebrew meetings, carrying the TV monitor and helping to set things up. The meetings now attracted more than one hundred enthusiasts and had been moved to the auditorium of the Stanford Linear Accelerator Center. Presiding with a pointer and a free-form manner was Lee Felsenstein, another embodiment of the merger between the world of computing and the counterculture. He was an engineering school dropout, a participant in the Free Speech Movement, and an antiwar activist. He had written for the alternative newspaper *Berkeley Barb* and then gone back to being a computer engineer.

Woz was usually too shy to talk in the meetings, but people would gather around his machine afterward, and he would proudly show off his progress. Moore had tried to instill in the Homebrew an ethos of swapping and sharing rather than commerce. "The theme of the club," Woz said, "was 'Give to help others.'" It was an expression of the hacker ethic that information should be free and all authority mistrusted. "I designed the Apple I because I wanted to give it away for free to other people," said Wozniak.

This was not an outlook that Bill Gates embraced. After he and Paul Allen had completed their BASIC interpreter for the Altair, Gates was appalled that members of the Homebrew were making copies of it and sharing it without paying him. So he wrote what would become a famous letter to the club: "As the majority of hobbyists must be aware, most of you steal your software. Is this fair? . . . One thing you do is prevent good software from being written. Who can afford to do professional work for nothing? . . . I would appreciate letters from anyone who wants to pay up."

Steve Jobs, similarly, did not embrace the notion that Wozniak's creations, be it a Blue Box or a computer, wanted to be free. So he convinced Wozniak to stop giving away copies of his schematics. Most people didn't have time to build it themselves anyway, Jobs argued. "Why don't we build and sell printed circuit boards to them?" It was an example of their symbiosis. "Every time I'd design something great, Steve would find a way to make money for us," said Wozniak. Wozniak admitted that he would have never thought of doing that on his own. "It never crossed my mind to sell computers. It was Steve who said, 'Let's hold them in the air and sell a few.'"

Jobs worked out a plan to pay a guy he knew at Atari to draw the circuit boards and then print up fifty or so. That would cost about $1,000, plus the fee to the designer. They could sell them for $40 apiece and perhaps clear a profit of $700. Wozniak was dubious that they could sell them all. "I didn't see how we would make our money back," he recalled. He was already in trouble with his landlord for bouncing checks and now had to pay each month in cash.

Jobs knew how to appeal to Wozniak. He didn't argue that they were sure to make money, but instead that they would have a fun adventure. "Even if we lose our money, we'll have a company," said Jobs as they were driving in his Volkswagen bus. "For once in our lives, we'll have a company." This was enticing to Wozniak, even more than any prospect of getting rich. He recalled, "I was excited to think about us like that. To be two best friends starting a company. Wow. I knew right then that I'd do it. How could I not?"

In order to raise the money they needed, Wozniak sold his HP 65 calculator for $500, though the buyer ended up stiffing him for half of that. For his part, Jobs sold his Volkswagen bus for $1,500. But the person who bought it came to find him two weeks later and said the engine had broken down, and Jobs agreed to pay for half of the repairs. Despite these little setbacks, they now had, with their own small savings thrown in, about $1,300 in working capital, the design for a product, and a plan. They would start their own computer company.

Apple Is Born

Now that they had decided to start a business, they needed a name. Jobs had gone for another visit to the All One Farm, where he had been pruning the Gravenstein apple trees, and Wozniak picked him up at the airport. On the ride down to Los Altos, they bandied around options. They considered some typical tech words, such as Matrix, and some neologisms, such as Executek, and some straightforward boring names, like Personal Computers Inc. The deadline for deciding was the next day, when Jobs wanted to start filing the papers. Finally Jobs proposed Apple Computer. "I was on one of my fruitarian diets," he explained. "I had just come back from the apple farm. It sounded fun, spirited, and not intimidating. Apple took the edge off the word 'computer.' Plus, it would get us ahead of Atari in the phone book." He told Wozniak that if a better name did not hit them by the next afternoon, they would just stick with Apple. And they did.

Apple. It was a smart choice. The word instantly signaled friendliness and simplicity. It managed to be both slightly off-beat and as normal as a slice of pie. There was a whiff of counterculture, back-to-nature earthiness to it, yet nothing could be more American. And the two words together—Apple Computer—provided an amusing disjuncture. "It doesn't quite make sense," said Mike Markkula, who soon thereafter became the first chairman of the new company. "So it forces your brain to dwell on it. Apple and computers, that doesn't go together! So it helped us grow brand awareness."

Wozniak was not yet ready to commit full-time. He was an HP company man at heart, or so he thought, and he wanted to keep his day job there. Jobs realized he needed an ally to help corral Wozniak and adjudicate if there was a disagreement. So he enlisted his friend Ron Wayne, the middle-aged engineer at Atari who had once started a slot machine company.

Wayne knew that it would not be easy to make Wozniak quit HP, nor was it necessary right away. Instead the key was to convince him that his computer designs would be owned by the Apple partnership. "Woz had a parental attitude toward the circuits he developed, and he wanted to be able to use them in other applications or let HP use them," Wayne said. "Jobs and I realized that these circuits would be the core of Apple. We spent two hours in a roundtable discussion at my apartment, and I was able to get Woz to accept this." His argument was that a great engineer would be remembered only if he teamed with a great marketer, and this required him to commit his designs to the partnership. Jobs was so impressed and grateful that he offered Wayne a 10% stake in the new partnership, turning him into a tie-breaker if Jobs and Wozniak disagreed over an issue.

"They were very different, but they made a powerful team," said Wayne. Jobs at times seemed to be driven by demons, while Woz seemed a naïf who was toyed with by angels. Jobs had a bravado that helped him get things done, occasionally by manipulating people. He could be charismatic, even mesmerizing, but also cold and brutal. Wozniak, in contrast, was shy and socially awkward, which made him seem childishly sweet. "Woz is very bright in some areas, but he's almost like a savant, since he was so stunted when it came to dealing with people he didn't know," said Jobs. "We were a good pair." It helped that Jobs was awed by Wozniak's engineering wizardry, and Wozniak was awed by Jobs's business drive. "I never wanted to deal with people and step on toes, but Steve could call up people he didn't know and make them do things," Wozniak recalled. "He could be rough on people he didn't think were smart, but he never treated me rudely, even in later years when maybe I couldn't answer a question as well as he wanted."

Even after Wozniak became convinced that his new computer design should become the property of the Apple partnership, he felt that he had to offer it first to HP, since he was working there. "I believed it was my duty to tell HP about what I had designed while working for them. That was the right thing and the ethical thing." So he demonstrated it to his managers in the spring of 1976. The senior executive at the meeting was impressed, and seemed torn, but he finally said it was not something that HP could develop. It was a hobbyist product, at least for now, and didn't fit into the company's high-quality market segments. "I was disappointed," Wozniak recalled, "but now I was free to enter into the Apple partnership."

On April 1, 1976, Jobs and Wozniak went to Wayne's apartment in Mountain View to draw up the partnership agreement. Wayne said he had some experience "writing in legalese," so he composed the three-page document himself. His "legalese" got the better of him. Paragraphs began with various flourishes: "Be it noted herewith . . . Be it further noted herewith . . . Now the refore [*sic*], in consideration of the respective assignments of interests . . ." But the division of shares and profits was clear—45%-45%-10%—and it was stipulated that any expenditures of more than $100 would require agreement of at least two of the partners. Also, the responsibilities were spelled out. "Wozniak shall assume both general and major responsibility for the conduct of Electrical Engineering; Jobs shall assume general responsibility for Electrical Engineering and Marketing, and Wayne shall assume major responsibility for Mechanical Engineering and Documentation." Jobs signed in lowercase script, Wozniak in careful cursive, and Wayne in an illegible squiggle.

Wayne then got cold feet. As Jobs started planning to borrow and spend more money, he recalled the failure of his own company. He didn't want to go through that again. Jobs and Wozniak had no personal assets, but Wayne (who worried about a global financial Armageddon) kept gold coins hidden in his mattress. Because they had structured Apple as a simple partnership rather than a corporation, the partners would be personally liable for the debts, and Wayne was afraid potential creditors would go after him. So he returned to the Santa Clara County office just eleven days later with a "statement of withdrawal" and an amendment to the partnership agreement. "By virtue of a re-assessment of understandings by and between all parties," it began, "Wayne shall hereinafter cease to function in the status of 'Partner.'" It noted that in payment for his 10% of the company, he received $800, and shortly afterward $1,500 more.

Had he stayed on and kept his 10% stake, in 2013 it would have been worth approximately $40 billion. Instead he was then living alone in a small home in Pahrump, Nevada, where he played the penny slot machines and lived off his social security check. He later claimed he had no regrets. "I made the best decision for me at the time. Both of them were real whirlwinds, and I knew my stomach and it wasn't ready for such a ride."

Jobs and Wozniak took the stage together for a presentation to the Homebrew Computer Club shortly after they signed Apple into existence. Wozniak held up one of their newly produced circuit boards and described the microprocessor, the eight kilobytes of memory, and the version of BASIC he had written. He also emphasized what he called the main thing: "a human-typable keyboard instead of a stupid, cryptic front panel with a bunch of lights and switches." Then it was Jobs's turn. He pointed out that the Apple, unlike the Altair, had all the essential components built in. Then he challenged them with a question: How much would people be willing to pay for such a wonderful machine? He was trying to get them to see the amazing value of the Apple. It was a rhetorical flourish he would use at product presentations over the ensuing decades.

The audience was not very impressed. The Apple had a cut-rate microprocessor, not the Intel 8080. But one important person stayed behind to hear more. His name was Paul Terrell, and in 1975 he had opened a computer store, which he dubbed the Byte Shop, on Camino Real in Menlo Park. Now, a year later, he had three stores and visions of building a national chain. Jobs was thrilled to give him a private demo. "Take a look at this," he said. "You're going to like what you see." Terrell was impressed enough to hand Jobs and Woz his card. "Keep in touch," he said.

"I'm keeping in touch," Jobs announced the next day when he walked barefoot into the Byte Shop. He made the sale. Terrell agreed to order fifty computers. But there was a condition: He didn't want just $50 printed circuit boards, for which customers would then have to buy all the chips and do the assembly. That might appeal to a few hard-core hobbyists, but not to most customers. Instead he wanted the boards to be fully assembled. For that he was willing to pay about $500 apiece, cash on delivery.

Jobs immediately called Wozniak at HP. "Are you sitting down?" he asked. Wozniak said he wasn't. Jobs nevertheless proceeded to give him the news. "I was shocked, just completely shocked," Wozniak recalled. "I will never forget that moment."

To fill the order, they needed about $15,000 worth of parts. Allen Baum, the third prankster from Homestead High, and his father agreed to loan them $5,000. Jobs tried to borrow more from a bank in Los Altos, but the manager looked at him and, not surprisingly, declined. He went to Haltek Supply and offered an equity stake in Apple in return for the parts, but the owner decided they were "a couple of young, scruffy-looking guys," and declined. Alcorn at Atari would sell them chips only if they paid cash up front. Finally, Jobs was able to convince the manager of Cramer Electronics to call Paul Terrell to confirm that he had really committed to a $25,000 order. Terrell was at a conference when he heard over a loudspeaker that he had an emergency call (Jobs had been persistent). The Cramer manager told him that two scruffy kids had just walked in waving an order from the Byte Shop. Was it real? Terrell confirmed that it was, and the store agreed to front Jobs the parts on thirty-day credit.

Garage Band

The Jobs house in Los Altos became the assembly point for the fifty Apple I boards that had to be delivered to the Byte Shop within thirty days, when the payment for the parts would come due. All available hands were enlisted: Jobs and Wozniak, plus Daniel Kottke, his ex-girlfriend Elizabeth Holmes (who had broken away from the cult she'd joined), and Jobs's pregnant sister, Patty. Her vacated bedroom as well as the kitchen table and garage were commandeered as work space. Holmes, who had taken jewelry classes, was given the task of soldering chips. "Most I did well, but I got flux on a few of them," she recalled. This didn't please Jobs. "We don't have a chip to spare," he railed, correctly. He shifted her to bookkeeping and paperwork at the kitchen table, and he did the soldering himself. When they completed a board, they would hand it off to Wozniak. "I would plug each assembled board into the TV and keyboard to test it to see if it worked," he said.

"If it did, I put it in a box. If it didn't, I'd figure what pin hadn't gotten into the socket right."

Paul Jobs suspended his sideline of repairing old cars so that the Apple team could have the whole garage. He put in a long old workbench, hung a schematic of the computer on the new plasterboard wall he built, and set up rows of labeled drawers for the components. He also built a burn box bathed in heat lamps so the computer boards could be tested by running overnight at high temperatures. When there was the occasional eruption of temper, an occurrence not uncommon around his son, Paul would impart some of his calm. "What's the matter?" he would say. "You got a feather up your ass?" In return he occasionally asked to borrow back the TV set so he could watch the end of a football game. During some of these breaks, Jobs and Kottke would go outside and play guitar on the lawn.

Clara Jobs didn't mind losing most of her house to piles of parts and houseguests, but she was frustrated by her son's increasingly quirky diets. "She would roll her eyes at his latest eating obsessions," recalled Holmes. "She just wanted him to be healthy, and he would be making weird pronouncements like, 'I'm a fruitarian and I will only eat leaves picked by virgins in the moonlight.'"

After a dozen assembled boards had been approved by Wozniak, Jobs drove them over to the Byte Shop. Terrell was a bit taken aback. There was no power supply, case, monitor, or keyboard. He had expected something more finished. But Jobs stared him down, and he agreed to take delivery and pay.

After thirty days Apple was on the verge of being profitable. "We were able to build the boards more cheaply than we thought, because I got a good deal on parts," Jobs recalled. "So the fifty we sold to the Byte Shop almost paid for all the material we needed to make a hundred boards." Now they could make a real profit by selling the remaining fifty to their friends and Homebrew compatriots.

Elizabeth Holmes officially became the part-time bookkeeper at $4 an hour, driving down from San Francisco once a week and figuring out how to port Jobs's checkbook into a ledger. In order to make Apple seem like a real company, Jobs hired an answering service, which would relay messages to his mother. Ron Wayne drew a logo, using the ornate line-drawing style of Victorian illustrated fiction, that featured Newton sitting under a tree framed by a quote from Wordsworth: "A mind forever voyaging through strange seas of thought, alone." It was a rather odd motto, one that fit Wayne's self-image more than Apple Computer. Perhaps a better Wordsworth line would have been the poet's description of those involved in the start of the French Revolution: "Bliss was it in that dawn to be alive / But to be young was very heaven!" As Wozniak later exulted, "We were participating in the biggest revolution that had ever happened, I thought. I was so happy to be a part of it."

Woz had already begun thinking about the next version of the machine, so they started calling their current model the Apple I. Jobs and Woz would drive up and down Camino Real trying to get the electronics stores to sell it. In addition to the fifty sold by the Byte Shop and almost fifty sold to friends, they were building another hundred for retail outlets. Not surprisingly, they had contradictory impulses: Wozniak wanted to sell them for about what it cost to build them, but Jobs wanted to make a serious profit. Jobs prevailed. He picked a retail price that was about three times what it cost to build the boards and a 33% markup over the $500 wholesale price that Terrell and other stores paid. The result was $666.66. "I was always into repeating digits," Wozniak said. "The phone number for my dial-a-joke service was 255-6666." Neither of them knew that in the Book of Revelation 666 symbolized the "number of the beast," but they soon were faced with complaints, especially after 666 was featured in that year's hit movie, *The Omen*. (In 2010 one of the original Apple I computers was sold at auction by Christie's for $213,000.)

The first feature story on the new machine appeared in the July 1976 issue of *Interface*, a now-defunct hobbyist magazine. Jobs and friends were still making them by hand in his house, but the article referred to him as the director of marketing and "a former private consultant to Atari." It made Apple sound like a real company. "Steve communicates with many of the computer clubs to keep his finger on the heartbeat of this young industry," the article reported, and it quoted him explaining, "If we can rap about their needs, feelings and motivations, we can respond appropriately by giving them what they want."

By this time they had other competitors, in addition to the Altair, most notably the IMSAI 8080 and Processor Technology Corporation's SOL-20. The latter was designed by Lee Felsenstein and Gordon French of the Homebrew Computer Club. They all had the chance to go on display during Labor Day weekend of 1976, at the first annual Personal Computer Festival, held in a tired hotel on the decaying boardwalk of Atlantic City, New Jersey. Jobs and Wozniak took a TWA flight to Philadelphia, cradling one cigar box with the Apple I and another with the prototype for the successor that Woz was working on. Sitting in the row behind them was Felsenstein, who looked at the Apple I and pronounced it "thoroughly unimpressive." Wozniak was unnerved by the conversation in the row behind him. "We could hear them talking in advanced business talk," he recalled, "using businesslike acronyms we'd never heard before."

Wozniak spent most of his time in their hotel room, tweaking his new prototype. He was too shy to stand at the card table that Apple had been assigned near the back of the exhibition hall. Daniel Kottke had taken the train down from Manhattan, where he was now attending Columbia, and he manned the table while Jobs walked the floor to inspect the competition. What he saw did not impress him. Wozniak, he felt reassured, was the best circuit engineer, and the Apple I (and surely its successor) could beat the competition in terms of functionality. However, the SOL-20 was better looking. It had a sleek metal case, a keyboard, a power supply, and cables. It looked as if it had been produced by grown-ups. The Apple I, on the other hand, appeared as scruffy as its creators.

CHAPTER SIX

THE APPLE II

Dawn of a New Age

An Integrated Package

As Jobs walked the floor of the Personal Computer Festival, he came to the realization that Paul Terrell of the Byte Shop had been right: Personal computers should come in a complete package. The next Apple, he decided, needed to have a great case and a built-in keyboard, and be integrated end to end, from the power supply to the software. "My vision was to create the first fully packaged computer," he recalled. "We were no longer aiming for the handful of hobbyists who liked to assemble their own computers, who knew how to buy transformers and keyboards. For every one of them there were a thousand people who would want the machine to be ready to run."

In their hotel room on that Labor Day weekend of 1976, Wozniak tinkered with the prototype of the new machine, to be named the Apple II, that Jobs hoped would take them to this next level. They brought the prototype out only once, late at night, to test it on the color projection television in one of the conference rooms. Wozniak had come up with an ingenious way to goose the machine's chips into creating color, and he wanted to see if it would work on the type of television that uses a projector to display on a movie-like screen. "I figured a projector might have a different color circuitry that would choke on my color method," he recalled. "So I hooked up the Apple II to this projector and it worked perfectly." As he typed on his keyboard, colorful lines and swirls burst on the screen across the room. The only outsider who saw this first Apple II was Jim Taylor, a sales manager for the VideoBeam television projector. He said he had looked at all the machines, and this was the one he would be buying.

To produce the fully packaged Apple II would require significant capital, so they considered selling the rights to a larger company. Jobs went to Al Alcorn and asked for the chance to pitch it to Atari's management. He set up a meeting with the company's president, Joe Keenan, who was a lot more conservative than Alcorn and Bushnell. "Steve goes in to pitch him, but Joe couldn't stand him," Alcorn recalled. "He didn't appreciate Steve's hygiene." Jobs was barefoot, and at one point put his feet up on a desk. "Not only are we not going to buy this thing," Keenan shouted, "but get your feet off my desk!" Alcorn recalled thinking, "Oh, well. There goes that possibility."

In September Chuck Peddle of the Commodore computer company came by the Jobs house to get a demo. "We'd opened Steve's garage to the sunlight, and he came in wearing a suit and a cowboy hat," Wozniak recalled. Peddle loved the Apple II, and he arranged a presentation for his top brass a few weeks later at Commodore headquarters. "You might want to buy us for a few hundred thousand dollars," Jobs said when they got there. Wozniak was stunned by this "ridiculous" suggestion, but Jobs persisted. The Commodore honchos called a few days later to say they had decided it would be cheaper to build their own machine. Jobs was not upset. He had checked out Commodore and decided that its leadership was "sleazy." Wozniak did not rue the lost money, but his engineering sensibilities were offended when the company came out with the Commodore PET nine months later. "It kind of sickened me. They made a real crappy product by doing it so quick. They could have had Apple."

The Commodore flirtation brought to the surface a potential conflict between Jobs and Wozniak: Were they truly equal in what they contributed to Apple and what they should get out of it? Jerry Wozniak, who exalted the value of engineers over mere entrepreneurs and marketers, thought most of the money should be going to his son. He confronted Jobs personally when he came by the Wozniak house. "You don't deserve shit," he told Jobs. "You haven't produced anything." Jobs began to cry, which was not unusual. He had never been, and would never be, adept at containing his emotions. He told Steve Wozniak that he was willing to call off the partnership. "If we're not fifty-fifty," he said to his friend, "you can have the whole thing." Wozniak, however, understood better than his father the symbiosis they had. If it had not been for Jobs, he might still be handing out schematics of his boards for free at the back of Homebrew meetings. It was Jobs who had turned his ingenious designs into a budding business, just as he had with the Blue Box. He agreed they should remain partners.

It was a smart call. To make the Apple II successful required more than just Wozniak's awesome circuit design. It would need to be packaged into a fully integrated consumer product, and that was Jobs's role.

He began by asking their erstwhile partner Ron Wayne to design a case. "I assumed they had no money, so I did one that didn't require any tooling and could be fabricated in a standard metal shop," he said. His design called for a Plexiglas cover attached by metal straps and a rolltop door that slid down over the keyboard.

Jobs didn't like it. He wanted a simple and elegant design, which he hoped would set Apple apart from the other machines, with their clunky gray metal cases. While haunting the appliance aisles at Macy's, he was struck by the Cuisinart food processors and decided that he wanted a sleek case made of light molded plastic. At a Homebrew meeting, he offered a local consultant, Jerry Manock, $1,500 to produce such a design. Manock, dubious about Jobs's appearance, asked for the money up front. Jobs refused, but Manock took the job anyway.

Within weeks he had produced a simple foam-molded plastic case that was uncluttered and exuded friendliness. Jobs was thrilled.

Next came the power supply. Digital geeks like Wozniak paid little attention to something so analog and mundane, but Jobs decided it was a key component. In particular he wanted—as he would his entire career—to provide power in a way that avoided the need for a fan. Fans inside computers were not Zen-like; they distracted. He dropped by Atari to consult with Alcorn, who knew old-fashioned electrical engineering. "Al turned me on to this brilliant guy named Rod Holt, who was a chain-smoking Marxist who had been through many marriages and was an expert on everything," Jobs recalled. Like Manock and others meeting Jobs for the first time, Holt took a look at him and was skeptical. "I'm expensive," Holt said. Jobs sensed he was worth it and said that cost was no problem. "He just conned me into working," said Holt, who ended up joining Apple full-time.

Instead of a conventional linear power supply, Holt built one like those used in oscilloscopes. It switched the power on and off not sixty times per second, but thousands of times; this allowed it to store the power for far less time, and thus throw off less heat. "That switching power supply was as revolutionary as the Apple II logic board was," Jobs later said. "Rod doesn't get a lot of credit for this in the history books, but he should. Every computer now uses switching power supplies, and they all rip off Rod's design." For all of Wozniak's brilliance, this was not something he could have done. "I only knew vaguely what a switching power supply was," Woz admitted.

Jobs's father had once taught him that a drive for perfection meant caring about the craftsmanship even of the parts unseen. Jobs applied that to the layout of the circuit board inside the Apple II. He rejected the initial design because the lines were not straight enough.

This passion for perfection led him to indulge his instinct to control. Most hackers and hobbyists liked to customize, modify, and jack various things into their computers. To Jobs, this was a threat to a seamless end-to-end user experience. Wozniak, a hacker at heart, disagreed. He wanted to include eight slots on the Apple II for users to insert whatever smaller circuit boards and peripherals they might want. Jobs insisted there be only two, for a printer and a modem. "Usually

I'm really easy to get along with, but this time I told him, 'If that's what you want, go get yourself another computer,'" Wozniak recalled. "I knew that people like me would eventually come up with things to add to any computer." Wozniak won the argument that time, but he could sense his power waning. "I was in a position to do that then. I wouldn't always be."

Mike Markkula

All of this required money. "The tooling of this plastic case was going to cost, like, $100,000," Jobs said. "Just to get this whole thing into production was going to be, like, $200,000." He went back to Nolan Bushnell, this time to get him to put in some money and take a minority equity stake. "He asked me if I would put $50,000 in and he would give me a third of the company," said Bushnell. "I was so smart, I said no. It's kind of fun to think about that, when I'm not crying."

Bushnell suggested that Jobs try Don Valentine, a straight-shooting former marketing manager at National Semiconductor who had founded Sequoia Capital, a pioneering venture capital firm. Valentine arrived at the Jobses' garage in a Mercedes wearing a blue suit, button-down shirt, and rep tie. His first impression was that Jobs looked and smelled odd. "Steve was trying to be the embodiment of the counter-culture. He had a wispy beard, was very thin, and looked like Ho Chi Minh."

Valentine, however, did not become a preeminent Silicon Valley investor by relying on surface appearances. What bothered him more was that Jobs knew nothing about marketing and seemed content to peddle his product to individual stores one by one. "If you want me to finance you," Valentine told him, "you need to have one person as a partner who understands marketing and distribution and can write a business plan." Jobs tended to be either bristly or solicitous when older people offered him advice. With Valentine he was the latter. "Send me three suggestions," he replied. Valentine did, Jobs met them, and he clicked with one of them, a man named Mike Markkula, who would end up playing a critical role at Apple for the next two decades.

Markkula was only thirty-three, but he had already retired after working at Fairchild and then Intel, where he made millions on his stock options when the chip maker went public. He was a cautious and shrewd man, with the precise moves of someone who had been a gymnast in high school, and he excelled at figuring out pricing strategies, distribution networks, marketing, and finance. Despite being slightly reserved, he had a flashy side when it came to enjoying his newly minted wealth. He built himself a house in Lake Tahoe and later an outsize mansion in the hills of Woodside. When he showed up for his first meeting at Jobs's garage, he was driving not a dark Mercedes like Valentine, but a highly polished gold Corvette convertible. "When I arrived at the garage, Woz was at the workbench and immediately began showing off the Apple II," Markkula recalled. "I looked past the fact that both guys needed a haircut and was amazed by what I saw on that workbench. You can always get a haircut."

Jobs immediately liked Markkula. "He was short and he had been passed over for the top marketing job at Intel, which I suspect made him want to prove himself." He also struck Jobs as decent and fair. "You could tell that if he could screw you, he wouldn't. He had a real moral sense to him." Wozniak was equally impressed. "I thought he was the nicest person ever," he recalled. "Better still, he actually liked what we had!"

Markkula proposed to Jobs that they write a business plan together. "If it comes out well, I'll invest," Markkula said, "and if not, you've got a few weeks of my time for free." Jobs began going to Markkula's house in the evenings, kicking around projections and talking through the night. "We made a lot of assumptions, such as about how many houses would have a personal computer, and there were nights we were up until 4 a.m.," Jobs recalled. Markkula ended up writing most of the plan. "Steve would say, 'I will bring you this section next time,' but he usually didn't deliver on time, so I ended up doing it."

Markkula's plan envisioned ways of getting beyond the hobbyist market. "He talked about introducing the computer to regular people in regular homes, doing things like keeping track of your favorite recipes or balancing your checkbook," Wozniak recalled. Markkula made a wild prediction: "We're going to be a Fortune 500 company in two years," he said. "This is the start of an industry. It happens once in a decade." It would take Apple seven years to break into the Fortune 500, but the spirit of Markkula's prediction turned out to be true.

Markkula offered to guarantee a line of credit of up to $250,000 in return for being made a one-third equity participant. Apple would incorporate, and he along with Jobs and Wozniak would each own 26% of the stock. The rest would be reserved to attract future investors. The three met in the cabana by Markkula's swimming pool and sealed the deal. "I thought it was unlikely that Mike would ever see that $250,000 again, and I was impressed that he was willing to risk it," Jobs recalled.

Now it was necessary to convince Wozniak to come on board full-time. "Why can't I keep doing this on the side and just have HP as my secure job for life?" he asked. Markkula said that wouldn't work, and he gave Wozniak a deadline of a few days to decide. "I felt very insecure in starting a company where I would be expected to push people around and control what they did," Wozniak recalled. "I'd decided long ago that I would never become someone authoritative." So he went to Markkula's cabana and announced that he was not leaving HP.

Markkula shrugged and said okay. But Jobs got very upset. He cajoled Wozniak; he got friends to try to convince him; he cried, yelled, and threw a couple of fits. He even went to Wozniak's parents' house, burst into tears, and asked Jerry for help. By this point Wozniak's father had realized there was real money to be made by capitalizing on the Apple II, and he joined forces on Jobs's behalf. "I started getting phone calls at work and home from my dad, my mom, my brother, and various friends," Wozniak recalled. "Every one of them told me I'd made the wrong decision." None of that worked. Then Allen Baum, their Buck Fry Club mate at Homestead High, called. "You really ought to go ahead and do it," he said. He argued that if he joined Apple full-time, he would not have to go into management or give up being an engineer. "That was exactly what I needed to hear," Wozniak later said. "I could stay at the bottom of the organization chart, as an engineer." He called Jobs and declared that he was now ready to come on board.

On January 3, 1977, the new corporation, the Apple Computer Co., was officially created, and it bought out the old partnership that had been formed by Jobs and Wozniak nine months earlier. Few people noticed. That month the Homebrew surveyed its members and found that, of the 181 who owned personal computers, only six owned an Apple. Jobs was convinced, however, that the Apple II would change that.

Markkula would become a father figure to Jobs. Like Jobs's adoptive father, he would indulge Jobs's strong will, and like his biological father, he would end up abandoning him. "Markkula was as much a father-son relationship as Steve ever had," said the venture capitalist Arthur Rock. He began to teach Jobs about marketing and sales. "Mike really took me under his wing," Jobs recalled. "His values were much aligned with mine. He emphasized that you should never start a company with the goal of getting rich. Your goal should be making something you believe in and making a company that will last."

Markkula wrote his principles in a one-page paper titled "The Apple Marketing Philosophy" that stressed three points. The first was *empathy*, an intimate connection with the feelings of the customer: "We will truly understand their needs better than any other company." The second was *focus*: "In order to do a good job of those things that we decide to do, we must eliminate all of the unimportant opportunities." The third and equally important principle, awkwardly named, was *impute*. It emphasized that people form an opinion about a company or product based on the signals that it conveys. "People *DO* judge a book by its cover," he wrote. "We may have the best product, the highest quality, the most useful software etc.; if we present them in a slipshod manner, they will be perceived as slipshod; if we present them in a creative, professional manner, we will *impute* the desired qualities."

For the rest of his career, Jobs would understand the needs and desires of customers better than any other business leader, he would focus on a handful of core products, and he would care, sometimes obsessively, about marketing and image and even the details of packaging. "When you open the box of an iPhone or iPad, we want that tactile experience to set the tone for how you perceive the product," he said. "Mike taught me that."

Regis McKenna

The first step in this process was convincing the Valley's premier publicist, Regis McKenna, to take on Apple as a client. McKenna was from a large working-class Pittsburgh family, and bred into his bones was a steeliness that he cloaked with charm. A college dropout, he had worked for Fairchild and National Semiconductor before starting his own PR and advertising firm. His two specialties were doling out exclusive interviews with his clients to journalists he had cultivated and coming up with memorable ad campaigns that created brand awareness for products such as microchips. One of these was a series of colorful magazine ads for Intel that featured racing cars and poker chips rather than the usual dull performance charts. These caught Jobs's eye. He called Intel and asked who created them. "Regis McKenna," he was told. "I asked them what Regis McKenna was," Jobs recalled, "and they told me he was a person." When Jobs phoned, he couldn't get through to McKenna. Instead he was transferred to Frank Burge, an account executive, who tried to put him off. Jobs called back almost every day.

Burge finally agreed to drive out to the Jobs garage. "Holy Christ, this guy is going to be something else," he recalled thinking. "What's the least amount of time I can spend with this clown without being rude." Then, when he was confronted with the unwashed and shaggy Jobs, two things hit him: "First, he was an incredibly smart young man. Second, I didn't understand a fiftieth of what he was talking about."

So Jobs and Wozniak were invited to have a meeting with, as his impish business cards read, "Regis McKenna, himself." This time it was the normally shy Wozniak who became prickly. McKenna glanced at an article Wozniak was writing about Apple and suggested that it was too technical and needed to be livened up. "I don't want any PR man touching my copy," Wozniak snapped. McKenna suggested it was time for them to leave his office. "But Steve called me back right away and said he wanted to meet again," McKenna recalled. "This time he came without Woz, and we hit it off."

McKenna had his team get to work on brochures for the Apple II. The first thing they did was to replace Ron Wayne's ornate Victorian woodcut-style logo, which ran counter to McKenna's colorful and playful advertising style. So an art director, Rob Janoff, was assigned to create a new one. "Don't make it cute," Jobs ordered. Janoff came up with a simple apple shape in two versions, one whole and the other with a bite taken out of it. The first looked too much like a cherry, so Jobs chose the one with a bite. He also picked a version that was striped in six colors, with psychedelic hues sandwiched between whole-earth green and sky blue, even though that made printing the logo significantly more expensive. Atop the brochure McKenna put a maxim, often attributed to Leonardo da Vinci, that would become the defining precept of Jobs's design philosophy: "Simplicity is the ultimate sophistication."

The First Launch Event

The introduction of the Apple II was scheduled to coincide with the first West Coast Computer Faire, to be held in April 1977 in San Francisco, organized by a Homebrew stalwart, Jim Warren. Jobs signed Apple up for a booth as soon as he got the information packet. He wanted to secure a location right at the front of the hall as a dramatic way to launch the Apple II, and so he shocked Wozniak by paying $5,000 in advance. "Steve decided that this was our big launch," said Wozniak. "We would show the world we had a great machine and a great company."

It was an application of Markkula's admonition that it was important to "impute" your greatness by making a memorable impression on people, especially when launching a new product. That was reflected in the care that Jobs took with Apple's display area. Other exhibitors had card tables and poster board signs. Apple had a counter draped in black velvet and a large pane of backlit Plexiglas with Janoff's new logo. They put on display the only three Apple IIs that had been finished, but empty boxes were piled up to give the impression that there were many more on hand.

Jobs was furious that the computer cases had arrived with tiny blemishes on them, so he had his handful of employees sand and polish them. The imputing even extended to gussying up Jobs and Wozniak. Markkula sent them to a San Francisco tailor for three-piece suits, which looked faintly ridiculous on them, like tuxes on teenagers. "Markkula explained how we would all have to dress up nicely, how we should appear and look, how we should act," Wozniak recalled.

It was worth the effort. The Apple II looked solid yet friendly in its sleek beige case, unlike the intimidating metal-clad machines and naked boards on the other tables. Apple got three hundred orders at the show, and Jobs met a Japanese textile maker, Mizushima Satoshi, who became Apple's first dealer in Japan.

The fancy clothes and Markkula's injunctions could not, however, stop the irrepressible Wozniak from playing some practical jokes. One program that he displayed tried to guess people's nationality from their last name and then produced the relevant ethnic jokes. He also created and distributed a hoax brochure for a new computer called the "Zaltair," with all sorts of fake ad-copy superlatives like "Imagine a car with five wheels." Jobs briefly fell for the joke and even took pride that the Apple II stacked up well against the Zaltair in the comparison chart. He didn't realize who had pulled the prank until eight years later, when Woz gave him a framed copy of the brochure as a birthday gift.

Mike Scott

Apple was now a real company, with a dozen employees, a line of credit, and the daily pressures that can come from customers and suppliers. It had even moved out of the Jobses' garage, finally, into a rented office on Stevens Creek Boulevard in Cupertino, about a mile from where Jobs and Wozniak went to high school.

Jobs did not wear his growing responsibilities gracefully. He had always been temperamental and bratty. At Atari his behavior had caused him to be banished to the night shift, but at Apple that was not possible. "He became increasingly tyrannical and sharp in his criticism," according to Markkula. "He would tell people, 'That design looks like shit.'" He was particularly rough on Wozniak's young programmers, Randy Wigginton and Chris Espinosa. "Steve would come in, take a quick look at what I had done, and tell me it was shit without having any idea what it was or why I had done it," said Wigginton, who was just out of high school.

There was also the issue of his hygiene. He was still convinced, against all evidence, that his vegan diets meant that he didn't need to use a deodorant or take regular showers. "We would have to literally put him out the door and tell him to go take a shower," said Markkula. "At meetings we had to look at his dirty feet." Sometimes, to relieve stress, he would soak his feet in the toilet, a practice that was not as soothing for his colleagues.

Markkula was averse to confrontation, so he decided to bring in a president, Mike Scott, to keep a tighter rein on Jobs. Markkula and Scott had joined Fairchild on the same day in 1967, had adjoining offices, and shared the same birthday, which they celebrated together each year. At their birthday lunch in February 1977, when Scott was turning thirty-two, Markkula invited him to become Apple's new president.

On paper he looked like a great choice. He was running a manufacturing line for National Semiconductor, and he had the advantage of being a manager who fully understood engineering. In person, however, he had some quirks. He was overweight, afflicted with tics and health problems, and so tightly wound that he wandered the halls with clenched fists. He also could be argumentative. In dealing with Jobs, that could be good or bad.

Wozniak quickly embraced the idea of hiring Scott. Like Markkula, he hated dealing with the conflicts that Jobs engendered. Jobs, not surprisingly, had more conflicted emotions. "I was only twenty-two, and I knew I wasn't ready to run a real company," he said. "But Apple was my baby, and I didn't want to give it up." Relinquishing any control was agonizing to him. He wrestled with the issue over long lunches at Bob's Big Boy hamburgers (Woz's favorite place) and at the Good Earth restaurant (Jobs's). He finally acquiesced, reluctantly.

Mike Scott, called "Scotty" to distinguish him from Mike Markkula, had one primary duty: managing Jobs. This was usually accomplished by Jobs's preferred mode of meeting, which was taking a walk together. "My very first walk was to tell him to bathe more often,"

Scott recalled. "He said that in exchange I had to read his fruitarian diet book and consider it as a way to lose weight." Scott never adopted the diet or lost much weight, and Jobs made only minor modifications to his hygiene. "Steve was adamant that he bathed once a week, and that was adequate as long as he was eating a fruitarian diet."

Jobs's desire for control and disdain for authority was destined to be a problem with the man who was brought in to be his regent, especially when Jobs discovered that Scott was one of the only people he had yet encountered who would not bend to his will. "The question between Steve and me was who could be most stubborn, and I was pretty good at that," Scott said. "He needed to be sat on, and he sure didn't like that." Jobs later said, "I never yelled at anyone more than I yelled at Scotty."

An early showdown came over employee badge numbers. Scott assigned #1 to Wozniak and #2 to Jobs. Not surprisingly, Jobs demanded to be #1. "I wouldn't let him have it, because that would stoke his ego even more," said Scott. Jobs threw a tantrum, even cried. Finally, he proposed a solution. He would have badge #0. Scott relented, at least for the purpose of the badge, but the Bank of America required a positive integer for its payroll system and Jobs's remained #2.

There was a more fundamental disagreement that went beyond personal petulance. Jay Elliot, who was hired by Jobs after a chance meeting in a restaurant, noted Jobs's salient trait: "His obsession is a passion for the product, a passion for product perfection." Mike Scott, on the other hand, never let a passion for the perfect take precedence over pragmatism. The design of the Apple II case was one of many examples. The Pantone company, which Apple used to specify colors for its plastic, had more than two thousand shades of beige. "None of them were good enough for Steve," Scott marveled. "He wanted to create a different shade, and I had to stop him." When the time came to tweak the design of the case, Jobs spent days agonizing over just how rounded the corners should be. "I didn't care how rounded they were," said Scott, "I just wanted it decided." Another dispute was over engineering benches. Scott wanted a standard gray; Jobs insisted on special-order benches that were pure white. All of this finally led to a showdown in front of Markkula about whether Jobs or Scott had the power to sign purchase orders; Markkula sided with Scott. Jobs also insisted that Apple be different in how it treated customers. He wanted a one-year warranty to come with the Apple II. This flabbergasted Scott; the usual warranty was ninety days. Again Jobs dissolved into tears during one of their arguments over the issue. They walked around the parking lot to calm down, and Scott decided to relent on this one.

Wozniak began to rankle at Jobs's style. "Steve was too tough on people. I wanted our company to feel like a family where we all had fun and shared whatever we made." Jobs, for his part, felt that Wozniak simply would not grow up. "He was very childlike. He did a great version of BASIC, but then never could buckle down and write the floating-point BASIC we needed, so we ended up later having to make a deal with Microsoft. He was just too unfocused."

But for the time being the personality clashes were manageable, mainly because the company was doing so well. Ben Rosen, the analyst whose newsletters shaped the opinions of the tech world, became an enthusiastic proselytizer for the Apple II. An independent developer came up with the first spreadsheet and personal finance program for personal computers, VisiCalc, and for a while it was available only on the Apple II, turning the computer into something that businesses and families could justify buying. The company began attracting influential new investors. The pioneering venture capitalist Arthur Rock had initially been unimpressed when Markkula sent Jobs to see him. "He looked as if he had just come back from seeing that guru he had in India," Rock recalled, "and he kind of smelled that way too." But after Rock scoped out the Apple II, he made an investment and joined the board.

The Apple II would be marketed, in various models, for the next sixteen years, with close to six million sold. More than any other machine, it launched the personal computer industry. Wozniak deserves the historic credit for the design of its awe-inspiring circuit board and related operating software, which was one of the era's great feats of solo invention. But Jobs was the one who integrated Wozniak's boards into a friendly package, from the power supply to the sleek case. He also created the company that sprang up around Wozniak's machines.

As Regis McKenna later said, "Woz designed a great machine, but it would be sitting in hobby shops today were it not for Steve Jobs." Nevertheless most people considered the Apple II to be Wozniak's creation. That would spur Jobs to pursue the next great advance, one that he could call his own.

CHAPTER SEVEN

CHRISANN AND LISA

He Who Is Abandoned . . .

Ever since they had lived together in a cabin during the summer after he graduated from high school, Chrisann Brennan had woven in and out of Jobs's life. When he returned from India in 1974, they spent time together at Robert Friedland's farm. "Steve invited me up there, and we were just young and easy and free," she recalled. "There was an energy there that went to my heart."

When they moved back to Los Altos, their relationship drifted into being, for the most part, merely friendly. He lived at home and worked at Atari; she had a small apartment and spent a lot of time at Kobun Chino's Zen center. By early 1975 she had begun a relationship with a mutual friend, Greg Calhoun. "She was with Greg, but went back to Steve occasionally," according to Elizabeth Holmes. "That was pretty much the way it was with all of us." Chrisann said that she was involved with Steve and Greg, but never at the same time.

Calhoun had been at Reed with Jobs, Friedland, Kottke, and Holmes. Like the others, he became deeply involved with Eastern spirituality, dropped out of Reed, and found his way to Friedland's farm. There he moved into an eight- by twenty-foot chicken coop that he converted into a little house by raising it onto cinderblocks and building a sleeping loft inside. In the spring of 1975 Brennan moved in with him, and the next year they decided to make their own pilgrimage to India. Jobs advised Calhoun not to take Brennan with him, saying that she would interfere with his spiritual quest, but they went together anyway. "I was just so impressed by what happened to Steve on his trip to India that I wanted to go there," she said.

Theirs was a serious trip, beginning in March 1976 and lasting almost a year. At one point they ran out of money, so Calhoun hitchhiked to Iran to teach English in Tehran. Brennan stayed in India, and when Calhoun's teaching stint was over they traveled to meet each other in the middle, in Afghanistan. The world was a very different place back then.

After a while their relationship frayed, and they returned from India separately. By the summer of 1977 Brennan had moved back to Los Altos, where she lived for a while in a cabin on the grounds of Kobun Chino's Zen center. By this time Jobs had moved out of his parents' house and was renting a $600 per month suburban ranch house in Cupertino with Daniel Kottke. It was an odd scene of free-spirited hippie types living in a tract house they dubbed Rancho Suburbia. "It was a four-bedroom house, and we occasionally rented one of the bedrooms out to all sorts of crazy people, including a stripper for a while," recalled Jobs. Kottke couldn't quite figure out why Jobs had not just gotten his own house, which he could have afforded by then. "I think he just wanted to have a roommate," Kottke speculated.

Even though her relationship with Jobs was sporadic, Brennan soon moved in as well. "Steve and I wanted to live together," Chrisann recalled despite the fact that "we were leery about doing so because some very real things were not working out between us." The house had two big bedrooms and two tiny ones. Jobs, not surprisingly, commandeered the largest of them, and Brennan (who was not really living with him) moved into the other big bedroom. "The two middle rooms were like for babies, and I didn't want either of them, so I moved into the living room and slept on a foam pad," said Kottke. They turned one of the small rooms into space for meditating. It was filled with foam packing material from Apple boxes. "Neighborhood kids used to come over and we would toss them in it and it was great fun," said Kottke, "but then some cats peed in the foam, and we had to get rid of it."

Living in the house at times rekindled the physical relationship between Brennan and Jobs, and within a few months she was pregnant. "Steve and I were in and out of a relationship for five years before I got pregnant," she said. "We didn't know how to be together and we didn't know how to be apart." When Greg Calhoun hitchhiked from Colorado to visit them on Thanksgiving 1977, Brennan told him the news: "Steve and I got back together, and now I'm pregnant, but now we are on again and off again, and I don't know what to do."

Calhoun noticed that Jobs was disconnected from the whole situation. He even tried to convince Calhoun to stay with them and come to work at Apple. "Steve was just not dealing with Chrisann or the pregnancy," he recalled. "He could be very engaged with you in one moment, but then very disengaged. There was a side to him that was frighteningly cold."

When Jobs did not want to deal with a distraction, he sometimes just ignored it, as if he could will it out of existence. At times he was able to distort reality not just for others but even for himself. In the case of Brennan's pregnancy, he simply shut it out of his mind. When confronted, he would say that he didn't know if he was the father, even though he admitted that he had been sleeping with her. "I wasn't sure it was my kid, because I was pretty sure I wasn't the only one she was sleeping with," he told me later. "She and I were not really even going out when she got pregnant. She just had a room in our house." Brennan had no doubt that Jobs was the father. She had not been involved with Greg or any other men at the time.

Was he lying to himself, or did he not know that he was the father? "I just think he couldn't access that part of his brain or the idea of being responsible," Kottke said. Elizabeth Holmes agreed: "He considered the option of parenthood and considered the option of not being a parent, and he decided to believe the latter. He had other plans for his life."

There was no discussion of marriage. "I knew that she was not the person I wanted to marry, and we would never be happy, and it wouldn't last long," Jobs later said. "I was all in favor of her getting an abortion, but she didn't know what to do. She thought about it repeatedly and decided not to, or I don't know that she ever really decided—I think time just decided for her." Brennan told me that it was her choice to have the baby: "He said he was fine with an abortion but never pushed for it." Interestingly, given his own background, he was adamantly against one option. "He strongly discouraged me putting the child up for adoption," she said.

There was a disturbing irony. Jobs and Brennan were both twenty-three, the same age that Joanne Schieble and Abdulfattah Jandali had been when they had Jobs. He had not yet tracked down his biological parents, but his adoptive parents had told him some of their tale. "I didn't know then about this coincidence of our ages, so it didn't affect my discussions with Chrisann," he later said. He dismissed the notion that he was somehow following his biological father's pattern of his girlfriend becoming pregnant when he was twenty-three, but he did admit that the ironic resonance gave him pause. "When I did find out that he was twenty-three when he got Joanne pregnant with me, I thought, whoa!"

The relationship between Jobs and Brennan quickly deteriorated. "Chrisann would get into this kind of victim mode, when she would say that Steve and I were ganging up on her," Kottke recalled. "Steve would just laugh and not take her seriously." Brennan was not, as even she later admitted, very emotionally stable. At one point she threw plates "as an expression of how terrible it had become between us." She said that Jobs kept provoking her with his callousness: "He was an enlightened being who was cruel." Kottke was caught in the middle. "Daniel didn't have that DNA of ruthlessness, so he was a bit flipped by Steve's behavior," according to Brennan. "He would go from 'Steve's not treating you right' to laughing at me with Steve."

Robert Friedland and his wife came to her rescue. "He heard that I was pregnant, and he said to come on up to their farm to have the baby," she recalled. "So I did." The Friedlands found an Oregon midwife to help with the delivery. On May 17, 1978, Brennan gave birth to a baby girl. Three days later Jobs flew up to be with them and help name the new baby. The practice on the commune was to give children Eastern spiritual names, but Steve and Chrisann insisted that she had been born in America and ought to have a name that fit.

They named her Lisa Nicole Brennan, and until she was nine she did not have the last name Jobs. And then he left to go back to work at Apple. "He didn't want to have anything to do with her or with me," said Brennan.

She and Lisa moved to a tiny, dilapidated house in back of a home in Menlo Park. They lived on welfare because Brennan did not feel up to suing for child support. Finally, the County of San Mateo sued Jobs to try to prove paternity and get him to take financial responsibility. At first Jobs was determined to fight the case. His lawyers wanted Kottke to testify that he had never seen them in bed together, and they tried to line up evidence that Brennan had been sleeping with other men. "At one point I yelled at Steve on the phone, 'You know that is not true,'" Brennan recalled. "He was going to drag me through court with a little baby and try to prove I was a whore and that anyone could have been the father of that baby."

A year after Lisa was born, Jobs agreed to take a paternity test. Brennan says he was legally forced to do so. In any event, Jobs knew that Apple would soon be going public and he decided it was best to get the issue resolved. DNA tests were new, and the one that Jobs took was done at UCLA. "I had read about DNA testing, and I was happy to do it to get things settled," he said. The results were pretty dispositive. "Probability of paternity . . . is 94.41%," the report read. The California courts ordered Jobs to start paying $385 a month in child support, sign an agreement admitting paternity, and reimburse the county $5,856 in back welfare payments. He was given visitation rights but for a long time didn't exercise them.

Even then Jobs continued at times to warp the reality around him. "He finally told us on the board," Arthur Rock recalled, "but he kept insisting that there was a large probability that he wasn't the father. He was delusional." He told a reporter for *Time*, Michael Moritz, that when you analyzed the statistics, it was clear that "28% of the male population in the United States could be the father." It was not only a false claim but an odd one. Worse yet, when Chrisann Brennan later heard what he said, she mistakenly thought that Jobs was hyperbolically claiming that she might have slept with 28% of the men in the United States. "He was trying to paint me as a slut or a whore," she recalled. "He spun the whore image onto me in order to not take responsibility."

Years later Jobs was remorseful for the way he behaved, one of the few times in his life he admitted as much:

> I wish I had handled it differently. I could not see myself as a father then, so I didn't face up to it. But when the test results showed she was my daughter, it's not true that I doubted it. I agreed to support her until she was eighteen and give some money to Chrisann as well. I found a house in Palo Alto and fixed it up and let them live there rent-free. Her mother found her great schools which I paid for. I tried to do the right thing. But if I could do it over, I would do a better job.

Once the case was resolved, Jobs began to move on with his life—maturing in some respects, though not all. He put aside drugs, eased away from being a strict vegan, and cut back the time he spent on Zen retreats. He began getting stylish haircuts and buying suits and shirts from the upscale San Francisco haberdashery Wilkes Bashford. And he settled into a serious relationship with one of Regis McKenna's employees, a beautiful Polynesian-Polish woman named Barbara Jasinski.

There was still, to be sure, a childlike rebellious streak in him. He, Jasinski, and Kottke liked to go skinny-dipping in Felt Lake on the edge of Interstate 280 near Stanford, and he bought a 1966 BMW R60/2 motorcycle that he adorned with orange tassels on the handlebars. He could also still be bratty. He belittled waitresses and frequently returned food with the proclamation that it was "garbage." At the company's first Halloween party, in 1979, he dressed in robes as Jesus Christ, an act of semi-ironic self-awareness that he considered funny but that caused a lot of eye rolling. Even his initial stirrings of domesticity had some quirks. He bought a proper house in the Los Gatos hills, which he adorned with a Maxfield Parrish painting, a Braun coffeemaker, and Henckels knives. But because he was so obsessive when it came to selecting furnishings, it remained mostly barren, lacking beds or chairs or couches. Instead his bedroom had a mattress in the center, framed pictures of Einstein and Maharaj-ji on the walls, and an Apple II on the floor.

CHAPTER EIGHT

XEROX AND LISA

Graphical User Interfaces

A New Baby

The Apple II took the company from Jobs's garage to the pinnacle of a new industry. Its sales rose dramatically, from 2,500 units in 1977 to 210,000 in 1981. But Jobs was restless. The Apple II could not remain successful forever, and he knew that, no matter how much he had done to package it, from power cord to case, it would always be seen as Wozniak's masterpiece. He needed his own machine. More than that, he wanted a product that would, in his words, make a dent in the universe.

At first he hoped that the Apple III would play that role. It would have more memory, the screen would display eighty characters across rather than forty, and it would handle uppercase and lowercase letters. Indulging his passion for industrial design, Jobs decreed the size and shape of the external case, and he refused to let anyone alter it, even as committees of engineers added more components to the circuit boards. The result was piggybacked boards with poor connectors that frequently failed. When the Apple III began shipping in May 1980, it flopped. Randy Wigginton, one of the engineers, summed it up: "The Apple III was kind of like a baby conceived during a group orgy, and later everybody had this bad headache, and there's this bastard child, and everyone says, 'It's not mine.'"

By then Jobs had distanced himself from the Apple III and was thrashing about for ways to produce something more radically different. At first he flirted with the idea of touchscreens, but he found himself frustrated. At one demonstration of the technology, he arrived late, fidgeted awhile, then abruptly cut off the engineers in the middle of their presentation with a brusque "Thank you." They were confused. "Would you like us to leave?" one asked. Jobs said yes, then berated his colleagues for wasting his time.

Then he and Apple hired two engineers from Hewlett-Packard to conceive a totally new computer. The name Jobs chose for it would have caused even the most jaded psychiatrist to do a double take: the Lisa. Other computers had been named after daughters of their designers, but Lisa was a daughter Jobs had abandoned and had not yet fully admitted was his. "Maybe he was doing it out of guilt," said Andrea Cunningham, who worked at Regis McKenna on public relations for the project. "We had to come up with an acronym so that we could claim it was not named after Lisa the child." The one they reverse-engineered was "local integrated systems architecture," and despite being meaningless it became the official explanation for the name. Among the engineers it was referred to as "Lisa: invented stupid acronym." Years later, when I asked about the name, Jobs admitted simply, "Obviously it was named for my daughter."

The Lisa was conceived as a $2,000 machine based on a sixteen-bit microprocessor, rather than the eight-bit one used in the Apple II. Without the wizardry of Wozniak, who was still working quietly on the Apple II, the engineers began producing a straightforward computer with a conventional text display, unable to push the powerful microprocessor to do much exciting stuff. Jobs began to grow impatient with how boring it was turning out to be.

There was, however, one programmer who was infusing the project with some life: Bill Atkinson. He was a doctoral student in neuroscience who had experimented with his fair share of acid. When he was asked to come work for Apple, he declined. But then Apple sent him a nonrefundable plane ticket, and he decided to use it and let Jobs try to persuade him. "We are inventing the future," Jobs told him at the end of a three-hour pitch. "Think about surfing on the front edge of a wave. It's really exhilarating. Now think about dog-paddling at the tail end of that wave. It wouldn't be anywhere near as much fun. Come down here and make a dent in the universe." Atkinson did.

With his shaggy hair and droopy moustache that did not hide the animation in his face, Atkinson had some of Woz's ingenuity along with Jobs's passion for awesome products. His first job was to develop a program to track a stock portfolio by auto-dialing the Dow Jones service, getting quotes, then hanging up. "I had to create it fast because there was a magazine ad for the Apple II showing a hubby at the kitchen table looking at an Apple screen filled with graphs of stock prices, and his wife is beaming at him—but there wasn't such a program, so I had to create one." Next he created for the Apple II a version of Pascal, a high-level programming language. Jobs had resisted, thinking that BASIC was all the Apple II needed, but he told Atkinson, "Since you're so passionate about it, I'll give you six days to prove me wrong." He did, and Jobs respected him ever after.

By the fall of 1979 Apple was breeding three ponies to be potential successors to the Apple II workhorse. There was the ill-fated Apple III. There was the Lisa project, which was beginning to disappoint Jobs. And somewhere off Jobs's radar screen, at least for the moment, there was a small skunkworks project for a low-cost machine that was being developed by a colorful employee named Jef Raskin, a former professor who had taught Bill Atkinson. Raskin's goal was to make an inexpensive "computer for the masses" that would be like an appliance—a self-contained unit with computer, keyboard, monitor, and software all together—and have a graphical interface. He tried to turn his colleagues at Apple on to a cutting-edge research center, right in Palo Alto, that was pioneering such ideas.

Xerox PARC

The Xerox Corporation's Palo Alto Research Center, known as Xerox PARC, had been established in 1970 to create a spawning ground for digital ideas. It was safely located, for better and for worse, three thousand miles from the commercial pressures of Xerox corporate headquarters in Connecticut. Among its visionaries was the scientist Alan Kay, who had two great maxims that Jobs embraced: "The best way to predict the future is to invent it" and "People who are serious about software should make their own hardware." Kay pushed the vision of a small personal computer, dubbed the "Dynabook," that would be easy enough for children to use. So Xerox PARC's engineers began to develop user-friendly graphics that could replace all of the command lines and DOS prompts that made computer screens intimidating. The metaphor they came up with was that of a desktop. The screen could have many documents and folders on it, and you could use a mouse to point and click on the one you wanted to use.

This graphical user interface—or GUI, pronounced "gooey"—was facilitated by another concept pioneered at Xerox PARC: bitmapping. Until then, most computers were character-based. You would type a character on a keyboard, and the computer would generate that character on the screen, usually in glowing greenish phosphor against a dark background. Since there were a limited number of letters, numerals, and symbols, it didn't take a whole lot of computer code or processing power to accomplish this. In a bitmap system, on the other hand, each and every pixel on the screen is controlled by bits in the computer's memory. To render something on the screen, such as a letter, the computer has to tell each pixel to be light or dark or, in the case of color displays, what color to be. This uses a lot of computing power, but it permits gorgeous graphics, fonts, and gee-whiz screen displays.

Bitmapping and graphical interfaces became features of Xerox PARC's prototype computers, such as the Alto, and its object-oriented programming language, Smalltalk. Jef Raskin decided that these features were the future of computing. So he began urging Jobs and other Apple colleagues to go check out Xerox PARC.

Raskin had one problem: Jobs regarded him as an insufferable theorist or, to use Jobs's own more precise terminology, "a shithead who sucks." So Raskin enlisted his friend Atkinson, who fell on the other side of Jobs's shithead/genius division of the world, to convince Jobs to take an interest in what was happening at Xerox PARC. What

Raskin didn't know was that Jobs was working on a more complex deal. Xerox's venture capital division wanted to be part of the second round of Apple financing during the summer of 1979. Jobs made an offer: "I will let you invest a million dollars in Apple if you will open the kimono at PARC." Xerox accepted. It agreed to show Apple its new technology and in return got to buy 100,000 shares at about $10 each.

By the time Apple went public a year later, Xerox's $1 million worth of shares were worth $17.6 million. But Apple got the better end of the bargain. Jobs and his colleagues went to see Xerox PARC's technology in December 1979 and, when Jobs realized he hadn't been shown enough, got an even fuller demonstration a few days later. Larry Tesler was one of the Xerox scientists called upon to do the briefings, and he was thrilled to show off the work that his bosses back east had never seemed to appreciate. But the other briefer, Adele Goldberg, was appalled that her company seemed willing to give away its crown jewels. "It was incredibly stupid, completely nuts, and I fought to prevent giving Jobs much of anything," she recalled.

Goldberg got her way at the first briefing. Jobs, Raskin, and the Lisa team leader John Couch were ushered into the main lobby, where a Xerox Alto had been set up. "It was a very controlled show of a few applications, primarily a word-processing one," Goldberg said. Jobs wasn't satisfied, and he called Xerox headquarters demanding more.

So he was invited back a few days later, and this time he brought a larger team that included Bill Atkinson and Bruce Horn, an Apple programmer who had worked at Xerox PARC. They both knew what to look for. "When I arrived at work, there was a lot of commotion, and I was told that Jobs and a bunch of his programmers were in the conference room," said Goldberg. One of her engineers was trying to keep them entertained with more displays of the word-processing program. But Jobs was growing impatient. "Let's stop this bullshit!" he kept shouting. So the Xerox folks huddled privately and decided to open the kimono a bit more, but only slowly. They agreed that Tesler could show off Smalltalk, the programming language, but he would demonstrate only what was known as the "unclassified" version. "It will dazzle [Jobs] and he'll never know he didn't get the confidential disclosure," the head of the team told Goldberg.

They were wrong. Atkinson and others had read some of the papers published by Xerox PARC, so they knew they were not getting a full description. Jobs phoned the head of the Xerox venture capital division to complain; a call immediately came back from corporate headquarters in Connecticut decreeing that Jobs and his group should be shown everything. Goldberg stormed out in a rage.

When Tesler finally showed them what was truly under the hood, the Apple folks were astonished. Atkinson stared at the screen, examining each pixel so closely that Tesler could feel the breath on his neck. Jobs bounced around and waved his arms excitedly. "He was hopping around so much I don't know how he actually saw most of the demo, but he did, because he kept asking questions," Tesler recalled. "He was the exclamation point for every step I showed." Jobs kept saying that he couldn't believe that Xerox had not commercialized the technology. "You're sitting on a gold mine," he shouted. "I can't believe Xerox is not taking advantage of this."

The Smalltalk demonstration showed three amazing features. One was how computers could be networked; the second was how object-oriented programming worked. But Jobs and his team paid little attention to these attributes because they were so amazed by the third feature, the graphical interface that was made possible by a bitmapped screen. "It was like a veil being lifted from my eyes," Jobs recalled. "I could see what the future of computing was destined to be."

When the Xerox PARC meeting ended after more than two hours, Jobs drove Bill Atkinson back to the Apple office in Cupertino. He was speeding, and so were his mind and mouth. "This is it!" he shouted, emphasizing each word. "We've got to do it!" It was the breakthrough he had been looking for: bringing computers to the people, with the cheerful but affordable design of an Eichler home and the ease of use of a sleek kitchen appliance.

"How long would this take to implement?" he asked.

"I'm not sure," Atkinson replied. "Maybe six months." It was a wildly optimistic assessment, but also a motivating one.

"Great Artists Steal"

The Apple raid on Xerox PARC is sometimes described as one of the biggest heists in the chronicles of industry. Jobs occasionally endorsed this view, with pride. As he once said, "Picasso had a saying—'good artists copy, great artists steal'—and we have always been shameless about stealing great ideas."

Another assessment, also sometimes endorsed by Jobs, is that what transpired was less a heist by Apple than a fumble by Xerox. "They were copier-heads who had no clue about what a computer could do," he said of Xerox's management. "They just grabbed defeat from the greatest victory in the computer industry. Xerox could have owned the entire computer industry."

Both assessments contain a lot of truth, but there is more to it than that. There falls a shadow, as T. S. Eliot noted, between the conception and the creation. In the annals of innovation, new ideas are only part of the equation. Execution is just as important.

Jobs and his engineers significantly improved the graphical interface ideas they saw at Xerox PARC, and then were able to implement them in ways that Xerox never could accomplish. For example, the Xerox mouse had three buttons, was complicated, cost $300 apiece, and didn't roll around smoothly; a few days after his second Xerox PARC visit, Jobs went to a local industrial design firm, IDEO, and told one of its founders, Dean Hovey, that he wanted a simple single-button model that cost $15, "and I want to be able to use it on Formica and my blue jeans." Hovey complied.

The improvements were in not just the details but the entire concept. The mouse at Xerox PARC could not be used to drag a window around the screen. Apple's engineers devised an interface so you could not only drag windows and files around, you could even drop them into folders. The Xerox system required you to select a command in order to do anything, ranging from resizing a window to changing the extension that located a file. The Apple system transformed the desktop metaphor into virtual reality by allowing you to directly touch, manipulate, drag, and relocate things. And Apple's engineers worked in tandem with its designers—with Jobs spurring them on daily—to improve the desktop concept by adding delightful icons and menus that pulled down from a bar atop each window and the capability to open files and folders with a double click.

It's not as if Xerox executives ignored what their scientists had created at PARC. In fact they did try to capitalize on it, and in the process they showed why good execution is as important as good ideas. In 1981, well before the Apple Lisa or Macintosh, they introduced the Xerox Star, a machine that featured their graphical user interface, mouse, bitmapped display, windows, and desktop metaphor. But it was clunky (it could take minutes to save a large file), costly ($16,595 at retail stores), and aimed mainly at the networked office market. It flopped; only thirty thousand were ever sold.

Jobs and his team went to a Xerox dealer to look at the Star as soon as it was released. But he deemed it so worthless that he told his colleagues they couldn't spend the money to buy one. "We were very relieved," he recalled. "We knew they hadn't done it right, and that we could—at a fraction of the price." A few weeks later he called Bob Belleville, one of the hardware designers on the Xerox Star team. "Everything you've ever done in your life is shit," Jobs said, "so why don't you come work for me?" Belleville did, and so did Larry Tesler.

In his excitement, Jobs began to take over the daily management of the Lisa project, which was being run by John Couch, the former HP engineer. Ignoring Couch, he dealt directly with Atkinson and Tesler to insert his own ideas, especially on Lisa's graphical interface design. "He would call me at all hours, 2 a.m. or 5 a.m.," said Tesler. "I loved it. But it upset my bosses at the Lisa division." Jobs was told to stop making out-of-channel calls. He held himself back for a while, but not for long.

One important showdown occurred when Atkinson decided that the screen should have a white background rather than a dark one. This would allow an attribute that both Atkinson and Jobs wanted: WYSIWYG, pronounced "wiz-ee-wig," an acronym for "What you see is what you get." What you saw on the screen was what you'd get when you printed it out. "The hardware team screamed bloody murder," Atkinson recalled. "They said it would force us to use a phosphor that was a lot less persistent and would flicker more." So Atkinson enlisted Jobs, who came down on his side. The hardware folks grumbled, but then went off and figured it out. "Steve wasn't much of an engineer himself, but he was very good at assessing people's answers. He could tell whether the engineers were defensive or unsure of themselves."

One of Atkinson's amazing feats (which we are so accustomed to nowadays that we rarely marvel at it) was to allow the windows on a screen to overlap so that the "top" one clipped into the ones "below" it. Atkinson made it possible to move these windows around, just like shuffling papers on a desk, with those below becoming visible or hidden as you moved the top ones. Of course, on a computer screen there are no layers of pixels underneath the pixels that you see, so there are no windows actually lurking underneath the ones that appear to be on top. To create the illusion of overlapping windows requires complex coding that involves what are called "regions." Atkinson pushed himself to make this trick work because he thought he had seen this capability during his visit to Xerox PARC. In fact the folks at PARC had never accomplished it, and they later told him they were amazed that he had done so. "I got a feeling for the empowering aspect of naïveté," Atkinson said. "Because I didn't know it couldn't be done, I was enabled to do it." He was working so hard that one morning, in a daze, he drove his Corvette into a parked truck and nearly killed himself. Jobs immediately drove to the hospital to see him. "We were pretty worried about you," he said when Atkinson regained consciousness. Atkinson gave him a pained smile and replied, "Don't worry, I still remember regions."

Jobs also had a passion for smooth scrolling. Documents should not lurch line by line as you scroll through them, but instead should flow. "He was adamant that everything on the interface had a good feeling to the user," Atkinson said. They also wanted a mouse that could easily move the cursor in any direction, not just up-down/left-right. This required using a ball rather than the usual two wheels. One of the engineers told Atkinson that there was no way to build such a mouse commercially. After Atkinson complained to Jobs over dinner, he arrived at the office the next day to discover that Jobs had fired the engineer. When his replacement met Atkinson, his first words were, "I can build the mouse."

Atkinson and Jobs became best friends for a while, eating together at the Good Earth most nights. But John Couch and the other professional engineers on his Lisa team, many of them buttoned-down HP types, resented Jobs's meddling and were infuriated by his frequent insults. There was also a clash of visions. Jobs wanted to build a VolksLisa, a simple and inexpensive product for the masses. "There was a tug-of-war between people like me, who wanted a lean machine, and those from HP, like Couch, who were aiming for the corporate market," Jobs recalled.

Both Mike Scott and Mike Markkula were intent on bringing some order to Apple and became increasingly concerned about Jobs's disruptive behavior. So in September 1980, they secretly plotted a reorganization. Couch was made the undisputed manager of the Lisa division. Jobs lost control of the computer he had named after his daughter. He was also stripped of his role as vice president for research and development. He was made non-executive chairman of the board. This position allowed him to remain Apple's public face, but it meant that he had no operating control. That hurt. "I was upset and felt abandoned by Markkula," he said. "He and Scotty felt I wasn't up to running the Lisa division. I brooded about it a lot."

CHAPTER NINE

GOING PUBLIC

A Man of Wealth and Fame

With Wozniak, 1981

Options

When Mike Markkula joined Jobs and Wozniak to turn their fledgling partnership into the Apple Computer Co. in January 1977, they valued it at $5,309. Less than four years later they decided it was time to take it public. It would become the most oversubscribed initial public offering since that of Ford Motors in 1956. By the end of December

1980, Apple would be valued at $1.79 billion. Yes, *billion*. In the process it would make three hundred people millionaires.

Daniel Kottke was not one of them. He had been Jobs's soul mate in college, in India, at the All One Farm, and in the rental house they shared during the Chrisann Brennan crisis. He joined Apple when it was headquartered in Jobs's garage, and he still worked there as an hourly employee. But he was not at a high enough level to be cut in on the stock options that were awarded before the IPO. "I totally trusted Steve, and I assumed he would take care of me like I'd taken care of him, so I didn't push," said Kottke. The official reason he wasn't given stock options was that he was an hourly technician, not a salaried engineer, which was the cutoff level for options. Even so, he could have justifiably been given "founder's stock," but Jobs decided not to. "Steve is the opposite of loyal," according to Andy Hertzfeld, an early Apple engineer who has nevertheless remained friends with him. "He's anti-loyal. He has to abandon the people he is close to."

Kottke decided to press his case with Jobs by hovering outside his office and catching him to make a plea. But at each encounter, Jobs brushed him off. "What was really so difficult for me is that Steve never told me I wasn't eligible," recalled Kottke. "He owed me that as a friend. When I would ask him about stock, he would tell me I had to talk to my manager." Finally, almost six months after the IPO, Kottke worked up the courage to march into Jobs's office and try to hash out the issue. But when he got in to see him, Jobs was so cold that Kottke froze. "I just got choked up and began to cry and just couldn't talk to him," Kottke recalled. "Our friendship was all gone. It was so sad."

Rod Holt, the engineer who had built the power supply, was getting a lot of options, and he tried to turn Jobs around. "We have to do something for your buddy Daniel," he said, and he suggested they each give him some of their own options. "Whatever you give him, I will match it," said Holt. Replied Jobs, "Okay. I will give him zero."

Wozniak, not surprisingly, had the opposite attitude. Before the shares went public, he decided to sell, at a very low price, two thousand of his options to each of forty different midlevel employees. Most of his beneficiaries made enough to buy a home. Wozniak bought a dream home for himself and his new wife, but she soon divorced him and kept the house. He also later gave shares outright to employees he felt had been shortchanged, including Kottke, Fernandez, Wigginton, and Espinosa. Everyone loved Wozniak, all the more so after his generosity, but many also agreed with Jobs that he was "awfully naïve and childlike." A few months later a United Way poster showing a destitute man went up on a company bulletin board. Someone scrawled on it "Woz in 1990."

Jobs was not naïve. He had made sure his deal with Chrisann Brennan was signed before the IPO occurred.

Jobs was the public face of the IPO, and he helped choose the two investment banks handling it: the traditional Wall Street firm Morgan Stanley and the untraditional boutique firm Hambrecht & Quist in San Francisco. "Steve was very irreverent toward the guys from Morgan Stanley, which was a pretty uptight firm in those days," recalled Bill Hambrecht. Morgan Stanley planned to price the offering at $18, even though it was obvious the shares would quickly shoot up. "Tell me what happens to this stock that we priced at eighteen?" Jobs asked the bankers. "Don't you sell it to your good customers? If so, how can you charge me a 7% commission?" Hambrecht recognized that there was a basic unfairness in the system, and he later went on to formulate the idea of a reverse auction to price shares before an IPO.

Apple went public the morning of December 12, 1980. By then the bankers had priced the stock at $22 a share. It went to $29 the first day. Jobs had come into the Hambrecht & Quist office just in time to watch the opening trades. At age twenty-five, he was now worth $256 million.

Baby You're a Rich Man

Before and after he was rich, and indeed throughout a life that included being both broke and a billionaire, Steve Jobs's attitude toward wealth was complex. He was an antimaterialistic hippie who capitalized on the inventions of a friend who wanted to give them away for free, and he was a Zen devotee who made a pilgrimage to India and then decided that his calling was to create a business. And yet somehow these attitudes seemed to weave together rather than conflict.

He had a great love for some material objects, especially those that were finely designed and crafted, such as Porsche and Mercedes cars, Henckels knives and Braun appliances, BMW motorcycles and Ansel Adams prints, Bösendorfer pianos and Bang & Olufsen audio equipment. Yet the houses he lived in, no matter how rich he became, tended not to be ostentatious and were furnished so simply they would have put a Shaker to shame. Neither then nor later would he travel with an entourage, keep a personal staff, or even have security protection. He bought a nice car, but always drove himself. When Markkula asked Jobs to join him in buying a Lear jet, he declined (though he eventually would demand of Apple a Gulfstream to use). Like his father, he could be flinty when bargaining with suppliers, but he didn't allow a craving for profits to take precedence over his passion for building great products.

Thirty years after Apple went public, he reflected on what it was like to come into money suddenly:

> I never worried about money. I grew up in a middle-class family, so I never thought I would starve. And I learned at Atari that I could be an okay engineer, so I always knew I could get by. I was voluntarily poor when I was in college and India, and I lived a pretty simple life even when I was working. So I went from fairly poor, which was wonderful, because I didn't have to worry about money, to being incredibly rich, when I also didn't have to worry about money.
>
> I watched people at Apple who made a lot of money and felt they had to live differently. Some of them bought a Rolls-Royce and various houses, each with a house manager and then someone to manage the house managers. Their wives got plastic surgery and turned into these bizarre people. This was not how I wanted to live. It's crazy. I made a promise to myself that I'm not going to let this money ruin my life.

He was not particularly philanthropic. He briefly set up a foundation, but he discovered that it was annoying to have to deal with the person he had hired to run it, who kept talking about "venture" philanthropy and how to "leverage" giving. Jobs became contemptuous of people who made a display of philanthropy or thinking they could reinvent it. Earlier he had quietly sent in a $5,000 check to help launch Larry Brilliant's Seva Foundation to fight diseases of poverty, and he even agreed to join the board. But when Brilliant brought some board members, including Wavy Gravy and Jerry Garcia, to Apple right after its IPO to solicit a donation, Jobs was not forthcoming. He instead worked on finding ways that a donated Apple II and a VisiCalc program could make it easier for the foundation to do a survey it was planning on blindness in Nepal.

His biggest personal gift was to his parents, Paul and Clara Jobs, to whom he gave about $750,000 worth of stock. They sold some to pay off the mortgage on their Los Altos home, and their son came over for the little celebration. "It was the first time in their lives they didn't have a mortgage," Jobs recalled. "They had a handful of their friends over for the party, and it was really nice." Still, they didn't consider buying a nicer house. "They weren't interested in that," Jobs said. "They had a life they were happy with." Their only splurge was to take a Princess cruise each year. The one through the Panama Canal "was the big one for my dad," according to Jobs, because it reminded him of when his Coast Guard ship went through on its way to San Francisco to be decommissioned.

With Apple's success came fame for its poster boy. *Inc.* became the first magazine to put him on its cover, in October 1981. "This man has changed business forever," it proclaimed. It showed Jobs with a neatly trimmed beard and well-styled long hair, wearing blue jeans and a dress shirt with a blazer that was a little too satiny. He was leaning on an Apple II and looking directly into the camera with the mesmerizing stare he had picked up from Robert Friedland. "When Steve Jobs speaks, it is with the gee-whiz enthusiasm of someone who sees the future and is making sure it works," the magazine reported.

Time followed in February 1982 with a package on young entrepreneurs. The cover was a painting of Jobs, again with his hypnotic stare. Jobs, said the main story, "practically singlehanded created the personal computer industry." The accompanying profile, written by Michael

Moritz, noted, "At 26, Jobs heads a company that six years ago was located in a bedroom and garage of his parents' house, but this year it is expected to have sales of $600 million. . . . As an executive, Jobs has sometimes been petulant and harsh on subordinates. Admits he: 'I've got to learn to keep my feelings private.' "

Despite his new fame and fortune, he still fancied himself a child of the counterculture. On a visit to a Stanford class, he took off his Wilkes Bashford blazer and his shoes, perched on top of a table, and crossed his legs into a lotus position. The students asked questions, such as when Apple's stock price would rise, which Jobs brushed off. Instead he spoke of his passion for future products, such as someday making a computer as small as a book. When the business questions tapered off, Jobs turned the tables on the well-groomed students. "How many of you are virgins?" he asked. There were nervous giggles. "How many of you have taken LSD?" More nervous laughter, and only one or two hands went up. Later Jobs would complain about the new generation of kids, who seemed to him more materialistic and careerist than his own. "When I went to school, it was right after the sixties and before this general wave of practical purposefulness had set in," he said. "Now students aren't even thinking in idealistic terms, or at least nowhere near as much." His generation, he said, was different. "The idealistic wind of the sixties is still at our backs, though, and most of the people I know who are my age have that ingrained in them forever."

CHAPTER TEN

THE MAC IS BORN

You Say You Want a Revolution

Jobs in 1982

Jef Raskin's Baby

Jef Raskin was the type of character who could enthrall Steve Jobs—
or annoy him. As it turned out, he did both. A philosophical guy who
could be both playful and ponderous, Raskin had studied computer
science, taught music and visual arts, conducted a chamber opera
company, and organized guerrilla theater. His 1967 doctoral thesis at
U.C. San Diego argued that computers should have graphical rather
than text-based interfaces. When he got fed up with teaching, he
rented a hot air balloon, flew over the chancellor's house, and shouted
down his decision to quit.

When Jobs was looking for someone to write a manual for the Apple II in 1976, he called Raskin, who had his own little consulting firm. Raskin went to the garage, saw Wozniak beavering away at a workbench, and was convinced by Jobs to write the manual for $50. Eventually he became the manager of Apple's publications department. One of Raskin's dreams was to build an inexpensive computer for the masses, and in 1979 he convinced Mike Markkula to put him in charge of a small development project code-named "Annie" to do just that. Since Raskin thought it was sexist to name computers after women, he redubbed the project in honor of his favorite type of apple, the McIntosh. But he changed the spelling in order not to conflict with the name of the audio equipment maker McIntosh Laboratory. The proposed computer became known as the Macintosh.

Raskin envisioned a machine that would sell for $1,000 and be a simple appliance, with screen and keyboard and computer all in one unit. To keep the cost down, he proposed a tiny five-inch screen and a very cheap (and underpowered) microprocessor, the Motorola 6809. Raskin fancied himself a philosopher, and he wrote his thoughts in an ever-expanding notebook that he called "The Book of Macintosh." He also issued occasional manifestos. One of these was called "Computers by the Millions," and it began with an aspiration: "If personal computers are to be truly personal, it will have to be as likely as not that a family, picked at random, will own one."

Throughout 1979 and early 1980 the Macintosh project led a tenuous existence. Every few months it would almost get killed off, but each time Raskin managed to cajole Markkula into granting clemency. It had a research team of only four engineers located in the original Apple office space next to the Good Earth restaurant, a few blocks from the company's new main building. The work space was filled with enough toys and radio-controlled model airplanes (Raskin's passion) to make it look like a day care center for geeks. Every now and then work would cease for a loosely organized game of Nerf ball tag. Andy Hertzfeld recalled, "This inspired everyone to surround their work area with barricades made out of cardboard, to provide cover during the game, making part of the office look like a cardboard maze."

The star of the team was a blond, cherubic, and psychologically intense self-taught young engineer named Burrell Smith, who worshipped the code work of Wozniak and tried to pull off similar dazzling feats. Atkinson discovered Smith working in Apple's service department and, amazed at his ability to improvise fixes, recommended him to Raskin. Smith would later succumb to schizophrenia, but in the early 1980s he was able to channel his manic intensity into weeklong binges of engineering brilliance.

Jobs was enthralled by Raskin's vision, but not by his willingness to make compromises to keep down the cost. At one point in the fall of 1979 Jobs told him instead to focus on building what he repeatedly called an "insanely great" product. "Don't worry about price, just specify the computer's abilities," Jobs told him. Raskin responded with a sarcastic memo. It spelled out everything you would want in the proposed computer: a high-resolution color display, a printer that worked without a ribbon and could produce graphics in color at a page per second, unlimited access to the ARPA net, and the capability to recognize speech and synthesize music, "even simulate Caruso singing with the Mormon tabernacle choir, with variable reverberation." The memo concluded, "Starting with the abilities desired is nonsense. We must start both with a price goal, and a set of abilities, and keep an eye on today's and the immediate future's technology." In other words, Raskin had little patience for Jobs's belief that you could distort reality if you had enough passion for your product.

Thus they were destined to clash, especially after Jobs was ejected from the Lisa project in September 1980 and began casting around for someplace else to make his mark. It was inevitable that his gaze would fall on the Macintosh project. Raskin's manifestos about an inexpensive machine for the masses, with a simple graphic interface and clean design, stirred his soul. And it was also inevitable that once Jobs set his sights on the Macintosh project, Raskin's days were numbered. "Steve started acting on what he thought we should do, Jef started brooding, and it instantly was clear what the outcome would be," recalled Joanna Hoffman, a member of the Mac team.

The first conflict was over Raskin's devotion to the underpowered Motorola 6809 microprocessor. Once again it was a clash between Raskin's desire to keep the Mac's price under $1,000 and Jobs's determination to build an insanely great machine. So Jobs began pushing for the Mac to switch to the more powerful Motorola 68000, which is what the Lisa was using. Just before Christmas 1980, he challenged Burrell Smith, without telling Raskin, to make a redesigned prototype that used the more powerful chip. As his hero Wozniak would have done, Smith threw himself into the task around the clock, working nonstop for three weeks and employing all sorts of breathtaking circuit design leaps. When he succeeded, Jobs was able to force the switch to the Motorola 68000, and Raskin had to brood and recalculate the cost of the Mac.

There was something larger at stake. The cheaper microprocessor that Raskin wanted would not have been able to accommodate all of the gee-whiz graphics—windows, menus, mouse, and so on—that the team had seen on the Xerox PARC visits. Raskin had convinced everyone to go to Xerox PARC, and he liked the idea of a bitmapped display and windows, but he was not as charmed by all the cute graphics and icons, and he absolutely detested the idea of using a point-and-click mouse rather than the keyboard. "Some of the people on the project became enamored of the quest to do everything with the mouse," he later groused. "Another example is the absurd application of icons. An icon is a symbol equally incomprehensible in all human languages. There's a reason why humans invented phonetic languages."

Raskin's former student Bill Atkinson sided with Jobs. They both wanted a powerful processor that could support whizzier graphics and the use of a mouse. "Steve had to take the project away from Jef," Atkinson said. "Jef was pretty firm and stubborn, and Steve was right to take it over. The world got a better result."

The disagreements were more than just philosophical; they became clashes of personality. "I think that he likes people to jump when he says jump," Raskin once said. "I felt that he was untrustworthy, and that he does not take kindly to being found wanting. He doesn't seem to like people who see him without a halo." Jobs was equally dismissive of Raskin. "Jef was really pompous," he said. "He didn't know much about interfaces. So I decided to nab some of his people who were really good, like Atkinson, bring in some of my own, take the thing over and build a less expensive Lisa, not some piece of junk."

Some on the team found Jobs impossible to work with. "Jobs seems to introduce tension, politics, and hassles rather than enjoying a buffer from those distractions," one engineer wrote in a memo to Raskin in December 1980. "I thoroughly enjoy talking with him, and I admire his ideas, practical perspective, and energy. But I just don't feel that he provides the trusting, supportive, relaxed environment that I need."

But many others realized that despite his temperamental failings, Jobs had the charisma and corporate clout that would lead them to "make a dent in the universe." Jobs told the staff that Raskin was just a dreamer, whereas he was a doer and would get the Mac done in a year. It was clear he wanted vindication for having been ousted from the Lisa group, and he was energized by competition. He publicly bet John Couch $5,000 that the Mac would ship before the Lisa. "We can make a computer that's cheaper and better than the Lisa, and get it out first," he told the team.

Jobs asserted his control of the group by canceling a brown-bag lunch seminar that Raskin was scheduled to give to the whole company in February 1981. Raskin happened to go by the room anyway and discovered that there were a hundred people there waiting to hear him; Jobs had not bothered to notify anyone else about his cancellation order. So Raskin went ahead and gave a talk.

That incident led Raskin to write a blistering memo to Mike Scott, who once again found himself in the difficult position of being a president trying to manage a company's temperamental cofounder and major stockholder. It was titled "Working for/with Steve Jobs," and in it Raskin asserted:

> He is a dreadful manager. . . . I have always liked Steve, but I have found it impossible to work for him. . . . Jobs regularly misses appointments. This is so well-known as to be almost a running joke. . . . He acts without thinking and with bad judgment. . . . He does not give credit where due. . . . Very often, when told of a new idea, he will immediately attack it and say that it is worthless or even stupid, and tell you that it was a waste of time to work on it. This alone is bad management, but if the idea is a good one he will soon be telling people about it as though it was his own.

That afternoon Scott called in Jobs and Raskin for a showdown in front of Markkula. Jobs started crying. He and Raskin agreed on only one thing: Neither could work for the other one. On the Lisa project, Scott had sided with Couch. This time he decided it was best to let Jobs win. After all, the Mac was a minor development project housed in a distant building that could keep Jobs occupied away from the main campus. Raskin was told to take a leave of absence. "They wanted to humor me and give me something to do, which was fine," Jobs recalled. "It was like going back to the garage for me. I had my own ragtag team and I was in control."

Raskin's ouster may not have seemed fair, but it ended up being good for the Macintosh. Raskin wanted an appliance with little memory, an anemic processor, a cassette tape, no mouse, and minimal graphics. Unlike Jobs, he might have been able to keep the price down to close to $1,000, and that may have helped Apple win market share. But he could not have pulled off what Jobs did, which was to create and market a machine that would transform personal computing. In fact we can see where the road not taken led. Raskin was hired by Canon to build the machine he wanted. "It was the Canon Cat, and it was a total flop," Atkinson said. "Nobody wanted it. When Steve turned the Mac into a compact version of the Lisa, it made it into a computing platform instead of a consumer electronic device."*

Texaco Towers

A few days after Raskin left, Jobs appeared at the cubicle of Andy Hertzfeld, a young engineer on the Apple II team, who had a cherubic face and impish demeanor similar to his pal Burrell Smith's. Hertzfeld recalled that most of his colleagues were afraid of Jobs "because of his spontaneous temper tantrums and his proclivity to tell everyone exactly what he thought, which often wasn't very favorable." But Hertzfeld was excited by him. "Are you any good?" Jobs asked the moment he walked in. "We only want really good people working on

---

* Raskin died of pancreatic cancer in 2005, not long after Jobs was diagnosed with the disease.

the Mac, and I'm not sure you're good enough." Hertzfeld knew how to answer. "I told him that yes, I thought that I was pretty good."

Jobs left, and Hertzfeld went back to his work. Later that afternoon he looked up to see Jobs peering over the wall of his cubicle. "I've got good news for you," he said. "You're working on the Mac team now. Come with me."

Hertzfeld replied that he needed a couple more days to finish the Apple II product he was in the middle of. "What's more important than working on the Macintosh?" Jobs demanded. Hertzfeld explained that he needed to get his Apple II DOS program in good enough shape to hand it over to someone. "You're just wasting your time with that!" Jobs replied. "Who cares about the Apple II? The Apple II will be dead in a few years. The Macintosh is the future of Apple, and you're going to start on it now!" With that, Jobs yanked out the power cord to Hertzfeld's Apple II, causing the code he was working on to vanish. "Come with me," Jobs said. "I'm going to take you to your new desk." Jobs drove Hertzfeld, computer and all, in his silver Mercedes to the Macintosh offices. "Here's your new desk," he said, plopping him in a space next to Burrell Smith. "Welcome to the Mac team!" The desk had been Raskin's. In fact Raskin had left so hastily that some of the drawers were still filled with his flotsam and jetsam, including model airplanes.

Jobs's primary test for recruiting people in the spring of 1981 to be part of his merry band of pirates was making sure they had a passion for the product. He would sometimes bring candidates into a room where a prototype of the Mac was covered by a cloth, dramatically unveil it, and watch. "If their eyes lit up, if they went right for the mouse and started pointing and clicking, Steve would smile and hire them," recalled Andrea Cunningham. "He wanted them to say 'Wow!'"

Bruce Horn was one of the programmers at Xerox PARC. When some of his friends, such as Larry Tesler, decided to join the Macintosh group, Horn considered going there as well. But he got a good offer, and a $15,000 signing bonus, to join another company. Jobs called him on a Friday night. "You have to come into Apple tomorrow morning," he said. "I have a lot of stuff to show you." Horn did, and Jobs hooked him. "Steve was so passionate about building this amazing device that

would change the world," Horn recalled. "By sheer force of his personality, he changed my mind." Jobs showed Horn exactly how the
plastic would be molded and would fit together at perfect angles, and
how good the board was going to look inside. "He wanted me to see
that this whole thing was going to happen and it was thought out from
end to end. Wow, I said, I don't see that kind of passion every day. So
I signed up."

Jobs even tried to reengage Wozniak. "I resented the fact that he
had not been doing much, but then I thought, hell, I wouldn't be here
without his brilliance," Jobs later told me. But as soon as Jobs was
starting to get him interested in the Mac, Wozniak crashed his new
single-engine Beechcraft while attempting a takeoff near Santa Cruz.
He barely survived and ended up with partial amnesia. Jobs spent time
at the hospital, but when Wozniak recovered he decided it was time
to take a break from Apple. Ten years after dropping out of Berkeley,
he decided to return there to finally get his degree, enrolling under the
name of Rocky Raccoon Clark.

In order to make the project his own, Jobs decided it should no
longer be code-named after Raskin's favorite apple. In various interviews, Jobs had been referring to computers as a bicycle for the mind;
the ability of humans to create a bicycle allowed them to move more
efficiently than even a condor, and likewise the ability to create computers would multiply the efficiency of their minds. So one day Jobs
decreed that henceforth the Macintosh should be known instead as
the Bicycle. This did not go over well. "Burrell and I thought this
was the silliest thing we ever heard, and we simply refused to use the
new name," recalled Hertzfeld. Within a month the idea was dropped.

By early 1981 the Mac team had grown to about twenty, and Jobs
decided that they should have bigger quarters. So he moved everyone to the second floor of a brown-shingled, two-story building about
three blocks from Apple's main offices. It was next to a Texaco station
and thus became known as Texaco Towers. In order to make the office
more lively, he told the team to buy a stereo system. "Burrell and I ran
out and bought a silver, cassette-based boom box right away, before he
could change his mind," recalled Hertzfeld.

Jobs's triumph was soon complete. A few weeks after winning his power struggle with Raskin to run the Mac division, he helped push out Mike Scott as Apple's president. Scotty had become more and more erratic, alternately bullying and nurturing. He finally lost most of his support among the employees when he surprised them by imposing a round of layoffs that he handled with atypical ruthlessness. In addition, he had begun to suffer a variety of afflictions, ranging from eye infections to narcolepsy. When Scott was on vacation in Hawaii, Markkula called together the top managers to ask if he should be replaced. Most of them, including Jobs and John Couch, said yes. So Markkula took over as an interim and rather passive president, and Jobs found that he now had full rein to do what he wanted with the Mac division.

CHAPTER ELEVEN

THE REALITY
DISTORTION FIELD

Playing by His Own Set of Rules

The original Mac team in 1984: George Crow, Joanna Hoffman, Burrell Smith, Andy Hertzfeld, Bill Atkinson, and Jerry Manock

When Andy Hertzfeld joined the Macintosh team, he got a briefing from Bud Tribble, the other software designer, about the huge amount of work that still needed to be done. Jobs wanted it finished by January 1982, less than a year away. "That's crazy," Hertzfeld said. "There's no way." Tribble said that Jobs would not accept any contrary facts. "The best way to describe the situation is a term from *Star Trek*," Tribble explained. "Steve has a reality distortion field." When Hertzfeld looked puzzled, Tribble elaborated. "In his presence, reality is malleable. He can convince anyone of practically anything. It wears off when he's not around, but it makes it hard to have realistic schedules."

Tribble recalled that he adopted the phrase from the "Menagerie" episodes of *Star Trek*, "in which the aliens create their own new world through sheer mental force." He meant the phrase to be a compliment as well as a caution: "It was dangerous to get caught in Steve's distortion field, but it was what led him to actually be able to change reality."

At first Hertzfeld thought that Tribble was exaggerating, but after two weeks of working with Jobs, he became a keen observer of the phenomenon. "The reality distortion field was a confounding mélange of a charismatic rhetorical style, indomitable will, and eagerness to bend any fact to fit the purpose at hand," he said.

There was little that could shield you from the force, Hertzfeld discovered. "Amazingly, the reality distortion field seemed to be effective even if you were acutely aware of it. We would often discuss potential techniques for grounding it, but after a while most of us gave up, accepting it as a force of nature." After Jobs decreed that the sodas in the office refrigerator be replaced by Odwalla organic orange and carrot juices, someone on the team had T-shirts made. "Reality Distortion Field," they said on the front, and on the back, "It's in the juice!"

To some people, calling it a reality distortion field was just a clever way to say that Jobs tended to lie. But it was in fact a more complex form of dissembling. He would assert something—be it a fact about world history or a recounting of who suggested an idea at a meeting—without even considering the truth. It came from willfully defying reality, not only to others but to himself. "He can deceive himself," said Bill Atkinson. "It allowed him to con people into believing his vision, because he has personally embraced and internalized it."

A lot of people distort reality, of course. When Jobs did so, it was often a tactic for accomplishing something. Wozniak, who was as congenitally honest as Jobs was tactical, marveled at how effective it could be. "His reality distortion is when he has an illogical vision of the future, such as telling me that I could design the Breakout game in just a few days. You realize that it can't be true, but he somehow makes it true."

When members of the Mac team got ensnared in his reality distortion field, they were almost hypnotized. "He reminded me of Rasputin," said Debi Coleman. "He laser-beamed in on you and didn't blink. It didn't matter if he was serving purple Kool-Aid. You drank it." But like Wozniak, she believed that the reality distortion field was empowering: It enabled Jobs to inspire his team to change the course of computer history with a fraction of the resources of Xerox or IBM. "It was a self-fulfilling distortion," she claimed. "You did the impossible, because you didn't realize it was impossible."

At the root of the reality distortion was Jobs's belief that the rules didn't apply to him. He had some evidence for this; in his childhood, he had often been able to bend reality to his desires. Rebelliousness and willfulness were ingrained in his character. He had the sense that he was special, a chosen one, an enlightened one. "He thinks there are a few people who are special—people like Einstein and Gandhi and the gurus he met in India—and he's one of them," said Hertzfeld. "He told Chrisann this. Once he even hinted to me that he was enlightened. It's almost like Nietzsche." Jobs never studied Nietzsche, but the philosopher's concept of the will to power and the special nature of the *Über*man came naturally to him. As Nietzsche wrote in *Thus Spoke Zarathustra*, "The spirit now wills his own will, and he who had been lost to the world now conquers the world." If reality did not comport with his will, he would ignore it, as he had done with the birth of his daughter and would do years later, when first diagnosed with cancer. Even in small everyday rebellions, such as not putting a license plate on his car and parking it in handicapped spaces, he acted as if he were not subject to the strictures around him.

Another key aspect of Jobs's worldview was his binary way of categorizing things. People were either "enlightened" or "an asshole." Their work was either "the best" or "totally shitty." Bill Atkinson, the Mac designer who fell on the good side of these dichotomies, described what it was like:

> It was difficult working under Steve, because there was a great polarity between gods and shitheads. If you were a god, you were up on a pedestal and could do no wrong. Those of us who were considered to be gods, as I was, knew that we were actually mortal and made bad engineering

decisions and farted like any person, so we were always afraid that we would get knocked off our pedestal. The ones who were shitheads, who were brilliant engineers working very hard, felt there was no way they could get appreciated and rise above their status.

But these categories were not immutable, for Jobs could rapidly reverse himself. When briefing Hertzfeld about the reality distortion field, Tribble specifically warned him about Jobs's tendency to resemble high-voltage alternating current. "Just because he tells you that something is awful or great, it doesn't necessarily mean he'll feel that way tomorrow," Tribble explained. "If you tell him a new idea, he'll usually tell you that he thinks it's stupid. But then, if he actually likes it, exactly one week later, he'll come back to you and propose your idea to you, as if he thought of it."

The audacity of this pirouette technique would have dazzled Diaghilev. "If one line of argument failed to persuade, he would deftly switch to another," Hertzfeld said. "Sometimes, he would throw you off balance by suddenly adopting your position as his own, without acknowledging that he ever thought differently." That happened repeatedly to Bruce Horn, the programmer who, with Tesler, had been lured from Xerox PARC. "One week I'd tell him about an idea that I had, and he would say it was crazy," recalled Horn. "The next week, he'd come and say, 'Hey I have this great idea'—and it would be my idea! You'd call him on it and say, 'Steve, I told you that a week ago,' and he'd say, 'Yeah, yeah, yeah' and just move right along."

It was as if Jobs's brain circuits were missing a device that would modulate the extreme spikes of impulsive opinions that popped into his mind. So in dealing with him, the Mac team adopted an audio concept called a "low pass filter." In processing his input, they learned to reduce the amplitude of his high-frequency signals. That served to smooth out the data set and provide a less jittery moving average of his evolving attitudes. "After a few cycles of him taking alternating extreme positions," said Hertzfeld, "we would learn to low pass filter his signals and not react to the extremes."

Was Jobs's unfiltered behavior caused by a lack of emotional sensitivity? No. Almost the opposite. He was very emotionally attuned, able to read people and know their psychological strengths and vulnerabilities. He could stun an unsuspecting victim with an emotional towel-snap, perfectly aimed. He intuitively knew when someone was faking it or truly knew something. This made him masterful at cajoling, stroking, persuading, flattering, and intimidating people. "He had the uncanny capacity to know exactly what your weak point is, know what will make you feel small, to make you cringe," Joanna Hoffman said. "It's a common trait in people who are charismatic and know how to manipulate people. Knowing that he can crush you makes you feel weakened and eager for his approval, so then he can elevate you and put you on a pedestal and own you."

Ann Bowers became an expert at dealing with Jobs's perfectionism, petulance, and prickliness. She had been the human resources director at Intel, but had stepped aside after she married its cofounder Bob Noyce. She joined Apple in 1980 and served as a calming mother figure who would step in after one of Jobs's tantrums. She would go to his office, shut the door, and gently lecture him. "I know, I know," he would say. "Well, then, please stop doing it," she would insist. Bowers recalled, "He would be good for a while, and then a week or so later I would get a call again." She realized that he could barely contain himself. "He had these huge expectations, and if people didn't deliver, he couldn't stand it. He couldn't control himself. I could understand why Steve would get upset, and he was usually right, but it had a hurtful effect. It created a fear factor. He was self-aware, but that didn't always modify his behavior."

Jobs became close to Bowers and her husband, and he would drop in at their Los Gatos Hills home unannounced. She would hear his motorcycle in the distance and say, "I guess we have Steve for dinner again." For a while she and Noyce were like a surrogate family. "He was so bright and also so needy. He needed a grown-up, a father figure, which Bob became, and I became like a mother figure."

There were some upsides to Jobs's demanding and wounding behavior. People who were not crushed ended up being stronger. They did better work, out of both fear and an eagerness to please. "His behavior can be emotionally draining, but if you survive, it works," Hoffman said. You could also push back—sometimes—and not only survive but thrive. That didn't always work; Raskin tried it, succeeded for a while, and then was destroyed. But if you were calmly confident, if Jobs sized you up and decided that you knew what you were doing, he would respect you. In both his personal and his professional life over the years, his inner circle tended to include many more strong people than toadies.

The Mac team knew that. Every year, beginning in 1981, it gave out an award to the person who did the best job of standing up to him. The award was partly a joke, but also partly real, and Jobs knew about it and liked it. Joanna Hoffman won the first year. From an Eastern European refugee family, she had a strong temper and will. One day, for example, she discovered that Jobs had changed her marketing projections in a way she found totally reality-distorting. Furious, she marched to his office. "As I'm climbing the stairs, I told his assistant I am going to take a knife and stab it into his heart," she recounted. Al Eisenstat, the corporate counsel, came running out to restrain her. "But Steve heard me out and backed down."

Hoffman won the award again in 1982. "I remember being envious of Joanna, because she would stand up to Steve and I didn't have the nerve yet," said Debi Coleman, who joined the Mac team that year. "Then, in 1983, I got the award. I had learned you had to stand up for what you believe, which Steve respected. I started getting promoted by him after that." Eventually she rose to become head of manufacturing.

One day Jobs barged into the cubicle of one of Atkinson's engineers and uttered his usual "This is shit." As Atkinson recalled, "The guy said, 'No it's not, it's actually the best way,' and he explained to Steve the engineering trade-offs he'd made." Jobs backed down. Atkinson taught his team to put Jobs's words through a translator. "We learned to interpret 'This is shit' to actually be a question that means, 'Tell me why this is the best way to do it.'" But the story had a coda, which Atkinson also found instructive. Eventually the engineer found an even better way to perform the function that Jobs had criticized. "He did it better because Steve had challenged him," said Atkinson, "which shows you can push back on him but should also listen, for he's usually right."

Jobs's prickly behavior was partly driven by his perfectionism and his impatience with those who made compromises in order to get a product out on time and on budget. "He could not make trade-offs well," said Atkinson. "If someone didn't care to make their product perfect, they were a bozo." At the West Coast Computer Faire in April 1981, for example, Adam Osborne released the first truly portable personal computer. It was not great—it had a five-inch screen and not much memory—but it worked well enough. As Osborne famously declared, "Adequacy is sufficient. All else is superfluous." Jobs found that approach to be morally appalling, and he spent days making fun of Osborne. "This guy just doesn't get it," Jobs repeatedly railed as he wandered the Apple corridors. "He's not making art, he's making shit."

One day Jobs came into the cubicle of Larry Kenyon, an engineer who was working on the Macintosh operating system, and complained that it was taking too long to boot up. Kenyon started to explain, but Jobs cut him off. "If it could save a person's life, would you find a way to shave ten seconds off the boot time?" he asked. Kenyon allowed that he probably could. Jobs went to a whiteboard and showed that if there were five million people using the Mac, and it took ten seconds extra to turn it on every day, that added up to three hundred million or so hours per year that people would save, which was the equivalent of at least one hundred lifetimes saved per year. "Larry was suitably impressed, and a few weeks later he came back and it booted up twenty-eight seconds faster," Atkinson recalled. "Steve had a way of motivating by looking at the bigger picture."

The result was that the Macintosh team came to share Jobs's passion for making a great product, not just a profitable one. "Jobs thought of himself as an artist, and he encouraged the design team to think of ourselves that way too," said Hertzfeld. "The goal was never to beat the competition, or to make a lot of money. It was to do the greatest thing possible, or even a little greater." He once took the team to see an exhibit of Tiffany glass in San Francisco because he believed they could learn from Louis Tiffany's example of creating great art that could be mass-produced. Recalled Bud Tribble, "We said to ourselves, 'Hey, if we're going to make things in our lives, we might as well make them beautiful.'"

Was all of his stormy and abusive behavior necessary? Probably not, nor was it justified. There were other ways to have motivated his team. Even though the Macintosh would turn out to be great, it was way behind schedule and way over budget because of Jobs's impetuous interventions. There was also a cost in brutalized human feelings, which caused much of the team to burn out. "Steve's contributions could have been made without so many stories about him terrorizing folks," Wozniak said. "I like being more patient and not having so many conflicts. I think a company can be a good family. If the Macintosh project had been run my way, things probably would have been a mess. But I think if it had been a mix of both our styles, it would have been better than just the way Steve did it."

But even though Jobs's style could be demoralizing, it could also be oddly inspiring. It infused Apple employees with an abiding passion to create groundbreaking products and a belief that they could accomplish what seemed impossible. They had T-shirts made that read "90 hours a week and loving it!" Out of a fear of Jobs mixed with an incredibly strong urge to impress him, they exceeded their own expectations. "I've learned over the years that when you have really good people you don't have to baby them," Jobs later explained. "By expecting them to do great things, you can get them to do great things. The original Mac team taught me that A-plus players like to work together, and they don't like it if you tolerate B work. Ask any member of that Mac team. They will tell you it was worth the pain."

Most of them agree. "He would shout at a meeting, 'You asshole, you never do anything right,'" Debi Coleman recalled. "It was like an hourly occurrence. Yet I consider myself the absolute luckiest person in the world to have worked with him."

CHAPTER TWELVE

THE DESIGN

Real Artists Simplify

A Bauhaus Aesthetic

Unlike most kids who grew up in Eichler homes, Jobs knew what they were and why they were so wonderful. He liked the notion of simple and clean modernism produced for the masses. He also loved listening to his father describe the styling intricacies of various cars. So from the beginning at Apple, he believed that great industrial design— a colorfully simple logo, a sleek case for the Apple II—would set the company apart and make its products distinctive.

The company's first office, after it moved out of his family garage, was in a small building it shared with a Sony sales office. Sony was famous for its signature style and memorable product designs, so Jobs would drop by to study the marketing material. "He would come in looking scruffy and fondle the product brochures and point out design features," said Dan'l Lewin, who worked there. "Every now and then, he would ask, 'Can I take this brochure?'" By 1980, he had hired Lewin.

His fondness for the dark, industrial look of Sony receded around June 1981, when he began attending the annual International Design Conference in Aspen. The meeting that year focused on Italian style, and it featured the architect-designer Mario Bellini, the filmmaker Bernardo Bertolucci, the car maker Sergio Pininfarina, and the Fiat heiress and politician Susanna Agnelli. "I had come to revere the Italian designers, just like the kid in *Breaking Away* reveres the Italian bikers," recalled Jobs, "so it was an amazing inspiration."

In Aspen he was exposed to the spare and functional design philosophy of the Bauhaus movement, which was enshrined by Herbert Bayer in the buildings, living suites, sans serif font typography, and furniture on the Aspen Institute campus. Like his mentors Walter Gropius and Ludwig Mies van der Rohe, Bayer believed that there should be no distinction between fine art and applied industrial design. The modernist International Style championed by the Bauhaus taught that design should be simple, yet have an expressive spirit. It emphasized rationality and functionality by employing clean lines and forms. Among the maxims preached by Mies and Gropius were "God is in the details" and "Less is more." As with Eichler homes, the artistic sensibility was combined with the capability for mass production.

Jobs publicly discussed his embrace of the Bauhaus style in a talk he gave at the 1983 design conference, the theme of which was "The Future Isn't What It Used to Be." He predicted the passing of the Sony style in favor of Bauhaus simplicity. "The current wave of industrial design is Sony's high-tech look, which is gunmetal gray, maybe paint it black, do weird stuff to it," he said. "It's easy to do that. But it's not great." He proposed an alternative, born of the Bauhaus, that was more true to the function and nature of the products. "What we're going to do is make the products high-tech, and we're going to package them cleanly so that you know they're high-tech. We will fit them in a small package, and then we can make them beautiful and white, just like Braun does with its electronics."

He repeatedly emphasized that Apple's products would be clean and simple. "We will make them bright and pure and honest about being high-tech, rather than a heavy industrial look of black, black, black, black, like Sony," he preached. "So that's our approach. Very simple, and we're really shooting for Museum of Modern Art quality. The way we're running the company, the product design, the advertising, it all comes down to this: Let's make it simple. Really simple."

Apple's design mantra would remain the one featured on its first brochure: "Simplicity is the ultimate sophistication."

Jobs felt that design simplicity should be linked to making products easy to use. Those goals do not always go together. Sometimes a design can be so sleek and simple that a user finds it intimidating or unfriendly to navigate. "The main thing in our design is that we have to make things intuitively obvious," Jobs told the crowd of design mavens. For example, he extolled the desktop metaphor he was creating for the Macintosh. "People know how to deal with a desktop intuitively. If you walk into an office, there are papers on the desk. The one on the top is the most important. People know how to switch priority. Part of the reason we model our computers on metaphors like the desktop is that we can leverage this experience people already have."

Speaking at the same time as Jobs that Wednesday afternoon, but in a smaller seminar room, was Maya Lin, twenty-three, who had been catapulted into fame the previous November when her Vietnam Veterans Memorial was dedicated in Washington, D.C. They struck up a close friendship, and Jobs invited her to visit Apple. "I came to work with Steve for a week," Lin recalled. "I asked him, 'Why do computers look like clunky TV sets? Why don't you make something thin? Why not a flat laptop?'" Jobs replied that this was indeed his goal, as soon as the technology was ready.

At that time there was not much exciting happening in the realm of industrial design, Jobs felt. He had a Richard Sapper lamp, which he admired, and he also liked the furniture of Charles and Ray Eames and the Braun products of Dieter Rams. But there were no towering figures energizing the world of industrial design the way that Raymond Loewy and Herbert Bayer had done. "There really wasn't much going on in industrial design, particularly in Silicon Valley, and Steve was very eager to change that," said Lin. "His design sensibility is sleek but not slick, and it's playful. He embraced minimalism, which came from his Zen devotion to simplicity, but he avoided allowing that to make his products cold. They stayed fun. He's passionate and super-serious about design, but at the same time there's a sense of play."

As Jobs's design sensibilities evolved, he became particularly attracted to the Japanese style and began hanging out with its stars, such as Issey Miyake. His Buddhist training was a big influence. "I have always found Buddhism, Japanese Zen Buddhism in particular, to be aesthetically sublime," he said. "The most sublime thing I've ever seen are the gardens around Kyoto. I'm deeply moved by what that culture has produced, and it's directly from Zen Buddhism."

Like a Porsche

Jef Raskin's vision for the Macintosh was that it would be like a boxy carry-on suitcase, which would be closed by flipping up the keyboard over the front screen. When Jobs took over the project, he decided to sacrifice portability for a distinctive design that wouldn't take up much space on a desk. He plopped down a phone book and declared, to the horror of the engineers, that it shouldn't have a footprint larger than that. So his design team of Jerry Manock and Terry Oyama began working on ideas that had the screen above the computer box, with a keyboard that was detachable.

One day in March 1981, Andy Hertzfeld came back to the office from dinner to find Jobs hovering over their one Mac prototype in intense discussion with the creative services director, James Ferris. "We need it to have a classic look that won't go out of style, like the Volkswagen Beetle," Jobs said. From his father he had developed an appreciation for the contours of classic cars.

"No, that's not right," Ferris replied. "The lines should be voluptuous, like a Ferrari."

"Not a Ferrari, that's not right either," Jobs countered. "It should be more like a Porsche!" Jobs owned a Porsche 928 at the time. When Bill Atkinson was over one weekend, Jobs brought him outside to admire the car. "Great art stretches the taste, it doesn't follow tastes," he told Atkinson. He also admired the design of the Mercedes. "Over the years, they've made the lines softer but the details starker," he said one day as he walked around the parking lot. "That's what we have to do with the Macintosh."

Oyama drafted a preliminary design and had a plaster model made. The Mac team gathered around for the unveiling and expressed their thoughts. Hertzfeld called it "cute." Others also seemed satisfied. Then Jobs let loose a blistering burst of criticism. "It's way too boxy, it's got to be more curvaceous. The radius of the first chamfer needs to be bigger, and I don't like the size of the bevel." With his new fluency in industrial design lingo, Jobs was referring to the angular or curved edge connecting the sides of the computer. But then he gave a resounding compliment. "It's a start," he said.

Every month or so, Manock and Oyama would present a new iteration based on Jobs's previous criticisms. The latest plaster model would be dramatically unveiled, and all the previous attempts would be lined up next to it. That not only helped them gauge the design's evolution, but it prevented Jobs from insisting that one of his suggestions had been ignored. "By the fourth model, I could barely distinguish it from the third one," said Hertzfeld, "but Steve was always critical and decisive, saying he loved or hated a detail that I could barely perceive."

One weekend Jobs went to Macy's in Palo Alto and again spent time studying appliances, especially the Cuisinart. He came bounding into the Mac office that Monday, asked the design team to go buy one, and made a raft of new suggestions based on its lines, curves, and bevels.

Jobs kept insisting that the machine should look friendly. As a result, it evolved to resemble a human face. With the disk drive built in below the screen, the unit was taller and narrower than most computers, suggesting a head. The recess near the base evoked a gentle chin, and Jobs narrowed the strip of plastic at the top so that it avoided the Neanderthal forehead that made the Lisa subtly unattractive. The patent for the design of the Apple case was issued in the name of Steve Jobs as well as Manock and Oyama. "Even though Steve didn't draw any of the lines, his ideas and inspiration made the design what it is," Oyama later said. "To be honest, we didn't know what it meant for a computer to be 'friendly' until Steve told us."

Jobs obsessed with equal intensity about the look of what would appear on the screen. One day Bill Atkinson burst into Texaco Towers all excited. He had just come up with a brilliant algorithm that could draw circles and ovals onscreen quickly. The math for making circles usually required calculating square roots, which the 68000 microprocessor didn't support. But Atkinson did a workaround based on the fact that the sum of a sequence of odd numbers produces a sequence of perfect squares (for example, 1 + 3 = 4, 1 + 3 + 5 = 9, etc.). Hertzfeld recalled that when Atkinson fired up his demo, everyone was impressed except Jobs. "Well, circles and ovals are good," he said, "but how about drawing rectangles with rounded corners?"

"I don't think we really need it," said Atkinson, who explained that it would be almost impossible to do. "I wanted to keep the graphics routines lean and limit them to the primitives that truly needed to be done," he recalled.

"Rectangles with rounded corners are everywhere!" Jobs said, jumping up and getting more intense. "Just look around this room!" He pointed out the whiteboard and the tabletop and other objects that were rectangular with rounded corners. "And look outside, there's even more, practically everywhere you look!" He dragged Atkinson out for a walk, pointing out car windows and billboards and street signs. "Within three blocks, we found seventeen examples," said Jobs. "I started pointing them out everywhere until he was completely convinced."

"When he finally got to a No Parking sign, I said, 'Okay, you're right, I give up. We need to have a rounded-corner rectangle as a primitive!'" Hertzfeld recalled, "Bill returned to Texaco Towers the following afternoon, with a big smile on his face. His demo was now drawing rectangles with beautifully rounded corners blisteringly fast." The dialogue boxes and windows on the Lisa and the Mac, and almost every other subsequent computer, ended up being rendered with rounded corners.

At the calligraphy class he had audited at Reed, Jobs learned to love typefaces, with all of their serif and sans serif variations, proportional spacing, and leading. "When we were designing the first Macintosh computer, it all came back to me," he later said of that class. Because the Mac was bitmapped, it was possible to devise an endless array of fonts, ranging from the elegant to the wacky, and render them pixel by pixel on the screen.

To design these fonts, Hertzfeld recruited a high school friend from suburban Philadelphia, Susan Kare. They named the fonts after the stops on Philadelphia's Main Line commuter train: Overbrook,

Merion, Ardmore, and Rosemont. Jobs found the process fascinating. Late one afternoon he stopped by and started brooding about the font names. They were "little cities that nobody's ever heard of," he complained. "They ought to be *world-class* cities!" The fonts were renamed Chicago, New York, Geneva, London, San Francisco, Toronto, and Venice.

Markkula and some others could never quite appreciate Jobs's obsession with typography. "His knowledge of fonts was remarkable, and he kept insisting on having great ones," Markkula recalled. "I kept saying, 'Fonts?!? Don't we have more important things to do?'" In fact the delightful assortment of Macintosh fonts, when combined with laser-writer printing and great graphics capabilities, would help launch the desktop publishing industry and be a boon for Apple's bottom line. It also introduced all sorts of regular folks, ranging from high school journalists to moms who edited PTA newsletters, to the quirky joy of knowing about fonts, which was once reserved for printers, grizzled editors, and other ink-stained wretches.

Kare also developed the icons, such as the trash can for discarding files, that helped define graphical interfaces. She and Jobs hit it off because they shared an instinct for simplicity along with a desire to make the Mac whimsical. "He usually came in at the end of every day," she said. "He'd always want to know what was new, and he's always had good taste and a good sense for visual details." Sometimes he came in on Sunday morning, so Kare made it a point to be there working. Every now and then, she would run into a problem. He rejected one of her renderings of a rabbit, an icon for speeding up the mouse-click rate, saying that the furry creature looked "too gay."

Jobs lavished similar attention on the title bars atop windows and documents. He had Atkinson and Kare do them over and over again as he agonized over their look. He did not like the ones on the Lisa because they were too black and harsh. He wanted the ones on the Mac to be smoother, to have pinstripes. "We must have gone through twenty different title bar designs before he was happy," Atkinson recalled. At one point Kare and Atkinson complained that he was making them spend too much time on tiny little tweaks to the title bar when they had bigger things to do. Jobs erupted. "Can you imagine looking at that every day?" he shouted. "It's not just a little thing, it's something we have to do right."

Chris Espinosa found one way to satisfy Jobs's design demands and control-freak tendencies. One of Wozniak's youthful acolytes from the days in the garage, Espinosa had been convinced to drop out of Berkeley by Jobs, who argued that he would always have a chance to study, but only one chance to work on the Mac. On his own, he decided to design a calculator for the computer. "We all gathered around as Chris showed the calculator to Steve and then held his breath, waiting for Steve's reaction," Hertzfeld recalled.

"Well, it's a start," Jobs said, "but basically, it stinks. The background color is too dark, some lines are the wrong thickness, and the buttons are too big." Espinosa kept refining it in response to Jobs's critiques, day after day, but with each iteration came new criticisms. So finally one afternoon, when Jobs came by, Espinosa unveiled his inspired solution: "The Steve Jobs Roll Your Own Calculator Construction Set." It allowed the user to tweak and personalize the look of the calculator by changing the thickness of the lines, the size of the buttons, the shading, the background, and other attributes. Instead of just laughing, Jobs plunged in and started to play around with the look to suit his tastes. After about ten minutes he got it the way he liked. His design, not surprisingly, was the one that shipped on the Mac and remained the standard for fifteen years.

Although his focus was on the Macintosh, Jobs wanted to create a consistent design language for all Apple products. So he set up a contest to choose a world-class designer who would be for Apple what Dieter Rams was for Braun. The project was code-named Snow White, not because of his preference for the color but because the products to be designed were code-named after the seven dwarfs. The winner was Hartmut Esslinger, a German designer who was responsible for the look of Sony's Trinitron televisions. Jobs flew to the Black Forest region to meet him and was impressed not only with Esslinger's passion but also his spirited way of driving his Mercedes at more than one hundred miles per hour.

Even though he was German, Esslinger proposed that there should be a "born-in-America gene for Apple's DNA" that would produce a

"California global" look, inspired by "Hollywood and music, a bit of rebellion, and natural sex appeal." His guiding principle was "Form follows emotion," a play on the familiar maxim that form follows function. He produced forty models of products to demonstrate the concept, and when Jobs saw them he proclaimed, "Yes, this is it!" The Snow White look, which was adopted immediately for the Apple IIc, featured white cases, tight rounded curves, and lines of thin grooves for both ventilation and decoration. Jobs offered Esslinger a contract on the condition that he move to California. They shook hands and, in Esslinger's not-so-modest words, "that handshake launched one of the most decisive collaborations in the history of industrial design." Esslinger's firm, frogdesign,* opened in Palo Alto in mid-1983 with a $1.2 million annual contract to work for Apple, and from then on every Apple product has included the proud declaration "Designed in California."

From his father Jobs had learned that a hallmark of passionate craftsmanship is making sure that even the aspects that will remain hidden are done beautifully. One of the most extreme—and telling— implementations of that philosophy came when he scrutinized the printed circuit board that would hold the chips and other components deep inside the Macintosh. No consumer would ever see it, but Jobs began critiquing it on aesthetic grounds. "That part's really pretty," he said. "But look at the memory chips. That's ugly. The lines are too close together."

One of the new engineers interrupted and asked why it mattered. "The only thing that's important is how well it works. Nobody is going to see the PC board."

Jobs reacted typically. "I want it to be as beautiful as possible, even if it's inside the box. A great carpenter isn't going to use lousy wood for the back of a cabinet, even though nobody's going to see it." In an

---

* The firm changed its name from frogdesign to frog design in 2000 and moved to San Francisco. Esslinger picked the original name not merely because frogs have the ability to metamorphose, but as a salute to its roots in the (f)ederal (r)epublic (o)f (g)ermany. He said that "the lowercase letters offered a nod to the Bauhaus notion of a non-hierarchical language, reinforcing the company's ethos of democratic partnership."

interview a few years later, after the Macintosh came out, Jobs again reiterated that lesson from his father: "When you're a carpenter making a beautiful chest of drawers, you're not going to use a piece of plywood on the back, even though it faces the wall and nobody will ever see it. You'll know it's there, so you're going to use a beautiful piece of wood on the back. For you to sleep well at night, the aesthetic, the quality, has to be carried all the way through."

From Mike Markkula he had learned the importance of packaging and presentation. People do judge a book by its cover, so for the box of the Macintosh, Jobs chose a full-color design and kept trying to make it look better. "He got the guys to redo it fifty times," recalled Alain Rossmann, a member of the Mac team who married Joanna Hoffman. "It was going to be thrown in the trash as soon as the consumer opened it, but he was obsessed by how it looked." To Rossmann, this showed a lack of balance; money was being spent on expensive packaging while they were trying to save money on the memory chips. But for Jobs, each detail was essential to making the Macintosh amazing.

When the design was finally locked in, Jobs called the Macintosh team together for a ceremony. "Real artists sign their work," he said. So he got out a sheet of drafting paper and a Sharpie pen and had all of them sign their names. The signatures were engraved inside each Macintosh. No one would ever see them, but the members of the team knew that their signatures were inside, just as they knew that the circuit board was laid out as elegantly as possible. Jobs called them each up by name, one at a time. Burrell Smith went first. Jobs waited until last, after all forty-five of the others. He found a place right in the center of the sheet and signed his name in lowercase letters with a grand flair. Then he toasted them with champagne. "With moments like this, he got us seeing our work as art," said Atkinson.

CHAPTER THIRTEEN

BUILDING THE MAC

The Journey Is the Reward

Competition

When IBM introduced its personal computer in August 1981, Jobs had his team buy one and dissect it. Their consensus was that it sucked. Chris Espinosa called it "a half-assed, hackneyed attempt," and there was some truth to that. It used old-fashioned command-line prompts and didn't support bitmapped graphical displays. Apple became cocky, not realizing that corporate technology managers might feel more comfortable buying from an established company like IBM rather than one named after a piece of fruit. Bill Gates happened to be visiting Apple headquarters for a meeting on the day the IBM PC was announced. "They didn't seem to care," he said. "It took them a year to realize what had happened."

Reflecting its cheeky confidence, Apple took out a full-page ad in the *Wall Street Journal* with the headline "Welcome, IBM. Seriously." It cleverly positioned the upcoming computer battle as a two-way contest between the spunky and rebellious Apple and the establishment Goliath IBM, conveniently relegating to irrelevance companies such as Commodore, Tandy, and Osborne that were doing just as well as Apple.

Throughout his career, Jobs liked to see himself as an enlightened rebel pitted against evil empires, a Jedi warrior or Buddhist samurai fighting the forces of darkness. IBM was his perfect foil. He cleverly cast the upcoming battle not as a mere business competition, but as a spiritual struggle. "If, for some reason, we make some giant mistakes and IBM wins, my personal feeling is that we are going to enter sort of a computer Dark Ages for about twenty years," he told an interviewer. "Once IBM gains control of a market sector, they almost always stop innovation." Even thirty years later, reflecting back on the competition, Jobs cast it as a holy crusade: "IBM was essentially Microsoft at its worst. They were not a force for innovation; they were a force for evil. They were like ATT or Microsoft or Google is."

Unfortunately for Apple, Jobs also took aim at another perceived competitor to his Macintosh: the company's own Lisa. Partly it was psychological. He had been ousted from that group, and now he wanted to beat it. He also saw healthy rivalry as a way to motivate his troops. That's why he bet John Couch $5,000 that the Mac would ship before the Lisa. The problem was that the rivalry became unhealthy. Jobs repeatedly portrayed his band of engineers as the cool kids on the block, in contrast to the plodding HP engineer types working on the Lisa.

More substantively, when he moved away from Jef Raskin's plan for an inexpensive and underpowered portable appliance and reconceived the Mac as a desktop machine with a graphical user interface, it became a scaled-down version of the Lisa that would likely undercut it in the marketplace.

Larry Tesler, who managed application software for the Lisa, realized that it would be important to design both machines to use many of the same software programs. So to broker peace, he arranged for Smith and Hertzfeld to come to the Lisa work space and demonstrate the Mac prototype. Twenty-five engineers showed up and were listening politely when, halfway into the presentation, the door burst open. It was Rich Page, a volatile engineer who was responsible for much of the Lisa's design. "The Macintosh is going to destroy the Lisa!" he shouted. "The Macintosh is going to ruin Apple!" Neither Smith nor Hertzfeld responded, so Page continued his rant. "Jobs wants to destroy Lisa because we wouldn't let him control it," he said, looking as if he were about to cry. "Nobody's going to buy a Lisa because they know the Mac is coming! But you don't care!" He stormed out of the room and slammed the door, but a moment later he barged back in briefly. "I know it's not your fault," he said to Smith and Hertzfeld. "Steve Jobs is the problem. Tell Steve that he's destroying Apple!"

Jobs did indeed make the Macintosh into a low-cost competitor to the Lisa, one with incompatible software. Making matters worse was that neither machine was compatible with the Apple II. With no one in overall charge at Apple, there was no chance of keeping Jobs in harness.

End-to-end Control

Jobs's reluctance to make the Mac compatible with the architecture of the Lisa was motivated by more than rivalry or revenge. There was a philosophical component, one that was related to his penchant for control. He believed that for a computer to be truly great, its hardware and its software had to be tightly linked. When a computer was open to running software that also worked on other computers, it would end up sacrificing some functionality. The best products, he believed, were "whole widgets" that were designed end-to-end, with the software closely tailored to the hardware and vice versa. This is what would distinguish the Macintosh, which had an operating system that worked only on its own hardware, from the environment that Microsoft was creating, in which its operating system could be used on hardware made by many different companies.

"Jobs is a strong-willed, elitist artist who doesn't want his creations mutated inauspiciously by unworthy programmers," explained ZDNet's editor Dan Farber. "It would be as if someone off the street added some brush strokes to a Picasso painting or changed the lyrics to a Dylan song." In later years Jobs's whole-widget approach would distinguish the iPhone, iPod, and iPad from their competitors. It resulted in awesome products. But it was not always the best strategy for dominating a market. "From the first Mac to the latest iPhone, Jobs's systems have always been sealed shut to prevent consumers from meddling and modifying them," noted Leander Kahney, author of *Cult of the Mac*.

Jobs's desire to control the user experience had been at the heart of his debate with Wozniak over whether the Apple II would have slots that allow a user to plug expansion cards into a computer's motherboard and thus add some new functionality. Wozniak won that argument: The Apple II had eight slots. But this time around it would be Jobs's machine, not Wozniak's, and the Macintosh would have limited slots. You wouldn't even be able to open the case and get to the motherboard. For a hobbyist or hacker, that was uncool. But for Jobs, the Macintosh was for the masses. He wanted to give them a controlled experience.

"It reflects his personality, which is to want control," said Berry Cash, who was hired by Jobs in 1982 to be a market strategist at Texaco Towers. "Steve would talk about the Apple II and complain, 'We don't have control, and look at all these crazy things people are trying to do to it. That's a mistake I'll never make again.'" He went so far as to design special tools so that the Macintosh case could not be opened with a regular screwdriver. "We're going to design this thing so nobody but Apple employees can get inside this box," he told Cash.

Jobs also decided to eliminate the cursor arrow keys on the Macintosh keyboard. The only way to move the cursor was to use the mouse. It was a way of forcing old-fashioned users to adapt to point-and-click navigation, even if they didn't want to. Unlike other product developers, Jobs did not believe the customer was always right; if they wanted to resist using a mouse, they were wrong.

There was one other advantage, he believed, to eliminating the cursor keys: It forced outside software developers to write programs specially for the Mac operating system, rather than merely writing generic software that could be ported to a variety of computers. That made for the type of tight vertical integration between application software, operating systems, and hardware devices that Jobs liked.

Jobs's desire for end-to-end control also made him allergic to proposals that Apple license the Macintosh operating system to other office equipment manufacturers and allow them to make Macintosh clones.

The new and energetic Macintosh marketing director Mike Murray proposed a licensing program in a confidential memo to Jobs in May 1982. "We would like the Macintosh user environment to become an industry standard," he wrote. "The hitch, of course, is that now one must buy Mac hardware in order to get this user environment. Rarely (if ever) has one company been able to create and maintain an industry-wide standard that cannot be shared with other manufacturers." His proposal was to license the Macintosh operating system to Tandy. Because Tandy's Radio Shack stores went after a different type of customer, Murray argued, it would not severely cannibalize Apple sales. But Jobs was congenitally averse to such a plan. His approach meant that the Macintosh remained a controlled environment that met his standards, but it also meant that, as Murray feared, it would have trouble securing its place as an industry standard in a world of IBM clones.

Machines of the Year

As 1982 drew to a close, Jobs came to believe that he was going to be *Time*'s Man of the Year. He arrived at Texaco Towers one day with the magazine's San Francisco bureau chief, Michael Moritz, and encouraged colleagues to give Moritz interviews. But Jobs did not end up on the cover. Instead the magazine chose "the Computer" as the topic for the year-end issue and called it "the Machine of the Year."

Accompanying the main story was a profile of Jobs, which was based on the reporting done by Moritz and written by Jay Cocks, an editor who usually handled rock music for the magazine. "With his smooth sales pitch and a blind faith that would have been the envy of the early Christian martyrs, it is Steven Jobs, more than anyone, who kicked open the door and let the personal computer move in," the story proclaimed. It was a richly reported piece, but also harsh at times—so harsh that Moritz (after he wrote a book about Apple and went on to be a partner in the venture firm Sequoia Capital with Don Valentine) repudiated it by complaining that his reporting had been "siphoned, filtered, and poisoned with gossipy benzene by an editor in New York whose regular task was to chronicle the wayward world of rock-and-roll music." The article quoted Bud Tribble on Jobs's "reality distortion field" and noted that he "would occasionally burst into tears at meetings." Perhaps the best quote came from Jef Raskin. Jobs, he declared, "would have made an excellent King of France."

To Jobs's dismay, the magazine made public the existence of the daughter he had forsaken, Lisa Brennan. He knew that Kottke had been the one to tell the magazine about Lisa, and he berated him in the Mac group work space in front of a half dozen people. "When the *Time* reporter asked me if Steve had a daughter named Lisa, I said 'Of course,'" Kottke recalled. "Friends don't let friends deny that they're the father of a child. I'm not going to let my friend be a jerk and deny paternity. He was really angry and felt violated and told me in front of everyone that I had betrayed him."

But what truly devastated Jobs was that he was not, after all, chosen as the Man of the Year. As he later told me:

> *Time* decided they were going to make me Man of the Year, and I was twenty-seven, so I actually cared about stuff like that. I thought it was pretty cool. They sent out Mike Moritz to write a story. We're the same age, and I had been very successful, and I could tell he was jealous and there was an edge to him. He wrote this terrible hatchet job. So the editors in New York get this story and say, "We can't make this guy Man of the Year." That really hurt. But it was a good lesson. It taught me to never get too excited about things like that, since the media is a circus anyway. They FedExed me the magazine, and I remember opening the package, thoroughly expecting to see my mug on the cover, and it was this computer sculpture thing. I thought, "Huh?" And then I read the article, and it was so awful that I actually cried.

In fact there's no reason to believe that Moritz was jealous or that he intended his reporting to be unfair. Nor was Jobs ever slated to be Man of the Year, despite what he thought. That year the top editors (I was then a junior editor there) decided early on to go with the computer rather than a person, and they commissioned, months in advance, a piece of art from the famous sculptor George Segal to be a gatefold cover image. Ray Cave was then the magazine's editor. "We never considered Jobs," he said. "You couldn't personify the computer, so that was the first time we decided to go with an inanimate object. We never searched around for a face to be put on the cover."

Apple launched the Lisa in January 1983—a full year before the Mac was ready—and Jobs paid his $5,000 wager to Couch. Even though he was not part of the Lisa team, Jobs went to New York to do publicity for it in his role as Apple's chairman and poster boy.

He had learned from his public relations consultant Regis McKenna how to dole out exclusive interviews in a dramatic manner. Reporters from anointed publications were ushered in sequentially for their hour with him in his Carlyle Hotel suite, where a Lisa computer was set on a table and surrounded by cut flowers. The publicity plan called for Jobs to focus on the Lisa and not mention the Macintosh, because speculation about it could undermine the Lisa. But Jobs couldn't help himself. In most of the stories based on his interviews that day—in *Time*, *Business Week*, the *Wall Street Journal*, and *Fortune*—the Macintosh was mentioned. "Later this year Apple will introduce a less powerful, less expensive version of Lisa, the Macintosh," *Fortune* reported. "Jobs himself has directed that project." *Business Week* quoted him as saying, "When it comes out, Mac is going to be the most incredible computer in the world." He also admitted that the Mac and the Lisa would not be compatible. It was like launching the Lisa with the kiss of death.

The Lisa did indeed die a slow death. Within two years it would be discontinued. "It was too expensive, and we were trying to sell it to big companies when our expertise was selling to consumers," Jobs later said. But there was a silver lining for Jobs: Within months of Lisa's launch, it became clear that Apple had to pin its hopes on the Macintosh instead.

Let's Be Pirates!

As the Macintosh team grew, it moved from Texaco Towers to the main Apple buildings on Bandley Drive, finally settling in mid-1983 into Bandley 3. It had a modern atrium lobby with video games, which

Burrell Smith and Andy Hertzfeld chose, and a Toshiba compact disc stereo system with MartinLogan speakers and a hundred CDs. The software team was visible from the lobby in a fishbowl-like glass enclosure, and the kitchen was stocked daily with Odwalla juices. Over time the atrium attracted even more toys, most notably a Bösendorfer piano and a BMW motorcycle that Jobs felt would inspire an obsession with lapidary craftsmanship.

Jobs kept a tight rein on the hiring process. The goal was to get people who were creative, wickedly smart, and slightly rebellious. The software team would make applicants play Defender, Smith's favorite video game. Jobs would ask his usual offbeat questions to see how well the applicant could think in unexpected situations. One day he, Hertzfeld, and Smith interviewed a candidate for software manager who, it became clear as soon as he walked in the room, was too uptight and conventional to manage the wizards in the fishbowl. Jobs began to toy with him mercilessly. "How old were you when you lost your virginity?" he asked.

The candidate looked baffled. "What did you say?"

"Are you a virgin?" Jobs asked. The candidate sat there flustered, so Jobs changed the subject. "How many times have you taken LSD?" Hertzfeld recalled, "The poor guy was turning varying shades of red, so I tried to change the subject and asked a straightforward technical question." But when the candidate droned on in his response, Jobs broke in. "Gobble, gobble, gobble, gobble," he said, cracking up Smith and Hertzfeld.

"I guess I'm not the right guy," the poor man said as he got up to leave.

For all of his obnoxious behavior, Jobs also had the ability to instill in his team an esprit de corps. After tearing people down, he would find ways to lift them up and make them feel that being part of the Macintosh project was an amazing mission. Every six months he would take most of his team on a two-day retreat at a nearby resort.

The retreat in September 1982 was at the Pajaro Dunes near Monterey. Fifty or so members of the Mac division sat in the lodge facing a fireplace. Jobs sat on top of a table in front of them. He spoke quietly for a while, then walked to an easel and began posting his thoughts.

The first was "Don't compromise." It was an injunction that would, over time, be both helpful and harmful. Most technology teams made trade-offs. The Mac, on the other hand, would end up being as "insanely great" as Jobs and his acolytes could possibly make it—but it would not ship for another sixteen months, way behind schedule. After mentioning a scheduled completion date, he told them, "It would be better to miss than to turn out the wrong thing." A different type of project manager, willing to make some trade-offs, might try to lock in dates after which no changes could be made. Not Jobs. He displayed another maxim: "It's not done until it ships."

Another chart contained a kōan-like phrase that he later told me was his favorite maxim: "The journey is the reward." The Mac team, he liked to emphasize, was a special corps with an exalted mission. Someday they would all look back on their journey together and, forgetting or laughing off the painful moments, would regard it as a magical high point in their lives.

At the end of the presentation someone asked whether he thought they should do some market research to see what customers wanted. "No," he replied, "because customers don't know what they want until we've shown them." Then he pulled out a device that was about the size of a desk diary. "Do you want to see something neat?" When he flipped it open, it turned out to be a mock-up of a computer that could fit on your lap, with a keyboard and screen hinged together like a notebook. "This is my dream of what we will be making in the mid- to late eighties," he said. They were building a company that would invent the future.

For the next two days there were presentations by various team leaders and the influential computer industry analyst Ben Rosen, with a lot of time in the evenings for pool parties and dancing. At the end, Jobs stood in front of the assemblage and gave a soliloquy. "As every day passes, the work fifty people are doing here is going to send a giant ripple through the universe," he said. "I know I might be a little hard to get along with, but this is the most fun thing I've done in my life."

Years later most of those in the audience would be able to laugh about the "little hard to get along with" episodes and agree with him that creating that giant ripple was the most fun they had in their lives.

The next retreat was at the end of January 1983, the same month the Lisa launched, and there was a shift in tone. Four months earlier Jobs had written on his flip chart: "Don't compromise." This time one of the maxims was "Real artists ship." Nerves were frayed. Atkinson had been left out of the publicity interviews for the Lisa launch, and he marched into Jobs's hotel room and threatened to quit. Jobs tried to minimize the slight, but Atkinson refused to be mollified. Jobs got annoyed. "I don't have time to deal with this now," he said. "I have sixty other people out there who are pouring their hearts into the Macintosh, and they're waiting for me to start the meeting." With that he brushed past Atkinson to go address the faithful.

Jobs proceeded to give a rousing speech in which he claimed that he had resolved the dispute with McIntosh audio labs to use the Macintosh name. (In fact the issue was still being negotiated, but the moment called for a bit of the old reality distortion field.) He pulled out a bottle of mineral water and symbolically christened the prototype onstage. Down the hall, Atkinson heard the loud cheer, and with a sigh joined the group. The ensuing party featured skinny-dipping in the pool, a bonfire on the beach, and loud music that lasted all night, which caused the hotel, La Playa in Carmel, to ask them never to come back.

Another of Jobs's maxims at the retreat was "It's better to be a pirate than to join the navy." He wanted to instill a rebel spirit in his team, to have them behave like swashbucklers who were proud of their work but willing to commandeer from others. As Susan Kare put it, "He meant, 'Let's have a renegade feeling to our group. We can move fast. We can get things done.'" To celebrate Jobs's birthday a few weeks later, the team paid for a billboard on the road to Apple headquarters. It read: "Happy 28th Steve. The Journey is the Reward.—The Pirates."

One of the Mac team's programmers, Steve Capps, decided this new spirit warranted hoisting a Jolly Roger. He cut a patch of black cloth and had Kare paint a skull and crossbones on it. The eye patch she put on the skull was an Apple logo. Late one Sunday night Capps climbed to the roof of their newly built Bandley 3 building and hoisted the flag on a scaffolding pole that the construction workers had left behind. It waved proudly for a few weeks, until members of the Lisa team, in a late-night foray, stole the flag and sent their Mac rivals a ransom note. Capps led a raid to recover it and was able to wrestle it from a secretary who was guarding it for the Lisa team. Some of the grown-ups overseeing Apple worried that Jobs's buccaneer spirit was getting out of hand. "Flying that flag was really stupid," said Arthur Rock. "It was telling the rest of the company they were no good." But Jobs loved it, and he made sure it waved proudly all the way through to the completion of the Mac project. "We were the renegades, and we wanted people to know it," he recalled.

Veterans of the Mac team had learned that they could stand up to Jobs. If they knew what they were talking about, he would tolerate the pushback, even admire it. By 1983 those most familiar with his reality distortion field had discovered something further: They could, if necessary, just quietly disregard what he decreed. If they turned out to be right, he would appreciate their renegade attitude and willingness to ignore authority. After all, that's what he did.

By far the most important example of this involved the choice of a disk drive for the Macintosh. Apple had a corporate division that built mass-storage devices, and it had developed a disk-drive system, code-named Twiggy, that could read and write onto those thin, delicate 5¼-inch floppy disks that older readers (who also remember Twiggy the model) will recall. But by the time the Lisa was ready to ship in the spring of 1983, it was clear that the Twiggy was buggy. Because the Lisa also came with a hard-disk drive, this was not a complete disaster. But the Mac had no hard disk, so it faced a crisis. "The Mac team was beginning to panic," said Hertzfeld. "We were using a single Twiggy drive, and we didn't have a hard disk to fall back on."

The team discussed the problem at the January 1983 retreat, and Debi Coleman gave Jobs data about the Twiggy failure rate. A few days later he drove to Apple's factory in San Jose to see the Twiggy being made. More than half were rejected. Jobs erupted. With his face flushed, he began shouting and sputtering about firing everyone who worked there. Bob Belleville, the head of the Mac engineering team, gently guided him to the parking lot, where they could take a walk and talk about alternatives.

One possibility that Belleville had been exploring was to use a new 3½-inch disk drive that Sony had developed. The disk was cased in sturdier plastic and could fit into a shirt pocket. Another option was to have a clone of Sony's 3½-inch disk drive manufactured by a smaller Japanese supplier, the Alps Electronics Co., which had been supplying disk drives for the Apple II. Alps had already licensed the technology from Sony, and if they could build their own version in time it would be much cheaper.

Jobs and Belleville, along with Apple veteran Rod Holt (the guy Jobs enlisted to design the first power supply for the Apple II), flew to Japan to figure out what to do. They took the bullet train from Tokyo to visit the Alps facility. The engineers there didn't even have a working prototype, just a crude model. Jobs thought it was great, but Belleville was appalled. There was no way, he thought, that Alps could have it ready for the Mac within a year.

As they proceeded to visit other Japanese companies, Jobs was on his worst behavior. He wore jeans and sneakers to meetings with Japanese managers in dark suits. When they formally handed him little gifts, as was the custom, he often left them behind, and he never reciprocated with gifts of his own. He would sneer when rows of engineers lined up to greet him, bow, and politely offer their products for inspection. Jobs hated both the devices and the obsequiousness. "What are you showing me *this* for?" he snapped at one stop. "This is a piece of crap! *Anybody* could build a better drive than this." Although most of his hosts were appalled, some seemed amused. They had heard tales of his obnoxious style and brash behavior, and now they were getting to see it in full display.

The final stop was the Sony factory, located in a drab suburb of Tokyo. To Jobs, it looked messy and inelegant. A lot of the work was done by hand. He hated it. Back at the hotel, Belleville argued for going with the Sony disk drive. It was ready to use. Jobs disagreed. He decided that they would work with Alps to produce their own drive, and he ordered Belleville to cease all work with Sony.

Belleville decided it was best to partially ignore Jobs, and he asked a Sony executive to get its disk drive ready for use in the Macintosh. If and when it became clear that Alps could not deliver on time, Apple would switch to Sony. So Sony sent over the engineer who had developed the drive, Hidetoshi Komoto, a Purdue graduate who fortunately possessed a good sense of humor about his clandestine task.

Whenever Jobs would come from his corporate office to visit the Mac team's engineers—which was almost every afternoon—they would hurriedly find somewhere for Komoto to hide. At one point Jobs ran into him at a newsstand in Cupertino and recognized him from the meeting in Japan, but he didn't suspect anything. The closest call was when Jobs came bustling onto the Mac work space unexpectedly one day while Komoto was sitting in one of the cubicles. A Mac engineer grabbed him and pointed him to a janitorial closet. "Quick, hide in this closet. Please! Now!" Komoto looked confused, Hertzfeld recalled, but he jumped up and did as told. He had to stay in the closet for five minutes, until Jobs left. The Mac engineers apologized. "No problem," he replied. "But American business practices, they are very strange. Very strange."

Belleville's prediction came true. In May 1983 the folks at Alps admitted it would take them at least eighteen more months to get their clone of the Sony drive into production. At a retreat in Pajaro Dunes, Markkula grilled Jobs on what he was going to do. Finally, Belleville interrupted and said that he might have an alternative to the Alps drive ready soon. Jobs looked baffled for just a moment, and then it became clear to him why he'd glimpsed Sony's top disk designer in Cupertino. "You son of a bitch!" Jobs said. But it was not in anger. There was a big grin on his face. As soon as he realized what Belleville and the other engineers had done behind his back, said Hertzfeld, "Steve swallowed his pride and thanked them for disobeying him and doing the right thing." It was, after all, what he would have done in their situation.

CHAPTER FOURTEEN

ENTER SCULLEY

The Pepsi Challenge

With John Sculley, 1984

The Courtship

Mike Markkula had never wanted to be Apple's president. He liked designing his new houses, flying his private plane, and living high off his stock options; he did not relish adjudicating conflict or curating high-maintenance egos. He had stepped into the role reluctantly, after he felt compelled to ease out Mike Scott, and he promised his wife the gig would be temporary. By the end of 1982, after almost two years, she gave him an order: Find a replacement right away.

Jobs knew that he was not ready to run the company himself, even though there was a part of him that wanted to try. Despite his arrogance, he could be self-aware. Markkula agreed; he told Jobs that he was still a bit too rough-edged and immature to be Apple's president. So they launched a search for someone from the outside.

The person they most wanted was Don Estridge, who had built IBM's personal computer division from scratch and launched a PC that, even though Jobs and his team disparaged it, was now outselling Apple's. Estridge had sheltered his division in Boca Raton, Florida, safely removed from the corporate mentality of Armonk, New York. Like Jobs, he was driven and inspiring, but unlike Jobs, he had the ability to allow others to think that his brilliant ideas were their own. Jobs flew to Boca Raton with the offer of a $1 million salary and a $1 million signing bonus, but Estridge turned him down. He was not the type who would jump ship to join the enemy. He also enjoyed being part of the establishment, a member of the Navy rather than a pirate. He was discomforted by Jobs's tales of ripping off the phone company. When asked where he worked, he loved to be able to answer "IBM."

So Jobs and Markkula enlisted Gerry Roche, a gregarious corporate headhunter, to find someone else. They decided not to focus on technology executives; what they needed was a consumer marketer who knew advertising and had the corporate polish that would play well on Wall Street. Roche set his sights on the hottest consumer marketing wizard of the moment, John Sculley, president of the Pepsi-Cola division of PepsiCo, whose Pepsi Challenge campaign had been an advertising and publicity triumph. When Jobs gave a talk to Stanford business students, he heard good things about Sculley, who had spoken to the class earlier. So he told Roche he would be happy to meet him.

Sculley's background was very different from Jobs's. His mother was an Upper East Side Manhattan matron who wore white gloves when she went out, and his father was a proper Wall Street lawyer. Sculley was sent off to St. Mark's School, then got his undergraduate degree from Brown and a business degree from Wharton. He had risen through the ranks at PepsiCo as an innovative marketer and advertiser, with little passion for product development or information technology.

Sculley flew to Los Angeles to spend Christmas with his two

teenage children from a previous marriage. He took them to visit a computer store, where he was struck by how poorly the products were marketed. When his kids asked why he was so interested, he said he was planning to go up to Cupertino to meet Steve Jobs. They were totally blown away. They had grown up among movie stars, but to them Jobs was a true celebrity. It made Sculley take more seriously the prospect of being hired as his boss.

When he arrived at Apple headquarters, Sculley was startled by the unassuming offices and casual atmosphere. "Most people were less formally dressed than PepsiCo's maintenance staff," he noted. Over lunch Jobs picked quietly at his salad, but when Sculley declared that most executives found computers more trouble than they were worth, Jobs clicked into evangelical mode. "We want to change the way people use computers," he said.

On the flight home Sculley outlined his thoughts. The result was an eight-page memo on marketing computers to consumers and business executives. It was a bit sophomoric in parts, filled with underlined phrases, diagrams, and boxes, but it revealed his newfound enthusiasm for figuring out ways to sell something more interesting than soda. Among his recommendations: "Invest in in-store merchandizing that romances the consumer with Apple's potential to enrich their life!" He was still reluctant to leave Pepsi, but Jobs intrigued him. "I was taken by this young, impetuous genius and thought it would be fun to get to know him a little better," he recalled.

So Sculley agreed to meet again when Jobs next came to New York, which happened to be for the January 1983 Lisa introduction at the Carlyle Hotel. After the full day of press sessions, the Apple team was surprised to see an unscheduled visitor come into the suite. Jobs loosened his tie and introduced Sculley as the president of Pepsi and a potential big corporate customer. As John Couch demonstrated the Lisa, Jobs chimed in with bursts of commentary, sprinkled with his favorite words, "revolutionary" and "incredible," claiming it would change the nature of human interaction with computers.

They then headed off to the Four Seasons restaurant, a shimmering haven of elegance and power. As Jobs ate a special vegan meal, Sculley described Pepsi's marketing successes. The Pepsi Generation campaign, he said, sold not a product but a lifestyle and an optimistic outlook. "I think Apple's got a chance to create an Apple Generation." Jobs enthusiastically agreed. The Pepsi Challenge campaign, in contrast, focused on the product; it combined ads, events, and public relations to stir up buzz. The ability to turn the introduction of a new product into a moment of national excitement was, Jobs noted, what he and Regis McKenna wanted to do at Apple.

When they finished talking, it was close to midnight. "This has been one of the most exciting evenings in my whole life," Jobs said as Sculley walked him back to the Carlyle. "I can't tell you how much fun I've had." When he finally got home to Greenwich, Connecticut, that night, Sculley had trouble sleeping. Engaging with Jobs was a lot more fun than negotiating with bottlers. "It stimulated me, roused my long-held desire to be an architect of ideas," he later noted. The next morning Roche called Sculley. "I don't know what you guys did last night, but let me tell you, Steve Jobs is ecstatic," he said.

And so the courtship continued, with Sculley playing hard but not impossible to get. Jobs flew east for a visit one Saturday in February and took a limo up to Greenwich. He found Sculley's newly built mansion ostentatious, with its floor-to-ceiling windows, but he admired the three hundred-pound custom-made oak doors that were so carefully hung and balanced that they swung open with the touch of a finger. "Steve was fascinated by that because he is, as I am, a perfectionist," Sculley recalled. Thus began the somewhat unhealthy process of a star-struck Sculley perceiving in Jobs qualities that he fancied in himself.

Sculley usually drove a Cadillac, but, sensing his guest's taste, he borrowed his wife's Mercedes 450SL convertible to take Jobs to see Pepsi's 144-acre corporate headquarters, which was as lavish as Apple's was austere. To Jobs, it epitomized the difference between the feisty new digital economy and the Fortune 500 corporate establishment. A winding drive led through manicured fields and a sculpture garden (including pieces by Rodin, Moore, Calder, and Giacometti) to a concrete-and-glass building designed by Edward Durell Stone. Sculley's huge office had a Persian rug, nine windows, a small private garden, a hideaway study, and its own bathroom. When Jobs saw the corporate fitness center, he was astonished that executives had an area, with its own whirlpool, separate from that of the regular employees. "That's weird," he said. Sculley hastened to agree. "As a matter of fact, I was against it, and I go over and work out sometimes in the employees' area," he said.

Their next meeting was a few weeks later in Cupertino, when Sculley stopped on his way back from a Pepsi bottlers' convention in Hawaii. Mike Murray, the Macintosh marketing manager, took charge of preparing the team for the visit, but he was not clued in on the real agenda. "PepsiCo could end up purchasing literally thousands of Macs over the next few years," he exulted in a memo to the Macintosh staff. "During the past year, Mr. Sculley and a certain Mr. Jobs have become friends. Mr. Sculley is considered to be one of the best marketing heads in the big leagues; as such, let's give him a good time here."

Jobs wanted Sculley to share his excitement about the Macintosh. "This product means more to me than anything I've done," he said. "I want you to be the first person outside of Apple to see it." He dramatically pulled the prototype out of a vinyl bag and gave a demonstration. Sculley found Jobs as memorable as his machine. "He seemed more a showman than a businessman. Every move seemed calculated, as if it was rehearsed, to create an occasion of the moment."

Jobs had asked Hertzfeld and the gang to prepare a special screen display for Sculley's amusement. "He's really smart," Jobs said. "You wouldn't believe how smart he is." The explanation that Sculley might buy a lot of Macintoshes for Pepsi "sounded a little bit fishy to me," Hertzfeld recalled, but he and Susan Kare created a screen of Pepsi caps and cans that danced around with the Apple logo. Hertzfeld was so excited he began waving his arms around during the demo, but Sculley seemed underwhelmed. "He asked a few questions, but he didn't seem all that interested," Hertzfeld recalled. He never ended up warming to Sculley. "He was incredibly phony, a complete poseur," he later said. "He pretended to be interested in technology, but he wasn't. He was a marketing guy, and that is what marketing guys are: paid poseurs."

Matters came to a head when Jobs visited New York in March 1983 and was able to convert the courtship into a blind and blinding romance. "I really think you're the guy," Jobs said as they walked through Central Park. "I want you to come and work with me. I can learn so much from you." Jobs, who had cultivated father figures in the past, knew just how to play to Sculley's ego and insecurities. It worked. "I was smitten by him," Sculley later admitted. "Steve was one of the brightest people I'd ever met. I shared with him a passion for ideas."

Sculley, who was interested in art history, steered them toward the Metropolitan Museum for a little test of whether Jobs was really willing to learn from others. "I wanted to see how well he could take coaching in a subject where he had no background," he recalled. As they strolled through the Greek and Roman antiquities, Sculley expounded on the difference between the Archaic sculpture of the sixth century B.C. and the Periclean sculptures a century later. Jobs, who loved to pick up historical nuggets he never learned in college, seemed to soak it in. "I gained a sense that I could be a teacher to a brilliant student," Sculley recalled. Once again he indulged the conceit that they were alike: "I saw in him a mirror image of my younger self. I, too, was impatient, stubborn, arrogant, impetuous. My mind exploded with ideas, often to the exclusion of everything else. I, too, was intolerant of those who couldn't live up to my demands."

As they continued their long walk, Sculley confided that on vacations he went to the Left Bank in Paris to draw in his sketchbook; if he hadn't become a businessman, he would be an artist. Jobs replied that if he weren't working with computers, he could see himself as a poet in Paris. They continued down Broadway to Colony Records on Forty-ninth Street, where Jobs showed Sculley the music he liked, including Bob Dylan, Joan Baez, Ella Fitzgerald, and the Windham Hill jazz artists. Then they walked all the way back up to the San Remo on Central Park West and Seventy-fourth, where Jobs was planning to buy a two-story tower penthouse apartment.

The consummation occurred outside the penthouse on one of the terraces, with Sculley sticking close to the wall because he was afraid of heights. First they discussed money. "I told him I needed $1 million in salary, $1 million for a sign-up bonus," said Sculley. Jobs claimed that would be doable. "Even if I have to pay for it out of my own pocket," he said. "We'll have to solve those problems, because you're the best person I've ever met. I know you're perfect for Apple, and Apple deserves the best." He added that never before had he worked for someone he really respected, but he knew that Sculley was the person who could teach him the most. Jobs gave him his unblinking stare.

Sculley uttered one last demurral, a token suggestion that maybe they should just be friends and he could offer Jobs advice from the sidelines. "Any time you're in New York, I'd love to spend time with you." He later recounted the climactic moment: "Steve's head dropped as he stared at his feet. After a weighty, uncomfortable pause, he issued a challenge that would haunt me for days. 'Do you want to spend the rest of your life selling sugared water, or do you want a chance to change the world?'"

Sculley felt as if he had been punched in the stomach. There was no response possible other than to acquiesce. "He had an uncanny ability to always get what he wanted, to size up a person and know exactly what to say to reach a person," Sculley recalled. "I realized for the first time in four months that I couldn't say no." The winter sun was beginning to set. They left the apartment and walked back across the park to the Carlyle.

The Honeymoon

Sculley arrived in California just in time for the May 1983 Apple management retreat at Pajaro Dunes. Even though he had left all but one of his dark suits back in Greenwich, he was still having trouble adjusting to the casual atmosphere. In the front of the meeting room, Jobs sat on the floor in the lotus position absentmindedly playing with the toes of his bare feet. Sculley tried to impose an agenda; he wanted to discuss how to differentiate their products—the Apple II, Apple III, Lisa, and Mac—and whether it made sense to organize the company around product lines or markets or functions. But the discussion descended into a free-for-all of random ideas, complaints, and debates.

At one point Jobs attacked the Lisa team for producing an unsuccessful product. "Well," someone shot back, "you haven't delivered the Macintosh! Why don't you wait until you get a product out before you start being critical?" Sculley was astonished. At Pepsi no one would have challenged the chairman like that. "Yet here, everyone began pig-piling on Steve." It reminded him of an old joke he had heard from one of the Apple ad salesmen: "What's the difference between Apple and the Boy Scouts? The Boy Scouts have adult supervision."

In the midst of the bickering, a small earthquake began to rumble the room. "Head for the beach," someone shouted. Everyone ran through the door to the water. Then someone else shouted that the previous earthquake had produced a tidal wave, so they all turned and ran the other way. "The indecision, the contradictory advice, the specter of natural disaster, only foreshadowed what was to come," Sculley later wrote.

One Saturday morning Jobs invited Sculley and his wife, Leezy, over for breakfast. He was then living in a nice but unexceptional Tudor-style home in Los Gatos with his girlfriend, Barbara Jasinski, a smart and reserved beauty who worked for Regis McKenna. Leezy had brought a pan and made vegetarian omelets. (Jobs had edged away from his strict vegan diet for the time being.) "I'm sorry I don't have much furniture," Jobs apologized. "I just haven't gotten around to it." It was one of his enduring quirks: His exacting standards of craftsmanship combined with a Spartan streak made him reluctant to buy any furnishings that he wasn't passionate about. He had a Tiffany lamp, an antique dining table, and a laser disc video attached to a Sony Trinitron, but foam cushions on the floor rather than sofas and chairs. Sculley smiled and mistakenly thought that it was similar to his own "frantic and Spartan life in a cluttered New York City apartment" early in his own career.

Jobs confided in Sculley that he believed he would die young, and therefore he needed to accomplish things quickly so that he would make his mark on Silicon Valley history. "We all have a short period of time on this earth," he told the Sculleys as they sat around the table that morning. "We probably only have the opportunity to do a few things really great and do them well. None of us has any idea how long we're going to be here, nor do I, but my feeling is I've got to accomplish a lot of these things while I'm young."

Jobs and Sculley would talk dozens of times a day in the early months of their relationship. "Steve and I became soul mates, near constant companions," Sculley said. "We tended to speak in half sentences and phrases." Jobs flattered Sculley. When he dropped by to hash something out, he would say something like "You're the only one who will understand." They would tell each other repeatedly, indeed so often that it should have been worrying, how happy they were to be with each other and working in tandem. And at every opportunity Sculley would find similarities with Jobs and point them out:

> We could complete each other's sentences because we were on the same wavelength. Steve would rouse me from sleep at 2 a.m. with a phone call to chat about an idea that suddenly crossed his mind. "Hi! It's me," he'd harmlessly say to the dazed listener, totally unaware of the time. I curiously had done the same in my Pepsi days. Steve would rip apart a presentation he had to give the next morning, throwing out slides and text. So had I as I struggled to turn public speaking into an important management tool during my early days at Pepsi. As a young executive, I was always impatient to get things done and often felt I could do them better myself. So did Steve. Sometimes I felt as if I was watching Steve playing me in a movie. The similarities were uncanny, and they were behind the amazing symbiosis we developed.

This was self-delusion, and it was a recipe for disaster. Jobs began to sense it early on. "We had different ways of looking at the world, different views on people, different values," Jobs recalled. "I began to realize this a few months after he arrived. He didn't learn things very quickly, and the people he wanted to promote were usually bozos."

Yet Jobs knew that he could manipulate Sculley by encouraging his belief that they were so alike. And the more he manipulated Sculley, the more contemptuous of him he became. Canny observers in the Mac group, such as Joanna Hoffman, soon realized what was happening and knew that it would make the inevitable breakup more explosive. "Steve made Sculley feel like he was exceptional," she said. "Sculley had never felt that. Sculley became infatuated, because Steve projected on him a whole bunch of attributes that he didn't really have. When it became clear that Sculley didn't match all of these projections, Steve's distortion of reality had created an explosive situation."

The ardor eventually began to cool on Sculley's side as well. Part of his weakness in trying to manage a dysfunctional company was his desire to please other people, one of many traits that he did not share with Jobs. He was a polite person; this caused him to recoil at Jobs's rudeness to their fellow workers. "We would go to the Mac building at eleven at night," he recalled, "and they would bring him code to show. In some cases he wouldn't even look at it. He would just take it and throw it back at them. I'd say, 'How can you turn it down?' And he would say, 'I know they can do better.'" Sculley tried to coach him. "You've got to learn to hold things back," he told him at one point. Jobs would agree, but it was not in his nature to filter his feelings through a gauze.

Sculley began to believe that Jobs's mercurial personality and erratic treatment of people were rooted deep in his psychological makeup, perhaps the reflection of a mild bipolarity. There were big mood swings; sometimes he would be ecstatic, at other times he was depressed. At times he would launch into brutal tirades without warning, and Sculley would have to calm him down. "Twenty minutes later, I would get another call and be told to come over because Steve is losing it again," he said.

Their first substantive disagreement was over how to price the Macintosh. It had been conceived as a $1,000 machine, but Jobs's design changes had pushed up the cost so that the plan was to sell it at $1,995. However, when Jobs and Sculley began making plans for a huge launch and marketing push, Sculley decided that they needed to charge $500 more. To him, the marketing costs were like any other production cost and needed to be factored into the price. Jobs resisted, furiously. "It will destroy everything we stand for," he said. "I want to make this a revolution, not an effort to squeeze out profits." Sculley said it was a simple choice: He could have the $1,995 price or he could have the marketing budget for a big launch, but not both.

"You're not going to like this," Jobs told Hertzfeld and the other engineers, "but Sculley is insisting that we charge $2,495 for the Mac instead of $1,995." Indeed the engineers were horrified. Hertzfeld pointed out that they were designing the Mac for people like themselves, and overpricing it would be a "betrayal" of what they stood for.

So Jobs promised them, "Don't worry, I'm not going to let him get away with it!" But in the end, Sculley prevailed. Even twenty-five years later Jobs seethed when recalling the decision: "It's the main reason the Macintosh sales slowed and Microsoft got to dominate the market." The decision made him feel that he was losing control of his product and company, and this was as dangerous as making a tiger feel cornered.

CHAPTER FIFTEEN

THE LAUNCH

A Dent in the Universe

The "1984" ad

Real Artists Ship

The high point of the October 1983 Apple sales conference in Hawaii was a skit based on a TV show called *The Dating Game.* Jobs played emcee, and his three contestants, whom he had convinced to fly to Hawaii, were Bill Gates and two other software executives, Mitch Kapor and Fred Gibbons. As the show's jingly theme song played, the three took their stools. Gates, looking like a high school sophomore, got wild applause from the 750 Apple salesmen when he said, "During

1984, Microsoft expects to get half of its revenues from software for the Macintosh." Jobs, clean-shaven and bouncy, gave a toothy smile and asked if he thought that the Macintosh's new operating system would become one of the industry's new standards. Gates answered, "To create a new standard takes not just making something that's a little bit different, it takes something that's really new and captures people's imagination. And the Macintosh, of all the machines I've ever seen, is the only one that meets that standard."

But even as Gates was speaking, Microsoft was edging away from being primarily a collaborator with Apple to being more of a competitor. It would continue to make application software, like Microsoft Word, for Apple, but a rapidly increasing share of its revenue would come from the operating system it had written for the IBM personal computer. The year before, 279,000 Apple IIs were sold, compared to 240,000 IBM PCs and its clones. But the figures for 1983 were coming in starkly different: 420,000 Apple IIs versus 1.3 million IBMs and its clones. And both the Apple III and the Lisa were dead in the water.

Just when the Apple sales force was arriving in Hawaii, this shift was hammered home on the cover of *Business Week*. Its headline: "Personal Computers: And the Winner Is . . . IBM." The story inside detailed the rise of the IBM PC. "The battle for market supremacy is already over," the magazine declared. "In a stunning blitz, IBM has taken more than 26% of the market in two years, and is expected to account for half the world market by 1985. An additional 25% of the market will be turning out IBM-compatible machines."

That put all the more pressure on the Macintosh, due out in January 1984, three months away, to save the day against IBM. At the sales conference Jobs decided to play the showdown to the hilt. He took the stage and chronicled all the missteps made by IBM since 1958, and then in ominous tones described how it was now trying to take over the market for personal computers: "Will Big Blue dominate the entire computer industry? The entire information age? Was George Orwell right about 1984?" At that moment a screen came down from the ceiling and showed a preview of an upcoming sixty-second television ad for the Macintosh. In a few months it was destined to make advertising history, but in the meantime it served its purpose of rallying Apple's demoralized sales force. Jobs had always been able to draw energy by imagining himself as a rebel pitted against the forces of darkness. Now he was able to energize his troops with the same vision.

There was one more hurdle: Hertzfeld and the other wizards had to finish writing the code for the Macintosh. It was due to start shipping on Monday, January 16. One week before that, the engineers concluded they could not make that deadline.

Jobs was at the Grand Hyatt in Manhattan, preparing for the press previews, so a Sunday morning conference call was scheduled. The software manager calmly explained the situation to Jobs, while Hertzfeld and the others huddled around the speakerphone holding their breath. All they needed was an extra two weeks. The initial shipments to the dealers could have a version of the software labeled "demo," and these could be replaced as soon as the new code was finished at the end of the month. There was a pause. Jobs did not get angry; instead he spoke in cold, somber tones. He told them they were really great. So great, in fact, that he knew they could get this done. "There's no way we're slipping!" he declared. There was a collective gasp in the Bandley building work space. "You guys have been working on this stuff for months now, another couple weeks isn't going to make that much of a difference. You may as well get it over with. I'm going to ship the code a week from Monday, with your names on it."

"Well, we've got to finish it," Steve Capps said. And so they did. Once again, Jobs's reality distortion field pushed them to do what they had thought impossible. On Friday Randy Wigginton brought in a huge bag of chocolate-covered espresso beans for the final three all-nighters. When Jobs arrived at work at 8:30 a.m. that Monday, he found Hertzfeld sprawled nearly comatose on the couch. They talked for a few minutes about a remaining tiny glitch, and Jobs decreed that it wasn't a problem. Hertzfeld dragged himself to his blue Volkswagen Rabbit (license plate: MACWIZ) and drove home to bed. A short while later Apple's Fremont factory began to roll out boxes emblazoned with the colorful line drawings of the Macintosh. Real artists ship, Jobs had declared, and now the Macintosh team had.

The "1984" Ad

In the spring of 1983, when Jobs had begun to plan for the Macintosh launch, he asked for a commercial that was as revolutionary and astonishing as the product they had created. "I want something that will stop people in their tracks," he said. "I want a thunderclap." The task fell to the Chiat/Day advertising agency, which had acquired the Apple account when it bought the advertising side of Regis McKenna's business. The person put in charge was a lanky beach bum with a bushy beard, wild hair, goofy grin, and twinkling eyes named Lee Clow, who was the creative director of the agency's office in the Venice Beach section of Los Angeles. Clow was savvy and fun, in a laid-back yet focused way, and he forged a bond with Jobs that would last three decades.

Clow and two of his team, the copywriter Steve Hayden and the art director Brent Thomas, had been toying with a tagline that played off the George Orwell novel: "Why 1984 won't be like *1984.*" Jobs loved it, and asked them to develop it for the Macintosh launch. So they put together a storyboard for a sixty-second ad that would look like a scene from a sci-fi movie. It featured a rebellious young woman outrunning the Orwellian thought police and throwing a sledgehammer into a screen showing a mind-controlling speech by Big Brother.

The concept captured the zeitgeist of the personal computer revolution. Many young people, especially those in the counterculture, had viewed computers as instruments that could be used by Orwellian governments and giant corporations to sap individuality. But by the end of the 1970s, they were also being seen as potential tools for personal empowerment. The ad cast Macintosh as a warrior for the latter cause—a cool, rebellious, and heroic company that was the only thing standing in the way of the big evil corporation's plan for world domination and total mind control.

Jobs liked that. Indeed the concept for the ad had a special resonance for him. He fancied himself a rebel, and he liked to associate himself with the values of the ragtag band of hackers and pirates he recruited to the Macintosh group. Even though he had left the apple commune in Oregon to start the Apple corporation, he still wanted to be viewed as a denizen of the counterculture rather than the corporate culture.

But he also realized, deep inside, that he had increasingly abandoned the hacker spirit. Some might even accuse him of selling out. When Wozniak held true to the Homebrew ethic by sharing his design for the Apple I for free, it was Jobs who insisted that they sell the boards instead. He was also the one who, despite Wozniak's reluctance, wanted to turn Apple into a corporation and not freely distribute stock options to the friends who had been in the garage with them. Now he was about to launch the Macintosh, a machine that violated many of the principles of the hacker's code: It was overpriced; it would have no slots, which meant that hobbyists could not plug in their own expansion cards or jack into the motherboard to add their own new functions; and it took special tools just to open the plastic case. It was a closed and controlled system, like something designed by Big Brother rather than by a hacker.

So the "1984" ad was a way of reaffirming, to himself and to the world, his desired self-image. The heroine, with a drawing of a Macintosh emblazoned on her pure white tank top, was a renegade out to foil the establishment. By hiring Ridley Scott, fresh off the success of *Blade Runner*, as the director, Jobs could attach himself and Apple to the cyberpunk ethos of the time. With the ad, Apple could identify itself with the rebels and hackers who thought differently, and Jobs could reclaim his right to identify with them as well.

Sculley was initially skeptical when he saw the storyboards, but Jobs insisted that they needed something revolutionary. He was able to get an unprecedented budget of $750,000 just to film the ad, which they planned to premiere during the Super Bowl. Ridley Scott made it in London using dozens of real skinheads among the enthralled masses listening to Big Brother on the screen. A female discus thrower was chosen to play the heroine. Using a cold industrial setting dominated by metallic gray hues, Scott evoked the dystopian aura of *Blade Runner*. Just at the moment when Big Brother announces "We shall prevail!" the heroine's hammer smashes the screen and it vaporizes in a flash of light and smoke.

When Jobs previewed the ad for the Apple sales force at the meeting in Hawaii, they were thrilled. So he screened it for the board at its December 1983 meeting. When the lights came back on in the boardroom, everyone was mute. Philip Schlein, the CEO of Macy's California, had his head on the table. Mike Markkula stared silently; at first it seemed he was overwhelmed by the power of the ad. Then he spoke: "Who wants to move to find a new agency?" Sculley recalled, "Most of them thought it was the worst commercial they had ever seen." Sculley himself got cold feet. He asked Chiat/Day to sell off the two commercial spots—one sixty seconds, the other thirty—that they had purchased.

Jobs was beside himself. One evening Wozniak, who had been floating into and out of Apple for the previous two years, wandered into the Macintosh building. Jobs grabbed him and said, "Come over here and look at this." He pulled out a VCR and played the ad. "I was astounded," Woz recalled. "I thought it was the most incredible thing." When Jobs said the board had decided not to run it during the Super Bowl, Wozniak asked what the cost of the time slot was. Jobs told him $800,000. With his usual impulsive goodness, Wozniak immediately offered, "Well, I'll pay half if you will."

He ended up not needing to. The agency was able to sell off the thirty-second time slot, but in an act of passive defiance it didn't sell the longer one. "We told them that we couldn't sell the sixty-second slot, though in truth we didn't try," recalled Lee Clow. Sculley, perhaps to avoid a showdown with either the board or Jobs, decided to let Bill Campbell, the head of marketing, figure out what to do. Campbell, a former football coach, decided to throw the long bomb. "I think we ought to go for it," he told his team.

Early in the third quarter of Super Bowl XVIII, the dominant Raiders scored a touchdown against the Redskins and, instead of an instant replay, television screens across the nation went black for an ominous two full seconds. Then an eerie black-and-white image of drones marching to spooky music began to fill the screen. More than ninety-six million people watched an ad that was unlike any they'd seen before. At its end, as the drones watched in horror the vaporizing of Big Brother, an announcer calmly intoned, "On January 24th, Apple

Computer will introduce Macintosh. And you'll see why 1984 won't be like '1984.'"

It was a sensation. That evening all three networks and fifty local stations aired news stories about the ad, giving it a viral life unprecedented in the pre–YouTube era. It would eventually be selected by both *TV Guide* and *Advertising Age* as the greatest commercial of all time.

Publicity Blast

Over the years Steve Jobs would become the grand master of product launches. In the case of the Macintosh, the astonishing Ridley Scott ad was just one of the ingredients. Another part of the recipe was media coverage. Jobs found ways to ignite blasts of publicity that were so powerful the frenzy would feed on itself, like a chain reaction. It was a phenomenon that he would be able to replicate whenever there was a big product launch, from the Macintosh in 1984 to the iPad in 2010. Like a conjurer, he could pull the trick off over and over again, even after journalists had seen it happen a dozen times and knew how it was done. Some of the moves he had learned from Regis McKenna, who was a pro at cultivating and stroking prideful reporters. But Jobs had his own intuitive sense of how to stoke the excitement, manipulate the competitive instincts of journalists, and trade exclusive access for lavish treatment.

In December 1983 he took his elfin engineering wizards, Andy Hertzfeld and Burrell Smith, to New York to visit *Newsweek* to pitch a story on "the kids who created the Mac." After giving a demo of the Macintosh, they were taken upstairs to meet Katharine Graham, the legendary proprietor, who had an insatiable interest in whatever was new. Afterward the magazine sent its technology columnist and a photographer to spend time in Palo Alto with Hertzfeld and Smith. The result was a flattering and smart four-page profile of the two of them, with pictures that made them look like cherubim of a new age. The article quoted Smith saying what he wanted to do next: "I want to build the computer of the 90's. Only I want to do it tomorrow." The article also described the mix of volatility and charisma displayed by his boss: "Jobs sometimes defends his ideas with highly vocal displays of temper that aren't always bluster; rumor has it that he has threatened to fire employees for insisting that his computers should have cursor keys, a feature that Jobs considers obsolete. But when he is on his best behavior, Jobs is a curious blend of charm and impatience, oscillating between shrewd reserve and his favorite expression of enthusiasm: 'Insanely great.'"

The technology writer Steven Levy, who was then working for *Rolling Stone*, came to interview Jobs, who urged him to convince the magazine's publisher to put the Macintosh team on the cover of the magazine. "The chances of Jann Wenner agreeing to displace Sting in favor of a bunch of computer nerds were approximately one in a googolplex," Levy thought, correctly. Jobs took Levy to a pizza joint and pressed the case: *Rolling Stone* was "on the ropes, running crummy articles, looking desperately for new topics and new audiences. The Mac could be its salvation!" Levy pushed back. *Rolling Stone* was actually good, he said, and he asked Jobs if he had read it recently. Jobs said that he had, an article about MTV that was "a piece of shit." Levy replied that he had written that article. Jobs, to his credit, didn't back away from the assessment. Instead he turned philosophical as he talked about the Macintosh. We are constantly benefiting from advances that went before us and taking things that people before us developed, he said. "It's a wonderful, ecstatic feeling to create something that puts it back in the pool of human experience and knowledge."

Levy's story didn't make it to the cover. But in the future, every major product launch that Jobs was involved in—at NeXT, at Pixar, and years later when he returned to Apple—would end up on the cover of either *Time, Newsweek*, or *Business Week*.

January 24, 1984

On the morning that he and his teammates completed the software for the Macintosh, Andy Hertzfeld had gone home exhausted and expected to stay in bed for at least a day. But that afternoon, after only six hours of sleep, he drove back to the office. He wanted to check in to see if there had been any problems, and most of his colleagues had done the same. They were lounging around, dazed but excited, when Jobs walked in. "Hey, pick yourselves up off the floor, you're not done yet!" he announced. "We need a demo for the intro!" His plan was to dramatically unveil the Macintosh in front of a large audience and have it show off some of its features to the inspirational theme from *Chariots of Fire*. "It needs to be done by the weekend, to be ready for the rehearsals," he added. They all groaned, Hertzfeld recalled, "but as we talked we realized that it would be fun to cook up something impressive."

The launch event was scheduled for the Apple annual stockholders' meeting on January 24—eight days away—at the Flint Auditorium of De Anza Community College. The television ad and the frenzy of press preview stories were the first two components in what would become the Steve Jobs playbook for making the introduction of a new product seem like an epochal moment in world history. The third component was the public unveiling of the product itself, amid fanfare and flourishes, in front of an audience of adoring faithful mixed with journalists who were primed to be swept up in the excitement.

Hertzfeld pulled off the remarkable feat of writing a music player in two days so that the computer could play the *Chariots of Fire* theme. But when Jobs heard it, he judged it lousy, so they decided to use a recording instead. At the same time, Jobs was thrilled with a speech generator that turned text into spoken words with a charming electronic accent, and he decided to make it part of the demo. "I want the Macintosh to be the first computer to introduce itself!" he insisted.

At the rehearsal the night before the launch, nothing was working well. Jobs hated the way the animation scrolled across the Macintosh screen, and he kept ordering tweaks. He also was dissatisfied with the stage lighting, and he directed Sculley to move from seat to seat to give his opinion as various adjustments were made. Sculley had never thought much about variations of stage lighting and gave the type of tentative answers a patient might give an eye doctor when asked which lens made the letters clearer. The rehearsals and changes went on for five hours, well into the night. "He was driving people insane, getting mad at the stagehands for every glitch in the presentation," Sculley recalled. "I thought there was no way we were going to get it done for the show the next morning."

Most of all, Jobs fretted about his presentation. Sculley fancied himself a good writer, so he suggested changes in Jobs's script. Jobs recalled being slightly annoyed, but their relationship was still in the phase when he was lathering on flattery and stroking Sculley's ego. "I think of you just like Woz and Markkula," he told Sculley. "You're like one of the founders of the company. They founded the company, but you and I are founding the future." Sculley lapped it up.

The next morning the 2,600-seat auditorium was mobbed. Jobs arrived in a double-breasted blue blazer, a starched white shirt, and a pale green bow tie. "This is the most important moment in my entire life," he told Sculley as they waited backstage for the program to begin. "I'm really nervous. You're probably the only person who knows how I feel about this." Sculley grasped his hand, held it for a moment, and whispered "Good luck."

As chairman of the company, Jobs went onstage first to start the shareholders' meeting. He did so with his own form of an invocation. "I'd like to open the meeting," he said, "with a twenty-year-old poem by Dylan—that's Bob Dylan." He broke into a little smile, then looked down to read from the second verse of "The Times They Are a-Changin'." His voice was high-pitched as he raced through the ten lines, ending with "For the loser now / Will be later to win / For the times they are a-changin'." That song was the anthem that kept the multimillionaire board chairman in touch with his counterculture self-image. He had a bootleg copy of his favorite version, which was from the live concert Dylan performed, with Joan Baez, on Halloween 1964 at Lincoln Center's Philharmonic Hall.

Sculley came onstage to report on the company's earnings, and the audience started to become restless as he droned on. Finally, he ended with a personal note. "The most important thing that has happened to me in the last nine months at Apple has been a chance to develop a friendship with Steve Jobs," he said. "For me, the rapport we have developed means an awful lot."

The lights dimmed as Jobs reappeared onstage and launched into a dramatic version of the battle cry he had delivered at the Hawaii sales conference. "It is 1958," he began. "IBM passes up a chance to buy a young fledgling company that has invented a new technology called xerography. Two years later, Xerox was born, and IBM has been kicking themselves ever since." The crowd laughed. Hertzfeld had heard versions of the speech both in Hawaii and elsewhere, but he was struck by how this time it was pulsing with more passion. After recounting other IBM missteps, Jobs picked up the pace and the emotion as he built toward the present:

> It is now 1984. It appears that IBM wants it all. Apple is perceived to be the only hope to offer IBM a run for its money. Dealers, after initially welcoming IBM with open arms, now fear an IBM-dominated and -controlled future and are turning back to Apple as the only force who can ensure their future freedom. IBM wants it all, and is aiming its guns at its last obstacle to industry control, Apple. Will Big Blue dominate the entire computer industry? The entire information age? Was George Orwell right?

As he built to the climax, the audience went from murmuring to applauding to a frenzy of cheering and chanting. But before they could answer the Orwell question, the auditorium went black and the "1984" commercial appeared on the screen. When it was over, the entire audience was on its feet cheering.

With a flair for the dramatic, Jobs walked across the dark stage to a small table with a cloth bag on it. "Now I'd like to show you Macintosh in person," he said. He took out the computer, keyboard, and mouse, hooked them together deftly, then pulled one of the new 3½-inch floppies from his shirt pocket. The theme from *Chariots of Fire* began to play. Jobs held his breath for a moment, because the demo had not worked well the night before. But this time it ran flawlessly. The word "MACINTOSH" scrolled horizontally onscreen, then underneath it the words "Insanely great" appeared in script, as if being slowly written by hand. Not used to such beautiful graphic displays, the audience quieted for a moment. A few gasps could be heard. And then, in rapid succession, came a series of screen shots: Bill Atkinson's QuickDraw graphics application followed by displays of different fonts, documents, charts, drawings, a chess game, a spreadsheet, and a rendering of Steve Jobs with a thought bubble containing a Macintosh.

When it was over, Jobs smiled and offered a treat. "We've done a lot of talking about Macintosh recently," he said. "But today, for the first time ever, I'd like to let Macintosh speak for itself." With that, he strolled back over to the computer, pressed the button on the mouse, and in a vibrato but endearing electronic deep voice, Macintosh became the first computer to introduce itself. "Hello. I'm Macintosh. It sure is great to get out of that bag," it began. The only thing it didn't seem to know how to do was to wait for the wild cheering and shrieks that erupted. Instead of basking for a moment, it barreled ahead. "Unaccustomed as I am to public speaking, I'd like to share with you a maxim I thought of the first time I met an IBM mainframe: Never trust a computer you can't lift." Once again the roar almost drowned out its final lines. "Obviously, I can talk. But right now I'd like to sit back and listen. So it is with considerable pride that I introduce a man who's been like a father to me, Steve Jobs."

Pandemonium erupted, with people in the crowd jumping up and down and pumping their fists in a frenzy. Jobs nodded slowly, a tight-lipped but broad smile on his face, then looked down and started to choke up. The ovation continued for five minutes.

After the Macintosh team returned to Bandley 3 that afternoon, a truck pulled into the parking lot and Jobs had them all gather next to it. Inside were a hundred new Macintosh computers, each personalized with a plaque. "Steve presented them one at a time to each team member, with a handshake and a smile, as the rest of us stood around cheering," Hertzfeld recalled. It had been a grueling ride, and many egos had been bruised by Jobs's obnoxious and rough management style. But neither Raskin nor Wozniak nor Sculley nor anyone else at the company could have pulled off the creation of the Macintosh. Nor would it likely have emerged from focus groups and committees. On the day he unveiled the Macintosh, a reporter from *Popular Science* asked Jobs what type of market research he had done. Jobs responded by scoffing, "Did Alexander Graham Bell do any market research before he invented the telephone?"

CHAPTER SIXTEEN

GATES AND JOBS

When Orbits Intersect

Jobs and Gates, 1991

The Macintosh Partnership

In astronomy, a binary system occurs when the orbits of two stars are linked because of their gravitational interaction. There have been analogous situations in history, when an era is shaped by the relationship and rivalry of two orbiting superstars: Albert Einstein and Niels Bohr in twentieth-century physics, for example, or Thomas Jefferson and Alexander Hamilton in early American governance. For the first thirty years of the personal computer age, beginning in the late 1970s, the defining binary star system was composed of two high-energy college dropouts both born in 1955.

Bill Gates and Steve Jobs, despite their similar ambitions at the confluence of technology and business, had very different personalities and backgrounds. Gates's father was a prominent Seattle lawyer, his mother a civic leader on a variety of prestigious boards. He became a tech geek at the area's finest private school, Lakeside High, but he was never a rebel, hippie, spiritual seeker, or member of the counterculture. Instead of a Blue Box to rip off the phone company, Gates created for his school a program for scheduling classes, which helped him get into ones with the right girls, and a car-counting program for local traffic engineers. He went to Harvard, and when he decided to drop out it was not to find enlightenment with an Indian guru but to start a computer software company.

Gates was good at computer coding, unlike Jobs, and his mind was more practical, disciplined, and abundant in analytic processing power. Jobs was more intuitive and romantic and had a greater instinct for making technology usable, design delightful, and interfaces friendly. He had a passion for perfection, which made him fiercely demanding, and he managed by charisma and scattershot intensity. Gates was more methodical; he held tightly scheduled product review meetings where he would cut to the heart of issues with lapidary skill. Both could be rude, but with Gates—who early in his career seemed to have a typical geek's flirtation with the fringes of the Asperger's scale—the cutting behavior tended to be less personal, based more on intellectual incisiveness than emotional callousness. Jobs would stare at people with a burning, wounding intensity; Gates sometimes had trouble making eye contact, but he was fundamentally humane.

"Each one thought he was smarter than the other one, but Steve generally treated Bill as someone who was slightly inferior, especially in matters of taste and style," said Andy Hertzfeld. "Bill looked down on Steve because he couldn't actually program." From the beginning of their relationship, Gates was fascinated by Jobs and slightly envious of his mesmerizing effect on people. But he also found him "fundamentally odd" and "weirdly flawed as a human being," and he was put off by Jobs's rudeness and his tendency to be "either in the mode of saying you were shit or trying to seduce you." For his part, Jobs found Gates unnervingly narrow. "He'd be a broader guy if he had dropped acid once or gone off to an ashram when he was younger," Jobs once declared.

Their differences in personality and character would lead them to opposite sides of what would become the fundamental divide in the digital age. Jobs was a perfectionist who craved control and indulged in the uncompromising temperament of an artist; he and Apple became the exemplars of a digital strategy that tightly integrated hardware, software, and content into a seamless package. Gates was a smart, calculating, and pragmatic analyst of business and technology; he was open to licensing Microsoft's operating system and software to a variety of manufacturers.

After thirty years Gates would develop a grudging respect for Jobs. "He really never knew much about technology, but he had an amazing instinct for what works," he said. But Jobs never reciprocated by fully appreciating Gates's real strengths. "Bill is basically unimaginative and has never invented anything, which is why I think he's more comfortable now in philanthropy than technology," Jobs said, unfairly. "He just shamelessly ripped off other people's ideas."

When the Macintosh was first being developed, Jobs went up to visit Gates at his office near Seattle. Microsoft had written some applications for the Apple II, including a spreadsheet program called Multiplan, and Jobs wanted to excite Gates and Co. about doing even more for the forthcoming Macintosh. Sitting in Gates's conference room, Jobs spun an enticing vision of a computer for the masses, with a friendly interface, which would be churned out by the millions in an automated California factory. His description of the dream factory sucking in the California silicon components and turning out finished Macintoshes caused the Microsoft team to code-name the project "Sand." They even reverse-engineered it into an acronym, for "Steve's amazing new device."

Gates had launched Microsoft by writing a version of BASIC, a programming language, for the Altair. Jobs wanted Microsoft to write a version of BASIC for the Macintosh, because Wozniak—despite much prodding by Jobs—had never enhanced his version of the Apple II's BASIC to handle floating-point numbers. In addition,

Jobs wanted Microsoft to write application software—such as spreadsheet, charting, and database programs—for the Macintosh. At the
time, Jobs was a king and Gates still a courtier: In 1982 Apple's annual
sales were $1 billion, while Microsoft's were a mere $32 million. Gates
signed on to do graphical versions of a new spreadsheet called Excel, a
word-processing program called Word, and BASIC.

Gates frequently went to Cupertino for demonstrations of the
Macintosh operating system, and he was not very impressed. "I remember the first time we went down, Steve had this app where it was
just things bouncing around on the screen," he said. "That was the only
app that ran." Gates was also put off by Jobs's attitude. "It was kind of
a weird seduction visit, where Steve was saying, 'We don't really need
you and we're doing this great thing, and it's under the cover.' He's in
his Steve Jobs sales mode, but kind of the sales mode that also says, 'I
don't need you, but I might let you be involved.'"

The Macintosh pirates found Gates hard to take. "You could tell
that Bill Gates was not a very good listener. He couldn't bear to have
anyone explain how something worked to him—he had to leap ahead
instead and guess about how he thought it would work," Hertzfeld recalled. They showed him how the Macintosh's cursor moved smoothly
across the screen without flickering. "What kind of hardware do you
use to draw the cursor?" Gates asked. Hertzfeld, who took great pride
that they could achieve their functionality solely using software, replied, "We don't have any special hardware for it!" Gates insisted that
it was necessary to have special hardware to move the cursor that way.
"So what do you say to somebody like that?" Bruce Horn, one of the
Macintosh engineers, later said. "It made it clear to me that Gates
was not the kind of person that would understand or appreciate the
elegance of a Macintosh."

Despite their mutual wariness, both teams were excited by the prospect that Microsoft would create graphical software for the Macintosh
that would take personal computing into a new realm, and they went
to dinner at a fancy restaurant to celebrate. Microsoft soon dedicated
a large team to the task. "We had more people working on the Mac
than he did," Gates said. "He had about fourteen or fifteen people. We
had like twenty people. We really bet our life on it." And even though

Jobs thought that they didn't exhibit much taste, the Microsoft programmers were persistent. "They came out with applications that were terrible," Jobs recalled, "but they kept at it and they made them better." Eventually Jobs became so enamored of Excel that he made a secret bargain with Gates: If Microsoft would make Excel exclusively for the Macintosh for two years, and not make a version for IBM PCs, then Jobs would shut down his team working on a version of BASIC for the Macintosh and instead indefinitely license Microsoft's BASIC. Gates smartly took the deal, which infuriated the Apple team whose project got canceled and gave Microsoft a lever in future negotiations.

For the time being, Gates and Jobs forged a bond. That summer they went to a conference hosted by the industry analyst Ben Rosen at a Playboy Club retreat in Lake Geneva, Wisconsin, where nobody knew about the graphical interfaces that Apple was developing. "Everybody was acting like the IBM PC was everything, which was nice, but Steve and I were kind of smiling that, hey, we've got something," Gates recalled. "And he's kind of leaking, but nobody actually caught on." Gates became a regular at Apple retreats. "I went to every luau," said Gates. "I was part of the crew."

Gates enjoyed his frequent visits to Cupertino, where he got to watch Jobs interact erratically with his employees and display his obsessions. "Steve was in his ultimate pied piper mode, proclaiming how the Mac will change the world and overworking people like mad, with incredible tensions and complex personal relationships." Sometimes Jobs would begin on a high, then lapse into sharing his fears with Gates. "We'd go down Friday night, have dinner, and Steve would just be promoting that everything is great. Then the second day, without fail, he'd be kind of, 'Oh shit, is this thing going to sell, oh God, I have to raise the price, I'm sorry I did that to you, and my team is a bunch of idiots.'"

Gates saw Jobs's reality distortion field at play when the Xerox Star was launched. At a joint team dinner one Friday night, Jobs asked Gates how many Stars had been sold thus far. Gates said six hundred. The next day, in front of Gates and the whole team, Jobs said that three hundred Stars had been sold, forgetting that Gates had just told everyone it was actually six hundred. "So his whole team starts looking at me like, 'Are you going to tell him that he's full of shit?' " Gates recalled. "And in that case I didn't take the bait." On another occasion Jobs and his team were visiting Microsoft and having dinner at the Seattle Tennis Club. Jobs launched into a sermon about how the Macintosh and its software would be so easy to use that there would be no manuals. "It was like anybody who ever thought that there would be a manual for any Mac application was the greatest idiot," said Gates. "And we were like, 'Does he really mean it? Should we not tell him that we have people who are actually working on manuals?' "

After a while the relationship became bumpier. The original plan was to have some of the Microsoft applications—such as Excel, Chart, and File—carry the Apple logo and come bundled with the purchase of a Macintosh. "We were going to get $10 per app, per machine," said Gates. But this arrangement upset competing software makers. In addition, it seemed that some of Microsoft's programs might be late. So Jobs invoked a provision in his deal with Microsoft and decided not to bundle its software; Microsoft would have to scramble to distribute its software as products sold directly to consumers.

Gates went along without much complaint. He was already getting used to the fact that, as he put it, Jobs could "play fast and loose," and he suspected that the unbundling would actually help Microsoft. "We could make more money selling our software separately," Gates said. "It works better that way if you're willing to think you're going to have reasonable market share." Microsoft ended up making its software for various other platforms, and it began to give priority to the IBM PC version of Microsoft Word rather than the Macintosh version. In the end, Jobs's decision to back out of the bundling deal hurt Apple more than it did Microsoft.

When Excel for the Macintosh was released, Jobs and Gates unveiled it together at a press dinner at New York's Tavern on the Green. Asked if Microsoft would make a version of it for IBM PCs, Gates did not reveal the bargain he had made with Jobs but merely answered that "in time" that might happen. Jobs took the microphone. "I'm sure 'in time' we'll all be dead," he joked.

The Battle of the GUI

At that time, Microsoft was producing an operating system, known as DOS, which it licensed to IBM and compatible computers. It was based on an old-fashioned command line interface that confronted users with surly little prompts such as C:\>. As Jobs and his team began to work closely with Microsoft, they grew worried that it would copy Macintosh's graphical user interface. Andy Hertzfeld noticed that his contact at Microsoft was asking detailed questions about how the Macintosh operating system worked. "I told Steve that I suspected that Microsoft was going to clone the Mac," he recalled.

They were right to worry. Gates believed that graphical interfaces were the future, and that Microsoft had just as much right as Apple did to copy what had been developed at Xerox PARC. As he freely admitted later, "We sort of say, 'Hey, we believe in graphics interfaces, we saw the Xerox Alto too.'"

In their original deal, Jobs had convinced Gates to agree that Microsoft would not create graphical software for anyone other than Apple until a year after the Macintosh shipped in January 1983. Unfortunately for Apple, it did not provide for the possibility that the Macintosh launch would be delayed for a year. So Gates was within his rights when, in November 1983, he revealed that Microsoft planned to develop a new operating system for IBM PCs featuring a graphical interface with windows, icons, and a mouse for point-and-click navigation. It would be called Windows. Gates hosted a Jobs-like product announcement, the most lavish thus far in Microsoft's history, at the Helmsley Palace Hotel in New York.

Jobs was furious. He knew there was little he could do about it—Microsoft's deal with Apple not to do competing graphical software was running out—but he lashed out nonetheless. "Get Gates down here immediately," he ordered Mike Boich, who was Apple's evangelist to other software companies. Gates arrived, alone and willing to discuss things with Jobs. "He called me down to get pissed off at me," Gates recalled. "I went down to Cupertino, like a command performance. I told him, 'We're doing Windows.' I said to him, 'We're betting our company on graphical interfaces.'"

They met in Jobs's conference room, where Gates found himself surrounded by ten Apple employees who were eager to watch their boss assail him. Jobs didn't disappoint his troops. "You're ripping us off!" he shouted. "I trusted you, and now you're stealing from us!" Hertzfeld recalled that Gates just sat there coolly, looking Steve in the eye, before hurling back, in his squeaky voice, what became a classic zinger. "Well, Steve, I think there's more than one way of looking at it. I think it's more like we both had this rich neighbor named Xerox and I broke into his house to steal the TV set and found out that you had already stolen it."

Gates's two-day visit provoked the full range of Jobs's emotional responses and manipulation techniques. It also made clear that the Apple-Microsoft symbiosis had become a scorpion dance, with both sides circling warily, knowing that a sting by either could cause problems for both. After the confrontation in the conference room, Gates quietly gave Jobs a private demo of what was being planned for Windows. "Steve didn't know what to say," Gates recalled. "He could either say, 'Oh, this is a violation of something,' but he didn't. He chose to say, 'Oh, it's actually really a piece of shit.'" Gates was thrilled, because it gave him a chance to calm Jobs down for a moment. "I said, 'Yes, it's a nice little piece of shit.'" So Jobs went through a gamut of other emotions. "During the course of this meeting, he's just ruder than shit," Gates said. "And then there's a part where he's almost crying, like, 'Oh, just give me a chance to get this thing off.'" Gates responded by becoming very calm. "I'm good at when people are emotional, I'm kind of less emotional."

As he often did when he wanted to have a serious conversation, Jobs suggested they go on a long walk. They trekked the streets of Cupertino, back and forth to De Anza college, stopping at a diner and then walking some more. "We had to take a walk, which is not one of my management techniques," Gates said. "That was when he began saying things like, 'Okay, okay, but don't make it too much like what we're doing.'"

As it turned out, Microsoft wasn't able to get Windows 1.0 ready for shipping until the fall of 1985. Even then, it was a shoddy product. It lacked the elegance of the Macintosh interface, and it had tiled windows rather than the magical clipping of overlapping windows that Bill Atkinson had devised. Reviewers ridiculed it and consumers spurned it. Nevertheless, as is often the case with Microsoft products, persistence eventually made Windows better and then dominant.

Jobs never got over his anger. "They just ripped us off completely, because Gates has no shame," Jobs told me almost thirty years later. Upon hearing this, Gates responded, "If he believes that, he really has entered into one of his own reality distortion fields." In a legal sense, Gates was right, as courts over the years have subsequently ruled. And on a practical level, he had a strong case as well. Even though Apple made a deal for the right to use what it saw at Xerox PARC, it was inevitable that other companies would develop similar graphical interfaces. As Apple found out, the "look and feel" of a computer interface design is a hard thing to protect.

And yet Jobs's dismay was understandable. Apple had been more innovative, imaginative, elegant in execution, and brilliant in design. But even though Microsoft created a crudely copied series of products, it would end up winning the war of operating systems. This exposed an aesthetic flaw in how the universe worked: The best and most innovative products don't always win. A decade later, this truism caused Jobs to let loose a rant that was somewhat arrogant and over-the-top, but also had a whiff of truth to it. "The only problem with Microsoft is they just have no taste, they have absolutely no taste," he said. "I don't mean that in a small way. I mean that in a big way, in the sense that they don't think of original ideas and they don't bring much culture into their product."

CHAPTER SEVENTEEN

ICARUS

What Goes Up . . .

Flying High

The launch of the Macintosh in January 1984 propelled Jobs into an even higher orbit of celebrity, as was evident during a trip to Manhattan he took at the time. He went to a party that Yoko Ono threw for her son, Sean Lennon, and gave the nine-year-old a Macintosh. The boy loved it. The artists Andy Warhol and Keith Haring were there, and they were so enthralled by what they could create with the machine that the contemporary art world almost took an ominous turn. "I drew a circle," Warhol exclaimed proudly after using MacPaint. Warhol insisted that Jobs take a computer to Mick Jagger. When Jobs arrived at the rock star's townhouse, Jagger seemed baffled. He didn't quite know who Jobs was. Later Jobs told his team, "I think he was on drugs. Either that or he's brain-damaged." Jagger's daughter Jade, however, took to the computer immediately and started drawing with MacPaint, so Jobs gave it to her instead.

He bought the top-floor duplex apartment that he'd shown Sculley in the San Remo on Manhattan's Central Park West and hired James Freed of I. M. Pei's firm to renovate it, but he never moved in. (He would later sell it to Bono for $15 million.) He also bought an old

Spanish colonial–style fourteen-bedroom mansion in Woodside, in the hills above Palo Alto, that had been built by a copper baron, which he moved into but never got around to furnishing.

At Apple his status revived. Instead of seeking ways to curtail Jobs's authority, Sculley gave him more: The Lisa and Macintosh divisions were folded together, with Jobs in charge. He was flying high, but this did not serve to make him more mellow. Indeed there was a memorable display of his brutal honesty when he stood in front of the combined Lisa and Macintosh teams to describe how they would be merged. His Macintosh group leaders would get all of the top positions, he said, and a quarter of the Lisa staff would be laid off. "You guys failed," he said, looking directly at those who had worked on the Lisa. "You're a B team. B players. Too many people here are B or C players, so today we are releasing some of you to have the opportunity to work at our sister companies here in the valley."

Bill Atkinson, who had worked on both teams, thought it was not only callous, but unfair. "These people had worked really hard and were brilliant engineers," he said. But Jobs had latched onto what he believed was a key management lesson from his Macintosh experience: You have to be ruthless if you want to build a team of A players. "It's too easy, as a team grows, to put up with a few B players, and they then attract a few more B players, and soon you will even have some C players," he recalled. "The Macintosh experience taught me that A players like to work only with other A players, which means you can't indulge B players."

For the time being, Jobs and Sculley were able to convince themselves that their friendship was still strong. They professed their fondness so effusively and often that they sounded like high school sweethearts at a Hallmark card display. The first anniversary of Sculley's arrival came in May 1984, and to celebrate Jobs lured him to a dinner party at Le Mouton Noir, an elegant restaurant in the hills southwest of Cupertino. To Sculley's surprise, Jobs had gathered the Apple board, its top managers, and even some East Coast investors. As they all congratulated him during cocktails, Sculley recalled, "a beaming Steve stood in the background, nodding his head up and down and wearing a Cheshire Cat smile on his face." Jobs began the dinner with a fulsome toast. "The happiest two days for me were when Macintosh shipped and when John Sculley agreed to join Apple," he said. "This has been the greatest year I've ever had in my whole life, because I've learned so much from John." He then presented Sculley with a montage of memorabilia from the year.

In response, Sculley effused about the joys of being Jobs's partner for the past year, and he concluded with a line that, for different reasons, everyone at the table found memorable. "Apple has one leader," he said, "Steve and me." He looked across the room, caught Jobs's eye, and watched him smile. "It was as if we were communicating with each other," Sculley recalled. But he also noticed that Arthur Rock and some of the others were looking quizzical, perhaps even skeptical. They were worried that Jobs was completely rolling him. They had hired Sculley to control Jobs, and now it was clear that Jobs was the one in control. "Sculley was so eager for Steve's approval that he was unable to stand up to him," Rock recalled.

Keeping Jobs happy and deferring to his expertise may have seemed like a smart strategy to Sculley. But he failed to realize that it was not in Jobs's nature to share control. Deference did not come naturally to him. He began to become more vocal about how he thought the company should be run. At the 1984 business strategy meeting, for example, he pushed to make the company's centralized sales and marketing staffs bid on the right to provide their services to the various product divisions. (This would have meant, for example, that the Macintosh group could decide not to use Apple's marketing team and instead create one of its own.) No one else was in favor, but Jobs kept trying to ram it through. "People were looking to me to take control, to get him to sit down and shut up, but I didn't," Sculley recalled. As the meeting broke up, he heard someone whisper, "Why doesn't Sculley shut him up?"

When Jobs decided to build a state-of-the-art factory in Fremont to manufacture the Macintosh, his aesthetic passions and controlling nature kicked into high gear. He wanted the machinery to be painted in bright hues, like the Apple logo, but he spent so much time going over paint chips that Apple's manufacturing director, Matt Carter, finally just installed them in their usual beige and gray. When Jobs took a tour, he ordered that the machines be repainted in the bright colors he wanted. Carter objected; this was precision equipment, and repainting the machines could cause problems. He turned out to be right. One of the most expensive machines, which got painted bright blue, ended up not working properly and was dubbed "Steve's folly." Finally Carter quit. "It took so much energy to fight him, and it was usually over something so pointless that finally I had enough," he recalled.

Jobs tapped as a replacement Debi Coleman, the spunky but good-natured Macintosh financial officer who had once won the team's annual award for the person who best stood up to Jobs. But she knew how to cater to his whims when necessary. When Apple's art director, Clement Mok, informed her that Jobs wanted the walls to be pure white, she protested, "You can't paint a factory pure white. There's going to be dust and stuff all over." Mok replied, "There's no white that's too white for Steve." She ended up going along. With its pure white walls and its bright blue, yellow, and red machines, the factory floor "looked like an Alexander Calder showcase," said Coleman.

When asked about his obsessive concern over the look of the factory, Jobs said it was a way to ensure a passion for perfection:

> I'd go out to the factory, and I'd put on a white glove to check for dust. I'd find it everywhere—on machines, on the tops of the racks, on the floor. And I'd ask Debi to get it cleaned. I told her I thought we should be able to eat off the floor of the factory. Well, this drove Debi up the wall. She didn't understand why. And I couldn't articulate it back then. See, I'd been very influenced by what I'd seen in Japan. Part of what I greatly admired there—and part of what we were lacking in our factory— was a sense of teamwork and discipline. If we didn't have the discipline to keep that place spotless, then we weren't going to have the discipline to keep all these machines running.

One Sunday morning Jobs brought his father to see the factory. Paul Jobs had always been fastidious about making sure that his craftsmanship was exacting and his tools in order, and his son was proud to show that he could do the same. Coleman came along to give the tour. "Steve was, like, beaming," she recalled. "He was so proud to show his father this creation." Jobs explained how everything worked, and his father seemed truly admiring. "He kept looking at his father, who touched everything and loved how clean and perfect everything looked."

Things were not quite as sweet when Danielle Mitterrand toured the factory. The Cuba-admiring wife of France's socialist president François Mitterrand asked a lot of questions, through her translator, about the working conditions, while Jobs, who had grabbed Alain Rossmann to serve as his translator, kept trying to explain the advanced robotics and technology. After Jobs talked about the just-in-time production schedules, she asked about overtime pay. He was annoyed, so he described how automation helped him keep down labor costs, a subject he knew would not delight her. "Is it hard work?" she asked. "How much vacation time do they get?" Jobs couldn't contain himself. "If she's so interested in their welfare," he said to her translator, "tell her she can come work here any time." The translator turned pale and said nothing. After a moment Rossmann stepped in to say, in French, "M. Jobs says he thanks you for your visit and your interest in the factory." Neither Jobs nor Madame Mitterrand knew what happened, Rossmann recalled, but her translator looked very relieved.

Afterward, as he sped his Mercedes down the freeway toward Cupertino, Jobs fumed to Rossmann about Madame Mitterrand's attitude. At one point he was going just over 100 miles per hour when a policeman stopped him and began writing a ticket. After a few minutes, as the officer scribbled away, Jobs honked. "Excuse me?" the policeman said. Jobs replied, "I'm in a hurry." Amazingly, the officer didn't get mad. He simply finished writing the ticket and warned that if Jobs was caught going over 55 again he would be sent to jail. As soon as the policeman left, Jobs got back on the road and accelerated to 100. "He absolutely believed that the normal rules didn't apply to him," Rossmann marveled.

His wife, Joanna Hoffman, saw the same thing when she accompanied Jobs to Europe a few months after the Macintosh was launched. "He was just completely obnoxious and thinking he could get away with anything," she recalled. In Paris she had arranged a formal dinner with French software developers, but Jobs suddenly decided he didn't want to go. Instead he shut the car door on Hoffman and told her he was going to see the poster artist Folon instead. "The developers were so pissed off they wouldn't shake our hands," she said.

In Italy, he took an instant dislike to Apple's general manager, a soft rotund guy who had come from a conventional business. Jobs told him bluntly that he was not impressed with his team or his sales strategy. "You don't deserve to be able to sell the Mac," Jobs said coldly. But that was mild compared to his reaction to the restaurant the hapless manager had chosen. Jobs demanded a vegan meal, but the waiter very elaborately proceeded to dish out a sauce filled with sour cream. Jobs got so nasty that Hoffman had to threaten him. She whispered that if he didn't calm down, she was going to pour her hot coffee on his lap.

The most substantive disagreements Jobs had on the European trip concerned sales forecasts. Using his reality distortion field, Jobs was always pushing his team to come up with higher projections. He kept threatening the European managers that he wouldn't give them any allocations unless they projected bigger forecasts. They insisted on being realistic, and Hoffmann had to referee. "By the end of the trip, my whole body was shaking uncontrollably," Hoffman recalled.

It was on this trip that Jobs first got to know Jean-Louis Gassée, Apple's manager in France. Gassée was among the few to stand up successfully to Jobs on the trip. "He has his own way with the truth," Gassée later remarked. "The only way to deal with him was to out-bully him." When Jobs made his usual threat about cutting down on France's allocations if Gassée didn't jack up sales projections, Gassée got angry. "I remember grabbing his lapel and telling him to stop, and then he backed down. I used to be an angry man myself. I am a recovering assaholic. So I could recognize that in Steve."

Gassée was impressed, however, at how Jobs could turn on the charm when he wanted to. François Mitterrand had been preaching the gospel of *informatique pour tous*—computing for all—and various academic experts in technology, such as Marvin Minsky and Nicholas Negroponte, came over to sing in the choir. Jobs gave a talk to the group at the Hotel Bristol and painted a picture of how France could move ahead if it put computers in all of its schools. Paris also brought out the romantic in him. Both Gassée and Negroponte tell tales of him pining over women while there.

Falling

After the burst of excitement that accompanied the release of Macintosh, its sales began to taper off in the second half of 1984. The problem was a fundamental one: It was a dazzling but woefully slow and underpowered computer, and no amount of hoopla could mask that. Its beauty was that its user interface looked like a sunny playroom rather than a somber dark screen with sickly green pulsating letters and surly command lines. But that led to its greatest weakness: A character on a text-based display took less than a byte of code, whereas when the Mac drew a letter, pixel by pixel in any elegant font you wanted, it required twenty or thirty times more memory. The Lisa handled this by shipping with more than 1,000K RAM, whereas the Macintosh made do with 128K.

Another problem was the lack of an internal hard disk drive. Jobs had called Joanna Hoffman a "Xerox bigot" when she fought for such a storage device. He insisted that the Macintosh have just one floppy disk drive. If you wanted to copy data, you could end up with a new form of tennis elbow from having to swap floppy disks in and out of the single drive. In addition, the Macintosh lacked a fan, another example of Jobs's dogmatic stubbornness. Fans, he felt, detracted from the calm of a computer. This caused many component failures and earned the Macintosh the nickname "the beige toaster," which did not enhance its popularity. It was so seductive that it had sold well enough for the first few months, but when people became more aware of its limitations, sales fell. As Hoffman later lamented, "The reality distortion field can serve as a spur, but then reality itself hits."

At the end of 1984, with Lisa sales virtually nonexistent and Macintosh sales falling below ten thousand a month, Jobs made a shoddy, and atypical, decision out of desperation. He decided to take the inventory of unsold Lisas, graft on a Macintosh-emulation program, and sell them as a new product, the "Macintosh XL." Since the Lisa had been discontinued and would not be restarted, it was an unusual instance of Jobs producing something that he did not believe in. "I was furious because the Mac XL wasn't real," said Hoffman. "It was just to blow the excess Lisas out the door. It sold well, and then we had to discontinue the horrible hoax, so I resigned."

The dark mood was evident in the ad that was developed in January 1985, which was supposed to reprise the anti-IBM sentiment of the resonant "1984" ad. Unfortunately there was a fundamental difference: The first ad had ended on a heroic, optimistic note, but the storyboards presented by Lee Clow and Jay Chiat for the new ad, titled "Lemmings," showed dark-suited, blindfolded corporate managers marching off a cliff to their death. From the beginning both Jobs and Sculley were uneasy. It didn't seem as if it would convey a positive or glorious image of Apple, but instead would merely insult every manager who had bought an IBM.

Jobs and Sculley asked for other ideas, but the agency folks pushed back. "You guys didn't want to run '1984' last year," one of them said. According to Sculley, Lee Clow added, "I will put my whole reputation, everything, on this commercial." When the filmed version, done by Ridley Scott's brother Tony, came in, the concept looked even worse. The mindless managers marching off the cliff were singing a funeral-paced version of the *Snow White* song "Heigh-ho, Heigh-ho," and the dreary filmmaking made it even more depressing than the storyboards portended. "I can't believe you're going to insult businesspeople across America by running that," Debi Coleman yelled at Jobs when she saw the ad. At the marketing meetings, she stood up to make her point about how much she hated it. "I literally put a resignation letter on his desk. I wrote it on my Mac. I thought it was an affront to corporate managers. We were just beginning to get a toehold with desktop publishing."

Nevertheless Jobs and Sculley bent to the agency's entreaties and ran the commercial during the Super Bowl. They went to the game together at Stanford Stadium with Sculley's wife, Leezy (who couldn't stand Jobs), and Jobs's new girlfriend, Tina Redse. When the commercial was shown near the end of the fourth quarter of a dreary game, the fans watched on the overhead screen and had little reaction. Across the country, most of the response was negative. "It insulted the very people Apple was trying to reach," the president of a market research firm told *Fortune*. Apple's marketing manager suggested afterward that the company might want to buy an ad in the *Wall Street Journal* apologizing. Jay Chiat threatened that if Apple did that his agency would buy the facing page and apologize for the apology.

Jobs's discomfort, with both the ad and the situation at Apple in general, was on display when he traveled to New York in January to do another round of one-on-one press interviews. Andy Cunningham, from Regis McKenna's firm, was in charge of hand-holding and logistics at the Carlyle. When Jobs arrived, he told her that his suite needed to be completely redone, even though it was 10 p.m. and the meetings were to begin the next day. The piano was not in the right place; the strawberries were the wrong type. But his biggest objection was that he didn't like the flowers. He wanted calla lilies. "We got into a big fight on what a calla lily is," Cunningham recalled. "I know what they are, because I had them at my wedding, but he insisted on having a different type of lily and said I was 'stupid' because I didn't know what a real calla lily was." So Cunningham went out and, this being New York, was able to find a place open at midnight where she could get the lilies he wanted. By the time they got the room rearranged, Jobs started objecting to what she was wearing. "That suit's disgusting," he told her. Cunningham knew that at times he just simmered with undirected anger, so she tried to calm him down. "Look, I know you're angry, and I know how you feel," she said.

"You have no fucking idea how I feel," he shot back, "no fucking idea what it's like to be me."

Thirty Years Old

Turning thirty is a milestone for most people, especially those of the generation that proclaimed it would never trust anyone over that age. To celebrate his own thirtieth, in February 1985, Jobs threw a lavishly formal but also playful—black tie and tennis shoes—party for one thousand in the ballroom of the St. Francis Hotel in San Francisco. The invitation read, "There's an old Hindu saying that goes, 'In the first 30 years of your life, you make your habits. For the last 30 years of your life, your habits make you.' Come help me celebrate mine."

One table featured software moguls, including Bill Gates and

Mitch Kapor. Another had old friends such as Elizabeth Holmes, who brought as her date a woman dressed in a tuxedo. Andy Hertzfeld and Burrell Smith had rented tuxes and wore floppy tennis shoes, which made it all the more memorable when they danced to the Strauss waltzes played by the San Francisco Symphony Orchestra.

Ella Fitzgerald provided the entertainment, as Bob Dylan had declined. She sang mainly from her standard repertoire, though occasionally tailoring a song like "The Girl from Ipanema" to be about the boy from Cupertino. When she asked for some requests, Jobs called out a few. She concluded with a slow rendition of "Happy Birthday."

Sculley came to the stage to propose a toast to "technology's foremost visionary." Wozniak also came up and presented Jobs with a framed copy of the Zaltair hoax from the 1977 West Coast Computer Faire, where the Apple II had been introduced. The venture capitalist Don Valentine marveled at the change in the decade since that time. "He went from being a Ho Chi Minh look-alike, who said never trust anyone over thirty, to a person who gives himself a fabulous thirtieth birthday with Ella Fitzgerald," he said.

Many people had picked out special gifts for a person who was not easy to shop for. Debi Coleman, for example, found a first edition of F. Scott Fitzgerald's *The Last Tycoon*. But Jobs, in an act that was odd yet not out of character, left all of the gifts in a hotel room. Wozniak and some of the Apple veterans, who did not take to the goat cheese and salmon mousse that was served, met after the party and went out to eat at a Denny's.

"It's rare that you see an artist in his 30s or 40s able to really contribute something amazing," Jobs said wistfully to the writer David Sheff, who published a long and intimate interview in *Playboy* the month he turned thirty. "Of course, there are some people who are innately curious, forever little kids in their awe of life, but they're rare." The interview touched on many subjects, but Jobs's most poignant ruminations were about growing old and facing the future:

> Your thoughts construct patterns like scaffolding in your mind. You are really etching chemical patterns. In most cases, people get stuck in those patterns, just like grooves in a record, and they never get out of them.

I'll always stay connected with Apple. I hope that throughout my life I'll sort of have the thread of my life and the thread of Apple weave in and out of each other, like a tapestry. There may be a few years when I'm not there, but I'll always come back. . . .

If you want to live your life in a creative way, as an artist, you have to not look back too much. You have to be willing to take whatever you've done and whoever you were and throw them away.

The more the outside world tries to reinforce an image of you, the harder it is to continue to be an artist, which is why a lot of times, artists have to say, "Bye. I have to go. I'm going crazy and I'm getting out of here." And they go and hibernate somewhere. Maybe later they re-emerge a little differently.

With each of those statements, Jobs seemed to have a premonition that his life would soon be changing. Perhaps the thread of his life would indeed weave in and out of the thread of Apple's. Perhaps it was time to throw away some of what he had been. Perhaps it was time to say "Bye, I have to go," and then reemerge later, thinking differently.

Exodus

Andy Hertzfeld had taken a leave of absence after the Macintosh came out in 1984. He needed to recharge his batteries and get away from his supervisor, Bob Belleville, whom he didn't like. One day he learned that Jobs had given out bonuses of up to $50,000 to engineers on the Macintosh team. So he went to Jobs to ask for one. Jobs responded that Belleville had decided not to give the bonuses to people who were on leave. Hertzfeld later heard that the decision had actually been made by Jobs, so he confronted him. At first Jobs equivocated, then he said, "Well, let's assume what you are saying is true. How does that change things?" Hertzfeld said that if Jobs was withholding the bonus as a reason for him to come back, then he wouldn't come back as a matter of principle. Jobs relented, but it left Hertzfeld with a bad taste.

When his leave was coming to an end, Hertzfeld made an appointment to have dinner with Jobs, and they walked from his office to an Italian restaurant a few blocks away. "I really want to return," he told Jobs. "But things seem really messed up right now." Jobs was vaguely annoyed and distracted, but Hertzfeld plunged ahead. "The software team is completely demoralized and has hardly done a thing for months, and Burrell is so frustrated that he won't last to the end of the year."

At that point Jobs cut him off. "You don't know what you're talking about!" he said. "The Macintosh team is doing great, and I'm having the best time of my life right now. You're just completely out of touch." His stare was withering, but he also tried to look amused at Hertzfeld's assessment.

"If you really believe that, I don't think there's any way that I can come back," Hertzfeld replied glumly. "The Mac team that I want to come back to doesn't even exist anymore."

"The Mac team had to grow up, and so do you," Jobs replied. "I want you to come back, but if you don't want to, that's up to you. You don't matter as much as you think you do, anyway."

Hertzfeld didn't come back.

By early 1985 Burrell Smith was also ready to leave. He had worried that it would be hard to quit if Jobs tried to talk him out of it; the reality distortion field was usually too strong for him to resist. So he plotted with Hertzfeld how he could break free of it. "I've got it!" he told Hertzfeld one day. "I know the perfect way to quit that will nullify the reality distortion field. I'll just walk into Steve's office, pull down my pants, and urinate on his desk. What could he say to that? It's guaranteed to work." The betting on the Mac team was that even brave Burrell Smith would not have the gumption to do that. When he finally decided he had to make his break, around the time of Jobs's birthday bash, he made an appointment to see Jobs. He was surprised to find Jobs smiling broadly when he walked in. "Are you gonna do it? Are you really gonna do it?" Jobs asked. He had heard about the plan.

Smith looked at him. "Do I have to? I'll do it if I have to." Jobs gave him a look, and Smith decided it wasn't necessary. So he resigned less dramatically and walked out on good terms.

He was quickly followed by another of the great Macintosh engineers, Bruce Horn. When Horn went in to say good-bye, Jobs told him, "Everything that's wrong with the Mac is your fault."

Horn responded, "Well, actually, Steve, a lot of things that are right with the Mac are my fault, and I had to fight like crazy to get those things in."

"You're right," admitted Jobs. "I'll give you 15,000 shares to stay." When Horn declined the offer, Jobs showed his warmer side. "Well, give me a hug," he said. And so they hugged.

But the biggest news that month was the departure from Apple, yet again, of its cofounder, Steve Wozniak. Wozniak was then quietly working as a midlevel engineer in the Apple II division, serving as a humble mascot of the roots of the company and staying as far away from management and corporate politics as he could. He felt, with justification, that Jobs was not appreciative of the Apple II, which remained the cash cow of the company and accounted for 70% of its sales at Christmas 1984. "People in the Apple II group were being treated as very unimportant by the rest of the company," he later said. "This was despite the fact that the Apple II was by far the largest-selling product in our company for ages, and would be for years to come." He even roused himself to do something out of character; he picked up the phone one day and called Sculley, berating him for lavishing so much attention on Jobs and the Macintosh division.

Frustrated, Wozniak decided to leave quietly to start a new company that would make a universal remote control device he had invented. It would control your television, stereo, and other electronic devices with a simple set of buttons that you could easily program. He informed the head of engineering at the Apple II division, but he didn't feel he was important enough to go out of channels and tell Jobs or Markkula. So Jobs first heard about it when the news leaked in the *Wall Street Journal*. In his earnest way, Wozniak had openly answered the reporter's questions when he called. Yes, he said, he felt that Apple had been giving short shrift to the Apple II division. "Apple's direction has been horrendously wrong for five years," he said.

Less than two weeks later Wozniak and Jobs traveled together to the White House, where Ronald Reagan presented them with the first National Medal of Technology. The president quoted what President Rutherford Hayes had said when first shown a telephone—"An amazing invention, but who would ever want to use one?"—and then quipped, "I thought at the time that he might be mistaken." Because of the awkward situation surrounding Wozniak's departure, Apple did not throw a celebratory dinner. So Jobs and Wozniak went for a walk afterward and ate at a sandwich shop. They chatted amiably, Wozniak recalled, and avoided any discussion of their disagreements.

Wozniak wanted to make the parting amicable. It was his style. So he agreed to stay on as a part-time Apple employee at a $20,000 salary and represent the company at events and trade shows. That could have been a graceful way to drift apart. But Jobs could not leave well enough alone. One Saturday, a few weeks after they had visited Washington together, Jobs went to the new Palo Alto studios of Hartmut Esslinger, whose company frogdesign had moved there to handle its design work for Apple. There he happened to see sketches that the firm had made for Wozniak's new remote control device, and he flew into a rage. Apple had a clause in its contract that gave it the right to bar frogdesign from working on other computer-related projects, and Jobs invoked it. "I informed them," he recalled, "that working with Woz wouldn't be acceptable to us."

When the *Wall Street Journal* heard what happened, it got in touch with Wozniak, who, as usual, was open and honest. He said that Jobs was punishing him. "Steve Jobs has a hate for me, probably because of the things I said about Apple," he told the reporter. Jobs's action was remarkably petty, but it was also partly caused by the fact that he understood, in ways that others did not, that the look and style of a product served to brand it. A device that had Wozniak's name on it and used the same design language as Apple's products might be mistaken for something that Apple had produced. "It's not personal," Jobs told the newspaper, explaining that he wanted to make sure that Wozniak's remote wouldn't look like something made by Apple. "We don't want to see our design language used on other products. Woz has to find his own resources. He can't leverage off Apple's resources; we can't treat him specially."

Jobs volunteered to pay for the work that frogdesign had already done for Wozniak, but even so the executives at the firm were taken aback. When Jobs demanded that they send him the drawings done for Wozniak or destroy them, they refused. Jobs had to send them a letter invoking Apple's contractual right. Herbert Pfeifer, the design director of the firm, risked Jobs's wrath by publicly dismissing his claim that the dispute with Wozniak was not personal. "It's a power play," Pfeifer told the *Journal*. "They have personal problems between them."

Hertzfeld was outraged when he heard what Jobs had done. He lived about twelve blocks from Jobs, who sometimes would drop by on his walks. "I got so furious about the Wozniak remote episode that when Steve next came over, I wouldn't let him in the house," Hertzfeld recalled. "He knew he was wrong, but he tried to rationalize, and maybe in his distorted reality he was able to." Wozniak, always a teddy bear even when annoyed, hired another design firm and even agreed to stay on Apple's retainer as a spokesman.

Showdown, Spring 1985

There were many reasons for the rift between Jobs and Sculley in the spring of 1985. Some were merely business disagreements, such as Sculley's attempt to maximize profits by keeping the Macintosh price high when Jobs wanted to make it more affordable. Others were weirdly psychological and stemmed from the torrid and unlikely infatuation they initially had with each other. Sculley had painfully craved Jobs's affection, Jobs had eagerly sought a father figure and mentor, and when the ardor began to cool there was an emotional backwash. But at its core, the growing breach had two fundamental causes, one on each side.

For Jobs, the problem was that Sculley never became a product person. He didn't make the effort, or show the capacity, to understand the fine points of what they were making. On the contrary, he found Jobs's passion for tiny technical tweaks and design details to be obsessive and counterproductive. He had spent his career selling sodas and snacks whose recipes were largely irrelevant to him. He wasn't naturally passionate about products, which was among the most damning sins that Jobs could imagine. "I tried to educate him about the details of engineering," Jobs recalled, "but he had no idea how products are created, and after a while it just turned into arguments. But I learned that my perspective was right. Products are everything." He came to see Sculley as clueless, and his contempt was exacerbated by Sculley's hunger for his affection and delusions that they were very similar.

For Sculley, the problem was that Jobs, when he was no longer in courtship or manipulative mode, was frequently obnoxious, rude, selfish, and nasty to other people. He found Jobs's boorish behavior as despicable as Jobs found Sculley's lack of passion for product details. Sculley was kind, caring, and polite to a fault. At one point they were planning to meet with Xerox's vice chair Bill Glavin, and Sculley begged Jobs to behave. But as soon as they sat down, Jobs told Glavin, "You guys don't have any clue what you're doing," and the meeting broke up. "I'm sorry, but I couldn't help myself," Jobs told Sculley. It was one of many such cases. As Atari's Al Alcorn later observed, "Sculley believed in keeping people happy and worrying about relationships. Steve didn't give a shit about that. But he did care about the product in a way that Sculley never could, and he was able to avoid having too many bozos working at Apple by insulting anyone who wasn't an A player."

The board became increasingly alarmed at the turmoil, and in early 1985 Arthur Rock and some other disgruntled directors delivered a stern lecture to both. They told Sculley that he was supposed to be running the company, and he should start doing so with more authority and less eagerness to be pals with Jobs. They told Jobs that he was supposed to be fixing the mess at the Macintosh division and not telling other divisions how to do their job. Afterward Jobs retreated to his office and typed on his Macintosh, "I will not criticize the rest of the organization, I will not criticize the rest of the organization . . ."

As the Macintosh continued to disappoint—sales in March 1985 were only 10% of the budget forecast—Jobs holed up in his office fuming or wandered the halls berating everyone else for the problems. His mood swings became worse, and so did his abuse of those around him. Middle-level managers began to rise up against him. The marketing chief Mike Murray sought a private meeting with Sculley at an industry conference. As they were going up to Sculley's hotel room, Jobs spotted them and asked to come along. Murray asked him not to. He told Sculley that Jobs was wreaking havoc and had to be removed from managing the Macintosh division. Sculley replied that he was not yet resigned to having a showdown with Jobs. Murray later sent a memo directly to Jobs criticizing the way he treated colleagues and denouncing "management by character assassination."

For a few weeks it seemed as if there might be a solution to the turmoil. Jobs became fascinated by a flat-screen technology developed by a firm near Palo Alto called Woodside Design, run by an eccentric engineer named Steve Kitchen. He also was impressed by another startup that made a touchscreen display that could be controlled by your finger, so you didn't need a mouse. Together these might help fulfill Jobs's vision of creating a "Mac in a book." On a walk with Kitchen, Jobs spotted a building in nearby Menlo Park and declared that they should open a skunkworks facility to work on these ideas. It could be called AppleLabs and Jobs could run it, going back to the joy of having a small team and developing a great new product.

Sculley was thrilled by the possibility. It would solve most of his management issues, moving Jobs back to what he did best and getting rid of his disruptive presence in Cupertino. Sculley also had a candidate to replace Jobs as manager of the Macintosh division: Jean-Louis Gassée, Apple's chief in France, who had suffered through Jobs's visit there. Gassée flew to Cupertino and said he would take the job if he got a guarantee that he would run the division rather than work under Jobs. One of the board members, Phil Schlein of Macy's, tried to convince Jobs that he would be better off thinking up new products and inspiring a passionate little team.

But after some reflection, Jobs decided that was not the path he wanted. He declined to cede control to Gassée, who wisely went back to Paris to avoid the power clash that was becoming inevitable. For the rest of the spring, Jobs vacillated. There were times when he wanted to assert himself as a corporate manager, even writing a memo urging cost savings by eliminating free beverages and first-class air travel, and other times when he agreed with those who were encouraging him to go off and run a new AppleLabs R&D group.

In March Murray let loose with another memo that he marked "Do not circulate" but gave to multiple colleagues. "In my three years at Apple, I've never observed so much confusion, fear, and dysfunction as in the past 90 days," he began. "We are perceived by the rank and file as a boat without a rudder, drifting away into foggy oblivion." Murray had been on both sides of the fence; at times he conspired with Jobs to undermine Sculley, but in this memo he laid the blame on Jobs. "Whether the *cause of* or *because of* the dysfunction, Steve Jobs now controls a seemingly impenetrable power base."

At the end of that month, Sculley finally worked up the nerve to tell Jobs that he should give up running the Macintosh division. He walked over to Jobs's office one evening and brought the human resources manager, Jay Elliot, to make the confrontation more formal. "There is no one who admires your brilliance and vision more than I do," Sculley began. He had uttered such flatteries before, but this time it was clear that there would be a brutal "but" punctuating the thought. And there was. "But this is really not going to work," he declared. The flatteries punctured by "buts" continued. "We have developed a great friendship with each other," he said, "but I have lost confidence in your ability to run the Macintosh division." He also berated Jobs for bad-mouthing him as a bozo behind his back.

Jobs looked stunned and countered with an odd challenge, that Sculley should help and coach him more: "You've got to spend more time with me." Then he lashed back. He told Sculley he knew nothing about computers, was doing a terrible job running the company, and had disappointed Jobs ever since coming to Apple. Then he began to cry. Sculley sat there biting his fingernails.

"I'm going to bring this up with the board," Sculley declared. "I'm going to recommend that you step down from your operating position of running the Macintosh division. I want you to know that." He urged Jobs not to resist and to agree instead to work on developing new technologies and products.

Jobs jumped from his seat and turned his intense stare on Sculley.

"I don't believe you're going to do that," he said. "If you do that, you're going to destroy the company."

Over the next few weeks Jobs's behavior fluctuated wildly. At one moment he would be talking about going off to run AppleLabs, but in the next moment he would be enlisting support to have Sculley ousted. He would reach out to Sculley, then lash out at him behind his back, sometimes on the same night. One night at 9 he called Apple's general counsel Al Eisenstat to say he was losing confidence in Sculley and needed his help convincing the board to fire him; at 11 the same night, he phoned Sculley to say, "You're terrific, and I just want you to know I love working with you."

At the board meeting on April 11, Sculley officially reported that he wanted to ask Jobs to step down as the head of the Macintosh division and focus instead on new product development. Arthur Rock, the most crusty and independent of the board members, then spoke. He was fed up with both of them: with Sculley for not having the guts to take command over the past year, and with Jobs for "acting like a petulant brat." The board needed to get this dispute behind them, and to do so it should meet privately with each of them.

Sculley left the room so that Jobs could present first. Jobs insisted that Sculley was the problem because he had no understanding of computers. Rock responded by berating Jobs. In his growling voice, he said that Jobs had been behaving foolishly for a year and had no right to be managing a division. Even Jobs's strongest supporter, Phil Schlein, tried to talk him into stepping aside gracefully to run a research lab for the company.

When it was Sculley's turn to meet privately with the board, he gave an ultimatum: "You can back me, and then I take responsibility for running the company, or we can do nothing, and you're going to have to find yourselves a new CEO." If given the authority, he said, he would not move abruptly, but would ease Jobs into the new role over the next few months. The board unanimously sided with Sculley. He was given the authority to remove Jobs whenever he felt the timing was right. As Jobs waited outside the boardroom, knowing full well that he was losing, he saw Del Yocam, a longtime colleague, and hugged him.

After the board made its decision, Sculley tried to be conciliatory. Jobs asked that the transition occur slowly, over the next few months, and Sculley agreed. Later that evening Sculley's executive assistant, Nanette Buckhout, called Jobs to see how he was doing. He was still in his office, shell-shocked. Sculley had already left, and Jobs came over to talk to her. Once again he began oscillating wildly in his attitude toward Sculley. "Why did John do this to me?" he said. "He betrayed me." Then he swung the other way. Perhaps he should take some time away to work on restoring his relationship with Sculley, he said. "John's friendship is more important than anything else, and I think maybe that's what I should do, concentrate on our friendship."

Plotting a Coup

Jobs was not good at taking no for an answer. He went to Sculley's office in early May 1985 and asked for more time to show that he could manage the Macintosh division. He would prove himself as an operations guy, he promised. Sculley didn't back down. Jobs next tried a direct challenge: He asked Sculley to resign. "I think you really lost your stride," Jobs told him. "You were really great the first year, and everything went wonderful. But something happened." Sculley, who generally was even-tempered, lashed back, pointing out that Jobs had been unable to get Macintosh software developed, come up with new models, or win customers. The meeting degenerated into a shouting match about who was the worse manager. After Jobs stalked out, Sculley turned away from the glass wall of his office, where others had been looking in on the meeting, and wept.

Matters began to come to a head on Tuesday, May 14, when the Macintosh team made its quarterly review presentation to Sculley and other Apple corporate leaders. Jobs still had not relinquished control of the division, and he was defiant when he arrived in the corporate boardroom with his team. He and Sculley began by clashing over what the division's mission was. Jobs said it was to sell more Macintosh machines. Sculley said it was to serve the interests of the Apple company as a whole. As usual there was little cooperation among the divisions;

for one thing, the Macintosh team was planning new disk drives that were different from those being developed by the Apple II division. The debate, according to the minutes, took a full hour.

Jobs then described the projects under way: a more powerful Mac, which would take the place of the discontinued Lisa; and software called FileServer, which would allow Macintosh users to share files on a network. Sculley learned for the first time that these projects were going to be late. He gave a cold critique of Murray's marketing record, Belleville's missed engineering deadlines, and Jobs's overall management. Despite all this, Jobs ended the meeting with a plea to Sculley, in front of all the others there, to be given one more chance to prove he could run a division. Sculley refused.

That night Jobs took his Macintosh team out to dinner at Nina's Café in Woodside. Jean-Louis Gassée was in town because Sculley wanted him to prepare to take over the Macintosh division, and Jobs invited him to join them. Belleville proposed a toast "to those of us who really understand what the world according to Steve Jobs is all about." That phrase—"the world according to Steve"—had been used dismissively by others at Apple who belittled the reality warp he created. After the others left, Belleville sat with Jobs in his Mercedes and urged him to organize a battle to the death with Sculley.

Months earlier, Apple had gotten the right to export computers to China, and Jobs had been invited to sign a deal in the Great Hall of the People over the 1985 Memorial Day weekend. He had told Sculley, who decided he wanted to go himself, which was just fine with Jobs. Jobs decided to use Sculley's absence to execute his coup. Throughout the week leading up to Memorial Day, he took a lot of people on walks to share his plans. "I'm going to launch a coup while John is in China," he told Mike Murray.

Seven Days in May

Thursday, May 23: At his regular Thursday meeting with his top lieutenants in the Macintosh division, Jobs told his inner circle about his plan to oust Sculley. He also confided in the corporate human resources director, Jay Elliot, who told him bluntly that the proposed rebellion wouldn't work. Elliot had talked to some board members and urged them to stand up for Jobs, but he discovered that most of the board was with Sculley, as were most members of Apple's senior staff. Yet Jobs barreled ahead. He even revealed his plans to Gassée on a walk around the parking lot, despite the fact that Gassée had come from Paris to take his job. "I made the mistake of telling Gassée," Jobs wryly conceded years later.

That evening Apple's general counsel Al Eisenstat had a small barbecue at his home for Sculley, Gassée, and their wives. When Gassée told Eisenstat what Jobs was plotting, he recommended that Gassée inform Sculley. "Steve was trying to raise a cabal and have a coup to get rid of John," Gassée recalled. "In the den of Al Eisenstat's house, I put my index finger lightly on John's breastbone and said, 'If you leave tomorrow for China, you could be ousted. Steve's plotting to get rid of you.'"

Friday, May 24: Sculley canceled his trip and decided to confront Jobs at the executive staff meeting on Friday morning. Jobs arrived late, and he saw that his usual seat next to Sculley, who sat at the head of the table, was taken. He sat instead at the far end. He was dressed in a well-tailored suit and looked energized. Sculley looked pale. He announced that he was dispensing with the agenda to confront the issue on everyone's mind. "It's come to my attention that you'd like to throw me out of the company," he said, looking directly at Jobs. "I'd like to ask you if that's true."

Jobs was not expecting this. But he was never shy about indulging in brutal honesty. His eyes narrowed, and he fixed Sculley with his unblinking stare. "I think you're bad for Apple, and I think you're the wrong person to run the company," he replied, coldly and slowly. "You really should leave this company. You don't know how to operate and never have." He accused Sculley of not understanding the product development process, and then he added a self-centered swipe: "I wanted you here to help me grow, and you've been ineffective in helping me."

As the rest of the room sat frozen, Sculley finally lost his temper. A childhood stutter that had not afflicted him for twenty years started to return. "I don't trust you, and I won't tolerate a lack of trust," he stammered. When Jobs claimed that he would be better than Sculley at running the company, Sculley took a gamble. He decided to poll the room on that question. "He pulled off this clever maneuver," Jobs recalled, still smarting twenty-five years later. "It was at the executive committee meeting, and he said, 'It's me or Steve, who do you vote for?' He set the whole thing up so that you'd kind of have to be an idiot to vote for me."

Suddenly the frozen onlookers began to squirm. Del Yocam had to go first. He said he loved Jobs, wanted him to continue to play some role in the company, but he worked up the nerve to conclude, with Jobs staring at him, that he "respected" Sculley and would support him to run the company. Eisenstat faced Jobs directly and said much the same thing: He liked Jobs but was supporting Sculley. Regis McKenna, who sat in on senior staff meetings as an outside consultant, was more direct. He looked at Jobs and told him he was not yet ready to run the company, something he had told him before. Others sided with Sculley as well. For Bill Campbell, it was particularly tough. He was fond of Jobs and didn't particularly like Sculley. His voice quavered a bit as he told Jobs he had decided to support Sculley, and he urged the two of them to work it out and find some role for Jobs to play in the company. "You can't let Steve leave this company," he told Sculley.

Jobs looked shattered. "I guess I know where things stand," he said, and bolted out of the room. No one followed.

He went back to his office, gathered his longtime loyalists on the Macintosh staff, and started to cry. He would have to leave Apple, he said. As he started to walk out the door, Debi Coleman restrained him. She and the others urged him to settle down and not do anything hasty. He should take the weekend to regroup. Perhaps there was a way to prevent the company from being torn apart.

Sculley was devastated by his victory. Like a wounded warrior, he retreated to Eisenstat's office and asked the corporate counsel to go for a ride. When they got into Eisenstat's Porsche, Sculley lamented, "I don't know whether I can go through with this." When Eisenstat asked what he meant, Sculley responded, "I think I'm going to resign."

"You can't," Eisenstat protested. "Apple will fall apart."

"I'm going to resign," Sculley declared. "I don't think I'm right for the company."

"I think you're copping out," Eisenstat replied. "You've got to stand up to him." Then he drove Sculley home.

Sculley's wife was surprised to see him back in the middle of the day. "I've failed," he said to her forlornly. She was a volatile woman who had never liked Jobs or appreciated her husband's infatuation with him. So when she heard what had happened, she jumped into her car and sped over to Jobs's office. Informed that he had gone to the Good Earth restaurant, she marched over there and confronted him in the parking lot as he was coming out with loyalists on his Macintosh team.

"Steve, can I talk to you?" she said. His jaw dropped. "Do you have any idea what a privilege it has been even to know someone as fine as John Sculley?" she demanded. He averted his gaze. "Can't you look me in the eyes when I'm talking to you?" she asked. But when Jobs did so—giving her his practiced, unblinking stare—she recoiled. "Never mind, don't look at me," she said. "When I look into most people's eyes, I see a soul. When I look into your eyes, I see a bottomless pit, an empty hole, a dead zone." Then she walked away.

Saturday, May 25: Mike Murray drove to Jobs's house in Woodside to offer some advice: He should consider accepting the role of being a new product visionary, starting AppleLabs, and getting away from headquarters. Jobs seemed willing to consider it. But first he would have to restore peace with Sculley. So he picked up the telephone and surprised Sculley with an olive branch. Could they meet the following afternoon, Jobs asked, and take a walk together in the hills above Stanford University. They had walked there in the past, in happier times, and maybe on such a walk they could work things out.

Jobs did not know that Sculley had told Eisenstat he wanted to quit, but by then it didn't matter. Overnight, he had changed his mind and decided to stay. Despite the blowup the day before, he was still eager for Jobs to like him. So he agreed to meet the next afternoon.

If Jobs was prepping for conciliation, it didn't show in the choice of movie he wanted to see with Murray that night. He picked *Patton,* the epic of the never-surrender general. But he had lent his copy of the tape to his father, who had once ferried troops for the general, so he drove to his childhood home with Murray to retrieve it. His parents weren't there, and he didn't have a key. They walked around the back, checked for unlocked doors or windows, and finally gave up. The video store didn't have a copy of *Patton* in stock, so in the end he had to settle for watching the 1983 film adaptation of Harold Pinter's *Betrayal*.

Sunday, May 26: As planned, Jobs and Sculley met in back of the Stanford campus on Sunday afternoon and walked for several hours amid the rolling hills and horse pastures. Jobs reiterated his plea that he should have an operational role at Apple. This time Sculley stood firm. It won't work, he kept saying. Sculley urged him to take the role of being a product visionary with a lab of his own, but Jobs rejected this as making him into a mere "figurehead." Defying all connection to reality, he countered with the proposal that Sculley give up control of the entire company to him. "Why don't you become chairman and I'll become president and chief executive officer?" he suggested. Sculley was struck by how earnest he seemed.

"Steve, that doesn't make any sense," Sculley replied. Jobs then proposed that they split the duties of running the company, with him handling the product side and Sculley handling marketing and business. But the board had not only emboldened Sculley, it had ordered him to bring Jobs to heel. "One person has got to run the company," he replied. "I've got the support and you don't."

On his way home, Jobs stopped at Mike Markkula's house. He wasn't there, so Jobs left a message asking him to come to dinner the following evening. He would also invite the core of loyalists from his Macintosh team. He hoped that they could persuade Markkula of the folly of siding with Sculley.

Monday, May 27: Memorial Day was sunny and warm. The Macintosh team loyalists—Debi Coleman, Mike Murray, Susan Barnes, and Bob Belleville—got to Jobs's Woodside home an hour before the scheduled dinner so they could plot strategy. Sitting on the patio as the sun set, Coleman told Jobs that he should accept Sculley's offer to be a product visionary and help start up AppleLabs. Of all the inner circle, Coleman was the most willing to be realistic. In the new organization plan, Sculley had tapped her to run the manufacturing division because he knew that her loyalty was to Apple and not just to Jobs. Some of the others were more hawkish. They wanted to urge Markkula to support a reorganization plan that put Jobs in charge.

When Markkula showed up, he agreed to listen with one proviso: Jobs had to keep quiet. "I seriously wanted to hear the thoughts of the Macintosh team, not watch Jobs enlist them in a rebellion," he recalled. As it turned cooler, they went inside the sparsely furnished mansion and sat by a fireplace. Instead of letting it turn into a gripe session, Markkula made them focus on very specific management issues, such as what had caused the problem in producing the FileServer software and why the Macintosh distribution system had not responded well to the change in demand. When they were finished, Markkula bluntly declined to back Jobs. "I said I wouldn't support his plan, and that was the end of that," Markkula recalled. "Sculley was the boss. They were mad and emotional and putting together a revolt, but that's not how you do things."

Tuesday, May 28: His ire stoked by hearing from Markkula that Jobs had spent the previous evening trying to subvert him, Sculley walked over to Jobs's office on Tuesday morning. He had talked to the board, he said, and he had its support. He wanted Jobs out. Then he drove to Markkula's house, where he gave a presentation of his reorganization plans. Markkula asked detailed questions, and at the end he gave Sculley his blessing. When he got back to his office, Sculley called the other members of the board, just to make sure he still had their backing. He did.

At that point he called Jobs to make sure he understood. The board had given final approval of his reorganization plan, which would proceed that week. Gassée would take over control of Jobs's beloved Macintosh as well as other products, and there was no other division for Jobs to run. Sculley was still somewhat conciliatory. He told Jobs that he could stay on with the title of board chairman and be a product visionary with no operational duties. But by this point, even the idea of starting a skunkworks such as AppleLabs was no longer on the table.

It finally sank in. Jobs realized there was no appeal, no way to warp the reality. He broke down in tears and started making phone calls—to Bill Campbell, Jay Elliot, Mike Murray, and others. Murray's wife, Joyce, was on an overseas call when Jobs phoned, and the operator broke in saying it was an emergency. It better be important, she told the operator. "It is," she heard Jobs say. When her husband got on the phone, Jobs was crying. "It's over," he said. Then he hung up.

Murray was worried that Jobs was so despondent he might do something rash, so he called back. There was no answer, so he drove to Woodside. No one came to the door when he knocked, so he went around back and climbed up some exterior steps and looked in the bedroom. Jobs was lying there on a mattress in his unfurnished room. He let Murray in and they talked until almost dawn.

Wednesday, May 29: Jobs finally got hold of a tape of *Patton*, which he watched Wednesday evening, but Murray prevented him from getting stoked up for another battle. Instead he urged Jobs to come in on Friday for Sculley's announcement of the reorganization plan. There was no option left other than to play the good soldier rather than the renegade commander.

Like a Rolling Stone

Jobs slipped quietly into the back row of the auditorium to listen to Sculley explain to the troops the new order of battle. There were a lot of sideways glances, but few people acknowledged him and none came over to provide public displays of affection. He stared without blinking at Sculley, who would remember "Steve's look of contempt" years later. "It's unyielding," Sculley recalled, "like an X-ray boring inside your bones, down to where you're soft and destructibly mortal." For a moment, standing onstage while pretending not to notice Jobs, Sculley thought back to a friendly trip they had taken a year earlier to Cambridge, Massachusetts, to visit Jobs's hero, Edwin Land. He had been dethroned from the company he created, Polaroid, and Jobs had said to Sculley in disgust, "All he did was blow a lousy few million and they took his company away from him." Now, Sculley reflected, he was taking Jobs's company away from him.

As Sculley went over the organizational chart, he introduced Gassée as the new head of a combined Macintosh and Apple II product group. On the chart was a small box labeled "chairman" with no lines connecting to it, not to Sculley or to anyone else. Sculley briefly noted that in that role, Jobs would play the part of "global visionary." But he didn't acknowledge Jobs's presence. There was a smattering of awkward applause.

Jobs stayed home for the next few days, blinds drawn, his answering machine on, seeing only his girlfriend, Tina Redse. For hours on end he sat there playing his Bob Dylan tapes, especially "The Times They Are a-Changin.'" He had recited the second verse the day he unveiled the Macintosh to the Apple shareholders sixteen months earlier. That verse ended nicely: "For the loser now / Will be later to win. . . ."

A rescue squad from his former Macintosh posse arrived to dispel the gloom on Sunday night, led by Andy Hertzfeld and Bill Atkinson. Jobs took a while to answer their knock, and then he led them to a room next to the kitchen that was one of the few places with any furniture. With Redse's help, he served some vegetarian food he had ordered. "So what really happened?" Hertzfeld asked. "Is it really as bad as it looks?"

"No, it's worse." Jobs grimaced. "It's much worse than you can imagine." He blamed Sculley for betraying him, and said that Apple would not be able to manage without him. His role as chairman, he complained, was completely ceremonial. He was being ejected from his Bandley 3 office to a small and almost empty building he nicknamed "Siberia." Hertzfeld turned the topic to happier days, and they began to reminisce about the past.

Earlier that week, Dylan had released a new album, *Empire Burlesque*, and Hertzfeld brought a copy that they played on Jobs's high-tech turntable. The most notable track, "When the Night Comes

Falling from the Sky," with its apocalyptic message, seemed appropriate for the evening, but Jobs didn't like it. It sounded almost disco, and he gloomily argued that Dylan had been going downhill since *Blood on the Tracks*. So Hertzfeld moved the needle to the last song on the album, "Dark Eyes," which was a simple acoustic number featuring Dylan alone on guitar and harmonica. It was slow and mournful and, Hertzfeld hoped, would remind Jobs of the earlier Dylan tracks he so loved. But Jobs didn't like that song either and had no desire to hear the rest of the album.

Jobs's overwrought reaction was understandable. Sculley had once been a father figure to him. So had Mike Markkula. So had Arthur Rock. That week all three had abandoned him. "It gets back to the deep feeling of being rejected at an early age," his friend and lawyer George Riley later said. "It's a deep part of his own mythology, and it defines to himself who he is." Jobs recalled years later, "I felt like I'd been punched, the air knocked out of me and I couldn't breathe."

Losing the support of Arthur Rock was especially painful. "Arthur had been like a father to me," Jobs said. "He took me under his wing." Rock had taught him about opera, and he and his wife, Toni, had been his hosts in San Francisco and Aspen. "I remember driving into San Francisco one time, and I said to him, 'God, that Bank of America building is ugly,' and he said, 'No, it's the best,' and he proceeded to lecture me, and he was right of course." Years later Jobs's eyes welled with tears as he recounted the story: "He chose Sculley over me. That really threw me for a loop. I never thought he would abandon me."

Making matters worse was that his beloved company was now in the hands of a man he considered a bozo. "The board felt that I couldn't run a company, and that was their decision to make," he said. "But they made one mistake. They should have separated the decision of what to do with me and what to do with Sculley. They should have fired Sculley, even if they didn't think I was ready to run Apple." Even as his personal gloom slowly lifted, his anger at Sculley, his feeling of betrayal, deepened.

The situation worsened when Sculley told a group of analysts that he considered Jobs irrelevant to the company, despite his title as chairman. "From an operations standpoint, there is no role either today or in the future for Steve Jobs," he said. "I don't know what he'll do." The blunt comment shocked the group, and a gasp went through the auditorium.

Perhaps getting away to Europe would help, Jobs thought. So in June he went to Paris, where he spoke at an Apple event and went to a dinner honoring Vice President George H. W. Bush. From there he went to Italy, where he drove the hills of Tuscany with Redse and bought a bike so he could spend time riding by himself. In Florence he soaked in the architecture of the city and the texture of the building materials. Particularly memorable were the paving stones, which came from Il Casone quarry near the Tuscan town of Firenzuola. They were a calming bluish gray. Twenty years later he would decide that the floors of most major Apple stores would be made of this sandstone.

The Apple II was just going on sale in Russia, so Jobs headed off to Moscow, where he met up with Al Eisenstat. Because there was a problem getting Washington's approval for some of the required export licenses, they visited the commercial attaché at the American embassy in Moscow, Mike Merin. He warned them that there were strict laws against sharing technology with the Soviets. Jobs was annoyed. At the Paris trade show, Vice President Bush had encouraged him to get computers into Russia in order to "foment revolution from below." Over dinner at a Georgian restaurant that specialized in shish kebab, Jobs continued his rant. "How could you suggest this violates American law when it so obviously benefits our interests?" he asked Merin. "By putting Macs in the hands of Russians, they could print all their newspapers."

Jobs also showed his feisty side in Moscow by insisting on talking about Trotsky, the charismatic revolutionary who fell out of favor and was ordered assassinated by Stalin. At one point the KGB agent assigned to him suggested he tone down his fervor. "You don't want to talk about Trotsky," he said. "Our historians have studied the situation, and we don't believe he's a great man anymore." That didn't help. When they got to the state university in Moscow to speak to computer students, Jobs began his speech by praising Trotsky. He was a revolutionary Jobs could identify with.

Jobs and Eisenstat attended the July Fourth party at the American embassy, and in his thank-you letter to Ambassador Arthur Hartman, Eisenstat noted that Jobs planned to pursue Apple's ventures in Russia more vigorously in the coming year. "We are tentatively planning on returning to Moscow in September." For a moment it looked as if Sculley's hope that Jobs would turn into a "global visionary" for the company might come to pass. But it was not to be. Something much different was in store for September.

CHAPTER EIGHTEEN

NeXT

Prometheus Unbound

The Pirates Abandon Ship

Upon his return from Europe in August 1985, while he was casting about for what to do next, Jobs called the Stanford biochemist Paul Berg to discuss the advances that were being made in gene splicing and recombinant DNA. Berg described how difficult it was to do experiments in a biology lab, where it could take weeks to nurture an experiment and get a result. "Why don't you simulate them on a computer?" Jobs asked. Berg replied that computers with such capacities were too expensive for university labs. "Suddenly, he was excited about the possibilities," Berg recalled. "He had it in his mind to start a new company.

He was young and rich, and had to find something to do with the rest of his life."

Jobs had already been canvassing academics to ask what their work-station needs were. It was something he had been interested in since 1983, when he had visited the computer science department at Brown to show off the Macintosh, only to be told that it would take a far more powerful machine to do anything useful in a university lab. The dream of academic researchers was to have a workstation that was both powerful and personal. As head of the Macintosh division, Jobs had launched a project to build such a machine, which was dubbed the Big Mac. It would have a UNIX operating system but with the friendly Macintosh interface. But after Jobs was ousted from the Macintosh division, his replacement, Jean-Louis Gassée, canceled the Big Mac.

When that happened, Jobs got a distressed call from Rich Page, who had been engineering the Big Mac's chip set. It was the latest in a series of conversations that Jobs was having with disgruntled Apple employees urging him to start a new company and rescue them. Plans to do so began to jell over Labor Day weekend, when Jobs spoke to Bud Tribble, the original Macintosh software chief, and floated the idea of starting a company to build a powerful but personal worksta-tion. He also enlisted two other Macintosh division employees who had been talking about leaving, the engineer George Crow and the controller Susan Barnes.

That left one key vacancy on the team: a person who could mar-ket the new product to universities. The obvious candidate was Dan'l Lewin, who at Apple had organized a consortium of universities to buy Macintosh computers in bulk. Besides missing two letters in his first name, Lewin had the chiseled good looks of Clark Kent and a Princetonian's polish. He and Jobs shared a bond: Lewin had written a Princeton thesis on Bob Dylan and charismatic leadership, and Jobs knew something about both of those topics.

Lewin's university consortium had been a godsend to the Mac-intosh group, but he had become frustrated after Jobs left and Bill Campbell had reorganized marketing in a way that reduced the role of direct sales to universities. He had been meaning to call Jobs when, that

Labor Day weekend, Jobs called first. He drove to Jobs's unfurnished mansion, and they walked the grounds while discussing the possibility of creating a new company. Lewin was excited, but not ready to commit. He was going to Austin with Campbell the following week, and he wanted to wait until then to decide. Upon his return, he gave his answer: He was in. The news came just in time for the September 13 Apple board meeting.

Although Jobs was still nominally the board's chairman, he had not been to any meetings since he lost power. He called Sculley, said he was going to attend, and asked that an item be added to the end of the agenda for a "chairman's report." He didn't say what it was about, and Sculley assumed it would be a criticism of the latest reorganization. Instead, when his turn came to speak, Jobs described to the board his plans to start a new company. "I've been thinking a lot, and it's time for me to get on with my life," he began. "It's obvious that I've got to do something. I'm thirty years old." Then he referred to some prepared notes to describe his plan to create a computer for the higher education market. The new company would not be competitive with Apple, he promised, and he would take with him only a handful of non-key personnel. He offered to resign as chairman of Apple, but he expressed hope that they could work together. Perhaps Apple would want to buy the distribution rights to his product, he suggested, or license Macintosh software to it.

Mike Markkula rankled at the possibility that Jobs would hire anyone from Apple. "Why would you take anyone at all?" he asked.

"Don't get upset," Jobs assured him and the rest of the board. "These are very low-level people that you won't miss, and they will be leaving anyway."

The board initially seemed disposed to wish Jobs well in his venture. After a private discussion, the directors even proposed that Apple take a 10% stake in the new company and that Jobs remain on the board.

That night Jobs and his five renegades met again at his house for dinner. He was in favor of taking the Apple investment, but the others convinced him it was unwise. They also agreed that it would be best if they resigned all at once, right away. Then they could make a clean break.

So Jobs wrote a formal letter telling Sculley the names of the five who would be leaving, signed it in his spidery lowercase signature, and drove to Apple the next morning to hand it to him before his 7:30 staff meeting.

"Steve, these are not low-level people," Sculley said.

"Well, these people were going to resign anyway," Jobs replied. "They are going to be handing in their resignations by nine this morning."

From Jobs's perspective, he had been honest. The five were not division managers or members of Sculley's top team. They had all felt diminished, in fact, by the company's new organization. But from Sculley's perspective, these were important players; Page was an Apple Fellow, and Lewin was a key to the higher education market. In addition, they knew about the plans for Big Mac; even though it had been shelved, this was still proprietary information. Nevertheless Sculley was sanguine. Instead of pushing the point, he asked Jobs to remain on the board. Jobs replied that he would think about it.

But when Sculley walked into his 7:30 staff meeting and told his top lieutenants who was leaving, there was an uproar. Most of them felt that Jobs had breached his duties as chairman and displayed stunning disloyalty to the company. "We should expose him for the fraud that he is so that people here stop regarding him as a messiah," Campbell shouted, according to Sculley.

Campbell admitted that, although he later became a great Jobs defender and supportive board member, he was ballistic that morning. "I was fucking furious, especially about him taking Dan'l Lewin," he recalled. "Dan'l had built the relationships with the universities. He was always muttering about how hard it was to work with Steve, and then he left." Campbell was so angry that he walked out of the meeting to call Lewin at home. When his wife said he was in the shower, Campbell said, "I'll wait." A few minutes later, when she said he was still in the shower, Campbell again said, "I'll wait." When Lewin finally came on the phone, Campbell asked him if it was true. Lewin acknowledged it was. Campbell hung up without saying another word.

After hearing the fury of his senior staff, Sculley surveyed the members of the board. They likewise felt that Jobs had misled them with his pledge that he would not raid important employees. Arthur Rock was especially angry. Even though he had sided with Sculley during the Memorial Day showdown, he had been able to repair his paternal relationship with Jobs. Just the week before, he had invited Jobs to bring his girlfriend up to San Francisco so that he and his wife could meet her, and the four had a nice dinner in Rock's Pacific Heights home. Jobs had not mentioned the new company he was forming, so Rock felt betrayed when he heard about it from Sculley. "He came to the board and lied to us," Rock growled later. "He told us he was thinking of forming a company when in fact he had already formed it. He said he was going to take a few middle-level people. It turned out to be five senior people." Markkula, in his subdued way, was also offended. "He took some top executives he had secretly lined up before he left. That's not the way you do things. It was ungentlemanly."

Over the weekend both the board and the executive staff convinced Sculley that Apple would have to declare war on its cofounder. Markkula issued a formal statement accusing Jobs of acting "in direct contradiction to his statements that he wouldn't recruit any key Apple personnel for his company." He added ominously, "We are evaluating what possible actions should be taken." Campbell was quoted in the *Wall Street Journal* as saying he "was stunned and shocked" by Jobs's behavior.

Jobs had left his meeting with Sculley thinking that things might proceed smoothly, so he had kept quiet. But after reading the newspapers, he felt that he had to respond. He phoned a few favored reporters and invited them to his home for private briefings the next day. Then he called Andy Cunningham, who had handled his publicity at Regis McKenna. "I went over to his unfurnished mansiony place in Woodside," she recalled, "and I found him huddled in the kitchen with his five colleagues and a few reporters hanging outside on the lawn." Jobs told her that he was going to do a full-fledged press conference and started spewing some of the derogatory things he was going to say. Cunningham was appalled. "This is going to reflect badly on you," she told him. Finally he backed down. He decided that he would give the reporters a copy of the resignation letter and limit any on-the-record comments to a few bland statements.

Jobs had considered just mailing in his letter of resignation, but Susan Barnes convinced him that this would be too contemptuous. Instead he drove it to Markkula's house, where he also found Al Eisenstat. There was a tense conversation for about fifteen minutes; then Barnes, who had been waiting outside, came to the door to retrieve him before he said anything he would regret. He left behind the letter, which he had composed on a Macintosh and printed on the new LaserWriter:

September 17, 1985

Dear Mike:

This morning's papers carried suggestions that Apple is considering removing me as Chairman. I don't know the source of these reports but they are both misleading to the public and unfair to me.

You will recall that at last Thursday's Board meeting I stated I had decided to start a new venture and I tendered my resignation as Chairman.

The Board declined to accept my resignation and asked me to defer it for a week. I agreed to do so in light of the encouragement the Board offered with regard to the proposed new venture and the indications that Apple would invest in it. On Friday, after I told John Sculley who would be joining me, he confirmed Apple's willingness to discuss areas of possible collaboration between Apple and my new venture.

Subsequently the Company appears to be adopting a hostile posture toward me and the new venture. Accordingly, I must insist upon the immediate acceptance of my resignation. . . .

As you know, the company's recent reorganization left me with no work to do and no access even to regular management reports. I am but 30 and want still to contribute and achieve.

After what we have accomplished together, I would wish our parting to be both amicable and dignified.

Yours sincerely, steven p. jobs

When a guy from the facilities team went to Jobs's office to pack up his belongings, he saw a picture frame on the floor. It contained a photograph of Jobs and Sculley in warm conversation, with an inscription from seven months earlier: "Here's to Great Ideas, Great Experiences, and a Great Friendship! John." The glass frame was shattered. Jobs had hurled it across the room before leaving. From that day, he never spoke to Sculley again.

Apple's stock went up a full point, or almost 7%, when Jobs's resignation was announced. "East Coast stockholders always worried about California flakes running the company," explained the editor of a tech stock newsletter. "Now with both Wozniak and Jobs out, those shareholders are relieved." But Nolan Bushnell, the Atari founder who had been an amused mentor ten years earlier, told *Time* that Jobs would be badly missed. "Where is Apple's inspiration going to come from? Is Apple going to have all the romance of a new brand of Pepsi?"

After a few days of failed efforts to reach a settlement with Jobs, Sculley and the Apple board decided to sue him "for breaches of fiduciary obligations." The suit spelled out his alleged transgressions:

> Notwithstanding his fiduciary obligations to Apple, Jobs, while serving as the Chairman of Apple's Board of Directors and an officer of Apple and pretending loyalty to the interests of Apple . . .
>
> (a) secretly planned the formation of an enterprise to compete with Apple;
>
> (b) secretly schemed that his competing enterprise would wrongfully take advantage of and utilize Apple's plan to design, develop and market the Next Generation Product . . .
>
> (c) secretly lured away key employees of Apple.

At the time, Jobs owned 6.5 million shares of Apple stock, 11% of the company, worth more than $100 million. He began to sell his shares, and within five months had dumped them all, retaining only one share so he could attend shareholder meetings if he wanted. He was furious, and that was reflected in his passion to start what was, no matter how he spun it, a rival company. "He was angry at Apple," said Joanna Hoffman, who briefly went to work for the new company. "Aiming at the educational market, where Apple was strong, was simply Steve being vengeful. He was doing it for revenge."

Jobs, of course, didn't see it that way. "I haven't got any sort of odd chip on my shoulder," he told *Newsweek*. Once again he invited his favorite reporters over to his Woodside home, and this time he did not have Andy Cunningham there urging him to be circumspect. He dismissed the allegation that he had improperly lured the five colleagues from Apple. "These people all called me," he told the gaggle of journalists who were milling around in his unfurnished living room. "They were thinking of leaving the company. Apple has a way of neglecting people."

He decided to cooperate with a *Newsweek* cover in order to get his version of the story out, and the interview he gave was revealing. "What I'm best at doing is finding a group of talented people and making things with them," he told the magazine. He said that he would always harbor affection for Apple. "I'll always remember Apple like any man remembers the first woman he's fallen in love with." But he was also willing to fight with its management if need be. "When someone calls you a thief in public, you have to respond." Apple's threat to sue him was outrageous. It was also sad. It showed that Apple was no longer a confident, rebellious company. "It's hard to think that a $2 billion company with 4,300 employees couldn't compete with six people in blue jeans."

To try to counter Jobs's spin, Sculley called Wozniak and urged him to speak out. "Steve can be an insulting and hurtful guy," he told *Time* that week. He revealed that Jobs had asked him to join his new firm—it would have been a sly way to land another blow against Apple's current management—but he wanted no part of such games and had not returned Jobs's phone call. To the *San Francisco Chronicle*, he recounted how Jobs had blocked frogdesign from working on his remote control under the pretense that it might compete with Apple products. "I look forward to a great product and I wish him success, but his integrity I cannot trust," Wozniak said.

To Be on Your Own

"The best thing ever to happen to Steve is when we fired him, told him to get lost," Arthur Rock later said. The theory, shared by many, is that the tough love made him wiser and more mature. But it's not that simple. At the company he founded after being ousted from Apple, Jobs was able to indulge all of his instincts, both good and bad. He was unbound. The result was a series of spectacular products that were dazzling market flops. *This* was the true learning experience. What prepared him for the great success he would have in Act III was not his ouster from his Act I at Apple but his brilliant failures in Act II.

The first instinct that he indulged was his passion for design. The name he chose for his new company was rather straightforward: Next. In order to make it more distinctive, he decided he needed a world-class logo. So he courted the dean of corporate logos, Paul Rand. At seventy-one, the Brooklyn-born graphic designer had already created some of the best-known logos in business, including those of *Esquire*, IBM, Westinghouse, ABC, and UPS. He was under contract to IBM, and his supervisors there said that it would obviously be a conflict for him to create a logo for another computer company. So Jobs picked up the phone and called IBM's CEO, John Akers. Akers was out of town, but Jobs was so persistent that he was finally put through to Vice Chairman Paul Rizzo. After two days, Rizzo concluded that it was futile to resist Jobs, and he gave permission for Rand to do the work.

Rand flew out to Palo Alto and spent time walking with Jobs and listening to his vision. The computer would be a cube, Jobs pronounced. He loved that shape. It was perfect and simple. So Rand decided that the logo should be a cube as well, one that was tilted at a 28° angle. When Jobs asked for a number of options to consider, Rand declared that he did not create different *options* for clients. "I will solve your problem, and you will pay me," he told Jobs. "You can use what I produce, or not, but I will not do options, and either way you will pay me."

Jobs admired that kind of thinking, so he made what was quite a gamble. The company would pay an astonishing $100,000 flat fee to get *one* design. "There was a clarity in our relationship," Jobs said. "He had a purity as an artist, but he was astute at solving business problems. He had a tough exterior, and had perfected the image of a curmudgeon, but he was a teddy bear inside." It was one of Jobs's highest praises: purity as an artist.

It took Rand just two weeks. He flew back to deliver the result to Jobs at his Woodside house. First they had dinner, then Rand handed him an elegant and vibrant booklet that described his thought process. On the final spread, Rand presented the logo he had chosen. "In its design, color arrangement, and orientation, the logo is a study in contrasts," his booklet proclaimed. "Tipped at a jaunty angle, it brims with the informality, friendliness, and spontaneity of a Christmas seal and the authority of a rubber stamp." The word "next" was split into two lines to fill the square face of the cube, with only the "e" in lowercase. That letter stood out, Rand's booklet explained, to connote "education, excellence . . . e = mc²."

It was often hard to predict how Jobs would react to a presentation. He could label it shitty or brilliant; one never knew which way he might go. But with a legendary designer such as Rand, the chances were that Jobs would embrace the proposal. He stared at the final spread, looked up at Rand, and then hugged him. They had one minor disagreement: Rand had used a dark yellow for the "e" in the logo, and Jobs wanted him to change it to a brighter and more traditional yellow. Rand banged his fist on the table and declared, "I've been doing this for fifty years, and I know what I'm doing." Jobs relented.

The company had not only a new logo, but a new name. No longer was it Next. It was NeXT. Others might not have understood the need to obsess over a logo, much less pay $100,000 for one. But for Jobs it meant that NeXT was starting life with a world-class feel and identity, even if it hadn't yet designed its first product. As Markkula had taught him, a great company must be able to impute its values from the first impression it makes.

As a bonus, Rand agreed to design a personal calling card for Jobs. He came up with a colorful type treatment, which Jobs liked, but they ended up having a lengthy and heated disagreement about the placement of the period after the "P" in Steven P. Jobs. Rand had placed the period to the right of the "P.", as it would appear if set in lead type.

Steve preferred the period to be nudged to the left, under the curve of the "P.", as is possible with digital typography. "It was a fairly large argument about something relatively small," Susan Kare recalled. On this one Jobs prevailed.

In order to translate the NeXT logo into the look of real products, Jobs needed an industrial designer he trusted. He talked to a few possibilities, but none of them impressed him as much as the wild Bavarian he had imported to Apple: Hartmut Esslinger, whose frogdesign had set up shop in Silicon Valley and who, thanks to Jobs, had a lucrative contract with Apple. Getting IBM to permit Paul Rand to do work for NeXT was a small miracle willed into existence by Jobs's belief that reality can be distorted. But that was a snap compared to the likelihood that he could convince Apple to permit Esslinger to work for NeXT.

This did not keep Jobs from trying. At the beginning of November 1985, just five weeks after Apple filed suit against him, Jobs wrote to Eisenstat and asked for a dispensation. "I spoke with Hartmut Esslinger this weekend and he suggested I write you a note expressing why I wish to work with him and frogdesign on the new products for NeXT," he said. Astonishingly, Jobs's argument was that he did not know what Apple had in the works, but Esslinger did. "NeXT has no knowledge as to the current or future directions of Apple's product designs, nor do other design firms we might deal with, so it is possible to inadvertently design similar looking products. It is in both Apple's and NeXT's best interest to rely on Hartmut's professionalism to make sure this does not occur." Eisenstat recalled being flabbergasted by Jobs's audacity, and he replied curtly. "I have previously expressed my concern on behalf of Apple that you are engaged in a business course which involves your utilization of Apple's confidential business information," he wrote. "Your letter does not alleviate my concern in any way. In fact it heightens my concern because it states that you have 'no knowledge as to the current or future directions of Apple's product designs,' a statement which is not true." What made the request all the more astonishing to Eisenstat was that it was Jobs who, just a year earlier, had forced frogdesign to abandon its work on Wozniak's remote control device.

Jobs realized that in order to work with Esslinger (and for a variety of other reasons), it would be necessary to resolve the lawsuit that

Apple had filed. Fortunately Sculley was willing. In January 1986 they reached an out-of-court agreement involving no financial damages. In return for Apple's dropping its suit, NeXT agreed to a variety of restrictions: Its product would be marketed as a high-end workstation, it would be sold directly to colleges and universities, and it would not ship before March 1987. Apple also insisted that the NeXT machine "not use an operating system compatible with the Macintosh," though it could be argued that Apple would have been better served by insisting on just the opposite.

After the settlement Jobs continued to court Esslinger until the designer decided to wind down his contract with Apple. That allowed frogdesign to work with NeXT at the end of 1986. Esslinger insisted on having free rein, just as Paul Rand had. "Sometimes you have to use a big stick with Steve," he said. Like Rand, Esslinger was an artist, so Jobs was willing to grant him indulgences he denied other mortals.

Jobs decreed that the computer should be an absolutely perfect cube, with each side exactly a foot long and every angle precisely 90 degrees. He liked cubes. They had gravitas but also the slight whiff of a toy. But the NeXT cube was a Jobsian example of design desires trumping engineering considerations. The circuit boards, which fitted nicely into the traditional pizza-box shape, had to be reconfigured and stacked in order to nestle into a cube.

Even worse, the perfection of the cube made it hard to manufacture. Most parts that are cast in molds have angles that are slightly greater than pure 90 degrees, so that it's easier to get them out of the mold (just as it is easier to get a cake out of a pan that has angles slightly greater than 90 degrees). But Esslinger dictated, and Jobs enthusiastically agreed, that there would be no such "draft angles" that would ruin the purity and perfection of the cube. So the sides had to be produced separately, using molds that cost $650,000, at a specialty machine shop in Chicago. Jobs's passion for perfection was out of control. When he noticed a tiny line in the chassis caused by the molds, something that any other computer maker would accept as unavoidable, he flew to Chicago and convinced the die caster to start over and do it perfectly. "Not a lot of die casters expect a celebrity to fly in," noted one of the engineers. Jobs also had the company buy a $150,000 sanding machine to remove all lines where the mold faces met and insisted that the magnesium case be a matte black, which made it more susceptible to showing blemishes.

Jobs had always indulged his obsession that the unseen parts of a product should be crafted as beautifully as its façade, just as his father had taught him when they were building a fence. This too he took to extremes when he found himself unfettered at NeXT. He made sure that the screws inside the machine had expensive plating. He even insisted that the matte black finish be coated onto the inside of the cube's case, even though only repairmen would see it.

Joe Nocera, then writing for *Esquire*, captured Jobs's intensity at a NeXT staff meeting:

> It's not quite right to say that he is sitting through this staff meeting, because Jobs doesn't sit through much of anything; one of the ways he dominates is through sheer movement. One moment he's kneeling in his chair; the next minute he's slouching in it; the next he has leaped out of his chair entirely and is scribbling on the blackboard directly behind him. He is full of mannerisms. He bites his nails. He stares with unnerving earnestness at whoever is speaking. His hands, which are slightly and inexplicably yellow, are in constant motion.

What particularly struck Nocera was Jobs's "almost willful lack of tact." It was more than just an inability to hide his opinions when others said something he thought dumb; it was a conscious readiness, even a perverse eagerness, to put people down, humiliate them, show he was smarter. When Dan'l Lewin handed out an organization chart, for example, Jobs rolled his eyes. "These charts are bullshit," he interjected. Yet his moods still swung wildly, as at Apple. A finance person came into the meeting and Jobs lavished praise on him for a "really, really great job on this"; the previous day Jobs had told him, "This deal is crap."

One of NeXT's first ten employees was an interior designer for the company's first headquarters, in Palo Alto. Even though Jobs had leased a building that was new and nicely designed, he had it completely gutted and rebuilt. Walls were replaced by glass, the carpets were replaced by light hardwood flooring. The process was repeated when NeXT moved to a bigger space in Redwood City in 1989. Even though the building was brand-new, Jobs insisted that the elevators be moved so that the entrance lobby would be more dramatic. As a centerpiece, Jobs commissioned I. M. Pei to design a grand staircase that seemed to float in the air. The contractor said it couldn't be built. Jobs said it could, and it was. Years later Jobs would make such staircases a feature at Apple's signature stores.

The Computer

During the early months of NeXT, Jobs and Dan'l Lewin went on the road, often accompanied by a few colleagues, to visit campuses and solicit opinions. At Harvard they met with Mitch Kapor, the chairman of Lotus software, over dinner at Harvest restaurant. When Kapor began slathering butter on his bread, Jobs asked him, "Have you ever heard of serum cholesterol?" Kapor responded, "I'll make you a deal. You stay away from commenting on my dietary habits, and I will stay away from the subject of your personality." It was meant humorously, but as Kapor later commented, "Human relationships were not his strong suit." Lotus agreed to write a spreadsheet program for the NeXT operating system.

Jobs wanted to bundle useful content with the machine, so Michael Hawley, one of the engineers, developed a digital dictionary. He learned that a friend of his at Oxford University Press had been involved in the typesetting of a new edition of Shakespeare's works. That meant that there was probably a computer tape he could get his hands on and, if so, incorporate it into the NeXT's memory. "So I called up Steve, and he said that would be awesome, and we flew over to Oxford together." On a beautiful spring day in 1986, they met in the publishing house's grand building in the heart of Oxford, where Jobs made an offer of $2,000 plus 74 cents for every computer sold in order to have the rights to Oxford's edition of Shakespeare. "It will be all gravy to you," he argued. "You will be ahead of the parade. It's never been done before." They agreed in principle and then went out to play skittles over beer at a nearby pub where Lord Byron used to drink. By the time it launched, the NeXT would also include a dictionary, a thesaurus, and the *Oxford Dictionary of Quotations*, making it one of the pioneers of the concept of searchable electronic books.

Instead of using off-the-shelf chips for the NeXT, Jobs had his engineers design custom ones that integrated a variety of functions on one chip. That would have been hard enough, but Jobs made it almost impossible by continually revising the functions he wanted it to do. After a year it became clear that this would be a major source of delay.

He also insisted on building his own fully automated and futuristic factory, just as he had for the Macintosh; he had not been chastened by that experience. This time too he made the same mistakes, only more excessively. Machines and robots were painted and repainted as he compulsively revised his color scheme. The walls were museum white, as they had been at the Macintosh factory, and there were $20,000 black leather chairs and a custom-made staircase, just as in the corporate headquarters. He insisted that the machinery on the 165-foot assembly line be configured to move the circuit boards from right to left as they got built, so that the process would look better to visitors who watched from the viewing gallery. Empty circuit boards were fed in at one end and twenty minutes later, untouched by humans, came out the other end as completed boards. The process followed the Japanese principle known as *kanban*, in which each machine performs its task only when the next machine is ready to receive another part.

Jobs had not tempered his way of dealing with employees. "He applied charm or public humiliation in a way that in most cases proved to be pretty effective," Tribble recalled. But sometimes it wasn't. One engineer, David Paulsen, put in ninety-hour weeks for the first ten months at NeXT. He quit when "Steve walked in one Friday afternoon and told us how unimpressed he was with what we were doing." When *Business Week* asked him why he treated employees so harshly, Jobs said it made the company better. "Part of my responsibility is to be a yardstick of quality. Some people aren't used to an environment where excellence is expected." But he still had his spirit and charisma. There were plenty of field trips, visits by akido masters, and off-site retreats. And he still exuded the pirate flag spunkiness. When Apple fired Chiat/Day, the ad firm that had done the "1984" ad and taken out the newspaper ad saying "Welcome IBM—seriously," Jobs took out a full-page ad in the *Wall Street Journal* proclaiming, "Congratulations Chiat/Day—Seriously . . . Because I can guarantee you: there is life after Apple."

Perhaps the greatest similarity to his days at Apple was that Jobs brought with him his reality distortion field. It was on display at the company's first retreat at Pebble Beach in late 1985. There Jobs pronounced that the first NeXT computer would be shipped in just eighteen months. It was already clear that this date was impossible, but he blew off a suggestion from one engineer that they be realistic and plan on shipping in 1988. "If we do that, the world isn't standing still, the technology window passes us by, and all the work we've done we have to throw down the toilet," he argued.

Joanna Hoffman, the veteran of the Macintosh team who was among those willing to challenge Jobs, did so. "Reality distortion has motivational value, and I think that's fine," she said as Jobs stood at a whiteboard. "However, when it comes to setting a date in a way that affects the design of the product, then we get into real deep shit." Jobs didn't agree: "I think we have to drive a stake in the ground somewhere, and I think if we miss this window, then our credibility starts to erode." What he did not say, even though it was suspected by all, was that if their targets slipped they might run out of money. Jobs had pledged $7 million of his own funds, but at their current burn rate that would run out in eighteen months if they didn't start getting some revenue from shipped products.

Three months later, when they returned to Pebble Beach for their next retreat, Jobs began his list of maxims with "The honeymoon is over." By the time of the third retreat, in Sonoma in September 1986, the timetable was gone, and it looked as though the company would hit a financial wall.

Perot to the Rescue

In late 1986 Jobs sent out a proposal to venture capital firms offering a 10% stake in NeXT for $3 million. That put a valuation on the entire company of $30 million, a number that Jobs had pulled out of thin air. Less than $7 million had gone into the company thus far, and there was little to show for it other than a neat logo and some snazzy offices. It had no revenue or products, nor any on the horizon. Not surprisingly, the venture capitalists all passed on the offer to invest.

There was, however, one cowboy who was dazzled. Ross Perot, the bantam Texan who had founded Electronic Data Systems, then sold it to General Motors for $2.4 billion, happened to watch a PBS documentary, *The Entrepreneurs*, which had a segment on Jobs and NeXT in November 1986. He instantly identified with Jobs and his gang, so much so that, as he watched them on television, he said, "I was finishing their sentences for them." It was a line eerily similar to one Sculley had often used. Perot called Jobs the next day and offered, "If you ever need an investor, call me."

Jobs did indeed need one, badly. But he was careful not to show it. He waited a week before calling back. Perot sent some of his analysts to size up NeXT, but Jobs took care to deal directly with Perot. One of his great regrets in life, Perot later said, was that he had not bought Microsoft, or a large stake in it, when a very young Bill Gates had come to visit him in Dallas in 1979. By the time Perot called Jobs, Microsoft had just gone public with a $1 billion valuation. Perot had missed out on the opportunity to make a lot of money and have a fun adventure. He was eager not to make that mistake again.

Jobs made an offer to Perot that was three times more costly than had quietly been offered to venture capitalists a few months earlier. For $20 million, Perot would get 16% of the equity in the company, after Jobs put in another $5 million. That meant the company would be valued at about $126 million. But money was not a major consideration for Perot. After a meeting with Jobs, he declared that he was in. "I pick the jockeys, and the jockeys pick the horses and ride them," he told Jobs. "You guys are the ones I'm betting on, so you figure it out."

Perot brought to NeXT something that was almost as valuable as his $20 million lifeline: He was a quotable, spirited cheerleader for the company, who could lend it an air of credibility among grown-ups. "In terms of a startup company, it's one that carries the least risk of any I've seen in 25 years in the computer industry," he told the *New York Times*. "We've had some sophisticated people see the hardware—it blew them away. Steve and his whole NeXT team are the darnedest bunch of per- fectionists I've ever seen."

Perot also traveled in rarefied social and business circles that com- plemented Jobs's own. He took Jobs to a black-tie dinner dance in San Francisco that Gordon and Ann Getty gave for King Juan Carlos I of Spain. When the king asked Perot whom he should meet, Perot immediately produced Jobs. They were soon engaged in what Perot later described as "electric conversation," with Jobs animatedly describ- ing the next wave in computing. At the end the king scribbled a note and handed it to Jobs. "What happened?" Perot asked. Jobs answered, "I sold him a computer."

These and other stories were incorporated into the mythologized story of Jobs that Perot told wherever he went. At a briefing at the National Press Club in Washington, he spun Jobs's life story into a Texas-size yarn about a young man

> so poor he couldn't afford to go to college, working in his garage at night, playing with computer chips, which was his hobby, and his dad— who looks like a character out of a Norman Rockwell painting—comes in one day and said, "Steve, either make something you can sell or go get a job." Sixty days later, in a wooden box that his dad made for him, the first Apple computer was created. And this high school graduate liter- ally changed the world.

The one phrase that was true was the one about Paul Jobs's look- ing like someone in a Rockwell painting. And perhaps the last phrase, the one about Jobs changing the world. Certainly Perot believed that. Like Sculley, he saw himself in Jobs. "Steve's like me," Perot told the *Washington Post*'s David Remnick. "We're weird in the same way. We're soul mates."

Gates and NeXT

Bill Gates was not a soul mate. Jobs had convinced him to produce software applications for the Macintosh, which had turned out to be hugely profitable for Microsoft. But Gates was one person who was resistant to Jobs's reality distortion field, and as a result he decided not to create software tailored for the NeXT platform. Gates went to California to get periodic demonstrations, but each time he came away unimpressed. "The Macintosh was truly unique, but I personally don't understand what is so unique about Steve's new computer," he told *Fortune.*

Part of the problem was that the rival titans were congenitally unable to be deferential to each other. When Gates made his first visit to NeXT's Palo Alto headquarters, in the summer of 1987, Jobs kept him waiting for a half hour in the lobby, even though Gates could see through the glass walls that Jobs was walking around having casual conversations. "I'd gone down to NeXT and I had the Odwalla, the most expensive carrot juice, and I'd never seen tech offices so lavish," Gates recalled, shaking his head with just a hint of a smile. "And Steve comes a half hour late to the meeting."

Jobs's sales pitch, according to Gates, was simple. "We did the Mac together," Jobs said. "How did that work for you? Very well. Now, we're going to do this together and this is going to be great."

But Gates was brutal to Jobs, just as Jobs could be to others. "This machine is crap," he said. "The optical disk has too high latency, the fucking case is too expensive. This thing is ridiculous." He decided then, and reaffirmed on each subsequent visit, that it made no sense for Microsoft to divert resources from other projects to develop applications for NeXT. Worse yet, he repeatedly said so publicly, which made others less likely to spend time developing for NeXT. "Develop for it? I'll piss on it," he told *InfoWorld.*

When they happened to meet in the hallway at a conference, Jobs started berating Gates for his refusal to do software for NeXT. "When you get a market, I will consider it," Gates replied. Jobs got angry. "It was a screaming battle, right in front of everybody," recalled Adele

Goldberg, the Xerox PARC engineer. Jobs insisted that NeXT was the next wave of computing. Gates, as he often did, got more expressionless as Jobs got more heated. He finally just shook his head and walked away.

Beneath their personal rivalry—and occasional grudging respect— was their basic philosophical difference. Jobs believed in an end-to-end integration of hardware and software, which led him to build a machine that was not compatible with others. Gates believed in, and profited from, a world in which different companies made machines that were compatible with one another; their hardware ran a standard operating system (Microsoft's Windows) and could all use the same software apps (such as Microsoft's Word and Excel). "His product comes with an interesting feature called incompatibility," Gates told the *Washington Post*. "It doesn't run any of the existing software. It's a super-nice computer. I don't think if I went out to design an incompatible computer I would have done as well as he did."

At a forum in Cambridge, Massachusetts, in 1989, Jobs and Gates appeared sequentially, laying out their competing worldviews. Jobs spoke about how new waves come along in the computer industry every few years. Macintosh had launched a revolutionary new approach with the graphical interface; now NeXT was doing it with object-oriented programming tied to a powerful new machine based on an optical disk. Every major software vendor realized they had to be part of this new wave, he said, "except Microsoft." When Gates came up, he reiterated his belief that Jobs's end-to-end control of the software and the hardware was destined for failure, just as Apple had failed in competing against the Microsoft Windows standard. "The hardware market and the software market are separate," he said. When asked about the great design that could come from Jobs's approach, Gates gestured to the NeXT prototype that was still sitting onstage and sneered, "If you want black, I'll get you a can of paint."

IBM

Jobs came up with a brilliant jujitsu maneuver against Gates, one that could have changed the balance of power in the computer industry forever. It required Jobs to do two things that were against his nature: licensing out his software to another hardware maker and getting into bed with IBM. He had a pragmatic streak, albeit a tiny one, so he was able to overcome his reluctance. But his heart was never fully in it, which is why the alliance would turn out to be short-lived.

It began at a party, a truly memorable one, for the seventieth birthday of the *Washington Post* publisher Katharine Graham in June 1987 in Washington. Six hundred guests attended, including President Ronald Reagan. Jobs flew in from California and IBM's chairman John Akers from New York. It was the first time they had met. Jobs took the opportunity to bad-mouth Microsoft and attempt to wean IBM from using its Windows operating system. "I couldn't resist telling him I thought IBM was taking a giant gamble betting its entire software strategy on Microsoft, because I didn't think its software was very good," Jobs recalled.

To Jobs's delight, Akers replied, "How would you like to help us?" Within a few weeks Jobs showed up at IBM's Armonk, New York, headquarters with his software engineer Bud Tribble. They put on a demo of NeXT, which impressed the IBM engineers. Of particular significance was NeXTSTEP, the machine's object-oriented operating system. "NeXTSTEP took care of a lot of trivial programming chores that slow down the software development process," said Andrew Heller, the general manager of IBM's workstation unit, who was so impressed by Jobs that he named his newborn son Steve.

The negotiations lasted into 1988, with Jobs becoming prickly over tiny details. He would stalk out of meetings over disagreements about colors or design, only to be calmed down by Tribble or Lewin. He didn't seem to know which frightened him more, IBM or Microsoft. In April Perot decided to play host for a mediating session at his Dallas headquarters, and a deal was struck: IBM would license the current version of the NeXTSTEP software, and if the managers liked it, they would use it on some of their workstations. IBM sent to Palo Alto a 125-page contract. Jobs tossed it down without reading it. "You don't get it," he said as he walked out of the room. He demanded a simpler contract of only a few pages, which he got within a week.

Jobs wanted to keep the arrangement secret from Bill Gates until the big unveiling of the NeXT computer, scheduled for October. But IBM insisted on being forthcoming. Gates was furious. He realized this could wean IBM off its dependence on Microsoft operating systems. "NeXTSTEP isn't compatible with anything," he raged to IBM executives.

At first Jobs seemed to have pulled off Gates's worst nightmare. Other computer makers that were beholden to Microsoft's operating systems, most notably Compaq and Dell, came to ask Jobs for the right to clone NeXT and license NeXTSTEP. There were even offers to pay a lot more if NeXT would get out of the hardware business altogether.

That was too much for Jobs, at least for the time being. He cut off the clone discussions. And he began to cool toward IBM. The chill became reciprocal. When the person who made the deal at IBM moved on, Jobs went to Armonk to meet his replacement, Jim Cannavino. They cleared the room and talked one-on-one. Jobs demanded more money to keep the relationship going and to license newer versions of NeXTSTEP to IBM. Cannavino made no commitments, and he subsequently stopped returning Jobs's phone calls. The deal lapsed. NeXT got a bit of money for a licensing fee, but it never got the chance to change the world.

The Launch, October 1988

Jobs had perfected the art of turning product launches into theatrical productions, and for the world premiere of the NeXT computer—on October 12, 1988, in San Francisco's Symphony Hall—he wanted to outdo himself. He needed to blow away the doubters. In the weeks leading up to the event, he drove up to San Francisco almost every day to hole up in the Victorian house of Susan Kare, NeXT's graphic designer, who had done the original fonts and icons for the Macintosh.

She helped prepare each of the slides as Jobs fretted over everything from the wording to the right hue of green to serve as the background color. "I like that green," he said proudly as they were doing a trial run in front of some staffers. "Great green, great green," they all murmured in assent.

No detail was too small. Jobs went over the invitation list and even the lunch menu (mineral water, croissants, cream cheese, bean sprouts). He picked out a video projection company and paid it $60,000 for help. And he hired the postmodernist theater producer George Coates to stage the show. Coates and Jobs decided, not surprisingly, on an austere and radically simple stage look. The unveiling of the black perfect cube would occur on a starkly minimalist stage setting with a black background, a table covered by a black cloth, a black veil draped over the computer, and a simple vase of flowers. Because neither the hardware nor the operating system was actually ready, Jobs was urged to do a simulation. But he refused. Knowing it would be like walking a tightrope without a net, he decided to do the demonstration live.

More than three thousand people showed up at the event, lining up two hours before curtain time. They were not disappointed, at least by the show. Jobs was onstage for three hours, and he again proved to be, in the words of Andrew Pollack of the *New York Times*, "the Andrew Lloyd Webber of product introductions, a master of stage flair and special effects." Wes Smith of the *Chicago Tribune* said the launch was "to product demonstrations what Vatican II was to church meetings."

Jobs had the audience cheering from his opening line: "It's great to be back." He began by recounting the history of personal computer architecture, and he promised that they would now witness an event "that occurs only once or twice in a decade—a time when a new architecture is rolled out that is going to change the face of computing." The NeXT software and hardware were designed, he said, after three years of consulting with universities across the country. "What we realized was that higher ed wants a personal mainframe."

As usual there were superlatives. The product was "incredible," he said, "the best thing we could have imagined." He praised the beauty of even the parts unseen. Balancing on his fingertips the foot-square circuit board that would be nestled in the foot-cube box, he enthused,

"I hope you get a chance to look at this a little later. It's the most beautiful printed circuit board I've ever seen in my life." He then showed how the computer could play speeches—he featured King's "I Have a Dream" and Kennedy's "Ask Not"—and send email with audio attachments. He leaned into the microphone on the computer to record one of his own. "Hi, this is Steve, sending a message on a pretty historic day." Then he asked those in the audience to add "a round of applause" to the message, and they did.

One of Jobs's management philosophies was that it is crucial, every now and then, to roll the dice and "bet the company" on some new idea or technology. At the NeXT launch, he boasted of an example that, as it turned out, would not be a wise gamble: having a high-capacity (but slow) optical read/write disk and no floppy disk as a backup. "Two years ago we made a decision," he said. "We saw some new technology and we made a decision to risk our company."

Then he turned to a feature that would prove more prescient. "What we've done is made the first real digital books," he said, noting the inclusion of the Oxford edition of Shakespeare and other tomes. "There has not been an advancement in the state of the art of printed book technology since Gutenberg."

At times he could be amusingly aware of his own foibles, and he used the electronic book demonstration to poke fun at himself. "A word that's sometimes used to describe me is 'mercurial,'" he said, then paused. The audience laughed knowingly, especially those in the front rows, which were filled with NeXT employees and former members of the Macintosh team. Then he pulled up the word in the computer's dictionary and read the first definition: "Of or relating to, or born under the planet Mercury." Scrolling down, he said, "I think the third one is the one they mean: 'Characterized by unpredictable changeableness of mood.'" There was a bit more laughter. "If we scroll down the thesaurus, though, we see that the antonym is 'saturnine.' Well what's that? By simply double-clicking on it, we immediately look that up in the dictionary, and here it is: 'Cold and steady in moods. Slow to act or change. Of a gloomy or surly disposition.'" A little smile came across his face as he waited for the ripple of laughter. "Well," he concluded, "I don't think 'mercurial' is so bad after all." After the applause, he used the quotations book to make a more subtle point, about his reality distortion field. The quote he chose was from Lewis Carroll's *Through the Looking Glass*. After Alice laments that no matter how hard she tries she can't believe impossible things, the White Queen retorts, "Why, sometimes I've believed as many as six impossible things before breakfast." Especially from the front rows, there was a roar of knowing laughter.

All of the good cheer served to sugarcoat, or distract attention from, the bad news. When it came time to announce the price of the new machine, Jobs did what he would often do in product demonstrations: reel off the features, describe them as being "worth thousands and thousands of dollars," and get the audience to imagine how expensive it really should be. Then he announced what he hoped would seem like a low price: "We're going to be charging higher education a single price of $6,500." From the faithful, there was scattered applause. But his panel of academic advisors had long pushed to keep the price to between $2,000 and $3,000, and they thought that Jobs had promised to do so. Some of them were appalled. This was especially true once they discovered that the optional printer would cost another $2,000, and the slowness of the optical disk would make the purchase of a $2,500 external hard disk advisable.

There was another disappointment that he tried to downplay: "Early next year, we will have our 0.9 release, which is for software developers and aggressive end users." There was a bit of nervous laughter. What he was saying was that the real release of the machine and its software, known as the 1.0 release, would not actually be happening in early 1989. In fact he didn't set a hard date. He merely suggested it would be sometime in the second quarter of that year. At the first NeXT retreat back in late 1985, he had refused to budge, despite Joanna Hoffman's pushback, from his commitment to have the machine finished in early 1987. Now it was clear it would be more than two years later.

The event ended on a more upbeat note, literally. Jobs brought onstage a violinist from the San Francisco Symphony who played Bach's A Minor Violin Concerto in a duet with the NeXT computer onstage. People erupted in jubilant applause. The price and the delayed release were forgotten in the frenzy. When one reporter asked him immediately afterward why the machine was going to be so late, Jobs replied, "It's not late. It's five years ahead of its time."

As would become his standard practice, Jobs offered to provide "exclusive" interviews to anointed publications in return for their promising to put the story on the cover. This time he went one "exclusive" too far, though it didn't really hurt. He agreed to a request from *Business Week*'s Katie Hafner for exclusive access to him before the launch, but he also made a similar deal with *Newsweek* and then with *Fortune*. What he didn't consider was that one of *Fortune*'s top editors, Susan Fraker, was married to *Newsweek*'s editor Maynard Parker. At the *Fortune* story conference, when they were talking excitedly about their exclusive, Fraker mentioned that she happened to know that *Newsweek* had also been promised an exclusive, and it would be coming out a few days before *Fortune*. So Jobs ended up that week on only two magazine covers. *Newsweek* used the cover line "Mr. Chips" and showed him leaning on a beautiful NeXT, which it proclaimed to be "the most exciting machine in years." *Business Week* showed him looking angelic in a dark suit, fingertips pressed together like a preacher or professor. But Hafner pointedly reported on the manipulation that surrounded her exclusive. "NeXT carefully parceled out interviews with its staff and suppliers, monitoring them with a censor's eye," she wrote. "That strategy worked, but at a price: Such maneuvering—self-serving and relentless—displayed the side of Steve Jobs that so hurt him at Apple. The trait that most stands out is Jobs's need to control events."

When the hype died down, the reaction to the NeXT computer was muted, especially since it was not yet commercially available. Bill Joy, the brilliant and wry chief scientist at rival Sun Microsystems, called it "the first Yuppie workstation," which was not an unalloyed compliment. Bill Gates, as might be expected, continued to be publicly dismissive. "Frankly, I'm disappointed," he told the *Wall Street Journal*. "Back in 1981, we were truly excited by the Macintosh when Steve showed it to us, because when you put it side-by-side with another computer, it was unlike anything anybody had ever seen before." The NeXT machine was not like that. "In the grand scope of things, most of these features are truly trivial." He said that Microsoft would continue its plans not to write software for the NeXT. Right after the announcement event, Gates wrote a parody email to his staff. "All reality has been completely suspended," it began. Looking back at it, Gates laughs that it may have been "the best email I ever wrote."

When the NeXT computer finally went on sale in mid-1989, the factory was primed to churn out ten thousand units a month. As it turned out, sales were about four hundred a month. The beautiful factory robots, so nicely painted, remained mostly idle, and NeXT continued to hemorrhage cash.

CHAPTER NINETEEN

PIXAR

Technology Meets Art

Ed Catmull, Steve Jobs, and John Lasseter, 1999

Lucasfilm's Computer Division

When Jobs was losing his footing at Apple in the summer of 1985, he went for a walk with Alan Kay, who had been at Xerox PARC and was then an Apple Fellow. Kay knew that Jobs was interested in the intersection of creativity and technology, so he suggested they go see a friend of his, Ed Catmull, who was running the computer division of George Lucas's film studio. They rented a limo and rode up to Marin County to the edge of Lucas's Skywalker Ranch, where Catmull and his little computer division were based. "I was blown away, and I came back and tried to convince Sculley to buy it for Apple," Jobs recalled. "But the folks running Apple weren't interested, and they were busy kicking me out anyway."

The Lucasfilm computer division made hardware and software for rendering digital images, and it also had a group of computer animators making shorts, which was led by a talented cartoon-loving executive named John Lasseter. Lucas, who had completed his first *Star Wars* trilogy, was embroiled in a contentious divorce, and he needed to sell off the division. He told Catmull to find a buyer as soon as possible.

After a few potential purchasers balked in the fall of 1985, Catmull and his colleague Alvy Ray Smith decided to seek investors so that they could buy the division themselves. So they called Jobs, arranged another meeting, and drove down to his Woodside house. After railing for a while about the perfidies and idiocies of Sculley, Jobs proposed that he buy their Lucasfilm division outright. Catmull and Smith demurred: They wanted an investor, not a new owner. But it soon became clear that there was a middle ground: Jobs could buy a majority of the division and serve as chairman but allow Catmull and Smith to run it.

"I wanted to buy it because I was really into computer graphics," Jobs recalled. "I realized they were way ahead of others in combining art and technology, which is what I've always been interested in." He offered to pay Lucas $5 million plus invest another $5 million to capitalize the division as a stand-alone company. That was far less than Lucas had been asking, but the timing was right. They decided to negotiate a deal.

The chief financial officer at Lucasfilm found Jobs arrogant and prickly, so when it came time to hold a meeting of all the players, he told Catmull, "We have to establish the right pecking order." The plan was to gather everyone in a room with Jobs, and then the CFO would come in a few minutes late to establish that he was the person running the meeting. "But a funny thing happened," Catmull recalled. "Steve started the meeting on time without the CFO, and by the time the CFO walked in Steve was already in control of the meeting."

Jobs met only once with George Lucas, who warned him that the people in the division cared more about making animated movies than they did about making computers. "You know, these guys are hell-bent on animation," Lucas told him. Lucas later recalled, "I did warn him that was basically Ed and John's agenda. I think in his heart he bought the company because that was his agenda too."

The final agreement was reached in January 1986. It provided that, for his $10 million investment, Jobs would own 70% of the company, with the rest of the stock distributed to Ed Catmull, Alvy Ray Smith, and the thirty-eight other founding employees, down to the reception- ist. The division's most important piece of hardware was called the Pixar Image Computer, and from it the new company took its name.

For a while Jobs let Catmull and Smith run Pixar without much interference. Every month or so they would gather for a board meet- ing, usually at NeXT headquarters, where Jobs would focus on the finances and strategy. Nevertheless, by dint of his personality and con- trolling instincts, Jobs was soon playing a stronger role. He spewed out a stream of ideas—some reasonable, others wacky—about what Pixar's hardware and software could become. And on his occasional visits to the Pixar offices, he was an inspiring presence. "I grew up a Southern Baptist, and we had revival meetings with mesmerizing but corrupt preachers," recounted Alvy Ray Smith. "Steve's got it: the power of the tongue and the web of words that catches people up. We were aware of this when we had board meetings, so we developed signals— nose scratching or ear tugs—for when someone had been caught up in Steve's distortion field and he needed to be tugged back to reality."

Jobs had always appreciated the virtue of integrating hardware and software, which is what Pixar did with its Image Computer and render- ing software. It also produced creative content, such as animated films and graphics. All three elements benefited from Jobs's combination of artistic creativity and technological geekiness. "Silicon Valley folks don't really respect Hollywood creative types, and the Hollywood folks think that tech folks are people you hire and never have to meet," Jobs later said. "Pixar was one place where both cultures were respected."

Initially the revenue was supposed to come from the hardware side. The Pixar Image Computer sold for $125,000. The primary cus- tomers were animators and graphic designers, but the machine also soon found specialized markets in the medical industry (CAT scan data could be rendered in three-dimensional graphics) and intelligence fields (for rendering information from reconnaissance flights and satellites). Because of the sales to the National Security Agency, Jobs had to get a security clearance, which must have been fun for the FBI agent assigned to vet him. At one point, a Pixar executive recalled, Jobs was called by the investigator to go over the drug use questions, which he answered unabashedly. "The last time I used that . . . ," he would say, or on occasion he would answer that no, he had actually never tried that particular drug.

Jobs pushed Pixar to build a lower-cost version of the computer that would sell for around $30,000. He insisted that Hartmut Esslinger design it, despite protests by Catmull and Smith about his fees. It ended up looking like the original Pixar Image Computer, which was a cube with a round dimple in the middle, but it had Esslinger's signature thin grooves.

Jobs wanted to sell Pixar's computers to a mass market, so he had the Pixar folks open up sales offices—for which he approved the design—in major cities, on the theory that creative people would soon come up with all sorts of ways to use the machine. "My view is that people are creative animals and will figure out clever new ways to use tools that the inventor never imagined," he later said. "I thought that would happen with the Pixar computer, just as it did with the Mac." But the machine never took hold with regular consumers. It cost too much, and there were not many software programs for it.

On the software side, Pixar had a rendering program, known as Reyes (Renders everything you ever saw), for making 3-D graphics and images. After Jobs became chairman, the company created a new language and interface, named RenderMan, that it hoped would become a standard for 3-D graphics rendering, just as Adobe's PostScript was for laser printing.

As he had with the hardware, Jobs decided that they should try to find a mass market, rather than just a specialized one, for the software they made. He was never content to aim only at the corporate or high-end specialized markets. "He would have these great visions of how RenderMan could be for everyman," recalled Pam Kerwin, Pixar's marketing director. "He kept coming up with ideas about how ordinary people would use it to make amazing 3-D graphics and photorealistic images." The Pixar team would try to dissuade him by saying that RenderMan was not as easy to use as, say, Excel or Adobe Illustrator. Then Jobs would go to a whiteboard and show them how to make it simpler and more user-friendly. "We would be nodding our heads and getting excited and say, 'Yes, yes, this will be great!'" Kerwin recalled. "And then he would leave and we would consider it for a moment and then say, 'What the heck was he thinking!' He was so weirdly charismatic that you almost had to get deprogrammed after you talked to him." As it turned out, average consumers were not craving expensive software that would let them render realistic images. RenderMan didn't take off.

There was, however, one company that was eager to automate the rendering of animators' drawings into color images for film. When Roy Disney led a board revolution at the company that his uncle Walt had founded, the new CEO, Michael Eisner, asked what role he wanted. Disney said that he would like to revive the company's venerable but fading animation department. One of his first initiatives was to look at ways to computerize the process, and Pixar won the contract. It created a package of customized hardware and software known as CAPS, Computer Animation Production System. It was first used in 1988 for the final scene of *The Little Mermaid*, in which King Triton waves good-bye to Ariel. Disney bought dozens of Pixar Image Computers as CAPS became an integral part of its production.

Animation

The digital animation business at Pixar—the group that made little animated films—was originally just a sideline, its main purpose being to show off the hardware and software of the company. It was run by John Lasseter, a man whose childlike face and demeanor masked an artistic perfectionism that rivaled that of Jobs. Born in Hollywood, Lasseter grew up loving Saturday morning cartoon shows. In ninth grade, he wrote a report on the history of Disney Studios, and he decided then how he wished to spend his life.

When he graduated from high school, Lasseter enrolled in the animation program at the California Institute of the Arts, founded by Walt Disney. In his summers and spare time, he researched the Disney archives and worked as a guide on the Jungle Cruise ride at Disneyland. The latter experience taught him the value of timing and pacing in telling a story, an important but difficult concept to master when creating, frame by frame, animated footage. He won the Student Academy Award for the short he made in his junior year, *Lady and the Lamp*, which showed his debt to Disney films and foreshadowed his signature talent for infusing inanimate objects such as lamps with human personalities. After graduation he took the job for which he was destined: as an animator at Disney Studios.

Except it didn't work out. "Some of us younger guys wanted to bring *Star Wars*–level quality to the art of animation, but we were held in check," Lasseter recalled. "I got disillusioned, then I got caught in a feud between two bosses, and the head animation guy fired me." So in 1984 Ed Catmull and Alvy Ray Smith were able to recruit him to work where *Star Wars*–level quality was being defined, Lucasfilm. It was not certain that George Lucas, already worried about the cost of his computer division, would really approve of hiring a full-time animator, so Lasseter was given the title "interface designer."

After Jobs came onto the scene, he and Lasseter began to share their passion for graphic design. "I was the only guy at Pixar who was an artist, so I bonded with Steve over his design sense," Lasseter said. He was a gregarious, playful, and huggable man who wore flowery Hawaiian shirts, kept his office cluttered with vintage toys, and loved cheeseburgers. Jobs was a prickly, whip-thin vegetarian who favored austere and uncluttered surroundings. But they were actually well-suited for each other. Lasseter was an artist, so Jobs treated him deferentially, and Lasseter viewed Jobs, correctly, as a patron who could appreciate artistry and knew how it could be interwoven with technology and commerce.

Jobs and Catmull decided that, in order to show off their hardware and software, Lasseter should produce another short animated film in 1986 for SIGGRAPH, the annual computer graphics conference. At the time, Lasseter was using the Luxo lamp on his desk as a model for graphic rendering, and he decided to turn Luxo into a lifelike character. A friend's young child inspired him to add Luxo Jr., and he showed a few test frames to another animator, who urged him to make sure he told a story. Lasseter said he was making only a short, but the animator reminded him that a story can be told even in a few seconds. Lasseter took the lesson to heart. *Luxo Jr.* ended up being just over two minutes; it told the tale of a parent lamp and a child lamp pushing a ball back and forth until the ball bursts, to the child's dismay.

Jobs was so excited that he took time off from the pressures at NeXT to fly down with Lasseter to SIGGRAPH, which was being held in Dallas that August. "It was so hot and muggy that when we'd walk outside the air hit us like a tennis racket," Lasseter recalled. There were ten thousand people at the trade show, and Jobs loved it. Artistic creativity energized him, especially when it was connected to technology.

There was a long line to get into the auditorium where the films were being screened, so Jobs, not one to wait his turn, fast-talked their way in first. *Luxo Jr.* got a prolonged standing ovation and was named the best film. "Oh, wow!" Jobs exclaimed at the end. "I really get this, I get what it's all about." As he later explained, "Our film was the only one that had art to it, not just good technology. Pixar was about making that combination, just as the Macintosh had been."

Luxo Jr. was nominated for an Academy Award, and Jobs flew down to Los Angeles to be there for the ceremony. It didn't win, but Jobs became committed to making new animated shorts each year, even though there was not much of a business rationale for doing so. As times got tough at Pixar, he would sit through brutal budget-cutting meetings showing no mercy. Then Lasseter would ask that the money they had just saved be used for his next film, and Jobs would agree.

Tin Toy

Not all of Jobs's relationships at Pixar were as good. His worst clash came with Catmull's cofounder, Alvy Ray Smith. From a Baptist background in rural north Texas, Smith became a free-spirited hippie computer imaging engineer with a big build, big laugh, and big personality—and occasionally an ego to match. "Alvy just glows, with a high color, friendly laugh, and a whole bunch of groupies at conferences," said Pam Kerwin. "A personality like Alvy's was likely to ruffle Steve. They are both visionaries and high energy and high ego. Alvy is not as willing to make peace and overlook things as Ed was."

Smith saw Jobs as someone whose charisma and ego led him to abuse power. "He was like a televangelist," Smith said. "He wanted to control people, but I would not be a slave to him, which is why we clashed. Ed was much more able to go with the flow." Jobs would sometimes assert his dominance at a meeting by saying something outrageous or untrue. Smith took great joy in calling him on it, and he would do so with a large laugh and a smirk. This did not endear him to Jobs.

One day at a board meeting, Jobs started berating Smith and other top Pixar executives for the delay in getting the circuit boards completed for the new version of the Pixar Image Computer. At the time, NeXT was also very late in completing its own computer boards, and Smith pointed that out: "Hey, you're even later with your NeXT boards, so quit jumping on us." Jobs went ballistic, or in Smith's phrase, "totally nonlinear." When Smith was feeling attacked or confrontational, he tended to lapse into his southwestern accent. Jobs started parodying it in his sarcastic style. "It was a bully tactic, and I exploded with everything I had," Smith recalled. "Before I knew it, we were in each other's faces—about three inches apart—screaming at each other."

Jobs was very possessive about control of the whiteboard during a meeting, so the burly Smith pushed past him and started writing on it. "You can't do that!" Jobs shouted.

"What?" responded Smith, "I can't write on your whiteboard? Bullshit." At that point Jobs stormed out.

Smith eventually resigned to form a new company to make software for digital drawing and image editing. Jobs refused him permission to use some code he had created while at Pixar, which further inflamed their enmity. "Alvy eventually got what he needed," said Catmull, "but he was very stressed for a year and developed a lung infection." In the end it worked out well enough; Microsoft eventually bought Smith's company, giving him the distinction of being a founder of one company that was sold to Jobs and another that was sold to Gates.

Ornery in the best of times, Jobs became particularly so when it became clear that all three Pixar endeavors—hardware, software, and animated content—were losing money. "I'd get these plans, and in the end I kept having to put in more money," he recalled. He would rail, but then write the check. Having been ousted at Apple and flailing at NeXT, he couldn't afford a third strike.

To stem the losses, he ordered a round of deep layoffs, which he executed with his typical empathy deficiency. As Pam Kerwin put it, he had "neither the emotional nor financial runway to be decent to people he was letting go." Jobs insisted that the firings be done immediately, with no severance pay. Kerwin took Jobs on a walk around the parking lot and begged that the employees be given at least two weeks notice. "Okay," he shot back, "but the notice is retroactive from two weeks ago." Catmull was in Moscow, and Kerwin put in frantic calls to him. When he returned, he was able to institute a meager severance plan and calm things down just a bit.

At one point the members of the Pixar animation team were trying to convince Intel to let them make some of its commercials, and Jobs became impatient. During a meeting, in the midst of berating an Intel marketing director, he picked up the phone and called CEO Andy Grove directly. Grove, still playing mentor, tried to teach Jobs a lesson: He supported his Intel manager. "I stuck by my employee," he recalled. "Steve doesn't like to be treated like a supplier."

Grove also played mentor when Jobs proposed that Pixar give Intel suggestions on how to improve the capacity of its processors to render 3-D graphics. When the engineers at Intel accepted the offer, Jobs sent an email back saying Pixar would need to be paid for its advice. Intel's chief engineer replied, "We have not entered into any financial arrangement in exchange for good ideas for our microprocessors in the past and have no intention for the future." Jobs forwarded the answer to Grove, saying that he found the engineer's response to be "extremely arrogant, given Intel's dismal showing in understanding computer graphics." Grove sent Jobs a blistering reply, saying that sharing ideas is "what friendly companies and friends do for each other." Grove added that he had often freely shared ideas with Jobs in the past and that Jobs should not be so mercenary. Jobs relented. "I have many faults, but one of them is not ingratitude," he responded. "Therefore, I have changed my position 180 degrees—we will freely help. Thanks for the clearer perspective."

Pixar was able to create some powerful software products aimed at average consumers, or at least those average consumers who shared Jobs's passion for designing things. Jobs still hoped that the ability to make super-realistic 3-D images at home would become part of the desktop publishing craze. Pixar's Showplace, for example, allowed users to change the shadings on the 3-D objects they created so that they could display them from various angles with appropriate shadows. Jobs thought it was incredibly compelling, but most consumers were content to live without it. It was a case where his passions misled him: The software had so many amazing features that it lacked the simplicity Jobs usually demanded. Pixar couldn't compete with Adobe, which was making software that was less sophisticated but far less complicated and expensive.

Even as Pixar's hardware and software product lines foundered, Jobs kept protecting the animation group. It had become for him a little island of magical artistry that gave him deep emotional pleasure, and he was willing to nurture it and bet on it. In the spring of 1988 cash was running so short that he convened a meeting to decree deep spending cuts across the board. When it was over, Lasseter and his animation group were almost too afraid to ask Jobs about authorizing some extra money for another short. Finally, they broached the topic and Jobs sat silent, looking skeptical. It would require close to $300,000 more out of his pocket. After a few minutes, he asked if there were any storyboards. Catmull took him down to the animation offices, and once Lasseter started his show—displaying his boards, doing the voices, showing his passion for his product—Jobs started to warm up.

The story was about Lasseter's love, classic toys. It was told from the perspective of a toy one-man band named Tinny, who meets a baby that charms and terrorizes him. Escaping under the couch, Tinny finds other frightened toys, but when the baby hits his head and cries, Tinny goes back out to cheer him up.

Jobs said he would provide the money. "I believed in what John was doing," he later said. "It was art. He cared, and I cared. I always said yes." His only comment at the end of Lasseter's presentation was, "All I ask of you, John, is to make it great."

Tin Toy went on to win the 1988 Academy Award for animated short films, the first computer-generated film to do so. To celebrate, Jobs took Lasseter and his team to Greens, a vegetarian restaurant in San Francisco. Lasseter grabbed the Oscar, which was in the center of the table, held it aloft, and toasted Jobs by saying, "All you asked is that we make a great movie."

The new team at Disney—Michael Eisner the CEO and Jeffrey Katzenberg in the film division—began a quest to get Lasseter to come back. They liked *Tin Toy*, and they thought that something more could be done with animated stories of toys that come alive and have human emotions. But Lasseter, grateful for Jobs's faith in him, felt that Pixar was the only place where he could create a new world of computer-generated animation. He told Catmull, "I can go to Disney and be a director, or I can stay here and make history." So Disney began talking about making a production deal with Pixar. "Lasseter's shorts were really breathtaking both in storytelling and in the use of technology," recalled Katzenberg. "I tried so hard to get him to Disney, but he was loyal to Steve and Pixar. So if you can't beat them, join them. We decided to look for ways we could join up with Pixar and have them make a film about toys for us."

By this point Jobs had poured close to $50 million of his own money into Pixar—more than half of what he had pocketed when he cashed out of Apple—and he was still losing money at NeXT. He was hard-nosed about it; he forced all Pixar employees to give up their options as part of his agreement to add another round of personal funding in 1991. But he was also a romantic in his love for what artistry and technology could do together. His belief that ordinary consumers would love to do 3-D modeling on Pixar software turned out to be wrong, but that was soon replaced by an instinct that turned out to be right: that combining great art and digital technology would transform animated films more than anything had since 1937, when Walt Disney had given life to Snow White.

Looking back, Jobs said that, had he known more, he would have focused on animation sooner and not worried about pushing the company's hardware or software applications. On the other hand, had he known the hardware and software would never be profitable, he would not have taken over Pixar. "Life kind of snookered me into doing that, and perhaps it was for the better."

CHAPTER TWENTY

A REGULAR GUY

Love Is Just a Four-Letter Word

Mona Simpson and her fiancé, Richard Appel, 1991

Joan Baez

In 1982, when he was still working on the Macintosh, Jobs met the famed folksinger Joan Baez through her sister Mimi Fariña, who headed a charity that was trying to get donations of computers for prisons, and through Mark Vermilion, who ran Baez's human rights foundation Humanitas. When Jobs donated some computers to them, he asked if he could meet Baez. A few weeks later he and Baez had lunch in Cupertino. "I wasn't expecting a lot, but she was really smart and funny," he recalled. At the time, he was nearing the end of his relationship with Barbara Jasinski. They had vacationed in Hawaii, shared a house in the Santa Cruz mountains, and even gone to one of Baez's concerts together. As his relationship with Jasinski flamed out, Jobs began getting more serious with Baez. He was twenty-seven and Baez was forty-one, but for a few years they had a romance. "It turned into a serious relationship between two accidental friends who became lovers," Jobs recalled in a somewhat wistful tone.

Elizabeth Holmes, Jobs's friend from Reed College, believed that one of the reasons he went out with Baez—other than the fact that she was beautiful and funny and talented—was that she had once been the lover of Bob Dylan. "Steve loved that connection to Dylan," she later said. Baez and Dylan had been lovers in the early 1960s, and they toured as friends after that, including with the Rolling Thunder Revue in 1975. (Jobs had the bootlegs of those concerts.)

When she met Jobs, Baez had a fourteen-year-old son, Gabriel, from her marriage to the antiwar activist David Harris. At lunch she told Jobs she was trying to teach Gabe how to type. "You mean on a typewriter?" Jobs asked. When she said yes, he replied, "But a typewriter is antiquated."

"If a typewriter is antiquated, what does that make me?" she asked. There was an awkward pause. As Baez later told me, "As soon as I said it, I realized the answer was so obvious. The question just hung in the air. I was just horrified."

Much to the astonishment of the Macintosh team, Jobs burst into the office one day with Baez and showed her the prototype of the Macintosh. They were dumbfounded that he would reveal the computer to an outsider, given his obsession with secrecy, but they were even more blown away to be in the presence of Joan Baez. He gave Gabe an Apple II, and he later gave Baez a Macintosh. On visits Jobs would show off the features he liked. "He was sweet and patient, but he was so advanced in his knowledge that he had trouble teaching me," she recalled.

He was a sudden multimillionaire; she was a world-famous celebrity, but sweetly down-to-earth and not all that wealthy. She didn't know what to make of him then, and still found him puzzling when she talked about him almost thirty years later. At one dinner early in their relationship, Jobs started talking about Ralph Lauren and his Polo Shop, which she admitted she had never visited. "There's a beautiful red dress there that would be perfect for you," he said, and then drove her to the store in the Stanford Mall. Baez recalled, "I said to myself, far out, terrific, I'm with one of the world's richest men and he wants me to have this beautiful dress." When they got to the store, Jobs bought a handful of shirts for himself and showed her the red dress. "You ought to buy it," he said. She was a little surprised, and told him she couldn't really afford it. He said nothing, and they left. "Wouldn't you think if someone had talked like that the whole evening, that they were going to get it for you?" she asked me, seeming genuinely puzzled about the incident. "The mystery of the red dress is in your hands. I felt a bit strange about it." He would give her computers, but not a dress, and when he brought her flowers he made sure to say they were left over from an event in the office. "He was both romantic and afraid to be romantic," she said.

When he was working on the NeXT computer, he went to Baez's house in Woodside to show her how well it could produce music. "He had it play a Brahms quartet, and he told me eventually computers would sound better than humans playing it, even get the innuendo and the cadences better," Baez recalled. She was revolted by the idea. "He was working himself up into a fervor of delight while I was shrinking into a rage and thinking, How could you defile music like that?"

Jobs would confide in Debi Coleman and Joanna Hoffman about his relationship with Baez and worry about whether he could marry someone who had a teenage son and was probably past the point of wanting to have more children. "At times he would belittle her as being an 'issues' singer and not a true 'political' singer like Dylan," said Hoffman. "She was a strong woman, and he wanted to show he was in control. Plus, he always said he wanted to have a family, and with her he knew that he wouldn't."

And so, after about three years, they ended their romance and drifted into becoming just friends. "I thought I was in love with her, but I really just liked her a lot," he later said. "We weren't destined to be together. I wanted kids, and she didn't want any more." In her 1989 memoir, Baez wrote about her breakup with her husband and why she never remarried: "I belonged alone, which is how I have been since then, with occasional interruptions that are mostly picnics." She did add a nice acknowledgment at the end of the book to "Steve Jobs for forcing me to use a word processor by putting one in my kitchen."

Finding Joanne and Mona

When Jobs was thirty-one, a year after his ouster from Apple, his mother Clara, who was a smoker, was stricken with lung cancer. He spent time by her deathbed, talking to her in ways he had rarely done in the past and asking some questions he had refrained from raising before. "When you and Dad got married, were you a virgin?" he asked. It was hard for her to talk, but she forced a smile. That's when she told him that she had been married before, to a man who never made it back from the war. She also filled in some of the details of how she and Paul Jobs had come to adopt him.

Soon after that, Jobs succeeded in tracking down the woman who had put him up for adoption. His quiet quest to find her had begun in the early 1980s, when he hired a detective who had failed to come up with anything. Then Jobs noticed the name of a San Francisco doctor on his birth certificate. "He was in the phone book, so I gave him a call," Jobs recalled. The doctor was no help. He claimed that his records had been destroyed in a fire. That was not true. In fact, right after Jobs called, the doctor wrote a letter, sealed it in an envelope, and wrote on it, "To be delivered to Steve Jobs on my death." When he died a short time later, his widow sent the letter to Jobs. In it, the doctor explained that his mother had been an unmarried graduate student from Wisconsin named Joanne Schieble.

It took another few weeks and the work of another detective to track her down. After giving him up, Joanne had married his biological father, Abdulfattah "John" Jandali, and they had another child, Mona. Jandali abandoned them five years later, and Joanne married a colorful ice-skating instructor, George Simpson. That marriage didn't last long either, and in 1970 she began a meandering journey that took her and Mona (both of them now using the last name Simpson) to Los Angeles.

Jobs had been reluctant to let Paul and Clara, whom he considered his real parents, know about his search for his birth mother. With a sensitivity that was unusual for him, and which showed the deep affection he felt for his parents, he worried that they might be offended. So he never contacted Joanne Simpson until after Clara Jobs died in early 1986. "I never wanted them to feel like I didn't consider them my parents, because they were totally my parents," he recalled. "I loved them so much that I never wanted them to know of my search, and I even had reporters keep it quiet when any of them found out." When Clara died, he decided to tell Paul Jobs, who was perfectly comfortable and said he didn't mind at all if Steve made contact with his biological mother.

So one day Jobs called Joanne Simpson, said who he was, and arranged to come down to Los Angeles to meet her. He later claimed it was mainly out of curiosity. "I believe in environment more than heredity in determining your traits, but still you have to wonder a little about your biological roots," he said. He also wanted to reassure Joanne that what she had done was all right. "I wanted to meet my biological mother mostly to see if she was okay and to thank her, because I'm glad I didn't end up as an abortion. She was twenty-three and she went through a lot to have me."

Joanne was overcome with emotion when Jobs arrived at her Los Angeles house. She knew he was famous and rich, but she wasn't exactly sure why. She immediately began to pour out her emotions. She had been pressured to sign the papers putting him up for adoption, she said, and did so only when told that he was happy in the house of his new parents. She had always missed him and suffered about what she had done. She apologized over and over, even as Jobs kept reassuring her that he understood, and that things had turned out just fine.

Once she calmed down, she told Jobs that he had a full sister, Mona Simpson, who was then an aspiring novelist in Manhattan. She had never told Mona that she had a brother, and that day she broke the news, or at least part of it, by telephone. "You have a brother, and he's wonderful, and he's famous, and I'm going to bring him to New York so you can meet him," she said. Mona was in the throes of finishing a novel about her mother and their peregrination from Wisconsin to Los

Angeles, *Anywhere but Here.* Those who've read it will not be surprised
that Joanne was somewhat quirky in the way she imparted to Mona
the news about her brother. She refused to say who he was—only that
he had been poor, had gotten rich, was good-looking and famous, had
long dark hair, and lived in California. Mona then worked at the *Paris
Review,* George Plimpton's literary journal housed on the ground floor
of his townhouse near Manhattan's East River. She and her coworkers
began a guessing game on who her brother might be. John Travolta?
That was one of the favorite guesses. Other actors were also hot prospects. At one point someone did toss out a guess that "maybe it's one
of those guys who started Apple computer," but no one could recall
their names.

The meeting occurred in the lobby of the St. Regis Hotel. "He was
totally straightforward and lovely, just a normal and sweet guy," Mona
recalled. They all sat and talked for a few minutes, then he took his
sister for a long walk, just the two of them. Jobs was thrilled to find that
he had a sibling who was so similar to him. They were both intense in
their artistry, observant of their surroundings, and sensitive yet strong-
willed. When they went to dinner together, they noticed the same
architectural details and talked about them excitedly afterward. "My
sister's a writer!" he exulted to colleagues at Apple when he found out.

When Plimpton threw a party for *Anywhere but Here* in late 1986,
Jobs flew to New York to accompany Mona to it. They grew increasingly close, though their friendship had the complexities that might be
expected, considering who they were and how they had come together.
"Mona was not completely thrilled at first to have me in her life and
have her mother so emotionally affectionate toward me," he later said.
"As we got to know each other, we became really good friends, and she
is my family. I don't know what I'd do without her. I can't imagine a
better sister. My adopted sister, Patty, and I were never close." Mona
likewise developed a deep affection for him, and at times could be very
protective, although she would later write an edgy novel about him,
A Regular Guy, that described his quirks with discomforting accuracy.

One of the few things they would argue about was her clothes.
She dressed like a struggling novelist, and he would berate her for not
wearing clothes that were "fetching enough." At one point his com-

ments so annoyed her that she wrote him a letter: "I am a young writer, and this is my life, and I'm not trying to be a model anyway." He didn't answer. But shortly after, a box arrived from the store of Issey Miyake, the Japanese fashion designer whose stark and technology-influenced style made him one of Jobs's favorites. "He'd gone shopping for me," she later said, "and he'd picked out great things, exactly my size, in flattering colors." There was one pantsuit that he had particularly liked, and the shipment included three of them, all identical. "I still remember those first suits I sent Mona," he said. "They were linen pants and tops in a pale grayish green that looked beautiful with her reddish hair."

The Lost Father

In the meantime, Mona Simpson had been trying to track down their father, who had wandered off when she was five. Through Ken Auletta and Nick Pileggi, prominent Manhattan writers, she was introduced to a retired New York cop who had formed his own detective agency. "I paid him what little money I had," Simpson recalled, but the search was unsuccessful. Then she met another private eye in California, who was able to find an address for Abdulfattah Jandali in Sacramento through a Department of Motor Vehicles search. Simpson told her brother and flew out from New York to see the man who was apparently their father.

Jobs had no interest in meeting him. "He didn't treat me well," he later explained. "I don't hold anything against him—I'm happy to be alive. But what bothers me most is that he didn't treat Mona well. He abandoned her." Jobs himself had abandoned his own illegitimate daughter, Lisa, and now was trying to restore their relationship, but that complexity did not soften his feelings toward Jandali. Simpson went to Sacramento alone.

"It was very intense," Simpson recalled. She found her father working in a small restaurant. He seemed happy to see her, yet oddly passive about the entire situation. They talked for a few hours, and he recounted that, after he left Wisconsin, he had drifted away from teaching and gotten into the restaurant business.

Jobs had asked Simpson not to mention him, so she didn't. But at one point her father casually remarked that he and her mother had had another baby, a boy, before she had been born. "What happened to him?" she asked. He replied, "We'll never see that baby again. That baby's gone." Simpson recoiled but said nothing.

An even more astonishing revelation occurred when Jandali was describing the previous restaurants that he had run. There had been some nice ones, he insisted, fancier than the Sacramento joint they were then sitting in. He told her, somewhat emotionally, that he wished she could have seen him when he was managing a Mediterranean restaurant north of San Jose. "That was a wonderful place," he said. "All of the successful technology people used to come there. *Even Steve Jobs.*" Simpson was stunned. "Oh, yeah, he used to come in, and he was a sweet guy, and a big tipper," her father added. Mona was able to refrain from blurting out, *Steve Jobs is your son!*

When the visit was over, she called Jobs surreptitiously from the pay phone at the restaurant and arranged to meet him at the Espresso Roma café in Berkeley. Adding to the personal and family drama, he brought along Lisa, now in grade school, who lived with her mother, Chrisann. When they all arrived at the café, it was close to 10 p.m., and Simpson poured forth the tale. Jobs was understandably astonished when she mentioned the restaurant near San Jose. He could recall being there and even meeting the man who was his biological father. "It was amazing," he later said of the revelation. "I had been to that restaurant a few times, and I remember meeting the owner. He was Syrian. Balding. We shook hands."

Nevertheless Jobs still had no desire to see him. "I was a wealthy man by then, and I didn't trust him not to try to blackmail me or go to the press about it," he recalled. "I asked Mona not to tell him about me."

She never did, but years later Jandali saw his relationship to Jobs mentioned online. (A blogger noticed that Simpson had listed Jandali as her father in a reference book and figured out he must be Jobs's father as well.) By then Jandali was married for a fourth time and working as a food and beverage manager at the Boomtown Resort and Casino just west of Reno, Nevada. When he brought his new wife, Roscille, to visit

Simpson in 2006, he raised the topic. "What is this thing about Steve Jobs?" he asked. She confirmed the story, but added that she thought Jobs had no interest in meeting him. Jandali seemed to accept that. "My father is thoughtful and a beautiful storyteller, but he is very, very passive," Simpson said. "He never contacted Steve."

Simpson turned her search for Jandali into a basis for her second novel, *The Lost Father*, published in 1992. (Jobs convinced Paul Rand, the designer who did the NeXT logo, to design the cover, but according to Simpson, "It was God-awful and we never used it.") She also tracked down various members of the Jandali family, in Homs and in America, and in 2011 was writing a novel about her Syrian roots. The Syrian ambassador in Washington threw a dinner for her that included a cousin and his wife who then lived in Florida and had flown up for the occasion.

Simpson assumed that Jobs would eventually meet Jandali, but as time went on he showed even less interest. In 2010, when Jobs and his son, Reed, went to a birthday dinner for Simpson at her Los Angeles house, Reed spent some time looking at pictures of his biological grandfather, but Jobs ignored them. Nor did he seem to care about his Syrian heritage. When the Middle East would come up in conversation, the topic did not engage him or evoke his typical strong opinions, even after Syria was swept up in the 2011 Arab Spring uprisings. "I don't think anybody really knows what we should be doing over there," he said when I asked whether the Obama administration should be intervening more in Egypt, Libya, and Syria. "You're fucked if you do and you're fucked if you don't."

Jobs did retain a friendly relationship with his biological mother, Joanne Simpson. Over the years she and Mona would often spend Christmas at Jobs's house. The visits could be sweet, but also emotionally draining. Joanne would sometimes break into tears, say how much she had loved him, and apologize for giving him up. It turned out all right, Jobs would reassure her. As he told her one Christmas, "Don't worry. I had a great childhood. I turned out okay."

Lisa

Lisa Brennan, however, did not have a great childhood. When she was young, her father almost never came to see her. "I didn't want to be a father, so I wasn't," Jobs later said, with only a touch of remorse in his voice. Yet occasionally he felt the tug. One day, when Lisa was three, Jobs was driving near the house he had bought for her and Chrisann, and he decided to stop. Lisa didn't know who he was. He sat on the doorstep, not venturing inside, and talked to Chrisann. The scene was repeated once or twice a year. Jobs would come by unannounced, talk a little bit about Lisa's school options or other issues, then drive off in his Mercedes.

But by the time Lisa turned eight, in 1986, the visits were occurring more frequently. Jobs was no longer immersed in the grueling push to create the Macintosh or in the subsequent power struggles with Sculley. He was at NeXT, which was calmer, friendlier, and headquartered in Palo Alto, near where Chrisann and Lisa lived. In addition, by the time she was in third grade, it was clear that Lisa was a smart and artistic kid, who had already been singled out by her teachers for her writing ability. She was spunky and high-spirited and had a little of her father's defiant attitude. She also looked a bit like him, with arched eyebrows and a faintly Middle Eastern angularity. One day, to the surprise of his colleagues, he brought her by the office. As she turned cartwheels in the corridor, she squealed, "Look at me!"

Avie Tevanian, a lanky and gregarious engineer at NeXT who had become Jobs's friend, remembers that every now and then, when they were going out to dinner, they would stop by Chrisann's house to pick up Lisa. "He was very sweet to her," Tevanian recalled. "He was a vegetarian, and so was Chrisann, but she wasn't. He was fine with that. He suggested she order chicken, and she did."

Eating chicken became her little indulgence as she shuttled between two parents who were vegetarians with a spiritual regard for natural foods. "We bought our groceries—our puntarella, quinoa, celeriac, carob-covered nuts—in yeasty-smelling stores where the women didn't dye their hair," she later wrote about her time with her mother. "But we sometimes tasted foreign treats. A few times we bought a hot, seasoned chicken from a gourmet shop with rows and rows of chickens turning on spits, and ate it in the car from the foil-lined paper bag with our fingers." Her father, whose dietary fixations came in fanatic waves, was more fastidious about what he ate. She watched him spit out a mouthful of soup one day after learning that it contained butter. After loosening up a bit while at Apple, he was back to being a strict vegan. Even at a young age Lisa began to realize his diet obsessions reflected a life philosophy, one in which asceticism and minimalism could heighten subsequent sensations. "He believed that great harvests came from arid sources, pleasure from restraint," she noted. "He knew the equations that most people didn't know: Things led to their opposites."

In a similar way, the absence and coldness of her father made his occasional moments of warmth so much more intensely gratifying. "I didn't live with him, but he would stop by our house some days, a deity among us for a few tingling moments or hours," she recalled. Lisa soon became interesting enough that he would take walks with her. He would also go rollerblading with her on the quiet streets of old Palo Alto, often stopping at the houses of Joanna Hoffman and Andy Hertzfeld. The first time he brought her around to see Hoffman, he just knocked on the door and announced, "This is Lisa." Hoffman knew right away. "It was obvious she was his daughter," she told me. "Nobody has that jaw. It's a signature jaw." Hoffman, who suffered from not knowing her own divorced father until she was ten, encouraged Jobs to be a better father. He followed her advice, and later thanked her for it.

Once he took Lisa on a business trip to Tokyo, and they stayed at the sleek and businesslike Okura Hotel. At the elegant downstairs sushi bar, Jobs ordered large trays of unagi sushi, a dish he loved so much that he allowed the warm cooked eel to pass muster as vegetarian. The pieces were coated with fine salt or a thin sweet sauce, and Lisa remembered later how they dissolved in her mouth. So, too, did the distance between them. As she later wrote, "It was the first time I'd felt, with him, so relaxed and content, over those trays of meat; the excess, the permission and warmth after the cold salads, meant a once inaccessible space had opened. He was less rigid with himself, even human under the great ceilings with the little chairs, with the meat, and me."

But it was not always sweetness and light. Jobs was as mercurial with Lisa as he was with almost everyone, cycling between embrace and abandonment. On one visit he would be playful; on the next he would be cold; often he was not there at all. "She was always unsure of their relationship," according to Hertzfeld. "I went to a birthday party of hers, and Steve was supposed to come, and he was very, very, late. She got extremely anxious and disappointed. But when he finally did come, she totally lit up."

Lisa learned to be temperamental in return. Over the years their relationship would be a roller coaster, with each of the low points elongated by their shared stubbornness. After a falling-out, they could go for months not speaking to each other. Neither one was good at reaching out, apologizing, or making the effort to heal, even when he was wrestling with repeated health problems. One day in the fall of 2010 he was wistfully going through a box of old snapshots with me, and paused over one that showed him visiting Lisa when she was young. "I probably didn't go over there enough," he said. Since he had not spoken to her all that year, I asked if he might want to reach out to her with a call or email. He looked at me blankly for a moment, then went back to riffling through other old photographs.

The Romantic

When it came to women, Jobs could be deeply romantic. He tended to fall in love dramatically, share with friends every up and down of a relationship, and pine in public whenever he was away from his current girlfriend. In the summer of 1983 he went to a small dinner party in Silicon Valley with Joan Baez and sat next to an undergraduate at the University of Pennsylvania named Jennifer Egan, who was not quite sure who he was. By then he and Baez had realized that they weren't destined to be forever young together, and Jobs found himself fascinated by Egan, who was working on a San Francisco weekly during her summer vacation. He tracked her down, gave her a call, and took her to Café Jacqueline, a little bistro near Telegraph Hill that specialized in vegetarian soufflés.

They dated for a year, and Jobs often flew east to visit her. At a Boston Macworld event, he told a large gathering how much in love he was and thus needed to rush out to catch a plane for Philadelphia to see his girlfriend. The audience was enchanted. When he was visiting New York, she would take the train up to stay with him at the Carlyle or at Jay Chiat's Upper East Side apartment, and they would eat at Café Luxembourg, visit (repeatedly) the apartment in the San Remo he was planning to remodel, and go to movies or (once at least) the opera.

He and Egan also spoke for hours on the phone many nights. One topic they wrestled with was his belief, which came from his Buddhist studies, that it was important to avoid attachment to material objects. Our consumer desires are unhealthy, he told her, and to attain enlightenment you need to develop a life of nonattachment and nonmaterialism. He even sent her a tape of Kobun Chino, his Zen teacher, lecturing about the problems caused by craving and obtaining things. Egan pushed back. Wasn't he defying that philosophy, she asked, by making computers and other products that people coveted? "He was irritated by the dichotomy, and we had exuberant debates about it," Egan recalled.

In the end Jobs's pride in the objects he made overcame his sensibility that people should eschew being attached to such possessions. When the Macintosh came out in January 1984, Egan was staying at her mother's apartment in San Francisco during her winter break from Penn. Her mother's dinner guests were astonished one night when Steve Jobs—suddenly very famous—appeared at the door carrying a freshly boxed Macintosh and proceeded to Egan's bedroom to set it up.

Jobs told Egan, as he had a few other friends, about his premonition that he would not live a long life. That was why he was driven and impatient, he confided. "He felt a sense of urgency about all he wanted to get done," Egan later said. Their relationship tapered off by the fall of 1984, when Egan made it clear that she was still far too young to think of getting married.

Shortly after that, just as the turmoil with Sculley was beginning to build at Apple in early 1985, Jobs was heading to a meeting when he stopped at the office of a guy who was working with the Apple Foundation, which helped get computers to nonprofit organizations. Sitting in his office was a lithe, very blond woman who combined a hippie aura of natural purity with the solid sensibilities of a computer consultant. Her name was Tina Redse. "She was the most beautiful woman I'd ever seen," Jobs recalled.

He called her the next day and asked her to dinner. She said no, that she was living with a boyfriend. A few days later he took her on a walk to a nearby park and again asked her out, and this time she told her boyfriend that she wanted to go. She was very honest and open. After dinner she started to cry because she knew her life was about to be disrupted. And it was. Within a few months she had moved into the unfurnished mansion in Woodside. "She was the first person I was truly in love with," Jobs later said. "We had a very deep connection. I don't know that anyone will ever understand me better than she did."

Redse came from a troubled family, and Jobs shared with her his own pain about being put up for adoption. "We were both wounded from our childhood," Redse recalled. "He said to me that we were misfits, which is why we belonged together." They were physically passionate and prone to public displays of affection; their make-out sessions in the NeXT lobby are well remembered by employees. So too were their fights, which occurred at movie theaters and in front of visitors to Woodside. Yet he constantly praised her purity and naturalness. As the well-grounded Joanna Hoffman pointed out when discussing Jobs's infatuation with the otherworldly Redse, "Steve had a tendency to look at vulnerabilities and neuroses and turn them into spiritual attributes."

When he was being eased out at Apple in 1985, Redse traveled with him in Europe, where he was salving his wounds. Standing on a bridge over the Seine one evening, they bandied about the idea, more romantic than serious, of just staying in France, maybe settling down, perhaps indefinitely. Redse was eager, but Jobs didn't want to. He was burned but still ambitious. "I am a reflection of what I do," he told her. She recalled their Paris moment in a poignant email she sent to him twenty-five years later, after they had gone their separate ways but retained their spiritual connection:

> We were on a bridge in Paris in the summer of 1985. It was overcast. We leaned against the smooth stone rail and stared at the green water rolling on below. Your world had cleaved and then it paused, waiting to rearrange itself around whatever you chose next. I wanted to run away from what had come before. I tried to convince you to begin a new life with me in Paris, to shed our former selves and let something else course through us. I wanted us to crawl through that black chasm of your broken world and emerge, anonymous and new, in simple lives where I could cook you simple dinners and we could be together every day, like children playing a sweet game with no purpose save the game itself. I like to think you considered it before you laughed and said "What could I do? I've made myself unemployable." I like to think that in that moment's hesitation before our bold futures reclaimed us, we lived that simple life together all the way into our peaceful old ages, with a brood of grandchildren around us on a farm in the south of France, quietly going about our days, warm and complete like loaves of fresh bread, our small world filled with the aroma of patience and familiarity.

The relationship lurched up and down for five years. Redse hated living in his sparsely furnished Woodside house. Jobs had hired a hip young couple, who had once worked at Chez Panisse, as housekeepers and vegetarian cooks, and they made her feel like an interloper. She would occasionally move out to an apartment of her own in Palo Alto, especially after one of her torrential arguments with Jobs. "Neglect is a form of abuse," she once scrawled on the wall of the hallway to their bedroom. She was entranced by him, but she was also baffled by how uncaring he could be. She would later recall how incredibly painful it was to be in love with someone so self-centered. Caring deeply about someone who seemed incapable of caring was a particular kind of hell that she wouldn't wish on anyone, she said.

They were different in so many ways. "On the spectrum of cruel to kind, they are close to the opposite poles," Hertzfeld later said. Redse's kindness was manifest in ways large and small; she always gave money to street people, she volunteered to help those who (like her father) were afflicted with mental illness, and she took care to make Lisa and even Chrisann feel comfortable with her. More than anyone, she helped persuade Jobs to spend more time with Lisa. But she lacked Jobs's ambition and drive. The ethereal quality that made her seem so spiritual to Jobs also made it hard for them to stay on the same wavelength. "Their relationship was incredibly tempestuous," said Hertzfeld. "Because of both of their characters, they would have lots and lots of fights."

They also had a basic philosophical difference about whether aesthetic tastes were fundamentally individual, as Redse believed, or universal and could be taught, as Jobs believed. She accused him of being too influenced by the Bauhaus movement. "Steve believed it was our job to teach people aesthetics, to teach people what they should like," she recalled. "I don't share that perspective. I believe when we listen deeply, both within ourselves and to each other, we are able to allow what's innate and true to emerge."

When they were together for a long stretch, things did not work out well. But when they were apart, Jobs would pine for her. Finally, in the summer of 1989, he asked her to marry him. She couldn't do it. It would drive her crazy, she told friends. She had grown up in a volatile household, and her relationship with Jobs bore too many similarities to that environment. They were opposites who attracted, she said, but the combination was too combustible. "I could not have been a good wife to 'Steve Jobs,' the icon," she later explained. "I would have sucked at it on many levels. In our personal interactions, I couldn't abide his unkindness. I didn't want to hurt him, yet I didn't want to stand by and watch him hurt other people either. It was painful and exhausting."

After they broke up, Redse helped found OpenMind, a mental health resource network in California. She happened to read in a psychiatric manual about Narcissistic Personality Disorder and decided that Jobs perfectly met the criteria. "It fits so well and explained so much of what we had struggled with, that I realized expecting him to be nicer or less self-centered was like expecting a blind man to see," she said. "It also explained some of the choices he'd made about his daughter Lisa at that time. I think the issue is empathy—the capacity for empathy is lacking."

Redse later married, had two children, and then divorced. Every now and then Jobs would openly pine for her, even after he was happily married. And when he began his battle with cancer, she got in touch again to give support. She became very emotional whenever she recalled their relationship. "Though our values clashed and made it impossible for us to have the relationship we once hoped for," she told me, "the care and love I felt for him decades ago has continued." Similarly, Jobs suddenly started to cry one afternoon as he sat in his living room reminiscing about her. "She was one of the purest people I've ever known," he said, tears rolling down his cheeks. "There was something spiritual about her and spiritual about the connection we had." He said he always regretted that they could not make it work, and he knew that she had such regrets as well. But it was not meant to be. On that they both agreed.

CHAPTER TWENTY-ONE

FAMILY MAN

At Home with the Jobs Clan

With Laurene Powell, 1991

Laurene Powell

By this point, based on his dating history, a matchmaker could have put together a composite sketch of the woman who would be right for Jobs. Smart, yet unpretentious. Tough enough to stand up to him, yet Zen-like enough to rise above turmoil. Well-educated and independent, yet ready to make accommodations for him and a family. Down-to-earth, but with a touch of the ethereal. Savvy enough to know how to manage him, but secure enough to not always need to.

And it wouldn't hurt to be a beautiful, lanky blonde with an easygoing sense of humor who liked organic vegetarian food. In October 1989, after his split with Tina Redse, just such a woman walked into his life.

More specifically, just such a woman walked into his classroom. Jobs had agreed to give one of the "View from the Top" lectures at the Stanford Business School one Thursday evening. Laurene Powell was a new graduate student at the business school, and a guy in her class talked her into going to the lecture. They arrived late and all the seats were taken, so they sat in the aisle. When an usher told them they had to move, Powell took her friend down to the front row and commandeered two of the reserved seats there. Jobs was led to the one next to her when he arrived. "I looked to my right, and there was a beautiful girl there, so we started chatting while I was waiting to be introduced," Jobs recalled. They bantered a bit, and Laurene joked that she was sitting there because she had won a raffle, and the prize was that he got to take her to dinner. "He was so adorable," she later said.

After the speech Jobs hung around on the edge of the stage chatting with students. He watched Powell leave, then come back and stand at the edge of the crowd, then leave again. He bolted out after her, brushing past the dean, who was trying to grab him for a conversation. After catching up with her in the parking lot, he said, "Excuse me, wasn't there something about a raffle you won, that I'm supposed to take you to dinner?" She laughed. "How about Saturday?" he asked. She agreed and wrote down her number. Jobs headed to his car to drive up to the Thomas Fogarty winery in the Santa Cruz mountains above Woodside, where the NeXT education sales group was holding a dinner. But he suddenly stopped and turned around. "I thought, wow, I'd rather have dinner with her than the education group, so I ran back to her car and said 'How about dinner *tonight*?'" She said yes. It was a beautiful fall evening, and they walked into Palo Alto to a funky vegetarian restaurant, St. Michael's Alley, and ended up staying there for four hours. "We've been together ever since," he said.

Avie Tevanian was sitting at the winery restaurant waiting with the rest of the NeXT education group. "Steve was sometimes unreliable, but when I talked to him I realized that something special had come up," he said. As soon as Powell got home, after midnight, she called her close friend Kathryn (Kat) Smith, who was at Berkeley, and left a message on her machine. "You will not believe what just happened to me!" it said. "You will not believe who I met!" Smith called back the next morning and heard the tale.

Powell later said that she wasn't focused on meeting Jobs and that the encounter had been pure serendipity. She went only because her friend wanted to go, and she was slightly confused as to who they were going to see. "I knew that Steve Jobs was the speaker, but the face I thought of was that of Bill Gates," she recalled. "I had them mixed up. This was 1989. He was working at NeXT, and he was not that big of a deal to me. I wasn't that enthused, but my friend was, so we went."

Laurene Powell had been born in New Jersey in 1963 and learned to be self-sufficient at an early age. Her father was a Marine Corps pilot who died a hero in a crash in Santa Ana, California; he had been leading a crippled plane in for a landing, and when it hit his plane he kept flying in an unsuccessful attempt to avoid a residential area rather than ejecting in time to save his life. Her mother's second marriage turned out to be a horrible situation, but she felt she couldn't leave because she had no means to support her large family. For ten years Laurene and her three brothers had to suffer in a tense household, keeping a good demeanor while compartmentalizing problems. She did well. "The lesson I learned was clear, that I always wanted to be self-sufficient," she said. "I took pride in that. My relationship with money is that it's a tool to be self-sufficient, but it's not something that is part of who I am."

After graduating from the University of Pennsylvania, she worked at Goldman Sachs as a fixed income trading strategist, dealing with enormous sums of money that she traded for the house account. Jon Corzine, her boss, tried to get her to stay at Goldman, but instead she decided the work was unedifying. "You could be really successful," she said, "but you're just contributing to capital formation." So after three years she quit and went to Florence, Italy, living there for eight months before enrolling in Stanford Business School.

After their Thursday night dinner, she invited Jobs over to her Palo Alto apartment on Saturday. Kat Smith drove down from Berkeley and pretended to be her roommate so she could meet him as well. Their relationship became very passionate. "They would kiss and make out," Smith said. "He was enraptured with her. He would call me on the phone and ask, 'What do you think, does she like me?' Here I am in this bizarre position of having this iconic person call me."

That New Year's Eve of 1989 the three went to Chez Panisse, the famed Alice Waters restaurant in Berkeley, along with Lisa, then eleven. Something happened at the dinner that caused Jobs and Powell to start arguing. They left separately, and Powell ended up spending the night at Kat Smith's apartment. At nine the next morning there was a knock at the door, and Smith opened it to find Jobs, standing in the drizzle holding some wildflowers he had picked. "May I come in and see Laurene?" he said. She was still asleep, and he walked into the bedroom. A couple of hours went by, while Smith waited in the living room, unable to go in and get her clothes. Finally, she put a coat on over her nightgown and went to Peet's Coffee to pick up some food. Jobs did not emerge until after noon. "Kat, can you come here for a minute?" he asked. They all gathered in the bedroom. "As you know, Laurene's father passed away, and Laurene's mother isn't here, and since you're her best friend, I'm going to ask you the question," he said. "I'd like to marry Laurene. Will you give your blessing?"

Smith clambered onto the bed and thought about it. "Is this okay with you?" she asked Powell. When she nodded yes, Smith announced, "Well, there's your answer."

It was not, however, a definitive answer. Jobs had a way of focusing on something with insane intensity for a while and then, abruptly, turning away his gaze. At work, he would focus on what he wanted to, when he wanted to, and on other matters he would be unresponsive, no matter how hard people tried to get him to engage. In his personal life, he was the same way. At times he and Powell would indulge in public displays of affection that were so intense they embarrassed people in their presence, including Kat Smith and Powell's mother. In the mornings at his Woodside mansion, he would wake Powell up by blasting the Fine Young Cannibals' "She Drives Me Crazy" on his tape deck. Yet at other times he would ignore her. "Steve would fluctuate between intense focus, where she was the center of the universe, to being coldly distant and focused on work," said Smith. "He had the power to focus like a laser beam, and when it came across you, you basked in the light of his attention. When it moved to another point of focus, it was very, very dark for you. It was very confusing to Laurene."

Once she had accepted his marriage proposal on the first day of 1990, he didn't mention it again for several months. Finally, Smith confronted him while they were sitting on the edge of a sandbox in Palo Alto. What was going on? Jobs replied that he needed to feel sure that Powell could handle the life he lived and the type of person he was. In September she became fed up with waiting and moved out.

For a while he sulked or ignored the situation. Then he thought he might still be in love with Tina Redse; he sent her roses and tried to convince her to return to him, maybe even get married. He was not sure what he wanted, and he surprised a wide swath of friends and even acquaintances by asking them what he should do. Who was prettier, he would ask, Tina or Laurene? Who did they like better? Who should he marry? In a chapter about this in Mona Simpson's novel *A Regular Guy*, the Jobs character "asked more than a hundred people who they thought was more beautiful." But that was fiction; in reality, it was probably fewer than a hundred. After a month of indecision, he gave Powell a diamond ring in October 1990, and she moved back in.

He ended up making the right choice. As Redse told friends, she never would have survived if she had gone back to Jobs, nor would their marriage. Even though he would pine about the spiritual nature of his connection to Redse, he had a far more solid relationship with Powell. He liked her, he loved her, he respected her, and he was comfortable with her. She would become a sensible and romantic anchor for his life. "He is the luckiest guy to have landed with Laurene, who is smart and can engage him intellectually and can sustain his ups and downs and tempestuous personality," said Joanna Hoffman. "Because she's not neurotic, Steve may feel that she is not as mystical as Tina or something. But that's silly." Andy Hertzfeld agreed. "Laurene looks a lot like Tina, but she is totally different because she is tougher and armor-plated. That's why the marriage works."

Jobs understood this as well. Despite his emotional turbulence and occasional meanness, the marriage would turn out to be enduring, marked by loyalty and faithfulness, overcoming the ups and downs and jangling emotional complexities it encountered.

In December Jobs took Powell to his favorite vacation spot, Kona Village in Hawaii. He had started going there nine years earlier when, stressed out at Apple, he had asked his assistant to pick out a place for him to escape. At first glance, he didn't like the cluster of sparse thatched-roof bungalows nestled on a beach on the big island of Hawaii. It was a family resort, with communal eating. But within hours he had begun to view it as paradise. There was a simplicity and spare beauty that moved him, and he returned whenever he could. He especially enjoyed being there that December with Powell. Their love had matured. The night before Christmas he again declared, even more formally, that he wanted to marry her. Soon another factor would drive that decision. While in Hawaii, Powell got pregnant. "We know exactly where it happened," Jobs later said with a laugh.

The Wedding, March 18, 1991

Avie Tevanian decided Jobs needed a bachelor's party. This was not as easy as it sounded. Jobs did not like to party and didn't have a gang of male buddies. He didn't even have a best man. So the party turned out to be just Tevanian and Richard Crandall, a computer science professor at Reed who had taken a leave to work at NeXT. Tevanian hired a limo, and when they got to Jobs's house, Powell answered the door dressed in a suit and wearing a fake moustache, saying that she wanted to come as one of the guys. It was just a joke, and soon the three bachelors, none of them drinkers, were rolling to San Francisco to see if they could pull off their own pale version of a bachelor party.

Tevanian had been unable to get reservations at Greens, the vegetarian restaurant at Fort Mason that Jobs liked, so he booked a very fancy restaurant at a hotel. "I don't want to eat here," Jobs announced as soon as the bread was placed on the table. He made them get up and walk out, to the horror of Tevanian, who was not yet used to Jobs's restaurant manners. He led them to Café Jacqueline in North Beach, the soufflé place that he loved, which was indeed a better choice. Afterward they took the limo across the Golden Gate Bridge to a bar in Sausalito, where all three ordered shots of tequila but only sipped them. "It was not great as bachelor parties go, but it was the best we could come up with for someone like Steve, and nobody else volunteered to do it," recalled Tevanian. Jobs was appreciative. He decided that he wanted Tevanian to marry his sister Mona Simpson. Though nothing came of it, the thought was a sign of affection.

Powell had fair warning of what she was getting into. As she was planning the wedding, the person who was going to do the calligraphy for the invitations came by the house to show them some options. There was no furniture for her to sit on, so she sat on the floor and laid out the samples. Jobs looked for a few minutes, then got up and left the room. They waited for him to come back, but he didn't. After a while Powell went to find him in his room. "Get rid of her," he said. "I can't look at her stuff. It's shit."

On March 18, 1991, Steven Paul Jobs, thirty-six, married Laurene Powell, twenty-seven, at the Ahwahnee Lodge in Yosemite National Park. Built in the 1920s, the Ahwahnee is a sprawling pile of stone, concrete, and timber designed in a style that mixed Art Deco, the Arts and Crafts movement, and the Park Service's love of huge fireplaces. Its best features are the views. It has floor-to-ceiling windows looking out on Half Dome and Yosemite Falls.

About fifty people came, including Steve's father Paul Jobs and sister Mona Simpson. She brought her fiancé, Richard Appel, a lawyer who went on to become a television comedy writer. (As a writer for *The Simpsons*, he named Homer's mother after his wife.) Jobs insisted that they all arrive by chartered bus; he wanted to control all aspects of the event.

The ceremony was in the solarium, with the snow coming down hard and Glacier Point just visible in the distance. It was conducted by Jobs's longtime Sōtō Zen teacher, Kobun Chino, who shook a stick, struck a gong, lit incense, and chanted in a mumbling manner that most guests found incomprehensible. "I thought he was drunk," said Tevanian. He wasn't. The wedding cake was in the shape of Half Dome, the granite crest at the end of Yosemite Valley, but since it was strictly vegan—

devoid of eggs, milk, or any refined products—more than a few of the
guests found it inedible. Afterward they all went hiking, and Powell's
three strapping brothers launched a snowball fight, with lots of tackling
and roughhousing. "You see, Mona," Jobs said to his sister, "Laurene is
descended from Joe Namath and we're descended from John Muir."

A Family Home

Powell shared her husband's interest in natural foods. While at business school, she had worked part time at Odwalla, the juice company,
where she helped develop the first marketing plan. After marrying
Jobs, she felt that it was important to have a career, having learned
from her childhood the need to be self-sufficient. So she started her
own company, Terravera, that made ready-to-eat organic meals and
delivered them to stores throughout northern California.

Instead of living in the isolated and rather spooky unfurnished
Woodside mansion, the couple moved into a charming and unpretentious house on a corner in a family-friendly neighborhood in old Palo
Alto. It was a privileged realm—neighbors would eventually include
the visionary venture capitalist John Doerr, Google's founder Larry
Page, and Facebook's founder Mark Zuckerberg, along with Andy
Hertzfeld and Joanna Hoffman—but the homes were not ostentatious,
and there were no high hedges or long drives shielding them from
view. Instead, houses were nestled on lots next to each other along flat,
quiet streets flanked by wide sidewalks. "We wanted to live in a neighborhood where kids could walk to see friends," Jobs later said.

The house was not the minimalist and modernist style Jobs would
have designed if he had built a home from scratch. Nor was it a large
or distinctive mansion that would make people stop and take notice as
they drove down his street in Palo Alto. It was built in the 1930s by a
local designer named Carr Jones, who specialized in carefully crafted
homes in the "storybook style" of English or French country cottages.

The two-story house was made of red brick, with exposed wood
beams and a shingle roof with curved lines; it evoked a rambling Cots-
wold cottage, or perhaps a home where a well-to-do Hobbit might

have lived. The one Californian touch was a mission-style courtyard framed by the wings of the house. The two-story vaulted-ceiling living room was informal, with a floor of tile and terra-cotta. At one end was a large triangular window leading up to the peak of the ceiling; it had stained glass when Jobs bought it, as if it were a chapel, but he replaced it with clear glass. The other renovation he and Powell made was to expand the kitchen to include a wood-burning pizza oven and room for a long wooden table that would become the family's primary gathering place. It was supposed to be a four-month renovation, but it took sixteen months because Jobs kept redoing the design. They also bought the small house behind them and razed it to make a backyard, which Powell turned into a beautiful natural garden filled with a profusion of seasonal flowers along with vegetables and herbs.

Jobs became fascinated by the way Carr Jones relied on old material, including used bricks and wood from telephone poles, to provide a simple and sturdy structure. The beams in the kitchen had been used to make the molds for the concrete foundations of the Golden Gate Bridge, which was under construction when the house was built. "He was a careful craftsman who was self-taught," Jobs said as he pointed out each of the details. "He cared more about being inventive than about making money, and he never got rich. He never left California. His ideas came from reading books in the library and *Architectural Digest*."

Jobs had never furnished his Woodside house beyond a few bare essentials: a chest of drawers and a mattress in his bedroom, a card table and some folding chairs in what would have been a dining room. He wanted around him only things that he could admire, and that made it hard simply to go out and buy a lot of furniture. Now that he was living in a normal neighborhood home with a wife and soon a child, he had to make some concessions to necessity. But it was hard. They got beds, dressers, and a music system for the living room, but items like sofas took longer. "We spoke about furniture in theory for eight years," recalled Powell. "We spent a lot of time asking ourselves, 'What is the purpose of a sofa?'" Buying appliances was also a philosophical task, not just an impulse purchase. A few years later, Jobs described to *Wired* the process that went into getting a new washing machine:

It turns out that the Americans make washers and dryers all wrong. The Europeans make them much better—but they take twice as long to do clothes! It turns out that they wash them with about a quarter as much water and your clothes end up with a lot less detergent on them. Most important, they don't trash your clothes. They use a lot less soap, a lot less water, but they come out much cleaner, much softer, and they last a lot longer. We spent some time in our family talking about what's the trade-off we want to make. We ended up talking a lot about design, but also about the values of our family. Did we care most about getting our wash done in an hour versus an hour and a half? Or did we care most about our clothes feeling really soft and lasting longer? Did we care about using a quarter of the water? We spent about two weeks talking about this every night at the dinner table.

They ended up getting a Miele washer and dryer, made in Germany. "I got more thrill out of them than I have out of any piece of high tech in years," Jobs said.

The one piece of art that Jobs bought for the vaulted-ceiling living room was an Ansel Adams print of the winter sunrise in the Sierra Nevada taken from Lone Pine, California. Adams had made the huge mural print for his daughter, who later sold it. At one point Jobs's housekeeper wiped it with a wet cloth, and Jobs tracked down a person who had worked with Adams to come to the house, strip it down a layer, and restore it.

The house was so unassuming that Bill Gates was somewhat baffled when he visited with his wife. "Do *all* of you live here?" asked Gates, who was then in the process of building a 66,000-square-foot mansion near Seattle. Even when he had his second coming at Apple and was a world-famous billionaire, Jobs had no security guards or live-in servants, and he even kept the back door unlocked during the day.

His only security problem came, sadly and strangely, from Burrell Smith, the mop-headed, cherubic Macintosh hardware engineer who had been Andy Hertzfeld's close friend. After leaving Apple, Smith descended into schizophrenia. He lived in a house down the street from Hertzfeld, and as his disorder progressed he began wandering the streets naked, at other times smashing the windows of cars and churches. He was put on strong medication, but it proved difficult to calibrate. At one point when his demons returned, he began going over to the Jobs house in the evenings, throwing rocks through the windows, leaving rambling letters, and once tossing a firecracker into the house. He was arrested, but the case was dropped when he went for more treatment. "Burrell was so funny and naïve, and then one April day he suddenly snapped," Jobs recalled. "It was the weirdest, saddest thing."

Jobs was sympathetic, and often asked Hertzfeld what more he could do to help. At one point Smith was thrown in jail and refused to identify himself. When Hertzfeld found out, three days later, he called Jobs and asked for assistance in getting him released. Jobs did help, but he surprised Hertzfeld with a question: "If something similar happened to me, would you take as good care of me as you do Burrell?"

Jobs kept his mansion in Woodside, about ten miles up into the mountains from Palo Alto. He wanted to tear down the fourteen-bedroom 1925 Spanish colonial revival, and he had plans drawn up to replace it with an extremely simple, Japanese-inspired modernist home one-third the size. But for more than twenty years he engaged in a slow-moving series of court battles with preservationists who wanted the crumbling original house to be saved. (In 2011 he finally got permission to raze the house, but by then he had no desire to build a second home.)

On occasion Jobs would use the semi-abandoned Woodside home, especially its swimming pool, for family parties. When Bill Clinton was president, he and Hillary Clinton stayed in the 1950s ranch house on the property on their visits to their daughter, who was at Stanford. Since both the main house and ranch house were unfurnished, Powell would call furniture and art dealers when the Clintons were coming and pay them to furnish the houses temporarily. Once, shortly after the Monica Lewinsky flurry broke, Powell was making a final inspection of the furnishings and noticed that one of the paintings was missing. Worried, she asked the advance team and Secret Service what had happened. One of them pulled her aside and explained that it was a painting of a dress on a hanger, and given the issue of the blue dress in the Lewinsky matter they had decided to hide it. (During one of his late-night phone conversations with Jobs, Clinton asked how he should handle the Lewinsky issue. "I don't know if you did it, but if so, you've got to tell the country," Jobs told the president. There was silence on the other end of the line.)

Lisa Moves In

In the middle of Lisa's eighth-grade year, her teachers called Jobs. There were serious problems, and it was probably best for her to move out of her mother's house. So Jobs went on a walk with Lisa, asked about the situation, and offered to let her move in with him. She was a mature girl, just turning fourteen, and she thought about it for two days. Then she said yes. She already knew which room she wanted: the one right next to her father's. When she was there once, with no one home, she had tested it out by lying down on the bare floor.

It was a tough period. Chrisann Brennan at one point got into a very heated argument with Steve about someone who was working at his house. When I asked her about her behavior and the allegations that led to Lisa's moving out of her house, she said that she had still not been able to process in her own mind what occurred during that period. But then she wrote me a long email that she said would help explain the situation:

> Do you know how Steve was able to get the city of Woodside to allow him to tear his Woodside home down? There was a community of people who wanted to preserve his Woodside house due to its historical value, but Steve wanted to tear it down and build a home with an orchard. Steve let that house fall into so much disrepair and decay over a number of years that there was no way to save it. The strategy he used to get what he wanted was to simply follow the line of least involvement and resistance. So by his doing nothing on the house, and maybe even leaving the windows open for years, the house fell apart. Brilliant, no? . . . In a similar way did Steve work to undermine my effectiveness AND my well being at the time when Lisa was 13 and 14 to get her

to move into his house. He started with one strategy but then it moved to another easier one that was even more destructive to me and more problematic for Lisa. It may not have been of the greatest integrity, but he got what he wanted.

Lisa lived with Jobs and Powell for all four of her years at Palo Alto High School, and she began using the name Lisa Brennan-Jobs. He tried to be a good father, but there were times when he was cold and distant. When Lisa felt she had to escape, she would seek refuge with a friendly family who lived nearby. Powell tried to be supportive, and she was the one who attended most of Lisa's school events.

By the time Lisa was a senior, she seemed to be flourishing. She joined the school newspaper, *The Campanile*, and became the coeditor. Together with her classmate Ben Hewlett, grandson of the man who gave her father his first job, she exposed secret raises that the school board had given to administrators. When it came time to go to college, she knew she wanted to go east. She applied to Harvard—forging her father's signature on the application because he was out of town—and was accepted for the class entering in 1996.

At Harvard Lisa worked on the college newspaper, *The Crimson*, and then the literary magazine, *The Advocate*. After breaking up with her boyfriend, she took a year abroad at King's College, London. Her relationship with her father remained tumultuous throughout her college years. When she would come home, fights over small things—what was being served for dinner, whether she was paying enough attention to her half-siblings—would blow up, and they would not speak to each other for weeks and sometimes months. The arguments occasionally got so bad that Jobs would stop supporting her. One year she borrowed money for her Harvard tuition from a married couple, both lawyers, who lived down the street in Palo Alto and whose house she stayed at sometimes. Later, Andy Hertzfeld lent Lisa $20,000 when she thought her father was not going to pay her tuition at a graduate writing program at Bennington College. "He was mad at me for making the loan," Hertzfeld recalled, "but he called early the next morning and had his accountant wire me the money."

There were, however, some nice times during those years, including one summer when Lisa came back home and performed at a benefit concert for the Electronic Frontier Foundation, an advocacy group that supports access to technology. The concert took place at the Fillmore Auditorium in San Francisco, which had been made famous by the Grateful Dead, Jefferson Airplane, and Jimi Hendrix. She sang Tracy Chapman's anthem "Talkin' bout a Revolution" ("Poor people are gonna rise up / And get their share") as her father stood in the back cradling his one-year-old daughter, Erin.

Jobs's ups and downs with Lisa continued after she moved to Manhattan as a freelance writer. Their problems were exacerbated because of Jobs's frustrations with Chrisann. He had bought a house for Chrisann to use in nearby Menlo Park, but Chrisann sold it and then proceeded to travel with a spiritual advisor and to live in Paris. Once the money ran out, she returned to San Francisco and became an artist creating "light paintings" and Buddhist mandalas. "I am a 'Connector' and a visionary contributor to the future of evolving humanity and the ascended Earth," she said on her website (which Hertzfeld maintained for her). "I experience the forms, color, and sound frequencies of sacred vibration as I create and live with the paintings." When Chrisann needed money for a bad sinus infection and dental problem, Jobs refused to give it to her, causing Lisa again to not speak to him for a few years. And thus the pattern would continue.

Mona Simpson used all of this, plus her imagination, as a springboard for her third novel, *A Regular Guy*, published in 1996. The book's title character is based on Jobs, and to some extent it adheres to reality: It depicts Jobs's quiet generosity to, and purchase of a special car for, a brilliant friend who had degenerative bone disease, and it accurately describes many unflattering aspects of his relationship with Lisa, including his original denial of paternity. But other parts are purely fiction; Chrisann had taught Lisa at a very early age how to drive, for example, but the book's scene of "Jane" driving a truck across the mountains alone at age five to find her father of course never happened. In addition, there are little details in the novel that, in journalist parlance, are too good to check, such as the head-snapping description of the character based on Jobs in the very first sentence: "He was a man too busy to flush toilets."

On the surface, the novel's fictional portrayal of Jobs seems harsh. Simpson describes her main character as unable "to see any need to pander to the wishes or whims of other people." His hygiene is also as dubious as that of the real Jobs. "He didn't believe in deodorant and often professed that with a proper diet and the peppermint castile soap, you would neither perspire nor smell." But the novel is lyrical and intricate on many levels, and by the end there is a fuller picture of a man who loses control of the great company he had founded and learns to appreciate the daughter he had abandoned. The final scene is of him dancing with his daughter.

Jobs later said that he never read the novel. "I heard it was about me," he told me, "and if it was about me, I would have gotten really pissed off, and I didn't want to get pissed at my sister, so I didn't read it." However, he told the *New York Times* a few months after the book appeared that he had read it and saw the reflections of himself in the main character. "About 25% of it is totally me, right down to the mannerisms," he told the reporter, Steve Lohr. "And I'm certainly not telling you which 25%." His wife said that, in fact, Jobs glanced at the book and asked her to read it for him to see what he should make of it.

Simpson sent the manuscript to Lisa before it was published, but at first she didn't read more than the opening. "In the first few pages, I was confronted with my family, my anecdotes, my things, my thoughts, myself in the character Jane," she noted. "And sandwiched between the truths was invention—lies to me, made more evident because of their dangerous proximity to the truth." Lisa was wounded, and she wrote a piece for the Harvard *Advocate* explaining why. Her first draft was very bitter, then she toned it down a bit before she published it. She felt violated by Simpson's friendship. "I didn't know, for those six years, that Mona was collecting," she wrote. "I didn't know that as I sought her consolations and took her advice, she, too, was taking." Eventually Lisa reconciled with Simpson. They went out to a coffee shop to discuss the book, and Lisa told her that she hadn't been able to finish it. Simpson told her she would like the ending. Over the years Lisa had an on-and-off relationship with Simpson, but it would be closer in some ways than the one she had with her father.

Children

When Powell gave birth in 1991, a few months after her wedding to Jobs, their child was known for two weeks as "baby boy Jobs," because settling on a name was proving only slightly less difficult than choosing a washing machine. Finally, they named him Reed Paul Jobs. His middle name was that of Jobs's father, and his first name (both Jobs and Powell insist) was chosen because it sounded good rather than because it was the name of Jobs's college.

Reed turned out to be like his father in many ways: incisive and smart, with intense eyes and a mesmerizing charm. But unlike his father, he had sweet manners and a self-effacing grace. He was creative— as a kid he liked to dress in costume and stay in character—and also a great student, interested in science. He could replicate his father's stare, but he was demonstrably affectionate and seemed not to have an ounce of cruelty in his nature.

Erin Siena Jobs was born in 1995. She was a little quieter and developed into a more introspective child with an emotional intelligence that gave her an acute sense of other people's feelings. She picked up her father's interest in design and architecture, but she also learned to keep a bit of an emotional distance, so as not to be hurt by his detachment.

The youngest child, Eve, was born in 1998, and she turned into a strong-willed, funny firecracker who, neither needy nor intimidated, knew how to handle her father, negotiate with him (and sometimes win), and even make fun of him. Her father joked that she's the one who will run Apple someday, if she doesn't become president of the United States.

In 1995 Oracle's CEO Larry Ellison threw a fortieth-birthday party for Jobs filled with tech stars and moguls. Ellison had become a close friend, and he would often take the Jobs family out on one of his many luxurious yachts. Reed started referring to him as "our rich friend," which was amusing evidence of how his father refrained from ostentatious displays of wealth. The lesson Jobs learned from his Buddhist days was that material possessions often cluttered life rather than enriched it. "Every other CEO I know has a security detail," he said. "They've even got them at their homes. It's a nutso way to live. We just decided that's not how we wanted to raise our kids."

CHAPTER TWENTY-TWO

TOY STORY

Buzz and Woody to the Rescue

Jeffrey Katzenberg

"It's kind of fun to do the impossible," Walt Disney once said. That was the type of attitude that appealed to Jobs. He admired Disney's obsession with detail and design, and he felt that there was a natural fit between Pixar and the movie studio that Disney had founded.

The Walt Disney Company had licensed Pixar's Computer Animation Production System, and that made it the largest customer for Pixar's computers. One day Jeffrey Katzenberg, the head of Disney's film division, invited Jobs down to the Burbank studios to see the technology in operation. As the Disney folks were showing him around, Jobs turned to Katzenberg and asked, "Is Disney happy with Pixar?" With great exuberance, Katzenberg answered yes. Then Jobs asked, "Do you think we at Pixar are happy with Disney?" Katzenberg said he assumed so. "No, we're not," Jobs said. "We want to do a film with you. That would make us happy."

Katzenberg was willing. He admired John Lasseter's animated shorts and had tried unsuccessfully to lure him back to Disney. So Katzenberg invited the Pixar team down to discuss partnering on a film. When Catmull, Jobs, and Lasseter got settled at the conference table, Katzenberg was forthright. "John, since you won't come work for me," he said, looking at Lasseter, "I'm going to make it work this way."

Just as the Disney company shared some traits with Pixar, so Katzenberg shared some with Jobs. Both were charming when they wanted to be, and aggressive (or worse) when it suited their moods or interests. Alvy Ray Smith, on the verge of quitting Pixar, was at the meeting. "Katzenberg and Jobs impressed me as a lot alike," he recalled. "Tyrants with an amazing gift of gab." Katzenberg was delightfully aware of this. "Everybody thinks I'm a tyrant," he told the Pixar team. "I *am* a tyrant. But I'm usually right." One can imagine Jobs saying the same.

As befitted two men of equal passion, the negotiations between Katzenberg and Jobs took months. Katzenberg insisted that Disney be given the rights to Pixar's proprietary technology for making 3-D animation. Jobs refused, and he ended up winning that engagement. Jobs had his own demand: Pixar would have part ownership of the film and its characters, sharing control of both video rights and sequels. "If that's what you want," Katzenberg said, "we can just quit talking and you can leave now." Jobs stayed, conceding that point.

Lasseter was riveted as he watched the two wiry and tightly wound principals parry and thrust. "Just to see Steve and Jeffrey go at it, I was in awe," he recalled. "It was like a fencing match. They were both masters." But Katzenberg went into the match with a saber, Jobs with a mere foil. Pixar was on the verge of bankruptcy and needed a deal with Disney far more than Disney needed a deal with Pixar. Plus, Disney could afford to finance the whole enterprise, and Pixar couldn't. The result was a deal, struck in May 1991, by which Disney would own the picture and its characters outright, have creative control, and pay Pixar about 12.5% of the ticket revenues. It had the option (but not the obligation) to do Pixar's next two films and the right to make (with or without Pixar) sequels using the characters in the film. Disney could also kill the film at any time with only a small penalty.

The idea that John Lasseter pitched was called "Toy Story." It sprang from a belief, which he and Jobs shared, that products have an essence to them, a purpose for which they were made. If the object were to have feelings, these would be based on its desire to fulfill its essence. The purpose of a glass, for example, is to hold water; if it had feelings, it would be happy when full and sad when empty. The essence of a computer screen is to interface with a human. The essence of a unicycle is to be ridden in a circus. As for toys, their purpose is to be played with by kids, and thus their existential fear is of being discarded or upstaged by newer toys. So a buddy movie pairing an old favorite toy with a shiny new one would have an essential drama to it, especially when the action revolved around the toys' being separated from their kid. The original treatment began, "Everyone has had the traumatic childhood experience of losing a toy. Our story takes the toy's point of view as he loses and tries to regain the single thing most important to him: to be played with by children. This is the reason for the existence of all toys. It is the emotional foundation of their existence."

The two main characters went through many iterations before they ended up as Buzz Lightyear and Woody. Every couple of weeks, Lasseter and his team would put together their latest set of storyboards or footage to show the folks at Disney. In early screen tests, Pixar showed off its amazing technology by, for example, producing a scene of Woody rustling around on top of a dresser while the light rippling in through a Venetian blind cast shadows on his plaid shirt—an effect that would have been almost impossible to render by hand. Impressing Disney with the plot, however, was more difficult. At each presentation by Pixar, Katzenberg would tear much of it up, barking out his detailed comments and notes. And a cadre of clipboard-carrying flunkies was on hand to make sure every suggestion and whim uttered by Katzenberg received follow-up treatment.

Katzenberg's big push was to add more edginess to the two main characters. It may be an animated movie called *Toy Story*, he said, but it should not be aimed only at children. "At first there was no drama, no real story, and no conflict," Katzenberg recalled. He suggested that Lasseter watch some classic buddy movies, such as *The Defiant Ones* and *48 Hours*, in which two characters with different attitudes are thrown together and have to bond. In addition, he kept pushing for what he called "edge," and that meant making Woody's character more jealous, mean, and belligerent toward Buzz, the new interloper in the toy box. "It's a toy-eat-toy world," Woody says at one point, after pushing Buzz out of a window.

After many rounds of notes from Katzenberg and other Disney execs, Woody had been stripped of almost all charm. In one scene he throws the other toys off the bed and orders Slinky to come help. When Slinky hesitates, Woody barks, "Who said your job was to think, spring-wiener?" Slinky then asks a question that the Pixar team members would soon be asking themselves: "Why is the cowboy so scary?" As Tom Hanks, who had signed up to be Woody's voice, exclaimed at one point, "This guy's a real jerk!"

Cut!

Lasseter and his Pixar team had the first half of the movie ready to screen by November 1993, so they brought it down to Burbank to show to Katzenberg and other Disney executives. Peter Schneider, the head of feature animation, had never been enamored of Katzenberg's idea of having outsiders make animation for Disney, and he declared it a mess and ordered that production be stopped. Katzenberg agreed. "Why is this so terrible?" he asked a colleague, Tom Schumacher. "Because it's not their movie anymore," Schumacher bluntly replied. He later explained, "They were following Katzenberg's notes, and the project had been driven completely off-track."

Lasseter realized that Schumacher was right. "I sat there and I was pretty much embarrassed with what was on the screen," he recalled. "It was a story filled with the most unhappy, mean characters that I've ever seen." He asked Disney for the chance to retreat back to Pixar and rework the script. Katzenberg was supportive.

Jobs did not insert himself much into the creative process. Given his proclivity to be in control, especially on matters of taste and design, this self-restraint was a testament to his respect for Lasseter and the other artists at Pixar—as well as for the ability of Lasseter and Catmull to keep him at bay. He did, however, help manage the relationship with Disney, and the Pixar team appreciated that. When Katzenberg and Schneider halted production on *Toy Story*, Jobs kept the work going with his own personal funding. And he took their side against Katzenberg. "He had *Toy Story* all messed up," Jobs later said.

"He wanted Woody to be a bad guy, and when he shut us down we kind of kicked him out and said, 'This isn't what we want,' and did it the way we always wanted."

The Pixar team came back with a new script three months later. The character of Woody morphed from being a tyrannical boss of Andy's other toys to being their wise leader. His jealousy after the arrival of Buzz Lightyear was portrayed more sympathetically, and it was set to the strains of a Randy Newman song, "Strange Things." The scene in which Woody pushed Buzz out of the window was rewritten to make Buzz's fall the result of an accident triggered by a little trick Woody initiated involving a Luxo lamp. Katzenberg & Co. approved the new approach, and by February 1994 the film was back in production.

Katzenberg had been impressed with Jobs's focus on keeping costs under control. "Even in the early budgeting process, Steve was very eager to do it as efficiently as possible," he said. But the $17 million production budget was proving inadequate, especially given the major revision that was necessary after Katzenberg had pushed them to make Woody too edgy. So Jobs demanded more in order to complete the film right. "Listen, we made a deal," Katzenberg told him. "We gave you business control, and you agreed to do it for the amount we offered." Jobs was furious. He would call Katzenberg by phone or fly down to visit him and be, in Katzenberg's words, "as wildly relentless as only Steve can be." Jobs insisted that Disney was liable for the cost overruns because Katzenberg had so badly mangled the original concept that it required extra work to restore things. "Wait a minute!" Katzenberg shot back. "We were helping you. You got the benefit of our creative help, and now you want us to pay you for that." It was a case of two control freaks arguing about who was doing the other a favor.

Ed Catmull, more diplomatic than Jobs, was able to reach a compromise new budget. "I had a much more positive view of Jeffrey than some of the folks working on the film did," he said. But the incident did prompt Jobs to start plotting about how to have more leverage with Disney in the future. He did not like being a mere contractor; he liked being in control. That meant Pixar would have to bring its own funding to projects in the future, and it would need a new deal with Disney.

As the film progressed, Jobs became ever more excited about it.

He had been talking to various companies, ranging from Hallmark to Microsoft, about selling Pixar, but watching Woody and Buzz come to life made him realize that he might be on the verge of transforming the movie industry. As scenes from the movie were finished, he watched them repeatedly and had friends come by his home to share his new passion. "I can't tell you the number of versions of *Toy Story* I saw before it came out," said Larry Ellison. "It eventually became a form of torture. I'd go over there and see the latest 10% improvement. Steve is obsessed with getting it right—both the story and the technology—and isn't satisfied with anything less than perfection."

Jobs's sense that his investments in Pixar might actually pay off was reinforced when Disney invited him to attend a gala press preview of scenes from *Pocahontas* in January 1995 in a tent in Manhattan's Central Park. At the event, Disney CEO Michael Eisner announced that *Pocahontas* would have its premiere in front of 100,000 people on eighty-foot-high screens on the Great Lawn of Central Park. Jobs was a master showman who knew how to stage great premieres, but even he was astounded by this plan. Buzz Lightyear's great exhortation— "To infinity and beyond!"—suddenly seemed worth heeding.

Jobs decided that the release of *Toy Story* that November would be the occasion to take Pixar public. Even the usually eager investment bankers were dubious and said it couldn't happen. Pixar had spent five years hemorrhaging money. But Jobs was determined. "I was nervous and argued that we should wait until after our second movie," Lasseter recalled. "Steve overruled me and said we needed the cash so we could put up half the money for our films and renegotiate the Disney deal."

To Infinity!

There were two premieres of *Toy Story* in November 1995. Disney organized one at El Capitan, a grand old theater in Los Angeles, and built a fun house next door featuring the characters. Pixar was given a handful of passes, but the evening and its celebrity guest list was very much a Disney production; Jobs did not even attend. Instead, the next night he rented the Regency, a similar theater in San Francisco, and held his own premiere. Instead of Tom Hanks and Steve Martin, the guests were Silicon Valley celebrities, such as Larry Ellison and Andy Grove. This was clearly Jobs's show; he, not Lasseter, took the stage to introduce the movie.

The dueling premieres highlighted a festering issue: Was *Toy Story* a Disney or a Pixar movie? Was Pixar merely an animation contractor helping Disney make movies? Or was Disney merely a distributor and marketer helping Pixar roll out its movies? The answer was somewhere in between. The question would be whether the egos involved, mainly those of Michael Eisner and Steve Jobs, could get to such a partnership.

The stakes were raised when *Toy Story* opened to blockbuster commercial and critical success. It recouped its cost the first weekend, with a domestic opening of $30 million, and it went on to become the top-grossing film of the year, beating *Batman Forever* and *Apollo 13*, with $192 million in receipts domestically and a total of $362 million worldwide. According to the review aggregator Rotten Tomatoes, 100% of the seventy-three critics surveyed gave it a positive review. *Time*'s Richard Corliss called it "the year's most inventive comedy," David Ansen of *Newsweek* pronounced it a "marvel," and Janet Maslin of the *New York Times* recommended it both for children and adults as "a work of incredible cleverness in the best two-tiered Disney tradition."

The only rub for Jobs was that reviewers such as Maslin wrote of the "Disney tradition," not the emergence of Pixar. After reading her review, he decided he had to go on the offensive to raise Pixar's profile. When he and Lasseter went on the *Charlie Rose* show, Jobs emphasized that *Toy Story* was a Pixar movie, and he even tried to highlight the historic nature of a new studio being born. "Since *Snow White* was released, every major studio has tried to break into the animation business, and until now Disney was the only studio that had ever made a feature animated film that was a blockbuster," he told Rose. "Pixar has now become the second studio to do that."

Jobs made a point of casting Disney as merely the distributor of a Pixar film. "He kept saying, 'We at Pixar are the real thing and you

Disney guys are shit,'" recalled Michael Eisner. "But we were the ones who made *Toy Story* work. We helped shape the movie, and we pulled together all of our divisions, from our consumer marketers to the Disney Channel, to make it a hit." Jobs came to the conclusion that the fundamental issue—Whose movie was it?—would have to be settled contractually rather than by a war of words. "After *Toy Story*'s success," he said, "I realized that we needed to cut a new deal with Disney if we were ever to build a studio and not just be a work-for-hire place." But in order to sit down with Disney on an equal basis, Pixar had to bring money to the table. That required a successful IPO.

The public offering occurred exactly one week after *Toy Story*'s opening. Jobs had gambled that the movie would be successful, and the risky bet paid off, big-time. As with the Apple IPO, a celebration was planned at the San Francisco office of the lead underwriter at 7 a.m., when the shares were to go on sale. The plan had originally been for the first shares to be offered at about $14, to be sure they would sell. Jobs insisted on pricing them at $22, which would give the company more money if the offering was a success. It was, beyond even his wildest hopes. It exceeded Netscape as the biggest IPO of the year. In the first half hour, the stock shot up to $45, and trading had to be delayed because there were too many buy orders. It then went up even further, to $49, before settling back to close the day at $39.

Earlier that year Jobs had been hoping to find a buyer for Pixar that would let him merely recoup the $50 million he had put in. By the end of the day the shares he had retained—80% of the company—were worth more than twenty times that, an astonishing $1.2 *billion*. That was about five times what he'd made when Apple went public in 1980. But Jobs told John Markoff of the *New York Times* that the money did not mean much to him. "There's no yacht in my future," he said. "I've never done this for the money."

The successful IPO meant that Pixar would no longer have to be dependent on Disney to finance its movies. That was just the leverage Jobs wanted. "Because we could now fund half the cost of our movies, I could demand half the profits," he recalled. "But more important, I wanted co-branding. These were to be Pixar as well as Disney movies."

Jobs flew down to have lunch with Eisner, who was stunned at his audacity. They had a three-picture deal, and Pixar had made only one. Each side had its own nuclear weapons. After an acrimonious split with Eisner, Katzenberg had left Disney and become a cofounder, with Steven Spielberg and David Geffen, of DreamWorks SKG. If Eisner didn't agree to a new deal with Pixar, Jobs said, then Pixar would go to another studio, such as Katzenberg's, once the three-picture deal was done. In Eisner's hand was the threat that Disney could, if that happened, make its own sequels to *Toy Story*, using Woody and Buzz and all of the characters that Lasseter had created. "That would have been like molesting our children," Jobs later recalled. "John started crying when he considered that possibility."

So they hammered out a new arrangement. Eisner agreed to let Pixar put up half the money for future films and in return take half of the profits. "He didn't think we could have many hits, so he thought he was saving himself some money," said Jobs. "Ultimately that was great for us, because Pixar would have ten blockbusters in a row." They also agreed on co-branding, though that took a lot of haggling to define. "I took the position that it's a Disney movie, but eventually I relented," Eisner recalled. "We start negotiating how big the letters in 'Disney' are going to be, how big is 'Pixar' going to be, just like four-year-olds." But by the beginning of 1997 they had a deal, for five films over the course of ten years, and even parted as friends, at least for the time being. "Eisner was reasonable and fair to me then," Jobs later said. "But eventually, over the course of a decade, I came to the conclusion that he was a dark man."

In a letter to Pixar shareholders, Jobs explained that winning the right to have equal branding with Disney on all the movies, as well as advertising and toys, was the most important aspect of the deal. "We want Pixar to grow into a brand that embodies the same level of trust as the Disney brand," he wrote. "But in order for Pixar to earn this trust, consumers must know that Pixar is creating the films." Jobs was known during his career for creating great products. But just as significant was his ability to create great companies with valuable brands. And he created two of the best of his era: Apple and Pixar.

CHAPTER TWENTY-THREE

THE SECOND COMING

What Rough Beast, Its Hour Come Round at Last . . .

Steve Jobs, 1996

Things Fall Apart

When Jobs unveiled the NeXT computer in 1988, there was a burst of excitement. That fizzled when the computer finally went on sale the following year. Jobs's ability to dazzle, intimidate, and spin the press began to fail him, and there was a series of stories on the company's woes. "NeXT is incompatible with other computers at a time when the industry is moving toward interchangeable systems," Bart Ziegler of Associated Press reported. "Because relatively little software exists to run on NeXT, it has a hard time attracting customers."

NeXT tried to reposition itself as the leader in a new category, personal workstations, for people who wanted the power of a workstation and the friendliness of a personal computer. But those customers were by now buying them from fast-growing Sun Microsystems. Revenues for NeXT in 1990 were $28 million; Sun made $2.5 billion that year. IBM abandoned its deal to license the NeXT software, so Jobs was forced to do something against his nature: Despite his ingrained belief that hardware and software should be integrally linked, he agreed in January 1992 to license the NeXTSTEP operating system to run on other computers.

One surprising defender of Jobs was Jean-Louis Gassée, who had bumped elbows with Jobs when he replaced him at Apple and subsequently been ousted himself. He wrote an article extolling the creativity of NeXT products. "NeXT might not be Apple," Gassée argued, "but Steve is still Steve." A few days later his wife answered a knock on the door and went running upstairs to tell him that Jobs was standing there. He thanked Gassée for the article and invited him to an event where Intel's Andy Grove would join Jobs in announcing that NeXTSTEP would be ported to the IBM/Intel platform. "I sat next to Steve's father, Paul Jobs, a movingly dignified individual," Gassée recalled. "He raised a difficult son, but he was proud and happy to see him onstage with Andy Grove."

A year later Jobs took the inevitable subsequent step: He gave up making the hardware altogether. This was a painful decision, just as it had been when he gave up making hardware at Pixar. He cared about all aspects of his products, but the hardware was a particular passion. He was energized by great design, obsessed over manufacturing details, and would spend hours watching his robots make his perfect machines. But now he had to lay off more than half his workforce, sell his beloved factory to Canon (which auctioned off the fancy furniture), and satisfy himself with a company that tried to license an operating system to manufacturers of uninspired machines.

By the mid-1990s Jobs was finding some pleasure in his new family life and his astonishing triumph in the movie business, but he despaired about the personal computer industry. "Innovation has virtually ceased," he told Gary Wolf of *Wired* at the end of 1995. "Microsoft dominates with very little innovation. Apple lost. The desktop market has entered the dark ages."

He was also gloomy in an interview with Tony Perkins and the editors of *Red Herring*. First, he displayed the "Bad Steve" side of his personality. Soon after Perkins and his colleagues arrived, Jobs slipped out the back door "for a walk," and he didn't return for forty-five minutes. When the magazine's photographer began taking pictures, he snapped at her sarcastically and made her stop. Perkins later noted, "Manipulation, selfishness, or downright rudeness, we couldn't figure out the motivation behind his madness." When he finally settled down for the interview, he said that even the advent of the web would do little to stop Microsoft's domination. "Windows has won," he said. "It beat the Mac, unfortunately, it beat UNIX, it beat OS/2. An inferior product won."

Apple Falling

For a few years after Jobs was ousted, Apple was able to coast comfortably with a high profit margin based on its temporary dominance in desktop publishing. Feeling like a genius back in 1987, John Sculley had made a series of proclamations that nowadays sound embarrassing. Jobs wanted Apple "to become a wonderful consumer products company," Sculley wrote. "This was a lunatic plan. . . . Apple would never be a consumer products company. . . . We couldn't bend reality to all our dreams of changing the world. . . . High tech could not be designed and sold as a consumer product."

Jobs was appalled, and he became angry and contemptuous as Sculley presided over a steady decline in market share for Apple in the early 1990s. "Sculley destroyed Apple by bringing in corrupt people and corrupt values," Jobs later lamented. "They cared about making money—for themselves mainly, and also for Apple—rather than making great products." He felt that Sculley's drive for profits came at the expense of gaining market share. "Macintosh lost to Microsoft because

Sculley insisted on milking all the profits he could get rather than improving the product and making it affordable." As a result, the profits eventually disappeared.

It had taken Microsoft a few years to replicate Macintosh's graphical user interface, but by 1990 it had come out with Windows 3.0, which began the company's march to dominance in the desktop market. Windows 95, which was released in 1995, became the most successful operating system ever, and Macintosh sales began to collapse. "Microsoft simply ripped off what other people did," Jobs later said. "Apple deserved it. After I left, it didn't invent anything new. The Mac hardly improved. It was a sitting duck for Microsoft."

His frustration with Apple was evident when he gave a talk to a Stanford Business School club at the home of a student, who asked him to sign a Macintosh keyboard. Jobs agreed to do so if he could remove the keys that had been added to the Mac after he left. He pulled out his car keys and pried off the four arrow cursor keys, which he had once banned, as well as the top row of F1, F2, F3 . . . function keys. "I'm changing the world one keyboard at a time," he deadpanned. Then he signed the mutilated keyboard.

During his 1995 Christmas vacation in Kona Village, Hawaii, Jobs went walking along the beach with his friend Larry Ellison, the irrepressible Oracle chairman. They discussed making a takeover bid for Apple and restoring Jobs as its head. Ellison said he could line up $3 billion in financing: "I will buy Apple, you will get 25% of it right away for being CEO, and we can restore it to its past glory." But Jobs demurred. "I decided I'm not a hostile-takeover kind of guy," he explained. "If they had asked me to come back, it might have been different."

By 1996 Apple's share of the market had fallen to 4% from a high of 16% in the late 1980s. Michael Spindler, the German-born chief of Apple's European operations who had replaced Sculley as CEO in 1993, tried to sell the company to Sun, IBM, and Hewlett-Packard. That failed, and he was ousted in February 1996 and replaced by Gil Amelio, a research engineer who was CEO of National Semiconductor. During his first year the company lost $1 billion, and the stock price, which had been $70 in 1991, fell to $14, even as the tech bubble was pushing other stocks into the stratosphere.

Amelio was not a fan of Jobs. Their first meeting had been in 1994, just after Amelio was elected to the Apple board. Jobs had called him and announced, "I want to come over and see you." Amelio invited him over to his office at National Semiconductor, and he later recalled watching through the glass wall of his office as Jobs arrived. He looked "rather like a boxer, aggressive and elusively graceful, or like an elegant jungle cat ready to spring at its prey." After a few minutes of pleasantries—far more than Jobs usually engaged in—he abruptly announced the reason for his visit. He wanted Amelio to help him return to Apple as the CEO. "There's only one person who can rally the Apple troops," Jobs said, "only one person who can straighten out the company." The Macintosh era had passed, Jobs argued, and it was now time for Apple to create something new that was just as innovative.

"If the Mac is dead, what's going to replace it?" Amelio asked. Jobs's reply didn't impress him. "Steve didn't seem to have a clear answer," Amelio later said. "He seemed to have a set of one-liners." Amelio felt he was witnessing Jobs's reality distortion field and was proud to be immune to it. He shooed Jobs unceremoniously out of his office.

By the summer of 1996 Amelio realized that he had a serious problem. Apple was pinning its hopes on creating a new operating system, called Copland, but Amelio had discovered soon after becoming CEO that it was a bloated piece of vaporware that would not solve Apple's needs for better networking and memory protection, nor would it be ready to ship as scheduled in 1997. He publicly promised that he would quickly find an alternative. His problem was that he didn't have one.

So Apple needed a partner, one that could make a stable operating system, preferably one that was UNIX-like and had an object-oriented application layer. There was one company that could obviously supply such software—NeXT—but it would take a while for Apple to focus on it.

Apple first homed in on a company that had been started by Jean-Louis Gassée, called Be. Gassée began negotiating the sale of Be to Apple, but in August 1996 he overplayed his hand at a meeting with Amelio in Hawaii. He said he wanted to bring his fifty-person team to Apple, and he asked for 15% of the company, worth about $500 million. Amelio was stunned. Apple calculated that Be was worth about $50 million. After a few offers and counteroffers, Gassée refused to budge from demanding at least $275 million. He thought that Apple had no alternatives. It got back to Amelio that Gassée said, "I've got them by the balls, and I'm going to squeeze until it hurts." This did not please Amelio.

Apple's chief technology officer, Ellen Hancock, argued for going with Sun's UNIX-based Solaris operating system, even though it did not yet have a friendly user interface. Amelio began to favor using, of all things, Microsoft's Windows NT, which he felt could be rejiggered on the surface to look and feel just like a Mac while being compatible with the wide range of software available to Windows users. Bill Gates, eager to make a deal, began personally calling Amelio.

There was, of course, one other option. Two years earlier *Macworld* magazine columnist (and former Apple software evangelist) Guy Kawasaki had published a parody press release joking that Apple was buying NeXT and making Jobs its CEO. In the spoof Mike Markkula asked Jobs, "Do you want to spend the rest of your life selling UNIX with a sugarcoating, or change the world?" Jobs responded, "Because I'm now a father, I needed a steadier source of income." The release noted that "because of his experience at Next, he is expected to bring a newfound sense of humility back to Apple." It also quoted Bill Gates as saying there would now be more innovations from Jobs that Microsoft could copy. Everything in the press release was meant as a joke, of course. But reality has an odd habit of catching up with satire.

Slouching toward Cupertino

"Does anyone know Steve well enough to call him on this?" Amelio asked his staff. Because his encounter with Jobs two years earlier had ended badly, Amelio didn't want to make the call himself. But as it turned out, he didn't need to. Apple was already getting incoming pings from NeXT. A midlevel product marketer at NeXT, Garrett

Rice, had simply picked up the phone and, without consulting Jobs, called Ellen Hancock to see if she might be interested in taking a look at its software. She sent someone to meet with him.

By Thanksgiving of 1996 the two companies had begun midlevel talks, and Jobs picked up the phone to call Amelio directly. "I'm on my way to Japan, but I'll be back in a week and I'd like to see you as soon as I return," he said. "Don't make any decision until we can get together." Amelio, despite his earlier experience with Jobs, was thrilled to hear from him and entranced by the possibility of working with him. "For me, the phone call with Steve was like inhaling the flavors of a great bottle of vintage wine," he recalled. He gave his assurance he would make no deal with Be or anyone else before they got together.

For Jobs, the contest against Be was both professional and personal. NeXT was failing, and the prospect of being bought by Apple was a tantalizing lifeline. In addition, Jobs held grudges, sometimes passionately, and Gassée was near the top of his list, despite the fact that they had seemed to reconcile when Jobs was at NeXT. "Gassée is one of the few people in my life I would say is truly horrible," Jobs later insisted, unfairly. "He knifed me in the back in 1985." Sculley, to his credit, had at least been gentlemanly enough to knife Jobs in the front.

On December 2, 1996, Steve Jobs set foot on Apple's Cupertino campus for the first time since his ouster eleven years earlier. In the executive conference room, he met Amelio and Hancock to make the pitch for NeXT. Once again he was scribbling on the whiteboard there, this time giving his lecture about the four waves of computer systems that had culminated, at least in his telling, with the launch of NeXT. He was at his most seductive, despite the fact that he was speaking to two people he didn't respect. He was particularly adroit at feigning modesty. "It's probably a totally crazy idea," he said, but if they found it appealing, "I'll structure any kind of deal you want—license the software, sell you the company, whatever." He was, in fact, eager to sell everything, and he pushed that approach. "When you take a close look, you'll decide you want more than my software," he told them. "You'll want to buy the whole company and take all the people."

A few weeks later Jobs and his family went to Hawaii for Christmas vacation. Larry Ellison was also there, as he had been the year before. "You know, Larry, I think I've found a way for me to get back into Apple and get control of it without you having to buy it," Jobs said as they walked along the shore. Ellison recalled, "He explained his strategy, which was getting Apple to buy NeXT, then he would go on the board and be one step away from being CEO." Ellison thought that Jobs was missing a key point. "But Steve, there's one thing I don't understand," he said. "If we don't buy the company, how can we make any money?" It was a reminder of how different their desires were. Jobs put his hand on Ellison's left shoulder, pulled him so close that their noses almost touched, and said, "Larry, this is why it's really important that I'm your friend. You don't need any more money."

Ellison recalled that his own answer was almost a whine: "Well, I may not need the money, but why should some fund manager at Fidelity get the money? Why should someone else get it? Why shouldn't it be us?"

"I think if I went back to Apple, and I didn't own any of Apple, and you didn't own any of Apple, I'd have the moral high ground," Jobs replied.

"Steve, that's really expensive real estate, this moral high ground," said Ellison. "Look, Steve, you're my best friend, and Apple is your company. I'll do whatever you want." Although Jobs later said that he was not plotting to take over Apple at the time, Ellison thought it was inevitable. "Anyone who spent more than a half hour with Amelio would realize that he couldn't do anything but self-destruct," he later said.

The big bakeoff between NeXT and Be was held at the Garden Court Hotel in Palo Alto on December 10, in front of Amelio, Hancock, and six other Apple executives. NeXT went first, with Avie Tevanian demonstrating the software while Jobs displayed his hypnotizing salesmanship. They showed how the software could play four video clips on the screen at once, create multimedia, and link to the Internet. "Steve's sales pitch on the NeXT operating system was dazzling," according to Amelio. "He praised the virtues and strengths as though he were describing a performance of Olivier as Macbeth."

Gassée came in afterward, but he acted as if he had the deal in his hand. He provided no new presentation. He simply said that the Apple team knew the capabilities of the Be OS and asked if they had any further questions. It was a short session. While Gassée was presenting, Jobs and Tevanian walked the streets of Palo Alto. After a while they bumped into one of the Apple executives who had been at the meetings. "You're going to win this," he told them.

Tevanian later said that this was no surprise: "We had better technology, we had a solution that was complete, and we had Steve." Amelio knew that bringing Jobs back into the fold would be a double-edged sword, but the same was true of bringing Gassée back. Larry Tesler, one of the Macintosh veterans from the old days, recommended to Amelio that he choose NeXT, but added, "Whatever company you choose, you'll get someone who will take your job away, Steve or Jean-Louis."

Amelio opted for Jobs. He called Jobs to say that he planned to propose to the Apple board that he be authorized to negotiate a purchase of NeXT. Would he like to be at the meeting? Jobs said he would. When he walked in, there was an emotional moment when he saw Mike Markkula. They had not spoken since Markkula, once his mentor and father figure, had sided with Sculley there back in 1985. Jobs walked over and shook his hand.

Jobs invited Amelio to come to his house in Palo Alto so they could negotiate in a friendly setting. When Amelio arrived in his classic 1973 Mercedes, Jobs was impressed; he liked the car. In the kitchen, which had finally been renovated, Jobs put a kettle on for tea, and then they sat at the wooden table in front of the open-hearth pizza oven. The financial part of the negotiations went smoothly; Jobs was eager not to make Gassée's mistake of overreaching. He suggested that Apple pay $12 a share for NeXT. That would amount to about $500 million. Amelio said that was too high. He countered with $10 a share, or just over $400 million. Unlike Be, NeXT had an actual product, real revenues, and a great team, but Jobs was nevertheless pleasantly surprised at that counteroffer. He accepted immediately.

One sticking point was that Jobs wanted his payout to be in cash. Amelio insisted that he needed to "have skin in the game" and take the payout in stock that he would agree to hold for at least a year. Jobs resisted. Finally, they compromised: Jobs would take $120 million in cash and $37 million in stock, and he pledged to hold the stock for at least six months.

As usual Jobs wanted to have some of their conversation while taking a walk. While they ambled around Palo Alto, he made a pitch to be put on Apple's board. Amelio tried to deflect it, saying there was too much history to do something like that too quickly. "Gil, that really hurts," Jobs said. "This was my company. I've been left out since that horrible day with Sculley." Amelio said he understood, but he was not sure what the board would want. When he was about to begin his negotiations with Jobs, he had made a mental note to "move ahead with logic as my drill sergeant" and "sidestep the charisma." But during the walk he, like so many others, was caught in Jobs's force field. "I was hooked in by Steve's energy and enthusiasm," he recalled.

After circling the long blocks a couple of times, they returned to the house just as Laurene and the kids were arriving home. They all celebrated the easy negotiations, then Amelio rode off in his Mercedes. "He made me feel like a lifelong friend," Amelio recalled. Jobs indeed had a way of doing that. Later, after Jobs had engineered his ouster, Amelio would look back on Jobs's friendliness that day and note wistfully, "As I would painfully discover, it was merely one facet of an extremely complex personality."

After informing Gassée that Apple was buying NeXT, Amelio had what turned out to be an even more uncomfortable task: telling Bill Gates. "He went into orbit," Amelio recalled. Gates found it ridiculous, but perhaps not surprising, that Jobs had pulled off this coup. "Do you really think Steve Jobs has anything there?" Gates asked Amelio. "I know his technology, it's nothing but a warmed-over UNIX, and you'll never be able to make it work on your machines." Gates, like Jobs, had a way of working himself up, and he did so now: "Don't you understand that Steve doesn't know anything about technology? He's just a super salesman. I can't believe you're making such a stupid decision. . . . He doesn't know anything about engineering, and 99% of what he says and thinks is wrong. What the hell are you buying that garbage for?"

Years later, when I raised it with him, Gates did not recall being that upset. The purchase of NeXT, he argued, did not really give Apple a new operating system. "Amelio paid a lot for NeXT, and let's be frank, the NeXT OS was never really used." Instead the purchase ended up bringing in Avie Tevanian, who could help the existing Apple operating system evolve so that it eventually incorporated the kernel of the NeXT technology. Gates knew that the deal was destined to bring Jobs back to power. "But that was a twist of fate," he said. "What they ended up buying was a guy who most people would not have predicted would be a great CEO, because he didn't have much experience at it, but he was a brilliant guy with great design taste and great engineering taste. He suppressed his craziness enough to get himself appointed interim CEO."

Despite what both Ellison and Gates believed, Jobs had deeply conflicted feelings about whether he wanted to return to an active role at Apple, at least while Amelio was there. A few days before the NeXT purchase was due to be announced, Amelio asked Jobs to rejoin Apple full-time and take charge of operating system development. Jobs, however, kept deflecting Amelio's request.

Finally, on the day that he was scheduled to make the big announcement, Amelio called Jobs in. He needed an answer. "Steve, do you just want to take your money and leave?" Amelio asked. "It's okay if that's what you want." Jobs did not answer; he just stared. "Do you want to be on the payroll? An advisor?" Again Jobs stayed silent. Amelio went out and grabbed Jobs's lawyer, Larry Sonsini, and asked what he thought Jobs wanted. "Beats me," Sonsini said. So Amelio went back behind closed doors with Jobs and gave it one more try. "Steve, what's on your mind? What are you feeling? Please, I need a decision now."

"I didn't get any sleep last night," Jobs replied.

"Why? What's the problem?"

"I was thinking about all the things that need to be done and about the deal we're making, and it's all running together for me. I'm really tired now and not thinking clearly. I just don't want to be asked any more questions."

Amelio said that wasn't possible. He needed to say something.

Finally Jobs answered, "Look, if you have to tell them something, just say advisor to the chairman." And that is what Amelio did.

The announcement was made that evening—December 20, 1996—
in front of 250 cheering employees at Apple headquarters. Amelio did as Jobs had requested and described his new role as merely
that of a part-time advisor. Instead of appearing from the wings of
the stage, Jobs walked in from the rear of the auditorium and ambled
down the aisle. Amelio had told the gathering that Jobs would be too
tired to say anything, but by then he had been energized by the applause. "I'm very excited," Jobs said. "I'm looking forward to get to
reknow some old colleagues." Louise Kehoe of the *Financial Times*
came up to the stage afterward and asked Jobs, sounding almost accusatory, whether he was going to end up taking over Apple. "Oh no,
Louise," he said. "There are a lot of other things going on in my life
now. I have a family. I am involved at Pixar. My time is limited, but
I hope I can share some ideas."

The next day Jobs drove to Pixar. He had fallen increasingly in love
with the place, and he wanted to let the crew there know he was still
going to be president and deeply involved. But the Pixar people were
happy to see him go back to Apple part-time; a little less of Jobs's focus
would be a good thing. He was useful when there were big negotiations, but he could be dangerous when he had too much time on his
hands. When he arrived at Pixar that day, he went to Lasseter's office
and explained that even just being an advisor at Apple would take up a
lot of his time. He said he wanted Lasseter's blessing. "I keep thinking
about all the time away from my family this will cause, and the time
away from the other family at Pixar," Jobs said. "But the only reason
I want to do it is that the world will be a better place with Apple in it."

Lasseter smiled gently. "You have my blessing," he said.

THE RESTORATION

The Loser Now Will Be Later to Win

Amelio calling up Wozniak as Jobs hangs back, 1997

Hovering Backstage

"It's rare that you see an artist in his thirties or forties able to really contribute something amazing," Jobs declared as he was about to turn thirty.

That held true for Jobs in his thirties, during the decade that began with his ouster from Apple in 1985. But after turning forty in 1995, he flourished. *Toy Story* was released that year, and the following year Apple's purchase of NeXT offered him reentry into the company he had founded. In returning to Apple, Jobs would show that even people over forty could be great innovators. Having transformed personal computers in his twenties, he would now help to do the same for music players, the recording industry's business model, mobile phones, apps, tablet computers, books, and journalism.

He had told Larry Ellison that his return strategy was to sell NeXT to Apple, get appointed to the board, and be there ready when CEO Gil Amelio stumbled. Ellison may have been baffled when Jobs insisted that he was not motivated by money, but it was partly true. He had neither Ellison's conspicuous consumption needs nor Gates's philanthropic impulses nor the competitive urge to see how high on the *Forbes* list he could get. Instead his ego needs and personal drives led him to seek fulfillment by creating a legacy that would awe people. A dual legacy, actually: building innovative products and building a lasting company. He wanted to be in the pantheon with, indeed a notch above, people like Edwin Land, Bill Hewlett, and David Packard. And the best way to achieve all this was to return to Apple and reclaim his kingdom.

And yet when the cup of power neared his lips, he became strangely hesitant, reluctant, perhaps coy.

He returned to Apple officially in January 1997 as a part-time advisor, as he had told Amelio he would. He began to assert himself in some personnel areas, especially in protecting his people who had made the transition from NeXT. But in most other ways he was unusually passive. The decision not to ask him to join the board offended him, and he felt demeaned by the suggestion that he run the company's operating system division. Amelio was thus able to create a situation in which Jobs was both inside the tent and outside the tent, which was not a prescription for tranquillity. Jobs later recalled:

> Gil didn't want me around. And I thought he was a bozo. I knew that before I sold him the company. I thought I was just going to be trotted out now and then for events like Macworld, mainly for show. That was fine, because I was working at Pixar. I rented an office in downtown Palo Alto where I could work a few days a week, and I drove up to Pixar for one or two days. It was a nice life. I could slow down, spend time with my family.

Jobs was, in fact, trotted out for Macworld right at the beginning of January, and this reaffirmed his opinion that Amelio was a bozo. Close to four thousand of the faithful fought for seats in the ballroom of the San Francisco Marriott to hear Amelio's keynote address. He was introduced by the actor Jeff Goldblum. "I play an expert in chaos theory in *The Lost World: Jurassic Park*," he said. "I figure that will qualify me to speak at an Apple event." He then turned it over to Amelio, who came onstage wearing a flashy sports jacket and a banded-collar shirt buttoned tight at the neck, "looking like a Vegas comic," the *Wall Street Journal* reporter Jim Carlton noted, or in the words of the technology writer Michael Malone, "looking exactly like your newly divorced uncle on his first date."

The bigger problem was that Amelio had gone on vacation, gotten into a nasty tussle with his speechwriters, and refused to rehearse. When Jobs arrived backstage, he was upset by the chaos, and he seethed as Amelio stood on the podium bumbling through a disjointed and endless presentation. Amelio was unfamiliar with the talking points that popped up on his teleprompter and soon was trying to wing his presentation. Repeatedly he lost his train of thought. After more than an hour, the audience was aghast. There were a few welcome breaks, such as when he brought out the singer Peter Gabriel to demonstrate a new music program. He also pointed out Muhammad Ali in the first row; the champ was supposed to come onstage to promote a website about Parkinson's disease, but Amelio never invited him up or explained why he was there.

Amelio rambled for more than two hours before he finally called onstage the person everyone was waiting to cheer. "Jobs, exuding confidence, style, and sheer magnetism, was the antithesis of the fumbling Amelio as he strode onstage," Carlton wrote. "The return of Elvis would not have provoked a bigger sensation." The crowd jumped to its feet and gave him a raucous ovation for more than a minute. The wilderness decade was over. Finally Jobs waved for silence and cut to the heart of the challenge. "We've got to get the spark back," he said. "The Mac didn't progress much in ten years. So Windows caught up. So we have to come up with an OS that's even better."

Jobs's pep talk could have been a redeeming finale to Amelio's frightening performance. Unfortunately Amelio came back onstage and resumed his ramblings for another hour. Finally, more than three hours after the show began, Amelio brought it to a close by calling Jobs back onstage and then, in a surprise, bringing up Steve Wozniak as well. Again there was pandemonium. But Jobs was clearly annoyed. He avoided engaging in a triumphant trio scene, arms in the air. Instead he slowly edged offstage. "He ruthlessly ruined the closing moment I had planned," Amelio later complained. "His own feelings were more important than good press for Apple." It was only seven days into the new year for Apple, and already it was clear that the center would not hold.

Jobs immediately put people he trusted into the top ranks at Apple. "I wanted to make sure the really good people who came in from NeXT didn't get knifed in the back by the less competent people who were then in senior jobs at Apple," he recalled. Ellen Hancock, who had favored choosing Sun's Solaris over NeXT, was on the top of his bozo list, especially when she continued to want to use the kernel of Solaris in the new Apple operating system. In response to a reporter's question about the role Jobs would play in making that decision, she answered curtly, "None." She was wrong. Jobs's first move was to make sure that two of his friends from NeXT took over her duties.

To head software engineering, he tapped his buddy Avie Tevanian. To run the hardware side, he called on Jon Rubinstein, who had done the same at NeXT back when it had a hardware division. Rubinstein was vacationing on the Isle of Skye when Jobs called him. "Apple needs some help," he said. "Do you want to come aboard?" Rubinstein did. He got back in time to attend Macworld and see Amelio bomb onstage. Things were worse than he expected. He and Tevanian would exchange glances at meetings as if they had stumbled into an insane asylum, with people making deluded assertions while Amelio sat at the end of the table in a seeming stupor.

Jobs did not come into the office regularly, but he was on the phone to Amelio often. Once he had succeeded in making sure that Tevanian, Rubinstein, and others he trusted were given top positions, he turned his focus onto the sprawling product line. One of his pet peeves was Newton, the handheld personal digital assistant that boasted hand-

writing recognition capability. It was not quite as bad as the jokes and
Doonesbury comic strip made it seem, but Jobs hated it. He disdained
the idea of having a stylus or pen for writing on a screen. "God gave
us ten styluses," he would say, waving his fingers. "Let's not invent
another." In addition, he viewed Newton as John Sculley's one major
innovation, his pet project. That alone doomed it in Jobs's eyes.

"You ought to kill Newton," he told Amelio one day by phone.

It was a suggestion out of the blue, and Amelio pushed back. "What
do you mean, kill it?" he said. "Steve, do you have any idea how expensive that would be?"

"Shut it down, write it off, get rid of it," said Jobs. "It doesn't matter
what it costs. People will cheer you if you got rid of it."

"I've looked into Newton and it's going to be a moneymaker,"
Amelio declared. "I don't support getting rid of it." By May, however,
he announced plans to spin off the Newton division, the beginning of
its yearlong stutter-step march to the grave.

Tevanian and Rubinstein would come by Jobs's house to keep him
informed, and soon much of Silicon Valley knew that Jobs was quietly
wresting power from Amelio. It was not so much a Machiavellian
power play as it was Jobs being Jobs. Wanting control was ingrained in
his nature. Louise Kehoe, the *Financial Times* reporter who had fore-
seen this when she questioned Jobs and Amelio at the December announcement, was the first with the story. "Mr. Jobs has become the
power behind the throne," she reported at the end of February. "He
is said to be directing decisions on which parts of Apple's operations
should be cut. Mr. Jobs has urged a number of former Apple colleagues
to return to the company, hinting strongly that he plans to take charge,
they said. According to one of Mr. Jobs' confidantes, he has decided
that Mr. Amelio and his appointees are unlikely to succeed in reviving
Apple, and he is intent upon replacing them to ensure the survival of
'his company.'"

That month Amelio had to face the annual stockholders meeting
and explain why the results for the final quarter of 1996 showed a
30% plummet in sales from the year before. Shareholders lined up at
the microphones to vent their anger. Amelio was clueless about how
poorly he handled the meeting. "The presentation was regarded as one

of the best I had ever given," he later wrote. But Ed Woolard, the former CEO of DuPont who was now the chair of the Apple board (Markkula had been demoted to vice chair), was appalled. "This is a disaster," his wife whispered to him in the midst of the session. Woolard agreed. "Gil came dressed real cool, but he looked and sounded silly," he recalled. "He couldn't answer the questions, didn't know what he was talking about, and didn't inspire any confidence."

Woolard picked up the phone and called Jobs, whom he'd never met. The pretext was to invite him to Delaware to speak to DuPont executives. Jobs declined, but as Woolard recalled, "the request was a ruse in order to talk to him about Gil." He steered the phone call in that direction and asked Jobs point-blank what his impression of Amelio was. Woolard remembers Jobs being somewhat circumspect, saying that Amelio was not in the right job. Jobs recalled being more blunt:

> I thought to myself, I either tell him the truth, that Gil is a bozo, or I lie by omission. He's on the board of Apple, I have a duty to tell him what I think; on the other hand, if I tell him, he will tell Gil, in which case Gil will never listen to me again, and he'll fuck the people I brought into Apple. All of this took place in my head in less than thirty seconds. I finally decided that I owed this guy the truth. I cared deeply about Apple. So I just let him have it. I said this guy is the worst CEO I've ever seen, I think if you needed a license to be a CEO he wouldn't get one. When I hung up the phone, I thought, I probably just did a really stupid thing.

That spring Larry Ellison saw Amelio at a party and introduced him to the technology journalist Gina Smith, who asked how Apple was doing. "You know, Gina, Apple is like a ship," Amelio answered. "That ship is loaded with treasure, but there's a hole in the ship. And my job is to get everyone to row in the same direction." Smith looked perplexed and asked, "Yeah, but what about the hole?" From then on, Ellison and Jobs joked about the parable of the ship. "When Larry relayed this story to me, we were in this sushi place, and I literally fell off my chair laughing," Jobs recalled. "He was just such a buffoon, and he took himself so seriously. He insisted that everyone call him Dr. Amelio. That's always a warning sign."

Brent Schlender, *Fortune*'s well-sourced technology reporter, knew Jobs and was familiar with his thinking, and in March he came out with a story detailing the mess. "Apple Computer, Silicon Valley's paragon of dysfunctional management and fumbled techno-dreams, is back in crisis mode, scrambling lugubriously in slow motion to deal with imploding sales, a floundering technology strategy, and a hemorrhaging brand name," he wrote. "To the Machiavellian eye, it looks as if Jobs, despite the lure of Hollywood—lately he has been overseeing Pixar, maker of *Toy Story* and other computer-animated films—might be scheming to take over Apple."

Once again Ellison publicly floated the idea of doing a hostile takeover and installing his "best friend" Jobs as CEO. "Steve's the only one who can save Apple," he told reporters. "I'm ready to help him the minute he says the word." Like the third time the boy cried wolf, Ellison's latest takeover musings didn't get much notice, so later in the month he told Dan Gillmore of the *San Jose Mercury News* that he was forming an investor group to raise $1 billion to buy a majority stake in Apple. (The company's market value was about $2.3 billion.) The day the story came out, Apple stock shot up 11% in heavy trading. To add to the frivolity, Ellison set up an email address, savapple@us.oracle.com, asking the general public to vote on whether he should go ahead with it.

Jobs was somewhat amused by Ellison's self-appointed role. "Larry brings this up now and then," he told a reporter. "I try to explain my role at Apple is to be an advisor." Amelio, however, was livid. He called Ellison to dress him down, but Ellison wouldn't take the call. So Amelio called Jobs, whose response was equivocal but also partly genuine. "I really don't understand what is going on," he told Amelio. "I think all this is crazy." Then he added a reassurance that was not at all genuine: "You and I have a good relationship." Jobs could have ended the speculation by releasing a statement rejecting Ellison's idea, but much to Amelio's annoyance, he didn't. He remained aloof, which served both his interests and his nature.

By then the press had turned against Amelio. *Business Week* ran a cover asking "Is Apple Mincemeat?"; *Red Herring* ran an editorial headlined "Gil Amelio, Please Resign"; and *Wired* ran a cover that showed the Apple logo crucified as a sacred heart with a crown of thorns and the headline "Pray." Mike Barnicle of the *Boston Globe*, railing against years of Apple mismanagement, wrote, "How can these nitwits still draw a paycheck when they took the only computer that didn't frighten people and turned it into the technological equivalent of the 1997 Red Sox bullpen?"

When Jobs and Amelio had signed the contract in February, Jobs began hopping around exuberantly and declared, "You and I need to go out and have a great bottle of wine to celebrate!" Amelio offered to bring wine from his cellar and suggested that they invite their wives. It took until June before they settled on a date, and despite the rising tensions they were able to have a good time. The food and wine were as mismatched as the diners; Amelio brought a bottle of 1964 Cheval Blanc and a Montrachet that each cost about $300; Jobs chose a vegetarian restaurant in Redwood City where the food bill totaled $72. Amelio's wife remarked afterward, "He's such a charmer, and his wife is too."

Jobs could seduce and charm people at will, and he liked to do so. People such as Amelio and Sculley allowed themselves to believe that because Jobs was charming them, it meant that he liked and respected them. It was an impression that he sometimes fostered by dishing out insincere flattery to those hungry for it. But Jobs could be charming to people he hated just as easily as he could be insulting to people he liked. Amelio didn't see this because, like Sculley, he was so eager for Jobs's affection. Indeed the words he used to describe his yearning for a good relationship with Jobs are almost the same as those used by Sculley. "When I was wrestling with a problem, I would walk through the issue with him," Amelio recalled. "Nine times out of ten we would agree." Somehow he willed himself to believe that Jobs really respected him: "I was in awe over the way Steve's mind approached problems, and had the feeling we were building a mutually trusting relationship."

Amelio's disillusionment came a few days after their dinner. During their negotiations, he had insisted that Jobs hold the Apple stock he got for at least six months, and preferably longer. That six months ended in June. When a block of 1.5 million shares was sold, Amelio called Jobs. "I'm telling people that the shares sold were not yours," he said. "Remember, you and I had an understanding that you wouldn't sell any without advising us first."

"That's right," Jobs replied. Amelio took that response to mean that Jobs had not sold his shares, and he issued a statement saying so. But when the next SEC filing came out, it revealed that Jobs had indeed sold the shares. "Dammit, Steve, I asked you point-blank about these shares and you denied it was you." Jobs told Amelio that he had sold in a "fit of depression" about where Apple was going and he didn't want to admit it because he was "a little embarrassed." When I asked him about it years later, he simply said, "I didn't feel I needed to tell Gil."

Why did Jobs mislead Amelio about selling the shares? One reason is simple: Jobs sometimes avoided the truth. Helmut Sonnenfeldt once said of Henry Kissinger, "He lies not because it's in his interest, he lies because it's in his nature." It was in Jobs's nature to mislead or be secretive when he felt it was warranted. But he also indulged in being brutally honest at times, telling the truths that most of us sugarcoat or suppress. Both the dissembling and the truth-telling were simply different aspects of his Nietzschean attitude that ordinary rules didn't apply to him.

Exit, Pursued by a Bear

Jobs had refused to quash Larry Ellison's takeover talk, and he had secretly sold his shares and been misleading about it. So Amelio finally became convinced that Jobs was gunning for him. "I finally absorbed the fact that I had been too willing and too eager to believe he was on my team," Amelio recalled. "Steve's plans to manipulate my termination were charging forward."

Jobs was indeed bad-mouthing Amelio at every opportunity. He couldn't help himself. But there was a more important factor in turning the board against Amelio. Fred Anderson, the chief financial officer, saw it as his fiduciary duty to keep Ed Woolard and the board informed of Apple's dire situation. "Fred was the guy telling me that cash was draining, people were leaving, and more key players were thinking of it," said Woolard. "He made it clear the ship was going to hit the sand soon, and even he was thinking of leaving." That added to the worries Woolard already had from watching Amelio bumble the shareholders meeting.

At an executive session of the board in June, with Amelio out of the room, Woolard described to current directors how he calculated their odds. "If we stay with Gil as CEO, I think there's only a 10% chance we will avoid bankruptcy," he said. "If we fire him and convince Steve to come take over, we have a 60% chance of surviving. If we fire Gil, don't get Steve back, and have to search for a new CEO, then we have a 40% chance of surviving." The board gave him authority to ask Jobs to return.

Woolard and his wife flew to London, where they were planning to watch the Wimbledon tennis matches. He saw some of the tennis during the day, but spent his evenings in his suite at the Inn on the Park calling people back in America, where it was daytime. By the end of his stay, his telephone bill was $2,000.

First, he called Jobs. The board was going to fire Amelio, he said, and it wanted Jobs to come back as CEO. Jobs had been aggressive in deriding Amelio and pushing his own ideas about where to take Apple. But suddenly, when offered the cup, he became coy. "I will help," he replied.

"As CEO?" Woolard asked.

Jobs said no. Woolard pushed hard for him to become at least the acting CEO. Again Jobs demurred. "I will be an advisor," he said. "Unpaid." He also agreed to become a board member—that was something he had yearned for—but declined to be the board chairman. "That's all I can give now," he said. After rumors began circulating, he emailed a memo to Pixar employees assuring them that he was not abandoning them. "I got a call from Apple's board of directors three weeks ago asking me to return to Apple as their CEO," he wrote. "I declined. They then asked me to become chairman, and I again declined. So don't worry—the crazy rumors are just that. I have no plans to leave Pixar. You're stuck with me."

Why did Jobs not seize the reins? Why was he reluctant to grab the job that for two decades he had seemed to desire? When I asked him, he said:

We'd just taken Pixar public, and I was happy being CEO there. I never knew of anyone who served as CEO of two public companies, even temporarily, and I wasn't even sure it was legal. I didn't know what I wanted to do. I was enjoying spending more time with my family. I was torn. I knew Apple was a mess, so I wondered: Do I want to give up this nice lifestyle that I have? What are all the Pixar shareholders going to think? I talked to people I respected. I finally called Andy Grove at about eight one Saturday morning—too early. I gave him the pros and the cons, and in the middle he stopped me and said, "Steve, I don't give a shit about Apple." I was stunned. It was then I realized that I *do* give a shit about Apple—I started it and it is a good thing to have in the world. That was when I decided to go back on a temporary basis to help them hire a CEO.

The claim that he was enjoying spending more time with his family was not convincing. He was never destined to win a Father of the Year trophy, even when he had spare time on his hands. He was getting better at paying heed to his children, especially Reed, but his primary focus was on his work. He was frequently aloof from his two younger daughters, estranged again from Lisa, and often prickly as a husband.

So what was the real reason for his hesitancy in taking over at Apple? For all of his willfulness and insatiable desire to control things, Jobs was indecisive and reticent when he felt unsure about something. He craved perfection, and he was not always good at figuring out how to settle for something less. He did not like to wrestle with complexity or make accommodations. This was true in products, design, and furnishings for the house. It was also true when it came to personal commitments. If he knew for sure a course of action was right, he was unstoppable. But if he had doubts, he sometimes withdrew, preferring not to think about things that did not perfectly suit him. As happened when Amelio had asked him what role he wanted to play, Jobs would go silent and ignore situations that made him uncomfortable.

This attitude arose partly out of his tendency to see the world in binary terms. A person was either a hero or a bozo, a product was either amazing or shit. But he could be stymied by things that were more complex, shaded, or nuanced: getting married, buying the right sofa, committing to run a company. In addition, he didn't want to be set up for failure. "I think Steve wanted to assess whether Apple could be saved," Fred Anderson said.

Woolard and the board decided to go ahead and fire Amelio, even though Jobs was not yet forthcoming about how active a role he would play as an advisor. Amelio was about to go on a picnic with his wife, children, and grandchildren when the call came from Woolard in London. "We need you to step down," Woolard said simply. Amelio replied that it was not a good time to discuss this, but Woolard felt he had to persist. "We are going to announce that we're replacing you."

Amelio resisted. "Remember, Ed, I told the board it was going to take three years to get this company back on its feet again," he said. "I'm not even halfway through."

"The board is at the place where we don't want to discuss it further," Woolard replied. Amelio asked who knew about the decision, and Woolard told him the truth: the rest of the board plus Jobs. "Steve was one of the people we talked to about this," Woolard said. "His view is that you're a really nice guy, but you don't know much about the computer industry."

"Why in the world would you involve Steve in a decision like this?" Amelio replied, getting angry. "Steve is not even a member of the board of directors, so what the hell is he doing in any of this conversation?" But Woolard didn't back down, and Amelio hung up to carry on with the family picnic before telling his wife.

At times Jobs displayed a strange mixture of prickliness and neediness. He usually didn't care one iota what people thought of him; he could cut people off and never care to speak to them again. Yet sometimes he also felt a compulsion to explain himself. So that evening Amelio received, to his surprise, a phone call from Jobs. "Gee, Gil, I just wanted you to know, I talked to Ed today about this thing and I really feel bad about it," he said. "I want you to know that I had absolutely nothing to do with this turn of events, it was a decision the board made, but they had asked me for advice and counsel." He told Amelio he respected him for having "the highest integrity of anyone I've ever met," and went on to give some unsolicited advice. "Take six months off," Jobs told him. "When I got thrown out of Apple, I immediately went back to work, and I regretted it." He offered to be a sounding board if Amelio ever wanted more advice.

Amelio was stunned but managed to mumble a few words of thanks. He turned to his wife and recounted what Jobs said. "In ways, I still like the man, but I don't believe him," he told her.

"I was totally taken in by Steve," she said, "and I really feel like an idiot."

"Join the crowd," her husband replied.

Steve Wozniak, who was himself now an informal advisor to the company, was thrilled that Jobs was coming back. (He forgave easily.) "It was just what we needed," he said, "because whatever you think of Steve, he knows how to get the magic back." Nor did Jobs's triumph over Amelio surprise him. As he told *Wired* shortly after it happened, "Gil Amelio meets Steve Jobs, game over."

That Monday Apple's top employees were summoned to the auditorium. Amelio came in looking calm and relaxed. "Well, I'm sad to report that it's time for me to move on," he said. Fred Anderson, who had agreed to be interim CEO, spoke next, and he made it clear that he would be taking his cues from Jobs. Then, exactly twelve years since he had lost power in a July 4 weekend struggle, Jobs walked back onstage at Apple.

It immediately became clear that, whether or not he wanted to admit it publicly (or even to himself), Jobs was going to take control and not be a mere advisor. As soon as he came onstage that day—wearing shorts, sneakers, and a black turtleneck—he got to work reinvigorating his beloved institution. "Okay, tell me what's wrong with this place," he said. There were some murmurings, but Jobs cut them off. "It's the products!" he answered. "So what's wrong with the products?" Again there were a few attempts at an answer, until Jobs broke in to hand down the correct answer. "The products *suck!*" he shouted. "There's no sex in them anymore!"

Woolard was able to coax Jobs to agree that his role as an advisor would be a very active one. Jobs approved a statement saying that he had "agreed to step up my involvement with Apple for up to 90 days, helping them until they hire a new CEO." The clever formulation that Woolard used in his statement was that Jobs was coming back "as an advisor leading the team."

Jobs took a small office next to the boardroom on the executive floor, conspicuously eschewing Amelio's big corner office. He got involved in all aspects of the business: product design, where to cut, supplier negotiations, and advertising agency review. He believed that he had to stop the hemorrhaging of top Apple employees, and to do so he wanted to reprice their stock options. Apple stock had dropped so low that the options had become worthless. Jobs wanted to lower the exercise price, so they would be valuable again. At the time, that was legally permissible, but it was not considered good corporate practice. On his first Thursday back at Apple, Jobs called for a telephonic board meeting and outlined the problem. The directors balked. They asked for time to do a legal and financial study of what the change would mean. "It has to be done fast," Jobs told them. "We're losing good people."

Even his supporter Ed Woolard, who headed the compensation committee, objected. "At DuPont we never did such a thing," he said.

"You brought me here to fix this thing, and people are the key," Jobs argued. When the board proposed a study that could take two months, Jobs exploded: "Are you nuts?!?" He paused for a long moment of silence, then continued. "Guys, if you don't want to do this, I'm not coming back on Monday. Because I've got thousands of key decisions to make that are far more difficult than this, and if you can't throw your support behind this kind of decision, I will fail. So if you can't do this, I'm out of here, and you can blame it on me, you can say, 'Steve wasn't up for the job.'"

The next day, after consulting with the board, Woolard called Jobs back. "We're going to approve this," he said. "But some of the board members don't like it. We feel like you've put a gun to our head." The options for the top team (Jobs had none) were reset at $13.25, which was the price of the stock the day Amelio was ousted.

Instead of declaring victory and thanking the board, Jobs continued to seethe at having to answer to a board he didn't respect. "Stop the train, this isn't going to work," he told Woolard. "This company is in shambles, and I don't have time to wet-nurse the board. So I need all of you to resign. Or else I'm going to resign and not come back on Monday." The one person who could stay, he said, was Woolard.

Most members of the board were aghast. Jobs was still refusing to commit himself to coming back full-time or being anything more than an advisor, yet he felt he had the power to force them to leave. The hard truth, however, was that he did have that power over them. They could not afford for him to storm off in a fury, nor was the prospect of remaining an Apple board member very enticing by then. "After all they'd been through, most were glad to be let off," Woolard recalled.

Once again the board acquiesced. It made only one request: Would he permit one other director to stay, in addition to Woolard? It would help the optics. Jobs assented. "They were an awful board, a terrible board," he later said. "I agreed they could keep Ed Woolard and a guy named Gareth Chang, who turned out to be a zero. He wasn't terrible, just a zero. Woolard, on the other hand, was one of the best board members I've ever seen. He was a prince, one of the most supportive and wise people I've ever met."

Among those being asked to resign was Mike Markkula, who in 1976, as a young venture capitalist, had visited the Jobs garage, fallen in love with the nascent computer on the workbench, guaranteed a $250,000 line of credit, and become the third partner and one-third owner of the new company. Over the subsequent two decades, he was the one constant on the board, ushering in and out a variety of CEOs. He had supported Jobs at times but also clashed with him, most notably when he sided with Sculley in the showdowns of 1985. With Jobs returning, he knew that it was time for him to leave.

Jobs could be cutting and cold, especially toward people who crossed him, but he could also be sentimental about those who had been with him from the early days. Wozniak fell into that favored category, of course, even though they had drifted apart; so did Andy Hertzfeld and a few others from the Macintosh team. In the end, Mike Markkula did as well. "I felt deeply betrayed by him, but he was like a father and I always cared about him," Jobs later recalled. So when the time came to ask him to resign from the Apple board, Jobs drove to Markkula's chateau-like mansion in the Woodside hills to do it personally.

As usual, he asked to take a walk, and they strolled the grounds to a redwood grove with a picnic table. "He told me he wanted a new board because he wanted to start fresh," Markkula said. "He was worried that I might take it poorly, and he was relieved when I didn't."

They spent the rest of the time talking about where Apple should focus in the future. Jobs's ambition was to build a company that would endure, and he asked Markkula what the formula for that would be. Markkula replied that lasting companies know how to reinvent themselves. Hewlett-Packard had done that repeatedly; it started as an instrument company, then became a calculator company, then a computer company. "Apple has been sidelined by Microsoft in the PC business," Markkula said. "You've got to reinvent the company to do some other thing, like other consumer products or devices. You've got to be like a butterfly and have a metamorphosis." Jobs didn't say much, but he agreed.

The old board met in late July to ratify the transition. Woolard, who was as genteel as Jobs was prickly, was mildly taken aback when Jobs appeared dressed in jeans and sneakers, and he worried that Jobs might start berating the veteran board members for screwing up. But Jobs merely offered a pleasant "Hi, everyone." They got down to the business of voting to accept the resignations, elect Jobs to the board, and empower Woolard and Jobs to find new board members.

Jobs's first recruit was, not surprisingly, Larry Ellison. He said he would be pleased to join, but he hated attending meetings. Jobs said it would be fine if he came to only half of them. (After a while Ellison was coming to only a third of the meetings. Jobs took a picture of him that had appeared on the cover of *Business Week* and had it blown up to life size and pasted on a cardboard cutout to put in his chair.)

Jobs also brought in Bill Campbell, who had run marketing at Apple in the early 1980s and been caught in the middle of the Sculley-Jobs clash. Campbell had ended up sticking with Sculley, but he had grown to dislike him so much that Jobs forgave him. Now he was the CEO of Intuit and a walking buddy of Jobs. "We were sitting out in the back of his house," recalled Campbell, who lived only five blocks from Jobs in Palo Alto, "and he said he was going back to Apple and wanted me on the board. I said, 'Holy shit, of course I will do that.'"

Campbell had been a football coach at Columbia, and his great talent, Jobs said, was to "get A performances out of B players." At Apple, Jobs told him, he would get to work with A players.

Woolard helped bring in Jerry York, who had been the chief financial officer at Chrysler and then IBM. Others were considered and then rejected by Jobs, including Meg Whitman, who was then the manager of Hasbro's Playskool division and had been a strategic planner at Disney. (In 1998 she became CEO of eBay, and she later ran unsuccessfully for governor of California.) Over the years Jobs would bring in some strong leaders to serve on the Apple board, including Al Gore, Eric Schmidt of Google, Art Levinson of Genentech, Mickey Drexler of the Gap and J. Crew, and Andrea Jung of Avon. But he always made sure they were loyal, sometimes loyal to a fault. Despite their stature, they seemed at times awed or intimidated by Jobs, and they were eager to keep him happy.

At one point he invited Arthur Levitt, the former SEC chairman, to become a board member. Levitt, who bought his first Macintosh in 1984 and was proudly "addicted" to Apple computers, was thrilled. He was excited to visit Cupertino, where he discussed the role with Jobs. But then Jobs read a speech Levitt had given about corporate governance, which argued that boards should play a strong and independent role, and he telephoned to withdraw the invitation. "Arthur, I don't think you'd be happy on our board, and I think it best if we not invite you," Levitt said Jobs told him. "Frankly, I think some of the issues you raised, while appropriate for some companies, really don't apply to Apple's culture." Levitt later wrote, "I was floored. . . . It's plain to me that Apple's board is not designed to act independently of the CEO."

Macworld Boston, August 1997

The staff memo announcing the repricing of Apple's stock options was signed "Steve and the executive team," and it soon became public that he was running all of the company's product review meetings. These and other indications that Jobs was now deeply engaged at Apple helped push the stock up from about $13 to $20 during July. It also created a frisson of excitement as the Apple faithful gathered for the August 1997 Macworld in Boston. More than five thousand showed up hours in advance to cram into the Castle convention hall of the Park Plaza hotel for Jobs's keynote speech. They came to see their returning hero—and to find out whether he was really ready to lead them again.

Huge cheers erupted when a picture of Jobs from 1984 was flashed on the overhead screen. "Steve! Steve! Steve!" the crowd started to chant, even as he was still being introduced. When he finally strode onstage—wearing a black vest, collarless white shirt, jeans, and an impish smile—the screams and flashbulbs rivaled those for any rock star. At first he punctured the excitement by reminding them of where he officially worked. "I'm Steve Jobs, the chairman and CEO of Pixar," he introduced himself, flashing a slide onscreen with that title. Then he explained his role at Apple. "I, like a lot of other people, are pulling together to help Apple get healthy again."

But as Jobs paced back and forth across the stage, changing the overhead slides with a clicker in his hand, it was clear that he was now in charge at Apple—and was likely to remain so. He delivered a carefully crafted presentation, using no notes, on why Apple's sales had fallen by 30% over the previous two years. "There are a lot of great people at Apple, but they're doing the wrong things because the plan has been wrong," he said. "I've found people who can't wait to fall into line behind a good strategy, but there just hasn't been one." The crowd again erupted in yelps, whistles, and cheers.

As he spoke, his passion poured forth with increasing intensity, and he began saying "we" and "I"—rather than "they"—when referring to what Apple would be doing. "I think you still have to think differently to buy an Apple computer," he said. "The people who buy them do think different. They are the creative spirits in this world, and they're out to change the world. *We* make tools for those kinds of people." When he stressed the word "we" in that sentence, he cupped his hands and tapped his fingers on his chest. And then, in his final peroration, he continued to stress the word "we" as he talked about Apple's future. "We too are going to think differently and serve the people who have been buying our products from the beginning. Because a lot of people think they're crazy, but in that craziness we see genius." During the prolonged standing ovation, people looked at each other in awe, and a few wiped tears from their eyes. Jobs had made it very clear that he and the "we" of Apple were one.

The Microsoft Pact

The climax of Jobs's August 1997 Macworld appearance was a bombshell announcement, one that made the cover of both *Time* and *Newsweek*. Near the end of his speech, he paused for a sip of water and began to talk in more subdued tones. "Apple lives in an ecosystem," he said. "It needs help from other partners. Relationships that are destructive don't help anybody in this industry." For dramatic effect, he paused again, and then explained: "I'd like to announce one of our first new partnerships today, a very meaningful one, and that is one with Microsoft." The Microsoft and Apple logos appeared together on the screen as people gasped.

Apple and Microsoft had been at war for a decade over a variety of copyright and patent issues, most notably whether Microsoft had stolen the look and feel of Apple's graphical user interface. Just as Jobs was being eased out of Apple in 1985, John Sculley had struck a surrender deal: Microsoft could license the Apple GUI for Windows 1.0, and in return it would make Excel exclusive to the Mac for up to two years. In 1988, after Microsoft came out with Windows 2.0, Apple sued. Sculley contended that the 1985 deal did not apply to Windows 2.0 and that further refinements to Windows (such as copying Bill Atkinson's trick of "clipping" overlapping windows) had made the infringement more blatant. By 1997 Apple had lost the case and various appeals, but remnants of the litigation and threats of new suits lingered. In addition, President Clinton's Justice Department was preparing a massive antitrust case against Microsoft. Jobs invited the lead prosecutor, Joel Klein, to Palo Alto. Don't worry about extracting a huge remedy against Microsoft, Jobs told him over coffee. Instead simply keep them tied up in litigation. That would allow Apple the opportunity, Jobs explained, to "make an end run" around Microsoft and start offering competing products.

Under Amelio, the showdown had become explosive. Microsoft refused to commit to developing Word and Excel for future Macintosh operating systems, which could have destroyed Apple. In defense of Bill Gates, he was not simply being vindictive. It was understandable that he was reluctant to commit to developing for a future Macintosh operating system when no one, including the ever-changing leadership at Apple, seemed to know what that new operating system would be. Right after Apple bought NeXT, Amelio and Jobs flew together to visit Microsoft, but Gates had trouble figuring out which of them was in charge. A few days later he called Jobs privately. "Hey, what the fuck, am I supposed to put my applications on the NeXT OS?" Gates asked. Jobs responded by "making smart-ass remarks about Gil," Gates recalled, and suggesting that the situation would soon be clarified.

When the leadership issue was partly resolved by Amelio's ouster, one of Jobs's first phone calls was to Gates. Jobs recalled:

> I called up Bill and said, "I'm going to turn this thing around." Bill always had a soft spot for Apple. We got him into the application software business. The first Microsoft apps were Excel and Word for the Mac. So I called him and said, "I need help." Microsoft was walking over Apple's patents. I said, "If we kept up our lawsuits, a few years from now we could win a billion-dollar patent suit. You know it, and I know it. But Apple's not going to survive that long if we're at war. I know that. So let's figure out how to settle this right away. All I need is a commitment that Microsoft will keep developing for the Mac and an investment by Microsoft in Apple so it has a stake in our success."

When I recounted to him what Jobs said, Gates agreed it was accurate. "We had a group of people who liked working on the Mac stuff, and we liked the Mac," Gates recalled. He had been negotiating with Amelio for six months, and the proposals kept getting longer and more complicated. "So Steve comes in and says, 'Hey, that deal is too complicated. What I want is a simple deal. I want the commitment and I want an investment.' And so we put that together in just four weeks."

Gates and his chief financial officer, Greg Maffei, made the trip to Palo Alto to work out the framework for a deal, and then Maffei returned alone the following Sunday to work on the details. When he arrived at Jobs's home, Jobs grabbed two bottles of water out of the refrigerator and took Maffei for a walk around the Palo Alto neighborhood. Both men wore shorts, and Jobs walked barefoot. As they sat in front of a Baptist church, Jobs cut to the core issues. "These are the things we care about," he said. "A commitment to make software for the Mac and an investment."

Although the negotiations went quickly, the final details were not finished until hours before Jobs's Macworld speech in Boston. He was rehearsing at the Park Plaza Castle when his cell phone rang. "Hi, Bill," he said as his words echoed through the old hall. Then he walked to a corner and spoke in a soft tone so others couldn't hear. The call lasted an hour. Finally, the remaining deal points were resolved. "Bill, thank you for your support of this company," Jobs said as he crouched on the empty stage. "I think the world's a better place for it."

During his Macworld keynote address, Jobs walked through the details of the Microsoft deal. At first there were groans and hisses from the faithful. Particularly galling was Jobs's announcement that, as part of the peace pact, "Apple has decided to make Internet Explorer its default browser on the Macintosh." The audience erupted in boos, and Jobs quickly added, "Since we believe in choice, we're going to be shipping other Internet browsers, as well, and the user can, of course, change their default should they choose to." There were some laughs and scattered applause. The audience was beginning to come around, especially when he announced that Microsoft would be investing $150 million in Apple and getting nonvoting shares.

But the mellower mood was shattered for a moment when Jobs made one of the few visual and public relations gaffes of his onstage career. "I happen to have a special guest with me today via satellite downlink," he said, and suddenly Bill Gates's face appeared on the huge screen looming over Jobs and the auditorium. There was a thin smile on Gates's face that flirted with being a smirk. The audience gasped in horror, followed by some boos and catcalls. The scene was such a brutal echo of the 1984 Big Brother ad that you half expected (and hoped?) that an athletic woman would suddenly come running down the aisle and vaporize the screenshot with a well-thrown hammer.

But it was all for real, and Gates, unaware of the jeering, began speaking on the satellite link from Microsoft headquarters. "Some of the most exciting work that I've done in my career has been the work that I've done with Steve on the Macintosh," he intoned in his high-pitched singsong. As he went on to tout the new version of Microsoft Office that was being made for the Macintosh, the audience quieted down and then slowly seemed to accept the new world order. Gates even was able to rouse some applause when he said that the new Mac versions of Word and Excel would be "in many ways more advanced than what we've done on the Windows platform."

Jobs realized that the image of Gates looming over him and the audience was a mistake. "I wanted him to come to Boston," Jobs later said. "That was my worst and stupidest staging event ever. It was bad because it made me look small, and Apple look small, and as if everything was in Bill's hands." Gates likewise was embarrassed when he saw the videotape of the event. "I didn't know that my face was going to be blown up to looming proportions," he said.

Jobs tried to reassure the audience with an impromptu sermon. "If we want to move forward and see Apple healthy again, we have to let go of a few things here," he told the audience. "We have to let go of this notion that for Apple to win Microsoft has to lose. . . . I think if we want Microsoft Office on the Mac, we better treat the company that puts it out with a little bit of gratitude."

The Microsoft announcement, along with Jobs's passionate reengagement with the company, provided a much-needed jolt for Apple. By the end of the day, its stock had skyrocketed $6.56, or 33%, to close at $26.31, twice the price of the day Amelio resigned. The one-day jump added $830 million to Apple's stock market capitalization. The company was back from the edge of the grave.

CHAPTER TWENTY-FIVE

THINK DIFFERENT

Jobs as iCEO

Enlisting Picasso

Here's to the Crazy Ones

Lee Clow, the creative director at Chiat/Day who had done the great "1984" ad for the launch of the Macintosh, was driving in Los Angeles in early July 1997 when his car phone rang. It was Jobs. "Hi, Lee, this is Steve," he said. "Guess what? Amelio just resigned. Can you come up here?"

Apple was going through a review to select a new agency, and Jobs was not impressed by what he had seen. So he wanted Clow and his firm, by then called TBWA\Chiat\Day, to compete for the business. "We have to prove that Apple is still alive," Jobs said, "and that it still stands for something special."

Clow said that he didn't pitch for accounts. "You know our work," he said. But Jobs begged him. It would be hard to reject all the others that were making pitches, including BBDO and Arnold Worldwide, and bring back "an old crony," as Jobs put it. Clow agreed to fly up to Cupertino with something they could show. Recounting the scene years later, Jobs started to cry.

> This chokes me up, this really chokes me up. It was so clear that Lee loved Apple so much. Here was the best guy in advertising. And he hadn't pitched in ten years. Yet here he was, and he was pitching his heart out, because he loved Apple as much as we did. He and his team had come up with this brilliant idea, "Think Different." And it was ten times better than anything the other agencies showed. It choked me up, and it still makes me cry to think about it, both the fact that Lee cared so much and also how brilliant his "Think Different" idea was. Every once in a while, I find myself in the presence of purity—purity of spirit and love—and I always cry. It always just reaches in and grabs me. That was one of those moments. There was a purity about that I will never forget. I cried in my office as he was showing me the idea, and I still cry when I think about it.

Jobs and Clow agreed that Apple was one of the great brands of the world, probably in the top five based on emotional appeal, but they needed to remind folks what was distinctive about it. So they wanted a brand image campaign, not a set of advertisements featuring products. It was designed to celebrate not what the computers could do, but what creative people could do with the computers. "This wasn't about processor speed or memory," Jobs recalled. "It was about creativity." It was directed not only at potential customers, but also at Apple's own employees: "We at Apple had forgotten who we were. One way to remember who you are is to remember who your heroes are. That was the genesis of that campaign."

Clow and his team tried a variety of approaches that praised the "crazy ones" who "think different." They did one video with the Seal song "Crazy" ("We're never gonna survive unless we get a little crazy"), but couldn't get the rights to it. Then they tried versions using a recording of Robert Frost reading "The Road Not Taken" and of Robin Williams's speeches from *Dead Poets Society*. Eventually they decided they needed to write their own text; their draft began, "Here's to the crazy ones."

Jobs was as demanding as ever. When Clow's team flew up with a version of the text, he exploded at the young copywriter. "This is shit!" he yelled. "It's advertising agency shit and I hate it." It was the first time the young copywriter had met Jobs, and he stood there mute. He never went back. But those who could stand up to Jobs, including Clow and his teammates Ken Segall and Craig Tanimoto, were able to work with him to create a tone poem that he liked. In its original sixty-second version it read:

> Here's to the crazy ones. The misfits. The rebels. The troublemakers. The round pegs in the square holes. The ones who see things differently. They're not fond of rules. And they have no respect for the status quo. You can quote them, disagree with them, glorify or vilify them. About the only thing you can't do is ignore them. Because they change things. They push the human race forward. And while some may see them as the crazy ones, we see genius. Because the people who are crazy enough to think they can change the world are the ones who do.

Jobs, who could identify with each of those sentiments, wrote some of the lines himself, including "They push the human race forward." By the time of the Boston Macworld in early August, they had produced a rough version. They agreed it was not ready, but Jobs used the concepts, and the "think different" phrase, in his keynote speech there. "There's a germ of a brilliant idea there," he said at the time. "Apple is about people who think outside the box, who want to use computers to help them change the world."

They debated the grammatical issue: If "different" was supposed to modify the verb "think," it should be an adverb, as in "think differently." But Jobs insisted that he wanted "different" to be used as a noun, as in "think victory" or "think beauty." Also, it echoed colloquial use, as in "think big." Jobs later explained, "We discussed whether it was correct before we ran it. It's grammatical, if you think about what we're trying to say. It's not think *the same*, it's think *different*. Think a little different, think a lot different, think different. 'Think *differently*' wouldn't hit the meaning for me."

In order to evoke the spirit of *Dead Poets Society*, Clow and Jobs wanted to get Robin Williams to read the narration. His agent said that Williams didn't do ads, so Jobs tried to call him directly. He got through to Williams's wife, who would not let him talk to the actor because she knew how persuasive he could be. They also considered Maya Angelou and Tom Hanks. At a fund-raising dinner featuring Bill Clinton that fall, Jobs pulled the president aside and asked him to telephone Hanks to talk him into it, but the president pocket-vetoed the request. They ended up with Richard Dreyfuss, who was a dedicated Apple fan.

In addition to the television commercials, they created one of the most memorable print campaigns in history. Each ad featured a black-and-white portrait of an iconic historical figure with just the Apple logo and the words "Think Different" in the corner. Making it particularly engaging was that the faces were not captioned. Some of them—Einstein, Gandhi, Lennon, Dylan, Picasso, Edison, Chaplin, King—were easy to identify. But others caused people to pause, puzzle, and maybe ask a friend to put a name to the face: Martha Graham, Ansel Adams, Richard Feynman, Maria Callas, Frank Lloyd Wright, James Watson, Amelia Earhart.

Most were Jobs's personal heroes. They tended to be creative people who had taken risks, defied failure, and bet their career on doing things in a different way. A photography buff, he became involved in making sure they had the perfect iconic portraits. "This is not the right picture of Gandhi," he erupted to Clow at one point. Clow explained that the famous Margaret Bourke-White photograph of Gandhi at the spinning wheel was owned by Time-Life Pictures and was not available for commercial use. So Jobs called Norman Pearlstine, the editor in chief of Time Inc., and badgered him into making an exception. He

A Portfolio of Diana Walker Photos

For almost thirty years, photographer Diana Walker
has had special access to her friend Steve Jobs.
Here is a selection from her portfolio.

1

At his home in Woodside, 1982: He was such a perfectionist that he had trouble buying furniture.

2

In his kitchen: "Coming back after seven months in Indian villages, I saw the craziness of the Western world as well as its capacity for rational thought."

3

At Stanford, 1982: "How many of you are virgins? How many of you have taken LSD?"

4

With the Lisa: "Picasso had a saying—'good artists copy, great artists steal'—and we have always been shameless about stealing great ideas."

5

With John Sculley in Central Park, 1984: "Do you want to spend the rest of your life selling sugared water, or do you want a chance to change the world?"

6

In his Apple office, 1982: Asked if he wanted to do market research, he said, "No, because customers don't know what they want until we've shown them."

7

At NeXT, 1988: Freed from the constraints at Apple, he indulged his own best and worst instincts.

8

With John Lasseter, August 1997: His cherubic face and demeanor masked an artistic perfectionism that rivaled that of Jobs.

At home working on his Boston Macworld speech after regaining command of
Apple, 1997: "In that craziness we see genius."

Sealing the Microsoft
deal by phone with
Gates: "Bill, thank
you for your support
of this company. I
think the world's a
better place for it."

At Boston Macworld, as Gates discusses their deal: "That was my worst and stupidest staging event ever. It made me look small."

With his wife, Laurene Powell, in their backyard in Palo Alto, August 1997: She was the sensible anchor in his life.

13

At his home office in Palo Alto, 2004: "I like living at the intersection of the humanities and technology."

From the Jobs Family Album

In August 2011, when Jobs was very ill, we sat in his room and went through wedding and vacation pictures for me to use in this book.

14

The wedding ceremony, 1991: Kobun Chino, Steve's Sōtō Zen teacher, shook a stick, struck a gong, lit incense, and chanted.

15

With his proud father Paul Jobs: After Steve's sister Mona tracked down their biological father, Steve refused ever to meet him.

LEFT: Cutting the cake in the shape of Half Dome with Laurene and his daughter from a previous relationship, Lisa Brennan.

BELOW: Laurene, Lisa, and Steve: Lisa moved into their home shortly afterward and stayed through her high school years.

Steve, Eve, Reed, Erin, and Laurene in Ravello, Italy, 2003: Even on vacation, he often withdrew into his work.

Dangling Eve in Foothills Park, Palo Alto: "She's a pistol and has the strongest will of any kid I've ever met. It's like payback."

19

20

With Laurene, Eve, Erin, and Lisa at the Corinth Canal in Greece, 2006: "For young people, this whole world is the same now."

With Erin in Kyoto,
2010: Like Reed
and Lisa, she got a
special trip to Japan
with her father.

21

22

With Reed in Kenya, 2007: "When I was diagnosed with cancer, I made my deal
with God or whatever, which was that I really wanted to see Reed graduate."

And just one more from Diana Walker: a 2004 portrait at his house in Palo Alto.

called Eunice Shriver to convince her family to release a picture that he loved, of her brother Bobby Kennedy touring Appalachia, and he talked to Jim Henson's children personally to get the right shot of the late Muppeteer.

He likewise called Yoko Ono for a picture of her late husband, John Lennon. She sent him one, but it was not Jobs's favorite. "Before it ran, I was in New York, and I went to this small Japanese restaurant that I love, and let her know I would be there," he recalled. When he arrived, she came over to his table. "This is a better one," she said, handing him an envelope. "I thought I would see you, so I had this with me." It was the classic photo of her and John in bed together, holding flowers, and it was the one that Apple ended up using. "I can see why John fell in love with her," Jobs recalled.

The narration by Richard Dreyfuss worked well, but Lee Clow had another idea. What if Jobs did the voice-over himself? "You really believe this," Clow told him. "You should do it." So Jobs sat in a studio, did a few takes, and soon produced a voice track that everyone liked. The idea was that, if they used it, they would not tell people who was speaking the words, just as they didn't caption the iconic pictures. Eventually people would figure out it was Jobs. "This will be really powerful to have it in your voice," Clow argued. "It will be a way to reclaim the brand."

Jobs couldn't decide whether to use the version with his voice or to stick with Dreyfuss. Finally, the night came when they had to ship the ad; it was due to air, appropriately enough, on the television premiere of *Toy Story*. As was often the case, Jobs did not like to be forced to make a decision. He told Clow to ship both versions; this would give him until the morning to decide. When morning came, Jobs called and told them to use the Dreyfuss version. "If we use my voice, when people find out they will say it's about me," he told Clow. "It's not. It's about Apple."

Ever since he left the apple commune, Jobs had defined himself, and by extension Apple, as a child of the counterculture. In ads such as "Think Different" and "1984," he positioned the Apple brand so that it reaffirmed his own rebel streak, even after he became a billionaire, and it allowed other baby boomers and their kids to do the same. "From when I first met him as a young guy, he's had the greatest intuition of the impact he wants his brand to have on people," said Clow.

Very few other companies or corporate leaders—perhaps none— could have gotten away with the brilliant audacity of associating their brand with Gandhi, Einstein, Picasso, and the Dalai Lama. Jobs was able to encourage people to define themselves as anticorporate, creative, innovative rebels simply by the computer they used. "Steve created the only lifestyle brand in the tech industry," Larry Ellison said. "There are cars people are proud to have—Porsche, Ferrari, Prius—because what I drive says something about me. People feel the same way about an Apple product."

Starting with the "Think Different" campaign, and continuing through the rest of his years at Apple, Jobs held a freewheeling three-hour meeting every Wednesday afternoon with his top agency, marketing, and communications people to kick around messaging strategy. "There's not a CEO on the planet who deals with marketing the way Steve does," said Clow. "Every Wednesday he approves each new commercial, print ad, and billboard." At the end of the meeting, he would often take Clow and his two agency colleagues, Duncan Milner and James Vincent, to Apple's closely guarded design studio to see what products were in the works. "He gets very passionate and emotional when he shows us what's in development," said Vincent. By sharing with his marketing gurus his passion for the products as they were being created, he was able to ensure that almost every ad they produced was infused with his emotion.

iCEO

As he was finishing work on the "Think Different" ad, Jobs did some different thinking of his own. He decided that he would officially take over running the company, at least on a temporary basis. He had been the de facto leader since Amelio's ouster ten weeks earlier, but only as an advisor. Fred Anderson had the titular role of interim CEO. On September 16, 1997, Jobs announced that he would take over that title, which inevitably got abbreviated as iCEO. His commitment was tentative: He took no salary and signed no contract. But he was not tentative in his actions. He was in charge, and he did not rule by consensus.

That week he gathered his top managers and staff in the Apple auditorium for a rally, followed by a picnic featuring beer and vegan food, to celebrate his new role and the company's new ads. He was wearing shorts, walking around the campus barefoot, and had a stubble of beard. "I've been back about ten weeks, working really hard," he said, looking tired but deeply determined. "What we're trying to do is not highfalutin. We're trying to get back to the basics of great products, great marketing, and great distribution. Apple has drifted away from doing the basics really well."

For a few more weeks Jobs and the board kept looking for a permanent CEO. Various names surfaced—George M. C. Fisher of Kodak, Sam Palmisano at IBM, Ed Zander at Sun Microsystems—but most of the candidates were understandably reluctant to consider becoming CEO if Jobs was going to remain an active board member. The *San Francisco Chronicle* reported that Zander declined to be considered because he "didn't want Steve looking over his shoulder, second-guessing him on every decision." At one point Jobs and Ellison pulled a prank on a clueless computer consultant who was campaigning for the job; they sent him an email saying that he had been selected, which caused both amusement and embarrassment when stories appeared in the papers that they were just toying with him.

By December it had become clear that Jobs's iCEO status had evolved from *interim* to *indefinite*. As Jobs continued to run the company, the board quietly deactivated its search. "I went back to Apple and tried to hire a CEO, with the help of a recruiting agency, for almost four months," he recalled. "But they didn't produce the right people. That's why I finally stayed. Apple was in no shape to attract anybody good."

The problem Jobs faced was that running two companies was brutal. Looking back on it, he traced his health problems back to those days:

It was rough, really rough, the worst time in my life. I had a young family. I had Pixar. I would go to work at 7 a.m. and I'd get back at 9 at night, and the kids would be in bed. And I couldn't speak, I literally couldn't, I was so exhausted. I couldn't speak to Laurene. All I could do was watch a half hour of TV and vegetate. It got close to killing me. I was driving up to Pixar and down to Apple in a black Porsche convertible, and I started to get kidney stones. I would rush to the hospital and the hospital would give me a shot of Demerol in the butt and eventually I would pass it.

Despite the grueling schedule, the more that Jobs immersed himself in Apple, the more he realized that he would not be able to walk away. When Michael Dell was asked at a computer trade show in October 1997 what he would do if he were Steve Jobs and taking over Apple, he replied, "I'd shut it down and give the money back to the shareholders." Jobs fired off an email to Dell. "CEOs are supposed to have class," it said. "I can see that isn't an opinion you hold." Jobs liked to stoke up rivalries as a way to rally his team—he had done so with IBM and Microsoft—and he did so with Dell. When he called together his managers to institute a build-to-order system for manufacturing and distribution, Jobs used as a backdrop a blown-up picture of Michael Dell with a target on his face. "We're coming after you, buddy," he said to cheers from his troops.

One of his motivating passions was to build a lasting company. At age twelve, when he got a summer job at Hewlett-Packard, he learned that a properly run company could spawn innovation far more than any single creative individual. "I discovered that the best innovation is sometimes the company, the way you organize a company," he recalled. "The whole notion of how you build a company is fascinating. When I got the chance to come back to Apple, I realized that I would be useless without the company, and that's why I decided to stay and rebuild it."

Killing the Clones

One of the great debates about Apple was whether it should have licensed its operating system more aggressively to other computer makers, the way Microsoft licensed Windows. Wozniak had favored that approach from the beginning. "We had the most beautiful operating system," he said, "but to get it you had to buy our hardware at twice the price. That was a mistake. What we should have done was calculate an appropriate price to license the operating system." Alan Kay, the star of Xerox PARC who came to Apple as a fellow in 1984, also fought hard for licensing the Mac OS software. "Software people are always multiplatform, because you want to run on everything," he recalled. "And that was a huge battle, probably the largest battle I lost at Apple."

Bill Gates, who was building a fortune by licensing Microsoft's operating system, had urged Apple to do the same in 1985, just as Jobs was being eased out. Gates believed that, even if Apple took away some of Microsoft's operating system customers, Microsoft could make money by creating versions of its applications software, such as Word and Excel, for the users of the Macintosh and its clones. "I was trying to do everything to get them to be a strong licensor," he recalled. He sent a formal memo to Sculley making the case. "The industry has reached the point where it is now impossible for Apple to create a standard out of their innovative technology without support from, and the resulting credibility of, other personal computer manufacturers," he argued. "Apple should license Macintosh technology to 3–5 significant manufacturers for the development of 'Mac Compatibles.'" Gates got no reply, so he wrote a second memo suggesting some companies that would be good at cloning the Mac, and he added, "I want to help in any way I can with the licensing. Please give me a call."

Apple resisted licensing out the Macintosh operating system until 1994, when CEO Michael Spindler allowed two small companies, Power Computing and Radius, to make Macintosh clones. When Gil Amelio took over in 1996, he added Motorola to the list. It turned out to be a dubious business strategy: Apple got an $80 licensing fee for each computer sold, but instead of expanding the market, the cloners cannibalized the sales of Apple's own high-end computers, on which it made up to $500 in profit.

Jobs's objections to the cloning program were not just economic, however. He had an inbred aversion to it. One of his core principles was that hardware and software should be tightly integrated. He loved to control all aspects of his life, and the only way to do that with computers was to take responsibility for the user experience from end to end.

So upon his return to Apple he made killing the Macintosh clones a priority. When a new version of the Mac operating system shipped in July 1997, weeks after he had helped oust Amelio, Jobs did not allow the clone makers to upgrade to it. The head of Power Computing, Stephen "King" Kahng, organized pro-cloning protests when Jobs appeared at Boston Macworld that August and publicly warned that the Macintosh OS would die if Jobs declined to keep licensing it out. "If the platform goes closed, it is over," Kahng said. "Total destruction. Closed is the kiss of death."

Jobs disagreed. He telephoned Ed Woolard to say he was getting Apple out of the licensing business. The board acquiesced, and in September he reached a deal to pay Power Computing $100 million to relinquish its license and give Apple access to its database of customers. He soon terminated the licenses of the other cloners as well. "It was the dumbest thing in the world to let companies making crappier hardware use our operating system and cut into our sales," he later said.

Product Line Review

One of Jobs's great strengths was knowing how to focus. "Deciding what *not* to do is as important as deciding what to do," he said. "That's true for companies, and it's true for products."

He went to work applying this principle as soon as he returned to Apple. One day he was walking the halls and ran into a young Wharton School graduate who had been Amelio's assistant and who said he was wrapping up his work. "Well, good, because I need someone to do grunt work," Jobs told him. His new role was to take notes as Jobs met with the dozens of product teams at Apple, asked them to explain what they were doing, and forced them to justify going ahead with their products or projects.

He also enlisted a friend, Phil Schiller, who had worked at Apple but was then at the graphics software company Macromedia. "Steve would summon the teams into the boardroom, which seats twenty, and they would come with thirty people and try to show PowerPoints, which Steve didn't want to see," Schiller recalled. One of the first things Jobs did during the product review process was ban PowerPoints. "I hate the way people use slide presentations instead of thinking," Jobs later recalled. "People would confront a problem by creating a presentation. I wanted them to engage, to hash things out at the table, rather than show a bunch of slides. People who know what they're talking about don't need PowerPoint."

The product review revealed how unfocused Apple had become. The company was churning out multiple versions of each product because of bureaucratic momentum and to satisfy the whims of retailers. "It was insanity," Schiller recalled. "Tons of products, most of them crap, done by deluded teams." Apple had a dozen versions of the Macintosh, each with a different confusing number, ranging from 1400 to 9600. "I had people explaining this to me for three weeks," Jobs said. "I couldn't figure it out." He finally began asking simple questions, like, "Which ones do I tell my friends to buy?"

When he couldn't get simple answers, he began slashing away at models and products. Soon he had cut 70% of them. "You are bright people," he told one group. "You shouldn't be wasting your time on such crappy products." Many of the engineers were infuriated at his slash-and-burn tactics, which resulted in massive layoffs. But Jobs later claimed that the good engineers, including some whose projects were killed, were appreciative. He told one staff meeting in September 1997, "I came out of the meeting with people who had just gotten their products canceled and they were three feet off the ground with excitement because they finally understood where in the heck we were going."

After a few weeks Jobs finally had enough. "Stop!" he shouted at one big product strategy session. "This is crazy." He grabbed a magic marker, padded to a whiteboard, and drew a horizontal and vertical line to make a four-squared chart. "Here's what we need," he continued. Atop the two columns he wrote "Consumer" and "Pro"; he labeled the two rows "Desktop" and "Portable." Their job, he said, was to make four great products, one for each quadrant. "The room was in dumb silence," Schiller recalled.

There was also a stunned silence when Jobs presented the plan to the September meeting of the Apple board. "Gil had been urging us to approve more and more products every meeting," Woolard recalled. "He kept saying we need more products. Steve came in and said we needed fewer. He drew a matrix with four quadrants and said that this was where we should focus." At first the board pushed back. It was a risk, Jobs was told. "I can make it work," he replied. The board never voted on the new strategy. Jobs was in charge, and he forged ahead.

The result was that the Apple engineers and managers suddenly became sharply focused on just four areas. For the professional desktop quadrant, they would work on making the Power Macintosh G3. For the professional portable, there would be the PowerBook G3. For the consumer desktop, work would begin on what became the iMac. And for the consumer portable, they would focus on what would become the iBook. The "i," Jobs later explained, was to emphasize that the devices would be seamlessly integrated with the Internet.

Apple's sharper focus meant getting the company out of other businesses, such as printers and servers. In 1997 Apple was selling StyleWriter color printers that were basically a version of the Hewlett-Packard DeskJet. HP made most of its money by selling the ink cartridges. "I don't understand," Jobs said at the product review meeting. "You're going to ship a million and not make money on these? This is nuts." He left the room and called the head of HP. Let's tear up our arrangement, Jobs proposed, and we will get out of the printer business and just let you do it. Then he came back to the boardroom and announced the decision. "Steve looked at the situation and instantly knew we needed to get outside of the box," Schiller recalled.

The most visible decision he made was to kill, once and for all, the Newton, the personal digital assistant with the almost-good handwriting-recognition system. Jobs hated it because it was Sculley's pet project, because it didn't work perfectly, and because he had an aversion to stylus devices. He had tried to get Amelio to kill it early in 1997 and succeeded only in convincing him to try to spin off the division. By late 1997, when Jobs did his product reviews, it was still around. He later described his thinking:

If Apple had been in a less precarious situation, I would have drilled down myself to figure out how to make it work. I didn't trust the people running it. My gut was that there was some really good technology, but it was fucked up by mismanagement. By shutting it down, I freed up some good engineers who could work on new mobile devices. And eventually we got it right when we moved on to iPhones and the iPad.

This ability to focus saved Apple. In his first year back, Jobs laid off more than three thousand people, which salvaged the company's balance sheet. For the fiscal year that ended when Jobs became interim CEO in September 1997, Apple lost $1.04 billion. "We were less than ninety days from being insolvent," he recalled. At the January 1998 San Francisco Macworld, Jobs took the stage where Amelio had bombed a year earlier. He sported a full beard and a leather jacket as he touted the new product strategy. And for the first time he ended the presentation with a phrase that he would make his signature coda: "Oh, and one more thing . . ." This time the "one more thing" was "Think Profit." When he said those words, the crowd erupted in applause. After two years of staggering losses, Apple had enjoyed a profitable quarter, making $45 million. For the full fiscal year of 1998, it would turn in a $309 million profit. Jobs was back, and so was Apple.

CHAPTER TWENTY-SIX

DESIGN PRINCIPLES

The Studio of Jobs and Ive

With Jony Ive and the sunflower iMac, 2002

Jony Ive

When Jobs gathered his top management for a pep talk just after he became iCEO in September 1997, sitting in the audience was a sensitive and passionate thirty-year-old Brit who was head of the company's design team. Jonathan Ive, known to all as Jony, was planning to quit. He was sick of the company's focus on profit maximization rather than product design. Jobs's talk led him to reconsider. "I remember very clearly Steve announcing that our goal is not just to make money but to make great products," Ive recalled. "The decisions you make based on that philosophy are fundamentally different from the ones we had been making at Apple." Ive and Jobs would soon forge a bond that would lead to the greatest industrial design collaboration of their era.

Ive grew up in Chingford, a town on the northeast edge of London. His father was a silversmith who taught at the local college. "He's a fantastic craftsman," Ive recalled. "His Christmas gift to me would be one day of his time in his college workshop, during the Christmas break when no one else was there, helping me make whatever I dreamed up." The only condition was that Jony had to draw by hand what they planned to make. "I always understood the beauty of things made by hand. I came to realize that what was really important was the care that was put into it. What I really despise is when I sense some carelessness in a product."

Ive enrolled in Newcastle Polytechnic and spent his spare time and summers working at a design consultancy. One of his creations was a pen with a little ball on top that was fun to fiddle with. It helped give the owner a playful emotional connection to the pen. For his thesis he designed a microphone and earpiece—in purest white plastic—to communicate with hearing-impaired kids. His flat was filled with foam models he had made to help him perfect the design. He also designed an ATM machine and a curved phone, both of which won awards from the Royal Society of Arts. Unlike some designers, he didn't just make beautiful sketches; he also focused on how the engineering and inner components would work. He had an epiphany in college when he was able to design on a Macintosh. "I discovered the Mac and felt I had a connection with the people who were making this product," he recalled. "I suddenly understood what a company was, or was supposed to be."

After graduation Ive helped to build a design firm in London, Tangerine, which got a consulting contract with Apple. In 1992 he moved to Cupertino to take a job in the Apple design department. He became the head of the department in 1996, the year before Jobs returned, but wasn't happy. Amelio had little appreciation for design. "There wasn't that feeling of putting care into a product, because we were trying to maximize the money we made," Ive said. "All they

wanted from us designers was a model of what something was supposed to look like on the outside, and then engineers would make it
as cheap as possible. I was about to quit."

When Jobs took over and gave his pep talk, Ive decided to stick
around. But Jobs at first looked around for a world-class designer from
the outside. He talked to Richard Sapper, who designed the IBM
ThinkPad, and Giorgetto Giugiaro, who designed the Ferrari 250 and
the Maserati Ghibli. But then he took a tour of Apple's design studio
and bonded with the affable, eager, and very earnest Ive. "We discussed
approaches to forms and materials," Ive recalled. "We were on the same
wavelength. I suddenly understood why I loved the company."

Ive reported, at least initially, to Jon Rubinstein, whom Jobs had
brought in to head the hardware division, but he developed a direct
and unusually strong relationship with Jobs. They began to have lunch
together regularly, and Jobs would end his day by dropping by Ive's design studio for a chat. "Jony had a special status," said Laurene Powell.
"He would come by our house, and our families became close. Steve
is never intentionally wounding to him. Most people in Steve's life are
replaceable. But not Jony."

Jobs described to me his respect for Ive:

> The difference that Jony has made, not only at Apple but in the world,
> is huge. He is a wickedly intelligent person in all ways. He understands
> business concepts, marketing concepts. He picks stuff up just like that,
> click. He understands what we do at our core better than anyone. If
> I had a spiritual partner at Apple, it's Jony. Jony and I think up most
> of the products together and then pull others in and say, "Hey, what do
> you think about this?" He gets the big picture as well as the most in-
> finitesimal details about each product. And he understands that Apple
> is a product company. He's not just a designer. That's why he works di-
> rectly for me. He has more operational power than anyone else at Apple
> except me. There's no one who can tell him what to do, or to butt out.
> That's the way I set it up.

Like most designers, Ive enjoyed analyzing the philosophy and
the step-by-step thinking that went into a particular design. For

Jobs, the process was more intuitive. He would point to models and sketches he liked and dump on the ones he didn't. Ive would then take the cues and develop the concepts Jobs blessed.

Ive was a fan of the German industrial designer Dieter Rams, who worked for the electronics firm Braun. Rams preached the gospel of "Less but better," *Weniger aber besser,* and likewise Jobs and Ive wrestled with each new design to see how much they could simplify it. Ever since Apple's first brochure proclaimed "Simplicity is the ultimate sophistication," Jobs had aimed for the simplicity that comes from conquering complexities, not ignoring them. "It takes a lot of hard work," he said, "to make something simple, to truly understand the underlying challenges and come up with elegant solutions."

In Ive, Jobs met his soul mate in the quest for true rather than surface simplicity. Sitting in his design studio, Ive described his philosophy:

> Why do we assume that simple is good? Because with physical products, we have to feel we can dominate them. As you bring order to complexity, you find a way to make the product defer to you. Simplicity isn't just a visual style. It's not just minimalism or the absence of clutter. It involves digging through the depth of the complexity. To be truly simple, you have to go really deep. For example, to have no screws on something, you can end up having a product that is so convoluted and so complex. The better way is to go deeper with the simplicity, to understand everything about it and how it's manufactured. You have to deeply understand the essence of a product in order to be able to get rid of the parts that are not essential.

That was the fundamental principle Jobs and Ive shared. Design was not just about what a product looked like on the surface. It had to reflect the product's essence. "In most people's vocabularies, design means veneer," Jobs told *Fortune* shortly after retaking the reins at Apple. "But to me, nothing could be further from the meaning of design. Design is the fundamental soul of a man-made creation that ends up expressing itself in successive outer layers."

As a result, the process of designing a product at Apple was integrally related to how it would be engineered and manufactured. Ive described one of Apple's Power Macs. "We wanted to get rid of anything other than what was absolutely essential," he said. "To do so required total collaboration between the designers, the product developers, the engineers, and the manufacturing team. We kept going back to the beginning, again and again. Do we need that part? Can we get it to perform the function of the other four parts?"

The connection between the design of a product, its essence, and its manufacturing was illustrated for Jobs and Ive when they were traveling in France and went into a kitchen supply store. Ive picked up a knife he admired, but then put it down in disappointment. Jobs did the same. "We both noticed a tiny bit of glue between the handle and the blade," Ive recalled. They talked about how the knife's good design had been ruined by the way it was manufactured. "We don't like to think of our knives as being glued together," Ive said. "Steve and I care about things like that, which ruin the purity and detract from the essence of something like a utensil, and we think alike about how products should be made to look pure and seamless."

At most other companies, engineering tends to drive the outer design elements of a product. The engineers set forth their specifications and requirements, and the designers then come up with cases and shells that will accommodate them. For Jobs, the process tended to work the other way. In the early days of Apple, Jobs had approved the design of the case of the original Macintosh, and the engineers had to make their boards and components fit.

After he was forced out, the process at Apple reverted to being engineer-driven. "Before Steve came back, engineers would say 'Here are the guts'—processor, hard drive—and then it would go to the designers to put it in a box," said Apple's marketing chief Phil Schiller. "When you do it that way, you come up with awful products." But when Jobs returned and forged his bond with Ive, the balance was again tilted toward the designers. "Steve kept impressing on us that the design was integral to what would make us great," said Schiller. "Design once again dictated the engineering, not just vice versa."

On occasion this could backfire, such as when Jobs and Ive insisted on using a solid piece of stainless steel for the edge of the iPhone 4 even when the engineers worried that it would compromise reception. But usually the distinctiveness of its designs—for the iMac, the iPod, the iPhone, and the iPad—would set Apple apart and lead to its triumphs in the years after Jobs returned.

Inside the Studio

The design studio where Jony Ive reigns, on the ground floor of Two Infinite Loop on the Apple campus, is shielded by tinted windows and a heavy clad, locked door. Just inside is a glass-booth reception desk where two assistants guard access. Even high-level Apple employees are not allowed in without special permission. Most of my interviews with Jony Ive for this book were held elsewhere, but one day in 2010 he arranged for me to spend an afternoon touring the studio and talking about how he and Jobs collaborate there.

To the left of the entrance is a bullpen of desks with young designers; to the right is the cavernous main room with six long steel tables for displaying and playing with works in progress. Beyond the main room is a computer-aided design studio, filled with workstations, that leads to a room with molding machines to turn what's on the screens into foam models. Beyond that is a robot-controlled spray-painting chamber to make the models look real. The look is sparse and industrial, with metallic gray décor. Leaves from the trees outside cast moving patterns of light and shadows on the tinted windows. Techno and jazz play in the background.

Almost every day when Jobs was healthy and in the office, he would have lunch with Ive and then wander by the studio in the afternoon. As he entered, he could survey the tables and see the products in the pipeline, sense how they fit into Apple's strategy, and inspect with his fingertips the evolving design of each. Usually it was just the two of them alone, while the other designers glanced up from their work but kept a respectful distance. If Jobs had a specific issue, he might call over the head of mechanical design or another of Ive's deputies. If something excited him or sparked some thoughts about corporate strategy, he might ask the chief operating officer Tim Cook or the marketing head Phil Schiller to come over and join them. Ive described the usual process:

> This great room is the one place in the company where you can look around and see everything we have in the works. When Steve comes in, he will sit at one of these tables. If we're working on a new iPhone, for example, he might grab a stool and start playing with different models and feeling them in his hands, remarking on which ones he likes best. Then he will graze by the other tables, just him and me, to see where all the other products are heading. He can get a sense of the sweep of the whole company, the iPhone and iPad, the iMac and laptop and everything we're considering. That helps him see where the company is spending its energy and how things connect. And he can ask, "Does doing this make sense, because over here is where we are growing a lot?" or questions like that. He gets to see things in relationship to each other, which is pretty hard to do in a big company. Looking at the models on these tables, he can see the future for the next three years.
>
> Much of the design process is a conversation, a back-and-forth as we walk around the tables and play with the models. He doesn't like to read complex drawings. He wants to see and feel a model. He's right. I get surprised when we make a model and then realize it's rubbish, even though based on the CAD [computer-aided design] renderings it looked great.
>
> He loves coming in here because it's calm and gentle. It's a paradise if you're a visual person. There are no formal design reviews, so there are no huge decision points. Instead, we can make the decisions fluid. Since we iterate every day and never have dumb-ass presentations, we don't run into major disagreements.

On this day Ive was overseeing the creation of a new European power plug and connector for the Macintosh. Dozens of foam models, each with the tiniest variation, have been cast and painted for inspection. Some would find it odd that the head of design would fret over something like this, but Jobs got involved as well. Ever since he had a special power supply made for the Apple II, Jobs has cared about not only the engineering but also the design of such parts. His name is listed on the patent for the white power brick used by the MacBook as well as its magnetic connector with its satisfying click. In fact he is listed as one of the inventors for 212 different Apple patents in the United States as of the beginning of 2011.

Ive and Jobs have even obsessed over, and patented, the packaging for various Apple products. U.S. patent D558572, for example, granted on January 1, 2008, is for the iPod Nano box, with four drawings showing how the device is nestled in a cradle when the box is opened. Patent D596485, issued on July 21, 2009, is for the iPhone packaging, with its sturdy lid and little glossy plastic tray inside.

Early on, Mike Markkula had taught Jobs to "impute"—to understand that people *do* judge a book by its cover—and therefore to make sure all the trappings and packaging of Apple signaled that there was a beautiful gem inside. Whether it's an iPod Mini or a MacBook Pro, Apple customers know the feeling of opening up the well-crafted box and finding the product nestled in an inviting fashion. "Steve and I spend a lot of time on the packaging," said Ive. "I love the process of unpacking something. You design a ritual of unpacking to make the product feel special. Packaging can be theater, it can create a story."

Ive, who has the sensitive temperament of an artist, at times got upset with Jobs for taking too much credit, a habit that has bothered other colleagues over the years. His personal feelings for Jobs were so intense that at times he got easily bruised. "He will go through a process of looking at my ideas and say, 'That's no good. That's not very good. I like that one,'" Ive said. "And later I will be sitting in the audience and he will be talking about it as if it was his idea. I pay maniacal attention to where an idea comes from, and I even keep notebooks filled with my ideas. So it hurts when he takes credit for one of my designs." Ive also has bristled when outsiders portrayed Jobs as the only ideas guy at Apple. "That makes us vulnerable as a company," Ive said earnestly, his voice soft. But then he paused to recognize the role Jobs in fact played. "In so many other companies, ideas and great design get lost in the process," he said. "The ideas that come from me and my team would have been completely irrelevant, nowhere, if Steve hadn't been here to push us, work with us, and drive through all the resistance to turn our ideas into products."

CHAPTER TWENTY-SEVEN

THE iMAC

Hello (Again)

Back to the Future

The first great design triumph to come from the Jobs-Ive collaboration was the iMac, a desktop computer aimed at the home consumer market that was introduced in May 1998. Jobs had certain specifications. It should be an all-in-one product, with keyboard and monitor and computer ready to use right out of the box. It should have a distinctive design that made a brand statement. And it should sell for $1,200 or so. (Apple had no computer selling for less than $2,000 at the time.) "He told us to go back to the roots of the original 1984 Macintosh, an all-in-one consumer appliance," recalled Schiller. "That meant design and engineering had to work together."

The initial plan was to build a "network computer," a concept championed by Oracle's Larry Ellison, which was an inexpensive terminal without a hard drive that would mainly be used to connect to the Internet and other networks. But Apple's chief financial officer Fred Anderson led the push to make the product more robust by adding a disk drive so it could become a full-fledged desktop computer for the home. Jobs eventually agreed.

Jon Rubinstein, who was in charge of hardware, adapted the microprocessor and guts of the PowerMac G3, Apple's high-end professional computer, for use in the proposed new machine. It would have a hard drive and a tray for compact disks, but in a rather bold move, Jobs and Rubinstein decided not to include the usual floppy disk drive. Jobs quoted the hockey star Wayne Gretzky's maxim, "Skate where the puck's going, not where it's been." He was a bit ahead of his time, but eventually most computers eliminated floppy disks.

Ive and his top deputy, Danny Coster, began to sketch out futuristic designs. Jobs brusquely rejected the dozen foam models they initially produced, but Ive knew how to guide him gently. Ive agreed that none of them was quite right, but he pointed out one that had promise. It was curved, playful looking, and did not seem like an unmovable slab rooted to the table. "It has a sense that it's just arrived on your desktop or it's just about to hop off and go somewhere," he told Jobs.

By the next showing Ive had refined the playful model. This time Jobs, with his binary view of the world, raved that he loved it. He took the foam prototype and began carrying it around the headquarters with him, showing it in confidence to trusted lieutenants and board members. In its ads Apple was celebrating the glories of being able to think different, yet until now nothing had been proposed that was much different from existing computers. Finally, Jobs had something new.

The plastic casing that Ive and Coster proposed was sea-green blue, later named bondi blue after the color of the water at a beach in Australia, and it was translucent so that you could see through to the inside of the machine. "We were trying to convey a sense of the computer being changeable based on your needs, to be like a chameleon," said Ive. "That's why we liked the translucency. You could have color but it felt so unstatic. And it came across as cheeky."

Both metaphorically and in reality, the translucency connected the inner engineering of the computer to the outer design. Jobs had always insisted that the rows of chips on the circuit boards look neat, even though they would never be seen. Now they would be seen. The casing would make visible the care that had gone into making all components of the computer and fitting them together. The playful design would convey simplicity while also revealing the depths that true simplicity entails.

Even the simplicity of the plastic shell itself involved great complexity. Ive and his team worked with Apple's Korean manufacturers to perfect the process of making the cases, and they even went to a jelly bean factory to study how to make translucent colors look enticing. The cost of each case was more than $60 per unit, three times that of a regular computer case. Other companies would probably have demanded presentations and studies to show whether the translucent case would increase sales enough to justify the extra cost. Jobs asked for no such analysis.

Topping off the design was the handle nestled into the iMac. It was more playful and semiotic than it was functional. This was a desktop computer; not many people were really going to carry it around. But as Ive later explained:

Back then, people weren't comfortable with technology. If you're scared of something, then you won't touch it. I could see my mum being scared to touch it. So I thought, if there's this handle on it, it makes a relationship possible. It's approachable. It's intuitive. It gives you permission to touch. It gives a sense of its deference to you. Unfortunately, manufacturing a recessed handle costs a lot of money. At the old Apple, I would have lost the argument. What was really great about Steve is that he saw it and said, "That's cool!" I didn't explain all the thinking, but he intuitively got it. He just knew that it was part of the iMac's friendliness and playfulness.

Jobs had to fend off the objections of the manufacturing engineers, supported by Rubinstein, who tended to raise practical cost considerations when faced with Ive's aesthetic desires and various design whims. "When we took it to the engineers," Jobs said, "they came up with thirty-eight reasons they couldn't do it. And I said, 'No, no, we're doing this.' And they said, 'Well, why?' And I said, 'Because I'm the CEO, and I think it can be done.' And so they kind of grudgingly did it."

Jobs asked Lee Clow and Ken Segall and others from the TBWA\Chiat\Day ad team to fly up to see what he had in the works. He brought them into the guarded design studio and dramatically unveiled Ive's translucent teardrop-shaped design, which looked like something from *The Jetsons*, the animated TV show set in the future. For a moment they were taken aback. "We were pretty shocked, but we couldn't be frank," Segall recalled. "We were really thinking, 'Jesus, do they know what they are doing?' It was so radical." Jobs asked them to suggest names. Segall came back with five options, one of them "iMac." Jobs didn't like any of them at first, so Segall came up with another list a week later, but he said that the agency still preferred "iMac." Jobs replied, "I don't hate it this week, but I still don't like it." He tried silk-screening it on some of the prototypes, and the name grew on him. And thus it became the iMac.

As the deadline for completing the iMac drew near, Jobs's legendary temper reappeared in force, especially when he was confronting manufacturing issues. At one product review meeting, he learned that the process was going slowly. "He did one of his displays of awesome fury, and the fury was absolutely pure," recalled Ive. He went around the table assailing everyone, starting with Rubinstein. "You know we're trying to save the company here," he shouted, "and you guys are screwing it up!"

Like the original Macintosh team, the iMac crew staggered to completion just in time for the big announcement. But not before Jobs had one last explosion. When it came time to rehearse for the launch presentation, Rubinstein cobbled together two working prototypes. Jobs had not seen the final product before, and when he looked at it onstage he saw a button on the front, under the display. He pushed it and the CD tray opened. "What the fuck is this?!?" he asked, though not as politely. "None of us said anything," Schiller recalled, "because he obviously knew what a CD tray was." So Jobs continued to rail. It was supposed to have a clean CD slot, he insisted, referring to the elegant slot drives that were already to be found in upscale cars. "Steve, this is exactly the drive I showed you when we talked about the components," Rubinstein explained. "No, there was never a tray, just a slot," Jobs insisted. Rubinstein didn't back down. Jobs's fury didn't abate. "I almost started crying, because it was too late to do anything about it," Jobs later recalled.

They suspended the rehearsal, and for a while it seemed as if Jobs might cancel the entire product launch. "Ruby looked at me as if to say, 'Am I crazy?'" Schiller recalled. "It was my first product launch with Steve and the first time I saw his mind-set of 'If it's not right we're not launching it.'" Finally, they agreed to replace the tray with a slot drive for the next version of the iMac. "I'm only going to go ahead with the launch if you promise we're going to go to slot mode as soon as possible," Jobs said tearfully.

There was also a problem with the video he planned to show. In it, Jony Ive is shown describing his design thinking and asking, "What computer would the Jetsons have had? It was like, the future yesterday." At that moment there was a two-second snippet from the cartoon show, showing Jane Jetson looking at a video screen, followed by another two-second clip of the Jetsons giggling by a Christmas tree. At a rehearsal a production assistant told Jobs they would have to remove the clips because Hanna-Barbera had not given permission to use them. "Keep it in," Jobs barked at him. The assistant explained that there were rules against that. "I don't care," Jobs said. "We're using it." The clip stayed in.

Lee Clow was preparing a series of colorful magazine ads, and when he sent Jobs the page proofs he got an outraged phone call in response. The blue in the ad, Jobs insisted, was different from that of the iMac. "You guys don't know what you're doing!" Jobs shouted. "I'm going to get someone else to do the ads, because this is fucked up." Clow argued back. Compare them, he said. Jobs, who was not in the office, insisted he was right and continued to shout. Eventually Clow got him to sit down with the original photographs. "I finally proved to him that the blue was the blue was the blue." Years later, on a Steve Jobs discussion board on the website Gawker, the following tale appeared from someone who had worked at the Whole Foods store in Palo Alto a few blocks from Jobs's home: "I was shagging carts one afternoon when I saw this silver Mercedes parked in a handicapped spot. Steve Jobs was inside screaming at his car phone. This was right before the first iMac was unveiled and I'm pretty sure I could make out, 'Not. Fucking. Blue. Enough!!!' "

As always, Jobs was compulsive in preparing for the dramatic unveiling. Having stopped one rehearsal because he was angry about the CD drive tray, he stretched out the other rehearsals to make sure the show would be stellar. He repeatedly went over the climactic moment when he would walk across the stage and proclaim, "Say hello to the new iMac." He wanted the lighting to be perfect so that the translucence of the new machine would be vivid. But after a few run-throughs he was still unsatisfied, an echo of his obsession with stage lighting that Sculley had witnessed at the rehearsals for the original 1984 Macintosh launch. He ordered the lights to be brighter and come on earlier, but that still didn't please him. So he jogged down the auditorium aisle and slouched into a center seat, draping his legs over the seat in front. "Let's keep doing it till we get it right, okay?" he said. They made another attempt. "No, no," Jobs complained. "This isn't working at all." The next time, the lights were bright enough, but they came on too late. "I'm getting tired of asking about this," Jobs growled. Finally, the iMac shone just right. "Oh! Right there! That's great!" Jobs yelled.

A year earlier Jobs had ousted Mike Markkula, his early mentor and partner, from the board. But he was so proud of what he had wrought with the new iMac, and so sentimental about its connection to the original Macintosh, that he invited Markkula to Cupertino for a private preview. Markkula was impressed. His only objection was to the new mouse that Ive had designed. It looked like a hockey puck, Markkula said, and people would hate it. Jobs disagreed, but Markkula was right. Otherwise the machine had turned out to be, as had its predecessor, insanely great.

The Launch, May 6, 1998

With the launch of the original Macintosh in 1984, Jobs had created a new kind of theater: the product debut as an epochal event, climaxed by a let-there-be-light moment in which the skies part, a light shines down, the angels sing, and a chorus of the chosen faithful sings "Hallelujah." For the grand unveiling of the product that he hoped would save Apple and again transform personal computing, Jobs symbolically chose the Flint Auditorium of De Anza Community College in Cupertino, the same venue he had used in 1984. He would be pulling out all the stops in order to dispel doubts, rally the troops, enlist support in the developers' community, and jump-start the marketing of the new machine. But he was also doing it because he enjoyed playing impresario. Putting on a great show piqued his passions in the same way as putting out a great product.

Displaying his sentimental side, he began with a graceful shout-out to three people he had invited to be up front in the audience. He had become estranged from all of them, but now he wanted them rejoined. "I started the company with Steve Wozniak in my parents' garage, and Steve is here today," he said, pointing him out and prompting applause. "We were joined by Mike Markkula and soon after that our first president, Mike Scott," he continued. "Both of those folks are in the audience today. And none of us would be here without these three guys." His eyes misted for a moment as the applause again built. Also in the audience were Andy Hertzfeld and most of the original Mac team. Jobs gave them a smile. He believed he was about to do them proud.

After showing the grid of Apple's new product strategy and going through some slides about the new computer's performance, he was ready to unveil his new baby. "This is what computers look like today," he said as a picture of a beige set of boxy components and monitor was projected on the big screen behind him. "And I'd like to take the privilege of showing you what they are going to look like from today on." He pulled the cloth from the table at center stage to reveal the new iMac, which gleamed and sparkled as the lights came up on cue. He pressed the mouse, and as at the launch of the original Macintosh, the screen flashed with fast-paced images of all the wondrous things the computer could do. At the end, the word "hello" appeared in the same playful script that had adorned the 1984 Macintosh, this time with the word "again" below it in parentheses: *Hello (again)*. There was thunderous applause. Jobs stood back and proudly gazed at his new Macintosh. "It looks like it's from another planet," he said, as the audience laughed. "A good planet. A planet with better designers."

Once again Jobs had produced an iconic new product, this one a harbinger of a new millennium. It fulfilled the promise of "Think Different." Instead of beige boxes and monitors with a welter of cables and a bulky setup manual, here was a friendly and spunky appliance, smooth to the touch and as pleasing to the eye as a robin's egg. You could grab its cute little handle and lift it out of the elegant white box and plug it right into a wall socket. People who had been afraid of computers now wanted one, and they wanted to put it in a room where others could admire and perhaps covet it. "A piece of hardware that blends sci-fi shimmer with the kitsch whimsy of a cocktail umbrella," Steven Levy wrote in *Newsweek*, "it is not only the coolest-looking computer introduced in years, but a chest-thumping statement that Silicon Valley's original dream company is no longer somnambulant." *Forbes* called it "an industry-altering success," and John Sculley later came out of exile to gush, "He has implemented the same simple strategy that made Apple so successful 15 years ago: make hit products and promote them with terrific marketing."

Carping was heard from only one familiar corner. As the iMac garnered kudos, Bill Gates assured a gathering of financial analysts visiting Microsoft that this would be a passing fad. "The one thing Apple's providing now is leadership in colors," Gates said as he pointed to a Windows-based PC that he jokingly had painted red. "It won't take long for us to catch up with that, I don't think." Jobs was furious, and he told a reporter that Gates, the man he had publicly decried for being completely devoid of taste, was clueless about what made the iMac so much more appealing than other computers. "The thing that our competitors are missing is that they think it's about fashion, and they think it's about surface appearance," he said. "They say, We'll slap a little color on this piece of junk computer, and we'll have one, too."

The iMac went on sale in August 1998 for $1,299. It sold 278,000 units in its first six weeks, and would sell 800,000 by the end of the year, making it the fastest-selling computer in Apple history. Most notably, 32% of the sales went to people who were buying a computer for the first time, and another 12% to people who had been using Windows machines.

Ive soon came up with four new juicy-looking colors, in addition to bondi blue, for the iMacs. Offering the same computer in five colors would of course create huge challenges for manufacturing, inventory, and distribution. At most companies, including even the old Apple, there would have been studies and meetings to look at the costs and benefits. But when Jobs looked at the new colors, he got totally psyched and summoned other executives over to the design studio. "We're going to do all sorts of colors!" he told them excitedly. When they left, Ive looked at his team in amazement. "In most places that decision would have taken months," Ive recalled. "Steve did it in a half hour."

There was one other important refinement that Jobs wanted for the iMac: getting rid of that detested CD tray. "I'd seen a slot-load drive on a very high-end Sony stereo," he said, "so I went to the drive manufacturers and got them to do a slot-load drive for us for the version of the iMac we did nine months later." Rubinstein tried to argue him out of the change. He predicted that new drives would come along that could burn music onto CDs rather than merely play them, and they would be available in tray form before they were made to work in slots. "If you go to slots, you will always be behind on the technology," Rubinstein argued.

"I don't care, that's what I want," Jobs snapped back. They were having lunch at a sushi bar in San Francisco, and Jobs insisted that they continue the conversation over a walk. "I want you to do the slot-load drive for me as a personal favor," Jobs asked. Rubinstein agreed, of course, but he turned out to be right. Panasonic came out with a CD drive that could rip and burn music, and it was available first for computers that had old-fashioned tray loaders. The effects of this would ripple over the next few years: It would cause Apple to be slow in catering to users who wanted to rip and burn their own music, but that would then force Apple to be imaginative and bold in finding a way to leapfrog over its competitors when Jobs finally realized that he had to get into the music market.

CHAPTER TWENTY-EIGHT

CEO

Still Crazy after All These Years

Tim Cook and Jobs, 2007

Tim Cook

When Steve Jobs returned to Apple and produced the "Think Different" ads and the iMac in his first year, it confirmed what most people already knew: that he could be creative and a visionary. He had shown that during his first round at Apple. What was less clear was whether he could run a company. He had definitely *not* shown that during his first round.

Jobs threw himself into the task with a detail-oriented realism that astonished those who were used to his fantasy that the rules of this universe need not apply to him. "He became a manager, which is different from being an executive or visionary, and that pleasantly surprised me," recalled Ed Woolard, the board chair who lured him back.

His management mantra was "Focus." He eliminated excess product lines and cut extraneous features in the new operating system software that Apple was developing. He let go of his control-freak desire to manufacture products in his own factories and instead outsourced the making of everything from the circuit boards to the finished computers. And he enforced on Apple's suppliers a rigorous discipline. When he took over, Apple had more than two months' worth of inventory sitting in warehouses, more than any other tech company. Like eggs and milk, computers have a short shelf life, so this amounted to at least a $500 million hit to profits. By early 1998 he had halved that to a month.

Jobs's successes came at a cost, since velvety diplomacy was still not part of his repertoire. When he decided that a division of Airborne Express wasn't delivering spare parts quickly enough, he ordered an Apple manager to break the contract. When the manager protested that doing so could lead to a lawsuit, Jobs replied, "Just tell them if they fuck with us, they'll never get another fucking dime from this company, ever." The manager quit, there was a lawsuit, and it took a year to resolve. "My stock options would be worth $10 million had I stayed," the manager said, "but I knew I couldn't have stood it—and he'd have fired me anyway." The new distributor was ordered to cut inventory 75%, and did. "Under Steve Jobs, there's zero tolerance for not performing," its CEO said. At another point, when VLSI Technology was having trouble delivering enough chips on time, Jobs stormed into a meeting and started shouting that they were "fucking dickless assholes." The company ended up getting the chips to Apple on time, and its executives made jackets that boasted on the back, "Team FDA."

After three months of working under Jobs, Apple's head of operations decided he could not bear the pressure, and he quit. For almost a year Jobs ran operations himself, because all the prospects he interviewed "seemed like they were old-wave manufacturing people," he recalled. He wanted someone who could build just-in-time factories and supply chains, as Michael Dell had done. Then, in 1998, he met Tim Cook, a courtly thirty-seven-year-old procurement and supply chain manager at Compaq Computers, who not only would become his operations manager but would grow into an indispensable back-stage partner in running Apple. As Jobs recalled:

> Tim Cook came out of procurement, which is just the right background for what we needed. I realized that he and I saw things exactly the same way. I had visited a lot of just-in-time factories in Japan, and I'd built one for the Mac and at NeXT. I knew what I wanted, and I met Tim, and he wanted the same thing. So we started to work together, and before long I trusted him to know exactly what to do. He had the same vision I did, and we could interact at a high strategic level, and I could just forget about a lot of things unless he came and pinged me.

Cook, the son of a shipyard worker, was raised in Robertsdale, Alabama, a small town between Mobile and Pensacola a half hour from the Gulf Coast. He majored in industrial engineering at Auburn, got a business degree at Duke, and for the next twelve years worked for IBM in the Research Triangle of North Carolina. When Jobs interviewed him, he had recently taken a job at Compaq. He had always been a very logical engineer, and Compaq then seemed a more sensible career option, but he was snared by Jobs's aura. "Five minutes into my initial interview with Steve, I wanted to throw caution and logic to the wind and join Apple," he later said. "My intuition told me that joining Apple would be a once-in-a-lifetime opportunity to work for a creative genius." And so he did. "Engineers are taught to make a decision analytically, but there are times when relying on gut or intuition is most indispensable."

At Apple his role became implementing Jobs's intuition, which he accomplished with a quiet diligence. Never married, he threw himself into his work. He was up most days at 4:30 sending emails, then spent an hour at the gym, and was at his desk shortly after 6. He scheduled Sunday evening conference calls to prepare for each week ahead. In a company that was led by a CEO prone to tantrums and withering blasts, Cook commanded situations with a calm demeanor, a soothing Alabama accent, and silent stares. "Though he's capable of mirth, Cook's default facial expression is a frown, and his humor is of the dry variety," Adam Lashinsky wrote in *Fortune*. "In meetings he's known for long, uncomfortable pauses, when all you hear is the sound of his tearing the wrapper off the energy bars he constantly eats."

At a meeting early in his tenure, Cook was told of a problem with one of Apple's Chinese suppliers. "This is really bad," he said. "Someone should be in China driving this." Thirty minutes later he looked at an operations executive sitting at the table and unemotionally asked, "Why are you still here?" The executive stood up, drove directly to the San Francisco airport, and bought a ticket to China. He became one of Cook's top deputies.

Cook reduced the number of Apple's key suppliers from a hundred to twenty-four, forced them to cut better deals to keep the business, convinced many to locate next to Apple's plants, and closed ten of the company's nineteen warehouses. By reducing the places where inventory could pile up, he reduced inventory. Jobs had cut inventory from two months' worth of product down to one by early 1998. By September of that year, Cook had gotten it down to six days. By the following September, it was down to an amazing two days' worth. In addition, he cut the production process for making an Apple computer from four months to two. All of this not only saved money, it also allowed each new computer to have the very latest components available.

Mock Turtlenecks and Teamwork

On a trip to Japan in the early 1980s, Jobs asked Sony's chairman, Akio Morita, why everyone in his company's factories wore uniforms. "He looked very ashamed and told me that after the war, no one had any clothes, and companies like Sony had to give their workers something to wear each day," Jobs recalled. Over the years the uniforms developed their own signature style, especially at companies such as Sony, and it became a way of bonding workers to the company. "I decided that I wanted that type of bonding for Apple," Jobs recalled.

Sony, with its appreciation for style, had gotten the famous designer

Issey Miyake to create one of its uniforms. It was a jacket made of ripstop nylon with sleeves that could unzip to make it a vest. "So I called Issey and asked him to design a vest for Apple," Jobs recalled. "I came back with some samples and told everyone it would be great if we would all wear these vests. Oh man, did I get booed off the stage. Everybody hated the idea."

In the process, however, he became friends with Miyake and would visit him regularly. He also came to like the idea of having a uniform for himself, because of both its daily convenience (the rationale he claimed) and its ability to convey a signature style. "So I asked Issey to make me some of his black turtlenecks that I liked, and he made me like a hundred of them." Jobs noticed my surprise when he told this story, so he gestured to them stacked up in the closet. "That's what I wear," he said. "I have enough to last for the rest of my life."

Despite his autocratic nature—he never worshipped at the altar of consensus—Jobs worked hard to foster a culture of collaboration at Apple. Many companies pride themselves on having few meetings. Jobs had many: an executive staff session every Monday, a marketing strategy session all Wednesday afternoon, and endless product review sessions. Still allergic to PowerPoints and formal presentations, he insisted that the people around the table hash out issues from various vantages and the perspectives of different departments.

Because he believed that Apple's great advantage was its integration of the whole widget—from design to hardware to software to content—he wanted all departments at the company to work together in parallel. The phrases he used were "deep collaboration" and "concurrent engineering." Instead of a development process in which a product would be passed sequentially from engineering to design to manufacturing to marketing and distribution, these various departments collaborated simultaneously. "Our method was to develop integrated products, and that meant our process had to be integrated and collaborative," Jobs said.

This approach also applied to key hires. He would have candidates meet the top leaders—Cook, Tevanian, Schiller, Rubinstein, Ive—rather than just the managers of the department where they wanted to work. "Then we all get together without the person and talk about whether they'll fit in," Jobs said. His goal was to be vigilant against "the bozo explosion" that leads to a company's being larded with second-rate talent:

> For most things in life, the range between best and average is 30% or so. The best airplane flight, the best meal, they may be 30% better than your average one. What I saw with Woz was somebody who was fifty times better than the average engineer. He could have meetings in his head. The Mac team was an attempt to build a whole team like that, A players. People said they wouldn't get along, they'd hate working with each other. But I realized that A players like to work with A players, they just didn't like working with C players. At Pixar, it was a whole company of A players. When I got back to Apple, that's what I decided to try to do. You need to have a collaborative hiring process. When we hire someone, even if they're going to be in marketing, I will have them talk to the design folks and the engineers. My role model was J. Robert Oppenheimer. I read about the type of people he sought for the atom bomb project. I wasn't nearly as good as he was, but that's what I aspired to do.

The process could be intimidating, but Jobs had an eye for talent. When they were looking for people to design the graphical interface for Apple's new operating system, Jobs got an email from a young man and invited him in. The applicant was nervous, and the meeting did not go well. Later that day Jobs bumped into him, dejected, sitting in the lobby. The guy asked if he could just show him one of his ideas, so Jobs looked over his shoulder and saw a little demo, using Adobe Director, of a way to fit more icons in the dock at the bottom of a screen. When the guy moved the cursor over the icons crammed into the dock, the cursor mimicked a magnifying glass and made each icon balloon bigger. "I said, 'My God,' and hired him on the spot," Jobs recalled. The feature became a lovable part of Mac OSX, and the designer went on to design such things as inertial scrolling for multi-touch screens (the delightful feature that makes the screen keep gliding for a moment after you've finished swiping).

Jobs's experiences at NeXT had matured him, but they had not mellowed him much. He still had no license plate on his Mercedes, and he still parked in the handicapped spaces next to the front door, sometimes straddling two slots. It became a running gag. Employees made signs saying, "Park Different," and someone painted over the handicapped wheelchair symbol with a Mercedes logo.

People were allowed, even encouraged, to challenge him, and sometimes he would respect them for it. But you had to be prepared for him to attack you, even bite your head off, as he processed your ideas. "You never win an argument with him at the time, but sometimes you eventually win," said James Vincent, the creative young adman who worked with Lee Clow. "You propose something and he declares, 'That's a stupid idea,' and later he comes back and says, 'Here's what we're going to do.' And you want to say, 'That's what I told you two weeks ago and you said that's a stupid idea.' But you can't do that. Instead you say, 'That's a great idea, let's do that.'"

People also had to put up with Jobs's occasional irrational or incorrect assertions. To both family and colleagues, he was apt to declare, with great conviction, some scientific or historical fact that had scant relationship to reality. "There can be something he knows absolutely nothing about, and because of his crazy style and utter conviction, he can convince people that he knows what he's talking about," said Ive, who described the trait as weirdly endearing. Yet with his eye for detail, Jobs sometimes correctly pounced on tiny things others had missed. Lee Clow recalled showing Jobs a cut of a commercial, making some minor changes he requested, and then being assaulted with a tirade about how the ad had been completely destroyed. "He discovered we had cut two extra frames, something so fleeting it was nearly impossible to notice," said Clow. "But he wanted to be sure that an image hit at the exact moment as a beat of the music, and he was totally right."

From iCEO to CEO

Ed Woolard, his mentor on the Apple board, pressed Jobs for more than two years to drop the *interim* in front of his CEO title. Not only was Jobs refusing to commit himself, but he was baffling everyone by taking only $1 a year in pay and no stock options. "I make 50 cents for showing up," he liked to joke, "and the other 50 cents is based on performance." Since his return in July 1997, Apple stock had gone from just under $14 to just over $102 at the peak of the Internet bubble at the beginning of 2000. Woolard had begged him to take at least a modest stock grant back in 1997, but Jobs had declined, saying, "I don't want the people I work with at Apple to think I am coming back to get rich." Had he accepted that modest grant, it would have been worth $400 million. Instead he made $2.50 during that period.

The main reason he clung to his *interim* designation was a sense of uncertainty about Apple's future. But as 2000 approached, it was clear that Apple had rebounded, and it was because of him. He took a long walk with Laurene and discussed what to most people by now seemed a formality but to him was still a big deal. If he dropped the *interim* designation, Apple could be the base for all the things he envisioned, including the possibility of getting Apple into products beyond computers. He decided to do so.

Woolard was thrilled, and he suggested that the board was willing to give him a massive stock grant. "Let me be straight with you," Jobs replied. "What I'd rather have is an airplane. We just had a third kid. I don't like flying commercial. I like to take my family to Hawaii. When I go east, I'd like to have pilots I know." He was never the type of person who could display grace and patience in a commercial airplane or terminal, even before the days of the TSA. Board member Larry Ellison, whose plane Jobs sometimes used (Apple paid $102,000 to Ellison in 1999 for Jobs's use of it), had no qualms. "Given what he's accomplished, we should give him five airplanes!" Ellison argued. He later said, "It was the perfect thank-you gift for Steve, who had saved Apple and gotten nothing in return."

So Woolard happily granted Jobs's wish, with a Gulfstream V, and also offered him fourteen million stock options. Jobs gave an unexpected response. He wanted more: twenty million options. Woolard was baffled and upset. The board had authority from the stockholders to give out only fourteen million. "You said you didn't want any, and we gave you a plane, which you did want," Woolard said.

"I hadn't been insisting on options before," Jobs replied, "but you

suggested it could be up to 5% of the company in options, and that's
what I now want." It was an awkward tiff in what should have been a
celebratory period. In the end, a complex solution was worked out that
granted him ten million shares in January 2000 that were valued at
the current price but timed to vest as if granted in 1997, plus another
grant due in 2001. Making matters worse, the stock fell with the burst
of the Internet bubble. Jobs never exercised the options, and at the end
of 2001 he asked that they be replaced by a new grant with a lower
strike price. The wrestling over options would come back to haunt the
company.

Even if he didn't profit from the options, at least he got to enjoy
the airplane. Not surprisingly he fretted over how the interior would
be designed. It took him more than a year. He used Ellison's plane as
a starting point and hired his designer. Pretty soon he was driving her
crazy. For example, Ellison's had a door between cabins with an open
button and a close button. Jobs insisted that his have a single button
that toggled. He didn't like the polished stainless steel of the buttons,
so he had them replaced with brushed metal ones. But in the end he
got the plane he wanted, and he loved it. "I look at his airplane and
mine, and everything he changed was better," said Ellison.

At the January 2000 Macworld in San Francisco, Jobs rolled out the
new Macintosh operating system, OSX, which used some of the software that Apple had bought from NeXT three years earlier. It was
fitting, and not entirely coincidental, that he was willing to incorporate
himself back at Apple at the same moment as the NeXT OS was incorporated into Apple's. Avie Tevanian had taken the UNIX-related
Mach kernel of the NeXT operating system and turned it into the Mac
OS kernel, known as Darwin. It offered protected memory, advanced
networking, and preemptive multitasking. It was precisely what the
Macintosh needed, and it would be the foundation of the Mac OS
henceforth. Some critics, including Bill Gates, noted that Apple ended
up not adopting the entire NeXT operating system. There's some truth
to that, because Apple decided not to leap into a completely new system but instead to evolve the existing one. Application software written for the old Macintosh system was generally compatible with or

easy to port to the new one, and a Mac user who upgraded would notice a lot of new features but not a whole new interface.

The fans at Macworld received the news with enthusiasm, of course, and they especially cheered when Jobs showed off the dock and how the icons in it could be magnified by passing the cursor over them. But the biggest applause came for the announcement he reserved for his "Oh, and one more thing" coda. He spoke about his duties at both Pixar and Apple, and said that he had become comfortable that the situation could work. "So I am pleased to announce today that I'm going to drop the interim title," he said with a big smile. The crowd jumped to its feet, screaming as if the Beatles had reunited. Jobs bit his lip, adjusted his wire rims, and put on a graceful show of humility. "You guys are making me feel funny now. I get to come to work every day and work with the most talented people on the planet, at Apple and Pixar. But these jobs are team sports. I accept your thanks on behalf of everybody at Apple."

CHAPTER TWENTY-NINE

APPLE STORES

Genius Bars and Siena Sandstone

New York's Fifth Avenue store

The Customer Experience

Jobs hated to cede control of anything, especially when it might affect the customer experience. But he faced a problem. There was one part of the process he didn't control: the experience of buying an Apple product in a store.

The days of the Byte Shop were over. Industry sales were shifting from local computer specialty shops to megachains and big box stores, where most clerks had neither the knowledge nor the incentive to explain the distinctive nature of Apple products. "All that the salesman cared about was a $50 spiff," Jobs said. Other computers were pretty generic, but Apple's had innovative features and a higher price tag. He didn't want an iMac to sit on a shelf between a Dell and a Compaq while an uninformed clerk recited the specs of each. "Unless we could find ways to get our message to customers at the store, we were screwed."

In great secrecy, Jobs began in late 1999 to interview executives who might be able to develop a string of Apple retail stores. One of the candidates had a passion for design and the boyish enthusiasm of a natural-born retailer: Ron Johnson, the vice president for merchandising at Target, who was responsible for launching distinctive-looking products, such as a teakettle designed by Michael Graves. "Steve is very easy to talk to," said Johnson in recalling their first meeting. "All of a sudden there's a torn pair of jeans and turtleneck, and he's off and running about why he needed great stores. If Apple is going to succeed, he told me, we're going to win on innovation. And you can't win on innovation unless you have a way to communicate to customers."

When Johnson came back in January 2000 to be interviewed again, Jobs suggested that they take a walk. They went to the sprawling 140-store Stanford Shopping Mall at 8:30 a.m. The stores weren't open yet, so they walked up and down the entire mall repeatedly and discussed how it was organized, what role the big department stores played relative to the other stores, and why certain specialty shops were successful.

They were still walking and talking when the stores opened at 10, and they went into Eddie Bauer. It had an entrance off the mall and another off the parking lot. Jobs decided that Apple stores should have only one entrance, which would make it easier to control the experience. And the Eddie Bauer store, they agreed, was too long and narrow. It was important that customers intuitively grasp the layout of a store as soon as they entered.

There were no tech stores in the mall, and Johnson explained why: The conventional wisdom was that a consumer, when making a major and infrequent purchase such as a computer, would be willing to drive to a less convenient location, where the rent would be cheaper. Jobs disagreed. Apple stores should be in malls and on Main Streets—in areas with a lot of foot traffic, no matter how expensive. "We may not be able to get them to drive ten miles to check out our products, but we can get them to walk ten feet," he said. The Windows users, in particular, had to be ambushed: "If they're passing by, they will drop in out of curiosity, if we make it inviting enough, and once we get a chance to show them what we have, we will win."

Johnson said that the size of a store signaled the importance of the brand. "Is Apple as big of a brand as the Gap?" he asked. Jobs said it was much bigger. Johnson replied that its stores should therefore be bigger. "Otherwise you won't be relevant." Jobs described Mike Markkula's maxim that a good company must "impute"—it must convey its values and importance in everything it does, from packaging to marketing. Johnson loved it. It definitely applied to a company's stores. "The store will become the most powerful physical expression of the brand," he predicted. He said that when he was young he had gone to the wood-paneled, art-filled mansion-like store that Ralph Lauren had created at Seventy-second and Madison in Manhattan. "Whenever I buy a polo shirt, I think of that mansion, which was a physical expression of Ralph's ideals," Johnson said. "Mickey Drexler did that with the Gap. You couldn't think of a Gap product without thinking of the great Gap store with the clean space and wood floors and white walls and folded merchandise."

When they finished, they drove to Apple and sat in a conference room playing with the company's products. There weren't many, not enough to fill the shelves of a conventional store, but that was an advantage. The type of store they would build, they decided, would benefit from having few products. It would be minimalist and airy and offer a lot of places for people to try out things. "Most people don't know Apple products," Johnson said. "They think of Apple as a cult. You want to move from a cult to something cool, and having an awesome store where people can try things will help that." The stores would impute the ethos of Apple products: playful, easy, creative, and on the bright side of the line between hip and intimidating.

The Prototype

When Jobs finally presented the idea, the board was not thrilled. Gateway Computers was going down in flames after opening suburban stores, and Jobs's argument that his would do better because they would be in more expensive locations was not, on its face, reassuring. "Think different" and "Here's to the crazy ones" made for good advertising slogans, but the board was hesitant to make them guidelines for corporate strategy. "I'm scratching my head and thinking this is crazy," recalled Art Levinson, the CEO of Genentech who joined the Apple board in 2000. "We are a small company, a marginal player. I said that I'm not sure I can support something like this." Ed Woolard was also dubious. "Gateway has tried this and failed, while Dell is selling direct to consumers without stores and succeeding," he argued. Jobs was not appreciative of too much pushback from the board. The last time that happened, he had replaced most of the members. This time, for personal reasons as well as being tired of playing tug-of-war with Jobs, Woolard decided to step down. But before he did, the board approved a trial run of four Apple stores.

Jobs did have one supporter on the board. In 1999 he had recruited the Bronx-born retailing prince Millard "Mickey" Drexler, who as CEO of Gap had transformed a sleepy chain into an icon of American casual culture. He was one of the few people in the world who were as successful and savvy as Jobs on matters of design, image, and consumer yearnings. In addition, he had insisted on end-to-end control: Gap stores sold only Gap products, and Gap products were sold almost exclusively in Gap stores. "I left the department store business because I couldn't stand not controlling my own product, from how it's manufactured to how it's sold," Drexler said. "Steve is just that way, which is why I think he recruited me."

Drexler gave Jobs a piece of advice: Secretly build a prototype of the store near the Apple campus, furnish it completely, and then hang out there until you feel comfortable with it. So Johnson and Jobs rented a vacant warehouse in Cupertino. Every Tuesday for six months, they convened an all-morning brainstorming session there, refining their retailing philosophy as they walked the space. It was the store equivalent of Ive's design studio, a haven where Jobs, with his visual approach, could come up with innovations by touching and seeing the options as they evolved. "I loved to wander over there on my own, just checking it out," Jobs recalled.

Sometimes he made Drexler, Larry Ellison, and other trusted friends come look. "On too many weekends, when he wasn't making me watch new scenes from *Toy Story*, he made me go to the warehouse and look at the mockups for the store," Ellison said. "He was obsessed by every detail of the aesthetic and the service experience. It got to the point where I said, 'Steve I'm not coming to see you if you're going to make me go to the store again.'"

Ellison's company, Oracle, was developing software for the handheld checkout system, which avoided having a cash register counter. On each visit Jobs prodded Ellison to figure out ways to streamline the process by eliminating some unnecessary step, such as handing over the credit card or printing a receipt. "If you look at the stores and the products, you will see Steve's obsession with beauty as simplicity—this Bauhaus aesthetic and wonderful minimalism, which goes all the way to the checkout process in the stores," said Ellison. "It means the absolute minimum number of steps. Steve gave us the exact, explicit recipe for how he wanted the checkout to work."

When Drexler came to see the prototype, he had some criticisms: "I thought the space was too chopped up and not clean enough. There were too many distracting architectural features and colors." He emphasized that a customer should be able to walk into a retail space and, with one sweep of the eye, understand the flow. Jobs agreed that simplicity and lack of distractions were keys to a great store, as they were to a product. "After that, he nailed it," said Drexler. "The vision he had was complete control of the entire experience of his product, from how it was designed and made to how it was sold."

In October 2000, near what he thought was the end of the process, Johnson woke up in the middle of a night before one of the Tuesday meetings with a painful thought: They had gotten something fundamentally wrong. They were organizing the store around each of Apple's main product lines, with areas for the PowerMac, iMac, iBook, and PowerBook. But Jobs had begun developing a new concept: the computer as a hub for all your digital activity. In other words, your computer might handle video and pictures from your cameras, and perhaps someday your music player and songs, or your books and magazines. Johnson's predawn brainstorm was that the stores should organize displays not just around the company's four lines of computers, but also around things people might want to do. "For example, I thought there should be a movie bay where we'd have various Macs and PowerBooks running iMovie and showing how you can import from your video camera and edit."

Johnson arrived at Jobs's office early that Tuesday and told him about his sudden insight that they needed to reconfigure the stores. He had heard tales of his boss's intemperate tongue, but he had not yet felt its lash—until now. Jobs erupted. "Do you know what a big change this is?" he yelled. "I've worked my ass off on this store for six months, and now you want to change everything!" Jobs suddenly got quiet. "I'm tired. I don't know if I can design another store from scratch."

Johnson was speechless, and Jobs made sure he remained so. On the ride to the prototype store, where people had gathered for the Tuesday meeting, he told Johnson not to say a word, either to him or to the other members of the team. So the seven-minute drive proceeded in silence. When they arrived, Jobs had finished processing the information. "I knew Ron was right," he recalled. So to Johnson's surprise, Jobs opened the meeting by saying, "Ron thinks we've got it all wrong. He thinks it should be organized not around products but instead around what people do." There was a pause, then Jobs continued. "And you know, he's right." He said they would redo the layout, even though it would likely delay the planned January rollout by three or four months. "We've only got one chance to get it right."

Jobs liked to tell the story—and he did so to his team that day—about how everything that he had done correctly had required a moment when he hit the rewind button. In each case he had to rework something that he discovered was not perfect. He talked about doing it on *Toy Story*, when the character of Woody had evolved into being a jerk, and on a couple of occasions with the original Macintosh. "If something isn't right, you can't just ignore it and say you'll fix it later," he said. "That's what other companies do."

When the revised prototype was finally completed in January 2001, Jobs allowed the board to see it for the first time. He explained the theories behind the design by sketching on a whiteboard; then he loaded board members into a van for the two-mile trip. When they saw what Jobs and Johnson had built, they unanimously approved going ahead. It would, the board agreed, take the relationship between retailing and brand image to a new level. It would also ensure that consumers did not see Apple computers as merely a commodity product like Dell or Compaq.

Most outside experts disagreed. "Maybe it's time Steve Jobs stopped thinking quite so differently," *Business Week* wrote in a story headlined "Sorry Steve, Here's Why Apple Stores Won't Work." Apple's former chief financial officer, Joseph Graziano, was quoted as saying, "Apple's problem is it still believes the way to grow is serving caviar in a world that seems pretty content with cheese and crackers." And the retail consultant David Goldstein declared, "I give them two years before they're turning out the lights on a very painful and expensive mistake."

Wood, Stone, Steel, Glass

On May 19, 2001, the first Apple store opened in Tyson's Corner, Virginia, with gleaming white counters, bleached wood floors, and a huge "Think Different" poster of John and Yoko in bed. The skeptics were wrong. Gateway stores had been averaging 250 visitors a week. By 2004 Apple stores were averaging 5,400 per week. That year the stores had $1.2 billion in revenue, setting a record in the retail industry for reaching the billion-dollar milestone. Sales in each store were tabulated every four minutes by Ellison's software, giving instant information on how to integrate manufacturing, supply, and sales channels.

As the stores flourished, Jobs stayed involved in every aspect. Lee Clow recalled, "In one of our marketing meetings just as the stores were opening, Steve made us spend a half hour deciding what hue of gray the restroom signs should be." The architectural firm of Bohlin Cywinski Jackson designed the signature stores, but Jobs made all of the major decisions.

Jobs particularly focused on the staircases, which echoed the one he had built at NeXT. When he visited a store as it was being constructed, he invariably suggested changes to the staircase. His name is listed as the lead inventor on two patent applications on the staircases, one for the see-through look that features all-glass treads and glass supports melded together with titanium, the other for the engineering system that uses a monolithic unit of glass containing multiple glass sheets laminated together for supporting loads.

In 1985, as he was being ousted from his first tour at Apple, he had visited Italy and been impressed by the gray stone of Florence's sidewalks. In 2002, when he came to the conclusion that the light wood floors in the stores were beginning to look somewhat pedestrian—a concern that it's hard to imagine bedeviling someone like Microsoft CEO Steve Ballmer—Jobs wanted to use that stone instead. Some of his colleagues pushed to replicate the color and texture using concrete, which would have been ten times cheaper, but Jobs insisted that it had to be authentic. The gray-blue Pietra Serena sandstone, which has a fine-grained texture, comes from a family-owned quarry, Il Casone, in Firenzuola outside of Florence. "We select only 3% of what comes out of the mountain, because it has to have the right shading and veining and purity," said Johnson. "Steve felt very strongly that we had to get the color right and it had to be a material with high integrity." So designers in Florence picked out just the right quarried stone, oversaw cutting it into the proper tiles, and made sure each tile was marked with a sticker to ensure that it was laid out next to its companion tiles. "Knowing that it's the same stone that Florence uses for its sidewalks assures you that it can stand the test of time," said Johnson.

Another notable feature of the stores was the Genius Bar. Johnson came up with the idea on a two-day retreat with his team. He had asked them all to describe the best service they'd ever enjoyed. Almost everyone mentioned some nice experience at a Four Seasons or Ritz-Carlton hotel. So Johnson sent his first five store managers through the Ritz-Carlton training program and came up with the idea of replicating something between a concierge desk and a bar. "What if we staffed the bar with the smartest Mac people," he said to Jobs. "We could call it the Genius Bar."

Jobs called the idea crazy. He even objected to the name. "You can't call them geniuses," he said. "They're geeks. They don't have the people skills to deliver on something called the genius bar." Johnson thought he had lost, but the next day he ran into Apple's general counsel, who said, "By the way, Steve just told me to trademark the name 'genius bar.'"

Many of Jobs's passions came together for Manhattan's Fifth Avenue store, which opened in 2006: a cube, a signature staircase, glass, and making a maximum statement through minimalism. "It was really Steve's store," said Johnson. Open 24/7, it vindicated the strategy of finding signature high-traffic locations by attracting fifty thousand visitors a week during its first year. (Remember Gateway's draw: 250 visitors a week.) "This store grosses more per square foot than any store in the world," Jobs proudly noted in 2010. "It also grosses more in total—absolute dollars, not just per square foot—than any store in New York. That includes Saks and Bloomingdale's."

Jobs was able to drum up excitement for store openings with the same flair he used for product releases. People began to travel to store openings and spend the night outside so they could be among the first in. "My then 14-year-old son suggested my first overnighter at Palo Alto, and the experience turned into an interesting social event," wrote Gary Allen, who started a website that caters to Apple store fans. "He and I have done several overnighters, including five in other countries, and have met so many great people."

In July 2011, a decade after the first ones opened, there were 326 Apple stores. The biggest was in London's Covent Garden, the tallest in Tokyo's Ginza. The average annual revenue per store was $34 million, and the total net sales in fiscal 2010 were $9.8 billion. But the stores did even more. They directly accounted for only 15% of Apple's revenue, but by creating buzz and brand awareness they indirectly helped boost everything the company did.

Even as he was fighting the effects of cancer in 2011, Jobs spent time envisioning future store projects, such as the one he wanted to build in New York City's Grand Central Terminal. One afternoon he showed me a picture of the Fifth Avenue store and pointed to the eighteen pieces of glass on each side. "This was state of the art in glass technology at the time," he said. "We had to build our own autoclaves to make the glass." Then he pulled out a drawing in which the eighteen panes were replaced by four huge panes. That is what he wanted to do next, he said. Once again, it was a challenge at the intersection of aesthetics and technology. "If we wanted to do it with our current technology, we would have to make the cube a foot shorter," he said. "And I didn't want to do that. So we have to build some new autoclaves in China."

Ron Johnson was not thrilled by the idea. He thought the eighteen panes actually looked better than four panes would. "The proportions we have today work magically with the colonnade of the GM Building," he said. "It glitters like a jewel box. I think if we get the glass too transparent, it will almost go away to a fault." He debated the point with Jobs, but to no avail. "When technology enables something new, he wants to take advantage of that," said Johnson. "Plus, for Steve, less is always more, simpler is always better. Therefore, if you can build a glass box with fewer elements, it's better, it's simpler, and it's at the forefront of technology. That's where Steve likes to be, in both his products and his stores."

CHAPTER THIRTY

THE DIGITAL HUB

From iTunes to the iPod

The original iPod, 2001

Connecting the Dots

Once a year Jobs took his most valuable employees on a retreat, which he called "The Top 100." They were picked based on a simple guideline: the people you would bring if you could take only a hundred people with you on a lifeboat to your next company. At the end of each retreat, Jobs would stand in front of a whiteboard (he loved whiteboards because they gave him complete control of a situation and they engendered focus) and ask, "What are the ten things we should be doing next?" People would fight to get their suggestions on the list.

Jobs would write them down, and then cross off the ones he decreed dumb. After much jockeying, the group would come up with a list of ten. Then Jobs would slash the bottom seven and announce, "We can only do three."

By 2001 Apple had revived its personal computer offerings. It was now time to think different. A set of new possibilities topped the what-next list on his whiteboard that year.

At the time, a pall had descended on the digital realm. The dot-com bubble had burst, and the NASDAQ had fallen more than 50% from its peak. Only three tech companies had ads during the January 2001 Super Bowl, compared to seventeen the year before. But the sense of deflation went deeper. For the twenty-five years since Jobs and Wozniak had founded Apple, the personal computer had been the centerpiece of the digital revolution. Now experts were predicting that its central role was ending. It had "matured into something boring," wrote the *Wall Street Journal*'s Walt Mossberg. Jeff Weitzen, the CEO of Gateway, proclaimed, "We're clearly migrating away from the PC as the centerpiece."

It was at that moment that Jobs launched a new grand strategy that would transform Apple—and with it the entire technology industry. The personal computer, instead of edging toward the sidelines, would become a "digital hub" that coordinated a variety of devices, from music players to video recorders to cameras. You'd link and sync all these devices with your computer, and it would manage your music, pictures, video, text, and all aspects of what Jobs dubbed your "digital lifestyle." Apple would no longer be just a computer company—indeed it would drop that word from its name—but the Macintosh would be reinvigorated by becoming the hub for an astounding array of new gadgets, including the iPod and iPhone and iPad.

When he was turning thirty, Jobs had used a metaphor about record albums. He was musing about why folks over thirty develop rigid thought patterns and tend to be less innovative. "People get stuck in those patterns, just like grooves in a record, and they never get out of them," he said. At age forty-five, Jobs was now about to get out of his groove.

FireWire

Jobs's vision that your computer could become your digital hub went back to a technology called FireWire, which Apple developed in the early 1990s. It was a high-speed serial port that moved digital files such as video from one device to another. Japanese camcorder makers adopted it, and Jobs decided to include it on the updated versions of the iMac that came out in October 1999. He began to see that FireWire could be part of a system that moved video from cameras onto a computer, where it could be edited and distributed.

To make this work, the iMac needed to have great video editing software. So Jobs went to his old friends at Adobe, the digital graphics company, and asked them to make a new Mac version of Adobe Premiere, which was popular on Windows computers. Adobe's executives stunned Jobs by flatly turning him down. The Macintosh, they said, had too few users to make it worthwhile. Jobs was furious and felt betrayed. "I put Adobe on the map, and they screwed me," he later claimed. Adobe made matters even worse when it also didn't write its other popular programs, such as Photoshop, for the Mac OSX, even though the Macintosh was popular among designers and other creative people who used those applications.

Jobs never forgave Adobe, and a decade later he got into a public war with the company by not permitting Adobe Flash to run on the iPad. He took away a valuable lesson that reinforced his desire for end-to-end control of all key elements of a system: "My primary insight when we were screwed by Adobe in 1999 was that we shouldn't get into any business where we didn't control both the hardware and the software, otherwise we'd get our head handed to us."

So starting in 1999 Apple began to produce application software for the Mac, with a focus on people at the intersection of art and technology. These included Final Cut Pro, for editing digital video; iMovie, which was a simpler consumer version; iDVD, for burning video or music onto a disc; iPhoto, to compete with Adobe Photoshop; GarageBand, for creating and mixing music; iTunes, for managing your songs; and the iTunes Store, for buying songs.

The idea of the digital hub quickly came into focus. "I first understood this with the camcorder," Jobs said. "Using iMovie makes your camcorder ten times more valuable." Instead of having hundreds of hours of raw footage you would never really sit through, you could edit it on your computer, make elegant dissolves, add music, and roll credits, listing yourself as executive producer. It allowed people to be creative, to express themselves, to make something emotional. "That's when it hit me that the personal computer was going to morph into something else."

Jobs had another insight: If the computer served as the hub, it would allow the portable devices to become simpler. A lot of the functions that the devices tried to do, such as editing the video or pictures, they did poorly because they had small screens and could not easily accommodate menus filled with lots of functions. Computers could handle that more easily.

And one more thing . . . What Jobs also saw was that this worked best when everything—the device, computer, software, applications, FireWire—was all tightly integrated. "I became even more of a believer in providing end-to-end solutions," he recalled.

The beauty of this realization was that there was only one company that was well-positioned to provide such an integrated approach. Microsoft wrote software, Dell and Compaq made hardware, Sony produced a lot of digital devices, Adobe developed a lot of applications. But only Apple did all of these things. "We're the only company that owns the whole widget—the hardware, the software and the operating system," he explained to *Time*. "We can take full responsibility for the user experience. We can do things that the other guys can't do."

Apple's first integrated foray into the digital hub strategy was video. With FireWire, you could get your video onto your Mac, and with iMovie you could edit it into a masterpiece. Then what? You'd want to burn some DVDs so you and your friends could watch it on a TV. "So we spent a lot of time working with the drive manufacturers to get a consumer drive that could burn a DVD," he said. "We were the first to ever ship that." As usual Jobs focused on making the product as simple as possible for the user, and this was the key to its success. Mike Evangelist, who worked at Apple on software design, recalled demonstrating to Jobs an early version of the interface. After looking at a bunch of screenshots, Jobs jumped up, grabbed a marker, and drew a simple rectangle on a whiteboard. "Here's the new application," he said. "It's got one window. You drag your video into the window. Then you click the button that says 'Burn.' That's it. That's what we're going to make." Evangelist was dumbfounded, but it led to the simplicity of what became iDVD. Jobs even helped design the "Burn" button icon.

Jobs knew digital photography was also about to explode, so Apple developed ways to make the computer the hub of your photos. But for the first year at least, he took his eye off one really big opportunity. HP and a few others were producing a drive that burned music CDs, but Jobs decreed that Apple should focus on video rather than music. In addition, his angry insistence that the iMac get rid of its tray disk drive and use instead a more elegant slot drive meant that it could not include the first CD burners, which were initially made for the tray format. "We kind of missed the boat on that," he recalled. "So we needed to catch up real fast."

The mark of an innovative company is not only that it comes up with new ideas first, but also that it knows how to leapfrog when it finds itself behind.

iTunes

It didn't take Jobs long to realize that music was going to be huge. By 2000 people were ripping music onto their computers from CDs, or downloading it from file-sharing services such as Napster, and burning playlists onto their own blank disks. That year the number of blank CDs sold in the United States was 320 million. There were only 281 million people in the country. That meant some people were *really* into burning CDs, and Apple wasn't catering to them. "I felt like a dope," he told *Fortune*. "I thought we had missed it. We had to work hard to catch up."

Jobs added a CD burner to the iMac, but that wasn't enough. His goal was to make it simple to transfer music from a CD, manage it on your computer, and then burn playlists. Other companies were already making music-management applications, but they were clunky and complex. One of Jobs's talents was spotting markets that were filled with second-rate products. He looked at the music apps that were available—including Real Jukebox, Windows Media Player, and one that HP was including with its CD burner—and came to a conclusion: "They were so complicated that only a genius could figure out half of their features."

That is when Bill Kincaid came in. A former Apple software engineer, he was driving to the Willow Springs track in California to race his Formula Ford sports car while (a bit incongruously) listening to National Public Radio. He heard a report about a portable music player called the Rio that played a digital song format called MP3. He perked up when the reporter said something like, "Don't get excited, Mac users, because it won't work with Macs." Kincaid said to himself, "Ha! I can fix that!"

To help him write a Rio manager for the Mac, he called his friends Jeff Robbin and Dave Heller, also former Apple software engineers. Their product, known as SoundJam, offered Mac users an interface for the Rio and software for managing the songs on their computer. In July 2000, when Jobs was pushing his team to come up with music-management software, Apple swooped in and bought SoundJam, bringing its founders back into the Apple fold. (All three stayed with the company, and Robbin continued to run the music software development team for the next decade. Jobs considered Robbin so valuable he once allowed a *Time* reporter to meet him only after extracting the promise that the reporter would not print his last name.)

Jobs personally worked with them to transform SoundJam into an Apple product. It was laden with all sorts of features, and consequently a lot of complex screens. Jobs pushed them to make it simpler and more fun. Instead of an interface that made you specify whether you were searching for an artist, song, or album, Jobs insisted on a simple box where you could type in anything you wanted. From iMovie the team adopted the sleek brushed-metal look and also a name. They dubbed it iTunes.

Jobs unveiled iTunes at the January 2001 Macworld as part of the digital hub strategy. It would be free to all Mac users, he announced.

"Join the music revolution with iTunes, and make your music devices ten times more valuable," he concluded to great applause. As his advertising slogan would later put it: *Rip. Mix. Burn.*

That afternoon Jobs happened to be meeting with John Markoff of the *New York Times*. The interview was going badly, but at the end Jobs sat down at his Mac and showed off iTunes. "It reminds me of my youth," he said as the psychedelic patterns danced on the screen. That led him to reminisce about dropping acid. Taking LSD was one of the two or three most important things he'd done in his life, Jobs told Markoff. People who had never taken acid would never fully understand him.

The iPod

The next step for the digital hub strategy was to make a portable music player. Jobs realized that Apple had the opportunity to design such a device in tandem with the iTunes software, allowing it to be simpler. Complex tasks could be handled on the computer, easy ones on the device. Thus was born the iPod, the device that would begin the transformation of Apple from being a computer maker into being the world's most valuable company.

Jobs had a special passion for the project because he loved music. The music players that were already on the market, he told his colleagues, "truly sucked." Phil Schiller, Jon Rubinstein, and the rest of the team agreed. As they were building iTunes, they spent time with the Rio and other players while merrily trashing them. "We would sit around and say, 'These things really stink,'" Schiller recalled. "They held about sixteen songs, and you couldn't figure out how to use them."

Jobs began pushing for a portable music player in the fall of 2000, but Rubinstein responded that the necessary components were not available yet. He asked Jobs to wait. After a few months Rubinstein was able to score a suitable small LCD screen and rechargeable lithium-polymer battery. The tougher challenge was finding a disk drive that was small enough but had ample memory to make a great music player. Then, in February 2001, he took one of his regular trips to Japan to visit Apple's suppliers.

At the end of a routine meeting with Toshiba, the engineers mentioned a new product they had in the lab that would be ready by that June. It was a tiny, 1.8-inch drive (the size of a silver dollar) that would hold five gigabytes of storage (about a thousand songs), and they were not sure what to do with it. When the Toshiba engineers showed it to Rubinstein, he knew immediately what it could be used for. A thousand songs in his pocket! Perfect. But he kept a poker face. Jobs was also in Japan, giving the keynote speech at the Tokyo Macworld conference. They met that night at the Hotel Okura, where Jobs was staying. "I know how to do it now," Rubinstein told him. "All I need is a $10 million check." Jobs immediately authorized it. So Rubinstein started negotiating with Toshiba to have exclusive rights to every one of the disks it could make, and he began to look around for someone who could lead the development team.

Tony Fadell was a brash entrepreneurial programmer with a cyberpunk look and an engaging smile who had started three companies while still at the University of Michigan. He had gone to work at the handheld device maker General Magic (where he met Apple refugees Andy Hertzfeld and Bill Atkinson), and then spent some awkward time at Philips Electronics, where he bucked the staid culture with his short bleached hair and rebellious style. He had come up with some ideas for creating a better digital music player, which he had shopped around unsuccessfully to RealNetworks, Sony, and Philips. One day he was in Colorado, skiing with an uncle, and his cell phone rang while he was riding on the chairlift. It was Rubinstein, who told him that Apple was looking for someone who could work on a "small electronic device." Fadell, not lacking in confidence, boasted that he was a wizard at making such devices. Rubinstein invited him to Cupertino.

Fadell assumed that he was being hired to work on a personal digital assistant, some successor to the Newton. But when he met with Rubinstein, the topic quickly turned to iTunes, which had been out for three months. "We've been trying to hook up the existing MP3 players to iTunes and they've been horrible, absolutely horrible," Rubinstein told him. "We think we should make our own version."

Fadell was thrilled. "I was passionate about music. I was trying to do some of that at RealNetworks, and I was pitching an MP3 player to Palm." He agreed to come aboard, at least as a consultant. After a few weeks Rubinstein insisted that if he was to lead the team, he had to become a full-time Apple employee. But Fadell resisted; he liked his freedom. Rubinstein was furious at what he considered Fadell's whining. "This is one of those life decisions," he told Fadell. "You'll never regret it."

He decided to force Fadell's hand. He gathered a roomful of the twenty or so people who had been assigned to the project. When Fadell walked in, Rubinstein told him, "Tony, we're not doing this project unless you sign on full-time. Are you in or out? You have to decide right now."

Fadell looked Rubinstein in the eye, then turned to the audience and said, "Does this always happen at Apple, that people are put under duress to sign an offer?" He paused for a moment, said yes, and grudgingly shook Rubinstein's hand. "It left some very unsettling feeling between Jon and me for many years," Fadell recalled. Rubinstein agreed: "I don't think he ever forgave me for that."

Fadell and Rubinstein were fated to clash because they both thought that they had fathered the iPod. As Rubinstein saw it, he had been given the mission by Jobs months earlier, found the Toshiba disk drive, and figured out the screen, battery, and other key elements. He had then brought in Fadell to put it together. He and others who resented Fadell's visibility began to refer to him as "Tony Baloney." But from Fadell's perspective, before he came to Apple he had already come up with plans for a great MP3 player, and he had been shopping it around to other companies before he had agreed to come to Apple. The issue of who deserved the most credit for the iPod, or should get the title Podfather, would be fought over the years in interviews, articles, web pages, and even *Wikipedia* entries.

But for the next few months they were too busy to bicker. Jobs wanted the iPod out by Christmas, and this meant having it ready to unveil in October. They looked around for other companies that were designing MP3 players that could serve as the foundation for Apple's work and settled on a small company named PortalPlayer. Fadell told the team there, "This is the project that's going to remold Apple, and ten years from now, it's going to be a music business, not a computer business." He convinced them to sign an exclusive deal, and his group began to modify PortalPlayer's deficiencies, such as its complex interfaces, short battery life, and inability to make a playlist longer than ten songs.

That's It!

There are certain meetings that are memorable both because they mark a historic moment and because they illuminate the way a leader operates. Such was the case with the gathering in Apple's fourth-floor conference room in April 2001, where Jobs decided on the fundamentals of the iPod. There to hear Fadell present his proposals to Jobs were Rubinstein, Schiller, Ive, Jeff Robbin, and marketing director Stan Ng. Fadell didn't know Jobs, and he was understandably intimidated. "When he walked into the conference room, I sat up and thought, 'Whoa, there's Steve!' I was really on guard, because I'd heard how brutal he could be."

The meeting started with a presentation of the potential market and what other companies were doing. Jobs, as usual, had no patience. "He won't pay attention to a slide deck for more than a minute," Fadell said. When a slide showed other possible players in the market, he waved it away. "Don't worry about Sony," he said. "We know what we're doing, and they don't." After that, they quit showing slides, and instead Jobs peppered the group with questions. Fadell took away a lesson: "Steve prefers to be in the moment, talking things through. He once told me, 'If you need slides, it shows you don't know what you're talking about.'"

Instead Jobs liked to be shown physical objects that he could feel, inspect, and fondle. So Fadell brought three different models to the conference room; Rubinstein had coached him on how to reveal them sequentially so that his preferred choice would be the pièce de résistance. They hid the mockup of that option under a wooden bowl at the center of the table.

Fadell began his show-and-tell by taking the various parts they were using out of a box and spreading them on the table. There were the 1.8-inch drive, LCD screen, boards, and batteries, all labeled with their cost and weight. As he displayed them, they discussed how the prices or sizes might come down over the next year or so. Some of the pieces could be put together, like Lego blocks, to show the options.

Then Fadell began unveiling his models, which were made of Styrofoam with fishing leads inserted to give them the proper weight. The first had a slot for a removable memory card for music. Jobs dismissed it as complicated. The second had dynamic RAM memory, which was cheap but would lose all of the songs if the battery ran out. Jobs was not pleased. Next Fadell put a few of the pieces together to show what a device with the 1.8-inch hard drive would be like. Jobs seemed intrigued. The show climaxed with Fadell lifting the bowl and revealing a fully assembled model of that alternative. "I was hoping to be able to play more with the Lego parts, but Steve settled right on the hard-drive option just the way we had modeled it," Fadell recalled. He was rather stunned by the process. "I was used to being at Philips, where decisions like this would take meeting after meeting, with a lot of PowerPoint presentations and going back for more study."

Next it was Phil Schiller's turn. "Can I bring out my idea now?" he asked. He left the room and returned with a handful of iPod models, all of which had the same device on the front: the soon-to-be-famous trackwheel. "I had been thinking of how you go through a playlist," he recalled. "You can't press a button hundreds of times. Wouldn't it be great if you could have a wheel?" By turning the wheel with your thumb, you could scroll through songs. The longer you kept turning, the faster the scrolling got, so you could zip through hundreds easily. Jobs shouted, "That's it!" He got Fadell and the engineers working on it.

Once the project was launched, Jobs immersed himself in it daily. His main demand was "Simplify!" He would go over each screen of the user interface and apply a rigid test: If he wanted a song or a function, he should be able to get there in three clicks. And the click should be intuitive. If he couldn't figure out how to navigate to something, or if it took more than three clicks, he would be brutal. "There would be times when we'd rack our brains on a user interface problem, and think we'd considered every option, and he would go, 'Did you think of this?'" said Fadell. "And then we'd all go, 'Holy shit.' He'd redefine the problem or approach, and our little problem would go away."

Every night Jobs would be on the phone with ideas. Fadell and the others would call each other up, discuss Jobs's latest suggestion, and conspire on how to nudge him to where they wanted him to go, which worked about half the time. "We would have this swirling thing of Steve's latest idea, and we would all try to stay ahead of it," said Fadell. "Every day there was something like that, whether it was a switch here, or a button color, or a pricing strategy issue. With his style, you needed to work with your peers, watch each other's back."

One key insight Jobs had was that as many functions as possible should be performed using iTunes on your computer rather than on the iPod. As he later recalled:

> In order to make the iPod really easy to use—and this took a lot of arguing on my part—we needed to limit what the device itself would do. Instead we put that functionality in iTunes on the computer. For example, we made it so you couldn't make playlists using the device. You made playlists on iTunes, and then you synced with the device. That was controversial. But what made the Rio and other devices so brain-dead was that they were complicated. They had to do things like make playlists, because they weren't integrated with the jukebox software on your computer. So by owning the iTunes software and the iPod device, that allowed us to make the computer and the device work together, and it allowed us to put the complexity in the right place.

The most Zen of all simplicities was Jobs's decree, which astonished his colleagues, that the iPod would not have an on-off switch. It became true of most Apple devices. There was no need for one. Apple's devices would go dormant if they were not being used, and they would wake up when you touched any key. But there was no need for a switch that would go "Click—you're off. Good-bye."

Suddenly everything had fallen into place: a drive that would hold a thousand songs; an interface and scroll wheel that would let you navigate a thousand songs; a FireWire connection that could sync a thousand songs in under ten minutes; and a battery that would last through a thousand songs. "We suddenly were looking at one another and saying, 'This is going to be so cool,'" Jobs recalled. "We knew how cool it was, because we knew how badly we each wanted one personally. And the concept became so beautifully simple: a thousand songs in your pocket." One of the copywriters suggested they call it a "Pod." Jobs was the one who, borrowing from the iMac and iTunes names, modified that to iPod.

The Whiteness of the Whale

Jony Ive had been playing with the foam model of the iPod and trying to conceive what the finished product should look like when an idea occurred to him on a morning drive from his San Francisco home to Cupertino. Its face should be pure white, he told his colleague in the car, and it should connect seamlessly to a polished stainless steel back. "Most small consumer products have this disposable feel to them," said Ive. "There is no cultural gravity to them. The thing I'm proudest of about the iPod is that there is something about it that makes it feel significant, not disposable."

The white would be not just white, but *pure* white. "Not only the device, but the headphones and the wires and even the power block," he recalled. "*Pure* white." Others kept arguing that the headphones, of course, should be black, like all headphones. "But Steve got it immediately, and embraced white," said Ive. "There would be a purity to it." The sinuous flow of the white earbud wires helped make the iPod an icon. As Ive described it:

There was something very significant and nondisposable about it, yet there was also something very quiet and very restrained. It wasn't wagging its tail in your face. It was restrained, but it was also crazy, with those flowing headphones. That's why I like white. White isn't just a neutral color. It is so pure and quiet. Bold and conspicuous and yet so inconspicuous as well.

Lee Clow's advertising team at TBWA\Chiat\Day wanted to celebrate the iconic nature of the iPod and its whiteness rather than create more traditional product-introduction ads that showed off the device's features. James Vincent, a lanky young Brit who had played in a band and worked as a DJ, had recently joined the agency, and he was a natural to help focus Apple's advertising on hip millennial-generation music lovers rather than rebel baby boomers. With the help of the art director Susan Alinsangan, they created a series of billboards and posters for the iPod, and they spread the options on Jobs's conference room table for his inspection.

At the far right end they placed the most traditional options, which featured straightforward photos of the iPod on a white background. At the far left end they placed the most graphic and iconic treatments, which showed just a silhouette of someone dancing while listening to an iPod, its white earphone wires waving with the music. "It understood your emotional and intensely personal relationship with the music," Vincent said. He suggested to Duncan Milner, the creative director, that they all stand firmly at the far left end, to see if they could get Jobs to gravitate there. When he walked in, he went immediately to the right, looking at the stark product pictures. "This looks great," he said. "Let's talk about these." Vincent, Milner, and Clow did not budge from the other end. Finally, Jobs looked up, glanced at the iconic treatments, and said, "Oh, I guess you like this stuff." He shook his head. "It doesn't show the product. It doesn't say what it is." Vincent proposed that they use the iconic images but add the tagline, "1,000 songs in your pocket." That would say it all. Jobs glanced back toward the right end of the table, then finally agreed. Not surprisingly he was soon claiming that it was his idea to push for the more iconic ads. "There were some skeptics around who asked, 'How's this going to actually sell an iPod?'" Jobs recalled. "That's when it came in handy to be the CEO, so I could push the idea through."

Jobs realized that there was yet another advantage to the fact that Apple had an integrated system of computer, software, and device. It meant that sales of the iPod would drive sales of the iMac. That, in turn, meant that he could take money that Apple was spending on iMac advertising and shift it to spending on iPod ads—getting a double bang for the buck. A triple bang, actually, because the ads would lend luster and youthfulness to the whole Apple brand. He recalled:

> I had this crazy idea that we could sell just as many Macs by advertising the iPod. In addition, the iPod would position Apple as evoking innovation and youth. So I moved $75 million of advertising money to the iPod, even though the category didn't justify one hundredth of that. That meant that we completely dominated the market for music players. We outspent everybody by a factor of about a hundred.

The television ads showed the iconic silhouettes dancing to songs picked by Jobs, Clow, and Vincent. "Finding the music became our main fun at our weekly marketing meetings," said Clow. "We'd play some edgy cut, Steve would say, 'I hate that,' and James would have to talk him into it." The ads helped popularize many new bands, most notably the Black Eyed Peas; the ad with "Hey Mama" is the classic of the silhouettes genre. When a new ad was about to go into production, Jobs would often have second thoughts, call up Vincent, and insist that he cancel it. "It sounds a bit poppy" or "It sounds a bit trivial," he would say. "Let's call it off." James would get flustered and try to talk him around. "Hold on, it's going to be great," he would argue. Invariably Jobs would relent, the ad would be made, and he would love it.

Jobs unveiled the iPod on October 23, 2001, at one of his signature product launch events. "Hint: It's not a Mac," the invitation teased. When it came time to reveal the product, after he described its technical capabilities, Jobs did not do his usual trick of walking over to a table and pulling off a velvet cloth. Instead he said, "I happen to have one right here in my pocket." He reached into his jeans and pulled out the gleaming white device. "This amazing little device holds a thousand songs, and it goes right in my pocket." He slipped it back in and ambled offstage to applause.

Initially there was some skepticism among tech geeks, especially about the $399 price. In the blogosphere, the joke was that iPod stood for "idiots price our devices." However, consumers soon made it a hit. More than that, the iPod became the essence of everything Apple was destined to be: poetry connected to engineering, arts and creativity intersecting with technology, design that's bold and simple. It had an ease of use that came from being an integrated end-to-end system, from computer to FireWire to device to software to content management. When you took an iPod out of the box, it was so beautiful that it seemed to glow, and it made all other music players look as if they had been designed and manufactured in Uzbekistan.

Not since the original Mac had a clarity of product vision so propelled a company into the future. "If anybody was ever wondering why Apple is on the earth, I would hold up this as a good example," Jobs told *Newsweek*'s Steve Levy at the time. Wozniak, who had long been skeptical of integrated systems, began to revise his philosophy. "Wow, it makes sense that Apple was the one to come up with it," Wozniak enthused after the iPod came out. "After all, Apple's whole history is making both the hardware and the software, with the result that the two work better together."

The day that Levy got his press preview of the iPod, he happened to be meeting Bill Gates at a dinner, and he showed it to him. "Have you seen this yet?" Levy asked. Levy noted, "Gates went into a zone that recalls those science fiction films where a space alien, confronted with a novel object, creates some sort of force tunnel between him and the object, allowing him to suck directly into his brain all possible information about it." Gates played with the scroll wheel and pushed every button combination, while his eyes stared fixedly at the screen. "It looks like a great product," he finally said. Then he paused and looked puzzled. "It's only for Macintosh?" he asked.

CHAPTER THIRTY-ONE

THE iTUNES STORE

I'm the Pied Piper

Warner Music

At the beginning of 2002 Apple faced a challenge. The seamless connection between your iPod, iTunes software, and computer made it easy to manage the music you already owned. But to get new music, you had to venture out of this cozy environment and go buy a CD or download the songs online. The latter endeavor usually meant foraying into the murky domains of file-sharing and piracy services. So Jobs wanted to offer iPod users a way to download songs that was simple, safe, and legal.

The music industry also faced a challenge. It was being plagued by a bestiary of piracy services—Napster, Grokster, Gnutella, Kazaa—that enabled people to get songs for free. Partly as a result, legal sales of CDs were down 9% in 2002.

The executives at the music companies were desperately scrambling, with the elegance of second-graders playing soccer, to agree on a common standard for copy-protecting digital music. Paul Vidich of Warner Music and his corporate colleague Bill Raduchel of AOL Time Warner were working with Sony in that effort, and they hoped

The iTunes Store 395

to get Apple to be part of their consortium. So a group of them flew to Cupertino in January 2002 to see Jobs.

It was not an easy meeting. Vidich had a cold and was losing his voice, so his deputy, Kevin Gage, began the presentation. Jobs, sitting at the head of the conference table, fidgeted and looked annoyed. After four slides, he waved his hand and broke in. "You have your heads up your asses," he pointed out. Everyone turned to Vidich, who struggled to get his voice working. "You're right," he said after a long pause. "We don't know what to do. You need to help us figure it out." Jobs later recalled being slightly taken aback, and he agreed that Apple would work with the Warner-Sony effort.

If the music companies had been able to agree on a standardized encoding method for protecting music files, then multiple online stores could have proliferated. That would have made it hard for Jobs to create an iTunes Store that allowed Apple to control how online sales were handled. Sony, however, handed Jobs that opportunity when it decided, after the January 2002 Cupertino meeting, to pull out of the talks because it favored its own proprietary format, from which it would get royalties.

"You know Steve, he has his own agenda," Sony's CEO Nobuyuki Idei explained to *Red Herring* editor Tony Perkins. "Although he is a genius, he doesn't share everything with you. This is a difficult person to work with if you are a big company. . . . It is a nightmare." Howard Stringer, then head of Sony North America, added about Jobs: "Trying to get together would frankly be a waste of time."

Instead Sony joined with Universal to create a subscription service called Pressplay. Meanwhile, AOL Time Warner, Bertelsmann, and EMI teamed up with RealNetworks to create MusicNet. Neither would license its songs to the rival service, so each offered only about half the music available. Both were subscription services that allowed customers to stream songs but not keep them, so you lost access to them if your subscription lapsed. They had complicated restrictions and clunky interfaces. Indeed they would earn the dubious distinction of becoming number nine on *PC World*'s list of "the 25 worst tech products of all time." The magazine declared, "The services' stunningly brain-dead features showed that the record companies still didn't get it."

At this point Jobs could have decided simply to indulge piracy. Free music meant more valuable iPods. Yet because he *really* liked music, and the artists who made it, he was opposed to what he saw as the theft of creative products. As he later told me:

> From the earliest days at Apple, I realized that we thrived when we created intellectual property. If people copied or stole our software, we'd be out of business. If it weren't protected, there'd be no incentive for us to make new software or product designs. If protection of intellectual property begins to disappear, creative companies will disappear or never get started. But there's a simpler reason: It's wrong to steal. It hurts other people. And it hurts your own character.

He knew, however, that the best way to stop piracy—in fact the only way—was to offer an alternative that was more attractive than the brain-dead services that music companies were concocting. "We believe that 80% of the people stealing stuff don't want to be, there's just no legal alternative," he told Andy Langer of *Esquire*. "So we said, 'Let's create a legal alternative to this.' Everybody wins. Music companies win. The artists win. Apple wins. And the user wins, because he gets a better service and doesn't have to be a thief."

So Jobs set out to create an "iTunes Store" and to persuade the five top record companies to allow digital versions of their songs to be sold there. "I've never spent so much of my time trying to convince people to do the right thing for themselves," he recalled. Because the companies were worried about the pricing model and unbundling of albums, Jobs pitched that his new service would be only on the Macintosh, a mere 5% of the market. They could try the idea with little risk. "We used our small market share to our advantage by arguing that if the store turned out to be destructive it wouldn't destroy the entire universe," he recalled.

Jobs's proposal was to sell digital songs for 99 cents—a simple and impulsive purchase. The record companies would get 70 cents of that.

Jobs insisted that this would be more appealing than the monthly subscription model preferred by the music companies. He believed that people had an emotional connection to the songs they loved. They wanted to *own* "Sympathy for the Devil" and "Shelter from the Storm," not just rent them. As he told Jeff Goodell of *Rolling Stone* at the time, "I think you could make available the Second Coming in a subscription model and it might not be successful."

Jobs also insisted that the iTunes Store would sell individual songs, not just entire albums. That ended up being the biggest cause of conflict with the record companies, which made money by putting out albums that had two or three great songs and a dozen or so fillers; to get the song they wanted, consumers had to buy the whole album. Some musicians objected on artistic grounds to Jobs's plan to disaggregate albums. "There's a flow to a good album," said Trent Reznor of Nine Inch Nails. "The songs support each other. That's the way I like to make music." But the objections were moot. "Piracy and online downloads had already deconstructed the album," recalled Jobs. "You couldn't compete with piracy unless you sold the songs individually."

At the heart of the problem was a chasm between the people who loved technology and those who loved artistry. Jobs loved both, as he had demonstrated at Pixar and Apple, and he was thus positioned to bridge the gap. He later explained:

> When I went to Pixar, I became aware of a great divide. Tech companies don't understand creativity. They don't appreciate *intuitive* thinking, like the ability of an A&R guy at a music label to listen to a hundred artists and have a feel for which five might be successful. And they think that creative people just sit around on couches all day and are undisciplined, because they've not seen how driven and disciplined the creative folks at places like Pixar are. On the other hand, music companies are completely clueless about technology. They think they can just go out and hire a few tech folks. But that would be like Apple trying to hire people to produce music. We'd get second-rate A&R people, just like the music companies ended up with second-rate tech people. I'm one of the few people who understands how producing technology requires intuition and creativity, and how producing something artistic takes real discipline.

Jobs had a long relationship with Barry Schuler, the CEO of the AOL unit of Time Warner, and began to pick his brain about how to get the music labels into the proposed iTunes Store. "Piracy is flipping everyone's circuit breakers," Schuler told him. "You should use the argument that because you have an integrated end-to-end service, from iPods to the store, you can best protect how the music is used."

One day in March 2002, Schuler got a call from Jobs and decided to conference-in Vidich. Jobs asked Vidich if he would come to Cupertino and bring the head of Warner Music, Roger Ames. This time Jobs was charming. Ames was a sardonic, fun, and clever Brit, a type (such as James Vincent and Jony Ive) that Jobs tended to like. So the Good Steve was on display. At one point early in the meeting, Jobs even played the unusual role of diplomat. Ames and Eddy Cue, who ran iTunes for Apple, got into an argument over why radio in England was not as vibrant as in the United States, and Jobs stepped in, saying, "We know about tech, but we don't know as much about music, so let's not argue."

Ames had just lost a boardroom battle to have his corporation's AOL division improve its own fledgling music download service. "When I did a digital download using AOL, I could never find the song on my shitty computer," he recalled. So when Jobs demonstrated a prototype of the iTunes Store, Ames was impressed. "Yes, yes, that's exactly what we've been waiting for," he said. He agreed that Warner Music would sign up, and he offered to help enlist other music companies.

Jobs flew east to show the service to other Time Warner execs. "He sat in front of a Mac like a kid with a toy," Vidich recalled. "Unlike any other CEO, he was totally engaged with the product." Ames and Jobs began to hammer out the details of the iTunes Store, including the number of times a track could be put on different devices and how the copy-protection system would work. They soon were in agreement and set out to corral other music labels.

Herding Cats

The key player to enlist was Doug Morris, head of the Universal Music Group. His domain included must-have artists such as U2, Eminem, and Mariah Carey, as well as powerful labels such as Motown and Interscope-Geffen-A&M. Morris was eager to talk. More than any other mogul, he was upset about piracy and fed up with the caliber of the technology people at the music companies. "It was like the Wild West," Morris recalled. "No one was selling digital music, and it was awash with piracy. Everything we tried at the record companies was a failure. The difference in skill sets between the music folks and technologists is just huge."

As Ames walked with Jobs to Morris's office on Broadway he briefed Jobs on what to say. It worked. What impressed Morris was that Jobs tied everything together in a way that made things easy for the consumer and also safe for the record companies. "Steve did something brilliant," said Morris. "He proposed this complete system: the iTunes Store, the music-management software, the iPod itself. It was so smooth. He had the whole package."

Morris was convinced that Jobs had the technical vision that was lacking at the music companies. "Of course we have to rely on Steve Jobs to do this," he told his own tech vice president, "because we don't have anyone at Universal who knows anything about technology." That did not make Universal's technologists eager to work with Jobs, and Morris had to keep ordering them to surrender their objections and make a deal quickly. They were able to add a few more restrictions to FairPlay, the Apple system of digital rights management, so that a purchased song could not be spread to too many devices. But in general, they went along with the concept of the iTunes Store that Jobs had worked out with Ames and his Warner colleagues.

Morris was so smitten with Jobs that he called Jimmy Iovine, the fast-talking and brash chief of Interscope-Geffen-A&M. Iovine and Morris were best friends who had spoken every day for the past thirty years. "When I met Steve, I thought he was our savior, so I immediately brought Jimmy in to get his impression," Morris recalled.

Jobs could be extraordinarily charming when he wanted to be, and he turned it on when Iovine flew out to Cupertino for a demo. "See how simple it is?" he asked Iovine. "Your tech folks are never going to do this. There's no one at the music companies who can make it simple enough."

Iovine called Morris right away. "This guy is unique!" he said. "You're right. He's got a turnkey solution." They complained about how they had spent two years working with Sony, and it hadn't gone anywhere. "Sony's never going to figure things out," he told Morris. They agreed to quit dealing with Sony and join with Apple instead. "How Sony missed this is completely mind-boggling to me, a historic fuckup," Iovine said. "Steve would fire people if the divisions didn't work together, but Sony's divisions were at war with one another."

Indeed Sony provided a clear counterexample to Apple. It had a consumer electronics division that made sleek products and a music division with beloved artists (including Bob Dylan). But because each division tried to protect its own interests, the company as a whole never got its act together to produce an end-to-end service.

Andy Lack, the new head of Sony music, had the unenviable task of negotiating with Jobs about whether Sony would sell its music in the iTunes Store. The irrepressible and savvy Lack had just come from a distinguished career in television journalism—a producer at CBS News and president of NBC—and he knew how to size people up and keep his sense of humor. He realized that, for Sony, selling its songs in the iTunes Store was both insane and necessary—which seemed to be the case with a lot of decisions in the music business. Apple would make out like a bandit, not just from its cut on song sales, but from driving the sale of iPods. Lack believed that since the music companies would be responsible for the success of the iPod, they should get a royalty from each device sold.

Jobs would agree with Lack in many of their conversations and claim that he wanted to be a true partner with the music companies. "Steve, you've got me if you just give me *something* for every sale of your device," Lack told him in his booming voice. "It's a beautiful device. But our music is helping to sell it. That's what true partnership means to me."

"I'm with you," Jobs replied on more than one occasion. But then he would go to Doug Morris and Roger Ames to lament, in a conspiratorial fashion, that Lack just didn't get it, that he was clueless about the music business, that he wasn't as smart as Morris and Ames. "In classic Steve fashion, he would agree to something, but it would never happen," said Lack. "He would set you up and then pull it off the table. He's pathological, which can be useful in negotiations. And he's a genius."

Lack knew that he could not win his case unless he got support from others in the industry. But Jobs used flattery and the lure of Apple's marketing clout to keep the other record labels in line. "If the industry had stood together, we could have gotten a license fee, giving us the dual revenue stream we desperately needed," Lack said. "We were the ones making the iPod sell, so it would have been equitable." That, of course, was one of the beauties of Jobs's end-to-end strategy: Sales of songs on iTunes would drive iPod sales, which would drive Macintosh sales. What made it all the more infuriating to Lack was that Sony could have done the same, but it never could get its hardware and software and content divisions to row in unison.

Jobs tried hard to seduce Lack. During one visit to New York, he invited Lack to his penthouse at the Four Seasons hotel. Jobs had already ordered a breakfast spread—oatmeal and berries for them both—and was "beyond solicitous," Lack recalled. "But Jack Welch taught me not to fall in love. Morris and Ames could be seduced. They would say, 'You don't get it, you're supposed to fall in love,' and they did. So I ended up isolated in the industry."

Even after Sony agreed to sell its music in the iTunes Store, the relationship remained contentious. Each new round of renewals or changes would bring a showdown. "With Andy, it was mostly about his big ego," Jobs claimed. "He never really understood the music business, and he could never really deliver. I thought he was sometimes a dick." When I told him what Jobs said, Lack responded, "I fought for Sony and the music industry, so I can see why he thought I was a dick."

Corralling the record labels to go along with the iTunes plan was not enough, however. Many of their artists had carve-outs in their contracts that allowed them personally to control the digital distribution of their music or prevent their songs from being unbundled from their albums and sold singly. So Jobs set about cajoling various top musicians, which he found fun but also a lot harder than he expected.

Before the launch of iTunes, Jobs met with almost two dozen major artists, including Bono, Mick Jagger, and Sheryl Crow. "He would call me at home, relentless, at ten at night, to say he still needed to get to Led Zeppelin or Madonna," Ames recalled. "He was determined, and nobody else could have convinced some of these artists."

Perhaps the oddest meeting was when Dr. Dre came to visit Jobs at Apple headquarters. Jobs loved the Beatles and Dylan, but he admitted that the appeal of rap eluded him. Now Jobs needed Eminem and other rappers to agree to be sold in the iTunes Store, so he huddled with Dr. Dre, who was Eminem's mentor. After Jobs showed him the seamless way the iTunes Store would work with the iPod, Dr. Dre proclaimed, "Man, somebody finally got it right."

On the other end of the musical taste spectrum was the trumpeter Wynton Marsalis. He was on a West Coast fund-raising tour for Jazz at Lincoln Center and was meeting with Jobs's wife, Laurene. Jobs insisted that he come over to the house in Palo Alto, and he proceeded to show off iTunes. "What do you want to search for?" he asked Marsalis. Beethoven, the trumpeter replied. "Watch what it can do!" Jobs kept insisting when Marsalis's attention would wander. "See how the interface works." Marsalis later recalled, "I don't care much about computers, and kept telling him so, but he goes on for two hours. He was a man possessed. After a while, I started looking at him and not the computer, because I was so fascinated with his passion."

Jobs unveiled the iTunes Store on April 28, 2003, at San Francisco's Moscone Center. With hair now closely cropped and receding, and a studied unshaven look, Jobs paced the stage and described how Napster "demonstrated that the Internet was made for music delivery." Its offspring, such as Kazaa, he said, offered songs for free. How do you compete with that? To answer that question, he began by describing the downsides of using these free services. The downloads were unreliable and the quality was often bad. "A lot of these songs are encoded by seven-year-olds, and they don't do a great job." In addition, there were no previews or album art. Then he added, "Worst of all it's stealing. It's best not to mess with karma."

Why had these piracy sites proliferated, then? Because, Jobs said, there was no alternative. The subscription services, such as Pressplay and MusicNet, "treat you like a criminal," he said, showing a slide of an inmate in striped prison garb. Then a slide of Bob Dylan came on the screen. "People want to own the music they love."

After a lot of negotiating with the record companies, he said, "they were willing to do something with us to change the world." The iTunes Store would start with 200,000 tracks, and it would grow each day. By using the store, he said, you can own your songs, burn them on CDs, be assured of the download quality, get a preview of a song before you download it, and use it with your iMovies and iDVDs to "make the soundtrack of your life." The price? Just 99 cents, he said, less than a third of what a Starbucks latte cost. Why was it worth it? Because to get the right song from Kazaa took about fifteen minutes, rather than a minute. By spending an hour of your time to save about four dollars, he calculated, "you're working for under the minimum wage!" And one more thing . . . "With iTunes, it's not stealing anymore. It's good karma."

Clapping the loudest for that line were the heads of the record labels in the front row, including Doug Morris sitting next to Jimmy Iovine, in his usual baseball cap, and the whole crowd from Warner Music. Eddy Cue, who was in charge of the store, predicted that Apple would sell a million songs in six months. Instead the iTunes Store sold a million songs in six *days.* "This will go down in history as a turning point for the music industry," Jobs declared.

Microsoft

"We were smoked."

That was the blunt email sent to four colleagues by Jim Allchin, the Microsoft executive in charge of Windows development, at 5 p.m. the day he saw the iTunes Store. It had only one other line: "How did they get the music companies to go along?"

Later that evening a reply came from David Cole, who was running Microsoft's online business group. "When Apple brings this to Windows (I assume they won't make the mistake of not bringing it to Windows), we will really be smoked." He said that the Windows team needed "to bring this kind of solution to market," adding, "That will require focus and goal alignment around an *end-to-end service* which delivers direct user value, something we don't have today." Even though Microsoft had its own Internet service (MSN), it was not used to providing end-to-end service the way Apple was.

Bill Gates himself weighed in at 10:46 that night. His subject line, "Apple's Jobs again," indicated his frustration. "Steve Jobs's ability to focus in on a few things that count, get people who get user interface right, and market things as revolutionary are amazing things," he said. He too expressed surprise that Jobs had been able to convince the music companies to go along with his store. "This is very strange to me. The music companies' own operations offer a service that is truly unfriendly to the user. Somehow they decide to give Apple the ability to do something pretty good."

Gates also found it strange that no one else had created a service that allowed people to buy songs rather than subscribe on a monthly basis. "I am not saying this strangeness means we messed up—at least if we did, so did Real and Pressplay and MusicNet and basically everyone else," he wrote. "Now that Jobs has done it we need to move fast to get something where the user interface and Rights are as good. . . . I think we need some plan to prove that, even though Jobs has us a bit flat footed again, we can move quick and both match and do stuff better." It was an astonishing private admission: Microsoft had again been caught flat-footed, and it would again try to catch up by copying Apple. But like Sony, Microsoft could never make it happen, even after Jobs showed the way.

Instead Apple continued to smoke Microsoft in the way that Cole had predicted: It ported the iTunes software and store to Windows. But that took some internal agonizing. First, Jobs and his team had to decide whether they wanted the iPod to work with Windows computers. Jobs was initially opposed. "By keeping the iPod for Mac only, it was driving the sales of Macs even more than we expected," he recalled.

But lined up against him were all four of his top executives: Schiller, Rubinstein, Robbin, and Fadell. It was an argument about what the future of Apple should be. "We felt we should be in the music player business, not just in the Mac business," said Schiller.

Jobs always wanted Apple to create its own unified utopia, a magical walled garden where hardware and software and peripheral devices worked well together to create a great experience, and where the success of one product drove sales of all the companions. Now he was facing pressure to have his hottest new product work with Windows machines, and it went against his nature. "It was a really big argument for months," Jobs recalled, "me against everyone else." At one point he declared that Windows users would get to use iPods "over my dead body." But still his team kept pushing. "This *needs* to get to the PC," said Fadell.

Finally Jobs declared, "Until you can prove to me that it will make business sense, I'm not going to do it." That was actually his way of backing down. If you put aside emotion and dogma, it was easy to prove that it made business sense to allow Windows users to buy iPods. Experts were called in, sales scenarios developed, and everyone concluded this would bring in more profits. "We developed a spreadsheet," said Schiller. "Under all scenarios, there was no amount of cannibalization of Mac sales that would outweigh the sales of iPods." Jobs was sometimes willing to surrender, despite his reputation, but he never won any awards for gracious concession speeches. "Screw it," he said at one meeting where they showed him the analysis. "I'm sick of listening to you assholes. Go do whatever the hell you want."

That left another question: When Apple allowed the iPod to be compatible with Windows machines, should it also create a version of iTunes to serve as the music-management software for those Windows users? As usual, Jobs believed the hardware and software should go together: The user experience depended on the iPod working in complete sync (so to speak) with iTunes software on the computer. Schiller was opposed. "I thought that was crazy, since we don't make Windows software," Schiller recalled. "But Steve kept arguing, 'If we're going to do it, we should do it right.'"

Schiller prevailed at first. Apple decided to allow the iPod to work with Windows by using software from MusicMatch, an outside company. But the software was so clunky that it proved Jobs's point, and Apple embarked on a fast-track effort to produce iTunes for Windows. Jobs recalled:

> To make the iPod work on PCs, we initially partnered with another company that had a jukebox, gave them the secret sauce to connect to the iPod, and they did a crappy job. That was the worst of all worlds, because this other company was controlling a big piece of the user experience. So we lived with this crappy outside jukebox for about six months, and then we finally got iTunes written for Windows. In the end, you just don't want someone else to control a big part of the user experience. People may disagree with me, but I am pretty consistent about that.

Porting iTunes to Windows meant going back to all of the music companies—which had made deals to be in iTunes based on the assurance that it would be for only the small universe of Macintosh users—and negotiate again. Sony was especially resistant. Andy Lack thought it another example of Jobs changing the terms after a deal was done. It was. But by then the other labels were happy about how the iTunes Store was working and went along, so Sony was forced to capitulate.

Jobs announced the launch of iTunes for Windows in October 2003. "Here's a feature that people thought we'd never add until this happened," he said, waving his hand at the giant screen behind him. "Hell froze over," proclaimed the slide. The show included iChat appearances and videos from Mick Jagger, Dr. Dre, and Bono. "It's a very cool thing for musicians and music," Bono said of the iPod and iTunes. "That's why I'm here to kiss the corporate ass. I don't kiss everybody's."

Jobs was never prone to understatement. To the cheers of the crowd, he declared, "iTunes for Windows is probably the best Windows app ever written."

Microsoft was not grateful. "They're pursuing the same strategy that they pursued in the PC business, controlling both the hardware and software," Bill Gates told *Business Week*. "We've always done things

a little bit differently than Apple in terms of giving people choice."
It was not until three years later, in November 2006, that Microsoft
was finally able to release its own answer to the iPod. It was called the
Zune, and it looked like an iPod, though a bit clunkier. Two years later
it had achieved a market share of less than 5%. Jobs was brutal about
the cause of the Zune's uninspired design and market weakness:

> The older I get, the more I see how much motivations matter. The
> Zune was crappy because the people at Microsoft don't really love music
> or art the way we do. We won because we personally love music. We
> made the iPod for ourselves, and when you're doing something for
> yourself, or your best friend or family, you're not going to cheese out. If
> you don't love something, you're not going to go the extra mile, work the
> extra weekend, challenge the status quo as much.

Mr. Tambourine Man

Andy Lack's first annual meeting at Sony was in April 2003, the same
week that Apple launched the iTunes Store. He had been made head
of the music division four months earlier, and had spent much of that
time negotiating with Jobs. In fact he arrived in Tokyo directly from
Cupertino, carrying the latest version of the iPod and a description of
the iTunes Store. In front of the two hundred managers gathered, he
pulled the iPod out of his pocket. "Here it is," he said as CEO Nobuyuki Idei and Sony's North America head Howard Stringer looked
on. "Here's the Walkman killer. There's no mystery meat. The reason
you bought a music company is so that you could be the one to make a
device like this. You can do better."

But Sony couldn't. It had pioneered portable music with the Walkman, it had a great record company, and it had a long history of making beautiful consumer devices. It had all of the assets to compete with
Jobs's strategy of integration of hardware, software, devices, and content sales. Why did it fail? Partly because it was a company, like AOL
Time Warner, that was organized into divisions (that word itself was
ominous) with their own bottom lines; the goal of achieving synergy

in such companies by prodding the divisions to work together was usually elusive.

Jobs did not organize Apple into semiautonomous divisions; he
closely controlled all of his teams and pushed them to work as one
cohesive and flexible company, with one profit-and-loss bottom line.
"We don't have 'divisions' with their own P&L," said Tim Cook. "We
run one P&L for the company."

In addition, like many companies, Sony worried about cannibalization. If it built a music player and service that made it easy for people
to share digital songs, that might hurt sales of its record division. One
of Jobs's business rules was to never be afraid of cannibalizing yourself.
"If you don't cannibalize yourself, someone else will," he said. So even
though an iPhone might cannibalize sales of an iPod, or an iPad might
cannibalize sales of a laptop, that did not deter him.

That July, Sony appointed a veteran of the music industry, Jay
Samit, to create its own iTunes-like service, called Sony Connect,
which would sell songs online and allow them to play on Sony's portable music devices. "The move was immediately understood as a
way to unite the sometimes conflicting electronics and content divisions," the New York Times reported. "That internal battle was seen by
many as the reason Sony, the inventor of the Walkman and the biggest
player in the portable audio market, was being trounced by Apple."
Sony Connect launched in May 2004. It lasted just over three years
before Sony shut it down.

Microsoft was willing to license its Windows Media software and
digital rights format to other companies, just as it had licensed out
its operating system in the 1980s. Jobs, on the other hand, would not
license out Apple's FairPlay to other device makers; it worked only on
an iPod. Nor would he allow other online stores to sell songs for use on
iPods. A variety of experts said this would eventually cause Apple to
lose market share, as it did in the computer wars of the 1980s. "If Apple
continues to rely on a proprietary architecture," the Harvard Business
School professor Clayton Christensen told Wired, "the iPod will likely
become a niche product." (Other than in this case, Christensen was one
of the world's most insightful business analysts, and Jobs was deeply

influenced by his book *The Innovator's Dilemma.*) Bill Gates made the same argument. "There's nothing unique about music," he said. "This story has played out on the PC."

Rob Glaser, the founder of RealNetworks, tried to circumvent Apple's restrictions in July 2004 with a service called Harmony. He had attempted to convince Jobs to license Apple's FairPlay format to Harmony, but when that didn't happen, Glaser just reverse-engineered it and used it with the songs that Harmony sold. Glaser's strategy was that the songs sold by Harmony would play on any device, including an iPod or a Zune or a Rio, and he launched a marketing campaign with the slogan "Freedom of Choice." Jobs was furious and issued a release saying that Apple was "stunned that RealNetworks has adopted the tactics and ethics of a hacker to break into the iPod." RealNetworks responded by launching an Internet petition that demanded "Hey Apple! Don't break my iPod." Jobs kept quiet for a few months, but in October he released a new version of the iPod software that caused songs bought through Harmony to become inoperable. "Steve is a one-of-a-kind guy," Glaser said. "You know that about him when you do business with him."

In the meantime Jobs and his team—Rubinstein, Fadell, Robbin, Ive—were able to keep coming up with new versions of the iPod that extended Apple's lead. The first major revision, announced in January 2004, was the iPod Mini. Far smaller than the original iPod—just the size of a business card—it had less capacity and was about the same price. At one point Jobs decided to kill it, not seeing why anyone would want to pay the same for less. "He doesn't do sports, so he didn't relate to how it would be great on a run or in the gym," said Fadell. In fact the Mini was what truly launched the iPod to market dominance, by eliminating the competition from smaller flash-drive players. In the eighteen months after it was introduced, Apple's market share in the portable music player market shot from 31% to 74%.

The iPod Shuffle, introduced in January 2005, was even more revolutionary. Jobs learned that the shuffle feature on the iPod, which played songs in random order, had become very popular. People liked to be surprised, and they were also too lazy to keep setting up and revising their playlists. Some users even became obsessed with figuring out whether the song selection was truly random, and if so, why their iPod kept coming back to, say, the Neville Brothers. That feature led to the iPod Shuffle. As Rubinstein and Fadell were working on creating a flash player that was small and inexpensive, they kept doing things like making the screen tinier. At one point Jobs came in with a crazy suggestion: Get rid of the screen altogether. "What?!?" Fadell responded. "Just get rid of it," Jobs insisted. Fadell asked how users would navigate the songs. Jobs's insight was that you wouldn't need to navigate; the songs would play randomly. After all, they were songs you had chosen. All that was needed was a button to skip over a song if you weren't in the mood for it. "Embrace uncertainty," the ads read.

As competitors stumbled and Apple continued to innovate, music became a larger part of Apple's business. In January 2007 iPod sales were half of Apple's revenues. The device also added luster to the Apple brand. But an even bigger success was the iTunes Store. Having sold one million songs in the first six days after it was introduced in April 2003, the store went on to sell seventy million songs in its first year. In February 2006 the store sold its one billionth song when Alex Ostrovsky, sixteen, of West Bloomfield, Michigan, bought Coldplay's "Speed of Sound" and got a congratulatory call from Jobs, bestowing upon him ten iPods, an iMac, and a $10,000 music gift certificate.

The success of the iTunes Store also had a more subtle benefit. By 2011 an important new business had emerged: being the service that people trusted with their online identity and payment information. Along with Amazon, Visa, PayPal, American Express, and a few other services, Apple had built up databases of people who trusted them with their email address and credit card information to facilitate safe and easy shopping. This allowed Apple to sell, for example, a magazine subscription through its online store; when that happened, Apple, not the magazine publisher, would have a direct relationship with the subscriber. As the iTunes Store sold videos, apps, and subscriptions, it built up a database of 225 million active users by June 2011, which positioned Apple for the next age of digital commerce.

CHAPTER THIRTY-TWO

MUSIC MAN

The Sound Track of His Life

Jimmy Iovine, Bono, Jobs, and The Edge, 2004

On His iPod

As the iPod phenomenon grew, it spawned a question that was asked of presidential candidates, B-list celebrities, first dates, the queen of England, and just about anyone else with white earbuds: "What's on your iPod?" The parlor game took off when Elisabeth Bumiller wrote a piece in the *New York Times* in early 2005 dissecting the answer that President George W. Bush gave when she asked him that question. "Bush's iPod is heavy on traditional country singers," she reported. "He has selections by Van Morrison, whose 'Brown Eyed Girl' is a Bush favorite, and by John Fogerty, most predictably 'Centerfield.'" She got

a *Rolling Stone* editor, Joe Levy, to analyze the selection, and he commented, "One thing that's interesting is that the president likes artists
who don't like him."

"Simply handing over your iPod to a friend, your blind date, or
the total stranger sitting next to you on the plane opens you up like a
book," Steven Levy wrote in *The Perfect Thing*. "All somebody needs
to do is scroll through your library on that click wheel, and, musically
speaking, you're naked. It's not just what you like—it's *who you are*."
So one day, when we were sitting in his living room listening to music,
I asked Jobs to let me see his. As we sat there, he flicked through his
favorite songs.

Not surprisingly, there were all six volumes of Dylan's bootleg series, including the tracks Jobs had first started worshipping when he
and Wozniak were able to score them on reel-to-reel tapes years before
the series was officially released. In addition, there were fifteen other
Dylan albums, starting with his first, *Bob Dylan* (1962), but going only
up to *Oh Mercy* (1989). Jobs had spent a lot of time arguing with Andy
Hertzfeld and others that Dylan's subsequent albums, indeed any of
his albums after *Blood on the Tracks* (1975), were not as powerful as
his early performances. The one exception he made was Dylan's track
"Things Have Changed" from the 2000 movie *Wonder Boys*. Notably his iPod did not include *Empire Burlesque* (1985), the album that
Hertzfeld had brought him the weekend he was ousted from Apple.

The other great trove on his iPod was the Beatles. He included
songs from seven of their albums: *A Hard Day's Night, Abbey Road,
Help!, Let It Be, Magical Mystery Tour, Meet the Beatles!* and *Sgt. Pepper's
Lonely Hearts Club Band*. The solo albums missed the cut. The Rolling
Stones clocked in next, with six albums: *Emotional Rescue, Flashpoint,
Jump Back, Some Girls, Sticky Fingers*, and *Tattoo You*. In the case of the
Dylan and the Beatles albums, most were included in their entirety.
But true to his belief that albums can and should be disaggregated,
those of the Stones and most other artists on his iPod included only
three or four cuts. His onetime girlfriend Joan Baez was amply repre-
sented by selections from four albums, including two different versions
of "Love Is Just a Four-Letter Word."

His iPod selections were those of a kid from the seventies with his heart in the sixties. There were Aretha, B. B. King, Buddy Holly, Buffalo Springfield, Don McLean, Donovan, the Doors, Janis Joplin, Jefferson Airplane, Jimi Hendrix, Johnny Cash, John Mellencamp, Simon and Garfunkel, and even The Monkees ("I'm a Believer") and Sam the Sham ("Wooly Bully"). Only about a quarter of the songs were from more contemporary artists, such as 10,000 Maniacs, Alicia Keys, Black Eyed Peas, Coldplay, Dido, Green Day, John Mayer (a friend of both his and Apple), Moby (likewise), U2, Seal, and Talking Heads. As for classical music, there were a few recordings of Bach, including the Brandenburg Concertos, and three albums by Yo-Yo Ma.

Jobs told Sheryl Crow in May 2003 that he was downloading some Eminem tracks, admitting, "He's starting to grow on me." James Vincent subsequently took him to an Eminem concert. Even so, the rapper missed making it onto Jobs's iPod. As Jobs said to Vincent after the concert, "I don't know . . ." He later told me, "I respect Eminem as an artist, but I just don't want to listen to his music, and I can't relate to his values the way I can to Dylan's."

His favorites did not change over the years. When the iPad 2 came out in March 2011, he transferred his favorite music to it. One afternoon we sat in his living room as he scrolled through the songs on his new iPad and, with a mellow nostalgia, tapped on ones he wanted to hear.

We went through the usual Dylan and Beatles favorites, then he became more reflective and tapped on a Gregorian chant, "Spiritus Domini," performed by Benedictine monks. For a minute or so he zoned out, almost in a trance. "That's really beautiful," he murmured. He followed with Bach's Second Brandenburg Concerto and a fugue from *The Well-Tempered Clavier*. Bach, he declared, was his favorite classical composer. He was particularly fond of listening to the contrasts between the two versions of the "Goldberg Variations" that Glenn Gould recorded, the first in 1955 as a twenty-two-year-old little-known pianist and the second in 1981, a year before he died. "They're like night and day," Jobs said after playing them sequentially one afternoon. "The first is an exuberant, young, brilliant piece, played so fast it's a revelation. The later one is so much more spare and stark. You sense a very deep soul who's been through a lot in life. It's deeper and wiser." Jobs

was on his third medical leave that afternoon when he played both versions, and I asked which he liked better. "Gould liked the later version
much better," he said. "I used to like the earlier, exuberant one. But
now I can see where he was coming from."

He then jumped from the sublime to the sixties: Donovan's "Catch
the Wind." When he noticed me look askance, he protested, "Donovan did some really good stuff, really." He punched up "Mellow Yellow," and then admitted that perhaps it was not the best example. "It
sounded better when we were young."

I asked what music from our childhood actually held up well these
days. He scrolled down the list on his iPad and called up the Grateful
Dead's 1969 song "Uncle John's Band." He nodded along with the lyrics: "When life looks like Easy Street, there is danger at your door." For
a moment we were back at that tumultuous time when the mellowness
of the sixties was ending in discord. "Whoa, oh, what I want to know
is, are you kind?"

Then he turned to Joni Mitchell. "She had a kid she put up for
adoption," he said. "This song is about her little girl." He tapped on
"Little Green," and we listened to the mournful melody and lyrics that
describe the feelings of a mother who gives up a child. "So you sign all
the papers in the family name / You're sad and you're sorry, but you're
not ashamed." I asked whether he still often thought about being put
up for adoption. "No, not much," he said. "Not too often."

These days, he said, he thought more about getting older than
about his birth. That led him to play Joni Mitchell's greatest song,
"Both Sides Now," with its lyrics about being older and wiser: "I've
looked at life from both sides now, / From win and lose, and still somehow, / It's life's illusions I recall, / I really don't know life at all." As
Glenn Gould had done with Bach's "Goldberg Variations," Mitchell
had recorded "Both Sides Now" many years apart, first in 1969 and
then in an excruciatingly haunting slow version in 2000. He played the
latter. "It's interesting how people age," he noted.

Some people, he added, don't age well even when they are young.
I asked who he had in mind. "John Mayer is one of the best guitar
players who's ever lived, and I'm just afraid he's blowing it big time,"
Jobs replied. Jobs liked Mayer and occasionally had him over for din-

ner in Palo Alto. When he was twenty-seven, Mayer appeared at the January 2004 Macworld, where Jobs introduced GarageBand, and he became a fixture at the event most years. Jobs punched up Mayer's hit "Gravity." The lyrics are about a guy filled with love who inexplicably dreams of ways to throw it away: "Gravity is working against me, / And gravity wants to bring me down." Jobs shook his head and commented, "I think he's a really good kid underneath, but he's just been out of control."

At the end of the listening session, I asked him a well-worn question: the Beatles or the Stones? "If the vault was on fire and I could grab only one set of master tapes, I would grab the Beatles," he answered. "The hard one would be between the Beatles and Dylan. Somebody else could have replicated the Stones. No one could have been Dylan or the Beatles." As he was ruminating about how fortunate we were to have all of them when we were growing up, his son, then eighteen, came in the room. "Reed doesn't understand," Jobs lamented. Or perhaps he did. He was wearing a Joan Baez T-shirt, with the words "Forever Young" on it.

Bob Dylan

The only time Jobs can ever recall being tongue-tied was in the presence of Bob Dylan. He was playing near Palo Alto in October 2004, and Jobs was recovering from his first cancer surgery. Dylan was not a gregarious man, not a Bono or a Bowie. He was never Jobs's friend, nor did he care to be. He did, however, invite Jobs to visit him at his hotel before the concert. Jobs recalled:

> We sat on the patio outside his room and talked for two hours. I was really nervous, because he was one of my heroes. And I was also afraid that he wouldn't be really smart anymore, that he'd be a caricature of himself, like happens to a lot of people. But I was delighted. He was as sharp as a tack. He was everything I'd hoped. He was really open and honest. He was just telling me about his life and about writing his songs. He said, "They just came through me, it wasn't like I was having

to compose them. That doesn't happen anymore, I just can't write them that way anymore." Then he paused and said to me with his raspy voice and little smile, "But I still can sing them."

The next time Dylan played nearby, he invited Jobs to drop by his tricked-up tour bus just before the concert. When Dylan asked what his favorite song was, Jobs said "One Too Many Mornings." So Dylan sang it that night. After the concert, as Jobs was walking out the back, the tour bus came by and screeched to a stop. The door flipped open. "So, did you hear my song I sang for you?" Dylan rasped. Then he drove off. When Jobs tells the tale, he does a pretty good impression of Dylan's voice. "He's one of my all-time heroes," Jobs recalled. "My love for him has grown over the years, it's ripened. I can't figure out how he did it when he was so young."

A few months after seeing him in concert, Jobs came up with a grandiose plan. The iTunes Store should offer a digital "boxed set" of every Dylan song ever recorded, more than seven hundred in all, for $199. Jobs would be the curator of Dylan for the digital age. But Andy Lack of Sony, which was Dylan's label, was in no mood to make a deal without some serious concessions regarding iTunes. In addition, Lack felt the price was too low and would cheapen Dylan. "Bob is a national treasure," said Lack, "and Steve wanted him on iTunes at a price that commoditized him." It got to the heart of the problems that Lack and other record executives were having with Jobs: He was getting to set the price points, not them. So Lack said no.

"Okay, then I will call Dylan directly," Jobs said. But it was not the type of thing that Dylan ever dealt with, so it fell to his agent, Jeff Rosen, to sort things out.

"It's a really bad idea," Lack told Rosen, showing him the numbers. "Bob is Steve's hero. He'll sweeten the deal." Lack had both a professional and a personal desire to fend Jobs off, even to yank his chain a bit. So he made an offer to Rosen. "I will write you a check for a million dollars tomorrow if you hold off for the time being." As Lack later explained, it was an advance against future royalties, "one of those accounting things record companies do." Rosen called back forty-five minutes later and accepted. "Andy worked things out with us and asked us not to do it, which we didn't," he recalled. "I think Andy gave us some sort of an advance to hold off doing it."

By 2006, however, Lack had stepped aside as the CEO of what was by then Sony BMG, and Jobs reopened negotiations. He sent Dylan an iPod with all of his songs on it, and he showed Rosen the type of marketing campaign that Apple could mount. In August he announced a grand deal. It allowed Apple to sell the $199 digital boxed set of all the songs Dylan ever recorded, plus the exclusive right to offer Dylan's new album, *Modern Times,* for pre-release orders. "Bob Dylan is one of the most respected poets and musicians of our time, and he is a personal hero of mine," Jobs said at the announcement. The 773-track set included forty-two rarities, such as a 1961 tape of "Wade in the Water" made in a Minnesota hotel, a 1962 version of "Handsome Molly" from a live concert at the Gaslight Café in Greenwich Village, the truly awesome rendition of "Mr. Tambourine Man" from the 1964 Newport Folk Festival (Jobs's favorite), and an acoustic version of "Outlaw Blues" from 1965.

As part of the deal, Dylan appeared in a television ad for the iPod, featuring his new album, *Modern Times.* This was one of the most astonishing cases of flipping the script since Tom Sawyer persuaded his friends to whitewash the fence. In the past, getting celebrities to do an ad required paying them a lot of money. But by 2006 the tables were turned. Major artists *wanted* to appear in iPod ads; the exposure would guarantee success. James Vincent had predicted this a few years earlier, when Jobs said he had contacts with many musicians and could pay them to appear in ads. "No, things are going to soon change," Vincent replied. "Apple is a different kind of brand, and it's cooler than the brand of most artists. We should talk about the opportunity we offer the bands, not pay them."

Lee Clow recalled that there was actually some resistance among the younger staffers at Apple and the ad agency to using Dylan. "They wondered whether he was still cool enough," Clow said. Jobs would hear none of that. He was thrilled to have Dylan.

Jobs became obsessed by every detail of the Dylan commercial. Rosen flew to Cupertino so that they could go through the album and pick the song they wanted to use, which ended up being "Someday

Baby." Jobs approved a test video that Clow made using a stand-in for Dylan, which was then shot in Nashville with Dylan himself. But when it came back, Jobs hated it. It wasn't distinctive enough. He wanted a new style. So Clow hired another director, and Rosen was able to convince Dylan to retape the entire commercial. This time it was done with a gently backlit cowboy-hatted Dylan sitting on a stool, strumming and singing, while a hip woman in a newsboy cap dances with her iPod. Jobs loved it.

The ad showed the halo effect of the iPod's marketing: It helped Dylan win a younger audience, just as the iPod had done for Apple computers. Because of the ad, Dylan's album was number one on the *Billboard* chart its first week, topping hot-selling albums by Christina Aguilera and Outkast. It was the first time Dylan had reached the top spot since *Desire* in 1976, thirty years earlier. *Ad Age* headlined Apple's role in propelling Dylan. "The iTunes spot wasn't just a run-of-the-mill celebrity-endorsement deal in which a big brand signs a big check to tap into the equity of a big star," it reported. "This one flipped the formula, with the all-powerful Apple brand giving Mr. Dylan access to younger demographics and helping propel his sales to places they hadn't been since the Ford administration."

The Beatles

Among Jobs's prized CDs was a bootleg that contained a dozen or so taped sessions of the Beatles revising "Strawberry Fields Forever." It became the musical score to his philosophy of how to perfect a product. Andy Hertzfeld had found the CD and made a copy of it for Jobs in 1986, though Jobs sometimes told folks that it had come from Yoko Ono. Sitting in the living room of his Palo Alto home one day, Jobs rummaged around in some glass-enclosed bookcases to find it, then put it on while describing what it had taught him:

> It's a complex song, and it's fascinating to watch the creative process as they went back and forth and finally created it over a few months. Lennon was always my favorite Beatle. [He laughs as Lennon stops during

the first take and makes the band go back and revise a chord.] Did you hear that little detour they took? It didn't work, so they went back and started from where they were. It's so raw in this version. It actually makes them sound like mere mortals. You could actually imagine other people doing this, up to this version. Maybe not writing and conceiving it, but certainly playing it. Yet they just didn't stop. They were such perfectionists they kept it going and going. This made a big impression on me when I was in my thirties. You could just tell how much they worked at this.

They did a bundle of work between each of these recordings. They kept sending it back to make it closer to perfect. [As he listens to the third take, he points out how the instrumentation has gotten more complex.] The way we build stuff at Apple is often this way. Even the number of models we'd make of a new notebook or iPod. We would start off with a version and then begin refining and refining, doing detailed models of the design, or the buttons, or how a function operates. It's a lot of work, but in the end it just gets better, and soon it's like, "Wow, how did they do that?!? Where are the screws?"

It was thus understandable that Jobs was driven to distraction by the fact that the Beatles were not on iTunes.

His struggle with Apple Corps, the Beatles' business holding company, stretched more than three decades, causing too many journalists to use the phrase "long and winding road" in stories about the relationship. It began in 1978, when Apple Computers, soon after its launch, was sued by Apple Corps for trademark infringement, based on the fact that the Beatles' former recording label was called Apple. The suit was settled three years later, when Apple Computers paid Apple Corps $80,000. The settlement had what seemed back then an innocuous stipulation: The Beatles would not produce any computer equipment and Apple would not market any music products.

The Beatles kept their end of the bargain; none of them ever produced any computers. But Apple ended up wandering into the music business. It got sued again in 1991, when the Mac incorporated the ability to play musical files, then again in 2003, when the iTunes Store was launched. The legal issues were finally resolved in 2007, when

Apple made a deal to pay Apple Corps $500 million for all worldwide rights to the name, and then licensed back to the Beatles the right to use Apple Corps for their record and business holdings.

Alas, this did not resolve the issue of getting the Beatles onto iTunes. For that to happen, the Beatles and EMI Music, which held the rights to most of their songs, had to negotiate their own differences over how to handle the digital rights. "The Beatles all want to be on iTunes," Jobs later recalled, "but they and EMI are like an old married couple. They hate each other but can't get divorced. The fact that my favorite band was the last holdout from iTunes was something I very much hoped I would live to resolve." As it turned out, he would.

Bono

Bono, the lead singer of U2, deeply appreciated Apple's marketing muscle. He was confident that his Dublin-based band was still the best in the world, but in 2004 it was trying, after almost thirty years together, to reinvigorate its image. It had produced an exciting new album with a song that the band's lead guitarist, The Edge, declared to be "the mother of all rock tunes." Bono knew he needed to find a way to get it some traction, so he placed a call to Jobs.

"I wanted something specific from Apple," Bono recalled. "We had a song called 'Vertigo' that featured an aggressive guitar riff that I knew would be contagious, but only if people were exposed to it many, many times." He was worried that the era of promoting a song through airplay on the radio was over. So Bono visited Jobs at home in Palo Alto, walked around the garden, and made an unusual pitch. Over the years U2 had spurned offers as high as $23 million to be in commercials. Now he wanted Jobs to use the band in an iPod commercial for free—or at least as part of a mutually beneficial package. "They had never done a commercial before," Jobs later recalled. "But they were getting ripped off by free downloading, they liked what we were doing with iTunes, and they thought we could promote them to a younger audience."

Any other CEO would have jumped into a mosh pit to have U2

in an ad, but Jobs pushed back a bit. Apple didn't feature recognizable people in the iPod ads, just silhouettes. (The Dylan ad had not yet been made.) "You have silhouettes of fans," Bono replied, "so couldn't the next phase be silhouettes of artists?" Jobs said it sounded like an idea worth exploring. Bono left a copy of the unreleased album, *How to Dismantle an Atomic Bomb*, for Jobs to hear. "He was the only person outside the band who had it," Bono said.

A round of meetings ensued. Jobs flew down to talk to Jimmy Iovine, whose Interscope records distributed U2, at his house in the Holmby Hills section of Los Angeles. The Edge was there, along with U2's manager, Paul McGuinness. Another meeting took place in Jobs's kitchen, with McGuinness writing down the deal points in the back of his diary. U2 would appear in the commercial, and Apple would vigorously promote the album in multiple venues, ranging from billboards to the iTunes homepage. The band would get no direct fee, but it would get royalties from the sale of a special U2 edition of the iPod. Bono believed, like Lack, that the musicians should get a royalty on each iPod sold, and this was his small attempt to assert the principle in a limited way for his band. "Bono and I asked Steve to make us a black one," Iovine recalled. "We weren't just doing a commercial sponsorship, we were making a co-branding deal."

"We wanted our own iPod, something distinct from the regular white ones," Bono recalled. "We wanted black, but Steve said, 'We've tried other colors than white, and they don't work.'" A few days later Jobs relented and accepted the idea, tentatively.

The commercial interspersed high-voltage shots of the band in partial silhouette with the usual silhouette of a dancing woman listening to an iPod. But even as it was being shot in London, the agreement with Apple was unraveling. Jobs began having second thoughts about the idea of a special black iPod, and the royalty rates were not fully pinned down. He called James Vincent, at Apple's ad agency, and told him to call London and put things on hold. "I don't think it's going to happen," Jobs said. "They don't realize how much value we are giving them, it's going south. Let's think of some other ad to do." Vincent, a lifelong U2 fan, knew how big the ad would be, both for the band and Apple, and begged for the chance to call Bono to try to get things on track. Jobs gave him Bono's mobile number, and he reached the singer in his kitchen in Dublin.

Bono was also having a few second thoughts. "I don't think this is going to work," he told Vincent. "The band is reluctant." Vincent asked what the problem was. "When we were teenagers in Dublin, we said we would never do naff stuff," Bono replied. Vincent, despite being British and familiar with rock slang, said he didn't know what that meant. "Doing rubbishy things for money," Bono explained. "We are all about our fans. We feel like we'd be letting them down if we went in an ad. It doesn't feel right. I'm sorry we wasted your time."

Vincent asked what more Apple could do to make it work. "We are giving you the most important thing we have to give, and that's our music," said Bono. "And what are you giving us back? Advertising, and our fans will think it's for you. We need something more." Vincent replied that the offer of the special U2 edition of the iPod and the royalty arrangement was a huge deal. "That's the most prized thing we have to give," he told Bono.

The singer said he was ready to try to put the deal back together, so Vincent immediately called Jony Ive, another big U2 fan (he had first seen them in concert in Newcastle in 1983), and described the situation. Then he called Jobs and suggested he send Ive to Dublin to show what the black iPod would look like. Jobs agreed. Vincent called Bono back, and asked if he knew Jony Ive, unaware that they had met before and admired each other. "Know Jony Ive?" Bono laughed. "I love that guy. I drink his bathwater."

"That's a bit strong," Vincent replied, "but how about letting him come visit and show how cool your iPod would be?"

"I'm going to pick him up myself in my Maserati," Bono answered. "He's going to stay at my house, I'm going to take him out, and I will get him really drunk."

The next day, as Ive headed toward Dublin, Vincent had to fend off Jobs, who was still having second thoughts. "I don't know if we're doing the right thing," he said. "We don't want to do this for anyone else." He was worried about setting the precedent of artists getting a royalty from each iPod sold. Vincent assured him that the U2 deal would be special.

"Jony arrived in Dublin and I put him up at my guest house, a serene place over a railway track with a view of the sea," Bono recalled. "He shows me this beautiful black iPod with a deep red click wheel, and I say okay, we'll do it." They went to a local pub, hashed out some of the details, and then called Jobs in Cupertino to see if he would agree. Jobs haggled for a while over each detail of the finances, and over the design, before he finally embraced the deal. That impressed Bono. "It's actually amazing that a CEO cares that much about detail," he said. When it was resolved, Ive and Bono settled into some serious drinking. Both are comfortable in pubs. After a few pints, they decided to call Vincent back in California. He was not home, so Bono left a message on his answering machine, which Vincent made sure never to erase. "I'm sitting here in bubbling Dublin with your friend Jony," it said. "We're both a bit drunk, and we're happy with this wonderful iPod and I can't even believe it exists and I'm holding it in my hand. Thank you!"

Jobs rented a theater in San Jose for the unveiling of the TV commercial and special iPod. Bono and The Edge joined him onstage. The album sold 840,000 copies in its first week and debuted at number one on the *Billboard* chart. Bono told the press afterward that he had done the commercial without charge because "U2 will get as much value out of the commercial as Apple will." Jimmy Iovine added that it would allow the band to "reach a younger audience."

What was remarkable was that associating with a computer and electronics company was the best way for a rock band to seem hip and appeal to young people. Bono later explained that not all corporate sponsorships were deals with the devil. "Let's have a look," he told Greg Kot, the *Chicago Tribune* music critic. "The 'devil' here is a bunch of creative minds, more creative than a lot of people in rock bands. The lead singer is Steve Jobs. These men have helped design the most beautiful art object in music culture since the electric guitar. That's the iPod. The job of art is to chase ugliness away."

Bono got Jobs to do another deal with him in 2006, this one for his Product Red campaign that raised money and awareness to fight AIDS in Africa. Jobs was never much interested in philanthropy, but he agreed to do a special red iPod as part of Bono's campaign. It was not a wholehearted commitment. He balked, for example, at using the campaign's signature treatment of putting the name of the company in parentheses with the word "red" in superscript after it, as in (APPLE)[RED]. "I don't want Apple in parentheses," Jobs insisted. Bono replied, "But Steve, that's how we show unity for our cause." The conversation got heated—to the F-you stage—before they agreed to sleep on it. Finally Jobs compromised, sort of. Bono could do what he wanted in his ads, but Jobs would never put Apple in parentheses on any of his products or in any of his stores. The iPod was labeled (PRODUCT)[RED], not (APPLE)[RED].

"Steve can be sparky," Bono recalled, "but those moments have made us closer friends, because there are not many people in your life where you can have those robust discussions. He's very opinionated. After our shows, I talk to him and he's always got an opinion." Jobs and his family occasionally visited Bono and his wife and four kids at their home near Nice on the French Riviera. On one vacation, in 2008, Jobs chartered a boat and moored it near Bono's home. They ate meals together, and Bono played tapes of the songs U2 was preparing for what became the *No Line on the Horizon* album. But despite the friendship, Jobs was still a tough negotiator. They tried to make a deal for another ad and special release of the song "Get On Your Boots," but they could not come to terms. When Bono hurt his back in 2010 and had to cancel a tour, Powell sent him a gift basket with a DVD of the comedy duo Flight of the Conchords, the book *Mozart's Brain and the Fighter Pilot*, honey from her beehives, and pain cream. Jobs wrote a note and attached it to the last item, saying, "Pain Cream—I love this stuff."

Yo-Yo Ma

There was one classical musician Jobs revered both as a person and as a performer: Yo-Yo Ma, the versatile virtuoso who is as sweet and profound as the tones he creates on his cello. They had met in 1981, when Jobs was at the Aspen Design Conference and Ma was at the Aspen Music Festival. Jobs tended to be deeply moved by artists who displayed purity, and he became a fan. He invited Ma to play at his wedding, but he was out of the country on tour. He came by the Jobs house a few years later, sat in the living room, pulled out his 1733 Stradivarius cello, and played Bach. "This is what I would have played for your wedding," he told them. Jobs teared up and told him, "You playing is the best argument I've ever heard for the existence of God, because I don't really believe a human alone can do this." On a subsequent visit Ma allowed Jobs's daughter Erin to hold the cello while they sat around the kitchen. By that time Jobs had been struck by cancer, and he made Ma promise to play at his funeral.

CHAPTER THIRTY-THREE

PIXAR'S FRIENDS

. . . and Foes

A Bug's Life

When Apple developed the iMac, Jobs drove with Jony Ive to show it to the folks at Pixar. He felt that the machine had the spunky personality that would appeal to the creators of Buzz Lightyear and Woody, and he loved the fact that Ive and John Lasseter shared the talent to connect art with technology in a playful way.

Pixar was a haven where Jobs could escape the intensity in Cupertino. At Apple, the managers were often excitable and exhausted, Jobs tended to be volatile, and people felt nervous about where they stood with him. At Pixar, the storytellers and illustrators seemed more serene and behaved more gently, both with each other and even with Jobs. In other words, the tone at each place was set at the top, by Jobs at Apple, but by Lasseter at Pixar.

Jobs reveled in the earnest playfulness of moviemaking and got passionate about the algorithms that enabled such magic as allowing computer-generated raindrops to refract sunbeams or blades of grass to wave in the wind. But he was able to restrain himself from trying to control the creative process. It was at Pixar that he learned to let other creative people flourish and take the lead. Largely it was because he loved Lasseter, a gentle artist who, like Ive, brought out the best in Jobs.

Jobs's main role at Pixar was deal making, in which his natural intensity was an asset. Soon after the release of *Toy Story*, he clashed with Jeffrey Katzenberg, who had left Disney in the summer of 1994 and joined with Steven Spielberg and David Geffen to start DreamWorks SKG. Jobs believed that his Pixar team had told Katzenberg, while he was still at Disney, about its proposed second movie, *A Bug's Life*, and that he had then stolen the idea of an animated insect movie when he decided to produce *Antz* at DreamWorks. "When Jeffrey was still running Disney animation, we pitched him on *A Bug's Life*," Jobs said. "In sixty years of animation history, nobody had thought of doing an animated movie about insects, until Lasseter. It was one of his brilliant creative sparks. And Jeffrey left and went to DreamWorks and all of a sudden had this idea for an animated movie about—Oh!—insects. And he pretended he'd never heard the pitch. He lied. He lied through his teeth."

Actually, not. The real story is a bit more interesting. Katzenberg never heard the *Bug's Life* pitch while at Disney. But after he left for DreamWorks, he stayed in touch with Lasseter, occasionally pinging him with one of his typical "Hey buddy, how you doing just checking in" quick phone calls. So when Lasseter happened to be at the Technicolor facility on the Universal lot, where DreamWorks was also located, he called Katzenberg and dropped by with a couple of colleagues. When Katzenberg asked what they were doing next, Lasseter told him. "We described to him *A Bug's Life*, with an ant as the main character, and told him the whole story of him organizing the other ants and enlisting a group of circus performer insects to fight off the grasshoppers," Lasseter recalled. "I should have been wary. Jeffrey kept asking questions about when it would be released."

Lasseter began to get worried when, in early 1996, he heard rumors that DreamWorks might be making its own computer-animated movie about ants. He called Katzenberg and asked him point-blank. Katzenberg hemmed, hawed, and asked where Lasseter had heard that. Lasseter asked again, and Katzenberg admitted it was true. "How could you?" yelled Lasseter, who very rarely raised his voice.

"We had the idea long ago," said Katzenberg, who explained that it had been pitched to him by a development director at DreamWorks.

"I don't believe you," Lasseter replied.

Katzenberg conceded that he had sped up *Antz* as a way to counter his former colleagues at Disney. DreamWorks' first major picture was to be *Prince of Egypt*, which was scheduled to be released for Thanksgiving 1998, and he was appalled when he heard that Disney was planning to release Pixar's *A Bug's Life* that same weekend. So he had rushed *Antz* into production to force Disney to change the release date of *A Bug's Life*.

"Fuck you," replied Lasseter, who did not normally use such language. He didn't speak to Katzenberg for another thirteen years.

Jobs was furious, and he was far more practiced than Lasseter at giving vent to his emotions. He called Katzenberg and started yelling. Katzenberg made an offer: He would delay production of *Antz* if Jobs and Disney would move *A Bug's Life* so that it didn't compete with *Prince of Egypt*. "It was a blatant extortion attempt, and I didn't go for it," Jobs recalled. He told Katzenberg there was nothing he could do to make Disney change the release date.

"Of course you can," Katzenberg replied. "You can move mountains. You taught me how!" He said that when Pixar was almost bankrupt, he had come to its rescue by giving it the deal to do *Toy Story*. "I was the one guy there for you back then, and now you're allowing them to use you to screw me." He suggested that if Jobs wanted to, he could simply slow down production on *A Bug's Life* without telling Disney. If he did, Katzenberg said, he would put *Antz* on hold. "Don't even go there," Jobs replied.

Katzenberg had a valid gripe. It was clear that Eisner and Disney were using the Pixar movie to get back at him for leaving Disney and starting a rival animation studio. "*Prince of Egypt* was the first thing we were making, and they scheduled something for our announced release date just to be hostile," he said. "My view was like that of the Lion King, that if you stick your hand in my cage and paw me, watch out."

No one backed down, and the rival ant movies provoked a press frenzy. Disney tried to keep Jobs quiet, on the theory that playing up the rivalry would serve to help *Antz*, but he was a man not easily muzzled. "The bad guys rarely win," he told the *Los Angeles Times*. In response, DreamWorks' savvy marketing maven, Terry Press, suggested, "Steve Jobs should take a pill."

Antz was released at the beginning of October 1998. It was not a bad movie. Woody Allen voiced the part of a neurotic ant living in a conformist society who yearns to express his individualism. "This is the kind of Woody Allen comedy Woody Allen no longer makes," *Time* wrote. It grossed a respectable $91 million domestically and $172 million worldwide.

A Bug's Life came out six weeks later, as planned. It had a more epic plot, which reversed Aesop's tale of "The Ant and the Grasshopper," plus a greater technical virtuosity, which allowed such startling details as the view of grass from a bug's vantage point. *Time* was much more effusive about it. "Its design work is so stellar—a wide-screen Eden of leaves and labyrinths populated by dozens of ugly, buggy, cuddly cutups—that it makes the DreamWorks film seem, by comparison, like radio," wrote Richard Corliss. It did twice as well as *Antz* at the box office, grossing $163 million domestically and $363 million worldwide. (It also beat *Prince of Egypt*.)

A few years later Katzenberg ran into Jobs and tried to smooth things over. He insisted that he had never heard the pitch for *A Bug's Life* while at Disney; if he had, his settlement with Disney would have given him a share of the profits, so it's not something he would lie about. Jobs laughed, and accepted as much. "I asked you to move your release date, and you wouldn't, so you can't be mad at me for protecting my child," Katzenberg told him. He recalled that Jobs "got really calm and Zen-like" and said he understood. But Jobs later said that he never really forgave Katzenberg:

> Our film toasted his at the box office. Did that feel good? No, it still felt awful, because people started saying how everyone in Hollywood was doing insect movies. He took the brilliant originality away from John, and that can never be replaced. That's unconscionable, so I've never trusted him, even after he tried to make amends. He came up to

me after he was successful with *Shrek* and said, "I'm a changed man, I'm finally at peace with myself," and all this crap. And it was like, give me a break, Jeffrey.

For his part, Katzenberg was much more gracious. He considered Jobs one of the "true geniuses in the world," and he learned to respect him despite their volatile dealings.

More important than beating *Antz* was showing that Pixar was not a one-hit wonder. *A Bug's Life* grossed as much as *Toy Story* had, proving that the first success was not a fluke. "There's a classic thing in business, which is the second-product syndrome," Jobs later said. It comes from not understanding what made your first product so successful. "I lived through that at Apple. My feeling was, if we got through our second film, we'd make it."

Steve's Own Movie

Toy Story 2, which came out in November 1999, was even bigger, with a $485 million gross worldwide. Given that Pixar's success was now assured, it was time to start building a showcase headquarters. Jobs and the Pixar facilities team found an abandoned Del Monte fruit cannery in Emeryville, an industrial neighborhood between Berkeley and Oakland, just across the Bay Bridge from San Francisco. They tore it down, and Jobs commissioned Peter Bohlin, the architect of the Apple stores, to design a new building for the sixteen-acre plot.

Jobs obsessed over every aspect of the new building, from the overall concept to the tiniest detail regarding materials and construction. "Steve had this firm belief that the right kind of building can do great things for a culture," said Pixar's president Ed Catmull. Jobs controlled the creation of the building as if he were a director sweating each scene of a film. "The Pixar building was Steve's own movie," Lasseter said.

Lasseter had originally wanted a traditional Hollywood studio, with separate buildings for various projects and bungalows for development teams. But the Disney folks said they didn't like their new campus because the teams felt isolated, and Jobs agreed. In fact he decided they should go to the other extreme: one huge building around a central atrium designed to encourage random encounters.

Despite being a denizen of the digital world, or maybe because he knew all too well its isolating potential, Jobs was a strong believer in face-to-face meetings. "There's a temptation in our networked age to think that ideas can be developed by email and iChat," he said. "That's crazy. Creativity comes from spontaneous meetings, from random discussions. You run into someone, you ask what they're doing, you say 'Wow,' and soon you're cooking up all sorts of ideas."

So he had the Pixar building designed to promote encounters and unplanned collaborations. "If a building doesn't encourage that, you'll lose a lot of innovation and the magic that's sparked by serendipity," he said. "So we designed the building to make people get out of their offices and mingle in the central atrium with people they might not otherwise see." The front doors and main stairs and corridors all led to the atrium, the café and the mailboxes were there, the conference rooms had windows that looked out onto it, and the six-hundred-seat theater and two smaller screening rooms all spilled into it. "Steve's theory worked from day one," Lasseter recalled. "I kept running into people I hadn't seen for months. I've never seen a building that promoted collaboration and creativity as well as this one."

Jobs even went so far as to decree that there be only two huge bathrooms in the building, one for each gender, connected to the atrium. "He felt that very, very strongly," recalled Pam Kerwin, Pixar's general manager. "Some of us felt that was going too far. One pregnant woman said she shouldn't be forced to walk for ten minutes just to go to the bathroom, and that led to a big fight." It was one of the few times that Lasseter disagreed with Jobs. They reached a compromise: there would be two sets of bathrooms on either side of the atrium on both of the two floors.

Because the building's steel beams were going to be visible, Jobs pored over samples from manufacturers across the country to see which had the best color and texture. He chose a mill in Arkansas, told it to blast the steel to a pure color, and made sure the truckers used caution not to nick any of it. He also insisted that all the beams be bolted together, not welded. "We sandblasted the steel and clear-coated it, so

you can actually see what it's like," he recalled. "When the steelwork-
ers were putting up the beams, they would bring their families on the
weekend to show them."

The wackiest piece of serendipity was "The Love Lounge." One of
the animators found a small door on the back wall when he moved into
his office. It opened to a low corridor that you could crawl through to
a room clad in sheet metal that provided access to the air-conditioning
valves. He and his colleagues commandeered the secret room, festooned it with Christmas lights and lava lamps, and furnished it with
benches upholstered in animal prints, tasseled pillows, a fold-up cocktail table, liquor bottles, bar equipment, and napkins that read "The
Love Lounge." A video camera installed in the corridor allowed oc-
cupants to monitor who might be approaching.

Lasseter and Jobs brought important visitors there and had them
sign the wall. The signatures include Michael Eisner, Roy Disney, Tim
Allen, and Randy Newman. Jobs loved it, but since he wasn't a drinker
he sometimes referred to it as the Meditation Room. It reminded him,
he said, of the one that he and Daniel Kottke had at Reed, but without
the acid.

The Divorce

In testimony before a Senate committee in February 2002, Michael
Eisner blasted the ads that Jobs had created for Apple's iTunes. "There
are computer companies that have full-page ads and billboards that
say: Rip, mix, burn," he declared. "In other words, they can create a
theft and distribute it to all their friends if they buy this particular
computer."

This was not a smart comment. It misunderstood the meaning of
"rip" and assumed it involved ripping someone off, rather than importing files from a CD to a computer. More significantly, it truly pissed
off Jobs, as Eisner should have known. That too was not smart. Pixar
had recently released the fourth movie in its Disney deal, *Monsters, Inc.*,
which turned out to be the most successful of them all, with $525 mil-

lion in worldwide gross. Disney's Pixar deal was again coming up for renewal, and Eisner had not made it easier by publicly poking a stick at his partner's eye. Jobs was so incredulous he called a Disney executive to vent: "Do you know what Michael just did to me?"

Eisner and Jobs came from different backgrounds and opposite coasts, but they were similar in being strong-willed and without much inclination to find compromises. They both had a passion for making good products, which often meant micromanaging details and not sugarcoating their criticisms. Watching Eisner take repeated rides on the Wildlife Express train through Disney World's Animal Kingdom and coming up with smart ways to improve the customer experience was like watching Jobs play with the interface of an iPod and find ways it could be simplified. Watching them manage people was a less edifying experience.

Both were better at pushing people than being pushed, which led to an unpleasant atmosphere when they started trying to do it to each other. In a disagreement, they tended to assert that the other party was lying. In addition, neither Eisner nor Jobs seemed to believe that he could learn anything from the other; nor would it have occurred to either even to fake a bit of deference by pretending to have anything to learn. Jobs put the onus on Eisner:

> The worst thing, to my mind, was that Pixar had successfully reinvented Disney's business, turning out great films one after the other while Disney turned out flop after flop. You would think the CEO of Disney would be curious how Pixar was doing that. But during the twenty-year relationship, he visited Pixar for a total of about two and a half hours, only to give little congratulatory speeches. He was never curious. I was amazed. Curiosity is very important.

That was overly harsh. Eisner had been up to Pixar a bit more than that, including visits when Jobs wasn't with him. But it was true that he showed little curiosity about the artistry or technology at the studio. Jobs likewise didn't spend much time trying to learn from Disney's management.

The open sniping between Jobs and Eisner began in the summer of 2002. Jobs had always admired the creative spirit of the great Walt Disney, especially because he had nurtured a company to last for generations. He viewed Walt's nephew Roy as an embodiment of this historic legacy and spirit. Roy was still on the Disney board, despite his own growing estrangement from Eisner, and Jobs let him know that he would not renew the Pixar-Disney deal as long as Eisner was still the CEO.

Roy Disney and Stanley Gold, his close associate on the Disney board, began warning other directors about the Pixar problem. That prompted Eisner to send the board an intemperate email in late August 2002. He was confident that Pixar would eventually renew its deal, he said, partly because Disney had rights to the Pixar movies and characters that had been made thus far. Plus, he said, Disney would be in a better negotiating position in a year, after Pixar finished *Finding Nemo*. "Yesterday we saw for the second time the new Pixar movie, *Finding Nemo*, that comes out next May," he wrote. "This will be a reality check for those guys. It's okay, but nowhere near as good as their previous films. Of course they think it is great." There were two major problems with this email: It leaked to the *Los Angeles Times*, provoking Jobs to go ballistic, and Eisner's assessment of the movie was wrong, very wrong.

Finding Nemo became Pixar's (and Disney's) biggest hit thus far. It easily beat out *The Lion King* to become, for the time being, the most successful animated movie in history. It grossed $340 million domestically and $868 million worldwide. Until 2010 it was also the most popular DVD of all time, with forty million copies sold, and spawned some of the most popular rides at Disney theme parks. In addition, it was a richly textured, subtle, and deeply beautiful artistic achievement that won the Oscar for best animated feature. "I liked the film because it was about taking risks and learning to let those you love take risks," Jobs said. Its success added $183 million to Pixar's cash reserves, giving it a hefty war chest of $521 million for the final showdown with Disney.

Shortly after *Finding Nemo* was finished, Jobs made Eisner an offer that was so one-sided it was clearly meant to be rejected. Instead of a fifty-fifty split on revenues, as in the existing deal, Jobs proposed a new arrangement in which Pixar would own outright the films it made and the characters in them, and it would merely pay Disney a 7.5% fee to distribute the movies. Plus, the last two films under the existing deal—*The Incredibles* and *Cars* were the ones in the works—would shift to the new distribution deal.

Eisner, however, held one powerful trump card. Even if Pixar didn't renew, Disney had the right to make sequels of *Toy Story* and the other movies that Pixar had made, and it owned all the characters, from Woody to Nemo, just as it owned Mickey Mouse and Donald Duck. Eisner was already planning—or threatening—to have Disney's own animation studio do a *Toy Story 3*, which Pixar had declined to do. "When you see what that company did putting out *Cinderella II*, you shudder at what would have happened," Jobs said.

Eisner was able to force Roy Disney off the board in November 2003, but that didn't end the turmoil. Disney released a scathing open letter. "The company has lost its focus, its creative energy, and its heritage," he wrote. His litany of Eisner's alleged failings included not building a constructive relationship with Pixar. By this point Jobs had decided that he no longer wanted to work with Eisner. So in January 2004 he publicly announced that he was cutting off negotiations with Disney.

Jobs was usually disciplined in not making public the strong opinions that he shared with friends around his Palo Alto kitchen table. But this time he did not hold back. In a conference call with reporters, he said that while Pixar was producing hits, Disney animation was making "embarrassing duds." He scoffed at Eisner's notion that Disney made any creative contribution to the Pixar films: "The truth is there has been little creative collaboration with Disney for years. You can compare the creative quality of our films with the creative quality of Disney's last three films and judge each company's creative ability yourselves." In addition to building a better creative team, Jobs had pulled off the remarkable feat of building a brand that was now as big a draw for moviegoers as Disney's. "We think the Pixar brand is now

the most powerful and trusted brand in animation." When Jobs called
to give him a heads-up, Roy Disney replied, "When the wicked witch
is dead, we'll be together again."

John Lasseter was aghast at the prospect of breaking up with Disney. "I was worried about my children, what they would do with the
characters we'd created," he recalled. "It was like a dagger to my heart."
When he told his top staff in the Pixar conference room, he started
crying, and he did so again when he addressed the eight hundred or
so Pixar employees gathered in the studio's atrium. "It's like you have
these dear children and you have to give them up to be adopted by
convicted child molesters." Jobs came to the atrium stage next and
tried to calm things down. He explained why it might be necessary to
break with Disney, and he assured them that Pixar as an institution had
to keep looking forward to be successful. "He has the absolute ability
to make you believe," said Oren Jacob, a longtime technologist at the
studio. "Suddenly, we all had the confidence that, whatever happened,
Pixar would flourish."

Bob Iger, Disney's chief operating officer, had to step in and do
damage control. He was as sensible and solid as those around him were
volatile. His background was in television; he had been president of the
ABC Network, which was acquired in 1996 by Disney. His reputation
was as a corporate suit, and he excelled at deft management, but he
also had a sharp eye for talent, a good-humored ability to understand
people, and a quiet flair that he was secure enough to keep muted. Unlike Eisner and Jobs, he had a disciplined calm, which helped him deal
with large egos. "Steve did some grandstanding by announcing that
he was ending talks with us," Iger later recalled. "We went into crisis
mode, and I developed some talking points to settle things down."

Eisner had presided over ten great years at Disney, when Frank
Wells served as his president. Wells freed Eisner from many management duties so he could make his suggestions, usually valuable and
often brilliant, on ways to improve each movie project, theme park
ride, television pilot, and countless other products. But after Wells
was killed in a helicopter crash in 1994, Eisner never found the right
manager. Katzenberg had demanded Wells's job, which is why Eisner
ousted him. Michael Ovitz became president in 1995; it was not a

pretty sight, and he was gone in less than two years. Jobs later offered his assessment:

> For his first ten years as CEO, Eisner did a really good job. For the last ten years, he really did a bad job. And the change came when Frank Wells died. Eisner is a really good creative guy. He gives really good notes. So when Frank was running operations, Eisner could be like a bumblebee going from project to project trying to make them better. But when Eisner had to run things, he was a terrible manager. Nobody liked working for him. They felt they had no authority. He had this strategic planning group that was like the Gestapo, in that you couldn't spend any money, not even a dime, without them approving it. Even though I broke with him, I had to respect his achievements in the first ten years. And there was a part of him I actually liked. He's a fun guy to be around at times—smart, witty. But he had a dark side to him. His ego got the better of him. Eisner was reasonable and fair to me at first, but eventually, over the course of dealing with him for a decade, I came to see a dark side to him.

Eisner's biggest problem in 2004 was that he did not fully fathom how messed up his animation division was. Its two most recent movies, *Treasure Planet* and *Brother Bear*, did no honor to the Disney legacy, or to its balance sheets. Hit animation movies were the lifeblood of the company; they spawned theme park rides, toys, and television shows. *Toy Story* had led to a movie sequel, a *Disney on Ice* show, a *Toy Story Musical* performed on Disney cruise ships, a direct-to-video film featuring Buzz Lightyear, a computer storybook, two video games, a dozen action toys that sold twenty-five million units, a clothing line, and nine different attractions at Disney theme parks. This was not the case for *Treasure Planet.*

"Michael didn't understand that Disney's problems in animation were as acute as they were," Iger later explained. "That manifested itself in the way he dealt with Pixar. He never felt he needed Pixar as much as he really did." In addition, Eisner loved to negotiate and hated to compromise, which was not always the best combination when dealing with Jobs, who was the same way. "Every negotiation needs to be resolved by compromises," Iger said. "Neither one of them is a master of compromise."

The impasse was ended on a Saturday night in March 2005, when Iger got a phone call from former senator George Mitchell and other Disney board members. They told him that, starting in a few months, he would replace Eisner as Disney's CEO. When Iger got up the next morning, he called his daughters and then Steve Jobs and John Lasseter. He said, very simply and clearly, that he valued Pixar and wanted to make a deal. Jobs was thrilled. He liked Iger and even marveled at a small connection they had: his former girlfriend Jennifer Egan and Iger's wife, Willow Bay, had been roommates at Penn.

That summer, before Iger officially took over, he and Jobs got to have a trial run at making a deal. Apple was coming out with an iPod that would play video as well as music. It needed television shows to sell, and Jobs did not want to be too public in negotiating for them because, as usual, he wanted the product to be secret until he unveiled it onstage. Iger, who had multiple iPods and used them throughout the day, from his 5 a.m. workouts to late at night, had already been envisioning what it could do for television shows. So he immediately offered ABC's most popular shows, *Desperate Housewives* and *Lost*. "We negotiated that deal in a week, and it was complicated," Iger said. "It was important because Steve got to see how I worked, and because it showed everyone that Disney could in fact work with Steve."

For the announcement of the video iPod, Jobs rented a theater in San Jose, and he invited Iger to be his surprise guest onstage. "I had never been to one of his announcements, so I had no idea what a big deal it was," Iger recalled. "It was a real breakthrough for our relationship. He saw I was pro-technology and willing to take risks." Jobs did his usual virtuoso performance, running through all the features of the new iPod, how it was "one of the best things we've ever done," and how the iTunes Store would now be selling music videos and short films. Then, as was his habit, he ended with "And yes, there is one more thing:" The iPod would be selling TV shows. There was huge applause. He mentioned that the two most popular shows were on ABC. "And who owns ABC? Disney! I know these guys," he exulted.

When Iger then came onstage, he looked as relaxed and as comfortable as Jobs. "One of the things that Steve and I are incredibly excited about is the intersection between great content and great technology," he said. "It's great to be here to announce an extension of our relation with Apple," he added. Then, after the proper pause, he said, "Not with Pixar, but with Apple."

But it was clear from their warm embrace that a new Pixar-Disney deal was once again possible. "It signaled my way of operating, which was 'Make love not war,'" Iger recalled. "We had been at war with Roy Disney, Comcast, Apple, and Pixar. I wanted to fix all that, Pixar most of all."

Iger had just come back from opening the new Disneyland in Hong Kong, with Eisner at his side in his last big act as CEO. The ceremonies included the usual Disney parade down Main Street. Iger realized that the only characters in the parade that had been created in the past decade were Pixar's. "A lightbulb went off," he recalled. "I'm standing next to Michael, but I kept it completely to myself, because it was such an indictment of his stewardship of animation during that period. After ten years of *The Lion King, Beauty and the Beast,* and *Aladdin,* there were then ten years of nothing."

Iger went back to Burbank and had some financial analysis done. He discovered that they had actually lost money on animation in the past decade and had produced little that helped ancillary products. At his first meeting as the new CEO, he presented the analysis to the board, whose members expressed some anger that they had never been told this. "As animation goes, so goes our company," he told the board. "A hit animated film is a big wave, and the ripples go down to every part of our business—from characters in a parade, to music, to parks, to video games, TV, Internet, consumer products. If I don't have wave makers, the company is not going to succeed." He presented them with some choices. They could stick with the current animation management, which he didn't think would work. They could get rid of management and find someone else, but he said he didn't know who that would be. Or they could buy Pixar. "The problem is, I don't know if it's for sale, and if it is, it's going to be a huge amount of money," he said. The board authorized him to explore a deal.

Iger went about it in an unusual way. When he first talked to Jobs, he admitted the revelation that had occurred to him in Hong Kong and how it convinced him that Disney badly needed Pixar. "That's why I just loved Bob Iger," recalled Jobs. "He just blurted it out. Now that's the dumbest thing you can do as you enter a negotiation, at least according to the traditional rule book. He just put his cards out on the table and said, 'We're screwed.' I immediately liked the guy, because that's how I worked too. Let's just immediately put all the cards on the table and see where they fall." (In fact that was not usually Jobs's mode of operation. He often began negotiations by proclaiming that the other company's products or services sucked.)

Jobs and Iger took a lot of walks—around the Apple campus, in Palo Alto, at the Allen and Co. retreat in Sun Valley. At first they came up with a plan for a new distribution deal: Pixar would get back all the rights to the movies and characters it had already produced in return for Disney's getting an equity stake in Pixar, and it would pay Disney a simple fee to distribute its future movies. But Iger worried that such a deal would simply set Pixar up as a competitor to Disney, which would be bad even if Disney had an equity stake in it. So he began to hint that maybe they should actually do something bigger. "I want you to know that I am really thinking out of the box on this," he said. Jobs seemed to encourage the advances. "It wasn't too long before it was clear to both of us that this discussion might lead to an acquisition discussion," Jobs recalled.

But first Jobs needed the blessing of John Lasseter and Ed Catmull, so he asked them to come over to his house. He got right to the point. "We need to get to know Bob Iger," he told them. "We may want to throw in with him and to help him remake Disney. He's a great guy." They were skeptical at first. "He could tell we were pretty shocked," Lasseter recalled.

"If you guys don't want to do it, that's fine, but I want you to get to know Iger before you decide," Jobs continued. "I was feeling the same as you, but I've really grown to like the guy." He explained how easy it had been to make the deal to put ABC shows on the iPod, and added, "It's night and day different from Eisner's Disney. He's straightforward, and there's no drama with him." Lasseter remembers that he and Catmull just sat there with their mouths slightly open.

Iger went to work. He flew from Los Angeles to Lasseter's house for dinner, and stayed up well past midnight talking. He also took Catmull out to dinner, and then he visited Pixar Studios, alone, with no entourage and without Jobs. "I went out and met all the directors one on one, and they each pitched me their movie," he said. Lasseter was proud of how much his team impressed Iger, which of course made him warm up to Iger. "I never had more pride in Pixar than that day," he said. "All the teams and pitches were amazing, and Bob was blown away."

Indeed after seeing what was coming up over the next few years—*Cars, Ratatouille, WALL-E*—Iger told his chief financial officer at Disney, "Oh my God, they've got great stuff. We've got to get this deal done. It's the future of the company." He admitted that he had no faith in the movies that Disney animation had in the works.

The deal they proposed was that Disney would purchase Pixar for $7.4 billion in stock. Jobs would thus become Disney's largest shareholder, with approximately 7% of the company's stock compared to 1.7% owned by Eisner and 1% by Roy Disney. Disney Animation would be put under Pixar, with Lasseter and Catmull running the combined unit. Pixar would retain its independent identity, its studio and headquarters would remain in Emeryville, and it would even keep its own email addresses.

Iger asked Jobs to bring Lasseter and Catmull to a secret meeting of the Disney board in Century City, Los Angeles, on a Sunday morning. The goal was to make them feel comfortable with what would be a radical and expensive deal. As they prepared to take the elevator from the parking garage, Lasseter said to Jobs, "If I start getting too excited or go on too long, just touch my leg." Jobs ended up having to do it once, but otherwise Lasseter made the perfect sales pitch. "I talked about how we make films, what our philosophies are, the honesty we have with each other, and how we nurture the creative talent," he recalled. The board asked a lot of questions, and Jobs let Lasseter answer most. But Jobs did talk about how exciting it was to connect art with technology. "That's what our culture is all about, just like at Apple," he said.

Before the Disney board got a chance to approve the merger, however, Michael Eisner arose from the departed to try to derail it. He called Iger and said it was far too expensive. "You can fix animation yourself," Eisner told him. "How?" asked Iger. "I know you can," said Eisner. Iger got a bit annoyed. "Michael, how come you say I can fix it, when you couldn't fix it yourself?" he asked.

Eisner said he wanted to come to a board meeting, even though he was no longer a member or an officer, and speak against the acquisition. Iger resisted, but Eisner called Warren Buffett, a big shareholder, and George Mitchell, who was the lead director. The former senator convinced Iger to let Eisner have his say. "I told the board that they didn't need to buy Pixar because they already owned 85% of the movies Pixar had already made," Eisner recounted. He was referring to the fact that for the movies already made, Disney was getting that percentage of the gross, plus it had the rights to make all the sequels and exploit the characters. "I made a presentation that said, here's the 15% of Pixar that Disney does not already own. So that's what you're getting. The rest is a bet on future Pixar films." Eisner admitted that Pixar had been enjoying a good run, but he said it could not continue. "I showed the history of producers and directors who had X number of hits in a row and then failed. It happened to Spielberg, Walt Disney, all of them." To make the deal worth it, he calculated, each new Pixar movie would have to gross $1.3 billion. "It drove Steve crazy that I knew that," Eisner later said.

After he left the room, Iger refuted his argument point by point. "Let me tell you what was wrong with that presentation," he began. When the board had finished hearing them both, it approved the deal Iger proposed.

Iger flew up to Emeryville to meet Jobs and jointly announce the deal to the Pixar workers. But before they did, Jobs sat down alone with Lasseter and Catmull. "If either of you have doubts," he said, "I will just tell them no thanks and blow off this deal." He wasn't totally sincere. It would have been almost impossible to do so at that point. But it was a welcome gesture. "I'm good," said Lasseter. "Let's do it." Catmull agreed. They all hugged, and Jobs wept.

Everyone then gathered in the atrium. "Disney is buying Pixar," Jobs announced. There were a few tears, but as he explained the deal, the staffers began to realize that in some ways it was a reverse acquisition. Catmull would be the head of Disney animation, Lasseter its chief creative officer. By the end they were cheering. Iger had been standing on the side, and Jobs invited him to center stage. As he talked about the special culture of Pixar and how badly Disney needed to nurture it and learn from it, the crowd broke into applause.

"My goal has always been not only to make great products, but to build great companies," Jobs later said. "Walt Disney did that. And the way we did the merger, we kept Pixar as a great company and helped Disney remain one as well."

CHAPTER THIRTY-FOUR

TWENTY-FIRST-CENTURY MACS

Setting Apple Apart

With the iBook, 1999

Clams, Ice Cubes, and Sunflowers

Ever since the introduction of the iMac in 1998, Jobs and Jony Ive had made beguiling design a signature of Apple's computers. There was a consumer laptop that looked like a tangerine clam, and a professional desktop computer that suggested a Zen ice cube. Like bell-bottoms that turn up in the back of a closet, some of these models looked better at the time than they do in retrospect, and they show a love of design that was, on occasion, a bit too exuberant. But they set Apple apart and provided the publicity bursts it needed to survive in a Windows world.

The Power Mac G4 Cube, released in 2000, was so alluring that one ended up on display in New York's Museum of Modern Art. An eight-inch perfect cube the size of a Kleenex box, it was the pure expression of Jobs's aesthetic. The sophistication came from minimalism. No buttons marred the surface. There was no CD tray, just a subtle slot. And as with the original Macintosh, there was no fan. Pure Zen. "When you see something that's so thoughtful on the outside you say, 'Oh, wow, it must be really thoughtful on the inside,'" he told *Newsweek*. "We make progress by eliminating things, by removing the superfluous."

The G4 Cube was almost ostentatious in its lack of ostentation, and it was powerful. But it was not a success. It had been designed as a high-end desktop, but Jobs wanted to turn it, as he did almost every product, into something that could be mass-marketed to consumers. The Cube ended up not serving either market well. Workaday professionals weren't seeking a jewel-like sculpture for their desks, and mass-market consumers were not eager to spend twice what they'd pay for a plain vanilla desktop. Jobs predicted that Apple would sell 200,000 Cubes per quarter. In its first quarter it sold half that. The next quarter it sold fewer than thirty thousand units. Jobs later admitted that he had overdesigned and overpriced the Cube, just as he had the NeXT computer. But gradually he was learning his lesson. In building devices like the iPod, he would control costs and make the trade-offs necessary to get them launched on time and on budget.

Partly because of the poor sales of the Cube, Apple produced disappointing revenue numbers in September 2000. That was just when the tech bubble was deflating and Apple's education market was declining. The company's stock price, which had been above $60, fell 50% in one day, and by early December it was below $15.

None of this deterred Jobs from continuing to push for distinctive, even distracting, new design. When flat-screen displays became commercially viable, he decided it was time to replace the iMac, the translucent consumer desktop computer that looked as if it were from a *Jetsons* cartoon. Ive came up with a model that was somewhat conventional, with the guts of the computer attached to the back of the flat screen. Jobs didn't like it. As he often did, both at Pixar and at

Apple, he slammed on the brakes to rethink things. There was something about the design that lacked purity, he felt. "Why have this flat display if you're going to glom all this stuff on its back?" he asked Ive. "We should let each element be true to itself."

Jobs went home early that day to mull over the problem, then called Ive to come by. They wandered into the garden, which Jobs's wife had planted with a profusion of sunflowers. "Every year I do something wild with the garden, and that time it involved masses of sunflowers, with a sunflower house for the kids," she recalled. "Jony and Steve were riffing on their design problem, then Jony asked, 'What if the screen was separated from the base like a sunflower?' He got excited and started sketching." Ive liked his designs to suggest a narrative, and he realized that a sunflower shape would convey that the flat screen was so fluid and responsive that it could reach for the sun.

In Ive's new design, the Mac's screen was attached to a movable chrome neck, so that it looked not only like a sunflower but also like a cheeky Luxo lamp. Indeed it evoked the playful personality of Luxo Jr. in the first short film that John Lasseter had made at Pixar. Apple took out many patents for the design, most crediting Ive, but on one of them, for "a computer system having a movable assembly attached to a flat panel display," Jobs listed himself as the primary inventor.

In hindsight, some of Apple's Macintosh designs may seem a bit too cute. But other computer makers were at the other extreme. It was an industry that you'd expect to be innovative, but instead it was dominated by cheaply designed generic boxes. After a few ill-conceived stabs at painting on blue colors and trying new shapes, companies such as Dell, Compaq, and HP commoditized computers by outsourcing manufacturing and competing on price. With its spunky designs and its pathbreaking applications like iTunes and iMovie, Apple was about the only place innovating.

Intel Inside

Apple's innovations were more than skin-deep. Since 1994 it had been using a microprocessor, called the PowerPC, that was made by a partnership of IBM and Motorola. For a few years it was faster than Intel's chips, an advantage that Apple touted in humorous commercials. By the time of Jobs's return, however, Motorola had fallen behind in producing new versions of the chip. This provoked a fight between Jobs and Motorola's CEO Chris Galvin. When Jobs decided to stop licensing the Macintosh operating system to clone makers, right after his return to Apple in 1997, he suggested to Galvin that he might consider making an exception for Motorola's clone, the StarMax Mac, but only if Motorola sped up development of new PowerPC chips for laptops. The call got heated. Jobs offered his opinion that Motorola chips sucked. Galvin, who also had a temper, pushed back. Jobs hung up on him. The Motorola StarMax was canceled, and Jobs secretly began planning to move Apple off the Motorola-IBM PowerPC chip and to adopt, instead, Intel's. This would not be a simple task. It was akin to writing a new operating system.

Jobs did not cede any real power to his board, but he did use its meetings to kick around ideas and think through strategies in confidence, while he stood at a whiteboard and led freewheeling discussions. For eighteen months the directors discussed whether to move to an Intel architecture. "We debated it, we asked a lot of questions, and finally we all decided it needed to be done," board member Art Levinson recalled.

Paul Otellini, who was then president and later became CEO of Intel, began huddling with Jobs. They had gotten to know each other when Jobs was struggling to keep NeXT alive and, as Otellini later put it, "his arrogance had been temporarily tempered." Otellini has a calm and wry take on people, and he was amused rather than put off when he discovered, upon dealing with Jobs at Apple in the early 2000s, "that his juices were going again, and he wasn't nearly as humble anymore." Intel had deals with other computer makers, and Jobs wanted a better price than they had. "We had to find creative ways to bridge the numbers," said Otellini. Most of the negotiating was done, as Jobs preferred, on long walks, sometimes on the trails up to the radio telescope known as the Dish above the Stanford campus. Jobs would start the walk by telling a story and explaining how he saw the history of computers evolving. By the end he would be haggling over price.

"Intel had a reputation for being a tough partner, coming out of the days when it was run by Andy Grove and Craig Barrett," Otellini said. "I wanted to show that Intel was a company you could work with." So a crack team from Intel worked with Apple, and they were able to beat the conversion deadline by six months. Jobs invited Otellini to Apple's Top 100 management retreat, where he donned one of the famous Intel lab coats that looked like a bunny suit and gave Jobs a big hug. At the public announcement in 2005, the usually reserved Otellini repeated the act. "Apple and Intel, together at last," flashed on the big screen.

Bill Gates was amazed. Designing crazy-colored cases did not impress him, but a secret program to switch the CPU in a computer, completed seamlessly and on time, was a feat he truly admired. "If you'd said, 'Okay, we're going to change our microprocessor chip, and we're not going to lose a beat,' that sounds impossible," he told me years later, when I asked him about Jobs's accomplishments. "They basically did that."

Options

Among Jobs's quirks was his attitude toward money. When he returned to Apple in 1997, he portrayed himself as a person working for $1 a year, doing it for the benefit of the company rather than himself. Nevertheless he embraced the idea of option megagrants—granting huge bundles of options to buy Apple stock at a preset price—that were not subject to the usual good compensation practices of board committee reviews and performance criteria.

When he dropped the "interim" in his title and officially became CEO, he was offered (in addition to the airplane) a megagrant by Ed Woolard and the board at the beginning of 2000; defying the image he cultivated of not being interested in money, he had stunned Woolard by asking for even more options than the board had proposed. But soon after he got them, it turned out that it was for naught. Apple stock cratered in September 2000—due to disappointing sales of the Cube plus the bursting of the Internet bubble—which made the options worthless.

Making matters worse was a June 2001 cover story in *Fortune* about overcompensated CEOs, "The Great CEO Pay Heist." A mug of Jobs, smiling smugly, filled the cover. Even though his options were underwater at the time, the technical method of valuing them when granted (known as a Black-Scholes valuation) set their worth at $872 million. *Fortune* proclaimed it "by far" the largest compensation package ever granted a CEO. It was the worst of all worlds: Jobs had almost no money that he could put in his pocket for his four years of hard and successful turnaround work at Apple, yet he had become the poster child of greedy CEOs, making him look hypocritical and undermining his self-image. He wrote a scathing letter to the editor, declaring that his options actually "are worth zero" and offering to sell them to *Fortune* for half of the supposed $872 million the magazine had reported.

In the meantime Jobs wanted the board to give him another big grant of options, since his old ones seemed worthless. He insisted, both to the board and probably to himself, that it was more about getting proper recognition than getting rich. "It wasn't so much about the money," he later said in a deposition in an SEC lawsuit over the options. "Everybody likes to be recognized by his peers. . . . I felt that the board wasn't really doing the same with me." He felt that the board should have come to him offering a new grant, without his having to suggest it. "I thought I was doing a pretty good job. It would have made me feel better at the time."

His handpicked board in fact doted on him. So they decided to give him another huge grant in August 2001, when the stock price was just under $18. The problem was that he worried about his image, especially after the *Fortune* article. He did not want to accept the new grant unless the board canceled his old options at the same time. But to do so would have adverse accounting implications, because it would be effectively repricing the old options. That would require taking a charge against current earnings. The only way to avoid this "variable accounting" problem was to cancel his old options at least six months after his new options were granted. In addition, Jobs started haggling with the board over how quickly the new options would vest.

It was not until mid-December 2001 that Jobs finally agreed to take the new options and, braving the optics, wait six months before his old ones were canceled. But by then the stock price (adjusting for a split) had gone up $3, to about $21. If the strike price of the new options was set at that new level, each would have thus been $3 less valuable. So Apple's legal counsel, Nancy Heinen, looked over the recent stock prices and helped to choose an October date, when the stock was $18.30. She also approved a set of minutes that purported to show that the board had approved the grant on that date. The backdating was potentially worth $20 million to Jobs.

Once again Jobs would end up suffering bad publicity without making a penny. Apple's stock price kept dropping, and by March 2003 even the new options were so low that Jobs traded in all of them for an outright grant of $75 million worth of shares, which amounted to about $8.3 million for each year he had worked since coming back in 1997 through the end of the vesting in 2006.

None of this would have mattered much if the *Wall Street Journal* had not run a powerful series in 2006 about backdated stock options. Apple wasn't mentioned, but its board appointed a committee of three members—Al Gore, Eric Schmidt of Google, and Jerry York, formerly of IBM and Chrysler—to investigate its own practices. "We decided at the outset that if Steve was at fault we would let the chips fall where they may," Gore recalled. The committee uncovered some irregularities with Jobs's grants and those of other top officers, and it immediately turned the findings over to the SEC. Jobs was aware of the backdating, the report said, but he ended up not benefiting financially. (A board committee at Disney also found that similar backdating had occurred at Pixar when Jobs was in charge.)

The laws governing such backdating practices were murky, especially since no one at Apple ended up benefiting from the dubiously dated grants. The SEC took eight months to do its own investigation, and in April 2007 it announced that it would not bring action against Apple "based in part on its swift, extensive, and extraordinary cooperation in the Commission's investigation [and its] prompt self-reporting." Although the SEC found that Jobs had been aware of the backdating, it cleared him of any misconduct because he "was unaware of the accounting implications."

The SEC did file complaints against Apple's former chief financial officer Fred Anderson, who was on the board, and general counsel Nancy Heinen. Anderson, a retired Air Force captain with a square jaw and deep integrity, had been a wise and calming influence at Apple, where he was known for his ability to control Jobs's tantrums. He was cited by the SEC only for "negligence" regarding the paperwork for one set of the grants (not the ones that went to Jobs), and the SEC allowed him to continue to serve on corporate boards. Nevertheless he ended up resigning from the Apple board.

Anderson thought he had been made a scapegoat. When he settled with the SEC, his lawyer issued a statement that cast some of the blame on Jobs. It said that Anderson had "cautioned Mr. Jobs that the executive team grant would have to be priced on the date of the actual board agreement or there could be an accounting charge," and that Jobs replied "that the board had given its prior approval."

Heinen, who initially fought the charges against her, ended up settling and paying a $2.2 million fine, without admitting or denying any wrongdoing. Likewise the company itself settled a shareholders' lawsuit by agreeing to pay $14 million in damages.

"Rarely have so many avoidable problems been created by one man's obsession with his own image," Joe Nocera wrote in the *New York Times*. "Then again, this is Steve Jobs we're talking about." Contemptuous of rules and regulations, he created a climate that made it hard for someone like Heinen to buck his wishes. At times, great creativity occurred. But people around him could pay a price. On compensation issues in particular, the difficulty of defying his whims drove some good people to make some bad mistakes.

The compensation issue in some ways echoed Jobs's parking quirk. He refused such trappings as having a "Reserved for CEO" spot, but he assumed for himself the right to park in the handicapped spaces. He wanted to be seen (both by himself and by others) as someone willing to work for $1 a year, but he also wanted to have huge stock grants bestowed upon him. Jangling inside him were the contradictions of a counterculture rebel turned business entrepreneur, someone who wanted to believe that he had turned on and tuned in without having sold out and cashed in.

ROUND ONE

Memento Mori

*At fifty (in center), with Eve and Laurene (behind cake), Eddy Cue
(by window), John Lasseter (with camera), and Lee Clow (with beard)*

Cancer

Jobs would later speculate that his cancer was caused by the grueling
year that he spent, starting in 1997, running both Apple and Pixar. As
he drove back and forth, he had developed kidney stones and other
ailments, and he would come home so exhausted that he could barely
speak. "That's probably when this cancer started growing, because my
immune system was pretty weak at that time," he said.

It is unclear whether exhaustion or a weak immune system could
have caused his cancer. However, his kidney problems did indirectly

452

lead to the detection of his cancer. In October 2003 he happened to run into the urologist who had treated him, and she asked him to get a CAT scan of his kidneys and ureter. It had been five years since his last scan. The new scan revealed nothing wrong with his kidneys, but it did show a shadow on his pancreas, so she asked him to schedule a pancreatic study. He didn't. As usual, he was good at willfully ignoring inputs that he did not want to process. But she persisted. "Steve, this is really important," she said a few days later. "You need to do this."

Her tone of voice was urgent enough that he complied. He went in early one morning, and after studying the scan, the doctors met with him to deliver the bad news that it was a tumor. One of them even suggested that he should make sure his affairs were in order, a polite way of saying that he might have only months to live. That evening they performed a biopsy by sticking an endoscope down his throat and into his intestines so they could put a needle into his pancreas and get a few cells from the tumor. Powell remembers her husband's doctors tearing up with joy. It turned out to be an islet cell or pancreatic neuro-endocrine tumor, which is rare but slower growing and thus more likely to be treated successfully. He was lucky that it was detected so early— as the by-product of a routine kidney screening—and thus could be surgically removed before it had definitely spread.

One of his first calls was to Larry Brilliant, whom he first met at the ashram in India. "Do you still believe in God?" Jobs asked him. Brilliant said that he did, and they discussed the many paths to God that had been taught by the Hindu guru Neem Karoli Baba. Then Brilliant asked Jobs what was wrong. "I have cancer," Jobs replied.

Art Levinson, who was on Apple's board, was chairing the board meeting of his own company, Genentech, when his cell phone rang and Jobs's name appeared on the screen. As soon as there was a break, Levinson called him back and heard the news of the tumor. He had a background in cancer biology, and his firm made cancer treatment drugs, so he became an advisor. So did Andy Grove of Intel, who had fought and beaten prostate cancer. Jobs called him that Sunday, and he drove right over to Jobs's house and stayed for two hours.

To the horror of his friends and wife, Jobs decided not to have surgery to remove the tumor, which was the only accepted medical approach. "I really didn't want them to open up my body, so I tried to see if a few other things would work," he told me years later with a hint of regret. Specifically, he kept to a strict vegan diet, with large quantities of fresh carrot and fruit juices. To that regimen he added acupuncture, a variety of herbal remedies, and occasionally a few other treatments he found on the Internet or by consulting people around the country, including a psychic. For a while he was under the sway of an herbal therapist who operated a natural healing clinic in southern California that stressed the use of organic herbs, juice fasts, frequent bowel cleansings, hydrotherapy, and the expression of all negative feelings.

"The big thing was that he really was not ready to open his body," Powell recalled. "It's hard to push someone to do that." She did try, however. "The body exists to serve the spirit," she argued. His friends repeatedly urged him to have surgery and chemotherapy. "Steve talked to me when he was trying to cure himself by eating horseshit and horseshit roots, and I told him he was crazy," Grove recalled. Levinson said that he "pleaded every day" with Jobs and found it "enormously frustrating that I just couldn't connect with him." The fights almost ruined their friendship. "That's not how cancer works," Levinson insisted when Jobs discussed his diet treatments. "You cannot solve this without surgery and blasting it with toxic chemicals." Even Dr. Dean Ornish, a pioneer in alternative and nutritional methods of treating diseases, took a long walk with Jobs and insisted that sometimes traditional methods were the right option. "You really need surgery," Ornish told him.

Jobs's obstinacy lasted for nine months after his October 2003 diagnosis. Part of it was the product of the dark side of his reality distortion field. "I think Steve has such a strong desire for the world to be a certain way that he wills it to be that way," Levinson speculated. "Sometimes it doesn't work. Reality is unforgiving." The flip side of his wondrous ability to focus was his fearsome willingness to filter out things he did not wish to deal with. This led to many of his great breakthroughs, but it could also backfire. "He has that ability to ignore stuff he doesn't want to confront," Powell explained. "It's just the way he's wired." Whether it involved personal topics relating to his family and marriage, or professional issues relating to engineering or business challenges, or health and cancer issues, Jobs sometimes simply didn't engage.

In the past he had been rewarded for what his wife called his "magical thinking"—his assumption that he could will things to be as he wanted. But cancer does not work that way. Powell enlisted everyone close to him, including his sister Mona Simpson, to try to bring him around. In July 2004 a CAT scan showed that the tumor had grown and possibly spread. It forced him to face reality.

Jobs underwent surgery on Saturday, July 31, 2004, at Stanford University Medical Center. He did not have a full "Whipple procedure," which removes a large part of the stomach and intestine as well as the pancreas. The doctors considered it, but decided instead on a less radical approach, a modified Whipple that removed only part of the pancreas.

Jobs sent employees an email the next day, using his PowerBook hooked up to an AirPort Express in his hospital room, announcing his surgery. He assured them that the type of pancreatic cancer he had "represents about 1% of the total cases of pancreatic cancer diagnosed each year, and can be cured by surgical removal if diagnosed in time (mine was)." He said he would not require chemotherapy or radiation treatment, and he planned to return to work in September. "While I'm out, I've asked Tim Cook to be responsible for Apple's day to day operations, so we shouldn't miss a beat. I'm sure I'll be calling some of you way too much in August, and I look forward to seeing you in September."

One side effect of the operation would become a problem for Jobs because of his obsessive diets and the weird routines of purging and fasting that he had practiced since he was a teenager. Because the pancreas provides the enzymes that allow the stomach to digest food and absorb nutrients, removing part of the organ makes it hard to get enough protein. Patients are advised to make sure that they eat frequent meals and maintain a nutritious diet, with a wide variety of meat and fish proteins as well as full-fat milk products. Jobs had never done this, and he never would.

He stayed in the hospital for two weeks and then struggled to regain his strength. "I remember coming back and sitting in that rocking chair," he told me, pointing to one in his living room. "I didn't have the energy to walk. It took me a week before I could walk around the block. I pushed myself to walk to the gardens a few blocks away, then further, and within six months I had my energy almost back."

Unfortunately the cancer had spread. During the operation the doctors found three liver metastases. Had they operated nine months earlier, they might have caught it before it spread, though they would never know for sure. Jobs began chemotherapy treatments, which further complicated his eating challenges.

The Stanford Commencement

Jobs kept his continuing battle with the cancer secret—he told everyone that he had been "cured"—just as he had kept quiet about his diagnosis in October 2003. Such secrecy was not surprising; it was part of his nature. What was more surprising was his decision to speak very personally and publicly about his cancer diagnosis. Although he rarely gave speeches other than his staged product demonstrations, he accepted Stanford's invitation to give its June 2005 commencement address. He was in a reflective mood after his health scare and turning fifty.

For help with the speech, he called the brilliant scriptwriter Aaron Sorkin (*A Few Good Men, The West Wing*). Jobs sent him some thoughts. "That was in February, and I heard nothing, so I ping him again in April, and he says, 'Oh, yeah,' and I send him a few more thoughts," Jobs recounted. "I finally get him on the phone, and he keeps saying 'Yeah,' but finally it's the beginning of June, and he never sent me anything."

Jobs got panicky. He had always written his own presentations, but he had never done a commencement address. One night he sat down and wrote the speech himself, with no help other than bouncing ideas off his wife. As a result, it turned out to be a very intimate and simple talk, with the unadorned and personal feel of a perfect Steve Jobs product.

Alex Haley once said that the best way to begin a speech is "Let me tell you a story." Nobody is eager for a lecture, but everybody loves a story. And that was the approach Jobs chose. "Today, I want to tell you three stories from my life," he began. "That's it. No big deal. Just three stories."

The first was about dropping out of Reed College. "I could stop taking the required classes that didn't interest me, and begin dropping in on the ones that looked far more interesting." The second was about how getting fired from Apple turned out to be good for him. "The heaviness of being successful was replaced by the lightness of being a beginner again, less sure about everything." The students were unusually attentive, despite a plane circling overhead with a banner that exhorted "recycle all e-waste," and it was his third tale that enthralled them. It was about being diagnosed with cancer and the awareness it brought:

> Remembering that I'll be dead soon is the most important tool I've ever encountered to help me make the big choices in life. Because almost everything—all external expectations, all pride, all fear of embarrassment or failure—these things just fall away in the face of death, leaving only what is truly important. Remembering that you are going to die is the best way I know to avoid the trap of thinking you have something to lose. You are already naked. There is no reason not to follow your heart.

The artful minimalism of the speech gave it simplicity, purity, and charm. Search where you will, from anthologies to YouTube, and you won't find a better commencement address. Others may have been more important, such as George Marshall's at Harvard in 1947 announcing a plan to rebuild Europe, but none has had more grace.

A Lion at Fifty

For his thirtieth and fortieth birthdays, Jobs had celebrated with the stars of Silicon Valley and other assorted celebrities. But when he turned fifty in 2005, after coming back from his cancer surgery, the surprise party that his wife arranged featured mainly his closest friends and professional colleagues. It was at the comfortable San Francisco home of some friends, and the great chef Alice Waters prepared salmon from Scotland along with couscous and a variety of garden-raised vegetables. "It was beautifully warm and intimate, with everyone and the kids all able to sit in one room," Waters recalled. The entertainment was comedy improvisation done by the cast of *Whose Line Is It Anyway?* Jobs's close friend Mike Slade was there, along with colleagues from Apple and Pixar, including Lasseter, Cook, Schiller, Clow, Rubinstein, and Tevanian.

Cook had done a good job running the company during Jobs's absence. He kept Apple's temperamental actors performing well, and he avoided stepping into the limelight. Jobs liked strong personalities, up to a point, but he had never truly empowered a deputy or shared the stage. It was hard to be his understudy. You were damned if you shone, and damned if you didn't. Cook had managed to navigate those shoals. He was calm and decisive when in command, but he didn't seek any notice or acclaim for himself. "Some people resent the fact that Steve gets credit for everything, but I've never given a rat's ass about that," said Cook. "Frankly speaking, I'd prefer my name never be in the paper."

When Jobs returned from his medical leave, Cook resumed his role as the person who kept the moving parts at Apple tightly meshed and remained unfazed by Jobs's tantrums. "What I learned about Steve was that people mistook some of his comments as ranting or negativism, but it was really just the way he showed passion. So that's how I processed it, and I never took issues personally." In many ways he was Jobs's mirror image: unflappable, steady in his moods, and (as the thesaurus in the NeXT would have noted) saturnine rather than mercurial. "I'm a good negotiator, but he's probably better than me because he's a cool customer," Jobs later said. After adding a bit more praise, he quietly added a reservation, one that was serious but rarely spoken: "But Tim's not a product person, per se."

In the fall of 2005, after returning from his medical leave, Jobs tapped Cook to become Apple's chief operating officer. They were flying together to Japan. Jobs didn't really *ask* Cook; he simply turned to him and said, "I've decided to make you COO."

Around that time, Jobs's old friends Jon Rubinstein and Avie

Tevanian, the hardware and software lieutenants who had been re-cruited during the 1997 restoration, decided to leave. In Tevanian's case, he had made a lot of money and was ready to quit working. "Avie is a brilliant guy and a nice guy, much more grounded than Ruby and doesn't carry the big ego," said Jobs. "It was a huge loss for us when Avie left. He's a one-of-a-kind person—a genius."

Rubinstein's case was a little more contentious. He was upset by Cook's ascendency and frazzled after working for nine years under Jobs. Their shouting matches became more frequent. There was also a substantive issue: Rubinstein was repeatedly clashing with Jony Ive, who used to work for him and now reported directly to Jobs. Ive was always pushing the envelope with designs that dazzled but were dif-ficult to engineer. It was Rubinstein's job to get the hardware built in a practical way, so he often balked. He was by nature cautious. "In the end, Ruby's from HP," said Jobs. "And he never delved deep, he wasn't aggressive."

There was, for example, the case of the screws that held the handles on the Power Mac G4. Ive decided that they should have a certain pol-ish and shape. But Rubinstein thought that would be "astronomically" costly and delay the project for weeks, so he vetoed the idea. His job was to deliver products, which meant making trade-offs. Ive viewed that approach as inimical to innovation, so he would go both above him to Jobs and also around him to the midlevel engineers. "Ruby would say, 'You can't do this, it will delay,' and I would say, 'I think we can,'" Ive recalled. "And I would know, because I had worked behind his back with the product teams." In this and other cases, Jobs came down on Ive's side.

At times Ive and Rubinstein got into arguments that almost led to blows. Finally Ive told Jobs, "It's him or me." Jobs chose Ive. By that point Rubinstein was ready to leave. He and his wife had bought property in Mexico, and he wanted time off to build a home there. He eventually went to work for Palm, which was trying to match Apple's iPhone. Jobs was so furious that Palm was hiring some of his former employees that he complained to Bono, who was a cofounder of a pri-vate equity group, led by the former Apple CFO Fred Anderson, that had bought a controlling stake in Palm. Bono sent Jobs a note back saying, "You should chill out about this. This is like the Beatles ring-ing up because Herman and the Hermits have taken one of their road crew." Jobs later admitted that he had overreacted. "The fact that they completely failed salves that wound," he said.

Jobs was able to build a new management team that was less con-tentious and a bit more subdued. Its main players, in addition to Cook and Ive, were Scott Forstall running iPhone software, Phil Schiller in charge of marketing, Bob Mansfield doing Mac hardware, Eddy Cue handling Internet services, and Peter Oppenheimer as the chief financial officer. Even though there was a surface sameness to his top team—all were middle-aged white males—there was a range of styles. Ive was emotional and expressive; Cook was as cool as steel. They all knew they were expected to be deferential to Jobs while also push-ing back on his ideas and being willing to argue—a tricky balance to maintain, but each did it well. "I realized very early that if you didn't voice your opinion, he would mow you down," said Cook. "He takes contrary positions to create more discussion, because it may lead to a better result. So if you don't feel comfortable disagreeing, then you'll never survive."

The key venue for freewheeling discourse was the Monday morn-ing executive team gathering, which started at 9 and went for three or four hours. The focus was always on the future: What should each product do next? What new things should be developed? Jobs used the meeting to enforce a sense of shared mission at Apple. This served to centralize control, which made the company seem as tightly integrated as a good Apple product, and prevented the struggles between divi-sions that plagued decentralized companies.

Jobs also used the meetings to enforce focus. At Robert Friedland's farm, his job had been to prune the apple trees so that they would stay strong, and that became a metaphor for his pruning at Apple. Instead of encouraging each group to let product lines proliferate based on marketing considerations, or permitting a thousand ideas to bloom, Jobs insisted that Apple focus on just two or three priorities at a time. "There is no one better at turning off the noise that is going on around him," Cook said. "That allows him to focus on a few things and say no to many things. Few people are really good at that."

In order to institutionalize the lessons that he and his team were learning, Jobs started an in-house center called Apple University. He hired Joel Podolny, who was dean of the Yale School of Management, to compile a series of case studies analyzing important decisions the company had made, including the switch to the Intel microprocessor and the decision to open the Apple Stores. Top executives spent time teaching the cases to new employees, so that the Apple style of decision making would be embedded in the culture.

In ancient Rome, when a victorious general paraded through the streets, legend has it that he was sometimes trailed by a servant whose job it was to repeat to him, "Memento mori": Remember you will die. A reminder of mortality would help the hero keep things in perspective, instill some humility. Jobs's memento mori had been delivered by his doctors, but it did not instill humility. Instead he roared back after his recovery with even more passion. The illness reminded him that he had nothing to lose, so he should forge ahead full speed. "He came back on a mission," said Cook. "Even though he was now running a large company, he kept making bold moves that I don't think anybody else would have done."

For a while there was some evidence, or at least hope, that he had tempered his personal style, that facing cancer and turning fifty had caused him to be a bit less brutish when he was upset. "Right after he came back from his operation, he didn't do the humiliation bit as much," Tevanian recalled. "If he was displeased, he might scream and get hopping mad and use expletives, but he wouldn't do it in a way that would totally destroy the person he was talking to. It was just his way to get the person to do a better job." Tevanian reflected for a moment as he said this, then added a caveat: "Unless he thought someone was really bad and had to go, which happened every once in a while."

Eventually, however, the rough edges returned. Because most of his colleagues were used to it by then and had learned to cope, what upset them most was when his ire turned on strangers. "Once we went to a Whole Foods market to get a smoothie," Ive recalled. "And this older woman was making it, and he really got on her about how she was doing it. Then later, he sympathized. 'She's an older woman and doesn't want to be doing this job.' He didn't connect the two. He was being a purist in both cases."

On a trip to London with Jobs, Ive had the thankless task of choosing the hotel. He picked the Hempel, a tranquil five-star boutique hotel with a sophisticated minimalism that he thought Jobs would love. But as soon as they checked in, he braced himself, and sure enough his phone rang a minute later. "I hate my room," Jobs declared. "It's a piece of shit, let's go." So Ive gathered his luggage and went to the front desk, where Jobs bluntly told the shocked clerk what he thought. Ive realized that most people, himself among them, tend not to be direct when they feel something is shoddy because they want to be liked, "which is actually a vain trait." That was an overly kind explanation. In any case, it was not a trait Jobs had.

Because Ive was so instinctively nice, he puzzled over why Jobs, whom he deeply liked, behaved as he did. One evening, in a San Francisco bar, he leaned forward with an earnest intensity and tried to analyze it:

> He's a very, very sensitive guy. That's one of the things that makes his antisocial behavior, his rudeness, so unconscionable. I can understand why people who are thick-skinned and unfeeling can be rude, but not sensitive people. I once asked him why he gets so mad about stuff. He said, "But I don't stay mad." He has this very childish ability to get really worked up about something, and it doesn't stay with him at all. But there are other times, I think honestly, when he's very frustrated, and his way to achieve catharsis is to hurt somebody. And I think he feels he has a liberty and a license to do that. The normal rules of social engagement, he feels, don't apply to him. Because of how very sensitive he is, he knows exactly how to efficiently and effectively hurt someone. And he does do that.

Every now and then a wise colleague would pull Jobs aside to try to get him to settle down. Lee Clow was a master. "Steve, can I talk to you?" he would quietly say when Jobs had belittled someone publicly. He would go into Jobs's office and explain how hard everyone was working. "When you humiliate them, it's more debilitating than stimulating," he said in one such session. Jobs would apologize and say he understood. But then he would lapse again. "It's simply who I am," he would say.

One thing that did mellow was his attitude toward Bill Gates. Microsoft had kept its end of the bargain it made in 1997, when it agreed to continue developing great software for the Macintosh. Also, it was becoming less relevant as a competitor, having failed thus far to replicate Apple's digital hub strategy. Gates and Jobs had very different approaches to products and innovation, but their rivalry had produced in each a surprising self-awareness.

For their All Things Digital conference in May 2007, the *Wall Street Journal* columnists Walt Mossberg and Kara Swisher worked to get them together for a joint interview. Mossberg first invited Jobs, who didn't go to many such conferences, and was surprised when he said he would do it if Gates would. On hearing that, Gates accepted as well.

Mossberg wanted the evening joint appearance to be a cordial discussion, not a debate, but that seemed less likely when Jobs unleashed a swipe at Microsoft during a solo interview earlier that day. Asked about the fact that Apple's iTunes software for Windows computers was extremely popular, Jobs joked, "It's like giving a glass of ice water to somebody in hell."

So when it was time for Gates and Jobs to meet in the green room before their joint session that evening, Mossberg was worried. Gates got there first, with his aide Larry Cohen, who had briefed him about Jobs's remark earlier that day. When Jobs ambled in a few minutes later, he grabbed a bottle of water from the ice bucket and sat down. After a moment or two of silence, Gates said, "So I guess I'm the representative from hell." He wasn't smiling. Jobs paused, gave him one of his impish grins, and handed him the ice water. Gates relaxed, and the tension dissipated.

The result was a fascinating duet, in which each wunderkind of the digital age spoke warily, and then warmly, about the other. Most memorably they gave candid answers when the technology strategist Lise Buyer, who was in the audience, asked what each had learned from observing the other. "Well, I'd give a lot to have Steve's taste," Gates answered. There was a bit of nervous laughter; Jobs had famously said, ten years earlier, that his problem with Microsoft was that it had absolutely no taste. But Gates insisted he was serious. Jobs was a "natural in terms of intuitive taste." He recalled how he and Jobs used to sit together reviewing the software that Microsoft was making for the Macintosh. "I'd see Steve make the decision based on a sense of people and product that, you know, is hard for me to explain. The way he does things is just different and I think it's magical. And in that case, wow."

Jobs stared at the floor. Later he told me that he was blown away by how honest and gracious Gates had just been. Jobs was equally honest, though not quite as gracious, when his turn came. He described the great divide between the Apple theology of building end-to-end integrated products and Microsoft's openness to licensing its software to competing hardware makers. In the music market, the integrated approach, as manifested in his iTunes-iPod package, was proving to be the better, he noted, but Microsoft's decoupled approach was faring better in the personal computer market. One question he raised in an offhand way was: Which approach might work better for mobile phones?

Then he went on to make an insightful point: This difference in design philosophy, he said, led him and Apple to be less good at collaborating with other companies. "Because Woz and I started the company based on doing the whole banana, we weren't so good at partnering with people," he said. "And I think if Apple could have had a little more of that in its DNA, it would have served it extremely well."

CHAPTER THIRTY-SIX

THE iPHONE

Three Revolutionary Products in One

An iPod That Makes Calls

By 2005 iPod sales were skyrocketing. An astonishing twenty million were sold that year, quadruple the number of the year before. The product was becoming more important to the company's bottom line, accounting for 45% of the revenue that year, and it was also burnishing the hipness of the company's image in a way that drove sales of Macs.

That is why Jobs was worried. "He was always obsessing about what could mess us up," board member Art Levinson recalled. The conclusion he had come to: "The device that can eat our lunch is the cell phone." As he explained to the board, the digital camera market was being decimated now that phones were equipped with cameras. The same could happen to the iPod, if phone manufacturers started to build music players into them. "Everyone carries a phone, so that could render the iPod unnecessary."

His first strategy was to do something that he had admitted in front of Bill Gates was not in his DNA: to partner with another company. He began talking to Ed Zander, the new CEO of Motorola, about making a companion to Motorola's popular RAZR, which was a cell phone and digital camera, that would have an iPod built in. Thus was born the ROKR. It ended up having neither the enticing minimalism of an iPod nor the convenient slimness of a RAZR. Ugly, difficult to load, and with an arbitrary hundred-song limit, it had all the hallmarks of a product that had been negotiated by a committee, which was counter to the way Jobs liked to work. Instead of hardware, software, and content all being controlled by one company, they were cobbled together by Motorola, Apple, and the wireless carrier Cingular. "You call this the phone of the future?" *Wired* scoffed on its November 2005 cover.

Jobs was furious. "I'm sick of dealing with these stupid companies like Motorola," he told Tony Fadell and others at one of the iPod product review meetings. "Let's do it ourselves." He had noticed something odd about the cell phones on the market: They all stank, just like portable music players used to. "We would sit around talking about how much we hated our phones," he recalled. "They were way too complicated. They had features nobody could figure out, including the address book. It was just Byzantine." George Riley, an outside lawyer for Apple, remembers sitting at meetings to go over legal issues, and Jobs would get bored, grab Riley's mobile phone, and start pointing out all the ways it was "brain-dead." So Jobs and his team became excited about the prospect of building a phone that they would want to use. "That's the best motivator of all," Jobs later said.

Another motivator was the potential market. More than 825 million mobile phones were sold in 2005, to everyone from grammar schoolers to grandmothers. Since most were junky, there was room for a premium and hip product, just as there had been in the portable music-player market. At first he gave the project to the Apple group that was making the AirPort wireless base station, on the theory that it was a wireless product. But he soon realized that it was basically a consumer device, like the iPod, so he reassigned it to Fadell and his teammates.

Their initial approach was to modify the iPod. They tried to use the trackwheel as a way for a user to scroll through phone options and, without a keyboard, try to enter numbers. It was not a natural fit. "We were having a lot of problems using the wheel, especially in getting it to dial phone numbers," Fadell recalled. "It was cumbersome." It was fine for scrolling through an address book, but horrible at inputting anything. The team kept trying to convince themselves that users would mainly be calling people who were already in their address book, but they knew that it wouldn't really work.

At that time there was a second project under way at Apple: a secret effort to build a tablet computer. In 2005 these narratives intersected, and the ideas for the tablet flowed into the planning for the phone. In other words, the idea for the iPad actually came before, and helped to shape, the birth of the iPhone.

Multi-touch

One of the engineers developing a tablet PC at Microsoft was married to a friend of Laurene and Steve Jobs, and for his fiftieth birthday he wanted to have a dinner party that included them along with Bill and Melinda Gates. Jobs went, a bit reluctantly. "Steve was actually quite friendly to me at the dinner," Gates recalled, but he "wasn't particularly friendly" to the birthday guy.

Gates was annoyed that the guy kept revealing information about the tablet PC he had developed for Microsoft. "He's our employee and he's revealing our intellectual property," Gates recounted. Jobs was also annoyed, and it had just the consequence that Gates feared. As Jobs recalled:

> This guy badgered me about how Microsoft was going to completely change the world with this tablet PC software and eliminate all notebook computers, and Apple ought to license his Microsoft software. But he was doing the device all wrong. It had a stylus. As soon as you have a stylus, you're dead. This dinner was like the tenth time he talked to me about it, and I was so sick of it that I came home and said, "Fuck this, let's show him what a tablet can really be."

Jobs went into the office the next day, gathered his team, and said, "I want to make a tablet, and it can't have a keyboard or a stylus." Users would be able to type by touching the screen with their fingers.

That meant the screen needed to have a feature that became known as multi-touch, the ability to process multiple inputs at the same time. "So could you guys come up with a multi-touch, touch-sensitive display for me?" he asked. It took them about six months, but they came up with a crude but workable prototype.

Jony Ive had a different memory of how multi-touch was developed. He said his design team had already been working on a multi-touch input that was developed for the trackpads of Apple's MacBook Pro, and they were experimenting with ways to transfer that capability to a computer screen. They used a projector to show on a wall what it would look like. "This is going to change everything," Ive told his team. But he was careful not to show it to Jobs right away, especially since his people were working on it in their spare time and he didn't want to quash their enthusiasm. "Because Steve is so quick to give an opinion, I don't show him stuff in front of other people," Ive recalled. "He might say, 'This is shit,' and snuff the idea. I feel that ideas are very fragile, so you have to be tender when they are in development. I realized that if he pissed on this, it would be so sad, because I knew it was so important."

Ive set up the demonstration in his conference room and showed it to Jobs privately, knowing that he was less likely to make a snap judgment if there was no audience. Fortunately he loved it. "This is the future," he exulted.

It was in fact such a good idea that Jobs realized that it could solve the problem they were having creating an interface for the proposed cell phone. That project was far more important, so he put the tablet development on hold while the multi-touch interface was adopted for a phone-size screen. "If it worked on a phone," he recalled, "I knew we could go back and use it on a tablet."

Jobs called Fadell, Rubinstein, and Schiller to a secret meeting in the design studio conference room, where Ive gave a demonstration of multi-touch. "Wow!" said Fadell. Everyone liked it, but they were not sure that they would be able to make it work on a mobile phone. They decided to proceed on two paths: P1 was the code name for the phone being developed using an iPod trackwheel, and P2 was the new alternative using a multi-touch screen.

A small company in Delaware called FingerWorks was already making a line of multi-touch trackpads. Founded by two academics at the University of Delaware, John Elias and Wayne Westerman, Finger-Works had developed some tablets with multi-touch sensing capabilities and taken out patents on ways to translate various finger gestures, such as pinches and swipes, into useful functions. In early 2005 Apple quietly acquired the company, all of its patents, and the services of its two founders. FingerWorks quit selling its products to others, and it began filing its new patents in Apple's name.

After six months of work on the trackwheel P1 and the multi-touch P2 phone options, Jobs called his inner circle into his conference room to make a decision. Fadell had been trying hard to develop the trackwheel model, but he admitted they had not cracked the problem of figuring out a simple way to dial calls. The multi-touch approach was riskier, because they were unsure whether they could execute the engineering, but it was also more exciting and promising. "We all know this is the one we want to do," said Jobs, pointing to the touchscreen. "So let's make it work." It was what he liked to call a bet-the-company moment, high risk and high reward if it succeeded.

A couple of members of the team argued for having a keyboard as well, given the popularity of the BlackBerry, but Jobs vetoed the idea. A physical keyboard would take away space from the screen, and it would not be as flexible and adaptable as a touchscreen keyboard. "A hardware keyboard seems like an easy solution, but it's constraining," he said. "Think of all the innovations we'd be able to adapt if we did the keyboard onscreen with software. Let's bet on it, and then we'll find a way to make it work." The result was a device that displays a numerical pad when you want to dial a phone number, a typewriter keyboard when you want to write, and whatever buttons you might need for each particular activity. And then they all disappear when you're watching a video. By having software replace hardware, the interface became fluid and flexible.

Jobs spent part of every day for six months helping to refine the display. "It was the most complex fun I've ever had," he recalled. "It was like being the one evolving the variations on 'Sgt. Pepper.'" A lot of features that seem simple now were the result of creative brainstorms.

For example, the team worried about how to prevent the device from playing music or making a call accidentally when it was jangling in your pocket. Jobs was congenitally averse to having on-off switches, which he deemed "inelegant." The solution was "Swipe to Open," the simple and fun on-screen slider that activated the device when it had gone dormant. Another breakthrough was the sensor that figured out when you put the phone to your ear, so that your lobes didn't accidentally activate some function. And of course the icons came in his favorite shape, the primitive he made Bill Atkinson design into the software of the first Macintosh: rounded rectangles. In session after session, with Jobs immersed in every detail, the team members figured out ways to simplify what other phones made complicated. They added a big bar to guide you in putting calls on hold or making conference calls, found easy ways to navigate through email, and created icons you could scroll through horizontally to get to different apps—all of which were easier because they could be used visually on the screen rather than by using a keyboard built into the hardware.

Gorilla Glass

Jobs became infatuated with different materials the way he did with certain foods. When he went back to Apple in 1997 and started work on the iMac, he had embraced what could be done with translucent and colored plastic. The next phase was metal. He and Ive replaced the curvy plastic PowerBook G3 with the sleek titanium PowerBook G4, which they redesigned two years later in aluminum, as if just to demonstrate how much they liked different metals. Then they did an iMac and an iPod Nano in anodized aluminum, which meant that the metal had been put in an acid bath and electrified so that its surface oxidized. Jobs was told it could not be done in the quantities they needed, so he had a factory built in China to handle it. Ive went there, during the SARS epidemic, to oversee the process. "I stayed for three months in a dormitory to work on the process," he recalled. "Ruby and others said it would be impossible, but I wanted to do it because Steve and I felt that the anodized aluminum had a real integrity to it."

Next was glass. "After we did metal, I looked at Jony and said that we had to master glass," said Jobs. For the Apple stores, they had created huge windowpanes and glass stairs. For the iPhone, the original plan was for it to have a plastic screen, like the iPod. But Jobs decided it would feel much more elegant and substantive if the screens were glass. So he set about finding a glass that would be strong and resistant to scratches.

The natural place to look was Asia, where the glass for the stores was being made. But Jobs's friend John Seeley Brown, who was on the board of Corning Glass in Upstate New York, told him that he should talk to that company's young and dynamic CEO, Wendell Weeks. So he dialed the main Corning switchboard number and asked to be put through to Weeks. He got an assistant, who offered to pass along the message. "No, I'm Steve Jobs," he replied. "Put me through." The assistant refused. Jobs called Brown and complained that he had been subjected to "typical East Coast bullshit." When Weeks heard that, he called the main Apple switchboard and asked to speak to Jobs. He was told to put his request in writing and send it in by fax. When Jobs was told what happened, he took a liking to Weeks and invited him to Cupertino.

Jobs described the type of glass Apple wanted for the iPhone, and Weeks told him that Corning had developed a chemical exchange process in the 1960s that led to what they dubbed "gorilla glass." It was incredibly strong, but it had never found a market, so Corning quit making it. Jobs said he doubted it was good enough, and he started explaining to Weeks how glass was made. This amused Weeks, who of course knew more than Jobs about that topic. "Can you shut up," Weeks interjected, "and let me teach you some science?" Jobs was taken aback and fell silent. Weeks went to the whiteboard and gave a tutorial on the chemistry, which involved an ion-exchange process that produced a compression layer on the surface of the glass. This turned Jobs around, and he said he wanted as much gorilla glass as Corning could make within six months. "We don't have the capacity," Weeks replied. "None of our plants make the glass now."

"Don't be afraid," Jobs replied. This stunned Weeks, who was good-humored and confident but not used to Jobs's reality distortion field. He tried to explain that a false sense of confidence would not overcome engineering challenges, but that was a premise that Jobs had repeatedly shown he didn't accept. He stared at Weeks unblinking. "Yes, you can do it," he said. "Get your mind around it. You can do it."

As Weeks retold this story, he shook his head in astonishment. "We did it in under six months," he said. "We produced a glass that had never been made." Corning's facility in Harrodsburg, Kentucky, which had been making LCD displays, was converted almost overnight to make gorilla glass full-time. "We put our best scientists and engineers on it, and we just made it work." In his airy office, Weeks has just one framed memento on display. It's a message Jobs sent the day the iPhone came out: "We couldn't have done it without you."

The Design

On many of his major projects, such as the first *Toy Story* and the Apple store, Jobs pressed "pause" as they neared completion and decided to make major revisions. That happened with the design of the iPhone as well. The initial design had the glass screen set into an aluminum case. One Monday morning Jobs went over to see Ive. "I didn't sleep last night," he said, "because I realized that I just don't love it." It was the most important product he had made since the first Macintosh, and it just didn't look right to him. Ive, to his dismay, instantly realized that Jobs was right. "I remember feeling absolutely embarrassed that he had to make the observation."

The problem was that the iPhone should have been all about the display, but in their current design the case competed with the display instead of getting out of the way. The whole device felt too masculine, task-driven, efficient. "Guys, you've killed yourselves over this design for the last nine months, but we're going to change it," Jobs told Ive's team. "We're all going to have to work nights and weekends, and if you want we can hand out some guns so you can kill us now." Instead of balking, the team agreed. "It was one of my proudest moments at Apple," Jobs recalled.

The new design ended up with just a thin stainless steel bezel that allowed the gorilla glass display to go right to the edge. Every part of the device seemed to defer to the screen. The new look was austere, yet also friendly. You could fondle it. It meant they had to redo the circuit boards, antenna, and processor placement inside, but Jobs ordered the change. "Other companies may have shipped," said Fadell, "but we pressed the reset button and started over."

One aspect of the design, which reflected not only Jobs's perfectionism but also his desire to control, was that the device was tightly sealed. The case could not be opened, even to change the battery. As with the original Macintosh in 1984, Jobs did not want people fiddling inside. In fact when Apple discovered in 2011 that third-party repair shops were opening up the iPhone 4, it replaced the tiny screws with a tamper-resistant Pentalobe screw that was impossible to open with a commercially available screwdriver. By not having a replaceable battery, it was possible to make the iPhone much thinner. For Jobs, thinner was always better. "He's always believed that thin is beautiful," said Tim Cook. "You can see that in all of the work. We have the thinnest notebook, the thinnest smartphone, and we made the iPad thin and then even thinner."

The Launch

When it came time to launch the iPhone, Jobs decided, as usual, to grant a magazine a special sneak preview. He called John Huey, the editor in chief of Time Inc., and began with his typical superlative: "This is the best thing we've ever done." He wanted to give *Time* the exclusive, "but there's nobody smart enough at *Time* to write it, so I'm going to give it to someone else." Huey introduced him to Lev Grossman, a savvy technology writer (and novelist) at *Time*. In his piece Grossman correctly noted that the iPhone did not really invent many new features, it just made these features a lot more usable. "But that's important. When our tools don't work, we tend to blame ourselves, for being too stupid or not reading the manual or having too-fat fingers. . . . When our tools are broken, we feel broken. And when somebody fixes one, we feel a tiny bit more whole."

For the unveiling at the January 2007 Macworld in San Francisco, Jobs invited back Andy Hertzfeld, Bill Atkinson, Steve Wozniak, and the 1984 Macintosh team, as he had done when he launched the iMac. In a career of dazzling product presentations, this may have been his best. "Every once in a while a revolutionary product comes along that changes everything," he began. He referred to two earlier examples: the original Macintosh, which "changed the whole computer industry," and the first iPod, which "changed the entire music industry." Then he carefully built up to the product he was about to launch: "Today, we're introducing three revolutionary products of this class. The first one is a widescreen iPod with touch controls. The second is a revolutionary mobile phone. And the third is a breakthrough Internet communications device." He repeated the list for emphasis, then asked, "Are you getting it? These are not three separate devices, this is one device, and we are calling it iPhone."

When the iPhone went on sale five months later, at the end of June 2007, Jobs and his wife walked to the Apple store in Palo Alto to take in the excitement. Since he often did that on the day new products went on sale, there were some fans hanging out in anticipation, and they greeted him as they would have Moses if he had walked in to buy the Bible. Among the faithful were Hertzfeld and Atkinson. "Bill stayed in line all night," Hertzfeld said. Jobs waved his arms and started laughing. "I sent him one," he said. Hertzfeld replied, "He needs six."

The iPhone was immediately dubbed "the Jesus Phone" by bloggers. But Apple's competitors emphasized that, at $500, it cost too much to be successful. "It's the most expensive phone in the world," Microsoft's Steve Ballmer said in a CNBC interview. "And it doesn't appeal to business customers because it doesn't have a keyboard." Once again Microsoft had underestimated Jobs's product. By the end of 2010, Apple had sold ninety million iPhones, and it reaped more than half of the total profits generated in the global cell phone market.

"Steve understands desire," said Alan Kay, the Xerox PARC pioneer who had envisioned a "Dynabook" tablet computer forty years earlier. Kay was good at making prophetic assessments, so Jobs asked him what he thought of the iPhone. "Make the screen five inches by eight inches, and you'll rule the world," Kay said. He did not know that the design of the iPhone had started with, and would someday lead to, ideas for a tablet computer that would fulfill—indeed exceed—his vision for the Dynabook.

CHAPTER THIRTY-SEVEN

ROUND TWO

The Cancer Recurs

The Battles of 2008

By the beginning of 2008 it was clear to Jobs and his doctors that his cancer was spreading. When they had taken out his pancreatic tumors in 2004, he had the cancer genome partially sequenced. That helped his doctors determine which pathways were broken, and they were treating him with targeted therapies that they thought were most likely to work.

He was also being treated for pain, usually with morphine-based analgesics. One day in February 2008 when Powell's close friend Kathryn Smith was staying with them in Palo Alto, she and Jobs took a walk. "He told me that when he feels really bad, he just concentrates on the pain, goes into the pain, and that seems to dissipate it," she recalled. That wasn't exactly true, however. When Jobs was in pain, he let everyone around him know it.

There was another health issue that became increasingly problematic, one that medical researchers didn't focus on as rigorously as they did cancer or pain. He was having eating problems and losing weight. Partly this was because he had lost much of his pancreas, which produces the enzymes needed to digest protein and other nutrients. It was also because both the cancer and the morphine reduced his appetite. And then there was the psychological component, which the doctors barely knew how to address: Since his early teens, he had indulged his weird obsession with extremely restrictive diets and fasts.

Even after he married and had children, he retained his dubious eating habits. He would spend weeks eating the same thing—carrot salad with lemon, or just apples—and then suddenly spurn that food and declare that he had stopped eating it. He would go on fasts, just as he did as a teenager, and he became sanctimonious as he lectured others at the table on the virtues of whatever eating regimen he was following. Powell had been a vegan when they were first married, but after her husband's operation she began to diversify their family meals with fish and other proteins. Their son, Reed, who had been a vegetarian, became a "hearty omnivore." They knew it was important for his father to get diverse sources of protein.

The family hired a gentle and versatile cook, Bryar Brown, who once worked for Alice Waters at Chez Panisse. He came each afternoon and made a panoply of healthy offerings for dinner, which used the herbs and vegetables that Powell grew in their garden. When Jobs expressed any whim—carrot salad, pasta with basil, lemongrass soup—Brown would quietly and patiently find a way to make it. Jobs had always been an extremely opinionated eater, with a tendency to instantly judge any food as either fantastic or terrible. He could taste two avocados that most mortals would find indistinguishable, and declare that one was the best avocado ever grown and the other inedible.

Beginning in early 2008 Jobs's eating disorders got worse. On some nights he would stare at the floor and ignore all of the dishes set out on the long kitchen table. When others were halfway through their meal, he would abruptly get up and leave, saying nothing. It was stressful for his family. They watched him lose forty pounds during the spring of 2008.

His health problems became public again in March 2008, when *Fortune* published a piece called "The Trouble with Steve Jobs." It revealed that he had tried to treat his cancer with diets for nine months and also investigated his involvement in the backdating of Apple stock options. As the story was being prepared, Jobs invited—summoned—

Fortune's managing editor Andy Serwer to Cupertino to pressure him to spike it. He leaned into Serwer's face and asked, "So, you've uncovered the fact that I'm an asshole. Why is that news?" Jobs made the same rather self-aware argument when he called Serwer's boss at Time Inc., John Huey, from a satellite phone he brought to Hawaii's Kona Village. He offered to convene a panel of fellow CEOs and be part of a discussion about what health issues are proper to disclose, but only if *Fortune* killed its piece. The magazine didn't.

When Jobs introduced the iPhone 3G in June 2008, he was so thin that it overshadowed the product announcement. In *Esquire* Tom Junod described the "withered" figure onstage as being "gaunt as a pirate, dressed in what had heretofore been the vestments of his invulnerability." Apple released a statement saying, untruthfully, that his weight loss was the result of "a common bug." The following month, as questions persisted, the company released another statement saying that Jobs's health was "a private matter."

Joe Nocera of the *New York Times* wrote a column denouncing the handling of Jobs's health issues. "Apple simply can't be trusted to tell the truth about its chief executive," he wrote in late July. "Under Mr. Jobs, Apple has created a culture of secrecy that has served it well in many ways—the speculation over which products Apple will unveil at the annual Macworld conference has been one of the company's best marketing tools. But that same culture poisons its corporate governance." As he was writing the column and getting the standard "a private matter" comment from all at Apple, he got an unexpected call from Jobs himself. "This is Steve Jobs," he began. "You think I'm an arrogant asshole who thinks he's above the law, and I think you're a slime bucket who gets most of his facts wrong." After that rather arresting opening, Jobs offered up some information about his health, but only if Nocera would keep it off the record. Nocera honored the request, but he was able to report that, while Jobs's health problems amounted to more than a common bug, "they weren't life-threatening and he doesn't have a recurrence of cancer." Jobs had given Nocera more information than he was willing to give his own board and shareholders, but it was not the full truth.

Partly due to concern about Jobs's weight loss, Apple's stock price drifted from $188 at the beginning of June 2008 down to $156 at the end of July. Matters were not helped in late August when *Bloomberg News* mistakenly released its prepackaged obituary of Jobs, which ended up on Gawker. Jobs was able to roll out Mark Twain's famous quip a few days later at his annual music event. "Reports of my death are greatly exaggerated," he said, as he launched a line of new iPods. But his gaunt appearance was not reassuring. By early October the stock price had sunk to $97.

That month Doug Morris of Universal Music was scheduled to meet with Jobs at Apple. Instead Jobs invited him to his house. Morris was surprised to see him so ill and in pain. Morris was about to be honored at a gala in Los Angeles for City of Hope, which raised money to fight cancer, and he wanted Jobs to be there. Charitable events were something Jobs avoided, but he decided to do it, both for Morris and for the cause. At the event, held in a big tent on Santa Monica beach, Morris told the two thousand guests that Jobs was giving the music industry a new lease on life. The performances—by Stevie Nicks, Lionel Richie, Erykah Badu, and Akon—went on past midnight, and Jobs had severe chills. Jimmy Iovine gave him a hooded sweatshirt to wear, and he kept the hood over his head all evening. "He was so sick, so cold, so thin," Morris recalled.

Fortune's veteran technology writer Brent Schlender was leaving the magazine that December, and his swan song was to be a joint interview with Jobs, Bill Gates, Andy Grove, and Michael Dell. It had been hard to organize, and just a few days before it was to happen, Jobs called to back out. "If they ask why, just tell them I'm an asshole," he said. Gates was annoyed, then discovered what the health situation was. "Of course, he had a very, very good reason," said Gates. "He just didn't want to say." That became more apparent when Apple announced on December 16 that Jobs was canceling his scheduled appearance at the January Macworld, the forum he had used for big product launches for the past eleven years.

The blogosphere erupted with speculation about his health, much of which had the odious smell of truth. Jobs was furious and felt violated. He was also annoyed that Apple wasn't being more active in pushing back. So on January 5, 2009, he wrote and released a misleading open letter. He claimed that he was skipping Macworld because he wanted to spend more time with his family. "As many of you know, I have been losing weight throughout 2008," he added. "My doctors think they have found the cause—a hormone imbalance that has been robbing me of the proteins my body needs to be healthy. Sophisticated blood tests have confirmed this diagnosis. The remedy for this nutritional problem is relatively simple."

There was a kernel of truth to this, albeit a small one. One of the hormones created by the pancreas is glucagon, which is the flip side of insulin. Glucagon causes your liver to release blood sugar. Jobs's tumor had metastasized into his liver and was wreaking havoc. In effect, his body was devouring itself, so his doctors gave him drugs to try to lower the glucagon level. He did have a hormone imbalance, but it was because his cancer had spread into his liver. He was in personal denial about this, and he also wanted to be in public denial. Unfortunately that was legally problematic, because he ran a publicly traded company. But Jobs was furious about the way the blogosphere was treating him, and he wanted to strike back.

He was very sick at this point, despite his upbeat statement, and also in excruciating pain. He had undertaken another round of cancer drug therapy, and it had grueling side effects. His skin started drying out and cracking. In his quest for alternative approaches, he flew to Basel, Switzerland, to try an experimental hormone-delivered radiotherapy. He also underwent an experimental treatment developed in Rotterdam known as peptide receptor radionuclide therapy.

After a week filled with increasingly insistent legal advice, Jobs finally agreed to go on medical leave. He made the announcement on January 14, 2009, in another open letter to the Apple staff. At first he blamed the decision on the prying of bloggers and the press. "Unfortunately, the curiosity over my personal health continues to be a distraction not only for me and my family, but everyone else at Apple," he said. But then he admitted that the remedy for his "hormone imbalance" was not as simple as he had claimed. "During the past week I have learned that my health-related issues are more complex than I originally thought." Tim Cook would again take over daily operations, but Jobs said that he would remain CEO, continue to be involved in major decisions, and be back by June.

Jobs had been consulting with Bill Campbell and Art Levinson, who were juggling the dual roles of being his personal health advisors and also the co-lead directors of the company. But the rest of the board had not been as fully informed, and the shareholders had initially been misinformed. That raised some legal issues, and the SEC opened an investigation into whether the company had withheld "material information" from shareholders. It would constitute security fraud, a felony, if the company had allowed the dissemination of false information or withheld true information that was relevant to the company's financial prospects. Because Jobs and his magic were so closely identified with Apple's comeback, his health seemed to meet this standard. But it was a murky area of the law; the privacy rights of the CEO had to be weighed. This balance was particularly difficult in the case of Jobs, who both valued his privacy and embodied his company more than most CEOs. He did not make the task easier. He became very emotional, both ranting and crying at times, when railing against anyone who suggested that he should be less secretive.

Campbell treasured his friendship with Jobs, and he didn't want to have any fiduciary duty to violate his privacy, so he offered to step down as a director. "The privacy side is so important to me," he later said. "He's been my friend for about a million years." The lawyers eventually determined that Campbell didn't need to resign from the board but that he should step aside as co-lead director. He was replaced in that role by Andrea Jung of Avon. The SEC investigation ended up going nowhere, and the board circled the wagons to protect Jobs from calls that he release more information. "The press wanted us to blurt out more personal details," recalled Al Gore. "It was really up to Steve to go beyond what the law requires, but he was adamant that he didn't want his privacy invaded. His wishes should be respected." When I asked Gore whether the board should have been more forthcoming at the beginning of 2009, when Jobs's health issues were far worse than shareholders were led to believe, he replied, "We hired outside counsel to do a review of what the law required and what the best practices

WALTER ISAACSON

were, and we handled it all by the book. I sound defensive, but the criticism really pissed me off."

One board member disagreed. Jerry York, the former CFO at Chrysler and IBM, did not say anything publicly, but he confided to a reporter at the *Wall Street Journal*, off the record, that he was "disgusted" when he learned that the company had concealed Jobs's health problems in late 2008. "Frankly, I wish I had resigned then." When York died in 2010, the *Journal* put his comments on the record. York had also provided off-the-record information to *Fortune*, which the magazine used when Jobs went on his third health leave, in 2011.

Some at Apple didn't believe the quotes attributed to York were accurate, since he had not officially raised objections at the time. But Bill Campbell knew that the reports rang true; York had complained to him in early 2009. "Jerry had a little more white wine than he should have late at night, and he would call at two or three in the morning and say, 'What the fuck, I'm not buying that shit about his health, we've got to make sure.' And then I'd call him the next morning and he'd say, 'Oh fine, no problem.' So on some of those evenings, I'm sure he got raggy and talked to reporters."

Memphis

The head of Jobs's oncology team was Stanford University's George Fisher, a leading researcher on gastrointestinal and colorectal cancers. He had been warning Jobs for months that he might have to consider a liver transplant, but that was the type of information that Jobs resisted processing. Powell was glad that Fisher kept raising the possibility, because she knew it would take repeated proddings to get her husband to consider the idea.

He finally became convinced in January 2009, just after he claimed his "hormonal imbalance" could be treated easily. But there was a problem. He was put on the wait list for a liver transplant in California, but it became clear he would never get one there in time. The number of available donors with his blood type was small. Also, the metrics used by the United Network for Organ Sharing, which establishes policies in the United States, favored those suffering from cirrhosis and hepatitis over cancer patients.

There is no legal way for a patient, even one as wealthy as Jobs, to jump the queue, and he didn't. Recipients are chosen based on their MELD score (Model for End-Stage Liver Disease), which uses lab tests of hormone levels to determine how urgently a transplant is needed, and on the length of time they have been waiting. Every donation is closely audited, data are available on public websites (optn.transplant.hrsa.gov/), and you can monitor your status on the wait list at any time.

Powell became the troller of the organ-donation websites, checking in every night to see how many were on the wait lists, what their MELD scores were, and how long they had been on. "You can do the math, which I did, and it would have been way past June before he got a liver in California, and the doctors felt that his liver would give out in about April," she recalled. So she started asking questions and discovered that it was permissible to be on the list in two different states at the same time, which is something that about 3% of potential recipients do. Such multiple listing is not discouraged by policy, even though critics say it favors the rich, but it is difficult. There were two major requirements: The potential recipient had to be able to get to the chosen hospital within eight hours, which Jobs could do thanks to his plane, and the doctors from that hospital had to evaluate the patient in person before adding him or her to the list.

George Riley, the San Francisco lawyer who often served as Apple's outside counsel, was a caring Tennessee gentleman, and he had become close to Jobs. His parents had both been doctors at Methodist University Hospital in Memphis, he was born there, and he was a friend of James Eason, who ran the transplant institute there. Eason's unit was one of the best and busiest in the nation; in 2008 he and his team did 121 liver transplants. He had no problem allowing people from elsewhere to multiple-list in Memphis. "It's not gaming the system," he said. "It's people choosing where they want their health care. Some people would leave Tennessee to go to California or somewhere else to seek treatment. Now we have people coming from California to Tennessee." Riley arranged for Eason to fly to Palo Alto and conduct the required evaluation there.

By late February 2009 Jobs had secured a place on the Tennessee list (as well as the one in California), and the nervous waiting began. He was declining rapidly by the first week in March, and the waiting time was projected to be twenty-one days. "It was dreadful," Powell recalled. "It didn't look like we would make it in time." Every day became more excruciating. He moved up to third on the list by mid-March, then second, and finally first. But then days went by. The awful reality was that upcoming events like St. Patrick's Day and March Madness (Memphis was in the 2009 tournament and was a regional site) offered a greater likelihood of getting a donor because the drinking causes a spike in car accidents.

Indeed, on the weekend of March 21, 2009, a young man in his midtwenties was killed in a car crash, and his organs were made available. Jobs and his wife flew to Memphis, where they landed just before 4 a.m. and were met by Eason. A car was waiting on the tarmac, and everything was staged so that the admitting paperwork was done as they rushed to the hospital.

The transplant was a success, but not reassuring. When the doctors took out his liver, they found spots on the peritoneum, the thin membrane that surrounds internal organs. In addition, there were tumors throughout the liver, which meant it was likely that the cancer had migrated elsewhere as well. It had apparently mutated and grown quickly. They took samples and did more genetic mapping.

A few days later they needed to perform another procedure. Jobs insisted against all advice they not pump out his stomach, and when they sedated him, he aspirated some of the contents into his lungs and developed pneumonia. At that point they thought he might die. As he described it later:

I almost died because in this routine procedure they blew it. Laurene was there and they flew my children in, because they did not think I would make it through the night. Reed was looking at colleges with one of Laurene's brothers. We had a private plane pick him up near

Dartmouth and tell them what was going on. A plane also picked up the girls. They thought it might be the last chance they had to see me conscious. But I made it.

Powell took charge of overseeing the treatment, staying in the hospital room all day and watching each of the monitors vigilantly. "Laurene was a beautiful tiger protecting him," recalled Jony Ive, who came as soon as Jobs could receive visitors. Her mother and three brothers came down at various times to keep her company. Jobs's sister Mona Simpson also hovered protectively. She and George Riley were the only people Jobs would allow to fill in for Powell at his bedside. "Laurene's family helped us take care of the kids—her mom and brothers were great," Jobs later said. "I was very fragile and not cooperative. But an experience like that binds you together in a deep way."

Powell came every day at 7 a.m. and gathered the relevant data, which she put on a spreadsheet. "It was very complicated because there were a lot of different things going on," she recalled. When James Eason and his team of doctors arrived at 9 a.m., she would have a meeting with them to coordinate all aspects of Jobs's treatment. At 9 p.m., before she left, she would prepare a report on how each of the vital signs and other measurements were trending, along with a set of questions she wanted answered the next day. "It allowed me to engage my brain and stay focused," she recalled.

Eason did what no one at Stanford had fully done: take charge of all aspects of the medical care. Since he ran the facility, he could coordinate the transplant recovery, cancer tests, pain treatments, nutrition, rehabilitation, and nursing. He would even stop at the convenience store to get the energy drinks Jobs liked.

Two of the nurses were from tiny towns in Mississippi, and they became Jobs's favorites. They were solid family women and not intimidated by him. Eason arranged for them to be assigned only to Jobs. "To manage Steve, you have to be persistent," recalled Tim Cook. "Eason managed Steve and forced him to do things that no one else could, things that were good for him that may not have been pleasant."

Despite all the coddling, Jobs at times almost went crazy. He chafed at not being in control, and he sometimes hallucinated or became angry. Even when he was barely conscious, his strong personality came through. At one point the pulmonologist tried to put a mask over his face when he was deeply sedated. Jobs ripped it off and mumbled that he hated the design and refused to wear it. Though barely able to speak, he ordered them to bring five different options for the mask and he would pick a design he liked. The doctors looked at Powell, puzzled. She was finally able to distract him so they could put on the mask. He also hated the oxygen monitor they put on his finger. He told them it was ugly and too complex. He suggested ways it could be designed more simply. "He was very attuned to every nuance of the environment and objects around him, and that drained him," Powell recalled.

One day, when he was still floating in and out of consciousness, Powell's close friend Kathryn Smith came to visit. Her relationship with Jobs had not always been the best, but Powell insisted that she come by the bedside. He motioned her over, signaled for a pad and pen, and wrote, "I want my iPhone." Smith took it off the dresser and brought it to him. Taking her hand, he showed her the "swipe to open" function and made her play with the menus.

Jobs's relationship with Lisa Brennan-Jobs, his daughter with Chrisann, had frayed. She had graduated from Harvard, moved to New York City, and rarely communicated with her father. But she flew down to Memphis twice, and he appreciated it. "It meant a lot to me that she would do that," he recalled. Unfortunately he didn't tell her at the time. Many of the people around Jobs found Lisa could be as demanding as her father, but Powell welcomed her and tried to get her involved. It was a relationship she wanted to restore.

As Jobs got better, much of his feisty personality returned. He still had his bile ducts. "When he started to recover, he passed quickly through the phase of gratitude, and went right back into the mode of being grumpy and in charge," Kat Smith recalled. "We were all wondering if he was going to come out of this with a kinder perspective, but he didn't."

He also remained a finicky eater, which was more of a problem than ever. He would eat only fruit smoothies, and he would demand that seven or eight of them be lined up so he could find an option that might satisfy him. He would touch the spoon to his mouth for a tiny taste and pronounce, "That's no good. That one's no good either." Finally Eason pushed back. "You know, this isn't a matter of taste," he lectured. "Stop thinking of this as food. Start thinking of it as medicine."

Jobs's mood buoyed when he was able to have visitors from Apple. Tim Cook came down regularly and filled him in on the progress of new products. "You could see him brighten every time the talk turned to Apple," Cook said. "It was like the light turned on." He loved the company deeply, and he seemed to live for the prospect of returning. Details would energize him. When Cook described a new model of the iPhone, Jobs spent the next hour discussing not only what to call it—they agreed on iPhone 3GS—but also the size and font of the "GS," including whether the letters should be capitalized (yes) and italicized (no).

One day Riley arranged a surprise after-hours visit to Sun Studio, the redbrick shrine where Elvis, Johnny Cash, B.B. King, and many other rock-and-roll pioneers recorded. They were given a private tour and a history lecture by one of the young staffers, who sat with Jobs on the cigarette-scarred bench that Jerry Lee Lewis used. Jobs was arguably the most influential person in the music industry at the time, but the kid didn't recognize him in his emaciated state. As they were leaving, Jobs told Riley, "That kid was really smart. We should hire him for iTunes." So Riley called Eddy Cue, who flew the boy out to California for an interview and ended up hiring him to help build the early R&B and rock-and-roll sections of iTunes. When Riley went back to see his friends at Sun Studio later, they said that it proved, as their slogan said, that your dreams can still come true at Sun Studio.

Return

At the end of May 2009 Jobs flew back from Memphis on his jet with his wife and sister. They were met at the San Jose airfield by Tim Cook and Jony Ive, who came aboard as soon as the plane landed. "You could see in his eyes his excitement at being back," Cook recalled. "He had fight in him and was raring to go." Powell pulled out a bottle of sparkling apple cider and toasted her husband, and everyone embraced.

Ive was emotionally drained. He drove to Jobs's house from the airport and told him how hard it had been to keep things going while he was away. He also complained about the stories saying that Apple's innovation depended on Jobs and would disappear if he didn't return. "I'm really hurt," Ive told him. He felt "devastated," he said, and underappreciated.

Jobs was likewise in a dark mental state after his return to Palo Alto. He was coming to grips with the thought that he might *not* be indispensable to the company. Apple stock had fared well while he was away, going from $82 when he announced his leave in January 2009 to $140 when he returned at the end of May. On one conference call with analysts shortly after Jobs went on leave, Cook departed from his unemotional style to give a rousing declaration of why Apple would continue to soar even with Jobs absent:

> We believe that we are on the face of the earth to make great products, and that's not changing. We are constantly focusing on innovating. We believe in the simple not the complex. We believe that we need to own and control the primary technologies behind the products that we make, and participate only in markets where we can make a significant contribution. We believe in saying no to thousands of projects, so that we can really focus on the few that are truly important and meaningful to us. We believe in deep collaboration and cross-pollination of our groups, which allow us to innovate in a way that others cannot. And frankly, we don't settle for anything less than excellence in every group in the company, and we have the self-honesty to admit when we're wrong and the courage to change. And I think, regardless of who is in what job, those values are so embedded in this company that Apple will do extremely well.

It sounded like something Jobs would say (and had said), but the press dubbed it "the Cook doctrine." Jobs was rankled and deeply depressed, especially about the last line. He didn't know whether to be proud or hurt that it might be true. There was talk that he might step aside and become chairman rather than CEO. That made him all the more motivated to get out of his bed, overcome the pain, and start taking his restorative long walks again.

A board meeting was scheduled a few days after he returned, and

Jobs surprised everyone by making an appearance. He ambled in and was able to stay for most of the meeting. By early June he was holding daily meetings at his house, and by the end of the month he was back at work.

Would he now, after facing death, be more mellow? His colleagues quickly got an answer. On his first day back, he startled his top team by throwing a series of tantrums. He ripped apart people he had not seen for six months, tore up some marketing plans, and chewed out a couple of people whose work he found shoddy. But what was truly telling was the pronouncement he made to a couple of friends late that afternoon. "I had the greatest time being back today," he said. "I can't believe how creative I'm feeling, and how the whole team is." Tim Cook took it in stride. "I've never seen Steve hold back from expressing his view or passion," he later said. "But that was good."

Friends noted that Jobs had retained his feistiness. During his recuperation he signed up for Comcast's high-definition cable service, and one day he called Brian Roberts, who ran the company. "I thought he was calling to say something nice about it," Roberts recalled. "Instead, he told me 'It sucks.'" But Andy Hertzfeld noticed that, beneath the gruffness, Jobs had become more honest. "Before, if you asked Steve for a favor, he might do the exact opposite," Hertzfeld said. "That was the perversity in his nature. Now he actually tries to be helpful."

His public return came on September 9, when he took the stage at the company's regular fall music event. He got a standing ovation that lasted almost a minute, then he opened on an unusually personal note by mentioning that he was the recipient of a liver donation. "I wouldn't be here without such generosity," he said, "so I hope all of us can be as generous and elect to become organ donors." After a moment of exultation—"I'm vertical, I'm back at Apple, and I'm loving every day of it"—he unveiled the new line of iPod Nanos, with video cameras, in nine different colors of anodized aluminum.

By the beginning of 2010 he had recovered most of his strength, and he threw himself back into work for what would be one of his, and Apple's, most productive years. He had hit two consecutive home runs since launching Apple's digital hub strategy: the iPod and the iPhone. Now he was going to swing for another.

CHAPTER THIRTY-EIGHT

THE iPAD

Into the Post-PC Era

You Say You Want a Revolution

Back in 2002, Jobs had been annoyed by the Microsoft engineer who kept proselytizing about the tablet computer software he had developed, which allowed users to input information on the screen with a stylus or pen. A few manufacturers released tablet PCs that year using the software, but none made a dent in the universe. Jobs had been eager to show how it should be done right—no stylus!—but when he saw the multi-touch technology that Apple was developing, he had decided to use it first to make an iPhone.

In the meantime, the tablet idea was percolating within the Macintosh hardware group. "We have no plans to make a tablet," Jobs declared in an interview with Walt Mossberg in May 2003. "It turns out people want keyboards. Tablets appeal to rich guys with plenty of other PCs and devices already." Like his statement about having a "hormone imbalance," that was misleading; at most of his annual Top 100 retreats, the tablet was among the future projects discussed. "We showed the idea off at many of these retreats, because Steve never lost his desire to do a tablet," Phil Schiller recalled.

The tablet project got a boost in 2007 when Jobs was considering ideas for a low-cost netbook computer. At an executive team brainstorming session one Monday, Ive asked why it needed a keyboard hinged to the screen; that was expensive and bulky. Put the keyboard on the screen using a multi-touch interface, he suggested. Jobs agreed. So the resources were directed to revving up the tablet project rather than designing a netbook.

The process began with Jobs and Ive figuring out the right screen size. They had twenty models made—all rounded rectangles, of course—in slightly varying sizes and aspect ratios. Ive laid them out on a table in the design studio, and in the afternoon they would lift the velvet cloth hiding them and play with them. "That's how we nailed what the screen size was," Ive said.

As usual Jobs pushed for the purest possible simplicity. That required determining what was the core essence of the device. The answer: the display screen. So the guiding principle was that everything they did had to defer to the screen. "How do we get out of the way so there aren't a ton of features and buttons that distract from the display?" Ive asked. At every step, Jobs pushed to remove and simplify.

At one point Jobs looked at the model and was slightly dissatisfied. It didn't feel casual and friendly enough, so that you would naturally scoop it up and whisk it away. Ive put his finger, so to speak, on the problem: They needed to signal that you could grab it with one hand, on impulse. The bottom of the edge needed to be slightly rounded, so that you'd feel comfortable just scooping it up rather than lifting it carefully. That meant engineering had to design the necessary connection ports and buttons in a simple lip that was thin enough to wash away gently underneath.

If you had been paying attention to patent filings, you would have noticed the one numbered D504889 that Apple applied for in March 2004 and was issued fourteen months later. Among the inventors listed were Jobs and Ive. The application carried sketches of a rectangular electronic tablet with rounded edges, which looked just the way the iPad turned out, including one of a man holding it casually in his left hand while using his right index finger to touch the screen.

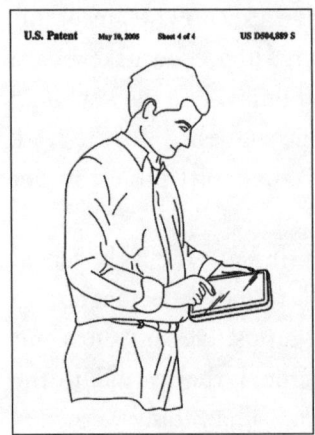

Since the Macintosh computers were now using Intel chips, Jobs initially planned to use in the iPad the low-voltage Atom chip that Intel was developing. Paul Otellini, Intel's CEO, was pushing hard to work together on a design, and Jobs's inclination was to trust him. His company was making the fastest processors in the world. But Intel was used to making processors for machines that plugged into a wall, not ones that had to preserve battery life. So Tony Fadell argued strongly for something based on the ARM architecture, which was simpler and used less power. Apple had been an early partner with ARM, and chips using its architecture were in the original iPhone. Fadell gathered support from other engineers and proved that it was possible to confront Jobs and turn him around. "Wrong, wrong, wrong!" Fadell shouted at one meeting when Jobs insisted it was best to trust Intel to make a good mobile chip. Fadell even put his Apple badge on the table, threatening to resign.

Eventually Jobs relented. "I hear you," he said. "I'm not going to go against my best guys." In fact he went to the other extreme. Apple licensed the ARM architecture, but it also bought a 150-person microprocessor design firm in Palo Alto, called P.A. Semi, and had it create a custom system-on-a-chip, called the A4, which was based on the ARM architecture and manufactured in South Korea by Samsung. As Jobs recalled:

> At the high-performance end, Intel is the best. They build the fastest chip, if you don't care about power and cost. But they build just the processor on one chip, so it takes a lot of other parts. Our A4 has the processor and the graphics, mobile operating system, and memory control all in the chip. We tried to help Intel, but they don't listen much. We've been telling them for years that their graphics suck. Every quarter we schedule a meeting with me and our top three guys and Paul Otellini. At the beginning, we were doing wonderful things together. They wanted this big joint project to do chips for future iPhones. There were two reasons we didn't go with them. One was that they are just really slow. They're like a steamship, not very flexible. We're used to going pretty fast. Second is that we just didn't want to teach them everything, which they could go and sell to our competitors.

According to Otellini, it would have made sense for the iPad to use Intel chips. The problem, he said, was that Apple and Intel couldn't agree on price. Also, they disagreed on who would control the design. It was another example of Jobs's desire, indeed compulsion, to control every aspect of a product, from the silicon to the flesh.

The Launch, January 2010

The usual excitement that Jobs was able to gin up for a product launch paled in comparison to the frenzy that built for the iPad unveiling on January 27, 2010, in San Francisco. The *Economist* put him on its cover robed, haloed, and holding what was dubbed "the Jesus Tablet." The *Wall Street Journal* struck a similarly exalted note: "The last time there was this much excitement about a tablet, it had some commandments written on it."

As if to underscore the historic nature of the launch, Jobs invited back many of the old-timers from his early Apple days. More poignantly, James Eason, who had performed his liver transplant the year before, and Jeffrey Norton, who had operated on his pancreas in 2004, were in the audience, sitting with his wife, his son, and Mona Simpson.

Jobs did his usual masterly job of putting a new device into context, as he had done for the iPhone three years earlier. This time he put up a screen that showed an iPhone and a laptop with a question mark in between. "The question is, is there room for something in the middle?" he asked. That "something" would have to be good at web browsing, email, photos, video, music, games, and ebooks. He drove a stake through the heart of the netbook concept. "Netbooks aren't better at anything!" he said. The invited guests and employees cheered. "But we have something that is. We call it the iPad."

To underscore the casual nature of the iPad, Jobs ambled over to a comfortable leather chair and side table (actually, given his taste, it was a Le Corbusier chair and an Eero Saarinen table) and scooped one up. "It's so much more intimate than a laptop," he enthused. He proceeded to surf to the *New York Times* website, send an email to Scott Forstall and Phil Schiller ("Wow, we really are announcing the iPad"), flip through a photo album, use a calendar, zoom in on the Eiffel Tower on Google Maps, watch some video clips (*Star Trek* and Pixar's *Up*), show off the iBook shelf, and play a song (Bob Dylan's "Like a Rolling Stone," which he had played at the iPhone launch). "Isn't that awesome?" he asked.

With his final slide, Jobs emphasized one of the themes of his life, which was embodied by the iPad: a sign showing the corner of Technology Street and Liberal Arts Street. "The reason Apple can create products like the iPad is that we've always tried to be at the intersection of technology and liberal arts," he concluded. The iPad was the digital reincarnation of the *Whole Earth Catalog*, the place where creativity met tools for living.

For once, the initial reaction was not a Hallelujah Chorus. The iPad was not yet available (it would go on sale in April), and some who watched Jobs's demo were not quite sure what it was. An iPhone on steroids? "I haven't been this let down since Snooki hooked up with The Situation," wrote *Newsweek*'s Daniel Lyons (who moonlighted as "The Fake Steve Jobs" in an online parody). Gizmodo ran a contributor's piece headlined "Eight Things That Suck about the iPad" (no multitasking, no cameras, no Flash . . .). Even the name came in for ridicule in the blogosphere, with snarky comments about feminine hygiene products and maxi pads. The hashtag "#iTampon" was the number-three trending topic on Twitter that day.

There was also the requisite dismissal from Bill Gates. "I still think that some mixture of voice, the pen and a real keyboard—in other words a netbook—will be the mainstream," he told Brent Schlender. "So, it's not like I sit there and feel the same way I did with the iPhone where I say, 'Oh my God, Microsoft didn't aim high enough.' It's a nice reader, but there's nothing on the iPad I look at and say, 'Oh, I wish Microsoft had done it.'" He continued to insist that the Microsoft approach of using a stylus for input would prevail. "I've been predicting a tablet with a stylus for many years," he told me. "I will eventually turn out to be right or be dead."

The night after his announcement, Jobs was annoyed and depressed. As we gathered in his kitchen for dinner, he paced around the table calling up emails and web pages on his iPhone.

> I got about eight hundred email messages in the last twenty-four hours. Most of them are complaining. There's no USB cord! There's no this, no that. Some of them are like, "Fuck you, how can you do that?" I don't usually write people back, but I replied, "Your parents would be so proud of how you turned out." And some don't like the iPad name, and on and on. I kind of got depressed today. It knocks you back a bit.

He did get one congratulatory call that day that he appreciated, from President Obama's chief of staff, Rahm Emanuel. But he noted at dinner that the president had not called him since taking office.

The public carping subsided when the iPad went on sale in April and people got their hands on it. Both *Time* and *Newsweek* put it on the cover. "The tough thing about writing about Apple products is that they come with a lot of hype wrapped around them," Lev Grossman wrote in *Time*. "The other tough thing about writing about Apple products is that sometimes the hype is true." His main reservation, a substantive one, was "that while it's a lovely device for consuming content, it doesn't do much to facilitate its creation." Computers, especially the Macintosh, had become tools that allowed people to make music, videos, websites, and blogs, which could be posted for the world to see. "The iPad shifts the emphasis from creating content to merely absorbing and manipulating it. It mutes you, turns you back into a passive consumer of other people's masterpieces." It was a criticism Jobs took to heart. He set about making sure that the next version of the iPad would emphasize ways to facilitate artistic creation by the user.

Newsweek's cover line was "What's So Great about the iPad? Everything." Daniel Lyons, who had zapped it with his "Snooki" comment at the launch, revised his opinion. "My first thought, as I watched Jobs run through his demo, was that it seemed like no big deal," he wrote. "It's a bigger version of the iPod Touch, right? Then I got a chance to use an iPad, and it hit me: I want one." Lyons, like others, realized that this was Jobs's pet project, and it embodied all that he stood for. "He has an uncanny ability to cook up gadgets that we didn't know we needed, but then suddenly can't live without," he wrote. "A closed system may be the only way to deliver the kind of techno-Zen experience that Apple has become known for."

Most of the debate over the iPad centered on the issue of whether its closed end-to-end integration was brilliant or doomed. Google was starting to play a role similar to the one Microsoft had played in the 1980s, offering a mobile platform, Android, that was open and could be used by all hardware makers. *Fortune* staged a debate on this issue in its pages. "There's no excuse to be closed," wrote Michael Copeland. But his colleague Jon Fortt rebutted, "Closed systems get a bad rap, but they work beautifully and users benefit. Probably no one in tech has proved this more convincingly than Steve Jobs. By bundling hardware, software, and services, and controlling them tightly, Apple is consistently able to get the jump on its rivals and roll out polished products." They agreed that the iPad would be the clearest test of this question since the original Macintosh. "Apple has taken its control-freak rep to a whole new level with the A4 chip that powers the thing," wrote Fortt. "Cupertino now has absolute say over the silicon, device, operating system, App Store, and payment system."

Jobs went to the Apple store in Palo Alto shortly before noon on April 5, the day the iPad went on sale. Daniel Kottke—his acid-dropping soul mate from Reed and the early days at Apple, who no longer harbored a grudge for not getting founders' stock options—made a point of being there. "It had been fifteen years, and I wanted to see him again," Kottke recounted. "I grabbed him and told him I was going to use the iPad for my song lyrics. He was in a great mood and we had a nice chat after all these years." Powell and their youngest child, Eve, watched from a corner of the store.

Wozniak, who had once been a proponent of making hardware and software as open as possible, continued to revise that opinion. As he often did, he stayed up all night with the enthusiasts waiting in line for the store to open. This time he was at San Jose's Valley Fair Mall, riding a Segway. A reporter asked him about the closed nature of Apple's ecosystem. "Apple gets you into their playpen and keeps you there, but there are some advantages to that," he replied. "I like open systems, but I'm a hacker. But most people want things that are easy to use. Steve's genius is that he knows how to make things simple, and that sometimes requires controlling everything."

The question "What's on your iPad?" replaced "What's on your iPod?" Even President Obama's staffers, who embraced the iPad as a mark of their tech hipness, played the game. Economic Advisor Larry Summers had the Bloomberg financial information app, Scrabble, and *The Federalist Papers.* Chief of Staff Rahm Emanuel had a slew of newspapers, Communications Advisor Bill Burton had *Vanity Fair* and one entire season of the television series *Lost,* and Political Director David Axelrod had Major League Baseball and NPR.

Jobs was stirred by a story, which he forwarded to me, by Michael Noer on *Forbes.com.* Noer was reading a science fiction novel on his iPad while staying at a dairy farm in a rural area north of Bogotá, Colombia, when a poor six-year-old boy who cleaned the stables came up to him. Curious, Noer handed him the device. With no instruction, and never having seen a computer before, the boy started using it intuitively. He began swiping the screen, launching apps, playing a pinball game. "Steve Jobs has designed a powerful computer that an illiterate six-year-old can use without instruction," Noer wrote. "If that isn't magical, I don't know what is."

In less than a month Apple sold one million iPads. That was twice as fast as it took the iPhone to reach that mark. By March 2011, nine months after its release, fifteen million had been sold. By some measures it became the most successful consumer product launch in history.

Advertising

Jobs was not happy with the original ads for the iPad. As usual, he threw himself into the marketing, working with James Vincent and Duncan Milner at the ad agency (now called TBWA/Media Arts Lab), with Lee Clow advising from a semiretired perch. The commercial they first produced was a gentle scene of a guy in faded jeans and sweatshirt reclining in a chair, looking at email, a photo album, the *New York Times*, books, and video on an iPad propped on his lap. There were no words, just the background beat of "There Goes My Love" by the Blue Van. "After he approved it, Steve decided he hated it," Vincent recalled. "He thought it looked like a Pottery Barn commercial." Jobs later told me:

> It had been easy to explain what the iPod was—a thousand songs in your pocket—which allowed us to move quickly to the iconic silhouette ads. But it was hard to explain what an iPad was. We didn't want to show it as a computer, and yet we didn't want to make it so soft that it looked like a cute TV. The first set of ads showed we didn't know what we were doing. They had a cashmere and Hush Puppies feel to them.

James Vincent had not taken a break in months. So when the iPad finally went on sale and the ads started airing, he drove with his family to the Coachella Music Festival in Palm Springs, which featured some of his favorite bands, including Muse, Faith No More, and Devo. Soon after he arrived, Jobs called. "Your commercials suck," he said. "The iPad is revolutionizing the world, and we need something big. You've given me small shit."

"Well, what do you want?" Vincent shot back. "You've not been able to tell me what you want."

"I don't know," Jobs said. "You have to bring me something new. Nothing you've shown me is even close."

Vincent argued back and suddenly Jobs went ballistic. "He just started screaming at me," Vincent recalled. Vincent could be volatile himself, and the volleys escalated.

When Vincent shouted, "You've got to tell me what you want," Jobs shot back, "You've got to show me some stuff, and I'll know it when I see it."

"Oh, great, let me write that on my brief for my creative people: I'll know it when I see it."

Vincent got so frustrated that he slammed his fist into the wall of the house he was renting and put a large dent in it. When he finally went outside to his family, sitting by the pool, they looked at him nervously. "Are you okay?" his wife finally asked.

It took Vincent and his team two weeks to come up with an array of new options, and he asked to present them at Jobs's house rather than the office, hoping that it would be a more relaxed environment. Laying storyboards on the coffee table, he and Milner offered twelve approaches. One was inspirational and stirring. Another tried humor, with Michael Cera, the comic actor, wandering through a fake house making funny comments about the way people could use iPads. Others featured the iPad with celebrities, or set starkly on a white background, or starring in a little sitcom, or in a straightforward product demonstration.

After mulling over the options, Jobs realized what he wanted. Not humor, nor a celebrity, nor a demo. "It's got to make a statement," he said. "It needs to be a manifesto. This is big." He had announced that the iPad would change the world, and he wanted a campaign that reinforced that declaration. Other companies would come out with copycat tablets in a year or so, he said, and he wanted people to remember that the iPad was the real thing. "We need ads that stand up and declare what we have done."

He abruptly got out of his chair, looking a bit weak but smiling. "I've got to go have a massage now," he said. "Get to work."

So Vincent and Milner, along with the copywriter Eric Grunbaum, began crafting what they dubbed "The Manifesto." It would be fast-paced, with vibrant pictures and a thumping beat, and it would proclaim that the iPad was revolutionary. The music they chose was Karen O's pounding refrain from the Yeah Yeah Yeahs' "Gold Lion." As the iPad was shown doing magical things, a strong voice declared, "iPad is thin. iPad is beautiful. . . . It's crazy powerful. It's magical. . . . It's video, photos. More books than you could read in a lifetime. It's already a revolution, and it's only just begun."

Once the Manifesto ads had run their course, the team again tried something softer, shot as day-in-the-life documentaries by the young filmmaker Jessica Sanders, who had directed the Manifesto ones. Jobs liked them—for a little while. Then he turned against them for the same reason he had reacted against the original Pottery Barn–style ads. "Dammit," he shouted, "they look like a Visa commercial, typical ad agency stuff."

He had been asking for ads that were different and new, but eventually he realized he did not want to stray from what he considered the Apple voice. For him, that voice had a distinctive set of qualities: simple, declarative, clean. "We went down that lifestyle path, and it seemed to be growing on Steve, and suddenly he said, 'I hate that stuff, it's not Apple,'" recalled Lee Clow. "He told us to get back to the Apple voice. It's a very simple, honest voice." And so they went back to a clean white background, with just a close-up showing off all the things that "iPad is . . ." and could do.

Apps

The iPad commercials were not about the device, but about what you could do with it. Indeed its success came not just from the beauty of the hardware but from the applications, known as apps, that allowed you to indulge in all sorts of delightful activities. There were thousands—and soon hundreds of thousands—of apps that you could download for free or for a few dollars. You could sling angry birds with the swipe of your finger, track your stocks, watch movies, read books and magazines, catch up on the news, play games, and waste glorious amounts of time. Once again the integration of the hardware, software, and store made it easy. But the apps also allowed the platform to be sort of open, in a very controlled way, to outside developers who wanted to create software and content for it—open, that is, like a carefully curated and gated community garden.

The apps phenomenon began with the iPhone. When it first came out in early 2007, there were no apps you could buy from outside developers, and Jobs initially resisted allowing them. He didn't want outsiders to create applications for the iPhone that could mess it up, infect it with viruses, or pollute its integrity.

Board member Art Levinson was among those pushing to allow iPhone apps. "I called him a half dozen times to lobby for the potential of the apps," he recalled. If Apple didn't allow them, indeed encourage them, another smartphone maker would, giving itself a competitive advantage. Apple's marketing chief Phil Schiller agreed. "I couldn't imagine that we would create something as powerful as the iPhone and not empower developers to make lots of apps," he recalled. "I knew customers would love them." From the outside, the venture capitalist John Doerr argued that permitting apps would spawn a profusion of new entrepreneurs who would create new services.

Jobs at first quashed the discussion, partly because he felt his team did not have the bandwidth to figure out all of the complexities that would be involved in policing third-party app developers. He wanted focus. "So he didn't want to talk about it," said Schiller. But as soon as the iPhone was launched, he was willing to hear the debate. "Every time the conversation happened, Steve seemed a little more open," said Levinson. There were freewheeling discussions at four board meetings.

Jobs soon figured out that there was a way to have the best of both worlds. He would permit outsiders to write apps, but they would have to meet strict standards, be tested and approved by Apple, and be sold only through the iTunes Store. It was a way to reap the advantage of empowering thousands of software developers while retaining enough control to protect the integrity of the iPhone and the simplicity of the customer experience. "It was an absolutely magical solution that hit the sweet spot," said Levinson. "It gave us the benefits of openness while retaining end-to-end control."

The App Store for the iPhone opened on iTunes in July 2008; the billionth download came nine months later. By the time the iPad went on sale in April 2010, there were 185,000 available iPhone apps. Most could also be used on the iPad, although they didn't take advantage of the bigger screen size. But in less than five months, developers had written twenty-five thousand new apps that were specifically configured for the iPad. By July 2011 there were 500,000 apps for both devices, and there had been more than fifteen billion downloads of them.

The App Store created a new industry overnight. In dorm rooms and garages and at major media companies, entrepreneurs invented new apps. John Doerr's venture capital firm created an iFund of $200 million to offer equity financing for the best ideas. Magazines and newspapers that had been giving away their content for free saw one last chance to put the genie of that dubious business model back into the bottle. Innovative publishers created new magazines, books, and learning materials just for the iPad. For example, the high-end publishing house Callaway, which had produced books ranging from Madonna's *Sex* to *Miss Spider's Tea Party*, decided to "burn the boats" and give up print altogether to focus on publishing books as interactive apps. By June 2011 Apple had paid out $2.5 billion to app developers.

The iPad and other app-based digital devices heralded a fundamental shift in the digital world. Back in the 1980s, going online usually meant dialing into a service like AOL, CompuServe, or Prodigy that charged fees for access to a carefully curated walled garden filled with content plus some exit gates that allowed braver users access to the Internet at large. The second phase, beginning in the early 1990s, was the advent of browsers that allowed everyone to freely surf the Internet using the hypertext transfer protocols of the World Wide Web, which linked billions of sites. Search engines arose so that people could easily find the websites they wanted. The release of the iPad portended a new model. Apps resembled the walled gardens of old. The creators could charge fees and offer more functions to the users who downloaded them. But the rise of apps also meant that the openness and linked nature of the web were sacrificed. Apps were not as easily linked or searchable. Because the iPad allowed the use of both apps and web browsing, it was not at war with the web model. But it did offer an alternative, for both the consumers and the creators of content.

Publishing and Journalism

With the iPod, Jobs had transformed the music business. With the iPad and its App Store, he began to transform all media, from publishing to journalism to television and movies.

Books were an obvious target, since Amazon's Kindle had shown there was an appetite for electronic books. So Apple created an iBooks Store, which sold electronic books the way the iTunes Store sold songs. There was, however, a slight difference in the business model. For the iTunes Store, Jobs had insisted that all songs be sold at one inexpensive price, initially 99 cents. Amazon's Jeff Bezos had tried to take a similar approach with ebooks, insisting on selling them for at most $9.99. Jobs came in and offered publishers what he had refused to offer record companies: They could set any price they wanted for their wares in the iBooks Store, and Apple would take 30%. Initially that meant prices were higher than on Amazon. Why would people pay Apple more? "That won't be the case," Jobs answered, when Walt Mossberg asked him that question at the iPad launch event. "The price will be the same." He was right.

The day after the iPad launch, Jobs described to me his thinking on books:

> Amazon screwed it up. It paid the wholesale price for some books, but started selling them below cost at $9.99. The publishers hated that— they thought it would trash their ability to sell hardcover books at $28. So before Apple even got on the scene, some booksellers were starting to withhold books from Amazon. So we told the publishers, "We'll go to the agency model, where you set the price, and we get our 30%, and yes, the customer pays a little more, but that's what you want anyway." But we also asked for a guarantee that if anybody else is selling the books

cheaper than we are, then we can sell them at the lower price too. So they went to Amazon and said, "You're going to sign an agency contract or we're not going to give you the books."

Jobs acknowledged that he was trying to have it both ways when it came to music and books. He had refused to offer the music companies the agency model and allow them to set their own prices. Why? Because he didn't have to. But with books he did. "We were not the first people in the books business," he said. "Given the situation that existed, what was best for us was to do this aikido move and end up with the agency model. And we pulled it off."

Right after the iPad launch event, Jobs traveled to New York in February 2010 to meet with executives in the journalism business. In two days he saw Rupert Murdoch, his son James, and the management of their *Wall Street Journal*; Arthur Sulzberger Jr. and the top executives at the *New York Times*; and executives at *Time, Fortune*, and other Time Inc. magazines. "I would love to help quality journalism," he later said. "We can't depend on bloggers for our news. We need real reporting and editorial oversight more than ever. So I'd love to find a way to help people create digital products where they actually can make money." Since he had gotten people to pay for music, he hoped he could do the same for journalism.

Publishers, however, turned out to be leery of his lifeline. It meant that they would have to give 30% of their revenue to Apple, but that wasn't the biggest problem. More important, the publishers feared that, under his system, they would no longer have a direct relationship with their subscribers; they wouldn't have their email address and credit card number so they could bill them, communicate with them, and market new products to them. Instead Apple would own the customers, bill them, and have their information in its own database. And because of its privacy policy, Apple would not share this information unless a customer gave explicit permission to do so.

Jobs was particularly interested in striking a deal with the *New York Times*, which he felt was a great newspaper in danger of declining because it had not figured out how to charge for digital content. "One of my personal projects this year, I've decided, is to try to help—whether they want it or not—the *Times*," he told me early in 2010. "I think it's important to the country for them to figure it out."

During his New York trip, he went to dinner with fifty top *Times* executives in the cellar private dining room at Pranna, an Asian restaurant. (He ordered a mango smoothie and a plain vegan pasta, neither of which was on the menu.) There he showed off the iPad and explained how important it was to find a modest price point for digital content that consumers would accept. He drew a chart of possible prices and volume. How many readers would they have if the *Times* were free? They already knew the answer to that extreme on the chart, because they were giving it away for free on the web already and had about twenty million regular visitors. And if they made it really expensive? They had data on that too; they charged print subscribers more than $300 a year and had about a million of them. "You should go after the midpoint, which is about ten million digital subscribers," he told them. "And that means your digital subs should be very cheap and simple, one click and $5 a month at most."

When one of the *Times* circulation executives insisted that the paper needed the email and credit card information for all of its subscribers, even if they subscribed through the App Store, Jobs said that Apple would not give it out. That angered the executive. It was unthinkable, he said, for the *Times* not to have that information. "Well, you can ask them for it, but if they won't voluntarily give it to you, don't blame me," Jobs said. "If you don't like it, don't use us. I'm not the one who got you in this jam. You're the ones who've spent the past five years giving away your paper online and not collecting anyone's credit card information."

Jobs also met privately with Arthur Sulzberger Jr. "He's a nice guy, and he's really proud of his new building, as he should be," Jobs said later. "I talked to him about what I thought he ought to do, but then nothing happened." It took a year, but in April 2011 the *Times* started charging for its digital edition and selling some subscriptions through Apple, abiding by the policies that Jobs established. It did, however, decide to charge approximately four times the $5 monthly charge that Jobs had suggested.

At the Time-Life Building, *Time*'s editor Rick Stengel played host. Jobs liked Stengel, who had assigned a talented team led by Josh Quittner to make a robust iPad version of the magazine each week. But he was upset to see Andy Serwer of *Fortune* there. Tearing up, he told Serwer how angry he still was about *Fortune*'s story two years earlier revealing details of his health and the stock options problems. "You kicked me when I was down," he said.

The bigger problem at Time Inc. was the same as the one at the *Times*: The magazine company did not want Apple to own its subscribers and prevent it from having a direct billing relationship. Time Inc. wanted to create apps that would direct readers to its own website in order to buy a subscription. Apple refused. When *Time* and other magazines submitted apps that did this, they were denied the right to be in the App Store.

Jobs tried to negotiate personally with the CEO of Time Warner, Jeff Bewkes, a savvy pragmatist with a no-bullshit charm to him. They had dealt with each other a few years earlier over video rights for the iPod Touch; even though Jobs had not been able to convince him to do a deal involving HBO's exclusive rights to show movies soon after their release, he admired Bewkes's straight and decisive style. For his part, Bewkes respected Jobs's ability to be both a strategic thinker and a master of the tiniest details. "Steve can go readily from the overarching principles into the details," he said.

When Jobs called Bewkes about making a deal for Time Inc. magazines on the iPad, he started off by warning that the print business "sucks," that "nobody really wants your magazines," and that Apple was offering a great opportunity to sell digital subscriptions, but "your guys don't get it." Bewkes didn't agree with any of those premises. He said he was happy for Apple to sell digital subscriptions for Time Inc. Apple's 30% take was not the problem. "I'm telling you right now, if you sell a sub for us, you can have 30%," Bewkes told him.

"Well, that's more progress than I've made with anybody," Jobs replied.

"I have only one question," Bewkes continued. "If you sell a subscription to my magazine, and I give you the 30%, who has the subscription—you or me?"

"I can't give away all the subscriber info because of Apple's privacy policy," Jobs replied.

"Well, then, we have to figure something else out, because I don't want my whole subscription base to become subscribers of yours, for you to then aggregate at the Apple store," said Bewkes. "And the next thing you'll do, once you have a monopoly, is come back and tell me that my magazine shouldn't be $4 a copy but instead should be $1. If someone subscribes to our magazine, we need to know who it is, we need to be able to create online communities of those people, and we need the right to pitch them directly about renewing."

Jobs had an easier time with Rupert Murdoch, whose News Corp. owned the *Wall Street Journal, New York Post*, newspapers around the world, Fox Studios, and the Fox News Channel. When Jobs met with Murdoch and his team, they also pressed the case that they should share ownership of the subscribers that came in through the App Store. But when Jobs refused, something interesting happened. Murdoch is not known as a pushover, but he knew that he did not have the leverage on this issue, so he accepted Jobs's terms. "We would prefer to own the subscribers, and we pushed for that," recalled Murdoch. "But Steve wouldn't do a deal on those terms, so I said, 'Okay, let's get on with it.' We didn't see any reason to mess around. He wasn't going to bend—and I wouldn't have bent if I were in his position—so I just said yes."

Murdoch even launched a digital-only daily newspaper, *The Daily*, tailored specifically for the iPad. It would be sold in the App Store, on the terms dictated by Jobs, at 99 cents a week. Murdoch himself took a team to Cupertino to show the proposed design. Not surprisingly, Jobs hated it. "Would you allow our designers to help?" he asked. Murdoch accepted. "The Apple designers had a crack at it," Murdoch recalled, "and our folks went back and had another crack, and ten days later we went back and showed them both, and he actually liked our team's version better. It stunned us."

The Daily, which was neither tabloidy nor serious, but instead a rather midmarket product like *USA Today*, was not very successful. But it did help create an odd-couple bonding between Jobs and Murdoch. When Murdoch asked him to speak at his June 2010 News Corp. annual management retreat, Jobs made an exception to his rule of never doing such appearances. James Murdoch led him in an after-dinner interview that lasted almost two hours. "He was very blunt and critical of what newspapers were doing in technology," Murdoch recalled. "He told us we were going to find it hard to get things right, because you're in New York, and anyone who's any good at tech works in Silicon Valley." This did not go down very well with the president of the Wall Street Journal Digital Network, Gordon McLeod, who pushed back a bit. At the end, McLeod came up to Jobs and said, "Thanks, it was a wonderful evening, but you probably just cost me my job." Murdoch chuckled a bit when he described the scene to me. "It ended up being true," he said. McLeod was out within three months.

In return for speaking at the retreat, Jobs got Murdoch to hear him out on Fox News, which he believed was destructive, harmful to the nation, and a blot on Murdoch's reputation. "You're blowing it with Fox News," Jobs told him over dinner. "The axis today is not liberal and conservative, the axis is constructive-destructive, and you've cast your lot with the destructive people. Fox has become an incredibly destructive force in our society. You can be better, and this is going to be your legacy if you're not careful." Jobs said he thought Murdoch did not really like how far Fox had gone. "Rupert's a builder, not a tearer-downer," he said. "I've had some meetings with James, and I think he agrees with me. I can just tell."

Murdoch later said he was used to people like Jobs complaining about Fox. "He's got sort of a left-wing view on this," he said. Jobs asked him to have his folks make a reel of a week of Sean Hannity and Glenn Beck shows—he thought that they were more destructive than Bill O'Reilly—and Murdoch agreed to do so. Jobs later told me that he was going to ask Jon Stewart's team to put together a similar reel for Murdoch to watch. "I'd be happy to see it," Murdoch said, "but he hasn't sent it to me."

Murdoch and Jobs hit it off well enough that Murdoch went to his Palo Alto house for dinner twice more during the next year. Jobs joked that he had to hide the dinner knives on such occasions, because he was afraid that his liberal wife was going to eviscerate Murdoch when he walked in. For his part, Murdoch was reported to have uttered a great line about the organic vegan dishes typically served: "Eating dinner at Steve's is a great experience, as long as you get out before the local restaurants close." Alas, when I asked Murdoch if he had ever said that, he didn't recall it.

One visit came early in 2011. Murdoch was due to pass through Palo Alto on February 24, and he texted Jobs to tell him so. He didn't know it was Jobs's fifty-sixth birthday, and Jobs didn't mention it when he texted back inviting him to dinner. "It was my way of making sure Laurene didn't veto the plan," Jobs joked. "It was my birthday, so she had to let me have Rupert over." Erin and Eve were there, and Reed jogged over from Stanford near the end of the dinner. Jobs showed off the designs for his planned boat, which Murdoch thought looked beautiful on the inside but "a bit plain" on the outside. "It certainly shows great optimism about his health that he was talking so much about building it," Murdoch later said.

At dinner they talked about the importance of infusing an entrepreneurial and nimble culture into a company. Sony failed to do that, Murdoch said. Jobs agreed. "I used to believe that a really big company couldn't have a clear corporate culture," Jobs said. "But I now believe it can be done. Murdoch's done it. I think I've done it at Apple."

Most of the dinner conversation was about education. Murdoch had just hired Joel Klein, the former chancellor of the New York City Department of Education, to start a digital curriculum division. Murdoch recalled that Jobs was somewhat dismissive of the idea that technology could transform education. But Jobs agreed with Murdoch that the paper textbook business would be blown away by digital learning materials.

In fact Jobs had his sights set on textbooks as the next business he wanted to transform. He believed it was an $8 billion a year industry ripe for digital destruction. He was also struck by the fact that many schools, for security reasons, don't have lockers, so kids have to lug a heavy backpack around. "The iPad would solve that," he said. His idea was to hire great textbook writers to create digital versions, and make them a feature of the iPad. In addition, he held meetings with

WALTER ISAACSON

the major publishers, such as Pearson Education, about partnering with Apple. "The process by which states certify textbooks is corrupt," he said. "But if we can make the textbooks free, and they come with the iPad, then they don't have to be certified. The crappy economy at the state level will last for a decade, and we can give them an opportunity to circumvent that whole process and save money."

CHAPTER THIRTY-NINE

NEW BATTLES

And Echoes of Old Ones

Google: Open versus Closed

A few days after he unveiled the iPad in January 2010, Jobs held a "town hall" meeting with employees at Apple's campus. Instead of exulting about their transformative new product, however, he went into a rant against Google for producing the rival Android operating system. Jobs was furious that Google had decided to compete with Apple in the phone business. "We did not enter the search business," he said. "They entered the phone business. Make no mistake. They want to kill the iPhone. We won't let them." A few minutes later, after the meeting moved on to another topic, Jobs returned to his tirade to attack Google's famous values slogan. "I want to go back to that other question first and say one more thing. This 'Don't be evil' mantra, it's bullshit."

Jobs felt personally betrayed. Google's CEO Eric Schmidt had been on the Apple board during the development of the iPhone and iPad, and Google's founders, Larry Page and Sergey Brin, had treated him as a mentor. He felt ripped off. Android's touchscreen interface was adopting more and more of the features—multi-touch, swiping, a grid of app icons—that Apple had created.

Jobs had tried to dissuade Google from developing Android. He had gone to Google's headquarters near Palo Alto in 2008 and gotten into a shouting match with Page, Brin, and the head of the Android development team, Andy Rubin. (Because Schmidt was then on the Apple board, he recused himself from discussions involving the iPhone.) "I said we would, if we had good relations, guarantee Google access to the iPhone and guarantee it one or two icons on the home screen," he recalled. But he also threatened that if Google continued to develop Android and used any iPhone features, such as multi-touch, he would sue. At first Google avoided copying certain features, but in January 2010 HTC introduced an Android phone that boasted multi-touch and many other aspects of the iPhone's look and feel. That was the context for Jobs's pronouncement that Google's "Don't be evil" slogan was "bullshit."

So Apple filed suit against HTC (and, by extension, Android), alleging infringement of twenty of its patents. Among them were patents covering various multi-touch gestures, swipe to open, double-tap to zoom, pinch and expand, and the sensors that determined how a device was being held. As he sat in his house in Palo Alto the week the lawsuit was filed, he became angrier than I had ever seen him:

> Our lawsuit is saying, "Google, you fucking ripped off the iPhone, wholesale ripped us off." Grand theft. I will spend my last dying breath if I need to, and I will spend every penny of Apple's $40 billion in the bank, to right this wrong. I'm going to destroy Android, because it's a stolen product. I'm willing to go to thermonuclear war on this. They are scared to death, because they know they are guilty. Outside of Search, Google's products—Android, Google Docs—are shit.

A few days after this rant, Jobs got a call from Schmidt, who had resigned from the Apple board the previous summer. He suggested they get together for coffee, and they met at a café in a Palo Alto shopping center. "We spent half the time talking about personal matters, then half the time on his perception that Google had stolen Apple's user interface designs," recalled Schmidt. When it came to the latter subject, Jobs did most of the talking. Google had ripped him off, he said in colorful language. "We've got you red-handed," he told Schmidt. "I'm not interested in settling. I don't want your money. If you offer me $5 billion, I won't want it. I've got plenty of money. I want you to stop using our ideas in Android, that's all I want." They resolved nothing.

Underlying the dispute was an even more fundamental issue, one that had unnerving historical resonance. Google presented Android as an "open" platform; its open-source code was freely available for multiple hardware makers to use on whatever phones or tablets they built. Jobs, of course, had a dogmatic belief that Apple should closely integrate its operating systems with its hardware. In the 1980s Apple had not licensed out its Macintosh operating system, and Microsoft eventually gained dominant market share by licensing its system to multiple hardware makers and, in Jobs's mind, ripping off Apple's interface.

The comparison between what Microsoft wrought in the 1980s and what Google was trying to do in 2010 was not exact, but it was close enough to be unsettling—and infuriating. It exemplified the great debate of the digital age: closed versus open, or as Jobs framed it, integrated versus fragmented. Was it better, as Apple believed and as Jobs's own controlling perfectionism almost compelled, to tie the hardware and software and content handling into one tidy system that assured a simple user experience? Or was it better to give users and manufacturers more choice and free up avenues for more innovation, by creating software systems that could be modified and used on different devices? "Steve has a particular way that he wants to run Apple, and it's the same as it was twenty years ago, which is that Apple is a brilliant innovator of closed systems," Schmidt later told me. "They don't want people to be on their platform without permission. The benefits of a closed platform is control. But Google has a specific belief that open is the better approach, because it leads to more options and competition and consumer choice."

So what did Bill Gates think as he watched Jobs, with his closed strategy, go into battle against Google, as he had done against Microsoft twenty-five years earlier? "There are some benefits to being more closed, in terms of how much you control the experience, and certainly at times he's had the benefit of that," Gates told me. But refusing to license the Apple iOS, he added, gave competitors like Android the chance to gain greater volume. In addition, he argued, competition among a variety of devices and manufacturers leads to greater consumer choice and more innovation. "These companies are not all building pyramids next to Central Park," he said, poking fun at Apple's Fifth Avenue store, "but they are coming up with innovations based on competing for consumers." Most of the improvements in PCs, Gates pointed out, came because consumers had a lot of choices, and that would someday be the case in the world of mobile devices. "Eventually, I think, open will succeed, but that's where I come from. In the long run, the coherence thing, you can't stay with that."

Jobs believed in "the coherence thing." His faith in a controlled and closed environment remained unwavering, even as Android gained market share. "Google says we exert more control than they do, that we are closed and they are open," he railed when I told him what Schmidt had said. "Well, look at the results—Android's a mess. It has different screen sizes and versions, over a hundred permutations." Even if Google's approach might eventually win in the marketplace, Jobs found it repellent. "I like being responsible for the whole user experience. We do it not to make money. We do it because we want to make great products, not crap like Android."

Flash, the App Store, and Control

Jobs's insistence on end-to-end control was manifested in other battles as well. At the town hall meeting where he attacked Google, he also assailed Adobe's multimedia platform for websites, Flash, as a "buggy" battery hog made by "lazy" people. The iPod and iPhone, he said, would never run Flash. "Flash is a spaghetti-ball piece of technology that has lousy performance and really bad security problems," he said to me later that week.

He even banned apps that made use of a compiler created by Adobe that translated Flash code so that it would be compatible with Apple's iOS. Jobs disdained the use of compilers that allowed developers to write their products once and have them ported to multiple operating systems. "Allowing Flash to be ported across platforms means things get dumbed down to the lowest common denominator," he said. "We spend lots of effort to make our platform better, and the developer doesn't get any benefit if Adobe only works with functions that every platform has. So we said that we want developers to take advantage of our better features, so that their apps work better on our platform than they work on anybody else's." On that he was right. Losing the ability to differentiate Apple's platforms—allowing them to become commoditized like HP and Dell machines—would have meant death for the company.

There was, in addition, a more personal reason. Apple had invested in Adobe in 1985, and together the two companies had launched the desktop publishing revolution. "I helped put Adobe on the map," Jobs claimed. In 1999, after he returned to Apple, he had asked Adobe to start making its video editing software and other products for the iMac and its new operating system, but Adobe refused. It focused on making its products for Windows. Soon after, its founder, John Warnock, retired. "The soul of Adobe disappeared when Warnock left," Jobs said. "He was the inventor, the person I related to. It's been a bunch of suits since then, and the company has turned out crap."

When Adobe evangelists and various Flash supporters in the blogosphere attacked Jobs for being too controlling, he decided to write and post an open letter. Bill Campbell, his friend and board member, came by his house to go over it. "Does it sound like I'm just trying to stick it to Adobe?" he asked Campbell. "No, it's facts, just put it out there," the coach said. Most of the letter focused on the technical drawbacks of Flash. But despite Campbell's coaching, Jobs couldn't resist venting at the end about the problematic history between the two companies. "Adobe was the last major third party developer to fully adopt Mac OS X," he noted.

Apple ended up lifting some of its restrictions on cross-platform compilers later in the year, and Adobe was able to come out with a Flash authoring tool that took advantage of the key features of Apple's iOS. It was a bitter war, but one in which Jobs had the better argument. In the end it pushed Adobe and other developers of compilers to make better use of the iPhone and iPad interface and its special features.

Jobs had a tougher time navigating the controversies over Apple's desire to keep tight control over which apps could be downloaded onto the iPhone and iPad. Guarding against apps that contained viruses or violated the user's privacy made sense; preventing apps that took users to other websites to buy subscriptions, rather than doing it through the iTunes Store, at least had a business rationale. But Jobs and his team went further: They decided to ban any app that defamed people, might be politically explosive, or was deemed by Apple's censors to be pornographic.

The problem of playing nanny became apparent when Apple rejected an app featuring the animated political cartoons of Mark Fiore, on the rationale that his attacks on the Bush administration's policy on torture violated the restriction against defamation. Its decision became public, and was subjected to ridicule, when Fiore won the 2010 Pulitzer Prize for editorial cartooning in April. Apple had to reverse itself, and Jobs made a public apology. "We're guilty of making mistakes," he said. "We're doing the best we can, we're learning as fast as we can—but we thought this rule made sense."

It was more than a mistake. It raised the specter of Apple's controlling what apps we got to see and read, at least if we wanted to use an iPad or iPhone. Jobs seemed in danger of becoming the Orwellian Big Brother he had gleefully destroyed in Apple's "1984" Macintosh ad. He took the issue seriously. One day he called the *New York Times* columnist Tom Friedman to discuss how to draw lines without looking like a censor. He asked Friedman to head an advisory group to help come up with guidelines, but the columnist's publisher said it would be a conflict of interest, and no such committee was formed.

The pornography ban also caused problems. "We believe we have a moral responsibility to keep porn off the iPhone," Jobs declared in an email to a customer. "Folks who want porn can buy an Android."

This prompted an email exchange with Ryan Tate, the editor of the tech gossip site Valleywag. Sipping a stinger cocktail one evening, Tate shot off an email to Jobs decrying Apple's heavy-handed control over which apps passed muster. "If Dylan was 20 today, how would he feel about your company?" Tate asked. "Would he think the iPad had the faintest thing to do with 'revolution'? Revolutions are about freedom."

To Tate's surprise, Jobs responded a few hours later, after midnight. "Yep," he said, "freedom from programs that steal your private data. Freedom from programs that trash your battery. Freedom from porn. Yep, freedom. The times they are a changin', and some traditional PC folks feel like their world is slipping away. It is."

In his reply, Tate offered some thoughts on Flash and other topics, then returned to the censorship issue. "And you know what? I don't want 'freedom from porn.' Porn is just fine! And I think my wife would agree."

"You might care more about porn when you have kids," replied Jobs. "It's not about freedom, it's about Apple trying to do the right thing for its users." At the end he added a zinger: "By the way, what have you done that's so great? Do you create anything, or just criticize others' work and belittle their motivations?"

Tate admitted to being impressed. "Rare is the CEO who will spar one-on-one with customers and bloggers like this," he wrote. "Jobs deserves big credit for breaking the mold of the typical American executive, and not just because his company makes such hugely superior products: Jobs not only built and then rebuilt his company around some very strong opinions about digital life, but he's willing to defend them in public. Vigorously. Bluntly. At two in the morning on a weekend." Many in the blogosphere agreed, and they sent Jobs emails praising his feistiness. Jobs was proud as well; he forwarded his exchange with Tate and some of the kudos to me.

Still, there was something unnerving about Apple's decreeing that those who bought their products shouldn't look at controversial political cartoons or, for that matter, porn. The humor site eSarcasm .com launched a "Yes, Steve, I want porn" web campaign. "We are dirty, sex-obsessed miscreants who need access to smut 24 hours a day," the site declared. "Either that, or we just enjoy the idea of an uncensored, open society where a techno-dictator doesn't decide what we can and cannot see."

• • •

At the time Jobs and Apple were engaged in a battle with Valleywag's affiliated website, Gizmodo, which had gotten hold of a test version of the unreleased iPhone 4 that a hapless Apple engineer had left in a bar. When the police, responding to Apple's complaint, raided the house of the reporter, it raised the question of whether control freakiness had combined with arrogance.

Jon Stewart was a friend of Jobs and an Apple fan. Jobs had visited him privately in February when he took his trip to New York to meet with media executives. But that didn't stop Stewart from going after him on *The Daily Show*. "It wasn't supposed to be this way! Microsoft was supposed to be the evil one!" Stewart said, only half-jokingly. Behind him, the word "appholes" appeared on the screen. "You guys were the rebels, man, the underdogs. But now, are you becoming The Man? Remember back in 1984, you had those awesome ads about overthrowing Big Brother? Look in the mirror, man!"

By late spring the issue was being discussed among board members. "There is an arrogance," Art Levinson told me over lunch just after he had raised it at a meeting. "It ties into Steve's personality. He can react viscerally and lay out his convictions in a forceful manner." Such arrogance was fine when Apple was the feisty underdog. But now Apple was dominant in the mobile market. "We need to make the transition to being a big company and dealing with the hubris issue," said Levinson. Al Gore also talked about the problem at board meetings. "The context for Apple is changing dramatically," he recounted. "It's not hammer-thrower against Big Brother. Now Apple's big, and people see it as arrogant." Jobs became defensive when the topic was raised. "He's still adjusting to it," said Gore. "He's better at being the underdog than being a humble giant."

Jobs had little patience for such talk. The reason Apple was being criticized, he told me then, was that "companies like Google and Adobe are lying about us and trying to tear us down." What did he think of the suggestion that Apple sometimes acted arrogantly? "I'm not worried about that," he said, "because we're not arrogant."

Antennagate: Design versus Engineering

In many consumer product companies, there's tension between the designers, who want to make a product look beautiful, and the engineers, who need to make sure it fulfills its functional requirements. At Apple, where Jobs pushed both design and engineering to the edge, that tension was even greater.

When he and design director Jony Ive became creative coconspirators back in 1997, they tended to view the qualms expressed by engineers as evidence of a can't-do attitude that needed to be overcome. Their faith that awesome design could force superhuman feats of engineering was reinforced by the success of the iMac and iPod. When engineers said something couldn't be done, Ive and Jobs pushed them to try, and usually they succeeded. There were occasional small problems. The iPod Nano, for example, was prone to getting scratched because Ive believed that a clear coating would lessen the purity of his design. But that was not a crisis.

When it came to designing the iPhone, Ive's design desires bumped into a fundamental law of physics that could not be changed even by a reality distortion field. Metal is not a great material to put near an antenna. As Michael Faraday showed, electromagnetic waves flow around the surface of metal, not through it. So a metal enclosure around a phone can create what is known as a Faraday cage, diminishing the signals that get in or out. The original iPhone started with a plastic band at the bottom, but Ive thought that would wreck the design integrity and asked that there be an aluminum rim all around. After that ended up working out, Ive designed the iPhone 4 with a steel rim. The steel would be the structural support, look really sleek, and serve as part of the phone's antenna.

There were significant challenges. In order to serve as an antenna, the steel rim had to have a tiny gap. But if a person covered that gap with a finger or sweaty palm, there could be some signal loss. The engineers suggested a clear coating over the metal to help prevent this, but again Ive felt that this would detract from the brushed-metal look. The issue was presented to Jobs at various meetings, but he thought the engineers were crying wolf. You can make this work, he said. And so they did.

And it worked, almost perfectly. But not totally perfectly. When the iPhone 4 was released in June 2010, it looked awesome, but a problem soon became evident: If you held the phone a certain way, especially using your left hand so your palm covered the tiny gap, you could lose your connection. It occurred with perhaps one in a hundred calls. Because Jobs insisted on keeping his unreleased products secret (even the phone that Gizmodo scored in a bar had a fake case around it), the iPhone 4 did not go through the live testing that most electronic devices get. So the flaw was not caught before the massive rush to buy it began. "The question is whether the twin policies of putting design in front of engineering and having a policy of supersecrecy surrounding unreleased products helped Apple," Tony Fadell said later. "On the whole, yes, but unchecked power is a bad thing, and that's what happened."

Had it not been the Apple iPhone 4, a product that had everyone transfixed, the issue of a few extra dropped calls would not have made news. But it became known as "Antennagate," and it boiled to a head in early July, when *Consumer Reports* did some rigorous tests and said that it could not recommend the iPhone 4 because of the antenna problem.

Jobs was in Kona Village, Hawaii, with his family when the issue arose. At first he was defensive. Art Levinson was in constant contact by phone, and Jobs insisted that the problem stemmed from Google and Motorola making mischief. "They want to shoot Apple down," he said.

Levinson urged a little humility. "Let's try to figure out if there's something wrong," he said. When he again mentioned the perception that Apple was arrogant, Jobs didn't like it. It went against his black-white, right-wrong way of viewing the world. Apple was a company of principle, he felt. If others failed to see that, it was their fault, not a reason for Apple to play humble.

Jobs's second reaction was to be hurt. He took the criticism personally and became emotionally anguished. "At his core, he doesn't do things that he thinks are blatantly wrong, like some pure pragmatists in our business," Levinson said. "So if he feels he's right, he will just charge ahead rather than question himself." Levinson urged him not to get depressed. But Jobs did. "Fuck this, it's not worth it," he told Levinson. Finally Tim Cook was able to shake him out of his lethargy. He quoted someone as saying that Apple was becoming the new Microsoft, complacent and arrogant. The next day Jobs changed his attitude. "Let's get to the bottom of this," he said.

When the data about dropped calls were assembled from AT&T, Jobs realized there was a problem, even if it was more minor than people were making it seem. So he flew back from Hawaii. But before he left, he made some phone calls. It was time to gather a couple of trusted old hands, wise men who had been with him during the original Macintosh days thirty years earlier.

His first call was to Regis McKenna, the public relations guru. "I'm coming back from Hawaii to deal with this antenna thing, and I need to bounce some stuff off of you," Jobs told him. They agreed to meet at the Cupertino boardroom at 1:30 the next afternoon. The second call was to the adman Lee Clow. He had tried to retire from the Apple account, but Jobs liked having him around. His colleague James Vincent was summoned as well.

Jobs also decided to bring his son Reed, then a high school senior, back with him from Hawaii. "I'm going to be in meetings 24/7 for probably two days and I want you to be in every single one because you'll learn more in those two days than you would in two years at business school," he told him. "You're going to be in the room with the best people in the world making really tough decisions and get to see how the sausage is made." Jobs got a little misty-eyed when he recalled the experience. "I would go through that all again just for that opportunity to have him see me at work," he said. "He got to see what his dad does."

They were joined by Katie Cotton, the steady public relations chief at Apple, and seven other top executives. The meeting lasted all afternoon. "It was one of the greatest meetings of my life," Jobs later said. He began by laying out all the data they had gathered. "Here are the facts. So what should we do about it?"

McKenna was the most calm and straightforward. "Just lay out the truth, the data," he said. "Don't appear arrogant, but appear firm and confident." Others, including Vincent, pushed Jobs to be more apologetic, but McKenna said no. "Don't go into the press conference with your tail between your legs," he advised. "You should just say: 'Phones aren't perfect, and we're not perfect. We're human and doing the best we can, and here's the data.'" That became the strategy. When the topic turned to the perception of arrogance, McKenna urged him not to worry too much. "I don't think it would work to try to make Steve look humble," McKenna explained later. "As Steve says about himself, 'What you see is what you get.'"

At the press event that Friday, held in Apple's auditorium, Jobs followed McKenna's advice. He did not grovel or apologize, yet he was able to defuse the problem by showing that Apple understood it and would try to make it right. Then he changed the framework of the discussion, saying that all cell phones had some problems. Later he told me that he had sounded a bit "too annoyed" at the event, but in fact he was able to strike a tone that was unemotional and straightforward. He captured it in four short, declarative sentences: "We're not perfect. Phones are not perfect. We all know that. But we want to make our users happy."

If anyone was unhappy, he said, they could return the phone (the return rate turned out to be 1.7%, less than a third of the return rate for the iPhone 3GS or most other phones) or get a free bumper case from Apple. He went on to report data showing that other mobile phones had similar problems. That was not totally true. Apple's antenna design made it slightly worse than most other phones, including earlier versions of the iPhone. But it was true that the media frenzy over the iPhone 4's dropped calls was overblown. "This is blown so out of proportion that it's incredible," he said. Instead of being appalled that he didn't grovel or order a recall, most customers realized that he was right.

The wait list for the phone, which was already sold out, went from two weeks to three. It remained the company's fastest-selling product ever. The media debate shifted to the issue of whether Jobs was right to assert that other smartphones had the same antenna problems. Even if the answer was no, that was a better story to face than one about whether the iPhone 4 was a defective dud.

Some media observers were incredulous. "In a bravura demonstration of stonewalling, righteousness, and hurt sincerity, Steve Jobs successfully took to the stage the other day to deny the problem, dismiss the criticism, and spread the blame among other smartphone makers," Michael Wolff of newser.com wrote. "This is a level of modern marketing, corporate spin, and crisis management about which you can only ask with stupefied incredulity and awe: How do they get away with it? Or, more accurately, how does he get away with it?" Wolff attributed it to Jobs's mesmerizing effect as "the last charismatic individual." Other CEOs would be offering abject apologies and swallowing massive recalls, but Jobs didn't have to. "The grim, skeletal appearance, the absolutism, the ecclesiastical bearing, the sense of his relationship with the sacred, really works, and, in this instance, allows him the privilege of magisterially deciding what is meaningful and what is trivial."

Scott Adams, the creator of the cartoon strip *Dilbert*, was also incredulous, but far more admiring. He wrote a blog entry a few days later (which Jobs proudly emailed around) that marveled at how Jobs's "high ground maneuver" was destined to be studied as a new public relations standard. "Apple's response to the iPhone 4 problem didn't follow the public relations playbook, because Jobs decided to rewrite the playbook," Adams wrote. "If you want to know what genius looks like, study Jobs' words." By proclaiming up front that phones are not perfect, Jobs changed the context of the argument with an indisputable assertion. "If Jobs had not changed the context from the iPhone 4 to all smartphones in general, I could make you a hilarious comic strip about a product so poorly made that it won't work if it comes in contact with a human hand. But as soon as the context is changed to 'all smartphones have problems,' the humor opportunity is gone. Nothing kills humor like a general and boring truth."

Here Comes the Sun

There were a few things that needed to be resolved for the career of Steve Jobs to be complete. Among them was an end to the Thirty Years' War with the band he loved, the Beatles. In 2007 Apple had settled its trademark battle with Apple Corps, the holding company of the Beatles, which had first sued the fledgling computer company over use of the name in 1978. But that still did not get the Beatles into the iTunes Store. The band was the last major holdout, primarily because it had not resolved with EMI music, which owned most of its songs, how to handle the digital rights.

By the summer of 2010 the Beatles and EMI had sorted things out, and a four-person summit was held in the boardroom in Cupertino. Jobs and his vice president for the iTunes Store, Eddy Cue, played host to Jeff Jones, who managed the Beatles' interests, and Roger Faxon, the chief of EMI music. Now that the Beatles were ready to go digital, what could Apple offer to make that milestone special? Jobs had been anticipating this day for a long time. In fact he and his advertising team, Lee Clow and James Vincent, had mocked up some ads and commercials three years earlier when strategizing on how to lure the Beatles on board.

"Steve and I thought about all the things that we could possibly do," Cue recalled. That included taking over the front page of the iTunes Store, buying billboards featuring the best photographs of the band, and running a series of television ads in classic Apple style. The topper was offering a $149 box set that included all thirteen Beatles studio albums, the two-volume "Past Masters" collection, and a nostalgia-inducing video of the 1964 Washington Coliseum concert.

Once they reached an agreement in principle, Jobs personally helped choose the photographs for the ads. Each commercial ended with a still black-and-white shot of Paul McCartney and John Lennon, young and smiling, in a recording studio looking down at a piece of music. It evoked the old photographs of Jobs and Wozniak looking at an Apple circuit board. "Getting the Beatles on iTunes was the culmination of why we got into the music business," said Cue.

CHAPTER FORTY

TO INFINITY

The Cloud, the Spaceship, and Beyond

The iPad 2

Even before the iPad went on sale, Jobs was thinking about what should be in the iPad 2. It needed front and back cameras—everyone knew that was coming—and he definitely wanted it to be thinner. But there was a peripheral issue that he focused on that most people hadn't thought about: The cases that people used covered the beautiful lines of the iPad and detracted from the screen. They made fatter what should be thinner. They put a pedestrian cloak on a device that should be magical in all of its aspects.

Around that time he read an article about magnets, cut it out, and handed it to Jony Ive. The magnets had a cone of attraction that could be precisely focused. Perhaps they could be used to align a detachable cover. That way, it could snap onto the front of an iPad but not have to engulf the entire device. One of the guys in Ive's group worked out how to make a detachable cover that could connect with a magnetic hinge. When you began to open it, the screen would pop to life like the face of a tickled baby, and then the cover could fold into a stand.

It was not high-tech; it was purely mechanical. But it was enchanting. It also was another example of Jobs's desire for end-to-end integration: The cover and the iPad had been designed together so that the magnets and hinge all connected seamlessly. The iPad 2 would have many improvements, but this cheeky little cover, which most other CEOs would never have bothered with, was the one that would elicit the most smiles.

Because Jobs was on another medical leave, he was not expected to be at the launch of the iPad 2, scheduled for March 2, 2011, in San Francisco. But when the invitations were sent out, he told me that I should try to be there. It was the usual scene: top Apple executives in the front row, Tim Cook eating energy bars, and the sound system blaring the appropriate Beatles songs, building up to "Revolution" and "Here Comes the Sun." Reed Jobs arrived at the last minute with two rather wide-eyed freshman dorm mates.

"We've been working on this product for a while, and I just didn't want to miss today," Jobs said as he ambled onstage looking scarily gaunt but with a jaunty smile. The crowd erupted in whoops, hollers, and a standing ovation.

He began his demo of the iPad 2 by showing off the new cover. "This time, the case and the product were designed together," he explained. Then he moved on to address a criticism that had been rankling him because it had some merit: The original iPad had been better at consuming content than at creating it. So Apple had adapted its two best creative applications for the Macintosh, GarageBand and iMovie, and made powerful versions available for the iPad. Jobs showed how easy it was to compose and orchestrate a song, or put music and special effects into your home videos, and post or share such creations using the new iPad.

Once again he ended his presentation with the slide showing the intersection of Liberal Arts Street and Technology Street. And this time he gave one of the clearest expressions of his credo, that true creativity and simplicity come from integrating the whole widget— hardware and software, and for that matter content and covers and salesclerks—rather than allowing things to be open and fragmented, as happened in the world of Windows PCs and was now happening with Android devices:

It's in Apple's DNA that technology alone is not enough. We believe that it's technology married with the humanities that yields us the result that makes our heart sing. Nowhere is that more true than in these post-PC devices. Folks are rushing into this tablet market, and they're looking at it as the next PC, in which the hardware and the software are done by different companies. Our experience, and every bone in our body, says that is not the right approach. These are post-PC devices that need to be even more intuitive and easier to use than a PC, and where the software and the hardware and the applications need to be intertwined in an even more seamless way than they are on a PC. We think we have the right architecture not just in silicon, but in our organization, to build these kinds of products.

It was an architecture that was bred not just into the organization he had built, but into his own soul.

After the launch event, Jobs was energized. He came to the Four Seasons hotel to join me, his wife, and Reed, plus Reed's two Stanford pals, for lunch. For a change he was eating, though still with some pickiness. He ordered fresh-squeezed juice, which he sent back three times, declaring that each new offering was from a bottle, and a pasta primavera, which he shoved away as inedible after one taste. But then he ate half of my crab Louie salad and ordered a full one for himself, followed by a bowl of ice cream. The indulgent hotel was even able to produce a glass of juice that finally met his standards.

At his house the following day he was still on a high. He was planning to fly to Kona Village the next day, alone, and I asked to see what he had put on his iPad 2 for the trip. There were three movies: *Chinatown*, *The Bourne Ultimatum*, and *Toy Story 3*. More revealingly, there was just one book that he had downloaded: *The Autobiography of a Yogi*, the guide to meditation and spirituality that he had first read as a teenager, then reread in India, and had read once a year ever since.

Midway through the morning he decided he wanted to eat something. He was still too weak to drive, so I drove him to a café in a shopping mall. It was closed, but the owner was used to Jobs knocking on the door at off-hours, and he happily let us in. "He's taken on a mission to try to fatten me up," Jobs joked. His doctors had pushed him to eat eggs as a source of high-quality protein, and he ordered an omelet. "Living with a disease like this, and all the pain, constantly reminds you of your own mortality, and that can do strange things to your brain if you're not careful," he said. "You don't make plans more than a year out, and that's bad. You need to force yourself to plan as if you will live for many years."

An example of this magical thinking was his plan to build a luxurious yacht. Before his liver transplant, he and his family used to rent a boat for vacations, traveling to Mexico, the South Pacific, or the Mediterranean. On many of these cruises, Jobs got bored or began to hate the design of the boat, so they would cut the trip short and fly to Kona Village. But sometimes the cruise worked well. "The best vacation I've ever been on was when we went down the coast of Italy, then to Athens—which is a pit, but the Parthenon is mind-blowing—and then to Ephesus in Turkey, where they have these ancient public lavatories in marble with a place in the middle for musicians to serenade." When they got to Istanbul, he hired a history professor to give his family a tour. At the end they went to a Turkish bath, where the professor's lecture gave Jobs an insight about the globalization of youth:

> I had a real revelation. We were all in robes, and they made some Turkish coffee for us. The professor explained how the coffee was made very different from anywhere else, and I realized, "So fucking what?" Which kids even in Turkey give a shit about Turkish coffee? All day I had looked at young people in Istanbul. They were all drinking what every other kid in the world drinks, and they were wearing clothes that look like they were bought at the Gap, and they are all using cell phones. They were like kids everywhere else. It hit me that, for young people, this whole world is the same now. When we're making products, there is no such thing as a Turkish phone, or a music player that young people in Turkey would want that's different from one young people elsewhere would want. We're just one world now.

After the joy of that cruise, Jobs had amused himself by beginning to design, and then repeatedly redesigning, a boat he said he wanted to build someday. When he got sick again in 2009, he almost canceled the project. "I didn't think I would be alive when it got done," he recalled. "But that made me so sad, and I decided that working on the design was fun to do, and maybe I have a shot at being alive when it's done. If I stop work on the boat and then I make it alive for another two years, I would be really pissed. So I've kept going."

After our omelets at the café, we went back to his house and he showed me all of the models and architectural drawings. As expected, the planned yacht was sleek and minimalist. The teak decks were perfectly flat and unblemished by any accoutrements. As at an Apple store, the cabin windows were large panes, almost floor to ceiling, and the main living area was designed to have walls of glass that were forty feet long and ten feet high. He had gotten the chief engineer of the Apple stores to design a special glass that was able to provide structural support.

By then the boat was under construction by the Dutch custom yacht builders Feadship, but Jobs was still fiddling with the design. "I know that it's possible I will die and leave Laurene with a half-built boat," he said. "But I have to keep going on it. If I don't, it's an admission that I'm about to die."

He and Powell would be celebrating their twentieth wedding anniversary a few days later, and he admitted that at times he had not been as appreciative of her as she deserved. "I'm very lucky, because you just don't know what you're getting into when you get married," he said. "You have an intuitive feeling about things. I couldn't have done better, because not only is Laurene smart and beautiful, she's turned out to be a really good person." For a moment he teared up. He talked about his other girlfriends, particularly Tina Redse, but said he ended up in the right place. He also reflected on how selfish and demanding he could be. "Laurene had to deal with that, and also with me being sick," he said. "I know that living with me is not a bowl of cherries."

Among his selfish traits was that he tended not to remember anniversaries or birthdays. But in this case, he decided to plan a surprise. They had gotten married at the Ahwahnee Hotel in Yosemite, and he decided to take Powell back there on their anniversary. But when Jobs called, the place was fully booked. So he had the hotel approach the people who had reserved the suite where he and Powell had stayed and ask if they would relinquish it. "I offered to pay for another weekend," Jobs recalled, "and the man was very nice and said, 'Twenty years, please take it, it's yours.'"

He found the photographs of the wedding, taken by a friend, and had large prints made on thick paper boards and placed in an elegant box. Scrolling through his iPhone, he found the note that he had composed to be included in the box and read it aloud:

We didn't know much about each other twenty years ago. We were guided by our intuition; you swept me off my feet. It was snowing when we got married at the Ahwahnee. Years passed, kids came, good times, hard times, but never bad times. Our love and respect has endured and grown. We've been through so much together and here we are right back where we started 20 years ago—older, wiser—with wrinkles on our faces and hearts. We now know many of life's joys, sufferings, secrets and wonders and we're still here together. My feet have never returned to the ground.

By the end of the recitation he was crying uncontrollably. When he composed himself, he noted that he had also made a set of the pictures for each of his kids. "I thought they might like to see that I was young once."

iCloud

In 2001 Jobs had a vision: Your personal computer would serve as a "digital hub" for a variety of lifestyle devices, such as music players, video recorders, phones, and tablets. This played to Apple's strength of creating end-to-end products that were simple to use. The company was thus transformed from a high-end niche computer company to the most valuable technology company in the world.

By 2008 Jobs had developed a vision for the next wave of the digital era. In the future, he believed, your desktop computer would no longer serve as the hub for your content. Instead the hub would move to "the cloud." In other words, your content would be stored on remote servers managed by a company you trusted, and it would be available for you to use on any device, anywhere. It would take him three years to get it right.

He began with a false step. In the summer of 2008 he launched a product called MobileMe, an expensive ($99 per year) subscription service that allowed you to store your address book, documents, pictures, videos, email, and calendar remotely in the cloud and to sync them with any device. In theory, you could go to your iPhone or any computer and access all aspects of your digital life. There was, however, a big problem: The service, to use Jobs's terminology, sucked. It was complex, devices didn't sync well, and email and other data got lost randomly in the ether. "Apple's MobileMe Is Far Too Flawed to Be Reliable," was the headline on Walt Mossberg's review in the *Wall Street Journal.*

Jobs was furious. He gathered the MobileMe team in the auditorium on the Apple campus, stood onstage, and asked, "Can anyone tell me what MobileMe is supposed to do?" After the team members offered their answers, Jobs shot back: "So why the fuck doesn't it do that?" Over the next half hour he continued to berate them. "You've tarnished Apple's reputation," he said. "You should hate each other for having let each other down. Mossberg, our friend, is no longer writing good things about us." In front of the whole audience, he got rid of the leader of the MobileMe team and replaced him with Eddy Cue, who oversaw all Internet content at Apple. As *Fortune*'s Adam Lashinsky reported in a dissection of the Apple corporate culture, "Accountability is strictly enforced."

By 2010 it was clear that Google, Amazon, Microsoft, and others were aiming to be the company that could best store all of your content and data in the cloud and sync it on your various devices. So Jobs redoubled his efforts. As he explained it to me that fall:

We need to be the company that manages your relationship with the cloud—streams your music and videos from the cloud, stores your pictures and information, and maybe even your medical data. Apple was the first to have the insight about your computer becoming a digital hub. So we wrote all of these apps—iPhoto, iMovie, iTunes—and tied in our devices, like the iPod and iPhone and iPad, and it's worked brilliantly. But over the next few years, the hub is going to move from your computer into the cloud. So it's the same digital hub strategy, but the hub's in a different place. It means you will always have access to your content and you won't have to sync.

It's important that we make this transformation, because of what Clayton Christensen calls "the innovator's dilemma," where people who invent something are usually the last ones to see past it, and we certainly don't want to be left behind. I'm going to take MobileMe and make it free, and we're going to make syncing content simple. We are building a server farm in North Carolina. We can provide all the syncing you need, and that way we can lock in the customer.

Jobs discussed this vision at his Monday morning meetings, and gradually it was refined to a new strategy. "I sent emails to groups of people at 2 a.m. and batted things around," he recalled. "We think about this a lot because it's not a job, it's our life." Although some board members, including Al Gore, questioned the idea of making MobileMe free, they supported it. It would be their strategy for attracting customers into Apple's orbit for the next decade.

The new service was named iCloud, and Jobs unveiled it in his keynote address to Apple's Worldwide Developers Conference in June 2011. He was still on medical leave and, for some days in May, had been hospitalized with infections and pain. Some close friends urged him not to make the presentation, which would involve lots of preparation and rehearsals. But the prospect of ushering in another tectonic shift in the digital age seemed to energize him.

When he came onstage at the San Francisco Convention Center, he was wearing a VONROSEN black cashmere sweater on top of his usual Issey Miyake black turtleneck, and he had thermal underwear beneath his blue jeans. But he looked more gaunt than ever. The crowd gave him a prolonged standing ovation—"That always helps, and I appreciate it," he said—but within minutes Apple's stock dropped more than $4, to $340. He was making a heroic effort, but he looked weak.

He handed the stage over to Phil Schiller and Scott Forstall to demo the new operating systems for Macs and mobile devices, then came back on to show off iCloud himself. "About ten years ago, we had one of our most important insights," he said. "The PC was going to become the hub for your digital life. Your videos, your photos, your music. But it has broken down in the last few years. Why?" He riffed about how hard it was to get all of your content synced to each of your devices. If you have a song you've downloaded on your iPad, a picture you've taken on your iPhone, and a video you've stored on your computer, you can end up feeling like an old-fashioned switchboard operator as you plug USB cables into and out of things to get the content shared. "Keeping these devices in sync is driving us crazy," he said to great laughter. "We have a solution. It's our next big insight. We are going to demote the PC and the Mac to be just a device, and we are going to move the digital hub into the cloud."

Jobs was well aware that this "big insight" was in fact not really new. Indeed he joked about Apple's previous attempt: "You may think, Why should I believe them? They're the ones who brought me MobileMe." The audience laughed nervously. "Let me just say it wasn't our finest hour." But as he demonstrated iCloud, it was clear that it would be better. Mail, contacts, and calendar entries synced instantly. So did apps, photos, books, and documents. Most impressively, Jobs and Eddy Cue had made deals with the music companies (unlike the folks at Google and Amazon). Apple would have eighteen *million* songs on its cloud servers. If you had any of these on any of your devices or computers— whether you had bought it legally or pirated it—Apple would let you access a high-quality version of it on all of your devices without having to go through the time and effort to upload it to the cloud. "It all just works," he said.

That simple concept—that everything would just work seamlessly— was, as always, Apple's competitive advantage. Microsoft had been advertising "Cloud Power" for more than a year, and three years earlier its chief software architect, the legendary Ray Ozzie, had issued a rallying cry to the company: "Our aspiration is that individuals will only need to license their media once, and use any of their . . . devices to access and enjoy their media." But Ozzie had quit Microsoft at the end of 2010, and the company's cloud computing push was never manifested in consumer devices. Amazon and Google both offered cloud services in 2011, but neither company had the ability to integrate the hardware and software and content of a variety of devices. Apple controlled every link in the chain and designed them all to work together: the devices, computers, operating systems, and application software, along with the sale and storage of the content.

Of course, it worked seamlessly only if you were using an Apple device and stayed within Apple's gated garden. That produced another benefit for Apple: customer stickiness. Once you began using iCloud, it would be difficult to switch to a Kindle or Android device. Your music and other content would not sync to them; in fact they might not even work. It was the culmination of three decades spent eschewing open systems. "We thought about whether we should do a music client for Android," Jobs told me over breakfast the next morning. "We put iTunes on Windows in order to sell more iPods. But I don't see an advantage of putting our music app on Android, except to make Android users happy. And I don't want to make Android users happy."

A New Campus

When Jobs was thirteen, he had looked up Bill Hewlett in the phone book, called him to score a part he needed for a frequency counter he was trying to build, and ended up getting a summer job at the instruments division of Hewlett-Packard. That same year HP bought some land in Cupertino to expand its calculator division. Wozniak went to work there, and it was on this site that he designed the Apple I and Apple II during his moonlighting hours.

When HP decided in 2010 to abandon its Cupertino campus, which was just about a mile east of Apple's One Infinite Loop headquarters, Jobs quietly arranged to buy it and the adjoining property. He admired the way that Hewlett and Packard had built a lasting company, and he prided himself on having done the same at Apple. Now he wanted a showcase headquarters, something that no West Coast technology company had. He eventually accumulated 150 acres, much of which had been apricot orchards when he was a boy, and threw himself into what would become a legacy project that combined his passion for design with his passion for creating an enduring company. "I want to leave a signature campus that expresses the values of the company for generations," he said.

He hired what he considered to be the best architectural firm in the world, that of Sir Norman Foster, which had done smartly engineered buildings such as the restored Reichstag in Berlin and 30 St. Mary Axe in London. Not surprisingly, Jobs got so involved in the planning, both the vision and the details, that it became almost impossible to settle on a final design. This was to be his lasting edifice, and he wanted to get it right. Foster's firm assigned fifty architects to the team, and every three weeks throughout 2010 they showed Jobs revised models and options. Over and over he would come up with new concepts, sometimes entirely new shapes, and make them restart and provide more alternatives.

When he first showed me the models and plans in his living room, the building was shaped like a huge winding racetrack made of three joined semicircles around a large central courtyard. The walls were floor-to-ceiling glass, and the interior had rows of office pods that allowed the sunlight to stream down the aisles. "It permits serendipitous and fluid meeting spaces," he said, "and everybody gets to participate in the sunlight."

The next time he showed me the plans, a month later, we were in Apple's large conference room across from his office, where a model of the proposed building covered the table. He had made a major change. The pods would all be set back from the windows so that long corridors would be bathed in sun. These would also serve as the common spaces. There was a debate with some of the architects, who wanted to allow the windows to be opened. Jobs had never liked the idea of people being able to open things. "That would just allow people to screw things up," he declared. On that, as on other details, he prevailed.

When he got home that evening, Jobs showed off the drawings at dinner, and Reed joked that the aerial view reminded him of male genitalia. His father dismissed the comment as reflecting the mind-set of a teenager. But the next day he mentioned the comment to the architects. "Unfortunately, once I've told you that, you're never going to be able to erase that image from your mind," he said. By the next time I visited, the shape had been changed to a simple circle.

The new design meant that there would not be a straight piece of glass in the building. All would be curved and seamlessly joined. Jobs had long been fascinated with glass, and his experience demanding huge custom panes for Apple's retail stores made him confident that it would be possible to make massive curved pieces in quantity. The planned center courtyard was eight hundred feet across (more than three typical city blocks, or almost the length of three football fields), and he showed it to me with overlays indicating how it could surround St. Peter's Square in Rome. One of his lingering memories was of the orchards that had once dominated the area, so he hired a senior arborist from Stanford and decreed that 80% of the property would be landscaped in a natural manner, with six thousand trees. "I asked him to make sure to include a new set of apricot orchards," Jobs recalled. "You used to see them everywhere, even on the corners, and they're part of the legacy of this valley."

By June 2011 the plans for the four-story, three-million-square-foot building, which would hold more than twelve thousand employees, were ready to unveil. He decided to do so in a quiet and unpublicized appearance before the Cupertino City Council on the day after he had announced iCloud at the Worldwide Developers Conference.

Even though he had little energy, he had a full schedule that day. Ron Johnson, who had developed Apple's stores and run them for more than a decade, had decided to accept an offer to be the CEO of J.C. Penney, and he came by Jobs's house in the morning to discuss his departure. Then Jobs and I went into Palo Alto to a small yogurt and oatmeal café called Fraiche, where he talked animatedly about possible future Apple products. Later that day he was driven to Santa Clara for the quarterly meeting that Apple had with top Intel executives, where they discussed the possibility of using Intel chips in future mobile devices. That night U2 was playing at the Oakland Coliseum, and Jobs had considered going. Instead he decided to use that evening to show his plans to the Cupertino Council.

Arriving without an entourage or any fanfare, and looking relaxed in the same black sweater he had worn for his developers conference speech, he stood on a podium with clicker in hand and spent twenty minutes showing slides of the design to council members. When a rendering of the sleek, futuristic, perfectly circular building appeared on the screen, he paused and smiled. "It's like a spaceship has landed," he said. A few moments later he added, "I think we have a shot at building the best office building in the world."

The following Friday, Jobs sent an email to a colleague from the distant past, Ann Bowers, the widow of Intel's cofounder Bob Noyce. She had been Apple's human resources director and den mother in the early 1980s, in charge of reprimanding Jobs after his tantrums and tending to the wounds of his coworkers. Jobs asked if she would come see him the next day. Bowers happened to be in New York, but she came by his house that Sunday when she returned. By then he was sick again, in pain and without much energy, but he was eager to show her the renderings of the new headquarters. "You should be proud of Apple," he said. "You should be proud of what we built."

Then he looked at her and asked, intently, a question that almost floored her: "Tell me, what was I like when I was young?"

Bowers tried to give him an honest answer. "You were very impetuous and very difficult," she replied. "But your vision was compelling. You told us, 'The journey is the reward.' That turned out to be true."

"Yes," Jobs answered. "I did learn some things along the way." Then, a few minutes later, he repeated it, as if to reassure Bowers and himself. "I did learn some things. I really did."

CHAPTER FORTY-ONE

ROUND THREE

The Twilight Struggle

Family Ties

Jobs had an aching desire to make it to his son's graduation from high school in June 2010. "When I was diagnosed with cancer, I made my deal with God or whatever, which was that I really wanted to see Reed graduate, and that got me through 2009," he said. As a senior, Reed looked eerily like his father at eighteen, with a knowing and slightly rebellious smile, intense eyes, and a shock of dark hair. But from his mother he had inherited a sweetness and painfully sensitive empathy that his father lacked. He was demonstrably affectionate and eager to please. Whenever his father was sitting sullenly at the kitchen table and staring at the floor, which happened often when he was ailing, the only thing sure to cause his eyes to brighten was Reed walking in.

Reed adored his father. Soon after I started working on this book, he dropped in to where I was staying and, as his father often did, suggested we take a walk. He told me, with an intensely earnest look, that his father was not a cold profit-seeking businessman but was motivated by a love of what he did and a pride in the products he was making.

After Jobs was diagnosed with cancer, Reed began spending his summers working in a Stanford oncology lab doing DNA sequencing to find genetic markers for colon cancer. In one experiment, he traced how mutations go through families. "One of the very few silver linings about me getting sick is that Reed's gotten to spend a lot of time studying with some very good doctors," Jobs said. "His enthusiasm for it is exactly how I felt about computers when I was his age. I think the biggest innovations of the twenty-first century will be the intersection of biology and technology. A new era is beginning, just like the digital one was when I was his age."

Reed used his cancer study as the basis for the senior report he presented to his class at Crystal Springs Uplands School. As he described how he used centrifuges and dyes to sequence the DNA of tumors, his father sat in the audience beaming, along with the rest of his family. "I fantasize about Reed getting a house here in Palo Alto with his family and riding his bike to work as a doctor at Stanford," Jobs said afterward.

Reed had grown up fast in 2009, when it looked as if his father was going to die. He took care of his younger sisters while his parents were in Memphis, and he developed a protective paternalism. But when his father's health stabilized in the spring of 2010, he regained his playful, teasing personality. One day during dinner he was discussing with his family where to take his girlfriend for dinner. His father suggested Il Fornaio, an elegant standard in Palo Alto, but Reed said he had been unable to get reservations. "Do you want me to try?" his father asked. Reed resisted; he wanted to handle it himself. Erin, the somewhat shy middle child, suggested that she could outfit a tepee in their garden and she and Eve, the younger sister, would serve them a romantic meal there. Reed stood up and hugged her. He would take her up on that some other time, he promised.

One Saturday Reed was one of the four contestants on his school's Quiz Kids team competing on a local TV station. The family—minus Eve, who was in a horse show—came to cheer him on. As the television crew bumbled around getting ready, his father tried to keep his impatience in check and remain inconspicuous among the parents sitting in the rows of folding chairs. But he was clearly recognizable in his trademark jeans and black turtleneck, and one woman pulled up a chair right next to him and started to take his picture. Without looking at her, he stood up and moved to the other end of the row. When Reed came on the set, his nameplate identified him as "Reed Powell." The host asked the students what they wanted to be when they grew up. "A cancer researcher," Reed answered.

Jobs drove his two-seat Mercedes SL55, taking Reed, while his wife followed in her own car with Erin. On the way home, she asked Erin why she thought her father refused to have a license plate on his car. "To be a rebel," she answered. I later put the question to Jobs. "Because people follow me sometimes, and if I have a license plate, they can track down where I live," he replied. "But that's kind of getting obsolete now with Google Maps. So I guess, really, it's just because I don't."

During Reed's graduation ceremony, his father sent me an email from his iPhone that simply exulted, "Today is one of my happiest days. Reed is graduating from High School. Right now. And, against all odds, I am here." That night there was a party at their house with close friends and family. Reed danced with every member of his family, including his father. Later Jobs took his son out to the barnlike storage shed to offer him one of his two bicycles, which he wouldn't be riding again. Reed joked that the Italian one looked a bit too gay, so Jobs told him to take the solid eight-speed next to it. When Reed said he would be indebted, Jobs answered, "You don't need to be indebted, because you have my DNA." A few days later *Toy Story 3* opened. Jobs had nurtured this Pixar trilogy from the beginning, and the final installment was about the emotions surrounding the departure of Andy for college. "I wish I could always be with you," Andy's mother says. "You always will be," he replies.

His middle daughter, Erin, had grown into a poised and attractive young woman, with a personal sensitivity more mature than her father's. She thought that she might want to be an architect, perhaps because of her father's interest in the field, and she had a good sense of design.

At one point as I was finishing this book, Powell told me that Erin wanted to give me an interview. It's not something that I would have requested, since she was then just turning sixteen, but I agreed. The point Erin emphasized was that she understood why her father was not always attentive, and she accepted that. "He does his best to be both a father and the CEO of Apple, and he juggles those pretty well," she said. "Sometimes I wish I had more of his attention, but I know the work he's doing is very important and I think it's really cool, so I'm fine. I don't really need more attention."

Jobs had promised to take each of his children on a trip of their choice when they became teenagers. Reed chose to go to Kyoto, knowing how much his father was entranced by the Zen calm of that beautiful city. Not surprisingly, when Erin turned thirteen, in 2008, she chose Kyoto as well. Her father's illness caused him to cancel the trip, so he promised to take her in 2010, when he was better. But that June he decided he didn't want to go. Erin was crestfallen but didn't protest. Instead her mother took her to France with family friends, and they rescheduled the Kyoto trip for July.

The whole family took off in early July for Kona Village, Hawaii, which was the first leg of the trip. But in Hawaii Jobs developed a bad toothache, which he ignored, as if he could will the cavity away. The tooth collapsed and had to be fixed. Then the iPhone 4 antenna crisis hit, and he decided to rush back to Cupertino, taking Reed with him. Powell and Erin stayed in Hawaii, hoping that Jobs would return and continue with the plans to take them to Kyoto.

Jobs did. While Reed took care of Eve back in Palo Alto, Erin and her parents stayed at the Tawaraya Ryokan, an inn of sublime simplicity that Jobs loved. "It was fantastic," Erin recalled.

Twenty years earlier Jobs had taken Erin's half-sister, Lisa Brennan-Jobs, to Japan when she was about the same age. Among her strongest memories was sharing with him delightful meals and watching him, usually such a picky eater, savor unagi sushi and other delicacies. Seeing him take joy in eating made Lisa feel relaxed with him for the first time. Erin recalled a similar experience: "Dad knew where he wanted to go to lunch every day. He told me he knew an incredible soba shop, and he took me there, and it was so good that it's been hard to ever eat soba again because nothing comes close." They also found a tiny neighborhood sushi restaurant, and Jobs tagged it on his iPhone as "best sushi I've ever had." Erin agreed.

They also visited Kyoto's famous Zen Buddhist temples; the one Erin loved most was Saihō-ji, known as the "moss temple" because of its Golden Pond surrounded by gardens featuring more than a hundred varieties of moss. "Erin was really really happy, which was deeply gratifying and helped improve her relationship with her father," Powell recalled. "She deserved that."

Their younger daughter, Eve, was spunky, self-assured, and in no way intimidated by her father. Her passion was horseback riding, and she became determined to make it to the Olympics. When a coach told her how much work it would require, she replied, "Tell me exactly what I need to do. I will do it." He did, and she began diligently following the program.

Eve was an expert at the difficult task of pinning her father down; she often called his assistant at work directly to make sure something got put on his calendar. She was also pretty good as a negotiator. One weekend in 2010, when the family was planning a trip, Erin wanted to delay the departure by half a day, but she was afraid to ask her father. Eve, then twelve, volunteered to take on the task, and at dinner she laid out the case to her father as if she were a lawyer before the Supreme Court. Jobs cut her off—"No, I don't think I want to"—but it was clear that he was more amused than annoyed. Later that evening Eve sat down with her mother and deconstructed the various ways that she could have made her case better.

Jobs came to appreciate her spirit—and see a lot of himself in her. "She's a pistol and has the strongest will of any kid I've ever met," he said. "It's like payback." He had a deep understanding of her personality, perhaps because it bore some resemblance to his. "Eve is more sensitive than a lot of people think," he explained. "She's so smart that she can roll over people a bit, so that means she can alienate people, and she finds herself alone. She's in the process of learning how to be who she is, but tempers it around the edges so that she can have the friends that she needs."

Jobs's relationship with his wife was sometimes complicated but always loyal. Savvy and compassionate, Laurene Powell was a stabilizing influence and an example of his ability to compensate for some of his selfish impulses by surrounding himself with strong-willed and sensible people. She weighed in quietly on business issues, firmly on family concerns, and fiercely on medical matters. Early in their marriage, she cofounded and launched College Track, a national after-school program that helps disadvantaged kids graduate from high school and get into college. Since then she had become a leading force in the education reform movement. Even though he tended to be generally dismissive of philanthropic endeavors, Jobs professed an admiration for his wife's work: "What she's done with College Track really impresses me."

In February 2010 Jobs celebrated his fifty-fifth birthday with just his family. The kitchen was decorated with streamers and balloons, and his kids gave him a red-velvet toy crown, which he wore. Now that he had recovered from a grueling year of health problems, he resumed his focus on his work. "I think it was hard on the family, especially the girls," Powell told me. "After two years of him being ill, he finally gets a little better, and they expected he would focus a bit on them, but he didn't." She wanted to make sure, she said, that both sides of his personality were reflected in this book and put into context. "Like many great men whose gifts are extraordinary, he's not extraordinary in every realm," she said. "He doesn't have social graces, such as putting himself in other people's shoes, but he cares deeply about empowering humankind, the advancement of humankind, and putting the right tools in their hands."

President Obama

On a trip to Washington in the early fall of 2010, Powell had met with some of her friends at the White House who told her that President Obama was going to Silicon Valley that October. She suggested that he might want to meet with her husband. Obama's aides liked the idea; it fit into his new emphasis on competitiveness. In addition, John Doerr, the venture capitalist who had become one of Jobs's close friends, had told a meeting of the President's Economic Recovery Advisory Board about Jobs's views on why the United States was losing its edge. He too suggested that Obama should meet with Jobs. So a half hour was put on the president's schedule for a session at the Westin San Francisco Airport.

There was one problem: When Powell told her husband, he said he didn't want to do it. He was annoyed that she had arranged it behind his back. "I'm not going to get slotted in for a token meeting so that he can check off that he met with a CEO," he told her. She insisted that Obama was "really psyched to meet with you." Jobs replied that if that were the case, then Obama should call and personally ask for the meeting. The standoff went on for five days. Jobs finally relented.

The meeting actually lasted forty-five minutes, and Jobs did not hold back. "You're headed for a one-term presidency," Jobs told Obama at the outset. To prevent that, he said, the administration needed to be a lot more business-friendly. He described how easy it was to build a factory in China, and said that it was almost impossible to do so these days in America, largely because of regulations and unnecessary costs.

Jobs also attacked America's education system, saying that it was hopelessly antiquated and crippled by union work rules. Until the teachers' unions were broken, there was almost no hope for education reform. Teachers should be treated as professionals, he said, not as industrial assembly-line workers. Principals should be able to hire and fire them based on how good they were. Schools should be staying open until at least 6 p.m. and be in session eleven months of the year. It was absurd, he added, that American classrooms were still based on teachers standing at a board and using textbooks. All books, learning materials, and assessments should be digital and interactive, tailored to each student and providing feedback in real time.

Jobs offered to put together a group of six or seven CEOs who could really explain the innovation challenges facing America, and the president accepted. So Jobs made a list of people for a Washington meeting to be held in December. Unfortunately, after Valerie Jarrett and other presidential aides had added names, the list had expanded to more than twenty, with GE's Jeffrey Immelt in the lead. Jobs sent Jarrett an email saying it was a bloated list and he had no intention of coming. In fact his health problems had flared anew by then, so he would not have been able to go in any case, as Doerr privately explained to the president.

In February 2011, Doerr began making plans to host a small dinner for President Obama in Silicon Valley. He and Jobs, along with their wives, went to dinner at Evvia, a Greek restaurant in Palo Alto, to draw up a tight guest list. The dozen chosen tech titans included Google's Eric Schmidt, Yahoo's Carol Bartz, Facebook's Mark Zuckerberg, Cisco's John Chambers, Oracle's Larry Ellison, Genentech's Art Levinson, and Netflix's Reed Hastings. Jobs's attention to the details of the dinner extended to the food. Doerr sent him the proposed menu, and he responded that some of the dishes proposed by the caterer—shrimp, cod, lentil salad—were far too fancy "and not who you are, John." He particularly objected to the dessert that was planned, a cream pie tricked out with chocolate truffles, but the White House advance staff overruled him by telling the caterer that the president liked cream pie. Because Jobs had lost so much weight that he was easily chilled, Doerr kept the house so warm that Zuckerberg found himself sweating profusely.

Jobs, sitting next to the president, kicked off the dinner by saying, "Regardless of our political persuasions, I want you to know that we're here to do whatever you ask to help our country." Despite that, the dinner initially became a litany of suggestions of what the president could do for the businesses there. Chambers, for example, pushed a proposal for a repatriation tax holiday that would allow major corporations to avoid tax payments on overseas profits if they brought them back to the United States for investment during a certain period. The president was annoyed, and so was Zuckerberg, who turned to Valerie Jarrett, sitting to his right, and whispered, "We should be talking about what's important to the country. Why is he just talking about what's good for him?"

Doerr was able to refocus the discussion by calling on everyone to suggest a list of action items. When Jobs's turn came, he stressed the need for more trained engineers and suggested that any foreign students who earned an engineering degree in the United States should be given a visa to stay in the country. Obama said that could be done only in the context of the "Dream Act," which would allow illegal aliens who arrived as minors and finished high school to become legal residents—something that the Republicans had blocked. Jobs found this an annoying example of how politics can lead to paralysis. "The president is very smart, but he kept explaining to us reasons why things can't get done," he recalled. "It infuriates me."

Jobs went on to urge that a way be found to train more American engineers. Apple had 700,000 factory workers employed in China, he said, and that was because it needed 30,000 engineers on-site to support those workers. "You can't find that many in America to hire," he said. These factory engineers did not have to be PhDs or geniuses; they simply needed to have basic engineering skills for manufacturing. Tech schools, community colleges, or trade schools could train them. "If you could educate these engineers," he said, "we could move more manufacturing plants here." The argument made a strong impression on the president. Two or three times over the next month he told his aides, "We've got to find ways to train those 30,000 manufacturing engineers that Jobs told us about."

Jobs was pleased that Obama followed up, and they talked by telephone a few times after the meeting. He offered to help create Obama's political ads for the 2012 campaign. (He had made the same offer in 2008, but he'd become annoyed when Obama's strategist David Axelrod wasn't totally deferential.) "I think political advertising is terrible. I'd love to get Lee Clow out of retirement, and we can come up with great commercials for him," Jobs told me a few weeks after the dinner. Jobs had been fighting pain all week, but the talk of politics energized him. "Every once in a while, a real ad pro gets involved, the way Hal Riney did with 'It's morning in America' for Reagan's reelection in 1984. So that's what I'd like to do for Obama."

Third Medical Leave, 2011

The cancer always sent signals as it reappeared. Jobs had learned that. He would lose his appetite and begin to feel pains throughout his body. His doctors would do tests, detect nothing, and reassure him that he still seemed clear. But he knew better. The cancer had its signaling pathways, and a few months after he felt the signs the doctors would discover that it was indeed no longer in remission.

Another such downturn began in early November 2010. He was in pain, stopped eating, and had to be fed intravenously by a nurse who came to the house. The doctors found no sign of more tumors, and they assumed that this was just another of his periodic cycles of fighting infections and digestive maladies. He had never been one to suffer pain stoically, so his doctors and family had become somewhat inured to his complaints.

He and his family went to Kona Village for Thanksgiving, but his eating did not improve. The dining there was in a communal room, and the other guests pretended not to notice as Jobs, looking emaciated, rocked and moaned at meals, not touching his food. It was a testament to the resort and its guests that his condition never leaked out. When he returned to Palo Alto, Jobs became increasingly emotional and morose. He thought he was going to die, he told his kids, and he would get choked up about the possibility that he would never celebrate any more of their birthdays.

By Christmas he was down to 115 pounds, which was more than fifty pounds below his normal weight. Mona Simpson came to Palo Alto for the holiday, along with her ex-husband, the television comedy writer Richard Appel, and their children. The mood picked up a bit. The families played parlor games such as Novel, in which participants try to fool each other by seeing who can write the most convincing fake opening sentence to a book, and things seemed to be looking up for a while. He was even able to go out to dinner at a restaurant with Powell a few days after Christmas. The kids went off on a ski vacation for New Year's, with Powell and Mona Simpson taking turns staying at home with Jobs in Palo Alto.

By the beginning of 2011, however, it was clear that this was not merely one of his bad patches. His doctors detected evidence of new tumors, and the cancer-related signaling further exacerbated his loss of appetite. They were struggling to determine how much drug therapy his body, in its emaciated condition, would be able to take. Every inch of his body felt like it had been punched, he told friends, as he moaned and sometimes doubled over in pain.

It was a vicious cycle. The first signs of cancer caused pain. The morphine and other painkillers he took suppressed his appetite. His pancreas had been partly removed and his liver had been replaced, so his digestive system was faulty and had trouble absorbing protein. Losing weight made it harder to embark on aggressive drug therapies. His emaciated condition also made him more susceptible to infections, as did the immunosuppressants he sometimes took to keep his body from rejecting his liver transplant. The weight loss reduced the lipid layers around his pain receptors, causing him to suffer more. And he was prone to extreme mood swings, marked by prolonged bouts of anger and depression, which further suppressed his appetite.

Jobs's eating problems were exacerbated over the years by his psychological attitude toward food. When he was young, he learned that he could induce euphoria and ecstasy by fasting. So even though he knew that he should eat—his doctors were begging him to consume high-quality protein—lingering in the back of his subconscious, he admitted, was his instinct for fasting and for diets like Arnold Ehret's fruit regimen that he had embraced as a teenager. Powell kept telling him that it was crazy, even pointing out that Ehret had died at fifty-six when he stumbled and knocked his head, and she would get angry when he came to the table and just stared silently at his lap. "I wanted him to force himself to eat," she said, "and it was incredibly tense at home." Bryar Brown, their part-time cook, would still come in the afternoon and make an array of healthy dishes, but Jobs would touch his tongue to one or two dishes and then dismiss them all as inedible. One evening he announced, "I could probably eat a little pumpkin pie," and the even-tempered Brown created a beautiful pie from scratch in an hour. Jobs ate only one bite, but Brown was thrilled.

Powell talked to eating disorder specialists and psychiatrists, but her husband tended to shun them. He refused to take any medications, or be treated in any way, for his depression. "When you have feelings," he said, "like sadness or anger about your cancer or your plight, to mask them is to lead an artificial life." In fact he swung to the other extreme. He became morose, tearful, and dramatic as he lamented to all around him that he was about to die. The depression became part of the vicious cycle by making him even less likely to eat.

Pictures and videos of Jobs looking emaciated began to appear online, and soon rumors were swirling about how sick he was. The problem, Powell realized, was that the rumors were true, and they were not going to go away. Jobs had agreed only reluctantly to go on medical leave two years earlier, when his liver was failing, and this time he also resisted the idea. It would be like leaving his homeland, unsure that he would ever return. When he finally bowed to the inevitable, in January 2011, the board members were expecting it; the telephone meeting in which he told them that he wanted another leave took only three minutes. He had often discussed with the board, in executive session, his thoughts about who could take over if anything happened to him, presenting both short-term and longer-term combinations of options. But there was no doubt that, in this current situation, Tim Cook would again take charge of day-to-day operations.

The following Saturday afternoon, Jobs allowed his wife to convene a meeting of his doctors. He realized that he was facing the type of problem that he never permitted at Apple. His treatment was fragmented rather than integrated. Each of his myriad maladies was being treated by different specialists—oncologists, pain specialists, nutritionists, hepatologists, and hematologists—but they were not being coordinated in a cohesive approach, the way James Eason had done in Memphis. "One of the big issues in the health care industry is the lack of caseworkers or advocates that are the quarterback of each team," Powell said. This was particularly true at Stanford, where nobody seemed in charge of figuring out how nutrition was related to pain care and to oncology. So Powell asked the various Stanford specialists to come to their house for a meeting that also included some outside doctors with a more aggressive and integrated approach, such as David Agus of USC. They agreed on a new regimen for dealing with the pain and for coordinating the other treatments.

Thanks to some pioneering science, the team of doctors had been able to keep Jobs one step ahead of the cancer. He had become one of the first twenty people in the world to have all of the genes of his cancer tumor as well as of his normal DNA sequenced. It was a process that, at the time, cost more than $100,000.

The gene sequencing and analysis were done collaboratively by teams at Stanford, Johns Hopkins, and the Broad Institute of MIT and Harvard. By knowing the unique genetic and molecular signature of Jobs's tumors, his doctors had been able to pick specific drugs that directly targeted the defective molecular pathways that caused his cancer cells to grow in an abnormal manner. This approach, known as molecular targeted therapy, was more effective than traditional chemotherapy, which attacks the process of division of all the body's cells, cancerous or not. This targeted therapy was not a silver bullet, but at times it seemed close to one: It allowed his doctors to look at a large number of drugs—common and uncommon, already available or only in development—to see which three or four might work best. Whenever his cancer mutated and repaved around one of these drugs, the doctors had another drug lined up to go next.

Although Powell was diligent in overseeing her husband's care, he was the one who made the final decision on each new treatment regimen. A typical example occurred in May 2011, when he held a meeting with George Fisher and other doctors from Stanford, the gene-sequencing analysts from the Broad Institute, and his outside consultant David Agus. They all gathered around a table at a suite in the Four Seasons hotel in Palo Alto. Powell did not come, but their son, Reed, did. For three hours there were presentations from the Stanford and Broad researchers on the new information they had learned about the genetic signatures of his cancer. Jobs was his usual feisty self. At one point he stopped a Broad Institute analyst who had made the mistake of using PowerPoint slides. Jobs chided him and explained why Apple's Keynote presentation software was better; he even offered to teach him how to use it. By the end of the meeting, Jobs and his team had gone through all of the molecular data, assessed the rationales for each of the potential therapies, and come up with a list of tests to help them better prioritize these.

One of his doctors told him that there was hope that his cancer, and others like it, would soon be considered a manageable chronic disease, which could be kept at bay until the patient died of something else.

"I'm either going to be one of the first to be able to outrun a cancer like this, or I'm going to be one of the last to die from it," Jobs told me right after one of the meetings with his doctors. "Either among the first to make it to shore, or the last to get dumped."

Visitors

When his 2011 medical leave was announced, the situation seemed so dire that Lisa Brennan-Jobs got back in touch after more than a year and arranged to fly from New York the following week. Her relationship with her father had been built on layers of resentment. She was understandably scarred by having been pretty much abandoned by him for her first ten years. Making matters worse, she had inherited some of his prickliness and, he felt, some of her mother's sense of grievance. "I told her many times that I wished I'd been a better dad when she was five, but now she should let things go rather than be angry the rest of her life," he recalled just before Lisa arrived.

The visit went well. Jobs was beginning to feel a little better, and he was in a mood to mend fences and express his affection for those around him. At age thirty-two, Lisa was in a serious relationship for one of the first times in her life. Her boyfriend was a struggling young filmmaker from California, and Jobs went so far as to suggest she move back to Palo Alto if they got married. "Look, I don't know how long I am for this world," he told her. "The doctors can't really tell me. If you want to see more of me, you're going to have to move out here. Why don't you consider it?" Even though Lisa did not move west, Jobs was pleased at how the reconciliation had worked out. "I hadn't been sure I wanted her to visit, because I was sick and didn't want other complications. But I'm very glad she came. It helped settle a lot of things in me."

Jobs had another visit that month from someone who wanted to repair fences. Google's cofounder Larry Page, who lived less than three blocks away, had just announced plans to retake the reins of the company from Eric Schmidt. He knew how to flatter Jobs: He asked if he could come by and get tips on how to be a good CEO. Jobs was still furious at Google. "My first thought was, 'Fuck you,'" he recounted. "But then I thought about it and realized that everybody helped me when I was young, from Bill Hewlett to the guy down the block who worked for HP. So I called him back and said sure." Page came over, sat in Jobs's living room, and listened to his ideas on building great products and durable companies. Jobs recalled:

> We talked a lot about focus. And choosing people. How to know who to trust, and how to build a team of lieutenants he can count on. I described the blocking and tackling he would have to do to keep the company from getting flabby or being larded with B players. The main thing I stressed was focus. Figure out what Google wants to be when it grows up. It's now all over the map. What are the five products you want to focus on? Get rid of the rest, because they're dragging you down. They're turning you into Microsoft. They're causing you to turn out products that are adequate but not great. I tried to be as helpful as I could. I will continue to do that with people like Mark Zuckerberg too. That's how I'm going to spend part of the time I have left. I can help the next generation remember the lineage of great companies here and how to continue the tradition. The Valley has been very supportive of me. I should do my best to repay.

The announcement of Jobs's 2011 medical leave prompted others to make a pilgrimage to the house in Palo Alto. Bill Clinton, for example, came by and talked about everything from the Middle East to American politics. But the most poignant visit was from the other tech prodigy born in 1955, the guy who, for more than three decades, had been Jobs's rival and partner in defining the age of personal computers.

Bill Gates had never lost his fascination with Jobs. In the spring of 2011 I was at a dinner with him in Washington, where he had come to discuss his foundation's global health endeavors. He expressed amazement at the success of the iPad and how Jobs, even while sick, was focusing on ways to improve it. "Here I am, merely saving the world from malaria and that sort of thing, and Steve is still coming up with amazing new products," he said wistfully. "Maybe I should have stayed in that game." He smiled to make sure that I knew he was joking, or at least half joking.

Through their mutual friend Mike Slade, Gates made arrangements to visit Jobs in May. The day before it was supposed to happen, Jobs's assistant called to say he wasn't feeling well enough. But it was rescheduled, and early one afternoon Gates drove to Jobs's house, walked through the back gate to the open kitchen door, and saw Eve studying at the table. "Is Steve around?" he asked. Eve pointed him to the living room.

They spent more than three hours together, just the two of them, reminiscing. "We were like the old guys in the industry looking back," Jobs recalled. "He was happier than I've ever seen him, and I kept thinking how healthy he looked." Gates was similarly struck by how Jobs, though scarily gaunt, had more energy than he expected. He was open about his health problems and, at least that day, feeling optimistic. His sequential regimens of targeted drug treatments, he told Gates, were like "jumping from one lily pad to another," trying to stay a step ahead of the cancer.

Jobs asked some questions about education, and Gates sketched out his vision of what schools in the future would be like, with students watching lectures and video lessons on their own while using the classroom time for discussions and problem solving. They agreed that computers had, so far, made surprisingly little impact on schools—far less than on other realms of society such as media and medicine and law. For that to change, Gates said, computers and mobile devices would have to focus on delivering more personalized lessons and providing motivational feedback.

They also talked a lot about the joys of family, including how lucky they were to have good kids and be married to the right women. "We laughed about how fortunate it was that he met Laurene, and she's kept him semi-sane, and I met Melinda, and she's kept me semi-sane," Gates recalled. "We also discussed how it's challenging to be one of our children, and how do we mitigate that. It was pretty personal." At one point Eve, who in the past had been in horse shows with Gates's daughter Jennifer, wandered in from the kitchen, and Gates asked her what jumping routines she liked best.

As their hours together drew to a close, Gates complimented Jobs on "the incredible stuff" he had created and for being able to save Apple in the late 1990s from the bozos who were about to destroy it. He even made an interesting concession. Throughout their careers they had adhered to competing philosophies on one of the most fundamental of all digital issues: whether hardware and software should be tightly integrated or more open. "I used to believe that the open, horizontal model would prevail," Gates told him. "But you proved that the integrated, vertical model could also be great." Jobs responded with his own admission. "Your model worked too," he said.

They were both right. Each model had worked in the realm of personal computers, where Macintosh coexisted with a variety of Windows machines, and that was likely to be true in the realm of mobile devices as well. But after recounting their discussion, Gates added a caveat: "The integrated approach works well when Steve is at the helm. But it doesn't mean it will win many rounds in the future." Jobs similarly felt compelled to add a caveat about Gates after describing their meeting: "Of course, his fragmented model worked, but it didn't make really great products. It produced crappy products. That was the problem. The big problem. At least over time."

"That Day Has Come"

Jobs had many other ideas and projects that he hoped to develop. He wanted to disrupt the textbook industry and save the spines of spavined students bearing backpacks by creating electronic texts and curriculum material for the iPad. He was also working with Bill Atkinson, his friend from the original Macintosh team, on devising new digital technologies that worked at the pixel level to allow people to take great photographs using their iPhones even in situations without much light. And he very much wanted to do for television sets what he had done for computers, music players, and phones: make them simple and elegant. "I'd like to create an integrated television set that is completely easy to use," he told me. "It would be seamlessly synced with all of your devices and with iCloud." No longer would users have to fiddle with complex remotes for DVD players and cable channels. "It will have the simplest user interface you could imagine. I finally cracked it."

But by July 2011, his cancer had spread to his bones and other parts of his body, and his doctors were having trouble finding targeted drugs that could beat it back. He was in pain, sleeping erratically, had little energy, and stopped going to work. He and Powell had reserved a sailboat for a family cruise scheduled for the end of that month, but those plans were scuttled. He was eating almost no solid food, and he spent most of his days in his bedroom watching television.

In August, I got a message that he wanted me to come visit. When I arrived at his house, at mid-morning on a Saturday, he was still asleep, so I sat with his wife and kids in the garden, filled with a profusion of yellow roses and various types of daisies, until he sent word that I should come in. I found him curled up on the bed, wearing khaki shorts and a white turtleneck. His legs were shockingly sticklike, but his smile was easy and his mind quick. "We better hurry, because I have very little energy," he said.

He wanted to show me some of his personal pictures and let me pick a few to use in the book. Because he was too weak to get out of bed, he pointed to various drawers in the room, and I carefully brought him the photographs in each. As I sat on the side of the bed, I held them up, one at a time, so he could see them. Some prompted stories; others merely elicited a grunt or a smile. I had never seen a picture of his father, Paul Jobs, and I was startled when I came across a snapshot of a handsome hardscrabble 1950s dad holding a toddler. "Yes, that's him," he said. "You can use it." He then pointed to a box near the window that contained a picture of his father looking at him lovingly at his wedding. "He was a great man," Jobs said quietly. I murmured something along the lines of "He would have been proud of you." Jobs corrected me: "He *was* proud of me."

For a while, the pictures seemed to energize him. We discussed what various people from his past, ranging from Tina Redse to Mike Markkula to Bill Gates, now thought of him. I recounted what Gates had said after he described his last visit with Jobs, which was that

Apple had shown that the integrated approach could work, but only "when Steve is at the helm." Jobs thought that was silly. "Anyone could make better products that way, not just me," he said. So I asked him to name another company that made great products by insisting on end-to-end integration. He thought for a while, trying to come up with an example. "The car companies," he finally said, but then he added, "Or at least they used to."

When our discussion turned to the sorry state of the economy and politics, he offered a few sharp opinions about the lack of strong leadership around the world. "I'm disappointed in Obama," he said. "He's having trouble leading because he's reluctant to offend people or piss them off." He caught what I was thinking and assented with a little smile: "Yes, that's not a problem I ever had."

After two hours, he grew quiet, so I got off the bed and started to leave. "Wait," he said, as he waved to me to sit back down. It took a minute or two for him to regain enough energy to talk. "I had a lot of trepidation about this project," he finally said, referring to his decision to cooperate with this book. "I was really worried."

"Why did you do it?" I asked.

"I wanted my kids to know me," he said. "I wasn't always there for them, and I wanted them to know why and to understand what I did. Also, when I got sick, I realized other people would write about me if I died, and they wouldn't know anything. They'd get it all wrong. So I wanted to make sure someone heard what I had to say."

He had never, in two years, asked anything about what I was putting in the book or what conclusions I had drawn. But now he looked at me and said, "I know there will be a lot in your book I won't like." It was more a question than a statement, and when he stared at me for a response, I nodded, smiled, and said I was sure that would be true. "That's good," he said. "Then it won't seem like an in-house book. I won't read it for a while, because I don't want to get mad. Maybe I will read it in a year—if I'm still around." By then, his eyes were closed and his energy gone, so I quietly took my leave.

• • •

As his health deteriorated throughout the summer, Jobs slowly began to face the inevitable: He would not be returning to Apple as CEO. So it was time for him to resign. He wrestled with the decision for weeks, discussing it with his wife, Bill Campbell, Jony Ive, and George Riley. "One of the things I wanted to do for Apple was to set an example of how you do a transfer of power right," he told me. He joked about all the rough transitions that had occurred at the company over the past thirty-five years. "It's always been a drama, like a third-world country. Part of my goal has been to make Apple the world's best company, and having an orderly transition is key to that."

The best time and place to make the transition, he decided, was at the company's regularly scheduled August 24 board meeting. He was eager to do it in person, rather than merely send in a letter or attend by phone, so he had been pushing himself to eat and regain strength. The day before the meeting, he decided he could make it, but he needed the help of a wheelchair. Arrangements were made to have him driven to headquarters and wheeled to the boardroom as secretly as possible.

He arrived just before 11 a.m., when the board members were finishing committee reports and other routine business. Most knew what was about to happen. But instead of going right to the topic on everyone's mind, Tim Cook and Peter Oppenheimer, the chief financial officer, went through the results for the quarter and the projections for the year ahead. Then Jobs said quietly that he had something personal to say. Cook asked if he and the other top managers should leave, and Jobs paused for more than thirty seconds before he decided they should. Once the room was cleared of all but the six outside directors, he began to read aloud from a letter he had dictated and revised over the previous weeks. "I have always said if there ever came a day when I could no longer meet my duties and expectations as Apple's CEO, I would be the first to let you know," it began. "Unfortunately, that day has come."

The letter was simple, direct, and only eight sentences long. In it he suggested that Cook replace him, and he offered to serve as chairman of the board. "I believe Apple's brightest and most innovative days are ahead of it. And I look forward to watching and contributing to its success in a new role."

There was a long silence. Al Gore was the first to speak, and he listed Jobs's accomplishments during his tenure. Mickey Drexler added that watching Jobs transform Apple was "the most incredible thing I've ever seen in business," and Art Levinson praised Jobs's diligence in ensuring that there was a smooth transition. Campbell said nothing, but there were tears in his eyes as the formal resolutions transferring power were passed.

Over lunch, Scott Forstall and Phil Schiller came in to display mockups of some products that Apple had in the pipeline. Jobs peppered them with questions and thoughts, especially about what capacities the fourth-generation cellular networks might have and what features needed to be in future phones. At one point Forstall showed off a voice recognition app. As he feared, Jobs grabbed the phone in the middle of the demo and proceeded to see if he could confuse it. "What's the weather in Palo Alto?" he asked. The app answered. After a few more questions, Jobs challenged it: "Are you a man or a woman?" Amazingly, the app answered in its robotic voice, "They did not assign me a gender." For a moment the mood lightened.

When the talk turned to tablet computing, some expressed a sense of triumph that HP had suddenly given up the field, unable to compete with the iPad. But Jobs turned somber and declared that it was actually a sad moment. "Hewlett and Packard built a great company, and they thought they had left it in good hands," he said. "But now it's being dismembered and destroyed. It's tragic. I hope I've left a stronger legacy so that will never happen at Apple." As he prepared to leave, the board members gathered around to give him a hug.

After meeting with his executive team to explain the news, Jobs rode home with George Riley. When they arrived at the house, Powell was in the backyard harvesting honey from her hives, with help from Eve. They took off their screen helmets and brought the honey pot to the kitchen, where Reed and Erin had gathered, so that they could all celebrate the graceful transition. Jobs took a spoonful of the honey and pronounced it wonderfully sweet.

That evening, he stressed to me that his hope was to remain as active as his health allowed. "I'm going to work on new products and marketing and the things that I like," he said. But when I asked how it really felt to be relinquishing control of the company he had built, his tone turned wistful, and he shifted into the past tense. "I've had a very lucky career, a very lucky life," he replied. "I've done all that I can do."

CHAPTER FORTY-TWO

LEGACY

The Brightest Heaven of Invention

*At the 2006 Macworld, in front of a slide of
him and Wozniak from thirty years earlier*

FireWire

His personality was reflected in the products he created. Just as the
core of Apple's philosophy, from the original Macintosh in 1984 to the
iPad a generation later, was the end-to-end integration of hardware
and software, so too was it the case with Steve Jobs: His passions, per-

fectionism, demons, desires, artistry, devilry, and obsession for control were integrally connected to his approach to business and the products that resulted.

The unified field theory that ties together Jobs's personality and products begins with his most salient trait: his intensity. His silences could be as searing as his rants; he had taught himself to stare without blinking. Sometimes this intensity was charming, in a geeky way, such as when he was explaining the profundity of Bob Dylan's music or why whatever product he was unveiling at that moment was the most amazing thing that Apple had ever made. At other times it could be terrifying, such as when he was fulminating about Google or Microsoft ripping off Apple.

This intensity encouraged a binary view of the world. Colleagues referred to the hero/shithead dichotomy. You were either one or the other, sometimes on the same day. The same was true of products, ideas, even food: Something was either "the best thing ever," or it was shitty, brain-dead, inedible. As a result, any perceived flaw could set off a rant. The finish on a piece of metal, the curve of the head of a screw, the shade of blue on a box, the intuitiveness of a navigation screen—he would declare them to "completely suck" until that moment when he suddenly pronounced them "absolutely perfect." He thought of himself as an artist, which he was, and he indulged in the temperament of one.

His quest for perfection led to his compulsion for Apple to have end-to-end control of every product that it made. He got hives, or worse, when contemplating great Apple software running on another company's crappy hardware, and he likewise was allergic to the thought of unapproved apps or content polluting the perfection of an Apple device. This ability to integrate hardware and software and content into one unified system enabled him to impose simplicity. The astronomer Johannes Kepler declared that "nature loves simplicity and unity." So did Steve Jobs.

This instinct for integrated systems put him squarely on one side of the most fundamental divide in the digital world: open versus closed. The hacker ethos handed down from the Homebrew Computer Club favored the open approach, in which there was little centralized control and people were free to modify hardware and software, share code, write to open standards, shun proprietary systems, and have content and apps that were compatible with a variety of devices and operating systems. The young Wozniak was in that camp: The Apple II he designed was easily opened and sported plenty of slots and ports that people could jack into as they pleased. With the Macintosh Jobs became a founding father of the other camp. The Macintosh would be like an appliance, with the hardware and software tightly woven together and closed to modifications. The hacker ethos would be sacrificed in order to create a seamless and simple user experience.

This led Jobs to decree that the Macintosh operating system would not be available for any other company's hardware. Microsoft pursued the opposite strategy, allowing its Windows operating system to be promiscuously licensed. That did not produce the most elegant computers, but it did lead to Microsoft's dominating the world of operating systems. After Apple's market share shrank to less than 5%, Microsoft's approach was declared the winner in the personal computer realm.

In the longer run, however, there proved to be some advantages to Jobs's model. Even with a small market share, Apple was able to maintain a huge profit margin while other computer makers were commoditized. In 2010, for example, Apple had just 7% of the revenue in the personal computer market, but it grabbed 35% of the operating profit.

More significantly, in the early 2000s Jobs's insistence on end-to-end integration gave Apple an advantage in developing a digital hub strategy, which allowed your desktop computer to link seamlessly with a variety of portable devices. The iPod, for example, was part of a closed and tightly integrated system. To use it, you had to use Apple's iTunes software and download content from its iTunes Store. The result was that the iPod, like the iPhone and iPad that followed, was an elegant delight in contrast to the kludgy rival products that did not offer a seamless end-to-end experience.

The strategy worked. In May 2000 Apple's market value was one-twentieth that of Microsoft. In May 2010 Apple surpassed Microsoft as the world's most valuable technology company, and by September 2011 it was worth 70% more than Microsoft. In the first quarter of

2011 the market for Windows PCs shrank by 1%, while the market for Macs grew 28%.

By then the battle had begun anew in the world of mobile devices. Google took the more open approach, and it made its Android operating system available for use by any maker of tablets or cell phones. By 2011 its share of the mobile market matched Apple's. The drawback of Android's openness was the fragmentation that resulted. Various handset and tablet makers modified Android into dozens of variants and flavors, making it hard for apps to remain consistent or make full use of its features. There were merits to both approaches. Some people wanted the freedom to use more open systems and have more choices of hardware; others clearly preferred Apple's tight integration and control, which led to products that had simpler interfaces, longer battery life, greater user-friendliness, and easier handling of content.

The downside of Jobs's approach was that his desire to delight the user led him to resist empowering the user. Among the most thoughtful proponents of an open environment is Jonathan Zittrain of Harvard. He begins his book *The Future of the Internet—And How to Stop It* with the scene of Jobs introducing the iPhone, and he warns of the consequences of replacing personal computers with "sterile appliances tethered to a network of control." Even more fervent is Cory Doctorow, who wrote a manifesto called "Why I Won't Buy an iPad" for Boing Boing. "There's a lot of thoughtfulness and smarts that went into the design. But there's also a palpable contempt for the owner," he wrote. "Buying an iPad for your kids isn't a means of jump-starting the realization that the world is yours to take apart and reassemble; it's a way of telling your offspring that even changing the batteries is something you have to leave to the professionals."

For Jobs, belief in an integrated approach was a matter of righteousness. "We do these things not because we are control freaks," he explained. "We do them because we want to make great products, because we care about the user, and because we like to take responsibility for the entire experience rather than turn out the crap that other people make." He also believed he was doing people a service: "They're busy doing whatever they do best, and they want us to do what we do best.

Their lives are crowded; they have other things to do than think about how to integrate their computers and devices."

This approach sometimes went against Apple's short-term business interests. But in a world filled with junky devices, inscrutable error messages, and annoying interfaces, it led to astonishing products marked by beguiling user experiences. Using an Apple product could be as sublime as walking in one of the Zen gardens of Kyoto that Jobs loved, and neither experience was created by worshipping at the altar of openness or by letting a thousand flowers bloom. Sometimes it's nice to be in the hands of a control freak.

Jobs's intensity was also evident in his ability to focus. He would set priorities, aim his laser attention on them, and filter out distractions. If something engaged him—the user interface for the original Macintosh, the design of the iPod and iPhone, getting music companies into the iTunes Store—he was relentless. But if he did not want to deal with something—a legal annoyance, a business issue, his cancer diagnosis, a family tug—he would resolutely ignore it. That focus allowed him to say no. He got Apple back on track by cutting all except a few core products. He made devices simpler by eliminating buttons, software simpler by eliminating features, and interfaces simpler by eliminating options.

He attributed his ability to focus and his love of simplicity to his Zen training. It honed his appreciation for intuition, showed him how to filter out anything that was distracting or unnecessary, and nurtured in him an aesthetic based on minimalism.

Unfortunately his Zen training never quite produced in him a Zen-like calm or inner serenity, and that too is part of his legacy. He was often tightly coiled and impatient, traits he made no effort to hide. Most people have a regulator between their mind and mouth that modulates their brutish sentiments and spikiest impulses. Not Jobs. He made a point of being brutally honest. "My job is to say when something sucks rather than sugarcoat it," he said. This made him charismatic and inspiring, yet also, to use the technical term, an asshole at times.

Andy Hertzfeld once told me, "The one question I'd truly love

Steve to answer is, 'Why are you sometimes so mean?' " Even his family members wondered whether he simply lacked the filter that restrains people from venting their wounding thoughts or willfully bypassed it. Jobs claimed it was the former. "This is who I am, and you can't expect me to be someone I'm not," he replied when I asked him the question. But I think he actually could have controlled himself, if he had wanted. When he hurt people, it was not because he was lacking in emotional awareness. Quite the contrary: He could size people up, understand their inner thoughts, and know how to relate to them, cajole them, or hurt them at will.

The nasty edge to his personality was not necessary. It hindered him more than it helped him. But it did, at times, serve a purpose. Polite and velvety leaders, who take care to avoid bruising others, are generally not as effective at forcing change. Dozens of the colleagues whom Jobs most abused ended their litany of horror stories by saying that he got them to do things they never dreamed possible. And he created a corporation crammed with A players.

The saga of Steve Jobs is the Silicon Valley creation myth writ large: launching a startup in his parents' garage and building it into the world's most valuable company. He didn't invent many things outright, but he was a master at putting together ideas, art, and technology in ways that invented the future. He designed the Mac after appreciating the power of graphical interfaces in a way that Xerox was unable to do, and he created the iPod after grasping the joy of having a thousand songs in your pocket in a way that Sony, which had all the assets and heritage, never could accomplish. Some leaders push innovations by being good at the big picture. Others do so by mastering details. Jobs did both, relentlessly. As a result he launched a series of products over three decades that transformed whole industries:

- The Apple II, which took Wozniak's circuit board and turned it into the first personal computer that was not just for hobbyists.
- The Macintosh, which begat the home computer revolution and popularized graphical user interfaces.

- *Toy Story* and other Pixar blockbusters, which opened up the miracle of digital imagination.
- Apple stores, which reinvented the role of a store in defining a brand.
- The iPod, which changed the way we consume music.
- The iTunes Store, which saved the music industry.
- The iPhone, which turned mobile phones into music, photography, video, email, and web devices.
- The App Store, which spawned a new content-creation industry.
- The iPad, which launched tablet computing and offered a platform for digital newspapers, magazines, books, and videos.
- iCloud, which demoted the computer from its central role in managing our content and let all of our devices sync seamlessly.
- And Apple itself, which Jobs considered his greatest creation, a place where imagination was nurtured, applied, and executed in ways so creative that it became the most valuable company on earth.

Was he smart? No, not exceptionally. Instead, he was a genius. His imaginative leaps were instinctive, unexpected, and at times magical. He was, indeed, an example of what the mathematician Mark Kac called a magician genius, someone whose insights come out of the blue and require intuition more than mere mental processing power. Like a pathfinder, he could absorb information, sniff the winds, and sense what lay ahead.

Steve Jobs thus became the greatest business executive of our era, the one most certain to be remembered a century from now. History will place him in the pantheon right next to Edison and Ford. More than anyone else of his time, he made products that were completely innovative, combining the power of poetry and processors. With a ferocity that could make working with him as unsettling as it was inspiring, he also built the world's most creative company. And he was able to infuse into its DNA the design sensibilities, perfectionism, and imagination that make it likely to be, even decades from now, the company that thrives best at the intersection of artistry and technology.

And One More Thing . . .

Biographers are supposed to have the last word. But this is a biography of Steve Jobs. Even though he did not impose his legendary desire for control on this project, I suspect that I would not be conveying the right feel for him—the way he asserted himself in any situation—if I just shuffled him onto history's stage without letting him have some last words.

Over the course of our conversations, there were many times when he reflected on what he hoped his legacy would be. Here are those thoughts, in his own words:

> My passion has been to build an enduring company where people were motivated to make great products. Everything else was secondary. Sure, it was great to make a profit, because that was what allowed you to make great products. But the products, not the profits, were the motivation. Sculley flipped these priorities to where the goal was to make money. It's a subtle difference, but it ends up meaning everything: the people you hire, who gets promoted, what you discuss in meetings.
>
> Some people say, "Give the customers what they want." But that's not my approach. Our job is to figure out what they're going to want before they do. I think Henry Ford once said, "If I'd asked customers what they wanted, they would have told me, 'A faster horse!'" People don't know what they want until you show it to them. That's why I never rely on market research. Our task is to read things that are not yet on the page.
>
> Edwin Land of Polaroid talked about the intersection of the humanities and science. I like that intersection. There's something magical about that place. There are a lot of people innovating, and that's not the main distinction of my career. The reason Apple resonates with people is that there's a deep current of humanity in our innovation. I think great artists and great engineers are similar, in that they both have a

desire to express themselves. In fact some of the best people working on the original Mac were poets and musicians on the side. In the seventies computers became a way for people to express their creativity. Great artists like Leonardo da Vinci and Michelangelo were also great at science. Michelangelo knew a lot about how to quarry stone, not just how to be a sculptor.

People pay us to integrate things for them, because they don't have the time to think about this stuff 24/7. If you have an extreme passion for producing great products, it pushes you to be integrated, to connect your hardware and your software and content management. You want to break new ground, so you have to do it yourself. If you want to allow your products to be open to other hardware or software, you have to give up some of your vision.

At different times in the past, there were companies that exemplified Silicon Valley. It was Hewlett-Packard for a long time. Then, in the semiconductor era, it was Fairchild and Intel. I think that it was Apple for a while, and then that faded. And then today, I think it's Apple and Google—and a little more so Apple. I think Apple has stood the test of time. It's been around for a while, but it's still at the cutting edge of what's going on.

It's easy to throw stones at Microsoft. They've clearly fallen from their dominance. They've become mostly irrelevant. And yet I appreciate what they did and how hard it was. They were very good at the business side of things. They were never as ambitious product-wise as they should have been. Bill likes to portray himself as a man of the product, but he's really not. He's a businessperson. Winning business was more important than making great products. He ended up the wealthiest guy around, and if that was his goal, then he achieved it. But it's never been my goal, and I wonder, in the end, if it was his goal. I admire him for the company he built—it's impressive—and I enjoyed working with him. He's bright and actually has a good sense of humor. But Microsoft never had the humanities and liberal arts in its DNA. Even when they saw the Mac, they couldn't copy it well. They totally didn't get it.

I have my own theory about why decline happens at companies like IBM or Microsoft. The company does a great job, innovates and becomes a monopoly or close to it in some field, and then the quality of the product becomes less important. The company starts valuing the great salesmen, because they're the ones who can move the needle on revenues, not the product engineers and designers. So the salespeople end up running the company. John Akers at IBM was a smart, eloquent, fantastic salesperson, but he didn't know anything about product. The same thing happened at Xerox. When the sales guys run the company, the product guys don't matter so much, and a lot of them just turn off. It happened at Apple when Sculley came in, which was my fault, and it happened when Ballmer took over at Microsoft. Apple was lucky and it rebounded, but I don't think anything will change at Microsoft as long as Ballmer is running it.

I hate it when people call themselves "entrepreneurs" when what they're really trying to do is launch a startup and then sell or go public, so they can cash in and move on. They're unwilling to do the work it takes to build a real company, which is the hardest work in business. That's how you really make a contribution and add to the legacy of those who went before. You build a company that will still stand for something a generation or two from now. That's what Walt Disney did, and Hewlett and Packard, and the people who built Intel. They created a company to last, not just to make money. That's what I want Apple to be.

I don't think I run roughshod over people, but if something sucks, I tell people to their face. It's my job to be honest. I know what I'm talking about, and I usually turn out to be right. That's the culture I tried to create. We are brutally honest with each other, and anyone can tell me they think I am full of shit and I can tell them the same. And we've had some rip-roaring arguments, where we are yelling at each other, and it's some of the best times I've ever had. I feel totally comfortable saying "Ron, that store looks like shit" in front of everyone else. Or I might say "God, we really fucked up the engineering on this" in front of the person that's responsible. That's the ante for being in the room: You've got to be able to be super honest. Maybe there's a better way, a gentlemen's club where we all wear ties and speak in this Brahmin language and velvet code-words, but I don't know that way, because I am middle class from California.

I was hard on people sometimes, probably harder than I needed to be. I remember the time when Reed was six years old, coming home, and I had just fired somebody that day, and I imagined what it was like for that person to tell his family and his young son that he had lost his job. It was hard. But somebody's got to do it. I figured that it was always my job to make sure that the team was excellent, and if I didn't do it, nobody was going to do it.

You always have to keep pushing to innovate. Dylan could have sung protest songs forever and probably made a lot of money, but he didn't. He had to move on, and when he did, by going electric in 1965, he alienated a lot of people. His 1966 Europe tour was his greatest. He would come on and do a set of acoustic guitar, and the audiences loved him. Then he brought out what became The Band, and they would all do an electric set, and the audience sometimes booed. There was one point where he was about to sing "Like a Rolling Stone" and someone from the audience yells "Judas!" And Dylan then says, "Play it fucking loud!" And they did. The Beatles were the same way. They kept evolving, moving, refining their art. That's what I've always tried to do—keep moving. Otherwise, as Dylan says, if you're not busy being born, you're busy dying.

What drove me? I think most creative people want to express appreciation for being able to take advantage of the work that's been done by others before us. I didn't invent the language or mathematics I use. I make little of my own food, none of my own clothes. Everything I do depends on other members of our species and the shoulders that we stand on. And a lot of us want to contribute something back to our species and to add something to the flow. It's about trying to express something in the only way that most of us know how—because we can't write Bob Dylan songs or Tom Stoppard plays. We try to use the talents we do have to express our deep feelings, to show our appreciation of all the contributions that came before us, and to add something to that flow. That's what has driven me.

Coda

One sunny afternoon, when he wasn't feeling well, Jobs sat in the garden behind his house and reflected on death. He talked about his experiences in India almost four decades earlier, his study of Buddhism, and his views on reincarnation and spiritual transcendence.

"I'm about fifty-fifty on believing in God," he said. "For most of my life, I've felt that there must be more to our existence than meets the eye."

He admitted that, as he faced death, he might be overestimating the odds out of a desire to believe in an afterlife. "I like to think that something survives after you die," he said. "It's strange to think that you accumulate all this experience, and maybe a little wisdom, and it just goes away. So I really want to believe that something survives, that maybe your consciousness endures."

He fell silent for a very long time. "But on the other hand, perhaps it's like an on-off switch," he said. "*Click!* And you're gone."

Then he paused again and smiled slightly. "Maybe that's why I never liked to put on-off switches on Apple devices."

EPILOGUE

In the summer of 2011, when he still thought that he would win another round in his battle against cancer, Steve Jobs suggested to me that I conclude this book with his resignation as Apple's CEO, which he planned to announce late that August. I had already given my publisher a draft of the manuscript, minus the ending. Just before I turned in the final revisions, I spent time with Jobs going over a lot of the stories that I used, including some that I thought he might not like. He had insisted that I write an unvarnished portrayal, so there were many anecdotes about his rough edges. I assured him that I had tried to put them into context, as one aspect of a complex and passionate personality that allowed him to change the world by believing that the ordinary rules didn't apply to him.

He was sanguine. He knew that he was not going down in history as the epitome of politeness, and it was better for him, he said, if the book didn't read like an officially sanctioned account. He told me that he would wait a while, maybe a year, before reading it. His confidence, or reality distortion field, was so strong that I was elated. For a moment I believed that he would be around in a year and would get the chance to read this book. He seemed so sure that he was going to regain his health and resume being active at Apple that I asked if he thought I should hold off publishing and see what happened. "No," he replied. "If I do something else amazing, that means you get to write a second volume." He smiled at that thought, then added, "Or at least a very long epilogue."

Sadly, this is a short epilogue.

• • •

On Monday, October 3, 2011, Steve Jobs realized that his time had come. He stopped talking about "making it to the next lily pad" in his effort to outrun his cancer and instead shifted his thoughts—with the suddenness that was typical whenever he changed his focus—to his impending death.

He had not before spoken about his funeral arrangements, and Laurene had assumed that he would want to be cremated. Over the years they had discussed, in an offhand manner, where they might like their ashes to be scattered. But on that Monday he declared that he did not like the idea of his body being cremated. He wanted to be buried in the cemetery near his parents.

Tuesday morning, Apple was introducing the new iPhone 4S with the Siri voice-recognition software that Steve had toyed with at his final board meeting. It was a relatively somber affair in the modest Town Hall Auditorium on the Apple campus; Steve's closest colleagues knew that he was doing badly. As soon as the event ended, Jony Ive, Eddy Cue, Tim Cook, and a few others got the phone call: Come to the house. And so that afternoon they did, taking their turns saying goodbye.

Jobs called his sister Mona Simpson and told her to hurry to Palo Alto. As she recalled in her eulogy, "His tone was affectionate, dear, loving, but like someone whose luggage was already strapped onto the vehicle, who was already on the beginning of his journey, even as he was sorry, truly deeply sorry, to be leaving us." He began saying farewell to her, but she said she was in a taxi to the airport and would be there soon. "I'm telling you now because I'm afraid you won't make it on time, honey," Jobs replied. His daughter Lisa flew in from New York; despite their uneven relationship over the years, she had always tried to be a good daughter, and she was. His sister Patty was there as well.

And thus it was that at the end, Steve Jobs was surrounded by a deeply loving family. He may not have always seemed like the best family man, as he often admitted. But any judgments must take into account results. As a business leader, he could be demanding and temperamental, but he forged a fanatically loyal team of colleagues, who loved him dearly. Likewise, as a family man, he could be abrupt and distracted, but he produced four well-grounded children who surrounded him with love at the end. That Tuesday afternoon, he kept staring into his children's eyes. At one point he looked at Patty and his children for a long time, then at Laurene, and finally gazed past them into the distance. "Oh wow," he said. "Oh wow. Oh wow."

Those were his final words before he drifted into unconsciousness sometime around two that afternoon. His breathing became heavy. "Even now, he had a stern, still handsome profile, the profile of an absolutist, a romantic," Mona recalled. "His breath indicated an arduous journey, some steep path, altitude." She and Laurene stayed up with him through the night. The next day—Wednesday, October 5, 2011—Steve Jobs died, with members of his family around him, touching him.

The news of his death unleashed an emotional outpouring around the world. Impromptu shrines were constructed in hundreds of cities and villages, even in Zuccotti Park, where Occupy Wall Street activists were protesting the malefactions of billionaire businessmen. It was fitting. Emotional outpourings are too often reserved for the deaths of drug-numbed rock stars and troubled princesses. It was refreshing to see an entrepreneur celebrated. He may have been a billionaire businessman, but he became so by crafting beautiful products that made lives more magical.

The day after Jobs died, Laurene and Mona went to the cemetery he had chosen and were driven around in a golf cart. There were no plots available next to those of Paul and Clara Jobs, and Laurene hated the other options that she was shown, where the headstones were crammed into rows on an undistinguished, flat piece of land. But like her husband, she was imaginative and willful. She pointed to a bucolic ridge crowned by one of the area's last remaining apricot orchards, the type of grove that Jobs had loved from his childhood. It wasn't available, she was told. There were no plans or permits to put burial plots there. That did not deter her. After much insistence, she convinced the cemetery director that her husband would eventually have his final resting place near the orchard. Steve would have been proud of her.

Laurene was able, then as always, to combine her husband's pristine taste with her own loving grace. The casket she had made was perfectly crafted and hinged, with no nails or screws. Pure and simple. At the private burial ceremony, it rested on one of the gray industrial tables from the serene design studio at Apple headquarters, where Jobs had spent so many afternoons. Jony Ive had arranged for the table to be brought to the graveside. There were fifty or so family members and friends in attendance, and some chose to share stories. Disney's Bob Iger, for example, told of taking a walk with Jobs around the Pixar campus just thirty minutes before the deal with Disney was to be announced. Jobs told him that his cancer had returned, and only Laurene and the doctors knew; he felt he had a duty to let Iger know in case he wanted to pull out of the deal. "It was an extraordinary gesture on his part," Iger said.

A formal memorial service was held on the evening of October 16 in Stanford's Memorial Church, which was bathed in candlelight for the occasion. Laurene and Jony Ive had worked together to get the look perfect. Among the hundred or so guests were Bill Clinton, Al Gore, Bill Gates, and Larry Page. From the past were members of the early Apple team, including Steve Wozniak and Andy Hertzfeld. Family members included his children and his sisters, Patty Jobs and Mona Simpson.

"Steve wanted me to play cello at his funeral," Yo Yo Ma said as the service began, "and I said I would prefer he speak at mine. As usual, he got his way." Ma played a Bach suite. Two other friends also performed. Bono sang "Every Grain of Sand," one of Jobs's Bob Dylan favorites. *In the fury of the moment I can see the Master's hand / In every leaf that trembles, in every grain of sand.* Joan Baez sang the mournful yet uplifting spiritual, "Swing Low, Sweet Chariot."

Each member of the family recounted a few stories or read a poem. "His mind was never a captive of reality," Laurene said. "He possessed an epic sense of possibility. He looked at things from the standpoint of perfection."

Mona Simpson, as befitting a novelist, had a finely crafted eulogy. "He was an intensely emotional man," she recalled. "Even ill, his taste, his discrimination, and his judgment held. He went through sixty-seven nurses before finding kindred spirits." She spoke of her brother's love of work and noted that "even in the last year, he embarked upon projects and elicited promises from his friends at Apple to finish them." She also, more personally, stressed his love of Laurene and all four of his children. Although he had achieved his wish of living to see Reed's graduation, he would not see his daughters' weddings. "He'd wanted to walk them down the aisle as he'd walked me the day of my wedding," she said. Those chapters would not be written. "We all—in the end—die in medias res. In the middle of a story. Of many stories."

The corporate memorial on the Apple campus was held three days later. Tim Cook, Al Gore , and Bill Campbell all spoke, but Jony Ive stole the show with a tribute both amusing and emotional. He told the story, as he had at the Stanford memorial, of Jobs being so finicky that whenever they checked into a hotel Ive would sit by the phone waiting for the inevitable call from him saying, "This hotel sucks, let's go." But Ive also captured the scattershot brilliance at the core of Jobs's genius when he described his boss tossing out ideas at a meeting. "Sometimes they were dopey. Sometimes they were truly dreadful. But sometimes they took the air from the room . . . bold, crazy, magnificent ideas, or quiet simple ones which, in their subtlety, their detail, were utterly profound."

The highlight of the service came from Jobs himself, speaking like a ghost hovering over the sunny courtyard. Cook described how Jobs had helped to craft the "Think Different" commercial when he was restored to Apple in 1997. Then the unused version that Jobs himself recorded—rather than the one read by Richard Dreyfuss—was played in public for the first time. From the loudspeakers came his distinctive voice, poignant and jarring as it wafted over the crowd. "Here's to the crazy ones. The misfits. The rebels. The troublemakers. The round pegs in the square holes. The ones who see things differently." It felt as if Jobs were back with them, earnest and emotional, describing himself. "They're not fond of rules. And they have no respect for the status quo. You can quote them, disagree with them, glorify or vilify them. About the only thing you can't do is ignore them." At that point his voice became slightly more emphatic, excited, as if he were sitting right in front of the crowd, his eyes again ablaze. It conjured up memories of what he sounded like when he was young, and how, as in his favorite Dylan song, he had remained forever young. "They push the human race forward." That was a line he had written himself. And then he delivered the famous summation, as fitting for that day as it is for this book. "While some may see them as the crazy ones, we see genius. Because the people who are crazy enough to think they can change the world are the ones who do."

ACKNOWLEDGMENTS

I'm deeply grateful to John and Ann Doerr, Laurene Powell, Mona Simpson, Leon Wieseltier, and Ken Auletta, all of whom provided invaluable support along the way. Alice Mayhew, who has been my editor at Simon & Schuster for thirty years, and Jonathan Karp, the publisher, both were extraordinarily diligent and attentive in shepherding this book, as was Amanda Urban, my agent. Crary Pullen was dogged in tracking down photos, and my assistant, Pat Zindulka, calmly facilitated things. I also want to thank my father, Irwin, and my daughter, Betsy, for reading the book and offering advice. When the original version of this book came out, it caused some wounded feelings, which was probably inevitable given what a complicated and extraordinary man Jobs was. For that I am sorry. It was not my intention. I am grateful to those who have been forgiving of my lapses and misperceptions and who have helped me make corrections or clear a few things up. And as always, I am most deeply indebted to my wife, Cathy, for her editing, suggestions, wise counsel, and so very much more.

SOURCES

Interviews (conducted 2009–2011)

Al Alcorn, Roger Ames, Fred Anderson, Bill Atkinson, Joan Baez, Marjorie Powell Barden, Jeff Bewkes, Bono, Ann Bowers, Stewart Brand, Chrisann Brennan, Larry Brilliant, John Seeley Brown, Tim Brown, Nolan Bushnell, Greg Calhoun, Bill Campbell, Berry Cash, Ed Catmull, Ray Cave, Lee Clow, Debi Coleman, Tim Cook, Katie Cotton, Eddy Cue, Andrea Cunningham, John Doerr, Millard Drexler, Jennifer Egan, Al Eisenstat, Michael Eisner, Larry Ellison, Philip Elmer-DeWitt, Gerard Errera, Tony Fadell, Jean-Louis Gassée, Bill Gates, Adele Goldberg, Craig Good, Austan Goolsbee, Al Gore, Andy Grove, Bill Hambrecht, Michael Hawley, Andy Hertzfeld, Joanna Hoffman, Elizabeth Holmes, Bruce Horn, John Huey, Jimmy Iovine, Jony Ive, Oren Jacob, Erin Jobs, Reed Jobs, Steve Jobs, Ron Johnson, Mitch Kapor, Susan Kare (email), Jeffrey Katzenberg, Pam Kerwin, Kristina Kiehl, Joel Klein, Daniel Kottke, Andy Lack, John Lasseter, Art Levinson, Steven Levy, Dan'l Lewin, Maya Lin, Yo-Yo Ma, Mike Markkula, John Markoff, Wynton Marsalis, Regis McKenna, Mike Merin, Bob Metcalfe, Doug Morris, Walt Mossberg, Rupert Murdoch, Mike Murray, Nicholas Negroponte, Dean Ornish, Paul Otellini, Norman Pearlstine, Laurene Powell, Josh Quittner, Tina Redse, George Riley, Brian Roberts, Arthur Rock, Jeff Rosen, Alain Rossmann, Jon Rubinstein, Phil Schiller, Eric Schmidt, Barry Schuler, Mike Scott, John Sculley, Andy Serwer, Mona Simpson, Mike Slade, Alvy Ray Smith, Gina Smith, Kathryn Smith, Rick Stengel, Larry Tesler, Avie Tevanian, Guy "Bud" Tribble, Don Valentine, Paul

Vidich, James Vincent, Alice Waters, Ron Wayne, Wendell Weeks, Ed Woolard, Stephen Wozniak, Del Yocam, Jerry York.

Bibliography

Amelio, Gil. *On the Firing Line.* HarperBusiness, 1998.

Berlin, Leslie. *The Man behind the Microchip.* Oxford, 2005.

Butcher, Lee. *The Accidental Millionaire.* Paragon House, 1988.

Carlton, Jim. *Apple.* Random House, 1997.

Cringely, Robert X. *Accidental Empires.* Addison Wesley, 1992.

Deutschman, Alan. *The Second Coming of Steve Jobs.* Broadway Books, 2000.

Elliot, Jay, with William Simon. *The Steve Jobs Way.* Vanguard, 2011.

Freiberger, Paul, and Michael Swaine. *Fire in the Valley.* McGraw-Hill, 1984.

Garr, Doug. *Woz.* Avon, 1984.

Hertzfeld, Andy. *Revolution in the Valley.* O'Reilly, 2005. (See also his website, folklore.org.)

Hiltzik, Michael. *Dealers of Lightning.* HarperBusiness, 1999.

Jobs, Steve. Smithsonian oral history interview with Daniel Morrow, April 20, 1995.

———. Stanford commencement address, June 12, 2005.

Kahney, Leander. *Inside Steve's Brain.* Portfolio, 2008. (See also his website, cultofmac.com.)

Kawasaki, Guy. *The Macintosh Way.* Scott, Foresman, 1989.

Knopper, Steve. *Appetite for Self-Destruction.* Free Press, 2009.

Kot, Greg. *Ripped.* Scribner, 2009.

Kunkel, Paul. *AppleDesign.* Graphis Inc., 1997.

Levy, Steven. *Hackers.* Doubleday, 1984.

———. *Insanely Great.* Viking Penguin, 1994.

———. *The Perfect Thing.* Simon & Schuster, 2006.

Linzmayer, Owen. *Apple Confidential 2.0.* No Starch Press, 2004.

Malone, Michael. *Infinite Loop.* Doubleday, 1999.

Markoff, John. *What the Dormouse Said.* Viking Penguin, 2005.

McNish, Jacquie. *The Big Score.* Doubleday Canada, 1998.

Moritz, Michael. *Return to the Little Kingdom.* Overlook Press, 2009. Originally published, without prologue and epilogue, as *The Little Kingdom* (Morrow, 1984).

Nocera, Joe. *Good Guys and Bad Guys.* Portfolio, 2008.

Paik, Karen. *To Infinity and Beyond!* Chronicle Books, 2007.

Price, David. *The Pixar Touch.* Knopf, 2008.

Rose, Frank. *West of Eden.* Viking, 1989.

Sculley, John. *Odyssey.* Harper & Row, 1987.

Sheff, David. "Playboy Interview: Steve Jobs." *Playboy*, February 1985.

Simpson, Mona. *Anywhere but Here.* Knopf, 1986.

———. *A Regular Guy.* Knopf, 1996.

Smith, Douglas, and Robert Alexander. *Fumbling the Future.* Morrow, 1988.

Stross, Randall. *Steve Jobs and the NeXT Big Thing.* Atheneum, 1993.

"Triumph of the Nerds," PBS Television, hosted by Robert X. Cringely, June 1996.

Wozniak, Steve, with Gina Smith. *iWoz.* Norton, 2006.

Young, Jeffrey. *Steve Jobs.* Scott, Foresman, 1988.

———, and William Simon. *iCon.* John Wiley, 2005.

NOTES

CHAPTER 1: CHILDHOOD

The Adoption: Interviews with Steve Jobs, Laurene Powell, Mona Simpson, Del Yocam, Greg Calhoun, Chrisann Brennan, Andy Hertzfeld. Moritz, 44–45; Young, 16–17; Jobs, Smithsonian oral history; Jobs, Stanford commencement address; Andy Behrendt, "Apple Computer Mogul's Roots Tied to Green Bay," (Green Bay) *Press Gazette*, Dec. 4, 2005; Georgina Dickinson, "Dad Waits for Jobs to iPhone," *New York Post* and *The Sun* (London), Aug. 27, 2011; Mohannad Al-Haj Ali, "Steve Jobs Has Roots in Syria," *Al Hayat*, Jan. 16, 2011; Ulf Froitzheim, "Porträt Steve Jobs," *Unternehmen*, Nov. 26, 2007.

Silicon Valley: Interviews with Steve Jobs, Laurene Powell. Jobs, Smithsonian oral history; Moritz, 46; Berlin, 155–177; Malone, 21–22.

School: Interview with Steve Jobs. Jobs, Smithsonian oral history; Sculley, 166; Malone, 11, 28, 72; Young, 25, 34–35; Young and Simon, 18; Moritz, 48, 73–74. Jobs's address was originally 11161 Crist Drive, before the subdivision was incorporated into the town from the county. Some sources mention that Jobs worked at both Haltek and another store with a similar name, Halted. When asked, Jobs says he can remember working only at Haltek.

CHAPTER 2: ODD COUPLE

Woz: Interviews with Steve Wozniak, Steve Jobs. Wozniak, 12–16, 22, 50–61, 86–91; Levy, *Hackers*, 245; Moritz, 62–64; Young, 28; Jobs, Macworld address, Jan. 17, 2007.

The Blue Box: Interviews with Steve Jobs, Steve Wozniak. Ron Rosenbaum, "Secrets of the Little Blue Box," *Esquire*, Oct. 1971. Wozniak answer, woz.org/

letters/general/03.html; Wozniak, 98–115. For slightly varying accounts, see
Markoff, 272; Moritz, 78–86; Young, 42–45; Malone, 30–35.

CHAPTER 3: THE DROPOUT

Chrisann Brennan: Interviews with Chrisann Brennan, Steve Jobs, Steve
Wozniak, Tim Brown. Moritz, 75–77; Young, 41; Malone, 39.

Reed College: Interviews with Steve Jobs, Daniel Kottke, Elizabeth Holmes.
Freiberger and Swaine, 208; Moritz, 94–100; Young, 55; "The Updated Book
of Jobs," *Time,* Jan. 3, 1983.

Robert Friedland: Interviews with Steve Jobs, Daniel Kottke, Elizabeth
Holmes. In September 2010 I met with Friedland in New York City to discuss
his background and relationship with Jobs, but he did not want to be quoted
on the record. McNish, 11–17; Jennifer Wells, "Canada's Next Billionaire,"
Maclean's, June 3, 1996; Richard Read, "Financier's Saga of Risk," *Mines and
Communities* magazine, Oct. 16, 2005; Jennifer Hunter, "But What Would
His Guru Say?" (Toronto) *Globe and Mail,* Mar. 18, 1988; Moritz, 96, 109;
Young, 56.

. . . Drop Out: Interviews with Steve Jobs, Steve Wozniak; Jobs, Stanford
commencement address; Moritz, 97.

CHAPTER 4: ATARI AND INDIA

Atari: Interviews with Steve Jobs, Al Alcorn, Nolan Bushnell, Ron Wayne.
Moritz, 103–104.

India: Interviews with Daniel Kottke, Steve Jobs, Al Alcorn, Larry Brilliant.

The Search: Interviews with Steve Jobs, Daniel Kottke, Elizabeth Holmes,
Greg Calhoun. Young, 72; Young and Simon, 31–32; Moritz, 107.

Breakout: Interviews with Nolan Bushnell, Al Alcorn, Steve Wozniak, Ron
Wayne, Andy Hertzfeld. Wozniak, 144–149; Young, 88; Linzmayer, 4.

CHAPTER 5: THE APPLE I

Machines of Loving Grace: Interviews with Steve Jobs, Bono, Stewart Brand.
Markoff, xii; Stewart Brand, "We Owe It All to the Hippies," *Time,* Mar. 1,
1995; Jobs, Stanford commencement address; Fred Turner, *From Counterculture
to Cyberculture* (Chicago, 2006).

The Homebrew Computer Club: Interviews with Steve Jobs, Steve Wozniak.
Wozniak, 152–172; Freiberger and Swaine, 99; Linzmayer, 5; Moritz, 144;

Steve Wozniak, "Homebrew and How Apple Came to Be," www.atariarchives .org; Bill Gates, "Open Letter to Hobbyists," Feb. 3, 1976.

Apple Is Born: Interviews with Steve Jobs, Steve Wozniak, Mike Markkula, Ron Wayne. Steve Jobs, address to the Aspen Design Conference, June 15, 1983, tape in Aspen Institute archives; Apple Computer Partnership Agreement, County of Santa Clara, Apr. 1, 1976, and Amendment to Agreement, Apr. 12, 1976; Bruce Newman, "Apple's Lost Founder," *San Jose Mercury News*, June 2, 2010; Wozniak, 86, 176–177; Moritz, 149–151; Freiberger and Swaine, 212–213; Ashlee Vance, "A Haven for Spare Parts Lives on in Silicon Valley," *New York Times*, Feb. 4, 2009; Paul Terrell interview, Aug. 1, 2008, mac-history.net.

Garage Band: Interviews with Steve Wozniak, Elizabeth Holmes, Daniel Kottke, Steve Jobs. Wozniak, 179–189; Moritz, 152–163; Young, 95–111; R. S. Jones, "Comparing Apples and Oranges," *Interface*, July 1976.

CHAPTER 6: THE APPLE II

An Integrated Package: Interviews with Steve Jobs, Steve Wozniak, Al Alcorn, Ron Wayne. Wozniak, 165, 190–195; Young, 126; Moritz, 169–170, 194–197; Malone, v, 103.

Mike Markkula: Interviews with Regis McKenna, Don Valentine, Steve Jobs, Steve Wozniak, Mike Markkula, Arthur Rock. Nolan Bushnell, keynote address at the ScrewAttack Gaming Convention, Dallas, July 5, 2009; Steve Jobs, talk at the International Design Conference at Aspen, June 15, 1983; Mike Markkula, "The Apple Marketing Philosophy" (courtesy of Mike Markkula), Dec. 1979; Wozniak, 196–199. See also Moritz, 182–183; Malone, 110–111.

Regis McKenna: Interviews with Regis McKenna, John Doerr, Steve Jobs. Ivan Raszl, "Interview with Rob Janoff," Creativebits.org, Aug. 3, 2009.

The First Launch Event: Interviews with Steve Wozniak, Steve Jobs. Wozniak, 201–206; Moritz, 199–201; Young, 139.

Mike Scott: Interviews with Mike Scott, Mike Markkula, Steve Jobs, Steve Wozniak, Arthur Rock. Young, 135; Freiberger and Swaine, 219, 222; Moritz, 213; Elliot, 4.

CHAPTER 7: CHRISANN AND LISA
Interviews with Chrisann Brennan, Steve Jobs, Elizabeth Holmes, Greg Calhoun, Daniel Kottke, Arthur Rock. Moritz, 285; "The Updated Book of Jobs," *Time,* Jan. 3, 1983; "Striking It Rich," *Time,* Feb. 15, 1982.

CHAPTER 8: XEROX AND LISA
A New Baby: Interviews with Andrea Cunningham, Andy Hertzfeld, Steve Jobs, Bill Atkinson. Wozniak, 226; Levy, *Insanely Great,* 124; Young, 168–170; Bill Atkinson, oral history, Computer History Museum, Mountain View, CA; Jef Raskin, "Holes in the Histories," *Interactions,* July 1994; Jef Raskin, "Hubris of a Heavyweight," *IEEE Spectrum,* July 1994; Jef Raskin, oral history, April 13, 2000, Stanford Library Department of Special Collections; Linzmayer, 74, 85–89.

Xerox PARC: Interviews with Steve Jobs, John Seeley Brown, Adele Goldberg, Larry Tesler, Bill Atkinson. Freiberger and Swaine, 239; Levy, *Insanely Great,* 66–80; Hiltzik, 330–341; Linzmayer, 74–75; Young, 170–172; Rose, 45–47; *Triumph of the Nerds,* PBS, part 3.

"Great Artists Steal": Interviews with Steve Jobs, Larry Tesler, Bill Atkinson. Levy, *Insanely Great,* 77, 87–90; *Triumph of the Nerds,* PBS, part 3; Bruce Horn, "Where It All Began" (1966), www.mackido.com; Hiltzik, 343, 367–370; Malcolm Gladwell, "Creation Myth," *New Yorker,* May 16, 2011; Young, 178–182.

CHAPTER 9: GOING PUBLIC
Options: Interviews with Daniel Kottke, Steve Jobs, Steve Wozniak, Andy Hertzfeld, Mike Markkula, Bill Hambrecht. "Sale of Apple Stock Barred," *Boston Globe,* Dec. 11, 1980.

Baby You're a Rich Man: Interviews with Larry Brilliant, Steve Jobs. Steve Ditlea, "An Apple on Every Desk," *Inc.,* Oct. 1, 1981; "Striking It Rich," *Time,* Feb. 15, 1982; "The Seeds of Success," *Time,* Feb. 15, 1982; Moritz, 292–295; Sheff.

CHAPTER 10: THE MAC IS BORN
Jef Raskin's Baby: Interviews with Bill Atkinson, Steve Jobs, Andy Hertzfeld, Mike Markkula. Jef Raskin, "Recollections of the Macintosh Project," "Holes in the Histories," "The Genesis and History of the Macintosh Project," "Reply to Jobs, and Personal Motivation," "Design Considerations for an

Anthropophilic Computer," and "Computers by the Millions," Raskin papers, Stanford University Library; Jef Raskin, "A Conversation," *Ubiquity*, June 23, 2003; Levy, *Insanely Great*, 107–121; Hertzfeld, 19; "Macintosh's Other Designers," *Byte*, Aug. 1984; Young, 202, 208–214; "Apple Launches a Mac Attack," *Time*, Jan. 30, 1984; Malone, 255–258.

Texaco Towers: Interviews with Andrea Cunningham, Bruce Horn, Andy Hertzfeld, Mike Scott, Mike Markkula. Hertzfeld, 19–20, 26–27; Wozniak, 241–242.

CHAPTER 11: THE REALITY DISTORTION FIELD

Interviews with Bill Atkinson, Steve Wozniak, Debi Coleman, Andy Hertzfeld, Bruce Horn, Joanna Hoffman, Al Eisenstat, Ann Bowers, Steve Jobs. Some of these tales have variations. See Hertzfeld, 24, 68, 161.

CHAPTER 12: THE DESIGN

A Bauhaus Aesthetic: Interviews with Dan'l Lewin, Steve Jobs, Maya Lin, Debi Coleman. Steve Jobs in conversation with Charles Hampden-Turner, International Design Conference in Aspen, June 15, 1983. (The design conference audiotapes are stored at the Aspen Institute. I want to thank Deborah Murphy for finding them.)

Like a Porsche: Interviews with Bill Atkinson, Alain Rossmann, Mike Markkula, Steve Jobs. "The Macintosh Design Team," *Byte*, Feb. 1984; Hertzfeld, 29–31, 41, 46, 63, 68; Sculley, 157; Jerry Manock, "Invasion of Texaco Towers," Folklore.org; Kunkel, 26–30; Jobs, Stanford commencement address; email from Susan Kare; Susan Kare, "World Class Cities," in Hertzfeld, 165; Laurence Zuckerman, "The Designer Who Made the Mac Smile," *New York Times*, Aug. 26, 1996; Susan Kare interview, Sept. 8, 2000, Stanford University Library, Special Collections; Levy, *Insanely Great*, 156; Hartmut Esslinger, *A Fine Line* (Jossey-Bass, 2009), 7–9; David Einstein, "Where Success Is by Design," *San Francisco Chronicle*, Oct. 6, 1995; Sheff.

CHAPTER 13: BUILDING THE MAC

Competition: Interview with Steve Jobs. Levy, *Insanely Great*, 125; Sheff; Hertzfeld, 71–73; *Wall Street Journal* advertisement, Aug. 24, 1981.

End-to-end Control: Interview with Berry Cash. Kahney, 241; Dan Farber, "Steve Jobs, the iPhone and Open Platforms," ZDNet.com, Jan. 13, 2007; Tim

Wu, *The Master Switch* (Knopf, 2010), 254–276; Mike Murray, "Mac Memo" to Steve Jobs, May 19, 1982 (courtesy of Mike Murray).

Machines of the Year: Interviews with Daniel Kottke, Steve Jobs, Ray Cave. "The Computer Moves In," *Time*, Jan. 3, 1983; "The Updated Book of Jobs," *Time*, Jan. 3, 1983; Moritz, 11; Young, 293; Rose, 9–11; Peter McNulty, "Apple's Bid to Stay in the Big Time," *Fortune*, Feb. 7, 1983; "The Year of the Mouse," *Time*, Jan. 31, 1983.

Let's Be Pirates! Interviews with Ann Bowers, Andy Hertzfeld, Bill Atkinson, Arthur Rock, Mike Markkula, Steve Jobs, Debi Coleman; email from Susan Kare. Hertzfeld, 76, 135–138, 158, 160, 166; Moritz, 21–28; Young, 295–297, 301–303; Susan Kare interview, Sept. 8, 2000, Stanford University Library; Jeff Goodell, "The Rise and Fall of Apple Computer," *Rolling Stone*, Apr. 4, 1996; Rose, 59–69, 93.

CHAPTER 14: ENTER SCULLEY

The Courtship: Interviews with John Sculley, Andy Hertzfeld, Steve Jobs. Rose, 18, 74–75; Sculley, 58–90, 107; Elliot, 90–93; Mike Murray, "Special Mac Sneak" memo to staff, Mar. 3, 1983 (courtesy of Mike Murray); Hertzfeld, 149–150.

The Honeymoon: Interviews with Steve Jobs, John Sculley, Joanna Hoffman. Sculley, 127–130, 154–155, 168, 179; Hertzfeld, 195.

CHAPTER 15: THE LAUNCH

Real Artists Ship: Interviews with Andy Hertzfeld, Steve Jobs. Video of Apple sales conference, Oct. 1983; "Personal Computers: And the Winner Is . . . IBM," *Business Week*, Oct. 3, 1983; Hertzfeld, 208–210; Rose, 147–153; Levy, *Insanely Great*, 178–180; Young, 327–328.

The "1984" Ad: Interviews with Lee Clow, John Sculley, Mike Markkula, Bill Campbell, Steve Jobs. Steve Hayden interview, *Weekend Edition*, NPR, Feb. 1, 2004; Linzmayer, 109–114; Sculley, 176.

Publicity Blast: Hertzfeld, 226–227; Michael Rogers, "It's the Apple of His Eye," *Newsweek*, Jan. 30, 1984; Levy, *Insanely Great*, 17–27.

January 24, 1984: Interviews with John Sculley, Steve Jobs, Andy Hertzfeld. Video of Jan. 1984 Apple shareholders meeting; Hertzfeld, 213–223; Sculley, 179–181; William Hawkins, "Jobs' Revolutionary New Computer," *Popular Science*, Jan. 1989.

CHAPTER 16: GATES AND JOBS

The Macintosh Partnership: Interviews with Bill Gates, Steve Jobs, Bruce Horn. Hertzfeld, 52–54; Steve Lohr, "Creating Jobs," *New York Times*, Jan. 12, 1997; *Triumph of the Nerds*, PBS, part 3; Rusty Weston, "Partners and Adversaries," *MacWeek*, Mar. 14, 1989; Walt Mossberg and Kara Swisher, interview with Bill Gates and Steve Jobs, *All Things Digital*, May 31, 2007; Young, 319–320; Carlton, 28; Brent Schlender, "How Steve Jobs Linked Up with IBM," *Fortune*, Oct. 9, 1989; Steven Levy, "A Big Brother?" *Newsweek*, Aug. 18, 1997.

The Battle of the GUI: Interviews with Bill Gates, Steve Jobs. Hertzfeld, 191–193; Michael Schrage, "IBM Compatibility Grows," *Washington Post*, Nov. 29, 1983; *Triumph of the Nerds*, PBS, part 3.

CHAPTER 17: ICARUS

Flying High: Interviews with Steve Jobs, Debi Coleman, Bill Atkinson, Andy Hertzfeld, Alain Rossmann, Joanna Hoffman, Jean-Louis Gassée, Nicholas Negroponte, Arthur Rock, John Sculley. Sheff; Hertzfeld, 206–207, 230; Sculley, 197–199; Young, 308–309; George Gendron and Bo Burlingham, "Entrepreneur of the Decade," *Inc.*, Apr. 1, 1989.

Falling: Interviews with Joanna Hoffman, John Sculley, Lee Clow, Debi Coleman, Andrea Cunningham, Steve Jobs. Sculley, 201, 212–215; Levy, *Insanely Great*, 186–192; Michael Rogers, "It's the Apple of His Eye," *Newsweek*, Jan. 30, 1984; Rose, 207, 233; Felix Kessler, "Apple Pitch," *Fortune*, Apr. 15, 1985; Linzmayer, 145.

Thirty Years Old: Interviews with Mallory Walker, Andy Hertzfeld, Debi Coleman, Elizabeth Holmes, Steve Wozniak, Don Valentine. Sheff.

Exodus: Interviews with Andy Hertzfeld, Steve Wozniak, Bruce Horn. Hertzfeld, 253, 263–264; Young, 372–376; Wozniak, 265–266; Rose, 248–249; Bob Davis, "Apple's Head, Jobs, Denies Ex-Partner Use of Design Firm," *Wall Street Journal*, Mar. 22, 1985.

Showdown, Spring 1985: Interviews with Steve Jobs, Al Alcorn, John Sculley, Mike Murray. Elliot, 15; Sculley, 205–206, 227, 238–244; Young, 367–379; Rose, 238, 242, 254–255; Mike Murray, "Let's Wake Up and Die Right," memo to undisclosed recipients, Mar. 7, 1985 (courtesy of Mike Murray).

Plotting a Coup: Interviews with Steve Jobs, John Sculley. Rose, 266–275; Sculley, ix–x, 245–246; Young, 388–396; Elliot, 112.

Seven Days in May: Interviews with Jean-Louis Gassée, Steve Jobs, Bill

Campbell, Al Eisenstat, John Sculley, Mike Murray, Mike Markkula, Debi Coleman. Bro Uttal, "Behind the Fall of Steve Jobs," *Fortune*, Aug. 5, 1985; Sculley, 249–260; Rose, 275–290; Young, 396–404.

Like a Rolling Stone: Interviews with Mike Murray, Mike Markkula, Steve Jobs, John Sculley, Bob Metcalfe, George Riley, Andy Hertzfeld, Tina Redse, Mike Merin, Al Eisenstat, Arthur Rock. Tina Redse email to Steve Jobs, July 20, 2010; "No Job for Jobs," AP, July 26, 1985; "Jobs Talks about His Rise and Fall," *Newsweek*, Sept. 30, 1985; Hertzfeld, 269–271; Young, 387, 403–405; Young and Simon, 116; Rose, 288–292; Sculley, 242–245, 286–287; letter from Al Eisenstat to Arthur Hartman, July 23, 1985 (courtesy of Al Eisenstat).

CHAPTER 18: NeXT

The Pirates Abandon Ship: Interviews with Dan'l Lewin, Steve Jobs, Bill Campbell, Arthur Rock, Mike Markkula, John Sculley, Andrea Cunningham, Joanna Hoffman. Patricia Bellew Gray and Michael Miller, "Apple Chairman Jobs Resigns," *Wall Street Journal*, Sept. 18, 1985; Gerald Lubenow and Michael Rogers, "Jobs Talks about His Rise and Fall," *Newsweek*, Sept. 30, 1985; Bro Uttal, "The Adventures of Steve Jobs," *Fortune*, Oct. 14, 1985; Susan Kerr, "Jobs Resigns," *Computer Systems News*, Sept. 23, 1985; "Shaken to the Very Core," *Time*, Sept. 30, 1985; John Eckhouse, "Apple Board Fuming at Steve Jobs," *San Francisco Chronicle*, Sept. 17, 1985; Hertzfeld, 132–133; Sculley, 313–317; Young, 415–416; Young and Simon, 127; Rose, 307–319; Stross, 73; Deutschman, 36; Complaint for Breaches of Fiduciary Obligations, *Apple Computer v. Steven P. Jobs and Richard A. Page*, Superior Court of California, Santa Clara County, Sept. 23, 1985; Patricia Bellew Gray, "Jobs Asserts Apple Undermined Efforts to Settle Dispute," *Wall Street Journal*, Sept. 25, 1985.

To Be on Your Own: Interviews with Arthur Rock, Susan Kare, Steve Jobs, Al Eisenstat. "Logo for Jobs' New Firm," *San Francisco Chronicle*, June 19, 1986; Phil Patton, "Steve Jobs: Out for Revenge," *New York Times*, Aug. 6, 1989; Paul Rand, NeXT Logo presentation, 1985; Doug Evans and Allan Pottasch, video interview with Steve Jobs on Paul Rand, 1993; Steve Jobs to Al Eisenstat, Nov. 4, 1985; Eisenstat to Jobs, Nov. 8, 1985; Agreement between Apple Computer Inc. and Steven P. Jobs, and Request for Dismissal of Lawsuit without Prejudice, filed in the Superior Court of California, Santa Clara County, Jan. 17, 1986; Deutschman, 47, 43; Stross, 76, 118–120, 245; Kunkel, 58–63; "Can He Do It Again?" *Business Week*, Oct. 24, 1988; Joe Nocera, "The Second

Coming of Steve Jobs," *Esquire*, Dec. 1986, reprinted in *Good Guys and Bad Guys* (Portfolio, 2008), 49; Brenton Schlender, "How Steve Jobs Linked Up with IBM," *Fortune*, Oct. 9, 1989.

The Computer: Interviews with Mitch Kapor, Michael Hawley, Steve Jobs. Peter Denning and Karen Frenkel, "A Conversation with Steve Jobs," *Communications of the Association for Computer Machinery*, Apr. 1, 1989; John Eckhouse, "Steve Jobs Shows Off Ultra-Robotic Assembly Line," *San Francisco Chronicle*, June 13, 1989; Stross, 122–125; Deutschman, 60–63; Young, 425; Katie Hafner, "Can He Do It Again?" *Business Week*, Oct. 24, 1988; *The Entrepreneurs*, PBS, Nov. 5, 1986, directed by John Nathan.

Perot to the Rescue: Stross, 102–112; "Perot and Jobs," *Newsweek*, Feb. 9, 1987; Andrew Pollack, "Can Steve Jobs Do It Again?" *New York Times*, Nov. 8, 1987; Katie Hafner, "Can He Do It Again?" *Business Week*, Oct. 24, 1988; Pat Steger, "A Gem of an Evening with King Juan Carlos," *San Francisco Chronicle*, Oct. 5, 1987; David Remnick, "How a Texas Playboy Became a Billionaire," *Washington Post*, May 20, 1987.

Gates and NeXT: Interviews with Bill Gates, Adele Goldberg, Steve Jobs. Brit Hume, "Steve Jobs Pulls Ahead," *Washington Post*, Oct. 31, 1988; Brent Schlender, "How Steve Jobs Linked Up with IBM," *Fortune*, Oct. 9, 1989; Stross, 14; Linzmayer, 209; "William Gates Talks," *Washington Post*, Dec. 30, 1990; Katie Hafner, "Can He Do It Again?" *Business Week*, Oct. 24, 1988; John Thompson, "Gates, Jobs Swap Barbs," *Computer System News*, Nov. 27, 1989.

IBM: Brent Schlender, "How Steve Jobs Linked Up with IBM," *Fortune*, Oct. 9, 1989; Phil Patton, "Out for Revenge," *New York Times*, Aug. 6, 1989; Stross, 140–142; Deutschman, 133.

The Launch, October 1988: Stross, 166–186; Wes Smith, "Jobs Has Returned," *Chicago Tribune*, Nov. 13, 1988; Andrew Pollack, "NeXT Produces a Gala," *New York Times*, Oct. 10, 1988; Brenton Schlender, "Next Project," *Wall Street Journal*, Oct. 13, 1988; Katie Hafner, "Can He Do It Again?" *Business Week*, Oct. 24, 1988; Deutschman, 128; "Steve Jobs Comes Back," *Newsweek*, Oct. 24, 1988; "The NeXT Generation," *San Jose Mercury News*, Oct. 10, 1988.

CHAPTER 19: PIXAR

Lucasfilm's Computer Division: Interviews with Ed Catmull, Alvy Ray Smith, Steve Jobs, Pam Kerwin, Michael Eisner. Price, 71–74, 89–101; Paik, 53–57, 226; Young and Simon, 169; Deutschman, 115.

Animation: Interviews with John Lasseter, Steve Jobs. Paik, 28–44; Price, 45–56.

Tin Toy: Interviews with Pam Kerwin, Alvy Ray Smith, John Lasseter, Ed Catmull, Steve Jobs, Jeffrey Katzenberg, Michael Eisner, Andy Grove. Steve Jobs email to Albert Yu, Sept. 23, 1995; Albert Yu to Steve Jobs, Sept. 25, 1995; Steve Jobs to Andy Grove, Sept. 25, 1995; Andy Grove to Steve Jobs, Sept. 26, 1995; Steve Jobs to Andy Grove, Oct. 1, 1995; Price, 104–114; Young and Simon, 166.

CHAPTER 20: A REGULAR GUY

Joan Baez: Interviews with Joan Baez, Steve Jobs, Joanna Hoffman, Debi Coleman, Andy Hertzfeld. Joan Baez, *And a Voice to Sing With* (Summit, 1989), 144, 380.

Finding Joanne and Mona: Interviews with Steve Jobs, Mona Simpson.

The Lost Father: Interviews with Steve Jobs, Laurene Powell, Mona Simpson, Ken Auletta, Nick Pileggi.

Lisa: Interviews with Chrisann Brennan, Avie Tevanian, Joanna Hoffman, Andy Hertzfeld. Lisa Brennan-Jobs, "Confessions of a Lapsed Vegetarian," *Southwest Review*, 2008; Young, 224; Deutschman, 76.

The Romantic: Interviews with Jennifer Egan, Tina Redse, Steve Jobs, Andy Hertzfeld, Joanna Hoffman. Deutschman, 73, 138. Mona Simpson's *A Regular Guy* is a novel loosely based on the relationship between Jobs, Lisa and Chrisann Brennan, and Tina Redse, who is the basis for the character named Olivia.

CHAPTER 21: FAMILY MAN

Laurene Powell: Interviews with Laurene Powell, Steve Jobs, Kathryn Smith, Avie Tevanian, Andy Hertzfeld, Marjorie Powell Barden.

The Wedding, March 18, 1991: Interviews with Steve Jobs, Laurene Powell, Andy Hertzfeld, Joanna Hoffman, Avie Tevanian, Mona Simpson. Simpson, *A Regular Guy*, 357.

A Family Home: Interviews with Steve Jobs, Laurene Powell, Andy Hertzfeld. David Weinstein, "Taking Whimsy Seriously," *San Francisco Chronicle*, Sept. 13, 2003; Gary Wolfe, "Steve Jobs," *Wired*, Feb. 1996; "Former Apple Designer Charged with Harassing Steve Jobs," AP, June 8, 1993.

Lisa Moves In: Interviews with Steve Jobs, Laurene Powell, Mona Simpson, Andy Hertzfeld. Lisa Brennan-Jobs, "Driving Jane," *Harvard Advocate*, Spring

1999; Simpson, *A Regular Guy,* 251; email from Chrisann Brennan, Jan. 19, 2011; Bill Workman, "Palo Alto High School's Student Scoop," *San Francisco Chronicle*, Mar. 16, 1996; Lisa Brennan-Jobs, "Waterloo," *Massachusetts Review*, Spring 2006; Deutschman, 258; Chrisann Brennan website, chrysanthemum .com; Steve Lohr, "Creating Jobs," *New York Times*, Jan. 12, 1997.

Children: Interviews with Steve Jobs, Laurene Powell.

CHAPTER 22: TOY STORY

Jeffrey Katzenberg: Interviews with John Lasseter, Ed Catmull, Jeffrey Katzenberg, Alvy Ray Smith, Steve Jobs. Price, 84–85, 119–124; Paik, 71, 90; Robert Murphy, "John Cooley Looks at Pixar's Creative Process," *Silicon Prairie News*, Oct. 6, 2010.

Cut! Interviews with Steve Jobs, Jeffrey Katzenberg, Ed Catmull, Larry Ellison. Paik, 90; Deutschman, 194–198; "Toy Story: The Inside Buzz," *Entertainment Weekly*, Dec. 8, 1995.

To Infinity! Interviews with Steve Jobs, Michael Eisner. Janet Maslin, "There's a New Toy in the House. Uh-Oh," *New York Times*, Nov. 22, 1995; "A Conversation with Steve Jobs and John Lasseter," *Charlie Rose*, PBS, Oct. 30, 1996; John Markoff, "Apple Computer Co-Founder Strikes Gold," *New York Times*, Nov. 30, 1995.

CHAPTER 23: THE SECOND COMING

Things Fall Apart: Interview with Jean-Louis Gassée. Bart Ziegler, "Industry Has Next to No Patience with Jobs' NeXT," AP, Aug. 19, 1990; Stross, 226–228; Gary Wolf, "The Next Insanely Great Thing," *Wired*, Feb. 1996; Anthony Perkins, "Jobs' Story," *Red Herring*, Jan. 1, 1996.

Apple Falling: Interviews with Steve Jobs, John Sculley, Larry Ellison. Sculley, 248, 273; Deutschman, 236; Steve Lohr, "Creating Jobs," *New York Times*, Jan. 12, 1997; Amelio, 190 and preface to the hardback edition; Young and Simon, 213–214; Linzmayer, 273–279; Guy Kawasaki, "Steve Jobs to Return as Apple CEO," *Macworld*, Nov. 1, 1994.

Slouching toward Cupertino: Interviews with Jon Rubinstein, Steve Jobs, Larry Ellison, Avie Tevanian, Fred Anderson, Larry Tesler, Bill Gates, John Lasseter. John Markoff, "Why Apple Sees Next as a Match Made in Heaven," *New York Times*, Dec. 23, 1996; Steve Lohr, "Creating Jobs," *New York Times*, Jan. 12, 1997; Rajiv Chandrasekaran, "Steve Jobs Returning to Apple," *Wash-*

ington Post, Dec. 21, 1996; Louise Kehoe, "Apple's Prodigal Son Returns," *Financial Times*, Dec. 23, 1996; Amelio, 189–201, 238; Carlton, 409; Linzmayer, 277; Deutschman, 240.

CHAPTER 24: THE RESTORATION

Hovering Backstage: Interviews with Steve Jobs, Avie Tevanian, Jon Rubinstein, Ed Woolard, Larry Ellison, Fred Anderson, email from Gina Smith. Sheff; Brent Schlender, "Something's Rotten in Cupertino," *Fortune*, Mar. 3, 1997; Dan Gillmore, "Apple's Prospects Better Than Its CEO's Speech," *San Jose Mercury News*, Jan. 13, 1997; Carlton, 414–416, 425; Malone, 531; Deutschman, 241–245; Amelio, 219, 238–247, 261; Linzmayer, 201; Kaitlin Quistgaard, "Apple Spins Off Newton," *Wired.com*, May 22, 1997; Louise Kehoe, "Doubts Grow about Leadership at Apple," *Financial Times*, Feb. 25, 1997; Dan Gillmore, "Ellison Mulls Apple Bid," *San Jose Mercury News*, Mar. 27, 1997; Lawrence Fischer, "Oracle Seeks Public Views on Possible Bid for Apple," *New York Times*, Mar. 28, 1997; Mike Barnicle, "Roadkill on the Info Highway," *Boston Globe*, Aug. 5, 1997.

Exit, Pursued by a Bear: Interviews with Ed Woolard, Steve Jobs, Mike Markkula, Steve Wozniak, Fred Anderson, Larry Ellison, Bill Campbell. Privately printed family memoir by Ed Woolard (courtesy of Woolard); Amelio, 247, 261, 267; Gary Wolf, "The World According to Woz," *Wired*, Sept. 1998; Peter Burrows and Ronald Grover, "Steve Jobs' Magic Kingdom," *Business Week*, Feb. 6, 2006; Peter Elkind, "The Trouble with Steve Jobs," *Fortune*, Mar. 5, 2008; Arthur Levitt, *Take on the Street* (Pantheon, 2002), 204–206.

Macworld Boston, August 1997: Steve Jobs, Macworld Boston speech, Aug. 6, 1997.

The Microsoft Pact: Interviews with Joel Klein, Bill Gates, Steve Jobs. Cathy Booth, "Steve's Job," *Time*, Aug. 18, 1997; Steven Levy, "A Big Brother?" *Newsweek*, Aug. 18, 1997. Jobs's cell phone call with Gates was reported by *Time* photographer Diana Walker, who shot the picture of him crouching onstage that appeared on the *Time* cover and in the photo section of this book.

CHAPTER 25: THINK DIFFERENT

Here's to the Crazy Ones: Interviews with Steve Jobs, Lee Clow, James Vincent, Norman Pearlstine. Cathy Booth, "Steve's Job," *Time*, Aug. 18, 1997; John Heilemann, "Steve Jobs in a Box," *New York*, June 17, 2007.

iCEO: Interviews with Steve Jobs, Fred Anderson. Video of Sept. 1997 staff meeting (courtesy of Lee Clow); "Jobs Hints That He May Want to Stay at Apple," *New York Times*, Oct. 10, 1997; Jon Swartz, "No CEO in Sight for Apple," *San Francisco Chronicle*, Dec. 12, 1997; Carlton, 437.

Killing the Clones: Interviews with Bill Gates, Steve Jobs, Ed Woolard. Steve Wozniak, "How We Failed Apple," *Newsweek*, Feb. 19, 1996; Linzmayer, 245–247, 255; Bill Gates, "Licensing of Mac Technology," a memo to John Sculley, June 25, 1985; Tom Abate, "How Jobs Killed Mac Clone Makers," *San Francisco Chronicle*, Sept. 6, 1997.

Product Line Review: Interviews with Phil Schiller, Ed Woolard, Steve Jobs. Deutschman, 248; Steve Jobs, speech at iMac launch event, May 6, 1998; video of Sept. 1997 staff meeting.

CHAPTER 26: DESIGN PRINCIPLES

Jony Ive: Interviews with Jony Ive, Steve Jobs, Phil Schiller. John Arlidge, "Father of Invention," *Observer* (London), Dec. 21, 2003; Peter Burrows, "Who Is Jonathan Ive?" *Business Week*, Sept. 25, 2006; "Apple's One-Dollar-a-Year Man," *Fortune*, Jan. 24, 2000; Rob Walker, "The Guts of a New Machine," *New York Times*, Nov. 30, 2003; Leander Kahney, "Design According to Ive," *Wired.com*, June 25, 2003.

Inside the Studio: Interview with Jony Ive. U.S. Patent and Trademark Office, online database, patft.uspto.gov; Leander Kahney, "Jobs Awarded Patent for iPhone Packaging," *Cult of Mac*, July 22, 2009; Harry McCracken, "Patents of Steve Jobs," *Technologizer.com*, May 28, 2009.

CHAPTER 27: THE iMAC

Back to the Future: Interviews with Phil Schiller, Avie Tevanian, Jon Rubinstein, Steve Jobs, Fred Anderson, Mike Markkula, Jony Ive, Lee Clow. Thomas Hormby, "Birth of the iMac," *Mac Observer*, May 25, 2007; Peter Burrows, "Who Is Jonathan Ive?" *Business Week*, Sept. 25, 2006; Lev Grossman, "How Apple Does It," *Time*, Oct. 16, 2005; Leander Kahney, "The Man Who Named the iMac and Wrote Think Different," *Cult of Mac*, Nov. 3, 2009; Levy, *The Perfect Thing*, 198; gawker.com/comment/21123257/; "Steve's Two Jobs," *Time*, Oct. 18, 1999.

The Launch, May 6, 1998: Interviews with Jony Ive, Steve Jobs, Phil Schiller, Jon Rubinstein. Steven Levy, "Hello Again," *Newsweek*, May 18, 1998; Jon

Swartz, "Resurgence of an American Icon," *Forbes*, Apr. 14, 2000; Levy, *The Perfect Thing*, 95.

CHAPTER 28: CEO

Tim Cook: Interviews with Tim Cook, Steve Jobs, Jon Rubinstein. Peter Burrows, "Yes, Steve, You Fixed It. Congratulations. Now What?" *Business Week*, July 31, 2000; Tim Cook, Auburn commencement address, May 14, 2010; Adam Lashinsky, "The Genius behind Steve," *Fortune*, Nov. 10, 2008; Nick Wingfield, "Apple's No. 2 Has Low Profile," *Wall Street Journal*, Oct. 16, 2006.

Mock Turtlenecks and Teamwork: Interviews with Steve Jobs, James Vincent, Jony Ive, Lee Clow, Avie Tevanian, Jon Rubinstein. Lev Grossman, "How Apple Does It," *Time*, Oct. 16, 2005; Leander Kahney, "How Apple Got Everything Right by Doing Everything Wrong," *Wired*, Mar. 18, 2008.

From iCEO to CEO: Interviews with Ed Woolard, Larry Ellison, Steve Jobs. Apple proxy statement, Mar. 12, 2001.

CHAPTER 29: APPLE STORES

The Customer Experience: Interviews with Steve Jobs, Ron Johnson. Jerry Useem, "America's Best Retailer," *Fortune*, Mar. 19, 2007; Gary Allen, "Apple Stores," ifoAppleStore.com.

The Prototype: Interviews with Art Levinson, Ed Woolard, Millard "Mickey" Drexler, Larry Ellison, Ron Johnson, Steve Jobs, Art Levinson. Cliff Edwards, "Sorry, Steve . . . ," *Business Week*, May 21, 2001.

Wood, Stone, Steel, Glass: Interviews with Ron Johnson, Steve Jobs. U.S. Patent Office, D478999, Aug. 26, 2003, US2004/0006939, Jan. 15, 2004; Gary Allen, "About Me," ifoapplestore.com.

CHAPTER 30: THE DIGITAL HUB

Connecting the Dots: Interviews with Lee Clow, Jony Ive, Steve Jobs. Sheff; Steve Jobs, Macworld keynote address, Jan. 9, 2001.

FireWire: Interviews with Steve Jobs, Phil Schiller, Jon Rubinstein. Steve Jobs, Macworld keynote address, Jan. 9, 2001; Joshua Quittner, "Apple's New Core," *Time*, Jan. 14, 2002; Mike Evangelist, "Steve Jobs, the Genuine Article," *Writer's Block Live*, Oct. 7, 2005; Farhad Manjoo, "Invincible Apple," *Fast Company*, July 1, 2010; email from Phil Schiller.

iTunes: Interviews with Steve Jobs, Phil Schiller, Jon Rubinstein, Tony

Fadell. Brent Schlender, "How Big Can Apple Get," *Fortune*, Feb. 21, 2005; Bill Kincaid, "The True Story of SoundJam," http://panic.com/extras/audionstory/popup-sjstory.html; Levy, *The Perfect Thing*, 49–60; Knopper, 167; Lev Grossman, "How Apple Does It," *Time*, Oct. 17, 2005; Markoff, xix.

The iPod: Interviews with Steve Jobs, Phil Schiller, Jon Rubinstein, Tony Fadell. Steve Jobs, iPod announcement, Oct. 23, 2001; Toshiba press releases, PR Newswire, May 10, 2000, and June 4, 2001; Tekla Perry, "From Podfather to Palm's Pilot," *IEEE Spectrum*, Sept. 2008; Leander Kahney, "Inside Look at Birth of the iPod," *Wired*, July 21, 2004; Tom Hormby and Dan Knight, "History of the iPod," *Low End Mac*, Oct. 14, 2005.

That's It! Interviews with Tony Fadell, Phil Schiller, Jon Rubinstein, Jony Ive, Steve Jobs. Levy, *The Perfect Thing*, 17, 59–60; Knopper, 169; Leander Kahney, "Straight Dope on the IPod's Birth," *Wired*, Oct. 17, 2006.

The Whiteness of the Whale: Interviews with James Vincent, Lee Clow, Steve Jobs. Wozniak, 298; Levy, *The Perfect Thing*, 73; Johnny Davis, "Ten Years of the iPod," *Guardian*, Mar. 18, 2011.

CHAPTER 31: THE iTUNES STORE

Warner Music: Interviews with Paul Vidich, Steve Jobs, Doug Morris, Barry Schuler, Roger Ames, Eddy Cue. Paul Sloan, "What's Next for Apple," *Business 2.0*, Apr. 1, 2005; Knopper, 157–161,170; Devin Leonard, "Songs in the Key of Steve," *Fortune*, May 12, 2003; Tony Perkins, interview with Nobuyuki Idei and Sir Howard Stringer, World Economic Forum, Davos, Jan. 25, 2003; Dan Tynan, "The 25 Worst Tech Products of All Time," *PC World*, Mar. 26, 2006; Andy Langer, "The God of Music," *Esquire*, July 2003; Jeff Goodell, "Steve Jobs," *Rolling Stone*, Dec. 3, 2003.

Herding Cats: Interviews with Doug Morris, Roger Ames, Steve Jobs, Jimmy Iovine, Andy Lack, Eddy Cue, Wynton Marsalis. Knopper, 172; Devin Leonard, "Songs in the Key of Steve," *Fortune*, May 12, 2003; Peter Burrows, "Show Time!" *Business Week*, Feb. 2, 2004; Pui-Wing Tam, Bruce Orwall, and Anna Wilde Mathews, "Going Hollywood," *Wall Street Journal*, Apr. 25, 2003; Steve Jobs, keynote speech, Apr. 28, 2003; Andy Langer, "The God of Music," *Esquire*, July 2003; Steven Levy, "Not the Same Old Song," *Newsweek*, May 12, 2003.

Microsoft: Interviews with Steve Jobs, Phil Schiller, Tim Cook, Jon Rubinstein, Tony Fadell, Eddy Cue. Emails from Jim Allchin, David Cole, Bill Gates,

Apr. 30, 2003 (these emails later became part of an Iowa court case and Steve Jobs sent me copies); Steve Jobs, presentation, Oct. 16, 2003; Walt Mossberg interview with Steve Jobs, All Things Digital conference, May 30, 2007; Bill Gates, "We're Early on the Video Thing," *Business Week*, Sept. 2, 2004.

Mr. Tambourine Man: Interviews with Andy Lack, Tim Cook, Steve Jobs, Tony Fadell, Jon Rubinstein. Ken Belson, "Infighting Left Sony behind Apple in Digital Music," *New York Times*, Apr. 19, 2004; Frank Rose, "Battle for the Soul of the MP3 Phone," *Wired*, Nov. 2005; Saul Hansel, "Gates vs. Jobs: The Rematch," *New York Times*, Nov. 14, 2004; John Borland, "Can Glaser and Jobs Find Harmony?" *CNET News*, Aug. 17, 2004; Levy, *The Perfect Thing*, 169.

CHAPTER 32: MUSIC MAN

On His iPod: Interviews with Steve Jobs, James Vincent. Elisabeth Bumiller, "President Bush's iPod," *New York Times*, Apr. 11, 2005; Levy, *The Perfect Thing*, 26–29; Devin Leonard, "Songs in the Key of Steve," *Fortune*, May 12, 2003.

Bob Dylan: Interviews with Jeff Rosen, Andy Lack, Eddy Cue, Steve Jobs, James Vincent, Lee Clow. Matthew Creamer, "Bob Dylan Tops Music Chart Again—and Apple's a Big Reason Why," *Ad Age*, Oct. 8, 2006.

The Beatles; Bono; Yo-Yo Ma: Interviews with Bono, John Eastman, Steve Jobs, Yo-Yo Ma, George Riley.

CHAPTER 33: PIXAR'S FRIENDS

A Bug's Life: Interviews with Jeffrey Katzenberg, John Lasseter, Steve Jobs. Price, 171–174; Paik, 116; Peter Burrows, "Antz vs. Bugs" and "Steve Jobs: Movie Mogul," *Business Week*, Nov. 23, 1998; Amy Wallace, "Ouch! That Stings," *Los Angeles Times*, Sept. 21, 1998; Kim Masters, "Battle of the Bugs," *Time*, Sept. 28, 1998; Richard Schickel, "Antz," *Time*, Oct. 12, 1998; Richard Corliss, "Bugs Funny," *Time*, Nov. 30, 1998.

Steve's Own Movie: Interviews with John Lasseter, Pam Kerwin, Ed Catmull, Steve Jobs. Paik, 168; Rick Lyman, "A Digital Dream Factory in Silicon Valley," *New York Times*, June 11, 2001.

The Divorce: Interviews with Mike Slade, Oren Jacob, Michael Eisner, Bob Iger, Steve Jobs, John Lasseter, Ed Catmull. James Stewart, *Disney War* (Simon & Schuster, 2005), 383; Price, 230–235; Benny Evangelista, "Parting

Slam by Pixar's Jobs," *San Francisco Chronicle*, Feb. 5, 2004; John Markoff and Laura Holson, "New iPod Will Play TV Shows," *New York Times*, Oct. 13, 2005.

CHAPTER 34: TWENTY-FIRST-CENTURY MACS

Clams, Ice Cubes, and Sunflowers: Interviews with Jon Rubinstein, Jony Ive, Laurene Powell, Steve Jobs, Fred Anderson, George Riley. Steven Levy, "Thinking inside the Box," *Newsweek*, July 31, 2000; Brent Schlender, "Steve Jobs," *Fortune*, May 14, 2001; Ian Fried, "Apple Slices Revenue Forecast Again," *CNET News*, Dec. 6, 2000; Linzmayer, 301; U.S. Design Patent D510577S, granted on Oct. 11, 2005.

Intel Inside: Interviews with Paul Otellini, Bill Gates, Art Levinson. Carlton, 436.

Options: Interviews with Ed Woolard, George Riley, Al Gore, Fred Anderson, Eric Schmidt. Geoff Colvin, "The Great CEO Heist," *Fortune*, June 25, 2001; Joe Nocera, "Weighing Jobs's Role in a Scandal," *New York Times*, Apr. 28, 2007; Deposition of Steven P. Jobs, Mar. 18, 2008, *SEC v. Nancy Heinen*, U.S. District Court, Northern District of California; William Barrett, "Nobody Loves Me," *Forbes*, May 11, 2009; Peter Elkind, "The Trouble with Steve Jobs," *Fortune*, Mar. 5, 2008.

CHAPTER 35: ROUND ONE

Cancer: Interviews with Steve Jobs, Laurene Powell, Art Levinson, Larry Brilliant, Dean Ornish, Bill Campbell, Andy Grove, Andy Hertzfeld.

The Stanford Commencement: Interviews with Steve Jobs, Laurene Powell. Steve Jobs, Stanford commencement address.

A Lion at Fifty: Interviews with Mike Slade, Alice Waters, Steve Jobs, Tim Cook, Avie Tevanian, Jony Ive, Jon Rubinstein, Tony Fadell, George Riley, Bono, Walt Mossberg, Steven Levy, Kara Swisher. Walt Mossberg and Kara Swisher interviews with Steve Jobs and Bill Gates, All Things Digital conference, May 30, 2007; Steven Levy, "Finally, Vista Makes Its Debut," *Newsweek*, Feb. 1, 2007.

CHAPTER 36: THE iPHONE

An iPod That Makes Calls: Interviews with Art Levinson, Steve Jobs, Tony Fadell, George Riley, Tim Cook. Frank Rose, "Battle for the Soul of the MP3 Phone," *Wired*, Nov. 2005.

Multi-touch: Interviews with Jony Ive, Steve Jobs, Tony Fadell, Tim Cook.

Gorilla Glass: Interviews with Wendell Weeks, John Seeley Brown, Steve Jobs.

The Design: Interviews with Jony Ive, Steve Jobs, Tony Fadell. Fred Vogelstein, "The Untold Story," *Wired*, Jan. 9, 2008.

The Launch: Interviews with John Huey, Nicholas Negroponte. Lev Grossman, "Apple's New Calling," *Time*, Jan. 22, 2007; Steve Jobs, speech, Macworld, Jan. 9, 2007; John Markoff, "Apple Introduces Innovative Cellphone," *New York Times*, Jan. 10, 2007; John Heilemann, "Steve Jobs in a Box," *New York*, June 17, 2007; Janko Roettgers, "Alan Kay: With the Tablet, Apple Will Rule the World," *GigaOM*, Jan. 26, 2010.

CHAPTER 37: ROUND TWO

The Battles of 2008: Interviews with Steve Jobs, Kathryn Smith, Bill Campbell, Art Levinson, Al Gore, John Huey, Andy Serwer, Laurene Powell, Doug Morris, Jimmy Iovine. Peter Elkind, "The Trouble with Steve Jobs," *Fortune*, Mar. 5, 2008; Joe Nocera, "Apple's Culture of Secrecy," *New York Times*, July 26, 2008; Steve Jobs, letter to the Apple community, Jan. 5 and Jan. 14, 2009; Doron Levin, "Steve Jobs Went to Switzerland in Search of Cancer Treatment," *Fortune.com*, Jan. 18, 2011; Yukari Kanea and Joann Lublin, "On Apple's Board, Fewer Independent Voices," *Wall Street Journal*, Mar. 24, 2010; Micki Maynard (Micheline Maynard), Twitter post, 2:45 p.m., Jan. 18, 2011; Ryan Chittum, "The Dead Source Who Keeps on Giving," *Columbia Journalism Review*, Jan. 18, 2011.

Memphis: Interviews with Steve Jobs, Laurene Powell, George Riley, Kristina Kiehl, Kathryn Smith. John Lauerman and Connie Guglielmo, "Jobs Liver Transplant," *Bloomberg*, Aug. 21, 2009.

Return: Interviews with Steve Jobs, George Riley, Tim Cook, Jony Ive, Brian Roberts, Andy Hertzfeld.

CHAPTER 38: THE iPAD

You Say You Want a Revolution: Interviews with Steve Jobs, Phil Schiller, Tim Cook, Jony Ive, Tony Fadell, Paul Otellini. All Things Digital conference, May 30, 2003.

The Launch, January 2010: Interviews with Steve Jobs, Daniel Kottke. Brent Schlender, "Bill Gates Joins the iPad Army of Critics," *bnet.com*, Feb. 10, 2010; Steve Jobs, keynote address in San Francisco, Jan. 27, 2010; Nick Summers, "Instant Apple iPad Reaction," *Newsweek.com*, Jan. 27, 2010; Adam Frucci, "Eight Things That Suck about the iPad" Gizmodo, Jan. 27, 2010; Lev Grossman, "Do We Need the iPad?" *Time*, Apr. 1, 2010; Daniel Lyons, "Think Really Different," *Newsweek*, Mar. 26, 2010; Techmate debate, *Fortune*, Apr. 12, 2010; Eric Laningan, "Wozniak on the iPad" TwiT TV, Apr. 5, 2010; Michael Shear, "At White House, a New Question: What's on Your iPad?" *Washington Post*, June 7, 2010; Michael Noer, "The Stable Boy and the iPad," *Forbes.com*, Sept. 8, 2010.

Advertising: Interviews with Steve Jobs, James Vincent, Lee Clow.

Apps: Interviews with Art Levinson, Phil Schiller, Steve Jobs, John Doerr.

Publishing and Journalism: Interviews with Steve Jobs, Jeff Bewkes, Rick Stengel, Andy Serwer, Josh Quittner, Rupert Murdoch. Ken Auletta, "Publish or Perish," *New Yorker*, Apr. 26, 2010; Ryan Tate, "The Price of Crossing Steve Jobs," Gawker, Sept. 30, 2010.

CHAPTER 39: NEW BATTLES

Google: Open versus Closed: Interviews with Steve Jobs, Bill Campbell, Eric Schmidt, John Doerr, Tim Cook, Bill Gates. John Abell, "Google's 'Don't Be Evil' Mantra Is 'Bullshit,' " *Wired*, Jan. 30, 2010; Brad Stone and Miguel Helft, "A Battle for the Future Is Getting Personal," *New York Times*, March 14, 2010.

Flash, the App Store, and Control: Interviews with Steve Jobs, Bill Campbell, Tom Friedman, Art Levinson, Al Gore. Leander Kahney, "What Made Apple Freeze Out Adobe?" *Wired*, July 2010; Jean-Louis Gassée, "The Adobe-Apple Flame War," *Monday Note*, Apr. 11, 2010; Steve Jobs, "Thoughts on Flash," Apple.com, Apr. 29, 2010; Walt Mossberg and Kara Swisher, Steve Jobs interview, All Things Digital conference, June 1, 2010; Robert X. Cringely (pseudonym), "Steve Jobs: Savior or Tyrant?" *InfoWorld*, Apr. 21, 2010; Ryan Tate, "Steve Jobs Offers World 'Freedom from Porn,' " Valleywag, May 15, 2010; JR Raphael, "I Want Porn," esarcasm.com, Apr. 20, 2010; Jon Stewart, *The Daily Show*, Apr. 28, 2010.

Antennagate: Design versus Engineering: Interviews with Tony Fadell, Jony Ive, Steve Jobs, Art Levinson, Tim Cook, Regis McKenna, Bill Campbell, James Vincent. Mark Gikas, "Why Consumer Reports Can't Recommend the iPhone4," *Consumer Reports*, July 12, 2010; Michael Wolff, "Is There Anything That Can Trip Up Steve Jobs?" *newser.com* and *vanityfair.com*, July 19, 2010; Scott Adams, "High Ground Maneuver," dilbert.com, July 19, 2010.

Here Comes the Sun: Interviews with Steve Jobs, Eddy Cue, James Vincent.

CHAPTER 40: TO INFINITY

The iPad 2: Interviews with Larry Ellison, Steve Jobs, Laurene Powell. Steve Jobs, speech, iPad 2 launch event, Mar. 2, 2011.

iCloud: Interviews with Steve Jobs, Eddy Cue. Steve Jobs, keynote address, Worldwide Developers Conference, June 6, 2011; Walt Mossberg, "Apple's Mobile Me Is Far Too Flawed to Be Reliable," *Wall Street Journal*, July 23, 2008; Adam Lashinsky, "Inside Apple," *Fortune*, May 23, 2011; Richard Waters, "Apple Races to Keep Users Firmly Wrapped in Its Cloud," *Financial Times*, June 9, 2011.

A New Campus: Interviews with Steve Jobs, Steve Wozniak, Ann Bowers. Steve Jobs, appearance before the Cupertino City Council, June 7, 2011.

CHAPTER 41: ROUND THREE

Family Ties: Interviews with Laurene Powell, Erin Jobs, Steve Jobs, Kathryn Smith, Jennifer Egan. Email from Steve Jobs, June 8, 2010, 4:55 p.m.; Tina Redse to Steve Jobs, July 20, 2010, and Feb. 6, 2011.

President Obama: Interviews with David Axelrod, Steve Jobs, John Doerr, Laurene Powell, Valerie Jarrett, Eric Schmidt, Austan Goolsbee.

Third Medical Leave, 2011: Interviews with Kathryn Smith, Steve Jobs, Larry Brilliant.

Visitors: Interviews with Steve Jobs, Bill Gates, Mike Slade.

CHAPTER 42: LEGACY

Jonathan Zittrain, *The Future of the Internet—And How to Stop It* (Yale, 2008), 2; Cory Doctorow, "Why I Won't Buy an iPad," Boing Boing, Apr. 2, 2010.

INDEX

Page numbers in *italics* refer to illustrations.

Abby Road (Beatles), 412
ABC, 219, 436, 438
Academy Awards, 244, 248
Adams, Ansel, 105, 276, 330
Adams, Scott, 523
Adobe, 241, 247, 381, 518
   Apple and, 514–16
Adobe Director, 363
Adobe Flash, 380, 514–15, 517
Adobe Illustrator, 242
Adobe Photoshop, 380
Adobe Premiere, 380
Advertising Age, 165, 418
Advocate, The, 279, 281
A4 (microchip), 492–93, 496
Agnelli, Susanna, 126
Aguilera, Christina, 418
Agus, David, 549
Airborne Express, 359
Air Force, U.S., 23
AirPort (base station), 466
Akers, John, 219, 231, 569
Akon (performer), 479

Aladdin (film), 439
Alcorn, Al, xiii, 42–43, 45, 52, 54,
   67, 72, 74, 195
Ali, Muhammad, 307
Alinsangan, Susan, 391
Allchin, Jim, 403
Allen, Gary, 376
Allen, Paul, 59, 61
Allen, Tim, 432
Allen, Woody, 429
All One Farm (commune), 39, 50,
   53, 59, 63, 103
All Things Digital conference,
   463
"All Watched Over by Machines
   of Loving Grace" (Brautigan),
   57
Alps Electronics Co., 146–47
Altair (personal computer), 59, 173
Alto (computer), 95
Amazon, 410, 531, 533
   Kindle of, 503, 534
   SJ on, 503–4

Amelio, Gil, xiii, 296–97, 327, 332,
    335, 336, 341
  Apple-NeXT deal and, 299–303
  Macworld gaffe of, 307–8, 339
  media and, 311–12
  Newton crisis and, 309, 338
  ouster of, 305–15, 324, 326
  ship parable of, 310
  SJ's first meeting with, 297–98,
    304, 316–17
American Express, 410
Ames, Roger, 398–99, 401, 402
Ames Research Center, 8–9
Anderson, Fred, 313, 316, 317,
    332, 349, 459
  backdated stock options
    controversy and, 450–51
Angelou, Maya, 330
"Annie" skunkworks project, 94,
    109
Ansen, David, 290
"Antennagate," 519–23
Antz (film), 427–30
Anywhere but Here (Simpson), 4,
    254–55
AOL, 502
AOL Time Warner, 394–95, 398,
    407
Apollo 13 (film), 290
Appel, Richard, *250*, 273, 547
Apple Computer Co., 54, 90, 132,
    207, 239, 295, 306–7, 308,
    317–22, 394–95, 409, 512
  Adobe and, 514–16
  Apple Corps lawsuits against,
    419–20, 523–24
  applications controlled by,
    516–17
  art-technology connection and,
    526–27

badge controversy in, 83
Blue Box and creation of, 27–30
business plan of, 76–77
collaborative culture of, 362–63
Cook Doctrine and, 488
Cook's role in, 360–61
design mantra of, 127
design philosophy of, 344–45
design studio of, 345–47
desktop concept and, 98–99
desktop publishing and, 295–96
incorporation of, 77–78
Intel chips adopted by, 446–48
IPO of, 102–4
logo of, xviii, 68–69, 79–80
Macintosh deal and, 324–25
Microsoft out-competed by,
    562–63
motto of, 69
name of, 63
NeXT and, 213–15, 217–18,
    221–22, 298–300, 305–6
original partnership of, 63–66,
    73
origins of, 61–63
product review process of,
    336–39
products of, 565–66
retreats of, 142–45, 147, 154–55,
    175, 398–99
Sculley's reorganization of,
    205–7
showcase headquarters of,
    534–35
SJ as interim CEO of, 332–33,
    364–65, 367
SJ ousted from, xvii–xviii, 202–6,
    215–16, 217
SJ's aesthetic and, 126–27
SJ-Scott dispute in, 83–84

SJ's resignations from, 215–16, 217, 303–4, 557–59, 563–64
SJ's return to, 306–8, 317–21
stock options controversy and, 365–66, 448–51, 477
turnover of board of, 318–20
uniforms idea and, 361–62
Wozniak's departure from, 192–93
Xerox "raided" by, 96–97, 98
Apple Corps, 419–20, 523–24
Apple Foundation, 263
Apple I computer, *56*, 63, 66, 163
early competition to, 69–70
first sales order for, 66–68
Wozniak and, 60–61, 67–68, 534
Apple II computer, 91, 93, 94, 109, 114, 125, 137, 138, 154, 173, 189, 192, 200, 207, 565
brochures of, 79–80
capitalization of, 72, 75, 77
circuit board of, 74–75
Commodore company and, 72–73
launch of, 80–81
Markkula and, 80–81
packaging of, 73–74
PC sales and, 160
peripherals and, 74–75
power supply of, 84, 146
sales of, 84, 92, 160
SJ's vision of, 71–72
Snow White ad for, 132–33
VisiCalc feature of, 84
warranty of, 84
Wozniak and, 80–81, 84–85, 92, 534, 562
Apple III computer, 92–94, 154
failure of, 92–93, 160
AppleLabs, 196–98, 203, 204–6

"Apple Marketing Philosophy, The" (Markkula), 78
Apple products, *see individual product names*
Apple Stores, 368–77, *368,* 461, 470, 472, 566
checkout design of, 372
on Fifth Avenue, 376–77, 514
first opening of, 374
floors of, 375
Gap and, 370
genius bar in, 375–76
minimalist nature of, 370
product organization in, 372–74
prototypes of, 371–74
staircases of, 375
success of, 374, 376
Apple University, 461
Arab Spring, 258
Architectural Digest, 275
ARM architecture, 492–93
Arnold Worldwide, 328
Aspen Institute, xvii, 126
Associated Press, 293
AT&T, 27, 136, 521
Atari, 42–45, 52, 53, 57, 63, 72, 74, 81, 217
SJ hired by, 83–84
Atkinson, Bill, xiii, 93–94, 95, 96–97, 99, 101, 110, 111, 113, *117,* 118, 122–23, 128–32, 134, 144, 179, 181, 207, 385, 470, 474, 554
Lisa Computer and, 99–101
overlapping windows concept of, 100, 323
QuickDraw program of, 169–70
SJ's worldview described by, 119–20

Atom (microchip), 492
Augmentation Research Center, 57
Auletta, Ken, 256
Autobiography of a Yogi (Yogananda), 35, 46–47, 527
Avon, 321, 481
Axelrod, David, 497, 546

Bach, Johann Sebastian, 413
Badu, Erykah, 479
Baez, Joan, 57, 153, 168, 261, 412, 415, 576
    SJ's romance with, 250–53
Ballmer, Steve, 375, 474, 569
Bank of America, 83
Barnes, Susan, 204, 212, 216
Barnicle, Mike, 312
Barrett, Craig, 448
Bartz, Carol, 545
BASIC (computer language), 59, 61, 66, 84, 94, 173, 174–75
Batman Forever (film), 290
Bauhaus movement, 126, 265, 372
Baum, Allen, 26, 60, 67, 77
Bay, Willow, 438
Bayer, Herbert, 126, 127
Beatles, 402, 412–13, 415, 418–19, 570
    in move to iTunes, 523–24
Beauty and the Beast (film), 439
Beck, Glenn, 508
Be company, 297–301
Be Here Now (Ram Dass), 34, 37, 52
Belleville, Bob, 99, 145–47, 190, 200, 204
Bellini, Mario, 126
Bell Labs, 9

Bell System Technical Manual, 27–28
Berg, Paul, 211–12
Berkeley Barb, 61
Bertelsmann, 395
Bertolucci, Bernardo, 126
Betrayal (Pinter), 204
Bewkes, Jeff, 506–7
Bezos, Jeff, 503
Big Mac (computer), 212, 214
Billboard, 418, 423
bitmapping concept, 95, 97, 111
BlackBerry, 469
Black Eyed Peas, 392, 413
Black-Scholes valuation, 449
Blade Runner (film), 163
Blood on the Tracks (Dylan), 52, 208, 412
Bloomberg News, 479, 497
Blue Box design, 27–30, 73
    SJ-Wozniak partnership and, 29–30
Blue Van, 498
Bob Dylan (Dylan), 412
Bohlin, Peter, 430
Bohlin Cywinski Jackson, 375
Bohr, Niels, 171
Boich, Mike, 177
Boing Boing, 563
Bono, 58, 180, 402, 406, 411, 424, 459–60
    iPod deal and, 420–23
"Book of Macintosh, The" (Raskin), 109
Boston Globe, 312
"Both Sides Now" (song), 414
Bourke-White, Margaret, 330
Bourne Ultimatum, The (film), 527
Bowers, Ann, 121, 537
Brand, Stewart, 58–59

Brandenburg Concertos (Bach), 413
Braun company, 132, 343
Brautigan, Richard, 57
Breaking Away (film), 126
Breakout (game), 118
Brennan, Chrisann, xiii, 5, 31–32, 41, 49, 86, 103, 104, 119, 257, 259, 265, 278–79, 280–81, 486
  pregnancy of, 88–90
  SJ's relationship with, 86–91
Brennan-Jobs, Lisa, xiii, 90, 140, 256, 257, 270, 541, 574
  Mona Simpson and, 281–82
  SJ's relationship with, 259–61, 265, 266, 278–82, 315, 486, 541, 551
Brilliant, Larry, 47, 106, 453
Brin, Sergey, 511–12
Brother Bear (film), 437
Brown, Bryar, 477, 548
Brown, John Seeley, 471
Brown, Tim, 32
"Brown Eyed Girl" (song), 411
Buffalo Springfield, 413
Buffett, Warren, 442
Bug's Life, A (film), 427–30
Bumiller, Elisabeth, 411–12
Burge, Frank, 79
Burroughs company, 20
Burton, Bill, 497
Bush, George H. W., 209
Bush, George W., 411, 516
Bushnell, Nolan, xiii, 42–44, 52–53, 54–55, 72, 75, 217
BusinessWeek, 141, 160, 166, 225, 236, 311, 320, 374, 406
Buyer, Lise, 463–64
Byron, George Gordon, Lord, 224
Byte Shop, 66–67, 68, 71, 368

Calder, Alexander, 151, 183
Calhoun, Greg, 5, 39, 51, 86–87, 88
California Motor Vehicle Department, 24
Callas, Maria, 330
Callaway (publisher), 502
Campanile, The, 279
Campbell, Bill, xiii, 164, 202, 206, 212–15, 320–21, 481, 482, 515, 557, 558, 577
Cannavino, Jim, 232
Canon, 294
  Cat computer of, 113
Capps, Steve, 144–45, 161
CAPS (Computer Animation Production System), 242, 284
Captain Crunch, *see* Draper, John
Carey Mariah, 399
Carlton, Jim, 307
Carroll, Lewis, 235
Cars (film), 435, 441
Carter, Matt, 182–83
Cash, Berry, 138
Cash, Johnny, 413, 487
Casone, Il (quarry), 375
"Catch the Wind" (song), 414
Catmull, Ed, xiii, 238–39, *238,* 240, 241, 243, 245–48, 284–85, 287, 288, 430, 440–41, 442
Cave, Ray, 140–41
CBS News, 400
cell phones, 465–66
"Centerfield" (song), 411
Cera, Michael, 499
Chambers, John, 545
Chang, Gareth, 319
Chaplin, Charlie, 330
Chapman, Tracy, 280
Chariots of Fire (film), 167, 169

Charlie Rose (TV show), 290
Chart (app), 176
Chiat, Jay, 187–88, 262
Chiat/Day advertising agency, 162,
    164, 225–26, 327
Chicago Tribune, 233, 423
China, People's Republic of, 200,
    201, 546
Chinatown (film), 527
Chino, Kobun, xiii, 49, 50, 86, 87,
    262, 273
Christensen, Clayton, 408–9, 532
Christie's, 69
Chrysler, 321, 482
Cinderella II (film), 435
Cingular, 466
Cisco, 545
CIT, 6
City of Hope (charity), 479
Clinton, Bill, 39, 277–78, 323, 330,
    552, 576
Clinton, Hillary, 277–78
Clow, Lee, xiii, 162, 164, 187, 327,
    364, 374, 391, 392, 417–18,
    452, 458, 462–63, 498, 500,
    521, 524, 546
  iMac and, 351, 352–53
  "Think Different" campaign
    and, 328–32
CNBC, 474
CNN, xvii
Coast Guard, U.S., 1–2, 6, 106
Coates, George, 233
Cocks, Jay, 139
Cohen, Larry, 463
Coldplay, 410, 413
Cole, David, 404
Coleman, Deborah "Debi," xiii,
    119, 122, 124, 145, 183–84,
    187, 189, 202, 204–5, 252

College Track, 543
Colorado, University of, 24
Comcast, 439, 489
Commodore, 72–73, 135
  PET computer of, 73
Compaq Computers, 232, 360,
    369, 374, 381, 446
CompuServe, 502
Computer Animation Production
    System (CAPS), 242, 284
computers, computing, 57–59
  closed-open debate and, 513,
    554, 561–62
  desktop concept and, 95, 98–99
  digital hub and evolution of,
    379–81
  first portable, 123
Consumer Reports, 520
Cook, Tim, xiii, 345–46, 358–59,
    362, 408, 455, 460, 461, 473,
    480–81, 485, 487, 489, 521,
    526, 549, 557–58, 574, 577
  "Doctrine" of, 488
  role of, 360–61, 458–59
Copeland, Michael, 496
Copland operating system, 297
Corliss, Richard, 290, 429
Corning Glass, 471–72
Corzine, Jon, 269
Coster, Danny, 349
Cotton, Katie, 521
Couch, John, 95, 99, 101, 112, 116,
    136, 141, 150
Cramer Electronics, 67
Crandall, Richard, 272
"Crazy" (song), 329
Cream Soda Computer, 25
Crimson, The, 279
Crittenden Middle School, 13
Crow, Cheryl, 402, 413

Crow, George, *117*, 212

Cue, Eddy, xiii, 398, 403, *452,* 460, 487, 524, 531, 533, 574

Cuisinart food processor, 73, 129

Cult of the Mac (Kahney), 138

Cunningham, Andrea "Andy," xiii, 93, 114, 188, 215, 218

Cutting Through Spiritual Materialism (Trungpa), 35

Daily, The, 507

Daily Show, The (TV show) 518

Dalai Lama, 332

"Dark Eyes" (song), 208

Darwin (operating system), 366

Dating Game (TV show), 159

Dead Poets Society (film), 329–30

Dean, James, 1, 6

De Anza Community College, 24, 32, 354

Defender (video game), 142

Defiant Ones (film), 286

Dell, Inc., 232, 369, 371, 374, 381, 446, 515

Dell, Michael, 334, 360, 479

Desire (Dylan), 418

desktop publishing industry, 131, 187, 515

Desperate Housewives (TV show), 438

Devo, 498

Dido, 413

Diet for a Small Planet (Lappé), 36

Digital Equipment PDP-8, 24

digital hub concept, 383, 463, 489, 530, 532–33, 562

   computer evolution and, 379–81

   iPod and, 384–85

Dilbert (cartoon), 523

Disney, Roy, 242, 432, 434–36, 439, 441

Disney, Walt, 242–43, 248, 284, 434, 442, 443, 569

Disney Channel, 291

Disney Co., 248, 284, 321

   ant movies rivalry and, 427–30

   Pixar's cobranding proposal and, 291–92

   Pixar's merger with, 432–43

   Pixar's *Toy Story* deal with, 284–88, 290–91

   Toy Story premieres and, 289–90

Disneyland, 243, 439

Disney on Ice, 437

Disney Studios, 242–43

Disney World, 433

Doctorow, Cory, 563

Doerr, John, 274, 501–2, 543, 545

Dr. Dre, 402, 406

Donovan, 413, 414

Doonesbury (comic strip), 309

Doors, 413

Draper, John (Captain Crunch), 27, 29

Dream Act, 545–46

DreamWorks SKG, 427–29

Drexler, Millard "Mickey," 321, 370, 371–72, 558

Dreyfuss, Richard, 330–31, 577

Dudman, Jack, 40

DuPont, 310, 318

Dylan, Bob, 25–26, 52, 153, 168, 189, 207–8, 212, 251, 330, 400, 402, 403, 412, 413, 421, 494, 561, 570, 576

   complete boxed set of, 416–18

   SJ's visit with, 415–16

Dynabook project, 95, 475

Eames, Charles and Ray, 127
Earhart, Amelia, 330
Eason, James, 483–85, 487,
    493–94, 549
eBay, 321
ebooks, 503
Economist, 493
Eddie Bauer (store), 369
Edge, The, 411, *411*, 420, 421,
    423
Edison, Thomas A., 330, 566
education reform movement,
    543–44
Egan, Jennifer, 261–63, 438
Egypt, 258
Ehret, Arnold, 36, 548
Eichler, Joseph, 7, 125
Einstein, Albert, xvii, xviii, xix, 91,
    119, 171, 330, 332
Eisenhower, Dwight D., 8
Eisenstat, Al, 122, 198, 201, 202–3,
    209–10, 216, 221
Eisner, Michael, xiv, 242, 289–92,
    428, 432–38, 441
    Disney-Pixar merger opposed
        by, 442
    ouster of, 426–27
    Senate testimony of, 432–33
    SJ's feud with, 432–35
Electric Kool-Aid Acid Test, The
    (Wolfe), 58
Electronic Data Systems, 227
Electronic Frontier Foundation,
    280
Electronic News, 10
Elias, John, 469
Eliot, T. S., 98
Elliot, Jay, 83, 197, 200–201, 206
Ellison, Larry, xiv, 282, 289–90,
    296, 299–300, 303, 306, 310,

311, 313, 320, 332, 333, 349,
    365, 372, 374, 545
Emanuel, Rahm, 495, 497
EMI Music, 395, 420, 524
Eminem, 399, 402, 413
Emotional Rescue (Rolling Stones),
    412
Empire Burlesque (Dylan), 207–8,
    412
Engelbart, Doug, 57–58
ENIAC, 23
Entrepreneurs, The (documentary),
    227
Esalen, 57
eSarcasm (website), 517
Espinosa, Chris, 81, 104, 132, 135
Esquire, 27, 219, 396, 478
Esslinger, Hartmut, 132, 193, 221,
    222, 241
est, 57
Estridge, Don, 149
Evangelist, Mike, 381–82
"Every Grain of Sand" (Dylan), 576

Facebook, 274, 545
Fadell, Tony, xiv, 385–89, 405, 409–
    10, 466–69, 473, 492, 520
Fairchild Semiconductor, 9–10, 76,
    79, 82, 568
FairPlay (management system),
    399, 408
Faith No More, 498
Faraday, Michael, 519
Farber, Dan, 137
Fariña, Mimi, 250
Feadship, 529
Federal Bureau of Investigation
    (FBI), 241
Federalist Papers, The, 497
Felsenstein, Lee, 61, 70

Fernandez, Bill, 25, 104
Ferrentino, Rick, 12–13
Ferris, James, 128
Few Good Men, A (film), 456
Feynman, Richard, 330
File (app), 176
FileServer (software), 200, 205
Final Cut Pro, 380
Financial Times, 304, 309
Finding Nemo (film), 434
Fine Young Cannibals, 270
FingerWorks, 469
Fiore, Mark, 516
FireWire, 380–81, 390, 393
Fisher, George M. C., 333, 482, 550
Fitzgerald, Ella, 153, 189
Fitzgerald, F. Scott, 189
Flashpoint (Rolling Stones), 412
flat-screen technology, 196
Flight of the Conchords, 424
Fogarty, Thomas, 268
Fogerty, John, 411
Forbes, 306, 355
Forbes.com, 497
Ford, Henry, 566, 567
Ford Motors, 102
Forstall, Scott, xiv, 460, 494, 533,
    558
Fortran (computer language), 24
Fortt, Jon, 496–97
Fortune, 77, 141, 187, 229, 236,
    311, 343, 361, 382, 449,
    477–78, 479, 482, 496, 504,
    506, 531
48 Hours (film), 286
Foster, Norman, 535
Fox News Channel, 507, 508
Fox Studios, 507
Fraker, Susan, 236
France, 185, 344

Franklin, Aretha, 413
Franklin, Benjamin, xvii, xix
Freed, James, 180
Free Speech Movement, 57, 61
French, Gordon, 59–60, 70
Friedland, Robert, xiv, 37–40, 42,
    45, 46, 50–51, 86, 89, 106, 460
Friedman, Tom, 516
frogdesign, 133, 193–94, 218,
    221–22
Frost, Robert, 329
Fuller, Buckminster, 58
*Future of the Internet—and How to
    Stop It, The* (Zittrain), 563

Gabriel, Peter, 307
Gage, Kevin, 395
Galvin, Chris, 447
Gandhi, Mohandas, 119, 330, 332
Gap, 321, 370–71
GarageBand, 380, 415, 526
Garcia, Jerry, 106
Gassée, Jean-Louis, xiv, 185, 196,
    200, 201, 205, 207, 212, 294,
    297–98, 299, 300–301
Gates, Bill, xiv, 10, 59, 61–62, 135,
    159–60, *171*, 227, 232, 245,
    269, 276, 297, 306, 324, 366,
    406–7, 409, 448, 465, 467,
    479, 553–54, 555, 576
  on Apple-Google dispute,
    513–14
  Apple-NeXT buyout reaction of,
    302–3
  background and personality of,
    171–72
  GUI debate and, 177–79
  iMac criticized by, 355–56
  iPad criticized by, 495
  iTunes Store reaction of, 404

Gates, Bill (*cont.*)
  Macworld conference and,
    325–26
  NeXT computer and, 229–30,
    236–37
  SJ contrasted with, 171–73
  SJ on, 568
  SJ's business relationship with,
    173–76
  SJ's personal relationship with,
    172–73, 175, 463–64
  SJ's sickbed visit with, 552–54
  at SJ's 30th birthday party,
    188–89
  worldview of, 230
Gates, Jennifer, 555
Gates, Melinda, 467, 554
Gateway Computers, 371, 374,
    376, 379
Gawker (website), 353, 479
Geffen, David, 292, 427
Genentech, 321, 371, 453, 545
General Magic, 385
General M.C. Meigs, USS, 2
General Motors, 227
"Get On Your Boots" (song), 424
Getty, Ann, 228
Getty, Gordon, 228
Giacometti, Alberto, 151
Gibbons, Fred, 159
Gillmore, Dan, 311
"Girl from Ipanema, The" (song),
    189
Giugiaro, Giorgetto, 342
Gizmodo (website), 495, 518, 520
Glaser, Rob, 409
Glavin, Bill, 195
Gnutella, 394
Gold, Stanley, 434
Goldberg, Adele, 96–97, 229–30

"Goldberg Variations" (Bach),
    413–14
Goldblum, Jeff, 307
"Gold Lion" (song), 500
Goldman Sachs, 269
Goldstein, David, 374
Goodell, Jeff, 397
Google, 47, 136, 274, 321, 496,
    502, 518, 531, 533, 534, 545,
    551, 561, 563, 568
  Android system of, 496, 511–14,
    516, 528, 534, 563
Gore, Al, 321, 450, 481, 518, 532,
    558, 576, 577
"gorilla glass," 471–72
Gould, Glenn, 413–14
Graham, Katharine, 165, 231
Graham, Martha, 330
Gran Trak 10 (game), 53
graphical user interface (GUI), 95,
    97, 98
  Macintosh-Microsoft conflict of,
    177–79
Grateful Dead, 57, 280, 414
Graves, Michael, 369
"Gravity" (song), 415
Graziano, Joseph, 374
Green Day, 413
Gretzky, Wayne, 349
Grokster, 394
Gropius, Walter, 126
Grossman, Lev, 473, 495–96
Grove, Andrew, 10, 246–47, 290,
    294, 315, 448, 453, 454, 479
Grunbaum, Eric, 500

Hafner, Katie, 236
Haley, Alex, 456
Hallicrafters, 23
Hallmark, 289

Haltek Supply, 17–18, 67
Hambrecht, Bill, 104
Hambrecht & Quist, 104
Hamilton, Alexander, 171
Hancock, Ellen, 299–300, 308
"Handsome Molly" (song), 417
Hanks, Tom, 287, 290, 330
Hanna-Barbera, 352
Hannity, Sean, 508
Hard Day's Night, A (Beatles), 412
Haring, Keith, 180
Harmony (music service), 409
Harris, David, 251
Harris, Gabriel, 251
Hartman, Arthur, 210
Hasbro, 321
Hastings, Reed, 545
Hawley, Michael, 224
Hayden, Steve, 162
Hayes, Rutherford, 193
HBO, 506
Heathkits, 16, 23
Heinen, Nancy, 450–51
Heller, Andrew, 231
Heller, Dave, 383
Help! (Beatles), 412
Hemingway, Ernest, 19
Hendrix, Jimi, 280, 413
Henry V (Shakespeare), xxi
Henson, Jim, 331
"Here Comes the Sun" (song),
    526
Hertzfeld, Andy, xiv, 5, 103,
    109, 115, 117–18, *117*, 120,
    141–42, 147, 152, 157, 165,
    169, 170, 172, 174, 177, 178,
    189, 194, 207–8, 260, 261,
    265, 271, 274, 276–77, 279,
    281, 319, 354, 385, 412, 418,
    474, 489, 564–65, 576

Macintosh computer and,
    113–14, 128–31, 136–37, 161,
    166–67, 190–91
Hewlett, Ben, 279
Hewlett, Bill, xix, 9, 17, 25,
    534–35, 552, 569
Hewlett-Packard (HP), xix, 52, 64,
    93, 296, 446, 459, 515, 534,
    552, 558–59, 568
    DeskJet printer of, 338
    Explorers Club of, 16–17, 28
    first product of, 9
    9100A computer of, 17
    SJ as employee of, 17
Hill, Imogene "Teddy," 13
Hinduism, 48, 57
Hoefler, Don, 10
Hoffman, Joanna, xiv, 110, *117*,
    121–22, 134, 156, 184–87,
    217–18, 226, 235, 252, 260,
    263, 271, 274
Holly, Buddy, 413
Holmes, Elizabeth, xiv, 34–35,
    38–39, 41, 49, 51–52, 67, 68,
    86, 88, 89, 189, 251
Holt, Rod, xiv, 74, 103, 146
Homebrew Computer Club,
    60–62, 64, 70, 78, 163, 561
Horn, Bruce, 96, 114–15, 120, 174,
    192
Hovey, Dean, 98
How to Dismantle an Atomic Bomb
    (U2), 421
HTC, 512
Huey, John, 473, 478

IBM, 119, 136, 139, 149, 160, 169,
    177, 294, 296, 321, 333, 334,
    361, 446–47, 482, 568
    Macintosh's rivalry with, 160

IBM (*cont.*)
  NeXT and, 231–32
  PC introduced by, 135
  ThinkPad of, 342
iBook, 338, 373, *444*, 494
iBooks Store, 503
iChat, 406, 431
iCloud, 530–34, 536, 555, 566
  competition and, 533–34
  MobileMe product and, 531–32, 533
  SJ's vision for, 531
  unveiling of, 532–33
Idei, Nobuyuki, 395, 407
iDVD, 380, 382, 403
iFund, 502
Iger, Robert, xiv, 436–43, 576
"I'm a Believer" (song), 413
iMac computer, 338, *340,* 345, 346, 348–56, 369, 373, 390, 426, 444, 470, 474, 515, 519
  casing of, 349–50
  CD burner of, 382–83
  CD tray debate and, 349, 351–52, 356–57, 382
  concept of, 349
  flat-screen technology and, 445–46
  Gates's criticism of, 355–56
  handle of, 350–51
  iPod and sales of, 391–92
  Ive and, 350–52, 356
  launch of, 354–55
  microprocessor of, 349
  mouse of, 353
  name of, 351
  prototype of, 349, 351–52
  sales of, 356
  specifications of, 348–49
Immelt, Jeffrey, 544

iMouse, 373
iMovie, 380, 381, 383, 403, 446, 526, 532
IMSAI 8080 (computer), 69–70
Inc., 106
Incredibles, The (film), 435
India, 37, 104
  SJ influenced by, 48–49
  SJ's sojourn in, 46–48, 570
inertial scrolling, 363
InfoWorld, 229
Innovator's Dilemma, The (Christensen), 409
Intel, 10, 76, 79, 121, 246, 294, 461, 493, 536–37, 568, 569
  Apple and, 446–48
  4004 chip of, 10
  8080 chip of, 60, 66
  in Macintosh computer, 492
Interface, 69
International Design Conference, 125–26
International Harvester, 2
International Style, 126
Internet, 300, 349, 402, 409, 474, 502
Internet Explorer, 325
Interscope-Geffen-A&M, 399, 421
Intuit, 320
Iovine, Jimmy, 399–400, 403, 411, 421, 423, 479
iPad, 78, 137, 339, 345, 346, 379, 408, 467, 511, 532, 555, 558, 562, 566
  apps phenomenon and, 500–503
  App Store and, 503, 505, 507
  ARM architecture and, 492–93
  case of, 491–92
  criticism of, 494–96

display screen of, 491
Gates's criticism of, 495
Grossman on, 495–96
launch of, 165, 493–94
Manifesto ad campaign and,
  498–500
publishing industry and, 504–6
sales of, 498
tablet project and, 490–91
textbook industry and, 509–10
iPad 2, 525–27
cover of, 525–26
launch of, 526
SJ's, 527
iPhone, 78, 137, 339, 344–45, 379,
  408, 459, 460, 492, 494, 511,
  512, 514, 532, 555, 562, 563,
  564, 566
antenna problem and, 519–23
apps phenomenon and, 501–2, 516
design of, 472–73
features of, 469–72
glass screen of, 470–72
initial application of, 466–67
iPod and, 466–67
Ive and, 519–23
launch of, 473–75
model 4 of, 518, 541
multi-touch technology and,
  467–69
onscreen keyboard of, 469
partnership and, 465–66
P1 and P2 routes of, 468–69
price of, 474
prototype of, 468
tablet computer idea and,
  467–68
3G model of, 478, 489
3GS model of, 487, 522
4S, introduction of, 574

iPhoto, 380, 532
iPod, 7, 137, 345, *378,* 384–90,
  394, 396, 407, 408, 440, 464,
  474, 503, 514, 516, 532, 534,
  562, 564, 565, 566
ad campaign for, 391–92
designing of, 387–88
development of, 384–85
digital hub concept and, 384–85
disc drive of, 384–85, 386
Fadell and, 385–89
Gates's first view of, 393
Harmony service of, 409
headphones of, 390
iconic whiteness of, 390–91
iMac sales and, 391–92
iPhone and, 466–67
Ive and, 390–91
Mini, 409
Nano, 347, 470, 489, 519
new versions of, 409
power switch of, 389–90
price of, 392–93
sales of, 410, 469
shuffle feature of, 409–10
SJ's selections on, 412–14
unveiling of, 392–93
user interface of, 388–89
U2 deal and, 420–22
video version of, 438–39
Windows and, 404–6
iPod Touch, 506
Italy, 185, 375
iTunes, 380, 385, 389–90, 394,
  432, 446, 464, 502, 532, 534,
  562
Beatles and, 419–20, 523–24
development of, 382–83
unveiling of, 383–84
Windows and, 404–6, 463

iTunes Store, 380, 407, 419, 438,
    501, 503, 516, 524, 562, 564,
    566
  creation of, 396–97
  data base of, 410
  Dylan boxed set offered by,
    416–18
  Gates's reaction to, 404
  initial idea for, 396–97
  iPod sales and, 400–401
  Microsoft's reaction to, 403–4
  music industry and, 398–402
  sales of, 403
  success of, 410
  technology-art gap and, 397–98
  unveiling of, 402–3
Ive, Jonathan "Jony," xiv, 340–52, 362,
    364, 372, 387, 398, 409, 426–27,
    446, 460, 461–62, 470, 472, 485,
    487–88, 491, 525, 574, 576, 577
  background of, 341
  design philosophy of, 342–43
  iMac and, 350–52, 356
  industrial designs of, 341–42
  iPhone antenna problem and,
    519–23
  iPod and, 390–91
  minimalist aesthetic of, 444–45
  on multi-touch feature, 468
  patents of, 346–47, 492
  SJ's collaboration with, 340–45,
    347
  SJ's relationship with, 342–43
  U2 deal and, 422–23

Jacob, Oren, 436
Jagger, Jade, 180
Jagger, Mick, 180, 402, 406
Jandali, Abdulfattah "John," xiv,
    3–4, 89, 253, 256–58

Jandali, Roscille, 257–58
Janoff, Rob, 80
Janov, Arthur, 50, 51
Jarrett, Valerie, 544–45
Jasinski, Barbara, 91, 155, 250–51
J. C. Penney, 536
J. Crew, 321
Jefferson, Thomas, 171
Jefferson Airplane, 57, 280, 413
Jetsons, The (TV show), 351–52,
    445
Jobs, Clara Hagopian, xiv, 1, 5, 8, 9,
    11–12, 50–51, 68
  background of, 2
  death of, 253–54
  SJ adopted by, 3
  SJ's money gift to, 106
Jobs, Erin, xiv, 280, 282, 425, 509,
    539, 558
  SJ's relationship with, 540–42
Jobs, Eve, xiv, 282, *452*, 497, 509,
    539, 553, 558
  SJ's relationship with, 542
Jobs, Patty, xiv, 5, 67, 255, 574, 575,
    576
Jobs, Paul Reinhold, xiv, 5–6, 14,
    15, 22, 50–51, 68, 125, 228,
    253, 254, 273, 294, 555
  background of, 1–2
  career of, 6–9
  in Macintosh factory tour,
    183–84
  SJ adopted by, xxxiv, 3
  SJ's money gift to, 106
  SJ's relationship with, 6, 8,
    11–12, 18–19
Jobs, Reed Paul, xiv, 258, 282, 315,
    415, 477, 484, 509, 521, 526,
    527, 536, 541, 550, 558, 569
  SJ's relationship with, 538–40

Jobs, Steven Paul, *21, 56, 108, 148, 293, 305, 340, 358, 490, 560*
achievements of, xx–xxi, 565–66
adoption trauma and, 4–5, 12, 50–51
AppleLabs proposal and, 196–98, 203–6
Apple-NeXT lawsuits and, 217–18, 221–22
assessment of, 565–67
attitude toward wealth of, 104–6, 448–49, 451
author's sickbed visit with, 555–56
aversion to authority of, 12, 19, 83
bachelor's party of, 272–73
birth mother found by, 253–55, 258
Blue Box partnership and, 29–30
business drive of, 54–55
calligraphy studied by, 40–41, 130
cancer of, xviii–xix, 266, 376, 415, 425, 452–56, 461, 476, 479–80, 482–84, 538–39, 546–51, 554
carbon microphone incident and, 10–11
as celebrity, 180–81
chairman role of, 207–9, 213, 225
charisma of, 31, 64, 112, 121, 172, 242, 245, 302, 564
childhood of, 5–12, 119
as college dropout, 40–41
commune living and, 38–39
controlling personality of, 74–75, 137–38, 182–83, 236, 245, 287, 288, 309, 315, 335–36, 365, 493

counterculture self-image of, 107, 162–63, 168, 331, 451
death of, 574–75
design aesthetic of, 80, 125–28, 239–40, 248
design passion of, 220–21
diet of, 14, 31, 35–36, 41, 51, 68, 82–83, 260, 454–55, 476–77, 548–49
Eastern spirituality interest of, 34–35, 48–52
education of, 12–20
electronics passion of, 10–11, 15–17, 19–20
fame of, 106–7
fasting practice of, 36, 476, 548
final resignation letter of, 557–59
first car of, 18
first computer seen by, 8
first desktop computer seen by, 17
first experience with electronics, 6–7
first girlfriend of, 31
first work experience of, 17–18
40th birthday party of, 282
50th birthday party of, 457–58
hallucinogenic drugs used by, 31–32, 35
health issues of, 333–34, 452–53, 456, 476
hygiene of, 82–83
illegitimate child of, 88–90, 256
India sojourn of, 46–48, 570
intensity of, xviii, 38, 172, 223, 561, 564
legacy of, 306, 534–35, 567–70
liver transplant of, 482–84, 489
low pass filter of, 120–21
LSD used by, 10, 41, 384

Index

Jobs, Steven Paul (*cont.*)
management focus mantra of, 359
marijuana used by, 18–19, 32
marriage of, 272–74
memorial services for, 576–77
in middle school, 13–14
mood swings of, 157, 195, 223, 548–49
music passion of, 19, 25–26
Narcissistic Personality Disorder ascribed to, 265–66
offensive behavior of, 5, 32, 43, 56, 64, 91, 101, 118, 119, 121–23, 124, 142, 146, 157, 166, 178, 195–96, 198, 223, 225, 461–62, 489, 565
Palo Alto home of, 274–77, 278
patents of, 375
perfectionism of, 74, 183, 315, 513, 561, 566
philanthropy and, 105–6, 423–24, 543
as prankster, 12–13, 16, 26
in primal scream therapy, 50
product launches and, 165–67
reality distortion field of, *see* reality distortion field
religion and, 14–15
resignation letters of, 215–16, 217, 557–59
Russia visit of, 209–10
selections on iPod of, 412–14
sense of abandonment of, 4–5, 12, 50–51
social awkwardness of, 13–14
stare of, 38, 106, 172, 191, 193, 201, 203, 206, 303
stock options matter and, 364–66, 448–50, 477

30th birthday celebration of, 188–90
Time profiles of, 106–7, 139–41
topography obsession of, 130–31
20th wedding anniversary of, 529–30
vegetarianism of, 35–36, 82, 96, 155, 185, 260, 312, 454
in White House visit, 192–93
whole-widget approach of, 137–38
worldview of, 119–20, 230, 315–16, 561
Wozniak's remote device episode and, 193–94
yacht planned by, 528–29
Zen Buddhism interest of, 15, 34–36, 41, 48–50, 128, 262, 564, 570

Johnson, Ron, xiv, 369–73, 377, 536
Jones, Carr, 275
Jones, Jeff, 524
Joplin, Janis, 57, 413
Joy, Bill, 236
Juan Carlos I, King of Spain, 228
Jump Back (Rolling Stones), 412
Jung, Andrea, 321, 481
Junod, Tom, 478
Justice Department, U.S., 323

Kac, Mark, 566
Kahney, Leander, 138
Kahng, Stephen "King," 336
kanban (manufacturing principle), 225
Kapor, Mitch, 159, 188–89, 224
Kare, Susan, 131–32, 144, 152, 221, 232–33
Karen O, 500

Katzenberg, Jeffrey, xiv, 248,
    284–87, 288, 292, 436
  ants movies rivalry and, 427–30
Kawasaki, Guy, 298
Kay, Alan, xv, 95, 238, 474–75
Kazaa, 394, 402
Keenan, Joe, 72
Kehoe, Louise, 304, 309
Kennedy, Bobby, 331
Kenyon, Larry, 123
Kepler, Johannes, 561
Kerwin, Pam, 241–42, 244–46, 431
Kesey, Ken, 57, 58
Keys, Alicia, 413
KGB, 209
Kincaid, Bill, 383
Kindle, 503, 534
King, B. B., 413, 487
King, Martin Luther, 330
King Lear (Shakespeare), 19
Kissinger, Henry, xx, 28–29, 313
Kitchen, Steve, 196
Klein, Joel, 323, 509
Kodak, 333
Komoto, Hidetoshi, 147
Kot, Greg, 423
Kottke, Daniel, xv, 38–39, 45,
    49–50, 51, 56, 67–68, 70, 86,
    87, 89, 90, 140, 432, 497
  Apple stock options issue and,
    103
  in India, 47
  SJ's friendship with, 34–36, 103
Kriegspiel (game), 35
Kumbh Mela (festival), 46

Lack, Andy, 400–401, 406, 407,
    416–17, 421
Lady and the Lamp (film), 243
Land, Edward, xix, 8, 207, 567

Lang, Don, 43
Lange, Larry, 10–11, 16–17
Langer, Andy, 396
Lappé, Frances Moore, 36
lasers, 15
Lashinsky, Adam, 361, 531
Lasseter, John, xv, *238*, 239, 240,
    244, 284–87, 289, 290, 291,
    304, 438, 446, *452*, 458
  animated film by, 247–48
  background of, 242–43
  Disney-Pixar merger and,
    440–43
  Pixar headquarters and, 430–32
  SJ's admiration of, 426–27
  "Toy Story" idea of, 285–86
Last Tycoon, The (Fitzgerald), 189
Lauren, Ralph, 251, 370
League for Spiritual Discovery
    (LSD), 33
Leary, Timothy, 33, 57–58
Led Zeppelin, 402
"Lemmings" (advertisement), 187
Lennon, John, 51, 330, 331, 374,
    524
Lennon, Sean, 180
Leonardo da Vinci, 80, 568
Let It Be (Beatles), 412
Levinson, Art, 321, 371, 447, 453,
    454, 465, 481, 501–2, 518,
    520–21, 558
Levitt, Arthur, 321
Levy, Joe, 412
Levy, Steven, 166, 355, 393, 412
Lewin, Dan'l, xv, 125, 214, 223,
    231
  NeXT and, 212–13, 224
Lewinsky, Monica, 277
Lewis, Jerry Lee, 487
Libya, 258

Life, 14–15
"Like a Rolling Stone" (song), 494, 570
Lin, Maya, 127
Lion King, The (film), 434, 439
Lisa Computer, 110–12, 129, 130, 144, 145, 150–51, 154, 181, 200
   Atkinson and, 99–101
   converted to Mac XLS, 186–87
   failure of, 141, 160, 186
   initial concept of, 93
   launch of, 141
   Macintosh's rivalry with, 136–37
   mouse of, 100–101
   name of, 93
   screen background of, 99–100
"Little Green" (song), 414
Little Mermaid, The (film), 242
Lockheed Missiles and Space Division, 9
Loewy, Raymond, 127
Lohr, Steve, 281
Los Angeles Times, 429
Lost (TV show), 438, 497
Lost Father, The (Simpson), 258
Lost World, The: Jurassic Park (film), 307
Lotus (software), 224
"Love Is Just a Four-Letter Word" (song), 412
"Love Lounge, The," 432
LSD, 19, 41, 57, 107
Lucas, George, 238–40, 243
Lucasfilm, 239–41, 243
Luxo Jr. (film), 243–44, 446
Lyons, Daniel, 494–95, 496

Ma, Yo-Yo, 413, 424–25, 576
MacBook, 347

MacBook Pro, 468
McCartney, Paul, 524
McCollum, John, 19–20, 21
Mac G4 Cube, 445, 448, 459
McGuinness, Paul, 421
Macintosh, xvii, 7, 41, 99, 207, 229, 230, 234, 239, 337, 348, 379, 396, 445, 463, 474, 513, 526, 554, 562, 563, 565, 569
   Baez shown prototype of, 251
   Bicycle proposed as name for, 115
   bundling proposal and, 176
   circuit board of, 133–34
   clones of, 335–36, 447
   design of, 127–28, 133–34
   desktop metaphor and, 127
   disk drive of, 145–47, 186, 200
   engineer team of, 113–15
   factory construction of, 182–84
   fonts of, 130–31
   Hertzfeld and, 113–14, 128–31, 161, 166–67, 190–91
   hidden craftsmanship of, 133–34
   icons of, 131
   Intel chip in, 492
   launch of, 160–61, 167–70, 353–54
   licensing proposals and, 138–39
   Lisa design team and, 181
   Lisa's rivalry with, 136–37
   media coverage of, 165–66
   Microsoft and, 173–75, 177–79
   name of, 109, 142
   nickname of, 186
   1984 ad campaign for, *159,* 160–65, 169, 187, 226, 325, 331, 516
   1985 ad campaign for, 187–88
   OSX system of, 366–67, 380
   packaging of, 134

price debate and, 157–58, 195

QuickDraw package of, 169–70

Raskin's vision for, 109–10, 128

research team of, 109–10

Russia sales of, 209–10

sales of, 186, 195, 295

screen of, 129–30

SJ-Gates relationship and, 173–76

SJ-Raskin clashes and, 110–14

SJ's end-to-end concept and, 137–39

SJ's European tour and, 184–85

team departures and, 190–92

title bar of, 131–32

McIntosh Laboratory, 109

McKenna, Regis, xv, 79, 85, 91, 93, 141, 151, 155, 162, 165, 188, 202, 215, 521–22

McLean, Don, 413

McLeod, Gordon, 508

MacPaint, 180

Macromedia, 336

Macworld, 298

Macworld conferences, 307–8, 322–26, 329, 336, 339, 366–67, 385, 415, 478, 479–80, 560

   Gates and, 325–26

   SJ's keynote speech at, 322–23, 325

Macy's, 73, 164, 196

Madonna, 402, 502

Maffei, Greg, 324–25

Magical Mystery Tour (Beatles), 412

Maharaj-ji (Neem Karoli Baba), 37, 45, 46, 91

Malone, Michael S., 14, 307

Manifesto (advertising campaign), 498–500

Manock, Jerry, 73–74, *117,* 128–29

Mansfield, Bob, 460

marijuana, 18–19

Markkula, Mike, xv, 63, 82, 84, 101, 102, 105, 109, 113, 116, 131, 134, 147, 148–49, 168, 192, 204, 205, 208, 213, 215, 220, 298, 301, 310, 347, 351, 355, 555

   Apple joined by, 75–76

   Apple left by, 319–20

   Apple II and, 80–81

   iMac preview and, 353

   1984 ad reaction of, 164

   SJ's relationship with, 78

Markoff, John, 57, 291, 384

Marsalis, Wynton, 402

Marshall, George, 457

Martin, Steve, 290

Maslin, Janet, 290

Mayer, John, 413

Meet the Beatles! (Beatles), 412

Mellencamp, John, 413

"Mellow Yellow" (song), 414

Merin, Mike, 209

Michelangelo, 568

microprocessor, 10

Microsoft, 84, 136, 137, 158, 245, 289, 295, 296, 320, 334, 381, 463, 464, 467, 474, 495, 513, 518, 531, 533–34, 561, 562, 568, 569

   federal lawsuit against, 323

   goes public, 227

   iTunes Store reaction of, 403–4

   Macintosh and, 173–75, 177–79, 324–25

   MSN service of, 407

   NeXT and, 229, 231–32, 236–37

   Sand project of, 173

Microsoft DOS, 177
Microsoft Excel, 174–76, 230, 323, 324, 326
Microsoft Media Player, 383
Microsoft Multiplan, 173
Microsoft Office, 326
Microsoft Windows, 177–79, 230, 335, 515, 528, 534, 554
  1.0, 323
  2.0, 323
  3.0, 296
  95, 291
  iPod and, 404–6
  iTunes and, 404–6, 463
  NT, 298
Microsoft Word, 160, 174, 176, 230, 324, 326
Microsoft Zune, 406–7, 409
Mies van der Rohe, Ludwig, 126
Milner, Duncan, 332, 391, 498–500
Minsky, Marvin, 185
Miss Spider's Tea Party (Madonna), 502
"Mr. Tambourine Man" (song), 417
Mitchell, George, 438, 442
Mitchell, Joni, 414
Mitterrand, Danielle, 184
Mitterrand, François, 184, 185
Miyake, Issey, 128, 256, 362, 532
MobileMe, 531–33
Moby-Dick (Melville), 19
Modern Times (Dylan), 417
Mok, Clement, 183
Monkees, 413
Monsters, Inc. (film), 432–33
Moore, Fred, 59–60, 61
Moore, Gordon, 9–10
Moore, Henry, 151

Moore's Law, 10
Morgan Stanley, 104
Morita, Akio, 361
Moritz, Michael, 90, 106–7, 139, 140
Morris, Doug, 399–401, 403, 479
Morrison, Van, 411
Mossberg, Walt, 379, 463, 491, 503, 531
MOS Technologies, 60
"Mother" (song), 51
Mother of All Demos, 58
Motorola, 335, 446–47, 465–66
  6800 microprocessor of, 60
  6809 microprocessor of, 109–10
  68000 microprocessor of, 110
Motorola Starmax, 447
Motown, 399
Mozart's Brain and the Fighter Pilot (Restak), 424
MP3 (music format), 383, 385–87
MTV, 166
Mucusless Diet Healing System (Ehret), 36
Müller, Marcel, 38
Mumford, Lewis, 57
Murdoch, James, 504, 508
Murdoch, Rupert, 504, 507–9
Murray, Joyce, 206
Murray, Mike, xv, 139, 152, 195–96, 197, 200, 203–4, 206
Muse (band), 498
Museum of Modern Art (New York), 445
music industry, 394–95, 398, 399–400, 503
MusicMatch, 406
MusicNet, 395, 403, 404
Myth of the Machine, The (Mumford), 57

Napster, 382, 394, 402

Narcissistic Personality Disorder, 265–66

NASDAQ, 379

National Aeronautics and Space Administration (NASA), 8–9

National Medal of Technology, 192–93

National Press Club, 228

National Security Agency, 241

National Semiconductor, 75, 79, 296, 297

NBC, 400

Negroponte, Nicholas, 185

Nepal, 106

netbook concept, 494

Netflix, 545

Netscape, 291

Neville Brothers, 410

Newman, Randy, 288, 432

News Corp., 507–8

newser.com, 523

Newsweek, 165–66, 218, 236, 290, 323, 355, 393, 445, 494, 495–96

Newton (Apple), 308–9, 338, 385

Newton, Isaac, 69

New York Post, 507

New York Times, 228, 233, 281, 290, 291, 384, 408, 411, 451, 478, 494, 498, 504–5, 516

NeXT, xviii, 166, 245, 246, 259, 268, 297, 363, 374, 445, 447, 458

   Apple and, 213–15, 217–18, 221–22, 298–300, 305–6

   Apple's staff "raid" on, 213–15

   bundled features of, 224–25, 234

   circuit board of, 222, 233–34

   design of, 222–23

   electronic book of, 234–35

   failure of, 293–94

   finances of, 226–28

   Gates and, 229–30, 236–37

   headquarters of, 223–24

   IBM and, 231–32

   idea behind, 211–12, 214

   late release of, 234–36

   launch of, 232–35

   Lewin and, 212–13, 224

   licensing issue and, 231–32

   logo of, 219–21

   matte finish of, 223

   Microsoft and, 236–37

   name of, 219

   NextStep system of, 231–32, 294

   operating system of, 366

   optical disk of, 234–35

   Perot and, 227–28

   price of, 235

   reaction to, 236

   retreats of, 226

   sales of, 237

   unseen craftsmanship in, 223

Ng, Stan, 387

Nicks, Stevie, 479

Nietzsche, Friedrich, 119

Nine Inch Nails, 397

1984 (Orwell), 162

Nocera, Joe, 223, 451, 478

Noer, Michael, 497–98

No Line on the Horizon (U2) 424

Norton, Jeffrey, 494

Novel (parlor game), 547

Noyce, Robert, 9–10, 121, 537

Obama, Barack, 495, 497, 556

   SJ's dinner for, 545–47

   SJ's meeting with, 543–45

Obama administration, 258

Oh Mercy (Dylan), 412
Omen, The (film), 69
"One Too Many Mornings" (song),
    416
Ono, Yoko, 180, 331, 374, 418
OpenMind (mental health
    network), 265
Oppenheimer, J. Robert, 363
Oppenheimer, Peter, 460, 557
Oracle, 282, 296, 349, 372, 545
Oregon Feeling Center, 50
O'Reilly, Bill, 508
Ornish, Dean, 454
Orwell, George, 160, 162, 169
Osborne, Adam, 123, 135
Ostrovsky, Alex, 410
Otellini, Paul, xv, 447–48, 492, 493
Otogawa, Kobun Chino, *see* Chino,
    Kobun
Outkast, 418
"Outlaw Blues" (song), 417
Ovitz, Michael, 436–37
Oxford Dictionary of Quotations, 225
Oxford University Press, 224
Oyama, Terry, 128–29
Ozzie, Ray, 533–34

Packard, David, xix, 9, 25, 306,
    534–35, 569
Page, Larry, 274, 511–12, 551–52,
    576
Page, Rich, 136–37, 212, 214
Palm, 459
Palmisano, Sam, 333
Panasonic, 356–57
Pantone company, 83
Paris Review, 255
Parker, Maynard, 236
Parrish, Maxfield, 91
Pascal (computer language), 94

P.A. Semi, 492–93
Patton, George S., 2
Patton (film), 203–4, 206
Paulsen, David, 225
PayPal, 410
PBS, 227
PC World, 395–96
Pearlstine, Norman, 330
Pearson Education, 511
Peddle, Chuck, 72
Pei, I. M., 180, 224
People's Computer Company, 59
PepsiCo., 149–52
    corporate headquarters of,
        151–52
Perfect Thing, The (Levy), 412
Perkins, Tony, 295, 395
Perot, Ross, 227–28, 231
Personal Computer Festival, 70, 71
Pfeifer, Herbert, 194
Philips Electronics, 385, 388
Picasso, Pablo, 330, 332
Pileggi, Nick, 256
Pininfarina, Sergio, 126
Pinter, Harold, 204
Pixar, xviii, 166, 242, 248, 304, 311,
    314, 322, 363, 450
    ant movies rivalry and, 427–30
    CAPS system of, 242
    digital animation business of,
        242–44
    Disney's merger with, 432–43
    Disney's *Toy Story* deal with,
        284–88, 290–91
    financial losses of, 245–48
    headquarters of, 430–32
    IPO of, 291
    mass market debate and, 241–42,
        247
    name of, 240

Reyes program of, 241
Showplace computer program
    of, 247
SJ's investment in, 248–49
Toy Story premiere and, 289–90
Pixar Image Computer, 240–41,
    242, 245
Plastic Ono Band, 51
Plato, 19
Playboy, 189
Plimpton, George, 255
Pocahontas (film), 289
Podolny, Joel, 461
Polaroid, xix, 8, 207, 567
Pollack, Andrew, 233
Polo Shop, 251–52
Pong (video game), 43, 52–54
Popular Electronics, 59
Popular Science, 170
PortalPlayer, 387
Portola Institute, 59
Powell, Laurene, xv, xviii, 267–83,
    267, 302, 365, 402, *452*, 467,
    476, 482, 497, 540–42, 553,
    558, 574, 575, 576
    background of, 269
    children of, 282–83
    College Track program and, 543
    marriage of, 272–74
    organic food company of, 274
    Palo Alto home of, 274–77, 278
    pregnancy of, 272
    SJ assessed by, 543–44
    SJ's cancer ordeal and, 453–55,
        483–86, 547–50, 555
    SJ's first meeting with, 268–69
    SJ's marriage proposal to, 270–72
    SJ's funeral arrangements, 574–76
    20th wedding anniversary of,
        529–30

PowerBook G3, 338, 373, 470
PowerBook G4, 470
Power Computing, 335–36
Power Macintosh G3, 338, 349,
    373
PowerPC (microprocessor), 446–
    47
President's Economic Recovery
    Advisory Board, 543–44
Presley, Elvis, 487
Press, Tony, 429
Pressplay, 395, 403, 404
primal scream therapy, 50, 51, 57
Prince of Egypt (film), 428–29
Processor Technology Corporation,
    70
Prodigy, 502
Product Red campaign, 423–24
publishing industry, 504–6

QuickDraw, 169–70
Quittner, Josh, 506

Radio Shack, 28, 139
Radius company, 335
Raduchel, Bill, 394
Ram Dass, Baba (Richard Alpert),
    34, 37
Rams, Dieter, 127, 132, 343
Rand, Paul, 219–21, 222
Raskin, Jef, 94, 95–96, 108–13,
    122, 140, 170
    Macintosh computer and,
        109–13, 128
    ouster of, 113
    SJ's clash with, 110–13
Ratatouille (film), 441
RAZR (cell phone), 465–66
Reagan, Ronald, 192–93, 231,
    546

reality distortion field, 38, 52, 117–20, 140, 145, 161, 175–76, 179, 185, 186, 191, 226, 229, 235, 240, 454, 471–72
   Wozniak on, 118–19
Real Jukebox, 383
RealNetworks, 385–86, 395
Red Herring, 295, 311, 395
Redse, Tina, 187, 207, 209, 268, 271, 529, 555
   SJ's relationship with, 263–66
Reed College, 33–36, 130, 432, 457
   SJ drops out of, 40–41
Regular Guy, A (Simpson), 255, 271, 280–82
Remnick, David, 228
RenderMan (computer language), 241–42
Revelation, Book of, 69
"Revolution" (song), 526
Reyes rendering program, 241
Reznor, Trent, 397
Rice, Garrett, 298–99
Richie, Lionel, 479
Riley, George, 208, 466, 483–84, 485, 487, 557, 558
Riney, Hal, 546
Rio (music player), 383, 384, 389, 409
"Road Not Taken, The" (Frost), 329
Robbin, Jeff, 383, 387, 405, 409
Roberts, Brian, 489
Roche, Gerry, 149
Rock, Arthur, xv, 78, 84, 90, 145, 182, 195, 198, 208, 215
Rock, Toni, 208
Rodin, Auguste, 151
ROKR, 466
Rolling Stone, 166, 397
Rolling Stones, 412, 415

Rolling Thunder Revue, 251
Rosen, Ben, 84, 143
Rosen, Jeff, 416–18
Rosenbaum, Ron, 27
Rossmann, Alain, 134, 184
Rotten Tomatoes, 290
Royal Society of the Arts, 341
Rubin, Andy, 512
Rubinstein, Jonathan "Ruby," xv, 308–9, 342, 362, 405, 409, 410, 468, 470
   Apple left by, 458–59
   iMac and, 349, 351–52, 356
   iPod and, 384–87

Samit, Jay, 408
Samsung, 493
Sam the Sham, 413
Sanders, Jessica, 500
"Sand" project, 173
San Francisco Chronicle, 218, 333
San Francisco Zen Center, 49
San Jose Mercury, 42
San Jose Mercury News, 311
San Jose swap meet, 18
Sapper, Richard, 127, 342
Sgt. Pepper's Lonely Heart Club Band (Beatles), 412
Satoshi, Mizushima, 81
Schieble, Arthur, 2–3
Schieble, Joanne, *see* Simpson, Joanne Schieble Jandali
Schiller, Phil, 336–37, 344, 348–49, 352, 362, 384, 387, 388, 405, 458, 460, 468, 491, 494, 501, 533, 558
Schlein, Philip, 164, 196, 198
Schlender, Brent, 311, 479, 495
Schmidt, Eric, 321, 450, 511, 512–14, 545, 551

Schneider, Peter, 287
Schuler, Barry, 398
Scott, Mike, xv, 82–84, 101, 113, 354
  badge number controversy and, 83
  ouster of, 115–16, 148
Scott, Ridley, 163, 165, 187
Scott, Tony, 187
Scrabble, 497
Sculley, John, xv, *148*, 167, 170, 180, 187, 213, 214, 222, 227, 228, 238, 263, 299, 301, 302, 309, 319, 320, 323, 338, 353, 355, 569
  and decline of Apple company, 295–96
  1984 ad and, 163–64
  pricing debate and, 157–58
  reorganization plan of, 205–7
  SJ and ouster of, 200–204, 207
  SJ's clashes with, 194–99, 216–17
  SJ's courtship of, 150–54
  at SJ's 30th birthday party, 189
  SJ's working relationship with, 155–57, 168, 181–82, 195, 199, 215
Sculley, Leezy, 155, 187, 203
Seal, 329
SEC (Securities and Exchange Commission), 313, 321, 481
  backdated stock options issue and, 450–51
Secret Service, 277
"Secrets of the Little Blue Box" (Rosenbaum), 27
Segal, George, 140
Segall, Ken, 329, 351
semiconductors, 9–10
Senate, U.S., 432–33

Sequoia Capital, 75, 139
Serwer, Andy, 478, 506
Seva Foundation, 106
Sex (Madonna), 502
Shakespeare, William, xxi, 19, 224, 234
"She Drives Me Crazy" (song), 270
Sheff, David, 189
"Shelter from the Storm" (song), 397
Shockley, William, 9
Showplace computer program, 247
Shrek (film), 430
Shriver, Eunice, 330–31
SIGGRAPH, 243–44
"Silicon Valley USA," 10
Simon and Garfunkel, 413
Simpson, George, 253
Simpson, Joanne Schieble Jandali, xv, 2–4, 89
  SJ's finding of, 253–55, 258
Simpson, Mona, xv, xix, 4, *250*, 254–58, 271, 273–74, 281–82, 455, 485, 494, 547–48, 574, 575, 576–77
  Jandali and, 256–58
  Lisa Brennan and, 282
  SJ's reconnection with, 255–56
Simpsons (TV show), 273
Skoll Foundation, 47
Slade, Mike, 458, 553
Smalltalk (computer language), 95, 96–97
Smith, Alvy Ray, xv, 239–41, 243, 285
  SJ's clash with, 244–45
Smith, Burrell, xv, 109–10, 113–15, *117*, 134, 136–37, 141–42, 165, 189, 191, 276–77
Smith, Gina, 310

Smith, Kathryn (Kat), 268–71, 476, 486
Smith, Wes, 233
Snow White (film), 187, 290
Snow White project, 132–33
Solaris operating system, 298, 308
SOL-20 (computer), 70
"Someday Baby" (song), 417–18
Some Girls (Rolling Stones), 412
Sonnenfeldt, Helmut, 313
Sonsini, Larry, 303
Sony, 125–26, 146–47, 361–62, 381, 385, 394–95, 404, 406, 408, 565
    music industry and, 394–95, 400–401
    Trinitron products of, 132, 155
Sony Connect, 408
Sony Walkman, 407
Sorkin, Aaron, 456
SoundJam, 383
Soviet Union, 8, 209
Spectra-Physics company, 15
Spielberg, Steven, 291, 427, 442
Spindler, Michael, 296, 335
"Spiritus Domini" (Gregorian chant), 413
Stalin, Joseph, 209
Stanford Linear Accelerator Center (SLAC), 28, 61
Stanford University, 9, 33, 57
    SJ's 2005 commencement address at, 456–57
Star Trek (TV show), 117–18, 494
Star Trek (video game), 44
Stengel, Rick, 506
Stewart, Jon, 508, 518
Sticky Fingers (Rolling Stones), 412
Stone, Edward Durell, 151
Stoppard, Tom, 570

"Strange Things" (song), 288
"Strawberry Fields Forever" (song), 418–19
Stringer, Howard, 395, 407
StyleWriter, 338
Sulzberger, Arthur, Jr., 504–5
Summers, Larry, 497
Sun Microsystems, 236, 294, 296, 308, 333
Sunnyvale Electronics, 28
Suzuki, Shunryu, 35, 49
"Swing Low, Sweet Chariot" (song), 576
Swisher, Kara, 463
Sylvania, 24
"Sympathy for the Devil" (song), 397
Syria, 3, 258

tablet computers, 467, 490–91
"Talkin' bout a Revolution" (song), 280
Talking Heads, 413
Tandy company, 135, 138
Tangerine (design company), 341
Tanimoto, Craig, 329
Target, 369
Tate, Ryan, 516–17
Tattoo You (Rolling Stones), 412
Taylor, Jim, 72
TBWA\Chiat\Day, 328, 351, 391
technology boom:
    counterculture and, 57
    hacker subculture and, 56–57
    microprocessor and, 10
    Moore's Law and, 10
    semiconductors and, 9–10
    10,000 Maniacs, 413
Terman, Frederick, 9
Terravera company, 274
Terrell, Paul, 66–67, 68

Tesler, Larry, 96–97, 99, 114, 120, 136, 301

Tevanian, Avadis "Avie," xvi, 259, 268, 272–74, 300–301, 303, 308–9, 362, 366, 458–59, 461

textbook industry, 509–10, 554

"There Goes My Love" (song), 498

"Things Have Changed" (song), 412

"Think Different" advertising campaign, vii, xviii, 328–32, 358

original Jobs version, 577

Thomas, Brent, 162

Thomas, Dylan, 19

Through the Looking Glass (Carroll), 235

Thurman, Mrs., 12

Thus Spoke Zarathustra (Nietzsche), 119

Tiffany, Louis, 123

Time, xvii, xviii, 90, 166, 218, 290, 323, 381, 383, 429, 473, 495, 504, 506

SJ profiled by, 106–7, 139–41

Time Inc., 330, 473, 478, 504, 506–7

Time-Life Pictures, 330

"Times They Are A-Changing, The" (Dylan), 168, 207

Time Warner, 506

Tin Toy (film), 248

Toshiba, 385, 386

touchscreens, 93

Toy Story (film), 285–91, 305, 311, 372, 373–74, 427, 428, 430, 434, 437, 472, 565

basic idea for, 285–86

blockbuster success of, 290–91

budgeting of, 288

premieres of, 289–90

reviews of, 290

revision of, 287–88

SJ's investment in, 287

television premiere of, 331

Toy Story 2 (film), 430

Toy Story 3 (film), 527, 540

Toy Story Musical, 437

Treasure Planet (film), 437

Tribble, Bud, 117–18, 120, 123, 140, 212, 225

Trips Festival, 58

Trotsky, Leon, 209

"Trouble with Steve Jobs, The" (*Fortune*), 477–78

Trungpa, Chögyam, 35

Turing, Alan, xviii

TV Guide, 165

Twain, Mark, 479

Twiggy, 145

Twitter, 495

"Uncle John's Band" (song), 414

United Network for Organ Sharing, 483

Universal Music Group, 395, 399, 479

UNIX operating system, 212, 297, 298

Up (film), 494

UPS, 219

U2, 399, 413, 537

iPod deal and, 420–22

U-2 spy plane, 8

United Way, 104

USA Today, 507

Valentine, Don, 75–76, 139, 189

Valleywag (website), 516–17, 518

Vanity Fair, 497

Varian Associates, 8, 9

Vatican, 28–29

"Vertigo" (song), 420

Vermilion, Mark, 250

Vidich, Paul, 394–95, 398

Vietnam Veterans Memorial, 127

Vietnam War, 34

"View from the Top" lectures, 268

Vincent, James, xvi, 332, 364, 391, 392, 398, 413, 417, 421–23, 498–500, 521–22, 524

Visa, 410

VisiCalc (finance program), 84

VLSI Technology, 359

"Wade in the Water" (song), 417

Wall-E (film), 441

Wall Street Journal, 135, 187–88, 192, 193, 215, 226, 236, 307, 379, 450, 463, 482, 493, 504, 507, 531

Wall Street Journal Digital Network, 508

Walt Disney Company, *see* Disney Co.

Warhol, Andy, 180

Warner Music, 394, 398, 403

Warnock, John, 515

Warren, Jim, 80

Washington Post, 228, 230, 231

Waters, Alice, 458, 477

Watson, James, 330

Wavy Gravy, 106

Wayne, Ron, xvi, 44, 52, 54, 63–64, 68–69, 73, 79–80

Weeks, Wendell, 471–72

Weitzen, Jeff, 379

Welch, Jack, 401

Wells, Frank, 436–37

Well-Tempered Clavier, The (Bach), 413

Wenner, Jann, 166

West Coast Computer Faire, 80, 123, 189

Westerman, Wayne, 469

Westgate Shopping Center, 32

Westinghouse, 9, 219

West Wing, The (TV show), 456

What the Dormouse Said (Markoff), 57

"When the Night Comes Falling From the Sky" (song), 207–8

Whitman, Meg, 321

Whole Earth Catalog, 57–59, 494

Whole Earth Truck Store, 58

Whose Line Is It Anyway? (TV show), 458

"Why I Won't Buy an iPad" (Doctorow), 563

Wigginton, Randy, 81–82, 92–93, 104, 161

Wikipedia, 386

Wilkes Bashford (store), 91

Williams, Robert, 329–30

Wired, 275–76, 295, 311–12, 317, 408, 466

Wolf, Gary, 295

Wolfe, Tom, 58

Wolff, Michael, 523

Wonder Boys (film), 412

Woodside Design, 196

Woolard, Ed, 310, 313, 314, 318–20, 336, 338, 359, 371

  options compensation issue and, 364–66, 448

"Wooly Bully" (song), 413

Wordsworth, William, 69

"Working for/with Steve Jobs" (Raskin), 112

Worldwide Developers Conference, 532–33, 536

Wozniak, Francis, 22

Wozniak, Jerry, 77

Wozniak, Stephen, xvi, *21*, 29, 32, 33, 59, 62, 69, 79, 93, 94, *102*, 110, 124, 132, 163, 168, 170, 217, *305*, 308, 317, 319, 334–35, 354, 363, 379, 393, 412, 464, 474, 524, *560*, 565, 576
  in air crash, 115
  Apple I design and, 61, 67–68, 534
  Apple II design and, 72–75, 80–81, 84–85, 92, 534, 562
  Apple left by, 192–93
  Apple partnership and, 63–65
  Apple's IPO and, 103–4
  background of, 21–22
  Blue Box designed by, 27–30, 81
  music passion of, 25–26
  personal computer vision of, 60–61
  Pong design and, 52–54
  as prankster, 23–29
  remote control device of, 193–94, 218, 221
  SJ contrasted with, 21–22, 40, 64
  on SJ's distortion of reality, 118–19
  SJ's first meeting with, 25
  SJ's friendship with, 21–23
  at SJ's 30th birthday party, 189
  in White House visit, 192–93
Wright, Frank Lloyd, 7, 330

Xerox, 95–96, 98, 119, 169, 195, 565, 566
  Alto GUI of, 177
  Star computer of, 99, 175–76
Xerox PARC, 94–96, 98–99, 100, 111, 114, 120, 177, 179, 474

Yahoo, 502, 545
Yeah Yeah Yeah (music group), 500
Yocam, Del, xvi, 4–5, 198, 202
Yogananda, Paramahansa, 35
York, Jerry, 321, 450, 482

Zaltair hoax, 81, 189
Zander, Ed, 333, 465
Zap, 53
ZDNet, 137
Zen Buddhism, 15, 34–35, 41, 57
Zen Mind, Beginner's Mind (Suzuki), 35, 49
Ziegler, Bart, 293
Zittrain, Jonathan, 563
Zuckerberg, Mark, 274, 545, 552

ILLUSTRATION CREDITS

Numbers in roman type refer to illustrations in the insert; numbers in *italics* refer to book pages.

Diana Walker—Contour by Getty Images: 1, 2, 3, 4, 5, 6, 7, 8, 9, 10, 11, 12, 13, 23

Courtesy of Steve Jobs: 14, 15, 17, 18, 19, 20, 21, 22, *facing p. 1* (top left and bottom right), *108, 250, 267, 293*

Courtesy of Kathryn Smith: 16

DPA/Landov: *21*

Courtesy of Daniel Kottke: *56*

Mark Richards: *71, 348*

Ted Thai/Polaris: *102*

Norman Seeff: *117, 148*

©Apple Inc. Used with permission. All rights reserved. Apple® and the Apple logo are registered trademarks of Apple Inc.: *159*

George Lange/Contour by Getty Images: *171*

Courtesy Pixar: *238*

Kim Kulish: *305*

John G. Mabanglo/AFP/Getty Images: *327*

Michael O'Neill: *340*

Monica M. Davey—EPA: *358*

Jin Lee/Bloomberg via Getty Images: *368*

Bob Pepping/Contra Costa Times/Zuma Press: *411*

Bebeto Matthews—AP: *444*

Courtesy of Mike Slade: *452*

Kimberly White—Reuters: *490*

John G. Mabanglo/EPA: *560*

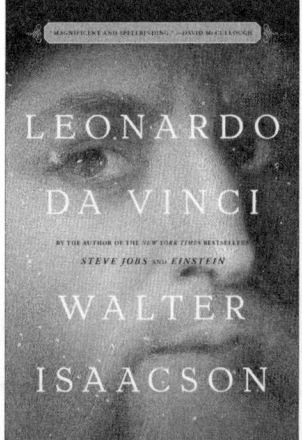

"This book will be widely and deservedly admired. It is excellently readable and combines the personal and the scientific aspects of Einstein's life in a graceful way."

—Gerald Holton, the Mallinckrodt Research Professor of Physics at Harvard University and author of *Einstein, History, and Other Passions*

"An excellent book . . . Isaacson's biography is well researched and contains a surprising amount of new information about its enigmatic subject. . . . Einstein emerges as a flesh-and-blood figure—a human with good qualities and flaws. Even Einstein scholars will likely find here facts they hadn't known. . . . A major and authoritative work on one of the most interesting figures in the history of science."

—Amir D. Aczel, *The Boston Globe*

"Isaacson has admirably succeeded in weaving together the complex threads of Einstein's personal and scientific life to paint a superb portrait."

—Arthur I. Miller, author of *Einstein, Picasso: Space, Time, and the Beauty That Havoc Causes*

"Delightful . . . The most comprehensive English-language biography of Einstein for a general readership . . . Isaacson weaves it all into a seamless narrative."

—Sharon Begley, *Newsweek*

"Isaacson has written a crisp, engaging, and refreshing biography, one that beautifully masters the historical literature and offers many new insights into Einstein's work and life."

—Diana Kormos Buchwald, the general editor of The Collected Papers of Albert Einstein and professor of history at Caltech

"Expansive in scope and exhaustively researched. . . . Isaacson skillfully sheds new light on Einstein's personality. . . . Superb."

—Bob Van Brocklin, *The Sunday Oregonian*

"With unmatched narrative skill, Isaacson has managed the extraordinary feat of preserving Einstein's monumental stature while at the same time bringing him to such vivid life that we come to feel as if he could be walking in our midst. This is a terrific work."

—Doris Kearns Goodwin, author of *Team of Rivals* and *No Ordinary Time*, winner of the Pulitzer Prize for history

Praise for *Einstein*

"An illuminating delight . . . This is a warm, insightful, affectionate portrait with a human and immensely charming Einstein at its core. . . . A wonderfully rounded portrait of the ever-surprising Einstein personality."

—Janet Maslin, *The New York Times*

"Once again Walter Isaacson has produced a most valuable biography of a great man about whom much has already been written. It helps that he has had access to important new material. He met the challenge of dealing with his subject as a human being and describing profound ideas in physics. His biography is a pleasure to read and makes the great physicist come alive."

—Murray Gell-Mann, winner of the 1969 Nobel Prize in Physics and author of *The Quark and the Jaguar*

"Brilliant . . . An illuminating biography of Einstein."

--*Vanity Fair*

"This book does an amazing job getting the science right and the man revealed."

—Sylvester James Gates Jr., the John S. Toll Professor of Physics at the University of Maryland

"A triumph . . . Isaacson understands Einstein and explains his discoveries while sharing riveting personal detail."

—*People* (4 stars)

"Isaacson has given us a life, not just a mind, perhaps the greatest in the twentieth century, but also a personality, as imperfect and fallible as all the rest of us. This unique combination of sheer brilliance and human uncertainty makes this one of the great biographies of our time."

—Joseph J. Ellis, author of *Founding Brothers: The Revolutionary Generation*

"A narrative masterpiece . . . This is a great read by a great writer about a great man—a biographical perfect storm."

—Michael Shermer, *The New York Sun*

"Isaacson has a lovely sense of the poetry of physics. . . . Utterly absorbing."

—Susan Larson, *The Times-Picayune* (New Orleans)

"Thoroughly researched and well written, *Einstein* does an excellent job of summarizing the concepts behind Einstein's theories. . . . Isaacson also does an excellent job illuminating Einstein's personality."

—Dennis O'Brien, *The Baltimore Sun*

"Isaacson has done a remarkable job conveying a sense of Einstein the man and also the fine details of Einstein's science. This is not only a compelling biography, one in which the next page always beckons, but an example of science writing at its best."

—Lawrence M. Krauss, the Ambrose Swasey Professor of Physics at Case Western Reserve and author of *Hiding in the Mirror*

"Isaacson brings the genius to life through letters, anecdotes, quotes and humor. . . . Isaacson has managed to make a science book read like a thriller."

—L. A. Lorek, *San Antonio Express-News*

"Isaacson's treatment of Einstein's scientific work is excellent: accurate, complete, and at just the right level of detail for the general reader. Taking advantage of the wealth of recently uncovered historical material, he has produced the most readable biography of Einstein yet."

—A. Douglas Stone, professor of physics at Yale

"Stimulating and provocative."

—Thomas L. Friedman, *The New York Times*

"Isaacson has triumphed . . . producing a thorough exploration of his subject's life, a skillful piece of scientific literature and a thumping good read. . . . It's one of the greatest stories of modern science and to his credit . . . Isaacson has done a first-rate job in telling it. This is, quite simply, a riveting read."

—Robin McKie, *The Guardian* (UK)

"Exemplary science writing . . . Isaacson exudes both a crisp precision and profundity that belie the difficulty of the physics Einstein created. He magisterially guides us through the man's expansive body of work that prefigured most modern physics. . . . Isaacson's tremendous scholarship in uncovering more of the less frequently discussed aspects of Einstein's character will stand as a benchmark for works to come."

—Joshua Roebke, *Seed*

"An accessible, fascinating account of one of the twentieth century's greatest figures . . . Like its subject, Walter Isaacson's ambitious biography of Albert Einstein radiates intelligence, wit and eloquence."
—Kathleen Krog, *The Miami Herald*

"A painstaking and reliable biography. You won't go wrong in reading and learning from it."
—Michael Dirda, *The Washington Post Book World*

"I found it hard to put down."
—Daniel Sutherland, *Chicago Tribune*

"A biography of Albert Einstein may seem daunting to many readers. Walter Isaacson gives you one that isn't. . . . Isaacson is a fluid writer whose narrative talents give Einstein an aura missing from many previous accounts of his life."
—Steve Weinberg, *The Houston Chronicle*

"Dramatic and revelatory."
—Bryan Appleyard, *Sunday Times* (London)

"Fascinating . . . a delicious read."
—Ian Stewart, *Winnipeg Free Press*

"Narrative nonfiction at its best . . . What the book also does is move the author up from the ranks of skilled narrator of history—one who seeks the story behind historical facts—and into the top tier of the craft to join the likes of David McCullough and Doris Kearns Goodwin."
—James Srodes, *The Washington Times*

"A fine, affectionate and determinedly lucid account of both Einstein's life and thought."
—Duane Davis, *Rocky Mountain News*

"A new biography offering hearty helpings alike of energy, mass, and light . . . To Isaacson's credit, *Einstein: His Life and Universe* conveys the dizzying concepts of physics in a way most lay readers can grasp."
—Erik Spanberg, *Christian Science Monitor*

"A triumphant biography . . . another coup for Isaacson."
—John Mark Eberhart, *The Kansas City Star*

ALSO BY WALTER ISAACSON

*The Innovators: How a Group of Hackers, Geniuses, and
Geeks Created the Digital Revolution*

Steve Jobs

American Sketches

Einstein: His Life and Universe

A Benjamin Franklin Reader

Benjamin Franklin: An American Life

Kissinger: A Biography

The Wise Men: Six Friends and the World They Made
(with Evan Thomas)

Pro and Con

ALSO BY WALTER ISAACSON

The Innovators: How a Group of Hackers, Geniuses, and Geeks Created the Digital Revolution

Steve Jobs

American Sketches

Einstein: His Life and Universe

A Benjamin Franklin Reader

Benjamin Franklin: An American Life

Kissinger: A Biography

The Wise Men: Six Friends and the World They Made
(with Evan Thomas)

Pro and Con

EINSTEIN

HIS LIFE
AND UNIVERSE

WALTER
ISAACSON

SIMON & SCHUSTER PAPERBACKS
New York   London   Toronto   Sydney   New Delhi

To my father,
the nicest, smartest, and most moral man I know

 SIMON & SCHUSTER PAPERBACKS
An Imprint of Simon & Schuster, Inc.
1230 Avenue of the Americas
New York, NY 10020

First Simon & Schuster paperback edition May 2008

SIMON & SCHUSTER PAPERBACKS and colophon are registered trademarks
of Simon & Schuster, Inc.

The Simon & Schuster Speakers Bureau can bring authors to your live event.
For more information or to book an event, contact the Simon & Schuster Speakers
Bureau at 1-866-248-3049 or visit our website at www.simonspeakers.com.

For information about special discounts for bulk purchases,
please contact Simon & Schuster Special Sales at
1-866-506-1949 or business@simonandschuster.com.

Frontispiece: Ullstein Bilderdienst/The Granger Collection, New York

Illustration credits are on page 679.

Manufactured in the United States of America

20

The Library of Congress has cataloged the hardcover edition as follows:
Isaacson, Walter.
  Einstein : his life and universe / Walter Isaacson.
    p. cm.
  Includes bibliographical references and index.
  1. Einstein, Albert, 1879–1955.   2. Physicists—Biography.   3. Einstein, Albert,
1879–1955—Friends and associates.   4. Relativity (Physics).   5. Unified field
theories.   I. Title.

QC16.E5I76 2007
530.092—dc22
[B]   2006051264

ISBN 978-0-7432-6473-0
ISBN 978-0-7432-6474-7 (pbk)
ISBN 978-1-4165-3932-2 (ebook)

In Santa Barbara, 1933

Life is like riding a bicycle.
To keep your balance you must keep moving.

—ALBERT EINSTEIN, IN A LETTER TO HIS SON EDUARD, FEBRUARY 5, 1930[1]

CONTENTS

Acknowledgments   xv

Main Characters   xix

CHAPTER ONE
The Light-Beam Rider   1

CHAPTER TWO
Childhood, 1879–1896   8

CHAPTER THREE
The Zurich Polytechnic, 1896–1900   32

CHAPTER FOUR
The Lovers, 1900–1904   50

CHAPTER FIVE
The Miracle Year: Quanta and Molecules, 1905   90

CHAPTER SIX
Special Relativity, 1905   107

CHAPTER SEVEN

The Happiest Thought, 1906–1909   140

CHAPTER EIGHT

The Wandering Professor, 1909–1914   158

CHAPTER NINE

General Relativity, 1911–1915   189

CHAPTER TEN

Divorce, 1916–1919   225

CHAPTER ELEVEN

Einstein's Universe, 1916–1919   249

CHAPTER TWELVE

Fame, 1919   263

CHAPTER THIRTEEN

The Wandering Zionist, 1920–1921   281

CHAPTER FOURTEEN

Nobel Laureate, 1921–1927   309

CHAPTER FIFTEEN

Unified Field Theories, 1923–1931   336

CHAPTER SIXTEEN

Turning Fifty, 1929–1931   357

CHAPTER SEVENTEEN

Einstein's God   384

CHAPTER EIGHTEEN

The Refugee, 1932–1933   394

CHAPTER NINETEEN
America, 1933–1939 425

CHAPTER TWENTY
Quantum Entanglement, 1935 448

CHAPTER TWENTY-ONE
The Bomb, 1939–1945 471

CHAPTER TWENTY-TWO
One-Worlder, 1945–1948 487

CHAPTER TWENTY-THREE
Landmark, 1948–1953 508

CHAPTER TWENTY-FOUR
Red Scare, 1951–1954 524

CHAPTER TWENTY-FIVE
The End, 1955 535

EPILOGUE
Einstein's Brain and Einstein's Mind 544

Sources 553
Notes 565
Index 643

ACKNOWLEDGMENTS

Diana Kormos Buchwald, the general editor of Einstein's papers, read this book meticulously and made copious comments and corrections through many drafts. In addition, she helped me get early and complete access to the wealth of new Einstein papers that became available in 2006, and guided me through them. She was also a gracious host and facilitator during my trips to the Einstein Papers Project at Caltech. She has a passion for her work and a delightful sense of humor, which would have pleased her subject.

Two of her associates were also very helpful in guiding me through the newly available papers as well as untapped riches in the older archival material. Tilman Sauer, who likewise checked and annotated this book, in particular vetted the sections on Einstein's quest for the equations of general relativity and his pursuit of a unified field theory. Ze'ev Rosenkranz, the historical editor of the papers, provided insights on Einstein's attitudes toward Germany and his Jewish heritage. He was formerly curator of the Einstein archives at Hebrew University in Jerusalem.

Barbara Wolff, who is now at those archives at Hebrew University, did a careful fact-checking of every page of the manuscript, making fastidious corrections large and small. She warned that she has a reputation as a nitpicker, but I am very grateful for each and every nit she found. I also appreciate the encouragement given by Roni Grosz, the curator there.

Brian Greene, the Columbia University physicist and author of *The*

Fabric of the Cosmos, was an indispensable friend and editor. He talked me through numerous revisions, honed the wording of the science passages, and read the final manuscript. He is a master of both science and language. In addition to his work on string theory, he and his wife, Tracy Day, are organizing an annual science festival in New York City, which will help spread the enthusiasm for physics so evident in his work and books.

Lawrence Krauss, professor of physics at Case Western Reserve and author of *Hiding in the Mirror,* also read my manuscript, vetted the sections on special relativity, general relativity, and cosmology, and offered many good suggestions and corrections. He, too, has an infectious enthusiasm for physics.

Krauss helped me enlist a protégé of his at Case, Craig J. Copi, who teaches relativity there. I hired him to do a thorough checking of the science and math, and I am grateful for his diligent edits.

Douglas Stone, professor of physics at Yale, also vetted the science in the book. A condensed matter theorist, he is writing what will be an important book on Einstein's contributions to quantum mechanics. In addition to checking my science sections, he helped me write the chapters on the 1905 light quanta paper, quantum theory, Bose-Einstein statistics, and kinetic theory.

Murray Gell-Mann, winner of the 1969 Nobel Prize in physics, was a delightful and passionate guide from the beginning to the end of this project. He helped me revise early drafts, edited and corrected the chapters on relativity and quantum mechanics, and helped draft sections that explained Einstein's objections to quantum uncertainty. With his combination of erudition and humor, and his feel for the personalities involved, he made the process a great joy.

Arthur I. Miller, emeritus professor of history and philosophy of science at University College, London, is the author of *Einstein, Picasso* and of *Empire of the Stars.* He read and reread the versions of my scientific chapters and helped with numerous revisions, especially on special relativity (about which he wrote a pioneering book), general relativity, and quantum theory.

Sylvester James Gates Jr., a physics professor at the University of Maryland, agreed to read my manuscript when he came out to Aspen for a conference on Einstein. He did a comprehensive edit filled with smart comments and rephrasing of certain scientific passages.

John D. Norton, a professor at the University of Pittsburgh, has specialized in tracing Einstein's thought process as he developed both special and then general relativity. He read these sections of my book, made edits, and offered useful comments. I am also grateful for guidance from two of his fellow scholars specializing in Einstein's development of his theories: Jürgen Renn of the Max Planck Institute in Berlin and Michel Janssen of the University of Minnesota.

George Stranahan, a founder of the Aspen Center for Physics, also agreed to read and review the manuscript. He was particularly helpful in editing the sections on the light quanta paper, Brownian motion, and the history and science of special relativity.

Robert Rynasiewicz, a philosopher of science at Johns Hopkins, read many of the science chapters and made useful suggestions about the quest for general relativity.

N. David Mermin, professor of theoretical physics at Cornell and author of *It's About Time: Understanding Einstein's Relativity,* edited and made corrections to the final version of the introductory chapter and chapters 5 and 6 on Einstein's 1905 papers.

Gerald Holton, professor of physics at Harvard, has been one of the pioneers in the study of Einstein, and he is still a guiding light. I am deeply flattered that he was willing to read my book, make comments, and offer generous encouragement. His Harvard colleague Dudley Herschbach, who has done so much for science education, also was supportive. Both Holton and Herschbach made useful comments on my draft and spent an afternoon with me in Holton's office going over suggestions and refining my descriptions of the historical players.

Ashton Carter, professor of science and international affairs at Harvard, kindly read and checked an early draft. Columbia University's Fritz Stern, author of *Einstein's German World,* provided encouragement and advice at the outset. Robert Schulmann, one of the original editors at the Einstein Papers Project, did likewise. And Jeremy Bernstein, who has written many fine books on Einstein, warned me how difficult the science would be. He was right, and I am grateful for that as well.

In addition, I asked two teachers of high school physics to give the book a careful reading to make sure the science was correct, and also comprehensible to those whose last physics course was in high school. Nancy Stravinsky Isaacson taught physics in New Orleans until, alas, Hurricane Katrina gave her more free time. David Derbes teaches physics at the University of Chicago Lab School. Their comments were very incisive and also aimed at the lay reader.

There is a corollary of the uncertainty principle that says that no matter how often a book is observed, some mistakes will remain. Those are my fault.

It also helped to have some nonscientific readers, who made very useful suggestions from a lay perspective on parts or all of the manuscript. These included William Mayer, Orville Wright, Daniel Okrent, Steve Weisman, and Strobe Talbott.

For twenty-five years, Alice Mayhew at Simon & Schuster has been my editor and Amanda Urban at ICM my agent. I can imagine no better partners, and they were again enthusiastic and helpful in their comments on the book. I also appreciate the help of Carolyn Reidy, David Rosenthal, Roger Labrie, Victoria Meyer, Elizabeth Hayes, Serena Jones, Mara Lurie, Judith Hoover, Jackie Seow, and Dana Sloan at Simon & Schuster. For their countless acts of support over the years, I am also grateful to Elliot Ravetz and Patricia Zindulka.

Natasha Hoffmeyer and James Hoppes translated for me Einstein's German correspondence and writing, especially the new material that had not yet been translated, and I appreciate their diligence. Jay Colton, who was photo editor for *Time*'s Person of the Century issue, also did a creative job tracking down pictures for this book.

I had two and a half other readers who were the most valuable of all. The first was my father, Irwin Isaacson, an engineer who instilled in me a love of science and is the smartest teacher I've ever had. I am grateful to him for the universe that he and my late mother created for me, and to my brilliant and wise stepmother, Julanne.

The other truly valuable reader was my wife, Cathy, who read every page with her usual wisdom, common sense, and curiosity. And the valuable half-a-reader was my daughter, Betsy, who as usual read selected portions of my book. The surety with which she made her pronouncements made up for the randomness of her reading. I love them both dearly.

MAIN CHARACTERS

MICHELE ANGELO BESSO (1873–1955). Einstein's closest friend. An engaging but unfocused engineer, he met Einstein in Zurich, then followed him to work at the Bern patent office. Served as a sounding board for the 1905 special relativity paper. Married Anna Winteler, sister of Einstein's first girlfriend.

NIELS BOHR (1885–1962). Danish pioneer of quantum theory. At Solvay conferences and subsequent intellectual trysts, he parried Einstein's enthusiastic challenges to his Copenhagen interpretation of quantum mechanics.

MAX BORN (1882–1970). German physicist and mathematician. Engaged in a brilliant, intimate correspondence with Einstein for forty years. Tried to convince Einstein to be comfortable with quantum mechanics; his wife, Hedwig, challenged Einstein on personal issues.

HELEN DUKAS (1896–1982). Einstein's loyal secretary, Cerberus-like guard, and housemate from 1928 until his death, and after that protector of his legacy and papers.

ARTHUR STANLEY EDDINGTON (1882–1944). British astrophysicist and champion of relativity whose 1919 eclipse observations dramatically confirmed Einstein's prediction of how much gravity bends light.

PAUL EHRENFEST (1880–1933). Austrian-born physicist, intense and insecure, who bonded with Einstein on a visit to Prague in 1912 and became a professor in Leiden, where he frequently hosted Einstein.

EDUARD EINSTEIN (1910–1965). Second son of Mileva Marić and Einstein. Smart and artistic, he obsessed about Freud and hoped to be a psychiatrist, but he succumbed to his own schizophrenic demons in his twenties and was institutionalized in Switzerland for much of the rest of his life.

ELSA EINSTEIN (1876–1936). Einstein's first cousin, second wife. Mother of Margot and Ilse Einstein from her first marriage to textile merchant Max Löwenthal. She and her daughters reverted to her maiden name, Einstein, after her 1908 divorce. Married Einstein in 1919. Smarter than she pretended to be, she knew how to handle him.

HANS ALBERT EINSTEIN (1904–1973). First son of Mileva Marić and Einstein, a difficult role that he handled with grace. Studied engineering at Zurich Polytechnic. Married Frieda Knecht (1895–1958) in 1927. They had two sons, Bernard (1930–) and Klaus (1932–1938), and an adopted daughter, Evelyn (1941–). Moved to the United States in 1938 and eventually became a professor of hydraulic engineering at Berkeley. After Frieda's death, married Elizabeth Roboz (1904–1995) in 1959. Bernard has five children, the only known great-grandchildren of Albert Einstein.

HERMANN EINSTEIN (1847–1902). Einstein's father, from a Jewish family from rural Swabia. With his brother Jakob, he ran electrical companies in Munich and then Italy, but not very successfully.

ILSE EINSTEIN (1897–1934). Daughter of Elsa Einstein from her first marriage. Dallied with adventurous physician Georg Nicolai and in 1924 married literary journalist Rudolph Kayser, who later wrote a book on Einstein using the pseudonym Anton Reiser.

LIESERL EINSTEIN (1902–?). Premarital daughter of Einstein and Mileva Marić. Einstein probably never saw her. Likely left in her Serbian mother's hometown of Novi Sad for adoption and may have died of scarlet fever in late 1903.

MARGOT EINSTEIN (1899–1986). Daughter of Elsa Einstein from her first marriage. A shy sculptor. Married Russian Dimitri Marianoff in 1930; no children. He later wrote a book on Einstein. She divorced him in 1937, moved in with Einstein at Princeton, and remained at 112 Mercer Street until her death.

MARIA "MAJA" EINSTEIN (1881–1951). Einstein's only sibling, and among his closest confidantes. Married Paul Winteler, had no children, and in 1938 moved without him from Italy to Princeton to live with her brother.

PAULINE KOCH EINSTEIN (1858–1920). Einstein's strong-willed and practical mother. Daughter of a prosperous Jewish grain dealer from Württemberg. Married Hermann Einstein in 1876.

ABRAHAM FLEXNER (1866–1959). American education reformer. Founded the Institute for Advanced Study in Princeton and recruited Einstein there.

PHILIPP FRANK (1884–1966). Austrian physicist. Succeeded his friend Einstein at German University of Prague and later wrote a book about him.

MARCEL GROSSMANN (1878–1936). Diligent classmate at Zurich Polytechnic who took math notes for Einstein and then helped him get a job in the patent office. As professor of descriptive geometry at the Polytechnic, guided Einstein to the math he needed for general relativity.

FRITZ HABER (1868–1934). German chemist and gas warfare pioneer who helped recruit Einstein to Berlin and mediated between him and Marić. A Jew who converted to Christianity in an attempt to be a good German, he preached to Einstein the virtues of assimilation, until the Nazis came to power.

CONRAD HABICHT (1876–1958). Mathematician and amateur inventor, member of the "Olympia Academy" discussion trio in Bern, and recipient of two famous 1905 letters from Einstein heralding forthcoming papers.

WERNER HEISENBERG (1901–1976). German physicist. A pioneer of quantum mechanics, he formulated the uncertainty principle that Einstein spent years resisting.

DAVID HILBERT (1862–1943). German mathematician who in 1915 raced Einstein to discover the mathematical equations for general relativity.

BANESH HOFFMANN (1906–1986). Mathematician and physicist who collaborated with Einstein in Princeton and later wrote a book about him.

PHILIPP LENARD (1862–1947). Hungarian-German physicist whose experimental observations on the photoelectric effect were explained by Einstein in his 1905 light quanta paper. Became an anti-Semite, Nazi, and Einstein hater.

HENDRIK ANTOON LORENTZ (1853–1928). Genial and wise Dutch physicist whose theories paved the way for special relativity. Became a father figure to Einstein.

MILEVA MARIĆ (1875–1948). Serbian physics student at Zurich Polytechnic who became Einstein's first wife. Mother of Hans Albert, Eduard, and Lieserl. Passionate and driven, but also brooding and increasingly gloomy, she triumphed over many, but not all, of the obstacles that then faced an aspiring female physicist. Separated from Einstein in 1914, divorced in 1919.

ROBERT ANDREWS MILLIKAN (1868–1953). American experimental physicist who confirmed Einstein's law of the photoelectric effect and recruited him to be a visiting scholar at Caltech.

HERMANN MINKOWSKI (1864–1909). Taught Einstein math at the Zurich Polytechnic, referred to him as a "lazy dog," and devised a mathematical formulation of special relativity in terms of four-dimensional spacetime.

GEORG FRIEDRICH NICOLAI, born Lewinstein (1874–1964). Physician, pacifist, charismatic adventurer, and seducer. A friend and doctor of Elsa Einstein and probable lover of her daughter Ilse, he wrote a pacifist tract with Einstein in 1915.

ABRAHAM PAIS (1918–2000). Dutch-born theoretical physicist who became a colleague of Einstein in Princeton and wrote a scientific biography of him.

MAX PLANCK (1858–1947). Prussian theoretical physicist who was an early patron of Einstein and helped recruit him to Berlin. His conservative instincts, both in life and in physics, made him a contrast to Einstein, but they remained warm and loyal colleagues until the Nazis took power.

ERWIN SCHRÖDINGER (1887–1961). Austrian theoretical physicist who was a pioneer of quantum mechanics but joined Einstein in expressing discomfort with the uncertainties and probabilities at its core.

MAURICE SOLOVINE (1875–1958). Romanian philosophy student in Bern who founded the "Olympia Academy" with Einstein and Habicht. Became Einstein's French publisher and lifelong correspondent.

LEÓ SZILÁRD (1898–1964). Hungarian-born physicist, charming and eccentric, who met Einstein in Berlin and patented a refrigerator with him. Conceived the nuclear chain reaction and cowrote the 1939 letter Einstein sent to President Franklin Roosevelt urging attention to the possibility of an atomic bomb.

CHAIM WEIZMANN (1874–1952). Russian-born chemist who emigrated to England and became president of the World Zionist Organization. In 1921, he brought Einstein to America for the first time, using him as the draw for a fundraising tour. Was first president of Israel, a post offered upon his death to Einstein.

THE WINTELER FAMILY. Einstein boarded with them while he was a student in Aarau, Switzerland. Jost Winteler was his history and Greek teacher; his wife, Rosa, became a surrogate mother. Of their seven children, Marie became Einstein's first girlfriend; Anna married Einstein's best friend, Michele Besso; and Paul married Einstein's sister, Maja.

HEINRICH ZANGGER (1874–1957). Professor of physiology at the University of Zurich. Befriended Einstein and Marić and helped mediate their disputes and divorce.

THE LIGHT-BEAM RIDER

"I promise you four papers," the young patent examiner wrote his friend. The letter would turn out to bear some of the most significant tidings in the history of science, but its momentous nature was masked by an impish tone that was typical of its author. He had, after all, just addressed his friend as "you frozen whale" and apologized for writing a letter that was "inconsequential babble." Only when he got around to describing the papers, which he had produced during his spare time, did he give some indication that he sensed their significance.[1]

"The first deals with radiation and the energy properties of light and is very revolutionary," he explained. Yes, it was indeed revolutionary. It argued that light could be regarded not just as a wave but also as a stream of tiny particles called quanta. The implications that would eventually arise from this theory—a cosmos without strict causality or certainty—would spook him for the rest of his life.

"The second paper is a determination of the true sizes of atoms." Even though the very existence of atoms was still in dispute, this was the most straightforward of the papers, which is why he chose it as the safest bet for his latest attempt at a doctoral thesis. He was in the process of revolutionizing physics, but he had been repeatedly thwarted in his efforts to win an academic job or even get a doctoral degree, which he hoped might get him promoted from a third- to a second-class examiner at the patent office.

The third paper explained the jittery motion of microscopic particles in liquid by using a statistical analysis of random collisions. In the process, it established that atoms and molecules actually exist.

"The fourth paper is only a rough draft at this point, and is an electrodynamics of moving bodies which employs a modification of the theory of space and time." Well, that was certainly more than inconsequential babble. Based purely on thought experiments—performed in his head rather than in a lab—he had decided to discard Newton's concepts of absolute space and time. It would become known as the Special Theory of Relativity.

What he did not tell his friend, because it had not yet occurred to him, was that he would produce a fifth paper that year, a short addendum to the fourth, which posited a relationship between energy and mass. Out of it would arise the best-known equation in all of physics: $E=mc^2$.

Looking back at a century that will be remembered for its willingness to break classical bonds, and looking ahead to an era that seeks to nurture the creativity needed for scientific innovation, one person stands out as a paramount icon of our age: the kindly refugee from oppression whose wild halo of hair, twinkling eyes, engaging humanity, and extraordinary brilliance made his face a symbol and his name a synonym for genius. Albert Einstein was a locksmith blessed with imagination and guided by a faith in the harmony of nature's handiwork. His fascinating story, a testament to the connection between creativity and freedom, reflects the triumphs and tumults of the modern era.

Now that his archives have been completely opened, it is possible to explore how the private side of Einstein—his nonconformist personality, his instincts as a rebel, his curiosity, his passions and detachments—intertwined with his political side and his scientific side. Knowing about the man helps us understand the wellsprings of his science, and vice versa. Character and imagination and creative genius were all related, as if part of some unified field.

Despite his reputation for being aloof, he was in fact passionate in both his personal and scientific pursuits. At college he fell madly in love with the only woman in his physics class, a dark and intense Serbian named Mileva Marić. They had an illegitimate daughter, then married and had two sons. She served as a sounding board for his scientific ideas and helped to check the math in his papers, but eventually their relationship disintegrated. Einstein offered her a deal. He would win the Nobel Prize someday, he said; if she gave him a divorce, he would give her the prize money. She thought for a week and accepted. Because his theories were so radical, it was seventeen years after his miraculous outpouring from the patent office before he was awarded the prize and she collected.

Einstein's life and work reflected the disruption of societal certainties and moral absolutes in the modernist atmosphere of the early twentieth century. Imaginative nonconformity was in the air: Picasso, Joyce, Freud, Stravinsky, Schoenberg, and others were breaking conventional bonds. Charging this atmosphere was a conception of the universe in which space and time and the properties of particles seemed based on the vagaries of observations.

Einstein, however, was not truly a relativist, even though that is how he was interpreted by many, including some whose disdain was tinged by anti-Semitism. Beneath all of his theories, including relativity, was a quest for invariants, certainties, and absolutes. There was a harmonious reality underlying the laws of the universe, Einstein felt, and the goal of science was to discover it.

His quest began in 1895, when as a 16-year-old he imagined what it would be like to ride alongside a light beam. A decade later came his miracle year, described in the letter above, which laid the foundations for the two great advances of twentieth-century physics: relativity and quantum theory.

A decade after that, in 1915, he wrested from nature his crowning glory, one of the most beautiful theories in all of science, the general theory of relativity. As with the special theory, his thinking had evolved through thought experiments. Imagine being in an enclosed elevator accelerating up through space, he conjectured in one of them. The effects you'd feel would be indistinguishable from the experience of gravity.

Gravity, he figured, was a warping of space and time, and he came up with the equations that describe how the dynamics of this curvature result from the interplay between matter, motion, and energy. It can be described by using another thought experiment. Picture what it would be like to roll a bowling ball onto the two-dimensional surface of a trampoline. Then roll some billiard balls. They move toward the bowling ball not because it exerts some mysterious attraction but because of the way it curves the trampoline fabric. Now imagine this happening in the four-dimensional fabric of space and time. Okay, it's not easy, but that's why we're no Einstein and he was.

The exact midpoint of his career came a decade after that, in 1925, and it was a turning point. The quantum revolution he had helped to launch was being transformed into a new mechanics that was based on uncertainties and probabilities. He made his last great contributions to quantum mechanics that year but, simultaneously, began to resist it. He would spend the next three decades, ending with some equations scribbled while on his deathbed in 1955, stubbornly criticizing what he regarded as the incompleteness of quantum mechanics while attempting to subsume it into a unified field theory.

Both during his thirty years as a revolutionary and his subsequent thirty years as a resister, Einstein remained consistent in his willingness to be a serenely amused loner who was comfortable not conforming. Independent in his thinking, he was driven by an imagination that broke from the confines of conventional wisdom. He was that odd breed, a reverential rebel, and he was guided by a faith, which he wore lightly and with a twinkle in his eye, in a God who would not play dice by allowing things to happen by chance.

Einstein's nonconformist streak was evident in his personality and politics as well. Although he subscribed to socialist ideals, he was too much of an individualist to be comfortable with excessive state control or centralized authority. His impudent instincts, which served him so well as a young scientist, made him allergic to nationalism, militarism, and anything that smacked of a herd mentality. And until Hitler caused him to revise his geopolitical equations, he was an instinctive pacifist who celebrated resistance to war.

His tale encompasses the vast sweep of modern science, from the infinitesimal to the infinite, from the emission of photons to the expansion of the cosmos. A century after his great triumphs, we are still living in Einstein's universe, one defined on the macro scale by his theory of relativity and on the micro scale by a quantum mechanics that has proven durable even as it remains disconcerting.

His fingerprints are all over today's technologies. Photoelectric cells and lasers, nuclear power and fiber optics, space travel, and even semiconductors all trace back to his theories. He signed the letter to Franklin Roosevelt warning that it may be possible to build an atom bomb, and the letters of his famed equation relating energy to mass hover in our minds when we picture the resulting mushroom cloud.

Einstein's launch into fame, which occurred when measurements made during a 1919 eclipse confirmed his prediction of how much gravity bends light, coincided with, and contributed to, the birth of a new celebrity age. He became a scientific supernova and humanist icon, one of the most famous faces on the planet. The public earnestly puzzled over his theories, elevated him into a cult of genius, and canonized him as a secular saint.

If he did not have that electrified halo of hair and those piercing eyes, would he still have become science's preeminent poster boy? Suppose, as a thought experiment, that he had looked like a Max Planck or a Niels Bohr. Would he have remained in their reputational orbit, that of a mere scientific genius? Or would he still have made the leap into the pantheon inhabited by Aristotle, Galileo, and Newton?[2]

The latter, I believe, is the case. His work had a very personal character, a stamp that made it recognizably his, the way a Picasso is recognizably a Picasso. He made imaginative leaps and discerned great principles through thought experiments rather than by methodical inductions based on experimental data. The theories that resulted were at times astonishing, mysterious, and counterintuitive, yet they contained notions that could capture the popular imagination: the relativity of space and time, $E=mc^2$, the bending of light beams, and the warping of space.

Adding to his aura was his simple humanity. His inner security was tempered by the humility that comes from being awed by nature. He could be detached and aloof from those close to him, but toward mankind in general he exuded a true kindness and gentle compassion.

Yet for all of his popular appeal and surface accessibility, Einstein also came to symbolize the perception that modern physics was something that ordinary laymen could not comprehend, "the province of priest-like experts," in the words of Harvard professor Dudley Herschbach.[3] It was not always thus. Galileo and Newton were both great geniuses, but their mechanical cause-and-effect explanation of the world was something that most thoughtful folks could grasp. In the eighteenth century of Benjamin Franklin and the nineteenth century of Thomas Edison, an educated person could feel some familiarity with science and even dabble in it as an amateur.

A popular feel for scientific endeavors should, if possible, be restored given the needs of the twenty-first century. This does not mean that every literature major should take a watered-down physics course or that a corporate lawyer should stay abreast of quantum mechanics. Rather, it means that an appreciation for the methods of science is a useful asset for a responsible citizenry. What science teaches us, very significantly, is the correlation between factual evidence and general theories, something well illustrated in Einstein's life.

In addition, an appreciation for the glories of science is a joyful trait for a good society. It helps us remain in touch with that childlike capacity for wonder, about such ordinary things as falling apples and elevators, that characterizes Einstein and other great theoretical physicists.[4]

That is why studying Einstein can be worthwhile. Science is inspiring and noble, and its pursuit an enchanting mission, as the sagas of its heroes remind us. Near the end of his life, Einstein was asked by the New York State Education Department what schools should emphasize. "In teaching history," he replied, "there should be extensive discussion of personalities who benefited mankind through independence of character and judgment."[5] Einstein fits into that category.

At a time when there is a new emphasis, in the face of global competition, on science and math education, we should also note the other part of Einstein's answer. "Critical comments by students should be taken in a friendly spirit," he said. "Accumulation of material should not stifle the student's independence." A society's competitive advantage will come not from how well its schools teach the multiplication and periodic tables, but from how well they stimulate imagination and creativity.

Therein lies the key, I think, to Einstein's brilliance and the lessons of his life. As a young student he never did well with rote learning. And later, as a theorist, his success came not from the brute strength of his mental processing power but from his imagination and creativity. He could construct complex equations, but more important, he knew that math is the language nature uses to describe her wonders. So he could visualize how equations were reflected in realities—how the electromagnetic field equations discovered by James Clerk Maxwell, for example, would manifest themselves to a boy riding alongside a light beam. As he once declared, "Imagination is more important than knowledge."[6]

That approach required him to embrace nonconformity. "Long live impudence!" he exulted to the lover who would later become his wife. "It is my guardian angel in this world." Many years later, when others thought that his reluctance to embrace quantum mechanics showed that he had lost his edge, he lamented, "To punish me for my contempt for authority, fate made me an authority myself."[7]

His success came from questioning conventional wisdom, challenging authority, and marveling at mysteries that struck others as mundane. This led him to embrace a morality and politics based on respect for free minds, free spirits, and free individuals. Tyranny repulsed him, and he saw tolerance not simply as a sweet virtue but as a necessary condition for a creative society. "It is important to foster individuality," he said, "for only the individual can produce the new ideas."[8]

This outlook made Einstein a rebel with a reverence for the harmony of nature, one who had just the right blend of imagination and wisdom to transform our understanding of the universe. These traits are just as vital for this new century of globalization, in which our success will depend on our creativity, as they were for the beginning of the twentieth century, when Einstein helped usher in the modern age.

CHAPTER TWO

CHILDHOOD

1879–1896

Maja, age 3, and Albert Einstein, 5

The Swabian

He was slow in learning how to talk. "My parents were so worried," he later recalled, "that they consulted a doctor." Even after he had begun using words, sometime after the age of 2, he developed a quirk that prompted the family maid to dub him "der Depperte," the dopey one, and others in his family to label him as "almost backwards." Whenever he had something to say, he would try it out on himself, whispering it softly until it sounded good enough to pronounce aloud. "Every sentence he uttered," his worshipful younger sister recalled, "no matter how routine, he repeated to himself softly, moving his lips." It was all very worrying, she said. "He had such difficulty with language that those around him feared he would never learn."[1]

His slow development was combined with a cheeky rebelliousness toward authority, which led one schoolmaster to send him packing and another to amuse history by declaring that he would never amount to much. These traits made Albert Einstein the patron saint of distracted school kids everywhere.² But they also helped to make him, or so he later surmised, the most creative scientific genius of modern times.

His cocky contempt for authority led him to question received wisdom in ways that well-trained acolytes in the academy never contemplated. And as for his slow verbal development, he came to believe that it allowed him to observe with wonder the everyday phenomena that others took for granted. "When I ask myself how it happened that I in particular discovered the relativity theory, it seemed to lie in the following circumstance," Einstein once explained. "The ordinary adult never bothers his head about the problems of space and time. These are things he has thought of as a child. But I developed so slowly that I began to wonder about space and time only when I was already grown up. Consequently, I probed more deeply into the problem than an ordinary child would have."³

Einstein's developmental problems have probably been exaggerated, perhaps even by himself, for we have some letters from his adoring grandparents saying that he was just as clever and endearing as every grandchild is. But throughout his life, Einstein had a mild form of echolalia, causing him to repeat phrases to himself, two or three times, especially if they amused him. And he generally preferred to think in pictures, most notably in famous thought experiments, such as imagining watching lightning strikes from a moving train or experiencing gravity while inside a falling elevator. "I very rarely think in words at all," he later told a psychologist. "A thought comes, and I may try to express it in words afterwards."⁴

Einstein was descended, on both parents' sides, from Jewish tradesmen and peddlers who had, for at least two centuries, made modest livings in the rural villages of Swabia in southwestern Germany. With each generation they had become, or at least so they thought, increasingly assimilated into the German culture that they loved. Although Jewish by cultural designation and kindred instinct, they displayed scant interest in the religion or its rituals.

Einstein regularly dismissed the role that his heritage played in shaping who he became. "Exploration of my ancestors," he told a friend late in life, "leads nowhere."[5] That's not fully true. He was blessed by being born into an independent-minded and intelligent family line that valued education, and his life was certainly affected, in ways both beautiful and tragic, by membership in a religious heritage that had a distinctive intellectual tradition and a history of being both outsiders and wanderers. Of course, the fact that he happened to be Jewish in Germany in the early twentieth century made him more of an outsider, and more of a wanderer, than he would have preferred— but that, too, became integral to who he was and the role he would play in world history.

Einstein's father, Hermann, was born in 1847 in the Swabian village of Buchau, whose thriving Jewish community was just beginning to enjoy the right to practice any vocation. Hermann showed "a marked inclination for mathematics,"[6] and his family was able to send him seventy-five miles north to Stuttgart for high school. But they could not afford to send him to a university, most of which were closed to Jews in any event, so he returned home to Buchau to go into trade.

A few years later, as part of the general migration of rural German Jews into industrial centers during the late nineteenth century, Hermann and his parents moved thirty-five miles away to the more prosperous town of Ulm, which prophetically boasted as its motto "Ulmenses sunt mathematici," the people of Ulm are mathematicians.[7]

There he became a partner in a cousin's featherbed company. He was "exceedingly friendly, mild and wise," his son would recall.[8] With a gentleness that blurred into docility, Hermann was to prove inept as a businessman and forever impractical in financial matters. But his docility did make him well suited to be a genial family man and good husband to a strong-willed woman. At age 29, he married Pauline Koch, eleven years his junior.

Pauline's father, Julius Koch, had built a considerable fortune as a grain dealer and purveyor to the royal Württemberg court. Pauline inherited his practicality, but she leavened his dour disposition with a teasing wit edged with sarcasm and a laugh that could be both infectious and wounding (traits she would pass on to her son). From all accounts, the match between Hermann and Pauline was a happy one, with her strong personality meshing "in complete harmony" with her husband's passivity.[9]

Their first child was born at 11:30 a.m. on Friday, March 14, 1879, in Ulm, which had recently joined, along with the rest of Swabia, the new German Reich. Initially, Pauline and Hermann had planned to name the boy Abraham, after his paternal grandfather. But they came to feel, he later said, that the name sounded "too Jewish."[10] So they kept the initial A and named him Albert Einstein.

Munich

In 1880, just a year after Albert's birth, Hermann's featherbed business foundered and he was persuaded to move to Munich by his brother Jakob, who had opened a gas and electrical supply company there. Jakob, the youngest of five siblings, had been able to get a higher education, unlike Hermann, and he had qualified as an engineer. As they competed for contracts to provide generators and electrical lighting to municipalities in southern Germany, Jakob was in charge of the technical side while Hermann provided a modicum of salesmanship skills plus, perhaps more important, loans from his wife's side of the family.[11]

Pauline and Hermann had a second and final child, a daughter, in November 1881, who was named Maria but throughout her life used instead the diminutive Maja. When Albert was shown his new sister for the first time, he was led to believe that she was like a wonderful toy that he would enjoy. His response was to look at her and exclaim, "Yes, but where are the wheels?"[12] It may not have been the most perceptive of questions, but it did show that during his third year his language challenges did not prevent him from making some memorable comments. Despite a few childhood squabbles, Maja was to become her brother's most intimate soul mate.

The Einsteins settled into a comfortable home with mature trees and an elegant garden in a Munich suburb for what was to be, at least through most of Albert's childhood, a respectable bourgeois existence. Munich had been architecturally burnished by mad King Ludwig II (1845–1886) and boasted a profusion of churches, art galleries, and concert halls that favored the works of resident Richard Wagner. In 1882, just after the Einsteins arrived, the city had about 300,000 residents, 85 percent of them Catholics and 2 percent of them Jewish, and it was the host of the first German electricity exhibition, at which electric lights were introduced to the city streets.

Einstein's back garden was often bustling with cousins and children. But he shied from their boisterous games and instead "occupied himself with quieter things." One governess nicknamed him "Father Bore." He was generally a loner, a tendency he claimed to cherish throughout his life, although his was a special sort of detachment that was interwoven with a relish for camaraderie and intellectual companionship. "From the very beginning he was inclined to separate himself from children his own age and to engage in daydreaming and meditative musing," according to Philipp Frank, a longtime scientific colleague.[13]

He liked to work on puzzles, erect complex structures with his toy building set, play with a steam engine that his uncle gave him, and build houses of cards. According to Maja, Einstein was able to construct card structures as high as fourteen stories. Even discounting the recollections of a star-struck younger sister, there was probably a lot of truth to her claim that "persistence and tenacity were obviously already part of his character."

He was also, at least as a young child, prone to temper tantrums. "At such moments his face would turn completely yellow, the tip of his nose snow-white, and he was no longer in control of himself," Maja remembers. Once, at age 5, he grabbed a chair and threw it at a tutor, who fled and never returned. Maja's head became the target of various hard objects. "It takes a sound skull," she later joked, "to be the sister of an intellectual." Unlike his persistence and tenacity, he eventually outgrew his temper.[14]

To use the language of psychologists, the young Einstein's ability to systemize (identify the laws that govern a system) was far greater than his ability to empathize (sense and care about what other humans are feeling), which have led some to ask if he might have exhibited mild symptoms of some developmental disorder.[15] However, it is important to note that, despite his aloof and occasionally rebellious manner, he did have the ability to make close friends and to empathize both with colleagues and humanity in general.

The great awakenings that happen in childhood are usually lost to memory. But for Einstein, an experience occurred when he was 4 or 5 that would alter his life and be etched forever in his mind—and in the history of science.

He was sick in bed one day, and his father brought him a compass. He later recalled being so excited as he examined its mysterious powers that he trembled and grew cold. The fact that the magnetic needle behaved as if influenced by some hidden force field, rather than through the more familiar mechanical method involving touch or contact, produced a sense of wonder that motivated him throughout his life. "I can still remember—or at least I believe I can remember—that this experience made a deep and lasting impression on me," he wrote on one of the many occasions he recounted the incident. "Something deeply hidden had to be behind things."[16]

"It's an iconic story," Dennis Overbye noted in *Einstein in Love*, "the young boy trembling to the invisible order behind chaotic reality." It has been told in the movie *IQ*, in which Einstein, played by Walter Matthau, wears the compass around his neck, and it is the focus of a children's book, *Rescuing Albert's Compass*, by Shulamith Oppenheim, whose father-in-law heard the tale from Einstein in 1911.[17]

After being mesmerized by the compass needle's fealty to an unseen field, Einstein would develop a lifelong devotion to field theories as a way to describe nature. Field theories use mathematical quantities, such as numbers or vectors or tensors, to describe how the conditions at any point in space will affect matter or another field. For example, in a gravitational or an electromagnetic field there are forces that could act on a particle at any point, and the equations of a field theory describe how these change as one moves through the region. The first paragraph of his great 1905 paper on special relativity begins with a consideration of the effects of electrical and magnetic fields; his theory of general relativity is based on equations that describe a gravitational field; and at the very end of his life he was doggedly scribbling further field equations in the hope that they would form the basis for a theory of everything. As the science historian Gerald Holton has noted, Ein-

stein regarded "the classical concept of the field the greatest contribution to the scientific spirit."[18]

His mother, an accomplished pianist, also gave him a gift at around
the same time, one that likewise would last throughout his life. She
arranged for him to take violin lessons. At first he chafed at the mechanical discipline of the instruction. But after being exposed to
Mozart's sonatas, music became both magical and emotional to him. "I
believe that love is a better teacher than a sense of duty," he said, "at
least for me."[19]

Soon he was playing Mozart duets, with his mother accompanying
him on the piano. "Mozart's music is so pure and beautiful that I see it
as a reflection of the inner beauty of the universe itself," he later told a
friend. "Of course," he added in a remark that reflected his view of
math and physics as well as of Mozart, "like all great beauty, his music
was pure simplicity."[20]

Music was no mere diversion. On the contrary, it helped him think.
"Whenever he felt that he had come to the end of the road or faced a
difficult challenge in his work," said his son Hans Albert, "he would
take refuge in music and that would solve all his difficulties." The violin thus proved useful during the years he lived alone in Berlin,
wrestling with general relativity. "He would often play his violin in his
kitchen late at night, improvising melodies while he pondered complicated problems," a friend recalled. "Then, suddenly, in the middle of
playing, he would announce excitedly, 'I've got it!' As if by inspiration,
the answer to the problem would have come to him in the midst of
music."[21]

His appreciation for music, and especially for Mozart, may have reflected his feel for the harmony of the universe. As Alexander
Moszkowski, who wrote a biography of Einstein in 1920 based on
conversations with him, noted, "Music, Nature, and God became intermingled in him in a complex of feeling, a moral unity, the trace of
which never vanished."[22]

Throughout his life, Albert Einstein would retain the intuition and
the awe of a child. He never lost his sense of wonder at the magic of
nature's phenomena—magnetic fields, gravity, inertia, acceleration,
light beams—which grown-ups find so commonplace. He retained the

ability to hold two thoughts in his mind simultaneously, to be puzzled when they conflicted, and to marvel when he could smell an underlying unity. "People like you and me never grow old," he wrote a friend later in life. "We never cease to stand like curious children before the great mystery into which we were born."[23]

School

In his later years, Einstein would tell an old joke about an agnostic uncle, who was the only member of his family who went to synagogue. When asked why he did so, the uncle would respond, "Ah, but you never know." Einstein's parents, on the other hand, were "entirely irreligious" and felt no compulsion to hedge their bets. They did not keep kosher or attend synagogue, and his father referred to Jewish rituals as "ancient superstitions."[24]

Consequently, when Albert turned 6 and had to go to school, his parents did not care that there was no Jewish one near their home. Instead he went to the large Catholic school in their neighborhood, the Petersschule. As the only Jew among the seventy students in his class, Einstein took the standard course in Catholic religion and ended up enjoying it immensely. Indeed, he did so well in his Catholic studies that he helped his classmates with theirs.[25]

One day his teacher brought a large nail to the class. "The nails with which Jesus was nailed to the cross looked like this," he said.[26] Nevertheless, Einstein later said that he felt no discrimination from the teachers. "The teachers were liberal and made no distinction based on denominations," he wrote. His fellow students, however, were a different matter. "Among the children at the elementary school, anti-Semitism was prevalent," he recalled.

Being taunted on his walks to and from school based on "racial characteristics about which the children were strangely aware" helped reinforce the sense of being an outsider, which would stay with him his entire life. "Physical attacks and insults on the way home from school were frequent, but for the most part not too vicious. Nevertheless, they were sufficient to consolidate, even in a child, a lively sense of being an outsider."[27]

When he turned 9, Einstein moved up to a high school near the center of Munich, the Luitpold Gymnasium, which was known as an enlightened institution that emphasized math and science as well as Latin and Greek. In addition, the school supplied a teacher to provide religious instruction for him and other Jews.

Despite his parents' secularism, or perhaps because of it, Einstein rather suddenly developed a passionate zeal for Judaism. "He was so fervent in his feelings that, on his own, he observed Jewish religious strictures in every detail," his sister recalled. He ate no pork, kept kosher dietary laws, and obeyed the strictures of the Sabbath, all rather difficult to do when the rest of his family had a lack of interest bordering on disdain for such displays. He even composed his own hymns for the glorification of God, which he sang to himself as he walked home from school.[28]

One widely held belief about Einstein is that he failed math as a student, an assertion that is made, often accompanied by the phrase "as everyone knows," by scores of books and thousands of websites designed to reassure underachieving students. It even made it into the famous "Ripley's Believe It or Not!" newspaper column.

Alas, Einstein's childhood offers history many savory ironies, but this is not one of them. In 1935, a rabbi in Princeton showed him a clipping of the Ripley's column with the headline "Greatest Living Mathematician Failed in Mathematics." Einstein laughed. "I never failed in mathematics," he replied, correctly. "Before I was fifteen I had mastered differential and integral calculus."[29]

In fact, he was a wonderful student, at least intellectually. In primary school, he was at the top of his class. "Yesterday Albert got his grades," his mother reported to an aunt when he was 7. "Once again he was ranked first." At the gymnasium, he disliked the mechanical learning of languages such as Latin and Greek, a problem exacerbated by what he later said was his "bad memory for words and texts." But even in these courses, Einstein consistently got top grades. Years later, when Einstein celebrated his fiftieth birthday and there were stories about how poorly the great genius had fared at the gymnasium, the school's current principal made a point of publishing a letter revealing how good his grades actually were.[30]

As for math, far from being a failure, he was "far above the school requirements." By age 12, his sister recalled, "he already had a predilection for solving complicated problems in applied arithmetic," and he decided to see if he could jump ahead by learning geometry and algebra on his own. His parents bought him the textbooks in advance so that he could master them over summer vacation. Not only did he learn the proofs in the books, he tackled the new theories by trying to prove them on his own. "Play and playmates were forgotten," she noted. "For days on end he sat alone, immersed in the search for a solution, not giving up before he had found it."[31]

His uncle Jakob Einstein, the engineer, introduced him to the joys of algebra. "It's a merry science," he explained. "When the animal that we are hunting cannot be caught, we call it X temporarily and continue to hunt until it is bagged." He went on to give the boy even more difficult challenges, Maja recalled, "with good-natured doubts about his ability to solve them." When Einstein triumphed, as he invariably did, he "was overcome with great happiness and was already then aware of the direction in which his talents were leading him."

Among the concepts that Uncle Jakob threw at him was the Pythagorean theorem (the square of the lengths of the legs of a right triangle add up to the square of the length of the hypotenuse). "After much effort I succeeded in 'proving' this theorem on the basis of the similarity of triangles," Einstein recalled. Once again he was thinking in pictures. "It seemed to me 'evident' that the relations of the sides of the right-angled triangles would have to be completely determined by one of the acute angles."[32]

Maja, with the pride of a younger sister, called Einstein's Pythagorean proof "an entirely original new one." Although perhaps new to him, it is hard to imagine that Einstein's approach, which was surely similar to the standard ones based on the proportionality of the sides of similar triangles, was completely original. Nevertheless, it did show Einstein's youthful appreciation that elegant theorems can be derived from simple axioms—and the fact that he was in little danger of failing math. "As a boy of 12, I was thrilled to see that it was possible to find out truth by reasoning alone, without the help of any outside experience," he told a reporter from a high school newspaper in Princeton years later. "I became more and more convinced that nature could be understood as a relatively simple mathematical structure."[33]

Einstein's greatest intellectual stimulation came from a poor medical student who used to dine with his family once a week. It was an old Jewish custom to take in a needy religious scholar to share the Sabbath meal; the Einsteins modified the tradition by hosting instead a medical student on Thursdays. His name was Max Talmud (later changed to Talmey, when he immigrated to the United States), and he began his weekly visits when he was 21 and Einstein was 10. "He was a pretty, dark-haired boy," remembered Talmud. "In all those years, I never saw him reading any light literature. Nor did I ever see him in the company of schoolmates or other boys his age."[34]

Talmud brought him science books, including a popular illustrated series called *People's Books on Natural Science*, "a work which I read with breathless attention," said Einstein. The twenty-one little volumes were written by Aaron Bernstein, who stressed the interrelations between biology and physics, and he reported in great detail the scientific experiments being done at the time, especially in Germany.[35]

In the opening section of the first volume, Bernstein dealt with the speed of light, a topic that obviously fascinated him. Indeed, he returned to it repeatedly in his subsequent volumes, including eleven essays on the topic in volume 8. Judging from the thought experiments that Einstein later used in creating his theory of relativity, Bernstein's books appear to have been influential.

For example, Bernstein asked readers to imagine being on a speeding train. If a bullet is shot through the window, it would seem that it was shot at an angle, because the train would have moved between the time the bullet entered one window and exited the window on the other side. Likewise, because of the speed of the earth through space, the same must be true of light going through a telescope. What was amazing, said Bernstein, was that experiments showed the same effect no matter how fast the source of the light was moving. In a sentence that, because of its relation to what Einstein would later famously conclude, seems to have made an impression, Bernstein declared, "Since each kind of light proves to be of exactly the same speed, the law of the speed of light can well be called the most general of all of nature's laws."

In another volume, Bernstein took his young readers on an imaginary trip through space. The mode of transport was the wave of an electric signal. His books celebrated the joyful wonders of scientific investigation and included such exuberant passages as this one written about the successful prediction of the location of the new planet Uranus: "Praised be this science! Praised be the men who do it! And praised be the human mind, which sees more sharply than does the human eye." [36]

Bernstein was, as Einstein would later be, eager to tie together all of nature's forces. For example, after discussing how all electromagnetic phenomena, such as light, could be considered waves, he speculated that the same may be true for gravity. A unity and simplicity, Bernstein wrote, lay beneath all the concepts applied by our perceptions. Truth in science consisted in discovering theories that described this underlying reality. Einstein later recalled the revelation, and the realist attitude, that this instilled in him as a young boy: "Out yonder there was this huge world, which exists independently of us human beings and which stands before us like a great, eternal riddle." [37]

Years later, when they met in New York during Einstein's first visit there, Talmud asked what he thought, in retrospect, of Bernstein's work. "A very good book," he said. "It has exerted a great influence on my whole development." [38]

Talmud also helped Einstein continue to explore the wonders of mathematics by giving him a textbook on geometry two years before he was scheduled to learn that subject in school. Later, Einstein would refer to it as "the sacred little geometry book" and speak of it with awe: "Here were assertions, as for example the intersection of the three altitudes of a triangle in one point, which—though by no means evident—could nevertheless be proved with such certainty that any doubt appeared to be out of the question. This lucidity and certainty made an indescribable impression upon me." Years later, in a lecture at Oxford, Einstein noted, "If Euclid failed to kindle your youthful enthusiasm, then you were not born to be a scientific thinker." [39]

When Talmud arrived each Thursday, Einstein delighted in showing him the problems he had solved that week. Initially, Talmud was able to help him, but he was soon surpassed by his pupil. "After a short time, a few months, he had worked through the whole book," Talmud recalled. "He thereupon devoted himself to higher mathematics ... Soon the flight of his mathematical genius was so high that I could no longer follow."[40]

So the awed medical student moved on to introducing Einstein to philosophy. "I recommended Kant to him," he recalled. "At that time he was still a child, only thirteen years old, yet Kant's works, incomprehensible to ordinary mortals, seemed to be clear to him." Kant became, for a while, Einstein's favorite philosopher, and his *Critique of Pure Reason* eventually led him to delve also into David Hume, Ernst Mach, and the issue of what can be known about reality.

Einstein's exposure to science produced a sudden reaction against religion at age 12, just as he would have been readying for a bar mitzvah. Bernstein, in his popular science volumes, had reconciled science with religious inclination. As he put it, "The religious inclination lies in the dim consciousness that dwells in humans that all nature, including the humans in it, is in no way an accidental game, but a work of lawfulness, that there is a fundamental cause of all existence."

Einstein would later come close to these sentiments. But at the time, his leap away from faith was a radical one. "Through the reading of popular scientific books, I soon reached the conviction that much in the stories of the Bible could not be true. The consequence was a positively fanatic orgy of freethinking coupled with the impression that youth is intentionally being deceived by the state through lies; it was a crushing impression."[41]

As a result, Einstein avoided religious rituals for the rest of his life. "There arose in Einstein an aversion to the orthodox practice of the Jewish or any traditional religion, as well as to attendance at religious services, and this he has never lost," his friend Philipp Frank later noted. He did, however, retain from his childhood religious phase a profound reverence for the harmony and beauty of what he called the mind of God as it was expressed in the creation of the universe and its laws.[42]

Einstein's rebellion against religious dogma had a profound effect on his general outlook toward received wisdom. It inculcated an allergic reaction against all forms of dogma and authority, which was to affect both his politics and his science. "Suspicion against every kind of authority grew out of this experience, an attitude which has never again left me," he later said. Indeed, it was this comfort with being a nonconformist that would define both his science and his social thinking for the rest of his life.

He would later be able to pull off this contrariness with a grace that was generally endearing, once he was accepted as a genius. But it did not play so well when he was merely a sassy student at a Munich gymnasium. "He was very uncomfortable in school," according to his sister. He found the style of teaching—rote drills, impatience with questioning—to be repugnant. "The military tone of the school, the systematic training in the worship of authority that was supposed to accustom pupils at an early age to military discipline, was particularly unpleasant."[43]

Even in Munich, where the Bavarian spirit engendered a less regimented approach to life, this Prussian glorification of the military had taken hold, and many of the children loved to play at being soldiers. When troops would come by, accompanied by fifes and drums, kids would pour into the streets to join the parade and march in lockstep. But not Einstein. Watching such a display once, he began to cry. "When I grow up, I don't want to be one of those poor people," he told his parents. As Einstein later explained, "When a person can take pleasure in marching in step to a piece of music it is enough to make me despise him. He has been given his big brain only by mistake."[44]

The opposition he felt to all types of regimentation made his education at the Munich gymnasium increasingly irksome and contentious. The mechanical learning there, he complained, "seemed very much akin to the methods of the Prussian army, where a mechanical discipline was achieved by repeated execution of meaningless orders." In later years, he would liken his teachers to members of the military. "The teachers at the elementary school seemed to me like drill sergeants," he said, "and the teachers at the gymnasium like lieutenants."

He once asked C. P. Snow, the British writer and scientist, whether he was familiar with the German word *Zwang*. Snow allowed that he was; it meant constraint, compulsion, obligation, coercion. Why? In his Munich school, Einstein answered, he had made his first strike against *Zwang*, and it had helped define him ever since.[45]

Skepticism and a resistance to received wisdom became a hallmark of his life. As he proclaimed in a letter to a fatherly friend in 1901, "A foolish faith in authority is the worst enemy of truth."[46]

Throughout the six decades of his scientific career, whether leading the quantum revolution or later resisting it, this attitude helped shape Einstein's work. "His early suspicion of authority, which never wholly left him, was to prove of decisive importance," said Banesh Hoffmann, who was a collaborator of Einstein's in his later years. "Without it he would not have been able to develop the powerful independence of mind that gave him the courage to challenge established scientific beliefs and thereby revolutionize physics."[47]

This contempt for authority did not endear him to the German "lieutenants" who taught him at his school. As a result, one of his teachers proclaimed that his insolence made him unwelcome in class. When Einstein insisted that he had committed no offense, the teacher replied, "Yes, that is true, but you sit there in the back row and smile, and your mere presence here spoils the respect of the class for me."[48]

Einstein's discomfort spiraled toward depression, perhaps even close to a nervous breakdown, when his father's business suffered a sudden reversal of fortune. The collapse was a precipitous one. During most of Einstein's school years, the Einstein brothers' company had been a success. In 1885, it had two hundred employees and provided the first electrical lights for Munich's Oktoberfest. Over the next few years, it won the contract to wire the community of Schwabing, a Munich suburb of ten thousand people, using gas motors to drive twin dynamos that the Einsteins had designed. Jakob Einstein received six patents for improvements in arc lamps, automatic circuit breakers, and electric meters. The company was poised to rival Siemens and other power companies then flourishing. To raise capital, the brothers mortgaged their homes, borrowed more than 60,000 marks at 10 percent interest, and went deeply in debt.[49]

But in 1894, when Einstein was 15, the company went bust after it lost competitions to light the central part of Munich and other locations. His parents and sister, along with Uncle Jakob, moved to northern Italy—first Milan and then the nearby town of Pavia—where the company's Italian partners thought there would be more fertile territory for a smaller firm. Their elegant home was torn down by a developer to build an apartment block. Einstein was left behind in Munich, at the house of a distant relative, to finish his final three years of school.

It is not quite clear whether Einstein, in that sad autumn of 1894, was actually forced to leave the Luitpold Gymnasium or was merely politely encouraged to leave. Years later, he recalled that the teacher who had declared that his "presence spoils the respect of the class for me" had gone on to "express the wish that I leave the school." An early book by a member of his family said that it was his own decision. "Albert increasingly resolved not to remain in Munich, and he worked out a plan."

That plan involved getting a letter from the family doctor, Max Talmud's older brother, who certified that he was suffering from nervous exhaustion. He used this to justify leaving the school at Christmas vacation in 1894 and not returning. Instead, he took a train across the Alps to Italy and informed his "alarmed" parents that he was never going back to Germany. Instead, he promised, he would study on his own and attempt to gain admission to a technical college in Zurich the following autumn.

There was perhaps one other factor in his decision to leave Germany. Had he remained there until he was 17, just over a year away, he would have been required to join the army, a prospect that his sister said "he contemplated with dread." So, in addition to announcing that he would not go back to Munich, he would soon ask for his father's help in renouncing his German citizenship. [50]

Aarau

Einstein spent the spring and summer of 1895 living with his parents in their Pavia apartment and helping at the family firm. In the process, he was able to get a good feel for the workings of magnets, coils, and generated electricity. Einstein's work impressed his family. On one occasion, Uncle Jakob was having problems with some calculations for a new machine, so Einstein went to work on it. "After my assistant engineer and I had been racking our brain for days, that young sprig had got the whole thing in just fifteen minutes," Jakob reported to a friend. "You will hear of him yet."[51]

With his love of the sublime solitude found in the mountains, Einstein hiked for days in the Alps and Apennines, including an excursion from Pavia to Genoa to see his mother's brother Julius Koch. Wherever he traveled in northern Italy, he was delighted by the non-Germanic grace and "delicacy" of the people. Their "naturalness" was a contrast to the "spiritually broken and mechanically obedient automatons" of Germany, his sister recalled.

Einstein had promised his family that he would study on his own to get into the local technical college, the Zurich Polytechnic.* So he bought all three volumes of Jules Violle's advanced physics text and copiously noted his ideas in the margins. His work habits showed his ability to concentrate, his sister recalled. "Even in a large, quite noisy group, he could withdraw to the sofa, take pen and paper in hand, set the inkstand precariously on the armrest, and lose himself so completely in a problem that the conversation of many voices stimulated rather than disturbed him."[52]

That summer, at age 16, he wrote his first essay on theoretical physics, which he titled "On the Investigation of the State of the Ether in a Magnetic Field." The topic was important, for the notion of the ether would play a critical role in Einstein's career. At the time, scientists conceived of light simply as a wave, and so they assumed that the universe must contain an all-pervasive yet unseen substance that was doing the rippling and thus propagating the waves, just as water was the medium rippling up and down and thus propagating the waves in an ocean. They dubbed this the ether, and Einstein (at least for the time being) went along with the assumption. As he put it in his essay,

---

* The official name of the institution was the Eidgenössische Polytechnische Schule. In 1911, it gained the right to grant doctoral degrees and changed its name to the Eidgenössische Technische Hochschule, or the Swiss Federal Institute of Technology, referred to as the ETH. Einstein, then and later, usually called it the Züricher Polytechnikum, or the Zurich Polytechnic.

"An electric current sets the surrounding ether in a kind of momentary motion."

The fourteen-paragraph handwritten paper echoed Violle's textbook as well as some of the reports in the popular science magazines about Heinrich Hertz's recent discoveries about electromagnetic waves. In it, Einstein made suggestions for experiments that could explain "the magnetic field formed around an electric current." This would be interesting, he argued, "because the exploration of the elastic state of the ether in this case would permit us a look into the enigmatic nature of electric current."

The high school dropout freely admitted that he was merely making a few suggestions without knowing where they might lead. "As I was completely lacking in materials that would have enabled me to delve into the subject more deeply than by merely meditating about it, I beg you not to interpret this circumstance as a mark of superficiality," he wrote.[53]

He sent the paper to his uncle Caesar Koch, a merchant in Belgium, who was one of his favorite relatives and occasionally a financial patron. "It is rather naïve and imperfect, as might be expected from such a young fellow like myself," Einstein confessed with a pretense of humility. He added that his goal was to enroll the following fall at the Zurich Polytechnic, but he was concerned that he was younger than the age requirement. "I should be at least two years older."[54]

To help him get around the age requirement, a family friend wrote to the director of the Polytechnic, asking for an exception. The tone of the letter can be gleaned from the director's response, which expressed skepticism about admitting this "so-called 'child prodigy.'" Nevertheless, Einstein was granted permission to take the entrance exam, and he boarded the train for Zurich in October 1895 "with a sense of well-founded diffidence."

Not surprisingly, he easily passed the section of the exam in math and science. But he failed to pass the general section, which included sections on literature, French, zoology, botany, and politics. The Polytechnic's head physics professor, Heinrich Weber, suggested that Einstein stay in Zurich and audit his classes. Instead, Einstein decided, on the advice of the college's director, to spend a year preparing at the cantonal school in the village of Aarau, twenty-five miles to the west.[55]

It was a perfect school for Einstein. The teaching was based on the philosophy of a Swiss educational reformer of the early nineteenth century, Johann Heinrich Pestalozzi, who believed in encouraging students to visualize images. He also thought it important to nurture the "inner dignity" and individuality of each child. Students should be allowed to reach their own conclusions, Pestalozzi preached, by using a series of steps that began with hands-on observations and then proceeded to intuitions, conceptual thinking, and visual imagery.[56] It was even possible to learn—and truly understand—the laws of math and physics that way. Rote drills, memorization, and force-fed facts were avoided.

Einstein loved Aarau. "Pupils were treated individually," his sister recalled, "more emphasis was placed on independent thought than on punditry, and young people saw the teacher not as a figure of authority, but, alongside the student, a man of distinct personality." It was the opposite of the German education that Einstein had hated. "When compared to six years' schooling at a German authoritarian gymnasium," Einstein later said, "it made me clearly realize how much superior an education based on free action and personal responsibility is to one relying on outward authority."[57]

The visual understanding of concepts, as stressed by Pestalozzi and his followers in Aarau, became a significant aspect of Einstein's genius. "Visual understanding is the essential and only true means of teaching how to judge things correctly," Pestalozzi wrote, and "the learning of numbers and language must be definitely subordinated."[58]

Not surprisingly, it was at this school that Einstein first engaged in the visualized thought experiment that would help make him the greatest scientific genius of his time: he tried to picture what it would be like to ride alongside a light beam. "In Aarau I made my first rather childish experiments in thinking that had a direct bearing on the Special Theory," he later told a friend. "If a person could run after a light wave with the same speed as light, you would have a wave arrangement which could be completely independent of time. Of course, such a thing is impossible."[59]

This type of visualized thought experiments—*Gedankenexperi-*

ment—became a hallmark of Einstein's career. Over the years, he would picture in his mind such things as lightning strikes and moving trains, accelerating elevators and falling painters, two-dimensional blind beetles crawling on curved branches, as well as a variety of contraptions designed to pinpoint, at least in theory, the location and velocity of speeding electrons.

While a student in Aarau, Einstein boarded with a wonderful family, the Wintelers, whose members would long remain entwined in his life. There was Jost Winteler, who taught history and Greek at the school; his wife, Rosa, soon known to Einstein as Mamerl, or Mama; and their seven children. Their daughter Marie would become Einstein's first girlfriend. Another daughter, Anna, would marry Einstein's best friend, Michele Besso. And their son Paul would marry Einstein's beloved sister, Maja.

"Papa" Jost Winteler was a liberal who shared Einstein's allergy to German militarism and to nationalism in general. His edgy honesty and political idealism helped to shape Einstein's social philosophy. Like his mentor, Einstein would become a supporter of world federalism, internationalism, pacifism, and democratic socialism, with a strong devotion to individual liberty and freedom of expression.

More important, in the warm embrace of the Winteler family, Einstein became more secure and personable. Even though he still fancied himself a loner, the Wintelers helped him flower emotionally and open himself to intimacy. "He had a great sense of humor and at times could laugh heartily," recalled daughter Anna. In the evenings he would sometimes study, "but more often he would sit with the family around the table." [60]

Einstein had developed into a head-turning teenager who possessed, in the words of one woman who knew him, "masculine good looks of the type that played havoc at the turn of the century." He had wavy dark hair, expressive eyes, a high forehead, and jaunty demeanor. "The lower half of his face might have belonged to a sensualist who found plenty of reasons to love life."

One of his schoolmates, Hans Byland, later wrote a striking description of "the impudent Swabian" who made such a lasting impression. "Sure of himself, his gray felt hat pushed back on his thick, black hair, he strode energetically up and down in the rapid, I might say crazy, tempo of a restless spirit which carries a whole world in itself. Nothing escaped the sharp gaze of the large bright brown eyes. Whoever approached him was captivated by his superior personality. A mocking curl of his fleshy mouth with its protruding lower lip did not encourage Philistines to fraternize with him."

Most notably, Byland added, young Einstein had a sassy, sometimes intimidating wit. "He confronted the world spirit as a laughing philosopher, and his witty sarcasm mercilessly castigated all vanity and artificiality."[61]

Einstein fell in love with Marie Winteler at the end of 1895, just a few months after he moved in with her parents. She had just completed teacher training college and was living at home while waiting to take a job in a nearby village. She was just turning 18, he was still 16. The romance thrilled both families. Albert and Marie sent New Year's greetings to his mother; she replied warmly, "Your little letter, dear Miss Marie, brought me immense joy."[62]

The following April, when he was back home in Pavia for spring break, Einstein wrote Marie his first known love letter:

> Beloved sweetheart!
> Many, many thanks sweetheart for your charming little letter, which made me endlessly happy. It was so wonderful to be able to press to one's heart such a bit of paper which two so dear little eyes have lovingly beheld and on which the dainty little hands have charmingly glided back and forth. I was now made to realize, my little angel, the meaning of homesickness and pining. But love brings much happiness—much more so than pining brings pain . . .
> My mother has also taken you to her heart, even though she does not know you; I only let her read two of your charming little letters. And she always laughs at me because I am no longer attracted to the girls who were supposed to have enchanted me so much in the past. You mean more to my soul than the whole world did before.

To which his mother penned a postscript: "Without having read this letter, I send you cordial greetings!"[63]

Although he enjoyed the school in Aarau, Einstein turned out to be an uneven student. His admission report noted that he needed to do remedial work in chemistry and had "great gaps" in his knowledge of

French. By midyear, he still was required to "continue with private lessons in French & chemistry," and "the protest in French remains in effect." His father was sanguine when Jost Winteler sent him the midyear report. "Not all its parts fulfill my wishes and expectations," he wrote, "but with Albert I got used to finding mediocre grades along with very good ones, and I am therefore not disconsolate about them."[64]

Music continued to be a passion. There were nine violinists in his class, and their teacher noted that they suffered from "some stiffness in bowing technique here and there." But Einstein was singled out for praise: "One student, by the name of Einstein, even sparkled by rendering an adagio from a Beethoven sonata with deep understanding." At a concert in the local church, Einstein was chosen to play first violin in a piece by Bach. His "enchanting tone and incomparable rhythm" awed the second violinist, who asked, "Do you count the beats?" Einstein replied, "Heavens no, it's in my blood."

His classmate Byland recalled Einstein playing a Mozart sonata with such passion—"What fire there was in his playing!"—that it seemed like hearing the composer for the first time. Listening to him, Byland realized that Einstein's wisecracking, sarcastic exterior was a shell around a softer inner soul. "He was one of those split personalities who know how to protect, with a prickly exterior, the delicate realm of their intense personal life."[65]

Einstein's contempt for Germany's authoritarian schools and militarist atmosphere made him want to renounce his citizenship in that country. This was reinforced by Jost Winteler, who disdained all forms of nationalism and instilled in Einstein the belief that people should consider themselves citizens of the world. So he asked his father to help him drop his German citizenship. The release came through in January 1896, and for the time being he was stateless.[66]

He also that year became a person without a religious affiliation. In the application to renounce his German citizenship, his father had written, presumably at Albert's request, "no religious denomination." It was a statement Albert would also make when applying for Zurich residency a few years later, and on various occasions over the ensuing two decades.

His rebellion from his childhood fling with ardent Judaism, coupled with his feelings of detachment from Munich's Jews, had alienated him from his heritage. "The religion of the fathers, as I encountered it in Munich during religious instruction and in the synagogue, repelled rather than attracted me," he later explained to a Jewish historian. "The Jewish bourgeois circles that I came to know in my younger years, with their affluence and lack of a sense of community, offered me nothing that seemed to be of value."[67]

Later in life, beginning with his exposure to virulent anti-Semitism in the 1920s, Einstein would begin to reconnect with his Jewish identity. "There is nothing in me that can be described as a 'Jewish faith,' " he said, "however I am happy to be a member of the Jewish people." Later he would make the same point in more colorful ways. "The Jew who abandons his faith," he once said, "is in a similar position to a snail that abandons his shell. He is still a snail."[68]

His renunciation of Judaism in 1896 should, therefore, be seen not as a clean break but as part of a lifelong evolution of his feelings about his cultural identity. "At that time I would not even have understood what leaving Judaism could possibly mean," he wrote a friend the year before he died. "But I was fully aware of my Jewish origin, even though the full significance of belonging to Jewry was not realized by me until later."[69]

Einstein ended his year at the Aarau school in a manner that would have seemed impressive for anyone except one of history's great geniuses, scoring the second highest grades in his class. (Alas, the name of the boy who bested Einstein is lost to history.) On a 1 to 6 scale, with 6 being the highest, he scored a 5 or 6 in all of his science and math courses as well as in history and Italian. His lowest grade was a 3, in French.

That qualified him to take a series of exams, written and oral, that would permit him, if he passed, to enter the Zurich Polytechnic. On his German exam, he did a perfunctory outline of a Goethe play and scored a 5. In math, he made a careless mistake, calling a number "imaginary" when he meant "irrational," but still got a top grade. In physics, he arrived late and left early, completing the two-hour test in an hour and fifteen minutes; he got the top grade. Altogether, he ended up with a 5.5, the best grade among the nine students taking the exams.

The one section on which he did poorly was French. But his three-paragraph essay was, to those of us today, the most interesting part of all of his exams. The topic was "Mes Projets d'avenir," my plans for the future. Although the French was not memorable, the personal insights were:

> If I am lucky and pass my exams, I will enroll in the Zurich Polytechnic. I will stay there four years to study mathematics and physics. I suppose I will become a teacher in these fields of science, opting for the theoretical part of these sciences.
>
> Here are the reasons that have led me to this plan. They are, most of all, my personal talent for abstract and mathematical thinking . . . My desires have also led me to the same decision. That is quite natural; everybody desires to do that for which he has a talent. Besides, I am attracted by the independence offered by the profession of science.[70]

In the summer of 1896, the Einstein brothers' electrical business again failed, this time because they bungled getting the necessary water rights to build a hydroelectric system in Pavia. The partnership was dissolved in a friendly fashion, and Jakob joined a large firm as an engineer. But Hermann, whose optimism and pride tended to overwhelm any prudence, insisted on opening yet another new dynamo business, this time in Milan. Albert was so dubious of his father's prospects that he went to his relatives and suggested that they not finance him again, but they did.[71]

Hermann hoped that Albert would someday join him in the business, but engineering held little appeal for him. "I was originally supposed to become an engineer," he later wrote a friend, "but the thought of having to expend my creative energy on things that make practical everyday life even more refined, with a bleak capital gain as the goal, was unbearable to me. Thinking for its own sake, like music!"[72] And thus he headed off to the Zurich Polytechnic.

CHAPTER THREE

THE ZURICH POLYTECHNIC

1896–1900

The Impudent Scholar

The Zurich Polytechnic, with 841 students, was mainly a teachers' and technical college when 17-year-old Albert Einstein enrolled in October 1896. It was less prestigious than the neighboring University of Zurich and the universities in Geneva and Basel, all of which could grant doctoral degrees (a status that the Polytechnic, officially named the Eidgenössische Polytechnische Schule, would attain in 1911 when it became the Eidgenössische Technische Hochschule, or ETH). Nevertheless, the Polytechnic had a solid reputation in engineering and science. The head of the physics department, Heinrich Weber, had recently procured a grand new building, funded by the electronics magnate (and Einstein Brothers competitor) Werner von Siemens. It housed showcase labs famed for their precision measurements.

Einstein was one of eleven freshmen enrolled in the section that provided training "for specialized teachers in mathematics and physics." He lived in student lodgings on a monthly stipend of 100 Swiss francs from his Koch family relatives. Each month he put aside 20 of those francs toward the fee he would eventually have to pay to become a Swiss citizen.[1]

Theoretical physics was just coming into its own as an academic discipline in the 1890s, with professorships in the field sprouting up across Europe. Its pioneer practitioners—such as Max Planck in Berlin,

Hendrik Lorentz in Holland, and Ludwig Boltzmann in Vienna—combined physics with math to suggest paths where experimentalists had yet to tread. Because of this, math was supposed to be a major part of Einstein's required studies at the Polytechnic.

Einstein, however, had a better intuition for physics than for math, and he did not yet appreciate how integrally the two subjects would be related in the pursuit of new theories. During his four years at the Polytechnic, he got marks of 5 or 6 (on a 6-point scale) in all of his theoretical physics courses, but got only 4s in most of his math courses, especially those in geometry. "It was not clear to me as a student," he admitted, "that a more profound knowledge of the basic principles of physics was tied up with the most intricate mathematical methods."[2]

That realization would sink in a decade later, when he was wrestling with the geometry of his theory of gravity and found himself forced to rely on the help of a math professor who had once called him a lazy dog. "I have become imbued with great respect for mathematics," he wrote to a colleague in 1912, "the subtler part of which I had in my simple-mindedness regarded as pure luxury until now." Near the end of his life, he expressed a similar lament in a conversation with a younger friend. "At a very early age, I made an assumption that a successful physicist only needs to know elementary mathematics," he said. "At a later time, with great regret, I realized that the assumption of mine was completely wrong."[3]

His primary physics professor was Heinrich Weber, the one who a year earlier had been so impressed with Einstein that, even after he had failed his entrance exam to the Polytechnic, he urged him to stay in Zurich and audit his lectures. During Einstein's first two years at the Polytechnic, their mutual admiration endured. Weber's lectures were among the few that impressed him. "Weber lectured on heat with great mastery," he wrote during their second year. "One lecture after another of his pleases me." He worked in Weber's laboratory "with fervor and passion," took fifteen courses (five lab and ten classroom) with him, and scored well in them all.[4]

Einstein, however, gradually became disenchanted with Weber. He felt that the professor focused too much on the historical foundations of physics, and he did not deal much with contemporary frontiers.

"Anything that came after Helmholtz was simply ignored," one contemporary of Einstein complained. "At the close of our studies, we knew all the past of physics but nothing of the present and future."

Notably absent from Weber's lectures was any exploration of the great breakthroughs of James Clerk Maxwell, who, beginning in 1855, developed profound theories and elegant mathematical equations that described how electromagnetic waves such as light propagated. "We waited in vain for a presentation of Maxwell's theory," wrote another fellow student. "Einstein above all was disappointed."[5]

Given his brash attitude, Einstein didn't hide his feelings. And given his dignified sense of himself, Weber bristled at Einstein's ill-concealed disdain. By the end of their four years together they were antagonists.

Weber's irritation was yet another example of how Einstein's scientific as well as personal life was affected by the traits deeply bred into his Swabian soul: his casual willingness to question authority, his sassy attitude in the face of regimentation, and his lack of reverence for received wisdom. He tended to address Weber, for example, in a rather informal manner, calling him "Herr Weber" instead of "Herr Professor."

When his frustration finally overwhelmed his admiration, Professor Weber's pronouncement on Einstein echoed that of the irritated teacher at the Munich gymnasium a few years earlier. "You're a very clever boy, Einstein," Weber told him. "An extremely clever boy. But you have one great fault: you'll never let yourself be told anything."

There was some truth to that assessment. But Einstein was to show that, in the jangled world of physics at the turn of the century, this insouciant ability to tune out the conventional wisdom was not the worst fault to have.[6]

Einstein's impertinence also got him into trouble with the Polytechnic's other physics professor, Jean Pernet, who was in charge of experimental and lab exercises. In his course Physical Experiments for Beginners, Pernet gave Einstein a 1, the lowest possible grade, thus earning himself the historic distinction of having flunked Einstein in a physics course. Partly it was because Einstein seldom showed up for the course. At Pernet's written request, in March 1899 Einstein was given an official "director's reprimand due to lack of diligence in physics practicum."[7]

Why are you specializing in physics, Pernet asked Einstein one day, instead of a field like medicine or even law? "Because," Einstein replied, "I have even less talent for those subjects. Why shouldn't I at least try my luck with physics?"[8]

On those occasions when Einstein did deign to show up in Pernet's lab, his independent streak sometimes got him in trouble, such as the day he was given an instruction sheet for a particular experiment. "With his usual independence," his friend and early biographer Carl Seelig reports, "Einstein naturally flung the paper in the waste paper basket." He proceeded to pursue the experiment in his own way. "What do you make of Einstein?" Pernet asked an assistant. "He always does something different from what I have ordered."

"He does indeed, Herr Professor," the assistant replied, "but his solutions are right and the methods he uses are of great interest."[9]

Eventually, these methods caught up with him. In July 1899, he caused an explosion in Pernet's lab that "severely damaged" his right hand and required him to go to the clinic for stitches. The injury made it difficult for him to write for at least two weeks, and it forced him to give up playing the violin for even longer. "My fiddle had to be laid aside," he wrote to a woman he had performed with in Aarau. "I'm sure it wonders why it is never taken out of the black case. It probably thinks it has gotten a stepfather."[10] He soon resumed playing the violin, but the accident seemed to make him even more wedded to the role of theorist rather than experimentalist.

Despite the fact that he focused more on physics than on math, the professor who would eventually have the most positive impact on him was the math professor Hermann Minkowski, a square-jawed, handsome Russian-born Jew in his early thirties. Einstein appreciated the way Minkowski tied math to physics, but he avoided the more challenging of his courses, which is why Minkowski labeled him a lazy dog: "He never bothered about mathematics at all."[11]

Einstein preferred to study, based on his own interests and passions, with one or two friends.[12] Even though he was still priding himself on being "a vagabond and a loner," he began to hang around the coffeehouses and attend musical soirees with a congenial crowd of bohemian soul mates and fellow students. Despite his reputation for detachment, he forged lasting intellectual friendships in Zurich that became important bonds in his life.

Among these was Marcel Grossmann, a middle-class Jewish math wizard whose father owned a factory near Zurich. Grossmann took copious notes that he shared with Einstein, who was less diligent about attending lectures. "His notes could have been printed and published," Einstein later marveled to Grossmann's wife. "When it came time to prepare for my exams, he would always lend me those notebooks, and they were my savior. What I would have done without these books I would rather not speculate on."

Together Einstein and Grossmann smoked pipes and drank iced coffee while discussing philosophy at the Café Metropole on the banks of the Limmat River. "This Einstein will one day be a great man," Grossmann predicted to his parents. He would later help make that prediction true by getting Einstein his first job, at the Swiss Patent Office, and then aiding him with the math he needed to turn the special theory of relativity into a general theory.[13]

Because many of the Polytechnic lectures seemed out of date, Einstein and his friends read the most recent theorists on their own. "I played hooky a lot and studied the masters of theoretical physics with a holy zeal at home," he recalled. Among those were Gustav Kirchhoff on radiation, Hermann von Helmholtz on thermodynamics, Heinrich Hertz on electromagnetism, and Boltzmann on statistical mechanics.

He was also influenced by reading a lesser-known theorist, August Föppl, who in 1894 had written a popular text titled *Introduction to Maxwell's Theory of Electricity*. As science historian Gerald Holton has pointed out, Föppl's book is filled with concepts that would soon echo in Einstein's work. It has a section on "The Electrodynamics of Moving Conductors" that begins by calling into question the concept of "absolute motion." The only way to define motion, Föppl notes, is relative to another body. From there he goes on to consider a question concerning the induction of an electric current by a magnetic field: "if it is all the same whether a magnet moves in the vicinity of a resting electric circuit or whether it is the latter that moves while the magnet is

at rest." Einstein would begin his 1905 special relativity paper by raising this same issue.[14]

Einstein also read, in his spare time, Henri Poincaré, the great
French polymath who would come tantalizingly close to discovering
the core concepts of special relativity. Near the end of Einstein's first
year at the Polytechnic, in the spring of 1897, there was a mathematics
conference in Zurich where the great Poincaré was due to speak. At the
last minute he was unable to appear, but a paper of his was read there
that contained what would become a famous proclamation. "Absolute
space, absolute time, even Euclidean geometry, are not conditions to be
imposed on mechanics," he wrote.[15]

The Human Side

One evening when Einstein was at home with his landlady, he
heard someone playing a Mozart piano sonata. When he asked who it
was, his landlady told him that it was an old woman who lived in the
attic next door and taught piano. Grabbing his violin, he dashed out
without putting on a collar or a tie. "You can't go like that, Herr Einstein," the landlady cried. But he ignored her and rushed into the
neighboring house. The piano teacher looked up, shocked. "Go on
playing," Einstein pleaded. A few moments later, the air was filled with
the sounds of a violin accompanying the Mozart sonata. Later, the
teacher asked who the intruding accompanist was. "Merely a harmless
student," her neighbor reassured her.[16]

Music continued to beguile Einstein. It was not so much an escape
as it was a connection: to the harmony underlying the universe, to the
creative genius of the great composers, and to other people who felt
comfortable bonding with more than just words. He was awed, both in
music and in physics, by the beauty of harmonies.

Suzanne Markwalder was a young girl in Zurich whose mother
hosted musical evenings featuring mostly Mozart. She played piano,
while Einstein played violin. "He was very patient with my shortcom-
ings," she recalled. "At the worst he used to say, 'There you are, stuck
like the donkey on the mountain,' and he would point with his bow to
the place where I had to come in.'"

What Einstein appreciated in Mozart and Bach was the clear architectural structure that made their music seem "deterministic" and, like his own favorite scientific theories, plucked from the universe rather than composed. "Beethoven created his music," Einstein once said, but "Mozart's music is so pure it seems to have been ever-present in the universe." He contrasted Beethoven with Bach: "I feel uncomfortable listening to Beethoven. I think he is too personal, almost naked. Give me Bach, rather, and then more Bach."

He also admired Schubert for his "superlative ability to express emotion." But in a questionnaire he once filled out, he was critical about other composers in ways that reflect some of his scientific sentiments: Handel had "a certain shallowness"; Mendelssohn displayed "considerable talent but an indefinable lack of depth that often leads to banality"; Wagner had a "lack of architectural structure I see as decadence"; and Strauss was "gifted but without inner truth."[17]

Einstein also took up sailing, a more solitary pursuit, in the glorious Alpine lakes around Zurich. "I still remember how when the breeze dropped and the sails drooped like withered leaves, he would take out his small notebook and he would start scribbling," recalled Suzanne Markwalder. "But as soon as there was a breath of wind he was immediately ready to start sailing again."[18]

The political sentiments he had felt as a boy—a contempt for arbitrary authority, an aversion to militarism and nationalism, a respect for individuality, a disdain for bourgeois consumption or ostentatious wealth, and a desire for social equality—had been encouraged by his landlord and surrogate father in Aarau, Jost Winteler. Now, in Zurich, he met a friend of Winteler's who became a similar political mentor: Gustav Maier, a Jewish banker who had helped arrange Einstein's first visit to the Polytechnic. With support from Winteler, Maier founded the Swiss branch of the Society for Ethical Culture, and Einstein was a frequent guest at their informal gatherings in Maier's home.

Einstein also came to know and like Friedrich Adler, the son of Austria's Social Democratic leader, who was studying in Zurich. Einstein later called him the "purest and most fervent idealist" he had ever met. Adler tried to get Einstein to join the Social Democrats. But it was not Einstein's style to spend time at meetings of organized institutions.[19]

His distracted demeanor, casual grooming, frayed clothing, and forgetfulness, which were later to make him appear to be the iconic absentminded professor, were already evident in his student days. He was known to leave behind clothes, and sometimes even his suitcase, when he traveled, and his inability to remember his keys became a running joke with his landlady. He once visited the home of family friends and, he recalled, "I left forgetting my suitcase. My host said to my parents, 'That man will never amount to anything because he can't remember anything.'"[20]

This carefree life as a student was clouded by the continued financial failings of his father, who, against Einstein's advice, kept trying to set up his own businesses rather than go to work for a salary at a stable company, as Uncle Jakob had finally done. "If I had my way, papa would have looked for salaried employment two years ago," he wrote his sister during a particularly gloomy moment in 1898 when his father's business seemed doomed to fail again.

The letter was unusually despairing, probably more than his parents' financial situation actually warranted:

> What depresses me most is the misfortune of my poor parents who have not had a happy moment for so many years. What further hurts me deeply is that as an adult man, I have to look on without being able to do anything. I am nothing but a burden to my family . . . It would be better off if I were not alive at all. Only the thought that I have always done what lay in my modest powers, and that I do not permit myself a single pleasure or distraction save for what my studies offer me, sustains me and sometimes protects me from despair.[21]

Perhaps this was all merely an attack of teenage angst. In any event, his father seemed to get through the crisis with his usual optimism. By the following February, he had won contracts for providing street lights to two small villages near Milan. "I am happy at the thought that the worst worries are over for our parents," Einstein wrote Maja. "If everyone lived such a way, namely like me, the writing of novels would never have been invented."[22]

Einstein's new bohemian life and old self-absorbed nature made it unlikely that he would continue his relationship with Marie Winteler, the sweet and somewhat flighty daughter of the family he had boarded with in Aarau. At first, he still sent her, via the mail, baskets of his laundry, which she would wash and then return. Sometimes there was not even a note attached, but she would cheerfully try to please him. In one letter she wrote of "crossing the woods in the pouring rain" to the post office to send back his clean clothes. "In vain did I strain my eyes for a little note, but the mere sight of your dear handwriting in the address was enough to make me happy."

When Einstein sent word that he planned to visit her, Marie was giddy. "I really thank you, Albert, for wanting to come to Aarau, and I don't have to tell you that I will be counting the minutes until that time," she wrote. "I could never describe, because there are no words for it, how blissful I feel ever since the dear soul of yours has come to live and weave in my soul. I love you for all eternity, sweetheart."

But he wanted to break off the relationship. In one of his first letters after arriving at the Zurich Polytechnic, he suggested that they refrain from writing each other. "My love, I do not quite understand a passage in your letter," she replied. "You write that you do not want to correspond with me any longer, but why not, sweetheart? . . . You must be quite annoyed with me if you can write so rudely." Then she tried to laugh off the problem: "But wait, you'll get some proper scolding when I get home."[23]

Einstein's next letter was even less friendly, and he complained about a teapot she had given him. "The matter of my sending you the stupid little teapot does not have to please you at all as long as you are going to brew some good tea in it," she replied. "Stop making that angry face which looked at me from all the sides and corners of the writing paper." There was a little boy in the school where she taught named Albert, she said, who looked like him. "I love him ever so much," she said. "Something comes over me when he looks at me and I always believe that you are looking at your little sweetheart."[24]

But then the letters from Einstein stopped, despite Marie's pleas. She even wrote his mother for advice. "The rascal has become frightfully lazy," Pauline Einstein replied. "I have been waiting in vain for

news for these last three days; I will have to give him a thorough talking-to once he's here."[25]

Finally, Einstein declared the relationship over in a letter to Marie's mother, saying that he would not come to Aarau during his academic break that spring. "It would be more than unworthy of me to buy a few days of bliss at the cost of new pain, of which I have already caused too much to the dear child through my fault," he wrote.

He went on to give a remarkably introspective—and memorable—assessment of how he had begun to avoid the pain of emotional commitments and the distractions of what he called the "merely personal" by retreating into science:

> It fills me with a peculiar kind of satisfaction that now I myself have to taste some of the pain that I brought upon the dear girl through my thoughtlessness and ignorance of her delicate nature. Strenuous intellectual work and looking at God's nature are the reconciling, fortifying yet relentlessly strict angels that shall lead me through all of life's troubles. If only I were able to give some of this to the good child. And yet, what a peculiar way this is to weather the storms of life—in many a lucid moment I appear to myself as an ostrich who buries his head in the desert sand so as not to perceive the danger.[26]

Einstein's coolness toward Marie Winteler can seem, from our vantage, cruel. Yet relationships, especially those of teenagers, are hard to judge from afar. They were very different from each other, particularly intellectually. Marie's letters, especially when she was feeling insecure, often descended into babble. "I'm writing a lot of rubbish, isn't that so, and in the end you'll not even read it to the finish (but I don't believe that)," she wrote in one. In another, she said, "I do not think about myself, sweetheart, that's quite true, but the only reason for this is that I do not think at all, except when it comes to some tremendously stupid calculation that requires, for a change, that I know more than my pupils."[27]

Whoever was to blame, if either, it was not surprising that they ended up on different paths. After her relationship with Einstein ended, Marie lapsed into a nervous depression, often missing days of teaching, and a few years later married the manager of a watch factory. Einstein, on the other hand, rebounded from the relationship by falling into the arms of someone who was just about as different from Marie as could be imagined.

Mileva Marić

Mileva Marić was the first and favorite child of an ambitious Serbian peasant who had joined the army, married into modest wealth, and then dedicated himself to making sure that his brilliant daughter was able to prevail in the male world of math and physics. She spent most of her childhood in Novi Sad, a Serbian city then held by Hungary,[28] and attended a variety of ever more demanding schools, at each of which she was at the top of her class, culminating when her father convinced the all-male Classical Gymnasium in Zagreb to let her enroll. After graduating there with the top grades in physics and math, she made her way to Zurich, where she became, just before she turned 21, the only woman in Einstein's section of the Polytechnic.

More than three years older than Einstein, afflicted with a congenital hip dislocation that caused her to limp, and prone to bouts of tuberculosis and despondency, Mileva Marić was known for neither her looks nor her personality. "Very smart and serious, small, delicate, brunette, ugly," is how one of her female friends in Zurich described her.

But she had qualities that Einstein, at least during his romantic scholar years, found attractive: a passion for math and science, a brooding depth, and a beguiling soul. Her deep-set eyes had a haunting intensity, her face an enticing touch of melancholy.[29] She would become, over time, Einstein's muse, partner, lover, wife, bête noire, and antagonist, and she would create an emotional field more powerful than that of anyone else in his life. It would alternately attract and repulse him with a force so strong that a mere scientist like himself would never be able to fathom it.

They met when they both entered the Polytechnic in October 1896, but their relationship took a while to develop. There is no sign, from their letters or recollections, that they were anything more than classmates that first academic year. They did, however, decide to go hiking together in the summer of 1897. That fall, "frightened by the new feelings she was experiencing" because of Einstein, Marić decided to leave the Polytechnic temporarily and instead audit classes at Heidelberg University.[30]

Her first surviving letter to Einstein, written a few weeks after she moved to Heidelberg, shows glimmers of a romantic attraction but also highlights her self-confident nonchalance. She addresses Einstein with the formal *Sie* in German, rather than the more intimate *du*. Unlike Marie Winteler, she teasingly makes the point that she has not been obsessing about him, even though he had written an unusually long letter to her. "It's now been quite a while since I received your letter," she said, "and I would have replied immediately and thanked you for the sacrifice of writing four long pages, would have also told of the joy you provided me through our trip together, but you said I should write to you someday when I happened to be bored. And I am very obedient, and I waited and waited for boredom to set in; but so far my waiting has been in vain."

Distinguishing Marić even more from Marie Winteler was the intellectual intensity of her letters. In this first one, she enthused over the lectures she had been attending of Philipp Lenard, then an assistant professor at Heidelberg, on kinetic theory, which explains the properties of gases as being due to the actions of millions of individual molecules. "Oh, it was really neat at the lecture of Professor Lenard yesterday," she wrote. "He is talking now about the kinetic theory of heat and gases. So, it turns out that the molecules of oxygen move with a velocity of over 400 meters per second, then the good professor calculated and calculated . . . and it finally turned out even though molecules do move with this velocity, they travel a distance of only 1/100 of a hairbreadth."

Kinetic theory had not yet been fully accepted by the scientific establishment (nor, for that matter, had even the existence of atoms and molecules), and Marić's letter indicated that she did not have a deep understanding of the subject. In addition, there was a sad irony: Lenard would be one of Einstein's early inspirations but later one of his most hateful anti-Semitic tormentors.

Marić also commented on ideas Einstein had shared in his earlier letter about the difficulty mortals have in comprehending the infinite. "I do not believe that the structure of the human brain is to be blamed for the fact that man cannot grasp infinity," she wrote. "Man is very capable of imagining infinite happiness, and he should be able to grasp the infinity of space—I think that should be much easier." There is a slight echo of Einstein's escape from the "merely personal" into the safety of scientific thinking: finding it easier to imagine infinite space than infinite happiness.

Yet Marić was also, it is clear from her letter, thinking of Einstein in a more personal way. She had even talked to her adoring and protective father about him. "Papa gave me some tobacco to take with me and I was supposed to hand it to you personally," she said. "He wanted so much to whet your appetite for our little land of outlaws. I told him all about you—you must absolutely come back with me someday. The two of you would really have a lot to talk about!" The tobacco, unlike Marie Winteler's teapot, was a present Einstein would likely have wanted, but Marić teased that she wasn't sending it. "You would have to pay duty on it, and then you would curse me." [31]

That conflicting admixture of playfulness and seriousness, of insouciance and intensity, of intimacy and detachment—so peculiar yet also so evident in Einstein as well—must have appealed to him. He urged her to return to Zurich. By February 1898, she had made up her mind to do so, and he was thrilled. "I'm sure you won't regret your decision," he wrote. "You should come back as soon as possible."

He gave her a thumbnail of how each of the professors was performing (admitting that he found the one teaching geometry to be "a little impenetrable"), and he promised to help her catch up with the aid of the lecture notes he and Marcel Grossmann had kept. The one problem was that she would probably not be able to get her "old pleasant room" at the nearby pension back. "Serves you right, you little runaway!" [32]

By April she was back, in a boarding house a few blocks from his, and now they were a couple. They shared books, intellectual enthusiasms, intimacies, and access to each other's apartments. One day, when he again forgot his key and found himself locked out of his own place, he went to hers and borrowed her copy of a physics text. "Don't be angry with me," he said in the little note he left her. Later that year, a similar note left for her added, "If you don't mind, I'd like to come over this evening to read with you."[33]

Friends were surprised that a sensuous and handsome man such as Einstein, who could have almost any woman fall for him, would find himself with a short and plain Serbian who had a limp and exuded an air of melancholy. "I would never be brave enough to marry a woman unless she were absolutely healthy," a fellow student said to him. Einstein replied, "But she has such a lovely voice."[34]

Einstein's mother, who had adored Marie Winteler, was similarly dubious about the dark intellectual who had replaced her. "Your photograph had quite an effect on my old lady," Einstein wrote from Milan, where he was visiting his parents during spring break of 1899. "While she studied it carefully, I said with the deepest sympathy: 'Yes, yes, she certainly is a clever one.' I've already had to endure much teasing about this."[35]

It is easy to see why Einstein felt such an affinity for Marić. They were kindred spirits who perceived themselves as aloof scholars and outsiders. Slightly rebellious toward bourgeois expectations, they were both intellectuals who sought as a lover someone who would also be a partner, colleague, and collaborator. "We understand each other's dark souls so well, and also drinking coffee and eating sausages, etcetera," Einstein wrote her.

He had a way of making the *etcetera* sound roguish. He closed another letter: "Best wishes etc., especially the latter." After being apart for a few weeks, he listed the things he liked to do with her: "Soon I'll be with my sweetheart again and can kiss her, hug her, make coffee with her, scold her, study with her, laugh with her, walk with her, chat with her, and ad infinitum!" They took pride in sharing a quirkiness. "I'm the same old rogue as I've always been," he wrote, "full of whims and mischief, and as moody as ever!"[36]

Above all, Einstein loved Marić for her mind. "How proud I will be to have a little Ph.D. for a sweetheart," he wrote to her at one point. Science and romance seemed to be interwoven. While on vacation with his family in 1899, Einstein lamented in a letter to Marić, "When I read Helmholtz for the first time I could not—and still cannot—believe that I was doing so without you sitting next to me. I enjoy working together and I find it soothing and also less boring."

Indeed, most of their letters mixed romantic effusions with scientific enthusiasms, often with an emphasis on the latter. In one letter, for example, he foreshadowed not only the title but also some of the concepts of his great paper on special relativity. "I am more and more convinced that the electrodynamics of moving bodies as it is presented today does not correspond to reality and that it will be possible to present it in a simpler way," he wrote. "The introduction of the term 'ether' into theories of electricity has led to the conception of a medium whose motion can be described without, I believe, being able to ascribe physical meaning to it."[37]

Even though this mix of intellectual and emotional companionship appealed to him, every now and then he recalled the enticement of the simpler desire represented by Marie Winteler. And with the tactlessness that masqueraded for him as honesty (or perhaps because of his puckish desire to torment), he let Marić know it. After his 1899 summer vacation, he decided to take his sister to enroll in school in Aarau, where Marie lived. He wrote Marić to assure her that he would not spend much time with his former girlfriend, but the pledge was written in a way that was, perhaps intentionally, more unsettling than reassuring. "I won't be going to Aarau as often now that the daughter I was so madly in love with four years ago is coming back home," he said. "For the most part I feel quite secure in my high fortress of calm. But I know that if I saw her a few more times, I would certainly go mad. Of that I am certain, and I fear it like fire."

But the letter goes on, happily for Marić, with a description of what they would do when they met back in Zurich, a passage in which Einstein showed once again why their relationship was so special. "The first thing we'll do is climb the Ütliberg," he said, referring to a high point just out of town. There they would be able to "take pleasure in unpacking our memories" of the things they had done together on other hiking trips. "I can already imagine the fun we will have," he wrote. Finally, with a flourish only they could have fully appreciated, he concluded, "And then we'll start in on Helmholtz's electromagnetic theory of light."[38]

In the ensuing months, their letters became even more intimate and passionate. He began calling her Doxerl (Dollie), as well as "my wild little rascal" and "my street urchin"; she called him Johannzel (Johnnie) and "my wicked little sweetheart." By the start of 1900, they were using the familiar *du* with one another, a process that began with a little note from her that reads, in full:

> My little Johnnie,
>   Because I like you so much, and because you're so far away that I can't give you a little kiss, I'm writing this letter to ask if you like me as much as I do you? Answer me immediately.
>
>   A thousand kisses from your
>   Dollie[39]

Graduation, August 1900

Academically, things were also going well for Einstein. In his intermediate exams in October 1898, he had finished first in his class, with an average of 5.7 out of a possible 6. Finishing second, with a 5.6, was his friend and math note-taker Marcel Grossmann.[40]

To graduate, Einstein had to do a research thesis. He initially proposed to Professor Weber that he do an experiment to measure how fast the earth was moving through the ether, the supposed substance that allowed light waves to propagate through space. The accepted wisdom, which he would famously destroy with his special theory of relativity, was that if the earth were moving through this ether toward or away from the source of a light beam, we'd be able to detect a difference in the observed speed of the light.

During his visit to Aarau at the end of his summer vacation of 1899, he worked on this issue with the rector of his old school there. "I had a good idea for investigating the way in which a body's relative motion with respect to the ether affects the velocity of the propagation of light," he wrote Marić. His idea involved building an apparatus that would use angled mirrors "so that light from a single source would be reflected in two different directions," sending one part of the beam in the direction of the earth's movement and the other part of the beam perpendicular to it. In a lecture on how he discovered relativity, Einstein recalled that his idea was to split a light beam, reflect it in different directions, and see if there was "a difference in energy depending on whether or not the direction was along the earth's motion through the ether." This could be done, he posited, by "using two thermoelectric piles to examine the difference of the heat generated in them."[41]

Weber rejected the proposal. What Einstein did not fully realize was that similar experiments had already been done by many others, including the Americans Albert Michelson and Edward Morley, and none had been able to detect any evidence of the perplexing ether—or that the speed of light varied depending on the motion of the observer or the light source. After discussing the topic with Weber, Einstein read a paper delivered the previous year by Wilhelm Wien, which briefly described thirteen experiments that had been conducted to detect the ether, including the Michelson-Morley one.

Einstein sent Professor Wien his own speculative paper on that topic and asked him to write him back. "He'll write me via the Polytechnic," Einstein predicted to Marić. "If you see a letter there for me, you may go ahead and open it." There is no evidence that Wien ever wrote back.[42]

Einstein's next research proposal involved exploring the link between the ability of different materials to conduct heat and to conduct electricity, something that was suggested by the electron theory. Weber apparently did not like that idea either, so Einstein was reduced, along with Marić, to doing a study purely on heat conduction, which was one of Weber's specialties.

Einstein later dismissed their graduation research papers as being of "no interest to me." Weber gave Einstein and Marić the two lowest essay grades in the class, a 4.5 and a 4.0, respectively; Grossmann, by comparison, got a 5.5. Adding annoyance to that injury, Weber said that Einstein had not written his on the proper regulation paper, and he forced him to copy the entire essay over again.[43]

Despite the low mark on his essay, Einstein was able to eke by with a 4.9 average in his final set of grades, placing him fourth in his class of five. Although history refutes the delicious myth that he flunked math in high school, at least it does offer as a consolation the amusement that he graduated college near the bottom of his class.

At least he graduated. His 4.9 average was just enough to let him get his diploma, which he did officially in July 1900. Mileva Marić, however, managed only a 4.0, by far the lowest in the class, and was not allowed to graduate. She determined that she would try again the following year.[44]

Not surprisingly, Einstein's years at the Polytechnic were marked by his pride at casting himself as a nonconformist. "His spirit of independence asserted itself one day in class when the professor mentioned a mild disciplinary measure just taken by the school's authorities," a classmate recalled. Einstein protested. The fundamental requirement of education, he felt, was the "need for intellectual freedom."[45]

Throughout his life, Einstein would speak lovingly of the Zurich Polytechnic, but he also would note that he did not like the discipline that was inherent in the system of examinations. "The hitch in this was, of course, that one had to cram all this stuff into one's mind for the examinations, whether one liked it or not," he said. "This coercion had such a deterring effect that, after I had passed the final examination, I found the consideration of any scientific problems distasteful to me for an entire year."[46]

In reality, that was neither possible nor true. He was cured within weeks, and he ended up taking with him some science books, including texts by Gustav Kirchhoff and Ludwig Boltzmann, when he joined his mother and sister later that July for their summer holiday in the Swiss Alps. "I've been studying a great deal," he wrote Marić, "mainly Kirchhoff's notorious investigations of the motion of the rigid body." He admitted that his resentment over the exams had already worn off. "My nerves have calmed down enough so that I'm able to work happily again," he said. "How are yours?"[47]

CHAPTER FOUR

THE LOVERS

1900–1904

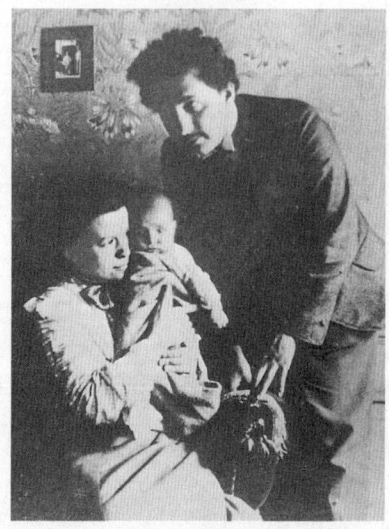

With Mileva and Hans Albert Einstein, 1904

Summer Vacation, 1900

Newly graduated, carrying his Kirchhoff and other physics books, Einstein arrived at the end of July 1900 for his family's summer vacation in Melchtal, a village nestled in the Swiss Alps between Lake Lucerne and the border with northern Italy. In tow was his "dreadful aunt," Julia Koch. They were met at the train station by his mother and sister, who smothered him with kisses, and then all piled into a carriage for the ride up the mountain.

As they neared the hotel, Einstein and his sister got off to walk. Maja confided that she had not dared to discuss with their mother his relationship with Mileva Marić, known in the family as "the Dollie affair" after his nickname for her, and she asked him to "go easy on Mama." It was not in Einstein's nature, however, "to keep my big mouth shut," as he later put it in his letter to Marić about the scene, nor was it in his nature to protect Marić's feelings by sparing her all the dramatic details about what ensued.[1]

He went to his mother's room and, after hearing about his exams, she asked him, "So, what will become of your Dollie now?"

"My wife," Einstein answered, trying to affect the same nonchalance that his mother had used in her question.

His mother, Einstein recalled, "threw herself on the bed, buried her head in the pillow, and wept like a child." She was finally able to regain her composure and proceeded to go on the attack. "You are ruining your future and destroying your opportunities," she said. "No decent family will have her. If she gets pregnant you'll really be in a mess."

At that point, it was Einstein's turn to lose his composure. "I vehemently denied we had been living in sin," he reported to Marić, "and scolded her roundly."

Just as he was about to storm out, a friend of his mother's came in, "a small, vivacious lady, an old hen of the most pleasant variety." They promptly segued into the requisite small talk: about the weather, the new guests at the spa, the ill-mannered children. Then they went off to eat and play music.

Such periods of storm and calm alternated throughout the vacation. Every now and then, just when Einstein thought that the crisis had receded, his mother would revisit the topic. "Like you, she's a book, but you ought to have a wife," she scolded at one point. Another time she brought up the fact that Marić was 24 and he was then only 21. "By the time you're 30, she'll be an old witch."

Einstein's father, still working back in Milan, weighed in with "a moralistic letter." The thrust of his parents' views—at least when applied to the situation of Mileva Marić rather than Marie Winteler—was that a wife was "a luxury" affordable only when a man was making a comfortable living. "I have a low opinion of that view of a relationship between a man and wife," he told Marić, "because it makes the wife and the prostitute distinguishable only insofar as the former is able to secure a lifelong contract."[2]

Over the ensuing months, there would be times when it seemed as if his parents had decided to accept their relationship. "Mama is slowly resigning herself," Einstein wrote Marić in August. Likewise in September: "They seem to have reconciled themselves to the inevitable. I think they will both come to like you very much once they get to know you." And once again in October: "My parents have retreated, grudgingly and with hesitation, from the battle of Dollie—now that they have seen that they'll lose it."[3]

But repeatedly, after each period of acceptance, their resistance would flare up anew, randomly leaping into a higher state of frenzy. "Mama often cries bitterly and I don't have a single moment of peace," he wrote at the end of August. "My parents weep for me almost as if I had died. Again and again they complain that I have brought misfortune upon myself by my devotion to you. They think you are not healthy."[4]

His parents' dismay had little to do with the fact that Marić was not Jewish, for neither was Marie Winteler, nor that she was Serbian, although that certainly didn't help her cause. Primarily, it seems, they considered her an unsuitable wife for many of the reasons that some of Einstein's friends did: she was older, somewhat sickly, had a limp, was plain looking, and was an intense but not a star intellectual.

All of this emotional pressure stoked Einstein's rebellious instincts and his passion for his "wild street urchin," as he called her. "Only now do I see how madly in love with you I am!" The relationship, as expressed in their letters, remained equal parts intellectual and emotional, but the emotional part was now filled with a fire unexpected from a self-proclaimed loner. "I just realized that I haven't been able to kiss you for an entire month, and I long for you so terribly much," he wrote at one point.

During a quick trip to Zurich in August to check on his job prospects, he found himself walking around in a daze. "Without you, I lack self-confidence, pleasure in my work, pleasure in life—in short, without you my life is not life." He even tried his hand at a poem for her, which began: "Oh my! That Johnnie boy! / So crazy with desire / While thinking of his Dollie / His pillow catches fire."[5]

Their passion, however, was an elevated one, at least in their minds. With the lonely elitism of young German coffeehouse denizens who have read the philosophy of Schopenhauer once too often, they unabashedly articulated the mystical distinction between their own rarefied spirits and the baser instincts and urges of the masses. "In the case of my parents, as with most people, the senses exercise a direct control over the emotions," he wrote her amid the family wars of August. "With us, thanks to the fortunate circumstances in which we live, the enjoyment of life is vastly broadened."

To his credit, Einstein reminded Marić (and himself) that "we mustn't forget that many existences like my parents' make our existence possible." The simple and honest instincts of people like his parents had ensured the progress of civilization. "Thus I am trying to protect my parents without compromising anything that is important to me— and that means you, sweetheart!"

In his attempt to please his mother, Einstein became a charming son at their grand hotel in Melchtal. He found the endless meals excessive and the "overdressed" patrons to be "indolent and pampered," but he dutifully played his violin for his mother's friends, made polite conversation, and feigned a cheerful mood. It worked. "My popularity among the guests here and my music successes act as a balm on my mother's heart."[6]

As for his father, Einstein decided that the best way to assuage him, as well as to draw off some of the emotional charge generated by his relationship with Marić, was to visit him back in Milan, tour some of his new power plants, and learn about the family firm "so I can take Papa's place in an emergency." Hermann Einstein seemed so pleased that he promised to take his son to Venice after the inspection tour. "I'm leaving for Italy on Saturday to partake of the 'holy sacraments' administered by my father, but the valiant Swabian* is not afraid."

Einstein's visit with his father went well, for the most part. A distant yet dutiful son, he had fretted mightily about each family financial crisis, perhaps even more than his father did. But business was good for the moment, and that lifted Hermann Einstein's spirits. "My father is a completely different man now that he has no more financial worries," Einstein wrote Marić. Only once did the "Dollie affair" intrude

---

* The phrase "valiant Swabian," used often by Einstein to refer to himself, comes from the poem "Swabian Tale" by Ludwig Uhland.

enough to make him consider cutting short his visit, but this threat so alarmed his father that Einstein stuck to the original plans. He seemed flattered that his father appreciated both his company and his willingness to pay attention to the family business.[7]

Even though Einstein occasionally denigrated the idea of being an engineer, it was possible that he could have followed that course at the end of the summer of 1900—especially if, on their trip to Venice, his father had asked him to, or if fate intervened so that he was needed to take his father's place. He was, after all, a low-ranked graduate of a teaching college without a teaching job, without any research accomplishments, and certainly without academic patrons.

Had he made such a choice in 1900, Einstein would have likely become a good enough engineer, but probably not a great one. Over the ensuing years he would dabble with inventions as a hobby and come up with some good concepts for devices ranging from noiseless refrigerators to a machine that measured very low voltage electricity. But none resulted in a significant engineering breakthrough or marketplace success. Though he would have been a more brilliant engineer than his father or uncle, it is not clear that he would have been any more financially successful.

Among the many surprising things about the life of Albert Einstein was the trouble he had getting an academic job. Indeed, it would be an astonishing nine years after his graduation from the Zurich Polytechnic in 1900—and four years after the miracle year in which he not only upended physics but also finally got a doctoral dissertation accepted—before he would be offered a job as a junior professor.

The delay was not due to a lack of desire on his part. In the middle of August 1900, between his family vacation in Melchtal and his visit to his father in Milan, Einstein stopped back in Zurich to see about getting a post as an assistant to a professor at the Polytechnic. It was typical that each graduate would find, if he wanted, some such role, and Einstein was confident it would happen. In the meantime, he rejected a friend's offer to help him get a job at an insurance company, dismissing it as "an eight hour day of mindless drudgery." As he told Marić, "One must avoid stultifying affairs."[8]

The problem was that the two physics professors at the Polytechnic were acutely aware of his impudence but not of his genius. Getting a job with Professor Pernet, who had reprimanded him, was not even a consideration. As for Professor Weber, he had developed such an allergy to Einstein that, when no other graduates of the physics and math department were available to become his assistant, he instead hired two students from the engineering division.

That left math professor Adolf Hurwitz. When one of Hurwitz's assistants got a job teaching at a high school, Einstein exulted to Marić: "This means I will become Hurwitz's servant, God willing." Unfortunately, he had skipped most of Hurwitz's classes, a slight that apparently had not been forgotten.[9]

By late September, Einstein was still staying with his parents in Milan and had not received an offer. "I plan on going to Zurich on October 1 to talk with Hurwitz personally about the position," he said. "It's certainly better than writing."

While there, he also planned to look for possible tutoring jobs that could tide them over while Marić prepared to retake her final exams. "No matter what happens, we'll have the most wonderful life in the world. Pleasant work and being together—and what's more, we now answer to no one, can stand on our own two feet, and enjoy our youth to the utmost. Who could have it any better? When we have scraped together enough money, we can buy bicycles and take a bike tour every couple of weeks."[10]

Einstein ended up deciding to write Hurwitz instead of visiting him, which was probably a mistake. His two letters do not stand as models for future generations seeking to learn how to write a job application. He readily conceded that he did not show up at Hurwitz's calculus classes and was more interested in physics than math. "Since lack of time prevented me from taking part in the mathematics seminar," he rather lamely said, "there is nothing in my favor except the fact that I attended most of the lectures offered." Rather presumptuously, he said he was eager for an answer because "the granting of citizenship in Zurich, for which I have applied, has been made conditional upon my proving that I have a permanent job."[11]

Einstein's impatience was matched by his confidence. "Hurwitz still hasn't written me more," he said only three days after sending his letter, "but I have hardly any doubt that I will get the position." He did not. Indeed, he managed to become the only person graduating in his section of the Polytechnic who was not offered a job. "I was suddenly abandoned by everyone," he later recalled.[12]

By the end of October 1900 he and Marić were both back in Zurich, where he spent most of his days hanging out at her apartment, reading and writing. On his citizenship application that month, he wrote "none" on the question asking his religion, and for his occupation he wrote, "I am giving private lessons in mathematics until I get a permanent position."

Throughout that fall, he was able to find only eight sporadic tutoring jobs, and his relatives had ended their financial support. But Einstein put up an optimistic front. "We support ourselves by private lessons, if we can ever pick up some, which is still very doubtful," he wrote a friend of Marić's. "Isn't this a journeyman's or even a gypsy's life? But I believe that we will remain cheerful in it as ever."[13] What kept him happy, in addition to Marić's presence, were the theoretical papers he was writing on his own.

Einstein's First Published Paper

The first of these papers was on a topic familiar to most school kids: the capillary effect that, among other things, causes water to cling to the side of a straw and curve upward. Although he later called this essay "worthless," it is interesting from a biographical perspective. Not only is it Einstein's first published paper, but it shows him heartily embracing an important premise—one not yet fully accepted—that would be at the core of much of his work over the next five years: that molecules (and their constituent atoms) actually exist, and that many natural phenomena can be explained by analyzing how these particles interact with one another.

During his vacation in the summer of 1900, Einstein had been reading the work of Ludwig Boltzmann, who had developed a theory of gases based on the behavior of countless molecules bouncing around. "The Boltzmann is absolutely magnificent," he enthused to Marić in September. "I am firmly convinced of the correctness of the principles of his theory, i.e., I am convinced that in the case of gases we are really dealing with discrete particles of definite finite size which move according to certain conditions."[14]

To understand capillarity, however, required looking at the forces acting between molecules in a liquid, not a gas. Such molecules attract one another, which accounts for the surface tension of a liquid, or the fact that drops hold together, as well as for the capillary effect. Einstein's idea was that these forces might be analogous to Newton's gravitational forces, in which two objects are attracted to each other in proportion to their mass and in inverse proportion to their distance from one another.

Einstein looked at whether the capillary effect showed such a relationship to the atomic weight of various liquid substances. He was encouraged, so he decided to see if he could find some experimental data to test the theory further. "The results on capillarity I recently obtained in Zurich seem to be entirely new despite their simplicity," he wrote Marić. "When we're back in Zurich we'll try to get some empirical data on this subject . . . If this yields a law of nature, we'll send the results to the *Annalen*."[15]

He did end up sending the paper in December 1900 to the *Annalen der Physik,* Europe's leading physics journal, which published it the following March. Written without the elegance or verve of his later papers, it conveyed what is at best a tenuous conclusion. "I started from the simple idea of attractive forces among the molecules, and I tested the consequences experimentally," he wrote. "I took gravitational forces as an analogy." At the end of the paper, he declares limply, "The question of whether and how our forces are related to gravitational forces must therefore be left completely open for the time being."[16]

The paper elicited no comments and contributed nothing to the history of physics. Its basic conjecture was wrong, as the distance dependence is not the same for differing pairs of molecules.[17] But it did get him published for the first time. That meant that he now had a printed article to attach to the job-seeking letters with which he was beginning to spam professors all over Europe.

In his letter to Marić, Einstein had used the term "we" when discussing plans to publish the paper. In two letters written the month after it appeared, Einstein referred to "our theory of molecular forces" and "our investigation." Thus was launched a historical debate over how much credit Marić deserves for helping Einstein devise his theories.

In this case, she mainly seemed to be involved in looking up some data for him to use. His letters conveyed his latest thoughts on molecular forces, but hers contained no substantive science. And in a letter to her best friend, Marić sounded as if she had settled into the role of supportive lover rather than scientific partner. "Albert has written a paper in physics that will probably be published very soon in the *Annalen der Physik*," she wrote. "You can imagine how very proud I am of my darling. This is not just an everyday paper, but a very significant one. It deals with the theory of liquids."[18]

Jobless Anguish

It had been almost four years since Einstein had renounced his German citizenship, and ever since then he had been stateless. Each month, he put aside some money toward the fee he would need to pay to become a Swiss citizen, a status he deeply desired. One reason was that he admired the Swiss system, its democracy, and its gentle respect for individuals and their privacy. "I like the Swiss because, by and large, they are more humane than the other people among whom I have lived," he later said.[19] There were also practical reasons; in order to work as a civil servant or a teacher in a state school, he would have to be a Swiss citizen.

The Zurich authorities examined him rather thoroughly, and they even sent to Milan for a report on his parents. By February 1901, they were satisfied, and he was made a citizen. He would retain that designation his entire life, even as he accepted citizenships in Germany (again), Austria, and the United States. Indeed, he was so eager to be a Swiss citizen that he put aside his antimilitary sentiments and presented himself, as required, for military service. He was rejected for having sweaty feet ("hyperidrosis ped"), flat feet ("pes planus"), and varicose veins ("varicosis"). The Swiss Army was, apparently, quite discriminating, and so his military service book was stamped "unfit."[20]

A few weeks after he got his citizenship, however, his parents insisted that he come back to Milan and live with them. They had decreed, at the end of 1900, that he could not stay in Zurich past Easter unless he got a job there. When Easter came, he was still unemployed.

Marić, not unreasonably, assumed that his summons to Milan was due to his parents' antipathy toward her. "What utterly depressed me was the fact that our separation had to come about in such an unnatural way, on account of slanders and intrigues," she wrote her friend. With an absentmindedness he was later to make iconic, Einstein left behind in Zurich his nightshirt, toothbrush, comb, hairbrush (back then he used one), and other toiletries. "Send everything along to my sister," he instructed Marić, "so she can bring them home with her." Four days later, he added, "Hold on to my umbrella for the time being. We'll figure out something to do with it later." [21]

Both in Zurich and then in Milan, Einstein churned out job-seeking letters, ever more pleading, to professors around Europe. They were accompanied by his paper on the capillary effect, which proved not particularly impressive; he rarely even received the courtesy of a response. "I will soon have graced every physicist from the North Sea to the southern tip of Italy with my offer," he wrote Marić. [22]

By April 1901, Einstein was reduced to buying a pile of postcards with postage-paid reply attachments in the forlorn hope that he would, at least, get an answer. In the two cases where these postcard pleas have survived, they have become, rather amusingly, prized collectors' items. One of them, to a Dutch professor, is now on display in the Leiden Museum for the History of Science. In both cases, the return-reply attachment was not used; Einstein did not even get the courtesy of a rejection. "I leave no stone unturned and do not give up my sense of humor," he wrote his friend Marcel Grossmann. "God created the donkey and gave him a thick skin." [23]

Among the great scientists Einstein wrote was Wilhelm Ostwald, professor of chemistry in Leipzig, whose contributions to the theory of dilution were to earn him a Nobel Prize. "Your work on general chemistry inspired me to write the enclosed article," Einstein said. Then flattery turned to plaintiveness as he asked "whether you might have use for a mathematical physicist." Einstein concluded by pleading: "I am without money, and only a position of this kind would enable me to continue my studies." He got no answer. Einstein wrote again two weeks later using the pretext "I am not sure whether I included my address" in the earlier letter. "Your judgment of my paper matters very much to me." There was still no answer.[24]

Einstein's father, with whom he was living in Milan, quietly shared his son's anguish and tried, in a painfully sweet manner, to help. When no answer came after the second letter to Ostwald, Hermann Einstein took it upon himself, without his son's knowledge, to make an unusual and awkward effort, suffused with heart-wrenching emotion, to prevail upon Ostwald himself:

> Please forgive a father who is so bold as to turn to you, esteemed Herr Professor, in the interest of his son. Albert is 22 years old, he studied at the Zurich Polytechnic for four years, and he passed his exam with flying colors last summer. Since then he has been trying unsuccessfully to get a position as a teaching assistant, which would enable him to continue his education in physics. All those in a position to judge praise his talents; I can assure you that he is extraordinarily studious and diligent and clings with great love to his science. He therefore feels profoundly unhappy about his current lack of a job, and he becomes more and more convinced that he has gone off the tracks with his career. In addition, he is oppressed by the thought that he is a burden on us, people of modest means. Since it is you whom my son seems to admire and esteem more than any other scholar in physics, it is you to whom I have taken the liberty of turning with the humble request to read his paper and to write to him, if possible, a few words of encouragement, so that he might recover his joy in living and working. If, in addition, you could secure him an assistant's position, my gratitude would know no bounds. I beg you to forgive me for my impudence in writing you, and my son does not know anything about my unusual step.[25]

Ostwald still did not answer. However, in one of history's nice ironies, he would become, nine years later, the first person to nominate Einstein for the Nobel Prize.

Einstein was convinced that his nemesis at the Zurich Polytechnic, physics professor Heinrich Weber, was behind the difficulties. Having hired two engineers rather than Einstein as his own assistant, he was apparently now giving him unfavorable references. After applying for a job with Göttingen professor Eduard Riecke, Einstein despaired to Marić: "I have more or less given up the position as lost. I cannot believe that Weber would let such a good opportunity pass without doing some mischief." Marić advised him to write Weber, confronting him directly, and Einstein reported back that he had. "He should at least know that he cannot do these things behind my back. I wrote to him that I know that my appointment now depends on his report alone."

It didn't work. Einstein again got turned down. "Riecke's rejection hasn't surprised me," he wrote Marić. "I'm completely convinced that Weber is to blame." He became so discouraged that, at least for the moment, he felt it futile to continue his search. "Under these circumstances it no longer makes sense to write further to professors, since, should things get far enough along, it is certain they would all enquire with Weber, and he would again give a poor reference." To Grossmann he lamented, "I could have found a job long ago had it not been for Weber's underhandedness."[26]

To what extent did anti-Semitism play a role? Einstein came to believe that it was a factor, which led him to seek work in Italy, where he felt it was not so pronounced. "One of the main obstacles in getting a position is absent here, namely anti-Semitism, which in German-speaking countries is as unpleasant as it is a hindrance," he wrote Marić. She, in turn, lamented to her friend about her lover's difficulties. "You know my sweetheart has a sharp tongue and moreover he is a Jew."[27]

In his effort to find work in Italy, Einstein enlisted one of the friends he had made while studying in Zurich, an engineer named Michele Angelo Besso. Like Einstein, Besso was from a middle-class Jewish family that had wandered around Europe and eventually settled in Italy. He was six years older than Einstein, and by the time they met he had already graduated from the Polytechnic and was working for an engineering firm. He and Einstein forged a close friendship that would last for the rest of their lives (they died within weeks of each other in 1955).

Over the years, Besso and Einstein would share both the most intimate personal confidences and the loftiest scientific notions. As Einstein wrote in one of the 229 extant letters they exchanged, "Nobody else is so close to me, nobody knows me so well, nobody is so kindly disposed to me as you are."[28]

Besso had a delightful intellect, but he lacked focus, drive, and dili-

gence. Like Einstein, he had once been asked to leave high school because of his insubordinate attitude (he sent a petition complaining
about a math teacher). Einstein called Besso "an awful weakling . . .
who cannot rouse himself to any action in life or scientific creation, but
who has an extraordinarily fine mind whose working, though disorderly, I watch with great delight."

Einstein had introduced Besso to Anna Winteler of Aarau, Marie's
sister, whom he ended up marrying. By 1901 he had moved to Trieste
with her. When Einstein caught up with him, he found Besso as smart,
as funny, and as maddeningly unfocused as ever. He had recently been
asked by his boss to inspect a power station, and he decided to leave the
night before to make sure that he arrived on time. But he missed his
train, then failed to get there the next day, and finally arrived on the
third day—"but to his horror realizes that he has forgotten what he's
supposed to do." So he sent a postcard back to the office asking them to
resend his instructions. It was the boss's assessment that Besso was
"completely useless and almost unbalanced."

Einstein's assessment of Besso was more loving. "Michele is an
awful schlemiel," he reported to Marić, using the Yiddish word for a
hapless bumbler. One evening, Besso and Einstein spent almost four
hours talking about science, including the properties of the mysterious
ether and "the definition of absolute rest." These ideas would burst into
bloom four years later, in the relativity theory that he would devise with
Besso as his sounding board. "He's interested in our research," Einstein
wrote Marić, "though he often misses the big picture by worrying
about petty considerations."

Besso had some connections that could, Einstein hoped, be useful.
His uncle was a mathematics professor at the polytechnic in Milan,
and Einstein's plan was to have Besso provide an introduction: "I'll
grab him by the collar and drag him to his uncle, where I'll do the talking myself." Besso was able to persuade his uncle to write letters on
Einstein's behalf, but nothing came of the effort. Instead, Einstein
spent most of 1901 juggling temporary teaching assignments and
some tutoring.[29]

It was Einstein's other close friend from Zurich, his classmate and
math note-taker Marcel Grossmann, who ended up finally getting

Einstein a job, though not one that would have been expected. Just when Einstein was beginning to despair, Grossmann wrote that there was likely to be an opening for an examiner at the Swiss Patent Office, located in Bern. Grossmann's father knew the director and was willing to recommend Einstein.

"I was deeply moved by your devotion and compassion, which did not let you forget your luckless friend," Einstein replied. "I would be delighted to get such a nice job and that I would spare no effort to live up to your recommendation." To Marić he exulted: "Just think what a wonderful job this would be for me! I'll be mad with joy if something should come of that."

It would take months, he knew, before the patent-office job would materialize, assuming that it ever did. So he accepted a temporary post at a technical school in Winterthur for two months, filling in for a teacher on military leave. The hours would be long and, worse yet, he would have to teach descriptive geometry, neither then nor later his strongest field. "But the valiant Swabian is not afraid," he proclaimed, repeating one of his favorite poetic phrases.[30]

In the meantime, he and Marić would have the chance to take a romantic vacation together, one that would have fateful consequences.

Lake Como, May 1901

"You absolutely must come see me in Como, you little witch," Einstein wrote Marić at the end of April 1901. "You'll see for yourself how bright and cheerful I've become and how all my brow-knitting is gone."

The family disputes and frustrating job search had caused him to be snappish, but he promised that was now over. "It was only out of nervousness that I was mean to you," he apologized. To make it up to her, he proposed that they should have a romantic and sensuous tryst in one of the world's most romantic and sensuous places: Lake Como, the grandest of the jewel-like Alpine finger lakes high on the border of Italy and Switzerland, where in early May the lush foliage bursts forth under majestic snow-capped peaks.

"Bring my blue dressing-gown so we can wrap ourselves up in it," he said. "I promise you an outing the likes of which you've never seen."[31]

Marić quickly accepted, but then changed her mind; she had received a letter from her family in Novi Sad "that robs me of all desire, not only for having fun, but for life itself." He should make the trip on his own, she sulked. "It seems I can have nothing without being punished." But the next day she changed her mind again. "I wrote you a little card yesterday while in the worst of moods because of a letter I received. But when I read your letter today I became a bit more cheerful, since I see how much you love me, so I think we'll take that trip after all." [32]

And thus it was that early on the morning of Sunday, May 5, 1901, Albert Einstein was waiting for Mileva Marić at the train station in the village of Como, Italy, "with open arms and a pounding heart." They spent the day there, admiring its gothic cathedral and walled old town, then took one of the stately white steamers that hop from village to village along the banks of the lake.

They stopped to visit Villa Carlotta, the most luscious of all the famous mansions that dot the shore, with its frescoed ceilings, a version of Antonio Canova's erotic sculpture *Cupid and Psyche,* and five hundred species of plants. Marić later wrote a friend how much she admired "the splendid garden, which I preserved in my heart, the more so because we were not allowed to swipe a single flower."

After spending the night in an inn, they decided to hike through the mountain pass to Switzerland, but found it still covered with up to twenty feet of snow. So they hired a small sleigh, "the kind they use that has just enough room for two people in love with each other, and a coachman stands on a little plank in the rear and prattles all the time and calls you 'signora,' " Marić wrote. "Could you think of anything more beautiful?"

The snow was falling merrily, as far as the eye could see, "so that this cold, white infinity gave me the shivers and I held my sweetheart firmly in my arms under the coats and shawls covering us." On the way down, they stomped and kicked at the snow to produce little avalanches, "so as to properly scare the world below." [33]

A few days later, Einstein recalled "how beautiful it was the last time you let me press your dear little person against me in that most natural way." [34] And in that most natural way, Mileva Marić became pregnant with Albert Einstein's child.

After returning to Winterthur, where he was a substitute teacher, Einstein wrote Marić a letter that made reference to her pregnancy. Oddly—or perhaps not oddly at all—he began by delving into matters scientific rather than personal. "I just read a wonderful paper by Lenard on the generation of cathode rays by ultraviolet light," he started. "Under the influence of this beautiful piece I am filled with such happiness and joy that I must share some of it with you." Einstein would soon revolutionize science by building on Lenard's paper to produce a theory of light quanta that explained this photoelectric effect. Even so, it is rather surprising, or at least amusing, that when he rhapsodized about sharing "happiness and joy" with his newly pregnant lover, he was referring to a paper on beams of electrons.

Only after this scientific exultation came a brief reference to their expected child, whom Einstein referred to as a boy: "How are you darling? How's the boy?" He went on to display an odd notion of what parenting would be like: "Can you imagine how pleasant it will be when we're able to work again, completely undisturbed, and with no one around to tell us what to do!"

Most of all, he tried to be reassuring. He would find a job, he pledged, even if it meant going into the insurance business. They would create a comfortable home together. "Be happy and don't fret, darling. I won't leave you and will bring everything to a happy conclusion. You just have to be patient! You will see that my arms are not so bad to rest in, even if things are beginning a little awkwardly."[35]

Marić was preparing to retake her graduation exams, and she was hoping to go on to get a doctorate and become a physicist. Both she and her parents had invested enormous amounts, emotionally and financially, in that goal over the years. She could have, if she had wished, terminated her pregnancy. Zurich was then a center of a burgeoning birth control industry, which included a mail-order abortion drug firm based there.

Instead, she decided that she wanted to have Einstein's child—even though he was not yet ready or willing to marry her. Having a child out of wedlock was rebellious, given their upbringings, but not uncommon. The official statistics for Zurich in 1901 show that 12 percent of births were illegitimate. Residents who were Austro-Hungarian, moreover, were much more likely to get pregnant while unmarried. In southern Hungary, 33 percent of births were illegitimate. Serbs had the highest rate of illegitimate births, Jews by far the lowest.[36]

The decision caused Einstein to focus on the future. "I will look for a position *immediately,* no matter how humble it is," he told her. "My scientific goals and my personal vanity will not prevent me from accepting even the most subordinate position." He decided to call Besso's father as well as the director of the local insurance company, and he promised to marry her as soon as he settled into a job. "Then no one can cast a stone on your dear little head."

The pregnancy could also resolve, or so he hoped, the issues they faced with their families. "When your parents and mine are presented with a fait accompli, they'll just have to reconcile themselves to it as best they can."[37]

Marić, bedridden in Zurich with pregnancy sickness, was thrilled. "So, sweetheart, you want to look for a job immediately? And have me move in with you!" It was a vague proposal, but she immediately pronounced herself "happy" to agree. "Of course it mustn't involve accepting a really bad position, darling," she added. "That would make me feel terrible." At her sister's suggestion she tried to convince Einstein to visit her parents in Serbia for the summer vacation. "It would make me so happy," she begged. "And when my parents see the two of us physically in front of them, all their doubts will evaporate."[38]

But Einstein, to her dismay, decided to spend the summer vacation again with his mother and sister in the Alps. As a result, he was not there to help and encourage her at the end of July 1901 when she retook her exams. Perhaps as a consequence of her pregnancy and personal situation, Mileva ended up failing for the second time, once again getting a 4.0 out of 6 and once again being the only one in her group not to pass.

Thus it was that Mileva Marić found herself resigned to giving up her dream of being a scientific scholar. She visited her home in Serbia—alone—and told her parents about her academic failure and her pregnancy. Before leaving, she asked Einstein to send her father a letter describing their plans and, presumably, pledging to marry her.

"Will you send me the letter so I can see what you've written?" she asked. "By and by I'll give him the necessary information, the unpleasant news as well."[39]

Disputes with Drude and Others

Einstein's impudence and contempt for convention, traits that were abetted by Marić, were evident in his science as well as in his personal life in 1901. That year, the unemployed enthusiast engaged in a series of tangles with academic authorities.

The squabbles show that Einstein had no qualms about challenging those in power. In fact, it seemed to infuse him with glee. As he proclaimed to Jost Winteler in the midst of his disputes that year, "Blind respect for authority is the greatest enemy of truth." It would prove a worthy credo, one suitable for being carved on his coat of arms if he had ever wanted such a thing.

His struggles that year also reveal something more subtle about Einstein's scientific thinking: he had an urge—indeed, a compulsion—to unify concepts from different branches of physics. "It is a glorious feeling to discover the unity of a set of phenomena that seem at first to be completely separate," he wrote to his friend Grossmann as he embarked that spring on an attempt to tie his work on capillarity to Boltzmann's theory of gases. That sentence, more than any other, sums up the faith that underlay Einstein's scientific mission, from his first paper until his last scribbled field equations, guiding him with the same sure sense that was displayed by the needle of his childhood compass.[40]

Among the potentially unifying concepts that were mesmerizing Einstein, and much of the physics world, were those that sprang from kinetic theory, which had been developed in the late nineteenth century by applying the principles of mechanics to phenomena such as heat transfer and the behavior of gases. This involved regarding a gas, for example, as a collection of a huge number of tiny particles—in this case, molecules made up of one or more atoms—that careen around freely and occasionally collide with one another.

Kinetic theory spurred the growth of statistical mechanics, which describes the behavior of a large number of particles using statistical calculations. It was, of course, impossible to trace each molecule and each collision in a gas, but knowing the statistical behavior gave a workable theory of how billions of molecules behaved under varying conditions.

Scientists proceeded to apply these concepts not only to the behavior of gases, but also to phenomena that occurred in liquids and solids, including electrical conductivity and radiation. "The opportunity arose to apply the methods of the kinetic theory of gases to completely different branches of physics," Einstein's close friend Paul Ehrenfest, himself an expert in the field, later wrote. "Above all, the theory was applied to the motion of electrons in metals, to the Brownian motion of microscopically small particles in suspensions, and to the theory of blackbody radiation." [41]

Although many scientists were using atomism to explore their own specialties, for Einstein it was a way to make connections, and develop unifying theories, between a variety of disciplines. In April 1901, for example, he adapted the molecular theories he had used to explain the capillary effect in liquids and applied them to the diffusion of gas molecules. "I've got an extremely lucky idea, which will make it possible to apply our theory of molecular forces to gases as well," he wrote Marić. To Grossmann he noted, "I am now convinced that my theory of atomic attractive forces can also be extended to gases." [42]

Next he became interested in the conduction of heat and electricity, which led him to study Paul Drude's electron theory of metals. As the Einstein scholar Jürgen Renn notes, "Drude's electron theory and Boltzmann's kinetic theory of gas do not just happen to be two arbitrary subjects of interest to Einstein, but rather they share an important common property with several other of his early research topics: they are two examples of the application of atomistic ideas to physical and chemical problems." [43]

Drude's electron theory posited that there are particles in metal that move freely, as molecules of gas do, and thereby conduct both heat and electricity. When Einstein looked into it, he was pleased with it in parts. "I have a study in my hands by Paul Drude on the electron theory, which is written to my heart's desire, even though it contains some very sloppy things," he told Marić. A month later, with his usual lack of deference to authority, he declared, "Perhaps I'll write to Drude privately to point out his mistakes."

And so he did. In a letter to Drude in June, Einstein pointed out what he thought were two mistakes. "He will hardly have anything sensible to refute me with," Einstein gloated to Marić, "because my objections are very straightforward." Perhaps under the charming illusion that showing an eminent scientist his purported lapses is a good method for getting a job, Einstein included a request for one in his letter.[44]

Surprisingly, Drude replied. Not surprisingly, he dismissed Einstein's objections. Einstein was outraged. "It is such manifest proof of the wretchedness of its author that no further comment by me is necessary," Einstein said when forwarding Drude's reply to Marić. "From now on I'll no longer turn to such people, and will instead attack them mercilessly in the journals, as they deserve. It is no wonder that little by little one becomes a misanthrope."

Einstein also vented his frustration to Jost Winteler, his father figure from Aarau, in a letter that included his declaration about a blind respect for authority being the greatest enemy of truth. "He responds by pointing out that another 'infallible' colleague of his shares his opinion. I'll soon make it hot for the man with a masterly publication."[45]

The published papers of Einstein do not identify this "infallible" colleague cited by Drude, but some sleuthing by Renn has turned up a letter from Marić that declares it to be Ludwig Boltzmann.[46] That explains why Einstein proceeded to immerse himself in Boltzmann's writings. "I have been engrossed in Boltzmann's works on the kinetic theory of gases," he wrote Grossmann in September, "and these last few days I wrote a short paper myself that provides the missing keystone in the chain of proofs that he started."[47]

Boltzmann, then at the University of Leipzig, was Europe's master of statistical physics. He had helped to develop the kinetic theory and defend the faith that atoms and molecules actually exist. In doing so, he found it necessary to reconceive the great Second Law of Thermodynamics. This law has many equivalent formulations. It says that heat flows naturally from hot to cold, but not the reverse. Another way to describe the Second Law is in terms of entropy, the degree of disorder and randomness in a system. Any spontaneous process tends to increase the entropy of a system. For example, perfume molecules drift out of an open bottle and into a room but don't, at least in our common experience, spontaneously gather themselves together and all drift back into the bottle.

The problem for Boltzmann was that mechanical processes, such as molecules bumping around, could each be reversed, according to Newton. So a spontaneous decrease in entropy would, at least in theory, be possible. The absurdity of positing that diffused perfume molecules could gather back into a bottle, or that heat could flow from a cold body to a hot one spontaneously, was flung against Boltzmann by opponents, such as Wilhelm Ostwald, who did not believe in the reality of atoms and molecules. "The proposition that all natural phenomena can ultimately be reduced to mechanical ones cannot even be taken as a useful working hypothesis: it is simply a mistake," Ostwald declared. "The irreversibility of natural phenomena proves the existence of processes that cannot be described by mechanical equations."

Boltzmann responded by revising the Second Law so that it was not absolute but merely a statistical near-certainty. It was theoretically possible that millions of perfume molecules could randomly bounce around in a way that they all put themselves back into a bottle at a certain moment, but that was exceedingly unlikely, perhaps trillions of times less likely than that a new deck of cards shuffled a hundred times would end up back in its pristine rank-and-suit precise order.[48]

When Einstein rather immodestly declared in September 1901 that he was filling in a "keystone" that was missing in Boltzmann's chain of proofs, he said he planned to publish it soon. But first, he sent a paper to the *Annalen der Physik* that involved an electrical method for investigating molecular forces, which used calculations derived from experiments others had done using salt solutions and an electrode.[49]

Then he published his critique of Boltzmann's theories. He noted that they worked well in explaining heat transfer in gases but had not yet been properly generalized for other realms. "Great as the achievements of the kinetic theory of heat have been in the domain of gas theory," he wrote, "the science of mechanics has not yet been able to produce an adequate foundation for the general theory of heat." His aim was "to close this gap."[50]

This was all quite presumptuous for an undistinguished Polytechnic student who had not been able to get either a doctorate or a job. Einstein himself later admitted that these papers added little to the body of physics wisdom. But they do indicate what was at the heart of his 1901 challenges to Drude and Boltzmann. Their theories, he felt, did not live up to the maxim he had proclaimed to Grossmann earlier that year about how glorious it was to discover an underlying unity in a set of phenomena that seem completely separate.

In the meantime, in November 1901, Einstein had submitted an attempt at a doctoral dissertation to Professor Alfred Kleiner at the University of Zurich. The dissertation has not survived, but Marić told a friend that "it deals with research into the molecular forces in gases using various known phenomena." Einstein was confident. "He won't dare reject my dissertation," he said of Kleiner, "otherwise the short-sighted man is of little use to me."[51]

By December Kleiner had not even responded, and Einstein started worrying that perhaps the professor's "fragile dignity" might make him uncomfortable accepting a dissertation that denigrated the work of such masters as Drude and Boltzmann. "If he dares to reject my dissertation, then I'll publish his rejection along with my paper and make a fool of him," Einstein said. "But if he accepts it, then we'll see what good old Herr Drude has to say."

Eager for a resolution, he decided to go see Kleiner personally. Rather surprisingly, the meeting went well. Kleiner admitted he had not yet read the dissertation, and Einstein told him to take his time. They then proceeded to discuss various ideas that Einstein was developing, some of which would eventually bear fruit in his relativity theory. Kleiner promised Einstein that he could count on him for a recommendation the next time a teaching job came up. "He's not quite as stupid as I'd thought," was Einstein's verdict. "Moreover, he's a good fellow."[52]

Kleiner may have been a good fellow, but he did not like Einstein's dissertation when he finally got around to reading it. In particular, he was unhappy about Einstein's attack on the scientific establishment. So he rejected it; more precisely, he told Einstein to withdraw it voluntarily, which permitted him to get back his 230 franc fee. According to a book written by Einstein's stepson-in-law, Kleiner's action was "out of consideration to his colleague Ludwig Boltzmann, whose train of reasoning Einstein had sharply criticized." Einstein, lacking such sensitivity, was persuaded by a friend to send the attack directly to Boltzmann.[53]

Lieserl

Marcel Grossmann had mentioned to Einstein that there was likely to be a job at the patent office for him, but it had not yet materialized. So five months later, he gently reminded Grossmann that he still needed help. Noticing in the newspaper that Grossmann had won a job teaching at a Swiss high school, Einstein expressed his "great joy" and then plaintively added, "I, too, applied for that position, but I did it only so that I wouldn't have to tell myself that I was too faint-hearted to apply."[54]

In the fall of 1901, Einstein took an even humbler job as a tutor at a little private academy in Schaffhausen, a village on the Rhine twenty miles north of Zurich. The work consisted solely of tutoring a rich English schoolboy who was there. To be taught by Einstein would someday seem a bargain at any price. But at the time, the proprietor of the school, Jacob Nüesch, was getting the bargain. He was charging the child's family 4,000 francs a year, while paying Einstein only 150 francs a month, plus providing room and board.

Einstein continued to promise Marić that she would "get a good husband as soon as this becomes feasible," but he was now despairing about the patent job. "The position in Bern has not yet been advertised so that I am really giving up hope for it."[55]

Marić was eager to be with him, but her pregnancy made it impossible for them to be together in public. So she spent most of November at a small hotel in a neighboring village. Their relationship was becoming strained. Despite her pleas, Einstein came only infrequently to visit her, often claiming that he did not have the spare money. "You'll surely surprise me, right?" she begged after getting yet another note canceling a visit. Her pleadings and anger alternated, often in the same letter:

If you only knew how terribly homesick I am, you would surely come. Are you really out of money? That's nice! The man earns 150 francs, has room and board provided, and at the end of the month doesn't have a cent to his name! . . . Don't use that as an excuse for Sunday, please. If you don't get any money by then, I will send you some . . . If you only knew how much I want to see you again! I think about you all day long, and even more at night.[56]

Einstein's impatience with authority soon pitted him against the proprietor of the academy. He tried to cajole his tutee to move to Bern with him and pay him directly, but the boy's mother balked. Then Einstein asked Nüesch to give him his meal money in cash so that he would not have to eat with his family. "You know what our conditions are," Nüesch replied. "There is no reason to deviate from them."

A surly Einstein threatened to find new arrangements, and Nüesch backed down in a rage. In a line that could be considered yet another maxim for his life, Einstein recounted the scene to Marić and exulted, "Long live impudence! It is my guardian angel in this world."

That night, as he sat down for his last meal at the Nüesch household, he found a letter for him next to his soup plate. It was from his real-life guardian angel, Marcel Grossmann. The position at the patent office, Grossmann wrote, was about to be advertised, and Einstein was sure to get it. Their lives were soon to be "brilliantly changed for the better," an excited Einstein wrote Marić. "I'm dizzy with joy when I think about it," he said. "I'm even happier for you than for myself. Together we'd surely be the happiest people on the earth."

That still left the issue of what to do about their baby, who was due to be born in less than two months, by early February 1902. "The only problem that would remain to be solved would be how to keep our Lieserl with us," Einstein (who had begun referring to their unborn child as a girl) wrote to Marić, who had returned home to have the baby at her parents' house in Novi Sad. "I wouldn't want to have to give her up." It was a noble intention on his part, yet he knew that it would be difficult for him to show up for work in Bern with an illegitimate child. "Ask your Papa; he's an experienced man, and knows the world better than your overworked, impractical Johnnie." For good measure, he declared that the baby, when born, "shouldn't be stuffed with cow milk, because it might make her stupid." Marić's milk would be more nourishing, he said.[57]

Although he was willing to consult Marić's family, Einstein had no intention of letting his own family know that his mother's worst fears about his relationship—a pregnancy and possible marriage—were materializing. His sister seemed to realize that he and Marić were secretly planning to be married, and she told this to members of the Winteler family in Aarau. But none of them showed any sign of suspecting that a child was involved. Einstein's mother learned about the purported engagement from Mrs. Winteler. "We are resolutely against Albert's relationship with Fraulein Marić, and we don't ever wish to have anything to do with her," Pauline Einstein lamented.[58]

Einstein's mother even took the extraordinary step of writing a nasty letter, signed also by her husband, to Marić's parents. "This lady," Marić lamented to a friend about Einstein's mother, "seems to have set as her life's goal to embitter as much as possible not only my life but also that of her son. I could not have thought it possible that there could exist such heartless and outright wicked people! They felt no compunctions about writing a letter to my parents in which they reviled me in a manner that was a disgrace."[59]

The official advertisement announcing the patent office opportunity finally appeared in December 1901. The director, Friedrich Haller, apparently tailored the specifications so that Einstein would get the job. Candidates did not need a doctorate, but they must have mechanical training and also know physics. "Haller put this in for my sake," Einstein told Marić.

Haller wrote Einstein a friendly letter making it clear that he was the prime candidate, and Grossmann called to congratulate him. "There's no doubt anymore," Einstein exulted to Marić. "Soon you'll be my happy little wife, just watch. Now our troubles are over. Only now that this terrible weight is off my shoulders do I realize how much I love you . . . Soon I'll be able to take my Dollie in my arms and call her my own in front of the whole world."[60]

He made her promise, however, that marriage would not turn them into a comfortable bourgeois couple: "We'll diligently work on science together so we don't become old philistines, right?" Even his sister, he felt, was becoming "so crass" in her approach to creature comforts. "You'd better not get that way," he told Marić. "It would be terrible. You must always be my witch and street urchin. Everyone but you seems foreign to me, as if they were separated from me by an invisible wall."

In anticipation of getting the patent-office job, Einstein abandoned the student he had been tutoring in Schaffhausen and moved to Bern in late January 1902. He would be forever grateful to Grossmann, whose aid would continue in different ways over the next few years. "Grossmann is doing his dissertation on a subject that is related to non-Euclidean geometry," Einstein noted to Marić. "I don't know exactly what it is."[61]

A few days after Einstein arrived in Bern, Mileva Marić, staying at her parents' home in Novi Sad, gave birth to their baby, a girl whom they called Lieserl. Because the childbirth was so difficult, Marić was unable to write to him. Her father sent Einstein the news.

"Is she healthy, and does she cry properly?" Einstein wrote Marić. "What are her eyes like? Which one of us does she more resemble? Who is giving her milk? Is she hungry? She must be completely bald. I love her so much and don't even know her yet!" Yet his love for their new baby seemed to exist mainly in the abstract, for it was not quite enough to induce him to make the train trip to Novi Sad.[62]

Einstein did not tell his mother, sister, or any of his friends about the birth of Lieserl. In fact, there is no indication that he *ever* told them about her. Never once did he publicly speak of her or acknowledge that she even existed. No mention of her survives in any correspondence, except for a few letters between Einstein and Marić, and these were suppressed and hidden until 1986, when scholars and the editors of his papers were completely surprised to learn of Lieserl's existence.*

But in his letter to Marić right after Lieserl's birth, the baby

---

* The letters were discovered by John Stachel of the Einstein Papers Project among a cache of four hundred family letters that were stored in a California safe deposit box by the second wife of Einstein's son Hans Albert Einstein, whose first wife had brought them to California after she went to Zurich to clean out Mileva Marić's apartment following her death in 1948.

brought out Einstein's wry side. "She's certainly able to cry already, but won't know how to laugh until much later," he said. "Therein lies a profound truth."

Fatherhood also focused him on the need to make some money while he waited to get the patent-office job. So the next day an ad appeared in the newspaper: "Private lessons in Mathematics and Physics . . . given most thoroughly by Albert Einstein, holder of the federal Polytechnic teacher's diploma . . . Trial lessons free."

Lieserl's birth even caused Einstein to display a domestic, nesting instinct not previously apparent. He found a large room in Bern and drew for Marić a sketch of it, complete with diagrams showing the bed, six chairs, three cabinets, himself ("Johnnie"), and a couch marked "look at that!" [63] However, Marić was not going to be moving into it with him. They were not married, and an aspiring Swiss civil servant could not be seen cohabitating in such a way. Instead, after a few months, Marić moved back to Zurich to wait for him to get a job and, as promised, marry her. She did not bring Lieserl with her.

Einstein and his daughter apparently never laid eyes on each other. She would merit, as we shall see, just one brief mention in their surviving correspondence less than two years later, in September 1903, and then not be referred to again. In the meantime, she was left back in Novi Sad with her mother's relatives or friends so that Einstein could maintain both his unencumbered lifestyle and the bourgeois respectability he needed to become a Swiss official.

There is a cryptic hint that the person who took custody of Lieserl may have been Marić's close friend, Helene Kaufler Savić, whom she had met in 1899 when they lived in the same rooming house in Zurich. Savić was from a Viennese Jewish family and had married an engineer from Serbia in 1900. During her pregnancy, Marić had written her a letter pouring out all of her woes, but she tore it up before mailing it. She was glad she had done so, she explained to Einstein two months before Lieserl's birth, because "I don't think we should say anything about Lieserl yet." Marić added that Einstein should write Savić a few words now and then. "We must now treat her very nicely. She'll have to help us in something important, after all."[64]

The Patent Office

As he was waiting to be offered the job at the patent office, Einstein ran into an acquaintance who was working there. The job was boring, the person complained, and he noted that the position Einstein was waiting to get was "the lowest rank," so at least he didn't have to worry that anyone else would apply for it. Einstein was unfazed. "Certain people find everything boring," Einstein told Marić. As for the disdain about being on the lowest rung, Einstein told her that they should feel just the opposite: "We couldn't care less about being on top!"[65]

The job finally came through on June 16, 1902, when a session of the Swiss Council officially elected him "provisionally as a Technical Expert Class 3 of the Federal Office for Intellectual Property with an annual salary of 3,500 francs," which was actually more than what a junior professor would make.[66]

His office in Bern's new Postal and Telegraph Building was near the world-famous clock tower over the old city gate (see p. 107). As he turned left out of his apartment on his way to work, Einstein walked past it every day. The clock was originally built shortly after the city was founded in 1191, and an astronomical contraption featuring the positions of the planets was added in 1530. Every hour, the clock would put on its show: out would come a dancing jester ringing bells, then a parade of bears, a crowing rooster, and an armored knight, followed by Father Time with his scepter and hourglass.

The clock was the official timekeeper for the nearby train station, the one from which all of the other clocks that lined the platform were synchronized. The moving trains arriving from other cities, where the local time was not always standardized, would reset their own clocks by looking up at the Bern clock tower as they sped into town.[67]

So it was that Albert Einstein would end up spending the most creative seven years of his life—even after he had written the papers that reoriented physics—arriving at work at 8 a.m., six days a week, and examining patent applications. "I am frightfully busy," he wrote a friend a few months later. "Every day I spend eight hours at the office and at least one hour of private lessons, and then, in addition, I do some scientific work." Yet it would be wrong to think that poring over applications for patents was drudgery. "I enjoy my work at the office very much, because it is uncommonly diversified."[68]

He soon learned that he could work on the patent applications so quickly that it left time for him to sneak in his own scientific thinking during the day. "I was able to do a full day's work in only two or three hours," he recalled. "The remaining part of the day, I would work out my own ideas." His boss, Friedrich Haller, was a man of good-natured, growling skepticism and genial humor who graciously ignored the sheets of paper that cluttered Einstein's desk and vanished into his drawer when people came to see him. "Whenever anybody would come by, I would cram my notes into my desk drawer and pretend to work on my office work."[69]

Indeed, we should not feel sorry for Einstein that he found himself exiled from the cloisters of academe. He came to believe that it was a benefit to his science, rather than a burden, to work instead in "that worldly cloister where I hatched my most beautiful ideas."[70]

Every day, he would do thought experiments based on theoretical premises, sniffing out the underlying realities. Focusing on real-life questions, he later said, "stimulated me to see the physical ramifications of theoretical concepts."[71] Among the ideas that he had to consider for patents were dozens of new methods for synchronizing clocks and coordinating time through signals sent at the speed of light.[72]

In addition, his boss Haller had a credo that was as useful for a creative and rebellious theorist as it was for a patent examiner: "You have to remain critically vigilant." Question every premise, challenge conventional wisdom, and never accept the truth of something merely because everyone else views it as obvious. Resist being credulous. "When you pick up an application," Haller instructed, "think that everything the inventor says is wrong."[73]

Einstein had grown up in a family that created patents and tried to apply them in business, and he found the process to be fulfilling. It reinforced one of his ingenious talents: the ability to conduct thought experiments in which he could visualize how a theory would play out in practice. It also helped him peel off the irrelevant facts that surrounded a problem.[74]

Had he been consigned instead to the job of an assistant to a professor, he might have felt compelled to churn out safe publications and be overly cautious in challenging accepted notions. As he later noted, originality and creativity were not prime assets for climbing academic ladders, especially in the German-speaking world, and he would have felt pressure to conform to the prejudices or prevailing wisdom of his patrons. "An academic career in which a person is forced to produce scientific writings in great amounts creates a danger of intellectual superficiality," he said.[75]

As a result, the happenstance that landed him on a stool at the Swiss Patent Office, rather than as an acolyte in academia, likely reinforced some of the traits destined to make him successful: a merry skepticism about what appeared on the pages in front of him and an independence of judgment that allowed him to challenge basic assumptions. There were no pressures or incentives among the patent examiners to behave otherwise.

The Olympia Academy

Maurice Solovine, a Romanian studying philosophy at the University of Bern, bought a newspaper while on a stroll one day during Easter vacation of 1902 and noticed Einstein's advertisement offering tutorials in physics ("trial lessons free"). A dapper dilettante with close-cropped hair and a raffish goatee, Solovine was four years older than Einstein, but he had yet to decide whether he wanted to be a philosopher, a physicist, or something else. So he went to the address, rang the bell, and a moment later a loud voice thundered "In here!" Einstein made an immediate impression. "I was struck by the extraordinary brilliance of his large eyes," Solovine recalled.[76]

Their first discussion lasted almost two hours, after which Einstein followed Solovine into the street, where they talked for a half-hour more. They agreed to meet the next day. At the third session, Einstein announced that conversing freely was more fun than tutoring for pay. "You don't have to be tutored in physics," he said. "Just come see me when you want and I will be glad to talk with you." They decided to read the great thinkers together and then discuss their ideas.

Their sessions were joined by Conrad Habicht, a banker's son and former student of mathematics at the Zurich Polytechnic. Poking a little fun at pompous scholarly societies, they dubbed themselves the Olympia Academy. Einstein, even though he was the youngest, was designated the president, and Solovine prepared a certificate with a drawing of an Einstein bust in profile beneath a string of sausages. "A man perfectly and clearly erudite, imbued with exquisite, subtle and elegant knowledge, steeped in the revolutionary science of the cosmos," the dedication declared.[77]

Generally their dinners were frugal repasts of sausage, Gruyère cheese, fruit, and tea. But for Einstein's birthday, Solovine and Habicht decided to surprise him by putting three plates of caviar on the table. Einstein was engrossed in analyzing Galileo's principle of inertia, and as he talked he took mouthful after mouthful of his caviar without seeming to notice. Habicht and Solovine exchanged furtive glances. "Do you realize what you've been eating?" Solovine finally asked.

"For goodness' sake," Einstein exclaimed. "So that was the famous caviar!" He paused for a moment, then added, "Well, if you offer gourmet food to peasants like me, you know they won't appreciate it."

After their discussions, which could last all night, Einstein would sometimes play the violin and, in the summertime, they occasionally climbed a mountain on the outskirts of Bern to watch the sunrise. "The sight of the twinkling stars made a strong impression on us and led to discussions of astronomy," Solovine recalled. "We would marvel at the sun as it came slowly toward the horizon and finally appeared in all of its splendor to bathe the Alps in a mystic rose." Then they would wait for the mountain café to open so they could drink dark coffee before hiking down to start work.

Solovine once skipped a session scheduled for his apartment because he was enticed instead to a concert by a Czech quartet. As a peace offering he left behind, as his note written in Latin proclaimed, "hard boiled eggs and a salutation." Einstein and Habicht, knowing how much Solovine hated tobacco, took revenge by smoking pipes and cigars in Solovine's room and piling his furniture and dishes on the bed. "Thick smoke and a salutation," they wrote in Latin. Solovine says he was "almost overwhelmed" by the fumes when he returned. "I thought I would suffocate. I opened the window wide and began to remove from the bed the mound of things that reached almost to the ceiling."[78]

Solovine and Habicht would become Einstein's lifelong friends, and he would later reminisce with them about "our cheerful 'Academy,'" which was less childish than those respectable ones which I later got to know at close quarters." In response to a joint postcard sent from Paris by his two colleagues on his seventy-fourth birthday, he paid tribute to it: "Your members created you to make fun of your long-established sister Academies. How well their mockery hit the mark I have learned to appreciate fully through long years of careful observation."[79]

The Academy's reading list included some classics with themes that Einstein could appreciate, such as Sophocles' searing play about the defiance of authority, *Antigone,* and Cervantes' epic about stubbornly tilting at windmills, *Don Quixote.* But mostly the three academicians read books that explored the intersection of science and philosophy: David Hume's *A Treatise of Human Nature,* Ernst Mach's *Analysis of the Sensations* and *Mechanics and Its Development,* Baruch Spinoza's *Ethics,* and Henri Poincaré's *Science and Hypothesis.*[80] It was from reading these authors that the young patent examiner began to develop his own philosophy of science.

The most influential of these, Einstein later said, was the Scottish empiricist David Hume (1711–1776). In the tradition of Locke and Berkeley, Hume was skeptical about any knowledge other than what could be directly perceived by the senses. Even the apparent laws of causality were suspect to him, mere habits of the mind; a ball hitting another may behave the way that Newton's laws predict time after time after time, yet that was not, strictly speaking, a reason to believe that it would happen that way the next time. "Hume saw clearly that certain concepts, for example that of causality, cannot be deduced from our perceptions of experience by logical methods," Einstein noted.

A version of this philosophy, sometimes called positivism, denied the validity of any concepts that went beyond descriptions of phenomena that we directly experience. It appealed to Einstein, at least initially. "The theory of relativity suggests itself in positivism," he said. "This line of thought had a great influence on my efforts, most specifically Mach and even more so Hume, whose *Treatise of Human Nature* I studied avidly and with admiration shortly before discovering the theory of relativity."[81]

Hume applied his skeptical rigor to the concept of time. It made no sense, he said, to speak of time as having an absolute existence that was independent of observable objects whose movements permitted us to define time. "From the succession of ideas and impressions we form the idea of time," Hume wrote. "It is not possible for time alone ever to make its appearance." This idea that there is no such thing as absolute time would later echo in Einstein's theory of relativity. Hume's specific thoughts about time, however, had less influence on Einstein than his more general insight that it is dangerous to talk about concepts that are not definable by perceptions and observations.[82]

Einstein's views on Hume were tempered by his appreciation for Immanuel Kant (1724–1804), the German metaphysician he had been introduced to, back when he was a schoolboy, by Max Talmud. "Kant took the stage with an idea that signified a step towards the solution of Hume's dilemma," Einstein said. Some truths fit into a category of "definitely assured knowledge" that was "grounded in reason itself."

In other words, Kant distinguished between two types of truths: (1) analytic propositions, which derive from logic and "reason itself" rather than from observing the world; for example, all bachelors are unmarried, two plus two equals four, and the angles of a triangle always add up to 180 degrees; and (2) synthetic propositions, which are based on experience and observations; for example, Munich is bigger than

Bern, all swans are white. Synthetic propositions could be revised by new empirical evidence, but not analytic ones. We may discover a black swan but not a married bachelor or (at least so Kant thought) a triangle with 181 degrees. As Einstein said of Kant's first category of truths: "This is held to be the case, for example, in the propositions of geometry and in the principle of causality. These and certain other types of knowledge . . . do not previously have to be gained from sense data, in other words they are a priori knowledge."

Einstein initially found it wondrous that certain truths could be discovered by reason alone. But he soon began to question Kant's rigid distinction between analytic and synthetic truths. "The objects with which geometry deals seemed to be of no different type than the objects of sensory perception," he recalled. And later he would reject outright this Kantian distinction. "I am convinced that this differentiation is erroneous," he wrote. A proposition that seems purely analytic—such as the angles of a triangle adding up to 180 degrees—could turn out to be false in a non-Euclidean geometry or in a curved space (such as would be the case in the general theory of relativity). As he later said of the concepts of geometry and causality, "Today everyone knows, of course, that the mentioned concepts contain nothing of the certainty, of the inherent necessity, which Kant had attributed to them."[83]

Hume's empiricism was carried a step further by Ernst Mach (1838–1916), the Austrian physicist and philosopher whose writings Einstein read at the urging of Michele Besso. He became one of the favorite authors of the Olympia Academy, and he helped to instill in Einstein the skepticism about received wisdom and accepted conventions that would become a hallmark of his creativity. Einstein would later proclaim, in words that could be used to describe himself as well, that Mach's genius was partly due to his "incorruptible skepticism and independence."[84]

The essence of Mach's philosophy was this, in Einstein's words: "Concepts have meaning only if we can point to objects to which they refer and to the rules by which they are assigned to these objects."[85] In other words, for a concept to make sense you need an operational definition of it, one that describes how you would observe the concept in operation. This would bear fruit for Einstein when, a few years later, he and Besso would talk about what observation would give meaning to the apparently simple concept that two events happened "simultaneously."

The most influential thing that Mach did for Einstein was to apply this approach to Newton's concepts of "absolute time" and "absolute space." It was impossible to define these concepts, Mach asserted, in terms of observations you could make. Therefore they were meaningless. Mach ridiculed Newton's "conceptual monstrosity of absolute space"; he called it "purely a thought-thing which cannot be pointed to in experience."[86]

The final intellectual hero of the Olympia Academy was Baruch Spinoza (1632–1677), the Jewish philosopher from Amsterdam. His influence was primarily religious: Einstein embraced his concept of an amorphous God reflected in the awe-inspiring beauty, rationality, and unity of nature's laws. But like Spinoza, Einstein did not believe in a personal God who rewarded and punished and intervened in our daily lives.

In addition, Einstein drew from Spinoza a faith in determinism: a sense that the laws of nature, once we could fathom them, decreed immutable causes and effects, and that God did not play dice by allowing any events to be random or undetermined. "All things are determined by the necessity of divine nature," Spinoza declared, and even when quantum mechanics seemed to show that was wrong, Einstein steadfastly believed it was right.[87]

Marrying Mileva

Hermann Einstein was not destined to see his son become anything more successful than a third-class patent examiner. In October 1902, when Hermann's health began to decline, Einstein traveled to Milan to be with him at the end. Their relationship had long been a mix of alienation and affection, and it concluded on that note as well. "When the end came," Einstein's assistant Helen Dukas later said, "Hermann asked all of them to leave the room, so he could die on his own."

Einstein felt, for the rest of his life, a sense of guilt about that moment, which encapsulated his inability to forge a true bond with his father. For the first time, he was thrown into a daze, "overwhelmed by a feeling of desolation." He later called his father's death the deepest shock he had ever experienced. The event did, however, solve one important issue. On his deathbed, Hermann Einstein gave his permission, finally, for his son to marry Mileva Marić.[88]

Einstein's Olympia Academy colleagues, Maurice Solovine and Conrad Habicht, convened in special session on January 6, 1903, to serve as witnesses at the tiny civil ceremony in the Bern registrar's office where Albert Einstein married Mileva Marić. No family members—not Einstein's mother or sister, nor Marić's parents—came to Bern. The tight group of intellectual comrades celebrated together at a restaurant that evening, and then Einstein and Marić went back to his apartment together. Not surprisingly, he had forgotten his key and had to wake his landlady.[89]

"Well, now I am a married man and I am living a very pleasant cozy life with my wife," he reported to Michele Besso two weeks later. "She takes excellent care of everything, cooks well, and is always cheerful." For her part, Marić* reported to her own best friend, "I am even closer to my sweetheart, if it is at all possible, than I was in our Zurich days." Occasionally she would attend sessions of the Olympia Academy, but mainly as an observer. "Mileva, intelligent and reserved, listened intently but never intervened in our discussions," Solovine recalled.

Nevertheless, clouds began to form. "My new duties are taking their toll," Marić said of her housekeeping chores and role as a mere onlooker when science was discussed. Einstein's friends felt that she was becoming even more gloomy. At times she seemed laconic, and distrustful as well. And Einstein, at least so he claimed in retrospect, had already become wary. He had felt an "inner resistance" to marrying Marić, he later claimed, but had overcome it out of a "sense of duty."

---

* Once married, she usually used the name Mileva Einstein-Marić. After they were divorced, she eventually resumed using Mileva Marić. To avoid confusion, I refer to her as Marić throughout.

Marić soon began to look for ways to restore the magic to their relationship. She hoped that they would escape the bourgeois drudgery that seemed inherent in the household of a Swiss civil servant and, instead, find some opportunity to recapture their old bohemian academic life. They decided—or at least so Marić hoped—that Einstein would find a teaching job somewhere far away, perhaps near their forsaken daughter. "We will try anywhere," she wrote to her friend in Serbia. "Do you think, for example, that in Belgrade people of our kind could find something?" Marić said they would do anything academic, even teaching German in a high school. "You see, we still have that old enterprising spirit."[90]

As far as we know, Einstein never went to Serbia to seek a job or to see his baby. A few months into their marriage, in August 1903, the secret cloud hovering over their lives suddenly cast a new pall. Marić received word that Lieserl, then 19 months old, had come down with scarlet fever. She boarded a train for Novi Sad. When it stopped in Salzburg, she bought a postcard of a local castle and jotted a note, which she mailed from the stop in Budapest: "It is going quickly, but it is hard. I don't feel at all well. What are you doing, little Jonzile, write me soon, will you? Your poor Dollie."[91]

Apparently, the child was given up for adoption. The only clue we have is a cryptic letter Einstein wrote Marić in September, after she had been in Novi Sad for a month: "I am very sorry about what happened with Lieserl. Scarlet fever often leaves some lasting trace behind. If only everything passes well. How is Lieserl registered? We must take great care, lest difficulties arise for the child in the future."[92]

Whatever the motivation Einstein may have had for asking the question, neither Lieserl's registration documents nor any other paper trace of her existence is known to have survived. Various researchers, Serbian and American, including Robert Schulmann of the Einstein Papers Project and Michele Zackheim, who wrote a book about searching for Lieserl, have fruitlessly scoured churches, registries, synagogues, and cemeteries.

All evidence about Einstein's daughter was carefully erased. Almost every one of the letters between Einstein and Marić in the summer and fall of 1902, many of which presumably dealt with Lieserl, were destroyed. Those between Marić and her friend Helene Savić during that period were intentionally burned by Savić's family. For the rest of their lives, even after they divorced, Einstein and his wife did all they could, with surprising success, to cover up not only the fate of their first child but her very existence.

One of the few facts that have escaped this black hole of history is that Lieserl was still alive in September 1903. Einstein's expression of worry, in his letter to Marić that month, about potential difficulties "for the child in the future," makes this clear. The letter also indicates that she had been given up for adoption by then, because in it Einstein spoke of the desirability of having a "replacement" child.

There are two plausible explanations about the fate of Lieserl. The first is that she survived her bout of scarlet fever and was raised by an adoptive family. On a couple of occasions later in his life, when women came forward claiming (falsely, it turned out) to be illegitimate children of his, Einstein did not dismiss the possibility out of hand, although given the number of affairs he had, this is no indication that he thought they might be Lieserl.

One possibility, favored by Schulmann, is that Marić's friend Helene Savić adopted Lieserl. She did in fact raise a daughter Zorka, who was blind from early childhood (perhaps a result of scarlet fever), was never married, and was shielded by her nephew from people who sought to interview her. Zorka died in the 1990s.

The nephew who protected Zorka, Milan Popović, rejects this possibility. In a book he wrote on the friendship and correspondence between Marić and his grandmother Helene Savić, *In Albert's Shadow*, Popović asserted, "A theory has been advanced that my grandmother adopted Lieserl, but an examination of my family's history renders this groundless." He did not, however, produce any documentary evidence, such as his aunt's birth certificate, to back up this contention. His mother burned most of Helene Savić's letters, including any that had dealt with Lieserl. Popović's own theory, based partly on the family stories recalled by a Serbian writer named Mira Alečković, is that Lieserl died of scarlet fever in September 1903, after Einstein's letter of that month. Michele Zackheim, in her book describing her hunt for Lieserl, comes to a similar conclusion.[93]

Whatever happened added to Marić's gloom. Shortly after Einstein died, a writer named Peter Michelmore, who knew nothing of Lieserl, published a book that was based in part on conversations with Einstein's son Hans Albert Einstein. Referring to the year right after their marriage, Michelmore noted, "Something had happened between the two, but Mileva would say only that it was 'intensely personal.' Whatever it was, she brooded about it, and Albert seemed to be in some ways responsible. Friends encouraged Mileva to talk about her problem and get it out in the open. She insisted that it was too personal and kept it a secret all her life—a vital detail in the story of Albert Einstein that still remains shrouded in mystery."[94]

The illness that Marić complained about in her postcard from Budapest was likely because she was pregnant again. When she found out that indeed she was, she worried that this would anger her husband. But Einstein expressed happiness on hearing the news that there would soon be a replacement for their daughter. "I'm not the least bit angry that poor Dollie is hatching a new chick," he wrote. "In fact, I'm happy about it and had already given some thought to whether I shouldn't see to it that you get a new Lieserl. After all, you shouldn't be denied that which is the right of all women."[95]

Hans Albert Einstein was born on May 14, 1904. The new child lifted Marić's spirits and restored some joy to her marriage, or so at least she told her friend Helene Savić: "Hop over to Bern so I can see you again and I can show you my dear little sweetheart, who is also named Albert. I cannot tell you how much joy he gives me when he laughs so cheerfully on waking up or when he kicks his legs while taking a bath."

Einstein was "behaving with fatherly dignity," Marić noted, and he spent time making little toys for his baby son, such as a cable car he constructed from matchboxes and string. "That was one of the nicest toys I had at the time and it worked," Hans Albert could still recall when he was an adult. "Out of little string and matchboxes and so on, he could make the most beautiful things."[96]

Milos Marić was so overjoyed with the birth of a grandson that he came to visit and offered a sizable dowry, reported in family lore (likely with some exaggeration) to be 100,000 Swiss francs. But Einstein declined it, saying he had not married his daughter for money, Milos Marić later recounted with tears in his eyes. In fact, Einstein was beginning to do well enough on his own. After more than a year at the patent office, he had been taken off probationary status.[97]

CHAPTER FIVE

THE MIRACLE YEAR:

Quanta and Molecules, 1905

At the Patent Office, 1905

Turn of the Century

"There is nothing new to be discovered in physics now," the revered Lord Kelvin reportedly told the British Association for the Advancement of Science in 1900. "All that remains is more and more precise measurement."[1] He was wrong.

The foundations of classical physics had been laid by Isaac Newton (1642–1727) in the late seventeenth century. Building on the discoveries of Galileo and others, he developed laws that described a very comprehensible mechanical universe: a falling apple and an orbiting moon were governed by the same rules of gravity, mass, force, and motion. Causes produced effects, forces acted upon objects, and in theory everything could be explained, determined, and predicted. As the mathematician and astronomer Laplace exulted about Newton's universe, "An intelligence knowing all the forces acting in nature at a given instant, as well as the momentary positions of all things in the universe, would be able to comprehend in one single formula the motions of the largest bodies as well as the lightest atoms in the world; to him nothing would be uncertain, the future as well as the past would be present to his eyes."[2]

Einstein admired this strict causality, calling it "the profoundest characteristic of Newton's teaching."[3] He wryly summarized the history of physics: "In the beginning (if there was such a thing) God created Newton's laws of motion together with the necessary masses and forces." What especially impressed Einstein were "the achievements of mechanics in areas that apparently had nothing to do with mechanics," such as the kinetic theory he had been exploring, which explained the behavior of gases as being caused by the actions of billions of molecules bumping around.[4]

In the mid-1800s, Newtonian mechanics was joined by another great advance. The English experimenter Michael Faraday (1791–1867), the self-taught son of a blacksmith, discovered the properties of electrical and magnetic fields. He showed that an electric current produced magnetism, and then he showed that a changing magnetic field could produce an electric current. When a magnet is moved near a wire loop, or vice versa, an electric current is produced.[5]

Faraday's work on electromagnetic induction permitted inventive entrepreneurs like Einstein's father and uncle to create new ways of combining spinning wire coils and moving magnets to build electricity generators. As a result, young Albert Einstein had a profound physical feel for Faraday's fields and not just a theoretical understanding of them.

The bushy-bearded Scottish physicist James Clerk Maxwell (1831–1879) subsequently devised wonderful equations that specified, among other things, how changing electric fields create magnetic fields and how changing magnetic fields create electrical ones. A changing electric field could, in fact, produce a changing magnetic field that could, in turn, produce a changing electric field, and so on. The result of this coupling was an electromagnetic wave.

Just as Newton had been born the year that Galileo died, so Einstein was born the year that Maxwell died, and he saw it as part of his mission to extend the work of the Scotsman. Here was a theorist who had shed prevailing biases, let mathematical melodies lead him into unknown territories, and found a harmony that was based on the beauty and simplicity of a field theory.

All of his life, Einstein was fascinated by field theories, and he described the development of the concept in a textbook he wrote with a colleague:

> A new concept appeared in physics, the most important invention since Newton's time: the field. It needed great scientific imagination to realize that it is not the charges nor the particles but the field in the space between the charges and the particles that is essential for the description of physical phenomena. The field concept proved successful when it led to the formulation of Maxwell's equations describing the structure of the electromagnetic field.[6]

At first, the electromagnetic field theory developed by Maxwell seemed compatible with the mechanics of Newton. For example, Maxwell believed that electromagnetic waves, which include visible light, could be explained by classical mechanics—if we assume that the universe is suffused with some unseen, gossamer "light-bearing ether" that serves as the physical substance that undulates and oscillates to propagate the electromagnetic waves, comparable to the role water plays for ocean waves and air plays for sound waves.

By the end of the nineteenth century, however, fissures had begun to develop in the foundations of classical physics. One problem was that scientists, as hard as they tried, could not find any evidence of our motion through this supposed light-propagating ether. The study of radiation—how light and other electromagnetic waves emanate from physical bodies—exposed another problem: strange things were happening at the borderline where Newtonian theories, which described the mechanics of discrete particles, interacted with field theory, which described all electromagnetic phenomena.

Up until then, Einstein had published five little-noted papers. They had earned him neither a doctorate nor a teaching job, even at a high school. Had he given up theoretical physics at that point, the scientific community would not have noticed, and he might have moved up the ladder to become the head of the Swiss Patent Office, a job in which he would likely have been very good indeed.

There was no sign that he was about to unleash an *annus mirabilis* the like of which science had not seen since 1666, when Isaac Newton, holed up at his mother's home in rural Woolsthorpe to escape the plague that was devastating Cambridge, developed calculus, an analysis of the light spectrum, and the laws of gravity.

But physics was poised to be upended again, and Einstein was poised to be the one to do it. He had the brashness needed to scrub away the layers of conventional wisdom that were obscuring the cracks in the foundation of physics, and his visual imagination allowed him to make conceptual leaps that eluded more traditional thinkers.

The breakthroughs that he wrought during a four-month frenzy from March to June 1905 were heralded in what would become one of the most famous personal letters in the history of science. Conrad Habicht, his fellow philosophical frolicker in the Olympia Academy, had just moved away from Bern, which, happily for historians, gave a reason for Einstein to write to him in late May.

> Dear Habicht,
>   Such a solemn air of silence has descended between us that I almost feel as if I am committing a sacrilege when I break it now with some inconsequential babble . . .
>   So, what are you up to, you frozen whale, you smoked, dried, canned piece of soul . . . ? Why have you still not sent me your dissertation? Don't you know that I am one of the 1½ fellows who would read it with interest and pleasure, you wretched man? I promise you four papers in return. The first deals with radiation and the energy properties of light and is very revolutionary, as you will see if you send me your work first. The second paper is a determination of the true sizes of atoms . . . The third proves that bodies on the order of magnitude 1/1000 mm, suspended in liquids, must already perform an observable random motion that is produced by thermal motion. Such movement of suspended bodies has actually been observed by physiologists who call it Brownian molecular motion. The fourth paper is only a rough draft at this point, and is an electrodynamics of moving bodies which employs a modification of the theory of space and time.[7]

Light Quanta, March 1905

As Einstein noted to Habicht, it was the first of these 1905 papers, not the famous final one expounding a theory of relativity, that deserved the designation "revolutionary." Indeed, it may contain the most revolutionary development in the history of physics. Its suggestion that light comes not just in waves but in tiny packets—quanta of light that were later dubbed "photons"—spirits us into strange scientific mists that are far murkier, indeed more spooky, than even the weirdest aspects of the theory of relativity.

Einstein recognized this in the slightly odd title he gave to the paper, which he submitted on March 17, 1905, to the *Annalen der Physik:* "On a Heuristic Point of View Concerning the Production and Transformation of Light."[8] Heuristic? It means a hypothesis that serves as a guide and gives direction in solving a problem but is not considered proven. From this first sentence he ever published about quantum theory until his last such sentence, which came in a paper exactly fifty years later, just before he died, Einstein regarded the concept of the quanta and all of its unsettling implications as heuristic at best: provisional and incomplete and not fully compatible with his own intimations of underlying reality.

At the heart of Einstein's paper were questions that were bedeviling physics at the turn of the century, and in fact have done so from the time of the ancient Greeks until today: Is the universe made up of particles, such as atoms and electrons? Or is it an unbroken continuum, as a gravitational or electromagnetic field seems to be? And if both methods of describing things are valid at times, what happens when they intersect?

Since the 1860s, scientists had been exploring just such a point of intersection by analyzing what was called "blackbody radiation." As anyone who has played with a kiln or a gas burner knows, the glow from a material such as iron changes color as it heats up. First it appears to radiate mainly red light; as it gets hotter, it glows more orange, and then white and then blue. To study this radiation, Gustav Kirchhoff and others devised a closed metal container with a tiny hole to let a little light escape. Then they drew a graph of the intensity of each wavelength when the device reached equilibrium at a certain temperature. No matter what the material or shape of the container's walls, the results were the same; the shape of the graphs depended only on the temperature.

There was, alas, a problem. No one could fully account for the basis of the mathematical formula that would produce the hill-like shape of these graphs.

When Kirchhoff died, his professorship at the University of Berlin was given to Max Planck. Born in 1858 into an ancient German family of great scholars, theologians, and lawyers, Planck was many things that Einstein was not: with his pince-nez glasses and meticulous dress, he was very proudly German, somewhat shy, steely in his resolve, conservative by instinct, and formal in his manner. "It is difficult to imagine two men of more different attitudes," their mutual friend Max Born later said. "Einstein a citizen of the whole world, little attached to the people around him, independent of the emotional background of the society in which he lived—Planck deeply rooted in the traditions of his family and nation, an ardent patriot, proud of the greatness of German history and consciously Prussian in his attitude to the state."[9]

His conservatism made Planck skeptical about the atom, and of particle (rather than wave and continuous field) theories in general. As he wrote in 1882, "Despite the great success that the atomic theory has so far enjoyed, ultimately it will have to be abandoned in favor of the assumption of continuous matter." In one of our planet's little ironies, Planck and Einstein would share the fate of laying the groundwork for quantum mechanics, and then both would flinch when it became clear that it undermined the concepts of strict causality and certainty they both worshipped.[10]

In 1900, Planck came up with an equation, partly using what he called "a fortuitous guess," that described the curve of radiation wavelengths at each temperature. In doing so he accepted that Boltzmann's statistical methods, which he had resisted, were correct after all. But the equation had an odd feature: it required the use of a constant, which was an unexplained tiny quantity (approximately 6.62607 x

10^{-34} joule-seconds), that needed to be included for it to come out right. It was soon dubbed Planck's constant, h, and is now known as one of the fundamental constants of nature.

At first Planck had no idea what, if any, physical meaning this mathematical constant had. But then he came up with a theory that, he thought, applied not to the nature of light itself but to the action that occurred when the light was absorbed or emitted by a piece of matter. He posited that the surface of anything that was radiating heat and light—such as the walls in a blackbody device—contained "vibrating molecules" or "harmonic oscillators," like little vibrating springs.[11] These harmonic oscillators could absorb or emit energy only in the form of discrete packets or bundles. These packets or bundles of energy came only in fixed amounts, determined by Planck's constant, rather than being divisible or having a continuous range of values.

Planck considered his constant a mere calculational contrivance that explained the process of emitting or absorbing light but did not apply to the fundamental nature of light itself. Nevertheless, the declaration he made to the Berlin Physical Society in December 1900 was momentous: "We therefore regard—and this is the most essential point of the entire calculation—energy to be composed of a very definite number of equal finite packages."[12]

Einstein quickly realized that quantum theory could undermine classical physics. "All of this was quite clear to me shortly after the appearance of Planck's fundamental work," he wrote later. "All of my attempts to adapt the theoretical foundation of physics to this knowledge failed completely. It was as if the ground had been pulled out from under us, with no firm foundation to be seen anywhere."[13]

In addition to the problem of explaining what Planck's constant was really all about, there was another curiosity about radiation that needed to be explained. It was called the photoelectric effect, and it occurs when light shining on a metal surface causes electrons to be knocked loose and emitted. In the letter he wrote to Marić right after he learned of her pregnancy in May 1901, Einstein enthused over a "beautiful piece" by Philipp Lenard that explored this topic.

Lenard's experiments found something unexpected. When he increased the *frequency* of the light—moving from infrared heat and red light up in frequency to violet and ultraviolet—the emitted electrons sped out with much more energy. Then, he increased the *intensity* of the light by using a carbon arc light that could be made brighter by a factor of 1,000. The brighter, more intense light had a lot more energy, so it seemed logical that the electrons emitted would have more energy and speed away faster. But that did not occur. More intense light produced more electrons, but the energy of each remained the same. This was something that the wave theory of light did not explain.

Einstein had been pondering the work of Planck and Lenard for four years. In his final paper of 1904, "On the General Molecular Theory of Heat," he discussed how the average energy of a system of molecules fluctuates. He then applied this to a volume filled with radiation, and found that experimental results were comparable. His concluding phrase was, "I believe that this agreement must not be ascribed to chance."[14] As he wrote to his friend Conrad Habicht just after finishing that 1904 paper, "I have now found in a most simple way the relation between the size of elementary quanta of matter and the wavelengths of radiation." He was thus primed, so it seems, to form a theory that the radiation field was made up of quanta.[15]

In his 1905 light quanta paper, published a year later, he did just that. He took the mathematical quirk that Planck had discovered, interpreted it literally, related it to Lenard's photoelectric results, and analyzed light as if it *really was* made up of pointlike particles—light quanta, he called them—rather than being a continuous wave.

Einstein began his paper by describing the great distinction between theories based on particles (such as the kinetic theory of gases) and theories that involve continuous functions (such as the electromagnetic fields of the wave theory of light). "There exists a profound formal difference between the theories that physicists have formed about gases and other ponderable bodies, and Maxwell's theory of electromagnetic processes in so-called empty space," he noted. "While we consider the state of a body to be completely determined by the positions and velocities of a very large, yet finite, number of atoms and electrons, we make use of continuous spatial functions to describe the electromagnetic state of a given volume."[16]

Before he made his case for a particle theory of light, he emphasized that this would *not* make it necessary to scrap the wave theory, which would continue to be useful as well. "The wave theory of light, which operates with continuous spatial functions, has worked well in the representation of purely optical phenomena and will probably never be replaced by another theory."

His way of accommodating both a wave theory and a particle theory was to suggest, in a "heuristic" way, that our observation of waves involve statistical averages of the positions of what could be countless particles. "It should be kept in mind," he said, "that the optical observations refer to time averages rather than instantaneous values."

Then came what may be the most revolutionary sentence that Einstein ever wrote. It suggests that light is made up of discrete particles or packets of energy: "According to the assumption to be considered here, when a light ray is propagated from a point, the energy is not continuously distributed over an increasing space but consists of a finite number of energy quanta which are localized at points in space and which can be produced and absorbed only as complete units."

Einstein explored this hypothesis by determining whether a volume of blackbody radiation, which he was now assuming consisted of discrete quanta, might in fact behave like a volume of gas, which he knew consisted of discrete particles. First, he looked at the formulas that showed how the entropy of a gas changes when its volume changes. Then he compared this to how the entropy of blackbody radiation changes as its volume changes. He found that the entropy of the radiation "varies with volume according to the same law as the entropy of an ideal gas."

He did a calculation using Boltzmann's statistical formulas for entropy. The statistical mechanics that described a dilute gas of particles was mathematically the same as that for blackbody radiation. This led Einstein to declare that the radiation "behaves thermodynamically as if it consisted of mutually independent energy quanta." It also provided a way to calculate the energy of a "particle" of light at a particular frequency, which turned out to be in accord with what Planck had found.[17]

Einstein went on to show how the existence of these light quanta could explain what he graciously called Lenard's "pioneering work" on the photoelectric effect. If light came in discrete quanta, then the energy of each one was determined simply by the frequency of the light multiplied by Planck's constant. If we assume, Einstein suggested, "that a light quantum transfers its entire energy to a single electron," then it follows that light of a higher frequency would cause the electrons to emit with more energy. On the other hand, increasing the intensity of the light (but not the frequency) would simply mean that more electrons would be emitted, but the energy of each would be the same.

That was precisely what Lenard had found. With a trace of humility or tentativeness, along with a desire to show that his conclusions had been deduced theoretically rather than induced entirely from experimental data, Einstein declared of his paper's premise that light consists of tiny quanta: "As far as I can see, our conception does not conflict with the properties of the photoelectric effect observed by Mr. Lenard."

By blowing on Planck's embers, Einstein had turned them into a flame that would consume classical physics. What precisely did Einstein produce that made his 1905 paper a discontinuous—one is tempted to say quantum—leap beyond the work of Planck?

In effect, as Einstein noted in a paper the following year, his role was that he figured out the physical significance of what Planck had discovered.[18] For Planck, a reluctant revolutionary, the quantum was a mathematical contrivance that explained how energy was emitted and absorbed when it interacted with matter. But he did not see that it related to a physical reality that was inherent in the nature of light and the electromagnetic field itself. "One can interpret Planck's 1900 paper to mean only that the quantum hypothesis is used as a *mathematical* convenience introduced in order to calculate a statistical distribution, not as a new *physical* assumption," write science historians Gerald Holton and Steven Brush.[19]

Einstein, on the other hand, considered the light quantum to be a feature of reality: a perplexing, pesky, mysterious, and sometimes maddening quirk in the cosmos. For him, these quanta of energy (which in 1926 were named photons)[20] existed even when light was moving through a vacuum. "We wish to show that Mr. Planck's determination of the elementary quanta is to some extent independent of his theory of blackbody radiation," he wrote. In other words, Einstein argued that the particulate nature of light was a property of the light itself and not just some description of how the light interacts with matter.[21]

Even after Einstein published his paper, Planck did not accept his leap. Two years later, Planck warned the young patent clerk that he had gone too far, and that quanta described a process that occurred during emission or absorption, rather than some real property of radiation in a vacuum. "I do not seek the meaning of the 'quantum of action' (light quantum) in the vacuum but at the site of absorption and emission," he advised.[22]

Planck's resistance to believing that the light quanta had a physical reality persisted. Eight years after Einstein's paper was published, Planck proposed him for a coveted seat in the Prussian Academy of Sciences. The letter he and other supporters wrote was filled with praise, but Planck added: "That he might sometimes have overshot the target in his speculations, as for example in his light quantum hypothesis, should not be counted against him too much."[23]

Just before he died, Planck reflected on the fact that he had long recoiled from the implications of his discovery. "My futile attempts to fit the elementary quantum of action somehow into classical theory continued for a number of years and cost me a great deal of effort," he wrote. "Many of my colleagues saw in this something bordering on a tragedy."

Ironically, similar words would later be used to describe Einstein. He became increasingly "aloof and skeptical" about the quantum discoveries he pioneered, Born said of Einstein. "Many of us regard this as a tragedy."[24]

Einstein's theory produced a law of the photoelectric effect that was experimentally testable: the energy of emitted electrons would depend on the frequency of the light according to a simple mathematical formula involving Planck's constant. The formula was subsequently shown to be correct. The physicist who did the crucial experiment was Robert Millikan, who would later head the California Institute of Technology and try to recruit Einstein.

Yet even after he verified Einstein's photoelectric formulas, Millikan still rejected the theory. "Despite the apparently complete success of the Einstein equation," he declared, "the physical theory on which it was designed to be the symbolic expression is found so untenable that Einstein himself, I believe, no longer holds to it."[25]

Millikan was wrong to say that Einstein's formulation of the photoelectric effect had been abandoned. In fact, it was specifically for discovering the law of the photoelectric effect that Einstein would win his only Nobel Prize. With the advent of quantum mechanics in the 1920s, the reality of the photon became a fundamental part of physics.

However, on the larger point Millikan was right. Einstein would increasingly find the eerie implications of the quantum—and of the wave-particle duality of light—to be deeply unsettling. In a letter he wrote near the end of his life to his dear friend Michele Besso, after quantum mechanics had been accepted by almost every living physicist, Einstein would lament, "All these fifty years of pondering have not brought me any closer to answering the question, What are light quanta?"[26]

Doctoral Dissertation on the Size of Molecules, April 1905

Einstein had written a paper that would revolutionize science, but he had not yet been able to earn a doctorate. So he tried one more time to get a dissertation accepted.

He realized that he needed a safe topic, not a radical one like quanta or relativity, so he chose the second paper he was working on, titled "A New Determination of Molecular Dimensions," which he completed on April 30 and submitted to the University of Zurich in July.[27]

Perhaps out of caution and deference to the conservative approach of his adviser, Alfred Kleiner, he generally avoided the innovative statistical physics featured in his previous papers (and in his Brownian motion paper completed eleven days later) and relied instead mainly on classical hydrodynamics.[28] Yet he was still able to explore how the behavior of countless tiny particles (atoms, molecules) are reflected in observable phenomena, and conversely how observable phenomena can tell us about the nature of those tiny unseen particles.

Almost a century earlier, the Italian scientist Amedeo Avogadro

(1776–1856) had developed the hypothesis—correct, as it turned out—that equal volumes of any gas, when measured at the same temperature and pressure, will have the same number of molecules. That led to a difficult quest: figuring out just how many this was.

The volume usually chosen is that occupied by a mole of the gas (its molecular weight in grams), which is 22.4 liters at standard temperature and pressure. The number of molecules under such conditions later became known as Avogadro's number. Determining it precisely was, and still is, rather difficult. A current estimate is approximately 6.02214×10^{23}. (This is a big number: that many unpopped popcorn kernels when spread across the United States would cover the country nine miles deep.)[29]

Most previous measurements of molecules had been done by studying gases. But as Einstein noted in the first sentence of his paper, "The physical phenomena observed in liquids have thus far not served for the determination of molecular sizes." In this dissertation (after a few math and data corrections were later made), Einstein was the first person able to get a respectable result using liquids.

His method involved making use of data about viscosity, which is how much resistance a liquid offers to an object that tries to move through it. Tar and molasses, for example, are highly viscous. If you dissolve sugar in water, the solution's viscosity increases as it gets more syrupy. Einstein envisioned the sugar molecules gradually diffusing their way through the smaller water molecules. He was able to come up with two equations, each containing the two unknown variables—the size of the sugar molecules and the number of them in the water—that he was trying to determine. He could then solve for these unknown variables. Doing so, he got a result for Avogadro's number that was 2.1×10^{23}.

That, unfortunately, was not very close. When he submitted his paper to the *Annalen der Physik* in August, right after it had been accepted by Zurich University, the editor Paul Drude (who was blissfully unaware of Einstein's earlier desire to ridicule him) held up its publication because he knew of some better data on the properties of sugar solutions. Using this new data, Einstein came up with a result that was closer to correct: 4.15×10^{23}.

A few years later, a French student tested the approach experimentally and discovered something amiss. So Einstein asked an assistant in Zurich to look at it all over again. He found a minor error, which when corrected produced a result of 6.56 x 10^{23}, which ended up being quite respectable.[30]

Einstein later said, perhaps half-jokingly, that when he submitted his thesis, Professor Kleiner rejected it for being too short, so he added one more sentence and it was promptly accepted. There is no documentary evidence for this.[31] Either way, his thesis actually became one of his most cited and practically useful papers, with applications in such diverse fields as cement mixing, dairy production, and aerosol products. And even though it did not help him get an academic job, it did make it possible for him to become known, finally, as Dr. Einstein.

Brownian Motion, May 1905

Eleven days after finishing his dissertation, Einstein produced another paper exploring evidence of things unseen. As he had been doing since 1901, he relied on statistical analysis of the random actions of invisible particles to show how they were reflected in the visible world.

In doing so, Einstein explained a phenomenon, known as Brownian motion, that had been puzzling scientists for almost eighty years: why small particles suspended in a liquid such as water are observed to jiggle around. And as a byproduct, he pretty much settled once and for all that atoms and molecules actually existed as physical objects.

Brownian motion was named after the Scottish botanist Robert Brown, who in 1828 had published detailed observations about how minuscule pollen particles suspended in water can be seen to wiggle and wander when examined under a strong microscope. The study was replicated with other particles, including filings from the Sphinx, and a variety of explanations was offered. Perhaps it had something to do with tiny water currents or the effect of light. But none of these theories proved plausible.

With the rise in the 1870s of the kinetic theory, which used the random motions of molecules to explain things like the behavior of gases, some tried to use it to explain Brownian motion. But because the suspended particles were 10,000 times larger than a water molecule, it seemed that a molecule would not have the power to budge the particle any more than a baseball could budge an object that was a half-mile in diameter.[32]

Einstein showed that even though one collision could not budge a particle, the effect of millions of random collisions per second could explain the jig observed by Brown. "In this paper," he announced in his first sentence, "it will be shown that, according to the molecular-kinetic theory of heat, bodies of a microscopically visible size suspended in liquids must, as a result of thermal molecular motions, perform motions of such magnitudes that they can be easily observed with a microscope."[33]

He went on to say something that seems, on the surface, somewhat puzzling: his paper was not an attempt to explain the observations of Brownian motion. Indeed, he acted as if he wasn't even sure that the motions he deduced from his theory were the same as those observed by Brown: "It is possible that the motions to be discussed here are identical with so-called Brownian molecular motion; however, the data available to me on the latter are so imprecise that I could not form a judgment on the question." Later, he distanced his work even further from intending to be an explanation of Brownian motion: "I discovered that, according to atomistic theory, there would have to be a movement of suspended microscopic particles open to observations, without knowing that observations concerning the Brownian motion were already long familiar."[34]

At first glance his demurral that he was dealing with Brownian motion seems odd, even disingenuous. After all, he had written Conrad Habicht a few months earlier, "Such movement of suspended bodies has actually been observed by physiologists who call it Brownian molecular motion." Yet Einstein's point was both true and significant: his paper did not start with the observed facts of Brownian motion and build toward an explanation of it. Rather, it was a continuation of his earlier statistical analysis of how the actions of molecules could be manifest in the visible world.

In other words, Einstein wanted to assert that he had produced a theory that was deduced from grand principles and postulates, not a

theory that was constructed by examining physical data (just as he had made plain that his light quanta paper had not *started* with the photo-electric effect data gathered by Philipp Lenard). It was a distinction he would also make, as we shall soon see, when insisting that his theory of relativity did not derive merely from trying to explain experimental results about the speed of light and the ether.

Einstein realized that a bump from a single water molecule would not cause a suspended pollen particle to move enough to be visible. However, at any given moment, the particle was being hit from all sides by thousands of molecules. There would be some moments when a lot more bumps happened to hit one particular side of the particle. Then, in another moment, a different side might get the heaviest barrage.

The result would be random little lurches that would result in what is known as a random walk. The best way for us to envision this is to imagine a drunk who starts at a lamppost and lurches one step in a random direction every second. After two such lurches he may have gone back and forth to return to the lamp. Or he may be two steps away in the same direction. Or he may be one step west and one step northeast. A little mathematical plotting and charting reveals an interesting thing about such a random walk: statistically, the drunk's distance from the lamp will be proportional to the square root of the number of seconds that have elapsed.[35]

Einstein realized that it was neither possible nor necessary to measure each zig and zag of Brownian motion, nor to measure the particle's velocity at any moment. But it was rather easy to measure the total distances of randomly lurching particles as these distances grew over time.

Einstein wanted concrete predictions that could be tested, so he used both his theoretical knowledge and experimental data about viscosity and diffusion rates to come up with precise predictions showing the distance a particle should move depending on its size and the temperature of the liquid. For example, he predicted, in the case of a particle with a diameter of one thousandth of a millimeter in water at 17 degrees centigrade, "the mean displacement in one minute would be about 6 microns."

Here was something that could actually be tested, and with great consequence. "If the motion discussed here can be observed," he wrote, "then classical thermodynamics can no longer be viewed as strictly valid." Better at theorizing than at conducting experiments, Einstein ended his paper with a charming exhortation: "Let us hope that a researcher will soon succeed in solving the problem presented here, which is so important for the theory of heat."

Within months, a German experimenter named Henry Seidentopf, using a powerful microscope, confirmed Einstein's predictions. For all practical purposes, the physical reality of atoms and molecules was now conclusively proven. "At the time atoms and molecules were still far from being regarded as real," the theoretical physicist Max Born later recalled. "I think that these investigations of Einstein have done more than any other work to convince physicists of the reality of atoms and molecules."[36]

As lagniappe, Einstein's paper also provided yet another way to determine Avogadro's number. "It bristles with new ideas," Abraham Pais said of the paper. "The final conclusion, that Avogadro's number can essentially be determined from observations with an ordinary microscope, never fails to cause a moment of astonishment even if one has read the paper before and therefore knows the punch line."

A strength of Einstein's mind was that it could juggle a variety of ideas simultaneously. Even as he was pondering dancing particles in a liquid, he had been wrestling with a different theory that involved moving bodies and the speed of light. A day or so after sending in his Brownian motion paper, he was talking to his friend Michele Besso when a new brainstorm struck. It would produce, as he wrote Habicht in his famous letter of that month, "a modification of the theory of space and time."

CHAPTER SIX

SPECIAL RELATIVITY

1905

The Bern Clock Tower

The Background

Relativity is a simple concept. It asserts that the fundamental laws of physics are the same whatever your state of motion.

For the *special* case of observers moving at a *constant velocity*, this concept is pretty easy to accept. Imagine a man in an armchair at home and a woman in an airplane gliding very smoothly above. Each can pour a cup of coffee, bounce a ball, shine a flashlight, or heat a muffin in a microwave and have the same laws of physics apply.

In fact, there is no way to determine which of them is "in motion" and which is "at rest." The man in the armchair could consider himself at rest and the plane in motion. And the woman in the plane could consider herself at rest and the earth as gliding past. There is no experiment that can prove who is right.

Indeed, there is no absolute right. All that can be said is that each is moving relative to the other. And of course, both are moving very rapidly relative to other planets, stars, and galaxies.*

The special theory of relativity that Einstein developed in 1905 applies only to this special case (hence the name): a situation in which the observers are moving at a constant velocity relative to one another—uniformly in a straight line at a steady speed—referred to as an "inertial reference system."[1]

It's harder to make the more general case that a person who is accelerating or turning or rotating or slamming on the brakes or moving in an arbitrary manner is not in some form of absolute motion, because coffee sloshes and balls roll away in a different manner than for people on a smoothly gliding train, plane, or planet. It would take Einstein a decade more, as we shall see, to come up with what he called a *general* theory of relativity, which incorporated accelerated motion into a theory of gravity and attempted to apply the concept of relativity to it.[2]

The story of relativity best begins in 1632, when Galileo articulated the principle that the laws of motion and mechanics (the laws of electromagnetism had not yet been discovered) were the same in all constant-velocity reference frames. In his *Dialogue Concerning the Two Chief World Systems,* Galileo wanted to defend Copernicus's idea that the earth does not rest motionless at the center of the universe with everything else revolving around it. Skeptics contended that if the earth was moving, as Copernicus said, we'd feel it. Galileo refuted this with a brilliantly clear thought experiment about being inside the cabin of a smoothly sailing ship:

> Shut yourself up with some friend in the main cabin below decks on some large ship, and have with you there some flies, butterflies, and other small flying animals. Have a large bowl of water with some fish in

---

* A person "at rest" on the equator is actually spinning with the earth's rotation at 1,040 miles per hour and orbiting with the earth around the sun at 67,000 miles per hour. When I refer to these observers being at a constant velocity, I am ignoring the change in velocity that arises from being on a rotating and orbiting planet, which would not affect most common experiments. (See Miller 1999, 25.)

it; hang up a bottle that empties drop by drop into a wide vessel beneath it. With the ship standing still, observe carefully how the little animals fly with equal speed to all sides of the cabin. The fish swim indifferently in all directions; the drops fall into the vessel beneath; and, in throwing something to your friend, you need throw it no more strongly in one direction than another, the distances being equal; jumping with your feet together, you pass equal spaces in every direction. When you have observed all these things carefully, have the ship proceed with any speed you like, so long as the motion is uniform and not fluctuating this way and that. You will discover not the least change in all the effects named, nor could you tell from any of them whether the ship was moving or standing still.[3]

There is no better description of relativity, or at least of how that principle applies to systems that are moving at a constant velocity relative to each other.

Inside Galileo's ship, it is easy to have a conversation, because the air that carries the sound waves is moving smoothly along with the people in the chamber. Likewise, if one of Galileo's passengers dropped a pebble into a bowl of water, the ripples would emanate the same way they would if the bowl were resting on shore; that's because the water propagating the ripples is moving smoothly along with the bowl and everything else in the chamber.

Sound waves and water waves are easily explained by classical mechanics. They are simply a traveling disturbance in some medium. That is why sound cannot travel through a vacuum. But it can travel through such things as air or water or metal. For example, sound waves move through room temperature air, as a vibrating disturbance that compresses and rarefies the air, at about 770 miles per hour.

Deep inside Galileo's ship, sound and water waves behave as they do on land, because the air in the chamber and the water in the bowls are moving at the same velocity as the passengers. But now imagine that you go up on deck and look at the waves out in the ocean, or that you measure the speed of the sound waves from the horn of another boat. The speed at which these waves come toward you depends on your motion relative to the medium (the water or air) propagating them.

In other words, the speed at which an ocean wave reaches you will depend on how fast you are moving through the water toward or away from the source of the wave. The speed of a sound wave relative to you will likewise depend on your motion relative to the air that's propagating the sound wave.

Those relative speeds add up. Imagine that you are standing in the ocean as the waves come toward you at 10 miles per hour. If you jump on a Jet Ski and head directly into the waves at 40 miles per hour, you will see them moving toward you and zipping past you at a speed (relative to you) of 50 miles per hour. Likewise, imagine that sound waves are coming at you from a distant boat horn, rippling through still air at 770 miles per hour toward the shore. If you jump on your Jet Ski and head toward the horn at 40 miles per hour, the sound waves will be moving toward you and zipping past you at a speed (relative to you) of 810 miles per hour.

All of this led to a question that Einstein had been pondering since age 16, when he imagined riding alongside a light beam: Does light behave the same way?

Newton had conceived of light as primarily a stream of emitted particles. But by Einstein's day, most scientists accepted the rival theory, propounded by Newton's contemporary Christiaan Huygens, that light should be considered a wave.

A wide variety of experiments had confirmed the wave theory by the late nineteenth century. For example, Thomas Young did a famous experiment, now replicated by high school students, showing how light passing through two slits produces an interference pattern that resembles that of water waves going through two slits. In each case, the crests and troughs of the waves emanating from each slit reinforce each other in some places and cancel each other out in some places.

James Clerk Maxwell helped to enshrine this wave theory when he successfully conjectured a connection between light, electricity, and magnetism. He came up with equations that described the behavior of electric and magnetic fields, and when they were combined they predicted electromagnetic waves. Maxwell found that these electromagnetic waves had to travel at a certain speed: approximately 186,000 miles per second.* That was the speed that scientists had already measured for light, and it was obviously not a mere coincidence.[4]

It became clear that light was the visible manifestation of a whole spectrum of electromagnetic waves. This includes what we now call AM radio signals (with a wavelength of 300 yards), FM radio signals (3 yards), and microwaves (3 inches). As the wavelengths get shorter (and the frequency of the wave cycles thus increases), they produce the spectrum of visible light, ranging from red (25 millionths of an inch) to violet (14 millionths of an inch). Even shorter wavelengths produce ultraviolet rays, X-rays, and gamma rays. When we speak of "light" and the "speed of light," we mean all electromagnetic waves, not just the ones that are visible to our eyes.

That raised some big questions: What was the medium that was propagating these waves? And their speed of 186,000 miles per second was a speed *relative to what*?

The answer, it seemed, was that light waves are a disturbance of an unseen medium, which was called the ether, and that their speed is relative to this ether. In other words, the ether was for light waves something akin to what air was for sound waves. "It appeared beyond question that light must be interpreted as a vibratory process in an elastic, inert medium filling up universal space," Einstein later noted.[5]

This ether, unfortunately, needed to have many puzzling properties. Because light from distant stars is able to reach the earth, the ether had to pervade the entire known universe. It had to be so gossamer and, shall we say, so ethereal that it had no effect on planets and feathers floating through it. Yet it had to be stiff enough to allow a wave to vibrate through it at an enormous speed.

All of this led to the great ether hunt of the late nineteenth century. If light was indeed a wave rippling through the ether, then you should see the waves going by you at a faster speed if you were moving *through*

---

* More precisely, 186,282.4 miles per second or 299,792,458 meters per second, in a vacuum. Unless otherwise specified, the "speed of light" is for light in a vacuum and refers to all electromagnetic waves, visible or not. This is also, as Maxwell discovered, the speed of electricity through a wire.

the ether toward the light source. Scientists devised all sorts of ingenious devices and experiments to detect such differences.

They used a variety of suppositions of how the ether might behave. They looked for it as if it were motionless and the earth passed freely through it. They looked for it as if the earth dragged parts of it along in a blob, the way it does its own atmosphere. They even considered the unlikely possibility that the earth was the only thing at rest with respect to the ether, and that everything else in the cosmos was spinning around, including the other planets, the sun, the stars, and presumably poor Copernicus in his grave.

One experiment, which Einstein later called "of fundamental importance in the special theory of relativity,"[6] was by the French physicist Hippolyte Fizeau, who sought to measure the speed of light in a moving medium. He split a light beam with a half-silvered angled mirror that sent one part of the beam through water in the direction of the water's flow and the other part against the flow. The two parts of the beam were then reunited. If one route took longer, then the crests and troughs of its waves would be out of sync with the waves of the other beam. The experimenters could tell if this happened by looking at the interference pattern that resulted when the waves were rejoined.

A different and far more famous experiment was done in Cleveland in 1887 by Albert Michelson and Edward Morley. They built a contraption that similarly split a light beam and sent one part back and forth to a mirror at the end of an arm facing in the direction of the earth's movement and the other part back and forth along an arm at a 90-degree angle to it. Once again, the two parts of the beam were then rejoined and the interference pattern analyzed to see if the path that was going up against the supposed ether wind would take longer.

No matter who looked, or how they looked, or what suppositions they made about the behavior of the ether, no one was able to detect the elusive substance. No matter which way anything was moving, the speed of light was observed to be exactly the same.

So scientists, somewhat awkwardly, turned their attention to coming up with explanations about why the ether existed but was undetectable in any experiment. Most notably, in the early 1890s Hendrik Lorentz—the cosmopolitan and congenial Dutch father figure of theoretical physics—and, independently, the Irish physicist George Fitzgerald came up with the hypothesis that solid objects contracted slightly when they moved through the ether. The Lorentz-Fitzgerald contraction would shorten everything, including the measuring arms used by Michelson and Morley, and it would do so by just the exact amount to make the effect of the ether on light undetectable.

Einstein felt that the situation "was very depressing." Scientists found themselves unable to explain electromagnetism using the Newtonian "mechanical view of nature," he said, and this "led to a fundamental dualism which in the long run was insupportable."[7]

Einstein's Road to Relativity

"A new idea comes suddenly and in a rather intuitive way," Einstein once said. "But," he hastened to add, "intuition is nothing but the outcome of earlier intellectual experience."[8]

Einstein's discovery of special relativity involved an intuition based on a decade of intellectual as well as personal experiences.[9] The most important and obvious, I think, was his deep understanding and knowledge of theoretical physics. He was also helped by his ability to visualize thought experiments, which had been encouraged by his education in Aarau. Also, there was his grounding in philosophy: from Hume and Mach he had developed a skepticism about things that could not be observed. And this skepticism was enhanced by his innate rebellious tendency to question authority.

Also part of the mix—and probably reinforcing his ability to both visualize physical situations and to cut to the heart of concepts—was the technological backdrop of his life: helping his uncle Jakob to refine the moving coils and magnets in a generator; working in a patent office that was being flooded with applications for new methods of coordinating clocks; having a boss who encouraged him to apply his skepticism; living near the clock tower and train station and just above the telegraph office in Bern just as Europe was using electrical signals to synchronize clocks within time zones; and having as a sounding board his engineer friend Michele Besso, who worked with him at the patent office, examining electromechanical devices.[10]

The ranking of these influences is, of course, a subjective judgment. After all, even Einstein himself could not be sure how the process unfolded. "It is not easy to talk about how I arrived at the theory of relativity," he said. "There were so many hidden complexities to motivate my thought."[11]

One thing we can note with some confidence is Einstein's main starting point. He repeatedly said that his path toward the theory of relativity began with his thought experiment at age 16 about what it would be like to ride at the speed of light alongside a light beam. This produced a "paradox," he said, and it troubled him for the next ten years:

> If I pursue a beam of light with the velocity c (velocity of light in a vacuum), I should observe such a beam of light as an electromagnetic field at rest though spatially oscillating. There seems to be no such thing, however, neither on the basis of experience nor according to Maxwell's equations. From the very beginning it appeared to me intuitively clear that, judged from the standpoint of such an observer, everything would have to happen according to the same laws as for an observer who, relative to the earth, was at rest. For how should the first observer know or be able to determine that he is in a state of fast uniform motion? One sees in this paradox the germ of the special relativity theory is already contained.[12]

This thought experiment did not necessarily undermine the ether theory of light waves. An ether theorist could imagine a frozen light beam. But it violated Einstein's intuition that the laws of optics should obey the principle of relativity. In other words, Maxwell's equations, which specify the speed of light, should be the same for all observers in constant-velocity motion. The emphasis that Einstein placed on this memory indicates that the idea of a frozen light beam—or frozen electromagnetic waves—seemed instinctively wrong to him.[13]

In addition, the thought experiment suggests that he sensed a conflict between Newton's laws of mechanics and the constancy of the speed of light in Maxwell's equations. All of this instilled in him "a state of psychic tension" that he found deeply unnerving. "At the very beginning, when the special theory of relativity began to germinate in me, I was visited by all sorts of nervous conflicts," he later recalled. "When young, I used to go away for weeks in a state of confusion."[14]

There was also a more specific "asymmetry" that began to bother him. When a magnet moves relative to a wire loop, an electric current is produced. As Einstein knew from his experience with his family's generators, the amount of this electric current is exactly the same whether the magnet is moving while the coil seems to be sitting still, or the coil is moving while the magnet seems to be sitting still. He also had studied an 1894 book by August Föppl, *Introduction to Maxwell's Theory of Electricity*. It had a section specifically on "The Electrodynamics of Moving Conductors" that questioned whether, when induction occurs, there should be any distinction between whether the magnet or the conducting coil is said to be in motion.[15]

"But according to the Maxwell-Lorentz theory," Einstein recalled, "the theoretical interpretation of the phenomenon is very different for the two cases." In the first case, Faraday's law of induction said that the motion of the magnet through the ether created an electric field. In the second case, Lorentz's force law said a current was created by the motion of the conducting coil through the magnetic field. "The idea that these two cases should essentially be different was unbearable to me," Einstein said.[16]

Einstein had been wrestling for years with the concept of the ether, which theoretically determined the definition of "at rest" in these electrical induction theories. As a student at the Zurich Polytechnic in 1899, he had written to Mileva Marić that "the introduction of the term 'ether' into theories of electricity has led to the conception of a medium whose motion can be described without, I believe, being able to ascribe physical meaning to it."[17] Yet that very month he was on vacation in Aarau working with a teacher at his old school on ways to detect the ether. "I had a good idea for investigating the way in which a body's relative motion with respect to the ether affects the velocity of the propagation of light," he told Marić.

Professor Weber told Einstein that his approach was impractical. Probably at Weber's suggestion, Einstein then read a paper by Wilhelm Wien that described the null results of thirteen ether-detection experiments, including those by Michelson and Morley and by

Fizeau.[18] He also learned about the Michelson-Morley experiment by reading, sometime before 1905, Lorentz's 1895 book, *Attempt at a Theory of Electrical and Optical Phenomena in Moving Bodies.* In this book, Lorentz goes through various failed attempts to detect the ether as a prelude to developing his theory of contractions.[19]

"Induction and Deduction in Physics"

So what effect did the Michelson-Morley results—which showed no evidence of the ether and no difference in the observed speed of light no matter in what direction the observer was moving—have on Einstein as he was incubating his ideas on relativity? To hear him tell it, almost none at all. In fact, at times he would even recollect (incorrectly) that he had not even known of the experiment before 1905. Einstein's inconsistent statements over the next fifty years about the influence of Michelson-Morley are useful in that they remind us of the caution needed when writing history based on dimming recollections.[20]

Einstein's trail of contradictory statements begins with an address he gave in Kyoto, Japan, in 1922, when he noted that Michelson's failure to detect an ether was "the first path that led me to what we call the principle of special relativity." In a toast at a 1931 dinner in Pasadena honoring Michelson, Einstein was gracious to the eminent experimenter, yet subtly circumspect: "You uncovered an insidious defect in the ether theory of light, as it then existed, and stimulated the ideas of Lorentz and Fitzgerald, out of which the Special Theory of Relativity developed."[21]

Einstein described his thought process in a series of talks with the Gestalt psychology pioneer Max Wertheimer, who later called the Michelson-Morley results "crucial" to Einstein's thinking. But as Arthur I. Miller has shown, this assertion was probably motivated by Wertheimer's goal of using Einstein's tale as a way to illustrate the tenets of Gestalt psychology.[22]

Einstein further confused the issue in the last few years of his life by giving a series of statements on the subject to a physicist named Robert Shankland. At first he said he had read of Michelson-Morley only *after* 1905, then he said he had read about it in Lorentz's book *before* 1905, and finally he added, "I guess I just took it for granted that it was true."[23]

That final point is the most significant one because Einstein made it often. He simply took for granted, by the time he started working seriously on relativity, that there was no need to review all the ether-drift experiments because, based on his starting assumptions, all attempts to detect the ether were doomed to failure.[24] For him, the significance of these experimental results was to reinforce what he already believed: that Galileo's relativity principle applied to light waves.[25]

This may account for the scant attention he gave to the experiments in his 1905 paper. He never mentioned the Michelson-Morley experiment by name, even where it would have been relevant, nor the Fizeau experiment using moving water. Instead, right after discussing the relativity of the magnet-and-coil movements, he merely flicked in a phrase about "the unsuccessful attempts to detect a motion of the earth relative to the light medium."

Some scientific theories depend primarily on induction: analyzing a lot of experimental findings and then finding theories that explain the empirical patterns. Others depend more on deduction: starting with elegant principles and postulates that are embraced as holy and then deducing the consequences from them. All scientists blend both approaches to differing degrees. Einstein had a good feel for experimental findings, and he used this knowledge to find certain fixed points upon which he could construct a theory.[26] But his emphasis was primarily on the deductive approach.[27]

Remember how in his Brownian motion paper he so oddly, yet accurately, downplayed the role that experimental findings played in what was essentially a theoretical deduction? There was a similar situation with his relativity theory. What he implied about Brownian motion he said explicitly about relativity and Michelson-Morley: "I was pretty much convinced of the validity of the principle before I knew of this experiment and its results."

Indeed, all three of his epochal papers in 1905 begin by asserting his intention to pursue a deductive approach. He opens each one by pointing out some oddity caused by jostling theories, rather than some unexplained set of experimental data. He then postulates grand principles while minimizing the role played by data, be it on Brownian motion or blackbody radiation or the speed of light.[28]

In a 1919 essay called "Induction and Deduction in Physics," he described his preference for the latter approach:

> The simplest picture one can form about the creation of an empirical science is along the lines of an inductive method. Individual facts are selected and grouped together so that the laws that connect them become apparent . . . However, the big advances in scientific knowledge originated in this way only to a small degree . . . The truly great advances in our understanding of nature originated in a way almost diametrically opposed to induction. The intuitive grasp of the essentials of a large complex of facts leads the scientist to the postulation of a hypothetical basic law or laws. From these laws, he derives his conclusions.[29]

His appreciation for this approach would grow. "The deeper we penetrate and the more extensive our theories become," he would declare near the end of his life, "the less empirical knowledge is needed to determine those theories."[30]

By the beginning of 1905, Einstein had begun to emphasize deduction rather than induction in his attempt to explain electrodynamics. "By and by, I despaired of the possibility of discovering the true laws by means of constructive efforts based on experimentally known facts," he later said. "The longer and the more despairingly I tried, the more I came to the conviction that only the discovery of a universal formal principle could lead us to assured results."[31]

The Two Postulates

Now that Einstein had decided to pursue his theory from the top down, by deriving it from grand postulates, he had a choice to make: What postulates—what basic assumptions of general principle— would he start with?[32]

His first postulate was the principle of relativity, which asserted that all of the fundamental laws of physics, even Maxwell's equations governing electromagnetic waves, are the same for all observers moving at constant velocity relative to each other. Put more precisely, they are the same for all inertial reference systems, the same for someone at rest relative to the earth as for someone traveling at a uniform velocity on a train or spaceship. He had nurtured his faith in this postulate beginning with his thought experiment about riding alongside a light beam: "From the very beginning it appeared to me intuitively clear that, judged from the standpoint of such an observer, everything would have to happen according to the same laws as for an observer who, relative to the earth, was at rest."

For a companion postulate, involving the velocity of light, Einstein had at least two options:

1. He could go with an emission theory, in which light would shoot from its source like particles from a gun. There would be no need for an ether. The light particles could zoom through emptiness. Their speed would be relative to the source. If this source was racing toward you, its emissions would come at you faster than if it was racing away. (Imagine a pitcher who can throw a ball at 100 miles per hour. If he throws it at you from a car racing toward you it will come at you faster than if he throws it from a car racing away.) In other words, starlight would be emitted from a star at 186,000 miles per second; but if that star was heading toward earth at 10,000 miles per second, the speed of its light would be 196,000 miles per second relative to an observer on earth.

2. An alternative was to postulate that the speed of light was a constant 186,000 miles per second irrespective of the motion of the source that emitted it, which was more consistent with a wave theory. By analogy with sound waves, a fire truck siren does not throw its sound at you faster when it's rushing toward you than it does when it's standing still. In either case, the sound travels through the air at 770 miles per hour.*

---

* If the source of sound is rushing toward you, the waves will not get to you any faster. However, in what is known as the Doppler effect, the waves will be compressed and the interval between them will be smaller. The decreased wavelength means a higher frequency, which results in a higher-pitched sound (or a lower one, when the siren passes by and starts moving away). A similar effect happens with light. If the source is moving toward you, the wavelength decreases (and frequency increases) so it is shifted to the blue end of the spectrum. Light from a source moving away will be red-shifted.

For a while, Einstein explored the emission theory route. This approach was particularly appealing if you conceived of light as behaving like a stream of quanta. And as noted in the previous chapter, that concept of light quanta was precisely what Einstein had propounded in March 1905, just when he was wrestling with his relativity theory.[33]

But there were problems with this approach. It seemed to entail abandoning Maxwell's equations and the wave theory. If the velocity of a light wave depended on the velocity of the source that emitted it, then the light wave must somehow encode within it this information. But experiments and Maxwell's equations indicated that was not the case.[34]

Einstein tried to find ways to modify Maxwell's equations so that they would fit an emission theory, but the quest became frustrating. "This theory requires that everywhere and in each fixed direction light waves of a different velocity of propagation should be possible," he later recalled. "It may be impossible to set up a reasonable electromagnetic theory that accomplishes such a feat."[35]

In addition, scientists had not been able to find any evidence that the velocity of light depended on that of its source. Light coming from any star seemed to arrive at the same speed.[36]

The more Einstein thought about an emission theory, the more problems he encountered. As he explained to his friend Paul Ehrenfest, it was hard to figure out what would happen when light from a "moving" source was refracted or reflected by a screen at rest. Also, in an emission theory, light from an accelerating source might back up on itself.

So Einstein rejected the emission theory in favor of postulating that the speed of a light beam was constant no matter how fast its source was moving. "I came to the conviction that all light should be defined by frequency and intensity alone, completely independently of whether it comes from a moving or from a stationary light source," he told Ehrenfest.[37]

Now Einstein had two postulates: "the principle of relativity" and this new one, which he called "the light postulate." He defined it carefully: "Light always propagates in empty space with a definite velocity V that is independent of the state of motion of the emitting body."[38]

For example, when you measure the velocity of light coming from the headlight of a train, it will always be a constant 186,000 miles per second, even if the train is rushing toward you or backing away from you.

Unfortunately, this light postulate seemed to be incompatible with the principle of relativity. Why? Einstein later used the following thought experiment to explain his apparent dilemma.

Imagine that "a ray of light is sent along the embankment" of a railway track, he said. A man standing on the embankment would measure its speed as 186,000 miles per second as it zipped past him. But now imagine a woman who is riding in a very fast train carriage that is racing away from the light source at 2,000 miles per second. We would assume that she would observe the beam to be zipping past her at only 184,000 miles per second. "The velocity of propagation of a ray of light relative to the carriage thus comes out smaller," Einstein wrote.

"But this result comes into conflict with the principle of relativity," he added. "For, like every other general law of nature, the law of the transmission of light must, according to the principle of relativity, be the same when the railway carriage is the reference body as it is when the embankment is the reference body." In other words, Maxwell's equations, which determine the speed at which light propagates, should operate the same way in the moving carriage as on the embankment. There should be no experiment you can do, including measuring the speed of light, to distinguish which inertial frame of reference is "at rest" and which is moving at a constant velocity.[39]

This was an odd result. A woman racing along the tracks toward or away from the source of a light beam should see that beam zip by her with the exact same speed as an observer standing on the embankment would see that same beam zip by him. The woman's speed relative to the train would vary, depending on whether she was running toward it or away from it. But her speed relative to the light beam coming from the train's headlight would be invariant. All of this made the two postulates, Einstein thought, "seemingly incompatible." As he later explained in a lecture on how he came to his theory, "the constancy of the velocity of light is not consistent with the law of the addition of velocities. The result was that I had to spend almost one year in fruitless thoughts."[40]

By combining the light postulate with the principle of relativity, it meant that an observer would measure the speed of light as the same whether the source was moving toward or away from him, or whether he was moving toward or away from the source, or both, or neither. The speed of light would be the same whatever the motion of the observer and the source.

That is where matters stood in early May 1905. Einstein had embraced the relativity principle and elevated it to a postulate. Then, with a bit more trepidation, he had adopted as a postulate that the velocity of light was independent of the motion of its source. And he puzzled over the apparent dilemma that an observer racing up a track toward a light would see the beam coming at him with the same velocity as when he was racing away from the light—and with the same velocity as someone standing still on the embankment would observe the same beam.

"In view of this dilemma, there appears to be nothing else to do than to abandon either the principle of relativity or the simple law of the propagation of light," Einstein wrote.[41]

Then something delightful happened. Albert Einstein, while talking with a friend, took one of the most elegant imaginative leaps in the history of physics.

"The Step"

It was a beautiful day in Bern, Einstein later remembered, when he went to visit his best friend Michele Besso, the brilliant but unfocused engineer he had met while studying in Zurich and then recruited to join him at the Swiss Patent Office. Many days they would walk to work together, and on this occasion Einstein told Besso about the dilemma that was dogging him.

"I'm going to give it up," Einstein said at one point. But as they discussed it, Einstein recalled, "I suddenly understood the key to the problem." The next day, when he saw Besso, Einstein was in a state of great excitement. He skipped any greeting and immediately declared, "Thank you. I've completely solved the problem."[42]

Only five weeks elapsed between that eureka moment and the day that Einstein sent off his most famous paper, "On the Electrodynamics of Moving Bodies." It contained no citations of other literature, no mention of anyone else's work, and no acknowledgments except for the charming one in the last sentence: "Let me note that my friend and colleague M. Besso steadfastly stood by me in my work on the problem discussed here, and that I am indebted to him for several valuable suggestions."

So what was the insight that struck him while talking to Besso? "An analysis of the concept of time was my solution," Einstein said. "Time cannot be absolutely defined, and there is an inseparable relation between time and signal velocity."

More specifically, the key insight was that two events that appear to be simultaneous to one observer will not appear to be simultaneous to another observer who is moving rapidly. And there is no way to declare that one of the observers is really correct. In other words, there is no way to declare that the two events are truly simultaneous.

Einstein later explained this concept using a thought experiment involving moving trains. Suppose lightning bolts strike the train track's embankment at two distant places, A and B. If we declare that they struck simultaneously, what does that mean?

Einstein realized that we need an operational definition, one we can actually apply, and that would require taking into account the speed of light. His answer was that we would define the two strikes as simultaneous if we were standing exactly halfway between them and the light from each reached us at the exact same time.

But now let us imagine how the event looks to a train passenger who is moving rapidly along the track. In a 1916 book written to explain this to nonscientists, he used the following drawing, in which the long train is the line on the top:

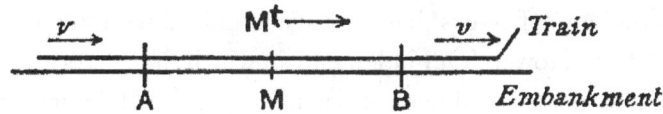

Suppose that at the exact instant (from the viewpoint of the person on the embankment) when lightning strikes at points A and B, there is a passenger at the midpoint of the train, M^t, just passing the observer who is at the midpoint alongside the tracks, M. If the train was motionless relative to the embankment, the passenger inside would see the lightning flashes simultaneously, just as the observer on the embankment would.

But if the train is moving to the right relative to the embankment, the observer inside will be rushing closer toward place B while the light signals are traveling. Thus he will be positioned slightly to the right by the time the light arrives; as a result, he will see the light from the strike at place B *before* he will see the light from the strike at place A. So he will assert that lightning hit at B before it did so at A, and the strikes were not simultaneous.

"We thus arrive at the important result: Events that are simultaneous with reference to the embankment are not simultaneous with respect to the train," said Einstein. The principle of relativity says that there is no way to decree that the embankment is "at rest" and the train "in motion." We can say only that they are in motion relative to each other. So there is no "real" or "right" answer. There is no way to say that any two events are "absolutely" or "really" simultaneous.[43]

This is a simple insight, but also a radical one. It means that *there is no absolute time.* Instead, all moving reference frames have their own relative time. Although Einstein refrained from saying that this leap was as truly "revolutionary" as the one he made about light quanta, it did in fact transform science. "This was a change in the very foundation of physics, an unexpected and very radical change that required all the courage of a young and revolutionary genius," noted Werner Heisenberg, who later contributed to a similar feat with his principle of quantum uncertainty.[44]

In his 1905 paper, Einstein used a vivid image, which we can imagine him conceiving as he watched the trains moving into the Bern station past the rows of clocks that were synchronized with the one atop the town's famed tower. "Our judgments in which time plays a part are always judgments of simultaneous events," he wrote. "If, for instance, I say, 'That train arrives here at 7 o'clock,' I mean something like this:

'The pointing of the small hand of my watch to 7 and the arrival of the train are simultaneous events.'" Once again, however, observers who are moving rapidly relative to one another will have a different view on whether two distant events are simultaneous.

The concept of absolute time—meaning a time that exists in "reality" and tick-tocks along independent of any observations of it—had been a mainstay of physics ever since Newton had made it a premise of his *Principia* 216 years earlier. The same was true for absolute space and distance. "Absolute, true, and mathematical time, of itself and from its own nature, flows equably without relation to anything external," he famously wrote in Book 1 of the *Principia*. "Absolute space, in its own nature, without relation to anything external, remains always similar and immovable."

But even Newton seemed discomforted by the fact that these concepts could not be directly observed. "Absolute time is not an object of perception," he admitted. He resorted to relying on the presence of God to get him out of the dilemma. "The Deity endures forever and is everywhere present, and by existing always and everywhere, He constitutes duration and space." [45]

Ernst Mach, whose books had influenced Einstein and his fellow members of the Olympia Academy, lambasted Newton's notion of absolute time as a "useless metaphysical concept" that "cannot be produced in experience." Newton, he charged, "acted contrary to his expressed intention only to investigate actual facts." [46]

Henri Poincaré also pointed out the weakness of Newton's concept of absolute time in his book *Science and Hypothesis,* another favorite of the Olympia Academy. "Not only do we have no direct intuition of the equality of two times, we do not even have one of the simultaneity of two events occurring in different places," he wrote. [47]

Both Mach and Poincaré were, it thus seems, useful in providing a foundation for Einstein's great breakthrough. But he owed even more, he later said, to the skepticism he learned from the Scottish philosopher David Hume regarding mental constructs that were divorced from purely factual observations.

Given the number of times in his papers that he uses thought experiments involving moving trains and distant clocks, it is also logical to surmise that he was helped in visualizing and articulating his thoughts by the trains that moved past Bern's clock tower and the rows of synchronized clocks on the station platform. Indeed, there is a tale that involves him discussing his new theory with friends by pointing to (or at least referring to) the synchronized clocks of Bern and the unsynchronized steeple clock visible in the neighboring village of Muni.[48]

Peter Galison provides a thought-provoking study of the technological ethos in his book *Einstein's Clocks, Poincaré's Maps*. Clock coordination was in the air at the time. Bern had inaugurated an urban time network of electrically synchronized clocks in 1890, and a decade later, by the time Einstein had arrived, finding ways to make them more accurate and coordinate them with clocks in other cities became a Swiss passion.

In addition, Einstein's chief duty at the patent office, in partnership with Besso, was evaluating electromechanical devices. This included a flood of applications for ways to synchronize clocks by using electric signals. From 1901 to 1904, Galison notes, there were twenty-eight such patents issued in Bern.

One of them, for example, was called "Installation with Central Clock for Indicating the Time Simultaneously in Several Places Separated from One Another." A similar application arrived on April 25, just three weeks before Einstein had his breakthrough conversation with Besso; it involved a clock with an electromagnetically controlled pendulum that could be coordinated with another such clock through an electric signal. What these applications had in common was that they used signals that traveled at the speed of light.[49]

We should be careful not to overemphasize the role played by the technological backdrop of the patent office. Although clocks are part of Einstein's description of his theory, his point is about the difficulties that observers *in relative motion* have in using light signals to synchronize them, something that was not an issue for the patent applicants.[50]

Nevertheless, it is interesting to note that almost the entire first two sections of his relativity paper deal directly and in vivid practical detail (in a manner so different from the writings of, say, Lorentz and Maxwell) with the two real-world technological phenomena he knew best. He writes about the generation of "electric currents of the same magnitude" due to the "equality of relative motion" of coils and magnets, and the use of "a light signal" to make sure that "two clocks are synchronous."

As Einstein himself stated, his time in the patent office "stimulated me to see the physical ramifications of theoretical concepts."[51] And Alexander Moszkowski, who compiled a book in 1921 based on conversations with Einstein, noted that Einstein believed there was "a definite connection between the knowledge acquired at the patent office and the theoretical results."[52]

"On the Electrodynamics of Moving Bodies"

Now let's look at how Einstein articulated all of this in the famous paper that the *Annalen der Physik* received on June 30, 1905. For all its momentous import, it may be one of the most spunky and enjoyable papers in all of science. Most of its insights are conveyed in words and vivid thought experiments, rather than in complex equations. There is some math involved, but it is mainly what a good high school senior could comprehend. "The whole paper is a testament to the power of simple language to convey deep and powerfully disturbing ideas," says the science writer Dennis Overbye.[53]

The paper starts with the "asymmetry" that a magnet and wire loop induce an electric current based only on their relative motion to one another, but since the days of Faraday there had been two different theoretical explanations for the current produced depending on whether it was the magnet or the loop that was in motion.[54] "The observable phenomenon here depends only on the relative motion of the conductor and the magnet," Einstein writes, "whereas the customary view draws a sharp distinction between the two cases in which either the one or the other of these bodies is in motion."[55]

The distinction between the two cases was based on the belief, which most scientists still held, that there was such a thing as a state of "rest" with respect to the ether. But the magnet-and-coil example, along with every observation made on light, "suggest that the phenomena of electrodynamics as well as of mechanics possess no properties corresponding to the idea of absolute rest." This prompts Einstein to raise "to the status of a postulate" the principle of relativity, which holds that the laws of mechanics and electrodynamics are the same in all reference systems moving at constant velocity relative to one another.

Einstein goes on to propound the other postulate upon which his theory was premised: the constancy of the speed of light "independent of the state of motion of the emitting body." Then, with the casual stroke of a pen, and the marvelously insouciant word "superfluous," the rebellious patent examiner dismissed two generations' worth of accrued scientific dogma: "The introduction of a 'light ether' will prove to be superfluous, inasmuch as the view to be developed here will not require a 'space at absolute rest.' "

Using these two postulates, Einstein explained the great conceptual step he had taken during his talk with Besso. "Two events which, viewed from a system of coordinates, are simultaneous, can no longer be looked upon as simultaneous events when envisaged from a system which is in motion relative to that system." In other words, there is no such thing as absolute simultaneity.

In phrases so simple as to be seductive, Einstein pointed out that time itself can be defined only by referring to simultaneous events, such as the small hand of a watch pointing to 7 as a train arrives. The obvious yet still astonishing conclusion: with no such thing as absolute simultaneity, there is no such thing as "real" or absolute time. As he later put it, "There is no audible tick-tock everywhere in the world that can be considered as time." [56]

Moreover, this realization also meant overturning the other assumption that Newton made at the beginning of his *Principia*. Einstein showed that if time is relative, so too are space and distance: "If the man in the carriage covers the distance w in a unit of time—*measured from the train*—then this distance—*as measured from the embankment*—is not necessarily also equal to w." [57]

Einstein explained this by asking us to picture a rod that has a certain length when it is measured while it is stationary relative to the observer. Now imagine that the rod is moving. How long is the rod?

One way to determine this is by moving alongside the rod, at the same speed, and superimposing a measuring stick on it. But how long would the rod be if measured by someone *not* in motion with it? In that

case, a way to measure the moving rod would be to determine, based on synchronized stationary clocks, the precise location of each end of the rod at a specific moment, and then use a stationary ruler to measure the distance between these two points. Einstein shows that these methods will produce *different* results.

Why? Because the two stationary clocks have been synchronized by a stationary observer. But what happens if an observer who is moving as fast as the rod tries to synchronize those clocks? She would synchronize them differently, because she would have a different perception of simultaneity. As Einstein put it, "Observers moving with the moving rod would thus find that the two clocks were not synchronous, while observers in the stationary system would declare the clocks to be synchronous."

Another consequence of special relativity is that a person standing on the platform will observe that time goes more slowly on a train speeding past. Imagine that on the train there is a "clock" made up of a mirror on the floor and one on the ceiling and a beam of light that bounces up and down between them. From the perspective of a woman on the train, the light goes straight up and then straight down. But from the perspective of a man standing on the platform, it appears that the light is starting at the bottom but moving on a diagonal to get to the ceiling mirror, which has zipped ahead a tiny bit, then bouncing down on a diagonal back to the mirror on the floor, which has in turn zipped ahead a tiny bit. For both observers, the speed of the light is the same (that is Einstein's great given). The man on the track observes the distance the light has to travel as being longer than the woman on the train observes it to be. Thus, from the perspective of the man on the track, time is going by more slowly inside the speeding train.[58]

Another way to picture this is to use Galileo's ship. Imagine a light beam being shot down from the top of the mast to the deck. To an observer on the ship, the light beam will travel the exact length of the mast. To an observer on land, however, the light beam will travel a diagonal formed by the length of the mast plus the distance (it's a *fast* ship) that the ship has traveled forward during the time it took the light to get from the top to the bottom of the mast. To both observers,

the speed of light is the same. To the observer on land, it traveled farther before it reached the deck. In other words, the exact same event (a
light beam sent from the top of the mast hitting the deck) took longer
when viewed by a person on land than by a person on the ship.[59]

This phenomenon, called time dilation, leads to what is known as
the twin paradox. If a man stays on the platform while his twin sister
takes off in a spaceship that travels long distances at nearly the speed of
light, when she returns she would be younger than he is. But because
motion is relative, this seems to present a paradox. The sister on the
spaceship might think it's her brother on earth who is doing the fast
traveling, and when they are rejoined she would expect to observe that
it was *he* who did not age much.

Could they each come back younger than the other one? Of course
not. The phenomenon does not work in both directions. Because the
spaceship does not travel at a *constant velocity,* but instead must turn
around, it's the twin on the spaceship, not the one on earth, who would
age more slowly.

The phenomenon of time dilation has been experimentally confirmed, even by using test clocks on commercial planes. But in our normal life, it has no real impact, because our motion relative to any other
observer is never anything near the speed of light. In fact, if you spent
almost your entire life on an airplane, you would have aged merely
0.00005 seconds or so less than your twin on earth when you returned,
an effect that would likely be counteracted by a lifetime spent eating
airline food.[60]

Special relativity has many other curious manifestations. Think
again about that light clock on the train. What happens as the train approaches the speed of light relative to an observer on the platform? It
would take almost forever for a light beam in the train to bounce from
the floor to the moving ceiling and back to the moving floor. Thus time
on the train would almost stand still from the perspective of an observer on the platform.

As an object approaches the speed of light, its apparent mass also
increases. Newton's law that force equals mass times acceleration still
holds, but as the apparent mass increases, more and more force will
produce less and less acceleration. There is no way to apply enough

force to push even a pebble faster than the speed of light. That's the ultimate speed limit of the universe, and no particle or piece of information can go faster than that, according to Einstein's theory.

With all this talk of distance and duration being relative depending on the observer's motion, some may be tempted to ask: So which observer is "right"? Whose watch shows the "actual" time elapsed? Which length of the rod is "real"? Whose notion of simultaneity is "correct"?

According to the special theory of relativity, all inertial reference frames are equally valid. It is not a question of whether rods *actually* shrink or time *really* slows down; all we know is that observers in different states of motion will measure things differently. And now that we have dispensed with the ether as "superfluous," there is no designated "rest" frame of reference that has preference over any other.

One of Einstein's clearest explanations of what he had wrought was in a letter to his Olympia Academy colleague Solovine:

> The theory of relativity can be outlined in a few words. In contrast to the fact, known since ancient times, that movement is perceivable only as *relative* movement, physics was based on the notion of *absolute* movement. The study of light waves had assumed that one state of movement, that of the light-carrying ether, is distinct from all others. All movements of bodies were supposed to be relative to the light-carrying ether, which was the incarnation of absolute rest. But after efforts to discover the privileged state of movement of this hypothetical ether through experiments had failed, it seemed that the problem should be restated. That is what the theory of relativity did. It assumed that there are no privileged physical states of movement and asked what consequences could be drawn from this.

Einstein's insight, as he explained it to Solovine, was that we must discard concepts that "have no link with experience," such as "absolute simultaneity" and "absolute speed."[61]

It is very important to note, however, that the theory of relativity does not mean that "everything is relative." It does not mean that everything is subjective.

Instead, it means that measurements of time, including duration and simultaneity, can be relative, depending on the motion of the observer. So can the measurements of space, such as distance and length.

But there is a union of the two, which we call spacetime, and that remains invariant in all inertial frames. Likewise, there are things such as the speed of light that remain invariant.

In fact, Einstein briefly considered calling his creation Invariance Theory, but the name never took hold. Max Planck used the term *Relativtheorie* in 1906, and by 1907 Einstein, in an exchange with his friend Paul Ehrenfest, was calling it *Relativitätstheorie*.

One way to understand that Einstein was talking about invariance, rather than declaring everything to be relative, is to think about how far a light beam would travel in a given period of time. That distance would be the speed of light multiplied by the amount of time it traveled. If we were on a platform observing this happening on a train speeding by, the elapsed time would appear shorter (time seems to move more slowly on the moving train), and the distance would appear shorter (rulers seem to be contracted on the moving train). But there is a relationship between the two quantities—a relationship between the measurements of space and of time—that remains invariant, whatever your frame of reference.[62]

A more complex way to understand this is the method used by Hermann Minkowski, Einstein's former math teacher at the Zurich Polytechnic. Reflecting on Einstein's work, Minkowski uttered the expression of amazement that every beleaguered student wants to elicit someday from condescending professors. "It came as a tremendous surprise, for in his student days Einstein had been a lazy dog," Minkowski told physicist Max Born. "He never bothered about mathematics at all."[63]

Minkowski decided to give a formal mathematical structure to the theory. His approach was the same one suggested by the time traveler on the first page of H. G. Wells's great novel *The Time Machine*, published in 1895: "There are really four dimensions, three which we call the three planes of Space, and a fourth, Time." Minkowski turned all events into mathematical coordinates in four dimensions, with time as the fourth dimension. This permitted transformations to occur, but the mathematical relationships between the events remained invariant.

Minkowski dramatically announced his new mathematical approach in a lecture in 1908. "The views of space and time which I wish to lay before you have sprung from the soil of experimental physics, and therein lies their strength," he said. "They are radical. Henceforth space by itself, and time by itself, are doomed to fade away into mere shadows, and only a kind of union of the two will preserve an independent reality."[64]

Einstein, who was still not yet enamored of math, at one point described Minkowski's work as "superfluous learnedness" and joked, "Since the mathematicians have grabbed hold of the theory of relativity, I myself no longer understand it." But he in fact came to admire Minkowski's handiwork and wrote a section about it in his popular 1916 book on relativity.

What a wonderful collaboration it could have been! But at the end of 1908, Minkowski was taken to the hospital, fatally stricken with peritonitis. Legend has it that he declared, "What a pity that I have to die in the age of relativity's development."[65]

Once again, it's worth asking why Einstein discovered a new theory and his contemporaries did not. Both Lorentz and Poincaré had already come up with many of the components of Einstein's theory. Poincaré even questioned the absolute nature of time.

But neither Lorentz nor Poincaré made the full leap: that there is no need to posit an ether, that there is no absolute rest, that time is relative based on an observer's motion, and so is space. Both men, the physicist Kip Thorne says, "were groping toward the same revision of our notions of space and time as Einstein, but they were groping through a fog of misperceptions foisted on them by Newtonian physics."

Einstein, by contrast, was able to cast off Newtonian misconceptions. "His conviction that the universe loves simplification and beauty, and his willingness to be guided by this conviction, even if it meant destroying the foundations of Newtonian physics, led him, with a clarity of thought that others could not match, to his new description of space and time."[66]

Poincaré never made the connection between the relativity of simultaneity and the relativity of time, and he "drew back when on the brink" of understanding the full ramifications of his ideas about local time. Why did he hesitate? Despite his interesting insights, he was too much of a traditionalist in physics to display the rebellious streak ingrained in the unknown patent examiner.[67] "When he came to the decisive step, his nerve failed him and he clung to old habits of thought and familiar ideas of space and time," Banesh Hoffmann said of Poincaré. "If this seems surprising, it is because we underestimate the boldness of Einstein in stating the principle of relativity as an axiom and, by keeping faith with it, changing our notion of space and time."[68]

A clear explanation of Poincaré's limitations and Einstein's boldness comes from one of Einstein's successors as a theoretical physicist at the Institute for Advanced Study in Princeton, Freeman Dyson:

> The essential difference between Poincaré and Einstein was that Poincaré was by temperament conservative and Einstein was by temperament revolutionary. When Poincaré looked for a new theory of electromagnetism, he tried to preserve as much as he could of the old. He loved the ether and continued to believe in it, even when his own theory showed that it was unobservable. His version of relativity theory was a patchwork quilt. The new idea of local time, depending on the motion of the observer, was patched onto the old framework of absolute space and time defined by a rigid and immovable ether. Einstein, on the other hand, saw the old framework as cumbersome and unnecessary and was delighted to be rid of it. His version of the theory was simpler and more elegant. There was no absolute space and time and there was no ether. All the complicated explanations of electric and magnetic forces as elastic stresses in the ether could be swept into the dustbin of history, together with the famous old professors who still believed in them.[69]

As a result, Poincaré expressed a principle of relativity that contained certain similarities to Einstein's, but it had a fundamental difference. Poincaré retained the existence of the ether, and the speed of light was, for him, constant only when measured by those at rest to this presumed ether's frame of reference.[70]

Even more surprising, and revealing, is the fact that Lorentz and Poincaré never were able to make Einstein's leap even *after* they read his paper. Lorentz still clung to the existence of the ether and its "at rest" frame of reference. In a lecture in 1913, which he reprinted in his 1920 book *The Relativity Principle,* Lorentz said, "According to Einstein, it is meaningless to speak of motion relative to the ether. He likewise denies the existence of absolute simultaneity. As far as this lecturer is concerned, he finds a certain satisfaction in the older interpretations, according to which the ether possesses at least some substantiality, space and time can be sharply separated, and simultaneity without further specification can be spoken of."[71]

For his part, Poincaré seems never to have fully understood Einstein's breakthrough. Even in 1909, he was still insisting that relativity theory required a third postulate, which was that "a body in motion suffers a deformation in the direction in which it was displaced." In fact, the contraction of rods is not, as Einstein showed, some separate hypothesis involving a real deformation, but rather the consequence of accepting Einstein's theory of relativity.

Until his death in 1912, Poincaré never fully gave up the concept of the ether or the notion of absolute rest. Instead, he spoke of the adoption of "the principle of relativity according to Lorentz." He never fully understood or accepted the basis of Einstein's theory. "Poincaré stood steadfast and held to his position that in the world of perceptions there was an absoluteness of simultaneity," notes the science historian Arthur I. Miller.[72]

His Partner

"How happy and proud I will be when the two of us together will have brought our work on the relative motion to a conclusion!" Einstein had written his lover Mileva Marić back in 1901.[73] Now it had been brought to that conclusion, and Einstein was so exhausted when he finished a draft in June that "his body buckled and he went to bed for two weeks," while Marić "checked the article again and again."[74]

Then they did something unusual: they celebrated together. As soon as he finished all four of the papers that he had promised in his memorable letter to Conrad Habicht, he sent his old colleague from the Olympia Academy another missive, this one a postcard signed by his wife as well. It read in full: "Both of us, alas, dead drunk under the table."[75]

All of which raises a question more subtle and contentious than that posed by the influences of Lorentz and Poincaré: What was Mileva Marić's role?

That August, they took a vacation together in Serbia to see her friends and family. While there, Marić was proud and also willing to accept part of the credit. "Not long ago we finished a very significant work that will make my husband world famous," she told her father, according to stories later recorded there. Their relationship seemed restored, for the time being, and Einstein happily praised his wife's help. "I need my wife," he told her friends in Serbia. "She solves all the mathematical problems for me."[76]

Some have contended that Marić was a full-fledged collaborator, and there was even a report, later discredited,[77] that an early draft version of his relativity paper had her name on it as well. At a 1990 conference in New Orleans, the American Association for the Advancement of Science held a panel on the issue at which Evan Walker, a physicist and cancer researcher from Maryland, debated John Stachel, the leader of the Einstein Papers Project. Walker presented the various letters referring to "our work," and Stachel replied that such phrases were clearly romantic politeness and that there was "no evidence at all that she contributed any ideas of her own."

The controversy, understandably, fascinated both scientists and the press. Columnist Ellen Goodman wrote a wry commentary in the *Boston Globe,* in which she judiciously laid out the evidence, and the *Economist* did a story headlined "The Relative Importance of Mrs. Einstein." Another conference followed in 1994 at the University of Novi Sad, where organizer Professor Rastko Maglić contended that it was time "to emphasize Mileva's merit in order to ensure a deserved place in the history of science for her." The public discussion culminated with a PBS documentary, *Einstein's Wife,* in 2003, that was generally balanced, although it gave unwarranted credence to the report that her name had been on the original manuscript.[78]

From all the evidence, Marić was a sounding board, though not as important in that role as Besso. She also helped check his math, although there is no evidence that she came up with any of the mathematical concepts. In addition, she encouraged him and (what at times was more difficult) put up with him.

For both the sake of colorful history and the emotional resonance it would have, it would be fun if we could go even further than this. But instead, we must follow the less exciting course of being confined to the evidence. None of their many letters, to each other or to friends, mentions a single instance of an idea or creative concept relating to relativity that came from Marić.

Nor did she ever—even to her family and close friends while in the throes of their bitter divorce—claim to have made any substantive contributions to Einstein's theories. Her son Hans Albert, who remained devoted to her and lived with her during the divorce, gave his own version that was reflected in a book by Peter Michelmore, and it seems to reflect what Marić told her son: "Mileva helped him solve certain mathematical problems, but no one could assist with the creative work, the flow of ideas."[79]

There is, in fact, no need to exaggerate Marić's contributions in order to admire, honor, and sympathize with her as a pioneer. To give her credit beyond what she ever claimed, says the science historian Gerald Holton, "only detracts both from her real and significant place in history and from the tragic unfulfillment of her early hopes and promise."

Einstein admired the pluck and courage of a feisty female physicist who had emerged from a land where women were generally not allowed to go into that field. Nowadays, when the same issues still reverberate across a century of time, the courage that Marić displayed by entering and competing in the male-dominated world of physics and math is what should earn her an admired spot in the annals of scientific history. This she deserves without inflating the importance of her collaboration on the special theory of relativity.[80]

The E=mc² *Coda, September 1905*

Einstein had raised the curtain on his miracle year in his letter to his Olympia Academy mate Conrad Habicht, and he celebrated its climax with his one-sentence drunken postcard to him. In September, he wrote yet another letter to Habicht, this one trying to entice him to come work at the patent office. Einstein's reputation as a lone wolf was somewhat artificial. "Perhaps it would be possible to smuggle you in among the patent slaves," he said. "You probably would find it relatively pleasant. Would you actually be ready and willing to come? Keep in mind that besides the eight hours of work, each day also has eight hours for fooling around, and then there's also Sunday. I would love to have you here."

As with his letter six months earlier, Einstein went on to reveal quite casually a momentous scientific breakthrough, one that would be expressed by the most famous equation in all of science:

> One more consequence of the electrodynamics paper has also crossed my mind. Namely, the relativity principle, together with Maxwell's equations, requires that mass be a direct measure of the energy contained in a body. Light carries mass with it. With the case of radium there should be a noticeable reduction of mass. The thought is amusing and seductive; but for all I know, the good Lord might be laughing at the whole matter and might have been leading me up the garden path.[81]

Einstein developed the idea with a beautiful simplicity. The paper that the *Annalen der Physik* received from him on September 27, 1905, "Does the Inertia of a Body Depend on Its Energy Content?," involved only three steps that filled merely three pages. Referring back to his special relativity paper, he declared, "The results of an electrodynamic investigation recently published by me in this journal lead to a very interesting conclusion, which will be derived here."[82]

Once again, he was deducing a theory from principles and postulates, not trying to explain the empirical data that experimental physicists studying cathode rays had begun to gather about the relation of mass to the velocity of particles. Coupling Maxwell's theory with the relativity theory, he began (not surprisingly) with a thought experiment. He calculated the properties of two light pulses emitted in opposite directions by a body at rest. He then calculated the properties of these light pulses when observed from a moving frame of reference. From this he came up with equations regarding the relationship between speed and mass.

The result was an elegant conclusion: mass and energy are different manifestations of the same thing. There is a fundamental interchangeability between the two. As he put it in his paper, "The mass of a body is a measure of its energy content."

The formula he used to describe this relationship was also strikingly simple: "If a body emits the energy L in the form of radiation, its mass decreases by L/V^2." Or, to express the same equation in a different manner: $L=mV^2$. Einstein used the letter L to represent energy until 1912, when he crossed it out in a manuscript and replaced it with the more common E. He also used V to represent the velocity of light, before changing to the more common c. So, using the letters that soon became standard, Einstein had come up with his memorable equation:

$$E=mc^2$$

Energy equals mass times the square of the speed of light. The speed of light, of course, is huge. Squared it is almost inconceivably bigger. That is why a tiny amount of matter, if converted completely into energy, has an enormous punch. A kilogram of mass would convert into approximately 25 billion kilowatt hours of electricity. More vividly: the energy in the mass of one raisin could supply most of New York City's energy needs for a day.[83]

As usual, Einstein ended by proposing experimental ways to confirm the theory he had just derived. "Perhaps it will prove possible," he wrote, "to test this theory using bodies whose energy content is variable to a high degree, e.g., salts of radium."

CHAPTER SEVEN

THE HAPPIEST THOUGHT

1906–1909

Recognition

Einstein's 1905 burst of creativity was astonishing. He had devised a revolutionary quantum theory of light, helped prove the existence of atoms, explained Brownian motion, upended the concept of space and time, and produced what would become science's best known equation. But not many people seemed to notice at first. According to his sister, Einstein had hoped that his flurry of essays in a preeminent journal would lift him from the obscurity of a third-class patent examiner and provide some academic recognition, perhaps even an academic job. "But he was bitterly disappointed," she noted. "Icy silence followed the publication."[1]

That was not exactly true. A small but respectable handful of physicists soon took note of Einstein's papers, and one of these turned out to be, as good fortune would have it, the most important possible admirer he could attract: Max Planck, Europe's revered monarch of theoretical physics, whose mysterious mathematical constant explaining blackbody radiation Einstein had transformed into a radical new reality of nature. As the editorial board member of *Annalen der Physik* responsible for theoretical submissions, Planck had vetted Einstein's papers, and the one on relativity had "immediately aroused my lively attention," he later recalled. As soon as it was published, Planck gave a lecture on relativity at the University of Berlin.[2]

Planck became the first physicist to build on Einstein's theory. In an article published in the spring of 1906, he argued that relativity conformed to the principle of least action, a foundation of physics that holds that light or any object moving between two points should follow the easiest path.[3]

Planck's paper not only contributed to the development of relativity theory; it also helped to legitimize it among other physicists. Whatever disappointment Maja Einstein had detected in her brother dissipated. "My papers are much appreciated and are giving rise to further investigations," he exulted to Solovine. "Professor Planck has recently written to me about that."[4]

The proud patent examiner was soon exchanging letters with the eminent professor. When another theorist challenged Planck's contention that relativity theory conformed to the principle of least action, Einstein took Planck's side and sent him a card saying so. Planck was pleased. "As long as the proponents of the principle of relativity constitute such a modest little band as is now the case," he replied to Einstein, "it is doubly important that they agree among themselves." He added that he hoped to visit Bern the following year and meet Einstein personally.[5]

Planck did not end up coming to Bern, but he did send his earnest assistant, Max Laue.* He and Einstein had already been corresponding about Einstein's light quanta paper, with Laue saying that he agreed with "your heuristic view that radiation can be absorbed and emitted only in specific finite quanta."

However, Laue insisted, just as Planck had, that Einstein was wrong to assume that these quanta were a characteristic of the radiation itself. Instead, Laue contended that the quanta were merely a description of the way that radiation was emitted or absorbed by a piece of matter. "This is not a characteristic of electromagnetic processes in a vacuum but rather of the emitting or absorbing matter," Laue wrote, "and hence radiation does not consist of light quanta as it says in section six of your first paper."[6] (In that section, Einstein had said that the

---

* Later, upon his father's death, he became Max von Laue.

radiation "behaves thermodynamically as if it consisted of mutually independent energy quanta.")

When Laue was preparing to visit in the summer of 1907, he was surprised to discover that Einstein was not at the University of Bern but was working at the patent office on the third floor of the Post and Telegraph Building. Meeting Einstein there did not lessen his wonder. "The young man who came to meet me made so unexpected an impression on me that I did not believe he could possibly be the father of the relativity theory," Laue said, "so I let him pass." After a while, Einstein came wandering through the reception area again, and Laue finally realized who he was.

They walked and talked for hours, with Einstein at one point offering a cigar that, Laue recalled, "was so unpleasant that I 'accidentally' dropped it into the river." Einstein's theories, on the other hand, made a pleasing impression. "During the first two hours of our conversation he overthrew the entire mechanics and electrodynamics," Laue noted. Indeed, he was so enthralled that over the next four years he would publish eight papers on Einstein's relativity theory and become a close friend.[7]

Some theorists found the amazing flurry of papers from the patent office to be uncomfortably abstract. Arnold Sommerfeld, later a friend, was among the first to suggest there was something Jewish about Einstein's theoretical approach, a theme later picked up by anti-Semites. It lacked due respect for the notion of order and absolutes, and it did not seem solidly grounded. "As remarkable as Einstein's papers are," he wrote Lorentz in 1907, "it still seems to me that something almost unhealthy lies in this unconstruable and impossible to visualize dogma. An Englishman would hardly have given us this theory. It might be here too, as in the case of Cohn, the abstract conceptual character of the Semite expresses itself."[8]

None of this interest made Einstein famous, nor did it get him any job offers. "I was surprised to read that you must sit in an office for eight hours a day," wrote yet another young physicist who was planning to visit. "History is full of bad jokes."[9] But because he had finally earned his doctorate, he had at least gotten promoted from a third-class to a second-class technical expert at the patent office, which came with a hefty 1,000-franc raise to an annual salary of 4,500 francs.[10]

His productivity was startling. In addition to working six days a week at the patent office, he continued his torrent of papers and reviews: six in 1906 and ten more in 1907. At least once a week he played in a string quartet. And he was a good father to the 3-year-old son he proudly labeled "impertinent." As Marić wrote to her friend Helene Savić, "My husband often spends his free time at home just playing with the boy."[11]

Beginning in the summer of 1907, Einstein also found time to dabble in what might have become, if the fates had been more impish, a new career path: as an inventor and salesman of electrical devices like his uncle and father. Working with Olympia Academy member Conrad Habicht and his brother Paul, Einstein developed a machine to amplify tiny electrical charges so they could be measured and studied. It had more academic than practical purpose; the idea was to create a lab device that would permit the study of small electrical fluctuations.

The concept was simple. When two strips of metal move close to each other, an electric charge on one will induce an opposite charge on the other. Einstein's idea was to use a series of strips that would induce the charge ten times and then transfer that to another disc. The process would be repeated until the original minuscule charge would be multiplied by a large number and thus be easily measurable. The trick was making the contraption actually work.[12]

Given his heritage, breeding, and years in the patent office, Einstein had the background to be an engineering genius. But as it turned out, he was better suited to theorizing. Fortunately, Paul Habicht was a good machinist, and by August 1907 he had a prototype of the *Maschinchen*, or little machine, ready to be unveiled. "I am astounded at the lightning speed with which you built the *Maschinchen*," Einstein wrote. "I'll show up on Sunday." Unfortunately, it didn't work. "I am driven by *murderous* curiosity as to what you're up to," Einstein wrote a month later as they tried to fix things.

Throughout 1908, letters flew back and forth between Einstein and the Habichts, filled with complex diagrams and a torrent of ideas for how to make the device work. Einstein published a description in a journal, which produced, for a while, a potential sponsor. Paul Habicht was able to build a better version by October, but it had trouble keeping a charge. He brought the machine to Bern, where Einstein commandeered a lab in one of the schools and dragooned a local mechanic. By November the machine seemed to be working. It took another year or so to get a patent and begin to make some versions for sale. But even then, it never truly caught hold or found a market, and Einstein eventually lost interest.[13]

These practical exploits may have been fun, but Einstein's glorious isolation from the priesthood of academic physicists was starting to have more drawbacks than advantages. In a paper he wrote in the spring of 1907, he began by exuding a joyful self-assurance about having neither the library nor the inclination to know what other theorists had written on the topic. "Other authors might have already clarified part of what I am going to say," he wrote. "I felt I could dispense with doing a literature search (which would have been very troublesome for me), especially since there is good reason to hope that others will fill this gap." However, when he was commissioned to write a major yearbook piece on relativity later that year, there was slightly less cockiness in his warning to the editor that he might not be aware of all the literature. "Unfortunately I am not in a position to acquaint myself about everything that has been published on this subject," he wrote, "because the library is closed in my free time."[14]

That year he applied for a position at the University of Bern as a *privatdozent*, a starter rung on the academic ladder, which involved giving lectures and collecting a small fee from anyone who felt like showing up. To become a professor at most European universities, it helped to serve such an apprenticeship. With his application Einstein enclosed seventeen papers he had published, including the ones on relativity and light quanta. He was also expected to include an unpublished paper known as a *habilitation* thesis, but he decided not to bother writing one, as this requirement was sometimes waived for those who had "other outstanding achievements."

Only one professor on the faculty committee supported hiring him without requiring him to write a new thesis, "in view of the important scientific achievements of Herr Einstein." The others disagreed, and the requirement was not waived. Not surprisingly, Einstein considered the matter "amusing." He did not write the special *habilitation* or get the post.[15]

The Equivalence of Gravity and Acceleration

Einstein's road to the general theory of relativity began in November 1907, when he was struggling against a deadline to finish an article for a science yearbook explaining his special theory of relativity. Two limitations of that theory still bothered him: it applied only to uniform constant-velocity motion (things felt and behaved differently if your speed or direction was changing), and it did not incorporate Newton's theory of gravity.

"I was sitting in a chair in the patent office at Bern when all of a sudden a thought occurred to me," he recalled. "If a person falls freely, he will not feel his own weight." That realization, which "startled" him, launched him on an arduous eight-year effort to generalize his special theory of relativity and "impelled me toward a theory of gravitation."[16] Later, he would grandly call it "the happiest* thought in my life."[17]

The tale of the falling man has become an iconic one, and in some accounts it actually involves a painter who fell from the roof of an apartment building near the patent office.[18] In fact, probably like other great tales of gravitational discovery—Galileo dropping objects from the Tower of Pisa and the apple falling on Newton's head[19]—it was embellished in popular lore and was more of a thought experiment than a real occurrence. Despite Einstein's propensity to focus on science rather than the merely personal, even he was not likely to watch a real human plunging off a roof and think of gravitational theory, much less call it the happiest thought in his life.

Einstein refined his thought experiment so that the falling man was in an enclosed chamber, such as an elevator in free fall above the earth.

---

* The German phrase he used was "der glücklichste Gedanke," which has usually been translated as "happiest" thought, but perhaps in this context is more properly translated as "luckiest" or "most fortunate."

In this falling chamber (at least until it crashed), the man would feel weightless. Any objects he emptied from his pocket and let loose would float alongside him.

Looking at it another way, Einstein imagined a man in an enclosed chamber floating in deep space "far removed from stars and other appreciable masses." He would experience the same perceptions of weightlessness. "Gravitation naturally does not exist for this observer. He must fasten himself with strings to the floor, otherwise the slightest impact against the floor will cause him to rise slowly towards the ceiling."

Then Einstein imagined that a rope was hooked onto the roof of the chamber and pulled up with a constant force. "The chamber together with the observer then begin to move 'upwards' with a uniformly accelerated motion." The man inside will feel himself pressed to the floor. "He is then standing in the chest in exactly the same way as anyone stands in a room of a house on our earth." If he pulls something from his pocket and lets go, it will fall to the floor "with an accelerated relative motion" that is the same no matter the weight of the object— just as Galileo discovered to be the case for gravity. "The man in the chamber will thus come to the conclusion that he and the chest are in a gravitational field. Of course he will be puzzled for a moment as to why the chest does not fall in this gravitational field. Just then, however, he discovers the hook in the middle of the lid of the chest and the rope which is attached to it, and he consequently comes to the conclusion that the chamber is suspended at rest in the gravitational field."

"Ought we to smile at the man and say that he errs in his conclusion?" Einstein asked. Just as with special relativity, there was no right or wrong perception. "We must rather admit that his mode of grasping the situation violates neither reason nor known mechanical laws." [20]

A related way that Einstein addressed this same issue was typical of his ingenuity: he examined a phenomenon that was so very well-known that scientists rarely puzzled about it. Every object has a "gravitational mass," which determines its weight on the earth's surface or, more generally, the tug between it and any other object. It also has an "inertial mass," which determines how much force must be applied to it in order to make it accelerate. As Newton noted, the inertial mass of an object is always the same as its gravitational mass, even though they are defined differently. This was obviously more than a mere coincidence, but no one had fully explained why.

Uncomfortable with two explanations for what seemed to be one phenomenon, Einstein probed the equivalence of inertial mass and gravitational mass using his thought experiment. If we imagine that the enclosed elevator is being accelerated upward in a region of outer space where there is no gravity, then the downward force felt by the man inside (or the force that tugs downward on an object hanging from the ceiling by a string) is due to *inertial* mass. If we imagine that the enclosed elevator is at rest in a gravitational field, then the downward force felt by the man inside (or the force that tugs downward on an object hanging from the ceiling by a string) is due to *gravitational* mass. But inertial mass always equals gravitational mass. "From this correspondence," said Einstein, "it follows that it is impossible to discover by experiment whether a given system of coordinates is accelerated, or whether . . . the observed effects are due to a gravitational field."[21]

Einstein called this "the equivalence principle."[22] The local effects of gravity and of acceleration are equivalent. This became a foundation for his attempt to generalize his theory of relativity so that it was not restricted just to systems that moved with a uniform velocity. The basic insight that he would develop over the next eight years was that "the effects we ascribe to gravity and the effects we ascribe to acceleration are both produced by one and the same structure."[23]

Einstein's approach to general relativity again showed how his mind tended to work:

- He was disquieted when there were two seemingly unrelated theories for the same observable phenomenon. That had been the case with the moving coil or moving magnet producing the same observable electric current, which he resolved with the special theory of relativity. Now it was the case with the differing definitions of inertial mass and gravitational mass, which he began to resolve by building on the equivalence principle.
- He was likewise uncomfortable when a theory made distinctions

that could not be observed in nature. That had been the case with observers in uniform motion: there was no way of determining who was at rest and who was in motion. Now it was also, apparently, the case for observers in accelerated motion: there was no way of telling who was accelerating and who was in a gravitational field.

- He was eager to generalize theories rather than settling for having them restricted to a special case. There should not, he felt, be one set of principles for the special case of constant-velocity motion and a different set for all other types of motion. His life was a constant quest for unifying theories.

In November 1907, working against the deadline imposed by the *Yearbook of Radioactivity and Electronics,* Einstein tacked on a fifth section to his article on relativity that sketched out his new ideas. "So far we have applied the principle of relativity . . . only to nonaccelerated reference systems," he began. "Is it conceivable that the principle of relativity applies to systems that are accelerated relative to each other?"

Imagine two environments, he said, one being accelerated and the other resting in a gravitational field.[24] There is no physical experiment you can do that would tell these situations apart. "In the discussion that follows, we shall therefore assume the complete physical equivalence of a gravitational field and a corresponding acceleration of the reference system."

Using various mathematical calculations that can be made about an accelerated system, Einstein proceeded to show that, if his notions were correct, clocks would run more slowly in a more intense gravitational field. He also came up with many predictions that could be tested, including that light should be bent by gravity and that the wavelength of light emitted from a source with a large mass, such as the sun, should increase slightly in what has become known as the gravitational redshift. "On the basis of some ruminating, which, though daring, does have something going for it, I have arrived at the view that the gravitational difference might be the cause of the shift to the red end of the spectrum," he explained to a colleague. "A bending of light rays by gravity also follows from these arguments."[25]

It would take Einstein another eight years, until November 1915, to work out the fundamentals of this theory and find the math to express it. Then it would take another four years before the most vivid of his predictions, the extent to which gravity would bend light, was verified by dramatic observations. But at least Einstein now had a vision, one that started him on the road toward one of the most elegant and impressive achievements in the history of physics: the general theory of relativity.

Winning a Professorship

By the beginning of 1908, even as such academic stars as Max Planck and Wilhelm Wien were writing to ask for his insights, Einstein had tempered his aspirations to be a university professor. Instead, he had begun, believe it or not, to seek work as a high school teacher. "This craving," he told Marcel Grossmann, who had helped him get the patent-office job, "comes only from my ardent wish to be able to continue my private scientific work under easier conditions."

He was even eager to go back to the Technical School in Winterhur, where he had briefly been a substitute teacher. "How does one go about this?" he asked Grossmann. "Could I possibly call on somebody and talk him into the great worth of my admirable person as a teacher and a citizen? Wouldn't I make a bad impression on him (no Swiss-German dialect, my Semitic appearance, etc.)?" He had written papers that were transforming physics, but he did not know if that would help. "Would there be any point in my stressing my scientific papers on that occasion?"[26]

He also responded to an advertisement for a "teacher of mathematics and descriptive geometry" at a high school in Zurich, noting in his application "that I would be ready to teach physics as well." He ended up deciding to enclose all of the papers he had written thus far, including the special theory of relativity. There were twenty-one applicants. Einstein did not even make the list of three finalists.[27]

So Einstein finally overcame his pride and decided to write a thesis in order to become a *privatdozent* at Bern. As he explained to the patron there who had supported him, "The conversation I had with you in the city library, as well as the advice of several friends, has induced me to change my decision for the second time and to try my luck with a *habilitation* at the University of Bern after all."[28]

The paper he submitted, an extension of his revolutionary work on light quanta, was promptly accepted, and at the end of February 1908, he was made a *privatdozent*. He had finally scaled the walls, or at least the outer wall, of academe. But his post neither paid enough nor was important enough for him to give up his job at the patent office. His lectures at the University of Bern thus became simply one more thing for him to do.

His topic for the summer of 1908 was the theory of heat, held on Tuesday and Saturday at 7 a.m., and he initially attracted only three attendees: Michele Besso and two other colleagues who worked at the postal building. In the winter session he switched to the theory of radiation, and his three coworkers were joined by an actual student named Max Stern. By the summer of 1909, Stern was the only attendee, and Einstein canceled his lecturing. He had, in the meantime, begun to adopt his professorial look: both his hair and clothing became a victim of nature's tendency toward randomness.[29]

Alfred Kleiner, the University of Zurich physics professor who helped Einstein get his doctorate, had encouraged him to pursue the *privatdozent* position.[30] He also had waged a long effort, which succeeded in 1908, to convince the Zurich authorities to increase the university's stature by creating a new position in theoretical physics. It was not a full professorship; instead, it was an associate professorship under Kleiner.

It was the obvious post for Einstein, but there was one obstacle. Kleiner had another candidate in mind: his assistant Friedrich Adler, a pale and passionate political activist who had become friends with Einstein when they were both at the Polytechnic. Adler, whose father was the leader of the Social Democratic Party in Austria, was more disposed to political philosophy than theoretical physics. So he went to see Kleiner one morning in June 1908, and the two of them concluded that Adler was not right for the job and Einstein was.

In a letter to his father, Adler recounted the conversation and said that Einstein "had no understanding how to relate to people" and had been "treated by the professors at the Polytechnic with outright contempt." But Adler said he deserved the job because of his genius and was likely to get it. "They have a bad conscience over how they treated him earlier. The scandal is being felt not only here but in Germany that such a man would have to sit in the patent office."[31]

Adler made sure that the Zurich authorities, and for that matter everyone else, knew that he was officially stepping aside for his friend. "If it is possible to get a man like Einstein for our university, it would be absurd to appoint me," he wrote. That resolved the political issue for the councilor in charge of education, who was a partisan Social Democrat. "Ernst would have liked Adler, since he was a fellow party member," Einstein explained to Michele Besso. "But Adler's statements about himself and me made it impossible."[32]

So, at the end of June 1908, Kleiner traveled from Zurich to Bern to audit one of Einstein's *privatdozent* lectures and, as Einstein put it, "size up the beast." Alas, it was not a great show. "I really did not lecture divinely," Einstein lamented to a friend, "partly because I was not well prepared, partly because being investigated got on my nerves a bit." Kleiner sat listening with a wrinkled brow, and after the lecture he informed Einstein that his teaching style was not good enough to qualify him for the professorship. Einstein calmly claimed that he considered the job "quite unnecessary."[33]

Kleiner went back to Zurich and reported that Einstein "holds monologues" and was "a long way from being a teacher." That seemed to end his chances. As Adler informed his powerful father, "The situation has therefore changed, and the Einstein business is closed." Einstein pretended to be sanguine. "The business with the professorship fell through, but that's all right with me," he wrote a friend. "There are enough teachers even without me."[34]

In fact Einstein was upset, and he became even more so when he heard that Kleiner's criticism of his teaching skills was being widely circulated, even in Germany. So he wrote to Kleiner, angrily reproaching him "for spreading unfavorable rumors about me." He was already finding it difficult to get a proper academic job, and Kleiner's assessment would make it impossible.

There was some validity to Kleiner's criticism. Einstein was never an inspired teacher, and his lectures tended to be regarded as disorganized until his celebrity ensured that every stumble he made was trans-formed into a charming anecdote. Nevertheless, Kleiner relented. He said that he would be pleased to help him get the Zurich job if he could only show "some teaching ability."

Einstein replied by suggesting that he come to Zurich to give a full-fledged (and presumably well-prepared) lecture to the physics society there, which he did in February 1909. "I was lucky," Einstein reported soon after. "Contrary to my habit, I lectured well on that occasion."[35] When he went to call on Kleiner afterward, the professor intimated that a job offer would soon follow.

A few days after Einstein returned to Bern, Kleiner provided his of-ficial recommendation to the University of Zurich faculty. "Einstein ranks among the most important theoretical physicists and has been recognized as such since his work on the relativity principle," he wrote. As for Einstein's teaching skills, he said as politely as possible that they were ripe for improvement: "Dr. Einstein will prove his worth also as a teacher, because he is too intelligent and too conscientious not to be open to advice when necessary."[36]

One issue was Einstein's Jewishness. Some faculty members con-sidered this a potential problem, but they were assured by Kleiner that Einstein did not exhibit the "unpleasant peculiarities" supposedly asso-ciated with Jews. Their conclusion is a revealing look at both the anti-Semitism of the time and the attempts to rise above it:

> The expressions of our colleague Kleiner, based on several years of per-sonal contact, were all the more valuable for the committee as well as for the faculty as a whole since Herr Dr. Einstein is an Israelite and since pre-cisely to the Israelites among scholars are inscribed (in numerous cases not entirely without cause) all kinds of unpleasant peculiarities of char-acter, such as intrusiveness, impudence, and a shopkeeper's mentality in the perception of their academic position. It should be said, however, that also among the Israelites there exist men who do not exhibit a trace of these disagreeable qualities and that it is not proper, therefore, to disqual-ify a man only because he happens to be a Jew. Indeed, one occasionally finds people also among non-Jewish scholars who in regard to a commer-cial perception and utilization of their academic profession develop qual-ities that are usually considered as specifically Jewish. Therefore, neither the committee nor the faculty as a whole considered it compatible with its dignity to adopt anti-Semitism as a matter of policy.[37]

The secret faculty vote in late March 1909 was ten in favor and one abstention. Einstein was offered his first professorship, four years after he had revolutionized physics. Unfortunately, his proposed salary was less than what he was making at the patent office, so he declined. Finally, the Zurich authorities raised their offer, and Einstein accepted. "So, now I too am an official member of the guild of whores," he exulted to a colleague.[38]

One person who saw a newspaper notice about Einstein's appointment was a Basel housewife named Anna Meyer-Schmid. Ten years earlier, when she was an unmarried girl of 17, they had met during one of Einstein's vacations with his mother at the Hotel Paradies. Most of the guests had seemed to him "philistines," but he took a liking to Anna and even wrote a poem in her album: "What should I inscribe for you here? / I could think of many things / Including a kiss / On your tiny little mouth / If you're angry about it / Do not start to cry / The best punishment / Is to give me one too." He signed it, "Your rascally friend."[39]

In response to a congratulatory postcard from her, Einstein replied with a polite and mildly suggestive letter. "I probably cherish the memory of the lovely weeks that I was allowed to spend near you in the Paradies more than you do," he wrote. "So now I've become such a big schoolmaster that my name is even mentioned in the newspapers. But I have remained a simple fellow." He noted that he had married his college friend Marić, but he gave her his office address. "If you ever happen to be in Zurich and have time, look me up there; it would give me great pleasure."[40]

Whether or not Einstein intended his response to hover uncertainly between innocence and suggestiveness, Anna's eyes apparently snapped it into the latter position. She wrote a letter back, which Marić intercepted. Her jealousy aroused, Marić then wrote a letter to Anna's husband claiming (wishfully more than truthfully) that Einstein was outraged by Anna's "inappropriate letter" and brazen attempt to rekindle a relationship.

Einstein ended up having to calm matters with an apology to the husband. "I am very sorry if I have caused you distress by my careless behavior," he wrote. "I answered the congratulatory card your wife sent me on the occasion of my appointment too heartily and thereby re-awakened the old affection we had for each other. But this was not done with impure intentions. The behavior of your wife, for whom I have the greatest respect, was totally honorable. It was wrong of my wife—and excusable only on account of extreme jealousy—to behave—without my knowledge—the way she did."

Although the incident itself was of no consequence, it marked a turn in Einstein's relationship with Marić. In his eyes, her brooding jealousy was making her darker. Decades later, still rankling at Marić's behavior, he wrote to Anna's daughter asserting, with a brutal bluntness, that his wife's jealousy had been a pathological flaw typical of a woman of such "uncommon ugliness."[41]

Marić indeed had a jealous streak. She resented not only her husband's flirtations with other women but also the time he spent with male colleagues. Now that he had become a professor, she succumbed to a professional envy that was understandable given her own curtailed scientific career. "With that kind of fame, he does not have much time left for his wife," she told her friend Helene Savić. "You wrote that I must be jealous of science. But what can you do? One gets the pearl, the other the box."

In particular, Marić worried that her husband's fame would make him colder and more self-centered. "I am very happy for his success, because he really does deserve it," she wrote in another letter. "I only hope that fame does not exert a detrimental influence on his human side."[42]

In one sense, Marić's worries proved unwarranted. Even as his fame increased exponentially, Einstein would retain a personal simplicity, an unaffected style, and at least a veneer of genial humility. But viewed from a different reference frame, there were transformations to his human side. Sometime around 1909, he began drifting apart from his wife. His resistance to chains and bonds increasingly led him to escape into his work while taking a detached approach to the realm he dismissed as "the merely personal."

On one of his last days working at the patent office, he received a large envelope with an elegant sheet covered in what seemed to be Latin calligraphy. Because it seemed odd and impersonal, he threw it

in the wastebasket. It was, in fact, an invitation to be one of those receiving an honorary doctorate at the July 1909 commemoration of the
founding of Geneva's university, and authorities there finally got a
friend of Einstein to persuade him to attend. Einstein brought only
a straw hat and an informal suit, so he stood out rather strangely, both
in the parade and at the opulent formal dinner that night. Amused by
the whole situation, he turned to the patrician seated next to him and
speculated about the austere Protestant Reformation leader who had
founded the university: "Do you know what Calvin would have done
had he been here?" The gentleman, befuddled, said no. Einstein
replied, "He would have erected an enormous stake and had us all
burnt for our sinful extravagance." As Einstein later recalled, "The man
never addressed another word to me."[43]

Light Can Be Wave and Particle

Also at the end of the summer of 1909, Einstein was invited to address the annual *Naturforscher* conference, the preeminent meeting of
German-speaking scientists, which was held that year in Salzburg. Organizers had put both relativity and the quantum nature of light on the
agenda, and they expected him to speak on the former. Instead, Einstein decided that he preferred to emphasize what he considered the
more pressing issue: how to interpret quantum theory and reconcile it
with the wave theory of light that Maxwell had so elegantly formulated.

After his "happiest thought" at the end of 1907 about how the
equivalence of gravity and acceleration might lead to a generalization
of relativity theory, Einstein had put that subject aside to focus instead
on what he called "the radiation problem" (i.e., quantum theory). The
more he thought about his "heuristic" notion that light was made up of
quanta, or indivisible packets, the more he worried that he and Planck
had wrought a revolution that would destroy the classical foundations
of physics, especially Maxwell's equations. "I have come to this pessimistic view mainly as a result of endless, vain efforts to interpret . . .
Planck's constant in an intuitive way," he wrote a fellow physicist early
in 1908. "I even seriously doubt that it will be possible to maintain the

general validity of Maxwell's equations."[44] (As it turned out, his love of Maxwell's equations was well placed. They are among the few elements of theoretical physics to remain unchanged by both the relativity and quantum revolutions that Einstein helped launch.)

When Einstein, still not officially a professor, arrived at the Salzburg conference in September 1909, he finally met Max Planck and other giants that he had known only through letters. On the afternoon of the third day, he stepped in front of more than a hundred famed scientists and delivered a speech that Wolfgang Pauli, who was to become a pioneer of quantum mechanics, later pronounced "one of the landmarks in the development of theoretical physics."

Einstein began by explaining how the wave theory of light was no longer complete. Light (or any radiation) could also be regarded, he said, as a beam of particles or packets of energy, which he said was akin to what Newton had posited. "Light has certain basic properties that can be understood more readily from the standpoint of the Newtonian emission theory than from the standpoint of the wave theory," he declared. "I thus believe that the next phase of theoretical physics will bring us a theory of light that can be interpreted as a kind of fusion of the wave and of the emission theories of light."

Combining particle theory with wave theory, he warned, would bring "a profound change." This was not a good thing, he feared. It could undermine the certainties and determinism inherent in classical physics.

For a moment, Einstein mused that perhaps such a fate could be avoided by accepting Planck's more limited interpretation of quanta: that they were features only of how radiation was emitted and absorbed by a surface rather than a feature of the actual light wave as it propagated through space. "Would it not be possible," he asked, "to retain at least the equations for the propagation of radiation and conceive only the processes of emission and absorption differently?" But after comparing the behavior of light to the behavior of gas molecules, as he had done in his 1905 light quanta paper, Einstein concluded that, alas, this was not possible.

As a result, Einstein said, light must be regarded as behaving like both an undulating wave and a stream of particles. "These two structural properties simultaneously displayed by radiation," he declared at the end of his talk, "should not be considered as mutually incompatible."[45]

It was the first well-conceived promulgation of the wave-particle duality of light, and it had implications as profound as Einstein's earlier theoretical breakthroughs. "Is it possible to combine energy quanta and the wave principles of radiation?" he merrily wrote to a physicist friend. "Appearances are against it, but the Almighty—it seems—managed the trick."[46]

A vibrant discussion followed Einstein's speech, led by Planck himself. Still unwilling to embrace the physical reality underlying the mathematical constant that he had devised nine years earlier, or to accept the revolutionary ramifications envisioned by Einstein, Planck now played protector of the old order. He admitted that radiation involved discrete "quanta, which are to be conceived as atoms of action." But he insisted that these quanta existed *only* as part of the process of radiation being emitted or absorbed. "The question is where to look for these quanta," he said. "According to Mr. Einstein, it would be necessary to conceive that free radiation in a vacuum, and thus the light waves themselves consist of atomistic quanta, and hence force us to give up Maxwell's equations. This seems to me a step that is not yet necessary."[47]

Within two decades, Einstein would assume a similar role as protector of the old order. Indeed, he was already looking for ways out of the eerie dilemmas raised by quantum theory. "I am very hopeful that I will solve the radiation problem, and that I will do so without light quanta," he wrote a young physicist he was working with.[48]

It was all too mystifying, at least for the time being. So as he moved up the professorial ranks in the German-speaking universities of Europe, he turned his attention back to the topic that was uniquely his own, relativity, and for a while became a refugee from the wonderland of the quanta. As he lamented to a friend, "The more successes the quantum theory enjoys, the sillier it looks."[49]

CHAPTER EIGHT

THE WANDERING PROFESSOR

1909–1914

Zurich, 1909

As a self-assured 17-year-old, Einstein had enrolled at the Zurich Polytechnic and met Mileva Marić, the woman he would marry. Now, in October 1909, at age 30, he was returning to that city to take up his post as a junior professor at the nearby University of Zurich.

Their homecoming restored, at least temporarily, some of the romance to their relationship. Marić was thrilled to be back in their original nesting ground, and by the end of their first month there she became pregnant again.

The apartment they rented was in a building where, they happily discovered, Friedrich Adler and his wife lived, and the couples became even closer friends. "They run a bohemian household," Adler wrote his father approvingly. "The more I talk to Einstein, the more I realize that my favorable opinion of him was justified."

The two men discussed physics and philosophy most evenings, often retreating to the attic of the three-story building so they would not be disturbed by children or spouses. Adler introduced Einstein to the work of Pierre Duhem, whose 1906 book *La Théorie Physique* Adler had just published in German. Duhem offered a more holistic approach than Mach did to the relationship between theories and experimental evidence, one that seemed to influence Einstein as he staked out his own philosophy of science.[1]

Adler particularly respected Einstein's "most independent" mind. There was, he told his father, a nonconformist streak in Einstein that reflected an inner security but not an arrogance. "We find ourselves in agreement on questions that the majority of physicists would not even understand," Adler boasted.[2]

Einstein tried to persuade Adler to focus on science rather than be enticed into politics. "Be a little patient," he said. "You will certainly be my successor in Zurich one day." (Einstein was already assuming that he would move on to a more prestigious university.) But Adler ignored the advice and decided to become an editor at the Social Democratic Party newspaper. Loyalty to a party, Einstein felt, meant surrendering some independence of thought. Such conformity confounded him. "How an intelligent man can subscribe to a party I find a complete mystery," Einstein later lamented about Adler.[3]

Einstein was also reunited with his former classmate and note-taker Marcel Grossmann, who had helped him get his job at the patent office and was now a professor of math at their old Polytechnic. Einstein would often visit Grossmann after lunch for help with the complex geometry and calculus he needed to extend relativity into a more general field theory.

Einstein was even able to forge a friendship with the other distinguished math professor at the Polytechnic, Adolf Hurwitz, whose classes he had often skipped and who had spurned his plea for a job. Einstein became a regular at the Sunday music recitals at Hurwitz's home. When Hurwitz told him during a walk one day that his daughter had been given a math homework problem she did not understand, Einstein showed up that afternoon to help her solve it.[4]

As Kleiner predicted, Einstein's teaching talents improved. He was not a polished lecturer, but instead used informality to his advantage. "When he took his chair in shabby attire with trousers too short for him, we were skeptical," recalled Hans Tanner, who attended most of Einstein's Zurich lectures. Instead of prepared notes, Einstein used a card-sized strip of paper with scribbles. So the students got to watch him develop his thoughts as he spoke. "We obtained some insight into his working technique," said Tanner. "We certainly appreciated this more than any stylistically perfect lecture."

At each step of the way, Einstein would pause and ask the students if they were following him, and he even permitted interruptions. "This comradely contact between teacher and student was, at that time, a rare occurrence," according to Adolf Fisch, another who attended the lectures. Sometimes he would take a break and let the students gather around him for casual conversation. "With an impulsiveness and naturalness he would take students by the arm to discuss things," recalled Tanner.

During one lecture, Einstein found himself momentarily stumped about the steps needed to complete a calculation. "There must be some silly mathematical transformation that I can't find for a moment," he said. "Can one of you gentlemen see it?" Not surprisingly, none of them could. So Einstein continued: "Then leave a quarter of a page. We won't lose any time." Ten minutes later, Einstein interrupted himself in the middle of another point and exclaimed, "I've got it." As Tanner later marveled, "During the complicated development of his theme he had still found time to reflect upon the nature of that particular mathematical transformation."

At the end of many of his evening lectures, Einstein would ask, "Who's coming to the Café Terasse?" There, with an informal cadre on a terrace overlooking the Limmat River, they would talk until closing time.

On one occasion, Einstein asked if anyone wanted to come back to his apartment. "This morning I received some work from Planck in which there must be a mistake," he said. "We could read it together." Tanner and another student took him up on the offer and followed him home. There they all pored over Planck's paper. "See if you can spot the fault while I make some coffee," he said.

After a while, Tanner replied, "You must be mistaken, Herr Professor, there is no error in it."

"Yes, there is," Einstein said, pointing to some discrepancies in the data, "for otherwise that and that would become that and that." It was a vivid example of Einstein's great strength: he could look at a complex mathematical equation, which for others was merely an abstraction, and picture the physical reality that lay behind it.

Tanner was astounded. "Let's write to Professor Planck," he suggested, "and tell him of the mistake."

Einstein had by then become slightly more tactful, especially with those he placed on a pedestal, such as Planck and Lorentz. "We won't tell him he made a mistake," he said. "The result is correct, but the proof is faulty. We'll simply write and tell him how the real proof should run. The main thing is the content, not the mathematics."[5]

Despite his work on his machine to measure electrical charges, Einstein had become a confirmed theorist rather than experimental physicist. When he was asked during his second year as a professor to supervise laboratory work, he was dismayed. He hardly dared, he told Tanner, "pick up a piece of apparatus for fear it might blow up." To another eminent professor he confided, "My fears regarding the laboratory were rather well founded."[6]

As he was finishing his first academic year at Zurich, in July 1910, Marić gave birth, again with difficulty, to their second son, named Eduard and called Tete. She was ill for weeks afterward. Her doctor, contending that she was overworked, suggested that Einstein find a way to make more money and pay for a maid. Marić was annoyed and protective. "Isn't it clear to anyone that my husband works himself half dead?" she said. Instead, her mother came down from Novi Sad to help.[7]

Throughout his life, Einstein would sometimes appear aloof toward his two sons, especially Eduard, who suffered from increasingly severe mental illness as he grew older. But when they were young, he tended to be a good father. "When my mother was busy around the house, father would put aside his work and watch over us for hours, bouncing us on his knee," Hans Albert later recalled. "I remember he would tell us stories—and he often played the violin in an effort to keep us quiet."

One of his strengths as a thinker, if not as a parent, was that he had the ability, and the inclination, to tune out all distractions, a category that to him sometimes included his children and family. "Even the loudest baby-crying didn't seem to disturb Father," Hans Albert said. "He could go on with his work completely impervious to noise."

One day his student Tanner came for a visit and found Einstein in his study poring over a pile of papers. He was writing with his right hand and holding Eduard with his left. Hans Albert was playing with toy bricks and trying to get his attention. "Wait a minute, I've nearly finished," Einstein said, as he handed Eduard to Tanner and kept scribbling his equations. "It gave me," said Tanner, "a glimpse into his immense powers of concentration."[8]

Prague, 1911

Einstein had been in Zurich less than six months when he received, in March 1910, a solicitation to consider a more prestigious job: a full professorship at the German part of the University of Prague. Both the university and the academic position were a step up; however, moving from the familiar and friendly Zurich to the less congenial Prague would be disruptive for his family. For Einstein, the professional considerations outweighed the personal ones.

He was again going through difficult periods at home. "The bad mood that you noticed in me had nothing to do with you," he wrote to his mother, who was now living in Berlin. "To dwell on the things that depress or anger us does not help in overcoming them. One must knock them down alone."

His scientific work, on the other hand, was giving him great pleasure, and he expressed excitement about his possible new opportunity. "It is most probable that I will be offered the position of full professor at a large university with a significantly better salary than I now have."[9]

When word of Einstein's possible move spread in Zurich, fifteen of his students, led by Hans Tanner, signed a petition urging officials there "to do your utmost to keep this outstanding researcher and teacher at our university." They stressed the importance of having a professor in "this newly created discipline" of theoretical physics, and they extolled him personally in effusive terms. "Professor Einstein has an amazing talent for presenting the most difficult problems of theoretical physics so clearly and so comprehensibly that it is a great delight for us to follow his lectures, and he is so good at establishing a perfect rapport with his audience."[10]

The Zurich authorities were so eager to keep him that they raised his salary from its current 4,500 francs, which was the same as he made as a patent examiner, to 5,500 francs. Those attempting to lure him to Prague, on the other hand, were having a more difficult time.

The faculty department at Prague had settled on Einstein as its first choice and forwarded the recommendation to the education ministry in Vienna. (Prague was then part of the Austro-Hungarian Empire, and such an appointment had to be approved by Emperor Franz Joseph and his ministers.) The report was accompanied by the highest possible recommendation from the best possible authority, Max Planck. Einstein's theory of relativity "probably exceeds in audacity everything that has been achieved so far in speculative science," Planck proclaimed. "This principle has brought about a revolution in our physical picture of the world that can be compared only to that produced by Copernicus." In a comment that might later have seemed prescient to Einstein, Planck added, "Non-Euclidean geometry is child's play by comparison."[11]

Planck's imprimatur should have been enough. But it wasn't. The ministry decided that it preferred the second-place candidate, Gustav Jaumann, who had two advantages: he was Austrian, and he was not Jewish. "I did not get the call to Prague," Einstein lamented to a friend in August. "I was proposed by the faculty, but because of my Semitic origin the ministry did not approve."

Jaumann, however, soon discovered that he was the faculty's second choice, and he erupted. "If Einstein has been proposed as the first choice because of the belief that he has greater achievements to his credit," he declared, "then I will have nothing to do with a university that chases after modernity and does not appreciate merit." So by October 1910, Einstein could confidently declare that his own appointment was "almost certain."

There was one final hurdle, also dealing with religion. Being a Jew was a disadvantage; being a nonbeliever who claimed *no* religion was a disqualifier. The empire required that all of its servants, including professors, be a member of some religion. On his official forms, Einstein had written that he had none. "Einstein is as unpractical as a child in cases like this," Friedrich Adler's wife noted.

As it turned out, Einstein's desire for the job was greater than his ornery impracticality. He agreed to write "Mosaic" as his faith, and he also accepted Austro-Hungarian citizenship, with the proviso that he was allowed to remain a Swiss citizen as well. Along with the German citizenship that he had forsaken but that would soon be foisted back on him, that meant he had held, off and on, three citizenships by the age of 32. In January 1911, he was officially appointed to the post, with a pay twice what he had been making before his recent raise. He agreed to move to Prague that March.[12]

Einstein had two scientific heroes he had never met—Ernst Mach and Hendrik Lorentz—and he was able to visit them both before his move to Prague. When he went to Vienna for his formal presentation to the ministers there, he called on Mach, who lived in a suburb of that city. The aging physicist and preacher of empiricism, who so deeply influenced the Olympia Academy and instilled in Einstein a skepticism about unobservable concepts such as absolute time, had a gnarly beard and gnarlier personality. "Please speak loudly to me," he barked when Einstein entered his room. "In addition to my other unpleasant characteristics I am also almost stone deaf."

Einstein wanted to convince Mach of the reality of atoms, which the old man had long rejected as being imaginary constructs of the human mind. "Let us suppose that by assuming the existence of atoms in a gas we were able to predict an observable property of this gas that could not be predicted on the basis of non-atomistic theory," Einstein asked. "Would you then accept such a hypothesis?"

"If with the help of the atomic hypothesis one could actually establish a connection between several observable properties which without it would remain isolated, then I should say that this hypothesis was an 'economical' one," Mach grudgingly replied.

It was not a full acceptance, but it was enough for Einstein. "For the moment Einstein was satisfied," his friend Philipp Frank noted. Nevertheless, Einstein began edging away from Mach's skepticism about any theories of reality not built on directly observable data. He developed, said Frank, "a certain aversion to the Machist philosophy."[13] It was the beginning of an important conversion.

Just before moving to Prague, Einstein went to the Dutch town of Leiden to meet Lorentz. Marić accompanied him, and they accepted an invitation to stay with Lorentz and his wife. Einstein wrote that he was looking forward to having a conversation on "the radiation problem," adding, "I wish to assure you in advance that I am not the orthodox light-quantizer for whom you take me."[14]

Einstein had long idolized Lorentz from afar. Just before he went to visit, he wrote a friend: "I admire this man like no other; I might say, I love him." The feeling was reinforced when they finally met. They stayed up late on Saturday night discussing such issues as the relationship between temperature and electrical conductivity.

Lorentz thought he had caught Einstein in a small mathematical mistake in one of his papers on light quanta, but in fact, as Einstein noted, it was simply "a one-time writing error" where he had left out a "$\frac{1}{2}$" that was included later in the paper.[15] Both the hospitality and "scientific stimulus" made Einstein effusive in his next letter. "You radiate so much goodness and benevolence," he wrote, "that the troubling conviction that I did not deserve the great kindness and honors could not even enter my mind during my stay at your house."[16]

Lorentz became, in the words of Abraham Pais, "the one father figure in Einstein's life." After his pleasant visit to Lorentz's study in Leiden, he would return whenever he could find an excuse. The atmosphere of such meetings was captured by their colleague Paul Ehrenfest:

> The best easy chair was carefully pushed in place next to the large work table for his esteemed guest. A cigar was given to him, and then Lorentz quietly began to formulate questions concerning Einstein's theory of the bending of light in a gravitational field . . . As Lorentz spoke on, Einstein began to puff less frequently on his cigar, and he sat more intently in his armchair. And when Lorentz had finished, Einstein bent over the slip of paper on which Lorentz had written mathematical formulas. The cigar was out, and Einstein pensively twisted his finger in a lock of hair over his right ear. Lorentz sat smiling at an Einstein completely lost in meditation, exactly the way that a father looks at a particularly beloved son—full of confidence that the youngster will crack the nut he has given him, but eager to see how. Suddenly, Einstein's head sat up joyfully; he had it. Still a bit of give and take, interrupting one another, a partial disagreement, very quick clarification and a complete mutual understanding, and then both men with beaming eyes skimming over the shining riches of the new theory.[17]

When Lorentz died in 1928, Einstein would say in his eulogy, "I stand at the grave of the greatest and noblest man of our times." And in 1953, for the celebration of the hundredth anniversary of Lorentz's birth, Einstein wrote an essay on his importance. "Whatever came from this supreme mind was as lucid and beautiful as a good work of art," he wrote. "He meant more to me personally than anybody else I have met in my lifetime."[18]

Marić was unhappy about moving to Prague. "I am not going there gladly and I expect very little pleasure," she wrote a friend. But initially, until the city's dirtiness and snobbishness became oppressive, their life there was nice enough. They had electric lighting in their home for the first time, and both the space and money for a live-in maid. "The people are haughty, shabby-genteel, or subservient, depending on their lot in life," Einstein said. "Many of them possess a certain grace."[19]

From Einstein's office at the university he could look down on a beautiful park with shady trees and manicured gardens. In the morning, it would be filled just with women, and in the afternoon just with men. Some walked alone as if deep in thought, Einstein noticed, while others clustered in groups holding animated arguments. Eventually, Einstein asked what the park was. It belonged, he was told, to an insane asylum. When he showed his friend Philipp Frank the view, Einstein commented ruefully, "Those are the madmen who do not occupy themselves with the quantum theory."[20]

The Einsteins became acquainted with Bertha Fanta, a delightfully cultured woman who hosted at her home a literary and musical salon for Prague's Jewish intelligentsia. Einstein was the ideal catch: a rising scholar who was willing, with equal gusto, to play the violin or discuss Hume and Kant, depending on the spirit of the occasion. Other habitués included the young writer Franz Kafka and his friend Max Brod.

In his book *The Redemption of Tycho Brahe*, Brod seemed to use (though he sometimes denied it) Einstein as the model for the character of Johannes Kepler, the brilliant astronomer who had been Brahe's assistant in Prague in 1600. The character is devoted to his scientific work and is always willing to throw away conventional thinking. But in the realm of the personal, he is protected from "the aberrations of feeling" by his aloof and abstracted air. "He had no heart and therefore nothing to fear from the world," Brod wrote. "He was not capable of emotion or love." When the novel came out, a fellow scientist, Walther Nernst, said to Einstein, "You are this man Kepler." [21]

Not really. Despite the image he sometimes cast as a loner, Einstein continued to establish, as he had back in Zurich and Bern, intimate friendships and emotional bonds, particularly with fellow thinkers and scientists. One such friend was Paul Ehrenfest, a young Jewish physicist from Vienna who was teaching at the University of St. Petersburg but feeling professionally stymied there because of his background. In early 1912, he embarked on a trip through Europe looking for a new job, and on his way toward Prague contacted Einstein, with whom he had been corresponding about gravity and radiation. "Do stay at my house so that we can make good use of the time," Einstein responded. [22]

When Ehrenfest arrived one rainy Friday afternoon in February, a cigar-puffing Einstein and his wife were at the train station to meet him. They all walked to a café, where they compared the great cities of Europe. When Marić left, the discussion turned to science, most notably statistical mechanics, and they continued talking as they walked to Einstein's office. "On the way to the institute, first argument about everything," Ehrenfest recorded in his diary of the seven days he spent in Prague.

Ehrenfest was a mousy and insecure man, but his eagerness for friendship and his love of physics made it easy for him to forge a bond with Einstein. [23] They both seemed to crave arguing about science, and Einstein later said that "within a few hours we were friends as if Nature created us for each other." Their intense discussions continued the next day, as Einstein explained his efforts to generalize his theory of relativity. On Sunday evening, they relaxed a bit by performing Brahms, with Ehrenfest on piano, Einstein on violin, and 7-year-old Hans Albert singing. "Yes we will be friends," Ehrenfest wrote in his diary that night. "Was awfully happy." [24]

Einstein was already thinking of leaving Prague, and he suggested Ehrenfest as a possible successor. But he "adamantly refuses to profess any religious affiliation," Einstein lamented. Unlike Einstein, who was willing to relent and write "Mosaic" on his official forms, Ehrenfest had abandoned Judaism and would not profess otherwise. "Your stubborn refusal to acknowledge any religious affiliation really *bugs* me," Einstein wrote him in April. "Drop it for your children's sake. After all, after becoming a professor here you could revert to this strange hobby horse of yours."[25]

Matters eventually came to a happy resolution when Ehrenfest accepted an offer, which Einstein had earlier received but declined, to replace the revered Lorentz, who was cutting back from full-time teaching at the University of Leiden. Einstein was thrilled, for it meant he would now have two friends there to visit regularly. It became, for Einstein, almost a second academic home and a way to escape the oppressive atmosphere he later found in Berlin. Almost every year for the next two decades, until 1933 when Ehrenfest committed suicide and Einstein moved to America, Einstein would make regular pilgrimages to see him and Lorentz in Leiden or at the seaside resorts nearby.[26]

The 1911 Solvay Conference

Ernest Solvay was a Belgian chemist and industrialist who reaped a fortune by inventing a method for making soda. Because he wanted to do something unusual yet useful with his money, and also because he had some odd theories of gravity that he wanted scientists to listen to, he decided to fund an elite gathering of Europe's top physicists. Scheduled for the end of October 1911, it eventually spawned a series of influential meetings, known as Solvay Conferences, that were held sporadically over the ensuing years.

Twenty of Europe's most famous scientists showed up at the Grand Hotel Metropole in Brussels. At 32, Einstein was the youngest. There was Max Planck, Henri Poincaré, Marie Curie, Ernest Rutherford, and Wilhelm Wien. The chemist Walther Nernst organized the event and acted as chaperone for the quirky Ernest Solvay. The kindly Hendrik Lorentz served as the chairman, as his fan Einstein put it, "with incomparable tact and unbelievable virtuosity."[27]

The focus of the conference was "the quantum problem," and Einstein was asked to present a paper on that topic, making him one of only eight "particularly competent members" thus honored. He expressed some annoyance, perhaps a bit more feigned than real, about the prestigious assignment. He dubbed the upcoming meeting "the witch's Sabbath" and complained to Besso, "My twaddle for the Brussels conference weighs down on me."[28]

Einstein's talk was titled "The Present State of the Problem of Specific Heats." Specific heat—the quantity of energy required to increase the temperature of a specific amount of substance by a certain amount—had been a specialty of Einstein's former professor and antagonist at the Zurich Polytechnic, Heinrich Weber. Weber had discovered some anomalies, especially at low temperatures, in the laws that were supposed to govern specific heat. Beginning in late 1906, Einstein had come up with what he called a "quantized" approach to the problem by surmising that the atoms in each substance could absorb energy only in discrete packets.

In his 1911 Solvay lecture, Einstein put these issues into the larger context of the so-called quantum problem. Was it possible, he asked, to avoid accepting the physical reality of these atomistic particles of light, which were like bullets aimed at the heart of Maxwell's equations and, indeed, all of classical physics?

Planck, who had pioneered the concept of the quanta, continued to insist that they came into play only when light was being emitted or absorbed. They were not a real-world feature of light itself, he argued. Einstein, in his talk to the conference, sorrowfully demurred: "These discontinuities, which we find so distasteful in Planck's theory, seem really to exist in nature."[29]

Really to exist in nature. It was, for Einstein, an odd phrase. To a pure proponent of Mach, or for that matter of Hume, the whole phrase "really to exist in nature" lacked clear meaning. In his special relativity theory, Einstein had avoided assuming the existence of such things as absolute time and absolute distance, because it seemed meaningless to say that they "really" existed in nature when they couldn't be observed. But henceforth, during the more than four decades in which he would express his discomfort with quantum theory, he increasingly sounded like a scientific realist, someone who believed that an underlying reality existed in nature that was independent of our ability to observe or measure it.

When he was finished, Einstein faced a barrage of challenges from Lorentz, Planck, Poincaré, and others. Some of what Einstein said, Lorentz rose to point out, "seems in fact to be totally incompatible with Maxwell's equations."

Einstein agreed, perhaps too readily, that "the quantum hypothesis is provisional" and that it "does not seem compatible with the experimentally verified conclusions of the wave theory." Somehow it was necessary, he told his questioners, to accommodate both wave and particle approaches to the understanding of light. "In addition to Maxwell's electrodynamics, which is essential to us, we must also admit a hypothesis such as that of quanta."[30]

It was unclear, even to Einstein, whether Planck was persuaded of the reality of quanta. "I largely succeeded in convincing Planck that my conception is correct, after he has struggled against it for so many years," Einstein wrote his friend Heinrich Zangger. But a week later, Einstein gave Zangger another report: "Planck stuck stubbornly to some undoubtedly wrong preconceptions."

As for Lorentz, Einstein remained as admiring as ever: "A living work of art! He was in my opinion the most intelligent of the theoreticians present." He dismissed Poincaré, who paid little attention to him, with a brusque stroke: "Poincaré was simply negative in general, and, all his acumen notwithstanding, he showed little grasp of the situation."[31]

Overall he gave low marks to the conference, where most of the time was spent bewailing rather than resolving quantum theory's threat to classical mechanics. "The congress in Brussels resembled the lamentations on the ruins of Jerusalem," he wrote Besso. "Nothing positive has come out of it."[32]

There was one interesting sideshow for Einstein: the romance between the widowed Marie Curie and the married Paul Langevin. Dignified and dedicated, Madame Curie was the first woman to win a Nobel Prize; she shared the 1903 physics prize with her husband and one other scientist for their work on radiation. Three years later, her husband was killed by a horse-drawn wagon. She was bereft, and so was her late husband's protégé, Langevin, who taught physics at the Sorbonne with the Curies. Langevin was trapped in a marriage with a wife who physically abused him, and soon he and Marie Curie were having an affair in a Paris apartment. His wife had someone break into it and steal their love letters.

Just as the Solvay Conference was getting under way, with both Curie and Langevin in attendance, the purloined letters began appearing in a Paris tabloid as a prelude to a sensational divorce case. In addition, at that very moment, it was announced that Curie had won the Nobel Prize in chemistry, for discovering radium and polonium.* A member of the Swedish Academy wrote her to suggest that she not appear to receive it, given the furor raised by her relationship with Langevin, but she coolly responded, "I believe there is no connection between my scientific work and the facts of private life." She headed to Stockholm and accepted the prize.[33]

The whole furor seemed silly to Einstein. "She is an unpretentious, honest person," he said, with "a sparkling intelligence." He also rather bluntly came to the conclusion, not justified, that she was not pretty enough to wreck anyone's marriage. "Despite her passionate nature," he said, "she is not attractive enough to represent a danger to anyone."[34]

More gracious was the sturdy letter of support he sent her later that month:

> Do not laugh at me for writing you without having anything sensible to say. But I am so enraged by the base manner in which the public is presently daring to concern itself with you that I absolutely must give vent to this feeling. I am impelled to tell you how much I have come to admire your intellect, your drive, and your honesty, and that I consider myself lucky to have made your personal acquaintance in Brussels. Anyone who does not number among these reptiles is certainly happy, now as before, that we have such personages among us as you, and Langevin too, real people with whom one feels privileged to be in contact. If the rabble continues to occupy itself with you, then simply don't read that hogwash, but rather leave it to the reptile for whom it has been fabricated.[35]

---

* Added to her 1903 physics prize, she thus became the first person to win Nobels in two different fields. The only other person to do so was Linus Pauling, who won for chemistry in 1954, and then won the 1962 Nobel Peace Prize for his fight against nuclear weapons testing.

Enter Elsa

As Einstein wandered around Europe giving speeches and basking in his rising renown, his wife stayed behind in Prague, a city she hated, and brooded about not being part of the scientific circles that she once struggled to join. "I would like to have been there and listened a little, and seen all these fine people," she wrote him after one of his talks in October 1911. "It is so long since we saw each other that I wonder if you will recognize me." She signed herself, "Deine alte D," your old D, as if she were still his Dollie, albeit a bit older.[36]

Her circumstances, perhaps combined with an innate disposition, caused her to become gloomy, even depressed. When Philipp Frank met her in Prague for the first time, he thought that she might be schizophrenic. Einstein concurred, and he later told a colleague that her gloominess "is doubtless traceable to a schizophrenic genetic disposition coming from her mother's family."[37]

Thus it was that Einstein's marriage was once again in an unstable state when he traveled alone to Berlin during the Easter holidays in 1912. There he became reacquainted with a cousin, three years older, whom he had known as a child.

Elsa Einstein* was the daughter of Rudolf ("the rich") Einstein and Fanny Koch Einstein. She was Einstein's cousin on both sides. Her father was the first cousin of Einstein's father, Hermann, and had helped fund his business. Her mother was the sister of Einstein's mother, Pauline (making Elsa and Albert first cousins). After Hermann's death, Pauline had moved in with Rudolf and Fanny Einstein for a few years, helping them keep house.

As children, Albert and Elsa had played together at the home of Albert's parents in Munich and on one occasion had shared a first artistic experience at the opera.[38] Since then, Elsa had been married, divorced, and now, at age 36, was living with her two daughters, Margot and Ilse, in the same apartment building as her parents.

---

* She was born Elsa Einstein, became Elsa Löwenthal during her brief marriage to a Berlin merchant, and was referred to as Elsa Einstein by Albert Einstein even before they married. For clarity, I refer to her as Elsa throughout.

The contrast with Einstein's wife was stark. Mileva Marić was exotic, intellectual, and complex. Elsa wasn't. Instead, she was conventionally handsome and domestically nurturing. She loved heavy German comfort foods and chocolate, which tended to give her a rather ample, matronly look. Her face was similar to her cousin's, and it would become strikingly more so as they aged.[39]

Einstein was looking for new companionship, and he first flirted with Elsa's sister. But by the end of his Easter visit, he had settled on Elsa as offering the comfort and nurturing that he now craved. The love he was seeking, it seems, was not wild romance but uncomplicated support and affection.

And Elsa, who revered her cousin, was eager to give it. When he returned to Prague, she wrote him right away—sending the letter to his office, not his home, and proposing a way they could correspond in secret. "How dear of you not to be too proud to communicate with me in such a way!" he responded. "I can't even begin to tell you how fond I have become of you during these few days." She asked him to destroy her letters, which he did. She, on the other hand, kept his responses for the rest of her life in a folder that she tied and later labeled "Especially beautiful letters from better days."[40]

Einstein apologized for his flirtation with her sister Paula. "It is hard for me to understand how I could have taken a fancy to her," he declared. "But it is in fact simple. She was young, a girl, and complaisant."

A decade earlier, when he was writing his love letters to Marić that celebrated their own rarefied and bohemian approach to life, Einstein would likely have lumped relatives such as Elsa into the category of "bourgeois philistines." But now, in letters that were almost as effusive as the ones he had written to Marić, he professed his new passion for Elsa. "I have to have someone to love, otherwise life is miserable," he wrote. "And this someone is you."

She knew how to make him defensive: she teased him for being under Marić's thumb and asserted that he was "henpecked." As she may have hoped, Einstein responded by protesting that he would show her otherwise. "Do not think about me in such a way!" he said. "I categorically assure you that I consider myself a full-fledged male. Perhaps I will sometime have the opportunity to prove it to you."

Spurred by this new affection and by the prospect of working in the world's capital of theoretical physics, Einstein developed a desire to move to Berlin. "The chances of getting a call to Berlin are, unfortunately, slight," he admitted to Elsa. But on his visit, he did what he could to increase his chances of someday getting a position there. In his notebook he listed appointments he had been able to get with important academic leaders, including the scientists Fritz Haber, Walther Nernst, and Emil Warburg.[41]

Einstein's son Hans Albert later recalled that it was just after his eighth birthday, in the spring of 1912, when he noticed that his parents' marriage was falling apart. But after returning to Prague from Berlin, Einstein seemed to develop qualms about his affair with his cousin. He tried, in two letters, to put an end to it. "There would only be confusion and misfortune if we were to give into our mutual attraction," he wrote Elsa.

Later that month, he tried to be even more definitive. "It will not be good for the two of us, as well as for the others, if we form a closer attachment. So, I am writing to you today for the last time and am submitting again to the inevitable, and you must do the same. You know that it is not hardness of heart or lack of feeling that makes me talk like this, because you know that, like you, I bear my cross without hope."[42]

Einstein and Marić shared one thing: a feeling that living among the middle-class German community in Prague had become wearisome. "These are not people with natural sentiments," he told Besso. They displayed "a peculiar mixture of snobbery and servility, without any kind of goodwill toward their fellow men." The water was undrinkable, the air was full of soot, and an ostentatious luxury was juxtaposed with misery on the streets. But what offended Einstein most were the artificial class structures. "When I come to the institute," he complained, "a servile man who smells of alcohol bows and says, 'your most humble servant.' "[43]

Marić worried that the bad water, milk, and air were hurting the health of their younger son, Eduard. He had lost his appetite and was not sleeping well. It was also now clear that her husband cared more about his science than his family. "He is tirelessly working on his problems; one can say that he lives only for them," she told her friend Helene Savić. "I must confess with a bit of shame that we are unimportant to him and take second place."[44]

So Einstein and his wife decided to return to the one place they thought could restore their relationship.

Zurich, 1912

The Zurich Polytechnic, where Einstein and Marić had blissfully shared their books and their souls, had been upgraded in June 1911 to a full university, now named the Eidgenössische Technische Hochschule (ETH), or the Swiss Federal Institute of Technology, with the right to grant graduate degrees. At 32 and by now quite famous in the world of theoretical physics, Einstein should have been an easy and obvious choice for one of the new professorships available there.

That possibility had been discussed a year earlier. Before he left for Prague, Einstein had made a deal with officials in Zurich. "I promised in private that I would advise them before accepting another offer from somewhere else, so that the administration of the Polytechnic could also make me an offer if they find it fit to do so," he told a Dutch professor who was trying to recruit him to Utrecht.[45]

By November 1911, Einstein had received such an offer from Zurich, or at least so he thought, and as a result he declined the offer to go to Utrecht. But the matter was not completely settled, because some of Zurich's education officials objected. They argued that a professor in theoretical physics was a "luxury," that there was not enough lab space to accommodate one, and that Einstein personally was not a good teacher.

Heinrich Zangger, a longtime friend who was a medical researcher in Zurich, intervened on Einstein's behalf. "A proper theoretical physicist is a necessity these days," he wrote in a letter to one of the top Swiss councilors. He also pointed out that in such a role Einstein "needs no laboratory." As for Einstein's teaching talents, Zangger provided a wonderfully nuanced and revealing description:

> He is not a good teacher for mentally lazy gentlemen who merely want to fill a notebook and then learn it by heart for an exam; he is not a

smooth talker, but anyone wishing to learn honestly how to develop his ideas in physics in an honest way, from deep within, and how to examine all premises carefully and see the pitfalls and the problems in his reflections, will find Einstein a first-class teacher, because all of this is expressed in his lectures, which force the audience to think along.[46]

Zangger wrote Einstein to express his outrage at the dithering in Zurich, and Einstein replied, "The dear Zurich folks can kiss my . . . [und die lieben Züricher können mich auch . . . (ellipses are in original letter)]." He told Zangger not to push the matter further. "Leave the Polytechnic* to God's inscrutable ways."[47]

Einstein, however, decided not to drop the matter but instead to push the Polytechnic through a light ruse. Officials at the university in Utrecht were just about to offer their open post to someone else, Peter Debye, when Einstein asked them to hold off. "I am turning to you with a strange request," he wrote. The Zurich Polytechnic had initially seemed very eager to recruit him, he said, and it had been proceeding with haste out of fear that he would go to Utrecht. "But if they were to learn in the near future that Debye is going to Utrecht, they would lose their fervor at once and keep me forever in suspense. I ask you therefore to wait a little longer with the official offer to Debye."[48]

Rather oddly, Einstein found himself needing letters of recommendation to secure a post at his own alma mater. Marie Curie wrote one. "In Brussels, where I attended a scientific conference in which Mr. Einstein also participated, I was able to admire the clarity of his intellect, the breadth of his information, and the profundity of his knowledge," she noted.[49]

Adding to the irony was that his other main letter of recommendation came from Henri Poincaré, the man who had almost come up with the special theory of relativity but still had not embraced it. Einstein was "one of the most original minds I have ever come across," he said. Particularly poignant was his description of Einstein's willingness, which Poincaré himself lacked, to make radical conceptual leaps:

---

* Although the school had been renamed, Einstein continued to call it the Polytechnic ("Polytechnikum") and, for clarity, I will continue to use this name.

"What I admire in him in particular is the facility with which he adapts himself to new concepts. He does not remain attached to classical principles, and, when presented with a problem in physics, is prompt to envision all the possibilities." Poincaré, however, could not resist asserting, perhaps with relativity in mind, that Einstein might not be right in all his theories: "Since he seeks in all directions one must expect the majority of the paths on which he embarks to be blind alleys."[50]

Soon it all worked out. Einstein would move back to Zurich in July 1912. He thanked Zangger for helping him to prevail "against all odds," and exulted, "I am enormously happy that we will be together again." Marić was thrilled as well. She thought that the return could help save both her sanity and their marriage. Even the children seemed happy to be out of Prague and back to the city of their birth. As Einstein put it in a postcard to another friend, "Great joy about it among us old folks and the two bear cubs."[51]

His departure caused a minor controversy in Prague. Newspaper articles noted that anti-Semitism at the university may have played a role. Einstein felt compelled to issue a public statement. "Despite all presumptions," he said, "I did not feel and did not notice any religious prejudice." The appointment of Philipp Frank, a Jew, as his successor, he added, confirmed that "such considerations" were not a major problem.[52]

Life in Zurich should have been glorious. The Einsteins were able to afford a modern six-room apartment with grand views. They were reunited with friends such as Zangger and Grossmann, and there was even one fewer adversary. "The fierce Weber has died, so it will be very pleasant from a personal point of view," Einstein wrote of their undergraduate physics professor and nemesis, Heinrich Weber.[53]

Once again there were musical gatherings at the home of math professor Adolf Hurwitz. The programs included not only Mozart, Einstein's favorite, but also Schumann, who was Marić's. On Sunday afternoons, Einstein would arrive with his wife and two little boys at the doorstep and announce, "Here comes the whole Einstein hen house."

Despite being back with such friends and diversions, Marić's depression continued to deepen, and her health to decline. She developed rheumatism, which made it hard for her to go out, especially when the streets became icy in winter. She attended the Hurwitz recitals less frequently, and when she did show up her gloom was increasingly evident. In February 1913, to entice her out, the Hurwitz family planned an all-Schumann recital. She came, but seemed paralyzed by pain, both mental and physical.[54]

Thus the atmosphere was ripe for a catalyst that would disrupt this unstable family situation. It came in the form of a letter. After almost a year of silence, Elsa Einstein wrote to her cousin.

The previous May, when he had declared that he was writing her "for the last time," Einstein had nonetheless given her the address of what would be his new office in Zurich. Now Elsa decided to send him a greeting for his thirty-fourth birthday, and she added a request for a picture of him and a recommendation of a good book she could read on relativity. She knew how to flatter.[55]

"There is no book on relativity that is comprehensible to the layman," he replied. "But what do you have a relativity cousin for? If you ever happen to be in Zurich, then we (without my wife, who is unfortunately very jealous) will take a nice walk, and I will tell you about all of those curious things that I discovered." Then he went a bit further. Instead of sending a picture, wouldn't it be better to see each other in person? "If you wish to make me truly happy, then arrange to spend a few days here sometime."[56]

A few days later, he wrote again, with word that he had instructed a photographer to send her a picture. He had been working on generalizing his theory of relativity, he reported, and it was exhausting. As he had a year earlier, he complained about being married to Marić: "What I wouldn't give to be able to spend a few days with you, but without my cross!" He asked Elsa if she would be in Berlin later that summer. "I would like to come for a short visit."[57]

It was therefore not surprising that Einstein was very receptive, a few months later, when the two towers of Berlin's scientific establishment—Max Planck and Walther Nernst—came to Zurich with an enticing proposal. Having been impressed by Einstein at the Solvay Conference of 1911, they had already been sounding out colleagues about getting him to Berlin.

The offer they brought with them, when they arrived with their wives on the night train from Berlin on July 11, 1913, had three impressive components: Einstein would be elected to a coveted vacancy in the Prussian Academy of Sciences, which would come with a hefty stipend; he would become the director of a new physics institute; and he would be made a professor at the University of Berlin. The package included a lot of money, and it was not nearly as much work as it may have seemed on the surface. Planck and Nernst made it clear that Einstein would have no required teaching duties at the university and no real administrative tasks at the institute. And though he would be required to accept German citizenship once again, he could keep his Swiss citizenship as well.

The visitors made their case during a long visit to Einstein's sunny office at the Polytechnic. He said he needed a few hours to think it over, though it is likely he knew he would accept. So Planck and Nernst took their wives on an excursion by funicular railway up one of the nearby mountains. With puckish amusement, Einstein told them he would be awaiting their return to the station with a signal. If he had decided to decline, he would be carrying a white rose, and if he was going to accept, a red rose (some accounts have the signal being a white handkerchief). When they stepped off the train, they happily discovered that he had accepted.[58]

That meant that Einstein would become, at 34, the youngest member of the Prussian Academy. But first Planck had to get him elected. The letter he wrote, which was also signed by Nernst and others, had the memorable but incorrect concession, quoted earlier, that "he might sometimes have overshot the target in his speculations, as for example in his light quantum hypothesis." But the rest of the letter was suffused with extravagant praise for each of his many scientific contributions. "Among the great problems abundant in modern physics, there is hardly one to which Einstein has not made a remarkable contribution."[59]

The Berliners were taking a risk, Einstein realized. He was being recruited not for his teaching skills (as he would not be teaching), nor for his administrative ones. And even though he had been publishing outlines and papers describing his ongoing efforts to generalize relativity, it was unclear whether he would succeed in that quest. "The Germans are gambling on me as they would on a prize-winning hen," he told a friend as they were leaving a party, "but I don't know if I can still lay eggs." [60]

Einstein, likewise, was taking a risk. He had a secure and lucrative post in a city and society that he, his wife, and his family loved. The Swiss personality agreed with him. His wife had a Slav's revulsion for all things Teutonic, and he had a similar distaste that had been ingrained in childhood. As a boy he had run away from Prussian-accented parades and Germanic rigidity. Only the opportunity to be gloriously coddled in the world capital of science could have compelled him to make such a move.

Einstein found the prospect thrilling and a bit amusing. "I am going to Berlin as an Academy-man without any obligations, rather like a living mummy," he wrote fellow physicist Jakob Laub. "I'm already looking forward to this difficult career!" [61] To Ehrenfest he admitted, "I accepted this odd sinecure because giving lectures gets on my nerves." [62] However, to the venerable Hendrik Lorentz in Holland Einstein displayed more gravitas: "I could not resist the temptation to accept a position in which I am relieved of all responsibilities so that I can give myself over completely to rumination." [63]

There was, of course, another factor that made the new job enticing: the chance to be with his cousin and new love, Elsa. As he would later admit to his friend Zangger, "She was the main reason for my going to Berlin, you know." [64]

The same evening that Planck and Nernst left Zurich, Einstein wrote Elsa an excited letter describing the "colossal honor" they had offered. "Next spring at the latest, I'll come to Berlin for good," he exulted. "I already rejoice at the wonderful times we will spend together!"

During the ensuing week, he sent two more such notes. "I rejoice at the thought that I will soon be coming to you," he wrote in the first. And a few days later: "Now we will be together and rejoice in each other!" It is impossible to know for sure what relative weight to assign to each of the factors enticing him to Berlin: the unsurpassed scientific community there, the glories and perks of the post he was offered, or the chance to be with Elsa. But at least to her he claimed it was primarily the latter. "I look forward keenly to Berlin, mainly because I look forward to *you*." [65]

Elsa had actually tried to help him get the offer. Earlier in the year, on her own initiative, she had dropped in on Fritz Haber, who ran the Kaiser Wilhelm Institute of Chemistry in Berlin, and let him know that her cousin might be open to a position that would bring him to Berlin. When he learned of Elsa's intervention, Einstein was amused. "Haber knows who he is dealing with. He knows how to appreciate the influence of a friendly female cousin . . . The nonchalance with which you dropped in on Haber is pure Elsa. Did you tell anyone about it, or did you consult only with your wicked heart? If only I could have looked on!" [66]

Even before Einstein moved to Berlin, he and Elsa began to correspond as if they were a couple. She worried about his exhaustion and sent him a long letter prescribing more exercise, rest, and a healthier diet. He responded by saying that he planned to "smoke like a chimney, work like a horse, eat without thinking, go for a walk *only* in really pleasant company."

He made clear, however, that she should not expect him to abandon his wife: "You and I can very well be happy with each other without her having to be hurt." [67]

Indeed, even amid his flurry of love letters with Elsa, Einstein was still trying to be a suitable family man. For his August 1913 vacation, he decided to take his wife and two sons hiking with Marie Curie and her two daughters. The plan was to go through the mountains of southeastern Switzerland down to Lake Como, where he and Marić had spent their most passionate and romantic moments twelve years earlier.

As it turned out, the sickly Eduard was unable to make the trip, and Marić stayed behind for a few days to get him settled with friends. Then she joined them as they neared Lake Como. During the hikes, Curie challenged Einstein to name all the peaks. They also talked science, especially when the children ran ahead. At one point Einstein stopped suddenly and grabbed Curie's arm. "You understand, what I need to know is exactly what happens to the passengers in an elevator when it falls into emptiness," he said, referring to his ideas about the equivalence of gravity and acceleration. As Curie's daughter noted later, "Such a touching preoccupation made the younger generation roar with laughter." [68]

Einstein then accompanied Marić and their children to visit her family in Novi Sad and at their summer house in Kać. On their final Sunday in Serbia, Marić took the children, without her husband, to be baptized. Hans Albert remembered later the beautiful singing; his brother, Eduard, only 3, was disruptive. As for their father, he seemed sanguine and bemused afterward. "Do you know what the result is?" he told Hurwitz. "They've turned Catholic. Well, it's all the same to me." [69]

The façade of familial harmony, however, masked the deterioration of the marriage. After his visit to Serbia and a stop in Vienna for his annual appearance at the conference of German-speaking physicists, Einstein continued on to Berlin, alone. There he was reunited with Elsa. "I now have someone I can think about with pure delight and I can live for," he told her. [70]

Elsa's home cooking, a hearty pleasure she lavished on him like a mother, became a theme in their letters. Their correspondence, like their relationship, was a stark contrast to that between Einstein and Marić a dozen years earlier. He and Elsa tended to write to each other about domestic comforts—food, tranquillity, hygiene, fondness—rather than about romantic bliss and planted kisses, or intimacies of the soul and insights of the intellect.

Despite such conventional concerns, Einstein still fancied their relationship could avoid sinking into a mundane pattern. "How nice it would be if one of these days we could share in managing a small bohemian household," he wrote. "You have no idea how charming such a life with very small needs and without grandeur can be!" [71] When Elsa gave him a hairbrush, he initially prided himself on his progress in personal grooming, but then he reverted to more slovenly ways and told her, only half jokingly, that it was to guard against the philistines and the bourgeoisie. Those were words he had used with Marić as well, but more earnestly.

Elsa wanted not only to domesticate Einstein but to marry him. Even before he moved to Berlin, she wrote to urge him to divorce Marić. It would become a running battle for years, until she finally won her way. But for the moment, Einstein was resistant. "Do you think," he asked her, "it is so easy to get a divorce if one does not have any proof of the other party's guilt?" She should accept that he had virtually separated from Marić even if he was not going to divorce her. "I treat my wife as an employee whom I cannot fire. I have my own bedroom and avoid being alone with her." Elsa was upset that Einstein did not want to marry her, and she was fearful of how an illicit relationship would affect her daughters, but Einstein insisted it was for the best.[72]

Marić was understandably depressed by the prospect of moving to Berlin. There she would have to deal with Einstein's mother, who had never liked her, and his cousin, whom she rightly suspected of being a rival. In addition, Berlin had sometimes been less tolerant to Slavs than it was even to Jews. "My wife whines to me incessantly about Berlin and her fear of the relatives," Einstein wrote Elsa. "Well, there is some truth in this." In another letter, when he noted that Marić was afraid of her, he added, "Rightly so I hope!"[73]

Indeed, by this point all of the women in his life—his mother, sister, wife, and kissing cousin—were at war with one another. As Christmas 1913 neared, Einstein's struggle to generalize relativity had the added benefit of being a way to avoid family emotions. The effort produced yet another eloquent restatement of how science could rescue him from the merely personal. "The love of science thrives under these circumstances," he told Elsa, "for it lifts me impersonally from the vale of tears into peaceful spheres."[74]

With the approach of the spring of 1914 and their move to Berlin, Eduard came down with an ear infection that made it necessary for Marić to take him to an Alpine resort to recover. "This has a good side," Einstein told Elsa. He would initially be traveling to Berlin alone, and "in order to savor that," he decided to skip a conference in Paris so that he could arrive earlier.

On one of their last evenings in Zurich, he and Marić went to the Hurwitz house for a farewell musical evening. Once again, the program featured Schumann, in an attempt to cheer her up. It didn't. She instead sat by herself in a corner and did not speak to anyone.[75]

Berlin, 1914

By April 1914, Einstein had settled into a spacious apartment just west of Berlin's city center. Marić had picked it out when she visited Berlin over Christmas vacation, and she arrived in late April, after Eduard's ear infection had subsided.[76]

The tensions in Einstein's domestic life were exacerbated by overwork and mental strain. He was settling into a new job—actually three new jobs—and still struggling with his fitful attempts to generalize his theory of relativity and tie it into a theory of gravity. That first April in Berlin, for example, he engaged in an intense correspondence with Paul Ehrenfest over ways to calculate the forces affecting rotating electrons in a magnetic field. He started writing a theory for such situations, then realized it was wrong. "The angel had unveiled itself halfway in its magnificence," he told Ehrenfest, "then on further unveiling a cloven hoof appeared and I ran away."

Even more revealing, perhaps more than he meant it to be, was his comment to Ehrenfest about his personal life in Berlin. "I really delight in my local relatives," he reported, "especially in a cousin of my age."[77]

When Ehrenfest came for a visit at the end of April, Marić had just arrived, and he found her gloomy and yearning for Zurich. Einstein, on the other hand, had thrown himself into his work. "He had the impression that the family was taking a bit too much of his time, and that he had the duty to concentrate completely on his work," his son Hans Albert later recollected about that fateful spring of 1914.[78]

Personal relationships involve nature's most mysterious forces. Outside judgments are easy to make and hard to verify. Einstein repeatedly and plaintively stressed to all of their mutual friends—especially the Bessos, Habers, and Zanggers—that they should try to see the breakup of his marriage from his perspective, despite his own apparent culpability.

It is probably true that he was not solely to blame. The decline of the marriage was a downward spiral. He had become emotionally withdrawn, Marić had become more depressed and dark, and each action reinforced the other. Einstein tended to avoid painful personal emotions by immersing himself in his work. Marić, for her part,

was bitter about the collapse of her own dreams and increasingly resentful of her husband's success. Her jealousy made her hostile toward
anyone else who was close to Einstein, including his mother (the feeling was reciprocal) and his friends. Her mistrustful nature was, understandably, to some extent an effect of Einstein's detachment, but it was
also a cause.

By the time they moved to Berlin, Marić had developed at least one
personal involvement of her own, with a mathematics professor in Zagreb named Vladimir Varićak, who had challenged Einstein's interpretations of how special relativity applied to a rotating disk. Einstein was
aware of the situation. "He had a kind of relationship with my wife,
which can't be held against either of them," he wrote to Zangger in
June. "It only made me feel my sense of isolation doubly painfully."[79]

The end came in July. Amid the turmoil, Marić moved with her two
boys into the house of Fritz Haber, the chemist who'd recruited Einstein and who ran the institute where his office was located. Haber had
his own experience with domestic discord. His wife, Clara, would end
up committing suicide the following year after a fight over Haber's participation in the war. But for the time being, she was Mileva Marić's
only friend in Berlin, and Fritz Haber became the intermediary as the
Einsteins' battles broke into the open.

Through the Habers, Einstein delivered to Marić in mid-July a
brutal cease-fire ultimatum. It was in the form of a proposed contract,
one in which Einstein's cold scientific approach combined with his
personal hostility and emotional alienation to produce an astonishing
document. It read in full:

Conditions.

A. You will make sure
   1. that my clothes and laundry are kept in good order;
   2. that I will receive my three meals regularly *in my room*;
   3. that my bedroom and study are kept neat, and especially that
      my desk is left for *my use only.*
B. You will renounce all personal relations with me insofar as they
   are not completely necessary for social reasons. Specifically, you
   will forego

      1. my sitting at home with you;

      2. my going out or traveling with you.

   C. You will obey the following points in your relations with me:

      1. you will not expect any intimacy from me, nor will you re-
         proach me in any way;

      2. you will stop talking to me if I request it;

      3. you will leave my bedroom or study immediately without
         protest if I request it.

   D. You will undertake not to belittle me in front of our children,
      either through words or behavior.[80]

Marić accepted the terms. When Haber delivered her response, Einstein insisted on writing to her again "so that you are completely clear about the situation." He was prepared to live together again "because I don't want to lose the children and I don't want them to lose me." It was out of the question that he would have a "friendly" relationship with her, but he would aim for a "businesslike" one. "The personal aspects must be reduced to a tiny remnant," he said. "In return, I assure you of proper comportment on my part, such as I would exercise to any woman as a stranger."[81]

Only then did Marić realize that the relationship was not salvageable. They all met at Haber's house on a Friday to work out a separation agreement. It took three hours. Einstein agreed to provide Marić and his children 5,600 marks a year, just under half of his primary salary. Haber and Marić went to a lawyer to have the contract drawn up; Einstein did not accompany them, but instead sent his friend Michele Besso, who had come from Trieste to represent him.[82]

Einstein left the meeting at Haber's house and went directly to the home of Elsa's parents, who were also his aunt and uncle. They arrived home late from dinner to find him there, and they received the news about the situation with "a mild distaste." Nevertheless, he ended up staying at their house. Elsa was on summer vacation in the Bavarian Alps with her two daughters, and Einstein wrote to inform her that he was now sleeping in her bed in the apartment upstairs. "It's peculiar how confusingly sentimental one gets," he told her. "It is just a bed like any other, as though you had never slept in it. And yet I find it comforting." She had invited him to visit her in the Bavarian Alps, but he said he could not, "for fear of damaging your reputation again."[83]

The way to a divorce had now been paved, he assured Elsa, and he called it "a sacrifice" he had made on her behalf. Marić would move back to Zurich and take custody of the two boys, and when they came to visit their father they could meet only on "neutral ground," not in any house he shared with Elsa. "This is justified," Einstein conceded to Elsa, "because it is not right to have the children see their father with a woman other than their own mother."

The prospect of parting with his children was devastating for Einstein. He pretended to be detached from personal sentiments, and sometimes he was. But he became deeply emotional as he imagined life apart from his sons. "I would be a real monster if I felt any other way," he wrote Elsa. "I have carried these children around innumerable times day and night, taken them out in their pram, played with them, romped around and joked with them. They used to shout with joy when I came; the little one cheered even now, because he was still too small to grasp the situation. Now they will be gone forever, and their image of their father is being spoiled."[84]

Marić and the two boys left Berlin, accompanied by Michele Besso, aboard the morning train to Zurich on Wednesday, July 29, 1914. Haber went to the station with Einstein, who "bawled like a little boy" all afternoon and evening. It was the most wrenching personal moment for a man who took perverse pride in avoiding personal moments. For all of his reputation of being inured to deep human attachments, he had been madly in love with Mileva Marić and bonded to his children. For one of the few times in his adult life, he found himself crying.

The next day he went to visit his mother, who cheered him up. She had never liked Marić and was delighted that she was gone. "Oh, if your poor Papa had only lived to see it!" she said about the separation. She even professed herself pleased for Elsa, although they had occasionally clashed. And Elsa's mother and father also seemed happy enough with the resolution, though they did express resentment that Einstein had been too financially generous to Marić, which meant the income left for him and Elsa might be "a bit meager."[85]

The whole ordeal left Einstein so drained that, despite what he had said to Elsa just a week earlier, he decided that he was not prepared to get married again. Thus he would not have to force the issue of a legal divorce, which Marić fiercely resisted. Elsa, still on vacation, was "bitterly disappointed" by the news. Einstein sought to reassure her. "For me there is no other female creature besides you," he wrote. "It is not a lack of true affection which scares me away again and again from marriage! Is it a fear of the comfortable life, of nice furniture, of the odium that I burden myself with or even of becoming some sort of contented bourgeois? I myself don't know; but you will see that my attachment to you will endure."

He insisted that she should not feel ashamed or let people pity her for consorting with a man who would not marry her. They would take walks together and be there for each other. Should she choose to offer even more, he would be grateful. But by not marrying, they would be protecting themselves from lapsing into a "contented bourgeois" existence and preventing their relationship "from becoming banal and from growing pale." To him, marriage was confining, which was a state he instinctively resisted. "I'm glad our delicate relationship does not have to founder on a provincial narrow-minded lifestyle."[86]

In the old days, Marić had been the type of soul mate who responded to such bohemian sentiments. Elsa was not such a person. A comfortable life with comfortable furniture appealed to her. So did marriage. She would accept his decision not to get married for a while, but not forever.

In the meantime, Einstein became embroiled in a long-distance battle with Marić over money, furniture, and the way she was allegedly "poisoning" their children against him.[87] And all around them, a chain reaction was taking Europe into the most incomprehensibly bloody war in its history.

Not surprisingly, Einstein reacted to all of this turmoil by throwing himself into his science.

CHAPTER NINE

GENERAL RELATIVITY

1911–1915

Light and Gravity

After Einstein formulated his special theory of relativity in 1905, he realized that it was incomplete in at least two ways. First, it held that no physical interaction can propagate faster than the speed of light; that conflicted with Newton's theory of gravity, which conceived of gravity as a force that acted instantly between distant objects. Second, it applied only to constant-velocity motion. So for the next ten years, Einstein engaged in an interwoven effort to come up with a new field theory of gravity and to generalize his relativity theory so that it applied to accelerated motion.[1]

His first major conceptual advance had come at the end of 1907, while he was writing about relativity for a science yearbook. As noted earlier, a thought experiment about what a free-falling observer would feel led him to embrace the principle that the local effects of being accelerated and of being in a gravitational field are indistinguishable.* A person in a closed windowless chamber who feels his feet pressed to the floor will not be able to tell whether it's because the chamber is in outer space being accelerated upward or because it is at rest in a gravitational

---

* See chapter 7. For purposes of this discussion, we are referring to a uniformly and rectilinearly accelerated reference frame and a static and homogeneous gravitational field.

field. If he pulls a penny from his pocket and lets it go, it will fall to the floor at an accelerating speed in either case. Likewise, a person who feels she is floating in the closed chamber will not know whether it's because the chamber is in free fall or hovering in a gravity-free region of outer space.[2]

This led Einstein to the formulation of an "equivalence principle" that would guide his quest for a theory of gravity and his attempt to generalize relativity. "I realized that I would be able to extend or generalize the principle of relativity to apply to accelerated systems in addition to those moving at a uniform velocity," he later explained. "And in so doing, I expected that I would be able to resolve the problem of gravitation at the same time."

Just as inertial mass and gravitational mass are equivalent, so too there is an equivalence, he realized, between all inertial effects, such as resistance to acceleration, and gravitational effects, such as weight. His insight was that they are both manifestations of the same structure, which we now sometimes call the inertio-gravitational field.[3]

One consequence of this equivalence is that gravity, as Einstein had noted, should bend a light beam. That is easy to show using the chamber thought experiment. Imagine that the chamber is being accelerated upward. A laser beam comes in through a pinhole on one wall. By the time it reaches the opposite wall, it's a little closer to the floor, because the chamber has shot upward. And if you could plot its trajectory across the chamber, it would be curved because of the upward acceleration. The equivalence principle says that this effect should be the same whether the chamber is accelerating upward or is instead resting still in a gravitational field. Thus, light should appear to bend when going through a gravitational field.

For almost four years after positing this principle, Einstein did little with it. Instead, he focused on light quanta. But in 1911, he confessed to Michele Besso that he was weary of worrying about quanta, and he turned his attention back to coming up with a field theory of gravity that would help him generalize relativity. It was a task that would take him almost four more years, culminating in an eruption of genius in November 1915.

In a paper he sent to the *Annalen der Physik* in June 1911, "On the

Influence of Gravity on the Propagation of Light," he picked up his insight from 1907 and gave it rigorous expression. "In a memoir published four years ago I tried to answer the question whether the propagation of light is influenced by gravitation," he began. "I now see that one of the most important consequences of my former treatment is capable of being tested experimentally." After a series of calculations, Einstein came up with a prediction for light passing through the gravitational field next to the sun: "A ray of light going past the sun would undergo a deflection of 0.83 second of arc."*

Once again, he was deducing a theory from grand principles and postulates, then deriving some predictions that experimenters could proceed to test. As before, he ended his paper by calling for just such a test. "As the stars in the parts of the sky near the sun are visible during total eclipses of the sun, this consequence of the theory may be observed. It would be a most desirable thing if astronomers would take up the question."[4]

Erwin Finlay Freundlich, a young astronomer at the Berlin University observatory, read the paper and became excited by the prospect of doing this test. But it could not be performed until an eclipse, when starlight passing near the sun would be visible, and there would be no suitable one for another three years.

So Freundlich proposed that he try to measure the deflection of starlight caused by the gravitational field of Jupiter. Alas, Jupiter did not prove big enough for the task. "If only we had a truly larger planet than Jupiter!" Einstein joked to Freundlich at the end of that summer. "But nature did not deem it her business to make the discovery of her laws easy for us."[5]

The theory that light beams could be bent led to some interesting questions. Everyday experience shows that light travels in straight lines. Carpenters now use laser levels to mark off straight lines and construct level houses. If a light beam curves as it passes through regions of changing gravitational fields, how can a straight line be determined?

---

* I am using the numbers in Einstein's original calculations. Subsequent data caused it to be revised to about 0.85 second of arc. Also, as we shall see, he later revised his theory to predict twice the bending. An arc-second, or second of arc, is an angle of $\frac{1}{3,600}$ of a degree.

One solution might be to liken the path of the light beam through a changing gravitational field to that of a line drawn on a sphere or on a surface that is warped. In such cases, the shortest line between two points is curved, a geodesic like a great arc or a great circle route on our globe. Perhaps the bending of light meant that the fabric of space, through which the light beam traveled, was curved by gravity. The shortest path through a region of space that is curved by gravity might seem quite different from the straight lines of Euclidean geometry.

There was another clue that a new form of geometry might be needed. It became apparent to Einstein when he considered the case of a rotating disk. As a disk whirled around, its circumference would be contracted in the direction of its motion when observed from the reference frame of a person not rotating with it. The diameter of the circle, however, would not undergo any contraction. Thus, the ratio of the disk's circumference to its diameter would no longer be given by pi. Euclidean geometry wouldn't apply to such cases.

Rotating motion is a form of acceleration, because at every moment a point on the rim is undergoing a change in direction, which means that its velocity (a combination of speed and direction) is undergoing a change. Because non-Euclidean geometry would be necessary to describe this type of acceleration, according to the equivalence principle, it would be needed for gravitation as well.[6]

Unfortunately, as he had proved at the Zurich Polytechnic, non-Euclidean geometry was not a strong suit for Einstein. Fortunately, he had an old friend and classmate in Zurich for whom it was.

The Math

When Einstein moved back to Zurich from Prague in July 1912, one of the first things he did was call on his friend Marcel Grossmann, who had taken the notes Einstein used when he skipped math classes at the Zurich Polytechnic. Einstein had gotten a 4.25 out of 6 in his two geometry courses at the Polytechnic. Grossmann, on the other hand, had scored a perfect 6 in both of his geometry courses, had written his dissertation on non-Euclidean geometry, published seven papers on that topic, and was now the chairman of the math department.[7]

"Grossmann, you've got to help me or I will go crazy," Einstein said. He explained that he needed a mathematical system that would express—and perhaps even help him discover—the laws that governed the gravitational field. "Instantly, he was all afire," Einstein recalled of Grossmann's response.[8]

Until then, Einstein's scientific success had been based on his special talent for sniffing out the underlying physical principles of nature. He had left to others the task, which to him seemed less exalted, of finding the best mathematical expressions of those principles, as his Zurich colleague Minkowski had done for special relativity.

But by 1912, Einstein had come to appreciate that math could be a tool for discovering—and not merely describing—nature's laws. Math was nature's playbook. "The central idea of general relativity is that gravity arises from the curvature of spacetime," says physicist James Hartle. "Gravity *is* geometry."[9]

"I am now working exclusively on the gravitation problem and I believe that, with the help of a mathematician friend here, I will overcome all difficulties," Einstein wrote to the physicist Arnold Sommerfeld. "I have gained enormous respect for mathematics, whose more subtle parts I considered until now, in my ignorance, as pure luxury!"[10]

Grossmann went home to think about the question. After consulting the literature, he came back to Einstein and recommended the non-Euclidean geometry that had been devised by Bernhard Riemann.[11]

Riemann (1826–1866) was a child prodigy who invented a perpetual calendar at age 14 as a gift for his parents and went on to study in the great math center of Göttingen, Germany, under Carl Friedrich Gauss, who had been pioneering the geometry of curved surfaces. This was the topic Gauss assigned to Riemann for a thesis, and the result would transform not only geometry but physics.

Euclidean geometry describes flat surfaces. But it does not hold true on curved surfaces. For example, the sum of the angles of a triangle on a flat page is 180°. But look at the globe and picture a triangle formed by the equator as the base, the line of longitude running from the equator to the North Pole through London (longitude 0°) as one side, and the line of longitude running from the equator to the North Pole through New Orleans (longitude 90°) as the third side. If you look at this on a globe, you will see that all three angles of this triangle are right angles, which of course is impossible in the flat world of Euclid.

Gauss and others had developed different types of geometry that could describe the surface of spheres and other curved surfaces. Riemann took things even further: he developed a way to describe a surface no matter how its geometry changed, even if it varied from spherical to flat to hyperbolic from one point to the next. He also went beyond dealing with the curvature of just two-dimensional surfaces and, building on the work of Gauss, explored the various ways that math could describe the curvature of three-dimensional and even four-dimensional space.

That is a challenging concept. We can visualize a curved line or surface, but it is hard to imagine what curved three-dimensional space would be like, much less a curved four dimensions. But for mathematicians, extending the concept of curvature into different dimensions is easy, or at least doable. This involves using the concept of the *metric*, which specifies how to calculate the distance between two points in space.

On a flat surface with just the normal x and y coordinates, any high school algebra student, with the help of old Pythagoras, can calculate the distance between points. But imagine a flat map (of the world, for example) that represents locations on what is actually a curved globe. Things get stretched out near the poles, and measurement gets more complex. Calculating the actual distance between two points on the map in Greenland is different from doing so for points near the equator. Riemann worked out ways to determine mathematically the distance between points in space no matter how arbitrarily it curved and contorted.[12]

To do so he used something called a tensor. In Euclidean geometry, a vector is a quantity (such as of velocity or force) that has both a magnitude and a direction and thus needs more than a single simple number to describe it. In non-Euclidean geometry, where space is curved, we need something more generalized—sort of a vector on steroids—in order to incorporate, in a mathematically orderly way, more components. These are called tensors.

A *metric tensor* is a mathematical tool that tells us how to calculate the distance between points in a given space. For two-dimensional maps, a metric tensor has three components. For three-dimensional space, it has six independent components. And once you get to that glorious four-dimensional entity known as spacetime, the metric tensor needs ten independent components.*

Riemann helped to develop this concept of the metric tensor, which was denoted as $g_{\mu\nu}$ and pronounced *gee-mu-nu*. It had sixteen components, ten of them independent of one another, that could be used to define and describe a distance in curved four-dimensional spacetime.[13]

The useful thing about Riemann's tensor, as well as other tensors that Einstein and Grossmann adopted from the Italian mathematicians Gregorio Ricci-Curbastro and Tullio Levi-Civita, is that they are *generally covariant*. This was an important concept for Einstein as he tried to generalize a theory of relativity. It meant that the relationships between their components remained the same even when there were arbitrary changes or rotations in the space and time coordinate system. In other words, the information encoded in these tensors could go through a variety of transformations based on a changing frame of reference, but the basic laws governing the relationship of the components to each other remained the same.[14]

Einstein's goal as he pursued his general theory of relativity was to find the mathematical equations describing two complementary processes:

---

* Here's how it works. If you are at some point in curved space and want to know the distance to a neighboring point—infinitesimally close—then things can be complicated if you have just the Pythagorean theorem and some general geometry to use. The distance to a nearby point to the north may need to be computed differently from the distance to one to the east or to one in the up direction. You need something comparable to a little scorecard at each point of space to tell you the distance to each of these points. In four-dimensional spacetime your scorecard will require ten numbers for you to be able to deal with all the questions pertaining to spacetime distances to nearby points. You need such a scorecard for every point in the spacetime. But once you have those scorecards, you can figure out the distance along any curve: just add up the distances along each infinitesimal bit using the scorecards as you pass them. These scorecards form the metric tensor, which is a field in spacetime. In other words, it is something defined at every point, but that can have differing values at every point. I am grateful to Professor John D. Norton for helping with this section.

1. How a gravitational field acts on matter, telling it how to move.
2. And in turn, how matter generates gravitational fields in space-time, telling it how to curve.

His head-snapping insight was that gravity could be defined as the curvature of spacetime, and thus it could be represented by a metric tensor. For more than three years he would fitfully search for the right equations to accomplish his mission.[15]

Years later, when his younger son, Eduard, asked why he was so famous, Einstein replied by using a simple image to describe his great insight that gravity was the curving of the fabric of spacetime. "When a blind beetle crawls over the surface of a curved branch, it doesn't notice that the track it has covered is indeed curved," he said. "I was lucky enough to notice what the beetle didn't notice."[16]

The Zurich Notebook, 1912

Beginning in that summer of 1912, Einstein struggled to develop gravitational field equations using tensors along the lines developed by Riemann, Ricci, and others. His first round of fitful efforts are preserved in a scratchpad notebook. Over the years, this revealing "Zurich Notebook" has been dissected and analyzed by a team of scholars including Jürgen Renn, John D. Norton, Tilman Sauer, Michel Janssen, and John Stachel.[17]

In it Einstein pursued a two-fisted approach. On the one hand, he engaged in what was called a "physical strategy," in which he tried to build the correct equations from a set of requirements dictated by his feel for the physics. At the same time, he pursued a "mathematical strategy," in which he tried to deduce the correct equations from the more formal math requirements using the tensor analysis that Grossmann and others recommended.

Einstein's "physical strategy" began with his mission to generalize the principle of relativity so that it applied to observers who were accelerating or moving in an arbitrary manner. Any gravitational field equation he devised would have to meet the following physical requirements:

- It must revert to Newtonian theory in the special case of weak and static gravitational fields. In other words, under certain normal conditions, his theory would describe Newton's familiar laws of gravitation and motion.
- It should preserve the laws of classical physics, most notably the conservation of energy and momentum.
- It should satisfy the principle of equivalence, which holds that observations made by an observer who is uniformly accelerating would be equivalent to those made by an observer standing in a comparable gravitational field.

Einstein's "mathematical strategy," on the other hand, focused on using generic mathematical knowledge about the metric tensor to find a gravitational field equation that was generally (or at least broadly) covariant.

The process worked both ways: Einstein would examine equations that were abstracted from his physical requirements to check their covariance properties, and he would examine equations that sprang from elegant mathematical formulations to see if they met the requirements of his physics. "On page after page of the notebook, he approached the problem from either side, here writing expressions suggested by the physical requirements of the Newtonian limit and energy-momentum conservation, there writing expressions naturally suggested by the generally covariant quantities supplied by the mathematics of Ricci and Levi-Civita," says John Norton.[18]

But something disappointing happened. The two groups of requirements did not mesh. Or at least Einstein thought not. He could not get the results produced by one strategy to meet the requirements of the other strategy.

Using his mathematical strategy, he derived some very elegant equations. At Grossmann's suggestion, he had begun using a tensor developed by Riemann and then a more suitable one developed by Ricci. Finally, by the end of 1912, he had devised a field equation using a tensor that was, it turned out, pretty close to the one that he would eventually use in his triumphant formulation of late November 1915. In other words, in his Zurich Notebook he had come up with what was quite close to the right solution.[19]

But then he rejected it, and it would stagnate in his discard pile for more than two years. Why? Among other considerations, he thought (somewhat mistakenly) that this solution did not reduce, in a weak and static field, to Newton's laws. When he tried it a different way, it did not meet the requirement of the conservation of energy and momentum. And if he introduced a coordinate condition that allowed the equations to satisfy one of these requirements, it proved incompatible with the conditions needed to satisfy the other requirement.[20]

As a result, Einstein reduced his reliance on the mathematical strategy. It was a decision that he would later regret. Indeed, after he finally returned to the mathematical strategy and it proved spectacularly successful, he would from then on proclaim the virtues—both scientific and philosophical—of mathematical formalism.[21]

The Entwurf *and Newton's Bucket, 1913*

In May 1913, having discarded the equations derived from the mathematical strategy, Einstein and Grossmann produced a sketchy alternative theory based more on the physical strategy. Its equations were constructed to conform to the requirements of energy-momentum conservation and of being compatible with Newton's laws in a weak static field.

Even though it did not seem that these equations satisfied the goal of being suitably covariant, Einstein and Grossmann felt it was the best they could do for the time being. Their title reflected their tentativeness: "Outline of a Generalized Theory of Relativity and of a Theory of Gravitation." The paper thus became known as the *Entwurf,* which was the German word they had used for "outline."[22]

For a few months after producing the *Entwurf,* Einstein was both pleased and depleted. "I finally solved the problem a few weeks ago," he wrote Elsa. "It is a bold extension of the theory of relativity, together with a theory of gravitation. Now I must give myself some rest, otherwise I will go kaput."[23]

However, he was soon questioning what he had wrought. And the more he reflected on the *Entwurf,* the more he realized that its equations did not satisfy the goal of being generally or even broadly covariant. In other words, the way the equations applied to people in arbitrary accelerated motion might not always be the same.

His confidence in the theory was not strengthened when he sat down with his old friend Michele Besso, who had come to visit him in June 1913, to study the implications of the *Entwurf* theory. They produced more than fifty pages of notes on their deliberations, each writing about half, which analyzed how the *Entwurf* accorded with some curious facts that were known about the orbit of Mercury.[24]

Since the 1840s, scientists had been worrying about a small but unexplained shift in the orbit of Mercury. The perihelion is the spot in a planet's elliptical orbit when it is closest to the sun, and over the years this spot in Mercury's orbit had slipped a tiny amount more—about 43 seconds of an arc each century—than what was explained by Newton's laws. At first it was assumed that some undiscovered planet was tugging at it, similar to the reasoning that had earlier led to the discovery of Neptune. The Frenchman who discovered Mercury's anomaly even calculated where such a planet would be and named it Vulcan. But it was not there.

Einstein hoped that his new theory of relativity, when its gravitational field equations were applied to the sun, would explain Mercury's orbit. Unfortunately, after a lot of calculations and corrected mistakes, he and Besso came up with a value of 18 seconds of an arc per century for how far Mercury's perihelion should stray, which was not even halfway correct. The poor result convinced Einstein not to publish the Mercury calculations. But it did not convince him to discard his *Entwurf* theory, at least not yet.

Einstein and Besso also looked at whether rotation could be considered a form of relative motion under the equations of the *Entwurf* theory. In other words, imagine that an observer is rotating and thus experiencing inertia. Is it possible that this is yet another case of relative motion and is indistinguishable from a case where the observer is at rest and the rest of the universe is rotating around him?

The most famous thought experiment along these lines was that described by Newton in the third book of his *Principia.* Imagine a bucket that begins to rotate as it hangs from a rope. At first the water in the bucket stays rather still and flat. But soon the friction from the bucket causes the water to spin around with it, and it assumes a concave shape. Why? Because inertia causes the spinning water to push outward, and therefore it pushes up the side of the bucket.

Yes, but if we suspect that all motion is relative, we ask: What is the water spinning relative to? Not the bucket, because the water is concave when it is spinning along with the bucket, and also when the bucket stops and the water keeps spinning inside for a while. Perhaps the water is spinning relative to nearby bodies such as the earth that exert gravitational force.

But imagine the bucket spinning in deep space with no gravity and no reference points. Or imagine it spinning alone in an otherwise empty universe. Would there still be inertia? Newton believed so, and said it was because the bucket was spinning relative to absolute space.

When Einstein's early hero Ernst Mach came along in the mid-nineteenth century, he debunked this notion of absolute space and argued that the inertia existed because the water was spinning relative to the rest of the matter in the universe. Indeed, the same effects would be observed if the bucket was still and the rest of the universe was rotating around it, he said.[25]

The general theory of relativity, Einstein hoped, would have what he dubbed "Mach's Principle" as one of its touchstones. Happily, when he analyzed the equations in his *Entwurf* theory, he concluded that they *did* seem to predict that the effects would be the same whether a bucket was spinning or was motionless while the rest of the universe spun around it.

Or so Einstein thought. He and Besso made a series of very clever calculations designed to see if indeed this was the case. In their notebook, Einstein wrote a joyous little exclamation at what appeared to be the successful conclusion of these calculations: "Is correct."

Unfortunately, he and Besso had made some mistakes in this work. Einstein would eventually discover those errors two years later and realize, unhappily, that the *Entwurf* did not in fact satisfy Mach's principle. In all likelihood, Besso had already warned him that this might be the case. In a memo that he apparently wrote in August 1913, Besso

suggested that a "rotation metric" was not in fact a solution permitted by the field equations in the *Entwurf*.

But Einstein dismissed these doubts, in letters to Besso as well as to Mach and others, at least for the time being.[26] If experiments upheld the theory, "your brilliant investigations on the foundations of mechanics will have received a splendid confirmation," Einstein wrote to Mach days after the *Entwurf* was published. "For it shows that inertia has its origin in some kind of interaction of the bodies, exactly in accordance with your argument about Newton's bucket experiment."[27]

What worried Einstein most about the *Entwurf*, justifiably, was that its mathematical equations did not prove to be generally covariant, thus deflating his goal of assuring that the laws of nature were the same for an observer in accelerated or arbitrary motion as they were for an observer moving at a constant velocity. "Regrettably, the whole business is still so very tricky that my confidence in the theory is still rather hesitant," he wrote in reply to a warm letter of congratulations from Lorentz. "The gravitational equations themselves unfortunately do not have the property of general covariance."[28]

He was soon able to convince himself, at least for a while, that this was inevitable. In part he did so through a thought experiment, which became known as the "hole argument,"[29] that seemed to suggest that the holy grail of making the gravitational field equations generally covariant was impossible to reach, or at least physically uninteresting. "The fact that the gravitational equations are not generally covariant, something that quite disturbed me for a while, is unavoidable," he wrote a friend. "It can easily be shown that a theory with generally covariant equations cannot exist if the demand is made that the field is mathematically completely determined by matter."[30]

For the time being, very few physicists embraced Einstein's new theory, and many came forth to denounce it.[31] Einstein professed pleasure that the issue of relativity "has at least been taken up with the requisite vigor," as he put it to his friend Zangger. "I enjoy controversies. In the manner of Figaro: 'Would my noble Lord venture a little dance? He should tell me! I will strike up the tune for him.' "[32]

Through it all, Einstein continued to try to salvage his *Entwurf* approach. He was able to find ways, or so he thought, to achieve enough covariance to satisfy most aspects of his principle about the equivalence of gravity and acceleration. "I succeeded in proving that the gravitational equations hold for arbitrarily moving reference systems, and thus that the hypothesis of the equivalence of acceleration and gravitational field is absolutely correct," he wrote Zangger in early 1914. "Nature shows us only the tail of the lion. But I have no doubt that the lion belongs with it even if he cannot reveal himself all at once. We see him only the way a louse that sits upon him would."[33]

Freundlich and the 1914 Eclipse

There was, Einstein knew, one way to quell doubts. He often concluded his papers with suggestions for how future experiments could confirm whatever he had just propounded. In the case of general relativity, this process had begun in 1911, when he specified with some precision how much he thought light from a star would be deflected by the gravity of the sun.

This was something that could, he hoped, be measured by photographing stars whose light passed close to the sun and determining whether there appeared to be a tiny shift in their position compared to when their light did not have to pass right by the sun. But this was an experiment that had to be done during an eclipse, when the starlight would be visible.

So it was not surprising that, with his theory arousing noisy attacks from colleagues and quiet doubts in his own mind, Einstein became keenly interested in what could be discovered during the next suitable total eclipse of the sun, which was due to occur on August 21, 1914. That would require an expedition to the Crimea, in Russia, where the path of the eclipse would fall.

Einstein was so eager to have his theory tested during the eclipse that, when it seemed there might be no money for such an expedition, he offered to pay part of the costs himself. Erwin Freundlich, the young Berlin astronomer who had read the light-bending predictions in Einstein's 1911 paper and become eager to prove him correct, was ready to take the lead. "I am extremely pleased that you have taken up the question of the bending of light with so much zeal," Einstein wrote him in early 1912. In August 1913, he was still bombarding the astronomer with encouragement. "Nothing more can be done by the theorists," he wrote. "In this matter it is only you, the astronomers, who can next year perform a simply invaluable service to theoretical physics."[34]

Freundlich got married in August 1913 and decided to take his honeymoon in the mountains near Zurich, in the hope that he could meet Einstein. It worked. When Freundlich described his honeymoon schedule in a letter, Einstein invited him over for a visit. "This is wonderful because it fits in with our plans," Freundlich wrote his fiancée, whose reaction to the prospect of spending part of her honeymoon with a theoretical physicist she had never met is lost to history.

When the newlyweds pulled into the Zurich train station, there was a disheveled Einstein wearing, as Freundlich's wife recalled, a large straw hat, with the plump chemist Fritz Haber at his side. Einstein brought the group to a nearby town where he was giving a lecture, after which he took them to lunch. Not surprisingly, he had forgotten to bring any money, and an assistant who had come along slipped him a 100 franc note under the table. For most of the day, Freundlich discussed gravity and the bending of light with Einstein, even when the group went on a nature hike, leaving his new wife to admire the scenery in peace.[35]

At his speech that day, which was on general relativity, Einstein pointed out Freundlich to the audience and called him "the man who will be testing the theory next year." The problem, however, was raising the money. At the time, Planck and others were trying to lure Einstein from Zurich to Berlin to become a member of the Prussian Academy, and Einstein used the courtship to write Planck and urge him to provide Freundlich the money to undertake the task.

In fact, on the very day that Einstein formally accepted the Berlin post and election to the Academy—December 7, 1913—he wrote Freundlich with the offer to reach into his own pocket. "If the Academy shies away from it, then we will get that little bit of mammon from private individuals," said Einstein. "Should everything fail, then I will pay for the thing myself out of the little bit that I have saved, at least the first 2,000 marks." The main thing, Einstein stressed, was that

Freundlich should proceed with his preparations. "Just go ahead and order the photographic plates, and do not let the time be squandered because of the money problem." [36]

As it turned out, there were enough private donations, mainly from the Krupp Foundation, to make the expedition possible. "You can imagine how happy I am that the external difficulties of your undertaking have now more or less been overcome," Einstein wrote. He added a note of confidence about what would be found: "I have considered the theory from every angle, and I have every confidence in the thing." [37]

Freundlich and two colleagues left Berlin on July 19 for the Crimea, where they were joined by a group from the Córdoba observatory in Argentina. If all went well, they would have two minutes to make photographs that could be used to analyze whether the starlight was deflected by the sun's gravity.

All did not go well. Twenty days before the eclipse, Europe tumbled into World War I and Germany declared war on Russia. Freundlich and his German colleagues were captured by the Russian army, and their equipment was confiscated. Not surprisingly, they were unable to convince the Russian soldiers that, with all of their powerful cameras and location devices, they were mere astronomers planning to gaze at the stars in order to better understand the secrets of the universe.

Even if they had been granted safe passage, it is likely that the observations would have failed. The skies were cloudy during the minutes of the eclipse, and an American group that was also in the region was unable to get any usable photographs. [38]

Yet the termination of the eclipse mission had a silver lining. Einstein's *Entwurf* equations were not correct. The degree to which gravity would deflect light, according to Einstein's theory at the time, was the same as that predicted by Newton's emission theory of light. But, as Einstein would discover a year later, the correct prediction would end up being twice that. If Freundlich had succeeded in 1914, Einstein might have been publicly proven wrong.

"My good old astronomer Freundlich, instead of experiencing a solar eclipse in Russia, will now be experiencing captivity there," Einstein wrote to his friend Ehrenfest. "I am concerned about him." [39]

There was no need to worry. The young astronomer was released in a prisoner exchange within weeks.

Einstein, however, had other reasons to worry in August 1914. His marriage had just exploded. His masterpiece theory still needed work. And now his native country's nationalism and militarism, traits that he had abhorred since childhood, had plunged it into a war that would cast him as a stranger in a strange land. In Germany, it would turn out, that was a dangerous position to be in.

World War I

The chain reaction that pushed Europe into war in August 1914 inflamed the patriotic pride of the Prussians and, in an equal and opposite reaction, the visceral pacifism of Einstein, a man so gentle and averse to conflict that he even disliked playing chess. "Europe in its madness has now embarked on something incredibly preposterous," he wrote Ehrenfest that month. "At such times one sees to what deplorable breed of brutes we belong."[40]

Ever since he ran away from Germany as a schoolboy and was exposed to the gauzy internationalism of Jost Winteler in Aarau, Einstein had harbored sentiments that disposed him toward pacifism, one-world federalism, and socialism. But he had generally shunned public activism.

World War I changed that. Einstein would never forsake physics, but he would henceforth be unabashedly public, for most of his life, in pushing his political and social ideals.

The irrationality of the war made Einstein believe that scientists in fact had a special duty to engage in public affairs. "We scientists in particular must foster internationalism," he said. "Unfortunately, we have had to suffer serious disappointments even among scientists in this regard."[41] He was especially appalled by the lockstep pro-war mentality of his three closest colleagues, the scientists who had lured him to Berlin: Fritz Haber, Walther Nernst, and Max Planck.[42]

Haber was a short, bald, and dapper chemist who was born Jewish but tried mightily to assimilate by converting, getting baptized, and adopting the dress, manner, and even pince-nez glasses of a proper Prussian. The director of the chemistry institute where Einstein had his office, he had been mediating the war between Einstein and Marić just as the larger war in Europe was breaking out. Although he hoped for a commission as an officer in the army, because he was an academic of Jewish heritage he had to settle for being made a sergeant.[43]

Haber reorganized his institute to develop chemical weapons for Germany. He had already found a way to synthesize ammonia from nitrogen, which permitted the Germans to mass-produce explosives. He then turned his attention to making deadly chlorine gas, which, heavier than air, would flow down into the trenches and painfully asphyxiate soldiers by burning through their throats and lungs. In April 1915, modern chemical warfare was inaugurated when some five thousand French and Belgians met that deadly fate at Ypres, with Haber personally supervising the attack. (In an irony that may have been lost on the inventor of dynamite, who endowed the prize, Haber won the 1918 Nobel in chemistry for his process of synthesizing ammonia.)

His colleague and occasional academic rival Nernst, bespectacled and 50, had his wife inspect his style as he practiced marching and saluting in front of their house. Then he took his private car and showed up at the western front to be a volunteer driver. Upon his return to Berlin, he experimented with tear gas and other irritants that could be used as a humane way to flush the enemy out of the trenches, but the generals decided they preferred the lethal approach that Haber was taking, so Nernst became part of that effort.

Even the revered Planck supported what he called Germany's "just war." As he told his students when they went off to battle, "Germany has drawn its sword against the breeding ground of insidious perfidy."[44]

Einstein was able to avoid letting the war cause a personal rift between him and his three colleagues, and he spent the spring of 1915 tutoring Haber's son in math.[45] But when they signed a petition defending Germany's militarism, he felt compelled to break with them politically.

The petition, published in October 1914, was titled "Appeal to the Cultured World" and became known as the "Manifesto of the 93," after the number of intellectuals who endorsed it. With scant regard for the truth, it denied that the German army had committed any attacks on civilians in Belgium and went on to proclaim that the war was necessary. "Were it not for German militarism, German culture would have been wiped off the face of the earth," it asserted. "We shall wage this fight to the very end as a cultured nation, a nation that holds the legacy of Goethe, Beethoven, and Kant no less sacred than hearth and home."[46]

It was no surprise that among the scientists who signed was the conservative Philipp Lenard, of photoelectric effect fame, who would later become a rabid anti-Semite and Einstein hater. What was distressing was that Haber, Nernst, and Planck also signed. As both citizens and scientists, they had a natural instinct to go along with the sentiments of others. Einstein, on the other hand, often displayed a natural inclination *not* to go along, which sometimes was an advantage both as a scientist and as a citizen.

A charismatic adventurer and occasional physician named Georg Friedrich Nicolai, who had been born Jewish (his original name was Lewinstein) and was a friend of both Elsa and her daughter Ilse, worked with Einstein to write a pacifist response. Their "Manifesto to Europeans" appealed for a culture that transcended nationalism and attacked the authors of the original manifesto. "They have spoken in a hostile spirit," Einstein and Nicolai wrote. "Nationalist passions cannot excuse this attitude, which is unworthy of what the world has heretofore called culture."

Einstein suggested to Nicolai that Max Planck, even though he had been one of the signers of the original manifesto, might also want to participate in their countermanifesto because of his "broad-mindedness and good will." He also gave Zangger's name as a possibility. But neither man, apparently, was willing to get involved. In an indication of the temper of the times, Einstein and Nicolai were able to garner only two other supporters. So they dropped their effort, and it was not published at the time.[47]

Einstein also became an early member of the liberal and cautiously pacifist New Fatherland League, a club that pushed for an early peace and the establishment of a federal structure in Europe to avoid future conflicts. It published a pamphlet titled "The Creation of the United

States of Europe," and it helped get pacifist literature into prisons and other places. Elsa went with Einstein to some of the Monday evening meetings until the group was banned in early 1916.[48]

One of the most prominent pacifists during the war was the French writer Romain Rolland, who had tried to promote friendship between his country and Germany. Einstein visited him in September 1915 near Lake Geneva. Rolland noted in his diary that Einstein, speaking French laboriously, gave "an amusing twist to the most serious of subjects."

As they sat on a hotel terrace amid swarms of bees plundering the flowering vines, Einstein joked about the faculty meetings in Berlin where each of the professors would anguish over the topic "why are we Germans hated in the world" and then would "carefully steer clear of the truth." Daringly, maybe even recklessly, Einstein openly said that he thought Germany could not be reformed and therefore hoped the allies would win, "which would smash the power of Prussia and the dynasty."[49]

The following month, Einstein got into a bitter exchange with Paul Hertz, a noted mathematician in Göttingen who was, or had been, a friend. Hertz was an associate member of the New Fatherland League with Einstein, but he had shied away from becoming a full member when it became controversial. "This type of cautiousness, not standing up for one's rights, is the cause of the entire wretched political situation," Einstein berated. "You have that type of valiant mentality the ruling powers love so much in Germans."

"Had you devoted as much care to understanding people as to understanding science, you would not have written me an insulting letter," Hertz replied. It was a telling point, and true. Einstein was better at fathoming physical equations than personal ones, as his family knew, and he admitted so in his apology. "You *must* forgive me, particularly since—as you yourself rightly say—I have *not* bestowed the same care to understanding people as to understanding science," he wrote.[50]

In November, Einstein published a three-page essay titled "My Opinion of the War" that skirted the border of what was permissible, even for a great scientist, to say in Germany. He speculated that there existed "a biologically determined feature of the male character" that was one of the causes of wars. When the article was published by the Goethe League that month, a few passages were deleted for safety's sake, including an attack on patriotism as potentially containing "the moral requisites of bestial hatred and mass murder."[51]

The idea that war had a biological basis in male aggression was a topic Einstein also explored in a letter to his friend in Zurich, Heinrich Zangger. "What drives people to kill and maim each other so savagely?" Einstein asked. "I think it is the sexual character of the male that leads to such wild explosions."

The only method of containing such aggression, he argued, was a world organization that had the power to police member nations.[52] It was a theme he would pick up again eighteen years later, in the final throes of his pure pacifism, when he engaged in a public exchange of letters with Sigmund Freud on both male psychology and the need for world government.

The Home Front, 1915

The early months of the war in 1915 made Einstein's separation from Hans Albert and Eduard more difficult, both emotionally and logistically. They wanted him to come visit them in Zurich for Easter that year, and Hans Albert, who was just turning 11, wrote him two letters designed to pull at his heart: "I just think: At Easter you're going to be here and we'll have a Papa again."

In his next postcard, he said that his younger brother told him about having a dream "that Papa was here." He also described how well he was doing in math. "Mama assigns me problems; we have a little booklet; I could do the same with you as well."[53]

The war made it impossible for him to come at Easter, but he responded to the postcards by promising Hans Albert that he would come in July for a hiking vacation in the Swiss Alps. "In the summer I will take a trip with just you alone for a fortnight or three weeks," he wrote. "This will happen every year, and Tete [Eduard] may also come along when he is old enough for it."

Einstein also expressed his delight that his son had taken a liking to geometry. It had been his "favorite pastime" when he was about the same age, he said, "but I had no one to demonstrate anything to me, so I had to learn it from books." He wanted to be with his son to help teach him math and "tell you many fine and interesting things about science and much else." But that would not always be possible. Perhaps they could do it by mail? "If you write me each time what you already know, I'll give you a nice little problem to solve." He sent along a toy for each of his sons, along with an admonition to brush their teeth well. "I do the same and am very happy now to have kept enough healthy teeth."[54]

But the tension in the family worsened. Einstein and Marić exchanged letters arguing about both money and vacation timing, and at the end of June a curt postcard came from Hans Albert. "If you're so unfriendly to her," he said of his mother, "I don't want to go with you." So Einstein canceled his planned trip to Zurich and instead went with Elsa and her two daughters to the Baltic sea resort of Sellin.

Einstein was convinced that Marić was turning the children against him. He suspected, probably correctly, that her hand was behind the postcards Hans Albert was sending, both the plaintive ones making him feel guilty for not being in Zurich and the sharper ones rejecting vacation hikes. "My fine boy had been alienated from me for a few years already by my wife, who has a vengeful disposition," he complained to Zangger. "The postcard I received from little Albert had been inspired, if not downright dictated, by her."

He asked Zangger, who was a professor of medicine, to check on young Eduard, who had been suffering ear infections and other ailments. "Please write me what is wrong with my little boy," he pleaded. "I'm particularly fondly attached to him; he was still so sweet to me and innocent."[55]

It was not until the beginning of September that he finally made it to Switzerland. Marić felt it would be proper for him to stay with her and the boys, despite the strain. They were, after all, still married. She had hopes of reconciling. But Einstein showed no interest in being with her. Instead, he stayed in a hotel and spent a lot of time with his friends Michele Besso and Heinrich Zangger.

As it turned out, he got a chance to see his sons only twice during the entire three weeks he was in Switzerland. In a letter to Elsa, he blamed his estranged wife: "The cause was mother's fear of the little ones becoming too dependent on me." Hans Albert let his father know that the whole visit made him feel uncomfortable.[56]

After Einstein returned to Berlin, Hans Albert paid a call on Zangger. The kindly medical professor, friends of all sides in the dispute, tried to work out an accord so that Einstein could visit his sons. Besso also played intermediary. Einstein could see his sons, Besso advised in a formal letter he wrote after consulting with Marić, but not in Berlin nor in the presence of Elsa's family. It would be best to do it at "a good Swiss inn," initially just with Hans Albert, where they could spend some time on their own free of all distractions. Over Christmas, Hans Albert was planning to visit Besso's family, and he suggested that perhaps Einstein could come then.[57]

The Race to General Relativity, 1915

What made the flurry of political and personal turmoil in the fall of 1915 so remarkable was that it highlighted Einstein's ability to concentrate on, and compartmentalize, his scientific endeavors despite all distractions. During that period, with great effort and anxiety, he was engaged in a competitive rush to what he later called the greatest accomplishment of his life.[58]

Back when Einstein had moved to Berlin in the spring of 1914, his colleagues had assumed that he would set up an institute and attract acolytes to work on the most pressing problem in physics: the implications of quantum theory. But Einstein was more of a lone wolf. Unlike Planck, he did not want a coterie of collaborators or protégés, and he preferred to focus on what again had become his personal passion: the generalization of his theory of relativity.[59]

So after his wife and sons left him for Zurich, Einstein moved out of their old apartment and rented one that was nearer to Elsa and the center of Berlin. It was a sparsely furnished bachelor's refuge, but still rather spacious: it had seven rooms on the third floor of a new five-story building.[60]

Einstein's study at home featured a large wooden writing table that was cluttered with piles of papers and journals. Padding around this hermitage, eating and working at whatever hours suited him, sleeping when he had to, he waged his solitary struggle.

Through the spring and summer of 1915, Einstein wrestled with his *Entwurf* theory, refining it and defending it against a variety of challenges. He began calling it "the general theory" rather than merely "a generalized theory" of relativity, but that did not mask its problems, which he kept trying to deflect.

He claimed that his equations had the greatest amount of covariance that was permissible given his hole argument and other strictures of physics, but he began to suspect that this was not correct. He also got into an exhausting debate with the Italian mathematician Tullio Levi-Civita, who pointed out problems with his handling of the tensor calculus. And there was still the puzzle of the incorrect result the theory gave for the shift in Mercury's orbit.

At least his *Entwurf* theory still successfully explained—or so he thought through the summer of 1915—rotation as being a form of *relative* motion, that is, a motion that could be defined only relative to the positions and motions of other objects. His field equations, he thought, were invariant under the transformation to rotating coordinates.[61]

Einstein was confident enough in his theory to show it off at a weeklong series of two-hour lectures, starting at the end of June 1915, at the University of Göttingen, which had become the preeminent center for the mathematical side of theoretical physics. Foremost among the geniuses there was David Hilbert, and Einstein was particularly eager—too eager, it would turn out—to explain all the intricacies of relativity to him.

The visit to Göttingen was a triumph. Einstein exulted to Zangger that he had "the pleasurable experience of convincing the mathematicians there thoroughly." Of Hilbert, a fellow pacifist, he added, "I met him and became quite fond of him." A few weeks later, after again reporting, "I was able to convince Hilbert of the general theory of relativity," Einstein called him "a man of astonishing energy and independence." In a letter to another physicist, Einstein was even more effusive: "In Göttingen I had the great pleasure of seeing that everything was understood down to the details. I am quite enchanted with Hilbert!"[62]

Hilbert was likewise enchanted with Einstein and his theory. So much so that he soon set out to see if he could beat Einstein to the goal of getting the field equations right. Within three months of his Göttingen lectures, Einstein was confronted with two distressing discoveries: that his *Entwurf* theory was indeed flawed, and that Hilbert was racing feverishly to come up with the correct formulations on his own.

Einstein's realization that his *Entwurf* theory was unraveling came from an accumulation of problems. But it culminated with two major blows in early October 1915.

The first was that, upon rechecking, Einstein found that the *Entwurf* equations did not actually account for rotation as he had thought.[63] He hoped to prove that rotation could be conceived of as just another form of relative motion, but it turned out that the *Entwurf* didn't actually prove this. The *Entwurf* equations were not, as he had believed, covariant under a transformation that uniformly rotated the coordinate axes.

Besso had warned him in a memo in 1913 that this seemed to be a problem. But Einstein had ignored him. Now, upon redoing his calculations, he was dismayed to see this pillar knocked away. "This is a blatant contradiction," he lamented to the astronomer Freundlich.

He assumed that the same mistake also accounted for his theory's inability to account fully for the shift in Mercury's orbit. And he despaired that he would not be able to find the problem. "I do not believe I am able to find the mistake myself, for in this matter my mind is too set in a deep rut."[64]

In addition, he realized that he had made a mistake in what was called his "uniqueness" argument: that the sets of conditions required by energy-momentum conservation and other physical restrictions uniquely led to the field equations in the *Entwurf*. He wrote Lorentz explaining in detail his previous "erroneous assertions."[65]

Added to these problems were ones he already knew about: the *Entwurf* equations were not generally covariant, meaning that they did not really make all forms of accelerated and nonuniform motion relative, and they did not fully explain Mercury's anomalous orbit. And now, as this edifice was crumbling, he could hear what seemed to be Hilbert's footsteps gaining on him from Göttingen.

Part of Einstein's genius was his tenacity. He could cling to a set of ideas, even in the face of "apparent contradiction" (as he put it in his 1905 relativity paper). He also had a deep faith in his intuitive feel for the physical world. Working in a more solitary manner than most other scientists, he held true to his own instincts, despite the qualms of others.

But although he was tenacious, he was not mindlessly stubborn. When he finally decided his *Entwurf* approach was untenable, he was willing to abandon it abruptly. That is what he did in October 1915.

To replace his doomed *Entwurf* theory, Einstein shifted his focus from the physical strategy, which emphasized his feel for basic principles of physics, and returned to a greater reliance on a mathematical strategy, which made use of the Riemann and Ricci tensors. It was an approach he had used in his Zurich notebooks and then abandoned, but on returning to it he found that it could provide a way to generate generally covariant gravitational field equations. "Einstein's reversal," writes John Norton, "parted the waters and led him from bondage into the promised land of general relativity."[66]

Of course, as always, his approach remained a mix of both strategies. To pursue a revitalized mathematical strategy, he had to revise the physical postulates that were the foundation for his *Entwurf* theory. "This was exactly the sort of convergence of physical and mathematical considerations that eluded Einstein in the Zurich notebook and in his work on the *Entwurf* theory," write Michel Janssen and Jürgen Renn.[67]

Thus he returned to the tensor analysis that he had used in Zurich, with its greater emphasis on the mathematical goal of finding equations that were generally covariant. "Once every last bit of confidence in the earlier theories had given way," he told a friend, "I saw clearly that it was only through general covariance theory, i.e., with Riemann's covariant, that a satisfactory solution could be found."[68]

The result was an exhausting, four-week frenzy during which Einstein wrestled with a succession of tensors, equations, corrections, and updates that he rushed to the Prussian Academy in a flurry of four Thursday lectures. It climaxed, with the triumphant revision of Newton's universe, at the end of November 1915.

Every week, the fifty or so members of the Prussian Academy gathered in the grand hall of the Prussian State Library in the heart of Berlin to address each other as "Your Excellency" and listen to fellow members pour forth their wisdom. Einstein's series of four lectures had been scheduled weeks earlier, but until they began—and even after they had begun—he was still working furiously on his revised theory.

The first was delivered on November 4. "For the last four years," he began, "I have tried to establish a general theory of relativity on the assumption of the relativity even of non-uniform motion." Referring to his discarded *Entwurf* theory, he said he "actually believed I had discovered the only law of gravitation" that conformed to physical realities.

But then, with great candor, he detailed all of the problems that theory had encountered. "For that reason, I completely lost trust in the field equations" that he had been defending for more than two years. Instead, he said, he had now returned to the approach that he and his mathematical caddy, Marcel Grossmann, had been using in 1912. "Thus I went back to the requirement of a more general covariance of the field equations, which I had left only with a heavy heart when I worked together with my friend Grossmann. In fact, we had then already come quite close to the solution."

Einstein reached back to the Riemann and Ricci tensors that Grossmann had introduced him to in 1912. "Hardly anyone who truly understands it can resist the charm of this theory," he lectured. "It signifies a real triumph of the method of the calculus founded by Gauss, Riemann, Christoffel, Ricci, and Levi-Civita."[69]

This method got him much closer to the correct solution, but his equations on November 4 were still not generally covariant. That would take another three weeks.

Einstein was in the throes of one of the most concentrated frenzies of scientific creativity in history. He was working, he said, "horrendously intensely."[70] In the midst of this ordeal, he was also still dealing with the personal crisis within his family. Letters arrived from both his wife and Michele Besso, who was acting on her behalf, that pressed the issue of his financial obligations and discussed the guidelines for his contact with his sons.

On the very day he turned in his first paper, November 4, he wrote an anguished—and painfully poignant—letter to Hans Albert, who was in Switzerland:

> I will try to be with you for a month every year so that you will have a father who is close to you and can love you. You can learn a lot of good things from me that no one else can offer you. The things I have gained from so much strenuous work should be of value not only to strangers but especially to my own boys. In the last few days I completed one of the finest papers of my life. When you are older, I will tell you about it.

He ended with a small apology for seeming so distracted: "I am often so engrossed in my work that I forget to eat lunch."[71]

Einstein also took time off from furiously revising his equations to engage in an awkward fandango with his erstwhile friend and competitor David Hilbert, who was racing him to find the equations of general relativity. Einstein had been informed that the Göttingen mathematician had figured out the flaws in the *Entwurf* equations. Worried about being scooped, he wrote Hilbert a letter saying that he himself had discovered the flaws four weeks earlier, and he sent along a copy of his November 4 lecture. "I am curious whether you will take kindly to this new solution," Einstein asked with a touch of defensiveness.[72]

Hilbert was not only a better pure mathematician than Einstein, he also had the advantage of not being as good a physicist. He did not get all wrapped up, the way Einstein did, in making sure that any new theory conformed to Newton's old one in a weak static field or that it obeyed the laws of causality. Instead of a dual math-and-physics strategy, Hilbert pursued mainly a math strategy, focusing on finding the equations that were covariant. "Hilbert liked to joke that physics was too complicated to be left to the physicists," notes Dennis Overbye.[73]

Einstein presented his second paper the following Thursday, November 11. In it, he used the Ricci tensor and imposed new coordinate conditions that allowed the equations thus to be generally covariant. As it turned out, that did not greatly improve matters. Einstein was still close to the final answer, but making little headway.[74]

Once again, he sent the paper off to Hilbert. "If my present modification (which does not change the equations) is legitimate, then gravitation must play a fundamental role in the composition of matter," Einstein said. "My own curiosity is interfering with my work!"[75]

The reply that Hilbert sent the next day must have unnerved Einstein. He said he was about ready to oblige with "an axiomatic solution to your great problem." He had planned to hold off discussing it until he explored the physical ramifications further. "But since you are so interested, I would like to lay out my theory in very complete detail this coming Tuesday," which was November 16.

He invited Einstein to come to Göttingen and have the dubious pleasure of personally hearing him lay out the answer. The meeting would begin at 6 p.m., and Hilbert helpfully provided Einstein with the arrival times of the two afternoon trains from Berlin. "My wife and I would be very pleased if you stayed with us."

Then, after signing his name, Hilbert felt compelled to add what must surely have been a tantalizing and disconcerting postscript. "As far as I understand your new paper, the solution given by you is entirely different from mine."

Einstein wrote four letters on November 15, a Monday, that give a glimpse into why he was suffering stomach pains. To his son Hans Albert, he suggested that he would like to travel to Switzerland around Christmas and New Year's to visit him. "Maybe it would be better if we were alone somewhere," such as at a secluded inn, he suggested to his son. "What do you think?"

He also wrote his estranged wife a conciliatory letter that thanked her for her willingness not "to undermine my relations with the boys." And he reported to their mutual friend Zangger, "I have modified the theory of gravity, having realized that my earlier proofs had a gap . . . I shall be glad to come to Switzerland at the turn of the year in order to see my dear boy."[76]

Finally, he replied to Hilbert and declined his invitation to visit Göttingen the next day. His letter did not hide his anxiety: "Your analysis interests me tremendously . . . The hints you gave in your messages awaken the greatest of expectations. Nevertheless, I must refrain from traveling to Göttingen for the moment . . . I am tired out and plagued by stomach pains . . . If possible, please send me a correction proof of your study to mitigate my impatience."[77]

Fortunately for Einstein, his anxiety was partly alleviated that week by a joyous discovery. Even though he knew his equations were not in final form, he decided to see whether the new approach he was taking would yield the correct results for what was known about the shift in Mercury's orbit. Because he and Besso had done the calculations once before (and gotten a disappointing result), it did not take him long to redo the calculations using his revised theory.

The answer, which he triumphantly announced in the third of his four November lectures, came out right: 43 arc-seconds per century.[78] "This discovery was, I believe, by far the strongest emotional experience in Einstein's scientific life, perhaps in all his life," Abraham Pais later said. He was so thrilled he had heart palpitations, as if "something had snapped" inside. "I was beside myself with joyous excitement," he told Ehrenfest. To another physicist he exulted: "The results of Mercury's perihelion movement fills me with great satisfaction. How helpful to us is astronomy's pedantic accuracy, which I used to secretly ridicule!"[79]

In the same lecture, he also reported on another calculation he had made. When he first began formulating general relativity eight years earlier, he had said that one implication was that gravity would bend light. He had previously figured that the bending of light by the gravitational field next to the sun would be approximately 0.83 arc-second, which corresponded to what would be predicted by Newton's theory when light was treated as if a particle. But now, using his newly revised theory, Einstein calculated that the bending of light by gravity would be twice as great, because of the effect produced by the curvature of spacetime. Therefore, the sun's gravity would bend a beam by about 1.7 arc-seconds, he now predicted. It was a prediction that would have to wait for the next suitable eclipse, more than three years away, to be tested.

That very morning, November 18, Einstein received Hilbert's new paper, the one that he had been invited to Göttingen to hear presented. Einstein was surprised, and somewhat dismayed, to see how similar it was to his own work. His response to Hilbert was terse, a bit cold, and clearly designed to assert the priority of his own work:

> The system you furnish agrees—as far as I can see—exactly with what I found in the last few weeks and have presented to the Academy. The difficulty was not in finding generally covariant equations . . . for this is easily achieved with Riemann's tensor . . . Three years ago with my friend Grossmann I had already taken into consideration the only covariant equations, which have now been shown to be the correct ones. We had distanced ourselves from it, reluctantly, because it seemed to me that the physical discussion yielded an incongruity with Newton's law. Today I am presenting to the Academy a paper in which I derive quantitatively out of general relativity, without any guiding hypothesis, the perihelion motion of Mercury. No gravitational theory has achieved this until now.[80]

Hilbert responded kindly and quite generously the following day, claiming no priority for himself. "Cordial congratulations on conquering perihelion motion," he wrote. "If I could calculate as rapidly as you, in my equations the electron would have to capitulate and the hydrogen atom would have to produce its note of apology about why it does not radiate."[81]

Yet the day after, on November 20, Hilbert sent in a paper to a Göttingen science journal proclaiming his own version of the equations for general relativity. The title he picked for his piece was not a modest one. "The Foundations of Physics," he called it.

It is not clear how carefully Einstein read the paper that Hilbert sent him or what in it, if anything, affected his thinking as he busily prepared his climactic fourth lecture at the Prussian Academy. Whatever the case, the calculations he had done the week earlier, on Mercury and on light deflection, helped him realize that he could avoid the constraints and coordinate conditions he had been imposing on his gravitational field equations. And thus he produced in time for his final lecture—"The Field Equations of Gravitation," on November 25, 1915—a set of covariant equations that capped his general theory of relativity.

The result was not nearly as vivid to the layman as, say, $E=mc^2$. Yet using the condensed notations of tensors, in which sprawling complexities can be compressed into little subscripts, the crux of the final Einstein field equations is compact enough to be emblazoned, as it indeed often has been, on T-shirts designed for proud physics students. In one of its many variations,[82] it can be written as:

$$R_{\mu\nu} - \tfrac{1}{2} g_{\mu\nu} R = 8\pi T_{\mu\nu}$$

The left side of the equation starts with the term $R_{\mu\nu}$, which is the Ricci tensor he had embraced earlier. The term $g_{\mu\nu}$ is the all-important metric tensor, and the term R is the trace of the Ricci tensor called the Ricci scalar. Together, this left side of the equation—which is now known as the Einstein tensor and can be written simply as $G_{\mu\nu}$—compresses together all of the information about how the geometry of spacetime is warped and curved by objects.

The right side describes the movement of matter in the gravitational field. The interplay between the two sides shows how objects curve spacetime and how, in turn, this curvature affects the motion of objects. As the physicist John Wheeler has put it, "Matter tells spacetime how to curve, and curved space tells matter how to move."[83]

Thus is staged a cosmic tango, as captured by another physicist, Brian Greene:

> Space and time become players in the evolving cosmos. They come alive. Matter here causes space to warp there, which causes matter over here to move, which causes space way over there to warp even more, and so on. General relativity provides the choreography for an entwined cosmic dance of space, time, matter, and energy.[84]

At last Einstein had equations that were truly covariant and thus a theory that incorporated, at least to his satisfaction, all forms of motion, whether it be inertial, accelerated, rotational, or arbitrary. As he proclaimed in the formal presentation of his theory that he published the following March in the *Annalen der Physik*, "The general laws of nature are to be expressed by equations that hold true for all systems of coordinates, that is they are covariant with respect to any substitutions whatever."[85]

Einstein was thrilled by his success, but at the same time he was worried that Hilbert, who had presented his own version five days earlier in Göttingen, would be accorded some of the credit for the theory. "Only one colleague has really understood it," he wrote to his friend

Heinrich Zangger, "and he is seeking to nostrify it (Abraham's expression) in a clever way." The expression "to nostrify" *(nostrifizieren)*, which had been used by the Göttingen-trained mathematical physicist Max Abraham, referred to the practice of nostrification by which German universities converted degrees granted by other universities into degrees of their own. "In my personal experience I have hardly come to know the wretchedness of mankind better." In a letter to Besso a few days later, he added, "My colleagues are acting hideously in this affair. You will have a good laugh when I tell you about it."[86]

So who actually deserves the primary credit for the final mathematical equations? The Einstein-Hilbert priority issue has generated a small but intense historical debate, some of which seems at times to be driven by passions that go beyond mere scientific curiosity. Hilbert presented a version of his equations in his talk on November 16 and a paper that he dated November 20, before Einstein presented his final equations on November 25. However, a team of Einstein scholars in 1997 found a set of proof pages of Hilbert's article, on which Hilbert had made revisions that he then sent back to the publisher on December 16. In the original version, Hilbert's equations differed in a small but important way from Einstein's final version of the November 25 lecture. They were not actually generally covariant, and he did not include a step that involved contracting the Ricci tensor and putting the resulting trace term, the Ricci scalar, into the equation. Einstein did this in his November 25 lecture. Apparently, Hilbert made a correction in the revised version of his article to match Einstein's version. His revisions, quite generously, also added the phrase "first introduced by Einstein" when he referred to the gravitational potentials.

Hilbert's advocates (and Einstein's detractors) respond with a variety of arguments, including that the page proofs are missing one part and that the trace term at issue was either unnecessary or obvious.

It is fair to say that both men—to some extent independently but each also with knowledge of what the other was doing—derived by November 1915 mathematical equations that gave formal expression to the general theory. Judging from Hilbert's revisions to his own page proofs, Einstein seems to have published the final version of these equations first. And in the end, even Hilbert gave Einstein credit and priority.

Either way, it was, without question, Einstein's theory that was being formalized by these equations, one that he had explained to Hilbert during their time together in Göttingen that summer. Even the physicist Kip Thorne, one of those who give Hilbert credit for producing the correct field equations, nonetheless says that Einstein deserves credit for the theory underlying the equations. "Hilbert carried out the last few mathematical steps to its discovery independently and almost simultaneously with Einstein, but Einstein was responsible for essentially everything that preceded these steps," Thorne notes. "Without Einstein, the general relativistic laws of gravity might not have been discovered until several decades later." [87]

Hilbert, graciously, felt the same way. As he stated clearly in the final published version of his paper, "The differential equations of gravitation that result are, as it seems to me, in agreement with the magnificent theory of general relativity established by Einstein." Henceforth he would always acknowledge (thus undermining those who would use him to diminish Einstein) that Einstein was the sole author of the theory of relativity.[88] "Every boy in the streets of Göttingen understands more about four-dimensional geometry than Einstein," he reportedly said. "Yet, in spite of that, Einstein did the work and not the mathematicians." [89]

Indeed, Einstein and Hilbert were soon friendly again. Hilbert wrote in December, just weeks after their dash for the field equations was finished, to say that with his support Einstein had been elected to the Göttingen Academy. After expressing his thanks, Einstein added, "I feel compelled to say something else to you." He explained:

> There has been a certain ill-feeling between us, the cause of which I do not want to analyze. I have struggled against the feeling of bitterness attached to it, with complete success. I think of you again with unmixed geniality and ask you to try to do the same with me. It is a shame when two real fellows who have extricated themselves somewhat from this shabby world do not afford each other mutual pleasure.[90]

They resumed their regular correspondence, shared ideas, and plotted to get a job for the astronomer Freundlich. By February Einstein was even visiting Göttingen again and staying at Hilbert's home.

Einstein's pride of authorship was understandable. As soon as he got printed copies of his four lectures, he mailed them out to friends. "Be sure you take a good look at them," he told one. "They are the most valuable discovery of my life." To another he noted, "The theory is of incomparable beauty."[91]

Einstein, at age 36, had produced one of history's most imaginative and dramatic revisions of our concepts about the universe. The general theory of relativity was not merely the interpretation of some experimental data or the discovery of a more accurate set of laws. It was a whole new way of regarding reality.

Newton had bequeathed to Einstein a universe in which time had an absolute existence that tick-tocked along independent of objects and observers, and in which space likewise had an absolute existence. Gravity was thought to be a force that masses exerted on one another rather mysteriously across empty space. Within this framework, objects obeyed mechanical laws that had proved remarkably accurate— almost perfect—in explaining everything from the orbits of the planets, to the diffusion of gases, to the jiggling of molecules, to the propagation of sound (though not light) waves.

With his special theory of relativity, Einstein had shown that space and time did not have independent existences, but instead formed a fabric of spacetime. Now, with his general version of the theory, this fabric of spacetime became not merely a container for objects and events. Instead, it had its own dynamics that were determined by, and in turn helped to determine, the motion of objects within it— just as the fabric of a trampoline will curve and ripple as a bowling ball and some billiard balls roll across it, and in turn the dynamic curving and rippling of the trampoline fabric will determine the path of the rolling balls and cause the billiard balls to move toward the bowling ball.

The curving and rippling fabric of spacetime explained gravity, its equivalence to acceleration, and, Einstein asserted, the general relativity of all forms of motion.[92] In the opinion of Paul Dirac, the Nobel laureate pioneer of quantum mechanics, it was "probably the greatest scientific discovery ever made." Another of the great giants of twentieth-century physics, Max Born, called it "the greatest feat of human thinking about nature, the most amazing combination of philosophical penetration, physical intuition and mathematical skill."[93]

The entire process had exhausted Einstein but left him elated. His marriage had collapsed and war was ravaging Europe, but Einstein was as happy as he would ever be. "My boldest dreams have now come true," he exulted to Besso. "*General* covariance. Mercury's perihelion motion wonderfully precise." He signed himself "contented but kaput."[94]

CHAPTER TEN

DIVORCE

1916–1919

With Elsa, June 1922

"The Narrow Whirlpool of Personal Experience"

As a young man, Einstein had predicted, in a letter to the mother of his first girlfriend, that the joys of science would be a refuge from painful personal emotions. And thus it was. His conquest of general relativity proved easier than finding the formulas for the forces swirling within his family.

Those forces were complex. At the very moment he was finalizing his field equations—the last week of November 1915—his son Hans Albert was telling Michele Besso that he wanted to spend time alone with his father over Christmas, preferably on Zugerberg mountain or someplace similarly isolated. But simultaneously, the boy was writing his father a nasty letter saying he did not want him to come to Switzerland at all.[1]

How to explain the contradiction? Hans Albert's mind seemed at times to display a duality—he was, after all, only 11—and he had powerfully conflicted attitudes toward his father. That was no surprise. Einstein was intense and compelling and at times charismatic. He was also aloof and distracted and had distanced himself, physically and emotionally, from the boy, who was guarded by a doting mother who felt humiliated.

The stubborn patience that Einstein displayed when dealing with scientific problems was equaled by his impatience when dealing with personal entanglements. So he informed the boy he was canceling the trip. "The unkind tone of your letter dismays me very much," Einstein wrote just days after finishing his last lecture on general relativity. "I see that my visit would bring you little joy, therefore I think it's wrong to sit in a train for two hours and 20 minutes."

There was also the question of a Christmas present. Hans Albert had become an avid little skier, and Marić gave him a set of equipment that cost 70 francs. "Mama bought them for me on condition that you also contribute," he wrote. "I consider them a Christmas present." This did not please Einstein. He replied that he would send him a gift in cash, "but I do think *that a luxury gift costing 70 francs does not match our modest circumstances,*" Einstein wrote, underlining the phrase.[2]

Besso put on what he called his "pastoral manner" to mediate. "You should not take serious offense at the boy," he said. The source of the friction was Marić, Besso believed, but he asked Einstein to remember that she was composed "not only of meanness but of goodness." He should try to understand, Besso urged, how difficult it was for Marić to deal with him. "The role as the wife of a genius is never easy."[3] In the case of Einstein, that was certainly true.

The anxiety surrounding Einstein's proposed visit was partly due to a misunderstanding. Einstein had assumed that the plan to have him and his son meet at the Bessos' had been arranged because Marić and Hans Albert wanted it that way. Instead, the boy had no desire to be a bystander while his father and Besso discussed physics. Just the opposite: he wanted his father to himself.

Marić ended up writing to clear up the matter, which Einstein appreciated. "I was likewise a bit disappointed that I would not get Albert to myself but only under Besso's protection," he said.

So Einstein reinstated his plan to visit Zurich, and he promised it would be one of many such trips to see his son. "[Hans] Albert* is now entering the age at which I can mean very much to him," he said. "I want mainly to teach him to think, judge and appreciate things objectively." A week later, in another letter to Marić, he reaffirmed that he was happy to make the trip, "for there is a faint chance that I'll please Albert by coming." He did, however, add rather pointedly, "See to it that he receives me fairly cheerfully. I am quite tired and overworked, and not capable of enduring new agitations and disappointments."[4]

It was not to be. Einstein's exhaustion lingered, and the war made the border crossing from Germany difficult. Two days before Christmas of 1915, when he was supposed to be departing for Switzerland, Einstein instead wrote his son a letter. "I have been working so hard in the last few months that I urgently need a rest during the Christmas holidays," he said. "Aside from this, coming across the border is very uncertain at present, since it has been almost constantly closed recently. That is why I must unfortunately deprive myself of visiting you now."

Einstein spent Christmas at home. That day, he took out of his satchel some of the drawings that Hans Albert had sent him and wrote the boy a postcard saying how much they pleased him. He would come for Easter, he promised, and he expressed delight that his son enjoyed playing piano. "Maybe you can practice something to accompany a violin, and then we can play at Easter when we are together."[5]

After he and Marić separated, Einstein had initially decided not to seek a divorce. One reason was that he had no desire to marry Elsa. Companionship without commitment suited him just fine. "The at-

---

* For clarity, I refer to the boy by both of his given names, Hans Albert, although his father invariably referred to him simply as Albert. At one point, Einstein wrote a letter to his son and signed it "Albert" instead of "Papa." In his next letter, he awkwardly began, "The explanation for the curious signature on my last letter is that, in my absent-mindedness, instead of signing my own name, I frequently sign for the person to whom the letter is addressed" (Einstein to Hans Albert Einstein, March 11 and 16, 1916).

tempts to force me into marriage come from my cousin's parents and is mainly attributable to vanity, though moral prejudice, which is still very much alive in the old generation, plays a part," Einstein wrote Zangger the day after presenting his climactic November 1915 lecture. "If I let myself become trapped, my life would become complicated, and above all it would probably be a heavy blow for my boys. Therefore, I must allow myself not to be moved either by my inclination or by tears, but must remain as I am." It was a resolution he repeated to Besso as well.[6]

Besso and Zangger agreed that he should not seek a divorce. "It is important that Einstein knows that his truest friends," Besso wrote Zangger, "would regard a divorce and subsequent remarriage as a great evil."[7]

But Elsa and her family kept pushing. So in February 1916, Einstein wrote Marić to propose—indeed, beg—that she agree to a divorce, "so that we can arrange the rest of our lives independently." The separation agreement they had worked out with the help of Fritz Haber, he suggested, could serve as the basis for a divorce. "It will surely be possible to have the details settled to your satisfaction," he promised. His letter also included instructions on how to keep their boys from suffering from calcium deficiency.[8]

When Marić resisted, Einstein became more insistent. "For you it involves a mere formality," he said. "For me, however, it is an imperative duty." He informed Marić that Elsa had two daughters whose reputations and chances of marriage were being compromised by "the rumors" that were circulating about the illicit relationship their mother was having with Einstein. "This weighs on me and ought to be redressed by a formal marriage," he told Marić. "Try to imagine yourself in my position for once."

As an enticement, he offered more money. "You would gain from this change," he told Marić. "I wish to do more than I had obligated myself to before." He would transfer 6,000 marks into a fund for the children and increase her payments to 5,600 marks annually. "By making myself such a frugal bed of straw, I am proving to you that my boys' well-being is closest to my heart, above all else in the world."

In return, he wanted the right to have his sons visit him in Berlin. They would not come into contact with Elsa, he pledged. He even added a somewhat surprising promise: he would not be living with Elsa even if they got married. Instead, he would keep his own apartment. "For I shall never give up the state of living alone, which has manifested itself as an indescribable blessing."

Marić did not consent to give him the right to have the boys visit him in Berlin. But she did tentatively agree—or at least so Einstein thought—to allow the start of divorce discussions.[9]

As he had promised Hans Albert, Einstein arrived in Switzerland in early April 1916 for a three-week Easter vacation, moving into a hotel near the Zurich train station. Initially, things went very well. The boys came to see him and greeted him joyously. From his hotel, he sent Marić a note of thanks:

> My compliments on the good condition of our boys. They are in such excellent physical and mental shape that I could not have wished for more. And I know that this is for the most part due to the proper upbringing you provide them. I am likewise thankful that you have not alienated me from the children. They came to meet me spontaneously and sweetly.

Marić sent word that she wanted to see Einstein herself. Her goal was to be assured that he truly wanted a divorce and was not merely being pressured by Elsa. Both Besso and Zangger tried to arrange such a meeting, but Einstein declined. "There would be no point in a conversation between us and it could serve only to reopen old wounds," he wrote in a note to Marić.[10]

Einstein took Hans Albert off alone, as the boy wished, for what was planned as a ten-day hiking excursion in a mountain resort overlooking Lake Lucerne. There they were caught in a late-season snowstorm that kept them confined to the inn, which initially pleased them both. "We are snowed in at Seelisberg but are enjoying ourselves immensely," Einstein wrote Elsa. "The boy delights me, especially with his clever questions and his undemanding way. No discord exists between us." Unfortunately, soon the weather, and perhaps also their enforced togetherness, became oppressive, and they returned to Zurich a few days early.[11]

Back in Zurich, the tensions revived. One morning, Hans Albert came to visit his father at the physics institute to watch an experiment. It was a pleasant enough activity, but as the boy was leaving for lunch, he urged his father to come by the house and at least pay a courtesy call on Marić.

Einstein refused. Hans Albert, who was just about to turn 12, became angry and said he would not come back for the completion of the experiment that afternoon unless his father relented. Einstein would not. "That's how it remained," he reported to Elsa a week later, on the day he left Zurich. "And I have seen neither of the children since."[12]

Marić subsequently went into an emotional and physical meltdown. She had a series of minor heart incidents in July 1916, accompanied by extreme anxiety, and her doctors told her to remain in bed. The children moved in with the Bessos, and then to Lausanne, where they stayed with Marić's friend Helene Savić, who was riding out the war there.

Besso and Zangger tried to get Einstein to come down from Berlin to be with his sons. But Einstein demurred. "If I go to Zurich, my wife will demand to see me," he wrote Besso. "This I would have to refuse, partly on an inalterable resolve partly also to spare her the agitation. Besides, you know that the personal relations between the children and me deteriorated so much during my stay at Easter (after a very promising start) that I doubt very much whether my presence would be reassuring for them."

Einstein assumed that his wife's illness was largely psychological and even, perhaps, partly faked. "Isn't it possible that nerves are behind it all?" he asked Zangger. To Besso, he was more blunt: "I have the suspicion that the woman is leading both of you kind-hearted men down the garden path. She is not afraid to use all means when she wants to achieve something. You have no idea of the natural craftiness of such a woman."[13] Einstein's mother agreed. "Mileva was never as sick as you seem to think," she told Elsa.[14]

Einstein asked Besso to keep him informed of the situation and made a stab at scientific humor by saying that his reports did not need to have logical "continuity" because "this is permissible in the age of quantum theory." Besso was not sympathetic; he wrote Einstein a sharp letter saying Marić's condition was not "a deception" but was instead caused by emotional stress. Besso's wife, Anna, was even harsher, adding a postscript to the letter that addressed Einstein with the formal *Sie*.[15]

Einstein backed down from his charge that Marić was faking illness, but railed that her emotional distress was unwarranted. "She leads a worry-free life, has her two precious boys with her, lives in a fabulous neighborhood, does what she likes with her time, and innocently stands by as the guiltless party," he wrote Besso.

Einstein was especially stung by the cold postscript, which he mistakenly thought came from Michele rather than Anna Besso. So he added his own postscript: "We have understood each other well for 20 years," he said. "And now I see you developing a bitterness toward me for the sake of a woman who has nothing to do with you. Resist it!" Later that day he realized he had mistaken Anna's harsh postscript for something her husband had written, and he quickly sent along another note apologizing to him.[16]

On Zangger's advice, Marić checked into a sanatorium. Einstein still resisted going to Zurich, even though his boys were at home alone with a maid, but he told Zangger he would change his mind "if you think it's appropriate." Zangger didn't. "The tension on both sides is too great," Zangger explained to Besso, who agreed.[17]

Despite his detached attitude, Einstein loved his sons and would always take care of them. Please let them know, he instructed Zangger, that he would take them under his wing if their mother died. "I would raise the two boys myself," he said. "They would be taught at home, as far as possible by me personally." In various letters over the next few months, Einstein described his different ideas and fantasies for home-schooling his sons, what he would teach, and even the type of walks they would take. He wrote Hans Albert to assure him that he was "constantly thinking of you both."[18]

But Hans Albert was so angry, or hurt, that he had stopped answering his father's letters. "I believe that his attitude toward me has fallen below the freezing point," Einstein lamented to Besso. "Under the given circumstances, I would have reacted in the same way." After three

letters to his son went unanswered in three months, Einstein plaintively wrote him: "Don't you remember your father anymore? Are we
never going to see each other again?"[19]

Finally, the boy replied by sending a picture of a boat he was constructing out of wood carvings. He also described his mother's return
from the sanatorium. "When Mama came home, we had a celebration.
I had practiced a sonata by Mozart, and Tete had learned a song."[20]

Einstein did make one concession to the sad situation: he decided
to give up asking Marić for a divorce, at least for the time being. That
seemed to aid her recovery. "I'll take care that she doesn't get any more
disturbance from me," he told Besso. "I have abandoned proceeding
with the divorce. Now on to scientific matters!"[21]

Indeed, whenever personal issues began to weigh on him, he took
refuge in his work. It shielded him, allowed him to escape. As he told
Helene Savić, likely with the intent that it get back to her friend Marić,
he planned to retreat into scientific reflection. "I resemble a farsighted
man who is charmed by the vast horizon and whom the foreground
bothers only when an opaque object prevents him from taking in the
long view."[22]

So even as the personal battle was raging, his science provided solace. In 1916, he began writing again about the quantum. He also wrote
a formal exposition of his general theory of relativity, which was far
more comprehensive, and slightly more comprehensible, than what
had poured forth in the weekly lectures during his race with Hilbert
the previous November.[23]

In addition, he produced an even more understandable version: a
book for the lay reader, *Relativity: The Special and the General Theory*,
that remains popular to this day. To make sure that the average person
would fathom it, he read every page out loud to Elsa's daughter Margot, pausing frequently to ask whether she indeed got it. "Yes, Albert,"
she invariably replied, even though (as she confided to others) she
found the whole thing totally baffling.[24]

This ability of science to be used as a refuge from painful personal
emotions was a theme of a talk he gave at a celebration of Max Planck's
sixtieth birthday. Putatively about Planck, it seemed to convey more

about Einstein himself. "One of the strongest motives that leads men to art and science is escape from everyday life with its painful crudity and hopeless dreariness," Einstein said. "Such men make this cosmos and its construction the pivot of their emotional life, in order to find the peace and security which they cannot find in the narrow whirlpool of personal experience."[25]

The Treaty

In early 1917, it was Einstein's turn to fall ill. He came down with stomach pains that he initially thought were caused by cancer. Now that his mission was complete, death did not frighten him. He told the astronomer Freundlich that he was not worried about dying because now he had completed his theory of relativity.

Freundlich, on the other hand, did worry about his friend, who was still only 38. He sent Einstein to a doctor, who diagnosed the problem as a chronic stomach malady, one that was exacerbated by wartime food shortages. He put him on a four-week diet of rice, macaroni, and zwieback bread.

These stomach ailments would lay him low for the next four years, then linger for the rest of his life. He was living alone and having trouble getting proper meals. From Zurich, Zangger sent packages to help satisfy the prescribed diet, but within two months Einstein had lost close to fifty pounds. Finally, by the summer of 1917, Elsa was able to rent a second apartment in her building, and she moved him in there to be her neighbor, charge, and companion.[26]

Elsa took great joy in foraging for the food he found comforting. She was resourceful and wealthy enough to commandeer the eggs and butter and bread he liked, even though the war made such staples hard to come by. Every day she cooked for him, doted on him, even found him cigars. Her parents helped as well by having them both over for comforting meals.[27]

The health of his younger son, Eduard, also was precarious. Once again he had fevers, and in early 1917 his lungs became inflamed. After receiving a pessimistic medical prognosis, Einstein lamented to

Besso, "My little boy's condition depresses me greatly. It is impossible that he will become a fully developed person. Who knows if it wouldn't be better for him if he could depart before coming to know life properly."

To Zangger, he ruminated about the "Spartan's method"—leaving sickly children out on a mountain to die—but then said he could not accept that approach. Instead, he promised to pay whatever it took to get Eduard care, and he told Zangger to send him to whatever treatment facility he thought best. "Even if you silently say to yourself that every effort is futile, send him anyway, so that my wife and my Albert think that something is being done."[28]

That summer, Einstein traveled back to Switzerland to take Eduard to a sanatorium in the Swiss village of Arosa. His ability to use science to rise above personal travails was illustrated in a letter he sent to his physicist friend Paul Ehrenfest: "The little one is very sickly and must go to Arosa for a year. My wife is also ailing. Worries and more worries. Nevertheless, I have found a nice generalization of the Sommerfeld-Epstein quantum law."[29]

Hans Albert joined his father on the journey to take Eduard to Arosa, and he then visited when Einstein was staying with his sister, Maja, and her husband, Paul Winteler, in Lucerne. There he found his father bedridden with stomach pains, but his uncle Paul took him hiking. Gradually, with a few rough patches, Einstein's relationship with his older son was being restored. "The letter from my Albert was the greatest joy I've had for the past year," he told Zangger. "I sense with bliss the intimate tie between us." Financial worries were also easing. "I received a prize of 1,500 crowns from the Viennese Academy, which we can use for Tete's cure."[30]

Now that he had moved into the same building as Elsa and she was nursing him back to health, it was inevitable that the issue of a divorce from Marić would arise again. In early 1918, it did. "My desire to put my private affairs in some state of order prompts me to suggest a divorce to you for a second time," he wrote. "I am resolved to do everything to make this step possible." This time his financial offer was even more generous. He would pay her 9,000 marks rather than what had now become a 6,000 annual stipend, with the provision that 2,000 would go into a fund for their children.*

Then he added an amazing new inducement. He was convinced, with good reason, that he would someday win the Nobel Prize. Even though the scientific community had not yet fully come to grips with special relativity, much less his new and unproven theory of general relativity, eventually it would. Or his groundbreaking insights into light quanta and the photoelectric effect would be recognized. And so he made a striking offer to Marić: "The Nobel Prize—in the event of the divorce and the event that it is bestowed upon me—would be ceded to you in full." [31]

It was a financially enticing wager. The Nobel Prize was then, as it is now, very lucrative, indeed huge. In 1918, it was worth about 135,000 Swedish kronor, or 225,000 German marks—more than 37 times what Marić was getting annually. In addition, the German mark was starting to collapse, but the Nobel would be paid in stable Swedish currency. Most poignantly, there would be some symbolic justice: she had helped Einstein with the math and proofreading and domestic support for his 1905 papers, and now she could reap some of the reward.

At first she was furious. "Exactly two years ago, such letters pushed me over the brink into misery, which I still can't get over," she replied. "Why do you torment me so endlessly? I really don't deserve this from you." [32]

But within a few days, she began to assess the situation more clinically. Her life had reached a low point. She suffered pains, anxieties, and depression. Her younger son was in a sanatorium. The sister who had come to help her succumbed to depression and had been committed to an asylum. And her brother, who was serving as a medic in the

---

* Einstein's salary after tax was 13,000 marks. Inflation was beginning to set in, and the value of the German mark had fallen from 24 cents in 1914 to 19 cents in January 1918. One mark at the time would buy two dozen eggs or four loaves of bread. (A year later, the mark would be worth only 12 cents, and when hyperinflation began to rage in January 1920 only 2 cents.) Marić's stipend of 6,000 marks in January 1918 was thus worth about $1,140, or just under $15,000 in inflation-adjusted 2006 dollars. His proposal was to increase this by 50 percent.

Austrian army, had been captured by the Russians. Perhaps an end to the battles with her husband and the chance of financial security might, in fact, be best for her. So she discussed the option with her neighbor Emil Zürcher, who was a lawyer and a friend.

A few days later she decided to take the deal. "Have your lawyer write Dr. Zürcher about how he envisions it, how the contract should be," she replied. "I must leave upsetting things to objective persons. I do not want to stand in the way of your happiness, if you are so resolved."[33]

The negotiations proceeded through letters and third parties through April. "I am curious what will last longer, the world war or our divorce proceedings," he complained lightly at one point. But as things were progressing the way he wanted, he merrily added, "In comparison, this little matter of ours is still much the more pleasant. Amiable greetings to you and kisses to the boys."

The main issue was money. Marić complained to a friend that Einstein was being stingy (in fact he wasn't) because of Elsa. "Elsa's very greedy," Marić charged. "Her two sisters are very rich, and she's always envious of them." Letters went back and forth over exactly how the prospective Nobel Prize money would be paid, what right the children would have to it, what would happen to it if she remarried, and even what compensation he would offer in the unlikely event that the prize was never awarded to him.[34]

Another contentious issue was whether his sons could visit him in Berlin. On barring that, Marić held firm.[35] Finally, at the end of April, he surrendered this final point. "I'm giving in about the children because I now believe you want to handle matters in a conciliatory manner," he said. "Maybe you will later take the view that the boys can come here without reservation. For the time being, I will see them in Switzerland."[36]

Given Marić's poor health, Einstein had tried to work out another option for the two boys: having them live in nearby Lucerne with his sister, Maja, and her husband, Paul Winteler. The Wintelers were willing to take custody of their nephews, and they took the train to Bern one day to see if this could be arranged. But when they arrived, Zanger was away, and they wanted his help before discussing things with

Marić. So Paul went over to see his feisty sister Anna, who was married to Michele Besso, to see if they could have a room for the night.

He had planned not to tell Anna the purpose of their mission, as she had a protective attitude toward Marić and a hair-trigger sense of righteous indignation. "But she guessed the purpose of our coming," Maja reported to Einstein, "and when Paul confirmed her suspicions a torrent of accusations, scoldings, and threats poured forth."[37]

So Einstein wrote a letter to Anna to try to enlist her support. Marić, he argued, was "incapable of running a household" given her condition. It would be best if Hans Albert went to live with Maja and Paul, he argued. Eduard could either do the same or stay in a mountain-air clinic until his health improved. Einstein would pay for it all, including Marić's costs in a sanatorium in Lucerne, where she could see her sons every day.

Unfortunately, Einstein made the mistake of ending the letter by pleading with Anna to help resolve the situation so that he could marry Elsa and end the shame that their relationship was causing her daughters. "Think of the two young girls, whose prospects of getting married are being hampered," he said. "Do put in a good word for me sometime to Miza [Marić] and make it clear to her how unkind it is to complicate the lives of others pointlessly."[38]

Anna shot back that Elsa was the one being selfish. "If Elsa had not wanted to make herself so vulnerable, she should not have run after you so conspicuously."[39]

In truth, Anna was quite difficult, and she soon had a falling out with Marić as well. "She tried to meddle in my affairs in a way that reveals potential human malice," Marić complained to Einstein. At the very least, this helped improve relations between the Einsteins. "I see from your letter that you also have had problems with Anna Besso," he wrote Marić just after they had agreed to the divorce terms. "She has written me such impertinent letters that I've put an end to further correspondence."[40]

It would be a few more months before the divorce decree could become final, but now that the negotiations were complete, everyone seemed relieved that there would be closure. Marić's health improved enough so that the children would remain with her,[41] and the letters

back and forth from Berlin and Zurich became friendlier. "A satisfactory relationship has formed between me and my wife through the
correspondence about the divorce!" he told Zangger. "A funny opportunity indeed for reconciliation." [42]

This détente meant that Einstein had an option for his summer
vacation of 1918: visit his children in Zurich, or have a less stressful
holiday with Elsa. He chose the latter, partly because his doctor recommended against the altitude, and for seven weeks he and Elsa stayed in
the Baltic Sea resort of Aarenshoop. He brought along some light
beach reading, Immanuel Kant's *Prolegomena*, spent "countless hours
pondering the quantum problem," and gloried in relaxing and recovering from his stomach ailments. "No telephones, no responsibilities, absolute tranquility," he wrote to a friend. "I am lying on the shore like a
crocodile, allowing myself to be roasted by the sun, never see a newspaper, and do not give a hoot about the so-called world." [43]

From this unlikely vacation, he sought to mollify Hans Albert, who
had written to say he missed his father. "Write me please why you aren't
coming, at least," he asked. [44] Einstein's explanation was sad and very
defensive:

> You can easily imagine why I could not come. This winter I was so sick
> that I had to lie in bed for over two months. Every meal must be cooked
> separately for me. I may not make any abrupt movements. So I'd have
> been allowed neither to go on a walk with you nor to eat at the hotel . . .
> Added to this is that I had quarreled with Anna Besso, and that I did not
> want to become a burden to Mr. Zangger again, and finally, that I
> doubted whether my coming mattered much to you. [45]

His son was understanding. He wrote him letters filled with news
and ideas, including a description and sketch of an idea he had for a
pendulum inside a monorail that would swing and break the electric
circuit whenever the train tilted too much.

Einstein had rebuked Hans Albert, unfairly, for not finding some
way to visit him in Germany during the vacation. That would have required Marić to waive the provision in their separation agreement that
barred such trips, and it would also have been sadly impractical. "My
coming to Germany would be almost more impossible than your com-

ing here," Hans Albert wrote, "because in the end I am the only one in the family who can shop for anything."[46]

So Einstein, yearning to be nearer to his boys, found himself briefly tempted to move back to Zurich. During his Baltic vacation that summer of 1918, he considered a combined offer from the University of Zurich and his old Zurich Polytechnic. "You can design your position here exactly as you wish," the physicist Edgar Meyer wrote. As Einstein jokingly noted to Besso, "How happy I would have been 18 years ago with a measly assistantship."[47]

Einstein admitted that he was tormented by the decision. Zurich was his "true home," and Switzerland was the only country for which he felt any affinity. Plus, he would be near his sons.

But there was one rub. If he moved close to his sons he would be moving close to their mother. Even for Einstein, who was good at shielding himself from personal emotions, it would be hard to set up household with Elsa in the same town as his first wife. "My major personal difficulties would persist if I pitched my tent in Zurich again," he told Besso, "although it does seem tempting to be close to my children."[48]

Elsa was also adamantly opposed to the prospect, even appalled. She begged Einstein to promise it would not happen. Einstein could be quite solicitous about Elsa's desires, and so he backed away from a full-time move to Zurich.

Instead, he did something he usually avoided: he compromised. He retained his position in Berlin but agreed to be a guest lecturer in Zurich, making month-long visits there twice a year. That, he thought, could give him the best of both worlds.

In what seemed like an excess of Swiss caution, the Zurich authorities approved the lecture contract, which paid Einstein his expenses but no fee, "by way of experiment." They were in fact wise; Einstein's lectures were initially very popular, but eventually attendance dwindled and they would be canceled after two years.

The Social Democrat

Which would finish first, Einstein had wondered half-jokingly to Marić, the world war or their divorce proceedings? As it turned out, both came to a messy resolution at the end of 1918. As the German Reich was crumbling that November, a revolt by sailors in Kiel mushroomed into a general strike and popular uprising. "Class canceled because of Revolution," Einstein noted in his lecture diary on November 9, the day that protestors occupied the Reichstag and the kaiser abdicated. Four days later, a worker-student revolutionary council took over the University of Berlin and jailed its deans and rector.

With the outbreak of war, Einstein had become, for the first time, an outspoken public figure, advocating internationalism, European federalism, and resistance to militarism. Now, the coming of the peace turned Einstein's political thinking toward more domestic and social issues.

From his youth as an admirer of Jost Winteler and a friend of Friedrich Adler, Einstein had been attracted to the ideal of socialism as well as that of individual freedom. The revolution in Berlin—led by a collection of socialists, workers' councils, communists, and others on the left—caused him to confront cases when these two ideals conflicted.

For the rest of his life Einstein would expound a democratic socialism that had a liberal, anti-authoritarian underpinning. He advocated equality, social justice, and the taming of capitalism. He was a fierce defender of the underdog. But to the extent that any revolutionaries edged over toward a Bolshevik desire to impose centralized control, or to the extent that a regime such as Russia's struck him as authoritarian, Einstein's instinctive love of individual liberty usually provoked a disdainful reaction.

"Socialism to him reflects the ethical desire to remove the appalling chasm between the classes and to produce a more just economic system," his stepson-in-law wrote of Einstein's attitudes during the 1920s. "And yet he cannot accept a socialist program. He appreciates the adventure of solitude and the happiness of freedom too much to welcome a system that threatens completely to eliminate the individual." [49]

It was an attitude that remained constant. "Einstein's basic political philosophy did not undergo any significant changes during his lifetime," said Otto Nathan, a socialist, who became a close friend and then literary executor after Einstein moved to America. "He welcomed the revolutionary development of Germany in 1918 because of his interest in socialism and particularly because of his profound and unqualified devotion to democracy. Basic to his political thinking was the recognition of the dignity of the individual and the protection of political and intellectual freedom."[50]

When the student revolutionaries in Berlin jailed their rector and deans, Einstein got to put this philosophy into practice. The physicist Max Born was in bed that day with the flu when his telephone rang. It was Einstein. He was heading over to the university to see what he could do to get the rector and deans released, and he insisted that Born get out of bed and join him. They also enlisted a third friend, the pioneering Gestalt psychologist Max Wertheimer, perhaps in the belief that his specialty might be more useful than theoretical physics in accomplishing the task.

The three took the tram from Einstein's apartment to the Reichstag, where the students were meeting. At first their way was blocked by a dense mob, but the crowd parted once Einstein was recognized, and they were ushered to a conference room where the student soviet was meeting.

The chairman greeted them and asked them to wait while the group finished hammering out their new statutes for governing the university. Then he turned to Einstein. "Before we come to your request to speak, Professor Einstein, may I be permitted to ask what you think of the new regulations?"

Einstein paused for a moment. Some people are innately conditioned to hedge their words, try to please their listeners, and enjoy the comfort that comes from conforming. Not Einstein. Instead, he responded critically. "I have always thought that the German university's most valuable institution is academic freedom, whereby the lecturers are in no way told what to teach, and the students are able to choose what lectures to attend, without much supervision and control," he said. "Your new statutes seem to abolish all of this. I would be very sorry if the old freedom were to come to an end." At that point, Born recalled, "the high and mighty young gentlemen sat in perplexed silence."

That did not help his mission. After some discussion, the students decided that they did not have the authority to release the rector and deans. So Einstein and company went off to the Reich chancellor's palace to seek out someone who did. They were able to find the new German president, who seemed harried and baffled and perfectly willing to scribble a note ordering the release.

It worked. The trio succeeded in springing their colleagues, and, as Born recalled, "We left the Chancellor's palace in high spirits, feeling that we had taken part in a historical event and hoping to have seen the last of Prussian arrogance." [51]

Einstein then went down the street to a mass meeting of the revived New Fatherland League, where he delivered a two-page speech that he had carried with him to his confrontation with the students. Calling himself "an old-time believer in democracy," he again made clear that his socialist sentiments did not make him sympathetic to Soviet-style controls. "All true democrats must stand guard lest the old class tyranny of the Right be replaced by a new class tyranny of the Left," he said.

Some on the left insisted that democracy, or at least multiparty liberal democracy, needed to be put aside until the masses could be educated and a new revolutionary consciousness take hold. Einstein disagreed. "Do not be seduced by feelings that a dictatorship of the proletariat is temporarily needed in order to hammer the concept of freedom into the heads of our fellow countrymen," he told the rally. Instead, he decried Germany's new left-wing government as "dictatorial," and he demanded that it immediately call open elections, "thereby eliminating all fears of a new tyranny as soon as possible." [52]

Years later, when Adolf Hitler and his Nazis were in power, Einstein would ruefully look back on that day in Berlin. "Do you still remember the occasion some 25 years ago when we went together to the Reichstag building, convinced that we could turn the people there into honest democrats?" he wrote Born. "How naïve we were for men of forty." [53]

Marrying Elsa

Just after the war ended, so did Einstein's divorce proceedings. As part of the process, he had to give a deposition admitting adultery. On December 23, 1918, he appeared before a court in Berlin, stood before a magistrate, and declared, "I have been living together with my cousin, the widow Elsa Einstein, divorced Löwenthal, for about 4½ years and have been continuing these intimate relations since then."[54]

As if to prove it, he brought Elsa when he traveled to Zurich the following month to deliver his first set of lectures there. His opening talks, unlike his later ones, were so well attended that, to Einstein's annoyance, an official was posted at the door to prevent unauthorized auditors from getting in. Hans Albert came to visit him at his hotel, presumably when Elsa was not there, and Einstein spent a few days in Arosa, where Eduard was still recuperating in a sanatorium.[55]

Einstein stayed in Zurich through February 14, when he stood before three local magistrates who granted his final divorce decree. It included the provisions regarding his prospective Nobel Prize award. In his deposition, Einstein had given his religion as "dissenter," but in the divorce decree the clerk designated him "Mosaic." Marić was also designated "Mosaic," even though she had been born and remained a Serbian Orthodox Christian.

As was customary, the decree included the order that "the Defendant [Einstein] is restrained from entering into a new marriage for the period of two years."[56] Einstein had no intention of obeying that provision. He had decided that he would marry Elsa, and he would end up doing so within four months.

His decision to remarry was accompanied by a drama that was, if true, weird even by the standards of his unusual family dynamics. It involved Elsa Einstein's daughter Ilse and the pacifist physician and adventurer Georg Nicolai.

Ilse, then 21, was the elder of Elsa's two daughters. Einstein had hired her as the secretary for the unbuilt Kaiser Wilhelm Institute of Physics that he was supposed to be creating (the only scientist who had been hired so far was his faithful astronomer Freundlich). A spirited, idealistic, swanlike beauty, Ilse's mystique was enhanced by the fact that as a child she had lost the use of an eye in an accident. Like a moth to flame, she was attracted to radical politics and fascinating men.

Thus it was not surprising that she fell for Georg Nicolai, who had collaborated with Einstein in 1914 on the pacifist response to the German intellectuals' "Appeal to the Cultured World." Among other things, Nicolai was a doctor specializing in electrocardiograms who had occasionally treated Elsa. A brilliant egomaniac with a serious sexual appetite, he had been born in Germany and had lived in Paris and Russia. During one visit to Russia, he kept a list of the women he had sex with, totaling sixteen in all, including two mother-daughter pairs.

Ilse fell in love with Nicolai and with his politics. In addition to being, at least briefly, his lover, she helped type and distribute his protest letters. She also helped persuade Einstein to support the publication of Nicolai's pacifist tome, *The Biology of War*, which included their ill-fated 1914 manifesto and a collection of liberal writings by Kant and other classical German authors.[57]

Einstein had initially supported this publishing project, but in early 1917 had labeled the idea "entirely hopeless." Nicolai, who had been drafted as a lowly medical orderly for the German army, somehow thought that Einstein would fund the endeavor, and he kept badgering him. "Nothing is more difficult than turning Nicolai down," Einstein wrote him, addressing him in the third person. "The man, who in other things is so sensitive that even grass growing is a considerable din to him, seems almost deaf when the sound involves a refusal."[58]

On one of Ilse's visits to see Nicolai, she told him that Einstein was now planning to marry her mother. Nicolai, an aficionado of the art of dating both mother and daughter, told Ilse that Einstein had it wrong. He should marry Ilse rather than her mother.

It is unclear what psychological game he was playing with his young lover's mind. And it is likewise unclear what psychological game she was playing with his mind, or her own mind, when she wrote him a detailed letter saying that the Ilse-or-Elsa question had suddenly become a real one for Einstein. The letter is so striking and curious it bears being quoted at length:

You are the only person to whom I can entrust the following and the only one who can give me advice . . . You remember that we recently spoke about Albert's and Mama's marriage and you told me that you thought a marriage between Albert and me would be more proper. I never thought seriously about it until yesterday. Yesterday, the question was suddenly raised about whether Albert wished to marry Mama or me. This question, initially posed half in jest, became within a few minutes a serious matter which must now be considered and discussed fully and completely. Albert himself is refusing to take any decision, he is prepared to marry either me or Mama. I know that Albert loves me very much, perhaps more than any other man ever will. He told me so himself yesterday. On the one hand, he might even prefer me as his wife, since I am young and he could have children with me, which naturally does not apply at all in Mama's case; but he is far too decent and loves Mama too much ever to mention it. You know how I stand with Albert. I love him very much; I have the greatest respect for him as a person. If ever there was true friendship and camaraderie between two beings of different types, those are quite certainly my feelings for Albert. I have never wished nor felt the least desire to be close to him physically. This is otherwise in his case—recently at least. He admitted to me once how difficult it is for him to keep himself in check. But now I do believe that my feelings for him are not sufficient for conjugal life . . . The third person still to be mentioned in this odd and certainly also highly comical affair would be Mother. For the present—because she does not yet firmly believe that I am really serious. She has allowed me to choose completely freely. If she saw that I could really be happy only with Albert, she would surely step aside out of love for me. But it would certainly be bitterly hard for her. And then I do not know whether it really would be fair if—after all her years of struggle—I were to compete with her over the place she had won for herself, now that she is finally at the goal. Philistines like the grandparents are naturally appalled about these new plans. Mother would supposedly be disgraced and other such unpleasant things . . . Albert also thought that if I did not wish to have a child of his it would be nicer for me not to be married to him. And I truly do not have this wish. It will seem peculiar to you that I, a silly little thing of a 20-year-old, should have to decide on such a serious matter; I can hardly believe it myself and feel very unhappy doing so as well. Help me! Yours, Ilse.[59]

She wrote a big note on top of the first page: "Please destroy this letter immediately after reading it!" Nicolai didn't.

Was it true? Was it half-true? Was the truth relative to the observer? The only evidence we have of Einstein's mother-daughter dithering is this one letter. No one else, then or in recollections, ever mentioned the issue. The letter was written by an intense and love-struck young woman to a dashing philanderer whose attentions she craved. Perhaps it was merely her fantasy, or her ploy to provoke Nicolai's jealousy. As with much of nature, especially human nature, the underlying reality, if there is such a thing, may not be knowable.

As it turned out, Einstein married Elsa in June 1919, and Ilse ended up remaining close to both of them.

Einstein's family relations seemed to be improving on all fronts. The very next month, he went to Zurich to see his boys, and he stayed with Hans Albert at his first wife's apartment while she was away. Elsa seemed worried about that arrangement, but he reassured her in at least two letters that Marić would not be around much. "Camping in the lioness's den is proving very worthwhile," he said in one, "and there's no fear of any incident happening." Together he and Hans Albert went sailing, played music, and built a model airplane together. "The boy gives me indescribable joy," he wrote Elsa. "He is very diligent and persistent in everything he does. He also plays piano very nicely." [60]

His relations with his first family were now so calm that, during his July 1919 visit, he once again thought that maybe he should move there with Elsa and her daughters. This completely flummoxed Elsa, who made her feelings very clear. Einstein backed down. "We're going to stay in Berlin, all right," he reassured her. "So calm down and never fear!" [61]

Einstein's new marriage was different from his first. It was not romantic or passionate. From the start, he and Elsa had separate bedrooms at opposite ends of their rambling Berlin apartment. Nor was it intellectual. Understanding relativity, she later said, "is not necessary for my happiness." [62]

She was, on the other hand, talented in practical ways that often eluded her husband. She spoke French and English well, which allowed her to serve as his translator as well as manager when he traveled. "I am not talented in any direction except perhaps as wife and mother," she said. "My interest in mathematics is mainly in the household bills." [63]

That comment reflects her humility and a simmering insecurity, but it sells her short. It was no simple task to play the role of wife and mother to Einstein, who required both, nor to manage their finances and logistics. She did it with good sense and warmth. Even though, every now and then, she succumbed to a few pretenses that came with their standing, she generally displayed an unaffected manner and self-aware humor, and in doing so she thus helped make sure that her husband retained those traits as well.

The marriage was, in fact, a solid symbiosis, and it served adequately, for the most part, the needs and desires of both partners. Elsa was an efficient and lively woman, who was eager to serve and protect him. She liked his fame, and (unlike him) did not try to hide that fact. She also appreciated the social standing it gave them, even if it meant she had to merrily shoo away reporters and other invaders of her husband's privacy.

He was as pleased to be looked after as she was to look after him. She told him when to eat and where to go. She packed his suitcases and doled out his pocket money. In public, she was protective of the man she called "the Professor" or even simply "Einstein."

That allowed him to spend hours in a rather dreamy state, focusing more on the cosmos than on the world around him. All of which gave her excitement and satisfaction. "The Lord has put into him so much that's beautiful, and I find him wonderful, even though life at his side is enervating and difficult," she once said.[64]

When Einstein was in one of his periods of intense work, as was often the case, Elsa "recognized the need for keeping all disturbing elements away from him," a relative noted. She would make his favorite meal of lentil soup and sausages, summon him down from his study, and then would leave him alone as he mechanically ate his meal. But when he would mutter or protest, she would remind him that it was important for him to eat. "People have centuries to find things out," she would say, "but your stomach, no, it will not wait for centuries."[65]

She came to know, from a faraway look in his eyes, when he was "seized with a problem," as she called it, and thus should not be disturbed. He would pace up and down in his study, and she would have food sent up. When his intense concentration was over, he would finally come down to the table for a meal and, sometimes, ask to go on a walk with Elsa and her daughters. They always complied, but they never initiated such a request. "It is he who has to do the asking," a newspaper reported after interviewing her, "and when he asks them for a walk they know that his mind is relieved of work."[66]

Elsa's daughter Ilse would eventually marry Rudolf Kayser, editor of the premier literary magazine in Germany, and they set up a house filled with art and artists and writers. Margot, who liked sculpting, was so shy that she would sometimes hide under the table when guests of her father arrived. She lived at home even after she married, in 1930, a Russian named Dimitri Marianoff. Both of these sons-in-law, it turned out, would end up writing florid but undistinguished books about the Einstein family.

For the time being, Einstein and Elsa and her two daughters lived together in a spacious and somberly furnished apartment near the center of Berlin. The wallpaper was dark green, the tablecloths white linen with lace embroidery. "One felt that Einstein would always remain a stranger in such a household," said his friend and colleague Philipp Frank, "a Bohemian as a guest in a bourgeois home."

In defiance of building codes, they converted three attic rooms into a garret study with a big new window. It was occasionally dusted, never tidied, and papers piled up under the benign gazes of Newton, Maxwell, and Faraday. There Einstein would sit in an old armchair, pad on his knee. Occasionally he would get up to pace, then he would sit back down to scribble the equations that would, he hoped, extend his theory of relativity into an explanation of the cosmos.[67]

CHAPTER ELEVEN

EINSTEIN'S UNIVERSE

1916–1919

In his Berlin home study

Cosmology and Black Holes, 1917

Cosmology is the study of the universe as a whole, including its size and shape, its history and destiny, from one end to the other, from the beginning to the end of time. That's a big topic. And it's not a simple one. It's not even simple to define what those concepts mean, or even if they have meaning. With the gravitational field equations in his general theory of relativity, Einstein laid the foundations for studying the nature of the universe, thereby becoming the primary founder of modern cosmology.

Helping him in this endeavor, at least in the early stages, was a profound mathematician and even more distinguished astrophysicist, Karl Schwarzschild, who directed the Potsdam Observatory. He read Einstein's new formulation of general relativity and, at the beginning of 1916, set about trying to apply it to objects in space.

One thing made Schwarzschild's work very difficult. He had volunteered for the German military during the war, and when he read Einstein's papers he was stationed in Russia, projecting the trajectory of artillery shells. Nevertheless, he was also able to find time to calculate what the gravitational field would be, according to Einstein's theory, around an object in space. It was the wartime counterpart to Einstein's ability to come up with the special theory of relativity while examining patent applications for the synchronization of clocks.

In January 1916, Schwarzschild mailed his result to Einstein with the declaration that it permitted his theory "to shine with increased purity." Among other things, it reconfirmed, with greater rigor, the success of Einstein's equations in explaining Mercury's orbit. Einstein was thrilled. "I would not have expected that the exact solution to the problem could be formulated so simply," he replied. The following Thursday, he personally delivered the paper at the Prussian Academy's weekly meeting.[1]

Schwarzschild's first calculations focused on the curvature of spacetime *outside* a spherical, nonspinning star. A few weeks later, he sent Einstein another paper on what it would be like *inside* such a star.

In both cases, something unusual seemed possible, indeed inevitable. If all the mass of a star (or any object) was compressed into a tiny enough space—defined by what became known as the Schwarzschild radius—then all of the calculations seemed to break down. At the center, spacetime would infinitely curve in on itself. For our sun, that would happen if all of its mass were compressed into a radius of less than two miles. For the earth, it would happen if all the mass were compressed into a radius of about one-third of an inch.

What would that mean? In such a situation, nothing within the Schwarzschild radius would be able to escape the gravitational pull, not even light or any other form of radiation. Time would also be part of the warpage as well, dilated to zero. In other words, a traveler nearing the Schwarzschild radius would appear, to someone on the outside, to freeze to a halt.

Einstein did not believe, then or later, that these results actually corresponded to anything real. In 1939, for example, he produced a paper that provided, he said, "a clear understanding as to why these 'Schwarzschild singularities' do not exist in physical reality." A few months later, however, J. Robert Oppenheimer and his student Hartland Snyder argued the opposite, predicting that stars could undergo a gravitational collapse.[2]

As for Schwarzschild, he never had the chance to study the issue further. Weeks after writing his papers, he contracted a horrible autoimmune disease while on the front, which ate away at his skin cells, and he died that May at age 42.

As scientists would discover after Einstein's death, Schwarzschild's odd theory was right. Stars *could* collapse and create such a phenomenon, and in fact they often did. In the 1960s, physicists such as Stephen Hawking, Roger Penrose, John Wheeler, Freeman Dyson, and Kip Thorne showed that this was indeed a feature of Einstein's general theory of relativity, one that was very real. Wheeler dubbed them "black holes," and they have been a feature of cosmology, as well as *Star Trek* episodes, ever since.[3]

Black holes have now been discovered all over the universe, including one at the center of our galaxy that is a few million times more massive than our sun. "Black holes are not rare, and they are not an accidental embellishment of our universe," says Dyson. "They are the only places in the universe where Einstein's theory of relativity shows its full power and glory. Here, and nowhere else, space and time lose their individuality and merge together in a sharply curved four-dimensional structure precisely delineated by Einstein's equations."[4]

Einstein believed that his general theory solved Newton's bucket issue in a way that Mach would have liked: inertia (or centrifugal forces) would not exist for something spinning in a completely empty universe.* Instead, inertia was caused only by rotation *relative* to all the other objects in the universe. "According to my theory, inertia is simply an interaction between masses, not an effect in which 'space' of itself is involved, separate from the observed mass," Einstein told Schwarzschild. "It can be put this way. If I allow all things to vanish, then ac-

---

* Chapter 14 describes Einstein's revision of this view in a 1920 lecture in Leiden.

cording to Newton the Galilean inertial space remains; following my interpretation, however, *nothing* remains."[5]

The issue of inertia got Einstein into a debate with one of the great astronomers of the time, Willem de Sitter of Leiden. Throughout 1916, Einstein struggled to preserve the relativity of inertia and Mach's principle by using all sorts of constructs, including assuming various "border conditions" such as distant masses along the fringes of space that were, by necessity, unable to be observed. As de Sitter noted, that in itself would have been anathema to Mach, who railed against postulating things that could not possibly be observed.[6]

By February 1917, Einstein had come up with a new approach. "I have completely abandoned my views, rightly contested by you," he wrote de Sitter. "I am curious to hear what you will have to say about the somewhat crazy idea I am considering now."[7] It was an idea that initially struck him as so wacky that he told his friend Paul Ehrenfest in Leiden, "It exposes me to the danger of being confined to a madhouse." He jokingly asked Ehrenfest for assurances, before he came to visit, that there were no such asylums in Leiden.[8]

His new idea was published that month in what became yet another seminal Einstein paper, "Cosmological Considerations in the General Theory of Relativity."[9] On the surface, it did indeed seem to be based on a crazy notion: space has no borders because gravity bends it back on itself.

Einstein began by noting that an absolutely infinite universe filled with stars and other objects was not plausible. There would be an infinite amount of gravity tugging at every point and an infinite amount of light shining from every direction. On the other hand, a finite universe floating at some random location in space was inconceivable as well. Among other things, what would keep the stars and energy from flying off, escaping, and depleting the universe?

So he developed a third option: a finite universe, but one without boundaries. The masses in the universe caused space to curve, and over the expanse of the universe they caused space (indeed, the whole four-dimensional fabric of spacetime) to curve completely in on itself. The system is closed and finite, but there is no end or edge to it.

One method that Einstein employed to help people visualize this notion was to begin by imagining two-dimensional explorers on a two-dimensional universe, like a flat surface. These "flatlanders" can wander in any direction on this flat surface, but the concept of going up or down has no meaning to them.

Now, imagine this variation: What if these flatlanders' two dimensions were still on a surface, but this surface was (in a way very subtle to them) gently curved? What if they and their world were still confined to two dimensions, but their flat surface was like the surface of a globe? As Einstein put it, "Let us consider now a two-dimensional existence, but this time on a spherical surface instead of on a plane." An arrow shot by these flatlanders would still seem to travel in a straight line, but eventually it would curve around and come back—just as a sailor on the surface of our planet heading straight off over the seas would eventually return from the other horizon.

The curvature of the flatlanders' two-dimensional space makes their surface finite, and yet they can find no boundaries. No matter what direction they travel, they reach no end or edge of their universe, but they eventually get back to the same place. As Einstein put it, "The great charm resulting from this consideration lies in the recognition that *the universe of these beings is finite and yet has no limits.*" And if the flatlanders' surface was like that of an inflating balloon, their whole universe could be expanding, yet there would still be no boundaries to it.[10]

By extension, we can try to imagine, as Einstein has us do, how three-dimensional space can be similarly curved to create a closed and finite system that has no edge. It's not easy for us three-dimensional creatures to visualize, but it is easily described mathematically by the non-Euclidean geometries pioneered by Gauss and Riemann. It can work for four dimensions of spacetime as well.

In such a curved universe, a beam of light starting out in any direction could travel what seems to be a straight line and yet still curve back on itself. "This suggestion of a finite but unbounded space is one of the greatest ideas about the nature of the world which has ever been conceived," the physicist Max Born has declared.[11]

Yes, but what is *outside* this curved universe? What's on the other side of the curve? That's not merely an unanswerable question, it's a meaningless one, just as it would be meaningless for a flatlander to ask what's outside her surface. One could speculate, imaginatively or mathematically, about what things are like in a fourth spatial dimension, but other than in science fiction it is not very meaningful to ask what's in a realm that exists outside of the three spatial dimensions of our curved universe.[12]

This concept of the cosmos that Einstein derived from his general theory of relativity was elegant and magical. But there seemed to be one hitch, a flaw that needed to be fixed or fudged. His theory indicated that the universe would have to be either expanding or contracting, not staying static. According to his field equations, a static universe was impossible because the gravitational forces would pull all the matter together.

This did not accord with what most astronomers thought they had observed. As far as they knew, the universe consisted only of our Milky Way galaxy, and it all seemed pretty stable and static. The stars appeared to be meandering gently, but not receding rapidly as part of an expanding universe. Other galaxies, such as Andromeda, were merely unexplained blurs in the sky. (A few Americans working at the Lowell Observatory in Arizona had noticed that the spectra of some mysterious spiral nebulae were shifted to the red end of the spectrum, but scientists had not yet determined that these were distant galaxies all speeding away from our own.)

When the conventional wisdom of physics seemed to conflict with an elegant theory of his, Einstein was inclined to question that wisdom rather than his theory, often to have his stubbornness rewarded. In this case, his gravitational field equations seemed to imply—indeed, screamed out—that the conventional thinking about a stable universe was wrong and should be tossed aside, just as Newton's concept of absolute time was.[13]

Instead, this time he made what he called a "slight modification" to his theory. To keep the matter in the universe from imploding, Einstein added a "repulsive" force: a little addition to his general relativity equations to counterbalance gravity in the overall scheme.

In his revised equations, this modification was signified by the Greek letter *lambda*, λ, which he used to multiply his metric tensor $g_{\mu\nu}$ in a way that produced a stable, static universe. In his 1917 paper, he was almost apologetic: "We admittedly had to introduce an extension of the field equations that is not justified by our actual knowledge of gravitation."

He dubbed the new element the "cosmological term" or the "cosmological constant" (*kosmologische Glied* was the phrase he used). Later,* when it was discovered that the universe was in fact expanding, Einstein would call it his "biggest blunder." But even today, in light of evidence that the expansion of the universe is accelerating, it is considered a useful concept, indeed a necessary one after all.[14]

During five months in 1905, Einstein had upended physics by conceiving light quanta, special relativity, and statistical methods for showing the existence of atoms. Now he had just completed a more prolonged creative slog, from the fall of 1915 to the spring of 1917, which Dennis Overbye has called "arguably the most prodigious effort of sustained brilliance on the part of one man in the history of physics." His first burst of creativity as a patent clerk had appeared to involve remarkably little anguish. But this later one was an arduous and intense effort, one that left him exhausted and wracked with stomach pains.[15]

During this period he generalized relativity, found the field equations for gravity, found a physical explanation for light quanta, hinted at how the quanta involved probability rather than certainty,† and came up with a concept for the structure of the universe as a whole. From the smallest thing conceivable, the quantum, to the largest, the cosmos itself, Einstein had proven a master.

The Eclipse, 1919

For general relativity, there was a dramatic experimental test that was possible, one that had the potential to dazzle and help heal a war-weary world. It was based on a concept so simple that everyone could understand it: gravity would bend light's trajectory. Specifically, Einstein predicted the degree to which light from a distant star would be

---

* See chapter 14 for Einstein's decision to renounce the term when he discovered the universe was expanding.

† Described in chapter 14.

observed to curve as it went through the strong gravitational field close to the sun.

To test this, astronomers would have to plot precisely the position of a star in normal conditions. Then they would wait until the alignments were such that the path of light from that star passed right next to the sun. Did the star's position seem to shift?

There was one exciting challenge. This observation required a total eclipse, so that the stars would be visible and could be photographed. Fortunately, nature happened to make the size of the sun and moon just properly proportional so that every few years there are full eclipses observable at times and places that make them ideally suited for such an experiment.

Einstein's 1911 paper, "On the Influence of Gravity on the Propagation of Light," and his *Entwurf* equations the following year, had calculated that light would undergo a deflection of approximately (allowing for some data corrections subsequently made) 0.85 arc-second when it passed near the sun, which was the same as would be predicted by an emission theory such as Newton's that treated light as particles. As previously noted, the attempt to test this during the August 1914 eclipse in the Crimea had been aborted by the war, so Einstein was saved the potential embarrassment of being proved wrong.

Now, according to the field equations he formulated at the end of 1915, which accounted for the curvature of spacetime caused by gravity, he had come up with *twice* that deflection. Light passing next to the sun should be bent, he said, by about 1.7 arc-seconds.

In his 1916 popular book on relativity, Einstein issued yet another call for scientists to test this conclusion. "Stars ought to appear to be displaced outwards from the sun by 1.7 seconds of arc, as compared with their apparent position in the sky when the sun is situated at another part of the heavens," he said. "The examination of the correctness or otherwise of this deduction is a problem of the greatest importance, the early solution of which is to be expected of astronomers."[16]

Willem de Sitter, the Dutch astrophysicist, had managed to send a copy of Einstein's general relativity paper across the English Channel in 1916 in the midst of the war and get it to Arthur Eddington, who was the director of the Cambridge Observatory. Einstein was not well-known in England, where scientists then took pride in either ignoring or denigrating their German counterparts. Eddington became an exception. He embraced relativity enthusiastically and wrote an account in English that popularized the theory, at least among scholars.

Eddington consulted with the Astronomer Royal, Sir Frank Dyson, and came up with the audacious idea that a team of English scientists should prove the theory of a German, even as the two nations were at war. In addition, it would help solve a personal problem for Eddington. He was a Quaker and, because of his pacifist faith, faced imprisonment for refusing military service in England. (In 1918, he was 35 years old, still subject to conscription.) Dyson was able to convince the British Admiralty that Eddington could best serve his nation by leading an expedition to test the theory of relativity during the next full solar eclipse.

That eclipse would occur on May 29, 1919, and Dyson pointed out that it would be a unique opportunity. The sun would then be amid the rich star cluster known as the Hyades, which we ordinary stargazers recognize as the center of the constellation Taurus. But it would not be convenient. The eclipse would be most visible in a path that stretched across the Atlantic near the equator from the coast of Brazil to Equatorial Africa. Nor would it be easy. As the expedition was being considered in 1918, there were German U-boats in the region, and their commanders were more interested in the control of the seas than in the curvature of the cosmos.

Fortunately, the war ended before the expeditions began. In early March 1919, Eddington sailed from Liverpool with two teams. One group split off to set up their cameras in the isolated town of Sobral in the Amazon jungle of northern Brazil. The second group, which included Eddington, sailed for the tiny island of Principe, a Portuguese colony a degree north of the equator just off the Atlantic coast of Africa. Eddington set up his equipment on a 500-foot bluff on the island's north tip.[17]

The eclipse was due to begin just after 3:13 p.m. local time on Principe and last about five minutes. That morning it rained heavily. But as the time of the eclipse approached, the sky started to clear. The heavens insisted on teasing and tantalizing Eddington at the most important minutes of his career, with the remaining clouds cloaking and then revealing the elusive sun.

"I did not see the eclipse, being too busy changing plates, except for one glance to make sure it had begun and another halfway through to see how much cloud there was," Eddington noted in his diary. He took sixteen photographs. "They are all good of the sun, showing a very remarkable prominence; but the cloud has interfered with the star images." In his telegram back to London that day, he was more telegraphic: "Through cloud, hopeful. Eddington."[18]

The team in Brazil had better weather, but the final results had to wait until all of the photographic plates from both places could be shipped back to England, developed, measured, and compared. That took until September, with Europe's scientific cognoscenti waiting eagerly. To some spectators, it took on the postwar political coloration of a contest between the English theory of Newton, predicting about 0.85 arc-second deflection, and the German theory of Einstein, predicting a 1.7 arc-seconds deflection.

The photo finish did not produce an immediately clear result. One set of particularly good pictures taken in Brazil showed a deflection of 1.98 arc-seconds. Another instrument, also at the Brazil location, produced photographs that were a bit blurrier, because heat had affected its mirror; they indicated a 0.86 deflection, but with a higher margin of error. And then there were Eddington's own plates from Principe. These showed fewer stars, so a series of complex calculations were used to extract some data. They seemed to indicate a deflection of about 1.6 arc-seconds.

The predictive power of Einstein's theory—the fact that it offered up a testable prediction—perhaps exercised a power over Eddington, whose admiration for the mathematical elegance of the theory caused him to believe in it deeply. He discarded the lower value coming out of Brazil, contending that the equipment was faulty, and with a slight bias toward his own fuzzy results from Africa got an average of just over 1.7 arc-seconds, matching Einstein's predictions. It wasn't the cleanest confirmation, but it was enough for Eddington, and it turned out to be valid. He later referred to getting these results as the greatest moment of his life.[19]

In Berlin, Einstein put on an appearance of nonchalance, but he could not completely hide his eagerness as he awaited word. The downward spiral of the German economy in 1919 meant that the elevator in his apartment building had been shut down, and he was preparing for a winter with little heat. "Much shivering lies ahead for the winter," he wrote his ailing mother on September 5. "There is still no news about the eclipse." In a letter a week later to his friend Paul Ehrenfest in Holland, Einstein ended with an affected casual question: "Have you by any chance heard anything over there about the English solar-eclipse observation?" [20]

Just by asking the question Einstein showed he was not quite as sanguine as he tried to appear, because his friends in Holland would certainly have already sent him such news if they had it. Finally they did. On September 22, 1919, Lorentz sent a cable based on what he had just heard from a fellow astronomer who had talked to Eddington at a meeting: "Eddington found stellar shift at solar limb, tentative value between nine-tenths of a second and twice that." It was wonderfully ambiguous. Was it a shift of 0.85 arc-second, as Newton's emission theory and Einstein's discarded 1912 theory would have it? Or twice that, as he now predicted?

Einstein had no doubts. "Today some happy news," he wrote his mother. "Lorentz telegraphed me that the British expeditions have verified the deflection of light by the sun." [21] Perhaps his confidence was partly an attempt to cheer up his mother, who was suffering from stomach cancer. But it is more likely that it was because he knew his theory was correct.

Einstein was with a graduate student, Ilse Schneider, shortly after Lorentz's news arrived. "He suddenly interrupted the discussion," she later recalled, and reached for the telegram that was lying on a window sill. "Perhaps this will interest you," he said, handing it to her.

Naturally she was overjoyed and excited, but Einstein was quite calm. "I *knew* the theory was correct," he told her.

But, she asked, what if the experiments had shown his theory to be wrong?

He replied, "Then I would have been sorry for the dear Lord; the theory is correct." [22]

As more precise news of the eclipse results spread, Max Planck was among those who gently noted to Einstein that it was good to have his own confidence confirmed by some actual facts. "You have already said many times that you never personally doubted what the result would be," Planck wrote, "but it is beneficial, nonetheless, if now this fact is indubitably established for others as well." For Einstein's stolid patron, the triumph had a transcendent aspect. "The intimate union between the beautiful, the true and the real has again been proved." Einstein replied to Planck with a veneer of humility: "It is a gift from gracious destiny that I have been allowed to experience this." [23]

Einstein's celebratory exchange with his closer friends in Zurich was more lighthearted. The physics colloquium there sent him a piece of doggerel:

> *All doubts have now been spent*
> *At last it has been found:*
> *Light is naturally bent*
> *To Einstein's great renown!* [24]

To which Einstein replied a few days later, referring to the eclipse:

> *Light and heat Mrs. Sun us tenders*
> *Yet loves not he who broods and ponders.*
> *So she contrives many a year*
> *How she may hold her secret dear!*
> *Now came the lunar visitor kind;*
> *For joy, she almost forgot to shine.*
> *Her deepest secrets too she lost*
> *Eddington, you know, has snapped a shot.* [25]

In defense of Einstein's poetic prowess, it should be noted that his verse works better in German, in which the last two lines end with "gekommen" and "aufgenommen."

The first unofficial announcement came at a meeting of the Dutch Royal Academy. Einstein sat proudly onstage as Lorentz described Eddington's findings to an audience of close to a thousand cheering students and scholars. But it was a closed meeting with no press, so the leaks about the results merely added to the great public anticipation leading up to the official announcement scheduled for two weeks later in London.

The distinguished members of the Royal Society, Britain's most venerable scientific institution, met along with colleagues from the Royal Astronomical Society on the afternoon of November 6, 1919, at Burlington House in Piccadilly, for what they knew was likely to be a historic event. There was only one item on the agenda: the report on the eclipse observations.

Sir J. J. Thomson, the Royal Society's president and discoverer of the electron, was in the chair. Alfred North Whitehead, the philosopher, had come down from Cambridge and was in the audience, taking notes. Gazing down on them from an imposing portrait in the great hall was Isaac Newton. "The whole atmosphere of tense interest was exactly that of the Greek drama," Whitehead recorded. "We were the chorus commenting on the decree of destiny . . . and in the background the picture of Newton to remind us that the greatest of scientific generalizations was, now, after more than two centuries, to receive its first modification." [26]

The Astronomer Royal, Sir Frank Dyson, had the honor of presenting the findings. He described in detail the equipment, the photographs, and the complexities of the calculations. His conclusion, however, was simple. "After a careful study of the plates, I am prepared to say that there can be no doubt that they confirm Einstein's prediction," he announced. "The results of the expeditions to Sobral and Principe leave little doubt that a deflection of light takes place in the neighborhood of the sun and that it is of the amount demanded by Einstein's generalized theory of relativity." [27]

There was some skepticism in the room. "We owe it to that great man to proceed very carefully in modifying or retouching his law of gravitation," cautioned Ludwig Silberstein, gesturing at Newton's portrait. But it was the commanding giant J. J. Thomson who set the tone. "The result is one of the greatest achievements of human thought," he declared. [28]

Einstein was back in Berlin, so he missed the excitement. He celebrated by buying a new violin. But he understood the historic impact of the announcement that the laws of Sir Isaac Newton no longer fully governed all aspects of the universe. "Newton, forgive me," Einstein later wrote, noting the moment. "You found the only way which, in your age, was just about possible for a man of highest thought and creative power."[29]

It was a grand triumph, but not one easily understood. The skeptical Silberstein came up to Eddington and said that people believed that only three scientists in the world understood general relativity. He had been told that Eddington was one of them.

The shy Quaker said nothing. "Don't be so modest, Eddington!" said Silberstein.

Replied Eddington, "On the contrary. I'm just wondering who the third might be."[30]

CHAPTER TWELVE

FAME

1919

With Charlie Chaplin and Elsa at the Hollywood
premiere of *City Lights,* January 1931

"Lights All Askew"

Einstein's theory of relativity burst into the consciousness of a world that was weary of war and yearning for a triumph of human transcendence. Almost a year to the day after the end of the brutal fighting, here was an announcement that the theory of a German Jew had been proven correct by an English Quaker. "Scientists belonging to two warring nations had collaborated again!" exulted the physicist Leopold Infeld. "It seemed the beginning of a new era."[1]

The Times of London carried stories on November 7 about the defeated Germans being summoned to Paris to face treaty demands from the British and French. But it also carried the following triple-decked headline:

REVOLUTION IN SCIENCE

New Theory of the Universe

NEWTONIAN IDEAS OVERTHROWN

"The scientific concept of the fabric of the Universe must be changed," the paper proclaimed. Einstein's newly confirmed theory will "require a new philosophy of the universe, a philosophy that will sweep away nearly all that has hitherto been accepted."[2]

The *New York Times* caught up with the story two days later.[3] Not having a science correspondent in London, the paper assigned the story to its golf expert, Henry Crouch, who at first decided to skip the Royal Society announcement, then changed his mind, but then couldn't get in. So he telephoned Eddington to get a summary and, somewhat baffled, asked him to repeat it in simpler words.[4]

Perhaps due to Eddington's enthusiasm in the retelling, or due to Crouch's enthusiasm in the reporting, Eddington's appraisal of Einstein's theory was enhanced to read "one of the greatest—perhaps the greatest—of achievements in the history of human thought."[5] But given the frenzy about to ensue, the headline was rather restrained:

ECLIPSE SHOWED GRAVITY VARIATION

Diversion of Light Rays Accepted as Affecting Newton's Principles.

HAILED AS EPOCHMAKING

British Scientist Calls the Discovery One of the Greatest of Human Achievements.

The following day, the *New York Times* apparently decided that it had been too restrained. So it followed up with an even more excited story, its six-deck headline a classic from the days when newspapers knew how to write classic headlines:

LIGHTS ALL ASKEW IN THE HEAVENS

Men of Science More or Less Agog Over Results of Eclipse Observations.

EINSTEIN THEORY TRIUMPHS

Stars Not Where They Seemed or Were Calculated to be, but Nobody Need Worry.

A BOOK FOR 12 WISE MEN

No More in All the World Could Comprehend It, Said Einstein When His Daring Publishers Accepted It.

For days the *New York Times*, with a bygone touch of merry populism, played up the complexity of the theory as an affront to common sense. "This news is distinctly shocking, and apprehensions for confidence even in the multiplication table will arise," it editorialized on November 11. The idea that "space has limits" was most assuredly silly, the paper decided. "It just doesn't, by definition, and that's the end of it—for common folk, however it may be for higher mathematicians." It returned to the theme five days later: "Scientists who proclaim that space comes to an end somewhere are under some obligation to tell us what lies beyond it."

Finally, a week after its first story, the paper decided that some words of calm, more amused than bemused, might be useful. "British scientists seem to have been seized with something like an intellectual panic when they heard of photographic verification of the Einstein theory," the paper pointed out, "but they are slowly recovering as they realize that the sun still rises—apparently—in the east and will continue to do so for some time to come."[6]

An intrepid correspondent for the newspaper in Berlin was able to get an interview with Einstein in his apartment on December 2, and in the process launched one of the apocryphal tales about relativity. After describing Einstein's top-floor study, the reporter asserted, "It was from this lofty library that he observed years ago a man dropping from a neighboring roof—luckily on a pile of soft rubbish—and escaping almost without injury. The man told Dr. Einstein that in falling he experienced no sensation commonly considered as the effect of gravity." That was how, the article said, Einstein developed a "sublimation or supplement" of Newton's law of gravity. As one of the stacked headlines of the article put it, "Inspired as Newton Was, But by the Fall of a Man from a Roof Instead of the Fall of an Apple."[7]

This was, in fact, as the newspaper would say, "a pile of soft rubbish." Einstein had done his thought experiment while working in the Bern patent office in 1907, not in Berlin, and it had not involved a person actually falling. "The newspaper drivel about me is pathetic," he wrote Zangger when the article came out. But he understood, and accepted, how journalism worked. "This kind of exaggeration meets a certain need among the public."[8]

There was, indeed, an astonishing public craving to understand relativity. Why? The theory seemed somewhat baffling, yes, but also very enticing in its mystery. Warped space? The bending of light rays? Time and space not absolute? The theory had the wondrous mix of *Huh?* and *Wow!* that can capture the public imagination.

This was lampooned in a Rea Irvin cartoon in the *New Yorker,* which showed a baffled janitor, fur-clad matron, doorman, kids, and others scratching their heads with wild surmise as they wandered down the street. The caption was a quote from Einstein: "People slowly accustomed themselves to the idea that the physical states of space itself were the final physical reality." As Einstein put it to Grossmann, "Now every coachman and waiter argues about whether or not relativity theory is correct."[9]

Einstein's friends found themselves besieged whenever they lectured on it. Leopold Infeld, who later worked with Einstein, was then a young schoolteacher in a small Polish town. "At the time, I did what hundreds of others did all over the world," he recalled. "I gave a public lecture on the theory of relativity, and the crowd that lined up on a cold winter night was so great that it could not be accommodated in the largest hall in town."[10]

The same thing happened to Eddington when he spoke at Trinity College, Cambridge. Hundreds jammed the hall, and hundreds more were turned away. In his attempt to make the subject comprehensible, Eddington said that if he was traveling at nearly the speed of light he would be only three feet tall. That made newspaper headlines. Lorentz likewise gave a speech to an overflow audience. He compared the earth to a moving vehicle as a way to illustrate some examples of relativity.[11]

Soon many of the greatest physicists and thinkers began writing their own books explaining the theory, including Eddington, von Laue, Freundlich, Lorentz, Planck, Born, Pauli, and even the philosopher and mathematician Bertrand Russell. In all, more than six hundred books and articles on relativity were published in the first six years after the eclipse observations.

Einstein himself had the opportunity to explain it in his own words in *The Times* of London, which commissioned him to write an article called "What Is the Theory of Relativity?"[12] The result was actually quite comprehensible. His own popular book on the subject, *Relativity: The Special and General Theory*, had first appeared in German in 1916. Now, in the wake of the eclipse observation, Einstein published it in English as well. Filled with many thought experiments that could be easily visualized, it became a best seller, with updated editions appearing over the ensuing years.

The Publicity Paradox

Einstein had just the right ingredients to be transformed into a star. Reporters, knowing that the public was yearning for a refreshing international celebrity, were thrilled that the newly discovered genius was not a drab or reserved academic. Instead, he was a charming 40-year-old, just passing from handsome to distinctive, with a wild burst of hair, rumpled informality, twinkling eyes, and a willingness to dispense wisdom in bite-sized quips and quotes.

His friend Paul Ehrenfest found the press attention rather ridiculous. "The startled newspaper ducks flutter up in a hefty bout of quacking," he joked. To Einstein's sister, Maja, who grew up at a time before people actually liked publicity, the attention was astonishing, and she assumed that he found it completely distasteful. "An article was published about you in a Lucerne paper!" she marveled, not fully appreciating that he had made front pages around the world. "I imagine this causes you much unpleasantness that so much is being written about you."[13]

Einstein indeed bemoaned his newfound fame, repeatedly. He was being "hounded by the press and other riff-raff," he complained to Max Born. "It's so dreadful that I can barely breathe anymore, not to mention getting around to any sensible work." To another friend, he painted an even more vivid picture of the perils of publicity: "Since the flood of newspaper articles, I've been so deluged with questions, invitations, and requests that I dream I'm burning in Hell and the postman is the Devil eternally roaring at me, hurling new bundles of letters at my head because I have not yet answered the old ones."[14]

Einstein's aversion to publicity, however, existed a bit more in theory than in reality. It would have been possible, indeed easy, for him to have shunned all interviews, pronouncements, pictures, and public appearances. Those who truly dislike the public spotlight do not turn up, as the Einsteins eventually would, with Charlie Chaplin on a red carpet at one of his movie premieres.

"There was a streak in him that enjoyed the photographers and the crowds," the essayist C. P. Snow said after getting to know him. "He had an element of the exhibitionist and the ham. If there had not been that element, there would have been no photographers and no crowds. Nothing is easier to avoid than publicity. If one genuinely doesn't want it, one doesn't get it."[15]

Einstein's response to adulation was as complex as that of the cosmos to gravity. He was attracted and repelled by the cameras, loved publicity and loved to complain about it. His love-hate relationship with fame and reporters might seem unusual until one reflects on how similar it was to the mix of enjoyment, amusement, aversion, and annoyance that so many other famous people have felt.

One reason that Einstein—unlike Planck or Lorentz or Bohr— became such an icon was because he looked the part and because he could, and would, play the role. "Scientists who become icons must not only be geniuses but also performers, playing to the crowd and enjoying public acclaim," the physicist Freeman Dyson (no relation to the Astronomer Royal) has noted.[16] Einstein performed. He gave interviews readily, peppered them with delightful aphorisms, and knew exactly what made for a good story.

Even Elsa, or perhaps *especially* Elsa, enjoyed the attention. She served as her husband's protector, fearsome in her bark and withering in her near-sighted gaze when unwanted intruders barged into his orbit. But even more than her husband, she reveled in the stature and deference that came with fame. She began charging a fee to photograph him, and she donated the money to charities that fed hungry children in Vienna and elsewhere.[17]

In the current celebrity-soaked age, it is hard to recall the extent to which, a century ago, proper people recoiled from publicity and disdained those who garnered it. Especially in the realm of science, focusing on the personal seemed discordant. When Einstein's friend Max Born published a book on relativity right after the eclipse observations, he included, in his first edition, a frontispiece picture of Einstein and a short biography of him. Max von Laue and other friends of both men were appalled. Such things did not belong in a scientific book, even a popular one, von Laue wrote Born. Chastened, Born left these elements out of the next edition.[18]

As a result, Born was dismayed when it was announced in 1920 that Einstein had cooperated on a forthcoming biography by a Jewish jour-

nalist, Alexander Moszkowski, who had mainly written humor and oc-
cult books. The book advertised itself, in the title, as being based on
conversations with Einstein, and in fact it was. During the war, the
gregarious Moszkowski had befriended Einstein, been solicitous of his
needs, and brought him into a semiliterary circle that hung around at a
Berlin café.

Born was a nonpracticing Jew eager to assimilate into German society, and he feared that the book would stoke the simmering anti-
Semitism. "Einstein's theories had been stamped as 'Jewish physics' by
colleagues," Born recalled, referring to the growing number of German
nationalists who had begun decrying the abstract nature and supposed
moral "relativism" inherent in Einstein's theories. "And now a Jewish
author, who had already published several books with frivolous titles,
came along and wanted to write a similar book on Einstein." So Born
and his wife, Hedwig, who never shied from berating Einstein,
launched a crusade with their friends to stop its publication.

"You must withdraw permission," Hedwig hectored, "at once and
by registered letter." She warned him that the "gutter press" would use
it to tarnish his image and portray him as a self-promoting Jew. "A
completely new and far worse wave of persecution will be unleashed."
The sin, she emphasized, was not what he said but the fact that he was
permitting any publicity for himself:

> If I did not know you well, I would certainly not concede innocent mo-
> tives under these circumstances. I would put it down to vanity. This
> book will constitute your moral death sentence for all but four or five of
> your friends. It could subsequently be the best *confirmation of the accusa-
> tion of self-advertisement.*[19]

Her husband weighed in a week later with a warning that all
of Einstein's anti-Semitic antagonists "will triumph" if he did not
block publication. "Your Jewish 'friends' [i.e., Moszkowski] will have
achieved what a pack of anti-Semites have failed to do."

If Moszkowski refused to back off, Born advised Einstein to get a
restraining order from the public prosecutor's office. "Make sure this is
reported in the newspapers," he said. "I shall send you the details of

where to apply." Like many of their friends, Born worried that Elsa was the one who was more susceptible to the lures of publicity. As he told Einstein, "In these matters you are a little child. We all love you, and you must obey judicious people (not your wife)."[20]

Einstein took the advice of his friends, up to a point, by sending Moszkowski a registered letter demanding that his "splendid" work not appear in print. But when Moszkowski refused to back down, Einstein did not invoke legal measures. Both Ehrenfest and Lorentz agreed that going to court would serve only to inflame the issue and make matters worse, but Born disagreed. "You can flee to Holland," he said, referring to the ongoing effort by Ehrenfest and Lorentz to lure him there, "but his Jewish friends who remained in Germany "would be affected by the stench."[21]

Einstein's detachment allowed him to affect an air of amusement rather than anxiety. "The whole affair is a matter of indifference to me, as is all the commotion, and the opinion of *each and every* human being," he said. "I will live through all that is in store for me like an unconcerned spectator."[22]

When the book came out, it made Einstein an easier target for anti-Semites, who used it to bolster their contention that he was a self-promoter trying to turn his science into a business.[23] But it did not cause much of a public commotion. There were, as Einstein noted to Born, no "earth tremors."

In retrospect, the controversy over publicity seems quaint and the book harmless fluff. "I have browsed through it a little, and find it not quite as bad as I had expected," Born later admitted. "It contains many rather amusing stories and anecdotes which are characteristic of Einstein."[24]

Einstein was able to resist letting his fame destroy his simple approach to life. On an overnight trip to Prague, he was afraid that dignitaries or curiosity-seekers would want to celebrate him, so he decided to stay with his friend Philipp Frank and his wife. The problem was that they actually lived in Frank's office suite at the physics laboratory, where Einstein had once worked himself. So Einstein slept on the sofa there. "This was probably not good enough for such a famous man,"

Frank recalled, "but it suited his liking for simple living habits and situations that contravened social conventions."

Einstein insisted that, on the way back from a coffeehouse, they buy food for dinner so that Frank's wife need not go shopping. They chose some calf's liver, which Mrs. Frank proceeded to cook on the Bunsen burner in the office laboratory. Suddenly Einstein jumped up. "What are you doing?" he demanded. "Are you boiling the liver in water?" Mrs. Frank allowed that was indeed what she was doing. "The boiling-point of water is too low," Einstein declared. "You must use a substance with a higher boiling-point such as butter or fat." From then on, Mrs. Frank referred to the necessity of frying liver as "Einstein's theory."

After Einstein's lecture that evening, there was a small reception given by the physics department at which several effusive speeches were made. When it was Einstein's turn to respond, he instead declared, "It will perhaps be pleasanter and more understandable if instead of making a speech I play a piece for you on the violin." He proceeded to perform a sonata by Mozart with, according to Frank, "his simple, precise and therefore doubly moving manner."

The next morning, before he could depart, a young man tracked him down at Frank's office and insisted on showing him a manuscript. On the basis of his $E=mc^2$ equation, the man insisted, it would be possible "to use the energy contained within the atom for the production of frightening explosives." Einstein brushed away the discussion, calling the concept foolish.[25]

From Prague, Einstein took the train to Vienna, where three thousand scientists and excited onlookers were waiting to hear him speak. At the station, his host waited for him to disembark from the first-class car but didn't find him. He looked to the second-class car down the platform, and could not find him there either. Finally, strolling from the third-class car at the far end of the platform was Einstein, carrying his violin case like an itinerant musician. "You know, I like traveling first, but my face is becoming too well known," he told his host. "I am less bothered in third class."[26]

"With fame I become more and more stupid, which of course is a very common phenomenon," Einstein told Zangger.[27] But he soon developed a theory that his fame was, for all of its annoyances, at least a welcome sign of the priority that society placed on people like himself:

> The cult of individual personalities is always, in my view, unjustified . . . It strikes me as unfair, and even in bad taste, to select a few for boundless admiration, attributing superhuman powers of mind and character to them. This has been my fate, and the contrast between the popular estimate of my achievements and the reality is simply grotesque. This extraordinary state of affairs would be unbearable but for one great consoling thought: it is a welcome symptom in an age, which is commonly denounced as materialistic, that it makes heroes of men whose ambitions lie wholly in the intellectual and moral sphere.[28]

One problem with fame is that it can engender resentment. Especially in academic and scientific circles, self-promotion was regarded as a sin. There was a distaste for those who garnered personal publicity, a sentiment that may have been exacerbated by the fact that Einstein was a Jew.

In the piece explaining relativity that he had written for *The Times* of London, Einstein humorously hinted at the issues that could arise. "By an application of the theory of relativity, today in Germany I am called a German man of science, and in England I am represented as a Swiss Jew," he wrote. "If I come to be regarded as a bête noire, the descriptions will be reversed, and I shall become a Swiss Jew for the Germans and a German man of science for the English!"[29]

It was not entirely facetious. Just months after he became world famous, the latter phenomenon occurred. He was told that he was to be given the prestigious gold medal of Britain's Royal Astronomical Society at the beginning of 1920, but a rebellion by a chauvinistic group of English purists forced the honor to be withheld.[30] Far more ominously, a small but growing group in his native country soon began vocally portraying him as a Jew rather than as a German.

"Lone Traveler"

Einstein liked to cast himself as a loner. Although he had an infectious laugh, like the barking of a seal, it could sometimes be wounding rather than warm. He loved being in a group playing music, discussing ideas, drinking strong coffee, and smoking pungent cigars. Yet there was a faintly visible wall that separated him from even family and close friends.[31] Starting with the Olympia Academy, he frequented many parlors of the mind. But he shied away from the inner chambers of the heart.

He did not like to be constricted, and he could be cold to members of his family. Yet he loved the collegiality of intellectual companions, and he had friendships that lasted throughout his life. He was sweet toward people of all ages and classes who floated into his ken, got along well with staffers and colleagues, and tended to be genial toward humanity in general. As long as someone put no strong demands or emotional burdens on him, Einstein could readily forge friendships and even affections.

This mix of coldness and warmth produced in Einstein a wry detachment as he floated through the human aspects of his world. "My passionate sense of social justice and social responsibility has always contrasted oddly with my pronounced lack of need for direct contact with other human beings and communities," he reflected. "I am truly a 'lone traveler' and have never belonged to my country, my home, my friends, or even my immediate family, with my whole heart; in the face of all these ties, I have never lost a sense of distance and a need for solitude."[32]

Even his scientific colleagues marveled at the disconnect between the genial smiles he bestowed on humanity in general and the detachment he displayed to the people close to him. "I do not know anyone as lonely and detached as Einstein," said his collaborator Leopold Infeld. "His heart never bleeds, and he moves through life with mild enjoyment and emotional indifference. His extreme kindness and decency are thoroughly impersonal and seem to come from another planet."[33]

Max Born, another personal and professional friend, noted the same trait, and it seemed to explain Einstein's ability to remain somewhat oblivious to the tribulations afflicting Europe during World War I. "For all his kindness, sociability and love of humanity, he was nevertheless totally detached from his environment and the human beings in it."[34]

Einstein's personal detachment and scientific creativity seemed to be subtly linked. According to his colleague Abraham Pais, this detachment sprang from Einstein's salient trait of "apartness," which led him to reject scientific conventional wisdom as well as emotional intimacies. It is easier to be a nonconformist and rebel, both in science and in a militaristic culture like Germany's, when you can detach yourself easily from others. "The detachment enabled him to walk through life immersed in thought," Pais said. It also allowed him—or compelled him—to pursue his theories in both a "single-minded and single-handed" manner.[35]

Einstein understood the conflicting forces in his own soul, and he seemed to think it was true for all people. "Man is, at one and the same time, a solitary being and a social being," he said.[36] His own desire for detachment conflicted with his desire for companionship, mirroring the struggle between his attraction and his aversion to fame. Using the jargon of psychoanalysis, the pioneering therapist Erik Erikson once pronounced of Einstein, "A certain alternation of isolation and outgoingness seems to have retained the character of a dynamic polarization."[37]

Einstein's desire for detachment was reflected in his extramarital relationships. As long as women did not make any claims on him and he felt free to approach them or not according to his own moods, he was able to sustain a romance. But the fear that he might have to surrender some of his independence led him to erect a shield.[38]

This was even more evident in his relationship with his family. He was not always merely cold, for there were times, especially when it came to Mileva Marić, that the forces of both attraction and repulsion raged inside him with a fiery heat. His problem, especially with his family, was that he was resistant to such strong feelings in others. "He had no gift for empathy," writes historian Thomas Levenson, "no ability to imagine himself into the emotional life of anyone else."[39] When confronted with the emotional needs of others, Einstein tended to retreat into the objectivity of his science.

The collapse of the German currency had caused him to urge Marić to move there, since it had become hard for him to afford her cost of living in Switzerland using depreciated German marks. But once the eclipse observations made him famous and more financially secure, he was willing to let his family stay in Zurich.

To support them, he had the fees from his European lecture trips sent directly to Ehrenfest in Holland, so that the money would not be converted into Germany's sinking currency. Einstein wrote Ehrenfest cryptic letters referring to his hard currency reserves as "results which you and I obtained here on Au ions" (i.e., gold).[40] The money was then disbursed by Ehrenfest to Marić and the children.

Shortly after his remarriage, Einstein visited Zurich to see his sons. Hans Albert, then 15, announced that he had decided to become an engineer.

"I think it's a disgusting idea," said Einstein, whose father and uncle had been engineers.

"I'm still going to become an engineer," replied the boy.

Einstein stormed away angry, and once again their relationship deteriorated, especially after he received a nasty letter from Hans Albert. "He wrote me as no decent person has ever written their father," he explained in a pained letter to his other son, Eduard. "It's doubtful I'll ever be able to take up a relationship with him again."[41]

But Marić by then was intent on improving rather than undermining his relationship with his sons. So she emphasized to the boys that Einstein was "a strange man in many ways," but he was still their father and wanted their love. He could be cold, she said, but also "good and kind." According to an account provided by Hans Albert, "Mileva knew that for all his bluff, Albert could be hurt in personal matters—and hurt deeply."[42]

By later that year, Einstein and his older son were again corresponding regularly about everything from politics to science. He also expressed his appreciation to Marić, joking that she should be happier now that she did not have to put up with him. "I plan on coming to Zurich soon, and we should put all the bad things behind us. You should enjoy what life has given you—like the wonderful children, the house, and that you are not married to me anymore."[43]

Hans Albert went on to enroll at his parents' alma mater, the Zurich Polytechnic, and became an engineer. He took a job at a steel company and then as a research assistant at the Polytechnic, studying hydraulics and rivers. Especially after he scored first in his exams, his father not only became reconciled, but proud. "My Albert has become a sound, strong chap," Einstein wrote Besso in 1924. "He is a total picture of a man, a first-rate sailor, unpretentious and dependable."

Einstein eventually said the same to Hans Albert, adding that he may have been right to become an engineer. "Science is a difficult profession," he wrote. "Sometimes I am glad that you have chosen a practical field, where one does not have to look for a four-leaf clover." [44]

One person who elicited strong and sustained personal emotions in Einstein was his mother. Dying from stomach cancer, she had moved in with him and Elsa at the end of 1919, and watching her suffer overwhelmed whatever human detachment he usually felt or feigned. When she died in February 1920, Einstein was exhausted by the emotions. "One feels right into one's bones what ties of blood mean," he wrote Zangger. Käthe Freundlich had heard him boast to her husband, the astronomer, that no death would affect him, and she was relieved that his mother's death proved that untrue. "Einstein wept like other men," she said, "and I knew that he could really care for someone." [45]

The Ripples from Relativity

For nearly three centuries, the mechanical universe of Isaac Newton, based on absolute certainties and laws, had formed the psychological foundation of the Enlightenment and the social order, with a belief in causes and effects, order, even *duty*. Now came a view of the universe, known as relativity, in which space and time were dependent on frames of reference. This apparent dismissal of certainties, an abandonment of faith in the absolute, seemed vaguely heretical to some people, perhaps even godless. "It formed a knife," historian Paul Johnson wrote in his sweeping history of the twentieth century, *Modern Times*, "to help cut society adrift from its traditional moorings." [46]

The horrors of the great war, the breakdown of social hierarchies, the advent of relativity and its apparent undermining of classical physics all seemed to combine to produce uncertainty. "For some years past, the entire world has been in a state of unrest, mental as well as physical," a Columbia University astronomer, Charles Poor, told the

New York Times the week after the confirmation of Einstein's theory was announced. "It may well be that the physical aspects of the unrest, the war, the strikes, the Bolshevist uprisings, are in reality the visible objects of some underlying deeper disturbance, worldwide in character. This same spirit of unrest has invaded science." [47]

Indirectly, driven by popular misunderstandings rather than a fealty to Einstein's thinking, *relativity* became associated with a new *relativism* in morality and art and politics. There was less faith in absolutes, not only of time and space, but also of truth and morality. In a December 1919 editorial about Einstein's relativity theory, titled "Assaulting the Absolute," the *New York Times* fretted that "the foundations of all human thought have been undermined." [48]

Einstein would have been, and later was, appalled at the conflation of relativity with relativism. As noted, he had considered calling his theory "invariance," because the physical laws of combined spacetime, according to his theory, were indeed invariant rather than relative.

Moreover, he was not a relativist in his own morality or even in his taste. "The word relativity has been widely misinterpreted as relativism, the denial of, or doubt about, the objectivity of truth or moral values," the philosopher Isaiah Berlin later lamented. "This was the opposite of what Einstein believed. He was a man of simple and absolute moral convictions, which were expressed in all he was and did." [49]

In both his science and his moral philosophy, Einstein was driven by a quest for certainty and deterministic laws. If his theory of relativity produced ripples that unsettled the realms of morality and culture, this was caused not by what Einstein believed but by how he was popularly interpreted.

One of those popular interpreters, for example, was the British statesman Lord Haldane, who fancied himself a philosopher and scientific scholar. In 1921, he published a book called *The Reign of Relativity,* which enlisted Einstein's theory to support his own political views on the need to avoid dogmatism in order to have a dynamic society. "Einstein's principle of the relativity of our measurements of space and time cannot be taken in isolation," he wrote. "When its import is considered it may well be found to have its counterpart in other domains of nature and of knowledge generally." [50]

Relativity theory would have profound consequences for theology, Haldane warned the archbishop of Canterbury, who immediately tried to comprehend the theory with only modest success. "The Archbishop," one minister reported to the dean of English science, J. J. Thomson, "can make neither head nor tail of Einstein, and protests that the more he listens to Haldane, and the more newspaper articles he reads on the subject, the less he understands."

Haldane persuaded Einstein to come to England in 1921. He and Elsa stayed at Haldane's grand London townhouse, where they found themselves completely intimidated by their assigned footman and butler. The dinner that Haldane hosted in Einstein's honor convened a pride of English intellectuals leonine enough to awe an Oxford senior common room. Among those present were George Bernard Shaw, Arthur Eddington, J. J. Thomson, Harold Laski, and of course the baffled archbishop of Canterbury, who got a personal briefing from Thomson in preparation.

Haldane seated the archbishop next to Einstein, so he got to pose his burning question directly to the source. What ramifications, His Grace inquired, did the theory of relativity have for religion?

The answer probably disappointed both the archbishop and their host. "None," Einstein said. "Relativity is a purely scientific matter and has nothing to do with religion."[51]

That was no doubt true. However, there was a more complex relationship between Einstein's theories and the whole witch's brew of ideas and emotions in the early twentieth century that bubbled up from the highly charged cauldron of modernism. In his novel *Balthazar*, Lawrence Durrell had his character declare, "The Relativity proposition was directly responsible for abstract painting, atonal music, and formless literature."

The relativity proposition, of course, was *not* directly responsible for any of this. Instead, its relationship with modernism was more mysteriously interactive. There are historical moments when an alignment of forces causes a shift in human outlook. It happened to art and philosophy and science at the beginning of the Renaissance, and again at the beginning of the Enlightenment. Now, in the early twentieth century, modernism was born by the breaking of the old strictures and verities. A spontaneous combustion occurred that included the works of Einstein, Picasso, Matisse, Stravinsky, Schoenberg, Joyce, Eliot, Proust, Diaghilev, Freud, Wittgenstein, and dozens of other path-breakers who seemed to break the bonds of classical thinking.[52]

In his book *Einstein, Picasso: Space, Time, and the Beauty That Causes Havoc*, the historian of science and philosophy Arthur I. Miller explored the common wellsprings that produced, for example, the 1905 special theory of relativity and Picasso's 1907 modernist masterpiece *Les Demoiselles d'Avignon*. Miller noted that both were men of great charm "yet who preferred emotional detachment." Each in his own way felt that something was amiss in the strictures that defined his field, and they were both intrigued by discussions of simultaneity, space, time, and specifically the writings of Poincaré.[53]

Einstein served as a source of inspiration for many of the modernist artists and thinkers, even when they did not understand him. This was especially true when artists celebrated such concepts as being "free from the order of time," as Proust put it in the closing of *Remembrance of Things Past*. "How I would love to speak to you about Einstein," Proust wrote to a physicist friend in 1921. "I do not understand a single word of his theories, not knowing algebra. [Nevertheless] it seems we have analogous ways of deforming Time."[54]

A pinnacle of the modernist revolution came in 1922, the year Einstein's Nobel Prize was announced. James Joyce's *Ulysses* was published that year, as was T. S. Eliot's *The Waste Land*. There was a midnight dinner party in May at the Majestic Hotel in Paris for the opening of *Renard*, composed by Stravinsky and performed by Diaghilev's *Ballets Russes*. Stravinsky and Diaghilev were both there, as was Picasso. So, too, were both Joyce and Proust, who "were destroying 19th century literary certainties as surely as Einstein was revolutionizing physics." The mechanical order and Newtonian laws that had defined classical physics, music, and art no longer ruled.[55]

Whatever the causes of the new relativism and modernism, the untethering of the world from its classical moorings would soon produce some unnerving reverberations and reactions. And nowhere was that mood more troubling than in Germany in the 1920s.

CHAPTER THIRTEEN

THE WANDERING ZIONIST

1920–1921

The motorcade in New York City, April 4, 1921

Kinship

In the article he wrote for *The Times* of London after the confirmation of his relativity theory, Einstein quipped that if things went bad the Germans would no longer consider him a compatriot but instead a Swiss Jew. It was a clever remark, made more so because Einstein knew, even then, that there was an odious smell of truth to it. That very week, in a letter to his friend Paul Ehrenfest, he described the mood in Germany. "Anti-Semitism is very strong here," he wrote. "Where is this all supposed to lead?"[1]

The rise of German anti-Semitism after World War I produced a counterreaction in Einstein: it made him identify more strongly with his Jewish heritage and community. At one extreme were German Jews such as Fritz Haber, who did everything they could, includ-

ing converting to Christianity, to assimilate, and they urged Einstein
to do the same. But Einstein took the opposite approach. Just when
he was becoming famous, he embraced the Zionist cause. He did
not officially join any Zionist organization, nor for that matter did
he belong to or worship at any synagogue. But he cast his lot in favor
of Jewish settlements in Palestine, a national identity among Jews
everywhere, and the rejection of assimilationist desires.

He was recruited by the pioneering Zionist leader Kurt Blumenfeld, who paid a call on Einstein in Berlin in early 1919. "With extreme
naïveté he asked questions," Blumenfeld recalled. Among Einstein's
queries: With their spiritual and intellectual gifts, why should Jews be
called on to create an agricultural nation-state? Wasn't nationalism the
problem rather than the solution?

Eventually, Einstein came around to the cause. "I am, as a human
being, an opponent of nationalism," he declared. "But as a Jew, I
am from today a supporter of the Zionist effort."[2] He also became,
more specifically, an advocate for the creation of a new Jewish university in Palestine, which eventually became Hebrew University in
Jerusalem.

Once he decided to abandon the postulate that all forms of nationalism were bad, he found it easy to embrace Zionism with greater enthusiasm. "One can be an internationalist without being indifferent to
members of one's tribe," he wrote a friend in October 1919. "The
Zionist cause is very close to my heart . . . I am glad that there should
be a little patch of earth on which our kindred brethren are not considered aliens."[3]

His support for Zionism put Einstein at odds with assimilationists. In April 1920, he was invited to address a meeting of one
such group that emphasized its members' loyalty to Germany, the
German Citizens of the Jewish Faith. He replied by accusing them
of trying to separate themselves from the poorer and less polished
eastern European Jews. "Can the 'Aryan' respect such pussyfooters?" he
chided.[4]

Privately declining the invitation was not enough. Einstein also felt
compelled to write a public attack on those who tried to fit in by talk-

ing "about religious faith instead of tribal affiliation."* In particular, he scorned what he called "the assimilatory" approach that sought "to overcome anti-Semitism by dropping nearly everything Jewish." This never worked; indeed, it "appears somewhat comical to a non-Jew," because the Jews are a people set apart from others. "The psychological root of anti-Semitism lies in the fact that the Jews are a group of people unto themselves," he wrote. "Their Jewishness is visible in their physical appearance, and one notices their Jewish heritage in their intellectual work."[5]

The Jews who practiced and preached assimilation tended to be those who took pride in their German or western European heritage. At the time (and through much of the twentieth century), they tended to look down on Jews from eastern Europe, such as Russia and Poland, who seemed less polished, refined, and assimilated. Although Einstein was German Jewish, he was appalled by those from his background who would "draw a sharp dividing line between eastern European Jews and western European Jews." The approach was doomed to backfire against all Jews, he argued, and it was not based on any true distinction. "Eastern European Jewry contains a rich potential of human talents and productive forces that can well stand the comparison to the higher civilization of western European Jews."[6]

Einstein was acutely aware, even more than the assimilationists, that anti-Semitism was not the result of rational causes. "In Germany today hatred of the Jews has taken on horrible expressions," he wrote in early 1920. Part of the problem was that inflation was out of control. The German mark had been worth about 12 cents at the beginning of 1919, which was half of its value from before the war but still manageable. But by the beginning of 1920, the mark was worth a mere 2 cents, and collapsing further each month.

In addition, the loss of the war had been humiliating. Germany had lost 6 million men and then was forced into surrendering land con-

---

* The word Einstein used was *Stammesgenossen*. Although *Stamm* generally means tribe, that translation can have some racial overtones. Some Einstein scholars have said that translations such as "kindred" or "clan" or "lineage" might be clearer.

taining half of its natural resources, plus all of its overseas colonies. Many proud Germans believed it must have been the result of betrayal. The Weimar Republic that had emerged after the war, though supported by liberals and pacifists and Jews such as Einstein, was disdained by much of the old order and even the middle class.

There was one group that could be easily cast as the alien and dark force most responsible for the humiliation facing a proud culture. "People need a scapegoat and make the Jews responsible," Einstein noted. "They are a target of instinctive resentment because they are of a different tribe."[7]

Weyland, Lenard, and the Antirelativists

The explosion of great art and ideas in Germany at the time, as Amos Elon wrote in his book *The Pity of It All*, was largely due to Jewish patrons and pioneers in a variety of fields. This was particularly true in science. As Sigmund Freud pointed out, part of the success of Jewish scientists was their "creative skepticism," which arose from their essential nature as outsiders.[8] What the Jewish assimilationists underestimated was the virulence with which many Germans, whom they considered to be their fellow countrymen, in fact saw them as essentially outsiders or, as Einstein put it, "a different tribe."

Einstein's first public collision with this anti-Semitism came in the summer of 1920. A shady German nationalist named Paul Weyland, an engineer by training, had turned himself into a polemicist with political aspirations. He was an active member of a right-wing nationalistic political party that pledged, in its 1920 official program, to "diminish the dominant Jewish influence showing up increasingly in government and in public."[9]

Weyland realized that Einstein, as a highly publicized Jew, had engendered resentment and jealousy. Likewise, his relativity theory was easy to turn into a target, because many people, including some scientists, were unnerved by the way it seemed to undermine absolutes and be built on abstract hypotheses rather than grounded in solid experiment. So Weyland published articles denouncing relativity as "a big hoax" and formed a ragtag (but mysteriously well-funded) organization grandly dubbed the Study Group of German Scientists for the Preservation of a Pure Science.

Joining with Weyland was an experimental physicist of modest reputation named Ernst Gehrcke, who for years had been assailing relativity with more vehemence than comprehension. Their group lobbed a few personal attacks at Einstein and the "Jewish nature" of relativity theory, then called a series of meetings around Germany, including a large rally at Berlin's Philharmonic Hall on August 24.

Weyland spoke first and, with the orotund rhetoric of a demagogue, accused Einstein of engaging in a "businesslike booming of his theory and his name." Einstein's penchant for publicity, wanted or not, was being used against him, as his assimilationist friends had warned. Relativity was a hoax, Weyland said, and plagiarized to boot. Gehrcke said much the same with a more technical gloss, reading from a written text. The meeting, reported the *New York Times,* "had a decidedly anti-Semitic complexion."[10]

In the middle of Gehrcke's talk, there arose from the audience a quiet murmur: *Einstein, Einstein.* He had come to see the circus and, averse neither to publicity nor controversy, laugh at the spectacle. As his friend Philipp Frank noted, "He always liked to regard events in the world around him as if he were a spectator in a theater." Sitting in the audience with his friend the chemist Walther Nernst, he cackled loudly at times and at the end pronounced the entire event "most amusing."[11]

But he was not truly amused, and he even briefly considered moving away from Berlin.[12] His anger aroused, he made the tactical mistake of responding with a highly charged diatribe that was published three days later on the front page of the *Berliner Tageblatt,* a liberal daily owned by Jewish friends. "I am well aware that the two speakers are unworthy of reply by my pen," he said, but then proceeded not to be restrained by that awareness. Gehrcke and Weyland had not been explicitly anti-Semitic, nor did they overtly criticize Jews in their speeches. But Einstein alleged that they would not have attacked his theory "if I were a German nationalist, with or without a swastika, instead of a Jew."[13]

Einstein spent most of his piece refuting Weyland and Gehrcke.

But he also attacked a more reputable physicist who was not at the meeting but had given support to the antirelativity cause: Philipp Lenard.

Winner of the 1905 Nobel Prize, Lenard had been a pioneer experimenter who described the photoelectric effect. Einstein had once admired him. "I have just read a wonderful paper by Lenard," Einstein had gushed to Marić back in 1901. "Under this beautiful piece I am filled with such happiness and joy that I absolutely must share some of it with you." After Einstein had published his first spate of seminal papers in 1905, citing Lenard by name in the one on light quanta, the two scientists had exchanged flattering letters.[14]

But as an ardent German nationalist, Lenard had become increasingly bitter about the British and the Jews, contemptuous of the publicity Einstein's theory was garnering, and vocal in his attacks on the "absurd" aspects of relativity. He had allowed his name to be used on brochures that were distributed at Weyland's meeting, and as a Nobel laureate he had worked behind the scenes to make sure that Einstein was not awarded the prize.

Because Lenard had refrained from showing up at the Philharmonic Hall rally, and because his published critiques of relativity had been academic in tone, Einstein did not need to attack him in his newspaper piece. But he did. "I admire Lenard as a master of experimental physics, but he has not yet produced anything outstanding in theoretical physics, and his objections to the general theory of relativity are of such superficiality that, up until now, I did not think it necessary to answer them," he wrote. "I intend to make up for this."[15]

Einstein's friends publicly supported him. A group that included von Laue and Nernst published a letter claiming, not altogether accurately, "Whoever is fortunate enough to be close to Einstein knows that he will never be surpassed in his . . . dislike of all publicity."[16]

Privately, however, his friends were appalled. He had been provoked into a display of public anger against those who should have remained unworthy of a reply by his pen, thus stirring up even more distasteful publicity. Max Born's wife, Hedwig, who had freely scolded Einstein about his treatment of his family, now lectured, "[You should] not have allowed yourself to be goaded into that rather unfortunate reply." He should show more respect, she said, for "the secluded temple of science."[17]

Paul Ehrenfest was even harsher. "My wife and I absolutely cannot believe that you yourself wrote some of the phrases in the article," he said. "If you really did write them down with your own hand, it proves that these damn pigs have finally succeeded in touching your soul. I urge you as strongly as I can not to throw one more word on this subject to that voracious beast, the public."[18]

Einstein was somewhat contrite. "Don't be too severe with me," he replied to the Borns. "Everyone must, from time to time, make a sacrifice on the altar of stupidity, to please the deity and mankind. And I did so thoroughly with my article."[19] But he made no apologies for flunking their standards of publicity avoidance. "I had to do this if I wanted to stay in Berlin, where every child recognizes me from photographs," he told Ehrenfest. "If one believes in democracy, then one must grant the public this much right as well."[20]

Not surprisingly, Lenard was outraged by Einstein's article. He insisted on an apology, as he had not even been part of the antirelativity rally. Arnold Sommerfeld, chairman of the German Physical Society, tried to mediate, and he urged Einstein "to write some conciliatory words to Lenard."[21] It was not to be. Einstein refused to back down, and Lenard ended up edging ever closer to being an outright anti-Semite and later a Nazi.

(There was one odd coda to this event. In 1953, according to declassified documents in Einstein's FBI file, a well-dressed German walked into the FBI field office in Miami and told the receptionist he had information that Einstein had admitted to being a communist in an article in *Berliner Tageblatt* in August 1920. The aspiring informer was none other than Paul Weyland, who had landed in Miami and was trying to emigrate after years of being a con man and swindler all over the world. J. Edgar Hoover's FBI was eagerly trying to prove, with no success, that Einstein was a communist, and took up the cause. After three months, the Bureau finally found the article and translated it. There was nothing about being a communist in it. Weyland was, nevertheless, granted American citizenship.)[22]

The public crossfire coming out of the antirelativity rally heightened interest in the upcoming annual meeting of German scientists, scheduled for late September in the spa town of Bad Nauheim. Both Einstein and Lenard were to attend, and Einstein had ended his newspaper response by proclaiming that, at his suggestion, a public discussion of relativity would occur there. "Anyone who can dare face a scientific forum can present his objections there," he said, tossing a gauntlet in Lenard's direction.

During the weeklong gathering in Bad Nauheim, Einstein stayed with Max Born in Frankfurt, twenty miles away, and the two men commuted to the resort town by train each day. The big showdown over relativity, at which both Einstein and Lenard were expected to participate, was on the afternoon of September 23. Einstein had forgotten to bring anything to write with, so he borrowed the pencil of the person next to him in order to take notes while Lenard talked.

Planck was in the chair, and by both his commanding presence and soothing words he was able to prevent any personal attacks. Lenard's objections to relativity were similar to those of many nontheorists. The theory was built on equations rather than observations, he said, and it "offends against the simple common sense of a scientist." Einstein replied that what "seems obvious" changes over time. That was true even of Galileo's mechanics.

It was the first time that Einstein and Lenard had met, but they did not shake hands or speak to each other. And though the official minutes of the meeting do not record it, Einstein apparently lost his equanimity at one point. "Einstein was provoked into making a caustic reply," Born recalled. And a few weeks later, Einstein wrote Born to assure him that he would "not allow myself to get excited again as in Nauheim."[23]

Finally, Planck was able to end the session, before any blood was drawn, with a limp joke. "Since the theory of relativity unfortunately has not so far been able to extend the absolute time available for this meeting," he said, " it must now be adjourned." The papers the next day were left without headlines, and the antirelativity movement subsided for the time being.[24]

As for Lenard, he distanced himself from the weird group of original antirelativists. "Unfortunately Weyland turned out to be a crook," he later said. But he did not let go of his own antipathy toward Einstein. After the Bad Nauheim meeting he became increasingly vitriolic and anti-Semitic in his attacks on Einstein and "Jewish science." He became a proponent of creating a "Deutsche Physik" that purged German physics of Jewish influences, which to him was exemplified by Einstein's relativity theory with its abstract, theoretical, and nonexperimental approach and its odor (at least to him) of a relativism that rejected absolutes, order, and certainties.

A few months later, at the beginning of January 1921, an obscure Munich party functionary picked up the theme. "Science, once our greatest pride, is today being taught by Hebrews," Adolf Hitler wrote in a newspaper polemic.[25] There were even ripples that made it across the Atlantic. That April, the *Dearborn Independent,* a weekly owned by automaker Henry Ford, a strong anti-Semite, blared a banner headline across the top of its front page. "Is Einstein a Plagiarist?" it accusingly asked.[26]

Einstein in America, 1921

Albert Einstein's exploding global fame and budding Zionism came together in the spring of 1921 for an event that was unique in the history of science, and indeed remarkable for any realm: a grand two-month processional through the eastern and midwestern United States that evoked the sort of mass frenzy and press adulation that would thrill a touring rock star. The world had never before seen, and perhaps never will again, such a scientific celebrity superstar, one who also happened to be a gentle icon of humanist values and a living patron saint for Jews.

Einstein had initially thought that his first visit to America might be a way to make some money in a stable currency in order to provide for his family in Switzerland. "I have demanded $15,000 from Princeton and Wisconsin," he told Ehrenfest. "It will probably scare them off. But if they do bite, I will be buying economic independence for myself—and that's not a thing to sniff at."

The American universities did not bite. "My demands were too high," he reported back to Ehrenfest.[27] So by February 1921, he had made other plans for the spring: he would present a paper at the third Solvay Conference in Brussels and give some lectures in Leiden at the behest of Ehrenfest.

It was then that Kurt Blumenfeld, leader of the Zionist movement in Germany, came by Einstein's apartment once again. Exactly two years earlier, Blumenfeld had visited Einstein and enlisted his support for the cause of creating a Jewish homeland in Palestine. Now he was coming with an invitation—or perhaps an instruction—in the form of a telegram from the president of the World Zionist Organization, Chaim Weizmann.

Weizmann was a brilliant biochemist who had emigrated from Russia to England, where he helped his adopted nation in the First World War by coming up with a bacterial method for more efficiently manufacturing the explosive cordite. During that war he worked under former prime minister Arthur Balfour, who was then first lord of the Admiralty. He subsequently helped to persuade Balfour, after he became foreign secretary, to issue the famous 1917 declaration in which Britain pledged to support "the establishment in Palestine of a national home for the Jewish people."

Weizmann's telegram invited Einstein to accompany him on a trip to America to raise funds to help settle Palestine and, in particular, to create Hebrew University in Jerusalem. When Blumenfeld read it to him, Einstein initially balked. He was not an orator, he said, and the role of simply using his celebrity to draw crowds to the cause was "an unworthy one."

Blumenfeld did not argue. Instead, he simply read Weizmann's telegram aloud again. "He is the president of our organization," Blumenfeld said, "and if you take your conversion to Zionism seriously, then I have the right to ask you, in Dr. Weizmann's name, to go with him to the United States."

"What you say is right and convincing," Einstein replied, to the "boundless astonishment" of Blumenfeld. "I realize that I myself am now part of the situation and that I must accept the invitation."[28]

Einstein's reply was indeed a cause for astonishment. He was already committed to the Solvay Conference and other lectures in Europe, he professed to dislike the public spotlight, and his fragile stomach had made him reluctant to travel. He was not a faithful Jew, and his allergy to nationalism kept him from being a pure and unalloyed Zionist.

Yet now he was doing something that went against his nature: accepting an implied command from a figure of authority, one that was based on his perceived bonds and commitments to other people. Why?

Einstein's decision reflected a major transformation in his life. Until the completion and confirmation of his general theory of relativity, he had dedicated himself almost totally to science, to the exclusion even of his personal, familial, and societal relationships. But his time in Berlin had made him increasingly aware of his identity as a Jew. His reaction to the pervasive anti-Semitism was to feel even more connected—indeed, inextricably connected—to the culture and community of his people.

Thus in 1921, he made a leap not of faith but of commitment. "I am really doing whatever I can for the brothers of my race who are treated so badly everywhere," he wrote Maurice Solovine.[29] Next to his science, this would become his most important defining connection. As he would note near the end of his life, after declining the presidency of Israel, "My relationship to the Jewish people has become my strongest human tie."[30]

One person who was not only astonished but dismayed by Einstein's decision was his friend and colleague in Berlin, the chemist Fritz Haber, who had converted from Judaism and assiduously assimilated in order to appear a proper Prussian. Like other assimilationists, he was worried (understandably) that a visit by Einstein to the great wartime enemy at the behest of a Zionist organization would reinforce the belief that Jews had dual loyalties and were not good Germans.

In addition, Haber had been thrilled that Einstein was planning to attend the Solvay Conference in Brussels, the first since the war. No other Germans had been invited, and his attendance was seen as a crucial step for the return of Germany to the larger scientific community.

"People in this country will see this as evidence of the disloyalty of the Jews," Haber wrote when he heard of Einstein's decision to visit America. "You will certainly sacrifice the narrow basis upon which the existence of professors and students of the Jewish faith at German universities rests." [31]

Haber apparently had the letter delivered by hand, and Einstein replied the same day. He took issue with Haber's way of regarding Jews as being people "of the Jewish faith" and instead, once again, cast the identity as being inextricably a matter of ethnic kinship. "Despite my emphatic internationalist beliefs, I have always felt an obligation to stand up for my persecuted and morally oppressed tribal companions," he said. "The prospect of establishing a Jewish university fills me with particular joy, having recently seen countless instances of perfidious and uncharitable treatment of splendid young Jews with attempts to deny their chances of education." [32]

And so it was that the Einsteins sailed from Holland on March 21, 1921, for their first visit to America. To keep things unpretentious and inexpensive, Einstein had said he was willing to travel steerage. The request was not granted, and he was given a nice stateroom. He also asked that he and Elsa be given separate rooms, both aboard the ship and at the hotels, so that he could work while on the trip. That request was granted.

It was, by all accounts, a pleasant Atlantic crossing, during which Einstein tried to explain relativity to Weizmann. Asked upon their arrival whether he understood the theory, Weizmann gave a delightful reply: "During the crossing, Einstein explained his theory to me every day, and by the time we arrived I was fully convinced that he really understands it." [33]

When the ship pulled up to the Battery in lower Manhattan on the afternoon of April 2, Einstein was standing on the deck wearing a faded gray wool coat and a black felt hat that concealed some but not all of his now graying shock of hair. In one hand was a shiny briar pipe; the other clutched a worn violin case. "He looked like an artist," the *New York Times* reported. "But underneath his shaggy locks was a scientific mind whose deductions have staggered the ablest intellects of Europe." [34]

As soon as they were permitted, dozens of reporters and cameramen rushed aboard. The press officer of the Zionist organization told

Einstein that he would have to attend a press conference. "I can't do that," he protested. "It's like undressing in public."[35] But he could, of course, and did.

First he obediently followed directions for almost a half hour as the photographers and newsreel men ordered him and Elsa to strike a variety of poses. Then, in the captain's cabin, he displayed more joy than reluctance as he conducted his first press briefing with all the wit and charm of a merry big-city mayor. "One could tell from his chuckling," the reporter from the *Philadelphia Public Ledger* wrote, "that he enjoyed it."[36] His questioners enjoyed it as well. The whole performance, sprinkled with quips and pithy answers, showed why Einstein was destined to become such a wildly popular celebrity.

Speaking through an interpreter, Einstein began with a statement about his hope "to secure the support, both material and moral, of American Jewry for the Hebrew University of Jerusalem." But the reporters were more interested in relativity, and the first questioner requested a one-sentence description of the theory, a request that Einstein would face at almost every stop on his trip. "All of my life I have been trying to get it into one book," he replied, "and *he* wants me to get it into one sentence!" Pressed to try, he provided a simple overview: "It is a theory of space and time as far as physics is concerned, which leads to a theory of gravitation."

What about those, especially in Germany, who attacked his theory? "No one of knowledge opposes my theory," he answered. "Those physicists who do oppose the theory are animated by political motives."

What political motives? "Their attitude is largely due to anti-Semitism," he replied.

The interpreter finally called the session to a close. "Well, I hope I have passed my examination," Einstein concluded with a smile.

As they were leaving, Elsa was asked if she understood relativity. "Oh, no, although he has explained it to me many times," she replied. "But it is not necessary to my happiness."[37]

Thousands of spectators, along with the fife and drum corps of the Jewish Legion, were waiting in Battery Park when the mayor and other dignitaries brought Einstein ashore on a police tugboat. As blue-and-white flags were waved, the crowd sang the *Star-Spangled Banner* and then the Zionist anthem *Hatikvah.*

The Einsteins and Weizmanns intended to head directly to the Hotel Commodore in Midtown. Instead, their motorcade wound through the Jewish neighborhoods of the Lower East Side late into the evening. "Every car had its horn, and every horn was put in action," Weizmann recalled. "We reached the Commodore at about 11:30, tired, hungry, thirsty and completely dazed."[38]

The following day Einstein entertained a steady procession of visitors and, with what the *Times* called "an unusual impression of geniality," he even held another press gathering. Why, he was asked, had he attracted such an unprecedented explosion of public interest? He professed to being puzzled himself. Perhaps a psychologist could determine why people who generally did not care for science had taken such an interest in him. "It seems psycho-pathological," he said with a laugh.[39]

Weizmann and Einstein were officially welcomed later in the week at City Hall, where ten thousand excited spectators gathered in the park to hear the speeches. Weizmann got polite applause. But Einstein, who said nothing, got a "tumultuous greeting" when he was introduced. "As Dr. Einstein left," the New York *Evening Post* reported, "he was lifted onto the shoulders of his colleagues and into the automobile, which passed in triumphal procession through a mass of waving banners and a roar of cheering voices."[40]

One of Einstein's visitors at the Commodore Hotel was a German immigrant physician named Max Talmey, whose name had been Max Talmud back when he was a poor student in Munich. This was the family friend who had first exposed the young Einstein to math and philosophy, and he was unsure whether the now famous scientist would remember him.

Einstein did. "He had not seen me or corresponded with me for nineteen years," Talmey later noted. "Yet as soon as I entered his room in the hotel, he exclaimed: 'You distinguish yourself through eternal youth!' "[41] They chatted about their days in Munich and their paths since. Einstein invited Talmey back various times during the course of his visit, and before he left even went to Talmey's apartment to meet his young daughters.

Even though he spoke in German about abstruse theories or stood silent as Weizmann tried to cajole money for Jewish settlements in Palestine, Einstein drew packed crowds wherever he went in New York. "Every seat in the Metropolitan Opera House, from the pit to the last row under the roof, was filled, and hundreds stood," reported the *Times* one day. About another lecture that week it likewise reported, "He spoke in German, but those anxious to see and hear the man who has contributed a new theory of space and time and motion to scientific conceptions of the universe filled every seat and stood in the aisles." [42]

After three weeks of lectures and receptions in New York, Einstein paid a visit to Washington. For reasons fathomable only by those who live in that capital, the Senate decided to debate the theory of relativity. Among the leaders asserting that it was incomprehensible were Pennsylvania Republican Boies Penrose, famous for once uttering that "public office is the last refuge of a scoundrel," and Mississippi Democrat John Sharp Williams, who retired a year later, saying, "I'd rather be a dog and bay at the moon than stay in the Senate another six years."

On the House side of the Capitol, Representative J. J. Kindred of New York proposed placing an explanation of Einstein's theories in the *Congressional Record*. David Walsh of Massachusetts rose to object. Did Kindred understand the theory? "I have been earnestly busy with this theory for three weeks," he replied, "and am beginning to see some light." But what relevance, he was asked, did it have to the business of Congress? "It may bear upon the legislation of the future as to general relations with the cosmos."

Such discourse made it inevitable that, when Einstein went with a group to the White House on April 25, President Warren G. Harding would be faced with the question of whether *he* understood relativity. As the group posed for cameras, President Harding smiled and confessed that he did not comprehend the theory at all. The *Washington Post* carried a cartoon showing him puzzling over a paper titled "Theory of Relativity" while Einstein puzzled over one on the "Theory of Normalcy," which was the name Harding gave to his governing philosophy. The *New York Times* ran a page 1 headline: "Einstein Idea Puzzles Harding, He Admits."

At a reception in the National Academy of Sciences on Constitution Avenue (which now boasts the world's most interesting statue of Einstein, a twelve-foot-high full-length bronze figure of him reclining),[43] he listened to long speeches from various honorees, including Prince Albert I of Monaco, who was an avid oceanographer, a North Carolina scholar of hookworms, and a man who had invented a solar stove. As the evening droned on, Einstein turned to a Dutch diplomat seated next to him and said, "I've just developed a new theory of eternity."[44]

By the time Einstein reached Chicago, where he gave three lectures and played violin at a dinner party, he had become more adept at answering irksome questions, particularly the most frequent one, which was sparked by the fanciful *New York Times* headline after the 1919 eclipse that only twelve people could understand his theory.

"Is it true only twelve great minds can understand your theory?" the reporter from the *Chicago Herald and Examiner* asked.

"No, no," Einstein replied with a smile. "I think the majority of scientists who have studied it can understand it."

He then proceeded to try to explain it to the reporter by using his metaphor about how the universe would look to a two-dimensional creature who spent its life moving on a surface of what turned out to be a globe. "It could travel for millions of years and would always return to its starting point," said Einstein. "It would never be conscious of what was above it or beneath it."

The reporter, being a good Chicago newspaperman, was able to spin a glorious tale, written in the third person, about the depths of his own confusion. "When the reporter came to he was vainly trying to light a three-dimensional cigarette with a three-dimensional match," the story concluded. "It began to trickle into his brain that the two-dimensional organism referred to was himself, and far from being the 13th Great Mind to comprehend the theory he was condemned henceforth to be one of the Vast Majority who live on Main Street and ride in Fords."[45]

When a reporter from the rival *Tribune* asked him the same question about only twelve people being able to understand his theory, Einstein again denied it. "Everywhere I go, someone asks me that question," he said. "It's absurd. Anyone who has had sufficient training in science can readily understand the theory." But this time Einstein made no attempt to explain it, nor did the reporter. "The *Tribune* regrets to inform its readers that it will be unable to present to them Einstein's theory of relativity," the article began. "After the professor explained that the most incidental discussion of the question would take from three to four hours, it was decided to confine the interview to other things."[46]

Einstein went on to Princeton, where he delivered a weeklong series of scientific lectures and received an honorary degree "for voyaging through strange seas of thought." Not only did he get a nice fee for the lectures (though apparently not the $15,000 he had originally sought), he also negotiated a deal while there that Princeton could publish his lectures as a book from which he would get a 15 percent royalty.[47]

At the behest of Princeton's president, all of Einstein's lectures were very technical. They included more than 125 complex equations that he scribbled on the blackboard while speaking in German. As one student admitted to a reporter, "I sat in the balcony, but he talked right over my head anyway."[48]

At a party following one of these lectures, Einstein uttered one of his most memorable and self-revealing quotes. Someone excitedly informed him that word had just arrived of a new set of experiments improving on the Michelson-Morley technique that seemed to show that the ether existed and the speed of light was variable. Einstein simply refused to accept it. He knew that his theory was correct. And so he calmly responded, "Subtle is the Lord, but malicious he is not."*

The mathematics professor Oswald Veblen, who was standing there, heard the remark and, when a new math building was built a decade later, asked Einstein for the right to carve the words on the stone mantel of the fireplace in the common room. Einstein happily sent back his approval and further explained to Veblen what he had meant:

---

* I have used the translation preferred by Abraham Pais. Einstein's words in German were, "Raffiniert ist der Herr Gott, aber boshaft ist er nicht."

"Nature hides her secret because of her essential loftiness, but not by means of ruse." [49]

The building, neatly enough, later became the temporary home of the Institute for Advanced Study, and Einstein would have an office there when he immigrated to Princeton in 1933. Near the end of his life, he was in front of the fireplace at a retirement party for the mathematician Hermann Weyl, a friend who had followed him from Germany to Princeton when the Nazis took power. Alluding to his frustration with the uncertainties of quantum mechanics, Einstein nodded to the quote and lamented to Weyl, "Who knows, perhaps He *is* a little malicious." [50]

Einstein seemed to like Princeton. "Young and fresh," he called it. "A pipe as yet unsmoked." [51] For a man who was invariably fondling new briar pipes, this was a compliment. It would not be a surprise, a dozen years hence, that he would decide to move there permanently.

Harvard, where Einstein went next, did not endear itself quite as well. Perhaps it was because Princeton President John Hibben had introduced him in German, whereas Harvard President A. Lawrence Lowell spoke to him in French. In addition, Harvard had invited Einstein to visit, but it did not invite him to give lectures.

Some charged that this slight was due to the influence of a rival Zionist group in America led by Louis Brandeis, a graduate of Harvard Law School, who had become the first Jewish Supreme Court justice. The allegation was so widespread that Brandeis's protégé Felix Frankfurter had to issue a public denial. That prompted an amused letter about the perils of assimilationism from Einstein to Frankfurter. It was "a Jewish weakness," he wrote, "always and eagerly to try to keep the Gentiles in good humor." [52]

The very assimilated Brandeis, who had been born in Kentucky and had turned himself into a proper Bostonian, was an example of the Jews from Germany whose families had arrived in the nineteenth century and tended to look down on the more recent immigrants from eastern Europe and Russia. For both political and personal reasons, Brandeis had clashed with Weizmann, a Russian Jew who had a more assertive and political approach toward Zionism. [53] The enthusiastic crowds that greeted Einstein and Weizmann on their trip were mainly made up of the eastern European Jews, while Brandeis and his ilk remained more aloof.

Most of Einstein's time during the two days he spent in Boston was devoted to appearances, rallies, and dinners (including a kosher banquet for five hundred) with Weizmann to drum up contributions for their Zionist cause. The *Boston Herald* reported on the reaction at one fund-raising event at a synagogue in Roxbury:

> The response was electrifying. Young girl ushers worked their way with difficulty through the crowded aisles, carrying long boxes. Bills of various denominations were rained into these receptacles. A prominent Jewess cried out ecstatically that she had eight sons who had been in the army and wanted to make some donation in proportion to their sacrifices. She held up her watch, a valuable imported timepiece, and slipped the rings from her hands. Others followed her example, and soon baskets and boxes filled with diamonds and other precious ornaments.[54]

While in Boston, Einstein was subjected to a pop quiz known as the Edison test. The inventor Thomas Edison was a practical man, getting crankier with age (he was then 74), who disparaged American colleges as too theoretical and felt the same about Einstein. He had devised a test he gave job applicants that, depending on the position being sought, included about 150 factual questions. How is leather tanned? What country consumes the most tea? What was Gutenberg's type made of?*

The *Times* called it "the ever-present Edison questionnaire controversy," and of course Einstein ran into it. A reporter asked him a question from the test. "What is the speed of sound?" If anyone understood the propagation of sound waves, it was Einstein. But he admitted that he did not "carry such information in my mind since it is readily available in books." Then he made a larger point designed to disparage Edison's view of education. "The value of a college education is not the learning of many facts but the training of the mind to think," he said.[55]

One remarkable feature of most stops on Einstein's grand tour was

---

* Governor Channing Cox had been thrust a version of the test earlier that week, and his first three responses were: Where does shellac come from? "From a can." What is a monsoon? "A funny-sounding word." Where do we get prunes? "Breakfast."

a noisy parade, which was rather unusual for a theoretical physicist. In Hartford, Connecticut, for example, the procession included more than a hundred automobiles headed by a band, a coterie of war veterans, and standard-bearers with the American and Zionist flags. More than fifteen thousand spectators lined the route. "North Main Street was jammed by crowds that struggled to get close to shake hands," the newspaper reported. "The crowds cheered wildly as Dr. Weizmann and Prof. Einstein stood up in the car to receive flowers." [56]

It was an astonishing scene, but it was exceeded in Cleveland. Several thousands thronged Union train depot to meet the visiting delegation, and the parade included two hundred honking and flag-draped cars. Einstein and Weizmann rode in an open car, preceded by a National Guard marching band and a cadre of Jewish war veterans in uniform. Admirers along the way grabbed on to Einstein's car and jumped on the running board, while police tried to pull them away. [57]

While in Cleveland, Einstein spoke at the Case School of Applied Science (now Case Western Reserve), where the famous Michelson-Morley experiments had been conducted. There he met privately, for more than an hour, with Professor Dayton Miller, whose new version of that experiment had provoked Einstein's skeptical response at the Princeton cocktail party. Einstein drew sketches of Miller's ether-drift models and urged him to continue refining his experiments. Miller remained dubious about relativity and partial to the ether, but other experiments eventually affirmed Einstein's faith that the Lord was indeed more subtle than malicious. [58]

The excitement, public outpouring, and dizzying superstar status conferred upon Einstein were unprecedented. But in financial terms, the tour was only a modest success for the Zionist movement. The poorer Jews and recent immigrants had poured out to see him and donated with enthusiasm. But few of the eminent and old-line Jews with great personal fortunes became part of the frenzy. They were, on the whole, more assimilated and less ardently Zionist. Weizmann had hoped to raise at least $4 million. By the end of the year, only $750,000 had actually been collected. [59]

Even after his trip to America, Einstein did not become a full-fledged member of the Zionist movement. He supported the general idea of Jewish settlements in Palestine, and especially Hebrew University in Jerusalem, but he never had a desire to relocate there himself nor to press for the creation of a Jewish nation-state. Instead, his connection was more visceral. He came to feel even more associated with the Jewish people, and he resented even more those who would forsake their roots in order to assimilate.

In this regard, he was part of a momentous trend that was reshaping Jewish identity, by choice and by imposition, in Europe. "Until a generation ago, Jews in Germany did not consider themselves as members of the Jewish people," he told a reporter on the day he was leaving America. "They merely considered themselves as members of a religious community." But anti-Semitism changed that, and there was a silver lining to that cloud, he thought. "The undignified mania of trying to adapt and conform and assimilate, which happens among many of my social standing, has always been very repulsive to me," he said.[60]

The Bad German

Einstein's trip to America indelibly cast him as he wanted to be: a citizen of the world, an internationalist, not a German. That image was reinforced by his trips to Germany's other two Great War enemies. On a visit to England, he spoke at the Royal Society and laid flowers on the grave of Isaac Newton in Westminster Abbey. In France, he charmed the public by lecturing in French and taking a mournful tour of the graves on the famous battlefields.

It was also a time of reconciliation with his family. That summer of 1921, he vacationed on the Baltic with his two boys, instilled in young Eduard a love of math, and then took Hans Albert to Florence. They had such a pleasant time that it helped further restore his relations with Marić. "I'm grateful that you've raised them to have a friendly regard for me," he wrote her. "In fact you've done an exemplary job all around." Most astonishingly, on his way home from Italy he visited Zurich and not only called on Marić but even considered staying in "the little upstairs room," as he called it, at her house there. They all got together with the Hurwitz family and had a musical evening as in the old days.[61]

But the mood was soon sullied by the continued collapse of the German mark, which made it harder for Einstein to support a family whose consumption was in Swiss currency. Before the war the mark had been worth 24 cents, but it had fallen to 2 cents by the beginning of 1920. At that time a mark could buy a loaf of bread. But then the bottom fell out of the currency. By the beginning of 1923, the price of a loaf went to 700 marks and by the end of that year cost 1 billion marks. Yes, 1 billion. In November 1923, a new currency, the Rentenmark, was introduced, backed by the government property; 1 trillion old marks equaled 1 new Rentenmark.

The German people increasingly cast around for scapegoats. They blamed internationalists and pacifists who had forced a surrender in the war. They blamed the French and English for imposing what was in fact an onerous peace. And, no surprise, they blamed the Jews. So Germany in the 1920s was not a good place or time to be an internationalist, pacifist, intellectual Jew.

The milestone that marked the passage of German anti-Semitism from being a nasty undercurrent to a public danger was the assassination of Walther Rathenau. From a wealthy Jewish family in Berlin (his father founded AEG, an electricity firm that competed with that of Einstein's father and then became a huge corporation), he served as a senior official in the war ministry, then reconstruction minister and finally foreign minister.

Einstein had read Rathenau's politics book in 1917, and over dinner told him, "I saw with astonishment and joy how extensive a meeting of minds there is between our outlooks on life." Rathenau returned the compliment by reading Einstein's popular explanation of relativity. "I do not say it comes easily to me, but certainly relatively easily," he joked. Then he peppered Einstein with some very insightful questions: "How does a gyroscope know that it is rotating? How does it distinguish the direction in space toward which it does not want to be tilted?"[62]

Although they became close friends, there was one issue that divided them. Rathenau opposed Zionism and thought, mistakenly, that Jews like himself could reduce anti-Semitism by thoroughly assimilating as good Germans.

In the hope that Rathenau could warm to the Zionist cause, Einstein introduced him to Weizmann and Blumenfeld. They met for discussions, both at Einstein's apartment and at Rathenau's grand manor in Berlin's Grunewald, but Rathenau remained unmoved.[63] The best course, he thought, was for Jews to take public roles and become part of Germany's power structure.

Blumenfeld argued that it was wrong for a Jew to presume to run the foreign affairs of another people, but Rathenau kept insisting that he was a German. It was an attitude that was "all too typical of assimilated German Jews," said Weizmann, who was contemptuous of German Jews who tried to assimilate, and especially of those courtiers who became what he dismissed as *Kaiserjuden*. "They seemed to have no idea that they were sitting on a volcano."[64]

As foreign minister in 1922, Rathenau supported German compliance with the Treaty of Versailles and negotiated the Treaty of Rappallo with the Soviet Union, which caused him to be among the first to be labeled by the fledgling Nazi Party as a member of a Jewish-communist conspiracy. On the morning of June 24, 1922, some young nationalists pulled alongside the open car in which Rathenau was riding to work, sprayed him with machine-gun fire, lobbed in a hand grenade, and then sped away.

Einstein was devastated by the brutal assassination, and most of Germany mourned. Schools, universities, and theaters were closed out of respect on the day of his funeral. A million people, Einstein included, paid tribute in front of the Parliament building.

But not everyone felt sympathy. Adolf Hitler called the killers German heroes. Likewise, at the University of Heidelberg, Einstein's antagonist Philipp Lenard decided to defy the day of mourning and give his regular lecture. A number of students showed up to cheer him, but a group of passing workers were so enraged that they dragged the professor from the class and were about to drop him in the Neckar River when police intervened.[65]

For Einstein, the assassination of Rathenau provided a bitter lesson: assimilation did not bring safety. "I regretted the fact that he became a government minister," Einstein wrote in a tribute he sent to a German magazine. "In view of the attitude that large numbers of educated Germans have towards Jews, I have always thought that the proper conduct of the Jews in public life should be one of proud reserve."[66]

Police warned Einstein that he might be next. His name appeared on the target lists prepared by Nazi sympathizers. He should leave Berlin, officials said, or at least avoid any public lectures.

Einstein moved temporarily to Kiel, took a leave of absence from his teaching duties, and wrote to Planck, backing out of the speech he was scheduled to give to the annual convention of German scientists. Lenard and Gehrcke had led a group of nineteen scientists who published a "Declaration of Protest" aimed at barring him from that convention, and Einstein realized that his fame had come back to haunt him. "The newspapers have mentioned my name too often, thus mobilizing the rabble against me," he explained in his note of apology to Planck.[67]

The months after Rathenau's assassination were "nerve-wracking," Einstein lamented to his friend Maurice Solovine. "I am always on the alert."[68] To Marie Curie he confided that he would probably quit his positions in Berlin and find someplace else to live. She urged him to stay and fight instead: "I think that your friend Rathenau would have encouraged you to make an effort."[69]

One option he considered briefly was a move to Kiel, on Germany's Baltic coast, to work at an engineering firm there run by a friend. He had already developed for the firm a new design for a navigational gyroscope, which it patented in 1922 and for which he was paid 20,000 marks in cash.

The firm's owner was surprised but thrilled when Einstein suggested that he might be willing to move there, buy a villa, and become an engineer rather than a theoretical physicist. "The prospect of a downright normal human existence in quietude, combined with the welcome chance of practical work in the factory, delights me," Einstein said. "Plus the wonderful scenery, sailing—enviable!"

But he quickly abandoned the idea, blaming it on Elsa's "horror" of any change. Elsa, for her part, pointed out, no doubt correctly, that it was really Einstein's own decision. "This business of quietude is an illusion," she wrote.[70]

Why didn't he leave Berlin? He had lived there for eight years, longer than anywhere since running away from Munich as a schoolboy. Anti-Semitism was rising, the economy collapsing, and Kiel was certainly not his only option. The light from his star was causing his friends in both Leiden and Zurich to try repeatedly to recruit him with lucrative job offers.

His inertia is hard to explain, but it is indicative of a change that became evident in both his personal life and his scientific work during the 1920s. He had once been a restless rebel who hopped from job to job, insight to insight, resisting anything that smacked of restraint. He had been repelled by conventional respectability. But now he personified it. From being a romantic youth who fancied himself a footloose bohemian he had settled, with but a few stabs at ironic detachment, into a bourgeois life with a doting hausfrau and a richly wallpapered home filled with heavy Biedermeier furniture. He was no longer restless. He was comfortable.

Despite his qualms about publicity and resolve to lie low, it was not in Einstein's nature to shy away from saying what he thought. Nor was he always able to resist demands that he play a public role. Thus he showed up at a huge pacifist rally in a Berlin public park on August 1, just five weeks after Rathenau's assassination. Although he did not speak, he agreed to be paraded around the rally in a car.[71]

Earlier that year, he had joined the League of Nations' International Committee on Intellectual Cooperation, which sought to promote a pacifist spirit among scholars, and he had persuaded Marie Curie to join as well. Its name and mission was sure to inflame German nationalists. So in the wake of the Rathenau assassination, Einstein declared that he wished to resign. "The situation here is that a Jew would do well to exercise restraint as regards his participation in political affairs," he wrote a League official. "In addition, I must say that I have no desire to represent people who would certainly not choose me as their representative."[72]

Even that small act of public reticence did not hold. Curie and the Oxford professor Gilbert Murray, a leader of the committee, begged him to stay a member, and Einstein promptly withdrew his resignation. For the next two years, he remained peripherally involved, but eventually he broke with the League, partly because it supported France's seizure of the Ruhr region after Germany was unable to make reparation payments.

He treated the League, as he did so many parts of life, with a slightly detached and amused air. Each member was supposed to give an address to Geneva University students, but Einstein gave a violin recital instead. One evening at a dinner, Murray's wife asked him why he remained so cheerful given the depravity of the world. "We must remember that this is a very small star," he responded, "and probably some of the larger and more important stars may be very virtuous and happy."[73]

Asia and Palestine, 1922–1923

The unpleasant atmosphere in Germany made Einstein willing to take the most extensive tour of his life, a six-month excursion beginning in October 1922 that would be the only time he would travel either to Asia or what is now Israel. Wherever he went, he was treated as a celebrity, arousing within him the usual mixed emotions. Upon arrival in Ceylon, the Einsteins were whisked away by a waiting rickshaw. "We rode in small one-man carriages drawn at a trot by men of Herculean strength yet delicate build," he noted in his travel diary. "I was bitterly ashamed to share responsibility for the abominable treatment accorded fellow human beings but was unable to do anything about it."[74]

In Singapore, almost the entire Jewish community of more than six hundred turned up at the dock, fortunately trailing no rickshaws. Einstein's target was the richest of them all, Sir Menasseh Meyer, who was born in Baghdad and made his fortune in the opium and real estate markets. "Our sons are refused admission to the universities of other nations," he declared in his speech seeking donations for Hebrew University. Not many of his listeners understood German, and Einstein called the event a "desperate calamity of language with good tasting cake." But it paid off. Meyer gave a sizable donation.[75]

Einstein's own take was even greater. His Japanese publisher and hosts paid him 2,000 pounds for his lecture series there. It was a huge success. Close to twenty-five hundred paying customers showed up for the first talk in Tokyo, which lasted four hours with translation, and more thronged the Imperial Palace to watch his arrival there to meet the emperor and empress.

Einstein was typically amused by it all. "No living person deserves this sort of reception," he told Elsa as they stood on the balcony of their hotel room at dawn listening to the cheers of a thousand people who had kept an all-night vigil hoping to glimpse him. "I'm afraid we're swindlers. We'll end up in prison yet." The German ambassador, with a bit of edge to his pen, reported that "the entire journey of the famous man has been mounted and executed as a commercial enterprise."[76]

Feeling sorry for his listeners, Einstein shortened his subsequent lecture to under three hours. But as he rode to the next city by train (passing along the way through Hiroshima), he could sense that something was amiss with his hosts. Upon asking what the problem was, he was politely told, "The persons who arranged the second lecture were insulted because it did not last four hours like the first one." Thenceforth, he lectured long to the patient Japanese audiences.

The Japanese people struck him as gentle and unpretentious, with a deep appreciation for beauty and ideas. "Of all the people I have met, I like the Japanese most, as they are modest, intelligent, considerate, and have a feel for art," he wrote his two sons.[77]

On his voyage back west, Einstein made his only visit to Palestine, a memorable twelve-day stay that included stops in Lod, Tel Aviv, Jerusalem, and Haifa. He was greeted with great British pomp, as if he were a head of state rather than a theoretical physicist. A cannon salute announced his arrival at the palatial residence of the British high commissioner, Sir Herbert Samuel.

Einstein, on the other hand, was typically unpretentious; he and Elsa arrived tired because he had insisted that they travel in the coach-class car of the overnight train from the coast rather than the first-class sleeping car that had been prepared for them. Elsa was so unnerved by the British formality that she went to bed early some nights to avoid ceremonial events. "When my husband commits a breach of etiquette, it is said it's because he's a man of genius," she complained. "In my case, however, it is attributed to lack of culture."[78]

Like Lord Haldane, Commissioner Samuel was a serious amateur in philosophy and science. Together he and Einstein walked the Old City of Jerusalem to that holiest shrine for religious Jews, the Western Wall (or Wailing Wall) that flanks Temple Mount. But Einstein's deepening love for his Jewish heritage did not instill any new appreciation for the Jewish religion. "Dull-minded tribal companions are praying, faces turned to the wall, rocking their bodies forward and back," he recorded in his diary. "A pitiful sight of men with a past but without a future."[79]

The sights of industrious Jewish people building a new land evinced a more positive reaction. One day he went to a reception for a Zionist organization, and the gates of the building were stormed by throngs who wanted to hear him. "I consider this the greatest day of my life," Einstein proclaimed in the excitement of the moment. "Before, I have always found something to regret in the Jewish soul, and that is the forgetfulness of its own people. Today, I have been made happy by the sight of the Jewish people learning to recognize themselves and to make themselves recognized as a force in the world."

The most frequent question Einstein was asked was whether he would someday return to Jerusalem to stay. He was unusually discreet in his replies, saying nothing quotable. But he knew, as he confided to one of his hosts, that if he came back he would be "an ornament" with no chance of peace or privacy. As he noted in his diary, "My heart says yes, but my reason says no."[80]

CHAPTER FOURTEEN

NOBEL LAUREATE

1921–1927

Einstein in Paris, 1922

The 1921 Prize

It seemed obvious that Einstein would someday win the Nobel Prize for Physics. He had, in fact, already agreed to transfer the money to his first wife, Mileva Marić, when that occurred. The questions were: When would it happen? and, For what?

Once it was announced—in November 1922, awarding him the prize for 1921—the questions were: What took so long? and, Why "especially for his discovery of the law of the photoelectric effect"?

It has been part of the popular lore that Einstein learned that he had finally won while on his way to Japan. "Nobel Prize for physics awarded to you. More by letter," read the telegram sent on November 10. In fact, he had been alerted as soon as the Swedish Academy made the decision in September, well before he left on his trip.

309

The chairman of the physics award committee, Svante Arrhenius, had heard that Einstein was planning to go to Japan in October, which meant that he would be away for the ceremony unless he postponed the trip. So he wrote Einstein directly and explicitly: "It will probably be very desirable for you to come to Stockholm in December." Expressing a principle of pre–jet travel physics, he added, "And if you are then in Japan that will be impossible."[1] Coming from the head of a Nobel Prize committee, it was clear what that meant. There are not a lot of other reasons for physicists to be summoned to Stockholm in December.

Despite knowing that he would finally win, Einstein did not see fit to postpone his trip. Partly it was because he had been passed over so often that it had begun to annoy him.

He had first been nominated for the prize in 1910 by the chemistry laureate Wilhelm Ostwald, who had rejected Einstein's pleas for a job nine years earlier. Ostwald cited special relativity, emphasizing that the theory involved fundamental physics and not, as some Einstein detractors argued, mere philosophy. It was a point that he reiterated over the next few years as he resubmitted the nomination.

The Swedish committee was mindful of the charge in Alfred Nobel's will that the prize should go to "the most important discovery or invention," and it felt that relativity theory was not exactly either of those. So it reported that it needed to wait for more experimental evidence "before one can accept the principle and in particular award it a Nobel prize."[2]

Einstein continued to be nominated for his work on relativity during most of the ensuing ten years, gaining support from distinguished theorists such as Wilhelm Wien, although not yet from a still-skeptical Lorentz. His greatest obstacle was that the committee at the time was leery of pure theorists. Three out of the committee's five members throughout the period from 1910 to 1922 were experimentalists from Sweden's Uppsala University, known for its fervent devotion to perfecting experimental and measuring techniques. "Swedish physicists with a strong experimentalist bias dominated the committee," notes Robert Marc Friedman, a historian of science in Oslo. "They held precision measurement as the highest goal for their discipline." That is one reason Max Planck had to wait until 1919 (when he was awarded the delayed prize for 1918) and why Henri Poincaré never won at all.[3]

The dramatic announcement in November 1919 that the eclipse observations had confirmed parts of Einstein's theory should have made 1920 his year. By then Lorentz was no longer such a skeptic. He along with Bohr and six other official nominators wrote in support of Einstein, mostly focusing on his completed theory of relativity. (Planck wrote in support as well, but his letter arrived after the deadline for consideration.) As Lorentz's letter declared, Einstein "has placed himself in the first rank of physicists of all time." Bohr's letter was equally clear: "One faces here an advance of decisive significance."[4]

Politics intervened. Up until then, the primary justifications for denying Einstein a Nobel had been scientific: his work was purely theoretical, it lacked experimental grounding, and it putatively did not involve the "discovery" of any new laws. After the eclipse observations, the explanation of the shift in Mercury's orbit, and other experimental confirmations, these arguments against Einstein were still made, but they were now tinged with more cultural and personal bias. To his critics, the fact that he had suddenly achieved superstar status as the most internationally celebrated scientist since the lightning-tamer Benjamin Franklin was paraded through the streets of Paris was evidence of his self-promotion rather than his worthiness of a Nobel.

This subtext was evident in the internal seven-page report prepared by Arrhenius, the committee chairman, explaining why Einstein should not win the prize in 1920. He noted that the eclipse results had been criticized as ambiguous and that scientists had not yet confirmed the theory's prediction that light coming from the sun would be shifted toward the red end of the spectrum by the sun's gravity. He also cited the discredited argument of Ernst Gehrcke, one of the anti-Semitic antirelativists who led the notorious 1920 rally against Einstein that summer in Berlin, that the shift in Mercury's orbit could be explained by other theories.

Behind the scenes, Einstein's other leading anti-Semitic critic, Philipp Lenard, was waging a crusade against him. (The following year, Lenard would propose Gehrcke for the prize!) Sven Hedin, a

Swedish explorer who was a prominent member of the Academy, later recalled that Lenard worked hard to persuade him and others that "relativity was really not a discovery" and that it had not been proven.[5]

Arrhenius's report cited Lenard's "strong critique of the oddities in Einstein's generalized theory of relativity." Lenard's views were couched as a criticism of physics that was not grounded in experiments and concrete discoveries. But there was a strong undercurrent in the report of Lenard's animosity to the type of "philosophical conjecturing" that he often dismissed as being a feature of "Jewish science."[6]

So the 1920 prize instead went to another Zurich Polytechnic graduate who was Einstein's scientific opposite: Charles-Edouard Guillaume, the director of the International Bureau of Weights and Measures, who had made his modest mark on science by assuring that standard measures were more precise and discovering metal alloys that had practical uses, including making good measuring rods. "When the world of physics had entered upon an intellectual adventure of extraordinary proportions, it was remarkable to find Guillaume's accomplishment, based on routine study and modest theoretical finesse, recognized as a beacon of achievement," says Friedman. "Even those who opposed relativity theory found Guillaume a bizarre choice."[7]

By 1921, the public's Einstein mania was in full force, for better or worse, and there was a groundswell of support for him from both theoreticians and experimentalists, Germans such as Planck and non-Germans such as Eddington. He garnered fourteen official nominations, far more than any other contender. "Einstein stands above his contemporaries even as Newton did," wrote Eddington, offering the highest praise a member of the Royal Society could muster.[8]

This time the prize committee assigned the task of doing a report on relativity to Allvar Gullstrand, a professor of ophthalmology at the University of Uppsala, who had won the prize for medicine in 1911. With little expertise in either the math or the physics of relativity, he criticized Einstein's theory in a sharp but unknowing manner. Clearly determined to undermine Einstein by any means, Gullstrand's fifty-page report declared, for example, that the bending of light was not a true test of Einstein's theory, that the results were not experimentally valid, and that even if they were there were still other ways to explain the phenomenon using classical mechanics. As for Mercury's orbit, he declared, "It remains unknown until further notice whether the Einstein theory can at all be brought into agreement with the perihelion experiment." And the effects of special relativity, he said, "lay below the limits of experimental error." As one who had made his name by devising precision optical measuring instruments, Gullstrand seemed particularly appalled by Einstein's theory that the length of rigid measuring rods could vary relative to moving observers.[9]

Even though some members of the full Academy realized that Gullstrand's opposition was unsophisticated, it was hard to overcome. He was a respected and popular Swedish professor, and he insisted both publicly and privately that the great honor of a Nobel should not be given to a highly speculative theory that was the subject of an inexplicable mass hysteria that would soon deflate. Instead of choosing someone else, the Academy did something that was less (or more?) of a public slap at Einstein: it voted to choose nobody and tentatively bank the 1921 award for another year.

The great impasse threatened to become embarrassing. His lack of a prize had begun to reflect more negatively on the Nobel than on Einstein. "Imagine for a moment what the general opinion will be fifty years from now if the name Einstein does not appear on the list of Nobel laureates," wrote the French physicist Marcel Brillouin in his 1922 nominating letter.[10]

To the rescue rode a theoretical physicist from the University of Uppsala, Carl Wilhelm Oseen, who joined the committee in 1922. He was a colleague and friend of Gullstrand, which helped him gently overcome some of the ophthalmologist's ill-conceived but stubborn objections. And he realized that the whole issue of relativity theory was so encrusted with controversy that it would be better to try a different tack. So Oseen pushed hard to give the prize to Einstein for "the discovery of the law of the photoelectric effect."

Each part of that phrase was carefully calculated. It was not a nomination for relativity, of course. In fact, despite the way it has been phrased by some historians, it was not for Einstein's theory of light quanta, even though that was the primary focus of the relevant 1905 paper. Nor was it for any *theory* at all. Instead, it was for the *discovery* of a *law*.

A report from the previous year had discussed Einstein's "*theory* of the photoelectric effect," but Oseen made clear his different approach with the title of his report: "Einstein's *Law* of the Photoelectric Effect" (emphasis added). In it, Oseen did not focus on the theoretical aspects of Einstein's work. He specified instead what he called a fundamental natural law, fully proven by experiment, that Einstein propounded: the mathematical description of how the photoelectric effect was explained by assuming that light was absorbed and emitted in discrete quanta, and the way this related to the frequency of the light.

Oseen also proposed that giving Einstein the prize delayed from 1921 would allow the Academy to use that as a basis for simultaneously giving Niels Bohr the 1922 prize, because his model of the atom built on the laws that explained the photoelectric effect. It was a clever coupled-entry ticket for making sure that the two greatest theoretical physicists of the time became Nobel laureates without offending the Academy's old-line establishment. Gullstrand went along. Arrhenius, who had met Einstein in Berlin and been charmed, was now also willing to accept the inevitable. On September 6, 1922, the Academy voted accordingly, and Einstein and Bohr were awarded the 1921 and 1922 prizes, respectively.

Thus it was that Einstein became the recipient of the 1921 Nobel Prize, in the words of the official citation, "for his services to theoretical physics, and especially for his discovery of the law of the photoelectric effect." In both the citation and the letter from the Academy's secretary officially informing Einstein, an unusual caveat was explicitly inserted. Both documents specified that the award was given "without taking into account the value that will be accorded your relativity and gravitation theories after these are confirmed in the future."[11] Einstein would not, as it turned out, ever win a Nobel for his work on relativity and gravitation, nor for anything other than the photoelectric effect.

There was a dark irony in using the photoelectric effect as a path to get Einstein the prize. His "law" was based primarily on observations made by Philipp Lenard, who had been the most fervent campaigner to have him blackballed. In his 1905 paper, Einstein had credited Lenard's "pioneering" work. But after the 1920 anti-Semitic rally in Berlin, they had become bitter enemies. So Lenard was doubly outraged that, despite his opposition, Einstein had won the prize and, worse yet, done so in a field that Lenard pioneered. He wrote an angry letter to the Academy, the only official protest it received, in which he said that Einstein misunderstood the true nature of light and was, in addition, a publicity-seeking Jew whose approach was alien to the true spirit of German physics.[12]

Einstein was traveling by train through Japan and missed the official award ceremony on December 10. After much controversy over whether he should be considered German or Swiss, the prize was accepted by the German ambassador, but he was listed as both nationalities in the official record.

The formal presentation speech by Arrhenius, the committee chair, was carefully crafted. "There is probably no physicist living today whose name has become so widely known as that of Albert Einstein," he began. "Most discussion centers on his theory of relativity." He then went on to say, almost dismissively, that "this pertains essentially to epistemology and has therefore been the subject of lively debate in philosophical circles."

After touching briefly on Einstein's other work, Arrhenius explained the Academy's position on why he had won. "Einstein's law of the photoelectrical effect has been extremely rigorously tested by the American Millikan* and his pupils and passed the test brilliantly," he said. "Einstein's law has become the basis of quantitative photochemistry in the same way as Faraday's law is the basis of electrochemistry."[13]

Einstein gave his official acceptance speech the following July at a Swedish science conference with King Gustav Adolf V in attendance. He spoke not about the photoelectric effect, but about relativity, and he

---

* Robert Andrews Millikan would win the Nobel Prize the following year, 1923, for experimental work on the photoelectric effect he had done at the University of Chicago. By then he had become director of the physics lab at the California Institute of Technology, and in the early 1930s he would bring Einstein there as a visiting scientist.

concluded by emphasizing the importance of his new passion, finding a unified field theory that would reconcile general relativity with electromagnetic theory and, if possible, with quantum mechanics.[14]

The prize money that year amounted to 121,572 Swedish kronor, or $32,250, which was more than ten times the annual salary of the average professor at the time. As per his divorce agreement with Marić, Einstein had part of it sent directly to Zurich to reside in a trust for her and their sons, and the rest went into an American account with the interest directed for her use.

This prompted another row. Hans Albert complained that the trust arrangement, which had previously been agreed to, made only the interest on the money accessible to the family. Once again, Zangger intervened and calmed the dispute. Einstein jokingly wrote to his sons, "You all will be so rich that some fine day I may ask you for a loan." The money was eventually used by Marić to buy three homes with rental apartments in Zurich.[15]

Newton's Bucket and the Ether Reincarnated

"Anything truly novel is invented only during one's youth," Einstein lamented to a friend after finishing his work on general relativity and cosmology. "Later one becomes more experienced, more famous—and more *blockheaded*."[16]

Einstein turned 40 in 1919, the year that the eclipse observations made him world-famous. For the next six years, he continued to make important contributions to quantum theory. But after that, as we shall see, he would begin to seem, if not blockheaded, at least a bit stubborn as he resisted quantum mechanics and embarked on a long, lonely, and unsuccessful effort to devise a unified theory that would subsume it into a more deterministic framework.

Over the ensuing years, researchers would discover new forces in nature, besides electromagnetism and gravity, and also new particles. These would make Einstein's attempts at unification all the more complex. But he would find himself less familiar with the latest data in experimental physics, and he thus would no longer have the same intuitive feel for how to wrest from nature her fundamental principles.

If Einstein had retired after the eclipse observations and devoted himself to sailing for the remaining thirty-six years of his life, would science have suffered? Yes, for even though most of his attacks on quantum mechanics did not prove to be warranted, he did serve to strengthen the theory by coming up with a few advances and also, less intentionally, by his ingenious but futile efforts to poke holes in it.

That raises another question: Why was Einstein so much more creative before the age of 40 than after? Partly, it is an occupational hazard of mathematicians and theoretical physicists to have their great breakthroughs before turning 40.[17] "The intellect gets crippled," Einstein explained to a friend, "but glittering renown is still draped around the calcified shell."[18]

More specifically, Einstein's scientific successes had come in part from his rebelliousness. There was a link between his creativity and his willingness to defy authority. He had no sentimental attachment to the old order, thus was energized by upending it. His stubbornness had worked to his advantage.

But now, just as he had traded his youthful bohemian attitudes for the comforts of a bourgeois home, he had become wedded to the faith that field theories could preserve the certainties and determinism of classical science. His stubbornness henceforth would work to his disadvantage.

It was a fate that he had begun fearing years before, not long after he finished his famous flurry of 1905 papers. "Soon I will reach the age of stagnation and sterility when one laments the revolutionary spirit of the young," he had worried to his colleague from the Olympia Academy, Maurice Solovine.[19]

Now, many triumphs later, there were young revolutionaries who felt this fate had indeed befallen him. In one of his most revealing remarks about himself, Einstein lamented, "To punish me for my contempt of authority, Fate has made me an authority myself."[20]

Thus it is not surprising that, during the 1920s, Einstein found himself scaling back on some of his bolder earlier ideas. For example, in his 1905 special relativity paper he had famously dismissed the concept of the ether as "superfluous." But after he finished his theory of general relativity, he concluded that the gravitational potentials in that theory characterized the physical qualities of empty space and served as a medium that could transmit disturbances. He began referring to this as a new way to conceive of an ether. "I agree with you that the general relativity theory admits of an ether hypothesis," he wrote Lorentz in 1916.[21]

In a lecture in Leiden in May 1920, Einstein publicly proposed a reincarnation, though not a rebirth, of the ether. "More careful reflection teaches us, however, that the special theory of relativity does not compel us to deny ether," he said. "We may assume the existence of an ether, only we must give up ascribing a definite state of motion to it."

This revised view was justified, he said, by the results of the general theory of relativity. He made clear that his new ether was different from the old one, which had been conceived as a medium that could ripple and thus explain how light waves moved through space. Instead, he was reintroducing the idea in order to explain rotation and inertia.

Perhaps he could have saved some confusion if he had chosen a different term. But in his speech he made clear that he was reintroducing the word intentionally:

> To deny the ether is ultimately to assume that empty space has no physical qualities whatever. The fundamental facts of mechanics do not harmonize with this view . . . Besides observable objects, another thing, which is not perceptible, must be looked upon as real, to enable acceleration or rotation to be looked upon as something real . . . The conception of the ether has again acquired an intelligible content, although this content differs widely from that of the ether of the mechanical wave theory of light . . . According to the general theory of relativity, space is endowed with physical qualities; in this sense, there exists an ether. Space without ether is unthinkable; for in such space there not only would be no propagation of light, but also no possibility of existence for standards of space and time (measuring-rods and clocks), nor therefore any spacetime intervals in the physical sense. But this ether may not be thought of as endowed with the qualities of ponderable media, as consisting of parts which may be tracked through time. The idea of motion may not be applied to it.[22]

So what was this reincarnated ether, and what did it mean for Mach's principle and for the question raised by Newton's bucket?* Einstein had initially enthused that general relativity explained rotation as being simply a motion *relative* to other objects in space, just as Mach had argued. In other words, if you were inside a bucket that was dangling in empty space, with no other objects in the universe, there would be no way to tell if you were spinning or not. Einstein even wrote to Mach saying he should be pleased that his principle was supported by general relativity.

Einstein had asserted this claim in a letter to Schwarzschild, the brilliant young scientist who had written to him from Germany's Russian front during the war about the cosmological implications of general relativity. "Inertia is simply an interaction between masses, not an effect in which 'space' of itself is involved, separate from the observed mass," Einstein had declared.[23] But Schwarzschild disagreed with that assessment.

And now, four years later, Einstein had changed his mind. In his Leiden speech, unlike in his 1916 interpretation of general relativity, Einstein accepted that his gravitational field theory implied that empty space had physical qualities. The mechanical behavior of an object hovering in empty space, like Newton's bucket, "depends not only on relative velocities but also on its state of rotation." And that meant "space is endowed with physical qualities."

As he admitted outright, this meant that he was now abandoning Mach's principle. Among other things, Mach's idea that inertia is caused by the presence of all of the distant bodies in the universe implied that these bodies could *instantly* have an effect on an object, even though they were far apart. Einstein's theory of relativity did not accept instant actions at a distance. Even gravity did not exert its force instantly, but only through changes in the gravitational field that obeyed the speed limit of light. "Inertial resistance to acceleration in relation to

---

* See page 119 for Newton's thought experiment about whether water rotating in a bucket in empty space would be subject to inertial pressure and thus press against the sides of the bucket. See page 251 for Einstein's 1916 view, which he was now revising, that an empty universe would have no inertia or fabric of spacetime.

distant masses supposes action at a distance," Einstein lectured. "Because the modern physicist does not accept such a thing as action at a distance, he comes back to the ether, which has to serve as medium for the effects of inertia."[24]

It is an issue that still causes dispute, but Einstein seemed to believe, at least when he gave his Leiden lecture, that according to general relativity as he now saw it, the water in Newton's bucket would be pushed up the walls even if it were spinning in a universe devoid of any other objects. "In contradiction to what Mach would have predicted," Brian Greene writes, "even in an otherwise empty universe, you *will* feel pressed against the inner wall of the spinning bucket . . . In general relativity, empty spacetime provides a benchmark for accelerated motion."[25]

The inertia pushing the water up the wall was caused by its rotation with respect to the metric field, which Einstein now reincarnated as an ether. As a result, he had to face the possibility that general relativity did not necessarily eliminate the concept of absolute motion, at least with respect to the metric of spacetime.[26]

It was not exactly a retreat, nor was it a return to the nineteenth-century concept of the ether. But it was a more conservative way of looking at the universe, and it represented a break from the radicalism of Mach that Einstein had once embraced.

This clearly made Einstein uncomfortable. The best way to eliminate the need for an ether that existed separately from matter, he concluded, would be to find his elusive unified field theory. What a glory that would be! "The contrast between ether and matter would fade away," he said, "and, through the general theory of relativity, the whole of physics would become a complete system of thought."[27]

Niels Bohr, Lasers, and "Chance"

By far the most important manifestation of Einstein's midlife transition from a revolutionary to a conservative was his hardening attitude toward quantum theory, which in the mid-1920s produced a radical new system of mechanics. His qualms about this new quantum mechanics, and his search for a unifying theory that would reconcile it with relativity and restore certainty to nature, would dominate—and to some extent diminish—the second half of his scientific career.

He had once been a fearless quantum pioneer. Together with Max Planck, he launched the revolution at the beginning of the century; unlike Planck, he had been one of the few scientists who truly believed in the physical reality of quanta—that light *actually* came in packets of energy. These quanta behaved at times like particles. They were indivisible units, not part of a continuum.

In his 1909 Salzburg address, he had predicted that physics would have to reconcile itself to a duality in which light could be regarded as both wave and particle. And at the first Solvay Conference in 1911, he had declared that "these discontinuities, which we find so distasteful in Planck's theory, seem really to exist in nature."[28]

This caused Planck, who resisted the notion that his quanta actually had a physical reality, to say of Einstein, in his recommendation that he be elected to the Prussian Academy, "His hypothesis of light quanta may have gone overboard." Other scientists likewise resisted Einstein's quantum hypothesis. Walther Nernst called it "probably the strangest thing ever thought up," and Robert Millikan called it "wholly untenable," even after confirming its predictive power in his lab.[29]

A new phase of the quantum revolution was launched in 1913, when Niels Bohr came up with a revised model for the structure of the atom. Six years younger than Einstein, brilliant yet rather shy and inarticulate, Bohr was Danish and thus able to draw from the work on quantum theory being done by Germans such as Planck and Einstein and also from the work on the structure of the atom being done by the Englishmen J. J. Thomson and Ernest Rutherford. "At the time, quantum theory was a German invention which had scarcely penetrated to England at all," recalled Arthur Eddington.[30]

Bohr had gone to study with Thomson in Cambridge. But the mumbling Dane and brusque Brit had trouble communicating. So Bohr migrated up to Manchester to work with the more gregarious Rutherford, who had devised a model of the atom that featured a positively charged nucleus around which tiny negatively charged electrons orbited.[31]

Bohr made a refinement based on the fact that these electrons did not collapse into the nucleus and emit a continuous spectrum of radiation, as classical physics would suggest. In Bohr's new model, which was based on studying the hydrogen atom, an electron circled a nucleus at certain permitted orbits in states with discrete energies. The atom could absorb energy from radiation (such as light) only in increments that would kick the electron up a notch to another permitted orbit. Likewise, the atom could emit radiation only in increments that would drop the electron down to another permitted orbit.

When an electron moved from one orbit to the next, it was a quantum leap. In other words, it was a disconnected and discontinuous shift from one level to another, with no meandering in between. Bohr went on to show how this model accounted for the lines in the spectrum of light emitted by the hydrogen atom.

Einstein was both impressed and a little jealous when he heard of Bohr's theory. As one scientist reported to Rutherford, "He told me that he had once similar ideas but he did not dare to publish them." Einstein later declared of Bohr's discovery, "This is the highest form of musicality in the sphere of thought." [32]

Einstein used Bohr's model as the foundation for a series of papers in 1916, the most important of which, "On the Quantum Theory of Radiation," was also formally published in a journal in 1917. [33]

Einstein began with a thought experiment in which a chamber is filled with a cloud of atoms. They are being bathed by light (or any form of electromagnetic radiation). Einstein then combined Bohr's model of the atom with Max Planck's theory of the quanta. If each change in an electron orbit corresponded to the absorption or emission of one light quantum, then—presto!—it resulted in a new and better way to derive Planck's formula for explaining blackbody radiation. As Einstein boasted to Michele Besso, "A brilliant idea dawned on me about radiation absorption and emission. It will interest you. An astonishingly simple derivation, I should say *the* derivation of Planck's formula. A thoroughly quantized affair." [34]

Atoms emit radiation in a spontaneous fashion, but Einstein theorized that this process could also be stimulated. A roughly simplified way to picture this is to suppose that an atom is already in a high-energy state from having absorbed a photon. If another photon with a particular wavelength is then fired into it, two photons of the same wavelength and direction can be emitted.

What Einstein discovered was slightly more complex. Suppose there is a gas of atoms with energy being pumped into it, say by pulses of electricity or light. Many of the atoms will absorb energy and go into a higher energy state, and they will begin to emit photons. Einstein argued that the presence of this cloud of photons made it even more likely that a photon of the same wavelength and direction as the other photons in the cloud would be emitted.[35] This process of stimulated emission would, almost forty years later, be the basis for the invention of the laser, an acronym for "light amplification by the stimulated emission of radiation."

There was one part of Einstein's quantum theory of radiation that had strange ramifications. "It can be demonstrated convincingly," he told Besso, "that the elementary processes of emission and absorption are directed processes."[36] In other words, when a photon pulses out of an atom, it does not do so (as the classical wave theory would have it) in all directions at once. Instead, a photon has momentum. In other words, the equations work only if each quantum of radiation is emitted in some particular direction.

That was not necessarily a problem. But here was the rub: *there was no way to determine which direction an emitted photon might go.* In addition, *there was no way to determine when it would happen.* If an atom was in a state of higher energy, it was possible to calculate the *probability* that it would emit a photon at any specific moment. But it was not possible to determine the moment of emission precisely. Nor was it possible to determine the direction. No matter how much information you had. It was all a matter of *chance,* like the roll of dice.

That was a problem. It threatened the strict determinism of Newton's mechanics. It undermined the certainty of classical physics and the faith that if you knew all the positions and velocities in a system you could determine its future. Relativity may have seemed like a radical idea, but at least it preserved rigid cause-and-effect rules. The quirky and unpredictable behavior of pesky quanta, however, was messing with this causality.

"It is a weakness of the theory," Einstein conceded, "that it leaves the time and direction of the elementary process to 'chance.' " The whole concept of chance—"*Zufall*" was the word he used—was so disconcerting to him, so odd, that he put the word in quotation marks, as if to distance himself from it.[37]

For Einstein, and indeed for most classical physicists, the idea that there could be a fundamental randomness in the universe—that events could just happen without a cause—was not only a cause of discomfort, it undermined the entire program of physics. Indeed, he never would become reconciled to it. "The thing about causality plagues me very much," he wrote Max Born in 1920. "Is the quantumlike absorption and emission of light ever conceivable in terms of complete causality?"[38]

For the rest of his life, Einstein would remain resistant to the notion that probabilities and uncertainties ruled nature in the realm of quantum mechanics. "I find the idea quite intolerable that an electron exposed to radiation should choose *of its own free will* not only its moment to jump off but also its direction," he despaired to Born a few years later. "In that case, I would rather be a cobbler, or even an employee of a gaming house, than a physicist."[39]

Philosophically, Einstein's reaction seemed to be an echo of the attitude displayed by the antirelativists, who interpreted (or misinterpreted) Einstein's relativity theory as meaning an end to the certainties and absolutes in nature. In fact, Einstein saw relativity theory as leading to a deeper description of certainties and absolutes—what he called invariances—based on the combination of space and time into one four-dimensional fabric. Quantum mechanics, on the other hand, would be based on true underlying uncertainties in nature, events that could be described only in terms of probabilities.

On a visit to Berlin in 1920, Niels Bohr, who had become the Copenhagen-based ringleader of the quantum mechanics movement, met Einstein for the first time. Bohr arrived at Einstein's apartment bearing Danish cheese and butter, and then he launched into a discussion of the role that chance and probability played in quantum mechanics. Einstein expressed his wariness of "abandoning continuity and causality." Bohr was bolder about going into that misty realm.

Abandoning strict causality, he countered to Einstein, was "the only way open" given the evidence.

Einstein admitted that he was impressed, but also worried, by Bohr's breakthroughs on the structure of the atom and the randomness it implied for the quantum nature of radiation. "I could probably have arrived at something like this myself," Einstein lamented, "but if all this is true then it means the end of physics."[40]

Although Einstein found Bohr's ideas disconcerting, he found the gangly and informal Dane personally endearing. "Not often in life has a human being caused me such joy by his mere presence as you did," he wrote Bohr right after the visit, adding that he took pleasure in picturing "your cheerful boyish face." He was equally effusive behind Bohr's back. "Bohr was here, and I am just as keen on him as you are," he wrote their mutual friend Ehrenfest in Leiden. "He is an extremely sensitive lad and moves around in this world as if in a trance."[41]

Bohr, for his part, revered Einstein. When it was announced in 1922 that they had won sequential Nobel Prizes, Bohr wrote that his own joy had been heightened by the fact that Einstein had been recognized first for "the fundamental contribution that you made to the special field in which I am working."[42]

On his journey home from delivering his acceptance speech in Sweden the following summer, Einstein stopped in Copenhagen to see Bohr, who met him at the train station to take him home by streetcar. On the ride, they got into a debate. "We took the streetcar and talked so animatedly that we went much too far," Bohr recalled. "We got off and traveled back, but again rode too far." Neither seemed to mind, for the conversation was so engrossing. "We rode to and fro," according to Bohr, "and I can well imagine what the people thought about us."[43]

More than just a friendship, their relationship became an intellectual entanglement that began with divergent views about quantum mechanics but then expanded into related issues of science, knowledge, and philosophy. "In all the history of human thought, there is no greater dialogue than that which took place over the years between Niels Bohr and Albert Einstein about the meaning of the quantum," says the physicist John Wheeler, who studied under Bohr. The social philosopher C. P. Snow went further. "No more profound intellectual debate has ever been conducted," he proclaimed.[44]

Their dispute went to the fundamental heart of the design of the cosmos: Was there an objective reality that existed whether or not we could ever observe it? Were there laws that restored strict causality to phenomena that seemed inherently random? Was everything in the universe predetermined?

For the rest of their lives, Bohr would sputter and fret at his repeated failures to convert Einstein to quantum mechanics. *Einstein, Einstein, Einstein,* he would mutter after each infuriating encounter. But it was a discussion that was conducted with deep affection and even great humor. On one of the many occasions when Einstein declared that God would not play dice, it was Bohr who countered with the famous rejoinder: Einstein, stop telling God what to do![45]

Quantum Leaps

Unlike the development of relativity theory, which was largely the product of one man working in near solitary splendor, the development of quantum mechanics from 1924 to 1927 came from a burst of activity by a clamorous congregation of young Turks who worked both in parallel and in collaboration. They built on the foundations laid by Planck and Einstein, who continued to resist the radical ramifications of the quanta, and on the breakthroughs by Bohr, who served as a mentor for the new generation.

Louis de Broglie, who carried the title of prince by virtue of being related to the deposed French royal family, studied history in hopes of being a civil servant. But after college, he became fascinated by physics. His doctoral dissertation in 1924 helped transform the field. If a wave can behave like a particle, he asked, shouldn't a particle also behave like a wave?

In other words, Einstein had said that light should be regarded not only as a wave but also as a particle. Likewise, according to de Broglie, a particle such as an electron could also be regarded as a wave. "I had a sudden inspiration," de Broglie later recalled. "Einstein's wave-particle dualism was an absolutely general phenomenon extending to all of physical nature, and that being the case the motion of all particles—photons, electrons, protons or any other—must be associated with the propagation of a wave." [46]

Using Einstein's law of the photoelectric affect, de Broglie showed that the wavelength associated with an electron (or any particle) would be related to Planck's constant divided by the particle's momentum. It turns out to be an incredibly tiny wavelength, which means that it's usually relevant only to particles in the subatomic realm, not to such things as pebbles or planets or baseballs.*

In Bohr's model of the atom, electrons could change their orbits (or, more precisely, their stable standing wave patterns) only by certain quantum leaps. De Broglie's thesis helped explain this by conceiving of electrons not just as particles but also as waves. Those waves are strung out over the circular path around the nucleus. This works only if the circle accommodates a whole number—such as 2 or 3 or 4—of the particle's wavelengths; it won't neatly fit in the prescribed circle if there's a fraction of a wavelength left over.

De Broglie made three typed copies of his thesis and sent one to his adviser, Paul Langevin, who was Einstein's friend (and Madame Curie's). Langevin, somewhat baffled, asked for another copy to send along to Einstein, who praised the work effusively. It had, Einstein said, "lifted a corner of the great veil." As de Broglie proudly noted, "This made Langevin accept my work." [47]

Einstein made his own contribution when he received in June of that year a paper in English from a young physicist from India named Satyendra Nath Bose. It derived Planck's blackbody radiation law by treating radiation as if it were a cloud of gas and then applying a statistical method of analyzing it. But there was a twist: Bose said that any two photons that had the same energy state were absolutely indistinguishable, in theory as well as fact, and should not be treated separately in the statistical calculations.

Bose's creative use of statistical analysis was reminiscent of Ein-

---

* The de Broglie wavelength of a baseball thrown at 90 mph would be about 10^{-34} meters, incredibly smaller than the size of an atom or even a proton, so infinitessimal as to be unobservable.

stein's youthful enthusiasm for that approach. He not only got Bose's paper published, he also extended it with three papers of his own. In them, he applied Bose's counting method, later called "Bose-Einstein statistics," to actual gas molecules, thus becoming the primary inventor of quantum-statistical mechanics.

Bose's paper dealt with photons, which have no mass. Einstein extended the idea by treating quantum particles *with mass* as being indistinguishable from one another for statistical purposes in certain cases. "The quanta or molecules are not treated as structures statistically independent of one another," he wrote.[48]

The key insight, which Einstein extracted from Bose's initial paper, has to do with how you calculate the probabilities for each possible state of multiple quantum particles. To use an analogy suggested by the Yale physicist Douglas Stone, imagine how this calculation is done for dice. In calculating the odds that the roll of two dice (A and B) will produce a lucky 7, we treat the possibility that A comes up 4 and B comes up 3 as one outcome, and we treat the possibility that A comes up 3 and B comes up 4 as a different outcome—thus counting each of these combinations as different ways to produce a 7. Einstein realized that the new way of calculating the odds of quantum states involved treating these not as two different possibilities, but only as one. A 4-3 combination was indistinguishable from a 3-4 combination; likewise, a 5-2 combination was indistinguishable from a 2-5.

That cuts in half the number of ways two dice can roll a 7. But it does not affect the number of ways they could turn up a 2 or a 12 (using either counting method, there is only one way to roll each of these totals), and it only reduces from five to three the number of ways the two dice could total 6. A few minutes of jotting down possible outcomes shows how this system changes the overall odds of rolling any particular number. The changes wrought by this new calculating method are even greater if we are applying it to dozens of dice. And if we are dealing with billions of particles, the change in probabilities becomes huge.

When he applied this approach to a gas of quantum particles, Einstein discovered an amazing property: unlike a gas of classical particles, which will remain a gas unless the particles attract one another, a gas of

quantum particles can condense into some kind of liquid even without a force of attraction between them.

This phenomenon, now called Bose-Einstein condensation,* was a brilliant and important discovery in quantum mechanics, and Einstein deserves most of the credit for it. Bose had not quite realized that the statistical mathematics he used represented a fundamentally new approach. As with the case of Planck's constant, Einstein recognized the physical reality, and the significance, of a contrivance that someone else had devised.[49]

Einstein's method had the effect of treating particles as if they had wavelike traits, as both he and de Broglie had suggested. Einstein even predicted that if you did Thomas Young's old double-slit experiment (showing that light behaved like a wave by shining a beam through two slits and noting the interference pattern) by using a beam of gas molecules, they would interfere with one another as if they were waves. "A beam of gas molecules which passes through an aperture," he wrote, "must undergo a diffraction analogous to that of a light ray."[50]

Amazingly, experiments soon showed that to be true. Despite his discomfort with the direction quantum theory was heading, Einstein was still helping, at least for the time being, to push it ahead. "Einstein is thereby clearly involved in the foundation of wave mechanics," his friend Max Born later said, "and no alibi can disprove it."[51]

Einstein admitted that he found this "mutual influence" of particles to be "quite mysterious," for they seemed as if they should behave independently. "The quanta or molecules are not treated as independent of one another," he wrote another physicist who expressed bafflement. In a postscript he admitted that it all worked well mathematically, but "the physical nature remains veiled."[52]

On the surface, this assumption that two particles could be treated as indistinguishable violated a principle that Einstein would nevertheless try to cling to in the future: the principle of separability, which as-

---

* In 1995, Bose-Einstein condensation was finally achieved experimentally by Eric A. Cornell, Wolfgang Ketterle, and Carl E. Wieman, who were awarded the 2001 Nobel Prize for this work.

serts that particles with different locations in space have separate, independent realities. One aim of general relativity's theory of gravity had been to avoid any "spooky action at a distance," as Einstein famously called it later, in which something happening to one body could instantly affect another distant body.

Once again, Einstein was at the forefront of discovering an aspect of quantum theory that would cause him discomfort in the future. And once again, younger colleagues would embrace his ideas more readily than he would—just as he had once embraced the implications of the ideas of Planck, Poincaré, and Lorentz more readily than they had.[53]

An additional step was taken by another unlikely player, Erwin Schrödinger, an Austrian theoretical physicist who despaired of discovering anything significant and thus decided to concentrate on being a philosopher instead. But the world apparently already had enough Austrian philosophers, and he couldn't find work in that field. So he stuck with physics and, inspired by Einstein's praise of de Broglie, came up with a theory called "wave mechanics." It led to a set of equations that governed de Broglie's wavelike behavior of electrons, which Schrödinger (giving half credit where he thought it was due) called "Einstein–de Broglie waves."[54]

Einstein expressed enthusiasm at first, but he soon became troubled by some of the ramifications of Schrödinger's waves, most notably that over time they can spread over an enormous area. An electron could not, in reality, be waving thus, Einstein thought. So what, in the real world, did the wave equation really represent?

The person who helped answer that question was Max Born, Einstein's close friend and (along with his wife, Hedwig) frequent correspondent, who was then teaching at Göttingen. Born proposed that the wave did not describe the behavior of the particle. Instead, he said that it described the *probability* of its location at any moment.[55] It was an approach that revealed quantum mechanics as being, even more than previously thought, fundamentally based on chance rather than causal certainties, and it made Einstein even more squeamish.[56]

Meanwhile, another approach to quantum mechanics had been developed in the summer of 1925 by a bright-faced 23-year-old hiking enthusiast, Werner Heisenberg, who was a student of Niels Bohr in

His parents, Pauline and
Hermann Einstein

In a Munich photo studio at age 14

Bottom left at the Aarau school, 1896

With Mileva Marić, ca. 1905

With Mileva and Hans Albert, 1905

Eduard, Mileva, and Hans Albert, 1914

7

With Conrad Habicht, left, and Maurice Solovine of the "Olympia Academy," ca. 1902

8

Anna Winteler Besso and Michele Besso

9

At the patent office in Bern during the miracle year, 1905

In Prague, 1912

Marcel Grossmann, who helped with
math at college and for general relativity

Hiking in Switzerland with Madame Curie, 1913

With the chemist Fritz Haber, assimilationist
and marriage mediator, July 1914

14

Watched over by Zionist leader Chaim
Weizmann in New York, April 1921

15

Meeting the press in New York, 1930

16

With Elsa at the Grand Canyon, February 1931

17

The 1911 Solvay Conference

18

The 1927 Solvay Conference

19

Receiving the Max Planck medal from its
namesake, 1929

20

In Leiden: Einstein, Ehrenfest, de Sitter in back;
Eddington and Lorentz in front; September 1923

21

With Paul Ehrenfest and Ehrenfest's son in Leiden

22

Niels Bohr and Einstein discussing quantum mechanics at Ehrenfest's home in Leiden, 1925, in a photo taken by Ehrenfest

23
Werner Heisenberg

24
Erwin Schrödinger

25
Max Born

26
Philipp Lenard

27

Vacationing on the Baltic Sea, 1928

28

Connecting to the cosmos

With Elsa and her daughter Margot, Berlin 1929

30

Margot and Ilse Einstein at the house in Caputh, 1929

31

In Caputh with his son Hans Albert and grandson
Bernhard, 1932

At the Mt. Wilson
Observatory near
Caltech, discovering
that the universe is
expanding, January 1931

32

Sailing against the
prevailing currents,
Long Island Sound,
1936

33

34

Welcoming Hans Albert to America, 1937

35

Margot, Einstein, and Helen Dukas being sworn in as U.S. citizens, October 1940

36

Receiving a telescope in the
backyard of 112 Mercer Street,
underneath the picture window
built for his study

37

With Kurt Gödel in Princeton, 1950

38

Princeton, 1953

Copenhagen and then of Max Born in Göttingen. As Einstein had done in his more radical youth, Heisenberg started by embracing Ernst Mach's dictum that theories should avoid any concepts that cannot be observed, measured, or verified. For Heisenberg this meant avoiding the concept of electron orbits, which could not be observed.

He relied instead on a mathematical approach that would account for something that *could* be observed: the wavelengths of the spectral lines of the radiation from these electrons as they lost energy. The result was so complex that Heisenberg gave his paper to Born and left on a camping trip with fellow members of his youth group, hoping that his mentor could figure it out. Born did. The math involved what are known as matrices, and Born sorted it all out and got the paper published.[57] In collaboration with Born and others in Göttingen, Heisenberg went on to perfect a matrix mechanics that was later shown to be equivalent to Schrödinger's wave mechanics.

Einstein politely wrote Born's wife, Hedwig, "The Heisenberg-Born concepts leave us breathless." Those carefully couched words can be read in a variety of ways. Writing to Ehrenfest in Leiden, Einstein was more blunt. "Heisenberg has laid a big quantum egg," he wrote. "In Göttingen they believe in it. I don't."[58]

Heisenberg's more famous and disruptive contribution came two years later, in 1927. It is, to the general public, one of the best known and most baffling aspects of quantum physics: the uncertainty principle.

It is impossible to know, Heisenberg declared, the precise *position* of a particle, such as a moving electron, and its precise *momentum* (its velocity times its mass) at the same instant. The more precisely the position of the particle is measured, the less precisely it is possible to measure its momentum. And the formula that describes the trade-off involves (no surprise) Planck's constant.

The very act of observing something—of allowing photons or electrons or any other particles or waves of energy to strike the object—affects the observation. But Heisenberg's theory went beyond that. An electron does not have a definite position or path until we observe it. This is a feature of our universe, he said, not merely some defect in our observing or measuring abilities.

The uncertainty principle, so simple and yet so startling, was a stake in the heart of classical physics. It asserts that there is no objective reality—not even an objective position of a particle—outside of our observations. In addition, Heisenberg's principle and other aspects of quantum mechanics undermine the notion that the universe obeys strict causal laws. Chance, indeterminacy, and probability took the place of certainty. When Einstein wrote him a note objecting to these features, Heisenberg replied bluntly, "I believe that indeterminism, that is, the nonvalidity of rigorous causality, is necessary."[59]

When Heisenberg came to give a lecture in Berlin in 1926, he met Einstein for the first time. Einstein invited him over to his house one evening, and there they engaged in a friendly argument. It was the mirror of the type of argument Einstein might have had in 1905 with conservatives who resisted his dismissal of the ether.

"We cannot observe electron orbits inside the atom," Heisenberg said. "A good theory must be based on directly observable magnitudes."

"But you don't seriously believe," Einstein protested, "that none but observable magnitudes must go into a physical theory?"

"Isn't that precisely what you have done with relativity?" Heisenberg asked with some surprise.

"Possibly I did use this kind of reasoning," Einstein admitted, "but it is nonsense all the same."[60]

In other words, Einstein's approach had evolved.

Einstein had a similar conversation with his friend in Prague, Philipp Frank. "A new fashion has arisen in physics," Einstein complained, which declares that certain things cannot be observed and therefore should not be ascribed reality.

"But the fashion you speak of," Frank protested, "was invented by you in 1905!"

Replied Einstein: "A good joke should not be repeated too often."[61]

The theoretical advances that occurred in the mid-1920s were shaped by Niels Bohr and his colleagues, including Heisenberg, into what became known as the Copenhagen interpretation of quantum mechanics. A property of an object can be discussed only in the context of how that property is observed or measured, and these observations are not simply aspects of a single picture but are complementary to one another.

In other words, there is no single underlying reality that is independent of our observations. "It is wrong to think that the task of physics is to find out how nature *is*," Bohr declared. "Physics concerns what we can *say* about nature." [62]

This inability to know a so-called "underlying reality" meant that there was no strict determinism in the classical sense. "When one wishes to calculate 'the future' from 'the present' one can only get statistical results," Heisenberg said, "since one can never discover every detail of the present." [63]

As this revolution climaxed in the spring of 1927, Einstein used the 200th anniversary of Newton's death to defend the classical system of mechanics based on causality and certainty. Two decades earlier, Einstein had, with youthful insouciance, toppled many of the pillars of Newton's universe, including absolute space and time. But now he was a defender of the established order, and of Newton.

In the new quantum mechanics, he said, strict causality seemed to disappear. "But the last word has not been said," Einstein argued. "May the spirit of Newton's method give us the power to restore union between physical reality and the profoundest characteristic of Newton's teaching—strict causality." [64]

Einstein never fully came around, even as experiments repeatedly showed quantum mechanics to be valid. He remained a realist, one who made it his creed to believe in an objective reality, rooted in certainty, that existed whether or not we could observe it.

"He does not play dice"

So what made Einstein cede the revolutionary road to younger radicals and spin into a defensive crouch?

As a young empiricist, excited by his readings of Ernst Mach, Einstein had been willing to reject any concepts that could not be observed, such as the ether and absolute time and space and simultaneity. But the success of his general theory convinced him that Mach's skepticism, even though it might be useful for weeding out superfluous concepts, did not provide much help in constructing new theories.

"He rides Mach's poor horse to exhaustion," Einstein complained to Michele Besso about a paper written by a mutual friend.

"We should not insult Mach's poor horse," Besso replied. "Didn't it make possible the tortuous journey through the relativities? And who knows, in the case of the nasty quanta, it may also carry Don Quixote de la Einsteina through it all!"

"You know what I think about Mach's little horse," Einstein wrote Besso in return. "It cannot give birth to anything living. It can only exterminate harmful vermin."[65]

In his maturity, Einstein more firmly believed that there was an objective "reality" that existed whether or not we could observe it. The belief in an external world independent of the person observing it, he repeatedly said, was the basis of all science.[66]

In addition, Einstein resisted quantum mechanics because it abandoned strict causality and instead defined reality in terms of indeterminacy, uncertainty, and probability. A true disciple of Hume would not have been troubled by this. There is no real reason—other than either a metaphysical faith or a habit ingrained in the mind—to believe that nature must operate with absolute certainty. It is just as reasonable, though perhaps less satisfying, to believe that some things simply happen by chance. Certainly, there was mounting evidence that on the subatomic level this was the case.

But for Einstein, this simply did not smell true. The ultimate goal of physics, he repeatedly said, was to discover the laws that strictly determine causes and effects. "I am very, very reluctant to give up complete causality," he told Max Born.[67]

His faith in determinism and causality reflected that of his favorite religious philosopher, Baruch Spinoza. "He was utterly convinced," Einstein wrote of Spinoza, "of the causal dependence of all phenomena, at a time when the success of efforts to achieve a knowledge of the causal relationship of natural phenomena was still quite modest."[68] It was a sentence that Einstein could have written about himself, emphasizing the temporariness implied by the word "still," after the advent of quantum mechanics.

Like Spinoza, Einstein did not believe in a personal God who interacted with man. But they both believed that a divine design was reflected in the elegant laws that governed the way the universe worked.

This was not merely some expression of faith. It was a principle that Einstein elevated (as he had the relativity principle) to the level of a postulate, one that guided him in his work. "When I am judging a theory," he told his friend Banesh Hoffmann, "I ask myself whether, if I were God, I would have arranged the world in such a way."

When he posed that question, there was one possibility that he simply could not believe: that the good Lord would have created beautiful and subtle rules that determined *most* of what happened in the universe, while leaving a few things completely to chance. It felt wrong. "If the Lord had wanted to do that, he would have done it thoroughly, and not kept to a pattern . . . He would have gone the whole hog. In that case, we wouldn't have to look for laws at all." [69]

This led to one of Einstein's most famous quotes, written to Max Born, the friend and physicist who would spar with him over three decades on this topic. "Quantum mechanics is certainly imposing," Einstein said. "But an inner voice tells me that it is not yet the real thing. The theory says a lot, but it does not really bring us any closer to the secrets of the Old One. I, at any rate, am convinced that He does not play dice." [70]

Thus it was that Einstein ended up deciding that quantum mechanics, though it may not be *wrong*, was at least *incomplete*. There must be a fuller explanation of how the universe operates, one that would incorporate both relativity theory and quantum mechanics. In doing so, it would not leave things to chance.

CHAPTER FIFTEEN

UNIFIED FIELD THEORIES

1923–1931

With Bohr at the 1930 Solvay Conference

The Quest

While others continued to develop quantum mechanics, un-daunted by the uncertainties at its core, Einstein persevered in his lonelier quest for a more complete explanation of the universe—a uni-fied field theory that would tie together electricity and magnetism and gravity and quantum mechanics. In the past, his genius had been in finding missing links between different theories. The opening sen-tences of his 1905 general relativity and light quanta papers were such examples.*

---

* From his 1905 special relativity paper: "It is well known that Maxwell's electrodynam-ics—as usually understood now—when applied to moving bodies leads to asymmetries that do not seem inherent in the phenomena. Take, for example, the electrodynamic

He hoped to extend the gravitational field equations of general relativity so that they would describe the electromagnetic field as well. "The mind striving after unification cannot be satisfied that two fields should exist which, by their nature, are quite independent," Einstein explained in his Nobel lecture. "We seek a mathematically unified field theory in which the gravitational field and the electromagnetic field are interpreted only as different components or manifestations of the same uniform field."[1]

Such a unified theory, he hoped, might make quantum mechanics compatible with relativity. He publicly enlisted Planck in this task with a toast at his mentor's sixtieth birthday celebration in 1918: "May he succeed in uniting quantum theory with electrodynamics and mechanics in a single logical system."[2]

Einstein's quest was primarily a procession of false steps, marked by increasing mathematical complexity, that began with his reacting to the false steps of others. The first was by the mathematical physicist Hermann Weyl, who in 1918 proposed a way to extend the geometry of general relativity that would, so it seemed, serve as a geometrization of the electromagnetic field as well.

Einstein was initially impressed. "It is a first-class stroke of genius," he told Weyl. But he had one problem with it: "I have not been able to settle my measuring-rod objection yet."[3]

Under Weyl's theory, measuring rods and clocks would vary depending on the path they took through space. But experimental observations showed no such phenomenon. In his next letter, after two more days of reflection, Einstein pricked his bubbles of praise with a wry putdown. "Your chain of reasoning is so wonderfully self-contained," he wrote Weyl. "Except for agreeing with reality, it is certainly a grand intellectual achievement."[4]

Next came a proposal in 1919 by Theodor Kaluza, a mathematics professor in Königsberg, that a fifth dimension be added to the four di-

---

interaction between a magnet and a conductor." From the 1905 light quanta paper: "A profound formal difference exists between the theories that physicists have formed about gases and other ponderable bodies, and Maxwell's theory of electromagnetic processes in so-called empty space."

mensions of spacetime. Kaluza further posited that this added spatial dimension was circular, meaning that if you head in its direction you get back to where you started, just like walking around the circumference of a cylinder.

Kaluza did not try to describe the physical reality or location of this added spatial dimension. He was, after all, a mathematician, so he didn't have to. Instead, he devised it as a mathematical device. The metric of Einstein's four-dimensional spacetime required ten quantities to describe all the possible coordinate relationships for any point. Kaluza knew that fifteen such quantities are needed to specify the geometry for a five-dimensional realm.[5]

When he played with the math of this complex construction, Kaluza found that four of the extra five quantities could be used to produce Maxwell's electromagnetic equations. At least mathematically, this might be a way to produce a field theory unifying gravity and electromagnetism.

Once again, Einstein was both impressed and critical. "A five-dimensional cylinder world never dawned on me," he wrote Kaluza. "At first glance I like your idea enormously."[6] Unfortunately, there was no reason to believe that most of this math actually had any basis in physical reality. With the luxury of being a pure mathematician, Kaluza admitted this and challenged the physicists to figure it out. "It is still hard to believe that all of these relations in their virtually unsurpassed formal unity should amount to the mere alluring play of a capricious accident," he wrote. "Should more than an empty mathematical formalism be found to reside behind these presumed connections, we would then face a new triumph of Einstein's general relativity."

By then Einstein had become a convert to the faith in mathematical formalism, which had proven so useful in his final push toward general relativity. Once a few issues were sorted out, he helped Kaluza get his paper published in 1921, and followed up later with his own pieces.

The next contribution came from the physicist Oskar Klein, son of Sweden's first rabbi and a student of Niels Bohr. Klein saw a unified field theory not only as a way to unite gravity and electromagnetism, but he also hoped it might explain some of the mysteries lurking in quantum mechanics. Perhaps it could even come up with a way to find "hidden variables" that could eliminate the uncertainty.

Klein was more a physicist than a mathematician, so he focused more than Kaluza had on what the physical reality of a fourth spatial dimension might be. His idea was that it might be coiled up in a circle, too tiny to detect, projecting out into a new dimension from every point in our observable three-dimensional space.

It was all quite ingenious, but it didn't turn out to explain much about the weird but increasingly well-confirmed insights of quantum mechanics or the new advances in particle physics. The Kaluza-Klein theories were put aside, although Einstein over the years would return to some of the concepts. In fact, physicists still do today. Echoes of these ideas, particularly in the form of extra compact dimensions, exist in string theory.

Next into the fray came Arthur Eddington, the British astronomer and physicist responsible for the famous eclipse observations. He refined Weyl's math by using a geometric concept known as an affine connection. Einstein read Eddington's ideas while on his way to Japan, and he adopted them as the basis for a new theory of his own. "I believe I have finally understood the connection between electricity and gravitation," he wrote Bohr excitedly. "Eddington has come closer to the truth than Weyl."[7]

By now the siren song of a unified theory had come to mesmerize Einstein. "Over it lingers the marble smile of nature," he told Weyl.[8] On his steamer ride through Asia, he polished a new paper and, upon arriving in Egypt in February 1923, immediately mailed it to Planck in Berlin for publication. His goal, he declared, was "to understand the gravitational and electromagnetic field as one."[9]

Once again, Einstein's pronouncements made headlines around the world. "Einstein Describes His Newest Theory," proclaimed the *New York Times*. And once again, the complexity of his approach was played up. As one of the subheads warned: "Unintelligible to Laymen."

But Einstein told the newspaper it was not all that complicated. "I can tell you in one sentence what it is about," the reporter quoted him as saying. "It concerns the relation between electricity and gravitation."

He also gave credit to Eddington, saying, "It is grounded on the theories of the English astronomer." [10]

In his follow-up articles that year, Einstein made explicit that his goal was not merely unification but finding a way to overcome the uncertainties and probabilities in quantum theory. The title of one 1923 paper stated the quest clearly: "Does the Field Theory Offer Possibilities for the Solution of Quanta Problems?" [11]

The paper began by describing how electromagnetic and gravitational field theories provide causal determinations based on partial differential equations combined with initial conditions. In the realm of the quanta, it may not be possible to choose or apply the initial conditions freely. Can we nevertheless have a causal theory based on field equations?

"Quite certainly," Einstein answered himself optimistically. What was needed, he said, was a method to "overdetermine" the field variables in the appropriate equations. That path of overdetermination became yet another proposed tool that he would employ, to no avail, in fixing what he persisted in calling the "problem" of quantum uncertainty.

Within two years, Einstein had concluded that these approaches were flawed. "My article published [in 1923]," he wrote, "does not reflect the true solution of this problem." But for better or worse, he had come up with yet another method. "After searching ceaselessly in the past two years, I think I have now found the true solution."

His new approach was to find the simplest formal expression he could of the law of gravitation in the absence of any electromagnetic field and then generalize it. Maxwell's theory of electromagnetism, he thought, resulted in a first approximation. [12]

He now was relying more on math than on physics. The metric tensor that he had featured in his general relativity equations had ten independent quantities, but if it were made nonsymmetrical there would be sixteen of them, enough to accommodate electromagnetism.

But this approach led nowhere, just like the others. "The trouble with this idea, as Einstein became painfully aware, is that there really is nothing in it that ties the 6 components of the electric and magnetic fields to the 10 components of the ordinary metric tensor that describes gravitation," says University of Texas physicist Steven Weinberg. "A Lorentz transformation or any other coordinate transformation will convert electric or magnetic fields into mixtures of electric and magnetic fields, but no transformation mixes them with the gravitational field." [13]

Undaunted, Einstein went back to work, this time trying an approach he called "distant parallelism." It permitted vectors in different parts of curved space to be related, and from that sprang new forms of tensors. Most wondrously (so he thought), he was able to come up with equations that did not require that pesky Planck constant representing quanta. [14]

"This looks old-fashioned, and my dear colleagues, and also you, will stick their tongues out because Planck's constant is not in the equations," he wrote Besso in January 1929. "But when they have reached the limit of their mania for the statistical fad, they will return full of repentance to the spacetime picture, and then these equations will form a starting point." [15]

What a wonderful dream! A unified theory without that rambunctious quantum. Statistical approaches turning out to be a passing mania. A return to the field theories of relativity. Tongue-sticking colleagues repenting!

In the world of physics, where quantum mechanics was now accepted, Einstein and his fitful quest for a unified theory were beginning to be seen as quaint. But in the popular imagination, he was still a superstar. The frenzy that surrounded the publication of his January 1929 five-page paper, which was merely the latest in a string of theoretical stabs that missed the mark, was astonishing. Journalists from around the world crowded around his apartment building, and Einstein was barely able to escape them to go into hiding at his doctor's villa on the Havel River outside of town. The *New York Times* had started the drumbeat weeks earlier with an article headlined "Einstein on Verge of Great Discovery: Resents Intrusion." [16]

Einstein's paper was not made public until January 30, 1929, but for the entire preceding month the newspapers printed a litany of leaks and speculation. A sampling of the headlines in the *New York Times*, for example, include these:

January 12: "Einstein Extends Relativity Theory / New Work Seeks to Unite Laws of Field of Gravitation and Electro-Magnetism / He Calls It His Greatest 'Book' / Took Berlin Scientist Ten Years to Prepare"

January 19: "Einstein Is Amazed at Stir Over Theory / Holds 100 Journalists at Bay for a Week / BERLIN—For the past week the entire press as represented here has concentrated efforts on procuring the five-page manuscript of Dr. Albert Einstein's 'New Field of Theory.' Furthermore, hundreds of cables from all parts of the world, with prepaid answers and innumerable letters asking for a detailed description or a copy of the manuscript have arrived."

January 25 (page 1): "Einstein Reduces All Physics to One Law / The New Electro-Gravitational Theory Links All Phenomena, Says Berlin Interpreter / Only One Substance Also / Hypothesis Opens Visions of Persons Being Able to Float in Air, Says N.Y.U. Professor / BERLIN—Professor Albert Einstein's newest work, 'A New Field Theory,' which will leave the press soon, reduces to one formula the basic laws of relativistic mechanics and of electricity, according to the person who has interpreted it into English."

Einstein got into the act from his Havel River hideaway. Even before his little paper was published, he gave an interview about it to a British newspaper. "It has been my greatest ambition to resolve the duality of natural laws into unity," he said. "The purpose of my work is to further this simplification, and particularly to reduce to one formula the explanation of the gravitational and electromagnetic fields. For this reason I call it a contribution to 'a unified field theory' . . . Now, but only now, we know that the force that moves electrons in their ellipses about the nuclei of atoms is the same force that moves our earth in its annual course around the sun."[17] Of course, it turned out that he did not know that, nor do we know that even now.

He also gave an interview to *Time*, which put him on its cover, the first of five such appearances. The magazine reported that, while the world waited for his "abstruse coherent field theory" to be made public, Einstein was plodding around his country hideaway looking "haggard, nervous, irritable." His sickly demeanor, the magazine explained, was due to stomach ailments and a constant parade of visitors. In addition, it noted, "Dr. Einstein, like so many other Jews and scholars, takes no physical exercise at all."[18]

The Prussian Academy printed a thousand copies of Einstein's paper, an unusually large number. When it was released on January 30, all were promptly sold, and the Academy went back to the printer for three thousand more. One set of pages was pasted in the window of a London department store, where crowds pushed forward to try to comprehend the complex mathematical treatise with its thirty-three arcane equations not tailored for window shoppers. Wesleyan University in Connecticut paid a significant sum for the handwritten manuscript to be deposited as a treasure in its library.

American newspapers were somewhat at a loss. The *New York Herald Tribune* decided to print the entire paper verbatim, but it had trouble figuring out how to cable all the Greek letters and symbols over telegraph machines. So it hired some Columbia physics professors to devise a coding system and then reconstruct the paper in New York, which they did. The *Tribune*'s colorful article about how they transmitted the paper was a lot more comprehensible to most readers than Einstein's paper itself.[19]

The *New York Times,* for its part, raised the unified theory to a religious level by sending reporters that Sunday to churches around the city to report on the sermons about it. "Einstein Viewed as Near Mystic," the headline declared. The Rev. Henry Howard was quoted as saying that Einstein's unified theory supported St. Paul's synthesis and the world's "oneness." A Christian Scientist said it provided scientific backing for Mary Baker Eddy's theory of illusive matter. Others hailed it as "freedom advanced" and a "step to universal freedom."[20]

Theologians and journalists may have been wowed, but physicists were not. Eddington, usually a fan, expressed doubts. Over the next year, Einstein kept refining his theory and insisting to friends that the equations were "beautiful." But he admitted to his dear sister that his work had elicited "the lively mistrust and passionate rejection of my colleagues."[21]

Among those who were dismayed was Wolfgang Pauli. Einstein's new approaches "betrayed" his general theory of relativity, Pauli sharply told him, and relied on mathematical formalism that had no relation to physical realities. He accused Einstein of "having gone over to the pure mathematicians," and he predicted that "within a year, if not before, you will have abandoned that whole distant parallelism, just as earlier you gave up the affine theory."[22]

Pauli was right. Einstein gave up the theory within a year. But he did not give up the quest. Instead, he turned his attention to yet another revised approach that would make more headlines but not more headway in solving the great riddle he had set for himself. "Einstein Completes Unified Field Theory," the *New York Times* reported on January 23, 1931, with little intimation that it was neither the first nor would it be the last time there would be such an announcement. And then again, on October 26 of that year: "Einstein Announces a New Field Theory."

Finally, the following January, he admitted to Pauli, "So you were right after all, you rascal."[23]

And so it went, for another two decades. None of Einstein's offerings ever resulted in a successful unified field theory. Indeed, with the discoveries of new particles and forces, physics was becoming *less* unified. At best, Einstein's effort was justified by the faint praise from the French mathematician Elie Joseph Cartan in 1931: "Even if his attempt does not succeed, it will have forced us to think about the great questions at the foundation of science."[24]

The Great Solvay Debates, 1927 and 1930

The tenacious rearguard action that Einstein waged against the onslaught of quantum mechanics came to a climax at two memorable Solvay Conferences in Brussels. At both he played the provocateur, trying to poke holes in the prevailing new wisdom.

Present at the first, in October 1927, were the three grand masters who had helped launch the new era of physics but were now skeptical of the weird realm of quantum mechanics it had spawned: Hendrik Lorentz, 74, just a few months from death, the winner of the Nobel for his work on electromagnetic radiation; Max Planck, 69, winner of the Nobel for his theory of the quantum; and Albert Einstein, 48, winner of the Nobel for discovering the law of the photoelectric effect.

Of the remaining twenty-six attendees, more than half had won or would win Nobel Prizes as well. The boy wonders of the new quantum mechanics were all there, hoping to convert or conquer Einstein: Werner Heisenberg, 25; Paul Dirac, 25; Wolfgang Pauli, 27; Louis de Broglie, 35; and from America, Arthur Compton, 35. Also there was Erwin Schrödinger, 40, caught between the young Turks and the older skeptics. And, of course, there was the old Turk, Niels Bohr, 42, who had helped spawn quantum mechanics with his model of the atom and become the staunch defender of its counterintuitive ramifications.[25]

Lorentz had asked Einstein to present the conference's report on the state of quantum mechanics. Einstein accepted, then balked. "After much back and forth, I have concluded that I am not competent to give such a report in a way that would match the current state of affairs," he replied. "In part it is because I do not approve of the purely statistical method of thinking on which the new theories are based." He then added rather plaintively, "I beg you not to be angry with me."[26]

Instead, Niels Bohr gave the opening presentation. He was unsparing in his description of what quantum mechanics had wrought. Certainty and strict causality did not exist in the subatomic realm, he said. There were no deterministic laws, only probabilities and chance. It made no sense to speak of a "reality" that was independent of our observations and measurements. Depending on the type of experiment chosen, light could be waves or particles.

Einstein said little at the formal sessions. "I must apologize for not having penetrated quantum mechanics deeply enough," he admitted at the very outset. But over dinners and late-night discussions, resuming again at breakfast, he would engage Bohr and his supporters in animated discourse that was leavened by affectionate banter about dice-playing deities. "One can't make a theory out of a lot of 'maybes,'" Pauli recalls Einstein arguing. "Deep down it is wrong, even if it is empirically and logically right."[27]

"The discussions were soon focused to a duel between Einstein and Bohr about whether atomic theory in its present form could be considered to be the ultimate solution," Heisenberg recalled.[28] As Ehrenfest told his students afterward, "Oh, it was delightful."[29]

Einstein kept lobbing up clever thought experiments, both in sessions and in the informal discussions, designed to prove that quantum mechanics did not give a complete description of reality. He tried to show how, through some imagined contraption, it would be possible, at least in concept, to measure all of the characteristics of a moving particle, with certainty.

For example, one of Einstein's thought experiments involved a beam of electrons that is sent through a slit in a screen, and then the positions of the electrons are recorded as they hit a photographic plate. Various other elements, such as a shutter to open and close the slit instantaneously, were posited by Einstein in his ingenious efforts to show that position and momentum could in theory be known with precision.

"Einstein would bring along to breakfast a proposal of this kind," Heisenberg recalled. He did not worry much about Einstein's machinations, nor did Pauli. "It will be all right," they kept saying, "it will be all right." But Bohr would often get worked up into a muttering frenzy.

The group would usually make their way to the Congress hall together, working on ways to refute Einstein's problem. "By dinner-time we could usually prove that his thought experiments did not contradict uncertainty relations," Heisenberg recalled, and Einstein would concede defeat. "But next morning he would bring along to breakfast a new thought experiment, generally more complicated than the previous one." By dinnertime that would be disproved as well.

Back and forth they went, each lob from Einstein volleyed back by Bohr, who was able to show how the uncertainty principle, in each instance, did indeed limit the amount of knowable information about a moving electron. "And so it went for several days," said Heisenberg. "In the end, we—that is, Bohr, Pauli, and I—knew that we could now be sure of our ground."[30]

"Einstein, I'm ashamed of you," Ehrenfest scolded. He was upset that Einstein was displaying the same stubbornness toward quantum mechanics that conservative physicists had once shown toward relativity. "He now behaves toward Bohr exactly as the champions of absolute simultaneity had behaved toward him."[31]

Einstein's own remarks, given on the last day of the conference, show that the uncertainty principle was not the only aspect of quantum mechanics that concerned him. He was also bothered—and later would become even more so—by the way quantum mechanics seemed to permit action at a distance. In other words, something that happened to one object could, according to the Copenhagen interpretation, instantly determine how an object located somewhere else would be observed. Particles separated in space are, according to relativity theory, independent. If an action involving one can immediately affect another some distance away, Einstein noted, "in my opinion it contradicts the relativity postulate." No force, including gravity, can propagate faster than the speed of light, he insisted.[32]

Einstein may have lost the debates, but he was still the star of the event. De Broglie had been looking forward to meeting him for the first time, and he was not disappointed. "I was particularly struck by his mild and thoughtful expression, by his general kindness, by his simplicity and by his friendliness," he recalled.

The two hit it off well, because de Broglie was trying, like Einstein, to see if there were ways that the causality and certainty of classical physics could be saved. He had been working on what he called "the theory of the double solution," which he hoped would provide a classical basis for wave mechanics.

"The indeterminist school, whose adherents were mainly young and intransigent, met my theory with cold disapproval," de Broglie recalled. Einstein, on the other hand, appreciated de Broglie's efforts, and he rode the train with him to Paris on his way back to Berlin.

At the Gare du Nord they had a farewell talk on the platform. Einstein told de Broglie that all scientific theories, leaving aside their mathematical expressions, ought to lend themselves to so simple a description "that even a child could understand them." And what could be *less* simple, Einstein continued, than the purely statistical interpretation of wave mechanics! "Carry on," he told de Broglie as they parted at the station. "You are on the right track!"

But he wasn't. By 1928, a consensus had formed that quantum mechanics was correct, and de Broglie relented and adopted that view. "Einstein, however, stuck to his guns and continued to insist that the purely statistical interpretation of wave mechanics could not possibly be complete," de Broglie recalled, with some reverence, years later.[33]

Indeed, Einstein remained the stubborn contrarian. "I admire to the highest degree the achievements of the younger generation of physicists that goes by the name quantum mechanics, and I believe in the deep level of truth of that theory," he said in 1929 when accepting the Planck medal from Planck himself. "But"—and there was always a *but* in any statement of support Einstein gave to quantum theory—"I believe that the restriction to statistical laws will be a passing one." [34]

The stage was thus set for an even more dramatic Solvay showdown between Einstein and Bohr, this one at the conference of October 1930. Theoretical physics has rarely seen such an interesting engagement.

This time, in his effort to stump the Bohr-Heisenberg group and restore certainty to mechanics, Einstein devised a more clever thought experiment. One aspect of the uncertainty principle, previously mentioned, is that there is a trade-off between measuring precisely the momentum of a particle and its position. In addition, the principle says that a similar uncertainty is inherent in measuring the energy involved in a process and the time duration of that process.

Einstein's thought experiment involved a box with a shutter that could open and shut so rapidly that it would allow only one photon to escape at a time. The shutter is controlled by a precise clock. The box is weighed exactly. Then, at a certain specified moment, the shutter opens and a photon escapes. The box is now weighed again. The relationship between energy and mass (remember, $E=mc^2$) permitted a precise determination of the energy of the particle. And we know, from the clock, its exact time of departing the system. So there!

Of course, physical limitations would make it impossible to actually *do* such an experiment. But in theory, did it refute the uncertainty principle?

Bohr was shaken by the challenge. "He walked from one person to another, trying to persuade them all that this could not be true, that it would mean the end of physics if Einstein was right," a participant recorded. "But he could think of no refutation. I will never forget the sight of the two opponents leaving the university club. Einstein, a majestic figure, walking calmly with a faint ironic smile, and Bohr trotting along by his side, extremely upset." [35] (See picture, page 336.)

It was one of the great ironies of scientific debate that, after a sleepless night, Bohr was able to hoist Einstein by his own petard. The thought experiment had not taken into account Einstein's own beautiful discovery, the theory of relativity. According to that theory, clocks in stronger gravitational fields run more slowly than those in weaker gravity. Einstein forgot this, but Bohr remembered. During the release of the photon, the mass of the box decreases. Because the box is on a spring scale (in order to be weighed), the box will rise a small amount in the earth's gravity. That small amount is precisely the amount needed to restore the energy-time uncertainty relation.

"It was essential to take into account the relationship between the rate of a clock and its position in a gravitational field," Bohr recalled. He gave Einstein credit for graciously helping to perform the calculations that, in the end, won the day for the uncertainty principle. But Einstein was never fully convinced. Even a year later, he was still churning out variations of such thought experiments.[36]

Quantum mechanics ended up proving to be a successful theory, and Einstein subsequently edged into what could be called his own version of uncertainty. He no longer denounced quantum mechanics as incorrect, only as incomplete. In 1931, he nominated Heisenberg and Schrödinger for the Nobel Prize. (They won in 1932 and 1933, along with Dirac.) "I am convinced that this theory undoubtedly contains a part of the ultimate truth," Einstein wrote in his nominating letter.

Part of the ultimate truth. There was still, Einstein felt, more to reality than was accounted for in the Copenhagen interpretation of quantum mechanics.

Its shortcoming was that it "makes no claim to describe physical reality itself, but only the *probabilities* of the occurrence of a physical reality that we view," he wrote that year in a tribute to James Clerk Maxwell, the master of his beloved field theory approach to physics. His piece concluded with a resounding realist credo—a direct denial of Bohr's declaration that physics concerns not what nature *is* but merely "what we can *say* about nature"—that would have raised the eyebrows of Hume, Mach, and possibly even a younger Einstein. He declared, "Belief in an external world independent of the perceiving subject is the basis of all natural science."[37]

Wresting Principles from Nature

In his more radical salad days, Einstein did not emphasize this credo. He had instead cast himself as an empiricist or positivist. In other words, he had accepted the works of Hume and Mach as sacred texts, which led him to shun concepts, like the ether or absolute time, that were not knowable through direct observations.

Now, as his opposition to the concept of an ether became more subtle and his discomfort with quantum mechanics grew, he edged away from this orthodoxy. "What I dislike in this kind of argumentation," the older Einstein reflected, "is the basic positivistic attitude, which from my point of view is untenable, and which seems to me to come to the same thing as Berkeley's principle, *Esse est percipi.*"*[38]

There was a lot of continuity in Einstein's philosophy of science, so it would be wrong to insist that there was a clean shift from empiricism to realism in his thinking.[39] Nonetheless, it is fair to say that as he struggled against quantum mechanics during the 1920s, he became less faithful to the dogma of Mach and more of a realist, someone who believed, as he said in his tribute to Maxwell, in an underlying reality that exists independently of our observations.

That was reflected in a lecture that Einstein gave at Oxford in June 1933, called "On the Method of Theoretical Physics," which sketched out his philosophy of science.[40] It began with a caveat. To truly understand the methods and philosophy of physicists, he said, "don't listen to their words, fix your attention on their deeds."

If we look at what Einstein did rather than what he was saying, it is clear that he believed (as any true scientist would) that the end product of any theory must be conclusions that can be confirmed by experience and empirical tests. He was famous for ending his papers with calls for these types of suggested experiments.

But how did he come up with the starting blocks for his theoretical

---

* "To be is to be perceived," meaning that it makes no sense to say that unperceived things—most famously Berkeley's example of trees in a forest "and no body by to perceive them"—actually exist (George Berkeley, *Principles of Human Knowledge,* section 23).

thinking—the principles and postulates that would launch his logical deductions? As we've seen, he did not usually start with a set of experimental data that needed some explanation. "No collection of empirical facts, however comprehensive, can ever lead to the formulation of such complicated equations," he said in describing how he had come up with the general theory of relativity.[41] In many of his famous papers, he made a point of insisting that he had not relied much on any specific experimental data—on Brownian motion, or attempts to detect the ether, or the photoelectric effect—to induce his new theories.

Instead, he generally began with postulates that he had abstracted from his understanding of the physical world, such as the equivalence of gravity and acceleration. That equivalence was not something he came up with by studying empirical data. Einstein's great strength as a theorist was that he had a keener ability than other scientists to come up with what he called "the general postulates and principles which serve as the starting point."

It was a process that mixed intuition with a feel for the patterns to be found in experimental data. "The scientist has to worm these general principles out of nature by discerning, when looking at complexes of empirical facts, certain general features."[42] When he was struggling to find a foothold for a unified theory, he captured the essence of this process in a letter to Hermann Weyl: "I believe that, in order to make any real progress, one would again have to find a general principle wrested from Nature."[43]

Once he had wrested a principle from nature, he relied on a byplay of physical intuition and mathematical formalism to march toward some testable conclusions. In his younger days, he sometimes disparaged the role that pure math could play. But during his final push toward a general theory of relativity, it was the mathematical approach that ended up putting him across the goal line.

From then on, he became increasingly dependent on mathematical formalism in his pursuit of a unified field theory. "The development of the general theory of relativity introduced Einstein to the power of abstract mathematical formalisms, notably that of tensor calculus," writes the astrophysicist John Barrow. "A deep physical insight orchestrated the mathematics of general relativity, but in the years that followed the balance tipped the other way. Einstein's search for a unified theory was characterized by a fascination with the abstract formalisms themselves." [44]

In his Oxford lecture, Einstein began with a nod to empiricism: "All knowledge of reality starts from experience and ends in it." But he immediately proceeded to emphasize the role that "pure reason" and logical deductions play. He conceded, without apology, that his success using tensor calculus to come up with the equations of general relativity had converted him to a faith in a mathematical approach, one that emphasized the simplicity and elegance of equations more than the role of experience.

The fact that this method paid off in general relativity, he said, "justifies us in believing that *nature is the realization of the simplest conceivable mathematical ideas.*" [45] That is an elegant—and also astonishingly interesting—creed. It captured the essence of Einstein's thought during the decades when mathematical "simplicity" guided him in his search for a unified field theory. And it echoed the great Isaac Newton's declaration in book 3 of the *Principia:* "Nature is pleased with simplicity."

But Einstein offered no proof of this creed, one that seems belied by modern particle physics. [46] Nor did he ever fully explain what, exactly, he meant by mathematical simplicity. Instead, he merely asserted his deep intuition that this is the way God would make the universe. "I am convinced that we can discover by means of purely mathematical constructions the concepts and the laws connecting them with each other," he claimed.

It was a belief—indeed, a faith—that he had expressed during his previous visit to Oxford, when in May 1931 he had been awarded an honorary doctorate there. In his lecture on that occasion, Einstein explained that his ongoing quest for a unified field theory was propelled by the lure of mathematical elegance, rather than the push of experimental data. "I have been guided not by the pressure from behind of experimental facts, but by the attraction in front from mathematical simplicity," he said. "It can only be hoped that experiments will follow the mathematical flag." [47]

Einstein likewise concluded his 1933 Oxford lecture by saying that he had come to believe that the mathematical equations of field theories were the best way to grasp "reality." So far, he admitted, this had not worked at the subatomic level, which seemed ruled by chance and probabilities. But he told his audience that he clung to the belief that this was not the final word. "I still believe in the possibility of a model of reality—that is to say, of a theory that represents things themselves and not merely the probability of their occurrence."[48]

His Greatest Blunder?

Back in 1917, when Einstein had analyzed the "cosmological considerations" arising from his general theory of relativity, most astronomers thought that the universe consisted only of our Milky Way, floating with its 100 billion or so stars in a void of empty space. Moreover, it seemed a rather stable universe, with stars meandering around but not expanding outward or collapsing inward in a noticeable way.

All of this led Einstein to add to his field equations a cosmological constant that represented a "repulsive" force (see page 254). It was invented to counteract the gravitational attraction that would, if the stars were not flying away from one another with enough momentum, pull all of them together.

Then came a series of wondrous discoveries, beginning in 1924, by Edwin Hubble, a colorful and engaging astronomer working with the 100-inch reflector telescope at the Mount Wilson Observatory in the mountains above Pasadena, California. The first was that the blur known as the Andromeda nebula was actually another galaxy, about the size of our own, close to a million light years away (we now know it's more than twice that far). Soon he was able to find at least two dozen even more distant galaxies (we now believe that there are more than 100 billion of them).

Hubble then made an even more amazing discovery. By measuring the red shift of the stars' spectra (which is the light wave counterpart to the Doppler effect for sound waves), he realized that the galaxies were moving away from us. There were at least two possible explanations for the fact that distant stars in all directions seemed to be flying away from us: (1) because we are the center of the universe, something that since the time of Copernicus only our teenage children believe; (2) because the entire metric of the universe was expanding, which meant that everything was stretching out in all directions so that all galaxies were getting farther away from one another.

It became clear that the second explanation was the case when Hubble confirmed that, in general, the galaxies were moving away from us at a speed that was proportional to their distance from us. Those twice as far moved away twice as fast, and those three times as far moved away three times as fast.

One way to understand this is to imagine a grid of dots that are each spaced an inch apart on the elastic surface of a balloon. Then assume that the balloon is inflated so that the surface expands to twice its original dimensions. The dots are now two inches away from each other. So during the expansion, a dot that was originally one inch away moved another one inch away. And during that same time period, a dot that was originally two inches away moved another two inches away, one that was three inches away moved another three inches away, and one that was ten inches away moved another ten inches away. The farther away each dot was originally, the faster it receded from our dot. And that would be true from the vantage point of each and every dot on the balloon.

All of which is a simple way to say that the galaxies are not merely flying away from us, but instead, the entire metric of space, or the fabric of the cosmos, is expanding. To envision this in 3-D, imagine that the dots are raisins in a cake that is baking and expanding in all directions.

On his second visit to America in January 1931, Einstein decided to go to Mount Wilson (conveniently up the road from Caltech, where he was visiting) to see for himself. He and Edwin Hubble rode in a sleek Pierce-Arrow touring car up the winding road. There at the top to meet him was the aging and ailing Albert Michelson, of ether-drift experiment fame.

It was a sunny day, and Einstein merrily played with the telescope's dials and instruments. Elsa came along as well, and it was explained to her that the equipment was used to determine the scope and shape of the universe. She reportedly replied, "Well, my husband does that on the back of an old envelope."[49]

The evidence that the universe was expanding was presented in the popular press as a challenge to Einstein's theories. It was a scientific drama that captured the public imagination. "Great stellar systems," an Associated Press story began, "rushing away from the earth at 7,300 miles a second, offer a problem to Dr. Albert Einstein." [50]

But Einstein welcomed the news. "The people at the Mt. Wilson observatory are outstanding," he wrote Besso. "They have recently found that the spiral nebulae are distributed approximately uniformly in space, and they show a strong Doppler effect, proportional to their distances, that one can readily deduce from general relativity theory without the 'cosmological' term."

In other words, the cosmological constant, which he had reluctantly concocted to account for a static universe, was apparently not necessary, for the universe was in fact expanding.* "The situation is truly exciting," he exulted to Besso. [51]

Of course, it would have been even more exciting if Einstein had trusted his original equations and simply announced that his general theory of relativity predicted that the universe is expanding. If he had done that, then Hubble's confirmation of the expansion more than a decade later would have had as great an impact as when Eddington confirmed his prediction of how the sun's gravity would bend rays of light. The Big Bang might have been named the Einstein Bang, and it would have gone down in history, as well as in the popular imagination, as one of the most fascinating theoretical discoveries of modern physics. [52]

As it was, Einstein merely had the pleasure of renouncing the cosmological constant, which he had never liked. [53] In a new edition of his popular book on relativity published in 1931, he added an appendix explaining why the term he had pasted into his field equations was, thankfully, no longer necessary. [54] "When I was discussing cosmological problems with Einstein," George Gamow later recalled, "he remarked

---

* As Eddington showed, the cosmological term probably would not have worked even if the universe had turned out to be static. Because it required such a delicate balance, any small disturbance would have caused a runaway expansion or contraction of the universe.

that the introduction of the cosmological term was the biggest blunder he ever made in his life."[55]

In fact, Einstein's blunders were more fascinating and complex than even the triumphs of lesser scientists. It was hard simply to banish the term from the field equations. "Unfortunately," says Nobel laureate Steven Weinberg, "it was not so easy just to drop the cosmological constant, because anything that contributes to the energy density of the vacuum acts just like a cosmological constant."[56]

It turns out that the cosmological constant not only was difficult to banish but is still needed by cosmologists, who use it today to explain the accelerating expansion of the universe.[57] The mysterious dark energy that seems to cause this expansion behaves as if it were a manifestation of Einstein's constant. As a result, two or three times each year fresh observations produce reports that lead with sentences along the lines of this one from November 2005: "The genius of Albert Einstein, who added a 'cosmological constant' to his equation for the expansion of the universe but then retracted it, may be vindicated by new research."[58]

CHAPTER SIXTEEN

TURNING FIFTY

1929–1931

Einstein's house in Caputh near Berlin

Caputh

Einstein wanted some solitude for his fiftieth birthday, a refuge from publicity. So in March 1929 he fled once again, as he had during the publication of his unified field theory paper of a few months earlier, to the gardener's cottage of an estate on the Havel River owned by Janos Plesch, a flamboyant and gossipy Hungarian-born celebrity doctor who had added Einstein to his showcase collection of patient-friends.

For days he lived by himself, cooking his own meals, while journalists and official well-wishers searched for him. His whereabouts became a matter of newspaper speculation. Only his family and assistant knew where he was, and they refused to tell even close friends.

Early on the morning of his birthday, he walked from this hideaway, which had no phone, to a nearby house to call Elsa. She started to wish him well on reaching the half-century mark, but he interrupted.

"Such a fuss about a birthday," he laughed. He was phoning about a matter involving physics, not the merely personal. He had made a small mistake in some calculations he had given to his assistant Walther Mayer, he told her, and he wanted her to take down the corrections and pass them along.

Elsa and her daughters came out that afternoon for a small, private celebration. She was dismayed to find him in his oldest suit, which she had hidden. "How did you manage to find it?" she asked.

"Ah," he replied, "I know all about those hiding places."[1]

The *New York Times,* as intrepid as ever, was the only paper that managed to track him down. A family member later recalled that Einstein's angry look drove the reporter away. That was not true. The reporter was smart and Einstein, despite his feigned fury, was as accommodating as usual. "Einstein Is Found Hiding on His Birthday" was the paper's headline. He showed the reporter a microscope he had been given as a gift, and the paper reported that he was like a "delighted boy" with a new toy.[2]

From around the world came other gifts and greetings. The ones that moved him the most were from ordinary people. A seamstress had sent him a poem, and an unemployed man had saved a few coins to get him a small packet of tobacco. The latter gift brought tears to his eyes and was the first for which he wrote a thank-you letter.[3]

Another birthday gift caused more problems. The city of Berlin, at the suggestion of the ever-meddling Dr. Plesch, decided to honor its most famous citizen by giving him lifelong rights to live in a country house that was part of a large lakeside estate that the city had acquired. There he would be able to escape, sail his wooden boat, and scribble his equations in serenity.

It was a generous and gracious gesture. It was also a welcome one. Einstein loved sailing and solitude and simplicity, but he owned no weekend retreat and had to store his sailboat with friends. He was thrilled to accept.

The house, in a classical style, was nestled in a park near the village of Cladow on a lake of the Havel River. Pictures of it appeared in the papers, and a relative called it "the ideal residence for a person of creative intellect and a man fond of sailing." But when Elsa went to inspect it, she found still living there the aristocratic couple who sold the estate to the city. They claimed that they had retained the right to live on the property. A study of the documents proved them right, and they could not be evicted.

So the city decided to give the Einsteins another part of the estate on which they could build their own home. But that, too, violated the city's purchase agreement. Pressure and publicity only hardened the resolve of the original family to block the Einsteins from building on the land, and it became an embarrassing front-page fiasco, especially after a third suggested alternative also proved unsuitable.

Finally it was decided that the Einsteins should simply find their own piece of land, and the city would buy it. So Einstein picked out a parcel, owned by some friends, farther out of town near a village just south of Potsdam called Caputh. It was in a sylvan spot between the Havel and a dense forest, and Einstein loved it. The mayor accordingly asked the assembly of city deputies to approve spending 20,000 marks to buy the property as the fiftieth birthday gift to Einstein.

A young architect drew up plans, and Einstein bought a small garden plot nearby. Then politics intervened. In the assembly, the right-wing German Nationalists objected, delayed the vote, and insisted that the proposal be put on a future agenda for a full debate. It became clear that Einstein personally would become the focus of that debate.

So he wrote a letter, tinged with amusement, declining the gift. "Life is very short," he told the mayor, "while the authorities work slowly. My birthday is already past, and I decline the gift." The headline the next day in the *Berliner Tageblatt* newspaper read, "Public Disgrace Complete / Einstein Declines."[4]

By this point, the Einsteins had fallen in love with the plot of land in Caputh, negotiated its purchase, and had a design for a house to build upon it. So they went ahead and bought it with their own money. "We have spent most of our savings," Elsa complained, "but we have our land."

The house they built was simple, with polished wood panels inside and unvarnished planks showing to the outside. Through a large picture window was a serene view of the Havel. Marcel Breuer, the famed Bauhaus furniture designer, had offered to do the interior design, but

Einstein was a man of conservative tastes. "I am not going to sit on furniture that continually reminds me of a machine shop or a hospital operating room," he said. Some leftover heavy pieces from the Berlin apartment were used instead.

Einstein's room on the ground floor had a spartan wooden table, a bed, and a small portrait of Isaac Newton. Elsa's room was also downstairs, with a shared bathroom between them. Upstairs were small rooms with sleeping niches for her two daughters and their maid. "I like living in the new little wooden house enormously, even though I am broke as a result," he wrote his sister shortly after moving in. "The sailboat, the sweeping view, the solitary fall walks, the relative quiet—it is a paradise."[5]

There he sailed the new twenty-three-foot boat his friends had given him for his birthday, the *Tümmler*, or Dolphin, which was built fat and solid to his specifications. He liked to go out on the water alone, even though he didn't swim. "He was absurdly happy as soon as he reached the water," recalled a visitor.[6] For hours he would let the boat drift and glide aimlessly as he gently toyed with the rudder. "His scientific thinking, which never leaves him even on the water, takes on the nature of a daydream," according to one relative. "Theoretical thinking is rich in imagination."[7]

Companions

Throughout Einstein's life, his relationships with women seemed subject to untamed forces. His magnetic appeal and soulful manner repeatedly attracted women. And even though he usually shielded himself from entangling commitments, he occasionally found himself caught in the swirl of a passionate attraction, just as he had been with Mileva Marić and even Elsa.

In 1923, after marrying Elsa, he had fallen in love with his secretary, Betty Neumann. Their romance was serious and passionate, according to newly revealed letters. That fall, while on a visit to Leiden, he wrote to suggest that he might take a job in New York, and she could come as his secretary. She would live there with him and Elsa, he fantasized. "I will convince my wife to allow this," he said. "We could live together forever. We could get a large house outside New York."

She replied by ridiculing both him and the idea, which prompted him to concede how much of a "crazy ass" he had been. "You have more respect for the difficulties of triangular geometry than I, old mathematicus, have."[8]

He finally terminated their romance with the lament that he "must seek in the stars" the true love that was denied to him on earth. "Dear Betty, laugh at me, the old donkey, and find somebody who is ten years younger than me and loves you just as much as I do."[9]

But the relationship lingered. The following summer, Einstein went to see his sons in southern Germany, and from there he wrote to his wife that he could not visit her and her daughters, who were at a resort nearby, because that would be "too much of a good thing." At the same time, he was writing Betty Neumann saying that he was going secretly to Berlin, but she should not tell anyone because if Elsa found out she "will fly back."[10]

After he built the house in Caputh, a succession of women friends visited him there, with Elsa's grudging acquiescence. Toni Mendel, a wealthy widow with an estate on the Wannsee, sometimes came sailing with him in Caputh, or he would pilot his boat up to her villa and stay late into the night playing the piano. They even went to the theater together in Berlin occasionally. Once when she picked Einstein up in her chauffeured limousine, Elsa got into a furious fight with him and would not give him any pocket money.

He also had a relationship with a Berlin socialite named Ethel Michanowski. She tagged along on one of his trips to Oxford, in May 1931, and apparently stayed in a local hotel. He composed a five-line poem for her one day on a Christ Church college notecard. "Long-branched and delicately strung, Nothing that will escape her gaze," it began. A few days later she sent him an expensive present, which was not appreciated. "The small package really angered me," he wrote. "You have to stop sending me presents incessantly . . . And to send something like that to an English college where we are surrounded by senseless affluence anyway!"[11]

When Elsa found out that Michanowski had visited Einstein in Oxford, she was furious, particularly at Michanowski for misleading her about where she was going. Einstein wrote from Oxford to tell Elsa to calm down. "Your dismay toward Frau M is totally groundless because she behaved completely according to the best Jewish-Christian morality," he said. "Here is the proof: 1) What one enjoys and doesn't harm others, one should do. 2) What one doesn't enjoy and only aggravates others, one should not do. Because of #1, she came with me, and because of #2 she didn't tell you anything about it. Isn't that impeccable behavior?" But in a letter to Elsa's daughter Margot, Einstein claimed that Michanowski's pursuit was unwanted. "Her chasing me is getting out of control," he wrote Margot, who was Michanowski's friend. "I don't care what people are saying about me, but for mother [Elsa] and for Frau M, it is better that not every Tom, Dick and Harry gossip about it." [12]

In his letter to Margot, he insisted that he was not particularly attached to Michanowski nor to most of the other women who flirted with him. "Of all the women, I am actually attached only to Frau L, who is perfectly harmless and respectable," he said, not so reassuringly. [13] That was a reference to a blond Austrian named Margarete Lebach, with whom he had a very public relationship. When Lebach visited Caputh, she brought pastries for Elsa. But Elsa, understandably, could not abide her, and she took to leaving the village to go shopping in Berlin on the days that Lebach came.

On one visit, Lebach left a piece of clothing in Einstein's sailboat, which caused a family row and prompted Elsa's daughter to urge her to force Einstein to end the relationship. But Elsa was afraid that her husband would refuse. He had let it be known that he believed that men and women were not naturally monogamous. [14] In the end, she decided that she was better off preserving what she could of their marriage. In other respects, it suited her aspirations. [15]

Elsa liked her husband, and she also revered him. She realized that she must accept him with all of his complexities, especially since her life as Mrs. Einstein included much that made her happy. "Such a genius should be irreproachable in every respect," she told the artist and etcher Hermann Struck, who did Einstein's portrait around the time of his fiftieth birthday (as he had done a decade earlier). "But nature does not behave this way. Where she gives extravagantly, she takes away extravagantly." The good and the bad had to be accepted as a whole. "You have to see him all of one piece," she explained. "God has given him so much nobility, and I find him wonderful, although life with him is exhausting and complicated, and not only in one way but in others."[16]

The most important other woman in Einstein's life was one who was completely discreet, protective, loyal, and not threatening to Elsa. Helen Dukas came to work as Einstein's secretary in 1928, when he was confined to bed with an inflamed heart. Elsa knew her sister, who ran the Jewish Orphans Organization, of which Elsa was honorary president. Elsa interviewed Dukas before allowing her to meet Einstein, and she felt that Dukas would be trustworthy and, more to the point, safe in all respects. She offered Dukas the job even before she had met Einstein.

When Dukas, then 32, was ushered into Einstein's sickroom in April 1928, he stretched out his hand and smiled, "Here lies an old child's corpse." From that moment until his death in 1955—indeed until her own death in 1982—the never-married Dukas was fiercely protective of his time, his privacy, his reputation, and later his legacy. "Her instincts were as infallible and straightforward as a magnetic compass," George Dyson later declared. Although she could display a pleasant smile and lively directness with those she liked, she was generally austere, hard-boiled, and at times quite prickly.[17]

More than a secretary, she could appear to intrusive outsiders as Einstein's pit bull—or, as he referred to her, his Cerberus, the guard dog at the gates of his own little kingdom of Hades. She would keep journalists at bay, shield him from letters she thought a waste of his time, and cover up any matters that she decreed should remain private. After a while, she became like a member of the family.

Another frequent visitor was a young mathematician from Vienna, Walther Mayer, who became an assistant and, in Einstein's words, "the calculator." Einstein collaborated with him on some unified field theory papers, and he called him "a splendid fellow who would have long had a professorship if he were not a Jew."[18]

Even Mileva Marić, who had gone back to using her maiden name after the divorce, started using the name Einstein again and was able to establish a strained but workable relationship with him. When he visited South America, he brought her back baskets of cactuses. Since she loved the plants, it was presumably meant as an amicable gift. On his visits to Zurich, he stayed at her apartment occasionally.

He even invited her to stay with him and Elsa when she came to Berlin, an arrangement that likely would have made every single person involved uncomfortable. But she wisely stayed with the Habers instead. Their relationship had improved so much, he told her, that he was now surprising his friends by recounting how well they were getting along. "Elsa is also happy that you and the boys are not hostile to her anymore," he added.[19]

Their two sons, he told Marić, were the best part of his inner life, a legacy that would remain after the clock of his own body had worn down. Despite this, or because of it, his relationship with his sons remained fraught with tensions. This was particularly true when Hans Albert decided to get married.

As if the gods wished to extract their revenge, the situation was similar to the one Einstein had put his own parents through when he decided to marry Mileva Marić. Hans Albert had fallen in love, while studying at the Zurich Polytechnic, with a woman nine years his senior named Frieda Knecht. Less than five feet tall, she was plain and had an abrupt manner but was very smart. Both Marić and Einstein, reunited by this cause, agreed that she was scheming, unattractive, and would likely produce physically unsuitable offspring. "I tried my best to convince him that marrying her would be crazy," he wrote Marić. "But it seems like he is totally dependent on her, so it was in vain."[20]

Einstein assumed that his son had been ensnared because he was shy and inexperienced with women. "She was the one to grab you first, and now you consider her to be the embodiment of femininity," he wrote Hans Albert. "That is the well-known way that women take advantage of unworldly people." So he suggested that an attractive woman would remedy such problems.

But Hans Albert was as stubborn as his father had been twenty-five years earlier, and he was determined to marry Frieda. Einstein conceded that he couldn't stop him, but he urged his son to promise not to have children. "And should you ever feel like you have to leave her, you should not be too proud to come talk to me," Einstein wrote. "After all, that day *will* come." [21]

Hans Albert and Frieda married in 1927, had children, and remained married until her death thirty-one years later. As Evelyn Einstein, their adopted daughter, recalled years later, "Albert had such a hell of a time with his parents over his own marriage that you would think he would have had the sense not to interfere with his son's. But no. When my father went to marry my mother, there was explosion after explosion." [22]

Einstein expressed his dismay about Hans Albert's marriage in letters to Eduard. "The deterioration of the race is a serious problem," Einstein wrote. "That is why I cannot forgive [Hans] Albert his sin. I instinctively avoid meeting him, because I cannot show him a happy face." [23]

But within two years, Einstein had begun to accept Frieda. The couple came to visit him in the summer of 1929, and he reported back to Eduard that he had made his peace. "She made a better impression than I had feared," he wrote. "He is really sweet with her. God bless those rose-colored spectacles." [24]

For his part, Eduard was becoming increasingly dreamy in his academic pursuits, and his psychological problems were becoming more apparent. He liked poetry and wrote doggerel and aphorisms that often had an edge to them, especially when the subject was his family. He played the piano, particularly Chopin, with a passion that was initially a welcome contrast to his usual lethargy but eventually became scary.

His letters to his father were equally intense, pouring out his soul about philosophy and the arts. Einstein responded sometimes tenderly, and occasionally with detachment. "I often sent my father rather rapturous letters, and several times got worried afterwards because he was of a cooler disposition," Eduard later recalled. "I learned only a lot later how much he treasured them."

Eduard went to Zurich University, where he studied medicine and planned to become a psychiatrist. He became interested in Sigmund Freud, whose picture he hung in his bedroom, and attempted his own self-analysis. His letters to his father during this period are filled with his efforts, often astute, to use Freud's theories to analyze various realms of life, including movies and music.

Not surprisingly, Eduard was especially interested in relationships between fathers and sons. Some of his comments were simple and poignant. "It's at times difficult to have such an important father, because one feels so unimportant," he wrote at one point. A few months later, he poured out more insecurities: "People who fill their time with intellectual work bring into the world sickly, nervous at times even completely idiotic children (for example, you me)."[25]

Later his comments became more complex, such as when he analyzed his father's famous lament that fate had punished him for his contempt for authority by making him an authority himself. Eduard wrote, "This means psychoanalytically that, because you didn't want to bend in front of your own father and instead fought with him, you had to become an authority in order to step into his place."[26]

Einstein met Freud when he came from Vienna to Berlin for New Year 1927. Freud, then 70, had cancer of the mouth and was deaf in one ear, but the two men had a pleasant talk, partly because they focused on politics rather than on their respective fields of study. "Einstein understands as much about psychology as I do about physics," Freud wrote to a friend.[27]

Einstein never asked Freud to meet or treat his son, nor did he seem impressed by the idea of psychoanalysis. "It may not always be helpful to delve into the subconscious," he once said. "Our legs are controlled by a hundred different muscles. Do you think it would help us to walk if we analyzed our legs and knew the exact purpose of each muscle and the order in which they work?" He certainly never expressed any interest in undergoing therapy himself. "I should like very much to remain in the darkness of not having been analyzed," he declared.[28]

Eventually, however, he did concede to Eduard, perhaps to make him happy, that there might be some merit to Freud's work. "I must admit that, through various little personal experiences, I am convinced at least of his main theses."[29]

While at the university, Eduard fell in love with an older woman, a trait that apparently ran in the family and might have amused Freud.

When the relationship came to a painful conclusion, he fell into a listless depression. His father suggested he find a dalliance with a younger "plaything." He also suggested that he find a job. "Even a genius like Schopenhauer was crushed by unemployment," he wrote. "Life is like riding a bicycle. To keep your balance you must keep moving." [30]

Eduard was unable to keep his balance. He began cutting classes and staying in his room. As he grew more troubled, Einstein's care and affection for him seemed to increase. There was a painful sweetness in his letters to his troubled son as he engaged with his ideas about psychology and wrestled with his enigmatic aphorisms.

"There is no meaning to life outside of life itself," Eduard declared in one of these aphorisms.

Einstein replied politely that he could accept this, "but that clarifies very little." Life for its own sake, Einstein went on, was hollow. "People who live in a society, enjoy looking into each other's eyes, who share their troubles, who focus their efforts on what is important to them and find this joyful—these people lead a full life." [31]

There was a knowing, self-referential quality in that exhortation. Einstein himself had little inclination or talent for sharing other people's troubles, and he compensated by focusing on what was important to him. "Tete really has a lot of myself in him, but with him it seems more pronounced," Einstein conceded to Marić. "He's an interesting fellow, but things won't be easy for him." [32]

Einstein visited Eduard in October 1930, and together with Marić tried to deal with his downward mental spiral. They played piano together, but to no avail. Eduard continued to slip into a darker realm. Soon after he left, the young man threatened to throw himself out of his bedroom window, but his mother restrained him.

The complex strands of Einstein's family life came together in an odd scene in November 1930. Four years earlier, a conniving Russian writer named Dimitri Marianoff had sought to meet Einstein. With great nerve and tenacity, he presented himself at Einstein's apartment and was able to convince Elsa to let him in. There he proceeded to charm Einstein by talking about Russian theater, and also to turn the head of Elsa's daughter Margot by engaging in a grand show of handwriting analysis.

Margot was so painfully shy that she often hid from strangers, but Marianoff's wiles soon brought her out of her shell. Their wedding occurred a few days after Eduard had tried to commit suicide, and a distraught Marić made an unannounced visit to Berlin to ask her former husband for help. Marianoff later described the scene at the end of his wedding ceremony: "As we came down the steps I noticed a woman standing near the portico. I would not have noticed her, except that she looked at us with such an intensely burning gaze that it impressed me. Margot said under her breath, 'It's Mileva.' " [33]

Einstein was shaken deeply by his son's illness. "This sorrow is eating up Albert," Elsa wrote. "He finds it difficult to cope with." [34]

There was, however, not much he could do. The morning after the wedding, he and Elsa left by train to Antwerp, from which they would sail for their second voyage to the United States. It was a hectic departure. Einstein got separated from Elsa at the Berlin station, then lost their train tickets. [35] But eventually they got everything together and embarked on what would be another triumphal American visit.

America Again

Einstein's second trip to America, beginning in December 1930, was supposed to be different from his first. This time, there would be no public frenzy or odd hoopla. Instead, he was coming for a two-month working visit as a research fellow at the California Institute of Technology. The officials who arranged it were eager to protect his privacy and, like his friends in Germany, they viewed any publicity as undignified.

As usual, Einstein seemed to agree—in theory. Once it was known that he was coming, he was swamped with dozens of telegrams each day with speaking offers and award invitations, all of which he declined. On the way over, he and his mathematical calculator, Walther Mayer, holed up, working on revisions to his unified field theory, in an upper-deck suite with a sailor guarding the door. [36]

He even decided that he would not disembark when his ship docked in New York. "I hate facing cameras and having to answer a crossfire of questions," he claimed. "Why popular fancy should seize on me, a scientist, dealing in abstract things and happy if left alone, is a manifestation of mass psychology that is beyond me."[37]

But by then the world, and especially America, had irrevocably entered the new age of celebrity. Aversion to fame was no longer considered natural. Publicity was still something that many proper people tended to avoid, but its lure had begun to be accepted. The day before his ship docked in New York, Einstein sent word that he had relented to reporters' requests and would hold a press conference and photo opportunity upon his arrival.[38]

It was "worse than the most fantastic expectation," he recorded in his travel diary. Fifty reporters plus fifty more cameramen swarmed aboard, accompanied by the German consul and his fat assistant. "The reporters asked exquisitely inane questions, to which I replied with cheap jokes, which were enthusiastically received."[39]

Asked to define the fourth dimension in a word, Einstein replied, "You will have to ask a spiritualist." Could he define relativity in one sentence? "It would take me three days to give a short definition."

There was, however, one question that he tried to answer seriously, and which he alas got wrong. It was about a politician whose party had risen from obscurity three months earlier to win 18 percent of the vote in the German elections. "What do you think of Adolf Hitler?" Einstein replied, "He is living on the empty stomach of Germany. As soon as economic conditions improve, he will no longer be important."[40]

Time magazine that week featured Elsa on its cover, wearing a sprightly hat and exulting in her role as wife of the world's most famous scientist. The magazine reported, "Because Mathematician Einstein cannot keep his bank account correctly," his wife had to balance his finances and handle the arrangements for the trip. "All these things I must do so that he will think he is free," she told the magazine. "He is all my life. He is worth it. I like being Mrs. Einstein very much."[41] One duty she assigned herself was to charge $1 for her husband's autograph and $5 for his photograph; she kept a ledger and donated the money to charities for children.

Einstein changed his mind about staying secluded aboard ship while it was docked in New York. In fact, he seemed to pop up everywhere. He celebrated Hanukkah with fifteen thousand people in

Madison Square Garden, toured Chinatown by car, lunched with the editorial board of the *New York Times*, was cheered when he arrived at the Metropolitan Opera to hear the sensational soprano Maria Jeritza sing *Carmen*, received the keys to the city (which Mayor Jimmy Walker quipped were given "relatively"), and was introduced by the president of Columbia University as "the ruling monarch of the mind."[42]

He also paid a visit to Riverside Church, a massive structure with a 2,100-seat nave, which had just been completed. It was a Baptist church, but above the west portal, carved in stone amid a dozen other great thinkers in history, was a full-length statue of Einstein. Harry Emerson Fosdick, the noted senior minister, met Einstein and Elsa at the door and gave them a tour. Einstein paused to admire a stained-glass window of Immanuel Kant in his garden, then asked about his own statue. "Am I the only living man among all these figures of the ages?" Dr. Fosdick, with a sense of gravity duly noted by the reporters present, replied, "That is true, Professor Einstein."

"Then I will have to be very careful for the rest of my life as to what I do and say," Einstein answered. Afterward, according to an article in the church bulletin, he joked, "I might have imagined that they could make a Jewish saint of me, but I never thought I'd become a Protestant one!"[43]

The church had been built with donations from John D. Rockefeller Jr., and Einstein arranged to have a meeting with the great capitalist and philanthropist. The purpose was to discuss the complex restrictions the Rockefeller foundations were putting on research grants. "The red tape," Einstein said, "encases the mind like the hands of a mummy."

They also discussed economics and social justice in light of the Great Depression. Einstein suggested that working hours be shortened so that, at least in his understanding of economics, more people would have a chance to be employed. He also said that lengthening the school year would help keep young people out of the workforce.

"Does not such an idea," Rockefeller asked, "impose an unwarranted restriction upon individual freedom?" Einstein replied that the current economic crisis justified measures like those taken during wartime. This gave Einstein the opportunity to propound his pacifist positions, which Rockefeller politely declined to share.[44]

His most memorable speech was a pacifist clarion call that he gave to the New History Society, in which he called for an "uncompromising war resistance and refusal to do military service under any circumstances." Then he issued what became a famous call for a brave 2 percent:

> The timid might say, "What's the use? We shall be sent to prison." To them I would reply: Even if only 2% of those assigned to perform military service should announce their refusal to fight . . . governments would be powerless, they would not dare send such a large number of people to jail.

The speech quickly became a manifesto for war resisters. Buttons that simply said "2%" began sprouting on the lapels of students and pacifists.* The *New York Times* headlined the story on page 1 and reprinted the speech in its entirety. One German paper also headlined it, but with less enthusiasm: "Einstein Begging for Military Service Objectors: Scientist's Unbelievable Publicity Methods in America."[45]

On the day he left New York, Einstein revised slightly one of the statements he had made upon his arrival. Asked again about Hitler, he declared that if the Nazis were ever able to gain control, he would consider leaving Germany.[46]

Einstein's ship headed to California through the Panama Canal. While his wife spent time at the hairdresser, Einstein dictated letters to Helen Dukas and worked on unified field theory equations with Walther Mayer. Although he complained about the "perpetual photographing" he had to endure from his fellow passengers, he did let one young man sketch him, and then he appended his own self-deprecating doggerel to turn it into a collector's item.

In Cuba, where he relished the warm weather, Einstein addressed the local Academy of Sciences. Then it was on to Panama, where a rev-

---

* The pacifists assumed that no other explanation was needed, but some contemporary accounts somehow thought the buttons referred to 2 percent beer.

olution was brewing that would depose a president who, it turned out, was also a graduate of the Zurich Polytechnic. That didn't stop officials from offering Einstein an elaborate welcome ceremony at which he was presented a hat that "an illiterate Ecuadorian Indian worked for six months weaving." On Christmas day, he broadcast holiday greetings to America via the ship's radio.[47]

When his ship docked in San Diego on the last morning of 1930, dozens of newsmen clambered aboard, with two of them falling off the ladder as they rushed their way onto the deck. Five hundred uniformed girls stood on the dock, waiting to serenade him. The gaudy arrival ceremony lasted four hours, filled with speeches and presentations.

Were there men, he was asked, living elsewhere in the universe? "Other beings, perhaps, but not men," he answered. Did science and religion conflict? Not really, he said, "though it depends, of course, on your religious views."[48]

Friends who saw all the arrival hoopla on newsreels back in Germany were astonished and somewhat appalled. "I am always very amused to see and hear you in the weekly newsreel," wrote the sharp-penned Hedwig Born, "being presented with a floral float containing lovely sea-nymphs in San Diego, and that sort of thing. However crazy things must look from the outside, I always have the feeling that the dear Lord knows what he's up to."[49]

It was on this trip, as noted in the previous chapter, that Einstein visited the Mount Wilson Observatory, was shown evidence of the expanding universe, and renounced the cosmological constant he had added to his general relativity equations. He also paid tribute to the aging Albert Michelson, carefully praising his famous experiments that detected no ether drift, without explicitly saying that they were a basis for his special theory of relativity.

Einstein soaked in a variety of the delights that southern California could offer. He attended the Rose Bowl parade, was given a special screening of *All Quiet on the Western Front*, and sunbathed nude in the Mojave desert while at a friend's house for the weekend. At a Hollywood studio, the special effects team filmed him pretending to drive a parked car, and then that evening amused him by showing how they made it seem as if he were zipping through Los Angeles, soaring up into the clouds, flying over the Rockies, and eventually landing in the German countryside. He even was offered some movie roles, which he politely declined.

He went sailing in the Pacific with Robert A. Millikan, Caltech's president, who Einstein noted in his diary "plays the role of God" at the university. Millikan was a physicist who had won the Nobel Prize in 1923 for, as the organization noted, having "verified experimentally Einstein's all-important photoelectric equation." He likewise verified Einstein's interpretation of Brownian motion. So it was understandable that, as he was building Caltech into one of the world's preeminent scientific institutions, he worked diligently to bring Einstein there.

Despite all they had in common, Millikan and Einstein were different enough in their personal outlooks that they were destined to have an awkward relationship. Millikan was so conservative scientifically that he resisted Einstein's interpretation of the photoelectric effect and his dismissal of the ether even after they were apparently verified by his own experiments. And he was even more conservative politically. A robust and athletic son of an Iowa preacher, he had a penchant for patriotic militarism that was as pronounced as Einstein's aversion to it.

Moreover, Millikan was enhancing Caltech through hefty donations from like-minded conservatives. Einstein's pacifist and socialist sentiments unnerved many of them, and they urged Millikan to restrain him from making pronouncements on earthly rather than cosmic issues. As Major General Amos Fried put it, they must avoid "aiding and abetting the teaching of treason to the youth of this country by being hosts to Dr. Albert Einstein." Millikan responded sympathetically by denouncing Einstein's call for military resistance and declaring that "the 2% comment, if he ever made it, is one which no experienced man could possibly have made."[50]

Millikan particularly disdained the crusading writer and union advocate Upton Sinclair, whom he called "the most dangerous man in California," and the actor Charlie Chaplin, who equaled Einstein in global celebrity and surpassed him in left-wing sentiments. Much to Millikan's dismay, Einstein promptly befriended both.

Einstein had corresponded with Sinclair about their shared commitment to social justice, and upon arriving in California was happy to accept his invitations to a variety of dinners, parties, and meetings. He even remained polite, though amused, while attending a farcical séance at Sinclair's home. When Mrs. Sinclair challenged his views on science and spirituality, Elsa chided her for having such presumption. "You know, my husband has the greatest mind in the world," she said. Mrs. Sinclair responded, "Yes, I know, but surely he doesn't know everything."[51]

During a tour of Universal Studios, Einstein mentioned that he had always wanted to meet Charlie Chaplin. So the studio boss called him, and he came right over to join the Einsteins for lunch in the commissary. The result, a few days later, was one of the most memorable scenes in the new era of celebrity: Einstein and Chaplin arriving together, dressed in black tie, with Elsa beaming, for the premiere of *City Lights*. As they were applauded on their way into the theater, Chaplin memorably (and accurately) noted, "They cheer me because they all understand me, and they cheer you because no one understands you."[52]

Einstein struck a more serious pose when he addressed the Caltech student body near the end of his stay. His sermon, grounded in his humanistic outlook, was on how science had not yet been harnessed to do more good than harm. During war it gave people "the means to poison and mutilate one another," and in peacetime it "has made our lives hurried and uncertain." Instead of being a liberating force, "it has enslaved men to machines" by making them work "long wearisome hours mostly without joy in their labor." Concern for making life better for ordinary humans must be the chief object of science. "Never forget this when you are pondering over your diagrams and equations!"[53]

The Einsteins took a train east across America for their return sail from New York. Along the way, they stopped at the Grand Canyon, where they were greeted by a contingent of Hopi Indians (employed by the concession stand at the canyon, though Einstein did not know that), who initiated him into their tribe as "the Great Relative" and gave him a bountiful feathered headdress that resulted in some classic photographs.[54]

When his train reached Chicago, Einstein gave a speech from its rear platform to a rally of pacifists who had come to celebrate him. Millikan must have been appalled. It was similar to the "2%" speech Einstein had given in New York. "The only way to be effective is through the revolutionary method of refusing military service," he declared. "Many who consider themselves good pacifists will not want to participate in such a radical form of pacifism; they will claim that patriotism prevents them from adopting such a policy. But in an emergency, such people cannot be counted on anyhow."[55]

Einstein's train pulled into New York City on the morning of March 1, and for the next sixteen hours Einstein mania reached new heights. "Einstein's personality, for no clear reason, triggers outbursts of a kind of mass hysteria," the German consul reported to Berlin.

Einstein first went to his ship, where four hundred members of the War Resisters' League were waiting to greet him. He invited them all on board and addressed them in a ballroom. "If in time of peace members of pacifist organizations are not ready to make sacrifices by opposing authorities at the risk of imprisonment, they will certainly fail in time of war, when only the most steeled and resolute person can be expected to resist." The crowd erupted in delirium, with overwrought pacifists rushing up to kiss his hand and touch his clothing.[56]

The socialist leader Norman Thomas was at the meeting, and he tried to convince Einstein that pacifism could not occur without radical economic reforms. Einstein disagreed. "It is easier to win over people to pacifism than to socialism," he said. "We should work first for pacifism, and only later for socialism."[57]

That afternoon, the Einsteins were taken to the Waldorf Hotel, where they had a sprawling suite in which they could meet a stream of visitors, such as Helen Keller and various journalists. Actually, it was two full suites connected by a grand private dining room. When one friend arrived that afternoon, he asked Elsa, "Where is Albert?"

"I don't know," she replied with some exasperation. "He always gets lost somewhere in all these rooms."

They finally found him wandering around, trying to find his wife. The ostentatious spread annoyed him. "I'll tell you what to do," the friend suggested. "Lock the second suite entirely off, and you will feel better." Einstein did, and it worked.[58]

That evening, he addressed a sold-out fund-raising dinner on behalf of the Zionist cause, and he finally made it back to his ship just before midnight. But even then his day was not over. A large crowd of young pacifists, chanting "No War Forever," cheered him wildly as he reached the pier. They later formed the Youth Peace Federation, and Einstein sent them a scrawled message of encouragement: "I wish you great progress in the radicalization of pacifism." [59]

Einstein's Pacifism

This radical pacifism had been building in Einstein throughout the 1920s. Even as he was retreating from the fore of physics, he was becoming, at age 50, more engaged in politics. His primary cause, at least until Adolf Hitler and his Nazis took power, was that of disarmament and resistance to war. "I am not only a pacifist," he told one interviewer on his trip to America. "I am a militant pacifist." [60]

He rejected the more modest approach taken by the League of Nations, the international organization formed after World War I, which the United States had declined to join. Instead of calling for complete disarmament, the League was nibbling at the margins by trying to define proper rules of engagement and arms control. When he was asked in January 1928 to attend one of the League's disarmament commissions, which was planning to study ways to limit gas warfare, he publicly proclaimed his disgust with such half measures:

> It seems to me an utterly futile task to prescribe rules and limitations for the conduct of war. War is not a game; hence one cannot wage war by rules as one would in playing games. Our fight must be against war itself. The masses of people can most effectively fight the institution of war by establishing an organization for the absolute refusal of military service. [61]

Thus he became one of the spiritual leaders of the growing movement led by War Resisters' International. "The international movement to refuse participation in any kind of war service is one of the most encouraging developments of our time," he wrote the London branch of that group in November 1928. [62]

Even as the Nazis began their rise to power, Einstein refused to admit, at least initially, that there might be exceptions to his pacifist postulate. What would he do, a Czech journalist asked, if another European war broke out and one side was clearly the aggressor? "I would unconditionally refuse all war service, direct or indirect, and would seek to persuade my friends to adopt the same position, regardless of how I might feel about the causes of any particular war," he answered.[63] The censors in Prague refused to allow the remark to be published, but it was made public elsewhere and enhanced Einstein's status as the standard-bearer of pacifist purists.

Such sentiments were not unusual at the time. The First World War had shocked people by being so astonishingly brutal and apparently unnecessary. Among those who shared Einstein's pacifism were Upton Sinclair, Sigmund Freud, John Dewey, and H. G. Wells. "We believe that everybody who sincerely wants peace should demand the abolition of military training for youth," they declared in a 1930 manifesto, which Einstein signed. "Military training is the education of the mind and body in the technique of killing. It thwarts the growth of man's will for peace."[64]

Einstein's advocacy of war resistance reached its peak in 1932, the year before the Nazis seized power. That year a General Disarmament Conference, organized by the League of Nations plus the United States and Russia, convened in Geneva.

Einstein initially had grand hopes that the conference, as he wrote in an article for the *Nation*, "will be decisive for the fate of the present generation and the one to come." But he warned that it must not merely content itself with feckless arms-limitation rules. "Mere agreements to limit armaments confer no protection," he said. Instead, there should be an international body empowered to arbitrate disputes and enforce the peace. "Compulsory arbitration must be supported by an executive force."[65]

His fears were realized. The conference became mired in such issues as how to calculate the offensive power of aircraft carriers in assessing an arms-control balance. Einstein showed up in Geneva in May, just as that topic was being tackled. When he appeared in the visitors' gallery, the delegates stopped their discussions and rose to applaud him. But Einstein was not pleased. That afternoon, he called a press conference at his hotel to denounce their timidity.

"One does not make war less likely to occur by formulating rules of warfare," he declared to dozens of excited journalists who abandoned the conference to cover his criticism. "We should be standing on rooftops, all of us, and denouncing this conference as a travesty!" He argued that it would be better for the conference to fail outright than to end with an agreement to "humanize war," which he considered a tragic delusion.[66]

"Einstein tended to become impractical once outside the scientific field," his novelist friend and fellow pacifist Romain Rolland commented. It is true that, given what was about to happen in Germany, disarmament was a chimera, and pacifist hopes were, to use a word sometimes flung at Einstein, naïve. Yet it should be noted that there was some merit to his criticisms. The arms-control acolytes in Geneva were no less naïve. They spent five years in futile, arcane debates as Germany rearmed itself.

Political Ideals

"Go One Step Further, Einstein!" the headline exhorted. It was on an essay, published in August 1931 as an open letter to Einstein, by the German socialist leader Kurt Hiller, one of many activists on the left who urged Einstein to expand his pacifism into a more radical politics. Pacifism was only a partial step, Hiller argued. The real goal was to advocate socialist revolution.

Einstein labeled the piece "rather stupid." Pacifism did not require socialism, and socialist revolutions sometimes led to the suppression of freedom. "I am not convinced that those who would gain power through revolutionary actions would act in accord with my ideals," he wrote to Hiller. "I also believe that the fight for peace must be pushed energetically, far ahead of any efforts to bring about social reforms."[67]

Einstein's pacifism, world federalism, and aversion to nationalism were part of a political outlook that also included a passion for social justice, a sympathy for underdogs, an antipathy toward racism, and a predilection toward socialism. But during the 1930s, as in the past, his wariness of authority, his fealty to individualism, and his fondness for personal freedom made him resist the dogmas of Bolshevism and communism. "Einstein was neither Red nor dupe," writes Fred Jerome, who has analyzed both Einstein's politics and the large dossier of material gathered on him by the FBI.[68]

This wariness of authority reflected the most fundamental of all of Einstein's moral principles: Freedom and individualism are necessary for creativity and imagination to flourish. He had demonstrated this as an impertinent young thinker, and he proclaimed the principle clearly in 1931. "I believe that the most important mission of the state is to protect the individual and to make it possible for him to develop into a creative personality," he said.[69]

Thomas Bucky, the son of a doctor who cared for Elsa's daughters, was 13 when he met Einstein in 1932, and they began what would become a longstanding discussion of politics. "Einstein was a humanist, socialist, and a democrat," he recalled. "He was completely anti-totalitarian, no matter whether it was Russian, German or South American. He approved of a combination of capitalism and socialism. And he hated all dictatorships of the right or left."[70]

Einstein's skepticism about communism was evident when he was invited to the 1932 World Antiwar Congress. Though putatively a pacifist group, it had become a front for Soviet communists. The official call for the conference, for example, denounced the "imperialist powers" for encouraging Japan's aggressive attitude toward the Soviet Union. Einstein refused to attend or support its manifesto. "Because of the glorification of Soviet Russia it includes, I cannot bring myself to sign it," he said.

He had come to some somber conclusions about Russia, he added. "At the top there appears to be a personal struggle in which the foulest means are used by power-hungry individuals acting from purely selfish motives. At the bottom there seems to be complete suppression of the individual and freedom of speech. One wonders whether life is worth living under such conditions." Perversely, when the FBI later compiled a secret dossier on Einstein during the Red Scare of the 1950s, one piece of evidence cited against him was that he had *supported*, rather than rejected, the invitation to be active in this world congress.[71]

One of Einstein's friends at the time was Isaac Don Levine, a Russian-born American journalist who had been sympathetic to the communists but had turned strongly against Stalin and his brutal regime as a columnist for the Hearst newspapers. Along with other defenders of civil liberties, including ACLU founder Roger Baldwin and Bertrand Russell, Einstein supported the publication of Levine's exposé of Stalinist horrors, *Letters from Russian Prisons*. He even provided an essay, written in longhand, in which he denounced "the regime of frightfulness in Russia." [72]

Einstein also read Levine's subsequent biography of Stalin, a fiercely critical exposé of the dictator's brutalities, and called it "profound." He saw in it a clear lesson about tyrannical regimes on both the left and the right. "Violence breeds violence," he wrote Levine in a letter of praise. "Liberty is the necessary foundation for the development of all true values." [73]

Eventually, however, Einstein began to break with Levine. Like many former communist sympathizers who swung over to the anticommunist cause, Levine had the zeal of a convert and an intensity that made it hard for him to appreciate any of the middle shades of the spectrum. Einstein, on the other hand, was too willing to accept, Levine felt, some aspects of Soviet repression as being an unfortunate byproduct of revolutionary change.

There were, indeed, many aspects of Russia that Einstein admired, including what he saw as its attempt to eliminate class distinctions and economic hierarchies. "I regard class differences as contrary to justice," he wrote in a personal statement of his credo. "I also consider that plain living is good for everybody, physically and mentally." [74]

These sentiments led Einstein to be critical of what he saw as the excessive consumption and disparities of wealth in America. As a result, he enlisted in a variety of racial and social justice movements. He took up, for example, the cause of the Scottsboro Boys, a group of young black men who were convicted of a gang rape in Alabama after a controversial trial, and of Tom Mooney, a labor activist imprisoned for murder in California. [75]

At Caltech, Millikan was upset with Einstein's activism, and wrote him to say so. Einstein responded diplomatically. "It cannot be my affair," he agreed, "to insist in a matter that concerns only the citizens of your country."[76] Millikan thought Einstein naïve in his politics, as did many people. To some extent he was, but it should be remembered that his qualms about the convictions of the Scottsboro Boys and Mooney proved justified, and his advocacy of racial and social justice turned out to be on the right side of history.

Despite his association with the Zionist cause, Einstein's sympathies extended to the Arabs who were being displaced by the influx of Jews into what would eventually be Israel. His message was a prophetic one. "Should we be unable to find a way to honest cooperation and honest pacts with the Arabs," he wrote Weizmann in 1929, "then we have learned absolutely nothing during our 2,000 years of suffering."[77]

He proposed, both to Weizmann and in an open letter to an Arab, that a "privy council" of four Jews and four Arabs, all independent-minded, be set up to resolve any disputes. "The two great Semitic peoples," he said, "have a great common future." If the Jews did not assure that both sides lived in harmony, he warned friends in the Zionist movement, the struggle would haunt them in decades to come.[78] Once again, he was labeled naïve.

The Einstein–Freud Exchange

When a group known as the Institute for Intellectual Cooperation invited him in 1932 to exchange letters with a thinker of his choice on issues relating to war and politics, Einstein picked as his correspondent Sigmund Freud, the era's other great intellectual and pacifist icon. Einstein began by proposing an idea that he had been refining over the years. The elimination of war, he said, required nations to surrender some of their sovereignty to a "supranational organization competent to render verdicts of incontestable authority and enforce absolute submission to the execution of its verdicts." In other words, some international authority more powerful than the League of Nations must be created.

Ever since he was a teenager rankling at German militarism, Einstein had been repulsed by nationalism. One of the fundamental postulates of his political view, which would remain invariant even after

Hitler's rise made him waver on the principles of pacifism, was his support for an international or "supranational" entity that would transcend the chaos of national sovereignty by imposing the resolution of disputes.

"The quest of international security," he wrote Freud, "involves the unconditional surrender by every nation, in a certain measure, of its liberty of action—its sovereignty that is to say—and it is clear that no other road can lead to such security." Years later, Einstein would become even more committed to this approach as a way to transcend the military dangers of the atomic age that he helped to spawn.

Einstein ended by posing a question to "the expert in the lore of human instincts." Because humans have within them a "lust for hatred and destruction," leaders can manipulate it to stir up militaristic passions. "Is it possible," Einstein asked, "to control man's mental evolution so as to make him secure against the psychosis of hate and destructiveness?"[79]

In a complex and convoluted response, Freud was bleak. "You surmise that man has in him an active instinct for hatred and destruction," he wrote. "I entirely agree." Psychoanalysts had come to the conclusion that two types of human instincts were woven together: "those that conserve and unify, which we call 'erotic' . . . and, secondly, the instincts to destroy and kill, which we assimilate as the aggressive or destructive instincts." Freud cautioned against labeling the first good and the second evil. "Each of these instincts is every whit as indispensable as its opposite, and all the phenomena of life derive from their activity, whether they work in concert or in opposition."

Freud thus came to a pessimistic conclusion:

> The upshot of these observations is that there is no likelihood of our being able to suppress humanity's aggressive tendencies. In some happy corners of the earth, they say, where nature brings forth abundantly whatever man desires, there flourish races whose lives go gently by; unknowing of aggression or constraint. This I can hardly credit; I would like further details about these happy folk. The Bolshevists, too, aspire to do away with human aggressiveness by insuring the satisfaction of material needs and enforcing equality between man and man. To me this hope seems vain. Meanwhile they busily perfect their armaments.[80]

Freud was not pleased with the exchange, and he joked that he doubted it would win either of them the Nobel Peace Prize. In any event, by the time it was ready for publication in 1933, Hitler had come to power. Thus the topic was suddenly moot, and only a few thousand copies were printed. Einstein, like a good scientist, was by then revising his theories based on new facts.

CHAPTER SEVENTEEN

EINSTEIN'S GOD

Santa Barbara beach, 1933

One evening in Berlin, Einstein and his wife were at a dinner party when a guest expressed a belief in astrology. Einstein ridiculed the notion as pure superstition. Another guest stepped in and similarly disparaged religion. Belief in God, he insisted, was likewise a superstition.

At this point the host tried to silence him by invoking the fact that even Einstein harbored religious beliefs.

"It isn't possible!" the skeptical guest said, turning to Einstein to ask if he was, in fact, religious.

"Yes, you can call it that," Einstein replied calmly. "Try and penetrate with our limited means the secrets of nature and you will find that, behind all the discernible laws and connections, there remains something subtle, intangible and inexplicable. Veneration for this force

384

beyond anything that we can comprehend is my religion. To that extent I am, in fact, religious."[1]

As a child, Einstein had gone through an ecstatic religious phase, then rebelled against it. For the next three decades, he tended not to pronounce much on the topic. But around the time he turned 50, he began to articulate more clearly—in various essays, interviews, and letters—his deepening appreciation of his Jewish heritage and, somewhat separately, his belief in God, albeit a rather impersonal, deistic concept of God.

There were probably many reasons for this, in addition to the natural propensity toward reflections about the eternal that can occur at age 50. The kinship he felt with fellow Jews due to their continued oppression reawakened some of his religious sentiments. But mainly, his beliefs seemed to arise from the sense of awe and transcendent order that he discovered through his scientific work.

Whether embracing the beauty of his gravitational field equations or rejecting the uncertainty in quantum mechanics, he displayed a profound faith in the orderliness of the universe. This served as a basis for his scientific outlook—and also his religious outlook. "The highest satisfaction of a scientific person," he wrote in 1929, is to come to the realization "that God Himself could not have arranged these connections any other way than that which does exist, any more than it would have been in His power to make four a prime number."[2]

For Einstein, as for most people, a belief in something larger than himself became a defining sentiment. It produced in him an admixture of confidence and humility that was leavened by a sweet simplicity. Given his proclivity toward being self-centered, these were welcome graces. Along with his humor and self-awareness, they helped him to avoid the pretense and pomposity that could have afflicted the most famous mind in the world.

His religious feelings of awe and humility also informed his sense of social justice. It impelled him to cringe at trappings of hierarchy or class distinction, to eschew excess consumption and materialism, and to dedicate himself to efforts on behalf of refugees and the oppressed.

Shortly after his fiftieth birthday, Einstein gave a remarkable interview in which he was more revealing than he had ever been about his religious thinking. It was with a pompous but ingratiating poet and propagandist named George Sylvester Viereck, who had been born in Germany, moved to America as a child, and then spent his life writing gaudily erotic poetry, interviewing great men, and expressing his complex love for his fatherland.

Having bagged interviews with people ranging from Freud to Hitler to the kaiser, which he would eventually publish as a book called *Glimpses of the Great,* he was able to secure an appointment to talk to Einstein in his Berlin apartment. There Elsa served raspberry juice and fruit salad; then the two men went up to Einstein's hermitage study. For reasons not quite clear, Einstein assumed Viereck was Jewish. In fact, Viereck proudly traced his lineage to the family of the kaiser, and he would later become a Nazi sympathizer who was jailed in America during World War II for being a German propagandist.[3]

Viereck began by asking Einstein whether he considered himself a German or a Jew. "It's possible to be both," replied Einstein. "Nationalism is an infantile disease, the measles of mankind."

Should Jews try to assimilate? "We Jews have been too eager to sacrifice our idiosyncrasies in order to conform."

To what extent are you influenced by Christianity? "As a child I received instruction both in the Bible and in the Talmud. I am a Jew, but I am enthralled by the luminous figure of the Nazarene."

You accept the historical existence of Jesus? "Unquestionably! No one can read the Gospels without feeling the actual presence of Jesus. His personality pulsates in every word. No myth is filled with such life."

Do you believe in God? "I'm not an atheist. The problem involved is too vast for our limited minds. We are in the position of a little child entering a huge library filled with books in many languages. The child knows someone must have written those books. It does not know how. It does not understand the languages in which they are written. The child dimly suspects a mysterious order in the arrangement of the books but doesn't know what it is. That, it seems to me, is the attitude of even the most intelligent human being toward God. We see the universe marvelously arranged and obeying certain laws but only dimly understand these laws."

Is this a Jewish concept of God? "I am a determinist. I do not believe in free will. Jews believe in free will. They believe that man shapes his own life. I reject that doctrine. In that respect I am not a Jew."

Is this Spinoza's God? "I am fascinated by Spinoza's pantheism, but I admire even more his contribution to modern thought because he is the first philosopher to deal with the soul and body as one, and not two separate things."

How did he get his ideas? "I'm enough of an artist to draw freely on my imagination. Imagination is more important than knowledge. Knowledge is limited. Imagination encircles the world."

Do you believe in immortality? "No. And one life is enough for me."[4]

Einstein tried to express these feelings clearly, both for himself and all of those who wanted a simple answer from him about his faith. So in the summer of 1930, amid his sailing and ruminations in Caputh, he composed a credo, "What I Believe." It concluded with an explanation of what he meant when he called himself religious:

> The most beautiful emotion we can experience is the mysterious. It is the fundamental emotion that stands at the cradle of all true art and science. He to whom this emotion is a stranger, who can no longer wonder and stand rapt in awe, is as good as dead, a snuffed-out candle. To sense that behind anything that can be experienced there is something that our minds cannot grasp, whose beauty and sublimity reaches us only indirectly: this is religiousness. In this sense, and in this sense only, I am a devoutly religious man.[5]

People found it evocative, even inspiring, and it was reprinted repeatedly in a variety of translations. But not surprisingly, it did not satisfy those who wanted a simple, direct answer to the question of whether he believed in God. As a result, getting Einstein to answer that question concisely replaced the earlier frenzy of trying to get him to give a one-sentence explanation of relativity.

A Colorado banker wrote that he had already gotten responses from twenty-four Nobel Prize winners to the question of whether they believed in God, and he asked Einstein to reply as well. "I cannot conceive of a personal God who would directly influence the actions of individuals or would sit in judgment on creatures of his own creation,"

Einstein scribbled on the letter. "My religiosity consists of a humble admiration of the infinitely superior spirit that reveals itself in the little that we can comprehend about the knowable world. That deeply emotional conviction of the presence of a superior reasoning power, which is revealed in the incomprehensible universe, forms my idea of God."[6]

A little girl in the sixth grade of a Sunday school in New York posed the question in a slightly different form. "Do scientists pray?" she asked. Einstein took her seriously. "Scientific research is based on the idea that everything that takes place is determined by laws of nature, and this holds for the actions of people," he explained. "For this reason, a scientist will hardly be inclined to believe that events could be influenced by a prayer, i.e. by a wish addressed to a supernatural Being."

That did not mean, however, there was no Almighty, no spirit larger than ourselves. As he went on to explain to the young girl:

Every one who is seriously involved in the pursuit of science becomes convinced that a spirit is manifest in the laws of the Universe—a spirit vastly superior to that of man, and one in the face of which we with our modest powers must feel humble. In this way the pursuit of science leads to a religious feeling of a special sort, which is indeed quite different from the religiosity of someone more naïve.[7]

For some, only a clear belief in a personal God who controls our daily lives qualified as a satisfactory answer, and Einstein's ideas about an impersonal cosmic spirit, as well as his theories of relativity, deserved to be labeled for what they were. "I very seriously doubt that Einstein himself really knows what he is driving at," Boston's Cardinal William Henry O'Connell said. But one thing seemed clear. It was godless. "The outcome of this doubt and befogged speculation about time and space is a cloak beneath which hides the ghastly apparition of atheism."[8]

This public blast from a cardinal prompted the noted Orthodox Jewish leader in New York, Rabbi Herbert S. Goldstein, to send a very direct telegram: "Do you believe in God? Stop. Answer paid. 50 words." Einstein used only about half his allotted number of words. It became the most famous version of an answer he gave often: "I believe in Spinoza's God, who reveals himself in the lawful harmony of all that exists, but not in a God who concerns himself with the fate and the doings of mankind."[9]

Einstein's response was not comforting to everyone. Some religious Jews, for example, noted that Spinoza had been excommunicated from the Jewish community of Amsterdam for holding these beliefs, and he had also been condemned by the Catholic Church for good measure. "Cardinal O'Connell would have done well had he not attacked the Einstein theory," said one Bronx rabbi. "Einstein would have done better had he not proclaimed his nonbelief in a God who is concerned with fates and actions of individuals. Both have handed down dicta outside their jurisdiction."[10]

Nevertheless, most people were satisfied, whether they fully agreed or not, because they could appreciate what he was saying. The idea of an impersonal God, whose hand is reflected in the glory of creation but who does not meddle in daily existence, is part of a respectable tradition in both Europe and America. It is to be found in some of Einstein's favorite philosophers, and it generally accords with the religious beliefs of many of America's founders, such as Jefferson and Franklin.

Some religious believers dismiss Einstein's frequent invocations of God as a mere figure of speech. So do some nonbelievers. There were many phrases he used, some of them playful, ranging from *der Herrgott* (the Lord God) to *der Alte* (the Old One). But it was not Einstein's style to speak disingenuously in order to appear to conform. In fact, just the opposite. So we should do him the honor of taking him at his word when he insists, repeatedly, that these oft-used phrases were not merely a semantic way of disguising that he was actually an atheist.

Throughout his life, he was consistent in deflecting the charge that he was an atheist. "There are people who say there is no God," he told a friend. "But what makes me really angry is that they quote me for support of such views."[11]

Unlike Sigmund Freud or Bertrand Russell or George Bernard Shaw, Einstein never felt the urge to denigrate those who believe in God; instead, he tended to denigrate atheists. "What separates me from most so-called atheists is a feeling of utter humility toward the unattainable secrets of the harmony of the cosmos," he explained.[12]

In fact, Einstein tended to be more critical of the debunkers, who

seemed to lack humility or a sense of awe, than of the faithful. "The fanatical atheists," he explained in a letter, "are like slaves who are still
feeling the weight of their chains which they have thrown off after
hard struggle. They are creatures who—in their grudge against traditional religion as the 'opium of the masses'—cannot hear the music of
the spheres."[13]

Einstein would later engage in an exchange on this topic with a
U.S. Navy ensign he had never met. Was it true, the sailor asked, that
Einstein had been converted by a Jesuit priest into believing in God?
That was absurd, Einstein replied. He went on to say that he considered the belief in a God who was a fatherlike figure to be the result of
"childish analogies." Would Einstein permit him, the sailor asked, to
quote his reply in his debates against his more religious shipmates?
Einstein warned him not to oversimplify. "You may call me an agnostic, but I do not share the crusading spirit of the professional atheist
whose fervor is mostly due to a painful act of liberation from the fetters
of religious indoctrination received in youth," he explained. "I prefer
the attitude of humility corresponding to the weakness of our intellectual understanding of nature and of our own being."[14]

How did this religious instinct relate to his science? For Einstein,
the beauty of his faith was that it informed and inspired, rather than
conflicted with, his scientific work. "The cosmic religious feeling," he
said, "is the strongest and noblest motive for scientific research."[15]

Einstein later explained his view of the relationship between science and religion at a conference on that topic at the Union Theological Seminary in New York. The realm of science, he said, was to
ascertain what was the case, but not evaluate human thoughts and actions about what *should* be the case. Religion had the reverse mandate.
Yet the endeavors worked together at times. "Science can be created
only by those who are thoroughly imbued with the aspiration toward
truth and understanding," he said. "This source of feeling, however,
springs from the sphere of religion."

The talk got front-page news coverage, and his pithy conclusion
became famous: "The situation may be expressed by an image: science
without religion is lame, religion without science is blind."

But there was one religious concept, Einstein went on to say, that science could not accept: a deity who could meddle at whim in the events of his creation or in the lives of his creatures. "The main source of the present-day conflicts between the spheres of religion and of science lies in this concept of a personal God," he argued. Scientists aim to uncover the immutable laws that govern reality, and in doing so they must reject the notion that divine will, or for that matter human will, plays a role that would violate this cosmic causality.[16]

This belief in causal determinism, which was inherent in Einstein's scientific outlook, conflicted not only with the concept of a personal God. It was also, at least in Einstein's mind, incompatible with human free will. Although he was a deeply moral man, his belief in strict determinism made it difficult for him to accept the idea of moral choice and individual responsibility that is at the heart of most ethical systems.

Jewish as well as Christian theologians have generally believed that people have this free will and are responsible for their actions. They are even free to choose, as happens in the Bible, to defy God's commands, despite the fact that this seems to conflict with a belief that God is all-knowing and all-powerful.

Einstein, on the other hand, believed, as did Spinoza,[17] that a person's actions were just as determined as that of a billiard ball, planet, or star. "Human beings in their thinking, feeling and acting are not free but are as causally bound as the stars in their motions," Einstein declared in a statement to a Spinoza Society in 1932.[18]

Human actions are determined, beyond their control, by both physical and psychological laws, he believed. It was a concept he drew also from his reading of Schopenhauer, to whom he attributed, in his 1930 "What I Believe" credo, a maxim along those lines:

> I do not at all believe in free will in the philosophical sense. Everybody acts not only under external compulsion but also in accordance with inner necessity. Schopenhauer's saying, "A man can do as he wills, but not will as he wills,"[19] has been a real inspiration to me since my youth; it has been a continual consolation in the face of life's hardships, my own and others', and an unfailing wellspring of tolerance.[20]

Do you believe, Einstein was once asked, that humans are free agents? "No, I am a determinist," he replied. "Everything is determined, the beginning as well as the end, by forces over which we have no control. It is determined for the insect as well as for the star. Human beings, vegetables, or cosmic dust, we all dance to a mysterious tune, intoned in the distance by an invisible player."[21]

This attitude appalled some friends, such as Max Born, who thought it completely undermined the foundations of human morality. "I cannot understand how you can combine an entirely mechanistic universe with the freedom of the ethical individual," he wrote Einstein. "To me a deterministic world is quite abhorrent. Maybe you are right, and the world is that way, as you say. But at the moment it does not really look like it in physics—and even less so in the rest of the world."

For Born, quantum uncertainty provided an escape from this dilemma. Like some philosophers of the time, he latched on to the indeterminacy that was inherent in quantum mechanics to resolve "the discrepancy between ethical freedom and strict natural laws."[22] Einstein conceded that quantum mechanics called into question strict determinism, but he told Born he still believed in it, both in the realm of personal actions and physics.

Born explained the issue to his high-strung wife, Hedwig, who was always eager to debate Einstein. She told Einstein that, like him, she was "unable to believe in a 'dice-playing' God." In other words, unlike her husband, she rejected quantum mechanics' view that the universe was based on uncertainties and probabilities. But, she added, "nor am I able to imagine that you believe—as Max has told me—that your 'complete rule of law' means that everything is predetermined, for example whether I am going to have my child inoculated."[23] It would mean, she pointed out, the end of all ethics.

In Einstein's philosophy, the way to resolve this issue was to look upon free will as something that was useful, indeed necessary, for a civilized society, because it caused people to take responsibility for their own actions. Acting *as if* people were responsible for their actions would, psychologically and practically, prompt them to act in a more responsible manner. "I am compelled to act as if free will existed," he explained, "because if I wish to live in a civilized society I must act responsibly." He could even hold people responsible for their good or evil, since that was both a pragmatic and sensible approach to life, while still believing intellectually that everyone's actions were prede-termined. "I know that philosophically a murderer is not responsible for his crime," he said, "but I prefer not to take tea with him."[24]

In defense of Einstein, as well as of both Max and Hedwig Born, it should be noted that philosophers through the ages have struggled, sometimes awkwardly and not very successfully, to reconcile free will with determinism and an all-knowing God. Whether Einstein was more or less adept than others at grappling with this knot, there is one salient fact about him that should be noted: he was able to develop, and to practice, a strong personal morality, at least toward humanity in gen-eral if not always toward members of his family, that was not hampered by all these irresolvable philosophical speculations. "The most impor-tant human endeavor is the striving for morality in our actions," he wrote a Brooklyn minister. "Our inner balance and even our existence depend on it. Only morality in our actions can give beauty and dignity to life."[25]

The foundation of that morality, he believed, was rising above the "merely personal" to live in a way that benefited humanity. There were times when he could be callous to those closest to him, which shows that, like the rest of us humans, he had flaws. Yet more than most peo-ple, he dedicated himself honestly and sometimes courageously to ac-tions that he felt transcended selfish desires in order to encourage human progress and the preservation of individual freedoms. He was generally kind, good-natured, gentle, and unpretentious. When he and Elsa left for Japan in 1922, he offered her daughters some advice on how to lead a moral life. "Use for yourself little," he said, "but give to others much."[26]

CHAPTER EIGHTEEN

THE REFUGEE

1932–1933

With Winston Churchill at his home, Chartwell, 1933

"Bird of Passage"

"Today I resolved to give up my Berlin position and shall be a bird of passage for the rest of my life," Einstein wrote in his travel diary. "I am learning English, but it doesn't want to stay in my old brain."[1]

It was December 1931, and he was sailing across the Atlantic for a third visit to America. He was in a reflective mood, aware that the course of science might be proceeding without him and that events in his native land might again make him rootless. When a ferocious storm, far greater than any he had ever witnessed, seized his ship, he recorded his thoughts in his travel diary. "One feels the insignificance of the individual," he wrote, "and it makes one happy."[2]

Yet Einstein was still torn about whether to forsake Berlin for good. It had been his home for seventeen years, Elsa's for even longer. Despite the challenge from Copenhagen, it was still the greatest center for theoretical physics in the world. For all of its dark political undercurrents, it remained a place where he was generally loved and revered, whether he was holding court in Caputh or taking his seat at the Prussian Academy.

In the meantime, his options continued to grow. This trip to America was for another two-month visiting professorship at Caltech, which Millikan was trying to turn into a permanent arrangement. Einstein's friends in Holland had for years also been trying to recruit him, and now so too was Oxford.

Soon after he settled into his rooms at the Athenaeum, the graceful faculty club at Caltech, yet another possibility arose. One morning, he was visited there by the noted American educator Abraham Flexner, who spent more than an hour walking the cloistered courtyard with him. When Elsa found them and summoned her husband to a luncheon engagement, he waved her off.

Flexner, who had helped reshape American higher education as an officer of the Rockefeller Foundation, was in the process of creating a "haven" where scholars could work without any academic pressures or teaching duties and, as he put it, "without being carried off in the maelstrom of the immediate."[3] Funded by a $5 million donation from Louis Bamberger and his sister Caroline Bamberger Fuld, who had the good fortune to sell their department store chain just weeks before the 1929 stock market crash, it would be named the Institute for Advanced Study and located in New Jersey, probably next to (but not formally affiliated with) Princeton University, where Einstein had already spent some enjoyable time.

Flexner had come to Caltech to get some ideas from Millikan, who (to his later regret) insisted he talk to Einstein. When Flexner finally set up such a meeting, he was impressed, he later wrote, with Einstein's "noble bearing, simply charming manner, and his genuine humility."

It was obvious that Einstein would be a perfect anchor and ornament for Flexner's new institute, but it would have been inappropriate for Flexner to make an offer on Millikan's home turf. Instead, they agreed that Flexner would visit Einstein in Europe to discuss matters further. Flexner claimed in his autobiography that, even after their

Caltech meeting, "I had no idea that he [Einstein] would be interested in being connected to the Institute." But that was belied by the letters he wrote to his patrons at the time, in which he referred to Einstein as an "unhatched chicken" whose prospects they needed to treat circumspectly.[4]

By then Einstein had grown slightly disenchanted with life in southern California. When he gave a speech to an international relations group, in which he denounced arms-control compromises and advocated complete disarmament, his audience seemed to treat him as celebrity entertainment. "The propertied classes here seize upon anything that might provide ammunition in the struggle against boredom," he noted in his diary. Elsa reflected his annoyance in a letter to a friend. "The affair was not only lacking in seriousness but was treated as a kind of social entertainment."[5]

As a result, he was dismissive when his friend Ehrenfest in Leiden wrote to ask for his help in getting a job in America. "I must tell you honestly that in the long term I would prefer to be in Holland rather than in America," Einstein replied. "Apart from the handful of really fine scholars, it is a boring and barren society that would soon make you shiver."[6]

Nevertheless, on this and other topics Einstein's mind was not a simple one. He clearly enjoyed America's freedom, excitement, and even (yes) the celebrity status it conferred upon him. Like many others, he could be critical of America yet also attracted to it. He could recoil at its occasional displays of crassness and materialism, yet find himself powerfully drawn to the freedoms and unvarnished individuality that were on the flip side of the same coin.

Soon after returning to Berlin, where the political situation had become even more unnerving, Einstein went to Oxford to give another series of lectures. Once again, he found its refined formality oppressive, especially in contrast to America. At the stultifying sessions of the governing body of Christ Church, his college at Oxford, he sat in the senior common room holding a notepad under the tablecloth so that he could scribble equations. He came to realize, once again, that America, for all of its lapses of taste and excesses of enthusiasm, offered freedoms he might never find again in Europe.[7]

Thus he was pleased when Flexner came, as promised, to continue the conversation they had started at the Athenaeum. Both men knew, from the outset, that it was not merely an abstract discussion but part of an effort to recruit Einstein. So Flexner was a bit disingenuous when he later wrote that it was only while they were pacing around the manicured lawns of Christ Church's Tom Quad that it "dawned on me" that Einstein might be interested in coming to the new institute. "If on reflection you conclude that it would give you the opportunities that you value," Flexner said, "you would be welcome on your own terms."[8]

The arrangement that would bring Einstein to Princeton was concluded the following month, June 1932, when Flexner visited Caputh. It was cool that day, and Flexner wore an overcoat, but Einstein was in summer clothes. He preferred, he joked, to dress "according to the season not according to the weather." They sat on the veranda of Einstein's beloved new cottage and spoke all afternoon and then through dinner, up until Einstein walked Flexner to the Berlin bus at 11 p.m.

Flexner asked Einstein how much he would expect to make. About $3,000, Einstein tentatively suggested. Flexner looked surprised. "Oh," Einstein hastened to add, "could I live on less?"

Flexner was amused. He had more, not less, in mind. "Let Mrs. Einstein and me arrange it," he said. They ended up settling on $10,000 per year. That was soon increased when Louis Bamberger, the primary backer, discovered that mathematician Oswald Veblen, the Institute's other jewel, was making $15,000 a year. Bamberger insisted that Einstein's salary be equal.

There was one additional deal point. Einstein insisted that his assistant, Walther Mayer, be given a job of his own as well. The previous year he had let authorities in Berlin know that he was entertaining offers in America that would provide for Mayer, something Berlin had been unwilling to do. Caltech had balked at this request, as did Flexner initially. But then Flexner relented.[9]

Einstein did not consider his post at the Institute a full-time job, but it was likely to be his primary one. Elsa delicately broached this in her letter to Millikan. "Will you, under the circumstances, still want my husband in Pasadena next winter?" she asked. "I doubt it."[10]

Actually, Millikan did want him, and they agreed that Einstein would come back again in January, before the Institute would be open in Princeton. Millikan was upset, however, that he had not finalized a long-term deal, and he realized that Einstein would end up being, at best, an occasional visitor to Caltech. As it turned out, the upcoming January 1933 trip that Elsa helped arrange would end up being his last trip to California.

Millikan vented his anger at Flexner. Einstein's connection with Caltech "has been laboriously built up during the past ten years," he wrote. As a result of Flexner's pernicious raid, Einstein would be spending his time at some new haven rather than a great center of experimental as well as theoretical physics. "Whether the progress of science in the U.S. will be advanced by such a move, or whether Professor Einstein's productivity will be increased by such a transfer, is at least debatable." He proposed, as a compromise, that Einstein split his time in America between the Institute and Caltech.

Flexner was not magnanimous in victory. He protested, falsely, that it was "altogether by accident" that he ended up in Oxford and speaking to Einstein, a tale that even his own memoirs later contradicted. As for sharing Einstein, Flexner declined. He claimed that he was looking after Einstein's interests. "I cannot believe that annual residence for brief periods at several places is sound or wholesome," he wrote. "Looking at the entire matter from Professor Einstein's point of view, I believe that you and all of his friends will rejoice that it has been possible to create for him a permanent post."[11]

For his part, Einstein was unsure how he would divide his time. He thought that he might be able to juggle visiting professorships in Princeton, Pasadena, and Oxford. In fact, he even hoped that he could keep his position in the Prussian Academy and his beloved cottage in Caputh, if things did not worsen in Germany. "I am not abandoning Germany," he announced when the Princeton post became public in August. "My permanent home will still be in Berlin."

Flexner spun the relationship the other way, telling the *New York Times* that Princeton would be Einstein's primary home. "Einstein will devote his time to the Institute," Flexner said, "and his trips abroad will be vacation periods for rest and meditation at his summer home outside of Berlin."[12]

As it turned out, the issue would be settled by events out of either man's control. Throughout the summer of 1932, the political situation in Germany darkened. As the Nazis continued to lose national elections but increase their share of the vote, the octogenarian president, Paul von Hindenburg, selected as chancellor the bumbling Franz von Papen, who tried to rule through martial authority. When Philipp Frank came to visit him in Caputh that summer, Einstein lamented, "I am convinced that a military regime will not prevent the imminent National Socialist [Nazi] revolution."[13]

As Einstein was preparing to leave for his third visit to Caltech in December 1932, he had to suffer one more indignity. The headlines about his future post in Princeton had aroused the indignation of the Woman Patriot Corporation, a once powerful but fading group of American self-styled guardians against socialists, pacifists, communists, feminists, and undesirable aliens. Although Einstein fit into only the first two of these categories, the women patriots felt sure that he fit into them all, with the possible exception of feminists.

The leader of the group, Mrs. Randolph Frothingham (who, given this context, seemed as if her distinguished family name had been conjured up by Dickens), submitted a sixteen-page typed memo to the U.S. State Department detailing reasons to "refuse and withhold such passport visa to Professor Einstein." He was a militant pacifist and communist who advocated doctrines that "would allow anarchy to stalk in unmolested," the memo charged. "*Not even Stalin himself* is affiliated with so many anarcho-communist international groups to promote this 'preliminary condition' of world revolution and ultimate anarchy as ALBERT EINSTEIN." (Emphasis and capitalization are in the original.)[14]

State Department officials could have ignored the memo. Instead, they put it into a file that would grow over the next twenty-three years into an FBI dossier of 1,427 pages of documents. In addition, they sent the memo to the U.S. consulate in Berlin so that officers there could interview Einstein and see if the charges were true before granting him another visa.

Initially, Einstein was quite amused when he read newspaper accounts of the women's allegations. He called up the Berlin bureau chief of United Press, Louis Lochner, who had become a friend, and gave him a statement that not only ridiculed the charges but also proved conclusively that he could not be accused of feminism:

> Never yet have I experienced from the fair sex such energetic rejection of all advances, or if I have, never from so many at once. But are they not right, these watchful citizenesses? Why should one open one's doors to a person who devours hard-boiled capitalists with as much appetite and gusto as the ogre Minotaur in Crete once devoured luscious Greek maidens—a person who is also so vulgar as to oppose every sort of war, except the inevitable one with his own wife? Therefore, give heed to your clever and patriotic women folk and remember that the capital of mighty Rome was once saved by the cackling of its faithful geese.[15]

The *New York Times* ran the story on its front page with the headline, "Einstein Ridicules Women's Fight on Him Here / Remarks Cackling Geese Once Saved Rome."[16] But Einstein was far less amused two days later when, as he and Elsa were packing to leave, he received a telephone call from the U.S. consular office in Berlin asking him to come by for an interview that afternoon.

The consul general was on vacation, so his hapless deputy conducted the interview, which Elsa promptly recounted to reporters.[17] According to the *New York Times*, which ran three stories the next day on the incident, the session started well enough but then degenerated.

"What is your political creed?" he was asked. Einstein gave a blank stare and then burst out laughing. "Well, I don't know," he replied. "I can't answer that question."

"Are you a member of any organization?" Einstein ran his hand through "his ample hair" and turned to Elsa. "Oh yes!" he exclaimed. "I am a War Resister."

The interview dragged on for forty-five minutes, and Einstein became increasingly impatient. When he was asked whether he was a sympathizer of any communist or anarchist parties, Einstein lost his temper. "Your countrymen invited me," he said. "Yes, begged me. If I am to enter your country as a suspect, I don't want to go at all. If you don't want to give me a visa, please say so."

Then he reached for his coat and hat. "Are you doing this to please yourselves," he asked, "or are you acting on orders from above?" Without waiting for an answer, he left with Elsa in tow.

Elsa let the papers know that Einstein had quit packing and had left Berlin for his cottage in Caputh. If he did not have a visa by noon the next day, he would cancel his trip to America. By late that night, the consulate issued a statement saying that it had reviewed the case and would issue a visa immediately.

As the *Times* correctly reported, "He is not a Communist and has declined invitations to lecture in Russia because he did not want to give the impression that he was in sympathy with the Moscow regime." What none of the papers reported, however, was that Einstein did agree to sign a declaration, requested by the consulate, that he was not a member of the Communist Party or any organization intent on overthrowing the U.S. government.[18]

"Einstein Resumes Packing for America," read the *Times* headline the next day. "From the deluge of cables reaching us last night," Elsa told reporters, "we know Americans of all classes were deeply disturbed over the case." Secretary of State Henry Stimson said that he regretted the incident, but he also noted that Einstein "was treated with every courtesy and consideration." As they left Berlin by train for Bremerhaven to catch their ship, Einstein joked about the incident and said that all had turned out well in the end.[19]

Pasadena, 1933

When the Einsteins left Germany in December 1932, he still thought that he might be able to return, but he wasn't sure. He wrote to his longtime friend Maurice Solovine, now publishing his works in Paris, to send copies "to me next April at my Caputh address." Yet when they left Caputh, Einstein said to Elsa, as if with a premonition, "Take a very good look at it. You will never see it again." With them on the steamer *Oakland* as it headed for California were thirty pieces of luggage, probably more than necessary for a three-month trip.[20]

Thus it was awkward, and painfully ironic, that the one public duty Einstein was scheduled to perform in Pasadena was to give a speech to celebrate German-American friendship. To finance Einstein's stay at Caltech, President Millikan had obtained a $7,000 grant from the Oberlaender Trust, a foundation that sought to promote cultural exchanges with Germany. The sole requirement was that Einstein would make "one broadcast which will be helpful to German-American relations." Upon Einstein's arrival, Millikan announced that Einstein was "coming to the United States on a mission of molding public opinion to better German-American relations,"[21] a view that may have surprised Einstein, with his thirty pieces of luggage.

Millikan usually preferred that his prize visitor avoid speaking on nonscientific matters. In fact, soon after Einstein arrived, Millikan forced him to cancel a speech he was scheduled to give to the UCLA chapter of the War Resisters' League, in which he had planned to denounce compulsory military service again. "There is no power on earth from which we should be prepared to accept an order to kill," he wrote in the draft of the speech he never gave.[22]

But as long as Einstein was expressing pro-German rather than pacifist sentiments, Millikan was happy for him to talk about politics—especially as there was funding involved. Not only had Millikan been able to secure the $7,000 Oberlaender grant by scheduling the speech, which was to be broadcast on NBC radio, he also had invited big donors to a black-tie dinner preceding it at the Athenaeum.

Einstein was such a draw that there was a wait list to buy tickets. Among those seated at Einstein's table was Leon Watters, a wealthy pharmaceutical manufacturer from New York. Noticing that Einstein looked bored, he reached across the woman seated between them to offer him a cigarette, which Einstein consumed in three drags. The two men subsequently became close friends, and Einstein would later stay at Watters's Fifth Avenue apartment when he visited New York from Princeton.

When the dinner was over, Einstein and the other guests went to the Pasadena Civic Auditorium, where several thousand people waited to hear his address. His text had been translated for him by a friend, and he delivered it in halting English.

After making fun of the difficulties of sounding serious while wearing a tuxedo, he proceeded to attack people who used words "laden with emotion" to intimidate free expression. "Heretic," as used during the Inquisition, was such a case, he said. Then he cited examples that had similar hateful connotations for people in a variety of countries: "the word Communist in America today, or the word bourgeoisie in Russia, or the word Jew for the reactionary group in Germany." Not all of these examples seemed calculated to please Millikan or his anticommunist and pro-German funders.

Nor was his critique of the current world crisis one that would appeal to ardent capitalists. The economic depression, especially in America, seemed to be caused, he said, mainly by technological advances that "decreased the need for human labor" and thereby caused a decline in consumer purchasing power.

As for Germany, he made a couple of attempts to express sympathy and earn Millikan's grant. America would be wise, he said, not to press too hard for continued payment of debts and reparations from the world war. In addition, he could see some justification in Germany's demand for military equality.

That did not mean, however, that Germany should be allowed to reintroduce mandatory military service, he hastened to add. "Universal military service means the training of youth in a warlike spirit," he concluded.[23] Millikan may have gotten his speech about Germany, but the price he paid was swallowing a few thoughts from the war resistance speech he had forced Einstein to cancel.

A week later, all of these items—German-American friendship, debt payments, war resistance, even Einstein's pacifism—were dealt a blow that would render them senseless for more than a decade. On January 30, 1933, while Einstein was safely in Pasadena, Adolf Hitler took power as the new chancellor of Germany.

Einstein initially seemed unsure what this meant for him. During the first week of February, he was writing letters to Berlin about how to calculate his salary for his planned return in April. His sporadic entries in his trip journal that week recorded only serious scientific discussions, such as on cosmic ray experiments, and frivolous social encounters, such as: "Evening Chaplin. Played Mozart quartets there. Fat lady whose occupation consists of making friends with all celebrities."[24]

By the end of February, however, with the Reichstag in flames and brownshirts ransacking the homes of Jews, things had become clearer. "Because of Hitler, I don't dare step on German soil," Einstein wrote one of his women friends.[25]

On March 10, the day before he left Pasadena, Einstein was strolling in the gardens of the Athenaeum. Evelyn Seeley of the *New York World Telegram* found him there in an expansive mood. They talked for forty-five minutes, and one of his declarations made headlines around the world. "As long as I have any choice in the matter, I shall live only in a country where civil liberty, tolerance and equality of all citizens before the law prevail," he said. "These conditions do not exist in Germany at the present time."[26]

Just as Seeley was leaving, Los Angeles was struck by a devastating earthquake—116 people were killed in the area—but Einstein barely seemed to notice. With the acquiescence of an indulgent editor, Seeley was able to end her article with a dramatic metaphor: "As he left for the seminar, walking across campus, Dr. Einstein felt the ground shaking under his feet."

In retrospect, Seeley would be saved from sounding too portentous by a drama that was occurring that very day back in Berlin, although neither she nor Einstein knew it. His apartment there, with Elsa's daughter Margot cowering inside, was raided twice that afternoon by the Nazis. Her husband, Dimitri Marianoff, was out doing errands and was almost trapped by one of the roving mobs of thugs. He sent word for Margot to get Einstein's papers to the French embassy and then meet him in Paris. She was able to do both. Ilse and her husband, Rudolph Kayser, successfully escaped to Holland. During the next two days, the Berlin apartment was ransacked three more times. Einstein would never see it again. But his papers were safe.[27]

On his train ride east from Caltech, Einstein reached Chicago on his fifty-fourth birthday. There he attended a Youth Peace Council rally, where speakers pledged that the pacifist cause should continue despite the events in Germany. Some left with the impression that he was in full agreement. "Einstein will never abandon the peace movement," one noted.

They were wrong. Einstein had begun to mute his pacifist rhetoric. At a birthday luncheon that day in Chicago, he spoke vaguely about the need for international organizations to keep the peace, but he refrained from repeating his calls for war resistance. He was similarly cautious a few days later at a New York reception for an anthology featuring his pacifist writings, *The Fight against War*. He mainly talked about the distressing turn of events in Germany. The world should make its moral disapproval of the Nazis known, he said, but he added that the German population itself should not be demonized.

It was unclear, even as he was about to sail, where he would now live. Paul Schwartz, the German consul in New York who had been Einstein's friend in Berlin, met with him privately to make sure that he did not plan to go back to Germany. "They'll drag you through the streets by the hair," he warned.[28]

His initial destination, where the ship would let him off, was Belgium, and he suggested to friends that he might go to Switzerland after that. When the Institute for Advanced Study opened the following year, he planned to spend four or five months there each year. Perhaps it would turn out to be even more. On the day before he sailed, he and Elsa slipped away to Princeton to look at houses they might buy.

The only place in Germany that he wanted to see again, he told family members, was Caputh. But on the journey across the Atlantic, he received word that the Nazis had raided his cottage under the pretense of looking for a cache of communist weaponry (there was none). Later they came back and confiscated his beloved boat on the pretense it might be used for smuggling. "My summer house was often honored by the presence of many guests," he said in a message from the ship. "They were always welcome. No one had any reason to break in."[29]

The Bonfires

The news of the raid on his Caputh cottage determined Einstein's relationship to his German homeland. He would never go back there.

As soon as his ship docked in Antwerp on March 28, 1933, he had a car drive him to the German consulate in Brussels, where he turned in his passport and (as he had done once before when a teenager) declared that he was renouncing his German citizenship. He also mailed a letter, written during the crossing, in which he submitted his resigna-

tion to the Prussian Academy. "Dependence on the Prussian government," he stated, "is something that, under the present circumstances,
I feel to be intolerable."[30]

Max Planck, who had recruited him to the Academy nineteen years
earlier, was relieved. "This idea of yours seems to be the only way that
would ensure for you an honorable severance of your relations with the
Academy," Planck wrote back with an almost audible sigh. He added
his gracious plea that "despite the deep gulf that divides our political
opinions, our personal amicable relations will never undergo any
change."[31]

What Planck was hoping to avoid, amid the flurry of anti-Semitic
diatribes against Einstein in the Nazi press, were formal disciplinary
hearings against Einstein, which some government ministers were demanding. That would cause Planck personal agony and the Academy
historic embarrassment. "Starting formal exclusion procedures against
Einstein would bring me into gravest conflicts of conscience," he wrote
an Academy secretary. "Even though on political matters a deep gulf
divides me from him, I am, on the other hand, absolutely certain that in
the history of centuries to come, Einstein's name will be celebrated as
one of the brightest stars that ever shone in the Academy."[32]

Alas, the Academy was not content to leave bad enough alone.
The Nazis were furious that he had preempted them by renouncing,
very publicly, with headlines in the papers, his citizenship and Academy membership before they could strip him of both. So a Nazi-
sympathizing secretary of the Academy issued a statement on its
behalf. Referring to the press reports of some of his comments in
America, which in fact had been very cautious, it denounced Einstein's
"participation in atrocity-mongering" and his "activities as an agitator
in foreign countries," concluding, "It has, therefore, no reason to regret
Einstein's withdrawal."[33]

Max von Laue, a longtime colleague and friend, protested. At a
meeting of the Academy later that week, he tried to get members to
disavow the secretary's action. But no other member would go along,
not even Haber, the converted Jew who had been one of Einstein's
closest friends and supporters.

Einstein was not willing to let such a slander pass. "I hereby declare that I have never taken any part in atrocity-mongering," he responded. He had merely spoken the truth about the situation in Germany, without resorting to purveying tales of atrocities. "I described the present state of affairs in Germany as a state of psychic distemper in the masses," he wrote.[34]

By then there was no doubt this was true. Earlier in the week, the Nazis had called for a boycott of all Jewish-owned businesses and stationed storm troopers outside of their stores. Jewish teachers and students were barred from the university in Berlin and their academic identification cards were confiscated. And the Nobel laureate Philipp Lenard, Einstein's longtime antagonist, declared in a Nazi newspaper, "The most important example of the dangerous influence of Jewish circles on the study of nature has been provided by Herr Einstein."[35]

The exchanges between Einstein and the Academy descended into petulance. An official wrote Einstein that, even if he had not actively spread slanders, he had failed to join "the side of the defenders of our nation against the flood of lies that has been let loose upon it . . . A good word from you in particular might have produced a great effect abroad." Einstein thought that absurd. "By giving such testimony in the present circumstances I would have been contributing, if only indirectly, to moral corruption and the destruction of all existing cultural values," he replied.[36]

The entire dispute was becoming moot. Early in April 1933, the German government passed a law declaring that Jews (defined as anyone with a Jewish grandparent) could not hold an official position, including at the Academy or at the universities. Among those forced to flee were fourteen Nobel laureates and twenty-six of the sixty professors of theoretical physics in the country. Fittingly, such refugees from fascism who left Germany or the other countries it came to dominate—Einstein, Edward Teller, Victor Weisskopf, Hans Bethe, Lise Meitner, Niels Bohr, Enrico Fermi, Otto Stern, Eugene Wigner, Leó Szilárd, and others—helped to assure that the Allies rather than the Nazis first developed the atom bomb.

Planck tried to temper the anti-Jewish policies, even to the extent of appealing to Hitler personally. "Our national policies will not be revoked or modified, even for scientists," Hitler thundered back. "If the dismissal of Jewish scientists means the annihilation of contemporary German science, then we shall do without science for a few years!" After that, Planck quietly went along and cautioned other scientists that it was not their role to challenge the political leadership.

Einstein could not bring himself to be angry at Planck, who was like an uncle as well as a patron. Even amid his angry exchanges with the Academy, he agreed to Planck's request that they keep their personal respect intact. "In spite of everything, I am happy that you greet me in old friendship and that even the greatest stresses have failed to cloud our mutual relations," he wrote, using the formal and respectful style he always used when writing to Planck. "These continue in their ancient beauty and purity, regardless of what, in a manner of speaking, is happening further below." [37]

Among those fleeing the Nazi purge was Max Born, who with his tart-tongued wife, Hedwig, ended up in England. "I have never had a particularly favorable opinion of the Germans," Einstein wrote when he received the news. "But I must confess that the degree of their brutality and cowardice came as something of a surprise."

Born took it all rather well, and he developed, like Einstein, a deeper appreciation for his heritage. "As regards my wife and children, they have only become conscious of being Jews or 'non-Aryans' (to use the delightful technical term) during the last few months, and I myself have never felt particularly Jewish," he wrote in his letter back to Einstein. "Now, of course, I am extremely conscious of it, not only because we are considered to be so, but because oppression and injustice provoke me to anger and resistance." [38]

Even more poignant was the case of Fritz Haber, friend to both Einstein and Marić, who thought that he had become German by converting to Christianity, affecting a Prussian air, and pioneering gas warfare for his Fatherland in the First World War. But with the new laws, even he was forced from his position at Berlin University and in the Academy, at age 64, just before he would have been eligible for a pension.

As if to atone for forsaking his heritage, Haber threw himself into organizing Jews who suddenly needed to find jobs outside of Germany. Einstein could not resist gigging him, in the bantering manner they had often used in their letters, about the failure of his theory of assimilation. "I can understand your inner conflicts," he wrote. "It is somewhat like having to give up a theory on which one has worked one's whole life. It is not the same for me because I never believed it in the least."[39]

In the process of helping his newfound tribal companions to emigrate, Haber became friends with the Zionist leader Chaim Weizmann. He even tried to mend a rift that had come between Weizmann and Einstein over Jewish treatment of the Arabs and the management of Hebrew University. "In my whole life I have never felt so Jewish as now!" he exulted, though that was not actually saying much.

Einstein replied by saying how pleased he was that "your former love for the blond beast has cooled off a bit." The Germans were all a bad breed, Einstein insisted, "except a few fine personalities (Planck 60% noble, and Laue 100%)." Now, in this time of adversity, they could at least take comfort that they were thrown together with their true kinsmen. "For me the most beautiful thing is to be in contact with a few fine Jews—a few millennia of a civilized past do mean something after all."[40]

Einstein would never again see Haber, who decided that he would try to make a new life at Hebrew University in Jerusalem, which Einstein had helped to launch. But in Basel, on his way there, Haber's heart gave out and he died.

Close to forty thousand Germans gathered in front of Berlin's opera house on May 10, 1933, as a parade of swastika-wearing students and beer-hall thugs carrying torches tossed books into a huge bonfire. Ordinary citizens poured forth carrying volumes looted from libraries and private homes. "Jewish intellectualism is dead," propaganda minister Joseph Goebbels, his face fiery, yelled from the podium. "The German soul can again express itself."

What happened in Germany in 1933 was not just a brutality perpetrated by thuggish leaders and abetted by ignorant mobs. It was also, as Einstein described, "the utter failure of the so-called intellectual aristocracy." Einstein and other Jews were ousted from what had been among the world's greatest citadels of open-minded inquiry, and those who remained did little to resist. It represented the triumph of the ilk of Philipp Lenard, Einstein's longtime anti-Semitic baiter, who was named by Hitler to be the new chief of Aryan science. "We must recognize that it is unworthy of a German to be the intellectual follower of a Jew," Lenard exulted that May. "Heil Hitler!" It would be a dozen years before Allied troops would fight their way in and oust him from that role.[41]

Le Coq sur Mer, 1933

Having found himself deposited in Belgium, more by the happenstance of ocean liner routes than by conscious choice, Einstein and his entourage—Elsa, Helen Dukas, Walther Mayer—set up household there for the time being. He was not, he realized after a little consideration, quite up for the emotional energy it would take to relocate his new family in Zurich alongside his old one. Nor was he ready to commit to Leiden or Oxford while he awaited his scheduled visit, or perhaps move, to Princeton. So he rented a house on the dunes of Le Coq sur Mer, a resort near Ostend, where he could contemplate, and Mayer could calculate, the universe and its waves in peace.

Peace, however, was elusive. Even by the sea he could not completely escape the threats of the Nazis. The newspapers reported that his name was on a list of assassination targets, and one rumor had it that there was a $5,000 bounty on his head. Upon hearing this, Einstein touched that head and cheerfully proclaimed, "I didn't know it was worth that much!" The Belgians took the danger more seriously and, much to his annoyance, assigned two beefy police officers to stand guard at the house.[42]

Philipp Frank, who still had Einstein's old job and office in Prague, happened to be passing through Ostend that summer and decided to pay a surprise visit. He asked local residents how to find Einstein and, despite all the security injunctions about giving out such information, was promptly directed to the cottage amid the dunes. As he approached, he saw two robust men, who certainly did not look like Einstein's usual visitors, in intense conversation with Elsa. Suddenly, as Frank later recalled, "the two men saw me, threw themselves at me and seized me."

Elsa, her face chalky white with fright, intervened. "They suspected you of being the rumored assassin."

Einstein found the entire situation quite hilarious, including the naïveté of the people in the neighborhood who kindly showed Frank the way to his house. Einstein described his exchange of letters with the Prussian Academy, which he had put into a folder with some lines of humorous verse he had composed for an imaginary response: "Thank you for your note so tender / It's typically German, like the sender."

When Einstein said that leaving Berlin had proved liberating, Elsa defended the city that she had loved for so long. "You often said to me after coming home from the physics colloquium that such a gathering of outstanding physicists is not to be found anywhere else."

"Yes," Einstein replied, "from a purely scientific point of view life in Berlin was often very nice. Nevertheless, I always had a feeling that something was pressing on me, and I always had a premonition that the end would not be good."[43]

With Einstein a free agent, offers flowed in from all over Europe. "I now have more professorships than rational ideas in my head," he told Solovine.[44] Although he had committed to spend at least a few months each year in Princeton, he began accepting these invitations somewhat promiscuously. He was never very good at declining requests.

Partly it was because the offers were enticing and he was flattered. Partly it was because he was still trying to leverage a better deal for his assistant, Walther Mayer. In addition, the offers became a way for him and the various universities to show their defiance of what the Nazis were doing to German academies. "You may feel that it would have been my duty not to accept the Spanish and French offers," he confessed to Paul Langevin in Paris, "however, such a refusal might have been misinterpreted since both invitations were, at least to some extent, political demonstrations that I considered important and did not want to spoil."[45]

His acceptance of a post at the University of Madrid made headlines in April. "Spanish Minister Announces Physicist Has Accepted Professorship," said the *New York Times*. "News Received with Joy." The paper pointed out that this should not affect his annual stints in

Princeton, but Einstein warned Flexner that it could if Mayer was not given a full rather than an associate professorship at the new Institute. "You will by now have learned through the press that I have accepted a chair at Madrid University," he wrote. "The Spanish government has given me the right to recommend to them a mathematician to be appointed as a full professor . . . I therefore find myself in a difficult position: either to recommend him for Spain or to ask you whether you could possibly extend his appointment to a full professorship." In case the threat was not clear enough, Einstein added, "His absence from the Institute might even create some difficulties for my own work." [46]

Flexner compromised. In a four-page letter, he cautioned Einstein about the perils of becoming too attached to one assistant, told tales of how that had worked out badly in other cases, but then relented. Although Mayer's title remained associate professor, he was given tenure, which was enough to secure the deal. [47]

Einstein also accepted or expressed interest in lectureships in Brussels, Paris, and Oxford. He was particularly eager to spend some time at the latter. "Do you think that Christ Church could find a small room for me?" he wrote his friend Professor Frederick Lindemann, a physicist there who would become an important adviser to Winston Churchill. "It need not be so grand as in the two previous years." At the end of the letter, he added a wistful little note: "I shall never see the land of my birth again." [48]

This raised one obvious question: Why did he not consider spending some time at Hebrew University in Jerusalem? After all, it was partly his baby. Einstein spent the spring of 1933 actively talking about starting up a new university, perhaps in England, that could serve as a refuge for displaced Jewish academics. Why wasn't he instead recruiting them for, and committing himself personally to, Hebrew University?

The problem was that for the previous five years, Einstein had been doing battle with administrators there, and it came to an untimely showdown in 1933, just as he and other professors were fleeing the Nazis. The target of his ire was the university's president, Judah Magnes, a former rabbi from New York who felt a duty to please his wealthy American backers, including on faculty appointments, even if this meant compromising on scholarly distinction. Einstein wanted the university to operate more in the European tradition, with the academic departments given great power over curriculum and tenured faculty decisions.[49]

While he was in Le Coq sur Mer, his frustrations with Magnes boiled over. "This ambitious and weak person surrounded himself with other morally inferior men," he wrote Haber in cautioning him about going to Hebrew University. He described it to Born as "a pigsty, complete charlatanism."[50]

Einstein's complaints put him at odds with the Zionist leader Chaim Weizmann. When Weizmann and Magnes sent him a formal invitation to join the Hebrew University faculty, he allowed his distaste to pour forth publicly. He told the press that the university was "unable to satisfy intellectual needs" and declared that he had thus rejected the invitation.[51]

Magnes must go, Einstein declared. He wrote Sir Herbert Samuel, the British high commissioner, who had been appointed to a committee to propose reforms, that Magnes had wrought "enormous damage" and that "if ever people want my collaboration, his immediate resignation is my condition." In June he said the same to Weizmann: "Only a decisive change of personnel would alter things."[52]

Weizmann was an adroit broken-field runner. He decided to turn Einstein's challenge into an opportunity to lessen Magnes's power. If he succeeded, then Einstein should feel compelled to join the faculty. On a trip to America later in June, he was asked why Einstein was not going to Jerusalem, where he surely belonged. He should indeed go there, Weizmann agreed, and he had been invited to do so. If he went to Jerusalem, Weizmann added, "he would cease to be a wanderer among the universities of the world."[53]

Einstein was furious. His reasons for not going to Jerusalem were well known to Weizmann, he said, "and he also knows under what circumstances I would be prepared to undertake work for the Hebrew University." That led Weizmann to appoint a committee that, he knew, would remove Magnes from direct control of the academic side of the university. He then announced, during a visit to Chicago, that Einstein's conditions had been met and therefore he should be coming to Hebrew University after all. "Albert Einstein has definitely decided to accept direction of the physics institute at the Hebrew University," the Jewish Telegraphic Agency reported, based on information from Weizmann.

It was a ruse by Weizmann that was not true and would never come to pass. But in addition to frightening Flexner in Princeton, it allowed the Hebrew University controversy to simmer down and for reforms to be made at the university.[54]

The End of Pacifism

Like a good scientist, Einstein could change his attitudes when confronted with new evidence. Among his deepest personal principles was his pacifism. But in early 1933, with Hitler's ascension, the facts had changed.

So Einstein forthrightly declared that he had come to the conclusion that absolute pacifism and military resistance were, at least for the moment, not warranted. "The time seems inauspicious for further advocacy of certain propositions of the radical pacifist movement," he wrote to a Dutch minister who wanted his support for a peace organization. "For example, is one justified in advising a Frenchman or a Belgian to refuse military service in the face of German rearmament?" Einstein felt the answer was now clear. "Frankly, I do not believe so."

Instead of pushing pacifism, he redoubled his commitment to a world federalist organization, like a League of Nations with real teeth, that would have its own professional army to enforce its decisions. "It seems to me that in the present situation we must support a supranational organization of force rather than advocate the abolition of all forces," he said. "Recent events have taught me a lesson in this respect."[55]

This met resistance from the War Resisters' International, an organization that he had long supported. Its leader, Lord Arthur Ponsonby, denounced the idea, calling it "undesirable because it is an admission that force is the factor that can resolve international disputes." Einstein disagreed. In the wake of the new threat arising in Germany, his new philosophy, he wrote, was "no disarmament without security."[56]

Four years earlier, while visiting Antwerp, Einstein had been invited to the Belgian royal palace by Queen Elisabeth,[57] the daughter of a Bavarian duke who was married to King Albert I. The queen loved music, and Einstein spent the afternoon playing Mozart with her, drinking tea, and attempting to explain relativity. Invited back the following year, he met her husband, the king, and became charmed by the least regal of all royals. "These two simple people are of a purity and goodness that is seldom to be found," he wrote Elsa. Once again he and the queen played Mozart, then Einstein was invited to stay and dine alone with the couple. "No servants, vegetarian, spinach with fried egg and potatoes," he recounted. "I liked it enormously, and I am sure that the feeling is mutual."[58]

Thus began a lifelong friendship with the Belgian queen. Later, his relationship with her would play a minor role in Einstein's involvement with the atomic bomb. But in July 1933, the issue at stake was pacifism and military resistance.

"The husband of the second violinist would like to talk to you on an urgent matter." It was a cryptic way for King Albert to identify himself that Einstein, but few others, would recognize. Einstein headed to the palace. On the king's mind was a case that was roiling his country. Two conscientious objectors were being held in jail for refusing service in the Belgian army, and international pacifists were pressuring Einstein to speak out on their behalf. This, of course, would cause problems.

The king hoped that Einstein would refrain from getting involved. Out of friendship, out of respect for the leader of a country that was hosting him, and also out of his new and sincere beliefs, Einstein agreed. He even went so far as to write a letter that he allowed to be made public.

"In the present threatening situation, created by the events in Germany, Belgium's armed forces can be regarded only as a means of defense, not an instrument of aggression," he declared. "And now, of all times, such defense forces are urgently needed."

Being Einstein, however, he felt compelled to add a few additional thoughts. "Men who, by their religious and moral convictions, are con-strained to refuse military service should not be treated as criminals," he argued. "They should be offered the alternative of accepting more onerous and hazardous work than military service." For example, they could be put to work as low-paid conscripts doing "mine labor, stoking furnaces aboard ships, hospital service in infectious disease wards or in certain sections of mental institutions."[59] King Albert sent back a warm note of gratitude, which politely avoided any discussions of al-ternative service.

When Einstein changed his mind, he did not try to hide the fact. So he also wrote a public letter to the leader of the pacifist group that was encouraging him to intervene in the Belgian case. "Until recently, we in Europe could assume that personal war resistance constituted an effective attack on militarism," he said. "Today we face an altogether different situation. In the heart of Europe lies a power, Germany, that is obviously pushing to war with all available means."

He even went so far as to proclaim the unthinkable: he himself would join the army if he were a young man.

> I must tell you candidly: Under today's conditions, if I were a Belgian, I would not refuse military service, but gladly take it upon me in the knowledge of serving European civilization. This does not mean that I am surrendering the principle for which I have stood heretofore. I have no greater hope than that the time may not be far off when refusal of military service will once again be an effective method of serving the cause of human progress.[60]

For weeks the story reverberated around the world. "Einstein Alters His Pacifist Views / Advises the Belgians to Arm Themselves Against the Threat of Germany," headlined the *New York Times*.[61] Einstein not only held firm, but explained himself more passionately in response to each successive attack.

> *To the French secretary of the War Resisters' International:* "My views have not changed, but the European situation has . . . So long as Ger-many persists in rearming and systematically indoctrinating its citi-zens for a war of revenge, the nations of western Europe depend,

unfortunately, on military defense. Indeed, I will go so far as to assert that if they are prudent, they will not wait, unarmed, to be attacked . . . I cannot shut my eyes to realities."[62]

To Lord Ponsonby, his pacifist partner from England: "Can you possibly be unaware of the fact that Germany is feverishly rearming and that the whole population is being indoctrinated with nationalism and drilled for war? . . . What protection, other than organized power, would you suggest?"[63]

To the Belgian War Resisters' Committee: "As long as no international police force exists, these countries must undertake the defense of culture. The situation in Europe has changed sharply within the past year; we should be playing into the hands of our bitterest enemies were we to close our eyes to this fact."[64]

To an American professor: "To prevent the greater evil, it is necessary that the lesser evil—the hated military—be accepted for the time being."[65]

And even a year later, to an upset rabbi from Rochester: "I am the same ardent pacifist I was before. But I believe that we can advocate refusing military service only when the military threat from aggressive dictatorships toward democratic countries has ceased to exist."[66]

After years of being called naïve by his conservative friends, now it was those on the left who felt that his grasp of politics was shaky. "Einstein, a genius in his scientific field, is weak, indecisive and inconsistent outside it," the dedicated pacifist Romain Rolland wrote in his diary.[67] The charge of inconsistency would have amused Einstein. For a scientist, altering your doctrines when the facts change is not a sign of weakness.

Farewell

The previous fall, Einstein had gotten a long, rambling, and, as often was the case, intensely personal letter from Michele Besso, one of his oldest friends. Most of it was about poor Eduard, Einstein's younger son, who had continued to succumb to his mental illness and was now confined to an asylum near Zurich. Einstein was pictured so often with his stepdaughters, but never with his sons, Besso noted. Why didn't he travel with them? Perhaps he could take Eduard on one of his trips to America and get to know him better.

Einstein loved Eduard. Elsa told a friend, "This sorrow is eating up Albert." But he felt that Eduard's schizophrenia was inherited from his mother's side, as to some extent it probably was, and there was little that he could do about it. That was also the reason he resisted psycho-analysis for Eduard. He considered it ineffective, especially in cases of severe mental illness that seemed to have hereditary causes.

Besso, on the other hand, had gone through psychoanalysis, and in his letter he was expansive and disarming, just as he had been back when they used to walk home from the patent office together more than a quarter-century earlier. He had his own problems in marriage, Besso said, referring to Anna Winteler, whom Einstein had introduced him to. But by forging a better relationship with his own son, he had made his marriage work and his life more meaningful.

Einstein replied that he hoped to take Eduard with him to visit Princeton. "Unfortunately, everything indicates that strong heredity manifests itself very definitely," he lamented. "I have seen that coming slowly but inexorably since Tete's youth. Outside influences play only a small part in such cases, compared to internal secretions, about which nobody can do anything."[68]

The tug was there, and Einstein knew that he had to, and wanted to, see Eduard. He was supposed to visit Oxford in late May, but he de-cided to delay the trip for a week so that he could go to Zurich and be with his son. "I could not wait six weeks before going to see him," he wrote Lindemann, asking his indulgence. "You are not a father, but I know you will understand."[69]

His relationship with Marić had improved so much that, when she heard he could not go back to Germany, she invited both him and Elsa to come to Zurich and live in her apartment building. He was pleas-antly surprised, and he stayed with her when he came alone that May. But his visit with Eduard turned out to be more wrenching than he had anticipated.

Einstein had brought with him his violin. Often he and Eduard had played together, expressing emotions with their music in ways they could not with words. The photograph of them on that visit is particu-larly poignant. They are sitting awkwardly next to each other, wearing suits, in what seems to be the visiting room of the asylum. Einstein is holding his violin and bow, looking away. Eduard is staring down intensely at a pile of papers, the pain seeming to contort his now fleshy face.

When Einstein left Zurich for Oxford, he was still assuming that he would be spending half of each ensuing year in Europe. What he did not know was that, as things would turn out, this would be the last time he would see his first wife and their younger son.

While at Oxford, Einstein gave his Herbert Spencer Lecture, in which he explained his philosophy of science, and then went to Glasgow, where he gave an account of his path toward the discovery of general relativity. He enjoyed the trip so much that, soon after his return to Le Coq sur Mer, he decided to go back to England in late July, this time at the invitation of one of his unlikeliest acquaintances.

British Commander Oliver Locker-Lampson was most things that Einstein was not. The adventurous son of a Victorian poet, he became a World War I aviator, leader of an armored division in Lapland and Russia, an adviser to Grand Duke Nicholas, and potential plotter in the murder of Rasputin. Now he was a barrister, journalist, and member of Parliament. He had studied in Germany, knew the language and the people, and had become, perhaps as a consequence, an early advocate for preparing to fight the Nazis. With an appetite for the interesting, he began writing Einstein, whom he had met only in passing once at Oxford, asking him to be his guest in England.

When Einstein accepted his offer, the dashing commander made the most of it. He took Einstein to see Winston Churchill, then suffering through his wilderness years as an opposition member of Parliament. At lunch in the gardens of Churchill's home, Chartwell, they discussed Germany's rearmament. "He is an eminently wise man," Einstein wrote Elsa that day. "It became clear to me that these people have made preparations and are determined to act resolutely and soon."[70] It sounded like an assessment from someone who had just eaten lunch with Churchill.

Locker-Lampson also brought Einstein to Austen Chamberlain, another advocate of rearmament, and former Prime Minister Lloyd

George. When he arrived at the home of the latter, Einstein was given the guest book to sign. When he got to the space for home address, he paused for a few moments, then wrote *ohne,* without any.

Locker-Lampson recounted the incident the next day when, with great flourish, he introduced a bill in Parliament, as Einstein watched from the visitors' gallery wearing a white linen suit, to "extend opportunities of citizenship for Jews." Germany was in the process of destroying its culture and threatening the safety of its greatest thinkers. "She has turned out her most glorious citizen, Albert Einstein," he said. "When he is asked to put his address in visitors' books he has to write, 'without any.' How proud this country must be to have offered him shelter at Oxford!"[71]

When he returned to his seaside cottage in Belgium, Einstein decided there was one issue he should clear up, or at least try to, before he embarked for America again. The Woman Patriot Corporation and others were still seeking to bar him as a dangerous subversive or communist, and he found their allegations to be both offensive and potentially problematic.

Because of his socialist sentiments, history of pacifism, and opposition to fascism, it was thought then—and throughout his life—that Einstein might be sympathetic to the Russian communists. Nor did it help that he had an earnest willingness to lend his name to almost any worthy-sounding manifesto or masthead that arrived in his mail, without always determining whether the groups involved might be fronts for other agendas.

Fortunately, his willingness to lend his name to sundry organizations was accompanied by an aversion to actually showing up for any meetings or spending time in comradely planning sessions. So there were not many political groups, and certainly no communist ones, in which he actually participated. And he made it a point never to visit Russia, because he knew that he could be used for propaganda purposes.

As his departure date neared, Einstein gave two interviews to make these points clear. "I am a convinced democrat," he told fellow German refugee Leo Lania for the *New York World Telegram.* "It is for this reason that I do not go to Russia, although I have received very cordial invitations. My voyage to Moscow would certainly be exploited by the rulers of the Soviets to profit their own political aims. Now I am an adversary of Bolshevism just as much as of fascism. I am against all dictatorships." [72]

In another interview, which appeared both in the *Times* of London and the *New York Times,* Einstein admitted that occasionally he had been "fooled" by organizations that pretended to be purely pacifist or humanitarian but "are in truth nothing less than camouflaged propaganda in the service of Russian despotism." He emphasized, "I have never favored communism and do not favor it now." The essence of his political belief was to oppose any power that "enslaves the individual by terror and force, whether it arises under a Fascist or Communist flag." [73]

These statements were made, no doubt, to tamp down any controversy in America about his alleged political leanings. But they had the added virtue of being true. He had occasionally been duped by groups whose agendas were not what they seemed, but he had, since childhood, kept as his guiding principle an aversion to authoritarianism, whether of the left or the right.

At the end of the summer, Einstein received some devastating news. Having recently separated from his wife and collaborator, his friend Paul Ehrenfest had gone to visit his 16-year-old son, who was in an Amsterdam institution with Down syndrome. He pulled out a gun, shot the boy in the face, taking out his eye but not killing him. Then he turned the gun on himself and committed suicide.

More than twenty years earlier, Ehrenfest, a wandering young Jewish physicist, had shown up in Prague, where Einstein was working, and asked for help finding a job. After visiting the cafés and talking physics for hours that day, the two men became deeply devoted friends. Ehrenfest's mind was very different from Einstein's in many ways. He had "an almost morbid lack of self-confidence," Einstein said, and was better at critically poking holes in existing theories than at building new ones. That made him a good teacher, "the best I have ever known," but his "sense of inadequacy, objectively unjustified, plagued him incessantly."

But there was one important way in which he was like Einstein. He could never make his peace with quantum mechanics. "To learn and teach things that one cannot fully accept in one's heart is always a difficult matter," Einstein wrote of Ehrenfest, "doubly difficult for a man of fanatical honesty."

Einstein, who knew what it was like to turn 50, followed this with a description that said as much about his own approach to quantum mechanics as it did about Ehrenfest's: "Added to this was the increasing difficulty of adapting to new thoughts which always confronts the man past fifty. I do not know how many readers of these lines will be capable of fully grasping that tragedy."[74] Einstein was.

Ehrenfest's suicide deeply unnerved Einstein, as did the increased intensity of the threats against his own life. His name had been falsely associated with a book attacking Hitler's terror; as was often the case, he had let his name be used as the honorary chair of a committee, which then published the book, but he had not read any of it. German papers headlined "Einstein's infamy" in red letters. One magazine pictured him on a list of enemies of the German regime, listed his "crimes," and concluded with the phrase "not yet hanged."

So Einstein decided to take Locker-Lampson up on his English hospitality yet again for the final month before his scheduled departure for America in October. Elsa, who wanted to stay behind in Belgium to pack, asked a reporter from the *Sunday Express* to arrange for Einstein to get to England safely. Being a good journalist, he accompanied Einstein on the trip himself and reported that on the channel crossing Einstein pulled out his notebook and went to work on his equations.

In a drama worthy of a James Bond movie, Locker-Lampson had two young female "assistants" take Einstein up to a secluded cottage he owned that was nestled on a coastal moor northeast of London. There he was swept into a slapstick whirl of secrecy and publicity. The two young women posed next to him holding hunting shotguns for a picture that was given to the press agencies, and Locker-Lampson declared, "If any unauthorized person comes near they will get a charge of buckshot." Einstein's own assessment of his security was less intimidating. "The beauty of my bodyguards would disarm a conspirator sooner than their shotguns," he told a visitor.

Among those who penetrated this modest security perimeter were a former foreign minister, who wanted to discuss the crisis in Europe;

Einstein's stepson-in-law, Dimitri Marianoff, who had come to inter-view him for an article he had sold to a French publication; Walther Mayer, who helped continue the Sisyphean task of finding unified field theory equations; and the noted sculptor Jacob Epstein, who spent three days making a beautiful bust of Einstein.

The only one who ran afoul of the female guards was Epstein, who asked if they would take one of the doors off its hinges so he could get a better angle for his sculpting. "They facetiously asked whether I would like the roof off next," he recalled. "I thought I should have liked that too, but I did not demand it as the attendant angels seemed to re-sent a little my intrusion into the retreat of their professor." After three days, however, the guardians warmed to Epstein, and everyone began drinking beer together at the end of his sittings.[75]

Einstein's humor stayed intact through it all. Among the letters he received in England was one from a man who had a theory that gravity meant that as the earth rotated people were sometimes upside down or horizontal. Perhaps that led people to do foolish things, he speculated, like falling in love. "Falling in love is not the most stupid thing that people do," Einstein scribbled on the letter, "but gravitation cannot be held responsible for it."[76]

Einstein's main appearance on this trip was a speech on October 3 in London's Royal Albert Hall, which was designed to raise money for displaced German scholars. Some suspected, no doubt with reason, that Locker-Lampson had hyped the security threat and publicity about Einstein's hideaway in order to promote ticket sales. If so, he was successful. All nine thousand seats were filled, and others jammed the aisles and lobbies. A thousand students acted as guides and guards against any pro-Nazi demonstration that might materialize (none did).

Einstein spoke, in English, about the current menace to freedom, but he was careful not to attack the German regime specifically. "If we want to resist the powers that threaten to suppress intellectual and in-dividual freedom, we must be clear what is at stake," he said. "Without such freedom there would have been no Shakespeare, no Goethe, no Newton, no Faraday, no Pasteur, no Lister." Freedom was a foundation for creativity.

He also spoke of the need for solitude. "The monotony of a quiet life stimulates the creative mind," he said, and he repeated a suggestion he had made when younger that scientists might be employed as light-house keepers so they could "devote themselves undisturbed" to think-ing.[77]

It was a revealing remark. For Einstein, science was a solitary pur-suit, and he seemed not to realize that for others it could be far more fruitful when pursued collaboratively. In Copenhagen and elsewhere, the quantum mechanics team had been building on one another's ideas with a frenzy. But Einstein's great breakthroughs had been those that could be done, with perhaps just an occasional sounding board and mathematical assistant, by someone in a Bern patent office, the garret of a Berlin apartment, or a lighthouse.

The ocean liner *Westmoreland,* which had sailed from Antwerp with Elsa and Helen Dukas aboard, picked up Einstein and Walther Mayer in Southampton on October 7, 1933. He did not think he would be away for long. In fact, he planned to spend another term at Christ Church, Oxford, the next spring. But although he would live for another twenty-two years, Einstein would never see Europe again.

CHAPTER NINETEEN

AMERICA

1933–1939

112 Mercer Street

Princeton

The ocean liner *Westmoreland,* which carried Einstein, at age 54, to what would become his new home country, arrived in New York Harbor on October 17, 1933. Waiting to meet him in the rain at the Twenty-third Street pier was an official committee led by his friend Samuel Untermyer, a prominent attorney, who carried some orchids he had grown, plus a group of cheerleaders that was scheduled to parade with him to a welcoming pageant.

Einstein and his entourage, however, were nowhere to be found. Abraham Flexner, the director of the Institute for Advanced Study, was obsessed with shielding him from publicity, whatever Einstein's quirky preferences might be. So he had sent a tugboat, with two Institute trustees, to spirit Einstein away from the *Westmoreland* as soon as it cleared quarantine. "Make no statement and give no interviews on any subject," he had cabled. To reiterate the message, he sent a letter with one of the trustees who greeted Einstein's ship. "Your safety in America depends upon silence and refraining from attendance at public functions," it said.[1]

Carrying his violin case, with a profusion of hair poking out from a wide-brimmed black hat, Einstein surreptitiously disembarked onto the tug, which then ferried him and his party to the Battery, where a car was waiting to whisk them to Princeton. "All Dr. Einstein wants is to be left in peace and quiet," Flexner told reporters.[2]

Actually, he also wanted a newspaper and an ice cream cone. So as soon as he had checked into Princeton's Peacock Inn, he changed into casual clothes and, smoking his pipe, went walking to a newsstand, where he bought an afternoon paper and chuckled over the headlines about the mystery of his whereabouts. Then he walked into an ice cream parlor, the Baltimore, pointed his thumb at the cone a young divinity student had just bought, and then pointed at himself. As the waitress made change for him, she announced, "This one goes in my memory book."[3]

Einstein was given a corner office in a university hall that served as the temporary headquarters of the Institute. There were eighteen scholars in residence then, including the mathematicians Oswald Veblen (nephew of the social theorist Thorstein Veblen) and John von Neumann, a pioneer of computer theory. When shown his office, he was asked what equipment he might need. "A desk or table, a chair, paper and pencils," he replied. "Oh yes, and a large wastebasket, so I can throw away all my mistakes."[4]

He and Elsa soon found a house to rent, which they celebrated by hosting a small musical recital featuring the works of Haydn and Mozart. The noted Russian violinist Toscha Seidel played lead, with Einstein as second fiddle. In return for some violin tips, Einstein tried to explain relativity theory to Seidel and made him some drawings of moving rods contracting in length.[5]

Thus began a proliferation of popular tales in town about Einstein's love for music. One involved Einstein playing in a quartet with violin virtuoso Fritz Kreisler. At a certain point they got out of sync. Kreisler stopped playing and turned to Einstein in mock exasperation. "What's the matter, professor, can't you count?"[6] More poignantly, there was an evening where a Christian prayer group gathered to make intercessions for persecuted Jews. Einstein surprised them by asking if he could come. He brought his violin and, as if offering a prayer, played a solo.[7]

Many of his performances were purely impromptu. That first Halloween, he disarmed some astonished trick-or-treaters, a group of 12-year-old girls who had come with the intent of playing a prank, by appearing at the door and serenading them with his violin. And at Christmastime, when members of the First Presbyterian Church came by to sing carols, he stepped out into the snow, borrowed a violin from one of the women, and accompanied them. "He was just a lovely person," one of them recalled.[8]

Einstein soon acquired an image, which grew into a near legend but was nevertheless based on reality, of being a kindly and gentle professor, distracted at times but unfailingly sweet, who wandered about lost in thought, helped children with their homework, and rarely combed his hair or wore socks. With his amused sense of self-awareness, he catered to such perceptions. "I'm a kind of ancient figure known primarily for his non-use of socks and wheeled out on special occasions as a curiosity," he joked. His slightly disheveled appearance was partly an assertion of his simplicity and partly a mild act of rebellion. "I have reached an age when, if someone tells me to wear socks, I don't have to," he told a neighbor.[9]

His baggy, comfortable clothes became a symbol of his lack of pretense. He had a leather jacket that he tended to wear to events both formal and informal. When a friend found out that he had a mild allergy to wool sweaters, she went to a surplus store and bought him some cotton sweatshirts, which he wore all the time. And his dismissive attitude toward haircuts and grooming was so infectious that Elsa, Margot, and his sister, Maja, all sported the same disheveled gray profusion.

He was able to make his rumpled-genius image as famous as Chaplin did the little tramp. He was kindly yet aloof, brilliant yet baffled. He floated around with a distracted air and a wry sensibility. He exuded honesty to a fault, was sometimes but not always as naïve as he seemed, cared passionately about humanity and sometimes about people. He would fix his gaze on cosmic truths and global issues, which allowed him to seem detached from the here and now. This role he played was not far from the truth, but he enjoyed playing it to the hilt, knowing that it was such a great role.

He had also, by then, adapted willingly to the role Elsa played, that of a wife who could be both doting and demanding, protective yet afflicted with occasional social aspirations. They had grown comfortable together, after some rough patches. "I manage him," she said proudly, "but I never let him know that I manage him."[10]

Actually, he knew, and he found it mildly amusing. He surrendered, for example, to Elsa's nagging that he smoked too much and on Thanksgiving bet her that he would be able to abstain from his pipe until the new year. When Elsa boasted of this at a dinner party, Einstein grumbled, "You see, I am no longer a slave to my pipe, but I am a slave to that woman." Einstein kept his word, but "he got up at daylight on New Year's morning, and he hasn't had his pipe out of his mouth since except to eat and sleep," Elsa told neighbors a few days after the deal was over.[11]

The greatest source of friction for Einstein came from Flexner's desire to protect him from publicity. Einstein was, as always, less fastidious about this than were his friends, patrons, and self-appointed protectors. An occasional flash of the limelight made his eyes twinkle. More important, he was willing and even eager to endure such indignities if he could use his fame to raise money and sympathy for the worsening plight of European Jews.

Such political activism made Einstein's penchant for publicity even more disconcerting to Flexner, an old-line and assimilated American Jew. It might provoke anti-Semitism, he thought, especially in Princeton, where the Institute was luring Jewish scholars into an environment that was, to say the least, socially wary of them.[12]

Flexner was particularly upset when Einstein, quite charmingly, agreed one Saturday to meet at his home with a group of boys from a Newark school who had named their science club after him. Elsa baked cookies, and when the discussion turned to Jewish political leaders, she noted, "I don't think there is any anti-Semitism in this country." Einstein agreed. It would have amounted to no more than a sweet visit, except that the adviser who accompanied the boys wrote a colorful account, focusing on Einstein's thoughts about the plight of Jews, that was bannered atop the front page of the Newark *Sunday Ledger*.[13]

Flexner was furious. "I simply want to protect him," he wrote in a sharp letter to Elsa, and he sent the Newark article to her with a stern note attached. "This is exactly the sort of thing that seems to me absolutely unworthy of Professor Einstein," he scolded. "It will hurt him in the esteem of his colleagues, for they will believe that he seeks such publicity, and I do not see how they can be convinced that such is not the case."[14]

Flexner went on to ask Elsa to dissuade her husband from being featured at a scheduled musical recital in Manhattan, which he had already accepted, that was to raise money for Jewish refugees. But like her husband, Elsa was not totally averse to publicity, nor to helping Jewish causes, and she resented Flexner's attempts at control. So she replied with a very frank refusal.

That provoked Flexner to send an astonishingly blunt letter the next day, which he noted he had discussed with the president of Princeton University. Echoing the sentiments of some of Einstein's European friends, including the Borns, Flexner warned Elsa that if Jews got too much publicity it would stoke anti-Semitism:

> It is perfectly possible to create anti-Semitic feeling in the United States. There is no danger that any such feeling would be created except by the Jews themselves. There are already signs which are unmistakable that anti-Semitism has increased in America. It is because I am myself a Jew and because I wish to help oppressed Jews in Germany that my efforts, though continuous and in a measure successful, are absolutely quiet and anonymous . . . The questions involved are the dignity of your husband and the Institute according to the highest American standards and the most effective way of helping the Jewish race in America and in Europe.[15]

That same day, Flexner wrote Einstein directly to make the case that Jews like themselves should keep a low profile because a penchant for publicity could arouse anti-Semitism. "I have felt this from the moment that Hitler began his anti-Jewish policy, and I have acted accordingly," he wrote. "There have been indications in American universities that Jewish students and Jewish professors will suffer unless the utmost caution is used."[16]

Not surprisingly, Einstein went ahead with his planned benefit recital in Manhattan, for which 264 guests paid $25 apiece to attend. It featured Bach's Concerto for Two Violins in D-minor and Mozart's G Major Quartet. It was even opened to the press. "He became so absorbed in the music," *Time* magazine reported, "that with a far-away look he was still plucking at the strings when the performance was all over."[17]

In his attempt to prevent such events, Flexner had begun intercepting Einstein's mail and declining invitations on his behalf. The stage was thus set for a showdown when Rabbi Stephen Wise of New York decided it would be a good idea to get Einstein invited to visit President Franklin Roosevelt, which Wise hoped would focus attention on Germany's treatment of Jews. "F.D.R. has not lifted a finger on behalf of the Jews of Germany, and this would be little enough," Wise wrote a friend.[18]

The result was a telephone call from Roosevelt's social secretary, Colonel Marvin MacIntyre, inviting Einstein to the White House. When Flexner found out, he was furious. He called the White House and gave a stern lecture to the somewhat surprised Colonel MacIntyre. All invitations must go through him, Flexner said, and on Einstein's behalf he declined.

For good measure, Flexner proceeded to write an official letter to the president. "I felt myself compelled this afternoon to explain to your secretary," Flexner said, "that Professor Einstein had come to Princeton for the purpose of carrying out his scientific work in seclusion and that it was absolutely impossible to make any exception which would inevitably bring him into public notice."

Einstein knew none of this until Henry Morgenthau, a prominent Jewish leader who was about to become treasury secretary, inquired about the apparent snub. Dismayed to discover Flexner's presumption, Einstein wrote to Eleanor Roosevelt, his political soul mate. "You can hardly imagine of what great interest it would have been for me to meet the man who is tackling with gigantic energy the greatest and most difficult problem of our time," he wrote. "However, as a matter of fact, no invitation whatever has reached me."

Eleanor Roosevelt answered personally and politely. The confusion came, she explained, because Flexner had been so adamant in his phone call to the White House. "I hope you and Mrs. Einstein will come sometime soon," she added. Elsa responded graciously. "First excuse my poor English please," she wrote. "Dr. Einstein and myself accept with feelings of gratitude your very kind invitation."

He and Elsa arrived at the White House on January 24, 1934, had dinner, and spent the night. The president was able to converse with them in passable German. Among other things, they discussed Roosevelt's marine prints and Einstein's love for sailing. The next morning, Einstein wrote an eight-line piece of doggerel on a White House note card to Queen Elisabeth of the Belgians marking his visit, but he made no public statements.[19]

Flexner's interference infuriated Einstein. He complained about it in a letter to Rabbi Wise—on which he put as his return address "Concentration Camp, Princeton"—and he sent a five-page litany of Flexner's meddling to the Institute's trustees. Either they must assure him that there would be no more "constant interference of the type that no self-respecting person would tolerate," Einstein threatened, or "I would propose that I discuss with you severing my relationship with your institute in a dignified manner."[20]

Einstein prevailed, and Flexner backed off. But as a result, he lost his influence with Flexner, whom he would later refer to as one of his "few enemies" in Princeton.[21] When Erwin Schrödinger, Einstein's fellow traveler in the minefields of quantum mechanics, arrived as a refugee in Princeton that March, he was offered a job at the university. But he wanted instead to be tapped for the Institute for Advanced Study. Einstein lobbied Flexner on his behalf, but to no avail. Flexner was doing him no more favors, even if it meant depriving the Institute of Schrödinger.

During his short stay in Princeton, Schrödinger asked Einstein if he was indeed going to come back to Oxford later that spring, as scheduled. He had called himself a "bird of passage" when heading off to Caltech in 1931, and it was unclear, perhaps even in his own mind, whether he saw this as a liberation or a lament. But now he found himself comfortable in Princeton, with no desire to take wing again.

"Why should an old fellow like me not enjoy peace and quiet for once?" he asked his friend Max Born. So he told Schrödinger to pass along his sincere regrets. "I am sorry to say that he asked me to write you a definite no," Schrödinger informed Lindemann. "The reason for his decision is really that he is frightened of all the ado and the fuss that would be laid upon him if he came to Europe." Einstein also worried that he would be expected to go to Paris and Madrid if he went to Oxford, "and I lack the courage to undertake all this." [22]

The stars had aligned to create for Einstein a sense of inertia, or at least a weariness of further wandering. In addition, Princeton, which he called a "pipe as yet unsmoked" on his first visit in 1921, captured him with its leafy charm and its neo-Gothic echoes of a European university town. "A quaint and ceremonious village of puny demigods strutting on stiff legs," he called it in a letter to Elisabeth, the queen mother of Belgium since the death of the king. "By ignoring certain social conventions, I have been able to create for myself an atmosphere conducive to study and free from distraction." [23]

Einstein particularly liked the fact that America, despite its inequalities of wealth and racial injustices, was more of a meritocracy than Europe. "What makes the new arrival devoted to this country is the democratic trait among the people," he marveled. "No one humbles himself before another person or class." [24]

This was a function of the right of individuals to say and think what they pleased, a trait that had always been important to Einstein. In addition, the lack of stifling traditions encouraged more creativity of the sort he had relished as a student. "American youth has the good fortune not to have its outlook troubled by outworn traditions," he noted. [25]

Elsa likewise loved Princeton, which was important to Einstein. She had taken such good care of him for so long that he had become more solicitous of her desires, particularly her nesting instinct. "The whole of Princeton is one great park with wonderful trees," she wrote a friend. "We might almost believe that we are in Oxford." The architecture and countryside reminded her of England, and she felt somewhat guilty that she was so comfortable while others back in Europe were suffering. "We are very happy here, perhaps too happy. Sometimes one has a bad conscience."[26]

So in April 1934, just six months after his arrival, Einstein announced that he was staying in Princeton indefinitely and assuming full-time status at the Institute. As it turned out, he would never live anywhere else for the remaining twenty-one years of his life. Nevertheless, he made appearances at the "farewell" parties that had been scheduled that month as fund-raisers for various of his favorite charities. These causes had become almost as important to him as his science. As he declared at one of the events, "Striving for social justice is the most valuable thing to do in life."[27]

Sadly, just when they had decided to settle in, Elsa had to travel back to Europe to care for her spirited and adventurous elder daughter, Ilse, who had dallied with the romantic radical Georg Nicolai and married the literary journalist Rudolf Kayser. Ilse was afflicted with what they thought was tuberculosis but what turned out to be leukemia, and her condition had taken a turn for the worse. Now she had gone to Paris to be nursed by her sister, Margot.

Insisting that her problems were mainly psychosomatic, Ilse resisted medications and turned instead to prolonged psychotherapy. Early during her illness, Einstein had tried to persuade her to go to a regular doctor, but she had refused. Now there was little that could be done as the whole family, absent Einstein himself, gathered by her bed in Margot's Paris apartment.

Ilse's death devastated Elsa. She "changed and aged," Margot's husband recalled, "almost beyond recognition." Instead of having Ilse's ashes deposited in a crypt, Elsa had them put in a sealed bag for her. "I cannot be separated," she said. "I have to have them." She then sewed the bag inside a pillow so that she could have them close to her on the trip home to America.[28]

Elsa also carried back cases of her husband's papers, which Margot had earlier smuggled from Berlin to Paris using French diplomatic channels and the anti-Nazi underground. To help get them into America, Elsa enlisted the help of a kindly neighbor from Princeton, Caroline Blackwood, who was on the same ship home.

Elsa had met the Blackwoods a few months earlier in Princeton, and they mentioned that they were going to Palestine and Europe and wished to meet some Zionist leaders.

"I didn't know you were Jews," Elsa said.

Mrs. Blackwood said that they actually were Presbyterian, but there was a deep connection between the Jewish heritage and the Christian, "and besides, Jesus was a Jew."

Elsa hugged her. "No Christian has ever said that to me in my life." She also asked for help in getting a German-language Bible, as they had lost theirs in the move from Berlin. Mrs. Blackwood found her a copy of Martin Luther's translation, which Elsa clasped to her heart. "I wish I had more faith," she told Mrs. Blackwood.

Elsa had taken note of what liner the Blackwoods were traveling on, and she purposely booked passage on it when she returned to America. One morning she brought Mrs. Blackwood into the ship's deserted lounge to ask a favor. Because she was not a citizen, she was afraid that her husband's papers might be held at the border. Would the Blackwoods bring them in?

They agreed, although Mr. Blackwood was careful not to lie on his customs declaration. "Material acquired in Europe for scholarly purposes," he wrote. Later, Einstein came over in the rain to the Blackwoods' shed to collect his papers. "Did I write this drivel?" he joked as he looked at one journal. But the Blackwoods' son, who was there, recalled that Einstein "was obviously deeply moved to have his books and papers in his hands."[29]

Ilse's death, accompanied in the summer of 1934 by Hitler's consolidation of power during the "Night of the Long Knives," severed the Einsteins' remaining bonds with Europe. Margot immigrated that year to Princeton, after she and her odd Russian husband separated. Hans Albert soon followed. She was "not longing for Europe at all," Elsa wrote Caroline Blackwood soon after returning. "I feel such a homelike feeling for this country."[30]

Recreations

When Elsa returned from Europe, she joined Einstein at a summer cottage he had rented in Watch Hill, Rhode Island, a quiet enclave on a peninsula near where Long Island Sound meets the Atlantic. It was perfect for sailing, which is why Einstein, at Elsa's urging, decided to summer there with his friend Gustav Bucky and his family.

Bucky was a physician, engineer, inventor, and pioneer of X-ray technology. A German who had gained American citizenship during the 1920s, he had met the Einsteins in Berlin. When Einstein came to America, his friendship with Bucky deepened; they even took out a joint patent on a device they came up with to control a photographic diaphragm, and Einstein testified as an expert witness for Bucky in a dispute over another invention.[31]

His son Peter Bucky happily spent time driving Einstein around, and he later wrote down some of his recollections in extensive notebooks. They provide a delightful picture of the mildly eccentric but deeply unaffected Einstein in his later years. Peter tells, for example, of driving in his convertible with Einstein when it suddenly started to rain. Einstein pulled off his hat and put it under his coat. When Peter looked quizzical, Einstein explained: "You see, my hair has withstood water many times before, but I don't know how many times my hat can."[32]

Einstein relished the simplicity of life in Watch Hill. He puttered around its lanes and even shopped for groceries with Mrs. Bucky. Most of all, he loved sailing his seventeen-foot wooden boat *Tinef,* which is Yiddish for a piece of junk. He usually went out on his own, aimlessly and often carelessly. "Frequently he would go all day long, just drifting around," remembered a member of the local yacht club who went to retrieve him on more than one occasion. "He apparently was just out there meditating."

As he had at Caputh, Einstein would drift with the breeze and sometimes scribble equations in his notebook when becalmed. "Once we all waited with growing concern for his return from an afternoon sail," Bucky recalls. "Finally, at 11 pm, we decided to send the Coast Guard out to search for him. The guardsmen found him in the Bay, not in the least concerned about his situation."

At one point a friend gave him an expensive outboard motor for emergency use. Einstein declined. He had a childlike delight about taking small risks—he still never took a life jacket even though he could not swim—and escaping to where he could be by himself. "To the average person, being becalmed for hours might be a terrible trial," said Bucky. "To Einstein, this could simply have provided more time to think."[33]

The sailing rescue sagas continued the following summer, when the Einsteins began renting in Old Lyme, Connecticut, also on Long Island Sound. One such tale even made the *New York Times*. "Relative Tide and Sand Bars Trap Einstein," read the headline. The young boys who saved him were invited to the house for raspberry juice.[34]

Elsa loved the Old Lyme house, although both she and her family found it a bit too imposing. It was set on twenty acres, with a tennis court and swimming pool, and the dining room was so large that they initially were afraid to use it. "Everything is so luxurious here that the first ten days—I swear to you—we ate in the pantry," Elsa wrote a friend. "The dining room was too magnificent for us."[35]

When the summers were over, the Einsteins would visit the Bucky family at their Manhattan home once or twice a month. Einstein would also stay, especially when he was by himself, at the home of the widower Leon Watters, the pharmaceutical company owner he had met in Pasadena. He once surprised Watters by arriving without a dressing gown or pajamas. "When I retire, I sleep as nature made me," he said. Watters recalled that he did, however, ask to borrow a pencil and notepad for his bedside.

Out of both politeness and his touch of vanity, Einstein found it hard to decline requests from artists and photographers who wanted him to pose. One weekend in April 1935, when he was staying with Watters, Einstein sat for two artists in one day. His first session was with the wife of Rabbi Stephen Wise, not known for her artistic ability. Why was he doing it? "Because she's a nice woman," he answered.

Later that day, Watters picked Einstein up to ferry him to Greenwich Village for a session with the Russian sculptor Sergei Konenkov, a practitioner of Soviet realism, who was producing what would be a distinguished bust of Einstein that is now at the Institute for Advanced Study. Einstein had been introduced to Konenkov through Margot, who was also a sculptor. Soon, all of them became friends with his wife, Margarita Konenkova, who, unbeknown to Einstein, was a Soviet spy.

In fact, Einstein would later become, after Elsa's death, romantically involved with her, which would end up creating, as we shall see, more complexities than he ever knew.[36]

Now that they had decided to stay in the United States, it made sense for Einstein to seek citizenship. When Einstein visited the White House, President Roosevelt had suggested that he should accept the offer of some congressmen to have a special bill passed on his behalf, but Einstein instead decided to go through the normal procedures. That meant leaving the country, so that he—and Elsa, Margot, and Helen Dukas—could come in not as visitors but as people seeking citizenship.

So in May 1935 they all sailed on the *Queen Mary* to Bermuda for a few days to satisfy these formalities. The royal governor was there to greet them when they arrived in Hamilton, and he recommended the island's two best hotels. Einstein found them stuffy and pretentious. As they walked through town, he saw a modest guest cottage, and that is where they ended up.

Einstein declined all official invitations from the Bermuda gentry and socialized instead with a German cook he met at a restaurant, who invited him to come sailing on his little boat. They were away for seven hours, and Elsa feared that Nazi agents may have nabbed her husband. But she found him at the cook's home, where he had gone to enjoy a dinner of German dishes.[37]

That summer, a house down the block from the one they were renting in Princeton went on sale. A modest white clapboard structure that peeked through a little front yard onto one of the town's pleasant tree-lined arteries, 112 Mercer Street was destined to become a world-famous landmark not because of its grandeur but because it so perfectly suited and symbolized the man who lived there. Like the public persona that he adopted in later life, the house was unassuming, sweet, charming, and unpretentious. It sat there right on a main street, highly visible yet slightly cloaked behind a veranda.

Its modest living room was a bit overwhelmed by Elsa's heavy German furniture, which had somehow caught up with them after all their wanderings. Helen Dukas commandeered the small library on the first floor as a workroom in which she dealt with Einstein's correspondence and took charge of the only telephone in the house (Princeton 1606 was the unlisted number).

Elsa oversaw the construction of a second-floor office for Einstein. They removed part of the back wall and installed a picture window that looked out on the long and lush backyard garden. Bookcases on both sides went up to the ceiling. A large wooden table, cluttered with papers and pipes and pencils, sat in the center with a view out of the window, and there was an easy chair where Einstein would sit for hours scribbling on a pad of paper in his lap.

The usual pictures of Faraday and Maxwell were tacked on the walls. There was also, of course, one of Newton, although after a while it fell off its hook. To that mix was added a fourth: Mahatma Gandhi, Einstein's new hero now that his passions were as much political as they were scientific. As a small joke, the only award displayed was a framed certificate of Einstein's membership in the Bern Scientific Society.

Besides his menagerie of women, the household was joined, over the years, by various pets. There was a parrot named Bibo, who required an unjustifiable amount of medical care; a cat named Tiger; and a white terrier named Chico that had belonged to the Bucky family. Chico was an occasional problem. "The dog is very smart," Einstein explained. "He feels sorry for me because I receive so much mail. That's why he tries to bite the mailman." [38]

"The professor does not drive," Elsa often said. "It's too complicated for him." Instead, he loved to walk, or, more precisely, shuffle, up Mercer Street each morning to his office at the Institute. People often snapped their heads when he passed, but the sight of him walking lost in thought was soon one of the well-known attractions of the town.

On his walk back home at midday, he would often be joined by three or four professors or students. Einstein would usually walk calmly and quietly, as if in a reverie, while they pranced around him, waved their arms, and tried to make their points. When they got to the house, the others would peel off, but Einstein sometimes just stood there thinking. Every now and then, unwittingly, he even started drifting back to the Institute. Dukas, always watching from her window, would come outside, take his arm, and lead him inside for his macaroni lunch. Then he would nap, dictate some answers to his mail, and pad up to his study for another hour or two of rumination about potential unified field theories.[39]

Occasionally, he would take rambling walks on his own, which could be dicey. One day someone called the Institute and asked to speak to a particular dean. When his secretary said that the dean wasn't available, the caller hesitantly asked for Einstein's home address. That was not possible to give out, he was informed. The caller's voice then dropped to a whisper. "Please don't tell anybody," he said, "but I *am* Dr. Einstein, I'm on my way home, and I've forgotten where my house is."[40]

This incident was recounted by the son of the dean, but like many of the tales about Einstein's distracted behavior it may have been exaggerated. The absentminded professor image fit him so nicely and naturally that it became reinforcing. It was a role that Einstein was happy to play in public and that his neighbors relished recounting. And like most assumed roles, there was a core of truth to it.

At one dinner where Einstein was being honored, for example, he got so distracted that he pulled out his notepad and began scribbling equations. When he was introduced, the crowd burst into a standing ovation, but he was still lost in thought. Dukas caught his attention and told him to get up. He did, but noticing the crowd standing and applauding, he assumed it was for someone else and heartily joined in. Dukas had to come over and inform him that the ovation was for him.[41]

In addition to the tales of the dreamy Einstein, another common theme was that of the kindly Einstein helping a child, usually a little girl, with her homework. The most famous of these involved an 8-year-old neighbor on Mercer Street, Adelaide Delong, who rang his bell and asked for help with a math problem. She carried a plate of homemade fudge as a bribe. "Come in," he said. "I'm sure we can solve it." He helped explain the math to her, but made her do her own homework. In return for the fudge, he gave her a cookie.

After that the girl kept reappearing. When her parents found out, they apologized profusely. Einstein waved them off. "That's quite unnecessary," he said. "I'm learning just as much from your child as she is learning from me." He loved to tell, with a twinkle in his eye, the tale of her visits. "She was a very naughty girl," he would laugh. "Do you know she tried to bribe me with candy?"

A friend of Adelaide's recalled going with her and another girl on one of these visits to Mercer Street. When they got up to his study, Einstein offered them lunch, and they accepted. "So he moved a whole bunch of papers from the table, opened four cans of beans with a can opener, and heated them on a Sterno stove one by one, stuck a spoon in each and that was our lunch," she recalled. "He didn't give us anything to drink."[42]

Later, Einstein famously told another girl who complained about her problems with math, "Do not worry about your difficulties in mathematics; I can assure you that mine are even greater." But lest it be thought he helped only girls, he hosted a group of senior boys from the Princeton Country Day School who were baffled by a problem on their math final exam.[43]

He also helped a 15-year-old boy at Princeton High School, Henry Rosso, who was doing poorly in a journalism course. His teacher had offered an A to anyone who scored an interview with Einstein, so Rosso showed up at Mercer Street but was rebuffed at the door. As he was slinking away, the milkman gave him a tip: Einstein could be found walking a certain route every morning at 9:30. So Rosso snuck out of school one day, positioned himself accordingly, and was able to accost Einstein as he wandered by.

Rosso was so flummoxed that he did not know what to ask, which may have been why he was doing poorly in the course. Einstein took pity on him and suggested questions. No personal topics, he insisted. Ask about math instead. Rosso was smart enough to follow his advice. "I discovered that nature was constructed in a wonderful way, and our task is to find out the mathematical structure of the nature itself," Einstein explained of his own education at age 15. "It is a kind of faith that helped me through my whole life."

The interview earned Rosso an A. But it also caused him a bit of dismay. He had promised Einstein that it would only be used in the school paper, but without his permission it got picked up by the Trenton newspaper and then others around the world, which provided yet another lesson in journalism.[44]

Elsa's Death

Soon after they moved into 112 Mercer Street, Elsa became afflicted with a swollen eye. Tests in Manhattan showed that it was a symptom of heart and kidney problems, and she was ordered to remain immobile in bed.

Einstein sometimes read to her, but mostly he threw himself more intently into his studies. "Strenuous intellectual work and looking at God's nature are the reconciling, fortifying yet relentlessly strict angels that shall lead me through all of life's troubles," he had written to the mother of his first girlfriend. Then as now, he could escape the complexity of human emotions by delving into the mathematical elegance that could describe the cosmos. "My husband sticks fearsomely to his calculations," Elsa wrote Watters. "I have never seen him so engrossed in his work."[45]

Elsa painted a warmer picture of her husband when writing to her friend Antonina Vallentin. "He has been so upset by my illness," she reported. "He wanders around like a lost soul. I never thought he loved me so much. And that comforts me."

Elsa decided that they would be better off if they went away for the summer, as they usually did, and so they rented a cottage on Saranac Lake in the Adirondack Mountains of New York. "I'm certain to get better there," she said. "If my Ilse walked into my room now, I would recover at once."[46]

It turned out to be an enjoyable summer, but by winter Elsa was again bedridden and getting weaker. She died on December 20, 1936.

Einstein was hit harder than he might have expected. In fact, he actually cried, as he had done when his mother died. "I had never seen him shed a tear," Peter Bucky reported, "but he did then as he sighed, 'Oh, I shall really miss her.' "[47]

Their relationship had not been a model romance. Before their marriage, Einstein's letters to her were filled with sweet endearments, but those disappeared over the years. He could be prickly and demanding at times, seemingly inured to her emotional needs, and occasionally a flirt or more with other women.

Yet beneath the surface of many romances that evolve into partnerships, there is a depth not visible to outside observers. Elsa and Albert Einstein liked each other, understood each other, and perhaps most important (for she, too, was actually quite clever in her own way) were amused by each other. So even if it was not the stuff of poetry, the bond between them was a solid one. It was forged by satisfying each other's desires and needs, it was genuine, and it worked in both directions.

Not surprisingly, Einstein found solace in his work. He admitted to Hans Albert that focusing was difficult, but the attempt provided him the means to escape the painfully personal. "As long as I am able to work, I must not and will not complain, because work is the only thing that gives substance to life." [48]

When he came to the office, he was "ashen with grief," his collaborator Banesh Hoffmann noted, but he insisted on delving into their work each day. He needed it more than ever, he said. "At first his attempts to concentrate were pitiful," Hoffmann recalled. "But he had known sorrow before and had learned that work was a precious antidote." [49] Together they worked that month on two major papers: one that explored how the bending of light by the gravitational fields of galaxies could create "cosmic lenses" that would magnify distant stars, and another that explored the existence of gravitational waves. [50]

Max Born learned of Elsa's death in a letter from Einstein in which it was mentioned almost as an afterthought in explaining why he had become less social. "I live like a bear in my cave, and really feel more at home than ever before in my eventful life," he told his old friend. "This bearlike quality has been further enhanced by the death of my woman comrade, who was better with other people than I am." Born later marveled at "the incidental way" in which Einstein broke the news of his wife's death. "For all his kindness, sociability and love of humanity," commented Born, "he was nevertheless totally detached from his environment and the human beings in it." [51]

That was not entirely true. For a self-styled bear in a cave, Einstein attracted a clan wherever he went. Whether it was walking home from the Institute, puttering around 112 Mercer Street, or sharing summer cottages and Manhattan weekends with the Watters or Bucky families, Einstein was rarely alone, except when he trundled up to his study. He could keep an ironic detachment and retreat into his own reveries, but he was a true loner only in his own mind.

After Elsa died, he still lived with Helen Dukas and his stepdaughter Margot, and soon thereafter his sister moved in. Maja had been living near Florence with her husband, Paul Winteler. But when Mussolini enacted laws in 1938 that withdrew resident status from all foreign Jews, Maja moved to Princeton on her own. Einstein, who loved her dearly and liked her immensely, was thrilled.

Einstein also encouraged Hans Albert, now 33, to come to America, at least for a visit. Their relationship had been rocky, but Einstein had come to admire the diligence of his son's engineering work, especially regarding the flow of rivers, a topic he had once studied himself.[52] He had also changed his mind and encouraged his son to have children, and he was now happy to have two young grandsons.

In October 1937, Hans Albert arrived for a three-month stay. Einstein met him at the pier, where they posed for photographs, and Hans Albert playfully lit a long Dutch pipe he had brought his father. "My father would like me to come here with my family," he said. "You know his wife died recently and he is all alone now."[53]

During the visit, young and eager Peter Bucky offered to drive Hans Albert across America so that he could visit universities and seek positions as an engineering professor. The trip, which covered ten thousand miles, took them to Salt Lake City, Los Angeles, Iowa City, Knoxville, Vicksburg, Cleveland, Chicago, Detroit, and Indianapolis.[54] Einstein reported to Mileva Marić how much he had enjoyed being with their son. "He has such a great personality," he wrote. "It is unfortunate that he has this wife, but what can you do if he's happy?"[55]

Einstein had written Frieda a few months earlier and suggested that she not accompany her husband on the trip.[56] But with his affection for Hans Albert fully restored, Einstein urged both of them to return together the following year, with their two children, and stay in America. They did. Hans Albert found a job studying soil conservation at a U.S. Department of Agriculture extension station in Clemson,

South Carolina, where he became an authority on alluvial transport by rivers. Displaying his father's taste, he built a simple wooden house, reminiscent of that in Caputh, in nearby Greenville, where he applied for American citizenship in December 1938.[57]

While his father was becoming more connected to his Jewish heritage, Hans Albert became, under the influence of his wife, a Christian Scientist. The rejection of medical care, as sometimes entailed by that faith, had tragic results. A few months after their arrival, their 6-year-old son, Klaus, contracted diphtheria and died. He was buried at a tiny new cemetery in Greenville. "The deepest sorrow loving parents can experience has come upon you," Einstein wrote in a condolence note. His relationship with his son became increasingly secure and even, at times, affectionate.

During the five years that Hans Albert lived in South Carolina, before moving to Caltech and then Berkeley, Einstein would occasionally take the train down to visit. There they would discuss engineering puzzles that reminded Einstein of his days at the Swiss patent office. In the afternoon, he would sometimes wander the roads and forests, often in dreamy thought, spawning colorful anecdotes from astonished locals who helped him find his way home.[58]

Because he was a mental patient, Eduard was not allowed to immigrate to America. As his illness progressed, his face became bloated, his speech slow. Marić increasingly had trouble allowing him back home, so his stays in the institution became more prolonged. Her sister Zorka, who had come to help care for them, descended into her own hell. After their mother died, she became an alcoholic, accidentally burned all the family money, which had been hidden in an old stove, and died a recluse in 1938 on a straw-covered floor surrounded only by her cats.[59] Marić lived on, through it all, in increasing despair.

Prewar Politics

In retrospect, the rise of the Nazis created a fundamental moral challenge for America. At the time, however, this was not so clear. That was especially true in Princeton, which was a conservative town, and at its university, which harbored a surprising number of students who shared the amorphous anti-Semitic attitude found among some in their social class. A survey of incoming freshmen in 1938 produced a result that is now astonishing, and should have been back then as well: Adolf Hitler polled highest as the "greatest living person." Albert Einstein was second.[60]

"Why do They Hate the Jews?" Einstein wrote in an article for the popular weekly *Collier's* that year. He used the article not just to explore anti-Semitism but also to explain how the social creed inbred in most Jews, which he personally tried to live by, was part of a long and proud tradition. "The bond that has united the Jews for thousands of years and that unites them today is, above all, the democratic ideal of social justice coupled with the ideal of mutual aid and tolerance among all men."[61]

His kinship with his fellow Jews, and his horror at the plight that was befalling them, plunged him into the effort for refugee relief. It was both a public and a private endeavor. He gave dozens of speeches for the cause, was feted at even more dinners, and even gave occasional violin recitals for the American Friends Service Committee or the United Jewish Appeal. One gimmick that organizers used was to have people write their checks to Einstein himself. He would then endorse them to the charity. The donor would thus have as a keepsake a cancelled check with Einstein's autograph.[62] He also quietly backed scores of individuals who needed financial guarantees in order to emigrate, especially as the United States made it harder to get visas.

Einstein also became a supporter of racial tolerance. When Marian Anderson, the black contralto, came to Princeton for a concert in 1937, the Nassau Inn refused her a room. So Einstein invited her to stay at his house on Mercer Street, in what was a deeply personal as well as a publicly symbolic gesture. Two years later, when she was barred from performing in Washington's Constitution Hall, she gave what became a historic free concert on the steps of the Lincoln Memorial. Whenever she returned to Princeton, she stayed with Einstein, her last visit coming just two months before he died.[63]

One problem with Einstein's willingness to sign on to various and sundry movements, appeals, and honorary chairmanships was that, as before, it opened him to charges that he was a dupe for those that were fronts for communists or other subversives. This purported sin was compounded, in the eyes of those who were suspicious about his loyalty, when he declined to sign on to some crusades that attacked Stalin or the Soviets.

For example, when his friend Isaac Don Levine, whose anticommunist writings Einstein had previously endorsed, asked him to sign a petition in 1934 condemning Stalin's murder of political prisoners, this time Einstein balked. "I, too, regret immensely that the Russian political leaders let themselves be carried away," Einstein wrote. "In spite of this, I cannot associate myself with your action. It will have no impact in Russia. The Russians have proved that their only aim is really the improvement of the lot of the Russian people."[64]

It was a gauzy view of the Russians and of Stalin's murderous regime, one that history would prove wrong. Einstein was so intent on fighting the Nazis, and so annoyed that Levine had shifted so radically from left to right, that he reacted strongly against those who would equate the Russian purges with the Nazi holocaust.

An even larger set of trials in Moscow began in 1936, involving supporters of the exiled Leon Trotsky, and again Einstein rebuffed some of his former friends from the left who had now swung to become ardently anticommunist. The philosopher Sidney Hook, a recovering Marxist, wrote Einstein, asking him to speak out in favor of the creation of an international public commission to assure that Trotsky and his supporters would get a fair hearing rather than merely a show trial. "There is no doubt that every accused person should be given an opportunity to establish his innocence," Einstein replied. "This certainly holds true for Trotsky." But how should this be accomplished? Einstein suggested it would best be done privately, without a public commission.[65]

In a very long letter, Hook tried to rebut each of Einstein's concerns, but Einstein lost interest in arguing with Hook and did not respond. So Hook phoned him in Princeton. He reached Helen Dukas, and somehow was able to make it through her defensive shield to set up an appointment.

Einstein received Hook cordially, brought him up to his study lair, smoked his pipe, and spoke in English. After listening to Hook again make his case, Einstein expressed sympathy but said he thought the whole enterprise was unlikely to succeed. "From my point of view," he proclaimed, "both Stalin and Trotsky are political gangsters." Hook later said that even though he disagreed with Einstein, "I could appreciate his reasons," especially because Einstein emphasized that he was "aware of what communists were capable of doing."

Wearing an old sweatshirt and no socks, Einstein walked Hook back to the train station. Along the way, he explained his anger at the Germans. They had raided his house in Caputh searching for communist weapons, he said, and found only a bread knife to confiscate. One remark he made turned out to be very prescient. "If and when war comes," he said, "Hitler will realize the harm he has done Germany by driving out the Jewish scientists."[66]

CHAPTER TWENTY

QUANTUM ENTANGLEMENT

1935

"Spooky Action at a Distance"

The thought experiments that Einstein had lobbed like grenades into the temple of quantum mechanics had done little damage to the edifice. In fact, they helped test it and permit a better understanding of its implications. But Einstein remained a resister, and he continued to conjure up new ways to show that the uncertainties inherent in the interpretations formulated by Niels Bohr, Werner Heisenberg, Max Born, and others meant that something was missing in their explanation of "reality."

Just before he left Europe in 1933, Einstein attended a lecture by Léon Rosenfeld, a Belgian physicist with a philosophical bent. When it was over, Einstein rose from the audience to ask a question. "Suppose two particles are set in motion towards each other with the same, very large, momentum, and they interact with each other for a very short time when they pass at known positions," he posited. When the particles have bounced far apart, an observer measures the momentum of one of them. "Then, from the conditions of the experiment, he will obviously be able to deduce the momentum of the other particle," Einstein said. "If, however, he chooses to measure the position of the first particle, he will be able to tell where the other particle is."

Because the two particles were far apart, Einstein was able to assert, or at least to *assume*, that "all physical interaction has ceased between them." So his challenge to the Copenhagen interpreters of quantum mechanics, posed as a question to Rosenfeld, was simple: "How can the final state of the second particle be influenced by a measurement performed on the first?"[1]

Over the years, Einstein had increasingly come to embrace the concept of realism, the belief that there is, as he put it, "a real factual situation" that exists "independent of our observations."[2] This belief was one aspect of his discomfort with Heisenberg's uncertainty principle and other tenets of quantum mechanics that assert that observations determine realities. With his question to Rosenfeld, Einstein was deploying another concept: locality.* In other words, if two particles are spatially distant from each other, anything that happens to one is independent from what happens to the other, and no signal or force or influence can move between them faster than the speed of light.

Observing or poking one particle, Einstein posited, could not *instantaneously* jostle or jangle another one far away. The only way an action on one system can affect a distant one is if some wave or signal or information traveled between them—a process that would have to obey the speed limit of light. That was even true of gravity. If the sun suddenly disappeared, it would not affect the earth's orbit for about eight minutes, the amount of time it would take the change in the gravitational field to ripple to the earth at the speed of light.

As Einstein said, "There is one supposition we should, in my opinion, absolutely hold fast: the *real factual situation* of the system S_2 is independent of what is done with the system S_1, which is spatially separated from the former."[3] It was so intuitive that it seemed obvious. But as Einstein noted, it was a "supposition." It had never been proven.

---

* There are two related concepts that Einstein uses. *Separability* means that different particles or systems that occupy different regions in space have an independent reality; *locality* means that an action involving one of these particles or systems cannot influence a particle or system in another part of space unless something travels the distance between them, a process limited by the speed of light.

To Einstein, realism and localism were related underpinnings of physics. As he declared to his friend Max Born, coining a memorable phrase, "Physics should represent a reality in time and space, free from spooky action at a distance."[4]

Once he had settled in Princeton, Einstein began to refine this thought experiment. His sidekick, Walther Mayer, less loyal to Einstein than Einstein was to him, had drifted away from the front lines of fighting quantum mechanics, so Einstein enlisted the help of Nathan Rosen, a 26-year-old new fellow at the Institute, and Boris Podolsky, a 49-year-old physicist Einstein had met at Caltech who had since moved to the Institute.

The resulting four-page paper, published in May 1935 and known by the initials of its authors as the EPR paper, was the most important paper Einstein would write after moving to America. "Can the Quantum-Mechanical Description of Physical Reality Be Regarded as Complete?" they asked in their title.

Rosen did a lot of the math, and Podolsky wrote the published English version. Even though they had discussed the content at length, Einstein was displeased that Podolsky had buried the clear conceptual issue under a lot of mathematical formalism. "It did not come out as well as I had originally wanted," Einstein complained to Schrödinger right after it was published. "Rather, the essential thing was, so to speak, smothered by the formalism."[5]

Einstein was also annoyed at Podolsky for leaking the contents to the *New York Times* before it was published. The headline read: "Einstein Attacks Quantum Theory / Scientist and Two Colleagues Find It Not 'Complete' Even though 'Correct.' " Einstein, of course, had occasionally succumbed to giving interviews about upcoming articles, but this time he declared himself dismayed by the practice. "It is my invariable practice to discuss scientific matters only in the appropriate forum," he wrote in a statement to the *Times,* "and I deprecate advance publication of any announcement in regard to such matters in the secular press."[6]

Einstein and his two coauthors began by defining their realist premise: "If without in any way disturbing a system we can predict with certainty the value of a physical quantity, then there exists an element of physical *reality* corresponding to this physical quantity."[7] In other words, if by some process we could learn with absolute certainty the position of a particle, and we have not disturbed the particle by observing it, then we can say the particle's position is real, that it exists in reality totally independent of our observations.

The paper went on to expand Einstein's thought experiment about two particles that have collided (or have flown off in opposite directions from the disintegration of an atom) and therefore have properties that are correlated. We can take measurements of the first particle, the authors asserted, and from that gain knowledge about the second particle "without in any way disturbing the second particle." By measuring the position of the first particle, we can determine precisely the position of the second particle. And we can do the same for the momentum. "In accordance with our criterion for reality, in the first case we must consider the quantity P as being an element of reality, in the second case the quantity Q is an element of reality."

In simpler words: at any moment the second particle, which we have not observed, has a position that is real and a momentum that is real. These two properties are features of reality that quantum mechanics does not account for; thus the answer to the title's question should be no, quantum mechanics' description of reality is not complete.[8]

The only alternative, the authors argued, would be to claim that the process of measuring the first particle affects the reality of the position and momentum of the second particle. "No reasonable definition of reality could be expected to permit this," they concluded.

Wolfgang Pauli wrote Heisenberg a long and angry letter. "Einstein has once again expressed himself publicly on quantum mechanics (together with Podolsky and Rosen—no good company, by the way)," he fumed. "As is well known, every time that happens it is a catastrophe."[9]

When the EPR paper reached Niels Bohr in Copenhagen, he realized that he had once again been cast in the role, which he played so well at the Solvay Conferences, of defending quantum mechanics from yet another Einstein assault. "This onslaught came down on us as a bolt from the blue," a colleague of Bohr's reported. "Its effect on Bohr was remarkable." He had often reacted to such situations by wandering around and muttering, "Einstein . . . Einstein . . . Einstein!" This time he added some collaborative doggerel as well: "Podolsky, Opodolsky, Iopodolsky, Siopodolsky . . ."[10]

"Everything else was abandoned," Bohr's colleague recalled. "We had to clear up such a misunderstanding at once." Even with such intensity, it took Bohr more than six weeks of fretting, writing, revising, dictating, and talking aloud before he finally sent off his response to EPR.

It was longer than the original paper. In it Bohr backed away somewhat from what had been an aspect of the uncertainty principle: that the mechanical disturbance caused by the act of observation was a cause of the uncertainty. He admitted that in Einstein's thought experiment, "there is no question of a mechanical disturbance of the system under investigation."[11]

This was an important admission. Until then, the disturbance caused by a measurement had been part of Bohr's physical explanation of quantum uncertainty. At the Solvay Conferences, he had rebutted Einstein's ingenious thought experiments by showing that the simultaneous knowledge of, say, position and momentum was impossible at least in part because determining one attribute caused a disturbance that made it impossible to then measure the other attribute precisely.

However, using his concept of complementarity, Bohr added a significant caveat. He pointed out that the two particles were part of one whole phenomenon. Because they have interacted, the two particles are therefore "entangled." They are part of one whole phenomenon or one whole system that has one quantum function.

In addition, the EPR paper did not, as Bohr noted, truly dispel the uncertainty principle, which says that it is not possible to know *both* the precise position and momentum of a particle *at the same moment*. Einstein is correct, that if we measure the *position* of particle A, we can indeed know the *position* of its distant twin B. Likewise, if we measure the *momentum* of A, we can know the *momentum* of B. However, even if we can *imagine* measuring the position and then the momentum of particle A, and thus ascribe a "reality" to those attributes in particle B, we cannot *in fact* measure *both* these attributes precisely at any one time for particle A, and thus we cannot know them both precisely for particle B. Brian Greene, discussing Bohr's response, has put it simply: "If you don't have both of these attributes of the right-moving particle in hand, you don't have them for the left-moving particle either. Thus there is no conflict with the uncertainty principle."[12]

Einstein continued to insist, however, that he had pinpointed an important example of the incompleteness of quantum mechanics by showing how it violated the principle of separability, which holds that two systems that are spatially separated have an independent existence. It likewise violated the related principle of locality, which says that an action on one of these systems cannot immediately affect the other. As an adherent of field theory, which defines reality using a spacetime continuum, Einstein believed that separability was a fundamental feature of nature. And as a defender of his own theory of relativity, which rid Newton's cosmos of spooky action at a distance and decreed instead that such actions obey the speed limit of light, he believed in locality as well.[13]

Schrödinger's Cat

Despite his success as a quantum pioneer, Erwin Schrödinger was among those rooting for Einstein to succeed in deflating the Copenhagen consensus. Their alliance had been forged at the Solvay Conferences, where Einstein played God's advocate and Schrödinger looked on with a mix of curiosity and sympathy. It was a lonely struggle, Einstein lamented in a letter to Schrödinger in 1928: "The Heisenberg-Bohr tranquilizing philosophy—or religion?—is so delicately contrived that, for the time being, it provides a gentle pillow for the true believer from which he cannot very easily be aroused."[14]

So it was not surprising that Schrödinger sent Einstein a congratulatory note as soon as he read the EPR paper. "You have publicly caught dogmatic quantum mechanics by its throat," he wrote. A few weeks later, he added happily, "Like a pike in a goldfish pond it has stirred everyone up."[15]

Schrödinger had just visited Princeton, and Einstein was still hoping, in vain, that Flexner might be convinced to hire him for the Institute. In his subsequent flurry of exchanges with Schrödinger, Einstein began conspiring with him on ways to poke holes in quantum mechanics.

"I do not believe in it," Einstein declared flatly. He ridiculed as "spiritualistic" the notion that there could be "spooky action at a distance," and he attacked the idea that there was no reality beyond our ability to observe things. "This epistemology-soaked orgy ought to burn itself out," he said. "No doubt, however, you smile at me and think that, after all, many a young whore turns into an old praying sister, and many a young revolutionary becomes an old reactionary."[16] Schrödinger did smile, he told Einstein in his reply, because he had likewise edged from revolutionary to old reactionary.

On one issue Einstein and Schrödinger diverged. Schrödinger did not feel that the concept of locality was sacred. He even coined the term that we now use, *entanglement*, to describe the correlations that exist between two particles that have interacted but are now distant from each other. The quantum states of two particles that have interacted must subsequently be described together, with any changes to one particle instantly being reflected in the other, no matter how far apart they now are. "Entanglement of predictions arises from the fact that the two bodies at some earlier time formed in a true sense *one* system, that is were interacting, and have left behind *traces* on each other," Schrödinger wrote. "If two separated bodies enter a situation in which they influence each other, and separate again, then there occurs what I have just called *entanglement* of our knowledge of the two bodies."[17]

Einstein and Schrödinger together began exploring another way— one that did not hinge on issues of locality or separation—to raise questions about quantum mechanics. Their new approach was to look at what would occur when an event in the quantum realm, which includes subatomic particles, interacted with objects in the macro world, which includes those things we normally see in our daily lives.

In the quantum realm, there is no definite location of a particle, such as an electron, at any given moment. Instead, a mathematical function, known as a wave function, describes the probability of finding the particle in some particular place. These wave functions also describe quantum states, such as the probability that an atom will, when observed, be decayed or not. In 1925, Schrödinger had come up with his famous equation that described these waves, which spread and smear throughout space. His equation defined the probability that a particle, when observed, will be found in a particular place or state.[18]

According to the Copenhagen interpretation developed by Niels Bohr and his fellow pioneers of quantum mechanics, until such an observation is made, the reality of the particle's position or state consists only of these probabilities. By measuring or observing the system, the observer causes the wave function to collapse and one distinct position or state to snap into place.

In a letter to Schrödinger, Einstein gave a vivid thought experiment showing why all this discussion of wave functions and probabilities, and of particles that have no definite positions until observed, failed his test of completeness. He imagined two boxes, one of which we know contains a ball. As we prepare to look in one of the boxes, there is a 50 percent chance of the ball being there. After we look, there is either a 100 percent or a 0 percent chance it is in there. But all along, *in reality*, the ball was in one of the boxes. Einstein wrote:

> I describe a state of affairs as follows: the probability is ½ that the ball is in the first box. Is that a complete description? NO: A complete statement is: the ball *is* (or is not) in the first box. That is how the characterization of the state of affairs must appear in a complete description. YES: Before I open them, the ball is by no means in *one* of the two boxes. Being in a definite box comes about only when I lift the covers.[19]

Einstein clearly preferred the former explanation, a statement of his realism. He felt that there was something incomplete about the second answer, which was the way quantum mechanics explained things.

Einstein's argument is based on what appears to be common sense. However, sometimes what seems to make sense turns out not to be a good description of nature. Einstein realized this when he developed his relativity theory; he defied the accepted common sense of the time and forced us to change the way we think about nature. Quantum mechanics does something similar. It asserts that particles do not have a definite state except when observed, and two particles can be in an entangled state so that the observation of one determines a property of the other instantly. As soon as any observation is made, the system goes into a fixed state.[20]

Einstein never accepted this as a complete description of reality, and along these lines he proposed another thought experiment to Schrödinger a few weeks later, in early August 1935. It involved a situation in which quantum mechanics would assign only probabilities, even though common sense tells us that there is *obviously* an underlying reality that exists with certainty. Imagine a pile of gunpowder that, due to the instability of some particle, will combust at some point, Einstein said. The quantum mechanical equation for this situation "describes a sort of blend of not-yet and already-exploded systems." But this is not "a *real* state of affairs," Einstein said, "for *in reality* there is just no intermediary between exploded and not-exploded."[21]

Schrödinger came up with a similar thought experiment—involving a soon-to-be-famous fictional feline rather than a pile of gunpowder—to show the weirdness inherent when the indeterminacy of the quantum realm interacts with our normal world of larger objects. "In a lengthy essay that I have just written, I give an example that is very similar to your exploding powder keg," he told Einstein.[22]

In this essay, published that November, Schrödinger gave generous credit to Einstein and the EPR paper for "providing the impetus" for his argument. It poked at a core concept in quantum mechanics, namely that the timing of the emission of a particle from a decaying nucleus is indeterminate until it is actually observed. In the quantum world, a nucleus is in a "superposition," meaning it exists simultaneously as being decayed and undecayed until it is observed, at which point its wave function collapses and it becomes either one or the other.

This may be conceivable for the microscopic quantum realm, but it is baffling when one imagines the intersection between the quantum realm and our observable everyday world. So, Schrödinger asked in his thought experiment, when does the system stop being in a superposition incorporating both states and snap into being one reality?

This question led to the precarious fate of an imaginary creature, which was destined to become immortal whether it was dead or alive, known as Schrödinger's cat:

> One can even set up quite ridiculous cases. A cat is penned up in a steel
> chamber, along with the following device (which must be secured
> against direct interference by the cat): in a Geiger counter there is a tiny

bit of radioactive substance, *so* small, that *perhaps* in the course of the hour one of the atoms decays, but also, with equal probability, perhaps none; if it happens, the counter tube discharges and through a relay releases a hammer which shatters a small flask of hydrocyanic acid. If one has left this entire system to itself for an hour, one would say that the cat still lives *if* meanwhile no atom has decayed. The psi-function of the entire system would express this by having in it the living and dead cat (pardon the expression) mixed or smeared out.[23]

Einstein was thrilled. "Your cat shows that we are in complete agreement concerning our assessment of the character of the current theory," he wrote back. "A psi-function that contains the living as well as the dead cat just cannot be taken as a description of a real state of affairs."[24]

The case of Schrödinger's cat has spawned reams of responses that continue to pour forth with varying degrees of comprehensibility. Suffice it to say that in the Copenhagen interpretation of quantum mechanics, a system stops being a superposition of states and snaps into a single reality when it is observed, but there is no clear rule for what constitutes such an observation. Can the cat be an observer? A flea? A computer? A mechanical recording device? There's no set answer. However, we do know that quantum effects generally are not observed in our everyday visible world, which includes cats and even fleas. So most adherents of quantum mechanics would not argue that Schrödinger's cat is sitting in that box somehow being both dead and alive until the lid is opened.[25]

Einstein never lost faith in the ability of Schrödinger's cat and his own gunpowder thought experiments of 1935 to expose the incompleteness of quantum mechanics. Nor has he received proper historical credit for helping give birth to that poor cat. In fact, he would later mistakenly give Schrödinger credit for both of the thought experiments in a letter that exposed the animal to being blown up rather than poisoned. "Contemporary physicists somehow believe that the quantum theory provides a description of reality, and even a *complete* description," Einstein wrote Schrödinger in 1950. "This interpretation is, however, refuted most elegantly by your system of radioactive atom + Geiger counter + amplifier + charge of gunpowder + cat in a box, in which the psi-function of the system contains the cat both alive and blown to bits." [26]

Einstein's so-called mistakes, such as the cosmological constant he added to his gravitational field equations, often turned out to be more intriguing than other people's successes. The same was true of his parries against Bohr and Heisenberg. The EPR paper would not succeed in showing that quantum mechanics was wrong. But it did eventually become clear that quantum mechanics was, as Einstein argued, incompatible with our commonsense understanding of locality—our aversion to spooky action at a distance. The odd thing is that Einstein, apparently, was far more right than he hoped to be.

In the years since he came up with the EPR thought experiment, the idea of entanglement and spooky action at a distance—the quantum weirdness in which an observation of one particle can instantly affect another one far away—has increasingly become part of what experimental physicists study. In 1951, David Bohm, a brilliant assistant professor at Princeton, recast the EPR thought experiment so that it involved the opposite "spins" of two particles flying apart from an interaction. [27] In 1964, John Stewart Bell, who worked at the CERN nuclear research facility near Geneva, wrote a paper that proposed a way to conduct experiments based on this approach. [28]

Bell was less than comfortable with quantum mechanics. "I hesitated to think it was wrong," he once said, "but I knew that it was rotten." [29] That, plus his admiration of Einstein, caused him to express some hope that Einstein rather than Bohr might be proven right. But when the experiments were undertaken in the 1980s by the French physicist Alain Aspect and others, they provided evidence that locality was not a feature of the quantum world. "Spooky action at a distance," or, more precisely, the potential entanglement of distant particles, was. [30]

Even so, Bell ended up appreciating Einstein's efforts. "I felt that Einstein's intellectual superiority over Bohr, in this instance, was enormous, a vast gulf between the man who saw clearly what was needed, and the obscurantist," he said. "So for me, it is a pity that Einstein's idea doesn't work. The reasonable thing just doesn't work." [31]

Quantum entanglement—an idea discussed by Einstein in 1935 as a way of undermining quantum mechanics—is now one of the weirder elements of physics, because it is so counterintuitive. Every year the evidence for it mounts, and public fascination with it grows. At the end of 2005, for example, the *New York Times* published a survey article called "Quantum Trickery: Testing Einstein's Strangest Theory," by Dennis Overbye, in which Cornell physicist N. David Mermin called it "the closest thing we have to magic."[32] And in 2006, the *New Scientist* ran a story titled "Einstein's 'Spooky Action' Seen on a Chip," which began:

> A simple semiconductor chip has been used to generate pairs of entangled photons, a vital step towards making quantum computers a reality. Famously dubbed "spooky action at a distance" by Einstein, entanglement is the mysterious phenomenon of quantum particles whereby two particles such as photons behave as one regardless of how far apart they are.[33]

Might this spooky action at a distance—where something that happens to a particle in one place can be instantly reflected by one that is billions of miles away—violate the speed limit of light? No, the theory of relativity still seems safe. The two particles, though distant, remain part of the same physical entity. By observing one of them, we may affect its attributes, and that is correlated to what would be observed of the second particle. But no information is transmitted, no signal sent, and there is no traditional cause-and-effect relationship. One can show by thought experiments that quantum entanglement cannot be used to send information instantaneously. "In short," says physicist Brian Greene, "special relativity survives by the skin of its teeth."[34]

During the past few decades, a number of theorists, including Murray Gell-Mann and James Hartle, have adopted a view of quantum mechanics that differs in some ways from the Copenhagen interpretation and provides an easier explanation of the EPR thought experiment. Their interpretation is based on alternative histories of the universe, coarse-grained in the sense that they follow only certain variables and ignore (or average over) the rest. These "decoherent" histories form a tree-like structure, with each of the alternatives at one time branching out into alternatives at the next time and so forth.

In the case of the EPR thought experiment, the position of one of the two particles is measured on one branch of history. Because of the common origin of the particles, the position of the other one is determined as well. On a different branch of history, the momentum of one of the particles may be measured, and the momentum of the other one is also determined. On each branch nothing occurs that violates the laws of classical physics. The information about one particle *implies* the corresponding information about the other one, but nothing *happens* to the second particle as a result of the measurement of the first one. So there is no threat to special relativity and its prohibition of instantaneous transmission of information. What is special about quantum mechanics is that the simultaneous determination of the position and the momentum of a particle is impossible, so if these two determinations occur, it must be on different branches of history.[35]

"Physics and Reality"

Einstein's fundamental dispute with the Bohr-Heisenberg crowd over quantum mechanics was not merely about whether God rolled dice or left cats half dead. Nor was it just about causality, locality, or even completeness. It was about reality.[36] Does it exist? More specifically, is it meaningful to speak about a physical reality that exists independently of whatever observations we can make? "At the heart of the problem," Einstein said of quantum mechanics, "is not so much the question of causality but the question of realism."[37]

Bohr and his adherents scoffed at the idea that it made sense to talk about what might be beneath the veil of what we can observe. All we can know are the results of our experiments and observations, not some ultimate reality that lies beyond our perceptions.

Einstein had displayed some elements of this attitude in 1905, back when he was reading Hume and Mach while rejecting such unobservable concepts as absolute space and time. "At that time my mode of thinking was much nearer positivism than it was later on," he recalled.

"My departure from positivism came only when I worked out the general theory of relativity." [38]

From then on, Einstein increasingly adhered to the belief that there *is* an objective classical reality. And though there are some consistencies between his early and late thinking, he admitted freely that, at least in his own mind, his realism represented a move away from his earlier Machian empiricism. "This credo," he said, "does not correspond with the point of view I held in younger years." [39] As the historian Gerald Holton notes, "For a scientist to change his philosophical beliefs so fundamentally is rare." [40]

Einstein's concept of realism had three main components:

1. His belief that a reality exists independent of our ability to observe it. As he put it in his autobiographical notes: "Physics is an attempt conceptually to grasp reality as it is thought independently of its being observed. In this sense one speaks of 'physical reality.'" [41]

2. His belief in separability and locality. In other words, objects are located at certain points in spacetime, and this separability is part of what defines them. "If one abandons the assumption that what exists in different parts of space has its own independent, real existence, then I simply cannot see what it is that physics is supposed to describe," he declared to Max Born. [42]

3. His belief in strict causality, which implies certainty and classical determinism. The idea that probabilities play a role in reality was as disconcerting to him as the idea that our observations might play a role in collapsing those probabilities. "Some physicists, among them myself, cannot believe," he said, "that we must accept the view that events in nature are analogous to a game of chance." [43]

It is possible to imagine a realism that has only two, or even just one, of these three attributes, and on occasion Einstein pondered such a possibility. Scholars have debated which of these three was most fundamental to his thinking. [44] But Einstein kept coming back to the hope, and faith, that all three attributes go together. As he said in a speech to a doctors convention in Cleveland near the end of his life, "Everything should lead back to conceptual objects in the realm of space and time and to lawlike relations that obtain for these objects." [45]

At the heart of this realism was an almost religious, or perhaps childlike, awe at the way all of our sense perceptions—the random sights and sounds that we experience every minute—fit into patterns, follow rules, and make sense. We take it for granted when these perceptions piece together to represent what seem to be external objects, and it does not amaze us when laws seem to govern the behavior of these objects.

But just as he felt awe when first pondering a compass as a child, Einstein was able to feel awe that there are rules ordering our perceptions, rather than pure randomness. Reverence for this astonishing and unexpected comprehensibility of the universe was the foundation for his realism as well as the defining character of what he called his religious faith.

He expressed this in a 1936 essay, "Physics and Reality," written on the heels of his defense of realism in the debates over quantum mechanics. "The very fact that the totality of our sense experiences is such that, by means of thinking, it can be put in order, this fact is one that leaves us in awe," he wrote. "The eternal mystery of the world is its comprehensibility . . . The fact that it is comprehensible is a miracle." [46]

His friend Maurice Solovine, with whom he had read Hume and Mach in the days of the Olympia Academy, told Einstein that he found it "strange" that he considered the comprehensibility of the world to be "a miracle or an eternal mystery." Einstein countered that it would be logical to assume that the opposite was the case. "Well, a priori, one should expect a chaotic world which cannot be grasped by the mind in any way," he wrote. "There lies the weakness of positivists and professional atheists." [47] Einstein was neither.

To Einstein, this belief in the existence of an underlying reality had a religious aura to it. That dismayed Solovine, who wrote to say that he had an "aversion" to such language. Einstein disagreed. "I have no better expression than 'religious' for this confidence in the rational nature of reality and in its being accessible, to some degree, to human reason.

When this feeling is missing, science degenerates into mindless empiricism."[48]

Einstein knew that the new generation viewed him as an out-of-touch conservative clinging to the old certainties of classical physics, and that amused him. "Even the great initial success of the quantum theory does not make me believe in a fundamental dice-game," he told his friend Max Born, "although I am well aware that our younger colleagues interpret this as a consequence of senility."[49]

Born, who loved Einstein dearly, agreed with the Young Turks that Einstein had become as "conservative" as the physicists of a generation earlier who had balked at his relativity theory. "He could no longer take in certain new ideas in physics which contradicted his own firmly held philosophical convictions."[50]

But Einstein preferred to think of himself not as a conservative but as (again) a rebel, a nonconformist, one with the curiosity and stubbornness to buck prevailing fads. "The necessity of conceiving of nature as an *objective reality* is said to be obsolete prejudice while the quantum theoreticians are vaunted," he told Solovine in 1938. "Each period is dominated by a mood, with the result that most men fail to see the tyrant who rules over them."[51]

Einstein pushed his realist approach in a textbook on the history of physics that he coauthored in 1938, *The Evolution of Physics.* Belief in an "objective reality," the book argued, had led to great scientific advances throughout the ages, thus proving that it was a useful concept even if not provable. "Without the belief that it is possible to grasp reality with our theoretical constructions, without the belief in the inner harmony of our world, there could be no science," the book declared. "This belief is and always will remain the fundamental motive for all scientific creation."[52]

In addition, Einstein used the text to defend the utility of field theories amid the advances of quantum mechanics. The best way to do that was to view particles not as independent objects but as a special manifestation of the field itself:

> There is no sense in regarding matter and field as two qualities quite different from each other . . . Could we not reject the concept of matter and build a pure field physics? We could regard matter as the regions in

space where the field is extremely strong. A thrown stone is, from this point of view, a changing field in which the states of the greatest field intensity travel through space with the velocity of the stone.[53]

There was a third reason that Einstein helped to write this textbook, a more personal one. He wanted to help Leopold Infeld, a Jew who had fled Poland, collaborated briefly in Cambridge with Max Born, and then moved to Princeton.[54] Infeld began working on relativity with Banesh Hoffmann, and he proposed that they offer themselves to Einstein. "Let's see if he'd like us to work with him," Infeld suggested.

Einstein was delighted. "We did all the dirty work of calculating the equations and so on," Hoffmann recalled. "We reported the results to Einstein and then it was like having a headquarters conference. Sometimes his ideas seemed to come from left field, to be quite extraordinary."[55] Working with Infeld and Hoffmann, Einstein in 1937 came up with elegant ways to explain more simply the motion of planets and other massive objects that produced their own curvatures of space.

But their work on unified field theory never quite gelled. At times, the situation seemed so hopeless that Infeld and Hoffmann became despondent. "But Einstein's courage never faltered, nor did his inventiveness fail him," Hoffmann recalled. "When excited discussion failed to break the deadlock, Einstein would quietly say in his quaint English, 'I will a little tink.'" The room would become silent, and Einstein would pace slowly up and down or walk around in circles, twirling a lock of his hair around his forefinger. "There was a dreamy, far-away, yet inward look on his face. No sign of stress. No outward indication of intense concentration." After a few minutes, he would suddenly return to the world, "a smile on his face and an answer to the problem on his lips."[56]

Einstein was so pleased with Infeld's help that he tried to get Flexner to give him a post at the Institute. But Flexner, who was annoyed that the Institute had already been forced to hire Walther Mayer, balked. Einstein even went to a fellows meeting in person, which he rarely did, to argue for a mere $600 stipend for Infeld, but to no avail.[57]

So Infeld came up with a plan to write a history of physics with Einstein, which was sure to be successful, and split the royalties. When he went to Einstein to pitch the idea, Infeld became incredibly tongue-tied, but he was finally able to stammer out his proposal. "This is not at all a stupid idea," Einstein said. "Not stupid at all. We shall do it."[58]

In April 1937, Richard Simon and Max Schuster, founders of the house that published this biography, drove out to Einstein's home in Princeton to secure the rights. The gregarious Schuster tried to win Einstein over with jokes. He had discovered something faster than the speed of light, he said: "The speed with which a woman arriving in Paris goes shopping."[59] Einstein was amused, or at least so Schuster recalled. In any event, the trip was successful, and the *Evolution of Physics*, which is in its forty-fourth printing, not only propagandized for the role of field theories and a faith in objective reality, it also made Infeld (and Einstein) more secure financially.

No one could accuse Infeld of being ungrateful. He later called Einstein "perhaps the greatest scientist and kindest man who ever lived." He also wrote a flattering biography of Einstein, while his mentor was still alive, that praised him for his willingness to defy conventional thinking in his quest for a unified theory. "His tenacity in sticking to a problem for years, in returning to the problem again and again—this is the characteristic feature of Einstein's genius," he wrote.[60]

Against the Current

Was Infeld right? Was tenacity the characteristic feature of Einstein's genius? To some extent he had always been blessed by this trait, especially in his long and lonely quest to generalize relativity. There was also ingrained in him, since his school days, a willingness to sail against the current and defy the reigning authorities. All of this was evident in his quest for a unified theory.

But even though he liked to claim that an analysis of empirical data had played a minimal role in the construction of his great theories, he had generally been graced with an intuitive feel for the insights and principles that could be wrested from nature based on current experiments and observations. This trait was now becoming less evident.

By the late 1930s, he was becoming increasingly detached from new experimental discoveries. Instead of the unification of gravity and electromagnetism, there was greater disunity as two new forces, the weak and the strong nuclear forces, were found. "Einstein chose to ignore those new forces, although they were not any less fundamental than the two which have been known about longer," his friend Abraham Pais recalled. "He continued the old search for a unification of gravitation and electromagnetism."[61]

In addition, a menagerie of new fundamental particles were discovered beginning in the 1930s. Currently there are dozens of them, ranging from bosons such as photons and gluons to fermions such as electrons, positrons, up quarks, and down quarks. This did not seem to bode well for Einstein's quest to unify everything. His friend Wolfgang Pauli, who joined him at the Institute in 1940, quipped about the futility of this quest. "What God has put asunder," he said, "let no man join together."[62]

Einstein found the new discoveries to be vaguely disconcerting, but he felt comfortable not putting much emphasis on them. "I can derive only small pleasure from the great discoveries, because for the time being they do not seem to facilitate for me an understanding of the foundations," he wrote Max von Laue. "I feel like a kid who cannot get the hang of the ABCs, even though, strangely enough, I do not abandon hope. After all, one is dealing here with a sphinx, not with a willing streetwalker."[63]

So Einstein beat on against the current, borne back ceaselessly into the past. He realized that he had the luxury to pursue his lonely course, something that would be too risky for younger physicists still trying to make their reputations.[64] But as it turned out, there were usually at least two or three younger physicists, attracted by Einstein's aura, willing to collaborate with him, even if the vast majority of the physics priesthood considered his search for a unified field theory to be quixotic.

One of these young assistants, Ernst Straus, remembers working on an approach that Einstein pursued for almost two years. One evening, Straus found, to his dismay, that their equations led to some conclusions that clearly could not be true. The next day, he and Einstein explored the issue from all angles, but they could not avoid the disappointing result. So they went home early. Straus was dejected, and he assumed that Einstein would be even more so. To his surprise, Einstein was as eager and excited as ever the next day, and he proposed yet another approach they could take. "This was the start of an entirely new theory, also relegated to the trash heap after a half-year's work and mourned no longer than its predecessor," Straus recalls.[65]

Einstein's quest was driven by his intuition that mathematical simplicity, an attribute he never fully defined though he felt he knew it when he saw it, was a feature of nature's handiwork.[66] Every now and then, when a particularly elegant formulation cropped up, he would exult to Straus, "This is so simple God could not have passed it up."

Enthusiastic letters to friends continued to pour forth from Princeton about the progress of his crusade against the quantum theorists who seemed wedded to probabilities and averse to believing in an underlying reality. "I am working with my young people on an extremely interesting theory with which I hope to defeat modern proponents of mysticism and probability and their aversion to the notion of reality in the domain of physics," he wrote Maurice Solovine in 1938.[67]

Likewise, headlines continued to emanate from Princeton on purported breakthroughs. "Soaring over a hitherto unscaled mathematical mountain-top, Dr. Albert Einstein, climber of cosmic Alps, reports having sighted a new pattern in the structure of space and matter," the distinguished *New York Times* science reporter William Laurence reported in a page 1 article in 1935. The same writer and the same paper reported on page 1 in 1939, "Albert Einstein revealed today that after twenty years of unremitting search for a law that would explain the mechanism of the cosmos in its entirety, reaching out from the stars and galaxies in the vastness of infinite space down to the mysteries within the heart of the infinitesimal atom, he has at last arrived within sight of what he hopes may be the 'Promised Land of Knowledge,' holding what may be the master key to the riddle of creation."[68]

The triumphs in his salad days had come partly from having an instinct that could sniff out underlying physical realities. He could intuitively sense the implications of the relativity of all motion, the constancy of the speed of light, and the equivalence of gravitational and inertial mass. From that he could build theories based on a feel for the physics. But he later became more reliant on a mathematical formalism, because it had guided him in his final sprint to complete the field equations of general relativity.

Now, in his quest for a unified theory, there seemed to be a lot of mathematical formalism but very few fundamental physical insights guiding him. "In his earlier search for the general theory, Einstein had been guided by his principle of equivalence linking gravitation with acceleration," said Banesh Hoffmann, a Princeton collaborator. "Where were the comparable guiding principles that could lead to the construction of a unified field theory? No one knew. Not even Einstein. Thus the search was not so much a search as a groping in the gloom of a mathematical jungle inadequately lit by physical intuition." Jeremy Bernstein later called it "like an all but random shuffling of mathematical formulas with no physics in view." [69]

After a while, the optimistic headlines and letters stopped emanating from Princeton, and Einstein publicly admitted that he was, at least for the time being, stymied. "I am not as optimistic," he told the *New York Times.* For years the paper had regularly headlined each of Einstein's purported breakthroughs toward a unified theory, but now its headline read, "Einstein Baffled by Cosmos Riddle."

Nonetheless, Einstein insisted that he still could not "accept the view that events in nature are analogous to a game of chance." And so he pledged to continue his quest. Even if he failed, he felt that the effort would be meaningful. "It is open to every man to choose the direction of his striving," he explained, "and every man may take comfort from the fine saying that the search for truth is more precious than its possession." [70]

Around the time of Einstein's sixtieth birthday, early in the spring of 1939, Niels Bohr came to Princeton for a two-month visit. Einstein remained somewhat aloof toward his old friend and sparring partner. They met at a few receptions, exchanged some small talk, but did not reengage in their old game of volleying thought experiments about quantum weirdness.

Einstein gave only one lecture during that period, which Bohr attended. It dealt with his latest attempts to find a unified field theory. At the end, Einstein fixed his eyes on Bohr and noted that he had long tried to explain quantum mechanics in such a fashion. But he made clear that he would prefer not to discuss the issue further. "Bohr was profoundly unhappy with this," his assistant recalled.[71]

Bohr had arrived in Princeton with a piece of scientific news that was related to Einstein's discovery of the link between energy and mass, $E=mc^2$. In Berlin, Otto Hahn and Fritz Strassman had gotten some interesting experimental results by bombarding heavy uranium with neutrons. These had been sent to their former colleague, Lise Meitner, who had just been forced to flee to Sweden because she was half Jewish. She in turn shared them with her nephew Otto Frisch, and they concluded that the atom had been split, two lighter nuclei created, and a small amount of lost mass turned into energy.

After they substantiated the results, which they dubbed *fission*, Frisch informed his colleague Bohr, who was about to leave for America. Upon his arrival in late January 1939, Bohr described the new discovery to colleagues, and it was discussed at a weekly gathering of physicists in Princeton known as the Monday Evening Club. Within days the results had been replicated, and researchers began churning out papers on the process, including one that Bohr wrote with a young untenured physics professor, John Archibald Wheeler.

Einstein had long been skeptical about the possibility of harnessing atomic energy or unleashing the power implied by $E=mc^2$. On a visit to Pittsburgh in 1934, he had been asked the question and replied that "splitting the atom by bombardment is something akin to shooting birds in the dark in a place where there are only a few birds." That produced a banner headline across the front page of the *Post-Gazette:* "Atom Energy Hope Is Spiked by Einstein / Efforts at Loosing Vast Force Is Called Fruitless / Savant Talked Here."[72]

With the news in early 1939 that it was, apparently, very possible to bombard and split an atomic nucleus, Einstein faced the question again. In an interview for his sixtieth birthday that March, he was asked whether mankind would find some use for the process. "Our results so far concerning the splitting of the atom do not justify the assumption of a practical utilization of the energies released," he replied. This time he was cautious, however, and went on to hedge his answer slightly. "There is no physicist with soul so poor who would allow this to affect his interest in this highly important subject."[73]

Over the next four months, his interest would indeed grow rapidly.

CHAPTER TWENTY-ONE

THE BOMB

1939–1945

With Leó Szilárd reenacting (in 1946) their 1939 meeting

The Letter

Leó Szilárd, a charming and slightly eccentric Hungarian physicist, was an old friend of Einstein's. While living in Berlin in the 1920s, they had collaborated on the development of a new type of refrigerator, which they patented but were unable to market successfully.[1] After Szilárd fled the Nazis, he made his way to England and then New York, where he worked at Columbia University on ways to create a nuclear chain reaction, an idea he had conceived while waiting at a stoplight in London a few years earlier. When he heard of the discovery of fission using uranium, Szilárd realized that element might be used to produce this potentially explosive chain reaction.

Szilárd discussed this possibility with his close friend Eugene Wigner, another refugee physicist from Budapest, and they began to worry that the Germans might try to buy up the uranium supplies of the Congo, which was then a colony of Belgium. But how, they asked themselves, could two Hungarian refugees in America find a way to warn the Belgians? Then Szilárd recalled that Einstein happened to be friends with that country's queen mother.

Einstein was spending the summer of 1939 in a rented cottage on the north fork of eastern Long Island, across the Great Peconic Bay from the villages of the Hamptons. There he sailed his small boat *Tinef,* bought sandals from the local department store, and played Bach with the store's owner.[2]

"We knew that Einstein was somewhere on Long Island but we didn't know precisely where," Szilárd recalled. So he phoned Einstein's Princeton office and was told he was renting the house of a Dr. Moore in the village of Peconic. On Sunday, July 16, 1939, they embarked on their mission with Wigner at the wheel (Szilárd, like Einstein, did not drive).

But when they arrived they couldn't find the house, and nobody seemed to know who Dr. Moore was. Just as they were ready to give up, Szilárd saw a young boy standing by the curb. "Do you, by any chance, know where Professor Einstein lives?" Like most people in town, even those who had no idea who Dr. Moore was, the boy did, and he led them up to a cottage near the end of Old Grove Road, where they found Einstein lost in thought.[3]

Sitting at a bare wooden table on the screen porch of the sparsely furnished cottage, Szilárd explained the process of how an explosive chain reaction could be produced in uranium layered with graphite by the neutrons released from nuclear fission. "I never thought of that!" Einstein interjected. He asked a few questions, went over the process for fifteen minutes, and then quickly grasped the implications. Instead of writing to the queen mother, Einstein suggested, perhaps they should write to a Belgian minister he knew.

Wigner, showing some sensible propriety, suggested that perhaps three refugees should not be writing to a foreign government about se-cret security matters without consulting with the State Department. In which case, they decided, perhaps the proper channel was a letter from Einstein, the only one of them famous enough to be heeded, to the

Belgian ambassador, with a cover letter to the State Department. With that tentative plan in mind, Einstein dictated a draft in German. Wigner translated it, gave it to his secretary to be typed, and then sent it to Szilárd.[4]

A few days later, a friend arranged for Szilárd to talk to Alexander Sachs, an economist at Lehman Brothers and a friend of President Roosevelt. Showing a bit more savvy than the three theoretical physicists, Sachs insisted that the letter should go right to the White House, and he offered to hand-deliver it.

It was the first time Szilárd had met Sachs, but his bold plan was appealing. "It could not do any harm to try this way," he wrote Einstein. Should they talk by phone or meet in person to revise the letter? Einstein replied that he should come back out to Peconic.

By that point Wigner had gone to California for a visit. So Szilárd enlisted, as driver and scientific sidekick, another friend from the amazing group of Hungarian refugees who were theoretical physicists, Edward Teller.[5] "I believe his advice is valuable, but also I think you might enjoy getting to know him," Szilárd told Einstein. "He is particularly nice."[6] Another plus was that Teller had a big 1935 Plymouth. So once again, Szilárd headed out to Peconic.

Szilárd brought with him the original draft from two weeks earlier, but Einstein realized that they were now planning a letter that was far more momentous than one asking Belgian ministers to be careful about Congolese uranium exports. The world's most famous scientist was about to tell the president of the United States that he should begin contemplating a weapon of almost unimaginable impact that could unleash the power of the atom. "Einstein dictated a letter in German," Szilárd recalled, "which Teller took down, and I used this German text as a guide in preparing two drafts of a letter to the President."[7]

According to Teller's notes, Einstein's dictated draft not only raised the question of Congo's uranium, but also explained the possibility of chain reactions, suggested that a new type of bomb could result, and urged the president to set up formal contact with physicists working on this topic. Szilárd then prepared and sent back to Einstein a 45-line version and a 25-line one, both dated August 2, 1939, "and left it up to

Einstein to choose which he liked best." Einstein signed them both in a small scrawl, rather than with the flourish he sometimes used.[8]

The longer version, which is the one that eventually reached Roosevelt, read in part:

> Sir:
>
> Some recent work by E. Fermi and L. Szilárd, which has been communicated to me in a manuscript, leads me to expect that the element uranium may be turned into a new and important source of energy in the immediate future. Certain aspects of this situation which has arisen seem to call for watchfulness and, if necessary, quick action on the part of the Administration. I believe therefore that it is my duty to bring to your attention the following facts and recommendations:
>
> . . . It may become possible to set up a nuclear chain reaction in a large mass of uranium, by which vast amounts of power and large quantities of new radium-like elements would be generated. Now it appears almost certain that this could be achieved in the immediate future.
>
> This new phenomena would also lead to the construction of bombs, and it is conceivable—though much less certain—that extremely powerful bombs of a new type may thus be constructed. A single bomb of this type, carried by boat and exploded in a port, might very well destroy the whole port together with some of the surrounding territory . . .
>
> In view of this situation you may think it desirable to have some permanent contact maintained between the administration and the group of physicists working on chain reactions in America.

It ended with a warning that German scientists might be pursuing a bomb. Once the letter had been written and signed, they still had to figure out who could best get it into the hands of President Roosevelt. Einstein was unsure about Sachs. They considered, instead, financier Bernard Baruch and MIT President Karl Compton.

More amazingly, when Szilárd sent back the typed version of the letter, he suggested that they use as their intermediary Charles Lindbergh, whose solo transatlantic flight twelve years earlier had made him a celebrity. All three of the refugee Jews were apparently unaware that the aviator had been spending time in Germany, was decorated the year before by the Nazi Hermann Göring with that nation's medal of honor, and was becoming an isolationist and Roosevelt antagonist.

Einstein had briefly met Lindbergh a few years earlier in New York, so he wrote a note of introduction, which he included when he returned the signed letters to Szilárd. "I would like to ask you to do me a favor of receiving my friend Dr. Szilárd and think very carefully about what he will tell you," Einstein wrote to Lindbergh. "To one who is outside of science the matter he will bring up may seem fantastic. However, you will certainly become convinced that a possibility is presented here which has to be very carefully watched in the public interest."[9]

Lindbergh did not respond, so Szilárd wrote him a reminder letter on September 13, again asking for a meeting. Two days later, they realized how clueless they had been when Lindbergh gave a nationwide radio address. It was a clarion call for isolationism. "The destiny of this country does not call for our involvement in European wars," Lindbergh began. Interwoven were hints of Lindbergh's pro-German sympathies and even some anti-Semitic implications about Jewish ownership of the media. "We must ask who owns and influences the newspaper, the news picture, and the radio station," he said. "If our people know the truth, our country is not likely to enter the war."[10]

Szilárd's next letter to Einstein stated the obvious: "Lindbergh is not our man."[11]

Their other hope was Alexander Sachs, who had been given the formal letter to Roosevelt that Einstein signed. Even though it was obviously of enormous importance, Sachs was not able to find the opportunity to deliver it for almost two months.

By then, events had turned what was an important letter into an urgent one. At the end of August 1939, the Nazis and Soviets stunned the world by signing their war alliance pact and proceeded to carve up Poland. That prompted Britain and France to declare war, starting the century's second World War. For the time being, America stayed neutral, or at least did not declare war. The country did, however, begin to rearm and to develop whatever new weapons might be necessary for its future involvement.

Szilárd went to see Sachs in late September and was horrified to discover that he still had not been able to schedule an appointment with Roosevelt. "There is a distinct possibility Sachs will be of no use to us," Szilárd wrote Einstein. "Wigner and I have decided to accord him ten days grace."[12] Sachs barely made the deadline. On the afternoon of Wednesday, October 11, he was ushered into the Oval Office carrying Einstein's letter, Szilárd's memo, and an eight-hundred-word summary he had written on his own.

The president greeted him jovially. "Alex, what are you up to?"

Sachs could be loquacious, which may be why the president's handlers made it hard for him to get an appointment, and he tended to tell the president parables. This time it was a tale about an inventor who told Napoleon that he would build him a new type of ship that could travel using steam rather than sails. Napoleon dismissed him as crazy. Sachs then revealed that the visitor was Robert Fulton and, so went the lesson, the emperor should have listened.[13]

Roosevelt responded by scribbling a note to an aide, who hurried off and soon returned with a bottle of very old and rare Napoleon brandy that Roosevelt said had been in his family for a while. He poured two glasses.

Sachs worried that if he left the memos and papers with Roosevelt, they might be glanced at and then pushed aside. The only reliable way to deliver them, he decided, was to read them aloud. Standing in front of the president's desk, he read his summation of Einstein's letter, parts of Szilárd's memo, and some other paragraphs from assorted historical documents.

"Alex, what you are after is to see that the Nazis don't blow us up," the president said.

"Precisely," Sachs replied.

Roosevelt called in his personal assistant. "This requires action," he declared.[14]

That evening, plans were drawn up for an ad hoc committee, coordinated by Dr. Lyman Briggs, director of the Bureau of Standards, the nation's physics laboratory. It met informally for the first time in Washington on October 21. Einstein was not there, nor did he want to be. He was neither a nuclear physicist nor someone who enjoyed proximity to political or military leaders. But his Hungarian émigré trio—Szilárd, Wigner, and Teller—were there to launch the effort.

The following week, Einstein received a polite and formal thank-you letter from the president. "I have convened a board," Roosevelt wrote, "to thoroughly investigate the possibilities of your suggestion regarding the element of uranium."[15]

Work on the atomic project proceeded slowly. Over the next few months, the Roosevelt administration approved only $6,000 for graphite and uranium experiments. Szilárd became impatient. He was becoming more convinced of the feasibility of chain reaction and more worried about reports he was getting from fellow refugees on the activity in Germany.

So in March 1940, he went to Princeton to see Einstein again. They composed another letter for Einstein to sign, which was addressed to Alexander Sachs but intended for him to convey to the president. It warned of all the work on uranium they heard was being done in Berlin. Given the progress being made in producing chain reactions with huge explosive potential, the letter urged the president to consider whether the American work was proceeding quickly enough.[16]

Roosevelt reacted by calling for a conference designed to spur greater urgency, and he told officials to make sure that Einstein could attend. But Einstein had no desire to be more involved. He replied by saying he had a cold—somewhat of a convenient excuse—and did not need to be at the meeting. But he did urge the group to get moving: "I am convinced of the wisdom and urgency of creating the conditions under which work can be carried out with greater speed and on a larger scale."[17]

Even if Einstein had wanted to take part in the meetings, which led to the Manhattan Project that developed the atom bomb, he may not have been welcome. Amazingly, the man who had helped get the project launched was considered, by some, to be too great a potential security risk to be permitted to know about the work.

Brigadier General Sherman Miles, the acting Army chief of staff who was organizing the new committee, sent a letter in July 1940 to J. Edgar Hoover, who had already been the director of the FBI for sixteen years and would remain so for another thirty-two. By addressing him by his national guard rank as "Colonel Hoover," the general was subtly pulling rank when it came to controlling intelligence decisions. But Hoover was assertive when Miles asked for a summary of information the Bureau had on Einstein.[18]

Hoover began by providing General Miles with the letter from Mrs. Frothingham's Woman Patriot Corporation, which had argued in

1932 that Einstein should be denied a visa and raised alarms about various pacifist and political groups he had supported.[19] The Bureau made no attempt to verify or assess any of the charges.

Hoover went on to say that Einstein had been involved in the World Antiwar Congress in Amsterdam in 1932, which had some European communists on its committee. This was the conference that Einstein, as noted earlier, had specifically and publicly declined to attend or even support; as he wrote the organizer, "Because of the glorification of Soviet Russia it includes, I cannot bring myself to sign it." Einstein had gone on in that letter to denounce Russia, where "there seems to be complete suppression of the individual and of freedom of speech." Nevertheless, Hoover implied that Einstein had supported the conference and was thus pro-Soviet.[20]

Hoover's letter had six more paragraphs making similar allegations about a variety of alleged Einstein associations, ranging from pacifist groups to those supporting Spain's loyalists. Appended was a biographical sketch filled with trivial misinformation ("has one child") and wild allegations. It called him "an extreme radical," which he certainly was not, and said he "has contributed to communist magazines," which he hadn't. General Miles was so taken aback by the memo that he wrote a note in the margin, warning, "There is some possibility of flameback" if it ever leaked.[21]

The conclusion of the unsigned biographical sketch was stark: "In view of this radical background, this office would not recommend the employment of Dr. Einstein on matters of a secret nature, without a very careful investigation, as it seems unlikely that a man of his background could, in such a short time, become a loyal American citizen." In a memo the following year, it was reported that the Navy had assented to giving Einstein a security clearance, but "the Army could not clear."[22]

Citizen Einstein

Just as the Army's decision was being made, Einstein was in fact eagerly doing something the likes of which he had not done for forty years, ever since he had saved up his money so that he could become a

Swiss citizen after leaving Germany. He was voluntarily and proudly becoming a citizen of the United States, a process that had begun five years earlier when he sailed to Bermuda so that he could return on an immigration visa. He still had his Swiss citizenship and passport, so he did not need to do this. But he wanted to.

He took his citizenship test on June 22, 1940, in front of a federal judge in Trenton. To celebrate the process, he agreed to give a radio interview as part of the immigration service's *I Am an American* series. The judge served lunch and had the radio folks set up in his chambers to make the process easier for Einstein.[23]

It was an inspiring day, partly because Einstein showed just what type of free-speaking citizen he would be. In his radio talk, he argued that, to prevent wars in the future, nations would have to give up some of their sovereignty to an armed international federation of nations. "A worldwide organization cannot insure peace effectively unless it has control over the entire military power of its members," he said.[24]

Einstein passed his test and he was sworn in—along with his step-daughter Margot, his assistant Helen Dukas, and eighty-six other new citizens—on October 1. Afterward, he praised America to the reporters covering his naturalization. The nation, he said, would prove that democracy is not just a form of government but "a way of life tied to a great tradition, the tradition of moral strength." Asked if he would renounce other loyalties, he joyously declared that he "would even renounce my cherished sailboat" if that were necessary.[25] It was not, however, necessary for him to renounce his Swiss citizenship, and he did not.

When he first arrived in Princeton, Einstein had been impressed that America was, or could be, a land free of the rigid class hierarchies and servility in Europe. But what grew to impress him more—and what made him fundamentally such a good American but also a controversial one—was the country's tolerance of free thought, free speech, and nonconformist beliefs. That had been a touchstone of his science, and now it was a touchstone of his citizenship.

He had forsaken Nazi Germany with the public pronouncement that he would not live in a country where people were denied the freedom to hold and express their own thoughts. "At that time, I did not understand how right I was in my choice of America as such a place," he wrote in an unpublished essay just after becoming a citizen. "On every side I hear men and women expressing their opinion on candidates for office and the issues of the day without fear of consequences."

The beauty of America, he said, was that this tolerance of each person's ideas existed without the "brute force and fear" that had arisen in Europe. "From what I have seen of Americans, I think that life would not be worth living to them without this freedom of self expression."[26] The depth of his appreciation for America's core value would help explain Einstein's cold public anger and dissent when, during the McCarthy era a few years later, the nation lapsed into a period marked by the intimidation of those with unpopular views.

More than two years after Einstein and his colleagues had urged attention to the possibility of building atomic weapons, the United States launched the supersecret Manhattan Project. It happened on December 6, 1941, which turned out to be, fittingly enough, the day before Japan launched its attack on Pearl Harbor that brought the nation into the war.

Because so many fellow physicists, such as Wigner, Szilárd, Oppenheimer, and Teller, had disappeared to obscure towns, Einstein was able to surmise that the bomb-making work he had recommended was now proceeding with greater urgency. But he was not asked to join the Manhattan Project, nor was he officially told about it.

There were many reasons he was not secretly summoned to places like Los Alamos or Oak Ridge. He was not a nuclear physicist or a practicing expert in the scientific issues at hand. He was, as noted, considered by some a security risk. And even though he had put aside his pacifist sentiments, he never expressed any desire or made any requests to enlist in the endeavor.

He was, however, offered a bit part that December. Vannevar Bush, the director of the Office of Scientific Research and Development, which oversaw the Manhattan Project, contacted Einstein through the man who had succeeded Flexner as the head of the Institute for Advanced Study in Princeton, Frank Aydelotte, and asked for his help on a problem involving the separation of isotopes that shared chemical traits. Einstein was happy to comply. Drawing on his old expertise in osmosis and diffusion, he worked on a process of gaseous diffusion in which uranium was converted into a gas and forced through filters. To preserve secrecy, he was not even allowed to have Helen Dukas or anyone else type up his work, so he sent it back in his careful handwriting.

"Einstein was very much interested in your problem, has worked on it for a couple of days and produced the solution, which I enclose," Aydelotte wrote Bush. "Einstein asks me to say that if there are other angles of the problem that you want him to develop or if you wish any parts of this amplified, you need only let him know and he will do anything in his power. I very much hope that you will make use of him in any way that occurs to you, because I know how deep is his satisfaction at doing anything which might be useful in the national effort." As an afterthought, Aydelotte added, "I hope you can read his handwriting."[27]

The scientists who received Einstein's paper were impressed, and they discussed it with Vannevar Bush. But in order for Einstein to be more useful, they said, he should be given more information about how the isotope separation fit in with other parts of the bomb-making challenge.

Bush refused. He knew that Einstein would have trouble getting a security clearance. "I do not feel that I ought to take him into confidence on the subject to the extent of showing just where this thing fits into the defense picture," Bush wrote Aydelotte. "I wish very much that I could place the whole thing before him and take him fully into confidence, but this is utterly impossible in view of the attitude of people here in Washington who have studied his whole history."[28]

Later, during the war, Einstein helped with less secret matters. A Navy lieutenant came to visit him at the Institute to enlist him in analyzing ordnance capabilities. He was enthusiastic. As Aydelotte noted, he had felt neglected since his brief flurry of work on uranium isotopes. Among the issues Einstein explored, as part of a $25-per-day consulting arrangement, were ways to shape the placement of sea mines in Japanese harbors, and his friend the physicist George Gamow got to come pick his brain on a variety of topics. "I am in the Navy, but not re-

quired to get a Navy haircut," Einstein joked to colleagues, who probably had trouble picturing him with a crew cut.[29]

Einstein also helped the war effort by donating a manuscript of
his special relativity paper to be auctioned off for a War Bond drive. It
was not the original version; he had thrown that away back when it
was published in 1905, not knowing it would ever be worth millions.
To re-create the manuscript, he had Helen Dukas read the paper
to him aloud as he copied down the words. "Did I really say it that
way?" he griped at one point. When Dukas assured him that he had,
Einstein lamented, "I could have put it much more simply." When he
heard that the manuscript, along with one other, had sold for $11.5
million, he declared that "economists will have to revise their theories
of value."[30]

Atomic Fears

The physicist Otto Stern, who had been one of Einstein's friends
since their days together in Prague, had been secretly working on the
Manhattan Project, mainly in Chicago, and had a good sense by the
end of 1944 that it would be successful. That December, he made a
visit to Princeton. What Einstein heard upset him. Whether or not the
bomb was used in the war, it would change the nature of both war and
peace forever. The policymakers weren't thinking about that, he and
Stern agreed, and they must be encouraged to do so before it was too
late.

So Einstein decided to write to Niels Bohr. They had sparred over
quantum mechanics, but Einstein trusted his judgment on more
earthly issues. Einstein was one of the few people to know that Bohr,
who was half Jewish, was secretly in the United States. When the
Nazis overran Denmark, he had made a daring escape by sailing with
his son in a small boat to Sweden. From there he had been flown to
Britain, given a fake passport with the name Nicholas Baker, then sent
to America to join the Manhattan Project at Los Alamos.

Einstein wrote to Bohr, using his real name, in care of Denmark's
embassy in Washington, and somehow the letter got to him. In it Ein-

stein described his worrisome talk with Stern about the dearth of thinking about how to control atomic weapons in the future. "The politicians do not appreciate the possibilities and consequently do not know the extent of the menace," Einstein wrote. Once again, he made his argument that it would take an empowered world government to prevent an arms race once the age of atomic weaponry arrived. "Scientists who know how to get a hearing with political leaders," Einstein urged, "should bring pressure on the political leaders in their countries in order to bring about an internationalization of military power."[31]

Thus began what would be the political mission that would dominate the remaining decade of Einstein's life. Since his days as a teenager in Germany, he had been repulsed by nationalism, and he had long argued that the best way to prevent wars was to create a world authority that had the right to resolve disputes and the military power to impose its resolutions. Now, with the impending advent of a weapon so awesome that it could transform both war and peace, Einstein viewed this approach as no longer an ideal but a necessity.

Bohr was unnerved by Einstein's letter, but not for the reason Einstein would have hoped. The Dane shared his desire for the internationalization of atomic weaponry, and he had advocated that approach in meetings with Churchill, and then with Roosevelt, earlier in the year. But instead of persuading them, he had prompted the two leaders to issue a joint order to their intelligence agencies saying that "enquiries should be made regarding the activities of Professor Bohr and steps taken to ensure that he is responsible for no leakage of information, particularly to the Russians."[32]

So upon receiving Einstein's letter, Bohr hurried to Princeton. He wanted to protect his friend by warning him to be circumspect, and he also hoped to repair his own reputation by reporting to government officials on what Einstein said.

During their private talk at the Mercer Street house, Bohr told Einstein that there would be "the most deplorable consequences" if anyone who knew about the development of the bomb shared that information. Responsible statesmen in Washington and London, Bohr assured him, were aware of the threat caused by the bomb as well as "the unique opportunity for furthering a harmonious relationship between nations."

Einstein was persuaded. He promised that he would refrain from sharing any information he had surmised and would urge his friends not do anything to complicate American or British foreign policy. And he immediately set out to make good on his word by writing a letter to Stern that was, for Einstein, remarkable in its circumspection. "I have the impression that one must strive seriously to be responsible, that one does best not to speak about the matter for the time being, and that it would in no way help, at the present moment, to bring it to public notice," he said. He was careful not to reveal anything, even that he had met with Bohr. "It is difficult for me to speak in such a nebulous way, but for the moment I cannot do anything else."[33]

Einstein's only intervention before the end of the war was prompted again by Szilárd, who came to visit in March 1945 and expressed anxiety about how the bomb might be used. It was clear that Germany, now weeks away from defeat, was not making a bomb. So why should the Americans rush to complete one? And shouldn't policymakers think twice about using it against Japan when it might not be needed to secure victory?

Einstein agreed to write another letter to President Roosevelt urging him to meet with Szilárd and other concerned scientists, but he went out of his way to feign ignorance. "I do not know the substance of the considerations and recommendations which Dr. Szilárd proposes to submit to you," Einstein wrote. "The terms of secrecy under which Dr. Szilárd is working at present do not permit him to give me information about his work; however, I understand that he now is greatly concerned about the lack of adequate contact between scientists who are doing this work and those members of your Cabinet who are responsible for formulating policy."[34]

Roosevelt never read the letter. It was found in his office after he died on April 12 and was passed on to Harry Truman, who in turn gave it to his designated secretary of state, James Byrnes. The result was a meeting between Szilárd and Byrnes in South Carolina, but Byrnes was neither moved nor impressed.

The atom bomb was dropped, with little high-level debate, on August 6, 1945, on the city of Hiroshima. Einstein was at the cottage he rented that summer on Saranac Lake in the Adirondacks, taking an afternoon nap. Helen Dukas informed him when he came down for tea. "Oh, my God," is all he said.[35]

Three days later, the bomb was used again, this time on Nagasaki. The following day, officials in Washington released a long history, compiled by Princeton physics professor Henry DeWolf Smyth, of the secret endeavor to build the weapon. The Smyth report, much to Einstein's lasting discomfort, assigned great historic weight for the launch of the project to the 1939 letter he had written to Roosevelt.

Between the influence imputed to that letter and the underlying relationship between energy and mass that he had formulated forty years earlier, Einstein became associated in the popular imagination with the making of the atom bomb, even though his involvement was marginal. *Time* put him on its cover, with a portrait showing a mushroom cloud erupting behind him with $E=mc^2$ emblazoned on it. In a story that was overseen by an editor named Whittaker Chambers, the magazine noted with its typical prose flair from the period:

> Through the incomparable blast and flame that will follow, there will be dimly discernible, to those who are interested in cause & effect in history, the features of a shy, almost saintly, childlike little man with the soft brown eyes, the drooping facial lines of a world-weary hound, and hair like an aurora borealis . . . Albert Einstein did not work directly on the atom bomb. But Einstein was the father of the bomb in two important ways: 1) it was his initiative which started U.S. bomb research; 2) it was his equation ($E = mc^2$) which made the atomic bomb theoretically possible.[36]

It was a perception that plagued him. When *Newsweek* did a cover on him, with the headline "The Man Who Started It All," Einstein offered a memorable lament. "Had I known that the Germans would not succeed in producing an atomic bomb," he said, "I never would have lifted a finger."[37]

Of course, neither he nor Szilárd nor any of their friends involved with the bomb-building effort, many of them refugees from Hitler's horrors, could know that the brilliant scientists they had left behind in Berlin, such as Heisenberg, would fail to unlock the secrets. "Perhaps I can be forgiven," Einstein said a few months before his death in a conversation with Linus Pauling, "because we all felt that there was a high probability that the Germans were working on this problem and they might succeed and use the atomic bomb and become the master race."[38]

CHAPTER TWENTY-TWO

ONE-WORLDER

1945–1948

Portrait by Philippe Halsman, 1947

Arms Control

For a few weeks after the dropping of the atom bomb, Einstein was uncharacteristically reticent. He fended off reporters who were knocking at his door in Saranac Lake, and he even declined to give a quote to his summer neighbor Arthur Hays Sulzberger, publisher of the *New York Times,* when he called.[1]

It was only as he was about to leave his summer rental in mid-September, more than a month after the bombs had been dropped, that Einstein agreed to discuss the issue with a wire service reporter who came calling. The point he stressed was that the bomb reinforced his longtime support for world federalism. "The only salvation for civilization and the human race lies in the creation of world government," he said. "As long as sovereign states continue

487

to have armaments and armaments secrets, new world wars will be inevitable."[2]

As in science, so it was in world politics for Einstein: he sought a unified set of principles that could create order out of anarchy. A system based on sovereign nations with their own military forces, competing ideologies, and conflicting national interests would inevitably produce more wars. So he regarded a world authority as realistic rather than idealistic, as practical rather than naïve.

He had been circumspect during the war years. He was a refugee in a nation that was using its military might for noble rather than nationalistic goals. But the end of the war changed things. So did the dropping of the atom bombs. The increase in the destructive power of offensive weaponry led to a commensurate increase in the need to find a world structure for security. It was time for him to become politically outspoken again.

For the remaining ten years of his life, his passion for advocating a unified governing structure for the globe would rival that for finding a unified field theory that could govern all the forces of nature. Although distinct in most ways, both quests reflected his instincts for transcendent order. In addition, both would display Einstein's willingness to be a nonconformist, to be serenely secure in challenging prevailing attitudes.

The month after the bombs were dropped, a group of scientists signed a statement urging that a council of nations be created to control atomic weaponry. Einstein responded with a letter to J. Robert Oppenheimer, who had so successfully led the scientific efforts at Los Alamos. He was pleased with the sentiments behind the statement, Einstein said, but he criticized the political recommendations as "obviously inadequate" because they retained sovereign nations as the ultimate powers. "It is unthinkable that we can have peace without a real governmental organization to create and enforce law on individuals in their international relations."

Oppenheimer politely pointed out that "the statements you attributed to me are not mine." They had been written by another group of scientists. He did, nevertheless, challenge Einstein's argument for a full-fledged world government: "The history of this nation up through the Civil War shows how difficult the establishment of a federal authority can be when there are profound differences in the values of the societies it attempts to integrate."[3] Oppenheimer thus became the first of many postwar realists to disparage Einstein for being allegedly too idealistic. Of course, one could flip his argument by noting that the Civil War showed in gruesome terms the danger of *not* having a secure federal authority instead of state military sovereignty when there are differences of values among member states.

What Einstein envisioned was a world "government" or "authority" that had a monopoly on military power. He called it a "supranational" entity, rather than an "international" one, because it would exist *above* its member nations rather than as a mediator among sovereign nations.[4] The United Nations, which was founded in October 1945, did not come close to meeting these criteria, Einstein felt.

Over the next few months, Einstein fleshed out his proposals in a series of essays and interviews. The most important arose from an exchange of fan letters he had with Raymond Gram Swing, a commentator on ABC radio. Einstein invited Swing to visit him in Princeton, and the result was an article by Einstein, as told to Swing, in the November 1945 issue of the *Atlantic* called "Atomic War or Peace."[5]

The three great powers—the United States, Britain, and Russia—should jointly establish the new world government, Einstein said in the article, and then invite other nations to join. Using a somewhat misleading phrase that was part of the popular debate of the time, he said that "the secret of the bomb" should be given to this new organization by Washington.[6] The only truly effective way to control atomic arms, he believed, was by ceding the monopoly on military power to a world government.

By then, in late 1945, the cold war was under way. America and Britain had begun to clash with Russia for imposing communist regimes in Poland and other eastern European areas occupied by the Red Army. For its part, Russia zealously sought a security perimeter and was neuralgic about any perceived attempt to interfere in its domestic affairs, which made its leaders resist surrendering any sovereignty to a world authority.

So Einstein sought to make it clear that the world government he envisioned would not try to impose a Western-style liberal democracy everywhere. He advocated a world legislature that would be elected directly by the people of each member country, in secret ballot, rather than appointed by the nation's rulers. However, "it should not be necessary to change the internal structure of the three great powers," he added as a reassurance to Russia. "Membership in a supranational security system should not be based on any arbitrary democratic standards."

One issue that Einstein could not resolve neatly was what right this world government would have to intervene in the internal affairs of nations. It must be able "to interfere in countries where a minority is oppressing a majority," he said, citing Spain as an example. Yet that caused him contortions about whether this standard applied to Russia. "One must bear in mind that the people in Russia have not had a long tradition of political education," he rationalized. "Changes to improve conditions in Russia had to be effected by a minority because there was no majority capable of doing so."

Einstein's efforts to prevent future wars were motivated not only by his old pacifist instincts but also, he admitted, by his guilty feelings about the role he had played in encouraging the atom bomb project. At a Manhattan dinner given by the Nobel Prize committee in December, he noted that Alfred Nobel, the inventor of dynamite, had created the award "to atone for having invented the most powerful explosives ever known up to his time." He was in a similar situation. "Today, the physicists who participated in forging the most formidable and dangerous weapon of all times are harassed by an equal feeling of responsibility, not to say guilt," he said.[7]

These sentiments prompted Einstein, in May 1946, to take on the most prominent public policy role in his career. He became chairman of the newly formed Emergency Committee of Atomic Scientists, which was dedicated to nuclear arms control and world government. "The unleashed power of the atom has changed everything save our modes of thinking," Einstein wrote in a fund-raising telegram that month, "and thus we drift towards unparalleled catastrophe."[8]

Leó Szilárd served as the executive director and did most of the organizational work. But Einstein, who served until the end of 1948, gave speeches, chaired meetings, and took his role seriously. "Our generation has brought into the world the most revolutionary force since prehistoric man's discovery of fire," he said. "This basic power of the universe cannot be fitted into the outmoded concept of narrow nationalisms."[9]

The Truman administration proposed a variety of plans for the international control of atomic power, but none were able, intentionally or not, to win the support of Moscow. As a result, the battle over the best approach quickly created a political divide.

On one side were those who celebrated the success of America and Britain in winning the race to develop such weapons. They saw the bomb as a guarantor of the freedoms of the West, and they wanted to guard what they saw as "the secret." On the other side were arms control advocates like Einstein. "The secret of the atomic bomb is to America what the Maginot Line was to France before 1939," he told *Newsweek*. "It gives us imaginary security, and in this respect it is a great danger."[10]

Einstein and his friends realized that the battle for public sentiment needed to be fought not only in Washington but also in the realm of popular culture. This led to an amusing—and historically illustrative—tangle in 1946 pitting them against Louis B. Mayer and a coterie of earnest Hollywood moviemakers.

It began when a Metro-Goldwyn-Mayer scriptwriter named Sam Marx asked if he could come to Princeton to get Einstein's cooperation on a docudrama about the making of the bomb. Einstein sent back word that he had no desire to help. A few weeks later Einstein got an anxious letter from an official with the Association of Manhattan Project Scientists saying that the movie seemed to be taking a very pro-military slant, celebrating the creation of the bomb and the security it gave to America. "I know that you will not want to lend your name to a picture which misrepresents the military and political implications of the bomb," the letter said. "I hope that you will see fit to make the use of your name conditional on your personal approval of the script."[11]

The following week Szilárd came to see Einstein about the issue, and soon a bevy of peace-loving physicists was bombarding him with concerns. So Einstein read the script and agreed to join the campaign to stop the movie. "The presentation of facts was so utterly misleading that I declined any cooperation or permission of the use of my name," he said.

He also sent a spiky letter to the famed mogul that attacked the proposed movie and also, for good measure, the tone of previous ones that Mayer had made. "Although I am not much of a moviegoer, I do know from the tenor of earlier films that have come out of your studio that you will understand my reasons," he wrote. "I find that the whole film is written too much from the point of view of the Army and the Army leader of the project, whose influence was not always in the direction which one would desire from the point of view of humanity."[12]

Mayer turned Einstein's letter over to the film's chief editor, who responded with a memo that Mayer sent back to Einstein. President Truman, it said, "was most anxious to have the picture made" and had personally read and approved the script, an argument not likely to reassure Einstein. "As American citizens we are bound to respect the viewpoint of our government." That, too, was not the best argument to use on Einstein. There followed an even less persuasive argument: "It must be realized that dramatic truth is just as compelling a requirement to us as veritable truth is to a scientist."

The memo concluded by promising that the moral issues raised by the scientists would be given a proper airing through the character of a fictional young scientist played by an actor named Tom Drake. "We selected among our young male players the one who best typifies earnestness and a spiritual quality," it said reassuringly. "You need only recall his performance in 'The Green Years.'"[13]

Not surprisingly, this did not turn Einstein around. When Sam Marx, the scriptwriter, wrote beseeching him to change his mind and allow himself to be portrayed, Einstein replied curtly: "I have explained my point of view in a letter to Mr. Louis Mayer." Marx was persistent. "When the picture is complete," he wrote back, "the audience will feel in greatest sympathy with the young scientist." And from later the same day: "Here is a new and revised script."[14]

The ending was not that hard to predict. The new script was more pleasing to the scientists, and they were not immune to the lure of being glorified on the big screen. Szilárd sent Einstein a telegram saying, "Have received new script from MGM and am writing that I have no objection to use of my name in it." Einstein relented. "Agree with use of my name on basis of the new script," he scribbled in English on the back of the telegram. The only change he requested was in the scene of Szilárd's 1939 visit to him on Long Island. The script said that he had not met Roosevelt before then, but he had.[15]

The Beginning or the End, which was the name of the movie, opened to good reviews in February 1947. "A sober, intelligent account of the development and deployment of the Atom Bomb," Bosley Crowther declared in the *New York Times*, "refreshingly free of propagandizing." Einstein was played by a character actor named Ludwig Stossel, who had a small part in *Casablanca* as a German Jew trying to get to America and would later have a flicker of fame in Swiss Colony wine commercials in the 1960s in which he spoke the tagline "That little old winemaker, me."[16]

Einstein's efforts on behalf of arms control and his advocacy of world government in the late 1940s got him tagged as woolly-headed and naïve. Woolly-headed he may have been, at least in appearance, but was it right to dismiss him as naïve?

Most Truman administration officials, even those working on behalf of arms control, thought so. William Golden was an example. An Atomic Energy Commission staffer who was preparing a report for Secretary of State George Marshall, he went to Princeton to consult with Einstein. Washington needed to try harder to enlist Moscow in an arms control plan, Einstein argued. Golden felt he was speaking "with almost childlike hope for salvation and without appearing to have thought through the details of his solution." He reported back to Marshall, "It was surprising, though perhaps it should not have been, that, out of his métier of mathematics, he seemed naïve in the field of international politics. The man who popularized the concept of a fourth dimension could think in only two of them in considerations of World Government."[17]

To the extent that Einstein was naïve, it was not because he had a benign view of human nature. Having lived in Germany in the first half of the twentieth century, there was little chance of that. When the famed photographer Philippe Halsman, who had escaped the Nazis with Einstein's help, asked whether he thought there would ever be lasting peace, Einstein answered, "No, as long as there will be man, there will be war." At that moment Halsman clicked his shutter and captured Einstein's sadly knowing eyes for what became a famous portrait (reproduced on page 487).[18]

Einstein's advocacy of an empowered world authority was based not on gooey sentiments but on this hardnosed assessment of human nature. "If the idea of world government is not realistic," he said in 1948, "then there is only one realistic view of our future: wholesale destruction of man by man."[19]

Like some of his scientific breakthroughs, Einstein's approach involved abandoning entrenched suppositions that others considered verities. National sovereignty and military autonomy had been an underpinning of the world order for centuries, just as absolute time and absolute space had been the underpinning of the cosmic order. To advocate transcending that approach was a radical idea, the product of a nonconformist thinker. But like many of Einstein's ideas that at first seemed so radical, it may have looked less so had it come to be accepted.

The world federalism that Einstein—and indeed many sober and established political leaders—advocated during the early years of America's atomic monopoly was not unthinkable. To the extent that he was naïve, it was because he put forth his idea in a simple fashion and did not consider complex compromises. Physicists are not used to trimming or compromising their equations in order to get them accepted. Which is why they do not make good politicians.

At the end of the 1940s, when it was becoming clear to him that the effort to control nuclear weaponry would fail, Einstein was asked what the next war would look like. "I do not know how the Third World War will be fought," he answered, "but I can tell you what they will use in the Fourth—rocks."[20]

Russia

Those who wanted international control of the bomb had one big issue to confront: how to deal with Russia. A growing number of

Americans, along with their elected leaders, came to view Moscow's communists as dangerously expansionist and deceitful. The Russians, for their part, did not seem all that eager for arms control or world governance either. They had deeply ingrained fears about their security, a desire for a bomb of their own, and leaders who recoiled at any hint of outside meddling in their nation's internal affairs.

There was a typical nonconformity in Einstein's attitudes toward Russia. He did not swing as far as many others did toward glorifying the Russians when they became allies during the war, nor did he swing as far toward demonizing them when the cold war began. But by the late 1940s, this put him increasingly outside mainstream American sentiments.

He disliked communist authoritarianism, but he did not see it as an imminent danger to American liberty. The greater danger, he felt, was rising hysteria about the supposed Red menace. When Norman Cousins, editor of the *Saturday Review* and the journalistic patron of America's internationalist intelligentsia, wrote a piece calling for international arms control, Einstein responded with a fan letter but added a caveat. "What I object to in your article is that you not only fail to oppose the widespread hysterical fear in our country of Russian aggression but actually encourage it," he said. "All of us should ask ourselves which of the two countries is objectively more justified in fearing the aggressive intentions of the other." [21]

As for the repression inside Russia, Einstein tended to offer only mild condemnations diluted by excuses. "It is undeniable that a policy of severe coercion exists in the political sphere," he said in one talk. "This may, in part, be due to the need to break the power of the former ruling class and to convert a politically inexperienced, culturally backward people into a nation well organized for productive work. I do not presume to pass judgment in these difficult matters." [22]

Einstein consequently became the target of critics who saw him as a Soviet sympathizer. Mississippi Congressman John Rankin said that Einstein's world government plan was "simply carrying out the Communist line." Speaking on the House floor, Rankin also denounced Einstein's science: "Ever since he published his book on relativity to try to convince the world that light had weight, he has capitalized on his reputation as a scientist . . . and has been engaged in communistic activities."[23]

Einstein continued his long-running exchanges on Russia with Sidney Hook, the social philosopher who had once been a communist and then become strongly anticommunist. These were not as exalted as his exchanges with Bohr, on either side, but they got as intense. "I am not blind to the serious weakness of the Russian system of government," Einstein replied to one of Hook's missives. "But it has, on the other side, great merits and it is difficult to decide whether it would have been possible for the Russians to survive by following softer methods."[24]

Hook took it upon himself to convince Einstein of the error of his ways and sent him long and rather frequent letters, most of which Einstein ignored. On the occasions he did answer, Einstein generally agreed that Russia's oppression was wrong, but he tended to balance such judgments by adding that it was also somewhat understandable. As he juggled it in one 1950 response:

> I do not approve of the interference by the Soviet government in intellectual and artistic matters. Such interference seems to me objectionable, harmful, and even ridiculous. Regarding the centralization of political power and the limitations of the freedom of action for the individual, I think that these restrictions should not exceed the limit demanded by security, stability, and the necessities resulting from a planned economy. An outsider is hardly able to judge the facts and possibilities. In any case it cannot be doubted that the achievements of the Soviet regime are considerable in the fields of education, public health, social welfare, and economics, and that the people as a whole have greatly gained by these achievements.[25]

Despite these qualified excuses for some of Moscow's behavior, Einstein was not the Soviet supporter that some tried to paint him. He had always rejected invitations to Moscow and rebuffed attempts by friends on the left to embrace him as a comrade. He denounced Moscow's repeated use of the veto at the United Nations and its resistance to the idea of world government, and he became even more critical when the Soviets made it clear that they had no appetite for arms control.

This was evident when an official group of Russian scientists attacked Einstein in a 1947 Moscow newspaper article, "Dr. Einstein's Mistaken Notions." His vision for a world government, they declared, was a plot by capitalists. "The proponents of a world super-state are asking us voluntarily to surrender independence for the sake of world government, which is nothing but a flamboyant signboard for the supremacy of capitalist monopolies," they wrote. They denounced Einstein for recommending a directly elected supranational parliament. "He has gone so far as to declare that if the Soviet Union refuses to join this new-fangled organization, other countries would have every right to go ahead without it. Einstein is supporting a political fad which plays into the hands of the sworn enemies of sincere international co-operation and enduring peace."[26]

Soviet sympathizers at the time were willing to follow almost any party line that Moscow dictated. Such conformity was not in Einstein's nature. When he disagreed with someone, he merrily said so. He was happy to take on the Russian scientists.

Although he reiterated his support for democratic socialist ideals, he rebutted the Russians' faith in communist dogma. "We should not make the mistake of blaming capitalism for all existing social and political evils, nor of assuming that the very establishment of socialism would be sufficient to cure the social and political ills of humanity," he wrote. Such thinking led to the "fanatical intolerance" that infected the Communist Party faithful, and it opened the way to tyranny.

Despite his criticisms of untrammeled capitalism, what repelled him more—and had repelled him his entire life—was repression of free thought and individuality. "Any government is evil if it carries within it the tendency to deteriorate into tyranny," he warned the Russian scientists. "The danger of such deterioration is more acute in a country in which the government has authority not only over the armed forces but also over every channel of education and information as well as over the existence of every single citizen."[27]

Just as his dispute with the Russian scientists was breaking, Einstein was working with Raymond Gram Swing to update the article in the *Atlantic* that they had done two years earlier. This time Einstein attacked Russia's rulers. Their reasons for not supporting a world government, he said, "quite obviously are pretexts." Their real fear was that their repressive communist command system might not survive in such an environment. "The Russians may be partly right about the difficulty of retaining their present social structure in a supranational regime, though in time they may be brought to see that this is a far lesser loss than remaining isolated from a world of law."[28]

The West should proceed with creating a world government without Russia, he said. They would eventually come around, he thought: "I believe that if this were done intelligently (rather than in clumsy Truman style!) Russia would cooperate once she realized that she was no longer able to prevent world government anyhow."[29]

From then on, Einstein seemed to take a perverse pride in disputing those who blamed the Russians for everything, and those who blamed them for nothing. When a left-leaning pacifist he knew sent him a book he had written on arms control, expecting Einstein's endorsement, he got instead a rebuff. "You have presented the whole problem as an advocate of the Soviet point of view," Einstein wrote, "but you have kept silent about everything which is not favorable for the Soviets (and this is not little)."[30]

Even his longtime pacifism developed a hard, realistic edge when it came to dealing with Russia, just as it had after the Nazis rose to power in Germany. Pacifists liked to think that Einstein's break with their philosophy in the 1930s was an aberration caused by the unique threat posed by the Nazis, and some biographers likewise treat it as a temporary anomaly.[31] But that minimizes the shift in Einstein's thinking. He was never again a pure pacifist.

When he was asked, for example, to join a campaign to persuade American scientists to refuse to work on atomic weapons, he not only declined but berated the organizers for advocating unilateral disarmament. "Disarmament cannot be effective unless all countries participate," he lectured. "If even one nation continues to arm, openly or secretly, the disarmament of the others will involve disastrous consequences."

Pacifists like himself had made a mistake in the 1920s by encouraging Germany's neighbors not to rearm, he explained. "This merely served to encourage the arrogance of the Germans." There were parallels now with Russia. "Similarly, your proposition would, if effective, surely lead to a serious weakening of the democracies," he wrote those pushing the antimilitary petition. "For we must realize that we are probably not able to exert any significant influence on the attitude of our Russian colleagues." [32]

He took a similar stance when his former colleagues in the War Resisters' League asked him to rejoin in 1948. They flattered him by quoting one of his old pacifist proclamations, but Einstein rebuffed them. "That statement accurately expresses the views I held on war resistance in the period from 1918 to the early thirties," he replied. "Now, however, I feel that policy, which involves the refusal of individuals to participate in military activities, is too primitive."

Simplistic pacifism could be dangerous, he warned, especially given the internal policies and external attitude of Russia. "The war resistance movement actually serves to weaken the nations with a more liberal type of government and, indirectly, to support the policies of the existing tyrannical governments," he argued. "Antimilitaristic activities, through refusal of military service, are wise only if they are feasible everywhere throughout the world. Individual antimilitarism is impossible in Russia." [33]

Some pacifists argued that world socialism, rather than world government, would be the best foundation for lasting peace. Einstein disagreed. "You say that socialism by its very nature rejects the remedy of war," Einstein replied to one such advocate. "I do not believe that. I can easily imagine that two socialist states might fight a war against each other." [34]

One of the early flashpoints of the cold war was Poland, where the occupying Red Army had installed a pro-Soviet regime without the open elections that Moscow had promised. When that new Polish government invited Einstein to a conference, they got a taste of his independence from party dogma. He politely explained that he no longer traveled overseas, and he sent a careful message that offered encouragement but also stressed his call for a world government.

The Poles decided to delete the parts about world government, which Moscow opposed. Einstein was furious, and he released his undelivered full message to the *New York Times*. "Mankind can gain protection against the danger of unimaginable destruction and wanton annihilation only if a supranational organization has alone the authority to produce or possess these weapons," it said. He also complained to the British pacifist who presided over the meeting that the communists were trying to enforce conformity to a party line: "I am convinced that our colleagues on the other side of the fence are completely unable to express their real opinions."[35]

The FBI Files

He had criticized the Soviet Union, refused to visit there, and opposed the sharing of atomic secrets unless a world government could be created. He had never worked on the bomb-making project and knew no classified information about its technology. Nevertheless, Einstein was unwittingly caught up in a chain of events that showed how suspicious, intrusive, and inept the FBI could be back then when pursuing the specter of Soviet communism.

The Red Scares and investigations into communist subversion originally had some legitimate justifications, but eventually they included bumbling inquisitions that resembled witch hunts. They began in earnest at the start of 1950, after America was stunned by news that the Soviets had developed their own bomb. During the first few weeks of that year, President Truman launched a program to build a hydrogen bomb, a refugee German physicist working in Los Alamos named Klaus Fuchs was arrested as a Soviet spy, and Senator Joseph McCarthy gave his famous speech, claiming that he had a list of card-carrying communists in the State Department.

As the head of the Emergency Committee of Atomic Scientists, Einstein had dismayed Edward Teller by not supporting the building of the hydrogen bomb. But Einstein also had not opposed it outright. When A. J. Muste, a prominent pacifist and socialist activist, asked him to join an appeal to delay construction of the new weapon, Einstein declined. "Your new proposal seems quite impractical to me," he said. "As long as competitive armament prevails, it will not be possible to halt the process in one country."[36] It was more sensible, he felt, to push for a global solution that included a world government.

The day after Einstein wrote that letter, Truman made his announcement of a full-scale effort to produce the H-bomb. From his Princeton home, Einstein taped a three-minute appearance for the premiere of a Sunday evening NBC show called *Today with Mrs. Roosevelt*. The former first lady had become a voice of progressivism after the death of her husband. "Each step appears as the inevitable consequence of the one that went before," he said of the arms race. "And at the end, looming ever clearer, lies general annihilation." The headline in the *New York Post* the next day was, "Einstein Warns World: Outlaw H-Bomb or Perish."[37]

Einstein made another point in his televised talk. He expressed his growing concern over the U.S. government's increased security measures and willingness to compromise the liberties of its citizens. "The loyalty of citizens, particularly civil servants, is carefully supervised by a police force growing more powerful every day," he warned. "People of independent thought are harassed."

As if to prove him right, J. Edgar Hoover, who hated communists and Eleanor Roosevelt with almost equal passion, the very next day called in the FBI's chief of domestic intelligence and ordered a report on Einstein's loyalty and possible communist connections.

The resulting fifteen-page document, produced two days later, listed thirty-four organizations, some purportedly communist fronts, that Einstein had been affiliated with or lent his name to, including the Emergency Committee of Atomic Scientists. "He is principally a pacifist and could be considered a liberal thinker," the memo concluded somewhat benignly, and it did not charge him with being either a communist or someone who gave information to subversives.[38]

Indeed, there was nothing that linked Einstein to any security threat. A reading of the dossier, however, makes the FBI agents look like Keystone Kops. They bumbled around, unable to answer questions such as whether Elsa Einstein was his first wife, whether Helen Dukas was a Soviet spy while in Germany, and whether Einstein had been responsible for bringing Klaus Fuchs into the United States. (In all three cases, the correct answer was no.)

The agents also tried to pin down a tip that Elsa had told a friend in California that they had a son by the name of Albert Einstein Jr. who was being held in Russia. In fact, Hans Albert Einstein was by then an engineering professor at Berkeley. Neither he nor Eduard, still in a Swiss sanatorium, had ever been to Russia. (If there was any basis to the rumor, it was that Elsa's daughter Margot had married a Russian, who returned there after they divorced, though the FBI never found that out.)

The FBI had been gathering rumors about Einstein ever since the 1932 screed from Mrs. Frothingham and her women patriots. Now it began systematically keeping track of that material in one growing dossier. It included such tips as one from a Berlin woman who sent him a mathematical scheme for winning the Berlin lottery and had concluded he was a communist when he did not respond to her.[39] By the time he died, the Bureau would amass 1,427 pages stored in fourteen boxes, all stamped *Confidential* but containing nothing incriminating.[40]

What is most notable, in retrospect, about Einstein's FBI file is not all the odd tips it contained, but the one relevant piece of information that was completely missing. Einstein did in fact consort with a Soviet spy, unwittingly. But the FBI remained clueless about it.

The spy was Margarita Konenkova, who lived in Greenwich Village with her husband, the Russian realist sculptor Sergei Konenkov, mentioned earlier. A former lawyer who spoke five languages and had an engaging way with men, so to speak, her job as a Russian secret agent was to try to influence American scientists. She had been introduced to Einstein by Margot, and she became a frequent visitor to Princeton during the war.

Out of duty or desire, she embarked on an affair with the widowed Einstein. One weekend during the summer of 1941, she and some friends invited him to a cottage on Long Island, and to everyone's surprise he accepted. They packed a lunch of boiled chicken, took the train from Penn Station, and spent a pleasant weekend during which Einstein sailed on the Sound and scribbled equations on the porch. At one point they went to a secluded beach to watch the sunset and almost got arrested by a local policeman who had no idea who Einstein was. "Can't you read," the officer said, pointing to a no-trespassing sign. He and Konenkova remained lovers until she returned to Moscow in 1945 at age 51.[41]

She succeeded in introducing him to the Soviet vice consul in New York, who was also a spy. But Einstein had no secrets to share, nor is there any evidence that he had any inclination at all to help the Soviets in any way, and he rebuffed her attempts to get him to visit Moscow.

The affair and potential security issue came to light not because of any FBI sleuthing but because a collection of nine amorous letters written by Einstein to Konenkova in the 1940s became public in 1998. In addition, a former Soviet spy, Pavel Sudoplatov, published a rather explosive but not totally reliable memoir in which he revealed that she was an agent code-named "Lukas."[42]

Einstein's letters to Konenkova were written the year after she left America. Neither she nor Sudoplatov, nor anyone else, ever claimed that Einstein passed along any secrets, wittingly or unwittingly. However, the letters do make clear that, at age 66, he was still able to be amorous in prose and probably in person. "I recently washed my hair myself, but not with great success," he said in one. "I am not as careful as you are."

Even with his Russian lover, however, Einstein made clear that he was not an unalloyed lover of Russia. In one letter he denigrated Moscow's militaristic May Day celebration, saying, "I watch these exaggerated patriotic exhibits with concern."[43] Any expressions of excess nationalism and militarism had always made him uncomfortable, ever since he had watched German soldiers march by when he was a boy, and Russia's were no different.

Einstein's Politics

Despite Hoover's suspicions, Einstein was a solid American citizen, and he considered his opposition to the wave of security and loyalty investigations to be a defense of the nation's true values. Tolerance of free expression and independence of thought, he repeatedly argued, were the core values that Americans, to his delight, most cherished.

His first two presidential votes had been cast for Franklin Roosevelt, whom he publicly and enthusiastically endorsed. In 1948, dismayed by Harry Truman's cold war policies, Einstein voted for the Progressive Party candidate Henry Wallace, who advocated greater cooperation with Russia and increased social welfare spending.

Throughout his life, Einstein was consistent in the fundamental premises of his politics. Ever since his student days in Switzerland, he had supported socialist economic policies tempered by a strong instinct for individual freedom, personal autonomy, democratic institutions, and protection of liberties. He befriended many of the democratic socialist leaders in Britain and America, such as Bertrand Russell and Norman Thomas, and in 1949 he wrote an influential essay for the inaugural issue of the *Monthly Review* titled "Why Socialism?"

In it he argued that unrestrained capitalism produced great disparities of wealth, cycles of boom and depression, and festering levels of unemployment. The system encouraged selfishness instead of cooperation, and acquiring wealth rather than serving others. People were educated for careers rather than for a love of work and creativity. And political parties became corrupted by political contributions from owners of great capital.

These problems could be avoided, Einstein argued in his article, through a socialist economy, if it guarded against tyranny and centralization of power. "A planned economy, which adjusts production to the needs of the community, would distribute the work to be done among all those able to work and would guarantee a livelihood to every man, woman, and child," he wrote. "The education of the individual, in addition to promoting his own innate abilities, would attempt to develop in him a sense of responsibility for his fellow-men in place of the glorification of power and success in our present society."

He added, however, that planned economies faced the danger of becoming oppressive, bureaucratic, and tyrannical, as had happened in communist countries such as Russia. "A planned economy may be accompanied by the complete enslavement of the individual," he warned. It was therefore important for social democrats who believed in individual liberty to face two critical questions: "How is it possible, in view of the far-reaching centralization of political and economic power, to

prevent bureaucracy from becoming all-powerful and overweening? How can the rights of the individual be protected?" [44]

That imperative—to protect the rights of the individual—was Einstein's most fundamental political tenet. Individualism and freedom were necessary for creative art and science to flourish. Personally, politically, and professionally, he was repulsed by any restraints.

That is why he remained outspoken about racial discrimination in America. In Princeton during the 1940s, movie theaters were still segregated, blacks were not allowed to try on shoes or clothes at department stores, and the student newspaper declared that equal access for blacks to the university was "a noble sentiment but the time had not yet come." [45]

As a Jew who had grown up in Germany, Einstein was acutely sensitive to such discrimination. "The more I feel an American, the more this situation pains me," he wrote in an essay called "The Negro Question" for *Pageant* magazine. "I can escape the feeling of complicity in it only by speaking out." [46]

Although he rarely accepted in person the many honorary degrees offered to him, Einstein made an exception when he was invited to Lincoln University, a black institution in Pennsylvania. Wearing his tattered gray herringbone jacket, he stood at a blackboard and went over his relativity equations for students, and then he gave a graduation address in which he denounced segregation as "an American tradition which is uncritically handed down from one generation to the next." [47] As if to break the pattern, he met with the 6-year-old son of Horace Bond, the university's president. That son, Julian, went on to become a Georgia state senator, one of the leaders of the civil rights movement, and chairman of the NAACP.

There was, however, one group for which Einstein could feel little tolerance after the war. "The Germans, as a whole nation, are responsible for these mass killings and should be punished as a people," he declared. [48] When a German friend, James Franck, asked him at the end of 1945 to join an appeal calling for a lenient treatment of the German economy, Einstein angrily refused. "It is absolutely necessary to prevent the restoration of German industrial policy for many years," he said. "Should your appeal be circulated, I shall do whatever I can to oppose it." When Franck persisted, Einstein became even more adamant. "The Germans butchered millions of civilians according to a well-prepared plan," he wrote. "They would do it again if only they were able to. Not a trace of guilt or remorse is to be found among them."[49]

Einstein would not even permit his books to be sold in Germany again, nor would he allow his name to be placed back on the rolls of any German scientific society. "The crimes of the Germans are really the most abominable ever to be recorded in the history of the so-called civilized nations," he wrote the physicist Otto Hahn. "The conduct of the German intellectuals—viewed as a class—was no better than that of the mob."[50]

Like many Jewish refugees, his feelings had a personal basis. Among those who suffered under the Nazis was his first cousin Roberto, son of Uncle Jakob. When German troops were retreating from Italy near the end of the war, they wantonly killed his wife and two daughters, then burned his home while he hid in the woods. Roberto wrote to Einstein, giving the horrible details, and committed suicide a year later.[51]

The result was that Einstein's national and tribal kinship became even more clear in his own mind. "I am not a German but a Jew by nationality," he declared as the war ended.[52]

Yet in ways that were subtle yet real, he had become an American as well. After settling in Princeton in 1933, he never once in the remaining twenty-two years of his life left the United States, except for the brief cruise to Bermuda that was necessary to launch his immigration process.

Admittedly, he was a somewhat contrarian citizen. But in that regard he was in the tradition of some venerable strands in the fabric of American character: fiercely protective of individual liberties, often cranky about government interference, distrustful of great concentrations of wealth, and a believer in the idealistic internationalism that gained favor among American intellectuals after both of the great wars of the twentieth century.

His penchant for dissent and nonconformity did not make him a worse American, he felt, but a better one. On the day in 1940 when he was naturalized as a citizen, Einstein had touched on these values in a radio talk. After the war ended, Truman proclaimed a day in honor of all new citizens, and the judge who had naturalized Einstein sent out thousands of form letters inviting anyone he had sworn in to come to a park in Trenton to celebrate. To the judge's amazement, ten thousand people showed up. Even more amazing, Einstein and his household decided to come down for the festivities. During the ceremony, he sat smiling and waving, with a young girl sitting on his lap, happy to be a small part of "I Am an American" Day.[53]

CHAPTER TWENTY-THREE

LANDMARK

1948–1953

With Israeli Prime Minister David Ben-Gurion in Princeton, 1951

The Endless Quest

The problems of the world were important to Einstein, but the problems of the cosmos helped him to keep earthly matters in perspective. Even though he was producing little of scientific significance, physics rather than politics would remain his defining endeavor until the day he died. One morning when walking to work with his scientific assistant and fellow arms control advocate Ernst Straus, Einstein mused at their ability to divide their time between the two realms. "But our equations are much more important to me," Einstein added. "Politics is for the present, while our equations are for eternity." [1]

Einstein had officially retired from the Institute for Advanced Study at the end of the war, when he turned 66. But he continued to work in a small office there every day, and he was still able to enlist the aid of loyal assistants willing to pursue what had come to be considered his quaint quest for a unified field theory.

Each weekday, he would wake at a civilized hour, eat breakfast and read the papers, and then around ten walk slowly up Mercer Street to the Institute, trailing stories both real and apocryphal. His colleague Abraham Pais recalled "one occasion when a car hit a tree after the driver suddenly recognized the face of the beautiful old man walking along the street, the black woolen knit cap firmly planted on his long white hair."[2]

Soon after the war ended, J. Robert Oppenheimer came from Los Alamos to take over as director of the Institute. A brilliant, chain-smoking theoretical physicist, he proved charismatic and competent enough to be an inspiring leader for the scientists who built the atomic bomb. With his charm and biting wit, he tended to produce either acolytes or enemies, but Einstein fell into neither category. He and Oppenheimer viewed each other with a mixture of amusement and respect, which allowed them to develop a cordial though not close relationship.[3]

When Oppenheimer first visited the Institute in 1935, he called it a "madhouse" with "solipsistic luminaries shining in separate and hapless desolation." As for the greatest of these luminaries, Oppenheimer declared, "Einstein is completely cuckoo," though he seemed to mean it in an affectionate way.[4]

Once they became colleagues, Oppenheimer became more adroit at dealing with his luminous charges and his jabs became more subtle. Einstein, he declared, was "a landmark but not a beacon," meaning he was admired for his great triumphs but attracted few apostles in his current endeavors, which was true. Years later, he provided another telling description of Einstein: "There was always in him a powerful purity at once childlike and profoundly stubborn."[5]

Einstein became a closer friend, and a walking partner, of another iconic figure at the Institute, the intensely introverted Kurt Gödel, a German-speaking mathematical logician from Brno and Vienna. Gödel was famous for his "incompleteness theory," a pair of logical proofs that purport to show that any useful mathematical system will have some propositions that cannot be proven true or false based on the postulates of that system.

Out of the supercharged German-speaking intellectual world, in which physics and mathematics and philosophy intertwined, three jarring theories of the twentieth century emerged: Einstein's relativity, Heisenberg's uncertainty, and Gödel's incompleteness. The surface similarity of the three words, all of which conjure up a cosmos that is tentative and subjective, oversimplifies the theories and the connections between them. Nevertheless, they all seemed to have philosophical resonance, and this became the topic of discussion when Gödel and Einstein walked to work together.[6]

They were very different personalities. Einstein was filled with good humor and sagacity, both qualities lacking in Gödel, whose intense logic sometimes overwhelmed common sense. This was on glorious display when Gödel decided to become a U.S. citizen in 1947. He took his preparation for the exam very seriously, studied the Constitution carefully, and (as might be expected by the formulator of the incompleteness theory) found what he believed was a logical flaw. There was an internal inconsistency, he insisted, that could allow the entire government to degenerate into tyranny.

Concerned, Einstein decided to accompany—or chaperone—Gödel on his visit to Trenton to take the citizenship test, which was to be administered by the same judge who had done so for Einstein. On the drive, he and a third friend tried to distract Gödel and dissuade him from mentioning this perceived flaw, but to no avail. When the judge asked him about the Constitution, Gödel launched into his proof that its internal inconsistency made a dictatorship possible. Fortunately, the judge, who by now cherished his connection to Einstein, cut Gödel off. "You needn't go into all that," he said, and Gödel's citizenship was saved.[7]

During their walks, Gödel explored some of the implications of relativity theory, and he came up with an analysis that called into question whether time, rather than merely being relative, could be said to exist at all. Einstein's equations, he figured, could describe a universe that was rotating rather than (or in addition to) expanding. In such a case, the relationship between space and time could become, mathematically, mixed up. "The existence of an objective lapse of time," he wrote, "means that reality consists of an infinity of layers of 'now' which come into existence successively. But if simultaneity is something relative, each observer has his own set of 'nows,' and none of these various layers can claim the prerogative of representing the objective lapse of time."[8]

As a result, Gödel argued, time travel would be possible. "By making a round trip on a rocket ship in a sufficiently wide curve, it is possible in these worlds to travel into any region of the past, present and future, and back again." That would be absurd, he noted, because then we could go back and chat with a younger version of ourselves (or, even more discomforting, our older version could come back and chat with us). "Gödel had achieved an amazing demonstration that time travel, strictly understood, was consistent with the theory of relativity," writes Boston University philosophy professor Palle Yourgrau in his book on Gödel's relationship with Einstein, *World Without Time*. "The primary result was a powerful argument that if time travel is possible, time itself is not."[9]

Einstein responded to Gödel's essay along with a variety of others that had been collected in a book, and he seemed to be mildly impressed but also not totally engaged by the argument. In his brief assessment, Einstein called Gödel's "an important contribution" but noted that he had thought of the issue long ago and "the problem here involved disturbed me already." He implied that although time travel may be true as a mathematical conceivability, it might not be possible in reality. "It will be interesting to weigh whether these are not to be excluded on physical grounds," Einstein concluded.[10]

For his part, Einstein remained focused on his own white whale, which he pursued not with the demonic drive of Ahab but the dutiful serenity of Ishmael. In his quest for a unified field theory, he still had no compelling physical insight—such as the equivalence of gravity and acceleration, or the relativity of simultaneity—to guide his way, so his endeavors remained a groping through clouds of abstract mathematical equations with no ground lights to orient him. "It's like being in an airship in which one can cruise around in the clouds but cannot see clearly how one can return to reality, i.e., earth," he lamented to a friend.[11]

His goal, as it had been for decades, was to come up with a theory that encompassed both the electromagnetic and the gravitational fields, but he had no compelling reason to believe that they in fact *had* to be part of the same unified structure, other than his intuition that nature liked the beauty of simplicity.

Likewise, he was still hoping to explain the existence of particles in terms of a field theory by finding permissible pointlike solutions to his field equations. "He argued that if one believed wholeheartedly in the basic idea of a field theory, matter should enter not as an interloper but as an honest part of the field itself," recalled one of his Princeton collaborators, Banesh Hoffmann. "Indeed, one might say that he wanted to build matter out of nothing but convolutions of spacetime." In the process he used all sorts of mathematical devices, but constantly searched for others. "I need more mathematics," he lamented at one point to Hoffmann.[12]

Why did he persist? Deep inside, such disjunctures and dualities—different field theories for gravity and electromagnetism, distinctions between particles and fields—had always discomforted him. Simplicity and unity, he intuitively believed, were hallmarks of the Old One's handiwork. "A theory is more impressive the greater the simplicity of its premises, the more different things it relates, and the more expanded its area of applicability," he wrote.[13]

In the early 1940s, Einstein returned for a while to the five-dimensional mathematical approach that he had adopted from Theodor Kaluza two decades earlier. He even worked on it with Wolfgang Pauli, the quantum mechanics pioneer, who had spent some of the war years in Princeton. But he could not get his equations to describe particles.[14]

So he moved on to a strategy dubbed "bivector fields." Einstein seemed to be getting a little desperate. This new approach, he admitted, might require surrendering the principle of locality that he had sanctified in some of his thought-experiments assaulting quantum mechanics.[15] In any event, it was soon abandoned as well.

Einstein's final strategy, which he pursued for the final decade of his life, was a resurrection of one he had tried during the 1920s. It used a Riemannian metric that was not assumed to be symmetric, which opened the way for sixteen quantities. Ten combinations of them were used for gravity, and the remaining ones for electromagnetism.

Einstein sent early versions of this work to his old comrade Schrödinger. "I am sending them to nobody else, because you are the only person known to me who is not wearing blinders in regard to the fundamental questions in our science," Einstein wrote. "The attempt depends on an idea that at first seems antiquated and unprofitable, the introduction of a non-symmetrical tensor . . . Pauli stuck his tongue out at me when I told him about it." [16]

Schrödinger spent three days poring over Einstein's work and wrote back to say how impressed he was. "You are after big game," he said.

Einstein was thrilled with such support. "This correspondence gives me great joy," he replied, "because you are my closest brother and your brain runs so similarly to mine." But he soon began to realize that the gossamer theories he was spinning were mathematically elegant but never seemed to relate to anything physical. "Inwardly I am not so certain as I previously asserted," he confessed to Schrödinger a few months later. "We have squandered a lot of time on this, and the result looks like a gift from the devil's grandmother." [17]

And yet he soldiered on, churning out papers and producing the occasional headline. When a new edition of his book, *The Meaning of Relativity,* was being prepared in 1949, he added the latest version of the paper he had shown Schrödinger as an appendix. The *New York Times* reprinted an entire page of complex equations from the manuscript, along with a front-page story headlined "New Einstein Theory Gives a Master Key to Universe: Scientist, after 30 Years' Work, Evolves Concept That Promises to Bridge Gap between the Star and the Atom." [18]

But Einstein soon realized that it still wasn't right. During the six weeks between when he submitted the chapter and when it went to the printers, he had second thoughts and revised it yet again.

In fact, he continued to revise the theory repeatedly, but to no avail. His growing pessimism was visible in the lamentations he sent to his old friend from the Olympia Academy days, Maurice Solovine, then

Einstein's publisher in Paris. "I shall never ever solve it," he wrote in 1948. "It will be forgotten and must later be rediscovered again." Then, the following year: "I am uncertain as to whether I was even on the right track. The current generation sees in me both a heretic and a reactionary who has, so to speak, outlived himself." And, with some resignation, in 1951: "The unified field theory has been put into retirement. It is so difficult to employ mathematically that I have not been able to verify it. This state of affairs will last for many more years, mainly because physicists have no understanding of logical and philosophical arguments."[19]

Einstein's quest for a unified theory was destined to produce no tangible results that added to the framework of physics. He was able to come up with no great insights or thought experiments, no intuitions about underlying principles, to help him visualize his goal. "No pictures came to our aid," his collaborator Hoffmann lamented. "It is intensely mathematical, and over the years, with helpers and alone, Einstein surmounted difficulty after difficulty, only to find new ones awaiting him."[20]

Perhaps the search was futile. And if it turns out a century from now that there is indeed no unified theory to be found, it will also look misconceived. But Einstein never regretted his dedication to it. When a colleague asked him one day why he was spending—perhaps squandering—his time in this lonely endeavor, he replied that even if the chance of finding a unified theory was small, the attempt was worthy. He had already made his name, he noted. His position was secure, and he could afford to take the risk and expend the time. A younger theorist, however, could not take such a risk, for he might thus sacrifice a promising career. So, Einstein said, it was his duty to do it.[21]

Einstein's repeated failures in seeking a unified theory did not soften his skepticism about quantum mechanics. Niels Bohr, his frequent sparring partner, came to the Institute for a stay in 1948 and spent part of his time writing an essay on their debates at the Solvay Conferences before the war.[22] Struggling with the article in his office one floor above Einstein's, he developed writer's block and called in Abraham Pais to help him. As Bohr paced furiously around an oblong table, Pais coaxed him and took notes.

When he got frustrated, Bohr sometimes would simply sputter the same word over and over. Soon he was doing so with Einstein's name. He walked to the window and kept muttering, over and over, "Einstein . . . Einstein . . ."

At one such moment, Einstein softly opened the door, tiptoed in, and signaled to Pais not to say anything. He had come to steal a bit of tobacco, which his doctor had ordered him not to buy. Bohr kept muttering, finally spurting out one last loud "Einstein" and then turning around to find himself staring at the cause of his anxieties. "It is an understatement to say that for a moment Bohr was speechless," Pais recalled. Then, after an instant, they all burst into laughter.[23]

Another colleague who tried and failed to convert Einstein was John Wheeler, Princeton University's renowned theoretical physicist. One afternoon he came by Mercer Street to explain a new approach to quantum theory (known as the sum-over-histories approach) that he was developing with his graduate student, Richard Feynman. "I had gone to Einstein with the hope to persuade him of the naturalness of the quantum theory when seen in this new light," Wheeler recalled. Einstein listened patiently for twenty minutes, but when it was over repeated his very familiar refrain: "I still cannot believe that the good Lord plays dice."

Wheeler showed his disappointment, and Einstein softened his pronouncement slightly. "Of course, I may be wrong," he said in a slow and humorous cadence. Pause. "But perhaps I have earned the right to make my mistakes." Einstein later confided to a woman friend, "I don't think I'll live to find out who is correct."

Wheeler kept coming back, sometimes bringing his students, and Einstein admitted that he found many of his arguments "sensible." But he was never converted. Near the end of his life, Einstein regaled a small group of Wheeler's students. When the talk turned to quantum mechanics, he once again tried to poke holes in the idea that our observations can affect and determine realities. "When a mouse observes," Einstein asked them, "does that change the state of the universe?"[24]

The Lion in Winter

Mileva Marić, her health deteriorating due to a succession of minor strokes, was still living in Zurich and trying to take care of their institutionalized son, Eduard, whose behavior had become increasingly erratic and violent. Financial problems again plagued her and revived the tension with her former husband. The portion of the money that he had put into trust for her in America from the Nobel Prize had slipped away during the Depression, and two of her three apartment houses had been sold to help pay for Eduard's care. By late 1946, Einstein was pushing to sell the remaining house and give control of the money to a legal guardian who would be appointed for Eduard. But Marić had the usufruct of the house and its proceeds, as well as power of attorney over it, and she was terrified of surrendering any control.[25]

One cold day later that winter, she slipped on the ice on the way to see Eduard and ended up lying unconscious until strangers found her. She knew she was going to die soon, and she had recurring nightmares about struggling through the snow, unable to reach Eduard. She was panicked about what would happen to him, and wrote heartwrenching letters to Hans Albert.[26]

Einstein succeeded in selling her house by early 1948, but with her power of attorney she blocked the proceeds from being sent to him. He wrote to Hans Albert, giving him all the details and promising him that, whatever happened, he would take care of Eduard "even if it costs me all my savings."[27] That May, Marić had a stroke and lapsed into a trance in which she repeatedly muttered only "No, no!" until she died three months later. The money from the sale of her apartment, 85,000 Swiss francs, was found under her mattress.

Eduard lapsed into a daze and never spoke of his mother again. Carl Seelig, a friend of Einstein's who lived nearby, visited him frequently and sent back regular reports to Einstein. Seelig hoped to get him to make contact with his son, but he never did. "There is something blocking me that I am unable to analyze fully," Einstein told Seelig. "I believe I would be arousing painful feelings of various kinds in him if I made an appearance in whatever form."[28]

Einstein's own health began to decline in 1948 as well. For years he had been plagued by stomach ailments and anemia, and late that year, after an attack of sharp pains and vomiting, he checked into the Jewish Hospital in Brooklyn. Exploratory surgery revealed an aneurysm in the abdominal aorta,* but doctors decided there was not much they could do about it. It was assumed, correctly, that it was likely to kill him one day, but in the meantime he could live on borrowed time and a healthy diet.[29]

To recuperate, he went on the longest trip he would make during his twenty-two years as a Princeton resident: down to Sarasota, Florida. For once, he successfully avoided publicity. "Einstein Elusive Sarasota Visitor," the local paper lamented.

Helen Dukas accompanied him. After Elsa's death, she had become even more of a loyal guardian, and she even shielded Einstein from letters written by Hans Albert's daughter, Evelyn. Hans Albert suspected that Dukas may have had an affair with his father, and said so to others. "On many occasions, Hans Albert told me of his long-held suspicion," family friend Peter Bucky later recalled. But others who knew Dukas found the suggestion to be implausible.[30]

By then, Einstein had become much friendlier with his son, now a respected engineering professor at Berkeley. "Whenever we met," Hans Albert later recalled of his trips east to see his father, "we mutually reported on all the interesting developments in our field and in our work." Einstein particularly loved learning about new inventions and solutions to puzzles. "Maybe both, inventions and puzzles, reminded him of the happy, carefree, and successful days at the patent office in Bern," said Hans Albert.[31]

Einstein's beloved sister, Maja, the closest intimate of his life, was also in declining health. She had come to Princeton when Mussolini enacted anti-Jewish laws, but her husband, Paul Winteler, from whom she had been drifting apart for many years,[32] moved to Switzerland to be with his own sister and her husband, Michele Besso. They corresponded often, but never rejoined one another.

---

* An aneurysm is the ballooning or dilation of a blood vessel, as if it were blistering. The abdominal aorta is one of the large arteries from the heart, in the region between the diaphragm and the abdomen.

Maja began, as Elsa had, to look more like Einstein, with radiating silver hair and a devilish smile. The inflection of her voice and the slightly skeptical wry tone she used when asking questions were similar to his. Although she was a vegetarian, she loved hot dogs, so Einstein decreed that they were a vegetable, and that satisfied her.[33]

Maja had suffered a stroke and, by 1948, was confined to bed most of the time. Einstein doted on her as he did no other person. Every evening he read aloud to her. Sometimes the fare was heavy, such as the arguments of Ptolemy against Aristarchus's opinion that the world rotates around the sun. "I could not help thinking of certain arguments of present-day physicists: learned and subtle, but without insight," he wrote Solovine about that evening. Other times, the readings were lighter but perhaps just as revealing, such as the evenings he read from *Don Quixote;* he sometimes compared his own quixotic parries against the prevailing windmills of science with that of the old knight with a ready lance.[34]

When Maja died in June 1951, Einstein was grief-stricken. "I miss her more than can be imagined," he wrote a friend. He sat on the back porch of his Mercer Street home for hours, pale and tense, staring into space. When his stepdaughter Margot came to console him, he pointed to the sky and said, as if reassuring himself, "Look into nature, and then you will understand it better."[35]

Margot had likewise left her husband, who responded by writing, as he had long wanted to, an unauthorized biography of Einstein. She worshipped Einstein, and each year they grew closer. He found her presence charming. "When Margot speaks," he said, "you see flowers growing."[36]

His ability to engender and feel such affection belied his reputation for being emotionally distant. Both Maja and Margot preferred living with him to living with their own husbands as they got older. He had been a difficult husband and father because he did not take well to any constricting bonds, but he could also be intense and passionate, both with family and friends, when he found himself engaged rather than confined.

Einstein was human, and thus both good and flawed, and the greatest of his failings came in the realm of the personal. He had lifelong friends who were devoted to him, and he had family members who doted on him, but there were also those few—Mileva and Eduard foremost among them—whom he simply walled out when the relationship became too painful.

As for his colleagues, they saw his kindly side. He was gentle and generous with partners and subordinates, both those who agreed with him and those who didn't. He had deep friendships lasting for decades. He was unfailingly benevolent to his assistants. His warmth, sometimes missing at home, radiated on the rest of humanity. So as he grew old, he was not only respected and revered by his colleagues, he was loved.

They honored him, with the blend of scientific and personal camaraderie he had enjoyed since his student days, at a seventieth birthday convocation upon his return from his Florida recuperation. Although the talks were supposed to focus on Einstein's science, most dwelled on his sweetness and humanity. When he walked in, there was a hush, then thunderous applause. "Einstein just had no sense at all about what absolute reverence there was for him," one of his assistants recalled.[37]

His closest friends at the Institute bought him a present, an advanced AM-FM radio and high-fidelity record player, which they installed in his home secretly when he was at work one day. Einstein was thrilled and used it not only for music but for news. In particular, he liked to catch Howard K. Smith's commentaries.

He had pretty much given up the violin by then. It was too hard on his aging fingers. Instead, he focused on the piano, which he was not quite as good at playing. Once, after repeatedly stumbling on a passage, he turned to Margot and smiled. "Mozart wrote such nonsense here," he said.[38]

He came to look even more like a prophet, with his hair getting longer, his eyes a bit sadder and more weary. His face grew more deeply etched yet somehow more delicate. It showed wisdom and wear but still a vitality. He was dreamy, as he was when a child, but also now serene.

"I am generally regarded as sort of a petrified object," he noted to Max Born, then a professor in Edinburgh, one of those friends whose affection had lasted so long. "I find this role not too distasteful, as it corresponds very well with my temperament . . . I simply enjoy giving more than receiving in every respect, do not take myself nor the doings of the masses seriously, am not ashamed of my weaknesses and vices, and naturally take things as they come with equanimity and humor."[39]

Israel's Presidency

Before the Second World War, Einstein had stated his opposition to a Jewish state when speaking to three thousand celebrants at a Manhattan hotel seder. "My awareness of the essential nature of Judaism resists the idea of a Jewish state with borders, an army, and a measure of temporal power," he said. "I am afraid of the inner damage Judaism will sustain—especially from the development of a narrow nationalism within our ranks. We are no longer the Jews of the Maccabee period."[40]

After the war, he took the same stance. When he testified in Washington in 1946 to an international committee looking into the situation in Palestine, he denounced the British for pitting Jews against Arabs, called for more Jewish immigration, but rejected the idea that the Jews should be nationalistic. "The State idea is not in my heart," he said in a quiet whisper that reverberated through the shocked audience of ardent Zionists. "I cannot understand why it is needed."[41] Rabbi Stephen Wise was flabbergasted that Einstein would break ranks with true Zionists at such a public hearing, and he got him to sign a clarifying statement that was, in fact, not clarifying at all.

Einstein was especially dismayed by the militaristic methods used by Menachem Begin and other Jewish militia leaders, and he joined with his occasional antagonist Sidney Hook to sign a petition in the *New York Times* denouncing Begin as a "terrorist" and "closely akin" to the fascists.[42] The violence was contrary to Jewish heritage. "We imitate the stupid nationalism and racial nonsense of the goyim," he wrote a friend in 1947.

But when the State of Israel was declared in 1948, Einstein wrote the same friend to say that his attitude had changed. "I have never considered the idea of a state a good one, for economic, political and military reasons," he conceded. "But now, there is no going back, and one has to fight it out."[43]

The creation of Israel caused him, yet again, to back away from the pure pacifism he had once embraced. "We may regret that we have to use methods that are repulsive and stupid to us," he wrote to a Jewish group in Uruguay, "but to bring about better conditions in the international sphere, we must first of all maintain our experience by all means at our disposal."[44]

Chaim Weizmann, the indefatigable Zionist who brought Einstein to America in 1921, had become Israel's first president, a prestigious but generally ceremonial post in a system that vested most power in the prime minister and cabinet. When he died in November 1952, a Jerusalem newspaper began urging that Einstein be tapped to replace him. Prime Minister David Ben-Gurion bowed to the pressure, and word quickly spread that Einstein would be asked.

It was an idea that was at once both astonishing and obvious—and also impractical. Einstein first learned of it from a small article in the *New York Times* a week after Weizmann's death. At first he and the women in his house laughed it off, but then reporters started to call. "This is very awkward, very awkward," he told a visitor. A few hours later, a telegram arrived from Israel's ambassador in Washington, Abba Eban. Could the embassy, it asked, send someone the next day to see him officially?

"Why should that man come all that way," Einstein lamented, "when I only will have to say no?"

Helen Dukas came up with the idea of simply giving Ambassador Eban a phone call. In those days, impromptu long-distance calls were somewhat novel. To her surprise, she was able to track Eban down in Washington and put him on the line with Einstein.

"I am not the person for that and I cannot possibly do it," Einstein said.

"I cannot tell my government that you phoned me and said no," Eban replied. "I have to go through the motions and present the offer officially."

Eban ended up sending a deputy, who handed Einstein a formal letter asking if he would take on the presidency. "Acceptance would entail moving to Israel and taking its citizenship," Eban's letter noted (presumably in case Einstein harbored any fantasy that he could preside over Israel from Princeton). Eban hastened to reassure Einstein, however: "Freedom to pursue your great scientific work would be afforded by a government and people who are fully conscious of the supreme significance of your labors." In other words, it was a job that would require his presence, but not much else.

Even though the offer seemed somewhat strange, it was a powerful testament to Einstein's unsurpassed standing as a hero of world Jewry. It "embodies the deepest respect which the Jewish people can repose in any of its sons," Eban said.

Einstein had already prepared his note of rejection, which he handed to Eban's envoy as soon as he arrived. "I have been a lawyer all my life," the visitor joked, "and I have never gotten a rebuttal before I have stated my case."

He was "deeply moved" by the offer, Einstein said in his prepared response, and "at once saddened and ashamed" that he would not accept it. "All my life I have dealt with objective matters, hence I lack both the natural aptitude and the experience to deal properly with people and to exercise official function," he explained. "I am the more distressed over these circumstances because my relationship with the Jewish people became my strongest human tie once I achieved complete clarity about our precarious position among the nations of the world."[45]

Offering Einstein the presidency of Israel was a clever idea, but Einstein was right to realize that sometimes a brilliant idea is also a very bad one. As he noted with his usual wry self-awareness, he did not have the natural aptitude to deal with people in the way the role would require, nor did he have the temperament to be an official functionary. He was not cut out to be either a statesman or a figurehead.

He liked to speak his mind, and he had no patience for the compromises necessary to manage, or even symbolically lead, complex organizations. Back when he was involved as a figurehead leader in the establishing of Hebrew University, he had not possessed the talent to handle, nor the temperament to ignore, all of the maneuverings involved. Likewise, he had more recently had the same unpleasant experiences with a group creating Brandeis University near Boston, which caused him to resign from that endeavor.[46]

In addition, he had never displayed a discernible ability to run any-thing. The only formal administrative duty he had ever undertaken was to head a new physics institute at the University of Berlin. He did little other than hire his stepdaughter to handle some clerical tasks and give a job to the astronomer trying to confirm his theories.

Einstein's brilliance sprang from being a rebel and nonconformist who recoiled at any attempt to restrain his free expression. Are there any worse traits for someone who is supposed to be a political concilia-tor? As he explained in a polite letter to the Jerusalem newspaper that had been campaigning for him, he did not want to face the chance that he would have to go along with a government decision that "might cre-ate a conflict with my conscience."

In society as in science, he was better off remaining a noncon-formist. "It is true that many a rebel has in the end become a figure of responsibility," Einstein conceded to a friend that week, "but I cannot bring myself to do so."[47]

Ben-Gurion was secretly relieved. He had begun to realize that the idea was a bad one. "Tell me what to do if he says yes!" he joked to his assistant. "I've had to offer the post to him because it's impossible not to. But if he accepts, we are in for trouble." Two days later, when Am-bassador Eban ran into Einstein at a black-tie reception in New York, he was happy that the issue was behind them. Einstein was not wear-ing socks.[48]

CHAPTER TWENTY-FOUR

RED SCARE

1951–1954

With J. Robert Oppenheimer, 1947

The Rosenbergs

The rush to build the H-Bomb, rising anticommunist fervor, and Senator Joseph McCarthy's increasingly untethered security investigations unnerved Einstein. The atmosphere reminded him of the rising Nazism and anti-Semitism of the 1930s. "The German calamity of years ago repeats itself," he lamented to the queen mother of Belgium in early 1951. "People acquiesce without resistance and align themselves with the forces for evil."[1]

He tried to maintain a middle ground between those who were reflexively anti-American and those who were reflexively anti-Soviet. On the one hand, he rebuked his collaborator Leopold Infeld, who wanted him to support statements by the World Peace Council, which Einstein rightly suspected was Soviet-influenced. "In my view they are more or less propaganda," he said. He did the same to a group of Russian students who pressed him to join a protest against what they alleged was America's use of biological weapons during the Korean War. "You cannot expect me to protest against incidents which possibly, and very probably, have never taken place," he replied.[2]

On the other hand, Einstein refrained from signing a petition circulated by Sidney Hook denouncing the perfidy of those who made such charges against America. He was enamored of neither extreme. As he put it, "Every reasonable person must strive to promote moderation and a more objective judgment."[3]

In what he presumed would be a quiet effort at promoting such moderation, Einstein wrote a private letter asking that Julius and Ethel Rosenberg, who had been convicted of turning over atomic secrets to the Soviets, be spared the death penalty. He had avoided making any statements about the case, which had divided the nation with a frenzy seldom seen before the advent of the cable-TV age. Instead, he sent the letter to the judge, Irving Kaufman, with a promise not to publicize it. Einstein did not contend that the Rosenbergs were innocent. He merely argued that a death penalty was too harsh in a case where the facts were murky and the outcome was driven more by popular hysteria than objectivity.[4]

In a reflection of the tenor of the time, Judge Kaufman took the private letter and turned it over to the FBI. Not only was it put into Einstein's file, but it was investigated to see if it could be construed as disloyalty. After three months, a report was sent to Hoover saying no further incriminating evidence had been found, but the letter remained in the file.[5]

When Judge Kaufman went ahead and imposed a death penalty, Einstein wrote to President Harry Truman, who was about to leave office, to ask him to commute the sentence. He drafted the letter first in German and then in English on the back of a piece of scrap paper that he had filled with a variety of equations that apparently, given how they trail off, led to nothing.[6] Truman bucked the decision to incoming President Eisenhower, who allowed the executions to proceed.

Einstein's letter to Truman was released publicly, and the *New York Times* ran a front-page story headlined "Einstein Supports Rosenberg

Appeal."[7] More than a hundred angry letters swept in from across the nation. "You need some common sense plus some appreciation for what America has given you," wrote Marian Rawles of Portsmouth, Virginia. "You place the Jew first and the United States second," said Charles Williams of White Plains, New York. From Corporal Homer Greene, serving in Korea: "You evidently like to see our GI's killed. Go to Russia or back where you came from, because I don't like Americans like you living off this country and making un-American statements."[8]

There were not as many positive letters, but Einstein did have a pleasant exchange with the liberal Supreme Court Justice William O. Douglas, who had unsuccessfully tried to stop the executions. "You have struggled so devotedly for the creation of a healthy public opinion in our troubled time," Einstein wrote in a note of appreciation. Douglas sent back a handwritten reply: "You have paid me a tribute which brightens the burdens of this dark hour—a tribute I will always cherish."[9]

Many of the critical letters asked Einstein why he was willing to speak out for the Rosenbergs but not for the nine Jewish doctors whom Stalin had put on trial as part of an alleged Zionist conspiracy to murder Russian leaders. Among those who publicly challenged what they saw as Einstein's double standard were the publisher of the *New York Post* and the editor of the *New Leader*.[10]

Einstein agreed that the Russian actions should be denounced. "The perversion of justice which manifests itself in all the official trials staged by the Russian government deserves unconditional condemnation," he wrote. He added that individual appeals to Stalin would probably not do much, but perhaps a joint declaration from a group of scholars would help. So he got together with the chemistry Nobel laureate Harold Urey and others to issue one. "Einstein and Urey Hit Reds' Anti-Semitism," the *New York Times* reported.[11] (After Stalin died a few weeks later, the doctors were freed.)

On the other hand, he stressed in scores of letters and statements that Americans should not let the fear of communism cause them to surrender the civil liberties and freedom of thought that they cherished. There were a lot of domestic communists in England, but the people there did not get themselves whipped into a frenzy by internal security investigations, he pointed out. Americans need not either.

William Frauenglass

Every year, Lord & Taylor department stores gave an award that, especially in the early 1950s, might have seemed unusual. It honored independent thinking, and Einstein, fittingly, won it in 1953 for his "nonconformity" in scientific matters.

Einstein took pride in that trait, which he knew had served him well over the years. "It gives me great pleasure to see the stubbornness of an incorrigible nonconformist warmly acclaimed," he said in his radio talk accepting the award.

Even though he was being honored for his nonconformity in the field of science, Einstein used the occasion to turn attention to the McCarthy-style investigations. For him, freedom in the realm of thought was linked to freedom in the realm of politics. "To be sure, we are concerned here with nonconformism in a remote field of endeavor," he said, meaning physics. "No Senatorial committee has as yet felt compelled to tackle the task of combating in this field the dangers that threaten the inner security of the uncritical or intimidated citizen."[12]

Listening to his talk was a Brooklyn schoolteacher, William Frauenglass, who had a month earlier been called to testify in Washington before a Senate Internal Security Subcommittee looking into communist influence in high schools. He had refused to talk, and now he wanted Einstein to say whether he had been right.

Einstein crafted a reply and told Frauenglass he could make it public. "The reactionary politicians have managed to instill suspicions of all intellectual efforts," he wrote. "They are now proceeding to suppress the freedom of teaching." What should intellectuals do against this evil? "Frankly, I can only see the revolutionary way of non-cooperation in the sense of Gandhi's," Einstein declared. "Every intellectual who is called before one of the committees ought to refuse to testify."[13]

Einstein's lifelong comfort in resisting prevailing winds made him serenely stubborn during the McCarthy era. At a time when citizens were asked to name names and testify at inquiries into their loyalty and that of their colleagues, he took a simple approach. He told people not to cooperate.

He felt, as he told Frauenglass, that this should be done based on the free speech guarantees of the First Amendment, rather than the "subterfuge" of invoking the Fifth Amendment's protection against possible self-incrimination. Standing up for the First Amendment was particularly a duty of intellectuals, he said, because they had a special role in society as preservers of free thought. He was still horrified that most intellectuals in Germany had not risen in resistance when the Nazis came to power.

When his letter to Frauenglass was published, there was an even greater public uproar than had been provoked by his Rosenberg appeal. Editorial writers across the nation pulled out all the stops for their denunciatory chords.

> The *New York Times:* "To employ unnatural and illegal forces of civil disobedience, as Professor Einstein advises, is in this case to attack one evil with another. The situation which Professor Einstein rebels against certainly needs correction, but the answer does not lie in defying the law."
>
> The *Washington Post:* "He has put himself in the extremist category by his irresponsible suggestion. He has proved once more that genius in science is no guarantee of sagacity in political affairs."
>
> The *Philadelphia Inquirer:* "It is particularly regrettable when a scholar of his attainments, full of honors, should permit himself to be used as an instrument of propaganda by the enemies of the country that has given him such a secure refuge . . . Dr. Einstein has come down from the stars to dabble in ideological politics, with lamentable results."
>
> The *Chicago Daily Tribune:* "It is always astonishing to find that a man of great intellectual power in some directions is a simpleton or even a jackass in others."
>
> The *Pueblo* (Colorado) *Star-Journal:* "He, of all people, should know better. This country protected him from Hitler." [14]

Ordinary citizens wrote as well. "Look in the mirror and see how disgraceful you look without a haircut like a wild man and wear a Russian wool cap like a Bolshevik," said Sam Epkin of Cleveland. The anticommunist columnist Victor Lasky sent a handwritten screed: "Your most recent blast against the institutions of this great nation finally convinces me that, despite your great scientific knowledge, you are an idiot, a menace to this country." And George Stringfellow of East Orange, New Jersey, noted incorrectly, "Don't forget that you left a communist country to come here where you could have freedom. Don't abuse that freedom sir."[15]

Senator McCarthy also issued a denunciation, though it seemed slightly muted due to Einstein's stature. "Anyone who advises Americans to keep secret information which they have about spies and saboteurs is himself an enemy of America," he said, not quite aiming directly at Einstein or what he had written.[16]

This time, however, there were actually more letters in support of Einstein. Among the more amusing ripostes came from his friend Bertrand Russell. "You seem to think that one should always obey the law, however bad," the philosopher wrote to the *New York Times*. "I am compelled to suppose that you condemn George Washington and hold that your country ought to return to allegiance to Her Gracious Majesty, Queen Elisabeth II. As a loyal Briton, I of course applaud this view; but I fear it may not win much support in your country." Einstein wrote Russell a thank-you letter, lamenting, "All the intellectuals in this country, down to the youngest student, have become completely intimidated."[17]

Abraham Flexner, now retired from the Institute for Advanced Study and living on Fifth Avenue, took the opportunity to restore his relationship with Einstein. "I am grateful to you as a native American for your fine letter to Mr. Frauenglass," he wrote. "American citizens in general will occupy a more dignified position if they absolutely refuse to say a word if questioned about their personal opinions and beliefs."[18]

Among the most poignant notes was from Frauenglass's teenage son, Richard. "In these troubled times, your statement is one that might alter the course of this nation," he said, which had a bit of truth to it. He noted that he would cherish Einstein's letter for the rest of his life, then added a P.S.: "My favorite subjects are your favorite too—math and physics. Now I am taking trigonometry."[19]

Passive Resistance

Dozens of dissenters subsequently begged Einstein to intervene on their behalf, but he declined. He had made his point and did not see the need to keep thrusting himself into the fray.

But one person did get through: Albert Shadowitz, a physics professor who had worked as an engineer during the war and helped form a union that was eventually expelled from the labor movement for having communists on its board. Senator McCarthy wanted to show that the union had ties to Moscow and had endangered the defense industry. Shadowitz, who had been a member of the Communist Party, decided to invoke the protections of the First, not the Fifth, Amendment, as Einstein had recommended to Frauenglass.[20]

Shadowitz was so worried about his plight that he decided to call Einstein for support. But Einstein's number was unlisted. So he got into his car in northern New Jersey, drove to Princeton, and showed up at Einstein's house, where he was met by the zealous guardian Dukas. "Do you have an appointment?" she demanded. He admitted he didn't. "Well, you can't just come in and speak to Professor Einstein," she declared. But when he explained his story, she stared at him for a while, then waved him in.

Einstein was wearing his usual attire: a baggy sweatshirt and corduroy trousers. He took Shadowitz upstairs to his study and assured him that his actions were right. He was an intellectual, and it was the special duty of intellectuals to stand up in such cases. "If you take this path then feel free to use my name in any way that you wish," Einstein generously offered.

Shadowitz was surprised by the blank check, but happy to use it. McCarthy's chief counsel, Roy Cohn, did the questioning as McCarthy listened during the initial closed hearing. Was he a communist? Shadowitz replied: "I refuse to answer that and I am following the advice of Professor Einstein." McCarthy suddenly took over the questioning. Did he know Einstein? Not really, Shadowitz answered, but I've met him. When the script was replayed in an open hearing, it made the same type of headlines, and provoked the same spurt of mail, as the Frauenglass case had.

Einstein believed he was being a good, rather than a disloyal, citizen. He had read the First Amendment and felt that upholding its spirit was at the core of America's cherished freedom. One angry critic sent him a copy of a card that contained what he called "The American Creed." It read, in part, "It is my duty to my country to love it; to support its Constitution; to obey its laws." Einstein wrote on the edge, "This is precisely what I have done." [21]

When the great black scholar W.E.B. Du Bois was indicted on charges stemming from helping to circulate a petition initiated by the World Peace Council, Einstein volunteered to testify as a character witness on his behalf. It represented a union of Einstein's sentiments on behalf of civil rights and of free speech. When Du Bois's lawyer informed the court that Einstein would appear, the judge rather quickly decided to dismiss the case. [22]

Another case hit closer to home: that of J. Robert Oppenheimer. After leading the scientists who developed the atom bomb and then becoming head of the Institute where Einstein still puttered in to work, Oppenheimer remained an adviser to the Atomic Energy Commission and kept his security clearance. By initially opposing the development of the hydrogen bomb, he had turned Edward Teller into an adversary, and he also alienated AEC commissioner Lewis Strauss. Oppenheimer's wife, Kitty, and his brother, Frank, had been members of the Communist Party before the war, and Oppenheimer himself had associated freely with party members and with scientists whose loyalty came under question. [23]

All of this prompted an effort in 1953 to strip Oppenheimer of his security clearance. It would have expired soon anyway, and everyone could have allowed the matter to be resolved quietly, but in the heated atmosphere neither Oppenheimer nor his adversaries wanted to back away from what they saw as a matter of principle. So a secret hearing was scheduled in Washington.

One day at the Institute, Einstein ran into Oppenheimer, who was preparing for the hearings. They chatted for a few minutes, and when Oppenheimer got to his car he recounted the conversation to a friend. "Einstein thinks that the attack on me is so outrageous that I should just resign," he said. Einstein considered Oppenheimer "a fool" for even answering the charges. Having served his country admirably, he had no obligations to subject himself to a "witch hunt." [24]

A few days after the secret hearings finally began—in April 1954, just as CBS journalist Edward R. Murrow was taking on Joseph McCarthy and the controversy over security investigations was at its height—they became public through a page-1 exclusive by James Reston of the *New York Times.*[25] The issue of the government's investigation of Oppenheimer's loyalty instantly became another polarizing public debate.

Warned that the story was about to break, Abraham Pais went to Mercer Street to make sure that Einstein was prepared for the inevitable press calls. He was bitterly amused when Pais told him that Oppenheimer continued to insist on a hearing rather than simply cutting his ties with the government. "The trouble with Oppenheimer is that he loves a woman who doesn't love him—the United States government," Einstein said. All Oppenheimer had to do, Einstein told Pais, was "go to Washington, tell the officials that they were fools, and then go home."[26]

Oppenheimer lost. The AEC voted that he was a loyal American but also a security risk and—one day before it would have expired anyway—revoked his clearance. Einstein visited him at the Institute the next day and found him depressed. That evening he told a friend that he did not "understand why Oppenheimer takes the business so seriously."

When a group of Institute faculty members circulated a petition affirming support for their director, Einstein immediately signed up. Others initially declined, some partly out of fear. This galvanized Einstein. He "put his 'revolutionary talents' into action to garner support," a friend recalled. After a few more meetings, Einstein had helped to convince or shame everyone into signing the statement.[27]

Lewis Strauss, Oppenheimer's AEC antagonist, was on the board of the Institute, which worried the faculty. Would he try to get Oppenheimer fired? Einstein wrote his friend Senator Herbert Lehman of New York, another trustee, calling Oppenheimer "by far the most capable Director the Institute has ever had." Dismissing him, he said, "would arouse the justified indignation of all men of learning."[28] The trustees voted to keep him.

Soon after the Oppenheimer affair, Einstein was visited in Princeton by Adlai Stevenson, the once and future Democratic nominee for president, who was a particular darling among intellectuals. Einstein expressed concern at the way politicians were whipping up fear of communism. Stevenson replied somewhat circumspectly. The Russians were, in fact, a danger. After some more gentle back and forth, Stevenson thanked Einstein for endorsing him in 1952. There was no need for thanks, Einstein replied, as he had done so only because he trusted Eisenhower even less. Stevenson said he found such honesty refreshing, and Einstein decided that he was not quite as pompous as he had originally seemed.[29]

Einstein's opposition to McCarthyism arose partly out of his fear of fascism. America's most dangerous internal threat, he felt, came not from communist subversives but from those who used the fear of communists to trample civil liberties. "America is incomparably less endangered by its own Communists than by the hysterical hunt for the few Communists that are here," he told the socialist leader Norman Thomas.

Even to people he did not know, Einstein expressed his disgust in unvarnished terms. "We have come a long way toward the establishment of a Fascist regime," he replied to an eleven-page letter sent to him by a New Yorker he had never met. "The similarity of general conditions here to those in the Germany of 1932 is quite obvious."[30]

Some colleagues worried that Einstein's vocal opinions would cause controversy for the Institute. Such concerns, he joked, made his hair turn gray. Indeed, he took a boyish American glee at his freedom to say whatever he felt. "I have become a kind of *enfant terrible* in my new homeland due to my inability to keep silent and to swallow everything that happens," he wrote Queen Mother Elisabeth. "Besides, I believe that older people who have scarcely anything to lose ought to be willing to speak out in behalf of those who are young and are subject to much greater restraint."[31]

He even announced, in tones both grave and a bit playful, that he would not have become a professor given the political intimidation that now existed. "If I were a young man again and had to decide how to make a living, I would not try to become a scientist or scholar or teacher," he intoned to Theodore White of the *Reporter* magazine. "I would rather choose to be a plumber or a peddler, in the hope of finding that modest degree of independence still available."[32]

That earned him an honorary membership card from a plumbers' union, and it sparked a national debate on academic freedom. Even slightly frivolous remarks made by Einstein carried a lot of momentum.

Einstein was right that academic freedom was under assault, and the damage done to careers was real. For example, David Bohm, a great theoretical physicist who worked with Oppenheimer and Einstein in Princeton and refined certain aspects of quantum mechanics, was called before the House Un-American Activities Committee, pleaded the Fifth Amendment, lost his job, and ended up moving to Brazil.

Nevertheless, Einstein's remark—and his litany of doom—turned out to be overstated. Despite his impolitic utterances, there was no serious attempt to muzzle him or threaten his job. Even the slapstick FBI efforts to compile a dossier on him did not curtail his free speech. At the end of the Oppenheimer investigation, both he and Einstein were still harbored safely in their haven in Princeton, free to think and speak as they chose. The fact that both men had their loyalty questioned and, at times, their security clearances denied was shameful. But it was not like Nazi Germany, not anything close, despite what Einstein sometimes said.

Einstein and some other refugees tended, understandably, to view McCarthyism as a descent into the black hole of fascism, rather than as one of those ebbs and flows of excess that happen in a democracy. As it turned out, American democracy righted itself, as it always has. McCarthy was relegated to his own disgrace in 1954 by Army lawyers, his Senate colleagues, President Eisenhower, and journalists such as Drew Pearson and Edward R. Murrow. When the transcript of the Oppenheimer case was published, it ended up hurting the reputation of Lewis Strauss and Edward Teller, at least within the academic and scientific establishment, as much as that of Oppenheimer.

Einstein was not used to self-righting political systems. Nor did he fully appreciate how resilient America's democracy and its nurturing of individual liberty could be. So for a while his disdain deepened. But he was saved from serious despair by his wry detachment and his sense of humor. He was not destined to die a bitter man.

THE END

1955

Intimations of Mortality

For his seventy-fifth birthday in March 1954, Einstein received from a medical center, unsolicited, a pet parrot that was delivered in a box to his doorstep. It had been a difficult journey, and the parrot seemed traumatized. At the time, Einstein was seeing a woman who worked in one of Princeton University's libraries named Johanna Fantova, whom he had met back in Germany in the 1920s. "The pet parrot is depressed after his traumatic delivery and Einstein is trying to cheer him up with his jokes, which the bird doesn't seem to appreciate," she wrote in the wonderful journal she kept of their dates and conversations.[1]

The parrot rebounded psychologically and was soon eating out of Einstein's hand, but it developed an infection. That necessitated a series of injections, and Einstein worried that the bird would not survive. But it was a tough bird, and after only two injections he bounced back.

Einstein likewise had repeatedly bounced back from bouts of anemia and stomach ailments. But he knew that the aneurysm on his abdominal aorta should soon prove fatal, and he began to display a peaceful sense of his own mortality. When he stood at the graveside and eulogized the physicist Rudolf Ladenberg, who had been his colleague in Berlin and then Princeton, the words seemed to be ones he felt personally. "Brief is this existence, as a fleeting visit in a strange house," he said. "The path to be pursued is poorly lit by a flickering consciousness."[2]

He seemed to sense that this final transition he was going through was at once natural and somewhat spiritual. "The strange thing about growing old is that the intimate identification with the here and now is slowly lost," he wrote his friend the queen mother of Belgium. "One feels transposed into infinity, more or less alone."[3]

After his colleagues updated, as a seventy-fifth birthday gift, the music system they had given him five years earlier, Einstein began repeatedly to play an RCA Victor recording of Beethoven's *Missa Solemnis*. It was an unusual choice for two reasons. He tended to regard Beethoven, who was not his favorite composer, as "too personal, almost naked."[4] Also, his religious instincts did not usually include these sorts of trappings. "I am a deeply religious nonbeliever," he noted to a friend who had sent him birthday greetings. "This is a somewhat new kind of religion."[5]

It was time for reminiscing. When his old friends Conrad Habicht and Maurice Solovine wrote a postcard from Paris recalling their time together in Bern, more than a half century earlier, as members of their self-proclaimed Olympia Academy, Einstein replied with a paean addressed to that bygone institution: "Though somewhat decrepit, we still follow the solitary path of our life by your pure and inspiring light." As he later lamented in another letter to Solovine, "The devil counts out the years conscientiously."[6]

Despite his stomach problems, he still loved to walk. Sometimes it was with Gödel to and from the Institute, at other times it was in the woods near Princeton with his stepdaughter Margot. Their relation-

ship had become even closer, but their walks were usually enjoyed in silence. She noticed that he was becoming mellower, both personally and politically. His judgments were mild, even sweet, rather than harsh.[7]

He had, in particular, made his peace with Hans Albert. Shortly after he celebrated his seventy-fifth birthday, his son turned 50. Einstein, thanks to a reminder from his son's wife, wrote him a letter that was slightly formal, as if created for a special occasion. But it contained a nice tribute both to his son and to the value of a life in science: "It is a joy for me to have a son who has inherited the main traits of my personality: the ability to rise above mere existence by sacrificing one's self through the years for an impersonal goal."[8] That fall, Hans Albert came east for a visit.

By then Einstein had finally discovered what was fundamental about America: it can be swept by waves of what may seem, to outsiders, to be dangerous political passions but are, instead, passing sentiments that are absorbed by its democracy and righted by its constitutional gyroscope. McCarthyism had died down, and Eisenhower had proved a calming influence. "God's own country becomes stranger and stranger," Einstein wrote Hans Albert that Christmas, "but somehow they manage to return to normality. Everything—even lunacy—is mass produced here. But everything goes out of fashion very quickly."[9]

Almost every day he continued to amble to the Institute to wrestle with his equations and try to push them a little closer toward the horizon of a unified field theory. He would come in with his new ideas, often clutching equations on scraps of paper he had scribbled the night before, and go over them with his assistant of that final year, Bruria Kaufman, a physicist from Israel.

She would write the new equations on a blackboard so they could ponder them together, and point out problems. Einstein would then try to counter them. "He had certain criteria by which to judge whether this is relevant to physical reality or not," she recounted. Even when they were defeated by the obstacles to a new approach, as they invariably were, Einstein remained optimistic. "Well, we've learned something," he would say as the clock ticked down.[10]

In the evening, he would often explain his last-ditch efforts to his companion, Johanna Fantova, and she would record them in her journal. The entries for 1954 were littered with hopes raised and dashed. February 20: "Thinks he found a new angle to his theory, something very important that would simplify it. Hopes he won't find any errors." February 21: "Didn't find any errors, but the new work isn't as exciting as he had thought the day before." August 25: "Einstein's equations are looking good—maybe something will come of them—but it's damned hard work." September 21: "He's making some progress with what was at first only a theory but is now looking good." October 14: "Found an error in his work today, which is a setback." October 24: "He calculated like crazy today but accomplished nothing."[11]

That year Wolfgang Pauli, the quantum mechanics pioneer, came to visit. Again the old debate over whether God would play dice was reengaged, as it had been a quarter-century earlier at the Solvay Conferences. Einstein told Pauli that he still objected to the fundamental tenet in quantum mechanics that a system can be defined only by specifying the experimental method of observing it. There was a reality, he insisted, that was independent of how we observed it. "Einstein has the philosophical prejudice that a state, termed 'real,' can be defined objectively under any circumstances, that is, without specification of the experimental arrangement used to examine the system," Pauli marveled in a letter to Max Born.[12]

He also clung to his belief that physics should be based, as he told his old friend Besso, "on the field concept, i.e., on continuous structures." Seventy years earlier, his awe at contemplating a compass caused him to marvel at the concept of fields, and they had guided his theories ever since. But what would happen, he worried to Besso, if field theory turned out to be unable to account for particles and quantum mechanics? "In that case *nothing* remains of my entire castle in the air, gravitation theory included."[13]

So even as Einstein apologized for his stubbornness, he proudly refused to abandon it. "I must seem like an ostrich who forever buries its head in the relativistic sand in order not to face the evil quanta," he wrote Louis de Broglie, another of his colleagues in the long struggle. He had found his gravitational theories by trusting an underlying principle, and that made him a "fanatic believer" that comparable methods would eventually lead to a unified field theory. "This should explain the ostrich policy," he wryly told de Broglie.[14]

He expressed this more formally in the concluding paragraph of his final updated appendix to his popular book, *Relativity: The Special and General Theory.* "The conviction prevails that the experimentally assured duality (corpuscular and wave structure) can be realized only by such a weakening of the concept of reality," he wrote. "I think that such a far-reaching theoretical renunciation is not for the present justified by our actual knowledge, and that one should not desist from pursuing to the end the path of the relativistic field theory."[15]

Bertrand Russell encouraged him to continue, in addition, the search for a structure that would ensure peace in the atomic age. They had both opposed the First World War, Russell recalled, and supported the Second. Now it was imperative to prevent a third. "I think that eminent men of science ought to do something dramatic to bring home to the governments the disasters that may occur," Russell wrote. Einstein replied by proposing a "public declaration" that they and perhaps a few other eminent scientists and thinkers could sign.[16]

Einstein set to work enlisting his old friend and sparring partner, Niels Bohr. "Don't frown like that!" Einstein joked, as if he were face-to-face with Bohr rather than writing to him in Copenhagen. "This has nothing to do with our old controversy on physics, but rather concerns a matter on which we are in complete agreement." Einstein admitted that his own name might carry some influence abroad, but not in America, "where I am known as a black sheep (and not merely in scientific matters)."[17]

Alas, Bohr declined, but nine other scientists, including Max Born, agreed to join the effort. Russell concluded the proposed document with a simple plea: "In view of the fact that in any future world war nuclear weapons will certainly be employed, and that such weapons threaten the continued existence of mankind, we urge the governments of the world to realize, and to acknowledge publicly, that their purpose cannot be furthered by a world war, and we urge them, consequently, to find peaceful means for the settlement of all matters of dispute between them."[18]

Einstein made it to his seventy-sixth birthday, but he was not well enough to come outside to wave to the reporters and photographers gathered in front of 112 Mercer Street. The mailman delivered presents, Oppenheimer came by with papers, the Bucky family brought some puzzles, and Johanna Fantova was there to record the events.

Among the presents was a tie sent by the fifth grade of the Farmingdale Elementary School in New York, which presumably had seen pictures of him and thought he could use one. "Neckties exist for me only as remote memories," he admitted politely in his letter of thanks.[19]

A few days later, he learned of the death of Michele Besso, the personal confessor and scientific sounding board he had met six decades earlier upon arriving as a student in Zurich. As if he knew that he had only a few more weeks, Einstein ruminated on the nature of death and time in the condolence letter he wrote to Besso's family. "He has departed from this strange world a little ahead of me. That means nothing. For us believing physicists, the distinction between past, present and future is only a stubborn illusion."

Einstein had introduced Besso to his wife, Anna Winteler, and he marveled as his friend made the marriage survive despite some difficult patches. Besso's most admirable personal trait, Einstein said, was to live in harmony with a woman, "an undertaking in which I twice failed rather miserably."[20]

One Sunday in April, the Harvard historian of science I. Bernard Cohen went to see Einstein. His face, deeply lined, struck Cohen as tragic, yet his sparkling eyes made him seem ageless. He spoke softly yet laughed loudly. "Every time he made a point that he liked," Cohen recalled, "he would burst into booming laughter."

Einstein was particularly amused by a scientific gadget, designed to show the equivalence principle, that he had recently been given. It was a version of the old-fashioned toy in which a ball that hangs by a string from the end of a stick has to be swung up so that it lands in a cup atop the stick. This one was more complex; the string tied to the ball went through the bottom of the cup and was attached to a loose spring inside the handle of the contraption. Random shaking would get the ball in the cup every now and then. The challenge: Was there a method that would get the ball in the cup every time?

As Cohen was leaving, a big grin came over Einstein's face as he said he would explain the answer to the gadget. "Now the equivalence principle!" he announced. He poked the stick upward until it almost touched the ceiling. Then he let it drop straight down. The ball, while in free fall, behaved as if it was weightless. The spring inside the contraption instantly pulled it into the cup.[21]

Einstein was now entering the last week of his life, and it is fitting that he focused on the matters most important to him. On April 11, he signed the Einstein-Russell manifesto. As Russell later declared, "He remained sane in a mad world."[22] Out of that document grew the Pugwash Conferences, in which scientists and thinkers gathered annually to discuss how to control nuclear weapons.

Later that same afternoon, Israeli Ambassador Abba Eban arrived at Mercer Street to discuss a radio address Einstein was scheduled to give to commemorate the seventh anniversary of the Jewish state. He would be heard, Eban told him, by as many as 60 million listeners. Einstein was amused. "So, I shall now have a chance to become world famous," he smiled.

After rattling around in the kitchen to make Eban a cup of coffee, Einstein told him that he saw the birth of Israel as one of the few political acts in his lifetime that had a moral quality. But he was concerned that the Jews were having trouble learning to live with the Arabs. "The attitude we adopt toward the Arab minority will provide the real test of our moral standards as a people," he had told a friend a few weeks earlier. He wanted to broaden his speech, which he was scribbling in German in a very tight and neat handwriting, to urge the creation of a world government to preserve peace.[23]

Einstein went in to work at the Institute the next day, but he had a pain in his groin and it showed on his face. Is everything all right? his assistant asked. Everything is all right, he replied, but I am not.

He stayed at home the following day, partly because the Israeli consul was coming and partly because he was still not feeling well. After the visitors left, he lay down for a nap. But Dukas heard him rush to the bathroom in the middle of the afternoon, where he collapsed. The doctors gave him morphine, which helped him sleep, and Dukas set up her bed right next to his so that she could put ice on his dehydrated lips throughout the night. His aneurysm had started to break.[24]

A group of doctors convened at his home the next day, and after some consultation they recommended a surgeon who might be able, though it was thought unlikely, to repair the aorta. Einstein refused. "It is tasteless to prolong life artificially," he told Dukas. "I have done my share, it is time to go. I will do it elegantly."

He did ask, however, whether he would suffer "a horrible death." The answer, the doctors said, was unclear. The pain of an internal hemorrhage could be excruciating. But it may take only a minute, or maybe an hour. To Dukas, who became overwrought, he smiled and said, "You're really hysterical—I have to pass on sometime, and it doesn't really matter when."[25]

Dukas found him the next morning in agony, unable to lift his head. She rushed to the telephone, and the doctor ordered him to the hospital. At first he refused, but he was told he was putting too much of a burden on Dukas, so he relented. The volunteer medic in the ambulance was a political economist at Princeton, and Einstein was able to carry on a lively conversation with him. Margot called Hans Albert, who caught a plane from San Francisco and was soon by his father's bedside. The economist Otto Nathan, a fellow German refugee who had become his close friend, arrived from New York.

But Einstein was not quite ready to die. On Sunday, April 17, he woke up feeling better. He asked Dukas to get him his glasses, papers, and pencils, and he proceeded to jot down a few calculations. He talked to Hans Albert about some scientific ideas, then to Nathan about the dangers of allowing Germany to rearm. Pointing to his equations, he lamented, half jokingly, to his son, "If only I had more mathematics."[26] For a half century he had been bemoaning both German nationalism and the limits of his mathematical toolbox, so it was fitting that these should be among his final utterances.

He worked as long as he could, and when the pain got too great he went to sleep. Shortly after one a.m. on Monday, April 18, 1955, the nurse heard him blurt out a few words in German that she could not understand. The aneurysm, like a big blister, had burst, and Einstein died at age 76.

At his bedside lay the draft of his undelivered speech for Israel Independence Day. "I speak to you today not as an American citizen and not as a Jew, but as a human being," it began.[27]

Also by his bed were twelve pages of tightly written equations, littered with cross-outs and corrections.[28] To the very end, he struggled to find his elusive unified field theory. And the final thing he wrote, before he went to sleep for the last time, was one more line of symbols and numbers that he hoped might get him, and the rest of us, just a little step closer to the spirit manifest in the laws of the universe.

$$U_{i\ h}^{\ n}\ U_{q\ k}^{\ q}\left(-\frac{16}{9}+\frac{2}{9}-\frac{4}{9}+\frac{2}{9}+\frac{2}{9}+\frac{2}{9}\right)+U_{k\ h}^{\ n}\ U_{q\ i}^{\ q}\left(\frac{4}{9}+\frac{2}{9}-\frac{4}{9}+\frac{2}{9}-\frac{1}{9}\mp\frac{1}{9}\right)$$

EINSTEIN'S BRAIN
AND EINSTEIN'S MIND

Einstein's study, as he left it

When Sir Isaac Newton died, his body lay in state in the Jerusalem chamber of Westminster Abbey, and his pallbearers included the lord high chancellor, two dukes, and three earls. Einstein could have had a similar funeral, glittering with dignitaries from around the world. Instead, in accordance with his wishes, he was cremated in Trenton on the afternoon that he died, before most of the world had heard the news. There were only twelve people at the crematorium, including Hans Albert Einstein, Helen Dukas, Otto Nathan, and four members of the Bucky family. Nathan recited a few lines from Goethe, and then took Einstein's ashes to the nearby Delaware River, where they were scattered.[1]

"No other man contributed so much to the vast expansion of 20th century knowledge," President Eisenhower declared. "Yet no other man was more modest in the possession of the power that is knowledge, more sure that power without wisdom is deadly." The *New York Times* ran nine stories plus an editorial about his death the next day: "Man stands on this diminutive earth, gazes at the myriad stars and upon billowing oceans and tossing trees—and wonders. What does it all mean? How did it come about? The most thoughtful wonderer who appeared among us in three centuries has passed on in the person of Albert Einstein."[2]

Einstein had insisted that his ashes be scattered so that his final resting place would not become the subject of morbid veneration. But there was one part of his body that was not cremated. In a drama that would seem farcical were it not so macabre, Einstein's brain ended up being, for more than four decades, a wandering relic.[3]

Hours after Einstein's death, what was supposed to be a routine autopsy was performed by the pathologist at Princeton Hospital, Thomas Harvey, a small-town Quaker with a sweet disposition and rather dreamy approach to life and death. As a distraught Otto Nathan watched silently, Harvey removed and inspected each of Einstein's major organs, ending by using an electric saw to cut through his skull and remove his brain. When he stitched the body back up, he decided, without asking permission, to embalm Einstein's brain and keep it.

The next morning, in a fifth-grade class at a Princeton school, the teacher asked her students what news they had heard. "Einstein died," said one girl, eager to be the first to come up with that piece of information. But she quickly found herself topped by a usually quiet boy who sat in the back of the class. "My dad's got his brain," he said.[4]

Nathan was horrified when he found out, as was Einstein's family. Hans Albert called the hospital to complain, but Harvey insisted that there may be scientific value to studying the brain. Einstein would have wanted that, he said. The son, unsure what legal and practical rights he now had in this matter, reluctantly went along.[5]

Soon Harvey was besieged by those who wanted Einstein's brain or a piece of it. He was summoned to Washington to meet with officials of the U.S. Army's pathology unit, but despite their requests he refused to show them his prized possession. Guarding it had become a mission. He finally decided to have friends at the University of Pennsylvania turn part of it into microscopic slides, and so he put Einstein's brain, now chopped into pieces, into two glass cookie jars and drove it there in the back of his Ford.

Over the years, in a process that was at once guileless as well as bizarre, Harvey would send off slides or chunks of the remaining brain to random researchers who struck his fancy. He demanded no rigorous studies, and for years none were published. In the meantime, he quit Princeton Hospital, left his wife, remarried a couple of times, and moved around from New Jersey to Missouri to Kansas, often leaving no forwarding address, the remaining fragments of Einstein's brain always with him.

Every now and then, a reporter would stumble across the story and track Harvey down, causing a minor media flurry. Steven Levy, then of *New Jersey Monthly* and later of *Newsweek,* found him in 1978 in Wichita, where he pulled a Mason jar of Einstein's brain chunks from a box labeled "Costa Cider" in the corner of his office behind a red plastic picnic cooler.[6] Twenty years later, Harvey was tracked down again, by Michael Paterniti, a free-spirited and soulful writer for *Harper's,* who turned his road trip in a rented Buick across America with Harvey and the brain into an award-winning article and best-selling book, *Driving Mr. Albert.*

Their destination was California, where they paid a call on Einstein's granddaughter, Evelyn Einstein. She was divorced, marginally employed, and struggling with poverty. Harvey's perambulations with the brain struck her as creepy, but she had a particular interest in one secret it might hold. She was the adopted daughter of Hans Albert and his wife Frieda, but the timing and circumstances of her birth were murky. She had heard rumors that made her suspect that possibly, just possibly, she might actually be Einstein's own daughter. She had been born after Elsa's death, when Einstein was spending time with a variety of women. Perhaps she had been the result of one of those liaisons, and he had arranged for her to be adopted by Hans Albert. Working with Robert Schulmann, an early editor of the Einstein papers, she hoped to see what could be learned by studying the DNA from Einstein's brain.

Unfortunately, it turned out that the way Harvey had embalmed the brain made it impossible to extract usable DNA. And so her questions were never answered.[7]

In 1998, after forty-three years as the wandering guardian of Einstein's brain, Thomas Harvey, by then 86, decided it was time to pass on the responsibility. So he called the person who currently held his old job as pathologist at Princeton Hospital and went by to drop it off.[8]

Of the dozens of people to whom Harvey doled out pieces of Einstein's brain over the years, only three published significant scientific studies. The first was by a Berkeley team led by Marian Diamond.[9] It reported that one area of Einstein's brain, part of the parietal cortex, had a higher ratio of what are known as glial cells to neurons. This could, the authors said, indicate that the neurons used and needed more energy.

One problem with this study was that his 76-year-old brain was compared to eleven others from men who had died at an average age of 64. There were no other geniuses in the sample to help determine if the findings fit a pattern. There was also a more fundamental problem: with no ability to trace the development of the brain over a lifetime, it was unclear which physical attributes might be the *cause* of greater intelligence and which might instead be the *effect* of years spent using and exercising certain parts of the brain.

A second paper, published in 1996, suggested that Einstein's cerebral cortex was thinner than in five other sample brains, and the density of his neurons was greater. Once again, the sample was small and evidence of any pattern was sketchy.

The most cited paper was done in 1999 by Professor Sandra Witelson and a team at McMaster University in Ontario. Harvey had sent her a fax, unprompted, offering samples for study. He was in his eighties, but he personally drove up to Canada by himself, transporting a hunk that amounted to about one-fifth of Einstein's brain, including the parietal lobe.

When compared to brains of thirty-five other men, Einstein's had a much shorter groove in one area of his inferior parietal lobe, which is thought to be key to mathematical and spatial thinking. His brain was also 15 percent wider in this region. The paper speculated that these traits may have produced richer and more integrated brain circuits in this region.[10]

But any true understanding of Einstein's imagination and intuition will not come from poking around at his patterns of glia and grooves. The relevant question was how his *mind* worked, not his brain.

The explanation that Einstein himself most often gave for his mental accomplishments was his curiosity. As he put it near the end of his life, "I have no special talents, I am only passionately curious."[11]

That trait is perhaps the best place to begin when sifting through the elements of his genius. There he is, as a young boy sick in bed, trying to figure out why the compass needle points north. Most of us can recall seeing such needles swing into place, but few of us pursue with passion the question of how a magnetic field might work, how fast it might propagate, how it could possibly interact with matter.

What would it be like to race alongside a light beam? If we are moving through curved space the way a beetle moves across a curved leaf, how would we notice it? What does it mean to say that two events are simultaneous? Curiosity, in Einstein's case, came not just from a desire to question the mysterious. More important, it came from a childlike sense of marvel that propelled him to question the familiar, those concepts that, as he once said, "the ordinary adult never bothers his head about."[12]

He could look at well-known facts and pluck out insights that had escaped the notice of others. Ever since Newton, for example, scientists had known that inertial mass was equivalent to gravitational mass. But Einstein saw that this meant that there was an equivalence between gravity and acceleration that would unlock an explanation of the universe.[13]

A tenet of Einstein's faith was that nature was not cluttered with extraneous attributes. Thus, there must be a purpose to curiosity. For Einstein, it existed because it created minds that question, which produced an appreciation for the universe that he equated with religious feelings. "Curiosity has its own reason for existing," he once explained. "One cannot help but be in awe when one contemplates the mysteries of eternity, of life, of the marvelous structure of reality."[14]

From his earliest days, Einstein's curiosity and imagination were expressed mainly through visual thinking—mental pictures and thought experiments—rather than verbally. This included the ability to visualize the physical reality that was painted by the brush strokes of mathematics. "Behind a formula he immediately saw the physical content, while for us it only remained an abstract formula," said one of his first students.[15] Planck came up with the concept of the quanta, which he viewed as mainly a mathematical contrivance, but it took Einstein to understand their physical reality. Lorentz came up with mathematical transformations that described bodies in motion, but it took Einstein to create a new theory of relativity based on them.

One day during the 1930s, Einstein invited Saint-John Perse to Princeton to find out how the poet worked. "How does the idea of a poem come?" Einstein asked. The poet spoke of the role played by intuition and imagination. "It's the same for a man of science," Einstein responded with delight. "It is a sudden illumination, almost a rapture. Later, to be sure, intelligence analyzes and experiments confirm or invalidate the intuition. But initially there is a great forward leap of the imagination."[16]

There was an aesthetic to Einstein's thinking, a sense of beauty. And one component to beauty, he felt, was simplicity. He had echoed Newton's dictum "Nature is pleased with simplicity" in the creed he declared at Oxford the year he left Europe for America: "Nature is the realization of the simplest conceivable mathematical ideas."[17]

Despite Occam's razor and other philosophical maxims along these lines, there is no self-evident reason this has to be true. Just as it is possible that God might actually play dice, so too it is possible that he might delight in Byzantine complexities. But Einstein didn't think so. "In building a theory, his approach had something in common with that of an artist," said Nathan Rosen, his assistant in the 1930s. "He would aim for simplicity and beauty, and beauty for him was, after all, essentially simplicity."[18]

He became like a gardener weeding a flower bed. "I believe what allowed Einstein to achieve so much was primarily a moral quality," said physicist Lee Smolin. "He simply cared far more than most of his colleagues that the laws of physics have to explain everything in nature co-herently and consistently."[19]

Einstein's instinct for unification was ingrained in his personality and reflected in his politics. Just as he sought a unified theory in science that could govern the cosmos, so he sought one in politics that could govern the planet, one that would overcome the anarchy of unfettered nationalism through a world federalism based on universal principles.

Perhaps the most important aspect of his personality was his will-ingness to be a nonconformist. It was an attitude that he celebrated in a foreword he wrote near the end of his life to a new edition of Galileo. "The theme that I recognize in Galileo's work," he said, "is the passion-ate fight against any kind of dogma based on authority."[20]

Planck and Poincaré and Lorentz all came close to some of the breakthroughs Einstein made in 1905. But they were a little too con-fined by dogma based on authority. Einstein alone among them was re-bellious enough to throw out conventional thinking that had defined science for centuries.

This joyous nonconformity made him recoil from the sight of Prussian soldiers marching in lockstep. It was a personal outlook that became a political one as well. He bristled at all forms of tyranny over free minds, from Nazism to Stalinism to McCarthyism.

Einstein's fundamental creed was that freedom was the lifeblood of creativity. "The development of science and of the creative activities of the spirit," he said, "requires a freedom that consists in the independ-ence of thought from the restrictions of authoritarian and social preju-dice." Nurturing that should be the fundamental role of government, he felt, and the mission of education.[21]

There was a simple set of formulas that defined Einstein's outlook. Creativity required being willing not to conform. That required nur-turing free minds and free spirits, which in turn required "a spirit of tol-erance." And the underpinning of tolerance was humility—the belief that no one had the right to impose ideas and beliefs on others.

The world has seen a lot of impudent geniuses. What made Ein-stein special was that his mind and soul were tempered by this humil-ity. He could be serenely self-confident in his lonely course yet also humbly awed by the beauty of nature's handiwork. "A spirit is manifest in the laws of the universe—a spirit vastly superior to that of man, and one in the face of which we with our modest powers must feel humble," he wrote. "In this way the pursuit of science leads to a religious feeling of a special sort."[22]

For some people, miracles serve as evidence of God's existence. For Einstein it was the absence of miracles that reflected divine providence. The fact that the cosmos is comprehensible, that it follows laws, is worthy of awe. This is the defining quality of a "God who reveals himself in the harmony of all that exists."[23]

Einstein considered this feeling of reverence, this cosmic religion, to be the wellspring of all true art and science. It was what guided him. "When I am judging a theory," he said, "I ask myself whether, if I were God, I would have arranged the world in such a way."[24] It is also what graced him with his beautiful mix of confidence and awe.

He was a loner with an intimate bond to humanity, a rebel who was suffused with reverence. And thus it was that an imaginative, impertinent patent clerk became the mind reader of the creator of the cosmos, the locksmith of the mysteries of the atom and the universe.

SOURCES

EINSTEIN'S CORRESPONDENCE AND WRITINGS

The Collected Papers of Albert Einstein, vols. 1–10. 1987–2006. Princeton: Princeton University Press. (Abbreviated CPAE)

    The founding editor was John Stachel. The current general editor is Diana Kormos Buchwald. Other editors over the years include David Cassidy, Robert Schulmann, Jürgen Renn, Martin Klein, A. J. Knox, Michel Janssen, Jósef Illy, Christoph Lehner, Daniel Kennefick, Tilman Sauer, Ze'ev Rosenkranz, and Virginia Iris Holmes.

    These volumes cover the years 1879–1920. Each volume comes in a German version and an English translation. The page numbers in each differ, but the document numbers are the same. In cases where I cite some information that is in one version but not the other (such as an editor's essay or footnote), I designate the volume and language version and cite the page number.

Albert Einstein Archives. (Abbreviated AEA)

    These archives are now at Hebrew University in Jerusalem with copies at the Einstein Papers Project at Caltech and in the Princeton University library. Documents from the archives are cited both by date and by the AEA folder (reel) and document number. In the case of most of the untranslated German documents, I have relied on translations made for me by James Hoppes and Natasha Hoffmeyer.

FREQUENTLY CITED WORKS

Abraham, Carolyn. 2001. *Possessing Genius.* New York: St. Martin's Press.
Aczel, Amir. 1999. *God's Equation: Einstein, Relativity, and the Expanding Universe.* New York: Random House.
————. 2002. *Entanglement: The Unlikely Story of How Scientists, Mathematicians, and Philosophers Proved Einstein's Spookiest Theory.* New York: Plume.
Baierlein, Ralph. 2001. *Newton to Einstein: The Trail of Light, an Excursion to the Wave-Particle Duality and the Special Theory of Relativity.* New York: Cambridge University Press.

Barbour, Julian, and Herbert Pfister, eds. 1995. *Mach's Principle: From Newton's Bucket to Quantum Gravity*. Boston: Birkhäuser.

Bartusiak, Marcia. 2000. *Einstein's Unfinished Symphony*. New York: Berkley.

Batterson, Steve. 2006. *Pursuit of Genius*. Wellesley, Mass.: A. K. Peters.

Beller, Mara, et al., eds. 1993. *Einstein in Context*. Cambridge, England: Cambridge University Press.

Bernstein, Jeremy. 1973. *Einstein*. Modern Masters Series. New York: Viking.

———. 1991. *Quantum Profiles*. Princeton: Princeton University Press.

———. 1996a. *Albert Einstein and the Frontiers of Physics*. New York: Oxford University Press.

———. 1996b. *A Theory for Everything*. New York: Springer-Verlag.

———. 2001. *The Merely Personal*. Chicago: Ivan Dee.

———. 2006. *Secrets of the Old One: Einstein, 1905*. New York: Copernicus.

Besso, Michele. 1972. *Correspondence 1903–1955*. In German with parallel French translation by Pierre Speziali. Paris: Hermann.

Bird, Kai, and Martin J. Sherwin. 2005. *American Prometheus: The Triumph and Tragedy of J. Robert Oppenheimer*. New York: Knopf.

Bodanis, David. 2000. *E=mc²: A Biography of the World's Most Famous Equation*. New York: Walker.

Bolles, Edmund Blair. 2004. *Einstein Defiant: Genius versus Genius in the Quantum Revolution*. Washington, D.C.: Joseph Henry.

Born, Max. 1978. *My Life: Recollections of a Nobel Laureate*. New York: Scribner's.

———. 2005. *Born-Einstein Letters*. New York: Walker Publishing. (Originally published in 1971, with new material for the 2005 edition)

Brian, Denis. 1996. *Einstein: A Life*. Hoboken, N.J.: Wiley.

———. 2005. *The Unexpected Einstein*. Hoboken, N.J.: Wiley.

Brockman, John, ed. 2006. *My Einstein*. New York: Pantheon.

Bucky, Peter. 1992. *The Private Albert Einstein*. Kansas City, Mo.: Andrews and McMeel.

Cahan, David. 2000. "The Young Einstein's Physics Education." In Howard and Stachel 2000.

Calaprice, Alice, ed. 2005. *The New Expanded Quotable Einstein*. Princeton: Princeton University Press.

Calder, Nigel. 1979. *Einstein's Universe: A Guide to the Theory of Relativity*. New York: Viking Press. (Reissued by Penguin Press in 2005)

Carroll, Sean M. 2003. *Spacetime and Geometry: An Introduction to General Relativity*. Boston: Addison-Wesley.

Cassidy, David C. 2004. *Einstein and Our World*. Amherst, N.Y.: Humanity Books.

Clark, Ronald. 1971. *Einstein: The Life and Times*. New York: HarperCollins.

Corry, Leo, Jürgen Renn, and John Stachel. 1997. "Belated Decision in the Hilbert-Einstein Priority Dispute." *Science* 278: 1270–1273.

Crelinsten, Jeffrey. 2006. *Einstein's Jury: The Race to Test Relativity*. Princeton: Princeton University Press.

Damour, Thibault. 2006. *Once upon Einstein*. Wellesley, Mass.: A. K. Peters.

Douglas, Vibert. 1956. *The Life of Arthur Stanley Eddington*. London: Thomas Nelson.

Dukas, Helen, and Banesh Hoffmann, eds. 1979. *Albert Einstein: The Human Side. New Glimpses from His Archives*. Princeton: Princeton University Press.

Dyson, Freeman. 2003. "Clockwork Science." (Review of Galison). *New York Review of Books*, Nov. 6.

Earman, John. 1978. *World Enough and Space-Time*. Cambridge, Mass.: MIT Press.

Earman, John, Clark Glymour, and Robert Rynasiewicz. 1982. "On Writing the History of Special Relativity." *Philosophy of Science Association Journal* 2: 403–416.

Earman, John, et al., eds. 1993. *The Attraction of Gravitation: New Studies in the History of General Relativity*. Boston: Birkhäuser.

Einstein, Albert. 1916. *Relativity: The Special and the General Theory*. (Written as a popular account, this book was published in German in December 1916. An authorized English translation was first published in 1920 by Methuen in London and Henry Holt in New York. It went through fifteen English-language editions in his lifetime, and he added appendixes up until 1952. It is available now from multiple publishers. The version I cite is the 1995 Random House edition. The book can be found at www.bartleby.com/173/ and at www.gutenberg.org/etext/5001.)

———. 1922a. *The Meaning of Relativity*. Princeton: Princeton University Press. (A technical exposition based on his 1921 lectures at Princeton. The fifth edition, published in 1954, contains an appendix revising his attempt at a unified field theory. The 2005 edition from Princeton University Press contains an introduction by Brian Greene.)

———. 1922b. *Sidelights on Relativity*. New York: Dutton.

———. 1922c. "How I Created the Theory of Relativity." Talk in Kyoto, Japan, Dec. 14. (I have used a new, corrected, and heretofore unpublished translation. Einstein's Kyoto talk was published in Japanese in 1923 by theoretical physicist Jun Ishiwara, who was present and took notes. His version was translated into English by Yoshimasa A. Ono and published in *Physics Today* in August 1982. This translation, which has been used by most previous writers on Einstein, is flawed, especially in the parts where Einstein refers to the Michelson-Morley experiments; see Ryoichi Itagaki, "Einstein's Kyoto Lecture," *Science* magazine, vol. 283, March 5, 1999. A proper and corrected translation by Prof. Itagaki will appear in a forthcoming volume of CPAE. I am grateful to Gerald Holton for providing me with a copy of this translation. See also Seiya Abiko, "Einstein's Kyoto Address," *Historical Studies in the Physical and Biological Sciences* 31 (2000): 1–35.)

———. 1934. *Essays in Science*. New York: Philosophical Library.

———. 1949a. *The World As I See It*. New York: Philosophical Library. (Based on *Mein Weltbild*, edited by Carl Seelig.)

———. 1949b. "Autobiographical Notes." In Schilpp 1949, 3–94.

———. 1950a. *Out of My Later Years*. New York: Philosophical Library.

———. 1950b. *Einstein on Humanism*. New York: Philosophical Library.

———. 1954. *Ideas and Opinions.* New York: Random House.

———. 1956. "Autobiographische Skizze." In Seelig 1956b.

Einstein, Albert, and Leopold Infeld. 1938. *The Evolution of Physics: The Growth of Ideas from Early Concepts to Relativity and Quanta.* New York: Simon & Schuster.

Einstein, Elizabeth Roboz. 1991. *Hans Albert Einstein: Reminiscences of Our Life Together.* Iowa City: University of Iowa Press.

Einstein, Maja. 1923. "Albert Einstein—A Biographical Sketch." CPAE 1: xv. (This sketch was originally written in 1923 as the start of a book she hoped to write, but it was never published by her. It tracks her brother's life only until 1905. See lorentz.phl.jhu.edu/AnnusMirabilis/AeReserveArticles/maja.pdf.)

Eisenstaedt, Jean, and A. J. Kox, eds. 1992. *Studies in the History of General Relativity.* Boston: Birkhäuser.

Elon, Amos. 2002. *The Pity of It All: A History of the Jews in Germany, 1743–1933.* New York: Henry Holt.

Elzinga, Aant. 2006. *Einstein's Nobel Prize.* Sagamore Beach, Mass.: Science History Publications.

Fantova, Johanna. "Journal of Conversations with Einstein, 1953–55." In Princeton University Einstein Papers archives and published as an appendix in Calaprice 2005. (For clarity and because the page numbers vary in different editions of Calaprice, I identify Fantova's entries by date.)

Federal Bureau of Investigation, Files on Einstein. Available through the Freedom of Information Act website, foia.fbi.gov/foiaindex/einstein.htm.

Feynman, Richard. 1997. *Six Not-So-Easy Pieces: Einstein's Relativity, Symmetry, and Space-Time.* Boston: Addison-Wesley.

———. 1999. *The Pleasure of Finding Things Out.* Cambridge, England: Perseus.

———. 2002. *The Feynman Lectures on Gravitation.* Boulder, Colo.: Westview Press.

Fine, Arthur. 1996. *The Shaky Game: Einstein, Realism, and the Quantum Theory.* Chicago: University of Chicago Press. (Revised edition of original 1986 publication.)

Flexner, Abraham. 1960. *An Autobiography.* New York: Simon & Schuster.

Flückiger, Max. 1974. *Albert Einstein in Bern.* Bern: Haupt.

Fölsing, Albrecht. 1997. *Albert Einstein: A Biography.* Translated and abridged by Ewald Osers. New York: Viking. (Original unabridged edition in German published in 1993.)

Frank, Philipp. 1947. *Einstein: His Life and Times.* Translated by George Rosen. New York: Da Capo Press. (Reprinted in 2002.)

———. 1957. *Philosophy of Science.* Saddle River, N.J.: Prentice-Hall.

French, A. P., ed. 1979. *Einstein: A Centenary Volume.* Cambridge, Mass.: Harvard University Press.

Friedman, Alan J., and Carol C. Donley. 1985. *Einstein as Myth and Muse.* Cambridge, England: Cambridge University Press.

Friedman, Robert Marc. 2005. "Einstein and the Nobel Committee." *Europhysics News,* July/Aug.

Galileo Galilei. 1632. *Dialogue Concerning the Two Chief World Systems: Ptolemaic and Copernican.* (I use the 2001 Modern Library edition translated by Stillman Drake, foreword by Albert Einstein, introduction by John Heilbron.)

Galison, Peter. 2003. *Einstein's Clocks, Poincaré's Maps.* New York: Norton.

Gamow, George. 1966. *Thirty Years That Shook Physics: The Story of Quantum Theory.* New York: Dover.

———. 1970. *My World Line.* New York: Viking.

———. 1993. *Mr. Tompkins in Paperback.* New York: Cambridge University Press.

Gardner, Martin. 1976. *The Relativity Explosion.* New York: Vintage.

Gell-Mann, Murray. 1994. *The Quark and the Jaguar.* New York: Henry Holt.

Goenner, Hubert. 2004. "On the History of Unified Field Theories." Living Reviews in Relativity website, relativity.livingreviews.org/.

———. 2005. *Einstein in Berlin.* Munich: Beck Verlag.

Goenner, Hubert, et al., eds. 1999. *The Expanding Worlds of General Relativity.* Boston: Birkhäuser.

Goldberg, Stanley. 1984. *Understanding Relativity: Origin and Impact of a Scientific Revolution.* Boston: Birkhäuser.

Goldsmith, Maurice, et al. 1980. *Einstein: The First Hundred Years.* New York: Pergamon Press.

Goldstein, Rebecca. 2005. *Incompleteness: The Proof and Paradox of Kurt Gödel.* New York: Atlas/Norton.

Greene, Brian. 1999. *The Elegant Universe: Superstrings, Hidden Dimensions, and the Quest for the Ultimate Theory.* New York: Norton.

———. 2004. *The Fabric of the Cosmos: Space, Time, and the Texture of Reality.* New York: Knopf.

Gribbin, John, and Mary Gribbin. 2005. *Annus Mirabilis: 1905, Albert Einstein, and the Theory of Relativity.* New York: Chamberlain Brothers.

Haldane, Richard. 1921. *The Reign of Relativity.* London: Murray. (Reprinted in 2003 by the University Press of the Pacific in Honolulu.)

Hartle, James. 2002. *Gravity: An Introduction to Einstein's General Relativity.* Boston: Addison-Wesley.

Hawking, Stephen. 1999. "A Brief History of Relativity." *Time,* Dec. 31.

———. 2001. *The Universe in a Nutshell.* New York: Bantam.

———. 2005. "Does God Play Dice?" Available at www.hawking.org.uk/lectures/lindex.html.

Hawking, Stephen, and Roger Penrose. 1996. *The Nature of Space and Time.* Princeton: Princeton University Press.

Heilbron, John. 2000. *The Dilemmas of an Upright Man: Max Planck and the Fortunes of German Science.* Cambridge, Mass.: Harvard University Press. (Revised edition of 1986 book.)

Heisenberg, Werner. 1958. *Physics and Philosophy.* New York: Harper.

———. 1971. *Physics and Beyond: Encounters and Conversations.* New York: Harper & Row.

———. 1989. *Encounters with Einstein.* Princeton: Princeton University Press.

Highfield, Roger, and Paul Carter. 1994. *The Private Lives of Albert Einstein*. New York: St. Martin's Press.

Hoffmann, Banesh, with the collaboration of Helen Dukas. 1972. *Albert Einstein: Creator and Rebel*. New York: Viking.

Hoffmann, Banesh. 1983. *Relativity and Its Roots*. New York: Scientific American Books.

Holmes, Frederick L., Jürgen Renn, and Hans-Jörg Rheinberger, eds. 2003. *Reworking the Bench: Research Notebooks in the History of Science*. Dordrecht: Kluwer.

Holton, Gerald. 1973. *Thematic Origins of Scientific Thought: Kepler to Einstein*. Cambridge, Mass.: Harvard University Press.

———. 2000. *Einstein, History, and Other Passions: The Rebellion against Science at the End of the Twentieth Century*. Cambridge, Mass.: Harvard University Press.

———. 2003. "Einstein's Third Paradise." *Daedalus* 132, no. 4 (fall): 26–34. Available at www.physics.harvard.edu/holton/3rdParadise.pdf.

Holton, Gerald, and Stephen Brush. 2004. *Physics, the Human Adventure*. New Brunswick, N.J.: Rutgers University Press.

Holton, Gerald, and Yehuda Elkana, eds. 1997. *Albert Einstein: Historical and Cultural Perspectives*. The Centennial Symposium in Jerusalem. Mineola, N.Y.: Dover Publications.

Howard, Don. 1985. "Einstein on Locality and Separability." *Studies in History and Philosophy of Science* 16: 171–201.

———. 1990a. "Einstein and Duhem." *Synthese* 83: 363–384.

———. 1990b. " 'Nicht sein kann was nicht sein darf,' or The Prehistory of EPR, 1909–1935. Einstein's Early Worries about the Quantum Mechanics of Composite Systems." In Arthur Miller, ed., *Sixty-two Years of Uncertainty: Historical, Philosophical, and Physical Inquiries into the Foundations of Quantum Mechanics*. New York: Plenum, 61–111.

———. 1993. "Was Einstein Really a Realist?" *Perspectives on Science* 1: 204–251.

———. 1997. "A Peek behind the Veil of Maya: Einstein, Schopenhauer, and the Historical Background of the Conception of Space as a Ground for the Individuation of Physical Systems." In John Earman and John D. Norton, eds., *The Cosmos of Science: Essays of Exploration*. Pittsburgh: University of Pittsburgh Press, 87–150.

———. 2004. "Albert Einstein, Philosophy of Science." *Stanford Encyclopedia of Philosophy*. Available at plato.stanford.edu/entries/einstein-philscience/.

———. 2005. "Albert Einstein as a Philosopher of Science." *Physics Today*, Dec., 34.

Howard, Don, and John Norton. 1993. "Out of the Labyrinth? Einstein, Hertz, and the Göttingen Answer to the Hole Argument." In Earman et al. 1993.

Howard, Don, and John Stachel, eds. 1989. *Einstein and the History of General Relativity*. Boston: Birkhäuser.

———, eds. 2000. *Einstein: The Formative Years, 1879–1909*. Boston: Birkhäuser.

Illy, József, ed. 2005, February. "Einstein Due Today." Manuscript. (Courtesy of the Einstein Papers Project, Pasadena. Includes newspaper clippings about Einstein's 1921 visit. Forthcoming publication planned as *Albert Meets America*. Baltimore: Johns Hopkins University Press.)

Infeld, Leopold. 1950. *Albert Einstein: His Work and Its Influence on Our World*. New York: Scribner's.

Jammer, Max. 1989. *The Conceptual Development of Quantum Mechanics*. Los Angeles: American Institute of Physics.

———. 1999. *Einstein and Religion: Physics and Theology*. Princeton: Princeton University Press.

Janssen, Michel. 1998. "Rotation as the Nemesis of Einstein's Entwurf Theory." In Goenner et al. 1999.

———. 2002. "The Einstein-Besso Manuscript: A Glimpse behind the Curtain of the Wizard." Available at www.tc.umn.edu/~janss011/.

———. 2004. "Einstein's First Systematic Exposition of General Relativity." Available at philsci-archive.pitt.edu/archive/00002123/01/annalen.pdf.

———. 2005. "Of Pots and Holes: Einstein's Bumpy Road to General Relativity." *Annalen der Physik* 14 (Supplement): 58–85.

———. 2006. "What Did Einstein Know and When Did He Know It? A Besso Memo Dated August 1913." Available at www.tc.umn.edu/~janss011/.

Janssen, Michel, and Jürgen Renn. 2004. "Untying the Knot: How Einstein Found His Way Back to Field Equations Discarded in the Zurich Notebook." Available at www.tc.umn.edu/~janss011/pdf%20files/knot.pdf.

Jerome, Fred. 2002. *The Einstein File: J. Edgar Hoover's Secret War against the World's Most Famous Scientist*. New York: St. Martin's Press.

Jerome, Fred, and Rodger Taylor. 2005. *Einstein on Race and Racism*. New Brunswick, N.J.: Rutgers University Press.

Kaku, Michio. 2004. *Einstein's Cosmos: How Albert Einstein's Vision Transformed Our Understanding of Space and Time*. New York: Atlas Books.

Kessler, Harry. 1999. *Berlin in Lights: The Diaries of Count Harry Kessler (1918–1937)*. Translated and edited by Charles Kessler. New York: Grove Press.

Klein, Martin J. 1970a. *Paul Ehrenfest: The Making of a Theoretical Physicist*. New York: American Elsevier.

———. 1970b. "The First Phase of the Bohr-Einstein Dialogue." *Historical Studies in the Physical Sciences* 2: 1–39.

Kox, A. J., and Jean Eisenstaedt, eds. 2005. *The Universe of General Relativity. Vol. II of Einstein Studies*. Boston: Birkhäuser.

Krauss, Lawrence. 2005. *Hiding in the Mirror*. New York: Viking.

Levenson, Thomas. 2003. *Einstein in Berlin*. New York: Bantam Books.

Levy, Steven. 1978. "My Search for Einstein's Brain." *New Jersey Monthly*, Aug.

Lightman, Alan. 1993. *Einstein's Dreams*. New York: Pantheon Books.

———. 1999. "A New Cataclysm of Thought." *Atlantic Monthly*, Jan.

———. 2005. *The Discoveries*. New York: Pantheon.

Lightman, Alan, et al. 1975. *Problem Book in Relativity and Gravitation*. Princeton: Princeton University Press.

Marianoff, Dimitri. 1944. *Einstein: An Intimate Study of a Great Man*. New York: Doubleday. (Marianoff married and then divorced Margot Einstein, a daughter of Einstein's second wife Elsa, and Einstein denounced this book.)

Mehra, Jagdish. 1975. *The Solvay Conferences on Physics: Aspects of the Development of Physics Since 1911*. Dordrecht: D. Reidel.

Mermin, N. David. 2005. *It's about Time: Understanding Einstein's Relativity*. Princeton: Princeton University Press.

Michelmore, Peter. 1962. *Einstein: Profile of the Man*. New York: Dodd, Mead.

Miller, Arthur I. 1981. *Albert Einstein's Special Theory of Relativity: Emergence (1905) and Early Interpretation (1905–1911)*. Boston: Addison-Wesley.

———. 1984. *Imagery in Scientific Thought*. Boston: Birkhäuser.

———. 1992. "Albert Einstein's 1907 Jahrbuch Paper: The First Step from SRT to GRT." In Eisenstaedt and Kox 1992, 319–335.

———. 1999. *Insights of Genius*. New York: Springer-Verlag.

———. 2001. *Einstein, Picasso: Space, Time and the Beauty That Causes Havoc*. New York: Basic Books.

———. 2005. *Empire of the Stars*. New York: Houghton Mifflin.

Misner, Charles, Kip Thorne, and John Archibald Wheeler. 1973. *Gravitation*. San Francisco: Freeman.

Moore, Ruth. 1966. *Niels Bohr: The Man, His Science, and the World They Changed*. New York: Knopf.

Moszkowski, Alexander. 1921. *Einstein the Searcher: His Work Explained from Dialogues with Einstein*. New York: Dutton.

Nathan, Otto, and Heinz Norden, eds. 1960. *Einstein on Peace*. New York: Simon & Schuster.

Neffe, Jürgen. 2005. *Einstein: Eine Biographie*. Hamburg: Rowohlt.

Norton, John D. 1984. "How Einstein Found His Field Equations." *Historical Studies in the Physical Sciences*. Reprinted in Howard and Stachel 1989, 101–159.

———. 1985. "What Was Einstein's Principle of Equivalence?" *Studies in History and Philosophy of Science* 16: 203–246. Reprinted in Howard and Stachel 1989, 5–47.

———. 1991. "Thought Experiments in Einstein's Work." In Tamara Horowitz and Gerald Massey, eds., *Thought Experiments in Science and Philosophy*. Savage, Md.: Rowman and Littlefield, 129–148.

———. 1993. "General Covariance and the Foundations of General Relativity: Eight Decades of Dispute." *Reports on Progress in Physics* 56: 791–858.

———. 1995a. "Eliminative Induction as a Method of Discovery: Einstein's Discovery of General Relativity." In Jarrett Leplin, ed., *The Creation of Ideas in Physics: Studies for a Methodology of Theory Construction*. Dordrecht: Kluwer, 29–69.

———. 1995b. "Did Einstein Stumble? The Debate over General Covariance." *Erkenntnis* 42: 223–245.

———. 1995c. "Mach's Principle before Einstein." Available at www.pitt.edu/~jdnorton/papers/MachPrinciple.pdf.

———. 2000. "Nature Is the Realization of the Simplest Conceivable Mathematical Ideas: Einstein and the Canon of Mathematical Simplicity." *Studies in the History and Philosophy of Modern Physics* 31: 135–170.

———. 2002. "Einstein's Triumph Over the Spacetime Coordinate System." *Dialogos* 79: 253–262.

————. 2004. "Einstein's Investigations of Galilean Covariant Electrodynamics prior to 1905." *Archive for History of Exact Sciences* 59: 45–105.

————. 2005a. "How Hume and Mach Helped Einstein Find Special Relativity." Available at www.pitt.edu/~jdnorton.

————. 2005b. "A Conjecture on Einstein, the Independent Reality of Spacetime Coordinate Systems and the Disaster of 1913." In Kox and Eisenstaedt 2005.

————. 2006a. "Einstein's Special Theory of Relativity and the Problems in the Electrodynamics of Moving Bodies That Led Him to It." Available at www.pitt.edu/~jdnorton/homepage/cv.html.

————. 2006b. "What Was Einstein's 'Fateful Prejudice'?" In Jürgen Renn, *The Genesis of General Relativity*, vol. 2. Dordrecht: Kluwer.

————. 2006c. "Atoms, Entropy, Quanta: Einstein's Miraculous Argument of 1905." Available at www.pitt.edu/~jdnorton.

Overbye, Dennis. 2000. *Einstein in Love: A Scientific Romance*. New York: Viking.

Pais, Abraham. 1982. *Subtle Is the Lord: The Science and Life of Albert Einstein*. New York: Oxford University Press.

————. 1991. *Niels Bohr's Times in Physics, Philosophy, and Polity*. Oxford: Clarendon Press.

————. 1994. *Einstein Lived Here: Essays for the Layman*. New York: Oxford University Press.

Panek, Richard. 2004. *The Invisible Century: Einstein, Freud, and the Search for Hidden Universes*. New York: Viking.

Parzen, Herbert. 1974. *The Hebrew University: 1925–1935*. New York: KTAV.

Paterniti, Michael. 2000. *Driving Mr. Albert*. New York: Dial.

Pauli, Wolfgang. 1994. *Writings on Physics and Philosophy*. Berlin: Springer-Verlag.

Penrose, Roger. 2005. *The Road to Reality*. New York: Knopf.

Poincaré, Henri. 1902. *Science and Hypothesis*. Available at spartan.ac.brocku.ca/~lward/Poincare/Poincare_1905_toc.html.

Popović, Milan. 2003. *In Albert's Shadow: The Life and Letters of Mileva Marić*. Baltimore: Johns Hopkins University Press.

Powell, Corey. 2002. *God in the Equation*. New York: Free Press.

Pyenson, Lewis. 1985. *The Young Einstein*. Boston: Adam Hilger.

Regis, Ed. 1988. *Who Got Einstein's Office?* New York: Addison-Wesley.

Reid, Constance. 1986. *Hilbert-Courant*. New York: Springer-Verlag.

Reiser, Anton. 1930. *Albert Einstein: A Biographical Portrait*. New York: Boni. (Reiser was the pseudonym of Rudoph Kayser, who married Ilse Einstein, the daughter of Einstein's second wife Elsa.)

Renn, Jürgen. 1994. "The Third Way to General Relativity." Max Planck Institute, www.mpiwg-berlin.mpg.de/Preprints/P9.pdf.

————. 2005a. "Einstein's Controversy with Drude and the Origin of Statistical Mechanics." In Howard and Stachel 2000.

————. 2005b. "Standing on the Shoulders of a Dwarf." In Kox and Eisenstaedt 2005.

————. 2005c. "Before the Riemann Tensor: The Emergence of Einstein's Double Strategy." In Kox and Eisenstaedt 2005.

———. 2005d. *Albert Einstein: Chief Engineer of the Universe. One Hundred Authors for Einstein.* Hoboken, N. J.: Wiley.

———. 2006. *Albert Einstein: Chief Engineer of the Universe. Einstein's Life and Work in Context and Documents of a Life's Pathway.* Hoboken, N. J.: Wiley.

Renn, Jürgen, and Tilman Sauer. 1997. "The Rediscovery of General Relativity in Berlin." Max Planck Institute, www.mpiwg-berlin.mpg.de/en/forschung/Preprints/P63.pdf.

———. 2003. "Errors and Insights: Reconstructing the Genesis of General Relativity from Einstein's Zurich Notebook." In Holmes et al. 2003, 253–268.

———. 2006. "Pathways out of Classical Physics: Einstein's Double Strategy in Searching for the Gravitational Field Equation." Available at www.hss.caltech.edu/~tilman/.

Renn, Jürgen, and Robert Schulmann, eds. 1992. *Albert Einstein and Mileva Marić: The Love Letters.* Princeton: Princeton University Press.

Rhodes, Richard. 1987. *The Making of the Atom Bomb.* New York: Simon & Schuster.

Rigden, John. 2005. *Einstein 1905: The Standard of Greatness.* Cambridge, England: Cambridge University Press.

Robinson, Andrew. 2005. *Einstein: A Hundred Years of Relativity.* New York: Abrams.

Rosenkranz, Ze'ev. 1998. *Albert through the Looking Glass: The Personal Papers of Albert Einstein.* Jerusalem: Hebrew University Press.

———. 2002. *The Einstein Scrapbook.* Baltimore: Johns Hopkins University Press.

Rowe, David E., and Robert Schulmann, eds. 2007. *Einstein's Political World.* Princeton: Princeton University Press.

Rozental, Stefan, ed. 1967. *Niels Bohr: His Life and Work As Seen by His Friends and Colleagues.* Hoboken, N. J.: Wiley.

Ryan, Dennis P., ed. 1987. *Einstein and the Humanities.* New York: Greenwood Press.

Ryckman, Thomas. 2005. *The Reign of Relativity.* Oxford: Oxford University Press.

Rynasiewicz, Robert. 1988. "Lorentz's Local Time and the Theorem of Corresponding States." *Philosophy of Science Association Journal* 1: 67–74.

———. 2000. "The Construction of the Special Theory: Some Queries and Considerations." In Howard and Stachel 2000.

Rynasiewicz, Robert, and Jürgen Renn. 2006. "The Turning Point for Einstein's Annus Mirabilis." *Studies in the History and Philosophy of Modern Physics* 37, Mar.

Sartori, Leo. 1996. *Understanding Relativity.* Berkeley: Univ. of California Press.

Sauer, Tilman. 1999. "The Relativity of Discovery: Hilbert's First Note on the Foundations of Physics." *Archive for History of Exact Sciences* 53: 529–575.

———. 2005. "Einstein Equations and Hilbert Action: What Is Missing on Page 8 of the Proofs for Hilbert's First Communication on the Foundations of Physics?" *Archive for History of Exact Sciences* 59: 577.

Sayen, Jamie. 1985. *Einstein in America: The Scientist's Conscience in the Age of Hitler and Hiroshima.* New York: Crown.

Schilpp, Paul Arthur, ed. 1949. *Albert Einstein: Philosopher-Scientist.* La Salle, Ill.: Open Court Press.

Seelig, Carl. 1956a. *Albert Einstein: A Documentary Biography.* Translated by Mervyn Savill. London: Staples Press. (Translation of *Albert Einstein: Eine Dokumentarische Biographie,* a revision of *Albert Einstein und die Schweiz.* Zürich: Europa-Verlag, 1952.)

———, ed. 1956b. *Helle Zeit, Dunkle Zeit: In Memoriam Albert Einstein.* Zürich: Europa-Verlag.

Singh, Simon. 2004. *Big Bang: The Origin of the Universe.* New York: Harper-Collins.

Solovine, Maurice. 1987. *Albert Einstein: Letters to Solovine.* New York: Philosophical Library.

Sonnert, Gerhard. 2005. *Einstein and Culture.* Amherst, N.Y.: Humanity Books.

Speziali, Maurice, ed. 1956. *Albert Einstein–Michele Besso, Correspondence 1903–1955.* Paris: Hermann.

Stachel, John. 1980. "Einstein and the Rigidly Rotating Disk." In A. Held, ed., *General Relativity and Gravitation: A Hundred Years after the Birth of Einstein.* New York: Plenum, 1–15.

———. 1987. "How Einstein Discovered General Relativity." In M. A. H. MacCallum, ed., *General Relativity and Gravitation: Proceedings of the 11th International Conference on General Relativity and Gravitation.* Cambridge, England: Cambridge University Press, 200–208.

———. 1989a. "The Rigidly Rotating Disk as the Missing Link in the History of General Relativity." In Howard and Stachel 1989.

———. 1989b. "Einstein's Search for General Covariance, 1912–1915." In Howard and Stachel 1989.

———. 1998. *Einstein's Miraculous Year: Five Papers That Changed the Face of Physics.* Princeton: Princeton University Press.

———. 2002a. *Einstein from "B" to "Z."* Boston: Birkhäuser.

———. 2002b. "What Song the Syrens Sang: How Did Einstein Discover Special Relativity?" In Stachel 2002a.

———. 2002c. "Einstein and Ether Drift Experiments." In Stachel 2002a.

Stern, Fritz. 1999. *Einstein's German World.* Princeton: Princeton University Press.

Talmey, Max. 1932. *The Relativity Theory Simplified, and the Formative Period of Its Inventor.* New York: Falcon Press.

Taylor, Edwin, and J. Archibald Wheeler. 1992. *Spacetime Physics: Introduction to Special Relativity.* New York: W. H. Freeman.

———. 2000. *Exploring Black Holes.* New York: Benjamin/Cummings.

Thorne, Kip. 1995. *Black Holes and Time Warps: Einstein's Outrageous Legacy.* New York: Norton.

Trbuhovic-Gjuric, Desanka. 1993. *In the Shadow of Albert Einstein.* Bern: Verlag Paul Haupt.

Vallentin, Antonina. 1954. *The Drama of Albert Einstein.* New York: Doubleday.

van Dongen, Jeroen. 2002. "Einstein's Unification: General Relativity and the Quest for Mathematical Naturalness." Ph.D. dissertation, Univ. of Amsterdam.

Viereck, George Sylvester. 1930. *Glimpses of the Great*. New York: Macauley. (Einstein profile first published as "What Life Means to Einstein," *Saturday Evening Post*, Oct. 26, 1929.)

Walter, Scott. 1998. "Minkowski, Mathematicians, and the Mathematical Theory of Relativity." In Goenner et al. 1999.

Weart, Spencer, and Gertrud Weiss Szilard, eds. 1978. *Leo Szilard: His Version of the Facts*. Cambridge, Mass.: MIT Press.

Weizmann, Chaim. 1949. *Trail and Error*. New York: Harper.

Wertheimer, Max. 1959. *Productive Thinking*. New York: Harper.

Whitaker, Andrew. 1996. *Einstein, Bohr and the Quantum Dilemma*. Cambridge, England: Cambridge University Press.

White, Michael, and John Gribbin.1994. *Einstein: A Life in Science*. New York: Dutton.

Whitrow, Gerald J. 1967. *Einstein: The Man and His Achievement*. London: BBC.

Wolfson, Richard. 2003. *Simply Einstein*. New York: Norton.

Yourgrau, Palle. 1999. *Gödel Meets Einstein*. La Salle, Ill.: Open Court Press.

———. 2005. *A World without Time: The Forgotten Legacy of Gödel and Einstein*. New York: Basic Books.

Zackheim, Michele. 1999. *Einstein's Daughter*. New York: Riverhead.

NOTES

Einstein's letters and writings through 1920 have been published in *The Collected Papers of Albert Einstein* series, and they are identified by the dates used in those volumes. Unpublished material that is in the Albert Einstein Archives (AEA) is identified using the folder (reel)-document numbering format of the archives. For some of the material, especially that previously unpublished, I have used translations made for me by James Hoppes and Natasha Hoffmeyer.

EPIGRAPH

1. Einstein to Eduard Einstein, Feb. 5, 1930. Eduard was suffering from deepening mental illness at the time. The exact quote is: "Beim Menschen ist es wie beim Velo. Nur wenn er faehrt, kann er bequem die Balance halten." A more literal translation is: "It is the same with people as it is with riding a bike. Only when moving can one comfortably maintain one's balance." Courtesy of Barbara Wolff, Einstein archives, Hebrew University, Jerusalem.

CHAPTER ONE: THE LIGHT-BEAM RIDER

1. Einstein to Conrad Habicht, May 18 or 25, 1905.
2. These ideas are drawn from essays I wrote in *Time*, Dec. 31, 1999, and *Discover*, Sept. 2004.
3. Dudley Herschbach, "Einstein as a Student," Mar. 2005, unpublished paper provided to the author. Herschbach says, "Efforts to improve science education and literacy face a root problem: science and mathematics are regarded not as part of the general culture, but rather as the province of priest-like experts. Einstein is seen as a towering icon, the exemplar par excellence of lonely genius. That fosters an utterly distorted view of science."
4. Frank 1957, xiv; Bernstein 1996b, 18.
5. Vivienne Anderson to Einstein, Apr. 27, 1953, AEA 60-714; Einstein to Vivienne Anderson, May 12, 1953, AEA 60-716.
6. Viereck, 377. See also Thomas Friedman, "Learning to Keep Learning," *New York Times*, Dec. 13, 2006.

7. Einstein to Mileva Marić, Dec. 12, 1901; Hoffmann and Dukas, 24. Hoffmann was Einstein's friend in the late 1930s in Princeton. He notes, "His early suspicion of authority, which never wholly left him, was to prove of decisive importance."
8. Einstein message for Ben Scheman dinner, Mar. 1952, AEA 28-931.

CHAPTER TWO: CHILDHOOD

1. Einstein to Sybille Blinoff, May 21, 1954, AEA 59-261; Ernst Straus, "Reminiscences," in Holton and Elkana, 419; Vallentin, 17; Maja Einstein, lviii.
2. See, for example, Thomas Sowell, *The Einstein Syndrome: Bright Children Who Talk Late* (New York: Basic Books, 2002).
3. Nobel laureate James Franck quoting Einstein in Seelig 1956b, 72.
4. Vallentin, 17; Einstein to psychologist Max Wertheimer, in Wertheimer, 214.
5. Einstein to Hans Muehsam, Mar. 4, 1953, AEA 60-604. Also: "I think we can dispense with this question of heritage," Einstein is quoted in Seelig 1956a, 11. See also Michelmore, 22.
6. Maja Einstein, xvi; Seelig 1956a, 10.
7. www.alemannia-judaica.de/synagoge_buchau.htm.
8. Einstein to Carl Seelig, Mar. 11, 1952, AEA 39-13; Highfield and Carter, 9.
9. Maja Einstein, xv; Highfield and Carter, 9; Pais 1982, 36.
10. Birth certificate, CPAE 1: 1; Fantova, Dec. 5, 1953.
11. Pais 1982, 36–37.
12. Maja Einstein, xviii. Maria was sometimes used as a stand-in for the name Miriam in Jewish families.
13. Frank 1947, 8.
14. Maja Einstein, xviii–xix; Fölsing, 12; Pais 1982, 37.
15. Some researchers view such a pattern as possibly being a mild manifestation of autism or Asperger's syndrome. Simon Baron-Cohen, the director of the Autism Research Center at Cambridge University, is among those who suggest that Einstein might have exhibited characteristics of autism. He writes that autism is associated with a "particularly intense drive to systemize and an unusually low drive to empathize." He also notes that this pattern "explains the 'islets of ability' that people with autism display in subjects like math or music or drawing—all skills that benefit from systemizing." See Simon Baron-Cohen, "The Male Condition," *New York Times*, Aug. 8, 2005; Simon Baron-Cohen, *The Essential Difference* (New York: Perseus, 2003), 167; Norm Ledgin, *Asperger's and Self-Esteem: Insight and Hope through Famous Role Models* (Arlington, TX: Future Horizons, 2002), chapter 7; Hazel Muir, "Einstein and Newton Showed Signs of Autism," *New Scientist*, Apr. 30, 2003; Thomas Marlin, "Albert Einstein and LD," *Journal of Learning Disabilities*, Mar. 1, 2000, 149. A Google search of Einstein + Asperger's results in 146,000 pages. I do not find such a long-distance diagnosis to be convincing. Even as a teenager, Einstein made close friends, had passionate relationships, enjoyed collegial discussions, communicated well verbally, and could empathize with friends and humanity in general.

16. Einstein 1949b, 9; Seelig 1956a, 11; Hoffmann 1972, 9; Pais 1982, 37; Vallentin, 21; Reiser, 25; Holton 1973, 359; author's interview with Shulamith Oppenheim, Apr. 22, 2005.
17. Overbye, 8; Shulamith Oppenheim, *Rescuing Albert's Compass* (New York: Crocodile, 2003).
18. Holton 1973, 358.
19. Fölsing, 26; Einstein to Philipp Frank, draft, 1940, CPAE 1, p. lxiii.
20. Maja Einstein, xxi; Bucky, 156; Einstein to Hans Albert Einstein, Jan. 8, 1917.
21. Hans Albert Einstein interview in Whitrow, 21; Bucky, 148.
22. Einstein to Paul Plaut, Oct. 23, 1928, AEA 28-65; Dukas and Hoffmann, 78; Moszkowski, 222. Einstein originally wrote that music and science "complement each other in the *release* they offer," but he later changed that to *Befriedigung*, or satisfaction, according to Barbara Wolff of Hebrew University.
23. Einstein to Otto Juliusburger, Sept. 29, 1942, AEA 38-238.
24. Clark, 25; Einstein 1949b, 3; Reiser, 28. (Anton Reiser was the pseudonym of Rudoph Kayser, who married Ilse Einstein, the daughter of Einstein's second wife, Elsa.)
25. Maja Einstein, xix, says he was 7; in fact he enrolled on Oct. 1, 1885, when he was 6.
26. According to the version later told by his stepson-in-law, the teacher then added that Jesus was nailed to the cross "by the Jews"; Reiser, 30. But Einstein's friend and physics colleague Philipp Frank makes a point of specifically noting that the teacher did not raise the role of the Jews; Frank 1947, 9.
27. Fölsing, 16; Einstein to unknown recipient, Apr. 3, 1920, CPAE 1: lx.
28. Reiser, 28–29; Maja Einstein, xxi; Seelig 1956a, 15; Pais 1982, 38; Fölsing, 20. Maja again has him only 8 when he enters the gymnasium, which he actually did in Oct. 1888, at age 9 and a half.
29. Brian 1996, 281. A Google search of *Einstein failed math*, performed in 2006, turned up close to 648,000 references.
30. Pauline Einstein to Fanny Einstein, Aug. 1, 1886; Fölsing, 18–20, citing Einstein to Sybille Blinoff, May 21, 1954, and Dr. H. Wieleitner in *Nueste Nachrichten*, Munich, Mar. 14, 1929.
31. Einstein to Sybille Blinoff, May 21, 1954, AEA 59-261; Maja Einstein, xx.
32. Frank 1947, 14; Reiser, 35; Einstein 1949b, 11.
33. Maja Einstein, xx; Bernstein 1996a, 24–27; Einstein interview with Henry Russo, *The Tower*, Princeton, Apr. 13, 1935.
34. Talmey, 164; Pais 1982, 38.
35. The first edition appeared in twelve volumes between 1853 and 1857. New editions, under a new title that is referred to in Maja's essay, appeared in the late 1860s. They were constantly updated. The version likely owned by Einstein had twenty-one volumes and was bound into four or five large books. The definitive study of this book's influence on Einstein is Frederick Gregory, "The Mysteries and Wonders of Science: Aaron Bernstein's *Naturwissenschaftliche Volksbücher* and the Adolescent Einstein," in Howard and Stachel 2000, 23–42. Maja Einstein, xxi; Einstein 1949b, 15; Seelig 1956a, 12.

36. Aaron Bernstein, *Naturwissenschaftliche Volksbücher*, 1870 ed., vols. 1, 8, 16, 19; Howard and Stachel 2000, 27–39.

37. Einstein 1949b, 5.

38. Talmey, 163. (Talmud wrote his small memoir after he had changed his name to Talmey in America.)

39. Einstein, "On the Method of Theoretical Physics," Herbert Spencer lecture, Oxford, June 10, 1933, in Einstein 1954, 270.

40. Einstein 1949b, 9, 11; Talmey, 163; Fölsing, 23 (he speculates that the "sacred" book may have been another text); Einstein 1954, 270.

41. Aaron Bernstein, vol. 12, cited by Frederick Gregory in Howard and Stachel 2000, 37; Einstein 1949b, 5.

42. Frank 1947, 15; Jammer, 15–29. "The meaning of a life of brilliant scientific activity drew on the remnants of his fervent first feelings of youthful religiosity," writes Gerald Holton in Holton 2003, 32.

43. Einstein 1949b, 5; Maja Einstein, xxi.

44. Einstein, "What I Believe," *Forum and Century* (1930): 194, reprinted as "The World As I See It," in Einstein 1954, 10. According to Philipp Frank, "He saw the parade as a movement of people compelled to be machines"; Frank 1947, 8.

45. Frank 1947, 11; Fölsing, 17; C. P. Snow, "Einstein," in *Variety of Men* (New York: Scribner's, 1966), 26.

46. Einstein to Jost Winteler, July 8, 1901.

47. Pais 1982, 17, 38; Hoffmann 1972, 24.

48. Maja Einstein, xx; Seelig 1956a, 15; Pais 1982, 38; Einstein draft to Philipp Frank, 1940, CPAE 1, p. lxiii.

49. Stefann Siemer, "The Electrical Factory of Jacob Einstein and Cie.," in Renn 2005b, 128–131; Pyenson, 40.

50. Overbye, 9–10; Einstein draft to Philipp Frank, 1940, CPAE 1, p. lxiii; Hoffmann, 1972, 25–26; Reiser, 40; Frank 1947, 16; Maja Einstein, xxi; Fölsing, 28–30.

51. Einstein to Marie Winteler, Apr. 21, 1896; Fölsing 34; *The Jewish Spectator*, Jan. 1969.

52. Frank 1947, 17; Maja Einstein, xxii; Hoffmann 1972, 27.

53. Einstein, "On the Investigation of the State of the Ether in a Magnetic Field," summer 1895, CPAE 1: 5.

54. Einstein to Caesar Koch, summer 1895.

55. Albin Herzog to Gustave Maier, Sept. 25, 1895, CPAE 1 (English), p. 7; Fölsing, 37; Seelig 1956a, 9.

56. This process of envisaging is what Kantian philosophers call *Anschauung*. See Miller 1984, 241–246.

57. Seelig 1956b, 56; Fölsing, 38.

58. Miller 2001, 47; Maja Einstein, xxii; Seelig 1956b, 9; Fölsing, 38; Holton, "On Trying to Understand Scientific Genius," in Holton 1973, 371.

59. Bucky, 26; Fölsing, 46. Einstein provides a fuller description in his "Autobiographical Notes," in Schilpp, 53.

60. Gustav Maier to Jost Winteler, Oct. 26, 1895, CPAE 1: 9; Fölsing, 39; Highfield and Carter, 22–24.
61. Vallentin, 12; Hans Byland, *Neue Bündner Zeitung*, Feb. 7, 1928, cited in Seelig 1956a, 14; Fölsing, 39.
62. Pauline Einstein to the Winteler family, Dec. 30, 1895, CPAE 1: 15.
63. Einstein to Marie Winteler, Apr. 21, 1896.
64. Entrance report, Aarau school, CPAE 1: 8; Aarau school record, CPAE 1: 10; Hermann Einstein to Jost Winteler, Oct. 29, 1995, CPAE 1: 11, and Dec. 30, 1895, CPAE 1: 14.
65. Report on a Music Examination, Mar. 31, 1896, CPAE 1: 17; Seelig 1956a, 15; Overbye, 13.
66. Release from Würtemberg citizenship, Jan. 28, 1896, CPAE 1: 16.
67. Einstein to Julius Katzenstein, Dec. 27, 1931, cited in Fölsing, 41.
68. *Israelitisches Wochenblatt*, Sept. 24, 1920; Einstein, "Why Do They Hate the Jews?," *Collier's*, Nov. 26, 1938.
69. Einstein to Hans Muehsam, Apr. 30, 1954, AEA 38-434; Fölsing 42.
70. Examination results, Sept. 18–21, 1896, CPAE 1: 20–27.
71. Overbye, 15; Maja Einstein, xvii.
72. Einstein to Heinrich Zangger, Aug. 11, 1918.

CHAPTER THREE: THE ZURICH POLYTECHNIC

1. Cahan, 42; editor's note, CPAE 1 (German), p. 44.
2. Einstein 1949b, 15.
3. Record and Grade Transcript, Oct. 1896–Aug. 1900, CPAE 1: 28; Bucky, 24; Einstein to Arnold Sommerfeld, Oct. 29, 1912; Fölsing, 50.
4. Einstein to Mileva Marić, Feb. 1898; Cahan, 64.
5. Louis Kollros, "Albert Einstein en Suisse," *Helvetica Physica*, Supplement 4 (1956): 22, in AEA 5-123; Adolf Frisch, in Seelig 1956a, 29; Cahan, 67; Clark, 55.
6. Seelig 1956a, 30; Overbye, 43; Miller 2001, 52; Charles Seife, "The True and the Absurd," in Brockman, 63.
7. Record and Grade Transcript, CPAE 1: 28.
8. Seelig 1956a, 30; Bucky, 25 (a slightly different version); Fölsing, 57.
9. Seelig 1956a, 30.
10. Einstein to Julia Niggli, July 28, 1899.
11. Seelig 1956a, 28; Whitrow, 5.
12. Einstein 1949b, 15–17.
13. Einstein interview in Bucky, 27; Einstein to Elizabeth Grossmann, Sept. 20, 1936, AEA 11-481; Seelig 1956a, 34, 207; Fölsing, 53.
14. Holton 1973, 209–212. Einstein's stepson-in-law Rudolph Kayser and colleague Philipp Frank both say that Einstein read Föppl in his spare time while at the Polytechnic.
15. Clark, 59; Galison, 32–34. Galison's book on Poincaré and Einstein is a fascinating exposition on how they developed their concepts and how Poincaré's

observations were "an anticipatory note to Einstein's special theory of relativity, a brilliant move by an author lacking the intellectual courage to pursue it to its logical, revolutionary end" (Galison, 34). Also very useful is Miller 2001, 200–204.

16. Seelig 1956a, 37; Whitrow, 5; Bucky, 156.
17. Miller 2001, 186; Hoffmann, 1972, 252; interview with Lili Foldes, *The Etude*, Jan. 1947, in Calaprice, 150; Einstein to Emil Hilb questionnaire, 1939, AEA 86-22; Dukas and Hoffmann, 76.
18. Seelig 1956a, 36.
19. Fölsing, 51, 67; Reiser, 50; Seelig 1956a, 9.
20. Clark, 50. Diana Kormos Buchwald points out that a careful examination of the picture of him at the Aarau school shows holes in his jacket.
21. Einstein to Maja Einstein, 1898.
22. Einstein to Maja Einstein, after Feb. 1899.
23. Marie Winteler to Einstein, Nov. 4–25, 1896.
24. Marie Winteler to Einstein, Nov. 30, 1896.
25. Pauline Einstein to Marie Winteler, Dec. 13, 1896.
26. Einstein to Pauline Winteler, May 1897.
27. Marie Winteler to Einstein, Nov. 4–25, Nov. 30.
28. Novi Sad, the cultural center of the Serbian people, had long been a "free royal city," then part of a Serbian autonomous region of the Hapsburg Empire. By the time Marić was born, it was in the Hungarian part of Austria-Hungary. Approximately 40 percent of the citizens there spoke Serbian when she was growing up, 25 percent spoke Hungarian, and about 20 percent spoke German. It is now the second largest city, after Belgrade, in the Republic of Serbia.
29. Desanka Trbuhovic-Gjuric, 9–38; Dord Krstic, "Mileva Einstein-Marić," in Elizabeth Einstein, 85; Overbye, 28–33; Highfield and Carter, 33–38; Marriage certificate, CPAE 5: 4.
30. Dord Krstic, "Mileva Einstein-Marić," in Elizabeth Einstein, 88 (Krstic's piece is based partly on interviews with school friends); Barbara Wolff, an expert on Einstein's life at the Hebrew University archives, says, "I imagine that Einstein was the main reason Mileva fled Zurich."
31. Mileva Marić to Einstein, after Oct. 20, 1897.
32. Einstein to Mileva Marić, Feb. 16, 1898.
33. Einstein to Mileva Marić, after Apr. 16, 1898, after Nov. 28, 1898.
34. Recollection of Suzanne Markwalder, in Seelig 1956a, 34; Fölsing, 71.
35. Einstein to Mileva Marić, Mar. 13 or 20, 1899.
36. Einstein to Mileva Marić, Aug. 10, 1899, Mar. 1899, Sept. 13, 1900.
37. Einstein to Mileva Marić, Sept. 13, 1900, early Aug. 1899, Aug. 10, 1899.
38. Einstein to Mileva Marić, ca. Sept. 28, 1899.
39. Mileva Marić to Einstein, 1900.
40. Intermediate Diploma Examinations, Oct. 21, 1898, CPAE 1: 42.
41. Einstein to Mileva Marić, Sept. 10, 1899; Einstein 1922c (see bibliography for explanation about this Dec. 14, 1922, lecture in Kyoto, Japan).

42. Einstein, 1922c; Reiser, 52; Einstein to Mileva Marić, ca. Sept. 28, 1899; Renn and Schulmann, 85, footnotes 11: 3, 11: 4. Wilhelm Wien's paper was delivered in Sept. 1898 in Düsseldorf and published in the *Annalen der Physik* 65, no. 3 of that year.
43. Einstein to Mileva Marić, Oct. 10, 1899; Seelig 1956a, 30; Fölsing, 68; Overbye, 55; final diploma examinations, CPAE 1: 67. The essay marks as recorded in CPAE are multiplied by 4 to reflect their weight in the final results.
44. Final diploma examinations, CPAE 1: 67.
45. Einstein to Walter Leich, Apr. 24, 1950, AEA 60-253; Walter Leich memo describing Einstein, Mar. 6, 1957, AEA 60-257.
46. Einstein, 1949b, 17.
47. Einstein to Mileva Marić, Aug. 1, 1900.

CHAPTER FOUR: THE LOVERS

1. Einstein to Mileva Marić, ca. July 29, 1900.
2. Einstein to Mileva Marić, Aug. 6, 1900.
3. Einstein to Mileva Marić, Aug. 1, Sept. 13, Oct. 3, 1900.
4. Einstein to Mileva Marić, Aug. 30, 1900.
5. Einstein to Mileva Marić, Aug. 1, Aug. 6, ca. Aug. 14, Aug. 20, 1900.
6. Einstein to Mileva Marić, Aug. 6, 1900.
7. Einstein to Mileva Marić, ca. Aug. 9, Aug. 14?, Aug. 20, 1900.
8. Einstein to Mileva Marić, ca. Aug. 9, ca. Aug. 14, 1900. Both of these letters came from this visit to Zurich.
9. Einstein to Mileva Marić, Sept. 13, 1900.
10. Einstein to Mileva Marić, Sept. 19, 1900.
11. Einstein to Adolf Hurwitz, Sept. 26, Sept. 30, 1900.
12. Einstein to Mileva Marić, Oct. 3, 1900; Einstein to Mrs. Marcel Grossmann, 1936; Seelig 1956a, 208.
13. Einstein's municipal citizenship application, Zurich, Oct. 1900, CPAE 1: 82; Einstein to Helene Kaufler, Oct. 11, 1900; minutes of the naturalization commission of Zurich, Dec. 14, 1900, CPAE 1: 84.
14. Einstein to Mileva Marić, Sept. 13, 1900.
15. Einstein to Mileva Marić, Oct. 3, 1900.
16. Einstein, "Conclusions Drawn from the Phenomena of Capillarity," *Annalen der Physik*, CPAE 2: 1, received Dec. 13, 1900, published Mar. 1, 1901. "The paper is very difficult to understand, not least because of the large number of obvious misprints; from its lack of clarity we can only assume that it had not been independently refereed . . . Yet it was an extraordinarily advanced paper for a recent graduate who was receiving no independent scientific advice." John N. Murrell and Nicole Grobert, "The Centenary of Einstein's First Scientific Paper," *The Royal Society* (London), Jan. 22, 2002, www.journals.royalsoc.ac.uk/app/home/content.asp.
17. Dudley Herschbach, "Einstein as a Student," Mar. 2005, unpublished paper provided to the author.

18. Einstein to Mileva Marić, Apr. 15, Apr. 30, 1901; Mileva Marić to Helene Savić, Dec. 20, 1900.
19. Einstein to G. Wessler, Aug. 24, 1948, AEA 59-26.
20. Maja Einstein, sketch, 19; Reiser, 63; minutes of the Municipal Naturalization Commission of Zurich, Dec. 14, 1900, CPAE 1: 84; Report of the Schweitzerisches Informationsbureau, Jan. 30, 1901, CPAE 1: 88; Military Service Book, Mar. 13, 1901, CPAE 1: 91.
21. Mileva Marić to Helene Savić, Dec. 20, 1900; Einstein to Mileva Marić, Mar. 23, Mar. 27, 1901.
22. Einstein to Mileva Marić, Apr. 4, 1901.
23. Einstein to Heike Kamerlingh Onnes, Apr. 12, 1901; Einstein to Marcel Grossmann, Apr. 14, 1901; Fölsing, 78; Clark, 66; Miller 2001, 68.
24. Einstein to Wilhelm Ostwald, Mar. 19, Apr. 3, 1901.
25. Hermann Einstein to Wilhelm Ostwald, Apr. 13, 1901.
26. Einstein to Mileva Marić, Mar. 23, Mar. 27, 1901; Einstein to Marcel Grossmann, Apr. 14, 1901.
27. Einstein to Mileva Marić, Mar. 27, 1901; Mileva Marić to Helene Savić, Dec. 9, 1901.
28. Einstein to Mileva Marić, Apr. 4, 1901; Einstein to Michele Besso, June 23, 1918; Overbye, 25; Miller 2001, 78; Fölsing, 115.
29. Einstein to Mileva Marić, Mar. 27, Apr. 4, 1901.
30. Einstein to Marcel Grossmann, Apr. 14, 1901; Einstein to Mileva Marić, Apr. 15, 1901.
31. Einstein to Mileva Marić, Apr. 30, 1901. The official translation is "blue nightshirt," but the word that Einstein actually used, *Schlafrock*, translates more accurately as "dressing gown."
32. Mileva Marić to Einstein, May 2, 1901.
33. Mileva Marić to Helene Savić, second half of May, 1901.
34. Einstein to Mileva Marić, second half of May, 1901.
35. Einstein to Mileva Marić, tentatively dated in CPAE as May 28?, 1901. The actual date is probably a week or so later.
36. Overbye, 77–78.
37. Einstein to Mileva Marić, July 7, 1901.
38. Mileva Marić to Einstein, after July 7, 1901 (published in CPAE vol. 8 as 1: 116, because it was discovered after vol. 1 had been printed).
39. Mileva Marić to Einstein, ca. July 31, 1901; Highfield and Carter, 80.
40. Einstein to Jost Winteler, July 8, 1901; Einstein to Marcel Grossmann, Apr. 14, 1901. The comparison to the compass needle comes from Overbye, 65.
41. Renn 2005a, 109. Jürgen Renn is the director of the Max Planck Institute for the History of Science in Berlin and an editor of the *Collected Papers of Albert Einstein*. I am grateful to him for help with this topic.
42. Einstein to Mileva Marić, Apr. 15, 1901; Einstein to Marcel Grossmann, Apr. 15, 1901.
43. Renn 2005a, 124.
44. Einstein to Mileva Marić, Apr. 4, ca. June 4, 1901. The letters to and from

Drude no longer exist, so it is not known precisely what Einstein's objections were.

45. Einstein to Mileva Marić, ca. July 7, 1901; Einstein to Jost Winteler, July 8, 1901.

46. Renn 2005a, 118. Renn's source notes say, "I gratefully acknowledge the kindness of Mr. Felix de Marez Oyens, from Christie's, who pointed my attention to the missing page of the letter by Einstein to Mileva Marić, ca. 8 July 1901. As, unfortunately, no copy of the page is available to me, my interpretation had to be based on a raw transcription of the passage in question."

47. Einstein to Marcel Grossmann, Sept. 6, 1901.

48. Overbye, 82–84. This includes a good synopsis of the Boltzmann-Ostwald dispute.

49. Einstein, "On the Thermodynamic Theory of the Difference in Potentials between Metals and Fully Dissociated Solutions of Their Salts," Apr. 1902. Renn does not mention this paper in his analysis of Einstein's dispute with Drude, and instead focuses only on the June 1902 paper.

50. Einstein, "Kinetic Theory of Thermal Equilibrium and the Second Law of Thermodynamics," June 1902; Renn 2005a, 119; Jos Uffink, "Insuperable Difficulties: Einstein's Statistical Road to Molecular Physics," *Studies in the History and Philosophy of Modern Physics* 37 (2006): 38; Clayton Gearhart, "Einstein before 1905: The Early Papers on Statistical Mechanics," *American Journal of Physics* (May 1990): 468.

51. Mileva Marić to Helene Savić, ca. Nov. 23, 1901; Einstein to Mileva Marić, Nov. 28, 1901.

52. Einstein to Mileva Marić, Dec. 17 and 19, 1901.

53. Receipt for the return of Doctoral Fees, Feb. 1, 1902, CPAE 1: 132; Fölsing, 88–90; Reiser, 69; Overbye, 91. From Einstein to Mileva Marić, ca. Feb. 8, 1902: "I'm explaining to [Conrad] Habicht the paper I submitted to Kleiner. He's very enthusiastic about my good ideas and is pestering me to send Boltzmann the part of the paper which relates to his book. I'm going to do it."

54. Einstein to Marcel Grossmann, Sept. 6, 1901.

55. Einstein to Mileva Marić, Nov. 28, 1901.

56. Mileva Marić to Einstein, Nov. 13, 1901; Highfield and Carter, 82.

57. Einstein to Mileva Marić, Dec. 12, 1901; Fölsing, 107; Zackheim, 35; Highfield and Carter, 86.

58. Pauline Einstein to Pauline Winteler, Feb. 20, 1902.

59. Mileva Marić to Helene Savić, ca. Nov. 23, 1901.

60. Einstein to Mileva Marić, Dec. 11 and 19, 1901.

61. Einstein to Mileva Marić, Dec. 28, 1901.

62. Einstein to Mileva Marić, Feb. 4, 1902, Dec. 12, 1901.

63. Einstein to Mileva Marić, Feb. 4, 1902.

64. Mileva Marić to Einstein, Nov. 13, 1901. For some context, see Popović, which includes a collection of letters between Marić and Savić collected by Savić's grandson.

65. Einstein to Mileva Marić, Feb. 17, 1902.
66. Swiss Federal Council to Einstein, June 19, 1902.
67. See Peter Galison's treatment of the synchronization of time in Europe at that period, in Galison, 222–248. Also, see chapter 6 below for a fuller discussion of the role this might have played in Einstein's development of special relativity.
68. Einstein to Hans Wohlwend, autumn 1902; Fölsing, 102.
69. Einstein interview, Bucky, 28; Reiser, 66.
70. Einstein to Michele Besso, Dec. 12, 1919.
71. Einstein interview, Bucky, 28; Einstein 1956, 12. Both say essentially the same thing, with variations in wording and translation. Reiser, 64.
72. Alas, as a rule, all applications were destroyed after eighteen years, and even though Einstein was by then world-famous, his comments on inventions were disposed of during the 1920s; Fölsing, 104.
73. Galison, 243; Flückiger, 27.
74. Fölsing, 103; C. P. Snow, "Einstein," in Goldsmith et al., 7.
75. Einstein interview, Bucky, 28; Einstein 1956, 12. See Don Howard, "A kind of vessel in which the struggle for eternal truth is played out," AEA Cedex-H.
76. Solovine, 6.
77. Maurice Solovine, Dedication of the Olympia Academy, "A.D. 1903," CPAE 2: 3.
78. Solovine, 11–14.
79. Einstein to Maurice Solovine, Nov. 25, 1948; Seelig 1956a, 57; Einstein to Conrad Habicht and Maurice Solovine, Apr. 3, 1953; Hoffmann 1972, 243.
80. The editors of Einstein's papers, in the introduction to vol. 2, xxiv–xxv, describe the books and specific editions read by the Olympia Academy.
81. Einstein to Moritz Schlick, Dec. 14, 1915. In a 1944 essay about Bertrand Russell, Einstein wrote, "Hume's clear message seemed crushing: the sensory raw material, the only source of our knowledge, through habit may lead us to belief and expectation but not to the knowledge and still less to the understanding of lawful relations." Einstein 1954, 22. See also Einstein, 1949b, 13.
82. David Hume, *Treatise on Human Nature*, book 1, part 2; Norton 2005a.
83. There are varying interpretations of Kant's *Critique of Pure Reason* (1781). I have tried here to stick closely to Einstein's own view of Kant. Einstein, "Remarks on Bertrand Russell's Theory of Knowledge," (1944) in Schilpp; Einstein 1954, 22; Einstein, 1949b, 11–13; Einstein, "On the Methods of Theoretical Physics," the Herbert Spencer lecture, Oxford, June 10, 1933, in Einstein 1954, 270; Mara Beller, "Kant's Impact on Einstein's Thought," in Howard and Stachel 2000, 83–106. See also Einstein, "Physics and Reality" (1936) in Einstein 1950a, 62; Yehuda Elkana, "The Myth of Simplicity," in Holton and Elkana, 221.
84. Einstein 1949b, 21.
85. Einstein, Obituary for Ernst Mach, Mar. 14, 1916, CPAE 6: 26.
86. Philipp Frank, "Einstein, Mach and Logical Positivism," in Schilpp, 272;

Overbye, 25, 100–104; Gerald Holton, "Mach, Einstein and the Search for Reality," *Daedalus* (spring 1968): 636–673, reprinted in Holton 1973, 221; Clark, 61; Einstein to Carl Seelig, Apr. 8, 1952; Einstein, 1949b, 15; Norton 2005a.

87. Spinoza, *Ethics*, part I, proposition 29 and passim; Jammer 1999, 47; Holton 2003, 26–34; Matthew Stewart, *The Courtier and the Heretic* (New York: Norton, 2006).

88. Pais 1982, 47; Fölsing, 106; Hoffmann 1972, 39; Maja Einstein, xvii; Overbye, 15–17.

89. Marriage Certificate, CPAE 5: 6; Miller 2001, 64; Zackheim, 47.

90. Einstein to Michele Besso, Jan. 22, 1903; Mileva Marić to Helene Savić, Mar. 1903; Solovine, 13; Seelig 1956a, 46; Einstein to Carl Seelig, May 5, 1952; AEA 39-20.

91. Mileva Marić to Einstein, Aug. 27, 1903; Zackheim, 50.

92. Einstein to Mileva Marić, ca. Sept. 19, 1903; Zackheim; Popović; author's discussions and e-mails with Robert Schulmann.

93. Popović, 11; Zackheim, 276; author's discussions and e-mails with Robert Schulmann.

94. Michelmore, 42.

95. Einstein to Mileva Marić, ca. Sept. 19, 1903.

96. Mileva Marić to Helene Savić, June 14, 1904; Popović, 86; Whitrow, 19.

97. Overbye, 113, citing Desanka Trbuhovic-Gjuric, *Im Schatten Albert Einstein* (Bern: Verlag Paul Haupt, 1993), 94.

CHAPTER FIVE: THE MIRACLE YEAR

1. This quote is attributed in a variety of books and sources to an address Lord Kelvin gave to the British Association for the Advancement of Science in 1900. I have not found direct evidence for it, which is why I qualify it as "reportedly" said. It is not in the two-volume biography by Silvanus P. Thompson, *The Life of Lord Kelvin* (New York: Chelsea Publishing, 1976), originally published in 1910.

2. Pierre-Simon Laplace, *A Philosophical Essay on Probabilities* (1820; reprinted, New York: Dover, 1951). This famous statement of determinism comes in the preface of a work devoted to probability theory. The fuller line is that in ultimate reality we have determinism, but in practice we have probabilities. The achievement of full knowledge is not reachable, he says, so we need probabilities.

3. Einstein, Letter to the Royal Society on Newton's bicentennial, Mar. 1927.

4. Einstein 1949b, 19.

5. For the influence of Faraday's induction theories on Einstein, see Miller 1981, chapter 3.

6. Einstein and Infeld, 244; Overbye, 40; Bernstein 1996a, 49.

7. Einstein to Conrad Habicht, May 18 or 25, 1905.

8. Sent on Mar. 17, 1905, and published in *Annalen der Physik* 17 (1905). I want to thank Yale professor Douglas Stone for help with this section.

9. Max Born, obituary for Max Planck, Royal Society of London, 1948.

10. John Heilbron, *The Dilemmas of an Upright Man* (Berkeley: University of California Press, 1986). Lucid explanations of Einstein's quantum paper, from which this section is drawn, include Gribbin and Gribbin; Bernstein 1996a, 2006; Overbye, 118–121; Stachel 1998; Rigden; A. Douglas Stone, "Genius and Genius²: Planck, Einstein and the Birth of Quantum Theory," Aspen Center for Physics, unpublished lecture, July 20, 2005.

11. Planck's approach was probably a bit more complex and involved assuming a group of oscillators and positing a total energy that is an integer multiple of a quantum unit. Bernstein 2006, 157–161.

12. Max Planck, speech to the Berlin Physical Society, Dec. 14, 1900. See Lightman 2005, 3.

13. Einstein 1949b, 46. Miller 1984, 112; Miller 1999, 50; Rynasiewicz and Renn, 5.

14. Einstein, "On the General Molecular Theory of Heat," Mar. 27, 1904.

15. Einstein to Conrad Habicht, Apr. 15, 1904. Jeremy Bernstein discussed the connections between the 1904 and 1905 papers in an e-mail, July 29, 2005.

16. Einstein, "On a Heuristic Point of View Concerning the Production and Transformation of Light," Mar. 17, 1905.

17. "We are startled, wondering what happened to the waves of light of the 19th century theory and marveling at how Einstein could see the signature of atomic discreteness in the bland formulae of thermodynamics," says the science historian John D. Norton. "Einstein takes what looks like a dreary fragment of the thermodynamics of heat radiation, an empirically based expression for the entropy of a volume of high-frequency heat radiation. In a few deft inferences he converts this expression into a simple, probabilistic formula whose unavoidable interpretation is that the energy of radiation is spatially localized in finitely many, independent points." Norton 2006c, 73. See also Lightman 2005, 48.

18. Einstein's paper in 1906 noted clearly that Planck had not grasped the full implications of the quantum theory. Apparently, Besso encouraged Einstein not to make this criticism of Planck too explicit. As Besso wrote much later, "In helping you edit your publications on the quanta, I deprived you of a part of your glory, but, on the other hand, I made a friend for you in Planck." Michele Besso to Einstein, Jan. 17, 1928. See Rynasiewicz and Renn, 29; Bernstein 1991, 155.

19. Holton and Brush, 395.

20. Gilbert Lewis coined the name "photon" in 1926. Einstein in 1905 discovered a quantum of light. Only later, in 1916, did he discuss the quantum's momentum and its zero rest mass. Jeremy Bernstein has noted that one of the most interesting discoveries Einstein did *not* make in 1905 was the photon. Jeremy Bernstein, letter to the editor, *Physics Today*, May 2006.

21. Gribbin and Gribbin, 81.

22. Max Planck to Einstein, July 6, 1907.
23. Max Planck and three others to the Prussian Academy, June 12, 1913, CPAE 5: 445.
24. Max Planck, *Scientific Autobiography* (New York: Philosophical Library, 1949), 44; Max Born, "Einstein's Statistical Theories," in Schilpp, 163.
25. Quoted in Gerald Holton, "Millikan's Struggle with Theory," *Europhysics News* 31 (2000): 3.
26. Einstein to Michele Besso, Dec. 12, 1951, AEA 7-401.
27. Completed Apr. 30, 1905, submitted to the University of Zurich on July 20, 1905, submitted to *Annalen der Physik* in revised form on Aug. 19, 1905, and published by *Annalen der Physik* Jan. 1906. See Norton 2006c and www.pitt.edu/~jdnorton/Goodies/Einstein_stat_1905/.
28. Jos Uffink, "Insuperable Difficulties: Einstein's Statistical Road to Molecular Physics," *Studies in the History and Philosophy of Modern Physics* 37 (2006): 37, 60.
29. bulldog.u-net.com/avogadro/avoga.html.
30. Rigden, 48–52; Bernstein 1996a, 88; Gribbin and Gribbin, 49–54; Pais 1982, 88.
31. Hoffmann 1972, 55; Seelig 1956b, 72; Pais 1982, 88–89.
32. Brownian motion introduction, CPAE 2 (German), p. 206; Rigden, 63.
33. Einstein, "On the Motion of Small Particles Suspended in Liquids at Rest Required by the Molecular-Kinetic Theory of Heat," submitted to the *Annalen der Physik* on May 11, 1905.
34. Einstein 1949b, 47.
35. The root mean square average is asymptotic to $\sqrt{2n/\pi}$. Good analyses of the relationship of random walks to Einstein's Brownian motion are in Gribbin and Gribbin, 61; Bernstein 2006, 117. I am grateful to George Stranahan of the Aspen Center for Physics for his help on the mathematics behind this relationship.
36. Einstein, "On the Theory of Brownian Motion," 1906, CPAE 2: 32 (in which he notes Seidentopf's results); Gribbin and Gribbin, 63; Clark, 89; Max Born, "Einstein's Statistical Theories," in Schilpp, 166.

CHAPTER SIX: SPECIAL RELATIVITY

1. Contemporary historical research on Einstein's special theory begins with Gerald Holton's essay, "On the Origins of the Special Theory of Relativity" (1960), reprinted in Holton 1973, 165. Holton remains a guiding light in this field. Most of his earlier essays are incorporated in his books *Thematic Origins of Scientific Thought: Kepler to Einstein* (1973), *Einstein, History and Other Passions* (2000), and *The Scientific Imagination*, Cambridge, Mass.: Harvard University Press, 1998.

   Einstein's popular description is his 1916 book, *Relativity: The Special and the General Theory*, and his more technical description is his 1922 book, *The Meaning of Relativity*.

For good explanations of special relativity, see Miller 1981, 2001; Galison; Bernstein 2006; Calder; Feynman 1997; Hoffmann 1983; Kaku; Mermin; Penrose; Sartori; Taylor and Wheeler 1992; Wolfson.

This chapter draws on these books along with the articles by John Stachel; Arthur I. Miller; Robert Rynasiewicz; John D. Norton; John Earman, Clark Glymour, and Robert Rynasiewicz; and Michel Janssen listed in the bibliography. See also Wertheimer 1959. Arthur I. Miller provides a careful and skeptical look at Max Wertheimer's attempt to reconstruct Einstein's development of special relativity as a way to explain Gestalt psychology; see Miller 1984, 189–195.

2. See Janssen 2004 for an overview of the arguments that Einstein's attempt to extend general relativity to arbitrary and rotating motion was not fully successful and perhaps less necessary than he thought.

3. Galileo Galilei, *Dialogue Concerning the Two Chief World Systems* (1632), translated by Stillman Drake, 186.

4. Miller 1999, 102.

5. Einstein, "Ether and the Theory of Relativity," address at the University of Leiden, May 5, 1920.

6. Ibid.; Einstein 1916, chapter 13.

7. Einstein, "Ether and the Theory of Relativity," address at the University of Leiden, May 5, 1920.

8. Einstein to Dr. H. L. Gordon, May 3, 1949, AEA 58-217.

9. See Alan Lightman's *Einstein's Dreams* for an imaginative and insightful fictional rumination on Einstein's discovery of special relativity. Lightman captures the flavor of the professional, personal, and scientific thoughts that might have been swirling in Einstein's mind.

10. Peter Galison, the Harvard science historian, is the most compelling proponent of the influence of Einstein's technological environment. Arthur I. Miller presents a milder version. Among those who feel that these influences are overstated are John Norton, Tilman Sauer, and Alberto Martinez. See Alberto Martinez, "Material History and Imaginary Clocks," *Physics in Perspective* 6 (2004): 224.

11. Einstein 1922c. I rely on a corrected translation of this 1922 lecture that gives a different view of what Einstein said; see bibliography for an explanation.

12. Einstein, 1949b, 49. For other versions, see Wertheimer, 214; Einstein 1956, 10.

13. Miller 1984, 123, has an appendix explaining how the 1895 thought experiment affected Einstein's thinking. See also Miller 1999, 30–31; Norton 2004, 2006b. In the latter paper, Norton notes, "[This] is untroubling to an ether theorist. Maxwell's equations *do* entail quite directly that the observer would find a frozen waveform; and the ether theorist does not expect frozen waveforms in our experience since we do not move at the velocity of light in the ether."

14. Einstein to Erika Oppenheimer, Sept. 13, 1932, AEA 25-192; Moszkowski, 4.

15. Gerald Holton was the first to emphasize Föppl's influence on Einstein, citing the memoir by his son-in-law Anton Reiser and the German edition of Philipp Frank's biography. Holton 1973, 210.

16. Einstein, "Fundamental Ideas and Methods of the Theory of Relativity" (1920), unpublished draft of an article for *Nature*, CPAE 7: 31. See also Holton 1973, 362–364; Holton 2003.

17. Einstein to Mileva Marić, Aug. 10, 1899.

18. Einstein to Mileva Marić, Sept. 10 and 28, 1899; Einstein 1922c.

19. Einstein to Robert Shankland, Dec. 19, 1952, says that he read Lorentz's book before 1905. In his 1922 Kyoto lecture (Einstein 1922c) he speaks of being a student in 1899 and says, "Just at that time I had a chance to read Lorentz's paper of 1895." Einstein to Michele Besso, Jan. 22?, 1903, says he is beginning "comprehensive, extensive studies in electron theory." Arthur I. Miller provides a good look at what Einstein had already learned. See Miller 1981, 85–86.

20. This section draws from Gerald Holton, "Einstein, Michelson, and the 'Crucial' Experiment," in Holton 1973, 261–286, and Pais 1982, 115–117. Both assess Einstein's varying statements. The historical approach has evolved over the years. For example, Einstein's longtime friend and fellow physicist Philipp Frank wrote in 1957, "Einstein started from the most prominent case in which the old laws of motion and light propagation had failed to yield to the observed facts: the Michelson experiment" (Frank 1957, 134). Gerald Holton, the Harvard historian of science, wrote in a letter to me about this topic (May 30, 2006): "Concerning the Michelson/Morley experiment, until three or four decades ago practically everyone wrote, particularly in textbooks, that there was a straight line between that experiment and Einstein's special relativity. All this changed of course when it became possible to take a careful look at Einstein's own documents on the matter . . . Even non-historians have long ago given up the idea that there was a crucial connection between that particular experiment and Einstein's work."

21. Einstein 1922c; Einstein toast to Albert Michelson, the Athenaeum, Caltech, Jan. 15, 1931, AEA 8-328; Einstein message to Albert Michelson centennial, Case Institute, Dec. 19, 1952, AEA 1-168.

22. Wertheimer, chapter 10; Miller 1984, 190.

23. Robert Shankland interviews and letters, Feb. 4, 1950, Oct. 24, 1952, Dec. 19, 1952. See also Einstein to F. G. Davenport, Feb. 9, 1954: "In my own development, Michelson's result has not had a considerable influence, I even do not remember if I knew of it at all when I wrote my first paper on the subject. The explanation is that I was, for general reasons, firmly convinced that there does not exist absolute motion."

24. Miller 1984, 118: "It was unnecessary for Einstein to review every extant ether-drift experiment, because in his view their results were ab initio [from the beginning] a foregone conclusion." This section draws on Miller's work and on suggestions he made to an earlier draft.

25. Einstein saw the null results of the ether-drift experiments as support for the

relativity principle, not (as is sometimes assumed) support for the postulate that light always moves at a constant velocity. John Stachel, "Einstein and Michelson: The Context of Discovery and Context of Justification," 1982, in Stachel 2002a.

26. Professor Robert Rynasiewicz of Johns Hopkins is among those who emphasize Einstein's reliance on inductive methods. Even though Einstein in his later career wrote often that he relied more on deduction than on induction, Rynasiewicz calls this "highly contentious." He argues instead, "My view of the annus mirabilis is that it is a triumph of what can be secured inductively in the way of fixed points from which to carry on despite the lack of a fundamental theory." Rynasiewicz e-mail to me, commenting on an earlier draft of this section, June 29, 2006.

27. Miller 1984, 117; Sonnert, 289.

28. Holton 1973, 167.

29. Einstein, "Induction and Deduction in Physics," *Berliner Tageblatt*, Dec. 25, 1919, CPAE 7: 28.

30. Einstein to T. McCormack, Dec. 9, 1952, AEA 36-549. McCormack was a Brown University undergraduate who had written Einstein a fan letter.

31. Einstein 1949b, 89.

32. The following analysis draws from Miller 1981 and from the work of John Stachel, John Norton, and Robert Rynasiewicz cited in the bibliography. Miller, Norton, and Rynasiewicz kindly read drafts of my work and suggested corrections.

33. Miller 1981, 311, describes a connection between Einstein's papers on light quanta and special relativity. In section 8 of his special relativity paper, Einstein discusses light pulses and declares, "It is remarkable that the energy and the frequency of a light complex vary with the state of motion of the observer in accordance with the same law."

34. Norton 2006a.

35. Einstein to Albert Rippenbein, Aug. 25, 1952, AEA 20-46. See also Einstein to Mario Viscardini, Apr. 28, 1922, AEA 25-301: "I rejected this hypothesis at that time, because it leads to tremendous theoretical difficulties (e.g., the explanation of shadow formation by a screen that moves relative to the light source)."

36. Mermin, 23. This was finally proven conclusively by Willem de Sitter's study of double stars that rotate around each other at great speeds, which was published in 1913. But even before then, scientists had noted that no evidence could be found for the theory that the velocity of light from moving stars, or any other source, varied.

37. Einstein to Paul Ehrenfest, Apr. 25, June 20, 1912. By taking this approach, Einstein was continuing to lay the foundation for a quandary about quantum theory that would bedevil him for the rest of his life. In his light quanta paper, he had praised the wave theory of light while at the same time proposing that light could also be regarded as particles. An emission theory of light could have fit nicely with that approach. But both facts and intuition made him abandon

that approach to relativity, just at the same moment he was finishing his light quanta paper. "To me, it is virtually inconceivable that he would have put forward two papers in the same year which depended upon hypothetical views of Nature that he felt were in contradiction with each other," says physicist Sir Roger Penrose. "Instead, he must have felt (correctly, as it turned out) that 'deep down' there was no real contradiction between the accuracy—indeed 'truth'—of Maxwell's wave theory and the alternative 'quantum' particle view that he put forward in the quantum paper. One is reminded of Isaac Newton's struggles with basically the same problem—some 300 years earlier—in which he proposed a curious hybrid of a wave and particle viewpoint in order to explain conflicting aspects of the behavior of light." Roger Penrose, foreword to *Einstein's Miraculous Year* (Princeton: Princeton University Press, 2005), xi. See also Miller 1981, 311.

38. Einstein, "On the Electrodynamics of Moving Bodies," June 30, 1905, CPAE 2: 23, second paragraph. Einstein originally used V for the constant velocity of light, but seven years later began using the term now in common use, c.

39. In section 2 of the paper, he defines the light postulate more carefully: "Every light ray moves in the 'rest' coordinate system with a fixed velocity V, independently of whether this ray of light is emitted by a body at rest or in motion." In other words, the postulate says that the speed of light is the same *no matter how fast the light source is moving*. Many writers, when defining the light postulate, confuse this with the stronger assertion that light always moves in any inertial frame at the same velocity no matter how fast the light source *or the observer* is moving toward or away from each other. That statement is also true, but it comes only by *combining* the relativity principle with the light postulate.

40. Einstein 1922c. In his popular 1916 book *Relativity: The Special and General Theory*, Einstein explains this in chapter 7, "The Apparent Incompatibility of the Law of Propagation of Light with the Principle of Relativity."

41. Einstein 1916, chapter 7.

42. Einstein 1922c; Reiser, 68.

43. Einstein 1916, chapter 9.

44. Einstein 1922c; Heisenberg 1958, 114.

45. Sir Isaac Newton, *Philosophiae Naturalis Principia Mathematica* (1689), books 1 and 2; Einstein, "The Methods of Theoretical Physics," Herbert Spencer lecture, Oxford, June 10, 1933, in Einstein 1954, 273.

46. Fölsing, 174–175.

47. Poincaré went on to reference himself, saying that he had discussed this idea in an article called "The Measurement of Time." Arthur I. Miller notes that Einstein's friend Maurice Solovine may have read this paper, in French, and discussed it with Einstein. Einstein would later cite it, and his analysis of the synchronizations of clocks reflects some of Poincaré's thinking. Miller 2001, 201–202.

48. Fölsing, 155: "He was observed gesticulating to friends and colleagues as he pointed to one of Bern's bell towers and then to one in the neighboring village of Muri." Galison, 253, picks up this tale. Both cite as their source Max Flück-

iger, *Einstein in Bern* (Bern: Paul Haupt, 1974), 95. In fact, Flückiger merely quotes a colleague saying that Einstein referred to these clocks as a hypothetical example. See Alberto Martinez, "Material History and Imaginary Clocks," *Physics in Perspective* 6 (2004): 229. Martinez does concede, however, that it is indeed interesting that there was a steeple clock in Muri not synchronized with the clocks in Bern and that Einstein referred to this in explaining the theory to friends.

49. Galison, 222, 248, 253; Dyson. Galison's thesis is based on his original research into the patent applications.

50. Norton 2006a, 3, 43: "Another oversimplification pays too much attention to the one part of Einstein's paper that especially fascinates us now: his ingenious use of light signals and clocks to mount his conceptual analysis of simultaneity. This approach gives far too much importance to notions that entered briefly only at the end of years of investigation . . . They are not necessary to special relativity or to the relativity of simultaneity." See also Alberto Martinez, "Material History and Imaginary Clocks," *Physics in Perspective* 6 (2004): 224–240; Alberto Martinez, "Railways and the Roots of Relativity," *Physics World*, Nov. 2003; Norton 2004. For a good assessment, which gives more credit to Galison's research and insights, see Dyson. Also see Miller 2001.

51. Einstein interview, Bucky, 28; Einstein 1956, 12.

52. Moszkowski, 227.

53. Overbye, 135.

54. Miller 1984, 109, 114. Miller 1981, chapter 3, explains the influence of Faraday's experiments with rotating magnets on Einstein's special theory.

55. Einstein, "On the Electrodynamics of Moving Bodies," *Annalen der Physik* 17 (Sept. 26, 1905). There are many available editions. For a web version, see www.fourmilab.ch/etexts/einstein/specrel/www/. Useful annotated versions include Stachel 1998; Stephen Hawking, ed., *Selections from the Principle of Relativity* (Philadelphia: Running Press, 2002); Richard Muller, ed., *Centennial Edition of* The Theory of Relativity (San Francisco: Arion Press, 2005).

56. Einstein, unused addendum to 1916 book *Relativity*, CPAE 6: 44a.

57. Einstein 1916.

58. Bernstein 2006, 71.

59. This example is lucidly described in Miller 1999, 82–83; Panek, 31–32.

60. James Hartle, lecture at the Aspen Center for Physics, June 29, 2005; British National Measurement Laboratory, report on time dilation experiments, spring 2005, www.npl.co.uk/publications/metromnia/issue18/.

61. Einstein to Maurice Solovine, undated, in Solovine, 33, 35.

62. Krauss, 35–47.

63. Seelig 1956a, 28. For a full mathematical description of the special theory, see Taylor and Wheeler 1992.

64. Pais, 1982, 151, citing Hermann Minkowski, "Space and Time," lecture at the University of Cologne, Sept. 21, 1908.

65. Clark, 159–60.

66. Thorne, 79. This is also explained well in Miller 2001, 200: "Neither Lorentz, Poincaré, nor any other physicist was willing to grant Lorentz's local time any physical reality . . . Only Einstein was willing to go beyond appearances." See also Miller 2001, 240: "Einstein inferred a meaning Poincaré did not. His thought experiment enabled him to *interpret* the mathematical formalism as a new theory of space and time, whereas for Poincaré it was a generalized version of Lorentz's electron theory." Miller has also explored this topic in "Scientific Creativity: A Comparative Study of Henri Poincaré and Albert Einstein," *Creativity Research Journal* 5 (1992): 385.

67. Arthur Miller e-mail to the author, Aug. 1, 2005.

68. Hoffmann 1972, 78. Prince Louis de Broglie, the quantum theorist who theorized that particles could behave as waves, said of Poincaré in 1954, "Yet Poincaré did not take the decisive step; he left to Einstein the glory of grasping all the consequences of the principle of relativity." See Schilpp, 112; Galison, 304.

69. Dyson.

70. Miller 1981, 162.

71. Holton 1973, 178; Pais 1982, 166; Galison, 304; Miller 1981. All four authors have done important work on Poincaré and the credit he deserves, from which some of this section is drawn. I am grateful to Prof. Miller for a copy of his paper "Why Did Poincaré Not Formulate Special Relativity in 1905?" and for helping to edit this section.

72. Miller 1984, 37–38; Henri Poincaré lecture, May 4, 1912, University of London, cited in Miller 1984, 37; Pais 1982, 21, 163–168. Pais writes: "In all his life, Poincaré never understood the basis of special relativity . . . It is apparent that Poincaré either never understood or else never accepted the Theory of Relativity." See also Galison, 242 and passim.

73. Einstein to Mileva Marić, Mar. 27, 1901.

74. Michelmore, 45.

75. Overbye, 139; Highfield and Carter, 114; Einstein and Mileva Marić to Conrad Habicht, July 20, 1905.

76. Overbye, 140; Trbuhovic-Gjuric, 92–93; Zackheim, 62.

77. The issue of whether Marić's name was in any way ever on a manuscript of the special theory is a knotted one, but it turns out that the single source for such reports, a late Russian physicist, never actually said precisely that, and there is no other evidence at all to support the contention. For an explanation, see John Stachel's appendix to the introduction of *Einstein's Miraculous Year*, centennial reissue edition (Princeton: Princeton University Press, 2005), lv.

78. "The Relative Importance of Einstein's Wife," *The Economist*, Feb. 24, 1990; Evan H. Walker, "Did Einstein Espouse His Spouse's Ideas?", *Physics Today*, Feb. 1989; Ellen Goodman, "Out from the Shadows of Great Men," *Boston Globe*, Mar. 15, 1990; *Einstein's Wife*, PBS, 2003, www.pbs.org/opb/einsteins wife/index.htm; Holton 2000, 191; Robert Schulmann and Gerald Holton, "Einstein's Wife," letter to the *New York Times Book Review*, Oct. 8, 1995; Highfield and Carter, 108–114; Svenka Savić, "The Road to Mileva Marić-Einstein," www.zenskestudie.edu.yu/wgsact/e-library/e-lib0027.html#_ftn1;

Christopher Bjerknes, *Albert Einstein: The Incorrigible Plagiarist*, home.com cast.net/~xtxinc/CIPD.htm; Alberto Martínez, "Arguing about Einstein's Wife," *Physics World*, Apr. 2004, physicsweb.org/articles/world/17/4/2/1; Alberto Martínez, "Handling Evidence in History: The Case of Einstein's Wife," *School Science Review*, Mar. 2005, 51–52; Zackheim, 20; Andrea Gabor, *Einstein's Wife: Work and Marriage in the Lives of Five Great Twentieth-Century Women* (New York: Viking, 1995); John Stachel, "Albert Einstein and Mileva Marić: A Collaboration That Failed to Develop," in H. Prycior et al., eds., *Creative Couples in Science* (New Brunswick, N.J.: Rutgers University Press, 1995), 207–219; Stachel 2002a, 25–37.

79. Michelmore, 45.
80. Holton 2000, 191.
81. Einstein to Conrad Habicht, June 30–Sept. 22, 1905 (almost certainly in early September, after returning from vacation and getting to work on the $E=mc^2$ paper).
82. Einstein, "Does the Inertia of a Body Depend on Its Energy Content?," *Annalen der Physik* 18 (1905), received Sept. 27, 1905, CPAE 2: 24.
83. For an insightful look at the background and ramifications of Einstein's equation, see Bodanis. Bodanis also has a useful website that includes further details: davidbodanis.com/books/emc2/notes/relativity/sigdev/index.html. The calculation about the mass of a raisin is in Wolfson, 156.

CHAPTER SEVEN: THE HAPPIEST THOUGHT

1. Maja Einstein, xxi.
2. Fölsing, 202; Max Planck, *Scientific Autobiography and Other Papers* (New York: Philosophical Library, 1949), 42.
3. More precisely, the definition that Richard Feynman uses in his *Lectures on Physics* (Boston: Addison-Wesley, 1989), 19-1 is, "Action in physics has a precise meaning. It is the time average of the kinetic energy of a particle minus the potential energy. The principle of least action then states that a particle will travel along the path that minimizes the difference between its kinetic and potential energies."
4. Fölsing, 203; Einstein to Maurice Solovine, Apr. 27, 1906; Einstein tribute to Planck, 1913, CPAE 2: 267.
5. Max Planck to Einstein, July 6, 1907; Hoffmann 1972, 83.
6. Max Laue to Einstein, June 2, 1906.
7. Hoffmann 1972, 84; Seelig 1956a, 78; Fölsing, 212.
8. Arnold Sommerfeld to Hendrik Lorentz, Dec. 26, 1907, in Diana Kormos Buchwald, "The First Solvay Conference," in *Einstein in Context* (Cambridge, England: Cambridge University Press, 1993), 64. Sommerfeld is referring to the German physicist Emil Cohn, an expert in electrodynamics.
9. Jakob Laub to Einstein, Mar. 1, 1908.
10. Swiss Patent Office to Einstein, Mar. 13, 1906.
11. Mileva Marić to Helene Savić, Dec. 1906.

12. Einstein, "A New Electrostatic Method for the Measurement of Small Quantities of Electricity," Feb. 13, 1908, CPAE 2: 48; Overbye, 156.

13. Einstein to Paul and/or Conrad Habicht, Aug. 16, Sept. 2, 1907, Mar. 17, June, July 4, Oct. 12, Oct. 22, 1908, Jan. 18, Apr. 15, Apr. 28, Sept. 3, Nov. 5, Dec. 17, 1909; Overbye, 156–158.

14. Einstein, "On the Inertia of Energy Required by the Relativity Principle," May 14, 1907, CPAE 2: 45; Einstein to Johannes Stark, Sept. 25, 1907.

15. Einstein to Bern Canton Education Department, June 17, 1907, CPAE 5: 46; Fölsing, 228.

16. Einstein 1922c.

17. Einstein, "Fundamental Ideas and Methods of Relativity Theory," 1920, unpublished draft of a paper for *Nature* magazine, CPAE 7: 31. The phrase he used was "glücklichste Gedanke meines Lebens."

18. "Einstein Expounds His New Theory," *New York Times*, Dec. 3, 1919.

19. Bernstein 1996a, 10, makes the point that Newton's thought experiments involving a falling apple and Einstein's involving an elevator "were liberating insights that revealed unexpected depths in commonplace experiences."

20. Einstein 1916, chapter 20.

21. Einstein, "The Fundaments of Theoretical Physics," *Science*, May 24, 1940, in Einstein 1954, 329. See also Sartori, 255.

22. Einstein first used the phrase in a paper he wrote for the *Annalen der Physik* in Feb. 1912, "The Speed of Light and the Statics of the Gravitational Field," CPAE 4: 3.

23. Janssen 2002.

24. The gravitational field would have to be static and homogeneous and the acceleration would have to be uniform and rectilinear.

25. Einstein, "On the Relativity Principle and the Conclusions Drawn from It," *Jahrbuch der Radioaktivität and Elektronik*, Dec. 4, 1907, CPAE 2: 47; Einstein to Willem Julius, Aug. 24, 1911.

26. Einstein to Marcel Grossmann, Jan. 3, 1908.

27. Einstein to the Zurich Council of Education, Jan. 20, 1908; Fölsing, 236.

28. Einstein to Paul Gruner, Feb. 11, 1908; Alfred Kleiner to Einstein, Feb. 8, 1908.

29. Flückiger, 117–121; Fölsing, 238; Maja Einstein, xxi.

30. Alfred Kleiner to Einstein, Feb. 8, 1908.

31. Friedrich Adler to Viktor Adler, June 19, 1908; Rudolph Ardelt, *Friedrich Adler* (Vienna: Österreichischer Bundesverlag, 1984), 165–194; Seelig 1956a, 95; Fölsing, 247; Overbye, 161.

32. Frank 1947, 75; Einstein to Michele Besso, Apr. 29, 1917.

33. Einstein to Jakob Laub, May 19, 1909; Reiser, 72.

34. Friedrich Adler to Viktor Adler, July 1, 1908; Einstein to Jakob Laub, July 30, 1908.

35. Einstein to Jakob Laub, May 19, 1909.

36. Alfred Kleiner, report to the faculty, Mar. 4, 1909; Seelig 1956a, 166; Pais 1982, 185; Fölsing, 249.

37. Alfred Kleiner, report to faculty, Mar. 4, 1909.
38. Einstein to Jakob Laub, May 19, 1909.
39. Einstein, verse in the album of Anna Schmid, Aug. 1899, CPAE 1: 49.
40. Einstein to Anna Meyer-Schmid, May 12, 1909.
41. Mileva Marić to Georg Meyer, May 23, 1909; Einstein to Georg Meyer, June 7, 1909; Einstein to Erika Schaerer-Meyer, July 27, 1951; Highfield and Carter, 125; Overbye, 164.
42. Mileva Marić to Helene Savić, late 1909, Sept. 3, 1909, in Popović, 26–27.
43. Seelig 1956a, 92; Dukas and Hoffmann, 5–7.
44. Einstein to Arnold Sommerfeld, Jan. 14, 1908. I am grateful to Douglas Stone of Yale, who helped me with Einstein's early work on the quanta.
45. Einstein lecture in Salzburg, "On the Development of Our Views Concerning the Nature and Constitution of Radiation," Sept. 21, 1909, CPAE 2: 60; Schilpp, 154; Armin Hermann, *The Genesis of the Quantum Theory* (Cambridge, Mass.: MIT Press, 1971), 66–69.
46. Einstein to Arnold Sommerfeld, July 1910. As Einstein's friend Banesh Hoffmann quipped in *The Strange Story of the Quantum* (New York: Dover, 1959), "They could but make the best of it, and went around with woebegone faces sadly complaining that on Mondays, Wednesdays, and Fridays they must look upon light as a wave; on Tuesdays, Thursdays and Saturdays, as a particle. On Sundays they simply prayed."
47. Discussion following Sept. 21, 1909, lecture in Salzburg, CPAE 2: 61.
48. Einstein to Jakob Laub, Nov. 4 and 11, 1910.
49. Einstein to Heinrich Zangger, May 20, 1912.

CHAPTER EIGHT: THE WANDERING PROFESSOR

1. The best and original work about Duhem's influence on Einstein is by Don Howard. See Howard 1990a, 2004.
2. Friedrich Adler to Viktor Adler, Oct. 28, 1909, in Fölsing, 258.
3. Seelig 1956a, 97.
4. Seelig 1956a, 113.
5. Seelig 1956a, 99–104; Brian 1996, 76.
6. Seelig 1956a, 102; Einstein to Arnold Sommerfeld, Jan. 19, 1909.
7. Overbye, 185; Miller 2001, 229–231.
8. Hans Albert Einstein interview, *Gazette and Daily* (York, Pa.), Sept. 20, 1948; Seelig 1956a, 104; Highfield and Carter, 129.
9. Einstein to Pauline Einstein, Apr. 28, 1910.
10. Student petition, University of Zurich, June 23, 1910, CPAE 5: 210.
11. Repeated in lecture by Max Planck, Columbia University, spring 1909; Pais 1982, 192; Fölsing, 271.
12. Einstein to Jakob Laub, Aug. 27, Oct. 11, 1910; Count Karl von Stürgkh to Einstein, Jan. 13, 1911; Frank 1947, 98–101; Clark, 172–176; Fölsing, 271–273; Pais 1982, 192.

13. Frank 1947, 104. Frank has the visit occuring in 1913, but in fact it occurred in Sept. 1910 when Einstein was in Vienna for his official interview about the Prague professorship. See notes in CPAE 5 (German version), p. 625.

14. Einstein to Hendrik Lorentz, Jan. 27, 1911.

15. Einstein to Jakob Laub, May 19, 1909.

16. Einstein to Hendrik Lorentz, Feb. 15, 1911.

17. Pais 1982, 8; Brian 1996, 78; Klein 1970a, 303. The Ehrenfest description is from a draft of his eulogy for Lorentz.

18. Einstein, "Address at the Grave of Lorentz" (1928), in Einstein 1954, 73; Einstein, "Message for Hundredth Anniversary of the Birth of Lorentz" (1953), in Einstein 1954, 73. See also Bucky, 114.

19. Mileva Marić to Helene Savić, Jan. 1911, in Popović, 30; Einstein to Heinrich Zangger, Apr. 7, 1911.

20. Frank 1947, 98.

21. Max Brod, *The Redemption of Tycho Brahe* (New York: Knopf, 1928); Seelig 1956a, 121; Clark, 179; Highfield and Carter, 138.

22. Einstein to Paul Ehrenfest, Jan. 26, Feb. 12, 1912.

23. Einstein, "Paul Ehrenfest: In Memoriam," written in 1934 for a Leiden almanac and reprinted in Einstein 1950a, 132.

24. Klein 1970a, 175–178; Seelig 1956a, 125; Fölsing, 294; Clark, 194; Brian 1996, 83; Highfield and Carter, 142.

25. Einstein to Paul Ehrenfest, Mar. 10, 1912; Einstein to Alfred Kleiner, Apr. 3, 1912; Einstein to Paul Ehrenfest, Apr. 25, 1912. Einstein to Heinrich Zangger, Mar. 17, 1912: "I would like to see him my successor here. But his fanatical atheism makes that impossible." Zangger's letter was part of material released in 2006 and is published as CPAE 5: 374a in a supplement to vol. 10.

26. Dirk van Delft, "Albert Einstein in Leiden," *Physics Today*, Apr. 2006, 57.

27. Einstein to Heinrich Zangger, Nov. 7, 1911.

28. An invitation from Ernest Solvay, June 9, 1911, CPAE 5: 269; Einstein to Michele Besso, Sept. 11, Oct. 21, 1911.

29. Einstein, "On the Present State of the Problem of Specific Heats," Nov. 3, 1911, CPAE 3: 26; the quote about "really exist in nature" appears on p. 421 of the English translation of vol. 3.

30. Discussion following Einstein lecture, Nov. 3, 1911, CPAE 3: 27.

31. Einstein to Heinrich Zangger, Nov. 7 and 15, 1911.

32. Einstein to Michele Besso, Dec. 26, 1911.

33. Bernstein 1996b, 125.

34. Einstein to Heinrich Zangger, Nov. 7, 1911.

35. Einstein to Marie Curie, Nov. 23, 1911. (This letter is included at the beginning of CPAE vol. 8, not vol. 5, where it would have fit chronologically had this letter been available when that volume was published.)

36. Mileva Marić to Einstein, Oct. 4, 1911.

37. Overbye, 201. Einstein's quote is from a letter to Carl Seelig, May 5, 1952.

38. Reiser, 126.

39. Highfield and Carter, 145.
40. Einstein to Elsa Einstein Löwenthal, Apr. 30, 1912; regarding her keeping the letters, CPAE 5: 389 (German edition), footnote 12.
41. Einstein to Elsa Einstein, Apr. 30, 1912; Einstein "scratch notebook," CPAE 3 (German edition), appendix A; CPAE 5: 389 (German edition), footnote 4.
42. Einstein to Elsa Einstein, May 7 and 12, 1912.
43. Einstein to Michele Besso, May 13, 1911; Einstein to Hans Tanner, Apr. 24, 1911; Einstein to Alfred and Clara Stern, Mar. 17, 1912.
44. Mileva Marić to Helene Savić, Dec. 1912, in Popović, 106.
45. Willem Julius to Einstein, Sept. 17, 1911; Einstein to Willem Julius, Sept. 22, 1911.
46. Heinrich Zangger to Ludwig Forrer, Oct. 9, 1911; CPAE 5: 291 (German edition), footnote 2; CPAE 5: 305 (German edition), footnote 2.
47. Einstein to Heinrich Zangger, Nov. 15, 1911.
48. Einstein to Willem Julius, Nov. 16, 1911.
49. Marie Curie, letter of recommendation, Nov. 17, 1911; Seelig 1956a, 134; Fölsing, 291; CPAE 5: 308 (German edition), footnote 3.
50. Henri Poincaré, letter of recommendation, Nov. 1911; Seelig 1956a, 135; Galison, 300; Fölsing, 291; CPAE 5: 308 (German edition), footnote 3.
51. Einstein to Alfred and Clara Stern, Feb. 2, 1912.
52. Articles appeared in Vienna's weekly paper *Montags-Revue* on July 29, 1912, and Prague's *Prager Tagblatt* on May 26 and Aug. 5, 1912. CPAE 5: 414 (German edition), footnotes 2, 3, 11; Einstein statement, Aug. 3, 1912.
53. Einstein to Ludwig Hopf, June 12, 1912.
54. Overbye, 234, 243; Highfield and Carter, 153; Seelig 1956a, 112.
55. In a letter from Einstein to Elsa Einstein, July 30, 1914, he recalls how she kidded him for including his new address in the May 7, 1912, letter in which he declared they must quit corresponding.
56. Einstein to Elsa Einstein, ca. Mar. 14, 1913.
57. Einstein to Elsa Einstein, Mar. 23, 1913.
58. Seelig 1956a, 244; Levenson, 2; CPAE 5: 451 (German edition), footnote 2; Clark, 213; Overbye, 248; Fölsing, 329. The editors of the collected papers use the white handkerchief, based on a letter by Nernst's daughter, while other accounts use the red rose, based on the account that Seelig was given.
59. Max Planck, Walther Nernst, Heinrich Rubens, and Emil Warburg to the Prussian Academy, June 12, 1913, CPAE 5: 445.
60. Seelig 1956a, 148.
61. Einstein to Jakob Laub, July 22, 1913.
62. Einstein to Paul Ehrenfest, late Nov. 1913.
63. Einstein to Hendrik Lorentz, Aug. 14, 1913.
64. Einstein to Heinrich Zangger, June 27, 1914, CPAE 8: 5a, released in 2006 and published as a supplement to CPAE vol. 10.
65. Einstein to Elsa Einstein, July 14, 19, before July 24, and Aug. 13, 1913.
66. Einstein to Elsa Einstein, after Aug. 11, 1913.
67. Einstein to Elsa Einstein, after Aug. 11 and Aug. 11, 1913.

68. Eve Curie, *Madame Curie* (New York: Doubleday, 1937), 284; Fölsing, 325; Highfield and Carter, 157.
69. The baptism took place at the St. Nicholas Church in Novi Sad on Sept. 21, 1913. Hans Albert Einstein to Dord Krstic, Nov. 5, 1970; Elizabeth Einstein, 97; Highfield and Carter, 159; Overbye, 255; Einstein to Heinrich Zangger, Sept. 20, 1913; Seelig 1956a, 113.
70. Einstein to Elsa Einstein, Oct. 10, 1913.
71. Einstein to Elsa Einstein, Oct. 16, 1913.
72. Einstein to Elsa Einstein, before Dec. 2, 1913.
73. Einstein to Elsa Einstein, after Dec. 21 and Aug. 11, 1913.
74. Einstein to Elsa Einstein, after Dec. 21, 1913.
75. Einstein to Elsa Einstein, after Feb. 11, 1914; Lisbeth Hurwitz diary, cited in Overbye, 265.
76. Marianoff, 1; Einstein to Mileva Marić, Apr. 2, 1914.
77. Einstein to Paul Ehrenfest, ca. Apr. 10, 1914; Paul Ehrenfest to Einstein, ca. Apr. 10, 1914; Highfield and Carter, 167.
78. Whitrow, 20.
79. Einstein to Heinrich Zangger, June 27, 1914, CPAE 8: 16a, made available in 2006 and printed in a supplement to vol. 10.
80. Einstein, Memorandum to Mileva Marić, ca. July 18, 1914, CPAE 8: 22. See also appendix, CPAE 8b (German edition), p. 1032, for a memo from Anna Besso-Winteler to Heinrich Zangger, Mar. 1918, about the Einstein breakup.
81. Einstein to Mileva Marić, ca. July 18 and July 18, 1914.
82. CPAE 8a: 26 (German edition), footnote 3; memo from Anna Besso-Winteler to Heinrich Zangger, Mar. 1918, CPAE 8b (German edition), p. 1032; Overbye, 268.
83. Einstein to Elsa Einstein, July 26, 1914.
84. Einstein to Elsa Einstein, after July 26, 1914.
85. Einstein to Elsa Einstein, July 30, 1914 (two letters); Michele Besso to Einstein, Jan. 17, 1928 (recalling the breakup); Pais 1982, 242; Fölsing, 338.
86. Einstein to Elsa Einstein, after Aug. 3, 1914.
87. Einstein to Mileva Marić, Sept. 15, 1914, contains the poisoning allegation. Many other letters in 1914 detail their struggle over money, furniture, and treatment of the children.

CHAPTER NINE: GENERAL RELATIVITY

1. Renn and Sauer 2006, 117.
2. The description of the equivalence principle follows the formulation that Einstein used in his yearbook article of 1907 and his comprehensive general relativity paper of 1916. Others have subsequently modified it slightly. See also Einstein, "Fundamental Ideas and Methods of Relativity Theory," 1920, unpublished draft of a paper for *Nature* magazine, CPAE 7: 31.
   Some of this chapter draws from a dissertation by one of the editors of the

Einstein Papers Project: Jeroen van Dongen, "Einstein's Unification: General Relativity and the Quest for Mathematical Naturalness," 2002. He provided a copy to me along with guidance and editing for this chapter. This chapter also follows the research findings of other scholars studying Einstein's general relativity work. I am grateful to van Dongen and others who met with me and helped me on this chapter, including Tilman Sauer, Jürgen Renn, John D. Norton, and Michel Janssen. This chapter draws on their work and also that of John Stachel, all listed in the bibliography.

3. Einstein, "The Speed of Light and the Statics of the Gravitational Field," *Annalen der Physik* (Feb. 1912), CPAE 4: 3; Einstein 1922c; Janssen 2004, 9. In his 1907 and 1911 papers, Einstein refers to it as the "equivalence hypothesis," but in this 1912 paper, he raises it to the status of an *Aequivalenzprinzip*.

4. Einstein, "On the Influence of Gravitation on the Propagation of Light," *Annalen der Physik* (June 21): 1911, CPAE 3: 23.

5. Einstein to Erwin Freundlich, Sept. 1, 1911.

6. Stachel 1989b.

7. Record and grade transcript, CPAE 1: 25; Adolf Hurwitz to Hermann Bleuler, July 27, 1900, CPAE 1: 67; Einstein to Mileva Marić, Dec. 28, 1901.

8. Fölsing, 314; Pais 1982, 212.

9. Hartle, 13.

10. Einstein to Arnold Sommerfeld, Oct. 29, 1912.

11. Einstein, foreword to the Czech edition of his popular book *Relativity*, 1923; see utf.mff.cuni.cz/Relativity/Einstein.htm. In it Einstein writes, "The decisive idea of the analogy between the mathematical formulation of the theory and the Gaussian theory of surfaces came to me only in 1912 after my return to Zurich, without being aware at that time of the work of Riemann, Ricci, and Levi-Civita. This was first brought to my attention by my friend Grossmann." Einstein 1922c: "I realized that the foundations of geometry have physical significance. My dear friend the mathematician Grossmann was there when I returned from Prague to Zurich. From him I learned for the first time about Ricci and later about Riemann."

12. Sartori, 275.

13. Amir Aczel, "Riemann's Metric," in Aczel 1999, 91–101; Hoffmann 1983, 144–151.

14. I am grateful to Tilman Sauer and Craig Copi for help with this section.

15. Janssen 2002; Greene 2004, 72.

16. Calaprice, 9; Flückiger, 121.

17. The Zurich Notebook is in CPAE 4: 10. An online facsimile is available at echo.mpiwg-berlin.mpg.de/content/relativityrevolution/jnul. See also Janssen and Renn.

18. Norton 2000, 147. See also Renn and Sauer 2006, 151. I am grateful to Tilman Sauer for his editing of this section.

19. Einstein, Zurich Notebook, CPAE 4: 10 (German edition), p. 39 has the first notations of what became known as the Einstein tensor.

20. An explanation of this dilemma is in Renn and Sauer 1997, 42–43. The

mystery of why Einstein in early 1913 could not find the correct gravitational tensor—and the issue of his understanding of coordinate condition options—is addressed nicely in Renn 2005b, 11–14. He builds on, and suggests some revisions to, the conclusions of Norton 1984.

21. Norton, Janssen, and Sauer have all suggested that Einstein's bad experience in 1913 of abandoning a mathematical strategy for a physical one, and his subsequent belated success with a mathematical strategy, is reflected in the views he expressed in his 1933 Spencer lecture at Oxford and also his approach in the later decades of his life to finding a unified field theory.

22. Einstein, "Outline [*Entwurf*] of a Generalized Theory of Relativity and of a Theory of Gravitation" (with Marcel Grossmann), before May 28, 1913, CPAE 4: 13; Janssen 2004; Janssen and Renn.

23. Einstein to Elsa Einstein, Mar. 23, 1913.

24. Einstein-Besso manuscript, CPAE 4: 14; Janssen, 2002.

25. Einstein, "On the Foundations of the General Theory of Relativity," *Annalen der Physik* (Mar. 6, 1918), CPAE 7: 4. A vivid explanation of Newton's bucket and how it connects to relativity is in Greene 2004, 23–74. Einstein is largely responsible for inferring how Mach would regard an empty universe. See Norton 1995c; Julian Barbour, "General Relativity as a Perfectly Machian Theory," Carl Hoefer, "Einstein's Formulation of Mach's Principle," and Hubert Goenner, "Mach's Principle and Theories of Gravity," all in Barbour and Pfister.

26. Janssen 2002, 14; Janssen 2004, 17; Janssen 2006. Janssen has done important work analyzing the Einstein-Besso collaborations of 1913. Reproductions of the Einstein-Besso manuscript and other related documents, along with an essay by Janssen on their significance, is in a 288-page catalogue from Christie's, which auctioned the originals on Oct. 4, 2002. (The 50-page Einstein-Besso manuscript sold for $595, 000.) For an example of how Einstein dismissed Besso's suggestion that the Minkowski metric in rotating coordinates wasn't a valid solution to the *Entwurf* field equations—and how Einstein kept feeling that the *Entwurf* did indeed comply with Mach's principle—see Einstein to Michele Besso, ca. Mar. 10, 1914.

27. Einstein to Ernst Mach, June 25, 1913; Misner, Thorne, and Wheeler, 544.

28. Einstein to Hendrik Lorentz, Aug. 14, 1913. But two days later, he writes Lorentz again to say that he has resigned himself to the belief that covariance is impossible: "Only now, after this ugly dark spot seems to have been eliminated, does the theory give me pleasure." Einstein to Hendrik Lorentz, Aug. 16, 1913.

29. The hole argument basically said that a generally covariant gravitational theory would be indeterministic. Generally covariant field equations could not determine the metric field uniquely. A full specification of the metric field outside of some small region that was devoid of matter, known as "the hole," would not be able to fix the metric field within that region. See Stachel 1989b; Norton 2005b; Janssen 2004.

30. Einstein to Ludwig Hopf, Nov. 2, 1913. See also Einstein to Paul Ehrenfest, Nov. 7, 1913: "It can be proved that *generally covariant* equations that deter-

mine the field completely from the matter tensor cannot exist at all. Can there be anything more beautiful than this, that the necessary specialization follows from the conservation laws? Thus, the conservation laws determine the surfaces that, from among all the surfaces, are to be privileged as coordinate surfaces. We can designate these privileged surfaces as planes, since we are left with linear substitutions as the only ones that are justified." Einstein's clearest explanation of the hole argument is "On the Foundations of the Generalized Theory of Relativity and the Theory of Gravitation," Jan. 1914, CPAE 4: 25.

31. When Einstein appeared at the annual convocation of German-speaking scientists in Sept. 1913, the rival gravitation theorist Gustav Mie rose to launch a "lively" attack on him and subsequently published a violent polemic that displayed a vitriol far beyond anything explained by scientific disagreements. Einstein also engaged in a bitter debate with Max Abraham, whose own gravitational theory Einstein had attacked with great relish throughout 1912. Report on the Vienna conference, Sept. 23, 1913, CPAE 4: 17.

32. Einstein to Heinrich Zangger, ca. Jan. 20, 1914.

33. Einstein to Heinrich Zangger, Mar. 10, 1914. Jürgen Renn has pointed out that the 1913–1915 period of defending and refining the *Entwurf*, even though it did not save that theory, did help Einstein to better understand the difficulties that seemed to bedevil the tensors he had explored in the mathematical strategy. "Practically all of the technical problems Einstein had encountered in the Zurich notebook with candidates derived from the Riemann tensor were actually resolved in this period in the course of his examination of problems associated with the *Entwurf* theory." Renn 2005b, 16.

34. Einstein to Erwin Freundlich, Jan. 8, 1912, mid-Aug. 1913; Einstein to George Hale, Oct. 14, 1913; George Hale to Einstein, Nov. 8, 1913.

35. Clark, 207.

36. Einstein to Erwin Freundlich, Dec. 7, 1913.

37. Einstein to Erwin Freundlich, Jan. 20, 1914.

38. Fölsing, 356–357.

39. Einstein to Paul Ehrenfest, Aug. 19, 1914.

40. Ibid.

41. Einstein to Paolo Straneo, Jan. 7, 1915.

42. For a good description from which this is drawn, see Levenson, especially 60–65.

43. Elon, 277, 303–304.

44. Fölsing, 344.

45. Einstein to Hans Albert Einstein, Jan. 25, 1915.

46. Nathan and Norden, 4; Elon, 326. Also translated as the "Manifesto to the Civilized World."

47. Einstein to Georg Nicolai, Feb. 20, 1915. The full text is in CPAE 6: 8, and Nathan and Norden, 5. Clark, 228, makes the case that some of the writing was Einstein's. See also Wolf William Zuelzer, *The Nicolai Case* (Detroit: Wayne State University Press, 1982); Overbye, 273; Levenson, 63; Fölsing, 346–347; Elon, 328.

48. Nathan and Norden, 9; Overbye, 275–276; Fölsing, 349; Clark, 238.
49. Einstein to Romain Rolland, Sept. 15, 1915; CPAE 8a: 118 (German edition), footnote 2; Romain Rolland diary, cited in Nathan and Norden, 16; Fölsing, 366.
50. Einstein to Paul Hertz, before Oct. 8, 1915; Paul Hertz to Einstein, Oct. 8, 1915; Einstein to Paul Hertz, Oct. 9, 1915.
51. Einstein, "My Opinion on the War," Oct. 23–Nov. 11, 1915, CPAE 6: 20.
52. Einstein to Heinrich Zangger, after Dec. 27, 1914, CPAE 8: 41a, in supplement to vol. 10.
53. Hans Albert Einstein to Einstein, two postcards, before Apr. 4, 1915, part of the family correspondence trust that was under seal until 2006. CPAE 8: 69a, 8: 69b, in supplement to vol. 10.
54. Einstein to Hans Albert Einstein, ca. Apr. 4, 1915.
55. Einstein to Heinrich Zangger, July 16, 1915.
56. Einstein to Elsa Einstein, Sept. 11, 1915; Einstein to Heinrich Zangger, Oct. 15, 1915; Einstein to Hans Albert Einstein, Nov. 4, 1915. For Einstein's complaint that he was barely able to see his boys during the Sept. 1916 visit, see Einstein to Mileva Marić, Apr. 1, 1916: "I hope that this time you will not again withhold the boys almost entirely from me."
57. Einstein to Heinrich Zangger, Oct. 15, 1915; Michele Besso to Einstein, ca. Oct. 30, 1915.
58. Once again, I have drawn on the works of Jürgen Renn, Tilman Sauer, John Stachel, Michel Janssen, and John D. Norton.
59. Horst Kant, "Albert Einstein and the Kaiser Wilhelm Institute for Physics in Berlin," in Renn 2005d, 168–170.
60. Wolf-Dieter Mechler, "Einstein's Residences in Berlin," in Renn 2005d, 268.
61. Janssen 2004, 29.
62. Einstein to Heinrich Zangger, July 7, ca. July 24, 1915; Einstein to Arnold Sommerfeld, July 15, 1915.
63. Specifically, the issue was whether the *Entwurf* field equations were invariant under the non-autonomous transformation to rotating coordinates in the case of the Minkowski metric in its standard diagonal form. Janssen 2004, 29.
64. Michele Besso memo to Einstein, Aug. 28, 1913; Janssen 2002; Norton 2000, 149; Einstein to Erwin Freundlich, Sept. 30, 1915.
65. Einstein to Hendrik Lorentz, Oct. 12, 1915. Einstein describes his October 1915 breakthroughs in a subsequent letter to Lorentz and another one to Arnold Sommerfeld. Einstein to Hendrik Lorentz, Jan. 1, 1916: "Trying times awaited me last fall as the inaccuracy of the older gravitational field equations gradually dawned on me. I had already discovered earlier that Mercury's perihelion motion had come out too small. In addition, I found that the equations were not covariant for substitutions corresponding to a uniform rotation of the new reference system. Finally, I found that the consideration I made last year on the determination of Lagrange's H function for the gravitational field was thoroughly illusory, in that it could easily be modified such that no restricting conditions had to be attached to H, thus making it possible to choose

it completely freely. In this way I came to the conviction that introducing adapted systems was on the wrong track and that a more broad-reaching covariance, preferably a *general* covariance, must be required. Now general covariance has been achieved, whereby nothing is changed in the subsequent specialization of the frame of reference . . . I had considered the current equations in essence already three years ago together with Grossmann, who had brought my attention to the Riemann tensor." Einstein to Arnold Sommerfeld, Nov. 28, 1915: "In the last month I had one of the most stimulating and exhausting times of my life, and indeed also one of the most successful. For I realized that my existing gravitational field equations were untenable! The following indications led to this: 1) I proved that the gravitational field on a uniformly rotating system does not satisfy the field equations. 2) The motion of Mercury's perihelion came to 18″ rather than 45″ per century. 3) The covariance considerations in my paper of last year do not yield the Hamiltonian function H. When it is properly generalized, it permits an arbitrary H. From this it was demonstrated that covariance with respect to 'adapted' coordinate systems was a flop."

66. Norton 2000, 152.
67. There is a subtle divergence of opinion among the group of general relativity historians about the extent of his purported shift from the physical to the mathematical strategy in Oct.–Nov. 1915. John Norton has argued that Einstein's "new tactic was to reverse his decision of 1913" and go back to a mathematical strategy, emphasizing a tensor analysis that would produce general covariance (Norton 2000, 151). Likewise, Jeroen van Dongen says the shift in tactics was clear: "Einstein immediately got hold of the way out of the *Entwurf*'s quagmire: he returned to the mathematical requirement of general covariance that he had abandoned in the Zurich notebook" (van Dongen, 25). Both scholars produce quotes from Einstein's later years in which he claims that the big lesson he learned was to trust a mathematical strategy. On the other side, Jürgen Renn and Michel Janssen say that Norton and van Dongen (and the older Einstein in his hazy memory) make too much of this shift. Physical considerations still played a major role in finding the final theory in Nov. 1915. "In our reconstruction, however, Einstein found his way back to the generally-covariant field equations by making one important adjustment to the *Entwurf* theory, a theory born almost entirely out of physical considerations . . . That mathematical considerations pointed in the same direction undoubtedly inspired confidence that this was the right direction, but guiding him along this path were physical not mathematical considerations" (Janssen and Renn, 13; the quote I use in the text is on p. 10). Also, Janssen 2004, 35: "Whatever he believed, said, or wrote about it later on, Einstein only discovered the mathematical high road to the Einstein field equations after he had already found these equations at the end of a poorly paved road through physics."
68. Einstein to Arnold Sommerfeld, Nov. 28, 1915.
69. Einstein, "On the General Theory of Relativity," Nov. 4, 1915, CPAE 6: 21.

70. Einstein to Michele Besso, Nov. 17, 1915; Einstein to Arnold Sommerfeld, Nov. 28, 1915.
71. Einstein to Hans Albert Einstein, Nov. 4, 1915.
72. Einstein to David Hilbert, Nov. 7, 1915.
73. Overbye, 290.
74. Einstein, "On the General Theory of Relativity (Addendum)," Nov. 11, 1915, CPAE 6: 22; Renn and Sauer 2006, 276; Pais 1982, 252.
75. Einstein to David Hilbert, Nov. 12, 1915.
76. Einstein to Hans Albert Einstein, Nov. 15, 1915; Einstein to Mileva Marić, Nov. 15, 1915; Einstein to Heinrich Zangger, Nov. 15, 1915 (released in 2006 and printed in supplement to vol. 10).
77. Einstein to David Hilbert, Nov. 15, 1915.
78. Einstein, "Explanation of the Perihelion Motion of Mercury from the General Theory of Relativity," Nov. 18, 1915, CPAE 6: 24.
79. Pais 1982, 253; Einstein to Paul Ehrenfest, Jan. 17, 1916; Einstein to Arnold Sommerfeld, Dec. 9, 1915.
80. Einstein to David Hilbert, Nov. 18, 1915.
81. David Hilbert to Einstein, Nov. 19, 1915.
82. The equation has been expressed in many ways. The one I use follows the formulation Einstein used in his 1921 Princeton lectures. The entire left-hand side of the equation can be expressed more compactly as what is now known as the Einstein tensor: $G_{\mu\nu}$.
83. Overbye, 293; Aczel 1999, 117; archive.ncsa.uiuc.edu/Cyberia/NumRel/EinsteinEquations.html#intro. A variation of Wheeler's quote is on p. 5 of the book he coauthored with Charles Misner and Kip Thorne, *Gravitation*.
84. Greene 2004, 74.
85. Einstein, "The Foundations of the General Theory of Relativity," *Annalen der Physik* (Mar. 20, 1916), CPAE 6: 30.
86. Einstein to Heinrich Zangger, Nov. 26, 1915; Einstein to Michele Besso, Nov. 30, 1915.
87. Thorne, 119.
88. For an analysis of Hilbert's contribution, see Sauer 1999, 529–575; Sauer 2005, 577–590. Papers describing Hilbert's revisions include Corry, Renn, and Stachel; Sauer 2005. For a flavor of the controversy, see also John Earman and Clark Glymour, "Einstein and Hilbert: Two Months in the History of General Relativity," *Archive for History of Exact Sciences* (1978): 291; A. A. Logunov, M. A. Mestvirishvili, and V. A. Petrov, "How Were the Hilbert-Einstein Equations Discovered?," *Uspekhi Fizicheskikh Nauk* 174, no. 6 (June 2004): 663–678; Christopher Jon Bjerknes, *Albert Einstein: The Incorrigible Plagiarist*, available at home.comcast.net/~xtxinc/AEIPBook.htm; John Stachel, "Anti-Einstein Sentiment Surfaces Again," *Physics World*, Apr. 2003, physicsweb.org/articles/review/16/4/2/1; Christopher Jon Bjerknes, "The Author of *Albert Einstein: The Incorrigible Plagiarist* Responds to John Stachel's Personal Attack," home.comcast.net/~xtxinc/Response.htm; Friedwardt Winterberg, "On 'Belated Decision in the Hilbert-Einstein Priority Dispute,'" *Zeitschrift*

fuer Naturforschung A, (Oct. 2004): 715–719, www.physics.unr.edu/faculty/ winterberg/Hilbert-Einstein.pdf; David Rowe, "Einstein Meets Hilbert: At the Crossroads of Physics and Mathematics," *Physics in Perspective* 3, no. 4 (Nov. 2001): 379.

89. Reid, 142. Although this comment is cited in other secondary sources as well, Tilman Sauer of the Einstein Papers Project, who is writing a book on Hilbert, says he has never found a primary source for it.

90. Einstein to David Hilbert, Dec. 20, 1915.

91. Einstein to Arnold Sommerfeld, Dec. 9, 1915; Einstein to Heinrich Zangger, Nov. 26, 1915.

92. It is a contentious question as to whether general relativity actually succeeds in making all forms of motion and all frames of reference equivalent. It can certainly be said that two observers in nonuniform relative motion can each legitimately view himself as "at rest" and the other as affected by a gravitational field. That does not necessarily mean (as Einstein sometimes seemed to believe and at other times not) that two observers in nonuniform relative motion are always physically equivalent, especially when it comes to rotation. See, for example, Norton 1995b, 223–245; Janssen 2004, 8–12; Don Howard, "Point Coincidences and Pointer Coincidences," in Goenner et al. 1999, 463; Robert Rynasiewicz, "Kretschmann's Analysis of Covariance and Relativity Principles," in Goenner et al. 1999, 431; Dennis Diek, "Another Look at General Covariance and the Equivalence of Reference Frames," *Studies in the History and Philosophy of Modern Physics* 37 (Mar. 2006): 174.

93. Fölsing, 374; Clark, 252.

94. Einstein to Michele Besso, Dec. 10, 1915.

CHAPTER TEN: DIVORCE

1. Michele Besso to Einstein, Nov. 29, 1915; Einstein to Michele Besso, Nov. 30, 1915; Neffe, 192.

2. Hans Albert Einstein to Einstein, before Nov. 30, 1915; Einstein to Hans Albert Einstein, Nov. 30, 1915.

3. Michele Besso to Einstein, Nov. 30, 1915. See also Einstein to Heinrich Zangger, Dec. 4, 1915: "The boy's soul is being systematically poisoned to make sure that he doesn't trust me."

4. Einstein to Mileva Marić, Dec. 1 and 10, 1915.

5. Einstein to Hans Albert Einstein, Dec. 23 and 25, 1915. Einstein wrote a similar postcard to Hans Albert on Dec. 18, 1915. Einstein to Hans Albert Einstein, Mar. 11, 1916.

6. Einstein to Heinrich Zangger, Nov. 26, 1915; Einstein to Michele Besso, Jan. 3, 1916.

7. Overbye, 300.

8. Einstein to Mileva Marić, Feb. 6, 1916.

9. Einstein to Mileva Marić, Mar. 12, Apr. 1, 1916; Neffe, 194.

10. Einstein to Mileva Marić, Apr. 1 and 8, 1916; Einstein to Michele Besso, Apr. 6, 1916; Michele Besso to Heinrich Zangger, Apr. 12, 1916, CPAE 8: 211 (German edition), footnote 2.

11. Einstein to Elsa Einstein, Apr. 12 and 15, 1916. See also Einstein to Elsa Einstein, Apr. 10, 1916, in the sealed family correspondence released in 2006, CPAE 8: 211a: "My relationship with him is becoming very warm."

12. Einstein to Elsa Einstein, Apr. 21, 1916. See also Einstein to Heinrich Zangger, July 11, 1916: "Following an exceedingly nice Easter excursion, the subsequent days in Zurich brought on a complete chilling in a way that is not quite explicable to me."

13. Einstein to Heinrich Zangger, July 11, 1916; Einstein to Michele Besso, July 14, 1916. See CPAE 8: 233 (German edition), footnote 4, for Zangger being the other person referred to in the letter.

14. Pauline Einstein to Elsa Einstein, Aug. 6, 1916, in Overbye, 301.

15. Einstein to Michele Besso, July 14, 1916; Michele Besso to Einstein, July 17, 1916; CPAE 8: 239 (German version), footnote 2.

16. Einstein to Michele Besso, July 21, 1916, two letters.

17. CPAE 8: 241 (German edition), footnotes 3, 4; Einstein to Heinrich Zangger, July 25, 1916; Heinrich Zangger to Michele Besso, July 31, 1916.

18. Einstein to Heinrich Zangger, Aug. 18, 1916; Einstein to Hans Albert Einstein, July 25, 1916. See also Einstein to Heinrich Zangger, Mar. 10, 1917.

19. Einstein to Michele Besso, Aug. 24, 1916; Einstein to Hans Albert Einstein, Sept. 26, 1916.

20. Hans Albert Einstein to Einstein, before Nov. 26, 1916.

21. Einstein to Michele Besso, Oct. 31, 1916.

22. Einstein to Helene Savić, Sept. 8, 1916.

23. Einstein, "The Foundation of the General Theory of Relativity," Mar. 20, 1916, CPAE 6: 30.

24. Einstein, *On the Special and the General Theory of Relativity*, Dec. 1916, CPAE 6: 42, and many popular editions; Michelmore, 63. For an Internet version of Einstein's book, see bartleby.com/173/ or www.gutenberg.org/etext/5001.

25. Einstein, "Principles of Research," 1918, in Einstein 1954, 224.

26. Einstein to Heinrich Zangger, Jan. 16, 1917; Clark, 241.

27. Clark, 248; Highfield and Carter, 183; Overbye, 327; Einstein to Paul Ehrenfest, Feb. 14, 1917; Einstein to Heinrich Zangger, Dec. 6, 1917.

28. Einstein to Michele Besso, Mar. 9, 1917; Einstein to Heinrich Zangger, Feb. 16 and Mar. 10, 1917.

29. Einstein to Paul Ehrenfest, May 25, 1917.

30. Einstein to Heinrich Zangger, June 12, 1917.

31. Einstein to Mileva Marić, Jan. 31, 1918.

32. Mileva Marić to Einstein, Feb. 9, 1918, from family trust correspondence, CPAE 8: 461a, in supplement to vol. 10.

33. Mileva Marić to Einstein, after Feb. 6, 1918. The Feb. 9 letter from the family trust correspondence, footnote 32 above, was unsealed in 2006. It clearly

comes before the one that was dated "after Feb. 6" by the Einstein papers editors.

34. Overbye, 338–339.
35. Mileva Marić to Einstein, Apr. 22, 1918.
36. Einstein to Mileva Marić, Apr. 15, 23, 26, 1918.
37. Maja Winteler-Einstein to Einstein, Mar. 6, 1918, family foundation correspondence, unsealed in 2006, CPAE 8: 475b, in supplement to vol. 10.
38. Einstein to Anna Besso, after Mar. 4, 1918.
39. Anna Besso to Einstein, after Mar. 4, 1918.
40. Mileva Marić to Einstein, before May 23, 1918; Einstein to Mileva Marić, June 4, 1918. See also Vero Besso (Anna and Michele's son) to Einstein, Mar. 28, 1918, family trust correspondence: "The postcard you sent to my mother was really not nice . . . Her words would not have offended you in any way if you had heard them yourself; you would just have laughed and would have toned down their sense a little."
41. Mileva Marić to Einstein, Mar. 17, 1918: "My state of health is now such that I can lie down quite well at home; although I can't get up, I can very well occupy myself quite a considerable amount with the children, and this makes me very happy and contributes much to my well-being." Einstein to Heinrich Zangger, May 8, 1918.
42. Einstein to Heinrich Zangger, May 8, 1918.
43. Einstein to Max Born, after June 29, 1918; Einstein to Michele Besso, July 29, 1918.
44. Einstein to Hans Albert Einstein, after June 4, 1918.
45. Einstein to Hans Albert Einstein, after June 19, 1918.
46. Hans Albert Einstein to Einstein, ca. July 17, 1918; Einstein to Eduard Einstein, ca. July 17, 1918.
47. Edgar Meyer to Einstein, Aug. 11, 1918; Einstein to Michele Besso, Aug. 20, 1918.
48. Einstein to Heinrich Zangger, Aug. 16, 1918; Einstein to Michele Besso, Sept. 6, 1918; Fölsing, 424.
49. Reiser, 140.
50. Nathan and Norden, 24. See also Rowe and Schulmann.
51. Born 2005, 145–147. My description relies on Born's recollection, which accompanies Einstein's references to the event in a letter to Born, Sept. 7, 1944. See also Bolles, 3–11; Seelig 1956a, 178; Fölsing, 423; Levenson, 198.
52. Einstein, "On the Need for a National Assembly," Nov. 13, 1918, CPAE 8: 14; Nathan and Norden, 25. Otto Nathan says that Einstein delivered these remarks to the student radicals at the university. There is no evidence of this, and Born does not mention it. The newspapers report it as a New Fatherland League speech later that day. See CPAE 8: 14 (German edition), footnote 2.
53. Einstein to Max Born, Sept. 7, 1944.
54. Einstein, Deposition in Divorce, Dec. 23, 1918, CPAE 8: 676.
55. Einstein to Mileva Marić and Hans Albert Einstein, Jan. 10, 1919; Einstein to Hedwig and Max Born, Jan. 15 and 19, 1919; Theodor Vetter to Einstein, Jan.

28, 1919. Vetter was the president of Zurich University, and he responded to Einstein's complaint about a guard being posted at the door of the lectures.

56. Divorce Decree, Feb. 14, 1919, CPAE 9: 6.

57. Overbye, 273–280.

58. Einstein to Georg Nicolai, ca. Jan. 22 and Feb. 28, 1917; Georg Nicolai to Einstein, Feb. 26, 1917.

59. Ilse Einstein to Georg Nicolai, May 22, 1918, CPAE 8: 545.

60. Einstein to Elsa Einstein, July 12 and 17, 1919.

61. Einstein to Elsa Einstein, July 28, 1919.

62. "Professor Einstein Here," *New York Times*, Apr. 3, 1921.

63. "Pronounced Sense of Humor," *New York Times*, Dec. 22, 1936.

64. Fölsing, 429; Highfield and Carter, 196.

65. Reiser, 127; Marianoff, 15, 174. Both of these authors married daughters of Elsa. Reiser's real name was Rudolph Kayser.

66. Elias Tobenkin, "How Einstein, Thinking in Terms of the Universe, Lives from Day to Day," *New York Evening Post*, Mar. 26, 1921.

67. Frank 1947, 219; Marianoff, 1; Fölsing, 428; Reiser, 193.

CHAPTER ELEVEN: EINSTEIN'S UNIVERSE

1. Overbye, 314; Einstein to Karl Schwarzschild, Jan. 9, 1916.

2. Einstein, "On a Stationary System with Spherical Symmetry Consisting of Many Gravitating Masses," *Annals of Mathematics*, 1939.

3. For a description of the history, math, and science of black holes, see Miller 2005; Thorne, 121–139.

4. Freeman Dyson in Robinson, 8–9.

5. Einstein to Karl Schwarzschild, Jan. 9, 1916.

6. CPAE vol. 8 brings together all of the correspondence between Einstein and de Sitter, with a good commentary on the dispute. Michel Janssen (uncredited author), "The Einstein–De Sitter–Weyl–Klein debate," CPAE 8a (German edition), p. 351.

7. Einstein to Willem de Sitter, Feb. 2, 1917.

8. Einstein to Paul Ehrenfest, Feb. 4, 1917.

9. Einstein, "Cosmological Considerations in the General Theory of Relativity," Feb. 8, 1917, CPAE 6: 43.

10. Einstein 1916, chapter 31.

11. Clark, 271.

12. For a delightful fictional tale along these lines (so to speak), see Edwin Abbott's *Flatland*, first published in 1880 and available in many paperback editions.

13. Edward W. Kold, "The Greatest Discovery Einstein Didn't Make," in Brockman, 205.

14. Lawrence Krauss and Michael Turner, "A Cosmic Conundrum," *Scientific American* (Sept. 2004): 71; Aczel 1999, 155; Overbye, 321. Einstein's famous blunder quote is from Gamow, 1970, 44.

15. Overbye, 327.
16. Einstein 1916, chapter 22.
17. There is a wonderful reprint now available in paperback of Eddington's classic book first published in 1920: Arthur Eddington, *Space, Time and Gravitation: An Outline of the General Relativity Theory* (Cambridge, England: Cambridge Science Classics, 1995). Page 141 describes the Principe expedition. See also an award-winning article: Matthew Stanley, "An Expedition to Heal the Wounds of War: 1919 Eclipse and Eddington as Quaker Adventurer," *Isis* 94 (2003): 57–89. A comprehensive account of all the tests is in Crelinsten.
18. Douglas, 40; Aczel 1999, 121–137; Clark, 285–287; Fölsing, 436–437; Overbye, 354–359.
19. Douglas, 40.
20. Einstein to Pauline Einstein, Sept. 5, 1919; Einstein to Paul Ehrenfest, Sept. 12, 1919.
21. Einstein to Pauline Einstein, Sept. 27, 1919; Bolles, 53.
22. Ilse Rosenthal-Schneider, *Reality and Scientific Truth: Discussions with Einstein, von Laue, and Planck* (Detroit: Wayne State University Press, 1980), 74. She reports mistakenly that the telegram was from Eddington when it was from Lorentz. Einstein's remark is famous, and is translated in many ways. The German sentence, as recorded by Rosenthal-Schneider, is "Da könnt' mir halt der Liebe Gott leid tun, die Theorie stimmt doch."
23. Max Planck to Einstein, Oct. 4, 1919; Einstein to Max Planck, Oct. 23, 1919.
24. Zurich Physics Colloquium to Einstein, Oct. 11, 1919.
25. Einstein to Zurich Physics Colloquium, Oct. 16, 1919.
26. Alfred North Whitehead, *Science and the Modern World* (1925; New York: Free Press, 1997), 13. See also pp. 29 and 113.
27. *The Times* of London, Nov. 7, 1919; Pais 1982, 307; Fölsing, 443; Clark, 289.
28. *The Times* of London, Nov. 7, 1919.
29. Einstein 1949b, 31. Purchase of violin is in Einstein to Paul Ehrenfest, Dec. 10, 1919.
30. Douglas, 41; Subrahmanyan Chandrasekhar, *Truth and Beauty: Aesthetics and Motivations in Science* (Chicago: University of Chicago Press, 1987), 117. (David Hilbert certainly would have been a third, though there were, of course, many others.) Chandrasekhar, who later worked with Eddington, told Jeremy Bernstein he heard this directly from Eddington; Bernstein 1973, 192.

CHAPTER TWELVE: FAME

1. Clark, 309. For a good overview, see David Rowe, "Einstein's Rise to Fame," Perimeter Institute, Oct. 15, 2005, www.mediasite.com.
2. "Fabric of the Universe," *The Times* of London, editorial, Nov. 7, 1919.
3. *New York Times*, Nov. 9, 1919.
4. Brian 1996, 100, from Meyer Berger, *The Story of the New York Times* (New York: Simon & Schuster, 1951), 251–252.
5. *New York Times*, Nov. 9, 1919.

6. The *New York Times* deserves praise, of course, for taking the theory seriously.

7. "Einstein Expounds His New Theory," *New York Times*, Dec. 3, 1919.

8. Einstein to Heinrich Zangger, Dec. 15, 1919.

9. Einstein to Marcel Grossmann, Sept. 12, 1920. Einstein went on to make the point to Grossmann that the issue, amid rising nationalism and anti-Semitism, had become politicized: "Their conviction is determined by what political party they belong to."

10. Leopold Infeld, "To Albert Einstein on His 75th Birthday," in Goldsmith et al., 24.

11. *New York Times*, Dec. 4 and 21, 1919.

12. *The Times* of London, Nov. 28, 1919.

13. Paul Ehrenfest to Einstein, Nov. 24, 1919; Maja Einstein to Einstein, Dec. 10, 1919.

14. Einstein to Max Born, Dec. 8, 1919; Einstein to Ludwig Hopf, Feb. 2, 1920.

15. C. P. Snow, "On Einstein," in *The Variety of Men* (New York: Scribner's, 1966), 108.

16. Freeman J. Dyson, "Wise Man," *New York Review of Books*, Oct. 20, 2005.

17. Clark, 296.

18. Born 2005, 41.

19. Hedwig Born to Einstein, Oct. 7, 1920.

20. Max Born to Einstein, Oct. 13, 1920.

21. Max Born to Einstein, Oct. 28, 1920.

22. Einstein to Max Born, Oct. 26, 1920. Einstein wrote to Maurice Solovine, when the book actually appeared a few months later, that Moszkowski was "abominable" and "wretched" and that "he committed a forgery" by using some of Einstein's letters in an unauthorized way to imply that Einstein had written an introduction to the book. Einstein to Maurice Solovine, Mar. 8 and 19, 1921. He was also dismayed when he heard that Hans Albert had bought it, and said, "I was unable to prevent its publication, and it has caused me a lot of grief"; Einstein to Hans Albert Einstein, June 18, 1921. See also Highfield and Carter, 199.

23. Brian 1996, 114–116; Moszkowski, 22–58.

24. Born 2005, 41.

25. Frank 1947, 171–174.

26. Michelmore, 95; Fölsing, 485.

27. Einstein to Heinrich Zangger, Dec. 24, 1919.

28. Einstein, "My First Impressions of the U.S.A.," *Nieuwe Rotterdamsche Courant*, July 4, 1921, CPAE 7, appendix D; Einstein 1954, 3–7.

29. Einstein, "Einstein on His Theory," *The Times* of London, Nov. 28, 1919.

30. Einstein to Hedwig and Max Born, Jan. 27, 1920; Einstein to Arthur Eddington, Feb. 2, 1920. Einstein graciously told an embarrassed Eddington, "The tragicomical outcome of the medal affair [is] insignificant compared to the self-sacrificing and fruitful labors you and your friends devoted to the theory of relativity and its verification."

31. Frida Bucky, quoted in Brian 1996, 230.

32. Einstein, "The World as I See It" (1930), in Einstein 1954, 8. A different translation is in Einstein 1949a, 3.
33. This appraisal appears with slight variations in Infeld, 118; Infeld, "To Albert Einstein on His 75th Birthday," in Goldsmith et al., 25; and in the *Bulletin of the World Federation of Scientific Workers*, July 1954.
34. Editorial note by Max Born in Born 2005, 127.
35. Abraham Pais, "Einstein and the Quantum Theory," *Reviews of Modern Physics* (Oct. 1979). See also Pais, "Einstein, Newton and Success," in French, 35; Pais 1982, 39.
36. Einstein, "Why Socialism?," *Monthly Review*, May 1949, reprinted in Einstein 1954, 151.
37. Erik Erikson, "Psychoanalytic Reflections on Einstein's Centenary," in Holton and Elkana, 151.
38. This idea is from Barbara Wolff of the Einstein archives at Hebrew University.
39. Levenson, 149.
40. Einstein to Paul Ehrenfest, Jan. 17, 1922; Fölsing, 482.
41. Einstein to Eduard Einstein, June 25, 1923, Einstein family correspondence trust, unpublished, letter in possession of Bob Cohn, who provided me a copy. Cohn is a collector of Einstein material. The letters in his possession have been translated by Dr. Janifer Stackhouse. I am grateful for their help.
42. Michelmore, 79.
43. Einstein to Mileva Marić, May 12, 1924, AEA 75-629.
44. Einstein to Michele Besso, Jan. 5, 1924, AEA 7-346; Einstein to Hans Albert Einstein, Mar. 7, 1924.
45. Einstein to Heinrich Zangger, Mar. 1920; Fölsing, 474; Highfield and Carter, 192; Clark, 243.
46. Paul Johnson, *Modern Times* (New York: HarperCollins, 1991), 1–3. This section is adapted from an essay I wrote when Einstein was chosen as *Time's* Person of the Century: "Who Mattered and Why," *Time*, Dec. 31, 1999. For a critique of this idea, which I also draw on in this section, see David Greenberg, "It Didn't Start with Einstein," *Slate*, Feb. 3, 2000, www.slate.com/id/74164/. Miller 2001 is also an important resource.
47. Charles Poor, professor of celestial mechanics, Columbia University, in the *New York Times*, Nov. 16, 1919.
48. *New York Times*, Dec. 7, 1919.
49. Isaiah Berlin, "Einstein and Israel," in Holton and Elkana, 282. See also, from his stepson-in-law Reiser, 158: "The word relativity was confused in lay circles and, today, is still confused with the word relativism. Einstein's work and personality, however, are far removed from the ambiguity and the concept of relativism, both in the theory of knowledge and in ethics . . . Ethical relativism, which denies all the generally obligatory moral norms, totally contradicts the high social idea which Einstein stands for and always follows."
50. Haldane, 123. For a contemporary book treating, in more sophisticated depth, many of the same topics, and sharing a title, see Ryckman 2005.
51. Frank 1947, 189–190; Clark, 339–340.

52. Gerald Holton, "Einstein's Influence on the Culture of Our Time," in Holton 2000, 127, and also Holton and Elkana, xi.
53. Miller 2001, especially 237–241.
54. Damour 34; Marcel Proust to Armand de Guiche, Dec. 1921.
55. Philip Courtenay, "Einstein and Art," in Goldsmith et al., 145; Richard Davenport-Hines, *Proust at the Majestic* (New York: Bloomsbury, 2006).

CHAPTER THIRTEEN: THE WANDERING ZIONIST

1. *The Times* of London, Nov. 28, 1919.
2. Kurt Blumenfeld, "Einstein and Zionism," in Seelig 1956b, 74; Kurt Blumenfeld, *Erlebte Judenfrage* (Stuttgart: Verlags-Anstalt, 1962), 127–128.
3. Einstein to Paul Epstein, Oct. 5, 1919.
4. Einstein to German Citizens of the Jewish Faith, Apr. 5, 1920, CPAE 7: 37.
5. Einstein, "Anti-Semitism: Defense through Knowledge," after Apr. 3, 1920, CPAE 7: 35.
6. Einstein, "Assimilation and Anti-Semitism," Apr. 3, 1920, CPAE 7: 34. See also Einstein, "Immigration from the East," Dec. 30, 1919, an article in *Berliner Tageblatt*, CPAE 7:29.
7. Einstein, "Anti-Semitism: Defense through Knowledge," after Apr. 3, 1920, CPAE 7: 35; Hubert Goenner, "The Anti-Einstein Campaign in Germany in 1920," in Beller et al., 107.
8. Elon, 277.
9. Hubert Goenner, "The Anti-Einstein Campaign in Germany in 1920," in Beller et al., 121.
10. *New York Times*, Aug. 29, 1920.
11. Frank 1947, 161; Clark, 318; Fölsing, 462; Brian 1996, 111.
12. "Einstein to Leave Berlin," *New York Times*, Aug. 29, 1920; the story, datelined Berlin, begins, "Local newspapers state that Professor Albert Einstein will leave the German capital on account of the many unfair attacks made against his relativity theory and himself."
13. Einstein, "My Response," Aug. 27, 1920, CPAE 7: 45.
14. See, in particular, Philipp Lenard to Einstein, June 5, 1909.
15. Einstein, "My Response," Aug. 27, 1920, CPAE 7: 45.
16. Seelig 1956a, 173.
17. Hedwig Born to Einstein, Sept. 8, 1920.
18. Paul Ehrenfest to Einstein, Sept. 2, 1920.
19. Einstein to Max and Hedwig Born, Sept. 9, 1920.
20. Einstein to Paul Ehrenfest, before Sept. 9, 1920.
21. Arnold Sommerfeld to Einstein, Sept. 11, 1920.
22. Jerome, 206–208, 256–257.
23. Born 2005, 35; Einstein to Max Born, Oct. 26, 1920.
24. Clark, 326–327; Fölsing, 467; Bolles, 73.
25. Fölsing, 523; Adolf Hitler, *Völkischer Beobachter*, Jan. 3, 1921.
26. *Dearborn* (Mich.) *Independent*, Apr. 30, 1921, on display at the "Chief Engi-

neer of the Universe" exhibit, Kronprinzenpalais, Berlin, May–Sept. 2005. A headline at the bottom of the page reads, "Jew Admits Bolshevism!"

27. Einstein to Paul Ehrenfest, Nov. 26, 1920, Feb. 12, 1921, AEA 9-545; Fölsing, 484. The Einstein letters after 1920 have not yet been published in the CPAE series, and I identify these unpublished letters by the Albert Einstein Archives (AEA) call numbers.

28. Clark, 465–466.

29. Einstein to Maurice Solovine, Mar. 8, 1921, AEA 9-555.

30. Einstein statement to Abba Eban, Nov. 18, 1952, AEA 28-943.

31. Fritz Haber to Einstein, Mar. 9, 1921, AEA 12-329.

32. Einstein to Fritz Haber, Mar. 9, 1921, AEA 12-331.

33. Seelig 1956a, 81; Fölsing, 500; Clark, 468.

34. *New York Times*, Apr. 3, 1921.

35. Illy, 29.

36. *Philadelphia Public Ledger*, Apr. 3, 1921.

37. These quotes and descriptions are taken from the Apr. 3, 1921, stories in the *New York Times, New York Call, Philadelphia Public Ledger*, and *New York American*.

38. Weizmann, 232.

39. "Einstein Sees End of Time and Space," *New York Times*, Apr. 4, 1921.

40. "City's Welcome for Dr. Einstein," *New York Evening Post*, Apr. 5, 1921.

41. Talmey, 174.

42. *New York Times*, Apr. 11 and 16, 1921.

43. The memorial, at the corner of Constitution Avenue and Twenty-second Street N.W. near the Mall, is a hidden treasure of Washington. (See picture on p. 605.) The sculptor was Robert Berks, who also did the bust of John Kennedy at the Kennedy Center nearby, and the landscape architect was James Van Sweden. On the tablet that Einstein holds are three equations, describing the photoelectric effect, general relativity, and of course $E=mc^2$. On the marble steps where the statue reclines are three quotes, including: "As long as I have any choice in the matter, I shall live only in a country where civil liberty, tolerance, and equality of all citizens before the law prevail." See www.nasonline.org.

44. *Washington Post*, Apr. 7, 1921; *New York Times*, Apr. 26 and 27, 1921; Frank 1947, 184. An account of the Academy dinner by Caltech astronomer Harlow Shapley is at the Einstein papers in Pasadena.

45. Charles MacArthur, "Einstein Baffled in Chicago: Seeks Pants in Only Three Dimensions, Faces Relativity of Trousers," *Chicago Herald and Examiner*, May 3, 1921.

46. *Chicago Daily Tribune*, May 3, 1921.

47. Memorandum of Agreement, Einstein and Princeton University Press, May 9, 1921. The deal was an exclusive one; no other venue in the United States was permitted to publish any of his lectures. The four lectures appeared as *The Meaning of Relativity*. It is now in its fifth edition.

48. *Philadelphia Evening Bulletin*, May 14, 1921.

49. Einstein to Oswald Veblen, Apr. 30, 1930, AEA 23-152. Pais 1982, 114, gives

a history of this phrase, which is recounted in a memo prepared for the Einstein archives by Einstein's secretary Helen Dukas. The fireplace is in room 202, the faculty lounge of what is now called Jones Hall at Princeton and was earlier known as Fine Hall, until that name moved to a newer math building.

50. Seelig 1956a, 183; Frank 1947, 285; Clark, 743.
51. *New York Times,* July 31, 1921.
52. Einstein to Felix Frankfurter, May 28, 1921, AEA 36-210.
53. See Ben Halpern, *A Clash of Heroes: Brandeis, Weizmann and American Zionism* (New York: Oxford University Press, 1987).
54. *Boston Herald,* May 19, 1921.
55. *New York Times,* May 18, 1921; Frank 1947, 185; Brian 1996, 129; Illy, 25–32.
56. *Hartford* (Conn.) *Daily Times,* May 23, 1921. Also, *Hartford Daily Courant,* May 23, 1921.
57. *Cleveland Press,* May 26, 1921.
58. Illy, 185.
59. Fölsing, 51.
60. Einstein, "How I Became a Zionist," interview in *Jüdische Rundschau,* June 21, 1921, conducted on May 30, CPAE 7: 57.
61. Einstein to Mileva Marić, Aug. 28, 1921, Einstein family trust correspondence, letter in possession of Bob Cohn. On this trip, in deference to Elsa's feelings, he decided at the last moment not to stay at Marić's apartment.
62. Einstein to Walther Rathenau, Mar. 8, 1917; Walther Rathenau to Einstein, May 10, 1917.
63. Reiser, 146, describes the Weizmann-Rathenau-Einstein discussions. See also Fölsing, 519; Elon, 364.
64. Weizmann, 288; Elon, 268.
65. Frank 1947, 192.
66. Reiser, 145.
67. Milena Wazeck, "Einstein on the Murder List," in Renn 2005d, 222; Einstein to Max Planck, July 6, 1922, AEA 19-300.
68. Einstein to Maurice Solovine, July 16, 1922, AEA 21-180.
69. Einstein to Marie Curie, July 4, 1922, AEA 34-773; Marie Curie to Einstein, July 7, 1922, AEA 34-775.

70. Fölsing, 521.
71. Nathan and Norden, 54.
72. Hermann Struck to Pierre Comert, July 12, 1922; Nathan and Norden, 59. (Einstein sent word to League press official Comert through their mutual friend, the painter Struck.)
73. Nathan and Norden, 70.
74. Einstein, "Travel Diary: Japan-Palestine-Spain," AEA 29-129. All quotes in this section from Einstein's diary are from this document.
75. Joan Bieder, "Einstein in Singapore," 2000, www.onthepage.org/outsiders/einstein_in_singapore.htm.
76. Fölsing, 527; Clark, 368; Brian 1996, 143; Frank 1947, 199.
77. Einstein to Hans Albert and Eduard Einstein, Dec. 12, 1922, AEA 75-620.
78. Frank 1947, 200.
79. Einstein, "Travel Diary: Japan-Palestine-Spain," AEA 29-129.
80. Clark, 477–480; Frank 1947, 200–201; Brian 1966, 145; Fölsing, 528–532.

CHAPTER FOURTEEN: NOBEL LAUREATE

1. Svante Arrhenius to Einstein, Sept. 1, 1922, AEA 6-353; Einstein to Svante Arrhenius, Sept. 20, 1922, AEA 6-354.
2. Pais 1982, 506–507; Elzinga, 82–84.
3. R. M. Friedman 2005, 129. See also Friedman's book, *The Politics of Excellence: Behind the Nobel Prize in Science* (New York: Henry Holt, 2001), especially chapter 7, "Einstein Must Never Get a Nobel Prize!"; Elzinga; Pais 1982, 502.
4. Pais 1982, 508; Hendrik Lorentz and Dutch colleagues to the Swedish Academy, Jan. 24, 1920; Niels Bohr to the Swedish Academy, Jan. 30, 1920; Elzinga, 134.
5. Brian 1996, 143, citing research and interviews by the writer Irving Wallace for his novel *The Prize*.
6. Elzinga, 144.
7. R. M. Friedman, 130. See also Pais 1982, 508.
8. Arthur Eddington to the Swedish Academy, Jan. 1, 1921.
9. Pais 1982, 509; R. M. Friedman, 131; Elzinga, 151.
10. Marcel Brillouin to the Swedish Academy, Jan. 1922; Arnold Sommerfeld to the Swedish Academy, Jan. 11, 1922.
11. Christopher Aurivillius to Einstein, Nov. 10, 1922. In another translation and version, the actual Nobel citation sent to Einstein includes the phrase "independent of the value that (after eventual confirmation) may be credited to the relativity and gravitation theory."
12. Elzinga, 182.
13. Svante Arrhenius, Nobel Prize presentation speech, Dec. 10, 1922, nobelprize.org/physics/laureates/1921/press.html.
14. Einstein, "Fundamental Ideas and Problems of the Theory of Relativity," Nobel lecture, July 11, 1923.
15. Einstein to Hans Albert and Eduard Einstein, Dec. 22, 1922, AEA 75-620.

The full story of the Nobel money was complex and over the years caused considerable disputes, as became clear in letters between Einstein and Marić released in 2006. According to the divorce agreement, the Nobel money was to go to a Swiss bank account. Marić was supposed to have use of the interest, but she could spend the capital only with Einstein's consent. In 1923, after consultation with a financial adviser, Einstein decided to place only part of the money in Switzerland and have the rest invested in an American account. That scared Marić and caused frictions that were calmed by friends. With Einstein's consent she bought a Zurich apartment house in 1924 using the Swiss money and a big loan. The rents covered the loan payments, as well as the maintenance of the house and a part of the family's livelihood. Two years later, again with Einstein's consent, Marić bought two more houses using another 40,000 Swiss francs from the Nobel money and an additional loan. The two new houses turned out to be bad investments and had to be sold to avoid endangering ownership of the first house, where Marić lived with Eduard. In the meantime, the Great Depression in America reduced the value of the account and investments made there. Einstein continued to pay considerable sums to Marić and Eduard, but Marić's fears for her financial security were understandable. At the end of the 1930s, Einstein created a holding company to buy from Marić the remaining apartment house, where she still lived, and to take over her debts in order to save the house from being repossessed by the bank. Marić could continue to live in the same apartment and receive the excess rental proceeds. In addition, Einstein sent a monthly contribution for Eduard's support. This arrangement lasted until the late 1940s, when Mileva was no longer able to care for the house and the income from the rents no longer covered the expenses. With Einstein's consent Marić sold the house but not the right to her apartment. The money from that sale was eventually found under Marić's mattress. Some critics have accused Einstein of allowing Marić to die impoverished. Although Marić at times certainly felt impoverished, Einstein did try to protect her and Eduard from financial worries, not only by paying what he was obliged to pay, but also by subsidizing their living expenses. I am grateful to Barbara Wolff of the Hebrew University Einstein archives for help researching this topic. See also Alexis Schwarzenbach, *Das verschmähte Genie: Albert Einstein und die Schweiz* (Berlin: DVA, 2003).

16. Einstein to Heinrich Zangger, Dec. 6, 1917.

17. "*All* the really great discoveries in *theoretical* physics—with a few exceptions that stand out because of their oddity—have been made by men *under thirty.*" Bernstein 1973, 89, emphasis in the original. Einstein finished his work on general relativity when he was 36, but his initial step, what he called his "happiest thought" about the equivalence of gravity and acceleration, came when he was 28. Max Planck was 42 when, in Dec. 1900, he gave his lecture on the quantum.

18. Einstein to Heinrich Zangger, Aug. 11, 1918; Clive Thompson, "Do Scientists Age Badly?," *Boston Globe*, Aug. 17, 2003. John von Neumann, a founder of modern computer science, once claimed that the intellectual

powers of mathematicians peaked at the age of 26. One study of a random group of scientists showed that 80 percent did their best work before their early forties.

19. Einstein to Maurice Solovine, Apr. 27, 1906.
20. Aphorism for a friend, Sept. 1, 1930, AEA 36-598.
21. Einstein to Hendrik Lorentz, June 17, 1916; Miller 1984, 55–56.
22. Einstein, "Ether and the Theory of Relativity," speech at University of Leiden, May 5, 1920, CPAE 7: 38.
23. Einstein to Karl Schwarzschild, Jan. 9, 1916.
24. Einstein, "Ether and the Theory of Relativity," speech at University of Leiden, May 5, 1920, CPAE 7: 38.
25. Greene 2004, 74.
26. Janssen 2004, 22. Einstein made this clearer in his 1921 Princeton lectures, but also continued to say, "It appears probable that Mach was on the right road in his thought that inertia depends on a mutual action of matter." Einstein 1922a, chapter 4.
27. Einstein, "Ether and the Theory of Relativity," speech at University of Leiden, May 5, 1920, CPAE 7: 38.
28. Einstein, "On the Present State of the Problem of Specific Heats," Nov. 3, 1911, CPAE 3: 26; the quote about "really exist in nature" appears on p. 421 of the English translation of vol. 3.
29. Robinson, 84–85.
30. Holton and Brush, 435.
31. Lightman 2005, 151.
32. Clark 202; George de Hevesy to Ernest Rutherford, Oct. 14, 1913; Einstein 1949b, 47.
33. Einstein, "Emission and Absorption of Radiation in Quantum Theory," July 17, 1916, CPAE 6: 34; Einstein, "On the Quantum Theory of Radiation," after Aug. 24, 1916, CPAE 6: 38, and also in *Physikalische Zeitschrift* 18 (1917). See Overbye, 304–306; Rigden, 141; Pais 1982, 404–412; Fölsing, 391; Clark, 265; Daniel Kleppner, "Rereading Einstein on Radiation," *Physics Today* (Feb. 2005): 30. In addition, in 1917 Einstein wrote a paper on the quantization of energy in mechanical theories called "On the Quantum Theorem of Sommerfeld and Epstein." It shows the problems that the classical quantum theory encountered when applied to mechanical systems we would now call chaotic. It was cited by earlier pioneers of quantum mechanics, but has since been largely forgotten. A good description of it and its importance in the development of quantum mechanics is Douglas Stone, "Einstein's Unknown Insight and the Problem of Quantizing Chaos," *Physics Today* (Aug. 2005).
34. Einstein to Michele Besso, Aug. 11, 1916.
35. I am grateful to Professor Douglas Stone of Yale for help with the wording of this.
36. Einstein to Michele Besso, Aug. 24, 1916.
37. Einstein, "On the Quantum Theory of Radiation," after Aug. 24, 1916, CPAE 6: 38.

38. Einstein to Max Born, Jan. 27, 1920.
39. Einstein to Max Born, Apr. 29, 1924, AEA 8-176.
40. Niels Bohr, "Discussion with Einstein," in Schilpp, 205–206; Clark, 202.
41. Einstein to Niels Bohr, May 2, 1920; Einstein to Paul Ehrenfest, May 4, 1920.
42. Niels Bohr to Einstein, Nov. 11, 1922, AEA 8-73.
43. Fölsing, 441.
44. John Wheeler, "Memoir," in French, 21; C. P. Snow, "Albert Einstein," in French, 3.
45. Bohr's quip is often quoted. One source I can find for it, in a less pithy fashion, is from Bohr's own descriptions of being with Einstein at the 1927 Solvay Conference: "Einstein mockingly asked us whether we could really believe that the providential authorities took recourse to dice-playing ('. . . ob der liebe Gott würfelt'), to which I replied by pointing at the great caution, already called for by ancient thinkers, in ascribing attributes to Providence in everyday language." Niels Bohr, "Discussion with Einstein," in Schilpp, 211. Werner Heisenberg, who was at these discussions, also recounts the quip: "To which Bohr could only answer: 'But still, it cannot be for us to tell God how he is to run the world.' " Heisenberg 1989, 117.
46. Holton and Brush, 447; Pais 1982, 436.
47. Pais 1982, 438. Wolfgang Pauli recalled, "In a discussion at the physics meeting in Innsbruck in the autumn of 1924, Einstein proposed to search for interference and diffraction phenomena with molecular beams." Pauli, 91.
48. Einstein, "Quantum Theory of Single-Atom Gases," part 1, 1924, part 2, 1925. This quote occurs in part 2, section 7. The manuscript of this paper was found in Leiden in 2005.
49. I am grateful to Professor Douglas Stone of Yale for helping to craft this section and explaining the fundamental importance of what Einstein did. A theoretical condensed matter physicist, he is writing a book on Einstein's contributions to quantum mechanics and how far-reaching they really were, despite Einstein's later rejection of the theory. According to Stone, "99% of the credit for this fundamental discovery called Bose-Einstein condensation is really owed to Einstein. Bose did not even realize that he had counted in a different way." Regarding the Nobel Prize for achieving Bose-Einstein condensation, see www.nobelprize.org/physics/laureates/2001/public.html.
50. Bernstein 1973, 217; Martin J. Klein, "Einstein and the Wave-Particle Duality," *Natural Philosopher* (1963): 26.
51. Max Born, "Einstein's Statistical Theories," in Schilpp, 174.
52. Einstein to Erwin Schrödinger, Feb. 28, 1925, AEA 22-2.
53. Don Howard, "Spacetime and Separability," 1996, AEA Cedex H; Howard 1985; Howard 1990b, 61–64; Howard 1997. The 1997 essay identifies the philosophy of Arthur Schopenhauer as an influence on Einstein's theories of spatial separability.
54. Bernstein 1996a, 138.
55. More precisely, it is the square of the wave function that is proportional to the probability. Holton and Brush, 452.

56. Einstein to Hedwig Born, Mar. 7, 1926, AEA 8-266; Einstein to Max Born, Dec. 4, 1926, AEA 8-180.

57. aip.org/history/heisenberg/p07.htm; Born 2005, 85.

58. Max Born to Einstein, July 15, 1925, AEA 8-177; Einstein to Hedwig Born, Mar. 7, 1926, AEA 8-178; Einstein to Paul Ehrenfest, Sept. 25, 1925, AEA 10-116.

59. Werner Heisenberg to Einstein, June 10, 1927, AEA 12-174.

60. Heisenberg 1971, 63; Gerald Holton, "Werner Heisenberg and Albert Einstein," *Physics Today* (2000), www.aip.org/pt/vol-53/iss-7/p38.html.

61. Frank 1947, 216.

62. Aage Petersen, "The Philosophy of Niels Bohr," *Bulletin of the Atomic Scientists* (Sept. 1963): 12.

63. Dugald Murdoch, *Niels Bohr's Philosophy of Physics* (Cambridge, England: Cambridge University Press, 1987), 47, citing the Niels Bohr Archives: Scientific Correspondence, 11: 2.

64. Einstein, "To the Royal Society on Newton's Bicentennial," Mar. 1927.

65. Einstein to Michele Besso, Apr. 29, 1917; Michele Besso to Einstein, May 5, 1917; Einstein to Michele Besso, May 13, 1917. For a good analysis, see Gerald Holton, "Mach, Einstein, and the Search for Reality," in Holton 1973, 240.

66. "Belief in an external world independent of the perceiving subject is the basis of all natural science." Einstein, "Maxwell's Influence on the Evolution of the Idea of Physical Reality," 1931, in Einstein 1954, 266.

67. Einstein to Max Born, Jan. 27, 1920.

68. Einstein's introduction to Rudolf Kayser, *Spinoza* (New York: Philosophical Library, 1946). Kayser was married to Einstein's stepdaughter and wrote a semi-authorized memoir of Einstein.

69. Fölsing, 703–704; Einstein to Fritz Reiche, Aug. 15, 1942, AEA 20-19.

70. Einstein to Max Born, Dec. 4, 1926, AEA 8-180.

CHAPTER FIFTEEN: UNIFIED FIELD THEORIES

1. Einstein, "Ideas and Problems of the Theory of Relativity," Nobel lecture, July 11, 1923. Available at nobelprize.org/nobel_prizes. This section draws from these papers on Einstein's unified field quest: van Dongen 2002, courtesy of the author; Tilman Sauer, "Dimensions of Einstein's Unified Field Theory Program," forthcoming in the *Cambridge Companion to Einstein*, courtesy of the author; Norton 2000; Goenner 2004.

2. Einstein, "The Principles of Research," a toast in honor of Max Planck, Apr. 26, 1918, CPAE 7: 7.

3. Einstein to Hermann Weyl, Apr. 6, 1918.

4. Einstein to Hermann Weyl, Apr. 8, 1918. In a letter to Heinrich Zangger, May 8, 1918, Einstein called Weyl's theory "ingenious" but "physically incorrect." It did, however, later become one of the recognized precursors of Yang-Mills gauge theory.

5. My description of the work of Kaluza and Klein relies on Krauss, 94–104,

which is an engaging book on the role extra dimensions have played in explaining the universe.

6. Einstein to Theodor Kaluza, Apr. 21, 1919.
7. Einstein to Niels Bohr, Jan. 10, 1923, AEA 8-74.
8. Einstein to Hermann Weyl, May 26, 1923, AEA 24-83.
9. Einstein, "On the General Theory of Relativity," Prussian Academy, Feb. 15, 1923.
10. *New York Times*, Mar. 27, 1923.
11. Pais 1982, 466; Einstein, "On the General Theory of Relativity," the Prussian Academy, Feb. 15, 1923.
12. Einstein, "Unified Field Theory of Gravity and Electricity," July 25, 1925; Hoffmann 1972, 225.
13. Steven Weinberg, "Einstein's Mistakes," *Physics Today* (Nov. 2005).
14. Einstein, "On the Unified Theory," Jan. 30, 1929.
15. Einstein to Michele Besso, Jan. 5, 1929, AEA 7-102.
16. *New York Times*, Nov. 4, 1928; Vallentin, 160.
17. Clark, 494; *London Daily Chronicle*, Jan. 26, 1929.
18. "Einstein's Field Theory," *Time*, Feb. 18, 1929. Einstein also appeared on *Time*'s cover on Apr. 4, 1938, July 1, 1946, and posthumously Feb. 19, 1979, and Dec. 31, 1999. Elsa appeared on the cover Dec. 22, 1930.
19. Fölsing, 605; Clark, 496; Brian 1996, 174.
20. *New York Times*, Feb. 4, 1929.
21. Einstein to Maja Winteler-Einstein, Oct. 22, 1929, AEA 29-409.
22. Wolfgang Pauli to Einstein, Dec. 19, 1929, AEA 19-163.
23. *New York Times*, Jan. 23, Oct. 26, 1931; Einstein to Wolfgang Pauli, Jan. 22, 1932, AEA 19-169.
24. Goenner 2004; Elie Cartan, "Absolute Parallelism and the Unified Theory," *Review Metaphysic Morale* (1931).
25. For a two-minute home movie of the conference shot by Irving Langmuir, the 1932 Nobel Prize winner in chemistry, see www.maxborn.net/index.php?page=filmnews.
26. Einstein to Hendrik Lorentz, Sept. 13, 1927, AEA 16-613.
27. Pauli, 121.
28. John Archibald Wheeler and Wojciech Zurek, *Quantum Theory and Measurement* (Princeton: Princeton University Press, 1983), 7.
29. Fölsing, 589; Pais 1982, 445, from Proceedings of the Fifth Solvay Conference.
30. Heisenberg 1989, 116.
31. Niels Bohr, "Discussion with Einstein," in Schilpp, 211–219, offers a detailed and loving description of the Solvay and other discussions; Otto Stern recollections, in Pais 1982, 445; Fölsing, 589.
32. "Reports and Discussions," in *Solvay Conference of 1927* (Paris: Gauthier-Villars, 1928), 102. See also Travis Norsen, "Einstein's Boxes," *American Journal of Physics*, vol. 73, Feb. 2005, pp. 164-176.
33. Louis de Broglie, "My Meeting with Einstein," in French, 15.

34. Einstein, "Speech to Professor Planck," Max Planck award ceremony, June 28, 1929.

35. Léon Rosenfeld, "Niels Bohr in the Thirties," in Rozental 1967, 132.

36. Niels Bohr, "Discussion with Einstein," in Schilpp, 225–229; Pais 1982, 447–448. I am grateful to Murray Gell-Mann and David Derbes for the phrasing of this section.

37. Einstein, "Maxwell's Influence on the Evolution of the Idea of Physical Reality," 1931, in Einstein 1954, 266.

38. Einstein, "Reply to Criticisms" (1949), in Schilpp, 669.

39. A fuller discussion of Einstein's realism is in chapter 20 of this book. For contrasting views on this issue, see Gerald Holton, "Mach, Einstein, and the Search for Reality," in Holton 1973, 219, 245 (he argues that there is a very clear change in Einstein's philosophy: "For a scientist to change his philosophical beliefs so fundamentally is rare"); Fine, 123 (he argues that "Einstein underwent a philosophical conversion, turning away from his positivist youth and becoming deeply committed to realism"); Howard 2004 (which argues, "Einstein was never an ardent 'Machian' positivist, and he was never a scientific realist"). This section also draws on van Dongen 2002 (he argues, "Broadly speaking, one can say that Einstein moved from Mach's empiricism, earlier in his career, to a strong realist position later on"). See also Anton Zeilinger, "Einstein and Absolute Reality," in Brockman, 121–131.

40. Einstein, "On the Method of Theoretical Physics," the Herbert Spencer lecture, Oxford, June 10, 1933, in Einstein 1954, 270.

41. Einstein 1949b, 89.

42. Einstein, "Principles of Theoretical Physics," inaugural address to the Prussian Academy, 1914, in Einstein 1954, 221.

43. Einstein to Hermann Weyl, May 26, 1923, AEA 24-83.

44. John Barrow, "Einstein as Icon," *Nature*, Jan. 20, 2005, 219. See also Norton 2000.

45. Einstein, "On the Method of Theoretical Physics," the Herbert Spencer lecture, Oxford, June 10, 1933, in Einstein 1954, 274.

46. Steven Weinberg, "Einstein's Mistakes," *Physics Today* (Nov. 2005): "Since Einstein's time, we have learned to distrust this sort of aesthetic criterion. Our experience in elementary-particle physics has taught us that any term in the field equations of physics that is allowed by fundamental principles is likely to be there in the equations."

47. Einstein, "Latest Developments of the Theory of Relativity," May 23, 1931, the third of three Rhodes Lectures at Oxford, this one coming on the day he was awarded his honorary doctorate there. Reprinted in the *Oxford University Gazette*, June 3, 1931.

48. Einstein, "On the Method of Theoretical Physics," Oxford, June 10, 1933, in Einstein 1954, 270.

49. Marcia Bartusiak, "Beyond the Big Bang," *National Geographic* (May 2005). Elsa's quip is widely reported but never fully sourced. See Clark, 526.

50. Associated Press, Dec. 30, 1930.

51. Einstein to Michele Besso, Mar. 1, 1931, AEA 7-125.
52. Greene 2004, 279: "That would certainly have ranked among the greatest discoveries—it may have been *the* greatest discovery—of all time." See also Edward W. Kolb, "The Greatest Discovery Einstein Didn't Make," in Brockman, 201.
53. Einstein, "On the Cosmological Problem of the General Theory of Relativity," Prussian Academy, 1931; "Einstein Drops Idea of 'Closed' Universe," *New York Times*, Feb. 5, 1931.
54. Einstein 1916, appendix IV (first appears in the 1931 edition).
55. Gamow 1970, 149.
56. Steven Weinberg, "The Cosmological Constant Problem," in *Morris Loeb Lectures in Physics* (Cambridge, Mass.: Harvard University Press 1988); Steven Weinberg, "Einstein's Mistakes," *Physics Today* (Nov. 2005); Aczel 1999, 167; Krauss 117; Greene 2004, 275–278; Dennis Overbye, "A Famous Einstein 'Fudge' Returns to Haunt Cosmology," *New York Times*, May 26, 1998; Jeremy Bernstein, "Einstein's Blunder," in Bernstein 2001, 86–89.
57. Lawrence Krauss of Case Western Reserve and Michael Turner of the University of Chicago have argued that an explanation of the universe requires use of a cosmological term that is different from the one Einstein added into his field equations and then discarded. Their version arises from quantum mechanics, not general relativity, and is based on the premise that even "empty" space does not necessarily possess zero energy. See Krauss and Turner, "A Cosmic Conundrum," *Scientific American* (Sept. 2004).
58. "Einstein's Cosmological Constant Predicts Dark Energy," *Universe Today*, Nov. 22, 2005. This particular headline was based on a research project known as the Supernova Legacy Survey (SNLS). According to a press release from Caltech, SNLS "aims to discover and examine 700 distant supernovae to map out the history of the expansion of the universe. The survey confirms earlier discoveries that the expansion of the universe proceeded more slowly in the past and is speeding up today. However, the crucial step forward is the discovery that Einstein's 1917 explanation of a constant energy term for empty space fits the new supernova data very well."

CHAPTER SIXTEEN: TURNING FIFTY

1. Vallentin, 163.
2. *New York Times*, Mar. 15, 1929.
3. Reiser, 205.
4. Reiser, 207; Frank 1947, 223; Fölsing, 611.
5. www.einstein-website.de/z_biography/caputh-e.html; Jan Otakar Fischer, "Einstein's Haven," *International Herald Tribune*, June 30, 2005; Fölsing, 612; Einstein to Maja Einstein, Oct. 22, 1929; Erika Britzke, "Einstein in Caputh," in Renn 2005d, 272.
6. Vallentin, 168.
7. Reiser, 221.

8. Einstein to Betty Neumann, Nov. 5 and 13, 1923. These letters are part of a set given to Hebrew University and are not catalogued in the Einstein archives.

9. Einstein to Betty Neumann, Jan. 11, 1924; Pais 1982, 320.

10. Einstein to Elsa Einstein, Aug. 14, 1924, part of sealed correspondence released in 2006; Einstein to Betty Neumann, Aug. 24, 1924. I am grateful to Ze'ev Rosenkranz of the Einstein archives in Jerusalem and Caltech for helping me find and translate these letters.

11. Einstein to Ethel Michanowski, May 16 and 24, 1931, in private collection.

12. Einstein to Elsa Einstein and Einstein to Margot Einstein, May 1931, part of sealed correspondence released in 2006. I am grateful for the help of Ze'ev Rosenkranz of the Einstein Papers Project for providing context and translation.

13. Einstein to Margot Einstein, May 1931, sealed correspondence released in 2006.

14. This is a sentiment that lasted through his life. Einstein to Eugenia Anderman, June 2, 1953, AEA 59-097: "You must be aware that most men (and many women) are by nature not monogamous. This nature is asserted more forcefully when tradition stands in the way."

15. Fölsing, 617; Highfield and Carter, 208; Marianoff, 186. (Note: Fölsing spells her name Lenbach, which is not correct according to the Einstein archive copies.)

16. Elsa Einstein to Hermann Struck, 1929.

17. George Dyson, "Helen Dukas: Einstein's Compass," in Brockman, 85–94 (George Dyson was the son of Freeman Dyson, a physicist at the Institute for Advanced Study in Princeton, and Dukas worked as his babysitter after Einstein died). See also Abraham Pais, "Eulogy for Helen Dukas," 1982, American Institute of Physics Library, College Park, Md.

18. Einstein to Maurice Solovine, Mar. 4, 1930, AEA 21-202.

19. Einstein to Mileva Marić, Feb. 23, 1927, AEA 75-742.

20. Ibid.

21. Einstein to Hans Albert Einstein, Feb. 2, 1927, AEA 75-738, and Feb. 23, 1927, AEA 75-739.

22. Highfield and Carter, 227.

23. Einstein to Eduard Einstein, Dec. 23, 1927, AEA 75-748.

24. Einstein to Eduard Einstein, July 10, 1929, AEA 75-782.

25. Eduard Einstein to Einstein, May 1, Dec. 10, 1926. Both are in sealed correspondence folders that were released in 2006 and not catalogued in the archives.

26. Eduard Einstein to Einstein, Dec. 24, 1935. Also in the sealed correspondence folders released in 2006 and not catalogued in the archives.

27. Sigmund Freud to Sandor Ferenczi, Jan. 2, 1927. For an analysis of the interwoven influence of Freud and Einstein, see Panek 2004.

28. Viereck, 374; Sayen, 134. See also Bucky, 113: "I have many doubts about some of his theories. I think Freud placed too much emphasis on dream theo-

ries. After all, a junk closet does not bring everything forth . . . On the other hand, Freud was very interesting to read and he was also very witty. I certainly do not mean to be overly critical."

29. Einstein to Eduard Einstein, 1936 or 1937, AEA 75-939.
30. Einstein to Eduard Einstein, Feb. 5, 1930, not catalogued; Highfield and Carter, 229, 234. See translation in epigraph source note on p. 565.
31. Einstein to Eduard Einstein, Dec. 23, 1927, AEA 75-748.
32. Einstein to Mileva Marić, Aug. 14, 1925, AEA 75-693.
33. Marianoff, 12. He apparently mistakes the year of his own wedding, as he refers to the fall of 1929 when it was in fact just before Einstein's second visit to the United States in late 1930. Barbara Wolff of the Einstein archives at Hebrew University says she believes this anecdote to be embellished.
34. Elsa Einstein to Antonina Vallentin, undated, in Vallentin, 196.
35. Einstein, Trip Diary to the U.S.A., Nov. 30, 1930, AEA 29-134.
36. "Einstein Works at Sea," *New York Times*, Dec. 5, 1930.
37. "Einstein Puzzled by Our Invitations," *New York Times*, Nov. 23, 1930.
38. "Einstein Consents to Face Reporters," *New York Times*, Dec. 10, 1930.
39. Einstein, Trip Diary, Dec. 11, 1930, AEA 29-134.
40. "Einstein on Arrival Braves Limelight for Only 15 Minutes," *New York Times*, Dec. 12, 1930.
41. "He Is Worth It," *Time*, Dec. 2, 1930.
42. Brian 1996, 204; "Einstein Receives Keys to the City," *New York Times*, Dec. 14, 1930.
43. "Einstein Saw His Statue in Church Here," *New York Times*, Dec. 28, 1930.
44. George Sylvester Viereck, profile of John D. Rockefeller, *Liberty*, Jan. 9, 1932; Nathan and Norden, 157. Einstein also mentions his visit to Rockefeller in a letter to Max Born, May 30, 1933, AEA 8-192.
45. Einstein, New History Society speech, Dec. 14, 1930, in Nathan and Norden, 117; "Einstein Advocates Resistance to War," *New York Times*, Dec. 15, 1930, p. 1; Fölsing, 635.
46. "Einstein Considers Seeking a New Home," Associated Press, Dec. 16, 1930.
47. Einstein, Trip Diary, Dec. 15–31, 1931, AEA 29-134; "Einstein Welcomed by Leaders of Panama," *New York Times*, Dec. 24, 1930; "Einstein Heard on Radio," *New York Times*, Dec. 26, 1930.
48. Brian 1996, 206.
49. Hedwig Born to Einstein, Feb. 22, 1931, AEA 8-190.
50. Amos Fried to Robert Millikan, Mar. 4, 1932; Robert Millikan to Amos Fried, Mar. 8, 1932; cited in Clark, 551.
51. Brian 1996, 216.
52. Seelig 1956a, 194. At the movie, Einstein "stared bewildered, utterly absorbed, like a child at a Christmas pantomime," according to a vivid report by Cissy Patterson, an ambitious young journalist who had also described him sunbathing nude. She would later own the *Washington Herald*. Brian 1996, 214, citing *Washington Herald*, Feb. 10, 1931.
53. Einstein address, Feb. 16, 1931, in Nathan and Norden, 122.

54. "At Grand Canyon Today," *New York Times*, Feb. 28, 1931; Einstein at Hopi House, www.hanksville.org/sand/Einstein.html.
55. "Einstein in Chicago Talks for Pacifism," *New York Times*, Mar. 4, 1931; Nathan and Norden, 123.
56. Fölsing, 641; Einstein talk to War Resisters' League, Mar. 1, 1931, in Nathan and Norden, 123.
57. Nathan and Norden, 124.
58. Marianoff, 184.
59. Einstein to Mrs. Chandler and the Youth Peace Federation, Apr. 5, 1931; Nathan and Norden, 124; Fölsing, 642. For an image of the note, see www .alberteinstein.info/db/ViewImage.do?DocumentID=21007&Page=1.
60. Einstein interview with George Sylvester Viereck, Jan. 1931, in Nathan and Norden, 125.
61. Einstein to Women's International League, Jan. 4, 1928, AEA 48-818.
62. Einstein to London chapter of War Resisters' International, Nov. 25, 1928; Einstein to the League for the Organization of Progress, Dec. 26, 1928.
63. Einstein statement, Feb. 23, 1929, in Nathan and Norden, 95.
64. Manifesto of the Joint Peace Council, Oct. 12, 1930; Nathan and Norden, 113.
65. Einstein, "The 1932 Disarmament Conference," *The Nation*, Sept. 23, 1931; Einstein 1954, 95; Einstein, "The Road to Peace," *New York Times*, Nov. 22, 1931.
66. Nathan and Norden, 168; "Einstein Assails Arms Conference," *New York Times*, May 24, 1931.
67. Einstein to Kurt Hiller, Aug. 21, 1931, AEA 46-693; Nathan and Norden, 143.
68. Jerome, 144. See in particular chapter 11, "How Red?"
69. Einstein, "The Road to Peace," *New York Times*, Nov. 22, 1931; Einstein 1954, 95.
70. Thomas Bucky interview with Denis Brian, in Brian 1996, 229.
71. Einstein to Henri Barbusse, June 1, 1932, AEA 34-543; Nathan and Norden, 175–179.
72. Einstein to Isaac Don Levine, after Jan. 1, 1925, AEA 28-29.00 (for image of handwritten document, see www.alberteinstein.info/db/ViewImage.do? DocumentID=21154&Page=1; Roger Baldwin and Isaac Don Levine, *Letters from Russian Prisons* (New York: Charles Boni, 1925); Robert Cottrell, *Roger Nash Baldwin and the American Civil Liberties Union* (New York: Columbia, 2001), 180.
73. Einstein to Isaac Don Levine, Mar. 15, 1932, AEA 50-922.
74. Einstein, "The World As I See It," originally published in 1930, reprinted in Einstein 1954, 8.
75. "Ask Pardon for Eight Negroes," *New York Times*, Mar. 27, 1932; "Einstein Hails Negro Race," *New York Times*, Jan. 19, 1932, citing an Einstein piece in the forthcoming *Crisis* magazine of Feb. 1932.
76. Brian 1996, 219.
77. Einstein to Chaim Weizmann, Nov. 25, 1929, AEA 33-411.

78. Einstein, "Letter to an Arab," Mar. 15, 1930; Einstein 1954, 172; Clark, 483; Fölsing, 623.

79. Einstein to Sigmund Freud, July 30, 1932, www.cis.vt.edu/modernworld/d/ Einstein.html.

80. Sigmund Freud to Einstein, Sept. 1932, www.cis.vt.edu/modernworld/d/ Einstein.html.

CHAPTER SEVENTEEN: EINSTEIN'S GOD

1. Charles Kessler, ed., *The Diaries of Count Harry Kessler* (New York: Grove Press, 2002), 322 (entry for June 14, 1927); Jammer 1999, 40. Jammer 1999 provides a thorough look at the biographical, philosophical, and scientific aspects of Einstein's religious thought.

2. Einstein, "Ueber den Gegenwertigen Stand der Feld-Theorie," 1929, AEA 4-38.

3. Neil Johnson, *George Sylvester Viereck: Poet and Propagandist* (Iowa City: University of Iowa Press, 1968); George S. Viereck, *My Flesh and Blood: A Lyric Autobiography with Indiscreet Annotations* (New York: Liveright, 1931).

4. Viereck, 372–378; Viereck first published the interview as "What Life Means to Einstein," *Saturday Evening Post*, Oct. 26, 1929. I have generally followed the translation and paraphrasing in Brian 2005, 185–186 and in Calaprice. See also Jammer 1999, 22.

5. Einstein, "What I Believe," originally written in 1930 and recorded for the German League for Human Rights. It was published as "The World As I See It" in *Forum and Century*, 1930; in *Living Philosophies* (New York: Simon & Schuster, 1931); in Einstein 1949a, 1–5; in Einstein 1954, 8–11. The versions are all translated somewhat differently and have slight revisions. For an audio version, see www.yu.edu/libraries/digital_library/einstein/credo .html.

6. Einstein to M. Schayer, Aug. 5, 1927, AEA 48-380; Dukas and Hoffmann, 66.

7. Einstein to Phyllis Wright, Jan. 24, 1936, AEA 52-337.

8. "Passover," *Time*, May 13, 1929.

9. Einstein to Herbert S. Goldstein, Apr. 25, 1929, AEA 33-272; "Einstein Believes in Spinoza's God," *New York Times*, Apr. 25, 1929; Gerald Holton, "Einstein's Third Paradise," *Daedalus* (fall 2002): 26–34. Goldstein was the rabbi of the Institutional Synagogue in Harlem and the longtime president of the Union of Orthodox Jewish Congregations of America.

10. Rabbi Jacob Katz of the Montefiore Congregation, quoted in *Time*, May 13, 1929.

11. Calaprice, 214; Einstein to Hubertus zu Löwenstein, ca. 1941, in Löwenstein's book, *Towards the Further Shore* (London: Victor Gollancz, 1968), 156.

12. Einstein to Joseph Lewis, Apr. 18, 1953, AEA 60-279.

13. Einstein to unknown recipient, Aug. 7, 1941, AEA 54-927.

14. Guy Raner Jr. to Einstein, June 10, 1948, AEA 57-287; Einstein to Guy Raner

Jr., July 2, 1945, AEA 57-288; Einstein to Guy Raner Jr., Sept. 28, 1949, AEA 57-289.

15. Einstein, "Religion and Science," *New York Times*, Nov. 9, 1930, reprinted in Einstein 1954, 36–40. See also Powell.

16. Einstein, speech to the Symposium on Science, Philosophy and Religion, Sept. 10, 1941, reprinted in Einstein 1954, 41; "Sees No Personal God," Associated Press, Sept. 11, 1941. A yellowed clipping of this story was given to me by Orville Wright, who was a young naval officer at the time and had kept it for sixty years; it had been passed around his ship and had notations from various sailors saying such things as, "Tell me, what do you think of this?"

17. "In the mind there is no absolute or free will, but the mind is determined by this or that volition, by a cause, which is also determined by another cause, and this again by another, and so on *ad infinitum*." Baruch Spinoza, *Ethics*, part 2, proposition 48.

18. Einstein, statement to the Spinoza Society of America, Sept. 22, 1932.

19. Sometimes translated as "A man can do what he wants, but not want what he wants." I cannot find this quote in Schopenhauer's writings. The sentiment, nevertheless, comports with Schopenhauer's philosophy. He said, for example, "A man's life, in all its events great and small, is as necessarily predetermined as are the movements of a clock." Schopenhauer, "On Ethics," in *Parerga and Paralipomena: Short Philosophical Essays* (New York: Oxford University Press, 2001), 2:227.

20. Einstein, "The World As I See It," in Einstein 1949a and Einstein 1954.

21. Viereck, 375.

22. Max Born to Einstein, Oct. 10, 1944, in Born 2005, 150.

23. Hedwig Born to Einstein, Oct. 9, 1944, in Born 2005, 149.

24. Viereck, 377.

25. Einstein to the Rev. Cornelius Greenway, Nov. 20, 1950, AEA 28-894.

26. Sayen, 165.

CHAPTER EIGHTEEN: THE REFUGEE

1. Einstein trip diary, Dec. 6, 1931, AEA 29-136.

2. Einstein trip diary, Dec. 10, 1931, AEA 29-141.

3. Flexner, 381–382; Batterson, 87–89.

4. Abraham Flexner to Robert Millikan, July 30, 1932, AEA 38-007; Abraham Flexner to Louis Bamberger, Feb. 13, 1932, in Batterson, 88.

5. Einstein trip diary, Feb. 1, 1932, AEA 29-141; Elsa Einstein to Rosika Schwimmer, Feb. 3, 1932; Nathan and Norden, 163.

6. Einstein to Paul Ehrenfest, Apr. 3, 1932, AEA 10-227.

7. Clark, 542, citing Sir Roy Harrod.

8. Flexner, 383.

9. Einstein to Abraham Flexner, July 30, 1932; Batterson, 149; Brian 1996, 232.

10. Elsa Einstein to Robert Millikan, June 22, 1932, AEA 38-002.

11. Robert Millikan to Abraham Flexner, July 25, 1932, AEA 38-006; Abraham Flexner to Robert Millikan, July 30, 1932, AEA 38-007; Batterson, 114.

12. "Einstein Will Head School Here," *New York Times*, Oct. 11, 1932, p. 1.

13. Frank 1947, 226.

14. Woman Patriot Corporation memo to the U.S. State Department, Nov. 22, 1932, contained in Einstein's FBI file, section 1, available at foia.fbi.gov /foiaindex/einstein.htm. This episode is nicely detailed in Jerome, 6–11.

15. Reprinted in Einstein 1954, 7. Einstein's relationship with Louis Lochner of United Press is detailed in Marianoff, 137.

16. *New York Times*, Dec. 4, 1932.

17. "Einstein's Ultimatum Brings a Quick Visa," "Consul Investigated Charge," and "Women Made Complaint," all in *New York Times*, Dec. 6, 1932; Sayen, 6; Jerome, 10.

18. This was uncovered by Richard Alan Schwartz of Florida International University, who did the original research into Einstein's FBI files. The versions he received were redacted by 25 percent. Fred Jerome was able to get fuller versions under the Freedom of Information Act, which he used in his book. Schwartz's articles on the topic include "The F.B.I. and Dr. Einstein," *The Nation*, Sept. 3, 1983, 168–173, and "Dr. Einstein and the War Department," *Isis* (June 1989): 281–284. See also Dennis Overbye, "New Details Emerge from the Einstein Files," *New York Times*, May 7, 2002.

19. "Einstein Resumes Packing," *New York Times*, Dec. 7, 1932; "Einstein Embarks, Jests about Quiz" and "Stimson Regrets Incident," *New York Times*, Dec. 11, 1932.

20. Einstein (from Caputh) to Maurice Solovine, Nov. 20, 1932, AEA 21-218; Frank 1947, 226; Pais 1982, 318, 450. Both Frank and Pais recount Einstein's prophetic words to Elsa about Caputh, and each likely heard the anecdote directly from them. Pais, among others, says they carried thirty pieces of luggage. Elsa, in her call to reporters after the U.S. consulate interrogation, said she had packed six trunks, but she may not have been finished packing, or may have been referring only to trunks, or may have understated the number so as not to inflame German authorities (or Pais may have been wrong). Barbara Wolff of the Einstein archives in Jerusalem thinks the tale that she packed thirty trunks is a fabrication, as is the tale that Einstein told her to "take a very good look at it" when they left Caputh (private correspondence with the author).

21. "Einstein Will Urge Amity with Germany," *New York Times*, Jan. 8, 1933.

22. Nathan and Norden, 208; Clark, 552.

23. "Einstein's Address on World Situation" (text of speech) and "Einstein Traces Slump to Machine," *New York Times*, Jan. 24, 1933.

24. Fölsing, 659.

25. Einstein to Margarete Lebach, Feb. 27, 1933, AEA 50-834.

26. Evelyn Seeley, interview with Einstein, *New York World-Telegram*, Mar. 11, 1933; Brian 1996, 243.

27. Marianoff, 142–144.

28. Michelmore, 180. Michelmore got much of his material from Hans Albert Einstein, though this quote may have been exaggerated.

29. Einstein, Statement against the Hitler regime, Mar. 22, 1933, AEA 28-235.

30. Einstein to the Prussian Academy, Mar. 28, 1933, AEA 36–55.

31. Max Planck to Einstein, Mar. 31, 1933.

32. Max Planck to Heinrich von Ficker, Mar. 31, 1933, cited in Fölsing, 663.

33. Prussian Academy declaration, Apr. 1, 1933. The exchanges are reprinted in Einstein 1954, 205–209.

34. Einstein to Prussian Academy, Apr. 5, 1933.

35. Frank 1947, 232.

36. Prussian Academy to Einstein, Apr. 7 and 13, 1933; Einstein to Prussian Academy, Apr. 12, 1933.

37. Max Planck to Einstein, Mar. 31, 1933, AEA 19-389; Einstein to Max Planck, Apr. 6, 1933, AEA 19-392.

38. Einstein to Max Born, May 30, 1933, AEA 8-192; Max Born to Einstein, June 2, 1933, AEA 8-193.

39. Einstein to Fritz Haber, May 19, 1933, AEA 12-378. For a good profile of the Einstein-Haber relationship and this final episode, see Stern, 156–160. Also very useful is John Cornwall, *Hitler's Scientists* (New York: Viking, 2003), 137–139.

40. Fritz Haber to Einstein, Aug. 1, 1933, AEA 385; Einstein to Fritz Haber, Aug. 8, 1933, AEA 12-388.

41. Einstein to Willem de Sitter, Apr. 5, 1933, AEA 20-575; Frank 1947, 232; Clark, 573.

42. Vallentin, 231.

43. Frank 1947, 240–242.

44. Einstein to Maurice Solovine, Apr. 23, 1933, AEA 21-223.

45. Einstein to Paul Langevin, May 5, 1933, AEA 15-394.

46. "Einstein Will Go to Madrid," *New York Times*, Apr. 11, 1933; Abraham Flexner to Einstein, Apr. 13, 1933, AEA 38-23; Pais 1982, 493.

47. Abraham Flexner to Einstein, Apr. 26 and 28, 1933, AEA 38-25, 38-26.

48. "Einstein Lists Contracts; Princeton, Paris, Madrid, Oxford Lectures Are Only Engagements," *New York Times*, Aug. 5, 1933; Einstein to Frederick Lindemann, May 1, 1933, AEA 16-372.

49. Hannoch Gutfreund, "Albert Einstein and Hebrew University," in Renn 2005d, 318.

50. Einstein to Fritz Haber, Aug. 9, 1933, AEA 37-109; Einstein to Max Born, May 30, 1933, AEA 8-192.

51. *Jewish Chronicle*, Apr. 8, 1933; Chaim Weizmann to Einstein, Apr. 3, 1933, AEA 33-425; Einstein to Paul Ehrenfest, June 14, 1933, AEA 10-255.

52. Einstein to Herbert Samuel, Apr. 15, 1933, AEA 21-17; Einstein to Chaim Weizmann, June 9, 1933, AEA 33-435.

53. "Weizmann Scores Einstein's Stand," *New York Times*, June 30, 1933.

54. "Albert Einstein Definitely Takes Post at Hebrew University," Jewish Tele-

graphic Agency, July 3, 1933; Abraham Flexner to Elsa Einstein, July 19, 1933, AEA 33-033; "Einstein Accepts Chair: Dr. Weizmann Announces He Has Made Peace with Hebrew University in Jerusalem," *New York Times,* July 4, 1933.

55. Einstein to the Rev. Johannes B. Th. Hugenholtz, July 1, 1933, AEA 50-320.

56. Nathan and Norden, 225.

57. The queen's name has been spelled Elizabeth in many books, but as carved on her statue and national monument in Brussels, and in most official sources, it is Elisabeth.

58. Einstein to Elsa Einstein, Nov. 1, 1930, uncatalogued new material provided to author.

59. Einstein to King Albert I of Belgium, Nov. 14, 1933, in Nathan and Norden, 230.

60. Einstein to Alfred Nahon, July 20, 1933, AEA 51-227.

61. *New York Times,* Sept. 10, 1933.

62. Einstein to E. Lagot, Aug. 28, 1933, AEA 50-477.

63. Einstein to Lord Ponsonby, Aug. 28, 1933, AEA 51-400.

64. Einstein to A. V. Frick, Sept. 9, 1933, AEA 36-567.

65. Einstein to G. C. Heringa, Sept. 11, 1933, AEA 50-199.

66. Einstein to P. Bernstein, Apr. 5, 1934, AEA 49-276.

67. Romain Rolland, Sept. 1933 diary entry, in Nathan and Norden, 232.

68. Michele Besso to Einstein, Sept. 18, 1932, AEA 7-130; Einstein to Michele Besso, Oct. 21, 1932, AEA 7-370.

69. Einstein to Frederick Lindemann, May 9, 1933, AEA 16-377.

70. Einstein to Elsa Einstein, July 21, 1933, AEA 143-250.

71. Locker-Lampson speech, House of Commons, July 26, 1933; "Einstein a Briton Soon: Home Secretary's Certificate Preferred to Palestine Citizenship," *New York Times,* July 29, 1933; Marianoff, 159.

72. *New York World Telegram,* Sept. 19, 1933, in Nathan and Norden, 234.

73. "Dr. Einstein Denies Communist Leanings," *New York Times,* Sept. 16, 1933; "Professor Einstein's Political Views," *Times* of London, Sept. 16, 1933, in Brian 1996, 251.

74. Einstein, Appreciation of Paul Ehrenfest, written in 1934 for a Leiden almanac and reprinted in Einstein 1950a, 236.

75. Clark, 600–605; Marianoff, 160–163; Jacob Epstein, *Let There Be Sculpture* (London: Michael Joseph, 1940), 78.

76. Dukas and Hoffmann, 56.

77. Einstein, "Civilization and Science," Royal Albert Hall, Oct. 3, 1933; *Times* of London, Oct. 4, 1933; Calaprice, 198; Clark, 610–611. Clark's version is more faithful to the way the speech was given than the written version, which had two references to Germany that Einstein, diplomatically, decided to omit.

CHAPTER NINETEEN: AMERICA

1. Abraham Flexner telegram to Einstein, Oct. 1933, AEA 38-049; Abraham Flexner to Einstein, Oct. 13, 1933, AEA 38-050.
2. "Einstein Arrives; Pleads for Quiet / Whisked from Liner by Tug at Quarantine," *New York Times*, Oct. 18, 1933.
3. "Einstein Views Quarters," *New York Times*, Oct. 18, 1933; Rev. John Lampe interview, in Clark, 614; "Einstein to Princeton," *Time*, Oct. 30, 1933.
4. Brian 1996, 251.
5. "Einstein Has Musicale," *New York Times*, Nov. 10, 1933. The sketches that Einstein made for Seidel are now in the Judah Magnes Museum, endowed by the president of Hebrew University with whom Einstein fought.
6. Bucky, 150.
7. Thomas Torrance, "Einstein and God," Center for Theological Inquiry, Princeton, ctinquiry.org/publications/reflections_volume_1/torrance.htm. Torrance says a friend related the tale to him.
8. Eleanor Drorbaugh interview with Jamie Sayen, in Sayen, 64, 74.
9. Sayen, 69; Bucky, 111; Fölsing, 732.
10. "Had Pronounced Sense of Humor," *New York Times*, Dec. 22, 1936.
11. Brian 1996, 265.
12. Abraham Flexner to Einstein, Oct. 13, 1933, in Regis, 34.
13. "Einstein, the Immortal, Shows Human Side," (Newark) *Sunday Ledger*, Nov. 12, 1933.
14. Abraham Flexner to Elsa Einstein, Nov. 14, 1933, AEA 38-055.
15. Abraham Flexner to Elsa Einstein, Nov. 15, 1933, AEA 38-059. Flexner also wrote to Herbert Maass, an Institute trustee, on Nov. 14, 1933: "I am beginning to weary a little of this daily necessity of 'sitting down' on Einstein and his wife. They do not know America. They are the merest children, and they are extremely difficult to advise and control. You have no idea the barrage of publicity I have intercepted." Batterson, 152.
16. Abraham Flexner to Einstein, Nov. 15, 1933, AEA 38-061.
17. "Fiddling for Friends," *Time*, Jan. 29, 1934; "Einstein in Debut as Violinist Here," *New York Times*, Jan. 18, 1934.
18. Stephen Wise to Judge Julian Mack, Oct. 20, 1933.
19. Col. Marvin MacIntyre report to the White House Social Bureau, Dec. 7, 1933, AEA 33-131; Abraham Flexner to Franklin Roosevelt, Nov. 3, 1933; Einstein to Eleanor Roosevelt, Nov. 21, 1933, AEA 33-129; Eleanor Roosevelt to Einstein, Dec. 4, 1933, AEA 33-130; Elsa Einstein to Eleanor Roosevelt, Jan. 16, 1934, AEA 33-132; Einstein to Queen Elisabeth of Belgium, Jan. 25, 1934, AEA 33-134; "Einstein Chats about Sea," *New York Times*, Jan. 26, 1934.
20. Einstein to Board of Trustees of the IAS, Dec. 1–31, 1933.
21. Johanna Fantova, Journal of conversations with Einstein, Jan. 23, 1954, in Calaprice, 354.

22. Einstein to Max Born, Mar. 22, 1934; Erwin Schrödinger to Frederick Lindemann, Mar. 29, 1934, Jan. 22, 1935.

23. Einstein to Queen Elisabeth of Belgium, Nov. 20, 1933, AEA 32-369. The line is usually translated as "puny demigods on stilts." The word Einstein uses, *stelzbeinig*, means stiff-legged, *as if* the legs were wooden stilts. It has nothing to do with height. Instead, it evokes the gait of a peacock.

24. Einstein, "The Negro Question," *Pageant*, Jan. 1946. In this essay, he was juxtaposing the generally democratic social tendency of Americans to the way they treated blacks. That became more of an issue for him than it was back in 1934, as will be noted later in this book.

25. Bucky, 45; "Einstein Farewell," *Time*, Mar. 14, 1932.

26. Vallentin, 235. See also Elsa Einstein to Hertha Einstein (wife of music historian Alfred Einstein, a distant cousin), Feb. 24, 1934, AEA 37-693: "The place is charming, altogether different from the rest of America . . . Here everything is tinged with Englishness—downright Oxford style."

27. "Einstein Cancels Trip Abroad," *New York Times*, Apr. 2, 1934.

28. Marianoff, 178. Other sources report that Ilse's ashes, or at least some of them, were brought to a cemetery in Holland, to a place chosen by the widower Rudi Kayser.

29. This entire story is from an interview given by the Blackwoods' son James to Denis Brian on Sept. 7, 1994, and is detailed in Brian 1996, 259–263.

30. Ibid. See also James Blackwood, "Einstein in the Rear-View Mirror," *Princeton History*, Nov. 1997.

31. "Einstein Inventor of Camera Device," *New York Times*, Nov. 27, 1936.

32. Bucky, 5. Bucky's book is written, in part, as a running conversation, though there are sections that actually draw from other Einstein interviews and writings.

33. Bucky, 16–21.

34. *New York Times*, Aug. 4, 1935; Brian 1996, 265, 280.

35. Vallentin, 237.

36. Brian 1996, 268.

37. Fölsing, 687; Brian 1996, 279.

38. Calaprice, 251.

39. Bucky, 25.

40. Clark, 622.

41. Pais 1982, 454.

42. Jon Blackwell, "The Genius Next Door," *The Trentonian*, www.capitalcentury.com/1933.html; Seelig 1956a, 193; Sayen, 78; Brian 1996, 330.

43. Einstein to Barbara Lee Wilson, Jan. 7, 1943, AEA 42-606; Dukas and Hoffmann, 8; "Einstein Solves Problem That Baffled Boys," *New York Times*, June 11, 1937.

44. "Einstein Gives Advice to a High School Boy," *New York Times*, Apr. 14, 1935; Sayen, 76.

45. Elsa Einstein to Leon Watters, Dec. 10, 1935, AEA 52-210.

46. Vallentin, 238.
47. Bucky, 13.
48. Einstein to Hans Albert Einstein, Jan. 4, 1937, AEA 75-926.
49. Hoffmann 1972, 231.
50. Einstein, "Lens-like Action of a Star by Deviation of Light in the Gravitational Field," *Science* (Dec. 1936); Einstein with Nathan Rosen, "On Gravitational Waves," *Journal of the Franklin Institute* (Jan. 1937). The gravitational wave paper was originally submitted to *Physical Review*. Editors there sent it to a referee, who noted flaws. Einstein was outraged, withdrew the paper, and had it published instead by the Franklin Institute. He then realized he was wrong after all (after the anonymous referee indirectly let him know), and he and Rosen juggled many modifications, just as Elsa was dying. Daniel Kinneflick uncovered the details of this saga and provides a fascinating acount in "Einstein versus the Physical Review," *Physics Today* (Sept. 2005).
51. Einstein to Max Born, Feb. 1937, in Born 2005, 128.
52. Einstein, "The Causes of the Formation of Meanders in the Courses of Rivers and of the So-Called Baer's Law," Jan. 7, 1926.
53. "Dr. Einstein Welcomes Son to America," *New York Times*, Oct. 13, 1937.
54. Bucky, 107.
55. Einstein to Mileva Marić, Dec. 21, 1937, AEA 75-938.
56. Einstein to Frieda Einstein, Apr. 11, 1937, AEA 75-929.
57. Robert Ettema and Cornelia F. Mutel, "Hans Albert Einstein in South Carolina," *Water Resources and Environmental History*, June 27, 2004; "Einstein's Son Asks Citizenship," *New York Times*, Dec. 22, 1938. He applied for citizenship on Dec. 21, 1938, at the U.S. District Court in Greenville, S.C. Some biographies have him living in Greensboro, N.C., at the time, but that is incorrect.
58. Einstein to Hans Albert and Frieda Einstein, Jan. 1939; James Shannon, "Einstein in Greenville," *The Beat* (Greenville, S.C.), Nov. 17, 2001.
59. Highfield and Carter, 242.
60. "Hitler Is 'Greatest' in Princeton Poll: Freshmen Put Einstein Second and Chamberlain Third," *New York Times*, Nov. 28, 1939. The story reports that this was for the second year in a row.
61. *Collier's*, Nov. 26, 1938; Einstein 1954, 191.
62. Sayen, 344; "Einstein Fiddles," *Time*, Feb. 3, 1941. *Time* reported of a little concert in Princeton for the American Friends Service Committee: "Einstein proved that he could play a slow melody with feeling, turn a trill with elegance, jigsaw on occasion. The audience applauded warmly. Fiddler Einstein smiled his broad and gentle smile, glanced at his watch in fourth-dimensional worriment, played his encore, peered at the watch again, retired."
63. Jerome, 77.
64. Einstein to Isaac Don Levine, Dec. 10, 1934, AEA 50-928; Isaac Don Levine, *Eyewitness to History* (New York: Hawthorne, 1973), 171.

65. Sidney Hook to Einstein, Feb. 22, 1937, AEA 34-731; Einstein to Sidney Hook, Feb. 23, 1937, AEA 34-735.
66. Sidney Hook, "My Running Debate with Einstein," *Commentary*, July 1982, 39.

CHAPTER TWENTY: QUANTUM ENTANGLEMENT

1. Hoffmann 1972, 190; Rigden, 144; Léon Rosenfeld, "Niels Bohr in the Thirties," in Rozental 1967, 127; N. P. Landsman, "When Champions Meet: Rethinking the Bohr–Einstein Debate," *Studies in the History and Science of Modern Physics* 37 (Mar. 2006): 212.
2. Einstein 1949b, 85.
3. Ibid.
4. Einstein to Max Born, Mar. 3, 1947, in Born 2005, 155 (not in AEA).
5. Einstein to Erwin Schrödinger, June 19, 1935, AEA 22-47.
6. *New York Times*, May 4 and 7, 1935; David Mermin, "My Life with Einstein," *Physics Today* (Jan. 2005).
7. Albert Einstein, Boris Podolsky, and Nathan Rosen, "Can Quantum-Mechanical Description of Physical Reality Be Regarded as Complete?," *Physical Review*, May 15, 1935 (received Mar. 25, 1935); www.drchinese .com/David/EPR.pdf.
8. Another formulation of the experiment would be for one observer to measure the position of a particle while at the "same moment" another observer measures the momentum of its twin. Then they compare notes and, supposedly, know the position and momentum of both particles. See Charles Seife, "The True and the Absurd," in Brockman, 71.
9. Aczel 2002, 117.
10. Whitaker, 229; Aczel 2002, 118.
11. Niels Bohr, "Can Quantum-Mechanical Description of Physical Reality Be Regarded as Complete?," *Physical Review*, Oct. 15, 1935 (received July 13, 1935).
12. Greene 2004, 102. Note that Arthur Fine says that the synopsis of EPR used by Bohr "is closer to a caricature of the EPR paper than it is to a serious reconstruction." Fine says that Bohr and other interpreters of Einstein feature a "criterion of reality" that Einstein in his own later writings on EPR does not feature, even though the EPR paper as written by Podolsky does talk about determining "an element of reality." Brian Greene's book is among those that do emphasize the "criterion of reality" element. See Arthur Fine, "The Einstein-Podolsky-Rosen Argument in Quantum Theory," *Stanford Encyclopedia of Philosophy*, plato.stanford.edu/entries/qt-epr/, and also: Fine 1996, chapter 3; Mara Beller and Arthur Fine, "Bohr's Response to EPR," in Jann Faye and Henry Folse, eds., *Niels Bohr and Contemporary Philosophy* (Dordrecht: Kluwer Academic, 1994), 1–31.
13. Arthur Fine has shown that Einstein's own critique of quantum mechanics

was not fully captured in the way that Podolsky wrote in the EPR paper, and especially in the way that Bohr and the "victors" described it. Don Howard has built on Fine's work and emphasized the issues of "separability" and "locality." See Howard 1990b.

14. Einstein to Erwin Schrödinger, May 31, 1928, AEA 22-22; Fine, 18.
15. Erwin Schrödinger to Einstein, June 7, 1935, AEA 22-45, and July 13, 1935, AEA 22-48.
16. Einstein to Erwin Schrödinger, June 19, 1935, AEA 22-47.
17. Erwin Schrödinger, "The Present Situation in Quantum Mechanics," third installment, Dec. 13, 1935, www.tu-harburg.de/rzt/rzt/it/QM/cat.html.
18. More specifically, Schrödinger's equation shows the rate of change over time of the mathematical formulation of the probabilities for the outcome of possible measurements made on a particle or system.
19. Einstein to Erwin Schrödinger, June 19, 1935, AEA 22-47.
20. I am grateful to Craig Copi and Douglas Stone for helping to compose this section.
21. Einstein to Erwin Schrödinger, Aug. 8, 1935, AEA 22-49; Arthur Fine, "The Einstein-Podolsky-Rosen Argument in Quantum Theory," *Stanford Encyclopedia of Philosophy*, plato.stanford.edu/entries/qt-epr/. Note that Arthur Fine uncovered some of the Einstein-Schrödinger correspondence. Fine, chapter 3.
22. Erwin Schrödinger to Einstein, Aug. 19, 1935, AEA 22-51.
23. Erwin Schrödinger, "The Present Situation in Quantum Mechanics," Nov. 29, 1935, www.tu-harburg.de/rzt/rzt/it/QM/cat.html.
24. Einstein to Erwin Schrödinger, Sept. 4, 1935, AEA 22-53. Schrödinger's paper had not been published, but Schrödinger included its argument in his Aug. 19, 1935, letter to Einstein.
25. en.wikipedia.org/wiki/Schrodinger's_cat.
26. Einstein to Erwin Schrödinger, Dec. 22, 1950, AEA 22-174.
27. David Bohm and Basil Huey, "Einstein and Non-locality in the Quantum Theory," in Goldsmith et al., 47.
28. John Stewart Bell, "On the Einstein-Podolsky-Rosen Paradox," *Physic* 1, no. 1 (1964).
29. Bernstein 1991, 20.
30. For an explanation of how Bohm and Bell set up their analysis, see Greene 2004, 99–115; Bernstein 1991, 76.
31. Bernstein 1991, 76, 84.
32. *New York Times*, Dec. 27, 2005.
33. *New Scientist*, Jan. 11, 2006.
34. Greene 2004, 117.
35. In the decoherent-histories formulation of quantum mechanics, the coarse graining is such that the histories don't interfere with one another: if A and B are mutually exclusive histories, then the probability of A or B is the sum of the probabilities of A and of B as it should be. These "decoherent" histories form a tree-like structure, with each of the alternatives at one time branching out into alternatives at the next time, and so forth. In this theory, there is much less em-

phasis on measurement than in the Copenhagen version. Consider a piece of mica in which there are radioactive impurities emitting alpha particles. Each emitted alpha particle leaves a track in the mica. The track is real, and it makes little difference whether a physicist or other human being or a chinchilla or a cockroach comes along to look at it. What is important is that the track is correlated with the direction of emission of the alpha particle and *could be used* to measure the emission. Before the emission takes place, all directions are equally probable and contribute to a branching of histories. I am grateful to Murray Gell-Mann for his help with this section. See also Gell-Mann, 135–177; Murray Gell-Mann and James Hartle, "Quantum Mechanics in the Light of Quantum Cosmology," in W. H. Zurek, ed., *Complexity, Entropy and the Physics of Information* (Reading, Mass.: Addison-Wesley, 1990), 425–459, and "Equivalent Sets of Histories and Multiple Quasiclassical Realms," May 1996, www.arxiv.org/abs/gr-qc/9404013. This view is derived from the many-worlds interpretation pioneered in 1957 by Hugh Everett.

36. The literature on Einstein and realism is fascinating. This section relies on the works of Don Howard, Gerald Holton, Arthur I. Miller, and Jeroen van Dongen cited in the bibliography.

   Don Howard has argued that Einstein was never a true Machian nor a true realist, and that his philosophy of science did not change much over the years. "On my view, Einstein was never an ardent 'Machian' positivist, and he was never a scientific realist, at least not in the sense acquired by the term 'scientific realist' in later twentieth-century philosophical discourse. Einstein expected scientific theories to have the proper empirical credentials, but he was no positivist; and he expected scientific theories to give an account of physical reality, but he was no scientific realist. Moreover, in both respects his views remained more or less the same from the beginning to the end of his career." Howard 2004.

   Gerald Holton, on the other side, argues that Einstein underwent "a pilgrimage from a philosophy of science in which sensationalism and empiricism were at the center, to one in which the basis was a rational realism . . . For a scientist to change his philosophical beliefs so fundamentally is rare" (Holton 1973, 219, 245). See also Anton Zeilinger, "Einstein and Absolute Reality," in Brockman, 123: "Instead of accepting only concepts that can be verified by observation, Einstein insisted on the existence of a reality prior to and independent of observation."

   Arthur Fine's *The Shaky Game* explores all sides of the issue. He develops for himself what he calls a "natural ontological attitude" that is neither realist nor antirealist, but instead "mediates between the two." Of Einstein he says, "I think there is no backing away from the fact that Einstein's so-called realism has a deeply empiricist core that makes it a 'realism' more nominal than real." Fine, 130, 108.

37. Einstein to Jerome Rothstein, May 22, 1950, AEA 22-54.
38. Einstein to Donald Mackay, Apr. 26, 1948, AEA 17-9.
39. Einstein 1949b, 11.

40. Gerald Holton, "Mach, Einstein and the Search for Reality," in Holton 1973, 245. Arthur I. Miller disagrees with some of Holton's interpretation. He stresses that Einstein's point was that for something to be real it should be measurable *in principle*, even if not actually measurable in real life, and he was content using thought experiments to "measure" something. Miller 1981, 186.

41. Einstein 1949b, 81.

42. Einstein to Max Born, comments on a paper, Mar. 18, 1948, in Born 2005, 161.

43. Einstein, "The Fundamentals of Theoretical Physics," *Science*, May 24, 1940; Einstein 1954, 334.

44. For example, Arthur Fine argues, "Causality and observer-independence were *primary* features of Einstein's realism, whereas a space/time representation was an important but *secondary* feature." Fine, 103.

45. Einstein, "Physics, Philosophy and Scientific Progress," *Journal of the International College of Surgeons* 14 (1950), AEA 1-163; Fine, 98.

46. Einstein, "Physics and Reality," *Journal of the Franklin Institute* (Mar. 1936), in Einstein 1954, 292. Gerald Holton says that this is more properly translated: "The eternally incomprehensible thing about the world is its comprehensibility"; see Holton, "What Precisely Is Thinking?," in French, 161.

47. Einstein to Maurice Solovine, Mar. 30, 1952, in Solovine, 131 (not in AEA).

48. Einstein to Maurice Solovine, Jan. 1, 1951, in Solovine, 119.

49. Einstein to Max Born, Sept. 7, 1944, in Born 2005, 146, and AEA 8-207.

50. Born 2005, 69. He put Einstein in the category of "conservative individuals who were unable to free their minds from the prevailing philosophical prejudices."

51. Einstein to Maurice Solovine, Apr. 10, 1938, in Solovine, 85.

52. Einstein and Infeld, 296.

53. Ibid., 241.

54. Born 2005, 118, 122.

55. Brian 1996, 289.

56. Hoffmann 1972, 231.

57. Regis, 35.

58. Leopold Infeld, *Quest* (New York: Chelsea, 1980), 309.

59. Brian 1996, 303.

60. Infeld, introduction to the 1960 edition of Einstein and Infeld; Infeld, 112–114.

61. Pais 1982, 23.

62. Vladimir Pavlovich Vizgin, *Unified Field Theories in the First Third of the 20th Century* (Basel: Birkhäuser, 1994), 218. Matthew 19:6, King James Version: "What therefore God hath joined together, let not man put asunder."

63. Einstein to Max von Laue, Mar. 23, 1934, AEA 16-101.

64. From Whitrow, xii: "Einstein agreed that the chance of success was very small but the attempt must be made. He himself had established his name; his position was assured, so he could afford to take the risk of failure. A young man

with his way to make in the world could not afford to take a risk by which he might lose a great career, so Einstein felt that in this matter he had a duty."

65. Hoffmann 1972, 227.
66. Arthur I. Miller, "A Thing of Beauty," *New Scientist*, Feb. 4, 2006.
67. Einstein to Maurice Solovine, June 27, 1938. See also Einstein to Maurice Solovine, Dec. 23, 1938, AEA 21-236: "I have come across a wonderful subject which I am studying enthusiastically with two young colleagues. It offers the possibility of destroying the statistical basis of physics, which I have always found intolerable. This extension of the general theory of relativity is of very great logical simplicity."
68. William Laurence, "Einstein in Vast New Theory Links Atoms and Stars in Unified System," *New York Times*, July 5, 1935; William Laurence, "Einstein Sees Key to Universe Near," *New York Times*, Mar. 14, 1939.
69. Hoffmann 1972, 227; Bernstein 1991, 157.
70. William Laurence, "Einstein Baffled by Cosmos Riddle," *New York Times*, May 16, 1940.
71. Fölsing, 704.
72. *Pittsburgh Post-Gazette*, Dec. 29, 1934.
73. William Laurence, "Einstein Sees Key to Universe Near," *New York Times*, Mar. 14, 1939.

CHAPTER TWENTY-ONE: THE BOMB

1. FBI interview with Einstein regarding Leó Szilárd, Nov. 1, 1940, obtained by Gene Dannen under the Freedom of Information Act, www.dannen.com/ein stein.html. It is ironic that the FBI had such an extensive and friendly interview with Einstein to check out Szilárd's worthiness for a security clearance, because Einstein had been denied such a clearance himself. See also Gene Dannen, "The Einstein-Szilárd Refrigerators," *Scientific American* (Jan. 1997).
2. Recollections of Chuck Rothman, son of David Rothman, www.sff.net/peo ple/rothman/einstein.htm.
3. Weart and Szilard 1978, 83–96; Brian 1996, 316.
4. An authoritative narrative is in Rhodes, 304–308.
5. See Kati Marton, *The Great Escape: Nine Hungarians Who Fled Hitler and Changed the World* (New York: Simon & Schuster, 2006).
6. Leó Szilárd to Einstein, July 19, 1933, AEA 76-532.
7. Some popular accounts suggest that Einstein merely signed a letter that Szilárd wrote and brought with him. Along these lines, Teller told the writer Ronald W. Clark in 1969 that Einstein had signed, with "very little comment," a letter that Szilárd and Teller had brought that day. See Clark, 673. This is contradicted, however, by Szilárd's own detailed description of that day and the notes of the conversation made by Teller that day. The notes and new draft letter in German as dictated by Einstein are in the Teller archives and reprinted in Nathan and Norden, 293. It is true that the letter dictated by Ein-

stein was based on a draft Szilárd brought that day, but that was a translation of the one Einstein had dictated two weeks earlier. Some accounts, including occasional comments made later by Einstein himself, try to minimize his role and say he simply signed a letter that someone else wrote. In fact, even though Szilárd prompted and propelled the discussions, Einstein was fully involved in writing the letter that he alone signed.

8. Einstein to Franklin Roosevelt, Aug. 2, 1939. The longer version is in the Franklin Roosevelt archives in Hyde Park, New York (with a copy in AEA 33-143), the shorter one in the Szilárd archives at the University of California, San Diego.

9. Clark, 676; Einstein to Leó Szilárd, Aug. 2, 1939, AEA 39-465; Leó Szilárd to Einstein, Aug. 9, 1939, AEA 39-467; Leó Szilárd to Charles Lindbergh, Aug. 14, 1939, Szilárd papers, University of California, San Diego, box 12, folder 5.

10. Charles Lindbergh, "America and European Wars," speech, Sept. 15, 1939, www.charleslindbergh.com/pdf/9_15_39.pdf.

11. Leó Szilárd to Einstein, Sept. 27, 1933, AEA 39-471. Lindbergh later did not recall getting any letters from Szilárd.

12. Leó Szilárd to Einstein, Oct. 3, 1939, AEA 39-473.

13. Moore, 268. The Napoleon tale is clearly one that Sachs or someone garbled, as Robert Fulton did in fact work on building ships for Napoleon, including a failed submarine; see Kirkpatrick Sale, *The Fire of His Genius* (New York: Free Press, 2001), 68–73.

14. Sachs told this tale to a U.S. Senate special committee on atomic energy hearing, Nov. 27, 1945. It is recounted in most histories of the atom bomb, including Rhodes, 313–314.

15. Franklin Roosevelt to Einstein, Oct. 19, 1939, AEA 33-192.

16. Einstein to Alexander Sachs, Mar. 7, 1940, AEA 39-475.

17. Einstein to Lyman Briggs, Apr. 25, 1940, AEA 39-484.

18. Sherman Miles to J. Edgar Hoover, July 30, 1940, in the FBI files on Einstein, foia.fbi.gov/einstein/einstein1a.pdf. A good analysis and context for these files is Jerome.

19. J. Edgar Hoover to Sherman Miles, Aug. 15, 1940.

20. Einstein to Henri Barbusse, June 1, 1932, AEA 34-543. The FBI refers to this conference with a different translation of its name, the World Congress against War.

21. Jerome, 28, 295 n. 6. The Miles note is on the copy in the National Archives but not the FBI files.

22. Jerome, 40–42.

23. Einstein, "This Is My America," unpublished, summer 1944, AEA 72-758.

24. "Einstein to Take Test," *New York Times*, June 20, 1940; "Einstein Predicts Armed League," *New York Times*, June 23, 1940.

25. "Einstein Is Sworn as Citizen of U.S.," *New York Times*, Oct. 2, 1940.

26. Einstein, "This Is My America," unpublished, summer 1944, AEA 72-758.

27. Frank Aydelotte to Vannevar Bush, Dec. 19, 1941; Clark, 684.

28. Vannevar Bush to Frank Aydelotte, Dec. 30, 1941.

29. Pais 1982,12; George Gamow, "Reminiscence," in French, 29; Fölsing, 715.

30. Sayen, 150; Pais 1982, 147. The manuscripts were purchased by the Kansas City Life Insurance Co. and were subsequently donated to the Library of Congress.

31. Einstein to Niels Bohr, Dec. 12, 1944, AEA 8-95.

32. Clark, 698.

33. Einstein to Otto Stern, Dec. 26, 1944, AEA 22-240; Clark, 699–700.

34. Einstein to Franklin Roosevelt, Mar. 25, 1945, AEA 33-109.

35. Sayen, 151.

36. *Time*, July 1, 1946. The portrait was by the longtime cover artist for the magazine, Ernest Hamlin Baker.

37. *Newsweek*, Mar. 10, 1947.

38. Linus Pauling report of conversation, Nov. 16, 1954, in Calaprice, 185.

CHAPTER TWENTY-TWO: ONE-WORLDER

1. Brian 1996, 345; Helen Dukas to Alice Kahler, Aug. 8, 1945: "One of the young reporters who was a guest at the Sulzbergers from the *New York Times* came over late at night . . . Arthur Sulzberger also called constantly for a statement. But no dice." Arthur Ochs Sulzberger Sr. told me that his father, Arthur Hays Sulzberger, and uncle David summered at Saranac Lake and knew Einstein.

2. United Press interview, Sept. 14, 1945, reprinted in *New York Times*, Sept. 15, 1945.

3. Einstein to J. Robert Oppenheimer (care of a post office box in Santa Fe near Los Alamos), Sept. 29, 1945, AEA 57-294; J. Robert Oppenheimer to Einstein, Oct. 10, 1945, AEA 57-296.

4. When he realized that Oppenheimer had not written the statement he considered too timid, Einstein wrote to the scientists in Oak Ridge, Tennessee, who actually had. In the letter, he explained his thoughts about what powers a world government should and should not have. "There would be no immediate need for member nations to subordinate their own tariff and immigration legislation to the authority of world government," he said. "In fact, I believe the sole function of world government should be to have a monopoly over military power." Einstein to John Balderston and other Oak Ridge scientists, Dec. 3, 1945, AEA 56-493.

5. It is reprinted in Nathan and Norden, 347, and Einstein 1954, 118. See also Einstein, "The Way Out," in *One World or None*, Federation of Atomic Scientists, 1946, www.fas.org/oneworld/index.html. The book is an important look at the ideas of scientists at the time—including Einstein, Oppenheimer, Szilárd, Wigner, and Bohr—on how to use world federalism to control nuclear arms.

6. Einstein realized there was no lasting "secret" of the bomb to protect. As he said later, "America has temporary superiority in armament, but it is certain that we have no lasting secret. What nature tells one group of men, she will tell

in time to any other group." Einstein, "The Real Problem Is in the Hearts of Men," *New York Times Magazine*, June 23, 1946.

7. Einstein, remarks at the Nobel Prize dinner, Hotel Astor, Dec. 10, 1945, in Einstein 1954, 115.

8. Einstein, ECAS fund-raising telegram, May 23, 1946. Material relating to this is in folder 40-11 of the Einstein archives. The history and archives of the ECAS can be found through www.aip.org/history/ead/chicago_ecas/20010108_content.html#top.

9. Einstein, ECAS letter, Jan. 22, 1947, AEA 40-606; Sayen, 213.

10. *Newsweek*, Mar. 10, 1947.

11. Richard Present to Einstein, Jan. 30, 1946, AEA 57-147.

12. Einstein to Dr. J. J. Nickson, May 23, 1946, AEA 57-150; Einstein to Louis B. Mayer, June 24, 1946, AEA 57-152.

13. Louis B. Mayer to Einstein, July 18, 1946, AEA 57-153; James McGuinness to Louis B. Mayer, July 16, 1946, AEA 57-154.

14. Sam Marx to Einstein, July 1, 1946, AEA 57-155; Einstein to Sam Marx, July 8, 1946, AEA 57-156; Sam Marx to Einstein, July 16, 1946, AEA 57-158.

15. Einstein to Sam Marx, July 19, 1946, AEA 57-162; Leó Szilárd telegram to Einstein, and Einstein note on reverse, July 27, 1946, AEA 57-163, 57-164.

16. Bosley Crowther, "Atomic Bomb Film Starts," *New York Times*, Feb. 21, 1947.

17. William Golden to George Marshall, June 9, 1947, Foreign Relations of the U.S.; Sayen, 196.

18. Halsman's quote from Einstein, recounted by Halsman's widow, is in *Time*'s Person of the Century issue, Dec. 31, 1999, which has the portrait he took (shown on p. 487) as the cover.

19. Einstein comment on the animated antiwar film, *Where Will You Hide?*, May 1948, AEA 28-817.

20. Einstein interview with Alfred Werner, *Liberal Judaism*, Apr.–May 1949.

21. Norman Cousins, "As 1960 Sees Us," *Saturday Review*, Aug. 5, 1950; Einstein to Norman Cousins, Aug. 2, 1950, AEA 49-453. (A weekly magazine is actually published one week earlier than it is dated.)

22. Einstein talk (via radio) to the Jewish Council for Russian War Relief, Oct. 25, 1942, AEA 28-571. See also, among many examples, Einstein unsent message regarding the May-Johnson Bill, Jan. 1946; in Nathan and Norden, 342; broadcast interview, July 17, 1947, in Nathan and Norden, 418.

23. "Rankin Denies Einstein A-Bomb Role," United Press, Feb. 14, 1950.

24. Einstein to Sidney Hook, Apr. 3, 1948, AEA 58-300; Sidney Hook, "My Running Debate with Einstein," *Commentary* (July 1982).

25. Einstein to Sidney Hook, May 16, 1950, AEA 59-1018.

26. "Dr. Einstein's Mistaken Notions," in *New Times* (Moscow), Nov. 1947, in Nathan and Norden, 443, and Einstein 1954, 134.

27. Einstein, Reply to the Russian Scientists, *Bulletin of Atomic Scientists* (the publication of the Emergency Committee that he chaired), Feb. 1948, in Einstein 1954, 135; "Einstein Hits Soviet Scientists for Opposing World Government," *New York Times*, Jan. 30, 1948.

28. Einstein, "Atomic War or Peace," part 2, *Atlantic Monthly*, Nov. 1947.

29. Einstein to Henry Usborne, Jan. 9, 1948, AEA 58-922.

30. Einstein to James Allen, Dec. 22, 1949, AEA 57-620.

31. Otto Nathan contributed to this phenomenon with the 1960 book of excerpts he coedited from Einstein's political writings, *Einstein on Peace*. Nathan, as the coexecutor with Helen Dukas of Einstein's literary estate, had a lot of influence over what was published early on. He was a committed socialist and pacifist. His collection is valuable, but in searching through the full Einstein archives, it becomes noticeable that he tended to leave out some material in which Einstein was critical of Russia or of radical pacifism. David E. Rowe and Robert Schulmann, in their own anthology of Einstein's political writings published in 2007, *Einstein's Political World*, provide a counterbalance. They stress that Einstein "was not tempted to give up free enterprise in favor of a rigidly planned economy, least of all at the price of basic freedoms," and they also emphasize the realistic and practical nature of Einstein's evolution away from pure pacifism.

32. Einstein to Arthur Squires and Cuthbert Daniel, Dec. 15, 1947, AEA 58-89.

33. Einstein to Roy Kepler, Aug. 8, 1948, AEA 58-969.

34. Einstein to John Dudzik, Mar. 8, 1948, AEA 58-108. See also Einstein to A. Amery, June 12, 1950, AEA 59-95: "However much I may believe in the necessity of socialism, it will not solve the problem of international security."

35. "Poles Issue Message by Einstein: He Reveals Quite Different Text," *New York Times*, Aug. 29, 1948; Einstein to Julian Huxley, Sept. 14, 1948, AEA 58-700; Nathan and Norden, 493.

36. Einstein to A. J. Muste, Jan. 30, 1950, AEA 60- 636.

37. *Today with Mrs. Roosevelt*, NBC, Jan. 12, 1950, www.cine-holocaust.de/cgi-bin/gdq?efw00fbw002802.gd; *New York Post*, Feb. 13, 1950.

38. D. M. Ladd to J. Edgar Hoover, Feb. 15, 1950, and V. P. Keay to H. B. Fletcher, Feb. 13, 1950, both in Einstein's FBI files, box 1a, foia.fbi.gov/foiaindex/einstein.htm. Fred Jerome's book *The Einstein File* offers an analysis. Jerome says that when making Einstein the Person of the Century, *Time* refrained from noting that he was a socialist: "As if the executives at *Time* decided to go so far but no farther, their article makes no mention of Einstein's socialist convictions." As the person who was the magazine's managing editor then, I can attest that the omission may indeed have been a lapse on our part, but it was not the result of a policy decision.

39. Gen. John Weckerling to J. Edgar Hoover, July 31, 1950, Einstein FBI files, box 2a.

40. See foia.fbi.gov/foiaindex/einstein.htm. Herb Romerstein and Eric Breindel in *The Venona Secrets* (New York: Regnery, 2000), an attack on Soviet espionage based on the "Venona" secret cables sent by Russian agents in the United States, have a section called "Duping Albert Einstein" (p. 398). It says that he was regularly willing to be listed as the "honorary chairman" of a variety of groups that were fronts for pro-Soviet agendas, but the authors say there is no evidence that he ever went to communist meetings or did anything other than

lend his name to various worthy-sounding organizations, with names like "Workers International Relief," that occasionally were part of the "front apparatus" of international Comintern leaders.

41. Marjorie Bishop, "Our Neighbors on Eighth Street," and Maria Turbow Lampard, introduction, in Sergei Konenkov, *The Uncommon Vision* (New Brunswick, N.J.: Rutgers University Press, 2000), 52–54, 192–195.

42. Pavel Sudoplatov, *Special Tasks*, updated ed. (Boston: Back Bay, 1995), appendix 8, p. 493; Jerome, 260, 283; Sotheby's catalogue, June 26, 1988; Robin Pogrebin, "Love Letters by Einstein at Auction," *New York Times*, June 1, 1998. The role of Konenkova has been confirmed by other sources.

43. Einstein to Margarita Konenkova, Nov. 27, 1945, June 1, 1946, uncatalogued.

44. Einstein, "Why Socialism?," *Monthly Review*, May 1949, reprinted in Einstein 1954, 151.

45. *Princeton Herald*, Sept. 25, 1942, in Sayen, 219.

46. Einstein, "The Negro Question," *Pageant*, Jan. 1946, in Einstein 1950a, 132.

47. Jerome, 71; Jerome and Taylor, 88–91; "Einstein Is Honored by Lincoln University," *New York Times*, May 4, 1946.

48. Einstein, "To the Heroes of the Warsaw Ghetto," 1944, in Einstein 1950a, 265.

49. Einstein to James Franck, Dec. 6, 1945, AEA 11-60; Einstein to James Franck, Dec. 30, 1945, AEA 11-64.

50. Einstein to Verlag Vieweg, Mar. 25, 1947, AEA 42-172; Einstein to Otto Hahn, Jan. 28, 1949, AEA 12-72.

51. Brian 1996, 340; Milton Wexler to Einstein, Sept. 17, 1944, AEA 55-48; Roberto Einstein (cousin) to Einstein, Nov. 27, 1944, AEA 55-49.

52. Einstein to Clara Jacobson, May 7, 1945, AEA 56-900.

53. Sayen, 219.

CHAPTER TWENTY-THREE: LANDMARK

1. Seelig 1956b, 71.

2. Pais 1982, 473.

3. See Bird and Sherwin.

4. J. Robert Oppenheimer to Frank Oppenheimer, Jan. 11, 1935, in Alice Smith and Charles Weiner, eds., *Robert Oppenheimer: Letters and Recollections* (Cambridge, Mass.: Harvard University Press, 1980), 190.

5. Sayen, 225; J. Robert Oppenheimer, "On Albert Einstein," *New York Review of Books*, Mar. 17, 1966.

6. Jim Holt, "Time Bandits," *New Yorker*, Feb. 28, 2005; Yourgrau 1999, 2005; Goldstein. Yourgrau 2005, 3, discusses the connections of incompleteness, relativity, and uncertainty to the zeitgeist. Holt's piece explains the insights they shared.

7. Goldstein, 232 n. 8, says that, alas, various research efforts have failed to discover the precise flaw Gödel thought he had discovered.

8. Kurt Gödel, "Relativity and Idealistic Philosophy," in Schilpp, 558.

9. Yourgrau 2005, 116.

10. Einstein, "Reply to Criticisms," in Schilpp, 687–688.

11. Einstein to Han Muehsam, June 15, 1942, AEA 38-337.

12. Hoffmann 1972, 240.

13. Einstein 1949b, 33.

14. Einstein and Wolfgang Pauli, "Non-Existence of Regular Solutions of Relativistic Field Equations," 1943.

15. Einstein and Valentine Bargmann, "Bivector Fields," 1944. He is sometimes referred to as Valentin, but in America he signed his name Valentine.

16. Einstein to Erwin Schrödinger, Jan. 22, 1946, AEA 22-93.

17. Erwin Schrödinger to Einstein, Feb. 19, 1946, AEA 22-94; Einstein to Erwin Schrödinger, Apr. 7, 1946, AEA 22-103; Einstein to Erwin Schrödinger, May 20, 1946, AEA 22-106; Einstein, "Generalized Theory of Gravitation," 1948, with subsequent addenda.

18. Einstein, *The Meaning of Relativity*, 1950 ed., appendix 2, revised again for the 1954 ed.; William Laurence, "New Theory Gives a Master Key to the Universe," *New York Times*, Dec. 27, 1949; William Laurence, "Einstein Publishes His Master Theory: Long-Awaited Chapter to Relativity Volume Is Product of 30 Years of Labor; Revised at Last Minute," *New York Times*, Feb. 15, 1950.

19. Einstein to Maurice Solovine, Nov. 25, 1948, AEA 21-256; Einstein to Maurice Solovine, Mar. 28, 1949, AEA 21-260; Einstein to Maurice Solovine, Feb. 12, 1951, AEA 21-277.

20. Tilman Sauer, "Dimensions of Einstein's Unified Field Theory Program," courtesy of the author; Hoffmann 1972, 239; I am grateful for the help of Sauer, who is doing research in Einstein's late work on field theories.

21. Whitrow, xii.

22. Niels Bohr, "Discussion with Einstein," in Schilpp, 199.

23. Abraham Pais, in Rozental 1967, 225; Clark, 742.

24. John Wheeler, "Memoir," in French, 21; John Wheeler, "Mentor and Sounding Board," in Brockman, 31; Einstein quoted in Johanna Fantova journal, Nov. 11, 1953. In letters to Besso in 1952, Einstein defended his stubbornness. He insisted that a complete description of nature would describe reality, or a "deterministic real state," rather than merely describe observations. "The orthodox quantum theoreticians generally refuse to admit the notion of a real state (based on positivist considerations). One thus ends up with a situation that resembles that of the good Bishop Berkeley." Einstein to Michele Besso, Sept. 10, 1952, AEA 7-412. A month later he noted that quantum theory declared that "laws don't apply to things, but only to what observation informs us about things . . . Now, I can't accept that." Einstein to Michele Besso, Oct. 8, 1952, AEA 7-414.

25. Einstein to Mileva Marić, Dec. 22, 1946, AEA 75-845.

26. Fölsing, 731; Highfield and Carter, 253; Brian 1996, 371; Einstein to Karl Zürcher, July 29, 1947.

27. Einstein to Hans Albert Einstein, Jan. 21, 1948, AEA 75-959.

28. Einstein to Carl Seelig, Jan. 4, 1954, AEA 39-59; Fölsing, 731.

29. Sayen, 221; Pais 1982, 475.

30. *Sarasota Tribune,* Mar. 2, 1949, AEA 30-1097; Bucky, 131. Jeremy Bernstein writes, "Anyone who spent five minutes with Miss Dukas would understand what a lunatic accusation this is." Bernstein 2001, 109.

31. Hans Albert Einstein interview, in Whitrow, 22.

32. "Trouble is brewing between Maja and Paul. They ought to divorce as well. Paul is supposedly having an affair and the marriage is quite in pieces. One shouldn't wait too long (as I did) . . . No mixed marriages are any good (Anna says: oh!)." Einstein to Michele Besso, Dec. 12, 1919. The half-joking reference to Anna was about Anna Winteler Besso, who was Michele Besso's wife and Paul Winteler's sister. The Wintelers were not Jewish; Besso and the Einsteins were.

33. Highfield and Carter, 248.

34. Einstein to Solovine, Nov. 25, 1948, AEA 21-256; Sayen, 134.

35. Einstein to Lina Kocherthaler, July 27, 1951, AEA 38-303; Sayen, 231.

36. "Einstein Repudiates Biography Written by His Ex-Son-in-Law," *New York Times,* Aug. 5, 1944; Frieda Bucky, "You Have to Ask Forgiveness," *Jewish Quarterly* (winter 1967–68), AEA 37-513.

37. "Einstein Extolled by 300 Scientists," *New York Times,* Mar. 20, 1949; Sayen, 227; Fölsing, 735.

38. Einstein to Queen Mother Elisabeth of Belgium, Jan. 6, 1951, AEA 32-400; Sayen, 139.

39. Einstein to Max Born, Apr. 12, 1949, AEA 8-223.

40. "3,000 Hear Einstein at Seder Service," *New York Times,* Apr. 18, 1938; Einstein, "Our Debt to Zionism," in Einstein 1954, 190.

41. "Einstein Condemns Rule in Palestine," *New York Times,* Jan. 12, 1946; Sayen, 235–237; Stephen Wise to Einstein, Jan. 14, 1946, AEA 35-258; Einstein to Stephen Wise, Jan. 14, 1946, AEA 35-260.

42. "Einstein Statement Assails Begin Party," *New York Times,* Dec. 3, 1948; "Einstein Is Assailed by Menachim Begin," *New York Times,* Dec. 7, 1948.

43. Einstein to Hans Muehsam, Jan. 22, 1947, AEA 38-360, and Sept. 24, 1948, AEA 38-379.

44. Einstein to Lina Kocherthaler, May 4, 1948, AEA 38-302.

45. Dukas interview, in Sayen, 245; Abba Eban to Einstein, Nov. 17, 1952, AEA 41-84; Einstein to Abba Eban, Nov. 18, 1952, AEA 28-943.

46. Einstein's travails with Hebrew University are recounted in Parzen 1974. For his relationship with Brandeis, see Abram Sacher, *Brandeis University* (Waltham, Mass.: Brandeis University Press, 1995), 22. The one place with which he had a great relationship was Yeshiva University. He was made the honorary chair of the fund-raising drive to build the College of Medicine there in 1952, and the following year allowed the medical college to be named after him. I am grateful to Edward Burns for providing information. See www.yu.edu/libraries/digital_library/einstein/panel10.html.

47. Einstein to *Maariv* newspaper editor Azriel Carlebach, Nov. 21, 1952, AEA 41-93; Sayen, 247; Nathan and Norden, 574; Einstein to Joseph Scharl, Nov. 24, 1952, AEA 41-107.

48. Yitzhak Navon, "On Einstein and the Presidency of Israel," in Holton and Elkana, 295.

CHAPTER TWENTY-FOUR: RED SCARE

1. Einstein to Queen Mother Elisabeth of Belgium, Jan. 6, 1951, AEA 32-400.
2. Einstein to Leopold Infeld, Oct. 28, 1952, AEA 14-173; Einstein to Russian students in Berlin, Apr. 1, 1952, AEA 59-218.
3. Einstein to T. E. Naiton, Oct. 9, 1952, AEA 60-664.
4. Einstein to Judge Irving Kaufman, Dec. 23, 1952, AEA 41-547.
5. Newark FBI Field Office to J. Edgar Hoover, Apr. 22, 1953, in Einstein FBI files, box 7.
6. Einstein to Harry Truman, with fifteen lines of equations on the other side, Jan. 11, 1953, AEA 41-551.
7. *New York Times*, Jan. 13, 1953.
8. Marian Rawles to Einstein, Jan. 14, 1953, AEA 41-629; Charles Williams to Einstein, Jan. 17, 1953, AEA 41-651; Homer Greene to Einstein, Jan. 15, 1953, AEA 41-588; Joseph Heidt to Einstein, Jan. 13, 1953, AEA 41-589.
9. Einstein to William Douglas, June 23, 1953, AEA 41-576; William Douglas to Einstein, June 30, 1953, AEA 41-577.
10. Generosa Pope Jr. to Einstein, Jan. 15, 1953, AEA 41-625; Daniel James to Einstein, Jan. 14, 1953, AEA 41-614.
11. Einstein to Daniel James, Jan. 15, 1953, AEA 60-696; *New York Times*, Jan. 22, 1953.
12. Einstein, Acceptance of the Lord & Taylor Award, May 4, 1953, AEA 28-979. In a letter to Dick Kluger, then a student editor of *The Daily Princetonian*, he wrote: "As long as a person has not violated the 'social contract' nobody has the right to inquire about his or her convictions. If this principal is not followed free intellectual development is not possible." Einstein to Dick Kluger, Sept. 17, 1953, in Kluger's possession.
13. Einstein to William Frauenglass, May 16, 1953, AEA 41-112; "Refuse to Testify Einstein Advises," *New York Times*, June 12, 1953; *Time*, June 22, 1953.
14. All of these editorials ran on June 13, 1953, except the Chicago editorial, which ran on June 15.
15. Sam Epkin to Einstein, June 15, 1953, AEA 41-409; Victor Lasky to Einstein, June 1953, AEA 41-441; George Stringfellow to Einstein, June 15, 1953, AEA 41-470.
16. *New York Times*, June 14, 1953.
17. Bertrand Russell to *New York Times*, June 26, 1953; Einstein to Bertrand Russell, June 28, 1953, AEA 33-195.
18. Abraham Flexner to Einstein, June 12, 1953, AEA 41-174; Shepherd Baum to Einstein, June 17, 1953, AEA 41-202.
19. Richard Frauenglass to Einstein, June 20, 1953, AEA 41-181.
20. Sarah Shadowitz, "Albert Shadowitz," *Globe and Mail* (Toronto), May 26, 2004. The author is the subject's daughter.

21. Sayen, 273–276; Permanent Subcommittee on Investigations, Committee on Government Operations, "Testimony of Albert Shadowitz," Dec. 14, 1953, and "Report on the Proceedings against Albert Shadowitz for Contempt of the Senate," July 16, 1954; Albert Shadowitz to Einstein, Dec. 14, 1953, AEA 41-659; Einstein to Albert Shadowitz, Dec. 15, 1953, AEA 41-660. Shadowitz was cleared in July 1955, two years after his testimony, after the fall of McCarthy.
22. Jerome and Taylor, 120–121.
23. Bird and Sherwin, 133, 495.
24. Ibid., 495.
25. James Reston, "Dr. Oppenheimer Suspended by A.E.C. in Security Review," *New York Times*, Apr. 13, 1954. On Sunday, Apr. 11, Joseph and Stewart Alsop, in their *New York Herald Tribune* column, had speculated that "leading physicists" were now a target of security investigations, but they did not mention Oppenheimer by name.
26. Pais 1982, 11; Bird and Sherwin, 502–504.
27. Johanna Fantova's journal, June 3, 16, 17, 1954, in Calaprice, 359.
28. Einstein to Herbert Lehman, May 19, 1954, AEA 6-236.
29. Johanna Fantova's journal, June 17, 1954, in Calaprice, 359.
30. Einstein to Norman Thomas, Mar. 10, 1954, AEA 61-549; Einstein to W. Stern, Jan. 14, 1954, AEA 61-470. See also Einstein to Felix Arnold, Mar. 19, 1954, AEA 59-118: "The current investigations are an incomparably greater danger to our society than those few communists in the country could ever be."
31. Johanna Fantova journal, Mar. 4, 1954, in Calaprice, 356; Einstein to Queen Mother Elisabeth of Belgium, Mar. 28, 1954, AEA 32-410.
32. Theodore White, "U.S. Science," *The Reporter*, Nov. 11, 1954. White went on to write *The Making of the President* series of books.

CHAPTER TWENTY-FIVE: THE END

1. Johanna Fantova journal, Mar. 19, 1954, in Calaprice, 356.
2. Einstein eulogy for Rudolf Ladenberg, Apr. 1, 1952, AEA 5-160.
3. Einstein to Jakob Ehrat, May 12, 1952, AEA 59-554; Einstein to Ernesta Marangoni, Oct. 1, 1952, AEA 60-406; Einstein to Queen Mother Elisabeth of Belgium, Jan. 12, 1953, AEA 32-405.
4. Einstein interview with Lili Foldes, *The Etude*, Jan. 1947; Calaprice, 150. Information about his repeated playing of this record was given to me by someone who knew Einstein in his later years.
5. Einstein to Hans Muehsam, Mar. 30, 1954, AEA 38-434.
6. Einstein to Conrad Habicht and Maurice Solovine, Apr. 3, 1953, AEA 21-294; Einstein to Maurice Solovine, Feb. 27, 1955, AEA 21-306.
7. Sayen, 294.
8. Einstein to Hans Albert Einstein, May 1, 1954, AEA 75-918.
9. Einstein to Hans Albert Einstein, unfinished letter, Dec. 28, 1954, courtesy of Bob Cohn, purchased at Christie's sale, Einstein Family Correspondence.

10. Gertrude Samuels, "Einstein, at 75, Is Still a Rebel," *New York Times Magazine*, Mar. 14, 1954.
11. Johanna Fantova journal, 1954, in Calaprice, 354–363.
12. Wolfgang Pauli to Max Born, Mar. 3, 1954, in Born 2005, 213.
13. Einstein to Michele Besso, Aug. 10, 1954, AEA 7-420.
14. Einstein to Louis de Broglie, Feb. 8, 1954, AEA 8-311.
15. Einstein 1916, final appendix to the 1954 ed., 178.
16. Bertrand Russell to Einstein, Feb. 11, 1955, AEA 33-199; Einstein to Bertrand Russell, Feb. 16, 1955, AEA 33-200.
17. Einstein to Niels Bohr, Mar. 2, 1955, AEA 33-204.
18. Bertrand Russell, "Manifesto by Scientists for Abolition of War," sent to Einstein on Apr. 5, 1955, AEA 33-209, and issued publicly July 9, 1955.
19. Einstein to Farmingdale Elementary School, Mar. 26, 1955, AEA 59-632; Alice Calaprice, ed., *Dear Professor Einstein* (New York: Prometheus, 2002), 219.
20. Einstein to Vero and Bice Besso, Mar. 21, 1955, AEA 7-245.
21. Eric Rogers, "The Equivalence Principle Demonstrated," in French, 131; I. Bernard Cohen, "An Interview with Einstein," *Scientific American* (July 1955).
22. Whitrow, 90; Einstein to Bertrand Russell, Apr. 11, 1955, AEA 33-212.
23. Einstein to Zvi Lurie, Jan. 5, 1955, AEA 60-388; Abba Eban, *An Autobiography* (New York: Random House, 1977), 191; Nathan and Norden, 640.
24. Helen Dukas, "Einstein's Last Days," AEA 39-71; Calaprice, 369; Pais 1982, 477.
25. Helen Dukas, "Einstein's Last Days," AEA 39-71; Helen Dukas to Abraham Pais, Apr. 30, 1955, in Pais 1982, 477.
26. Michelmore, 261.
27. Nathan and Norden, 640.
28. Einstein, final calculations, AEA 3-12. The final page can be viewed at www.alberteinstein.info/db/ViewImage.do?DocumentID=34430&Page=12.

EPILOGUE: EINSTEIN'S BRAIN AND EINSTEIN'S MIND

1. Michelmore, 262. Einstein's will, which was witnessed by the logician Kurt Gödel, among others, gave Helen Dukas $20,000, most of his personal belongings and books, and the income from his royalties until she died, which she did in 1982. Hans Albert received only $10,000; he died while a visiting lecturer in Woods Hole, Mass., in 1973, survived by a son and daughter. Einstein's other son, Eduard, received $15,000 to assure his continued care at the Zurich asylum, where he died in 1965. His stepdaughter Margot got $20,000 and the Mercer Street house, which was actually already in her name, and she died there in 1986. Dukas and Otto Nathan were made literary executors, and they guarded his reputation and papers so zealously that biographers and the editors of his collected papers would for years be stymied when they attempted to print anything verging on the merely personal.
2. "Einstein the Revolutionist," *New York Times*, Apr. 19, 1955; *Time*, May 2,

1955. The lead story in the extra edition of *The Daily Princetonian* was written by R. W. "Johnny" Apple, a future *Times* correspondent.

3. The weird tale has produced two fascinating books: Carolyn Abraham's *Possessing Genius*, a comprehensive account of the odyssey of Einstein's brain, and Michael Paterniti's *Driving Mr. Albert*, a delightful narrative of a ride across America with Einstein's brain in the trunk of a rented Buick. There have also been some memorable articles, including Steven Levy's "My Search for Einstein's Brain," *New Jersey Monthly*, August 1978; Gina Maranto's "The Bizarre Fate of Einstein's Brain," *Discover*, May 1985; Scott McCartney, "The Hidden Secrets of Einstein's Brain Are Still a Mystery," *Wall Street Journal*, May 5, 1994. In addition, Einstein's ophthalmologist Henry Abrams happened to wander into the autopsy room, and he ended up taking with him his former patient's eyeballs, which he subsequently kept in a New Jersey safe deposit box.

4. Abraham, 22. Abraham interviewed the grown girl in 2000.

5. "Son Asked Study of Einstein's Brain," *New York Times*, Apr. 20, 1955; Abraham, 75. Harvey had indicated that he was going to send the brain to Montefiore Medical Center in New York to oversee the studies. But as doctors there waited in anticipation, he changed his mind and decided to keep it to himself. The dispute made headlines. "Doctors Row over Brain of Dr. Einstein," reported the *Chicago Daily Tribune*. Abraham, 83, citing *Chicago Daily Tribune*, Apr. 20, 1955.

6. Levy 1978. See also www.echonyc.com/~steven/einstein.html.

7. See Abraham, 214–230, for an account of this issue.

8. Bill Toland, "Doctor Kept Einstein's Brain in Jar 43 Years: Seven Years Ago, He Got 'Tired of the Responsibility,' " *Pittsburgh Post-Gazette*, Apr. 17, 2005.

9. Marian Diamond, "On the Brain of a Scientist," *Experimental Neurology* 88 (1985); www.newhorizons.org/neuro/diamond_einstein.htm.

10. Sandra Witelson et al., "The Exceptional Brain of Albert Einstein," *Lancet*, June 19, 1999; Lawrence K. Altman, "Key to Intellect May Lie in Folds of Einstein's Brain," *New York Times*, June 18, 1999; www.fhs.mcmaster.ca/psychiatryneuroscience/faculty/witelson; Steven Pinker, "His Brain Measured Up," *New York Times*, June 24, 1999.

11. Einstein to Carl Seelig, Mar. 11, 1952, AEA 39-013. See also Bucky, 29: "I am not more gifted than anybody else. I am just more curious than the average person, and I will not give up on a problem until I have found the proper solution."

12. Seelig 1956a, 70.

13. Born 1978, 202.

14. Einstein to William Miller, quoted in *Life* magazine, May 2, 1955, in Calaprice, 261.

15. Hans Tanner, quoted in Seelig 1956a, 103.

16. André Maurois, *Illusions* (New York: Columbia University Press, 1968), 35, courtesy of Eric Motley. Perse was the pseudonym of Marie René Auguste Alexis Léger, who won the Nobel Prize for literature in 1960.

17. Newton's *Principia*, book 3; Einstein, "On the Method of Theoretical

Physics," the Herbert Spencer lecture, Oxford, June 10, 1933, in Einstein 1954, 274.

18. Clark, 649.

19. Lee Smolin, "Einstein's Lonely Path," *Discover* (Sept. 2004).

20. Einstein's foreword to Galileo Galilei, *Dialogue Concerning the Two Chief World Systems* (Berkeley: University of California Press, 2001), xv.

21. Einstein, "Freedom and Science," in Ruth Anshen, ed., *Freedom, Its Meaning* (New York: Harcourt, Brace, 1940), 92, reprinted in part in Einstein 1954, 31.

22. Einstein to Phyllis Wright, Jan. 24, 1936, AEA 52-337.

23. Einstein to Herbert S. Goldstein, Apr. 25, 1929, AEA 33-272. For a discussion of Maimonides and divine providence in Jewish thought, see Marvin Fox, *Interpreting Maimonides* (Chicago: University of Chicago Press, 1990), 229–250.

24. Banesh Hoffmann, in Harry Woolf, ed., *Some Strangeness in the Proportion* (Saddle River, N.J.: Addison-Wesley, 1980), 476.

INDEX

Page numbers in *italics* refer to illustrations.

Abraham, Max, 221, 592*n*
Abrams, Henry, 640*n*
acceleration, 108, 145–49, 155, 181–82, 188–92, 199, 201–2, 223, 319–20, 511, 548, 607*n*
"action at a distance," 319–20, 330, 346–47, 448–53, 454, 458
Adler, Friedrich, 38–39, 150–51, 156, 158–59, 163, 240
AEG, 302
affine connection, 339, 344
African-Americans, 445, 505, 531
Agriculture Department, U.S., 443–44
Albert I, King of Belgium, 415–16, 432
Albert I, Prince of Monaco, 296
Alečković, Mira, 87
algebra, 17
All Quiet on the Western Front, 372
American Association for the Advancement of Science, 136
"American Creed, The," 530–31
American Friends Service Committee, 445, 624*n*
ammonia, 206
AM radio signals, 111
Analysis of the Sensations (Mach), 81
analytic propositions, 82–83
Anderson, Marian, 445
Andromeda galaxy, 254, 353
Annalen der Physik, 57, 58, 70, 94, 102, 127, 138, 140, 190–91, 220
Antigone (Sophocles), 81

anti-Semitism, 3, 15, 30, 43, 61, 142, 149, 152, 163–64, 177, 183, 207, 269–71, 281–308, 311–12, 315, 359, 403–10, 427, 428–30, 443, 444–45, 469, 475, 505, 517, 524, 567*n*, 601*n*
"Appeal to the Cultured World" ("Manifesto of the 93") (1914), 206–7, 244
Arabs, 381, 409, 520, 541
Aristarchus, 518
Aristotle, 5
arms control, 487–95, 498, 500–501
Army, U.S., 478
Arrhenius, Svante, 310, 311, 312, 314
Aspect, Alain, 458
Associated Press, 355
Association of Manhattan Project Scientists, 491
astrology, 384
astronomy, 5, 191, 202–5, 218, 253, 254–62, 267, 269, 275–76, 311, 316, 317, 353–56
atheism, 386, 388–90, 462, 587*n*
Atlantic, 489, 497
atomic bomb, 5, 272, 382, 415, 469–76, 480–86, 489–90, 497–98, 500, 509, 525, 629*n*–32*n*
Atomic Energy Commission (AEC), 531–32
"Atomic War or Peace" (Einstein), 489–90, 497–98

atomic weight, 57

atoms:

existence of, 2, 43, 56, 57, 70, 93, 94, 95, 101, 103, 104, 140, 164, 169, 255

gas, 164, 323, 480–81

momentum and position in, 323, 346, 348–49

nucleus of, 322, 456

splitting of (nuclear fission), 469–72

structure of, 314, 321–22, 325, 345, 456

subatomic particles of, 316, 322–33, 334, 345, 352, 353, 454, 459–60, 463–64, 512, 538, 625n, 627n

Attempt at a Theory of Electrical and Optical Phenomena in Moving Bodies (Lorentz), 116–17

Austro-Hungarian Empire, 163–64

autism, 566n

Avogadro, Amedeo, 101–2

Avogadro's number, 101–3, 106

Aydelotte, Frank, 480–81

Bach, Johann Sebastian, 29, 38, 420, 472

Bad Nauheim conference (1920), 287–89

Baldwin, Roger, 380

Balfour, Arthur, 290

Ballets Russes, 280

Balthazar (Durrell), 279

Bamberger, Louis, 395, 397

Baron-Cohen, Simon, 566n

Barrow, John, 351–52

Baruch, Bernard, 474

Beethoven, Ludwig van, 29, 38, 207, 536

Begin, Menachem, 520

Beginning or the End, The, 491–93

Belgian War Resisters' Committee, 417

Belgium, 168, 471–73

Bell, John Stewart, 458

Ben-Gurion, David, *508,* 521, 523

Berkeley, George, 81, 350

Berks, Robert, 604n

Berlin, Isaiah, 278

Berlin, University of, 14, 168, 178–81, 184–89, 201, 202, 203–11, 212, 213, 215–16, 217, 218–21, 224, 227n, 228–32, 234, 236, 237, 241–42, 246–48, 249, 259, 261–62, 271, 277, 280, 281–89, 301–6, 307, 315, 318, 356–59, 362, 363, 364, 381–83, 384, 387–89, 392, 394–95, 399–401, 403, 408, 411, 471, 523, 601n

Berliner Tageblatt, 285–88, 359

Berlin Physical Society, 96

Bern, University of, 142, 144–53

Bern Clock Tower, *107,* 113, 124, 125–26

Bern Scientific Society, 438

Bernstein, Aaron, 18–19, 567n

Bernstein, Jeremy, 468, 576n

Besso, Anna Winteler, 27, 62, 231, 237, 418, 517, 540, 636n

Besso, Michele Angelo, 27, 61–62, 66, 83, 85, 101, 106, 113, 122, 126, 128, 136, 150, 151, 169, 170, 174, 184, 186, 190, 199, 200–201, 210, 211, 213, 215, 218, 221, 224, 225, 226, 227, 228, 229, 230–31, 234, 237, 239, 277, 322, 323, 334, 341, 355, 417, 418, 517, 538, 540, 576n, 591n, 636n

Bethe, Hans, 407

Bible, 20, 386, 391, 434

Bibo (Einstein's parrot), 438, 535–36

Big Bang theory, 355

Biology of War, The (Nicolai), 244

birth control, 65–66

bivector fields, 512

Bizet, Georges, 370

blackbody radiation, 68, 94–95, 96, 98, 99–100, 118, 322

black holes, 250–52

Blackwood, Caroline, 433–34

Blumenfeld, Kurt, 282, 290, 303

Bohm, David, 458, 534

Bohr, Niels:
  atomic model of, 314, 321–22, 325,
    345
  Einstein's disputes with, 269,
    324–26, 344–49, 496, 514–15,
    539, 609n
  at Institute for Advanced Study,
    514–15
  in Manhattan Project, 482–84
  Nobel Prize awarded to, 325
  photograph of, *336*
  quantum mechanics supported by,
    324–26, 332–33, 344–49, 448,
    451–52, 458, 468–69, 514–15,
    626n
  reputation of, 5, 269, 311, 330–31,
    325, 338, 407
Boltzmann, Ludwig, 33, 49, 56–57, 67,
    68, 69–72, 98
Bond, Horace, 505
Bond, Julian, 505
"border conditions," 252–54, 265–66
Born, Hedwig, 270, 286–87, 330, 331,
    372, 392, 393, 408, 429
Born, Max, 95, 100, 106, 132, 223–24,
    241–42, 253, 267, 268, 269–70,
    274, 286, 287, 288, 324, 329, 330,
    331, 334, 335, 392, 393, 408, 413,
    429, 432, 442, 448, 450, 461, 463,
    464, 519–20, 538, 539
Bose, Satyendra Nath, 327–29, 609n
Bose-Einstein condensation, 328–29,
    609n
Bose-Einstein statistics, 327–28
Boston Globe, 136
Boston Herald, 299
Brahe, Tycho, 166
Brahms, Johannes, 167
Brandeis, Louis, 298
Brandeis University, 522
Breuer, Marcel, 359–60
Briggs, Lyman, 476
Brillouin, Marcel, 313
British Association for the
    Advancement of Science, 90, 575n

Brod, Max, 166–67
Broglie, Louis de, 326–27, 330, 345,
    347, 538–39, 583n
Brown, Robert, 103, 104
Brownian motion, 68, 93, 101, 103–6,
    117, 118, 140, 351, 373, 577n
Brush, Steven, 99
Bucky, Gustav, 435, 438, 540, 544
Bucky, Peter, 435–36, 441, 443, 517
Bucky, Thomas, 379
Bush, Vannevar, 480, 481
Byland, Hans, 27–28
Byrnes, James, 484

calculus, 16, 93
California Institute of Technology
    (Caltech), 315n, 368, 373, 374,
    380–81, 395–98, 399, 401–4, 431,
    444
Calvin, John, 155
Cambridge University, 267
Canova, Antonio, 64
capillary effect, 56–58, 59, 68
capitalism, 497, 504
Carmen (Bizet), 370
Cartan, Elie Joseph, 344
Casablanca, 493
Case Western University, 300
cathode rays, 65
Catholic Church, 389
centrifugal force, 251–52
cerebral cortex, 547
Cervantes Saavedra, Miguel de, 81, 518
Chamberlain, Austen, 419–20
Chambers, Whittaker, 485
Chaplin, Charlie, *263,* 268, 373, 374,
    403, 427
chemical weapons, 206
Chicago Daily Tribune, 528
Chicago Herald and Examiner, 296
Chicago Tribune, 296–97
Chico (Einstein's terrier), 438
chlorine gas, 206
Chopin, Frédéric, 365
Christian Science, 444

Christoffel van de Hulst, Hendrik, 215
Churchill, Winston, *394,* 412, 419, 483
City Lights, 263, 374
civil rights movement, 505, 531
Civil War, U.S., 488–89
Cohen, I. Bernard, 540–41
Cohn, Roy, 530
cold war, 499–500, 504
Collier's, 445
Columbia University, 370, 471
communism, 287, 379–80, 399–401,
    403, 420–21, 445–47, 478,
    489–90, 494–503, 524–34, 550,
    633n–34n
compasses, 13, 67, 462, 538, 548
complementarity, 452–53
Compton, Arthur, 345
Compton, Karl, 474
Concerto for Two Violins in D-minor
    (Bach), 430
condensation, 328–29
Congolese uranium exports, 471–73
Congressional Record, 295
constant velocity, 107–9, 114, 118–19,
    127–31, 145, 148, 189, 201
Constitution, U.S., 510, 527–28,
    530–31, 534
contraction, 112–13, 116
Copenhagen interpretation, 332–33,
    347, 349, 424, 449, 453, 455, 457,
    459–60, 626n–27n
Copernicus, Nicolaus, 108, 112, 163,
    353
Córdoba observatory, 204
Cornell, Eric A., 329n
cosmic rays, 403
"Cosmological Considerations in the
    General Theory of Relativity"
    (Einstein), 252–53
cosmological constant, 254–55,
    353–56, 372, 613n
cosmology, 223–24, 248, 249–62,
    265–66, 353–56, 372, 442,
    510–11, 613n
Cousins, Norman, 495

covariance, 195, 198–202, 212, 213,
    218–22, 224, 591n–92n, 594n
Cox, Channing, 299n
"Creation of the United States of
    Europe, The," 207–8
Critique of Pure Reason (Kant), 20, 574n
Crouch, Henry, 264
Crowther, Bosley, 493
Cupid and Psyche (Canova), 64
Curie, Marie, 168, 176, 181–82, 304,
    305, 327

Dearborn Independent, 289
death penalty, 525–26
Debye, Peter, 176
"Declaration of Protest," 304
decoherent histories, 459–60,
    626n–27n
Delong, Adelaide, 439–40
democracy, 240, 242, 287, 420, 423–24,
    479–80, 489–90, 499, 503–7, 537
Demoiselles d'Avignon, Les (Picasso),
    280
Depression, Great, 370–71, 516, 607n
determinism, 84, 156, 316, 317,
    320–21, 323–25, 331–33, 334,
    340, 345, 347, 349, 455, 575n
"Deutsch Physik" ("German Physics"),
    289, 315, 405–10
Dewey, John, 377
Diaghilev, Serge, 280
*Dialogue Concerning the Two Chief
    World Systems* (Galileo), 108–9
Diamond, Marian, 547
differential calculus, 61
diffusion, 105, 223, 481–82
Dirac, Paul, 223, 345, 349
distant parallelism, 341, 343–44
DNA, 546–47
"Does the Field Theory Offer
    Possibilities for the Solution of
    Quanta Problems?" (Einstein), 340
"Does the Inertia of a Body Depend on
    Its Energy Content?" (Einstein),
    138–39

Dongen, Jeroen von, 594*n*
Don Quixote (Cervantes), 81, 518
Doppler effect (red shift), 119*n*, 148, 254, 311, 353–56
double stars, 580*n*
Douglas, William O., 526
Drake, Tom, 492
"Dr. Einstein's Mistaken Notions," 497
Driving Mr. Albert (Paterniti), 546, 640*n*
Drude, Paul, 68–69, 71, 102
Du Bois, W. E. B., 531
Duhem, Pierre, 158
Dukas, Helen, 84, 363, 371, 410, 424, 437–39, 443, 446, 479, 481, 482, 485, 501, 517, 521, 530, 541–42, 544, 633*n*, 636*n*, 639*n*
Durrell, Lawrence, 279
Dutch Royal Academy, 260–61
Dyson, Frank, 257, 261, 269
Dyson, Freeman, 134, 251, 269
Dyson, George, 363

E=mc², 2, 5, 137–39, 140, 219, 272, 348, 469–70, 485, 604*n*
Eban, Abba, 521–22, 523, 541
echolalia, 9
eclipses, 5, 191, 202–5, 218, 255–62, 267, 269, 275–76, 311, 316, 317
Economist, 136
Eddington, Arthur Stanley, 256–62, 264, 267, 279, 312, 321, 339, 340, 343, 355*n*, 600*n*, 601*n*
Eddy, Mary Baker, 343
Edison, Thomas, 6, 299
Edison test, 299
Ehrenfest, Paul, 68, 120, 132, 165, 167–68, 180, 184, 204, 205, 218, 234, 252, 259, 268, 271, 276, 281, 287, 289, 325, 331, 345, 396, 421–22
Einstein, Albert:
  in Aarau, Germany, 25–31, 40, 46, 113, 115
  at Aarenshoop resort, 238–39
  absentmindedness of, 39, 44, 59, 203, 227*n*, 426–28, 435–36, 437, 438–41, 519
  academic career of, 149–52, 158–63, 175–88, 239, 304–5, 368, 394–412, 431–32
  academic positions sought by, 54–56, 57, 58–63, 65, 66, 67, 69, 78, 86, 92, 140, 142, 144–45, 149–53
  aloofness of, 2, 5, 12–13, 41, 44, 100, 150–51, 154, 161–62, 184–86, 226, 231, 232–33, 271, 273–77, 280, 441–43, 516, 518, 519–20
  anemia of, 517, 536
  aneurysm of, 516–17, 536, 541–43
  in Antwerp, 368
  arms control supported by, 487–95, 498, 500–501
  in Arosa, Switzerland, 234, 243
  assimilation opposed by, 205–6, 280–84, 291, 302–4, 386, 408–10, 428
  astrology and spiritualism as viewed by, 374, 384
  atheism as viewed by, 386, 388–90, 462, 587*n*
  Austro-Hungarian citizenship of, 163–64
  authority questioned by, 2, 7, 8–9, 12–13, 20–22, 29, 34, 38, 49, 54–55, 67–72, 73, 113, 180, 240, 317, 378–79, 550
  autograph of, 369, 445
  awards and honors received by, 3, 60, 101, 154–55, 235, 236, 243, 280, 297, 309–16, 337, 348, 352, 368, 387, 438, 490, 505, 516, 533–34, 606*n*, 607*n*
  at Bad Nauheim conference, 287–89
  in Belgium, 168–71, 289–91, 344–49, 405, 410–22
  as Berlin University professor, 14, 168, 178–81, 184–89, 201, 202, 203–11, 212, 213, 215–16, 217, 218–21, 224, 227*n*, 228–32, 234,

Einstein, Albert *(cont.)*
  236, 237, 241–42, 246–48, 259,
    261–62, 271, 277, 280, 281–89,
    301–6, 307, 315, 318, 356–59,
    362, 363, 364, 381–83, 384,
    387–89, 392, 394–95, 399–401,
    403, 411, 471, 523, 601*n*
  in Bermuda, 437, 479, 506
  as Bern resident, 75–89, 124,
    125–26, 141–55, 167, 184–88
  as Bern University professor,
    144–53
  biographies of, 269–71, 465, 478,
    498, 518, 601*n*, 639*n*
  birth of, 11, 91–92
  Bohr's disputes with, 269, 324–26,
    344–49, 496, 514–15, 539, 609*n*
  brain of, 545–48, 640*n*
  busts of, 423, 436
  in California, 263, 268, 315, 354–55,
    368, 371, 372–74, 380–81, 384,
    395–98, 399, 401–4, 431
  at Caltech, 315*n*, 368, 373, 374,
    380–81, 395–98, 399, 401–4,
    431
  Caputh cottage of, 357–60, *357*, 361,
    362, 387, 395, 397, 398, 399, 401,
    405, 444, 447, 619*n*
  Central America visited by, 364,
    371–72
  in Ceylon, 306
  in Chicago, 374–75, 404–5
  childhood of, 8–31, 67, 114, 180,
    205, 385, 462, 483, 538, 548
  in Cleveland, 300, 461–62
  communism as viewed by, 287,
    379–80, 399–401, 403, 420–21,
    445–47, 478, 489–90, 494–503,
    524–34, 550, 633*n*–34*n*
  compass given to, 13, 67, 462, 538,
    548
  correspondence of, 1, 3, 39–47,
    50–53, 93, 94, 97, 104, 106, 131,
    135, 137–38, 143–44, 165, 170,
    171, 174, 184, 355, 360–61,

  405–6, 408–9, 411, 415–16, 417,
    421–22; *see also specific*
    correspondents
  correspondence of (Berlin), 184, 201,
    202, 203–4, 205, 208, 209–11,
    212, 213, 215–16, 217, 218–21,
    224, 227*n*, 230–32, 234, 237, 242,
    259, 271, 277, 286, 307, 318, 362,
    363, 381–83, 387–89, 392, 601*n*
  correspondence of (Princeton),
    430–31, 438, 441, 442, 467, 478,
    482–83, 484, 500–501, 503, 513,
    519–20, 524–29, 537, 539, 540,
    636*n*
  cremation of, 544, 545
  in Cuba, 371
  daily walks of, 438–39, 442–43, 509,
    536–37
  death of, 88, 94, 251, 445, 541–45
  death threats against, 410–11,
    422–23, 437
  democracy supported by, 240, 242,
    287, 420, 423–24, 479–80,
    489–90, 499, 503–7, 537
  economic views of, 370–71, 375, 380,
    403, 504–5, 633*n*
  education as viewed by, 6–7, 21–22,
    26, 290, 292, 293, 299, 550
  education of, 8–9, 15–49, 54–56, 60,
    113, 115, 150–51, 565*n*
  engineering background of, 23–24,
    31, 53–54, 91, 113, 115, 126–27,
    143–44, 161, 276–77, 304, 435,
    443, 444, 517
  English spoken by, 394, 402, 446,
    464, 525
  essays of, 208–9, 380, 479–80,
    489–90, 497–98, 504
  eyeballs of, 640*n*
  fame and reputation of, 2, 5–6, 136,
    140–42, 149, 151–52, 154, 163,
    166, 168–69, 172, 175, 176–77,
    196, 240, 247, 263–316, 339–44,
    357–59, 363, 368–76, 396, 403,
    426–30, 445, 472–73, 517,

520–23, 525–34, 540, 541,
544–45, 633*n*, 639*n*

as father, 75–76, 86–88, 143, 161–62,
174–75, 186, 187, 209–11,
215–16, 225–40, 243, 246, 274,
276–77, 301, 417–19

FBI file on, 287, 379, 399, 477–78,
500–503, 525, 534, 629*n*

FDR letter written by, 473–78, 484,
485, 629*n*–30*n*

FDR's meeting with, 430–31, 493

fiftieth birthday of, 357–59, 362–63

film portrayal of, 491–93

financial situation of, 22–23, 32, 39,
72–73, 88–89, 162–63, 164, 179,
186, 187, 188, 204, 210, 215, 226,
228, 233, 234–36, 244, 275–76,
289–90, 297, 302, 306–7, 309,
316, 359, 397, 403, 465, 478–79,
607*n*, 639*n*

foreign tour of, 306–8, 309, 310, 315

France visited by, 301, *309*, 311

free speech supported by, 479–80,
524–34

free will as viewed by, 387, 388,
391–93, 618*n*, 635*n*

French spoken by, 208, 301

friendships of, 12–13, 35–36, 61–62,
79–81, 85, 104, 137–39, 142, 143,
167–68, 184, 185, 206, 208, 222,
228, 231, 260, 269–71, 274–75,
286–87, 294–95, 305, 363, 364,
408, 421–22, 518–19, 536, 540,
542, 566*n*

generosity and kindness of, 5, 186,
187, 188, 210, 215, 226, 228,
234–36, 275–76, 302, 309, 316,
427–30, 438–41, 445, 516,
518–19, 607*n*

at Geneva Disarmament
Conference, 377–78

German citizenship of, 23, 29, 58,
164, 405, 406

German culture as viewed by, 21–22,
23, 24, 26, 180, 205–9, 239–42,

275, 282–84, 401–3, 414, 447,
505–6, 542

German spoken by, 149, 297, 306,
431, 542–43

in Glasgow, 419

"God does not play dice" quote of, 4,
326, 335, 392, 515, 538, 549, 609*n*

as grandfather, 443, 444

grief experienced by, 84–85, 277,
417–19, 441–42, 518

gyroscope improvement by, 304

hand injured by, 35

at Havel River villa, 341–42, 357–58

heart inflammation of, 363

Herbert Spencer Lecture given by,
419, 591*n*

hiking trips of, 24, 42, 46, 80–81,
181–82, 203, 209, 210, 217, 225,
229

in Hollywood, 263, 268, 372–73, 374

honorary degrees awarded to,
154–55, 352, 505

ill health of, 13, 35, 217, 233, 234,
238, 255, 291, 342, 363, 516–17,
519, 536, 541–42, 548

immigration visa of, 399–401, 437,
477, 479

individual freedom supported by,
433, 445–47, 478–80, 503–7,
524–34, 537, 550, 637*n*

at Institute for Advanced Study,
298, 395–98, 402, 405, 410,
411–12, 425–26, 428, 431–32,
436, 438, 439, 442–43, 450, 453,
464, 466, 468–69, 480, 508–9,
514–15, 532, 536, 537, 541, 622*n*

intellectual development of, 1–2,
8–9, 12, 78–84

as internationalist, 205–9, 240, 282,
291, 301, 302, 305, 378, 381–82,
386, 479, 482–83, 487–500, 541,
601*n*, 631*n*

interviews with, 266, 342, 385–87,
420–21, 423, 428–29, 440–41,
450, 469–70

Einstein, Albert *(cont.)*
    inventions of, 143–44, 161, 304, 435, 471
    Israeli presidency offered to, 520–23
    in Japan, 306–7, 309, 310, 315, 339, 393
    Jewish background of, 3, 9–10, 11, 15, 16, 18, 20–21, 29–30, 43, 52, 61, 142, 149, 152, 163–64, 177, 183, 207, 243, 263, 269–71, 273, 281–308, 311–12, 315, 342, 359, 381, 385, 403–10, 412–14, 420, 427, 428–30, 444–45, 447, 505–6, 520–23, 541, 543, 567n
    Jewish refugees aided by, 429–30, 445
    in Kiel, Germany, 304, 305
    Kyoto address of, 116
    at Lake Como, 63–64
    at Le Coq sur Mer, Belgium, 410–22
    lectures given by, 150–52, 159–60, 168–71, 175–76, 179, 203, 212, 214–15, 218, 219–20, 223, 228, 232, 239, 272, 295, 296, 297, 298, 306–7, 318–20, 321, 350–53, 361–62, 396–97, 469
    in Leiden, 164–66, 168, 318–20, 360–61
    in London, 279, 301
    as loner, 12, 15, 24, 35–36, 38, 52, 137, 211, 357–60, 363, 423–24, 431–32, 435–36, 442–43, 551
    love life of, 27, 28, 40–47, 153–54, 243, 275, 360–64, 437, 441–42, 502–4, 517, 535, 538, 540, 546–47
    magazine and newspaper articles by, 267, 281, 285–88, 377, 445, 489–90, 497–98
    manifestos signed by, 207, 539, 541
    McCarthyism opposed by, 480, 500, 524–34, 537, 550
    in Melchtal, Switzerland, 50–51, 53, 54

    Mercer Street home of, *425*, 437–43, 445, 483, 509, 515, 518, 530, 532, 540–41, 639n
    in Milan, 45, 58–63
    militarism opposed by, 4, 205–9, 240, 275, 371, 373, 375, 381–83, 414–17, 419–20, 488, 494, 498–99, 520
    as military consultant, 481–82
    military service avoided by, 23, 58
    moral principles of, 378–79, 387, 388, 391–93, 541, 549–50, 602n, 618n, 635n
    in Munich, 11–23, 294, 305, 483
    music system as gift to, 519, 536
    nationalism opposed by, 4, 205–9, 240, 282, 291, 301, 302, 305, 378, 381–82, 386, 479, 482–83, 487–491, 601n
    nervous strain of, 184, 217–18, 255
    newspaper advertisement placed by, 76, 79
    Newton admired by, 248, 301, 360, 423, 438
    Newton compared with, 5, 6, 90–91, 93, 312, 333, 352, 544, 549, 581n
    in New York City, *281*, 292–95, 369–71, 375–76, 402, 443
    Nobel Prize awarded to, 3, 60, 101, 235, 236, 243, 280, 309–16, 337, 387, 490, 516, 606n, 607n
    as nonconformist, 4, 7, 15, 20–22, 35–36, 38–39, 49, 52–53, 67, 74–75, 76, 85–86, 158, 159, 182, 248, 271–72, 305, 317, 347–48, 463, 523, 527, 550
    nuclear weapons opposed by, 482–84, 487–95, 539, 541, 631n–32n
    offices of, 166, 298, 426, 438, 508–9
    at Old Lyme, Conn. cottage, 436
    ordinance capabilities analyzed by, 481–82

organizations joined by, 207–8,
305–6, 399, 400, 445–46, 490–91,
500, 501, 633*n*–34*n*
at Oxford University, 350–53,
361–62, 396–97, 410, 412, 418–20,
422–24, 431, 432, 549, 591*n*
as pacifist, 4, 23, 58, 205–9, 212, 302,
305, 371, 373, 374–78, 381–83,
396, 399–401, 402, 403, 404–5,
414–17, 421, 483, 490, 498–99,
501, 521, 633*n*
in Palestine, 306, 307–8
in Panama, 371–72
papers of, 75*n*, 86, 136, 404, 433–34,
633*n*, 639*n*
in Paris, *309*, 311
as patent examiner, 1, 3, 36, 62–63,
72, 74, 76, 77–79, 84, 85–86, 89,
90, 92–93, 113, 122, 126, 128,
137–38, 140, 141, 142–43, 149,
150, 151, 154–55, 159, 250, 255,
266, 424, 444, 517, 551
patents awarded to, 304, 435, 471
in Pavia, Italy, 23–25
at Peconic, N.Y. cottage, 472
personal enemies of, 207, 285–87,
304, 314–15, 405–10
personality of, 2–3, 4, 12–15, 21,
27–28, 34, 38, 39, 41, 46, 49,
50–51, 54–55, 84–85, 142,
150–51, 154, 161–62, 166–67,
173, 208, 211–12, 214, 247–48,
268–69, 273–77, 280, 285–89,
357–63, 364, 417–19, 441–43,
509, 518–20, 549–50, 566*n*, 635*n*
personal problems avoided by, 154,
166–67, 174–75, 183, 184–86,
187, 188, 208, 215–16, 224, 225,
231, 232–33, 234, 239, 273–77,
441–42
pets owned by, 438, 535–36
philosophy studied by, 20, 52–53,
79–84, 113, 164, 166, 238,
334–35, 387, 388–89, 391,
460–61, 518, 627*n*

photographs of, *ix, 8, 50, 90*, 178,
225, 249, 263, 269, *281*, 287, 293,
309, 336, 369, 371, 374, *394*,
418–19, 436, 443, *471, 487*,
493–94, *508, 524*
physical appearance of, 2, 5, 27–28,
39, 79–80, 142, 150, 159, 182,
347, 426, 447, 518, 530
piano played by, 519
in Pittsburgh, 469
Planck medal awarded to, 348
as plumbers' union honorary
member, 533–34
political views of, 4, 38–39, 58, 159,
205–9, 239–42, 274, 287, 373,
375, 378–83, 385, 399–401,
420–21, 438, 444–47, 477–80,
487–507, 508, 523, 524–34, 539,
541, 550, 633*n*–34*n*
portraits of, 362–63, 436
as Prague University professor,
162–68, 173, 175–77, 192, 421,
482
press coverage of, 136, 153, 263–66,
269–71, 273, 277–78, 285–87,
288, 289–301, 304, 339–44, 355,
357, 358, 363, 369, 370, 371, 377,
378, 390, 398, 399–400, 401, 406,
411–12, 413, 414, 416, 420–21,
422, 423, 425–26, 428–30, 436,
440–41, 450, 451, 459, 467, 468,
469–70, 479, 485, 487, 491,
499–500, 513, 517, 521, 525–26,
528, 545, 615*n*, 622*n*, 624*n*,
631*n*
as Princeton resident, 425–27,
431–32, 437–41, 444–45
privatdozent appointment of, 144–53
public addresses by, 116, 166,
168–71, 172, 232–33, 242,
282–83, 290, 295, 296, 297,
306–7, 315–16, 318, 368, 371,
373, 374–75, 376, 390–91, 396,
401–5, 423–24, 445, 461–62, 491,
541, 543

Einstein, Albert *(cont.)*
 racism opposed by, 378, 380, 381,
  445, 505, 520, 531
 radio broadcasts of, 372, 402, 479,
  506–7, 527, 541
 religious convictions of, 15, 16,
  20–21, 29–30, 56, 163–64,
  167–68, 182, 243, 282–83, 372,
  384–93, 462, 536, 548, 550–51,
  587*n*
 Royal Albert Hall speech of, 423–24
 sailboats owned by, 360, 435, 472,
  479
 sailing as pastime of, 38, 246, 304,
  317, 358, 360, 361, 362, 373, 387,
  405, 435–36, 437, 472, 479, 502–3
 salary of, 186, 235*n*, 397, 403
 in Salzburg, 321
 at Saranac Lake cottage, 441, 485,
  487
 in Sarasota, Fla., 517, 519
 in Schaffhausen, Germany, 72–73,
  75
 security clearance for, 399–401, 420,
  477–78, 480, 481–84, 500–503,
  629*n*
 at Sellin sea resort, 210
 sense of humor of, 27, 28, 46,
  230–31, 385, 438, 518, 519,
  540–41
 seventy-fifth birthday of, 535, 536
 seventy-sixth birthday of, 540
 in Singapore, 306
 sixtieth birthday of, 468, 469–70
 smoking by, 44, 142, 168, 181, 274,
  292, 298, 402, 446
 socialist ideals of, 4, 38–39, 205,
  239–42, 373, 375, 378–81,
  399–401, 420, 499, 504–5,
  633*n*
 socks not worn by, 427, 447, 523
 Soviet Union as viewed by, 379–80,
  420–21, 446–47, 478, 489–90,
  494–503, 504, 524–25, 526, 633*n*
 statues of, 296, 370, 604*n*

 stomach problems of, 217, 233, 234,
  238, 255, 291, 342, 516–17, 536
 stubbornness of, 144, 211–12, 214,
  259–60, 316, 347–48, 364, 509,
  538–39, 550, 635*n*
 students of, 150, 159–62, 211
 study of, 211–12, 247–48, *249*, 360,
  386, 438, 440, 443, 446, *544*
 as substitute teacher, 63, 65, 149
 Swabian background of, 9–10, 27,
  34, 53*n*, 63
 Swiss citizenship of, 29, 32, 55, 56,
  58, 76, 164, 478–79
 telephone owned by, 438, 530
 television appearance of, 501
 travel diaries of, 240, 306, 308, 369,
  373, 394, 396
 as tutor, 55, 56, 62, 72–73, 75, 76, 78,
  79–80, 206, 439–40
 "2%" speech of, 371, 373, 375
 U.S. as viewed by, 380, 478–80, 500,
  524–34, 537, 550
 as U.S. citizen, 59, 437, 478–80,
  503–7, 510, 530–31, 543
 as U.S. resident, 168, 298, 424,
  425–47
 U.S. visited by, 263, 281, 289–301,
  354–55, 368–76, 394, 395–96,
  398, 399, 431
 in Venice, 53–54
 in Vienna, 164, 182, 272, 587*n*
 violin played by, 14, 29, 35, 37–38,
  53, 80, 143, 159, 161, 166, 167,
  177, 227, 261–62, 272, 292, 296,
  306, 403, 415, 418–19, 426–27,
  430, 472, 519, 624*n*
 at Watch Hill, R. I. cottage, 434–36
 will of, 639*n*
 in Winterhur, Germany, 63, 65,
  149
 world government supported by,
  209, 301, 479, 487–500, 541, 631*n*
 as Zionist, 281–84, 289–301, 302–3,
  306, 307–8, 376, 381, 409,
  412–14, 520–23, 526, 541

in Zurich, 24, 25–26, 30, 31, 32–49,
54–59, 60, 115, 149–53, 152,
158–63, 167, 175–83, 192, 203,
210–11, 229–30, 234, 239, 246,
276, 301, 364, 367, 410, 418–19
as Zurich Polytechnic professor,
150–51, 158, 175–83, 192, 203,
239
as Zurich Polytechnic student, 24,
25–26, 30, 31, 32–49, 54–56, 60,
115
as Zurich University professor,
150–53, 158–63, 167, 239
Einstein, Albert, as physicist:
assistants of, 358, 363, 368, 371, 397,
410, 411, 412, 423, 424, 450,
463–65, 508, 509, 537, 549
conservative reaction of, 316–21,
333–35, 346, 350–53, 460–70,
514, 538–39
as cosmologist, 223–24, 248,
249–62, 265–66, 353–56, 372,
442, 510–11, 613n
creativity and genius of, 1–2, 3, 4–6,
7, 14–15, 21, 67, 106, 122, 124,
128, 134, 140–42, 149, 156, 163,
176–77, 215, 223–24, 253, 255,
316–18, 320, 333, 336, 350,
351–52, 424, 465, 538–39,
547–51, 570n, 607n–8n
doctoral dissertation of, 1, 54, 71–72,
92, 101–3, 142–43, 150
early investigations by, 24–25,
56–58, 67–72
experimental verification by, 5,
34–35, 47–48, 57, 58, 100–101,
103, 104–5, 106, 116–18, 125,
138, 139, 158, 161, 316–17, 350,
351, 465–66, 549
habilitation thesis of, 144–45,
149–50
inductive method of, 116–18, 191,
350–52, 579n–81n
intuitive approach of, 113–18, 119,
131, 133, 142, 145, 146–47, 155,

197–98, 201–2, 214, 250–51,
259–60, 297–98, 316–18, 333–34,
346, 350–52, 449, 465–68,
538–39, 549–50, 580n–81n
as mathematician, 3, 16–20, 30–31,
33, 48, 55, 56, 63, 76, 99, 132, 133,
137, 149, 160, 192, 209–10, 216,
222, 235, 338–39, 439–40, 441,
450, 542, 549, 624n
"miracle year" of (1905), 1–2, 54,
90–106, 140, 317, 550
papers published by, 1–2, 3, 13, 46,
56–58, 59, 69, 70, 92–106, 117,
122–35, 138–39, 140, 141, 142,
144, 286, 315, 317, 322, 328,
339–44, 350, 351, 442, 571n,
573n, 580n–81n, 608n, 624n; *see
also specific papers*
as scientific realist, 169, 323–25,
333–35, 349, 350–53, 385,
450–51, 455, 460–65, 538–39,
612n, 627n, 628n, 635n
skepticism of, 67–72, 78–79, 100,
113, 125, 164, 169, 284, 333–34,
350, 460–61
as theoretical physicist, 3, 7, 24–25,
32–37, 43, 44, 47–48, 59, 91–93,
99, 104–5, 106, 113, 143, 147–48,
150, 152, 156, 160, 161, 162, 175,
203, 304, 310–11, 312, 314,
316–18, 350–53, 360, 538–39,
607n–8n
thought experiments
(Gedankenexperiment) of, 2, 3–4, 5,
26–27, 78, 79, 114, 121, 122–27,
138, 142, 145–46, 147, 190, 201,
267, 322, 345–46, 348–49,
448–60, 468, 512, 514, 583n
visual thinking by, 17, 26, 93, 114,
121, 122–27, 142, 549
work habits of, 24, 38, 142, 159–62,
165, 175–76, 181, 184, 211–12,
247–48, 426, 508–9
see also quantum mechanics;
relativity; unified field theory

Einstein, Eduard "Tete":
  childhood of, 161–62, 177, 181, 182,
    209–11, 232
  correspondence of, *ix*, 276, 307,
    365–66
  education of, 365–66
  Einstein's relationship with, 161–62,
    181, 182, 185, 186, 187, 196,
    209–11, 228–29, 230, 235,
    236–37, 243, 246, 276, 301, 316,
    365–67, 417–19, 444, 516, 519,
    639*n*
  ill health of, 174, 181, 183, 184,
    233–34, 235
  mental illness of, 365–68, 417–19,
    565*n*
  piano played by, 365, 367
  in sanatoriums, 234, 235, 243,
    417–19, 444, 502, 516, 639*n*
Einstein, Elsa Löwenthal:
  in Belgium, 410–11
  in Berlin, 172–74, 178, 180–81, 207,
    208, 304, 394, 400–401, 411, 619*n*
  at Caputh cottage, 358–59, 361,
    362
  correspondence of, 173, 174, 178,
    180–81, 182, 186–87, 198,
    210–11, 396, 419, 441–42
  death of, 441–42, 624*n*
  as Einstein's cousin, 172, 178, 181,
    183
  Einstein's fame and, 263, 269, 271,
    307, 357–58, 369, 374, 375, 386
  Einstein's marriage to, 182–83, 188,
    227–28, 237, 239, 243–48, 277,
    292, 304, 360–63, 418, 428,
    441–42, 501, 502
  Einstein's papers recovered by,
    433–34
  Einstein's relationship with, 172–74,
    178, 180–83, 186–87, 210,
    227–28, 233, 237, 238–39,
    243–48, 293, 427
  first marriage of, 172*n*, 243
  Jewish background of, 433–34

personality of, 173–74, 182, 247–48,
    442
  photographs of, *225, 263,* 293
  as Princeton resident, 405, 426, 427,
    428–29, 431, 432–33, 437
  as U.S. resident, 424, 434, 437
  U.S. visited by, 292, 293, 354, 395,
    396
Einstein, Evelyn, 365, 517, 546–47
Einstein, Fanny Koch, 172
Einstein, Frieda Knecht, 364–65, 443,
    546
Einstein, Hans Albert:
  childhood of, 75*n*, 88, 137, 143,
    161–62, 167, 177, 181, 182,
    209–11, 225–26
  as Christian Scientist, 444
  correspondence of, 225, 231–32, 307,
    364–65, 516
  Einstein's death and, 542, 544,
    545
  Einstein's relationship with, 14, 143,
    167, 174, 181, 182, 184, 185, 186,
    187, 209–11, 215–16, 225–40,
    243, 246, 276–77, 301, 316,
    364–65, 417, 442, 443–44, 517,
    537, 601*n*, 639*n*
  engineering career of, 276–77,
    443–44, 502, 517, 639*n*
  financial situation of, 316
  marriage of, 364–65, 443
  personality of, 364–65, 443
  photograph of, *50*
  piano played by, 227
  scientific ability of, 209–10
  as U.S. resident, 434, 443–44, 502
Einstein, Hermann, 10–11, 13, 15, 16,
    22–23, 31, 32, 39, 51, 52, 53–54,
    58–59, 60, 74, 84–85, 91, 143,
    172, 187, 302
Einstein, Ilse, 172, 207, 228, 243–46,
    248, 393, 404, 433, 441
Einstein, Jakob, 11, 17, 22–24, 31, 32,
    39, 91, 113, 143, 506
Einstein, Klaus, 444

Einstein, Lieserl, 3, 63–67, 72–77, 86–88

Einstein, Margot, 172, 228, 232, 248, 362, 367–68, 393, 404, 433, 434, 436, 443, 479, 502, 519, 536–37, 639*n*

Einstein, Maria "Maja," *8,* 11, 12, 16, 17, 23, 24, 39, 49, 50, 59, 66, 74, 75, 85, 140, 141, 234, 236–37, 268, 343, 427, 443, 517–18, 636*n*

Einstein, Mileva Marić, *see* Marić, Mileva

Einstein, Paula, 173

Einstein, Pauline Koch, 10–11, 14, 15, 16, 23, 39, 40–41, 45, 49, 50–52, 53, 58–59, 66, 74, 85, 162, 172, 183, 187, 230, 259, 277, 441

Einstein, Picasso: Space, Time, and the Beauty That Causes Havoc (Miller), 280

Einstein, Roberto, 506

Einstein, Rudolf, 172

Einstein Brothers, 32

Einstein–de Broglie waves, 330

Einstein in Love (Overbye), 13

Einstein on Peace (Nathan and Norden, eds.), 633

Einstein Papers Project, 75*n,* 86, 136

Einstein-Russell manifesto, 539, 541

Einstein's Clocks, Poincaré's Maps (Galison), 126, 569*n*–70*n*

Einstein's Wife (PBS show), 136

Einstein tensor, 220

Eisenhower, Dwight D., 525, 533, 534, 544–45

electrical charges, 143–44, 161

electrical conductivity, 68, 70, 127, 165, 336*n*–37*n*

electrical induction, 115

electric current (electricity), 25, 46, 68, 91, 110, 111*n,* 115, 323

electrodynamics, 2, 46, 118, 127–28, 138, 170, 315, 336*n*–37*n*

electromagnetic field, 7, 13, 19, 24–25, 36–37, 91, 92, 94, 97, 108, 110–11, 114, 134, 141–42, 315–16, 337, 338–41, 344, 466, 512–13

electromechanical devices, 113, 126, 142–43

electrons, 68, 94, 96–97, 184, 219, 261, 321–22, 326–27, 330, 331, 332, 346, 466, 583*n*

Eliot, T. S., 280

Elisabeth, Queen of Belgium, 415, 431, 432, 533, 536

Elon, Amos, 284

Emergency Committee of Atomic Scientists, 490–91, 500, 501

empiricism, 164, 350, 352, 612*n,* 627*n*

energy:
    conservation of, 197, 198, 213, 592*n*
    dark, 356
    kinetic, 43, 67–72, 91, 97, 103–4
    mass converted to, 2, 5, 137–39, 272, 348, 469–70, 485
    molecular, 97
    potential, 584*n*

Enlightenment, 277, 279

entanglement, 454, 455, 458–59

entropy, 69–70

Entwurf approach, 198–202, 204, 212, 213–14, 215, 216, 256, 591*n,* 592*n,* 594*n*

Epkin, Sam, 528

EPR paper, "Can the Quantum-Mechanical Description of Physical Reality Be Regarded as Complete?" (Einstein, Podolsky, and Rosen), 450–53, 456, 458, 459–60, 625*n*–26*n*

Epstein, Jacob, 423

equivalence principle, 147–48, 190, 197, 351, 540–41, 589*n*

Erikson, Erik, 275

Esse est percipi principle, 350

ether, 24–25, 47–48, 62, 92, 105, 111–13, 115–17, 119, 128, 131, 133, 135, 297, 300, 317–20, 332, 351, 373, 578*n,* 579*n*–80*n*

Ethics (Spinoza), 81
Euclidean geometry, 17, 19–20, 33, 37, 44, 63, 75, 83, 192, 193–94, 209–10
Evolution of Physics, The (Einstein and Infeld), 463–65

Fanta, Bertha, 166
Fantova, Johanna, 535, 538, 540
Faraday, Michael, 91, 115, 127, 248, 315, 423, 438
Farmingdale Elementary School, 540
Federal Bureau of Investigation (FBI), 287, 379, 399, 477–78, 500–503, 525, 534, 629n
Fermi, Enrico, 407, 474
Feynman, Richard, 515, 584n
"Field Equations of Gravitation" (Einstein), 219–20
field theory, 13–14, 92, 94, 95, 317, 612n
    of relativity, 159, 189, 197–98, 200–201, 212–24, 254–55, 336–37, 353, 468, 591n–92n, 594n
    see also unified field theory
Fifth Amendment, 528, 530, 534
Fight against War, The, 405
Fine, Arthur, 627n
First Amendment, 527–28, 530
Fisch, Adolf, 160
Fitzgerald, George, 113, 116
fixed states, 455–56
Fizeau, Hippolyte, 112, 116, 117
"flatlanders," 252–53
Flexner, Abraham, 395–98, 412, 425–26, 428–31, 453, 464, 480, 529, 622n
FM radio signals, 111
Föppl, August, 36–37, 115, 579n
Ford, Henry, 289
Fosdick, Harry Emerson, 370
"Foundations of Physics, The" (Hilbert), 219
Franck, James, 505–6

Frank, Philipp, 12, 20, 164, 166, 172, 177, 248, 271–72, 285, 332, 399, 410–11, 567n, 579n
Frankfurter, Felix, 298
Franklin, Benjamin, 311, 389
Franklin Institute, 624n
Franz Joseph, Emperor of Austria, 163
Frauenglass, Richard, 529
Frauenglass, William, 527–29, 530
frequencies:
    light, 96–97, 99, 119, 314
    sound, 119n
Freud, Sigmund, 3, 209, 284, 365–66, 377, 381–83, 386, 389, 614n–15n
Freundlich, Erwin Finlay, 191, 202–5, 213, 222, 233, 243, 267
Freundlich, Käthe, 277
Fried, Amos, 373
Friedman, Robert Marc, 310, 312
Frisch, Otto, 469
Frothingham, Mrs. Randolph, 399, 477, 502
Fuchs, Karl, 500, 501–2
Fuld, Caroline Bamberger, 395
Fulton, Robert, 476, 630n

galaxies, 254, 353–56, 442
Galileo, 5, 6, 80, 90, 91, 108–9, 117, 128–29, 145, 146, 251–52, 288, 550
Galison, Peter, 126, 569n–70n, 578n
gamma rays, 111
Gamow, George, 355–56, 481
Gandhi, Mohandas K., 438, 527
gases:
    atomic structure of, 164, 323, 480–81
    condensation of, 328–29
    diffusion of, 223
    molecular theory of, 43, 56–57, 67–72, 91, 97, 103–4, 156, 328–29
    volume of, 98, 101–3
Gauss, Carl Friedrich, 193–94, 215, 253, 589n

Gedankenexperiment (thought
experiments), 2, 3–4, 5, 26–27, 78,
79, 114, 121, 122–27, 138, 142,
145–46, 147, 190, 201, 267, 322,
345–46, 348–49, 448–60, 468,
512, 514, 583*n*
Gehrcke, Ernst, 285–86, 304, 311
Gell-Mann, Murray, 459–60
General Disarmament Conference
(1932), 377–78
generators, electric, 91, 115
Geneva, University of, 154–55, 306
geodesic lines, 192
geometry:
Euclidean, 17, 19–20, 33, 37, 44,
63, 75, 83, 149, 192, 193–94,
209–10
non-Euclidean, 163, 192, 193–96,
253
propositions of, 83
of relativity, 192, 222, 337
German Citizens of the Jewish Faith,
282
Gestalt psychology, 116, 241
glial cells, 547
Glimpses of the Great (Viereck), 386
G Major Quartet (Mozart), 430
God, 4, 16, 20, 84, 91, 125, 297–98,
326, 335, 352, 384–93, 466, 515,
538, 549, 550–51, 609*n*
Gödel, Kurt, 509–11, 536, 634*n*, 639*n*
Goebbels, Joseph, 409
Goethe, Johann Wolfgang von, 30, 207,
423, 544
Goethe League, 209
Golden, William, 493
Goldstein, Herbert S., 388–89
Goodman, Ellen, 136
Göring, Hermann, 474
Göttingen, University of, 212, 222, 331
Göttingen Academy, 222
gravitation, gravity:
acceleration and, 145–49, 155,
181–82
field of, 13, 19, 94, 146, 319–20, 349

light bent by, 5, 148–49, 165,
189–92, 202–5, 218, 219, 255–62,
266, 312–13, 355, 442
Newtonian laws of, 2, 57, 81–82, 84,
90–91, 93, 110, 113, 114, 118–19,
125, 128, 130–31, 133, 145,
146–47, 156, 189, 197, 198,
199–201, 204, 214, 216, 218, 223,
251–52, 256, 258, 259, 261–62,
264, 266, 277, 280, 318–20, 323,
333, 352, 453, 548
in quantum mechanics, 349, 449,
458
relativity and, 145–49, 155, 181–82,
189–97, 198, 199–202, 215,
216–22, 223, 249, 250–62, 266,
293, 314, 319–20, 337, 347, 349,
468, 511, 538–39, 548, 590*n*–94*n*,
607*n*
solar, 191, 202–5, 218
stellar, 250–52
in unified field theory, 338–41, 385,
466, 511, 512–13, 538
waves of, 442, 624*n*
great circle routes, 192
Great Depression, 370–71, 516, 607*n*
Greene, Brian, 220, 320, 452–53, 459
Greene, Homer, 526
Grossmann, Marcel, 36, 44, 47, 48, 59,
61, 62–63, 71, 72, 73, 74, 75, 149,
159, 177, 192–93, 195, 196, 197,
198, 215, 219, 267, 589*n*, 594*n*,
601*n*
Guillaume, Charles-Edouard, 312
Gullstrand, Allvar, 312–13, 314
"gunpowder experiment," 456,
457–58
Gustav Adolf V, King of Sweden,
315
gyroscopes, 304

Haber, Clara, 185
Haber, Fritz, 174, 181, 184, 185, 186,
203, 205–7, 228, 281–82, 291–92,
406, 408–9, 413

Habicht, Conrad, 80–81, 85, 93, 94, 97, 104, 106, 135, 137–38, 143–44, 536

Habicht, Paul, 143–44

habilitation thesis, 144–45, 149–50

Hahn, Otto, 469, 506

Haldane, Richard Burdon, Lord, 278–79, 307

Haller, Friedrich, 74, 78–79

Halsman, Philippe, *487*, 493–94

Handel, George Frideric, 38

Harding, Warren G., 295–96

harmonic oscillators, 96

Hartle, James, 193, 459

Harvard University, 298

Harvey, Thomas, 545–48, 640*n*

Hawking, Stephen, 251

Haydn, Franz Joseph, 426

heat:
    conduction of, 48, 67–68, 70–71
    kinetic theory of, 104
    radiation of, 96, 576*n*

Hebrew University, 290, 292, 293, 301, 306, 409, 412–14, 522

Hedin, Sven, 311–12

Heidelberg, University of, 42–44

Heisenberg, Werner, 124, 330–33, 345, 348, 349, 448, 451, 453, 458, 485, 510

Helmholtz, Hermann von, 34, 36, 45–46

Herschbach, Dudley, 6

Hertz, Heinrich, 25, 36

Hertz, Paul, 208

Hibben, John, 298

Hilbert, David, 212–22, 232

Hiller, Kurt, 378

Hindenburg, Paul von, 399

Hiroshima bombing (1945), 484–85

Hitler, Adolf, 4, 242, 289, 303, 369, 371, 376–77, 381–82, 383, 386, 403–5, 407–8, 410, 414, 422, 429–30, 434, 445, 447, 485, 528

Hoffmann, Banesh, 22, 134, 335, 442, 464, 468, 512, 514, 586*n*

"hole argument," 201, 591*n*–92*n*

Hollywood, *263*, 268, 372–73, 374, 491–93

Holton, Gerald, 13–14, 99, 137, 461, 579*n*, 612*n*, 627*n*, 628*n*

Hook, Sidney, 446–47, 496, 520, 525

Hoover, J. Edgar, 287, 477–78, 501, 503, 525

Hopi Indians, 374

House Un-American Activities Committee (HUAC), 534

Howard, Don, 627*n*

Howard, Henry, 343

Hubble, Edward, 353–55

Hume, David, 20, 81–82, 113, 125, 166, 169, 334, 349, 350, 460

Hurwitz, Adolf, 55–56, 177, 178, 183, 301

Huygens, Christiaan, 110

Hyades, 257

hydrodynamics, 101

hydrogen, 219, 322

hydrogen bomb, 500–501, 524, 531

"I Am an American Day," 507

I Am an American series, 479

In Albert's Shadow (Popović), 87

incompleteness theory, 509–10

individual freedom, 433, 445–47, 478–80, 503–7, 524–34, 537, 550, 637*n*

"Induction and Deduction in Physics" (Einstein), 118

inertia, 80, 107–9, 118–19, 131, 146–47, 190, 199–201, 251–52, 318–20, 468, 548

inertial reference system, 107–9

inertio-gravitational field, 190

Infeld, Leopold, 263, 267, 274, 463–65, 524–25

inferior parietal lobe, 547–48

Institute for Advanced Study, 298, 395–98, 402, 405, 410, 411–12, 425–26, 428, 431–32, 436, 438,

439, 442–43, 450, 453, 464, 466,
468–69, 480, 508–9, 514–15, 532,
536, 537, 541, 622*n*
Institute for Intellectual Cooperation,
381–83
integral calculus, 16
interference patterns, 112, 329
International Bureau of Weights and
Measures, 312
International Committee on
Intellectual Cooperation, 305–6
*Introduction to Maxwell's Theory of
Electricity* (Föppl), 36–37, 115
invariances, 131–32, 324
IQ, 13
Irvin, Rea, 266–67
isolationism, 474, 475
isotopes, 480–81
Israel, 306, 307–8, 381, 520–23, 541,
543

Janssen, Michel, 196, 214, 594*n*
Japan, 306–7, 309, 310, 315, 339, 379,
393, 481
Jaumann, Gustav, 163
Jefferson, Thomas, 389
Jeritza, Maria, 370
Jerome, Fred, 379, 633*n*
Jesus Christ, 386, 434, 567*n*
Jewish Hospital (Brooklyn), 517
Jewish Legion, 293–94
Jewish Orphans Organization, 363
Jewish Telegraph Agency, 414
Jews:
    assimilation of, 205–6, 280–84, 291,
    302–4, 386, 408–10, 428
    Einstein's identification with, 3,
    9–10, 11, 15, 16, 18, 20–21,
    29–30, 43, 52, 61, 142, 149, 152,
    163–64, 177, 183, 207, 243, 263,
    269–71, 273, 281–308, 311–12,
    315, 342, 359, 381, 385, 403–10,
    412–14, 420, 427, 428–30,
    444–45, 447, 505–6, 520–23, 541,
    543, 567*n*

    prejudice against, 3, 15, 30, 43, 61,
    142, 149, 152, 163–64, 177, 183,
    207, 269–71, 281–308, 311–12,
    315, 359, 403–10, 427, 428–30,
    443, 444–45, 469, 475, 505, 517,
    524, 567*n*, 601*n*
    Zionist movement for, 281–84,
    289–301, 302–3, 306, 307–8, 376,
    381, 409, 412–14, 520–23, 526,
    541
Johnson, Paul, 277
Joyce, James, 3, 280
Jupiter, 191

Kafka, Franz, 166
Kaiser Wilhelm Institute of Physics,
243
Kaluza, Theodor, 337–38, 339, 512
Kant, Immanuel, 20, 82–83, 166, 207,
238, 244, 370, 574*n*
Kaufman, Bruria, 537
Kaufman, Irving, 525
Kayser, Ilse Einstein, 172, 207, 228,
243–46, 248, 393, 404, 433,
441
Kayser, Rudolf, 248, 404, 433
Keller, Helen, 375
Kelvin, William Thomson, Lord, 90,
575*n*
Kepler, Johannes, 166–67
Ketterle, Wolfgang, 329*n*
Kindred, J. J., 295
kinetic energy, 43, 67–72, 91, 97, 103–4
Kirchhoff, Gustav, 36, 49, 50, 94–95
Klein, Oskar, 338–39
Kleiner, Alfred, 71–72, 101, 150,
151–52
Koch, Caesar, 25
Koch, Julia, 50
Koch, Julius, 10, 24
Konenkov, Sergei, 436, 503
Konenkova, Margarita, 436–37, 503–4
Korean War, 525
Kreisler, Fritz, 426–27
Krupp Foundation, 204

Ladenberg, Rudolf, 536
Lagrange, Joseph-Louis, Count, 593*n*
Lake Como, 63–64, 181–82
Lake Lucerne, 229
Langevin, Paul, 170–71, 327, 411
Lania, Leo, 420–21
Laplace, Pierre-Simon, Marquis de, 90–91, 575*n*
lasers, 5, 323
Laski, Harold, 279
Lasky, Victor, 528
Laub, Jakob, 180
Laue, Max von, 141–42, 267, 269, 286, 406, 409, 466
Laurence, William, 467
League of Nations, 305–6, 376, 377, 381, 414
least action principle, 141, 584*n*
Lebach, Margarete, 362
Lehman, Herbert, 532
Leiden, University of, 168
Leiden Museum for the History of Science, 59
Lenard, Philipp, 43, 65, 96–99, 105, 207, 285–89, 303, 304, 311–12, 314–15, 407, 409–10
Letters from a Russian Prison (Levine), 380
Levenson, Thomas, 275
Levi-Civita, Tullio, 195, 197, 212, 215, 589*n*
Levine, Isaac Don, 380, 446
Levy, Steven, 546
Lewis, Gilbert, 576*n*
light:
    absorption of, 96, 100, 169, 314, 322, 324
    bending of, 5, 148–49, 165, 189–92, 202–5, 218, 219, 255–62, 266, 312–13, 355, 442
    dual (particle-wave) nature of, 97–98, 100, 155–57, 170, 321, 326–29, 539, 580*n*–81*n*, 583*n*, 586*n*

emission of, 94–96, 99–100, 119–20, 156, 204, 256, 259, 314, 322–24
    ether as medium for, 92, 111–13, 115–16, 119, 317–20
    frequencies of, 96–97, 99, 119, 314
    interference patterns of, 112, 329
    propagation of, 119–22, 190–91, 223, 317–20
    quantum (particle) theory of, 1, 65, 93, 94–101, 105, 110, 120–22, 124, 140, 141–42, 144, 150, 155–57, 165, 168–71, 179, 190, 235, 255, 256, 286, 313–14, 318–20, 321, 326–33, 337*n*, 539, 580*n*–81*n*, 583*n*, 586*n*
    radiation of, 1, 68, 92, 93, 94–101, 115, 141–42, 150, 155–57, 165, 322–24, 331, 576*n*
    redshift of, 119*n*, 148, 254, 311, 353–56
    relativity and, 120–22, 124, 141–42, 190, 255, 256, 318–20, 321, 580*n*–81*n*, 583*n*
    spectrum of, 93, 322, 331
    speed of, 18–19, 47–48, 78, 105, 106, 110–12, 114, 116–17, 118, 119–22, 123, 126, 128–30, 132, 138, 139, 189, 250, 252, 267, 297, 319, 347, 468, 548, 578*n*, 579*n*–80*n*, 581*n*
    split beams of, 47–48, 112
    ultraviolet, 65, 111
    in vacuum, 97, 99, 111*n*, 114, 157
    wavelengths of, 9, 65, 94–95, 97, 111, 322, 323, 331
    wave theory of, 1, 19, 24, 26, 34, 46, 47–48, 94–95, 97–98, 109–12, 119, 155–57, 170, 318, 323, 329, 578*n*
Lincoln University, 505
Lindbergh, Charles, 474–75
Lindemann, Frederick, 412, 418, 432
liquids:
    molecular structure of, 2, 56–58, 68
    temperature of, 105–6
    viscosity of, 102, 105

Lloyd George, David, 419–20

local effects, 189–90, 583*n*

locality principle, 448–53, 454, 458, 461, 512, 626*n*

Lochner, Louis, 399–400

Locke, John, 81

Locker-Lampson, Oliver, 419–20, 422–423

logic, 81–84

Lord & Taylor department stores, 527

Lorentz, Hendrik, 32–33, 112–13, 115, 116–17, 126, 133, 142, 161, 164–66, 168, 170, 180, 201, 213, 259, 260–61, 267, 269, 271, 310, 311, 318, 330, 341, 344, 549, 550, 583*n*, 591*n*, 593*n*, 600*n*

Lorentz transformation, 341

Los Alamos laboratory, 480, 488

Lowell, A. Lawrence, 298

Lowell Observatory, 254

Luitpold Gymnasium, 16–18, 21–22, 23

Luther, Martin, 434

McCarthy, Joseph, 500, 524, 529, 530, 531–32, 534

McCarthyism, 480, 500, 524–34, 537, 550

Mach, Ernst, 20, 81, 82, 83–84, 113, 125, 158, 164, 169, 200, 201, 251, 252, 319, 320, 331, 333–34, 349, 350, 460, 461, 462, 591*n*, 612*n*, 627*n*

MacIntyre, Marvin, 430

Madison Square Garden, 369–70

Madrid, University of, 411–12, 432

Maginot Line, 491

Maglić, Rastko, 136

Magnes, Judah, 412–14

magnetic field (magnetism), 13, 24–25, 91, 110, 115, 117, 127, 184, 185, 336, 548

Maier, Gustav, 38

Manhattan Project, 477, 480–86, 491

"Manifesto of the 93" ("Appeal to the Cultured World") (1914), 206–7, 244

"Manifesto to Europeans," 207

Marianoff, Dimitri, 248, 367–68, 404, 423, 502

Marianoff, Margot Einstein, 172, 228, 232, 248, 362, 367–68, 393, 404, 433, 434, 436, 443, 479, 502, 519, 536–37, 639*n*

Marić, Mileva:
  in Berlin, 183, 184–88
  correspondence of, 7, 39, 42–47, 50–53, 54, 55–58, 60–61, 62, 63, 65, 66–67, 68, 69, 72–76, 77, 86, 96, 115, 136, 137, 173, 210, 215, 217, 227, 237–38, 246, 286, 367, 443, 598*n*
  death of, 75*n*, 516
  depressions of, 177–78, 183, 184–85
  Einstein's divorce from, 3, 85*n*, 87, 137, 182–83, 187, 225–40, 243, 275–76, 301, 309, 316, 363–64
  as Einstein's intellectual companion, 2–3, 7, 41–47, 57–58, 74–75, 135–37, 173, 188, 235, 360, 583*n*
  Einstein's marriage to, 2–3, 42, 65, 74–75, 76, 84–89, 136, 143, 153–54, 158, 172, 173, 174–75, 177–78, 181, 182–88, 205, 206, 209–11, 360, 519
  Einstein's reconciliation with, 301, 363–64, 367–68, 418, 419, 516
  Einstein's separation from, 184–88, 205, 206, 209–11, 215, 217, 224, 225–40
  financial situation of, 186, 187, 188, 210, 215, 226, 228, 234–36, 275–76, 302, 309, 316, 516, 607*n*
  at Heidelberg University, 42–44
  ill health of, 161, 177–78, 229–30, 232, 237, 516, 598*n*
  at Lake Como (1901), 63–64
  in Leyden, 164–65

Marić, Mileva (*cont.*)
  as mathematician and physicist, 2,
    42–46, 48, 49, 55, 135–37, 235,
    583*n*
  as mother, 63–67, 88, 96, 158, 161,
    186, 187, 367–68, 516, 598*n*
  as Orthodox Christian, 243
  personality of, 42, 43–44, 88,
    153–54, 172, 173, 177–78, 183,
    184–85
  photographs of, 45, *50*
  physical appearance of, 42, 45, 154
  in Prague, 166, 172
  pregnancies of, 63–67, 88, 96, 158,
    161
  relativity theory and, 135–37, 235,
    583*n*
  rental properties of, 316, 516, 607*n*
  Serbian background of, 42, 52, 64,
    66–67, 86–88, 136, 180, 182, 243
  in Zurich, 2, 42–46, 48, 49, 158,
    177–78, 180, 187, 209–11, 246,
    275–76, 301, 316, 364, 367, 418,
    419, 444, 516, 607*n*
  at Zurich Polytechnic, 2, 42–46, 48,
    49, 158
Marić, Milos, 89
Markwalder, Suzanne, 37, 38
Marshall, George, 493
Marx, Sam, 491–93
Maschinchen device, 143–44, 161
mass:
  energy converted from, 2, 5, 137–39,
    272, 348, 469–70, 485
  gravitational vs. inertial, 146–47,
    468, 548
  Newtonian laws of, 90, 91, 130–31
  in quantum mechanics, 348–49
  relativity and, 250–51, 252, 468,
    548
matrix mechanics, 331
Matthau, Walter, 13
Maxwell, James Clerk, 7, 34, 91–92, 97,
    110–11, 114, 115, 118, 120, 121,
    126, 138, 155–56, 157, 169, 170,

248, 336*n*–37*n*, 338, 340, 349,
    350, 438
Maxwell equations, 115, 118, 120, 121,
    138, 155–56, 157, 169, 170,
    336*n*–37*n*, 338, 549, 578*n*, 581*n*
Mayer, Louis B., 491–92
Mayer, Walther, 358, 363, 368, 371,
    397, 410, 411, 412, 423, 424, 450,
    464
Meaning of Relativity, The (Einstein),
    513, 577*n*
mechanics:
  classical, 91, 92, 109, 113, 114,
    127–28
  laws of, 127–28
  matrix, 331
  quantum, *see* quantum mechanics
  statistical, 67–70, 98, 99, 101, 103–6,
    167, 255, 327–29, 333, 341, 345,
    347–48, 629*n*
  wave, 329–30, 331, 347, 454–55, 456
Mechanics and Its Development (Mach),
    81
Meitner, Lise, 407, 469
Mendel, Toni, 361
Mercury, 199, 212, 213, 218–19, 223,
    224, 250, 311, 313, 593*n*–94*n*
Mermin, N. David, 459
metals, 68
metric tensors, 194–98, 200–201,
    212–22, 254–55, 320, 340–41,
    351, 352, 512–13, 590*n*–91*n*
Metro-Goldwyn-Mayer (MGM),
    491–93
Metropolitan Opera House, 295, 370
Meyer, Edgar, 239
Meyer, Menasseh, 306
Meyer-Schmid, Anna, 153–54
Michanowski, Ethel, 361–62
Michelmore, Peter, 88, 137
Michelson, Albert, 48, 112, 113, 115,
    116–17, 297, 300, 354, 372,
    579*n*–80*n*
microwaves, 111
Mie, Gustav, 592*n*

Miles, Sherman, 477–78
militarism, 4, 205–9, 240, 275, 371, 373, 375, 381–83, 414–17, 419–20, 488, 494, 498–99, 520
Milky Way, 254, 353
Miller, Arthur I., 116, 135, 280, 578n, 581n, 628n
Miller, Dayton, 300
Millikan, Robert Andrews, 100–101, 212, 315, 321, 373, 380–81, 395–98, 402, 403
Minkowski, Hermann, 35, 132–33, 193, 591n
Missa Solemnis (Beethoven), 536
modernism, 3, 277–80
Modern Times (Johnson), 277
molecules:
    attraction of, 56–57
    existence of, 43, 56, 67, 70, 103, 104
    gas, 43, 56–57, 67–72, 91, 103, 156, 328–29
    liquid, 2, 56–58, 68
    motion of, 2, 68, 91, 93, 97, 101, 103–6, 117, 118, 140, 156, 223, 351, 373, 577n
    size of, 101–3
momentum, 323, 346, 348–49, 448–53, 459–60, 626n–27n
Monday Evening Club, 469
Monthly Review, 504
Mooney, Tom, 380, 381
moral relativism, 270, 277–80, 602n
Morgenthau, Henry, 430
Morley, Edward, 48, 112, 113, 115, 116–17, 297, 300, 579n
Moscow show trials, 446
Moszkowski, Alexander, 14, 127, 269–71, 601n
motion:
    absolute, 320
    Brownian, 68, 93, 101, 103–6, 117, 118, 140, 351, 373, 577n
    laws of, 90–91

molecular, 2, 68, 91, 93, 97, 101, 103–6, 117, 118, 140, 156, 223, 351, 373, 577n
relative, 36, 93, 107–9, 127–31, 133, 134, 135, 145–46, 197, 199–201, 212, 213, 215, 220, 223, 318–20, 467
rotation and, 192, 199–201, 212, 213, 251–52, 318–20, 510–11, 593n–94n, 596n
spontaneous, 69–70
Mount Wilson Observatory, 353–55, 372
Mozart, Wolfgang Amadeus, 14, 29, 37–38, 177, 232, 272, 403, 415, 426, 430, 519
Murray, Gilbert, 305
Murrow, Edward R., 531–32, 534
Mussolini, Benito, 443, 517
Muste, A. J., 500–501
mutual influence, 329–30
"My Opinion of the War" (Einstein), 208–9

Nagasaki bombing (1945), 485
Napoleon I, Emperor of France, 476, 630n
Nassau Inn, 445
Nathan, Otto, 240–41, 542, 544, 545, 633n, 639n
Nation, 377
National Academy of Sciences, 296
National Association for the Advancement of Colored People (NAACP), 505
nationalism, 4, 205–9, 240, 282, 291, 301, 302, 305, 378, 381–82, 386, 479, 482–83, 487–491, 601n
nature:
    atomic model of, 2, 43, 56, 70, 93, 94, 95, 101, 103, 104, 140, 164, 169, 255
    causality in, 1, 81–84, 90–91, 95, 216, 323–26, 332, 333, 334, 345, 347, 460, 461

nature (*cont.*)
  harmonious arrangement of, 3, 4, 13–14, 20, 37–38, 78, 297–98, 388–89, 548, 549–51
  objective reality in, 323–26, 331–35, 352–53, 460–65, 538–39
  physical existence of, 169–70, 251–52, 321, 326–33, 337, 345–46, 347, 349, 350, 352–53, 448–70, 538, 625*n*
  simplicity of, 82–83, 99, 349, 512, 549
  see also physics
Naturforscher conference (1909), 155
Navy, U.S., 478, 481–82
Nazi Germany, 471–73, 479, 485–86, 498–99, 534
Nazism, 242, 287, 298, 303, 371, 376–78, 386, 399, 403–10, 411, 412, 414–17, 423, 433–34, 437, 444–45, 446, 447, 471–73, 474, 479, 485–86, 498–99, 505–6, 524, 528, 533, 534, 550
Nazi-Soviet Nonaggression Pact (1939), 475
NBC, 402, 501
nebulae, 254, 355
"Negro Question, The" (Einstein), 505
Neptune, 199
Nernst, Walther, 167, 168, 174, 178–79, 205, 206–7, 285, 286, 321
Neumann, Betty, 360–61
Neumann, John von, 426, 607*n*–8*n*
neurons, 547
neutrons, 469, 472
Newark *Sunday Ledger,* 429
"New Determination of Molecular Dimensions, A" (Einstein), 101–3
New Fatherland League, 207–8, 242
New History Society, 371
New Leader, 526
New Scientist, 459
Newsweek, 485, 491

Newton, Isaac:
  "bucket experiment" of, 199–201, 251–52, 318–20
  calculus developed by, 93
  Einstein compared with, 5, 6, 90–91, 93, 312, 333, 352, 544, 549, 581*n*
  Einstein's admiration for, 248, 301, 360, 423, 438
  gravitational laws of, 2, 57, 81–82, 84, 90–91, 93, 110, 113, 114, 118–19, 125, 128, 130–31, 133, 145, 146–47, 156, 189, 197, 198, 199–201, 204, 214, 216, 218, 223, 251–52, 256, 258, 259, 261–62, 264, 266, 277, 280, 318–20, 323, 333, 352, 453, 548
  Principia of, 125, 128, 199–201, 352
New Yorker, 266–67
New York *Evening Post,* 294
New York Herald Tribune, 343
New York Post, 501, 526
New York Times, 264–66, 277–78, 285, 292, 294, 296, 299, 339–42, 343, 344, 358, 370, 398, 400, 411–12, 416, 421, 436, 450, 459, 467, 468, 487, 493, 499–500, 513, 520, 521, 525–26, 528, 529, 532, 545, 631*n*
New York World Telegram, 404, 420
Nicolai, Georg Friedrich, 207, 243–46, 433
Night of the Long Knives, 434
Nobel, Alfred, 310, 490
Nobel Prize, 3, 60, 101, 206, 235, 236, 243, 280, 286, 309–16, 325, 329, 337, 344–45, 349, 373, 383, 387, 407, 490, 516, 606*n*, 607*n*
non-symmetrical tensors, 512–13
Norden, Heinz, 633
Norton, John D., 195*n*, 196, 197, 214, 576*n*, 594*n*
Novi Sad, Serbia, 42, 64, 73, 75, 76–77, 86–88, 136, 161, 182, 570*n*
Novi Sad, University of, 136
nuclear fission, 469–72

nuclear weapons, 482–84, 487–95, 539, 541, 631*n*–32*n*

Nüesch, Jacob, 72, 73

Oakland, 401

Oberlaender Trust, 401–3

Occam's razor, 549

O'Connell, William Henry, 388, 389

Office of Scientific Research and Development, U.S., 480

Olympia Academy, 79–84, 85, 93, 125, 131, 135, 143, 164, 274, 317, 462, 513, 536

"On a Heuristic Point of View Concerning the Production and Transformation of Light" (Einstein), 94–101, 105

"On the Electrodynamics of Moving Bodies" (Einstein), 122–35

"On the Influence of Gravity on the Propagation of Light" (Einstein), 190–91, 256

"On the Investigation of the State of Ether in a Magnetic Field" (Einstein), 24–25

"On the Method of Theoretical Physics" (Einstein), 350–53

"On the Molecular Theory of Heat" (Einstein), 97

"On the Quantum Theorem of Sommerfeld and Epstein" (Einstein), 608*n*

"On the Quantum Theory of Radiation" (Einstein), 322–24

Oppenheim, Shulamith, 13

Oppenheimer, Frank, 531

Oppenheimer, J. Robert, 251, 480, 488–89, 509, *524,* 531–32, 534, 540, 631*n,* 638*n*

Oppenheimer, Kitty, 531

optics, 98, 114

Oseen, Carl Wilhelm, 313–14

osmosis, 480–81

Ostwald, Wilhelm, 59–60, 70, 310

"Outline of a Generalized Theory of Relativity and a Theory of Gravitation" *(Entwurf* approach) (Einstein), 198–202, 204, 212, 213–14, 215, 216, 256, 591*n,* 592*n,* 594*n*

Overbye, Dennis, 13, 127, 216, 255, 459

Oxford University, 350–53, 361–62, 396–97, 410, 412, 418–20, 422–24, 431, 432, 549, 591*n*

pacifism, 4, 23, 58, 205–9, 212, 302, 305, 371, 373, 374–78, 381–83, 396, 399–401, 402, 403, 404–5, 414–17, 421, 483, 490, 498–99, 501, 521, 633*n*

Pageant, 505

Pais, Abraham, 106, 165, 218, 275, 297*n,* 466, 509, 514–15, 532, 619*n*

Panama Canal, 371

Papen, Franz von, 399

paradoxes, 114–15, 130

parietal cortex, 547–48

particle (quantum) theory, 1, 65, 93, 94–101, 105, 110, 120–22, 124, 140, 141–42, 144, 150, 155–57, 165, 168–71, 179, 190, 235, 255, 256, 286, 313–14, 318–20, 321, 326–33, 337*n,* 539, 580*n*–81*n,* 583*n,* 586*n*

Pasadena Civic Auditorium, 402–3

Pasteur, Louis, 423

Paterniti, Michael, 546, 640*n*

Patterson, Cissy, 615*n*

Paul, Saint, 343

Pauli, Wolfgang, 156, 267, 343–44, 345, 346, 451, 466, 538

Pauling, Linus, 171*n,* 486

Peacock Inn, 426

Pearl Harbor attack (1941), 480

Pearson, Drew, 534

Penrose, Boies, 295

Penrose, Roger, 251, 581*n*

People's Books on Natural Science (Bernstein), 18–19, 567*n*

perihelion, 199, 212, 213, 218–19, 223, 224, 250, 311, 313, 593*n*–94*n*

Pernet, Jean, 34–35, 54–55

Perse, Saint-John, 549

Pestalozzi, Johann Heinrich, 26

Petersschule, 15–16

Philadelphia Inquirer, 528

Philadelphia Public Ledger, 293

philosophy, 20, 52–53, 79–84, 113, 164, 166, 238, 334–35, 387, 388–89, 391, 460–61, 518, 627*n*

photoelectric effect, 65, 96–101, 105, 207, 235, 286, 309, 313–15, 327, 344, 351, 373

photographic diaphragm, 435

photons, 94, 99, 101, 322–24, 326–33, 349, 459, 466, 576*n*

Physical Review, 624*n*

physics:
  absolutes in, 2, 37, 82, 84, 111, 124–25, 128, 169, 200, 223, 266, 277, 288, 320, 333, 460
  classical, 90–92, 96, 99, 100, 101, 109, 113, 114, 125, 156, 169, 197, 277, 280, 312–13, 317, 322, 323, 324, 332, 333, 347, 461, 463
  deductive method for, 116–18
  experimental, 34–35, 47–48, 57, 161, 286, 310–11, 312, 314
  "German," 289, 315, 405–10
  heuristic approach to, 94, 98, 155
  historical development of, 33–34, 90–92
  inductive method for, 116–18, 191, 350–52, 579*n*–81*n*
  "Jewish," 142, 269–71, 284–89, 311–12, 315
  laws of, 17–19, 57, 69–70, 84, 90–91, 107–8, 193, 196–97, 216–17, 220, 223–24, 277, 278, 312–13, 386, 388, 510–11, 549–50
  particle, 316, 326–27, 334, 345, 352, 353, 463–64, 512, 538

  popular understanding of, 5–7, 18, 263–80, 355, 567*n*
  scientific realism in, 169, 323–25, 333–35, 349, 350–53, 385, 450–51, 455, 460–65, 538–39, 612*n*, 627*n*, 628*n*, 635*n*
  theoretical, 33–34, 35, 91–93, 99, 150, 152, 156, 161, 162, 175, 203, 212, 286, 310–11, 312, 314, 348, 407
  unified conception of, 3, 4, 13–14, 67, 70–71, 148, 352, 550
  see also quantum mechanics; relativity; unified field theory

"Physics and Reality" (Einstein), 462–63

Picasso, Pablo, 3, 5, 280

Pittsburgh *Post-Gazette*, 469

Pity of It All, The (Elon), 284

Planck, Max, 5, 32, 95–100, 132, 140–41, 149, 155, 156, 157, 160–61, 163, 168, 169, 170, 178–79, 203, 205, 206–7, 211, 232–33, 260, 267, 269, 288, 304, 310–11, 321, 322, 326, 327, 329, 330, 331, 344, 337, 339, 344, 406, 407–8, 409, 550, 549, 576*n*

Planck medal, 348

Planck's constant *(h)*, 95–96, 99, 155, 157, 327, 331

planetary orbits, 199, 212, 213, 218–19, 223, 224, 250, 311, 313, 593*n*–94*n*

Plesch, Janos, 357–58

Podolsky, Boris, 450–53, 456, 458, 459–60, 625*n*–26*n*

Poincaré, Henri, 81, 125, 133–34, 135, 168, 170, 176–77, 311, 330, 550, 569*n*–70*n*, 581*n*

Poland, 499

polonium, 171

Ponsonby, Arthur, 414–15, 417

Poor, Charles, 277–78

Popović, Milan, 87

positivism, 82, 350, 460–61, 462, 609*n*, 627*n*

Postal and Telegraph Building (Bern), 77, 142
postulates, 118–22, 127–28, 134, 191, 252, 335, 347, 581*n*
potential energy, 584*n*
Prague, University of, 162–68, 173, 175–77, 192, 421, 482
"Present State of the Problem of Specific Heats, The" (Einstein), 169–71
Princeton Country Day School, 440
Princeton Hospital, 545, 546, 547
Princeton University, 289, 297–98, 395, 399, 444–45
Principe Island, 257–58, 261
Principia (Newton), 125, 128, 199–201, 352
Principles of Human Knowledge (Berkeley), 350*n*
privatdozent appointments, 144–53
probability, 84, 255, 323–25, 328–29, 330, 332, 333–35, 338–39, 345, 347, 349, 353, 392, 454–56, 461, 462, 515, 626*n*–27*n*
Prolegomena (Kant), 238
Proust, Marcel, 280
Prussian Academy of Sciences, 100, 179, 203, 214–15, 218, 219–20, 250, 321, 343, 395, 398, 405–7, 408, 411
psi-functions, 457–58
Ptolemy, 518
Pueblo (Colorado) *Star-Journal*, 528
Pugwash Conferences, 541
Pythagoras, 194
Pythagorean theorem, 17, 195*n*

quantum mechanics, 320–35, 448–70
  "action at a distance" in, 319–20, 330, 346–47, 448–53, 454, 458
  Bohr's contributions to, 324–26, 332–33, 344–49, 448, 451–52, 458, 468–69, 514–15, 626*n*
  causality in, 345, 347, 460, 461
  complementarity in, 452–53

  Copenhagen interpretation of, 332–33, 347, 349, 424, 449, 453, 455, 457, 459–60, 626*n*–27*n*
  decoherent histories in, 459–60, 626*n*–27*n*
  Einstein's contributions to, 3, 4, 5, 22, 94–101, 140, 144, 155–57, 168–71, 211, 234, 235, 238, 316, 321, 322–33, 608*n*
  Einstein's criticism of, 4, 7, 22, 84, 94, 157, 166, 298, 316, 317, 320–35, 344–53, 385, 421–22, 448–70, 514–15, 538, 609*n*, 625*n*–29*n*, 635*n*
  entanglement in, 454, 455, 458–59
  "EPR paper" on, 450–53, 456, 458, 459–60, 625*n*–26*n*
  experimental support for, 329, 333, 458
  fixed states in, 455–56
  gravitation in, 349, 449, 458
  "gunpowder experiment" for, 456, 457–58
  incompleteness of, 450–53, 457
  locality principle in, 448–53, 454, 458, 461, 512, 626*n*
  mass in, 348–49
  momentum and position in, 323, 346, 348–49, 448–53, 459–60, 626*n*–27*n*
  Newton's laws and, 323, 333, 453
  observation in, 331–33, 345, 349, 448–70, 515, 538, 625*n*, 635*n*
  physical reality in, 169–70, 321, 326–33, 345–46, 347, 349, 448–70, 538, 625*n*
  probability in, 84, 255, 323–25, 328–29, 330, 332, 333–35, 338–39, 345, 347, 349, 353, 392, 454–56, 461, 462, 515, 626*n*–27*n*
  psi-functions in, 457–58
  relativity compared with, 5, 168–71, 320–21, 323, 326, 332, 334–37, 346, 347, 453, 459, 460

quantum mechanics (*cont.*)
Schrödinger equation for, 454–55, 626*n*
"Schrödinger's cat" and, 453–60
scientific collaboration on, 326–33, 424, 451–52, 453
separability in, 449–50, 453, 454, 461, 609*n*, 626*n*
Solvay conference debates on, 344–49, 452, 453, 514, 538, 609*n*
spacetime continuum in, 348–49, 450, 453, 455, 461–62
"spooky action at a distance" in, 448–53, 454, 458
statistical calculations for, 327–29, 333, 341, 345, 347–48, 629*n*
of subatomic particles, 322–24, 326–33, 454, 459–60, 625*n*, 627*n*
sum-over-histories approach to, 515
superposition in, 456–60
thought experiments (*Gedankenexperiment*) for, 345–46, 348–49, 448–60, 468, 512
unified field theory vs., 4, 315–16, 320–21, 336–38, 340, 341, 349, 453, 468–69, 538
"Quantum Trickery: Testing Einstein's Strangest Theory" (Overbye), 459
Queen Mary, 437

racism, 378, 380, 381, 445, 505, 520, 531
radio signals, 111
radium, 138, 139, 171
randomness, 2, 84, 103–6, 577*n*
"random walk," 105, 577*n*
Rankin, John, 495–96
Rapallo Treaty (1922), 303
Rathenau, Walther, 302–4, 305
Rawles, Marian, 526
reason, 81–84
Redemption of Tycho Brahe, The (Brod), 166–67
Red Scare, 379, 480, 500–503, 524–34, 537, 550

redshift, 119*n*, 148, 254, 311, 353–56
refrigerators, 471
Reign of Relativity, The (Haldane), 278–79
relativity, 107–49, 189–224, 249–62
acceleration in, 108, 145–49, 155, 181–82, 188–92, 199, 201–2, 223, 319–20, 511, 548, 607*n*
"action at a distance" and, 319–20, 330
black holes and, 250–52
"border conditions" in, 252–54, 265–66
causality in, 216, 323, 324, 332
complexity of, 6, 262, 265–67, 295–97
conceptual breakthroughs in, 107–13, 122–27, 138, 145–49, 176–77, 211–24, 266, 316–18, 467–68, 538–39, 548
constant velocity in, 107–9, 114, 118–19, 127–31, 145, 148, 189, 201
cosmological implications of, 223–24, 248, 249–62, 265–66, 353–56, 372, 442, 510–11, 613*n*
cosmological term (λ) in, 254–55, 353–56, 372, 613*n*
covariance in, 195, 198–202, 212, 213, 218–22, 224, 591*n*–92*n*, 594*n*
development of, 9, 14, 26, 47–48, 62, 71, 93, 94, 107–39
Einstein's intuitive approach to, 113–18, 119, 131, 133, 142, 145, 146–47, 197–98, 201–2, 214, 250–51, 259–60, 297–98, 316–18, 333–34, 346, 351–52, 467–68, 538–39, 580*n*–81*n*
Einstein's lectures on, 212, 214–15, 218, 219–20, 223, 228, 232, 272, 295, 296, 297, 298, 306–7
energy conservation in, 197, 198, 213, 592*n*

Entwurf approach for, 198–202, 204, 212, 213–14, 215, 216, 256, 591n, 592n, 594n

equivalence principle in, 147–48, 190, 197, 351, 540–41, 589n

ether concept and, 111–13, 115–17, 119, 128, 131, 133, 135, 297, 300, 317–20, 332, 351, 373, 578n, 579n–80n

experimental support for, 47–48, 112, 115–18, 130, 147–48, 191, 199, 202–5, 212, 213, 251, 255–62, 264, 267, 288, 310–12, 314, 351, 353–56, 579n–80n

as field theory, 159, 189, 197–98, 200–201, 212–24, 254–55, 336–37, 353, 468, 591n–92n, 594n

general theory of, 3, 13, 14, 36, 83, 108, 145–49, 155, 159, 178, 179–80, 183, 189–224, 232, 235, 249–62, 291, 311, 312, 317, 318–20, 330, 333–34, 336–38, 340, 351–56, 372, 419, 460, 467–68, 589n–96n, 607n

geometry of, 192, 222, 337

gravitation and, 145–49, 155, 181–82, 189–97, 198, 199–202, 215, 216–22, 223, 249, 250–62, 266, 293, 314, 319–20, 337, 347, 349, 468, 511, 538–39, 548, 590n–94n, 607n

Hilbert's equations for, 212–22, 232

"hole argument" in, 201, 591n–92n

inductive method for, 116–18, 191, 579n–81n

inertia in, 107–9, 118–19, 131, 146–47, 190, 199–201, 251–52, 318–20, 468, 548

invariances in, 131–32, 324

as "Jewish physics," 142, 269–71, 284–89, 311–12, 315

least action principle and, 141, 584n

light bending in, 5, 148–49, 165, 189–92, 202–5, 218, 219, 255–62, 266, 312–13, 355

local effects in, 189–90, 583n

magnetic fields in, 184, 185

manuscripts of, 136, 482, 583n

mass in, 250–51, 252, 468, 548

mathematical strategy for, 196, 197–98, 214, 594n

mathematics of, 36, 127, 132, 133, 136, 137, 149, 159, 191n, 192–99, 211–24, 250, 251, 288, 337, 340, 351, 352, 468, 510–11, 590n–91n, 594n

Maxwell equations and, 115, 118, 120, 121, 138, 155–56, 157, 169, 170, 336n–37n, 338, 549, 578n, 581n

measurement in, 128–29, 313, 337

Mercury perihelion confirmed by, 199, 212, 213, 218–19, 223, 224, 250, 311, 313, 593n–94n

metric tensors used in, 194–98, 200–201, 212–22, 254–55, 320, 340, 351, 352, 590n–91n

modernism and, 3, 277–80

moral relativism contrasted with, 270, 277–80, 602n

motion in, 36, 93, 107–9, 127–31, 133, 134, 135, 145–46, 197, 199–201, 212, 213, 215, 220, 223, 318–20, 467

Newtonian laws modified by, 114, 118–19, 125, 133, 145, 146–47, 189, 197, 198, 199–201, 204, 214, 216, 218, 223, 251–52, 256, 258, 259, 261–62, 264, 266, 277, 280, 548

observational frames of reference in, 114, 116, 118–19, 121–22, 130–32, 148, 277, 333, 511, 581n, 594n, 596n

papers published on, 122–35, 138–39, 144, 190–91, 198–202, 214, 215, 219, 220, 223, 252–55, 256, 317–18, 580n, 582n

paradoxes in, 114–15, 130

relativity (*cont.*)
    particle theory and, 120–22, 124,
        141–42, 190, 255, 256, 318–20,
        321, 580*n*–81*n*, 583*n*
    physical laws in, 107–8, 196–97,
        216–17, 223–24, 277, 278,
        312–13, 510–11
    physical strategy for, 196–97,
        213–14, 591*n*, 594*n*
    popular explanations of, 123–24,
        133, 144, 145, 148, 178, 189, 232,
        256, 263–67, 277–80, 284–86,
        287, 293, 296–97, 302, 355, 369,
        387, 426, 513, 539, 577*n*
    postulates of, 118–22, 127–28, 134,
        191, 252, 335, 347, 581*n*
    public reaction to, 263–80, 355
    quantum mechanics compared with,
        5, 168–71, 320–21, 323, 326, 332,
        334–37, 346, 347, 453, 459, 460
    relativity principle in, 118–19, 120,
        121–22, 124, 126, 127–35, 138,
        148, 201, 250–54, 318–20, 323,
        332, 335, 347, 349, 467, 510–11,
        579*n*–80*n*, 581*n*
    rest as concept in, 127–28, 133, 134
    rotation in, 192, 199–201, 212, 213,
        251–52, 318–20, 593*n*–94*n*, 596*n*
    scientific acceptance of, 132–35,
        140–42, 163, 176–77, 201,
        223–24, 256–57, 263–66, 284–89,
        309–16, 510, 606*n*
    scientific opposition to, 142, 269–71,
        273, 284–89, 309–16, 324, 388,
        389, 495
    simultaneous events in
        (synchronicity), 123–27, 129, 131,
        134–35, 333, 346, 511, 548,
        581*n*–82*n*
    singularities in, 250–52
    space as concept in (spacetime), 93,
        125, 128, 131–35, 140, 169, 192,
        193–96, 200, 218, 220, 223,
        250–62, 265–66, 277, 278, 296,
        318, 319, 333, 510–11, 548

    special theory of, 2, 5, 13, 26, 36–37,
        46, 47–48, 93, 106, 107–37, 138,
        148, 149, 169, 176, 185, 189, 193,
        235, 250, 255, 310, 313, 317–18,
        336*n*–37*n*, 482, 570*n*, 578*n*–83*n*
    speed of light in, 110–12, 114,
        116–17, 118, 119–22, 123, 126,
        128–30, 132, 138, 139, 189, 250,
        252, 267, 297, 319, 347, 468, 548,
        578*n*, 579*n*–80*n*, 581*n*
    starlight verification of (eclipses), 5,
        191, 202–5, 218, 255–62, 267,
        269, 275–76, 311, 316, 317
    thought experiments
        (*Gedankenexperiment*) for, 2, 3–4,
        5, 114, 121, 122–27, 138, 142,
        145–46, 147, 190, 201, 267, 583*n*
    time as concept in, 93, 113, 122,
        123–27, 128, 130–35, 140, 148,
        169, 223, 250, 251, 266, 277, 318,
        333, 349, 510–11, 581*n*–82*n*
    train analogies for, 123–26, 128–30
    twin paradox in, 130
    unified field theory and, 336–38
    "uniqueness" argument in, 213
    velocity in, 114, 192
    wave theory and, 109–12, 578*n*
    Zurich Notebook for, 196–98, 214,
        592*n*, 594*n*
*Relativity: The Special and General
    Theory* (Einstein), 232, 256, 267,
    355, 539, 577*n*
religion, 15, 16, 20–21, 29–30, 56,
    163–64, 167–68, 182, 243,
    282–83, 372, 384–93, 462, 536,
    548, 550–51, 587*n*
Remembrance of Things Past (Proust),
    280
Renard (Stravinsky), 280
Renn, Jürgen, 68, 196, 214, 573*n*, 592*n*,
    594*n*
Rentenmark currency, 302
Rescuing Albert's Compass
    (Oppenheim), 13
rest, 127–28, 133, 134

Reston, James, 532
Ricci-Curbastro, Gregorio, 195, 196,
    197, 214, 215, 216, 220, 221, 589n
Riecke, Eduard, 60–61
Riemann, Bernhard, 193–94, 195, 196,
    214, 215, 219, 253, 513–14, 589n,
    594n
river flows, 276–77, 443–44
Riverside Church, 370
Rockefeller, John D., Jr., 370–71
Rockefeller Foundation, 395
Rolland, Romain, 208, 378, 417
Roosevelt, Eleanor, 430–31, 501
Roosevelt, Franklin D., 5, 430–31, 437,
    473–78, 483, 484, 485, 493, 504,
    629n–30n
Rosen, Nathan, 450–53, 456, 458,
    459–60, 549, 624n, 625n–26n
Rosenberg, Julius and Ethel, 525–26,
    528
Rosenfeld, Léon, 448, 449
Rosso, Henry, 440–41
rotation, 192, 199–201, 212, 213,
    251–52, 318–20, 510–11,
    593n–94n, 596n
Rowe, David E., 633n
Royal Albert Hall, 423–24
Royal Astronomical Society, 261,
    273
Royal Society, 261, 264, 301, 312
Russell, Bertrand, 267, 380, 389, 504,
    529, 539, 541
Rutherford, Ernest, 168, 321, 322
Rynasiewicz, Robert, 580n

Sachs, Alexander, 473–76, 477, 630n
Samuel, Herbert, 307–8
Sauer, Tilman, 196
Savić, Helene Kaufler, 76–77, 86–87,
    88, 143, 154, 174–75, 230, 232
Savić, Zorka, 87, 444
scarlet fever, 86, 87
Schneider, Ilse, 259
Schopenhauer, Arthur, 52, 367, 391,
    609n, 618n

Schrödinger, Erwin, 330, 331, 345,
    349, 431, 432, 450, 453–60, 513,
    626n
Schrödinger equation, 454–55, 626n
"Schrödinger's cat," 453–60
Schubert, Franz, 38
Schulmann, Robert, 86, 546, 633n
Schumann, Robert, 177, 178, 183
Schuster, Max, 465
Schwartz, Paul, 405
Schwarzschild, Karl, 249–52, 319
Schwarzschild radius, 250
Science and Hypothesis (Poincaré), 81,
    125
Scottsboro Boys, 380, 381
Second Law of Thermodynamics,
    69–70
Seeley, Evelyn, 404
Seelig, Carl, 35, 516
segregation, racial, 445, 505
Seidel, Toscha, 426
separability principle, 329–30, 449–50,
    453, 454, 461, 609n, 626n
Shadowitz, Albert, 530
Shakespeare, William, 423
Shaky Game, The (Fine), 627n
Shankland, Robert, 116–17
Shaw, George Bernard, 279, 389
Siemens, Werner von, 32
Silberstein, Ludwig, 261, 262
Simon, Richard, 465
simultaneous events in (synchronicity),
    83–84, 123–27, 129, 131, 134–35,
    333, 346, 511, 548, 581n–82n
Sinclair, Upton, 373–74, 377
singularities, 250–52
Sitter, Willem de, 252, 256, 580n
skepticism, 67–72, 78–79, 100, 113,
    125, 164, 169, 284, 333–34, 350,
    460–61
Smith, Howard K., 519
Smolin, Lee, 549–50
Smyth, Henry DeWolf, 485
Snow, C. P., 21–22, 268–69, 325–26
Snyder, Hartland, 251

Social Democratic Party, 38–39, 150, 151, 159, 239–42

socialism, 4, 38–39, 205, 239–42, 373, 375, 378–81, 399–401, 420, 499, 504–5, 633n

Society for Ethical Culture, 38

solar eclipse (1914), 202–5

solar eclipse (1919), 5, 218, 255–62

solar mass, 250

Solovine, Maurice, 79–81, 85, 131, 141, 291, 304, 317, 401, 411, 462, 463, 467, 513–14, 536, 581n, 601n

Solvay, Ernest, 168

Solvay Conference (1911), 168–71, 178, 321

Solvay Conference (1921), 289–90, 291

Solvay Conference (1927), *336*, 344–48, 450, 452, 453, 514, 538, 609n

Solvay Conference (1930), 348–49, 450, 452, 453, 514, 538

Sommerfeld, Arnold, 142, 193, 234, 287, 593n, 594n

Sommerfeld-Einstein quantum law, 234

Sophocles, 81

sound waves, 92, 109–10, 119, 224, 299

Soviet Union, 379–80, 420–21, 446–47, 478, 489–90, 494–503, 504, 524–25, 526, 633n

space, spacetime:
absolute, 2, 37, 84, 111, 125, 128, 169, 200, 223, 266, 277, 333, 460

curved, 3–4, 5, 83, 192, 193–96, 220, 250–62, 266, 341, 464, 548

as emptiness (void), 97, 99, 111n, 114, 157, 319–20

five-dimensional, 337–38

four-dimensional, 4, 132, 324, 338, 369

in quantum mechanics, 348–49, 450, 453, 455, 461–62

relativity and, 93, 125, 128, 131–35, 140, 169, 192, 193–96, 200, 218, 220, 223, 250–62, 265–66, 277,

278, 296, 318, 319, 333, 510–11, 548

three-dimensional, 252–53, 296, 339

two-dimensional, 4, 252–54, 296

in unified field theory, 337–38, 341, 512

Spanish Civil War, 478, 490

spectrum, light, 93, 322, 331

Spinoza, Baruch, 81, 84, 334–35, 387, 388–89, 391

Spinoza Society, 391

spiral nebulae, 254, 355

spiritualism, 374

spontaneous motion, 69–70

"spooky action at a distance," 448–53, 454, 458

Stachel, John, 75n, 136, 196

Stalin, Joseph, 380, 399, 446–47, 526

Star Trek, 251

State Department, U.S., 399–401, 472–73, 500

statistical mechanics, 2, 67–70, 98, 99, 101, 103–6, 167, 255, 327–29, 333, 341, 345, 347–48, 629n

Stern, Max, 150

Stern, Otto, 407, 482–83, 484

Stevenson, Adlai, 532–33

Stimson, Henry, 401

Stone, Douglas, 328, 609n

Stossel, Ludwig, 493

Strassman, Fritz, 469

Straus, Ernst, 466–67, 508

Strauss, Lewis, 531, 532, 534

Strauss, Richard, 38

Stravinsky, Igor, 3, 280

Stringfellow, George, 528–29

string theory, 339

Struck, Hermann, 362–63

Study Group of German Scientists for the Preservation of a Pure Science, 284–85

Sudoplatov, Pavel, 503

sugar solutions, 102

Sulzberger, Arthur Hays, 487, 631n

sum-over-histories approach, 515

Sunday Express, 422
Supernova Legacy Survey (SNLS), 613
superposition, 456–60
surface tension, 57
"Swabian Tale" (Uhland), 53*n*
Swing, Raymond Gram, 489, 497–98
Swiss Patent Office, 1, 3, 36, 62–63, 72,
    74, 76, 77–79, 84, 85–86, 89, *90,*
    92–93, 113, 122, 126, 128,
    137–38, 140, 141, 142–43, 149,
    150, 151, 154–55, 159, 250, 255,
    266, 424, 444, 517, 551
synthetic propositions, 82–83
Szilárd, Leó, 407, 471–76, *471,* 480,
    484, 485, 490, 491, 492–93,
    629*n*–30*n*

Talmud, 386
Talmud (Talmey), Max, 18, 19–20, 23,
    82, 294–95
Tanner, Hans, 159, 160–62
Taurus, 257
Teller, Edward, 407, 473, 476, 480, 500,
    531, 534, 629*n*
temperature, 105–6, 165
Théorie Physique, La (Duhem), 158
thermodynamics, 69–70, 98, 105–6,
    141–42, 576*n*
Thomas, Norman, 375, 504
Thomson, J. J., 261, 279, 321
Thorne, Kip, 133, 222, 251
thought experiments
    (Gedankenexperiment), 2, 3–4, 5,
    26–27, 78, 79, 114, 121, 122–27,
    138, 142, 145–46, 147, 190, 201,
    267, 322, 345–46, 348–49,
    448–60, 468, 512, 514, 583*n*
Tiger (Einstein's cat), 438
time:
    absolute, 2, 37, 82, 84, 124–25, 128,
        169, 223, 266, 277, 288, 333,
        460
    duration of, 130–32
    as fourth dimension, 132
    local, 134

    in relativity theory, 93, 113, 122,
        123–27, 128, 130–35, 140, 148,
        169, 223, 250, 251, 266, 277, 318,
        333, 349, 510–11, 581*n*–82*n*
    travel in, 511
Time, 342, 369, 430, 485, 624*n,* 633*n*
Time Machine, The (Wells), 132
Times (London), 263–64, 267, 273,
    281, 421
Tinef (Einstein's sailboat), 435, 472, 479
Today with Mrs. Roosevelt, 501
Treatise of Human Nature, A (Hume),
    81, 82
Trotsky, Leon, 446–47
Truman, Harry S., 484, 491, 492, 493,
    500, 504, 507, 525–26
Tümmler (Einstein's sailboat), 360
twin paradox, 130

Uhland, Ludwig, 53*n*
ultraviolet light, 65, 111
Ulysses (Joyce), 280
uncertainty principle, 124, 331–33,
    349, 449, 452–53, 510
unified field theory, 336–44
    affine connection in, 339, 344
    bivector fields in, 512
    complexity of, 339–44
    distant parallelism in, 341, 343–44
    Einstein's formulation of, 4, 13–14,
        67, 316, 320, 336–44, 350–53,
        358, 368, 371, 410, 423, 466–69,
        508–9, 511–14, 537–39, 542, 543
    electromagnetism in, 338–41, 466,
        512–13
    experimental verification of, 351, 352
    gravitation in, 338–41, 385, 466,
        511, 512–13, 538
    Kaluza-Klein formulation for,
        337–39
    mathematical approach of, 67,
        337–44, 351–52, 358, 363, 368,
        423, 466–67, 511–14, 538–39,
        542, 543, 591*n*
    metric tensors in, 340–41, 512–13

unified field theory (*cont.*)
  non-symmetric tensors in, 512–13
  papers published on, 338, 339–44,
    357, 363, 513
  physical reality of, 337–38, 340, 342,
    343–44, 511–12, 513, 537–39
  press coverage of, 339–44, 467, 468,
    513
  quantum mechanics vs., 4, 315–16,
    320–21, 336–38, 340, 341, 349,
    453, 468–69, 538
  relativity and, 336–38
  scientific validity of, 316, 343–44,
    511–14, 537–39, 628n–29n
  spacetime in, 337–38, 341, 512
  for subatomic particles, 463–64, 512,
    538
  unified concept of, 3, 4, 13–14, 67,
    70–71, 148, 342, 550
Union Theological Seminary, 390–91
"uniqueness" argument, 213
United Jewish Appeal, 445
United Nations, 489, 496
Universal Studios, 374
universe:
  alternative histories of, 459–60
  Big Bang theory of, 355
  dark energy in, 356
  expansion of, 253, 353–56, 372, 510
  galaxies of, 254, 353–56, 442
  limits of, 252–54
  metric of, 353–54
  rotation of, 510–11
Untermyer, Samuel, 425
Uppsala, University of, 310–11
uranium, 469, 471–73
Urey, Harold, 526
Utrecht, University of, 175, 176

Vallentin, Antonina, 441
Varićak, Vladimir, 185
Veblen, Oswald, 297–98, 397, 426
vectors, 194
velocity, 107–9, 114, 118–19, 127–31,
  145, 148, 189, 192, 201

"Venona" secret cables, 633n
Versailles Treaty (1919), 303
Viennese Academy, 234
Viereck, George Sylvester, 385–87
Villa Carlotta, 64
Violle, Jules, 24, 25
viscosity, 102, 105
volume, 98, 101–3

Wagner, Richard, 11–12, 38
Waldorf Hotel, 375
Walker, Evan, 136
Walker, Jimmy, 370
Wallace, Henry, 504
Walsh, David, 295
War Bonds, 482
Warburg, Emil, 174
War Resisters' International, 414–17
War Resisters' League, 375, 376, 400,
  402, 499
Washington, George, 529
Washington Post, 295–96, 528
Waste Land, The (Eliot), 280
water waves, 92, 109–10
Watters, Leon, 402, 436, 441, 443
wavelengths, 65, 94–95, 97, 111, 322,
  323, 331
wave mechanics, 329–30, 331, 347,
  454–55, 456
wave theory, 1, 19, 24, 26, 34, 46,
  47–48, 94–95, 97–98, 109–12,
  119, 155–57, 170, 318, 323, 329,
  578n
Weber, Heinrich, 25, 32, 33–34, 47–48,
  55, 60–61, 115, 169, 177
weight and weightlessness, 145–46, 190
Weimar Republic, 284
Weinberg, Steven, 340–41, 356
Weisskopf, Victor, 407
Weizmann, Chaim, 290, 294, 295,
  298–99, 300, 303, 381, 409,
  413–14, 520
Wells, H. G., 132, 377
Wertheimer, Max, 116, 241–42
Wesleyan University, 343

Westmoreland, 424, 425–26
Weyl, Hermann, 298, 337, 339, 351
Weyland, Paul, 284–86, 287, 288–89
"What I Believe" (Einstein), 387, 391
"What Is the Theory of Relativity?"
     (Einstein), 267
Wheeler, John Archibald, 220, 251,
     325, 469, 515
White, Theodore, 533
Whitehead, Alfred North, 261
"Why do They Hate the Jews?"
     (Einstein), 445
"Why Socialism?" (Einstein), 504
Wieman, Carl E., 329n
Wien, Wilhelm, 48, 115–16, 149, 168,
     310
Wigner, Eugene, 407, 471–73, 475,
     476, 480
Wilhelm II, Emperor of Germany, 386
Williams, Charles, 526
Williams, John Sharp, 295
Winteler, Anna, 27, 62, 231, 237, 418,
     517, 540, 636n
Winteler, Jost, 27, 29, 38, 67, 69, 205,
     240
Winteler, Maria Einstein "Maja," *8,* 11,
     12, 16, 17, 23, 24, 39, 49, 50, 59,
     66, 74, 75, 85, 140, 141, 234,
     236–37, 268, 343, 427, 443,
     517–18, 636n
Winteler, Marie, 27, 28, 40–42, 43, 44,
     46, 51, 52
Winteler, Paul, 27, 234, 236–37, 443,
     517, 518, 636n
Winteler, Rosa, 27
Wise, Stephen, 430, 431, 436, 520
Witelson, Sandra, 547–48
Woman Patriot Corporation, 399–401,
     420, 477–78
World Antiwar Congress (1932), 379,
     478

world government, 209, 301, 479,
     487–500, 541, 631n
World Peace Council, 524–25, 531
World War I, 188, 204, 205–9, 224,
     227, 233, 239–40, 250, 251,
     256–57, 274, 277, 283–84, 290,
     376, 377, 408, 539
World War II, 386, 475, 491, 539
World Without Time (Yourgrau),
     511
World Zionist Organization, 290
Wright, Orville, 618n

X-rays, 111, 435

Yearbook of Radioactivity and Electronics,
     144, 145, 148, 189
Yeshiva University, 636n
Young, Thomas, 329
Yourgrau, Palle, 511
Youth Peace Foundation, 376, 404–5
Ypres, Battle of, 206

Zackheim, Michele, 86, 88
Zangger, Heinrich, 170, 175–76, 177,
     180, 184, 185, 201, 202, 207, 209,
     210, 211, 212, 217, 220–21, 228,
     229, 231, 233, 234, 236–37, 266,
     272, 277, 316
Zionism, 281–84, 289–301, 302–3,
     306, 307–8, 376, 381, 409,
     412–14, 520–23, 526, 541
Zürcher, Emil, 236
Zurich, University of, 101–3, 150–53,
     158–63, 167, 239, 365
Zurich Notebook, 196–98, 214, 592n,
     594n
Zurich Polytechnic, 2, 24, 25–26, 30,
     31, 32–49, 54–56, 60, 115,
     150–51, 158, 175–83, 239,
     276–77, 372

ABOUT THE AUTHOR

Walter Isaacson is the CEO of the Aspen Institute. He has been chairman and CEO of CNN and managing editor of *Time* magazine. He is the author of *Benjamin Franklin: An American Life* and *Kissinger: A Biography,* and he is the coauthor with Evan Thomas of *The Wise Men: Six Friends and the World They Made.* He lives with his wife and daughter in Washington, D.C.

ILLUSTRATION CREDITS

Numbers in roman type refer to illustrations in the insert; numbers in *italics* refer to book pages.

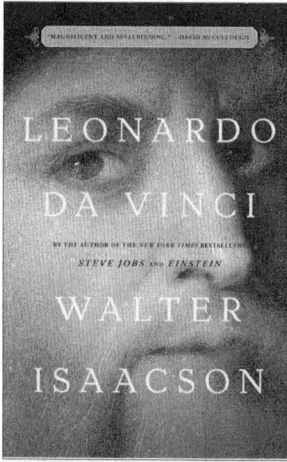
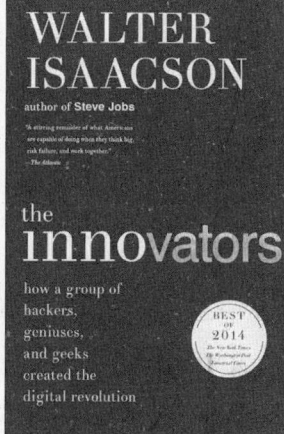

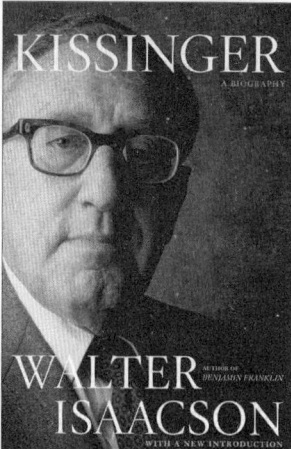

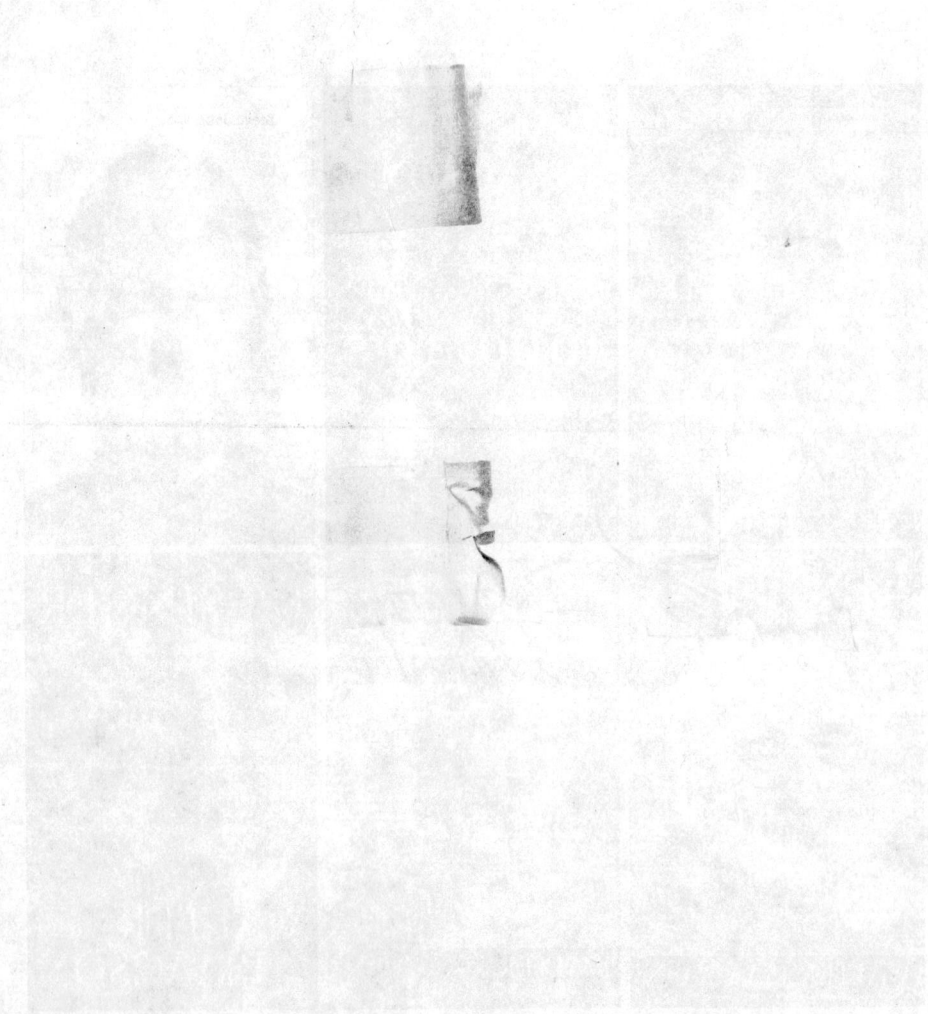

Praise for *Benjamin Franklin*

"Isaacson's . . . will probably supplant Van Doren's as the standard single-volume biography of Franklin."

—Gordon S. Wood, *The New York Review of Books*

"Given the nature and accomplishments of the man, any biography of Benjamin Franklin has to be a chronicle of a half-dozen or more lives in one, all lived with amazing energy, and all extremely interesting. And so, happily, it is in this splendid new look at the incomparable Franklin, who remains one of those Americans about whom we can never know enough. Walter Isaacson writes with great vitality, intelligence, and a clear-eyed understanding of the worlds of politics, the press, and the human equations of high-level diplomacy. This is a book I've looked forward to for a long time and that I've found wholly enthralling from beginning to end."

—David McCullough

"A full-length portrait virtually assured to bring Franklin's remarkable career before a sizable readership. . . . *Benjamin Franklin: An American Life* . . . is a thoroughly researched, crisply written, convincingly argued chronicle that is also studded with little nuggets of fresh information. . . . Isaacson's most impressive chapter, a little tour de force of historical synthesis, focuses on Franklin's role during the Paris peace negotiations that ended the War of Independence. . . . A prime candidate for the authoritative Franklin of our time."

—Joseph J. Ellis, *The New York Times Book Review*

"Franklin once said, 'Let all men know thee, but no man know thee thoroughly.' Every biographer has probed the meaning of that dictum but no one with greater insight than Walter Isaacson. Isaacson gives us the measure of the man in all his relations with the people he let know him: with friends and enemies, with wife and children, with statesmen, philosophers, and diplomats. The result is a complete picture of an extraordinary human being and the company he kept."

—Edmund S. Morgan

"An immensely readable telling of a remarkable life. . . . An indispensable and highly entertaining addition to the long afterlife of Benjamin Franklin."

—John Freeman, *The Atlanta Journal-Constitution*

"Walter Isaacson's splendid *Benjamin Franklin* is both an absorbing narrative biography and an acute assessment of the man and his impact on his times and on posterity. After all, Franklin, the man who did so much to invent America, is the most modern of the Founding Fathers and vividly embodies the virtues and contradictions of the national character."

—Arthur Schlesinger, Jr.

"Isaacson has crafted a wonderfully written biography, and his treatment of Franklin's youth and rise to prominence is insightful and imaginative. It sparkles as well in chronicling some areas of Franklin's life following his retirement, especially the evolution of his views on religion and slavery, and his troubled and insensitive relationships with members of his family. . . . The most readable full-length Franklin biography available."

—John Ferling, *The Washington Post Book World*

"Walter Isaacson has given us a Ben Franklin for the ages. In this marvelous, groundbreaking book, Franklin stands on center stage in the drama of America's founding—where he has long deserved to stand. The reader will fall in love with this high-spirited, larger-than-life character who, above all the founders, was the most committed—in practice and in theory—to the common man."

—Doris Kearns Goodwin

"[A] solid new biography. . . . Isaacson's account of Franklin's diplomacy during and after the Revolutionary War—diplomacy that produced, first, an alliance with France that made the American victory possible and, second, a peace treaty that confirmed the victory—is the fullest in any of the Franklin biographies."

—H. W. Brands, *Los Angeles Times Book Review*

"One of the clearer and more accurate, as well as perhaps the most entertaining, biography of Franklin since the founding father's own autobiography some 200 years ago."

—Ted Dreiter, *The Saturday Evening Post*

"Isaacson has written a biography worthy of its subject, with a plain, straightforward tone that its subject would likely have approved. This volume is well documented, but it also saunters, making it both diverting and informative."

—Tracy Lee Simmons, *National Review*

"The man we encounter in *Benjamin Franklin*—funny, pragmatic, and self-aware—seems like one of us, or at least someone we'd like to be.... Excellent."

—Malcolm Jones, *Newsweek*

"*Benjamin Franklin* is first-rate popular biography, worthy of David McCullough at his best—deeply researched and written in prose that's accessible, friendly and intelligent. The book is a labor of love about a most lovable, and important, fellow."

—Bob Frost, *San Jose Mercury News*

"Marvelous.... A mesmerizing account of Franklin's diverse and extraordinary achievements.... An enthralling one-volume overview of Franklin that should be on the reading list of anyone who is curious about the years leading up to and just after the founding of our nation."

—Bob Van Brocklin, *The Sunday Oregonian*

"Isaacson's vivid and readable narrative gives a clear account of Franklin's scientific work, of his extraordinary career as a social innovator, of his labors as a diplomat and statesman, and of the vagaries of his love life."

—Robin Blackburn, *The Nation*

"Invigorating.... A fresh and organic telling of Franklin's life.... Isaacson's narrative is lively, meticulously researched, and well-paced, shifting easily from science and philosophy to the frivolity of Franklin's Paris years to his famous sly humor."

—David Takami, *The Seattle Times*

"With its exhaustive research laid out in a straightforward and readable manner, with its comprehensive appendixes and its many insightful and surprising conclusions about its subject and his era, Isaacson's book is eminently useful as an important study for anyone curious about the dawning of the American mind."

—Charlie Mount, *Forbes*

"Walter Isaacson understands that spin is the essence of Franklin, and so in his immensely readable new biography he builds his portrait around the great diplomat's skills for myth-making and subterfuge. It is not a revisionist biography, but a celebratory one that depicts Franklin as, among other things, America's first public relations genius.... An indispensable and highly entertaining addition to the long afterlife of Benjamin Franklin."

—John Freeman, *The Cleveland Plain Dealer*

"Isaacson has produced an entertaining, compassionate, and evenhanded look into the mind and life of our most personable founding father. . . . Settle down with a copy of his Franklin biography and rediscover what being American is really all about."

—Dorman T. Shindler, *The Denver Post*

"Franklin is center stage, and he couldn't be more alive, approachable, practical and winking."

—Patrick Beach, *The Austin American-Statesman*

"Compelling. . . . Isaacson is an accomplished writer, and he tells a wonderful story. The book is copiously researched, but it wears its scholarship easily. The writing, whether about diplomatic negotiations or scientific experiments, is clear, direct, and even humorous—a touch Franklin would have appreciated. Scholars and lay readers alike will appreciate this nuanced and thoughtful volume."

—Terry W. Hartle, *The Christian Science Monitor*

"Benjamin Franklin was the most accomplished man of his age. That is the point of Walter Isaacson's superbly written and most accomplished account and assessment of that man. It is told with great gusto, facts that have purpose and point, anecdotes that are revealing and robust. As Poor Richard might have said: Only the truly great among us deserve truly great books about us. Both Isaacson's subject and book meet that test."

—Jim Lehrer

"Meticulously researched and lucid. . . . This balanced assessment of Franklin explores his flaws as well as his successes. A warts-and-all approach to Franklin's life humanizes the man rather than diminishes him. . . . [A] remarkable book. . . . Definitive."

—Marc Horton, *Edmonton (Alberta) Journal*

"Engaging. . . . Franklin's importance as a scientist probably will come as a revelation to readers who think of him as a kite-flying dabbler. . . . Written in lively, colloquial prose, *Benjamin Franklin* will appeal to the same large body of readers who made David McCullough's *John Adams* a huge bestseller. Like that book, it transforms marble men into flesh-and-blood figures, complex and admirable if hardly perfect. . . . A good read."

—Fritz Lanham, *Houston Chronicle*

"Superb. Isaacson has a keen eye for the genius of a man whose fingerprints lie everywhere in our history."

—*Publishers Weekly* (starred)

Kissinger: A Biography

The Wise Men: Six Friends and the World They Made
(with Evan Thomas)

Pro and Con

BENJAMIN FRANKLIN

AN AMERICAN LIFE

WALTER ISAACSON

SIMON & SCHUSTER PAPERBACKS

New York London Toronto Sydney

SIMON & SCHUSTER PAPERBACKS
Rockefeller Center
1230 Avenue of the Americas
New York, NY 10020

First Simon & Schuster paperback edition 2004

SIMON AND SCHUSTER PAPERBACKS and colophon are
registered trademarks of Simon & Schuster, Inc.

For information about special discounts for bulk purchases,
please contact Simon & Schuster Special Sales:
1-800-456-6798 or business@simonandschuster.com.

Designed by Jaime Putorti

Manufactured in the United States of America

30 29 28 27

The Library of Congress has cataloged the hardcover edition as follows:
Isaacson, Walter.
  Benjamin Franklin : an American life / Walter Isaacson.
    p. cm.
  Includes bibliographical references and index.
  1. Franklin, Benjamin, 1706–1790. 2. Statesmen—United States—Biography.
3. United States—Politics and government—1775–1783. 4. United States—
Politics and government—1783–1789. 5. Scientists—United States—Biography.
6. Inventors—United States—Biography. 7. Printers—United States—Biography.
I. Title.
E302.6F8I83   2003
973.3'092—dc21
[B]   2003050463

ISBN-13: 978-0-684-80761-4
ISBN-10:   0-684-80761-0
ISBN-13: 978-0-7432-5807-4 (Pbk)
ISBN-13:   0-7432-5807-X (Pbk)

To Cathy and Betsy, as always . . .

CONTENTS

CHAPTER ONE

Benjamin Franklin and the Invention of America   *1*

CHAPTER TWO

Pilgrim's Progress: Boston, 1706–1723   *5*

CHAPTER THREE

Journeyman: Philadelphia and London, 1723–1726   *36*

CHAPTER FOUR

Printer: Philadelphia, 1726–1732   *52*

CHAPTER FIVE

Public Citizen: Philadelphia, 1731–1748   *102*

CHAPTER SIX

Scientist and Inventor: Philadelphia, 1744–1751   *129*

CHAPTER SEVEN

Politician: Philadelphia, 1749–1756   *146*

CHAPTER EIGHT

Troubled Waters: London, 1757–1762   *175*

CHAPTER NINE
Home Leave: Philadelphia, 1763–1764   206

CHAPTER TEN
Agent Provocateur: London, 1765–1770   219

CHAPTER ELEVEN
Rebel: London, 1771–1775   252

CHAPTER TWELVE
Independence: Philadelphia, 1775–1776   290

CHAPTER THIRTEEN
Courtier: Paris, 1776–1778   325

CHAPTER FOURTEEN
Bon Vivant: Paris, 1778–1785   350

CHAPTER FIFTEEN
Peacemaker: Paris, 1778–1785   382

CHAPTER SIXTEEN
Sage: Philadelphia, 1785–1790   436

CHAPTER SEVENTEEN
Epilogue   471

CHAPTER EIGHTEEN
Conclusions   476

Cast of Characters   495
Chronology   503
Currency Conversions   506
Acknowledgments   507
Sources and Abbreviations   510
Notes   515
Index   563

BENJAMIN
FRANKLIN

AN AMERICAN LIFE

CHAPTER ONE

BENJAMIN FRANKLIN AND THE INVENTION OF AMERICA

His arrival in Philadelphia is one of the most famous scenes in autobiographical literature: the bedraggled 17-year-old runaway, cheeky yet with a pretense of humility, straggling off the boat and buying three puffy rolls as he wanders up Market Street. But wait a minute. There's something more. Peel back a layer and we can see him as a 65-year-old wry observer, sitting in an English country house, writing this scene, pretending it's part of a letter to his son, an illegitimate son who has become a royal governor with aristocratic pretensions and needs to be reminded of his humble roots.

A careful look at the manuscript peels back yet another layer. Inserted into the sentence about his pilgrim's progress up Market Street is a phrase, written in the margin, in which he notes that he passed by the house of his future wife, Deborah Read, and that "she, standing at the door, saw me and thought I made, as I certainly did, a most awkward ridiculous appearance." So here we have, in a brief paragraph, the multilayered character known so fondly to his author as Benjamin Franklin: as a young man, then seen through the eyes of his older self, and then through the memories later recounted by his wife. It's all topped off with the old man's deft little affirmation—"as I certainly did"—in which his self-deprecation barely cloaks the pride he felt regarding his remarkable rise in the world.[1]

Benjamin Franklin is the founding father who winks at us. George Washington's colleagues found it hard to imagine touching the austere general on the shoulder, and we would find it even more so today. Jefferson and Adams are just as intimidating. But Ben Franklin, that ambitious urban entrepreneur, seems made of flesh rather than of marble, addressable by nickname, and he turns to us from history's stage with eyes that twinkle from behind those newfangled spectacles. He speaks to us, through his letters and hoaxes and autobiography, not with orotund rhetoric but with a chattiness and clever irony that is very contemporary, sometimes unnervingly so. We see his reflection in our own time.

He was, during his eighty-four-year-long life, America's best scientist, inventor, diplomat, writer, and business strategist, and he was also one of its most practical, though not most profound, political thinkers. He proved by flying a kite that lightning was electricity, and he invented a rod to tame it. He devised bifocal glasses and clean-burning stoves, charts of the Gulf Stream and theories about the contagious nature of the common cold. He launched various civic improvement schemes, such as a lending library, college, volunteer fire corps, insurance association, and matching grant fund-raiser. He helped invent America's unique style of homespun humor and philosophical pragmatism. In foreign policy, he created an approach that wove together idealism with balance-of-power realism. And in politics, he proposed seminal plans for uniting the colonies and creating a federal model for a national government.

But the most interesting thing that Franklin invented, and continually reinvented, was himself. America's first great publicist, he was, in his life and in his writings, consciously trying to create a new American archetype. In the process, he carefully crafted his own persona, portrayed it in public, and polished it for posterity.

Partly, it was a matter of image. As a young printer in Philadelphia, he carted rolls of paper through the streets to give the appearance of being industrious. As an old diplomat in France, he wore a fur cap to portray the role of backwoods sage. In between, he created an image for himself as a simple yet striving tradesman, assiduously honing the virtues—diligence, frugality, honesty—of a good shopkeeper and beneficent member of his community.

But the image he created was rooted in reality. Born and bred a member of the leather-aproned class, Franklin was, at least for most of his life, more comfortable with artisans and thinkers than with the established elite, and he was allergic to the pomp and perks of a hereditary aristocracy. Throughout his life he would refer to himself as "B. Franklin, printer."

From these attitudes sprang what may be Franklin's most important vision: an American national identity based on the virtues and values of its middle class. Instinctively more comfortable with democracy than were his fellow founders, and devoid of the snobbery that later critics would feel toward his own shopkeeping values, he had faith in the wisdom of the common man and felt that a new nation would draw its strength from what he called "the middling people." Through his self-improvement tips for cultivating personal virtues and his civic-improvement schemes for furthering the common good, he helped to create, and to celebrate, a new ruling class of ordinary citizens.

The complex interplay among various facets of Franklin's character—his ingenuity and unreflective wisdom, his Protestant ethic divorced from dogma, the principles he held firm and those he was willing to compromise—means that each new look at him reflects and refracts the nation's changing values. He has been vilified in romantic periods and lionized in entrepreneurial ones. Each era appraises him anew, and in doing so reveals some assessments of itself.

Franklin has a particular resonance in twenty-first-century America. A successful publisher and consummate networker with an inventive curiosity, he would have felt right at home in the information revolution, and his unabashed striving to be part of an upwardly mobile meritocracy made him, in social critic David Brooks's phrase, "our founding Yuppie." We can easily imagine having a beer with him after work, showing him how to use the latest digital device, sharing the business plan for a new venture, and discussing the most recent political scandals or policy ideas. He would laugh at the latest joke about a priest and a rabbi, or about a farmer's daughter. We would admire both his earnestness and his self-aware irony. And we would relate to the way he tried to balance, sometimes uneasily, the pursuit of reputation, wealth, earthly virtues, and spiritual values.[2]

Some who see the reflection of Franklin in the world today fret about a shallowness of soul and a spiritual complacency that seem to permeate a culture of materialism. They say that he teaches us how to live a practical and pecuniary life, but not an exalted existence. Others see the same reflection and admire the basic middle-class values and democratic sentiments that now seem under assault from elitists, radicals, reactionaries, and other bashers of the bourgeoisie. They regard Franklin as an exemplar of the personal character and civic virtue that are too often missing in modern America.

Much of the admiration is warranted, and so too are some of the qualms. But the lessons from Franklin's life are more complex than those usually drawn by either his fans or his foes. Both sides too often confuse him with the striving pilgrim he portrayed in his autobiography. They mistake his genial moral maxims for the fundamental faiths that motivated his actions.

His morality was built on a sincere belief in leading a virtuous life, serving the country he loved, and hoping to achieve salvation through good works. That led him to make the link between private virtue and civic virtue, and to suspect, based on the meager evidence he could muster about God's will, that these earthly virtues were linked to heavenly ones as well. As he put it in the motto for the library he founded, "To pour forth benefits for the common good is divine." In comparison to contemporaries such as Jonathan Edwards, who believed that men were sinners in the hands of an angry God and that salvation could come through grace alone, this outlook might seem somewhat complacent. In some ways it was, but it was also genuine.

Whatever view one takes, it is useful to engage anew with Franklin, for in doing so we are grappling with a fundamental issue: How does one live a life that is useful, virtuous, worthy, moral, and spiritually meaningful? For that matter, which of these attributes is most important? These are questions just as vital for a self-satisfied age as they were for a revolutionary one.

CHAPTER TWO

PILGRIM'S PROGRESS

Boston, 1706–1723

THE FRANKLINS OF ECTON

During the late Middle Ages, a new class emerged in the villages of rural England: men who possessed property and wealth but were not members of the titled aristocracy. Proud but without great pretension, assertive of their rights as members of an independent middle class, these freeholders came to be known as franklins, from the Middle English word "frankeleyn," meaning freeman.[1]

When surnames gained currency, families from the upper classes tended to take on the titles of their domains, such as Lancaster or Salisbury. Their tenants sometimes resorted to invocations of their own little turf, such as Hill or Meadows. Artisans tended to take their name from their labor, be it Smith or Taylor or Weaver. And for some families, the descriptor that seemed most appropriate was Franklin.

The earliest documented use of that name by one of Benjamin Franklin's ancestors, at least that can be found today, was by his great-great-grandfather Thomas Francklyne or Franklin, born around 1540 in the Northamptonshire village of Ecton. His independent spirit became part of the family lore. "This obscure family of ours was early in the Reformation," Franklin later wrote, and "were sometimes in danger of trouble on account of their zeal against popery." When Queen Mary I was engaged in her bloody crusade to reestablish the Roman Catholic Church, Thomas Franklin kept the banned English Bible tied to the underside of a stool. The stool could be turned over on a lap so the Bible could be read aloud, but then instantly hidden whenever the apparitor rode by.[2]

The strong yet pragmatic independence of Thomas Franklin, along with his clever ingenuity, seems to have been passed down through four generations. The family produced dissenters and non-conformists who were willing to defy authority, although not to the point of becoming zealots. They were clever craftsmen and inventive blacksmiths with a love of learning. Avid readers and writers, they had deep convictions—but knew how to wear them lightly. Sociable by nature, the Franklins tended to become trusted counselors to their neighbors, and they were proud to be part of the middling class of in-dependent shopkeepers and tradesmen and freeholders.

It may be merely a biographer's conceit to think that a person's character can be illuminated by rummaging among his family roots and pointing out the recurring traits that culminate tidily in the per-sonality at hand. Nevertheless, Franklin's family heritage seems a fruitful place to begin a study. For some people, the most important formative element is place. To appreciate Harry Truman, for example, you must understand the Missouri frontier of the nineteenth century; likewise, you must delve into the Hill Country of Texas to fathom Lyndon Johnson.[3] But Benjamin Franklin was not so rooted. His her-itage was that of a people without place—the youngest sons of middle-class artisans—most of whom made their careers in towns different from those of their fathers. He is thus best understood as a product of lineage rather than of land.

Moreover, Franklin thought so as well. "I have ever had a pleasure in obtaining any little anecdotes of my ancestors," reads the opening sentence in his autobiography. It was a pleasure he would indulge when he journeyed to Ecton as a middle-aged man to interview dis-tant relatives, research church records, and copy inscriptions from family tombstones.

The dissenting streak that ran in his family, he discovered, involved more than just matters of religion. Thomas Franklin's father had been active, according to lore, as a legal advocate on the side of the common man in the controversy over the practice known as enclosure, under which the landed aristocracy closed off their estates and prevented poorer farmers from grazing their herds there. And Thomas's son Henry spent a year in prison for writing some poetry that, as one descendant noted, "touched the character of some great man." The inclination to defy the elite, and to write mediocre poetry, was to last a few more generations.

Henry's son Thomas II also displayed traits that would later be evident in his famous grandson. He was a gregarious soul who loved reading, writing, and tinkering. As a young man, he built from scratch a clock that worked throughout his life. Like his father and grandfather, he became a blacksmith, but in small English villages the smith took on a variety of tasks. According to a nephew, he "also practiced for diversion the trade of a turner [turning wood with a lathe], a gunsmith, a surgeon, a scrivener, and wrote as pretty a hand as ever I saw. He was a historian and had some skill in astronomy and chemistry."[4]

His eldest son took over the blacksmith business and also prospered as a school owner and a solicitor. But this is a story about youngest sons: Benjamin Franklin was the youngest son of the youngest sons for five generations. Being the last of the litter often meant having to strike out on your own. For people like the Franklins, that generally meant leaving villages such as Ecton that were too tiny to support more than one or two practitioners of each trade and moving to a larger town where they could secure an apprenticeship.

It was not unusual—especially in the Franklin family—for younger brothers to be apprenticed to older ones. So it was that Thomas II's youngest son, Josiah Franklin,* left Ecton in the 1670s for the nearby Oxfordshire market town of Banbury and bound himself to a pleasant older brother named John, who had set up shop there as a silk and cloth dyer. After the dour days of Cromwell's protectorate, the restoration under King Charles II led to a brief flowering of the garment industry.

While in Banbury, Josiah was swept up in the second great religious convulsion to hit England. The first had been settled by Queen Elizabeth: the English church would be Protestant rather than

---

* See page 495 for thumbnail descriptions of the main characters in this book.

Roman Catholic. Yet she and her successors subsequently faced pressure from those who wanted to go even further and to "purify" the church of all Roman Catholic traces. The Puritans, as these Calvinist dissenters who advocated this purge of papist vestiges came to be known, were particularly vocal in Northamptonshire and Oxfordshire. They stressed congregational self-governance, emphasized the sermon and Bible study over the liturgy and ritual, and disdained much of the Anglican Church's adornments as lingering pollutants from the Church of Rome. Despite their puritanical views on personal morality, their sect appealed to some of the more intellectual members of the middle class because it emphasized the value of meetings, discussions, sermons, and a personal understanding of the Bible.

By the time Josiah arrived in Banbury, the town was torn by the struggle over Puritanism. (During one of the more physical battles, a mob of Puritans toppled Banbury's famous cross.) The Franklin family was divided as well, though less bitterly. John and Thomas III remained loyal to the Anglican Church; their younger brothers, Josiah and Benjamin (sometimes called Benjamin the Elder to distinguish him from his famous nephew), became dissenters. But Josiah was never fanatic in pursuing theological disputes. There is no record of any family feud over the issue.[5]

ERRAND INTO THE WILDERNESS

Franklin would later claim that it was a desire "to enjoy the exercise of their religion with freedom" that led his father, Josiah, to emigrate to America. To some extent, this was true. The end of Cromwell's Puritan rule and the restoration of the monarchy in 1660 had led to restrictions on the Puritan faithful, and dissenting ministers were forced from their pulpits.

But Josiah's brother, Benjamin the Elder, was probably right in attributing the move more to economic than religious factors. Josiah was not zealous about his faith. He was close to his father and older brother John, both of whom remained Anglican. "All evidence suggests that it was a spirit of independence, coupled with a kind of intellectual liveliness and earthy practicality, rather than controlling doctrinal persuasions, that led the only two Franklins, Benjamin the Elder and Josiah, who became Puritans, to follow that course," wrote Arthur Tourtellot, author of a comprehensive book about the first seventeen years of Franklin's life.[6]

Josiah's greater concern was supporting his family. At age 19, he married a friend from Ecton, Anne Child, and brought her to Banbury. In quick succession, they had three children. With his apprenticeship over, he worked on salary in his brother's shop. But there was not enough business to support both fast-growing Franklin families, and the law made it impossible for Josiah to go into a new trade without serving another apprenticeship. As Benjamin the Elder put it, "Things not succeeding there according to his mind, with the leave of his friends and father he went to New England in the year 1683."

The story of the Franklin family migration, like the story of Benjamin Franklin, gives a glimpse into the formation of the American character. Among the great romantic myths about America is that, as schoolbooks emphasize, the primary motive of its settlers was freedom, particularly religious freedom.

Like most romantic American myths, it contains a lot of truth. For many in the seventeenth-century wave of Puritan migration to Massachusetts, as in the subsequent migratory waves that made America, the journey was primarily a religious pilgrimage, one that involved fleeing persecution and pursuing freedom. And like most romantic American myths, it also glosses over some significant realities. For many other Puritan migrants, as for many in subsequent waves, the journey was primarily an economic quest.

But to set up such a sharp dichotomy is to misunderstand the Puritans—and America. For most Puritans, ranging from rich John Winthrop to poor Josiah Franklin, their errand into the wilderness was propelled by considerations of both faith and finance. The Massachusetts Bay Colony was, after all, established by investors such as Winthrop to be a chartered commercial enterprise as well as to create a heavenly "city upon a hill." These Puritans would not have made an either/or distinction between spiritual and secular motives. For among the useful notions that they bequeathed to America was a Protestant ethic that taught that religious freedom and economic freedom were linked, that enterprise was a virtue, and that financial success need not preclude spiritual salvation.[7]

Instead, the puritans were contemptuous of the old Roman Church's monastic belief that holiness required withdrawal from worldly economic concerns, and they preached that being industrious was a heavenly as well as earthly imperative. What the literary historian Perry Miller calls "the paradox of Puritan materialism and immateriality" was not paradoxical to the Puritans. Making money was a way to glorify God. As Cotton Mather put it in his famous sermon "A Christian at His Calling," delivered five years before Franklin was born, it was important to attend to "some settled business, wherein a Christian should spend most of his time so that he may glorify God by doing good for others, and getting of good for himself." The Lord, quite conveniently, smiled on those who were diligent in their earthly calling and, as Poor Richard's almanac would later note, "helped those who helped themselves."[8]

And thus the Puritan migration established the foundation for some characteristics of Benjamin Franklin, and of America itself: a belief that spiritual salvation and secular success need not be at odds, that industriousness is next to godliness, and that free thought and free enterprise are integrally related.

A MAN OF SOLID JUDGMENT

Josiah Franklin was 25 years old when, in August 1683, he set sail for America with his wife, two toddlers, and a baby girl only a few months old. The voyage, in a squat frigate crammed with a hundred passengers, took more than nine weeks, and it cost the family close to £15, which was about six months' earnings for a tradesman such as Josiah. It was, however, a sensible investment. Wages in the New World were two to three times higher, and the cost of living was lower.[9]

The demand for brightly dyed fabrics and silks was not great in a frontier town, especially a Puritan one such as Boston. Indeed, it was a legal offense to wear clothing that was considered too elaborate. But unlike in England, there was no law requiring a person to serve a long apprenticeship before going into a trade. So Josiah chose a new one that had far less glamour but far more utility: that of a tallow chandler, rendering animal fat into candles and soap.

It was a shrewd choice. Candles and soap were just evolving from luxuries into staples. The odiferous task of making lye from ashes and simmering it for hours with fat was one that even the heartiest of frontier housewives were willing to pay someone else to do. Cattle, once a rarity, were being slaughtered more often, making mass manufacture of tallow possible. Yet the trade was uncrowded. One register of professions in Boston just before Josiah arrived lists twelve cobblers, eleven tailors, three brewers, but only one tallow chandler.

He set up shop and residence in a rented two-and-a-half-story clapboard house, only thirty feet by twenty, on the corner of Milk Street and High Street (now Washington Street). The ground floor was only one room, with a kitchen in a separate tiny structure added in the back. Like other Boston houses, it had small windows so that it would be easier to keep warm, but it was brightly painted to make it seem more cheerful.[10]

Across the street was the South Church, newest and most liberal (relatively speaking) of Boston's three Puritan congregations. Josiah was admitted to membership, or permitted to "own the covenant," two years after his arrival.

Church membership was, for the Puritans at least, a social leveler. Although he was merely a struggling tradesman, Josiah was able, because of his membership in the South Church, to become friends with such colony luminaries as Simon Bradstreet, the onetime governor, and Judge Samuel Sewall, a Harvard fellow and diligent diarist.

A trusted and paternalistic figure, Josiah rose within Boston's Puritan/civic hierarchy. In 1697, he was tapped to become a tithingman, the name for the moral marshals whose job it was to enforce attendance and attention at Sunday services and to keep an eye out for "nightwalkers, tipplers, Sabbath breakers . . . or whatever else tending toward debauchery, irreligion, profaneness and atheism." Six years later, he was made a constable, one of eleven people who helped oversee the tithingmen. Although the posts were unpaid, Josiah practiced the art, which his son would perfect, of marrying public virtue with

private profit: he made money by selling candles to the night watchmen he oversaw.[11]

In his autobiography, Benjamin Franklin gives a lapidary description of his father:

> He had an excellent constitution of body, was of middle stature, but
> well set and very strong. He was ingenious, could draw prettily, was
> skilled a little in music and had a clear pleasing voice, so that when he
> played Psalm tunes on his violin and sung withal as he sometimes did in
> an evening after the business of the day was over, it was extremely
> agreeable to hear. He had a mechanical genius too, and on occasion was
> very handy in the use of other tradesmen's tools. But his great excel-
> lence lay in a sound understanding, and solid judgment in prudential
> matters, both in private and public affairs . . . I remember well his
> being frequently visited by leading people, who consulted him for his
> opinion in affairs of the town or of the church . . . He was also much
> consulted by private persons about their affairs when any difficulty oc-
> curred, and frequently chosen an arbitrator between contending par-
> ties.[12]

This description was perhaps overly generous. It is contained, after
all, in an autobiography designed in part to instill filial respect in Benjamin's own son. As we shall see, Josiah, wise though he undoubtedly
was, had limited horizons. He tended to dampen his son's educational,
professional, and even poetic aspirations.

Josiah's most prominent trait was captured in a phrase, deeply Puritan in its fealty to both industriousness and egalitarianism, that
would be inscribed on his tombstone by his son: "Diligence in thy calling." It came from Josiah's favorite piece of Solomonic wisdom
(Proverbs 22:29), a passage that he would quote often to his son:
"Seest thou a man diligent in his calling, he shall stand before Kings."
As Franklin would recall when he was 78, with the wry mixture of
light vanity and amused self-awareness that pervades his autobiography, "I from thence considered industry as a means of obtaining
wealth and distinction, which encouraged me, though I did not think
that I should ever literally stand before kings, which, however, has
since happened; for I have stood before five, and even had the honor of
sitting down with one, the King of Denmark, to dinner."[13]

As Josiah prospered, his family grew; he would have seventeen children over a period of thirty-four years. Such fecundity was common among the robust and lusty Puritans: the Rev. Samuel Willard, pastor of the South Church, had twenty children; the famous theologian Cotton Mather had fifteen. Children tended to be a resource rather than a burden. They helped around the house and shop by handling most of the menial chores.[14]

To the three children who accompanied them from England, Josiah and Anne Franklin quickly added two more, both of whom lived to adulthood: Josiah Jr., born in 1685, and Anne Jr., born in 1687. Then, however, death struck brutally. Three times over the next eighteen months, Josiah made the procession across Milk Street to the South Church burial grounds: first in 1688 for a newborn son who died after five days; then in 1689 for his wife, Anne, who died a week after delivering another son; then for that son who died after another week. (One-quarter of all Boston newborns at the time died within a week.)

It was not unusual for men in colonial New England to outlive two or three wives. Of the first eighteen women who came to Massachusetts in 1628, for example, fourteen died within a year. Nor was it considered callous for a bereaved husband to remarry quickly. In fact, as in the case of Josiah, it was often considered an economic necessity. At the age of 31, he had five children to raise, a trade to tend, and a shop to keep. He needed a robust new wife, and he needed her quickly.

A VIRTUOUS WOMAN

Like the Franklins, the Folger (originally Foulgier) family was rebellious but also practical, and they shared the same mix of religious and economic restlessness. Descended from reformist Flemish Protestants who had fled to England in the sixteenth century, the Folgers were among the first wave of emigrants to depart for Massachusetts when Charles I and his Archbishop of Canterbury, William Laud, began cracking down on the Puritans. The family of John Folger, including his 18-year-old son Peter, sailed for Boston in 1635, when the town was a mere five years old.

On the voyage over, Peter met a young servant girl named Mary Morrill, who was indentured to one of the Puritan ministers aboard. After their arrival, Peter was able to buy her freedom for £20 and take her as his wife.

Having found religious and personal freedom, the Folgers were restless for economic opportunities. From Boston they moved to a new settlement up the river called Dedham, then to Watertown, and finally to Nantucket Island, where Peter became the schoolmaster. Most of the inhabitants were Indians, and he learned their language, taught them English, and attempted (with great success) to convert them to Christianity. Rebellious in nature, he underwent his own conversion and became a Baptist, which meant that the faithful Indians whom he had led to Christianity now had to follow him through a ritual that required total immersion.

Displaying the robust resistance to authority that ran in both the Folger and Franklin families, Peter was the sort of rebel destined to transform colonial America. As clerk of the court on Nantucket, he was at one point jailed for disobeying the local magistrate during a struggle between the island's wealthy shareholders and its growing middle class of shopkeepers and artisans.[15]

He also wrote a near-seditious pamphlet, in verse, sympathizing with the Indians during what became known as King Philip's War in 1676. The war, he declared, was the result of God's anger at the intolerance of the Puritan ministers in Boston. His passion overpowered his poetic talents: "Let Magistrates and Ministers / consider what they do; / Let them repeal those evil laws, / and break those bonds in two." Later, his grandson Benjamin Franklin would pronounce that the poem was "written with manly freedom and a pleasing simplicity."[16]

Peter and Mary Folger had ten children, the youngest of whom, Abiah, was born in 1667. When she was 21 and still unmarried, she moved to Boston to live with an older sister and her husband, who were members of the South Church. Although raised as a Baptist, Abiah joined the congregation shortly after her arrival. By July 1689, when the well-respected tallow chandler Josiah Franklin went there to bury his wife, Abiah was a faithful parishioner.[17]

Less than five months later, on November 25, 1689, they were married. Both were the youngest children in a large brood. Together they would live to unusually ripe ages—he to 87, she to 84. And their longevity was among the many traits they would bequeath to their famous youngest son, who himself would live to be 84. "He was a pious and prudent man, she a discreet and virtuous woman," Benjamin would later inscribe on their tombstone.

Over the next twelve years, Josiah and Abiah Franklin had six children: John (born 1690), Peter (1692), Mary (1694), James (1697), Sarah (1699), and Ebenezer (1701). Along with those from Josiah's first marriage, that made eleven children, all still unmarried, crammed into the tiny Milk Street house that also contained the tallow, soap, and candle equipment.

It might seem impossible to keep a watchful eye on so large a brood in such circumstances, and the Franklin tale provides tragic evidence that this was so. When he was a toddler of 16 months, Ebenezer drowned in a tub of his father's suds. Later that year, in 1703, the Franklins had another son, but he also died as a child.

So even though their next son, Benjamin, would spend his youth in a house with ten older siblings, the youngest of them would be seven years his senior. And he would have two younger sisters, Lydia (born 1708) and Jane (1712), looking up to him.

A SPUNKY LAD

Benjamin Franklin was born and baptized on the same day, a Sunday, January 17, 1706.* Boston was by then 76 years old, no longer a Puritan outpost but a thriving commercial center filled with preachers, merchants, seamen, and prostitutes. It had more than a thousand

---

* See page 503 for a concise chronology of events in this book. Franklin's birthdate of January 17, 1706, and all dates unless otherwise noted, are according to the Georgian calendar in use today. Until 1752, Britain and her colonies were still using the Julian calendar, which then differed by eleven days. In addition, they considered March 25, rather than January 1, to be the first day of a new year. Thus, under the Old Style calendar of the time, Franklin's birth was recorded as Sunday, January 6, 1705. Likewise, George Washington was born on February 11, 1731, on the Old Style calendar, but his birthday is now considered to be February 22, 1732.

homes, a thousand ships registered at its harbor, and seven thousand inhabitants, a figure that was doubling every twenty years.

As a kid growing up along the Charles River, Franklin was, he recalled, "generally the leader among the boys." One of their favorite gathering places was a salt marsh near the river's mouth, which had become a quagmire due to their constant trampling. Under Franklin's lead, the friends built themselves a wharf with stones intended for the construction of a house nearby. "In the evening when the workmen were gone home, I assembled a number of my playfellows, and we worked diligently like so many emmets, sometimes two or three to a stone, until we brought them all to make our little wharf." The next morning, he and the other culprits were caught and punished.

Franklin recounted the tale in his autobiography to illustrate, he said, his father's maxim "that nothing was useful which was not honest."[18] Yet, like many of Franklin's attempts at self-deprecation, the anecdote seems less designed to show how bad a boy he was than how good a leader he was. Throughout his life, he took palpable pride in his ability to organize cooperative endeavors and public-spirited projects.

Franklin's childhood days playing along the Charles River also instilled a lifelong love for swimming. Once he had learned and taught his playmates, he tinkered with ways to make himself go faster. The size of people's hands and feet, he realized, limited how much water they could push and thus their propelling power. So he made two oval palettes, with holes for his thumbs, and (as he explained in a letter to a friend) "I also fitted to the soles of my feet a kind of sandals." With these paddles and flippers, he could speed through the water.

Kites, as he would later famously show, could also be useful. Sending one aloft, he stripped, waded into a pond, floated on his back, and let it pull him. "Having then engaged another boy to carry my clothes round the pond," he recalled, "I began to cross the pond with my kite, which carried me quite over without the least fatigue and with the greatest pleasure imaginable."[19]

One childhood incident that he did not include in his autobiography, though he would recount it more than seventy years later for the amusement of his friends in Paris, occurred when he encountered a boy blowing a whistle. Enchanted by the device, he gave up all the coins in his pocket for it. His siblings proceeded to ridicule him, saying he had paid four times what it was worth. "I cried with vexation," Franklin recalled, "and the reflection gave me more chagrin than the whistle gave me pleasure." Frugality became for him not only a virtue but also a pleasure. "Industry and frugality," he wrote in describing the theme of Poor Richard's almanacs, are "the means of procuring wealth and thereby securing virtue."[20]

When Benjamin was 6, his family moved from the tiny two-room house on Milk Street, where fourteen children had been raised, to a larger home and shop in the heart of town, on Hanover and Union Streets. His mother was 45, and that year (1712) she gave birth to the last of her children, Jane, who was to become Benjamin's favorite sibling and lifelong correspondent.

Josiah Franklin's new house, coupled with the dwindling number of children still living with him, allowed him to entertain interesting guests for dinner. "At his table," Benjamin recalled, "he liked to have, as often as he could, some sensible friend or neighbor to converse with, and always took care to start some ingenious or useful topic for discourse which might tend to improve the minds of his children."

The conversations were so engrossing, Franklin claims in his autobiography, that he took "little or no notice" of what was served for dinner. This training instilled in him a "perfect inattention" to food for the rest of his life, a trait he deemed "a great convenience," albeit one that seems belied by the number of recipes of American and French culinary delights among his papers.[21]

The new home also allowed the Franklins to accommodate Josiah's brother Benjamin, who emigrated from England in 1715 when he was 65 and his namesake was 9. Like Josiah, the elder Benjamin found the New World inhospitable to his craft of silk dyeing, but unlike Josiah, he did not have the drive to learn a new trade. So he sat around the Franklin house writing bad poetry (including a 124-quatrain autobiography) and a useful family history, attending and transcribing sermons, amusing his nephew, and gradually getting on his brother's nerves.[22]

Uncle Benjamin stayed with the Franklins for four years, easily outlasting his welcome with his brother, if not with his nephew. Finally, he moved in with his own son Samuel, a cutler who had also immigrated to Boston. Years later, the younger Benjamin would write to his sister Jane and humorously recount the "disputes and misunderstandings" that grew between their father and uncle. The lesson his father drew was that visits from distant relatives "could not well be short enough for them to part good friends." In Poor Richard's almanac, Franklin would later put it more pithily: "Fish and guests stink after three days."[23]

EDUCATION

The plan for young Benjamin was to have him study for the ministry, Josiah's tenth son anointed as his tithe to the Lord. Uncle Benjamin was strongly supportive; among the many benefits of this plan was that it gave him something to do with his stash of secondhand sermons. For decades, he had scouted out the best preachers and transcribed their words in a neat shorthand of his own device. His nephew later noted with wry amusement that he "proposed to give me all his shorthand volumes, I suppose as a stock to set up with."

To prepare him for Harvard, Josiah sent his son, at age 8, to Boston Latin School, where Cotton Mather had studied and his son Samuel was then enrolled. Even though he was among the least privileged students, Franklin excelled in his first year, rising from the middle of the class to the very top, and then was jumped a grade ahead. Despite this success, Josiah abruptly changed his mind about sending him to Harvard. "My father," Franklin wrote, "burdened with a numerous family, was unable without inconvenience to support the expense of a college education."

This economic explanation is unsatisfying. The family was well-off enough, and there were fewer Franklin children being supported at home (only Benjamin and his two younger sisters) than had been the case for many years. There was no tuition at the Latin School, and as the top of his class he would easily have won a scholarship to Harvard. Of the forty-three students who entered the college when Franklin would have, only seven were from wealthy families; ten were sons of tradesmen, and four were orphans. The university at that time spent approximately 11 percent of its budget for financial aid, more than it does today.[24]

Most likely there was another factor. Josiah came to believe, no doubt correctly, that his youngest son was not suited for the clergy. Benjamin was skeptical, puckish, curious, irreverent, the type of person who would get a lifelong chuckle out of his uncle's notion that it would be useful for a new preacher to start his career with a cache of used sermons. Anecdotes about his youthful intellect and impish nature abound, but there are none that show him as pious or faithful.

Just the opposite. A tale related by his grandson, but not included in the autobiography, shows Franklin to be cheeky not only about religion but also about the wordiness in worship that was a hallmark of Puritan faith. "Dr. Franklin, when a child, found the long graces used by his father before and after meals very tedious," his grandson reported. "One day after the winter's provisions had been salted— 'I think, Father,' said Benjamin, 'if you were to say Grace over the whole cask—once for all—it would be a vast saving of time.'"[25]

So Benjamin was enrolled for a year at a writing and arithmetic academy two blocks away run by a mild but businesslike master named George Brownell. Franklin excelled in writing but failed math, a scholastic deficit he never fully remedied and that, combined with his lack of academic training in the field, would eventually condemn him to be merely the most ingenious scientist of his era rather than transcending into the pantheon of truly profound theorists such as Newton.

What would have happened if Franklin had, in fact, received a formal academic education and gone to Harvard? Some historians such as Arthur Tourtellot argue that he would have been stripped of his "spontaneity," "intuitive" literary style, "zest," "freshness," and the "unclutteredness" of his mind. And indeed, Harvard has been known to do that and worse to some of its charges.

But the evidence that Franklin would have so suffered is weak and does not do justice either to him or to Harvard. Given his skeptical turn of mind and allergy to authority, it is unlikely that Franklin would have become, as planned, a minister. Of the thirty-nine who were in what would have been his class, fewer than half eventually joined the clergy. His rebellious nature may even have been enhanced rather than repressed; the college administrators were at the time wrestling mightily with the excessive partying, eating, and drinking that was infecting the campus.

One aspect of Franklin's genius was the variety of his interests, from science to government to diplomacy to journalism, all of them approached from a very practical rather than theoretical angle. Had he gone to Harvard, this diversity in outlook need not have been lost, for the college under the liberal John Leverett was no longer under the firm control of the Puritan clergy. By the 1720s it offered famous courses in physics, geography, logic, and ethics as well as the classics and theology, and a telescope atop Massachusetts Hall made it a center for astronomy. Fortunately, Franklin acquired something that was perhaps just as enlightening as a Harvard education: the training and experiences of a publisher, printer, and newspaperman.

APPRENTICE

At age 10, with but two years of schooling, Franklin went to work full time in his father's candle and soap shop, replacing his older brother John, who had served his term as an apprentice and left to set up his own business in Rhode Island. It was not pleasant work— skimming rendered tallow from boiling cauldrons of fat was particularly noxious, and cutting wicks and filling molds was quite mindless—and Franklin made clear his distaste for it. More ominously, he expressed his "strong inclination for the sea," even though his brother Josiah Jr. had recently been lost to its depths.

Fearing that his son would "break loose and go to sea," Josiah took him on long walks through Boston to see other craftsmen, so that he could "observe my inclination and endeavor to fix it on some trade that would keep me on land." This instilled in Franklin a lifelong appreciation for craftsmen and tradesmen. His passing familiarity with an array of crafts also helped make him an accomplished tinkerer, which served him in good stead as an inventor.

Josiah eventually concluded that Benjamin would be best as a cutler, making knives and grinding blades. So he was, at least for a few days, apprenticed to Uncle Benjamin's son Samuel. But Samuel demanded an apprenticeship fee that struck Josiah as unreasonable, especially given the history of both hospitality and aggravation that existed between him and the elder Benjamin.[26]

Instead, almost by default rather than design, young Benjamin ended up apprenticed in 1718, at age 12, to his brother James, 21, who had recently returned from training in England to set up as a printer. At first, the willful young Benjamin balked at signing the indenture papers; he was a little older than usual for starting an apprenticeship, and his brother demanded a nine-year term instead of the typical seven years. Eventually, Benjamin signed on, though he was not destined to stay indentured until he was 21.

During his time in London, James saw how Grub Street balladeers would churn out odes and hawk them in the coffeehouses. So he promptly put Benjamin to work not only pushing type but also producing poetry. With encouragement from his uncle, young Franklin wrote two works based on news stories, both dealing with the sea: one about a family killed in a boating accident, and the other about the killing of the pirate known as Blackbeard. They were, as Franklin recalled, "wretched stuff," but they sold well, which "flattered my vanity."[27]

Herman Melville would one day write that Franklin was "everything but a poet." His father, no romantic, in fact preferred it that way, and he put an end to Benjamin's versifying. "My father discouraged me by ridiculing my performances and telling me verse-makers were generally beggars; so I escaped being a poet, most probably a very bad one."

When Franklin began his apprenticeship, Boston had only one newspaper: *The Boston News-Letter*, which had been launched in 1704 by a successful printer named John Campbell, who was also the town's postmaster. Then, as today, there was an advantage in the media business to controlling both content and distribution. Campbell was able to join forces with a network of fellow postmasters running from New Hampshire to Virginia. His books and papers were sent along the route for free—unlike those of other printers—and the postmasters in his network would send him a steady stream of news items. In addition, because he held an official position he could proclaim that his paper was "published by authority," an important certification at a time when the press did not pride itself on independence.

The link between being the postmaster and a newspaper publisher was so natural that when Campbell lost the former job, his successor as postmaster, William Brooker, assumed that he would also take over the newspaper. Campbell, however, kept hold of it, which prompted Brooker to launch, in December 1719, a rival: *The Boston Gazette.* He hired James Franklin, the cheapest of the town's printers, to produce it for him.

But after two years, James lost the contract to print the *Gazette,* and he did something quite audacious. He launched what was then the only truly independent newspaper in the colonies and the first with literary aspirations. His weekly *New England Courant* would very explicitly *not* be "published by authority."[28]

The *Courant* would be remembered by history mainly because it contained the first published prose of Benjamin Franklin. And James would become known for being the harsh and jealous master described in his brother's autobiography. In fairness, however, the *Courant* ought to be remembered on its own as America's first fiercely independent newspaper, a bold, antiestablishment journal that helped to create the nation's tradition of an irreverent press. "It was the first open effort to defy the norm," literary historian Perry Miller has written.[29]

Defying authority in Boston at that time meant defying the Mathers and the role of the Puritan clergy in secular life, a cause James took up on the first page of his paper's first edition. Unfortunately, the battle he chose was over inoculation for smallpox, and he happened to pick the wrong side.

Smallpox epidemics had devastated Massachusetts at regular intervals in the ninety years since its founding. A 1677 outbreak wiped out seven hundred people, 12 percent of the population. During the epidemic of 1702, during which three of his children were stricken but survived, Cotton Mather began studying the disease. A few years later, he was introduced to the practice of inoculation by his black slave, who had undergone the procedure in Africa and showed Mather his scar. Mather checked with other blacks in Boston and found that inoculation was a standard practice in parts of Africa.

Just before James Franklin's *Courant* made its debut in 1721, the HMS *Seahorse* arrived from the West Indies carrying what would become a new wave of smallpox. Within months, nine hundred of Boston's ten thousand inhabitants would be dead. Mather, trained as a physician before becoming a preacher, sent a letter to the ten practicing doctors in Boston (only one of whom had a medical degree) summarizing his knowledge of the African inoculation and urging that they adopt the practice. (Mather had evolved quite far from the superstitions that had led him to support Salem's witch hunts.)

Most of the doctors rejected the notion, and (with little justification other than a desire to prick at the pretensions of the preachers) so did James Franklin's new newspaper. The first issue of the *Courant* (August 7, 1721) contained an essay by a young friend of James's, John Checkley, a sassy Oxford-educated Anglican. He singled out for his sally the Puritan clergy, who "by teaching and practicing what's Orthodox, pray hard against sickness, yet preach up the Pox!" The issue also carried a diatribe by the town's only physician who actually had a medical degree, Dr. William Douglass, who dismissed inoculation as "the practice of Greek old women" and called Mather and his fellow ministerial proponents "six gentlemen of piety and learning profoundly ignorant of the matter." It was the first example, and a robust one at that, of a newspaper attacking the ruling establishment in America.[30]

Increase Mather, the family's aging patriarch, thundered, "I cannot but pity poor Franklin, who though but a young man, it may be speedily he must appear before the judgment seat of God." Cotton Mather, his son, wrote a letter to a rival paper denouncing the "notorious, scandalous paper called the *Courant,* full-freighted with nonsense, unmanliness, railery," and comparing its contributors to the Hell-Fire Club, a well-known clique of dapper young heretics in London. Cotton's cousin, a preacher named Thomas Walter, weighed in by writing a scathing piece entitled "The Anti-*Courant.*"

Knowing full well that this public spat would sell papers, and eager

to profit from both sides of an argument, James Franklin quite happily
took on the job of publishing and selling Thomas Walter's rebuttal.
However, the escalating personal nature of the controversy began to
unsettle him. After a few weeks, he announced in an editor's note that
he had banned Checkley from his paper for letting the feud get too
vindictive. Henceforth, he promised, the *Courant* would aim to be "innocently diverting" and would publish opinions on either side of the
inoculation controversy as long as they were "free from malicious reflections."[31]

Benjamin Franklin managed to stay out of his brother's smallpox
battle with the Mather family, and he never mentioned it in his autobiography or letters, a striking omission that suggests that he was not
proud of the side the paper chose. He later became a fervent advocate
of inoculation, painfully and poignantly espousing the cause right
after his 4-year-old son, Francis, died of the pox in 1736. And he
would, both as an aspiring boy of letters and as a striver who sought
the patronage of influential elders, end up becoming Cotton Mather's
admirer and, a few years later, his acquaintance.

BOOKS

The print trade was a natural calling for Franklin. "From a child I
was fond of reading," he recalled, "and all the little money that came
into my hands was ever laid out in books." Indeed, books were the
most important formative influence in his life, and he was lucky to
grow up in Boston, where libraries had been carefully nurtured since
the *Arabella* brought fifty volumes along with the town's first settlers in
1630. By the time Franklin was born, Cotton Mather had built a private library of almost three thousand volumes rich in classical and scientific as well as theological works. This appreciation of books was
one of the traits shared by the Puritanism of Mather and the Enlightenment of Locke, worlds that would combine in the character of Benjamin Franklin.[32]

Less than a mile from Mather's library was the small bookshelf of
Josiah Franklin. Though certainly modest, it was still notable that an

uneducated chandler would have one at all. Fifty years later, Franklin could still recall its titles: Plutarch's *Lives* ("which I read abundantly"), Daniel Defoe's *An Essay upon Projects,* Cotton Mather's *Bonifacius: Essays to Do Good,* and an assortment of "books in polemic divinity."

Once he began working in his brother's print shop, Franklin was able to sneak books from the apprentices who worked for booksellers, as long as he returned the volumes clean. "Often I sat up in my room reading the greatest part of the night, when the book was borrowed in the evening and to be returned early in the morning, lest it should be missed or wanted."

Franklin's favorite books were about voyages, spiritual as well as terrestrial, and the most notable of these was about both: John Bunyan's *Pilgrim's Progress,* the saga of the tenacious quest by a man named Christian to reach the Celestial City, which was published in 1678 and quickly became popular among Puritans and other dissenters. As important as its religious message, at least for Franklin, was the refreshingly clean and sparse prose style it offered in an age when writing had become clotted by the richness of the Restoration. "Honest John was the first that I know of," Franklin correctly noted, "who mixed narration and dialogue, a method of writing very engaging to the reader."

A central theme of Bunyan's book—and of the passage from Puritanism to Enlightenment, and of Franklin's life—was contained in its title: *progress,* the concept that individuals, and humanity in general, move forward and improve based on a steady increase of knowledge and the wisdom that comes from conquering adversity. Christian's famous opening phrase sets the tone: "As I walked through the wilderness of this world . . ." Even for the faithful, this progress was not solely the handiwork of the Lord but also the result of a human struggle, by individuals and communities, to triumph over obstacles.

Likewise, another Franklin favorite—and one must pause to marvel at a 12-year-old with such tastes in leisure pursuits—was Plutarch's *Lives,* which is also based on the premise that individual endeavor can change the course of history for the better. Plutarch's heroes, like Bunyan's Christian, are honorable men who believe that their personal strivings are intertwined with the progress of humanity. History is a tale, Franklin came to believe, not of immutable forces but of human endeavors.

This outlook clashed with some of the tenets of Calvinism, such as the essential depravity of man and the predestination of his soul, which Franklin would eventually abandon as he edged his way closer to the less daunting deism that became the creed of choice during the Enlightenment. Yet, there were many aspects of Puritanism that made a lasting impression, most notably the practical, sociable, community-oriented aspects of that religion.

These were expressed eloquently in a work that Franklin often cited as a key influence: *Bonifacius: Essays to Do Good,* one of the few gentle tracts of the more than four hundred written by Cotton Mather. "If I have been," Franklin wrote to Cotton Mather's son almost seventy years later, "a useful citizen, the public owes the advantage of it to that book." Franklin's first pen name, Silence Dogood, paid homage both to the book and to a famous sermon by Mather, "Silentiarius: The Silent Sufferer."

Mather's tract called on members of the community to form voluntary associations to benefit society, and he personally founded a neighborhood improvement group, known as Associated Families, which Benjamin's father joined. He also urged the creation of Young Men Associated clubs and of Reforming Societies for the Suppression of Disorders, which would seek to improve local laws, provide charity for the poor, and encourage religious behavior.[33]

Mather's ideas were influenced by Daniel Defoe's *An Essay upon Projects,* which was another favorite book of Franklin's. Published in 1697, it proposed for London many of the sort of community projects that Franklin would later launch in Philadelphia: fire insurance associations, voluntary seamen's societies to create pensions, schemes to provide welfare for the elderly and widows, academies to educate the children of the middle class, and (with just a touch of Defoe humor) institutions to house the mentally retarded paid for by a tax on authors because they happened to get a greater share of intelligence at birth just as the retarded happened to get less.[34]

Among Defoe's most progressive notions was that it was "barbarous" and "inhumane" to deny women equal education and rights, and *An Essay upon Projects* contains a diatribe against such sexism. Around that time, Franklin and "another bookish lad" named John Collins began engaging each other in debates as an intellectual sport. Their first topic was the education of women, with Collins opposing it. "I took the contrary side," Franklin recalled, not totally out of conviction but "perhaps a little for dispute sake."

As a result of his mock debates with Collins, Franklin began to tailor for himself a persona that was less contentious and confrontational, which made him seem endearing and charming as he grew older—or, to a small but vocal cadre of enemies, manipulative and conniving. Being "disputatious," he concluded, was "a very bad habit" because contradicting people produced "disgusts and perhaps enmities." Later in his life he would wryly say of disputing: "Persons of good sense, I have since observed, seldom fall into it, except lawyers, university men, and men of all sorts that have been bred at Edinburgh."

Instead, after stumbling across some rhetoric books that extolled Socrates' method of building an argument through gentle queries, he "dropped my abrupt contradiction" style of argument and "put on the humbler enquirer" of the Socratic method. By asking what seemed to be innocent questions, Franklin would draw people into making concessions that would gradually prove whatever point he was trying to assert. "I found this method the safest for myself and very embarrassing to those against whom I used it; therefore, I took a delight in it." Although he later abandoned the more annoying aspects of a Socratic approach, he continued to favor gentle indirection rather than confrontation in making his arguments.[35]

SILENCE DOGOOD

Part of his debate with Collins over the education of women was waged by exchanging letters, and his father happened to read them. Though Josiah did not take sides in the dispute (he achieved his own semblance of fairness by providing little formal education to any of his children of either sex), he did criticize his son for his weak and unpersuasive writing style. In reaction, the precocious young teen devised for himself a self-improvement course with the help of a volume of *The Spectator* that he found.

The Spectator, a London daily that flourished in 1711–12, featured deft essays by Joseph Addison and Richard Steele probing the vanities and values of contemporary life. The outlook was humanistic and enlightened, yet light. As Addison put it, "I shall endeavor to enliven Morality with Wit, and to temper Wit with Morality."

As part of his self-improvement course, Franklin read the essays, took brief notes, and laid them aside for a few days. Then he tried to recreate the essay in his own words, after which he compared his composition to the original. Sometimes he would jumble up the notes he took, so that he would have to figure out on his own the best order to build the essay's argument.

He turned some of the essays into poetry, which helped him (so he thought) expand his vocabulary by forcing him to search for words that had similar meanings but different rhythms and sounds. These, too, he turned back into essays after a few days, comparing them to see where he had diverged from the original. When he found his own version wanting, he would correct it. "But I sometimes had the pleasure of fancying that in certain particulars of small import I had been lucky enough to improve the method or the language, and this encouraged me to think that I might possibly in time come to be a tolerable English writer, of which I was extremely ambitious."[36]

More than making himself merely "tolerable" as a writer, he became the most popular writer in colonial America. His self-taught style, as befitting a protégé of Addison and Steele, featured a fun and conversational prose that was lacking in poetic flourish but powerful in its directness.

Thus was born Silence Dogood. James Franklin's *Courant*, which was modeled on *The Spectator*, featured sassy pseudonymous essays, and his print shop attracted a congregation of clever young contributors who liked to hang around and praise each other's prose. Benjamin was eager to become part of the crowd, but he knew that James, already jealous of his upstart young brother, was unlikely to encourage him. "Hearing their conversations, and their accounts of the approbation their papers were received with, I was excited to try my hand among them."

So one night, Franklin, disguising his handwriting, wrote an essay and slipped it under the printing house door. The cadre of Couranteers who gathered the next day lauded the anonymous submission, and Franklin had the "exquisite pleasure" of listening as they decided to feature it on the front page of the issue out the next Monday, April 2, 1722.

The literary character Franklin invented was a triumph of imagination. Silence Dogood was a slightly prudish widowed woman from a rural area, created by a spunky unmarried Boston teenager who had never spent a night outside of the city. Despite the uneven quality of the essays, Franklin's ability to speak convincingly as a woman was remarkable, and it showed both his creativity and his appreciation for the female mind.

The echoes of Addison are apparent from the outset. In Addison's first *Spectator* essay, he wrote, "I have observed that a reader seldom peruses a book with pleasure 'til he knows whether the writer of it be a black or a fair man, of a mild or choleric disposition, married or a bachelor." Franklin likewise began by justifying an autobiographical introduction from his fictitious narrator: "It is observed, that the generality of people, nowadays, are unwilling either to commend or dispraise what they read, until they are in some measure informed who or what the author of it is, whether he be poor or rich, old or young, a scholar or a leather apron man."

One reason the Silence Dogood essays are so historically notable is that they were among the first examples of what would become a quintessential American genre of humor: the wry, homespun mix of folksy tales and pointed observations that was perfected by such Franklin descendants as Mark Twain and Will Rogers. For example, in the second of the essays, Silence Dogood tells how the minister to whom she was apprenticed decided to make her his wife: "Having made several unsuccessful fruitless attempts on the more topping sort of our sex, and being tired with making troublesome journeys and visits to no purpose, he began unexpectedly to cast a loving eye upon me . . . There is certainly scarce any part of a man's life in which he appears more silly and ridiculous than when he makes his first onset in courtship."

Franklin's portrayal of Mrs. Dogood exhibits a literary dexterity that was quite subtle for a 16-year-old boy. "I could easily be persuaded to marry again," he had her declare. "I am courteous and affable, good humored (unless I am first provoked) and handsome, and sometimes witty." The flick of the word "sometimes" is particularly deft. In describing her beliefs and biases, Franklin had Mrs. Dogood assert an attitude that would, with his encouragement, become part of the emerging American character: "I am . . . a mortal enemy to arbitrary government and unlimited power. I am naturally very jealous for the rights and liberties of my country; and the least appearance of an encroachment on those invaluable privileges is apt to make my blood boil exceedingly. I have likewise a natural inclination to observe and reprove the faults of others, at which I have an excellent faculty." It was as good a description of the real Benjamin Franklin—and, indeed, of a typical American—as is likely to be found anywhere.[37]

Of the fourteen Dogood essays that Franklin wrote between April and October 1722, the one that stands out both as journalism and self-revelation is his attack on the college he never got to attend. Most of the classmates he had bested at Boston Latin had just entered Harvard, and Franklin could not refrain from lampooning them and their institution. The form he used was an allegorical narrative cast as a dream. In doing so, he drew on, and perhaps was mildly parodying, Bunyan's *Pilgrim's Progress,* also an allegorical journey set as a dream. Addison had used the form somewhat clumsily in an issue of *The Spectator* that Franklin read, which recounted the dream of a banker about an allegorical virgin named Public Credit.[38]

In the essay, Mrs. Dogood recounts falling asleep under an apple tree while she mulls over whether to send her son to Harvard. As she journeys in her dream toward this temple of learning, she makes a discovery about those who send sons there: "Most of them consulted their own purses instead of their children's capacities: so that I observed a great many, yea, the most part of those who were traveling thither were little better than Dunces and Blockheads." The gate of the temple, she finds, is guarded by "two sturdy porters named Riches and Poverty," and only those who meet the approval of the former could get in. Most of the students are content to dally with the figures called Idleness and Ignorance. "They learn little more than how to carry themselves handsomely, and enter a room genteelly (which might as well be acquired at a dancing school), and from thence they return, after abundance of trouble and charge, as great blockheads as ever, only more proud and self-conceited."

Picking up on the proposals of Mather and Defoe for voluntary civic associations, Franklin devoted two of his Silence Dogood essays to the topic of relief for single women. For widows like herself, Mrs. Dogood proposes an insurance scheme funded by subscriptions from married couples. The next essay extended the idea to spinsters. A "friendly society" would be formed that would guarantee £500 "in ready cash" to any member who reaches age 30 and is still not married. The money, Mrs. Dogood notes, would come with a condition: "No woman, who after claiming and receiving, has had the good fortune to marry, shall entertain any company [by praising] her husband above the space of one hour at a time upon pain of returning one half the money into the office for the first offense, and upon the second offense to return the remainder." In these essays, Franklin was being gently satirical rather than fully serious. But his interest in civic associations would later find more earnest expression, as we shall see, when he became established as a young tradesman in Philadelphia.

Franklin's vanity was further fed during that summer of 1722, when his brother was jailed for three weeks—without trial—by Massachusetts authorities for the "high affront" of questioning their competence in pursuing pirates. For three issues, Benjamin got to put out the paper.

He boasts in his autobiography that "I had the management of the paper, and I made bold to give our rulers some rubs in it, which my brother took very kindly, while others began to consider me in an unfavorable light as a young genius that had a turn for libeling and satire." In fact, other than a letter to the readers written from prison by James, nothing in Benjamin's three issues directly challenged the civil authorities. The closest he came was having Mrs. Dogood quote in full an essay from an English newspaper that defended free speech.

"Without freedom of thought there can be no such thing as wisdom," it declared, "and no such thing as public liberty without freedom of speech."[39]

The "rubs" that Franklin remembered came a week after his brother's return from prison. Writing as Silence Dogood, he unleashed a piercing attack on the civil authorities, perhaps the most biting of his entire career. The question that Mrs. Dogood posed was "Whether a Commonwealth suffers more by hypocritical pretenders to religion or by the openly profane?"

Unsurprisingly, Franklin's Mrs. Dogood argued that "some late thoughts of this nature have inclined me to think that the hypocrite is the most dangerous person of the two, especially if he sustains a post in the government." The piece attacked the link between the church and the state, which was the very foundation of the Puritan commonwealth. Governor Thomas Dudley, who moved from the ministry to the law, is cited (though not by name) as an example: "The most dangerous hypocrite in a Commonwealth is one who leaves the gospel for the sake of the law. A man compounded of law and gospel is able to cheat a whole country with his religion and then destroy them under color of law."[40]

By the fall of 1722, Franklin was running short of ideas for Silence Dogood. Worse yet, his brother was beginning to suspect the provenance of the pieces. In her thirteenth submission, Silence Dogood noted that she had overheard a conversation one night in which a gentleman had said, "Though I wrote in the character of a woman, he knew me to be a man; but, continued he, he has more need of endeavoring a reformation in himself than spending his wit in satirizing others." The next Dogood would be Franklin's last. When he revealed Mrs. Dogood's true identity, it raised his stature among the Couranteers but "did not quite please" James. "He thought, probably with reason, that it tended to make me too vain."

Silence Dogood had been able to get away with an attack on hypocrisy and religion, but when James penned a similar piece in January 1723, he landed in trouble yet again. "Of all knaves," he wrote, "the religious knave is the worst." Religion was important, he wrote, but, using words that would describe the lifelong attitude of his younger brother, he added, "too much of it is worse than none at all." The local authorities, noting "that the tendency of the said paper is to mock religion," promptly passed a resolution that required James to submit each issue to the authorities for approval before publication. James defied the order with relish.

The General Court responded by forbidding James Franklin from publishing the *Courant*. At a secret meeting in his shop, it was decided that the best way around the order was to continue to print the paper, but without James as its publisher. On Monday, February 11, 1723, there appeared atop the *Courant* the masthead: "Printed and sold by Benjamin Franklin."

Benjamin's *Courant* was more cautious than that of his brother. An editorial in his first issue denounced publications that were "hateful" and "malicious," and it declared that henceforth the *Courant* would be "designed purely for the diversion and merriment of the reader" and to "entertain the town with the most comical and diverting incidents of human life." The master of the paper, the editorial declared, would be the Roman god Janus, who could look two ways at once.[41]

The next few issues, however, hardly lived up to that billing. Most articles were slightly stale dispatches containing foreign news or old speeches. There was only one essay that was clearly written by Franklin, a wry musing on the folly of titles such as Viscount and Master. (His aversion to hereditary and aristocratic titles would be a theme throughout his life.) After a few weeks, James returned to the helm of the *Courant*, in fact if not officially, and he resumed treating Benjamin as an apprentice, subject to occasional beatings, rather than as a brother and fellow writer. Such treatment "demeaned me too much," Franklin recalled, and he became eager to move on. He had an urge for independence that he would help to make a hallmark of the American character.

THE RUNAWAY

Franklin managed his escape by taking advantage of a ruse his brother had contrived. When James had pretended to turn over the *Courant* to Benjamin, he signed an official discharge of his apprenticeship to make the transfer seem legitimate. But he then made Benjamin sign a new apprentice agreement that would be kept secret. A few months later, Benjamin decided to run away. He assumed, correctly, that his brother would realize that it was unwise to try to enforce the secret indenture.

Benjamin Franklin left behind a brother whose paper would slowly fail and whose reputation would eventually be reduced to a tarnished historical footnote. James was doomed by his brother's sharp pen to be remembered "for the blows his passion too often urged him to bestow upon me." Indeed, his significance in Franklin's life is described in a brusque footnote in the *Autobiography*, written during Franklin's time as a colonial agent fighting British rule: "I fancy his harsh and tyrannical treatment of me might be a means of impressing me with that aversion to arbitrary power that has stuck to me through my whole life."

James deserved better. If Franklin learned an "aversion to arbitrary power" from him, it was not merely because of his alleged tyrannical style but because he had set an example by challenging, with bravery and spunk, Boston's ruling elite. James was the first great fighter for an independent press in America, and he was the most important journalistic influence on his younger brother.

He was also an important literary influence. Silence Dogood may have been, in Benjamin's mind, modeled on Addison and Steele, but in fact she more closely resembled, in her down-home vernacular and common-touch perceptions, Abigail Afterwit, Jack Dulman, and the other pseudonymous characters that had been created for the *Courant* by James.

Benjamin's break with his brother was fortunate for his career. As great as it was to be raised in Boston, it would likely have become a constricting town for a free-spirited deist who had not attended Harvard. "I had already made myself a little obnoxious to the governing party," he later wrote, "and it was likely I might if I stayed soon bring myself into scrapes." His mockery of religion meant that he was pointed to on the streets "with horror by good people as an infidel or atheist." All in all, it was a good time for him to leave both his brother and Boston behind.[42]

It was a tradition among American pioneers, when their communities became too confining, to strike out for the frontier. But Franklin was a different type of American rebel. The wilderness did not beckon. Instead, he was enticed by the new commercial centers, New York and Philadelphia, that offered the chance to become a self-made success. John Winthrop may have led his Puritan band on an errand into the wilderness; Franklin, on the other hand, was part of a new breed leading an errand into the Market streets.

Afraid that his brother would try to detain him, Franklin had a friend secretly book him passage on a sloop for New York using the cover story that it was for a boy who needed to sneak away because he "had an intrigue with a girl of bad character" (or, as Franklin put it in an earlier draft, "had got a naughty girl with child"). Selling some of his books to pay for the fare, the 17-year-old Franklin set sail in a fair wind on the evening of Wednesday, September 25, 1723. The following Monday, the *New England Courant* carried a succinct, slightly sad little ad: "James Franklin, printer in Queen Street, wants a likely lad for an Apprentice."[43]

CHAPTER THREE

JOURNEYMAN

Philadelphia and London, 1723–1726

KEIMER'S SHOP

As a young apprentice, Franklin had read a book extolling vegetarianism. He embraced the diet, but not just for moral and health reasons. His main motive was financial: it enabled him to take the money his brother allotted him for food and save half for books. While his coworkers went off for hearty meals, Franklin ate biscuits and raisins and used the time for study, "in which I made the greater progress from that greater clearness of head and quicker apprehension which usually attend temperance in eating and drinking."[1]

But Franklin was a reasonable soul, so wedded to being rational that he became adroit at rationalizing. During his voyage from Boston to New York, when his boat lay becalmed off Block Island, the crew caught and cooked some cod. Franklin at first refused any, until the aroma from the frying pan became too enticing. With droll self-awareness, he later recalled what happened:

> I balanced some time between principle and inclination until I recollected that when the fish were opened, I saw smaller fish taken out of their stomachs. "Then," thought I, "if you eat one another, I don't see why we may not eat you." So I dined upon cod very heartily and have since continued to eat as other people, returning only now and then occasionally to a vegetable diet.

From this he drew a wry, perhaps even a bit cynical, lesson that he expressed as a maxim: "So convenient a thing it is to be a reasonable creature, since it enables one to find or make a reason for everything one has a mind to do."[2]

Franklin's rationalism would make him an exemplar of the Enlightenment, the age of reason that flourished in eighteenth-century Europe and America. He had little use for the fervor of the religious age into which he was born, nor for the sublime sentiments of the Romantic period that began budding near the end of his life. But like Voltaire, he was able to poke fun at his own efforts, and that of humanity in general, to be guided by reason. A recurring theme in his autobiography, as well as in his tales and almanacs, was his amusement at man's ability to rationalize what was convenient.

At 17, Franklin was physically striking: muscular, barrel-chested, open-faced, and almost six feet tall. He had the happy talent of being at ease in almost any company, from scrappy tradesmen to wealthy merchants, scholars to rogues. His most notable trait was a personal magnetism; he attracted people who wanted to help him. Never shy, and always eager to win friends and patrons, he gregariously exploited this charm.

On his runaway journey, for example, he met the sole printer in New York, William Bradford, who had published editorials supporting James Franklin's fight against the "oppressors and bigots" in Boston. Bradford had no job to offer, but he suggested that the young runaway continue on to Philadelphia and seek work with his son Andrew Bradford, who ran the family print shop and weekly newspaper there.

Franklin arrived at Philadelphia's Market Street wharf on a Sunday morning ten days after his departure from Boston. In his pocket he had nothing more than a Dutch dollar and about a shilling in copper, the latter of which he gave to the boatmen to pay for his passage. They tried to decline it, because Franklin had helped with the rowing, but he insisted. He also gave away two of the three puffy rolls he bought to a mother and child he had met on the journey. "A man [is] sometimes more generous when he has little money than when he has plenty," he later wrote, "perhaps through fear of being thought to have but little."[3]

From his first moments in Philadelphia, Franklin cared about such appearances. American individualists sometimes boast of not worrying about what others think of them. Franklin, more typically, nurtured his reputation, as a matter of both pride and utility, and he became the country's first unabashed public relations expert. "I took care not only to be in *reality* industrious and frugal," he later wrote, "but to avoid all *appearances* of the contrary" (his emphasis). Especially in his early years as a young tradesman, he was, in the words of the critic Jonathan Yardley, "a self-created and self-willed man who moved through life at a calculated pace toward calculated ends."[4]

With a population of two thousand, Philadelphia was then America's second-largest village after Boston. Envisioned by William Penn as a "green country town," it featured a well-planned grid of wide streets lined with brick houses. In addition to the original Quakers who had settled there fifty years earlier, the city named for brotherly love had attracted raucous and entrepreneurial German, Scotch, and Irish immigrants who turned it into a lively marketplace filled with shops and taverns. Though its economy was sputtering and most of its streets were dirty and unpaved, the tone set by both the Quakers and subsequent immigrants was appealing to Franklin. They tended to be diligent, unpretentious, friendly, and tolerant, especially compared to the Puritans of Boston.

The morning after his arrival, rested and better dressed, Franklin called on Andrew Bradford's shop. There he found not only the young printer but also his father, William, who had come from New York on horseback and made it there faster. Andrew had no immediate work for the runaway, so William brought him around to see the town's other printer, Samuel Keimer—a testament both to Franklin's charming ability to enlist patrons and to the peculiar admixture of cooperation and competition so often found among American tradesmen.

Keimer was a disheveled and quirky man with a motley printing operation. He asked Franklin a few questions, gave him a composing stick to assess his skills, and then promised to employ him as soon as he had more work. Not knowing that William was the father of his competitor, Keimer volubly described his plans for luring away most of Andrew Bradford's business. Franklin stood by silently, marveling at the elder Bradford's craftiness. After Bradford left, Franklin recalled, Keimer "was greatly surprised when I told him who the old man was."

Even after this inauspicious introduction, Franklin was able to get work from Keimer while he lodged with the younger Bradford. When Keimer finally insisted that he find living quarters that were less of a professional conflict, he fortuitously was able to rent a room from John Read, the father of the young girl who had been so amused by his appearance the day he straggled off the boat. "My chest and clothes being come by this time, I made rather a more respectable appearance in the eyes of Miss Read than I had done when she first happened to see me eating my roll in the street," he noted.[5]

Franklin thought Keimer an "odd fish," but he enjoyed having sport with him as they shared their love for philosophical debate. Franklin honed the Socratic method he found so useful for winning arguments without antagonizing opponents. He would ask Keimer questions that seemed innocent and tangential but eventually exposed his logical fallacies. Keimer, who was prone to embracing eclectic religious beliefs, was so impressed that he proposed they establish a sect together. Keimer would be in charge of the doctrines, such as not trimming one's beard, and Franklin would be in charge of defending them. Franklin agreed with one condition: that vegetarianism be part of the creed. The experiment ended after three months when Keimer, ravenous, gave in to temptation and ate an entire roast pig by himself one evening.

Franklin's magnetism attracted not only patrons but also friends. With his clever mind, disarming wit, and winning smile, he became a popular member of the town's coterie of young tradesmen. His clique included three young clerks: Charles Osborne, Joseph Watson, and James Ralph. Ralph was the most literary of the group, a poet convinced both of his own talent and of the need to be self-indulgent in order to be a great artist. Osborne, a critical lad, was jealous and invariably belittled Ralph's efforts. On one of their long walks by the river, during which the four friends read their work to one another, Ralph had a poem he knew Osborne would criticize. So he got Franklin to read the poem as if it were his own. Osborne, falling for the ruse, heaped praise on it, teaching Franklin a rule of human nature that served him well (with a few exceptions) throughout his career: people are more likely to admire your work if you're able to keep them from feeling jealous of you.[6]

AN UNRELIABLE PATRON

The most fateful patron Franklin befriended was Pennsylvania's effusive governor Sir William Keith, a well-meaning but feckless busybody. They met as a result of a passionate letter Franklin had written to a brother-in-law explaining why he was happy in Philadelphia and had no desire to return to Boston or let his parents know where he was. The relative showed the letter to Governor Keith, who expressed surprise that a missive so eloquent had been written by a lad so young. The governor, who realized that both of the established printers in his province were wretched, decided to seek out Franklin and encourage him.

When Governor Keith, dressed in all his finery, marched up the street to Keimer's print shop, the disheveled owner bustled out to greet him. To his surprise, Keith asked to see Franklin, whom he proceeded to lavish with compliments and an invitation to join him for a drink. Keimer, Franklin later noted, "stared like a pig poisoned."[7]

Over fine Madeira at a nearby tavern, Governor Keith offered to help Franklin set up on his own. He would use his influence, Keith promised, to get him the province's official business and would write Franklin's father a letter exhorting him to help finance his son. Keith followed up with invitations to dinner, further flattery, and continued encouragement. So, with a fulsome letter from Keith in hand and dreams of a familial reconciliation followed by fame and fortune, Franklin was ready to face his family again. He boarded a ship heading for Boston in April 1724.

It had been seven months since he had run away, and his parents were not even sure that he was still alive, so they were thrilled by his return and welcomed him warmly. Franklin had not, however, yet learned his lesson about the pitfalls of pride and of provoking jealousy.

He sauntered down to the print shop of his jilted brother James, proudly sporting a "genteel new suit," a fancy watch, and £5 of silver coins bulging his pocket. James looked him up and down, turned on his heels, and silently went back to work.

Franklin could not refrain from flaunting his new status. As James stewed, he regaled the shop's young journeymen with tales of his happy life in Philadelphia, spread his silver coins on the table for them to admire, and gave them money to buy drinks. James later told their mother he could never forget nor forgive the offense. "In this, however, he was mistaken," Franklin recalled.

His family's old antagonist Cotton Mather was more receptive, and instructive. He invited young Franklin over, chatted with him in his magnificent library, and let it be known that he forgave him for the barbs that had appeared in the *Courant*. As they were making their way out, they went through a narrow passage and Mather suddenly warned, "Stoop! Stoop!" Franklin, not understanding the exhortation, bumped his head on a low beam. As was his wont, Mather turned it into a homily: "Let this be a caution to you not always to hold your head so high. Stoop, young man, stoop—as you go through this world—and you'll miss many hard thumps." As Franklin later recalled to Mather's son, "This advice, thus beat into my head, has frequently been of use to me, and I often think of it when I see pride mortified and misfortunes brought upon people by carrying their heads too high." Although the lesson was a useful counterpoint to his showy visit to his brother's print shop, he failed to include it in his autobiography.[8]

Governor Keith's letter and proposal surprised Josiah Franklin. But after considering it for a few days, he decided it was imprudent to fund a rather rebellious runaway who was only 18. Though he was proud of the patronage his son had attracted and the industriousness he had shown, Josiah knew that Benjamin was still impudent.

Seeing no chance of a reconciliation between his two sons, Josiah did give his blessing for Benjamin to return to Philadelphia, with the exhortation "to behave respectfully to the people there . . . and avoid lampooning and libeling, to which he thought I had too much inclination." If he was able by "steady industry and prudent parsimony" to save almost enough to open his own shop by the time he was 21, Josiah promised he would help fund the rest.

Franklin's old friend John Collins, entranced by his tales, decided to leave Boston as well. But once in Philadelphia, the two teenagers had a falling-out. Collins, academically brighter than Franklin but less disciplined, soon took to drink. He borrowed money from Franklin and began to resent him. One day, when they were boating with friends on the Delaware, Collins refused to row his turn. Others in the boat were willing to let it pass, but not Franklin, who scuffled with him, grabbed him by the crotch, and threw him overboard. Each time Collins swam up to the boat, Franklin and the others would row it away a few feet more while insisting that he promise to take his turn at the oars. Proud and resentful, Collins never agreed, but they finally allowed him back in. He and Franklin barely spoke after that, and Collins ended up going to Barbados, never repaying the money he had borrowed.

In the course of a few months, Franklin had learned from four people—James Ralph, James Franklin, Cotton Mather, and John Collins—lessons about rivalry and resentments, pride and modesty. Throughout his life, he would occasionally make enemies, such as the Penn family, and jealous rivals, such as John Adams. But he did so less than most men, especially men so accomplished. A secret to being more revered than resented, he learned, was to display (at least when he could muster the discipline) a self-deprecating humor, unpretentious demeanor, and unaggressive style in conversation.[9]

Josiah Franklin's refusal to fund his son's printing venture did not dampen Governor Keith's enthusiasm. "Since he will not set you up, I will do it myself," he grandly promised. "I am resolved to have a good printer here." He asked Franklin for a list of what equipment was necessary—Franklin estimated it would cost about £100—and then suggested that Franklin should sail to London so that he could personally pick out the fonts and make contacts. Keith pledged letters of credit to pay for both the equipment and the voyage.[10]

The adventurous Franklin was thrilled. In the months leading up to his planned departure, he dined frequently with the governor.

Whenever he asked for the promised letters of credit, they were not ready, but Franklin felt no reason to worry.

At the time, Franklin was courting his landlady's daughter, Deborah Read. Despite his sexual appetites, he was practical about what he wanted in a wife. Deborah was rather plain, but she offered the prospect of comfort and domesticity. Franklin offered a lot as well, in addition to his husky good looks and genial charm. He had transformed himself from the bedraggled runaway she first spotted wandering up Market Street into one of the town's most promising and eligible young tradesmen, one who had found favor with the governor and popularity with his peers. Deborah's father had recently died, which put her mother into financial difficulty and made her open to the prospect of a good marriage for her daughter. Nevertheless, she was wary of allowing her to marry a suitor who was preparing to leave for London. She insisted that marriage wait until he returned.

LONDON

In November 1724, just over a year after arriving in Philadelphia, Franklin set sail for London. Traveling with him was the boy who had replaced Collins as his unreliable best friend, the aspiring poet James Ralph, who was leaving behind a wife and child. Franklin still had not received the letters of credit from Governor Keith, but he was assured that they would be sent on board in the final bag of dispatches.

Only after he arrived in London, on Christmas Eve, did Franklin discover the truth. The flighty governor had supplied no letters of credit nor recommendation. Franklin, puzzled, consulted a fellow passenger named Thomas Denham, a prominent Quaker merchant who had befriended him on the voyage. Denham explained to Franklin that Keith was incorrigibly capricious, and he "laughed at the idea of the Governor's giving me a letter of credit, having, as he said, no credit to give." For Franklin, it was an insight into human foibles rather than evil. "He wished to please everybody," Franklin later said of Keith, "and having little to give, he gave expectations."[11]

Taking Denham's advice, Franklin decided to make the best of his situation. London was enjoying a golden age of peace and prosperity, one particularly appealing to an intellectually ambitious young printer. Among those then brightening the world of London letters were Swift, Defoe, Pope, Richardson, Fielding, and Chesterfield.

With the dreamy wastrel Ralph under his wing, Franklin found cheap lodgings and a job at a famous printing house, Samuel Palmer's. Ralph tried to get work as an actor, then as a journalist or clerk. He failed on all fronts, borrowing money from Franklin all the while.

It was an odd-couple symbiosis of the type often found between ambitious, practical guys and their carefree, romantic pals: Franklin diligently made the money, Ralph made sure they spent it all on the theater and other amusements, including occasional "intrigues with low women." Ralph quickly forgot his own wife and child in Philadelphia, and Franklin followed suit by ignoring his engagement to Deborah and writing her only once.

The friendship exploded, not surprisingly, over a woman. Ralph fell in love with a pleasant but poor young milliner, moved in with her, then was finally motivated to find work as a teacher in a village school in Berkshire. He wrote Franklin often, sending installments of a bad epic poem along with requests that Franklin look after his girlfriend. That he did all too well. He lent her money, comforted her loneliness, and then ("being at the time under no religious restraint") tried to seduce her. Ralph returned in a fury, broke off their friendship, and declared that the transgression released him from the duty of paying back any debts, which amounted to £27.[12]

Franklin later concluded that the loss of money he was owed was balanced by the loss of the burden of having Ralph as a friend. A pattern was emerging. Beginning with Collins and Ralph, Franklin easily made casual friends, intellectual companions, useful patrons, flirty admirers, and circles of genial acquaintances, but he was less good at nurturing lasting bonds that involved deep personal commitments or emotional relationships, even within his own family.

CALVINISM AND DEISM

While at Palmer's, Franklin helped print an edition of William Wollaston's *The Religion of Nature Delineated*, an Enlightenment tract that argued that religious truths were to be gleaned through the study of science and nature rather than through divine revelation. With the intellectual spunk that comes from being youthful and untutored, Franklin decided that Wollaston was right in general but wrong in parts, and he set out his own thinking in a piece he wrote early in 1725 called "A Dissertation on Liberty and Necessity, Pleasure and Pain."

In it, Franklin strung together theological premises with logical syllogisms to get himself quite tangled up. For example: God is "all wise, all good, all powerful," he posited. Therefore, everything that exists or happens is with his consent. "What He consents to must be good, because He is good; therefore evil doth not exist."

Furthermore, happiness existed only as a contrast to unhappiness, and one could not exist without the other. Therefore, they balanced out: "Since pain naturally and infallibly produces a pleasure in proportion to it, every individual creature must, in any state of life, have an equal quantity of each." Along the way, Franklin disproved (to his own satisfaction at least) the concept of an immortal soul, the possibility of free will, and the fundamental Calvinist tenet that people are destined to be either saved or damned. "A creature can do nothing but what is good," he declared, and all "must be equally esteemed by the Creator."[13]

Franklin's "Dissertation" does not belong in the annals of sophisticated philosophy. Indeed, it was, as he later conceded, so shallow and unconvincing as to be embarrassing. He printed a hundred copies, called it an "erratum," and burned as many as he could retrieve.

In his defense, philosophers greater and more mature than Franklin have, over the centuries, gotten lost when trying to sort out the question of free will and reconcile it with that of an all-knowing God. And many of us can perhaps remember—or would cringe at being reminded of—our papers or freshmen dorm disquisitions from when we were 19. Yet even as he matured, Franklin would never develop into a rigorous, first-rank philosopher on the order of such contemporaries as Berkeley and Hume. Like Dr. Johnson, he was more comfortable exploring practical thoughts and real-life situations than metaphysical abstractions or deductive proofs.

The primary value of his "Dissertation" lies in what it reveals about Franklin's fitful willingness to abandon Puritan theology. As a young man, he had read John Locke, Lord Shaftesbury, Joseph Addison, and others who embraced the freethinking religion and Enlightenment philosophy of deism, which held that each individual could best discover the truth about God through reason and studying nature, rather than through blind faith in received doctrines and divine revelation. He also read more orthodox tracts that defended the dogmas of Calvinism against such heresies, but he found them less convincing. As he wrote in his autobiography, "The arguments of the deists which were quoted to be refuted appeared to me much stronger than the refutations."[14]

Nevertheless, he soon came to the conclusion that a simple and complacent deism had its own set of drawbacks. He had converted Collins and Ralph to deism, and they soon wronged him without moral compunction. Likewise, he came to worry that his own freethinking had caused him to be cavalier toward Deborah Read and others. In a classic maxim that typifies his pragmatic approach to religion, Franklin declared of deism, "I began to suspect that this doctrine, though it might be true, was not very useful."

Although divine revelation "had no weight with me," he decided that religious practices were beneficial because they encouraged good behavior and a moral society. So he began to embrace a morally fortified brand of deism that held God was best served by doing good works and helping other people.

It was a philosophy that led him to renounce much of the doctrine of the Puritans and other Calvinists, who preached that salvation came through God's grace alone and could not be earned by doing good deeds. That possibility, they believed, was lost when Adam rejected God's covenant of good works and it was replaced by a covenant of grace in which the saved were part of an elect predetermined by God. To a budding rationalist and pragmatist like Franklin, the covenant of grace seemed "unintelligible" and, even worse, "not beneficial."[15]

A PLAN FOR MORAL CONDUCT

After a year at Palmer's, Franklin got a better-paying job at a far larger printing house, John Watts's. There the pressmen drank pint after pint of watery beer throughout the day to keep them fortified. With his penchant for temperance and frugality, Franklin tried to convince his fellow workers that they could get their nourishment better by eating porringers of hot-water gruel with bread. Thus he became known as the "Water American," admired for his strength, clear head, and ability to lend them money when they had used up their weekly pay at the alehouses.

Despite his abstinence, the workers at Watts's insisted that he pay a five-shilling initiation fee used for drinks. When he was promoted from the pressroom to the composition room, he was called on to pay yet another initiation, but this time he refused. As a result, he was treated as an outcast and subjected to small mischiefs. Finally, after three weeks, he relented and paid up, "convinced of the folly of being on ill terms" with his workmates. He promptly regained his popularity, earning the reputation of "a pretty good riggite," someone whose jocularity and ability as a "verbal satirist" earned him respect.

One of the least shy men imaginable, Franklin was as sociable in London as he had been in Boston and Philadelphia. He frequented the roundtables hosted by minor literary luminaries of the day, and he sought out introductions to various interesting people. Among his earliest surviving letters is one he sent to Sir Hans Sloane, secretary of the Royal Society. Franklin wrote that he had brought from America a purse made of asbestos, and he wondered if Sloane might want to buy it. Sloane paid a call on Franklin, brought the lad back to his Bloomsbury Square home to show off his collection, and bought the purse for a handsome sum. Franklin also made a deal to borrow books from a neighborhood bookseller.

Ever since, as a young boy, he had invented some paddles and flippers to propel himself across Boston harbor, Franklin had been fascinated by swimming. He studied one of the first books on the subject, *The Art of Swimming*, written in 1696 by a Frenchman named Melchisedec Thevenot, which helped to popularize the breaststroke.

(The crawl did not catch on for more than another century.) Franklin perfected variations on the motions for swimming both on the surface and underwater, "aiming at the graceful and easy as well as the useful."

Among the friends he taught to swim was a fellow young printer named Wygate. One day, during a boat trip on the Thames with Wygate and others, Franklin decided to show off. He stripped, leaped into the river, and swam back and forth to the bank using a variety of strokes. One member of the party offered to fund a swim school for Franklin. Wygate, for his part, "grew more and more attached" to him, and he proposed that they travel around Europe together as journey-men printers and teachers. "I was once inclined to it," Franklin re-called, "but, mentioning it to my good friend Mr. Denham, with whom I often spent an hour when I had leisure, he dissuaded me from it, advising me to think only of returning to Pennsylvania, which he was now about to do."[16]

Denham, the Quaker merchant Franklin had met on the voyage over, was planning to open a general store once back in Philadelphia, and he offered to pay Franklin's passage if he would agree to sign on as his clerk at £50 a year. It was less than he was making in London, but it offered him the chance both to return to America and to become es-tablished as a merchant, a vocation more exalted than that of printer. Together they set sail in July 1726.

Franklin had been burned in the past by his attraction to romantic rogues (Keith, Collins, Ralph) of dubious character. Denham, on the other hand, was a man of integrity. He had left England years earlier deeply in debt, made a small fortune in America, and on his return to England threw a lavish dinner for his old creditors. After thanking them profusely, he told them all to look under their plates. There they discovered full repayment plus interest. Henceforth, Franklin would find himself more attracted to people who were practical and reliable rather than dreamy and romantic.

To perfect the art of becoming such a reliable person, Franklin wrote out a "Plan for Future Conduct" during his eleven-week voyage back to Philadelphia. It would be the first of many personal credos that laid out pragmatic rules for success and made him the patron saint of self-improvement guides. He lamented that because he had never outlined a design for how he should conduct himself, his life so far had been somewhat confused. "Let me, therefore, make some resolutions, and some form of action, that, henceforth, I may live in all respects like a rational creature." There were four rules:

1. It is necessary for me to be extremely frugal for some time, till I have paid what I owe.
2. To endeavor to speak truth in every instance; to give nobody expectations that are not likely to be answered, but aim at sincerity in every word and action—the most amiable excellence in a rational being.
3. To apply myself industriously to whatever business I take in hand, and not divert my mind from my business by any foolish project of suddenly growing rich; for industry and patience are the surest means of plenty.
4. I resolve to speak ill of no man whatever.[17]

Rule 1 he had already mastered. Rule 3 he likewise had little trouble following. As for 2 and 4, he would henceforth preach them diligently and generally make a show of practicing them, though he would sometimes be better at the show than the practicing.

On his voyage home, the 20-year-old Franklin indulged what would be a lifelong scientific curiosity. He experimented on the small crabs he found on some seaweed, calculated his distance from London based on the timing of a lunar eclipse, and studied the habits of dolphins and flying fish.

His journal of the voyage also reveals his talent for observing human nature. When he heard the tale of a former governor of the Isle of Wight who had been considered saintly yet was known to be a knave by the keeper of his castle, Franklin concluded that it was impossible for a dishonest person, no matter how cunning, to completely conceal his character. "Truth and sincerity have a certain distinguishing native luster about them which cannot be perfectly counterfeited; they are like fire and flame, that cannot be painted."

While gambling at checkers with some shipmates, he formulated an "infallible rule," which was that "if two persons equal in judgment play for a considerable sum, he that loves money most shall lose; his anxiety for the success of the game confounds him." The rule, he decided, applied to other battles; a person who is too fearful will end up performing defensively and thus fail to seize offensive advantages.

He also developed theories about the sociable yearnings of men, ones that applied particularly to himself. One of the passengers was caught cheating at cards, and the others sought to fine him. When the fellow resisted paying, they decided on an even tougher punishment: he would be ostracized and completely shunned until he relented. Finally the miscreant paid the fine in order to end his excommunication. Franklin concluded:

> Man is a sociable being, and it is, for aught I know, one of the worst punishments to be excluded from society. I have read abundance of fine things on the subject of solitude, and I know it is a common boast in the mouths of those that affect to be thought wise that they are never less alone than when alone. I acknowledge solitude an agreeable refreshment to a busy mind; but were these thinking people obliged to be always alone, I am apt to think they would quickly find their very being insupportable to them.

One of the fundamental sentiments of the Enlightenment was that there is a sociable affinity, based on the natural instinct of benevolence, among fellow humans, and Franklin was an exemplar of this outlook. The opening phrase of the passage—"Man is a sociable being"—would turn out to be a defining credo of his long life. Later in the voyage, they encountered another vessel. Franklin noted:

> There is really something strangely cheering to the spirits in the meeting of a ship at sea, containing a society of creatures of the same species and in the same circumstances with ourselves, after we had been long separated and excommunicated as it were from the rest of mankind. I saw so many human countenances and I could scarce refrain from that kind of laughter which proceeds from some degree of inward pleasure.

His greatest happiness, however, came when he finally glimpsed the American shore. "My eyes," he wrote, "were dimmed with the suffusion of two small drops of joy." With his deepened appreciation of community, his scientific curiosity, and his rules for leading a practical life, Franklin was ready to settle down and pursue success in the city that, more than Boston or London, he now realized was his true home.[18]

CHAPTER FOUR

PRINTER

Philadelphia, 1726–1732

A SHOP OF HIS OWN

Franklin was a natural shopkeeper: clever, charming, astute about human nature, and eager to succeed. He became, as he put it, "an expert at selling" when he and Denham opened a general store on Water Street shortly after their return to Philadelphia in late 1726. Denham served as both a mentor and a surrogate parent to the aspiring 20-year-old. "We lodged and boarded together; he counseled me as a father, having a sincere regard for me. I respected and loved him."[1]

But Franklin's dreams of becoming a prosperous merchant ended after a few months, when Denham took ill and later died. In his oral will, he forgave Franklin the £10 he still owed for his ocean passage, but he did not leave him the business they had built. With no money and few prospects, Franklin swallowed his pride and accepted an offer from the eccentric Keimer to come back to his print shop, this time as the manager.[2]

Because there was no foundry in America for casting type, Franklin contrived one of his own by using Keimer's letters to make lead molds. He thus became the first person in America to manufacture type. One of the most popular contemporary typefaces, a sans-serif font known as Franklin Gothic that is often used in newspaper headlines, was named after him in 1902.

When Keimer began to assert his power, the aversion to arbitrary authority that was part of Franklin's heritage and breeding flared. One day, there was a commotion outside of the shop, and Franklin poked his head out of the window to watch. Keimer, who was on the street below, shouted at him to mind his own business. The public nature of the rebuke was humiliating, and Franklin quit on the spot. But after a few days, Keimer came begging for him to return, and Franklin did. They each needed the other, at least for the time being.

Keimer had won the right to print a new issue of paper currency for the New Jersey assembly, and only Franklin had the skills to do the job properly. He contrived a copperplate press to make bills so ornate they could not easily be counterfeited, and together they traveled to Burlington. Once again, it was young Franklin, the willing and witty conversationalist, rather than his slovenly master, who befriended the dignitaries. "My mind, having been much more improved by reading than Keimer's, I suppose it was for that reason my conversation seemed more valued. They had me to their houses, introduced me to their friends, and showed me much civility."[3]

The relationship with Keimer was not destined to last. Franklin, ever striving and chafing, realized that he was being used. Keimer was paying him to train the four "cheap hands" who worked at the shop with the intention of laying him off once they were in shape. Franklin, in turn, was willing to use Keimer. He and one of those apprenticed hands, Hugh Meredith, made secret plans to open a competing print shop, funded by Meredith's father, once Meredith's servitude was completed. Though not an outright devious scheme, it did not fully comport with Franklin's high-minded pledge to "aim at sincerity in every word and action."

Meredith, 30, was fond of reading but also of alcohol. His father, a Welsh-bred farmer, took a liking to Franklin, especially because he had persuaded his son to abstain (at least temporarily) from drinking. He agreed to provide the funding necessary (£200) for the two young men to set up a partnership, Franklin's contribution being his own talent. They sent to London for equipment,* which arrived early in 1728,

---

* The fonts that Franklin ordered were those created in the early 1720s by the famed London type-maker William Caslon, and they are the model for the Adobe Caslon typeface used for the text in this book.

shortly after the New Jersey job was completed and Meredith's indenture had expired.

The two partners bid farewell to the hapless Keimer, leased a house on Market Street, set up shop, and promptly served their first customer, a farmer referred by a friend. "This country man's five shillings, being our first fruits and coming so seasonably, gave me more pleasure than any crown I have since earned."

Their business succeeded largely because of Franklin's diligence. When they were hired by a group of Quakers to print 178 pages of their history, the rest to be printed by Keimer, Franklin did not leave the shop each night until he had completed a four-page folio, often working past eleven. One night, just as he was finishing that day's sheet, the plate dropped and broke; Franklin stayed overnight to redo it. "This industry visible to our neighbors began to give us character and credit," Franklin noted. One of the town's prominent merchants told members of his club, "The industry of that Franklin is superior to anything I ever saw of the kind; I see him still at work when I go home from club, and he is at work again before his neighbors are out of bed."

Franklin became an apostle of being—and, just as important, of appearing to be—industrious. Even after he became successful, he made a show of personally carting the rolls of paper he bought in a wheelbarrow down the street to his shop, rather than having a hired hand do it.[4]

Meredith, on the other hand, was far from industrious, having taken again to drink. In addition, his father had paid only half of the money he had committed for their equipment, which prompted threatening letters from the suppliers. Franklin found two friends who were willing to finance him, but only if he dumped Meredith. Fortunately, Meredith realized that he was better off returning to farming. All ended well: Meredith let Franklin buy him out of their partnership, headed off to the Carolinas, and later wrote letters describing the countryside there, which Franklin published.

And so Franklin finally had a print shop of his own. More to the point, he had a career. Printing and its related endeavors—publisher, writer, newspaperman, postmaster—began to seem not merely a job but an interesting calling, both noble and fun. In his long life he would have many other careers: scientist, politician, statesman, diplomat. But henceforth he always identified himself the way he would do sixty years later in the opening words of his last will and testament: "I, Benjamin Franklin of Philadelphia, printer."[5]

THE JUNTO

Franklin was the consummate networker. He liked to mix his civic life with his social one, and he merrily leveraged both to further his business life. This approach was displayed when he formed a club of young workingmen in the fall of 1727, shortly after his return to Philadelphia, that was commonly called the Leather Apron Club and officially dubbed the Junto.

Franklin's small club was composed of enterprising tradesmen and artisans, rather than the social elite who had their own fancier gentlemen's clubs. At first, the members went to a local tavern for their Friday evening meetings, but soon they were able to rent a house of their own. There they discussed issues of the day, debated philosophical topics, devised schemes for self-improvement, and formed a network for the furtherance of their own careers.

The enterprise was typical of Franklin, who seemed ever eager to organize clubs and associations for mutual benefit, and it was also typically American. As the nation developed a shopkeeping middle class, its people balanced their individualist streaks with a propensity to form clubs, lodges, associations, and fraternal orders. Franklin epitomized this Rotarian urge and has remained, after more than two centuries, a symbol of it.

Franklin's Junto initially had twelve young members, among them his printing partner Hugh Meredith; George Webb, a witty but imprudent runaway Oxford student who was also apprenticed to Keimer; Thomas Godfrey, a glassworker and amateur mathematician; Joseph Breintnall, a scrivener and poetry lover; Robert Grace, a generous and pun-loving man with some family money; and William Coleman, a clear-headed and good-hearted clerk with exacting morals, who later became a distinguished merchant.

Besides being amiable club mates, the Junto members often proved

helpful to one another personally and professionally. Godfrey boarded
at Franklin's shop and his wife cooked for them. Breintnall was the
friend who procured the Quaker printing commission. And Grace
and Coleman funded Franklin when he broke with Meredith.

The tone Franklin set for Junto meetings was earnest. Initiates
were required to stand, lay their hand on their breast, and answer
properly four questions: Do you have disrespect for any current member? Do you love mankind in general regardless of religion or profession? Do you feel people should ever be punished because of their
opinions or mode of worship? Do you love and pursue truth for its
own sake?

Franklin was worried that his fondness for conversation and eagerness to impress made him prone to "prattling, punning and joking,
which only made me acceptable to trifling company." Knowledge, he
realized, "was obtained rather by the use of the ear than of the
tongue." So in the Junto, he began to work on his use of silence and
gentle dialogue.

One method, which he had developed during his mock debates
with John Collins in Boston and then when discoursing with Keimer,
was to pursue topics through soft, Socratic queries. That became the
preferred style for Junto meetings. Discussions were to be conducted
"without fondness for dispute or desire of victory." Franklin taught his
friends to push their ideas through suggestions and questions, and to
use (or at least feign) naïve curiosity to avoid contradicting people in a
manner that could give offense. "All expressions of positiveness in
opinion or of direct contradiction," he recalled, "were prohibited
under small pecuniary penalties." It was a style he would urge on the
Constitutional Convention sixty years later.

In a witty newspaper piece called "On Conversation," which he
wrote shortly after forming the Junto, Franklin stressed the importance of deferring, or at least giving the appearance of deferring, to
others. Otherwise, even the smartest comments would "occasion envy
and disgust." His secret for how to win friends and influence people
read like an early Dale Carnegie course: "Would you win the hearts of
others, you must not seem to vie with them, but to admire them. Give
them every opportunity of displaying their own qualifications, and

when you have indulged their vanity, they will praise you in turn and prefer you above others . . . Such is the vanity of mankind that minding what others say is a much surer way of pleasing them than talking well ourselves."[6]

Franklin went on to catalog the most common conversational sins "which cause dislike," the greatest being "talking overmuch . . . which never fails to excite resentment." The only thing amusing about such people, he joked, was watching two of them meet: "The vexation they both feel is visible in their looks and gestures; you shall see them gape and stare and interrupt one another at every turn, and watch with utmost impatience for a cough or pause, when they may crowd a word in edgeways."

The other sins on his list were, in order: seeming uninterested, speaking too much about your own life, prying for personal secrets ("an unpardonable rudeness"), telling long and pointless stories ("old folks are most subject to this error, which is one chief reason their company is so often shunned"), contradicting or disputing someone directly, ridiculing or railing against things except in small witty doses ("it's like salt, a little of which in some cases gives relish, but if thrown on by handfuls spoils all"), and spreading scandal (though he would later write lighthearted defenses of gossip).

The older he got, the more Franklin learned (with a few notable lapses) to follow his own advice. He used silence wisely, employed an indirect style of persuasion, and feigned modesty and naïveté in disputes. "When another asserted something that I thought an error, I denied myself the pleasure of contradicting him." Instead, he would agree in parts and suggest his differences only indirectly. "For these fifty years past no one has ever heard a dogmatical expression escape me," he recalled when writing his autobiography. This velvet-tongued and sweetly passive style of circumspect argument would make him seem sage to some, insinuating and manipulative to others, but inflammatory to almost nobody. The method would also become, often with a nod to Franklin, a staple in modern management guides and self-improvement books.

Though the youngest member of the Junto, Franklin was, by dint of his intellectual charisma and conversational charm, not only its founder but its driving force. The topics discussed ranged from the social to the scientific and metaphysical. Most of them were earnest, some were quirky, and all were intriguing. Did importing indentured servants make America more prosperous? What made a piece of writing good? Why did condensation form on a cold mug? What accounted for happiness? What is wisdom? Is there a difference between knowledge and prudence? If a sovereign power deprives a citizen of his rights, is it justifiable for him to resist?

In addition to such topics of debate, Franklin laid out a guide for the type of conversational contributions each member could usefully make. There were twenty-four in all, and because their practicality is so revealing of Franklin's purposeful approach, they are worth excerpting at length:

1. Have you met with anything in the author you last read remarkable or suited to be communicated to the Junto? . . .
2. What new story have you lately heard agreeable for telling in conversation?
3. Hath any citizen in your knowledge failed in his business lately, and what have you heard of the cause?
4. Have you lately heard of any citizen's thriving well, and by what means?
5. Have you lately heard how any present rich man, here or elsewhere, got his estate?
6. Do you know of any fellow citizen who has lately done a worthy action deserving praise and imitation? Or who has committed an error proper for us to be warned against and avoid?
7. What unhappy effects of intemperance have you lately observed or heard? Of imprudence? Of passion? Or of any other vice or folly? . . .
12. Hath any deserving stranger arrived in town since last meeting that you heard of? And what have you heard of his character or merits? And whether you think it lies in the power of the Junto to oblige him or encourage him as he deserves? . . .

14. Have you lately observed any defect in the laws of your country of which it would be proper to move the legislature for an amendment?
15. Have you lately observed any encroachments on the just liberties of the people?
16. Has anybody attacked your reputation lately, and what can the Junto do toward securing it?
17. Is there any man whose friendship you want and which the Junto or any of them can procure for you? . . .
20. In what manner can the Junto or any of them assist you in any of your honorable designs?[7]

Franklin used the Junto as a launching pad for a variety of his public-service ideas. Early on, the group discussed whether Pennsylvania should increase its supply of paper currency, a proposal Franklin heartily favored because he thought it would benefit the economy and, of course, his own printing business. (Franklin and, by extension, the Junto were particularly fond of things that could help the public as well as themselves.) When the Junto moved into its own rented rooms, it created a library of books pooled from its members, which later formed the foundation for America's first subscription library. Out of the Junto also came Franklin's proposals for establishing a tax to pay for neighborhood constables, for creating a volunteer fire force, and for establishing the academy that later became the University of Pennsylvania.

Many of the rules and proposed queries for the Junto were similar to, though a bit less judgmental than, those that Cotton Mather had devised for his neighborhood benevolent societies a generation earlier in Boston. One of Mather's, for example, was: "Is there any particular person whose disorderly behavior may be so scandalous and so notorious that we may do well to send unto the said person our charitable admonitions?" Daniel Defoe's essay "Friendly Societies" and John Locke's "Rules of a Society which Met Once a Week for the Improvement of Useful Knowledge," both of which Franklin had read, also served as models.[8]

But, for the most part, with its earnest tenor and emphasis on self-improvement, the Junto was a product of Franklin's own persona and part of his imprint on the American personality. It flourished with him at the helm for thirty years. Although it operated in relative secrecy, so many people sought to join that Franklin empowered each member to form his own spinoff club. Four or five affiliates flourished, and the Junto served as an extension and amplification of Franklin's gregarious civic nature. Like Franklin himself, it was practical, industrious, inquiring, convivial, and middle-brow philosophical. It celebrated civic virtue, mutual benefits, the improvement of self and society, and the proposition that hardworking citizens could do well by doing good. It was, in short, Franklin writ public.

THE BUSY-BODY ESSAYS

Frugal and industrious, with a network of Junto members to steer business his way, Franklin was doing modestly well as one of three printers in a town that would naturally have supported only two. But he had learned from his apprentice days in Boston that true success would come if he had not only a printing operation but also his own content and distribution network. His competitor Andrew Bradford published the town's only newspaper, which was paltry but profitable, and that helped Bradford's printing business by giving him clout with the merchants and politicians. He also was the postmaster, which gave him some control over what papers got distributed plus first access to news from afar.

Franklin decided to take Bradford on, and over the next decade he would succeed by building a media conglomerate that included production capacity (printing operations, franchised printers in other cities), products (a newspaper, magazine, almanac), content (his own writings, his alter ego Poor Richard's, and those of his Junto), and distribution (eventually the whole of the colonial postal system).

First came the newspaper. Franklin decided to launch a competitor to Bradford's *American Weekly Mercury*, but he made the mistake of confiding his plan to George Webb, a fellow member of the Junto who was an apprentice at Keimer's print shop. Webb, to Franklin's dismay, told Keimer, who immediately launched a slapdash newspaper of his own, to which he gave the unwieldly name *The Universal Instructor in All Arts and Sciences, and Pennsylvania Gazette.* Franklin realized that it would be difficult to launch a third paper right away, and he did not have the funds. So he came up with a plan to first crush Keimer's paper by using the most powerful weapon at his disposal: the fact that he was the best writer in Philadelphia, and probably, at 23, the most amusing writer in all of America. (Carl Van Doren, a Franklin biographer and great literary critic of the 1930s, flatly declared of Franklin that in 1728, "he was the best writer in America." The closest rival for that title at the time would probably be the preacher Jonathan Edwards, who was certainly more intense and literary, though far less felicitous and amusing.)

In a competitive bank shot, Franklin decided to write a series of anonymous letters and essays, along the lines of the Silence Dogood pieces of his youth, for Bradford's *Mercury* to draw attention away from Keimer's new paper. The goal was to enliven, at least until Keimer was beaten, Bradford's dull paper, which in its ten years had never published any such features.

The first two pieces were attacks on poor Keimer, who was serializing entries from an encyclopedia. His initial installment included, innocently enough, an entry on abortion. Franklin pounced. Using the pen names "Martha Careful" and "Celia Shortface," he wrote letters to Bradford's paper feigning shock and indignation at Keimer's offense. As Miss Careful threatened, "If he proceeds farther to expose the secrets of our sex in that audacious manner [women would] run the hazard of taking him by the beard in the next place we meet him." Thus Franklin manufactured the first recorded abortion debate in America, not because he had any strong feelings on the issue, but because he knew it would help sell newspapers.

The next week Franklin launched a series of classic essays signed "Busy-Body," which Bradford published on his front page with a large byline. Franklin wrote at least four on his own and two others in part before turning the series over to fellow Junto member Joseph Breintnall. "By this means the attention of the public was fixed on that paper, and Keimer's proposals, which we burlesqued and ridiculed, were disregarded."[9]

The Busy-Body began by cleverly establishing the inadequacies of Bradford's paper ("frequently very dull") and declaring his intention to make it (at least temporarily) better. He would do so by being a scold and tattle, in the tradition of the character Isaac Bickerstaff that the English essayist Richard Steele had created, thus adding gossip columnist to the list of Franklin's American firsts. He readily admitted that much of this was "nobody's business," but "out of zeal for the public good," he volunteered "to take nobody's business wholly into my own hands." Some might find themselves offended, he warned. Yet, he pointed out what was, and is, the basic appeal of gossip: "As most people delight in censure when they themselves are not the objects of it, if any are offended at my publicly exposing their private vices, I promise they shall have the satisfaction, in a very little time, of seeing their good friends and neighbors in the same circumstances."

Keimer responded with a fusty admonition that the Busy-Body series might initially raise for readers of Bradford's paper the "expectation that they would now have some entertainment for their money," but they would soon feel "a secret grief to see the reputation of their neighbors blasted." When the Busy-Body merrily continued to publish his barbs, the excitable Keimer became more shrill. He responded with limp doggerel: "You hinted at me in your paper. Which now has made me draw my rapier. With scornful eye, I see your hate. And pity your unhappy fate." He paired this with a convoluted tale called "Hue and Cry after the Busy-Body," portraying Franklin and Breintnall as a two-headed monster, with Franklin described as "every Ape's epitome . . . as threadbare as his great coat, and skull as thick as his shoe soles." [10]

Keimer thus became one of Franklin's first outspoken foes. The betrayal, the press war, the dueling essays would all be repeated a decade later when Franklin and Bradford each decided to start magazines.

Sadly for those who enjoy titillation, the Busy-Body essays in fact failed to deliver much gossip. Instead, they tended to be clever tales with thinly disguised real-life counterparts (in one instance, a reader took the effort to publish a key to whom each character referred). Franklin employed what is now a standard disingenuous disclaimer:

"If any bad characters happen to be drawn in the course of these papers, they mean no particular person."

The final Busy-Body that was mainly written by Franklin made fun of treasure seekers who used divining rods and dug up the woods looking for buried pirate loot. "Men otherwise of very good sense have been drawn into this practice through an overweening desire of sudden wealth," he wrote, "while the rational and almost certain methods of acquiring riches by industry and frugality are neglected." The fable, an attack on the get-rich-quick schemes of the time, went on to preach Franklin's favorite theme: slow and steady diligence is the true way to wealth. He ended by quoting what his imaginary friend Agricola said on giving his son a parcel of land: "I assure thee I have found a considerable quantity of gold by digging there; thee mayst do the same. But thee must carefully observe this, Never to dig more than plow deep."

The essay had a second half that advocated more paper currency for Pennsylvania. Franklin wrote most of it, with a small section written by Breintnall. Franklin implied that those who opposed more paper currency were trying to protect their own financial interests, though he of course had his own financial interest in the approval of more printing work. He also launched the first of what would be many attacks on the province's Proprietors, the Penn family, and their appointed governor, by implying that they were trying to make the bulk of Pennsylvania's residents "their tenants and vassals." This ending was deleted in most editions of Bradford's newspaper, perhaps because Bradford was allied with the Penn family and their party.[11]

Another reason for pulling back the snide section on paper currency was that Franklin had produced a far more thoughtful essay on the subject, which he discussed in the Junto and published as a pamphlet the following week. "A Modest Enquiry into the Nature and Necessity of a Paper Currency" was Franklin's first serious analysis of public policy, and it holds up a lot better than his metaphysical musings on religion. Money was a concept he had a solid feel for, unlike theological abstractions.

Franklin argued that the lack of enough currency caused interest rates to rise, kept wages low, and increased dependence on imports. Creditors and big landowners opposed an increase in currency for self-ish reasons, he charged, but "those who are lovers of trade and delight to see manufactures encouraged will be for having a large addition to our currency." Franklin's key insight was that hard currency, such as silver and gold, was not the true measure of a nation's wealth: "The riches of a country are to be valued by the quantity of labor its inhabi-tants are able to purchase, and not by the quantity of silver and gold they possess."

The essay was very popular, except among the wealthy, and it helped to persuade the legislature to adopt the proposed increase in paper currency. Although Bradford got the first commission to print some of the money, Franklin was given the next round of work. In the spirit of what Poor Richard would call "doing well by doing good," Franklin was not averse to mingling his private interests with his pub-lic ones. His friends in the legislature, "who considered I had been of some service, thought it fit to reward me by employing me in printing the money—a very profitable job and a great help to me. This was an-other advantage gained by my being able to write."[12]

THE PENNSYLVANIA GAZETTE

Franklin's scheme to put Keimer out of business, which was aided by the quirky printer's own incompetence and inability to ignore barbs, soon succeeded. He fell into debt, was briefly imprisoned, fled to Barbados, and as he was leaving sold his newspaper to Franklin. Jettisoning the serialized encyclopedia and part of the paper's un-wieldy name, Franklin became the proud publisher of *The Pennsylva-nia Gazette* in October 1729. In his first letter to his readers, he announced that "there are many who have long desired to see a good newspaper in Pennsylvania," thus taking a poke at both Keimer and Bradford.[13]

There are many types of newspaper editors. Some are crusading ideologues who are blessed with strong opinions, partisan passions, or a desire to challenge authority. Benjamin's brother James was in this category. Some are the opposite: they like power and their proximity to it, and are comfortable with the established order and feel vested in it. Franklin's Philadelphia competitor Andrew Bradford was such.

And then there are those who are charmed and amused by the world and delight in charming and amusing others. They tend to be skeptical of both orthodoxies and heresies, and they are earnest in their desire to seek truth and promote public betterment (as well as sell papers). There fits Franklin. He was graced—and afflicted—with the trait so common to journalists, especially ones who have read Swift and Addison once too often, of wanting to participate in the world while also remaining a detached observer. As a journalist he could step out of a scene, even one that passionately engaged him, and comment on it, or on himself, with a droll irony. The depths of his beliefs were often concealed by his knack for engaging in a knowing wink.

Like most other newspapers of the time, Franklin's *Pennsylvania Gazette* was filled not only with short news items and reports on public events, but also with amusing essays and letters from readers. What made his paper a delight was its wealth of this type of correspondence, much of it written under pseudonyms by Franklin himself. This gimmick of writing as if from a reader gave Franklin more leeway to poke fun at rivals, revel in gossip, circumvent his personal pledge to speak ill of no one, and test-drive his evolving philosophies.

In a classic canny maneuver, Franklin corrected an early typo—he had reported that someone "died" at a restaurant when he meant to say "dined" at it—by composing a letter from a fictitious "J.T." who discoursed on other amusing misprints. For example, one edition of the Bible quoted David as saying he was "wonderfully mad" rather than "made," which caused an "ignorant preacher to harangue his audience for half an hour on the subject of spiritual madness." Franklin then went on (under the guise of J.T.) to praise Franklin's own paper, point out a similar typo made by his rival Bradford, criticize Bradford for being generally sloppier, and (with delicious irony) praise Franklin for not criticizing Bradford: "Your paper is most commonly very correct, and yet you were never known to triumph upon it by publicly ridiculing and exposing the continual blunders of your contemporary." Franklin even turned his false modesty into a maxim to forgive his typo: "Whoever accustoms himself to pass over in silence the faults of his neighbors shall meet with much better quarter from the world when he happens to fall into a mistake himself."[14]

The Franklin–Bradford newspaper war also included disputes over scoops and stolen stories. "When Mr. Bradford publishes after us," Franklin wrote in one editor's note, "and has occasion to take an Article or two out of the Gazette, which he is always welcome to do, he is desired not to date his paper a day before ours lest readers should imagine we take from him, which we always carefully avoid."

Their competition had been going on for a year when Franklin set out to win from Bradford the job of being the official printer for the Pennsylvania Assembly. He had already begun cultivating some of the members, especially those in the faction that resisted the power of the Penn family and its upper-crust supporters. After Bradford printed the governor's address to the Assembly in a "coarse and blundering manner," Franklin saw his opening. He printed the same message "elegantly and correctly," as he put it, and sent it to each of the members. "It strengthened the hands of our friends in the House," Franklin later recalled, "and they voted us their printers."[15]

Even as he became more political, Franklin resisted making his newspaper fiercely partisan. He expressed his credo as a publisher in a famous *Gazette* editorial "Apology for Printers," which remains one of the best and most forceful defenses of a free press.

The opinions people have, Franklin wrote, are "almost as various as their faces." The job of printers is to allow people to express these differing opinions. "There would be very little printed," he noted, if publishers produced only things that offended nobody. At stake was the virtue of free expression, and Franklin summed up the Enlightenment position in a sentence that is now framed on newsroom walls: "Printers are educated in the belief that when men differ in opinion, both sides ought equally to have the advantage of being heard by the public; and that when Truth and Error have fair play, the former is always an overmatch for the latter."

"It is unreasonable to imagine that printers approve of everything they print," he went on to argue. "It is likewise unreasonable what some assert, That printers ought not to print anything but what they approve; since . . . an end would thereby be put to free writing, and the world would afterwards have nothing to read but what happened to be the opinions of printers."

With a wry touch, he reminded his readers that publishers are in business both to make money and inform the public. "Hence they cheerfully service all contending writers that pay them well," even if they don't agree with the writers' opinions. "If all people of different opinions in this province would engage to give me as much for not printing things they don't like as I could get by printing them, I should probably live a very easy life; and if all printers everywhere were so dealt by, there would be very little printed."

It was not in Franklin's nature, however, to be dogmatic or extreme about any principle; he generally gravitated toward a sensible balance. The rights of printers, he realized, were balanced by their duty to be responsible. Thus, even though printers should be free to publish offensive opinions, they should generally exercise discretion. "I myself have constantly refused to print anything that might countenance vice or promote immorality, though . . . I might have got much money. I have also always refused to print such things as might do real injury to any person."

One such example involved a customer who asked the young printer to publish a piece in the *Gazette* that Franklin found "scurrilous and defamatory." In his effort to decide whether he should take the customer's money even though it violated his principles, Franklin subjected himself to the following test:

> To determine whether I should publish it or not, I went home in the evening, purchased a twopenny loaf at the baker's, and with the water from the pump made my supper; I then wrapped myself up in my great-coat, and laid down on the floor and slept till morning, when, on another loaf and a mug of water, I made my breakfast. From this regimen I feel no inconvenience whatever. Finding I can live in this manner, I have formed a determination never to prostitute my press to the purposes of corruption and abuse of this kind for the sake of gaining a more comfortable subsistence.

Franklin ended his "Apology for Printers" with a fable about a father and son traveling with a donkey. When the father rode and made his son walk, they were criticized by those they met; likewise, they were criticized when the son rode and made the father walk, or when they both rode the donkey, or when neither did. So finally, they decided to throw the donkey off a bridge. The moral, according to Franklin, was that it is foolish to try to avoid all criticism. Despite his "despair of pleasing everybody," Franklin concluded, "I shall not burn my press or melt my letters."[16]

Along with such high-minded principles, Franklin employed some more common strategies to push papers. One ever reliable method, which had particular appeal to the rather raunchy unmarried young publisher, was the time-honored truth that sex sells. Franklin's *Gazette* was spiced with little leering and titillating items. In the issue a week after his "Apology for Printers," for example, Franklin wrote about a husband who caught his wife in bed with a man named Stonecutter, tried to cut off the interloper's head with a knife, but only wounded him. Franklin ends with a smirking pun about castration: "Some people admire that when the person offended had so fair and suitable opportunity, it did not enter his head to turn St-n-c-tt-r himself."

The next issue had a similar short item about an amorous constable who had "made an agreement with a neighboring female to *watch* with her that night." The constable makes the mistake of climbing into the window of a different woman, whose husband was in another room. Reported Franklin: "The good woman perceiving presently by the extraordinary fondness of her bedfellow that it could not possibly be her husband, made so much disturbance as to wake the good man, who finding somebody had got into his place without his leave began to lay about him unmercifully."

And then there was the story of the sex-starved woman who wanted to divorce her husband because he could not satisfy her. She "at times industriously solicited most of the magistrates" to gain sympathy for her plight. After her husband was medically examined, however, she moved back in with him. "The report of the physicians (who in form examined his *abilities* and allowed him in every respect to be *sufficient*) gave her but small satisfaction," Franklin wrote. "Whether any experiments *more satisfactory* have been tried, we cannot say; but it seems she now declares it as her opinion that 'George is as good as de best.' " In another passing reference to sexual virility, which was also his first published notice of lightning, Franklin reported about a bolt that melted the pewter button on the pants of a young lad, adding: " 'Tis well nothing else thereabouts was made of pewter."

Writing as "The Casuist," Franklin even helped to pioneer the genre of sexual and moral advice columns. (Although the literal definition of the word "casuistry" refers to the application of moral principles to everyday conduct, Franklin used it, with a touch of irony, in its more colloquial sense, which implies a slightly off-kilter or misleading application of those principles.) One letter from a reader, or from Franklin pretending to be a reader, posed the following dilemma: Suppose a person discovers that his wife has been seduced by his neighbor, and suppose he has reason to believe that if he reveals this to his neighbor's wife, then she might agree to have sex with him, "is he justifiable in doing it?" Franklin, writing as the Casuist, gave an earnest answer. If the questioner were a Christian, he would know that he should "return not evil for evil, but repay evil with good." And if he is not a Christian but instead "one who would make reason the rule of his actions," he would come to the same conclusion: "such practices can produce no good to society."[17]

Franklin also knew another maxim of journalism: crime stories sell, particularly when they are outlandish. In a report on the death of a young girl, for example, he provided the mix of reporting and outrage later perfected by racier tabloids. The case involved a couple who were charged with murdering the man's daughter from a previous marriage by neglecting her, forcing her "to lie and rot in her nastiness," giving her "her own excrements to eat," and "turning her out of doors." The child died, but a physician testified she would have died anyway from other ailments she had, so the judge sentenced the couple merely to be burned on the hand. Franklin raged at the "pathetic" ruling and delivered his own harsh verdict that the couple "had not only acted contrary to the particular law of all nations, but had even broken the universal law of nature."[18]

A third reliable method of selling papers was through a light and rather innocent willingness to gossip and scandalmonger. In his first Busy-Body essay for Bradford, Franklin had defended the value of nosiness and tattling. Now that he had his own paper, he made it clear that the *Gazette* was pleased, indeed proud, to continue this service. Using the same tone as the Busy-Body, Franklin wrote an anonymous letter to his paper defending gossip, backbiting, and censure "by showing its usefulness and the great good it does to society.

"It is frequently the means of preventing powerful, politic, ill-designing men from growing too popular," he wrote. "All-examining Censure, with her hundred eyes and her thousand tongues, soon discovers and as speedily divulges in all quarters every least crime or foible that is part of their true character. This clips the wings of their ambition." Gossip can also, he noted, promote virtue, as some people are motivated more by fear of public humiliation than they are by inner moral principles. " *'What will the world say of me if I act thus?'* is often a reflection strong enough to enable us to resist the most powerful temptation to vice or folly. This preserves the integrity of the wavering, the honesty of the covetous, the sanctity of some of the religious, and the chastity of all virgins."

It is amusing that Franklin, though he was willing to impugn the innate resolve of "all" virgins, protected himself by impugning only "some" religious people. In addition, he showed a somewhat cynical side by implying that most people act virtuously not because of an inner goodness, but because they are afraid of public censure.[19]

The following week Franklin defended the value of gossip in another letter, even more flavorful, purportedly penned by the aptly named Alice Addertongue. Franklin, who was then 26, had his fictional Alice identify herself, with an edge of irony, as a "young girl of about thirty-five." She lived at home with her mother and, she said, "find it my duty as well as inclination to exercise my talent at censure for the good of my country folks."

After taking a swipe at a "silly" piece in Bradford's *Mercury* that criticized women for being gossipy, Alice recounts how she once found herself at odds with her mother on this issue. "She argued that scandal spoiled all good conversation, and I insisted without it there could be no such thing." As a result, she was banished to the kitchen when visitors came for tea. While her mother engaged guests in high-minded discourse in the parlor, Alice regaled a few young friends with tales of a neighbor's intrigue with his maid. Hearing the laughter, her mother's friends began drifting from the parlor into the kitchen to partake in the gossip. Her mother finally joined them. "I have long thought that if you would make your paper a vehicle of scandal, you would *double the number of your subscribers.*"

Franklin's playful defenses of busybodies, among the most amusing pieces he ever wrote, set a lighthearted tone for his paper. Because of his gregarious personality and fascination with human nature, he appreciated tales about people's foibles and behavior, and he understood why others did as well. But he was, of course, only half-serious in his defense of gossip. The other part of his personality was more earnest: he continually resolved to speak ill of nobody. As a result, he toyed in the *Gazette* with the argument for gossip, but he did not really indulge in it much. For example, in one issue he noted that he had gotten a letter describing the disagreements and conduct of a certain couple, "but for charitable reasons the said letter is at present thought not fit to be published."[20]

Likewise, he was ambiguous when writing about drinking. He was a temperate man who nevertheless enjoyed the joviality of taverns. In one famous *Gazette* piece, destined to become a poster in countless pubs, he produced a "Drinker's Dictionary" listing 250 or so synonyms for being drunk: "Addled . . . afflicted . . . biggy . . . boozy . . . busky . . . buzzey . . . cherubimical . . . cracked . . . halfway to Concord . . ." Yet he also frightened readers with colorful news accounts of the deaths of drunks, and he wrote editorials on the "poisonous" effect of spirits. As a printer in London, he had lectured coworkers that strong drink made them less industrious; as an editor in Philadelphia, he continued this crusade.[21]

Franklin also perfected the art of poking fun at himself. He realized, as have subsequent American humorists, that a bit of wry self-deprecation could make him seem more endearing. In one small item in the *Gazette,* he recounted how "a certain printer" was walking along the wharf when he slipped and stuck his leg into a barrel of tar. His awkward escape resembled the saying about being "as nimble as a bee in a tarbarrel." Franklin ended the item with a little play on words: " 'Tis true he was no Honey Bee, nor yet a Humble Bee, but a Boo-bee he may be allowed to be, namely B.F."[22]

By the early 1730s, Franklin's business was thriving. He started building an extended little empire by sending his young workers, once they had served their time with him, to set up partnership shops in places ranging from Charleston to Hartford. He would supply the presses and part of the expenses, as well as some content for the publications, and in return take a portion of the revenue.

A PRACTICAL MARRIAGE

Now that he had established himself in business, Franklin found himself in want of a good wife. Bachelorhood was frowned on in colonial America, and Franklin had a sexual appetite that he knew required discipline. So he set out to find himself a mate, preferably one with a dowry attached.

Boarding at his house was a friend from the Junto, glazier and mathematician Thomas Godfrey, and his wife, who tended to their meals and homemaking. Mrs. Godfrey proposed a match with one of her nieces, whom Franklin found "very deserving," and a courtship ensued. Dowries being common, Franklin sought to negotiate his through Mrs. Godfrey: approximately £100, the amount he still owed on his printing business. When the girl's family replied that they could not spare that much, Franklin suggested rather unromantically that they could mortgage their home.

The girl's family promptly broke off the relationship, either out of outrage or (as Franklin suspected) in the hope that the courtship had gone so far that they would elope without a dowry. Resentful, Franklin refused to have anything more to do with the girl, even after Mrs. Godfrey suggested they were open to negotiations.

Not only did the courtship end, so did yet another Franklin friendship. Godfrey moved out, quit the Junto, and eventually turned over the printing of his little almanac to Franklin's competitor, Bradford. Years later, Franklin wrote dismissively about the man who once shared his house, club, and presumably affection. Godfrey "was not a pleasing companion, as like most great mathematicians I have met with he expected unusual precision in everything said, or was forever denying or distinguishing upon trifles to the disturbance of all conversation."

Franklin's annoyance also led him to satirize the situation in the *Gazette* not long thereafter, using the pseudonym Anthony Afterwit. The "honest tradesman" complains that when he was courting his wife, her father hinted that he could be in for a nice dowry, and he "formed several fine schemes" of how to spend the money. "When the old gentleman saw I was pretty well engaged, and that the match was too far gone to be easily broke off, he . . . forbid me the house and told his daughter that if she married me he would not give her a farthing." Afterwit, unlike the real Franklin, elopes. "I have since learned that there are old curmudgeons besides him who have this trick to marry their daughters and yet keep what they might well spare."

(The Anthony Afterwit essay had an interesting side effect. His fictional wife, Abigail Afterwit, was the name of a character that had been created almost a decade earlier by Franklin's estranged brother, James, in the *New England Courant.* James, who had since moved to Rhode Island, reprinted the Anthony Afterwit piece in his own paper along with a reply from a Patience Teacraft. Benjamin in turn reprinted the reply in his Philadelphia paper, and the following year he visited his brother for an emotional reconciliation. James's health was failing, and he begged his younger brother to look after his 10-year-old son. That Benjamin did, arranging for his education and taking him on as an apprentice. A dominant theme in Franklin's autobiography is that of making mistakes and then making amends, as if he were a moral bookkeeper balancing his accounts. Running away from his brother was, Franklin noted, "one of the first errata of my life." Helping James's son was the way to set the ledger back into balance. "Thus it was that I made my brother ample amends for the service I had deprived him of by leaving him so early.")

After his courtship of Mrs. Godfrey's niece was scuttled, Franklin scouted around for other possible brides, but he discovered that young printers were not valued enough to command a sure dowry. He could not expect money unless it was to marry a woman "I should not otherwise think agreeable." In his autobiography, which he began years later as a letter to the illegitimate son he fathered while looking for a wife, Franklin wrote a memorable line: "In the meantime, that hard-to-be-governed passion of youth had hurried me frequently into intrigues with low women that fell in my way, which were attended with some expense and great inconvenience."[23]

Deborah Read, the girl who had laughed at him when he first straggled into Philadelphia, was also in a rather desperate situation. After Franklin left her to live in London, she had received only one curt letter from him. So she made the mistake of marrying a charming but unreliable potter named John Rogers. He was unable to make a living, and Deborah soon heard rumors that he had abandoned a wife in England. So she moved back in with her mother, and Rogers stole a slave and absconded to the West Indies, leaving behind a load of debt. Although there were reports he had died there in a brawl, these were unconfirmed, which meant Deborah would have difficulty legally re-marrying. Bigamy was a crime punishable by thirty-nine lashes and life imprisonment.

Since the death of Deborah's father, her mother had been eking out a living by selling homemade medicines. An advertising bill, printed by Franklin, notes: "The widow Read . . . continues to make and sell her well-known ointment for the itch, with which she has cured abundance of people . . . It also kills or drives away all sorts of lice in once or twice using." Franklin frequently visited the Reads, advised them on business matters, and took pity on the dejected Deborah. He faulted himself for her plight, though Mrs. Read kindly took most of the blame for not having let them marry before he left for London. Fortunately for all, according to Franklin, "our mutual affection was revived."

Around that time, Franklin developed a method for making difficult decisions. "My way is to divide a sheet of paper by a line into two columns, writing over the one *Pro* and the other *Con*," he later recalled. Then he would list all the arguments on each side and weigh how important each was. "Where I find two, one on each side, that seem equal, I strike them both out; if I find a reason *pro* equal to some two reasons *con*, I strike out the three." By this bookkeeper's calculus, it became clear to him "where the balance lies."

However exactly he came to his decision, the balance of considerations eventually tipped toward Deborah, and in September 1730 they began living together as a married couple. There was no official ceremony. Instead, they entered into a type of common-law arrangement that served to protect them from charges of bigamy if Rogers unexpectedly reappeared. But he never did. Franklin viewed his union with Deborah, like his reconciliation with his brother, as an example of his rectifying an earlier error. "Thus I corrected that great erratum as well as I could," Franklin later wrote of his mistreatment of the younger Deborah.

Franklin is often described as (or accused of) being far more practical than romantic, a man of the head rather than heart. The tale of his common-law marriage to Deborah provides some support for this view. But it also illustrates some complexities of Franklin's character: his desire to tame his hard-to-govern passions by being practical, and the genuine fondness he felt for kindred companions. He was not given to starry-eyed soulful commitments or poetic love; instead, his emotional attachments tended to be the more prosaic bonds of affection that grew out of partnership, self-interest, collaboration, camaraderie, and good-humored kinship.

A wife who brought with her a dowry would have likely also brought expensive social airs and aspirations. Instead, Franklin found "a good and faithful helpmate" who was frugal and practical and devoid of pretensions, traits that he later noted were far more valuable to a rising tradesman. Their union remained mutually useful, if not deeply romantic, until Deborah's death forty-four years later. As Franklin would soon have Poor Richard pronounce in his almanac: "Keep your eyes wide open before marriage, half shut afterwards."[24]

WILLIAM

There was one major complication facing the new marriage. Around that time, Franklin fathered and took sole custody of an illegitimate son named William, which was probably the "great inconvenience" that he coldly wrote in his autobiography was the result of consorting with "low women."

The identity of William's mother is one of history's delicious mysteries, a source of speculation among scholars. Franklin never revealed the secret, nor did William, if he knew. In fact, even the date of his birth is unclear. Let's start there.

Most historians say that William was born sometime between April 12, 1730, and April 12, 1731. This is based on a letter Franklin wrote to his own mother on April 12, 1750, referring to William as "now 19 years of age, a tall, proper youth, and much of a beau."

Willard Sterne Randall in *A Little Revenge,* a fascinating but somewhat speculative account of Franklin's troubled relationship with his son, questions this. In September 1746, William left home with an ensign's commission on a military expedition to Canada, and Randall argues that he was unlikely to have been only 15 or 16. Perhaps, in writing his mother, Franklin was shaving a year or two off William's age to make him seem legitimate. Likewise, the meticulous Franklin scholar J. A. Leo Lemay, on his Web site detailing Franklin's life, surmises he was born in 1728 or 1729, as do some nineteenth-century biographers.

However, we know that before he was allowed to enlist, perhaps sometime in early 1746, William tried to run away to sea, and his father had to fetch him home from a ship in the harbor, which indicates that he indeed might have been not any older than 15 or 16 at the time (his father had considered running off to sea at age 12, and did run away to Philadelphia at 17). Sheila Skemp's comprehensive biography of William makes it seem quite logical that he embarked with the military at 16, well after he finished his schooling. In addition, William was responsible for the belief reported in a magazine that he was 82 when he died in 1813 (which would place his birth in late 1730 or early 1731).

On balance, because neither man ever denied William's illegitimacy, it makes sense to believe that Franklin was telling the truth to his mother when he referred to William's age, and it makes equal sense to believe that William was never (intentionally or not) misleading about his age. Based on these assumptions, it is likely that William was born around the time that Deborah began living with Franklin in late 1730.[25]

That being the case, might Deborah actually have been his mother, as some scholars speculate? Might the common-law marriage have been partly occasioned by her pregnancy, while William's origin was left murky in case Rogers reappeared and charged her with bigamy and adultery? As Carl Van Doren muses, "There was bound to be a scandal. But of course it would be less if the child appeared to be Franklin's and an unknown mother's. The lusty philosopher could take all the blame."

But this theory doesn't bear much scrutiny. If Deborah had been pregnant and given birth, there would surely be some friends and relatives, including her mother, who would have known. As H. W. Brands puts it, "Even after the passage of years precluded any further concerns about Rogers, Debbie declined to claim William as her own—an omission impossible to imagine in any mother, let alone one who had to watch from close at hand while her son spent his life labeled a bastard." On the contrary, she was openly hostile to him. According to a clerk who later worked for the Franklins, Deborah referred to William as "the greatest villain upon earth" and heaped upon him "invectives in the foulest terms I ever heard from a gentlewoman."[26]

During a heated election in 1764, William's paternity became an issue. One abusive pamphlet charged that he was the son of a prostitute named Barbara who was subsequently exploited by the Franklins as a maid until she died and was buried in an unmarked grave. Given the scurrilous nature of that campaign and the unlikelihood that any of the Franklins could have abided having William's real mother around as their maid, this also seems implausible.

The best explanation comes from a 1763 letter about William, rediscovered more than two centuries later, which was written by George Roberts, a prosperous Philadelphia merchant who was a close family friend. " 'Tis generally known here his birth is illegitimate and his mother not in good circumstances," Roberts wrote to a friend in London, "but the report of her begging bread in the streets of this city is without the least foundation in truth. I understand some small pro-

vision is made by him for her, but her being none of the most agreeable women prevents particular notice being shown, or the father and
son acknowledging any connection with her." As Roberts was probably in a position to know, and as he had no ulterior motive, we are left
with this as the likeliest scenario.[27]

A FRUGAL MATE

In his autobiography (which extols the virtues of "industry" and
"frugality" a total of thirty-six times), Franklin wrote of his wife, "It
was lucky for me that I had one as much disposed to industry and frugality as myself." He gives her even more credit in a letter written later,
near the end of his life: "Frugality is an enriching virtue, a virtue I
could never acquire in myself, but I was lucky enough to find it in a
wife, who thereby became a fortune to me." For Franklin, this passed
for true love. Deborah helped at the print shop, stitched pamphlets,
and purchased rags for papermaking. At least initially, they had no servants, and Franklin ate his bread-and-milk porridge each morning
from a twopenny bowl.

In later years, after a conflicted Franklin had developed some taste
for finery while still clinging to his admiration for frugality, he wryly
recounted a little lapse on Deborah's part that showed "how luxury
will enter families and make a progress, in spite of principle." One day
he arrived at breakfast to find it served in a china bowl with a silver
spoon. Deborah had bought them at the "enormous sum" of 23 shillings, with "no other excuse or apology to make but that she thought
her husband deserved a silver spoon and china bowl as well as any of
his neighbors." With a droll mix of pride and disdain, Franklin recalled how, over many years, as their wealth grew, they ended up with
china and furnishings worth several hundred pounds.

When the young Franklin heard that his little sister Jane was planning to marry, he wrote her a letter that reflected his view that a good
wife should be frugal and industrious. He had thought about sending
her a tea table, he said, but his practical nature got the better of him.
"When I considered that the character of a good housewife was far

preferable to that of being only a pretty gentlewoman, I concluded to send you a spinning-wheel." As Poor Richard would soon phrase it in his first almanac: "Many estates are spent in the getting/ Since women for tea forsook spinning and knitting."[28]

The virtue of frugality was also one of young Franklin's favorite themes in his newspaper writings. In Anthony Afterwit's letter, after complaining about having to elope with no dowry, he goes on to ridicule his wife for adopting the airs and spending habits of a gentlewoman. First she pays for a fancy mirror, which then requires a nice table under it, then a tea service, and then a clock. Facing mounting debts, Anthony decides to sell these things when his wife leaves town to visit relatives. To replace the fancy furniture, he buys a spinning wheel and some knitting needles. He asks the *Gazette* to publish the letter so that she will read it before she returns and thus be prepared. "If she can conform to this new scheme of living, we shall be the happiest couple perhaps in the province." And then, as a reward, he might let her have the nice mirror back.

Less sexist than most men of his day, Franklin also aimed his barbs at men. Afterwit's letter was answered two weeks later by one from another Franklin creation, Celia Single. With the delightful gossipy voice of his other female characters, such as Silence Dogood and Alice Addertongue, Single recounts a visit to a friend whose husband is trying to replicate Afterwit's approach. A raucous argument ensues. "There is neither sin nor shame in knitting a pair of stockings," the husband says. She replies, "There are poor women enough in town that can knit." Single finally leaves, "knowing that a man and his wife are apt to quarrel more violently when before strangers than when by themselves." She later hears that the knitting thread ended up in the fireplace.

Single (or rather Franklin) goes on to admonish Franklin for publishing more tales of self-indulgent women than men. "If I were disposed to be censorious, I could furnish you with instances enough," she says, then proceeds to rattle off a long list of men who waste their time playing pool, dice, or checkers and buying fancy clothes. Finally, Franklin has her cleverly poke at his veil of pseudonymity. "There are holes enough to be picked in your coat as well as others; and those who are affronted by the satires you may publish will not consider so much who wrote as who printed."[29]

On a more serious and less modern note, Franklin published, four weeks after he married, "Rules and Maxims for Promoting Matrimonial Happiness." He began with a paean to marriage, "the surest and most lasting foundation of comfort and love." However, the folly of some who enter into it often makes it "a state of the most exquisite wretchedness and misery." He apologized for aiming his advice at women, as men were in fact more faulty, "but the reason is because I esteem them better disposed to receive and practice it."

Among his rules: avoid all thoughts of managing your husband, never deceive him or make him uneasy, accept that he "is a man not an angel," "resolve every morning to be good-natured and cheerful," remember the word "obey" in your marriage vows, do not dispute with him, and "deny yourself the trivial satisfaction of having your own will." A woman's power and happiness, Franklin wrote, "has no other foundation than her husband's esteem and love." Therefore, a wife should "share and soothe his cares, and with the utmost diligence conceal his infirmities." And when it comes to sex: "Let the tenderness of your conjugal love be expressed with such decency, delicacy and prudence as that it may appear plainly and thoroughly distinct from the designing fondness of a harlot."[30]

Franklin's essays and fictional letters make it clear that he entered into his union with Deborah holding some traditional views on matrimony: wives should be supportive, households should be run frugally and industriously. Fortunately for him, Deborah tended to share those views. In general, she had plain tastes, a willingness to work, and a desire to please her spouse. Of course, as he might have pointed out, the same could be said of him at the time.

And so they settled into a partnership that was both more and less than a conventional marriage. A tireless collaborator both in the house and at work, Deborah handled most of the accounts and expanded their shop's inventory to include ointments made by her mother, crown soap made by Franklin's Boston relatives, coffee, tea, chocolate, saffron, cheese, fish, and various other sundries. She strained her eyes

binding books and sewing clothes by candlelight. And though her
spelling and choice of words reflected her lack of education—the sex-
ton of the church was noted as the "seck stone" and one customer was
called "Mary the Papist"—her copious entries in their shop book are a
delightful record of the times.

Franklin's affection for her grew from his pride at her industry;
many years later, when he was in London arguing before the House of
Commons that unfair taxes would lead to boycotts of British manufacturers, he asserted that he had never been prouder than when he
was a young tradesman and wore only clothes that had been made by
his wife.

But Deborah was not merely a submissive or meek partner to the
man she often addressed (as he did her) as "my dear child" and whom
she sometimes publicly called "Pappy." She had a fierce temper, which
Franklin invariably defended. "Don't you know that all wives are in the
right?" he asked a nephew who was having a dispute with Deborah.
Soon after their marriage, he wrote a piece called "A Scolding Wife,"
in which he defended assertive women by saying they tended to be
"active in the business of the family, special good housewives, and very
careful of their husband's interests."[31]

The only extant painting of Deborah makes her appear to be a sensible and determined woman, plump and plain but not unattractive. In
a letter he wrote her years later from London, he described a mug he
was sending and compared it to her: "I fell in love with it at first sight,
for I thought it looked like a fat, jolly dame, clean and tidy, with a neat
blue and white calico gown on, good natured and lovely, and just put
me in mind of—somebody."

It was a relationship that did not inspire great romantic verse, but it
did produce an endearing ballad that he put into the mouth of Poor
Richard. In it, Franklin paid tribute to "My Plain Country Joan" and
blessed the day he made her his own. Among the lyrics:

> *Not a word of her shape, or her face, or her eyes,*
> *Of flames or of darts shall you hear:*
> *Though I beauty admire, 'tis virtue I prize,*
> *Which fades not in seventy years . . .*

In peace and good order my household she guides,
  Right careful to save what I gain;
Yet cheerfully spends, and smiles on the friends
  I've the pleasure to entertain . . .
The best have some faults, and so has my Joan,
  But then they're exceedingly small,
And now, I'm used to 'em, they're so like my own.
  I can scarcely feel them at all.

Over the years, Franklin would outgrow Deborah in many ways. Though they shared values, he was far more worldly and intellectual than she was, or ever wanted to be. There is some evidence that she may have been born in Birmingham and brought to America as a young child, but during her adult life she seems never to have spent a night away from Philadelphia, and she lived most of her life on Market Street within two blocks of the house where she was raised.

Franklin, on the other hand, loved to travel, and although he would, in later years, occasionally express some hope that she would accompany him, he knew that she was not so inclined. He seemed to sense that she would not be socially comfortable in his new realms. So, in this regard, they respected each other's independence, perhaps to a fault. For fifteen of the last seventeen years of Deborah's life, Franklin would be away, including when she died. Nevertheless, their mutual affection, respect, and loyalty—and their sense of partnership—would endure.[32]

FRANCIS

Two years into their marriage, in October 1732, Deborah gave birth to a son. Francis Folger Franklin, known as Franky, was doted on by both parents: he had his portrait painted when still a baby, and his father advertised for a tutor to teach both his children when Francis was 2 and William about 4. For the rest of his life, Franklin would marvel at the memory of how precocious, curious, and special Franky was.

These were, alas, destined to be only sorrowful memories. In one of the few searing tragedies of Franklin's life, Franky died of smallpox just after his fourth birthday. On his grave, Franklin chose a simple epitaph: "The delight of all who knew him."

The bitter irony was that Franklin had become a fervent advocate of smallpox vaccinations after they had been ridiculed in the *New England Courant* when Franklin worked there for his brother. In the years preceding Franky's birth, he had editorialized in the *Pennsylvania Gazette* in support of inoculations and published statistics showing how effective they were. In 1730, for example, he wrote an account of a Boston epidemic in which most people who had been vaccinated were spared.

He had planned to inoculate Franky, but he had delayed doing so because the boy had been ill with the flux. In a sad announcement that appeared in his paper a week after the boy's death, Franklin denied rumors that he died from being vaccinated. "I do hereby sincerely declare that he was not inoculated, but received the distemper in the common way of infection." He went on to declare his belief that inoculation was "a safe and beneficial practice."

The memory of Franky was one of the few things ever to cause Franklin painful reflections. When his sister Jane wrote to him in London years later with happy news about his grandsons, Franklin responded that it "brings often afresh to my mind the idea of my son Franky, though now dead thirty-six years, whom I have seldom since seen equaled in everything, and whom to this day I cannot think of without a sigh."[33]

Adding to the poignancy, Franklin had written for his paper, while Franky was still alive, an unusually deep rumination on "The Death of Infants," which was occasioned by the death of a neighbor's child. Drawing on his observations of the tiny Franky, he described the magical beauty of babies: "What curious joints and hinges on which limbs are moved to and fro! What an inconceivable variety of nerves, veins, arteries, fibers, and little invisible parts are found in every member! . . . What endless contrivances to secure life, to nourish nature, and to propagate the same to future animals!" How could it be, Franklin then asked, that "a good and merciful Creator should produce myriads of such exquisite machines to no other end or purpose but to be deposited in the dark chambers of the grave" before they were old enough to know good from evil or to serve their fellow man and their God? The answer, he admitted, was "beyond our mortal ken" to understand. "When nature gave us tears, she gave us leave to weep."[34]

DEFINING HIS GOD

When we last took Franklin's spiritual pulse in London, he had written his ill-conceived "Dissertation on Liberty and Necessity," which attacked the idea of free will and much of Calvinist theology, and then he had repudiated the pamphlet as an embarrassing "erratum." That left him in a religious quandary. He no longer believed in the received dogmas of his Puritan upbringing, which taught that man could achieve salvation only through God's grace rather than through good works. But he was uncomfortable embracing a simple and unenhanced version of deism, the Enlightenment-era creed that reason and the study of nature (instead of divine revelation) tell us all we can know about our Creator. The deists he knew, including his younger self, had turned out to be squirrelly in their morals.

On his return to Philadelphia, Franklin showed little interest in organized religion and even less in attending Sunday services. Still, he continued to hold some basic religious beliefs, among them "the existence of the Deity" and that "the most acceptable service of God was doing good to man." He was tolerant toward all sects, particularly those that worked to make the world a better place, and he made sure "to avoid all discourse that might tend to lessen the good opinion another might have of his own religion." Because he believed that churches were useful to the community, he paid his annual subscription to support the town's Presbyterian minister, the Rev. Jedediah Andrews.[35]

One day, Andrews prevailed on him to sample his Sunday sermons, which Franklin did for five weeks. Unfortunately, he found them "uninteresting and unedifying since not a single moral principle was inculcated or enforced, their aim seeming to be rather to make us good Presbyterians than good citizens." On his final visit, the reading from the Scripture (Philippians 4:8) related to virtue. It was a topic dear to Franklin's heart, and he hoped that Andrews would expound on the concept in his sermon. Instead, the minister focused only on dogma and doctrine, without offering any practical thoughts about virtue. Franklin was "disgusted," and he reverted to spending his Sundays reading and writing on his own.[36]

Franklin began to clarify his religious beliefs through a series of essays and letters. In them, he adopted a creed that would last the rest of his life: a virtuous, morally fortified, and pragmatic version of deism. Unlike most pure deists, he concluded that it was useful (and thus probably correct) to believe that a faith in God should inform our daily actions; but like other deists, his faith was devoid of sectarian dogma, burning spirituality, deep soul-searching, or a personal relationship to Christ.[37]

The first of these religious essays was a paper "for my own private use," written in November 1728, entitled "Articles of Belief and Acts of Religion." Unlike his London dissertation, which was clogged with convoluted imitations of analytic philosophy, it was elegant and sparse. He began with a simple affirmation: "I believe there is one Supreme most perfect being."[38]

It was an important statement, because some mushier deists shied even from going that far. As Diderot once quipped, a deist is someone who has not lived long enough to become an atheist. Franklin lived very long, and despite the suspicions of John Adams and others that he was a closet atheist, he repeatedly and indeed increasingly asserted his belief in a supreme God.

In the deist tradition, Franklin's Supreme Being was somewhat distant and uninvolved in our daily travails. "I imagine it great vanity in me to suppose that the Supremely Perfect does in the least regard such an inconsiderable nothing as man," he wrote. He added his belief that this "Infinite Father" was far above wanting our praise or prayers.

There is in all humans, however, a desire and a deeply felt duty to worship a more intimate God, Franklin surmised. Therefore, he wrote, the Supreme Being causes there to be lesser and more personal gods for mortal men to worship. Franklin thus has it both ways: combining the deist concept of God as a distant First Cause with the belief of other religions that worship a God who is directly involved in people's lives. The result is a Supreme Being that can be manifest in various ways, depending on the needs of different worshipers.

Some commentators, most notably A. Owen Aldridge, read this literally as Franklin's embracing some sort of polytheism, with a bevy of lesser gods overseeing various realms and planets. Occasionally throughout his life, Franklin would refer to "the gods," but these later references are quite casual and colloquial, and Franklin seems to be speaking more figuratively than literally in his 1728 paper. As Kerry Walters writes in *Benjamin Franklin and His Gods,* "It is an error to presume they point to a literal polytheism. Such a conclusion is as philosophically bizarre as it is textually unwarranted." (Given the difficulties Franklin sometimes seems to have in believing in one God, it seems unlikely he could find himself believing in many.)[39]

Franklin went on to outline how he viewed and worshiped his own personal God. This involved offering suitable prayers, and Franklin produced a whole liturgy that he had composed. It also required acting virtuously, and Franklin engaged in a moral calculus that was very pragmatic and even somewhat utilitarian: "I believe He is pleased and delights in the happiness of those He has created; and since without virtue man can have no happiness in this world, I firmly believe He delights to see me virtuous."

In a paper he subsequently read to his friends in the Junto, Franklin elaborated his religious beliefs by exploring the issue of "divine providence," the extent to which God gets involved in worldly matters. The Puritans believed in a detailed and intimate involvement, called "special providence," and regularly prayed to God for very specific intercessions. As Calvin himself put it, "Supposing that He remains tranquilly in heaven without caring for the world outrageously deprives God of all effective power." Most deists, on the other hand, believed in a "general providence," in which God expresses his will through the laws of nature he set in motion instead of by micromanaging our daily lives.

As was typical, Franklin sought a pragmatic resolution in his Junto talk, which he called "On the Providence of God in the Government of the World." He began by apologizing to "my intimate pot companions" for being rather "unqualified" to speak on spiritual matters. His study of nature, he said, convinced him that God created the universe and was infinitely wise, good, and powerful. He then explored four possibilities: (1) God predetermined and predestined everything that happens, eliminating all possibility of free will; (2) He left things to proceed according to natural laws and the free will of His creatures, and never interferes; (3) He predestined some things and left some things to free will, but still never interferes; (4) "He sometimes interferes by His particular providence and sets aside the effects which would otherwise have been produced by any of the above causes."[40]

Franklin ended up settling on the fourth option, but not because he could prove it; instead, it resulted from a process of elimination and a sense of which belief would be most useful for people to hold. Any of the first three options would mean that God is not infinitely powerful or good or wise. "We are then necessarily driven into the fourth supposition," he wrote. He admitted that many find it contradictory to believe both that God is infinitely powerful and that men have free will (it was the conundrum that stymied him in the London dissertation he wrote and then renounced). But if God is indeed all powerful, Franklin reasoned, he surely is able to find a way to give the creatures he made in his image some of his free will.

Franklin's conclusion had, as might be expected, practical consequences: people should love God and "pray to Him for His favor and protection." He did not, however, stray too far from deism; he placed little faith in the use of prayers for specific personal requests or miracles. In an irreverent letter he later wrote to his brother John, he calculated that 45 million prayers were offered in all of New England seeking victory over a fortified French garrison in Canada. "If you do not succeed, I fear I shall have but an indifferent opinion of Presbyterian prayers in such cases as long as I live. Indeed, in attacking strong towns I should have more dependence on *works* than on *faith*."

Above all, Franklin's beliefs were driven by pragmatism. The final sentence of his Junto talk stressed that it was socially useful for people to believe in the version of divine providence and free will that he proposed: "This religion will be a powerful regulator of our actions, give us peace and tranquility within our own minds, and render us benevolent, useful and beneficial to others."[41]

Not all of Franklin's religious musings were this earnest. Around the time of his Junto paper, he wrote for his newspaper a tale called "A Witch Trial at Mount Holly," which was a delightful parody of Puritan mystical beliefs clashing with scientific experimentation. The accused witches were to be subjected to two tests: weighed on a scale against the Bible, and tossed in the river with hands and feet bound to see if they floated. They agree to submit to these tests—on the condition that two of the accusers take the same test. With colorful details of all the ridiculous pomp, Franklin described the process. The accused and accusers all succeed in outweighing the Bible. But both of the accused and one of the accusers fail to sink in the river, thus indicating that they are witches. The more intelligent spectators conclude from this that most people naturally float. The others are not so sure, and they resolve to wait until summer when the experiment could be tried with the subjects unclothed.[42]

Franklin's freethinking unnerved his family. When his parents wrote of their concern over his "erroneous opinions," Franklin replied with a letter that spelled out a religious philosophy, based on tolerance and utility, that would last his life. It would be vain, he wrote, for any person to insist that "all the doctrines he holds are true and all he rejects are false." The same could be said of the opinions of different religions as well. They should be evaluated, the young pragmatist said, by their utility: "I think opinions should be judged by their influences and effects; and if a man holds none that tend to make him less virtuous or more vicious, it may be concluded that he holds none that are dangerous, which I hope is the case with me." He had little use for the doctrinal distinctions his mother worried about. "I think vital religion has always suffered when orthodoxy is more regarded than virtue. And the Scripture assures me that at the last day we shall not be examined by what we *thought*, but what we *did* . . . that we did good to our fellow creatures. See Matth 26." His parents, a bit more versed in the Scripture, probably caught that he meant Matthew 25. They did, nonetheless, eventually stop worrying about his heresies.[43]

THE MORAL PERFECTION PROJECT

Franklin's historical reputation has been largely shaped, for disciples and detractors alike, by his account in his autobiography of the famous project he launched to attain "moral perfection." This rather odd endeavor, which involved sequentially practicing a list of virtues, seems at once so earnest and mechanical that one cannot help either admiring him or ridiculing him. As the novelist D. H. Lawrence later sneered, "He made himself a list of virtues, which he trotted inside like a gray nag in a paddock."

So it's important to note the hints of irony and self-deprecation in his droll recollection, written when he was 79, of what he wryly dubbed "the bold and arduous project of arriving at moral perfection." His account has touches of the amused-by-his-younger-self tone to be found in the diverting little tales he wrote in France at the same time that he was writing this part of his autobiography. Yet it should also be noted that, as a young man, he seemed to approach his moral perfection program with an endearing sincerity, and even as an old man seemed proud of its worthiness.

Franklin began his quest around the time he ended his unsatisfactory visits to Presbyterian services and started spelling out his own religious creed. The endeavor was typically pragmatic. It contained no abstract philosophizing nor any reference to religious doctrines. As he later noted with pride, it was not merely an exhortation to be virtuous, it was also a practical guide on how to achieve that goal.

First he made a list of twelve virtues he thought desirable, and to each he appended a short definition:

Temperance: Eat not to dullness; drink not to elevation.

Silence: Speak not but what may benefit others or yourself; avoid trifling conversation.

Order: Let all your things have their places; let each part of your business have its time.

Resolution: Resolve to perform what you ought; perform without fail what you resolve.

Frugality: Make no expense but to do good to others or yourself; (i.e., waste nothing).

Industry: Lose no time; be always employed in something useful; cut off all unnecessary actions.

Sincerity: Use no hurtful deceit; think innocently and justly,
and, if you speak, speak accordingly.

Justice: Wrong none by doing injuries, or omitting the benefits
that are your duty.

Moderation: Avoid extremes; forbear resenting injuries so much
as you think they deserve.

Cleanliness: Tolerate no uncleanliness in body, clothes, or habi-
tation.

Tranquility: Be not disturbed at trifles, or at accidents common
or unavoidable.

Chastity: Rarely use venery but for health or offspring, never to
dullness, weakness, or the injury of your own or another's
peace or reputation.

A Quaker friend "kindly" informed him that he had left something
off: Franklin was often guilty of "pride," the friend said, citing many
examples, and could be "overbearing and rather insolent." So Franklin
added "humility" to be the thirteenth virtue on his list. "Imitate Jesus
and Socrates."[44]

The descriptions, such as the notably lenient one for chastity, were
rather revealing. So too was the endeavor itself. It was also, in its passion for self-improvement through diligent resolve, enchantingly
American.

Franklin's focus was on traits that could help him succeed in this
world, instead of ones that would exalt his soul for the hereafter.
"Franklin celebrated a characteristically bourgeois set of virtues,"
writes social theorist David Brooks. "These are not heroic virtues.
They don't fire the imagination or arouse the passions like the aristocratic love of honor. They are not particularly spiritual virtues. But
they are practical and they are democratic."

The set of virtues was also, as Edmund Morgan and others have

pointed out, somewhat selfish. It did not include benevolence or charity, for example. But in fairness, we must remember that this was a
young tradesman's plan for self-improvement, not a full-blown statement of his morality. Benevolence was and would continue to be a
motivating ideal for him, and charity, as Morgan notes, "was actually
the guiding principle of Franklin's life." The fundamental tenet of his
morality, he repeatedly declared, was "The most acceptable service to
God is doing good to man."[45]

Mastering all of these thirteen virtues at once was "a task of more
difficulty than I had imagined," Franklin recalled. The problem was
that "while my care was employed in guarding against one fault, I was
often surprised by another." So he decided to tackle them like a person
who, "having a garden to weed, does not attempt to eradicate all the
bad herbs at once, which would exceed his reach and his strength, but
works on one of the beds at a time."

On the pages of a little notebook, he made a chart with seven red
columns for the days of the week and thirteen rows labeled with his
virtues. Infractions were marked with a black spot. The first week he
focused on temperance, trying to keep that line clear while not worrying about the other lines. With that virtue strengthened, he could turn
his attention to the next one, silence, hoping that the temperance line
would stay clear as well. In the course of the year, he would complete
the thirteen-week cycle four times.

"I was surprised to find myself so much fuller of faults than I had
imagined," he dryly noted. In fact, his notebook became filled with
holes as he erased the marks in order to reuse the pages. So he transferred his charts to ivory tablets that could be more easily wiped clean.

His greatest difficulty was with the virtue of order. He was a sloppy
man, and he eventually decided that he was so busy and had such a
good memory that he didn't need to be too orderly. He likened himself
to the hurried man who goes to have his ax polished but after a while
loses patience and declares, "I think I like a speckled ax best." In addition, as he recounted with amusement, he developed another convenient rationalization: "Something that pretended to be reason was
every now and then suggesting to me that such extreme nicety as I ex-

acted of myself might be a kind of foppery in morals, which if it were known would make me ridiculous; that a perfect character might be attended with the inconvenience of being envied and hated."

Humility was also a problem. "I cannot boast of much success in acquiring the *reality* of this virtue, but I had a good deal with regard to the *appearance* of it," he wrote, echoing what he had said about how he had acquired the appearance of industry by carting his own paper through the streets of Philadelphia. "There is perhaps no one of our natural passions so hard to subdue as pride; disguise it, struggle with it, beat it down, stifle it, mortify it as much as one pleases, it is still alive and will every now and then peep out and show itself." This battle against pride would challenge—and amuse—him for the rest of his life. "You will see it perhaps often in this history. For even if I could conceive that I had completely overcome it, I would probably be proud of my humility."

Indeed, he would always indulge a bit of pride in discussing his moral perfection project. Fifty years later, as he flirted with the ladies of France, he would pull out the old ivory slates and show off his virtues, causing one French friend to exult at touching "this precious booklet."[46]

ENLIGHTENMENT CREED

This plan for pursuing virtue, combined with the religious outlook that he had simultaneously been formulating, laid the foundation for a lifelong creed. It was based on pragmatic humanism and a belief in a benevolent but distant deity who was best served by being benevolent to others. Franklin's ideas never ripened into a profound moral or religious philosophy. He focused on understanding virtue rather than God's grace, and he based his creed on rational utility rather than religious faith.

His outlook contained some vestiges of his Puritan upbringing, most notably an inclination toward frugality, lack of pretense, and a belief that God appreciates those who are industrious. But he detached these concepts from Puritan orthodoxy about the salvation of the elect and from other tenets that he did not consider useful in improving earthly conduct. His life shows, the Yale scholar A. Whitney Griswold has noted, "what Puritan habits detached from Puritan beliefs were capable of achieving."

He was also far less inward-looking than Cotton Mather or other Puritans. Indeed, he poked fun at professions of faith that served little worldly purpose. As A. Owen Aldridge writes, "The Puritans were known for their constant introspection, fretting about sins, real or imaginary, and agonizing about the uncertainty of their salvation. Absolutely none of this soul-searching appears in Franklin. One can scrutinize his work from first page to last without finding a single note of spiritual anxiety."[47]

Likewise, he had little use for the sentimental subjectivity of the Romantic era, with its emphasis on the emotional and inspirational, that began rising in Europe and then America during the later part of his life. As a result, he would be criticized by such Romantic exemplars as Keats, Carlyle, Emerson, Thoreau, Poe, and Melville.[48]

Instead, he fit squarely into the tradition—indeed, was the first great American exemplar—of the Enlightenment and its Age of Reason. That movement, which rose in Europe in the late seventeenth century, was defined by an emphasis on reason and observable experience, a mistrust of religious orthodoxy and traditional authority, and an optimism about education and progress. To this mix, Franklin added elements of his own pragmatism. He was able (as novelist John Updike and historian Henry Steele Commager, among others, have noted) to appreciate the energies inherent in Puritanism and to liberate them from rigid dogma so they could flower in the freethinking atmosphere of the Enlightenment.[49]

In his writings about religion over the next five decades, Franklin rarely displayed much fervor. This is largely because he felt it was futile to wrestle with theological questions about which he had no empirical evidence and thus no rational basis for forming an opinion. Thunderbolts from heaven were, for him, something to be captured by a kite string and studied.

As a result, he was a prophet of tolerance. Focusing on doctrinal disputes was divisive, he felt, and trying to ascertain divine certainties was beyond our mortal ken. Nor did he think that such endeavors were socially useful. The purpose of religion should be to make men better and to improve society, and any sect or creed that did so was fine with him. Describing his moral improvement project in his autobiography, he wrote, "There was in it no mark of any of the distinguishing tenets of any particular sect. I had purposely avoided them; for, being fully persuaded of the utility and excellency of my method, and that it might be serviceable to people in all religions, and intending some time or other to publish it, I would not have any thing in it that should prejudice any one, of any sect, against it."

This simplicity of Franklin's creed meant that it was sneered at by sophisticates and disqualified from inclusion in the canon of profound philosophy. Albert Smyth, who compiled volumes of Franklin's papers in the nineteenth century, proclaimed, "His philosophy never got beyond the homely maxims of worldly prudence." But Franklin freely admitted that his religious and moral views were not based on profound analysis or metaphysical thinking. As he declared to a friend later in life, "The great uncertainty I found in metaphysical reasonings disgusted me, and I quitted that kind of reading and study for others more satisfactory."

What he found more satisfactory—more than metaphysics or poetry or exalted romantic sentiments—was looking at things in a pragmatic and practical way. Did they have beneficial consequences? For him, there was a connection between civic virtue and religious virtue, between serving his fellow man and honoring God. He was unashamed by the simplicity of this creed, as he explained in a sweet letter to his wife. "God is very good to us," he wrote. "Let us . . . show our sense of His goodness to us by continuing to do good to our fellow creatures." [50]

POOR RICHARD AND THE WAY TO WEALTH

Poor Richard's Almanack, which Franklin began publishing at the end of 1732, combined the two goals of his doing-well-by-doing-good philosophy: the making of money and the promotion of virtue. It became, in the course of its twenty-five-year run, America's first great humor classic. The fictional Poor Richard Saunders and his nagging wife, Bridget (like their predecessors Silence Dogood, Anthony After-wit, and Alice Addertongue), helped to define what would become a dominant tradition in American folk humor: the naïvely wicked wit and homespun wisdom of down-home characters who seem to be charmingly innocent but are sharply pointed about the pretensions of the elite and the follies of everyday life. Poor Richard and other such characters "appear as disarming plain folk, the better to convey wicked insights," notes historian Alan Taylor. "A long line of humorists—from Davy Crockett and Mark Twain to Garrison Keillor—still re-work the prototypes created by Franklin."[51]

Almanacs were a sweet source of annual revenue for a printer, easily outselling even the Bible (because they had to be bought anew each year). Six were being published in Philadelphia at the time, two of which were printed by Franklin: Thomas Godfrey's and John Jerman's. But after falling out with Godfrey over his failed matchmak-ing and losing Jerman to his rival Andrew Bradford, Franklin found himself in the fall of 1732 with no almanac to help make his press profitable.

So he hastily assembled his own. In format and style, it was like other almanacs, most notably that of Titan Leeds, who was publish-ing, as his father had before him, Philadelphia's most popular version. The name Poor Richard, a slight oxymoron pun, echoed that of *Poor Robin's Almanack,* which had been published by Franklin's brother James. And Richard Saunders happened to be the real name of a noted almanac writer in England in the late seventeenth century.[52]

Franklin, however, added his own distinctive flair. He used his pseudonym to permit himself some ironic distance, and he ginned up a running feud with his rival Titan Leeds by predicting and later fabri-cating his death. As his ad in the *Pennsylvania Gazette* immodestly promised:

> Just published for 1733: *Poor Richard: An Almanack* containing the lunations, eclipses, planets motions and aspects, weather, sun and moon's rising and setting, highwater, etc. besides many pleasant and witty verses, jests and sayings, author's motive of writing, prediction of the death of his friend Mr. Titan Leeds . . . By Richard Saunders, philomath, printed and sold by B. Franklin, price 3s. 6d per dozen.[53]

Years later, Franklin would recall that he regarded his almanac as a "vehicle for conveying instruction among the common folk" and therefore filled it with proverbs that "inculcated industry and frugality as the means of procuring wealth and thereby securing virtue." At the time, however, he also had another motive, about which he was quite forthright. The beauty of inventing a fictional author was that he could poke fun at himself by admitting, only half in jest, through the pen of Poor Richard, that money was his main motivation. "I might in this place attempt to gain thy favor by declaring that I write almanacks with no other view than that of the public good; but in this I should not be sincere," Poor Richard began his first preface. "The plain truth of the matter is, I am excessive poor, and my wife . . . has threatened more than once to burn all my books and Rattling-Traps (as she calls my instruments) if I do not make some profitable use of them for the good of my family."[54]

Poor Richard went on to predict "the inexorable death" of his rival Titan Leeds, giving the exact day and hour. It was a prank borrowed from Jonathan Swift. Leeds fell into the trap, and in his own almanac for 1734 (written after the date of his predicted death) called Franklin a "conceited scribbler" who had "manifested himself a fool and a liar." Franklin, with his own printing press, had the luxury of reading Leeds before he published his own 1734 edition. In it, Poor Richard responded that all of these defamatory protestations indicate that the real Leeds must indeed be dead and his new almanac a hoax by someone else. "Mr. Leeds was too well bred to use any man so indecently and scurrilously, and moreover his esteem and affection for me was extraordinary."

In his almanac for 1735, Franklin again ridiculed his "deceased" rival's sharp responses—"Titan Leeds when living would not have used me so!"—and also caught Leeds in a language mishap. Leeds had declared it was "untrue" that he had himself predicted that he would "survive until" the date in question. Franklin retorted that if it were untrue that he survived until then, he must therefore be "really defunct and dead." " 'Tis plain to everyone that reads his last two almanacks," Poor Richard jibed, "no man living would or could write such stuff."[55]

Even after Leeds in fact did die in 1738, Franklin did not relent.

He printed a letter from Leeds's ghost admitting "that I did actually die at that time, precisely at the hour you mentioned, with a variation only of 5 minutes, 53 seconds." Franklin then had the ghost make a prediction about Poor Richard's other rival: John Jerman would convert to Catholicism in the coming year. Franklin kept up this jest for four years, even while he had, once again, the contract to print Jerman's almanac. Jerman's good humor finally ran out, and in 1743 he took his business back to Bradford. "The reader may expect a reply from me to R—— S——rs alias B—— F——ns way of proving me no Protestant," he wrote, adding that because "of that witty performance [he] shall not have the benefit of my almanack for this year."[56]

Franklin had fun hiding behind the veil of Poor Richard, but he also occasionally enjoyed poking through the veil. In 1736 he had Poor Richard deny rumors that he was just a fiction. He would not, he said, "have taken any notice of so idle a report if it had not been for the sake of my printer, to whom my enemies are pleased to ascribe my productions, and who it seems is as unwilling to father my offspring as I am to lose credit of it." The following year, Poor Richard blamed his printer (Franklin) for causing some mistakes in the weather forecasts by moving them around to fit in holidays. And in 1739, he lamented that his printer was pocketing his profits, but added, "I do not grudge it him; he is a man I have great regard for."

Richard and Bridget Saunders did, in many ways, reflect Benjamin and Deborah Franklin. In the almanac for 1738, Franklin had the fictional Bridget take a turn at writing the preface for Poor Richard. This was shortly after Deborah Franklin had bought her husband the china breakfast bowl, and it came at the time when Franklin's newspaper pieces were poking fun at the pretensions of wives who acquire a taste for fancy tea services. Bridget Saunders announced to the reader that year that she read the preface her husband had composed, discovered he had "been slinging some of his old skits at me," and tossed it away. "Cannot I have a little fault or two but all the country must see it in print! They have already been told at one time that I am proud, another time that I am loud, and that I have a new petticoat, and abundance of such kind of stuff. And now, forsooth! all the world must know that Poor Dick's wife has lately taken a fancy to drink a little tea

now and then." Lest the connection be missed, she noted that the tea
was "a present from the printer."[57]

Poor Richard's delightful annual prefaces never, alas, became as famous as the maxims and sayings that Franklin scattered in the margins of his almanacs each year, such as the most famous of all: "Early
to bed and early to rise, makes a man healthy, wealthy and wise."
Franklin would have been amused by how faithfully these were
praised by subsequent advocates of self-improvement, and he would
likely have been even more amused by the humorists who later poked
fun at them. In a sketch with the ironic title "The Late Benjamin
Franklin," Mark Twain jibed, "As if it were any object to a boy to be
healthy and wealthy and wise on such terms. The sorrow that that
maxim has cost me, through my parents, experimenting on me with it,
tongue cannot tell. The legitimate result is my present state of general
debility, indigence, and mental aberration. My parents used to have
me up before nine o'clock in the morning sometimes when I was a
boy. If they had let me take my natural rest where would I have been
now? Keeping store, no doubt, and respected by all." Groucho Marx,
in his memoirs, also picked up the theme: " 'Early to bed, early to rise,
makes a man you-know-what.' This is a lot of hoopla. Most wealthy
people I know like to sleep late, and will fire the help if they are disturbed before three in the afternoon . . . You don't see Marilyn Monroe getting up at six in the morning. The truth is, I don't see Marilyn
Monroe getting up at any hour, more's the pity."[58]

Most of Poor Richard's sayings were not, in fact, totally original, as
Franklin freely admitted. They "contained the wisdom of many ages
and nations," he said in his autobiography, and he noted in the final
edition "that not a tenth part of the wisdom was my own." Even a near
version of his "early to bed and early to rise" maxim had appeared in a
collection of English proverbs a century earlier.[59]

Franklin's talent was inventing a few new maxims and polishing up
a lot of older ones to make them pithier. For example, the old English
proverb "Fresh fish and new-come guests smell, but that they are three
days old" Franklin made: "Fish and visitors stink in three days." Likewise, "A muffled cat is no good mouser" became "The cat in gloves

catches no mice." He took the old saying "Many strokes fell great oaks" and gave it a sharper moral edge: "Little strokes fell great oaks." He also sharpened "Three may keep a secret if two of them are away" into "Three may keep a secret if two of them are dead." And the Scottish saying that "a listening damsel and a speaking castle shall never end with honor" was turned into "Neither a fortress nor a maidenhead will hold out long after they begin to parley."[60]

Even though most of the maxims were adopted from others, they offer insight into his notions of what was useful and amusing. Among the best are:

> He's a fool that makes his doctor his heir . . . Eat to live, and not live to eat . . . He that lies down with dogs shall rise up with fleas . . . Where there's marriage without love, there will be love without marriage . . . Necessity never made a good bargain . . . There's more old drunkards than old doctors . . . A good example is the best sermon . . . None preaches better than the ant, and she says nothing . . . A Penny saved is Twopence clear . . . When the well's dry we know the worth of water . . . The sleeping fox catches no poultry . . . The used key is always bright . . . He that lives on hope dies farting [he later wrote it as "dies fasting," and the early version may have been a misprint] . . . Diligence is the mother of good luck . . . He that pursues two hares at once does not catch one and lets the other go . . . Search others for their virtues, thy self for thy vices . . . Kings and bears often worry their keepers . . . Haste makes waste . . . Make haste slowly . . . He who multiplies riches multiplies cares . . . He's a fool that cannot conceal his wisdom . . . No gains without pains . . . Vice knows she's ugly, so puts on her mask . . . The most exquisite folly is made of wisdom spun too fine . . . Love your enemies, for they will tell you your faults . . . The sting of a reproach is the truth of it . . . There's a time to wink as well as to see . . . Genius without education is like silver in the mine . . . There was never a good knife made of bad steel . . . Half the truth is often a great lie . . . God helps them that help themselves.

What distinguished Franklin's almanac was its sly wit. As he was completing his 1738 edition, he wrote a letter in his newspaper, using the pen name "Philomath," that poked at his rivals by giving sarcastic advice about writing almanacs. A requisite talent, he said, "is a sort of gravity, which keeps a due medium between dullness and nonsense."

This is because "grave men are taken by the common people for wise men." In addition, the author "should write sentences and throw out hints that neither himself nor anybody else can understand." As examples, he cited some phrases used by Titan Leeds.[61]

In his final edition, completed while on his way to England in 1757, Franklin would sum things up with a fictional speech by an old man named Father Abraham who strings together all of Poor Richard's adages about the need for frugality and virtue. But Franklin's wry tone was, even then, still intact. Poor Richard, who is standing in the back of the crowd, reports at the end: "The people heard it, and approved the doctrine, and immediately practiced the contrary."[62]

All of this made Poor Richard a success and his creator wealthy. The almanac sold ten thousand copies a year, surpassing its Philadelphia rivals. John Peter Zenger, whose famous 1735 libel trial was covered by Franklin's paper, bought thirty-six dozen one year. James's widow sold about eighty dozen a year. Father Abraham's speech compiling Poor Richard's sayings was published as *The Way to Wealth* and became, for a time, the most famous book to come out of colonial America. Within forty years, it was reprinted in 145 editions and seven languages; the French one was entitled *La Science du Bonhomme Richard*. Through the present, it has gone through more than thirteen hundred editions.

Like Franklin's moral perfection project and *Autobiography*, the sayings of Poor Richard have been criticized for revealing the mind of a penny-saving prig. "It has taken me many years and countless smarts to get out of that barbed wire moral enclosure that Poor Richard rigged up," wrote D. H. Lawrence. But that misses the humor and irony, as well as the nice mix of cleverness and morality, that Franklin deftly brewed. It also mistakenly confuses Franklin with the characters he created. The real Franklin was not a moral prude, and he did not dedicate his life to accumulating wealth. "The general foible of mankind," he told a friend, is "in the pursuit of wealth to no end." His goal was to help aspiring tradesmen become more diligent, and thus more able to be useful and virtuous citizens.

Poor Richard's almanacs do provide some useful insights into Franklin, especially into his wit and outlook. But by half hiding behind a fictional cutout, Franklin once again followed his Junto rule of revealing his thinking only through indirection. In that, he was acting according to the advice he put in Poor Richard's mouth. "Let all men know thee, but no man know thee thoroughly: Men freely ford that see the shallows." [63]

CHAPTER FIVE

PUBLIC CITIZEN

Philadelphia, 1731–1748

ORGANIZATIONS FOR THE COMMON GOOD

The essence of Franklin is that he was a civic-minded man. He cared more about public behavior than inner piety, and he was more interested in building the City of Man than the City of God. The maxim he had proclaimed on his first trip back from London—"Man is a sociable being"—was reflected not only in his personal collegiality, but also in his belief that benevolence was the binding virtue of society. As Poor Richard put it, "He that drinks his cider alone, let him catch his horse alone."

This gregarious outlook would lead him, as a twentysomething printer during the 1730s, to use his Junto to launch a variety of community organizations, including a lending library, fire brigade, and night watchmen corps, and later a hospital, militia, and college. "The good men may do separately," he wrote, "is small compared with what they may do collectively."

Franklin picked up his penchant for forming do-good associations from Cotton Mather and others, but his organizational fervor and galvanizing personality made him the most influential force in instilling this as an enduring part of American life. "Americans of all ages, all stations in life, and all types of dispositions are forever forming associations," Tocqueville famously marveled. "Hospitals, prisons and schools take shape this way."

Tocqueville came to the conclusion that there was an inherent struggle in America between two opposing impulses: the spirit of rugged individualism versus the conflicting spirit of community and association building. Franklin would have disagreed. A fundamental aspect of Franklin's life, and of the American society he helped to create, was that individualism and communitarianism, so seemingly contradictory, were interwoven. The frontier attracted barn-raising pioneers who were ruggedly individualistic as well as fiercely supportive of their community. Franklin was the epitome of this admixture of self-reliance and civic involvement, and what he exemplified became part of the American character.[1]

Franklin's subscription library, which was the first of its type in America, began when he suggested to his Junto that each member bring books to the clubhouse so that the others could use them. It worked well enough, but money was needed to supplement and care for the collection. So he decided to recruit subscribers who would pay dues for the right to borrow books, most of which would be imported from London.

The Library Company of Philadelphia was incorporated in 1731, when Franklin was 27. Its motto, written by Franklin, reflected the connection he made between goodness and godliness: *Communiter Bona profundere Deum est* (To pour forth benefits for the common good is divine).

Raising funds was not easy. "So few were the readers at the time in Philadelphia and the majority of us so poor that I was not able with great industry to find more than fifty persons, mostly young tradesmen, willing to pay." In doing so, he learned one of his pragmatic lessons about jealousy and modesty: he found that people were reluctant to support a "proposer of any useful project that might be supposed to raise one's reputation." So he put himself "as much as I could out of sight" and gave credit for the idea to his friends. This method worked so well that "I ever after practiced it on such occasions." People will eventually give you the credit, he noted, if you don't try to claim it at the time. "The present little sacrifice of your vanity will afterwards be amply repaid."

The choice of books, recommended by learned Philadelphians such as James Logan, a wealthy fur trader and gentleman scholar whom Franklin got the chance to befriend for this purpose, reflected Franklin's practical nature. Of the first forty-five bought, there were nine on science, eight on history, and eight on politics; most of the rest were reference books. There were no novels, dramas, poetry, or great literature, other than two classics (Homer and Virgil).

Franklin spent an hour or two each day reading the books in the library, "and thus repaired in some degree the loss of the learned education my father once intended for me." His involvement also helped him climb socially: the Junto was composed mainly of poor tradesmen, but the Library Company allowed Franklin to elicit the patronage of some of the more distinguished gentlemen of the town and also begin a lifelong friendship with Peter Collinson, a London merchant who agreed to help acquire the books. Eventually, the idea of local subscription libraries caught on in the rest of the colonies, and so did the benefits. "These libraries have improved the general conversation of the Americans," Franklin later noted, and "made the common tradesmen and farmers as intelligent as most gentlemen from other countries." The Library Company thrives to this day. With 500,000 books and 160,000 manuscripts, it remains a significant historical repository and is the oldest cultural institution in the United States.[2]

Franklin often floated his ideas for civic improvements by writing under a pseudonym for his paper. Using the name Pennsylvanus, he wrote a description of the "brave men" who volunteer to fight fires, and suggested that those who didn't join them should help bear the expense of ladders, buckets, and pumps. A year later, in an essay he read to the Junto and subsequently published as a letter to his newspaper, he proposed the formation of a fire company. Again taking care not to claim credit, he pretended the letter was written by an old man (who, in declaring that "an ounce of prevention is worth a pound of cure," sounded quite like Poor Richard). Philadelphia had a lot of spirited volunteers, he noted, but they lacked "order and method." They should therefore consider following the example of Boston, he said, and organize into fire-fighting clubs with specific duties. Always a stickler for specifics, Franklin helpfully enumerated these duties in great detail: there should be wardens, who carry "a red staff of five feet," as well as axmen and hookmen and other specialties.

"This was much spoken of as a useful piece," Franklin recalled in his autobiography, so he set about organizing the Union Fire Company, which was incorporated in 1736. He was fastidious in detailing its rules and the fines that would be levied for infractions. This being a Franklin scheme, it included a social component as well; they met for dinner once a month "for a social evening together discussing and communicating such ideas as occurred to us on the subject of fires." So many people wanted to join that, like the Junto, it spawned sister fire companies around town.

Franklin remained actively involved in the Union Fire Company for years. In 1743, the *Gazette* carried a little notice: "Lost at the late fire on Water Street, two leather buckets, marked B. Franklin & Co. Whoever brings them to the printer hereof shall be satisfied for their trouble." Fifty years later, when he returned from Paris after the Revolution, he would gather the four remaining members of the company, along with their leather buckets, for meetings.[3]

Franklin also sought to improve the town's ineffective police forces. At the time, the ragtag groups of watchmen were managed by constables who either enlisted neighbors or dunned them a fee to avoid service. This resulted in roaming gangs that made a little money and, Franklin noted, spent most of the night getting drunk. Once again, Franklin suggested a solution in a paper he wrote for his Junto. It proposed that full-time watchmen be funded by a property tax levied according to the value of each home, and it included one of the first arguments in America for progressive taxation. It was unfair, he wrote, that "a poor widow housekeeper, all of whose property to be guarded by the watch did not perhaps exceed the value of fifty pounds, paid as much as the wealthiest merchant, who had thousands of pounds worth of goods in his stores."

Unlike the fire associations, these police patrols were conceived as a government function and needed Assembly approval. Consequently, they did not get formed until 1752, "when the members of our clubs were grown more in influence." By that time, Franklin was an assemblyman, and he helped draft the detailed legislation on how the watchmen would be organized.[4]

THE FREEMASONS

One fraternal association, more exalted than the Junto, already existed in Philadelphia, and it seemed perfectly tailored to Franklin's aspirations: the Grand Lodge of Free and Accepted Masons. Freemasonry, a semisecret fraternal organization based on the ancient rituals and symbols of the stone-cutting guilds, had been founded in London in 1717, and its first Philadelphia lodge cropped up in 1727. Like Franklin, the Freemasons were dedicated to fellowship, civic works, and nonsectarian religious tolerance. They also represented, for Franklin, another step up the social ladder; many of the town's top merchants and lawyers were Freemasons.

Social mobility was not very common in the eighteenth century. But Franklin proudly made it his mission—indeed, helped it become part of America's mission—that a tradesman could rise in the world and stand before kings. This was not always easy, and at first he had trouble getting invited to join the Freemasons. So he began printing small, favorable notices about them in his newspaper. When that did not work, he tried a tougher tactic. In December 1730, he ran a long article that purported, based on the papers of a member who had just died, to uncover some of the secrets of the organization, including the fact that most of the secrets were just a hoax.

Within a few weeks, he was invited to join, after which the *Gazette* retracted its December article and printed some small, flattering notices. Franklin became a faithful Freemason. In 1732, he helped draft the bylaws of the Philadelphia lodge, and two years later became the Grand Master and printed its constitution.[5]

Franklin's fealty to the Freemasons embroiled him in a scandal that illustrated his aversion to confronting people. In the summer of 1737, a naïve apprentice named Daniel Rees wanted to join the group. A gang of rowdy acquaintances, not Freemasons, sought to have sport with him and concocted a ritual filled with weird oaths, purgatives, and butt kissing. When they told Franklin of their prank, he laughed and asked for a copy of the fake oaths. A few days later, the hooligans enacted another ceremony, where the hapless Rees was accidentally burned to death by a bowl of flaming brandy. Franklin was not involved, but he was called as a witness in the subsequent manslaughter trial. The newspaper printed by his rival Andrew Bradford, no friend of either Franklin or Freemasonry, charged that Franklin was indirectly responsible because he encouraged the tormentors.

Responding in his own paper, Franklin admitted that he initially laughed at the prank. "But when they came to those circumstances of their giving him a violent purge, leading him to kiss T's posteriors, and administering him the diabolical oath which R——n read to us, I grew indeed serious." His credibility, however, was not helped by the fact that he had asked to see the oath and then merrily showed it to friends.

News of the tragedy, and Franklin's involvement, was published in anti-Mason papers throughout the colonies, including the Boston *News Ledger,* and reached his parents. In a letter, he sought to allay his mother's concerns about the Freemasons. "They are in general a very harmless sort of people," he wrote, "and have no principles or practices that are inconsistent with religion or good manners." He did concede, however, that she had a right to be displeased that they did not admit women.[6]

THE GREAT AWAKENING

Although he was nondoctrinaire to the point of being little more than a deist, Franklin remained interested in religion, particularly its social effects. During the 1730s, he became enthralled by two preachers, the first an unorthodox freethinker like himself, the other an evangelical revivalist whose fiery conservatism ran counter to most of what Franklin believed.

Samuel Hemphill was a young preacher from Ireland who, in 1734, came to Philadelphia to work as a deputy at the Presbyterian church that Franklin had sporadically visited. More interested in preaching about morality than Calvinist doctrines, Hemphill started drawing large crowds, including a curious Franklin, who found "his sermons pleasing me, as they had little of the dogmatical kind, but inculcated strongly the practice of virtue." That dearth of dogma did not endear Hemphill to the church elders, however. Jedediah Andrews, the senior minister whose sermons had bored Franklin, complained that Hemphill had been imposed on his church and that "free thinkers, deists, and nothings, getting a scent of him, flocked to him." Soon Hemphill was brought before the synod on charges of heresy.

As the trial began, Franklin came to his defense with a deft article purporting to be a dialogue between two local Presbyterians. Mr. S., representing Franklin, listens as Mr. T. complains about how the "new-fangled preacher" talks too much about good works. "I do not love to hear so much of morality; I am sure it will carry no man to heaven."

Mr. S. rejoins that it is what "Christ and his Apostles used to preach." The Bible makes it clear, he says, that God would have us lead "virtuous, upright and good-doing lives."

But, asks Mr. T., isn't faith rather than virtue the path to salvation?

"Faith is recommended as a means of producing morality," Franklin's mouthpiece Mr. S. replies, adding heretically, "That from such faith alone salvation may be expected appears to me to be neither a Christian doctrine nor a reasonable one."

As a believer in tolerance, Franklin might have been expected to tolerate the Presbyterians' imposing whatever doctrine they wanted on their own preachers, but instead he had Mr. S. argue that they should not adhere to their orthodoxies. "No point of faith is so plain as that morality is our duty," Mr. S. concludes, echoing Franklin's core philosophy. "A virtuous heretic shall be saved before a wicked Christian."

It was a typical Franklin effort at persuasion: clever, indirect, and using fabricated characters to make his point. But when the synod unanimously censured and suspended Hemphill, Franklin shed his usual velvet gloves and, as he put it, "became his zealous partisan." He published an anonymous pamphlet (and, unlike his newspaper dialogue, made sure that the pamphlet remained anonymous) filled with uncharacteristic anger. Not only did he offer detailed theological rebuttals to each of the synod's charges, but he accused its members of "malice and envy."

Hemphill's accusers responded with their own pamphlet, which prompted Franklin to write another, even more vitriolic anonymous response that hurled phrases like "bigotry and prejudice" and "pious fraud." In a subsequent poem, he labeled Hemphill's critics "Rev. Asses."

It was a rare violation by Franklin of his Junto rule of avoiding direct contradiction or argumentation, one that was all the more odd because in the past he had cheerily forsaken any claim to care much about doctrinal disputes. His resentment of the entrenched, pious clerical establishment seemed to get the better of his temper.

Franklin's defense became more difficult when Hemphill was exposed as having plagiarized many of his sermons. Nevertheless, Franklin still stuck by him, explaining later that "I rather approved his giving us good sermons composed by others, than bad ones of his own manufacture, though the latter was the practice of our common teachers." In the end, Hemphill left town and Franklin quit the Presbyterian congregation for good.[7]

The Hemphill affair occurred just as an emotional tide of revivalism, known as the Great Awakening, began sweeping America. Fervent Protestant traditionalists, most notably Jonathan Edwards, were whipping congregants into spiritual frenzies and convulsive conversions with tales of fire and brimstone. As Edwards told his congregation in the most famous of his "terror" sermons, "Sinners in the Hands of an Angry God," the only thing that kept them from eternal damnation was the inexplicable grace of "the God that holds you over the pit of Hell, much as one holds a spider or some loathsome insect over fire."

Nothing could have been further from Franklin's theology. Indeed, Edwards and Franklin, the two preeminent Americans of their generation, can be viewed, Carl Van Doren noted, as "symbols of the hostile movements that strove for the mastery of their age." Edwards and the Great Awakeners sought to recommit America to the anguished spirituality of Puritanism, whereas Franklin sought to bring it into an Enlightenment era that exalted tolerance, individual merit, civic virtue, good deeds, and rationality.[8]

Thus, it might seem surprising, indeed somewhat odd, that Franklin became enthralled by George Whitefield, the most popular of the Great Awakening's roving preachers, who arrived in Philadelphia in 1739. The English evangelist had been an unhappy soul at Pembroke College, Oxford, and then had a "new birth" into Methodism and later Calvinism. He was doctrinally pure in his insistence that salvation came only through God's grace, but he was nevertheless deeply involved in charitable work, and his year-long tour through America was to raise money for an orphanage in Georgia. He raised more money than any other cleric of his time for philanthropies, which included schools, libraries, and almshouses across Europe and America. So perhaps it was not so surprising that Franklin took a liking to him though never embraced his theology.

Whitefield's nightly outdoor revival meetings in Philadelphia (by then America's largest town, with a population of thirteen thousand) drew huge crowds, and Franklin, sensing a great story, covered him lavishly in the *Pennsylvania Gazette*. "On Thursday," he reported, "the Rev. Mr. Whitefield began to preach from the Court House gallery in this city, about six at night, to nearly 6,000 people before him in the street, who stood in an awful silence to hear him." The crowds grew throughout his week-long visit, and Whitefield returned to the city three more times during his year-long American crusade.

Franklin was awed. He published accounts of Whitefield's appearances in forty-five weekly issues of his *Gazette,* and eight times he turned over his entire front page to reprints of the sermons. Franklin recounted in his autobiography, with a wryness born only after years of detachment, the enthusiasm that infected him at the time:

> I happened soon after to attend one of his sermons, in the course of which I perceived he intended to finish with a collection, and I silently resolved he should get nothing from me. I had in my pocket a handful of copper money, three or four silver dollars, and five pistoles in gold. As he proceeded I began to soften, and concluded to give the coppers. Another stroke of his oratory made me ashamed of that, and determined me to give the silver; and he finished so admirably, that I emptied my pocket wholly into the collector's dish, gold and all.

Franklin was also impressed with the transforming effect that Whitefield had on Philadelphia's citizenry. "Never did the people show so great a willingness to attend sermons," he reported in the *Gazette*. "Religion is become the subject of most conversation. No books are in request but those of piety."[9]

The financial implications of that last observation were not lost on Franklin. He met with Whitefield and arranged a deal to be the primary publisher of his sermons and journals, which no doubt added to his zeal to publicize him. After Whitefield's first visit, Franklin ran an advertisement soliciting orders for a series of Whitefield's sermons at two shillings a volume. A few months later, he ran a notice that he had received so many orders that those "who have paid or who bring the money in their hands will have the preference."

Thousands were sold, which helped to make Franklin rich and Whitefield famous. Franklin also published ten editions of Whitefield's journals, each five times more expensive than his almanac, and enlisted a sales force of eleven printers he knew throughout the colonies to make them bestsellers. His sister-in-law Anne Franklin of Newport took a shipment of 250. During 1739–41, more than half the books that Franklin printed were by or about Whitefield.

Some historians have consequently concluded that Franklin's passion for Whitefield was merely pecuniary. But that is too simplistic. As was often the case, Franklin was able to weave together seamlessly his financial interests with his civic desires and personal enthusiasms. He had a companionable personality, and he was genuinely attracted by Whitefield's mesmerizing charisma and charitable bent. He invited Whitefield to stay at his home, and when the preacher praised the invitation as being "for Christ's sake," Franklin corrected him: "Don't let me be mistaken; it was not for Christ's sake, but for your sake."

In addition, despite their theological differences, Franklin was attracted to Whitefield because he was shaking up the local establishment. Franklin's long-standing disdain for the religious elite led him to enjoy the discomfort and schisms caused by the intrusion of wildly popular itinerant preachers onto their turf. The tolerant Franklin was pleased that Whitefield's supporters had erected, with Franklin's financial support, a large new hall that, among other uses, could provide a pulpit to anyone of any belief, "so that even if the Mufti of Constantinople were to send a missionary to preach Mohammedanism to us, he would find a pulpit at his service."[10]

Franklin's populist delight at the discomfort of the elite was evident in the way he stoked up a controversy about a letter sent to the *Gazette* by some of the town's gentry, who wrote that Whitefield had not "met with great success among the better sort of people." The next week, using the pen name "Obadiah Plainman," Franklin ridiculed the use of the phrase "the better sort of people" and its implication that Whitefield's supporters were "the meaner sort, the mob or the rabble." Mr. Plainman said that he and his friends were proud to call themselves part of the rabble, but they hated it when people who styled themselves "better sort" used such terms and implied that common folks were "a stupid herd."

A haughty-sounding gentleman named Tom Trueman (or perhaps, given the name, Franklin pretending to be such a gentleman) wrote the next week to William Bradford's more upscale newspaper to deny that such offense was intended and to accuse Mr. Plainman of fancying himself a leader of the town's common folks. Franklin, again replying as Mr. Plainman, said he was merely "a poor ordinary" craftsman who, after his labors, "instead of going to the alehouse, I amuse myself with the books of the Library Company." As such, he rankled at those who proclaimed themselves to be of the better sort and "look on the rest of their fellow subjects with contempt." Though he was rising in the world in a way that would have allowed him, if he were so inclined, to put on aristocratic airs, Franklin was still allergic to snobbery and proud to be a Plainman defending the middling people.[11]

By the fall of 1740, Franklin showed signs of cooling slightly toward Whitefield, though not toward the profits that came from publishing him. The preacher's efforts to make him a "new born" believer in Calvinist orthodoxy wore thin, and valuable patrons among the Philadelphia gentry began to denounce the *Gazette*'s ardent flackery. In response to such criticism, Franklin printed an editorial denying (unconvincingly) any bias and restating his philosophy, first propounded in his 1731 "Apology for Printers," that "when truth has fair play, it will always prevail over falsehood." But he also included in the issue a letter from a preacher who criticized Whitefield's "enthusiastic ravings," and he subsequently published two pamphlets harshly attacking Whitefield as well as one giving Whitefield's response. The letters in Franklin's *Gazette*, 90 percent of which had been favorable to Whitefield in the first nine months of 1740, tipped mostly negative beginning in September, though the pieces written by Franklin remained positive.

Albeit with less ardor, Franklin continued to support Whitefield over the ensuing years, and they maintained an affectionate correspondence until the preacher's death in 1770. In his autobiography, written after Whitefield died, Franklin added a dose of ironic detachment to his warm recollections. He recounted one sermon he attended where, rather than being moved by Whitefield's words, Franklin spent the time calculating how far his voice carried. And as for Whitefield's effect on his spiritual life, Franklin wryly recalled, "He used, indeed, sometimes to pray for my conversion, but never had the satisfaction of believing that his prayers were heard." [12]

PUBLISHING WARS

As Franklin's publishing business grew, his competition with the town's other printer, Andrew Bradford, intensified. Throughout the early 1730s, they had poked fun at errors in each other's papers and sparred over such matters as the death of the aspiring young Freemason and the preachings of Samuel Hemphill. There was a political and social basis to the rivalry. The well-born Bradford and his *American Weekly Mercury* were aligned with Pennsylvania's "Proprietary faction," which supported the Penn family and their appointed governors. The leather-aproned Franklin and his *Pennsylvania Gazette* were more antiestablishment and tended to support the rights of the elected Assembly.

Their politics clashed during the 1733 reelection campaign of the Assembly's speaker, Andrew Hamilton, an anti-Proprietary leader who had helped Franklin wrest the government printing job from Bradford. Franklin admired Hamilton's antiaristocratic populism. "He was no friend to power," Franklin wrote. "He was the poor man's friend." Bradford, on the other hand, printed fervent attacks on Hamilton. Among them was an essay "On Infidelity," which was aimed at Hamilton but designed to wound Franklin as well. Another accused Hamilton of insulting the Penn family and abusing his power as head of the loan office.

Franklin came to Hamilton's defense with a dignified yet damning rebuttal. Cast as an account of a "Half-Hour's Conversation" with Hamilton, the piece skewered Bradford for sins ranging from malapropism (using "contemptibly" when he meant "contemptuously") to hiding behind the cloak of anonymity ("seeing it was commonly agreed to be wrote by nobody, he thought nobody should regard it"). Hamilton comes across as a polite Junto visitor with a touch of Poor Richard. "Throw enough dirt," he laments, "and some will stick." [13]

Hamilton won reelection, and in 1736 he got Franklin chosen as the clerk of the Assembly. Again, public service and private profit were combined. The clerkship, Franklin freely admitted, "gave me a better opportunity of keeping up an interest among the members, which secured to me the business of printing the votes, laws, paper money, and other occasional jobs for the public, that, on the whole, were very profitable."

It also taught him a useful trick for seducing opponents. After one rich and well-bred member spoke against him, Franklin decided to win him over:

> I did not, however, aim at gaining his favor by paying any servile respect to him, but, after some time, took this other method. Having heard that he had in his library a certain very scarce and curious book, I wrote a note to him, expressing my desire of perusing that book, and requesting he would do me the favor of lending it to me for a few days. He sent it immediately, and I returned it in about a week with another note, expressing strongly my sense of the favor. When we next met in the House, he spoke to me (which he had never done before), and with great civility; and he ever after manifested a readiness to serve me on all occasions, so that we became great friends, and our friendship continued to his death. This is another instance of the truth of an old maxim I had learned, which says, "He that has once done you a kindness will be more ready to do you another, than he whom you yourself have obliged." [14]

Franklin's competition with Bradford had one interesting aspect that might seem unusual but was, then as now, somewhat common. Even as they competed against each other in some areas, like modern media barons they cooperated in others. For example, in 1733, even as they were bitter opponents in the Hamilton election, they formed a joint venture to share the risk of publishing an expensive Psalm book. At Bradford's suggestion, Franklin handled the printing, Bradford supplied the paper, they split the costs, and each got half of the five hundred copies that were made.[15]

In his competition with Bradford, Franklin had one big disadvantage. Bradford was the postmaster of Philadelphia, and he used that position to deny Franklin the right, at least officially, to send his *Gazette* through the mail. Their ensuing struggle over the issue of open carriage was an early example of the tension that often still exists between those who create content and those who control distribution systems.

At one point, Franklin got Col. Alexander Spotswood, the postmaster for the colonies, to order Bradford to run an open system that would carry rival papers. But Bradford continued to make it difficult for Franklin's papers to get carriage, forcing Franklin to bribe the postal riders. Franklin worried not only about the expense but also about the public perception. Because Bradford controlled the Philadelphia post, Franklin wrote, "it was imagined he had better opportunities of obtaining news, [and] his paper was thought a better distributor of advertisements than mine."

Franklin was able to wrest the Philadelphia postmastership away when it was discovered that Bradford had been sloppy in his bookkeeping. Colonel Spotswood, with Franklin's encouragement, withdrew Bradford's commission in 1737 and offered the job to Franklin. "I accepted it readily," Franklin noted, "and found it of great advantage, for though the salary was small, it facilitated the correspondence that improved my newspaper, increased the number demanded, as well as the advertisements to be inserted, so that it came to afford me a very considerable income." Bradford's paper declined accordingly.

Instead of retaliating, Franklin allowed Bradford's *Mercury* to be carried through the mails along with the *Gazette* and others—at least initially. In his autobiography, Franklin congratulated himself for being so open. In fact, however, that policy lasted just two years. Because Bradford never settled the accounts from his tenure as Philadelphia postmaster, Spotswood sent Franklin an order to "commence suit against him" and "no longer suffer to be carried by the Post any of his newspapers."

Bradford had to resort to Franklin's old habit of bribing the postal riders to deliver his papers unofficially. Franklin knew this and tolerated it, just as Bradford had earlier tolerated it for Franklin. But even this partial indulgence by Franklin was not to last.[16]

In 1740, he and Bradford became involved in a race to start the first general-interest magazine in America. Franklin came up with the idea, but once again he was betrayed by a confidant, just as happened when he first planned to launch a newspaper. As a wiser Poor Richard would pointedly proclaim in his 1741 almanac, "If you would keep your secret from an enemy, tell it not to a friend."

This time the turncoat was a lawyer named John Webbe, who had contributed essays to the *Gazette* and had been chosen by Franklin to file the suit against Bradford that Colonel Spotswood ordered. Franklin described the magazine to Webbe and offered him the job of editor. But Webbe took the idea to Bradford and struck a better deal. On November 6, 1740, Bradford announced plans for *The American Magazine.* One week later, Franklin published his own plans for *The General Magazine.*

In his announcement, Franklin denounced Webbe's betrayal. "This Magazine . . . was long since projected," he wrote. "It would not, indeed, have been published quite so soon, were it not that a Person, to whom the scheme was communicated in confidence, has thought fit to advertise it in the last *Mercury* . . . and reap the Advantage of it wholly to himself." The ensuing spat led Franklin to ban completely Bradford's paper from the mails. It also turned the question of postal access into a public issue.

Webbe responded in the *Mercury* the next week with a sharp counterattack of his own. He particularly objected to one of Franklin's less endearing traits: his clever and often sly way of implying allegations rather than saying them outright. Franklin's indirection, "like the slyness of a pickpocket," was more "dastardly" than the audacity of a "direct liar," Webbe wrote. "The strokes being oblique and indirect, a man cannot so easily defend himself against them." Franklin liked to believe that his method of using indirect insinuation was less offensive than confrontational argument, but it sometimes led to even greater enmity and a reputation for crafty deceit.

Franklin did not respond. With an exquisite sense of how to goad Webbe and Bradford, he merely reprinted his original notice in his next issue of the *Gazette,* including the same allegation of Webbe's duplicity. This led Webbe to publish another screed in the *Mercury.* Once again, Franklin showed infuriating restraint: he did not respond, but again reprinted his original notice and allegation.

Webbe escalated the dispute in the December 4 *Mercury* with an allegation guaranteed to draw a response from Franklin. "Since my first letter," Webbe wrote, Franklin had "taken upon him to deprive the *Mercury* of the benefit of the Post." Franklin replied the following week with a somewhat disingenuous explanation. It had been a year, he said, since Bradford's *Mercury* had been barred free use of the mails. This had nothing to do with the dispute over the magazines. Instead, it was at the direct order of Colonel Spotswood. To prove his point, Franklin printed Spotswood's letter. He said that Bradford and Webbe knew this to be the case, Webbe in particular, as he had been the lawyer Franklin retained to file the suit.

Webbe replied by laying out the history of the postal practices. Yes, he conceded, Spotswood had ordered Franklin to stop carrying Bradford's paper. But, as Franklin well knew, the riders had continued to carry it unofficially. Moreover, Webbe charged, Franklin himself had confided to people that he permitted this arrangement because it helped assure that Bradford would take care not to print anything too harmful to Franklin. "He had declared," wrote Webbe, "that as he favored Mr. Bradford by permitting the Postman to distribute his Papers, he had him therefore under his thumb."

The public debate over postal practices quieted down as each side raced to put out its magazine. In the end, Bradford and Webbe won by three days. Their *American Magazine* came off the press February 13, 1741, and Franklin's *General Magazine* appeared on the 16th.

The word *magazine*, as then used, tended to mean a collection drawn from newspapers and other places. The contents of Franklin's, patterned after London's ten-year-old *Gentleman's Magazine*, were surprisingly dry: official proclamations, reports on government proceedings, discussion of paper currency issues, some smatterings of poetry, and a report about Whitefield's orphanage.

The formula failed. Bradford's magazine folded in three months, Franklin's in six. No memorable writing from Franklin came out of this process, except a poem he wrote parodying in Irish dialect one of the advertisements in Bradford's magazine. But the competition to launch the magazine did kindle Franklin's interest in the power of the postal system.[17]

SALLY FRANKLIN

In 1743, eleven years after the birth of their short-lived son, Franky, the Franklins had a baby girl. Named Sarah after Deborah's mother, and called Sally, she delighted and charmed both of her parents. When she was 4, Franklin wrote his mother that "your granddaughter is the greatest lover of her book and school of any child I ever knew." Two years later, he provided a similar report: "Sally grows a fine girl, and is extremely industrious with her needle and delights in her books. She is of most affectionate temper, and perfectly dutiful and obliging, to her parents and to all. Perhaps I flatter myself too much, but I have hopes that she will prove an ingenious, sensible, notable and worthy woman."

Franklin half-seriously pushed the notion that his young daughter might someday marry the son of William Strahan, a London printer who was one of his English correspondents. (In this he was not sexist: he also tried to fix up his son, William, and later his two grandsons with children of his English and French friends, all to no avail.) His descriptions of Sally in his letters to Strahan reveal both his affection for her and the traits he looked for in a daughter. "She discovers daily the seeds and tokens of industry and economy, and in short, of every female virtue," he wrote when she was 7. Six years later, he wrote,

"Sally is indeed a very good girl, affectionate, dutiful, and industrious, has one of the best hearts, and though not a wit, is for one of her years by no means deficient in understanding."

In one of his childhood debates with John Collins, Franklin had argued in favor of giving girls as well as boys an education, a case he reiterated as Silence Dogood. He practiced these preachings to some degree with Sally, with a predictable emphasis on practical subjects. He made sure she was taught reading, writing, and arithmetic. At her request, he got her French lessons, though her interest soon waned. He also insisted that she learn accounting; when a publishing partner he had in Charleston died and his wife had to take over the business, it reinforced in Franklin the practical view that girls should be taught accounting "as likely to be of more use to them and their children in case of widowhood than either music or dancing."

When Sally was only 8, Franklin imported from England a large shipment of books for her. The idea was that she would be in charge of selling them at his print shop, but presumably she might also learn something from them herself. Included in the order were three dozen manuals from the Winchester School, four dictionaries, and two dozen copies of a collection of "tales and fables with prudential maxims."

For the most part, however, Franklin urged Sally to perfect her domestic skills. One day, after watching as she tried unsuccessfully to sew a buttonhole, he arranged for his tailor to come give her lessons. She never got the formal academic training that he provided William. And when he drew up plans to establish an academy in Philadelphia, Sally was 6, but he made no provision for it to educate girls.[18]

With only one daughter (and an illegitimate stepson), Deborah's was an unusually small brood for a robust woman in colonial days; she was one of seven children, Franklin's father had seventeen in his two marriages, and the average family at the time had about eight. Franklin wrote glowingly of children and had Poor Richard sing praises to the look of a pregnant woman. In satires such as "Polly Baker" and serious essays such as "Observations on the Increase of Mankind," he extolled the benefits of fecundity. So the Franklins' paucity of children does not appear to reflect a deliberate decision; instead, it indicated either that they lacked abundant intimacy or found conceiving not always easy, or a combination of both. Whatever the cause, it would eventually give Franklin more leeway to retire from his business early to pursue scientific endeavors and far-flung diplomatic journeys. It also, perhaps, contributed to his lifelong practice of befriending younger people—women in particular—and forging relationships with them as if they were his children.[19]

POLLY BAKER

Franklin's attitudes toward women can be characterized as somewhat enlightened in the context of his time, but only somewhat. What is clear, however, is that he genuinely liked women, enjoyed their company and conversation, and was able to take them seriously as well as flirt with them. During Sally's early childhood, he wrote two famous essays that, in different ways, amusingly combined his lenient attitude toward unmarried sex with his appreciative attitude toward women.

"Advice to a Young Man on the Choice of a Mistress," written in 1745, is now quite famous, but it was suppressed by Franklin's grandson and other compilers of his papers throughout the nineteenth century as being too indecent to print. Franklin began the little essay by extolling marriage as being "the proper remedy" for sexual urges. But, if his reader "will not take this counsel" and yet still finds "sex inevitable," he advised that "in all your amours you should prefer old women to young ones."

Franklin then provided a saucy list of eight reasons: because they have more knowledge, they make better conversation; as they lose their looks, they learn a thousand useful services "to maintain their influence over men"; "there is no hazard of children"; they are more discreet; they age from the head down, so even after their face grows wrinkled their lower bodies stay firm, "so that covering all above with a basket, and regarding only what is below the girdle, it is impossible of two women to know an old one from a young one"; it is less sinful to debauch an older woman than a virgin; there is less guilt, because the older woman will be made happy whereas the younger one will be made miserable. Finally, Franklin produces the cheeky kicker to the piece: "Lastly, they are so grateful!!"[20]

"The Speech of Polly Baker" is a tale of sex and woe told from a woman's point of view, a literary device often used by Franklin with a dexterity that displayed his ability to appreciate the other sex. It purports to recount the speech of a young woman on trial for having a fifth illegitimate child. First published in London, it was then frequently reprinted in England and America without people's realizing that it was fiction. Thirty years would pass before Franklin revealed that he had written it as a hoax.

The light humor of the piece hides the fact that it is actually a sharp attack on hypocritical customs and unfair attitudes toward women and sex. Polly argues that she has been doing good by obeying God's injunction to be fruitful and multiply. "I have brought five fine children into the world, at the risk of my life; I have maintained them well by my own industry." Indeed, she complains, she could have maintained them a little better were it not for the fact that the court kept fining her. "Can it be a crime (in the nature of things I mean) to add to the number of the King's subjects in a new country that really wants people? I own it, I should think it a praiseworthy rather than a punishable action."

Franklin, who had fathered an illegitimate child but taken responsibility for it, is particularly scathing about the double standard that subjects Polly, but not the men who had sex with her, to humiliation. As Polly says, "I readily consented to the only proposal of marriage that ever was made me, which was when I was a virgin; but too easily confiding in the person's sincerity that made it, I unhappily lost my own honor by trusting his; for he got me with child, and then forsook me. That very person you all know; he is now become a magistrate of this county."

By doing her duty to bring children into the world, despite the fact that no one would marry her and despite the public disgrace, she argued that she deserved, "in my humble opinion, instead of a whipping, to have a statue erected to my memory." The court, Franklin wrote, was so moved by the speech that she was acquitted, and one of the judges married her the next day.[21]

THE AMERICAN PHILOSOPHICAL SOCIETY

Franklin was among the first to view the British settlements in America not only as separate colonies but also as part of a potentially unified nation. That was, in part, because he was far less parochial than most Americans. He had traveled from one colony to another, formed alliances with printers from Rhode Island to South Carolina, and gathered news for his paper and magazine by reading widely other American publications. Now, as the postmaster in Philadelphia, his connections to other colonies were easier, and his curiosity about them grew.

In a May 1743 circular, "A Proposal for Promoting Useful Knowledge Among the British Plantations in America," he proposed what was, in effect, an intercolonial Junto, to be called the American Philosophical Society. The idea had been discussed by the naturalist John Bartram, among others, but Franklin had the printing press, the inclination, and the postal contacts to pull it all together. It would be based in Philadelphia and include scientists and thinkers from other cities. They would share their studies by post, and abstracts would be sent to each member four times a year.

As with the detailed charter he created for the Junto, Franklin was very specific about the type of subjects to be explored, which were, unsurprisingly, more practical than purely theoretical: "newly discovered plants, herbs, trees, roots, their virtues, uses, etc.; . . . improvements of vegetable juices, such as ciders, wines, etc.; new methods of curing or preventing diseases; . . . improvements in any branch of mathematics . . . new arts, trades, and manufactures . . . surveys, maps and charts . . . methods of improving the breeds of animals . . . and all philosophical experiments that let light into the nature of things." Franklin volunteered to serve as secretary.

By the spring of 1744 the society began meeting regularly. The pedantic mathematician Thomas Godfrey was a member, indicating that his feud with Franklin over dowries and almanacs was over. One of the most important members was Cadwallader Colden, a scholar and official from New York whom Franklin had met on his travels the year before. They were to become lifelong friends and spur each other's scientific interests. Their club was not very active at first—Franklin complained that its members were "very idle gentlemen"—but it eventually grew into a learned society that thrives to this day.[22]

THE PENNSYLVANIA MILITIA

Most of the voluntary associations that Franklin had thus far formed—the Junto, library, philosophical society, even fire squad—had not usurped the core functions of government. (When he came up with a plan for a police patrol, he had suggested that the Assembly enact and control it.) But in 1747, he proposed something that was, though he may not have realized it, far more radical: a military force that would be independent of Pennsylvania's colonial government.

Franklin's plan for a volunteer Pennsylvania militia arose because of the feckless response by the colony's government to the ongoing threats from France and her Indian allies. Ever since 1689, the intermittent wars between Britain and France had been played out in America, with each side enlisting various Indian tribes and thuggish privateers to gain advantage. The latest American installment was known as King George's War (1744–48), which was an offshoot of Europe's War of Austrian Succession and a quaint British struggle with Spain known as the War of Jenkins's Ear (after a British smuggler who had that body part removed by the Spanish). Among those Americans who marched off toward Canada to fight the French and Indians on behalf of the British in 1746 was William Franklin, then perhaps 16 or so, whose father realized it was futile to resist the wanderlust he himself had felt at that age.

William never saw any action, but the war soon threatened the safety of Philadelphia when French and Spanish privateers began raiding towns along the Delaware River. The Assembly, dominated by pacifist Quakers, dithered and failed to authorize any defenses. Franklin was appalled by the unwillingness of the various groups in the colony—Quakers and Anglicans and Presbyterians, city and country folks—to work together. So in November 1747, he stepped into the breach by writing a vibrant pamphlet entitled "Plain Truth," signed by "a Tradesman of Philadelphia."

His description of the havoc that a privateer raid might wreak sounded like a Great Awakening terror sermon:

> On the first alarm, terror will spread over all . . . The man that has a wife and children will find them hanging on his neck, beseeching him with tears to quit the city . . . Sacking the city will be the first, and burning it, in all probability, the last act of the enemy . . . Confined to your houses, you will have nothing to trust but the enemy's mercy . . . Who can, without the utmost horror, conceive the miseries of the latter when your persons, fortunes, wives and daughters shall be subject to the wanton and unbridled rage, rapine and lust.

With a small pun on the word "Friends," Franklin first blamed the Quakers of the Assembly: "Should we entreat them to consider, if not as Friends, at least as legislators, that protection is as truly due from the government to the people." If their pacifist principles prevent them from acting, he said, they should step aside. He then turned on the "great and rich men" of the Proprietary faction, who were refusing to act because of their "envy and resentment" toward the Assembly.

So who could save the colony? Here came Franklin's great rallying cry for the new American middle class. "We, the middling people," he wrote proudly, using the phrase twice in the pamphlet. "The tradesmen, shopkeepers and farmers of this province and city!"

He then proceeded to spin an image that would end up applying to much of his work over the ensuing years. "At present we are like separate filaments of flax before the thread is formed, without strength because without connection," he declared. "But Union would make us strong."

Of particular note was his populist insistence that there be no class distinctions. The militia would be organized by geographic area instead of social strata. "This," he said, "is intended to prevent people's sorting themselves into companies according to their ranks in life, their quality or station. It is designed to mix the great and the small together . . . There should be no distinction from circumstance, but all be on the level." In another radically democratic approach, Franklin proposed that each of the new militia companies elect its own officers rather than have them appointed by the governor or Crown.

Franklin concluded with an offer to draw up proposals for a militia if his plea was well received. It was. "The pamphlet had a sudden and surprising effect," he later wrote. So, a week later, in an annotated article in his newspaper, he presented his plans for a militia, filled with his typical detailed description of its organization, training, and rules. Even though he was never an avid or effective public orator, he agreed to address a crowd of his fellow middling people at a sail-making loft and then, two days later, spoke to a more upscale audience of "gentlemen, merchants and others" at the New Hall that had been built for Whitefield.[23]

Soon some ten thousand men from all over the colony had signed up and formed themselves into more than one hundred companies. Franklin's local company in Philadelphia elected him their colonel, but he declined the post by saying he was "unfit." Instead, he served as a "common soldier" and regularly took his turn patrolling the batteries he had helped build along the Delaware River banks. He also amused himself by designing an array of insignia and mottos for the various companies.

To furnish the Militia Association with cannons and equipment, Franklin organized a lottery that raised £3,000. The artillery had to be purchased from New York, and Franklin led a delegation to convince Gov. George Clinton to approve the sale. As Franklin recounted with some amusement:

> He at first refused us peremptorily; but at dinner with his council, where there was great drinking of Madeira wine, as the custom of that place then was, he softened by degrees, and said he would lend us six. After a few more bumpers he advanced to ten; and at length he very good-naturedly conceded eighteen. They were fine cannon, eighteen-pounders, with their carriages, which we soon transported and mounted on our battery.

Franklin did not quite realize how radical it was for a private association to take over from the government the right to create and control a military force. His charter, both in its spirit and wording, faintly foreshadowed a declaration that would come three decades later. "Being thus unprotected by the government under which we live," he wrote, "we do hereby, for our mutual defense and security, and for the security of our wives, children and estates . . . form ourselves into an Association."

Thomas Penn, the colony's Proprietor, understood the implications of Franklin's actions. "This association is founded on a contempt to government," he wrote the clerk of the governor's council, "a part little less than treason." In a subsequent letter, he called Franklin "a sort of tribune of the people," and lamented: "He is a dangerous man and I should be very glad [if] he inhabited any other country, as I believe him of a very uneasy spirit."

By the summer of 1748, the threat of war had passed and the Militia Association disbanded, without any attempt by Franklin to capitalize on his new power and popularity. But the lessons he learned stayed with him. He realized that the colonists might have to fend for themselves instead of relying on their British governors, that the powerful elites deserved no deference, and that "we the middling people" of workers and tradesmen should be the proud sinews of the new land. It also reinforced his core belief that people, and perhaps someday colonies, could accomplish more when they joined together rather than remained separate filaments of flax, when they formed unions rather than stood alone.[24]

RETIREMENT

Franklin's print shop had by then grown into a successful, vertically integrated media conglomerate. He had a printing press, publishing house, newspaper, an almanac series, and partial control of the postal system. The successful books he had printed ranged from Bibles and psalters to Samuel Richardson's novel *Pamela,* a tale whose mix of raciness and moralism probably appealed to him. (Franklin's 1744 reprint of *Pamela* was the first novel published in America.) He also had built a network of profitable partnerships and franchises from Newport and New York to Charleston and Antigua. Money flowed in, much of which he invested, quite wisely, in Philadelphia property. "I experienced," he recalled, "the truth of the observation, that after getting the first £100, it is more easy to get the second."

Accumulating money, however, was not Franklin's goal. Despite the pecuniary spirit of Poor Richard's sayings and the penny-saving reputation they later earned Franklin, he did not have the soul of an acquisitive capitalist. "I would rather have it said," he wrote his mother, " 'He lived usefully,' than, 'He died rich.' "

So, in 1748 at age 42—which would turn out to be precisely the midpoint of his life—he retired and turned over the operation of his printing business to his foreman, David Hall. The detailed partnership deal Franklin drew up would leave him rich enough by most people's standards: it provided him with half of the shop's profits for the next eighteen years, which would amount to about £650 annually. Back then, when a common clerk made about £25 a year, that was enough to keep him quite comfortable. He saw no reason to keep plying his trade to make even more. Now he would have, he wrote Cadwallader Colden, "leisure to read, study, make experiments, and converse at large with such ingenious and worthy men as are pleased to honor me with their friendship."[25]

Up until then, Franklin had proudly considered himself a leather-apron man and common tradesman, devoid and even contemptuous of aristocratic pretenses. Likewise, that is how he would portray himself again in the late 1760s, when his antagonism to British authority grew (and his hopes for high patronage posts were dashed), and that is how he would cast himself in his autobiography, which he began writing in 1771. It was also the role he would play later in life as a revolutionary patriot, fur-capped envoy, and fervent foe of hereditary honors and privileges.

However, on his retirement, and intermittently over the next decade or so, he would occasionally fancy himself a refined gentleman. In his groundbreaking study *The Radicalism of the American Revolution*, historian Gordon Wood calls him "one of the most aristocratic of the founding fathers." That assessment is perhaps a bit too sweeping or stretches the definition of aristocrat, for even during the years right after his retirement Franklin eschewed most elitist pretensions and remained populist in most of his local politics. But his retirement did indeed usher in a period in his life when he had aspirations to be, if not part of the aristocracy, at least, as Wood says, "a gentleman philosopher and public official" with a veneer of "enlightened gentility."[26]

Franklin's ambivalent flirtation with a new social status was captured on canvas when Robert Feke, a popular self-taught painter from Boston, arrived in Philadelphia that year. He produced the earliest known portrait of Franklin (now at Harvard's Fogg Art Museum), and it shows him garbed as a gentleman with a velvet coat, ruffled shirt, and wig. Yet, compared to Feke's other subjects that year, Franklin had himself portrayed in a rather simple way, devoid of social ostentation. "He is represented in an almost painfully plain and unpretentious manner," notes art historian Wayne Craven, an expert on colonial portraiture. "Franklin's plainness is not accidental: both the portrait painter and his subject would have agreed that this was the most appropriate way to represent a member of colonial mercantile society who was successful, but not actually wealthy."

Franklin was not aspiring, by his retirement, to become merely an idle gentleman of leisure. He left his print shop because he was, in fact, eager to focus his undiminished ambition on other pursuits that beckoned: first science, then politics, then diplomacy and statecraft. As Poor Richard said in his almanac that year, "Lost time is never found again."[27]

CHAPTER SIX

SCIENTIST AND INVENTOR

Philadelphia, 1744–1751

STOVES, STORMS, AND CATHETERS

Even when he was young, Franklin's intellectual curiosity and his Enlightenment-era awe at the orderliness of the universe attracted him to science. During his voyage home from England at age 20, he had studied dolphins and calculated his location by analyzing a lunar eclipse, and in Philadelphia he had used his newspaper, almanac, the Junto, and the philosophical society to discuss natural phenomena. His scientific interests would continue throughout his life, with research into the Gulf Stream, meteorology, the earth's magnetism, and refrigeration.

His most intense immersion into science was during the 1740s, and it reached a peak in the years right after he retired from business in 1748. He had neither the academic training nor the grounding in math to be a great theorist, and his pursuit of what he called his "scientific amusements" caused some to dismiss him as a mere tinkerer. But during his life he was celebrated as the most famous scientist alive, and recent academic studies have restored his place in the scientific pantheon. As Harvard professor Dudley Herschbach declares, "His work on electricity was recognized as ushering in a scientific revolution comparable to those wrought by Newton in the previous century or by Watson and Crick in ours."[1]

Franklin's scientific inquiries were driven, primarily, by pure cu-

riosity and the thrill of discovery. Indeed, there was joy in his antic curiosity, whether it was using electricity jolts to cook turkeys or whiling
away his time as Assembly clerk by constructing complex "magic
squares" of numbers where the rows, columns, and diagonals all added
up to the same sum.

Unlike in some of his other pursuits, he was not driven by pecuniary motives; he declined to patent his famous inventions, and he
took pleasure in freely sharing his findings. Nor was he motivated
merely by his quest for the practical. He acknowledged that his magic
squares were "incapable of useful application," and his initial interest
in electricity was prompted more by fascination than a quest for utility.

He did, however, always keep in mind the goal of making science
useful, just as Poor Richard's wife had made sure that he did something practical with all his old "rattling traps." In general, he would
begin a scientific inquiry driven by pure intellectual curiosity and then
seek a practical application for it.

Franklin's study of how dark fabrics absorb heat better than bright
ones is an example of this approach. These experiments (which were
begun in the 1730s with his Junto colleague Joseph Breintnall, based
on the theories of Isaac Newton and Robert Boyle) included putting
cloth patches of different colors on snow and determining how much
the sun heated each by measuring the melting. Later, in describing the
experiments, he turned his mind to the practical consequences, among
them that "black clothes are not so fit to wear in a hot sunny climate"
and that the walls of fruit sheds should be painted black. In reporting
these conclusions, he famously noted: "What signifies philosophy that
does not apply to some use?"[2]

A far more significant instance of Franklin's application of scientific theory for practical purpose was his invention, in the early 1740s,
of a wood-burning stove that could be built into fireplaces to maximize heat while minimizing smoke and drafts. Using his knowledge
of convection and heat transfer, Franklin came up with an ingenious
(and probably too complex) design.

The stove was constructed so that heat and smoke from the fire
rose to warm an iron plate on top, then were carried by convection
down a channel that led under the wall of the hearth and finally up

through the chimney. In the process, the fire heated an inner metal chamber that drew clean cool air up from the basement, warmed it, and let it out through louvers into the room. That was the theory.

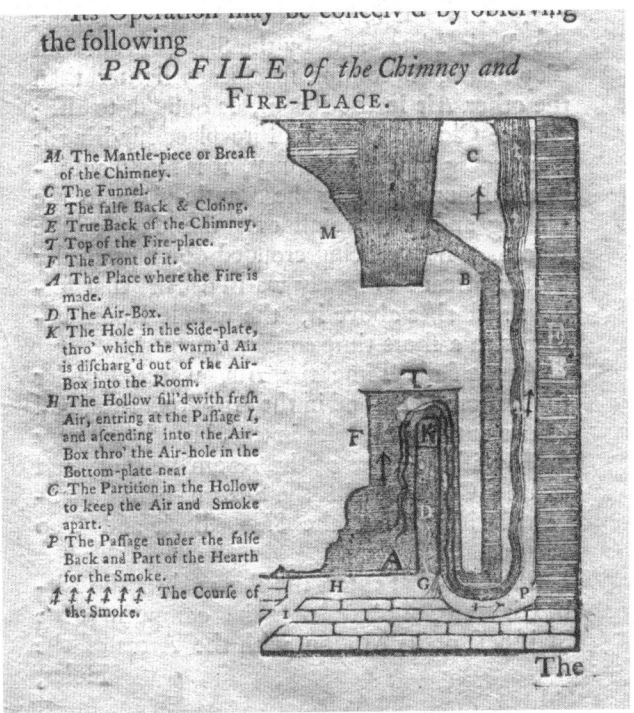

In 1744, he had a fellow Junto member who was an ironworker manufacture the new stove, and he got two of his brothers and several other friends to market them throughout the northeast. The promotional pamphlet Franklin wrote was filled with both science and salesmanship. He explained in detail how warm air expands to take up more space than cold, how it is lighter, and how heat radiates whereas smoke is carried only by air. He then included testimonials about his new design and touted that it minimized cold drafts and smoke, thus reducing the chance of fevers and coughs. It would also save on fuel, he advertised.

The new Pennsylvania Fireplaces, as he called them, were initially somewhat popular, at £5 apiece, and papers around the colonies were filled with testimonials. "They ought to be called, both in justice and gratitude, Mr. Franklin's stoves," declared one letter writer in the *Boston Evening Post*. "I believe all who have experienced the comfort and benefit of them will join with me that the author of this happy invention merits a statue."

The governor of Pennsylvania was among the enthusiastic, and he offered Franklin what could have been a lucrative patent. "But I declined it," Franklin noted in his autobiography. "As we enjoy great advantages from the invention of others, we should be glad of an opportunity to serve others by any invention of ours, and this we should do freely and generously." It was a noble and sincere sentiment.

An exhaustive study by one scholar shows that Franklin's design eventually proved less practical and popular than he hoped. Unless the chimney and lower channels were hot, there was not enough convection to keep the smoke from being forced back into the room. That made getting started a problem. Sales tapered off, manufacturing ceased within two decades, and most models were modified by their owners to eliminate the back channel and chamber. Throughout the rest of his life, Franklin would refine his theories about chimney and fireplace designs. But what is today commonly known as the Franklin Stove is a far simpler contraption than what he originally envisioned.[3]

Franklin also combined science and mechanical practicality by devising the first urinary catheter used in America, which was a modification of a European invention. His brother John in Boston was gravely ill and wrote Franklin of his desire for a flexible tube to help him urinate. Franklin came up with a design, and instead of simply describing it he went to a Philadelphia silversmith and oversaw its construction. The tube was thin enough to be flexible, and Franklin included a wire that could be stuck inside to stiffen it while it was inserted and then be gradually withdrawn as the tube reached the point where it needed to bend. His catheter also had a screw component that allowed it to be inserted by turning, and he made it collapsible so that it would be easier to withdraw. "Experience is necessary for the right using of all new tools or instruments, and that will perhaps suggest some improvements," Franklin told his brother.

The study of nature also continued to interest Franklin. Among his most noteworthy discoveries was that the big East Coast storms known as northeasters, whose winds come from the northeast, actually move in the opposite direction from their winds, traveling up the coast from the south. On the evening of October 21, 1743, Franklin looked forward to observing a lunar eclipse he knew was to occur at 8:30. A violent storm, however, hit Philadelphia and blackened the sky. Over the next few weeks, he read accounts of how the storm caused damage from Virginia to Boston. "But what surprised me," he later told his friend Jared Eliot, "was to find in the Boston newspapers an account of the observation of that eclipse." So Franklin wrote his brother in Boston, who confirmed that the storm did not hit until an hour after the eclipse was finished. Further inquiries into the timing of this and other storms up and down the coast led him to "the very singular opinion," he told Eliot, "that, though the course of the wind is from the northeast to the southwest, yet the course of the storm is from the southwest to the northeast." He further surmised, correctly, that rising air heated in the south created low-pressure systems that drew winds from the north. More than 150 years later, the great scholar William Morris Davis proclaimed, "With this began the science of weather prediction."[4]

Dozens of other scientific phenomena also engaged Franklin's interest during this period. For example, he exchanged letters with his friend Cadwallader Colden on comets, the circulation of blood, perspiration, inertia, and the earth's rotation. But it was a parlor-trick show in 1743 that launched him on what would be by far his most celebrated scientific endeavor.

ELECTRICITY

On a visit to Boston in the summer of 1743, Franklin happened to be entertained one evening by a traveling scientific showman from Scotland named Dr. Archibald Spencer. (In his autobiography, Franklin gets the name and year wrong, saying it was a Dr. Spence in 1746.) Spencer specialized in amazing demonstrations that verged on amusement shows. He depicted Newton's theories of light and displayed a machine that measured blood flow, both interests of Franklin's. But more important, he performed electricity tricks, such as creating static electricity by rubbing a glass tube and drawing sparks from the feet of a boy hanging by silk cords from the ceiling. "Being on a subject quite new to me," Franklin recalled, "they equally surprised and pleased me."

In the previous century, Galileo and Newton had demystified gravity. But that other great force of the universe, electricity, was understood little better than it had been by the ancients. There were people, such as Dr. Spencer, who played with it to perform spectacles. The Abbé Nollet, court scientist to France's King Louis XV, had linked 180 soldiers and then 700 monks and made them jump in unison for the court's amusement by sending through them a jolt of static electricity. But Franklin was the perfect person to turn electricity from a parlor trick into a science. That task demanded not a mathematical or theoretical scholar, but instead a clever and ingenious person who had the curiosity to perform practical experiments, plus enough mechanical talent and time to tinker with a lot of contraptions.

A few months after Franklin returned to Philadelphia, Dr. Spencer came to town. Franklin acted as his agent, advertised his lectures, and sold tickets from his shop. His Library Company also received, early in 1747, a long glass tube for generating static electricity, along with papers describing some experiments, from its agent in London, Peter Collinson. In his letter thanking Collinson, Franklin was effusive in describing the fun he was having with the device: "I never was before engaged in any study that so totally engrossed my attention." He commissioned a local glassblower and silversmith to make more such gadgets, and he enlisted his Junto friends to join in the experimenting.[5]

Franklin's first serious experiments involved collecting an electric charge and then studying its properties. He had his friends draw charges from the spinning glass tube and then touch each other to see if sparks flew. The result was the discovery that electricity was "not *created* by the friction, but *collected* only." In other words, a charge could be drawn into person A and out of person B, and the electric fluid would flow back if the two people touched each other.

To explain what he meant, he invented some new terms in a letter to Collinson. "We say B is electrised *positively;* A *negatively:* or rather

B is electrised *plus* and A *minus.*" He apologized to the Englishman for the new coinage: "These terms we may use until your philosophers give us better."

In fact, these terms devised by Franklin are the ones we still use today, along with other neologisms that he coined to describe his findings: battery, charged, neutral, condense, and conductor. Part of Franklin's importance as a scientist was the clear writing he employed. "He has written equally for the uninitiated as well as the philosopher," the early nineteenth-century English chemist Sir Humphry Davy noted, "and he has rendered his details as amusing as well as perspicuous."

Until then, electricity had been thought to involve two types of fluids, called vitreous and resinous, that could be created independently. Franklin's discovery that the generation of a positive charge was accompanied by the generation of an equal negative charge became known as the conservation of charge and the single-fluid theory of electricity. The concepts reflected Franklin's bookkeeper mentality, which was first expressed in his London "Dissertation" positing that pleasure and pain are always in balance.

It was a breakthrough of historic proportions. "As a broad generalization that has withstood the test of 200 years of fruitful application," Harvard professor I. Bernard Cohen has pronounced, "Franklin's law of conservation of charge must be considered to be of the same fundamental importance to physical science as Newton's law of conservation of momentum."

Franklin also discovered an attribute of electrical charges—"the wonderful effects of points"—that would soon lead to his most famous practical application. He electrified a small iron ball and dangled a cork next to it, which was repelled based on the strength of the ball's charge. When he brought the tip of a pointed piece of metal near the ball, it drew away the charge. But a blunt piece of metal did not draw a charge or spark as easily, and if it was insulated instead of grounded, did not draw a charge at all.

Franklin continued his experiments by capturing and storing electric charges in a primitive form of capacitor called, after the Dutch town where it was invented, a Leyden jar. These jars had a metal foil on the outside; on the inside, separated from the foil by the glass insulation, was lead or water or metal that could be charged up through a wire. Franklin showed that when the inside of the jar was charged, the outside foil had an equal and opposite charge.

Also, by pouring out the water and metal inside a charged Leyden jar and not being able to elicit a spark, he found that the charge did not actually reside in them; instead, he correctly concluded, it was the glass itself that held the charge. So he lined up a series of glass plates flanked by metal, charged them up, wired them together, and created (and gave a name to) a new device: "what we called an electrical battery."[6]

Electricity also energized his antic sense of fun. He created a charged metal spider that leaped around like a real one, he electrified the iron fence around his house to produce sparks that amused visitors, and he rigged a picture of King George II to produce a "high-treason" shock when someone touched his gilded crown. "If a ring of persons take the shock among them," Franklin joked, "the experiment is called The Conspirators." Friends flocked to see his shows, and he reinforced his reputation for playfulness. (In one of the weirder scenes in Thomas Pynchon's novel *Mason & Dixon*, Franklin lines up some young men in a tavern to jolt them from his battery, shouting "All hold hands, Line of Fops.")

As the summer of 1749 approached and the rising humidity made experiments more difficult, Franklin decided to suspend them until the fall. Although his findings were of great historical significance, he had yet to put them to practical use. He lamented to Collinson that he was "chagrined a little that we have hitherto been able to discover nothing in the way of use to mankind." Indeed, after many revised theories and a couple of painful shocks that knocked him senseless, the only "use discovered of electricity," said the man who was always trying to tackle his own pride, was that "it may help make a vain man humble."

The end of the experimenting season gave an occasion for a "party of pleasure" on the banks of the river. Franklin described it in a letter to Collinson: "A turkey is to be killed for our dinners by the electrical shock; and roasted by the electrical jack, before a fire kindled by the electrified bottle; while the healths of all the famous electricians in England, France and Germany are to be drank in electrified bumpers, under the discharge of guns from the electrical battery."

The frivolity went well. Though turkeys proved harder to kill than chickens, Franklin and friends finally succeeded by linking together a big battery. "The birds killed in this manner eat uncommonly tender," he wrote, thus becoming a culinary pioneer of fried turkey. As for doing something more practical, there would be time for that in the fall.[7]

SNATCHING LIGHTNING FROM THE SKY

In the journal he kept for his experiments, Franklin noted in November 1749 some intriguing similarities between electrical sparks and lightning. He listed twelve of them, including "1. Giving light. 2. Color of the light. 3. Crooked directions. 4. Swift motion. 5. Being conducted by metals. 6. Crack or noise in exploding . . . 9. Destroying animals . . . 12. Sulpherous smell."

More important, he made a connection between this surmise about lightning and his earlier experiments on the power of pointed metal objects to draw off electrical charges. "Electrical fluid is attracted by points. We do not know whether this property is in lightning. But since they agree in all particulars wherein we can already compare them, is it not probable they agree likewise in this?" To which he added a momentous rallying cry: *"Let the experiment be made."*

For centuries, the devastating scourge of lightning had generally been considered a supernatural phenomenon or expression of God's will. At the approach of a storm, church bells were rung to ward off the bolts. "The tones of the consecrated metal repel the demon and avert storm and lightning," declared St. Thomas Aquinas. But even the most religiously faithful were likely to have noticed this was not very effective. During one thirty-five-year period in Germany alone during the mid-1700s, 386 churches were struck and more than one hundred bell ringers killed. In Venice, some three thousand people were killed when tons of gunpowder stored in a church was hit. As Franklin later recalled to Harvard professor John Winthrop, "The lightning seems to strike steeples of choice and at the very time the bells are ringing; yet still they continue to bless the new bells and jangle the old ones whenever it thunders. One would think it was now time to try some other trick."[8]

Many scientists, including Newton, had noted the apparent connection between lightning and electricity. But no one had declared "Let the experiment be made," nor laid out a methodical test, nor thought of the practicality of tying this all in with the power of pointed metal rods.

Franklin first sketched out his theories about lightning in April 1749, just before his end-of-season turkey fry. The water vapors in a cloud can be electrically charged, he surmised, and the positive ones will separate from the negative ones. When such "electrified clouds pass over," he added, "high trees, lofty towers, spires, masts of ships . . . draw the electrical fire and the whole cloud discharges." It was not a bad guess, and it led to some practical advice: "Dangerous therefore it is to take shelter under a tree during a thunder gust." It also led to the most famous of all his experiments.[9]

Before he tried to conduct his proposed experiments himself, Franklin described them in two famous letters to Collinson in 1750, which were presented to the Royal Society in London and then widely published. The essential idea was to use a tall metal rod to draw some of the electrical charge from a cloud, just as he had used a needle to draw off the charge of an iron ball in his lab. He detailed his proposed experiment:

> On the top of some high tower or steeple, place a kind of sentry box big enough to contain a man and an electrical stand. From the middle of the stand, let an iron rod rise . . . upright 20 or 30 feet, pointed very sharp at the end. If the electrical stand be kept clean and dry, a man standing on it when such clouds are passing low might be electrified and afford sparks, the rod drawing fire to him from the cloud. If any danger to the man be apprehended (though I think there would be none) let him stand on the floor of his box, and now and then bring near to the rod the loop of a wire that has one end fastened to the leads; he holding it by a wax handle [i.e., insulating him from it]. So the sparks, if the rod is electrified, will strike from the rod to the wire and not affect him.

Franklin's one mistake was thinking that there would be no danger, as at least one European experimenter fatally discovered. His suggestion of using a wire held with an insulating wax handle was a smarter approach.

If his suppositions held true, Franklin wrote in another letter to Collinson, then lightning rods could tame one of the greatest natural dangers people faced. "Houses, ships and even towns and churches may be effectually secured from the stroke of lightning by their means," he predicted. "The electrical fire would, I think, be drawn out of a cloud silently." He wasn't certain, however. "This may seem whimsical, but let it pass for the present until I send the experiments at large."[10]

Franklin's letters were excerpted in London by *The Gentleman's Magazine* in 1750 and then published as an eighty-six-page booklet the following year. More significant, they were translated into French in early 1752 and became a sensation. King Louis XV asked that the lab tests be performed for him, which they were in February by three Frenchmen who had translated Franklin's experiments, led by the naturalists Comte de Buffon and Thomas-François D'Alibard. The king was so excited that he encouraged the group to try Franklin's proposed lightning rod experiment. As a letter to London's Royal Society noted, "These applauses of his Majesty having excited in Messieurs de Buffon, D'Alibard and de Lor a desire of verifying the conjectures of Mr. Franklin upon the analogy of thunder and electricity, they prepared themselves for making the experiment."

In the village of Marly on the northern outskirts of Paris, the Frenchmen constructed a sentry box with a 40-foot iron rod and dragooned a retired soldier to play Prometheus. On May 10, 1752, just after 2 in the afternoon, a storm cloud passed over and the soldier was able to draw sparks as Franklin had predicted. An excited local prior grabbed the insulated wire and repeated the experiment six times, shocking himself once but surviving to celebrate the success. Within weeks it was replicated dozens of times across France. "M. Franklin's idea has ceased to be a conjecture," D'Alibard reported to the French Royal Academy. "Here it has become a reality."

Though he did not yet know it, Franklin had become an international sensation. An ecstatic Collinson wrote from London that "the Grand Monarch of France strictly commands" that his scientists convey "compliments in an express manner to Mr. Franklin of Philadelphia for the useful discoveries in electricity and application of the pointed rods to prevent the terrible effects of thunderstorms."[11]

The following month, before word of the French success reached America, Franklin came up with his own ingenious way to conduct the experiment, according to accounts later written by himself and his friend the scientist Joseph Priestley. He had been waiting for the steeple of Philadelphia's Christ Church to be finished, so he could use its high vantage point. Impatient, he struck on the idea of using instead a kite, a toy he had enjoyed flying and experimenting with since his boyhood days in Boston. To do the experiment in some secrecy, he enlisted his son, William, to help fly the silk kite. A sharp wire protruded from its top and a key was attached near the base of the wet string, so that a wire could be brought near it in an effort to draw sparks.

Clouds passed over to no effect. Franklin began to despair when he suddenly saw some of the strands of the string stiffen. Putting his knuckle to the key, he was able to draw sparks (and, notably, to survive). He proceeded to collect some of the charge in a Leyden jar and found it had the same qualities as electricity produced in a lab. "Thereby the sameness of electrical matter with that of lightning," he reported in a letter the following October, was "completely demonstrated."

Franklin and his kite were destined to be celebrated not just in the annals of science but also in popular lore. Benjamin West's famous 1805 painting, *Franklin Drawing Electricity from the Sky*, mistakenly shows him as a wrinkled sage rather than a lively 46-year-old, and an equally famous nineteenth-century Currier and Ives print shows William as a little boy rather than a man of about 21.

Even among scientific historians, there is some mystery about Franklin's celebrated kite flying. Although it supposedly took place in June 1752, before word had reached him of the French tests a few weeks earlier, Franklin made no public declaration of it for months. He did not mention it in the letters he wrote Collinson that summer, and he apparently did not tell his friend Ebenezer Kinnersley, who was lecturing on electricity in Philadelphia at the time. Nor did he publicly report his kite experiment even when word reached him, probably in late July or August, of the French success. His *Pennsylvania Gazette* for August 27, 1752, reprinted a letter about the French experiments, but it made no mention that Franklin and his son had already privately confirmed the results.

The first public report came in October, four months after the fact, in a letter Franklin wrote to Collinson and printed in his *Pennsylvania Gazette*. "As frequent mention is made in the public papers from Europe of the success of the Philadelphia Experiment for drawing the electric fire from the clouds," he wrote, "it may be agreeable to the curious to be informed that the same experiment has succeeded in Philadelphia, though made in a different and more easy manner." He went on to describe the details of constructing the kite and other apparatus, but in an oddly impersonal way, never using the first person to say explicitly that he and his son had carried it out themselves. He ended by expressing pleasure that the success of his experiments in France had prompted the installation of lightning rods there, and he made a point of noting that "we had before placed them upon our academy and state house spires." The same issue of the paper advertised the new edition of *Poor Richard's Almanack*, with an account of "how to secure houses, etc., from lightning."

A more colorful and personal account of the kite flying, including the details about William's involvement, appeared in Joseph Priestley's *The History and Present State of Electricity*, first published in 1767. "It occurred to him that, by means of a common kite, he could have a readier and better access to the regions of thunder than by any spire whatever," Priestley wrote of Franklin, and "he took the opportunity of the first approaching thunder storm to take a walk into a field, in which there was a shed convenient for his purpose." Priestley, a noted English scientist, based his account on information directly from Franklin, whom he first met in London in 1766. Franklin supplied Priestley with scientific material and vetted the manuscript, which ends with the flat declaration: "This happened in June 1752, a month after the electricians in France had verified the same theory, but before he had heard of anything they had done."[12]

The delay by Franklin in reporting his kite experiment has led

some historians to wonder if he truly did it that summer, and one recent book even charges that his claim was a "hoax." Once again, the
meticulous I. Bernard Cohen has done an exhaustive job of historical
sleuthing. Drawing on letters, reports, and the fact that lightning rods
were erected in Philadelphia that summer, he concludes after forty
pages of analysis that "there is no reason to doubt that Franklin had
conceived and executed the kite experiment before hearing the news
of the French performance." He goes on to say that it was performed
"not only by Franklin but by others," and he adds that "we may with
confidence conclude that Franklin performed the lightning kite experiment in June 1752, and that soon after, in late June or July 1752, it
was in Philadelphia that the first lightning rods ever to be erected were
put in service." [13]

Indeed, it is unreasonable, I think, to believe that Franklin fabricated the June date or other facts of his kite experiment. There is no
case of his ever embellishing his scientific achievements, and his description and the account by Priestley contain enough specific color
and detail to be convincing. Had he wanted to embellish, Franklin
could have claimed that he flew his kite before the French scientists
carried out their version of his experiment; instead, he generously admitted that the French scientists were the first to prove his theory.
And Franklin's son, with whom he later had a vicious falling-out,
never contradicted the well-told tale of the kite.

So why did he delay reporting what may be his most famous scientific feat? There are many explanations. Franklin almost never printed
immediate accounts of his experiments in his newspaper, or elsewhere. He usually waited, as he likely did in this case, to prepare a full
account rather than a quick announcement. These often took him a
while to write out and then recopy; he did not publicly report his 1748
experiments, for example, until his letter to Collinson in April 1749,
and there was a similar delay in conveying his results for the following
year.

He also may have feared being ridiculed if his initial findings
turned out to be wrong. Priestley, in his history of electricity, cited
such worries as being the reason Franklin flew his kite secretly. Indeed,
even as the experiments were being carried out that summer, many

scientists and commentators, including the Abbé Nollet, were calling them foolish. He thus may have been waiting, as Cohen speculates, to repeat and perfect the experiments. Another possibility, suggested by Van Doren, is that he wanted the revelation to coincide with the publication of the article about lightning rods in his new almanac edition that October.[14]

Whatever his reason for delaying the report of his experiment, Franklin was prompted that summer to convince the citizens of Philadelphia to erect at least two grounded lightning rods on high buildings, which were apparently the first in the world to be used for protection. That September, he also erected a rod on his own house with an ingenious device to warn of the approaching of a storm. The rod, which he described in a letter to Collinson, was grounded by a wire connected to the pump of a well, but he left a six-inch gap in the wire as it passed by his bedroom door. In the gap were a ball and two bells that would ring when a storm cloud electrified the rod. It was a typical combination of amusement, research, and practicality. He used it to draw charges for his experiments, but the gap was small enough to allow the safe discharge if lightning actually struck. Deborah, however, was less amused. Years later, when Franklin was living in London, he responded to her complaint by instructing her, "if the ringing frightens you," to close the bell gap with a metal wire so the rod would protect the house silently.

In some circles, especially religious ones, Franklin's findings stirred controversy. The Abbé Nollet, jealous, continued to denigrate his ideas and claimed that the lightning rod was an offense to God. "He speaks as if he thought it presumption in man to propose guarding himself against the thunders of Heaven!" Franklin wrote a friend. "Surely the thunder of Heaven is no more supernatural than the rain, hail or sunshine of Heaven, against the inconvenience of which we guard by roofs and shades without scruple."

Most of the world soon agreed, and lightning rods began sprouting across Europe and the colonies. Franklin was suddenly a famous man. Harvard and Yale gave him honorary degrees in the summer of 1753, and London's Royal Society made him the first person living outside of Britain to receive its prestigious gold Copley Medal. His reply to the Society was typically witty: "I know not whether any of your learned body have attained the ancient boasted art of multiplying gold; but you have certainly found the art of making it infinitely more valuable."[15]

A PLACE IN THE PANTHEON

In describing to Collinson how metal points draw off electrical charges, Franklin ventured some theories on the underlying physics. But he admitted that he had "some doubts" about these conjectures, and he added his opinion that learning *how* nature acted was more important than knowing the theoretical reasons *why:* "Nor is it much importance to us to know the manner in which nature executes her laws; it is enough if we know the laws themselves. It is of real use to know that china left in the air unsupported will fall and break; but how it comes to fall and why it breaks are matters of speculation. It is a pleasure indeed to know them, but we can preserve our china without it."

This attitude, and his lack of grounding in theoretical math and physics, is why Franklin, ingenious as he was, was no Galileo or Newton. He was a practical experimenter more than a systematic theorist. As with his moral and religious philosophy, Franklin's scientific work was distinguished less for its abstract theoretical sophistication than for its focus on finding out facts and putting them to use.

Still, we should not minimize the theoretical importance of his discoveries. He was one of the foremost scientists of his age, and he conceived and proved one of the most fundamental concepts about nature: that electricity is a single fluid. "The service which the one-fluid theory has rendered to the science of electricity," wrote the great nineteenth-century British physicist J. J. Thompson, who discovered the electron 150 years after Franklin's experiments, "can hardly be overestimated." He also came up with the distinction between insulators and conductors, the idea of electrical grounding, and the concepts of capacitors and batteries. As Van Doren notes, "He found electricity a curiosity and left it a science."

Nor should we underestimate the practical significance of proving that lightning, once a deadly mystery, was a form of electricity that could be tamed. Few scientific discoveries have been of such immediate service to humanity. The great German philosopher Immanuel Kant called him the "new Prometheus" for stealing the fire of heaven. He quickly became not only the most celebrated scientist in America and Europe, but also a popular hero. In solving one of the universe's greatest mysteries, he had conquered one of nature's most terrifying dangers.

But as much as he loved his scientific pursuits, Franklin felt that they were no more worthy than endeavors in the field of public affairs. Around this time, his friend the politician and naturalist Cadwallader Colden also retired and declared his intention to devote himself full time to "philosophical amusements," the term used in the eighteenth century for scientific experiments. "Let not your love of philosophical amusements have more than its due weight with you," Franklin urged in response. "Had Newton been pilot but of a single common ship, the finest of his discoveries would scarce have excused or atoned for his abandoning the helm one hour in time of danger; how much less if she had carried the fate of the Commonwealth."

So Franklin would soon apply his scientific style of reasoning— experimental, pragmatic—not only to nature but also to public affairs. These political pursuits would be enhanced by the fame he had gained as a scientist. The scientist and statesman would henceforth be interwoven, each strand reinforcing the other, until it could be said of him, in the two-part epigram that the French statesman Turgot composed, "He snatched lightning from the sky and the scepter from tyrants."[16]

CHAPTER SEVEN

POLITICIAN

Philadelphia, 1749–1756

THE ACADEMY AND THE HOSPITAL

The ingenious lad who did not get to go to Harvard, who skewered that college's pretensions with ill-disguised envy as a teenage essayist, and whose thirst for knowledge had made him the best self-taught writer and scientist of his times had for years nurtured the dream of starting a college of his own. He had discussed the idea in his Junto back in 1743, and after his retirement he became further motivated by the joy he found in science and reading. So in 1749 he published a pamphlet on "Proposals Relating to the Education of Youth in Pennsylvania" that described, with his usual indulgence in detail, why an academy was needed, what it should teach, and how the funds might be raised.

This was not to be a religiously affiliated, elite bastion like the four colleges (Harvard, William & Mary, Yale, and Princeton) that already existed in the colonies. The focus, as to be expected from Franklin, would be on practical instruction, such as writing, arithmetic, accounting, oratory, history, and business skills, with "regard being had to the several professions for which they are intended." Earthly virtues should be instilled; students would live "plainly, temperately and frugally" and be "frequently exercised in running, leaping, wrestling and swimming."

Franklin's plan was that of an educational reformer taking on the rigid classicists. The new academy should not, he felt, train scholars merely to glorify God or to seek learning for its own sake. Instead, what should be cultivated was "an inclination joined with an ability to serve mankind, one's country, friends and family." That, Franklin declared in conclusion, "should indeed be the great *aim* and *end* of all learning."

The pamphlet was crammed with footnotes citing ancient scholars and his own experience on everything from swimming to writing style. Like any good Enlightenment thinker, Franklin loved order and precise procedures. He had displayed this penchant by outlining, in the most minute detail imaginable, his rules for running the Junto, Masonic lodge, library, American Philosophical Society, fire corps, constable patrol, and militia. His proposal for the academy was an extreme example, crammed with exhaustive procedures on the best ways to teach everything from pronunciation to military history.

Franklin quickly raised £2,000 in donations (though not the £5,000 he recalled in his autobiography), drew up a constitution that was as detailed as his original proposal, and was elected president of the board. He also happened to be on the board of the Great Hall that had been built for the Rev. Whitefield, which had fallen into disuse as religious revivalism waned. He was thus able to negotiate a deal to have the new academy take over the building, divide it into floors and classrooms, and leave some space available for visiting preachers and a free school for poor children.

The academy opened in January 1751 as the first nonsectarian college in America (by 1791 it came to be known as the University of Pennsylvania). Franklin's reformist instincts were thwarted at times. Most of the trustees were from the wealthy Anglican establishment, and they voted over his objection to choose as the school's rector the Latin rather than English master. William Smith, a flighty minister from Scotland whom Franklin had befriended, was made the provost, but he and Franklin soon had a bitter falling-out over politics. Nonetheless, Franklin remained a trustee for the rest of his life and considered the college one of his proudest achievements.[1]

Soon after the college opened, Franklin moved on to his next project, raising money for a hospital. The public appeal he published in the

Gazette, which vividly described the moral duty people have to help the sick, contained the typical Franklin ringing refrain: "The good particular men may do separately in relieving the sick is small compared with what they may do collectively."

Raising money was difficult, so he concocted a clever scheme: he got the Assembly to agree that, if £2,000 could be raised privately, it would be matched by £2,000 from the public purse. The plan, Franklin recalled, gave people "an additional motive to give, since every man's donation would be doubled." Political opponents would later criticize Franklin for being too conniving, but he took great joy in this example of his cleverness. "I do not remember any of my political maneuvers the success of which gave me at the time more pleasure, or that in after thinking about it I more easily excused myself for having made use of cunning."[2]

AN AMERICAN POLITICAL PHILOSOPHY

By coming up with what is now known as the matching grant, Franklin showed how government and private initiative could be woven together, which remains to this day a very American approach. He believed in volunteerism and limited government, but also that there was a legitimate role for government in fostering the common good. By working through public-private partnerships, he felt, governments could have the best impact while avoiding the imposition of too much authority from above.

There were other streaks of conservatism, albeit what would now be labeled compassionate conservatism, in Franklin's political style. He believed very much in order, and it would end up taking a lot to radicalize him into an American revolutionary. Though charitable and very much a civic activist, he was wary of the unintended consequences of too much social engineering.

This was reflected in a ruminative letter on human nature he sent to his London friend Peter Collinson. "Whenever we attempt to mend the scheme of providence," Franklin wrote, "we had need be very circumspect lest we do more harm than good." Perhaps even welfare for the poor was an example. He asked whether "the laws peculiar to England which compel the rich to maintain the poor have not given the latter a dependence." It was "godlike" and laudable, he added, "to relieve the misfortunes of our fellow creatures," but might it not in the end "provide encouragements for laziness"? He added a cautionary tale about the New Englanders who decided to get rid of blackbirds that were eating the corn crop. The result was that the worms the blackbirds used to eat proliferated and destroyed the grass and grain crops.

But these were questions more than assertions. In his political philosophy, as in his religion and science, Franklin was generally non-ideological, indeed allergic to anything smacking of dogma. Instead, he was, as in most aspects of his life, interested in finding out what worked. As one writer noted, he exemplified the Enlightenment's "regard for reason and nature, its social consciousness, its progressivism, its tolerance, its cosmopolitanism, and its bland philanthropy." He had an empirical temperament that was generally averse to sweeping passions, and he espoused a kindly humanism that emphasized the somewhat sentimental (but still quite real) earthly goal of "doing good" for his fellow man.[3]

What made him a bit of a rebel, and later much more of one, was his inbred resistance to establishment authority. Not awed by rank, he was eager to avoid importing to America the rigid class structure of England. Instead, even as a retired would-be gentleman, he continued in his writings and letters to extol the diligence of the middling class of tradesmen, shopkeepers, and leather-aprons.

Out of this arose a vision of America as a nation where people, whatever their birth or social class, could rise (as he did) to wealth and status based on their willingness to be industrious and cultivate their virtues. In this regard, his ideal was more egalitarian and democratic than even Thomas Jefferson's view of a "natural aristocracy," which sought to pluck selected men with promising "virtues and talents" and groom them to be part of a new leadership elite. Franklin's own idea was more expansive: he believed in encouraging and providing opportunities for all people to succeed based on their diligence, hard work, virtue, and ambition. His proposals for what became the University of Pennsylvania (in contrast to Jefferson's for the University of Virginia) were aimed not at filtering a new elite but at encouraging and enriching all "aspiring" young men.

Franklin's political attitudes, along with his religious and scientific ones, fit together into a rather coherent outlook. But just as he was not a profound religious or scientific theorist—no Aquinas or Newton—neither was he a profound political philosopher on the order of a Locke or even a Jefferson. His strength as a political thinker, as in other fields, was more practical than abstract.

This was evident in one of his most important political tracts, "Observations Concerning the Increase of Mankind," which he wrote in 1751. The abundance of unsettled land in America, he said, led to a faster population growth. This was not a philosophical surmise but an empirical calculation. He observed that the colonists were only half as likely as the English to remain unmarried, that they married younger (around age 20), and that they averaged twice as many children (approximately eight). Thus, he concluded, America's population would double every twenty years and surpass that of England in one hundred years.

He turned out to be right. America's population surpassed that of England by 1851, and kept doubling every two decades until the frontier ran out at the end of that century. Adam Smith cited Franklin's tract in his 1776 classic, *The Wealth of Nations,* and Thomas Malthus, famous for his gloomy views on overpopulation and inevitable poverty, also used Franklin's calculations.

Franklin, however, was no Malthusian pessimist. He believed that, at least in America, increased productivity would keep ahead of population growth, thus making everyone better off as the country grew. In fact, he predicted (also correctly) that what would restrain America's population growth in the future was likely to be wealth rather than poverty, because richer people tended to be more "cautious" about getting married and having children.

Franklin's most influential argument—one that would play a significant role in the struggles ahead—was against the prevailing British mercantilist desire to restrain manufacturing in America. Parliament had just passed a bill prohibiting ironworks in America, and it held fast to an economic system based on using the colonies as a source of raw materials and a market for finished products.

Franklin countered that America's abundance of open land would preclude the development of a large pool of cheap urban labor. "The danger, therefore, of these colonies interfering with their Mother Country in trades that depend on labor, manufactures, etc., is too re-mote to require the attention of Great Britain." Britain would soon be unable to supply all of America's needs. "Therefore Britain should not too much restrain manufactures in her colonies. A wise and good mother will not do it. To distress is to weaken, and weakening the children weakens the whole family."[4]

The seriousness of this tract on imperial affairs was balanced by a satirical one he wrote around the same time. Britain had been expelling convicts to America, which it justified as a way to help the colonies grow. Writing as Americanus in the *Gazette*, Franklin sarcas-tically noted that "such a tender parental concern in our Mother Country for the welfare of her children calls aloud for the highest re-turns of gratitude." So he proposed that America ship a boatload of rattlesnakes back to England. Perhaps the change of climate might tame them, which is what the British had claimed would happen to the convicts. Even if not, the British would get the better deal, "for the rattlesnake gives warning before he attempts his mischief, which the convict does not."[5]

SLAVERY AND RACE

One great moral issue historians must wrestle with when assessing America's Founders is slavery, and Franklin was wrestling with it as well. Slaves made up about 6 percent of Philadelphia's population at the time, and Franklin had facilitated the buying and selling of them through ads in his newspaper. "A likely Negro woman to be sold. En-quire at the Widow Read's," read one such ad on behalf of his mother-in-law. Another offered for sale "a likely young Negro fellow" and ended with the phrase "enquire of the printer hereof." He personally owned a slave couple, but in 1751 he decided to sell them because, as he told his mother, he did not like having "Negro servants" and he found them uneconomical. Nevertheless, he would later, at times, have a slave as a personal servant.

In "Observations on the Increase of Mankind," he attacked slavery on economic grounds. Comparing the costs and benefits of owning a slave, he concluded that it made no sense. "The introduction of slaves," he wrote, was one of the things that "diminish a nation." But he mainly focused on the ill effects to the owners rather than the immorality done to the slaves. "The whites who have slaves, not laboring, are enfeebled," he said. "Slaves also pejorate the families that use them; white children become proud, disgusted with labor."

The tract was, in fact, quite prejudiced in places. He decried German immigration, and he urged that America be settled mainly by whites of English descent. "The number of purely white people in the world is proportionally very small," he wrote. "Why increase the sons of Africa by planting them in America, where we have so fair an opportunity, by excluding all blacks and tawneys, of increasing the lovely white and red? But perhaps I am partial to the complexion of my country, for such kind of partiality is natural to mankind."

As the final sentence indicates, he was beginning to reexamine his "partiality" to his own race. In the first edition of "Observations," he remarked on "almost every slave being by nature a thief." When he reprinted it eighteen years later, he changed it to say that they became thieves "from the nature of slavery." He also omitted the entire section about the desirability of keeping America mainly white.[6]

What helped shift his attitude was another of his philanthropic endeavors. In the late 1750s, he became active in an organization that established schools for black children in Philadelphia and then elsewhere in America. After visiting the Philadelphia school in 1763, he would write a reflective letter about his previous prejudices:

> I was on the whole much pleased, and from what I then saw have conceived a higher opinion of the natural capacities of the black race than I had ever before entertained. Their apprehension seems as quick, their memory as strong, and their docility in every respect equal to that of white children. You will wonder perhaps that I should ever doubt it, and I will not undertake to justify all my prejudices.[7]

In his later life, as we shall see, he became one of America's most active abolitionists, one who denounced slavery on moral grounds and helped advance the rights of blacks.

As indicated by the phrase he used in "Observations" about increasing "the lovely white and red" faces in America, Franklin's feelings about the Indians were generally positive. He marveled, in a letter to Collinson, that the simplicity of the Indians' wilderness life had a romantic appeal. "They have never shown any inclination to change their manner of life for ours," he wrote. "When an Indian child has been brought up among us, taught our language and habituated to our customs, yet if he goes to see his relations and make one Indian ramble with them, there is no persuading him ever to return."

White people also sometimes feel this preference for the Indians' way of living, Franklin noted. When white children were captured and raised by Indians, then later returned to white society, "in a short time they become disgusted with our manner of life, and the care and pains that are necessary to support it, and take the first good opportunity of escaping again into the woods."

He also told the story of some Massachusetts commissioners who invited the Indians to send a dozen of their youth to study free at Harvard. The Indians replied that they had sent some of their young braves to study there years earlier, but on their return "they were absolutely good for nothing, being neither acquainted with the true methods for killing deer, catching beaver, or surprising an enemy." They offered instead to educate a dozen or so white children in the ways of the Indians "and make men of them."[8]

ASSEMBLYMAN, INDIAN DIPLOMAT, AND POSTMASTER

Serving as clerk of the Pennsylvania Assembly, as he had since 1736, frustrated Franklin. Unable to take part in the debates, he amused himself by concocting his numerical magic squares. So when one of the members from Philadelphia died in 1751, Franklin readily accepted election to the seat (and passed on the clerkship to his unemployed son, William). "I conceived my becoming a member would enlarge my powers of doing good," he recalled, but then admitted: "I would not, however, insinuate that my ambition was not flattered."[9]

Thus began Franklin's career in politics, which would last for most of thirty-seven years until his retirement as president of the Pennsylvania Executive Council. As a private citizen, he had proposed various civic improvement schemes, such as the library, fire corps, and police patrol. Now, as a member of the Assembly, he could do even more to be, as he put it, "a great promoter of useful projects."

The quintessence of these was his effort to sweep, pave, and light the city streets. The endeavor began when he became bothered by the dust in front of his house, which faced the farmers' market. So he found "a poor industrious man" who was willing to sweep the block for a monthly fee and then wrote a paper that described all the benefits of hiring him. Houses on the block would remain cleaner, he noted, and shops would attract more customers. He sent the paper around to his neighbors, who all agreed to contribute a portion of the street sweeper's pay each month. The beauty of the scheme was that it opened the way for grander civic improvements. "This raised a general desire to have all the streets paved," Franklin recalled, "and made the people more willing to submit to a tax for that purpose."

As a result, Franklin was able to draw up a bill in the Assembly to pay for street paving, and he accompanied it with a proposal to install street lamps in front of each house. With his love of science and detail, Franklin even worked on a design for the lamps. The globes imported from London, he noticed, did not have a vent on the bottom to allow air in, which meant the smoke collected and darkened the glass. Franklin invented a new model with vents and a chimney, so that the lamp remained clean and bright. He also designed the style of lamp, common today, that had four flat panes of glass rather than one globe, making it easier to repair if broken. "Some may think these trifling matters not worth minding," Franklin said, but they should remember that "human felicity is produced . . . by little advantages that occur every day."[10]

There were, of course, more momentous issues to debate. The Assembly was dominated by Quakers, who were generally pacifist and frugal. They were often at odds with the family of the Proprietors, led by the great William Penn's not-so-great son Thomas, who didn't help relations when he married an Anglican and drifted away from the Quaker faith. The main concerns of the Proprietors were getting more land from the Indians and making sure that their property remained exempt from taxation.

(Pennsylvania was a Proprietary colony, which meant that it was governed by a private family that owned most of the unsettled land. In 1681, Charles II granted such a charter to William Penn, in repayment of a debt. A majority of the colonies started out as Proprietary ones, but by the 1720s most had become Royal colonies directly ruled by the king and his ministers. Only Pennsylvania, Maryland, and Delaware remained under their Proprietors until the Revolution.)

Two big issues faced Pennsylvania at the time: forging good relations with the Indians and protecting the colony from the French. These were related, because alliances with the Indians became all the more important whenever the recurring wars with the French flared up.

Remaining on good terms with the Indians required significant sums of money for gifts, and colonial defense was also costly. This led to complex political struggles in Pennsylvania. The Quakers opposed military spending on principle, and the Penns (acting through a series of appointed lackey governors) opposed anything that would cost them much money or subject their lands to taxes.

Franklin had been instrumental in finessing these issues in 1747, when he formed the voluntary militia. But by the early 1750s, tensions with France over control of the Ohio valley were rising again and would soon erupt into the French and Indian War (an offshoot of what was known in Europe as the Seven Years' War). The situation would lead Franklin to take two momentous initiatives that were to shape not only his political career but also the destiny of America:

- He became an increasingly fervent opponent of the Proprietors, and eventually of the British, as they stubbornly asserted their right to control the taxes and government of the colony, a stance that reflected his anti-authoritarian and populist sentiments.

- He became a leader of the effort to get the colonies, heretofore truculently independent of one another, to join together and unite for common purposes, which reflected his penchant for forging associations, his nonparochial view of America, and his belief that people could accomplish more when they worked together than when they stood separately.

The process began in 1753, when Franklin was appointed one of three commissioners from Pennsylvania to attend a summit conference with a congregation of Indian leaders at Carlisle, halfway between Philadelphia and the Ohio River. The goal was to secure the allegiance of the Delaware Indians, who were angry with the Penns for cheating them in what was known as the "Walking Purchase." (An old deed had given the Penns a tract of Indian land that was defined as what a man could walk in a day and a half, and Thomas Penn had hired three fleet runners to sprint for thirty-six hours, thus claiming far more land than intended.) Allied on the side of the Pennsylvanians were the Six Nations of the Iroquois confederacy, which included the Mohawk and Seneca tribes.

More than a hundred Indians came to the Carlisle conference. After the Pennsylvanians presented the traditional string of wampum, in this case, a whopping £800 worth of gifts,* the Iroquois chief Scaroyady proposed a peace plan. The white settlers should pull back to the east of the Appalachians, and their traders should be regulated to operate honestly and sell the Indians more ammunition and less rum. They also wanted assurances that the English would help defend them from the French, who were militarizing the Ohio valley.

The Pennsylvanians ended up pledging little more than a stricter regulation of their traders, which eventually caused the Delaware to drift over to the French side. On the last night, Franklin saw a frightening display of the dangers of rum. The Pennsylvanians had refused to offer the Indians any until the summit was over, and when the ban was lifted, a bacchanal erupted. As Franklin described the scene:

---

* Roughly equivalent to $128,000 in 2002 dollars. See page 506 for currency equivalents.

They had made a great bonfire in the middle of the square. They were all drunk, men and women, quarreling and fighting. Their dark-colored bodies, half naked, seen only by the gloomy light of the bonfire, running after and beating one another with firebrands, accompanied by their horrid yellings, formed a scene the most resembling our ideas of hell that could well be imagined.

Franklin and his fellow commissioners wrote an angry report decrying the white traders who regularly sold rum to the Indians. By doing so they threatened to "to keep these poor Indians continually under the force of liquor" and "entirely estrange the affections of the Indians from the English." [11]

Upon his return, Franklin learned that he had been appointed by the British government to share, along with William Hunter of Virginia, the top post office job in America, known as the Deputy Postmaster for the Colonies. He had been eagerly seeking the position for two years and had even authorized Collinson to spend up to £300 lobbying on his behalf in London. "However," Franklin joked, "the less it costs the better, as it is for life only, which is an uncertain tenure."

His quest was driven by his usual mix of motives: control of the post would allow him to invigorate the American Philosophical Society, improve his publishing network by placing friends and relatives in postal jobs across America, and perhaps make some money. He installed his son as Philadelphia's postmaster, and he later gave jobs in various towns to his brothers Peter and John, John's stepson, his sister Jane's son, two of Deborah's relatives, and his New York printing partner James Parker.

Franklin drew up typically detailed procedures for running the service more efficiently, established the first home-delivery system and dead letter office, and took frequent inspection tours. Within a year, he had cut to one day the delivery time of a letter from New York to Philadelphia. The reforms were costly, and he and Hunter incurred £900 in debt over their first four years. But then they started turning a profit, earning at least £300 a year apiece.

By 1774, when the British fired him for his rebellious political stances, he would be making more than £700 a year. But an even greater benefit of the job, both to him and history, was that it furthered Franklin's conception of the disparate American colonies as a potentially unified nation with shared interests and needs.[12]

THE ALBANY PLAN FOR
AN AMERICAN UNION

The summit of Pennsylvanians and Indians at Carlisle had done nothing to deter the French. Their goal was to confine the British settlers to the East Coast by building a series of forts along the Ohio River that would create a French arc from Canada to Louisiana. In response, Virginia's governor sent a promising young soldier named George Washington to the Ohio valley in late 1753 to demand that the French vacate. He failed, but his vivid account of the mission made him a hero and a colonel. The following spring, he began a series of haphazard raids against the French forts that would grow into a full-scale war.

Britain's ministers had been wary of encouraging too much cooperation among their colonies, but the French threat now made it necessary. The Board of Trade in London thus asked each colony to send delegates to a conference in Albany, New York, in June 1754. They would have two missions: meeting with the Iroquois confederation to reaffirm their allegiance and discussing among themselves ways to create a more unified colonial defense.

Cooperation among the colonies did not come naturally. Some of their assemblies declined the invitation, and most of the seven that accepted instructed their delegates to avoid any plan for colonial confederation. Franklin, on the other hand, was always eager to foster more unity. "It would be a very strange thing," he had written his friend James Parker in 1751, "if six nations of ignorant savages [the Iroquois] could be capable of forming a scheme for such a union . . . and yet that a like union should be impracticable for ten or a dozen English colonies, to whom it is more necessary."

In his letter to Parker, Franklin sketched out a structure for colonial cooperation: there should be, he said, a General Council with delegates from all the colonies, in rough proportion to the amount each paid in taxes to the general treasury, and a governor appointed by the king. The meeting sites should rotate among the various colonial capitals, so delegates could better understand the rest of America, and money would be raised by a tax on liquor. Typically, he felt the council should arise voluntarily rather than being imposed by London. The best way to get it going, he thought, was to pick a handful of smart men to visit influential people throughout the colonies and enlist support. "Reasonable, sensible men can always make a reasonable scheme appear such to other reasonable men."

When news of Washington's defeats reached Philadelphia in May 1754, just before the Albany conference, Franklin wrote an editorial in the *Gazette*. He blamed the French success "on the present disunited state of the British colonies." Next to the article he printed the first and most famous editorial cartoon in American history: a snake cut into pieces, labeled with names of the colonies, with the caption: "Join, or Die." [13]

Franklin was one of the four commissioners (along with the Proprietor's private secretary, Richard Peters, Thomas Penn's nephew John, and Assembly Speaker Isaac Norris) chosen to represent Pennsylvania at the Albany Conference. The Assembly, to his regret, had gone on record against "propositions for a union of the colonies," but Franklin was undeterred. He carried with him, as he left Philadelphia, a paper he had written called "Short Hints towards a Scheme for Uniting the Northern Colonies." It had one modification from the union plan that he had described in his earlier letter to James Parker: because the colonial assemblies seemed recalcitrant, perhaps it would be best, if and when the commissioners in Albany adopted such a plan, to send it back to London "and an act of Parliament obtained for establishing it."

On a stopover in New York, Franklin shared with friends the plan he had drafted. In the meantime, Peters and others went shopping for the £500 of wampum the Assembly had authorized as gifts for the Indians: blankets, ribbons, gunpowder, guns, vermilion for face paint, kettles, and cloth. Then, on June 9, they left on a well-laden sloop for Albany with "a pipe of the oldest and best Madeira wine to be got." [14]

Before the Indians arrived, the twenty-four colonial commissioners gathered for their own discussions. New York governor James De-

Lancey proposed a plan to build two western forts, but it stalled because the delegates could not agree to share the costs. So a motion was passed, likely at Franklin's instigation, that a committee be appointed "to prepare and receive plans or schemes for the union of the colonies." Franklin was one of seven named to the committee, which offered a perfect venue for him to gather support for the plan he had in his pocket.

In the meantime, the Indians arrived led by the Mohawk chief Tiyanoga, also known as Hendrick Peters. He was scornful. The Six Nations had been neglected, he said, "and when you neglect business, the French take advantage of it." In another tirade he added, "Look at the French! They are men, they are fortifying everywhere. But, we are ashamed to say it, you are all like women."

After a week of discussions, the commissioners made a series of promises to the Indians: There would be more consultation on settlements and trade routes, certain land sales would be investigated, and laws would be passed to restrict the rum trade. The Indians, with little choice, accepted the presents and declared their covenant chain with the English to be "solemnly renewed." Franklin was not impressed. "We brightened the chain with them," he wrote Peter Collinson, "but in my opinion no assistance is to be expected from them in any dispute with the French until by a complete union among ourselves we are able to support them in case they should be attacked."

In his effort to forge such a union at Albany, Franklin's key ally was a wealthy Massachusetts shipping merchant named Thomas Hutchinson. (Remember the name; he was later to become a fateful foe.) The plan that their committee approved was based on the one Franklin had written. There would be a national congress composed of representatives selected by each state roughly in proportion to their population and wealth. The executive would be a "President General" appointed by the king.

At its core was a somewhat new concept that became known as federalism. A "General Government" would handle matters such as national defense and westward expansion, but each colony would keep its own constitution and local governing power. Though he was sometimes dismissed as more of a practitioner than a visionary, Franklin in Albany had helped to devise a federal concept—orderly, balanced, and enlightened—that would eventually form the basis for a unified American nation.

On July 10, more than a week after the Indians had left Albany, the full group of commissioners finally voted on the plan. Some New York delegates opposed it, as did Isaac Norris, the Quaker leader of Pennsylvania's Assembly, but it nevertheless passed rather easily. Only a few revisions had been made to the scheme sketched out in the "Short Hints" that Franklin had carried with him to Albany, and he accepted them in the spirit of compromise. "When one has so many different people with different opinions to deal with in a new affair," he explained to his friend Cadwallader Colden, "one is obliged sometimes to give up some smaller points in order to obtain greater." It was a sentiment he would express in similar words when he became the key conciliator at the Constitutional Convention thirty-three years later.

The commissioners decided that the plan should be sent both to the colonial assemblies and to Parliament for approval, and Franklin promptly launched a public campaign on its behalf. This included a spirited exchange of open letters with Massachusetts governor William Shirley, who argued that the king rather than the colonial assemblies should choose the federal congress. Franklin replied with a principle that would be at the heart of the struggles ahead: "It is supposed an undoubted right of Englishmen not to be taxed but by their own consent given through their representatives."

It was to no avail. The Albany Plan was rejected by all of the colonial assemblies for usurping too much of their power, and it was shelved in London for giving too much power to voters and encouraging a dangerous unity among the colonies. "The assemblies did not adopt it as they all thought there was too much *prerogative* in it," Franklin recalled, "and in England it was judged to have too much of the *democratic.*"

Looking back on it near the end of his life, Franklin was convinced that the acceptance of his Albany Plan could have prevented the Revolution and created a harmonious empire. "The colonies so united would have been sufficiently strong to have defended themselves," he reasoned. "There would then have been no need of troops from England; of course the subsequent pretence for taxing America, and the bloody contest it occasioned, would have been avoided."

On that score he was probably mistaken. Further conflicts over Britain's right to tax her colonies and keep them subservient were almost inevitable. But for the next two decades, Franklin would struggle to find a harmonious solution even as he became more convinced of the need for the colonies to unite.[15]

CATHERINE RAY

After the Albany Conference, Franklin embarked on a tour of his postal realms that culminated in a visit to Boston. He had not been back there since before his mother's death two years earlier, and he spent time with his sprawling family, arranging jobs and apprenticeships. While staying with his brother John, he met an entrancing young woman who became the first intriguing example of his many amorous and romantic—but probably never consummated—flirtations.

Catherine Ray was a lively and fresh 23-year-old from Block Island, whose sister was married to John Franklin's stepson. Franklin, then 48, was immediately both charmed and charming. She was a great talker; so too was Franklin, when he wanted to flatter, and he was also a great listener. They played a game where he tried to guess her thoughts; she called him a conjurer and relished his attention. She made sugarplums; he insisted they were the best he'd ever eaten.

When it came time, after a week, for her to leave Boston to visit another sister in Newport, he decided to accompany her. Along the way, their poorly shod horses had trouble on the icy hills; they got caught in cold rains and on one occasion took a wrong turn. But they would recall, years later, the fun they had talking for hours, exploring ideas, gently flirting. After two days with her family in Newport, he saw her off on the boat to Block Island. "I stood on the shore," he wrote her shortly afterward, "and looked after you, until I could no longer distinguish you, even with my glass."

He left for Philadelphia slowly and with reluctance, loitering on the way for weeks. When he finally arrived home, there was a letter from her. Over the next few months he would write her six times, and through the course of their lives more than forty letters would pass between them. Franklin didn't save most of her letters, perhaps out of prudence, but the correspondence that does survive reveals a remarkable friendship and provides insights into Franklin's relations with women.

From reading their letters, and reading between the lines, one gets the impression that Franklin made a few playful advances that Caty gently deflected, and he seemed to respect her all the more for it. "I write this during a Northeaster storm of snow," he said in the first one he sent after their meeting. "The snowy fleeces which are pure as your virgin innocence, white as your lovely bosom—and as cold." In a letter a few months later, he spoke of life, math, and the role of "multiplication" in marriage, adding roguishly: "I would gladly have taught you that myself, but you thought it was time enough, and wouldn't learn."

Nevertheless, Caty's letters to him were filled with ardor. "Absence rather increases than lessens my affections," she wrote. "Love me one thousandth part so well as I do you." She was soulful and tearful in her letters, which conveyed her affection for him yet also described the men who were courting her. She begged him to destroy them after he had finished reading them. "I have said a thousand things that nothing should have tempted me to say."

Franklin reassured her that he would be discreet. "You may write freely everything you think fit, without the least apprehension of any person's seeing your letters but myself," he promised. "I know very well that the most innocent expressions of warm friendship . . . between persons of different sexes are liable to be misinterpreted by suspicious minds." That, he explained, was why he was being circumspect in his own letters. "Though you say more, I say less than I think."

And so we are left with a set of surviving letters that are filled with nothing more than tantalizing flirtations. She sent him some sugarplums that she had marked with (one assumes) a kiss. "They are every one sweetened as you used to like," she said. He replied, "The plums came safe, and were so sweet from the cause you mentioned that I could scarce taste the sugar." He spoke of the "pleasures of life" and noted that "I still have them all in my power." She wrote of spinning a long strand of thread, and he replied, "I wish I had hold of one end of it, to pull you to me."

How did his loyal and patient wife, Deborah, fit into this type of long-distance flirtation? Oddly enough, he seemed to use her as a shield, both with Caty and the other young women he later toyed with, to keep his relationships just on the safe side of propriety. He invariably invoked Deborah's name and praised her virtues in almost every letter he wrote to Caty. It was as if he wanted Caty to keep her ardor in perspective and to realize that, though his affection was real, his flirtations were merely playful. Or, perhaps, once his sexual advances had been rebuffed, he wanted to show (or to pretend) that they had not been serious. "I almost forgot I had a home," he wrote to Caty in describing his trip back from their first encounter. But soon he began "to think of and wish for home, and as I drew nearer I found the attraction stronger and stronger." So he sped ever faster, he wrote, "to my own house and to the arms of my good old wife and children, where I remain, thanks to God."

Later that fall, he was even more explicit in reminding Caty that he was a married man. When she sent him a present of cheese, he replied, "Mrs. Franklin was very proud that a young lady should have so much regard for her old husband as to send such a present. We talk of you every time it comes to table." Indeed, there was an interesting aspect to this and subsequent letters he wrote to her: they revealed less about the nature of his relationship with Caty than about the relationship, less passionate but deeply comfortable, that he had with his wife. As he told Caty, "She is sure you are a sensible girl and . . . talks of bequeathing me to you as a legacy. But I ought to wish you a better, and hope she will live these hundred years; for we are grown old together, and if she has any faults I am so used to them that I don't perceive them . . . Let us join in wishing the old lady a long life and happy."

Instead of merely continuing their flirtation, Franklin also began to provide Caty with paternal exhortations about duty and virtue. "Be a good girl," he urged, "until you get a good husband; then stay at home, and nurse the children, and live like a Christian." He hoped that when he next visited her, he would find her surrounded by "plump, juicy, blushing pretty little rogues, like their mama." And so it happened. The next time they met, she was married to William Greene, a future governor of Rhode Island, with whom she would have six children.[16]

So what are we to make of their relationship? Clearly, there were sweet hints of romantic attraction. But unless Franklin was dissembling in his letters in order to protect her reputation (and his), the joy came from fun fancies rather than physical realities. It was probably typical of the many flirtations he would have with younger women over the years: slightly naughty in a playful way, flattering to both parties, filled with intimations of intimacy, engaging both the heart and the mind. Despite a reputation for lecherousness that he did little to dispel, there is no evidence of any serious sexual affair he had after his marriage to Deborah.

Claude-Anne Lopez, a former editor of the Franklin Papers project at Yale, has spent years researching his private life. Her analysis of the type of relationships he had with women such as Catherine Ray seems both astute and credible:

> A romance? Yes, but a romance in the Franklinian manner, somewhat risqué, somewhat avuncular, taking a bold step forward and an ironic step backward, implying that he is tempted as a man but respectful as a friend. Of all shades of feeling, this one, the one the French call *amitié amoureuse*—a little beyond the platonic but short of the grand passion—is perhaps the most exquisite.[17]

Franklin only occasionally forged intimate bonds with his male friends, who tended to be either intellectual companions or jovial club colleagues. But he relished being with women, and he formed deep and lasting relationships with many. For him, such relationships were not a sport or trifling amusement, despite how they might appear, but a pleasure to be savored and respected. Throughout his life, Franklin would lose many male friends, but he never lost a female one, including Caty Ray. As he would tell her thirty-five years later, just a year before he died, "Among the felicities of my life I reckon your friendship."[18]

SUPPLYING GENERAL BRADDOCK

When he returned to Philadelphia in early 1755 after his dalliance with Caty Ray, Franklin was able, for the moment, to forge a workable relationship with most of the political leaders there. The Proprietors had appointed a new governor, Robert Hunter Morris, and Franklin assured him that he would have a comfortable tenure "if you will only take care not to enter into any dispute with the Assembly." Morris responded half-jokingly. "You know I love disputing," he said. "It is one of my greatest pleasures." Nevertheless, he promised to "if possible avoid them."

Franklin likewise worked hard to avoid disputes with the new governor, especially when it involved the issue of protecting Pennsylvania's frontier. So he was pleased when the British decided to send Gen. Edward Braddock to America with the mission of pushing the French out of the Ohio valley, and he supported Governor Morris's request that the Assembly appropriate funds to supply the troops.

Once again, the members insisted that the Proprietors' estates be taxed. Franklin proposed some clever schemes involving loans and excise taxes designed to break the impasse, but he was not able to resolve the issue right away. So he took on the mission of finding other ways to make sure that Braddock got the necessary supplies.

A delegation of three governors—Morris of Pennsylvania, Shirley of Massachusetts, and DeLancey of New York—had been chosen to meet with the general on his arrival in Virginia. The Pennsylvania Assembly wanted Franklin to be part of the delegation, as did his friend Governor Shirley, and Franklin was eager to be involved. So he joined the group wearing his postmaster hat, ostensibly to help arrange ways to facilitate Braddock's communications. Along the way, he impressed his fellow delegation members with his scientific curiosity. Encountering a small whirlwind, Franklin rode his horse into it, studied its effects, and even tried to break it up with his whip.[19]

General Braddock was brimming with arrogance. "I see nothing that can obstruct my march to Niagara," he crowed. Franklin cautioned that he should be wary of Indian ambushes. Replied Braddock:

"These savages may be a formidable enemy to your raw American militia, but upon the king's regular and disciplined troops, sir, it is impossible they would make any impression." As Franklin later recalled, "He had too much self-confidence."

What he lacked, besides humility, were supplies. Because the Americans had come up with only a fraction of the horses and wagons promised, he declared his intention to return home. Franklin interceded. Pennsylvanians would rally to his cause, he said. The general promptly designated Franklin to be in charge of procuring the equipment.

The broadsides that Franklin wrote advertising Braddock's need to hire horses and wagons played on fear, self-interest, and patriotism. The general had proposed to seize the horses and compel Americans into service, he said, but had been prevailed on instead to try "fair and equitable means." The terms were good, Franklin argued: "The hire of these wagons and horses will amount to upwards of £30,000, which will be paid you in silver and gold and the King's money." As an inducement, he assured the farmers that "the service will be light and easy." Finally came a threat that if voluntary offers did not come, "your loyalty will be strongly suspected," "violent measures will probably be used," and a "Hussar with a body of soldiers will immediately enter the province."

Franklin acted selflessly, indeed remarkably so. When the farmers said they were unwilling to trust the financial pledges of an unknown general, Franklin gave his personal bond that they would receive full payment. His son, William, helped him sign up the farmers, and within two weeks they had procured 259 horses and 150 wagons.[20]

General Braddock was thrilled with Franklin's performance, and the Assembly profusely commended him as well. But Governor Morris, not heeding Franklin's advice to avoid disputes, could not resist attacking the Assembly for being of little help. This upset Franklin, but he still tried to be a conciliator. "I am heartily sick of our present situation: I like neither the governor's conduct nor the Assembly's," he wrote his London friend Collinson, "and having some share in the confidence of both, I have endeavored to reconcile them, but in vain."

Ever collegial, Franklin was able to remain on good personal terms with the governor for the time being. "You must go home with me and spend the evening," Morris said one day on meeting him on the street. "I am to have some company that you will like." One guest told the tale of Sancho Panza, who, when offered a government, requested that his subjects be blacks so that he could sell them if they gave him trouble. "Why do you continue to side with these damned Quakers?" he asked Franklin. "Had not you better sell them? The Proprietors would give you a good price." Franklin replied, "The governor has not yet *blacked* them enough."

Though everyone laughed, the fissures were deepening. By attempting to blacken the reputation of the Assembly, Franklin later wrote, Morris had "negrofied himself." Morris likewise had begun to distrust Franklin. In a letter to Proprietor Thomas Penn, he charged that Franklin was "as much a favorer of the unreasonable claims of American assemblies as any man whatever." [21]

In the meantime, Braddock was confidently marching west. Most Philadelphians were sure that he would prevail, and they even launched a collection to buy fireworks to celebrate. Franklin, more cautious, refused to contribute. "The events of war are subject to great uncertainty," he warned.

His worries were warranted. The British army was ambushed and routed, and Braddock was killed along with two-thirds of his soldiers. "Who would have thought it?" Braddock whispered to an aide just before he died. Among the few survivors was the American colonel George Washington, who had two horses shot out from under him and four bullets pierce his clothing.

Adding to Franklin's distress was the financial exposure he faced because of the loans he had personally guaranteed. These "amounted to near £20,000, which to pay would have ruined me," he recalled. Just as the farmers began to sue him, Massachusetts governor Shirley, now the general of the British troops, came to his rescue and ordered that the farmers be paid from the army's funds.

Braddock's disaster increased the threat from the French and Indians, and it deepened the political rift in Philadelphia. The Assembly quickly passed a bill appropriating £50,000 for defense, but again it insisted a tax be placed on all lands, "those of the proprietors not excepted." Governor Morris rejected it, demanding that the word "not" be changed to "only."

Franklin was furious. No longer casting himself as a mediator, he wrote the reply that the Assembly sent to Morris. He called the governor a "hateful instrument of reducing a free people to the abject state of vassalage," and he accused Proprietor Thomas Penn of "taking advantage of public calamity" and trying "to force down their throats laws of imposition abhorrent to common justice and common reason."

Franklin became particularly enraged when he learned that Morris was required by a secret clause in his commission as governor to reject any tax on the Proprietary estates. In another message from the Assembly a week later, responding to Morris's objection to the use of the word "vassalage," Franklin wrote of Penn: "Our lord would have us defend his estate at our own expense! This is not merely vassalage, it is worse than any vassalage we have heard of; it is something we have no adequate name for; it is even more slavish than slavery itself." In a subsequent message, he added what would become a revolutionary cry: "Those who would give up essential liberty to purchase a little temporary safety deserve neither liberty nor safety."

In the end, a series of patchwork compromises was reached. The Proprietors, on gauging the Assembly's anger, agreed to a voluntary contribution of £5,000 to supplement whatever the Assembly raised. Although that defused the immediate crisis, the principle remained unresolved. More significant, for himself and for history, Franklin had abandoned his long-standing aversion to dispute. Henceforth he would become an increasingly fervent foe of the Proprietors.[22]

COLONEL FRANKLIN OF THE MILITIA

The issue of how to pay for frontier defense had been settled, for the time being, by the uneasy compromises between the Assembly and the Proprietors. To Franklin fell the task of figuring out how to spend the money and raise a militia. He pushed through a bill to create a force that was purely voluntary, thus securing the support of the Quakers, and then published an imaginary discourse designed to rally support for the plan. One character, objecting to the idea that the

Quakers did not have to join, declares, "Hang me if I'll fight to save the Quakers." Replies his friend: "That is to say you won't pump ship, because it will save the rats as well as yourself."

Franklin's plan was modeled on the Association Militia he had organized in 1747, but this time it would be under the aegis of the government. Once again, he spelled out at length the details of training, organization, and election of officers. In one letter he also came up with a very specific scheme for using dogs as scouts. "They should be large, strong and fierce," he wrote, "and every dog led in a slip strong to prevent them tiring themselves by running out and in and discovering the party by barking at squirrels."

Governor Morris grudgingly accepted Franklin's militia bill, though he disliked the provisions making it voluntary and allowing the democratic election of officers. Even more distressing was that Franklin had become the de facto leader and most powerful man in the colony. "Since Mr. Franklin has put himself at the head of the Assembly," Morris warned Penn, his followers "are using every means in their power, even while their country is invaded, to wrest the government out of your hands." For his part, Franklin had developed a burning contempt for Morris. "This man is half a madman," he wrote the Assembly's lobbyist in London.[23]

The Proprietors' fears were not calmed when Franklin donned a military uniform and, along with his son, headed to the frontier to oversee the construction of a line of stockades. He spent the week of his fiftieth birthday, in January 1756, camping at the Lehigh Gap and dining on the provisions that his dutiful wife had sent. "We have enjoyed your roast beef and this day began on the roast veal," he wrote her. "Citizens that have their dinners hot know nothing of good eating; we find it in much greater perfection when the kitchen is four score miles from the dining room."

Franklin enjoyed his stint as a frontier commander. Among his clever accomplishments was devising a reliable method for getting the five hundred soldiers under his command to attend worship services: he assigned to the militia's chaplain the task of doling out the daily allotments of rum right after his services. "Never were prayers more generally and punctually attended." He also found time to observe and record, in his wry way, the customs of the local Moravians, who believed in arranged marriages. "I objected if the matches were not made by the mutual choice of the parties, some of them may chance to be very unhappy," Franklin recounted. " 'And so they may,' answered my informer, 'if you let the parties choose for themselves,' which indeed I could not deny."[24]

After seven weeks on the frontier, Franklin returned to Philadelphia. Despite the worries of the Proprietors and their governor, he had little desire to play the hero on horseback or parlay his popularity into political power. Indeed, he hurried his return so that he arrived late at night to avoid the triumphant welcome that his supporters had planned.

He did not, however, decline when the militia's Philadelphia regiment elected him their colonel. Governor Morris, who had reluctantly sought Franklin's help during the crisis, balked at approving the selection. But he had little choice, as Franklin's militia bill called for the democratic selection of officers, and after a few weeks he grudgingly assented.

Throughout his life, Franklin would find himself torn (and amused) by the conflict between his professed desire to acquire the virtue of humility and his natural thirst for acclaim. His tenure as a colonel was no exception. He could not refrain from indulging his vanity by scheduling a grand public review of his troops. More than a thousand marched past his Market Street house with great pomp and ceremony. Each company arrived to the sounds of fifes and oboes, showed off their freshly painted cannons, and then fired off a volley to herald the arrival of the next company. The shots, he later noted wryly, "shook down and broke several glasses of my electrical apparatus."

When he left a few weeks later on a postal inspection trip, "the officers of my regiment took it into their heads that it would be proper for them to escort me out of town." They drew their swords and accompanied him to the ferry, which infuriated Thomas Penn when he read of it in London. "This silly affair," Franklin noted, "greatly increased his rancor against me . . . and he instanced this parade with my officers as a proof of my having an intention to take the government of the province out of his hands by force." Franklin was likewise "chagrined" by the display, or at least so he said in retrospect. "I had not been previously acquainted with the project or I should have prevented it, being naturally averse to the assuming of state on any occasion."

In fairness to Franklin, he was never the type of person who liked to revel in public ceremony or the pomposity and perks of power. When Penn and his allies sought to neutralize him by forming rival militias in Philadelphia and then convincing the king's ministers to nullify his militia act, Franklin responded by readily surrendering his commission. In a reflective letter to his friend Peter Collinson, he admitted that he enjoyed the public affection but realized that he should not allow it to go to his head. "The people happen to love me," he wrote, but then added, "Forgive your friend a little vanity, as it's only between ourselves . . . You are now ready to tell me that popular favor is a most uncertain thing. You are right. I blush at having valued myself so much upon it."[25]

A NEW MISSION

Franklin's days as a dexterous politician, one who was willing and able to seek pragmatic compromises in times of crisis, were temporarily over. At the height of earlier tensions, he had enjoyed occasional amiable consultations and social interactions with Governor Morris, but that was no longer the case. Morris and others in the Proprietary faction were doing whatever they could to humiliate him, and for a while he talked of moving to Connecticut or even out west to help start a colony in the Ohio region.

So his postal inspection trip to Virginia was a welcome respite, one he extended for as long as possible. From Williamsburg he wrote to his wife that he was "as gay as a bird, not beginning yet to long for home, the worry of perpetual business being fresh in my memory." He met with Colonel Washington and other acquaintances, marveled at the size of the peaches, accepted an honorary degree from William & Mary, and rode through the countryside inspecting postal accounts at a leisurely pace.

When he finally returned home after more than a month, the atmosphere of Philadelphia was even more polarized. The Proprietors' secretary, Richard Peters, conspired with William Smith, whom Franklin had recruited to run the Pennsylvania Academy, to oust him from the presidency of that board. Smith had been writing harsh attacks on Franklin, and the two men stopped speaking to each other, another in the line of rifts he had with male friends.

Late that summer of 1756, there was a brief period of hope for restored civility when a professional military man, William Denny, replaced Morris as governor. All sides hastened to greet and embrace him. At his festive inaugural dinner, he took Franklin aside to a private room and tried to cultivate him. Drinking liberally from a decanter of Madeira, Denny profusely flattered Franklin, which was a smart approach, and then tried to bribe him with financial promises, which wasn't. If Franklin's opposition abated, Denny promised, he could "depend on adequate acknowledgments and recompenses." Franklin replied that "my circumstances, thanks to God, were such as to make proprietary favors unnecessary to me."

Denny was less fastidious about financial inducements. Like his predecessor, he confronted the Assembly by rejecting bills that taxed the Proprietary estates, but he later reversed himself, without permission from the Penns, on being offered a generous salary by the Assembly.

The Assembly, in the meantime, decided that the obstinacy of the Proprietors could no longer be tolerated. In January 1757, the members voted to send Franklin to London as their agent. His goal, at least initially, would be to lobby the Proprietors to be more accommodating to the Assembly over taxation and other matters, and then, if that failed, to take up the Assembly's cause with the British government.

Peters, the Proprietors' secretary, was worried. "B.F.'s view is to effect a change of government," he wrote Penn in London, "and considering the popularity of his character and the reputation gained by his electricity discoveries, which will introduce him into all sorts of company, he may prove a dangerous enemy." Penn was more sanguine. "Mr. Franklin's popularity is nothing here," he replied. "He will be looked upon coldly by great people."

In fact, Peters and Penn would both turn out to be right. Franklin set sail in June 1757 with the firm belief that the colonists should forge a closer union among themselves and be accorded their full rights and liberties as subjects of the British Crown. But he held these views as a proud and loyal Englishman, one who sought to strengthen his majesty's empire rather than seek independence for the American colonies. Only much later, after he was indeed looked on coldly by great people in London, would Franklin prove a dangerous enemy to the imperial cause.[26]

TROUBLED WATERS

London, 1757–1762

MRS. STEVENSON'S LODGER

As he crossed the Atlantic in the summer of 1757, Franklin noticed something about the other ships in the convoy. Most roiled the water with large wakes. One day, however, the ocean behind two of them was oddly tranquil. Ever inquisitive, he asked about the phenomenon. "The cooks," he was told, "have been emptying their greasy water through the scuppers, which has greased the sides of those ships."

The explanation did not satisfy Franklin. Instead, he recalled reading about how Pliny the Elder, the first-century Roman senator and scientist, had calmed agitated water by pouring oil on it. In the ensuing years, Franklin would engage in a variety of oil-and-water experiments, and he even devised a parlor trick where he stilled waves by touching them with a cane that contained a hidden cruet of oil. The metaphor, though obvious, is too good to resist: Franklin, by nature, liked to find ingenious ways to calm turbulent waters. But during his time as a diplomat in England, this instinct would fail him.[1]

Also during the crossing, his ship narrowly avoided being wrecked on the Scilly Isles when it sought to evade French privateers in the fog. Franklin described his grateful reaction in a letter home to his wife. "Were I a Roman Catholic, perhaps I should on this occasion vow to build a chapel to some saint," he wrote. "But as I am not, if I were to vow at all, it should be to build a *lighthouse*." Franklin always took pride in his instinct for practical solutions, but that too would fail him in England.[2]

Franklin's return to London at age 51 came almost thirty-three years after his first visit there as a teenage printer. His mission as Pennsylvania's agent was to mix lobbying with deft diplomacy. Unfortunately, his usual observational skills, his sense of practicality and prudence, and his soothing temperament and cool head would be overwhelmed by frustration and then bitterness. Yet, even as his diplomatic mission foundered, there would be aspects of his life in London—the company of cosmopolitan intellectuals who doted on him, the creation of a contented home life similar to his in Philadelphia—that would make it hard for him to tear himself away. He initially thought his work would be done in five months, but he ended up staying more than five years, and then, after a brief interlude back home, another ten.

Franklin arrived in London in July accompanied by his son, William, then about 26, and two slaves who had been their household servants. They were met by his longtime pen pal Peter Collinson, the London Quaker merchant and botanist, who had helped procure books for the Junto's first library and later published Franklin's letters on electricity. Collinson put Franklin up at his stately home just north of London and immediately invited over others, such as the printer William Strahan, who were likewise delighted finally to meet in person the now-legendary man they had known only through years of correspondence.[3]

After a few days, Franklin found lodgings (including a room for his electricity experiments) in a cozy but convenient four-story row house on Craven Street, nestled between the Strand and the Thames River just off what is now Trafalgar Square, a short walk from the ministries of Whitehall. His landlady was a sensible and unpretentious middle-aged widow named Margaret Stevenson. With her he would form a familial relationship, at once both curious and mundane, that replicated the marriage of comforting convenience that he enjoyed with Deborah in Philadelphia. His London friends often treated Franklin and Mrs. Stevenson as a couple, inviting them together to dinners and inquiring after them both in letters. Though it is possible that their re-

lationship had some sexual aspect, there was no particular passion, and it provoked very little gossip or scandal in London.[4]

More complex was his relation with her daughter Mary, known as Polly. She was a lively and endearing 18-year-old with the sort of inquisitive intellect that Franklin loved in women. In some respects, Polly served as the London counterpart to his daughter, Sally. He treated her in an avuncular, and sometimes even paternal, manner, instructing her on life and morals as well as science and education. But she was also an English version of Caty Ray, a pretty young woman of playful demeanor and lively mind. His letters to her were flirtatious at times, and he flattered her with the focused attention that he lavished on women he liked.

Franklin spent hours talking to Polly, whose eager curiosity enchanted him, and then, when she went to live with an aunt in the country, carried on an astonishing correspondence. During his years in London, he wrote to her far more often than he wrote to his family. Some of the letters were flirtatious. "Not a day passes in which I do not think of you," he wrote less than a year after their first meeting. She sent him little gifts. "I have received the garters you have so kindly knit for me," he said in one letter. "They are of the only sort that I can wear, having worn none of any kind for 20 years, until you began to supply me . . . Be assured that I shall think as often of you in the wearing as you did of me in the making."

As with Caty Ray, his relationship with Polly was an engagement of the mind as much as the heart. He wrote to her at great length and in sophisticated detail about how barometers work, colors absorb heat, electricity is conducted, waterspouts are formed, and the moon affects tidal flows. Eight of these letters were later included in a revised edition of his electricity papers.

He also worked with Polly to come up with what was essentially a correspondence course to teach her a variety of subjects. "Our easiest method of proceeding, I think, will be for you to read some books I may recommend to you," he suggested. "Those will furnish matter for your letters to me and, in consequence, of mine also to you." Such intellectual tutoring was, for him, the ultimate way to flatter a young woman. As he ended one letter to her, "After writing six folio pages of philosophy to a young girl, is it necessary to finish such a letter with a compliment? Is not such a letter of itself a compliment? Does it not say, She has a mind thirsty after knowledge and capable of receiving it?"[5]

His one concern was that Polly would take her studies *too* seriously. Even though he appreciated her mind, Franklin flinched when she hinted at her desire to devote herself to learning at the expense of getting married and raising a family. So he provided her with some paternal prodding. In response to her suggestion that she might "live single" the rest of her life, he lectured her about the "duty" of a woman to raise a family:

> There is, however, a prudent moderation to be used in studies of this kind. The knowledge of nature may be ornamental, and it may be useful, but if to attain an eminence in that we neglect the knowledge and practice of essential duties, we deserve reprehension. For there is no rank in natural knowledge of equal dignity and importance with that of being a good parent, a good child, a good husband, or wife.

Polly took the injunction to heart. "Thank you my dear preceptor for your indulgence in satisfying my curiosity," she replied. "As my greatest ambition is to render myself amiable in your eyes, I will be careful never to transgress the bounds of moderation you prescribe." And then, over the next few weeks, they proceeded to engage in an extensive colloquy, filled with both factual research and various theories, of how the tides affect the flow of water at the mouth of a river.[6]

Polly would eventually marry, have three children, and then become widowed, but through it all she remained extraordinarily close to Franklin. As he would write to her in 1783, near the end of his life, "Our friendship has been all clear sunshine, without the least cloud in its hemisphere." And she would be at his bedside when he died, thirty-three years after their first meeting.[7]

Margaret and Polly Stevenson provided a replica of the family he left in Philadelphia, just as comfortable and more intellectually stimulating. So what did this mean for his real family? Franklin's English friend William Strahan expressed concern. He wrote Deborah to try to persuade her to join her husband in London. The opposite of the peripatetic Franklin, she had no desire to travel and was deeply afraid of the sea. Strahan assured her that no one had ever been killed crossing from Philadelphia to London, not mentioning that this statistic ignored that many had been killed on similar routes. The trip would also be a great experience for Sally, Strahan went on to urge.

That was the sweet part of the letter, the carrots designed to entice. But it was followed, almost rudely, by some jarringly presumptuous advice, which was courteously cloaked but contained barely concealed warnings that reflected Strahan's knowledge of Franklin's nature: "Now madam, as I know the ladies here consider him in exactly the same light I do, upon my word I think that you should come over with all convenient speed to look after your interest; not but that I think him as faithful to his Joan [Franklin's poetic nickname for Deborah] as any man breathing, but who knows what repeated and strong temptation may in time, and while he at so great a distance from you, accomplish." In case Deborah missed the point, Strahan dropped a poison-tinged reassurance at the very end of his letter: "I cannot take my leave of you without informing you that Mr. F. has the good fortune to lodge with a very discreet gentlewoman who is particularly careful of him, who attended him during a very severe cold with an assiduity, concern and tenderness which, perhaps, only yourself could equal; so that I don't think you could have a better substitute until you come over to take him under your own protection."[8]

Franklin was fond of Deborah, relied on her, and respected her solid and simple manner, but he knew that she would be out of place in this more sophisticated London world. So he seemed somewhat ambivalent about the prospect of enticing her to England—and typically realistic about the likelihood. "[Strahan] has offered to lay me a considerable wager that a letter he wrote to you will bring you immediately over here," he wrote. "I tell him I will not pick his pocket, for I am sure there is no inducement strong enough to prevail with you to cross the seas." When she replied that she would indeed be staying in Philadelphia, Franklin showed little grief. "Your answer to Mr. Strahan was just what it should be; I was very much pleased with it. He fancied his rhetoric and art would certainly bring you over."

In his letters home, Franklin walked a fine line of assuring Deborah that he was well looked after, but also reassuring her that he missed her love. After falling ill a few months after his arrival, he wrote, "I have made your compliments to Mrs. Stevenson. She is indeed very obliging, takes great care of my health, and is very diligent when I am in any way indisposed; but yet I have a thousand times wished you with me, and my little Sally . . . There is a great difference in sickness between being nursed with that tender attention which proceeds from sincere love."

Accompanying the letter was an assortment of gifts, some of which, he told her, were chosen by Mrs. Stevenson. The shipment included china, four of London's "newest but ugliest" silver salt ladles, "a little instrument to core apples, another to make little turnips out of great ones," a basket for Sally from Mrs. Stevenson, garters for Deborah that had been knit by Polly ("who favored me with a pair of the same kind"), carpets, blankets, tablecloths, gown fabric chosen for Deborah by Mrs. Stevenson, candle snuffers, and enough other items to assuage any guilt.[9]

Deborah was generally sanguine about the women in Franklin's life. She supplied him with all the news and gossip from home, including the latest she had heard from Caty Ray asking for advice about (of all things) her love life. "I am glad to hear that Miss Ray is well, and that you correspond," Franklin replied, though he urged her not to "be forward in giving advice in such cases."

Their correspondence, for the most part, contained little of the emotional or intellectual content to be found in the letters Franklin exchanged with Polly or Caty Ray or later with his female friends in Paris. Nor did he discourse much with her on political matters, the way he did with his sister Jane Mecom. Although his letters conveyed what seems to be a sincere fondness for Deborah and for the practical nature of their partnership, there were no signs of the more profound partnership that is so evident, for example, in John Adams's correspondence with his wife, Abigail.

Eventually, as Franklin's mission stretched on, Deborah's letters to him would become more bereft and self-pitying, especially after her mother died in a horrible kitchen fire in 1760. Shortly after, she wrote in her awkward way about her loneliness and her worries about rumors she had heard about him and other women. Franklin's reply, though reassuring, was phrased in a coolly abstract manner. "I am concerned that so much trouble should be given you by idle reports," he wrote. "Be satisfied, my dear, that while I have my senses, and God vouchsafes me his protection, I shall do nothing unworthy the character of an honest man, and one that loves his family." [10]

FRANKLIN'S LONDON WORLD

With 750,000 inhabitants and growing rapidly, London in the 1750s was the largest city in Europe and second only to Beijing (pop: 900,000) in the world. It was cramped and dirty, filled with disease and prostitutes and crime, and had long been stratified into an upper class of titled aristocrats and a lower class of impoverished workers who struggled with starvation. Yet it was also vibrant and cosmopolitan, and by the 1750s it had an emerging middle class of merchants and industrialists as well as a growing coffeehouse society of intellectuals, writers, scientists, and artists. Although Philadelphia was the largest city in America, it was a tiny village by comparison, with only 23,000 inhabitants (about the size of Franklin, Wisconsin, or Franklin, Massachusetts, today).

In the cosmopolitan mix of old and new classes that made up London, Franklin quickly found favor among the intellectual and literary set. But despite his reputation for social climbing, he showed little inclination to court the members of the Tory aristocracy, and the feeling was mutual. He liked to be among people with lively minds and simple virtues, and he had an inbred aversion to powerful establishments and idle elites. One of his first visits was to the press where he had once worked. There he bought buckets of beer and drank toasts to the "success of printing."

Strahan and Collinson formed the nucleus of a new set of friends that replicated for Franklin his old Junto but with more sophistication and distinction. He had been corresponding with Strahan, a printer and part-owner of the London *Chronicle*, since 1743, when Strahan provided a letter of recommendation for his apprentice, David Hall, whom Franklin hired and later made his partner. They had exchanged more than sixty letters before they even met, and when they finally did, Strahan was smitten by the larger-than-life Franklin. "I never saw a man who was, in every respect, so perfectly agreeable to me," he wrote Deborah Franklin. "Some are amiable in one view, some in another, he in all."

Collinson, the merchant with whom he had corresponded about electricity, introduced Franklin to the Royal Society, which had already elected him its first American member a year before he arrived. Through Collinson he met Dr. John Fothergill, one of London's foremost physicians, who became his doctor and helped advise him on dealing with the Penns, and also Sir John Pringle, a crusty Scottish professor of moral philosophy and later royal physician, who became his traveling companion. Collinson also brought him into the Honest Whigs, a discussion club of pro-American liberal intellectuals. Among its members, Franklin befriended Joseph Priestley, who wrote the history of electricity that secured Franklin's reputation and went on to isolate oxygen, and Jonathan Shipley, the Bishop of St. Asaph, at whose home Franklin would write much of his autobiography.[11]

Franklin also got in touch with the wayward friend of his youth, James Ralph, who had been his companion on his earlier trip to London, during which they had a falling-out over money and a woman. Ralph's character hadn't changed much. Franklin carried from Philadelphia a letter to Ralph written by the daughter he had abandoned, who was now the mother of ten children. But Ralph didn't want his own English wife and daughter to learn of his connections to America, so he refused to write back. He merely told Franklin to pass along his "great affection." Franklin had little to do with Ralph after that.[12]

For the fashionable gentlemen of the aristocracy, elegant eating and gambling clubs, such as White's and later Brookes's and Boodle's, were starting to spring up in St. James's. For the burgeoning new class of writers, journalists, professionals, and intellectuals whose company Franklin preferred, there were the coffeehouses. London had more than five hundred at the time. They contained newspapers and periodicals for the patrons to read and tables around which discussion clubs could be formed. Fellows of the Royal Society tended to meet at the

Grecian coffeehouse in the Strand, just a short walk from Craven Street. The Club of Honest Whigs met on alternate Thursdays at St. Paul's coffeehouse. Others, such as the Massachusetts and Pennsylvania coffeehouses, provided an American connection. Franklin, always fond of clubs and the occasional glass of Madeira, frequented these and others.[13]

And thus he created an embracing new set of friends and hangouts that replicated the joys of the Junto and provided him with a modest power base among the city's intellectuals. But it was, as Thomas Penn had predicted, a somewhat limited power base. The Proprietor had reassured his own allies, after Franklin's appointment, that he might find favor among those who cared about his scientific experiments, but these middle-class Whiggish intellectuals were not the ones who would decide Pennsylvania's fate. "There are very few of any consequence that have heard of his electrical experiments, those matters being attended to by a particular set of people," Penn wrote. "But it is quite another sort of people who are to determine the dispute between us." Indeed it was.[14]

BATTLING THE PENNS

Franklin came to London not only as a loyalist to the Crown but as an enthusiast for the empire, of which he felt that America was an integral part. But he soon found out that he labored under a misconception. He believed that His Majesty's subjects who happened to live in the colonies were not second-class citizens. Instead, he felt they should have all the rights of any British subject, including that of electing assemblies with legislative and tax-writing powers similar to those of Parliament. The Penns might not see it that way, but certainly the enlightened British ministers would, he believed, help him pressure the Penns to revise their autocratic ways.

That is why it was a rude surprise to Franklin when, shortly after his arrival, he met Lord Granville, the president of the Privy Council, the group of top ministers who acted for the king. "You Americans have wrong ideas of the nature of your constitution," Lord Granville said. The instructions given to colonial governors were "the law of the land," and colonial legislatures had no right to ignore them. Franklin replied that "this was new doctrine to me." The colonial charters specified that the laws were to be made by the colonial assemblies, he argued; although the governors could veto them, they could not dictate them. "He assured me that I was totally mistaken," recalled Franklin, who was so alarmed that he wrote the conversation down verbatim as soon as he returned to Craven Street.[15]

Franklin's interpretation had merit. Years earlier, Parliament had rejected a clause that would give the power of law to governors' instructions. But the rebuke from Granville, who happened to be an in-law of the Penns, served as a warning that the Proprietors' interpretation had support in court circles.

A few days later, in August 1757, Franklin began a series of meetings with the primary Proprietor, Thomas Penn, and his brother Richard. He was already acquainted with Thomas, who had lived for a while in Philadelphia and even had bookplates printed at Franklin's shop (though Franklin's account books show he did not pay all of his bills). Initially, the sessions were cordial; both sides proclaimed their desire to be reasonable. But as Franklin later noted, "I suppose each party had its own idea of what should be meant by *reasonable*."[16]

The Penns asked for the Assembly's case in writing, which Franklin produced in two days. Entitled "Heads of Complaint," Franklin's memo demanded that the appointed governor be allowed "use of his best discretion," and it called the Proprietors' demand to be exempt from the taxes that helped defend their land "unjust and cruel." More provocative than its substance was the informal style Franklin used; he did not address the paper to the Penns directly or use their correct title of "True and Absolute Proprietaries."

Offended by the snub, the Penns advised Franklin that he should henceforth deal only through their lawyer, Ferdinand John Paris. Franklin refused. He considered Paris a "proud, angry man," who had developed a "mortal enmity" toward him. The impasse served the Proprietors' ends; for a year they avoided giving any response while waiting for legal rulings from the government's lawyers.[17]

Franklin's famous ability to be calm and congenial abandoned him at a rancorous meeting with Thomas Penn in January 1758. At issue was Penn's right to veto the Assembly's appointment of a set of commissioners to deal with the Indians. But Franklin used the meeting to assert the broader claim that the Assembly had powers in Pennsylvania comparable to those that Parliament had in Britain. He argued that Penn's revered father, William Penn, had expressly given such rights to Pennsylvania's Assembly in his 1701 "Charter of Privileges" granted to the colonists.

Thomas replied that the royal charter held by his father did not give him the power to make such a grant. "If my father granted privileges he was not by the royal charter empowered to grant," Penn said, "nothing can be claimed by such a grant."

Franklin replied, "If then your father had no right to grant the privileges he pretended to grant, and published all over Europe as granted, those who came to settle in the province . . . were deceived, cheated and betrayed."

"The royal charter was no secret," Penn responded. "If they were deceived, it was their own fault."

Franklin was not entirely correct. William Penn's 1701 charter in fact declared that the Pennsylvania Assembly would have the "power and privileges of an assembly, according to the rights of the free-born subjects of England, and as is usual in any of the King's Plantations in America," and thus was subject to some interpretation. Franklin was nevertheless furious. In a vivid description of the row, written to Assembly Speaker Isaac Norris, Franklin used words that would later, when the letter leaked public, destroy any chance he had to be an effective lobbyist with the Proprietors: "[Penn spoke] with a kind of triumphing, laughing insolence, such as a low jockey might do when a purchaser complained that he had cheated him in a horse. I was astonished to see him thus meanly give up his father's character, and conceived at that moment a more cordial and thorough contempt for him than I have ever before felt for any man living."

Franklin found his face growing warm, his temper starting to rise. So he was careful to say little that would betray his emotions. "I made no other answer," he recalled, "than that the poor people were no lawyers themselves, and confiding in his father, did not think it necessary to consult any."[18]

The venomous meeting was a turning point in Franklin's mission. Penn refused any further personal negotiations, described Franklin as looking like a "malicious villain," and declared that "from this time I will not have any conversation with him on any pretence." Whenever they subsequently ran into one another, Franklin reported, "there appears in his wretched countenance a strange mixture of hatred, anger, fear and vexation."

Abandoning his usual pragmatism, Franklin began to vent his anger to allies back in Pennsylvania. "My patience with the Proprietors is almost, though not quite, spent," he wrote his Pennsylvania ally Joseph Galloway. He was, along with his son, preparing to publish a history of the Pennsylvania disputes, one "in which the Proprietors will be gibbeted up as they deserve, to rot and stink in the nostrils of posterity."[19]

Franklin's ability to act as an agent was thus pretty much over, at least for the time being. He was nevertheless still able to provide his Philadelphia friends with inside intelligence, such as advance word that the Penns were planning to fire Gov. William Denny, who had violated his instructions by allowing a compromise that taxed the Proprietary estates. "It was to have been kept a secret from me," he wrote Deborah, adding with a bit of Poor Richard's wit: "So you may make a secret of it too, if you please, and oblige all your friends with it."

He also was effective, as he had been since a teenager, at using the press to wage a propaganda campaign. Writing anonymously in Strahan's paper, the London *Chronicle,* he decried the actions of the Penns as being contrary to the interests of Britain. A letter signed by William Franklin, but clearly written with the help of his father, attacked the Penns more personally, and it was reprinted in a book on the history of Pennsylvania that Franklin helped compile.[20]

As the summer of 1758 approached, Franklin faced two choices: he could return home to his family, as planned, but his mission would have been a failure. Or he could, instead, spend his time traveling through England and enjoying the acclaim he found among his intellectual admirers.

There is no sign that Franklin found it a difficult decision. "I have no prospect of returning until next Spring," he reported to Deborah rather coolly that June. He would spend the summer, he reported, wandering the countryside. "I depend chiefly on these intended journeys for the establishment of my health." As for Deborah's complaints about her own health, Franklin was only mildly solicitous: "It gives me concern to receive such frequent accounts of your being indisposed; but we both of us grow in years, and must expect our constitutions, though tolerably good in themselves, will by degrees give way to the infirmities of age."

His letters remained, as always, kindly and chatty but hardly romantic. They tended to be paternalistic, perhaps a bit condescending at times, and they were certainly not as intellectually engaging as those to his sister Jane Mecom or Polly Stevenson. But they do convey some genuine fondness and even devotion. He appreciated Deborah's sensible practicality and the accommodating nature of their partnership. And for the most part, she seemed accepting of the arrangement they had made long ago and generally content about staying ensconced in her comfortable home and familiar neighborhood, rather than having to follow him on his far-flung travels. Their correspondence contained, until near the end, only occasional reproaches from either side, and he dutifully provided gossip, instructions about how to dismantle his lightning rod bells, and some old-fashioned advice about women and politics. "You are very prudent not to engage in party disputes," he wrote at one point. "Women should never meddle in them except in endeavors to reconcile their husbands, brothers and friends, who happen to be on contrary sides. If your sex can keep cool, you may be a means of cooling ours the sooner."

Franklin was likewise solicitous, but again only mildly so, about the daughter he had left behind. He expressed his happiness at receiving a portrait of Sally, and he sent her a white hat and cloak, some sundries, and a buckle made of French paste stones. "They cost three guineas, and are said to be cheap at that price," he wrote. If he felt the tug of his family, it was not particularly strong, because he had a mirror one in London. As he noted in a cavalier postscript to a rambling letter to Deborah that June, "Mrs. Stevenson and her daughter desire me to present their respects."[21]

WILLIAM AND THE FAMILY TREE

William Franklin, perhaps in reaction to being referred to regularly by his family's enemies as a base-born bastard, had a yearning for social status that was far greater than his father's. Among the most thumbed of his books was one titled *The True Conduct of Persons of Quality*, and in London he liked to frequent the fashionable homes of the young earls and dukes instead of the coffeehouses and intellectual salons favored by his father. Both in his social world and in his legal studies at the Inns of Court, where his father enrolled him, William would eventually be tugged toward a more Tory and loyalist outlook. But the change would be gradual, fitful, and filled with personal conflicts.

Before leaving Philadelphia, William had been courting a well-born young debutante named Elizabeth Graeme. Her father, Dr. Thomas Graeme, a physician and member of the Governor's Council, owned a grand home on Society Hill and a three-hundred-acre country estate considered the finest in the Philadelphia area. Her mother was the stepdaughter of Benjamin Franklin's unreliable patron Governor Keith. The relationship between the Graemes and the Franklins was strained; Dr. Graeme had felt insulted when the elder Franklin did not initially enlist him to run the staff of the new Philadelphia Hospital, and he was a close friend of the Penn family in its struggle with the Assembly.

Nevertheless, with the grudging assent of Dr. Graeme, the relationship had progressed to the point where Elizabeth tentatively accepted William's offer of marriage. She was 18, he close to ten years older. It came with a stipulation: William would withdraw from any involvement in politics. She refused, however, to accompany him to London or to marry him before he left. They would, both agreed, await his return to be married.

Once in England, William's ardor for her apparently cooled far more than his ardor for politics. After a short note on his arrival, he did not write her again for five months. Gone were the flowery clichés he had once penned about their love, replaced instead with descriptions of the joy of "this bewitching country." Worse yet, he proudly sent her the political screed he had signed in the London *Chronicle* attacking the Proprietors, and he went so far as to solicit her opinion of how the article was received back in Philadelphia.

Thus ended the relationship. She waited months before sending a cold and bitter response, which labeled him "a collection of party malice." The next day he replied, through a mutual friend, that the fault lay with her fickleness and he would be glad to see her find happiness with another man. For his part, William was finding his own happiness, both with the fashionable ladies of London and, too much his father's son, occasionally with prostitutes and other women of low repute.[22]

Benjamin Franklin, who had mixed emotions about the relationship, seemed unfazed by the breakup. His own hope was that his son would marry Polly Stevenson. There was little chance of that, as William's social aspirations were higher than those of his father. Indeed, William was developing social and financial airs that had begun to worry Franklin. So he began an effort, which would later become a theme in the section of his autobiography that was written ostensibly as a letter to his son, to restrain William from putting on upper-class pretensions. It would ultimately prove futile and become, as much as politics, a cause of their estrangement.

Years earlier, Franklin had warned William not to expect much of an inheritance. "I have assured him that I intend to spend what little I have myself," he wrote his own mother. Once in England, Franklin kept a meticulous account of all of William's expenses—including meals, lodging, clothing, and books—with the understanding that they were advances that must someday be repaid. By 1758, even as he was pampering himself a bit with a carriage at Pennsylvania's expense, Franklin was warning his son to be more frugal on meals and to avoid becoming attached to a high style of London living. William, who was traveling with friends in the south of England, was cowed. "I am extremely obliged to you for your care in supplying me with money," he wrote, adding that he had changed his lodgings for something "much for the worse, though cheaper."[23]

As part of his effort to keep his son rooted in his "middling" heritage, Franklin took him on a genealogical excursion during the summer of 1758. They traveled to Ecton, about sixty miles northwest of London, where generations of Franklins had lived before Josiah had migrated to America. Still living nearby was Franklin's first cousin Mary Franklin Fisher, daughter of Josiah's brother Thomas. She was "weak with age," Franklin noted, but "seems to have been a very smart, sensible woman."

At the parish church, the Franklins uncovered two hundred years of birth, marriage, and death records of their family. The rector's wife entertained them with stories of Franklin's uncle Thomas, whose life bore some resemblance to that of his nephew. As Franklin reported to Deborah:

> [Thomas Franklin was] a very leading man in all county affairs, and much employed in public business. He set on foot a subscription for erecting chimes in their steeple, and completed it, and we heard them play. He found out an easy method of saving their village meadows from being drowned, as they used to be sometimes by the river, which method is still in being . . . His advice and opinion were sought for on all occasions, by all sorts of people, and he was looked upon, she said, by some, as something of a conjuror. He died just four years before I was born, on the same day of the same month."

Franklin may have noted that the description "conjuror" was the same that Caty Ray had once used about him. And William, impressed by the coincidence of dates, surmised that a "transmigration" had occurred.

At the cemetery, as William copied data from the gravestones, Franklin's servant, Peter, used a hard brush to scour off the moss. Franklin's account of the scene is a reminder that, as enlightened as he would eventually become, he had brought with him to England two slaves. He viewed them, however, more as old family servants than as property. When one of them left soon after they arrived in England, Franklin did not try to force his return, as British law would have allowed. His response to Deborah, when she asked about their welfare later, is revealing:

> Peter continues with me, and behaves as well as I can expect in a
> country where there are many occasions of spoiling servants, if they are

ever so good. He has as few faults as most of them, [but I see them] with only one eye and hear with only one ear; so we rub on pretty comfortably. King, that you enquire after, is not with us. He ran away from our house, near two years ago, while we were absent in the country; but was soon found in Suffolk, where he had been taken in the service of a lady that was very fond of the merit of making him a Christian and contributing to his education and improvement.[24]

As he felt about Peter, so too he felt about slavery for the time being: he saw the faults with only one eye, heard them with only one ear, and rubbed along pretty comfortably, though increasingly less so. The evolution of his views on slavery and race was indeed continuing. He would soon be elected to the board of an English charitable group, the Associates of Dr. Bray, dedicated to building schools for blacks in the colonies.

With William in tow, Franklin spent that spring and summer of 1758 wandering England to soak up the hospitality and acclaim of his intellectual admirers. On a visit to Cambridge University, he conducted a series of experiments on evaporation with the renowned chemist John Hadley. Franklin had previously studied how liquids produce different refrigeration effects based on how quickly they evaporate. With Hadley he experimented using ether, which evaporates very quickly. In a 65-degree room, they repeatedly coated a thermometer bulb with ether and used a bellows to evaporate it. "We continued this operation, one of us wetting the ball, and another of the company blowing on it with the bellows to quicken the evaporation, the mercury sinking all the time until it came down to 7, which is 25 degrees below the freezing point," Franklin wrote. "From this experiment one may see the possibility of freezing a man to death on a warm summer's day." He also speculated, correctly, that summer breezes do not by themselves cool people; instead, the cooling effect comes from the increased evaporation of human perspiration caused by the breeze.

His study of heat and refrigeration, though not as seminal as his work on electricity, continued throughout his life. In addition to his evaporation experiments, they included further studies of how different colors absorb heat from light, how materials such as metal that conduct electricity are also good at transmitting heat, and how to bet-

ter design stoves. As usual, his strength was devising not abstract theories but practical applications that could improve everyday life.[25]

His visit to Cambridge made such an impression that he was invited back later that summer to view the university's commencement.
"My vanity was not a little gratified by the particular regard shown
me," he admitted to Deborah. But that regard was not awaiting him
when he returned to London in the fall.[26]

THE PENNS RESPOND

In November 1758, more than a year after Franklin had submitted
his "Heads of Complaint," the Penns finally responded. Snubbing
Franklin, they had their lawyer, Ferdinand Paris, write directly to the
Pennsylvania Assembly, with a copy to Franklin, and then followed
with a letter of their own to the Assembly.

On the issue of the Assembly's power, the Proprietors held firm:
their instructions to their governors were inviolable, and the charter
"gives the power to make laws to the Proprietary." The Assembly
could provide only "advice and consent." On the issue of taxation,
however, the Penns held open the possibility of some compromise.
"They are very ready to have the annual income of their estate inquired into," Paris wrote, and consider some contributions based on
what "is in its nature taxable."

The murky response, which offered no concrete assurances of any
real money, prompted Franklin to write seeking clarification. But a key
aspect of the Proprietors' position was that they would not deal with
him anymore. Paris pointedly told the Assembly that they had not
chosen a "person of candor" to be their agent. And the Penns, in their
own letter, said that further negotiations would require "a very different representation." To emphasize the point, Paris visited Franklin
personally to deliver the Penns' message that "we do not think it necessary to keep up a correspondence with a gentleman who acknowl-
edges he is not empowered to conclude proper measures." Franklin
"answered not a word," Paris reported, and "looked as if much disappointed."

"Thus a final end is put to all further negotiation between them and me," Franklin wrote Assembly Speaker Norris. His mission stymied, he could have returned home and let others work out the details of a compromise on taxation. So he made a halfhearted offer to resign. "The House will see," he wrote Norris, "that if they propose to continue treating with the Proprietors, it will be necessary to recall me and appoint another person or persons for that service who are likely to be more acceptable or more pliant than I am, or, as the Proprietors express it, persons of candor."

But Franklin did not recommend this approach. His usual pragmatic instincts fell prey to sentiments he had once tried to train himself to avoid, such as bitterness, wounded pride, emotionalism, and political fervor. He proposed, instead, a radically different alternative: attempting to take Pennsylvania away from the Penns and turning it into a Crown colony under the king and his ministers. "If the House, grown at length sensible of the dangers to the liberties of the people necessarily arising from such growing power and property in one family with such principles, shall think it expedient to have the government and property in different hands, and for that purpose shall desire that the Crown would take the province into its immediate care, I believe that point might without much difficulty be carried." With some eagerness he concluded, "In that I think I could still do service."[27]

There was no reason to believe that England's ministers would meddle with the Proprietary charter or strike a blow for democracy in the colonies. So why did Franklin fixate on an ill-considered, and ill-fated, crusade to turn Pennsylvania into a royal colony? Part of the problem was that his animosity toward the Penns had blurred his peripheral vision. To the Yale historian Edmund Morgan, this "prolonged fit of political blindness" seems surprising, even puzzling. "Franklin's preoccupation, not to say obsession, with the Proprietary prerogatives not only wasted his immense talents but obscured his vision and his perceptions of what was politically feasible," he writes.

Yet Franklin's actions can be explained, at least partly, by his enthusiasm for the glory of the king's growing empire. "Once we fully accept the fact that Franklin between 1760 and 1764 was an enthusiastic and unabashed royalist who did not and could not foresee the breakup of the Empire, then much of the surprise, confusion and mystery of his behavior in these years falls away," argues Brown University professor Gordon Wood.[28]

Others in America were quicker than Franklin to realize that it was the prevailing attitude among most British leaders, and not merely the Proprietors, that the colonies ought to be subservient both politically and economically. Franklin's allies in the Pennsylvania Assembly, however, shared his belief that the struggle was with the Proprietors, and they agreed he should stay to fight them. So, with no personal desire to leave England, he launched assaults against the Penns on three fronts.

The first involved the Penns' handling of Indian affairs. Franklin had long been sympathetic to the rights of the Indians, especially the Delawares, who felt that the Penns had cheated them of land. In the fall of 1758, he submitted a brief on the Delawares' behalf to the Privy Council. In it, he echoed his use of the phrase "low jockey" that he knew had already enraged the Penns. The Penns, he wrote, had extended their holdings "by such arts of jockeyship [that] gave the Indians the worst of opinions of the English." Little came of Franklin's advocacy, but he helped publicize the case to score propaganda points against the way the Penns managed their colony.[29]

Franklin's second line of attack involved a libel case the Pennsylvania Assembly had won against William Smith, the provost of the Academy who had become Franklin's political adversary. When Smith appealed to the Privy Council in London for a reversal, Franklin turned the case into a larger struggle on behalf of the Assembly's rights. Ferdinand Paris represented Smith, arguing that "the Assembly of Pennsylvania was not a Parliament nor had anything near so much power as the House of Commons had." In June 1759, the Privy Council ruled against Franklin. On a narrow point, it noted that the Assembly in question had adjourned and a new one been voted in, so the current Assembly had no case. More ominously, it noted that "inferior assemblies" like those in the colonies "must not be compared in power or privileges to the House of Commons."[30]

On the third issue Franklin was somewhat more successful. It involved the case of Gov. William Denny, who had violated his instruction in a number of cases by approving bills that taxed the Proprietors' estates. The Penns, alleging with some evidence that Denny had been bribed, not only recalled him but also appealed to the Privy Council to have the bills nullified.

An initial advisory opinion by the Board of Trade went against Franklin and the Assembly. But something surprising happened when the Privy Council heard the appeal. Lord Mansfield, a member of the Council, beckoned Franklin to join him in the clerk's office while the lawyers were arguing. Was he really of the opinion that the taxes could be levied in such a way that did not injure the Penn estates?

"Certainly," Franklin replied.

"Then," said Lord Mansfield, "you can have little objection to enter into an engagement to assure that point."

"None at all," said Franklin.

Thus a compromise was reached. Franklin agreed that the Assembly's tax bill would exclude the "unsurveyed wastelands" belonging to the Proprietors and would tax unsettled land at a rate "no higher than similar land owned by others." By reverting to his old pragmatism, Franklin had won a partial victory. But the compromise did not settle permanently the issue of the Assembly's power, nor did it restore harmony between it and the Proprietors.[31]

The compromise also did nothing to further Franklin's crusade to strip the Penns of their proprietorship of Pennsylvania. Quite the contrary. In all of its rulings, the Privy Council showed no inclination to alter the charter of the Proprietors, nor had Franklin succeeded in whipping up any public support for such a course. Once again, he faced a situation in which there was little more he could achieve in England and no real reason he could not return home. Yet once again, Franklin felt no inclination to leave.

"DENSEST HAPPINESS"

Among Franklin's greatest joys were his summer travels. In 1759, he and William went to Scotland, their path paved with introductions to the intellectual elite from William Strahan and John Pringle, both Edinburgh natives. He stayed at the manor of Sir Alexander Dick, a renowned physician and scientist, and there met the greats of the

Scottish Enlightenment: the economist Adam Smith, the philosopher David Hume, and the jurist and historian Lord Kames.

One night at dinner, Franklin regaled the guests with one of his best literary hoaxes, a biblical chapter he fabricated called the Parable against Persecution. It told of Abraham giving food and shelter to a 198-year-old man, then throwing him out when he said he did not believe in Abraham's God. The parable concluded:

> And at midnight God called upon Abraham, saying, Abraham where is the stranger?
> And Abraham answered and said, Lord, he would not worship thee; neither would he call upon thy name. Therefore have I driven him out before my face into the wilderness.
> And God said, Have I borne with him these hundred ninety and eight years, and nourished him, and clothed him, notwithstanding his rebellion against me, and couldst thou not, that art thyself a sinner, bear with him one night?[32]

The guests, charmed by Franklin and his philosophy of tolerance, asked him to send them copies, which he did. It was also at this time that Franklin wrote Hume about the tale of the dispute over a Maypole, which involved a Lord Mareschal who had been asked to opine on whether all forms of damnation were for eternity. Franklin compared it to the plight of a mayor in a Puritan Massachusetts village who was called on to resolve a dispute between those who wanted to erect a Maypole and others who considered it blasphemous:

> He heard their altercation with great patience, and then gravely determined thus: You that are for having no Maypole shall have no Maypole; and you that are for having a Maypole shall have a Maypole. Get about your business and let me hear no more of this quarrel. So methinks Lord Mareschal might say: You that are for no more damnation than is proportioned to your offenses, have my consent that it may be so; and you that are for being damned eternally, G——d eternally d——n you all, and let me hear no more of your disputes.[33]

David Hume was the greatest British philosopher of his era and one of the most important logical and analytic thinkers of all time. He had already written the two seminal tracts, *A Treatise of Human Nature* and *Essays Concerning Human Understanding,* that are now considered among the most important works in the development of empirical thought, placing him in the pantheon with Locke and Berkeley. When Franklin met him, he was completing the six-volume *History of England* that would make him rich and famous.

Franklin assiduously courted him and helped convert him to the colonial cause. "I am not a little pleased to hear of your change of sentiments in some particulars relating to America," Franklin subsequently wrote him, adding as flattery, "I know no one that has it more in his power to rectify" the British misunderstandings. Of one of Hume's essays favoring free trade with the colonies, Franklin enthused that it would have "a good effect in promoting a certain interest too little thought of by selfish man . . . I mean the interest of humanity, or common good of mankind."

Franklin and Hume also shared an interest in language. When Hume berated him for coining new words, Franklin agreed to quit using the terms "colonize" and "unshakeable." But he lamented that "I cannot but wish the usage of our tongue permitted making new words when we want them." For example, Franklin argued, the word "inaccessible" was not nearly as good as coining a new word such as "uncomeatable." Hume's response to this suggestion is unknown, but it did nothing to diminish his ardent admiration for his new friend. "America has sent us many good things, gold, silver, sugar, tobacco, indigo," he wrote back. "But you are the first philosopher, and indeed the first great man of letters, for whom we are beholden to her."[34]

During his visit to Scotland, Franklin also became friends with Henry Home, Lord Kames, whose interests ranged from farming and science to literary criticism and history. Among the things they discussed on their horseback rides through the countryside was the need for Britain to keep control of Canada, which had been wrested from the French earlier that year when an Anglo-American force captured Quebec in one of the decisive battles of the French and Indian War. Franklin pushed the case "not merely as I am a colonist, but as I am a Briton." As he wrote Kames soon after his departure, "The future grandeur and stability of the British Empire lie in America." For all his problems with the Penns, he had not yet turned into a rebel.

The visit to Scotland was capped by Franklin's acceptance of an honorary doctorate from the University of St. Andrews. As the crimson silk and white satin robe was draped over his shoulder, Franklin was read a citation praising "the rectitude of his morals and sweetness of his life and conversation." It added, "By his ingenious inventions and successful experiments, with which he has enriched the science of natural philosophy and more especially of electricity which heretofore was little known, [he has] acquired so much praise throughout the world as to deserve the greatest honors in the Republic of Letters." Thereafter, he was often referred to, even by himself, as Dr. Franklin.

The time he spent in Scotland, he wrote Lord Kames on his way home, "was six weeks of the densest happiness I have met with in any part of my life." This was, perhaps, a small exaggeration. But it helped explain why he was not hurrying back to Philadelphia.[35]

Indeed, by early 1760, Franklin was beginning to harbor some hope that Deborah and Sally would join him in England. His dream, now that he realized William was unlikely to marry Polly Stevenson, was another middle-class union: to have Sally marry William Strahan's son Billy. It was a match he had fantasized about when Sally was a mere toddler and Strahan was someone he knew only through his letters. Although arranged marriages were no longer prevalent, they were not uncommon, and Strahan proposed in writing a plan to unite their children. Franklin passed it along to Deborah tentatively, assuming that it was unlikely to entice her over:

> I received the enclosed some time since from Mr. Strahan. I afterwards spent an evening in conversation with him on the subject. He was very urgent with me to stay in England and prevail with you to move hither with Sally. He proposed several advantageous schemes to me which appeared reasonably founded. His family is a very agreeable one; Mrs. Strahan a sensible and good woman, the children of amiable characters and particularly the young man, who is sober, ingenious and industrious, and a desirable person.
>
> In point of circumstances there can be no objection, Mr. Strahan being in so thriving a way as to lay up a thousand pounds every year

from the profits of his business, after maintaining his family and paying all charges . . . I gave him, however, two reasons why I could not think of removing hither. One my affection to Pennsylvania, and long established friendships and other connections there. The other your invincible aversion to crossing the seas.

Sally was almost 17, and the union held out the promise of a comfortable life in a smart and fun circle. But Franklin left the decision up to his wife. "I thanked him for the regard shown us in the proposal, but gave him no expectation that I should forward the letters," he wrote. "So you are at liberty to answer or not as you think proper." There is no indication that Deborah was tempted in the least.[36]

As for William, Franklin was not only a bad matchmaker, he was an even worse role model. Around this time, probably in February 1760, William followed in his father's steps by siring an illegitimate son, William Temple Franklin, known as Temple. His mother was apparently a woman of the streets who (like William's own mother) seems never to have been heard from again. William accepted paternity, but instead of promptly finding a wife and taking him home (as his own father had done), he sent the child to be raised secretly by a foster family.[37]

Temple would eventually become a treasured grandchild to Benjamin Franklin, who oversaw his education and then brought him under his wing as a personal secretary. Later, when his grandfather and father were on opposite sides during the Revolutionary War, Temple would become a pawn in a heart-wrenching struggle for his loyalty and devotion, one that Benjamin Franklin would win at great personal cost. But for the time being, he was kept out of sight while William enjoyed the social whirl of London and more excursions with his celebrated father.

The most memorable was a trip to the continent in the summer of 1761. Because Britain was still at war with France, they traveled instead to Holland and Flanders. Franklin noted with pleasure that the observance of religion there was not as strict as in America, especially when it came to observing Sundays as the Sabbath. "In the afternoon, both high and low went to the play or the opera, where there was plenty of singing, fiddling and dancing," he reported to a Connecticut friend. "I looked around for God's judgments but saw no signs of them." He concluded, with a touch of amusement, that this provided evidence that the Lord did not care so much about preventing pleasure on the Sabbath as the strict Puritans would have people believe. The happiness and prosperity in Flanders, he wrote, "would almost make one suspect that the Deity is not so angry at that offense as a New England justice."

Franklin's fame as a scientist meant that he was celebrated wherever he went. In Brussels, Prince Charles of Lorrains showed them the equipment he had bought to replicate Franklin's electricity experiments. And in Leyden, a meeting of the world's two great electricians occurred: Franklin spent time with Pieter van Musschenbroek, inventor of the Leyden jar. The professor said he was about to publish a book that would make use of a letter Franklin had sent him about electricity, but alas, he died just two weeks after the Franklins left.[38]

CANADA AND EMPIRE

Franklin cut short his trip to the continent to come back to London to attend the coronation of King George III in September 1761. Still very much a proud British royalist, he harbored high hopes for the new king and fancied that he might protect the colonies from the tyranny of the Proprietors.

In America, the French and Indian War had pretty much ended, with England and her colonies capturing control of Canada and many of the Caribbean sugar islands belonging to France and Spain. In Europe, however, the broader struggle between Britain and France, known as the Seven Years' War, would not be resolved until a Treaty of Paris was signed in 1763. Franklin's ardor for the expansion of the king's empire led him to continue his crusade to convince Britain to keep control of Canada, rather than cede it back to France in return for some Caribbean islands as part of a negotiated settlement. In an anonymous article in Strahan's London *Chronicle,* he used his old trick of parody and produced ten facetious reasons why Canada *should* be restored to France. Among them:

We should restore Canada because an uninterrupted trade with the Indians throughout a vast country, where the communication by water is so easy, would increase our commerce, already too great . . .

We should restore it lest, through a greater plenty of beaver, broad-brimmed hats become cheaper to that unmannerly sect, the Quakers.

We should restore Canada that we may soon have another war, and another opportunity of spending two or three millions a year in America, there being great danger of our growing too rich.

On a far more serious note, he produced a fifty-eight-page pamphlet entitled "The Interest of Great Britain Considered with Regard to Her Colonies," in which he argued that keeping control of Canada would benefit the British Empire and help protect its American colonies from constant harassment by the French and their Indian allies. "To leave the French in possession of Canada when it is in our power to remove them," he wrote, "seems neither safe nor prudent."

The pamphlet dwelled in great detail on the issue of Canada, but it also raised an even more important topic: the relationship between Britain and her colonies. Franklin wrote as a man who was still a loyal, indeed an ardent, supporter of the empire, "happy as we now are under the best of Kings." The inhabitants of the colonies, he argued, were "anxious for the glory of her crown, the extent of her power and commerce, the welfare and future repose of the whole British people." The best way to assure continued harmony, he wrote, was to provide safe and abundant land so that the colonies could expand.

Franklin had a theory about the underlying cause of the growing friction between Britain and her colonies, one that he first expressed nine years earlier in his "Observations Concerning the Increase of Mankind." The conflicts, he believed, grew from the attitude of the British mercantilists, who had something in common with the Proprietors: they viewed the colonies as a market to be exploited. Consequently, they opposed the development of manufacturing in the colonies as well as greater rights of self-government. In the pamphlet, he noted his fear that this attitude could even provoke "the future independence of our colonies."

The best way to make America prosperous without turning it into a manufacturing center, Franklin said, was to keep Canada and thus

assure there was always an abundance of land for the colonists to settle. "No man who can have a piece of land of his own, sufficient by his
labor to subsist his family in plenty, is poor enough to be a manufacturer and work for a master," he wrote. "Hence while there is enough
land in America for our people, there can never be manufacturers of
any amount or value." An expanding America would thus always provide a market for British goods.

He also argued that, as long as Britain avoided "tyranny and oppression," there was no danger of the colonies rebelling. "While the
government is mild and just, while important civil and religious rights
are secure, such subjects will be dutiful and obedient." Then he provided a metaphor that drew from his studies of turbulent waters: "The
waves do not rise, but when the winds blow."

Britain would therefore be best served, he concluded, by treating
the people of the colonies as full citizens of the empire, with the same
liberties and rights and economic aspirations. He would, in the end,
fail to sell the British ministry on this expansive vision of imperial harmony. But he and others who argued for Britain's retention of Canada
did prevail.[39]

BITTERSWEET FAREWELL

In the summer of 1762, five years after his arrival, Franklin finally
decided it was time to return home. He was torn. He loved his life in
England, both the acclaim (he had just been awarded an honorary
doctorate at Oxford) and the friends and surrogate family he had
made.

But the decision was made a bit easier because he assumed that he
would soon be back. "The attraction of *reason* is at present for the
other side of the water, but that of *inclination* will be for this side," he
wrote Strahan. "You know which usually prevails." Indeed, his inclination to be in England would prevail again within two years. He was,
however, too optimistic about both his personal and public life when
he added, "I shall probably make but this one vibration and settle here
forever. Nothing will prevent it if I can, as I hope I can, prevail with
Mrs. F. to accompany me."[40]

William was ready to return as well, and he needed a job. He had applied for appointment as deputy secretary of North Carolina and inquired about opportunities in the customs service and the Caribbean. But luck and good connections ended up producing something surprisingly better. The royal governor of New Jersey had just been recalled, and his presumed replacement decided to decline the post. Acting quietly to avoid alerting the Penns, William successfully lobbied for the job with the help of his father's friend John Pringle, who was the doctor and close adviser of the new prime minister, Lord Bute. When news of the pending appointment became public, the Penns surreptitiously tried to derail it by spreading word that he was a bastard, but to no avail.

William's appointment was partly an attempt by Bute and others to assure the loyalty of William's famous father, but there is no sign that the elder Franklin did much to help his son. Years later, Franklin would tell his friends in France that he had tried to dissuade his son from pursuing the post, or any appointed patronage position, by telling him of the time as a child when he had paid too much for a whistle. "Think of what the whistle may one day cost you," he said to William. "Why not become a joiner or a wheelwright, if the estate I leave you is not enough? The man who lives by his labor is at least free." William, however, had become infatuated with the title "excellency" as a way to emerge from his father's shadow.[41]

In possession of a public job, William was in need of a wife. So, at the same time he was securing his appointment, he was making plans to marry a sweet and well-born planter's daughter, Elizabeth Downes, a fixture of high Tory society whom he had met at the balls of London. His father had trouble extinguishing all hope that William would marry Polly Stevenson, but he finally gave his "consent and approbation" to the marriage.

In a letter to his sister Jane, Franklin professed to be pleased by William's new appointment and even more by his marriage. "The lady is of so amiable a character that the latter gives me more pleasure than the former, though I have no doubt but that he will make as good a governor as husband, for he has good principles and good dispositions, and I think is not deficient in good understanding." Yet Franklin, usually so fond of younger ladies and surrogate family members, did not warm up to Elizabeth, and never would.

Franklin was, in fact, unenthusiastic about, perhaps even bothered by, his son's successes. William's marriage to an upper-class woman was a declaration of independence, and his appointment as governor meant he was no longer subservient to his father. Indeed, it meant that William, then about 31, would have a station in life higher than his father's, one that would likely reinforce his son's unattractive tendency to adopt elitist airs and pretenses.

A cloud was coming over the horizon, and there was no lightning rod to defuse its emotional charge. The first signs of the tension that would develop between father and son came when Franklin decided to sail from England without him on August 24, 1762—the very day the news of William's pending appointment appeared in the papers and less than two weeks before his scheduled wedding. On September 4, William married Elizabeth Downes at the fashionable St. George's Church on Hanover Square, without his father in attendance. A few days later, he went to St. James's Palace, where he kissed the ring of young King George III and received his royal commission. His father, who had rushed back to London from Flanders a year earlier to witness George III's coronation, was not there. Then William and Elizabeth sailed for New Jersey, leaving William's secret son, Temple, behind in England.

With the cool detachment he could display toward his family, Franklin never expressed any sorrow or apologies for missing these momentous events in his son's life. In his parting letter to Polly Stevenson, on the other hand, he expressed great emotion and regret that she had not become his daughter-in-law. Writing from a "wretched inn" in Portsmouth, using the third person, he lamented that he "once flattered himself" that she "might become his own in the tender relation of a child, but can now entertain such pleasing hopes no more." Yet, though his son had not married her, Franklin promised that his paternal love would be undiminished. With more emotion than he ever used in his letters to his real daughter, he bid Polly farewell. "Adieu, my dearest child: I will call you so. Why should I not call you so, since I love you with all the tenderness, all the fondness of a father?"[42]

Franklin's mission to London had produced mixed results. The dispute over taxing the Proprietors had reached a compromise for the moment, and the end of the French and Indian War had calmed the larger disagreements over raising funds for colonial defense. Unresolved, however, was the underlying question of colonial governance. For Franklin, who saw himself equally as a Briton and an American, the answer was obvious. The powers of the colonial assemblies should evolve to mirror those of Parliament, and Englishmen on either side of the ocean should enjoy the same liberties. After five years in England, however, he had begun to realize that the Penns were not the only ones who saw things differently.

On his voyage home, Franklin resumed his study of the calming effect of oil on water, this time with more disturbing metaphorical implications. The lanterns aboard his ship had a thick layer of oil that floated atop a layer of water. The surface was always calm and flat, so viewed from above, it would seem that the oil had stilled the roiling water. But when the lantern was viewed from the side, so that both layers could be seen, it became evident that, as Franklin recorded, "the water under the oil was in great commotion." Even though oil could give the appearance of stilling turbulence, the water beneath the surface was still "rising and falling in irregular waves." This underlying turbulence, Franklin realized, was not something that could easily be calmed, even by the most judicious application of oil.[43]

CHAPTER NINE

HOME LEAVE

Philadelphia, 1763–1764

THE PERIPATETIC POSTMASTER

When William Franklin arrived in Philadelphia in February 1763, three months after his father's arrival, any tension between the two men quickly dissipated. He and his new wife stayed four days at Franklin's house, recovering from their frightful winter crossing, and then father and son set off for New Jersey. The local gentry came out in sleighs to escort them to Perth Amboy, a tiny village of two hundred homes, during a driving snowstorm. After William took his oath of office there, they traveled to repeat the ceremony in the colony's other capital, Burlington, where the festivities concluded "with bonfires, ringing of bells, firing of guns."

In Philadelphia, Franklin's enemies were appalled that his son had won a royal appointment. But Proprietor Thomas Penn, writing from London, suggested it might have a calming effect. "I am told you will find Mr. Franklin more tractable, and I believe we shall," he said. "His son must obey instructions, and what he is ordered to do the father cannot well oppose in Pennsylvania."[1]

That would turn out to be wishful thinking, because Franklin (at least for the time being) saw a distinction between instructions issued by the Proprietor and those issued by the king. Nevertheless, his first year back in America would be a peaceful one. He was, indeed, far more tractable about Pennsylvania politics—partly because he was less engaged by politics, and partly because he was less engaged by life in Pennsylvania. Always invigorated by travel and the pursuit of diverse interests, and clearly not wedded to the hearth and home he had forsaken for five years, Franklin left in April on a seven-month, 1,780-mile postal inspection tour that took him from Virginia to New Hampshire.

In Virginia, he performed one of those acts of quiet generosity that led him to have, even in controversial times, more loyal friends than enemies. His partner as colonial postmaster, William Hunter, had died, leaving a destitute illegitimate son. Franklin was asked by one of Hunter's friends to take care of the boy and oversee his education. It was a difficult assignment, and Franklin expressed some reluctance. "Like other older men, I begin in most things to consult my ease," he noted. "But I shall with pleasure undertake the charge you propose to me." With both an illegitimate son and grandson of his own, he was sensitive to the situation, and he noted that Hunter would have done the same for him.[2]

Franklin hoped that Hunter's death would mean that, after twenty-four years of service, he would become the sole postmaster in the colonies, as his original commission stipulated. That was not to be. Despite Franklin's ardent appeal to his superiors in London, Virginia's governor was able to secure the appointment of his secretary, John Foxcroft, as Franklin's new partner. Franklin's more collegial nature returned to the fore, and he forged a friendship with Foxcroft on his visit to Virginia. There was much work to be done. With Canada now part of the British Empire, they set up a system for extending mail delivery to Montreal. They also arranged for packet ships to the West Indies and for postal riders to travel at night. A letter sent from Philadelphia to Boston could receive a reply within six days, and a round-trip to New York could be done within twenty-four hours, a service that seems remarkable even now.

Foxcroft joined Franklin on a brief visit to Philadelphia, and then they left for New York and a tour of the northern post offices. Franklin ardently wanted Deborah to come. If she could learn to share his love for travel and curiosity about the world, he felt, she might even agree to accompany him to London someday. Not surprisingly, she again refused to be uprooted; she was as independent in her own way as he was in his. But their relationship was close enough that he gave her permission to open any mail he got from England, "as it must give you pleasure to see that people who knew me there so long and so intimately retain so sincere of a regard for me." There was more than vanity involved: the letters might, he hoped, soften her resistance to visiting England.[3]

In Deborah's stead, he took their daughter, Sally, then 19, on his tour. It would serve as her coming-out party. In New Jersey they stayed with William and Elizabeth, who took them to formal parties as well as pleasant excursions to the countryside. They then traveled by boat to Newport, where Sally had the pleasure (and it did indeed turn out to be that) of meeting her father's long-ago flirtation Caty, now Catherine Ray Greene, a married mother of two girls. (Never one to forget the women who had become parts of his extended family, he also exchanged letters with Polly Stevenson on the trip, noting that "the tender filial regard you constantly express for your old friend is particularly engaging.")[4]

Franklin dislocated his shoulder falling from his carriage, and Sally was willing to linger in Newport so that she and Caty could nurse him. But he was eager to press on to Boston. They stayed there for two months, Franklin living with his sister Jane Mecom and Sally with her cousins, who owned a harpsichord. "I would not have her lose her practice," Franklin explained to Jane, adding sweetly, "and then I shall be more with my dear sister."

During much of his stay in Boston, Franklin was confined to the house. He had suffered another fall, on a short trip to New Hampshire, and once again dislocated his shoulder. With most of his Boston relatives now dead, and his own stamina at age 57 diminished, his letters turned more reflective and less flirtatious. "I am not yet able to travel rough roads," he lamented to Caty. Nevertheless, he still harbored hopes of traveling to England again. "No friend can wish me more in England than I do myself," he wrote Strahan. "But before I go, everything I am concerned in must be settled here as to make another return to America unnecessary."[5]

When he got back to Philadelphia in November, he would find it harder than ever to settle affairs in a way that would allow him a sedentary retirement in England. More ferocious political turmoil, and four more crossings of the Atlantic, lay ahead. Franklin's seven-month tour of the colonies, along with the time he had spent in England, put him in a unique position to play a role in the coming storms. As a publishing magnate and then as a postmaster, he was one of the few to view America as a whole. To him, the colonies were not merely disparate entities. They were a new world with common interests and ideals.

During his postal trip, Franklin made plans and issued instructions for the construction of a new three-story brick home on Market Street, just steps from the spot where Deborah had first spotted him as a runaway lad. Since their common-law marriage in 1730, they had lived in at least six rented houses, but never one that they owned. Now, for the first time, they would have room to enjoy all the finery they had acquired since Deborah had bought him his first china breakfast bowl: the armonica and harpsichord, the stove and scientific equipment, the library and lace curtains.

Was Franklin becoming domesticated? In some ways, despite his love of travel and sometimes distant relationship to his own household, the aging runaway had always been a rather domestic soul, wherever he had lived. He loved his Junto and clubs, his regular routine, and the surrogate domestic arrangements he had made in England. He had also remained somewhat solicitous, even caring, about his wife and daughter, as well as his relatives, even as he indulged his wanderlust. Whether his new house was intended for his own enjoyment or mainly for that of his family was unclear, perhaps even to himself, but his love of projects led him to be deeply involved in all the details, down to the quality of the doorknobs and hinges.

Despite what he had written Strahan, the conflict about which side of the ocean he would inhabit was still unresolved. Deborah, for sure, still had no desire to live more than a few hundred yards from where she had been raised. "My mother is so averse to going to sea that I believe my father will never be induced to see England again," William wrote in his own letter to Strahan. "He is now building a house to live in himself." Franklin had also flirted with the idea of getting a land grant in Ohio, looking west rather than east. By late in 1763, he was confessing to Strahan that he was baffled about where he would spend his remaining years: "We shall see in a little time how things will turn out."[6]

THE PAXTON BOYS

Franklin's future plans would depend, in part, on the conduct of Pennsylvania's new governor, John Penn, who was a nephew of Proprietor Thomas Penn and had been a delegate with Franklin to the Albany Conference. Franklin was hopeful. "He is civil," he wrote to Collinson, "so I think we shall have no personal difference, at least I will give him no occasion."

The first issue that Penn and the Pennsylvania Assembly faced was frontier defense. The British victory in the French and Indian War had not fully secured peace with all of the Indians, and settlers in the west were being plagued by raids led by the Ottawa chief known as Pontiac. By the fall of 1763, the fighting had subsided, but not the resentments of many of Pennsylvania's rough-hewn backwoodsmen.

These erupted on December 14, when a mob of more than fifty frontiersmen from around the town of Paxton murdered six unarmed Indians, all of them peaceful, converted Christians. Two weeks later, an even larger mob slaughtered fourteen more Indians who had been harbored for their safety in a nearby workhouse.

The "Paxton Boys," as the growing mob of frontiersmen came to be called, declared that their next stop was Philadelphia, where more than 140 other peaceful Indians were being sheltered. They threatened to kill not only the Indians but also any whites who protected them, including prominent Quakers. This provoked some Quakers to set aside pacifism and take up arms, and it led others to flee the city.

The uprising threatened to become the most serious crisis Pennsylvania had ever faced, a full-fledged social and religious civil war. On one side were the frontiersmen, mainly Presbyterians, plus their working-class sympathizers in town, including many German Lutherans and Scots-Irish Presbyterians. On the other side were Philadelphia's old-line Quakers, with their pacifist proclivities and desire to trade with the Indians. The Quakers, despite being now easily out-numbered by the new German immigrants, dominated the Assembly and repeatedly resisted spending much for frontier defense. For a change, Philadelphia's upper-class Anglican merchants, who tended to support the Proprietors in their fights with the Assembly, found themselves allied with the Quakers, at least temporarily.

A virulent pamphlet war ensued. Philadelphia's Presbyterians, supporting their backwoods brethren, assailed the Quakers for coddling the Indians and refusing to allow the frontiersmen the proper representation in the Assembly that was decreed in the charter. Franklin responded with his own pamphlet in late January 1764. Entitled "A Narrative of the Late Massacres in Lancaster County," it was among the most emotional pieces he ever wrote.

He began his screed with poignant profiles of each of the Indians killed, which stressed their gentle personalities and used their English names. "These poor, defenseless creatures were immediately fired upon, stabbed and hatcheted to death!" he wrote, describing the massacre in gory detail. The eldest Indian was "cut to pieces in his bed," the others "scalped and otherwise horribly mangled."

Franklin went on to describe the second massacre two weeks later in even more horrid terms:

> Being without the least weapon for defense, they divided into their little families, the children clinging to their parents. They fell on their knees, protested their innocence, declared their love to the English, and that, in their whole lives, they had never done them injury; and in this posture they all received the hatchet! Men, women and little children— were every one inhumanly murdered!—in cold blood!

To the Paxton Boys, all Indians were alike and there was no need to treat them as individuals. "Whoever proclaimed war," their spokesman declared, "with part of a nation, and not with the whole?" Franklin, on the other hand, used his pamphlet to denounce prejudice and make the case for individual tolerance that was at the core of his political creed. "If an Indian injures me, does it follow that I may revenge that injury on all Indians?" he asked. "The only crime of these poor wretches seems to have been that they had a reddish brown skin and black hair." It was immoral, he argued, to punish an individual as revenge for what others of his race, tribe, or group may have done. "Should any man with a freckled face and red hair kill a wife or child of mine, [by this reasoning] it would be right for me to revenge it by killing all the freckled red-haired men, women and children I could afterwards anywhere meet."

To reinforce his point, he provided historical examples of how various other people—Jews, Muslims, Moors, blacks, and Indians—had all shown a greater morality and tolerance in similar situations. It was necessary, Franklin concluded, for the entire province to stand up to the Paxton Boys as they prepared to march on Philadelphia and to bring them to justice. Ignoring the slight inconsistency in his argument, he warned of the collective guilt all whites would otherwise share: "The guilt will lie on the whole land till justice is done on the murderers."[7]

The pamphlet would later damage Franklin politically, for it reflected his underlying prejudice against the German settlers as well as his lifelong distaste for Presbyterian-Calvinist dogma. He showed little sympathy for the grievances of the frontiersmen, calling them "barbarous men" who had acted "to the eternal disgrace of their country and color." Though a populist in many ways, he was wary of the rabble. His outlook, as usual, was from the perspective of a new middle class: distrustful both of the unwashed mob and of the entrenched elites.

On Saturday, February 4, a week or so after Franklin's pamphlet was published, Gov. John Penn called a mass meeting on the State House grounds as the Paxton Boys headed toward the city. At first he took a strong stand. He ordered the arrest of the mob leaders, deployed British troops, and asked the crowd to join the militia companies that Franklin and others were organizing. Even many Quakers took up arms, though most of the town's Presbyterians refused.

At midnight on Sunday, the mob of 250 reached Germantown, just north of the city. Church bells pealed alarms, and amid the chaos a surprising alliance was formed. Governor Penn, Franklin wrote a friend, "did me the honor, on an alarm, to run to my house at midnight, with his counselors at his heels, for advice, and made it his headquarters for some time." Penn went so far as to offer Franklin control of the militia, but Franklin prudently declined. "I chose to carry a musket and strengthen his authority by setting an example of obedience to his orders."[8]

Franklin and others, including many Quakers, wanted the governor to order an attack. Instead, Penn decided to send a delegation of seven city leaders, including Franklin, to meet with the Paxton Boys. "The fighting face we put on and the reasonings we used with the insurgents," Franklin later recalled, "restored quiet to the city." The mob agreed to disperse if they could send some of their leaders into town to present their grievances.

As the tension with the Paxton Boys receded, the antagonism between Franklin and Penn resumed. Franklin took a hard line. He wanted the governor and Assembly, acting jointly, to confront the Paxton delegation together and hold them accountable for the massacres. The governor, however, realized the political advantage he could gain by forging an alliance with the Presbyterians and Germans who sympathized with the frontiersmen (and who were offended by the harsh slurs Franklin had written about them). So he met with the Paxton delegation in private, listened to them courteously, and agreed not to press charges against them. He also, at their suggestion, instituted a policy of offering a bounty for any Indian scalps, male or female.

Franklin was livid. "These things bring him and his government into sudden contempt," he wrote a friend. "All regard for him in the Assembly is lost. All hopes of happiness under a Proprietary government are at an end." The feeling was mutual. In a letter to his uncle, the Proprietor Thomas Penn, Gov. John Penn wrote an equally strong condemnation of Franklin: "There will never be any prospect of ease and happiness while that villain has the liberty of spreading about the poison of that inveterate malice and ill nature which is deeply implanted in his own black heart."

A darkness had indeed begun to infect Franklin's usually optimistic heart. Feeling confined by Philadelphia and its foul politics, restless at home, and finding few scientific or professional diversions, he lost some of his amused, wry demeanor. His letters contained harsh rather than humorous assessments of politics and even gloomier personal passages. To the medical doctor John Fothergill, a Quaker friend living in London, Franklin wrote, "Do you please yourself with the fancy that you are doing good? You are mistaken. Half the lives you save are not worth saving, as being useless; and almost the other half ought not to be saved, as being mischievous."[9]

FIGHTING THE PROPRIETORS AGAIN

And so the fights between governor and Assembly resumed, more heated than ever. They clashed over control of militia appointments, a lighthouse, and, of course, taxes. When the Assembly passed a bill taxing the Proprietors' estates, which followed the general outline but not the precise formula of the Privy Council compromise, Franklin wrote a message from the Assembly to the governor warning that the consequences of vetoing the bill "will undoubtedly add to that load of obloquy and guilt the Proprietary family is already burdened with and bring their government into (if possible) still greater contempt." The governor vetoed it.[10]

At stake was not just principle but power. Franklin realized that the Proprietary party now had strong support from the frontiersmen and their Scots-Irish and German kinsmen. That reignited his resolve to continue pursuing, against all odds, his dream of convincing the British to revoke the Proprietors' charter and make Pennsylvania a Crown colony.

Most people in Pennsylvania still did not share his fervor for a royal rather than Proprietary government. The members of Philadelphia's merchant aristocracy were friends with the Penns. The Presbyterian frontiersmen and ethnic working class had forged a new alliance after the Paxton Boys affair, plus they feared a royal takeover would bring the official establishment of the Church of England, which their dissenting families had fled. Even many prominent Quakers such as Isaac Norris and Israel Pemberton, who tended to be Franklin's allies, were leery of a new charter that might remove some of the religious liberties that the late William Penn had secured long ago. With his stubborn crusade, Franklin was succeeding in dividing his friends and uniting his enemies.

Likewise, in London there was no more support for a royal takeover than there had been when Franklin began his crusade as an agent there. Lord Hyde, Franklin's boss at the British postal department, wrote that even those royal ministers who might like to "get their hands on" the colony were not willing to take on the Penn family. He publicly warned Franklin, a royal appointee, that "all officers of the crown are expected to assist government." Franklin made a little joke of the warning, noting that he would "not be Hyde-bound."[11]

Nevertheless, Franklin still enjoyed effective control of the Assembly, and in March 1764 he pushed through a series of twenty-six resolutions—a "necklace of resolves," he called them—calling for the end of Proprietary government. The Proprietors, he wrote, had acted in ways that were "tyrannical and inhuman." They had used the Indian threat "to extort privileges from the people . . . with the knife of savages at their throat." The final resolution declared that the Assembly would consult citizens as to whether a "humble address" should be sent to the king "praying that he would be graciously pleased to take the people of this province under his immediate protection and government."

The result was a petition drive asking for the ouster of the Proprietors. Franklin printed copies in English and German, and even created a slightly different version for the Quaker community, but his supporters could garner merely thirty-five hundred signers. Opponents of the change were eventually able to come up with fifteen thousand on their own petitions.

Once again, a pamphlet war broke out. Franklin's contribution, "Cool Thoughts on the Present Situation," was more heated than its title implied. He was not, at least for now, detached enough to employ his old tools of humor, satire, indirection, and gentle wryness in argument. His pamphlet attacked the Proprietors for truckling to the Paxton Boys and for being unable to manage the colony. "Religion has happily nothing to do with our present differences, though great pains is taken to lug it into the squabble," he wrote, not altogether correctly.

In any case, he continued, the Crown rather than the Proprietors was most likely to protect religious liberties.

Franklin's newest opponent was John Dickinson, a young lawyer who was the son-in-law of the great Quaker eminence, Isaac Norris. Dickinson had been a friend of Franklin's and no great fan of the Proprietors, but he rationally argued that the safeguards of the Penn charter should not be lightly abandoned, nor should it be assumed that the royal ministers would be more enlightened than the Proprietors. Norris, unwilling to be caught in the crossfire, feigned sickness and resigned as Assembly speaker in May. Franklin was elected to the post.

Franklin also faced a more vitriolic older opponent: Chief Justice William Allen, who had also once been a friend but whose ardent support of the Proprietors had long ago led to a bitter break. When Allen returned from a trip to England in August, Franklin paid him a visit as "an overture." In front of other guests, Allen denounced his assault on the Proprietors. A switch to a royal government, he said, would cost Pennsylvania £100,000, and it had no support in London.

As the October 1 Assembly elections neared, the pamphlet war turned vicious as Franklin's foes sought to thwart his bid for reelection. One anonymous offering, entitled "What is Sauce for a Goose is also Sauce for a Gander," raked up every possible allegation against Franklin—most notably, that his son, William, was the bastard child of a "kitchen wench" named Barbara. It also reprinted, and embellished a bit, various anti-German passages Franklin had written earlier. And it accused him, falsely but vociferously, of buying honorary degrees, seeking a royal governorship for himself, and stealing his electricity experiments from other scientists.

Another broadside painted him as an excitable lecher:

> *Franklin, though plagued with fumbling age,*
> *Needs nothing to excite him,*
> *But is too ready to engage,*
> *When younger arms invite him.*[12]

Modern election campaigns are often criticized for being negative, and today's press is slammed for being scurrilous. But the most brutal of modern attack ads pale in comparison to the barrage of pamphlets in the 1764 Assembly election. Pennsylvania survived them, as did Franklin, and American democracy learned that it could thrive in an atmosphere of unrestrained, even intemperate, free expression. As the election of 1764 showed, American democracy was built on a foundation of unbridled free speech. In the centuries since then, the nations that have thrived have been those, like America, that are most comfortable with the cacophony, and even occasional messiness, that comes from robust discourse.

Election Day was as wild as the pamphlets. Throngs of voters clogged the State House steps throughout the day of October 1, and the lines remained long well past midnight. Franklin's supporters were able to force the polls to stay open until dawn as they roused anyone they could find who had not yet voted. It was a tactical mistake. The Proprietary party sent workers up to Germantown to round up even more supporters. Franklin finished thirteenth out of fourteen candidates vying for the eight seats in Philadelphia.

His faction, however, kept control of the Assembly, which promptly voted to submit to the British ministers the petition against the Proprietors. And as a consolation prize that was perhaps better than a victory, it voted 19–11 to send Franklin back to England as an agent to present it.

That prompted a new flurry of pamphlets. Dickinson declared that Franklin would be ineffectual because he was hated by the Penns, disdained by the king's ministers, and "extremely disagreeable to a very great number of the serious and reputable inhabitants" of Pennsylvania. Chief Justice Allen labeled him "the most unpopular and odious name in the province . . . delirious with rage, disappointment and malice." But now that he was heading back to England, Franklin's even temper started to return. "I am now to take leave (perhaps a last leave) of the country I love," he wrote in response. "I wish every kind of prosperity to my friends, and I forgive my enemies."[13]

Once again, his wife declined to accompany him to England. Nor would she permit him to take their daughter. So why was he so willing to leave home again? Partly because he missed London, and partly because he felt depressed and confined by Philadelphia.

There was also a loftier reason. Franklin had been developing a vision of an American future that went beyond even wresting Pennsylvania from the Proprietors. It involved a greater union among the colonies, along the lines of his Albany Plan, and a more equal relationship between the colonies and the mother country as part of a greater British Empire. That could include, he suggested, representation in Parliament. Responding to reports that Britain might propose taxes on the colonies, he wrote to Richard Jackson, whom he had left behind in London as Pennsylvania's other agent, a suggested response: "If you choose to tax us, give us members in your legislature, and let us be one people."

As he prepared to leave for England in November 1764, Franklin wrote a letter to his daughter. It included paternal exhortations to be "dutiful and tender towards your good mama" and typical Franklin advice, such as "to acquire those useful accomplishments arithmetic and bookkeeping." But it also contained a more serious note. "I have many enemies," he said. "Your slightest indiscretions will be magnified into crimes, in order the more sensibly to wound and afflict me. It is therefore the more necessary for you to be extremely circumspect in all your behavior that no advantage may be given to their malevolence."

He also had many supporters. More than three hundred cheered him as he left Philadelphia for his ship. Cannons were fired as a send-off, and a song was sung to the tune of "God Save the King," with the new ending "Franklin on thee we fix / God save us all." He told some friends that he expected to be gone only a few months, others that he might never return. It is not clear which prediction, if either, he truly believed, but as it turned out, neither proved correct.[14]

CHAPTER TEN

AGENT PROVOCATEUR

London, 1765–1770

AN EXTENDED FAMILY

Mrs. Stevenson was out when Franklin arrived, unannounced, at his old home on Craven Street, and her maid did not know where to find her. "So I sat me down and waited her return," Franklin recalled in a letter to her daughter, Polly. "She was a good deal surprised to find me in her parlor." Surprised, perhaps, but prepared. His rooms had been left vacant, for his English friends and surrogate family had no doubt he would someday return.[1]

It would be just a short visit, he led his real wife, and perhaps even himself, to believe. He wanted to be back home by the end of the summer, he wrote Deborah soon after his arrival. "A few months, I hope, will finish affairs here to my wish, and bring me to that retirement and repose with my little family." She had heard that many times before. He would, in fact, never see her again. Despite her pleas and declining health, he would continue his increasingly futile mission for more than ten years, right up to the eve of the Revolution.

That mission involved complex balancing acts that would test all of Franklin's wiles. On the one hand, he was still a committed royalist who wanted to stay in favor with the king's ministers in order to wrest Pennsylvania from the hated Penns. He also had personal motives: protecting his postmastership, perhaps achieving an even higher appointment, and pursuing his dream of a land grant. On the other hand, once it became clear that the British government had little sympathy for colonial rights, he would have to scramble to reestablish his reputation as an American patriot.[2]

In the meantime, Franklin had the pleasure of settling back into the life he loved in London. Sir John Pringle, the distinguished physician, had become his best friend. They played chess, made the rounds to their regular coffeehouse clubs, and soon got into the habit of taking summer trips together. The great Samuel Johnson biographer James Boswell was another acquaintance. After dropping in on one of their chess games, Boswell noted in his journal that Pringle had "a peculiar sour manner," but that Franklin was, as always, "all jollity and pleasantry." Franklin and Mrs. Stevenson resumed their relationship of domestic convenience, and Polly, still living with an aunt in the countryside, remained an object of Franklin's paternal affection and intellectual flirtation.

He picked Polly as his first potential convert to a new phonetic alphabet that he had invented in a quixotic quest to simplify English spelling. It is easy to see why it did not catch on. "Kansider chis alfabet, and giv mi instanses af syts Inlis uyrds and saunds az iu mee hink kannat perfektlyi bi eksprest byi it," went one of his more comprehensible sentences. After a long reply that is near impossible to translate, in which she halfheartedly says the alphabet "myit bi uv syrvis," she lapses into standard English to conclude, "With ease & with sincerity, I can in the old way subscribe myself . . ."

It was a measure of their intellectual bonding that Polly would indulge this linguistic fantasy as faithfully as she did. Franklin's phonetic reform showed little of his usual regard for utility, and it took his passion for social improvement to radical extremes. It required the invention of six new letters for which there were no printing fonts, and it dropped six other letters that Franklin considered superfluous. Answering Polly's many objections, he insisted that the difficulty in learning the new spellings would be overcome by the logic behind them, and he dismissed her concerns that the words would be divorced from their etymological roots and thus lose their power. But he soon gave up the endeavor. Years later, he turned his scheme over to Noah Webster. The famed lexicographer reprinted Franklin's letters to

Polly in his 1789 book *Dissertations on the English Language* (which he dedicated to Franklin) and called the project "deeply interesting," but added, "Whether it will be defeated by insolence and prejudice remains for my countrymen to determine."[3]

Franklin brought his grandson, Temple, the illegitimate son of his own illegitimate son, out of anonymity and into his odd domestic orbit on Craven Street. The relationship was weird, even by Franklin family standards. The boy, who was 4 when Franklin reestablished contact, had been cared for by a series of women who sent itemized bills for his expenses (haircuts, inoculations, clothes) to Mrs. Stevenson, who then sought reimbursement from William in New Jersey. In all of his letters to Deborah at the time, filled with details of various friends and acquaintances, Franklin never mentioned Temple. But by the time the boy turned 9, William was asking, in a quite cowardly way, whether his son could be brought to live with him in America. "He might then take his proper name and be introduced as the son of a poor relation, for whom I stood Godfather and intended to bring up as my own."

Foreshadowing a later struggle for the boy's allegiance, Franklin instead took him under his own wing. On Craven Street he was known merely as "William Temple," and Franklin enrolled him in a school run by William Strahan's brother-in-law, an eccentric educator who shared Franklin's passion for spelling reform. Even though Temple became part of the extended Stevenson family, they pretended (at least publicly) to be unaware of his exact provenance.

(As late as 1774, in a letter describing a wedding in which he was an usher, Polly would refer to him as "Mr. Temple, a young gentleman who is at school here and is under the care of Dr. Franklin." Not until later, after Franklin and his grandson returned to America and Temple took up his true last name, did Polly confess that she suspected all along that there was some relationship. "I rejoiced to hear he has the addition of Franklin [to his name], which I always knew he had some right to.")[4]

THE STAMP ACT OF 1765

Back in Philadelphia, Franklin was still seen as a "tribune of the people" and a defender of their rights. When word finally reached there in March 1765 of his safe arrival in London, bells were rung "almost all night," his supporters "ran about like mad men," and copious quantities of "libations" were drunk to his health. But their joy would be fleeting. Franklin was about to become embroiled in a controversy over the notorious Stamp Act, which would require a tax stamp on every newspaper, book, almanac, legal document, and deck of cards.[5]

It was the first time that Parliament had proposed a major internal tax on the colonies. Franklin believed that Parliament had the right to impose external taxes, such as duties and tariffs, to regulate trade. But he thought it unwise, perhaps even unconstitutional, for Parliament to levy an internal tax on people who had no representation in that assembly. Nevertheless, he did not fight the Stamp Act proposal with much vigor. Instead, he tried to play conciliator.

He and a small group of colonial agents met in February 1765 with George Grenville, the prime minister, who explained that the high cost of the Indian wars made some tax on the colonies necessary. What was a better way to levy it? Franklin argued that it should be done in the "usual constitutional way," which meant by a request from the king to the various colonial legislatures, who alone had the power to tax their own inhabitants. Would Franklin and his fellow agents, Grenville asked, be able to commit that the colonies would agree to the proper amount and how to apportion it among themselves? Franklin and the others admitted that they could make no firm commitment.

Franklin offered another alternative a few days later. It stemmed from his long-standing desire, both as a rather sophisticated economic theorist and as a printer, to have more paper currency circulating in America. Parliament, he proposed, could authorize new bills of credit that would be issued to borrowers at 6 percent interest. These paper bills would serve as legal tender and circulate like currency, thus increasing America's money supply, and Britain would collect the interest instead of levying direct internal taxes. "It will operate as a general tax on the colonies, and yet not an unpleasing one," said Franklin. "The rich, who handle most money, would in reality pay most of the tax." Grenville was, in Franklin's words, "besotted with his stamp scheme," and dismissed the idea. This may have been fortunate for Franklin, as he later heard that even his friends in Philadelphia disliked his paper credit idea as well.[6]

When the Stamp Act passed in March, Franklin made the mistake of taking a pragmatic attitude. He recommended that his good friend John Hughes be appointed the collection officer in Pennsylvania. "Your undertaking to execute it may make you unpopular for a time, but your acting with coolness and steadiness and with every circumstance in your power of favor to the people will by degrees reconcile them," he mistakenly argued in a letter to Hughes. "In the meantime, a firm loyalty to the Crown and faithful adherence to the government of this nation will always be the wisest course for you and I to take, whatever may be the madness of the populace." In his desire to remain on decent terms with the royal ministers, Franklin badly underestimated the madness of the populace back home.

Thomas Penn, on the other hand, played the situation cleverly. He refused to offer his own candidate for stamp collector, saying that if he did so "the people might suppose we were consenting to the laying this load upon them." John Dickinson, Franklin's young adversary as the leader of the Proprietary party in the Assembly, drew up a declaration of grievances against the Stamp Act that resoundingly passed.[7]

It was one of Franklin's worst political misjudgments. His hatred of the Penns blinded him to the fact that most of his fellow Pennsylvanians hated taxes imposed from London more. "I took every step in my power to prevent the passing of the Stamp Act," he claimed unconvincingly to his Philadelphia friend Charles Thomson, "but the tide was too strong against us." He then went on to argue the case for pragmatism: "We might well have hindered the sun's setting. That we could not do. But since it is down, my friend, and it may be long before it rises again, let us make as good a night of it as we can. We may still light candles."

The letter, which became public, was a public relations disaster for Franklin. Thomson replied that Philadelphians, rather than being willing to light candles, were ready to launch "the works of darkness." By September, it was clear that this could include mob violence. "A sort of frenzy or madness has got such hold of the people of all ranks that I fancy some lives will be lost before this fire is put out," a frightened Hughes wrote the man who had gotten him what had become an unenviable job.[8]

Franklin's printing partner, David Hall, sent a similar warning. "The spirit of the people is so violently against everyone they think has the least concern with the Stamp law," he wrote. Angry Philadelphians had "imbibed the notion that you had a hand in the framing of it, which has occasioned you many enemies." He added that he would be afraid for Franklin's safety if he were to return. A cartoon printed in Philadelphia showed the devil whispering in Franklin's ear: "Thee shall be agent, Ben, for all my dominions."[9]

The frenzy climaxed one evening in late September 1765 when a mob gathered at a Philadelphia coffeehouse. Leaders of the rabble accused Franklin of advocating the Stamp Act, and they set out to level his new home, along with those of Hughes and other Franklin supporters. "If I live until tomorrow morning, I shall give you a farther account," Hughes wrote in a log he later sent Franklin.

Deborah dispatched their daughter to New Jersey for safety. But ever the homebound stalwart, she refused to flee. Her cousin Josiah Davenport arrived with more than twenty friends to help defend her. Her account of that night, while harrowing, is also a testament to her strength. She described it in a letter to her husband:

> Toward night I said he [cousin Davenport] should fetch a gun or two, as we had none. I sent to ask my brother to come and bring his gun. Also we made one room the magazine. I ordered some sort of defense upstairs as I could manage myself. I said when I was advised to remove that I was very sure you had done nothing to hurt anybody, nor I had not given any offense to any person at all. Nor would I be made uneasy by anybody. Nor would I stir.

Franklin's house and his wife were saved when a group of supporters, dubbed the White Oak Boys, gathered a force to confront the mob. If Franklin's house was destroyed, they declared, so too would be the homes of anyone involved. Finally, the mob dispersed. "I honor much the spirit and courage you showed," he wrote Deborah after hearing of her ordeal. "The woman deserves a good house that is determined to defend it."[10]

The Stamp Act crisis sparked a radical transformation in American affairs. A new group of colonial leaders, who bristled at being subservient to England, were coming to the fore, especially in Virginia and Massachusetts. Even though most Americans harbored few separatist or nationalist sentiments until 1775, the clash between imperial control and colonial rights was erupting on a variety of fronts. Young Patrick Henry, 29, rose in Virginia's House of Burgesses to decry taxation without representation. "Caesar had his Brutus, Charles the First his Cromwell, and George the Third . . ." He was interrupted by shouts of "Treason!" before he could finish, but it was clear that some colonists were becoming deadly serious. Soon he would find an ally in Thomas Jefferson. In Boston, a group that would take the name the Sons of Liberty met at a distillery and attacked the homes of the Massachusetts tax commissioner and Gov. Thomas Hutchinson. Among the rising patriots there who would eventually become rebels were a young merchant named John Hancock, a fiery agitator named Samuel Adams, and his sour lawyer cousin John Adams.

For the first time since the Albany Conference of 1754, leaders from different parts of America were galvanized into thinking as a collective unit. A congress of nine colonies, including Pennsylvania, was held in New York in October. Not only did it urge the repeal of the Stamp Act, it denied the right of Parliament to levy internal taxes on the colonies. The motto they adopted was the one Franklin had written as a cartoon caption more than a decade earlier, as he sought to rally unity at Albany: "Join, or Die."

From his distance in London, Franklin was slow to join the frenzy. "The rashness of the Assembly in Virginia is amazing," he wrote Hughes. "I hope, however, that ours will keep within the bounds of prudence and moderation." For the time being, he was still more in sympathy with Governor Hutchinson of Massachusetts, later a great enemy. Both were reasonable men appalled by mob rule, and in this case threatened by it. "When you and I were at Albany ten years ago,"

Hutchinson wrote him, "we did not propose a union for such purposes as these."[11]

Franklin's moderation was due in part to his temperament, his love of Britain, and his dreams of a harmonious empire. It was in his nature to be a smooth operator rather than a revolutionary. He liked witty discussion over Madeira, and he hated disorder and mob behavior. The fine wines and meals contributed not only to his gout, but also to his blurred vision about the animosity that was building back home. Perhaps more important, he was making one last attempt to turn Pennsylvania into a royal rather than Proprietary colony.

It was always an unlikely quest, now all the more so because of the turmoil over the Stamp Act, which made royal rule less popular in Pennsylvania and made colonial pleadings less popular in London. In November 1765, a year after Franklin's arrival and just as he was absorbing the damage done to his reputation by his waffling over the Stamp Act, the Privy Council officially deferred action on the anti-Penn petition he had brought. Franklin initially believed (or at least publicly professed) that this was merely a temporary setback. But he soon came to realize that Thomas Penn was correct when he wrote to his nephew, Gov. John Penn, that the action meant the issue was dead "forever."[12]

SPIN CYCLE

By the end of 1765, with his reputation as a defender of colonial rights in tatters because of his equivocation over the Stamp Act, Franklin faced one of the great challenges in the annals of political damage control. He began with a letter-writing campaign. To his partner David Hall and others, he strongly denied that he had ever supported the act. He also had prominent London Quakers write on his behalf. "I can safely aver that Benjamin Franklin did all in his power to prevent the Stamp Act from passing," John Fothergill wrote a Philadelphia friend. "He asserted the rights and privileges of America with the utmost firmness." Hall reprinted the letter in the *Pennsylvania Gazette*.

Franklin felt the best way to force repeal, one that appealed to his

Poor Richard penchant for frugality and self-reliance, was for Americans to boycott British imports and refrain from transactions that would require use of the stamps. This approach would also rally British tradesmen and manufacturers, hurt by the loss of exports, to the cause of repeal. Writing anonymously as "Homespun" in a British paper, he ridiculed the notion that Americans could not get by without such British imports as tea. If need be, they would make tea from corn. "Its green ears roasted are a delicacy beyond expression."[13]

Franklin's two sardonic essays signed Homespun were among at least thirteen attacks on the Stamp Act that he published in a three-month period. In one hoax, signed "A Traveler," he claimed that America had no need of British wool because "the very tails of the American sheep are so laden with wool that each has a car or wagon on four little wheels to support and keep it from trailing on the ground." Writing as "Pacificus Secundus," he resorted to his old tactic of scathing satire by pretending to support the idea that military rule be imposed in the colonies. It would take only fifty thousand British soldiers at a cost of merely £12 million a year. "It may be objected that by ruining our colonies, killing one half the people, and driving the rest over the mountains, we may deprive ourselves of their custom for our manufacturers; but a moment's consideration will satisfy us that since we have lost so much of our European trade, it can be only the demand in America that keeps up and has of late so greatly enhanced the price of those manufacturers, and therefore a stop put to that demand will be an advantage to all of us, as we may thereafter buy our own goods cheaper." The only downside for England, he noted, was that "multitudes of our poor may starve for want of employment."[14]

(As has been frequently noted, Franklin often wrote anonymously or using a pseudonym, beginning as a young teen when he wrote as Silence Dogood and then as the Busy-Body, Alice Addertongue, Poor Richard, Homespun, and others. Sometimes, he was trying to be truly anonymous; at other times, he was wearing only a thin mask. This practice was not unusual, indeed it was quite common, among writers of the eighteenth century, including such Franklin heroes as Addison, Steele, and Defoe. "Scarce one part in ten of the valuable books which are published are with the author's name," Addison once declared, with a bit of exaggeration. At the time, writing anonymously was considered cleverer, less vulgar, and less likely to lead to libel or sedition charges. Gentlemen sometimes thought it was beneath their stature to have their names on pamphlets and press pieces. The practice also assured that dissenting political and religious writings were rebutted on their merits rather than by personal attacks.) [15]

Franklin also produced a political cartoon, a counterpart to his "Join, or Die," that showed a bloodied and dismembered British Empire, its limbs labeled with the names of colonies. The motto underneath, "Give a Penny to Belisarius," referred to the Roman general who oppressed his provinces and died in poverty. He had the cartoon printed on note cards, hired a man to hand them out in front of Parliament, and sent one to his sister Jane Mecom. "The moral," he told her, "is that the colonies may be ruined, but that Britain would thereby be maimed." Enforcing the Stamp Act, he warned one British minister, would end up "creating a deep-rooted aversion between the two countries and laying the foundation of a future total separation." [16]

Still a loyal Briton, Franklin was eager to prevent such a split. His preferred solution was colonial representation in Parliament. In a set of notes he prepared for his meetings with ministers, Franklin jotted down the argument: "Representation useful two ways. It brings information and knowledge to the great council. It conveys back to the remote parts of the empire the reasons of public conduct . . . It will forever preserve the union which otherwise may be various ways broken."

But he also warned that the time to seize that opportunity was passing. "The time has been when the colonies would have esteemed it a great advantage as well as honor to them to be permitted to send members to Parliament," he wrote a friend in January 1766. "The time is now come when they are indifferent about it, and will probably not ask it, though they might accept it if offered them; and the time will come when they will certainly refuse it."

Short of representation in Parliament, Franklin wrote, "the next best thing" would be the traditional method of requesting funds to be appropriated by each of the colonial legislatures. In the notes he wrote for his conversation with ministers, he suggested a third alternative that would be a step toward independence for the colonies: "empowering them to send delegates from each Assembly to a common council." In other words, the American colonies would form their own federal legislature rather than be subject to the laws of Parliament. The only thing that would then unite the two parts of the British Empire would be loyalty to the king. It derived from the plan he had proposed more than a decade earlier; next to this idea in his notes he wrote the phrase "Albany Plan."[17]

On February 13, 1766, Franklin got the chance to present his case directly to Parliament. His dramatic appearance was a masterpiece of both lobbying and theater, helpfully choreographed by his supporters in that body. In one afternoon of highly charged testimony, he would turn himself into the foremost spokesman for the American cause and brilliantly restore his reputation back home.

Many of the 174 questions directed at him were scripted in advance by leaders of the new Whig ministry of Lord Rockingham, which was sympathetic to the colonies and was looking for a way out of the Stamp Act debacle. Others were more hostile. Through it all, Franklin was cogent and calm. The questioning was begun by a member whose manufacturing business had been hurt by the breakdown in trade, who asked Franklin whether the Americans already paid taxes voluntarily to Britain. "Certainly many, and very heavy taxes," he replied, and he went on to recount their history in detail (though leaving out some of the disputes over taxing of Proprietary lands).

An adversary broke in. "Are not the colonies," he asked, "very able to pay the Stamp duty?" Replied Franklin: "There is not gold and silver enough in the colonies to pay the stamp duty for one year."

Grenville, who had proposed the act, defended it by asking whether Franklin didn't agree that the colonies should pay for the defense provided them by royal forces. The Americans, Franklin countered, had defended themselves, and by doing so had defended British interests as well. "The colonies raised, clothed and paid, during the last war, near 25,000 men and spent many millions," he explained, adding that only a small portion had been reimbursed.

The larger issue, Franklin stressed, was how to promote harmony within the British Empire. Before the Stamp Act was imposed, asked a supporter named Grey Cooper, "What was the temper of America towards Great Britain?"

Franklin: The best in the world. They submitted willingly to the government of the Crown, and paid, in all their courts, obedience to the acts of Parliament . . . They cost you nothing in forts, citadels, garrisons or armies to keep them in subjection. They were governed by this country at the expense of only a little pen, ink and paper. They were led by a thread. They had not only a respect but an affection for Great Britain; for its laws, its customs and manners, and even a fond- ness for its fashions, which greatly increased the commerce.

Cooper: And what is their temper now?

Franklin: Oh, very much altered.

Cooper: In what light did the people of America used to consider the Parliament?

Franklin: They considered the Parliament as the great bulwark and security of their liberties.

Cooper: And have they not still the same respect?

Franklin: No, it is greatly lessened.

Once again, Franklin emphasized a distinction between external and internal taxes. "I have never heard any objection to the right of laying duties to regulate commerce. But a right to lay internal taxes was never supposed to be in Parliament, as we are not represented there."

Would America submit to a compromise? No, said Franklin, it was a matter of principle. So only military force could compel them to pay the Stamp Tax?

"I do not see how a military force could be applied to that pur- pose," Franklin answered.

Question: Why may it not?

Franklin: Suppose a military force is sent into America. They will find nobody in arms. What are they then to do? They cannot force a man to take stamps who chooses to do without them. They will not find a rebellion; they may indeed make one.

The finale came when supporters of the Stamp Act tried to dismiss the distinction between external and internal taxes. If the colonies successfully opposed an internal tax, might they later start opposing tariffs and other external taxes?

"They never have hitherto," replied Franklin. "Many arguments have lately been used here to show them that there is no difference . . . At present they do not reason so. But in time they may possibly be convinced by these arguments."

It was a dramatic ending, and a foreboding one. In making a distinction between internal taxes and external tariffs, Franklin was again taking a stance more moderate and pragmatic than some emerging American leaders, including most members of the Massachusetts Assembly, who rankled at the prospect of heavy import duties levied by London. But the Boston Tea Party was still almost eight years in the future. On both sides of the Atlantic, there was great rejoicing when Parliament promptly repealed the Stamp Act, even though it laid the ground for future conflict by adding a Declaratory Act stating that Parliament had the right "in all cases whatsoever" to enact laws for the colonies.[18]

Franklin had displayed, with steely words cloaked in velvet, both reason and resolve. For a generally reluctant public speaker, it was the longest sustained oratorical performance of his life. He made his case less through eloquence than through a persuasive persistence in focusing the debate on the realities that existed in America. Even one of his diehard opponents told him afterward, Franklin recorded, "that he liked me from that day for the spirit I showed in defense of my country." Famed in Britain as a writer and scientist, he was now widely recognized as America's most effective spokesman. He also became, in effect, the ambassador for America in general; besides representing Pennsylvania, he was soon named the agent for Georgia, and then New Jersey and Massachusetts.

In Philadelphia, his reputation was fully restored. His friend William Strahan helped assure that by sending a transcript of the testimony back to David Hall for publication there. "To this examination," Strahan wrote, "more than to anything else, you are indebted to the speedy and total repeal of this odious law." Salutes were fired from a barge christened *The Franklin,* and at the taverns there were free drinks and presents to all those who arrived with news of the triumph from England. "Your enemies at last began to be ashamed of their base insinuations and to acknowledge that the colonies are under obligation to you," Charles Thomson wrote.[19]

SALLY AND RICHARD BACHE

The battle served to remind Franklin about the virtues of the wife he had left back home, or at least to feel guiltier about his neglect of her. Deborah's frugality and self-reliance were symbols of America's ability to sacrifice rather than submit to an unfair tax. Now that it was repealed, Franklin rewarded her with a shipment of gifts: fourteen yards of Pompadour satin (he noted that it "cost eleven shillings a yard"), two dozen gloves, a silk negligee and petticoat for Sally, a Turkish rug, cheeses, a corkscrew, and some tablecloths and curtains, which he politely informed her had been selected by Mrs. Stevenson. In the letter accompanying the gifts, he wrote:

> My Dear Child,
>   As the Stamp Act is at length repealed, I am willing you should have a new gown, which you may suppose I did not send sooner as I knew you would not like to be finer than your neighbors, unless in a gown of your own spinning. Had the trade between the two countries totally ceased, it was a comfort to me to recollect that I had once been clothed from head to foot in woolen and linen of my wife's manufacture, that I was never prouder of any dress in my life, and that she and her daughter might do it again if necessary.

Perhaps, he jovially noted, some of the cheese would be left for him to enjoy by the time he got home. But even though he had turned 60 during the repeal battle and his work in England seemed done, Franklin was not ready to return. Instead, he made plans to spend the summer of 1766 visiting Germany with his friend the physician Sir John Pringle.[20]

Deborah's letters to her husband, awkward though they were, convey both her strength and her loneliness: "I partake of none of the diversions. I stay at home and flatter myself that the next packet will bring me a letter from you." She coped with his absence and the political tensions by cleaning the house, she said, and she tried hard (perhaps on his instructions) not to bother him with her worries about political matters. "I have wrote several letters to you one almost every day but then I could not forbear saying something to you about public affairs then I would destroy it and then begin again and burn it again and so on." Describing their newly completed house, she reported that she had not yet hung his pictures because she feared driving nails into the wall without his approval. "There is great odds between a man's being at home and abroad as everybody is afraid that they shall do wrong so every thing is left undone."

His letters, in return, were generally businesslike, focusing mainly on the details of the house. "I could have wished to have been present at the finishing of the kitchen," he wrote. "I think you will scarce know how to work it, the several contrivances to carry off steam and smell and smoke not being fully explained to you." He issued detailed instructions for how to paint each room and occasionally made tantalizing references to his eventual homecoming: "If that iron [furnace] is not set, let it alone till my return, when I shall bring a more convenient copper one." [21]

At the end of 1766, his printing partnership with David Hall expired after eighteen years. The end came with a bit of acrimony. Hall had become less ardent about using the pages of the *Pennsylvania Gazette* to attack the Proprietors, and two of Franklin's friends helped fund a new printer and paper to take up the cause. Hall considered this a breach of the spirit of their partnership agreement, even though it had expired. "Though you are not absolutely prohibited from being any farther concerned in the printing business in this place, yet so much is plainly implied," he wrote plaintively.

Franklin replied from London that the new rival print shop had been "set on foot without my knowledge or participation, and the first notice I had of it was by reading the advertisement in your paper." He professed his deep affection for Hall and said he had no disagreements with his politics or editorial policies, even if some of his political allies felt otherwise. "I never thought you of any party, and as you never blamed me for the side I took in public affairs, so I never censured you for not taking the same, believing as I do that every man has and ought to enjoy a perfect liberty of judging for himself in such matters."

Still, he felt compelled to add that their original agreement did not in fact prevent him from competing now that it had expired: "I could not possibly foresee 18 years beforehand that I should at the end of that term be so rich as to live without business." Then he added a veiled threat, wrapped in a promise, by saying that he had been offered a chance to become a partner in the rival business but would refrain from doing so as long as Hall provided some more of what Franklin thought he was owed. "I hope I shall have no occasion to do it," he said of the possibility that he would join with Hall's rival. "I know there must be a very great sum due to me from our customers, and I hope much more of it will be recovered by you for me than you apprehend." If so, Franklin promised, that money along with his other income would allow him to stay retired. "My circumstances will be sufficiently affluent, especially as I am not inclined to much expense. In this case I have no purpose of being again concerned in printing." [22]

The expiration of the partnership meant that Franklin would lose about £650 in income a year, which stoked his sense of economy. His life in London was a middle-class mix of frugality and indulgence. Although he did not entertain or live in the grand style that might be expected of someone of his stature, he liked to travel, and his accounts show that he ordered top-quality beer for his home at 30 shillings a barrel (a sharp contrast to his first stay in London, when he preached the virtues of bread and water over beer). His efforts at economy were mainly directed at his wife. In June of 1767 he wrote her:

> A great source of our income is cut off, and if I should lose the post office, which . . . is far from being unlikely, we should be reduced to our rents and interests of money for a subsistence, which will by no means afford the chargeable housekeepings and entertainments we have been used to. For my own part I live here as frugally as possible not to be destitute of the comforts of life, making no dinners for anybody and contenting myself with a single dish when I dine at home; and yet such is the dearness of living here that my expenses amaze me. I see too by the sums you have received in my absence that yours are very great, and I am very sensible that your situation naturally brings you a great many

visitors, which occasion an expense not easily to be avoided ... But when people's incomes are lessened, if they cannot proportionally lessen their outgoings they must come to poverty.[23]

What made the letter particularly cold was that it was written in response to the news that their daughter had fallen in love and hoped for his approval to marry. Sally had grown into a distinguished fixture in Philadelphia society, attending all the balls and even riding in the carriage of Franklin's adversary Governor Penn. But she fell in love with a man who seemed to be of questionable character and financial security.

Richard Bache, the suitor in question, had emigrated from England to work as an importer and marine insurance broker with his brother in New York, and then he headed to Philadelphia to open a dry goods store on Chestnut Street. Charming to women but hapless in business, Bache had been engaged to Sally's best friend, Margaret Ross. When Margaret became fatally ill, she made a deathbed request for Sally to take care of Bache for her, and Sally was quite willing to oblige.[24]

For Deborah, deciding what to do in her husband's absence was an overwhelming responsibility. "I am obliged to be father and mother," she wrote Franklin, with a tinge of accusation. "I hope I act to your satisfaction, I do so according to my best judgment."

Surely, this should have precipitated Franklin's return. He remained, however, distant from his family. The only time he had hastened home to Philadelphia was when his son was planning to marry—in London. "As I am in doubt whether I shall be able to return this summer," he wrote Deborah, "I would not occasion a delay in her happiness if you thought the match a proper one." Permitting himself to be indulgent from afar, he sent Sally two summer hats with the letter.

A few weeks later, he sent his long sermon about saving money. "Do not make an expensive feasting wedding," he wrote Deborah, "but conduct everything with frugality and economy, which our circumstances really now require." She should make clear to Bache, he added, that they would provide a nice but not excessive dowry:

I hope his expectations are not great of any fortune to be had with our daughter before our death. I can only say that if he proves a good husband to her, and a good son to me, he shall find me as good a father as I can be. But at present I suppose you would agree with me that we cannot do more than fit her out handsomely in clothes and furniture not exceeding in the whole five hundred pounds of value.[25]

Then came more disturbing news. At Franklin's request, William checked into Bache's financial situation and discovered it was in shambles. Worse yet, he learned that Margaret Ross's father had previously found the same thing and denied them permission to marry. "Mr. Bache had often attempted to deceive him [Ross] about his circumstances," William reported. "In short, he is a mere fortune hunter who wants to better his circumstances by marrying into a family that will support him." He ended the letter with a request: "Do burn this." Franklin didn't.

So the marriage was put on hold, and Bache tried to explain himself to Franklin in a letter. It was true, he admitted, that he had suffered a severe financial reversal, but he claimed it was not his fault. He had unfairly been left holding the bills for a merchant ship that suffered in the Stamp Act boycott.[26]

"I love my daughter perhaps as well as ever a parent did a child," Franklin replied with perhaps some exaggeration. "But I have told you before that my estate is small, scarce a sufficiency for the support of me and my wife . . . Unless you can convince her friends of the probability of your being able to maintain her properly, I hope you will not persist in a proceeding that may be attended with ruinous consequences to you both." Franklin wrote Deborah the same day to say that he assumed Bache would now back off. "The misfortune that has lately happened to his affairs," said Franklin, "will probably induce him to forbear entering hastily" into a marriage. He suggested that Sally might, instead, want to visit England, where she could meet other men, such as William Strahan's son.[27]

Though Franklin's sentiments were clear, his letters did not outright forbid his daughter from getting married. Perhaps he felt that, because he was unwilling to come home to deal with the matter, he had neither the moral right nor practical ability to issue any decrees.

Detached from his family by distance, he also remained rather emotionally detached.

Further complicating the odd family dynamics, Mrs. Stevenson decided to weigh in. Having lived with Franklin, she felt herself to be Deborah's soul mate, and she wrote to share her sympathy. Franklin, she reported, was in a foul humor. Stung by his temper, she consoled herself by buying some silk and making a petticoat for his daughter, even though she had never met her. Indeed, she confided, she was so excited by the possible wedding that she had wanted to buy even more gifts, but Franklin had forbidden it. She longed for the opportunity to sit down and chat, she told Deborah. "I truly think your expectations of seeing Mr. Franklin from time to time has been too much for a tender affectionate wife to bear."[28]

Ignoring the family drama back in Philadelphia, Franklin escaped in August 1767 for a summer vacation to France. "I have stayed too long in London this summer, and now sensibly feel the want of my usual journey to preserve my health," he wrote Deborah. His mood was so sour that, on the way, he "engaged in perpetual disputes with the innkeepers," he told Polly. He and his traveling companion, John Pringle, were upset that their carriage was rigged in such a way that they had little view of the countryside. The coachman's explanation of the rationale, Franklin groused, "made me, as upon a hundred other occasions, almost wish that mankind had never been endowed with a reasoning faculty, since they know so little how to make use of it."

When they got to Paris, however, things improved. He was intrigued by how the ladies there applied their rouge, which he chose to share in great detail in a letter to Polly rather than to his own daughter. "Cut a hole of three inches in diameter in a piece of paper, place it on the side of your face in such a manner as that the top of the hole may be just under your eye; then with a brush dipped in the color paint face and paper together, so when the paper is taken off there will remain a round patch of red."[29]

Franklin was feted as a celebrity in France, where electrical experimenters were known as *franklinistes*, and he and Pringle were invited to Versailles to attend a grand *couvert* (public supper) with King Louis XV and Queen Marie. "He spoke to both of us very graciously and cheerfully," Franklin reported to Polly. Despite his travails with England's ministers, however, he stressed he was still loyal "in thinking my own King and Queen the very best in the world and the most amiable."

Versailles was magnificent but negligently maintained, he noted, "with its shabby half brick walls and broken windows." Paris, on the other hand, had some pristine qualities that appealed to his affection for civic improvement schemes. The streets were swept daily so they were "fit to walk in," unlike those of London, and the water was made "as pure as that of the best spring by filtering it through cisterns filled with sand." While his daughter was preparing for a wedding without him, Franklin was getting new tailored clothes and "a little bag wig" that made him look "twenty years younger," he told Polly. The trip had done so much to invigorate his health, he joked, that "I was once very near to making love to my friend's wife." [30]

On his return from France, Franklin promptly wrote charming letters to Polly and others, but only a short note home. He seemed miffed that the letters from Philadelphia carried little news of his daughter, other than that she was "disappointed" that her marriage plans were put in limbo. He assured Deborah that he had been "extremely hearty and well ever since my return," and then deigned to inquire about his daughter's welfare.

By that time, though he did not know it, Sally and Richard had already gone ahead and gotten married. In October 1767, as recorded in the *Pennsylvania Chronicle* (the new rival to Franklin's old *Gazette*), "Mr. Richard Bache, of this city, merchant, was married to Miss Sally Franklin, the only daughter of the celebrated Doctor Franklin, a young lady of distinguished merit. The next day all the shipping in the harbor displayed their colors on this happy occasion." [31]

There is no sign that Franklin ever expressed regret for missing the wedding of his only daughter. In December, his sister Jane Mecom wrote to offer congratulations on the "marriage of your beloved daughter to a worthy gentleman whom she loves and is the only one that can make her happy." Franklin replied the following February in a cool manner: "She has pleased herself and her mother, and I hope she will do well; but I think they should have seen some better prospect than they have, before they married, how the family was to be maintained."[32]

In his occasional letters over the next few months, Franklin would send his love to Deborah and Sally, but he never made any overtures to Bache. Finally, in August 1768, Franklin wrote Bache admitting him into the family. "Loving son," he began promisingly, before turning a bit cool. "I thought the step you had taken, to engage yourself in the charge of a family while your affairs bore so unpromising an aspect with regard to the probable means of maintaining it, a very rash and precipitate one." This was why, Franklin explained, he had not answered Bache's earlier letters. "I could say nothing agreeable: I did not choose to write what I thought, being unwilling to give pain where I could not give pleasure." But at the end of the one-paragraph letter, Franklin softened somewhat. "Time has made me easier," he said. "My best wishes attend you, and that if you prove a good husband and son, you will find me an affectionate father." In a one-sentence postscript, he gave his love to Sally and noted that he was sending her a new watch.

Deborah was thrilled. In a note she sent when forwarding Franklin's letter to Bache, who was visiting Boston, she wrote, "Mr. Bache (or my son Bache), I give you joy: although there are no fine speeches as some would make, your father (or so I will call him) and you, I hope, will have many happy days together."[33]

Deborah got even better news from Franklin at the beginning of 1769. His health was very good, he wrote, but "I know that according to the course of nature I cannot at most continue much longer." He had just turned 63. Therefore, he was "indulging myself in no future prospect except one, that of returning to Philadelphia, there to spend the evening of my life with my friends and family." Sally and her husband came back from Boston hoping to find Franklin there. But he was still not ready, despite what he had written, to return.

Nor did he return that spring when he learned that Deborah had suffered a small stroke. "These are bad symptoms in advanced life and augur danger," her doctor wrote to Franklin. He consulted his traveling companion, John Pringle, who was physician to the queen, and forwarded his advice to Deborah. For once expressing slight impatience with her wayward husband, she disparaged the advice and said that her condition was largely caused by "dissatisfied distress" brought on by his prolonged absence: "I was only unable to bear any more and so I fell and could not get up again."

Even good news could not yet entice him back to Philadelphia. When he heard that Sally was pregnant that summer, he conveyed his affection by sending a little luxury: six caudle cups, which were used by pregnant women to share a brew of wine, bread, and spice. Sally missed no opportunity for seeking his affection. The child, born in August 1769, was named Benjamin Franklin Bache. Franklin would turn out to be closer to his grandchildren than his children; Benny Bache, like his cousin Temple, would eventually become part of his retinue. In the meantime, he sent his best wishes and instructions to make sure that Benny was inoculated for smallpox.[34]

THE SURROGATE FAMILY

In his family life, as in the rest of his personal life, Franklin clearly did not look for deep commitments. He did, however, have a need for domestic comfort and intellectual stimulation. That is what he found with his surrogate family in London. On Craven Street there was a cleverness and spirit that was absent on Market Street. His landlady, Mrs. Stevenson, was livelier than Deborah, her daughter, Polly, a bit smarter than Sally. And in September 1769, just after Franklin returned from France, Polly found a suitor who was more distinguished than Bache.

William Hewson was a good catch for Polly, who by then was 30 and still unmarried. He was on the verge of what would be a prominent career as a medical researcher and lecturer. "He must be clever because he thinks as *we* do," Polly gushed in a letter from the country home where she was staying. "I should not have you or my mother surprised if I should run off with this young man; to be sure it would be an imprudent step at the discreet age of 30."

Amid these half-jokes, Polly played coy with Franklin by confessing (or feigning) her lack of enthusiasm for marrying Hewson. "He may be too young," she told her older admirer. She was filled with happiness, she added, but she couldn't be sure whether "this flight might be owing to this new acquaintance or to the joy of hearing my old one [meaning Franklin, who had been in Paris] is returned to this country."

Franklin's reply, written the very next day, contained more flirtations than felicitations. "If the truth were known, I have reason to be jealous of this insinuating handsome young physician." He would flatter his vanity, he said, and "turn a deaf ear to reason" by deciding "to suppose you were in spirits because of my safe return."

For almost a year, Polly held off getting married because Franklin refused to advise her to accept Hewson's proposal. Finally, in May 1770, Franklin wrote that he had no objections. It was hardly an overwhelming endorsement. "I am sure you are a much better judge in this affair of your own than I can possibly be," he said, adding that the match appeared "a rational one." As for her worry that she would not bring much of a financial dowry, Franklin could not resist noting that "I should think you a fortune sufficient for me without a shilling."[35]

Although he had missed the weddings of both his own children, this was one Franklin made sure not to miss. Even though it was held in midsummer, when he usually traveled abroad, he was there to walk Polly down the aisle and play the role of her father. A few weeks later, he professed to be pleased that she was happy, but he confessed that he was "now and then in low spirits" at the prospect of having lost her friendship. Fortunately for all, it was not to be. He became close to the new couple, and he and Polly would exchange more than 130 more letters during their lifelong friendship.

Indeed, a few months after their wedding, Polly and William Hewson came to stay with Franklin while Mrs. Stevenson spent one of her long weekends visiting friends in the country. Together they published a fake newspaper to mark the occasion. *The Craven Street Gazette* for Saturday, September 22, 1770, reported on the departure of "Queen Margaret" and Franklin's ensuing grumpiness. "The GREAT person (so called from his enormous size) . . . could hardly be comforted this morning, though the new ministry promised him roasted shoulder of mutton and potatoes for his dinner." Franklin, it was reported, was also miffed that Queen Margaret had taken the keys to a closet so that he could not find his ruffled shirts, which prevented him from going to St. James's Palace for Coronation Day. "Great clamors were made on this occasion against her Majesty . . . The shirts were afterwards found, tho' too late, in another place."

For four days, the newspaper poked fun at various Franklin foibles: how he violated his sermons about saving fuel by making a fire in his bedroom when everyone else was out, how he vowed to fix the front door but gave up because he was unable to decide whether it required buying a new lock or a new key, and how he pledged to go to church on Sunday. "It is now found by sad experience that good resolutions are easier made than executed," Sunday's edition reported. "Notwithstanding yesterday's solemn Order of Council, nobody went to church today. It seems the GREAT person's broad-built bulk lay so long abed that breakfast was not over until it was too late." The moral of the tale could have been written by Poor Richard: "It seems a vain thing to hope reformation from the example of our great folks."

One particularly intriguing entry seems to refer to a woman living nearby with whom Franklin had an unrequited flirtation. That Sunday, Franklin pretended to visit her: "Dr. Fatsides made 469 turns in his dining room, as the exact distance of a visit to the lovely Lady Barwell, whom he did not find at home, so there was no struggle for and against a kiss, and he sat down to dream in his easy chair that he had it without any trouble." By the third day of Mrs. Stevenson's absence, the *Gazette* was reporting that Dr. Fatsides "begins to wish for her Majesty's return."

That final edition contained one of Franklin's inimitable letters to the editor, signed with the pseudonym "Indignation," decrying the food and conditions. Referring to Polly and her husband, it railed: "If these nefarious wretches continue in power another week, the nation will be ruined—undone!—totally undone if the Queen does not return; or (which is better) turn them all out and appoint me and my friends to succeed them." It was answered by "A Hater of Scandal," who wrote that the surly Franklin had been offered a wonderful dinner of beef ribs and had rejected it, saying "that beef does not with him perspire well, but makes his back itch, to his no small vexation now that he hath lost the little Chinese ivory hand at the end of the stick, commonly called a scratchback, presented to him by Her Majesty."[36]

Franklin was able to indulge on Craven Street the many eccentricities he had developed. One of these was taking hour-long "air baths" early each morning, during which he would open his windows and "sit in my chamber without any clothes whatever." Another was engaging in little flirtations. The famous painter Charles Willson Peale recounted how he once visited Craven Street unannounced and found "the Doctor was seated with a young lady on his knee." The lady in question was probably Polly, though the sketch Peale later made of the scene is ambiguous.[37]

Eventually, Polly and William Hewson moved into Craven Street and brought with them Hewson's skeletons, "prepared fetuses," and other tools for his medical research. Later, Franklin and Mrs. Stevenson moved a few doors away. Their odd relationship was reflected in a crotchety letter Franklin wrote her during one of her regular escapes to visit friends in the country. Reminding her of Poor Richard's adage that guests become tiresome after three days, he urged her to return on the next stagecoach. But lest she think he was too dependent on her, he spelled out his contentment at being alone. "I find such a satisfaction in being a little more my own master, going anywhere and doing anything just when and how I please," he claimed. "This happiness however is perhaps too great to be conferred on any but Saints and holy hermits. Sinners like me, I might have said us, are condemned to live together and tease one another."[38]

HILLSBOROUGH AND
THE TOWNSHEND DUTIES

In his dramatic testimony arguing for repeal of the Stamp Act, Franklin made a serious misjudgment: he said that Americans recognized Parliament's right to impose external taxes, such as tariffs and export duties, just not internal taxes that were collected on transactions inside the country. He repeated the argument in April 1767, writing as "A Friend to Both Countries" and then as "Benevolus" in a London paper. In an effort to soothe troubled relations, he recounted all the times that Americans had been very accommodating in helping to raise money for the defense of the empire. "The colonies submit to pay all external taxes laid upon them by way of duty on merchandise imported into their country and never disputed the authority of Parliament to lay such duties," he wrote.[39]

Charles Townshend, the new chancellor of the exchequer, had been among those who grilled Franklin in Parliament about his acceptance of external but not internal taxes. The distinction was complete "nonsense," Townshend felt, but he decided to pretend to please the colonies—or call their bluff—by adopting it. In a brilliant speech that earned him the nickname "Champagne Charlie" because it was delivered while he was half-drunk, he laid out a plan for import duties on glass, paper, china, paint colors, and tea. Making matters worse, part of the money raised would be used to pay royal governors, thus freeing them from dependence on colonial legislatures.

Once again, as with the passage of the Stamp Act, Franklin expressed little concern when the Townshend duties passed in June 1767, and he did not realize how far he lagged behind the growing radicalism in parts of the colonies. Outrage at the new duties grew particularly strong in the port city of Boston, where the Sons of Liberty, led by Samuel Adams, effectively roused sentiments with dances around a "Liberty Tree" near the common. Adams got the Massachusetts Assembly to draft a circular letter to the rest of the colonies that petitioned for repeal of the act. The British ministry demanded that the letter be rescinded and sent troops to Boston after the Assembly refused.

When reports of American anger reached him in London, Franklin remained rather moderate and wrote a series of essays calling for "civility and good manners" on both sides. To friends in Philadelphia, he expressed his disapproval of the radicalism growing in Boston; in articles published in England, he tried hard—indeed, too hard—to pull off an adroit feat of ambidexterity.

His juggling act was reflected in a long, anonymous essay he wrote in January 1768 for the London *Chronicle,* called "Causes of the American Discontents." Written from the perspective of an Englishman, it explained the Americans' belief that their own legislatures should control all revenue measures, and it added in a squirrelly manner, "I do not undertake here to support these opinions." His goal, he averred, was to let people "know what ideas the Americans have." In doing so, Franklin tried to have it both ways: he warned that America's fury at being taxed by Parliament could tear apart the empire, then pretended to lament these "wild ravings" as something "I do not pretend to support." [40]

His reaction was similar when he read a set of anonymous articles, published in Philadelphia, called "Letters from a Farmer in Pennsylvania." At the time, Franklin did not know that they were written by John Dickinson, his adversary in Philadelphia's battles over the Proprietors. Dickinson's letters conceded that Parliament had a right to regulate trade, but he argued that it could not use that right to raise revenues from the colonies without their consent. Franklin arranged to have the letters published as a pamphlet in London in May 1768 and wrote an introduction. But he refrained from fully endorsing their arguments. "How far these sentiments are right or wrong I do not pretend at present to judge."

By then, Franklin had begun to realize that his distinction between external and internal taxes was probably unworkable. "The more I have thought and read on the subject," he wrote William in March, "the more I find myself confirmed in my opinion that no middle doctrine can be well maintained." There were only two alternatives: "that Parliament has a power to make *all* laws for us, or that it has the power to make *no laws* for us." He was beginning to lean toward the latter, but he admitted that he was unsure. [41]

Franklin's inelegant dance around the issue of parliamentary power during the first half of 1768 caused his contemporaries (as well as subsequent historians) to come to different conclusions about what he really believed or what games he was playing. In fact, there were many factors jangling in his mind: he sincerely hoped that moderation and reason would lead to a restoration of harmony between Britain and the colonies; he wanted to make one last attempt to wrest Pennsylvania from the Proprietors; and he was still pursuing land deals that required the favor of the British government. Above all, as he admitted in some letters, his views were in flux and he was still trying to make up his mind.

There was one other complicating factor. His desire to help resolve the disputes, combined with his ambition, led him to hope that he might be appointed an official in the British ministry overseeing colonial affairs. Lord Hillsborough had just been named secretary of state of that ministry, and Franklin thought (incorrectly) that he might turn out to be friendly to the colonies. "I do not think this nobleman in general an enemy to America," he wrote a friend in January. In a letter to his son, Franklin admitted the more personal ambition. "I am told there is talk of getting me appointed undersecretary to Lord Hillsborough," he said. His chances, he admitted, were slim: "It is a settled point here that I am too much of an American."

That was the crux of Franklin's dilemma. He had rendered himself suspect, he noted in a letter to a friend, "in England of being too much of an American, and in America of being too much of an Englishman." With his dreams for a harmonious and growing British Empire, he still hoped that he could be both. "Being born and bred in one of the countries and having lived long and made many agreeable connections in the other, I wish all prosperity to both," he proclaimed. Thus, he was intrigued, even hopeful, about securing a government job in which he could try to hold the two parts of the empire together.[42]

When Hillsborough consolidated his power by becoming the head of the board of trade as well as colonial secretary, Franklin won support from other British ministers who felt that giving him a government post would provide some balance. Most notable was Lord North, who had become chancellor of the exchequer after Townshend's death. Franklin met with him in June and professed to have plans to return to America. He added, however, that "I should stay with pleasure if I could any ways be useful to government." North took the hint, and he began trying to line up backing for his appointment.

It was not to be. Franklin's hope of joining the British government ended abruptly when he had a long and contentious meeting with Lord Hillsborough in August 1768. Hillsborough declared that he had no intention of appointing Franklin and would instead choose as his deputy John Pownall, a loyal bureaucrat. Franklin was dismayed. Pownall "seems to have a strong bias against us," he wrote Joseph Galloway, his ally in the Pennsylvania Assembly. Adding injury to insult, Hillsborough also rejected once and for all any further consideration of the petition to remove Pennsylvania from Proprietary rule. With two of his main goals dashed, Franklin was ready to abandon his moderation in the colonies' battles with Parliament. The turning point had been reached.[43]

THE AMERICAN PATRIOT

With the situation clarified in his own mind, Franklin took up his pen to wage an essay war against Hillsborough and the Townshend duties. Most of his articles were anonymous, but this time he did little to disguise his authorship. He even signed one of them, with clear frankness, "Francis Lynn." Relations between Britain and America had been amicable, he argued, "until the idea of taxing us by the power of Parliament unfortunately entered the heads of your ministers." He claimed that the colonies had no desire to rebel against the king, but misguided ministers were likely "to convert millions of the King's loyal subjects into rebels for the sake of establishing a newly-claimed power in Parliament to tax a distant people." Something must be done. "Is there not one wise and good man to be found in Britain who can propose some conciliating measure that may prevent this mischief?" In another piece, written as if from a concerned Englishman, he proposed seven "queries" to be considered "by those gentlemen who are for vigorous measures with the Americans." Among them: "Why must they be stripped of their property without their consent?" As for Hillsborough personally, Franklin labeled him "our new Haman."[44]

His opponents returned the fire. One article signed by "Machiavel" in the *Gazetteer* called it a "burlesque on patriotism" that so many Americans were "filling newspapers and consecrating trees to liberty" with lamentations about being taxed while at the same time surreptitiously recommending their friends for appointments and "trying to obtain offices" for themselves. Machiavel provided a list of fifteen such hypocrites, with Franklin the postmaster at the top. Franklin responded (anonymously) that the Americans were attacking Parliament, not the king. "Being loyal subjects to their sovereign, the Americans think they have as good a right to enjoy offices under him in America as a Scotchman has in Scotland or an Englishman in England."

Throughout 1769, Franklin became increasingly worried that the situation would lead to a rupture. America could not be subjugated by British troops, he argued, and it soon would be strong enough to win its own independence. If that happened, Britain would be sorry that it missed the opportunity to create a system of imperial harmony. To make his point, he published a parable in January 1770 about a young lion cub and a large English dog traveling together on a ship. The dog picked on the lion cub and "frequently took its food by force." But the lion grew and eventually became stronger than the dog. One day, in response to all the insults, it smashed the dog with "a stunning blow," leaving the dog "regretting that he had not rather secured its friendship than provoked its enmity." The parable was "humbly inscribed" to Lord Hillsborough.[45]

Many in Parliament were seeking a compromise. One proposal was to remove most of the Townshend duties, leaving only the one on tea as a way to assert the principle that Parliament retained the right to regulate trade and tariffs. It was the type of pragmatic solution that in earlier days would have appealed to Franklin. But he was now in no mood for moderation. "It is not the sum paid in that duty on tea that is complained of as a burden, but the principle of the act," he wrote Strahan. A partial repeal "may inflame matters still more" and lead to "some mad action" and an escalation that "will thus go on to complete the separation."[46]

Separatist sentiments were, in fact, already being inflamed, especially in Boston. On March 5, 1770, a young apprentice insulted one of the redcoats sent to enforce the Townshend duties, a fight broke out, bells rang, and a swarm of armed and angry Bostonians came out in force. "Fire and be damned," the crowd taunted. The British soldiers did. Five Americans ended up dead in what soon became known as the Boston Massacre.

Parliament went ahead with the partial repeal of the Townshend duties that month, leaving a duty on tea. In a letter to his Philadelphia friend Charles Thomson, which was promptly published throughout the colonies, Franklin urged a continued boycott of all British manufactured goods. America, he argued, must be "steady and persevere in our resolutions."

Franklin had finally caught up with the more ardent patriotism spreading through the colonies, most notably Massachusetts. Writing to Samuel Cooper, a Boston minister, he declared that Parliament had no authority to tax the colonies or order British troops there: "In truth they have no such right, and their claim is founded only on usurpation."

Still, like many Americans, he was not yet willing to advocate a total break with Britain. The solution, he felt, was a new arrangement in which the colonial assemblies would remain loyal to the king but no longer be subservient to Britain's Parliament. As he told Cooper, "Let us therefore hold fast our loyalty to our King (who has the best disposition toward us, and has a family interest in our prosperity) as that steady loyalty is the most probable means of securing us from the arbitrary power of a corrupt Parliament that does not like us and conceives itself to have an interest in keeping us down and fleecing us." It was an elegant formula for commonwealth governance. Alas, it was based on the unproven assumption that the king would be more sympathetic to colonial rights than was Parliament.[47]

Franklin's letter to Cooper, widely published, helped to secure him an appointment by the Massachusetts lower house to be its agent in London as well. In January 1771, he paid a call on Lord Hillsborough to present those new credentials. Although the minister was dressing for court, he cheerfully had Franklin admitted to his chambers. But when Franklin mentioned his new appointment, Hillsborough sneered. "I must set you right there, Mr. Franklin. You are not agent."

"I do not understand your lordship," replied Franklin. "I have the appointment in my pocket."

Hillsborough maintained that Massachusetts governor Hutchinson had vetoed the bill appointing Franklin.

"There was no such bill," said Franklin. "It is a vote of the House."

"The House of Representatives has no right to appoint an agent," Hillsborough angrily retorted. "We shall take no notice of agents but such as are appointed by Acts of Assembly to which the governor gives his assent."

Hillsborough's argument was clearly specious. Franklin had, of course, been appointed as the agent of the Pennsylvania Assembly without the consent of the Penn family's governors there. The minister was trying to eliminate the right of the people to choose their own agents in London, and Franklin was appalled. "I cannot conceive, my lord, why the consent of the *governor* should be thought necessary to the appointment of an agent for the *people*."

The discussion went downhill from there. Hillsborough, turning pale, launched into a tirade about how his "firmness" was necessary to bring order to the rebellious colonials. To which Franklin added a personal insult: "It is, I believe, of no great importance whether the appointment is acknowledged or not, for I have not the least conception that an agent *at present* can be of any use to any of the colonies. I shall therefore give your lordship no farther trouble." At that point, Franklin abruptly departed and went home to write down a transcript of the discussion.[48]

Hillsborough "took great offense at some of my last words, which he calls extremely rude and abusive," Franklin reported to Samuel Cooper in Boston. "I find that he did not mistake me."

Initially, Franklin pretended to be unconcerned about Hillsborough's enmity. "He is not a whit better liked by his colleagues in the ministry than he is by me," Franklin claimed in his letter to Cooper. In another letter, he described Hillsborough as "proud, supercilious, extremely conceited of his political knowledge and abilities (such as they are), fond of everyone that can stoop to flatter him, and inimical to all that dare tell him disagreeable truths." The only reason he remained in power, Franklin surmised, was that the other ministers had "difficulty of knowing how to dispose of or what to do with a man of his wrong-headed bustling energy."

Nevertheless, it soon became clear that the showdown with Hillsborough depressed Franklin. His friend Strahan noticed that he had become "very reserved, which adds greatly to his natural inactivity and there is no getting him to take part in anything." It also made him far more pessimistic about the eventual outcome of America's growing tensions with Britain. One could see in Parliament's actions "the seeds sown of a total disunion of the two countries," he reported to the Massachusetts Committee on Correspondence, which brought out the more radical side of him. "The bloody struggle will end in absolute slavery to America, or ruin to Britain by the loss of her colonies."[49]

Despite such pessimistic feelings, Franklin still hoped for a reconciliation. He urged the Massachusetts Assembly to avoid passing an "open denial and resistance" to Parliament's authority and instead adopt a strategy designed "gradually to wear off the assumed authority of Parliament over America." He even went so far as to advise Cooper that it might "be prudent in us to indulge the Mother Country in this concern for her own honor." And he continued to urge a policy of loyalty to the Crown, if not to Parliament.

This led some of his enemies to accuse him of being too conciliatory. "The Dr. is not the dupe but the instrument of Lord Hillsborough's treachery," the ambitious Virginian Arthur Lee wrote to his friend Samuel Adams. Lee went on to accuse Franklin of wanting to cling to his postmastership and keep his son in office. All of this explained, he said, "the temporizing conduct he has always held in American affairs."

Lee had his own motives: he wanted Franklin's job as agent in London. But Franklin still had the support of most Massachusetts patriots, including (at least for the time being) Samuel Adams. Adams ignored Lee's letter, allowed it to leak, and Franklin's friends in Boston, including Thomas Cushing and Samuel Cooper, assured him of their support. Lee's attack, Cooper wrote, served to "confirm the opinion of your importance, while it shows the baseness of its author." But it also highlighted the difficulty that Franklin faced in attempting, as he had during the Stamp Act crisis, to be both a loyal Briton and an American patriot.[50]

CHAPTER ELEVEN

REBEL

London, 1771–1775

THE VACATIONS OF 1771

As the summer of 1771 approached, Franklin decided to forsake the world of public affairs for the time being. He had been stymied, at least for the moment, in all of his political missions: the fight against the Proprietors and then Parliament, his pursuit of a land grant and a royal appointment. But he was still not ready to return home. So, instead, he escaped the pressures of politics in the manner he loved best, by taking an extended series of trips that lasted until the end of the year: to England's industrial midland and north in May, to a friend's estate in southern England in June and again in August, and then to Ireland and Scotland in the fall.

On his rambles in May, Franklin visited the village of Clapham, where there was a large pond. It was a windy day and the water was rough, so he decided to test his theories about the calming effect of oil. Using just a teaspoon, he watched in amazement as it "produced an instant calm" that extended gradually to make a "quarter of the pond, perhaps half an acre, as smooth as a looking glass."

Although Franklin would continue to study the effect of oil on water seriously, he also found ways to have fun by turning it into a conjuring trick. "After this, I contrived to take with me, whenever I went into the country, a little oil in the upper hollow joint of my bamboo cane," he wrote. On a visit to the house of Lord Shelburne, he was walking by a stream with a group of friends, including the great actor David Garrick and the visiting French philosopher the Abbé Morellet, and told them he could still the waves. He walked upstream, waved his cane three times, and the surface of the stream calmed. Only later did he show off his cane and explain the magic.[1]

His tour of midland and north England in the company of two fellow scientists gave Franklin the chance to study the Industrial Revolution that was booming there. He visited an iron and tin factory in Rotherham, the metal casting shops of Birmingham, and a silk mill in Derby where 63,700 reels were turning constantly "and the twist process is tended by children of about 5 to 7 years old." In Manchester, he "embarked in a luxurious horse-drawn boat" owned by the Duke of Bridgewater that, befitting the peer's name, took him onto an aqueduct that crossed a river before ending in a coal mine. Near Leeds they called on the scientist Joseph Priestley, "who made some very pretty electrical experiments" for them and then described the various gases he had been discovering.

Franklin had denounced England's mercantile trading laws, which were designed to suppress manufacturing in her colonies, by arguing (a bit disingenuously) that she would never have to fear that America would become an industrial competitor. In his letters from his tour in 1771, however, he sent detailed advice about creating silk, clothing, and metal industries that would make the colonies self-sufficient. He had become "more and more convinced," he wrote his Massachusetts friend Thomas Cushing, of the "impossibility" that England would be able to keep up with America's growing demand for clothing. "Necessity therefore, as well as prudence, will soon induce us to seek resources in our own industry."

Franklin returned to London briefly in early June "in time to be at Court for the King's birthday," he wrote Deborah. Despite his disagreements with Parliament's taxation policies, he was still a loyal supporter of George III. "While we are declining the usurped authority of Parliament," he wrote Cushing that week, "I wish to see a steady dutiful attachment to the King and his family maintained among us."[2]

After a fortnight in London, Franklin headed to the south of England, where he visited his friend Jonathan Shipley at his Tudor manor in Twyford, just outside Winchester. Shipley was an Anglican bishop in Wales, but he spent most of his time in Twyford with his wife and five spirited daughters. It was such a delightful visit (Franklin might well have defined delight as an intellectually stimulating country house filled with five spirited young women) that he lamented that he had to leave after a week to attend to the correspondence that had been piling up in London. In his thank-you note to the Shipleys, which included a present of dried apples from America, Franklin complained that he had to "breathe with reluctance the smoke of London" and said he hoped to get back to the "sweet air of Twyford" for a longer visit later that summer.[3]

THE AUTOBIOGRAPHY

Franklin, at 65, had begun to think about family matters more. He felt affection for all of his kin, despite the fact—or perhaps, as he himself speculated, because of the fact—that he continued to live far away from them. In a long letter to his sole surviving sibling, Jane Mecom, that summer, he praised her for getting along well with her Philadelphia in-laws and, in a telling passage, reflected on how much easier it was for relatives to remain friendly from afar. "Our father, who was a very wise man, used to say nothing was more common than for those who loved one another at a distance to find many causes of dislike when they came together." A good example, he noted, was the relationship their father had with his brother Benjamin. "Though I was a child I still remember how affectionate their correspondence was" while Benjamin remained in England. But when Uncle Benjamin moved to Boston, they began to engage in "disputes and misunderstandings."

Franklin also wrote Jane about Sally Franklin, a 16-year-old who had joined his surrogate family on Craven Street. Sally was the only child of a second cousin who had continued the Franklin family's textile dyeing business in Leicestershire. Accompanying the letter was a detailed family tree showing how they were all descendants of Thomas Franklin of Ecton and noting that Sally was the last in England to bear the family name.

His interest in family was further piqued when he happened to visit one of his favorite used-book shops in London. The dealer showed him a collection of old political pamphlets that were filled with annotations. Franklin was amazed to discover that they had belonged to his Uncle Benjamin. "I suppose he parted with them when he left England," Franklin wrote in a letter to another cousin. He promptly bought them.[4]

So, in late July, when he was finally free to return to Twyford for a longer stay with the Shipleys, he was in a reflective mood. His career was at an impasse, and the history of his family was on his mind. Thus, the stage was set for the first installment of the most enduring of his literary efforts, *The Autobiography of Benjamin Franklin*.

"Dear son," he began, casting his account as a letter to William, whom he had not seen for seven years. The epistolary guise gave him the opportunity to be chatty and casual in his prose. He pretended, at least initially, that this was merely a personal communication rather than a work of literature. "I used to write more methodically," he said in a paragraph he inserted into the text after rereading some of the rambling genealogical digressions he had composed on the first day. "But one does not dress for private company as for a public ball."

Was the autobiography really just for the private company of his son? No. It was clear from the outset that Franklin was writing for public consumption as well. The family information that would most interest his son was omitted completely: the identity and description of William's own mother. Nor did Franklin write the letter on regular stationery; instead, he used the left half of large folio sheets, leaving the right half blank for revisions and additions.

At the beginning of his second day of writing, he stopped to make an outline of his entire career, showing his intention to construct a full memoir. Also, that second morning, he used the blank right-hand columns of his first pages to insert a long section justifying the "vanity" of his decision to "indulge the inclination so natural in old men to be talking of themselves." His goal, he declared, was to describe how he rose from obscurity to prominence and to provide some useful hints about how he succeeded, expressing hope that others might find them suitable to be imitated.

This was obviously directed at an audience beyond that of his son, who was already 40 and the governor of New Jersey. There was, however, a subtext directed at him: William had taken on airs since becoming a governor, and he was far more enamored of the aristocracy and establishment than his father. The autobiography would be a reminder of their humble origins and a paean to hard work, thrift, shopkeeping values, and the role of an industrious middle class that resisted rather than emulated the pretensions of the well-born elite.

For almost three weeks, Franklin wrote by day and then read aloud portions to the Shipleys in the evening. Because the work was cast as a letter, and because it was read aloud, Franklin's prose took on the voice of a lovable old raconteur. Lacking in literary flair, with nary a metaphor nor poetic flourish, the narrative flowed as a string of wry anecdotes and instructive lessons. Occasionally, when he found himself writing with too much pride about an event, he would revise it by adding a self-deprecating comment or ironic aside, just as would a good after-dinner storyteller.

The result was one of Franklin's most delightful literary creations: the portrait he painted of his younger self. The novelist John Updike has memorably called it an "elastically insouciant work, full of cheerful contradictions and humorous twists—a fond look back upon an earlier self, giving an intensely ambitious young man the benefit of the older man's relaxation."

With a mix of wry detachment and amused self-awareness, Franklin was able to keep his creation at a bit of a distance, to be modestly revealing but never deeply so. Amid all the enlightening anecdotes, he included few intimations of inner torment, no struggles of the soul or reflections of the deeper spirit. More pregnant than profound, his recollections provide a cheerful look at a simple approach to life that only hints at the deeper meanings he found in serving his fellow man and thus his God. What he wrote had little pretension other than pretending to poke fun at all pretensions. It was the work of a gregarious man who loved to recount stories, turn them into down-home parables that could lead to a better life, and delve into the shallows of simple lessons.

To some, this simplicity is its failing. The great literary critic Charles Angoff declares that "it is lacking in almost everything necessary to a really great work of *belles lettres:* grace of expression, charm of personality, and intellectual flight." But surely it is unfair to say that it lacks charm of personality, and as the historian Henry Steele Commager points out, its "artless simplicity, lucidity, homely idiom, freshness and humor have commended it anew to each generation of readers." Indeed, read with an unjaundiced eye, it is a pure delight as well as an archetype of homespun American literature. And it was destined to become, through hundreds of editions published in almost every language, the world's most popular autobiography.

In this age of instant memoirs, it is important to note that Franklin was producing something relatively new for his time. St. Augustine's *Confessions* had mainly been about his religious conversion, and Rousseau's *Confessions* had not yet been published. "There had been almost no famous autobiographies before Franklin, and he had no models," writes Carl Van Doren. That is not entirely true. Among those who had already published some form of autobiography were Benvenuto Cellini, Lord Herbert of Cherbury, and Bishop Gilbert Burnet. But Van Doren is correct when he says that Franklin "wrote for a middle class which had few historians. His book was the first masterpiece of autobiography by a self-made man." The closest model that he had, in terms of narrative style, was one of his favorite books, John Bunyan's allegorical dream, *A Pilgrim's Progress.* But Franklin's was the story of a very real pilgrim, albeit a lapsed one, in a very real world.

By the time he had to leave Twyford in mid-August, he had finished the first of four installments in what would later become known as the *Autobiography.* It took him through his years as a young printer engaged in civic endeavors and ended with the founding of the Philadelphia library and its offshoots in 1731. Only in his last lines did he let a note of politics creep in. "These libraries," he noted, "have made the common tradesmen and farmers as intelligent as most gentlemen from other countries, and perhaps have contributed in some degree to the stand so generally made throughout the colonies in defense of their privileges." It would be thirteen years before, at the urging of friends, he would pick up that part of the tale.[5]

Always eager to create a family wherever he could find one, Franklin took the Shipley's youngest daughter, Kitty, 11, under his wing and brought her in his coach back to London, where she was going to school. Along the way, they chatted about the type of man each of the Shipley daughters would marry. Kitty felt all of her sisters deserved a very rich merchant or aristocrat. As for herself, Kitty coquettishly allowed, "I like an old man, indeed I do, and somehow or another all the old men take to me." Perhaps she should marry a younger man, Franklin suggested, "and let him grow old upon your hands, because you'll like him better and better every year as he grows older." Kitty replied that she would prefer to marry someone already older, "and then you know I may be a rich young widow."

Another lifelong flirtation was born. He had his wife send over a squirrel from Philadelphia as a pet for all the Shipley girls. When the creature met an untimely end a year later in the jaws of a dog, Franklin composed a flowery epitaph and then added a simpler one that would become famous: "Here Skugg/Lies snug/As a bug/In a rug." His affection for Kitty would be immortalized fifteen years later when Franklin, then 80, wrote for her a little essay on "The Art of Procuring Pleasant Dreams."

On his last evening at Twyford, the Shipleys had insisted on throwing a birthday party, in absentia, for his Philadelphia grandson, 2-year-old Benjamin Franklin Bache. "That he may be as good as his grandfather," Mrs. Shipley said in her toast. Franklin responded that he hoped that Benny would, in fact, turn out much better. To which Bishop Shipley added, "We will compound the matter and be contented if he should not prove *quite* so good."[6]

The odd thing about all this affection for Benny was that Franklin had never met him, nor showed much of an inclination to do so. He had not even met the boy's father. But at that moment, Richard Bache was arriving in England on a mission to find his famous father-in-law. Bache appeared unannounced on Craven Street, where Mrs. Stevenson joyously greeted him. Franklin, however, had already departed, after little more than a week in London, for another extended vacation.

IRELAND AND SCOTLAND

Traveling with Richard Jackson, Pennsylvania's other agent in England, Franklin left in late August 1771 for three months in Ireland and Scotland, hoping to see if the relationship those countries were trying to forge within the British Empire might serve as a model for America. There were some promising signs. When they visited the Irish Parliament, Jackson was accorded the right to sit in the chamber because he was a member of England's Parliament. On seeing the famous Franklin, the Speaker proposed that, because he represented American legislatures, he should be accorded such a privilege as well. "The whole House gave a loud, unanimous Aye," Franklin reported to Cushing. "I esteemed it a mark of respect for our country."

On the other hand, much of what he saw in Ireland distressed him. England severely regulated Irish trade, and absentee English landlords exploited Irish tenant farmers. "They live in wretched hovels of mud and straw, are clothed in rags, and subsist chiefly on potatoes," he noted. His shock at the disparity between rich and poor made him all the more proud that America was building a vibrant middle class. The strength of America, he wrote, was its proud freeholders and tradesmen, who had the right to vote on public affairs and ample opportunity to feed and clothe their families.[7]

While in Dublin, Franklin happened to run into his nemesis, Lord Hillsborough, whose family estate was in northern Ireland. Surprisingly, Hillsborough insisted that he and Jackson stop by on their way to Scotland. Franklin was conflicted. "As it might afford an opportunity of saying something on American affairs," he wrote one friend, "I concluded to comply with his invitation." But he subsequently wrote his son that he had "determined not to go." As it turned out, Jackson insisted on going, and Franklin could not find another coach so had to follow along.

It was an astonishingly friendly visit. At Hillsborough's house, Franklin was "detained by a thousand civilities" for almost a week. The minister "seemed attentive to everything that might make my stay in his house agreeable." That even included "putting his own cloak about my shoulders when I went out, that I might not take cold."

In discussing Ireland's poverty, Hillsborough blamed it on England for restraining manufacturing there. Wasn't the same true, Franklin asked, about England's policy toward America? To Franklin's pleasure, Hillsborough responded that "America ought not to be restrained in manufacturing." He even suggested a subsidy for American silk industries and winemaking. He would be pleased to hear Franklin's "opinion and advice" on that, as well as on how to form a government for Newfoundland. Would Franklin consider these issues and when he returned to London "favor him with my sentiments?"

"Does not all this seem extraordinary to you?" he wrote his son. In a letter to Thomas Cushing, he suggested there might be a more cynical explanation. Hillsborough's behavior might be "meant only, by patting and stroking the horse, to make him more patient when the reins are drawn tighter and the spurs set deeper into his sides." Or, perhaps "he apprehended an approaching storm and was desirous of lessening beforehand the number of enemies he had so imprudently created."[8]

Franklin arrived, through storms and floods, in Edinburgh late on a Saturday and spent one night "lodged miserably" at an inn. "But that excellent Christian, David Hume, agreeable to the precepts of the gospel, has received the stranger and I now live with him," Franklin reported the next day. His old friend Hume had built a new house, and he took pride that the sheep's head soup made by his cook was the best in Europe. The talk at the table was also enviable: philosophy (Hume had recently befriended Rousseau in Paris), history, and the plight of the American colonies.

After ten days, Franklin traveled west toward Glasgow to see Lord Kames, his other favorite Scottish philosopher. Kames was also a great botanist who cultivated arbors of diverse trees; the ones Franklin planted on his visit are alive today. On his way back to Edinburgh, Franklin stopped at the Carron iron works, where James Watt was developing the steam engine, so that he could continue his study of industrialization. Among the ordnance they saw being cast, some of which would be used against the colonies in a few years, were cannons that weighed up to thirty-two tons.

Back at Hume's house in Edinburgh, Franklin spent another few days enjoying the intellectual circle there. He met with Adam Smith, who reportedly showed him some early chapters of the *Wealth of Nations* that he was then writing. Perhaps suspecting that they would never see their American friend again, Hume hosted a farewell dinner that included a variety of Franklin's favorite Scottish academics and writers, including Lord Kames.[9]

MEETING BACHE

Franklin had planned to stay longer with Hume, but two letters caught up with him while he was there. One was from his son-in-law, Richard Bache. Having missed Franklin in London, he wrote, he had gone to visit his own parents in Preston, a city in the north of England near Manchester. The other was from Polly. "Mr. Bache is at Preston, where he will wait with the pleasing expectation of seeing you on your return. We were all very much pleased with him." So Franklin hastened his departure for London and decided to visit his new in-law on the way.

Sally Franklin Bache, not surprisingly, was fretting back in Philadelphia about how her husband and father would get along. "If it should not be as cordial as I could wish," she wrote Richard, "I know when you consider it is my father, your goodness to and affection for me will make you try a little to gain his esteem and friendship." As it turned out, her fears were unfounded. "I can," Bache joyously wrote Deborah, "with great satisfaction, tell you that he received me with open arms and with a degree of affection I did not expect." He was particularly pleased that everyone told him he looked like Franklin, a revelation in those pre-Freudian times that was not seen as a reflection of Sally's taste in a husband. "I should be glad to be like him in any respect," Bache enthused.

Indeed, the old charmer wowed everyone in Bache's family, particularly his mother, Mary Bache, a "stately" and "serious" widow of 68, who had borne twenty children. During the visit, she stayed up until midnight talking to Franklin. A few weeks later, Franklin sent her a thank-you note with some oysters and (his vanity not fully conquered) a portrait of himself. Mrs. Bache carried it back and forth from the parlor to the dining room so she could view it all the time. "It is so like the original you cannot imagine with what pleasure we look at it, as we can perceive in it the likeness of my son as well as yourself."[10]

Bache traveled back to London with Franklin, stayed with him for a while on Craven Street, and tried hard to please. "His behavior here has been agreeable to me," Franklin told Deborah. But his affection did not extend to offering Bache the help he sought in winning a public appointment, such as customs inspector. "I am of the opinion that almost any profession a man has been educated in is preferable to an office held . . . subject to the caprices of superiors." Instead, he advised Bache to go home, become a merchant "selling only for ready cash," and to "always be close" to his wife. This advice, it must be remembered, came from a man who had lived across an ocean from his wife for much of fifteen years and had been clinging to his appointment as a royal postmaster.

As for Sally, he advised that she should learn accounting (always a theme) and help her husband out. "In keeping a store, if it be where you dwell, you can be serviceable to him as your mother was to me; for you are not deficient in that capacity, and I hope are not too proud." The Baches, ever mindful, would end up living in Deborah's house, opening a store in one of Franklin's Market Street buildings, and advertising "for cash only" a variety of silks and textiles for sale. When this dry goods shop turned out to be, as Bache complained to Franklin, a "sorry concern," he converted it to a "wine and grocery business," which also fared poorly. It was not the status or situation a woman of Sally's education and Bache's ambition felt was their due, but they followed Franklin's injunction to be not too proud.[11]

Deborah wrote Franklin so often about their grandson Benny that one can detect a note of caution creeping into his responses: "I can see you are quite in love with him, and your happiness wrapped up in his." He praised her for not stepping in during an argument when Sally was trying to discipline Benny: "I feared, from your fondness of him, that he would be too much humored, and perhaps spoiled."

He felt differently, however, about spoiling Polly Stevenson's new son, William Hewson, who had been born that spring. "Pray let him have everything he likes," he had written to Polly. "It gives [children] a pleasant air and . . . the face is ever after the handsomer for it." In the same letter, he responded sanguinely to Polly's teasing news that her mother had a new male friend. "I have been used to rivals," replied Franklin, "and scarce ever had a friend or a mistress in my whole life that other people did not like as well as myself."

Within two years, Billy Hewson had become Franklin's surrogate grandson. Responding to yet another letter from his wife describing their own grandson, Franklin wrote: "In return for your history of your *grandson*, I must give you a little of the history of my *godson*. He is now 21 months old, very strong and healthy, begins to speak a little, and even to sing. He was with us a few days last week, grew fond of me, and would not be contented to sit down to breakfast without coming to call Pa." He did deign to add, however, that watching Billy "makes me long to be at home to play with Ben."[12]

MORE SCIENCE AND INVENTION

When he poured the teaspoon of oil on the pond in Clapham and noted that it spread for a half acre, Franklin had come close to a discovery that would not be made for another century: determining the size of a molecule. If he had taken the volume of the teaspoon of oil (2 cubic centimeters) and divided it by the half-acre area it covered (2,000 square meters), he would have arrived at a ballpark figure (10^{-7} centimeters) for the thickness of an oil molecule. As Charles Tanford noted in his wonderful book, *Ben Franklin Stilled the Waves,* "Franklin had actually correctly determined the scale of magnitude of molecular dimensions, the first person ever to do so, but he did not recognize it."

Franklin was always better at practical applications than theoretical analysis. Rather than speculate about the size of molecules, he looked for uses for his oil-and-water experiments. Might it be possible to save ships from dangerous waves by dumping oil into the ocean? With three friends from the Royal Academy, he went to Portsmouth to see. "The experiment," Franklin reported, "had not the success we wished." The surface ripples were smoothed, but not the force of the underlying surges (another metaphor, perhaps). His report on his failed experiment was deemed useful enough, however, to be published in the *Philosophical Transactions* of the Royal Society.[13]

Throughout his time in England, whenever he could escape the demands of politics, he continued his scientific inquiries. After he wired some lightning rods on St. Paul's Cathedral, the keepers of the royal munitions asked him to propose ways to protect their buildings from lightning as well. This again embroiled Franklin in a dispute over whether lightning rods should have pointed or rounded tops; Franklin insisted on pointed ones, but (perhaps for political reasons) King George changed them to rounded ones after the American Revolution. Franklin also devised a system of hot-water pipes to keep the House of Commons warm.

Other excursions into science and invention during his years in London included:

- *The Cause of Colds:* Although germs and viruses had yet to be discovered, Franklin was one of the first to argue that colds and flu "may possibly be spread by contagion" rather than cold air. "Traveling in our severe winters, I have often suffered cold sometimes to the extremity only short of freezing, but this did not make me catch cold," he wrote the Philadelphia physician Benjamin Rush in 1773. "People often catch cold from one another when shut up together in close rooms, coaches, etc., and when sitting near and conversing so as to breathe in each other's transpiration." The best defense was fresh air. Throughout his life, Franklin liked good ventilation and open windows, even in the midst of winter.[14]

- *The Study of Exercise:* One way to prevent colds, he argued, was regular exercise. The best way to measure exercise, he argued, was not by its duration but "by the degree of warmth it produces in the body." This was one of the first theories linking exercise to calories of heat. For example, he explained, walking a mile up and down stairs produced five times more body warmth than walking a mile on a level surface. When swinging weights, Franklin calculated that this raised his pulse from 60 to 100 beats per minute. Again, he rightly calculated that body "warmth generally increases with quickness of pulse."[15]

- *Lead Poisoning:* As a printer, Franklin had noticed that the handling of hot lead type often caused a stiffness or paralysis. He also noticed that people in certain trades were prone to a severe illness called "dry belly ache." A friend added a clue by noting that people who drank rum from stills that used metal coils also got the disease. Acting as an epidemiologist, Franklin became one of the first to discover the cause of this malady. "It affects among tradesmen those that use lead, however different their trades, as glazers, type-founders, plumbers, potters, white-lead makers and painters." He suggested, among other things, that the coils of stills should be made of pure tin, instead of pewter that includes lead.[16]
- *Ships in Canals:* When visiting Holland, Franklin and his friend Sir John Pringle, president of the Royal Society, were told that ships passing through shallow canals went more slowly than those in deeper canals. This was because, Franklin surmised, each time a boat moved one length of distance, it would have to displace an amount of water equal to the space that her hull took up under the water. That water would then have to pass alongside or underneath the boat. If the passage underneath was constrained by being shallow, more water would have to rush past the sides of the boat, thus slowing her down. Here was a scientific theory that had enormous practical importance. So Franklin reacted accordingly. "I determined to make an experiment of this," he wrote Pringle. He built a fourteen-foot wooden trough that was six inches wide and deep, and in it he put a little boat that was tugged by a silk thread. The thread was placed over a pulley and pulled by the weight of a small coin. He repeatedly timed how fast the toy boat moved when the water was at various depths. The results showed that it took 20 percent more power or time to move a boat through a shallow canal than a deeper one.[17]
- *The Saltiness of Oceans:* At the time, the prevailing opinion about why the oceans were salty was that they had originally been filled with fresh water, but over the eons they accumu-

lated the salts and minerals that were dumped into them by rivers. Franklin surmised, in a letter to his brother Peter, that there was just as much evidence for the other hypothesis: "All the water on this globe was originally salt, and the fresh water we find in springs and rivers is the produce of distillation." As it turns out, Franklin was incorrect in this case. The oceans, over the centuries, have been getting saltier.[18]

- *The Armonica:* Among the most amusing of his inventions was a musical instrument he called the armonica. It was based on the common practice of bored dinner guests, and some musicians, of producing a resonant tone by moving a wet finger around the rim of a glass. Franklin attended a concert in England of music performed on wineglasses, and in 1761 he perfected the idea by taking thirty-seven glass bowls of different sizes and attaching them to a spindle. He rigged up a foot pedal and flywheel to spin the contraption, which allowed him to produce various tones by pressing on the glass pieces with his wet fingers. In a letter to an Italian electrician, Franklin described the new instrument in minute detail. "It is an instrument," he said, "that seems peculiarly adapted to Italian music, especially that of the soft and plaintive kind." Franklin's armonica was quite a rage for a while. Marie Antoinette took lessons on it, Mozart and Beethoven wrote pieces for it, and its haunting tones became popular at weddings. But it tended to produce melancholia, perhaps from lead poisoning, and it eventually went out of fashion.[19]

SOCIAL PHILOSOPHY

Over the years, Franklin had been developing a social outlook that, in its mixture of liberal, populist, and conservative ideas, would become one archetype of American middle-class philosophy. He exalted hard work, individual enterprise, frugality, and self-reliance. On the other hand, he also pushed for civic cooperation, social compassion, and voluntary community improvement schemes. He was equally distrustful of the elite and the rabble, of ceding power to a well-born establishment or to an unruly mob. With his shopkeeper's values, he cringed at class warfare. Bred into his bones was a belief in social mobility and the bootstrap values of rising through hard work.

His innate conservatism about government intervention and welfare was evident in the series of questions he had posed to Peter Collinson in 1753 (see pp. 148–49). Back then, he had asked whether laws "which compel the rich to maintain the poor have not given the latter a dependence" and "provide encouragements for laziness."[20]

To Collinson these points were raised as questions. But in his essays in the late 1760s and early 1770s, Franklin asserted his conservatism more forcefully. Most notable was an anonymous piece entitled "On the Laboring Poor," which he signed "Medius," from the Latin word for "middle," and published in *The Gentleman's Magazine* in 1768. In the essay, he chastised writers who stirred up the rabble by claiming that the poor were oppressed by the rich. "Will you admit a word or two on the other side of the question?" he asked. The condition of the poor in England was the best in Europe, he argued. Why? Because in England there was legislation to help support the poor. "This law was not made by the poor. The legislators were men of fortune . . . They voluntarily subjected their own estates, and the estates of others, to a payment of a tax for the maintenance of the poor."

These laws were compassionate. But he warned that they could have unintended consequences and promote laziness: "I fear the giving mankind a dependence on anything for support in age or sickness, besides industry and frugality during youth and health, tends to flatter our natural indolence, to encourage idleness and prodigality, and thereby to promote and increase poverty, the very evil it was intended to cure."

Not only did he warn against welfare dependency, but he offered his own version of the trickle-down theory of economics. The more money made by the rich and by all of society, the more money that would make its way down to the poor. "The rich do not work for one another . . . Everything that they or their families use and consume is the produce of the laboring poor." The rich spend their money in ways that enrich the laboring poor: clothing and furniture and dwellings. "Our laboring poor receive annually the whole of the clear revenues of the nation." He also debunked the idea of imposing a higher minimum wage: "A law might be made to raise their wages; but if our manufactures are too dear, they might not vend abroad."[21]

His economic conservatism was balanced, however, by his fundamental moral belief that actions should be judged by how much they benefit the common good. Policies that encouraged hard work were good, but not because they led to great accumulations of private wealth; they were good because they increased the total well-being of a community and the dignity of every aspiring individual. People who acquired more wealth than they needed had a duty to help others and to create civic institutions that promoted the success of others. "His ideal was of a prosperous middle class whose members lived simple lives of democratic equality," writes James Campbell. "Those who met with greater economic success in life were responsible to help those in genuine need; but those who from lack of virtue failed to pull their own weight could expect no help from society."[22]

To this philosophical mix Franklin added an increasingly fervent advocacy of the traditional English liberal values of individual rights and liberties. He had not yet, however, completed his evolution on the great moral question of slavery. As an agent for some of the colonies, including Georgia, he found himself awkwardly and unconvincingly defending America against British attacks that slavery made a mockery of the colonists' demands for liberty.

In 1770, he published anonymously a "Conversation on Slavery" in which the American participant tries to defend himself against charges of hypocrisy. Only "one family in a hundred" in America has slaves, and of those, "many treat their slaves with great humanity." He also argued that the condition of the "working poor" in England "seems something a little like slavery." At one point, the speaker's argument even lapses into racism: "Perhaps you imagine the Negroes to be a mild tempered, tractable kind of people. Some of them are indeed so. But the majority are of a plotting disposition, dark, sullen, malicious, revengeful and cruel in the highest degree."[23]

In his desire to defend America at all costs, Franklin had produced what was one of the worst arguments he ever wrote. Even his facts were wrong. The proportion of slave-owning families in America was not one in a hundred, but close to one in nine (47,664 families out of a total 410,636 American families owned slaves in 1790). Making his argument morally as well as factually weak was the fact that, even as he tried to argue that slave owning was an aberration, Franklin's own family was among those who still kept slaves. Although the two slaves who had accompanied him on his first trip to England were no longer with him, one or two continued to be part of Deborah's Philadelphia household.[24]

His views, however, were still evolving. Two years after he wrote the "Conversation," Franklin began corresponding with the ardent Philadelphia abolitionist Anthony Benezet. He used some of Benezet's arguments in a 1772 piece he wrote for the London *Chronicle* in which he decried, using stronger language than ever, the "constant butchery of the human species by this pestilent detestable traffic in the bodies and souls of men." He even edged closer to Benezet's argument that slavery itself—not merely the importation of new slaves—had to be abolished. "I am glad to hear that the disposition against keeping Negroes grows more general in North America," he wrote Benezet. "I hope in time it will be taken into consideration and suppressed by the legislature."

Franklin wrote in a similar vein to his friend the Philadelphia physician Benjamin Rush. "I hope in time that the friends to liberty and humanity will get the better of a practice that has so long disgraced our nation and religion." Yet it is important to note that, both to Benezet and to Rush, Franklin included the same qualifying phrase: "in time." For Franklin, support for complete abolition of slave ownership (rather than merely ending the importation of slaves) would come only in time, only after the Revolution.[25]

DEFEATING HILLSBOROUGH

Lord Hillsborough's solicitous warmth in Ireland, which had so baffled Franklin, soon dissipated. "When I had been a little while returned to London," Franklin wrote his son, "I waited on him to thank him for his civilities in Ireland." The porter informed Franklin that the minister was "not at home." Franklin left his card and returned another day to hear the same response, even though Franklin knew Hillsborough was indeed receiving guests that day. He tried the next week, then the next, to no avail. "The last time was on a levee day, when a number of carriages were at his door. My coachman, driving up, alighted and was opening the coach door when the porter, seeing me, came out and surlily chid the coachman for opening the door before he had enquired whether my lord was at home; and then, turning to me, said: 'My lord is not at home.' I have never since been nigh him, and we have only abused one another at a distance."

Hillsborough "threw me away as an orange that would yield no juice and therefore not worth more squeezing," Franklin complained. Again he considered returning to Philadelphia. "I grow homesick," he wrote William. But there was still one factor that kept him from leaving England in fury. Against all odds, he remained hopeful that he could secure for himself (and friends, family, and partners) a western land grant along the Ohio.[26]

To that end, he had been involved with a variety of partnerships, including ones called the Illinois Company and then the Indiana Company, that had failed to win support in London. In the summer of 1769, Franklin helped organize a consortium so powerful that he was convinced it would be able to outmaneuver Lord Hillsborough. The Grand Ohio Company, as it was named, included a collection of some of London's richest and most prominent names, most notably Thomas and Richard Walpole. For a while, it seemed the group, known as the Walpole Company, was destined for success. But in the summer of 1770, Hillsborough managed to have the scheme tabled for more study.

The Walpole group, however, was able to keep its prospects alive by spreading around ownership shares to an array of top ministers, including the lord chancellor and the president of the Privy Council. By the spring of 1772, Hillsborough could delay the matter no longer. Even the king let Hillsborough know that he expected the matter to be considered. In April, the board of trade sent the land application to the Privy Council with a recommendation that it be denied. But the Privy Council, two months later, held its own hearing, attended by Franklin, Walpole, and many of their influential shareholders. Hillsborough threatened to resign if it was approved, a prospect that likely hurt his case because many on the council were eager, in Franklin's words, "to mortify him." And they did. The grant was approved, and Hillsborough resigned.

Franklin and friends would never end up getting their land grant; the growing tensions between Britain and the colonies intervened. "The affair of the grant goes on but slowly," he wrote a friend the following year. "I begin to be a little of the sailor's mind when they were handing a cable out of a store into a ship, and one of them said: ' 'Tis a long, heavy cable. I wish we could see the end of it.' 'Damn me,' says another, 'if I believe it has any end; somebody has cut it off.' "

Still, Franklin had succeeded in ousting his nemesis. "At length we have gotten rid of Lord Hillsborough," he exulted to William. Hillsborough, in turn, called Franklin "one of the most mischievous men in England." Yet, in that odd way they had of cloaking their enmity in occasional bouts of feigned cordiality, the two men made peace when they happened upon each other at Oxford the following summer. Hillsborough made a point of bowing and complimenting Franklin. "In return for this extravagance," Franklin reported to William, "I complimented him on his son's performance in the theatre, though indeed it was but indifferent; so that account was settled. For as people say when they are angry: 'If he strikes me, I'll strike him again'; I sometimes think it might be right to say: 'If he flatters me, I'll flatter him again.' "[27]

THE HUTCHINSON LETTERS

"There has lately fallen into my hands part of a correspondence that I have reason to believe laid the foundation of most if not all our present grievances." With these fateful words, written to his Massachusetts supporter Thomas Cushing in December 1772, Franklin stirred up a tempest that would lead to his final break with Britain. Enclosed was a batch of letters, six of them written by Massachusetts governor Thomas Hutchinson, a Boston merchant from an old Puritan family, who had once been Franklin's friend when they had put together the Albany Plan for colonial union in 1754. The letters had been given to Franklin surreptitiously by an unnamed member of Parliament, and he forwarded them to Cushing with the injunction that they not be made public.

Hutchinson's letters were filled with advice on how to subdue colonial unrest. "There must be an abridgment of what are called English liberties," he had written. When they were published in Boston (John and Samuel Adams, with the acquiescence of Thomas Cushing, made sure that they were, despite Franklin's request that they not be), they stoked the growing fury of the radical patriots there.

This was the opposite of what Franklin had intended. His aim was to calm the rebellious sentiments by privately showing Cushing and a few other leaders that England's misguided policies had been caused by bad advice from people such as Hutchinson more than by unreasonable hatred for America. The letters, he believed, might even promote a "tendency . . . towards a reconciliation," which is what, he later claimed, "I earnestly wished."[28]

Indeed, most of Franklin's missives in early 1773 were designed to decrease tensions. "I hope that great care will be taken to keep our people quiet," he wrote Cushing in March, "since nothing is more wished for by our enemies than that by insurrections we would give a good pretence for increasing the military among us and putting us under more severe restraints." When the Massachusetts Assembly passed a resolution declaring that it was not subservient to Parliament, Franklin similarly urged the English to refrain from overreacting. "In my opinion, it would be better and more prudent to take no notice of it," he wrote Colonial Secretary Lord Dartmouth, who had replaced Hillsborough. "It is words only."[29]

To make his point without stirring up more animosity, Franklin reverted to his youthful love of satire in two anonymous propaganda pieces he wrote for the English papers in September 1773. The first was entitled "Rules by Which a Great Empire May be Reduced to a Small One." Noting that "an ancient sage" (it was the Greek admiral and ruler Themistocles) had once boasted that he knew how to turn a little city into a great one, the essay listed twenty ways to do the reverse to an empire. Among them:

In the first place, gentlemen, you are to consider that a great
    empire, like a great cake, is most easily diminished at the
    edges.

Take special care the provinces are never incorporated with the
    Mother Country, that they do not enjoy the same common
    rights, the same privileges in commerce, and that they are
    governed by severer laws, all of your enacting, without allow-
    ing them any share in the choice of legislators.

However peaceably your colonies have submitted to your gov-
    ernment, shown their affection to your interest, and patiently
    borne their grievances, you are to suppose them always in-
    clined to revolt, and treat them accordingly. Quarter troops
    among them, who by their insolence may provoke the rising
    of mobs . . . Like the husband who uses his wife ill from sus-
    picion, you may in time convert your suspicions into realities.

Whenever the injured come to the capital with complaints . . .
    punish such suitors with long delay, enormous expense, and a
    final judgment in favor of the oppressor.

Resolve to harass them with novel taxes. They will probably
    complain to your Parliaments that they are taxed by a body
    in which they have no representative, and that this is con-
    trary to common right . . . Let the Parliaments flout their
    claims . . . and treat the petitioners with utmost contempt.

The list, reflecting the indignities that had been perpetrated on
America, went on at length: send them "prodigals" and "petty-fogging
lawyers" to govern them, "perplex their commerce with infinite regulations," appoint "insolent" tax collectors, and garrison your troops in
their homes rather than on the frontier where they can be of use. If
you follow these rules for diminishing your colonies, the essay concluded, you will "get rid of the trouble of governing them." It was
signed "Q.E.D.," the initials for the Latin phrase *quod erat demon-
strandum* (which was to be demonstrated), used at the end of a philosophical argument to note the proposition was proved.[30]

Two weeks later, Franklin published an even broader parody of

Britain's treatment of America, "An Edict by the King of Prussia." A thinly disguised hoax, it purported to be a declaration issued by King Frederick II. Whereas the Germans had long ago created the first settlements in England and had lately protected it in the war against France, they had decided "that a revenue should be raised from said colonies in Britain." So Prussia was levying 4.5 percent duties on all English imports and exports, and it was prohibiting the creation of any further manufacturing plants in England. The edict added that the felons in German jails "shall be emptied out" and sent to England "for the better peopling of that country." Lest anyone be so thick as to miss the point, it concluded by noting that all of these measures should be considered "just and reasonable" in England because they were "copied" from the rules imposed by the British Parliament on the American colonies.[31]

When his "Edict" appeared, Franklin had the pleasure of being a guest at the country estate of Lord Le Despencer, who, as postmaster general of Britain, was Franklin's boss and had become his friend. Le Despencer was, in Van Doren's words, a "seasoned old sinner" who had restored a former abbey where he gathered dissolute friends for, as rumor had it, blasphemous rites and an occasional orgy. Franklin befriended him in 1772, when Le Despencer had become a bit more respectable, and helped him compile a simplified and deistic version of the Book of Common Prayer. (In his reformist zeal, Franklin had recently written a "more concise" version of the Lord's Prayer as well.)

Franklin was chatting in the breakfast parlor with Le Despencer and others when a guest "came running in to us out of breath" with the morning papers and exclaimed, "Here's the King of Prussia claiming a right to this kingdom!" Franklin feigned innocence as the story was read aloud.

"Damn his impudence," one of those present proclaimed.

But as the reading neared its end, another guest began to sense the hoax. "I'll be hanged if this is not some of your American jokes upon us," he said to Franklin. The reading, Franklin noted, "ended with abundance of laughing and a general verdict that it was a fair hit."

Franklin proudly described the parodies in a letter to William. He preferred the one on "Rules," he said, because of the "quantity and variety of the matter contained and a kind of spirited ending of each paragraph," but others preferred the "Edict." He boasted, "I am not suspected as the author, except by one or two friends, and have heard the latter ['Edict'] spoken of in the highest terms as the keenest and severest piece that has appeared here for a long time."

His letter to William, however, was not wholly jovial. Slowly, inevitably, a rift was widening between the increasingly radical American agent and the royal governor with upper-class friends and aspirations. "Parliament has no right to make any law whatever binding on the colonies," Franklin argued in the letter. "I know your sentiments differ from mine on these subjects. You are a thorough government man."[32]

IN THE COCKPIT

"I want much to hear how that tea is received," Franklin worriedly wrote a friend in late 1773. Parliament had added to the indignity of its continued tariff on tea by passing new regulations that gave the corrupt East India Company a virtual monopoly over the trade. Franklin urged calm, but the radicals of Boston, led by Sam Adams and the Sons of Liberty, did not. On December 16, 1773, after a mass rally in the Old South Church, some fifty patriots disguised as Mohawk Indians went down to the wharves and dumped 342 chests of tea worth £10,000 into the sea.

Franklin was shocked by "the act of violent injustice on our part." His sympathies for the colonial cause were not enough to overcome his basic conservatism about rabble rule. The shareholders of the East India Company "are not our adversaries," he declared. It was wrong "to destroy private property."[33]

As Boston was having its tea party, England was being roiled by recriminations from the release of the purloined Hutchinson letters. Franklin had expressed surprise that "my name has not been heard" in connection with the affair and added his "wish it may continue unknown." But in December, two men engaged in an inconclusive duel in Hyde Park after one accused the other of leaking the letters. When a rematch seemed imminent, Franklin felt he had to step forward. "I

alone am the person who obtained and transmitted to Boston the letters in question," he wrote in a letter to the London *Chronicle* on
Christmas Day. But he did not apologize. These were not "private letters between friends," he claimed, but were "written by public officers
to persons in public station." They were designed to "incense the
Mother Country against her colonies."[34]

Franklin's role in publicizing purloined copies gave ammunition to
those in Britain who saw him as a troublemaker. In early January, he
was summoned to appear before the Privy Council in a famed room
known as the Cockpit, because cockfights had been held there during
the time of Henry VIII. The ostensible reason was to hear testimony
on a petition from the Massachusetts Assembly to remove Hutchinson from the governorship. The questioning, however, quickly focused
on whether the letters from Hutchinson, which had been presented as
evidence by Franklin, were private and how they were obtained.

Franklin was surprised to find at the hearing the solicitor general,
Alexander Wedderburn, a nasty and ambitious prosecutor who had
voted against the repeal of the Stamp Act and possessed (in the words
of his prime minister Lord North) "an accommodating conscience." It
was clear that the political issue of the petition against Hutchinson
was being turned into a legal case against Franklin for making his letters public. The government, Wedderburn said pointedly, had "the
right of inquiring how they were obtained."

"I thought this had been a matter of politics and not of law,"
Franklin told the committee, "and I have not brought any counsel."

"Dr. Franklin may have the assistance of counsel, or go on without
it, as he shall choose," said one of the lords on the council.

"I desire to have counsel," Franklin replied. Asked how long he
needed to prepare his case, Franklin answered, "Three weeks."

It was not a fun three weeks for Franklin. News of the Boston Tea
Party reached England, further undermining sympathy for the American cause. He was called "an incendiary" and, he noted, "the papers
were filled with invectives against me." There were even hints that he
might be jailed. His fellow shareholders in the Walpole group expressed fear that his involvement would hurt their case for a land
grant, so he wrote them that "I do therefore desire that you will strike

my name out of the list of your Associates." (The letter, it should be noted, was cleverly phrased so that he did not, in fact, actually resign; he remained a secret shareholder without voting rights.)[35]

When the Privy Council reconvened in the Cockpit on January 29, 1774, the showdown made the original use of that room seem tame. "All the courtiers were invited," Franklin noted, "as to an entertainment." The packed crowd of councilors and spectators ranged from the Archbishop of Canterbury to the revenge-hungry Lord Hillsborough, with but a few friends of Franklin—including Edmund Burke, Lord Le Despencer, and Joseph Priestley—there to lend him moral support. Franklin later said it was like a "bull baiting."

Wedderburn, that man of sharp tongue, was both clever and brutal in his hour-long tirade. He called Franklin the "prime conductor"—an allusion to his electric fame—of the agitation against the British government. Instead of focusing on the merits of the Massachusetts petition, he homed in on the purloined letters. "Private correspondence has hitherto been held sacred," he raged. "He has forfeited all the respect of societies and of men." With a zinging wit, he added, "He will henceforth call it a libel to be called a man of letters." In addition to wit there was ample invective. Burke called Wedderburn's attack a "furious Phillipic," and another spectator called it "a torrent of virulent abuse."

Amid his fury, Wedderburn scored some valid points. Ridiculing Franklin's argument that Hutchinson's desire to keep the letters secret was an admission he had something to hide, the solicitor correctly noted that Franklin had kept his own involvement in the affair secret for almost a year. "He kept himself concealed until he nearly occasioned the murder" of an innocent man, he said, referring to the duel in Hyde Park. Pounding the council table until (according to Jeremy Bentham) it "groaned under the assault," Wedderburn accused Franklin of wanting to be governor himself.

The crowd cheered and jeered, but Franklin betrayed not the slightest emotion as he stood at the edge of the room wearing a plain suit made of blue Manchester velvet. Edward Bancroft, a friend of Franklin's (who later spied on him in Paris), described his behavior: "The Doctor was dressed in a full suit of spotted Manchester velvet, and stood conspicuously erect, without the smallest movement of any part of his body. The muscles of his face had been previously composed as to afford a placid tranquil expression of countenance, and he did not suffer the slightest alteration of it to appear."

At the finale of his speech, Wedderburn called Franklin forward as a witness and declared, "I am ready to examine him." The official records of the proceedings notes, "Dr. Franklin being present remained silent, but declared by his counsel that he did not choose to be examined." Silence had often been his best weapon, making him seem wise or benign or serene. On this occasion, it made him look stronger than his powerful adversaries, contemptuous rather than contrite, condescending rather than cowed.[36]

The Privy Council, as expected, rejected the Massachusetts petition against Hutchinson, calling it "groundless, vexatious and scandalous." The next day, Franklin was informed by letter that his old friend Lord Le Despencer "found it necessary" to remove him from his job as American postmaster. This infuriated him, for he was proud of having made the colonial system efficient and profitable, and he wrote a terse note to William suggesting that he leave his governorship and become a farmer. "It is an honester and more honorable, because a more independent, employment." To his sister Jane, he was more ruminative: "I am deprived of my office. Don't let this give you any uneasiness. You and I have almost finished the journey of life; we are now but a little way from home, and have enough in our pocket to pay the post chaises."[37]

Fearing that he might be arrested or his papers confiscated, Franklin slipped down to the Thames near Craven Street a few days after the Cockpit hearing. Carrying a trunk of his papers, he took a boat upriver to a friend's house in Chelsea, where he laid low for a few days. When the danger passed, he returned to Craven Street and resumed receiving guests. "I do not find that I have lost a single friend on the occasion," he noted. "All have visited me repeatedly with affectionate assurances of unaltered respect." At their request, he wrote a very long and detailed account of the Hutchinson affair, but then did not publish it, noting that "such censures I have generally passed over in silence."[38]

He did, however, continue his torrent of anonymous publications. Indulging an atypical but, given the circumstances, understandable desire to be boastful, he wrote a semianonymous piece (signed *Homo Trium Literarum,* a "Man of Letters," the insulting pun Wedderburn had hurled at him) that declared that "the admirers of Dr. Franklin in England are much shocked at Mr. Wedderburn's calling him a thief." He noted that the French, in the preface to his scientific papers just published there, also called him a thief: "To steal from the Heaven its sacred fire he taught." In an unsigned description of the Cockpit hearings, published in a Boston paper, he claimed of himself that "the Doctor came by these letters honorably, his intention in sending them was virtuous: to lessen the breach between Britain and the colonies." [39]

His satires and sarcasm became ever more biting. In one essay, written after General Gage had been sent to replace Hutchinson as governor in Massachusetts, he suggested that Britain "without delay introduce into North America a government absolutely and entirely military." That would "so intimidate the Americans" that they would happily submit to all taxes. "When the colonists are drained of their last shilling," he added, "they should be sold to the best bidder," such as Spain or France. In another piece, he proposed a policy for General Gage to assure that more rebels did not arise in America: "all the males there be castrated." For good measure, the "ringleaders" such as John Hancock and Sam Adams "should be shaved quite close." Among the side benefits, he added, were that it would be useful to the opera and it would reduce the number of people emigrating from Britain to America. [40]

Once again, the question arose: Why not finally head home? His wife was near death, he was a political outcast. Once again, he resolved to do so. As soon as he settled the post office accounts, he told friends; by May, he promised Richard Bache. And once again, he ended up not returning. For the rest of 1774, Franklin stayed in England with little to do, no official business to conduct, no ministers to lobby. Even the king found it curious.

"Where is Dr. Franklin?" His Majesty asked Lord Dartmouth that summer.

"I believe, sir, he is in town. He was going to America, but I fancy he is not gone."

"I heard," said the king, "he was going to Switzerland."

"I think," Lord Dartmouth replied, "there has been such a report."

In fact, he had stayed close to Craven Street, venturing out rarely, seeing mainly close friends. As he would write to his sister in September, "I have seen no minister since January, nor had the least communication with them." [41]

THE BREACH WITH WILLIAM

The impending clash between Britain and America inevitably foreshadowed a personal one between Franklin and his loyalist son. Tormented about the former prospect, Franklin remained callous about the latter.

William, on the other hand, agonized mightily as he tried to balance his duties as a son with those of being the royal governor of New Jersey. In his letters to his father after the Cockpit fight, he hoped to curry favor by flattering him, reassuring him, and cajoling him to come home. "Your popularity in this country, whatever it may be on the other side, is greatly beyond what it ever was," William wrote in May. "You may depend when you return here on being received with every mark of regard and affection." He made clear, however, that he had no intention of resigning his governorship, despite his father's occasional suggestions that he do so.

Caught in the middle was the printer William Strahan, one of Franklin's closest friends in England, who had become a confidant of the younger Franklin as well. He urged William to be his own man, to stick to loyalist positions, and to let the ministers know that he would not let his father's views interfere with his allegiance to the government he served.

William heeded the advice. Shortly after writing the solicitous letter to his father, he wrote one to Lord Dartmouth, the colonial secretary. "His Majesty may be assured that I will omit nothing in my power to keep this province quiet," he promised. Then he added pointedly, "No attachment or connections shall ever make me swerve from the duty of my station." Translation: his loyalty to his father would not tug him away from his loyalty to Britain. Lord Dartmouth promptly responded with reassurances: "I should do injustice to my own sentiments of your character and conduct in supposing you could be induced by any consideration whatever to swerve from the duty you owe the King."

William went further than merely offering professions of fealty. He opened what he called a "secret and confidential" correspondence with Lord Dartmouth that provided information about American sentiments. Support was growing throughout the colonies to aid Massachusetts, he warned, in reaction to the British decision to blockade Boston's port. A meeting of colonial delegates, which would become known as the First Continental Congress, had been scheduled for Philadelphia in September. William made clear which side he was on. The proposed gathering, he declared, was "absurd if not unconstitutional," and he doubted that it would lead to a mass boycott of British goods.[42]

His father disagreed on all counts. He had been recommending a continental congress for more than a year, he felt strongly that it should call for a boycott, and he was confident that it would. In that case, he wrote gleefully to William, "the present ministry will certainly be knocked up." He also chided William for clinging to his governorship and, typically, cast the issue in pecuniary as well as political terms. By remaining dependent on the salary of a governor, said Franklin, he would never be able to pay off the debts he owed his father. In addition, the changing political climate meant "you will find yourself in no comfortable situation and perhaps wish you had soon disengaged yourself." It was signed, simply, "B. Franklin."[43]

Even though he knew his letters were being opened and read by British authorities, Franklin forcefully urged his American supporters to take a firm stand. The Continental Congress, he wrote, must vote "immediately to stop all commerce with this country, both exports and imports . . . until you have obtained redress." At stake was "no less than whether Americans, and their endless generations, shall enjoy the common rights of mankind or be worse than eastern slaves."

In those days, when it could take up to two months for the mail to be delivered overseas, there were a lot of crossed letters. William continued to try to convince his father that a continental congress was a bad idea. "There is no foreseeing the consequences that may result from such a Congress." Instead, Bostonians should make restitution for the tea they destroyed, and then "they might get their port opened in a few months."

Franklin had actually expressed, a few months earlier, similar sentiments about how Bostonians would be prudent to pay restitution for their tea party. "Such a step will remove much of the prejudice now entertained against us," he had written Cushing in March. It infuriated him, however, to be given such a lecture by his son, and in September he wrote a crushing response rebutting William point by point. Britain had "extorted many thousands of pounds" from the colonies unconstitutionally. "Of this money they ought to make restitution." The argument ended in insult: "But you, who are a thorough courtier, see everything with government eyes."

Franklin wrote his son again in October, making many of the same arguments and then turning personal: he pointedly noted that his son was behind in paying back the money he had loaned him over the years and would not likely be able to do so if he remained a royal governor.[44]

For a while there was no answer. Then, on Christmas eve of 1774, William sent his father a letter of brutal sadness and pain. Deborah had died, with Franklin not there.

"I came here on Thursday last to attend the funeral of my poor old mother, who died Monday," he began, referring to his stepmother.

Franklin's dutiful and long-suffering wife had been pining away since her stroke five years earlier. "I find myself growing very feeble very fast," she had written in 1772. For most of 1774, she had been too weak to write at all. Oblivious, Franklin had continued to send off short notes to her, some paternalistic and others businesslike, that contained breezy references to his own health, greetings from the Stevenson family, and admonitions for not writing him.

"A very respectable number of the inhabitants were at the funeral," William continued. Clearly wanting his father to feel guilty, he described his last visit with Deborah that October. "She told me that she never expected to see you unless you returned this winter, that she was sure she would not live until next summer. I heartily wish you had happened to have come over in the fall, as I think her disappointment preyed a good deal on her spirits."

At the end of the letter, William turned plaintive as he beseeched his father to leave England. "You are looked upon with an evil eye in that country, and are in no small danger of being brought into trouble for your political conduct," William warned. "You had certainly better return while you are able to bear the fatigues of the voyage to a country where the people revere you." He also ached to see his own son, Temple, now 14, and he begged Franklin to bring him to America. "I hope to see you and him in the spring and that you will spend some time with me."[45]

THE HOWE–CHATHAM SECRET TALKS

As his wife was dying that December, Franklin was enjoying a flirtatious series of chess matches with a fashionable woman he had just met in London. But the games were not merely social. They were part of a secret last-ditch effort by some members of Britain's Whig opposition to stave off a revolution by the colonies.

The process had begun in August, when he received a request to call on Lord Chatham, formerly William Pitt the Elder, who had served two stints as prime minister and been known as "the Great Commoner" until unwisely accepting a peerage as the Earl of Chatham. The great Whig orator was a steadfast supporter of America. By 1774, he was ailing and out of government, but he had decided to reengage in public affairs as an outspoken opponent of Lord North and his policy of colonial repression.

Lord Chatham received Franklin warmly, professed full support for the resistance by the colonies to British taxation, and said he "hoped they would continue firm." Franklin responded by urging Chatham to join with other Whig "Wise Men" to oust the "present set of bungling ministers" and form a government that would restore the "union and harmony between Britain and her colonies."

That was not likely, Chatham said. There were too many in England who felt that there could be no further concessions because "America aimed at setting up for itself an independent state."

"America did not aim at independence," Franklin claimed. "I assured him that, having more than once traveled almost from one end of the continent to the other, and kept a great variety of company, eating, drinking and conversing with them freely, I never had heard in any conversation, from any person drunk or sober, the least expression of a wish for separation."

Franklin was not being fully forthright. It had been ten years since he had traveled in America, and he knew full well that a small but growing number of radical colonists, drunk and sober, desired independence. He had even begun entertaining that possibility himself. Josiah Quincy Jr., a zealous Boston patriot and son of an old Franklin friend, visited him that fall and reported that they had discussed "total emancipation" of the colonies as an increasingly likely outcome.[46]

The next act in the drama began with a curious invitation from a well-connected society matron who let it be known that she wanted to play chess with Franklin. The woman in question was Caroline Howe, the sister of Adm. Richard Howe and Gen. William Howe. They would eventually end up the commanders of England's naval and land forces during the Revolution, but at the time they were both somewhat sympathetic to the American cause. (Their sister was the widow of a distant cousin, Richard Howe, and thus known as Mrs. Howe.)[47]

When Franklin called on Mrs. Howe in early December, he found her "of very sensible conversation and pleasing behavior." They enjoyed a few games and Franklin "most readily" accepted an invitation to play again a few days later. This time, the conversation wandered. They discussed her interest in math, which Franklin noted was "a little unusual in ladies," and then Mrs. Howe turned to politics.

"What is to be done," she asked, "about this dispute between Great Britain and her colonies?"

"They should kiss and be friends," replied Franklin.

"I have often said that I wished the government would employ you to settle the dispute," she said. "I am sure nobody could do it so well. Don't you think that the thing is practicable?"

"Undoubtedly, madam, if the parties are disposed to reconciliation," he responded. "The two countries really have no clashing interests." It was a matter that "reasonable people might settle in half an hour." He added, however, that "the ministers will never think of employing me in that good work; they choose rather to abuse me."

"Aye," she agreed, "they have behaved shamefully to you. And indeed some of them are now ashamed of it themselves."

Later that same evening, Franklin dined with two old friends, the Quakers John Fothergill and David Barclay, who made the same plea that he act as a mediator. "Put pen to paper," they urged him, and draft a plan for reconciliation.

And so he did. His "Hints for a Conversation" included seventeen points, among them: Massachusetts would pay for the destroyed tea, the tea duties would be repealed, the regulations on colonial manufacturing would be reconsidered, all money raised by trade duties would go to the colonial treasuries, no troops would be stationed in a colony without the approval of its legislature, and all powers of taxation would reside with the colonial legislatures rather than Parliament. His friends asked permission to show the list to some "moderate ministers," and Franklin agreed.

These private negotiations were interrupted in mid-December, when Franklin finally received the resolutions that had been approved by the First Continental Congress. At its meeting in Philadelphia, which lasted until late October, the rump assembly had reasserted America's loyalty to the Crown—but not to Parliament. In addition, it voted a boycott of British goods if Parliament did not repeal its coercive acts.

Many of the colonial agents in London refused to have anything to do with the resolutions when they arrived. So Franklin and the other agents from Massachusetts took it upon themselves to deliver them to Lord Dartmouth, who "told us it was a decent and proper petition and cheerfully undertook to present it to his Majesty."

On Christmas day, Franklin visited Mrs. Howe for another chess match. As soon as he arrived, she mentioned that her brother, Admiral Lord Richard Howe, wanted to meet him. "Will you give me leave to send for him?" she asked.

Franklin readily agreed, and soon he was listening as Lord Howe showered him with compliments. "No man could do more towards reconciling our differences," the admiral told him. He asked Franklin to offer some suggestions, which he would then communicate to the proper ministers.

Franklin, wary of being caught in the middle, noted that the Continental Congress had made clear what the colonies wanted. But he agreed to another secret session a week later, again under the guise of visiting Mrs. Howe to play chess.

This time, the meeting was not quite as cordial. Lord Howe asked Franklin if he thought it might be useful for England to send an emissary to America to seek an accommodation. It might "be of great use," Franklin responded, as long as the person was one of "rank and dignity."

Mrs. Howe interjected by nominating her brother for such a role, subtly noting that there was talk of sending over their other brother, the army general, on a less peaceful mission. "I wish, brother, you were to be sent thither on such a service," she said. "I should like that much better than General Howe's going to command the army there."

"I think, madam," Franklin said pointedly, "they ought to provide for General Howe some more honorable employment."

Lord Howe then pulled out a piece of paper and asked if Franklin knew anything about it. It was a copy of the "Hints for a Conversation" that he had prepared. Franklin said that his role in drawing up the paper was supposed to be a secret, but he readily owned up to having been the originator. Howe replied that he "was rather sorry" to find that the propositions were Franklin's, because there was no likelihood that the ministers would accept them. He urged Franklin to reconsider the proposals and come up with a new plan "that would be acceptable." Mrs. Howe could recopy it in her own hand, so that the authorship would be kept secret. If Franklin did so, Lord Howe hinted, he could "expect any reward in the power of the government to bestow."

Franklin bristled at the implied bribe. "This to me was what the French call 'spitting in the soup,' " he later noted. Nevertheless, Franklin found himself trusting Lord Howe and decided to play along. "I liked his manner," he noted, "and found myself disposed to place great confidence in him."

The paper he sent to Mrs. Howe the next day made no substantive concessions. Instead, it merely restated the American position and declared them necessary "to cement a cordial union." Although the talks with Howe continued fitfully through February, fueled mainly by the admiral's ambition to be chosen as an envoy, they never moved much closer to a solution.

In the meantime, Franklin was engaged in a variety of other back-channel talks and negotiations, most notably with Lord Chatham. The former prime minister invited him to his country house to show him a series of proposals he planned to put before Parliament, and then visited him for two hours on Craven Street for further discussions. Lord Chatham's presence at Franklin's humble boarding-house—his coach waiting very visibly in the narrow street outside the door—caused quite a stir in the neighborhood. "Such a visit from so great a man, on so important a business, flattered not a little my vanity," Franklin admitted. It was particularly savory because it fell precisely on the first anniversary of his humiliation in the Cockpit.

The compromise that Chatham proposed, as the two men sat together in the tiny parlor of Mrs. Stevenson's house, would permit Parliament to regulate imperial trade and to send troops to America. But only the colonial legislatures would have the right to impose taxes, and the Continental Congress would be given official and permanent standing. Although Franklin did not approve of all its particulars, he readily agreed to lend his support by being present when Chatham presented the plan to the House of Lords on February 1.

Chatham gave an eloquent explanation of his proposals, and Lord Dartmouth responded for the government by saying they were of "such weight and magnitude as to require much consideration." For a moment, Franklin felt that all of his back-channel talks and lobbying might be bearing fruit.

Then Lord Sandwich, who as first lord of the admiralty had taken a hard line on colonial affairs, took the floor. In a "petulant, vehement speech," he attacked Chatham's bill and then turned his aim on Franklin. He could not believe, he said, that the plan came from the pen of an English peer. Instead, it appeared to him the work of some American. As Franklin recounted the scene: "Turning his face to me,

[he] said he fancied he had in his eye the person who drew it up, one of the bitterest and most mischievous enemies this country had ever known. This drew the eyes of many lords upon me; but . . . I kept my countenance as immovable as if my features had been made of wood."

Chatham replied that the plan was his own, but he was not ashamed to have consulted "a person so perfectly acquainted with the whole of American affairs as the gentleman alluded to and so injuriously reflected on." He then proceeded to heap praise on Franklin as a person "whom all Europe held in high estimation for his knowledge and wisdom and ranked with our Boyles and Newtons; who was an honor not to the English nation only but to human nature." Franklin later wrote to his son, with perhaps a bit of feigned humility, "I found it harder to stand this extravagant compliment than the preceding equally extravagant abuse."[48]

But Chatham was not only out of power, he was out of touch. Lord Dartmouth quickly abandoned his initial openness and agreed with Lord Sandwich that the bill should be rejected immediately, which it was. "Chatham's bill," Franklin wrote to a Philadelphia friend, "was treated with as much contempt as they could have shown to a ballad offered by a drunken porter."[49]

For the next few weeks, Franklin engaged in a flurry of further meetings designed to salvage some compromise. But by early March 1775, as he finally prepared to leave England, his patience had run out. He drew up an insolent petition to Lord Dartmouth demanding British reparations for the blockade of Boston Harbor. When he showed it to his friend and land deal partner Thomas Walpole, "he looked at it and me several times alternately, as if he apprehended me a little out of my senses." Franklin returned to his senses and decided not to submit the petition.

Instead, he played a small role in one of the final and most eloquent pleas for peace. He spent the afternoon of March 19 with the great Whig orator and philosopher Edmund Burke. Three days later, Burke rose in Parliament to give his famous but futile "On Conciliation with America" speech. "A great empire and little minds go ill together," he proclaimed.

By then, Franklin was already on the Philadelphia packet ship

heading west from Portsmouth. He had spent his last day in London with his old friend and scientific partner Joseph Priestley. People who did not know Franklin, Priestley wrote, sometimes found him reserved, even cold. But that day, as they discussed the looming war and read from the newspapers, he grew very emotional. For a while, the tears in his eyes made it impossible for him to read.[50]

CHAPTER TWELVE

INDEPENDENCE

Philadelphia, 1775–1776

CHOOSING SIDES

Just as his son, William, had helped him with his famed kite-flying experiment, now William's son, Temple, lent a hand as he lowered the homemade thermometer into the ocean. Three or four times a day, they would take the temperature and record it on a chart. Franklin had learned from his Nantucket cousin, the whaling captain Timothy Folger, about the course of the Gulf Stream. During the latter half of his six-week voyage home, after writing a detailed account of his futile negotiations, Franklin turned his attention to studying it. The maps he published and the temperature measurements he made are included on the NASA Web site, which notes how remarkably similar they are to the infrared data gathered by modern satellites.[1]

The voyage was notably calm, but in America the long-brewing storm had begun. On the night of April 18, 1775, while Franklin was in midocean, a contingent of British redcoats headed north from Boston to arrest the tea party planners Samuel Adams and John Hancock and capture the munitions stockpiled by their supporters. Paul Revere spread the alarm, as did others less famously. When the redcoats reached Lexington, seventy American "minutemen" were there to meet them.

"Disperse, ye rebels," the British major ordered. At first they did. Then a shot was fired. In the ensuing skirmish, eight Americans were killed. The victorious redcoats marched on to Concord, where, as Emerson put it, "the embattled farmers stood, and fired the shot heard round the world." (Somehow, the poor Lexington fighters lost out in Emerson's poetic version of history, just as William Dawes and other messengers got slighted in Longfellow's "Paul Revere's Ride.") On their day-long retreat back to Boston, more than 250 redcoats were killed or wounded by American militiamen.

When Franklin landed in Philadelphia with his 15-year-old grandson on May 5, delegates were beginning to gather there for the Second Continental Congress. Bells were rung to celebrate his arrival. "Dr. Franklin is highly pleased to find us arming and preparing for the worst events," wrote one reporter. "He thinks nothing else can save us from the most abject slavery."

America was indeed arming and preparing. Among those arriving in Philadelphia that week, with his uniform packed and ready, was Franklin's old military comrade, George Washington, who had become a plantation squire in Virginia after the French and Indian War. Close to a thousand militiamen on horse and foot met him at the outskirts of Philadelphia, and a military band played patriotic songs as his carriage rode into town. Yet there was still no consensus, except among the radical patriots in the Massachusetts delegation, about whether the war that had just erupted should be waged for independence or merely for the assertion of American rights within a British Empire that could still be preserved. For that question to be resolved would take another year, though not for Franklin.

Franklin was selected a member of the Congress the day after his arrival. Nearing 70, he was by far the oldest. Most of the sixty-two others who convened in the Pennsylvania statehouse—such as Thomas Jefferson and Patrick Henry from Virginia and John Adams and John Hancock from Massachusetts—had not even been born when Franklin first went to work there more than forty years earlier.

Franklin moved to the house on Market Street that he had designed but never known, the one where Deborah had been living without him for the past ten years. His daughter, Sally, took care of his housekeeping needs, her husband, Richard Bache, remained dutiful, and their two children, Ben and Will, provided amusement. "Will has

got a little gun, marches with it, and whistles at the same time by way
of fife," Franklin wrote.[2]

For the time being, Franklin kept quiet about whether or not he favored independence, and he avoided the taverns where the other delegates spent the evenings debating the topic. He diligently attended
sessions and committee meetings, said little, and then went home to
dine with his family. Beginning what would become a long and conflicted association with Franklin, the loquacious and ambitious John
Adams complained that the older man was treated with reverence
even as he was "sitting in silence, a great part of the time fast asleep in
his chair."

Many of the younger, hotter-tempered delegates had never witnessed Franklin's artifice of silence, his trick of seeming sage by saying
nothing. They knew him by reputation as the man who had successfully argued in Parliament against the Stamp Act, not realizing that
oratory did not come naturally to him. So rumors began to circulate.
What was his game? Was he a secret loyalist?

Among the suspicious was William Bradford, who had taken over
the printing business and newspaper of his father, Franklin's first patron and later competitor. Some of the delegates, he confided to the
young James Madison, "begin to entertain a great suspicion that Dr.
Franklin came rather as a spy than as a friend, and that he means to
discover our weak side and make his peace with the ministers."[3]

In fact, Franklin was biding his time through much of May because there were two people, both very close to him, whom he first
wanted to convert to the American rebel cause. One was Joseph Galloway, his old ally in the struggle against the Penns, who had acted as
his lieutenant and surrogate for ten years in the Pennsylvania Assembly. During the First Continental Congress, Galloway had proposed
the creation of an American congress that would have power parallel
to that of Parliament, with both loyal to the king. It was a plan for an
imperial union along the lines that Franklin had supported at the Albany Conference and later, but the Congress peremptorily rejected it.
Sulking, Galloway had declined an appointment to the Second Continental Congress.

By early 1775, Franklin had come to believe it was too late for a plan like Galloway's to work. Nevertheless, he tried to persuade Galloway to join him as a member of the new Congress. It was wrong to quit public life, he wrote, "at a time when your abilities are so much wanted." Initially, he also gave Galloway no more clue than he had given others about where he stood on the question of independence. "People seemed at a loss what party he would take," Galloway later recalled.[4]

The other person Franklin hoped to convert to the revolutionary cause was someone even closer to him.

THE SUMMIT AT TREVOSE

New Jersey governor William Franklin, still loyal to the British ministry and embroiled in disputes with his own legislature, read of his father's return to Philadelphia in the papers. It was, he wrote Strahan, "quite unexpected news to me." He was eager to meet with his father and to reclaim his son, Temple. First, however, he had to endure a special session of the New Jersey legislature he had called for May 15. Shortly after it ended in rancor, the three generations of Franklins—father and son and a poor grandson caught in the middle—were finally reunited.[5]

Franklin and his son chose a neutral venue for their summit: Trevose, the grand fieldstone manor house of Joseph Galloway in Bucks County, just north of Philadelphia. Surprisingly, given the intensely emotional nature of the meeting, neither they nor Galloway apparently ever wrote about it. The only source for what transpired is, ironically, the diary of Thomas Hutchinson, the Massachusetts governor whose letters Franklin had purloined; in his diary, Hutchinson recorded an account of the meeting Galloway gave three years later, when both men were exiled loyalists in England.

The evening started awkwardly, with embraces and then small talk. At one point, William pulled Galloway aside to say that he had avoided, until now, seriously talking politics with his father. But after a while, "the glass having gone around freely" and much Madeira consumed, they confronted their political disagreements. "Well, Mr. Galloway," Franklin asked his longtime ally, "you are really of the mind that I ought to promote a reconciliation?"

Galloway was indeed of such a mind, but Franklin would hear none of it. He had brought with him the long letter he had written to William during his Atlantic crossing, which detailed his futile attempts at negotiating a reconciliation. Although Galloway had already heard portions of it, Franklin again read most of it aloud and told of the abuse he had suffered. Galloway volleyed with his own horror stories about how anonymous radicals had sent him a noose for proposing a plan to save the British union. A revolution, he stressed, would be suicidal.

William argued that it was best for them all to remain neutral, but his father was not moved. As Hutchinson later recorded, he "opened himself and declared in favor of measures for attaining to independence" and "exclaimed against the corruption and dissipation of the kingdom." William responded with anger, but also with a touch of concern for his father's safety. If he intended "to set the colonies in flame," William hoped, he should "take care to run away by the light of it."[6]

So William rode back to New Jersey, defeated and dejected, to resume his duties as royal governor. With him was his son, Temple. The one issue that Benjamin and William had settled at Trevose was that the boy would spend the summer in New Jersey, then return to Philadelphia to be enrolled in the college his grandfather had founded there. William had hoped to send him to King's College (now Columbia) in New York, but Benjamin scuttled that plan because it had become a hotbed of English loyalism. Temple was soon to be caught in a tug-of-war between two men who vied for his loyalty. He eagerly sought to please them both, but he was fated to find that impossible.

FRANKLIN THE REBEL

It is hard to pinpoint precisely when America crossed the threshold of deciding that complete independence from Britain was necessary and desirable. It is even difficult to determine when that tipping point came for specific individuals. Franklin, who for ten years had juggled hope and despair that a breach could be avoided, made his own private declaration to his family during their summit at Trevose. By early July 1775, precisely a year before his fellow American patriots made their own stance official, he was ready to come out publicly.

There were many specific events that pushed Franklin across the line to rebellion: personal slights, dashed hopes, betrayals, and the accretion of hostile British acts. But it is also important to take note of the core causes of Franklin's evolution and, by extension, that of a people he had come to exemplify.

When Englishmen such as his father had immigrated to a new land, they had bred a new type of people. As Franklin repeatedly stressed in his letters to his son, America should not replicate the rigid ruling hierarchies of the Old World, the aristocratic structures and feudal social orders based on birth rather than merit. Instead, its strength would be its creation of a proud middling people, a class of frugal and industrious shopkeepers and tradesmen who were assertive of their rights and proud of their status.

Like many of these new Americans, Franklin chafed at authority, which is why he had run away from his brother's print shop in Boston. He was not awed by established elites, whether they be the Mathers or the Penns or the peers in the House of Lords. He was cheeky in his writings and rebellious in his manner. And he had imbibed the philosophy of the new Enlightenment thinkers, who believed that liberty and tolerance were the foundation for a civil society.

For a long time he had cherished a vision of imperial harmony in which Britain and America could both flourish in one great expanding empire. But he felt that it would work only if Britain stopped subjugating Americans through mercantile trading rules and taxes imposed from afar. Once it was clear that Britain remained intent on subordinating its colonies, the only course left was independence.

The bloody Battle of Bunker Hill and the burning of Charleston, both in June 1775, further inflamed the hostility that Franklin and his fellow patriots felt toward the British. Nevertheless, most members of the Continental Congress were not quite as far down the road to revolution. Many colonial legislatures, including Pennsylvania's, had instructed their delegates to resist any calls for independence. The captain of the cautious camp was Franklin's long-time adversary John Dickinson, who still refrained from erecting a lightning rod on his house.

On July 5, Dickinson pushed through the Congress one last appeal to the king, which became known as the Olive Branch Petition. Blaming the troubles on the perfidies of "irksome" and "delusive" ministers, it "beseeched" the king to come to America's rescue. The Congress also passed a Declaration of the Causes and Necessity for Taking Up Arms, in which it proclaimed "that we mean not to dissolve that union which has so long and so happily subsisted between us, and which we sincerely wish to see restored."

Like the other delegates, Franklin agreed for the sake of consensus to sign the Olive Branch Petition. But he made his own rebellious sentiments public the same day. The outlet he chose was quite odd: a letter to his long-time London friend and fellow printer, William Strahan. No longer addressing him as "dear Straney," he wrote in cold and calculated fury:

> Mr. Strahan,
>   You are a Member of Parliament, and one of that Majority which has doomed my country to destruction. You have begun to burn our towns, and murder our people. Look upon your hands! They are stained with the blood of your relations! You and I were long friends: You are now my enemy, and I am, Yours,
>   B. Franklin.

What made the famous letter especially odd was that Franklin allowed it to be circulated and publicized—but he never sent it. Instead, it was merely an artifice for making his sentiments clear to his fellow Americans.

In fact, Franklin wrote Strahan a much mellower letter two days later, which he actually sent. "Words and arguments are now of no use," he said in tones more sorrowful than angry. "All tends to a separation." Just as he had not mailed the angrier version, Franklin did not keep a copy of the milder letter in his papers.[7]

(Franklin ended up remaining close friends with Strahan, who four years earlier had declared that "though we differ we do not disagree." The very day Franklin wrote his unsent note, Strahan wrote one from London lamenting the possibility that the looming war would lead to "the ultimate ruin of the whole of the most glorious fabric of civil and religious government that ever existed." They continued to correspond throughout 1775, with Strahan begging Franklin to return to England "with proposals of accommodation." Franklin responded in October by suggesting that Strahan "send us over fair proposals of peace, if you choose it, and nobody will be more ready than myself to promote their acceptation: for I make it a rule not to mix personal resentments with public business." He signed the letter, as Strahan had signed his, "your affectionate and humble servant." A year later, when he arrived in Paris as an American envoy, Franklin would receive a gift of Stilton cheese that Strahan sent over from London.)[8]

Franklin wrote his two other close British friends on July 7 as well. To Bishop Shipley, he railed against England's tactics of stirring up slaves and Indians against the colonists, and then he apologized for the angry tone of his letter. "If a temper naturally cool and phlegmatic can, in old age, which often cools the warmest, be thus heated, you will judge by that of the general temper here, which is now little short of madness."[9]

To Joseph Priestley, he lamented that the Olive Branch Petition was destined to be rejected. "We have carried another humble petition to the crown, to give Britain one more chance, one opportunity more of recovering the friendship of the colonies; which however I think she has not sense enough to embrace, and so I conclude she has lost them for ever." The letter to Priestley also offered a glimpse into Franklin's workday and the mood of relative frugality in the colonies:

> My time was never more fully employed. In the morning at 6, I am at the committee of safety, appointed by the assembly to put the province in a state of defense; which committee holds till near 9, when I am at the congress, and that sits till after 4 in the afternoon . . . Great frugality and great industry are now become fashionable here: Gentlemen who used to entertain with two or three courses, pride themselves

now in treating with simple beef and pudding. By these means, and the stoppage of our consumptive trade with Britain, we shall be better able to pay our voluntary taxes for the support of our troops.[10]

Liberated by his private break with his son and his public break with Strahan, Franklin became one of the most ardent opponents of Britain in the Continental Congress. He served on a committee to draft a declaration to be issued by General Washington, and the result was so strong that the Congress was afraid to pass or publish it. The document clearly came from Franklin's pen. It contained phrases he had used before to refute Britain's claims of having funded the defense of the colonies ("groundless assertions and malicious calumnies"), and it even concluded by seriously comparing the American-British relationship to the one between Britain and Saxony ("her mother country"), a comparison he had earlier made facetiously in his parody "An Edict by the King of Prussia." In an even more strongly worded preamble to a congressional resolution on privateering that he drafted but never submitted, Franklin accused Britain of "the practice of every injustice which avarice could dictate or rapacity execute" and of "open robbery, declaring by a solemn act of Parliament that all our estates are theirs."[11]

No longer was there any doubt, even among his detractors, where Franklin stood. Ever eager, like many Virginians, to hear about Franklin, Madison wrote to Bradford to see if the rumors of his ambivalence persisted. "Has anything further been whispered relative to the conduct of Dr. Franklin?" Bradford confessed that opinions had changed. "The suspicions against Dr. Franklin have died away. Whatever was his design at coming over here, I believe he has now chosen his side and favors our cause."

Likewise, John Adams reported to his wife, Abigail, that Franklin was now squarely in their revolutionary camp. "He does not hesitate at our boldest measures, but rather seems to think us too irresolute." The jealous orator could not suppress a slight resentment that the British believed that American opposition was "wholly owing" to Franklin, "and I suppose their scribblers will attribute the temper and proceedings of this Congress to him."[12]

FRANKLIN'S FIRST ARTICLES OF CONFEDERATION PLAN

For the colonies to cross the threshold of rebellion, they needed to begin conceiving of themselves as a new nation. To become independent of Britain, they had to become less independent of each other. As one of the most traveled and least parochial of colonial leaders, Franklin had long espoused some form of confederation, beginning with his Albany Plan of 1754.

That plan, which was never adopted, envisioned an intercolonial Congress that would be loyal to the king. Now, in 1775, Franklin put forth the idea again, but with one big difference: although his plan allowed for the possibility that the new confederation would remain part of the king's empire, it was designed to work even if the empire broke apart.

The Articles of Confederation and Perpetual Union that he presented to the Congress on July 21, like his Albany Plan, contained the seeds of the great conceptual breakthrough that would eventually define America's federal system: a division of powers between a central government and those of the states. Franklin, however, was ahead of his time. His proposed central government was very powerful, indeed more powerful than the one eventually created by the actual Articles of Confederation that the Congress began to draft the following year.

Much of the wording in Franklin's proposal was drawn from New England confederation plans that stretched back to one forged by settlements in Massachusetts and Connecticut in 1643. But the scope and powers went far beyond anything previously proposed. "The Name of the Confederacy shall henceforth be The United Colonies of North America," Franklin's detailed thirteen articles began. "The said United Colonies hereby severally enter into a firm League of Friendship with each other, binding on themselves and their posterity, for their common defense against their enemies, for the security of their liberties and properties, the safety of their persons and families, and their mutual and general welfare."[13]

Under Franklin's proposal, the Congress would have only a single chamber, in which there would be proportional representation from each state based on population. It would have the power to levy taxes, make war, manage the military, enter into foreign alliances, settle disputes between colonies, form new colonies, issue a unified currency, establish a postal system, regulate commerce, and enact laws "necessary to the general welfare." Franklin also proposed that, instead of a single president, the Congress appoint a twelve-person "executive council" whose members would serve for staggered three-year terms.

Franklin included an escape provision: in the event that Britain accepted all of America's demands and made financial reparation for all of the damage it had done, the union could be dissolved. Otherwise, "this confederation is to be perpetual."

As Franklin fully realized, this pretty much amounted to a declaration of independence from Britain and a declaration of dependence by the colonies on each other, neither of which had widespread support yet. So he read his proposal into the record but did not force a vote on it. He was content to wait for history, and the rest of the Continental Congress, to catch up with him.

By late August, when it was time for Temple to return from New Jersey to Philadelphia, William tentatively suggested that he could accompany the boy there. Franklin, uncomfortable at the prospect of his loyalist son arriving in town while the rebellious Congress was in session, decided instead to fetch Temple himself.[14]

Temple was lanky, fun-loving, and as disorganized as most 15-year-olds. Much correspondence was spent reuniting him with personal items he had left in the wrong place. As his stepmother noted, "You are extremely unlucky in your clothes." William tried hard to keep up the pretense of family harmony and included kind words about Franklin in all his letters to Temple. He also tried to keep up with Temple's frequent requests for more money; in the tug-of-war for his affections, the lad got fewer lectures about frugality than other members of his family had.

Once again, Franklin surrounded himself with the sort of domestic menagerie he found so comfortable: his daughter and her husband, their two children (Benny, 6, and William, 2), Temple, and eventually Jane Mecom, his sole surviving sibling. In none of the letters we have from that time is Deborah mentioned; life on Market Street seemed to go along without her.

For the time being, Franklin was able to close out his accounts, literally and symbolically, with his counterpart family back in London. He sent Mrs. Stevenson a £1,000 payment for his back rent, and stiffly warned her to invest it in a piece of land instead of stocks. "Britain having begun a war with us, which I apprehend is not likely soon to be ended," he wrote, "there is great probability of these stocks falling headlong."

For her part, Mrs. Stevenson sunk into "weak spirits" pining for his return. "Without the animating hope of spending the remainder of life with you," a friend of hers wrote Franklin, "she would be very wretched indeed." In his jovial way, Franklin once again proposed an arranged marriage, this time between his grandson Benny and Polly Stevenson's daughter, Elizabeth Hewson.[15]

A TRIP TO CAMBRIDGE

Franklin had been serving his country, as it headed toward revolution, in roles befitting a man of his age: diplomat, elder statesman, sage, and dozing delegate. But he still had the inclination and talent for hands-on management, organizing things and making them happen in a practical way.

He was the obvious choice to chair a committee to figure out how to replace the British-run postal system and then become, as he did in July, America's new postmaster general. The job paid a handsome £1,000 per year, but Franklin's patriotism overwhelmed his frugality: he donated the salary to care for wounded soldiers. "Men can be as diligent with us from zeal for the public good as with you for thousands per annum," he wrote Priestley. "Such is the difference between uncorrupted new states and corrupted old ones." His penchant for nepotism, however, remained intact. Richard Bache became the financial comptroller of the new system.

Franklin was also put in charge of establishing a system of paper currency, one of his long-standing passions. As usual, he immersed himself in many of the details. Using his botanical knowledge of the vein structures of different types of leaves, he personally drew the leaf designs for the various notes to make them harder to counterfeit. Once again, Bache benefited: he was one of those Franklin selected to oversee the printing.

Franklin's other assignments included heading up the effort to collect lead for munitions, devising ways to manufacture gunpowder, and serving on committees to deal with the Indians and to promote trade with Britain's enemies. In addition, he was made president of Pennsylvania's own defense committee. In that capacity, he oversaw construction of a secret system of underwater obstructions to prevent enemy warships from navigating the Delaware River and wrote detailed proposals, filled with historical precedents, for using pikes and even bows and arrows (reminiscent of the suggestions he had made in 1755 for using dogs) to compensate for the colonial shortage of gunpowder. The idea of using arrows might seem quirky, but he justified it in a letter to Gen. Charles Lee in New York. Among the reasons he offered: "A man may shoot as truly with a bow as with a common musket . . . He can discharge four arrows in the same time of charging and discharging one bullet . . . A flight of arrows, seen coming upon them, terrifies and disturbs the enemies' attention to their business . . . An arrow striking in any part of a man puts him hors du combat till it is extracted." [16]

Given his age and physical infirmities, Franklin might have been expected to contribute his expertise from the comfort of Philadelphia. But among his attributes was a willingness, indeed an eagerness, to be involved in practical details rather than detached theorizing. He was also, both as a teen and as a septuagenarian, revitalized by travel. Thus, he would find himself embarked on missions for the Congress in October 1775 and the following March.

The October trip came in response to an appeal from General Washington, who had taken command of the motley Massachusetts militias and was struggling to make them, along with various undisciplined backwoodsmen who had arrived from other colonies, into the nucleus of a true continental army. With little equipment and declining morale, it was questionable whether he could hold his troops together through the winter. So the Congress appointed a committee to look into the situation, which was about all it could do, and Franklin agreed to serve as its head.

On the eve of his departure, Franklin wrote two of his British friends to emphasize that America was determined to prevail. "If you flatter yourselves with beating us into submission, you know neither the people nor the country," he told David Hartley. To Joseph Priestley, he provided a bit of math for one of their friends to ponder: "Britain, at the expense of three millions, has killed 150 Yankees this campaign, which is £20,000 a head . . . During the same time, 60,000 children have been born in America. From these data his mathematical head will easily calculate the time and expense necessary to kill us all."[17]

Franklin and his two fellow committee members met with General Washington in Cambridge for a week. Discipline was a big problem, and Franklin approached it in his usual meticulous manner by drawing up (as he had done two decades earlier for Pennsylvania's militia) incredibly detailed methods and procedures. His list of prescribed punishments, for example, included between twenty and thirty-nine lashes for sentries caught sleeping, a fine of a month's pay for an officer absent without leave, seven days' confinement with only bread and water for an enlisted man absent without leave, and the death penalty for mutiny. The rations for each man were spelled out in similar detail: a pound of beef or salt fish per day, a pound of bread, a pint of milk, a quart of beer or cider, and so on, down to the amount of soap and candles.[18]

As they were preparing to leave, Washington asked the committee to stress to the Congress "the necessity of having money constantly and regularly sent." That was the colonies' greatest challenge, and Franklin provided a typical take on how raising £1.2 million a year could be accomplished merely through more frugality. "If 500,000 families will each spend a shilling a week less," he explained to Bache, "they may pay the whole sum without otherwise feeling it. Forbearing to drink tea saves three-fourths of the money, and 500,000 women doing each threepence worth of spinning or knitting in a week will pay the rest." For his own part, Franklin forked over his postmaster's salary plus £100 that Mrs. Stevenson had helped raise in London for

the American wounded. He also collected from the Massachusetts
Assembly the money it owed him for his services as their London
agent, and that he kept.[19]

At a dinner during the trip, he met John Adams's wife, Abigail, who
was later to be disparaging about Franklin but on that night was
charmed. Her description in a letter to her husband shows that she had
a good insight into his demeanor, though not his religious convictions:

> I found him social but not talkative, and when he spoke something
> useful dropped from his tongue. He was grave, yet pleasant and affable.
> You know I make some pretensions to physiognomy, and I thought I
> could read into his countenance the virtues of his heart; among which
> patriotism shone in its full luster, and with that is blended every virtue
> of a Christian: for a true patriot must be a religious man.[20]

On his way back to Philadelphia, Franklin stopped in Rhode Island to meet his sister Jane Mecom. She had fled British-occupied
Boston and taken refuge with Franklin's old friend Catherine Ray
Greene and her husband. Caty's house now included dozens of refugee relatives and friends, and Franklin worried that Jane "must be a
great burden to that hospitable house." In fact, as Claude-Anne Lopez
notes, "Jane and Caty, a generation apart in age, a world in circumstances and temperament, had a marvelous rapport." Just as Franklin
was wont to find surrogate daughters for himself, Jane took to treating
Caty as one. ("Would to God I had such a one!" she wrote Caty, even
though Jane in fact had a daughter of her own from whom she was estranged.)[21]

Franklin reciprocated. When he picked up Jane, he convinced
Caty's 10-year-old son, Ray, to come with them back to Philadelphia
and enroll with Temple at the college there. The carriage ride through
Connecticut and New Jersey was a delight for Jane. "My dear brother's
conversation was more than the equivalent of all the fine weather
imaginable," she reported to Caty. The good feelings were so strong
that they were able to overcome any political tensions when they made
a brief stop at the governor's mansion in Perth Amboy to call on
William.

It would turn out to be the last time Franklin would see his son other than a final tense meeting in England ten years later. But neither man knew that at the time, and they kept the meeting short. "We would willingly have detained them longer," William's wife wrote Temple, "but Papa was anxious to get home." [22]

Back in Philadelphia, a group of Marine units were being organized to try to capture British arms shipments. Franklin noticed that one of their drummers had painted a rattlesnake on his drum emblazoned with the words "Don't tread on me." In an anonymous article, filled with bold humor and a touch of venom, Franklin suggested that this should be the symbol and motto of America's fight. The rattlesnake, Franklin noted, had no eyelids, and "may therefore be esteemed an emblem of vigilance." It also never initiated an attack nor surrendered once engaged, and "is therefore an emblem of magnanimity and true courage." As for the rattles, the snake on the drum had thirteen of them, "exactly the number of the colonies united in America; and I recollected too that this was the only part of the snake which increased in number." Christopher Gadsen, a delegate to the Congress from South Carolina, picked up the suggestion in Franklin's article and subsequently designed a yellow flag with a rattlesnake emblazoned "Don't Tread on Me." It was flown in early 1776 by America's first Marine units and later by many other militias. [23]

CANADA

Undertaking a mission to the Boston area in autumn was understandable: it was an easy enough trip to the town of his birth. The Congress's decision to send him on his second mission, and his willingness to agree, was less explicable. In March 1776, Franklin, now 70, embarked on a brutal trip to Quebec.

A combined American force, led in part by the still-patriotic Benedict Arnold, had invaded Canada with the goal of preventing Britain from launching an expedition down the Hudson and splitting the colonies. Trapped and under siege, the American forces had spent the winter freezing and begging the Congress for reinforcements. Once more, the Congress responded by appointing a committee, again with Franklin at the head.

On their first day of travel, Franklin and his fellow commissioners passed just north of Perth Amboy, where William kept up the pretense of governing even though local rebels restricted his movements. Franklin did not visit. His son was now an enemy. Indeed, William showed where his loyalties now were: he sent back to London all the information he had been able to gather on his father's mission. "Dr. Franklin," he noted, planned to "prevail on the Canadians to enter into the Confederacy with the other colonies." Yet, in his letters to Temple, William poured out his sorrow and fears. Was the old man healthy enough to survive the journey? Was there a way to dissuade him from going? "Nothing ever gave me more pain than his undertaking that journey."

By the time he reached Saratoga, where they paused to wait for the ice on the lakes to clear, Franklin realized that he in fact might not survive. "I have undertaken a fatigue that at my time of life may prove too much for me," he wrote Josiah Quincy. "So I sit down to write to a few friends by way of farewell." But he soldiered on and, after an arduous month of travel that included time spent sleeping on the floors of abandoned houses, finally reached Montreal. Along the way, he picked up a soft marten fur cap that he would later make famous when, as an envoy in Paris, he wore it as part of his pose as a simple frontier sage.[24]

Despite the disarray of his forces, Benedict Arnold hosted Franklin and his fellow commissioners at a grand supper graced by a profusion of young French ladies. Alas, Franklin was in no shape to enjoy it. "I suffered much from a number of large boils," he later wrote. "In Canada, my legs swelled and I apprehended a dropsy."

The military situation was equally bad. America's besieged army had expected the committee to bring needed funds, and there was great discouragement when they discovered this was not the case. Franklin's delegation hoped, on the other hand, that it would be able to raise funds from the local Canadians, but that proved impossible. Franklin personally provided £353 in gold from his own pocket to Arnold, a nice gesture that bought him some affection while doing little to solve the situation.

Franklin had been instructed to try to entice Quebec into joining the American rebellion, but he decided not to even try. "Until the arrival of money, it seems improper to propose the federal union of this province with the others," he reported, "as the few friends we have here will scarce venture to exert themselves in promoting it until they see our credit recovered and a sufficient army arrived."

When reports came that more British ships were on their way, the Canadians became even less hospitable. The committee reached what was an inevitable conclusion: "If money cannot be had to support your army here with honor, so as to be respected instead of being hated by the people, we repeat it as our firm and unanimous opinion that it is better immediately to withdraw."

Exhausted and feeling defeated, Franklin spent the month of May struggling to make it back to Philadelphia. "I find I grow daily more feeble," he wrote. When he arrived home, his gout was so bad that he could not leave his house for days. It seemed he had performed his last mission for his country.

But his strength gradually returned, spurred by a visit from General Washington and by some tidings of a big event that was about to occur. His poor health, he wrote Washington on June 21, "has kept me from Congress and company almost ever since you left us, so that I know little of what has passed there except that a Declaration of Independence is preparing."[25]

THE PATH TO THE DECLARATION

Until 1776, most colonial leaders believed—or politely pretended to believe—that America's dispute was with the king's misguided ministers, not with the king himself nor the Crown in concept. To declare independence, they had to convince their countrymen, and themselves, to take the daunting leap of abandoning this distinction. One thing that helped them do so was the publication, in January of that year, of an anonymous forty-seven-page pamphlet entitled *Common Sense.*

In prose that drew its power, as Franklin's often did, from being unadorned, the author argued that there was no "natural or religious reason [for] the distinction of men into kings and subjects." Hereditary rule was a historic abomination. "Of more worth is one honest man to society and in the sight of God, than all the crowned ruffians that ever lived." Thus, there was only one path for Americans: "Every thing that is right or natural pleads for separation."

Within weeks of its appearance in Philadelphia, the pamphlet sold an astonishing 120,000 copies. Many thought Franklin the author, for it reflected his blunt sentiments about the corruption of hereditary power. In fact, Franklin's hand was more indirect: the real author was a cheeky young Quaker from London named Thomas Paine, who had failed as a corset maker, been fired as a tax clerk, and then gained an introduction to Franklin, who, not surprisingly, took a liking to him. When Paine decided he wanted to immigrate to America and become a writer, Franklin procured him passage and wrote to Richard Bache in 1774 asking him to help get Paine a job. Soon he was working for a Philadelphia printer and honing his skills as an essayist. When Paine showed him the manuscript for *Common Sense,* Franklin offered his wholehearted support along with a few suggested revisions.[26]

Paine's pamphlet galvanized the forces favoring outright revolution. Cautious colonial legislatures became less so, revising their instructions to their delegates so that they now were permitted to consider the question of independence. On June 7, as Franklin recuperated, Virginia's Richard Henry Lee, brother of his once and future rival Arthur Lee, put the motion on the table, to wit: "These United Colonies are, and of right ought to be, free and independent states."

Although the Congress put off a vote on the motion for a few weeks, it took one immediate step toward independence that affected the Franklins personally: ordering the removal of all royal governments in the colonies. Patriotic new provincial congresses asserted themselves, and the one in New Jersey, on June 15, 1776, declared that Gov. William Franklin was "an enemy of the liberties of this country." In deference to the fact that he was a Franklin, the order for William's arrest did suggest that he be handled "with all the delicacy and tenderness which the nature of the business can possibly admit."

William was in no mood for delicacy or tenderness. The speech he made at his trial on June 21 was so defiant that one of the judges described it as "every way worthy of his exalted birth," referring to his illegitimacy rather than to his famous paternity. For his part, the elder

Franklin was not acting particularly paternal. His letter to Washington that noted the preparation of a declaration of independence was written on the same day that his son was being tried, but Franklin didn't mention it. Nor did he say or do anything to help his son when the Continental Congress, three days later, voted to have him imprisoned in Connecticut.

Thus, the words that William wrote on the eve of his confinement to his own son, who was now firmly ensconced in his grandfather's custody, read so painfully generous: "God bless you, my dear boy; be dutiful and attentive to your grandfather, to whom you owe great obligation." Then he concluded with a bit of forced optimism: "If we survive the present storm, we may all meet and enjoy the sweets of peace with the greater relish."[27]

They would, in fact, survive the storm, and indeed all meet again, but never to relish the sweets of peace together. The wounds of 1776 would prove too deep.

EDITING JEFFERSON

As the Congress prepared to vote on the question of independence, it appointed a committee for what, in hindsight, would turn out to be a momentous task, but one that at the time did not seem so important: drafting a declaration that explained the decision. It included Franklin, of course, and Thomas Jefferson and John Adams, as well as Connecticut merchant Roger Sherman and New York lawyer Robert Livingston.[28]

How was it that Jefferson, at 33, got the honor of drafting the document? His name was listed first on the committee, signifying that he was the chairman, because he had gotten the most votes and because he was from Virginia, the colony that had proposed the resolution. His four colleagues had other committee assignments that they considered to be more important, and none of them realized that the document would eventually become viewed as a text akin to scripture.

For his part, Adams mistakenly thought he had already secured his place in history by writing the preamble to a May 10 resolution that called for the dismantling of royal authority in the colonies, which he proclaimed incorrectly would be regarded by historians as "the most important resolution that ever was taken in America." Years later, in his pompous way, he would claim that Jefferson wanted him to be the declaration's writer, but that he had convinced the younger man to do the honors, arguing: "Reason first, you are a Virginian, and a Virginian ought to appear at the head of this business. Reason second, I am obnoxious, suspected, and unpopular. You are very much otherwise. Reason third, you can write ten times better than I can." Jefferson's recollection was quite different. The committee "unanimously pressed on myself alone to make the draught," he later wrote.[29]

As for Franklin, he was still laid up in bed with boils and gout when the committee first met. Besides, he later told Jefferson, "I have made it a rule, whenever in my power, to avoid becoming the draughtsman of papers to be reviewed by a public body."

And thus it was that Jefferson had the glorious honor of composing, on a little lap desk he had designed, some of the most famous phrases in history while sitting alone in a second-floor room of a home on Market Street just a block from Franklin's home. "When in the course of human events . . ." he famously began. Significantly, what followed was an attack not on the British government (i.e., the ministers) but on the British state incarnate (i.e., the king). "To attack the king was," historian Pauline Maier notes, "a constitutional form. It was the way Englishmen announced revolution."[30]

The document Jefferson drafted was in some ways similar to what Franklin would have written. It contained a highly specific bill of particulars against the British, and it recounted, as Franklin had often done, the details of America's attempts to be conciliatory despite England's repeated intransigence. Indeed, Jefferson's words echoed some of the language that Franklin had used earlier that year in a draft resolution that he never published:

> Whereas, whenever kings, instead of protecting the lives and properties of their subjects, as is their bounden duty, do endeavor to perpetrate the destruction of either, they thereby cease to be kings, become tyrants, and dissolve all ties of allegiance between themselves and their people; we hereby further solemnly declare, that whenever it shall appear clearly to us, that the King's troops and ships now in America, or

hereafter to be brought there, do, *by his Majesty's orders,* destroy any town or the inhabitants of any town or place in America, or that the savages have been by the same orders hired to assassinate our poor out-settlers and their families, we will from that time renounce all allegiance to Great Britain, so long as that kingdom shall submit to him, or any of his descendants, as its sovereign.[31]

Jefferson's writing style, however, was different from Franklin's. It was graced with rolling cadences and mellifluous phrases, soaring in their poetry and powerful despite their polish. In addition, Jefferson drew on a depth of philosophy not found in Franklin. He echoed both the language and grand theories of English and Scottish Enlightenment thinkers, most notably the concept of natural rights propounded by John Locke, whose *Second Treatise on Government* he had read at least three times. And he built his case, in a manner more sophisticated than Franklin would have, on a contract between government and the governed that was founded on the consent of the people.

Jefferson also, it should be noted, borrowed freely from the phrasings of others, including the resounding Declaration of Rights in the new Virginia constitution that had just been drafted by his fellow planter George Mason, in a manner that today might subject him to questions of plagiarism but back then was considered not only proper but learned. Indeed, when the cranky John Adams, jealous of the acclaim that Jefferson had gotten, did point out years later that there were no new ideas in the Declaration and that many of the phrases had been lifted from others, Jefferson retorted: "I did not consider it as any part of my charge to invent new ideas altogether and to offer no sentiment which had ever been expressed before."[32]

When he had finished a draft and incorporated some changes from Adams, Jefferson sent it to Franklin on the morning of Friday, June 21. "Will Doctor Franklin be so good as to peruse it," he wrote in his cover note, "and suggest such alterations as his more enlarged view of the subject will dictate?"[33] People were much more polite to editors back then.

Franklin made only a few changes, some of which can be viewed written in his own hand on what Jefferson referred to as the "rough draft" of the Declaration. (This remarkable document is at the Library of Congress and on its Web site.) The most important of his edits was small but resounding. He crossed out, using the heavy backslashes that he often employed, the last three words of Jefferson's phrase "We hold these truths to be sacred and undeniable" and changed them to the words now enshrined in history: "We hold these truths to be self-evident."[34]

The idea of "self-evident" truths was one that drew less on John Locke, who was Jefferson's favored philosopher, than on the scientific determinism espoused by Isaac Newton and on the analytic empiricism of Franklin's close friend David Hume. In what became known as "Hume's fork," the great Scottish philosopher, along with Leibniz and others, had developed a theory that distinguished between synthetic truths that describe matters of fact (such as "London is bigger than Philadelphia") and analytic truths that are self-evident by virtue of reason and definition ("The angles of a triangle equal 180 degrees"; "All bachelors are unmarried"). By using the word "sacred," Jefferson had asserted, intentionally or not, that the principle in question—the equality of men and their endowment by their creator with inalienable rights—was an assertion of religion. Franklin's edit turned it instead into an assertion of rationality.

Franklin's other edits were less felicitous. He changed Jefferson's "reduce them to arbitrary power" to "reduce them under absolute despotism," and he took out the literary flourish in Jefferson's "invade and deluge us in blood" to make it more sparse: "invade and destroy us." And a few of his changes seem somewhat pedantic. "Amount of their salaries" became "amount and payment of their salaries."[35]

On July 2, the Continental Congress finally took the momentous step of voting for independence. Pennsylvania was one of the last states to hold out; until June, its legislature had instructed its delegates to "utterly reject" any actions "that may cause or lead to a separation from our Mother Country." But under pressure from a more radical rump legislature, the instructions were changed. Led by Franklin, Pennsylvania's delegation, with conservative John Dickinson abstaining, joined the rest of the colonies in voting for independence.

As soon as the vote was completed, the Congress formed itself into a committee of the whole to consider Jefferson's draft Declaration. They were not so light in their editing as Franklin had been. Large sections were eviscerated, most notably the one that criticized the king for perpetuating the slave trade. The Congress also, to its credit, cut by more than half the draft's final five paragraphs, in which Jefferson had begun to ramble in a way that detracted from the document's power.[36]

Jefferson was distraught. "I was sitting by Dr. Franklin," he recalled, "who perceived that I was not insensible to these mutilations." But the process (in addition to in fact improving the great document) had the delightful consequence of eliciting from Franklin, who sought to console Jefferson, one of his most famous little tales. When he was a young printer, a friend starting out in the hat-making business wanted a sign for his shop. As Franklin recounted:

> He composed it in these words, "John Thompson, hatter, makes and sells hats for ready money," with a figure of a hat subjoined. But he thought he would submit it to his friends for their amendments. The first he showed it to thought the word "Hatter" tautologous, because followed by the words "makes hats," which showed he was a hatter. It was struck out. The next observed that the word "makes" might as well be omitted, because his customers would not care who made the hats ... He struck it out. A third said he thought the words "for ready money" were useless, as it was not the custom of the place to sell on credit. Everyone who purchased expected to pay. They were parted with; and the inscription now stood, "John Thompson sells hats." "Sells hats!" says his next friend; "why, nobody will expect you to give them away. What then is the use of that word?" It was stricken out, and "hats" followed, the rather as there was one painted on the board. So his inscription was reduced ultimately to "John Thompson," with the figure of a hat subjoined."[37]

At the official signing of the parchment copy on August 2, John Hancock, the president of the Congress, penned his name with his famous flourish. "There must be no pulling different ways," he declared. "We must all hang together." According to the early American historian Jared Sparks, Franklin replied: "Yes, we must, indeed, all hang together, or most assuredly we shall all hang separately." Their lives, as well as their sacred honor, had been put on the line.[38]

CONSTITUTIONAL IDEAS

Having declared the collective colonies a new nation, the Second Continental Congress now needed to create, from scratch, a new system of government. So it began work on what would become the Articles of Confederation. The document was not completed until late 1777, and it would take another four years before all the colonies ratified it, but the basic principles were decided during the weeks following the declaration of independence.

In the Articles of Confederation plan he had submitted a year earlier, Franklin proposed a strong central government run by a popularly elected congress based on proportional representation. By temperament and upbringing, he was among the most democratic of the colonial leaders. Most of his ideas did not prevail in the new Articles, but the arguments he made in the debate—and in the concurrent meetings at which the Pennsylvania Assembly wrote a new constitution for that state—were eventually to prove influential.

One of the core issues, then and throughout American history, was whether they were creating a confederacy of sovereign states or a single unified nation. More specifically: Should each state have one vote in Congress, or should representation be in proportion to population? Franklin, not surprisingly, favored the latter, not merely because he was from a big state, but also because he felt that the power of the national congress should come from the people and not from the states. In addition, giving small states the same representation as large ones would be unfair. "A confederation upon such iniquitous principles will never last long," he correctly predicted.

As the argument got heated, Franklin attempted to add some levity. The smaller states had argued that they would be overwhelmed by the larger ones if there was proportional representation. Franklin replied that some Scots had said, at the time of the union with England, that they would meet Jonah's fate of being swallowed by a whale, but so many Scots ended up being part of the government "that it was found, in the event, that Jonah had swallowed the whale." Jefferson noted that the Congress laughed heartily enough to regain its humor. Nevertheless, it voted to keep the system of one vote per state.

Franklin initially threatened to persuade Pennsylvania not to join the confederation, but he eventually backed down.

Another issue was whether slaves should be counted as part of a state's population for the purpose of assessing its tax liability. No, argued one South Carolina delegate, slaves were not population but property, more akin to sheep than to people. This drew a rebuke from Franklin: "There is some difference between them and sheep: Sheep will never make any insurrections."[39]

At the same time the Congress was debating the new Articles, Pennsylvania was holding its own state constitutional convention, conveniently in the same building. Franklin was unanimously chosen as its president, and his main contribution was to push for a legislature composed of only one house. The idea of balancing the power of a directly elected legislature with an indirectly chosen "upper" house, he contended, was a vestige of the aristocratic and elitist system against which America was rebelling. Franklin likened a legislature with two branches to "the fabled" snake with two heads: "She was going to a brook to drink, and in her way was to pass through a hedge, a twig of which opposed her direct course; one head chose to go on the right side of the twig, the other on the left; so that time was spent in the contest, and, before the decision was completed, the poor snake died with thirst." His fingerprints were also visible in the list of qualifications that Pennsylvania's officeholders must meet: unlike in other states, they did not have to own property, but they should have a "firm adherence to justice, moderation, temperance, industry and frugality."

Franklin's preference for a unicameral legislature would eventually be discarded both by Pennsylvania and the United States, but it was greeted with great acclaim in France, which implemented it (with dubious results) after its own revolution. Another ultrademocratic proposal Franklin made to the Pennsylvania convention was that the state's Declaration of Rights discourage large holdings of property or concentrations of wealth as "a danger to the happiness of mankind." That also ended up being too radical for the convention.

In his spare time, Franklin served on a variety of congressional committees. He helped design, for example, the Great Seal of the new nation, working once again with Jefferson and Adams. Jefferson proposed a scene of the children of Israel being led through the wilderness, and Adams suggested a depiction of Hercules. Franklin's proposal was to have the motto *E Pluribus Unum* on the front and an ornate scene on the reverse of Pharaoh being engulfed by the Red Sea with the phrase "Rebellion to Tyrants is obedience to God." Jefferson then embraced Franklin's plan, and much of it was adopted by the Congress.[40]

MEETING LORD HOWE AGAIN

Franklin's negotiations in London with Adm. Richard Howe—the ones that began under the cover of chess matches at Howe's sister's house at the end of 1774—had ended in failure, but they did not destroy the respect the two men felt for each other. What particularly frustrated Lord Howe was that the impasse had dashed his dream of being designated a peace envoy to the colonies. By July 1776, the admiral was commander of all British forces in America, with his brother, Gen. William Howe, in charge of the ground troops. In addition, he had gotten his wish of being commissioned to try to negotiate a reconciliation. He carried with him a detailed proposal that offered a truce, pardons for the rebel leaders (with John Adams secretly exempted), and promises of rewards for any American who helped restore peace.

Because the British did not recognize the Continental Congress as a legitimate body, Lord Howe was unsure where to direct his proposals. So when he reached Sandy Hook, New Jersey, he sent a letter to Franklin, whom he addressed as "my worthy friend." He had "hopes of being serviceable," Howe declared, "in promoting the establishment of lasting peace and union with the colonies."[41]

Franklin had the letter read to the Congress and was granted permission to reply, which he did on July 30. It was an adroit and eloquent response, one that made clear America's determination to remain independent yet set in motion a fascinating final attempt to avert an all-out revolution.

"I received safe the letters your Lordship so kindly forwarded to me, and beg you to accept my thanks," Franklin began with requisite civility. But his letter quickly turned heated, even resurrecting the phrase "deluge us in blood" that he had edited out of Jefferson's draft of the Declaration:

> Directing pardons to be offered to the colonies, who are the very parties injured, expresses indeed that opinion of our ignorance, baseness and insensibility which your uninformed and proud nation has long been pleased to entertain of us; but it can have no other effect than that of increasing our resentments. It is impossible we should think of submission to a government that has with the most wanton barbarity and cruelty burnt our defenseless towns in the midst of winter, excited the savages to massacre our peaceful farmers, and our slaves to murder their masters, and is even now bringing foreign mercenaries to deluge our settlements with blood.

Skillfully, however, Franklin included in his letter more than mere fury. With great sorrow and poignancy, he went on to recall how they had worked together to prevent an irreparable breach. "Long did I endeavor, with unfeigned and unwearied zeal, to preserve from breaking that fine and noble china vase, the British empire; for I knew that, being once broken, the separate parts could not retain even their share of the strength or value that existed in the whole," he wrote. "Your Lordship may possibly remember the tears of joy that wet my cheek when, at your good sister's in London, you once gave me expectations that a reconciliation might soon take place."

Perhaps, Franklin intimated, peace talks could be useful. It was not likely. It would require that Howe be willing to treat Britain and America "as distinct states." Franklin said he doubted that Howe had such authority. But if Britain wanted to make peace with an independent America, Franklin offered, "I think a treaty for that purpose is not yet quite impracticable." He ended on a graceful personal note, declaring "the well-founded esteem and, permit me to say, affection which I shall always have for your Lordship."[42]

Howe was understandably taken aback by the terms of Franklin's response. The messenger who delivered it reported the "surprise" on his face and his comment that "his old friend had expressed himself very warmly." When the messenger asked if he wanted to send a reply, "he declined, saying the doctor had grown too warm, and if he expressed his sentiments fully to him, he should only give him pain, which he wished to avoid."

Howe waited two weeks, as the British outmaneuvered General Washington's forces on Long Island, before sending a carefully worded and exceedingly polite response to his "worthy friend." In it, the admiral admitted that he did not have the authority "to negotiate a reunion with America under any other description than as subject to the crown of Great Britain." Nevertheless, he said, a peace was possible under terms that the Congress had laid out in its Olive Branch Petition to the king a year earlier, which included all of the colonial demands for autonomy yet still preserved some form of union under the Crown. Although he had refrained from being explicit "in my public declaration," he now made clear that the peace he envisioned would be "of mutual interest to both countries." In other words, America would be treated as a separate country within the framework of the empire.[43]

This was what Franklin had envisioned for years. Yet it was, after July 4, likely too late. Franklin now felt so. Even more fervently, John Adams and others in his radical faction felt that way. So there was much discussion and dissent within the Congress about whether Franklin should even keep the correspondence alive. Howe forced the issue by paroling a captured American general and sending him to Philadelphia with an invitation for the Congress to send an unofficial delegation for talks before "a decisive blow was struck."

Three members—Franklin, Adams, and Edward Rutledge of South Carolina—were appointed to meet with Howe to hear what he had to say. The inclusion of Adams (who had warned the Congress that, in his biographer David McCullough's words, Howe's messenger was "a decoy duck sent to seduce Congress into renunciation of independence") was a safeguard that Franklin would not revert to his old peace-seeking habits.

With perhaps a hint of irony, Franklin proposed that the meeting could take place in the governor's mansion at Perth Amboy, which had lately been vacated by his captive son, or alternatively on Staten Island. Howe chose the latter. On the way there, the committee spent the night in New Brunswick, where the inn was so full that Franklin and Adams were forced to share a bed. The result was a somewhat farcical night, recorded by Adams in his diary, which gave a delightful glimpse at Franklin's personality and the odd-couple relationship he had over the years with Adams.

Adams was suffering from a cold, and as they went to bed he shut the small window in their room. "Oh!" said Franklin. "Don't shut the window. We shall be suffocated."

Adams replied that he was afraid of the evening air.

"The air within this chamber will soon be, and is indeed now, worse than that outdoors," Franklin replied. "Come! Open the window and come to bed, and I will convince you. I believe you are not acquainted with my theory of colds."

Adams reopened the window and "leaped into bed," a sight that must have been worth beholding. Yes, he said, he had read Franklin's letters (see p. 264) arguing that nobody got colds from cold air, but the theory was inconsistent with his own experience. Would Franklin please explain?

Adams, with a touch of wryness unusual for him, recorded: "The Doctor then began a harangue, upon air and cold and respiration and perspiration, with which I was so much amused that I soon fell asleep, and left him and his philosophy together." In addition to winning the argument over leaving open the window, it should be noted that Franklin, perhaps as a result, did not catch Adams's cold.[44]

When Howe sent a barge to ferry the American delegation to Staten Island, he instructed his officer to stay behind as a hostage. Franklin and his committee brought the officer with them as a gesture of confidence in Howe's honor. Although Howe marched his guests past a double line of menacing Hessian mercenaries, the three-hour meeting on September 11 was cordial, and the Americans were treated to a feast of good claret, ham, tongue, and mutton.

Howe pledged that the colonies could have what they had requested in the Olive Branch Petition: control over their own legislation and taxes, and "a revisal of any of the plantation laws by which the colonists may be aggrieved." The British, he said, were still kindly disposed toward the Americans: "When an American falls, England feels it." He felt the same, even more strongly. If America fell, he said, "I should feel and lament it like the loss of a brother."

Adams recorded Franklin's retort: "Dr. Franklin, with an easy air and collected countenance, a bow, a smile and all that naiveté which sometimes appeared in his conversation and is often observed in his writings, replied, 'My Lord, we will do our utmost endeavors to save your Lordship that mortification.' "

The dispute that was causing this horrible war, Howe insisted, was merely about the method Britain should use in raising taxes from America. Franklin replied, "That we never refused, upon requisition."

America offered other sources of strength to the empire, Howe continued, including "her men." Franklin, whose writings on population growth Howe knew well, agreed. "We have a pretty considerable manufactury of men."

Why then, Howe asked, was it not possible "to put a stop to these ruinous extremities?"

Because, Franklin replied, it was too late for any peace that required a return to allegiance to the king. "Forces have been sent out and towns have been burnt," he said. "We cannot now expect happiness under the domination of Great Britain. All former attachments have been obliterated." Adams, likewise, "mentioned warmly his own determination not to depart from the idea of independency."

The Americans suggested that Howe send home for authority to negotiate with them as an independent nation. That was a "vain" hope, replied Howe.

"Well, my Lord," said Franklin, "as America is to expect nothing but upon unconditional submission . . ."

Howe interrupted. He was not demanding submission. But it was clear, he acknowledged, that no accommodation was possible, at least for now, and he apologized that "the gentlemen had the trouble of coming so far to so little purpose."[45]

TO FRANCE, WITH TEMPLE AND BENNY

Within two weeks of his return from meeting Lord Howe, Franklin was chosen, by a congressional committee acting in great secrecy, to embark on the most dangerous, complex, and fascinating of all his

public missions. He was to cross the Atlantic yet again to become an envoy in Paris, with the goal of cajoling from France, now enjoying a rare peace with Britain, the aid and alliance without which it was unlikely that America could prevail.

It was an odd appointment. Elderly and ailing, Franklin was now happily ensconced, finally, in a family nest that actually included members of his own brood. But there was a certain logic, from the Congress's perspective, to the choice. Though he had visited there only twice, he was the most famous and revered American in France. In addition, as a member of the Congress's Committee of Secret Correspondence, Franklin had held confidential talks over the past year with a variety of French intermediaries. Among them was Julien de Bonvouloir, an agent personally approved by the new king, Louis XVI. Franklin met with him three times in December 1775, and came away with the impression, though Bonvouloir was scrupulously circumspect, that France would be willing to support, at least secretly, the American rebellion.[46]

Two other commissioners were also chosen for the mission to France: Silas Deane, a merchant and congressional delegate from Connecticut who had already been sent to Paris in March 1776, and Thomas Jefferson. When Jefferson begged off for family reasons, his place was given to the cantankerous Virginian Arthur Lee, who had taken over Franklin's duties as a colonial agent in London.

Franklin professed to accept the assignment reluctantly. "I am old and good for nothing," he said to his friend Benjamin Rush, who was sitting next to him in the Congress. "But as the storekeepers say of their remnants of cloth, I am but a fag end, and you may have me for what you are pleased to give."[47]

Yet, knowing Franklin—with his love for travel, attraction to new experiences, taste for Europe, and (perhaps) his proclivity to run away from awkward situations—it is likely that he welcomed the assignment, and there is some evidence that he sought it. During the Secret Committee's deliberations the previous month, he had written a "Sketch of Propositions for Peace" with England, which the committee ended up not using. In his draft, Franklin noted his own inclination for going back to England:

322 WALTER ISAACSON

> Having such propositions to make, or any powers to treat of peace, will furnish a pretence for B.F.'s going to England, where he has many friends and acquaintances, particularly among the best writers and ablest speakers in both Houses of Parliament; he thinks he shall be able when there, if the terms are not accepted, to work up such a division of sentiments in the nation as to greatly weaken its exertions against the United States.[48]

His meeting with Lord Howe, which occurred after he had drafted this memo, made a mission to England less enticing, especially compared to the possibilities of Paris. From his previous visits he knew that he would love Paris, and it would certainly be safer than remaining in America with the outcome of war so unclear (Howe was edging closer to Philadelphia at the time). A few of Franklin's enemies, including the British ambassador to Paris and some American loyalists, thought he was finding a pretense to flee the danger. Even his friend Edmund Burke, the pro-American philosopher and member of Parliament, thought so. "I will never believe," he said, "that he is going to conclude a long life, which has brightened every hour it continued, with so foul and dishonorable flight."[49]

Such suspicions were probably too harsh. If personal safety were his prime concern, a wartime crossing of an ocean controlled by the enemy's navy at age 70 while plagued with gout and kidney stones was not the most logical course. As with all of Franklin's decisions about crossing the Atlantic, this one involved many conflicting emotions and desires. But surely the opportunity to serve his country in a task for which there was no American better equipped, and the chance to live and be feted in Paris, were simple enough reasons to explain his decision. As he prepared for his departure, he withdrew more than £3,000 from his bank account and lent it to the Congress for prosecuting the war.

His grandson Temple had been spending the summer taking care of his forlorn stepmother in New Jersey. The arrest of her husband had left Elizabeth Franklin, who was fragile in the best of times, completely distraught. "I can do nothing but sigh and cry," she wrote her sister-in-law Sally Bache in July. "My hand shakes to such a degree that I can scarcely hold a pen." In pleading with Temple to come stay with her, she complained of the "unruly soldiers" who surrounded her mansion. "They have been extremely rude, insolent and abusive to me and have terrified me almost out of my senses." They even, she added, tried to steal Temple's pet dog.[50]

Temple arrived at his stepmother's house at the end of July, typically forgetting some of his clothes on the way. ("There seems to be," his grandfather wrote, "a kind of fatality attending the conveyance of your things between Amboy and Philadelphia.") The elder Franklin sent along some money for Elizabeth, but she begged for something more. Couldn't he "sign a parole" so that William would be permitted to return to his family? "Consider, my Dear and Honored Sir, that I am now pleading the cause of your son and my beloved husband." Franklin refused, and he dismissed her pitiful complaints about her plight by noting that others were suffering far worse at the hands of the British. Nor did he make any effort to see her when he passed through Amboy on his way to meet Lord Howe. Ever since her marriage to his son, he had shown little desire to befriend her, visit her, or correspond with her, much less engage in any of the flatteries he usually lavished on younger women.[51]

Temple was more sympathetic. In early September, he made plans to travel to Connecticut so he could visit his captive father and bring him a letter from Elizabeth. But Franklin forbade him to go, saying that it was important for him to resume his studies in Philadelphia soon. Temple kept pushing. He had no secret information, just a letter he wanted to deliver. His grandfather remained unmoved. "You are mistaken in imagining that I am apprehensive of your carrying dangerous intelligence to your father," he chided. "You would have been more in the right if you could have suspected me of a little tender concern for your welfare." If Elizabeth wanted to write her husband, he added, she could do so in care of the Connecticut governor, and he even included some franked stationery for that purpose.

Franklin, in fact, realized that his grandson had other motives— one bad, the other honorable—for wanting to go see his father: "I rather think the project takes its rise from your own inclination to ramble and disinclination for returning to college, joined with a desire I do not blame of seeing a father you have so much reason to love."

Not blaming him for wanting to see his father? Saying he had so much reason to love him? For Franklin, such sentiments with regard to William were somewhat surprising, even poignant. They did, however, come in a letter that had denied William's son the right to visit him.[52]

The dispute became moot less than a week later. Careful about keeping the news of his appointment as envoy to France secret, Franklin was cryptic. "I hope you will return hither immediately and your mother will make no objections to it," he wrote. "Something offering here that will be much to your advantage."

In deciding to take Temple to France, Franklin never consulted with Elizabeth, who would die a year later without seeing her husband or stepson again. Nor did he inform William, who did not learn until later of the departure of his sole son, a lad he had gotten to know for only a year. It is a testament to the powerful personal force exerted by Benjamin Franklin, a man so often callous about the feelings of his family, that William was so pitifully accepting of the situation. "If the old gentleman has taken the boy with him," he wrote to his forlorn wife, "I hope it is only to put him in some foreign university."[53]

Franklin also decided to take along his other grandson, Benny Bache. So it was an odd trio that set sail on October 27, 1776, aboard a cramped but speedy American warship aptly named *Reprisal:* a restless old man about to turn 71, plagued by poor health but still ambitious and adventurous, heading for a friendless land from whence he was convinced he would never return, accompanied by a high-spirited, frivolous lad of about 17 and a brooding, eager-to-please child who had just turned 7. The experience in Europe would be good for his grandchildren, he hoped, and their presence would be comforting to him. Two years later, writing of Temple but using words that applied to both boys, Franklin explained one reason he wanted them along: "If I die, I have a child to close my eyes."[54]

CHAPTER THIRTEEN

COURTIER

Paris, 1776–1778

THE WORLD'S MOST FAMOUS AMERICAN

The rough winter crossing aboard the *Reprisal,* though a fast thirty days, "almost demolished me," Franklin later recalled. The salt beef brought back his boils and rashes, the other food was too tough for his old teeth, and the small frigate pitched so violently that he barely slept. So, on sighting the coast of Brittany, an exhausted Franklin, unwilling to wait for winds to take him closer to Paris, had a fishing boat ferry him and his two bewildered grandchildren to the tiny village of Auray. Until he could get to Paris by coach, he wrote John Hancock, he would avoid taking "a public character" and try to keep a low profile, "thinking it prudent first to know whether the court is ready and willing to receive ministers publicly from the Congress."[1]

France was not a place, however, where the world's most famous American would find, nor truly seek, anonymity. When his carriage reached Nantes, the city feted him at a hastily arranged grand ball, where Franklin reigned as a celebrity philosopher-statesman and Temple marveled at the height of the women's ornately adorned coiffures. After seeing Franklin's soft fur cap, the ladies of Nantes began wearing wigs that imitated it, a style that became known as the *coiffure à la Franklin.*

To the French, this lightning-defying scientist and tribune of liberty who had unexpectedly appeared on their shores was a symbol both of the virtuous frontier freedom romanticized by Rousseau and of the Enlightenment's reasoned wisdom championed by Voltaire. For more than eight years he would play his roles to the hilt. In a clever and deliberate manner, leavened by the wit and joie de vivre the French so adored, he would cast the American cause, through his own personification of it, as that of the natural state fighting the corrupted one, the enlightened state fighting the irrational old order.

Into his hands, almost as much as those of Washington and others, had been placed the fate of the Revolution. Unless he could secure the support of France—its aid, its recognition, its navy—America would find it difficult to prevail. Already the greatest American scientist and writer of his time, he would display a dexterity that would make him the greatest American diplomat of all times. He played to the romance as well as the reason that entranced France's *philosophes*, to the fascination with America's freedom that captivated its public, and to the cold calculation of national interest that moved its ministers.

With its 440-year tradition of regular wars with England, France was a ripe potential ally, especially because it yearned to avenge the loss it suffered in the most recent American outcropping of these struggles, the Seven Years' War. Just before he left, Franklin learned that France had agreed to send some aid to the American rebels secretly through a cutout commercial entity.

But convincing France to do more was not going to be easy. The nation was now financially strapped, ostensibly at peace with Britain, and understandably cautious about betting big on a country that, after Washington's precipitous retreat from Long Island, looked like a loser. In addition, neither Louis XVI nor his ministers were instinctive champions of America's desire, which might prove contagious, to cast off hereditary monarchs.

Among Franklin's cards was his fame, and he was among a long line of statesmen, from Richelieu to Metternich to Kissinger, to realize that with celebrity came cachet, and with that came influence. His lightning theories had been proved in France in 1752, his collected works published there in 1773, and a new edition of Poor Richard's *The Way to Wealth*, entitled *La Science du Bonhomme Richard*, was published soon after his arrival and reprinted four times in two years. His fame was so great that people lined the streets hoping to get a glimpse of his entry into Paris on December 21, 1776.

Within weeks, all of fashionable Paris seemed to desire some display of his benign countenance. Medallions were struck in various sizes, engravings and portraits were hung in homes, and his likeness graced snuffboxes and signet rings. "The numbers sold are incredible," he wrote his daughter, Sally. "These, with the pictures, busts and prints (of which copies upon copies are spread everywhere), have made your father's face as well known as that of the moon." The fad went so far as to mildly annoy, though still amuse, the king himself. He gave the Comtesse Diane de Polignac, who had bored him often with her praise of Franklin, a Sèvres porcelain chamber pot with his cameo embossed inside.[2]

"His reputation was more universal than that of Leibniz, Frederick or Voltaire, and his character more loved and esteemed," John Adams would recall many years later, after his own jealousy of Franklin's fame had somewhat subsided. "There was scarcely a peasant or a citizen, a valet de chambre, coachman or footman, a lady's chambermaid or a scullion in the kitchen who was not familiar with Franklin's name."[3]

The French even tried to claim him as one of their own. He always assumed, as noted at the beginning of this book, that his surname came from the class of landowning English freemen known as franklins, and he was almost surely correct. But the *Gazette* of Amiens reported that the name Franquelin was common in the province of Picardie, from which many families had emigrated to England.

Various groups of French philosophers, in addition to the disciples of Voltaire and Rousseau, also made intellectual claims on him. Most notable were the physiocrats, who pioneered the field of economics and developed the doctrine of laissez-faire. The group became for him a new Junto, and he wrote essays for their monthly journal.

One of the most famous physiocrats, Pierre-Samuel Du Pont de Nemours (who emigrated in 1799 and with his son founded the Du-Pont chemical company), described his friend Franklin in almost mythic terms. "His eyes reveal a perfect equanimity," he wrote, "and his lips the smile of an unalterable serenity." Others were awed by the fact that he dressed so plainly and wore no wig. "Everything in him announced the simplicity and the innocence of primitive morals," marveled one Parisian, who added the perfect French compliment about his love of silence: "He knew how to be impolite without being rude."

His taciturnity and unadorned dress led many to mistake him for a Quaker. One French cleric reported shortly after Franklin's arrival, "This Quaker wears the full dress of his sect. He has a handsome physiognomy, glasses always on his eyes, very little hair, a fur cap, which he always wears." It was an impression he did little to correct, for Franklin knew that fascination about the Quakers was fashionable in France. Voltaire had famously extolled their peaceful simplicity in four of his "Letters on England," and as Carl Van Doren has noted, "Paris admired the sect for its gentle and resolute merits."[4]

Franklin was well aware of, and amused by, the image he created for himself. Picture me, he wrote a friend, "very plainly dressed, wearing my thin gray straight hair that peeps out under my only coiffure, a fine fur cap, which comes down to my forehead almost to my spectacles. Think how this must appear among the powdered heads of Paris." It was a very different image from the one he had adopted, and wrote Polly about, during his first visit in 1767, when he bought "a little bag wig" and had his tailor "transform me into a Frenchman."[5]

Indeed, his new rustic look was partly a pose, the clever creation of America's first great image-maker and public relations master. He wore his soft marten fur cap, the one he had picked up on his trip to Canada, during most of his social outings, including when he was received at the famous literary salon of Madame du Deffand shortly after his arrival, and it became a feature in the portraits and medallions of him. The cap, like that worn by Rousseau, served as his badge of homespun purity and New World virtue, just as his ever-present spectacles (also featured in portraits) became an emblem of wisdom. It helped him play the part that Paris imagined for him: that of the noble frontier philosopher and simple backwoods sage—even though he had lived most of his life on Market Street and Craven Street.

Franklin reciprocated France's adoration. "I find them a most amiable nation to live with," he wrote Josiah Quincy. "The Spaniards are

by common opinion supposed to be cruel, the English proud, the Scotch insolent, the Dutch avaricious, etc., but I think the French have no national vice ascribed to them. They have some frivolities, but they are harmless." As he put it to a Boston relative, "This is the civilest nation upon earth."[6]

FRANKLIN'S COURT AT PASSY

In England, Franklin had set up a cozy household with a surrogate family. In France, he quickly assembled not merely a household but a miniature court. It was situated, both figuratively and geographically, between the salons of Paris and the palace at Versailles, and it would grow to include not only the requisite new family but also a visiting cast of fellow commissioners, deputies, spies, intellectuals, courtiers, and flirtatious female admirers.

The village of Passy, where Franklin reigned over this coterie, was a collection of villas and chateaux about three miles from the center of Paris on the edge of the Bois de Boulogne. One of the finest of these estates was owned by Jacques-Donatien Leray de Chaumont, a nouveau riche merchant who had made a fortune trading in the East Indies and was now motivated—by sincere sympathies as well as the prospect of profit—to associate himself with the American cause. He offered, initially at no rent, rooms and board to Franklin and his crowd, and his Passy compound became America's first foreign embassy.

It was an idyllic arrangement for Franklin. He had a "fine house" and a "large garden to walk in" as well as an "abundance of acquaintances," he wrote to Mrs. Stevenson. The only thing missing was "that order and economy in my family that reigned in it when under your direction," he added, giving only the slightest hint that he might like her to come over and be his household partner again. But it was not a suggestion that he pushed, for he found himself quite comfortable with a new set of domestic and female companions. "I never remember to have seen my grandfather in better health," Temple wrote Sally. "The air of Passy and the warm bath three times a week have made quite a young man out of him. His pleasing gaiety makes everybody in love with him, especially the ladies, who permit him always to kiss them."

Chaumont's main house (on which Franklin erected a lightning rod) was set amid chains of pavilions, formal gardens, stately terraces, and an octagonal pond that overlooked the Seine. Dinners, served at 2 P.M., were seven-course extravaganzas, and Franklin built a wine collection that soon included more than one thousand bottles of Bordeaux, champagne, and sherry. The witty Madame Chaumont served as hostess, and her eldest daughter became Franklin's "ma femme." He also took a fancy to the teenage daughter of the seigneur of the village, whom he referred to wishfully as his "mistress." (When she ended up marrying the Marquis de Tonnerre, Madame Chaumont punned, "All the rods of Mr. Franklin could not prevent the lightning [in French, *tonnerre*] from falling on Mademoiselle.")

Through his trading companies, Chaumont procured supplies for the American cause, including saltpeter and uniforms. Because he emulated Poor Richard's injunction to do well by doing good, many questioned his motives. "He would grasp, if he could, the commerce of the thirteen colonies for himself alone," wrote one newspaper.[7]

Chaumont also served as Franklin's publicist. He commissioned the great Italian sculptor Giovanni Battista Nini to produce a series of Franklin medallions and the king's portraitist Joseph-Siffrèd Duplessis to do a majestic oil painting of him. Franklin's favorite, the Duplessis now hangs in a room atop the grand stairway of New York's Metropolitan Museum (others by Duplessis are in Washington's National Portrait Gallery and elsewhere).

Benny was placed in a nearby boarding school, where he quickly mastered French; he came to dine, occasionally with some American classmates, with his grandfather every Sunday. Jonathan Williams, a grandnephew, arrived from England and for a while was entrusted to oversee commercial transactions. Temple served as Franklin's very loyal aide, though not a great one; he became a bit of a playboy who had yet to master most of his grandfather's thirteen virtues.

Franklin, who was kept busy wrestling with the complexities of arms shipments and commercial transactions, would need whatever loyalty and family support he could muster, as he would find himself working alongside one co-commissioner who was corrupt, another who hated everyone, a secretary who was a spy, a cook who was an embezzler, and a landlord who hoped to be a profiteer.

Of the motley lot, the corrupt commissioner, who was in fact quite congenial and not all that dishonest, was Franklin's favorite. Silas Deane of Connecticut had arrived in France in July 1776, five months before Franklin, and helped arrange France's first secret shipment of aid. In that endeavor, he worked with a most unlikely middleman: Pierre-Augustin Caron de Beaumarchais, a diplomatic dabbler, would-be profiteer, and the world-famous dramatist who had just written *The Barber of Seville* and was soon to write *The Marriage of Figaro*. Like Beaumarchais, Deane seemed to have sticky fingers and inscrutable accounting methods. He would be recalled in a year to face, and fail, a congressional audit. But Franklin remained friendly throughout.

The great antagonist amid this menagerie, to Deane and then to Franklin, was the third American commissioner, Arthur Lee of Virginia. He was suspicious of all around him to the point of paranoia, a trait only partly vindicated by the fact that he was right in many cases. He had been jealous of Franklin since serving with him as a colonial agent in London (and being part of a rival land scheme syndicate). Along with his brothers, William Lee and Richard Henry Lee, he was behind many of the rumors casting doubts on Franklin's loyalty and character.

As soon as he had succeeded in exposing, with some justification, Deane's dubious transactions, Lee embarked on a campaign, with no justification, to cast doubt on Franklin. "I am more and more satisfied that the old doctor is concerned in the plunder," he wrote his brother. He later noted, this time with a bit more justification, that Franklin was "more devoted to pleasure than would become even a young man in his station."[8]

Having once thought Franklin too soft on England, Lee now thought him too soft on France. He was also convinced that nearly everyone at Passy was a spy or a crook, and he fretted over every detail down to the color of the uniforms being sent to America and the fact that Deane had gotten rooms closer to Franklin's.

On rare occasions, Lee and Franklin put aside their animosity as they discussed their common cause. One evening at Passy, Franklin regaled him at length with the grand tale of July 1776, all of which Lee, who had been in London at the time, recorded reverentially in his diary. It was "a miracle in human affairs," Franklin recounted, one that would result in "the greatest revolution the world ever saw."

By early 1778, however, Lee and Franklin would barely be speaking to each other. "I have a right to know your reasons for treating me thus," Lee wrote, after a barrage of his resentful letters had gone unanswered. Franklin let loose with the angriest words he is known to have ever written:

> Sir: It is true I have omitted answering some of your letters. I do not like to answer angry letters. I hate disputes. I am old, cannot have long to live, have much to do and no time for altercation. If I have often received and borne your magisterial snubbings and rebukes without reply, ascribe it to the right causes, my concern for the honor & success of our mission, which would be hurt by our quarrelling, my love of peace, my respect for your good qualities, and my pity of your sick mind, which is forever tormenting itself, with its jealousies, suspicions & fancies that others mean you ill, wrong you, or fail in respect for you. If you do not cure your self of this temper it will end in insanity, of which it is the symptomatic forerunner, as I have seen in several instances. God preserve you from so terrible an evil: and for His sake pray suffer me to live in quiet.

As with his other famous angry letter, the one calling his friend Strahan an enemy, Franklin did not send this one. Although he meant every word of it, he was generally averse to altercations, and was now, as he noted, too old for them. Instead, on the following day, he wrote Lee a slightly milder response. In the revised version, he again admitted that he had not answered some of Lee's letters, "particularly your angry ones in which you with very magisterial airs schooled and documented me as if I had been one of your domestics." Instead, he had burned these letters, he said, because "I saw in the strongest light the importance of our living in a decent civility towards each other." He complained to Deane, "I bear all his rebukes with patience for the good of the service, but it goes a little hard on me."[9]

Lee attracted like-minded visitors who proved equally annoying.

His brother William had been sent as envoy to Austria but, not being received there, ended up in Paris. So, too, did Ralph Izard, a wealthy and jealous South Carolina planter, who came after finding himself unwelcome as an envoy in Tuscany. When Izard took the side of the Lees, Franklin retaliated with an anonymous satire, "The Petition of the Letter Z, Commonly called Ezzard, Zed, or Izard." In it the letter Z complains about being "placed at the tail end of the alphabet" and "totally excluded from the word WISE."[10]

BANCROFT THE SPY

Arthur Lee was particularly vituperative toward Edward Bancroft, the secretary of the American delegation. Bancroft was an intriguing character in all senses of those two words. Born in Massachusetts in 1744, he had been tutored as a young man by Silas Deane and then went to work at age 19 on a plantation in Guiana, where he wrote about tropical plants and patented a textile dye made from a native black oak bark. In 1767, at age 23, he moved to London, where he became a physician and stock speculator. There he befriended Franklin, who sponsored his election to the Royal Society and paid him to gather intelligence on British leaders. When Deane was preparing to leave for France in March 1776, he was instructed by Franklin to "procure a meeting with Mr. Bancroft by writing a letter to him, under cover to Mr. Griffiths at Turnham Green near London, and desiring him to come over to you." Bancroft arrived in Paris in July, just as Deane did, and began working for his former tutor.[11]

When Franklin arrived later that year, he made Bancroft the secretary of the delegation. What he did not know (and what historians were only to discover a century later by turning up secret documents in London archives) was that Bancroft had recently begun working as a highly active British secret agent.

The British Secret Service, which was spending close to £200,000 per year by 1777 to gather intelligence, was run by a quick-witted man named William Eden, later Lord Auckland. Overseeing his operations in France was a New Hampshire native, Paul Wentworth, who had moved to London in the 1760s and made money by speculating in stocks and buying land in the West Indies and South America, including the plantation in Guiana where Bancroft had worked as a young medical researcher.

Wentworth in turn recruited Bancroft to be one of his many spies in Paris, and in December 1776 they entered into a formal agreement, using the flimsy code name "Dr. Edward Edwards" for Bancroft. "Dr. Edwards engages to correspond with P. Wentworth to communicate to him whatever may come to his knowledge in the following subjects," the memo began. It then went on for ten paragraphs to detail the information that Bancroft would provide. This included:

> The progress of the treaty with France and of the assistance expected . . . The same with Spain and of every other court in Europe . . . The means of obtaining credit, effect and money and the channels and agents used . . . Franklin's and Deane's correspondence with Congress in secret . . . Descriptions of the ships and cargoes, the time of sailing and the ports bound to . . . The intelligence that may arrive from America.

Every week, the genial and urbane Bancroft would provide his secret reports by writing between the lines of fake love letters in an invisible ink. The British spymasters had a special chemical wash that could make the writing visible. Bancroft would put the letters in a bottle with a string attached and, at 9:30 every Tuesday evening, drop it in the hollow of a tree near the south terrace of the Tuileries Gardens, where it would be picked up by a messenger from the British embassy. The instructions for the drop were explicit: "The bottle to be sealed and tied by the neck with a common twine, about half a yard in length, the other end of which to be fastened to a peg of wood . . . the peg into the ground on the west side." For these services he was initially paid £500 annually, but he performed so well that his stipend rose to £1,000, which was on top of the £1,000 per year he was making as secretary to Franklin's American delegation. He also made a lot of money on the side by using his inside information to speculate in the stock markets.[12]

The hundreds of secret reports that Bancroft sent to the British were filled with sensitive information on the transactions of the

Americans in Passy, the discussion they held with French ministers, the schedules of arms shipments being sent to America, and other military matters. He told, for example, of Lafayette's departure for America in April 1777, listed the French officers accompanying him, and revealed that he was leaving from the Spanish port of San Sebastian and heading "directly to Port Royal South Carolina." He also warned that the French were "ordering eight to ten ships of war to protect the trade of the colonies near the coast of France and to remove the British cruisers," and in September 1777 added that "four ships of war are sailed from Toulons to join the Brest fleet." The following year, in April 1778, he sent word that the French Admiral Count d'Estaing was sailing from Toulon to join the American war effort "and commands a fleet of 17 ships of the line and frigates to destroy or secure the English fleet." In his letter the next week, he revealed that "the Brest fleet is nearly ready" and noted the possibility that "Count Broglio [a noted French marshal] is to conduct an invasion of England." [13]

Franklin and Deane trusted Bancroft so fully that they often had him travel secretly to London to gather intelligence there. He would use these trips to convey some of his most sensitive espionage to the British, and then return with information that seemed valuable but was in fact planted by his spymasters. The British were so intent on keeping his cover that on one trip to London, in March 1777, they pretended to arrest him and briefly imprison him for being an American agent. "Dr. Bancroft is arrested in London for corresponding with and assisting us," a distraught Deane informed the Congress, and he added, "I feel more for Dr. Bancroft than I can express." In what seemed a nice miracle, Bancroft was released from prison within weeks and allowed to go back to work in Passy. [14]

Arthur Lee soon became suspicious of his loyalties. "The notorious character of Dr. Bancroft as a stock-jobber is perfectly known to you," he wrote Franklin and Adams after learning that he was being sent on yet another secret mission to London in February 1779. "His living in open defiance of decency and religion you are no strangers to; nor to his enmity against me." More seriously, Lee cited material that indicated Bancroft was a spy: "I have evidence in my possession that makes me consider Dr. Bancroft as a criminal with regard to the United States."

Because he was paranoid about almost everyone, Lee's suspicions were generally ignored. He was not, however, paranoid enough to realize that his own private secretary was also a spy. Among the papers buried in the British Library are secret transcripts of more than a dozen of Lee's most sensitive letters as well as a memo informing the head of the spy service that their agent "stole Lee's journal and copied the information."[15]

Through it all, Franklin remained sanguine about the possibility of spies in his midst, even though, shortly after his arrival, he had been warned to be wary by a Philadelphia woman then living in Paris. "You are surrounded with spies who watch your every movement," she wrote. With an eye more to extolling his virtues than addressing the problem, he sent what became a famous response:

> I have long observed one rule which prevents any inconveniences from such practices. It is simply this: to be concerned in no affairs I should blush to have made public, and to do nothing but what spies may see and welcome. When a man's actions are just and honorable, the more they are known, the more his reputation is increased and established. If I was sure, therefore, that my valet de place was a spy, as he probably is, I think I should probably not discharge him for that, if in other respects I liked him.[16]

On one level, Franklin's answer was naïve, for Bancroft's treachery led to ships being endangered. (As it turned out, there is no direct evidence that any were consequently lost: Lafayette sailed safely, the British were not able to act quickly enough to block d'Estaing's passage through the Straits of Gibraltar, and Broglio did not invade England.) On another level, however, Franklin was shrewd, for he would end up using his assumption that there were spies in his midst to play the English off against the French when serious negotiations began.

REALISM AND IDEALISM

France's foreign minister, the Comte de Vergennes, was a dowdy professional diplomat, portly and lacking in pretense, but in the words

of Susan Mary Alsop, whose book *Yankees at the Court* is a delightful portrayal of the period, "he was a human and affectionate man and a shrewd judge of character." He would, indeed, be both affectionate and shrewd in his dealings with Franklin. He was never fully accepted socially at the court of Louis XVI because his wife was bourgeois, but he admired those sensible middle-class qualities in her and presumably found them agreeable in Franklin as well.[17]

Vergennes was very much a realist in his view of international relations, an outlook he summarized pithily in 1774, when he declared that "the influence of every power is measured by the opinion one has of its intrinsic force." He was also ardently anti-British, which helped make him sympathetic to the American cause.

In the spring of 1776, just before Franklin's arrival, Vergennes had composed for the king a set of proposals that argued in unvarnished terms what France's policy should be: "England is the natural enemy of France; and she is an avid enemy, ambitious, unjust, brimming with bad faith; the permanent and cherished object of her policy is the humiliation and ruin of France." America, he said, needed French support to prevail. It was in France's interest, economically and politically, to try to cripple England by embracing the new nation. He presented these proposals to Louis XVI and his cabinet—which included the comptroller of finances, Anne-Robert-Jacques Turgot, who was to become Franklin's friend and fan—in the gold-gilded Council Chamber of Versailles.

Turgot and the other ministers were worried about France's tight finances and lack of preparedness, so they urged caution. The king approved a compromise: France would lend some support to America, but only secretly. Vergennes's letters on the subject, it was decided, would be dictated to his 15-year-old son, whose handwriting would not be identifiable if they fell into the wrong hands.[18]

Franklin first met Vergennes later that year, on December 28, 1776, at a secret session in Paris, just days after his arrival. With Deane and Lee at his side, Franklin pushed forcefully, and perhaps a bit too quickly, for a French alliance. The foreign minister complimented Franklin on his knowledge and wit, but he made no commitments other than to say that he would consider a memo on the subject if Franklin wished to write one. In his notes that evening, he described Franklin as "intelligent but circumspect," and in a letter to his ambassador in London he noted, "His conversation is gentle and honest, he appears to be a man of much talent."[19]

Franklin accepted Vergennes's suggestion that he write a memo, and in it he emphasized the realistic balance-of-power calculus that he knew the French minister would appreciate. If France and her ally Spain joined the American cause, Britain would lose her colonies, her possessions in the West Indies, and the "commerce that has rendered her so opulent," thus reducing her to a "state of weakness and humiliation." America would be willing to "guarantee in the firmest manner" that France and Spain could keep any of the West Indian islands Britain lost. But if France balked, then America might be "reduced to the necessity of ending the war by an accommodation" with Britain. "Delay may be attended with fatal consequences."[20]

But Franklin realized that appealing to a cold calculus of interests was only part of the equation. Better than most other diplomats in the nation's history, he understood that America's strength in world affairs would come from a unique mix that included idealism as well as realism. When woven together, as they would later be in policies ranging from the Monroe Doctrine to the Marshall Plan, they were the warp and woof of a resilient foreign policy. "America's great historical moments," writes historian Bernard Bailyn, "have occurred when realism and idealism have been combined, and no one knew this better than Franklin."[21]

As he would prove in France, Franklin not only knew how to play a calculated balance-of-power game like the best practitioner of realpolitik, but he also knew how to play with his other hand the rousing chords of America's exceptionalism, the sense that America stood apart from the rest of the world because of its virtuous nature. Both the hard power that came from its strategic might and the soft power that flowed from the appeal of its ideals and culture would, he realized, be equally important in assuring its influence. In his diplomacy, as in his personal business, he was "a man who believed in the power of reason and the reality of virtue," declared the writer and mathematician Condorcet, who became one of his best French friends.

1

Franklin's birthplace on Milk Street in Boston,
across from the Old South Church.

Deborah Franklin, circa 1759,
by Benjamin Wilson.

2

William Franklin, circa 1790,
by Mather Brown.

3

Sarah "Sally" Franklin Bache, 1793, by John Hoppner.

4

Jean-Antoine Houdon's famous bust of Franklin.

5

Francis Folger Franklin, circa 1736, who died of smallpox at age 4.

6

Poor Richard, 1733.

AN

Almanack

For the Year of Chrift

1733,

Being the Firft after LEAP YEAR:

And makes fince the Creation	Years
By the Account of the Eaftern *Greeks*	7241
By the Latin Church, when ⊙ ent. ♈	6932
By the Computation of *W. W.*	5742
By the *Roman* Chronology	5682
By the *Jewifh* Rabbies	5494

Wherein is contained

The Lunations, Eclipfes, Judgment of
the Weather, Spring Tides, Planets Motions &
mutual Afpects, Sun and Moon's Rifing and Setting, Length of Days, Time of High Water,
Fairs, Courts, and obfervable Days.
Fitted to the Latitude of Forty Degrees,
and a Meridian of Five Hours Weft from *London*,
but may without fenfible Error, ferve all the adjacent Places, even from *Newfoundland* to *South-
Carolina*.

By *RICHARD SAUNDERS*, Philom.

PHILADELPHIA:

Printed and fold by *B. FRANKLIN*, at the New
Printing-Office near the Market.

Poor Richard's first edition.

Benjamin Franklin Drawing Electricity from the Sky,
by Benjamin West.

PROFILE of the Chimney and FIRE-PLACE.

M The Mantle-piece or Breaſt of the Chimney.
C The Funnel.
B The falſe Back & Cloſing.
E True Back of the Chimney.
T Top of the Fire-place.
F The Front of it.
A The Place where the Fire is made.
D The Air-Box.
K The Hole in the Side-plate, thro' which the warm'd Air is diſcharg'd out of the Air-Box into the Room.
H The Hollow fill'd with freſh Air, entring at the Paſſage *I*, and aſcending into the Air-Box thro' the Air-hole in the Bottom-plate near
G The Partition in the Hollow to keep the Air and Smoke apart.
P The Paſſage under the falſe Back and Part of the Hearth for the Smoke.
↑↑↑↑↑ The Courſe of the Smoke.

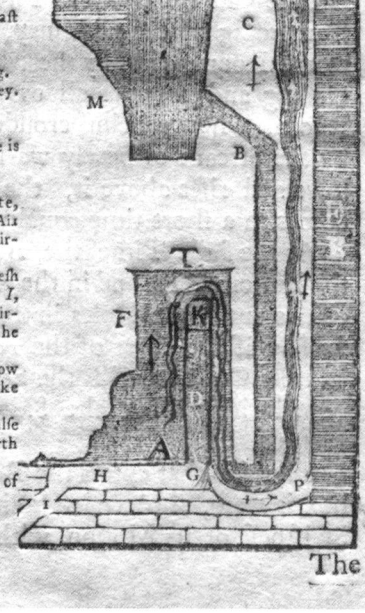

Franklin's diagram for his stove, 1744.

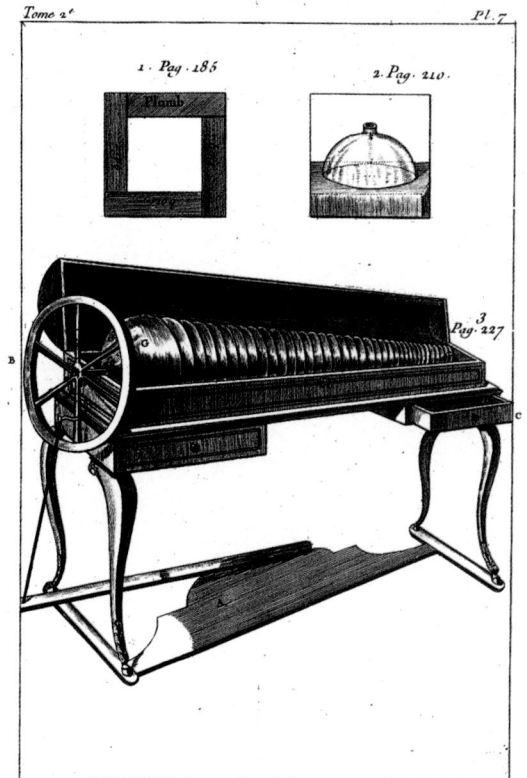

The glass armonica, Franklin's musical invention.

A chart of the Gulf Stream based on Franklin's notes.

12

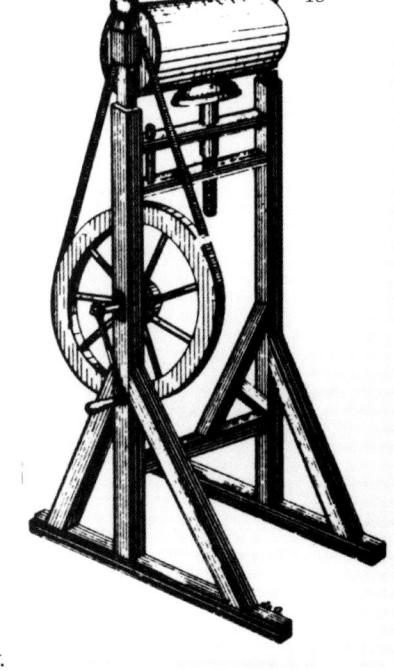

13

Franklin's battery of Leyden jars.

Franklin's machine for
collecting static electricity.

The first portrait of Franklin, as a simple gentleman,
by Robert Feke, 1748.

15

Franklin's foe, Thomas Penn,
Pennsylvania's Proprietor.

The Pennsylvania Statehouse, 1778.   16

17

Franklin's house on Craven
Street, London.

Franklin's friend William Strahan,
by Joshua Reynolds.

18

19

JOIN, or DIE.

America's first political cartoon,
produced by Franklin.

20

Franklin in London, studying under the gaze of Newton, by David Martin, 1766.

21

Charles Willson Peale made this sketch after walking in on Franklin kissing a girl, perhaps Polly Stevenson, on Craven Street.

Franklin standing silent as he is humiliated in London's cockpit in 1774.

22

A Declaration by the Representatives of the UNITED STATES OF AMERICA, in General Congress assembled.

When in the course of human events it becomes necessary for one people to dissolve the political bands which have connected them with another, and to assume among the powers of the earth the separate and equal station to which the laws of nature & of nature's god entitle them, a decent respect to the opinions of mankind requires that they should declare the causes which impel them to the separation.

We hold these truths to be self-evident; that all men are created equal, that they are endowed by their creator with inherent & inalienable rights; that among these are life, liberty, & the pursuit of happiness; that to secure these rights, governments are instituted among men, deriving their just powers from the consent of the governed; that whenever any form of government becomes destructive of these ends, it is the right of the people to alter

23

Edits by Franklin and Adams of Jefferson's rough draft of the Declaration of Independence; Franklin's heavy backslashes change "sacred and undeniable" to "self-evident."

Congress debates the Declaration, with Franklin dozing, center.

The famous portrait by Siffrèd Duplessis, 1778.

25

Engraving based on the portrait, circa 1778, by Rosalie Filleul, one of Franklin's lady friends in Paris, who wrote that she would "look forward to kissing" him, and was later guillotined during the French Revolution.

26

Franklin and the ladies of Paris.

28

A view of Passy.

Franklin in his famous marten fur cap.

29

30

Engraving of Madame Helvétius.

The American negotiators at the peace talks with Britain in Paris, in an unfinished painting by Benjamin West, 1783: Temple Franklin, Henry Laurens, Benjamin Franklin, John Adams, John Jay.

A mural in the U.S. Capitol of Franklin under his Mulberry tree during the Constitutional Convention, with Alexander Hamilton, James Wilson, and James Madison.

THE CONSTITUTIONAL CONVENTION · 1787

So, after writing Vergennes a memo infused with classic diplomatic realism, Franklin settled down in Passy to pursue the gambit of drawing power from America's idealism. He arranged for the inspiring documents coming out of America—including the constitution he had written for Pennsylvania—to be translated and published as a way of winning hearts and minds in France and elsewhere. "All Europe is for us," he wrote the Committee of Secret Correspondence in a letter that explained his rationale for publishing those documents. Then he went on to give a classic formulation of the lure of America's ideals: "Tyranny is so generally established in the rest of the world that the prospect of an asylum in America for those who love liberty gives general joy, and our cause is esteemed the cause of all mankind." He ended by echoing the shining "city upon a hill" metaphor used by the great American exceptionalists from John Winthrop to Ronald Reagan. "We are fighting for the dignity and happiness of human nature," he proclaimed. "Glorious it is for the Americans to be called by Providence to this post of honor." A few weeks later, he wrote in a similar vein to a Boston friend, concluding, "It is a common observation here that our cause is the cause of all mankind, and that we are fighting for their liberty in defending our own."[22]

Franklin's public diplomacy strategy puzzled Vergennes. "I really do not know what Franklin has come to do here," he wrote. "At the beginning we thought he had all sorts of projects, but all of a sudden he has shut himself up in sanctuary with the *philosophes*." The French minister rejected America's proposal for an immediate alliance, deflected requests for further meetings, and kept his distance from Franklin for a few months, waiting to see how the war evolved. He did, however, quietly offer some aid: France would make another secret loan to America and allow its ports to be used by American merchant ships.

Franklin also waged his public relations campaign, as he had in England, with some anonymous pieces in the press. The most powerful was a brutal parody, along the lines of "An Edict by the King of Prussia," that he wrote shortly after his first meeting with Vergennes. It purported to be a letter to the commander of the Hessian troops in America from a German count who got paid a bounty for the death of each of the soldiers he sent over. Because Britain had decided not to pay for any wounded soldiers, only for those who died, the count encouraged his commander to make sure that as many died as possible:

> I do not mean by this that you should assassinate them; we should be humane, my dear Baron, but you may insinuate to the surgeons with entire propriety that a crippled man is a reproach to their profession, and that there is no wiser course than to let every one of them die when he ceases to be fit to fight . . . You will therefore promise promotion to all who expose themselves; you will exhort them to seek glory in the midst of dangers.

He also used his wit to parry the propaganda reports being spread by the British ambassador, Lord Stormont. Asked about one of these reports, Franklin retorted, "It is not a truth; it is only a Stormont." After that, he and fashionable Paris began using the ambassador's name as a verb, "stormonter," a weak pun on the French verb *mentir*, meaning "to lie." [23]

Wild rumors began to circulate about Franklin's various strategies and schemes in France. One British spy (not Bancroft) reported that Franklin was preparing "a great number of reflecting mirrors" that would be placed on the Calais coast to focus the heat from the sun on the British navy, thus destroying it. That would be followed by an electric shock sent over a cross-channel chain that would disrupt the entire British island. The New Jersey *Gazette* went further: Franklin was inventing an electrical apparatus that could shift landmasses and a method of using oil that could still the waves in one place while stirring up tempests in another. [24]

Alas, what he was actually doing was more mundane, such as coping with European supplicants who sought commissions to serve as officers in the American army. His collected letters are clogged with requests, more than four hundred in all, some valiant and others vain. "Not a day passes in which I have not a number of soliciting visits, besides letters," he complained. "You can have no conception how I am harassed." There was the mother who offered up three of her flock of sons, the Dutch surgeon who wanted to study bodies that had been blown apart, and the Benedictine monk who promised to pray for America if it would pay off his gambling debts. Franklin's favorite was a less than effusive recommendation he received from a mother, which began: "Sir, If in your America one knows the secret of how to reform a detestable subject who has been the cross of his family . . ."

The case of one such supplicant showed how Franklin's difficulty in saying no made him an easy mark. An Irishman living in Paris named William Parsons wrote Franklin a pitiful letter describing his unfortunate plight and begging for a commission to join the American army. Franklin did not offer him a recommendation, but he did lend him fifteen guineas, which Parsons then absconded with to England, leaving his poor wife behind. When the wife wrote Franklin a sad letter accusing him of causing her husband to leave, Franklin denied that he had given him any encouragement, wrote off the fifteen-guinea loan, and sent along another guinea to help the wife buy food. For the next three months, she peppered him with pleas for even more relief.

Not all the supplicants were vagabonds. Franklin was able to find, among those seeking commissions, a few great officers to recommend: the Marquis de Lafayette, Baron von Steuben (whose rank in the Prussian army Franklin inflated in his eagerness to get General Washington to take him), and Count Pulaski, a famed Polish fighter who became a heroic brigadeer general for America. Nevertheless, Washington quickly grew testy about the number of aspiring officers Franklin was sending his way. "Our corps being already formed and fully officered," he wrote, "every new arrival is only a source of embarrassment to Congress and myself and of disappointment and chagrin to the gentlemen who come over."

So Franklin tried as best he could to reject most of the commission seekers or provide them only with letters that used such phrases as "goes over at his own expense, contrary to my advice." To cope with the constant flood of requests, or perhaps merely to make fun of them, Franklin even composed a form letter which he had printed up. "The bearer of this, who is going to America, presses me to give him a letter of recommendation, though I know nothing of him, not even his name," it read. "I must refer you to himself for his character and merits, with which he is certainly better acquainted than I can possibly be."[25]

In September 1777, Franklin and his fellow commissioners went to press Vergennes again for French recognition and, as if to conceal the weakness of their position, to request seven times more aid than had already been given. It was an inauspicious meeting for two reasons. Before it even happened, the spying Bancroft had leaked details of the planned request to Ambassador Stormont, who protested it to Vergennes, who then chided the Americans for being so unguarded. In addition, shortly after the meeting, news arrived that British General Howe had captured Philadelphia.

Howe's success was a personal blow for Franklin. His house on Market Street was commandeered by a British captain named John André, who, as the Baches took refuge in the countryside, stole his electrical equipment, books, musical instruments, and an elegant portrait of him that had been painted by Benjamin Wilson in 1759. (It was returned from England in 1906 and now hangs on the second floor of the White House.)

For America, it threatened to be an even worse blow. Howe was in Philadelphia and General Burgoyne was heading down the Hudson; if and when the two British armies linked, New England would be cut off from the rest of the colonies.

Nonetheless, Franklin kept his equanimity. Told of Howe's triumph, he replied, "You mistake the matter. Instead of Howe taking Philadelphia, Philadelphia has taken Howe." On one level it seemed a flippant bon mot. On another, it was a shrewd assessment. If Burgoyne was slowed in his move down the Hudson, and if Howe did not press northward to reinforce him, both could end up isolated.

Arthur Lee wanted to use America's precarious position to present an ultimatum to the French: either they join America in a military alliance immediately or else America would be forced to reconcile with Britain. "Dr. Franklin was of a different position," Lee recorded in his journal. "The effect of such a declaration," Franklin argued, "might make them abandon us in despair or anger." He felt that America would eventually gain a position that would make it in France's own interest to want an alliance.

He was right. Shortly before noon on December 4, a messenger from America galloped into the courtyard of Passy bearing a message from the front. Franklin asked if, as he had already heard, Philadelphia had fallen. "Yes, sir," said the messenger. Franklin turned his back.

"But, sir, I have greater news than that," said the messenger. "General Burgoyne and his whole army are prisoners!" Burgoyne had been defeated at the Battle of Saratoga, and now Howe was indeed isolated.[26]

The very dramatic dramatist Beaumarchais, who happened to be at Passy at the time, was eager to use the inside news to speculate in the stock markets; he raced back to Paris at such a high speed that his cabriolet overturned, fracturing his arm. Bancroft also immediately scurried off, heading for London to consult with his spymasters (he would also have speculated, but the news reached London before he did).

Franklin, far calmer than his odd friends, wrote up a news release filled with little details and large exaggerations: "Mail arrived from Philadelphia at Dr. Franklin's house in Passy after 34 days. On October 14th General Burgoyne was forced to lay down his arms, 9200 men killed or taken prisoner . . . General Howe is in Philadelphia, where he is imprisoned. All communication with his fleet is cut off."

Howe was not in fact trapped, nor was America on the verge of victory. Still, the British surrender at Saratoga was a great turning point on the battlefield and—because Franklin knew that power on the battlefield correlated to power at the bargaining table—it was a great turning point for his diplomatic efforts. The note he wrote to Vergennes that afternoon was more restrained than his news release. "We have the honor to acquaint your Excellency," it began, "with advice of the total reduction of the force under General Burgoyne."

Two days later, Louis XVI from his chamber at Versailles put his royal assent on a gilt-edged paper, prepared for him by Vergennes, that invited the Americans to resubmit their request for a formal alliance. In delivering the message, Vergennes's secretary added that "it could be done none too soon."[27]

THE TREATIES OF FRIENDSHIP AND ALLIANCE

After a full year of deflecting requests for an alliance, the French were suddenly impatient as 1777 drew to a close. They were prodded not only by America's success at Saratoga and the completion of their own naval rearmament program, but also by a new gambit by Franklin. He began to play the French and British off against one another and to let each side discover—and here is where he relied on the spies he knew were in his midst—how eager the other side was for a deal.

Franklin wrote a renewed proposal for a French-American alliance on December 7, Temple delivered it the next day, and within a week the three American commissioners were meeting with Vergennes. The French quickly agreed to full recognition of America and treaties of trade and alliance. There was one caveat: France needed the approval of Spain, as the two countries had pledged in the Bourbon family pact of 1761 to act in concert. Vergennes sent his courier to Madrid and promised the Americans they would have a response in three weeks.

In the meantime, the British sent to Paris the most trusted envoy they could muster, Paul Wentworth, their able spymaster. At the time, Wentworth was angry with his secret agent Bancroft for sending inside information to his stock speculating partner before sending it to Wentworth, who also was a speculator. King George III, upset by the bad news that his spies were giving him, denounced them all as untrustworthy stock manipulators, but he reluctantly approved Wentworth's secret peace mission.

Wentworth arrived in Paris in mid-December, just as the Americans were meeting with Vergennes, and sent a missive to Silas Deane that was worthy of a British spy: a gentleman who wished to meet him, it said, could be found the next morning in a coach at a specified place on the road to Passy, or later at an exhibition in the Luxembourg Gallery, or at the public baths on the Seine, where Deane would find a note giving the room number to use. Deane sent a reply worthy of an American: he would be in his office, where he would be happy to see anyone who wanted to come by.[28]

At dinner with Deane, Wentworth proposed a plan for reconciliation between Britain and her colonies. America would have its own Congress, would be subject to Parliament only in matters of foreign policy and trade, and all the offensive acts passed since 1763 would be repealed. He also offered personal inducements—knighthoods, peerages, jobs, money—to Deane or any American who helped secure such a peace.

Franklin at first refused to meet with Wentworth. But then word came of Spain's answer to France's proposal for an alliance with America. Somewhat surprisingly, the Spanish king had rejected the plan and declared that Spain saw no reason to recognize America. It would now be up to France to act alone, if it so chose.

So, during the first week of 1778, Franklin applied pressure. He let word leak to the press that British emissaries were in town and that they might reach a pact with the Americans if the French did not do so promptly. Such a pact, the stories went, might even include American support for Britain's efforts to capture France's islands in the West Indies. He also agreed to meet with Wentworth on January 6, though he made him promise not to offer any personal bribes.

Wentworth's report back to London was written in the clumsy code that might be expected from an agent who had tried to set up a secret rendezvous in a bathhouse: "I called on 72 [Franklin] yesterday, and found him very busy with his nephew [either Jonathan Williams or, more likely, Temple] who was directed to leave the room, and we remained together two hours before 51 [Deane] joined us, when the conversation ceased." Wentworth added that he had offered to Franklin an unsigned letter that spoke of the possibility of "unqualified 107," which was the code he used for independence. "[Franklin] said it was a very interesting, sensible letter," Wentworth reported, "and applauded the candor, good sense and benevolent spirit of it." Then he added the kicker: "Pity it did not come a little sooner."

Not quite sure who was spying on whom, Franklin pursued the cleverly naïve approach he had described a year earlier. It was in his interest that the British discover (as they did through their spy Bancroft) how close the Americans were to a deal with France. And it was in his interest that the French discover (as they did through their own constant surveillance of Wentworth) that the Americans were having discussions with a British emissary. Everything he said to Wentworth he was happy to have the French overhear. As Yale historian Jonathan Dull has noted, "The ineptitude of the British government presented Franklin with a chance to play one of his best diplomatic roles: the innocent who may not be so innocent as he pretends."[29]

Indeed, Franklin's meeting with Wentworth seemed to prod the French. Two days later, Vergennes's secretary called on the Americans. He had only one question: "What is necessary to be done to give such satisfaction to the American commissioners as to engage them not to listen to any proposition from England for a new connection with that country?" Thanks to Franklin's maneuvers as well as the victory of Saratoga, the French now wanted an alliance as eagerly as America did.

Franklin personally wrote out the answer: "The commissioners have long since proposed a treaty of amity and commerce which is not yet concluded. The immediate conclusion of that treaty will remove the uncertainty they are under with regard to it and give them such a reliance on the friendship of France as to reject firmly all propositions made to them of peace from England which have not for their basis the entire freedom and independence of America."

That was all the French now needed to hear. Franklin was told that the king would assent to the treaties—one on friendship and trade, the other creating a military alliance—even without the participation of Spain. France made one stipulation: America could not make peace with Britain in the future without France's consent. And so the treaties of friendship and alliance were won.

The treaties had an important aspect: they did not violate the idealistic view, held by Franklin and others, that America, in its virgin purity, should avoid becoming entangled in foreign alliances or European spheres of influence. The commercial rights that the Americans granted were mutual, nonexclusive, and permitted a system of open and free trade with other nations. "No monopoly of our trade was granted," Franklin pointed out in a letter to the Congress. "None are given to France but what we are at liberty to grant to any other nation."[30]

The American commissioners met in Paris on February 5, 1778, for the signing of the treaty. Vergennes's secretary had a cold, however, so the ceremony was put off for a day. At both gatherings, Franklin appeared without his usual brown coat. Instead, he wore a suit of blue Manchester velvet that was faded and a bit worn. Silas Deane, finding this puzzling, asked why. "To give it a little revenge," Franklin answered. "I wore this coat the day Wedderburn abused me at Whitehall." It had been four years since his humiliation in the Cockpit, and he had saved the suit for such an occasion.[31]

Standing near Franklin, ready to assist, was his supposedly loyal secretary, Edward Bancroft. The British spy took the document, made a copy, hired a special messenger, and got it to the ministers in London within forty-two hours. He had already, two weeks earlier, written coded letters in invisible ink that provided the outline of what the treaty would contain plus the intelligence that a French convoy of three ships and two war frigates was preparing to leave Quiberon to bring the document back to an anxious American Congress. He also sent word that "we have just received a letter from the Prussian ministry to say that the King of Prussia will immediately follow France in acknowledging the independency of America."

Years later, when he was haggling with the British over back pay, Bancroft wrote a secret memo telling the foreign secretary that this was "information for which many individuals here would, for purposes of speculation, have given me more than all that I have received from the government." In fact, Bancroft had indeed used this information to make money speculating on the markets. He had sent £420 to his stock partner in England, the Philadelphia-born merchant Samuel Wharton, and provided him word of the impending treaties so that it could be used to short stocks. "The bulls in the alley are likely to be left in the lurch," he wrote in one secret missive to Wharton, using invisible ink. That letter was intercepted by the English spy service, but others made it through to Wharton and also to their other partner, the British banker Thomas Walpole. Bancroft ended up making £1,000 in the transactions.[32]

Louis XVI made the Franco-American treaties official by receiving the three commissioners at Versailles on March 20. Crowds gathered at the palace gates to catch a glimpse of the famous American, and they shouted "Vive Franklin" as his coach passed through the gold-crested gates.

Among those in the courtyard were, according to Susan Mary Alsop, the "officious porters" who rented out to visitors the ceremonial swords that were generally required for admission to the palace. The other American commissioners each wore one, along with the other items of official court dress. But not Franklin. Seeing no reason to abandon the simple style that had served him well, he dressed in a plain brown suit with his famous spectacles as his only adornment. He did not wear a sword and, when he discovered that the wig he had bought for the occasion did not sit well on his head, decided to forsake it as well. "I should have taken him for a big farmer," wrote one female observer, "so great was his contrast with the other diplomats, who were all powdered, in full dress, and splashed all over with gold and ribbons."

His one fashion concession to the occasion was that he did not wear his fur cap but instead carried a hat of pure white under his arm. "Is that white hat a symbol of liberty?" asked Madame du Deffand, the old aristocrat at whose salon Franklin had worn his fur cap. Whether or not he meant it to be, white hats for men were soon in vogue in Paris, as everything else Franklin wore was wont to become.

When Franklin was ushered into the king's bedchamber at noon, after the official levee, Louis XVI was in a posture of prayer. "I hope that this will be for the good of both nations," he said, giving a royal imprimatur to America's status as an independent nation. On a personal note, he added, "I am very satisfied with your conduct since you arrived in my kingdom."

After a midafternoon dinner hosted by Vergennes, Franklin had the honor, if not pleasure, of being allowed to stand next to the queen, the famously haughty Marie-Antoinette, as she played at the gambling tables. Alone among the throng at Versailles, she seemed to have little appreciation for the man who, she had been told, had once been "a printer's foreman." As she noted dismissively, a man of that background would never have been able to rise so high in Europe. Franklin would have proudly agreed.[33]

Franklin's diplomatic triumph would help seal the course of the Revolution. It would also alter the world's balances of power, not just between France and England, but also—though France certainly did not intend it to—between republicanism and monarchy.

"Franklin had won," writes Carl Van Doren, "a diplomatic campaign equal in results to Saratoga." The Yale historian Edmund Morgan goes even further, calling it "the greatest diplomatic victory the United States has ever achieved." With the possible exception of the creation of the NATO alliance, that assessment may be true, though it partly points up the paucity of American successes over the years at bargaining tables, whether in Versailles after World War I or in Paris at the end of the Vietnam War. At the very least, it can be said that Franklin's triumph permitted America the possibility of an outright victory in its war for independence while conceding no lasting entanglements that would encumber it as a new nation.

Before word of the treaty reached Philadelphia, the Congress had been debating whether to consider the new peace offers that had arrived from Britain. Now, after only two days of deliberation, it decided instead to ratify the alliance with France. "You cannot conceive what joy the treaties with France have diffused among all true Americans," Franklin's friend Samuel Cooper wrote from Massachusetts.[34]

CHAPTER FOURTEEN

BON VIVANT

Paris, 1778–1785

JOHN ADAMS

In April 1778, shortly after the American treaties with France had been signed, John Adams arrived in Paris to replace the recalled Silas Deane as one of the three American commissioners. The French were not thrilled by the switch. "Mr. Deane," reported Edward Bancroft to his spymasters in London, "is highly esteemed here and his successor J. Adams is much distrusted." Bancroft reported that Adams was also unhappy. "Adams is heartily disappointed to find everything done and talks of returning."

When they served together in the Congress, Adams had initially distrusted Franklin, then gone through a blender of emotions: bemusement, resentment, admiration, and jealousy. On their trip to negotiate with Lord Howe on Staten Island (when they shared a bed and open window), he had found Franklin both amusing and annoying. So, when he arrived in Paris, it was probably inevitable that he and Franklin would, as they did, enjoy and suffer a complex mix of disdain and grudging admiration for one another.

Some have found the relationship baffling: Did Adams resent or respect Franklin? Did Franklin find Adams maddening or solid? Did they like or dislike each other? The answer, which is not all that baffling because it is often true of the relationship between two great and strong people, is that they felt all of these conflicting emotions about each other, and more.

They were both very smart, but otherwise they had quite different personalities. Adams was unbending and outspoken and argumentative, Franklin charming and taciturn and flirtatious. Adams was rigid in his personal morality and lifestyle, Franklin famously playful. Adams learned French by poring over grammar books and memorizing a collection of funeral orations; Franklin (who cared little about the grammar) learned the language by lounging on the pillows of his female friends and writing them amusing little tales. Adams felt comfortable confronting people, whereas Franklin preferred to seduce them, and the same was true of the way they dealt with nations.

Adams, who was 42 when he arrived, was thirty years younger than Franklin and about five years younger than Franklin's son, William. More sensitive to insults, real and imagined, Adams came to feel more strongly about Franklin than vice versa. At times, he was driven almost to distraction by Franklin's insouciance and self-indulgence. "He envied—and suspected—people with no rough edges, people who moved easily in the finer circles," Berkeley historian Robert Middlekauff writes of Adams in his textured study *Benjamin Franklin and His Enemies.* He was "incapable of the easy gesture, and incapable too of the small hypocrisies that carry other men through life." David McCullough, in his masterly biography of Adams, is more sympathetic and balanced about him, but he too conveys the rich complexity of his attitudes toward Franklin.[1]

Most of Adams's resentments were occasioned by ill-disguised jealousy at being overshadowed. Franklin had "a monopoly of reputation here and an indecency in displaying it," Adams complained to a friend after a few months in Paris. But in reading some of the unkind things he had to say about Franklin, it is important to note that at one time or another, Adams hurled a few nasty adjectives at just about everyone he met. (For instance, he once described George Washington as a "muttonhead.") Despite their personal friction, Adams and Franklin were bound together by their shared patriotism and their ardor for America's independence.

Franklin took Adams under his wing at Passy, enrolled 10-year-old
John Quincy Adams at Benny Bache's boarding school, and took his
new colleague on all of his social and cultural rounds, including his
grand embrace of Voltaire at the Académie. On Adams's first day at
Passy, Franklin brought him along to dine at the home of Jacques Turgot, the former finance minister, and then on subsequent days to the
salons of the various women whose seductive styles entranced Franklin and appalled Adams.

Even more appalling to the puritanical Adams was Franklin's living and work style. He was disturbed by what he assumed to be the
cost of the luxurious accommodations at Passy, then even more upset
when he learned that the ambitious Chaumont was charging them no
rent. Soon after his arrival, Adams vented in his diary about the difficulty of getting Franklin to focus on work:

> I found out that the business of our commission would never be
> done unless I did it . . . The life of Dr. Franklin was a scene of continual
> dissipation . . . It was late when he breakfasted, and as soon as breakfast
> was over, a crowd of carriages came to his levee . . . some philosophers,
> academicians, and economists; some of his small tribe of humble
> friends in the literary way whom he employed to translate some of his
> ancient compositions, such as his Bonhomme Richard and for what I
> know his Polly Baker, etc., but by far the greater part were women and
> children, come to have the honor to see the great Franklin, and to have
> the pleasure of telling stories about his simplicity, his bald head . . .
> He was invited to dine every day and never declined unless we had
> invited company to dine with us. I was always invited with him, till I
> found it necessary to send apologies, that I might have some time to
> study the French language and do the business of the mission. Mr.
> Franklin kept a horn book always in his pocket in which he minuted all
> his invitations to dinner, and Mr. Lee said it was the only thing in
> which he was punctual . . . In these agreeable and important occupa-
> tions and amusements the afternoon and evening was spent, and he
> came home at all hours from nine to twelve o'clock at night.[2]

One of Franklin's French friends put a more positive spin on his
work habits: "He would eat, sleep, work whenever he saw fit, according to his needs, so that there never was a more leisurely man, though
he certainly handled a tremendous amount of business." These two
descriptions of Franklin's style reveal not just differing views about

him but also differing views about work. Franklin was always industrious, and in America he famously believed in also giving the *appearance* of being industrious. But in France, where the appearance of pleasure was more valued, Franklin knew how to adopt the style. As Claude-Anne Lopez notes, "In colonial America it was sinful to look idle, in France it was vulgar to look busy."[3]

One day, a Frenchman asked Adams whether he was surprised that Franklin never attended any religious services. "No," Adams replied laughing, "because Mr. Franklin has no . . ." Adams did not finish the sentence for fear of seeming too blasphemous.

"Mr. Franklin adores only great nature," said the Frenchman, "which has interested a great many people of both sexes in his favor."

"Yes," replied Adams, "all the atheists, deists and libertines, as well as all the philosophers and ladies, are in his train."

"Yes," the Frenchman continued, "he is celebrated as the great philosopher and the great legislator of America."

Adams was unable to control his resentment. "He is a great philosopher, but as a legislator of America he has done very little," he told the Frenchman. "It is universally believed in France, England and all Europe that his electric wand has accomplished all this revolution, but nothing is more groundless . . . He did not even make the constitution of Pennsylvania, bad as it is." (Adams, who was not as much of a democrat as Franklin and believed in checks on the power of the people, strongly objected to the unicameral legislature.)[4]

After a few years, Franklin would tire of Adams and declare that he was "sometimes, and in some things, absolutely out of his senses." But for the time being, he found Adams tolerable, at times even admirable. And he was happy to make him part of his social set, despite Adams's minimal enthusiasm for such frivolities.[5]

VOLTAIRE

The *philosophes* of France were, like Franklin, eager to engage in the real world rather than lose themselves in abstruse metaphysics. Their secular version of the Bible was the *Encyclopédie* compiled by Diderot, which included articles by Turgot on economics, Montesquieu on politics, Rousseau on the arts, Condorcet on sciences, and Helvétius on man. Reigning as their king and god—or perhaps neither, as he was skeptical of both—was Voltaire, a man who contributed anonymously to the *Encyclopédie* but prominently to the intellectual life of France.

Voltaire and Franklin were, at least in the mind of the French public, soul mates. Both were aging embodiments of the wit and reason of the Enlightenment, playful yet pointed parodists, debunkers of orthodoxy and pretense, disciples of deism, tribunes of tolerance, and apostles of revolution. So it was inevitable not only that the two sages would meet but also that their meetings would, even more than the one between Franklin and the king himself, capture the public imagination.[6]

By early 1778, Voltaire was 84 and ailing, and there had even been stories that he had died. (His retort, even better than Mark Twain's similar one, was that the reports were true, only premature.) In February, Franklin paid a ceremonial visit to his home and asked him to give his blessing to 7-year-old Benny Bache. As twenty awed disciples watched and shed "tears of tenderness," Voltaire put his hands on the boy's head and pronounced in English, "God and Liberty." According to Condorcet, one of the witnesses, he added, "This is the only appropriate benediction for the grandson of Monsieur Franklin."

Some derided the rather histrionic display. One of Paris's more caustic papers accused them of "playing out a scene" of "puerile adulation," and when former Massachusetts governor Hutchinson heard of the "God and Liberty" benediction, he remarked that it was "difficult to say which of those words had been most used to bad purposes." Mainly, however, the encounter was reverentially publicized throughout Europe.[7]

Franklin and Voltaire staged an even more dramatic meeting at the Académie Royale on April 29 of that year. Franklin was dressed with trademark simplicity: plain coat, no wig, and no adornments other than his spectacles. Voltaire, who would die within a month, was gaunt and frail. The crowd demanded that they give each other a French embrace, an act that evoked, in the words of Condorcet, such "noisy acclamation one would have said it was Solon who embraced

Sophocles." The comparison to the great Greek philosophers, one famous for his laws and the other for his literature, was proclaimed throughout Europe, as eyewitness John Adams reported with his typical mix of awe and resentment:

> There was a general cry that M. Voltaire and M. Franklin should be introduced to each other. This was no satisfaction; there must be something more. Neither of our philosophers seemed to divine what was wished or expected; they however took each other by the hand. But this was not enough. The clamor continued until the explanation came out: Il faut s'embrasser à la française. The two aged actors upon this great theater of philosophy and frivolity then embraced each other by hugging one another in their arms and kissing each other's cheeks, and then the tumult subsided. And the cry immediately spread through the kingdom, and I suppose all over Europe: Qu'il est charmant de voir embrasser Solon et Sophocles.[8]

The Académie served as one of Franklin's bases among the intellectual elite of Paris. Another was a remarkable Masonic lodge known, in honor of the muses, as the Lodge of the Nine Sisters. Freemasonry in France was evolving from being just a set of businessmen's social clubs, which is what it mainly was in America, and was becoming part of the movement led by the *philosophes* and other freethinkers who challenged the orthodoxies of both the church and the monarchy. Claude-Adrien Helvétius, a very freethinking *philosophe,* had first envisioned a superlodge in Paris that would be filled with the greatest writers and artists. When he died, his widow, Madame Helvétius (about whom we will soon hear a lot more), helped fund its creation in 1776.

Franklin and Voltaire joined the Lodge of the Nine Sisters in April 1778, the same month as their public meeting at the Académie. The lodge provided Franklin with influential supporters and enjoyable evenings. But it was risky. Both the king and the clerics were wary of the renegade lodge—and of Franklin's membership in it.

The controversy surrounding the lodge was heightened when, in November 1778, it held a memorial service for Voltaire, who, on his deathbed a few months earlier, had waved off priests seeking to give him last rites. Some friends, such as Condorcet and Diderot, thought it wise to avoid the ceremony. But Franklin not only attended, he took part in it.

The hall was draped in black, lit only dimly by candles. There were songs, speeches, and poems attacking the clergy and absolutism in all forms. Voltaire's niece presented a bust by Houdon. (Houdon, a member, also did a bust of Franklin for the lodge, which is now in the Philadelphia Museum of Art.) Then a flame of light revealed a grand painting of the apotheosis of Voltaire emerging from his tomb to be presented in heaven by the goddesses of Truth and Benevolence. Franklin took the Masonic wreath from his head and solemnly laid it at the foot of the painting. Everyone then adjourned to the banquet room, where the first toast included a tribute to Franklin—"the captive thunder dying at his feet"—and to America.

Louis XVI, though a Mason himself, was annoyed by the spectacle and worked through the other Masonic lodges to have the Nine Sisters expelled. After months of controversy, the situation was resolved when the Nine Sisters reorganized itself and Franklin took over as its Venerable, or Grand Master. During the ensuing years, Franklin would induct many Americans into the lodge, including his grandson Temple, the spy Edward Bancroft, and the naval warrior John Paul Jones. He also helped create from within the lodge a group somewhat akin to his American Philosophical Society, known as the Société Apollonienne.[9]

MADAME BRILLON

As fascinating as the freemasons and *philosophes* were, it was not for his male friends that Franklin was famous in France. Among his many reputations was that of a legendary and lecherous old lover who had many mistresses among the ladies of Paris. The reality, truth be told, was somewhat less titillating. His famed female friends were mistresses only of his mind and soul. Yet that hardly made their relationships less interesting.

The first of these was with a talented and high-strung neighbor in Passy, Madame Brillon de Jouy, an accomplished musician who was noted for her performances on the harpsichord and the new pianos that were becoming fashionable in France. When she first met Franklin in the spring of 1777, she worried that she had been too shy to make a good impression. So the next day she asked a mutual friend to send her some of the Scottish melodies she knew Franklin loved. "I would try to play them and compose some in the same style!" she wrote. "I do wish to provide the great man with some moments of relaxation from his occupations, and also to have the pleasure of seeing him."

Thus began their intense companionship, which soon became sexually charged and the fodder for much gossip. Adams and others were shocked by what Madame Brillon called her "sweet habit of sitting on your lap" and by stories of their late nights spent together. "I am certain you have been kissing my wife," her husband once wrote Franklin.

Yet Monsieur Brillon added in his letter, "My dear Doctor, let me kiss you back in return." Franklin's relationship with Madame Brillon, like so many of his others with distinguished ladies, was complex and never fully consummated. It was, as Claude-Anne Lopez has ably described, an *amitié amoureuse* in which Franklin had to settle for playing the role of "Cher Papa," an oddly flirtatious father.[10]

Madame Brillon, who was 33 when she met Franklin, was buffeted by conflicting passions and variable moods. Her husband, twenty-four years her senior (but fourteen years younger than Franklin), was wealthy, doting, and unfaithful. She had two daughters with beautiful singing voices and lived in one of the most elegant estates in Passy, yet she was prone to fits of depression and self-pity. Although she spoke no English, she and Franklin exchanged more than 130 letters during their eight-year relationship, and she was able not only to enchant him but also to manipulate him.

She did so by composing and playing music for him, creating a salon around him, and writing him flattering letters in French and in the third person. "It is," she declared, "a real source of joy for her to think that she can sometimes amuse Mr. Franklin, whom she loves and esteems as he deserves." When the Americans won the Battle of Saratoga, she composed a triumphal overture entitled "Marche des Insurgents" (which is still sometimes performed) and played it for him in a private concert. They also flirted over the chessboard. "She is still a little miffed," Madame Brillon teasingly wrote of herself, "about the six games of chess he won so inhumanly and she warns him she will spare nothing to get her revenge."[11]

By March 1778, after months of just music and chess, Franklin was ready for something more. So he shocked her with some of his libertine theology and challenged her to save his soul. "You were kind enough," she wrote, now comfortable in the first person, "to entrust me with your conversion." Her propositions were promising, even suggestive. "I know my penitent's weak spot, I shall tolerate it! As long as he loves God, America, and me above all things, I absolve him of all of his sins, present, past and *future*."

Madame Brillon went on to describe the seven cardinal sins, merrily noting that he had conquered well the first six, ranging from pride to sloth. When she got to the seventh, the sin of lust, she became a bit coy: "The seventh—I shall not name it. All great men are tainted with it . . . You have loved, my dear brother; you have been kind and lovable; you have been loved in return! What is so damnable about that?"

"She promises to lead me to heaven along a road so delicious," Franklin exulted in his reply to her. "I am in raptures when I think of being absolved of the *future* sins." Turning to the Ten Commandments, he argued that there were actually two others that should be included: to multiply and fill the earth, and to love one another. He had always obeyed those two very well, he argued, and should not that "compensate for my having so often failed to respect one of the ten? I mean the one which forbids us to covet thy neighbor's wife, a commandment which (I confess) I have consistently violated."[12]

Alas, Madame Brillon took that cue to beat a hasty retreat. "I dare not decide the question without consulting that neighbor whose wife you covet," she wrote, referring to her husband. There was, she explained, a double standard she must obey. "You are a man, I am a woman, and while we might think along the same lines, we must speak and act differently. Perhaps there is no great harm in a man having desires and yielding to them; a woman may have desires, but she must not yield."

Little did she know that her own husband was engaging in this double standard. Once again, it was John Adams who recorded the situation in shocked detail after Franklin took him to dine with "a large company of both sexes" at the Brillons. Madame Brillon struck Adams as "one of the most beautiful women of France," her husband as "a rough kind of country squire." Among the crowd was a "very plain and clumsy" woman. "I afterwards learned both from Dr. Franklin and his grandson," Adams noted, "that this woman was the amie of Mr. Brillon." He also surmised, this time incorrectly, that Madame Brillon was having an affair with another neighbor. "I was astonished that these people could live together in such apparent friendship and indeed without cutting each other's throats. But I did not know the world."

A year later, Madame Brillon found out about her husband's affair with this "clumsy" young woman, Mademoiselle Jupin, who was the governess of the Brillon girls. She banished the young woman from the house, and then began to fear that she might take a job as Franklin's housekeeper. After Franklin assured her, in a closed-door session at his office, that he had no intention of hiring the woman, Madame Brillon wrote him a relieved letter. "My soul is calmer, my dear Papa, since it has unburdened itself into yours, since it does not fear anymore that Mlle J—— might settle down with you and be your torment."[13]

Even before this fit of jealousy, Madame Brillon had begun a crusade to stop Franklin from turning his attentions to other women, despite being unwilling to satisfy his ardor. "When you scatter your friendship, as you have done, my friendship does not diminish, but from now on I shall try to be somewhat sterner to your faults," she threatened.

In a forceful yet seductive reply, Franklin argued that she had no right to be so possessive. "You renounce and totally exclude all that might be of the flesh in our affection, allowing me only some kisses, civil and honest, such as you might grant your little cousins," he chided. "What am I receiving that is so special as to prevent me from giving the same to others?"

He included in the letter a proposed nine-article treaty of "peace, friendship and love" between the two of them. It began with articles that she would accept, followed by ones declaring pretty much the opposite that he would accept. The former included one saying that "Mr.

F. shall come to her whenever she sends for him" and another saying that he would "stay with her as long as she pleases." His stipulations, on the other hand, included one saying that "he will go away from Madame B's whenever he pleases," and another that "he will stay away as long as he pleases." The final article of the treaty was one on his side: "That he will love any other woman as far as he finds her amiable." He added, however, that he was "without much hope" that she would agree to this final provision, and in any event "I despair of finding any other woman that I could love with equal tenderness."[14]

In describing his sexual desires, Franklin could be quite salacious. "My poor little boy, whom you ought to have cherished, instead of being fat and jolly like those in your elegant drawings, is thin and starved for want of the nourishment that you inhumanely deny him." Madame Brillon continued the colloquy by calling him an Epicurean, who "wants a fat chubby love," and herself a Platonist, who "tries to blunt his little arrows." In another suggestive letter, he told a fable about a man who refused to lend out his horses to a friend. He was not like that. "You know that I am ready to sacrifice my beautiful big horses."

After dozens of such sensuous parries and thrusts had passed between them, at least on paper, Madame Brillon ended up rejecting once and for all his desires for a more corporeal love. In return, she also abandoned her attempt to prevent him from seeking it elsewhere. "Platonism may not be the gayest sect, but it is a convenient defense for the fair sex," she wrote. "Hence, the lady, who finds it congenial, advises the gentleman to fatten up his favorite at other tables than hers, which will always offer too meager a diet for his greedy appetites."[15]

The letter, which concluded with an invitation for tea the next day, did not end their relationship. Instead, it took on another form: Madame Brillon declared that she would henceforth like to play the role of an adoring daughter, and she assigned to him the role of a loving father.

> It is to her father that this tender and loving daughter is speaking; I had a father once, the best of men, he was my first, my closest friend. I lost him too soon! You have often asked me: "Couldn't I take the place of those you regret?" And you have told me about the humane custom

of certain savages who adopt their prisoners of war and put them in the place of their own dead relatives. You have taken in my heart the place of that father.

Franklin, either out of desire or necessity, formally agreed. "I accept with infinite pleasure, my dear friend, the proposal you make, with such kindness, of adopting me as your father," he wrote. Then he turned philosophical. It was, as he had said of Benny and Temple, important for him, now that he was separated from his own "affectionate daughter" in Philadelphia, to have always some child with him "to take care of me during my life and tenderly close my eyelids when I must take my last rest." He would work hard, he promised, to play the role properly. "I love you as a father, with all my heart. It is true that I sometimes suspect that heart of wanting to go further, but I try to conceal it from myself."[16]

The transformation of their relationship evoked from Franklin one of his most wistful and self-revealing little tales, *The Ephemera,* written to her after a stroll in the garden. (The theme came from an article he had printed in the *Pennsylvania Gazette* fifty years earlier.) He had happened to overhear, he wrote, a lament by one of the tiny short-lived flies who realized that his seven hours on this planet were nearing an end.

> I have seen generations born, flourish and expire. My present friends are the children and grandchildren of the friends of my youth, who are now, alas, no more! And I must soon follow them; for by the course of nature, though still in health, I cannot expect to live above seven or eight minutes longer. What now avails all my toil and labor in amassing honey-dew on this leaf, which I cannot live to enjoy! . . .
>
> My Friends would comfort me with the idea of a name they say I shall leave behind me; and they tell me I have lived long enough, to nature and to glory. But what will fame be to an Ephemere who no longer exists? . . .
>
> To me, after all my eager pursuits, no solid pleasures now remain, but the reflection of a long life spent in meaning well, the sensible conversation of a few good Lady-Ephemeres, and now and then a kind smile and a tune from the ever-amiable BRILLANTE. [In the original French version, the final words more clearly refer to the recipient: "toujours amiable Brillon."][17]

Throughout his remaining years in France, and even in letters after his return to America, Franklin would stay emotionally attached to Madame Brillon. Their new arrangement still allowed him such liberties as playing chess with a mutual friend, late into the night, in her bathroom, while she soaked in her tub and watched. But it was, as bathtub chess games go, rather innocent; the tub was covered, as was the style, by a wooden plank. "I'm afraid that we may have made you very uncomfortable by keeping you so long in the bath," he apologized the next day, adding a wry little promise: "Never again will I consent to start a chess game with the neighbor in your bathing room. Can you forgive me this indiscretion?" She certainly could. "No, my good papa, you did not do me any ill yesterday," she replied. "I get so much pleasure from seeing you that it made up for the little fatigue of having come out of the bath a little too late."

Having forsaken the possibility of an earthly romance, they amused themselves by promising themselves one in heaven. "I give you my word," she teased him at one point, "that I will become your wife in paradise on the condition that you will not make too many conquests among the heavenly maidens while you are waiting for me. I want a faithful husband when I take one for eternity."

More than almost anyone, she could articulate what made him so charming to women, "that gaiety and that gallantry that cause all women to love you, because you love them all." With both insight and affection, she declared, "You combine the kindest heart with the soundest moral teaching, a lively imagination, and that droll roguishness which shows that the wisest of men allows his wisdom to be perpetually broken against the rocks of femininity."[18]

In the ensuing years, Franklin would help guide Madame Brillon through her bouts of depression, and he would try, as we shall see, to encourage a marriage between Temple and either of her daughters. But increasingly, by 1779, he was turning more of his attention toward another woman, one with an even more fascinating household, who lived in the neighboring village of Auteuil.

MADAME HELVÉTIUS

Anne-Catherine de Ligniville d'Autricourt was born to one of the great aristocratic families of Lorraine, but she was the tenth of twenty children and thus lacked a dowry. So when she was 15 and of marriageable age, she was sent off to a convent. As it turned out, she certainly did not have the temperament for a cloistered life nor, for that matter, the funds. At age 30, her pension ran out and so did she, to Paris, where she was taken in by a kindly aunt who had left her husband, become a novelist, and created a salon filled with bright and slightly bohemian intellectuals.

There Anne-Catherine's vivacity and beauty attracted many suitors, most notably the economist Turgot, eight years her junior, who would later become France's comptroller and a friend of Franklin. Turgot was engaging but not wealthy enough, so she instead married someone more established, Claude-Adrien Helvétius.

Helvétius was one of France's fifty or so Farmers General, a royal-chartered group with the very lucrative assignment of collecting taxes and holding leases. Once he had made his fortune, Helvétius set out to satisfy his social and intellectual aspirations. So the rich financier married the poor aristocrat and became, as mentioned above, a noted philosopher who helped plan the Nine Sisters Masonic Lodge. His great work, *De l'Esprit* (1758), was a controversial espousal of godless hedonism, which argued that the love of pleasure motivated human activity. Around him he gathered the stars of the Enlightenment, including Diderot, Condorcet, Hume on his occasional visits from Edinburgh, and Turgot, still in favor though spurned as a suitor.

When Helvétius died in 1771, five years before Franklin's arrival, his widow Anne-Catherine, now Madame Helvétius, married off their two daughters to men of their own choosing, gave each of them one of the family chateaux, and bought a rambling farm in Auteuil near Passy. She was lively, outgoing and, as befitted her aristocratic birth but impoverished upbringing, somewhat of a free-spirited bohemian who enjoyed projecting an earthy aura. There is an oft-repeated remark that has been attributed to many but was likely first famously uttered by the writer Fontenelle, who was in his late nineties when he frequented her salon. Beholding Madame Helvétius in one of her more casual states of undress, he proclaimed, "Oh, to be seventy again!"

At Auteuil she cultivated a free-spirited garden that was devoid of all French formality, a collection of ducks and dogs that formed a noisy and motley menagerie, and a salon that displayed many of the same attributes. Friends brought her rare plants, unusual pets, and provocative ideas, and she nurtured them all at what became jokingly known as "l'Académie d'Auteuil."[19]

Living with Madame Helvétius were two priests and one acolyte:

- The Abbé André Morellet, a noted political economist and contributor to the *Encyclopédie*, in his late forties who had first befriended Franklin in 1772 at the English house party where he played the trick of stilling the waves with his magic cane, and who shared his love for fine wine, song, economic theories, and practical inventions.
- The Abbé Martin Lefebvre de la Roche, in his late thirties, a former Benedictine whom (in Morellet's words) "Helvétius had after a fashion secularized."
- Pierre-Jean-Georges Cabanis, a bachelor poet in his early twenties, who translated Homer, studied medicine, wrote a book on hospitals, and revered Franklin, whose tales and anecdotes he faithfully recorded.

"We discoursed of morality, of politics, and of philosophy," la Roche recalled. "Notre Dame d'Auteuil excited your coquetry, and the Abbé Morellet wrangled over the cream and ushered his arguments to prove what we did not believe."[20]

It was Turgot, still smitten by Madame Helvétius, who first brought Franklin to visit her in 1778, when she was nearly 60 but still both lively and beautiful. Her domestic menagerie, filled with banter and intellectual irreverence, was perfectly tailored to Franklin's tastes, and shortly thereafter he wrote her a letter in which he described her electromagnetism:

I have in my way been trying to form some hypothesis to account for your having so many friends and of such various kinds. I see that statesmen, philosophers, historians, poets and men of learning of all sorts attach themselves to you as straws to a fine piece of amber . . . We find in your sweet society that charming benevolence, that amiable attention to oblige, that disposition to please and be pleased, which we do not always find in the society of one another . . . In your company, we are not only pleased with you, but better pleased with one another and with ourselves.[21]

Not surprisingly, John Adams was shocked by both Madame Helvétius and her household when Franklin brought him for a visit. The two abbots, he sniped, "I suppose have as much power to pardon a sin as they have to commit one." Of the moral "absurdities" at the house he commented, "No kind of republican government can ever exist with such national manners." His wife, Abigail, was even more horrified when she visited later, and she described Madame Helvétius with a delightfully vicious pen:

Her hair was frizzled; over it she had a small straw hat, with a dirty gauze handkerchief behind . . . She carried on the chief of the conversation at dinner, frequently locking her hand into the Doctor's, and sometimes spreading her arms upon the arms of both the gentlemen's chairs, then throwing her arms carelessly upon the Doctor's neck . . . I was highly disgusted, and never wish for an acquaintance with ladies of this cast. After dinner, she threw herself on a settee, where she showed more than her feet. She had a little lap-dog, who was, next to the doctor, her favorite. This she kissed, and when he wet the floor she wiped it up with her shirt.[22]

Franklin did more than flirt with Madame Helvétius; by September 1779, he was ardently proposing marriage in a way that was more than half-serious but retained enough ironic detachment to preserve their dignities. "If that Lady likes to pass her days with him, he in turn would like to pass his nights with her," he wrote through Cabanis, using the third person. "As he has already given her many of his days, though he has so few left to give, she appears ungrateful never to have given him a single one of her nights, which steadily pass as a pure loss, without giving happiness to anyone except Poupon [her dog]."[23]

She led him on lightly. "I hoped that after putting such pretty things on paper," she scrawled, "you would come and tell me some." He continued his quest in a clever, yet still humorously detached, fashion by composing for her two little tales. The first was written in the voice of the flies living in his apartment. They complain about the dangers they faced from the spiders at Passy and thank her for making him clean out their webs. "There only remains one thing for us to wish," they conclude. "It is to see both of you forming at last but one ménage."[24]

Turgot, now more jealous than amused by Franklin, counseled her to decline his marriage proposals, which she did. Franklin nevertheless renewed his suit with one of his most famous tales, "The Elysian Fields," in which he recounted a dream about going to heaven and discussing the matter with her late husband and his late wife, who had themselves married. Praising Madame Helvétius's looks over those of his departed wife, he suggested they take revenge:

> Vexed by your barbarous resolution, announced so positively last evening, to remain single all your life in respect to your dear husband, I went home, fell on my bed, and, believing myself dead, found myself in the Elysian Fields . . . [M. Helvétius] received me with great courtesy, having known me for some time, he said, by the reputation I had there. He asked me a thousand things about the war, and about the present state of religion, liberty, and the government in France. You ask nothing then of your dear friend Madame H——; nevertheless she still loves you excessively and I was at her place but an hour ago.
>
> Ah! said he, you make me remember my former felicity.—But it is necessary to forget it in order to be happy here. During several of the early years, I thought only of her. Finally I am consoled. I have taken another wife. The most like her that I could find. She is not, it is true, so completely beautiful, but she has as much good sense, a little more of Spirit, and she loves me infinitely. Her continual study is to please me; and she has actually gone to hunt the best Nectar and the best Ambrosia in order to regale me this evening; remain with me and you will see her.
>
> . . . At these words the new Madame H—— entered with the Nectar: at which instant I recognized her to be Madame F——, my old American friend. I reclaimed to her. But she told me coldly, "I have been your good wife forty-nine years and four months, nearly a half century; be content with that. Here I have formed a new connection, which will endure to eternity."

Offended by this refusal of my Eurydice, I suddenly decided to leave these ungrateful spirits, to return to the good earth, to see again the sunshine and you. Here I am! Let us revenge ourselves.[25]

Beneath the frivolity lurked a sincere desire—his friends thought so, as did his friendly rival Turgot—yet it was expressed with a flair that made it seem safe and clever. Always uncomfortable with deep emotional bonds, Franklin performed the perfect distancing trick. Instead of conducting his suit in secret, which would have given it a dangerous seriousness, he took it public by publishing the story on his private press a few months later. By doing so, he put his heart out for all to see, and there it could dance safely in the realm between sincerity and self-deprecating playfulness. "Franklin somehow never committed himself wholly in love," notes Claude-Anne Lopez. "A part of him was always holding back and watching the proceedings with irony."

It was all too much, both the seriousness and the public playfulness, for Madame Helvétius. She fled in June 1780 to spend the summer in Tours with the hope, according to a letter Turgot wrote a mutual friend, "that she may forget, if possible, all the turmoil that has tormented her." He added that the vacation was best "not only for her own tranquility, but also to reestablish it in that other head [i.e., Franklin's] that has agitated so ill-advisedly."[26]

As for Franklin, the deft dance of half-serious flirtations, unrequited though they were, had a rejuvenating effect on his body and spirit. "I do not find that I grow any older," he wrote a friend that spring. "Being arrived at 70, and considering that by traveling further in the same road I should probably be led to the grave, I stopped short, turned about, and walked back again; which having done these four years, you may now call me 66."[27]

THE BAGATELLES

One product of Franklin's flirtations at Passy and Auteuil was the collection of fables and tales—such as "The Ephemera," "The Flies," and "The Elysian Fields," mentioned above—that he wrote to amuse his friends. He called them bagatelles, the French term for a sprightly little musical piece, and he published many of them on the private press he installed at Passy. They were similar to little stories he had written in the past, such as "The Trial of Polly Baker," but the dozen or so written in Passy have a slight French accent to them.

They have been the subject of much critical fawning. "Franklin's bagatelles combine delight with moral truth," declares Alfred Owen Aldridge. "They are among the world's masterpieces of light litera-ture." Not exactly. Their value lies more in the glimpse they give into Franklin's personality than in their literary merit, which is somewhat slight. They are jeux d'esprit, as fun as a five-finger exercise. Most dis-play Franklin's typical wry self-awareness, though some are a bit heavy-handed in their attempt to teach a moral lesson.[28]

The most amusing is "Dialogue between the Gout and Mr. Frank-lin," a precursor to the old Alka Seltzer commercial in which a man is berated by his stomach. When he was bedridden by the malady in Oc-tober 1780, Madame Brillon wrote him a poem, "Le Sage et la Goutte," that implied that his malady was caused by his love for "one pretty mistress, sometimes two, three, four." Among the lines:

> "Moderation, dear Doctor," said the Gout,
> "Is no virtue for which you stand out.
> You like food, you like ladies' sweet talk,
> You play chess when you should walk."

Franklin replied one midnight with a long and rollicking dialogue in which the gout chided him for his indulgences and also, because Franklin liked to be instructive, prescribed a course of exercise and fresh air:

MR. F.: Eh! oh! eh! What have I done to merit these cruel suffer-ings?

THE GOUT: Many things; you have ate and drank too freely, and too much indulged those legs of yours in their indolence.

MR. F.: Who is it that accuses me?

THE GOUT: It is I, even I, the Gout.

MR. F.: What! my enemy in person?

THE GOUT: No, not your enemy.

MR. F.: I repeat it, my enemy; for you would not only torment my body to death, but ruin my good name; you reproach me as a glutton and a tippler; now all the world, that knows me, will allow that I am neither the one nor the other.

THE GOUT: The world may think as it pleases; it is always very complaisant to itself, and sometimes to its friends; but I very well know that the quantity of meat and drink proper for a man who takes a reasonable degree of exercise, would be too much for another who never takes any . . .

If your situation in life is a sedentary one, your amusements, your recreation, at least, should be active. You ought to walk or ride; or, if the weather prevents that, play at billiards. But let us examine your course of life. While the mornings are long, and you have leisure to go abroad, what do you do? Why, instead of gaining an appetite for breakfast by salutary exercise, you amuse yourself with books, pamphlets, or newspapers, which commonly are not worth the reading. Yet you eat an inordinate breakfast, four dishes of tea with cream, and one or two buttered toasts, with slices of hung beef, which I fancy are not things the most easily digested.

Immediately afterwards you sit down to write at your desk, or converse with persons who apply to you on business. Thus the time passes till one, without any kind of bodily exercise. But all this I could pardon, in regard, as you say, to your sedentary condition. But what is your practice after dinner? Walking in the beautiful gardens of those friends with whom you have dined would be the choice of men of sense; yours is to be fixed down to chess, where you are found engaged for two or three hours!

. . . You know M. Brillon's gardens, and what fine walks they contain; you know the handsome flight of an hundred steps which lead from the terrace above to the lawn below. You have been in the practice of visiting this amiable family twice a week, after dinner, and it is a maxim of your own, that "a man may take as much exercise in walking a mile up and down stairs, as in ten on level ground." What an opportunity was here for you to have had exercise in both these ways! Did you embrace it, and how often?

MR. F.: I cannot immediately answer that question.

THE GOUT: I will do it for you; not once.[29]

He sent the bagatelle to Madame Brillon along with a letter that, in a cheeky way, rebutted her poem's contention "that mistresses have had a share in producing this painful malady." As he pointed out, "When I was a young man and enjoyed more of the favors of the fair sex than I do at present, I had no gout. Hence, if the ladies of Passy had shown more of that Christian charity that I have so often recommended to you in vain, I should not be suffering from the gout right now." Sex had become, by then, a topic of banter rather than of tension for them. "I will do my best for you, in a spirit of Christian charity," she wrote back, "but to the exclusion of *your* brand of Christian charity."

Franklin used his bagatelles as a way to improve his language skills; he would translate them back and forth, show them to friends like the Abbé de la Roche, and then incorporate corrections. He wrote his famous story about paying too much for a whistle as a child, for example, in two columns, the left in French and the right in English, with space in the margins for revisions. Because Madame Brillon spoke no English, Franklin sent her the French versions of his writings, often showing her the corrections others had made.

She was looser about grammar than about morals. "The corrector of your French spoiled your work," she said of the edits la Roche made to the gout dialogue. "Leave your works as they are, use words that say things, and laugh at grammarians, who by their purity weaken all your sentences." For example, Franklin often coined new French words, such as "indulger" (meaning "to indulge"), which his friends would then revise. Madame Brillon, however, found these neologisms charming. "A few purists might quibble with us, because those birds weigh words on a scale of cold erudition," she wrote, but "since you seem to express yourself more forcefully than a grammarian, my judgment goes in your favor."[30]

Franklin found it particularly difficult to master the language's masculine and feminine distinctions, and he even jokingly put the word "masculines" in the feminine form, and "feminines" in the masculine when complaining about the need to look such things up in the dictionary. "For sixty years now [since age 16], masculine and feminine things—and I am not talking about modes and tenses—have been giving me a lot of trouble," he noted wryly. "It will make me all the happier to go to paradise where, they say, all such distinctions will be abolished."

So how good was Franklin's French? By 1780, he was speaking and writing with great flourish and gusto, though not always with proper pronunciation and grammar. That approach appealed to most of his friends there, particularly the women, but not surprisingly, it offended John Adams. "Dr. Franklin is reported to speak French very well, but I find upon attending to him critically that he does not speak it grammatically," Adams chided. "He acknowledged to me that he was wholly inattentive to grammar. His pronunciation, too, upon which the French gentlemen and ladies complimented him very highly, and which he seemed to think pretty well, I soon found out was very inaccurate."[31]

The bagatelle that most enchanted his French friends, entitled "Conte," was a parable about religious tolerance. A French officer who is about to die recounts a dream in which he arrives at the gates of heaven and watches St. Peter ask people about their religion. The first replies that he is a Catholic, and St. Peter says, "Take your place there among the Catholics." A similar procedure follows for an Anglican and a Quaker. When the officer confesses that he has no religion, St. Peter is indulgent: "You can come in anyway; just find a place for yourself wherever you can." (Franklin seems to have revised the manuscript a few times to make his point about tolerance clear, and in one version expressed it more forcefully as: "Enter anyway and take any place you wish.")[32]

The tale echoed many of Franklin's previous light writings advocating religious tolerance. Although Franklin's belief in a benevolent God was becoming stronger as he grew older, the French intellectuals admired the fact that he did not embrace any religious sect. "Our freethinkers have adroitly sounded him on his religion," one acquaintance wrote, "and they maintain that they have discovered he is one of their own, that is that he had none at all."[33]

CHESS AND FARTS

One of Franklin's famous passions was chess, as evidenced by the late-night match he played in Madame Brillon's bathroom. He saw the game as a metaphor for both diplomacy and life, a point that he made explicit in a bagatelle he wrote in 1779 on "The Morals of Chess," which was based on an essay he had drafted in 1732 for his Philadelphia Junto. "The game of chess is not merely an idle amusement," he began. "Several very valuable qualities of the mind, useful in the course of human life, are to be acquired or strengthened by it. For life is a kind of chess, in which we have often points to gain and competitors or adversaries to contend with."

Chess, he said, taught foresight, circumspection, caution, and the importance of not being discouraged. There was also an important etiquette to be practiced: never hurry your opponent, do not try to deceive by pretending to have made a bad move, and never gloat in victory: "Moderate your desire of victory over your adversary, and be pleased with the one over yourself." There were even times when it was prudent to let an opponent retract a bad move: "You may indeed happen to lose the game to your opponent, but you will win what is better, his esteem." [34]

During one of Franklin's late-night chess matches in Passy, a messenger arrived with an important set of dispatches from America. Franklin waved him off until the game was finished. Another time, he was playing with his equal, the Duchess of Bourbon, who made a move that inadvertently exposed her king. Ignoring the rules of the game, he promptly captured it. "Ah," said the duchess, "we do not take Kings so." Replied Franklin in a famous quip: "We do in America." [35]

One night in Passy he was absorbed in a game when the candles flickered out. Refusing to quit, he sent his opponent to find more. The man quickly returned with a surprised look and the news that it was already light outside. Franklin threw open the shutters. "You are right, it is daytime," he said. "Let's go to bed."

The incident was the inspiration for a bagatelle he wrote about his surprise at discovering that the sun rose and poured forth light at 6 in the morning. By this stage in his life, it should be noted, he no longer shared Poor Richard's belief in being early to bed and early to rise. He declared that this discovery would surprise his readers, "who with me have never seen any signs of sunshine before noon." This led him to conclude that if people would simply get up much earlier, they could save a lot of money on candles. He even included some pseudo-scientific calculations of what could be saved by this "Economical Project" if during the summer months Parisians would shift their sleeping time seven hours earlier: close to 97 million livres, "an immense sum that the city of Paris might save every year by the economy of using sunshine instead of candles."

Franklin concluded by bestowing the idea on the public without any request for royalty or reward. "I expect only to have the honor of it," he declared. He ended up with far more honor than he could have imagined: most histories of the invention of Daylight Savings Time credit the idea to this essay by Franklin, even though he wrote it mockingly and did not come up with the idea of actually shifting clocks by an hour during the summer.[36]

The essay, which parodied both human habits and scientific treatises, reflected (as did his writings as a youth) the influence of Jonathan Swift. "It was the type of irony Swift would have written in place of 'A Modest Proposal' if he had spent five years in the company of Mmes. Helvétius and Brillon," notes Alfred Owen Aldridge.[37]

A similar scientific spoof, even more fun and famous (or perhaps notorious), was the mock proposal he made to the Royal Academy of Brussels that they study the causes and cures of farting. Noting that the academy's leaders, in soliciting questions to study, claimed to "esteem utility," he suggested a "serious enquiry" that would be worthy of "this enlightened age":

> It is universally well known that in digesting our common food, there is created or produced in the bowels of human creatures a great quantity of wind. That the permitting this air to escape and mix with the atmosphere is usually offensive to the company from the fetid smell that accompanies it. That all well-bred people therefore, to avoid giving such offense, forcibly restrain the efforts of nature to discharge that wind. That so retained contrary to nature, it not only gives frequently great present pain, but occasions future diseases . . .

> Were it not for the odiously offensive smell accompanying such escapes, polite people would probably be under no more restraint in discharging such wind in company than they are in spitting or in blowing their noses. My Prize Question therefore should be, To discover some drug wholesome and not disagreeable, to be mixed with our common food or sauces, that shall render the natural discharges of wind from our bodies, not only inoffensive, but agreeable as perfumes.

With a pretense of scientific seriousness, Franklin proceeded to explain how different foods and minerals change the odor of farts. Might not a mineral such as lime work to make the smell pleasant? "This is worth the experiment!" There would be "immortal honor" attached to whoever made the discovery, he argued, for it would be far more "useful [than] those discoveries in science that have heretofore made philosophers famous." All the works of Aristotle and Newton, he noted, do little to help those plagued by gas. "What comfort can the vortices of Descartes give to a man who has whirlwinds in his bowels!" The invention of a fart perfume would allow hosts to pass wind freely with the comfort that it would give pleasure to their guests. Compared to this luxury, he said with a bad pun, previous discoveries "are, all together, scarcely worth a Fart-hing."

Although he printed this farce privately at his press in Passy, Franklin apparently had qualms and never released it publicly. He did, however, send it to friends, and he noted in particular that it might be of interest to one of them, the famous chemist and gas specialist Joseph Priestley, "who is apt to give himself airs."[38]

Yet another delightful essay of mock science was written as a letter to the Abbé Morellet. It celebrated the wonders of wine and the glories of the human elbow:

> We hear of the conversion of water into wine at the marriage in Cana as a miracle. But this conversion is, through the goodness of God, made every day before our eyes. Behold the rain which descends from heaven upon our vineyards; there it enters the roots of the vines, to be changed into wine; a constant proof that God loves us, and loves to see us happy. The miracle in question was performed only to hasten the operation.

As for the human elbow, Franklin explained, it was important that it be located at the right place, otherwise it would be hard to drink wine. If Providence had placed the elbow too low on the arm, it would be hard for the forearm to reach the mouth. Likewise, if the elbow had been placed too high, the forearm would overshoot the mouth. "But by the actual situation, we are enabled to drink at our ease, the glass going exactly to the mouth. Let us, then, with glass in hand, adore this benevolent wisdom; let us adore and drink!"[39]

FAMILY MATTERS

Where did this new circle of ersatz family members leave Franklin's actual family? At a distance. His daughter, Sally, who adored him, wrote of her diligence in restoring their house in Philadelphia after the British had withdrawn in May 1778. But whereas the letters from his French lady friends began "Cher Papa," most of those from his real daughter began more stiffly, with "Dear and honored sir." His replies, addressed to "Dear Sally" and occasionally "My Dear Child," often expressed delight about the exploits of his grandchildren. But sometimes even his compliments were freighted with exhortations. "If you knew how happy your letters make me," he lectured at one point, "I think you would write oftener."

In early 1779, Sally wrote of the high price of goods in America and how she was busy spinning her own tablecloths. Unfortunately, however, she made the mistake of adding that she had been invited to a ball in honor of General Washington and had sent to France for pins, lace, and feathers so she could look fashionable. "There never was so much dressing and pleasure going on," she exulted to her father, and she added that she hoped he would send her some accessories so that she could take pride in showing off his taste.

At the time, Franklin was writing his sweet bagatelles to his French friends and promising Polly Stevenson a pair of diamond earrings if one of his lottery tickets won. But he responded with dismay at Sally's plea for a few luxuries. "Your sending for long black pins, and lace, and feathers! disgusted me as much as if you had put salt in my strawberries," he chided. "The spinning, I see, is laid aside, and you are to be dressed for the ball! You seem not to know, my dear daughter, that, of all the dear things in this world, idleness is the dearest." He sent her some of the items she had requested "that are useful and necessary," but added a dose of homespun advice, with just a touch of his humor, about the frivolous fineries. "If you wear your cambric ruffles as I do, and take care not to mend the holes, they will come in time to be lace; and feathers, my dear girl, may be had in America from every cock's tail."[40]

Clearly hurt, she replied with a detailed description of how industrious and frugal she was being, and she tried to work back into his graces by sending over some homespun American silk for him to present from her to Queen Marie-Antoinette. Knowing her father's desire to promote the local silk industry, she noted, "It will show what can be sent from America."

It was a sweet gesture, with all the elements—industriousness, selflessness, promotion of American products, gratitude toward France—that should have appealed to Franklin. Alas, the silk was stained by salt water on the way over and, worse yet, her father scoffed at the entire scheme. "I wonder how, having yourself scarce shoes to your feet, it would come into your head to give clothes to a Queen," he wrote back. "I shall see if the stains can be covered by dyeing it and make summer suits of it for myself, Temple and Benny." He did, however, end on a kinder and gentler note. "All the things you order will be sent, for you continue to be a good girl, and spin and knit your family stockings."[41]

Franklin's heart proved far softer when it came to news about his grandchildren. In late 1779, Sally had a fourth child and, in hopes of pleasing Franklin, baptized the boy Louis, after the French king. The name was so unusual in America that people had to inquire whether the child was a boy or girl. When her son Willy recited the Lord's Prayer after a nightmare and addressed it to Hercules, she asked her father for his advice: "Whether it is best to instruct him in a little religion or let him pray a little longer to Hercules?" Franklin replied, with a hint of humor, that she should teach him "to direct his worship more properly, for the deity of Hercules is now quite out of fashion." Sally complied. A little later she wrote that Willy was learning his Bible well and that he had "an extraordinary memory" for all literature. "He has learned the speech of Anthony over Caesar's body, which he can scarcely speak without tears." Her daughter, Elizabeth, she added, was fond of looking at the picture of her grandfather "and has frequently tried to tempt you to walk out of the frame to play with her with a piece of apple pie, the thing of all others she likes best."[42]

Sally also found a project that enabled her to earn Franklin's unvarnished approval. With Washington's army suffering in tattered uniforms in December 1779, she rallied the women of Philadelphia to raise donations, buy cloth, and sew more than two thousand shirts for the beleaguered troops. "I am very busily employed in cutting out and making shirts . . . for our brave soldiers," she reported. When Washington tried to pay cash for even more shirts, the ladies refused it and kept working for free. "I hope you will approve of what we have done," she wrote, clearly fishing for an expression of praise. Franklin, of course, did approve. He wrote back commending her for her "amor patrie," and he had an account of her activities published in France.[43]

Her son Benny also felt the vagaries of Franklin's affection, even though the boy had been snatched from the bosom of the Bache family to accompany him to Europe. After two years at a boarding school near Passy, where he saw his grandfather but once a week, the quiet 9-year-old was packed off to an academy in Geneva, where he would not see him for more than four years. Despite his love of the French, Franklin felt that a Catholic monarchy was not the best place to educate his grandson, he wrote Sally, "as I intend him for a Presbyterian as well as a Republican."[44]

Benny was taken to Geneva by a French diplomat, Philibert Cramer, who was a publisher of Voltaire. Hungry as ever for affection and a father figure, Benny latched on to Cramer, who died suddenly a few months later. So he lived for a while with Cramer's widow, Catherine, and then was left in the charge of Gabriel Louis de Marignac, a former poet and military officer who ran the academy.

Horribly lonely, Benny begged that his brother William, or his former Passy classmate John Quincy Adams, be sent to join him. At the very least, could he please have a picture of Franklin and some news?

Franklin, ever willing to send out his portrait, obliged with one, along with the news of Sally's success in supplying shirts to Washington's troops. "Be diligent in your studies that you also may be qualified to do service to your country and be worthy of so good a mother," he wrote. He also sent word that four of Benny's former Passy schoolmates had died of smallpox, and he should be thankful he had been inoculated as a child. Yet even his expressions of affection contained a note of contingency. "I shall always love you very much if you continue to be a good boy," he closed one letter.[45]

Benny did well his first year and even won the school prize for translating Latin into French. Franklin sent him some money so that he could host the celebration the prizewinner traditionally gave for his classmates. He also asked Polly Stevenson, still in London, to pick out some books for Benny in English, as he was showing signs of losing that language. Polly, knowing how to flatter her friend, picked out a book that included mentions of Franklin.[46]

But Benny eventually fell into the funk of a depressed adolescent, perhaps because Franklin never visited, nor did Temple, nor was he brought back to Passy for vacations. He turned shy and indolent, reported Madame Cramer, who continued to keep an eye on him. "He has an excellent heart; he is sensible, reasonable, he is serious, but he has neither gaiety nor vivacity; he is cold, he has few needs, no fantasies." He didn't play cards, never got in fights, and showed no signs that he would ever display "great talents" or "passions." (In this prediction she was wrong, for in later life Benny would become a crusading newspaper editor.) When she reminded Benny that he had won the Latin prize and was clearly capable of being a good student, "he answered coldly that it had been sheer luck," she wrote Franklin. And when she offered to request for him a larger allowance from his grandfather, he showed no interest.

Benny's parents became worried, and Richard Bache timidly suggested that perhaps Franklin could find time to go see him. "It would give us pleasure to hear that you had found leisure enough to visit him at Geneva," Bache wrote, noting that "the journey might conduce to your health." But it was a tentative suggestion made almost apologetically. "I suspect your time has been more importantly employed," he quickly added. Madame Cramer, for her part, suggested that at the very least he could write Benny more frequently.[47]

Franklin did not find time to travel to Geneva, but he did compose for him one of his didactic little essays that proclaimed the virtues of education and diligence. Those who study hard, he wrote, "live comfortably in good houses," whereas those who are idle and neglect their schoolwork "are poor and dirty and ragged and ignorant and vicious and live in miserable cabins and garrets." Franklin liked the lesson so much that he made a copy and sent it to Sally, who gushed that "Willy shall get it by heart." Benny, on the other hand, did not even acknowledge receiving it. So Franklin sent him another copy and ordered him to translate it into French and send it back to assure he understood it.[48]

Finally, Benny found a friend who brought him out of his torpor: Samuel Johonnot, the grandson of Franklin's Boston friend the Rev. Samuel Cooper. A "turbulent and factious" lad, he was expelled from the school in Passy, and Franklin arranged to send him to the Geneva academy. He was a smart student, placing first in the class and spurring Benny to come in a respectable third.

Socially, Johonnot's effect on Benny was even more pronounced. He began to develop more of his family's rebellious streak. At one point, a cat killed one of their pet guinea pigs, and they resolved to kill a cat, any cat, in revenge, which they did. Benny went to his first dance, which unnerved him so much that he was relieved when a fire across the street brought it to an abrupt end, but then he went to another dance and a third, where he enjoyed himself thoroughly. He wrote to his grandfather that he was now having fun, told of his butterfly-hunting and grape-harvesting expeditions, and was even so bold to hint that he would, after all, like a larger allowance. That, and a watch, "a good golden one." It would be practical, he assured his grandfather, and he promised to take good care of it.

Franklin responded the way he had to Sally's request for lace and feathers: "I cannot afford to give gold watches to children," he wrote. "You should not tease me for expensive things that can be of little or no service to you." He was also appalled when young Johonnot asked that he and Benny be allowed to come back to Paris. That elicited another stern admonition sent to Johonnot but directed at both boys: "It is time for you to think of establishing a character for manly steadiness."[49]

It was an injunction that should have been addressed to his other grandson, Temple, who had gone to France to continue his own education but had neither enrolled in a college nor taken a course. Temple's work for the American delegation was competent enough, but he spent most of his time hunting, riding, partying, and chasing women. Hoping to help him settle down with both a dowry and a job, Franklin proposed a marriage between his roguish grandson and the Brillons' elder daughter, Cunégonde.

This was nothing new. An incorrigible but never successful matchmaker, Franklin was incessantly trying, usually with ironic half-seriousness, to marry off his children and grandchildren to those of his friends. This time, however, he was wholly serious, indeed earnestly plaintive. His letter making the formal proposal, awkwardly written in a French that was uncorrected by his friends, declared that Madame Brillon was a daughter to him and expressed hope that her daughter would become one as well. He said that Temple, whom the Brillons called Franklinet, had agreed to the proposal, especially after Franklin promised to "remain in France until the end of my days" if the marriage took place. After repeating his desire to have children nearby "to close my eyes when I die," he went on to extol the virtues of Temple, "who has no vices" and "has what it takes to become, in time, a distinguished man."

Knowing Temple well, the Brillons may not have fully agreed with that assessment. They certainly did not agree to the marriage proposal. The main excuse they gave was that Temple was not a Catholic. That gave Franklin an opening to write, as he had often done before, about the need for religious tolerance and how all religions had at their core the same basic principles. (Among the five he listed in his letter was his own oft-stated religious credo, "The best service to God is doing good to men.")

Madame Brillon agreed, in her reply, that "there is only one religion and one morality." Nevertheless, she and her husband refused to assent to the marriage. "We are obliged to submit to the customs of our country," she said. M. Brillon was looking to retire from his posi-

tion as a tax receiver-general and wanted a son-in-law who could succeed him. "This position is the most important of our assets," she
wrote, ignoring that she had frequently complained to Franklin that
she was trapped in an arranged marriage made for financial reasons.
"It calls for a man who knows the laws and customs of our country, a
man of our religion."

Franklin realized that M. Brillon's objections might be caused by
something more than merely Temple's religion. "There may be other
objections he has not communicated to me," he wrote Madame Brillon, "and I ought not give him trouble." For his part, Temple embarked
on a year-long series of affairs with women high and low, including a
French countess and an Italian, until suddenly falling in love, albeit
briefly, with the Brillons' younger daughter, who was only 15. This
time M. Brillon seemed ready to approve of the alliance, and even offered a job and dowry, but the fickle Temple had already moved on to
other women, including a married mistress who would, eventually,
end up making him the third generation of Franklins to bear an illegitimate son.[50]

CHAPTER FIFTEEN

PEACEMAKER

Paris, 1778–1785

MINISTER PLENIPOTENTIARY

By the summer of 1778, it had become clear to all three American commissioners that there should be only one person in charge. Not only was it difficult for the three of them to agree on policies, Franklin told the Congress, but it was now even difficult for them to work in the same house together. Even their servants were quarreling. In addition, the French had appointed a minister plenipotentiary to America, and protocol demanded that the new nation reciprocate with an appointee of similar rank. Arthur Lee nominated himself and conspired with his brothers to win the prize. John Adams more graciously suggested to friends that Franklin, despite his work habits and softness toward France, would be best. Franklin did not overtly push for the job, but he did strongly ask the Congress, in July 1778, to "separate us."

The French did Franklin's lobbying for him. They let it be known that he was their choice, and the Congress complied in September by electing him the sole minister plenipotentiary. The vote was 12–1, the dissenting state being Pennsylvania, where his enemies questioned his loyalty and that of his grandson Temple, the son of an imprisoned loyalist governor.[1]

Word of his appointment did not reach Paris until February 1779, for the war and the winter hindered the passage of American ships.

When it did, Arthur Lee sulked and refused to hand over his papers to Franklin. As for Adams, his biographer David McCullough writes, "The new arrangement was exactly what Adams had recommended and the news was to leave him feeling more miserable than ever." He soon left Paris, at least for the time being, to make his way back to Massachusetts.

Franklin was suffering from the gout and could not immediately present his new credentials, but in late March he paid a call on the king and his ministers. Mindful of Adams's hurt feelings, Franklin worked to keep their relationship cordial. He wrote Adams a polite and amusing letter in which he described his rounds at Versailles and complained that "the fatigue however was a little too much for my feet and disabled me for near another week." In his own letters, Adams kept up a collegial façade, and he even expressed some support for Franklin's deep fealty to the French, despite his own doubts about the wisdom of becoming too aligned with them. "I am much pleased with your reception at court in the new character," he replied, "and I do not doubt that your opinion of the good will of this court to the United States is just."

Adams's fragile equanimity was shaken, however, when Franklin and the French decided to commandeer the ship that was supposed to take him home and assign it to be part of the fleet that John Paul Jones planned to use against the British (of which more below). Well aware that Adams was impatiently waiting at the port of Nantes to set sail, Franklin was apologetic, and he even got the powerful French naval minister Antoine de Sartine to write a letter explaining the decision. Another ship would be assigned to take him home as soon as feasible, Franklin promised, and it would allow Adams the benefit of traveling with the new French minister to the United States.

Adams pretended to be understanding: "The public service must not be obstructed for the private convenience of an individual, and the honor of a passage with the new Ambassador should be a compensation to me for the loss of the prospect of so speedy a return home." Showing just a touch of the polite hypocrisy that he was generally famed for lacking, Adams even went so far as to ask Franklin to "oblige me much by making my compliments [to] Madame Brillon and Madame Helvétius, ladies for whose characters I have a great respect."

But as he brooded in port, Adams became increasingly bitter. After dining with Jones, he declared that the captain was a man of "eccentricities and irregularities," and he grew furious at the thought that Jones and Franklin were conspiring to delay his trip home. "It is decreed that I shall endure all sorts of mortifications," he wrote in his diary. "Do I see that these people despise me, or do I see that they dread me?" Inevitably, he began to ascribe dark motives to Franklin. Simmering in self-importance, Adams began to suspect that Franklin was hindering his return because he feared the "dangerous truths" he might reveal. "Does the Old Conjurer dread my voice in Congress?" Adams wrote in his diary. "He had some reason, for he has often heard it there, a terror to evil doers."

Franklin was blithely oblivious of Adams's dark suspicions, and he carried on trying to be cordial in his letters. "I shall take care to present your respects to the good ladies you mention," he cheerfully promised. He even agreed, after three strident requests from Adams, that the new ship might go directly to Boston, rather than accommodating the French minister by going to Philadelphia first. But it was to no avail. New specters of distrust had infected Adams's mind, and they were destined to haunt his relationship with Franklin when he returned the following year.[2]

While Adams simmered, Arthur Lee and his brothers declared open war on Franklin back in America. Lee circulated a letter accusing Franklin of "weaving little plots" and "sowing pernicious dissension," and he also made sure that the Congress saw the flurry of accusatory letters to Franklin, questioning his honor, that he and Ralph Izard had written earlier that year.

Warned by his son-in-law, Richard Bache, of all these intrigues, Franklin was able to dismiss the resentments of the Lees. "My too great reputation," he wrote, "grieve those unhappy gentlemen, unhappy in their tempers and in the dark, uncomfortable passions of jealousy, anger, suspicion, envy and malice."

He was, however, far more wounded by Bache's reports that Lee and his allies were attacking Temple, for he loved his grandson with a blindness that was unusual for him. "Izard, Lees & company," Bache wrote, "lay some stress upon your employing as a private secretary your grandson whom they hold unfit to be trusted because of his father's principles." Then he added ominously, "They have had some thoughts of bringing a motion to have him removed." In a separate note, Sally Bache confided that her husband had been afraid to inform Franklin of this campaign against Temple because he knew it would upset him.

It certainly did. "Methinks it is rather some merit that I have rescued a valuable young man from the danger of being a Tory," he wrote Richard. Then he let loose a cry of anger at the thought that Temple might be recalled:

> It is enough that I have lost my *son;* would they add my *grandson!* An old man of seventy, I undertook a winter voyage at the command of the Congress, and for the public service, with no other attendant to take care of me. I am continued here in a foreign country, where, if I am sick, his filial attention comforts me, and if I die, I have a child to close my eyes and take care of my remains.

In a letter to Sally at the same time, he repeated these sentiments and added that trying to deprive him of Temple would be cruel but futile. "I should not part with the child, but with the employment," he threatened. "But I am confident that, whatever may be proposed by weak or malicious people, the Congress is too wise and too good to think of treating me in that manner." The Congress was indeed supportive. There was no serious effort to have Temple dismissed, and he remained the secretary to the American delegation.[3]

Temple was about 19 at the time, still a roguish lad who worked hard but had earned the deep respect of few besides his grandfather. As the controversy swirled around him in the summer of 1779, he decided to prove his mettle by taking part in an audacious mission with Lafayette to launch a surprise attack on Britain itself.

The French general, less than three years older than Temple, had recently returned from serving under George Washington. By this time, the Revolution had reached an unsteady stalemate, with British troops under Sir Henry Clinton still ensconced in New York but doing little for the time being other than conducting hit-and-run raids. So Lafayette, on arriving back in Paris, hatched his audacious plan to attack the British mainland, and he shared it with Franklin and the French military. "I admire much the activity of your genius," Franklin wrote. "It is certain that the coasts of England and Scotland are extremely open and defenseless." He conceded that he did not know enough about military strategy to "presume upon advising it." But he could give encouragement. "Many instances of history prove that in war, attempts thought to be impossible do often, for that very reason, become possible and practicable because nobody expects them."

Lafayette was eager to have Temple at his side. "We will be always together during the campaign, which I do assure you gives me great pleasure," he wrote the young man. For his part, Temple, ever the dandy, fretted about his rank, his title, his commission, and his uniform. He wanted to be commissioned as an officer rather than merely as a volunteer, and he insisted on the right to wear the epaulettes of an officer, even though Lafayette advised against it. Just as all these issues were being settled, the land invasion was called off by the French military.

Franklin professed to be disappointed. "I flattered myself," he wrote Lafayette, "that he might possibly catch from you some tincture of those engaging manners that make you so much the delight of all that know you." Once again, Temple's chance to make a name for himself on his own was scuttled.[4]

JOHN PAUL JONES

One component of the proposed invasion of Britain did proceed, and it inserted a colorful character into Franklin's life. When Lafayette was first planning his mission, Franklin told him that "much will depend on a prudent and brave sea commander who knows the coasts." They settled instead for a commander who was, as Franklin was already well aware, more brave than prudent: John Paul Jones.

Born John Paul, the son of a Scottish landscape designer, he had shipped off to sea at age 13, served as the first mate of a slave vessel, and soon commanded his own merchant ship. But the hotheaded captain, who throughout his career was prone to provoking mutinies, got into trouble by flogging a crew member who later died and then, after being exonerated, running his sword through yet another crew member who was threatening an insurrection. So he fled to Virginia, changed his last name to Jones, and at the beginning of the Revolution won a commission in America's motley navy of ex-privateers and adventurers. By 1778, he was making his reputation by conducting daring attacks along the English and Scottish coasts.

On one of these raids, Jones decided to kidnap a Scottish earl, but the man was away taking the waters down in Bath, so the crew instead forced his wife to hand over the family silver. In a fit of noble guilt, Jones decided to buy the booty from his crew so that he could return it to the family, and he wrote a flowery letter to the earl declaring his intention, copies of which he circulated to various friends, including Franklin, who had by then assumed the difficult task of acting as his American overseer as well as his occasional host in Passy. Franklin tried to help Jones resolve the problem, but it led to such a convoluted exchange of letters with the outraged earl and his baffled wife that the silver was not returned until after the end of the war.

Franklin decided that the impetuous captain would do more good, or less harm, if he focused his raids on the Channel Islands instead. "The Jersey privateers do us a great deal of mischief," he wrote to Jones in May 1778. "It has been mentioned to me that your small vessel, commanded by so brave an officer, might render great service by following them where greater ships dare not venture." He added that the suggestion came "from high authority," meaning the great French naval minister Antoine Sartine.[5]

Jones, not so easily managed, replied that his ship, *Ranger*, was too "crank and slow," and it would require promises of great reward for him to convince his men to undertake more missions. But he knew how to flatter Franklin: he sent him a copy of his battle journals, which Franklin read avidly. So, without permission from his fellow commissioners or from France, Franklin decided that Jones should be given command of a ship that had just been built for the Americans in Amsterdam. Alas, the nervous Dutch, who were trying to remain neutral, scuttled the plan, especially after the British, who had learned of it through their spy Bancroft, applied pressure.

Franklin was finally able to help secure for Jones, in February 1779, an old forty-gun man-of-war named the *Duras,* which Jones promptly rechristened the *Bonhomme Richard* in his patron's honor. Jones was so thrilled that he paid a visit to Passy that month to thank Franklin and his landlord Chaumont, who had helped supply Jones with uniforms and funds. There was perhaps another reason for the visit: Jones may have been having an illicit affair with Madame de Chaumont.[6]

During this stay, an incident occurred that, as played out in subsequent letters, resembled a French farce. A wizened old woman, who was the wife of the Chaumonts' gardener, alleged that Jones tried to rape her. Franklin made a passing allusion to the alleged incident in a postscript to a subsequent letter, and Jones mistakenly assumed that "the mystery you so delicately mention" referred to the controversy that surrounded his killing of the rebellious crew member years earlier. So he provided a long and anguished account of that old travail.

Confused and somewhat amused by Jones's detailed explanation of impaling the mutineer, Franklin replied that he had never heard that story and informed Jones that the "mystery" he alluded to referred, instead, to an allegation made by the gardener's wife that Jones had "attempted to ravish her" in the bushes of the estate at "about 7 o'clock the evening before your departure." The woman had recounted the horror in great detail, "some of which are not fit for me to write," and three of her sons had declared that they "were determined to kill you." But Jones should not worry: everyone at Passy found the tale to be the subject of great merriment. It "occasioned some laughing," wrote Franklin, "the old woman being one of the grossest, coarsest, dirtiest and ugliest that one may find in a thousand." Madame Chaumont, whose own familiarity with Jones's sexual appetites did not prevent her from a great display of French insouciance, declared that "it gave a high idea of the strength of appetite and courage of the Americans."

They all ended up concluding, Franklin assured Jones, that it must have been a case of mistaken identity. As part of the Mardi Gras festivities, a chamber girl had apparently dressed up in one of his uniforms and, so they surmised, attacked the gardener's wife as a prank. It seems quite implausible that the gardener's wife, even in the dimness of early evening, could have been so easily fooled—not even their friend Beaumarchais would have attempted such a cross-dressing rape scene in *The Marriage of Figaro*—but the explanation was satisfactory enough that the event was not mentioned in subsequent letters.[7]

All of this occurred just as Franklin was helping to plan the proposed sneak attack on Britain by Jones and Lafayette, who had both arrived at Passy and were spending hours warily assessing one another under Franklin's worried eye. Both officers were proud, and they were soon struggling over matters large and small, ranging from who would be in charge of various aspects of the invasion to whether their men would eat at the same tables. Franklin resorted to his most indirect manner in trying to soothe Jones. "It has been observed that joint expeditions of land and sea forces often miscarry through jealousies and misunderstandings between the officers of different corps," he pointed out. Then, saying almost the opposite of what he truly felt, he added, "Knowing you both as I do and your just manner of thinking on these occasions, I am confident nothing of the kind can happen between you." But Franklin made it clear that he was concerned, quite understandably, about Jones's temperament. "A cool, prudent conduct" was necessary, he cautioned. Jones must remember that Lafayette was the ranking officer, and it would be "a kind of trial of your abilities and of your fitness in temper and disposition for acting in concert with others."

In his formal set of instructions to Jones, Franklin was even more explicit in ordering him to show restraint, especially in light of his crew's previous plundering of the Scottish earl's silver. "Although the English have wantonly burnt many defenseless towns in America, you are not to follow this example, unless where a reasonable ransom is refused; in which case your own generous feelings, as well as this instruction, will induce you to give timely notice of your intention, so that sick and ancient persons, women and children, may be first removed." Replied Jones, "Your liberal and noble minded instructions would make a coward brave."[8]

When Lafayette's part of the mission was scrapped, Franklin and the French decided that Jones should proceed with a purely naval attack, which he did in September 1779. The result was the fabled sea battle between the *Bonhomme Richard* and the much better-equipped *Serapis.* When the British captain, after applying a fierce pounding, asked him to surrender, Jones replied, at least according to legend, "I have not yet begun to fight!" As Jones put it in his vivid and detailed account of the battle to Franklin, "I answered him in the most determined negative."

Jones was able to lash the *Bonhomme Richard* into a death grip with the *Serapis,* and his men scrambled up the masts to lob grenades into the ammunition holds of the enemy ship. After a three-hour battle, in which half of his three hundred crew members were killed or wounded, Jones captured control of the *Serapis* just before the *Bonhomme Richard* sank. "The scene was dreadful beyond the reach of language," he wrote Franklin. "Humanity cannot but recoil and lament that war should be capable of producing such fatal consequences."

Franklin took great pride in Jones's success, and they became even closer friends. "Scarce anything was talked of at Paris and Versailles but your cool conduct and persevering bravery during that terrible conflict," he replied. He helped to get Jones, who was desperately eager to gain social respect, initiated into the Nine Sisters Masonic Lodge, and he accompanied him on a triumphal visit to the king at Versailles. Franklin even got embroiled in Jones's lengthy and bitter disputes with the insubordinate Pierre Landais, captain of the *Alliance,* which was supposed to be part of Jones's fleet. Landais had failed to come to the rescue during the battle with the *Serapis,* and in fact had actually fired on the *Bonhomme Richard.* For the next two years, Franklin and Jones fought with Landais, who was supported by Arthur Lee, over who should be the captain of the *Alliance.* When Landais finally commandeered the vessel and sailed away, a beleaguered Franklin decided it was best to let others sort it all out. He had other things in France to deal with.[9]

FRIEND OF THE COURT

The absence of John Adams from Paris, so pleasing both to Franklin and the French court, was too good to last. He had left, in a mood even more sour than usual, after Franklin was made the sole minister to France, but he had been home only a few months when the Congress decided to send him back to Paris. His new official mission was to negotiate a peace accord with the British, if and when the time ever became ripe. As the time was not, in fact, ripe for such talks, Adams contented himself by meddling in Franklin's duties.

This thoroughly annoyed the French foreign minister Vergennes. When Adams proposed, on his arrival in February 1780, to make public his authority to negotiate with the British, Vergennes invoked the American promise not to act independently of France. He should say and do nothing. "Above all," Vergennes sternly instructed him, "take the necessary precautions that the object of your commission remain unknown to the Court of London."[10]

Franklin was also annoyed. Adams's return threatened to disrupt his careful cultivation of the French court, and it reminded him of the attacks on his reputation that had long been waged by the Adams and Lee family factions in the Congress. In a ruminative mood, he wrote Washington a letter that ostensibly offered reassurance about the general's reputation but clearly reflected his worries about his own. "I must soon quit the scene," Franklin wrote, in an unusually introspective way, referring not to his post in France but his life in this world. Washington's own great reputation in France, he said, was "free from those little shades that the jealousy and envy of a man's countrymen and contemporaries are ever endeavoring to cast over living merit." It was clear that he was trying to reassure not only Washington but also himself that history would ignore "the feeble voice of those groveling passions."[11]

More specifically, Franklin sought to explain, to himself and his friends (and also to history), why Adams rather than he had been chosen to negotiate any potential peace with Britain. Just as Adams was arriving, Franklin wrote a letter to his old friend David Hartley, a member of Parliament with whom he had previously discussed prisoner exchanges and peace feelers. Hartley had proposed a ten-year truce between Britain and America. Franklin replied that it was his "private opinion" that a truce might make sense, but he noted that "neither you nor I are at present authorized" to negotiate such matters.

That authority now resided with Adams, and Franklin put his own spin on the Congress's choice: "If the Congress have therefore entrusted to others rather than to me the negotiations for peace, when such shall be set on foot, as has been reported, it is perhaps because they may have heard of a very singular opinion of mine, that there hardly ever existed such a thing as a bad peace, or a good war, and that I might therefore easily be induced to make improper concessions."[12]

Franklin had indeed often used the phrase about there being no such thing as a bad peace or a good war, and he would repeat it to dozens of other friends after the Revolution ended. It is sometimes used as an antiwar slogan and cited to cast Franklin as one of history's noble pacifists. But that is misleading. Throughout his life, Franklin supported wars when he felt they were warranted; he had helped form militias in Philadelphia and raised supplies for the battles with the French and Indians. Though he had initially worked to avert the Revolution, he supported it strongly when he decided that independence was inevitable. The sentiments in his letter were aimed both at Hartley and at history. He wanted to explain why he had not been chosen as a peace negotiator. Perhaps more intriguing, he also wanted to let his friends in Britain know that he could eventually provide a good channel, better than Adams, if the talks ever began.[13]

In the meantime, Franklin was ardently committed to the French alliance, more so than most of his American colleagues. This led to a great public rift with Adams after his return in early 1780. Previously, the tension between the two men had been based more on their differences in personality and style, but this one was caused by a fundamental disagreement over policy: whether or not America should show gratitude, allegiance, and fealty to France.

In the early days of the Revolution, both men shared a somewhat isolationist or exceptionalist view, one that has since been a thread throughout American history: the United States should never be a supplicant in seeking support from other nations, and it should be coy and cautious about entering into entangling foreign alliances. Even after he began his love affair with France in 1777, Franklin restated this principle. "I have never yet changed the opinion I gave in Congress that a virgin state should preserve the virgin character, and not go about suitoring for alliances," he assured Arthur Lee. In negotiating the alliance with France, he had successfully resisted making any concessions that would give a monopoly over American trade or favors.

Once the treaties were signed in early 1778, however, Franklin became a strong believer in showing gratitude and loyalty. In the words of diplomatic historian Gerald Stourzh, he "extolled the magnanimity and generosity of France in terms which at times touch on the slightly ridiculous." America's fealty to France, in Franklin's view, was based on idealism as well as realism, and he described it in moral terms rather than merely in the cold calculus of commercial advantages and European power balances. "This is really a generous nation, fond of glory, and particularly that of protecting the oppressed," he declared of France in a letter to the Congress. "Telling them their *commerce* will be advantaged by our success, and that it is their *interest* to help us, seems as much to say, 'help us and we shall not be obliged to you.' Such indiscreet and improper language has been sometimes held here by some of our people, and produced no good effects."[14]

Adams, on the other hand, was much more of a cold realist. He felt that France had supported America because of its own national interests—weakening Britain, gaining a lucrative new trading relationship—and neither side owed the other any moral gratitude. France, he correctly predicted, would help America only up to a point; it wanted the new nation to break with Britain but not to become so strong that it no longer needed France's support. Franklin showed too much subservience to the court, Adams felt, and on his return in 1780 he forcefully propounded this view. "We ought to be cautious," Adams wrote the Congress in April, "how we magnify our ideas and exaggerate our expressions of the generosity and magnanimity of any of those powers."

Vergennes, not surprisingly, was eager to deal only with Franklin, and by the end of July 1780 he had exchanged enough strained correspondence with Adams—on everything from American currency revaluation to the deployment of the French navy—that he felt justified in sending him a stinging letter that managed to be both formally diplomatic and undiplomatic at the same time. On behalf of the court of Louis XVI, he declared, "The King did not stand in need of your solicitations to direct his attentions to the interests of the United States." In other words, France would not deal with Adams any longer.[15]

Vergennes informed Franklin of this decision and sent him copies of all his testy correspondence with Adams, with the request that Franklin "lay the whole before Congress." In his reply, Franklin was exceedingly candid with Vergennes, indeed dangerously so, in revealing his own frustration with Adams. "It was from his particular indiscretion alone, and not from any instructions received by him, that he has given such just cause of displeasure." Franklin went on to explicitly distance himself from Adams's activities. "He has never yet communicated to me more of his business in Europe than I have seen in the newspapers," Franklin told Vergennes. "I live upon terms of civility with him, not of intimacy." He concluded by promising to send the Congress the offending Adams correspondence that Vergennes had supplied.

Although Franklin could have, and perhaps should have, dispatched the letters without comment, he took the opportunity to write ("with reluctance") a letter of his own to the Congress that detailed his disagreement with Adams. Their dispute was partly due to a difference in style. Adams believed in blunt assertions of American interests, whereas Franklin favored suasion and diplomatic charm. But the dispute was also caused by a fundamental difference in philosophy. Adams believed that America's foreign policy should be based on realism; Franklin believed that it should also include an element of idealism, both as a moral duty and as a component of America's national interests. As Franklin put it in his letter:

> Mr. Adams . . . thinks, as he tells me himself, that America has been too free in expressions of gratitude to France; for that she is more obliged to us than we to her; and that we should show spirit in our applications. I apprehend that he mistakes his ground, and that this Court is to be treated with decency and delicacy. The King, a young and virtuous prince, has, I am persuaded, a pleasure in reflecting on the generous benevolence of the action in assisting an oppressed people, and proposes it as a part of the glory of his reign. I think it right to increase this

pleasure by our thankful acknowledgments, and that such an expression
of gratitude is not only our duty, but our interest.[16]

With the British not yet ready to deal with him and the French no
longer willing to deal with him, Adams once again left Paris feeling
resentful. And Franklin once again tried to keep their disagreements
from becoming personal. He wrote to Adams in Holland, where he
had gone to try to elicit a loan for America, and commiserated about
the difficulties of that task. "I have long been humiliated," he said,
"with the idea of our running from court to court begging for money
and friendship." And in a subsequent letter complaining about how
long France was taking to answer his own requests, Franklin wryly
wrote Adams: "I have, however, two of the Christian graces, faith and
hope. But my faith is only that of which the apostle speaks, the evidence of things not seen." If their mutual endeavors failed, he added,
"I shall be ready to break, run away, or go to prison with you, as it shall
please God."[17]

America's need for more money had indeed become quite desperate by the end of 1780. Earlier in the year, the British commander Sir
Henry Clinton had sailed south from New York, with General Cornwallis as his deputy, to launch an attack on Charleston, South Carolina. It succeeded in May, and Cornwallis set up a British command
there after Clinton returned to New York. Also that summer, the troubled American general Benedict Arnold had turned coat in a way that
made his name synonymous with treachery. "Our present situation,"
Washington wrote Franklin in October of that year, "makes one of two
things essential to us: a peace, or the most vigorous aid of our allies,
particularly in the article of money."

Franklin thus resorted to all of his wiles—personal pleadings
mixed with appeals to idealism and national interests—in his application to Vergennes in February 1781. "I am grown old," he said, adding
that his illness made it probable that he would soon retire. "The present conjuncture is critical." If more money did not come soon, the
Congress could lose its influence, the new government would be still-
born, and England would recover control over America. That, he
warned, would tilt the balance of power in a way that "will enable

them to become the Terror of Europe and to exercise with impunity that insolence which is so natural to their nation."[18]

His request was audacious: 25 million livres.* In the end, France agreed to provide 6 million, which was a great victory for Franklin and enough money to keep American hopes alive.

Franklin, however, was disheartened. Back home, his enemies were being as vindictive as ever. "The political salvation of America depends upon the recalling of Dr. Franklin," Ralph Izard wrote Richard Lee. Even Vergennes expressed some doubts that made their way back to the Congress. "Although I have a high esteem for M. Franklin," he wrote to his minister in Philadelphia, "I am nevertheless obliged to concede that his age and his love of tranquility produce an apathy incompatible with the affairs in his charge." Izard pushed a recall vote that was supported by the Lee–Adams faction. Although Franklin easily survived, the Congress did decide to send a special envoy to take over the work of handling future financial transactions.

So, in March, after receiving word of France's new loan, Franklin informed the Congress that he was ready to resign. "I have passed my 75th year," he wrote, adding that he was plagued by gout and weakness. "I do not know that my mental faculties are impaired; perhaps I shall be the last to discover that." Having served in public life for fifty years, he had received "honor sufficient to satisfy any reasonable ambition, and I have no other left but that of repose, which I hope Congress will grant me."

He included one personal request: that the members find a job for his grandson Temple, who had passed up the chance to study law so that he could serve his country in Paris. "If they shall think fit to employ him as a secretary to their minister at any European court, I am

---

* This is the rough equivalent of $130 million in purchasing power in 2002 U.S. dollars. In 1780, there were about 23.5 livres to the British pound, and £1 in 1780 had the same purchasing power as £83 in 2002. Although the American Congress had begun issuing paper currency denominated in dollars by 1780, the states continued to issue their own currencies, often in pounds. Rapid changes in the value of all American currencies during the Revolution made them difficult to compare to European currencies. By 1786, an ounce of gold cost $19 or £4.2, making £1 worth $4.52, which became the semiofficial exchange rate in 1790. See page 506 for more currency conversion data.[19]

persuaded they will have reason to be satisfied with his conduct, and I shall be thankful for his appointment as a favor to me."[20]

PEACE COMMISSIONER

The Congress refused Franklin's offer to resign. Instead, in what came as a pleasant surprise, he was not only kept on as minister to France, he was also given an additional role: one of the five commissioners to handle the peace negotiations with Britain if and when the time came for an end to the war. The others were John Adams (who originally had been designated the sole negotiator and was at the time still in Holland), Thomas Jefferson (who again declined the overseas assignment for personal reasons), South Carolina planter-merchant Henry Laurens (who was captured at sea by the British and imprisoned in the Tower of London), and New York lawyer John Jay.

Franklin's selection was controversial, and it came partly because of pressure from Vergennes. Despite his doubts about Franklin's energy, the French minister instructed his envoy in Philadelphia to lobby on his behalf and inform the Congress that his conduct "is as zealous and patriotic as it is wise and circumspect." Vergennes also asked the Congress to require that the new delegation take no steps without France's approval. The Congress complied by giving its commissioners strict instructions "to make the most candid and confidential communications upon all subjects to the ministers of our generous ally, the King of France; to undertake nothing in the negotiations for peace or truce without their knowledge and concurrence."[21]

Adams was appalled at being so shackled to France's will, and he called the instructions "shameful." Jay agreed, declaring that by "casting herself into the arms of the King of France" America would not "advance either her interest or her reputation." Franklin, on the other hand, was pleased with the instructions to follow France's guidance. "I have had so much experience of his majesty's goodness to us," he wrote the Congress, "and of the sincerity of this upright and able minister [Vergennes], that I cannot but think the confidence well and judiciously placed and that it will have happy effects."[22]

He was heartened as well by a personal triumph. Over the objections of even such friends as Silas Deane, he was able to get Temple appointed as the secretary to the new delegation. The honor of his new appointment, and the rejection of his resignation, rejuvenated him. "I call this continuance an honor," he wrote a friend, "and I really esteem it to be greater than my first appointment, when I consider that all the interest of my enemies . . . were not sufficient to prevent it."

He even wrote another friendly letter to Adams, whose own commission to negotiate with Britain had been diluted by the addition of the new delegation. Their mutual appointments, Franklin told Adams, were a great honor, but he wryly lamented that they were likely to be criticized for whatever they accomplished. "I have never known a peace made, even the most advantageous, that was not censured as inadequate," he said. " 'Blessed are the peacemakers' is, I suppose, to be understood in the other world, for in this they are frequently cursed."[23]

As a master of the relationship between power and diplomacy, Franklin knew that it would be impossible to win at the negotiating table what was unwinnable on the battlefield. He had been able to negotiate an alliance with France only after America had won the Battle of Saratoga in 1777; he would be able to negotiate a suitable peace with Britain only after America and its French allies won an even more decisive victory.

That problem was solved in October 1781. The British general Lord Cornwallis had marched north from Charleston, seeking to engage General Washington's forces, and had taken his stand at Yorktown, Virginia. France's support proved critical: Lafayette moved to Cornwallis's southern flank to prevent a retreat, a French fleet arrived at the mouth of the Chesapeake to preclude an escape by sea, French artillery arrived from Rhode Island, and nine thousand French soldiers joined eleven thousand Americans under General Washington's command. Two four-hundred-man columns, one French and the other American, began the allied assault and bombardment, which continued day and night with such intensity that when Cornwallis sent out a drummer on October 17 to signal his willingness to surrender, it took a while for him to get noticed. It had been four years since the battle of Saratoga, six and a half since Lexington and Concord. On November 19, word of the allied triumph at Yorktown reached Vergennes, who sent a note to Franklin that he reprinted on his press at Passy and distributed the following dawn.

Although the war seemed effectively over, Franklin was cautious. Until the present ministry resigned, there was always the chance that Britain would renew the struggle. "I remember that, when I was a boxing boy, it was allowed, even after an adversary said he had enough, to give him a rising blow," he wrote Robert Morris, the American finance minister. "Let ours be a douser."[24]

Lord North's government finally collapsed in March 1782, replaced by one headed by Lord Rockingham. Peace talks between America and Britain could now begin. Franklin, it so happened, was the only one of the five American commissioners who was then in Paris. So, for the next few months, until Jay and then Adams finally arrived, he would handle the negotiations on his own. In doing so, he would face two complicating factors:

- America had pledged to coordinate its diplomacy with France and her allies, rather than negotiate with London separately. But the British wanted direct talks leading to a separate peace with America. Franklin, on the surface, would initially insist on acting in concert with the French. But behind the scenes, he would arrange for private and direct peace negotiations with the British.
- The Rockingham government had two rival ministers, Foreign Secretary Charles Fox and Colonial Secretary Lord Shelburne, each of whom sent their own negotiators to Paris. Franklin would maneuver to ensure that Shelburne's envoy, whom he liked better and found more malleable, was given a commission to negotiate with the Americans.

THE NEGOTIATIONS BEGIN

"Great affairs sometimes take their rise from small circumstances," Franklin recorded in the journal he began of the 1782 peace negotiations. In this case, it was a chance meeting between his old flame Madame Brillon and an Englishman named Lord Cholmondeley, who was a friend of Shelburne. Madame Brillon sent Cholmondeley to call on Franklin in Passy, and through him Franklin sent his regards to the new colonial secretary. Franklin had known and liked Shelburne since at least 1766, when he lobbied him about getting a western land grant and made occasional visits to his grand country manor in Wiltshire. Madame Helvétius also played a small role; Shelburne had just sent her some gooseberry bushes, and Franklin wrote politely that they had arrived "in excellent order."[25]

Shelburne responded by dispatching Richard Oswald, a retired one-eyed London merchant and former slave trader who had once lived in America, to begin negotiating with Franklin. Oswald arrived on April 15 and immediately tried to convince Franklin that America could get a quicker and better deal if it negotiated independently of the French. Franklin was not yet willing. "I let him know," he wrote, "that America would not treat but in concert with France." Instead, he took Oswald to Versailles the next day to meet with Vergennes, who proposed to host a general peace conference of all the warring parties in Paris.[26]

On the way back from Versailles, Oswald argued again for a separate peace. Once the issue of American independence was settled by negotiations, he said, it should not be held up while matters relating only to France and Spain (including the ownership of Gibraltar) were still being disputed. He added an implicit threat: if France became involved and made too many demands, England would continue the war and finance it by stopping payment on its public debt.

The issue of independence, Franklin pointedly replied, had already been settled back in 1776. Britain should simply acknowledge it, rather than offer to negotiate it. As for reneging on their debt in order to renew the war, Franklin made no reply. "I did not desire to discourage their stopping payment, which I considered as cutting the throat of their public credit," he wrote in his journal. "Such menaces were besides an encouragement with me, remembering the old adage that *they who threaten are afraid.*"

Instead, Franklin suggested that Britain consider offering reparations to America, especially to "those who had suffered by the scalping and burning parties" that England had enlisted the Indians to wage. "Nothing could have a greater tendency to conciliate," he said, and that would lead to the renewal of commerce that Britain both needed and desired.

He even suggested a specific reparations proposal: Britain should offer to cede control of Canada. The money Britain could make from the Canadian fur trade, after all, was tiny compared to what it would save by not having to defend Canada. It was also far less than Britain could make through the renewed commerce with America that would flow from a friendly settlement. In addition, the money that America made from selling open land in Canada could be used to compensate the patriots whose homes had been destroyed by British troops and also the British loyalists whose estates had been confiscated by the Americans.

Behind France's back, Franklin was playing a wily balance-of-power game. He knew that France, despite her enmity toward Britain, did not want it to cede control of Canada to America. That would make America's borders more secure, reduce its tensions with Britain, and lessen its need for a friendship with France. If England continued to hold Canada, Franklin explained to Oswald, it "would necessarily oblige us to cultivate and strengthen our union with France." In his report to Vergennes about his conversation with Oswald, Franklin did not mention that he had suggested the ceding of Canada. It was the first small indication that Franklin, despite his insistence that he would work hand in glove with the French, would be willing to act unilaterally when warranted.

As usual, Franklin was speaking from notes he had prepared, and Oswald "begged" to be trusted with them so he could show them to Shelburne. After some hesitation, Franklin agreed. Oswald was charmed by Franklin's trust, and Franklin found Oswald to be sensible and devoid of guile. "We parted exceeding good friends," he noted.

Franklin had one regret about the paper he entrusted to Oswald: its hint that compensation might be due to the British loyalists in America whose property had been confiscated. So he published on his Passy press, and sent to Adams and others, a fake issue of a Boston newspaper that purported to describe, in gruesome detail, the horrors that the British had perpetrated on innocent Americans. His goal was to emphasize that no sympathy was due the British loyalists, and that it was the Americans who deserved compensation. The fake edition was cleverly convincing. It featured a description of a shipment of American scalps purportedly sent by the Seneca Indians to England and a letter that he pretended was from John Paul Jones. To make it more realistic, he even included fake little ads about a new brick house for sale in south Boston and a missing bay mare in Salem.[27]

Britain agreed to Vergennes's proposal for an all-parties peace conference, but that meant sending a new envoy, one who represented the foreign secretary Charles Fox rather than the colonial secretary Shelburne. The new envoy's name was not auspicious: Thomas Grenville, the son of the despised George Grenville who had imposed the Stamp Act back in 1765. But Fox, who had long been sympathetic to the American side, assured Franklin that the young Grenville, a mere 27, was to be trusted. "I know your liberality of mind too well to be afraid that any prejudices against Mr. Grenville's *name* may prevent you from esteeming those excellent qualities of heart and head which belong to him, or from giving the fullest credit to the sincerity of his wishes for peace."[28]

When Grenville arrived in early May, Franklin immediately took him to Versailles, where the young Englishman made the mistake of suggesting to Vergennes that if "England gave America independence," France should give back some of the Caribbean islands it had conquered and a peace could be quickly settled.

With the hint of a smile, Vergennes turned on the novice English diplomat and belittled his offer of independence. "America," he said, "did not ask it of you. There is Mr. Franklin. He will answer you as to that point."

"To be sure," said Franklin, "we do not consider ourselves as under any necessity of bargaining for such a thing that is our own and which we have bought at the expense of much blood and treasure."

Like Oswald, Grenville hoped to be able to convince Franklin to negotiate a separate peace with Britain rather than remain linked to France's demands as well. To that end, he visited Passy a few days later and warned that France "might insist on" provisions that were not related to the treaty she had made with America. If that happened, America should not feel obligated by that treaty to "continue the war to obtain such points for her."

As he had done with Oswald, Franklin refused to make such a concession. "I gave a little more of my sentiments on the general subject of benefits, obligations and gratitude," Franklin noted. People who wanted to get out of obligations often "became ingenious in finding out reasons and arguments" to do so, but America would not follow that route. Even if a person borrows money from another and then repays it, he still owes gratitude: "He has discharged the money debt, but the obligation remains."

This was stretching the idea of gratitude rather far, replied Grenville, for France was the party that actually benefited from America's separation from Britain. Franklin insisted that he felt so strongly about the "generous and noble manner" in which France had supported America that "I could never suffer myself to think of such reasonings for lessening the obligations."[29]

Grenville further annoyed Franklin by trying to hide the fact that his commission gave him the authority to negotiate only with France and not directly with the United States, which Britain did not yet recognize as an independent country. Franklin confronted him on this point at the beginning of June. Why did his commission not explicitly authorize him, Franklin asked, to deal directly with the United States? As Franklin reported to Adams the next day, "He could not explain this to my satisfaction, but said he believed the omission was occasioned by their copying an old commission." That, of course, did not convince Franklin. He insisted that Grenville get a new commission before any negotiation could begin. This was not merely a nicety of protocol, as Franklin well knew. He was insisting that the British tacitly accept America's independence as a precondition for talks. "I imagine there is a reluctance in their King to take this first step," he wrote Adams, "as the giving such a commission would itself be a kind of acknowledgment of our independence."[30]

Franklin was willing to work in concert with France, but he had no intention of allowing Britain to insist that France negotiate on America's behalf. Vergennes agreed. "They want to treat with us for you. But this the King [of France] will not agree to. He thinks it not consistent with the dignity of your state. You will treat for yourselves." All that was necessary, Vergennes added, was "that the treaties go hand in hand and are signed the same day."

Wittingly or not, Vergennes had given Franklin tacit permission to begin separate discussions with the British. Because the British were very eager to have such talks, and because there were two British negotiators vying to conduct them, Franklin had a lot of leverage. When Grenville returned to Passy at the beginning of June to argue once again for direct talks, this time Franklin decided "to evade the discussion" rather than reject the idea.

"If Spain and Holland and even if France should insist on unreasonable terms," Grenville asked, "can it be right that America should be dragged on in a war for their interests only?"

It was "unnecessary to enter at present into considerations of that kind," Franklin replied. "If any of the other powers should make extravagant demands," he continued enticingly, "it would then be time enough to consider what our obligations were."

Because Grenville was so eager to get direct talks underway, he was willing to tell Franklin, confidentially, that he was "instructed to acknowledge the independence of America previous to the commencement of the treaty." Oswald was also eager for direct talks to begin, and he came to Passy two days later to hint that he would be willing to serve as Britain's negotiator if Franklin preferred. He was coy. He was not trying to supplant Grenville, he insisted, for he was old and had no need for further glory. But it was clear to Franklin that he was now in the happy position of having a choice between two hungry suitors.

Oswald was more sophisticated than Grenville, and he was able to appear both more eager and more threatening. Peace was "absolutely necessary" for Britain, he confided. "Our enemies may now do what they please with us; they have the ball at their foot." On the other hand, there were those back in London who were "a little too much elated" by Britain's recent victory over the French navy in a major battle in the West Indies. If he and Franklin did not act soon, they might prevail in prolonging the war. There had even been serious discussions, Oswald warned, of ways to finance further fighting by canceling debt payment only on bonds of more than £1,000, which would not upset most of the population.

Franklin noted that he viewed this "as a kind of intimidation." Yet Oswald was able to soften Franklin through flattery. "He repeatedly mentioned the great esteem the ministers had for me," Franklin recorded. "They depended on me for the means of extricating the nation from its present desperate situation; that perhaps no single man had ever in his hands an opportunity of doing so much good as I had at present."

Oswald further endeared himself to Franklin by seeming to agree with him privately on what should be in a treaty. When Franklin railed against the idea of paying compensation to loyalists whose estates had been confiscated, saying that such a demand would elicit a contrary one from America demanding reparations for all the towns the British had burned, Oswald confidentially said that he personally felt the same. He also said that he agreed with Franklin that Britain should cede Canada to America. It was as if he were competing with young Grenville in an audition for the job of being Britain's negotiator and trying to win Franklin's recommendation.

Indeed, oddly enough, he was. He showed Franklin a memo that Shelburne had written that offered to give Oswald, if Franklin wished it, a commission to be the special negotiator with America. Shelburne wrote that he was willing to give Oswald any authority "which Dr. Franklin and he may judge conducive to a final settlement of things between Great Britain and America." That way, Shelburne's memo added, Britain could forge a peace with America "in a very different manner from the peace between Great Britain and France, who have always been at enmity with each other."

Oswald coyly noted that Grenville was "a very sensible young gentleman," and he was perfectly willing to leave it to him to conduct the negotiations in concert with France. However, if Franklin thought it would be "useful" to have Oswald deal directly with the Americans, he was "content to give his time and service."

Franklin was happy to accept. Oswald's "knowledge of America," he noted, meant that he would be better than Grenville "in persuading

the ministry to things reasonable." Franklin asked Oswald whether he
would prefer to negotiate with all the countries, including France, or
to negotiate with America alone. Oswald's answer, obviously, was the
latter. "He said he did not choose to be concerned in treating with the
foreign powers," Franklin noted. "If he accepted any commission, it
should be that of treating with America." Franklin agreed to write
Shelburne secretly recommending that course.[31]

Partly, Franklin was motivated by his affection for Oswald, who
was his age, and his lack of affection for the younger Grenville, who
had annoyed Franklin by leaking to the London *Evening Post* an inaccurate account of one of their meetings. "Mr. Oswald, an old man,
seems now to have no desire but that of being useful in doing good,"
Franklin noted. "Mr. Grenville, a young man, naturally desirous of acquiring a reputation, seems to aim at that of being an able negotiator."
Franklin, though still ambitious at 76, now believed in the moderating
effects of old age.

Although Franklin had made a great show of insisting that the
French be involved in all negotiations, he had come to believe that it
was now in America's interest to have its own separate and private
channel with Britain. So, when he went to Versailles in mid-June, a
week after his momentous meeting with Oswald, he was less candid
than usual with Vergennes. "We spoke of all [Britain's] attempts to
separate us, and the prudence of holding together and treating in concert," he recorded. This time, however, he held back some information. He did not detail Oswald's offer to have a private negotiating
channel or his suggestion that Britain cede Canada to America.

Nor was Franklin fully candid with the Congress, which had instructed its peace commissioners, with Franklin's approval, not to do
anything without France's full knowledge and support. In a letter in
late June to Robert Livingston, the new American foreign secretary,
Franklin reported that Britain had sent over two envoys, Oswald and
Grenville, and he claimed that he had rejected their attempts to split
America from France. "They had at first some hopes of getting the
belligerent powers to treat separately, one after another, but finding
that impracticable, they have, after several messages sent to and fro,
come to a resolution of treating with all together for a general peace."

The very next day, however, he reiterated his desire for a separate channel in a letter he wrote for Oswald to give to Shelburne: "I cannot but hope that it is still intended to vest you with [authority] respecting the treaty with America."

Britain was likewise engaging in back-channel intrigue. In addition to holding informal discussions with the French, it sent envoys directly to the Congress trying to urge members to accept some form of dominion status for America that would permit separate parliaments loyal to a common king. When Franklin heard of these overtures, he wrote another letter to Livingston warning that they must be forcefully resisted. "The King hates us most cordially," he declared. If he were allowed "any degree of power or government" over America, "it will soon be extended by corruption, artifice, and force, until we are reduced to absolute subjection."[32]

FRANKLIN'S PEACE PLAN

At the beginning of July, the negotiating situation was simplified by the death of Lord Rockingham. Shelburne took over as prime minister, Fox resigned as foreign secretary, and Grenville was recalled. The time was right for Franklin to make an informal, but precise, peace offer to Oswald, which he did on July 10.

His proposal was divided into two parts, "necessary" provisions and "advisable" ones. Four fell into the former category: independence for America that was "full and complete in every sense," the removal of all British troops, secure boundaries, and fishing rights off the Canadian coast. In the advisable category were four suggested provisions: payment of reparations for the destruction in America, an acknowledgment of British guilt, a free trade agreement, and the ceding of Canada to the United States.

Oswald immediately sent Shelburne all the details, but Franklin kept the proposals private and never recorded them. Nor did he consult with, or even inform, Vergennes about the offer he had made to Oswald.[33]

Thus, with clear vision and a bit of conniving, Franklin had set the stage for the final negotiations that would end the Revolutionary War.

Shelburne promptly informed Oswald that the suggestions were "unequivocal proofs of Dr. Franklin's sincerity." Britain was willing, he
said, to affirm America's independence as a preliminary to negotiations, and it should "be done decidedly so as to avoid future risks of
enmity." If America would drop the "advisable" provisions, Shelburne
said, and "those called necessary alone retained as the ground of discussion," then he was confident that a treaty could be "speedily concluded." Although it would take a few more months, that is in essence
what happened.[34]

The final resolution was delayed, however, when Franklin was
struck by "cruel gout" and kidney stones, which incapacitated him for
much of August and September. John Jay, who had finally arrived in
Paris, took over as the lead negotiator. The flinty New Yorker objected
that the wording of Oswald's commission, which authorized him to
negotiate "with the said colonies and plantations," was not much better than Grenville's had been, and he demanded that Oswald get a
clear statement that he was dealing with an independent nation before
talks proceeded further.

When Jay and Franklin went to call on Vergennes, the French
minister advised that it did not seem necessary to insist that Oswald's
commission contain a clear declaration of America's sovereignty.
Franklin, who likewise gave his opinion that Oswald's commission
"would do," was thrilled by Vergennes's tacit approval for the British-
American negotiations to proceed, which he interpreted as a magnanimous and supportive gesture showing France's "gracious goodwill."

Jay's interpretation, more sinister but more correct, was that Vergennes did not want Britain to recognize American independence except as part of a comprehensive peace settlement involving France and
Spain. "This Court chooses to postpone an acknowledgment of our
independence by Britain," Jay reported to the Congress, "in order to
keep us under their direction" until all the demands of France and
Spain were met. "I ought to add that Dr. Franklin does not see the
conduct of this Court in the light I do."[35]

Jay's skepticism about France's motives led to a heated argument
with Franklin when they returned to Passy from Versailles that
evening. Jay was especially angry, he told Franklin, that Vergennes

had brought up Spain's desire to claim some of the land between the Allegheny Mountains and the Mississippi River. Franklin fully agreed that Spain should not be permitted to "coop us up," but he gave Jay one of his gentle lectures about the wisdom of assuming that a friend like France was acting in good faith until there was hard evidence to the contrary. France was not trying to hold up negotiations, as Jay kept angrily insisting; instead, Franklin argued, Vergennes had shown a willingness to speed them along by not objecting to the wording of Oswald's commission.

But Jay's suspicions were reinforced when he learned that Vergennes had sent a deputy on a secret mission to London. Trusting neither the French nor Franklin, Jay joined in the back-channel fandango by dispatching a secret envoy of his own to London. What made this especially intriguing was that the man he sent was Benjamin Vaughan, Franklin's longtime friend and publisher, who had come to Paris to visit Franklin and do what he could to promote peace.

Jay asked Vaughan to tell Lord Shelburne that Oswald's commission needed to state unambiguously that he was to negotiate with "the United States." Such an explicit acknowledgment of American independence at the outset, Jay promised, would help "cut the cords" that bound America to France. Shelburne, eager to conclude a peace before his government toppled, was willing to go far enough to satisfy Jay. In mid-September his cabinet granted Oswald a new commission "to treat with the commissioners appointed by the colonies under the title of 13 united states," and it reaffirmed that American independence could be acknowledged as a preliminary to further discussions.

So, on October 5, with Jay and Franklin both satisfied and back in harmony, official negotiations began. Oswald presented his formal new commission, and Jay presented a proposed treaty that was very similar to the one Franklin had informally offered in July. The only addition to Franklin's four "necessary" points was a provision that was sure to please Britain, though not France or Spain: that both Britain and America would have free navigation rights on the Mississippi.

Their momentum, however, was slowed for a few weeks after Britain succeeded in beating back a French-Spanish attack on Gibraltar, thus emboldening their ministers. To stiffen Oswald's backbone,

Shelburne sent over Henry Strachey, a cabinet officer who had served as Admiral Howe's secretary. Just as he arrived, so did John Adams, yet again, to assume his role as a member of the American delegation.

Adams was as blunt as ever, filled with suspicions and doubting everyone's character but his own. Even Lafayette, who had become Franklin's close confidant, was immediately slammed by Adams as a "mongrel character" of "unlimited ambition" who was "panting for glory." Adams also displayed, in a public and undiplomatic way, his personal distrust of Vergennes by not calling on him for almost three weeks, until the minister "caused him to be reminded of" his duty to do so. (Vergennes, who was as smooth as Adams was rough, baffled the wary Adams by laying on a lavish dinner and plying him with fine wines and Madeira.)[36]

Adams likewise initially balked at paying a courtesy call on Franklin, who was pretty much confined to Passy with the gout and kidney stones, even though they had managed to exchange civil letters during Adams's mission in Holland. "He could not bear to go near him," Matthew Ridley, an American merchant in Paris, recorded in his diary. Ridley, who was a friend of both men, finally convinced Adams that it was necessary.

Adams felt particularly spiteful because he had recently learned about the letter Franklin had written to the Congress, at the behest of Vergennes, which had led to his earlier recall. Franklin had been motivated by "base jealousy" and "sordid envy," Adams told a friend. That was a complete misreading of Franklin, who had acted more out of annoyance than jealousy and whose occasional vices did not include an excess of envy.

Whatever the cause, Adams was filled with anger by the time he arrived back in Paris. "That I have no friendship for Franklin I avow," he wrote. "That I am incapable of having any with a man of his moral sentiments I avow." In his diary, Adams had even more to say: "Franklin's cunning will be to divide us. To this end he will provoke, he will insinuate, he will intrigue, he will maneuver."[37]

So it was a great testament to Franklin's charm that, as it turned out, he got along rather well with Adams once they settled down to work. When Adams bluntly told him, during the visit he finally made to Passy, that he agreed with Jay's tougher attitude toward France, "the Doctor heard me patiently, but said nothing." And at a meeting of the three commissioners the next day, Franklin serenely agreed with Adams and Jay that it made sense to meet with the British negotiators without coordinating with the French. Turning to Jay he said, "I am of your opinion and will go on with these gentlemen in the business without consulting this [France's] Court."

Franklin's willingness to negotiate without consulting France was not new; he had begun pursuing that approach before Jay and Adams arrived in Paris. But he made it seem that he was doing it partly in deference to the views of his two fellow commissioners, which served to soften Adams's attitude. Franklin "has gone on with us in entire harmony and unanimity," Adams happily recorded in his diary, "and has been able and useful, both by his sagacity and his reputation, in the whole negotiation."

For his part, Franklin continued to feel the same mixture of admiration and annoyance toward Adams that he had long held. As he would put it to Livingston a few months later, once the negotiations were over, "He means well for his country, is always an honest man, often a wise one, but sometimes and in some things, absolutely out of his senses."[38]

On October 30, Adams's forty-seventh birthday, the American negotiators and their British counterparts launched an intense week of negotiations, which started at eleven each morning and continued through late suppers most evenings. The British readily accepted the four "necessary points" that Franklin had proposed back in July, but not the "advisable points," such as the ceding of Canada. The main disputes they faced that week were:

- Fishing rights off Newfoundland: This was a major issue for Adams, who, as David McCullough points out, was eloquent in his sermons on "New England's ancient stake in the sacred codfish." Franklin was likewise firm on the point, and he provided an economic argument: the money that Americans made from fishing would be spent on British manufactures once friendship was restored. "Are you afraid there is not fish enough," he asked, "or that we should catch too many?" The British conceded the point, to the dismay of France, which was hoping to win special fishing rights of its own. (When Franklin was accused by his enemies in America of favoring the French position and opposing a demand for American fishing rights, he wrote Jay and Adams asking them to attest to his firmness; Jay graciously complied, and Adams did so more grudgingly.) [39]

- Prewar debts still owed by Americans to British merchants: Franklin and Jay felt they should be renounced, because Britain had taken or destroyed so much American property. Adams, however, insisted that such debts be honored, and his view prevailed.

- The western boundary: With his lifelong vision of American expansion, Franklin insisted that no other nation should have rights to the land between the Alleghenies and the Mississippi. As Jay recorded, "He has invariably declared it to be his opinion that we should insist on the Mississippi as our Western boundary." Again, this is not something that France or Spain would have supported at a general peace conference. But Britain was happy to accept the river as the western boundary along with free navigation rights for both nations.

- Compensation for the British loyalists in America whose estates had been confiscated: This was the most contentious issue, and Franklin made it even more so. He justified his implacable stance on moral grounds. The loyalists had helped cause the war, and their losses were far less than those suffered by American patriots whose property had been destroyed by the British. But his stubbornness also had a personal component. Among the most visible loyalists were his former friend Joseph Galloway and, more notably, his estranged son, William. Franklin's anger toward his son, and his desire to prove it publicly, had a major impact on his attitude toward the loyalist claims, and it added a painful personal poignancy to the final weeks of negotiations.

William, who had been released from his Connecticut captivity through a prisoner exchange in September 1778, had been living in British-occupied New York, where he served as the president of the Board of Associated Loyalists. In that capacity, he had encouraged a series of small but brutal raids on American forces. One of these resulted in the lynching murder of an American captain, and General Washington had responded by threatening to hang one of his British prisoners, a young and very well-connected officer named Charles Asgill, if the perpetrators were not brought to justice.

Asgill's friends and family used their great influence to try to save his life, and Shelburne sent a personal appeal to Franklin to intercede. Franklin sharply refused. Washington's aim was "to obtain the punishment of a deliberate murderer," he replied. "If the English refuse to deliver up or punish this murderer, it is saying that they choose to preserve him rather than Captain Asgill. It seems to me therefore that the application should be made to the English ministers."[40]

The issue became more personal for Franklin when a British court-martial acquitted the accused British soldier on the grounds that he was merely following orders. That prompted outraged Americans to demand the arrest of the person who had issued those orders: William Franklin. So, in August 1782, twenty years after his arrival in America as New Jersey governor, William prudently fled back to London, where he arrived in late September, just as his father's final round of peace negotiations with Oswald were beginning.

The meddlesome Vaughan further complicated matters by urging Shelburne to be solicitous toward William. He informed the prime minister that Temple Franklin had, when Vaughan discussed it with him in Passy, "intimated hopes to see something done for his father," and Vaughan later added his own belief, very mistaken, that doing so would have a "seasonable effect" on Benjamin Franklin's disposition toward Britain. So Shelburne met with William and promised to do all he could to help both him and the loyalists. Franklin was chagrined when he learned of all this, and was especially angry when he discovered that Vaughan's misguided interference had come at the behest of young Temple, who had interceded on his father's behalf without telling his grandfather.[41]

Franklin expressed his sentiments, as he often did, in a short fable. There was once, he wrote, a great lion, king of the forest, who "had among his subjects a body of faithful dogs." But the lion king, "influenced by evil counselors," went to war with them. "A few of them, of a mongrel race, derived from a mixture of wolves and foxes, corrupted by royal promises of great rewards, deserted the honest dogs and joined their enemies." When the dogs won their freedom, the wolves and foxes of the king's council gathered to argue for compensation to the mongrels who had remained loyal. But a horse arose, "with a boldness and freedom that became the nobleness of his nature," and argued that any reward for fratricide was unjust and would lead only to further wars. "The council had sense enough," Franklin concluded, "to resolve that the demand be rejected." [42]

In the final days of the negotiations, Franklin became even more obdurate against any compensation for the loyalists, even as Adams and Jay showed some willingness to compromise on the issue. In the past, Adams had accused Franklin of being untrustworthy because of his supposed sympathy toward his loyalist son. Now he was baffled that Franklin was being so belligerent in the other direction. "Dr. Franklin is very staunch against the Tories," he noted in his diary, "more decided on this point than Mr. Jay or myself."

Given the influence of the loyalist emigrants now living in Britain, Shelburne knew that his ministry might fall if he did nothing to satisfy their claims. His negotiators pushed until the very last day, but Franklin threatened to scuttle the entire treaty over this point. He pulled from his pocket a paper that resurrected his own demand that Britain, if it wanted any recompense for the loyalists' estates, must pay for all of the American towns destroyed, goods taken, cargo captured, villages burned, and even his own looted library in Philadelphia.

The British were forced to relent. After hearing Franklin's diatribe, they retired to an adjacent room, huddled, and returned to say they would accept instead a somewhat meaningless promise that the Congress would "earnestly recommend" to the individual states that they make whatever restitution each of them saw fit for the loyalists' estates confiscated there. The Americans knew that the states would end up doing little, so they agreed, but Franklin still insisted on one caveat, aimed at William: the recommendation would not apply to loyalists who had "borne arms against the said United States."

The next morning, November 30, 1782, the American negotiators, along with their secretary, Temple Franklin, met with the British in Oswald's suite at the Grand Hotel Muscovite to sign the provisional treaty that, in effect, ended the Revolutionary War. In a nod to the obligations owed France, the pact would not become formally binding "until terms of a peace shall be agreed upon between Great Britain and France." That would take another nine months. But the treaty had an immediate and irrevocable import that was contained in its opening line, which declared the United States "to be free, sovereign and independent."

That afternoon, the American negotiators all went to Passy, where Franklin hosted a celebratory dinner. Even John Adams was feeling mellower, at least for the time being. He conceded to his friend Matthew Ridley that Franklin had "behaved well and nobly."[43]

PLACATING THE FRENCH

To Franklin fell the difficult duty of explaining to Vergennes why the Americans had breached their obligations to France, and their instructions from the Congress, by agreeing to a treaty without consulting him. After sending Vergennes a copy of the signed accord, which he stressed was provisional, Franklin called on him at Versailles the following week. The French minister remarked, coolly but politely, that "proceeding in this abrupt signature of the articles" was not "agreeable to the [French] King" and that the Americans "had not been particularly civil." Nevertheless, Vergennes did allow that the Americans had done well by themselves, and he noted that "our conversation was amicable."

Only when Franklin followed up with a brash request for yet another French loan, along with the information that he was transmitting the peace accord to the Congress, did Vergennes take the opportunity to protest officially. It was lacking in propriety, he wrote Franklin, for him "to hold out a certain hope of peace to America without even informing yourself on the state of negotiation on our part." America was under an obligation not to consider ratifying any peace until France had also come to terms with Britain. "You have all your life performed your duties," Vergennes continued. "I pray you to consider how you propose to fulfill those which are due to the King."[44]

Franklin's response, which has been called "a diplomatic masterpiece" and "one of the most famous of all diplomatic letters," combined a few dignified expressions of contrition with appeals to France's national interest. "Nothing has been agreed in the preliminaries contrary to the interests of France," he noted, not entirely correctly, "and no peace is to take place between us and England until you have concluded yours." Using a French word that roughly translates as "propriety," Franklin sought to minimize the American transgression:

> In not consulting you before they were signed, we have been guilty of neglecting a point of *bienséance*. But, as this was not from want of respect for the King, whom we all love and honor, we hope it will be excused, and that the great work, which has hitherto been so happily conducted, is so nearly brought to perfection, and is so glorious to his reign, will not be ruined by a single indiscretion of ours.

He went on, undaunted, to press his case for another loan. "Certainly the whole edifice sinks to the ground immediately if you refuse on that account to give us any further assistance." With that came both a plea and an implied threat: making a public issue of the transgression, he warned, could hurt the mutual interests of both countries. "The English, I just now learn, flatter themselves they have already divided us. I hope this little misunderstanding will therefore be kept a secret, and that they will find themselves totally mistaken."[45]

Vergennes was stunned by Franklin's letter, a copy of which he sent to his ambassador in Philadelphia. "You may imagine my astonishment," he wrote. "I think it proper that the most influential members of Congress should be informed of the very irregular conduct of their commissioners in regard to us." He did not blame Franklin personally, except to say that "he has yielded too easily to the bias of his colleagues." Vergennes went on to lament, correctly, that the new nation was not one that would enter into entangling alliances. "We shall be but poorly paid for all that we have done for the United States," he complained, "and for securing to them a national existence."

There was little Vergennes could do. Forcing a showdown, as Franklin had subtly warned, would drive the Americans into an even faster and closer alliance with Britain. So, reluctantly, he let the matter drop, instructed his envoy not to file an official protest with the Congress, and even agreed to supply yet another French loan.[46]

"Two great diplomatic duelists had formally crossed swords," Carl Van Doren noted, "and the philosopher had exquisitely disarmed the minister." Yes, but perhaps a better analogy would be to Franklin's own favorite game of chess. From his opening gambit that led to America's treaty of alliance with France to the endgame that produced a peace with England while preserving French friendship, Franklin mastered a three-dimensional game against two aggressive players by exhibiting great patience when the pieces were not properly aligned and carefully exploiting strategic advantages when they were.[47]

Franklin had been instrumental in shaping the three great documents of the war: the Declaration of Independence, the alliance with France, and the treaty with England. Now he turned his thoughts to peace. "All wars are follies, very expensive, and very mischievous ones," he wrote Polly Stevenson. "When will mankind be convinced of this, and agree to settle their differences by arbitration? Were they to do it, even by the cast of a die, it would be better than by fighting and destroying each other." To Joseph Banks, one of the many old friends from England he wrote in celebration, he asserted yet again his famous, albeit somewhat misleading, credo: "There never was a good war or a bad peace."[48]

BENNY AND TEMPLE

Rather than return home immediately, Franklin decided to relish his newly earned peace and leisure by enjoying the friends, family, and intellectual pursuits available to him in the idyllic setting of Passy. His grandson Benny had been languishing at his school in Geneva, which had recently been thrown into political turmoil over plans to give full

voting rights to all citizens. Now that his diplomatic duties had subsided, Franklin decided to permit Benny to come back to Passy for a
vacation during the summer of 1783, his first since leaving four years
earlier.[49]

Reunited at last with the grandfather he was so eager to impress,
Benny was completely charmed. Franklin was "very different from
other old persons," he told a visitor, "for they are fretful and complaining and dissatisfied, and my grandpapa is laughing and cheerful like a
young person." Their new proximity also warmed Franklin. Benny
was "so well grown," he wrote the boy's parents, "and so much improved in his learning and behavior." To Polly Stevenson he wrote,
"He gains every day upon my affections."

That summer, during which Benny turned 14, his grandfather took
him to the Seine for swimming lessons, and his cousin Temple taught
him fencing and dancing. Temple also impressed him by pretending to
kill a mouse with helium, then reviving him, then killing him for good
with an electric spark from one of Franklin's batteries. "I am sure my
cousin would pass for a conjurer in America," Benny wrote his parents.[50]

Benny had been sickly and depressed at school, Franklin learned,
and the political situation in Geneva remained volatile. So he decided
that the boy need not return, even though he had left his clothes and
books there. He had earlier considered sending Benny to school in
England under the care of Polly Stevenson, who had been excited by
the prospect. Now, worried that Benny was losing his command of
English, he raised the possibility with Polly more seriously. "Would
that still be convenient to you?" he asked. "He is docile and of gentle
manners, ready to receive and follow good advice, and will set no bad
example to your *other* children." Polly was wary but willing. "I fear he
will think us so unpolished he will scarcely be able to endure us," she
replied, "but if English cordiality will make amends for French refinement, we may have some chance of making him happy."[51]

Franklin, who had grown ever more fond of Benny, instead decided that he should stay in Passy. "He showed such an unwillingness
to leave me, and Temple such a fondness for retaining him, that I concluded to keep him," Franklin explained to Polly in a letter at the end
of 1783. "He behaves very well, and we love him very much."

Perhaps, with his felicity in language, Benny could become a diplomat, Franklin thought. That would require, however, getting him a public appointment, something that was proving difficult for Temple. He had once told Richard Bache, just as he had told his son, William, and many others, that it was demeaning to be dependent on a government appointment. Now he expressed the same sentiment to Richard again, this time in a letter about his son Benny: "I have determined to give him a trade that he may have something to depend on, and not be obliged to ask favors or offices of anybody."[52]

The trade Franklin chose was the obvious one. His private little printing press at Passy was busy that autumn turning out editions of his bagatelles, so he was delighted when the boy eagerly started to work there. A master founder was hired to teach him how to cast type, and by spring Franklin had persuaded François Didot, the greatest and most artistic printer in France, to take him on as a student. Benny was destined to follow in Franklin's footsteps, not only as a printer but also eventually as a newspaper editor.

As for Temple, Franklin was reduced to asking for favors and offices. As he was enjoying the sweet summer of 1783, he wrote to Foreign Secretary Livingston yet another plaintive plea on poor Temple's behalf:

> He has now gone through an apprenticeship of near seven years in the ministerial business, and is very capable of serving the States in that line, as possessing all the requisites of knowledge, zeal, activity, language, and address . . . But it is not my custom to solicit employments for myself, or any of my family, and I shall not do it in this case. I only hope, that if he is not to be employed in your new arrangement, I may be informed of it as soon as possible, that, while I have strength left for it, I may accompany him in a tour to Italy, returning through Germany, which I think he may make to more advantage with me than alone, and which I have long promised to afford him, as a reward for his faithful service, and his tender filial attachment to me.

Temple did not get a ministerial posting, nor did his grandfather take him on a grand tour. Instead, he emulated his grandfather (and father) in a less laudable way than Benny. After failing to marry either of the Brillons' daughters, Temple became involved with a married woman who lived near Passy, Blanchette Caillot, whose husband was a successful actor. With her he fathered an illegitimate son, Theodore. In a cruel irony, the child died from smallpox, the disease that had taken the only legitimate son among three generations of Franklins.

Theodore Franklin, the illegitimate son of the illegitimate son of Franklin's own illegitimate son, was, albeit briefly, the last male-line descendant of Benjamin Franklin, who would in the end leave no family line bearing his name.[53]

BALLOON MANIA

Among the diversions Benny enjoyed with his grandfather in the summer and fall of 1783 were the grand spectacles of the first balloon flights. The age of air travel began in June when two brothers, Joseph and Etienne Montgolfier, launched an unmanned hot-air balloon near Lyons that rose to a height of six thousand feet. The Franklins were not there, but they did witness in late August the first unmanned flight using hydrogen. A scientist named Jacques Charles launched a twelve-foot-diameter silk balloon filled with hydrogen produced by pouring oil of vitriol over fiery iron filings. With great fanfare, it took off from Paris in front of fifty thousand spectators and floated for more than forty-five minutes before landing in a village more than fifteen miles away. "The country people who saw it fall were frightened," Franklin wrote Sir Joseph Banks, president of the Royal Society, "and attacked it with stones and knives so that it was much mangled."

The race was then on to produce the first *manned* flight, and it was won on November 21 by the Montgolfiers with their hot-air model. As a huge crowd cheered and countless women fainted, the balloon took off with two champagne-toting noblemen, who initially found themselves snared by some tree branches. "I was then in great pain for the men, thinking them in danger of being thrown out or burnt," Franklin reported. But soon they were free and gliding their way over the Seine, and after twenty minutes they landed on the other side and popped their corks in triumph. Franklin was among the distinguished scientists who signed the official certification of the historic flight the following evening, when the Montgolfiers called on him at Passy.

The Montgolfiers believed that the lift was caused not just by hot air but also by smoke, so they instructed their "aeronauts" to ply the fire with wet straw and wool. Franklin, however, was more partial to Charles's "inflammable air" model using hydrogen, and he helped to finance the first manned flight in such a balloon. It took place ten days later. As Franklin watched from his carriage parked near the Tuileries Gardens (his gout preventing him from joining the throng on the wet grass), Charles and a partner flew for more than two hours and landed safely twenty-seven miles away. Once again, Franklin provided a report to the Royal Society through Banks: "I had a pocket glass, with which I followed it until I lost sight, first of the men, then of the car, and when I last saw the balloon it appeared no bigger than a walnut."

Ever since the days of his electricity experiments, Franklin believed that science should be pursued initially for pure fascination and curiosity, and then practical uses would eventually flow from what was discovered. At first, he was reluctant to guess what practical use might come of balloons, but he was convinced that experimenting with them would someday, as he told Banks, "pave the way to some discoveries in natural philosophy of which at present we have no conception." There could be, he noted in another letter, "important consequences that no one can foresee." More famous was his pithier expression of the same sentiment, made in response to a spectator who asked what use this new balloon thing could be. "What is the use," he replied, "of a new-born baby?"[54]

Because the English saw no utility in ballooning and because they were a bit too proud to follow the French, they did not join in the excitement. "I see an inclination in the more respectable part of the Royal Society to guard against the Ballomania [until] some experiment likely to prove beneficial either to society or science is proposed," Banks wrote. Franklin scoffed at this attitude. "It does not seem to me a good reason to decline prosecuting a new experiment which apparently increases the power of man over matter until we can see to what use that power may be applied," he replied. "When we have learned to manage it, we may hope some time or other to find uses for it, as men have done for magnetism and electricity, of which the first experiments were mere matters of amusement." By early the following year, he had come up with one possibility for a practical use: balloons might serve as a way to wage war, or even better, as a way to preserve peace. "Convincing sovereigns of the folly of wars may perhaps be one effect, since it will be impracticable for the most potent of them to guard his dominions," he wrote to his friend Jan Ingenhousz, the Dutch scientist and physician.

Mainly, however, Franklin contented himself with enjoying the craze and all the entertainments surrounding it. Exhibition flights of fanciful balloons, decorated and gilded in glorious patterns, became the rage in Paris that season, and they even influenced hats and hairstyles, fashions and dances. Temple Franklin and Benny Bache produced their own miniature models. And Franklin wrote one of his typical parodies, which, like many of his early ones, used the anonymous voice of a fictional woman. "If you want to fill your balloons with an element ten times lighter than inflammable air," she wrote to one of the newspapers, "you can find a great quantity of it, and ready made, in the promises of lovers and of courtiers."[55]

EMINENCE GRISE

Even as he indulged in the frivolities of prerevolutionary Paris, Franklin focused much of his writing on his egalitarian, antielitist ideas for building a new American society based on middle-class virtues. His daughter, Sally, sent him newspaper clippings about the formation of a hereditary order of merit called the Society of the Cincinnati, which was headed by General Washington and open to distinguished officers of the American army who would pass the title down to their eldest sons. Franklin, replying at the beginning of 1784, ridiculed the concept. The Chinese were right, he said, to honor the parents of people who earned distinction, for they had some role in it. But honoring a worthy person's descendants, who had nothing to do with achieving the merit, "is not only groundless and absurd but often hurtful to that posterity." Any form of hereditary aristocracy or nobility was, he declared, "in direct opposition to the solemnly declared sense of their country."

He also, in the letter, ridiculed the symbol of the new Cincinnati order, a bald eagle, which had also been selected as a national symbol. That provoked one of Franklin's most famous riffs about America's values and the question of a national bird:

> I wish the bald eagle had not been chosen as the representative of our country; he is a bird of bad moral character, he does not get his living honestly; you may have seen him perched on some dead tree, near the river where, too lazy to fish for himself, he watches the labors of the fishing-hawk . . . The turkey is, in comparison, a much more respectable bird, and a true original native of America . . . He is (though a little vain and silly, it is true, but not the worse emblem for that) a bird of courage, and would not hesitate to attack a grenadier of the British guards.[56]

Franklin heard so frequently from people who wanted to emigrate to America that in early 1784 he printed a pamphlet, in French and English, designed to encourage the more industrious of them while discouraging those who sought a life of upper-class leisure. His essay, "Information to Those Who Would Remove to America," is one of the clearest expressions of his belief that American society should be based on the virtues of the middle (or "mediocre," as he sometimes called them, meaning it as a word of praise) classes, of which he still considered himself a part.

There were few people in America either as poor or as rich as those in Europe, he said. "It is rather a general happy mediocrity that prevails." Instead of rich proprietors and struggling tenants, "most people cultivate their own lands" or follow some craft or trade. Franklin was particularly harsh on those who sought hereditary privilege or who had "no other quality to recommend him but his birth." In America, he said, "people do not enquire of a stranger, What is he? but, What can he do?" Reflecting his own pride in discovering that he had hardworking forebears rather than aristocratic ones, he said that a true American "would think himself more obliged to a genealogist who could prove for him that his ancestors and relations for ten generations had been ploughmen, smiths, carpenters, turners, weavers, tanners or even shoemakers, and consequently that they were useful members of society, than if he could only prove that they were Gentlemen, doing nothing of value but living idly on the labor of others."

424   WALTER ISAACSON

America was creating a society, Franklin proclaimed, where a "mere man of Quality" who does not want to work would be "despised and disregarded," while anyone who has a useful skill would be honored. All of this made for a better moral clime. "The almost general mediocrity of fortune that prevails in America, obliging its people to follow some business for subsistence, those vices that arise usually from idleness are in a great measure prevented," he concluded. "Industry and constant employment are great preservatives of morals and virtue." He purported to be describing the way America was, but he was also subtly prescribing what he wanted it to become. All in all, it was his best paean to the middle-class values he represented and helped to make integral to the new nation's character.[57]

Franklin's affection for the middle class and its virtues of hard work and frugality meant that his social theories tended to be a blend of conservatism (as we have seen, he was dubious of generous welfare laws that led to dependency among the poor) and populism (he was opposed to the privileges of inheritance and to wealth idly gained through ownership of large estates). In 1784, he expanded on these ideas by questioning the morality of excess personal luxuries.

"I have not," he lamented to Benjamin Vaughan, "thought of a remedy for luxury." On the one hand, the desire for luxury spurred people to work hard. He recalled how his wife had once given a fancy hat to a country girl, and soon all the other girls in the village were working hard spinning mittens in order to earn money to buy fancy hats. This appealed to his utilitarian sentiments: "Not only the girls were made happier by having fine caps, but the Philadelphians by the supply of warm mittens." However, too much time spent seeking luxuries was wasteful and "a public evil." So he suggested that America should impose heavy duties on the importation of frivolous fineries.[58]

His antipathy to excess wealth also led him to defend high taxes, especially on luxuries. A person had a "natural right" to all he earned that was necessary to support himself and his family, he wrote finance minister Robert Morris, "but all property superfluous to such purposes is the property of the public, who by their laws have created it." Likewise, to Vaughan, he argued that cruel criminal laws had been wrought by those who sought to protect excess ownership of property.

"Superfluous property is the creature of society," he said. "Simple and mild laws were sufficient to guard the property that was merely necessary." [59]

To some of his contemporaries, both rich and poor, Franklin's social philosophy seemed an odd mix of conservative and radical beliefs. In fact, however, it formed a very coherent leather-apron outlook. Unlike many subsequent revolutions, the American was not a radical rebellion by an oppressed proletariat. Instead, it was led largely by propertied and shopkeeping citizens whose rather bourgeois rallying cry was "No taxation without representation." Franklin's blend of beliefs would become part of the outlook of much of America's middle class: its faith in the virtues of hard work and frugality, its benevolent belief in voluntary associations to help others, its conservative opposition to handouts that led to laziness and dependency, and its slightly ambivalent resentment of unnecessary luxury, hereditary privileges, and an idle landowning leisure class.

The end of the war permitted the resumption of amiable correspondence with old friends in England, most notably his fellow printer William Strahan, to whom he had written the famous but unsent letter nine years earlier declaring "You are now my enemy." By 1780, he had mellowed enough to draft a letter signed "Your formerly affectionate friend," which he then changed to "Your long affectionate humble servant." By 1784, he was signing himself "Most affectionately."

Once again, they debated Franklin's theories that top government officials should serve without pay and that England's society and government were inherently corrupt. Now, however, the tone was bantering as Franklin suggested that the Americans, who "have some remains of affection" for the British, perhaps should help govern *them*. "If you have not sense and virtue enough left to govern yourselves," he wrote, "dissolve your present old crazy constitution and send members to Congress." Lest Strahan not realize he was joking, Franklin confessed, "You will say my advice smells of Madeira. You are right. This foolish letter is mere chitchat between ourselves over the second bottle." [60]

Franklin also spent the early summer of 1784 adding more to his memoirs. He had written about 40 percent of what would become his famous *Autobiography* at Bishop Shipley's in Twyford in 1771. Now he responded to a request from Vaughan, who said that Franklin's story would help to explain the "manners of a rising people," and in Passy wrote what would become another 10 percent of that work. His focus at the time was on the need to build a new American character, and most of the section he wrote in 1784 was devoted to an explanation of the famous self-improvement project in which he sought to train himself in the thirteen virtues ranging from frugality and industry to temperance and humility.

His Passy friends were especially thrilled by the tale of the slate booklet Franklin used to record his efforts at acquiring these virtues. Franklin, who still had not fully acquired all aspects of humility, proudly showed off the tablets to Cabanis, the young physician who lived with Madame Helvétius. "We touched this precious booklet," Cabanis exulted in his journal. "We held it in our hands. Here was, in a way, the chronological story of Franklin's soul!"[61]

In his spare time, Franklin perfected one of his most famous and useful inventions: bifocal glasses. Writing to a friend in August 1784, he announced himself "happy in the invention of Double Spectacles, which, serving for distant objects as well as near ones, make my eyes as useful to me as ever they were." A few months later, in response to a request for more information about "your invention," Franklin provided details:

> The same convexity of glass through which a man sees clearest and best at the distance proper for reading is not the best for greater distances. I therefore had formerly two pair of spectacles, which I shifted occasionally, as in traveling I sometimes read, and often wanted to regard the prospects. Finding this change troublesome, and not always sufficiently ready, I had the glasses cut and half of each kind associated in the same circle. By this means, as I wear my spectacles constantly, I have only to move my eyes up or down, as I want to see distinctly far or near, the proper glasses being always ready.[62]

A portrait by Charles Willson Peale, done in 1785, shows him wearing his new spectacles.

Because of his renown both as a scientist and a rationalist, Franklin was appointed by the king in 1784 to a commission to investigate the theories of Friedrich Anton Mesmer, whose advocacy of a new method of healing led to the new word "mesmerize." (Another member of Franklin's commission, Dr. Joseph-Ignace Guillotin, would also have his name turned into a neologism during the French Revolution.) A flamboyant healer from Vienna, Mesmer believed that maladies were caused by the artificial disruption of a universal fluid emitted by heavenly bodies and they could be cured by the techniques of animal magnetism he had discovered. His treatment involved putting patients around huge oak tubs filled with glass and iron filings while a healer, carrying an iron wand, magnetized and mesmerized them. In a sign that the Enlightenment was losing its grip, Mesmerism became wildly popular in Paris, replacing ballooning as the fad of the moment, with adherents that included Lafayette, Temple Franklin, and Queen Marie-Antoinette.

Many of the commission's meetings were held in Passy, where Franklin himself, in the name of science, submitted to the treatments. In his diary, 14-year-old Benny recorded one session where Mesmer's disciples, "after having magnetized many sick persons . . . are gone into the garden to magnetize some trees." It was clear that the power of suggestion could produce some strange effects. The commissioners, however, decided that "our role was to keep cool, rational and open-minded." So they blindfolded the patients, not letting them know whether or not they were being treated by Mesmer's doctors. "We discovered we could influence them ourselves so that their answers were the same, whether they had been magnetized or not." They concluded that Mesmer was a fraud and what was at work was, at they put it in their report, "the power of imagination." An unpublished annex to the report did note that the treatment was powerful at sexually stimulating young women when "titillations délicieuses" were applied.

Franklin wrote to Temple, who was no longer a disciple of Mesmer, that the report had roundly debunked the theories. "Some think it will put an end to Mesmerism," he said, "but there is a wonderful deal of credulity in the world, and deceptions as absurd have supported themselves for ages."[63]

FINALE

One source of despair for Franklin was that, in negotiating treaties with other European nations, he had to work with John Adams again. He was worried, he told one friend, about "what will be the offspring of a coalition between my ignorance and his positiveness." Adams's brief period of mellowness had lasted for only a few months after the signing of the provisional peace with Britain, and he subsequently resumed his backbiting. Franklin was an "unintelligible politician," Adams wrote Robert Livingston. "If this gentleman and the marble Mercury in the garden of Versailles were in nomination for an embassy, I would not hesitate to give my vote for the statue, upon the principle that it would do no harm."

So Franklin was thrilled when Thomas Jefferson, who had twice resisted congressional commissions to join Franklin and Adams as a minister in Paris, finally relented and arrived there in August 1784. Jefferson was everything that Adams was not: diplomatic and charming, partial to France, secure rather than jealous, a lover of women and social gaiety with no Puritan prudishness. He was also a philosopher, inventor, and scientist whose Enlightenment curiosity meshed perfectly with Franklin's.

To make matters even better, Jefferson was fully aware of the darkness that infected Adams. James Madison had written him to complain that Adams's letters were "a display of his vanity, his prejudice against the French court and his venom against Dr. Franklin." Jefferson replied, "He hates Franklin, he hates Jay, he hates the French, he hates the English. To whom will he adhere?"

Jefferson shared Franklin's belief that idealism and realism should both play a role in foreign policy: "The best interest of nations, like men, was to follow the dictates of conscience," he declared. And unlike Adams, he completely revered Franklin. "More respect and veneration attached to the character of Dr. Franklin in France than to that of any other person, foreign or native," he wrote, and he proclaimed Franklin "the greatest man and ornament of the age." When word spread, a few months later, that he was being tapped to replace Franklin, Jefferson gave his famed reply: "No one can replace him, Sir, I am only his successor."[64]

Jefferson dined often with Franklin, played chess with him, and listened to his lectures about the loyalty America owed France. His calming presence even helped Franklin and Adams get along better, and the three men who had worked together on the Declaration now worked together at Passy almost every day throughout September preparing for new European treaties and commercial pacts. There was, in fact, a lot that the three patriots could agree on. They shared a faith in free trade, open covenants, and the need to end the mercantilist system of repressive commercial arrangements and restrictive spheres of influence. As Adams, with uncharacteristic generosity, noted, "We proceeded with wonderful harmony, good humor and unanimity."

For both men and nations, it was a season of reconciliation. If Franklin could repair his relationship with Adams, there was even hope that he could do so with his son. "Dear and honored father," William wrote from England that summer. "Ever since the termination of the unhappy contest between Great Britain and America, I have been anxious to write to you, and to endeavor to revive that affectionate intercourse and connection which, until the commencement of the late troubles, had been the pride and happiness of my life."

It was a noble, gracious, and plaintive gesture from a son who, through it all, had never said anything bad about his estranged father nor stopped loving him. But William was still a Franklin, and he could not bring himself to admit that he had been in the wrong, nor to apologize. "If I have been mistaken, I cannot help it. It is an error of judgment that the maturest reflection I am capable of cannot rectify; and I verily believe were the same circumstances to occur again tomorrow, my conduct would be exactly similar to what it was." He offered to come to Paris if his father did not want to come to England so they could settle their issues with "a personal interview."[65]

Franklin's response revealed his pain, but it also offered some hints of hope. He began by saying he was "glad to find that you desire to revive the affectionate intercourse," and he even brought himself to add, "it will be agreeable to me." Yet he immediately segued from love to anger:

> Indeed nothing has ever hurt me so much and affected me with such keen sensations as to find myself deserted in my old age by my only son; and not only deserted, but to find him taking up arms against me, in a cause, wherein my good fame, fortune and life were all at stake. You conceived, you say, that your duty to your King and regard for your country required this. I ought not to blame you for differing in senti- ment with me in public affairs. We are men, all subject to errors. Our opinions are not in our own power; they are formed and governed much by circumstances, that are often as inexplicable as they are irresistible. Your situation was such that few would have censured your remaining neuter, *though there are natural duties which precede political ones* [empha- sis is Franklin's].

Then he caught himself. "This is a disagreeable subject," he wrote. "I drop it." It would not be convenient, he added, to "have you come here at the present." Instead, Temple would be sent to London to act as an intermediary. "You may confide to your son the family affairs you wish to confer upon with me." Then, a bit condescendingly, he added, "I trust you will prudently avoid introducing him to company that it may be improper for him to be seen with." Temple may have been Wil- liam's son, but Franklin made it clear who controlled him.[66]

At 24, Temple had little of his grandfather's wisdom but possessed a lot more of the normal emotions that bind families, even estranged ones. He had long been hoping, he wrote a London friend, to return there to "embrace my father." On his visit to England, he nevertheless was careful to show fealty to his grandfather, even asking for permis- sion before accompanying his father on a trip to the seashore.

After a few weeks, Franklin began to fear that Temple might be forsaking him for his father, and he chided him for not writing enough. "I have waited with impatience the arrival of every post. But not a word." Among other things, Franklin complained, this was em- barrassing him with those who kept asking whether he had heard from Temple: "Judge what I must feel, what they must think, and tell me what I am to think of such neglect." Of all the members of his family, Temple alone could cause such jealousy and possessiveness.

For his part, Temple was thoroughly enjoying himself. He was treated as a celebrity prince: feted by the Royal Society, the Lord Mayor, and various ladies who held teas in his honor. He had his portrait painted by Gilbert Stuart, and a friend gave him a list of the best bootmakers and tailors, adding, "And when lewd, go to the following safe girls who I think are quite handsome."[67]

Temple was not able to resolve the issues dividing his father and grandfather, but he was able to accomplish another part of his mission: enticing Polly Stevenson to come to Passy. Now 45, she had been widowed for a decade, and her mother, Franklin's longtime landlady and companion, had died a year earlier. (She "loved you with the most ardent affection," Polly had written when conveying the sad news.) Franklin had written Polly that she must come see him soon, for he was now like a building that required "so many repairs that in a little time the Owner will find it cheaper to pull it down and build a new one." By the end of the summer of 1784, his letters had become even more plaintive. "Come, my dear friend, live with me while I stay here, and go with me, if I do go, to America."[68]

In early December 1784, many people converged on Passy and provided for Franklin, during his final winter in France, a most satisfying version of the hybrid families, real and adopted, he so loved to assemble around him. There to pamper him were Temple and Benny, Polly and her three children, Thomas Jefferson and other great minds, plus Mesdames Brillon and Helvétius along with their wonderful retinues. "For a fragile moment," note Claude-Anne Lopez and Eugenia Herbert, "his various 'families' were almost in perfect poise, drawing closer in a network of good will of which he was the center."[69]

Polly was amused by Temple on first seeing him again in London after ten years, and she joked with Franklin about how he had tried to keep the boy's lineage secret back then. "We see a strong resemblance of you, and indeed saw it when we did not think ourselves at liberty to say we did, as we pretended to be as ignorant as you supposed we were, or chose that we should be." That gave her an opportunity to chide them both a bit: "I believe you may have been handsomer than your grandson is, but then you never were so genteel."

But close familiarity with Temple did not, except in his grandfather's case, necessarily breed fondness, and Polly became somewhat disenchanted with him after their arrival in Passy. "He has such a love of dress," she wrote a relative, "and is so absorbed in self-importance and so engaged in the pursuit of pleasure that he is not an amiable or respectable character."

Benny, on the other hand, with the benefit of his Geneva education and natural eagerness to please, struck Polly as "sensible and manly in his manner without the slightest tincture of the coxcomb." He wore his hair like an English lad rather than a French fop, and "with the simplicity of his dress retains a lovely simplicity of character." Temple might look more like Franklin, but Benny—who swam in the Seine, flew kites with a passion, took Polly on tours of Paris, and yet was ever diligent in his printing work—resembled him more "in mind."[70]

ADIEU

There were times, indeed many of them, when Franklin wrote of his inclination not to disrupt this little paradise, but instead to remain in France and die among those who so loved and pleased him. His gout and his kidney stones made the prospect of an ocean voyage something to dread, while the embers of his passions for the ladies of Paris were something he could still savor. In May 1785, he wrote a friend recalling one of his favorite old drinking songs:

> *May I govern my Passions with an absolute sway,*
> *Grow wiser and better as my Strength wears away,*
> *Without Gout or Stone, by a gentle Decay.*

"But what signifies our wishing?" he asked. "I have sung that wishing song a thousand times, when I was young, and now find, at fourscore, that the three contraries have befallen me, being subject to the gout and the stone, and not being yet master of all my passions."

Nevertheless, when word reached him that month that the Congress had at long last accepted his resignation and that Temple was not being offered an overseas assignment, Franklin decided it was time to go home. From Passy he wrote Polly, who had returned to England, begging her to accompany him. He had taken the liberty of reserving a spacious cabin for her whole family. "You may never have so good an opportunity." For the time being at least, she decided to stay in England.

He sent word of his travel plans to his sister Jane and explained, "I have continued to work until late in the day; 'tis time I should go home, and go to bed." Such metaphors had begun to creep into his writing, and he expanded on them to his friend David Hartley, who had helped him during his many negotiations. "We were long fellow laborers in the best of all works, the work of peace," he wrote. "I leave you still in the field, but having finished my day's work, I am going home *to go to bed*! Wish me a good night's rest, as I do you a pleasant evening. Adieu!"[71]

The farewells at Passy were dramatic and tearful. "Every day of my life I shall remember that a great man, a sage, has wanted to be my friend," Madame Brillon wrote after their final meeting. "If it ever pleases you to remember the woman who loved you the most, think of me."

Madame Helvétius was not to be outdone. "Come back, my dear friend, come back to us," she wrote in a letter dispatched to catch up with him as he boarded his boat. To each of his friends went a gift that was to become a relic: Cabanis got the hollow cane that magically stilled the waves, the Abbé Morellet a tool chest and armchair, and his landlord Chaumont a table that could be ingeniously raised and lowered. (He also gave Chaumont a bill for the improvements he had made to his apartments, including installing a lightning rod and fixing the chimney "to cure it of its intolerable malady of smoke.")

To ease his travel to the port of Le Havre, Queen Marie-Antoinette sent her personal enclosed litter borne by surefooted Spanish mules. Her husband, King Louis XVI, sent a miniature portrait of himself surrounded by 408 small diamonds. Franklin also exchanged gifts with Vergennes, who noted to an aide that "the United States will never have a more zealous and more useful servant than M. Franklin."[72]

On the day he left Passy, July 12, Benny recorded in his diary, "A mournful silence reigned around him, broken only by a few sobs."

Jefferson had come to see him off, and he later recalled: "The ladies smothered him with embraces, and on his introducing me as his successor, I told him I wished he would transfer these privileges to me, but he answered, 'You are too young a man.'"[73]

Franklin's plan was to cross the English Channel and then determine whether he felt he could endure an ocean crossing. If not, he would ferry back to Le Havre, and the Queen's litter, which waited there for word, would carry him back to Passy.

As usual, however, travel was a tonic rather than travail for Franklin, and he turned out to be the only passenger not to get sick during the rough channel crossing. When they arrived in Southampton, he and his party went to visit a hot saltwater spa where, he noted in his journal, he bathed in the springs "and, floating on my back, fell asleep, and slept near an hour by my watch, without sinking or turning!"[74]

There was one last dramatic scene to be played out, one last emotional moment, before he could set sail on his eighth and final crossing of the Atlantic. For four days he stayed at the Star Inn in Southampton, so that he could receive some of his old English friends and bid them a final farewell. Bishop Shipley came, along with his daughter Kitty. So did Benjamin Vaughan, his back-channel missions for Jay and Temple forgiven, who was preparing to publish a new edition of his friend's writings. There were grand dinners and celebrations, which he described in his journal as "very affectionate."

But the main person who had come to see him at the Star Inn got only a brusque mention in his journal. "Met my son, who arrived from London the evening before," Franklin noted. There was no reconciliation, no recorded tears or affection, just a cold negotiation over debts and property.

Franklin had regained full control over Temple by then, and he drove a hard bargain on his grandson's behalf. He insisted that William sell his New Jersey farm to Temple for less than he had paid, and he applied against the purchase price the decades of debts, carefully recorded, that William still owed him. He also took title to all of William's land claims in New York. Having taken William's son from him, he was now extracting his wealth and his connections to America.

This final reunion of three generations of Franklin men, so fraught with father-son tensions, ended so coldly that none of them ever saw fit to discuss it. Franklin's journal offers not a word of detail, nor is there any record of his ever writing or telling about it. He and his son never corresponded again. William wrote a letter to his half-sister, Sally, four days later, but amazingly, he rambled on about her children and a portrait he was trying to send her without ever describing the climactic scene. The closest he came, at the end of the long letter, was to lament, in discussing how everyone would soon be in Philadelphia, that "my fate has thrown me on a different side of the globe." Even decades later, after his father and grandfather had both died and he finally got around to producing a collection of his grandfather's life and works, Temple provided only a desultory and unrevealing phrase noting that at Southampton, Franklin "had the satisfaction of seeing his son, the former Governor of New Jersey."[75]

William was not invited to the farewell party aboard his father's vessel on the evening of July 27. Fully revitalized by travel and showing no remorse over the cool parting with his son, Franklin stayed up with his friends until 4 A.M. When he awoke late that morning, his friends were gone, his two grandsons were with him, and his ship was already under sail for home.

CHAPTER SIXTEEN

SAGE

Philadelphia, 1785–1790

HOME AT LAST

On this, his final voyage across the ocean, Franklin felt no need to study, or even to mention, the calming effect of oil on troubled waters. Nor, despite his many promises to friends, did he bring himself to work on his memoirs, which he had begun as a letter to the "dear son" he had just forsaken.

Instead, he indulged the passion that both relaxed and invigorated his mind: scientific inquiries awash with experimental details and practical consequences. The result was a forty-page gusher of observations and theories on a wide variety of maritime topics, replete with charts and drawings and data tables. At one point he paused, admitted that "the garrulity of an old man has got hold of me," and then sailed forth. "I think I might as well now, once and for all, empty my nautical budget."

That budget was a full one: theories, illustrated with diagrams, on how to design hulls to minimize their resistance to wind as well as water; descriptions of his old experiments, along with proposals for new ones, on the effects of air currents on objects of various shapes; how to rig up sliced playing cards to gauge the effects of wind; how to translate that experiment into one using sails and booms; ways to use pulleys to prevent anchor cables from breaking; an analysis of how ships fill with water after a leak; proposals for compartmentalizing hulls the way the Chinese did; tales from history about endangered ships that sank and those that survived, with speculations as to why; learned comparisons of Eskimo kayaks, Chinese rowboats, Indian canoes, Bermuda sloops, and Pacific island proas; proposals for building water propellers and air propellers; and more, much more, for page after page, diagram after diagram.

He also turned his attention to the Gulf Stream again, this time devising an experiment to test whether it extended to the depths or was more like a warm river flowing near the surface of the ocean. An empty bottle with a cork in its mouth was lowered to thirty-five fathoms, at which point the water pressure pushed the cork in and allowed the bottle to fill. The water gathered from that depth was six degrees cooler than that on the surface. A similar experiment using a keg with two valves found the water on the bottom, even at only eighteen fathoms, to be twelve degrees cooler than the water at the surface. He provided temperature charts and maps, along with the suggestion that a "thermometer may be a useful instrument to a navigator," that could help captains catch a ride on the Gulf Stream going eastbound and avoid it westbound, thus potentially saving a week or more of travel.[1]

In addition, Franklin wrote papers, equally long and filled with experimental findings, on how to cure smoky chimneys and how to build better stoves. From a modern vantage these treatises might seem obsessive in their immersion into details, but it must be remembered that they addressed one of the most serious issues of the time: the choking soot that plagued most homes and cities. It was, altogether, his most prodigious scientific outpouring since his electricity experiments of 1752. And like those previous studies, the ones he produced during his ocean crossing of 1785 showed his unique appreciation—that of an ingenious man if not a genius—for combining scientific theory, technical invention, clever experiments, and practical utility.[2]

When Franklin and his two grandchildren arrived at Philadelphia's Market Street wharf in September 1785, sixty-two years after he had first straggled ashore there as a 17-year-old runaway, "we were received by a crowd of people with huzzas and accompanied with acclamations quite to my door." Cannons boomed, bells rang, Sally embraced him, and tears ran down Temple's cheeks. Long worried about the damage the Lees and Adamses may have done to his reputation, Franklin was much relieved. "The affectionate welcome I meet with from my fellow citizens is far beyond my expectation," he proudly wrote John Jay.[3]

Gathered around him now at his Market Street home, even more than at Passy, would be that glorious assembly of family both real and adopted he always relished. There was his ever-dutiful daughter, Sally, who would play the role of his housekeeper, and her husband, Richard Bache, never successful but always accommodating. In addition to Benny and Willy, there were now four new Bache children—"four little prattlers who cling about the knees of their grandpapa and afford me great pleasure"—with another soon on the way. And within a year, Polly Stevenson would make good on her promise to come over, along with her three children. "As to my domestic circumstances," Franklin wrote Bishop Shipley, "they are at present as happy as I could wish them. I am surrounded by my offspring, a dutiful and affectionate daughter in my house, with six grandchildren."[4]

Benny enrolled at the Philadelphia Academy his grandfather had founded (by then renamed the University of the State of Pennsylvania), and on his graduation in 1787 became a full-time printer. Franklin was delighted, almost too much so. He built Benny a shop, helped him choose and cast fonts, and suggested books for him to publish. His knack for creating bestsellers like Poor Richard's almanacs, however, had given way to a desire for more edifying and educational tomes, and Benny eventually began to squirm, just a bit, at his hovering presence. Yet he loyally served as Franklin's secretary and scrivener.

Temple tried to turn himself into a gentleman farmer on the New Jersey estate that had just been wrested from his father, but he was temperamentally unsuited to caring much about crops and herds. In an ill-conceived attempt to create a showcase chateau, he pestered his French friends to send him specimen deer (American venison he declared tasteless), hunting dogs, and costumes for his workers. After the deer kept dying en route, Temple reverted to his urban dandy ways and spent most of his time on the party circuit in Philadelphia, while his grandfather, the only person to dote on him, continued his futile efforts to win him a ministerial appointment.

Though less mobile than before, Franklin was as clubbable as he had been as a young tradesman, and the few surviving members of his old associations resumed their gatherings, often at his house. There were only four left of the volunteer fire company he founded in 1736, but Franklin dug out his bucket and convened a meeting. The American Philosophical Society, which sometimes held sessions in his dining room, elected Temple a new member in 1786, along with most of the intellectual friends Franklin had made in Europe over the years: le Veillard, la Rochefoucauld, Condorcet, Ingenhousz, and Cabanis. To apply the same earnest curiosity to "the arduous and complicated science of government" that the philosophical society applied to the science of nature, Franklin organized a companion group, the Society for Political Inquiries, whose members included his young activist friends such as Thomas Paine.

Franklin had reached an age when he no longer fretted about squandering his time. For hours on end, he would play cribbage or cards with friends, which caused him, he wrote Polly, to have brief twinges of guilt. "But another reflection comes to relieve me, whispering: 'You know the soul is immortal; why then should you be such a niggard of a little time, when you have a whole eternity before you?' So being easily convinced and, like other reasonable creatures, satisfied with a small reason when it is in favor of doing what I have a mind to, I shuffle the cards again, and begin another game."[5]

Finding the well-stocked farmers' market, which now extended to the third block of Market Street where he lived, an easier source of produce than growing his own, he turned his vegetable patch into a pocket Passy garden with gravel paths, shrubs, and a shady mulberry tree. As one visitor recorded the new domestic scene, "We found him in his garden, sitting up a grassplot, under a very large mulberry tree, with several other gentlemen and two or three ladies . . . The tea table was spread under the tree, and Mrs. Bache, who is the only daughter of the Doctor, and lives with him, served it out to the company. She had three of her children about her. They seemed to be excessively fond of their grandpapa."[6]

It was a lifestyle that kept the gout at bay and, for the time being, his kidney stones from worsening. He suffered pain only when he was walking or "making water," he wrote Veillard. "As I live temperately, drink no wine, and use daily the exercise of the dumb-bell, I flatter myself that the stone is kept from augmenting so much as it might otherwise do, and that I may still continue to find it tolerable. People who live long, who will drink the cup of life to the very bottom, must expect to meet with some of the usual dregs."

Twenty-two years earlier, he had personally overseen each detail of the construction of his new house on Market Street, and he even instructed Deborah from afar about the specifics of its decoration and furnishing. But he had lived in it for only brief intervals, and now he found it far too cramped for his extended family, club meetings, and entertaining. It was time, he decided, to embark on a new building spree.

Despite his age, he found the prospect enticing. He took joy in the details of design and craftsmanship, he had a passion for modern improvements and contrivances, and he relished the thrill of construction. As he wrote Veillard, he derived pleasure from overseeing the "bricklayers, carpenters, stone-cutters, painters, glaziers," whose craft he had first admired as a child in Boston. Plus, he knew that real estate was a good investment; housing values were rising fast, as were rents.[7]

His plan was to demolish three older houses he owned on Market Street and replace them with two larger ones. He had wooed Deborah in one of them and worked as a fledgling printer in another, but nostalgia was not among his stronger sentiments. He was forced to change his plans, however, by a challenge to their property lines. "My neighbor disputing my bounds, I have been obliged to postpone until that dispute is settled by law," he wrote his sister Jane in Boston. "In the meantime, the workmen and materials being ready, I have ordered an addition to the house I live in, it being too small for our growing family."

The new three-story wing, designed to meld seamlessly with the existing house, was thirty-three feet long and sixteen feet wide, which enlarged his space by a third. On the ground floor was a long dining room able to seat twenty-four, and on the third floor were new bedrooms. The finest feature, which connected by a passage to "my best old bedchamber," was a library that took up the entire second floor. With shelves from floor to ceiling, it accommodated 4,276 volumes, making it what one visitor claimed (with some exaggeration) "the largest and by far the best private library in America." As he confessed to Jane, "I hardly know how to justify building a library at an age that will soon oblige me to quit it, but we are apt to forget that we are grown old, and building is an amusement."[8]

Eventually he was able to build the two new houses as well, one of which became Benny's printing shop, and he designed an arched passageway between them into the courtyard in front of his own renovated home, which was set back from Market Street. All the new construction allowed him to put into practice the various fire safety ideas he had advocated over the years. None of the wooden beams in one room connected directly to those in another, the floors and stairs were tightly plastered, and a trapdoor opened to the roof so "one may go out and wet the shingles in case of a neighboring fire." He was satisfied to discover, during the renovation of his main house, that a bolt had melted the tip of its old lightning rod while he was in France, but the house had remained unscathed, "so that at length the invention has been of some use to the inventor."[9]

Besides all his books, his new library boasted a variety of scientific paraphernalia, including his electricity equipment and a glass machine that exhibited the flow of blood through the body. For his reading comfort, Franklin built a great armchair set on rockers with an overhead fan that was powered by a foot pedal. Among his musical instruments were an armonica, a harpsichord, a "glassichord" similar to his armonica, a viola, and bells.

From James Watt, the famed Birmingham steam engine maker, he imported, and made some improvements on, the first rudimentary copying machine. Documents would be written with a slow-drying ink made of gum arabic and then pressed on sheets of moist tissue paper to make copies for as long as the ink was still wet, usually a full day. Franklin, who had first used the machine in Passy, liked it so much that he ordered another that he gave to Jefferson.[10]

Franklin took special pride in one particularly handy invention, a mechanical arm that could retrieve and replace books from upper shelves. He wrote a description of it, filled with drawings and diagrams and instructive tips, that was as detailed as the scientific trea-

tises he had written on his ocean crossing. It was typical of Franklin.
Throughout his life, he loved immersing himself in minutiae and
trivia in a manner so obsessive that it might today be described as
geeky. He was meticulous in describing every technical detail of his
inventions, be it the library arm, stove, or lightning rod. In his essays,
ranging from his arguments against hereditary honors to his discussions of trade, he provided reams of detailed calculations and historical
footnotes. Even in his most humorous parodies, such as his proposal
for the study of farts, the cleverness was enhanced by his inclusion of
mock-serious facts, trivia, calculations, and learned precedents.[11]

This penchant was on display in its most charming manner in a
long letter he wrote to his young friend Kitty Shipley, daughter of the
bishop, on the art of procuring pleasant dreams. It contained all of his
theories, some more sound than others, on nutrition, exercise, fresh
air, and health. Exercise should precede meals, he advised, not follow
them. There should be a constant supply of fresh air in the bedroom;
Methuselah, he reminded, always slept outdoors. He propounded a
thorough, though not scientifically valid, theory of how air in a stifled
room gets saturated and thus prevents people's pores from expelling
"putrid particles." After a full discourse on the science and pseudo-
science, he provided three important ways to avoid unpleasant dreams:

1. By eating moderately, less perspirable matter is produced in
   a given time; hence the bed-clothes receive it longer before
   they are saturated, and we may therefore sleep longer before
   we are made uneasy by their refusing to receive any more.
2. By using thinner and more porous bed-clothes, which will
   suffer the perspirable matter more easily to pass through
   them, we are less incommoded, such being longer tolerable.
3. When you are awakened by this uneasiness, and find you
   cannot easily sleep again, get out of bed, beat up and turn
   your pillow, shake the bed-clothes well, with at least twenty
   shakes, then throw the bed open and leave it to cool; in the
   meanwhile, continuing undressed, walk about your chamber till your skin has had time to discharge its load, which it
   will do sooner as the air may be dried and colder. When you

begin to feel the cool air unpleasant, then return to your bed, and you will soon fall asleep, and your sleep will be sweet and pleasant . . . If you happen to be too indolent to get out of bed, you may, instead of it, lift up your bed-clothes with one arm and leg, so as to draw in a good deal of fresh air, and by letting them fall force it out again. This, re-peated twenty times, will so clear them of the perspirable matter they have imbibed, as to permit your sleeping well for some time afterwards. But this latter method is not equal to the former. Those who do not love trouble, and can afford to have two beds, will find great luxury in rising, when they wake in a hot bed, and going into the cool one.

He concluded on a sweet note: "There is a case in which the most punctual observance of them will be totally fruitless. I need not men-tion this case to you, my dear friend, but my account of the art would be imperfect without it. The case is, when the person who desires to have pleasant dreams has not taken care to preserve, what is necessary above all things, A GOOD CONSCIENCE."[12]

Pennsylvania was prospering at the time. "The crops are plentiful," he wrote a friend, "working people have plenty of employ." Yet, as usual, the state's politicians were split into two factions. On one side were the populists, made up mainly of local shopkeepers and rural farmers, who supported the very democratic state constitution, with its directly elected unicameral legislature, that Franklin had helped write; on the other side were those more frightened of rabble rule, in-cluding middle- and upper-class property owners. Franklin fit philo-sophically in both camps, both sought his support, and both he obliged. So both nominated him for the state executive council and then its presidency, the equivalent of the governorship, to which he was elected almost unanimously.[13]

Pleased to find that he was still so popular, Franklin took great pride in his election. "Old as I am," he told a nephew, "I am not yet grown insensible with respect to reputation." To Bishop Shipley he conceded that "the remains of ambition from which I had imagined myself free" had successfully seduced him.

He also enjoyed the fact that, after years of watching his reputation be pricked by partisan attacks, he could gain prestige by being above the fray. "He has destroyed party rage in our state," gushed Benjamin Rush after dining with him, "or to borrow an allusion from one of his discoveries, his presence and advice, like oil upon troubled waters, have composed the contending waves of faction." It was a talent that would soon serve him and his nation very well.[14]

THE CONSTITUTIONAL CONVENTION OF 1787

The need for a new federal constitution became apparent, to those who wanted to notice, just a few months after the ratification of the Articles of Confederation back in 1781, when a messenger reached the Congress with the wondrous news of the victory at Yorktown. There was no money in the national treasury to pay the messenger's expenses, so the members had to pull coins from their own pockets. Under the Articles, the Congress had no power to levy taxes, or do much of anything else. Instead, it attempted to requisition money from the states, the way colonial leaders had once wished the king would do, and the states, as the king and his ministers had once feared, often did not respond.

By 1786, the situation was ominous. A former Revolutionary War officer named Daniel Shays led a rebellion of poor farmers in western Massachusetts against tax and debt collections, and there were worries that the anarchy would spread. The Congress, which was then meeting in New York, had been wandering from venue to venue, often unable to pay its bills or sometimes muster a quorum. The thirteen states were indulging in their independence not only from Britain but also from one another. New York imposed fees on all vessels coming from New Jersey, which retaliated by taxing a New York harbor lighthouse on Sandy Hook. Other states were in the process of being formed— including one called Franklin, later renamed Tennessee—that struggled to sort out their potential relationship with the existing states. When the settlers who wished to form the new state of Franklin sought his advice on how to deal with the rival claims of North Carolina, he told them to submit the whole matter to the Congress, which everyone knew would do little good.[15]

After Maryland and Virginia were unable to resolve some border and navigation disputes, a multistate conference was convened in Annapolis to address them along with larger issues of trade and cooperation. Only five states attended and little was accomplished, but James Madison and Alexander Hamilton, along with others who saw the need for a stronger national government, used the gathering to call for a federal convention, ostensibly designed merely to amend the Articles of Confederation. It was scheduled for Philadelphia in May 1787.

The stakes were enormous, as Franklin, who was selected as one of Pennsylvania's delegates, made clear in a letter he sent to Jefferson in Paris: "Our federal constitution is generally thought defective, and a convention, first proposed by Virginia, and since recommended by Congress, is to assemble here next month, to revise it and propose amendments . . . If it does not do good it will do harm, as it will show that we have not the wisdom enough among us to govern ourselves."[16]

So they gathered in the abnormally hot and humid summer of 1787 to draft, in deepest secrecy, a new American constitution that would turn out to be the most successful ever written by human hand. The men there formed, in Jefferson's famous assessment later, "an assembly of demi-gods." If so, they were mainly young ones. Hamilton and Charles Pinckney were 29. (Vain about his age as well as his wealth, Pinckney pretended to be but 24 so he could pass for the youngest member, who was in fact Jonathan Dayton of New Jersey, 26.) At 81, Franklin was the oldest member by fifteen years and exactly twice the average age of the rest of the members.[17]

When General Washington arrived in town on May 13, his first act was to pay a call on Franklin, who opened his new dining room along with a cask of dark beer to entertain him. Among the many roles that Philadelphia's celebrated sage played at the convention was that of symbolic host. His garden and shady mulberry tree, just a few hundred yards from the statehouse, became a respite from the debates, a place where delegates could talk over tea, hear Franklin's tales, and be calmed into a mood of compromise. Among the sixteen grand murals in the U.S. Capitol's Great Experiment Hall depicting scenes of historical importance, from the Mayflower Compact to the suffragette marches, is a garden scene of Hamilton, Madison, and James Wilson talking to Franklin under the shade of his mulberry tree.

If his health permitted and ambition desired, Franklin could have been the only person other than Washington with a chance of becoming the chairman of the convention. He chose instead to be the one to nominate Washington. Unfortunately, heavy rains and a flare-up of his kidney stones made him miss the opening day, May 25, so he asked another member of his delegation to nominate Washington. In his journal of the convention, Madison recorded that "the nomination came with particular grace from Pennsylvania, as Dr. Franklin alone could have been thought of as a competitor."

On Monday, May 28, Franklin arrived to take his seat at one of the fourteen round tables in the East Room of the statehouse, where he had spent so many years. According to some later accounts, it was a grand entrance: to minimize his pain, he was reportedly transported the block from his home in an enclosed sedan chair he had brought from Paris, which was carried by four prisoners from the Walnut Street jail. They held the chair aloft on flexible rods and walked slowly to prevent any painful jostling.[18]

Franklin's benign countenance and venerable grace as he took his seat every morning, and his preference for wry storytelling over argumentative oratory, added a calming presence. "He exhibits daily a spectacle of transcendent benevolence by attending the convention punctually," said Benjamin Rush, who added that Franklin had declared the convention "the most august and respectable assembly he was ever in."

Franklin could be doddering at times, a bit unfocused in his speeches, and occasionally baffling in a few of his suggestions. Still, the delegates usually respected him and always indulged him. This mix of feelings was tellingly recorded by one member, William Pierce of Georgia:

> Dr. Franklin is well known to be the greatest philosopher of the present age; all the operations of nature he seems to understand, the very heavens obey him, and the clouds yield up their lightning to be

imprisoned in his rod. But what claim he has to be a politician, posterity must determine. It is certain that he does not shine much in public council. He is no speaker, nor does he seem to let politics engage his attention. He is, however, a most extraordinary man, and tells a story in a style more engaging than anything I ever heard.

Over the ensuing four months, many of Franklin's pet proposals—a unicameral legislature, prayers, an executive council instead of president, no salaries for officeholders—were politely listened to and, sometimes with a bit of embarrassment, tabled. However, he brought to the convention floor three unique and crucial strengths that made him central to the historic compromise that saved the nation.

First, he was far more comfortable with democracy than most of the delegates, who tended to regard the word and concept as dangerous rather than desirable. "The evils we experience," declared Elbridge Gerry of Massachusetts, "flow from the excess of democracy." The people, Roger Sherman of Connecticut concurred, "should have as little to do as may be possible about government." Franklin was at the other end of the spectrum. Though averse to rabble rule, he favored direct elections, trusted the average citizen, and resisted anything resembling elitism. The constitution he had drafted for Pennsylvania, with its popularly elected single-chamber legislature, was the most democratic of all the new states'.

Second, he was, by far, the most traveled of the delegates, and he knew not only the nations of Europe but the thirteen states, appreciating both what they had in common and how they differed. As a postmaster he had helped bind America together. He was one of the few men equally at home visiting the Carolinas as Connecticut—both places where he had once franchised print shops—and he could discuss, as he had done, indigo farming with a Virginia planter and trade economics with a Massachusetts merchant.

Third, and what would prove most important of all, he embodied a spirit of Enlightenment tolerance and pragmatic compromise. "Both sides must part with some of their demands," he preached at one point, in a phrase that would be his mantra. "We are sent hither to *consult*, not to *contend*, with each other," he said at another. "His disarmingly candid manner masked a very complex personality," the con-

stitutional historian Richard Morris has written, "but his accommodating nature would time after time conciliate jarring interests."[19]

These three attributes proved invaluable in resolving the core issues facing the convention. The greatest of these was whether America would remain thirteen separate states or become one nation, or—if
the demigods could prove so ingenious—some magical combination
of both, as Franklin had first suggested in his Albany Plan of Union
back in 1754. This issue was manifest in various specific ways: Would
Congress be directly elected by the people or chosen by the state legislatures? Would representation be based on population or be equal for
each state? Would the national government or the state governments
be sovereign?

America was deeply split on this set of issues. Some people, Franklin initially among them, were in favor of creating a supreme national
government and reducing the states to a subordinate role. On the
other side were those fervently opposed to any surrender of state sovereignty, which had been enshrined in the Articles of Confederation.
The call for the convention expressly declared that its purpose would
be to revise the Articles, not abandon them. The most radical proponents of states' rights even refused to attend. "I smell a rat," declared
Patrick Henry. Samuel Adams justified his own absence by saying, "I
stumble at the threshold. I meet with a national government instead of
a federal union of sovereign states."[20]

The Virginia delegation, led by Madison and Edmund Randolph,
arrived in Philadelphia early and proceeded to do just what the states'
rights camp feared: they proposed scrapping the Articles entirely and
starting afresh with a new constitution for a strong national government. It would be headed by a very powerful House of Representatives
elected directly by the people based on proportional representation.
The House would select members of an upper chamber, the president,
and the judiciary.

Franklin had long favored a legislature with only one directly
elected house, seeing little reason to place checks on the democratic
will of the people, and he had designed such a system in Pennsylvania.
But in its first week the convention decided this was, in fact, too democratic by half. Madison recorded: " 'The national Legislature ought

to consist of two branches' was agreed to without debate or dissent, except that of Pennsylvania, given probably from complaisance to Dr. Franklin, who was understood to be partial to a single House of Legislation." One modification was made to the Virginia plan. To give the state governments some stake in the new Congress, the delegates decided that the upper chamber, dubbed the Senate after the Roman precedent, would be chosen by the state legislatures rather than by the House of Representatives. (This procedure remained in effect until 1913.)[21]

The central issue, however, remained unresolved. Would votes in the houses of Congress be in proportion to population or, as per the Articles of Confederation, equal for each state? The dispute was not only a philosophical one between proponents of a strong national government and those who favored protecting the rights of the states. It was also a power struggle: little states, such as Delaware and New Jersey, feared they would be overwhelmed by the big states such as Virginia and New York.

The debate grew heated, threatening to break up the convention, and on June 11 Franklin decided it was time to try to restore a spirit of compromise. He had written his speech in advance and because of his health asked another delegate to read it aloud. "Until this point [about] the proportion of representation came before us," he began, "our debates were carried on with great coolness and temper." After making his plea that members consult rather than contend, he expressed a sentiment that he had preached for much of his life, starting with the rules he had written for his Junto sixty years earlier, about the dangers of being too assertive in debate. "Declarations of a fixed opinion, and of determined resolution never to change it, neither enlighten nor convince us," he said. "Positiveness and warmth on one side, naturally beget their like on the other." He had personally been willing, he said, to revise many of his opinions, including the desirability of a unicameral legislature. Now it was time for all members to compromise.

Franklin went on to propose a few suggestions, some of them sensible, others rather odd. He defended the idea of proportional representation with the historical example of how Scotland, despite its smaller representation in the British Parliament, had avoided being overwhelmed by England. Then, with his love of detail, he provided a lengthy mathematical set of calculations showing how smaller states could garner enough votes to match the power of larger ones. There were other remedies to be considered. Perhaps the larger states could give up some of their land to the smaller ones. "If it should be found necessary to diminish Pennsylvania, I should not be averse to the giving a part of it to New Jersey, and another to Delaware." But if that was not feasible, he suggested an even more complex option: there could be equal tax contributions requisitioned from each state, and equal votes in Congress from each state on how to spend this money, then a supplemental requisition from larger states, with proportional votes in Congress on how to spend that fund.[22]

Franklin's speech was long, complex, and at times baffling. Were these all serious suggestions or were some of them merely theoretical discourses? Members seemed not to know. He made no motion to vote on his suggestion for adjusting borders or creating separate treasury funds, nor did any of the other delegates. More important than his specific ideas was his tone of moderation and conciliation. His speech, with its openness to new ideas and absence of one-sided advocacy, provided time for tempers to cool, and his call for creative compromises had an effect.

A few minutes later, Roger Sherman of Connecticut rose to suggest another possible approach: the House of Representatives would be apportioned by population and the Senate would have equal votes for each state. William Samuel Johnson, also of that state, explained the thinking behind what would become known as the Connecticut Compromise. The new country was, in some ways, "one political society," but in other ways it was a federation of separate states, yet these two concepts need not conflict, for they could be combined as "halves of a unique whole." There was, however, little discussion of the plan. By a 6–5 vote, the idea was rejected, for the time being, in favor of proportional representation in both chambers.

As the days grew even hotter, so again did the dispute over representation. William Paterson of New Jersey proposed a counterplan, based on amending the Articles rather than supplanting them, that featured a single-house legislature in which each state, large or small, would have one vote. The larger states were able to defeat that idea, but the debate grew so intense that one Delaware delegate suggested that, if the large states sought to impose a national government, "the small ones will find some foreign ally of more honor and good faith, who will take them by the hand and do them justice."

Once again it was time for Franklin to try to restore equanimity, and this time he did so in an unexpected way. In a speech on June 28, he suggested that they open each session with a prayer. With the convention "groping as it were in the dark to find political truth," he said, "how has it happened that we have not hitherto once thought of humbly applying to the Father of lights to illuminate our understandings?" Then he added, in a passage destined to become famous, "The longer I live, the more convincing proofs I see of this truth—that God governs in the affairs of men. And if a sparrow cannot fall to the ground without his notice, is it probable that an empire can rise without his aid?"

Franklin was a believer, even more so as he grew older, in a rather general and at times nebulous divine providence, the principle that God had a benevolent interest in the affairs of men. But he never showed much faith in the more specific notion of special providence, which held that God would intervene directly based on personal prayer. So the question arises: Did he make his proposal for prayer out of a deep religious faith or out of a pragmatic political belief that it would encourage calm in the deliberations?

There was, as usual, probably an element of both, but perhaps a bit more of the latter. Franklin was never known to pray publicly himself, and he rarely attended church. Yet he thought it useful to remind this assembly of demigods that they were in the presence of a God far greater, and that history was watching as well. To succeed, they had to be awed by the magnitude of their task and be humbled, not assertive. Otherwise, he concluded, "we shall be divided by our little, partial, local interests, our projects will be confounded, and we ourselves shall become a reproach and a by-word down to future ages."[23]

Hamilton warned that the sudden hiring of a chaplain might frighten the public into thinking that "embarrassments and dissensions within the convention had suggested this measure." Franklin replied that a sense of alarm outside the hall might help rather than hurt the deliberations within. Another objection was raised: that there was no money to pay a chaplain. The idea was quietly shelved. On the bottom of his copy of his speech, Franklin appended a note of marvel: "The convention, except three or four persons, thought prayers unnecessary!"[24]

The time had come for Franklin to propose more earthly measures. Two days after his prayer speech—on Saturday, June 30—he helped to set in motion the process that would break the impasse and, to a large extent, shape the new nation. Others had discussed compromises, and now it was time to insist on one and to propose it.

First Franklin succinctly stated the problem: "The diversity of opinions turns on two points. If a proportional representation takes place, the small States contend that their liberties will be in danger. If an equality of votes is to be put in its place, the large States say their money will be in danger."

Then he gently emphasized, in a homespun analogy that drew on his affection for craftsmen and construction, the importance of compromise: "When a broad table is to be made, and the edges of planks do not fit, the artist takes a little from both, and makes a good joint. In like manner here, both sides must part with some of their demands."

Finally, he incorporated a workable compromise into a specific motion. Representatives to the lower House would be popularly elected and apportioned by population, but in the Senate "the Legislatures of the several States shall choose and send an equal number of Delegates." The House would have primary authority over taxes and spending, the Senate over the confirmation of executive officers and matters of state sovereignty.[25]

The convention proceeded to appoint a committee, which included Franklin, to draw up the details of this compromise, and by a close vote it was finally adopted, in much the form Franklin had proposed, on July 16. "This was Franklin's great victory in the Convention," declares Van Doren, "that he was the author of the compromise which held the delegates together."

That, perhaps, gives him a bit too much credit. He was not the author of the idea, nor the first to suggest it. It grew from proposals by

Sherman of Connecticut and others. Franklin's role, nonetheless, was crucial. He embodied the spirit and issued the call for compromise, he selected the most palatable option available and refined it, and he wrote the motion and picked the right moment to offer it. His prestige, his neutrality, and his eminence made it easier for all to swallow. The artisan had taken a little from all sides and made a joint good enough to hold together a nation for centuries.

A few days after he offered his compromise, Franklin hosted some of the delegates for tea in his garden, including Elbridge Gerry of Massachusetts, a leading skeptic of unfettered democracy. But Franklin's shaded garden was a place where controversies could be cooled. Gerry invited along a Massachusetts minister named Manasseh Cutler, a portly and congenial character who was in town pushing the territorial schemes of the Ohio Company, which he had helped found. In his journal Cutler noted that "my knees smote together" at the prospect of meeting the celebrated sage, but he was immediately put at ease by Franklin's unassuming style. "I was highly delighted with the extensive knowledge he appeared to have of every subject, the brightness of his memory, and clearness and vivacity of all his mental faculties, notwithstanding his age," Cutler recorded. "His manners are perfectly easy, and every thing about him seems to diffuse an unrestrained freedom and happiness. He has an incessant vein of humor, accompanied with an uncommon vivacity, which seems as natural and involuntary as his breathing."

Discovering that Cutler was an avid botanist, Franklin produced a curiosity he had just received, a ten-inch snake with two perfectly formed heads preserved in a vial. Imagine what would happen, Franklin speculated with amusement, if one head of the snake attempted to go to the left of a twig and the other head went to the right and they could not agree. He was about to compare this to an issue that had just been debated at the convention, but some of the other delegates stopped him. "He seemed to forget that everything in the convention was to be kept a profound secret," Cutler noted. "But the secrecy of convention matters was suggested to him, which stopped him, and deprived me of the story he was going to tell."

The point Franklin was about to make, no doubt, was the same one he had made in the Pennsylvania state convention in 1776, when he argued against a two-chamber legislature because it might fall prey to the fate of the fabled two-headed snake that died of thirst when its heads could not agree on which way to pass a twig. Indeed, in a paper he wrote in 1789 extolling Pennsylvania's unicameral legislature, he again referred to what he called "the famous political fable of the snake with two heads." He had come to accept, however, that in forging the compromise needed to create a national Congress, two heads could be better than one.[26]

On other issues as well, Franklin was usually on the side favoring fewer fetters on direct democracy. He opposed, for example, giving the president a veto over acts of Congress, which he saw as the repository of the people's will. Colonial governors, he reminded the delegates, had used that power to extort more influence and money whenever the legislature wanted a measure approved. When Hamilton favored making the president a near-monarch to be chosen for life, Franklin noted that he provided living proof that a person's life sometimes lasted longer than his mental and physical prime. Instead, it would be more democratic to relegate the president to the role of average citizen after his term. The argument that "returning to the mass of the people was degrading," he said, "was contrary to republican principles. In free Governments the rulers are the servants, and the people their superiors and sovereigns. For the former therefore to return among the latter was not to degrade but to promote them."

Likewise, he argued that Congress should have the power to impeach the president. In the past, when impeachment was not possible, the only method people had for removing a corrupt ruler was through assassination, "in which he was not only deprived of his life but of the opportunity of vindicating his character." Franklin also felt that it would be more democratic for executive power to reside with a small council, as it did in Pennsylvania, rather than one man. This was a hard debate to have with Washington sitting in the chair, as it was widely assumed that he would be the first president. So Franklin noted diplomatically that the first man to take the office would likely be benevolent, but the person who came next (perhaps he had a sense that it could be John Adams) might harbor more autocratic tendencies. On this issue Franklin lost, but the convention did decide to institutionalize the role of the Cabinet.

He also advocated, unsuccessfully, the direct election of federal judges, instead of permitting the president or Congress to select them. As usual, he made his argument by telling a tale. It was the practice in Scotland for judges to be nominated by that country's lawyers, who always selected the ablest of the profession in order to get rid of him and share his practice among themselves. In America, it would be in the best interest of voters "to make the best choice," which was the way it should be.[27]

Many of the delegates believed strongly that only those who owned substantial property should be eligible for office, as was the case in most states other than Pennsylvania. Young Charles Pinckney of South Carolina went so far as to propose that the wealth requirement for president should be $100,000, until it was pointed out that this might exclude Washington. Franklin rose and, in Madison's words, "expressed his dislike of everything that tended to debase the spirit of the common people." His democratic sensibilities were offended by any suggestion that the Constitution "should betray a great partiality to the rich." On the contrary, he said, "some of the greatest rogues I was ever acquainted with, were the richest rogues." Likewise, he spoke out against any property requirements on the right to vote. "We should not depress the virtue and public spirit of our common people." On these issues he was successful.[28]

On only one issue did Franklin take what could be considered the less democratic position, though he did not recognize it as such. Federal officials, he argued, should serve without pay. In *The Radicalism of the American Revolution,* historian Gordon Wood contends that Franklin's proposal reflected the "classical sentiments of aristocratic leadership." Even John Adams, generally less democratic in his outlook, wrote from London that under such a policy "all offices would be monopolized by the rich, the poor and middling ranks would be excluded and an aristocratic despotism would immediately follow."

Franklin, I think, did not intend for his proposal to be elitist or exclusionary, but instead saw it as a way to limit corrupting influences. In his many letters on the subject, he never considered, though he should have, that his plan might limit the jobs to those who could afford to work for free. Indeed, he seemed quite oblivious to this argument. Instead, he based his position on his faith in citizen volunteers and his long-standing belief that a pursuit of profit had corrupted English government. It was a case he had made in an exchange of letters with William Strahan three years earlier, and he used almost the exact same language on the floor of the convention:

> There are two passions which have a powerful influence in the affairs of men. These are *ambition* and *avarice;* the love of power and the love of money. Separately, each of these has great force in prompting men to action; but, when united in view of the same object, they have in many minds the most violent effects . . . And of what kind are the men that will strive for this profitable preeminence, through all the bustle of cabal, the heat of contention, the infinite mutual abuse of parties, tearing to pieces the best of characters? It will not be the wise and moderate, the lovers of peace and good order, the men fittest for the trust. It will be the bold and the violent, the men of strong passions and indefatigable activity in their selfish pursuits.

On this issue he found almost no support, and the idea was put aside with no debate. "It was treated with great respect," Madison recorded, "but rather for the author of it than from any conviction of its expediency or practicability." [29]

There were, through the long and hot summer, some occasions for humor. Gouverneur Morris of Pennsylvania, who wrote with a taut and serious pen but at times acted as the congressional jester, was dared by Hamilton, for the price of a dinner, to slap the austere and intimidating Washington on the shoulder and say, "My dear general, how happy I am to see you look so well!" Morris did, but after weathering the look from Washington's face declared that he would not do so again for a thousand dinners. Elbridge Gerry, arguing against a large standing army, lasciviously compared it to a standing penis: "An excellent assurance of domestic tranquility, but a dangerous temptation to foreign adventure." [30]

When it was all over, many compromises had been made, including on the issue of slavery. Some members were distressed because they felt that the final result usurped too much state sovereignty, others because they thought it did not create a strong enough national government. The cantankerous Luther Martin of Maryland sneered contemptuously that they had concocted a "perfect medley," and left before the final vote.

He was right, except for his contemptuous sneer. The medley was, indeed, as close to perfect as mortals could have achieved. From its profound first three words, "We the people," to the carefully calibrated compromises and balances that followed, it created an ingenious system in which the power of the national government as well as that of the states derived directly from the citizenry. And thus it fulfilled the motto on the nation's great seal, suggested by Franklin in 1776, of *E Pluribus Unum*, out of many one.

With the wisdom of a patient chess player and the practicality of a scientist, Franklin realized that they had succeeded not because they were self-assured, but because they were willing to concede that they might be fallible. "We are making experiments in politics," he wrote la Rochefoucauld. To Du Pont de Nemours he confessed, "We must not expect that a new government may be formed as a game of chess may be played, by a skillful hand, without a fault."[31]

Franklin's final triumph was to express these sentiments with a wry but powerful charm in a remarkable closing address to the convention. The speech was a testament to the virtue of intellectual tolerance and to the evil of presumed infallibility, and it proclaimed for the ages the enlightened creed that became central to America's freedom. They were the most eloquent words Franklin ever wrote—and perhaps the best ever written by anyone about the magic of the American system and the spirit of compromise that created it:

> I confess that I do not entirely approve this Constitution at present; but sir, I am not sure I shall never approve it: For, having lived long, I have experienced many instances of being obliged, by better information or fuller consideration, to change opinions even on important subjects, which I once thought right, but found to be otherwise. It is therefore that, the older I grow, the more apt I am to doubt my own judgment and pay more respect to the judgment of others.
>
> Most men, indeed as well as most sects in religion, think themselves in possession of all truth, and that wherever others differ from them, it is so far error. Steele, a Protestant, in a dedication, tells the Pope that

the only difference between our two churches in their opinions of the certainty of their doctrine is, the Romish Church is infallible, and the Church of England is never in the wrong. But, though many private persons think almost as highly of their own infallibility as of that of their sect, few express it so naturally as a certain French lady, who, in a little dispute with her sister said: "I don't know how it happens, sister, but I meet with nobody but myself that is *always* in the right."

In these sentiments, sir, I agree to this Constitution with all its faults—if they are such—because I think a general government necessary for us . . . I doubt, too, whether any other convention we can obtain may be able to make a better Constitution; for, when you assemble a number of men, to have the advantage of their joint wisdom, you inevitably assemble with those men all their prejudices, their passions, their errors of opinion, their local interests, and their selfish views. From such an assembly can a perfect production be expected?

It therefore astonishes me, sir, to find this system approaching so near to perfection as it does; and I think it will astonish our enemies, who are waiting with confidence to hear that our councils are confounded like those of the builders of Babel, and that our States are on the point of separation, only to meet hereafter for the purpose of cutting one another's throats. Thus I consent, sir, to this Constitution because I expect no better, and because I am not sure that it is not the best.

He concluded by pleading that, "for the sake of our posterity, we shall act heartily and unanimously." To that end, he made a motion that the convention adopt the device of declaring that the document had been accepted by all of the states, which would allow even the minority of delegates who dissented to sign it. "I cannot help expressing a wish that every member of the convention who may still have objections to it, would, with me, on this occasion, doubt a little of his own infallibility, and, to make manifest our unanimity, put his name to this instrument."[32]

And so it was that when Franklin finished, most of the delegates, even some with doubts, heeded his urgings and lined up by state delegation for the historic signing. As they did so, Franklin turned their attention to the sun carved on the back of Washington's chair and observed that painters often found it difficult to distinguish in their art a rising sun from a setting one. "I have," he said, "often in the course of the session, and the vicissitudes of my hopes and fears as to its issue, looked at that behind the President without being able to tell whether it was rising or setting. But now at length I have the happiness to know that it is a rising and not a setting sun."

According to a tale recorded by James McHenry of Maryland, he made his point in a pithier way to an anxious lady named Mrs. Powel, who accosted him outside the hall. What type of government, she asked, have you delegates given us? To which he replied, "A republic, madam, if you can keep it."[33]

The historian Clinton Rossiter has called Franklin's closing speech "the most remarkable performance of a remarkable life," and the Yale scholar Barbara Oberg calls it "the culmination of Franklin's life as a propagandist, persuader and cajoler of people." With his deft and self-deprecating use of double negatives—"I am not sure I shall never approve it," "I am not sure that it is not the best"—he emphasized the humility and appreciation for human fallibility that was necessary to form a nation. Opponents attacked Franklin's compromising approach as lacking in principle, yet that was the point of his message. "A stand for compromise," Oberg points out, "is not the stuff of heroism, virtue, or moral certainty. But it is the essence of the democratic process."[34]

Throughout his life, Franklin had, by his thoughts and activities, helped to lay the foundation for the democratic republic that this Constitution enshrined. He had begun as a young man by teaching his fellow tradesmen ways to become virtuous, diligent, and responsible citizens. Then he sought to enlist them in associations—Juntos, libraries, fire departments, neighborhood patrols, and militias—for their mutual benefit and the good of the common community. Later, he created networks, from the postal service to the American Philosophical Society, designed to foster the connections that would integrate an emerging nation. Finally, in the 1750s, he began pushing the colonies to gain strength through unity, to stand together for common purposes in a way that helped shape a national identity.

Since that time, he had been instrumental in shaping every major document that led to the creation of the new republic. He was the only person to sign all four of its founding papers: the Declaration of Independence, the treaty with France, the peace accord with Britain, and the Constitution. In addition, he devised the first federal scheme for America, the unfulfilled Albany Plan of 1754, under which the separate states and a national government would have shared power. And the Articles of Confederation he proposed in 1775 were a closer approximation of the final Constitution than were the weak and ill-fated alternative Articles adopted in 1781.

The Constitution, wrote Henry May in his book *The Enlightenment in America,* reflected "all the virtues of the moderate Enlightenment, and also one of its faults: the belief that everything can be settled by compromise." For Franklin, who embodied the Enlightenment and its spirit of compromise, this was hardly a fault. For him, compromise was not only a practical approach but a moral one. Tolerance, humility, and a respect for others required it. On almost every issue for more than two centuries, this supposed fault has served the Constitution, and the nation it formed, quite well. There was only one great issue that could not, then or later, be solved by constitutional compromise: slavery. And that indeed was the issue on which Franklin, as his life neared its end, chose to take an uncompromising stand.[35]

ENDGAME

Franklin's role in the miracle at Philadelphia could have been a fitting finale to a career spent creating the possibility of a free and democratic republic, and for most people, or at least most people of his era approaching 82, it would have been enough to sate any ambition. Now he could, if he wanted, retire from public life knowing that he was widely revered and had outlasted any enemies. Nevertheless, a month after personally presenting a copy of the new federal Constitution to the Pennsylvania Assembly, he accepted reelection for a third one-year term as the state's president. "It was my intention to decline serving another year as president, that I might be at liberty to take a trip to Boston in the spring," he wrote his sister. "I have now upwards of fifty years employed in public offices."

He would, in fact, never travel nor see his sister again. His kidney stones and her health, he noted, made it so they would have to be satisfied by letters rather than visits. In addition, as he freely admitted, his pride made him still appreciate public recognition. "It is no small pleasure to me, and I suppose it will give my sister pleasure, that after such long trial of me, I should be elected a third time by my fellow citizens," he wrote. "This universal and unbounded confidence of a whole people flatters my vanity much more than a peerage could do."

Franklin's letters to his sister were filled with such candid comments, especially during his later years. At one point he scolded that "your Post Office is very badly managed" and decried her propensity to get into little feuds. This led to an amusing riff on how the Franklins "were always subject to being a little miffy." What had happened, he asked, to the Folger cousins in Nantucket? "They are wonderfully shy. But I admire their honest plainness of speech. About a year ago I invited two of them to dine with me. Their answer was that they would—if they could not do better. I suppose they did better, for I never saw them afterwards."[36]

To Noah Webster, the famous lexicographer who had dedicated his *Dissertations on the English Language* to him, Franklin lamented the loose new word usages infecting the language, a common complaint of curmudgeonly writers but a bit atypical of the jovial Franklin, who had once taken pleasure in inventing new English words and, with even more pleasure, amusing the ladies of Paris with new French ones. "I find a verb formed from the substantive *notice;* 'I should not have *noticed* this, were it not that the gentleman, etc.' Also another verb from the substantive *advocate;* 'the Gentleman who *advocates* or who has *advocated* that motion, etc.' Another from the substantive *progress,* the most awkward and abominable of the three; 'the committee, having *progressed,* resolved to adjourn . . . If you should happen to be of my opinion with respect to these innovations, you will use your authority in reprobating them."[37]

He also finally resumed work on his autobiography. He had written 87 manuscript pages in Twyford in 1771, and then added 12 more in Passy in 1784. Writing steadily from August 1788 until May of the following year, he completed another 119 pages, which brought him up to his arrival in England as a colonial agent. "I omit all facts and transactions that may not have a tendency to benefit the young reader," he wrote to Vaughan. His purpose was still to provide a self-help manual for America's ambitious middle class by describing "my success in emerging from poverty" and "the advantages of certain modes of conduct which I observed."[38]

By now he was facing ever greater pain from his kidney stones, and he resorted to using laudanum, a tincture of opium and alcohol. "I am so interrupted by extreme pain, which obliges me to have recourse to opium, that between the effects of both, I have but little time in which I can write anything," he complained to Vaughan. He also worried that what he had written was not worth publishing. "Give me your candid opinion whether I had best publish it or suppress it," he asked, "for I am grown so old and feeble in mind, as well as body, that I cannot place any confidence in my own judgment." He had now begun to dictate the work to Benny rather than write it by hand, but he was able to complete only a few more pages.

Friends sent him various home remedies for kidney stones, including a suggestion from Vaughan, which amused Franklin, that a small dose of hemlock might work. At times, he could be cheerful enough about his maladies and repeat his maxim that those who "drink to the bottom of the cup must expect to meet some of the dregs," as he did to his old friend Elizabeth Partridge. He was still, he said, "joking, laughing and telling merry stories, as when you first knew me, a young man about fifty."[39]

Yet Franklin was becoming resigned to the fact that he did not have much longer to live, and his letters took on a tone of sanguine farewell. "Hitherto this long life has been tolerably happy," he wrote to Caty Ray Greene, the girl who had captured his mind and heart thirty-five years earlier. "If I were allowed to live it over again, I should make no objection, only wishing for leave to do what authors do in a second edition of their works, correct some of my errata." When Washington became president that year, Franklin wrote to him that it made him glad he was still alive: "For my own personal ease, I should have died two years ago; but, though those years have been spent in excruciating pain, I am pleased that I have lived them, since they have brought me to see our present situation."[40]

He was also sanguine about the revolution now welling up in his beloved France. The explosion of democratic sentiments was producing "mischief and trouble," he noted, but he assumed that it would lead to greater democracy and eventually a good constitution. So most of his letters to his French friends were inappropriately lighthearted. "Are you still living?" he wrote the French scientist Jean-Baptiste Le Roy, his friend and Passy neighbor, in late 1789. "Or have the mob of Paris mistaken the head of a monopolizer of knowledge for a monopolizer of corn, and paraded it about the streets upon a pole?" (It was also in this letter that he famously noted that "nothing can be said to be certain except death and taxes.") He assured Louis-Guillaume le Veillard, his neighbor and closest friend in Passy, that it was all for the good. "When the fermentation is over and the troubling parts subsided, the wine will be fine and good, and cheer the hearts of those that drink it." [41]

Franklin was wrong, sadly wrong, about the French Revolution, though he would not live long enough to learn it. Le Veillard would soon lose his life to the guillotine. So would Lavoisier the chemist, who had worked with him on the Mesmer investigation. Condorcet, the economist who had accompanied Franklin to his famed meetings with Voltaire, would be imprisoned and poison himself in his cell. And la Rochefoucauld, who had translated the state constitutions for Franklin and engaged him in a lively correspondence since his departure, would be stoned to death by a mob.

SLAVERY

In the very last year of his life, Franklin was to embark on one final public mission, a moral crusade that would help ameliorate one of the few blemishes on a life spent fighting for freedom. Throughout much of the eighteenth century, slavery had been an institution that few whites questioned. Even in brotherly Philadelphia, ownership continued to climb until about 1760, when almost 10 percent of the city's population were slaves. But views had begun to evolve, especially after the ringing words of the Declaration and the awkward compromises of the Constitution. George Mason of Virginia, despite the fact that he owned two hundred slaves, called the institution "pernicious" at the Constitutional Convention and declared that "every master of slaves is a petty tyrant; they bring the judgment of heaven on a country."

Franklin's views had been evolving as well. He had, as we have seen, owned one or two household slaves off and on for much of his life, and as a young publisher he had carried ads for slave sales. But he had also published, in 1729, one of the nation's first antislavery pieces and had joined the Associates of Dr. Bray to establish schools for blacks in America. Deborah had enrolled her house servants in the Philadelphia school, and after visiting it Franklin had spoken of his "higher opinions of the natural capacities of the black race." In his 1751 "Observations on the Increase of Mankind," he attacked slavery strongly, but mainly from an economic perspective rather than a moral one. In expressing sympathy for the Philadelphia abolitionist Anthony Benezet in the 1770s, he had agreed that the importation of new slaves should end immediately, but he qualified his support for outright abolition by saying it should come "in time." As an agent for Georgia in London, he had defended the right of that colony to keep slaves. But he preached, in articles such as his 1772 "The Somerset Case and the Slave Trade," that one of Britain's great sins against America was foisting slavery on it.

Franklin's conversion culminated in 1787, when he accepted the presidency of the Pennsylvania Society for Promoting the Abolition of Slavery. The group tried to persuade him to present a petition against slavery at the Constitutional Convention, but knowing the delicate compromises being made between north and south, he kept silent on the issue. After that, however, he became outspoken.

One of the arguments against immediate abolition, which Franklin had heretofore accepted, was that it was not practical or safe to free hundreds of thousands of adult slaves into a society for which they were not prepared. (There were about seven hundred thousand slaves in the United States out of a total population of four million in 1790.) So his abolition society dedicated itself not only to freeing slaves but also to helping them become good citizens. "Slavery is such an atrocious debasement of human nature that its very extirpation, if not performed with solicitous care, may sometimes open a source of serious evils," Franklin wrote in a November 1789 address to the public from the society. "The unhappy man, who has long been treated as a brute animal, too frequently sinks beneath the common standard of the human species. The galling chains that bind his body do also fetter his intellectual faculties and impair the social affections of his heart."

As was typical of Franklin, he drew up for the society a meticulously detailed charter and procedures "for improving the condition of free blacks." There would be a twenty-four-person committee divided into four subcommittees:

> A Committee of Inspection, who shall superintend the morals, general conduct, and ordinary situation of the free Negroes, and afford them advice and instruction . . .
>
> A Committee of Guardians, who shall place out children and young people with suitable persons, that they may (during a moderate time of apprenticeship or servitude) learn some trade or other business . . .
>
> A Committee of Education, who shall superintend the school instruction of the children and youth of the free blacks. They may either influence them to attend regularly the schools already established in this city, or form others with this view . . .
>
> A Committee of Employ, who shall endeavor to procure constant employment for those free Negroes who are able to work; as the want of this would occasion poverty, idleness, and many vicious habits.[42]

On behalf of the society, Franklin presented a formal abolition petition to Congress in February 1790. "Mankind are all formed by the same Almighty Being, alike objects of his care, and equally designed for the enjoyment of happiness," it declared. The duty of Congress was to secure "the blessings of liberty to the People of the United States," and this should be done "without distinction of color." Therefore, Congress should grant "liberty to those unhappy men who alone in this land of freedom are degraded into perpetual bondage."[43]

Franklin and his petition were roundly denounced by the defenders of slavery, most notably Congressman James Jackson of Georgia, who declared on the House floor that the Bible had sanctioned slavery and, without it, there would be no one to do the hard and hot work on plantations. It was the perfect setup for Franklin's last great parody, written less than a month before he died.

He had begun his literary career sixty-eight years earlier when, as a 16-year-old apprentice, he pretended to be a prudish widow named Silence Dogood, and he made a subsequent career of enlightening readers with similar hoaxes such as "The Trial of Polly Baker" and "An Edict from the King of Prussia." In the spirit of the latter of these essays, he anonymously published in a local newspaper, with appropriate scholarly source citations, a purported speech given by a member of the divan of Algiers one hundred years earlier.

It bore a scathing mirror resemblance to Congressman Jackson's speech. "God is great, and Mahomet is his prophet," it began realistically. Then it went on to attack a petition by a purist sect asking for an end to the practice of capturing and enslaving European Christians to work in Algeria: "If we forbear to make slaves of their people, who in this hot climate are to cultivate our lands? Who are to perform the common labors of our city, and in our families?" An end to the slavery of "infidels" would cause land values to fall and rents to sink by half.

> Who is to indemnify their masters for their loss? Will the state do it? Is our Treasury sufficient? . . . And if we set our slaves free, what is to be done with them? Few of them will return to their countries; they know too well the greater hardships they must there be subject to; they will not embrace our holy religion; they will not adopt our manners; our people will not pollute themselves by intermarrying with them. Must we maintain them as beggars in our streets, or suffer our properties to be the prey of their pillage? For men long accustomed to slavery will not work for a livelihood when not compelled.
>
> And what is there so pitiable in their present condition? . . . Here they are brought into a land where the sun of Islamism gives forth its light, and shines in full splendor, and they have an opportunity of making themselves acquainted with the true doctrine, and thereby saving their immortal souls . . . While serving us, we take care to provide them with every thing, and they are treated with humanity. The laborers in their own country are, as I am well informed, worse fed, lodged, and clothed . . .

> How grossly are they mistaken in imagining slavery to be disallowed by the Koran! Are not the two precepts, to quote no more, "Masters, treat your Slaves with kindness; Slaves, serve your Masters with cheerfulness and Fidelity," clear proofs to the contrary? . . . Let us then hear no more of this detestable proposition, the manumission of Christian slaves, the adoption of which would, by depreciating our lands and houses, and thereby depriving so many good citizens of their properties, create universal discontent, and provoke insurrections.[44]

In his parody, Franklin recorded that the Algerian divan ended up rejecting the petition. Congress, likewise, decided that it did not have the authority to act on Franklin's abolition petition.

TO BED

It is not surprising that, at the end of their lives, many people take stock of their religious beliefs. Franklin had never fully joined a church nor subscribed to a sectarian dogma, and he found it more useful to focus on earthly issues rather than spiritual ones. When he narrowly escaped a shipwreck as he neared the English coast in 1757, he had joked to Deborah that, "Were I a Roman Catholic, perhaps I should on this occasion vow to build a chapel to some saint; but as I am not, if I were to vow at all, it should be to build a *lighthouse*." Likewise, when a town in Massachusetts named itself Franklin in 1785 and asked him to donate a church bell, he told them to forsake the steeple and build a library, for which he sent "books instead of a bell, sense being preferable to sound."[45]

As he grew older, Franklin's amorphous faith in a benevolent God seemed to become more firm. "If it had not been for the justice of our cause and the consequent interposition of Providence, in which we had faith, we must have been ruined," he wrote Strahan after the war. "If I had ever before been an atheist, I should now have been convinced of the Being and government of a Deity!"[46]

His support for religion tended to be based on his belief that it was useful and practical in making people behave better, rather than because it was divinely inspired. He wrote a letter, possibly sent in 1786 to Thomas Paine, in response to a manuscript that ridiculed religious devotion. Franklin begged the recipient not to publish his heretical treatise, but he did so on the grounds that the arguments could have harmful practical effects, not on the grounds that they were false. "You yourself may find it easy to live a virtuous life without the assistance afforded by religion," he said, "but think how great a proportion of mankind consists of weak and ignorant men and women, and of in-experienced and inconsiderate youth of both sexes, who have need of the motives of religion to restrain them from vice." In addition, he noted, the personal consequences for the author would likely be odi-ous. "He that spits against the wind, spits in his own face." If the letter was indeed addressed to Paine, it had an effect. He had long been for-mulating the virulent attack on organized religious faith that he would later title *The Age of Reason,* but he held off publishing it for another seven years, until near the end of his life.[47]

The most important religious role Franklin played—and it was an exceedingly important one in shaping his enlightened new republic—was as an apostle of tolerance. He had contributed to the building funds of each and every sect in Philadelphia, including £5 for the Congregation Mikveh Israel for its new synagogue in April 1788, and he had opposed religious oaths and tests in both the Pennsylvania and federal constitutions. During the July 4 celebrations in 1788, Franklin was too sick to leave his bed, but the parade marched under his win-dow. For the first time, as per arrangements that Franklin had over-seen, "the clergy of different Christian denominations, with the rabbi of the Jews, walked arm in arm."[48]

His final summation of his religious thinking came the month be-fore he died, in response to questions from the Rev. Ezra Stiles, presi-dent of Yale. Franklin began by restating his basic creed: "I believe in one God, Creator of the Universe. That he governs it by his Provi-dence. That he ought to be worshipped. That the most acceptable ser-vice we render to him is doing good to his other children." These beliefs were fundamental to all religions; anything else was mere em-bellishment.

Then he addressed Stiles's question about whether he believed in Jesus, which was, he said, the first time he had ever been asked directly. The system of morals that Jesus provided, Franklin replied, was "the best the world ever saw or is likely to see." But on the issue of whether Jesus was divine, he provided a surprisingly candid and wry response. "I have," he declared, "some doubts as to his divinity; though it is a question I do not dogmatize upon, having never studied it, and think it needless to busy myself with it now, when I expect soon an opportunity of knowing the truth with less trouble."[49]

The last letter Franklin ever wrote was, fittingly, to Thomas Jefferson, his spiritual heir as the nation's foremost apostle of the Enlightenment's faith in reason, experiment, and tolerance. Jefferson had come to call at Franklin's bedside and provide news of their beleaguered friends in France. "He went over all in succession," Jefferson noted, "with a rapidity and animation almost too much for his strength." Jefferson praised him for getting so far in his memoirs, which he predicted would be very instructive. "I cannot say much of that," replied Franklin, "but I will give you a sample." Then he pulled out a page that described the last weeks of his negotiations in London to avert the war, which he insisted that Jefferson keep as a memento.

Jefferson followed up by asking about an arcane issue that needed resolving: Which maps had been used to draw America's western boundaries in the Paris peace talks? After Jefferson left, Franklin studied the matter and then wrote his final letter. His mind was clear enough to describe, with precision, the decisions they had made and the maps they had used regarding various rivers running into the Bay of Passamaquoddy.[50]

Soon after he finished the letter, Franklin's fever and chest pains began to worsen. For ten days he was confined to bed with a heavy cough and labored breathing. Sally and Richard Bache attended to him, as did Temple and Benny. Polly Stevenson was there as well, pressing him to make a clearer proclamation of his religious faith, pleased that he had a picture of the Day of Judgment by his bedside. Only once during that period was he able to rise briefly, and he asked that his bed be made up so that he could "die in a decent manner." Sally expressed hope that he was recovering, that he might live many years longer. "I hope not," he calmly replied.[51]

Then an abscess in his lung burst, making it impossible for him to talk. Benny approached his bed, and his grandfather reached out to hold his hand for a long time. At eleven that evening, April 17, 1790, Franklin died at the age of 84.

Back in 1728, when he was a fledgling printer imbued with the pride that he believed an honest man should have in his trade, Franklin had composed for himself, or at least for his amusement, a cheeky epitaph that reflected his wry perspective on his pilgrim's progress through this world:

> *The body of*
> *B. Franklin, Printer;*
> *(Like the cover of an old book,*
> *Its contents worn out,*
> *and stripped of its lettering and gilding)*
> *Lies here, food for worms.*
> *But the work shall not be lost:*
> *For it will, (as he believed) appear once more,*
> *In a new and more elegant edition,*
> *Revised and corrected*
> *By the Author.*[52]

Shortly before he died, however, he prescribed something simpler to be placed over the grave site that he would share with his wife. His tombstone should be, he wrote, a marble slab "six feet long, four feet wide, plain, with only a small molding round the upper edge, and this inscription: Benjamin and Deborah Franklin."[53]

Close to twenty thousand mourners, more than had ever before gathered in Philadelphia, watched as his funeral procession made its way to the Christ Church burying ground, a few blocks from his home. In front marched the clergymen of the city, all of them, of every faith.

CHAPTER SEVENTEEN

EPILOGUE

William Franklin: In his will, Franklin bequeathed to his only surviving son nothing more than some worthless land claims in Canada and the forgiveness of any debts he still owed him. "The part he acted against me in the late war, which is of public notoriety, will account for my leaving him no more of an estate he endeavored to deprive me of." William, who thought he had already paid off his debts by deeding over his New Jersey lands, complained about the "shameful injustice" of the will, and for the remaining twenty-five years of his life never returned to America. But he still revered his father's memory, and he did not permit himself another harsh public word about him. Indeed, when his own son, Temple, dithered in producing an edition of Franklin's life and writings, William began work on one of his own, which he hoped would honor his father by showing the "turn of his mind and variety of his knowledge." It was not to be. He had married his Irish landlady, Mary D'Evelyn, but after she died in 1811 he was a broken and lonely man. He died three years later, estranged from his son, suffering in what he called "that solitary state which is most repugnant to my nature."[1]

Temple Franklin: Having inherited a nice share of his grandfather's estate and all of his important papers, Temple returned to England in 1792 and reunited temporarily with his father. Still a charming but aimless rogue, he chafed under his father's pressure to get married and work on Franklin's papers, and he brought the family's dysfunctionality to new heights. He had another illegitimate child, a daughter named Ellen, whose mother was the younger sister of William's new wife, and then he broke bitterly with them all and ran away to Paris, leaving little Ellen Franklin to be raised by William, who was both her uncle and grandfather. For fourteen years, Temple neither reestablished contact with his father nor published the papers of his grandfather, even as unauthorized portions of the *Autobiography* appeared in France. Finally, in 1812, he wrote his father to say he was about to publish the papers and wanted to come to London to consult with him. William, who remembered the cool response he had gotten when he wrote a similar letter to his own father twenty-eight years earlier, was overjoyed. "I shall be happy to see you," he said, "not being able to bear the thought of dying in enmity with one so nearly connected." But Temple never came to England. Instead, in 1817, he published the *Autobiography* (without the final installment) and a haphazard collection of some of his grandfather's papers. He lived the next six years in Paris with yet another mistress, an Englishwoman named Hannah Collyer, whom he married a few months before he died in 1823. She later brought many of Franklin's precious papers back to London, where they were rediscovered in 1840 in the shop of a tailor who was using them as patterns. The papers that Temple abandoned in Philadelphia were scattered to various souvenir hunters until the American Philosophical Society began the process of collecting them in the 1860s.[2]

Sally and Richard Bache: Franklin's loyal daughter and her husband got most of his property, including the Market Street houses, on the condition that Richard "set free his Negro man Bob." (He did, but Bob took to drink, couldn't support himself, and asked to be restored to slavery; the Baches declined, but they let him live in their home for the rest of his life.) Sally was also given the Louis XVI miniature encircled with diamonds, with the stipulation that she not turn "any of those diamonds into ornaments either for herself or daughters and thereby introduce or countenance the expensive, vain and useless fashion of wearing jewels in this country." She sold the diamonds to fulfill her lifelong desire to see England. With her husband, she went to stay with William, with whom she had always remained close. On their return, the Baches settled on a farm in Delaware.

Benjamin Bache: Inheriting Franklin's printing equipment and many of his books, he followed in his grandfather's steps by launching, seventy years after the *New England Courant* was first published, a crusading Jeffersonian newspaper, *The American Aurora.* The paper became fiercely partisan on behalf of those who believed, with a passion that surpassed even Franklin's, in pro-French and democratic policies, and it attacked Washington and then Adams for creating imperial presidencies. It was, for a while, the most popular paper in America, and has been the subject of two recent books. His politics caused a rift with his parents, as did his decision to marry against their wishes a feisty woman named Margaret Markoe. In 1798, he was arrested for sedition and for libeling Adams, but before he could stand trial he died of yellow fever at age 29. By then he was so estranged from his parents that his sisters had to sneak away to see him during his final illness. Margaret promptly married her late husband's pressman, an argumentative Irishman named William Duane, and they kept the *Aurora* going. One of Benny's sisters, Deborah Bache, then married one of Duane's sons from his first marriage.[3]

Polly Stevenson: She inherited nothing more than a silver tankard from the man she had revered for thirty-three years, and she soon became disenchanted with all branches of his family and all things American. When her second son, Tom, went back to England (accompanied by Willie Bache, to study medicine), she wrote him longing letters about her desire to return home as well. But she died in 1795, before she had the chance. Tom ended up back in Philadelphia, where he became a successful doctor; his brother William and sister Eliza stayed in America as well, and they all raised happy families.

The aspiring tradesmen of Boston and Philadelphia: The most unusual provision in the codicil to Franklin's will was a trust he established. He noted that, unlike the other founders of the country, he was born poor and had been helped in his rise by those who supported him as a struggling artisan. "I wish to be useful even after my death, if possible, in forming and advancing other young men that may be serviceable to their country." So he designated the £2,000 he had earned as President of Pennsylvania—citing his often expressed belief that officials should serve without pay—to be split between the towns of Boston and Philadelphia and provided as loans, "at 5 percent per annum, to such young married artificers" who had served apprenticeships and were now seeking to establish their own businesses. With his usual obsession with detail, he described precisely how the loans and repayments would work, and he calculated that after one hundred years, the annuities would each be worth £131,000. At that time, the cities could spend £100,000 of it on public projects, keeping the remainder in the trust, which after another hundred years of loans and compounded interest would, he calculated, be worth £4,061,000. At that point, the money would go into the public treasury.

Did it work as he envisioned? In Boston it had to be modified as the apprenticeship system went out of fashion, but the loans were made according to the spirit of his bequest and, after one hundred years, the fund was worth about $400,000, a little bit less than he had calculated. At that point a trade school, Franklin Union (now the Benjamin Franklin Institute of Technology), was founded with three-fourths of the money plus a matching bequest from Andrew Carnegie, who considered Franklin a hero; the rest remained in the trust. A century later, that amount had grown to nearly $5 million, not quite the equivalent of £4 million but still a sizable sum. As per Franklin's will, the fund was then disbursed. After a legal struggle that was settled by an act of the legislature, the funds went to the Benjamin Franklin Institute of Technology.

In Philadelphia, the bequest did not accumulate quite as well. A century after his death, it totaled $172,000, about one-quarter of what he had projected. Of that sum, three-fourths went to establish Philadelphia's Franklin Institute, still a thriving science museum, with the remainder continued as a loan fund for young tradesmen, much of it given as home mortgages. A century later, in 1990, this fund had reached $2.3 million. Why was it less than half of what Boston had? One Philadelphia partisan charged that Boston had turned its fund into "a savings company for the rich." By focusing on loans to poor individuals, as Franklin intended, Philadelphia had not been as successful in getting repayments.

At that point, Philadelphia Mayor Wilson Goode suggested, one assumes jokingly, that the Ben Franklin money be used to pay for a party featuring *Ben* Vereen and Aretha *Franklin*. Others, more serious, proposed it be used to promote tourism, which caused a popular uproar. The mayor finally appointed a panel of historians, and the state divvied up the money in accordance with their general recommendations. Among the recipients were the Franklin Institute, a variety of community libraries and fire companies, and a group called the Philadelphia Academies that funds scholarships at vocational training programs in the city schools. When the 2001 scholarships were announced, a *Philadelphia Inquirer* columnist pointed out that the diversity among the thirty-four names—including Abimael Acaedevo, Muhammed Hogue, Zrakpa Karpoleh, David Kusiak, Pedro Lopez, and Rany Ly—would have delighted their benefactor. He most certainly would have smiled at one of the small but appropriate examples of his legacy that occurred at that year's Tour de Sol, a race of experimental cars. Some of these scholarship recipients from a poor high school in West Philadelphia used a $4,300 grant from the father of electricity to build a battery-powered car that won the race's Power of Dreams award.[4]

CHAPTER EIGHTEEN

CONCLUSIONS

HISTORY'S REFLECTIONS

"Mankind divides into two classes," the *Nation* magazine declared in 1868: the "natural-born lovers" and the "natural-born haters" of Benjamin Franklin. One reason for this split is that he does not, despite what some commentators claim, embody the American character. Instead, he embodies one aspect of it. He represents one side of a national dichotomy that has existed since the days when he and Jonathan Edwards stood as contrasting cultural figures.[1]

On one side were those, like Edwards and the Mather family, who believed in an anointed elect and in salvation through God's grace alone. They tended to have a religious fervor, a sense of social class and hierarchy, and an appreciation for exalted values over earthly ones. On the other side were the Franklins, those who believed in salvation through good works, whose religion was benevolent and tolerant, and who were unabashedly striving and upwardly mobile.

Out of this grew many related divides in the American character, and Franklin represents one strand: the side of pragmatism versus romanticism, of practical benevolence versus moral crusading. He was on the side of religious tolerance rather than evangelical faith. The side of social mobility rather than an established elite. The side of middle-class virtues rather than more ethereal noble aspirations.

During the three centuries since his birth, the changing assessments of Franklin have tended to reveal less about him than about the values of the people judging him and their attitudes toward a striving middle class. From an august historical stage filled with far less accessible founders, he turned to each new generation with a half-smile and spoke directly in whatever vernacular was in vogue, infuriating some and beguiling others. His reputation thus tended to reflect, or refract, the attitudes of each succeeding era.

In the years right after his death, as personal antagonisms faded, reverence for him grew. Even William Smith, who had battled him in the legislature and on the board of the Academy, gave a respectful eulogy at a memorial service in 1791, in which he dismissed their "unhappy divisions and disputes" and focused instead on Franklin's philanthropy and science. When his daughter afterward said she doubted he believed "one-tenth of what you said of old Ben lightning-rod," he merely laughed heartily.[2]

Franklin's other occasional antagonist, John Adams, likewise mellowed. "Nothing in life has mortified or grieved me more than the necessity which compelled me to oppose him so often as I have," he wrote in a remarkably anguished reassessment in 1811. His earlier harsh criticisms, Adams explained, were in some ways a testament to Franklin's greatness: "Had he been an ordinary man, I should never have taken the trouble to expose the turpitude of his intrigues." He even cast Franklin's lack of religious commitment, which he had once derided as verging on atheism, in a more favorable light: "All sects considered him, and I believe justly, a friend to unlimited toleration." At times, Adams charged, Franklin was hypocritical, a poor negotiator, and a misguided politician. But his essay also included some of the most nuanced words of appreciation written by any contemporary:

> Franklin had a great genius, original, sagacious and inventive, capable of discoveries in science no less than of improvement in the fine arts and the mechanical arts. He had a vast imagination . . . He had wit at will. He had a humor that, when he pleased, was delicate and delightful. He had a satire that was good-natured or caustic, Horace or Juvenal, Swift or Rabelais, at his pleasure. He had talents for irony, allegory

and fable that he could adapt with great skill to the promotion of moral
and political truth. He was a master of that infantile simplicity which
the French call naiveté, which never fails to charm.[3]

By this time, Franklin's view of the central role of the middle class
in American life had triumphed, despite the qualms of those who felt
that this represented a trend toward vulgarization. "By absorbing the
gentility of the aristocracy and the work of the working class, the middling sorts gained a powerful moral hegemony over the whole society,"
historian Gordon Wood noted. He was describing America in the
early 1800s, but he could also have been describing Franklin personally.

Franklin's reputation was further enhanced when his grandson
Temple finally produced an edition of his papers in 1817. Adams
wrote to Temple that his collection "seemed to make me live over
again my life at Passy," which could have been read ambiguously by
those who knew of their bitter feuding at Passy had he not added:
"There is scarce a scratch of his pen that is not worth preserving."
Francis, Lord Jeffrey, a founder of the *Edinburgh Review,* extolled
Franklin's writings for their "homely jocularity," their attempt to "persuade the multitude to virtue," and above all for their emphasis on the
humanistic values that defined the Enlightenment. "This self-taught
American is the most rational, perhaps, of all philosophers. He never
loses sight of common sense in any of his speculations."[4]

This Age of Enlightenment, however, was being replaced in the
early 1800s by a literary era that valued romanticism more than rationality. With the shift came a profound reversal, especially among
those of presumed higher sensibilities, in attitudes toward Franklin.
The romantics admired not reason and intellect but deep emotion,
subjective sensibility, and imagination. They exalted the heroic and
the mystical rather than tolerance and rationality. Their haughty criticisms decimated the reputations of Franklin, Voltaire, Swift, and
other Enlightenment thinkers.[5]

The great romantic poet John Keats was among the many who assaulted Franklin for his lowly sensibilities. He was, Keats wrote his
brother in 1818, "full of mean and thrifty maxims" and a "not sublime

man." Keats's friend and early publisher, the poet and editor Leigh Hunt, heaped scorn on Franklin's "scoundrel maxims" and charged that he was "at the head of those who think that man lives by bread alone." He had "few passions and no imagination," Leigh's indictment continued, and he encouraged mankind to a "love of wealth" that was stripped of "higher callings" or of "heart and soul." Along these lines, Thomas Carlyle, the Scottish critic so in love with romantic heroism, scorned Franklin as "the father of all Yankees," which was perhaps not as denigrating as Carlyle meant it to be.[6]

American transcendentalists such as Thoreau and Emerson, who shared the romantic poets' allergic reaction to rationalism and materialism, also found Franklin too mundane for their rarefied tastes. The more earthy and middle-class backwoodsmen still revered Franklin's *Autobiography*—it was the one book that Davy Crockett carried with him to his death at the Alamo—but a backwoodsman as refined as Thoreau had no place for it when heading off to Walden Pond. Indeed, the first chapter of his Walden journal, on economy, has tables and charts that subtly satirize those used by Franklin. Edgar Allen Poe, in his story "The Business Man," likewise poked glancingly at Franklin and other "methodical" men in describing the rise and methods of his aptly named antihero Peter Proffit.

Franklin appears by name in Herman Melville's semihistorical 1855 novel *Israel Potter*. In the narrative he comes across as a shallow spouter of maxims. But Melville, addressing the reader directly, apologized and noted that Franklin was not quite as one-dimensional as the book portrays him. "Seeking here to depict him in his less exalted habitudes, the narrator feels more as if he were playing with one of the sage's worsted hose than reverentially handling the honored hat which once oracularly sat on his brow." Melville's own judgment on Franklin was that for better or worse, he was very versatile. "Having carefully weighed the world, Franklin could act any part in it." He lists the dozens of pursuits in which Franklin excelled, and then he adds, in the quintessential romantic critique, "Franklin was everything but a poet." (Franklin would have agreed. He wrote that he "approved [of] amusing one's self with poetry now and then, so far as to improve one's language, but no further.")[7]

Emerson provided a similar mixed assessment. "Franklin was one of the most sensible men that ever lived," he wrote his aunt, and was "more useful, more moral and more pure" than Socrates. But he went on to lament, "Franklin's man is a frugal, inoffensive, thrifty citizen, but savors of nothing heroic." Nathaniel Hawthorne has one of his young characters complain that Franklin's maxims "are all about getting money or saving it," in response to which Hawthorne himself observes that there is some virtue in the sayings but that they "teach men but a small portion of their duties."[8]

Along with the rise of romanticism came a growing disdain, among those for whom "bourgeois" would become a term of contempt, for Franklin's beloved urban middle class and its shopkeeping values. It was a snobbery that would come to be shared by very disparate groups: proletarians and aristocrats, radical workers and leisured landowners, Marxists and elitists, intellectuals and anti-intellectuals. Flaubert declared that hatred of the bourgeoisie "is the beginning of all virtue," which was precisely the opposite of what Franklin had preached.[9]

But with the publication of fuller editions of his papers, Franklin's reputation began to revive. After the Civil War, the growth of industry and the onset of the Gilded Age made the times ripe for the glorification of his ideas, and for the next three decades he was the most popular subject of American biography. The 130 novels by Horatio Alger, which would eventually sell twenty million copies, made tales of virtuous boys who rose from rags to riches popular again. Franklin's reputation was also elevated by the emergence of that distinctly American philosophy known as pragmatism, which holds, as Franklin had, that the truth of any proposition, whether it be a scientific or moral or theological or social one, is based on how well it correlates with experimental results and produces a practical outcome.

Mark Twain, a literary heir who cloaked his humor in the same homespun cloth, had a wonderful time poking friendly fun at Franklin, who "prostituted his talents to the invention of maxims and aphorisms calculated to inflict suffering upon the rising generation of all subsequent ages . . . boys who might otherwise have been happy." But

Twain was actually a grudging admirer, and even more so were the great capitalists who took Franklin's maxims seriously.[10]

The industrialist Thomas Mellon, who erected a statue of Franklin in his bank's headquarters, declared that Franklin had inspired him to leave his family's farm near Pittsburgh and go into business. "I regard the reading of Franklin's *Autobiography* as the turning point of my life," he wrote. "Here was Franklin, poorer than myself, who by industry, thrift and frugality had become learned and wise, and elevated to wealth and fame . . . The maxims of 'poor Richard' exactly suited my sentiments. I read the book again and again, and wondered if I might not do something in the same line by similar means." Andrew Carnegie was similarly stimulated. Not only did Franklin's success story provide him guidance in business, it also inspired his philanthropy, especially his devotion to the creation of public libraries.[11]

Franklin was praised as "the first great American" by the definitive historian of that period, Frederick Jackson Turner. "His life is the story of American common-sense in its highest form," he wrote in 1887, "applied to business, to politics, to science, to diplomacy, to religion, to philanthropy." He also was championed by the period's most influential editor, William Dean Howells of *Harper's* magazine. "He was a very great man," Howells wrote in 1888, "and the objects to which he dedicated himself with an unfailing mixture of motive were such as concerned the immediate comfort of men and the advancement of knowledge." Despite the fact that he was "cynically incredulous of ideals and beliefs sacred to most of us," he was "instrumental in promoting the moral and material welfare of the race."[12]

The pendulum again swung against Franklin in the 1920s, as Gilded Age individualism fell out of intellectual favor. Max Weber famously dissected America's middle-class work ethic from a quasi-Marxist perspective in *The Protestant Ethic and the Spirit of Capitalism*, which quoted Franklin (and Poor Richard) extensively as a prime example of the "philosophy of avarice." "All Franklin's moral attitudes," wrote Weber, "are colored with utilitarianism," and he accused Franklin of believing only in "the earning of more and more money combined with the strict avoidance of all spontaneous engagement of life."

The literary critic Van Wyck Brooks distinguished between America's highbrow and lowbrow cultures, and he placed Franklin as the founder of the latter. He exemplified, Brooks said, a "catchpenny opportunism" and a "two-dimensional wisdom." The poet William Carlos Williams added that he was "our wise prophet of chicanery." And in his novel *Babbitt*, Sinclair Lewis belittled bourgeois values and civic boosterism. In a barb aimed at Franklin's oft-stated creed, Lewis wrote: "If you had asked Babbitt what his religion was, he would have answered in sonorous Boosters' Club rhetoric, 'My religion is to serve my fellow men, to honor my brother as myself, and to do my bit to make life happier for one and all.' "[13]

The most vicious and amusing—and in most ways, misguided—attack on Franklin came in 1923 from the English critic and novelist D. H. Lawrence. His essay is, at times, a stream-of-consciousness rant that assaults Franklin for the unromantic and bourgeois nature of the virtues reflected in his *Autobiography:*

> Doctor Franklin. Snuff-colored little man! Immortal soul and all! The immortal soul part was a sort of cheap insurance policy. Benjamin had no concern, really, with the immortal soul. He was too busy with social man . . . I do not like him.
>
> I can remember, when I was a little boy, my father used to buy a scrubby yearly almanac with the sun and moon and stars on the cover. And it used to prophesy bloodshed and famine. But also crammed in corners it had little anecdotes and humorisms, with a moral tag. And I used to have my little priggish laugh at the woman who counted her chickens before they were hatched and so forth, and I was convinced that honesty was the best policy, also a little priggishly. The author of these bits was Poor Richard, and Poor Richard was Benjamin Franklin, writing in Philadelphia well over a hundred years before. And probably I haven't got over those Poor Richard tags yet. I rankle still with them. They are thorns in young flesh.
>
> Because, although I still believe that honesty is the best policy, I dislike policy altogether; though it is just as well not to count your chickens before they are hatched, it's still more hateful to count them with gloating when they are hatched. It has taken me many years and countless smarts to get out of that barbed wire moral enclosure that Poor Richard rigged up . . .
>
> Which brings us right back to our question, what's wrong with Benjamin, that we can't stand him? . . . I am a moral animal. And I'm going

to remain such. I'm not going to be turned into a virtuous little automaton as Benjamin would have me . . . And now I, at least, know why I can't stand Benjamin. He tries to take away my wholeness and my dark forest, my freedom.

As part of the essay, Lawrence rewrote Franklin's thirteen virtues to make them more to his romantic liking. Instead of Franklin's definition of industry ("Be always employed in something useful") Lawrence substituted "Serve the Holy Ghost; never serve mankind." Instead of Franklin's definition of justice ("Wrong none by doing injuries"), Lawrence proclaimed, "The only justice is to follow the sincere intuition of the soul, angry or gentle."

It is a bracing essay, but it should be noted that Lawrence, in addition to having an odd and self-indulgent definition of justice, aimed his assault not on the real-life Franklin but on the character he created in Poor Richard and in the *Autobiography*. In addition, Lawrence got a few facts wrong, among them attributing to Franklin the maxim "Honesty is the best policy," which sounds like him but actually is from Cervantes, just as the one about not counting unhatched chickens is from Aesop.[14]

Lawrence's approach was echoed in a more substantive, if less dramatic, attack on Franklin's bourgeois Babbittry by Charles Angoff in his *Literary History of the American People*, published in 1931. Carlyle's description of Franklin as the father of all the Yankees was, Angoff declared, a "libel against the tribe" that had produced fine writers such as Hawthorne and Thoreau. "It would be more accurate to call Franklin the father of all the Kiwanians," Angoff sneered, and he was brutal about what he saw as the "low order" of Franklin's thinking:

> Franklin represented the least praiseworthy qualities of the inhabitants of the new world: miserliness, fanatical practicality, and lack of interest in what are usually known as spiritual things. Babbittry was not a new thing in America, but he made a religion of it, and by his tremendous success with it grafted it upon the American people so securely that the national genius is still suffering from it . . . Not a word about nobility, not a word about honor, not a word about grandeur of soul, not a word about charity of mind! . . . He had a cheap and shabby soul, and the upper levels of the mind were far beyond his reach.[15]

The Great Depression of the 1930s reminded people that the virtues of industry and frugality, of helping others and making sure that the community held together, did not deserve to be dismissed as trivial and mundane. Franklin's reputation again made a comeback. The pragmatist philosopher Herbert Schneider, in his book *The Puritan Mind,* pointed out that the previous attacks had mainly been on *Poor Richard's* preachings rather than on how Franklin really lived his life, which did not focus on the pursuit of wealth for its own sake.

Carl Van Doren, Schneider's colleague at Columbia, in 1938 fleshed out this point in his glorious literary biography of Franklin. "He moved through this world in a humorous mastery of it," Van Doren concluded. And the great historian of science, I. Bernard Cohen, began his lifelong work of showing that Franklin's scientific achievements placed him in the pantheon with Newton. Franklin's experiments, he wrote in 1941, "afforded a basis for the explanation for all the known phenomena of electricity." [16]

Franklin also became the patron saint of the self-help movement. Dale Carnegie studied the *Autobiography* when writing *How to Win Friends and Influence People,* which, after its publication in 1937, helped launch a craze that persists to this day for books featuring simple rules and secrets about how to succeed in business and in life. As E. Digby Baltzell, a sociologist of America's elite, has noted, Franklin's *Autobiography* was "the first and greatest manual of careerist Babbittry ever written." [17]

Stephen Covey, the guru of the genre, referred to Franklin's system in developing his bestseller *The Seven Habits of Highly Effective People,* and a national chain of stores now sell "FranklinCovey Organizers" and other paraphernalia featuring Franklin's ideas. By the beginning of the twenty-first century, the self-help shelves of bookstores were filled with titles such as *Ben's Book of Virtues: Ben Franklin's Simple Weekly Plan for Success and Happiness; Ben Franklin's 12 Rules of Management: The Founding Father of American Business Solves Your Toughest Problems; Benjamin Franklin's the Art of Virtue: His Formula for Successful Living; The Ben Franklin Factor: Selling One to One;* and *Healthy, Wealthy and Wise: Principals for Successful Living from the Life of Benjamin Franklin.* [18]

In the academic world, Franklin was the subject of generally favorable books as the three hundredth anniversary of his birth approached. In *The First American,* H. W. Brands of Texas A&M sympathetically described the evolution of Franklin's character in a solid and balanced narrative biography. "To genius he joined a passion for virtue," he concluded. In 2002, Edmund S. Morgan, the retired and revered Sterling Professor of History at Yale, wrote a wonderfully astute character analysis based on an exhaustive reading of Franklin's papers. "We may discover," Morgan declared, "a man with a wisdom about himself that comes only to the great of heart."[19]

In the popular imagination, Franklin came to be viewed as a figure of fun, rather than as the serious thinker admired by Hume or the political manipulator resented by Adams. During an era that was at times trivial and untroubled, filled with sexual winks and unfettered entrepreneurship, Franklin was enlisted into the spirit. He became a jovial lecher dabbling in statecraft in such plays as *1776* and *Ben Franklin in Paris,* a sprightly old spokesman for everything from cookies to mutual funds, and a genial sage whose adages were designed to entertain rather than intimidate aspiring young workers.

"Today we know Benjamin Franklin mainly from an old advertising image: an elderly man in knickers, long coat, and spectacles, with a bald crown and long hair—a zealot foolishly determined to fly a kite during a thunderstorm," the historian Alan Taylor has written. "He no longer arouses either controversy or adulation—merely laughter. We only dimly sense his importance in the nineteenth and early twentieth centuries as the paragon of, and the pattern for, American middle-class values."[20]

To the social commentator David Brooks, this anodyne version of Franklin embodies both the entrepreneurial and moral tenor of America at the beginning of the twenty-first century. He was the one historic figure from the American pantheon, Brooks wrote, "who would be instantly at home in an office park."

> He'd probably join the chorus of all those techno-enthusiasts who claim that the internet and bio-tech breakthroughs are going to transform life on earth wonderfully; he shared that passion for progress. At the same time, he'd be completely at home with the irony and gen-

tle cynicism that is the prevailing conversational tone in those buildings . . .

But then, Franklin would be at home in much of contemporary
America. He'd share the values of the comfortably middle class; he was
optimistic, genial, and kind, and his greatest flaw was his self-approving
complacency. One can easily picture him traipsing through a shopping
mall enchanted by the cheerful abundance and the clever marketing. At
the same time, he'd admire all the effort young Americans put into civic
activism, and the way older Americans put religion to good use through
faith-based community organizations.

Franklin had been unfairly attacked over the years, Brooks concluded, by romantics whose real targets were capitalism and middle-
class morality. "But now the main problem is excess Franklinism,
and we've got to figure out how to bring to today's America the
tragic sense and the moral gravity that was so lacking in its Founding
Yuppie."[21]

THE LEDGER BOOK

This perceived lack of moral gravity and spiritual depth is the most
serious charge against Franklin. In both his life and his writings, he
sometimes displayed a lack of commitment, anguish, poetry, or soul. A
sentence he wrote to his sister Jane in 1771 captured this complacency
and dearth of passion: "Upon the whole, I am much disposed to like
the world as I find it, and to doubt my own judgment as to what would
mend it."[22]

His religious beliefs, especially early in life, were largely a calculus
of what credos would prove useful for people to believe, rather than an
expression of sincere inner convictions. Deism was appealing, but he
discovered it was not all that helpful, so he gave it a moral gloss and
seldom troubled his soul with questions about grace, salvation, the divinity of Christ, or other profound issues that did not lend themselves
to practical inquiry. He was at the other extreme from the anguished
soul-searching Puritans. As he had no factual evidence about what
was divinely inspired, he settled instead for the simple creed that the
best way to serve God was doing good to others.

His moral beliefs were likewise plain and earthly, focused on practical ways to benefit others. He espoused the middle-class virtues of a shopkeeper, and he had little interest in proselytizing about higher ethical aspirations. He wrestled more with what he called "errata" than he did with sin.

As a scientist, he had a feel for the mechanical workings of the world but little appreciation for abstract theories or the sublime. He was a great experimenter and clever inventor, with an emphasis on things useful. But he had neither the temperament nor the training to be a profound conceptualizer.

In most of the endeavors of his soul and mind, his greatness sprang more from his practicality than from profundity or poetry. In science he was more an Edison than a Newton, in literature more a Twain than a Shakespeare, in philosophy more a Dr. Johnson than a Bishop Berkeley, and in politics more a Burke than a Locke.

In his personal life as well, there was likewise a lack of soulful commitment and deep passion. He frequented many antechambers, but few inner chambers. His love of travel reflected the spirit of a young runaway, one who had run from his family in Boston, from Deborah when he first thought of marrying, and from William just before his wedding. Throughout his life he had few emotional bonds tying him to any one place, and he seemed to glide through the world the way he glided through relationships.

His friendships with men often ended badly: his brother James, his friends John Collins and James Ralph, his printing partners Samuel Keimer and Hugh Meredith. He was a sociable man who liked clubs that offered enlightening conversations and activities, but the friendships he formed with his fellow men were more affable than intimate. He had a genial affection for his wife, but not enough love to prevent him from spending fifteen of the last seventeen years of their marriage an ocean away. His relationship with her was a practical one, as was the case with his London landlady, Margaret Stevenson. With his many women admirers, he preferred flirting rather than making serious commitments, and he retreated into playful detachment at any sign of danger. His most passionate relationship was with his son William, but that fire turned into ice. Only to his grandson Temple did he show unalloyed affection.

He could also, despite his professed belief in the virtue of sincerity, come across as conniving. He wrote his first hoax at 16 and the last on his deathbed; he misled his employer Samuel Keimer when scheming to start a newspaper; he perfected indirection as a conversational artifice; and he utilized the appearance of virtue as well as its reality. "In a place and a time that celebrated sincerity while practicing insincerity, Franklin seemed far too accomplished at the latter," Taylor notes. "Owing to his smooth manner and shifting tactics, Franklin invited suspicions far beyond his actual intent to trick."[23]

All of which has led some critics to dismiss even Franklin's civic accomplishments as the mundane aspirations of a shallow soul. The apotheosis of such criticism is in Vernon Parrington's famous *Main Currents in American Thought:*

> A man who is less concerned with the golden pavements of the City of God than that the cobblestones on Chestnut Street in Philadelphia should be well and evenly laid, who troubles less to save his soul from burning hereafter than to protect his neighbors' houses by organizing an efficient fire-company, who is less regardful of the light that never was on sea or land than of a new-model street lamp to light the steps of a belated wayfarer—such a man, obviously, does not reveal the full nature of human aspiration.[24]

It is Parrington's haughty use of the word "obviously" that provides us with a good launching point for a defense of Franklin. "Obviously," perhaps, to Parrington and others of rarefied sensibility whose contributions to society are not so mundane as a library, university, fire company, bifocals, stove, lightning rod, or, for that matter, democratic constitutions. Their disdain is in part a yearning for the loftier ideals that could sometimes seem lacking in Franklin's soul. Yet it is also, in part, a snobbery about the earthly concerns and middle-class values that he appreciated.

So how are we, as Franklin the bookkeeper would have wished, to balance the ledger fairly? As he did in his own version of a moral calculus, we can list all the Pros on the other side and determine if, as I think is the case, they outweigh the Cons.

First we must rescue Franklin from the schoolbook caricature of a genial codger flying kites in the rain and spouting homespun maxims about a penny saved being a penny earned. We must also rescue him from the critics who would confuse him with the character he carefully crafted in his *Autobiography*.[25]

When Max Weber says that Franklin's ethics are based only on the earning of more money, and when D.H. Lawrence reduces him to a man who pinched pennies and morals, they betray the lack of even a passing familiarity with the man who retired from business at 42, dedicated himself to civic and scientific endeavors, gave up much of his public salaries, eschewed getting patents on his inventions, and consistently argued that the accumulation of excess wealth and the idle indulgence in frivolous luxuries should not be socially sanctioned. Franklin did not view penny saving as an end in itself but as a path that permitted young tradesmen to be able to display higher virtues, community spirit, and citizenship. "It is hard for an empty sack to stand upright," both he and Poor Richard proclaimed.[26]

To assess Franklin properly, we must view him, instead, in all his complexity. He was not a frivolous man, nor a shallow one, nor a simple one. There are many layers to peel back as he stands before us so coyly disguised, both to history and to himself, as a plain character unadorned by wigs and other pretensions.

Let's begin with the surface layer, the Franklin who serves as a lightning rod for the Jovian bolts from those who disdain middle-class values. There is something to be said—and Franklin said it well and often—for the personal virtues of diligence, honesty, industry, and temperance, especially when they are viewed as a means toward a nobler and more benevolent end.

The same is true of the civic virtues Franklin both practiced and preached. His community improvement associations and other public endeavors helped to create a social order that promoted the common good. Few people have ever worked as hard, or done as much, to inculcate virtue and character in themselves and their communities.[27]

Were such efforts mundane, as Parrington and some others charge? Perhaps in part, but in his autobiography, after recounting his effort to pave Philadelphia's streets, Franklin provided an eloquent defense against such aspersions:

Some may think these trifling matters not worth minding or relating; but when they consider that though dust blown into the eyes of a single person, or into a single shop on a windy day, is but of small importance, yet the great number of the instances in a populous city, and its frequent repetitions give it weight and consequence, perhaps they will not censure very severely those who bestow some attention to affairs of this seemingly low nature. Human felicity is produced not so much by great pieces of good fortune that seldom happen, as by little advantages that occur every day.[28]

Likewise, although a religious faith based on fervor can be inspiring, there is also something admirable about a religious outlook based on humility and openness. Charles Angoff has charged that "his main contribution to the religious question was little more than a good-natured tolerance." Well, perhaps so, but the concept of good-natured religious tolerance was in fact no small advance for civilization in the eighteenth century. It was one of the greatest contributions to arise out of the Enlightenment, more indispensable than that of the most profound theologians of the era.

In both his life and his writings, Franklin became a preeminent proponent of this creed of tolerance. He developed it with great humor in his tales and with an earnest depth in his life and letters. In a world that was then (as, alas, it still is now) bloodied by those who seek to impose theocracies, he helped to create a new type of nation that could draw strength from its religious pluralism. As Garry Wills argued in his book *Under God,* this "more than anything else, made the United States a new thing on earth."[29]

Franklin also made a more subtle religious contribution: he detached the Puritan spirit of industriousness from the sect's rigid dogma. Weber, with his contempt for middle-class values, disdained the Protestant ethic, and Lawrence felt that Franklin's demystified version of it could not sate the dark soul. This ethic was, however, instrumental in instilling the virtue and character that built a nation. "He remade the Puritan in him into a zealous bourgeois," writes John Updike, whose novels explore these very themes, "and certainly this is his main meaning for the American psyche: a release into the Enlightenment of the energies cramped under Puritanism." As Henry Steele

Commager declared in *The American Mind*, "In a Franklin could be merged the virtues of Puritanism without its defects, the illumination of the Enlightenment without its heat."[30]

So, does Franklin deserve the accolade, accorded by his great contemporary David Hume, of America's "first philosopher"? To some extent, he does. Disentangling morality from theology was an important achievement of the Enlightenment, and Franklin was its avatar in America. In addition, by relating morality to everyday human consequences, Franklin laid the foundation for the most influential of America's homegrown philosophies, pragmatism. His moral and religious thinking, when judged in the context of his actions, writes James Campbell, "becomes a rich philosophical defense of service to advance the common good." What it lacked in spiritual profundity, it made up for in practicality and potency.[31]

What about the charge that Franklin was too much of a compromiser instead of a heroic man of principle? Yes, he played both sides for a few years in the 1770s, when he was trying to mediate between England and America. Yes, he was somewhat squishy in dealing with the Stamp Act. He had taught himself as a young tradesman to avoid disputatious assertions, and his habit of benignly smiling while he listened to all sorts of people made him seem at times duplicitous or insinuating.

But once again, there's something to be said for Franklin's outlook, for his pragmatism and occasional willingness to compromise. He believed in having the humility to be open to different opinions. For him that was not merely a practical virtue, but a moral one as well. It was based on the tenet, so fundamental to most moral systems, that every individual deserves respect. During the Constitutional Convention, for example, he was willing to compromise some of his beliefs to play a critical role in the conciliation that produced a near-perfect document. It could not have been accomplished if the hall had contained only crusaders who stood on unwavering principle. Compromisers may not make great heroes, but they do make great democracies.

More important, Franklin did in fact believe, uncompromisingly, in a few high principles—very important ones for shaping a new nation—that he stuck to throughout his life. Having learned from his brother a resistance to establishment power, he was ever unwavering in his opposition to arbitrary authority. That led him to be unflinching in opposing the unfair tax policies the Penns tried to impose, even when it would have served his personal advantage to go along. It also meant that, despite his desire to find a compromise with Britain during the 1770s, he adhered firmly to the principle that American citizens and their legislatures must not be treated as subservient.

Similarly, he helped to create, and came to symbolize, a new political order in which rights and power were based not on the happenstance of heritage but on merit and virtue and hard work. He rose up the social ladder, from runaway apprentice to dining with kings, in a way that would become quintessentially American. But in doing so he resolutely resisted, as a matter of principle, sometimes to a fur-capped extreme, taking on elitist pretensions.

Franklin's belief that he could best serve God by serving his fellow man may strike some as mundane, but it was in truth a worthy creed that he deeply believed and faithfully followed. He was remarkably versatile in this service. He devised legislatures and lightning rods, lotteries and lending libraries. He sought practical ways to make stoves less smoky and commonwealths less corrupt. He organized neighborhood constabularies and international alliances. He combined two types of lenses to create bifocals and two concepts of representation to foster the nation's federal compromise. As his friend the French statesman Turgot said in his famous epigram, *Eripuit cœlo fulmen sceptrumque tyrannis*, he snatched lightning from the sky and the scepter from tyrants.

All of this made him the most accomplished American of his age and the most influential in inventing the type of society America would become. Indeed, the roots of much of what distinguishes the nation can be found in Franklin: its cracker-barrel humor and wisdom; its technological ingenuity; its pluralistic tolerance; its ability to weave together individualism and community cooperation; its philosophical pragmatism; its celebration of meritocratic mobility; the idealistic streak ingrained in its foreign policy; and the Main Street (or Market Street) virtues that serve as the foundation for its civic values. He was egalitarian in what became the American sense: he approved of individuals making their way to wealth through diligence and talent, but opposed giving special privileges to people based on their birth.

His focus tended to be on how ordinary issues affect everyday lives, and on how ordinary people could build a better society. But that did not make him an ordinary man. Nor did it reflect a shallowness. On the contrary, his vision of how to build a new type of nation was both revolutionary and profound. Although he did not embody each and every transcendent or poetic ideal, he did embody the most practical and useful ones. That was his goal, and a worthy one it was.

Through it all, he trusted the hearts and minds of his fellow leather-aprons more than he did those of any inbred elite. He saw middle-class values as a source of social strength, not as something to be derided. His guiding principle was a "dislike of everything that tended to debase the spirit of the common people." Few of his fellow founders felt this comfort with democracy so fully, and none so intuitively.

From the age of 21, when he first gathered his Junto, he held true to a fundamental ideal with unwavering and at times heroic fortitude: a faith in the wisdom of the common citizen that was manifest in an appreciation for democracy and an opposition to all forms of tyranny. It was a noble ideal, one that was transcendent and poetic in its own way.

And it turned out to be, as history proved, a practical and useful one as well.

CAST OF CHARACTERS

JOHN ADAMS (1735–1826). Massachusetts patriot, second U.S. president. Worked with Franklin editing Jefferson's draft of the Declaration of Independence and negotiating with Lord Howe in 1776. Arrived in Paris April 1778 to work with Franklin as commissioner, left March 1779, returned February 1780, left for Holland August 1780, returned for final peace talks with Britain October 1782.

WILLIAM ALLEN (1704–1780). Pennsylvania merchant and chief justice who was initially a friend but broke with Franklin by supporting the Proprietors.

BENJAMIN "BENNY" FRANKLIN BACHE (1769–1798). Son of Sally and Richard Bache, traveled to Paris with grandfather Franklin and cousin Temple in 1776, sent to school in Geneva, learned printing in Passy, set up by Franklin as a printer in Philadelphia, published antifederalist paper *The American Aurora*, arrested for libeling President John Adams. Died of yellow fever at 29.

RICHARD BACHE (1737–1811). Struggling merchant who married Franklin's daughter, Sally, in 1767. They had seven children who survived infancy: Benjamin, William, Louis, Elizabeth, Deborah, Sarah, and Richard.

EDWARD BANCROFT (1745–1821). Massachusetts-born physician and stock speculator who met Franklin in London, became secretary to the American commission in France during the American Revolution, and turned out to be a British spy.

PIERRE-AUGUSTIN CARON DE BEAUMARCHAIS (1732–1799). Dramatic dramatist, stock speculator, and arms dealer. Helped arrange French aid to America during the Revolution and became a friend of Franklin's in Passy. Wrote *The Barber of Seville* in 1775 and *Figaro* in 1784.

ANDREW BRADFORD (1686–1742). Philadelphia printer and publisher of *American Weekly Mercury*, became a competitor of Franklin's and supported the Proprietary elite.

WILLIAM BRADFORD (1663–1752). Pioneering printer in New York whom Franklin met when running away from Boston and who introduced him to his son Andrew in Philadelphia.

ANNE-LOUISE BOIVIN D'HARDANCOURT BRILLON DE JOUY (1744–1824). Franklin's neighbor in Passy, an accomplished harpsichordist who became one of Franklin's favorite female friends. Wrote "Marche des Insurgents" to commemorate American victory at Saratoga.

WILLIAM PITT THE ELDER, EARL OF CHATHAM (1708–1778). As the "Great Commoner," was prime minister during Seven Years' War, 1756–63. Accepted peerage in 1766. Opposed repressive Tory measures. Negotiated with Franklin in early 1776, parking his carriage outside Mrs. Stevenson's boarding house.

JACQUES-DONATIEN LERAY DE CHAUMONT (1725–1803). Merchant, aspiring war profiteer, and former slave trader. Franklin's landlord in Passy.

CADWALLADER COLDEN (1688–1776). New York politician and naturalist. Corresponded frequently with Franklin about experiments and science.

PETER COLLINSON (1694–1768). London merchant and scientist who helped Franklin set up the library and furnished him with electricity tracts and equipment.

MARIE-JEAN-ANTOINE-NICOLAS CARITAT, MARQUIS DE CONDORCET (1743–1794). Mathematician and biographer, contributor to Diderot's *Encyclopédie*. Franklin's close friend in Paris. Poisoned during the French Revolution.

SAMUEL COOPER (1725–1783). Boston politician and minister. An advocate of independence and close confidant of Franklin.

THOMAS CUSHING (1725–1788). Massachusetts politician and its speaker of the House 1766–74. A frequent correspondent of Franklin's and the recipient of the Hutchinson letters.

SILAS DEANE (1737–1789). Connecticut diplomat and merchant. Went to France in July 1776, just before Franklin, to solicit support. Became an ally of Franklin's but antagonized Arthur Lee, who accused him of corruption and helped to force his recall.

WILLIAM DENNY (1709–1765). British army officer who was the Penns' appointed governor 1756–59.

FRANCIS DASHWOOD, BARON LE DESPENCER (1708–1781). British politician and, from 1766 to 1781, the postmaster who protected and then had to fire his friend Franklin as the deputy postmaster for America. At his country house, Franklin had the pleasure of hearing his hoax "An Edict from the King of Prussia" fool people.

JOHN DICKINSON (1732–1808). Philadelphia politician who opposed Franklin in the fight with the Proprietors and was more cautious about independence. Wrote "Letters from a Pennsylvania Farmer," which Franklin (not knowing who was the author) helped publish in London.

JOHN FOTHERGILL (1712–1780). Quaker physician in London. Published Franklin's electricity papers in 1751 and served as his doctor in England. "I can hardly conceive that a better man has ever lived," Franklin once said.

ABIAH FOLGER FRANKLIN (1667–1752). Married Josiah Franklin in 1689 and had ten children, including Benjamin.

BENJAMIN FRANKLIN "THE ELDER" (1650–1727). The brother of Franklin's father Josiah. Encouraged his nephew (unsuccessfully) in poetry and preaching and came to live in Boston in 1715 as a retired widower.

DEBORAH READ FRANKLIN (1705?–1774). Franklin's loyal, common-

law wife. May have been born in Birmingham, but was raised on Market Street in Philadelphia and never left that neighborhood for the rest of her life. First saw Franklin in October 1723 when he straggled off the boat into Philadelphia. Married John Rogers, who abandoned her. Entered common-law union with Franklin in 1730. Served as bookkeeper and manager of print shop. Defended home during Stamp Act riots. Two children: Francis "Franky," who died at age 4, and Sarah "Sally," who in many ways resembled her.

JAMES FRANKLIN (1697–1735). Franklin's brother and early master. Started *New England Courant* in 1721 and was a pioneer in provocative American journalism.

JANE FRANKLIN [MECOM] (1712–1794). Franklin's youngest sister and favorite sibling.

JOHN FRANKLIN (1690–1756). Franklin's brother. Became a soap and candle maker in Rhode Island and then (with Franklin's help) the postmaster in Boston. Franklin made a flexible catheter for him.

JOSIAH FRANKLIN (1657–1745). A silk dyer born in Ecton, England. Emigrated to America in 1683, where he became a candle maker. Had seven children by his first wife, Anne Child, and ten (inluding Benjamin Franklin) by his second wife, Abiah Folger Franklin.

SARAH "SALLY" FRANKLIN [BACHE] (1743–1808). Loyal only daughter. Married Richard Bache in 1767. Served as hostess and homemaker when Franklin returned to Philadelphia in 1776 and 1785. Like her mother, she never traveled to Europe with him, but she did travel to Boston with him in 1763.

[WILLIAM] TEMPLE FRANKLIN (ca. 1760–1823). Illegitimate son of William Franklin. Grandfather helped to raise and educate him, brought him back to America in 1775, took him to Paris in 1776, retained his loyalty in struggle with the boy's father. Had his own illegitimate children. Published a haphazard collection of his grandfather's writings.

WILLIAM FRANKLIN (ca. 1730–1813). Illegitimate son raised by Franklin. Accompanied him to England, became a Tory sympathizer, appointed royal governor of New Jersey, remained loyal to the Crown, and irrevocably split with his father.

JOSEPH GALLOWAY (ca. 1731–1803). Philadelphia politician and longtime ally of Franklin in fight with the Proprietors. His home, Trevose, was the site of a tense meeting between Franklin and his son. Remained loyal to the Crown and split with Franklin during the Revolution.

DAVID HALL (1714–1772). Recommended by William Strahan, moved from London in 1744 to become Franklin's shop foreman and in 1748 took over running the business as managing partner.

ANDREW HAMILTON (ca. 1676–1741). Speaker of the Pennsylvania Assembly for much of the 1730s. Defended John Peter Zenger in his libel trial and usually supported Franklin.

JAMES HAMILTON (1710–1783). Andrew's son. Governor of Pennsylvania 1748–54 and 1759–63. As a Mason, trustee of the Library Company and the Academy, he was Franklin's friend, but they were often politically opposed.

ANNE-CATHERINE DE LIGNIVILLE HELVÉTIUS (1719–1800). Franklin's close friend in Auteuil, near Passy. Franklin proposed marriage, more than half-seriously, in 1780. Widowed in 1771 from noted philosopher and wealthy farmer-general Claude-Adrien Helvétius.

LORD RICHARD HOWE (1726–1799). British admiral. Joined the Royal Navy at age 14 and became commander in America. First negotiated with Franklin secretly under cover of chess games at his sister's in late 1775. Met Franklin and Adams on Staten Island in September 1776.

WILLIAM HOWE (1729–1814). Younger brother of Admiral Lord Richard Howe. Fought in the French and Indian War and then the Battle of Bunker Hill. In 1775, replaced General Thomas Gage as the commander of British land troops in the colonies, serving under the overall command of his brother. Became Viscount Howe in 1799.

DAVID HUME (1711–1776). Scottish historian and philosopher. With Locke and Berkeley, one of the greatest British empirical analysts. Franklin befriended him in London and visited him in Edinburgh in 1759 and 1771.

THOMAS HUTCHINSON (1711–1780). Originally a friend of Franklin's and an ally at the Albany Conference of 1754. Became royal governor of Massachusetts in 1771. House burned during Stamp Act crisis, and Franklin wrote him sympathetically. But in 1773, Franklin got hold of some of his letters and sent them to allies in Massachusetts, which caused Franklin to face a grilling by British ministers in the Cockpit.

HENRY HOME, LORD KAMES (1696–1782). Scottish judge and moral philosopher, with interests in farming and science and history, whom Franklin first met on his 1759 trip to Scotland.

SAMUEL KEIMER (ca. 1688–1742). London printer. Moved to Philadelphia in 1722 and gave Franklin his first job there the following year. Franklin had a stormy relationship with him and became his competitor; Keimer left for Barbados in 1730.

SIR WILLIAM KEITH (1680–1749). Governor of Pennsylvania 1717–26. Became an unreliable patron to Franklin in 1724 and sent him to London without a letter of credit he had promised. Keith was fired when he defied the Proprietors. Eventually imprisoned as a debtor in the Old Bailey, where he died.

ARTHUR LEE (1740–1792). Virginia politician and diplomat. Began his personal opposition to Franklin while both were in London in late 1760s. His disputes with Franklin intensified when both were commissioners in Paris in 1777. Remained a Franklin foe along with his powerful brothers: William, Richard Henry, and Francis Lightfoot Lee.

JEAN-BAPTISTE LE ROY (1720–1800). French scientist. Shared Franklin's interest in electricity and became his close friend in Paris.

ROBERT LIVINGSTON (1746–1813). New York statesman, foreign secretary of the United States 1781–83.

JAMES LOGAN (1674–1751). Prominent Philadelphia Quaker and gentleman, whom Franklin befriended as an adviser to the library.

COTTON MATHER (1663–1728). Prominent Puritan clergyman and famed witch-hunter. Succeeded his father, Increase Mather, as pastor of Boston's Old North Church. His writings inspired Franklin's civic projects.

HUGH MEREDITH (ca. 1697–ca. 1749). Printer at Keimer's shop. Became a member of Franklin's Junto and then his first partner in 1728. But when he resumed drinking, Franklin bought him out in 1730, and he left for North Carolina.

ABBÉ ANDRÉ MORELLET (1727–1819). Economist, contributor to the *Encyclopédie*, and lover of wine. Met Franklin in 1772 at Lord Shelburne house party, where Franklin did his trick stilling waves with oil. Part of Madame Helvétius's circle.

ROBERT HUNTER MORRIS (ca. 1700–1764). The Penns' governor in Pennsylvania 1754–56. Fought with Franklin over taxing the Proprietors' estates. Son of New Jersey governor Lewis Morris.

JEAN-ANTOINE NOLLET (1700–1770). French scientist and electrician. Jealous opponent of Franklin's theories.

ISAAC NORRIS (1701–1766). Philadelphia merchant, speaker of the Assembly 1750–64; allied with Franklin in opposition to the Proprietors.

THOMAS PAINE (1737–1809). Failed corset-maker and a tax clerk in England. Charmed Franklin, who provided a letter of introduction to Richard Bache, which led to a job as a journalist and printer in Philadelphia. Wrote *Common Sense* in January 1776, which paved the way for the Declaration of Independence. Wrote *The Age of Reason*, but delayed publishing it until 1794, perhaps after Franklin warned that people would find it heretical.

JAMES PARKER (ca. 1714–1770). New York printer, fled an apprenticeship with William Bradford, and Franklin set him up in New York as a printing partner, local postmaster, and then comptroller of the postal system. Franklin corresponded with him about a plan for union before the Albany Conference.

JOHN PENN (1729–1785). Grandson of Pennsylvania founder William Penn. Served as his family's governor there for most of 1763–76. Went with Franklin to Albany Conference in 1754, solicited Franklin's help during Paxton Boys riots, but soon was a political foe over Proprietary rights and taxes.

THOMAS PENN (1702–1775). Son of William and uncle of John Penn. Became, in 1746, the primary Proprietor of Pennsylvania, based in London with his brother Richard. One of Franklin's foremost political enemies.

RICHARD PETERS (ca. 1704–1776). Anglican clergyman. Came to Pennsylvania in 1734 as the right hand of the Penn family. Became one of Franklin's adversaries even as they worked together building the Academy.

JOSEPH PRIESTLEY (1733–1804). Theologian who turned to science. Met Franklin in 1765. Wrote a history of electricity (1767) that stressed Franklin's work. Isolated oxygen and other gases.

SIR JOHN PRINGLE (1707–1782). Physician who became Franklin's close English friend and traveling companion.

CATHERINE "CATY" RAY [GREENE] (1731–1794). Met Franklin on his 1754 trip to New England and became his first major young female flirtation. Married in 1758 to William Greene, who became governor of Rhode Island, but remained a friend of Franklin and his family. (She signed her name "Caty," but Franklin tended to address her as "Katy" or "Katie.")

LOUIS-ALEXANDRE, DUC DE LA ROCHEFOUCAULD (1743–1792). Scientist and nobleman. Translated the American state constitutions for publication in France at Franklin's request. Stoned to death during the French Revolution.

EARL OF SHELBURNE (1737–1805). English friend at whose house party Franklin did his oil-on-water trick. Later, colonial secretary and prime minister during Franklin's 1782 British-American peace talks.

JONATHAN SHIPLEY, BISHOP OF ST. ASAPH (1714–1788). Anglican bishop at whose house, Twyford, near Winchester, Franklin began his autobiography.

WILLIAM SHIRLEY (1694–1771). London lawyer. Moved to Boston as governor of Massachusetts 1741–57 and briefly as commander of British troops. He and Franklin corresponded after the Albany Conference of 1754 on the shape an American colonial union should take.

WILLIAM SMITH (1727–1803). English clergyman and writer. Recruited by Franklin in the early 1750s for the new Philadelphia Academy, where he was made provost. Became an ardent supporter of the Proprietors and bitterly split with Franklin.

MARGARET STEVENSON (1706–1783). Franklin's landlady on Craven Street, off the Strand, and occasional companion in London.

MARY "POLLY" STEVENSON [HEWSON] (1739–1795). Mrs. Stevenson's daughter. Longtime flirtatious young friend and intellectual companion to Franklin. Married in 1770 to medical researcher William Hewson. Widowed in 1774. Visited Franklin in Passy in 1785. Moved to Philadelphia in 1786 to be at his deathbed.

WILLIAM STRAHAN (1715–1785). London printer who became Franklin's close friend via letters before even meeting him in person. Sent David Hall to be his partner. Franklin wrote but did not send a famous "you are my enemy" letter to him during the American Revolution, but they actually remained friends.

CHARLES THOMSON (1729–1824). Irish-born teacher. Franklin gave him a job at the Philadelphia Academy and got him involved in Pennsylvania politics. Served as Franklin's eyes and ears while Franklin was in London. Later became the secretary to Congress 1774–89.

ANNE-ROBERT-JACQUES TURGOT (1727–1781). Economist, finance minister to Louis XVI, Franklin's friend and occasional rival for the affections of Madame Helvétius. Wrote the famous epigram: *Eripuit cœlo fulmen sceptrumque tyrannis,* He snatched lightning from the sky and the scepter from tyrants.

BENJAMIN VAUGHAN (1751–1835). Diplomat and associate of Lord Shelburne. Compiled many of Franklin's papers in 1779 and helped to negotiate with him the final peace treaties with Britain.

LOUIS-GUILLAUME LE VEILLARD (1733–1794). Proprietor of a famed water spa. Franklin's neighbor at Passy. Guillotined during the French Revolution.

CHARLES GRAVIER, COMTE DE VERGENNES (1717–1787). French foreign minister 1774–87, with whom Franklin negotiated an alliance.

THOMAS WALPOLE (1727–1803). British banker and MP, nephew of Prime Minister Robert Walpole. Formed with Franklin the Grand Ohio Co. to seek an American land grant and later speculated on stocks, using inside information from Edward Bancroft.

PAUL WENTWORTH (ca. 1740–1793). Britain's spymaster in France who recruited Edward Bancroft. Born in New Hampshire, moved to London in the 1760s, became rich on stocks and land purchases in Guyana, and met with Franklin in Paris in December 1777 to try to scuttle American treaty with France.

SAMUEL WHARTON (1732–1800). Philadelphia-born merchant. Moved to London in 1769 and became involved in land deal schemes and stock speculations with Thomas Walpole.

GEORGE WHITEFIELD (1714–1770). Evangelist. Joined the Wesley movement while at Pembroke College, Oxford. Made seven trips to America as one of the foremost of the Great Awakening revivalist preachers and was supported by Franklin in Philadelphia in 1739.

CHRONOLOGY

1706   Born in Boston on Jan. 17 (Jan. 6, 1705, Old Style).

1714   Attends Boston Latin.

1715   Attends Brownell's school.

1716   Begins working at father's candle shop.

1718   Apprenticed to brother James.

1722   Writes Silence Dogood essays.

1723   Runs away to Philadelphia. Works for Keimer.

1724   Moves to London.

1725   "A Dissertation on Liberty and Necessity, Pleasure and Pain"

1726   Returns to Philadelphia. Works with Denham.

1727   Rejoins Keimer's print shop.

1728   Opens his own print shop with Hugh Meredith.

1729   Writes Busy-Body essays. Buys *Pennsylvania Gazette.*

1730   Enters common-law marriage with Deborah Read. William born?

1731   Joins Freemasons. Founds library.

1732   Francis born. Launches *Poor Richard's Almanack.*

1733   Moral perfection project.

1735   Controversy over preacher Hemphill.

1736   Clerk of Pennsylvania Assembly. Francis dies. Forms Union Fire Co.

1737   Made Philadelphia postmaster.

1739   Becomes friends with evangelist Whitefield.

1741   Launches *General Magazine,* which fails. Designs stove.

1743   Sarah ("Sally") born. Launches American Philosophical Society.

1745   Collinson sends electricity pamphlets and glass tube.

1746   Summer of electricity experiments.

1747   Writes *Plain Truth.* Organizes militia.

1748   Retires from printing business.

1749   Writes proposal for the Academy (University of Pennsylvania).

1751   Electricity writings published in London. Elected to Pennsylvania Assembly.

1752   Kite and lightning experiment.

1753   Becomes joint postmaster for America. Carlisle Indian summit.

1754 French and Indian War begins. Albany Plan of Union.

1755 Supplies Gen. Braddock. Passes militia bill. Fights Proprietors.

1756 Night watchmen and street lighting bills passed.

1757 Leaves for London as agent. Writes "Way to Wealth" and last *Poor Richard's Almanack*. Moves in with Mrs. Stevenson on Craven Street.

1758 Visits Ecton to research ancestry with William.

1759 Visits northern England and Scotland. English and American troops capture Quebec.

1760 Urges Britain to keep Canada. Privy Council gives partial victory in fight with Penns. Travels in England with William.

1761 Travels to Flanders and Holland with William.

1762 Returns to Philadelphia. William made royal governor of New Jersey, marries.

1763 Begins new Market Street house. Postal inspection trip from Virginia to New England. French and Indian War ends.

1764 Paxton Boys crisis. Defeated in bitter Assembly election. Returns to London as agent.

1765 Stamp Act passes.

1766 Testifies against Stamp Act in Parliament. Act repealed. Partnership with David Hall expires.

1767 Townshend duties imposed. Travels to France.

1768 Wages press crusade in London on behalf of the colonies.

1769 Second visit to France.

1770 Townshend duties repealed except on tea. Made agent for Massachusetts.

1771 Showdown with Hillsborough. Begins *Autobiography*. Visits Ireland and Scotland. Meets son-in-law, Bache.

1772 Secretly sends purloined Hutchinson letters to Boston.

1773 Writes parodies "Rules by Which a Great Empire May Be Reduced to a Smaller One" and "Edict of the King of Prussia." Boston Tea Party.

1774 Cockpit showdown over Hutchinson letters. Dismissed as postmaster. Coercive Acts passed. Begins peace discussions with both Lord Chatham and Lord Howe. Deborah dies.

1775 Returns to Philadelphia. Battles of Lexington and Concord. Elected to Second Continental Congress. Proposes first Articles of Confederation.

1776 William removed as royal governor, imprisoned in Connecticut. Canada mission. Declaration of Independence. Meets with Lord Howe on Staten Island. Goes to France with Temple and Benny.

1777 Settles in Passy, feted throughout Paris.

1778 Treaties of alliance and commerce with France. William released from captivity and moves to loyalist New York.

1779 Becomes sole minister to France. Salons of Mesdames Brillon and Helvétius. John Paul Jones's *Bonhomme Richard* defeats the *Serapis*.

1780 Adams returns, then Franklin helps get him dismissed as commissioner. British capture Charleston.

1781 Adams returns to Paris again as minister to negotiate with Britain. Franklin is then appointed (with Jay and others) to join Adams in that commission. Cornwallis surrenders at Yorktown.

1782 Negotiates, with Adams and Jay, peace treaty with Britain. William returns to London.

1783 Balloon flights.

1784 Mesmer commission. Polly Stevenson visits Passy.

1785 Last meeting with William. Returns to Philadelphia.

1786 Builds addition to Market Street house.

1787 Constitutional Convention. Elected president of Pennsylvania Society for Promoting the Abolition of Slavery.

1790 Dies on Apr. 17 at age 84.

CURRENCY CONVERSIONS

Rough equivalents of eighteenth-century currencies in today's value based on price index comparisons of a bundle of consumer products:

1706

The British pound was the standard currency in America.

£1 in 1706 had the same purchasing power as £104 (or $161) in 2002.

A fine ounce of gold cost £4.35.

1750

The British pound was still the standard currency in America, but some colonies (including Pennsylvania at Franklin's behest) were printing paper currency denominated in pounds that varied somewhat in value.

£1 in 1750 had the same purchasing power as £103 (or $160) in 2002.

A fine ounce of gold cost £4.25.

1790

The dollar was becoming the standard currency in the United States, and an official exchange rate was established. The gold price of the pound remained fixed, but its consumer purchasing power had fallen.

The exchange rate was £1 equals $4.55 equals 23.5 French livres.

A fine ounce of gold cost £4.25 or $19.50.

£1 in 1790 had the same purchasing power as £70 in 2002.

$1 in 1790 had the same purchasing power as $19.26 in 2002.

The changes in purchasing power of the pound and dollar from 1790 are not comparable.

Sources: Economic History Services, eh.net/hmit ; John McCusker, *How Much Is That in Real Money?* (New Castle, Del.: Oak Knoll Press, 2001).

ACKNOWLEDGMENTS

Alice Mayhew at Simon & Schuster has been a diligent editor and gracious friend for twenty years and, now, three books. Her detailed notes and valuable edits on all my manuscripts are treasured possessions. She has always been rigorous about, among other things, shaping a logical narrative, and her energy in handling this book was unflagging and deeply appreciated. Amanda Urban at ICM has likewise been a valued friend and agent for all these years. She read my earliest drafts and offered good suggestions and warm encouragement, as well as an occasional guest room in which to work.

To help ensure that my facts were as correct as possible and that I did not inadvertently fail to give due citations, I hired Carole Le Faivre-Rochester to vet my manuscript, sources, and credit notes. For twenty-four years, she worked at the American Philosophical Society, which Franklin founded and which has done great work in preserving his papers, and she retired as the editor of that society in 2001. She was industrious in digging out material and making useful suggestions.

One of the joys of working on Franklin was meeting the generous and humorous Claude-Anne Lopez, who was a longtime editor at Yale compiling his papers and is the author of many delightful books and articles about him. She graciously agreed to read parts of the manuscript and edited the three chapters on his years in France, about which she is both an expert and an enthusiast.

Ms. Lopez suggested that I try to dig out information about Edward Bancroft's spying activities on Franklin. To help in that task, I hired Susan Ann Bennett, a researcher in London who, among other things, wrote "Benjamin Franklin of Craven Street" when she was a curator at the RSA (formerly, the Royal Society of Arts). I am very grateful for her diligent work, transcriptions, and intelligent sleuthing at the British Library, where some of Bancroft's reports in code and invisible ink are stored.

I am also grateful to the editors at Yale who continue the task of producing what I think must be the greatest collection of anyone's papers ever. Their thirty-seventh volume, which goes through August 1782, is due out at the same time as this book and should be bought by everyone interested in Franklin. They were gracious in letting me study their manuscript of that work as well as their early drafts of volumes 38, 39, and 40. I particularly enjoyed a vibrant lunch I had in New

Haven with Ms. Lopez and some core members of the current team, including Ellen Cohen, Judith Adkins, Jonathan Dull, Karen Duval, and Kate Ohno.

Also at that lunch was the justly venerated Edmund Morgan, retired Sterling Professor of History at Yale, who had written his own wonderful book analyzing Franklin and his papers. Professor Morgan has been kindly, beneficent, generous, and exceedingly helpful in the tradition of our subject. He graciously offered to read parts of my manuscript, and he provided suggestions and encouragement about my theme and concluding chapter. I tried to take a different approach from his by writing a chronological narrative biography, but I do not pretend to have matched his insights. Those who find my book interesting, and more important those who don't, should buy and read his, if they haven't already.

Márcia Baliscano is the director of the Franklin House on Craven Street in London, soon to be (we all hope) a fitting museum. With enormous skill and intellectual rigor, along with a diligence that would have dazzled even Franklin, she painstakingly dissected my entire manuscript and made scores of invaluable suggestions. In addition, she was very helpful in hosting me on Craven Street, and she did her duty by energetically enlisting me and others to her cause. One of her board members is Lady Joan Reid, a great repository of Franklin information. I deeply appreciate her willingness to volunteer for the arduous task of reading my manuscript and being both meticulous and unflinching in her crusade to separate facts from lore. In doing so, she expended not only an enormous amount of time and intellectual energy, but also a huge pile of colored Post-it notes filled with suggestions. Someday, I hope, she will write a book about Franklin's London circle of friends.

Part of the pleasure of writing about Franklin is meeting his aficionados. Foremost among them is a group called the Friends of Franklin, based in Philadelphia, which hosts lunches, organizes seminars, and publishes the delightful *Franklin Gazette*. (To join, go to www.benfranklin2006.org) I want to thank Kathleen DeLuca, the executive secretary, for her hospitality. The group is working with the Franklin Institute, the American Philosophical Society, the Library Company of Philadelphia, the Philadelphia Museum of Art, the University of Pennsylvania, and the Pew Charitable Trust to organize a celebration and exhibition, under the direction of Connover Hunt, that will culminate with Franklin's three hundredth birthday in January 2006.

I am deeply indebted to Strobe Talbott, who has long been a friend and inspiration. He helped to shape and carefully edit both *The Wise Men,* which I coauthored in 1986, and a biography of Henry Kissinger that I published in 1992. This time, he volunteered again to read my manuscript, and he came back with a wealth of helpful suggestions and comments. Stephen Smith, one of the most deft editors I have ever known, also read the entire manuscript and offered useful perspectives and ideas. Evan Thomas, my coauthor on *The Wise Men,* spotted some mistakes I made about John Paul Jones, about whom he has written a great book. Steven Weisman read a draft and provided very insightful suggestions. Many other friends have given wise counsel, among them: James Kelly, Richard Stengel, Priscilla Painton and Tim Smith, Elisabeth Bumiller, Andrew and Betsy Lack, David and Sherrie Westin.

Elliot Ravetz, my former assistant at *Time,* helped me get started by giving me my first collection of Franklin papers, inspired me later with a bust of Franklin, offered comments on my manuscript, and has been an earnest compatriot. I am also grateful to Tosca Laboy and Ashley Van Buren at CNN, who are both truly wonderful people.

My father and stepmother, Irwin and Julanne Isaacson, also read and edited my manuscript. They are, along with my late mother, Betsy Isaacson, the smartest people I have ever known.

Most of all, I am grateful to my wife, Cathy, and daughter, Betsy. Cathy read through what I wrote with enormous care and was invaluable in sharpening the themes and spotting some problems. But that is merely a tiny fraction of what she did as my partner in this book and in life. As for Betsy, after a bit of prodding, she faithfully plowed through some of the manuscript. Parts of it she admitted were interesting (as befitting a 12-year-old, she liked the section on ballooning) and other parts (like that on the Constitutional Convention) she declared boring, which I guess was a help, especially to readers who were thus treated to shortened versions of a few of these sections. They both make everything not only possible but worthwhile.

None of these people, of course, deserve blame for any errors or lapses that I have undoubtedly made. In a May 23, 1785, letter to his friend George Whatley, Franklin said about his life, "I shall not object to a new edition of mine; hoping however that the errata of the last may be corrected." I feel the same of this book.

SOURCES AND ABBREVIATIONS

Except where otherwise noted, Franklin's writings cited are in the Franklin Papers edited at Yale (see below) and the CD-ROM by the Packard Humanities Institute.

In using Internet addresses, please note that the periods, commas, hyphens, and semicolons used below to separate entries should not be included as part of a URL.

ABBREVIATIONS USED IN SOURCE NOTES

People

BF	=	Benjamin Franklin
DF	=	Deborah Franklin, wife
JM	=	Jane Franklin Mecom, sister
MS	=	Margaret Stevenson, London landlady
PS	=	Mary "Polly" Stevenson [Hewson], landlady's daughter
RB	=	Richard Bache, son-in-law
SF	=	Sarah "Sally" Franklin [Bache], daughter
TF	=	[William] Temple Franklin, grandson
WF	=	William Franklin, son

Franklin's Writings

Autobiography = *The Autobiography of Benjamin Franklin.*

For the reader's convenience, page citations refer to the most commonly available edition, the Signet Classic paperback (New York: Penguin Putnam, 2001), which is primarily based on a version prepared by Max Farrand (Berkeley: University of California Press, 1949).

There are more than 150 editions of this classic. The one that best shows his revisions is the "Genetic Text" edited by J. A. Leo Lemay and P. M. Zall (Knoxville: University of Tennessee Press, 1981), which is also to be found in the Norton Critical Edition, edited by Lemay and Zall (New York: Norton, 1986), referred to in the notes below as the Lemay/Zall Autobiography and Norton Autobiography, respectively. The authoritative edition produced by Leonard Labaree and the other editors of the Franklin Papers at Yale (New Haven: Yale University Press, 1964), referred to below as the Yale Autobiography, is based directly on Franklin's handwritten manuscript and includes useful annotations and a history of various versions.

Searchable electronic versions of the autobiography can be found on the Internet at ushistory.org/franklin/autobiography/index.htm; cedarcottage.com/eBooks/benfrank.rtf; earlyamerica.com/lives/franklin/index.html; odur.let.rug.nl/~usa/B/bfranklin/frank.htm; etext.lib.virginia.edu/toc/modeng/public/Fra2Aut.html; eserver.org/books/franklin/.

Lib. of Am. = *Benjamin Franklin Writings*
with notes by J. A. Leo Lemay (New York: Library of America, 1987). This 1,560-page volume has an authoritative collection of Franklin's most important writings along with source notes and annotations. It includes important revisions to the Franklin canon by Lemay that update the work of the Yale editors of Franklin's papers. A searchable electronic version of much of the text is on the Internet at www.historycarper.com/resources/twobf1/contents.htm .

Pa. Gazette = The *Pennsylvania Gazette*
Searchable electronic versions are on the Internet at www.accessible.com/about.htm; etext.lib.virginia.edu/pengazet.html; www.historycarper.com/resources/twobf2/pg29-30.htm .

Papers = *The Papers of Benjamin Franklin*
(New Haven: Yale, 1959–). This definitive and extraordinary series of annotated volumes, produced at Yale in conjunction with the American Philosophical Society, was begun under Leonard Labaree. Recent members of the distinguished team of editors include Ellen Cohn, Judith Adkins, Jonathan Dull, Karen Duval, Leslie Lindenauer, Claude-Anne Lopez, Barbara Oberg, Kate Ohno, and Michael Sletcher. By 2003, the team had reached volume 37, which goes through August 1782. All correspondence and writings cited below, unless otherwise noted, refer to versions in the Papers. See: www.yale.edu/franklinpapers .

Papers CD = CD-ROM of the *Papers of Benjamin Franklin*
prepared by the Packard Humanities Institute in cooperation with the Yale editors. These include all of Franklin's known writings, including material from 1783 to 1790 that has not yet been published. It is searchable by phrase, correspondent, and chronology, but it does not include the valuable annotations by the Yale editors. I am grateful to David Packard and his staff for giving me a version of the CD-ROM before its release.

Poor Richard's = *Poor Richard's: An Almanack*
by Benjamin Franklin. Many versions are available, and quotations are cited by year in the notes below. Searchable electronic versions can be found on the Internet at www.sage-advice.com/Benjamin_Franklin.htm ; www.ku.edu/carrie/stacks/authors.franklin.html ; itech.fgcu.edu/faculty/wohlpart/alra/franklin.htm ; and www.swarthmore.edu/SocSci/bdorsey1/41docs/52-fra.html .

Silence Dogood = The Silence Dogood essays
The complete editions of the *New England Courant*, including these essays, are at ushistory.org/franklin/courant .

Smyth *Writings* = *The Writings of Benjamin Franklin*
edited by Albert Henry Smyth, first published in 1907 (New York: Macmillan, 1905–7; reprinted New York: Haskell House, 1970). Until the Yale editions, this 10-volume work had been a definitive collection of Franklin's papers.

Sparks = *The Works of Benjamin Franklin* and the *Life of Benjamin Franklin*
by Jared Sparks (Boston: Tappan, Whittemore and Mason, 1840). Sparks was a Harvard history professor and president who published a 10-volume collection of Franklin's papers and a biography in 1836–40; www.ushistory.org/franklin/biography/index.htm .

Temple *Writings* = *Memoirs of the Life and Writings of Benjamin Franklin*
by [William] Temple Franklin, 3 volumes (London: Henry Colburn, 1818).

Other Frequently Cited Sources

Adams Diary = *The Diary and Autobiography of John Adams*
edited by L. H. Butterfield (Cambridge: Harvard University Press, 1961).

Adams Letters = *Adams Family Correspondence*
edited by L. H. Butterfield (Cambridge: Harvard University Press, 1963–73).

Aldridge *French* = *Franklin and His French Contemporaries*
by Alfred Owen Aldridge (New York: NYU Press, 1957).

Aldridge *Nature* = *Benjamin Franklin and Nature's God*
by Alfred Owen Aldridge (Durham, N.C.: Duke University Press, 1967).

Alsop = *Yankees at the Court*
by Susan Mary Alsop (Garden City, N.Y.: Doubleday, 1982).

Bowen = *The Most Dangerous Man in America*
by Catherine Drinker Bowen (Boston: Little, Brown, 1974).

Brands = *The First American*
by H. W. Brands (New York: Doubleday, 2000).

Buxbaum = *Benjamin Franklin and the Zealous Presbyterians*
by Melvin Buxbaum (University Park: Pennsylvania State University Press, 1975).

Campbell = *Recovering Benjamin Franklin*
by James Campbell (Chicago: Open Court, 1999).

Clark = *Benjamin Franklin*
by Ronald W. Clark (New York: Random House, 1983).

Cohen = *Benjamin Franklin's Science*
by I. Bernard Cohen (Cambridge: Harvard University Press, 1990).

Faÿ = *Franklin: The Apostle of Modern Man*
by Bernard Faÿ (Boston: Little, Brown, 1929).

Fleming = *The Man Who Dared the Lightning*
by Thomas Fleming (New York: Morrow, 1971).

Hawke = *Franklin*
by David Freeman Hawke (New York: Harper & Row, 1976).

Jefferson Papers = *Papers of Thomas Jefferson*
edited by Julian Boyd (Princeton: Princeton University Press, 1950–).

Lemay *Internet Doc* = "Benjamin Franklin: A Documentary History"
by J. A. Leo Lemay, University of Delaware, www.english.udel.edu/lemay/franklin .

Lemay *Reappraising* = *Reappraising Benjamin Franklin*
edited by J. A. Leo Lemay (Newark: University of Delaware Press, 1993).

Lopez *Cher* = *Mon Cher Papa*
by Claude-Anne Lopez (New Haven: Yale University Press, 1966).

Lopez *Life* = *My Life with Benjamin Franklin*
by Claude-Anne Lopez (New Haven: Yale University Press, 2002).

Lopez *Private* = *The Private Franklin*
by Claude-Anne Lopez and Eugenia Herbert (New York: Norton, 1975).

McCullough = *John Adams*
by David McCullough (New York: Simon & Schuster, 2001).

Middlekauff = *Benjamin Franklin and His Enemies*
by Robert Middlekauff (Berkeley: University of California Press, 1996).

Morgan *Franklin* = *Benjamin Franklin*
by Edmund S. Morgan (New Haven: Yale University Press, 2002).

Morgan *Devious* = *The Devious Dr. Franklin: Benjamin Franklin's Years in London*
by David Morgan (Macon, Ga.: Mercer University Press, 1996).

Parton = *Life and Times of Benjamin Franklin*
by James Parton, 2 volumes (New York: Mason Brothers, 1865).

PMHB = *Pennsylvania Magazine of History and Biography*

Randall = *A Little Revenge*
by Willard Sterne Randall (New York: William Morrow, 1984).

Sanford = *Benjamin Franklin and the American Character*
edited by Charles Sanford (Boston: Heath, 1955).

Sappenfield = *A Sweet Instruction: Franklin's Journalism as a Literary Apprenticeship*
by James Sappenfield (Carbondale: Southern Illinois University Press, 1973).

Schoenbrun = *Triumph in Paris*
by David Schoenbrun (New York: Harper & Row, 1976).

Skemp *William* = *William Franklin*
by Sheila Skemp (New York: Oxford University Press, 1990).

Skemp *Benjamin* = *Benjamin and William Franklin*
by Sheila Skemp (New York: St. Martin's, 1994).

Smith = *Franklin and Bache: Envisioning the Enlightened Republic*
by Jeffery A. Smith (New York: Oxford University Press, 1990).

Stourzh = *Benjamin Franklin and American Foreign Policy*
by Gerald Stourzh (Chicago: University of Chicago Press, 1954).

Tourtellot = *Benjamin Franklin: The Shaping of Genius, the Boston Years*
by Arthur Tourtellot (Garden City, N.Y.: Doubleday, 1977).

Van Doren = *Benjamin Franklin*
by Carl Van Doren (New York: Viking, 1938). The page numbers are the same
in the Penguin USA paperback edition, 1991 and subsequent reprints.

Walters = *Benjamin Franklin and His Gods*
by Kerry S. Walters (Urbana: University of Illinois Press, 1998).

Wright = *Franklin of Philadelphia*
by Esmond Wright (Cambridge: Harvard University Press, 1986).

NOTES

CHAPTER 1

1. For a description of the writing of the *Autobiography*, see pages 254–57 and chapter 11 note 5 on page 542.

2. David Brooks, "Our Founding Yuppie," *Weekly Standard*, Oct. 23, 2000, 31. The word "meritocracy" is an argument-starter, and I have employed it sparingly in this book. It is often used loosely to denote a vision of social mobility based on merit and diligence, like Franklin's. The word was coined by British social thinker Michael Young (later to become, somewhat ironically, Lord Young of Darlington) in his 1958 book *The Rise of the Meritocracy* (New York: Viking Press) as a dismissive term to satirize a society that misguidedly created a new elite class based on the "narrow band of values" of IQ and educational credentials. The Harvard philosopher John Rawls, in *A Theory of Justice* (Cambridge: Harvard University Press, 1971), 106, used it more broadly to mean a "social order [that] follows the principle of careers open to talents." The best description of the idea is in Nicholas Lemann's *The Big Test: The Secret History of the American Meritocracy* (New York: Farrar, Straus & Giroux, 1999), a history of educational aptitude tests and their effect on American society. In Franklin's time, Enlightenment thinkers (such as Jefferson in his proposals for creating the University of Virginia) advocated replacing the hereditary aristocracy with a "natural aristocracy," whose members would be plucked from the masses at an early age based on "virtues and talents" and groomed for leadership. Franklin's idea was more expansive. He believed in encouraging and providing opportunities for all people to succeed as best they could based on their diligence, hard work, virtue, and talent. As we shall see, his proposals for what became the University of Pennsylvania (in contrast to Jefferson's for the University of Virginia) were aimed not at filtering a new elite but at encouraging and enriching all "aspiring" young men. Franklin was propounding a more egalitarian and democratic approach than Jefferson by proposing a system that would, as Rawls (p. 107) would later prescribe, assure that "resources for education are not to be allotted solely or necessarily mainly according to their return as estimated in productive trained abilities, but also according to their worth in enriching the personal and social life of citizens." (Translation: He cared not simply about making

society as a whole more productive, but also about making each individual more enriched.)

CHAPTER 2

1. Autobiography 18; Josiah Franklin to BF, May 26, 1739; editor's note in Papers 2:229; Tourtellot 12. Franklin provides a footnote in the Autobiography showing how the noun and surname "franklin" was used in fifteenth-century England. Some analysts, as well as his French fans, have pointed out that Franquelin was a common name in the province of Picardie, France, in the fifteenth century, and his ancestors may have come from there. His father, Josiah Franklin, wrote, "Some think we are of a French extract which was formerly called Franks; some of a free line (frank line), a line free from that vassalage which was common to subjects in the days of old; some from a bird of long red legs." Franklin's own assessment that his surname came from the class of English freemen called *franklins* is almost surely the correct explanation, and just as important, it was the one he believed. The *Oxford English Dictionary* defines *franklin* as "A class of landowners, of free but not noble birth, and ranking next below the gentry." It is derived from the Middle English word *frankeleyn,* meaning a freeman or freeholder. See Chaucer's "The Franklin's Tale," or "The Frankeleyn's Tale," www.librarius.com/cantales.htm .

2. Autobiography 20; Josiah Franklin to BF, May 26, 1739. The tale of the Bible and stool is in the letter from Josiah Franklin, but BF writes that he heard it from his uncle Benjamin. For a full genealogy, see Papers 1:xlix. The Signet edition of the Autobiography, based on a version prepared by Max Farrand (Berkeley: University of California Press, 1949), uses a somewhat different phrase: "Our humble family early embraced the Reformation."

3. As David McCullough does in *Truman* (New York: Simon & Schuster, 1992) and Robert Caro in *The Path to Power* (New York: Knopf, 1982).

4. Autobiography 20; "A short account of the Family of Thomas Franklin of Ecton," by Benjamin Franklin the elder (uncle of BF), Yale University Library; Benjamin Franklin the Elder's commonplace book, cited in Papers, vol. 1; Tourtellot 18.

5. BF to David Hume, May 19, 1762.

6. Tourtellot 42.

7. John Winthrop, "A Model of Christian Charity" (1630), www.winthropsociety.org/charity.htm ; Perry Miller, *Errand into the Wilderness* (Cambridge: Harvard University Press, 1956). See also Andrew Delbanco, *The Puritan Ordeal* (Cambridge: Harvard University Press, 1989); Edmund Morgan, *Visible Saints: The History of a Puritan Idea* (New York: NYU Press, 1963); Herbert Schneider, *The Puritan Mind* (Ann Arbor: University of Michigan Press, 1958).

8. Perry Miller, "Benjamin Franklin and Jonathan Edwards," in *Major Writers of America* (New York: Harcourt Brace, 1962), 84; Tourtellot 41; Cotton Mather, "A Christian at His Calling," 1701, personal.pitnet.net/primarysources/mather.html ;

Poor Richard's, 1736 (drawn from Aesop's "Hercules and the Wagoner," ca. 550 B.C., and Algernon Sidney's *Discourses on Government,* 1698, among other antecedents).

9. Tourtellot 47–52; Nian Sheng Huang, "Franklin's Father Josiah: Life of a Colonial Boston Tallow Chandler, 1657–1745" (Philadelphia: Transactions of the American Philosophical Society, 2000) vol. 90, pt. 3.

10. Lemay *Internet Doc* for 1657–1705; a drawing of the house is in Papers 1:4.

11. Edmund Morgan, *The Puritan Family* (New York: Harper & Row, 1966); Mark Van Doren and Samuel Sewall, eds., *Samuel Sewall's Diary* (New York: Macy-Masius, 1927), 208.

12. Autobiography 24.

13. Autobiography 25, 91.

14. Tourtellot 86; Lopez *Private* 5–7.

15. Alexander Starbuck, *The History of Nantucket* (New York: Heritage, 1998), 53, 91, cited in Tourtellot 104.

16. Peter Folger, "A Looking Glass for the Times," reprinted in Tourtellot 106; Autobiography 23.

17. The genealogy of the Franklin and Folger families is in Papers 1:xlix.

18. Autobiography 23. The Farrand/Signet edition uses the phrase: "that which was not honest could not be truly useful."

19. BF to Barbeu Dubourg, April 1773; Tourtellot 161.

20. BF to Madame Brillon, Nov. 10, 1779 (known as the bagatelle of The Whistle); Autobiography 107; Pierre Jean Georges Cabanis, in *Complete Works* (Paris: Bossange frères, 1823), 5:222, records it as a lesson learned from his family.

21. Autobiography 24; Lopez *Private* 7.

22. Benjamin Franklin the elder, "To My Name, 1713," Paper 1:3–5; BF to JM, July 17, 1771; Parton 32–38; Tourtellot 139–40; Autobiography 20.

23. Autobiography 22; BF to JM, July 17, 1771; Lopez *Private,* 9.

24. Autobiography 22; Tourtellot 156. Boston Latin School was then generally called the South Grammar School.

25. Temple *Writings,* 1: 447.

26. Autobiography 25–26.

27. Autobiography 27; *Boston Post,* Aug. 7, 1940, cited in Papers 1:6–7. No authenticated copies of these two poems are known to have survived. The Franklin Papers 1:6–7 quote a few possible verses that may have been his.

28. Lemay *Internet Doc* for 1719–20, citing *Early Boston Booksellers,* by George Emery Littlefield (Boston: Antiquarian Society, 1900), 150–55; Tourtellot 230–32. Franklin incorrectly states that the *Courant* was the second newspaper in Boston. See Yale Autobiography 67n.

29. Perry Miller, *The New England Mind: From Colony to Province* (Cambridge: Harvard University Press, 1983), 344. See also E. Digby Baltzell, *Puritan Boston and Quaker Philadelphia* (New York: Free Press, 1979).

30. John Blake, "The Inoculation Controversy in Boston: 1721–1722," *New England Quarterly* (1952): 489–506; *New England Courant,* Aug. 7, 1721, and following, ushistory.org/franklin/courant ; Tourtellot 252.

31. Lemay *Internet Doc* for 1721; Perry Miller, *The New England Mind: From Colony to Province*, 337.

32. Autobiography 26. Analysis of Franklin's childhood reading can be found in Parton 1:44–51, 60–72; Ralph Ketcham, *Benjamin Franklin* (New York: Washington Square Press, 1965), 8–31; Tourtellot 166.

33. Autobiography 27; BF to Samuel Mather, July 7, 1773, May 12, 1784; John Bunyan, *Pilgrim's Progress*, 1678, www.ccel.org/b/bunyan/progress/; Plutarch, *Parallel Lives*, ca. A.D. 100, ibiblio.org/gutenberg/etext96/plivs10.txt ; Cotton Mather, *Bonifacius*, also known as *Essays to Do Good* and *An Essay upon the Good*, 1710, edweb.sdsu.edu/people/DKitchen/new_655/mather.htm ; Tourtellot 187–89.

34. Daniel Defoe, *An Essay upon Projects*, 1697, ibiblio.org/gutenberg/etext03/esprj10.txt ; Tourtellot 185.

35. Autobiography 28.

36. *The Spectator*, Mar. 13, 1711, harvest.rutgers.edu/projects/spectator/markup.html ; Autobiography 29.

37. *The Spectator*, Mar. 1, 1711; Silence Dogood #1, Apr. 2, 1722; Silence Dogood #2, Apr. 16, 1722; Silence Dogood #3, Apr. 30, 1722; ushistory.org/franklin/courant ; Papers 1:8–11. These dates, unlike others, are in the Old Style because they refer to editions of the *Courant* as dated at the time.

38. Silence Dogood #4, May 14, 1722; *The Spectator*, Mar. 3, 1711.

39. Autobiography 34; *New England Courant*, June 18, 25, July 2, 9, 1722. The excerpt is from *The London Journal*.

40. *New England Courant*, July 16, 23, 1722.

41. *New England Courant*, Sept. 14, 1722, Feb. 11, 1723; Autobiography 33. Franklin compresses the chronology by recalling that his name went on top of the paper right after his brother's release from jail, which was in July 1722; in fact, it occurred after James got into another dispute in January 1723. Oddly, his name remained atop the paper until at least 1726, which was three years after he had run away to Philadelphia. See *New England Courant*, June 25, 1726, and Yale Autobiography 70n.

42. Autobiography 34–35.

43. Claude-Anne Lopez, an editor of Franklin's papers at Yale, discovered a scrap of paper on which Franklin, in 1783, jotted down some dates and places designed to pinpoint his itinerary of sixty years earlier. In the Norton edition of the Autobiography, J. A. Leo Lemay and P. M. Zall note that the only boat leaving Boston for New York that week was a sloop on September 25. Franklin's editing of the "naughty girl" passage is noted in the Signet edition, 35. James Franklin's forlorn ad appears in *New England Courant*, Sept. 30, 1723.

CHAPTER 3

1. *The Way to Health* was written by Thomas Tryon (1634–1703) and first published in 1683; Autobiography 29.

2. Autobiography 49.

3. Autobiography 38.

4. Autobiography 79; Jonathan Yardley, review of Edmund Morgan's *Benjamin Franklin,* in *Washington Post Book World,* Sept. 15, 2002, 2.

5. Autobiography 41.

6. Autobiography 52.

7. Autobiography 42. Franklin later politely revised the phrase in his autobiography to read, "stared with astonishment." Lemay/Zall Autobiography provides a complete look at the original manuscript and all of its revisions. The governors sent to Pennsylvania were sometimes referred to as lieutenant governors.

8. Franklin recounted this tale twice to Mather's son: BF to Samuel Mather, July 7, 1773, and May 12, 1784.

9. Autobiography 104.

10. Autobiography 48.

11. Autobiography 54.

12. Autobiography 55–58.

13. "A Dissertation on Liberty and Necessity, Pleasure and Pain," 1725, Papers 1:58; Campbell 101–3.

14. Autobiography 70; Campbell 91–135.

15. Autobiography 92; Poor Richard Improved, 1753; Papers 4:406. See also Alfred Owen Aldridge, "The Alleged Puritanism of Benjamin Franklin," in Lemay *Reappraising* 370; Aldridge *Nature;* Campbell 99. For good descriptions of the evolution of Franklin's religious thought, see Walters; Buxbaum. See also chapter 7 of this book.

16. Autobiography 63.

17. "Plan of Conduct," 1726, Papers 1:99; Autobiography 183.

18. "Journal of a Voyage," July 22–Oct. 11, 1726, Papers 1:72–99. The idea that "affability and sociability" were core tenets of the Enlightenment is explained well in Gordon Wood, *The Radicalism of the American Revolution* (New York: Random House, 1991), 215–6.

CHAPTER 4

1. Autobiography 64. For overviews of life in Philadelphia, see Carl Bridenbaugh and Jessica Bridenbaugh, *Rebels and Gentlemen: Philadelphia in the Age of Franklin* (New York: Oxford University Press, 1942); E. Digby Baltzell, *Puritan Boston and Quaker Philadelphia* (New York: Free Press, 1979). For a good overview of Franklin's work as a printer, see C. William Miller, *Benjamin Franklin's Philadelphia Printing 1728–1766* (Philadelphia: American Philosophical Society, 1974).

2. The chronology in the Autobiography is not quite correct. Denham took ill in the spring of 1727 but did not die until July 1728. Lemay/Zall Autobiography 41.

3. Autobiography 69; Brands 87–89; Van Doren 71–73.

4. Autobiography 71–79; Brands 91; Lemay/Zall Autobiography 49. The

Quaker history was written by William Sewel. Franklin records that he published forty sheets of folio, which would have been 160 pages, but in fact he produced 178 pages and Keimer the remaining 532 pages.

5. Last Will and Codicil, June 23, 1789, Papers CD 46:u20.

6. Whitfield J. Bell Jr., *Patriot Improvers* (Philadelphia: American Philosophical Society, 1999), vol. 1; Autobiography 72–73; "On Conversation," Pa. Gazette, Oct. 15, 1730. Dale Carnegie, in his book *How to Win Friends and Influence People* (1937; New York: Pocket Books, 1994), draws on Franklin's rules for conversation. Carnegie's first two rules for "How to Win People to Your Way of Thinking" are: "The only way to get the best of an argument is to avoid it" and "Show respect for the other person's opinions. Never say, 'You're wrong.' " In his section on "How to Change People without Giving Offense or Arousing Resentment," he instructs: "Call attention to people's mistakes indirectly" and "Ask questions instead of giving direct orders." Carnegie's book has sold more than 15 million copies.

7. Autobiography 96; "Rules for a Club for Mutual Improvement," 1727; "Proposals and Queries to be Asked the Junto," 1732.

8. BF to Samuel Mather, May 17, 1784; Van Doren 75; Cotton Mather, "Religious Societies," 1724; Lemay/Zall Autobiography 47n. See also Mitchell Breitwieser, *Cotton Mather and Benjamin Franklin* (Cambridge: Cambridge University Press, 1984).

9. Autobiography 74; *American Weekly Mercury*, Jan. 28, 1729 (Shortface and Careful); Papers 1:112; Brands 101; Van Doren 94; Sappenfield 49–55.

10. Busy-Body #1, *American Weekly Mercury*, Feb. 4, 1729; Sappenfield 51; *The Universal Instructor . . . and Pennsylvania Gazette*, Feb. 25, Mar. 13, 1729; Papers 1:115–27.

11. Busy-Body #3, *American Weekly Mercury*, Feb. 18, 1729; Busy-Body #4, *American Weekly Mercury*, Feb. 25, 1789; Busy-Body #8, *American Weekly Mercury*, Mar. 28, 1729. Lemay's masterly notes in the Library of America's edition of Franklin's *Writings* (p. 1524) describe which parts Franklin wrote and what was withdrawn in Busy-Body #8.

12. "A Modest Enquiry into the Nature and Necessity of a Paper Currency," Apr. 3, 1729; Autobiography 77–78. Franklin draws on William Petty's 1662 work, *A Treatise of Taxes and Contributions*, www.socsci.mcmaster.ca/~econ/ugcm/3113/petty/taxes.txt .

13. "The Printer to the Reader," Pa. Gazette, Oct. 2, 1729.

14. "Printer's Errors," Pa. Gazette, Mar. 13, 1730.

15. Pa. Gazette, Mar. 19, 1730; Autobiography 75.

16. "Apology for Printers," Pa. Gazette, June 10, 1731; Clark 49; Isaiah Thomas, *The History of Printing in America* (1810; Albany: Munsell, 1874), 1: 237.

17. Pa. Gazette, June 17, 24, July 29, 1731, Feb. 15, June 19, July 3, 1732.

18. Pa. Gazette, Oct. 24, 1734; not in the Yale Papers, but later ascribed to the Franklin canon by Lemay, see Lib. of Am. 233–34.

19. Pa. Gazette, Sept. 7, 1732. For an analysis of Franklin's journalistic treatment of crime and scandal, see Ronald Bosco, "Franklin Working the Crime Beat," Lemay *Reappraising*, 78–97.

20. Pa. Gazette, Sept. 12, 1732, Jan. 27, 1730.

21. "Death of a Drunk," Pa. Gazette, Dec. 7, 1732; "On Drunkenness," Feb. 1, 1733; "A Meditation on a Quart Mugg," July 19, 1733; "The Drinker's Dictionary," Jan. 13, 1737. In Silence Dogood #12 (Sept. 10, 1722), Franklin had his sassy widow defend moderate drinking and condemn excess, drawing on Richard Steele's essays in London's *Tatler*. See Robert Arnor, "Politics and Temperance," in Lemay *Reappraising*, 52–77.

22. Pa. Gazette, Sept. 23, 1731.

23. Autobiography 34, 80, 72; "Anthony Afterwit," Pa. Gazette, July 10, 1732.

24. Autobiography 64, 81; Faÿ 135; Brands 106–9; Lopez *Private*, 23–24; BF to Joseph Priestley, Sept. 19, 1772; Poor Richard's, 1738. The first volume of the Papers 1:1xii in 1959 said Deborah was born in Philadelphia in 1708, but that thinking was revised after Francis James Dallett published a paper the following year called "Dr. Franklin's In-Laws," which is cited in Papers 8:139. Dallett's evidence indicates that Deborah was born in 1705 or 1706, maybe in Philadelphia but more likely in Birmingham, from which she emigrated to Philadelphia with her family in about 1711. See Edward James et al., *Notable American Women 1607–1950* (Cambridge: Harvard University Press, 1971), 1:663, entry on Deborah Franklin by Leonard Labaree, the initial editor of the Yale Papers. If she did cross the ocean at age 5 or so, it may have caused her lifelong aversion to ever crossing (or even seeing) it again. For a good analysis, see J. A. Leo Lemay, "Recent Franklin Scholarship," *PMHB* 76.2 (Apr. 2002): 336.

25. BF to "honoured mother" Abiah Franklin, Apr. 12, 1750; Lemay *Internet Doc* for 1728; Parton 1:177, 198–99; Randall 43; Skemp *William*, 4–5, 10; Brands 110, 243; *Gentleman's Magazine* (1813), in Papers 3:474n. The Yale editors of Franklin's papers say in volume 1 (published in 1959) that William was born circa 1731, but by volume 3 (published in 1961) they note the controversy (Papers 3:89n) and suggest that perhaps he was born earlier; however, in their edition of the Autobiography, published in 1964, they reiterate "circa 1731" as the year of his birth.

26. Van Doren 93, 231; Brands 110, 243. See also Charles Hart, "Who Was the Mother of Franklin's Son?" *PMHB* (July 1911): 308–14; Paul Leicester Ford, *Who Was the Mother of Franklin's Son?* (New York: Century, 1889).

27. Van Doren 91; Lopez *Private*, 22–23; Clark 41; Roberts letter, Papers 2:370n.; Bell, *Patriot Improvers*, 1:277–80.

28. Autobiography 92; BF to JM, Jan. 6, 1727; Poor Richard's, 1733.

29. "Anthony Afterwit," Pa. Gazette, July 10, 1732; "Celia Single," Pa. Gazette, July 24, 1732.

30. "Rules and Maxims for Promoting Matrimonial Happiness," Pa. Gazette, Oct. 8, 1730, Lib. of Am. 151. This piece is not included by the Yale editors, but Lemay and others subsequently attributed it to Franklin.

31. Lopez *Private*, 31–37; BF to James Read, Aug. 17, 1745; "A Scolding Wife," Pa. Gazette, July 5, 1733.

32. BF to Deborah Franklin, Feb. 19, 1758; "I Sing My Plain Country Joan," 1742; Francis James Dallett, "Dr. Franklin's In-Laws," cited in Papers 8:139;

Leonard Labaree, "Deborah Franklin," in *Notable American Women 1607–1950,* ed. Edward James et al. (Cambridge: Harvard University Press 1971), 1:663.

33. Autobiography 112; BF to JM, Jan. 13, 1772; Pa. Gazette, Dec. 23–30, 1736; Van Doren 126; Clark 43; Brands 154–55. Franklin had editorialized in favor of smallpox inoculations in his paper before Francis was born: Pa. Gazette, May 14, 28, 1730, Mar. 4, 1731.

34. "The Death of Infants," Pa. Gazette, June 20, 1734, ascribed to the Franklin canon by Lemay, Lib. of Am. 228.

35. Franklin writes in the Autobiography (p. 92) that he was "educated as a Presbyterian," but the Puritan sect in Boston into which he was baptized in fact became what is now called the Congregational Church. Both Presbyterians and Congregationalists generally follow the doctrines of John Calvin. See Yale Autobiography 145n. For more on Jedediah Andrews, see Richard Webster, *A History of the Presbyterian Church in America, from Its Origin until the Year 1760* (Philadelphia: J. M. Wilson, 1857), 105–12. For more on Franklin and the Presbyterians, see chapter 5, n. 7.

36. Autobiography 92–94.

37. Deism can be an amorphous concept. Despite his qualms about the consequences of unenhanced deism, Franklin did not shy from the word in labeling his beliefs. I use the word, as he did, to describe the Enlightenment-era philosophy that (1) rejects the belief that faith depends on received or revealed religious doctrines; (2) does not emphasize an intimate or passionate spiritual relationship with God or Christ; (3) believes in a rather impersonal Creator who set in motion the universe and all its laws; (4) holds that reason and the study of nature tells us all we can know about the Creator. See Walters; "Franklin's Life in Deism," in Campbell 110–26; Kerry Walters, *The American Deists* (Lawrence: University of Kansas Press, 1992); Buxbaum; A. Owen Aldridge, "Enlightenment and Awakening in Franklin and Edwards," in *Benjamin Franklin, Jonathan Edwards,* ed. Barbara Oberg and Harry Stout (New York: Oxford University Press, 1997), 27–41; Aldridge, "The Alledged Puritanism of Benjamin Franklin," in Lemay *Reappraising,* 362–71; Aldridge, *Nature;* Douglas Anderson, *The Radical Enlightenments of Benjamin Franklin* (Baltimore: Johns Hopkins University Press, 1997); Baltzell, *Puritan Boston and Quaker Philadelphia;* Larzer Ziff, *Puritanism in America* (New York: Viking, 1973); Donald Meyer, "Franklin's Religion," in *Critical Essays,* ed. Melvin Buxbaum (Boston: Hall, 1987), 147–67; Perry Miller, *Nature's Nation* (Cambridge: Harvard University Press, 1967); Mark Noll, *America's God* (New York: Oxford University Press, 2002); Simon Blackburn, *The Oxford Dictionary of Philosophy* (Oxford: Oxford University Press, 1994).

38. "Articles of Belief and Acts of Religion," Nov. 20, 1728, Papers 1:101.

39. Walters 8, 84–86. Walters's book is the most direct argument that Franklin was not espousing a literal polytheism. The opposite view is expressed in A. Owen Aldridge's comprehensive *Benjamin Franklin and Nature's God.* Read figuratively, Franklin seems to be saying that different denominations and religions each have their own gods: there is the God of the Puritans, who is different from Franklin's own God, or the God of the Methodists, of the Jews, of the Anabaptists, or, for that

matter, of the Hindus, Muslims, and ancient Greeks. These different gods arise because of differing perspectives (producing what Walters calls Franklin's "theistic perspectivism"). Franklin believed that the idea of a God as Creator and first cause is common to all religions, and thus can be assumed true. But different religions and sects add their own expressions and concepts, none of which we can really know to be true or false, but that lead to the existence of a multiplicity of gods that allow a more personal relationship with their believers. This interpretation comports with Franklin's comment in his essay that these gods can sometimes disappear as times and cultures evolve. "It may be that after many ages, they are changed and others supply their places."

40. "On the Providence of God in the Government of the World," Papers 1:264. The Yale editors posit 1732 as its date. A. Owen Aldridge, Leo Lemay, and others persuasively argue, based on a letter Franklin later wrote about it, that it was actually 1730; BF to Benjamin Vaughan, Nov. 9, 1779. See Aldridge *Nature,* 34–40; Lemay *Internet Doc* for 1730. The Library of America edition of Franklin's writings accepts the 1730 date. Wilhelm Niesel, *The Theology of Calvin* (Philadelphia: Westminster Press, 1956), 70; John Calvin, *Commentaries,* "On Paul's Epistle to the Romans" (1539), www.ccel.org/c/calvin/comment3/comm_vol38/htm/TOC.htm .

41. Walters 98; Campbell 109–11; Aldridge *Nature,* 25–38; BF to John Franklin, May 1745.

42. "A Witch Trial at Mount Holly," Pa. Gazette, Oct. 22, 1730.

43. BF to Josiah and Abiah Franklin, Apr. 13, 1738. When his beloved sister Jane also conveyed her misgivings about his emphasis on good works rather than prayer, he offered a similar mix of explanation and mild reassurance. "I am so far from thinking that God is not to be worshipped that I have composed and wrote a whole book of devotions for my own use," he says, and then urges tolerance. "There are some things in your New England doctrines and worship which I do not agree with, but I do not therefore condemn them . . . I would only have you make me the same allowances." BF to JM, July 28, 1743.

44. Autobiography 94–105, 49; D. H. Lawrence, "Benjamin Franklin," in *Studies in Classic American Literature* (New York: Viking, 1923), 10–16, xroads. virginia.edu/~HYPER/LAWRENCE/dhlch02.htm .

45. Randy Cohen, "Best Wishes," *New York Times Magazine,* June 30, 2002; David Brooks, *Bobos in Paradise* (New York: Simon & Schuster, 2000), 64; Morgan *Franklin,* 23; Autobiography 104.

46. Autobiography 94–105, 49; Sappenfield 187–88; Lopez *Private,* 24; Lopez *Cher,* 277. The French friend was the scientist Pierre-Georges Cabanis, *Complete Works* (Paris: Bossange frères, 1825), 2:348.

47. Cotton Mather, "Two Brief Discourses," 1701; A. Whitney Griswold, "Two Puritans on Prosperity," 1934, in Sanford 42; Campbell 99, 166–74; Ziff, *Puritanism in America,* 218; Aldridge, "The Alleged Puritanism of Benjamin Franklin," in Lemay *Reappraising,* 370; Lopez *Private,* 104. Perry Miller notes: "This child of New England Puritanism simply dumped the whole theological preoccupation overboard; but, not the slightest ceasing to be a Puritan, went about his business"; see "Ben Franklin, Jonathan Edwards," *Major Writers of America* (New York: Har-

court Brace, 1962), 86. See chapter 4, n. 37 for sources on deism and the Enlightenment.

48. See chapter 18 for details of the Romantic-era view of Franklin.

49. John Updike, "Many Bens," *The New Yorker,* Feb. 22, 1988, 115; Henry Steele Commager, *The American Mind* (New Haven: Yale University Press, 1950), 26.

The strongest argument that Franklin was a pure exemplar of the Enlightenment is in historian Carl Becker's masterful essay on him in the *Dictionary of American Biography* (New York: Scribner's, 1933), in which he called Franklin "a true child of the Enlightenment, not indeed of the school of Rousseau, but of Defoe and Pope and Swift, of Fontenelle and Montesquieu and Voltaire. He spoke their language, although with a homely accent . . . He accepted without question all the characteristic ideas [of the Enlightenment]: its healthy, clarifying skepticism; its passion for freedom and its humane sympathies; its preoccupation with the world that is evident to the senses; its profound faith in common sense, in the efficacy of Reason for the solution of human problems and the advancement of human welfare." See also Stuart Sherman, "Franklin and the Age of Enlightenment," in Sanford.

50. Autobiography 139; Albert Smyth, *American Literature* (Philadelphia: Eldredge, 1889), 20; BF to Benjamin Vaughan, Nov. 9, 1779; BF to DF, June 4, 1765. For additional words of disgust about metaphysics, see BF to Thomas Hopkinson, Oct. 16, 1746. For a fuller assessment of Franklin's religious and moral beliefs, see the final chapter of this book. The ideas here draw in part from the following: Campbell 25, 34–36, 137, 165, 169–72, 286; Charles Angoff, *Literary History of the American People* (New York: Knopf, 1931), 295–310; Van Wyck Brooks, *America's Coming of Age* (Garden City, N.Y.: Anchor, 1934), 3–7; Lopez *Private,* 26; Alan Taylor, "For the Benefit of Mr. Kite," *The New Republic,* Mar. 19, 2001, 39; Vernon Parrington, *Main Currents in American Thought* (New York: Harcourt, 1930), 1:178; David Brooks, "Our Founding Yuppie," *The Weekly Standard,* Oct. 23, 2000, 31. "In its naive simplicity this hardly seems worthy of study as a philosophy," writes Herbert Schneider, "yet as a moral regime and outline of the art of virtue, it has a clarity and a power that command respect." Herbert Schneider, *The Puritan Mind* (Ann Arbor: University of Michigan Press, 1958), 246.

51. Alan Taylor, "For the Benefit of Mr. Kite," 39.

52. Poor Richard's 1733–58, by Franklin, plus editor's note in Papers 1:280; Faÿ 159–73; Sappenfield 121–77; Brands 124–31. There was also a real Richard Saunders who appears in the account books as a customer of Franklin's. Van Doren 107.

53. Pa. Gazette, Dec. 28, 1732.

54. Poor Richard's, 1733; Autobiography 107.

55. Poor Richard's, 1734, 1735; Titan Leeds's *American Almanack,* 1734; Jonathan Swift, "Predictions for the Ensuing Year by Isaac Bickerstaff, esq.," 1708, ftp://sailor.gutenberg.org/pub/gutenberg/etext97/bstaf10.txt . Swift's piece was a parody of an almanac by John Partridge; he predicted Partridge's death, and then engaged in a running jest similar to the one Franklin perpetrated on Leeds.

56. Poor Richard's, 1734, 1735, 1740; Papers 2:332n; Sappenfield 143; Brands 126.

57. Poor Richard's, 1736, 1738, 1739. See also the verses by "Bridget Saunders, my duchess" about lazy men in 1734 ("God in his mercy may do much to save him/ But woe to the poor wife whose lot is to have him"), which "Poor Richard" prints as a response to his own 1733 verses about lazy women.

58. Mark Twain, "The Late Benjamin Franklin," *The Galaxy,* July 1870, www.twainquotes.com/Galaxy/187007e.html ; Groucho Marx, *Groucho and Me* (New York: Random House, 1959), 6.

59. For an exhaustive study of the provenance of "early to bed and early to rise" see Wolfgang Mieder, "Early to Bed and Early to Rise," in the Web-based journal *De Proverbio,* www.utas.edu.au/docs/flonta/DP,1,1,95/FRANKLIN.html . *Bartlett's Familiar Quotations* (1882; Boston: Little, Brown, 2002) in its thirteenth edition (1955) and previous editions attributes the phrase to Franklin but also cites John Clarke's *Proverbs* (1639); it drops the reference to Clarke in subsequent editions.

60. The most detailed work on the origins of the maxims is Robert Newcombe, "The Sources of Benjamin Franklin's Sayings of Poor Richard," Ph.D. diss., University of Maryland, 1957. See also Papers 1:281–82; Van Doren 112–13; Wright 54; Frances Barbour, *A Concordance to the Sayings in Franklin's Poor Richard* (Detroit: Gale Research, 1974). Franklin's greatest reliance is on Jonathan Swift, James Howell's *Proverbs* (1659), and Thomas Fuller's *Gnomologia* (1732).

61. Philomath (BF), "Talents Requisite in an Almanac Writer," Pa. Gazette, Oct. 20, 1737. "Philomath" was a term used for almanac writers.

62. *Poor Richard Improved,* 1758.

63. Autobiography 107; Wright 55; Van Doren 197; D. H. Lawrence, "Benjamin Franklin," 14; BF to William Strahan, June 2, 1750; Poor Richard's, 1743.

CHAPTER 5

1. Poor Richard's, 1744; "Appeal for the Hospital," Pa. Gazette, Aug. 8, 1751; Alexis de Tocqueville, *Democracy in America* (1835; New York: Doubleday, 1969), 513; "Inside Main Street USA," *New York Times,* Aug. 27, 1995; John Van Horne, "Collective Benevolence for the Common Good," in Lemay *Reappraising,* 432. The two books that most influenced Franklin to form associations for the public good were Daniel Defoe's *An Essay upon Projects* (1697) and Cotton Mather's *Bonifacius: Essays to do Good* (1710).

2. Autobiography 90–91, 82; Faÿ 149; "The Library Company of Philadelphia," www.librarycompany.org ; Morgan *Franklin,* 56. The list of first books is in *PMHB* 300 (1906): 300.

3. "Brave Men at Fires," Pa. Gazette, Dec. 1, 1733; Autobiography 115; "On Protection of Towns from Fire," Pa. Gazette, Feb. 4, 1735; notice in Pa. Gazette, Jan. 27, 1743; Van Doren 130; Brands 135–37; Hawke 53.

4. Autobiography 115; Brands 214.

526

Notes for Pages 106–114

5. Faÿ 137; Pa Gazette, Dec. 30, 1730; Clark 44; Pennsylvania Grand Lodge Web site, www.pagrandlodge.org ; Julius Sachse, *Benjamin Franklin's Account with the Lodge of Masons* (Kila, Mont.: Kessinger, 1997).

6. Van Doren 134; Faÿ 180; Brands 152–54; BF to Joseph and Abiah Franklin, Apr. 13, 1738; Pa. Gazette, Feb. 7 (dated Feb. 15), 1738.

7. Autobiography 111; "Dialogue Between Two Presbyterians," Pa. Gazette, Apr. 10, 1735; "Observations on the Proceedings against Mr. Hemphill," July 1735, Papers 2:37; BF, "A Letter to a Friend in the Country," Sept. 1735, Papers 2:65; Jonathan Dickinson, "A Vindication of the Reverend Commission of the Synod," Sept. 1735, and "Remarks Upon the Defense of Rev. Hemphill's Observations," Nov. 1735; "A Defense of Mr. Hemphill's Observations," Oct. 1735. The pieces by Franklin, along with annotations about the affair and Dickinson's presumed authorship of the essays attributed to him, are in Papers 2:27–91. Franklin's fascinating battle over Hemphill has been recounted in many good historical studies, from which this section draws: Bryan LeBeau, "Franklin and the Presbyterians," *Early American Review* (summer 1996), earlyamerica.com/review/summer/franklin/; Merton Christensen, "Franklin on the Hemphill Trial: Deism versus Presbyterian Orthodoxy," *William and Mary Quarterly* (July 1953): 422–40; William Barker, "The Hemphill Case, Benjamin Franklin and Subscription to the Westminster Confession," *American Presbyterians* 69 (winter 1991); Aldridge *Nature*, 86–98; Buxbaum 93–104.

8. Campbell 97; Barbara Oberg and Harry Stout, eds., *Benjamin Franklin, Jonathan Edwards* (New York: Oxford University Press, 1997), 119; Carl Van Doren, *Benjamin Franklin and Jonathan Edwards* (New York: Scribner's, 1920), introduction; Jonathan Edwards, "Sinners in the Hands of an Angry God," delivered at Enfield, Conn., July 8, 1741, douglass.speech.nwu.edu/edwa_a45.htm ; Jack Hitt, "The Great Divide: It's Not Left and Right. It's Meritocrats and Valuecrats," *New York Times Magazine,* Dec. 31, 2000, 14.

9. Pa. Gazette, Nov. 15, 1739, May 22, 1740, June 12, 1740; Autobiography 116–20; Buxbaum 93–142; Brands 138–48; Hawke 57. Buxbaum presents an exhaustive analysis of all the items Franklin printed on Whitefield.

10. Frank Lambert, "Subscribing for Profits and Piety," *William and Mary Quarterly* (July 1993): 529–48; Harry Stout, "George Whitefield and Benjamin Franklin," *Massachusetts Historical Society* 103 (1992):9–23; David Morgan, "A Most Unlikely Friendship," *The Historian* 47 (1985): 208–18; Autobiography 118.

11. "Obadiah Plainman," Pa. Gazette, May 15, 29, 1740, Lib. of Am. 275–83, 1528; *American Weekly Mercury,* May 22, 1740. The editors of the Yale Papers do not include the Obadiah Plainman letters as Franklin's. But Leo Lemay convincingly argues that he wrote them, and he included them in the Library of America collection. Likewise, it seems possible that Franklin, as was his wont, stoked the controversy by writing the opposing letters from "Tom Trueman."

12. "Letter to a Friend in the Country" and "Statement of Editorial Policy," Pa. Gazette, July 24, 1740; Autobiography 118.

13. "Obituary of Andrew Hamilton," Pa. Gazette, Aug. 6, 1741; "Half-Hour's Conversation with a Friend," Pa. Gazette, Nov. 16, 1733.

14. Sappenfield 86–93; Autobiography 113–14.

15. C. William Miller, *Benjamin Franklin's Philadelphia Printing: A Descriptive Bibliography* (Philadelphia: American Philosophical Society, 1984), 32; James Green, *Benjamin Franklin as Publisher and Bookseller,* in Lemay *Reappraising,* 101. Green was a distinguished curator at the Library Company, and his notes on exhibitions of Franklin's books are useful.

16. Walter Isaacson, "Info Highwayman," *Civilization* (Mar. 1995): 48; Autobiography 114.

17. Sappenfield 93–105; Pa. Gazette, Nov. 13, Dec. 11, 1740; *American Weekly Mercury,* Nov. 20, 27, Dec. 4, 18, 1740; Papers, vol. 2; Frank Mott, *A History of American Magazines* (New York: Appleton, 1930), 1:8–27.

18. BF to Abiah Franklin, Oct. 16, 1747, Apr. 12, 1750; Lopez *Private,* 70–79; Autobiography 109; BF to William Strahan, June 2, 1750, Jan. 31, 1757; Clark 62, 139; Mrs. E. D. Gillespie (daughter of Sally Franklin Bache), *A Book of Remembrance* (Philadelphia: Lippincott, 1901), cited in Clark 17; Silence Dogood #5, *New England Courant,* May 28, 1722; DF to Margaret Strahan, Dec. 24, 1751; "A Petition of the Left Hand," 1785, in Lib. of Am. 1115 and Papers CD 43:u611.

In addition to half-seriously trying to fix Sally up with Strahan's son Billy, Franklin hoped his son, William, would marry Polly Stevenson, the daughter of his London landlady; that his grandson William Temple Franklin would marry the son of his Paris lady friend Mme. Brillon; and that Sally's son Benjamin Bache would marry Polly Stevenson's daughter. A harsher assessment of Franklin's treatment of Sally and the education he provided her can be found in an essay by Larry Tise, "Liberty and the Rights of Women," in the collection he edited, *Benjamin Franklin and Women* (University Park: Pennsylvania State University Press, 2000), 37–49.

19. Lopez *Private,* 34; Poor Richard's, 1735. "Reply to a Piece of Advice," Pa. Gazette, Mar, 4, 1735, praises marriage and children. The Yale editors of Franklin Papers tentatively attribute it to him, partly because it is signed "A.A.," initials he often used. Papers 2:21.

20. "Advice to a Young Man on the Choice of a Mistress," also known as "Old Mistress Apologue," June 25, 1745. A description of its publishing history is in Papers 3:27–31, and in the introduction to Larry Tise, *Benjamin Franklin and Women.*

21. "Speech of Polly Baker," *General Advertiser,* Apr. 15, 1747; Sappenfield 64. Franklin revealed his authorship in about 1778 at a dinner with the Abbé Raynal in Paris, where the authenticity of the famous speech was being debated. Franklin told the group, "I am going to set you straight. When I was young and printed a newspaper, it sometimes happened, when I was short of material to fill my sheet, that I amused myself by making up stories, and that of Polly Baker is one of the number." Papers 3:121–22.

22. "A Proposal for Promoting Useful Knowledge," May 14, 1743, Papers 2:378; *The Beginnings of the APS* (Philadelphia: APS Proceedings, 1944), 277–89; Edward C. Carter III, *One Grand Pursuit* (Philadelphia: American Philosophical Society, 1993); American Philosophical Society, www.amphilsoc.org .

Franklin had a love for writing very detailed charters, rules, and procedures for organizations. Among the groups he did this for were the Junto, Masonic lodge, fire company, police patrol, American Philosophical Society, Pennsylvania militia, Academy, postal service, and society for the abolition of slavery. This penchant also helped him draw up the Albany plan for union, the discipline regulations for the colonial army, and the first proposed articles of confederation.

23. Autobiography 121–23; "Plain Truth," Nov. 17, 1747; "Form of Association," Nov. 24, 1747; Papers 3:187, with historical notes. See chapter 4 for the issue of whether William was 16 or perhaps a bit older.

24. Autobiography 123; Richard Peters to Thomas Penn, Nov. 29, 1747, Papers 3:214; Penn to Peters, Mar. 30, June 9, 1748, Papers 3:186; "The Necessity of Self Defense," Pa. Gazette, Dec. 29, 1747 (in Lib. of Am. but not Yale papers); Brands 179–88; Wright 77–81; Hawke 75–80.

25. Wright 52; Van Doren 122; Autobiography 120, 92; "Articles of Agreement with David Hall," Jan. 1, 1748; Brands 188, 380; Clark 62; BF to Abiah Franklin, Apr. 12, 1750; BF to Cadwallader Colden, Sept. 29, 1748; Poor Richard's, 1744.

The year he retired, Franklin wrote and published an essay called "Advice to a Young Tradesman, Written by an Old One," in which he restated much of the philosophy of Poor Richard and the Autobiography: "The way to wealth, if you desire it, is as plain as the way to market. It depends chiefly on two words, Industry and Frugality; i.e., waste neither time nor money, but make the best use of both." Papers 3:304.

26. Gordon S. Wood, *The Radicalism of the American Revolution* (New York: Random House, 1991), 77, 85–86, 199. I tend to disagree with Wood's thesis to the extent that he portrays Franklin as a man of aristocratic aspirations whose leather-apron image was mainly affected after his social ambitions were dashed. The evidence in favor of giving more weight than Wood does to the view of Franklin as a proud member of the middle class is, I hope, detailed throughout this book. Even during the period right after his retirement, which Wood says was the prime period of his "aristocratic" aspirations, Franklin's politics remained rather populist and his civic endeavors had a common touch. Nevertheless, Wood provides an interesting assessment that merits consideration as a counterpoint to the approach taken by other historians. And because Wood contends that Franklin's aristocratic attitude was manifest primarily during the period from 1748 to the late 1760s (plus when he advocated at the Constitutional Convention that officeholders serve without pay), his thesis can be given weight without entirely rejecting the view that for most of his life Franklin was, as he claimed, a proud part of "we, the middling people." Wood also uses a somewhat broader definition of aristocracy than others do; he includes in it not only titled nobility and hereditary classes but also wealthy commoners who hold themselves out to be gentlemen. Wood's thesis reminds us, correctly I think, that one of Franklin's goals, beginning with his creation of the lending library, was to help members of the middling class take on some of the qualities of the enlightened gentry. (It should also be noted that the classical definition of aristocracy denoted a system of rule by the best, rather than a hereditary class system of social hierarchy and titles based on birth, which is what the term came to mean in England by Franklin's time.)

27. Wayne Craven, "The British and American Portraits of Benjamin Franklin," in Lemay *Reappraising,* 249; Charles Sellers, *Benjamin Franklin in Portraiture* (New Haven: Yale University Press, 1962); Poor Richard's, 1748.

CHAPTER 6

1. Dudley Herschbach, "Dr. Franklin's Scientific Amusements," *Harvard Magazine* (Nov. 1995): 36, and in the *Bulletin of the American Academy of Arts and Sciences* (Oct. 1994): 23. Herschbach, the Baird Professor of Science at Harvard, won the Nobel Prize for chemistry in 1958.

The most important academic studies on Franklin's science were done by the eminent scientific historian Harvard's I. Bernard Cohen. These include *Benjamin Franklin's Science* (Cambridge: Harvard University Press, 1990); *Science and the Founding Fathers* (New York: Norton, 1995), and *Franklin and Newton* (Philadelphia: American Philosophical Society, 1956). Also useful are Charles Tanford, *Ben Franklin Stilled the Waves* (Durham, N.C.: Duke University Press, 1989); Nathan Goodman, ed., *The Ingenious Dr. Franklin* (Philadelphia: University of Pennsylvania Press, 1931), which is a collection of Franklin's scientific letters and essays; J. L. Heilbron, "Franklin as an Enlightened Natural Philosopher," and Heinz Otto Sibum, "The Bookkeeper of Nature," in Lemay *Reappraising.*

2. "Magic Squares," BF to Peter Collinson, 1750; BF to PS, Sept. 20, 1761; Cohen 159–71; Brands 630. Cohen dates the heat experiments of Franklin and Breintnall from 1729 to 1737 based on letters and Junto notes, and traces the theories back to Newton and Boyle, accounts of which Franklin had read.

3. "An Account of the New Invented Pennsylvania Fire-Places," 1744, Papers 2:419–46 (with historical notes by the paper's editors); Autobiography 128; Lemay *Reappraising,* 201–3; letter to the *Boston Evening Post,* Sept. 8, 1746, first rediscovered and noted in Lemay *Internet Doc* for 1746; Brands 167; Samuel Edgerton Jr., "The Franklin Stove," in Cohen 199–211. Edgerton, an art historian at the University of Pennsylvania, shows that the stove was not as practical or popular as other historians assume.

4. BF to John Franklin, Dec. 8, 1752; "Origin of Northeast Storms," BF to Jared Eliot, Feb. 13, 1750; BF to Jared Eliot, July 16, 1747; BF to Alexander Small, May 12, 1760; John Cox, *The Storm Watchers* (New York: Wiley, 2002), 5–7.

5. Cohen 40–65; BF to Collinson, Mar. 28, 1747; Autobiography 164; Bowen 47–49. Cohen provides detailed evidence on the dates of Dr. Spencer's lectures, their content, Collinson's gift, and the errors Franklin made in later recalling the chronology.

6. BF to Collinson, May 25, July 28, 1747, Apr. 29, 1749; Cohen 22–26; I. Bernard Cohen, *Franklin and Newton,* 303; Clark 71. J. L. Heilbrun and Heinz Otto Sibum, in Lemay's *Reappraising,* 196–242, emphasize the "bookkeeping" nature of Franklin's theories.

7. BF to Collinson, Apr. 29, 1749, Feb. 4, 1750; Brands 199; Thomas Pynchon, *Mason & Dixon* (New York: Holt, 1997), 294.

8. BF to John Lining, Mar. 18, 1755; BF to Collinson, Mar. 2, 1750; BF to John Winthrop, July 2, 1768; Hawke 86–88; Cohen 121; Van Doren 156–70; Brands 198–202. Andrew White, "History of Warfare of Science with Theology in Christendom," www.human-nature.com/reason/white/chap11.html . Among those, in addition to Newton, who had already noted the similarities between electrical sparks and lightning were Francis Hauksbee, Samuel Wall, John Freke, Johann Heinrich Winkler, and Franklin's antagonist the Abbé Nollet; see Clark 79–80. None, however, had proposed serious experiments to assess the hypothesis.

9. BF to John Mitchell, Apr. 29, 1749.

10. BF to Collinson, July 29, Mar. 2, 1750.

11. *The Gentleman's Magazine,* Jan., May 1750; *Experiments and Observations on Electricity, Made at Philadelphia in America, by Mr. Benjamin Franklin* (London: 1750, 1756, and subsequent editions); Abbé Guillaume Mazéas to Stephen Hales, May 20, 1752, Papers 4:315 and *Philosophical Transactions of the Royal Society* (1751–52); Autobiography 165–67; Clark 3–5, 83; Cohen 70–72.

12. "The Kite Experiment," Pa. Gazette, Oct. 19, 1752; Papers 4:360–65 has a footnote explaining historical issues; Pa. Gazette, Aug. 27, Oct. 19, 1752; Cohen 68–77; Joseph Priestley, *The History and Present State of Electricity* (1767), www.ushistory.org/franklin/kite/index.htm ; Hawke 103–6.

13. Cohen 66–109; Van Doren 164; Tom Tucker, *Bolt of Fate* (New York: Public Affairs, 2003). Tucker charges that "It's possible that . . . Franklin dreamed up his own kite claim" and that it was all a "hoax" akin to his literary ones. His book does not address the detailed evidence I. Bernard Cohen cites on this question and is, I think, unpersuasive. Franklin's kite description is in no ways similar to his literary hoaxes, and if untrue would have been an outright lie rather than a hoax. Tucker also makes the odd allegation that Franklin's description of his sentry box experiment was a death threat to the president of London's Royal Society. He also charges that Franklin may have been lying when he publicly reported in 1752 that two lightning rods had been erected on public buildings in Philadelphia that summer (a report that was published in the Royal Society's journal and would, it seems, have been challenged at the time if it were false). The comprehensive analysis by Cohen, a professor of the history of science who is the foremost authority on Franklin's electricity work, addresses fully and more convincingly the issues surrounding Franklin's sentry box, kite, and lightning rods. Other articles about whether Franklin flew the kite that summer include Abbott L. Rotch, "Did Franklin Fly His Electrical Kite before He Invented the Lighting Rod?" *American Antiquarian Society Proceedings,* 1907; Alexander McAdie, "The Date of Franklin's Kite Experiment," *American Antiquarian Society Proceedings,* 1925.

14. Cohen 66–109; Van Doren 165–70. Van Doren says that the possibility that Franklin fabricated or embellished his kite experiment would be "quite out of keeping with his record in science, in which he elsewhere appears always truthful and unpretending."

15. BF to Collinson, Sept. 1753; BF to DF, June 10, 1758; Dudley Herschbach, "Ben Franklin's Scientific Amusements," *Harvard Magazine* (Nov. 1995): 44; BF to Cadwallader Colden, Apr. 12, 1753; BF to Royal Society, May 29, 1754.

16. BF to Collinson, July 29, 1750; Van Doren 171; J. J. Thompson, *Recollections and Reflections* (London: Bell, 1939), 252; BF to Cadwallader Colden, Oct. 11, 1750; Turgot epigram, 1781: *Eripuit cœlo fulmen, sceptrumque tyrannis.*

CHAPTER 7

1. "On the Need for an Academy," Pa. Gazette, Aug. 24, 1749; "Proposals Relating to the Education of Youth in Pennsylvania," Oct. 1749; BF to Cadwallader Colden, Nov. 1749; Constitutions of the Publick Academy, Nov. 13, 1749; Autobiography 121, 129–31; Van Doren 193; University of Pennsylvania history, www.archives.upenn.edu/histy/genlhistory/brief.html . (The school was originally called the Academy of Philadelphia, then the College of Philadelphia, then in 1779 it was taken over by the state and became the University of the State of Pennsylvania, and finally in 1791 it was named the University of Pennsylvania.)

2. "Appeal for the Hospital," Pa. Gazette, Aug. 8, 1751; Autobiography 134.

3. BF to Peter Collinson, May 9, 1753; Stuart Sherman, "Franklin and the Age of Enlightenment," in Sanford 75. See also chapter 4, n. 49.

For more on Franklin's political thought, see Paul Conner, *Poor Richard's Politicks* (New York: Oxford University Press, 1965), and Francis Jennings, *Benjamin Franklin: Politician* (New York: Norton, 1996).

4. "Observations Concerning the Increase of Mankind," 1751, Papers 4:225; Conner 69–87; Hawke 95.

5. "Felons and Rattlesnakes," Pa. Gazette, May 9, 1751.

6. "Observations Concerning the Increase of Mankind," 1751; BF to Abiah Franklin, Apr. 12, 1750; John Van Horne, "Collective Benevolence," in Lemay *Reappraising,* 433–36; Lopez *Private,* 291–302.

7. BF to John Waring, Dec. 17, 1763.

8. BF to Peter Collinson, May 9, 1753.

9. Autobiography 131.

10. Autobiography 132.

11. Autobiography 132; Report of the Treaty of Carlisle, Nov. 1, 1753; Minutes of the Provincial Council of Pennsylvania, Nov. 15, 1753.

12. Autobiography 140; BF to Collinson, May 21, 1751; John Franklin to BF, Nov. 26, 1753; "Procedures for Postmasters," 1753, Papers 5:162–77; post office finances, Aug. 10, 1753, Papers 5:18; Wright 85; Hawke 114; Brands 243–45; Clark 100; Lopez *Private,* 53.

13. BF to James Parker, Mar. 20, 1751; Pa. Gazette, May 9, 1754.

14. "Commission to Treat With the Indians," Pa. Assembly, May 13, 1754, Papers 5:275; "Short Hints towards a Scheme for Uniting the Northern Colonies," in BF to James Alexander and Cadwallader Colden, June 8, 1754, Papers 5:335.

15. BF to Peter Collinson, July 29, 1754; BF to Cadwallader Colden, July 14, 1754; "Plan of Proposed Union," July 10, 1754; Autobiography 141–42; BF to William Shirley, Dec. 4, 22, 1754.

For overviews: Bernard Bailyn, *The Ordeal of Thomas Hutchinson* (Cambridge:

Harvard University Press, 1974); Robert Newbold, *The Albany Congress and Plan of Union* (New York: Vantage, 1955), 95–105; Morgan *Franklin*, 83–90; Hawke 116–23; Brands 234–40; Wright 89–94. The most colorful popular account is in Catherine Drinker Bowen, *The Most Dangerous Man in America* (Boston: Little, Brown, 1974), 91–162.

There is a scholarly dispute on how to apportion credit for the final plan between Franklin and Hutchinson. In a letter years later, Hutchinson referred to it as his plan, but in a history book he wrote that "the plan for a general union was projected by Benjamin Franklin." Indeed, the final plan was very similar in structure and phrasing to the "Short Hints" paper that Franklin prepared before arriving at Albany. See Papers 5:335; Wright 92. For a pro-Hutchinson view, see Lawrence Gipson, *The British Empire before the American Revolution* (New York: Knopf, 1936–69), 5:126–38.

16. BF to John Franklin, Mar. 16, 1755; BF to Catherine Ray, Mar. 4, Mar.–Apr., Sept. 11, Oct. 16, 1755; Catherine Ray to BF, June 28, 1755. (She signed her name "Caty," but Franklin tended to address her as "Katy" or "Katie.")

17. The best analysis is in Lopez *Private*, 55–57, and Lopez *Life*, 25–29. The quote from Lopez is from the former book, but it is repeated in similar form in the latter. See also William Roelker, *Benjamin Franklin and Catherine Ray Greene* (Philadelphia: American Philosophical Society, 1949). Also worth noting is J. A. Leo Lemay's astute analysis in *PMHB* 126:2 (Apr. 2002): 336: "Biographers who read Franklin's flirtations as serious attempts to have sexual affairs seem to me to be either unsophisticated about human psychology or as prudish as John Adams in Paris."

18. BF to Catherine Ray, Mar. 2, 1789.

19. Autobiography 143–47; Hawke 124–62; BF to Peters, Sept. 17, 1754; BF to Collinson, Aug. 25, 1755.

20. Autobiography 151–52, 148–51; "Advertisement for Wagons," Apr. 26, 1755; Papers 6:19. (It is misdated in the Autobiography.)

21. BF to Peter Collinson, June 26, 1755; Autobiography 144; Robert Hunter Morris to Thomas Penn, June 16, 1755.

22. Autobiography 154–56; Assembly reply to Governor Morris, Aug. 8, 19, Nov. 11, 1755.

23. Autobiography 156; Brands 262; Pa. Gazette, Dec. 18, 1755; BF to James Read, Nov. 2, 1755; BF to Richard Partridge, Nov. 27, 1755.

24. BF to DF, Jan. 25, 1756; Autobiography 160–62; Brands 267–69; J. Bennett Nolan, *General Benjamin Franklin* (Philadelphia: University of Pennsylvania Press, 1936), 62.

25. Autobiography 162–63; Brands 270–71; BF to Collinson, Nov. 5, 1756.

26. BF to George Whitefield, July 2, 1756; BF to DF, Mar. 25, 1756; Autobiography 169; Assembly reply, by BF, Oct. 29, 1756; Assembly appointment of Franklin, Jan. 29, Feb. 3, 1757, Papers 7:109; Wright 105; Thomas Penn to Richard Peters, May 14, 1757.

CHAPTER 8

1. BF to William Brownrigg, Nov. 7, 1773; "Everything is soothed by oil," Pliny the Elder (A.D. 23–79) wrote in his work *Natural History,* book 2, section 234. He was, in addition to being a scientist and senator, a commander of the Roman imperial fleet near Naples, and was killed at an eruption of Mount Vesuvius.

2. BF to DF, July 17, 1757; Autobiography 175–77.

3. Lopez *Private,* 86.

4. The Craven Street house where Franklin spent most of his time, now number 36, still exists, and in 2003 work began on converting it into a small museum. The plan is to have each of the tiny rooms feature a different aspect of his stay in London: his diplomacy, science, social life, and writings. The house, which has a nineteenth-century brick façade but is otherwise structurally similar to the way it was in Franklin's time, is a few hundred yards from Charing Cross station and Trafalgar Square. www.thersa.org/franklin/default.html ; www.rsa.org.uk/projects/ project_closeup.asp?id=1001 ; www.cs.mdx.ac.uk/wrt/Siteview/project.html .

5. BF to PS May 4, 1759, and undated 1759, May 1, Sept. 13, 1760.

6. BF to PS, Sept. 13, 1759, May 1, June 11 (includes the "prudent moderation" excerpt), Sept. 13, and undated Nov., 1760; PS to BF, June 23, 1760, undated Aug., and Sept. 16, 1760. See also their letters throughout 1761–62.

7. BF to PS, Jan. 27, 1783; Wright 110; Clark 140; Lopez *Private,* 83; Randall 123.

8. William Strahan to DF, Dec. 13, 1757.

9. BF to DF, Jan. 14, Feb. 19, June 10, 1758; Lopez *Private,* 80; Clark 142–43, 147.

10. BF to DF, Nov. 22, Dec. 3, 1757, June 10, 1758, June 27, 1760; Lopez *Private,* 172.

11. Verner Crane, "The Club of Honest Whigs," *William and Mary Quarterly* 23 (1966): 210; Leonard Labaree, "Benjamin Franklin's British Friendships," *Proceedings of the American Philosophical Society* 108 (1964): 423; Clark 142; Brands 279; Morgan *Devious,* 15; Hawke 163.

12. Strahan to DF, Dec. 13, 1757; BF to DF, Nov. 27, 1757.

13. Wright 114–15, 216–17.

14. Thomas Penn to Richard Peters, May 14, 1757.

15. Autobiography 177–79.

16. Autobiography 178.

17. Autobiography 179; "Heads of Complaint," BF to the Penns, Aug. 20, 1757; answer to "Heads of Complaint" by Ferdinand John Paris, Nov. 28, 1758, Papers 8:184; Cecil Currey, *Road to Revolution* (Garden City, N.Y.: Anchor, 1968), 35.

18. "Pennsylvania Charter of Privileges," Oct. 28, 1701, www.constitution.org/ bcp/penncharpriv.htm ; BF to Isaac Norris, Jan. 14, 1758; Clark 144; Middlekauff 65–66; Brands 301.

19. Thomas Penn to Richard Peters, July 5, 1758; BF to Joseph Galloway, Feb. 17, 1758; Brands 302; Wright 117.

20. WF to the Printer of the *Citizen,* from the Pennsylvania Coffee-house in London, Sept. 16, 1757.

21. BF to DF, June 10, 1758; Skemp *William,* 30–31.

22. Lopez *Private,* 61–69; Skemp *William,* 24–26, 37; Randall 102–15; WF to Elizabeth Graeme, Feb. 26, Apr. 7, Dec. 9, 1757; WF to Margaret Abercrombie, Oct. 24, 1758. *The True Conduct of Persons of Quality* was written by Nicolas Rémond des Cours and translated from the French and published in London in 1694.

23. BF to Abiah Franklin, Apr. 12, 1750; WF to BF, Sept. 3, 1758.

24. BF to DF, Sept. 6, 1758, Aug. 29, 1759.

25. Dr. Thomas Bray, "Society for the Propagation of the Gospel in Foreign Parts Among the Negroes in the Colonies," docsouth.dsi.internet2.edu/church/ pierre/pierre.html ; BF to John Lining, Apr. 14, 1757, June 17, 1758; BF to Cadwallader Colden, Feb. 25, 1763.

26. BF to DF, Sept. 6, 1758.

27. Answer to Heads of Complaint by Ferdinand John Paris, Nov. 28, 1758; Thomas and Richard Penn to the Assembly, Nov. 28, 1758; BF to Isaac Norris, Jan. 19, 1759. See Papers 8:178–86; Middlekauff 68–70; Hawke 173; Morgan *Devious,* 38.

28. Morgan *Franklin,* 102, 130; Gordon Wood, "Wise Men," *New York Review,* Sept. 26, 2002, 44. In this review of Morgan's book, Wood argues that Franklin's actions can be readily explained by his loyalty to the Crown, and he faults Morgan for being blinded by hindsight when he accuses Franklin of blindness. "His account of Franklin seems at times subtly infused with what historians call 'whiggism,' the anachronistic foreshortening that makes the past an anticipation of the future," Wood writes. On balance, I feel that Franklin's anger at the Proprietors did, in fact, cause him to lose his perspective at a time when others, both supporters and foes of the Penns, were able to see more clearly that there was not enough support on either side of the ocean to turn Pennsylvania into a royal colony and that the fundamental problem was the general attitude among British leaders that the colonies ought to be economically and politically submissive.

29. BF to the Privy Council, Sept. 20, 1758; Hawke 176.

30. BF to Thomas Leech, May 13, 1758; Hawke 169, 177; Papers 8:60.

31. Autobiography 180; Report of the Board of Trade, June 24, 1760, in Papers 9:125–73; Privy Council order, Sept. 2, 1760; Morgan *Devious,* 56–57; Middlekauff 73.

32. Brands 305–6; "A Parable on Brotherly Love," 1755, Papers 6:124; BF to Lord Kames, May 3, 1760.

33. BF to David Hume, May 19, 1762.

34. BF to David Hume, Sept. 27, 1760; David Hume to BF, May 10, 1762.

35. BF to Lord Kames, Jan. 3, 1760; Brands 287; St. Andrew's citation, Oct. 1, 1759, Papers 8:277.

36. BF to DF, Mar. 5, 1760.

37. Temple Franklin's tombstone refers to his birthdate as Feb. 22, 1762, but

family correspondence indicates that he was born in February 1760. Lopez *Private*, 93; Van Doren 290.

38. BF to Jared Ingersoll, Dec. 11, 1762; WF to SF, Oct. 10, 1761.

39. "Humorous Reasons for Restoring Canada," London *Chronicle*, Dec. 27, 1759; "The Interest of Great Britain Considered," Apr. 1760, Papers 9:59–100; Jack Greene, "Pride, Prejudice and Jealousy," in Lemay *Reappraising*, 125.

40. BF to William Strahan, Aug. 23, 1762.

41. Aldridge *French*, 169, from Pierre Cabanis, *Complete Works* (Paris: Bossange frères, 1825), 5:222.

42. Temple Franklin, "Memoirs of Benjamin Franklin," 1:75; Randall 180; Skemp *William*, 38; Brands 328; BF to JM, Nov. 25, 1752; BF to PS, Aug. 11, 1762.

43. BF to John Pringle, Dec. 1, 1762.

CHAPTER 9

1. Skemp *William*, 48; Thomas Penn to James Hamilton, Sept. 1762; Clark 170.

2. BF to Benjamin Waller, Aug. 1, 1763.

3. BF to Lord Bessborough, Oct. 1761; Lopez *Private*, 100; BF to DF, June 16, 1763.

4. BF to PS, June 10, 1763; Lopez *Private*, 100.

5. Hawke 202; BF to JM, June 19, 1763; BF to Catherine Ray Greene, Aug. 1, 1763; BF to William Strahan, Aug. 8, 1763.

6. Lopez *Private*, 114; WF to William Strahan, Apr. 25, 1763; BF to William Strahan, Dec. 19, 1763.

7. BF to Peter Collinson, Dec. 19, 1763; "A Narrative of the Late Massacres, in Lancaster County, of a Number of Indians, Friends of this Province, by Persons Unknown," Jan. 1764; Van Doren 307; Hawke 208; Brands 352.

There is an interesting historical dispute over Franklin's sympathies for the Indians and prejudice toward the frontier Presbyterians and ethnic Germans. Buxbaum 185–219 is among those who play up Franklin's prejudice toward Presbyterians and take him to task for making the Indians seem "human beings not essentially different from Englishmen." Brooke Hindle, in "The March of the Paxton Boys," *William and Mary Quarterly* (Oct. 1946), takes a similar approach. They are opposed by Francis Jennings in *Benjamin Franklin: Politician* (New York: Norton, 1996), 158–59. He calls Buxbaum "learnedly confused" and accuses Hindle of "absolute ignorance" and of making "bigoted asinine" comments.

8. BF to John Fothergill, Mar. 14, 1764; BF to Richard Jackson, Feb. 11, 1764; Hawke 208.

9. BF to Lord Kames, June 2, 1765; John Penn to Thomas Penn, May 5, 1764; BF to John Fothergill, Mar. 14, 1764; Hawke 211; Brands 356; Van Doren 311.

10. Assembly reply to the governor, Mar. 24, 1764.

11. Van Doren 314; Buxbaum 192; Cecil Currey, *Road to Revolution* (Garden City, N.Y.: Anchor, 1968), 58.

12. Resolutions of the Pennsylvania Assembly, Mar. 24, 1764; "Cool Thoughts on the Present Situation of Our Public Affairs," Apr. 12, 1764; BF to Richard Jackson, Mar. 14, 29, Sept. 1, 1764; BF to William Strahan, Mar. 30, 1764; J. Philip Gleason, "A Scurrilous Election and Franklin's Reputation," *William and Mary Quarterly* (Oct. 1961); Brands 357; Van Doren 313; Morgan *Devious*, 80–83. The anti-Franklin pamphlets are in Papers 11:381.

13. Hawke 225; Brands 358; Van Doren 316; Buxbaum 12; "Remarks on a Late Protest," Nov. 5, 1764.

14. BF to Richard Jackson, May 1, 1764; BF to SF, Nov. 8, 1764; Hawke 222–26.

CHAPTER 10

1. BF to PS, Dec. 12, 1764.

2. BF to DF, Dec. 27, 1764, Feb. 9, 14, 1765. For good overviews on Franklin's mission, see Middlekauff; Morgan *Devious;* Cecil Currey, *Road to Revolution* (Garden City, N.Y.: Anchor, 1968); Theodore Draper, *The Struggle for Power* (New York: Times Books, 1996); Edmund Morgan and Helen Morgan, *The Stamp Act Crisis* (Chapel Hill: University of North Carolina Press, 1953).

3. BF to PS, July 20, 1768; PS to BF, Sept. 26, 1768; Noah Webster to BF, May 24, 1786; BF to Webster, June 18, 1786; Van Doren 426; Noah Webster, *Dissertations on the English Language: With Notes, Historical and Critical, to Which Is Added, by Way of Appendix, an Essay on a Reformed Mode of Spelling, with Dr. Franklin's Arguments on That Subject* (Boston: Isaiah Thomas, 1789), edweb.sdsu.edu/people/DKitchen/new_655/webster_language.htm .

4. Lopez *Private*, 152; WF to BF, Jan. 2, 1769; PS to Barbara Hewson, Oct. 4, 1774; PS to BF, Sept. 5, 1776.

5. Cadwalader Evans to BF, Mar. 15, 1765; John Penn to Thomas Penn, Mar. 16, 1765; Morgan *Devious*, 94.

6. BF to Joseph Galloway, Oct. 11, 1766; Morgan *Devious*, 102. Morgan and Morgan, *The Stamp Act Crisis*, 89–91; Brands 360–63; Van Doren 320.

7. BF to John Hughes, Aug. 9, 1765; Morgan *Devious*, 106; Thomas Penn to William Allen, July 13, 1765.

8. BF to Charles Thomson, July 11, 1765; Morgan *Devious*, 105; Charles Thomson to BF, Sept. 24, 1765; John Hughes to BF, Sept. 17, 1765.

9. David Hall to BF, Sept. 6, 1765; Morgan *Devious*, 106; Wright 188.

10. Samuel Wharton to BF, Oct. 13, 1765; John Hughes to BF, Sept. 12, 1765; DF to BF, Sept. 22, 1765; Morgan *Devious*, 107; BF to DF, Nov. 9, 1765; Brands 368.

11. Patrick Henry to the Virginia House of Delegates, May 30, 1765; BF to John Hughes, Aug. 9, 1765; Thomas Hutchinson to BF, Nov. 18, 1765; Brands 368.

12. BF to Pennsylvania Assembly committee, Apr. 12, 1766; Thomas Penn to John Penn, Nov. 30, 1765.

13. BF to David Hall, Nov. 9, 1765; BF to Joseph Galloway, Oct. 11, 1766; John Fothergill to James Pemberton, Feb. 27, 1766; "Defense of Indian Corn and a Reply," *The Gazetteer*, Jan. 2, 15, 1766.

14. *Public Advertiser*, May 22, 1765, Jan. 2, 1766.

15. William Warner, "Enlightened Anonymity," University of California Santa Barbara, lecture, Mar. 8, 2002, dc-mrg.english.ucsb.edu/conference/2002/documents/william_warner_anon.html .

16. BF to JM, Mar. 1, 1766; BF to WF, Nov. 9, 1765; Brands 373; Hawke 235–37.

17. BF to unknown recipient, Jan. 6, 1766; see also BF to Cadwalader Evans, May 1766; Wright 187; Van Doren 333.

18. Testimony to the House of Commons, Feb. 13, 1766, Papers 13:129–62; Brands 374–76; Van Doren 336–52.

19. William Strahan to David Hall, May 10, 1766; Joseph Galloway to BF, May 23, June 7, 1766; Charles Thomson to BF, May 20, 1766; Van Doren 353; Clark 195; Hawke 242.

20. BF to DF, Apr. 6, 1766.

21. DF to BF, Feb. 10, Oct. 8, 13, 1765; BF to DF, June 4, 1765; Lopez *Private*, 126.

22. David Hall to BF, Jan. 27, 1767; BF to Hall, Apr. 14, 1767.

23. BF to DF, June 22, 1767.

24. Lopez *Private*, 134, citing E. D. Gillespie, *A Book of Remembrance* (Philadelphia: Lippincott, 1901), 25.

25. DF to BF, Apr. 25, 1767; BF to DF, May 23, June 22, 1767; Brands 390; Hawke 255.

26. WF to BF, May 1767; RB to BF, May 21, 1767; Brands 391.

27. BF to RB, Aug. 5, 1767; BF to DF, Aug. 5, 1767.

28. MS to DF, Sept. 18, 1767; Lopez *Private*, 139.

29. BF to DF, Aug. 28, 1767; BF to PS, Sept. 14, 1767.

30. BF to PS, Aug. 28, 1767; Van Doren 367–69.

31. BF to DF, Nov. 2, 17, 1767; BF to PS, Oct. 9, 1767; Brands 395–96; Van Doren 368; Hawke 258.

32. JM to BF, Dec. 1, 1767; BF to JM, Feb. 21, 1768.

33. BF to RB, Aug. 13, 1768; BF to DF, Aug. 9, 1768; Lopez *Private*, 141.

34. BF to DF, Jan. 26, 1769; Thomas Bond to BF, June 7, 1769; DF to BF, Nov. 27, 1769; Van Doren 404; Lopez *Private*, 143; Brands 456.

35. PS to BF, Sept. 1, 1769; BF to PS, Sept. 2, 1769, May 31, 1770; Lopez *Private*, 154.

36. "Craven Street Gazette," Sept. 22–25, 1770, in Papers 17:220–26.

37. BF to Barbeu Dubourg, July 28, 1768; Lopez *Private*, 27.

38. BF to MS, Nov. 3, 1772, misdated 1767 in Papers.

39. "A Friend to Both Countries," London *Chronicle*, Apr. 9, 1767; "Be-

nevolous," London *Chronicle,* Apr. 11, 1767; Brands 386; Hawke 252; Cecil Currey, *Road to Revolution,* 222.

40. "Causes of the American Discontents before 1768," London *Chronicle,* Jan. 7, 1768. Although it was anonymous, Franklin indicated his authorship by using as an epigram a line he had used in his 1760 piece on "The Interest of Great Britain Considered": "The waves never rise but when the winds blow." With his interest in waves, both scientific and political, he enjoyed this metaphor.

41. "Preface to Letters from a Farmer," by N.N. (BF), May 8, 1768, Papers 15:110; BF to WF, Mar. 13, 1768.

42. BF to Joseph Galloway, Jan. 9, 1768; BF to WF, Jan. 9, 1768; BF to unknown recipient, Nov. 28, 1768; Lib. of Am. 839; Clark 211.

43. BF to Joseph Galloway, July 2, Dec. 13, 1768; BF to WF, July 2, 1768; Hawke 263, 268; Brands 408.

44. To Thomas Crowley, by "Francis Lynn" (BF), *Public Advertiser,* Oct. 21, 1768; "On Civil War," signed N.N. (BF), *Public Advertiser,* Aug. 25, 1768; "Queries," by "NMCNPCH" (BF), London *Chronicle,* Aug. 18, 1768; "On Absentee Governors," by Twilight (BF), *Public Advertiser,* Aug. 27, 1768.

45. "An American" (BF) to the *Gazetteer,* Jan. 17, 1769; "A Lion's Whelp," *Public Advertiser,* Jan. 2, 1770.

46. BF to William Strahan, Nov. 29, 1769.

47. BF to Charles Thomson, Mar. 18, 1770; BF to Samuel Cooper, June 8, 1770.

48. Franklin's account of audience with Hillsborough, Jan. 16, 1771, Papers 18:9; Hawke 290; Brands 431–34.

49. BF to Samuel Cooper, Feb. 5, June 10, 1771; Strahan to WF, Apr. 3, 1771; BF to Massachusetts Committee of Correspondence, May 15, 1771; Hawke 294–95; Van Doren 387–88.

50. BF to Thomas Cushing, June 10, 1771; Arthur Lee to Sam Adams, June 10, 1771, in Richard Henry Lee, *The Life of Arthur Lee* (Boston: Wells and Lilly, 1829); Samuel Cooper to BF, Aug. 25, 1771; Brands 437–38.

CHAPTER 11

1. BF to William Brownrigg, Nov. 7, 1773; Charles Tanford, *Ben Franklin Stilled the Waves* (Durham, N.C.: Duke University Press, 1989), 29; Van Doren 419.

2. Jonathan Williams (BF's nephew), "Journal of a Tour Through Northern England," May 28, 1771, Papers 18:113; BF to Thomas Cushing, June 10, 1771; BF to DF, June 5, 1771; Hawke 295; Brands 438.

3. BF to Jonathan Shipley, June 24, 1771.

4. BF to JM, July 17, 1771; BF to Samuel Franklin, July 19, 1771.

5. John Updike, "Many Bens," *New Yorker,* Feb. 22, 1988, 112; Charles Angoff, *A Literary History of the American People* (New York: Knopf, 1931); Van Doren 415.

Lemay/Zall Autobiography provides a complete look at the original manuscript and all of its revisions. The edition produced by Leonard Labaree and the other editors of the Franklin Papers at Yale (New Haven: Yale University Press, 1964) is authoritative, filled with useful annotations, and has an introduction that gives a good history of the manuscript. Carl Van Doren, *Benjamin Franklin's Autobiographical Writings* (1945; New York: Viking, 2002), 208–11, and Van Doren's biography of Franklin, 414–15, describe Franklin's process of writing. Also valuable are various articles by J. A. Leo Lemay: "The Theme of Vanity in Franklin's Autobiography," in Lemay *Reappraising*, 372, and "Franklin and the Autobiography," *Eighteenth Century Studies* (1968): 200. For good analyses of the manuscript, which is available at the Huntington Library, see P. M. Zall, "The Manuscript of Franklin's Autobiography," *Huntington Library Quarterly* 39 (1976); P. M. Zall, "A Portrait of the Autobiographer as an Old Artificer," in *The Oldest Revolutionary*, ed. J. A. Leo Lemay (Philadelphia: University of Pennsylvania Press, 1976), 53. The Norton Critical edition (New York: Norton, 1968), which was edited by Lemay and Zall, contains a bibliography of scholarly articles as well as excerpts of criticism. See also Ormond Seavey, *Becoming Benjamin Franklin: The Autobiography and the Life* (University Park: Pennsylvania State University Press, 1988); Henry Steele Commager, introduction to the Modern Library edition (New York: Random House, 1944); Daniel Aaron, introduction to the Library of America edition (New York: Vintage, 1990).

The memoir written by Lord Herbert of Cherbury (1583–1648) had been published by Franklin's friend Horace Walpole in 1764, seven years before Franklin began his own work. Gilbert Burnet was a great English clergyman and historian who described the revolution of 1688 in his *History of My Own Time,* a copy of which was owned by Franklin's Library Company.

6. BF to Anna Shipley, Aug. 13, 1771; BF to Georgiana Shipley, Sept. 26, 1772; BF to DF, Aug. 14, 1771; Van Doren 416–17.

7. BF to Thomas Cushing, Jan. 13, 1772; BF to Joshua Babcock, Jan. 13, 1772; Brands 440.

8. BF to Thomas Cushing, Jan. 13, 1772; BF to WF, Jan. 30, 1772.

9. J. Bennett Nolan, *Benjamin Franklin in Scotland and Ireland* (Philadelphia: University of Pennsylvania Press, 1956). This small book is a detailed and well-researched account of Franklin's activities on these trips. There is some disagreement about whether Adam Smith showed Franklin chapters of the *Wealth of Nations,* published in 1776, but one of Smith's relatives said this was the case.

10. PS to BF, Oct. 31, 1771; SF to RB, Dec. 2, 1771; RB to DF, Dec. 3, 1771; Mary Bache to BF, Dec. 3, 1771, Feb. 5, 1772; Lopez *Private*, 143–44.

11. BF to DF, Jan. 28, 1772; BF to SF, Jan. 29, 1772; Lopez *Private*, 146; RB to BF, Apr. 6, 1773; Van Doren 392; Brands 455.

12. BF to DF, Oct. 3, 1770; BF to PS, Nov. 25, 1771; BF to DF, Feb. 2, 1773; Brands 456; Van Doren 404, 411.

13. BF to William Brownrigg, Nov. 7, 1773; Stanford 78–80; C. H. Giles, "Franklin's Teaspoon of Oil," *Chemistry & Industry* (1961): 1616–34; Stephen Thompson, "How Small Is a Molecule?" *SHiPS News,* Jan. 1994, www1.umn.edu/ships/words/avogadro.htm ; "Measuring Molecules: The Pond on Clapham Common," www.rosepetruck.chem.brown.edu/Chem10-01/Lab3/Chem10_lab3.htm .

14. BF to Benjamin Rush, July 14, 1773.

15. BF to WF, Aug. 19, 1772.

16. BF to Cadwalader Evans, Feb. 20, 1768.

17. BF to John Pringle, May 10, 1768.

18. BF to Peter Franklin, May 7, 1760.

19. BF to Giambatista Beccaria, July 13, 1762; www.gigmasters.com/armonica/index.asp .

20. Franklin to Collinson, May 9, 1753.

21. Medius (BF), "On the Labouring Poor," *The Gentleman's Magazine*, Apr. 1768.

22. Campbell 236.

23. "A Conversation on Slavery," *Public Advertiser*, Jan. 30, 1770.

24. Lopez *Private*, 292–98; Gary Nash, "Slaves and Slaveowners in Colonial Philadelphia," *William and Mary Quarterly* (Apr. 1973): 225–56. Lopez and Herbert say that one out of five families owned slaves, which is wrong; however, it is true that slaves accounted for roughly one-fifth of the population in 1790, which is not quite the same thing. According to the 1790 census, the first conducted in America, the country had a population of 3,893,874, of which 694,207 were slaves. There were 410,636 families, of which 47,664 owned slaves. In 1750, it is estimated there were 1.2 million people in the thirteen colonies, of which 236,000 were slaves. See fisher.lib.virginia.edu/census/; www.eh.net/encyclopedia/wahl.slavery.us.php; Stanley Engerman and Eugene Genovese, *Race and Slavery in the Western Hemisphere: Quantitative Studies* (Princeton: Princeton University Press, 1975).

25. Anthony Benezet to BF, Apr. 27, 1772; BF to Anthony Benezet, Aug. 22, 1772; BF to Benjamin Rush, July 14, 1773; "The Somerset Case and the Slave Trade," London *Chronicle*, June 20, 1772; Lopez *Private*, 299.

26. BF to WF, Jan. 30, Aug. 19, 1772.

27. BF to WF, Aug. 17, 1772, July 14, 1773; BF to Joseph Galloway, Apr. 6, 1773; Van Doren 394–98.

28. BF to Thomas Cushing, Dec. 2, 1772; BF, *Tract Relative to the Affair of the Hutchinson Letters*, 1774, Papers 21:414. An excellent account of the affair is in Bernard Bailyn, *The Ordeal of Thomas Hutchinson* (Cambridge: Harvard University Press, 1974), 221–49. See also Brands 452; Van Doren 461; Wright 224.

29. BF to Thomas Cushing, Mar. 9, May 6, 1773.

30. "Rules by Which a Great Empire May Be Reduced to a Small One," *Public Advertiser*, Sept. 11, 1773.

31. "An Edict by the King of Prussia," *Public Advertiser*, Sept. 23, 1773.

32. Baron Le Despencer, "Franklin's Contributions to an Abridged Version of a Book of Common Prayer," Aug. 5, 1773, Dashwood Papers, Bodleian Library, Oxford, Papers 20:343; "A New Version of the Lord's Prayer," Papers 15:299; BF to WF, Oct. 6, 1773. Sir Francis Dashwood became Lord Le Despencer in 1763.

33. BF to Joseph Galloway, Nov. 3, 1773; BF to Thomas Cushing, Feb. 2, 1774.

34. BF to Thomas Cushing, July 25, 1773; BF to London *Chronicle*, Dec. 25, 1773, Papers 20:531; BF, *Tract Relative to the Affair of the Hutchinson Letters*, 1774, Papers 21:414; Bailyn, *The Ordeal of Thomas Hutchinson*, 255.

35. BF to Thomas Cushing, Feb. 15, 1774; BF to Thomas Walpole, Jan. 12, 1774; Van Doren 462–63.

36. The record of hearings and the speech by Wedderburn, Jan. 29, 1774, are in Papers 21:37. There are numerous reconstructions, notably, Fleming 248–50; Hawke 324–27; Brands 470–74; Van Doren 462–76.

37. BF to Thomas Cushing, Feb. 15, 1774; BF to WF, Feb. 2, 1774; BF to JM, Feb. 17, 1774.

38. BF to Jan Ingenhousz, Mar. 18, 1774; "A Tract Relative to the Hutchinson Letters," 1774, Papers 21:414; Hawke 327; Van Doren 477.

39. Homo Trium Literarum (A Man of Letters, BF), "The Reply," *Public Advertiser,* Feb. 16, 1774; Boston *Gazette,* Apr. 25, 1774; Brands 477–78.

40. *Public Advertiser,* Apr. 15, May 21, 1774.

41. BF to RB, Feb. 17, 1774; Hawke 329; BF to JM, Sept. 26, 1774.

42. WF to BF, May 3, 1774; WF to Lord Dartmouth, May 31, 1774; Lord Dartmouth to WF, July 6, 1774; Randall 282–84.

43. BF to WF, June 30, May 7, 1774. The May 7 letter is dated 1775, and many authors accept that it was written then, which was just a couple of days after Franklin's arrival back in America. In fact, it seems to be misdated, as the Yale editors have concluded. On May 7, 1775, a Sunday, he did not write any other letters, but on May 7, 1774, he was busily engaged in correspondence. The letter fits into the pattern of letters he was writing at that time.

44. BF to undisclosed recipient, July 27, 1774; BF to Thomas Cushing, Mar. 22, 1774; WF to BF, July 5, 1774; BF to WF, Sept. 7, Oct. 12, 1774.

45. BF to DF, Sept. 10, 1774; WF to BF, Dec. 24, 1774.

46. "Journal of the Negotiations in London," BF to WF, Mar. 22, 1775, in Papers 21:540; Sparks, ch. 8.

47. Morgan *Devious,* 241.

48. This section is drawn from Franklin's Mar. 22, 1775, journal (cited above) of negotiations and the notes he inserted into it, Papers 21:540. Also, BF to Charles Thomson, Feb. 5, Mar. 13, 1775; BF to Thomas Cushing, Jan. 28, 1775; BF to Joseph Galloway, Feb. 5, 25, 1775; Thomas Walpole to BF, Mar. 16, 1775; Van Doren 495–523.

49. BF to Charles Thomson, Feb. 5, 1775.

50. Van Doren 521, citing J. T. Rutt, ed., *The Life and Correspondence of Joseph Priestley* (1817; New York: Thoemmes Press, 1999), 1:227.

CHAPTER 12

1. "Benjamin Franklin and the Gulf Stream," podaac.jpl.nasa.gov/kids/history.html .

2. BF to TF, June 13, 1775; Brands 499.

3. Adams Diary 2:127; William Rachel, ed., *Papers of James Madison* (Chicago: University of Chicago Press, 1962), 1:149; Lopez *Private,* 200; Van Doren 530; Hawke 351; Brands 499.

4. BF to Joseph Galloway, Feb. 25, May 8, 1775; Van Doren 527; Peter Hutchinson, ed., *The Diary of Thomas Hutchinson* (1884; Boston: Houghton Mifflin, 1991), 2:237.

5. WF to William Strahan, May 7, 1775. There is some uncertainty about when the Franklins first reunited. Some assume it was within days of Benjamin Franklin's return, though I find no evidence for this. See Hawke 292, and Clark 273. Sheila Skemp, in two books about William Franklin, concludes that William remained in New Jersey until the end of the May 15–16 legislative session and traveled to Pennsylvania for the first time shortly thereafter. See Skemp *William*, 167, 173; Skemp *Benjamin*, 127. Brands 524 accepts that chronology. Also, see ch. 11 n. 43 regarding the May 7 letter from Benjamin to William Franklin that some authors (notably Hawke 349), though not the Yale editors, date as being written in 1775, just after Franklin's arrival.

6. Peter Hutchinson, *The Diary of Thomas Hutchinson*, 2: 237; Hawke 349; Skemp *William*, 173–79; Fleming 292; Lopez *Private*, 199. See also Bernard Bailyn, *The Ordeal of Thomas Hutchinson* (Cambridge: Harvard University Press, 1974).

7. BF to William Strahan, unsent, July 5, 1775; BF to Strahan, July 7, 1775, quoted by Strahan to BF, Sept. 6, 1775.

8. William Strahan to BF, July 5, Sept. 6, Oct. 4, 1775; BF to Strahan, Oct. 3, 1775; Lopez *Private*, 198; Clark 276–77.

9. BF to Jonathan Shipley, July 7, 1775.

10. BF to Joseph Priestley, July 7, 1775.

11. "Intended Vindication and Offer from Congress to Parliament," July 1775, in Smyth *Writings*, 412–20 and Papers 22:112; Proposed preamble, before Mar. 23, 1776, Papers 22:388.

12. Adams to Abigail Adams, July 23, 1775; Brands 500; Hawke 354.

13. "Proposed Articles of Confederation," July 21, 1775, Papers 22:120; www.yale.edu/lawweb/avalon/contcong/07-21-75.htm ; Articles of Confederation of the United Colonies of New England, May 19, 1643, religiousfreedom.lib. virginia.edu/sacred/colonies_of_ne_1643.html .

14. WF to BF, Aug. 14, Sept. 6, 1775; Lopez *Private*, 202; Skemp *William*, 181.

15. BF to MS, July 17, 1775; Lopez *Private*, 201; Dorothea Blount to BF, Apr. 19, 1775.

16. BF to Joseph Priestley, July 7, 1775; BF to Charles Lee, Feb. 11, 1776; Van Doren 532–36.

17. BF to David Hartley, Oct. 3, 1775; BF to Joseph Priestley, July 7, Oct. 3, 1775.

18. Minutes of Conference with General Washington, Oct. 18–24, 1775, in Papers 22:224.

19. BF to RB, Oct. 19, 1775.

20. Abigail to John Adams, Nov. 5, 1775, Adams Letters, 1:320; Van Doren 537.

21. Lopez *Private*, 204; JM to Catherine Ray Greene, Nov. 24, 1775.

22. JM to Catherine Ray Greene, Nov. 24, 1775; Elizabeth Franklin to TF, Nov. 9, 1775.

23. "The Rattle-Snake as a Symbol of America," by An American Guesser (BF), Pa. Journal, Dec. 27, 1775; www.crwflags.com/fotw/flags/us-ratt.html .

24. WF to TF, Mar. 14, June 3, 1776; WF to Lord Germain, Mar. 28, 1776; BF to Josiah Quincy, Apr. 15, 1776.

25. Franklin's Journal in Passy, Oct. 4, 1778; BF to Charles Carroll and Samuel Chase, May 27, 1776; Allan Everest, ed., *The Journal of Charles Carroll* (1776; New York: Champlain–Upper Hudson Bicentennial Commission, 1976), 50; BF to John Hancock, May 1, 8, 1776; BF to George Washington, June 21, 1776; Brands 506–8; Van Doren 542–46; Clark 281–84.

26. BF to RB, Sept. 30, 1774; Thomas Paine, *Common Sense,* Feb. 14, 1776, www.bartleby.com/133/.

27. WF to TF, June 25, 1776; Skemp *William,* 206–15.

28. The literature on the writing of the Declaration of Independence is voluminous. This section draws from Pauline Maier, *American Scripture* (New York: Knopf, 1997); Garry Wills, *Inventing America* (Garden City, N.Y.: Doubleday, 1978); and Carl Becker, *The Declaration of Independence* (New York: Random House, 1922; Vintage paperback, 1970). See also McCullough, 119–36; Adams Diary 2:392, 512–15; Jefferson to James Madison, Aug. 30, 1823, in Jefferson Papers 10:267–69; drafts and revisions of the Declaration of Independence, www.walika.com/sr/drafting.htm . See also n. 34 below.

29. Adams Diary 3:336, 2:512–15; Jefferson Papers 1:299; Maier 100; "Thomas Jefferson's Recollection," www.walika.com/sr/jeff-tells.htm .

30. Maier, *American Scripture,* 38.

31. Sparks, ch. 9 n. 62; Preamble to a Congressional Resolution, Papers 22:322. The document in Sparks's work is more complete than the one in the Franklin papers.

32. Becker, *The Declaration of Independence,* 24–25; Adams Diary 2:512; Jefferson Papers 7:304.

33. Jefferson to BF, June 21, 1776.

34. The "original rough draught" of the Declaration shows the evolution of the text from the initial "fair copy" draft by Thomas Jefferson to the final text adopted by Congress. It can be viewed at the Library of Congress and on the Internet at www.loc.gov/exhibits/treasures/trt001.html and www.lcweb.loc.gov/exhibits/declara/declara4.html . See also odur.let.rug.nl/~usa/D/1776-1800/independence/doitj.htm and www.walika.com/sr/drafting.htm .

I am grateful to Gerhard Gawalt, the historian of the Library of Congress, for personally showing me the "original rough draft" and sharing his knowledge about each of the edit changes. I am also grateful to James Billington, Librarian of Congress, and Mark Roosa, the director of preservation, who arranged the presentation. Dr. Gawalt has edited and written a preface to an updated version of a useful illustrated book showing the various drafts: Julian Boyd, *The Declaration of Independence: The Evolution of the Text* (1945; Washington, D.C.: Library of Congress, 1999).

35. Franklin's alterations are noted in Becker, *The Declaration of Independence*, 142; Van Doren 550; Maier, *American Scripture*, 136. See also Wills, *Inventing America*, 181 and passim. Wills does not discuss Franklin's role in changing Jefferson's words to "self-evident," but he does discuss the definition used by Locke. Wills also gives a fascinating analysis of the influences of the Scottish Enlightenment philosophers.

36. Maier, *American Scripture*, appendix C, 236–40, shows all of the revisions made by Congress. Garry Wills argues that the changes made did not improve the document as much as other scholars have contended; Wills, *Inventing America*, 307 and passim.

37. Thomas Jefferson to Robert Walsh, Dec. 4, 1818, Jefferson Papers 18:169.

38. Sparks 1:408, ch. 9.

39. Franklin speech of July 31, 1776, in Adams Diary 2:245; Van Doren 557–58.

40. Smyth *Writings*, 10:57; Papers CD 46:u344 has the speech reused in his Nov. 3, 1789, remarks on the Pennsylvania Constitution. For a description of Franklin's design of the Great Seal, see James Hutson, Sara Day, and Jaroslav Pelikan, *Religion and the Founding of the American Republic* (Washington, D.C.: Library of Congress, 1998), 50–52; Jefferson Papers, LCMS-27748, 181–82.

41. Richard Howe to BF, written June 20, sent July 12, 1776.

42. BF to Lord Howe, July 30, 1776.

43. Howe's remarks in Papers 22:518; Richard Howe to BF, Aug. 16, 1776.

44. Adams Diary 3:418.

45. Many accounts were written of the Staten Island summit: the notes of Henry Strachey (Howe's secretary) in the New York Public Library and reprinted elsewhere; report to Congress of the committee to confer with Lord Howe, in Smyth *Writings*, 6:465 and elsewhere; Adams Diary 3:79, 3:418–22; Papers 22:518–20; Howe's report to Lord Germain, Sept. 20, 1776, in the London Public Records Office and reprinted in *Documents of the American Revolution* (Dublin: Irish Academic Press, 1981); John Adams to Abigail Adams, Sept. 14, 1776, in Adams Letters 2:124. See also Parton 2:148; Van Doren 558–62; Clark 287–91; Brands 518–19; McCullough 156–58.

46. Alsop 30–31.

47. BF to Benjamin Rush, Sept. 27, 1776.

48. "Sketch of Propositions for Peace," written sometime between Sept. 26 and Oct. 25, 1776, Papers 22:630; Smyth *Writings*, 454; Cecil Currey, *Code Number 72* (Englewood Cliffs, N.J.: Prentice-Hall, 1972), 73; Van Doren 553.

49. Currey *Code Number 72*, 77–78; Edward Hale Sr. and Edward Hale Jr., *Franklin in France* (Boston: Roberts Brothers, 1888), 1:67.

50. Elizabeth Franklin to SF, July 12, 1776; Elizabeth Franklin to TF, July 16, 1776.

51. BF to TF, Sept. 19, 1776; Elizabeth Franklin to BF, Aug. 6, 1776; Skemp *William*, 217.

52. BF to TF, Sept. 19, 22, 1776; TF to BF, Sept. 21, 1776.

53. BF to TF, Sept. 28, 1776; WF to Elizabeth Franklin, Nov. 25, 1776.

54. BF to RB, June 2, 1779.

CHAPTER 13

1. Franklin's Passy journal, Oct. 4, 1778; BF to SF, May 10, 1785; BF to John Hancock, Dec. 8, 1776. He was writing to Hancock in his capacity as president of Congress.

Franklin's social life in Paris has, not surprisingly, inspired many books. The most delightful include Lopez *Cher;* Aldridge *French;* Alsop; Schoenbrun. An older work of some value is Edward Hale Sr. and Edward Hale Jr., *Franklin in France* (Boston: Roberts Brothers, 1888). It was also the subject of a musical, *Ben Franklin in Paris,* by Mark Sandrich Jr. and Sidney Michaels, which premiered Oct. 27, 1964, and ran for 215 performances.

2. BF to SF, June 3, 1779; Aldridge *French,* 43; Van Doren 632. The tale of the chamber pot given by the king to Comtesse Diane de Polignac comes from the memoirs of Madame Henriette de Campan, the lady-in-waiting to Marie-Antoinette. It is well enough known that it was told by the French ambassador at a ceremony in the Benjamin Franklin room of the U.S. State Department; see: www.info-france-usa.org/news/statmnts/1998/amba0910.asp. However, Claude-Anne Lopez tells me, "It comes from a very unreliable source, a snobbish sourpuss, and my guess is that it's not true." That said, Lopez included it without qualification in her own book, Lopez *Cher,* 184.

3. *The Boston Patriot,* May 15, 1811, in Charles Francis Adams, ed., *The Works of John Adams* (Boston: Little, Brown, 1856) 1:660; Lopez *Cher,* 13; Wright 270.

4. Aldridge *French,* 23, 66, 115, 43, 61; Voltaire, "Letters on England" (1733), www.literatureproject.com/letters-Voltaire ; Van Doren 570; Abbé Flamarens to *Mémoires Secret,* Jan. 17, 1777.

5. BF to Emma Thompson, Feb. 8, 1777; BF to PS, Aug. 28, 1767.

6. BF to Josiah Quincy, Apr. 22, 1779; BF to Elizabeth Partridge, Oct. 11, 1776.

7. BF to MS, Jan. 25, 1779; Alsop 76–94; Lopez *Cher,* 123–36; Aldridge *French,* 196–99. Temple's letter is from Randall 455, citing TF to SF, Nov. 25, 1777. The quote from Madame Chaumont is from Adams Diary 4:64. I am grateful to Professor Thomas Schaeper of St. Bonaventure University for his help and his delightful, though hard to find, biography of Franklin's landlord, *France and America in the Revolutionary Era: The Life of Jacques-Donatien Leray de Chaumont, 1725–1803* (Providence, R.I.: Berghahn, 1995).

8. Arthur Lee to Richard Lee, Sept. 12, 1778; BF to Congress, Dec. 7, 1780; Charles Isham, *The Silas Deane Papers* (New York: New-York Historical Society, 1890). For more on the Silas Deane papers in the Connecticut Historical Society in Hartford and a biographical sketch, see www.chs.org/library/ead/htm_faids/deans1789.htm#OB1.3 .

9. BF to Arthur Lee, Apr. 3 (unsent), 4, 1778; Van Doren 598.

10. "Petition of the Letter Z," 1778, Papers 28:517.

11. "Instructions to Silas Deane," Mar. 2, 1776, from Congress's Committee of Secret Correspondence, signed by BF and others and apparently written by BF, Papers 22:369; Sidney Edelstein, "Notes on the Wet-Processing Industry: The Dual Life of Edward Bancroft," *American Dyestuff Reporter* (Oct. 25, 1954).

12. "Engagement of Dr. Edwards to correspond with P. Wentworth and Lord Stormont, and the means of conducting that correspondence," Dec. 13, 1776, British Library, London, Auckland Papers, additional manuscripts 34,413 (hereafter cited as Auckland Papers, Add Mss); Edward Bancroft memo to the Marquis of Camarthen, Sept. 17, 1784, Foreign Office papers, 4:3, Public Records Office, London.

Some of the material is available in *Material Relating to the American Revolution from the Auckland Papers* (Yorkshire, England: EP Microform, 1974) and in Benjamin Stevens, ed., *Facsimiles of Manuscripts in European Archives Relating to America, 1773–1783* (25 volumes published in 1898, copies in the Franklin collection in Yale's Sterling Library). Please note the acknowledgment to Susan Ann Bennett, who provided research help in London finding and transcribing some of the documents cited in this section.

I am also grateful to the Central Intelligence Agency's Center for the Study of Intelligence for providing the declassified paper by John Vaillancourt, "Edward Bancroft (@Edwd.Edwards) Estimable Spy," *Studies in Intelligence* (winter 1961): A53–A67. See also Lewis Einstein, *Divided Loyalties* (Boston: Ayer, 1933), 3–48; Cecil Currey, *Code Number 72* (Englewood Cliffs, N.J.: Prentice-Hall, 1972); Samuel Bemis, "The British Secret Service and the French-American Alliance," *American Historical Review* 29.3 (Apr. 1924). There is also a historical novel, fun but heavily fictionalized, on Bancroft: Arthur Mullin, *Spy: America's First Double Agent, Dr. Edward Bancroft* (Santa Barbara, Calif.: Capra Press, 1987).

Currey argues that Franklin's loyalties (and Deane's) were also suspect. It's an interesting and fact-filled book, but I think its analysis is unconvincing. Jonathan Dull, in *Franklin the Diplomat* (Philadelphia: Transactions of the American Philosophical Society, 1982), 1:72, 36, and passim, convincingly argues that Franklin was oblivious to Bancroft's dealings and that Deane was involved in stock speculating but not in spying with Bancroft.

13. Auckland papers, Add Mss 34413, f330 and 402; 46490, f64; 34413, f405–7; Paul Wentworth to the Earl of Suffolk (the minister in charge of the northern department), quoting a secret letter from "Dr. Edwards," Sept. 19, 1777, in the Stevens *Facsimiles* at Yale noted above.

14. Silas Deane to Robert Morris for Congress, Mar. 16, 1777; Isham, *The Silas Deane Papers*, 2:24.

15. Arthur Lee to BF and John Adams, Feb. 7, 1779; Auckland Papers, Add Mss, 46490, f52 and f57.

16. Juliana Ritchie to BF, Jan. 12, 1777; BF to Juliana Ritchie, Jan. 19, 1777.

17. Alsop 20.

18. Dull, *Franklin the Diplomat*, 1:72, 9; Alsop 35–40, from Henri Doniol, *His-*

tory of the Participation of France in the Establishment of the United States (Paris: Imprimerie Nationale, 1866), 1:244.

The best overviews of Franklin's diplomacy in France, in addition to Dull's book cited above, include Jonathan Dull, *A Diplomatic History of the American Revolution* (New Haven: Yale University Press, 1987); Jonathan Dull, *The French Navy and American Independence* (Princeton: Princeton University Press, 1975); Richard Morris, *The Peacemakers* (New York: Harper & Row, 1965); Samuel Flagg Bemis, *The Diplomacy of the American Revolution* (New York: Appleton, 1935); Stourzh; Ronald Hoffman and Peter Albert, eds., *Diplomacy and Revolution* (Charlottesville: University of Virginia Press, 1981). For original documents, see Francis Wharton, ed., *Revolutionary Diplomatic Correspondence of the United States* (Washington, D.C.: GPO, 1889). See also Orville Murphy, *Charles Gravier, Comte de Vergennes* (Albany: State University of New York Press, 1982).

19. Vergennes, Dec. 28, 1776, in Papers 23:113n; Vergennes to the Marquis de Noailles, Jan. 10, 1777, in Clark 306.

20. BF to Vergennes, Jan. 5, 1777; Doniol, *History of the Participation of France,* 1:20; Stourzh 137.

21. Bernard Bailyn, *Realism and Idealism in American Foreign Policy* (Princeton: Institute of Advanced Studies, 1994), 13, reprinted in Bernard Bailyn, *To Begin the World Anew* (New York: Knopf, 2003).

22. BF to Committee of Secret Correspondence, Apr. 9, 1777; BF to Samuel Cooper, May 1, 1777; Brands 532; Stourzh 3. For a contemporary discussion of "hard power" versus "soft power," see Joseph Nye, *The Paradox of American Power* (New York: Oxford University Press, 2002). The "city upon a hill" image comes from Jesus' Sermon on the Mount, Matthew 5:14: "Ye are the light of the world. A city that is set on an hill cannot be hid." It was used by John Winthrop in the sermon, "A Model of Christian Charity," that he preached on Mar. 22, 1630, on the *Arabella* while heading to America. Ronald Reagan used the image throughout his political career, most notably as the title of a Jan. 25, 1974, speech to the Conservative Political Action Committee, in his first 1980 debate with Jimmy Carter, in a 1980 debate with John Anderson, in his 1984 speech to the Republican Convention, and in his 1989 farewell speech.

23. "The Sale of the Hessians," Feb. 18, 1777, Lib. of Am. 917; Papers 23:480; Van Doren 577. I am grateful to Claude-Anne Lopez for pointing out to me the weak French pun.

24. Alsop 77; *New Jersey Gazette,* Oct. 2, 1777, quoted in Clark 325.

25. William Parsons to BF, Aug. 4, 1778; Mrs. Parsons to BF, Aug. 12, 17, Oct. 2, Nov. 2, 1778; BF to Mrs. Parsons, Aug. 12, 1778; BF to George Washington, Mar. 29, Sept. 4, 1777; Washington to BF, Aug. 17, 1777; "Model of a Letter of Recommendation," by BF, Apr. 2, 1777; Van Doren 578; Clark 335. In the Sept. 4, 1777, letter to Washington, Franklin refers to Baron von Steuben as Baron de Steuben and inflates his rank from captain to lieutenant general. The spy Bancroft reported back to London that they had "received a resolve of Congress directing all their ministers" to discourage French mercenaries unless they spoke English, which "may enable us to cut short the solicitation with which we have for a long time al-

most been persecuted to death by thousands of officers wanting employment in America"; Edward Bancroft to Paul Wentworth, June 1777, Auckland papers, Add MSS 46490, f64.

26. Arthur Lee's journal, Nov. 27, 1777, in Richard Lee, *Life of Arthur Lee* (Boston: Wells and Lilly, 1829), 1:354; Hale and Hale, *Benjamin Franklin in France,* 1:159; Papers 25:234n.

27. Franklin statement, Dec. 4, 1777; BF to Vergennes, Dec. 4, 1777; Lee, *Life of Arthur Lee,* 1:357; Alsop 93–94; Doniol, *History of the Participation of France,* 2:625. See also Dull, *A Diplomatic History of the American Revolution,* 89. Dull argues that for months the French had been planning to enter the war against Britain in early 1778 once their naval rearmament program permitted; the American victory at Saratoga, he contends, was not a major factor. Others dispute this view. See Claude Van Tyne, "Influences Which Determined the French Government to Make Their Treaty with America," *American Historical Review* 21 (1915–16): 528, cited by Dull.

28. Alsop 103; Cecil Currey, *Code Number 72* (Englewood Cliffs, N.J.: Prentice-Hall, 1972), 175–92. Currey devotes an entire chapter to the Wentworth meeting. It seems somewhat overdrawn in its assessment of Franklin's duplicity, but it is carefully annotated and researched. See also James Perkins, *France and the American Revolution* (New York: Franklin, 1970), 203–4.

29. Paul Wentworth to William Eden, Dec. 25, 1777, Jan. 7, 1778; Van Doren 592; Currey, *Code Number 72,* 186; Dull, *Franklin the Diplomat,* 29.

30. BF to Thomas Cushing, for Congress, Feb. 27, 1778.

31. R. M. Bache, "Franklin's Ceremonial Coat," *PMHB* 23 (1899); 444–52, quote is on 450.

32. Edward Bancroft to Paul Wentworth, as deciphered, Jan. 22, 28, 1778, Auckland Papers, Add Mss 46491, f1 and f1b; Edward Bancroft memo to the Marquis of Camarthen, Sept. 17, 1784, Foreign Office papers 4:3, Public Records Office, London; Edward Bancroft to Thomas Walpole, under cover to Mr. White, with two pages of invisible ink, Nov. 3, 1777, Auckland Papers, Add Mss 34414, f.304; Edward Bancroft note, unsigned and undated, sent to Samuel Wharton, with two pages of white ink, November 1777, Auckland Papers, Add Mss 34414, f.306; Samuel Wharton letters to Edward Bancroft, 1778, Auckland Papers, Add Mss 321, ff6–35; Silas Deane's accounts with Edward Bancroft, Feb, 1778, Aug. 1779, the Connecticut Historical Society, Hartford, series 4, folder 9.12.

Jonathan Dull discusses Bancroft's stock manipulations in *Franklin the Diplomat,* 33–36, and notes that Silas Deane, although in his opinion not a spy, was also able to make money by speculating with Wharton on Bancroft's inside information. Also in on the scheme was Thomas Walpole, the wealthy and well-connected London banker who had tried with Franklin to win a land grant in Ohio. Deane died of poisoning in 1789 as he was preparing to sail from London to Canada, and some have speculated that he was murdered by Bancroft, an expert in poisons.

33. Lopez *Cher,* 179–83; Alsop 108–10; Van Doren 595; Clark 341.

34. Van Doren 593; Edmund Morgan, *The Birth of the Republic* (Chicago: University of Chicago Press, 1956), 83; Gordon Wood, "Not So Poor Richard," *The*

New York Review of Books, June 6, 1996; Samuel Cooper to BF, May 14, 1778. See also Samuel Cooper to BF, July 1, 1778, in which the Boston clergyman describes how the treaty thwarted England's attempts to lure Congress into a reconciliation and how information sent by Franklin and Adams about a British convoy of eleven warships would be passed along, presumably to warn French admiral d'Estaing.

CHAPTER 14

1. Edward Bancroft, "most secret extracts," Apr. 2, 16, 1778, British Library, Auckland papers, Add MSS 34413, f405–7; Middlekauff 171; McCullough 197, 204, 208, 239. Middlekauff's chapter on Adams in his book, pp. 171–202, is a vivid look at the vagaries of their relationship. McCullough, 210–15, provides an authoritative assessment of their feelings about each other, with some deference to Adams.

2. Adams to James Lovell, Feb. 20, 1779, Adams Letters 4:118–19; Middlekauff 189.

3. Lopez *Private,* 237; Lopez *Cher,* 9. The quote is from Pierre-Jean-Georges Cabanis, *Complete Works* (Paris: Bossange frères, 1825), 2:267.

4. Brands 547–48; Adams Diary 2:391, 4:69.

5. BF to Robert Livingston, July 22, 1783.

6. Diderot, editor, *Encyclopédie,* www.lib.uchicago.edu/efts/ARTFL/projects/encyc/; Alsop 13; Harold Nicolson, *The Age of Reason* (London: Constable, 1960), 268.

7. Most accounts say, I think mistakenly, that it was Temple who received the benediction. Smith 60, 187 traces the mystery and convincingly concludes that the "boy" was actually his younger grandson Benny, who was 7 at the time, rather than Temple, who was about 18. Aldridge *French,* 10, says it was Temple, but in his later writings, including *Voltaire and the Century of Light* (Princeton: Princeton University Press, 1975), 399, he revises his opinion. Claude-Anne Lopez tells me that Temple used a wax seal with the phrase "God and Liberty," which leads her to believe it may have been Temple. See also Voltaire to the Abbé Gaultier, Feb. 21, 1778, in *The Works of Voltaire* (Paris: Didot, 1829), 1:290; Hutchinson Diary and Letters 2:276. The newspaper quoted is *Les Mémoires Secret,* Feb. 22, 1778, in Aldridge *French,* 10.

8. Aldridge *French,* 12; Adams Diary 3:147; Van Doren 606.

9. Lopez *Life,* 148–57; Van Doren 655–56; Lemay *Reappraising,* 145.

10. Lopez *Cher,* 34, 29. As one of the Yale editors, Lopez's specialty was analyzing Franklin's papers from his period in France. Her translations, astute assessments, and personal discussions with me informed this chapter.

11. Madame Brillon to BF, July 30, 1777.

12. Madame Brillon to BF, Mar. 7, 1778; BF to Madame Brillon, Mar. 10, 1778.

13. Madame Brillon to BF, May 3, 8, 1779; Lopez *Cher,* 40, 61–62; Adams Letters 4:46; Brands 552.

14. BF to Madame Brillon, July 27, 1778. Lib. of Am. uses a version dated 1782,

and some sources have the final article worded differently. The version I have used is from the Yale Papers and the American Philosophical Society; Papers 27:164.

15. Madame Brillon to BF, Mar. 16, 17, 18, Apr. 26, June 9, July 27, Sept. 13, 17, 1778; BF to Madame Brillon, July 27, Sept. 1, 15, 1778.

16. Madame Brillon to BF, Sept. 13, 1778; BF to Madame Brillon, Sept. 15, 1778; Lopez *Cher*, 29–121.

17. "The Ephemera," Sept. 20, 1778, Lib. of Am. 922; A. Owen Aldridge, "Sources for Franklin's Ephemera," *New England Quarterly* 27 (1954): 388.

18. BF to Madame Brillon, Nov. 29, 1777; Madame Brillon to BF, Nov. 30, 1777 (the chess game partner was their neighbor Louis-Guillaume le Veillard); Papers 25:204, 25:218); Madame Brillon to BF, Dec. 10, 15, 20, 1778; BF to Madame Brillon, Dec. 11?, 1778.

19. Lopez *Cher*, 243–48. Lopez draws on Antoine Guillois, *Le Salon de Madame Helvétius* (Paris: Calmann Levy, 1894). Claude-Adrien Helvétius, *De l'Esprit* (Paris, 1758; English translation, *Essays on the Mind*, London, 1759); it was publicly burned in Paris but also one of the most widely read books of its time. See gallica.bnf.fr/Fonds_textes/T0088614.htm ; www.aei.ca/~anbou/mhelv.html .

20. Aldridge *French*, 162; Gilbert Chinard, "Abbé Lefebvre de la Roche's Recollections of Benjamin Franklin," *Proceedings of the American Philosophical Society* (1950).

21. BF to Madame Helvétius, Oct. 31, 1778.

22. Aldridge *French*, 165; Adams Papers 2:55.

23. BF to Madame Helvétius, through Cabanis, Sept. 19, 1779. It is possible that Poupon was a cat, but we know she had a dog and this is more likely.

24. "The Flies," Papers 34:220; Lib. of Am., 991 (the date of this piece is unknown and in dispute); Lopez *Cher*, 260. See also Lopez *Cher*, 371n.32 arguing that some biographers "overdramatize" Franklin's proposal to Madame Helvétius whereas others discount it too much.

25. "The Elysian Fields," Dec. 7, 1778, Lib. of Am. 924.

26. Turgot to Pierre du Pont de Nemours, June 24, 1780, in Lopez *Cher*, 170.

27. BF to Thomas Bond, Mar. 16, 1780.

28. Aldridge *French*, 183. For a good assessment, see Richard Amacher, *Franklin's Wit and Folly: The Bagatelles* (New Brunswick, N.J.: Rutgers University Press, 1953).

29. Poem from Madame Brillon to BF, Oct., 1780, translation in Lopez *Cher*, 78; "Dialogue with the Gout," Oct. 22, 1780.

30. Madame Brillon to BF, Nov. 18, 26, 1780; Lopez *Cher*, 79–81; Aldridge *French*, 166.

31. Lopez *Cher*, 25–26.

32. "Conte," dated Dec. 1778 in Papers 28:308 and early 1779 by Lemay in Lib. of Am. 938; Aldridge *French*, 173; Lopez *Cher*, 90.

33. Abbé Flamarens, Jan. 15, 1777, in Aldridge *French*, 61.

34. "The Morals of Chess," June 28, 1779; Papers 29:750–56 also includes the Junto notes he made in 1732. See also Jacques Barbeu-Dubourg to BF, July 3, 1779, which mentions a "refutation" of Franklin's points.

35. Aldridge *French,* 197; Jefferson Papers 18:168.

36. "An Economical Project," *Journal of Paris,* Apr. 26, 1784; Poor Richard's, 1735. See also http://www.standardtime.com ; http://www.energy.ca.gov/daylight saving.html ; http ://webexhibits.org/daylightsaving .

37. Aldridge *French,* 178

38. "To the Royal Academy of ***," May 19, 1780, or after, Lib. of Am. 952. See also, Carl Japsky, ed., *Fart Proudly* (Columbus, Ohio: Enthea Press, 1990).

39. BF to the Abbé Morellet, ca. July 5, 1779.

40. SF to BF, Jan. 17, 1779; BF to SF, June 3, 1779. General Howe had been re-placed by Sir Henry Clinton, who evacuated his British troops from Philadelphia in May 1778 to concentrate on the defense of New York. General Washington tried and failed to stop the British in a battle in Monmouth County, New Jersey, and Clinton's troops safely ensconced themselves in New York.

41. SB to BF, Sept. 14, 1779; BF to SB, Mar. 16, 1780. See the poignant chapter "No Watch for Benny, No Feathers for Sally," in Lopez *Private,* 215–32.

42. SF to BF, Jan. 17, Sept. 25, 1779, Sept. 8, 1780; BF to SF, June 3, 1779.

43. RB to BF, July 28, 1780; SF to BF, Sept. 9, 1780; BF to RB and SF, Oct. 4, 1780.

44. BF to SF, June 3, 1779.

45. BF to Benjamin Bache, Aug. 19, 1779, Apr. 16, 1781. For a well-researched and insightful assessment of their relationship, see Smith, in particular 67–70, 77–82. Also Lopez *Private,* 221–30.

46. BF to Benjamin Bache, Jan. 25, 1782. See also May 3, 30, Aug. 19, 1779, July 18, 1780. Gabriel Louis de Marignac to BF, Nov. 20, 1781.

47. Catherine Cramer to BF, May 15, 1781; RB to BF, July 22, 1780.

48. BF to Benjamin Bache, Sept. 25, 1780; SB to BF, Jan. 14, 1781.

49. Benjamin Bache to BF, Jan. 30, 1783; BF to Benjamin Bache, May 2, 1783; BF to Johonnot, Jan. 26, 1782.

50. BF to the Brillons, Apr. 20, Oct. 30, 1781; Madame Brillon to BF, Apr. 20, Oct. 20, 1781; Lopez *Cher,* 91–101.

CHAPTER 15

1. BF to James Lovell (for Congress), July 22, 1778; Richard Bache to BF, Oct. 22, 1778; Van Doren 609.

2. BF to John Adams, Apr. 3, 24, May 10, June 5, 1779; John Adams to BF, Apr. 13, 29, May 14, 17, 1779; Middlekauff 190–92; McCullough 210–14; Schoenbrun 229.

3. RB to BF, Oct. 8, 22, 1778; BF to RB, June 2, 1779; BF to SF, June 3, 1779.

4. BF to Lafayette, Mar. 22, Oct. 1, 1779; Lafayette to BF, July 12, 1779; Lafayette to TF, Sept. 7, 1779. See also Harlowe Giles Unger, *Lafayette* (New York: Wiley, 2002).

5. BF to Lafayette, Mar. 22, 1779; BF to John Paul Jones, May 27, June 1, 10, 1778. See also Evan Thomas, *John Paul Jones* (New York: Simon & Schuster, 2003).

Evan Thomas graciously provided an early copy of his manuscript, which helped inform this section, and he read and helped to correct this section.

6. Samuel Eliot Morison, *John Paul Jones* (Annapolis, Md.: Naval Institute Press, 1959), 156 and passim. Alsop 176 also says that "all the world knew of the love affair between the dashing officer and Madame de Chaumont." But Evan Thomas in his biography points out that there is no concrete evidence of this.

7. John Paul Jones to BF, Mar. 6, 1779; BF to Jones, Mar. 14, 1779.

8. BF to John Paul Jones, Apr. 27, 1779; Jones to BF, May 1, 1779.

9. John Paul Jones to BF, May 26, Oct. 3, 1779; BF to Jones, Oct. 15, 1779. As Evan Thomas points out, it is very unclear whether Jones actually uttered his famous "I have not yet begun to fight."

10. Vergennes to Adams, Feb. 15, 1780; McCullough 232.

11. BF to George Washington, Mar. 5, 1780.

12. BF to David Hartley, Feb. 2, 1780.

13. For Franklin's use of the phrase "no bad peace or good war," see BF to Jonathan Shipley, June 10, 1782; BF to Joseph Banks, July 27, 1783; BF to Josiah Quincy, Sept. 11, 1783; BF to Rodolphe-Ferdinand Grand, Mar. 5, 1786.

14. BF to Arthur Lee, Mar. 21, 1777; Stourzh 160; BF to Robert Livingston, Mar. 4, 1782.

15. John Adams to Congress, Apr. 18, 1780, Adams Letters 3:151; Vergennes to John Adams, July 29, 1780, Adams Letters 3:243; McCullough 241.

16. Vergennes to BF, July 31, 1780; BF to Vergennes, Aug. 3, 1780; BF to Samuel Huntington (for Congress), Aug. 9, 1780. Adams was still rehashing this disagreement decades later in an article in the *Boston Patriot,* May 15, 1811; see Stourzh 159.

17. BF to John Adams, Oct. 2, 1780, Feb. 22, 1781. Adams replied with a gloomy camaraderie, saying he had accepted some bills "relying on your virtues and graces of Faith and Hope." John Adams to BF, Apr. 10, 1781.

18. Washington to BF, Oct. 9, 1780; BF to Vergennes, Feb. 13, 1781.

19. For currency conversion data see page 507. See also: Thomas Schaeper, *France and America in the Revolutionary Era* (Providence: Bergham Books, 1995), 348; John McCusker, *How Much Is That in Real Money?* (New Castle, Del.: Oak Knoll Press, 2001); Economic History Services, http://eh.net/hmit/; Inflation Conversion Factors, www.orst.edu/Dept/pol_sci/fac/sahr/cf166502.pdf .

20. Ralph Izard to Richard Lee, Oct. 15, 1780; Vergennes to la Luzerne, Feb. 19, 1781; Stourzh 153; BF to Samuel Huntington (for Congress), Mar. 12, 1781.

21. Vergennes to la Luzerne, Dec. 4, 1780; Stourzh 167.

22. Stourzh 168; BF to Samuel Huntington (for Congress), Sept. 13, 1781.

23. BF to William Carmichael, Aug. 24, 1781; BF to John Adams, Oct. 12, 1781.

24. BF to Robert Morris, Mar. 7, 1782.

25. Madame Brillon to BF, Jan. 20, Feb. 1, 1782; BF to Shelburne, Mar. 22, Apr. 18, 1782; BF to Vergennes, Apr. 15, 1782. See also BF to WF, Sept. 12, 27, Oct. 11, 1766, June 13, Aug. 28, 1767, for discussions of Franklin's early meetings with Shelburne.

26. "Journal of Peace Negotiations," May 9–July 1, 1782, Papers CD 37:191. This forty-page journal is a detailed description of all the talks and meetings Franklin had up until an attack of the gout caused him to quit keeping the journal on July 1. The following narrative is drawn from this journal as well as the letters he included in it.

Much of this information is also based on the forthcoming volume 37 of the Franklin Papers, due to be published in late 2003, which covers March 16–September 15, 1782. It adds notes and assessments about Franklin's writings, which were already available on the Papers CD and elsewhere. I am grateful to the Yale editors for letting me read the manuscript in the fall of 2002. The editors also provided access to the drafts of volumes 38 and 39, due out in 2004, which cover the conclusion of the negotiations.

27. "Supplement to the *Boston Independent Chronicle*," a hoax by BF, Mar. 12, 1782. The Yale editors provide a detailed assessment of this document for the forthcoming volume 37 of the Papers. Among the people he sent it to was James Hutton, an English friend, who replied, "That article in the Boston paper must be romance, all of it invention, cruel forgery I hope and believe. Bales of scalps!!! Neither the King nor his old ministers . . . are capable of such atrocities." Nevertheless, at least one London magazine (*Public Advertiser*, Sept. 27, 1782) reprinted parts of it as true. BF to James Hutton, July 7, 1782; James Hutton to BF, July 23, 1782, Papers 37:443, 37:503.

28. "Journal of Peace Negotiations"; Shelburne to BF, Apr. 28, 1782; Charles Fox to BF, May 1, 1782.

29. Richard Morris, *The Peacemakers* (New York: Harper & Row, 1965), 274, points out that Grenville and Oswald did not report Franklin's strong refusals to consider a separate peace, but instead reported back hints that he might be open to it.

30. BF to John Adams, June 2, 1782.

31. "Journal of Peace Negotiations"; BF to Shelburne, Apr. 18, May 10, 13, 1782; Shelburne to BF, Apr. 28, 1782; BF to Charles James Fox, May 10, 1782; BF to John Adams, Apr. 20, May 2, 8, 1782; BF to Henry Laurens, Apr. 20, 1782.

32. BF to Robert Livingston, June 25, 29, 1782; BF to Richard Oswald, June 25, 1782. Franklin's journal ends July 1.

33. Richard Oswald to Lord Shelburne, July 10, 1782; BF to Richard Oswald, July 12, 1782; BF to Vergennes, July 24, 1782.

34. Lord Shelburne to Richard Oswald, July 27, 1782; Wright 314.

35. John Jay to Robert Livingston, Sept. 18, Nov. 17, 1782; Stourzh 178; BF to Lafayette, Sept. 17, 1782.

36. Vergennes to la Luzerne, Dec. 19, 1782; McCullough 280.

37. Middlekauff 197; Herbert Klinghoffer, "Matthew Ridley's Diary during the Peace Negotiations of 1782," *William and Mary Quarterly* 20.1 (January 1963): 123; John Adams to Edmund Jennings, July 20, 1782, in McCullough 276; Adams Letters 3:38; Wright 315.

38. John Adams to BF, Sept. 13, 1783; McCullough 277; Wright 316; Stourzh 177; BF to Robert Livingston, July 22, 1783.

39. BF to John Jay, Sept. 10, 1783; John Adams to BF, Sept. 13, 1783; McCullough 282.

40. Samuel Cooper to BF, July 15, 1782; Robert Livingston to BF, June 23, 1782; BF to Richard Oswald, July 28, 1782; Fleming 455.

41. Benjamin Vaughan to Lord Shelburne, July 31, Dec. 10, 1782.

42. "Apologue," Nov. 1782, Lib. of Am. 967; Smyth *Writings,* 8:650.

43. Adams Diaries 3:37; Middlekauff 198; Klinghoffer, "Matthew Ridley's Diary," 132.

44. Vergennes to la Luzerne, Dec. 19, 1782; Vergennes to BF, Dec. 15, 1782.

45. BF to Vergennes, Dec. 17, 1782; Stourzh 178. The dispute, it so happens, hardly remained a secret: Edward Bancroft, still a spy, promptly sent the letter to the British ministers.

46. Vergennes to la Luzerne, Dec. 19, 1782. A few months later, when Foreign Secretary Robert Livingston asked him about the French objections, Franklin replied, "I do not see, however, that they have much reason to complain of that Transaction. Nothing was stipulated to their Prejudice, and none of the Stipulations were to have Force, but by a subsequent Act of their own . . . I long since satisfied Count de Vergennes about it here. We did what appeared to all of us best at the Time, and, if we have done wrong, the Congress will do right, after hearing us, to censure us." Franklin told Livingston he felt that the French advice on fishing rights was merely designed to assure that a deal was made. Adams felt the French were making the suggestions because they did not want America to succeed in getting the fishing rights. It is in this letter that Franklin chides Adams for his lack of gratitude toward France and calls him "in some things completely out of his senses." BF to Robert Livingston, July 22, 1783.

47. Van Doren 696–97.

48. BF to PS, Jan. 27, 1783; BF to Joseph Banks, July 27, 1783.

49. BF to Benjamin Bache, June 23, 1783; Robert Pigott to BF, June 27, 1783; Smith 79.

50. Dorcas Montgomery to SB, July 23, 1783; BF to PS, Sept. 7, 1783; BF to SF, July 27, 1783; Benjamin Bache to RB and SF, Oct. 30, 1783; Smith 80–82.

51. BF to PS, 1782, Jan. 8, Sept. 7, 1783; PS to BF, Sept. 28, 1783.

52. BF to PS, Dec. 26, 1783; BF to RB, Nov. 11, 1783; Van Doren 709.

53. BF to Robert Livingston, July 22, 1783; Lopez *Cher,* 314.

54. BF to Joseph Banks, Aug. 30, Nov. 21, Dec. 1, 1783. A vivid account of the ballooning race and craze is in Lopez *Cher,* 215–22, which cites Gaston Tissandier, *Histoire des ballons et des aéronautes célèbres, 1783–1800* (Paris: Launette, 1887). See also Lopez *Private,* 267; www.ballooning.org/ballooning/timeline.html ; www.balloonzone.com/history.html .

55. Joseph Banks to BF, Nov. 7, 1783; BF to Joseph Banks, Nov. 21, 1783; BF to Jan Ingenhousz, Jan. 16, 1784; Lopez *Cher,* 222, contains Franklin's parody letter.

56. BF to SF, Jan. 26, 1784.

57. "Information to Those Who Would Remove to America," Feb. 1784; Lib. of Am. 975; Morgan *Franklin,* 297. In a letter to me commenting on some draft sections of this book, Edmund Morgan noted: Franklin's "description is mainly accu-

rate but at the same time a statement of what he values in the country and hopes to see perpetuated or magnified" (Dec. 2, 2002).

58. BF to Benjamin Vaughan, July 26, 1784.

59. BF to Robert Morris, Dec. 25, 1783; BF to Benjamin Vaughan, Mar. 14, 1785.

60. BF to Strahan, Jan. 24, 1780, Feb. 16, Aug. 19, 1784.

61. Lopez *Cher,* 277–79; Pierre Cabanis, *Complete Works* (Paris: Bossange frères, 1825), 2:348.

62. BF to George Whatley, Aug. 21, 1784, May 23, 1785.

63. BF to TF, Aug. 25, 1784. There are many books and articles on Mesmer. The best, as it relates to Franklin, is the chapter in Lopez *Life,* 114–26. See also Robert Darnton, *Mesmerism and the End of the Enlightenment in France* (Cambridge: Harvard University Press, 1968); Lopez *Cher,* 163–73; Van Doren 713–14.

64. Willard Sterne Randall, *Thomas Jefferson* (New York: Henry Holt, 1993), 370–400; John Adams to Robert Livingston, May 25, 1783, James Madison to Thomas Jefferson, Feb. 11, 1783, Jefferson to Madison, Feb. 14, 1783, all quoted in Middlekauff 200–201.

65. WF to BF, July 22, 1784.

66. BF to WF, Aug. 16, 1784.

67. BF to TF, Oct. 2, 1784; Lopez *Private,* 258.

68. BF to PS, Mar. 19, Aug. 15, 1784.

69. Lopez *Private,* 272.

70. PS to BF, Oct. 25, 1784; PS to Barbara Hewson, Jan. 25, 1785; Lopez *Private,* 269.

71. BF to PS, July 4, 1785; BF to JM, July 13, 1785; BF to David Hartley, July 5, 1785.

72. Vergennes to François Barbé de Marbois, May 10, 1785; BF to John Jay, Sept. 21, 1785.

73. Lopez *Cher,* 137–39; Lopez *Private,* 275; Fawn Brodie, *Thomas Jefferson* (New York: Norton, 1974), 425.

74. Franklin trip journal, July 13–28, 1785, Papers CD 43:310.

75. WF to SF, Aug. 1, 1785; Temple *Writings,* 2:165. In a letter to John Jay, Sept. 21, 1785, he describes how Shipley and others visited him in Southampton, but does not mention William.

CHAPTER 16

1. "Maritime Observations," BF to David Le Roy, Aug. 1785, Papers CD 41:384.

2. "Causes and Cure of Smoky Chimneys," BF to Jan Ingenhousz, Aug. 28, 1785; "Description of a New Stove," by BF, Aug. 1785, Papers CD 43:380.

3. BF journal, Sept. 14, 1785, unpublished, Papers CD 43:310; BF to John Jay, Sept. 21, 1785.

4. BF to Jonathan Shipley, Feb. 24, 1786.

5. BF to Polly Stevenson, May 6, 1786.

6. Manasseh Cutler, diary excerpt of July 13, 1787, in Smyth *Writings,* 10:478.

7. BF to Louis-Guillaume le Veillard, Apr. 15, 1787; BF to Ferdinand Grand, Apr. 22, 1787.

8. BF to JM, Sept. 21, 1786; Manasseh Cutler, diary excerpt of July 13, 1787, in Smyth *Writings,* 10:478. When he died, the 4,276 volumes in his library were valued at just over £184. See "An inventory and appraisement of the goods and chattels of the estate of Benjamin Franklin," Bache papers, Castle Collection, American Philosophical Society, Philadelphia.

9. BF to JM, Sept. 20, 1787; BF to Professor Landriani, Oct. 14, 1787.

10. BF to James Woodmason, July 25, 1780, in which he discusses with the London stationer the "new-invented art of copying" and orders three rudimentary machines from him for delivery to Passy. The machines from Woodmason came from Watt's factory, and the stationer insisted that Franklin pay in advance before they were ordered. In a letter of Nov. 1, 1780, he tells Franklin he is sending three new machines and provides instructions for how to use the ink; Papers CD 33:579. See also Copying machine history, http://www.inc.com/articles/it/computers_networks/peripherals/2000.html .

11. "Description of An Instrument for Taking Down Books from High Shelves," Jan. 1786, Papers CD 43:873; Lib. of Am. 1116.

12. BF to Catherine (Kitty) Shipley, May 2, 1786; Lib. of Am. 1118.

13. BF to David Hartley, Oct. 27, 1785.

14. BF to Jonathan Williams, Feb. 16, 1786; to Jonathan Shipley, Feb. 24, 1786; Brands 661.

15. BF to William Cocke, Aug. 12, 1786.

16. BF to Thomas Jefferson, Apr. 19, 1787.

17. www.nara.gov/exhall/charters/constitution/confath.html .

Much of the following relies on Max Farrand, ed., *Records of the Federal Convention* (New Haven: Yale University Press, 1937) and, in particular, *Madison's Journals.* There are many editions of this masterful narrative. Among the most convenient are the searchable versions on the Web, including www.yale.edu/lawweb/avalon/debates/debcont.htm , and www.constitution.org/dfc/dfc_000.htm .

For good analysis of Franklin's role at the convention, see William Carr, *The Oldest Delegate* (Newark: University of Delaware Press, 1990); Gordon Wood, *The Creation of the American Public* (Chapel Hill: University of North Carolina Press, 1969); Clinton Rossiter, *1787: The Grand Convention* (New York: Macmillan, 1966); Catherine Drinker Bowen, *Miracle at Philadelphia* (Boston: Little, Brown, 1966); Richard Morris, *The Forging of the Union* (New York: Harper & Row, 1987).

18. The oft-told story of Franklin arriving at the convention in a sedan chair is described most vividly in Catherine Drinker Bowen's *Miracle at Philadelphia,* 34. See also Smyth *Writings,* 10:477; Brands 674; Van Doren 741. The careful scholar J. A. Leo Lemay writes that no evidence exists that Franklin was carried in a sedan chair to any meeting of the convention. See Lemay, "Recent Franklin Scholarship,

with a Note on Franklin's Sedan Chair," *PMHB* 76:2 (Apr. 2002): 339–40. In fact, however, there is an unpublished letter written by his daughter, Sally, to his grandson Temple during the convention in which she reports: "Your Grand Father was just getting into his Chair to go to convention when I told him I had received your letter" (SB to TF, undated in 1787, Papers CD 45:u350). We know that Franklin was feeling poorly at the outset of the convention, though not throughout it, and also that he owned a sedan chair. The list of items in his estate ("An inventory and appraisement of the goods and chattels of the estate of Benjamin Franklin," Bache papers, Castle Collection, American Philosophical Society, Philadelphia) lists a "Sedan Chair" valued at £20, and it is also listed as part of the items sold from Franklin's house on May 25, 1792, two years after his death (*Dunlap's American Daily Advertiser*, May 21, 1792, copy in the American Philosophical Society, also reprinted in *PMHB* 23 [1899]: 123). We also know that a friend requested permission to borrow "his sedan chair" in 1788 (Mrs. Powel to BF, unpublished, June 16, 1788, Papers CD 45:558). Thus, I think it is reasonable to believe the reports that he was carried in the chair to the convention that first day, May 28. However, Lemay makes the good point that it is unlikely that he regularly used the sedan chair to get to the convention. As Franklin wrote to his sister in September, "The daily exercise of going and returning from the state house has done me good" (BF to JM, Sept. 20, 1787, Papers CD, 45:u167). One friend wrote in late 1786, "Except for the stone, which prevents his using exercise except in walking in the house up and down stairs and sometime to the state-house, [he] still retains his health, spirits and memory" (Samuel Vaughan to Richard Price, Nov. 4, 1786, *Massachusetts Historical Society Proceedings*, 21.17 [May 1903]: 355).

19. Benjamin Rush to Richard Price, June 2, 1787, *Massachusetts Historical Society Proceedings* 21.17 (May 1903): 361. For Pierce's speech, see Farrand's Records of the Convention, 3:91; Franklin speeches, June 30, June 11, Madison's journal; Morris, *The Forging of the Union*, 272.

20. Bowen 18.

21. Madison journal, May 31, 1787.

22. Madison journal, June 11, 1787.

23. Madison journal, June 28, 1787.

24. "Motion For Prayers," by BF, June 28, 1787; Madison's journal, Farrand, 1:452; Papers CD 45:u77; Smyth *Writings*, 9:600.

25. Madison journal, June 30, 1787.

26. Manasseh Cutler journal, July 13, 1787, in Smyth *Writings*, 10:478; "Queries and Remarks Respecting Alterations in the Constitution of Pennsylvania," Nov. 3, 1789, Smyth *Writings*, 10:57.

27. Madison journal, July 26, 20, June 5, 1787.

28. Madison journal, Aug. 7, 10, 1787.

29. Madison journal, June 2, 1787; BF to Benjamin Strahan, Feb. 16, Aug. 19, 1784; Gordon S. Wood, *The Radicalism of the American Revolution* (New York: Random House, 1991), 199. See also chapter 5 n. 25; McCullough 400.

30. Farrand's Records of Convention, 3:85; Samuel Eliot Morison, *Oxford History of the American People* (New York: Oxford University Press, 1965), 1:398.

31. BF to la Rochefoucauld, Oct. 22, 1788; BF to Pierre Du Pont de Nemours, June 9, 1788.

32. Franklin closing speech, Sept. 17, 1787, Papers CD 45:ul61. There are a few versions of this speech, including a draft version, a copy, and Madison's notes, each with minor variations. The one quoted here is that used by the Yale editors of Franklin's papers.

33. Farrand's Records of Convention, 3:85; see memory.loc.gov/ammem/amlaw/lwfr.html .

34. Barbara Oberg, "Plain, Insinuating, Persuasive," in Lemay *Reappraising,* 176, 189; Rossiter, *1787: The Grand Convention,* 234.

35. Roger Rosenblatt, *Where We Stand* (New York: Harcourt, 2002), 70, citing Henry May, *The Enlightenment in America* (New York: Oxford University Press, 1976). The only major founding document Franklin did not sign was the Articles of Confederation, as he was then in France. Roger Sherman signed the Declaration of Independence, the Articles of Confederation, and the Constitution, as well as the Declaration of 1774, but he did not sign either of the treaties.

36. BF to JM, Nov. 4, 1787, Aug. 3, 1789.

37. BF to Noah Webster, Dec. 26, 1789.

38. BF to Benjamin Vaughan, Oct. 24, 1788; see also BF to Louis-Guillaume Le Veillard, Oct. 24, 1788.

39. BF to Benjamin Vaughan, June 3, Nov. 2, 1798; BF to Elizabeth Partridge, Nov. 25, 1788.

40. BF to Catherine Ray Greene, Mar. 2, 1789; BF to George Washington, Sept. 18, 1789.

41. BF to Jean Baptiste Le Roy, Nov. 13, 1789; BF to Louis-Guillaume le Veillard, Oct. 24, 1788.

42. "An Address to the Public," Nov. 9, 1789, Smyth *Writings,* 10:66. Mason quote is in Farrand's Records of the Convention, 2:370.

43. Pennsylvania Society for the Abolition of Slavery, Petition to Congress, by BF, Feb. 12, 1790.

44. "Sidi Mehemet Ibrahim on the Slave Trade," BF to *Federal Gazette,* Mar. 23, 1790.

45. See chapter 11; BF to Richard Price, Mar. 18, 1785.

46. BF to William Strahan, Aug. 19, 1784.

47. BF to unknown recipient, July 3, 1786, Smyth *Writings,* 9:520; the same letter, dated Dec. 13, 1757, Papers 7:293; Thomas Paine, *The Age of Reason,* first fully published in 1794, www.ushistory.org/paine/; libertyonline.hypermall.com/Paine/AOR-Frame.html .

The Yale editors of the Franklin Papers note, "Both the date and the addressee of this letter have been subjects of much difference of opinion. Each of the three surviving manuscript versions bears a different date line. That on the draft, in Franklin's hand, has been heavily scratched out, probably long after the letter was written, by someone other than Franklin." That draft, now at the Library of Congress, has a note by Franklin calling it "Rough of letter dissuading ——— from publishing his piece." Jared Sparks, one of the earliest editors and biographers, deciphered the blacked-out line as "Phila., July 3, 1786," and he published it as addressed to Thomas Paine (Sparks 10:281). Sparks writes, "When a skeptical writer, who is supposed to have been Thomas Paine, showed him in manuscript a work written against religion, he urged him earnestly not to publish it, but to burn it; objecting to his arguments as fallacious, and to his principles as poisoned with the seeds of vice, without tending to any imaginable good." John Bigelow in *The Works of Benjamin Franklin* (New York: Putnam's, 1904) and Smyth *Writings*, 9:520, also use that date. For a contrary assessment written by a student of Sparks's, see Moncure Conway, *The Life of Thomas Paine* (New York: Putnam's, 1892), vii–viii.

The Yale editors (Papers 7:293n, published in 1963) called that dating "plausible" but give six other possible years, ranging from 1751 to 1787. They tentatively use the 1757 date based on a transcription in French that appears to have been written and dated by the clerk Franklin used while living in Passy. In their note, however, they say, "The editors have not been able to identify any particular 'infidel' who might have sent Franklin a manuscript in 1757, nor have they located any particular tract which might be evidence that his advice against publication was disregarded." The Yale editors, when I asked them in 2002, said that they remain uncertain about the date. In a letter to me commenting on some draft sections of this book, Dec. 2, 2002, Edmund Morgan wrote, "Your suggestion that it was written in 1786 to Paine makes more sense to me than the reasons offered by the former editors for placing it in 1757."

My belief that the 1786 date is likely and that it was sent to Paine is based on the following. As early as 1776, Paine had expressed his "contempt" for the Bible and told John Adams, "I have some thoughts of publishing my thoughts on religion, but I believe it will be best to postpone it to the latter part of my life" (John Keane, *Tom Paine* [Boston: Little, Brown, 1995], 390). By 1786, Paine was writing frequently to Franklin (Sept. 23, Dec. 31, 1785, Mar. 31, June 6, 14, 1786) and even using the courtyard in front of Franklin's house to display a bridge design Paine had made. In *The Age of Reason*, Paine favorably mentions Franklin five times ("The Proverbs which are said to be of Solomon's . . . [are] not more wise and economical than those of the American Franklin"). He echoes the more general aspects of Franklin's deist creed by saying that he believes in God and that the "moral duty of man" is to practice God's beneficence "toward each other." But he also engages in many heretical attacks on organized religion that would have elicited Franklin's cautious response. He says that churches "appear to me to be no other than human inventions set up to terrify and enslave mankind and monopolize power and profit." He also says that "the theory of what is called the Christian church sprung out of the tale of heathen mythology" and decries Christian theology for its "absurdity." And he begins his book by indicating that he had considered publishing his thoughts earlier but was dissuaded: "It has been my intention, for several years past, to publish my thoughts upon religion. I am well aware of the difficulties that attend the subject, and from that consideration had reserved it to a more advanced period of life."

48. Archives of Congregation Mikveh Israel, Apr. 30, 1788 (Franklin's gift is one of the three largest of forty-four, and he is on top of the subscriber list), www.mikvehisrael.org/gifs/frank2.jpg ; BF to John Calder, Aug. 21, 1784.

49. BF to Ezra Stiles, Mar. 9, 1790.

50. BF to Thomas Jefferson, Apr. 8, 1790.

51. Reports of Dr. John Jones and Benjamin Rush, in Sparks and elsewhere; Pa. Gazette, Apr. 21, 1790; Benjamin Bache to Margaret Markoe, May 2, 1790.

52. Epitaph, 1728; this is the version Temple Franklin published. See Papers CD 41:u539. Franklin also produced slightly edited versions, including one that ends "Corrected and amended/By the author" (Papers 1:109a).

53. Last will and testament, plus codicil, June 23, 1789, Papers CD 46:u20.

CHAPTER 17

1. Last will and testament, plus codicil, June 23, 1789, Papers CD 46:u20; Skemp *William,* 275. The will and codicil are at www.sln.fi.edu/franklin/family/lastwill.html .

2. WF to TF, July 3, 1789; Skemp *William,* 275; Lopez *Private,* 309. A full and authorized English edition of Franklin's autobiography was not published until 1868.

3. The two great books on Benjamin Bache and his paper are Jeffery A. Smith, *Franklin and Bache: Envisioning the Enlightened Republic* (New York: Oxford University Press, 1990), and Richard Rosenfeld, *American Aurora* (New York: St. Martin's, 1997). See also Bernard Faÿ, *The Two Franklins* (Boston: Little, Brown, 1933).

4. Patricia Nealon, "Ben Franklin Trust to Go to State, City," *Boston Globe,* Dec. 7, 1993, A22; Clark DeLeon, "Divvying Up Ben," *Philadelphia Inquirer,* Feb. 7, 1993, B2; Tom Ferrick Jr., "Ben Franklin's Gift Keeps Giving," *Philadelphia Inquirer,* Jan. 27, 2002, B1; Tour de Sol Web site, www.nesea.org/transportation/tour ; *The Franklin Gazette,* printed by the Friends of Franklin Inc., www.benfranklin2006.org (spring 2002); Philadelphia Academies Annual Report 2001 and Web site, www.academiesinc.org . Web sites on Franklin's bequest include www.philanthropyroundtable.org/magazines/2000-01/lastpage.html ; www.cs.appstate.edu/~sjg/class/1010/wc/finance/benfranklin.html ; www.lehighvalleyfoundation.org/support.html#BenFranklin .

CHAPTER 18

1. *The Nation,* July 9, 1868, reprinted in Norton Autobiography 270. See also Nian-Sheng Huang, *Benjamin Franklin in American Thought and Culture, 1790–1990* (Philadelphia: American Philosophical Society, 1994).

2. The Provost Smith papers, *Pennsylvania Gazette,* Apr. 1997, www.upenn.edu/gazette/0497/.

3. John Adams, *Boston Patriot,* May 15, 1811.

4. Gordon Wood, *The Radicalism of the American Revolution* (New York: Vintage, 1991), 347; John Adams to TF, May 5, 1817; Francis, Lord Jeffrey, *Edinburgh Review* 8 (1806), in Norton Autobiography 253. Jeffrey was reviewing an earlier unauthorized edition of the writings and autobiography.

5. Robert Spiller, "Franklin and the Art of Being Human," *Proceedings of the American Philosophical Society* 100.4 (Aug. 1956): 304.

6. John Keats to George and Georgiana Keats, Oct. 31, 1818; Leigh Hunt, *Autobiography* (New York: Harper, 1850), 1:130–32; both reprinted in Norton Autobiography 257, 266.

7. Herman Melville, *Israel Potter* (1855; New York: Library of America, 1985), chapter 8, http://www.melville.org/hmisrael.htm ; Autobiography 45.

8. Emerson's Journals 1:375, quoted in Campbell 35; Nathaniel Hawthorne, *Works,* 12:189, cited in Yale Autobiography 13.

9. David Brooks, "Among the Bourgeoisophobes," *The Weekly Standard,* Apr. 15, 2002.

10. Mark Twain, "The Late Benjamin Franklin," *The Galaxy,* July 1870.

11. Jim Powell, "How Benjamin Franklin's *Autobiography* inspired all kinds of people to help themselves," www.libertystory.net/LSCONNFRAN.htm .

12. Frederick Jackson Turner, essay in *The Dial,* May 1887; William Dean Howells, "Editor's Study," *Harper's,* Apr. 1888; reprinted in Norton Autobiography.

13. Max Weber, *The Protestant Ethic and the Spirit of Capitalism,* first published (in German) in 1904 and revised in 1920 (New York: Harper Collins, 1930), 52–53; Van Wyck Brooks, *America's Coming of Age,* originally published in 1915 as an essay (Garden City, N.Y.: Doubleday, 1934); William Carlos Williams, *In the Grain* (New York: New Directions, 1925), 153; Sinclair Lewis, *Babbitt,* first published in 1922, chapter 16, section 3, see www.bartleby.com/162/16.html .

14. D. H. Lawrence, "Benjamin Franklin," *Studies in Classic American Literature* (New York: Viking, 1923), 10–16, xroads.virginia.edu/~HYPER/LAWRENCE/dhlch02.htm ; Cervantes, *Don Quixote,* part 2, chapter 33; Aesop, "The Milkmaid and the Pail." Franklin did cite the maxim "Honesty is the best policy" in a letter to Edward Bridgen, Oct. 2, 1779, but it was part of a list of maxims that could be on coins, and he did not claim it as his own.

15. Charles Angoff, *A Literary History of the American People* (New York: Knopf, 1931), 296–308.

16. Herbert Schneider, *The Puritan Mind* (New York: Henry Holt, 1930); Van Doren 782; I. Bernard Cohen, *Benjamin Franklin's Experiments* (Cambridge: Harvard University Press, 1941), 73.

17. For more on Dale Carnegie's *How to Win Friends and Influence People* (1937; New York: Pocket Books, 1994), see ch. 4 n. 6, above; E. Digby Baltzell, *Puritan Boston and Quaker Philadelphia* (New York: Free Press, 1979), 55.

18. FranklinCovey Web site, www.franklincovey.com ; Grady McAllister, "An Unhurried Look at Time Management," vasthead.com/Time/tm_papl.html. Peter Jennings and Todd Brewster, *In Search of America* (New York: Hyperion, 2002), chapter 3, reports on an interesting class discussion by Baylor professor Blaine McCormick about Franklin as the founding father of business books.

19. Brands 715; Morgan *Franklin*, 314.

20. Alan Taylor, "For the Benefit of Mr. Kite," *The New Republic,* Mar. 19, 2001, 39. The play *1776,* by Sherman Edwards and Peter Stone, opened at Broadway's 46th Street Theater on Mar. 16, 1969, ran for 1,217 performances, and was made into a film in 1972; Howard Da Silva played Franklin on both stage and screen. *Ben Franklin in Paris,* by Mark Sandrich Jr. and Sidney Michaels, opened at the Lunt-Fontanne Theater on Oct. 27, 1964, and ran for 215 performances with Robert Preston playing Franklin.

21. David Brooks, "Our Founding Yuppie," *The Weekly Standard,* Oct. 23, 2000, 32, 35.

22. BF to JM, July 17, 1771.

23. Taylor, "For the Benefit of Mr. Kite," 39.

24. Vernon Parrington, *Main Currents in American Thought* (New York: Harcourt, 1930), 1:178.

25. Taylor, "For the Benefit of Mr. Kite," 39.

26. Poor Richard's, 1750; BF to Louis Le Veillard, Mar. 6, 1786; Autobiography 107 (all use the "empty sack" line).

27. Brooks, "Our Founding Yuppie," 35.

28. Autobiography 139.

29. Angoff, *A Literary History of the American People,* 306; Garry Wills, *Under God* (New York: Simon & Schuster, 1990), 380.

30. Henry Steele Commager, *The American Mind* (New Haven: Yale University Press, 1950), 26; John Updike, "Many Bens," *New Yorker,* Feb. 22, 1988, 115.

31. David Hume to BF, May 10, 1762; Campbell 356.

INDEX

abolition, 269, 464–67
abortion issue, 61
Adams, Abigail, 180, 298
  BF described by, 304
  Madame Helvétius described by,
    365
Adams, John, 2, 42, 85, 180, 225, 272,
    291, 292, 298, 304, 316, 327, 335,
    382, 398, 454, 455, 473, 485, 495,
    498, 536n, 553n, 563n
  BF reassessed by, 477–78
  BF's relationship with, 318–19,
    350–53, 355, 371, 383–84,
    392–94, 428–29
  Great Seal and, 315–16
  in Paris mission, 350–53, 355, 365,
    371, 390–92, 428
  in peace negotiations, 397, 399, 403,
    410–12, 414, 415, 558n
  in Staten Island summit, 318–20
  Vergennes and, 391, 393–94
  and writing of Declaration of
    Independence, 309–10, 311
Adams, John Quincy, 352, 377
Adams, Samuel, 244, 251, 272, 275,
    279, 290, 448
Addison, Joseph, 28, 29, 30, 34, 46, 65,
    227–28
"Advice to a Young Man on the Choice
  of a Mistress" (Franklin), 120–21
"Advice to a Young Tradesman,
  Written by an Old One"
  (Franklin), 532n

Aesop, 483
Age of Reason, 93
Age of Reason, The (Paine), 468, 499,
    563n
Albany Plan, 158–62, 210, 218, 225,
    229, 271, 292, 299, 448, 460, 498,
    499, 500, 532n, 536n
  federalism concept and, 160–61
  Indians and, 158–61
  unified colonies idea and, 158, 160
Aldridge, Alfred Owen, 86, 93, 368,
    373, 526n
Alger, Horatio, 480
Allen, William, 216–17, 495
Alliance, 390
almanacs, 95
alphabet, phonetic, 220–21
Alsop, Susan Mary, 336–37, 348
American Aurora, 473, 495
American Magazine, 116–18
American Mind, The (Commager), 491
American Philosophical Society,
    122–23, 147, 157, 356, 439, 459,
    472, 532n
American Revolution, 199, 344, 425
  Albany Plan and, 161–62
  battles of, see specific battles
  Canada invaded in, 305–7
  financial problems in, 303–4
  independence question and, 294–96
  Olive Branch Petition in, 296–97
  onset of, 290–91
  Philadelphia captured in, 342

American Revolution (*cont.*)
  Staten Island summit in, 316–20
  treaty ending, 415
American Weekly Mercury, 60, 61, 70,
    113, 115–16, 117, 495
analytic truths, 312
André, John, 342
Andrews, Jedediah, 84–85, 108
Anglican Church, 7–8, 214, 458
Anglo-American peace negotiations of
    1782:
  Adams-BF rift and, 392–95
  Adams in, 397, 399, 403, 410–12,
    414, 415, 558*n*
  "advisable" points in, 407–8, 411
  American delegation to, 397–98,
    399
  assessment of diplomacy in, 417
  BF's peace proposal in, 407–8
  British back-door overtures in, 407
  compensation for loyalists in, 401–2,
    405, 412, 414–15
  fishing rights in, 407, 411–12,
    558*n*
  French protest of, 415–17
  Hartley's ten-year truce proposal in,
    391–92
  independence debate in, 400, 403–4,
    407–8
  Jay in, 408–9, 411–12, 414
  "necessary" points in, 407–8, 411
  official opening of, 409–10
  Oswald-BF talks in, 400–402,
    404–6
  prewar debts in, 412
  reparations issue in, 400–401, 405,
    407
  separate peace as issue in, 400,
    402–6, 408–9, 411, 557*n*
  signing of treaty in, 415
  Spain and, 408–9, 412
  status of Canada in, 401, 405, 406,
    407, 411
  Temple Franklin and, 397–98
  Thomas Grenville-BF talks in,
    402–6
  Vaughan's secret mission and, 409
  western boundary in, 412
  Yorktown Battle and, 398–99
Angoff, Charles, 257, 483, 490
"Anti-Courant, The" (Walter), 23
"Apology for Printers" (Franklin),
    66–68, 112–13
Aquinas, Saint Thomas, 137, 150
Arabella, 24
Aristotle, 374
armonica, 266, 441
Arnold, Benedict, 305–6, 395
"Articles of Belief and Acts of
    Religion" (Franklin), 85
Articles of Confederation and
    Perpetual Union, 299–300, 314,
    444, 445, 448, 449, 460
"Art of Procuring Pleasant Dreams,
    The" (Franklin), 258
Art of Swimming, The (Thevenot),
    47–48
Asgill, Charles, 413
Associated Families, 26
Associates of Dr. Bray, 191, 464
Augustine, Saint, 257
Austria, 333
Austrian Succession, War of, 123
*Autobiography of Benjamin Franklin,
    The* (Franklin), 34, 100, 479, 481,
    482–83, 489
  Updike on, 256
  writing of, 255–57, 425–26, 461–62

Babbitt (Lewis), 482
Bache, Benjamin Franklin, 240, 258,
    262–63, 291, 300, 301, 324, 330,
    361, 422, 427, 431, 433, 462, 469,
    495, 531*n*
  death of, 473
  described, 432
  education of, 377–79, 438
  personality of, 378–80, 432
  in return to Passy, 417–19
  in training as printer, 419, 438
  Voltaire's blessing of, 354
Bache, Deborah, 473, 495
Bache, Elizabeth, 377, 495
Bache, Louis, 376, 495

Bache, Mary, 261
Bache, Richard (father), 235–36,
   238–39, 258, 261–62, 279,
   300, 301–2, 303, 308, 378–79,
   384–85, 419, 438, 469, 472–73,
   495, 499
Bache, Richard (son), 495
Bache, Sarah (BF's granddaughter),
   495
Bache, Sarah Franklin "Sally" (BF's
   daughter), 120, 177, 180, 198–99,
   208, 232, 235, 240, 261, 262, 291,
   300, 322, 329, 378, 422, 435, 437,
   438, 439, 469, 495, 497, 531*n*,
   561*n*
   BF's correspondence with, 187, 262,
      327, 375–77, 379, 385
   BF's "luxury" letter to, 375–77
   in BF's will, 472–73
   birth of, 118–19
   marriage of, 238–39
Bache, William, 291–92, 300, 376–77,
   379, 438, 473, 495
bagatelles, 367–71, 375
Bailyn, Bernard, 338
balloon fad, 420–22
Bancroft, Edward, 277–78, 333–36,
   342, 343, 344, 345, 347, 350, 356,
   388, 495, 501, 550*n*, 551*n*–52*n*
Banks, Joseph, 417, 420, 421
Barber of Seville, The (Beaumarchais),
   331, 495
Barclay, David, 285
Bartram, John, 122
Beaumarchais, Pierre-Augustin Caron
   de, 331, 343, 389, 495
Becker, Carl, 528*n*
Beethoven, Ludwig van, 266
Benezet, Anthony, 269, 464
Ben Franklin in Paris (Sandrich and
   Michaels), 485, 566*n*
Ben Franklin Stilled the Waves
   (Tanford), 263
Benjamin Franklin and His Enemies
   (Middlekauff), 351
Benjamin Franklin and His Gods
   (Walters), 86

Benjamin Franklin and Nature's God
   (Aldridge), 526*n*–27*n*
Benjamin Franklin Institute of
   Technology, 474
Bentham, Jeremy, 277
Berkeley, George, 45, 197, 498
bifocal glasses, 2, 426, 492
Board of Associated Loyalists, 413
Board of Trade, London, 158, 195
Bob (Bache family slave), 472
Bonhomme Richard, 388, 390
Bonifacius: Essays to Do Good (C.
   Mather), 25–26, 529*n*
Bonvouloir, Julien de, 321
Boston, Mass., 244
   in BF's will, 474–75
   British blockade of, 281, 288
   in eighteenth century, 15–16
   libraries of, 24
   Puritan hierarchy of, 11–12
   smallpox epidemic in, 22–23, 83
Boston Evening Post, 132
Boston Gazette, 22
Boston Latin School, 18, 30
Boston Massacre, 248
Boston *News Ledger*, 107
Boston News-Letter, 21–22
Boston Tea Party, 231, 275, 276, 282
Boswell, James, 220
Bourbon, Duchess of, 372
Boyle, Robert, 130
Braddock, Edward, 166–67
Bradford, Andrew, 37–38, 60, 69, 72,
   95, 97, 107, 495
   BF's rivalry with, 61–62, 64, 65–66,
      113–17
Bradford, William (father), 37, 38–39,
   112, 495, 499
Bradford, William (son), 292, 298
Bradstreet, Simon, 11
Brands, H. W., 77, 485
Breintnall, Joseph, 55–56, 61, 62, 63,
   130
Bridgewater, Duke of, 253
Brillon de Jouy, Anne-Louise, 356–62,
   368, 370, 372, 373, 380–81, 384,
   431, 433, 495, 531*n*

Brillon de Jouy, Cunégonde, 380
Brillon de Jouy, Monsieur, 357, 380–81
Broglio, Count, 335, 336
Brooker, William, 22
Brooks, David, 3, 90, 485–86
Brooks, Van Wyck, 482
Brownell, George, 19
Buffon, Comte de, 139
Bunker Hill, Battle of, 295, 498
Bunyan, John, 25, 30, 257
Burgoyne, John, 342–43
Burke, Edmund, 277, 288, 322
Burnet, Gilbert, 257
"Business Man, The" (Poe), 479
Busy-Body Essays, 60–64, 69, 227
Bute, Lord, 203

Cabanis, Pierre-Jean-Georges, 364,
     365, 426, 433, 439
Cabinet, U.S., 455
Caillot, Blanchette, 420
Calvin, John, 86, 526n
Calvinism, 26, 44–46, 110
Cambridge mission, 302–4
Cambridge University, 191–92
Campan, Henriette de, 549n
Campbell, James, 268, 491
Campbell, John, 21–22
Canada, 123, 158, 197, 328, 471
     in Anglo-American peace
          negotiations, 401, 405–7, 411
     Britain's retention of, 200–202
     Quebec expedition and, 305–7
Carlyle, Thomas, 93, 479, 483
Carlyle conference, 156–57, 158
Carnegie, Andrew, 474, 481, 524n
Carnegie, Dale, 524n
Caslon, William, 53n
"Casuist, The" (BF pen name), 69
"Causes of the American Discontents"
     (Franklin), 244–45
Cellini, Benvenuto, 257
Cervantes, Miguel de, 483
Channel Islands, 387
Charles, Jacques, 420–21
Charles, Prince of Lorrains, 200
Charles I, King of England, 13

Charles II, King of England, 7, 155
Charleston, S.C., 295, 395
Chatham, Lord, *see* Pitt, William
Chaumont, Jacques-Donatien Leray
     de, 329–30, 352, 388, 433, 496
Chaumont, Madame de, 330, 388
Checkley, John, 23, 24
chess, 357–58, 372–73
Chesterfield, Earl of, 44
Child, Anne, *see* Franklin, Anne Child
Cholmondeley, Lord, 400
"Christian at His Calling, A"
     (C. Mather), 10
Cincinnati, Society of, 422–23
Civil War, U.S., 480
Clinton, George, 125
Clinton, Henry, 385, 395
Cohen, I. Bernard, 135, 142, 143, 484,
     534n
Colden, Cadwallader, 122–23, 127,
     133, 145, 161, 496
Coleman, William, 55–56
colleges, 2, 102, 146–47, 149–50
Collins, John, 27, 42, 43, 44, 46, 48,
     56, 119, 487
Collinson, Peter, 104, 157, 176,
     181–82, 267, 496
     BF's correspondence with, 134, 135,
          136, 138, 139–40, 141, 142, 143,
          144, 148–49, 150, 160, 167, 172,
          210
Collyer, Hannah, 472
Commager, Henry Steele, 93, 257,
     491
Committee on Correspondence,
     Massachusetts, 251
common cold, 2, 264
Common Sense (Paine), 307–8, 499
community associations, 26–27, 31,
     102
Concord, Battle of, 291, 399
Condorcet, Marie-Jean Caritat,
     Marquis de, 338, 354–55, 363,
     439, 463, 495
Confessions (Rousseau), 257
Confessions (St. Augustine), 257
Congregation Mikveh Israel, 468

Congress, U.S., 465, 467
see also House of Representatives,
U.S.; Senate, U.S.
Connecticut, 299
Connecticut Compromise, 450
Constitution, U.S., 458, 459–60, 463
Constitutional Convention of 1787,
56, 161, 444–60, 491
BF's closing address to, 457–59
BF's role in, 445–48, 453, 459–60
BF's speeches in, 449–50, 451,
457–58
bicameral legislature as issue in, 447,
448–49, 450
colonial discord and, 444–45
Connecticut Compromise in, 450
delegates to, 445
election of judges as issue in, 455
executive powers debated in, 454–55
impeachment powers in, 454
payment of legislators debated in,
455–56, 532n
prayer as issue in, 451–52
property requirements debated in,
455
representation debated in, 447,
448–51, 452
signing of Constitution in, 458–60
slavery as issue in, 456–57, 460,
464
states' rights in, 448–49
two-headed snake fable and, 453–54
Virginia plan in, 449
Washington in, 445, 446, 454, 455,
456, 458
"Conte" (Franklin), 371
Continental Congress (1774), 281–82,
285–87, 292
Continental Congress (1775), 291–93,
382, 385, 392, 393, 395, 416, 432,
444
and Articles of Confederation,
299–300, 314
BF's assignments for, 301–2
BF selected as delegate to, 291
BF's Paris mission and, 321
Cambridge mission and, 302–4

Committee of Secret
Correspondence of, 321, 339
Declaration of Independence edited
in, 313
financial problems of, 303–4
Franco-American treaty ratified by,
349
Great Seal adopted by, 315–16
peace negotiations and, 406–8,
415
Quebec expedition and, 305–6
representation question in, 314
roots of federal system in, 299
royal congresses removed by, 308
Staten Island summit and, 316–17
vote for independence in, 312–13
"Conversation on Slavery" (Franklin),
268–69
"Cool Thoughts on the Present
Situation" (Franklin), 215–16
Cooper, Grey, 230
Cooper, Samuel, 249, 349, 379, 496
Copley Medal, 143
copperplate press, 53
Cornwallis, Charles, Lord, 395, 398
Covey, Stephen, 484
Cramer, Catherine, 377, 378–79
Cramer, Philibert, 377
Craven, Wayne, 128
Craven Street Gazette, 241–42
Crockett, Davy, 95, 479
Cromwell, Oliver, 7–8
Cushing, Thomas, 251, 253, 260,
271–72, 282, 496
Cutler, Manasseh, 453

D'Alibard, Thomas-François, 139
Dallett, Francis James, 525n
Dartmouth, William Legge, Lord,
272, 279–81, 285, 287–88
BF's secret correspondence with,
280–81
Davenport, Josiah, 224
Davis, William Morris, 133
Davy, Humphry, 135
Dawes, William, 291
Dayton, Jonathan, 445

Deane, Silas, 321, 331–32, 335, 337,
    344–45, 347, 350, 398, 496, 550*n*,
    552*n*
"Death of Infants, The" (Franklin),
    83–84
Declaration of Independence, 317,
    417, 459, 463, 495, 499
    Adams and, 309–10, 311
    BF's editing of, 311–12
    BF's influence on, 310–11
    congressional editing of, 313,
        547*n*
    official signing of, 313
    "self-evident truths" phrase in, 312,
        548*n*
    slave trade in, 313
    writing of, 309–10, 547*n*
Declaration of Rights, 311, 315
Declaration of the Causes and
    Necessity for Taking Up Arms,
    296
Declaratory Act, 231
Deffand, Marie de Vichy-Chamrond,
    Marquise du, 328, 348
Defoe, Daniel, 25, 26–27, 31, 44, 59,
    227, 528*n*, 529*n*
deism, 26, 486
    BF's interpretation of, 46, 84–87,
        526*n*, 563*n*,
    "general providence" concept in,
        86–87
DeLancey, James, 159–60, 166
de la Roche, Martin Lefebvre, 364,
    370
Delaware, 155, 449, 450, 451
Delaware Indians, 156, 194
De l'Esprit (C.-A. Helvétius), 363
democracy, 3, 217, 447, 493
Denham, Thomas, 43, 48, 52
Denny, William, 173, 186, 194–95,
    496
Descartes, René, 374
D'Evelyn, Mary, 471
"Dialogue Between the Gout and
    Mr. Franklin, The" (Franklin),
    368–70
Dick, Alexander, 195

Dickinson, John, 216–17, 223, 245,
    296, 312, 496
Dictionary of American Biography, 528*n*
Diderot, Denis, 85, 353, 355, 363, 495
Didot, François, 419
"Dissertation on Liberty and Necessity,
    Pleasure and Pain, A" (Franklin),
    45–46, 84, 135
Dissertations on the English Language
    (Webster), 220–21, 461
divine providence, 86–87
"Dogood, Silence" (pen name), 26,
    28–33, 79, 94, 119, 227, 466
"Don't Tread on Me" flag, 305
Douglass, William, 23
Downes, Elizabeth, *see* Franklin,
    Elizabeth Downes
"Dr. Franklin's In-Laws" (Dallett),
    525*n*
"Drinker's Dictionary" (Franklin), 71
Duane, William, 473
Dudley, Thomas, 32
Dull, Jonathan, 346, 552*n*
"Dulman, Jack" (pseudonym), 34
Duplessis, Joseph-Siffrèd, 330
Du Pont de Nemours, Pierre-Samuel,
    327–28, 457
Duras, 388

East India Company, 275
Eden, William, 333
"Edict by the King of Prussia, An"
    (Franklin), 274, 298, 339, 466,
    496
Edinburgh Review, 478
Edwards, Jonathan, 4, 61, 109, 476
electricity, 133–44, 484
    BF's importance to field of, 144–45
    BF's kite experiments in, 140–42,
        534*n*
    and coinage of new terms, 134–35
    criticism of BF and, 142–43
    French experiments in, 139–40
    lightning and, 137–40
    single-fluid theory of, 135, 144
    Spencer's experiments in, 133–34
    storage of, 135–36

Eliot, Jared, 133
Elizabeth I, Queen of England, 7–8
"Elysian Fields, The" (Franklin),
    366–67
Emerson, Ralph Waldo, 93, 291, 479
    BF assessed by, 480
enclosure practice, 6–7
Encyclopédie, 353–54, 364, 495, 499
Enlightenment, 24, 25, 44–46, 50, 84,
    109, 149, 295, 311, 326, 354, 363,
    427, 447, 460, 469, 478, 490, 491,
    528*n*–29*n*
    Age of Reason in, 93
    BF as exemplar of, 37
    BF's creed of, 92–94
    free press and, 66
Enlightenment in America, The (May),
    460
Ephemera, The (Franklin), 361, 367
*Essays Concerning Human
    Understanding* (Hume), 197
Essay Upon Projects, An (Defoe), 25,
    26–27, 529*n*
Estaing, Jean-Baptiste, Comte d', 335,
    336, 553*n*
exercise, 264

Farmers General, 363
federalism, concept of, 160–61
Feke, Robert, 128
Fielding, Henry, 44
fire corps, 2, 59, 102, 104–5, 147, 154
First American, The (Brands), 485
Fisher, Mary Franklin, 190
Flaubert, Gustave, 480
"Flies, The" (Franklin), 367
Folger, Abiah, *see* Franklin, Abiah
    Folger
Folger, John, 13
Folger, Mary Morrill, 14
Folger, Peter, 13–14
Folger, Timothy, 290
Fontenelle, Bernard Le Bovier de,
    363–64, 528*n*
Fothergill, John, 182, 214, 226, 285,
    496
Fox, Charles, 399, 402, 407

Foxcroft, John, 207
France, 123, 155, 156, 158, 166, 199,
    274, 279, 315, 321
    adoration of BF in, 325–29
    BF's mission to, *see* Paris mission of
        1776–1785
    BF's 1767 vacation in, 237–38
    electricity experiments in, 139–40
    freemasonry in, 355–56
    peace negotiations and, *see* Anglo-
        American peace negotiations of
        1782
Franklin, Abiah Folger (BF's mother),
    14–15, 496, 497
Franklin, Anne (BF's half-sister), 13
Franklin, Anne (BF's sister-in-law),
    111
Franklin, Anne Child, 9, 13, 497
Franklin, Benjamin:
    abolitionist views of, 269, 464–67
    air baths of, 243
    America as viewed by, 149–50,
        217–18
    appearance as a concern of, 38, 54,
        92, 353
    appointed postmaster general, 301
    on bald eagle as national symbol,
        422–23
    birth of, 15
    books as passion of, 24–27
    in Cambridge mission, 302–4
    in Canada mission, 305–7
    character of, 3–4, 24, 75
    chess loved by, 372–73
    childhood of, 15–17
    colonial unity as theme of, 156,
        158–59
    conservatism of, 148, 267–68
    curiosity of, 49, 129–30, 166
    death of, 469–70
    as debater, 27, 39, 56–57
    decision-making method of, 74–75
    and decision to run away, 33, 35
    as deist, 46, 84–85, 107, 526*n*, 563*n*,
    demeanor of, 42, 213–14, 304
    described, 37, 43, 304, 327–28, 348
    diplomatic style of, 337–38

Franklin, Benjamin (*cont.*)
  domesticity of, 209
  eccentricities of, 243
  education of, 18–20, 526n
  elected assembly speaker, 216
  elected militia colonel, 171–72
  epitaph of, 470
  as essayist, 28–33, 45
  eulogy for, 477
  fame of, 139–40, 143, 200, 326
  family background of, 5–6, 9, 13–15
  family history as interest of, 254–55
  federalism concept of, 160–61
  final letter of, 469
  first London sojourn of, 43–51
  first published prose of, 22
  flirtatious relationships of, 162–65,
      177–79, 220, 241–43, 258, 283,
      284–87, 356–62, 487, 499, 500,
      536n
  foreign missions of, *see* London
      mission of 1757–1762;
      London mission of 1765–1775;
      Paris mission of 1776–1785
  as Freemason, 106–7
  on free press, 66–67
  on free speech, 31–32
  as freethinker, 46, 88
  as frontier commander, 170–71
  frugality of, 17, 47, 49, 78, 92, 227,
      266, 297–98
  funeral of, 470
  as gossip columnist, 62
  health of, 239, 302, 306–7, 310, 321,
      322, 324, 325, 368, 383, 395, 396,
      408, 410, 421, 432, 439–40, 446,
      460–61, 462, 468, 469–70
  Hemphill affair and, 107–9
  honorary degrees of, 143, 172, 198,
      202
  house renovated by, 440–41
  humor of, 2, 29, 42–43, 71–72, 92,
      95, 99, 106–7, 121, 340, 477
  illegitimate son of, *see* Franklin,
      William
  income and wealth of, 100, 111,
      126–27, 157, 234, 301, 474

  independence favored by, 292,
      294–95, 298
  Keith as patron of, 40–41
  land grant sought by, 209–10, 219,
      245–46, 270–71, 276–77, 552n
  languages as interest of, 197, 370–71
  laudanum used by, 462
  lecherous reputation of, 356, 485
  library of, 440–41
  liturgy composed by, 86
  as lowbrow, 482
  as loyalist, 193, 201, 203, 226, 253,
      281
  on luxury, 424–25
  magazine started by, 116–18
  making mistakes and amends as
      theme of, 73
  on marriage, 80
  maxims of, 4, 17, 27, 37, 65–66,
      98–99, 101, 102, 478–81
  and method for winning over
      opponents, 114–15
  middle class values of, 3, 212, 268,
      424–25, 476, 478, 480, 487, 488,
      493
  mistakes-amends theme of, 73
  moral beliefs of, 486–87, 491
  national identity of, 2, 3
  nepotism of, 301–2
  as networker, 55
  new American archetype created by,
      2
  new house of, 209–10
  new words coined by, 134–35, 197,
      370–71, 461
  as observer of human nature, 49–50
  onset of political career of, 153–54
  pen names used by, 34, 69, 70–71,
      73, 80, 104, 112, 151, 242, 243,
      267, 530n; *see also* Busy-Body
      Essays; "Dogood, Silence"; *Poor
      Richard's Almanack*
  personality of, 19–20, 39, 42–43, 44,
      52, 71, 75, 102, 111, 319, 351,
      357, 367, 368, 392, 447–48
  personal magnetism of, 37, 39
  as philosopher, 45

poetry of, 21, 27, 81–82, 109
political cartoon produced by, 228
political philosophy of, 148–50
in popular imagination, 485, 488–89
portraits of, 128, 330, 342, 356, 426
practical advice and exhortations of, 41, 56–57, 69, 80
pragmatism of, 2, 87–88, 92–94, 130, 144, 145, 421–22, 476, 491, 492–93
pride of, 1, 92, 460–61
print shop of, 53–55
progress as theme of, 25–26
public persona of, 2–3, 27, 60
as public speaker, 231
racism of, 152–53, 268
Rees scandal and, 106–7
religious beliefs of, 19–20, 26, 32–33, 44–45, 46, 84–88, 92–94, 107–11, 371, 380, 451, 467–69, 486, 491, 526n–27n, 563n
in retirement from printing trade, 126–28
as royalist, 193–94, 200, 201, 218, 219, 246, 249
in runaway journey, 36–38
scientific paraphernalia of, 441
self-deprecation of, 1, 71–72
self-help movement and, 484
self-improvement theme of, 41, 48–49
sexual appetite of, 43, 72, 120–21
sexuality in writings of, 68–69, 360, 370
slaves owned by, 151–52, 176, 190–91, 269
small family of, 119–20
social philosophy of, 266–67, 425
Socratic method used by, 27, 39, 56–57
Supreme Being as viewed by, 85–86
surname of, 5, 520n
swimming as interest of, 16, 47
and taste for finery, 78
temperance of, 47, 71

tolerance as creed of, 93–94, 108, 196, 211, 295, 371, 380, 468, 476, 490
vanity of, 31–32, 171, 172, 208, 461
as vegetarian, 36, 39
virtues as defined and practiced by, 2–4, 89–91, 426, 483
as "Water American," 47
whistle incident and, 16–17, 203
will of, 470–74
women and, 44, 119–21, 163–65, 176–77, 362
work habits of, 352–53
writing influences on, 28–30, 34, 373
writing style of, 27–30, 135, 311
young people and, 119–20
Assessments, 459–60, 476–91
by academic world, 485
by Adams, 477–78
by Emerson, 480
by intellectuals, 481–82, 489
Marxist, 481, 489
by Melville, 480
of personal life, 487
in popular imagination, 485, 488–89
in post–Civil War era, 480–81
by romanticists, 478–79, 480, 486
as scientist, 144–45
by transcendentalists, 479
in twentieth century, 481–84
Civic Activities
BF on, 490
colleges, 2, 102, 146–47, 149–50
community associations, 26–27, 31, 102
fire brigade, 2, 59, 102, 104–5, 147, 154
fund-raising, 2
hospitals, 102, 147–48
insurance association, 2, 31
Junto, *see* Junto (Leather Apron Club)
libraries, 2, 4, 59, 102, 103–4, 147, 154, 257–58, 492, 532n
militia, 102, 123–26, 147, 155, 169–72, 392, 532n

Franklin, Benjamin (*cont.*)
  moral perfection project, 89–92, 94
  police patrols, 59, 105–6, 147, 154
  post office reform, 157, 207
  self-improvement and, 3, 484
  street maintenance, 154, 489
  welfare, 148–49, 267–68
  Inventions
  bifocal glasses, 2, 426, 492
  copperplate press design, 53
  copy machine design, 441
  daylight savings idea, 372–73
  hot water system design, 264
  light globe model, 154
  lightning rod, 141–43, 441, 442, 492
  mechanical arm, 441–42
  musical instrument, 266
  new words, 134–35, 197, 370–71,
    461
  phonetic alphabet, 220–21
  storage battery, 135–36
  stove, 2, 130–31, *131*, 441, 492
  street lamp design, 154
  swimming pads, 16, 47
  typeface, 52
  urinary catheter, 132, 497
  Scientific Interests, 129–45
  air currents, 436
  assessment of, 144–45, 487
  BF's writing style and, 135
  color, 191
  common cold, 2, 264
  electricity, *see* electricity
  evaporation, 191
  Gulf Stream, 2, 129, 290, 437
  heat, 130, 191–92, 264
  hull design, 436–37
  importance and significance of,
    144–45
  lead poisoning, 265
  magnetism, 129
  maritime topics, 436–37
  meteorology, 129, 132–33
  mock essays on, 372–75
  population growth, 150–51
  pragmatism of, 130, 144, 145, 192,
    421–22, 437

  refrigeration, 129, 191
  saltiness of oceans, 265–66
  ship speeds in canals, 265
  smoky chimneys, 437
  study of exercise, 264
  weather forecasting, 132–33
Franklin, Benjamin (BF's uncle), 8–9,
    17–18, 21, 254, 255, 496, 520*n*
Franklin, Deborah Read (BF's wife), 1,
    43, 44, 46, 77, 97, 143, 157, 209,
    217, 261, 269, 291, 300–301, 440,
    464, 496–97, 525*n*
  BF on, 78
  BF's common-law marriage with,
    74–75
  BF's correspondence with, 179–81,
    182, 186–87, 190–91, 192,
    198–99, 219, 221, 224–25,
    232–36, 237, 238, 253, 262, 263,
    467
  BF's flirtations and, 164
  BF's relationship with, 80–82,
    164, 176, 179–80, 187, 207–8,
    487
  children of, 82, 118–20; *see also*
    specific children
  death of, 282–83
  home defended by, 224–25
  personality of, 80–81
  Strahan's letters to, 178–79, 182
  stroke suffered by, 239–40
Franklin, Ebenezer (BF's brother),
    15
Franklin, Elizabeth Downes (BF's
    daughter-in-law), 203–4, 208,
    322–23, 324
Franklin, Ellen (BF's granddaughter),
    472
Franklin, Francis Folger (Franky) (BF's
    son), 4, 82–83, 118, 497
Franklin, Henry (BF's great-
    grandfather), 7
Franklin, James (BF's brother), 15,
    22–24, 28–29, 31–32, 35, 37, 42,
    64, 95, 100, 497, 522*n*
  BF's break with, 33–34, 41
  BF's reconciliation with, 73

Franklin, Jane (BF's sister), 157, 180, 187, 208, 300, 304, 497, 527*n*
   BF's correspondence with, 17, 18, 78–79, 83, 203, 228, 238–39, 257, 278, 280, 433, 440, 461, 486
Franklin, John (BF's brother), 15, 20, 87, 132, 157, 162, 497
Franklin, John (BF's uncle), 7, 8
Franklin, Josiah (BF's father), 7, 20–21, 27–28, 190, 496, 497, 520*n*
   BF's description of, 12
   BF's education and, 18–19
   BF's printing venture and, 41–42
   in chandler trade, 10–11
   character of, 12
   children of, 13, 15, 17
   first marriage of, 9
   library of, 24–25
   in migration to America, 9–11
   second marriage of, 13, 14–15
Franklin, Josiah, Jr. (BF's half-brother), 13, 20
Franklin, Mary (BF's sister), 15
Franklin, Peter (BF's brother), 15, 157, 266
Franklin, Sally (BF's cousin), 254
Franklin, Samuel (BF's cousin), 18, 21
Franklin, Sarah (BF's sister), 15
Franklin, Sarah "Sally," *see* Bache, Sarah Franklin "Sally"
Franklin, Theodore (BF's great-grandson), 420
Franklin, Thomas (BF's great-great-grandfather), 5–6, 254
Franklin, Thomas, II (BF's grandfather), 7
Franklin, Thomas, III (BF's uncle), 8, 190
Franklin, William (BF's son), 75, 82, 118, 119, 123, 153, 157, 170, 206, 208, 216, 236, 290, 351, 419, 473, 487, 531*n*, 546*n*
   age of, 76–78, 525*n*
   appointed governor of New Jersey, 203–4
   Asgill affair and, 412–13

   BF's correspondence with, 245, 255, 270–71, 274–75, 278, 280, 281–83, 288, 295, 429–30
   BF's relationship with, 189, 204, 275, 280–83, 293–94, 304–5, 306, 412–15, 429–31, 434–35, 497
   in BF's will, 471
   in Braddock expedition, 167
   death of, 471
   in flight to England, 413
   Graeme courtship and, 188–89
   illegitimate children of, 199, 472
   kite experiment and, 140–41, 147
   in London mission, 175, 186, 188–90, 191, 195–96, 198–99, 203–4
   loyalist outlook of, 188–89, 256, 275, 306
   marriage of, 203–4
   in Scotland, 195–96
   Shelburne's meeting with, 413
   Temple Franklin's relationship with, 221, 283, 293, 294, 300, 306, 309, 323–24, 413, 430–31, 434, 435, 471, 472
   in Trevose meeting, 293–95
   trial of, 308–9
Franklin, William Temple (BF's grandson), 204, 345, 362, 376, 382, 396, 418, 422, 427, 437, 439, 469, 478, 495, 497, 531*n*, 553*n*, 561*n*
   appointed to peace delegation, 397–98
   BF's relationship with, 221, 240, 290, 361, 487
   birth of, 199
   dandyish behavior of, 330, 419–20, 438
   illegitimate son of, 420
   Lee-BF feud and, 385–86
   in Paris mission, 322–25, 329, 330, 344, 356, 385–86, 415
   peace negotiations and, 397–98
   Polly Stevenson and, 431–32
   in visit to England, 430–31

Franklin, William Temple (BF's grandson) (*cont.*)
  William Franklin's relationship with, 221, 283, 293, 294, 300, 306, 309, 323–24, 413, 430–31, 434, 435, 471, 472
Franklin, The (barge), 231–32
"Franklin Covey Organizers," 484
Franklin Drawing Electricity From the Sky (West), 140
Franklin family:
  derivation of name, 5, 520*n*
  dissenting streak of, 6–7
  genealogical records of, 189–90
  in migration to America, 9, 13–14
  religion and, 8–9
  traits of, 6, 14
Franklin Gothic (typeface), 52
Franklin Institute, 474, 475
Franklin Union, 474
Frederick II, King of Prussia, 274, 327
Freemasons, 106–7, 355
free press, 66–67
free speech, 31–32, 217
free will, 45, 87–88
Freke, John, 534*n*
French and Indian War, 155, 197, 200, 205, 210, 498
French Revolution, 427, 495, 500
  BF's perception of, 462–63
"Friendly Societies" (Defoe), 59

Gadsen, Christopher, 305
Gage, Thomas, 279, 498
Galileo Galilee, 134, 144
Galloway, Joseph, 186, 247, 292–94, 412, 497
Garrick, David, 253
Gazette (Amiens), 327
Gazetteer, 247
General Magazine, 116–18
Gentleman's Magazine, 118, 139, 267
George II, King of England, 136
George III, King of England, 200, 204, 253, 264, 279–80, 344
Georgia, 231, 268, 464
Germany, 137, 232

Gerry, Elbridge, 447, 453, 456
Gibraltar, 400, 409
Gilded Age, 480, 481
"God and Liberty" benediction, 354
Godfrey, Mrs. Thomas, 72
Godfrey, Thomas, 55–56, 72–73, 95, 122
Goode, Wilson, 475
Grace, Robert, 55–56
Graeme, Elizabeth, 188–89
Graeme, Thomas, 188
Grand Lodge of Free and Accepted Masons, 106
Grand Ohio Company, 270, 453, 501
Granville, Lord, 183–84
Great Awakening, 107–13, 501
Great Britain, 15*n*, 123, 150–51, 155, 199, 200–201, 220, 264, 271, 273–74, 326, 464
  BF's effort to join government of, 246–47
  BF's Paris mission and, 333–36, 342–45, 347, 382, 551*n*–52*n*
  in peace negotiations, *see* Anglo-American peace negotiations of 1782
  Staten Island summit and, 316–20
Great Depression, 484
Great Seal, 315–16, 457
Greene, Catherine Ray, 162–65, 166, 177, 180, 190, 208, 304, 462, 499–500
Greene, William, 165, 500
Grenville, George, 222–23, 229, 402
Grenville, Thomas, 402–6, 407, 408, 557*n*
Griswold, A. Whitney, 93
Guillotin, Joseph-Ignace, 427
Gulf Stream, 2, 129, 290, 437

Hadley, John, 191
Hall, David, 127, 181–82, 224, 226, 231, 233–34, 497, 500
Hamilton, Alexander, 445, 446, 451–52, 454, 456
Hamilton, Andrew, 113–14, 497
Hamilton, James, 497

Hancock, John, 225, 279, 290, 291, 313, 325

Harper's, 481

Hartley, David, 303, 391, 392, 433

Harvard College, 18, 19–20, 30, 143

Hauksbee, Francis, 534*n*

Hawthorne, Nathaniel, 480, 483

"Heads of Complaint" (Franklin), 184, 192

Hell-Fire Club, 23

Helvétius, Anne-Catherine, 355, 363–67, 373, 384, 426, 431, 433, 498, 499, 500

Helvétius, Claude-Adrien, 354–55, 363, 364, 366, 498

Hemphill, Samuel, 107–9, 113, 530*n*

Henry, Patrick, 225, 291, 448

Henry VIII, King of England, 276

Herbert, Eugenia, 431

Herbert of Cherbury, Lord, 257

Herschbach, Dudley, 129

Hewson, Elizabeth, 301, 473

Hewson, Mary Stevenson "Polly," 180, 189, 198, 203, 243, 301, 375, 378, 417, 438, 469, 500, 531*n*
    BF's correspondence with, 177–78, 187, 204–5, 208, 219, 221, 237–38, 261, 263, 328, 418, 432–33, 439
    death of, 473
    marriage of, 240–41
    Temple Franklin and, 431–32

Hewson, Tom, 473

Hewson, William (father), 240–41, 243, 500

Hewson, William (son), 262–63, 473

Hillsborough, Lord, 246–47, 249–50, 251, 259–60, 269–71, 277

"Hints for a Conversation" (Franklin), 285–86

History and Present State of Electricity, The (Priestley), 141

History of England (Berkeley), 197

Homer, 104

Honest Whigs, 182, 183

hospitals, 102, 147–48

hot-air balloons, 420–22

Houdon, Jean-Antoine, 356

House of Burgesses, Virginia, 225

House of Commons, British, 81, 194, 264

House of Lords, British, 287

House of Representatives, Massachusetts, 249–50

House of Representatives, U.S., 448, 450, 452, 466

Howe, Caroline, 284–87

Howe, Richard, 284, 322, 410, 495, 498
    BF's Staten Island summit with, 316–20

Howe, William, 284–87, 316, 342, 498

Howells, William Dean, 481

How to Win Friends and Influence People (Carnegie), 524*n*

"Hue and Cry after the Busy-Body" (Keimer), 62

Hughes, John, 223–25

hull design, 436–37

Hume, David, 45, 196–97, 260–61, 312, 363, 485, 491, 498

"Hume's fork," 312

Hunt, Leigh, 479

Hunter, William, 157, 207

Hutchinson, Thomas, 160, 249, 293, 294, 354, 536*n*
    purloined letters of, 271–80, 498
    Stamp Act crisis and, 225–26

Hutton, James, 557*n*

Hyde, Lord, 215

Illinois Company, 270

Indiana Company, 270

Indians, 123, 153, 297, 302, 539*n*
    Albany Plan and, 158–61
    in Carlyle conference, 156–57
    Paxton Boys uprising and, 210–14
    Proprietors and, 155–56, 194
    see also specific tribes

Industrial Revolution, 253

"Information to Those Who Would Remove to America" (Franklin), 423

Ingenhousz, Jan, 422, 439

insurance associations, 2, 31
"Interest of Great Britain Considered
    with Regard to Her Colonies"
    (Franklin), 201, 542*n*
Ireland, 252
Iroquois confederacy, 156–57, 158
Israel Potter (Melville), 479
Izard, Ralph, 333, 384–85, 396

Jackson, James, 466
Jackson, Richard, 218, 259
Jay, John, 397, 408–9, 411–12, 428,
    434, 438
Jefferson, Thomas, 2, 149–50, 225,
    291, 314, 317, 321, 397, 431, 434,
    441, 445, 469, 495, 519*n*, 547*n*
  Declaration of Independence
    written by, 309–13
  Great Seal and, 315–16
  in Paris mission, 428–29
Jeffrey, Francis, Lord, 478
Jenkins Ear, War of, 123
Jerman, John, 95, 97
Jews, 468
Johnson, Lyndon B., 6
Johonnot, Samuel, 379–80
Jones, John Paul, 356, 383–84, 385–90,
    402
  background of, 386–87
  Lafayette's proposed attack and,
    385–86, 389
  rape incident and, 388–89
  in *Serapis* fight, 390
Johnson, Samuel (writer), 45, 220
Johnson, William Samuel (convention
    delegate), 450
Junto (Leather Apron Club), 55–60,
    63, 72, 101, 109, 146, 147, 183,
    372, 449, 493, 499, 532*n*
  BF's religious talk to, 86–88
  debating style of, 56–57
  members of, 55–56
  models for, 59
  as reflection of BF's persona, 59–60
  subscription library of, 103–4
  topics guide of, 58–59
Jupin, Mademoiselle, 359

Kames, Henry Home, Lord, 196,
    197–98, 260, 261, 498
Kant, Immanuel, 145
Keats, John, 93, 478–79
Keillor, Garrison, 95
Keimer, Samuel, 38–39, 52–54, 56,
    60–61, 62–63, 64, 487–88, 498,
    499
Keith, William, 40–41, 42, 43, 48, 188,
    498
King (BF's slave), 191
King George's War, 123
King Philip's War, 14
Kinnersley, Ebenezer, 140
Kissinger, Henry A., 326

Lafayette, Marquis de, 335, 336, 341,
    385–86, 389, 410, 427
laissez-faire, doctrine of, 327
Landais, Pierre, 390
La Rochefoucauld, Louis-Alexandre
    de, 439, 457, 463, 500
"Late Benjamin Franklin, The"
    (Twain), 98
Laud, William, 13
Laurens, Henry, 397
Lavoisier, Antoine-Laurent, 463
Lawrence, D. H., 89, 100, 482–83,
    489, 490
lead poisoning, 265
Leather Apron Club, *see* Junto
    (Leather Apron Club)
Le Despencer, Francis Dashwood,
    Lord, 274, 277–78, 496
Lee, Arthur, 308, 321, 337, 342, 393,
    496
  Bancroft suspected of spying by,
    335–36
  BF's conflicts with, 251, 331–33,
    382–83, 384, 390, 498
Lee, Charles, 302
Lee, Francis Lightfoot, 498
Lee, Richard Henry, 308, 331, 396,
    498
Lee, William, 331, 333, 498
Leeds, Titan, 95, 96–97, 100
Leibniz, Gottfried Wilhelm, 312, 327

Lemay, J. A. Leo, 76, 522*n*, 530*n*, 561*n*
Le Roy, Jean-Baptiste, 463, 498
"Letters from a Farmer in
  Pennsylvania" (Dickinson), 245,
  496
"Letters on England" (Voltaire), 328
Leverett, John, 20
Lewis, Sinclair, 482
Lexington, Battle of, 290, 291, 399
Leyden jar, 135–36, 200
Liberty Tree, 244
libraries, 2, 4, 59, 102, 103–4, 147, 154,
  257–58, 492, 532*n*
Library Company of Philadelphia,
  103–4, 112, 134
lightning rod, 141–43, 441, 442,
  492
Literary History of the American People
  (Angoff), 483
Little Revenge, A (Randall), 76
Lives (Plutarch), 25–26
Livingston, Robert, 309, 406, 407, 411,
  419, 428, 498, 558*n*
Locke, John, 24, 46, 59, 150, 311, 312,
  498
Lodge of the Nine Sisters, 355–56,
  363, 390
Logan, James, 104, 498
London, 43–44, 181, 238
London Board of Trade, 158, 195
London *Chronicle*, 181, 186, 200, 244,
  269, 276
London *Evening Post*, 406
London mission of 1757–1762,
  175–205
  BF-Deborah Franklin
    correspondence in, 178–81,
    186–87, 190–91, 192, 198–99
  BF-Penn confrontations in, 183–86,
    192–95
  BF's circle of friends in, 181–83
  BF's departure for, 173–74
  BF's genealogical excursion in,
    189–90
  BF's Scotland trip in, 195–98
  BF's surrogate family in, 178–79,
    187

BF's travels through England in,
  186–91
BF's trip to continent in, 199–200
Canada retention as issue in,
  200–202
results of, 205
royal charter debate in, 185
taxation as issue in, 184, 186, 205
William Franklin in, 175, 186,
  188–90, 191, 195–96, 198–99,
  203–4
London mission of 1765–1775,
  219–89
  Bache-Sally Franklin romance in,
    235–40
  Bache's visit in, 261–63
  BF as colonial spokesman in,
    228–31
  BF-Deborah Franklin
    correspondence in, 219, 221,
    224–25, 232–36, 237, 238, 253,
    262, 263
  BF's cockpit ordeal in, 276–79
  BF's invention interests in, 264, 266
  BF's motives in, 219–20, 245–46
  BF's scientific experiments in,
    263–65
  BF's social outlook and, 266–69
  BF's surrogate family in, 219,
    240–43, 254, 262–63
  BF's vacation in France in, 237–38
  BF's vacation of 1771 in, 252–61
  BF-William Franklin rift in, 280–83
  Deborah Franklin's death and,
    282–83
  Hillsborough-BF confrontations in,
    246–47, 249–50, 251, 259–60,
    269–71, 277
  Howe-Chatham secret talks in,
    283–84
  Hutchinson letters affair in,
    271–80
  Stamp Act crisis in, 222–26
  Stamp Act repeal battle in, 226–32
  Townshend duties controversy in,
    243–45, 247–49
Longfellow, Henry Wadsworth, 291

Lopez, Claude-Anne, 165, 304, 353, 357, 367, 431, 549*n*

Louis XV, King of France, 139, 237–38

Louis XVI, King of France, 321, 326, 337, 343, 346, 347–48, 356, 393–94, 404, 433, 472, 500

McCullough, David, 318, 351, 383, 411

McHenry, James, 459

Madison, James, 292, 298, 428, 445, 446, 448–49, 455, 456

"magazine," 118

magnetism, 129

Maier, Paul, 310

Main Currents in American Thought (Parrington), 488

Malthus, Thomas, 150

Mansfield, William Murray, Lord, 195

"Marche des Insurgents" (Brillon), 357, 495

Mareschal, Lord, 196

Marie, Queen of France, 237

Marie Antoinette, Queen of France, 266, 348, 376, 427, 433

Marignac, Gabriel Louis de, 377

Markoe, Margaret, 473

Marriage of Figaro, The (Beaumarchais), 331, 389, 495

Marshall Plan, 338

Martin, Luther, 457

Mary I, Queen of England, 5

Maryland, 155, 445

Mason, George, 311, 463–64

Mason & Dixon (Pynchon), 136

Massachusetts, 231, 249, 281, 285, 291, 299

anti-tax rebellion in, 444

Stamp Act crisis in, 225

Massachusetts Assembly, 231, 244, 272, 276, 304

Massachusetts Bay Colony, 9

Massachusetts Committee on Correspondence, 251

Massachusetts House of Representatives, 249–50

matching grant, concept of, 148

Mather, Cotton, 10, 13, 18, 25, 26, 31, 41, 42, 59, 93, 102, 499, 529*n*

library of, 24

smallpox controversy and, 22–24

Mather, Increase, 23, 499

Mather, Samuel, 18

May, Henry, 460

mechanical arm, 441–42

Mecom, Jane, *see* Franklin, Jane

Mellon, Thomas, 481

Melville, Herman, 21, 93, 479

BF assessed by, 480

Meredith, Hugh, 53–54, 55, 487, 499

"meritocracy," 519*n*

Mesmer, Friedrich Anton, 427, 463

meteorology, 129, 132–33

Methodism, 110

Metternich, Klemens von, 326

middle class, 5, 423, 532*n*

values of, 3, 212, 268, 424–25, 476, 478, 480, 487, 488, 493

Middlekauff, Robert, 351

militia, 102, 123–26, 147, 155, 169–72, 392, 532*n*

Militia Association, 125, 170

Miller, Perry, 10, 22, 527*n*

"minutemen," 290

Mississippi River, 409, 412

"Modest Enquiry into the Nature and Necessity of a Paper Currency, A" (Franklin), 63–64

"Modest Proposal, A" (Swift), 373

Mohawk Indians, 156, 160

Monroe Doctrine, 338

Montesquieu, Baron de la Brède et de, 353–54, 528*n*

Montgolfier, Etienne, 420–21

Montgolfier, Joseph, 420–21

moral perfection project, 89–92, 94

"Morals of Chess, The" (Franklin), 372

Morellet, André, 253, 364, 374, 433, 499

Morgan, Edmund, 90–91, 193, 349, 485, 563*n*

Morrill, Mary, *see* Folger, Mary Morrill

Morris, Gouverneur, 456

Morris, Lewis, 499
Morris, Richard, 447–48
Morris, Robert, 399, 424
Morris, Robert Hunter, 166, 167–68,
    170, 171, 172, 499
Mozart, Wolfgang Amadeus, 266
Musschenbroek, Pieter van, 200

"Narrative of the Late Massacres in
    Lancaster County, A" (Franklin),
    211–12
Nation, 476
Native Americans, *see* Indians
natural rights, concept of, 311
Netherlands, 387–88, 404
New England Courant, 22, 34, 35, 41,
    73, 83, 473, 497
  "Silence Dogood" essays in, 28–33
  smallpox dispute in, 23–24
Newfoundland, 260, 411
New Jersey, 53–54, 206, 231, 293, 444,
    449, 450
  William Franklin appointed
    governor of, 203–4
New Jersey Gazette, 340
Newton, Isaac, 19, 129, 130, 133, 134,
    135, 138, 144, 145, 150, 312, 374,
    484, 534n
New York, 444, 449
Nine Sisters, Lodge of, 355–56, 363,
    390
Nini, Giovanni Battista, 330
Nollet, Abbé, 134, 143, 499, 534n
Norris, Isaac, 159, 161, 185, 193, 214,
    216, 499
North, Lord, 246, 276, 283, 399
North Carolina, 203, 444–45

Oberg, Barbara, 459
"Observations on the Increase of
    Mankind" (Franklin), 119, 150,
    152–53, 201, 464
Ohio valley, 155–56, 166
Olive Branch Petition, 296–97, 318,
    319
"On Conciliation with America"
    (Burke), 288

"On Conversation" (Franklin), 56
"On Infidelity" (Bradford), 114
"On the Laboring Poor" (Franklin),
    267
"On the Providence of God in the
    Government of the World"
    (Franklin), 86–88
Osborne, Charles, 39–40
Oswald, Richard, 400, 401, 403,
    404–10, 413, 415, 557n
Ottawa Indians, 210
Oxford University, 202

Paine, Thomas, 307–8, 439, 467–68,
    499, 563n
Palmer, Samuel, 44, 47
Pamela (Richardson), 126
paper currency, 63–64, 222–23, 301–2,
    396n
Paris, 238
Paris, Ferdinand John, 184
Paris, Treaty of (1763), 200
Paris mission of 1776–1785:
  Adams-BF rift and, 392–95
  Adams in, 350–53, 355, 365, 371,
    382–84, 390–94, 428
  Adams's return to, 390–92
  American commissioners in,
    331–33
  balloon fad in, 420–21
  Bancroft's spying activities in,
    333–36, 342, 343, 344, 345, 347,
    382, 551n–52n
  BF appointed minister
    plenipotentiary in, 382–83
  BF's appointment to, 320–21
  and BF's arrival in France, 325–29
  BF's attempted resignation from,
    396–97
  BF's bagatelles in, 367–71
  BF's departure from, 433–35
  BF's diplomatic style in, 337–39
  BF's flirtatious relationships in,
    356–62, 364–67, 372
  BF's household in, 329–30
  BF's mock scientific essays in,
    372–75

Paris mission of 1776–1785 (_cont._)
  BF's public relations campaign in,
    339–40
  BF's resignation from, 432
  BF's writing of _Autobiography_ in,
    425–26
  commission-seeking supplicants in,
    340–42
  French loans in, 395–96, 415–17
  French policy in, 337–38
  Jefferson in, 428–29
  Lee-BF feud in, 384–85
  Lodge of Nine Sisters controversy
    in, 355–56
  Mesmer commission investigation
    in, 426–27
  military alliance treaty in, 346–49,
    392–93
  new European treaties in, 429
  peace negotiations in, _see_ Anglo-
    American peace negotiations of
    1782
  planned attack on Britain in,
    385–86, 389
  proposed Franco-American alliance
    in, 339, 342, 344
  realism and idealism in, 336–43,
    393, 428–29
  Spain's rejection of treaty in, 344–45
  Temple Franklin in, 322–25, 329,
    330, 344, 356, 385–86, 415
  trade and friendship treaty in, 344,
    346–49, 392–93
  Wentworth's secret mission and,
    344–46
Parker, James, 157–59, 192, 194, 499
Parliament, British, 150–51, 159, 161,
    183–84, 205, 218, 222, 225, 272,
    275, 285, 287–88, 292, 298
  colonial representation in, 228–29
  Scotland in, 449–50
  taxation power of, 245, 247–49
  see also House of Commons, British;
    House of Lords, British
Parliament, Irish, 259
Parrington, Vernon, 488, 489
Parsons, William, 341

Partridge, Elizabeth, 462
Paterson, William, 450–51
"Paul Revere's Ride" (Longfellow), 291
Paxton Boys, 210–14, 499
peace negotiations, _see_ Anglo-
    American peace negotiations of
    1782
Peale, Charles Willson, 243, 426
Pemberton, Israel, 214
Penn, John, 159, 210, 212–13, 226,
    235, 499
Penn, Richard, 184, 499
Penn, Thomas, 126, 155, 156, 159,
    168, 183, 206, 210, 213, 223, 226,
    499
  BF on, 169
  BF's conflict with, 184–86
Penn, William, 38, 155, 214–15,
    499
  royal charter of, 185
pen names, 34, 69, 70–71, 73, 80, 104,
    112, 151, 242, 243, 267, 530n
  see also Busy-Body Essays; "Dogood,
    Silence"; _Poor Richard's Almanack_
Penn family, 42, 63, 66, 113, 114, 194,
    203, 205, 215, 250, 492
Pennsylvania, 59, 63, 225, 450, 454
  BF elected president of, 443, 460–61
  BF's efforts to change colonial status
    of, 155, 183–86, 192–95, 214–17,
    226
  BF's militia proposal for, 123–25
  colonial defense as issue in, 155,
    168–69
  constitution of, 314, 315, 443, 447,
    468
  Continental Congress and, 295–96
  independence question and, 295–96,
    312
  Indians' relations with, 155–56
  Paxton Boys uprising in, 210–14
  royal charter of, 185
  unicameral legislature of, 443, 447,
    449
Pennsylvania, University of, 59,
    146–48, 149–50, 173, 438, 499,
    500, 519n

Pennsylvania Assembly, 66, 105, 159,
161, 192, 213, 223, 250, 292, 314,
460, 497, 499
  BF as clerk of, 114, 153
  BF elected speaker of, 216
  BF elected to, 153–54
  BF's militia proposal and, 123–24
  Braddock's Ohio campaign and,
  166–67
  "Charter of Privileges" of, 185
  colonial status as issue in, 214–17
  defense issues and, 167–68, 210–11
  election of 1733 and, 113–14, 115
  election of 1764 and, 216–17
  hospital scheme and, 148
  Quakers in, 154–55, 211
  taxation of Proprietors and, 173,
  194–95, 214
Pennsylvania Chronicle, 238
Pennsylvania Executive Council, 154
Pennsylvania Fireplaces, 131–32
Pennsylvania Gazette, 64–72, 79, 83,
105, 106, 147–48, 151, 226, 233,
361
  "Apology for Printers" in, 66–68
  first political cartoon in, 159
  gossip in, 69–70
  humor in, 71–72
  lightning experiments in, 141
  Poor Richard's Almanack
  advertisements in, 95–96
  postal service dispute and, 115–16,
  117
  readers' essays and letters in, 65, 69
  sexual references in, 68–69
  Whitefield in, 110–13
Pennsylvania Society for Promoting
the Abolition of Slavery, 464–65
Peter (BF's slave), 190–91
Peters, Richard, 159, 173, 499
"Petition of the Letter Z, Commonly
Called Ezzard, Zed, or Izard"
(Franklin), 333
Philadelphia, Pa., 1, 123
  BF's 1723 arrival in, 37–38
  BF's 1785 arrival in, 437–38
  in BF's will, 474–75

British capture of, 342
Freemasons in, 106
Great Awakening in, 110
lightning rods erected in, 143
population of, 151, 181
slavery in, 151, 463
Philadelphia Academies, 475
Philadelphia Academy, *see*
  Pennsylvania, University of
Philadelphia Inquirer, 475
philosophes, 355
Philosophical Transactions (Royal
  Society of London), 263
phonetic alphabet, 220–21
physiocrats, 327
Pierce, William, 446–47
Pilgrim's Progress (Bunyan), 25, 30, 257
Pinckney, Charles, 445
Pitt, William (the Elder), 283–84,
  287–88, 496
"Plain Truth" (Franklin), 123–24
"Plan for Future Conduct" (Franklin),
  48–49
Pliny the Elder, 175
Plutarch, 25–26
Poe, Edgar Allan, 93, 479
police patrols, 59, 105–6, 147, 154
Polignac, Diane de, 327, 549*n*
"Polly Baker" (Franklin), 119, 121,
  368, 466, 531*n*
polytheism, 86, 526*n*
Pontiac (Ottawa chief), 210
Poor Richard's Almanack, 94–101
  BF's motive for, 96
  final edition of, 100
  format and style of, 95, 100–101
  lightning rod ad in, 141
  maxims and sayings in, 98–99
  sly wit of, 99–100
  success of, 100
Poor Robin's Almanack, 95
Pope, Alexander, 44, 528*n*
population growth, 150–51
postal system, 60
  BF as postmaster of, 157
  BF-Bradford access dispute and,
  115–17

postal system (*cont.*)
    BF's inspection tours of, 172–73,
        207–9
    BF's reforms of, 157, 207
    dead letter office of, 157
    home delivery system of, 157
Powel, Mrs., 459
Pownall, John, 247
pragmatism, 480, 491, 492–93
Presbyterians, 84–85, 109, 526*n*, 539*n*
    Paxton Boys uprising and, 210–11,
        213
Priestley, Joseph, 140–42, 182, 253,
    277, 289, 297, 301, 303, 374,
    499
Princeton University, 146
Pringle, John, 182, 195, 203, 220, 232,
    237, 239, 265, 499
Privy Council, British, 183, 194, 195,
    214, 226
    BF's Cockpit ordeal in, 276–78,
        279
progressive taxation, 105
"Proposal for Promoting Useful
    Knowledge Among the British
    Plantations in America, A"
    (Franklin), 122
"Proposals Relating to the Education
    of Youth in Pennsylvania"
    (Franklin), 146–47
Proprietors, 201, 233, 495, 496, 497,
    498, 499
    BF's colonial status dispute with,
        155, 183–86, 192–95, 214–17,
        226
    Indians and, 155–56, 194
    taxation as issue and, 166, 168–69,
        173, 184, 186, 214
*Protestant Ethic and the Spirit of
    Capitalism, The* (Weber), 481
Prussia, 347
Pulaski, Casimir, 341
Puritan Mind, The (Schneider), 484
Puritans, Puritanism, 8–10, 19–20, 25,
    26, 109, 486, 490–91, 527*n*
    BF's rejection of, 45–46, 84, 92–93
    in Boston, 11–12

in migration to America, 9–10
    Protestant ethic of, 10
    special providence dogma of, 86
Pynchon, Thomas, 136

Quakers, 38, 54, 123, 124, 169–70, 215
    Paxton Boys uprising and, 210–11,
        213
    in Pennsylvania Assembly, 154–55,
        211
Quincy, Josiah, Jr., 284, 306, 328

race, 151–53, 191, 268
*Radicalism of the American Revolution,
    The* (Wood), 127–28, 455
Ralph, James, 39, 42, 43–44, 46, 48,
    182, 487
Randall, Willard Sterne, 76
Randolph, Edmund, 448
Ranger, 387
Rawls, John, 519*n*
Ray, Catherine, *see* Greene, Catherine
    Ray
Raynal, Abbé, 531*n*
Read, Deborah, *see* Franklin, Deborah
    Read
Read, John, 39
Reagan, Ronald, 339
Rees, Daniel, 106–7
Reforming Societies for the
    Suppression of Disorders, 26
refrigeration, 129, 191
religion, 19–20, 26, 44–45, 46, 84–88,
    92–94, 371, 380, 467–69, 486,
    491, 526*n*–27*n*, 563*n*
    BF on, 32–33, 85–86
    divine providence in, 86–88, 451
    Great Awakening and, 107–13
    Junto talk on, 86–88
    Supreme Being in, 85–86
    see also deism; Puritans, Puritanism
Religion of Nature Delineated, The
    (Wollaston), 44–45
Reprisal, 324, 325
Revere, Paul, 290
Revolutionary War, *see* American
    Revolution

Richardson, Samuel, 44, 126
Richelieu, Cardinal, 326
Ridley, Matthew, 410, 415
Roberts, George, 77–78
Rockingham, Lord, 229, 399, 407
Rogers, John, 74, 77, 497
Rogers, Will, 29
Roman Catholic Church, 5–8, 10
Romantic era, romanticism, 93,
    478–79
Ross, Margaret, 235–36
Rossiter, Clinton, 459
Rousseau, Jean-Jacques, 257, 260, 326,
    327, 328, 354, 528*n*
Royal Academy, French, 139, 354, 355
Royal Academy of Brussels, 373
Royal Society of London, 47, 138, 139,
    263, 333, 420, 421, 431, 534*n*
  BF elected to, 182–83
  BF honored by, 143–44
"Rules and Maxims for Promoting
    Matrimonial Happiness"
    (Franklin), 80
"Rules by Which a Great Empire May
    be Reduced to a Small One"
    (Franklin), 272, 272–75
"Rules of a Society which Met Once a
    Week for the Improvement of
    Useful Knowledge" (Locke), 59
Rush, Benjamin, 264, 269, 321, 444,
    446
Rutledge, Edward, 318

"Sage et la Goutte, Le" (Brillon), 368
St. Andrews, University of, 198
Sandwich, Lord, 287–88
Saratoga, Battle of, 343, 344, 346, 357,
    398–99, 552*n*
Sartine, Antoine de, 383, 387
Saxony, 298
Scaroyady (Iroquois chief), 156
Schneider, Herbert, 484
"Scolding Wife, A" (Franklin), 81
Scotland, 195–98, 252, 449–50, 455
Seahorse, HMS, 23
Second Treatise on Government (Locke),
    311

Secret Service, British, 333
self-help movement, 3, 484
Senate, U.S., 449, 450, 452
Seneca Indians, 156, 402
Serapis, HMS, 390
*Seven Habits of Highly Effective People,
    The* (Covey), 484
1776 (Edwards and Stone), 485, 566*n*
Seven Years' War, 155, 200, 326, 495
Sewall, Samuel, 11
Shaftesbury, Lord, 46
Shays, Daniel, 444
Shelburne, Lord, 252, 399, 400, 401,
    405, 406–10, 413, 414, 499, 500
Sherman, Roger, 309, 447, 450, 453
Shipley, Jonathan, 182, 253–54, 255,
    257, 258, 297, 426, 434, 438, 443,
    500
Shipley, Kitty, 258, 434
  BF's "pleasant dreams" letter to,
    442–43
Shipley, Mrs. Jonathan, 258
Shirley, William, 161, 166, 500
"Short Hints towards a Scheme for
    Uniting the Northern Colonies"
    (Franklin), 159, 161
"Silentiarius: The Silent Sufferer" (C.
    Mather), 26
silk industry, 376
single-fluid theory, 135, 144
"Sinners in the Hands of an Angry
    God" (Edwards), 109
Six Nations, 156, 160
Skemp, Sheila, 76
"Sketch of Propositions for Peace"
    (Franklin), 321–22
slavery, 151–53, 463–67, 544*n*
  and BF as slave owner, 151–52, 176,
    190–91, 269
  BF's "Conversation" on, 268–69
  in Constitutional Convention,
    456–57, 460, 464
  in Declaration of Independence,
    313
  representation question and, 315
Sloane, Hans, 47
smallpox, 22–23, 82–83, 378, 420

Smith, Adam, 150, 196, 260–61
Smith, William, 147, 173, 194, 477,
    500
Smyth, Albert, 94
Société Apollonienne, 356
Society for Political Inquiries, 439
Society of the Cincinnati, 422–23
Socrates, 354–55
Socratic method, 27, 39, 56–57
Solon, 354–55
"Somerset Case and the Slave Trade,
    The" (Franklin), 464
Sons of Liberty, 225, 244, 275
South Carolina, 315
Spain, 123, 200, 279, 346, 400, 404,
    408–9, 412
    Franco-American treaty rejected by,
        344–45
Sparks, Jared, 313, 563*n*
Spectator, 28, 29
Spencer, Archibald, 133–34
Spotswood, Alexander, 115–17
Stamp Act, 222–32, 243, 276, 402,
    491, 498
    repeal of, 226–32
states' rights, 448
Steele, Richard, 28, 34, 62, 227, 457,
    525*n*
Steuben, Friedrich von, Baron, 341,
    551*n*
Stevenson, Margaret, 176–77, 178,
    180, 187, 219, 220, 221, 232, 237,
    258, 301, 303–4, 329, 431, 487,
    500
Stevenson, Mary "Polly," *see* Hewson,
    Mary Stevenson "Polly"
Stiles, Ezra, 468
storage battery, 135–36
Stormont, Lord, 340, 342
Stourzh, Gerald, 393
stove design, 2, 130–31, *131*, 441,
    492
Strachey, Henry, 410
Strahan, Billy, 198, 531*n*
Strahan, William, 118, 176, 181, 186,
    195, 198, 221, 236, 280, 293, 467,
    497, 531*n*

BF's correspondence with, 202, 208,
    209–10, 231, 296–97, 425, 456,
    500
BF's "you are my enemy" letter to,
    296–97, 500
Deborah Franklin's correspondence
    with, 178–79, 182
Stuart, Gilbert, 431
Swift, Jonathan, 44, 65, 96, 373, 478,
    528*n*
swimming pads, 16, 47
synthetic truths, 312

Tanford, Charles, 263
Tatler, 525*n*
taxes, taxation:
    in Constitutional Convention, 184,
        186, 205
    exterior-interior distinction of,
        230–31, 243–45
    progressive, 105
    property, 105
    of Proprietors, 166, 168–69, 173,
        184, 186, 214
    representation and, 161, 222, 230
    Shays' rebellion and, 444
    Townshend duties and, 243–45
Taylor, Alan, 95, 485, 488
Temple, William, *see* Franklin, William
    Temple
Tennessee, 444–45
Themistocles, 272
Thevenot, Melchisedec, 47–48
Thompson, J. J., 144
Thomson, Charles, 223–24, 232, 249,
    500
Thoreau, Henry David, 93, 479,
    483
Tiyanoga (Hendrick Peters), 160
Tocqueville, Alexis de, 102–3
Tonnerre, Marquis de, 330
Tour de Sol, 475
Tourtellot, Arthur, 9, 19
Townshend, Charles, 244, 246
Townshend duties, 243–45
    BF's essay on, 247–49
transcendentalists, 479

Treatise of Human Nature, A (Hume), 197

Trevose summit, 293–94, 295

True Conduct of Persons of Quality, The, 188

Truman, Harry, 6

Turgot, Anne-Robert-Jacques, 145, 337, 352, 363, 364, 366–67, 492, 500

Turner, Frederick Jackson, 481

Twain, Mark, 29, 95, 98, 354, 480–81

typeface, 52

Under God (Wills), 490

Union Fire Company, 105

United States, 383, 403, 415
  bald eagle as national symbol of, 422–23

Universal Instructor in all Arts and Sciences, and Pennsylvania Gazette, The, 60–61

Updike, John, 93
  on BF's *Autobiography,* 256
  on BF's transformation of Puritanism, 490

urinary catheter, 132, 497

Van Doren, Carl, 61, 77, 143, 144, 257, 274, 328, 349, 417, 452, 484

Vaughan, Benjamin, 409, 413, 424, 426, 434, 461–62, 500

vegetarianism, 36, 39

Veillard, Louis-Guillaume le, 439, 440, 463

Vergennes, Comte de, 336–39, 342–43, 346–48, 396, 397, 399, 433, 500–501, 558*n*
  Adams and, 391, 393–94
  Anglo-American peace negotiations and, 400–402, 404, 406, 408–9, 410, 415–17
  BF's first meeting with, 337–38

Virgil, 104

Virginia, 309, 445, 449
  BF's postal inspection trips to, 172–73, 207

constitution of, 311
  Stamp Act crisis in, 225

Virginia, University of, 149, 519*n*

Virginia House of Burgesses, 225

virtues, BF's definitions of, 89–91

Voltaire, 37, 326, 327, 328, 352, 353–55, 377, 463, 478, 528*n*

"Walking Purchase," 156

Wall, Samuel, 534*n*

Walpole, Richard, 270

Walpole, Robert, 501

Walpole, Thomas, 270, 288, 347, 501, 552*n*

Walpole Company, 270

Walter, Thomas, 23, 24

Walters, Kerry, 86, 527*n*

War of Austrian Succession, 123

War of Jenkins Ear, 123

Washington, George, 2, 15*n*, 291, 298, 302, 307, 309, 318, 326, 341, 351, 375, 377, 378, 385, 391, 413, 473
  BF and, 172, 303
  BF's correspondence with, 395, 462, 551*n*
  Cincinnati Society and, 422
  at Constitutional Convention, 445–46, 454, 455, 456, 458
  in Ohio Valley missions, 158–59, 168
  at Yorktown, 398

Watson, Joseph, 39

Watt, James, 260, 441, 560*n*

Watts, John, 47

Way to Wealth, The (Franklin), 100, 326

Wealth of Nations, The (A. Smith), 150, 261

weather forecasting, 132–33

Webb, George, 55, 60

Webbe, John, 116–17

Weber, Max, 481, 489, 490

Webster, Noah, 220–21, 461

Wedderburn, Alexander, 276–78, 279, 347

welfare, 148–49, 267–68

Wentworth, Paul, 333–34, 344–46, 501, 552*n*

West, Benjamin, 140
Wharton, Samuel, 347, 501, 552*n*
Whigs, 229, 283
Whitefield, George, 110–13, 118, 125, 147, 501
White Oak Boys, 224–25
Willard, Samuel, 12
William & Mary, 146, 172
Williams, Jonathan, 345
Williams, William Carlos, 482
Wills, Garry, 490, 548*n*
Wilson, Benjamin, 342
Wilson, James, 446
Winchester School, 119
Winkler, Johann Heinrich, 534*n*
Winthrop, John, 9, 35, 137, 339

"Witch Trial at Mount Holly, A" (Franklin), 88
Wollaston, William, 44–45
Wood, Gordon, 127–28, 193–94, 455, 478, 532*n*, 538*n*
Wygate (printer), 48

Yale University, 143, 165
Yankees at the Court (Alsop), 337
Yardley, Jonathan, 38
Yorktown, Battle of, 398–99, 444
Young, Michael, 519*n*
Young Men Associated clubs, 26

Zall, P. M., 522*n*
Zenger, John Peter, 100, 497

ABOUT THE AUTHOR

Walter Isaacson is the president of the Aspen Institute. He has been the chairman and CEO of CNN and the managing editor of *Time* magazine. He is the author of *Kissinger: A Biography* and the coauthor, with Evan Thomas, of *The Wise Men: Six Friends and the World They Made.* He lives with his wife and daughter in Washington, D.C.

ILLUSTRATION CREDITS

Numbers in roman type refer to illustrations in the insert; *italics* refer to book pages.

Courtesy of The Bostonian Society/Old State House: 1
American Philosophical Society: 2, 11, 12, 17, 21, 26, 29
Private Collection: 3, 6
The Metropolitan Museum of Art, Catharine Lorillard Wolfe Collection, Wolfe
    Fund, 1901 (01.20). Photograph © 1998 The Metropolitan Museum of
    Art: 4
© Réunion des Musées Nationaux/Art Resource, NY: 5, 27
Philadelphia Museum of Art: Gift of Mr. and Mrs. Wharton Sinkler: 8
Courtesy of the Chapin Library of Rare Books, Williams College: 9, *131*
Franklin Collection, Yale University Library: 10, 30
© Bettmann/Corbis: 13, 16, 19
Courtesy of the Harvard University Portrait Collection, Bequest of Dr. John
    Collins Warren, 1856: 14
Courtesy of The Historical Society of Pennsylvania Collection, Atwater Kent
    Museum of Philadelphia: 15, 24
By courtesy of the National Portrait Gallery, London: 18
Courtesy of the Pennsylvania Academy of Fine Arts, Philadelphia. Gift of Maria
    McKean Allen and Phebe Warren Downes through the bequest of their
    mother Elizabeth Wharton McKean: 20
© Huntington Library/SuperStock: 22
Library of Congress: 23
The Metropolitan Museum of Art, The Friedsam Collection, Bequest of Michael
    Friedsam, 1931 (32.100.132). Photograph © 1981 The Metropolitan
    Museum of Art: 25
Leonard Labaree et al., eds., *The Papers of Benjamin Franklin* (36 vols. to date, New
    Haven and London: Yale University Press, 1959–), vol. XXIII: 28
Courtesy of the Winterthur Museum, Gift of Henry Francis du Pont: 31
The Architect of the Capitol: 32

Additional photo research by Alexandra Truitt and Jerry Marshall, Picture
    Research & Editing.

A NOTE ON TYPE

This book is set in Adobe Caslon type, designed in 1990 by Carol Twombly, which is known for its elegance, dignity, regularity, and legibility. It is based on a typeface originally created in the early 1720s by the preeminent London punch-cutter and type-maker William Caslon. Benjamin Franklin imported Caslon's type for his print shop in Philadelphia, championed it, and chose it for the first printing of the Declaration of Independence.

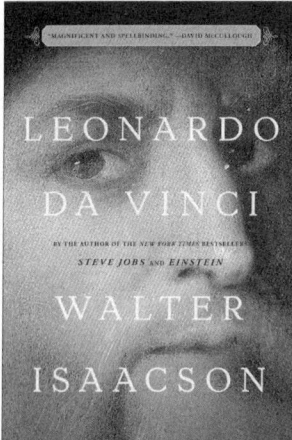
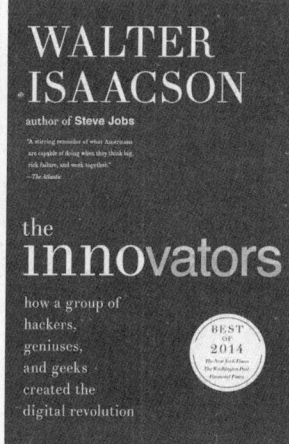

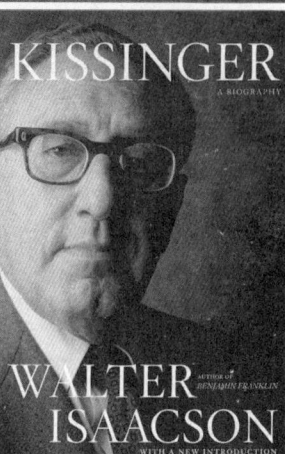